COMICS VALUES ANNUAL: 1995 EDITION
The Comic Books Price Guide

COMICS VALUES ANNUAL: 1995 EDITION
The Comic Books Price Guide

Alex G. Malloy

Wallace-Homestead Book Company
Radnor, Pennsylvania

Published in Radnor, Pennsylvania 19089, by Wallace-Homestead,
a division of Chilton Book Company

Designed by Stuart W. Wells III

Manufactured in the United States of America

Wallace-Homestead ISBN: 0-87069-725-0
ISSN: 1062-4503

1 2 3 4 5 6 7 8 9 0 3 2 1 0 9 8 7 6 5 4

Contents

Preface

By Alex G. Malloy

The comics industry has seen a leveling off during the last eighteen months. After a record setting summer in 1993, reality set in throughout the industry. During the summer, publishers produced more new comics than collectors could absorb. Many speculators seeking immediate dividends on their investments left comic collecting after realizing that these new books were not going to increase in value, causing many small dealers to be caught with excess issues.

Some small stores even closed up shop while many survivors are still feeling the after-effects. Many comic book shop owners are diversifying to protect themselves from another drop in sales. Collecting back issues of comic books has fallen flat as a result of all this chaos within the industry.

What are some of the other results after the "Summer of Glut" in 1993? First, the distributors made delayed comic products returnable if thirty days late in an attempt to protect shop owners from getting stuck with unwanted books. Second, publishers and distributors are expanding their product lines and seeking new avenues to generate lost revenues by creating new comic book fans. Decorating arcades and living rooms across the country, new video games featuring superheroes continue to grow in popularity. In addition, comic-related cartoons made for television are once again popular. Third, action figures, PVC (Polyvinyl chloride) figures, games, buttons, watches, and many other comic-related toy items now are available in comic stores. Fourth, the biggest increase in sales may be the booming comic card industry. Young kids and adults collect all the new cards with great enthusiasm!

The biggest and largest publisher in the comics industry for some time has been Marvel Comics, which is now feeling an unprecedented surge of competition. The added competition has caused Marvel to expand into new venues. Having opened an office in Japan, Marvel wants to expand into the Japanese market. The House of Ideas is also distributing comics for both Disney and Harvey Comics. Marvel has also bought Toy Biz, a leading toy manufacturer, and Fleer Corporation, a leading card company, hoping to expand and increase revenue. At the current time, the *X-Men* cartoon on Saturday mornings is the number one-rated Saturday morning show. During the fall, a new animated *Spider-Man* TV show will appear, along with the *Marvel Action Hour*, featuring the Fantastic Four and Iron Man. (What's next? A Marvel theme park?) Nevertheless, all of these added ventures by Marvel will surely create new comic collectors and increase Marvel's profits, to the delight of its shareholders.

Despite the slump of sales industry-wide, DC has made tremendous strides since the 1993-94 *Comics Values Annual.* Sales of Superman and Batman titles have brought in many new readers and increased DC's market share and fan base. The Vertigo books, an adult comic book line, is an enormous success, which attracts new readers to comic book stores. DC also produces superb comic cards through SkyBox, which are very popular with collectors. One of the best trends for DC has been its ability to produce excellent crossover comics: Batman/Punisher, Batman/Spawn, and Batman/Predator. For the Distinguished Competition, Jonah Hex is also an emerging popular character from the 1970s.

In the future, *Jonah Hex* comics may very well increase in price as collectors seek out Hex books. A third Batman movie with Jim Carrey (star of TV's *"In Living Color"* and the movie *Ace Ventura*) as the Riddler is expected within the next two years and will most likely make millions in worldwide profits (and increased comic sales!).

Appearing in theaters during the summer of 1994, Carrey starred in *The Mask*, a movie based on the comic book of the same title by Dark Horse Comics. Another comic that reached the big time was *The Crow* by James O'Barr (who is so popular that his new sight-unseen property *Gothic* is movie bound). Valiant Comics has been bought by Akklaim, the video game manufacturers, with new merchandise surely following.

Image Comics continues to thrive and appears to be a huge player for years to come. Jim Lee's *WildC.A.T.S.* is now a Saturday morning cartoon series and will compete for viewers with Marvel's popular *X-Men* cartoon. Todd McFarlane has a new line of *Spawn* action figures and Rob Liefeld's *Youngblood* is being touted as the next toy line.

Jim Shooter with Defiant Comics is exploring Spanish comics with *Prudence & Caution*. If this is successful, a whole new untapped audience will be created.

Females with an attitude, such as Vampirella, Lady Death, and Shi, have become a buzz-word around the industry. *Bone,* a cult character, continues to grow in popularity and his appearences in *Disney Adventures* will certainly help!

The entire industry, though, is looking ahead as comics become more available to the entire population. Blockbuster now sells comic books and the Chicago, based Moondog's has emerged as the prime mover in nationwide store chains in malls across the country. Heroes World Distribution has expanded into Hong Kong while the biggest, Diamond Comics Distribution, has gobbled up another property, Comics Unlimited. The chief executive officer and founder, Steve Geppi, has also opened Diamond International Galleries.

On the whole, gimmicks appear to have slowed down as collectors have shown less and less interest in 3-D covers and holograms in the back issue market. Though, the strongest areas of collectibility and gimmicks are the limited edition Gold and Platinum books that are immediately hot and continue to command a good price in the back issue market.

The auction houses of Sotheby's and Christie's have been a prime avenue of sparkling Golden Age interest. The old key issues and even title runs are seeing renewed interest as many issues have risen in price during the past eighteen months. At the 1993 Sotheby's auction, *Amazing Fantasy* #15 commanded a $39,000 price tag. The scarcity of Golden Age comics, even in lesser grades, has moved the values upward. The last Golden Age books available at bargain-level prices appear to be the precomic code comics. These are well written and have just enough spice to attract guys and gals alike.

* * *

A few words about using this book might be appropriate at this point. As you may already have noticed, we have decided to segment our listings just as the industry itself is segmented: DC, Marvel, Golden Age, Independent Color, Independent Black & White, Classics Illustrated, and Underground Comix; each has its own section complete with comprehensive listings of each particular division.

Wherever necessary, cross-referencing has been provided. We feel this style of listing greatly enhances the ease of usage of our *Comics Values Annual: 1994-95*. When seeking information about a particular title, simply turn to the section indicated, follow alphabetically, and you'll find prices, artist listings, and any other significant information you may need. All abbreviations used in our listings are easily found in our handy fold-out index.

Thank you to the staff at Attic Books; without their time, patience, and effort, this project would have never been completed:

John (Onions & Cheese) Laub, Editor

Louis (Psycho) Porter, Assistant Editor

Brian (3BK) Kelly, Copy Editor

Dean (Roid Boy) Sasso, Editorial Consultant

Roderick (Worm) Malloy, Marketing Director

Stuart (Solid Citizen) Wells, Photo Manipulator Extraordinaire

Heidi (Hair Color) Shaw, Production Assistant

Sandy (Deep) Fryer, Production Assistant

Steve (Ooh Me Back!) Thomas, Cover Editor

And a Special Thanks for Assistance to:

Maureen McTigue, DC Comics; Robert J. Sodaro; Dana Kelly; Pat Callanan; Scott Hilgeneck; Meredith S. Woodwell; Mark Haverty; Don Bouchard; Matt Sanger; Jeff Smith; Gary Ramos; Donald W. Riordan; Thomas J. Mulvey; Walt Dittrich; Phil Mateer; Katie Hoeing; Ron Goulart; Jeff Juliard; Buddy Scalera; Monica Nofi; and Troy Vozzella, Chilton Book Company.

Greetings from the Editor

By John Laub

I must make a confession before you read any further: watching football every Sunday afternoon is my passion and love in life now, not collecting comic books. However, that doesn't prevent me from believing that Superman can fly faster than a speeding bullet, that Spider-Man's strength is proportionate to that of any arachnid, or that Solar can traverse time and space without breaking a sweat.

For years, I collected comic books and even bought the first issue of the X-Men for $20 (now worth $3,600) in 1982. Collecting comics helped me learn how to read and how to understand the value of money by budgeting the income I made as a paper boy. They also paid for my education when I went to graduate school to pursue master's degree in history, which I completed in 1991.

I can still remember the thrill when my Mom would drive me to the Southbury Pharmacy every Wednesday to buy the latest comic books. When I collected comics, there were no comic shops and no preservation materials available. I had to keep my comics in boxes that my Dad brought home for me from work and in large zip-lock bags my Mom bought for me at the grocery store. I also remember attending my first convention in Hartford, Connecticut and trying to negotiate with a dealer to sell me *X-Men* #51 for $10 instead of $12. Much to my regret, he wouldn't budge on the price so I finally gave in.

But enough reminiscing about my childhood. Now, I must thank everyone for buying this year's edition of *Comics Values Annual: 1994-95*. I have been employed for another year in a job that every twelve-year-old comic fan dreams about (actually many twenty-seven-year old men also fantasize about it). Where else could I earn a living in which knowing Wolverine's origin is more valuable than a degree in chemical engineering?

To everyone unfamiliar with *Comics Values Annual*, you now hold the third (and best) edition in your hands; it is the third one that I have edited for Attic Books, Ltd. During the past three years, I have worked diligently to bring these books to press and put them in the hands of collectors and fans.

I came on board in September 1991, fresh out of graduate school, when *Comics Values Annual* was only an idea of Alex G. Malloy's and a contract with Chilton Book Company for completion by March 1992. Of course, I had our monthly magazine, *Comics Values Monthly*, as an outline and guide, but little else. The final product seemed as impossible (and improbable) as Patrick Buchanan and Gore Vidal agreeing on which course of action is best for our country to ensure another generation of Americans good health-care, access to higher education, and equal (and fair) employment opportunities.

My first task required the laborious and tedious exercise of researching every Golden Age comic. Having never read an issue from my father's generation, the chore proved more difficult than I had imagined. When my assignment was completed after three months,

I needed an assistant to help me decipher all of my notes and put them in a legible format for collectors. Luckily, my best friend and beer-drinking buddy from college ,3BK, who hung on the telephone with Jeff Smith, remained unemployed after graduating with a bachelor's degree in English. I asked if he would be willing to work with me despite the low salary and the fact that we worked out of a garage without heat (which we resolved a couple of months later). Grudgingly, he accepted, and we completed the first *Comics Values Annual* in March 1992.

The 1993-94 edition was much easier and sold very well across the country. Looking back, I would love to make hundreds of changes to improve both, but only in comics can we go back in time and correct our past mistakes.

An extensive market research project concluded that an October publication would be much better received and anticipated by comic fans. After numerous meetings of the marketing and editorial teams, we decided to take a break in between the second and third issues and make some changes to improve *Comics Values Annual: 1994-95*.

In this edition, our regional reporters discuss the many changes in the comics industry, which comics (and companies) were hot and which were not during the past year; Bob Sodaro examines the Dynamic Changes in the DC Universe; Phil Mateer looks at The World's Greatest Comic Magazine!; Ron Goulart provides background information on DC's *The Golden Age* from 1993 and pays tribute to Jack Kirby: The King of Comics; Jeff Juliard and Buddy Scalera take a peek at the success of Image Comics; 3BK talks with *Bone* creator Jeff Smith; and Jeff Juliard explores Classics Illustrated.

Remember to hug your Dad, buy *Marvels*, send flowers to Mom, save Triton, kiss your Grandma, vote Democratic, read comics, end racism, give peace a chance, explore Taoism, provide health-care for the masses, question authority, give *Comics Values Annual:1994-95* to a friend for Christmas, love your children, collect *Bone*, support higher education, appreciate Barry Bonds' grace on the diamond, promote diversity, and accept everyone for their uniqueness.

MAKING THE GRADE

By Buddy Scalera

When comic collecting established itself as a source of income for savvy investors, it became clear that it was necessary to institute guidelines. Among these guidelines was the practice of grading comics fairly and evenly. Comic book values are established by a number of criteria, including scarcity, condition, and popularity. Grading is necessary in determining the true value of a particular issue.

For the purpose of brevity (and sanity), we shall explore the eight standard comic grades: mint, near mint, very fine, fine, very good, good, fair, and poor. Clearly, these eight grades could be split into even finer categories when haggling over an exceptionally rare or coveted Golden Age comic. In most cases, however, comic books can be evaluated using the eight standard grades.

New comic book collectors benefit most from learning how to assess the prospective value of a comic. These collectors protect themselves from being fleeced by unscrupulous dealers or hucksters. Yet, a majority of dealers, especially store owners, can be considered reliable judges of comic grade. Because comic retail may be their primary source of income, certain dealers are particularly adept at noticing comic book imperfections, especially in issues they intend to purchase. As such, hobbyists and collectors must understand that dealers need to make a minimum profit on their investments. Buying collectible comics entails certain risks. Therefore, dealers must scrutinize a comic to determine if the particular book will stand a chance of resale. Well-preserved comics are invariably more desirable to dealers because they are more desirable to collectors.

Despite the pop subcultural craze of comic book collecting, very old, well-preserved comics remain coveted collector's items. There are basically two reasons for this. The primary reason is that, in most cases, many people did not save their comic books for future generations. They read them and discarded them. Comic books were considered harmless ephemera for children. When these children outgrew their comics, their parents often threw them away. If everybody kept all of their comics, comics would not be valuable because everybody would have them scattered about the house!

The second reason that comics are collectible is because of their condition. This is a basic tenet of all collectibles. A car is more valuable with its original paint. A baseball card is more valuable if it has not been marred by bicycle spokes. Coke bottles, stamps, coins, and toys in good condition are all more valuable than their abused counterparts. Comic books are no exception.

It is a sad but basic fact of life that nothing lasts forever. Not metal nor rubber nor uranium! Everything has a shelf life, so to speak, and paper is no exception. The fact that paper comes from trees makes its life especially short by comparison. Paper is sensitive to light, heat, moisture, draught, pressure, impact, and just about every force of nature or man. Although paper has been a longtime tool of man, it is still downright delicate.

In spite of its shortcomings, paper has always been one of man's favorite inventions. Paper is cheap and plentiful, which are two cornerstones of effective capitalism. It is also a nearly perfect medium for written or drawn mass communications, which is why it is used for comic books. As mentioned, comic books were not designed to be preserved for fifty or more years. Rather, they were intended as unpretentious entertainment. As such, comic books were printed on rather cheap paper, usually the stock used for newspapers. Only the covers were privy to special glossy paper stocks.

Mint

Finding old comics in mint condition is rare or almost impossible. Mint condition comics usually fetch prices higher than price guide listings. Mint comics can sell for 120% or more of *Comics Values Annual* listed prices. The reason for this is the strict criteria reserved for mint comics.

Mint comics are perfect comics and allow no room for imperfections. Pages and covers must be free of discoloration, wear, and wrinkles. A mint comic is one that looks like it just rolled off the press. Staples and spine must meet perfectly without cover "rollover." The cover must be crisp, bright, and trimmed perfectly. The staples must not be rusted and the cover should not have any visible creases.

The interior pages of a mint comic are equally crisp and new. A mint comic must not show any signs of age or decay. Because of the paper stock used on many older comics, acid and oxygen cause interior pages to yellow and flake. It is much harder to find pre-1970 mint comics because of inferior storage techniques and materials. In the early days of collecting, few people anticipated that the very boxes and bags in which they stored their comics were contributing to decay. Acid from bags, backing boards, and boxes ate away at many comics.

Near Mint

A near mint comic and a mint comic are close siblings, with their differences slight, even to an experienced eye. Most of the new comics on the shelf of the local comic shop are in near mint condition. These are comics that have been handled gingerly to preserve the original luster of the book.

Near mint comics are bright, clean copies with no major or minor defects. Slight stress lines near the staples and perhaps a very minor printing defect are permissible. Corners must still be sharp and devoid of creases. Interior pages of newsprint stock should show almost no discernible yellowing. Near mint comics usually trade for 100% of the suggested *Comics Values Annual* listed prices.

Very Fine

A very fine comic is one that is routinely found on the shelves and back issue bins of most good direct market comic shops. This grade comic has few defects, none of them major. Stress around the staples of a very fine comic are visible but not yet radical enough to create wrinkles. Both the cover and interior pages should still be crisp and sharp, devoid of flaking and creases. Interior pages may be slightly yellowed from age.

Most high-quality older comics graded as very fine can obtain 80-90% of *Comics Val-*

ues Annual listed prices. Newer comics graded as very fine get about 70-85% because many near mint copies probably exist. Despite that, very fine comics are desirable for most collectors.

Fine

Fine comics are often issues that may have been stored carefully under a bed or on a shelf by a meticulous collector. This grade of comic is also very desirable because it shows little wear and retains much of its original sharpness. The cover may be slightly off center from rollover. The cover retains less of its original gloss and may even possess a chip or wrinkle. The corners should be sharp but may also have a slight crease. Yellowing begins to creep into the interior pages of a comic graded as fine.

Fine comics are respectable additions to collections and sell for about 40-60% of the listed prices.

Very Good

A very good comic may have been an issue passed around or read frequently. This grade is the common condition of older books. Its cover will probably have lost some luster and may have two or three creases around the staples or edges. The corners of the book may begin to show the beginnings of minor rounding and chipping, but it is by no means a damaged or defaced comic. Comics in very good condition sell for about 30-40% of *Comics Values Annual* listed prices.

Good

A good comic is one that has been well read and is beginning to show its age. Although both front and back covers are still attached, a good grade comic may have a number of serious wrinkles and chips. The corners and edges of this grade comic may show clear signs of rounding and flaking. There should be no major tears in a good comic nor should any pages be clipped out or missing. Interior pages may be fairly yellowed and brittle. Good comics sell for about 15-25% of the *Comics Values Annual* listed prices.

Fair

A fair comic is one that has definitely seen better days and has considerably limited resale value for most collectors. This comic may be soiled and damaged on the cover and interior. Fair comics should be completely intact and may only be useful as a comic to lend to friends. Fair comics sell for about 10-20% of the *Comics Values Annual* listed prices.

Poor

Comics in poor condition are generally unsuitable for collecting or reading because they range from damaged to unrecognizable. Poor comics may have been water damaged, attacked by a small child, or worse, perhaps, gnawed on by the family pet! Interior and exterior pages may be cut apart or missing entirely. A poor comic sells for about 5-15% of the *Comics Values Annual* listed price.

Sniffing Out Grades

Despite everything that is mentioned about comic grading, the process remains relative to the situation. A comic that seems to be in very good condition may actually be a restored copy. A restored copy is generally considered to be in between the grade it was previous to restoration and the grade it has become. Many collectors avoid restored comics entirely.

Each collector builds his collection around what he believes is important. Some want every issue of a particular series or company. Others want every issue of a favorite artist or writer. Because of this, many collectors will purchase lower-grade comics to fill out a series or to try out a new series. Mint and near mint comics are usually much more desirable to hard-core collectors. Hobbyists and readers may find the effort and cost of collecting only high-grade comics financially prohibitive.

Getting artists or writers to autograph comics has also become a source of major dispute. Some collectors enjoy signed comics and others consider those very comics defaced! The current trends indicate that most collectors do enjoy signed comics. A signature does not usually change the grade of the comic.

As mentioned, comic grading is a subjective process that must be agreed upon by the buyer and seller. Buyers will often be quick to note minor defects in order to negotiate a better price. Sellers are sometimes selectively blind to their comic's defects. *Comics Values Annual: 1994-95* provides this grading guide as a protection for both parties.

GIVING IT ALL AWAY

By Robert J. Sodaro

If you're looking to build your comics collection and you've already latched onto all of the so-called hot comics currently available, you might want to pick up something a little different. However, you don't want to pick up just any book; you want something that will not only appeal to you but will prove to be a worthwhile investment as well. What to do? What to do?

Well, there's hope, as there is a whole genre of books that fills these criteria. These "giveaway" or "custom" books feature flagship superheroes and/or name talent and are generally produced not for newsstand or direct sales but for a specific market. These give-aways often find their way into the fan market, but unless you know about them, they'll probably slip by unnoticed. Generally speaking, they are very affordable.

These specialty comics run the gamut in respect to form, content, and purpose. They range from comics packed in games or toys to public-service comics proselytizing an awareness message to comics that are independently produced to hawk a product, store, or consumer goods. They also range in size and shape from the standard comic book size to mini-comics that fit in the palm of your hand. As diverse as they are, they all have two things in common: they adapt the comic book medium to pitch a message and they are usually distributed free to a target market.

While this article does not purport to list every giveaway comic ever published, it offers a cross section of the genre. It should be noted that in today's market, some companies specifically produce a limited number of their comics with enhanced covers to be given away as promotional items. While some of these could technically be considered "give-aways," they are not covered in depth in this article.

Still, as they have become a legitimate part of the market, they do warrant inclusion in this piece, if only by way of a cursory mention. Some of these specialty giveaways include the following: a platinum cover produced by Marvel for *Spider-Man* #1; a platinum bagged *Superman* #75 produced by DC; and given to fans and retailers by Valiant, gold-foil comics for "meritorious service or dedication" to the company. Malibu, Image, Lightning, and other publishers have likewise produced enhanced versions of their standard comics.

Marvel issued a *Magneto* #0 as a special promo for fans. The comic featured a pair of Claremont/Bolton Magneto stories that had been in the early issues of *X-Men Classic*. A special gold-cover version of *Uncanny X-Men* #307 was shipped to fans who mailed in the card from the 1993 *X-Men* board game.

Then there is the question of modern-day ashcan comics. Of the modern-day, promotional ashcans, many are not full comics but rather sketchbooks with text material designed to tantalize the fan. Typical ashcans include a Jae Lee *Hellshock* that was distributed at a couple of recent Great Eastern Cons.

Marvel has jumped in with both feet and produced numerous ashcans promoting upcoming or ongoing series. These include *Spider-Man*, *Force Works*, *War Machine*, *The Hulk*, *New Warriors*, *X-Men 2099*, and *Generation X*. In spite of the fact that a number of these bear cover prices (generally 75 cents), these ashcans have frequently been given away at conventions by Marvel.

Marvel has also produced a number of full-sized "ashcans" that have been bound into their regular, monthly books. One sixteen-page promo even pushed the upcoming *Spider-Man Animated* FOX-TV series, and it came polybagged with an animation cel!

Marvel pushed the promo ashcan giveaway into the twenty-first century when it offered up the first "electronic" ashcan: *Ghost Rider 2099* was designed as a computerized download from the on-line service CompuServe.

Marvel-Style Specialty Books with a Message

As might be expected, the company with the widest range of giveaways is Marvel Comics. One reason is that Marvel has an entire department specifically dedicated to producing custom comics. The best known of these comics has been distributed free since it appeared in 1984, has never been out of print, and, as of 1990, has a circulation that topped fifteen million. This comic featured Spider-Man and Power Pack and was produced in conjunction with the National Committee for the Prevention of Child Abuse (NCPCA).

The comic features two tales, one starring Spidey and the second with the Power Pack kids. The first story deals with Spidey coming to the aid of a young boy who was being sexually molested by his baby-sitter. During the course of the story, Spidey revealed that as a young boy, he too was sexually molested by an older boy. In the backup story, the four Power kids come to the defense of a schoolmate who is being molested by her father.

This hugely successful comic has been distributed to social service centers around the country and has also been printed in various newspapers over the past eight years. It was followed by two more comics: one dealing with emotional abuse (1987) and a second with physical abuse (1990).

A fourth in the series, released in early 1994 and offered for sale via a mail-in coupon found in many Marvel comics, was done in conjunction with the NCPCA, with proceeds from the sale of the book benefiting NCPCA. This story takes place within Marvel continuity, features Hulk and Venom, and was written by Peter David.

Other Marvel specialty comics that promote a safety or public service message include *The Amazing Spider-Man vs. the Prodigy* (1976); *Captain America and the Campbell Kids* in battle against The Energy Drainers (1980), *Spider-Man, Storm, and Power Man vs. Smokescreen* (1982); *Captain America and the Asthma Monster* (1987); *Adventures in Reading starring the Amazing Spider-Man* (1990); a five-part Spidey series *Skating on Thin Ice*, *Double Trouble*, *Hit and Run* (with Ghost Rider), *Chaos in Calgary* (with the Texas Rangers), and *Deadball Field of Screams* (with the Montreal Expos; 1990-93); and the two-part *Captain America Goes to War Against Drugs* (1990-93).

All of these comics, while ostensibly public service books, are subsidized by various companies, sometimes with the intent to hype a product of the sponsoring company. The first book mentioned is the most unusual, as it is a minicomic sponsored by Planned Parenthood. In it, Marvel's web-slinger battles the Prodigy, an alien who is utilizing his hypnotic powers to convince teenagers that having unprotected sex doesn't mean they are going to get pregnant. It is Prodigy's hope that if enough teenagers have indiscriminate sexual relations, many will bear children that he will then kidnap for slave labor.

The book helps to dispel many of the myths about sex. The story is followed by a couple of text pages filled with facts about sex and babies, homosexuality, and venereal disease. There are also a couple of ads aimed at teens for textbooks about sexual matters.

Next up was an energy-awareness book where Cap and a group of children battle a trio of villains intent on disrupting the world's energy supply. Between chapters, the Campbell Soup kids offer energy-saving tips and puzzles and games with a conservation theme. In a book sponsored by the American Cancer Society, Spidey helps a young athlete kick a smoking habit as the web-slinger and company battle Smokescreen.

In a book sponsored by Glaxo, Inc. (the makers of an antiasthma medicine), Cap again teams up with children to battle a villain who wants to give asthma to everyone in a twisted retribution for his own childhood asthma condition! In the sequel (*Return of the Asthma Monster*), the monster returns to exact revenge, only to be foiled once more by Cap and his young helpers. Spidey's *Adventure in Reading* book (Sponsored by the Literacy Volunteers of America) encourages kids to read.

Keeping with the tone of the non-Comics Code Authority-approved newsstand *Amazing Spider-Man* #96 (circa 1971), there have been a number of antidrug comics in Marvel's custom-comics program. In the first issue, Spidey pursues Electro to Winnipeg, Canada, where he gets involved with a kids' hockey team when one of the players begins to dabble in drugs.

The first four of these antidrug books were rereleased for specialty-shop distribution in 1993. The for-sale comics differ slightly from the original giveaways in that the giveaways state they are a "$1.25 Can. value" (issue #5 has a $1.60 Can. value), and their cover numbering is larger than is standard for comics. The for-sale versions sport cover prices and normal-sized numbering.

In the first issue of Cap's drug-awareness series, he busts up a drug ring attempting to hook a Little League team on drugs. It has been reprinted a number of times with different sponsors (the FBI, Waldbaums, and several insurance companies). The second installment costars the New Warriors and has Colleen Doran art.

Glen Herdling, who edits Marvel's line of Custom Comics, acknowledged that most companies or organizations that request custom comics initially ask for Marvel's best-known characters, Spider-Man and the X-Men. So he is always pleased when he can steer groups to characters that would be more appropriate to their cause, as he did in the case of the Namorita comic produced for the Arise Foundation and Metro-Dade Police Department. The book promoted not only environmental awareness but also drug awareness. Another good match was a Daredevil comic produced for the Gas Appliance Manufacturers Association proclaiming the dangers of natural gas vapors.

Also in 1993, Marvel produced a pair of comics for the National Action Council for Minorities in Engineering, Inc. These books highlighted the fact that minorities have not only the right but also the abilities necessary to achieve equality in the engineering world.

One of the most ambitious giveaways Marvel ever attempted was a *Spider-Man vs. Venom* comic featuring Daredevil. This was the first giveaway designed to directly affect Marvel continuity. In the Spidey/Venom comic DD travels, as lawyer Matt Murdock, to the supervillain prison known as the Vault. His purpose is to defend Venom, with Spidey as a hostile witness for the defense. Interested fans were able to acquire this book by sending a donation of $5 or more to UNICEF. The book had a heavy-stock, raised-imprint cover, and bound inside the comic was a full-color poster.

The Marvel Newspaper Syndicate

Between 1979 and 1983, Marvel issued a number of comic books as inserts in various newspapers. These stories, mostly starring Spider-Man and featuring the Hulk, were sponsored by local department stores (Sanger Harris, May D&F, The Jones Store), and bore the logo of the store as well as the newspaper. These newspapers included the *Columbus Dispatch, Chicago Tribune, Dallas Times-Herald, The San Antonio Express News, Denver Post, Tulsa World,* and *Kansas City Star.*

All of these stories had Peter Parker traveling to the city in question on assignment for *The Daily Bugle* and Spidey getting involved in an adventure of some sort. Occasionally, the costars were real people (the Dallas Cowboys' cheerleaders showed up in one!) and some of the action would occur in the department store.

One newspaper supplement featured the X-Men at the Texas State Fair. In this 1983 adventure, Magneto and the X-Men travel to the State Fair to recruit Daniel Wiley (aka Eques). Daniel's just-manifested power is that he can transform himself into a Centaur. He initially sides with Magneto until Magneto's battle with the X-Men inadvertently endangers some horses. Daniel switches sides, later choosing to stay in Dallas tending to his horses rather than joining the X-Men.

All in all, these stories are fairly entertaining and are worth collecting for their novelty nature. Also of note are the ads in these books, as many of them sport Spidey or the Hulk hawking the item. Some even offer special Marvel-related products.

Superheroes as Sales Tools

As celebrity spokespeople are all the rage in standard ads, why not hire on a comic book hero to pitch your product, especially if it's aimed at kids? Well, giveaway comics in this area fall into two categories. First, there are the comics that are simply packed into comic-related toys, and second there are the comics that are designed as mailaways for noncomic items. The following fall under the first category: a sixteen-page Evel Knievel comic for a Knievel model produced by Marvel and Ideal and a number of comics/assembly instructions produced by Aurora for its line of hero models. These comics included Tonto, the Lone Ranger, Spider-Man, and Hulk.

In 1981, Amurol Products Company issued a short-lived line of minicomics that came packed with bubble gum. Each of the Marvel comics delivered a brief version of the hero's origin plus a short battle with one of their foes while the Archie book served up a typical story of Archie accidentally dating both Betty and Veronica.

Since 1978, Pez has issued dispensers with superhero heads and, naturally, they packed a short strip with the dispenser. In 1989, Marvel packed a comic with Paragon Software's computer games. These giveaways offered insight into the play of the games. Paragon only packed comics in their first two games, *Dr. Doom's Revenge* (with Cap and Spidey) and *The Uncanny X-Men.* Both of the comics came rolled up and stuffed in all versions of the games (Commodore 64, IBM-PC, etc.).

Pushing its own product, in 1982, Marvel issued a sixteen-page all newsprint, color comic that promoted comic book collecting for fun and profit. This comic was itself adapted from Sunshine Comics' *Comics for Fun, Comics for Profit,* which was published in 1979.

Filling the second category are the following comics, most of which star Spidey: All detergent (1979); Aim toothpaste (1980); Acme and Dingo boots (1980, co-starring Jessica Drew as Spider Woman; Seven-Eleven (1981, with Hulk, Captain America, and Spider-Woman); and a second Aim comic in 1982. Marvel also issued a pair of *Kool-Aid Man* comics (1983 and 1984) plus *The Adventures of Quik Bunny* (1984, costarring Spidey).

In 1992, in conjunction with Charleston Chew, Marvel issued an anthology flip book starring Spidey, the Silver Surfer, Wolverine, and Ghost Rider. A second Charleston Chew comic starring the Avengers followed in 1993 and had a set of uncut trading cards bound in.

Perhaps the most unusual Marvel giveaway was the Ghost Rider comic issued by Kay-Bee toy stores. Given the nature of Ghost Rider, it was a surprise to everyone that Kay-Bee was actually interested in the demonic character! This comic was available with the purchase of a Spider-Man or X-Men video game.

Of course, since Marvel characters do so well promoting their own products, Marvel enlisted their support in 1993 to promote upcoming Marvel titles. To this end, Marvel produced a pair of convention promos entitled *Marvel Live*. These books are full-color, glossy sixteen-pagers (#0 adds a card-stock cover) combining art and color photos pumping upcoming projects and their creators.

In 1993, Marvel also launched a pair of successful X-Men related promotional tie-ins with Pizza Hut. The first (a four-part series) included specially designed place mats, plastic cups, and single-serving pizza boxes. The second offered a two-part mini, a pair of trading cards, and a couple of videotapes of the animated X-Men series. Each tape had a pair of episodes, with additional footage of Stan Lee, Scott Lobdell, and Fabian Nicieza talking about the characters.

A veritable explosion of Marvel-related giveaways occurred in 1993. In addition to those already mentioned, there was a four-issue minicomic series, featuring Spidey, Jubilee, Wolverine, Hulk, Silver Surfer, and Dr. Doom found in boxes of Drakes cakes; and an X-Men comic produced in cooperation with Stridex medicated pads. There was also a mini, *The Adventures of Apple and Cinnamon*, which was packed in boxes of Apple and Cinnamon Cheerios, and four G.I. Joe minis produced for Hasbro.

Nomextra and Kevlor was an especially interesting comic that Marvel produced for DuPont in 1993. Unlike most of its other custom comics, Marvel actually created a pair of superheroes for DuPont (Nomextra and Kevlor are materials developed by DuPont to fight fires). In the comic, Nomextra and Kevlor are a pair of fire fighters who gain superpowers and use them in the course of their jobs.

A couple of last-minute additions to this section include a four-page promo done strictly as a Revlon sales gimmick (astute fans will recall that Ronald Perlman, who owns the lion's share of Marvel stock, is the chief executive officer of Revlon).

One of the most notorious comic book insert/giveaway comics was the initial Marvel Mart catalogue. This catalogue was inserted into the direct edition of *X-Men Adventures*, volume 2, #4. The comic-cum-catalogue was designed to showcase a number of Marvel-related items that were then available via mail order.

Big Giveaways in the Minimarket

In 1988, Marvel issued a special line of minicomics that was designed to be given away as Halloween treats. These sixteen-page comics stripped away nonessential parts of the stories and compressed the rest into a cohesive tale. The comics came four to a polybagged set, featuring heroes from the main line (Spidey, X-Men, Cap), plus characters from their Star line of kid's comics. These were sold to consumers who were encouraged to give them away on Halloween instead of candy.

Another mini that Marvel issued came bound inside *Esquire* and *Eye* magazines (1969). This mini appeared in an unusual size (6 3/4" by 5") and reprinted *Amazing Spider-Man* #42. The final page, which is in black and white, appears on the inside back cover and a classic Romita Spidey pose is featured on the back cover. Near as can be determined, this is probably the first customized comic issued by Marvel.

Marvel in the Bull Market

Late in 1990, Marvel Comics was purchased by Ronald Perlman, CEO of Revlon, who brought the company public and traded its stock on the New York Stock Exchange. While this action didn't directly affect the average fan, it did result in a new type of giveaway, as Marvel began to issue its quarterly and annual reports in the form of comics. Since going public, Marvel has issued ten such reports. All of them are designed to look like comics with appropriate covers and the Marvel logo in the upper left corner. Some are comic-sized on standard cover-quality paper while others are magazine-sized card stock.

That rounds out Marvel's rather extensive contributions to the giveaway market, but it proves to be merely the tip of the depth and breadth of books currently available in this genre.

DC and the Atari Force

Back in the early 1980s, when the Atari 2600 video-game system was king, DC Comics entered into a copublishing agreement with Atari, wherein DC acquired the rights to publish *Atari Force*. However, the flip side of this arrangement was that DC also produced a number of minicomics that came packed in several Atari games. This resulted in two series of forty-eight page minis: the aforementioned *Atari Force* and *Swordquest*.

The five comics were in *Defender*, *Berzerk*, *Star Raiders*, *Phoenix,* and *Galaxian*, with a special full-sized insert bound into *Teen Titans* #27. As an interesting aside, the five minis all read like regular comics while the *Liberator* story from *Titans* #27 was actually more akin to a printed video game. Since the Atari craze is long past, these comics (sans the games) are not only much cheaper but probably fairly easy to locate.

DC was far more successful integrating its *Swordquest* comics with the video game series of the same name. As conceived, *Swordquest* would have encompassed four games and comics (*Earthworld*, *Fireworld*, *Waterworld*, and *Windworld*). It would be necessary to read the four comics for clues to the game play, and each game would build on the last. The last two games and comics never saw the light of day, which is really too bad, as they featured some very fine George Perez artwork.

Two other Atari comics deserve mention here, one by DC and one by an independent. The DC comic was for *Centipede*. The second comic, *Yars' Revenge*, was a nine-pager that told the story of how the alien flylike race of Yars came to be and must now defend its world from invaders.

As integrated packages go, the *Swordquest* series, along with *Centipede* and *Yars'*

Revenge, were very successful packages and probably served as a model to the Marvel/ Paragon games and comics that followed.

Inserts, Giveaways, and Minis

A few of the other DC giveaways include a pair of drug-awareness comics starring the Teen Titans, a couple of Tandy/Radio Shack related comics (one a giveaway Superman and the other bound into *Action* #509), a set of four minis that came packed with McDonald's Happy Meals, a special promotional copy of *Birth of the Demon*-a Batman graphic novel, and their latest, a set of minis that came packed in Kellogg's Cinnamon Mini-Buns Cereal. There is also at least one *Batman and Robin* mini from the 1970s that must have come packaged with a toy or game, although the exact product is unknown.

The twin *Titans* comics appeared in 1983, and were produced in cooperation with the President's Drug Awareness Campaign, with the first comic cosponsored by IBM and the second by the American Soft Drink Industry. Both comics were stories about high school kids and drugs, and both offered a section at the end that explained the dangers of drugs.

The Radio Shack comics dealt with a group of children who assisted the Man of Steel in catching crooks while learning about the "astounding" abilities of the TRS-80 personal computer. The stand-alone giveaway is a thirty two-pager while the insert runs only 28 pages.

The four DC/Warner/McDonalds' minis appeared in 1991 during a cross promotion with the fast-food chain. Each comic came packed with a PVC of a Warner Bros. cartoon character and each character also came with a snap-on costume of a DC character depicting the toons as Super Bugs, Taz-Flash, Bat-Duck, and Wonder Pig.

The four DC/Kellogg minis have sixteen pages and spotlight a different DC hero-*Flash vs. Dr. Polaris*, *Justice League vs. Amazo*, *Wonder Woman and the Star Riders vs. Purrsia*, and *Superman vs. Metallo*. The cereal box sports a picture of Superman and proclaims that the comic is inside.

A trio of comics DC issued spotlighted their Vertigo line, as well as the Darknight Detective. *Vertigo*, a standard-sized, black-and-white sixteen-page book, featured some text features of the horror/adult-only line, serving up segments of the *Death* miniseries and *Sandman: Mystery Theater*. In the same vein, *The Birth of the Demon* giveaway delivered the first twelve pages of the graphic novel. The third comic is a reprinting of the Death/AIDS insert that ran in a number of DC comics in 1992.

In the comic, Death explains, in a straight forward, adult fashion, what AIDS is, how it can be contracted, and how to avoid getting it. She winds up her talk by explaining how to use a condom and then demonstrates how to put one on, utilizing the time-honored method of a condom and a banana. DC reprinted it in 1993 and distributed it to health organizations, schools, and youth groups.

News from Riverdale High

As one would expect of a company with an image as wholesome as Archie, they are very much involved with creating themed giveaway books of a public-service nature. We'll run down a handful of them.

Archie churned out a sizable number of books in conjunction with Tandy and distributed through Radio Shack. These stories read much like Hardy Boy stories, as the kids get caught up in all sorts of adventures and wind up using Radio Shack products to crack the cases. All the stories carry positive messages, contain no real violence, and promote Tandy computers and electronic gear.

A second series of Tandy comics, entitled *Electronics*, acts like a type of junior encyclopedia, serving up all sorts of information about some aspect or other of the electronic field. While these comics don't specifically pitch Tandy products, it's in the company's interest to have this stuff lying around the store to entice buyers to spend more money on doodads. Radio Shack still periodically issues comics.

In 1990, Archie and the gang finally got into the Tandy/Radio Shack act in a comic that delved into the history of electronics. Other Archie giveaways include a comic promoting fishing in New York and one promoting ham radios, produced in conjunction with the American Radio Relay League.

Giveaways from the Rest of the Market

In the interest of brevity, we'll talk specifically about the giveaways I have in my own collection to show the varied uses and publishers of such items.

Beginning in the comic book field, Valiant has made use of giveaways for their zero-numbered comics (*Magnus*, *Harbinger*, *Rai*), as well as different methods of acquiring them. In the case of *Magnus*, readers had to clip out a special card and mail it in to receive *Magnus* #0 and complete a set of trading cards. With *Harbinger*, there were two ways to receive the zero issue. The first was by clipping the coupon in each issue and the second was to purchase the Harbinger trade paperback. Likewise, the trade paperback collection of Rai included a special *Rai* comic.

Valiant has also produced a number of custom comics that were never intended for the comics market. These comics have not utilized any Valiant heroes and had a extremely specific and highly targeted audience (Kraft Macaroni and Cheese and Franco American's Spaghettios are just two of the comics Valiant has produced).

Dark Horse has produced quite a number of mini-comics that have been rolled up and packaged with the line of Aliens action figures. These comics each deliver a story that relates in some manner to the figure with which they are packaged. The company has also produced several promo comics that have been given away at past San Diego comic conventions.

Taboo #6 included a special sixteen-page *Sweeney Todd* comic by Neil Gaiman and Michael Zulli that served as a prequel to the story that began serialization in issue #7. Felix Comics (publishers of *Felix the Cat*) issued a sixteen-page tie-in to the eponymous Hudson Soft NES video game.

One of the most unusual "comic" giveaways came out of Comico in 1987. The company produced a slick, magazine-sized, color catalogue for Jordan Marsh. This was a catalogue that promoted various articles of clothing for an on-going sale and was mailed out to all Jordan Marsh credit card holders.

Prior to cashing in their superhero chips, Majestic issued a number of ashcan giveaways spotlighting their books *Legacy* and *S.T.A.T.* There are at least three different *Legacy* ashcans, one with a pink cover that delivers six pages from the first issue, and two that showcase six pages from the second (with blue and black covers). *S.T.A.T.*, likewise, has six pages from that comic. Sky Comics has also issued a number of ashcan giveaways promoting their books. One, entitled *Sky Zero*, showcases short segments from several titles (*Seeker*, *Blood & Roses*, *Tempered Steele*, *Dead Kid*, *Morgana X*, and *Ashley Dust*). This has a glossy, card-stock cover and gold-embossed lettering. A second ashcan spotlights *Seeker*.

In 1978, Paragon Productions produced a 16-pager for Captain D's (a restaurant) that told of the battle of Hampton Roads between the Monitor and the Merrimac. In 1992, Denny's likewise issued a children's menu that utilized the Jetsons. The first family in space appeared in the menu itself, as well as in a three-page story inserted into the menu. In 1981 the New York Thoroughbred Racing Association commissioned Mike Roy Enterprises to produce a sixteen-page comic that talked about various aspects of horse racing. MRC issued a comic promoting their Lightning Racers, a line of slot cars. In 1989, Instant Quaker Oatmeal included a sixteen-page mini in its packages. The comic starred Popeye and company and told us we should all eat Quaker Oats. In a neat turn, Popeye shuns his usual spinach in favor of Quaker Oats!

Even the state of Connecticut got into the act by publishing *The Adventures of Ray Cycle*, featuring an ecologically minded superhero and designed to help promote its recycling campaign. Issued in 1988 the comic gives the origin of Ray and expounds the need for recycling. The comic is distributed throughout the school system by Ray himself (actually an actor who dresses up as Ray and delivers a forty-five minute talk on recycling).

In addition to the video game/comic book giveaways already mentioned, Infocom, one of the major players in the field, included comics in a couple of games it issued in the 1980s. These comics appeared in *The Leather Goddess of Phobos* and *Trinity*.

What It All Means

Regardless of what some would have you believe, comics are more than just guys in long underwear pounding each other senseless. As this article has indicated, there are many uses for comics. Given the correct sponsors and causes, and with the right marketing spin, comics can be used to educate people about a social ill or to pitch products. However, since most public service comics tend to have very high print runs and multiple reprintings, they are not considered highly collectible.

Still, many of these comics are quite interesting to read. In the case of the public service comics, it is not recommended that collectors seek out and hoard them, for if they do, the comics will never reach their intended readers. Nevertheless, if as a fan, you wanted a single copy of each of these comics, there is nothing wrong with attempting to acquire one for your own collection.

Batman and Joker © DC Comics

COMICS VALUES ANNUAL: 1994-95
The Comic Books Price Guide

REGIONAL REPORTS

Pat Callanan
Cave Comics
Newtown, CT
Northeast

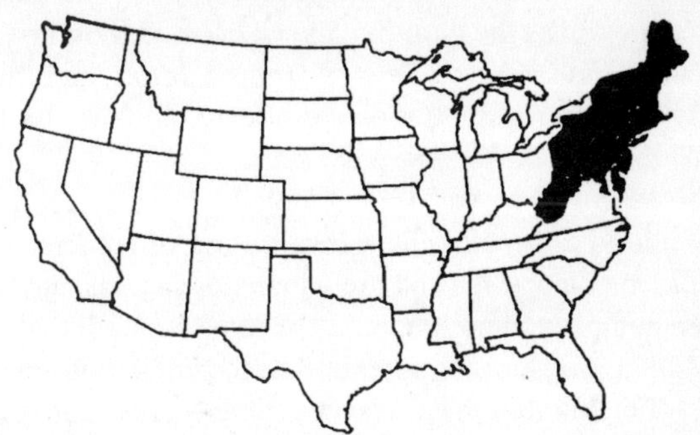

After the Crash of 1993, comic sales in our general area are off. This was a correction that had to happen: the comic industry had become bloated with too many books and too many limited, embossed, bagged, chromium, die-cut, special editions.

The speculator geeks had pumped up sales of new companies with their get-rich-quick, low-print-run, what's-hot-this-week mind-set. This was not good!

When the bottom finally fell out, it fell hard and fast. It caught many retailers with their pants down. Suddenly they had boxes and boxes of worthless books. Many could not afford these losses and were forced out of business.

But the hobby survives. Let's not forget that's what it is: something we do for fun. We collect comics because we love the characters. Now, I'll get off my soapbox and give a year in review.

DC

1993 was a banner year for DC. It they did seemed to go right. The "Death of Superman," the breaking of Batman, and the success of the Vertigo line were the highlights of a great year. *Golden Age*, *Power of Shazam*, *Batman: Red Rain,* and the *Elseworlds* stories reinforced DC's leadership in the quality comics field.

The success of Batman and Superman had a secondary effect on the market. They brought back a large number of the baby boomers who had not picked up a comic in decades. These returning fans are now becoming regular readers.

Marvel

1993 was not one of Marvel's better years. While the X-books remained strong, most other titles sagged. Marvel UK and the Clive Barker books were major disappointments! The Punisher and Spider-Man lines both saw a large decline in readers. Ghost Rider and the rest of the Midnight Sons have also suffered.

On the brighter side, *Marvels*, *Daredevil: Man Without Fear*, and *Deadpool* were very successful. The *Fantastic Four*, *Daredevil*, and the *Hulk* were some others that gained ground this year.

It seemed that Marvel's biggest problems this year were too many books (and too many marginal books cutting into sales). There was only so much money to go around, and when it came time to drop books, Marvel took the biggest hit.

Other Publishers

This seemed to be a telling year for Image Comics. While *Spawn* sales remained steady, the rest of the titles faltered. Even the much-anticipated Batman/Spawn did not sell as well as the monthly *Spawn* book. All of the Extreme Studios books are off dramatically. *Shadowhawk*, *Savage Dragon*, *Maxx*, and *Pitt* are all fading. The *WildC.A.T.S.* and *Cyberforce* regular series are slowly climbing back up the sales chart while *Gen*^{13} and *Kindred* are off to very good starts.

1993 was a year of incredible highs and now the deepest of lows for Valiant Comics. While it still maintains a loyal group of readers, sales in general are down 60-70%. It started as a peewee and grew to major success, but because all of the speculators have left, the company is no longer at the same strength that it was originally. It's too bad because Valiant produces high-quality, well-written books that deserve to be read, not invested in.

For Malibu, the Ultraverse titles started out strong but have since settled back to (at least) respectable levels. *Prime* and *Rune* are the leaders, with *Mantra*, *Sludge*, and *Solution* close behind. The Bravura imprint started out strong and remained strong. *Breed* and *Dreadstar* are the most popular of the titles so far.

Other books of note: *Bone*, *Bone*, *Bone*. Did I mention *Bone*? This has been a breakthrough year for many of the smaller press books. Interest in *Bone* has jump, started other books, such as *Starchild*, *Distant Soil*, *Windows*, and *Hate*.

Cerebus remains the godfather of the small press and still sells very well. The Elfquest books made great strides this year with very good new titles and regular shipping.

The success of these books are the real story this year. These books are the soul of what I like about comic collecting-if you put out a good, well, written book, it will be appreciated. A good story can carry bad art, but great art can't save a bad story.

Scott Hilgeneck
Back to the Past Comics
Livonia, MI
North Central

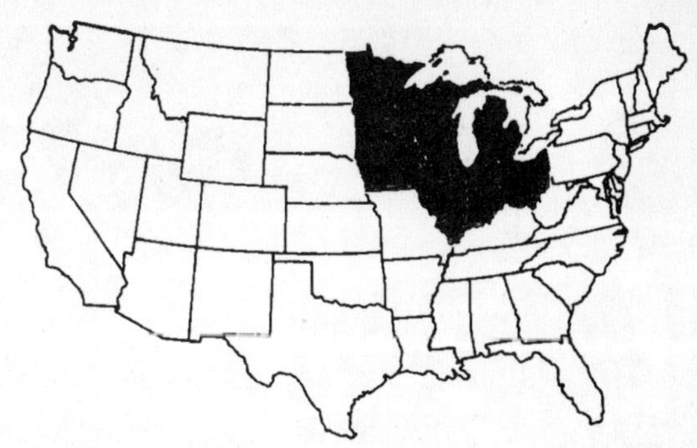

DC

1993 turned out to be the year that DC reclaimed a lot of market share, and 1994 may well be the year that DC gives Marvel a good hard run for first place! Superman's line of books is very strong and has remained so for the entire year.

Our only concern is why they decided to remove the current major event from ongoing continuity entirely by creating a separate Doomsday title. So while Supes is fighting out the current crisis in Metropolis, he's also calmly zipping across the galaxy because he's been having bad dreams. It's a little flimsy!

Batman is, of course, second in line for major events of 1993. What started as an ultra-hot read quickly grew cool due to confusion on the reader's part as to what books needed to be read to follow the storyline. The multitude of "Knightquest" stories crossed too many titles for too long a period. We also heard a huge sigh of frustration from readers when Bruce Wayne got healed within the space of a page and a half! What could have been a major milestone of a book turned out to be pretty soft.

We look forward to the end of the whole Jean Paul issue soon but fear that many readers who would have been there got lost in the interim. Maybe Batman's editorial staff would consider a triangle system like Superman next time.

The Vertigo Imprint introduced at the start of 1993 was just the right thing at the right time. Many older readers who might not have gotten a chance to read alternative books from independent publishers were exposed to Vertigo's mainstream alternative mix. We now see a growing following for these titles. Lastly, we applaud DC's sparsity of special covers. The books that do have them tend to actually be special issues! Weird, huh?

Marvel

In review, we got mixed results from Marvel's performance in 1993. While sales on top books remained very strong throughout the year, we're getting more and more feedback from readers that storylines are nonexistent or entirely rehashed! And, from a dealer's standpoint, what help has Marvel exhibited as industry leader to refresh and drive the comics industry into the future?

Never before have we seen such a greedy, bridge-burning attitude than from these guys this year. Misleading solicitations caused over ordering on pointless product, large-scale dumping of consumer-level trading cards (i.e., WalMart) and direct competition on back issue sales; and pointedly ignoring questions on where they're taking their business has caused many dealers to question where their bread and butter will be coming from in 1994.

On the upside, however, are less flashy covers and the fact that Marvel has some really

DAVE
HOOVER

fantastic characters waiting for some good solid writing. Depending on the attitude we see in 1994, they could strengthen the #1 position or lose it entirely.

Other Publishers

Was this the year of too many new universes or what? Who won and who lost? While there are still several players and not everything has shaken out yet, we have some observations and predictions.

Ultraverse has clearly been the Rookie of the Year. It has shown a great marketing direction and pulled a good market share. Dark Horse's Comic's Greatest World was a sleeper and caused some early speculation that it had come and gone, but it is steadily gaining ground as we move into its second summer weekly push.

Dark Horse's licensed lines (*Aliens*, *Predator*, *Indiana Jones*, *Star Wars*, etc.) are also making a very good showing. Although Defiant and Continuity started relatively strong, our customers quickly grew tired of Jim Shooter's constant industry posturing and Continuity's inconsistent shipping schedule. (Thus, Defiant remained so towards sales and Continuity didn't have any!)

As we also predicted early in 1993, Image has gained its second wind and some business maturity and has stabilized its print runs and recently published some hot books. Is this for real this time? We'll wait and see.

Valiant has continued to slow since dropping the artificially high print runs based on speculation. We've noticed a lot of Valiant readers moving to Ultraverse. New readers are just not interested in Valiant's convoluted storylines. Lastly, a big round of applause to small press publishers who garnered a lot of public notice this year. *Vampirella*, *Bone*, *Lady Death*, and *Bru-Hed* were all instant sellouts.

Silver Age

Sales on high-grade Silver Age issues were very brisk and picked up throughout 1993. However, mid-to-lower-grade issues mostly sat around and collected dust. We've noticed a definite shift toward later years in the category, as early issues have shot up beyond the means of the average collector. Dell and Dell Four-Color photo covers have really gotten hot, as well as later Marvel issues. DC Silver Age is pretty even throughout the period.

Golden Age

Because of the price tags, we haven't seen a lot of key issues in this period, but we've noticed many collectors looking for less-renowned issues from this age. Values on secondary Golden Age properties are definitely rising as the average collector turns his attention to them.

Additional Comments

We think 1993 will be remembered as the year the baseball card dealers realized that they weren't going to make a million dollars overnight in the comics industry and backed out.

We weren't sorry to see them go! Even though we all experienced a few pangs with the shudders the business went through and the multitude of products throughout the summer and fall of 1993, it was a good period of growth, and we experienced many new faces coming through the doors.

Meredith S. Woodwell
Zanadu Comics
Seattle, WA
Northwest

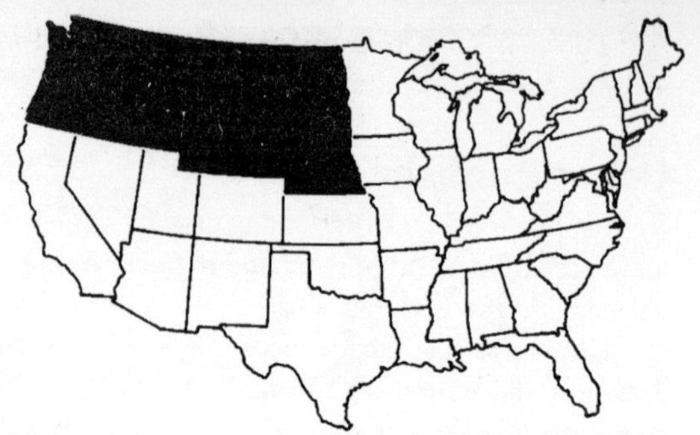

Overwhelmed by the vast quantity of books being produced, the overabundance of glitzy, high-priced covers, rocketing back issue prices, and progressive late shipping of their favorite titles, fans began leaving the marketplace in droves.

September 1993 through March 1994 were some of the leanest months this industry has seen in a long time. Now we hear how publishers are tightening their editorial control, focusing on quality and character-driven stories, and slimming down their product lines. The result? "It was the best of times, it was the worst of times." pretty well sums up this last year in the comics industry.

DC

1993 roared in with the "Reign of Superman" and "Batman: Knightfall" storylines from DC and the arrival of a new superhero universe-DC's Milestone. Reasons? Overcrowding in the marketplace caused DC to trim some of its "deadweight" titles and focus its energies on the core titles that have been their strength for so many years.

Thus, we see the continued success of the Superman, Batman, Green Lantern, and the Justice League titles. Horror (Vertigo titles) is making a comeback! Some titles that ran out of steam for DC were *Deathstroke*, *The Heckler*, and the *Demon* (not even Garth Ennis's writing has helped).

DC books that are sure to be big sellers are early "Zero Hour" tie-ins (*Valor*, *LSH*, *Legionnaires*) and "Crisis on Infinite Earth" back issues. *Sandman* and *Hellblazer* should be big while Gaiman and Ennis finish their runs.

Marvel

"Daredevil: Fall from Grace" was a big seller from the House of Ideas. The speculator market was at its peak with instant sellouts of *Moon Knight* #55-58 featuring artwork by wunderkind Steven Platt. All of the X-books remained solid. The *Fantastic Four*, *Daredevil*, and *Captain America* all gained new directions, which so far seem to be working.

Marvel UK and Frontier lines are dead. However, comics to look out for from Marvel are *Captain America* and *Fantastic Four*.

There has been a general downtrend in the market. Some of this drop-off may be due to cover-price increases (up to 20%) by Marvel and DC, which comprise 60% of the current market.

For fans on a fixed budget, this means cutting out those marginal titles, usually the low-end books, so they can keep buying their favorites, usually the high-end books.

Thus, sales on low-end comic books decline, while the high-end sales remain steady.

Bloodshot © Voyager Communications

Increased competition from high-volume discount stores such as WalMart may also be a factor.

Other Publishers

This year showed some interesting developments in the independent comics with Malibu's Ultraverse, Dark Horses's Comics Greatest World creating new universes, and Valiant back issues pulling in $100 plus.

Two new creator-owned imprints from Dark Horse and Malibu (Legends and Bravura, respectively) have been welcomed to wide acclaim. This expansion leads to a greater diversity of product available within the market.

We've already seen the establishment of other media (*Star Wars*), humor (*Bone*), and horror (Vertigo). How long until we have romances and Westerns gaining popularity, too? Not only does this type of diversification mean more variety for current comics readers but it also means we have a better chance of capturing the attention of some noncomics readers and pulling them into our little slice of heaven.

Independent books for whom the bell tolls: Dark Horse *Spike Lee* comics, *Atlas,* and *Hammer of God*; Image's *Trencher, Spoof, and Images of Shadowhawk*; Valiant's *Archer and Armstrong* (Barry Windsor-Smith left big shoes to fill) and *Eternal Warrior*.

Comics to look out for: Jeff Smith's *Bone*; James Owen's *Starchild*; anything from the Legend and Bravura imprints; anything from *Star Wars, The Crow, The Mask, and Tank Girl*; and Defiant's "Schism." (Remember what "Unity" did for Valiant sales?)

Mark Haverty & Don Bouchard Crisis Comics Winooski, VT

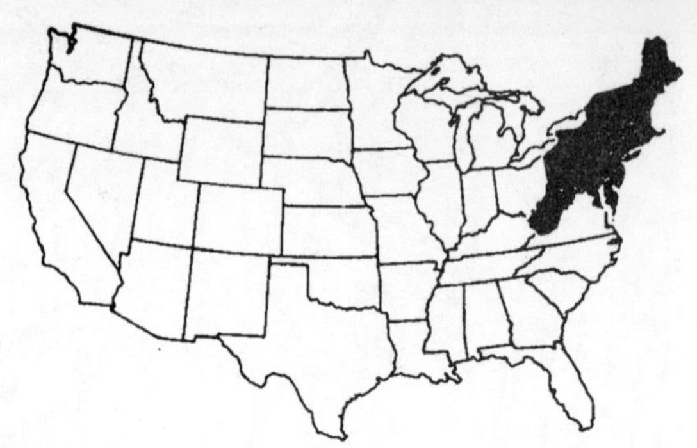

Northeast

DC

Without DC, there would not have been a light at the end of the tunnel for over ordered books. DC Comics has been great at bringing new people into the stores! They killed off Superman, they brought him back; they broke the Bat's back; and they are responsible for two of the greatest adaptations of comic book characters in other media-*Batman: The Animated Series* and *Lois and Clark*. All of these things have brought people back to a hobby that they had left years ago. And this time, they have kids; kids who also like the books! We, like many other stores, have a subscription service, and we have had more people become regular subscription customers because of the Superman titles than any other title.

DC is also at the forefront when it comes to new books. When a new Marvel comes out, the usual reaction is "Why?" Not with DC. Why? Because DC still puts an effort into its books. The company logo in the corner is no longer enough to sell a book. Marvel doesn't know this yet but DC does.

Superboy was beautiful. It is one of the best new books in years. *Steel* has also been very well done. *Robin* is the best Batman book out. *Catwoman* is also well done, more so when she isn't involved with the anti-Bat, Az-Bat, or whatever his name is! We didn't expect much from *Damage*, but we're pleasantly surprised. And then there was *The Ray: The Ray* was great! Anyone out there who hasn't tried these titles should.

The outlook for DC is great. "Zero Hour" is one of the most talked-about crossovers in years. *Crisis on Infinite Earths* was a great series, but DC dropped the ball and made a mess again. With "Zero Hour" and "Zero Month" DC will have a new beginning, another chance to start over right.

Marvel

It's Marvel only in name, as the things that made it great are no longer there. The X-books still sell, but not the same as they used to, and to a whole new market. The X-books cater to a lower age group now, the one that watches the cartoon. (As a side note: Marvel should learn from DC that you don't have to butcher storylines and characters to make a comic into a cartoon. Hey, guys, watch *Batman* if you want to learn something!) The X-Men were built on strong characterization and long, drawn-out plotlines. Chris Claremont's *X-Men* was a mature superhero book, a team book that an adult could feel good about reading and a kid could love as well. Bob Harras and Marvel have abandoned the adults!

Marvel is also trying to drown us all in its books again this year, as it continues the mighty Marvel tradition of beating a hot character to death. Four Spidey books, two (two!!) reprint books, a quarterly, and a future book. And they still think that they need at

JIM BALENT '94

least four Spidey miniseries this year, along with one for that incredibly popular character, the Black Cat (if the cover says "Because you demanded it!" I won't be able to control myself). They are beating Venom to death as well. Sales have dropped after every series. If Marvel wants a regular Venom out on the market, there are two things it should do. First, it should make it a monthly book, as people tire quickly of perpetual minis. (A perfect example of this is Dark Horse's *Aliens*.) Second, it needs to decide if Venom is a good guy or a bad guy. Each miniseries says the opposite of the one before! Try making him into a good guy, and people won't read and won't care.

One Marvel book that has not been a disappointment is *Wolverine*. This new storyline by Larry Hama has been great. The art by Adam Kubert makes this book not only great to read but great to look at as well.

Other Publishers

Let's start off with Image. Image is becoming what it always should have been-monthly. The books are finally getting here on time, and this does help. The only problem now is getting Mr. McFarlane, who used to be the most consistent, back on schedule. Spawn/Batman was great, with an excellent story by Frank Miller. *Spawn* was also great in the hands of Grant Morrison and Greg Capullo.

Then there is Platt. *Prophet* is great. I would just like to take this moment to thank the people at Extreme for Prophet 4A, the Platt cover. Less than 20% of all covers being done by Platt sure helps a book go up in value (we got $20 for it). Many people didn't look at *Newmen* because they thought it would be another "Liefeld-clone." It wasn't. It was a very enjoyable book with a good story and beautiful art. Try it. You'll thank us later!

Valiant has been great for retailers. It has consistent sales and will not glut the market. Also, it shows that it truly does care about the retailers. Paul Fairchild from Valiant calls our store and many others every few months to see what is hot on the market, and he does not mean just his stuff. This shows a deep concern and appreciation for the dealers who help them. (And they don't have a Valiant Mart!) *Ninjak* is a well-written title, and I hope that people don't stop getting it because Quesada walked. *Dr. Mirage* continues to be a well-written and well-drawn title and is not only one of Valiant's best titles but one of the best overall.

People talk about how well the Ultraverse is doing. For us, after one month, the books died. We are lucky to sell more than two copies of any given title from the Ultraverse! The books may be well done but people are turned off to Ultraverse because of the rigid continuity.

Yes, Valiant does this also, but Valiant grew slowly. Malibu did not, and that is where it made its mistake. Had it waited four to six months between the launch of new titles, Malibu would be the king of the hill.

Dark Horse is a consistent seller, very similar to Valiant. Dark Horse has built up a core following and (while still trying to gain new readers) caters to them. Dark Horse has done a great job with the Star Wars line. Tom Veitch has done an excellent job telling the tales of Luke, Leia, Han, Lando, and company. *Star Wars* still sells without Tom's name but not as well. We have had at least two different people tell us that they want only Veitch *Star Wars* on their subscriptions. Finally, we would like to mention Dave Sim and *Cerebus*. Many people talk about all of the new and wonderful black-and-white books out there. Well, Dave is the father of them all. *Cerebus* is, every month, one of the best black-and-white books in existence. Dave, if you read this, thank you!

Gary Ramos
California Comics
Covina, CA
Southwest

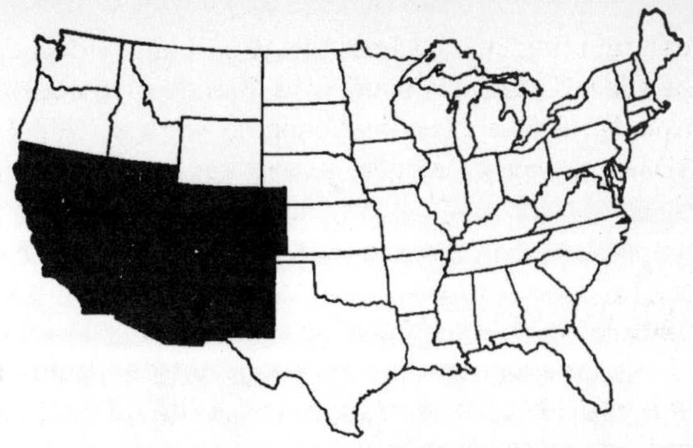

DC

Without a doubt, the Batman/Spawn crossover created the best-selling DC books of the year. We sold out immediately, restocked, and sold out again and again! All of our Superman orders are consistently high. *Superman*, *Adventures of Superman*, *Man of Steel,* and especially *Action* are definitely our best-selling DC titles. *Detective*, *Legends of the Dark Knight*, *Shadow of the Bat*, and *Batman* are also very steady in terms of year-long sales. Other DC titles that did well for us during the past year were *Green Lantern* #46-50, *Catwoman* #1, *Robin* #1, *Sandman*, and all Elseworlds titles.

The DC back issue market was fairly strong. Many customers picked up back issue "Knightfall" titles, as well as "Death of Superman," all Doomsday issues, and "Funeral for a Friend" parts 1-8. *Spectre* and *Green Arrow* are also showing strong back issue support. *Anima*, *Darkstars*, *Outsiders*, *Gunfire*, and *Black Orchid* were our worst-selling DC titles.

Marvel

Marvel, I'm sure, has had a very profitable year. It constitutes (and will probably continue to do so) the bulk of our new and back issue sales. Our best-selling Marvel titles throughout the year are, without a doubt, *X-Men* and *Uncanny X-Men*, with *Wolverine* in the next place. *Spider-Man*, *Amazing Spider-Man*, *Web of Spider-Man*, *Spectacular Spider-Man*, and *Spider-Man 2099* are very consistent-selling Marvel titles, as are *Silver Surfer*, *Avengers*, *Hulk*, and *Fantastic Four*.

Other Marvel titles that did well for us in the past year were the *Marvels* #1-4, *Gambit* #1 and #2, *Venom* #1-6, *Daredevil* #319-325, *Fantastic Four* #381, *Sabretooth* #1-4, all *Punisher* "Suicide Run" issues, *Beavis and Butthead*, *Ren and Stimpy*, *Daredevil: Man Without Fear,* all first issue *2099* titles, as well as all *Marvel Unlimited* first issues. These were red hot at the time of release and were very profitable for us. The Marvel back issue market was very strong this year. We've sold many back issues of *Ren and Stimpy*, *Moon Knight* #55-57, *Fantastic Four* #381, *Wolverine*, *Daredevil*, *Spider-Man*, and *Punisher*.

But nothing can compare to the unbelievable back issue sales of *Uncanny X-Men*, *X-Factor*, and/or any X-Men related titles or crossovers! Our customers buy these recent or older back issue *X-Men* as if they were in scarce supply. During our sales, they brought them up to the counter in stacks!

Other Publishers

It must have been a wild ride this year for many of the better known independents as sales have plummeted to an all-time low, with the exception of Image (of course!). Our year-long sales on *Spawn*, *WildC.A.T.S.*, *Cyberforce*, *Pitt*, and *Savage Dragon* are still reasonably high, though nowhere as high as when the company first emerged. Our preorders on *Wetworks* were very high, but our best-selling single independent comic was Spawn/Batman. *Spawn* was and is our most successful monthly independent title, with *WildC.A.T.S.* coming in at second place. *Sin City* remains the cult favorite and Defiant is dead!

Preorders in the past months for Valiant and Ultraverse are almost nonexistent, with the exception of *Ninjak* and *Turok* from Valiant. Dark Horse sales are low but consistent. It would appear that many of our customers have lost faith in the independents.

Back issue sales this past year were favorable for *Spawn*, *WildC.A.T.S.*, *Cyberforce*, *Pitt*, *Gen* [13], *Kindred*, *Simpsons*, *Star Wars* (Dark Horse), *Vampirella*, *Jurassic Park*, and older *Dark Horse Presents*.

Grifter and Backlash © Wildstorm Productions

Donald W. Riordan
Future Dreams
Portland, OR
Northwest

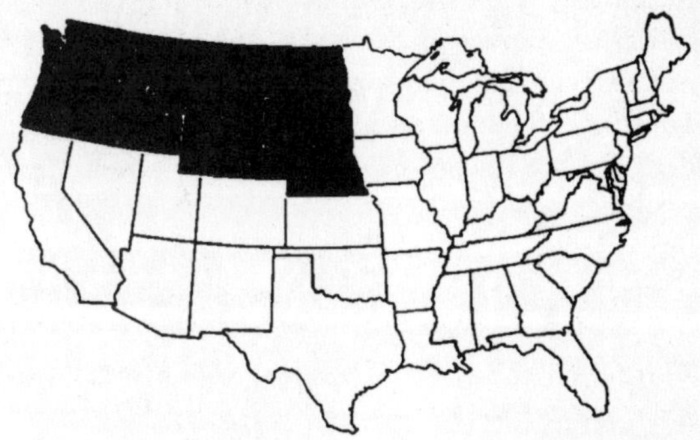

DC

The renovation of the flagship titles at DC continued with the "Reign of the Supermen" and Batman's "Knightfall." New issue sales with these heroes held strong through most of the year. This was partly due to the big change momentum and partly due to better-than-average storytelling. Let's all hope for the best when DC overhauls the entire line! Batman/Grendel made a very strong showing in sales and reader interest.

"Sword of Azrael" back issues shot up in price before gently falling back down, as demand was satisfied for many by the trade paperback edition. In fact, DC should be congratulated for rushing to market recent story collections at a reasonable price. It makes good sense in both sales and happy readers.

Other titles that held high interest included the following: *The Ray*, *Animal Man*, *The Demon*, *Golden Age*, *Kid Eternity*, *Outsiders*, *Sandman*, *Death*, *Shade the Changing Man*, and *Books of Magic*. We saw a jump in requests for key Silver Age DC's, including the war titles. Demand, of course, far outstripped supplies, pushing prices up again. The Milestone line is not selling as well as it should. Do yourself a favor and take a look!

Marvel

A tremendous amount of product was shipped from Marvel during 1993, but the X titles and Spider titles continue to produce the strongest sales. Many Marvel titles that used to always be strong, steady sellers have dropped down to their core readership level. New readers are not picking them up because most books are, at best, an average read with average artwork.

One exception to this trend is the Unlimited line of titles. They are better, and the sales and growing readership prove it. Sales are down on Marvel UK, Ghost Rider Family, Clive Barker Family, 2099 titles, Punisher titles, and the Avenger Groups. Marvel has had spectacular success when it puts out top-notch, limited-run stories like *Daredevil: Man Without Fear* and *Marvels*. And everyone was caught short of *Moon Knight* #55-57 because Marvel didn't know what it had and failed to promote the work of Stephen Platt properly! Marvel will always bring in great new talent, but perhaps now is the time to develop some methods of keeping the best talent around a bit longer.

Other Publishers

Cerebus is selling steadily. The interesting trend here is that more customers are dropping the monthly in favor of waiting for the trade paperback collections. *Bone* is a hit! Fun to read and look at. *Love & Rockets* is steady and way too far apart. *The Crow* back issues are in high demand. *Elfquest* titles are also very steady as new issues but very

littleback issue interest exists. *Hate* and *Eightball* are steady sellers, as are back issues of *Faust* and *Cry for Dawn*.

Spawn, new and back issues, is still on the top of the sales charts. Interest in other Image titles consistently wanes in the long gaps between issues. The readers are speaking with their dollars as sales continue to drop. The books continue to look sharp and can give any average Marvel a run for its money. If they want to see a growth in readership, the books must come out on time!

Valiant has more and more issues entering the marketplace. Their current titles are average at best, and they have very few new readers. Dark Horse fans have strong interest in the great *Star Wars* issues and readership is growing on the Comics Greatest World titles. Interest in Aliens and Predator titles is fading, but another movie may help. *The Mask* is receiving additional interest due to the 1994 movie starring Jim Carrey. Malibu Ultraverse has better than average sales but shows weak growth in a very crowded market.

Thomas J. Mulvey
Jolly Roger's Comics
Arlington, VA
Southeast

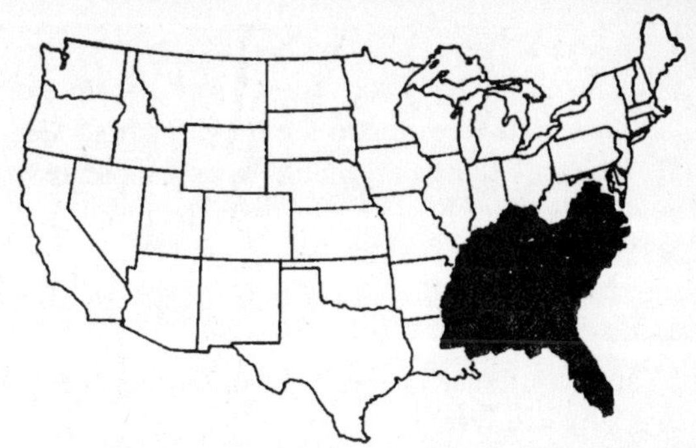

DC

Milestone launched onto the comic scene with the not-so-friendly hoods from Blood Syndicate, the ever-cool *Hardware*, and the mighty *Icon*. Well done, gentlemen! My hat's off to you and your creations! DC's other half, Vertigo, steamed on to bring us a new line with *Sandman Mystery Theater* and items such as *Sebastion O*. Comics aren't just for kids anymore!

With good stories, popularity, and the Death Statue, the desire was seen for more *Sandman* stories. A really interesting item was "Newstime," the magazine that covered the death of a great legend. (Great profits also, but that wasn't covered!)

Other crime fighters were getting bogged down with maniacal killers as Batman was having a bad week with his own brand of injustice. The Legionnaires arrived with new talent, and the artwork of Chris Sprouse continued on, giving a fresh feeling to a new book.

DC was very active at the time with the return of Supermen. These items kept the readers going with great action and good art. Stories filled the reader with that burning question, "Who is the real man of steel?"

As for artwork, Mike Grell displayed some fantastic art on *Green Arrow* covers while "mental art" was painted by the master hand of Neil Gaiman on his *Sandman* series.

DC gained strength from Batman's fall and Superman's return. Vertigo (as well as Milestone) comics grew in popularity and are still holding fast. With the *Golden Age* comic book leading the charge, *Elseworlds* later took the point in 1994.

Marvel

Marvel delivered a hellish surprise with *Hellstorm* and a sticky surprise at $3.95 for *Spider-Man Unlimited*. Is it the price or the comic that's unlimited? The big man with the bigger guns "bodyslid" into our lives with the enhanced cover to *Cable* #1. Now that looks like the real thing and not a later Image clone!

Whatever happened to that awesome spider armor from *Web of Spiderman* #100?

Marvel gave us another holy war as *Infinity Crusade* asked the eternal question: What is really good and do really we need it?

The most impressive thing to come about sprung from the pages of the X-Men. *X-Men Unlimited* ($3.95 again) had great stories and very nice visuals. I don't like the X-Men that much but this book won me over. For good writing, just pick up a Peter David *Hulk*. Nuff said!

A new player showed his 90s style as the powerful *Thunderstrike* plowed into our imagination. The "Fatal Attractions" X-Men storyline continued on and X-Men abounded as *X-Men 2099* leapt into the fray. Without fear, so did *Daredevil: Man Without Fear.*

The only thing that should have been feared was the lame line of Marvel/British titles, and Wolverine should have known fear as he lost the indestructible metal in his body from #75.

The *Marvels* book took the industry by storm. "Fatal Attractions" from the X-books rocked the universe and *Punisher* went off on "Suicide Run." Who can forget *Daredevil*'s "Fall from Grace" series? Last, but not least, was the popular *Gambit* miniseries with work by Lee Weeks.

Other Publishers

The independent scene looked stronger with *Aliens: Colonial Marines* and books such as *Cry for Dawn.* Now half of *CFD* is going to Sirius (a new publishing house). Does this make the other half silly?

Speaking of silly, let's look at Image! *Maxx* plopped onto the floor fully purple with no lower jaw. One neat thing was the Cerebus appearance in *Spawn* #10. At least we had good works by other companies as *Terminal Drift* by Neotek gave us cyberpunk at its best. Valiant also gave us a good book with *Rai and the Future Force.*

For the second quarter of the year, there was an onslaught of books from Image. With titles such as *Bloodstrike*, *Brigade*, *1963*, *Shaman's Tears*, and the Frank Miller-styled *Deathblow*, the flood of comics hits us all full force.

Little-known books crept in and held on with incredible stories and entertaining artwork. Two such books are *Sugarvirus*, a delectable vampire book from jolly old England, and *Bone*. *Bone* caught everyone with their orders down and surged forward to catch the readers, attention.

A favorite comic that later became a Sega video game reappeared in a collected format called *Chakan the Forever Man.*

By the summer, Image/Valiant buying had reached an all-time high. The rage was on for both companies. Unfortunately, because Image was so damn late, most shops got screwed with late arrivals that were not returnable! Stores were forced to swallow thousands of dollars in lost revenue from boxes deep of unsold Image. Thanks guys!

Deathmate was the perfect name for that book. Not only was it high-priced, but we had to wait again for Image to do its part. Valiant came out, sold well, and moved on.

To enhance your reading pleasure, Valiant released the *Valiant Vision* kits. Those new 3-D glasses were excellent! The colors came out best on *Ninjak* #1 and *Bloodshot* #0.

At least Defiant came out on time. *Plasm* had a slower start than we expected but has held on, for now. A fine concept turned partial reality was *Donna Matrix*, a fully computer- generated comic. Where's #2? Most people don't get to see *The Dark*. This book comes out very slowly but holds a strong grip on its readership.

Malibu had a surprise for us all with its new Ultraverse line. Sales were low at first, but demand grew as more people started getting into *Prime*, *Hardcase*, *Mantra*, *Freex*, *Strangers*, and *Exiles*.

Dark Horse has the right idea with *The Shadow*. Good book and a movie too, starring Alec Baldwin. Also from Dark Horse, now we finally get *Tales of the Jedi* in our greedy hands. Another noteworthy independent (reaching all ages) was Bongo Comics' *Simpsons* and *Itchy and Scratchy*.

YOU DON'T KNOW WHAT YOU'RE SAYING, HARDCASE! BUT THAT'S OKAY.

FROM NOW ON NOBODY'S GOING TO SAY THAT *PRIME* ACTS LIKE A *KID*... OR EVEN A *TEENAGER*.

THEY'RE JUST GOING TO SAY THAT *PRIME* ACTS LIKE A *HERO!*

THE ADVENTURES OF THE **NEW PRIME** WILL CONTINUE IN PRIME #17

... WHILE PRIME AND HARDCASE WORK TOGETHER EVERY MONTH IN THE ULTRAVERSE'S NEWEST ULTRA-COMIC...

ULTRAFORCE!

50

Walt Dittrich
Sin City Comics
Las Vegas, NV
Southwest

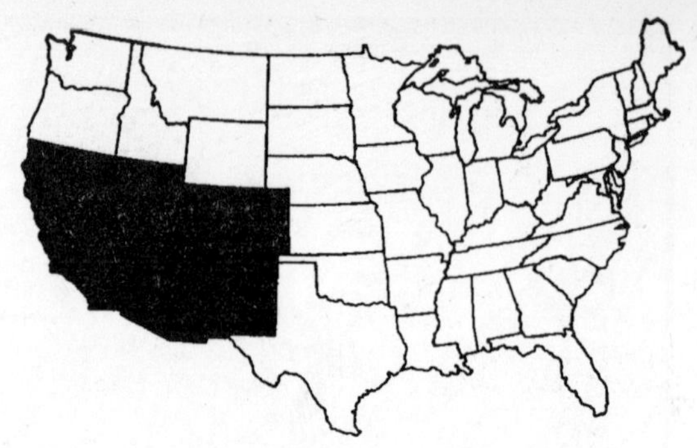

DC

This past year, we've seen the return of Superman, the fall of Batman, the "fall" of Hal Jordan, the formations of "Zero Hour," and several very successful new titles (*Steel*, *Superboy*, *Supergirl*, *Robin*, *Catwoman*)-all amounting to a tremendous year for DC. I see it only getting better! "Zero Hour's" zero-issue month in August should result in many new DC readers picking up titles they never would have before, and in the end, I'm sure many will stay for the long run.

I am very impressed with DC's marketing, more so than its stories or artwork (which are both much better than they're given credit for). DC's marketing department, which used to be based just on Batman and Superman, has enticed readers to pick up their books, many for the first time, and get interested.

I'm sure DC will always put out duds like *Gunfire*, but when you're selling out of titles like *Justice League*, *Guy Gardner*, and *Valor*(!), something is really clicking.

I'd like to make a prediction that this time next year, DC's market share is going to be within a few percentage points of Marvel (as opposed to the five to ten points that they differ now). The *Batman* cartoon and *Superman* TV show are both great, but how about getting more cartoons out like Marvel and Image? Get even more attention to these great books!

Marvel

If it weren't for the X-titles and the (I believe) soon-to-be-hot-again Spider-Man titles, DC would surpass Marvel. These poor guys! The Marvel Mart catastrophe has upset many retailers. I hear from more and more that they (the retailers) are not going to recommend Marvel titles and they're going to cut orders back just to cover club members. This is coming at a time when DC is ready to pounce.

The big powerhouse that was Marvel got complacent, which allowed companies like Image, Malibu, and Valiant to eat up its market share! Now Marvel seems to be stumbling to get those readers back. Marvel UK didn't do it and the Barkerverse didn't do it. Marvel doesn't have enough mature reader titles like *Sachs and Violens* to bring in new readers (hint, hint).

So what do they do? Bring on more X-titles. Hey, if something works, don't fix it! Another *Deadpool* series, *Generation X*, *Bishop* limited series, *Rogue* limited series-all coming out shortly and all sure to be sellouts.

Rather than have one X-Men crossover, this summer Marvel is doing a few smaller crossovers that, of course, will lead into the big event-*Generation X*. If it can keep this title from becoming another *New Mutants*, we'll all be happy.

Marvel believes Spider-Man hasn't had enough problems, so it's running him through the ringer. Several fans have started paying attention, but there's going to have to be more high-profile events to get more people involved now rather than have another "Fall from Grace" prologue on our hands. Sure, they sell well as back issues, but who wants to rake people over the coals with high back issue prices when we could have sold them when they were new, if the customer had known what was going on.

Other Publishers

We've seen the exodus of the speculators (thank gosh!). Now let's get back down to the basics: good stories with good artwork. Leading the way: Ultraverse, without a doubt, the best new universe in a long, long time. When Malibu starts shipping these books on time, look for interest to increase even further (yes, it is possible!). Great ad campaigns outside the comics realm continue to bring in new comic readers.

Likewise, mature reader titles like those from Dark Horse and Innovation (a great loss when they closed) just continuously garner more interest for our fantastic hobby.

Glut this past year? Maybe. Mayhaps it wouldn't have been a glut if enough high-quality product had come out. Though the bigger companies should work toward that goal, it seems the independent companies do it best.

With Quesada off *Ninjak*, Valiant would be done for were it not for this "Chaos Effect." "The Next Unity" won't make them explode like its predecessor but hopefully will hook enough new readers, or at least bring back the old ones, to make it worthwhile.

This year, the hottest titles are going to be scantily clad female books. A trend has already begun with *Lady Death*, *Vengeance of Vampirella*, *Shi*, *Penthouse Comix,* and (where can I get it?) *Gen* ^{13}. Selling out like crazy down here! DC's even catching on with its *Vamps* Vertigo title.

I only hope retailers properly display these books to avoid bad press from some mother whose kid was able to purchase *Vampirella: A Scarlett Thirst.* It's just a fad, like black-and-whites a few years back, but if it attracts new readers it can't be bad.

DYNAMIC CHANGES

IN THE DC UNIVERSE

By Robert J. Sodaro

Things change. Sometimes for better, sometimes for worse; and sometimes they just change.

Nowhere could this be more evident than by viewing the recent history of DC Comics. In 1992, Superman, the grandfather to this entire industry, died, proving once and for all that "Yes, Virginia, the good guys don't always win."

Despite a huge increase in sales for the entire comics industry, complaints reached the DC offices because of the enormous amount of national media attention. "A lot of people were complaining about the hype DC generated from the death of Superman," said Superman group editor Mike Carlin. "All we did was put out our order forms!"

Within days of the special bagged edition, *Superman* #75 hitting the racks, new customers stormed comic book shops across the country, and prices for the issue skyrocketed to as high as $100 in some stores. "We were just writing stories," Carlin said. "And quite honestly, if something that we published for $2.50 goes for $100, we don't get a penny of it."

While the epic battle of Superman versus Doomsday equaled that of any champion's from the *Odyssey* or the *Iliad*, Batman got a raw deal as he was battered from pillar to post by every criminal in Arkham Asylum and had his back broken by a hoodlum on supersteriods.

Batman's good name and rep were then further tarnished by his handpicked replacement (Azrael), who turned out not to be a savior in an armored batsuit but an off-kilter anti hero who was so into following his own lights that he suited up, spaced out, and went psycho!

According to Batman group editor Denny O'Neil, it is possible to alter a legend. "After fifty-five years, we're not bound by the rules anymore," he stated. "We're manipulating our audience's expectations and *using them against them.*" O'Neil went on to say that after the *Batman* movies and the animated TV show, there was a perception that the comic book character was running out of steam.

O'Neil was determined to do something that would change that perception. So even before news broke about Superman's impending demise, he laid the foundations for the fall and rise of the son of the night. "If you bring about the downfall of a character, you either have to bring him back or kill him," O'Neil revealed.

He went on to say that he always had the intention of bringing back Bruce Wayne as the Batman, but he wanted to really shake up the readership. "We were prepared to go as long as three years," he said. "Change is acceptable, so long as it is done for a good story and not just for the sake of change."

For store owners across the country, the "Death of Superman" and the "Knightfall" story lines brought in new customers and increased sales on DC titles. "The Death of Su-

Superman and Doomsday © DC Comics

perman' brought many new people into the stores," said Laurie Messer of Odin's Cosmic Bookshelf in Lilburn, Georgia. "The Knightfall" story lines also did wonderful, but 'Knightquest', which followed the 'Knightfall' series, was drawn out a little bit longer than the customers wanted and sales dropped off."

Mike Laz of Moondog's in Mt. Prospect, Illinois also agrees. "'The Death of Superman' and 'Knightfall' story lines brought new customers into our stores and increased our sales greatly," he said. "People who heard about the death of Superman or that Batman broke his back immediately came off the street looking for those comic books."

Looking back at the phenomenon created by the "Death of Superman," Laz believes that its success derived from an abundance of mass-media hype along with excellent continuity and good writing, which created additional interest that lasted after the first issue.

As for the future collectibility of the "Death of Superman" and "Knightfall" comics, Laz contends that they will always be available for the collectors at reasonable prices in the future. "Overall, there has been a steady decline in back issue market interest of both story lines," Laz said. "During the last few months, there has not been much change in prices on those books; fans will be able to buy them at below price guide value. The availability of trade paperbacks also hurts interest in back issues. People come into the store all the time looking to sell the 'Death of Superman' and 'Knightfall' comics, but we don't buy them because we have enough issues in stock."

Rising from the ashes of "Knightfall," the (somewhat) newly created character of Azrael assumed the Caped Crusader's costume. Hobbyists once frenzied pursuit of Azrael appearances, however, may be dead. "I believe that interest in Azrael is dead; the party is over," Laz said. "Collectors stopped buying the 'Knightquest' series halfway through the story line and came back to the Batman books, Knightsend, only because Bruce Wayne returned."

While store owners' and comics fans' collective heads were still reeling, the third in a seemingly ongoing series of punches then landed as Hal Jordan destroyed every Lantern Corps member in the universe! When Green Lantern delivered his own unique version of Johnny Paycheck's classic work tune, *"Take this Job and Shove It"*, the upsetting factor was that Hal Jordan had always been that part of us that followed all the rules, even when we didn't actually understand (or particularly like) them.

He was the part of our mass consciousness that kept order flowing in our society. Hal Jordan was the kind of guy who would sit in his car at midnight at a red light waiting for it to change rather than run it. He was an uptight, buttoned-down accountant in spandex.

But if we stop to think about it long enough, he actually had the coolest power ever.

Sure, Superman was the most powerful guy on the planet, but he was an alien! The only reason he was so strong was because of our yellow sun. If he had stayed on his native Krypton, he would have been an everyday, anonymous Joe just like the rest of us. Batman was the coolest because he had no special powers (he knew everything and could beat the stuffing out of every hood in town), but he was rich beyond belief, which puts him a little bit out of touch with the rest of us.

Green Lantern had that cool ring. Yeah, the ring. It could do anything he wanted it to do: make scissors, a sledgehammer, even a disembodied hand. Not only that, it automatically protected its wearer from all sorts of permanent harm. All he had to do was charge it up every couple of days or so. "In brightest day, in blackest night." Now there was a power to have. You could fly, go underwater, out in space, anything. Sure, he had to toe the line for those bald, blue-skinned, alien midgets, but what the heck! Everybody's got a boss, right?

But Hal Jordan's true bosses (the evil DC editors) really turned the tables on poor Mr. Jordan. So what if Hal's got the mightiest weapon in the whole universe? His hometown of Coast City has just been turned into fifty square miles of industrial waste, and everybody living in it is just a memory!

In a fit of paranoid depression, Hal strikes out at the most powerful authority he knows and heads straight at the heart and soul of the Green Lantern Corps: the planet OA. On the way, many of the other Corps' members fall to the might of Jordan's power ring, regrettably including one of his oldest and closest friends, Tomar-Re. Hal's oldest enemy, Sinestro, meets his maker after confronting Green Lantern; Kilowag, who taught Jordan to use the power of the ring, is also murdered by Jordan.

On OA, he taps the energy battery of the ring's power and becomes one with it and its awesome energies. After destroying the power battery and *all the other members of the Corps*, Green Lantern leaves OA to find his destiny. The last remaining Guardian, Ganthet, appoints the power of the ring to the last remaining Lantern in the Corps, Kyle Rayner.

So, Green Lantern became, essentially, a mad-dog mass murderer, and the character was irrevocably changed.

Once again, new shoppers rushed through the doors to grab their copies of the *Green Lantern*. "'Emerald Twilight' did real well, and actually got people to read *Guy Gardner*!" Messer said. "However, a lot of people dropped *Green Lantern* completely after the story line concluded."

Conversely, in Illinois and Vermont, it appeared that comic fans still followed the exploits of the power ring. "There are a lot of new readers still following the *Green Lantern* book," Laz said.

"Readers have stayed with the Green Lantern titles and like them," said Mark Haverty of Crisis Comics in Winooski, Vermont.

Greg Bazaz of M&M Comics feels that the 'Emerald Twilight' story line was terrific and one of the best available to fans during the past year. He also thinks the collectibility of *Green Lantern* issues #46-50 will remain high even if their value doesn't increase significantly. "The title is still holding people's attention even after Hal Jordan disappeared," Bazaz said. "It will not increase in price very much over the course of the next year, but it is definitely worth buying to read. In the long run, comic books that are fun to read are always sought by collectors."

Superman, Lazurus-like, rose from the dead. Batman's back will eventually mend, and we'll be seeing him answering the Batsignal once more, but Hal Jordan as the Green Lantern is gone forever.

Kevin Dooley, Green Lantern's editor, agreed. "We wanted to do some exciting stories; to do some exciting things," he said. "Green Lantern was the kind of character that people would go, 'Oh yeah, my dad read Green Lantern.' We wanted to make him interesting for readers in the '90s."

Recent events in the DC Universe have boosted the company's market share and new fans have joined the loyal DC legions in bunches. "The other companies don't seem to be picking up new customers the way DC has recently," Haverty said.

For those of us who have been around comic books for a few years, this new style of writing shakes the foundation of the one thing we were alway sure about in funny books: we knew that the good guys were going to win.

Superman was going to nab Lex Luthor, Batman was going to toss the Joker in the slammer, and Green Lantern was going to save the day. If not today, then perhaps tomor-

Batman, Nightwing and Robin © DC Comics

OH GOD.
KILOWOG.
I'M...SO SORRY.
Green Lantern © DC Comics

row and definitely the day after. Because, eventually, good will win out.

We can't really say that any more. Supes is back, but he's not quite the Boy Scout that he used to be, and Bruce will pull the gray-and-blue cowl over his head once again, and someone will eventually fear no evil and slip on that green-hewed ring once again, but are these heroes truly the ones that we remember?

Well, if they are not, do they actually have to be? If Superman was always the same as he ever was, why bother reading the book? Which is just the problem that Superman group editor Mike Carlin was faced with a couple of years ago. Why indeed?

"We aren't the doddering old dinosaur that everyone thought we were," O'Neil stated with grim finality, and he's right.

If DC can kill off Superman, cripple Batman, and psychologically destroy Green Lantern, then the comics world isn't as cut and dried as perhaps we once thought. And if these three heroes, arguably the oldest, most respected, and best-known superheroes the world has ever known, can be bent, folded, spindled, and mutilated, what can happen to the rest?

Will Hawkman's wings be clipped? Will Flash break a leg? Will Wonder Woman marry and settle down? Will Aquaman get the hook? How will we hold up to the vagaries of tomorrow?

Who knows? Yet still, with our comics future just a little less secure, the rules of order just a tad out of whack, doesn't our future become just that much more romantic? Is there perhaps just a little more of a thrill in the air? Can't you feel the excitement a touch more?

If all the above scenarios are true, then isn't our hobby that much more interesting than it was just a few years ago? While it is not this writer's intention to sanction wholesale slaughter of heroes, it is fair to say that stories where every aspect of the ending isn't necessarily a foregone conclusion make far more interesting reading than ones where the conclusion is a straight-up lock.

Where does that bring us? Right here. Right now. On the cutting edge of tomorrow. Here on this date, at this point in time, we stand together on the precipice of the cliff at the edge of the known comics universe world and gaze over the edge into the great unknown, where anything at all can happen, and it probably will.

ACTION
June, 1938

1 JoS,I&O:Superman;Rescues Evelyn Curry from electric chair . 85,000.00
2 JoS,V:Emil Norvell 7,500.00
3 JoS,V:Thorton Blakely . . . 6,750.00
4 JoS,V:Coach Randall 3,500.00
5 JoS,Emergency of Vallegho Dam 3,500.00
6 JoS,I:Jimmy Olsen, V:Nick Williams 3,400.00
7 JoS,V:Derek Niles 5,000.00
8 JoS,V:Gimpy 3,000.00
9 JoS,A:Det.Captain Reilly . 2,900.00
10 JoS,Superman fights for prison reform 4,500.00
11 JoS,Disguised as Homer Ramsey 1,650.00
12 JoS,Crusade against reckless drivers 1,650.00

Action Comics #13 © DC Comics, Inc.

13 JoS,I:Ultra Humanite 2,500.00
14 JoS,BKa,V:Ultra Humanite, B:Clip Carson 1,500.00
15 JoS,BKa,Superman in Kidtown 2,100.00
16 JoS,BKa,Crusade against Gambling 1,200.00
17 JoS,BKa,V:Ultra Humanite 1,800.00
18 JoS,BKa,V:Mr.Hamilton O:Three Aces 1,200.00
19 JoS,BKa,V:Ultra Humanite B:Superman (c) 1,600.00
20 JoS,BKa,V:Ultra Humanite 1,500.00
21 JoS,BKa,V:Ultra Humanite . 900.00
22 JoS,BKa,War between Toran and Galonia 900.00
23 JoS,BKa,SMo,I:Lex Luthor 1,900.00
24 JoS,BKa,BBa,SMo,FG,Meets Peter Carnahan 850.00
25 JoS,BKa,BBa,SMo,V:Medini 850.00
26 JoS,BKa,V:Clarence Cobalt 850.00
27 JoS,BKa,V:Mr & Mrs.Tweed 800.00
28 JoS,BKa,JBu,V:Strongarm Bandit 800.00
29 JoS,BKa,V:Martin 800.00
30 JoS,BKa,V:Zolar 800.00
31 JoS,BKa,JBu,V:Baron Munsdorf 650.00
32 JoS,BKa,JBu,I:Krypto Ray Gun V:Mr.Preston 650.00
33 JoS,BKa,JBu,V:Brett Hall, O:Mr. America 650.00
34 JoS,BKa,V:Jim Laurg 600.00
35 JoS,BKa,V:Brock Walter . . . 600.00
36 JoS,BKa,V:Stuart Pemberton 550.00
37 JoS,BKa,V:Commissioner Kennedy, O:Congo Bill 550.00
38 JoS,BKa,V:Harold Morton . . 550.00
39 JoS,BKa,Meets Britt Bryson 550.00
40 JoS,BKa,Meets Nancy Thorgenson 550.00
41 JoS,BKa,V:Ralph Cowan, E:Clip Carson 450.00
42 V:Lex Luthor,I&O:Vigilante . 800.00
43 V:Dutch O'Leary,Nazi(c) . . . 600.00
44 V:Prof. Steffens,Nazi(c) . . . 600.00
45 V:Count Von Henzel, I:Stuff,Nazi(c), ... 600.00
46 V:The Domino 550.00
47 V:Lex Luthor-1st app w/super powers,I:Powerstone 575.00
48 V:The Top 550.00
49 I:Puzzler 575.00
50 Meets Stan Doborak 550.00
51 I:Prankster 550.00
52 V:Emperor of America 550.00
53 JBu,V:Night-Owl 550.00
54 JBu,Meets Stanley Finchcomb 400.00
55 JBu,V:Cartoonist Al Hatt . . . 400.00
56 V:Emil Loring 400.00
57 V:Prankster 400.00
58 JBu,V:Adonis 400.00
59 I:Susie Thompkins,Lois Lane's niece 400.00
60 JBu,Lois Lane-Superwoman! 450.00
61 JBu,Meets Craig Shaw 350.00
62 JBu,V:Admiral Von Storff . . 350.00
63 JBu,V:Professor Praline . . . 350.00
64 I:Toyman 400.00
65 JBu,V:Truman Treadwell . . . 350.00
66 JBu,V:Mr.Annister 350.00
67 JBu,Superman School for Officer's Training 350.00
68 A:Susie Thompkins 350.00
69 V:Prankster 350.00
70 JBu,V:Thinker 350.00
71 Superman Valentine's Day Special 300.00
72 V:Mr. Sniggle 300.00
73 V:Lucius Spruce 300.00
74 Meets Adelbert Dribble 300.00
75 V:Johnny Aesop 300.00
76 A Voyage with Destiny 300.00
77 V:Prankster 300.00
78 The Chef of Bohemia 300.00
79 JBu,A:J. Wilbur Wolfingham 300.00
80 A:Mr. Mxyzptlk (2nd App) . . 500.00
81 Meets John Nicholas 300.00
82 JBu,V:Water Sprite 300.00
83 I:Hocus and Pocus 300.00
84 JBu,V:Dapper Gang 300.00
85 JBu,V:Toyman 300.00
86 JBu,V:Wizard of Wokit 300.00
87 V:Truck Hijackers 300.00
88 A:Hocus and Pocus 300.00
89 V:Slippery Andy 300.00
90 JBu,V:Horace Rikker and the Amphi-Bandits 300.00
91 JBu,V:Davey Jones 275.00
92 JBu,V:Nowmie Norman 275.00
93 Superman Christmas story . 275.00
94 JBu,V:Bullwer 'Bull' Rylie . . 275.00
95 V:Prankster 275.00
96 V:Mr. Twister 275.00
97 A:Hocus and Pocus 275.00
98 V:Mr. Mxyzptlk, A:Susie Thompkins 275.00
99 V:Keith Langwell 275.00
100 I:Inspector Erskine Hawkins 675.00
101 V:Specs Dour,A-Bomb(c) . 400.00
102 V:Mr. Mxyzptlk 285.00
103 V:Emperor Quexo 285.00
104 V:Prankster 285.00
105 Superman Christmas story 285.00
106 Clark Kent becomes Baron Edgestream 285.00
107 JBu,A:J.Wilbur Wolfingham 285.00
108 JBu,V:Vince Vincent 285.00
109 V:Prankster 285.00
110 A:Susie Thompkins 285.00
111 Cameras in the Clouds . . . 285.00
112 V:Mr. Mxyzptlk 285.00
113 Just an Ordinary Guy 275.00
114 V:Mike Chesney 275.00
115 Meets Arthur Parrish 275.00
116 A:J. Wilbur Wolfingham . . . 275.00
117 Superman Christmas story 275.00
118 The Execution of Clark Kent 275.00
119 Meets Jim Banning 275.00
120 V:Mike Foss 275.00
121 V:William Sharp 275.00
122 V:Charley Carson 275.00
123 V:Skid Russell 275.00
124 Superman becomes radioactive 300.00
125 V:Lex Luthor 375.00
126 V:Chameleon 275.00
127 JKu,Superman on Truth or Consequences 350.00
128 V:'Aces' Deucey 275.00
129 Meets Gob-Gob 275.00
130 V:Captain Kidder 275.00
131 V:Lex Luthor 275.00
132 Superman meets George Washington 275.00
133 V:Emma Blotz 275.00
134 V:Paul Strong 275.00
135 V:John Morton 275.00
136 Superman Show-Off! 275.00
137 Meets Percival Winter 275.00
138 Meets Herbert Hinkle 275.00
139 Clark Kent...Daredevil! . . . 275.00
140 Superman becomes Hermit 275.00
141 V:Lex Luthor 275.00
142 V:Dan the Dip 275.00
143 Dates Nikki Larve 275.00
144 O:Clark Kent reporting for Daily Planet 300.00
145 Meets Merton Gloop 275.00
146 V:Luthor 275.00
147 V:'Cheeks' Ross 275.00
148 Superman, Indian Chief . . 275.00
149 The Courtship on Krypton! 275.00
150 V:Morko 275.00
151 V:Mr.Mxyzptlk,Lex Luthor and Prankster 275.00
152 I:Metropolis Shutterbug Society 275.00
153 V:Kingpin 275.00
154 V:Harry Reed 275.00
155 V:Andrew Arvin 275.00
156 Lois Lane becomes Superwoman,V:Lex Luthor 275.00
157 V:Joe Striker 275.00
158 V:Kane Korrell O:Superman (retold) 500.00
159 Meets Oswald Whimple . . 250.00
160 I:Minerva Kent 250.00
161 Meets Antara 250.00
162 V:'IT!' 250.00
163 Meets Susan Semple 250.00
164 Meets Stefan Andriessen . 250.00
165 V:Crime Czar 250.00
166 V:Lex Luthor 250.00
167 V:Prof. Nero 250.00
168 O:Olaf 250.00
169 Caveman Clark Kent! 250.00
170 V:Mad Artist of Metropolis . 250.00
171 The Secrets of Superman . 250.00
172 Lois Lane..Witch! 250.00
173 V:Dragon Lang 250.00
174 V:Miracle Twine Gang . . . 250.00
175 V:John Vinden 250.00
176 V:Billion Dollar Marvin Gang 250.00
177 V:General 250.00
178 V:Prof. Sands 250.00

All comics prices listed are for *Near Mint* condition.

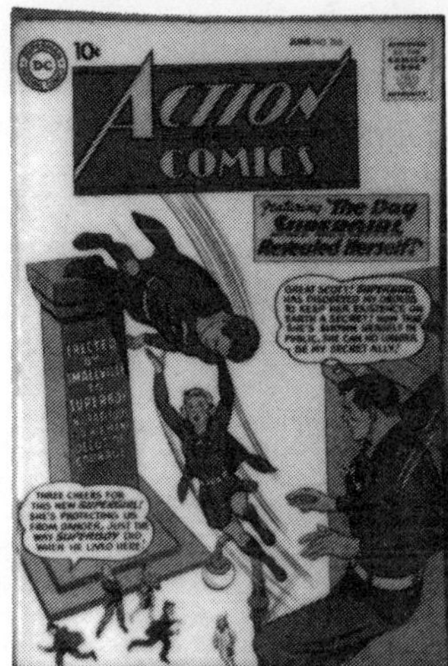

Action Comics #265 © DC Comics, Inc.

179 Superman in Mapleville . . . 250.00
180 V:Syndicate of Five 225.00
181 V:Diamond Dave Delaney . 225.00
182 The Return from Planet Krypton 225.00
183 V:Lex Luthor 225.00
184 Meets Donald Whitmore . . 225.00
185 V:Issah Pendleton 225.00
186 The Haunted Superman . . 225.00
187 V:Silver 225.00
188 V:Cushions Raymond gang 225.00
189 Meets Mr.&Mrs. John Vandeveir 225.00
190 V:Mr. Mxyzptlk 225.00
191 V:Vic Vordan 225.00
192 Meets Vic Vordan 225.00
193 V:Beetles Brogan 225.00
194 V:Maln 225.00
195 V:Tiger Woman 225.00
196 Superman becomes Mental Man 225.00
197 V:Stanley Stark 225.00
198 The Six Lives of Lois Lane 225.00
199 V:Lex Luthor 225.00
200 V:Morwatha 225.00
201 V:Benny the Brute 225.00
202 Lois Lane's X-Ray Vision . 225.00
203 Meets Pietro Paresca 225.00
204 Meets Sam Spulby 225.00
205 Sergeant Superman 225.00
206 Imaginary story featuring Lois Lane 225.00
207 Four Superman Medals! . 225.00
208 V:Mr. Mxyzptlk 225.00
209 V:'Doc' Winters 225.00
210 V:Lex Luthor,I:Superman Land 225.00
211 Superman Spectaculars . . 200.00
212 V:Thorne Varden 200.00
213 V:Paul Paxton 200.00
214 Superman,Sup.Destroyer! . 200.00
215 I:Superman of 2956 . . . . . 200.00
216 A:Jor-El 200.00
217 Meets Mr&Mrs.Roger Bliss 200.00
218 I:Super-Ape from Krypton . 200.00
219 V:Art Shaler 200.00
220 The Interplanetary Olympics 200.00
221 V:Jay Vorrell 150.00
222 The Duplicate Superman . 150.00
223 A:Jor-El 150.00
224 I:Superman Island 150.00
225 The Death of Superman . . 175.00
226 V:Lex Luthor 150.00
227 The Man with the Triple X-Ray Eyes 150.00
228 A:Superman Museum 150.00
229 V:Dr. John Haley 150.00
230 V:Bart Wellins 150.00
231 Sir Jimmy Olsen, Knight of Metropolis 150.00
232 Meets Johnny Kirk 150.00
233 V:Torm 150.00
234 Meets Golto 150.00
235 B:Congo Bill, B:Tommy Tomorrow 150.00
236 A:Lex Luthor 150.00
237 V:Nebula Gang 150.00
238 I:King Krypton,the Gorilla . 150.00
239 'Superman's New Face' . . 150.00
240 V:Superman Sphinx 150.00
241 WB,A:Batman,Fortress of Solitude (Fort Superman) . . 150.00
242 I&O:Brainiac 800.00
243 Lady and the Lion 125.00
244 CS,A:Vul-Kor,Lya-La 125.00
245 WB,V:Kak-Kul 125.00
246 WB,A:Krypton Island 125.00
247 WB,Superman Lost Parents 125.00
248 B&I:Congorilla 125.00
249 AP,A:Lex Luthor 125.00
250 WB,'The Eye of Metropolis' 125.00
251 AP,E:Tommy Tomorrow . . 125.00
252 I&O:Supergirl 900.00
253 B:Supergirl 225.00
254 I:Adult Bizarro 175.00
255 I:Bizarro Lois 125.00
256 'Superman of the Future' . . 75.00
257 WB,JM,V:Lex Luthor 75.00
258 A:Cosmic Man 75.00
259 A:Lex Luthor,Superboy 75.00
260 A:Mighty Maid 75.00
261 I:Streaky,E:Congorilla 75.00
262 A:Bizarro 60.00
263 O:Bizarro World 75.00
264 V:Bizarro 60.00
265 A:Hyper-Man 60.00
266 A:Streaky,Krypto 60.00
267 JM,3rd A:Legion,I:Invisible Kid 300.00
268 WB,A:Hercules 60.00
269 A:Jerro 60.00
270 CS,JM,A:Batman 60.00
271 A:Lex Luthor 60.00
272 A:Aquaman 50.00
273 A:Mr.Mxyzptlk 50.00
274 A:Superwoman 50.00
275 WB,JM,V:Braimiac 50.00
276 JM,6th A:Legion,I:Brainiac 5, Triplicate Girl,Bouncing Boy 135.00
277 CS,JM,V:Lex Luthor 50.00
278 CS,Perry White Becomes Master Man 50.00
279 JM,V:Hercules,Samson 50.00
280 CS,JM,V:Braniac, A:Congorilla 50.00
281 JM,A:Krypto 50.00
282 JM,V:Mxyzptlk 50.00
283 CS,JM,A:Legion of Super Outlaws 55.00
284 A:Krypto,Jerro 55.00
285 JM,Supergirl Existence Revealed, C:Legion (12th app.) 65.00
286 CS,JM,V:Lex Luthor 30.00
287 JM,A:Legion 30.00
288 JM,A:Mon-El 28.00
289 JM,A:Adult Legion 28.00
290 JM,C:Phantom Girl 28.00
291 JM,V:Mxyzptlk 28.00
292 JM,I:Superhorse 22.00
293 JM,O:Comet-Superhorse . . . 60.00
294 JM,V:Lex Luthor 22.00
295 CS,JM,O:Lex Luthor 24.00
296 V:Super Ants 22.00
297 CS,JM,A:Mon-El 22.00
298 CS,JM,V:Lex Luthor 22.00
299 O:Superman Robots 22.00
300 JM,A:Mxyzptlk 30.00

Action Comics #309 © DC Comics, Inc.

301 JM,O:Superhorse 15.00
302 JM,O:Superhorse 15.00
303 Red Kryptonite Story 15.00
304 CS,JM,I&O:Black Flame . . . 16.00
305 O:Supergirl 15.00
306 JM,C:Mon-El,Brainiac 5 . . . 15.00
307 CS,JM,A:Saturn Girl 15.00
308 V:Hercules 15.00
309 CS,A:Batman,JFK,Legion . . 17.00
310 CS,JM,I:Jewel Kryptonite . . 14.00
311 CS,JM,O:Superhorse 14.00
312 CS,JM,V:Metallo-Superman 14.00
313 JM,A:Supergirl,Lex Luthor, Batman 14.00
314 JM,A:Justice League 14.00
315 JM,V:Zigi,Zag 14.00
316 JM,A:Zigi,Zag,Zyra 14.00
317 JM,V:Lex Luthor 14.00
318 CS,JM,A:Brainiac 14.00
319 CS,JM,A:Legion,V:L.Luthor . 14.00
320 CS,JM,V:Atlas,Hercules . . . 14.00
321 CS,JM,A:Superhorse 14.00
322 JM,'Coward of Steel' 14.00
323 JM,A:Superhorse 14.00
324 JM,A:Abdul 14.00
325 CS,JM,SkyscraperSuperman 14.00
326 CS,JM,V:Legion of Super Creatures 14.00
327 CS,JM,C:Brainiac 14.00
328 JM,Hands of Doom 14.00
329 JM,V:Drang 14.00
330 CS,JM,Krypto 14.00
331 CS,V:Dr.Supernatural 14.00
332 CS,A:Brainiac 14.00
333 A:Lex Luthor 14.00
334 A:L.Luthor,(giant) 16.00
335 CSV:Lex Luthor 11.00
336 CS,O:Akvar 11.00
337 CS,V:Tiger Gang 11.00
338 CS,JM,V:Muto 11.00
339 CSV:Muto,Brainiac 11.00
340 JM,I:Parasite 12.00
341 CS,V:Vakox,A:Batman 9.00
342 WB,JM,V:Brainiac 9.00
343 WB,V:Eterno 9.00
344 WB,JM,A:Batman 9.00
345 A:Allen Funt 9.00
346 WB,JM, ... 9.00
347 A:Supergirl (giant size) 11.00
348 WB,JM,V:Acid Master 8.00
349 WB,JM,V:Dr.Kryptonite 8.00
350 A:JLA 8.00

351 WB,I:Zha-Vam 8.00
352 WB,V:Zha-Vam 8.00
353 WB,JM,V:Zha-Vam 8.00
354 JM,A:Captain Incredible 8.00
355 WB,JM,V:Lex Luthor 8.00
356 WB,JM,V:Jr. Annihilitor 8.00
357 WB,JM,V:Annihilitor 8.00
358 NA(c),CS,JM,A:Superboy . . . 8.00
359 NA(c),CS,KS,C:Batman 8.00
360 A:Supergirl,(giant size) 9.00
361 A:Parasite 7.00
362 RA,KS,V:Lex Luthor 7.00

Action Comics #313 © DC Comics, Inc.

363 RA,KS,V:Lex Luthor 7.00
364 RA,KS,V:Lex Luthor 7.00
365 A:Legion & J.L.A. 7.00
366 RA,KS,A:J.L.A. 7.00
367 NA(c),CS,KS,A:Supergirl 7.00
368 CS,KS,V:Mxyzptlk 7.00
369 CS,KS,Superman's Greatest
Blunder 7.00
370 NA(c),CS,KS, ... 7.00
371 NA(c),CS,KS, ... 7.00
372 NA(c),CS,KS, ... 7.00
373 A:Supergirl,(giant size) 10.00
374 NA(c),CS,KS,V:Super Thief . . 6.00
375 CS,KS,The Big Forget 6.00
376 CS,KS,E:Supergirl 6.00
377 CS,KS,B:Legion 6.00
378 CS,KS,V:Marauder 6.00
379 CS,JA,MA,V:Eliminator 6.00
380 KS,Confessions of Superman 6.00
381 CS,Dictators of Earth 6.00
382 CS,Clark Kent-Magician 6.00
383 CS,The Killer Costume 6.00
384 CS,The Forbidden Costume . 6.00
385 CS,The Mortal Superman . . . 6.00
386 CS,Home For Old Supermen 6.00
387 CS,A:Legion,Even
Supermen Die 6.00
388 CS,A:Legion,Puzzle of
The Wild Word 6.00
389 A:Legion,The Kid Who
Struck Out Superman 6.00
390 CS,'Self-Destruct Superman' . 6.00
391 CS,Punishment of
Superman's Son 6.00
392 CS,E:Legion 6.00
393 CS,MA,RA,A:Super Houdini . 4.50
394 CS,MA 4.50
395 CS,MA,A:Althera 4.50
396 CS,MA 4.50
397 CS,MA,Imaginary Story 4.50
398 NA(c),CS,MA,I:Morgan Edge . 5.00
399 NA(c),CS,MA,A:Superbaby . . 4.50
400 NA(c),CS,MA,Kandor Story . . 5.00
401 CS,MA,V:Indians 3.50
402 NA(c),CS,MA,V:Indians 3.50
403 CS,MA,Vigilante rep. 3.50
404 CS,MA,Aquaman rep 3.50
405 CS,MA,Vigilante rep. 3.50
406 CS,MA,Atom & Flash rep. . . . 3.50
407 CS,MA,V:Lex Luthor 3.50
408 CS,MA,Atom rep. 3.50
409 CS,MA,T.Tommorrow rep. . . . 3.50
410 CS,MA,T.Tommorrow rep. . . . 3.50
411 CS,MA,O:Eclipso rep. 5.00
412 CS,MA,Eclipso rep. 4.00
413 CS,MA,V:Brainiac 3.50
414 CS,MA,B:Metamorpho 3.50
415 CS,MA,V:Metroplis Monster . 3.50
416 CS,MA, ... 3.50
417 CS,MA,V:Luthor 3.50
418 CS,MA,V:Luthor,
E:Metamorpho 3.50
419 CS,MA,CI,DG,I:HumanTarget 3.50
420 CS,MA,DG,V:Towbee 3.50
421 CS,MA,B:Green Arrow 4.00
422 CS,DG,O:Human Target 3.00
423 CS,MA,DG,A:Lex Luthor 3.00
424 CS,MA,Green Arrow 3.50
425 CS,DD,NA,DG,B:Atom 3.50
426 CS,MA,Green Arrow 3.00
427 CS,MA,DD,DG,Atom 3.00
428 CS,MA,DG,Luthor 3.00
429 CS,BO,DG,C:JLA 3.00
430 CS,MA,DD,DG,Atom 2.75
431 CS,MA,Green Arrow 3.00
432 CS,MA,DG,Toyman 2.50
433 CS,BO,DD,DG,A:Atom 2.50
434 CS,DD,Green Arrow 3.00
435 FM(c),CS,DD,DG,Atom 2.50
436 CS,DD,Green Arrow 3.00
437 CS,DG,Green Arrow,
(100 page giant) 4.00
438 CS,BO,DD,Atom 2.50
439 CS,BO,DD,Atom 2.50
440 1st MGr Green Arrow 7.50
441 CS,BO,MGr,A:Green Arrow,
Flash,R:Krypto 6.00
442 CS,MS,MGr,Atom 3.00
443 CS,A:JLA(100 pg.giant) 4.50
444 MGr,Green Arrow 3.50
445 MGr,Green Arrow 3.50
446 MGr,Green Arrow 3.50
447 CS,BO,RB,KJ,Atom 2.50
448 CS,BO,DD,JL,Atom 2.50
449 CS,BO 2.50
450 MGr,Green Arrow 2.75
451 MGr,Green Arrow 2.75
452 CS,MGr,Green Arrow 2.75
453 CS,Atom 2.50
454 CS,E:Atom 2.50
455 CS,Green Arrow 2.75
456 CS,MGr,Green Arrow 2.75
457 CS,MGr,Green Arrow 2.75
458 CS,MGr,I:Black Rock 2.75
459 CS,BO,Blackrock 2.50
460 CS,I:Karb-Brak 2.50
461 CS,V:Karb-Brak 2.50
462 CS,V:Karb-Brak 2.50
463 CS,V:Karb-Brak 2.50
464 CS,KS,V:Pile-Driver 2.50
465 CS,FMc,Luthor 2.50
466 NA(c),CS,V:Luthor 2.50
467 CS,V:Mzyzptlk 2.50
468 NA(c),CS,FMc,V:Terra-Man . . 2.50
469 CS,TerraMan 2.50
470 CS,Flash Green Lantern 2.50
471 CS,V:Phantom Zone Female . 2.50
472 CS,V:Faora Hu-Ul 2.50
473 NA(c),CS,Phantom Zone
Villians 2.50
474 KS,V:Doctor Light 2.50
475 KS,V:Karb-Brak,A:Vartox . . . 2.50
476 KS,V:Vartox 2.50
477 CS,DD,Land Lords of Earth . . 2.50
478 CS,Earth's Last 2.50
479 CS 2.50
480 CS,A:JLA,V:Amazo 2.50
481 CS,A:JLA,V:Amazo 2.50
482 CS,Amazo 2.50
483 CS,Amazo,JLA 2.50
484 CS,W:Earth 2 Superman
& Lois Lane 3.00
485 NA(c),CS,rep.Superman#233 2.50
486 GT,KS,V:Lex Luthor 2.50
487 CS,AS,O:Atom 2.75
488 CS,AS,A:Air Wave 2.50
489 CS,AS,A:JLA,Atom 2.50
490 CS,Brainiac 2.50
491 CS,A:Hawkman 2.50
492 CS,'Superman's After Life' . . 2.50
493 CS,A:UFO 2.50
494 CS, ... 2.50
495 CS 2.50
496 CS,A:Kandor 2.50
497 CS 2.50
498 CS,Vartox 2.50
499 CS,Vartox 2.50
500 CS,Superman's Life Story
A:Legion 3.50
501 KS 2.00
502 CS,A:Supergirl,Gal.Golem . . . 2.00
503 CS,'A Save in Time' 2.00
504 CS,'The Power and Choice' . 2.00
505 CS 2.00
506 CS 2.00
507 CS,A:Jonathan Kent 2.00
508 CS,A:Jonathan Kent 2.00
509 CS,JSn,DG 2.25
510 CS,Luthor 2.00
511 CS,AS,V:Terraman,
A:Air Wave 2.00
512 CS,RT,V:Luthor,A:Air Wave . 2.00
513 CS,RT,V:Krell,A:Air Wave . . 2.00
514 CS,RT,V:Brainiac,A:Atom . . . 2.00
515 CS,AS,A:Atom 2.00
516 CS,AS,V:Luthor,A:Atom 2.00
517 CS,DH,A:Aquaman 2.00
518 CS,DH,A:Aquaman 2.00
519 CS,DH,A:Aquaman 2.00
520 CS,DH,A:Aquaman 2.00
521 CS,AS,I:Vixen,A:Atom 2.00
522 CS,AS,A:Atom 2.00
523 CS,AS,A:Atom 2.00
524 CS,AS,A:Atom 2.00
525 JSon,FMc,AS,I:Neutron,
A:Air Wave 2.00
526 JSon,AS,V:Neutron 2.00
527 CS,AS,I:Satanis,A:Aquaman . 2.50
528 CS,AS,V:Brainiac,A:Aq'man . 2.00
529 GP(c),CS,DA,AS,A:Aquaman,
V:Brainiac 2.00
530 CS,DA,Brainiac 2.00
531 JSon,FMc,AS,A:Atom 2.00
532 CS,C:New Teen Titans 2.00
533 CS,V:The. 2.00
534 CS,AS,V:Satanis,A:Air Wave . 2.00
535 GK(c),JSon,AS,
A:Omega Men 2.00
536 JSon,AS,FMc,A:Omega Men . 2.00
537 IN,CS,AS,V:Satanis
A:Aquaman 2.00
538 IN,AS,FMc,V:Satanis,
A:Aquaman 2.00
539 KG(c),GK,AS,DA,A:Flash,
Atom,Aquaman 2.00
540 GK,AS,V:Satanis 2.00
541 GK,V:Satanis 2.00
542 AS,V:Vandal Savage 2.00
543 CS,V:Vandal Savage 2.00
544 CS,MA,GK,GP,45th Anniv.
D:Ardora,Lexor 3.00
545 GK,Brainiac 2.00
546 GK,A:JLA,New Teen Titans . . 2.00
547 GK(c),CS 2.00
548 GK(c),AS,Phantom Zone 2.00
549 GK(c),AS, ... 2.00
550 AS(c),GT, ... 2.00
551 GK,Starfire becomes Red
Star 2.00
552 GK,Forgotten Heroes
(inc.Animal Man) 10.00

553 GK,Forgotten Heroes(inc. Animal Man) 9.00
554 GK 1.75
555 CS,A:Parasite (X-over Supergirl #20) 1.75
556 CS,KS,C:Batman 1.75
557 CS,Terra-man 1.75
558 KS 1.75
559 KS,AS 1.75
560 AS,KG,BO,A:Ambush Bug . . 1.75
561 KS,WB,Toyman 1.75
562 KS,Queen Bee 1.75
563 AS,KG,BO,A:Ambush Bug . . 1.75
564 AS,V:Master Jailer 1.75
565 KG,KS,BO,A:Ambush Bug . . 1.75
566 BO(i),MR 1.75
567 KS,AS,PB 1.75
568 CS,AW,AN 1.75
569 IN 1.75
570 KS 1.75
571 BB(c),AS,A:Thresh 222 . . . . . 1.75
572 WB,BO 1.75
573 KS,BO,AS 1.75
574 KS 1.75
575 KS,V:Intellax 1.75
576 KS,Earth's Sister Planet 1.75
577 KG,BO,V:Caitiff 1.75
578 KS,Parasite 1.75
579 KG,BO,Asterix Parody 1.75
580 GK(c),KS,Superman's Failure 1.75
581 DCw(c),KS,Superman Requires Legal aid 1.75
582 AS,KS,Superman's Parents Alive 2.00
583 CS,KS,AMo(s),Last Pre Crisis Superman 10.00
584 JBy,DG,A:NewTeenTitans, I:Modern Age Superman. 3.00
585 JBy,DG,Phantom Stranger . . 2.50
586 JBy,DG,Legends,V:New Gods,Darkseid 2.50
587 JBy,DG,Demon 2.50
588 JBy,DG,Hawkman 2.50
589 JBy,DG,Gr.Lant.Corp. 2.50
590 JBy,DG,Metal Men 2.50
591 JBy,V:Superboy,A:Legion . . . 2.50
592 JBy,Big Barda 2.50
593 JBy,Mr. Miracle 2.50
594 JBy,A:Booster Gold 2.50
595 JBy,A:M.Manhunter, I:Silver Banshee 2.50
596 JBy,A:Spectre,Millenium 2.50
597 JBy,L.Starr(i),Lois V:Lana . . . 2.50
598 JBy,TyT,I:Checkmate 3.50
599 RA,JBy(i),A:MetalMen, BonusBook 2.50
600 JBy,GP,KS,JOy,DG,CS,MA, MMi,A:Wonder Woman; Man-Bat,V:Darkseid 8.00

Becomes: ACTION WEEKLY

601 GK,DSp,CS,DJu,TD, B:Superman,Gr.Lantern, Blackhawk,Deadman,Secret Six,Wilddog 1.50
602 GP(c),GK,DSp,CS,DJu,TD . . 1.50
603 GK,CS,DsP,DJu,TD 1.50
604 GK,DSp,CS,DJu,TD 1.50
605 NKu/AKu(c),GK,DSp,CS, DJu,TD 1.50
606 DSp,CS,DJu,TD 1.50
607 SLi(c),TD,DSp,CS,DJu 1.50
608 DSp,CS,DJu,TD,E:Blackhawk 1.50
609 BB(c),DSp,DJu,TD,CS, E:Wild Dog,B:Black Canary . . . 1.50
610 KB,DJu,CS,DSp,TD,CS A:Phantom Stranger 2.00
611 AN(c),DJu,DSp,CS,BKi,TD, BKi,B:Catwoman 3.00
612 PG(c),DSp,CS,BKi,TD, E:Secret Six,Deadman 2.50
613 MK(c),BKi,CS,MA,TGr, Nightwing,B:Phantom Stranger 2.50
614 TG,CS,Phantom Stranger E:Catwoman 2.50
615 MMi(c),CS,MA,BKi,TGr, Blackhawk,B:Wild Dog 1.50
616 ATh(c),CS,MA,E:Bl.Canary . . 1.50
617 CS,MA,JO,A:Ph.Stranger . . . 1.50
618 JBg(c),CS,MA,JKo,TD, B:Deadman,E:Nightwing 1.50
619 CS,MA,FS,FMc,KJo,TD,FMc, B:Sinister Six. 1.50
620 CS,MA,FS,FMc,KJo,TD 1.50
621 JO(c),CS,MA,FS,FMc,KJo, TD,MBr,E:Deadman 1.50
622 RF(c),MBr,TL,CS,MA,FS, FMc,A:Starman,E:Wild Dog,Blackhawk 1.50
623 MBr,TD,CS,MA,FS,FMc,JL, JKo,A:Ph.Stranger, B:Deadman,Shazam 1.50
624 AD(c),MBr,FS,FMc,CS,MA, TD,B:Black Canary 1.50
625 MBr,FS,FMc,CS,MA, TD,FMc, ... 1.50
626 MBr,FS,FMc,CS,MA,JKo,TD, E:Shazam,Deadman 1.50
627 GK(c),MBr,RT,FS,FMc,CS, MA,TMd,B:Nightwing,Speedy . 1.75
628 TY(c),MBr,RT,TMd,CS,MA, FS,FMc,B:Blackhawk 1.50
629 CS,MA,MBr,RT,FS,FMc,TMd . 1.50
630 CS,MA,MBr,RT,FS,FMc,TMd, E:Secret Six 1.50
631 JS(c),CS,MA,MBr,RT,TMd, B:Phantom Stranger 1.50
632 TGr(c),CS,MA,MBr,RT,TMd, . 1.50
633 CS,MA,MBr,RT,TMd 1.50
634 CS,MA,MBr,RT,TMd,E:Ph.Stranger, Nightwing/Speedy,Bl.hawk . . . 1.50
635 CS,MA,MBr,RT,EB,E:Black Canary,Green Lantern 1.50
636 DG(c),CS,MA,NKu,MPa,FMc, B:Demon,Wild Dog,Ph.Lady, Speedy,A:Phantom Stranger . . 1.75
637 CS,MA,KS,FMc,MPa, B:Hero Hotline 1.50
638 JK(c),CS,MA,KS,FMc,MPa, . . 1.50
639 CS,MA,KS,FMc,MPa 1.50
640 CS,KS,MA,FS,FMc,MPa, E:Speedy,Hero Hotline 1.50
641 CS,MA,JL,DG,MPa,E:Demon, Phant.Lady,Superman,Wild Dog, A:Ph.Stranger,Hum.Target . . . 1.75
642 GK,SD,ATi,CS,JAp,JM,CI,KN, Green Lantern,Superman 1.50

Becomes: ACTION COMICS

643 B:RSt(s),GP,BBr,V:Intergang . 2.50
644 GP,BBr,V:Matrix 2.00
645 GP,BBr,I:Maxima 2.00
646 KG,V:Alien Creature, A:Brainiac 2.00
647 GP,KGa,BBr,V:Brainiac 2.00
648 GP,KGa,BBr,V:Brainiac 2.00
649 GP,KGa,BBr,V:Brainiac 2.00
650 JOy,BBr,CS,BMc,GP,KGa, ATi,DJu,A:JLA,C:Lobo 3.00
651 GP,KGa,BBr,Day of Krypton Man #3,V:Maxima 3.00
652 GP,KGa,BBr,Day of Krypton Man #6,V:Eradicator 3.00
653 BMc,BBr,D:Amanda 2.00
654 BMc,BBr,A:Batman Part 3 . . . 2.50
655 BMc,BBr,V:Morrisson,Ma Kent's Photo Album 2.00
656 BMc,BBr,Soul Search #1, V:Blaze 2.00
657 KGa,BBr,V:Toyman 2.00
658 CS,Sinbad Contract #3 . . . . . 2.00
659 BMc,BBr,K.Krimson Kryptonite #3 . . . . 3.00
660 BMc,BBr,D:Lex Luthor 2.00
661 BMc,BBr,A:Plastic Man 2.00
662 JOy,JM,TG,BMc,V:Silver Banshee,Clark tells Lois his identity 3.00
662a 2nd printing 2.00
663 BMc,Time & Time Again Pt.2, A:JSA,Legion 2.00

Action Comics #662 © DC Comics, Inc.

664 BMc,Time & Time Again Pt.5 2.00
665 TG,V:Baron Sunday 2.00
666 EH,Red Glass Trilogy Pt.3 . . 2.00
667 JOy,JM,TG,ATi,DJu,Revenge of the Krypton Man Pt.4 . . . . . 2.25
668 BMc,Luthor confirmed dead . 2.00
669 BMc,V:Intergang,A:Thorn . . . 2.00
670 BMc,A:Waverider,JLA,JLE . . 2.00
671 KD,Blackout Pt.2 . . . . 2.00
672 BMc,Superman Meets Lex Luthor II 2.00
673 BMc,V:Hellgramite 2.00
674 BMc,Panic in the Sky (Prologue) R:Supergirl(Matrix) 4.00
675 BMc,Panic in the Sky #4, V:Brainiac 3.00
676 B:KK(s),JG,A:Supergirl,Lex Luthor II 1.75
677 JG,Supergirl V:Superman . . . 1.75
678 JG,O:Lex Luthor II 1.75
679 JG,I:Shellshock 1.75
680 JG,Blaze/Satanus War Pt.2 . . 1.75
681 JG,V:Hellgramite 1.75
682 DAb,TA,V:Hi-Tech 1.75
683 JG,I:Jackal,C:Doomsday 6.00
683a 2nd printing 1.50
684 JG,Doomsday Part 4. . . . . . 12.00
684a 2nd printing 1.75
685 JG,Funeral for a Friend#2 . . . 4.00
686 JG,Funeral for a Friend#6 . . . 4.00
687 JG,Reign of Superman #1,Direct Sales,Die-Cut(c),Mini-Poster, F:Last Son of Krypton 3.00
687a newsstand Ed. 1.75
688 JG,V:Guy Gardner 2.00
689 JG,V:Man of Steel,A:Superboy, Supergirl,R:Real Superman . . . 6.00
690 JG,Cyborg Vs. Superboy . . . 2.50
691 JG,A:All Supermen,V:Cyborg Superman,Mongul 3.50
692 JG,A:Superboy,Man of Steel . 1.75
693 JG,A:Last Son of Krypton . . . 1.75
694 JG,Spilled Blood#2,V:Hi-Tech 1.75
695 JG,Foil(c),I:Cauldron,A:Lobo . 2.75
695a Newsstand Ed. 1.75
696 JG,V:Alien,C:Doomsday 2.50
697 JG,Bizarro's World#3, V:Bizarro 1.75
698 JG,A:Lex Luthor 1.75
699 JG,A:Project Cadmus 1.50
700 JG,Fall of Metropolis#1 . . . . . 3.25
701 JG,Fall of Metropolis#5,

V:Luthor . . . 1.50
Ann.#1 AAd,DG,A:Batman . . . 4.00
Ann.#2 MMi,CS,GP,JOy,DJu,BBr, V:Mongul . . . 5.00
Ann.#3 TG,Armageddon X-over . . 3.00
Ann.#4 Eclipso,A:Captain Marvel . . . 3.00
Ann.#5 MZ(c),I:Loose Cannon . . . 2.75
Gold.Ann.rep.#1 . . . 1.50

Adam Strange, Book One
© DC Comics, Inc.

ADAM STRANGE

1 NKu,A.Strange on Rann . . . 5.00
2 NKu,Wanted:Adam Strange . . . 4.50
3 NKu,final issue . . . 4.50

ADVANCED DUNGEONS & DRAGONS

1 JD,I:Onyx,Priam,Timoth, Cybriana,Vajra,Luna . . . 12.00
2 JD,V:Imgig Zu,I:Conner . . . 10.00
3 JD,V:Imgig Zu . . . 9.00
4 JD,V:Imgig Zu,I:Kyriani . . . 7.00
5 JD,Spirit of Myrrth I . . . 7.00
6 JD,Spirit of Myrrth II . . . 7.00
7 JD,Spirit of Myrrth III . . . 5.50
8 JD,Spirit of Myrrth IV . . . 5.50
9 JD,Catspawn Quartet I . . . 5.50
10 JD,Catspawn Quartet II . . . 4.50
11 JD,Catspawn Quartet III . . . 4.50
12 JD,Catspawn Quartet IV . . . 4.50
13 JD,Spell Games I . . . 4.50
14 JD,Spell Games II . . . 4.50
15 JD,Spell Games III . . . 4.00
16 JD,Spell Games IV . . . 4.00
17 JD,RM,Kyriani's Story I . . . 4.00
18 JD,RM,Kyriani's Story II . . . 4.00
19 JD,RM,Luna I . . . 4.00
20 JD,RM,Luna II . . . 4.00
21 JD,RM,Luna III . . . 4.00
22 JD,RM,Luna IV . . . 4.00
23 TMd,RM,Siege Dragons I . . . 3.00
24 Scavengers . . . 2.50
25 JD,RM,Centaur Village . . . 2.00
26 JD,Timoth the Centaur . . . 2.00
27 JD,Kyriani,Dragons Eye #1 . . . 2.00
28 JD,Dragons Eye #2 . . . 2.00
29 JD,RM,Dragons Eye #3 . . . 2.00
30 JD,RM,Carril's Killer Revealed . . . 2.00
31 TMd,Onyx'Father Pt.1 . . . 2.00
32 TMd,Onyx'Father Pt.2 . . . 2.00
33 JD,Waterdeep Pt.1 . . . 2.00
34 JD,Waterdeep Pt.2 . . . 2.00
35 JD,RM,Waterdeep Pt.3 . . . 1.75
36 JD,RM,final issue . . . 1.75
Ann.#1 JD,RM,Tmd . . . 5.50

ADVENTURE COMICS

November 1938
[Prev: New Comics]

32 CF(c) . . . 1,400.00
33 . . . 700.00
34 FG(c) . . . 700.00
35 FG(c) . . . 700.00
36 Giant Snake(c) . . . 700.00
37 Rampaging Elephant(c) . . . 700.00
38 Tiger(c) . . . 700.00
39 Male Bondage(c) . . . 750.00
40 CF(c),1st app. Sandman . 17,500.00
41 Killer Shark(c) . . . 2,000.00
42 CF,Sandman(c) . . . 2,500.00
43 CF(c) . . . 1,400.00
44 CF,Sandman(c) . . . 2,400.00
45 FG(c) . . . 1,400.00
46 CF,Sandman(c) . . . 2,400.00
47 Sandman (c) . . . 1,400.00
48 1st app.& B:Hourman . . . 9,500.00
49 . . . 1,000.00
50 Hourman(c) . . . 1,000.00
51 BBa(c),Sandman(c) . . . 1,200.00
52 BBa(c),Hourman(c) . . . 1,200.00
53 BBa(c),1st app. Minuteman . 850.00
54 BBa(c),Hourman(c) . . . 850.00
55 BBa(c),same . . . 850.00
56 BBa(c),same . . . 850.00
57 BBa(c),same . . . 850.00
58 BBa(c),same . . . 850.00
59 BBa(c),same . . . 850.00
60 Sandman(c) . . . 1,200.00
61 CF(c),JBu,Sandman(c) . . . 6,500.00
62 JBu(c),JBu,Starman(c) . . . 750.00
63 JBu(c),JBu,same . . . 750.00
64 JBu(c),JBu,same . . . 750.00
65 JBu(c),JBu,same . . . 750.00
66 JBu(c),JBu,O:Shining Knight, Starman(c) . . . 1,000.00
67 JBu(c),JBu,O:Mist . . . 750.00
68 JBu(c),JBu,same . . . 750.00
69 JBu(c),JBu,1st app. Sandy, Starman(c) . . . 1,000.00
70 JBu(c),JBu,Starman(c) . . . 800.00
71 JBu(c),JBu,same . . . 800.00
72 JBu(c),S&K,JBu, Sandman . . . 5,000.00
73 S&K(c),S&K,I:Manhunter . . 5,400.00
74 S&K(c),S&K,You can't Escape your Fate-The Sandman . . . 950.00
75 S&K(c),S&K,Sandman and Sandy Battle Thor in 'Villian from Valhalla' . . . 950.00
76 S&K(c),Sandman(c),S&K . . 950.00
77 S&K,(c),S&K,same . . . 950.00
78 S&K(c),S&K,same . . . 950.00
79 S&K(c),S&K,Manhunter in 'Cobras of the Deep' . . . 950.00
80 S&K(c),Sandman(c),S&K . . 950.00
81 S&K(c),MMe,S&K,same . . . 900.00
82 S&K(c),S&K,Sandman X-Mas story . . . 900.00
83 S&K(c),S&K,Sandman Boxing(c),E:Hourman . . . 900.00
84 S&K(c),S&K . . . 900.00
85 S&K(c),S&K,Sandman in 'The Amazing Dreams of Gentleman Jack' . . . 900.00
86 S&K(c),Sandman(c) . . . 900.00
87 S&K(c),same . . . 900.00
88 S&K(c),same . . . 900.00
89 S&K(c),same . . . 900.00
90 S&K(c),same . . . 900.00
91 S&K(c),JK . . . 550.00
92 S&K(c), . . . 400.00
93 S&K(c),Sandman in 'Sleep for Sale' . . . 400.00

Adventure Comics #40
© DC Comics, Inc.

94 S&K(c),Sandman(c) . . . 400.00
95 S&K(c),same . . . 400.00
96 S&K(c),same . . . 400.00
97 S&K(c),same . . . 400.00
98 JK(c),Sandman in 'Hero of Dreams' . . . 400.00
99 JK(c) . . . 400.00
100 . . . 700.00
101 S&K(c) . . . 400.00
102 S&K(c) . . . 400.00
103 B:Superboy stories,(c),BU: Johnny Quick,Aquaman,Shining Knight,Green Arrow . . . 1,600.00
104 S&S,ToyTown USA . . . 550.00
105 S&S,Palace of Fantasy . . 375.00
106 S&S,Weather Hurricane . . 375.00
107 S&S,The Sky is the Limit . 375.00
108 S&S,Proof of the Proverbs 375.00
109 S&S,You Can't Lose . . . 375.00
110 S&S,The Farmer Takes it Easy . . . 375.00
111 S&S,The Whiz Quiz Club . 350.00
112 S&S,Super Safety First . . . 350.00
113 S&S,The 33rd Christmas . 350.00
114 S&S,Superboy Spells Danger . . . 350.00
115 S&S,The Adventure of Jaguar Boy . . . 350.00
116 S&S,JBu,Superboy Toy Tester . . . 350.00
117 S&S,JBu,Miracle Plane . . . 350.00
118 S&S,JBu,The Quiz Biz Broadcast . . . 350.00
119 WMo,JBu,Superboy Meets Girls . . . 350.00
120 S&S,JBu,A:Perry White; I:Ringmaster . . . 375.00
121 S&S,Great Hobby Contest 300.00
122 S&S,Superboy-Super-Magician . . . 300.00
123 S&S,Lesson For a Bully . . 300.00
124 S&S,Barbed Wire Boys Town . . . 300.00
125 S&S,The Weight Before Christmas . . . 300.00
126 S&S,Superboy:Crime Fighting Poet . . . 300.00
127 MMe,O:Shining Knight; Super Bellboy . . . 335.00
128 WMo,How Clark Kent Met Lois Lane' . . . 300.00
129 WMo,Pupils of/the Past . . . 300.00
130 WMo,Superboy Super

Adventure Comics #51
© DC Comics, Inc.

Salesman 300.00
131 WMo,The Million Dollar Athlete 250.00
132 WMo,Superboy Super Cowboy 250.00
133 WMo,Superboy's Report Card 250.00
134 WMo,Silver Gloves Sellout 250.00
135 WMo,The Most Amazing of All Boys 250.00
136 WMo,My Pal Superboy . . . 250.00
137 WMo,Treasure of Tondimo 250.00
138 WMo,Around the World in Eighty Minutes 250.00
139 WMo,Telegraph Boy 250.00
140 Journey to the Moon 250.00
141 WMo,When Superboy Lost His Powers 250.00
142 WMo,The Man Who Walked With Trouble 275.00
143 WMo,The Superboy Savings Bank,A:Wooden Head Jones 275.00
144 WMo,The Way to Stop Superboy 275.00
145 WMo,Holiday Hijackers . . . 275.00
146 The Substitute Superboy . . 275.00
147 Clark Kent,Orphan 275.00
148 Superboy Meets Mummies 275.00
149 Fake Superboys 275.00
150 FF,Superboy's Initiation . . 350.00
151 FF,No Hunting(c) 350.00
152 Superboy Hunts For a Job 275.00
153 FF,Clark Kent,Boy Hobo . . 350.00
154 The Carnival Boat Crimes 225.00
155 FF,Superboy-Hollywood Actor 325.00
156 The Flying Peril 225.00
157 FF,The Worst Boy in Smallville 325.00
158 The Impossible Task 225.00
159 FF,Superboy Millionaire? . 325.00
160 Superboy's Phoney Father 225.00
161 FF 325.00
162 'The Super-Coach of Smallville High!' 225.00
163 FF,'Superboy's Phoney Father' 335.00
164 Discovers the Secret of a Lost Indian Tribe! 210.00
165 'Superboy's School for Stunt Men!' 210.00
166 'The Town That Stole Superboy' 210.00
167 'Lana Lang, Super-Girl!' . . 210.00
168 'The Boy Who Out Smarted Superboy' 210.00
169 'Clark Kent's Private Butler' 210.00
170 'Lana Lang's Big Crush' . . 185.00
171 'Superboy's Toughest Tasks!' 185.00
172 'Laws that Backfired' 185.00
173 'Superboy's School of Hard Knocks' 185.00
174 'The New Lana Lang!' 185.00
175 'Duel of the Superboys' . . . 185.00
176 'Superboy's New Parents!' 185.00
177 'Hot-Rod Chariot Race!' . . 185.00
178 'Boy in the Lead Mask' . . . 185.00
179 'The World's Whackiest Inventors' 185.00
180 Grand Prize o/t Underworld 185.00
181 'Mask for a Hero' 175.00
182 The Super Hick from Smallville' 160.00
183 'Superboy and Cleopatra' . 160.00
184 'The Shutterbugs of Smallville' 160.00
185 'The Mythical Monster' . . . 160.00
186 . . . . 160.00
187 '25th Century Superboy' . . 160.00
188 'The Bull Fighter from Smallville' 160.00
189 Girl of Steel(Lana Lang) . . 160.00
190 The Two Clark Kents 160.00
191 . . . . 160.00
192 'The Coronation of Queen Lana Lang' 160.00
193 'Superboy's Lost Costume' 160.00
194 'Super-Charged Superboy' 160.00
195 'Lana Lang's Romance on Mars!' 160.00
196 'Superboy vs. King Gorilla' 160.00

Adventure Comics #321
© DC Comics, Inc.

197 V:Juvenile Gangs 160.00
198 'The Super-Carnival from Space' 160.00
199 'Superboy meets Superlad' 160.00
200 'Superboy and the Apes!' . 325.00
201 'Safari in Smallville!' 225.00
202 'Superboy City, U.S.A.' . . . 225.00
203 'Uncle Superboy!' 275.00
204 'The Super-Brat of Smallville' 225.00
205 'The Journey of the Second Superboy!' 225.00
206 'The Impossible Creatures' 225.00
207 'Smallville's Worst Athlete' 225.00
208 'Rip Van Winkle of Smallville?' 225.00
209 'Superboy Week!' 225.00
210 I:Krypto,'The Superdog from Krypton' 2,400.00
211 'Superboy's Most Amazing Dream!' 175.00
212 'Superboy's Robot Twin' . . 175.00
213 'The Junior Jury of Smallville!' 175.00
214 A:Krypto 175.00
215 'The Super-Hobby of Superboy' 175.00
216 'The Wizard City' 175.00
217 'Superboy's Farewell to Smallville' 175.00
218 'The Two World's of Superboy' 175.00
219 The Rip Van Wrinkle of Smallville 175.00
220 The Greatest Show on Earth A:Krypto 175.00
221 'The Babe of Steel' 150.00
222 'Superboy's Repeat Performance' 150.00
223 'Hercules Junior' 150.00
224 'Pa Kent Superman' 150.00
225 'The Bird with Super-Powers' 150.00
226 'Superboy's Super Rival!' . 150.00
227 'Good Samaritan of Smallville' 150.00
228 'Clark Kent's Body Guard' . 150.00
229 . . . . 150.00
230 'The Secret of the Flying Horse' 150.00
231 'The Super-Feats of Super-Baby!' 150.00
232 'The House where Superboy was Born' 150.00
233 'Joe Smith, Man of Steel!' . 150.00
234 'The 1,001 Rides of Superboy!' 150.00
235 'The Confessions of Superboy!' 150.00
236 'Clark Kent's Super-Dad!' . 150.00
237 Robot War of Smallville! . . 150.00
238 'The Secret Past of Superboy's Father' 150.00
239 'The Super-Tricks of the Dog of Steel' 150.00
240 'The Super Teacher From Krypton' 150.00
241 'The Super-Outlaw of Smallville' 150.00
242 'The Kid From Krypton' . . . 150.00
243 'The Super Toys From Krypton' 150.00
244 'The Poorest Family in Smallville' 150.00
245 'The Mystery of Monster X' 150.00
246 'The Girl Who Trapped Superboy!' 150.00
247 I&O:Legion 3,400.00
248 Green Arrow 120.00
249 CS,Green Arrow 120.00
250 JK,Green Arrow 120.00
251 JK,Green Arrow 120.00
252 JK,Green Arrow 120.00
253 JK,1st Superboy & Robin T.U 175.00
254 JK,Green Arrow 120.00
255 JK,Green Arrow 120.00
256 JK,O:Green Arrow 400.00
257 CS,LE,A:Hercules,Samson 100.00
258 LE,Aquaman,Superboy . . . 100.00
259 I:Crimson Archer 100.00
260 1st S.A. O:Aquaman 400.00
261 GA,A:Lois Lane 75.00
262 O:Speedy 80.00
263 GA,Aquaman,Superboy . . . 75.00

264 GA,A:Robin Hood 75.00
265 GA,Aquaman,Superboy . . . 75.00
266 GA,I:Aquagirl 75.00
267 N:Legion(2nd app.) 1000.00
268 I:Aquaboy 75.00
269 I:Aqualad,E:Green Arrow . 130.00
270 2nd A:Aqualad,B:Congorilla . 75.00
271 O:Lex Luthor rtd 140.00
272 I:Human Flying Fish 56.00
273 Aquaman,Superboy 56.00
274 Aquaman,Superboy 56.00
275 O:Superman/Batman T.U. rtd 100.00

Adventure Comics #377
© DC Comics, Inc.

276 Superboy,3rd A:Metallo 50.00
277 Aquaman,Superboy 50.00
278 Aquaman,Superboy 50.00
279 CS,Aquaman,Superboy 50.00
280 CS,A:Lori Lemaris 50.00
281 Aquaman,Superboy E:Congorilla 50.00
282 5th A:Legion,I:Starboy . . . 150.00
283 I:Phantom Zone 65.00
284 CS,JM,Aquaman,Superboy . 32.00
285 WB,B:Bizarro World 70.00
286 I:Bizarro Mxyzptlk 65.00
287 I:Dev-Em,Bizarro Perry White, Jimmy Olsen 40.00
288 A:Dev-Em 35.00
289 Superboy 32.00
290 8th A:Legion,O&J:Sunboy, I:Brainiac 5 . . . . 100.00
291 A:Lex Luthor 28.00
292 Superboy,I:Bizarro Lucy Lane, Lana Lang 28.00
293 CS,O&I:Marv-El,I:Bizarro Luthor 60.00
294 I:Bizarro M.Monroe,JFK . . . 60.00
295 I:Bizarro Titano 35.00
296 A:Ben Franklin,George Washington 30.00
297 Lana Lang Superboy Sister . 30.00
298 The Fat Superboy 30.00
299 I:Gold Kryptonite 35.00
300 B:Legion,J:Mon-El, E:Bizarro World 300.00
301 CS,O:Bouncing Boy 80.00
302 CS,Legion 50.00
303 I:Matter Eater Lad 55.00
304 D:Lightning Lad 55.00
305 A:Chameleon Boy 50.00
306 I:Legion of Sub.Heroes 40.00

Adventure Comics #420
© DC Comics, Inc.

307 I:Element Lad 45.00
308 I:Light Lass 45.00
309 I:Legion of Super Monsters . 37.00
310 A:Mxyzptlk 37.00
311 CS,V:Legion of Substiue Heroes 26.00
312 R:Lightning Lad 28.00
313 CS,J:Supergirl 26.00
314 A:Hitler 26.00
315 A:Legion of Substitute Heroes 26.00
316 O:Legion 28.00
317 I&J:Dreamgirl 28.00
318 Legion 28.00
319 Legion 25.00
320 A:Dev-Em 25.00
321 I:Time Trapper 27.00
322 JF,A:Legion of Super Pets . 20.00
323 JF,BU:Kypto 20.00
324 JF,I:Legion of Super Outlaws 20.00
325 JF,V:Lex Luthor 20.00
326 BU:Superboy 20.00
327 I&J:Timber Wolf 30.00
328 Legion 17.00
329 I:Legion of Super Bizarros . . 19.00
330 Legion 17.00
331 Legion 16.00
332 Legion 16.00
333 Legion 16.00
334 Legion 15.00
335 Legion 15.00
336 Legion 14.00
337 Legion 14.00
338 Legion 15.00
339 Legion 15.00
340 I:Computo 17.00
341 CS,D:Triplicate Girl (becomes Duo Damsel) 12.00
342 CS,Star Boy expelled 10.00
343 CS,V:Lords of Luck 10.00
344 CS,Super Stalag pt.1. . . . . . 10.00
345 CS,Super Stalag pt.2 . . . . . 10.00
346 CS,I&J:Karate Kid,Princess Projectra,I:Nemesis Kid 13.00
347 CS,Legion 10.00
348 I:Dr.Regulus 12.00
349 CS,I:Rond Vidar 11.00
350 CS,I:White Witch 12.00
351 CS,R:Star Boy 10.00
352 CS,I:Fatal Fire 10.00
353 CS,D:Ferro Lad 15.00
354 CS,Adult Legion 10.00
355 CS,J:Insect Queen 10.00
356 CS,Five Legion Orphans 8.00
357 CS,I:Controller 8.00
358 I:Hunter 8.00
359 CS,Outlawed Legion pt.1 . . . 8.00
360 CS,Outlawed Legion pt.2 . . . 8.00
361 I:Dominators (30th century) . . 9.00
362 I:Dr.Mantis Morto 8.00
363 V:Dr.Mantis Morlo 8.00
364 A:Legion of Super Pets 8.00
365 CS,I:Shadow Lass, V:Fatal Five 9.00
366 CS,J:Shadow Lass 7.00
367 N:Legion H.Q.,I:Dark Circle . . 9.00
368 CS 7.00
369 CS,JAb,I:Mordru 8.00
370 CS,JAb,V:Mordru 7.00
371 CS,JAb,I:Chemical King 9.00
372 CS,JAb,J:Timber Wolf, Chemical King, ... 9.00
373 I:Tornado Twins 7.00
374 WM,I:Black Mace 7.00
375 I:Wanderers 8.00
376 Execution of Cham.Boy 7.00
377 Heroes for Hire 7.00
378 Twelve Hours to Live 7.00
379 Burial In Space 7.00
380 The Amazing Space Odyssey of the Legion,E:Legion 7.00
381 The Supergirl Gang C:Batgirl,B:Supergirl 3.00
382 NA(c),The Superteams Split Up,A:Superman 3.00
383 NA(c),Please Stop my Funeral, A:Superman,Comet,Streaky . . 4.00
384 KS,The Heroine Haters, A:Superman 3.00
385 Supergirl's Big Sister 3.00
386 The Beast That Loved Supergirl 3.00
387 Wolfgirl of Stanhope; A:Superman;V:Lex Luthor 3.00
388 Kindergarten Criminal; V:Luthor,Brainiac 3.00
389 A:Supergirl's Parents, V:Brainiac 3.00
390 Linda Danvers Superstar (80 page giant) 6.00
391 The Super Cheat;A:Comet . . 3.00
392 Supergirls Lost Costume 3.00
393 KS,Unwanted Supergirl 3.00
394 KS,Heartbreak Prison 3.00
395 Heroine in Haunted House . . 3.00
396 Mystery o/t Super Orphan . . . 3.00
397 Now Comes Zod,N:Supergirl, V:Luthor 3.00
398 Maid of Doom,A:Superman, Streaky,Krypto,Comet 3.00
399 CI,Johnny Dee,Hero Bum . . . 3.00
400 MSy,35th Anniv.,Return of the Black Flame 3.50
401 MSy,JAb,The Frightened Supergirl,V:Lex Luthor 2.50
402 MSy,JAb,TD,I:Starfire, Dr.Kangle 2.50
403 68 page giant 6.00
404 MSy,JAb,V:Starfire 2.25
405 V:Starfire,Dr.Kangle 2.25
406 MSy,JAb,Suspicion 2.25
407 MSy,JAb,Suspicion Confirmed N:Supergirl 2.25
408 The Face at the Window 2.25
409 MSy,DG,Legion rep. 2.25
410 N:Supergirl 2.25
411 CI,N:Supergirl 2.50
412 rep.Strange Adventures #180 (I:Animal Man). 5.00
413 GM,JKu,rep Hawkman 2.00
414 Animal Man rep. 4.00
415 BO,GM,CI,Animal Man rep. . . 3.00
416 CI,All women issue,giantsize . 3.50
417 GM,inc.rep.Adventure #161, Frazetta art. 2.00

418 ATh,Black Canary 2.00
419 ATh,Black Canary 2.00
420 Animal Man rep. 3.00
421 MSy,Supergirl 2.00
422 MSy,Supergirl 2.00
423 MSy,Supergirl 2.00
424 MSy,E:Supergirl,A:JLA 2.00
425 AN,ATh,I:Captain Fear 2.00
426 MSy,DG,JAp,Vigilante 2.00
427 TD, ... 7.50
428 TD,I:Black Orchid 6.00
429 TD,AN,Black Orchid 5.00
430 A:Black Orchid 3.50
431 JAp,ATh,B:Spectre 2.50
432 JAp,AN,A:Spectre,Capt.Fear . 2.50
433 JAp,AN 2.50
434 JAp 2.50
435 MGr(1st work),JAp,Aquaman . 3.50
436 JAp,MGr,Aquaman 3.00
437 JAp,MGr,Aquaman 3.00
438 JAp,HC,DD,7 Soldiers 1.75
439 JAp 1.75
440 JAp,O:New Spectre 1.75
441 JAp,B:Aquaman 1.75
442 JAp,A:Aquaman 1.75
443 JAp 1.75
444 JAp 1.75
445 JAp,RE,JSon,Creeper 1.75
446 JAp,RE,JSon,Creeper 1.75
447 JAp,RE,JSon,Creeper 1.75
448 JAp,Aquaman 1.75
449 JAp,MN,TA,Jonn J'onz 1.50
450 JAp,MN,TA,Supergirl 1.50
451 JAp,MN,TA,Hawkman 1.50
452 JAp,Aquaman 1.50
453 MA,CP,JRu,B:Superboy
& Aqualad 1.50
454 CP,DG,A:Kryptonite Kid 1.50
455 CP,DG,A:Kryptonite Kid
E:Aqualad 1.50
456 JSon,JA 1.50
457 JSon,JA,JO,B:Eclipso 3.50
458 JSon,JAp,JO,BL,E:Superboy
& Eclipso 3.00
459 IN,FMc,JAp,JSon,DN,JA,A:Wond.
Woman,New Gods,Green Lantern,
Flash,Deadman,(giant size) . . . 2.00
460 IN,FMc,JAp,DN,DA,JSon,JA,
D:Darkseid 1.75
461 IN,FMc,JAp,JSon,DN,JA,
B:JSA & Aquaman 2.50
462 IN,FMc,DH,JL,DG,JA,
D:Earth 2,Batman 4.00
463 DH,JL,JSon,FMc 1.50
464 DH,JAp,JSon,DN,DA,
Deadman 1.75
465 DN,JSon,DG,JL 1.50
466 MN,JL,JSon,DN,DA 1.50
467 JSon,SD,RT,I:Starman
B:Plastic Man 1.50
468 SD,JSon 1.50
469 SD,JSon,O:Starman 1.50
470 SD,JSon,O:Starman 1.50
471 SD,JSon,I:Brickface 1.50
472 SD,RT,JSon 1.50
473 SD,RT,JSon 1.50
474 SD,RT,JSon 1.50
475 BB(c),SD,RT,JSon,DG,
B:Aquaman 1.50
476 SD,RT,JSon,DG 1.50
477 SD,RT,JSon,DG 1.50
478 SD,RT,JSon,DG 1.50
479 CI,DG,JSon,Dial H For Hero,
E:Starman and Aquaman 1.50
480 CI,DJ,B:Dial H for Hero 1.50
481 CI,DJ 1.50
482 CI,DJ,DH 1.50
483 CI,DJ,DH 1.50
484 GP(c),CI,DJ,DH, ... 1.50
485 GP(c),CI,DJ, ... 1.50
486 GP(c),DH,RT,TVE, ... 1.50
487 CI,DJ,DH 1.50
488 CI,DJ,TVE 1.50
489 CI,FMc,TVE 1.50
490 GP(c),CI,E:Dial H for Hero . . 1.50
491 KG(c),DigestSize,DN,
Shazam,rep other material . . . 1.50
492 KG(c),DN,E:Shazam 1.50
493 KG(c),GT,B:Challengers of
the Unknown,reprints 1.50
494 KG(c),GT,Challengers,
reprints 1.50
495 ATh,reprints,Challengers 1.75
496 GK(c),ATh,reprints,
Challengers 1.75
497 ATh,DA,reps.,E:Challengers . 1.75
498 GK(c),reprints,Rep.Legion . . . 1.50
499 GK(c),reprints,Rep 1.50
500 KG(c),Legion reprints,Rep . . . 1.50
501 reprints,Rep 1.50
502 reprints,Rep 1.50
503 reprints,final issue 1.50

ADVENTURES OF ALAN LADD
October-November, 1949

1 Ph(c) 500.00
2 Ph(c) 300.00
3 Ph(c) 200.00
4 Ph(c) 200.00

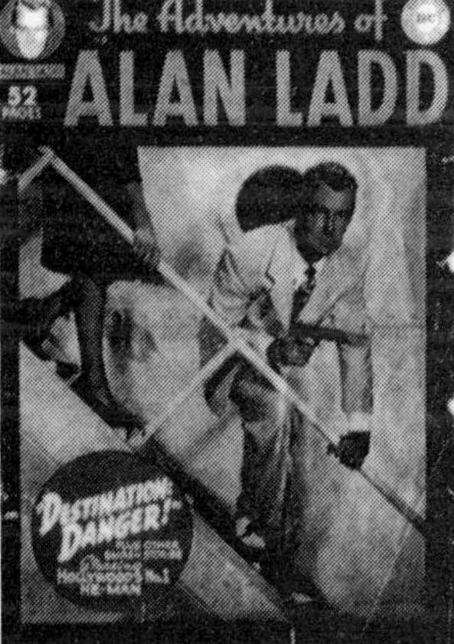

Alan Ladd #5 © DC Comics, Inc.

5 Ph(c),inc.Destination Danger 175.00
6 Ph(c) 175.00
7 . . . . 175.00
8 Grand Duchess takes over . 175.00
9 Deadlien in Rapula,
February-March, 1951 . . . . 175.00

ADVENTURES OF BOB HOPE
February-March, 1951

1 Ph(c) 800.00
2 Ph(c) 400.00
3 Ph(c) 275.00
4 Ph(c) 250.00
5 thru 10 . . . . @200.00
11 thru 20 . . . . @125.00
21 thru 40 . . . . @85.00
41 thru 90 . . . . @50.00
91 thru 93 . . . . @20.00
94 C:Aquaman 22.00
95 thru 105 . . . . @20.00
106 NA 30.00
107 NA 30.00
108 NA 30.00
109 NA 30.00

Bob Hope #11 © DC Comics, Inc.

ADVENTURES OF DEAN MARTIN AND JERRY LEWIS
July-August, 1952

1 . . . . 500.00
2 . . . . 250.00
3 thru 10 . . . . @125.00
11 thru 20 . . . . @75.00
21 thru 40 . . . . @45.00

Becomes:

ADVENTURES OF JERRY LEWIS

41 thru 55 . . . . @30.00
56 thru 69 . . . . @25.00
70 thru 87 . . . . @15.00
88 A:Bob Hope 18.00
89 thru 91 . . . . @15.00
92 C:Superman 30.00
93 thru 96 . . . . @15.00
97 A:Batman & Joker 30.00
98 thru 100 . . . . @15.00
101 thru 104 NA . . . . @25.00
105 A:Superman 20.00
106 thru 111 . . . . @8.00
112 A:Flash 15.00
113 thru 116 . . . . @8.00
117 A:Wonder Woman 10.00
118 thru 124 . . . . @6.00

ADVENTURES OF FORD FAIRLANE

1 DH,DG 1.50
2 DH 1.50
3 DH 1.50
4 DH 1.50

ADVENTURES OF THE OUTSIDERS
(see BATMAN & THE OUTSIDERS)

ADVENTURES OF OZZIE AND HARRIET
October-November, 1949

1 Ph(c) 500.00
2 . . . . 250.00
3 . . . . 200.00
4 . . . . 200.00
5 June-July, 1950 . . . . 200.00

ADVENTURES OF REX, THE WONDERDOG

January-February, 1952

1 ATh 600.00
2 ATh 300.00
3 ATh 250.00
4 . . . . 175.00
5 . . . . 175.00
6 thru 11 . . . . @125.00
12 thru 20 . . . . @75.00
21 thru 46 . . . . @50.00

ADVENTURES OF SUPERBOY

(See: SUPERBOY)

ADVENTURES OF SUPERMAN

(See: SUPERMAN)

AGENT LIBERTY SPECIAL

1 DAb,O:Agent Liberty 2.00

ALIEN NATION

1 JBi,movie adaption 2.50

ALL-AMERICAN COMICS

April, 1939

1 B:Hop Harrigan,Scribbly,Mutt&Jeff, Red,White&Blue,Bobby Thatcher, Skippy,Daiseybelle,Mystery Men of Mars,Toonerville 2,750.00
2 B:Ripley's Believe It or Not . 850.00
3 Hop Harrigan (c) 600.00

All-American Comics #4
© DC Comics, Inc.

4 Flag(c) 600.00
5 B:The American Way 600.00
6 ShM(c),Fredric Marchin in 'The American Way' 550.00
7 E:Bobby Thatcher,C.H. Claudy's 'A Thousand Years in a Minute' 550.00
8 B:Ultra Man 800.00
9 . . . . 550.00
10 ShM(c),E:The American Way, Santa-X-Mas(c) 550.00
11 Ultra Man(c) 500.00
12 E:Toonerville Folks 500.00
13 'The Infra Red Des'Royers' . 500.00

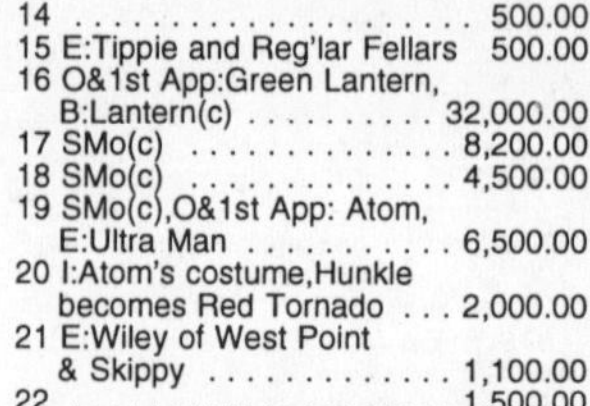

14 . . . . 500.00
15 E:Tippie and Reg'lar Fellars 500.00
16 O&1st App:Green Lantern, B:Lantern(c) 32,000.00
17 SMo(c) 8,200.00
18 SMo(c) 4,500.00
19 SMo(c),O&1st App: Atom, E:Ultra Man 6,500.00
20 I:Atom's costume,Hunkle becomes Red Tornado . . . 2,000.00
21 E:Wiley of West Point & Skippy 1,100.00
22 . . . . 1,500.00

All-American Comics #23
© DC Comics, Inc.

23 E:Daieybelle 1,500.00
24 E:Ripley's Believe It or Not 1,200.00
25 O&1st App:Dr. Mid-Nite . . 4,500.00
26 O&I:Sargon the Sorcerer . 1,500.00
27 I:Doiby Dickles 1,800.00
28 . . . . 750.00
29 ShM(c) 750.00
30 ShM(c) 750.00
31 . . . . 750.00
32 . . . . 550.00
33 . . . . 550.00
34 . . . . 550.00
35 Doiby discovers Lantern's ID 550.00
36 . . . . 550.00
37 . . . . 550.00
38 . . . . 550.00
39 . . . . 550.00
40 . . . . 550.00
41 . . . . 500.00
42 . . . . 500.00
43 . . . . 500.00
44 'I Accuse the Green Lantern!' 500.00
45 . . . . 500.00
46 . . . . 500.00
47 Hop Harrigan meets the Enemy,(c) 500.00
48 . . . . 500.00
49 . . . . 500.00
50 E:Sargon 500.00
51 'Murder Under the Stars' . . . 450.00
52 . . . . 450.00
53 Green Lantern delivers the Mail 450.00
54 . . . . 450.00
55 'The Riddle of the Runaway Trolley' 450.00
56 V:Elegant Esmond 450.00
57 V:The Melancholy Men 450.00
58 . . . . 450.00
59 'The Story of the Man Who

All-American Comics #53
© DC Comics, Inc.

Couldn't Tell The Truth' . . . 450.00
60 . . . . 450.00
61 O:Soloman Grundy,'Fighters Never Quit' 1,800.00
62 'Da Distrik Attorney' 350.00
63 . . . . 350.00
64 'A Bag of Assorted Nuts!' . . 350.00
65 'The Man Who Lost Wednesday' 350.00
66 'The Soles of Manhattan!' . . 350.00
67 V:King Shark 350.00
68 Meets Napoleon&Joe Safeen 350.00
69 'Backwards Man!' 350.00
70 JKu,I:Maximillian O'Leary, V:Colley, the Leprechaun . . 350.00
71 E:Red,White&Blue,'The Human Bomb' 325.00
72 B:Black Pirate 325.00
73 B:Winkey,Blinky&Noddy, 'Mountain Music Mayhem' . . 325.00
74 . . . . 325.00
75 . . . . 325.00
76 'Spring Time for Doiby' 325.00
77 Hop Harrigan(c) 325.00
78 . . . . 325.00
79 . . . . 325.00
80 . . . . 325.00
81 . . . . 325.00
82 . . . . 325.00
83 . . . . 325.00
84 'The Adventure of the Man with Two Faces' 325.00
85 . . . . 300.00
86 V:Crime of the Month Club . 300.00
87 'The Strange Case of Professor Nobody' 300.00
88 'Canvas of Crime' 300.00
89 O:Harlequin 300.00
90 O:Icicle 300.00
91 'Wedding of the Harlequin' . 300.00
92 'The Icicle goes South' 300.00
93 'The Double Crossing Decoy' 300.00
94 A:Harlequin 300.00
95 'The Unmasking of the Harlequin' 300.00
96 ATh(c),'Solve the Mystery of the Emerald Necklaces!' . 300.00
97 ATh(c),'The Country Fair Crimes' 300.00
98 ATh,ATh(c),'End of Sports!' . 300.00
99 ATh,ATh(c),E:Hop Harrigan 300.00

100 ATh,I:Johnny Thunder . . . 650.00
101 ATh,ATh(c),E:Mutt and Jeff 550.00
102 ATh,ATh(c),E:Green Lantern 650.00

Becomes:

ALL-AMERICAN WESTERN

103 A:Johnny Thunder,'The City Without Guns,'All Johnny Thunder stories 250.00
104 ATh(c),'Unseen Allies' 200.00
105 ATh(c),'Hidden Guns' 150.00
106 ATh(c),'Snow Mountain Ambush' 125.00
107 ATh(c),'Cheyenne Justice' . 150.00
108 ATh(c),'Vengeance of the Silver Bullet' 125.00
109 ATh(c),'Secret of Crazy River' 125.00
110 ATh(c),'Ambush at Scarecrow Hills' 125.00
111 ATh(c),'Gun-Shy Sheriff' . . 125.00
112 ATh(c),'Double Danger' . . . 125.00
113 ATh(c),'Johnny Thunder Indian Chief' 150.00
114 ATh(c),'The End of Johnny Thunder' 125.00
115 ATh(c),'Cheyenne Mystery' 125.00
116 ATh(c),'Buffalo Raiders of the Mesa' 125.00
117 ATh(c),V:Black Lightnin . . . 100.00
118 ATh(c),'Challenge of the Aztecs' 100.00
119 GK(c),'The Vanishing Gold Mine' 100.00
120 GK(c),'Ambush at Painted Mountain' 100.00
121 ATh(c),'The Unmasking of Johnny Thunder' 100.00
122 ATh(c),'The Real Johnny Thunder' 100.00
123 GK(c),'Johnny Thunder's Strange Rival' 100.00
124 ATh(c),'The Iron Horse's Last Run' 100.00
125 ATh(c),'Johnny Thunder's Last Roundup' 100.00
126 ATh(c),'Phantoms of the Desert' 100.00

Becomes:

ALL-AMERICAN MEN OF WAR

127 (0) 500.00
128 (1) 350.00
2 JGr(c),Killer Bait 300.00
3 Pied Piper of Pyong-Yang . 300.00
4 JGr(c),The Hills of Hate . . . 300.00
5 One Second to Zero 175.00
6 IN(c),Jungle Killers 175.00
7 IN(c),Beach to Hold 175.00
8 IN(c),Sgt. Storm Cloud 175.00
9 . . . . 175.00
10 . . . . 175.00
11 JGr(c),Dragon's Teeth 175.00
12 . . . . 150.00
13 JGr(c),Lost Patrol 150.00
14 IN(c),Pigeon Boss 150.00
15 JGr(c),Flying Roadblock . . . 150.00
16 JGr(c),The Flying Jeep 150.00
17 JGr(c),Booby Trap Ridge . . 150.00
18 JKu(c),The Ballad of Battling Bells 150.00
19 JGr(c),IN,Torpedo Track . . . 125.00
20 JGr(c),JKu,Lifenet to Beach Road 125.00
21 JGr(c),IN,RH,The Coldest War 125.00
22 JGr(c),IN,JKu,Snipers Nest . 125.00
23 JGr(c),The Silent War 125.00
24 JGr(c),The Thin Line 125.00
25 JGr(c),IN,For Rent-One Foxhole 125.00
26 . . . . 125.00
27 JGr(c),RH,Fighting Pigeon . 125.00

All-American Men of War #8
© DC Comics, Inc.

All-American Men of War #13
© DC Comics, Inc.

28 JGr(c),RA,JKu,Medal for A Dog 125.00
29 IN(c),JKu,Battle Bridges . . . 135.00
30 JGr(c),RH,Frogman Hunt . . 125.00
31 JGr(c),Battle Seat 135.00
32 JGr(c),RH,Battle Station . . . 135.00
33 JGr(c),IN,Sky Ambush 125.00
34 JGr(c),JKu,No Man's Alley . 125.00
35 JGr(c),IN, Battle Call 90.00
36 JGr(c),JKu,Battle Window . . . 90.00
37 JGr(c),JKu,The Big Stretch . . 90.00
38 JGr(c),RH,JKu,The Floating Sentinel 90.00
39 JGr(c),JKu,The Four Faces of Sgt. Fay 90.00
40 JGr(c),IN,Walking Helmet . . . 90.00
41 JKu(c),RH,JKu,The 50-50 War 75.00
42 JGr(c),JKu,Battle Arm 75.00
43 JGr(c),JKu,Command Post . . 75.00
44 JKu(c),The Flying Frogman . . 75.00
45 JGr(c),RH,Combat Waterboy . 75.00
46 JGr(c),IN,RH,Tank Busters . . 75.00
47 JGr(c),JKu,MD,Battle Freight . 75.00
48 JGr(c),JKu,MD,Roadblock . . . 75.00
49 JGr(c),Walking Target 75.00
50 IN,RH,Bodyguard For A Sub . 75.00
51 JGr(c),RH,Bomber's Moon . . 50.00
52 JKu(c),RH,MD,Back Seat Driver 50.00
53 JKu(c),JKu,Night Attack 50.00
54 JKu(c),IN,Diary of a Fighter Pilot 50.00
55 JKu(c),RH,Split-Second Target 50.00
56 JKu,IN,RH,Frogman Jinx . . . 50.00
57 Pick-Up for Easy Co. 50.00
58 JKu(c),RH,MD,A Piece of Sky 50.00
59 JGr(c),JKu,The Hand of War . 50.00
60 JGr(c),The Time Table 50.00
61 JGr(c),IN,MD,Blind Target . . . 50.00
62 JGr(c),RH,RA,No(c) 50.00
63 JGr(c),JKu,Frogman Carrier . 50.00
64 JKu(c),JKu,RH,The Other Man's War 50.00
65 JGr(c),JKu,MD,Same Old Sarge 50.00
66 JGr(c),The Walking Fort 50.00
67 JGr(c),RH,A:Gunner&Sarge, The Cover Man 100.00
68 JKu(c),Gunner&Sarge, The Man & The Gun 50.00
69 JKu(c),A:Tank Killer, Bazooka Hill 50.00
70 JKu(c),IN,Pigeon Without Wings 50.00
71 JGr(c),A:Tank Killer,Target For An Ammo Boy 50.00
72 JGr(c),A:Tank Killer,T.N.T. Broom 50.00
73 JGr(c),JKu,No Detour 50.00
74 The Minute Commandos 50.00
75 JKu(c),Sink That Flattop 50.00
76 JKu(c),A:Tank Killer, Just One More Tank 50.00
77 JKu(c),IN,MD,Big Fish-little Fish 50.00
78 JGr(c),Tin Hat for an Iron Man 50.00
79 JKu(c),RA,Showdown Soldier 50.00
80 JGr(c),RA,The Medal Men . . 50.00
81 JGr(c),IN,Ghost Ship of Two Wars 25.00
82 IN(c),B:Johnny Cloud, The Flying Chief 25.00
83 IN(c),Fighting Blind 25.00
84 IN(c),Death Dive 25.00
85 RH(c),Battle Eagle 25.00
86 JGr(c),Top-Gun Ace 25.00
87 JGr(c),Broken Ace 25.00
88 JGr(c),The Ace of Vengeance 25.00
89 JGr(c),The Star Jockey 25.00
90 JGr(c),Wingmate of Doom . . . 25.00
91 RH(c),Two Missions To Doom 25.00
92 JGr(c),The Battle Hawk 25.00
93 RH(c),The Silent Rider 25.00
94 RH(c),Be Brave-Be Silent . . . 25.00
95 RH(c),Second Sight For a Pilot 25.00
96 RH(c),The Last Flight of Lt. Moon 25.00
97 IN(c),A 'Target' Called Johnny 25.00
98 The Time-Bomb Ace 25.00
99 IN(c),The Empty Cockpit 25.00
100 RH(c),Battle o/t Sky Chiefs 25.00
101 RH(c),Death Ship of Three Wars 15.00
102 JKu(c),Blind Eagle-Hungry Hawk 15.00
103 IN(c),Battle Ship-Battle Heart 15.00
104 JKu(c),The Last Target 15.00
105 IN(c),Killer Horse-Ship 15.00

106 IN(c),Death Song For A Battle Hawk 15.00
107 IN(c),Flame in the Sky 15.00
108 IN(c),Death-Dive of the Aces 15.00
109 IN(c),The Killer Slot 15.00
110 RH(c),The Co-Pilot was Death 15.00
111 RH(c),E:Johnny Cloud, Tag– You're Dead 15.00
112 RH(c),B:Balloon Buster,Lt. Steve Savage-Balloon Buster 15.00
113 JKu(c),The Ace of Sudden Death 15.00
114 JKu(c),The Ace Who Died Twice 15.00
115 IN(c),A:Johnny Cloud, Deliver One Enemy Ace-Handle With Care 15.00
116 JKu(c),A:Baloon Buster, Circle of Death 15.00
117 September-October, 1966 . . 15.00

All-Flash #7 © DC Comics, Inc.

ALL-FLASH
Summer, 1941

1 EHi,O:Flash,I:The Monocle 6,000.00
2 EHi,The Adventure of Roy Revenge 1,200.00
3 EHi,The Adventure of Misplaced Faces 800.00
4 EHi,Tale of the Time Capsule 625.00
5 EHi,The Case of the Patsy Colt! Last Quarterly 500.00
6 EHi,The Ray that Changed Men's Souls 475.00
7 EHi,Adventures of a Writers Fantasy, House of Horrors . 475.00
8 EHi,Formula to Fairyland! . . 475.00
9 EHi,Adventure of the Stolen Telescope 475.00
10 EHi,Case of the Curious Cat 475.00
11 EHi,Troubles come in Doubles 400.00
12 EHi,Tumble INN to Trouble, Becomes Quarterly on orders from War Production Board O:The Thinker 400.00
13 EHi,I:The King 400.00
14 EHi,I:Winky,Blinky & Noddy Green Lantern (c) 500.00
15 EHi,Secrets of a Stranger . . 400.00
16 EHi,A:The Sinister 400.00
17 Tales of the Three Wishes . 400.00
18 A:Winlky,Blinky&Noddy B:Mutt & Jeff reprints 400.00

All-Flash #13 © DC Comics, Inc.

19 No Rest at the Rest Home . 400.00
20 A:Winky, Blinky & Noddy . 400.00
21 I:Turtle, ... 300.00
22 The Money Doubler,E:Mutt & Jeff reprints 300.00
23 The Bad Men of Bar Nothing 300.00
24 I:Worry Wart,3 Court Clowns Get Caught 300.00
25 I:Slapsy Simmons, Flash Jitterbugs 300.00
26 I:The Chef,The Boss,Shrimp Coogan,A:Winky, Blinky & Noddy 350.00
27 A:The Thinker,Gangplank Gus story 300.00
28 A:Shrimp Coogan,Winky, Blinky & Noddy 300.00
29 The Thousand-Year Old Terror, A:Winky,Blinky & Noddy . . . 300.00
30 The Vanishing Snowman . 300.00
31 A:Black Hat,The Planet of Sport 300.00
32 I:Fiddler,A:Thinker December-January, 1947 . . 450.00

ALL FUNNY COMICS
Winter, 1943

1 Genius Jones 250.00
2 same 100.00
3 same 75.00
4 same 75.00
5 thru 10 . . . . @75.00
11 Genius Jones 40.00
12 same 40.00
13 same 40.00
14 . . . . 30.00
15 . . . . 40.00
16 A:DC Superheroes 125.00
17 thru 22 . . . . @30.00
23 May-June, 1948 . . . . 30.00

ALL-STAR COMICS
Summer, 1940

1 B:Flash,Hawkman,Hourman,Sandman, Spectre,Red White & Blue 8,000.00
2 B:Green Lantern and Johnny Thunder 3,000.00
3 First meeting of Justice Society with Flash as Chairman . 18,000.00
4 First mission of JSA 3,200.00
5 V:Mr. X,I:Hawkgirl 3,100.00
6 Flash leaves 2,100.00

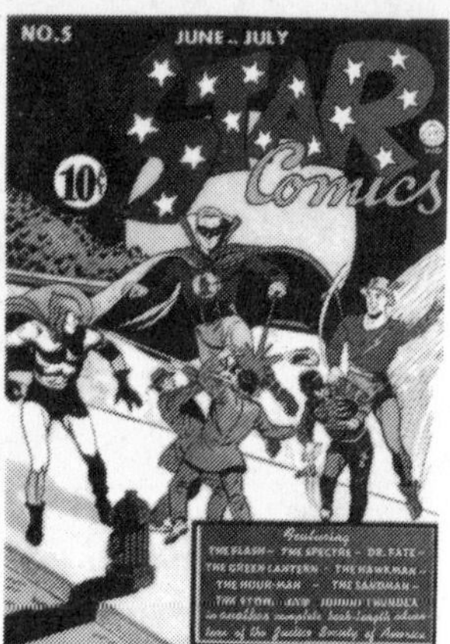

All-Star Comics #5 © DC Comics, Inc.

7 Green Lantern becomes Chairman, L:Hourman, C:Superman, Batman & Flash 2,000.00
8 I:Wonder Women;Starman and Dr. Mid-Nite join,Hawkman becomes chairman 7,500.00
9 JSA in Latin America 1,700.00
10 C:Flash & Green Lantern, JSA Time Travel story . . . 1,600.00
11 Wonder Women joins; I:Justice Battalion 1,400.00
12 V:Black Dragon society . . . 1,400.00
13 V:Hitler 1,350.00
14 JSA in occupied Europe . . 1,350.00
15 I:Brain Wave,A:JSA's Girl Friends 1,400.00
16 Propaganda/relevance issue 1,000.00
17 V:Brain Wave 1,000.00
18 I:King Bee 1,100.00
19 Hunt for Hawkman 1,000.00
20 I:Monster 1,000.00
21 Time travel story 900.00
22 Sandman and Dr. Fate leave, I:Conscience, the Good Fairy 900.00
23 I:Psycho-Pirate 900.00
24 Propaganda/relevance issue, A:Conscience&Wildcat,Mr.Terrific; L:Starman & Spectre; Flash & Green Lantern return 900.00
25 JSA whodunit issue 800.00
26 V:Metal Men from Jupiter . . 800.00
27 Handicap issue,A:Wildcat . . 800.00
28 Ancient curse comes to life . 700.00
29 I:Landor from 25th century . 700.00
30 V:Brain Wave 700.00
31 V:Zor 700.00
32 V:Psycho-Pirate 700.00
33 V:Soloman Grundy,A:Doiby Dickles, Last appearance Thunderbolt 1,500.00
34 I:Wizard 650.00
35 I:Per Degaton 650.00
36 A:Superman and Batman . 1,500.00
37 I:Injustice Society of the World 850.00
38 V:Villians of History, A:Black Canary 900.00
39 JSA in magic world, Johnny Thunder leaves . . . 600.00
40 A:Black Canary,Junior Justice Society of America 600.00
41 Black Canary joins,A:Harlequin, V:Injustice Society

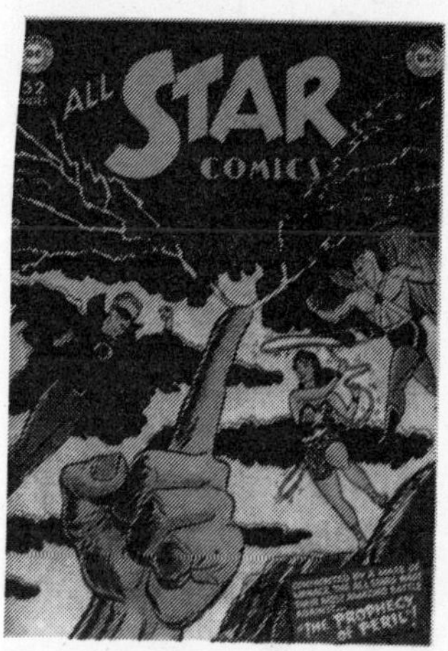

All-Star Comics #41 © DC Comics, Inc.

of the World	600.00
42 I:Alchemist	625.00
43 V:Interdimensional gold men	625.00
44 I:Evil Star	650.00
45 Crooks develop stellar JSA powers	600.00
46 Comedy issue	600.00
47 V:Billy the Kid	600.00
48 Time Travel story	600.00
49 V:Comet-being invaders	600.00
50 V:College classmate of Flash	650.00
51 V:Diamond men from center of the Earth	600.00
52 JSA disappears from Earth for years	600.00
53 Time Travel issue	600.00
54 Circus issue	600.00
55 JSA fly to Jupiter	600.00
56 V:Chameleons from 31st Century	600.00
57 I:Key	700.00

Becomes:

ALL STAR WESTERN
April-May 1951

58 Trigger Twins	250.00
59	125.00
60	125.00
61 thru 64 ATh	100.00
65 thru 66	@100.00
67 GK,B:Johnny Thunder	125.00
68 thru 81	@55.00
82 thru 98	@45.00
99 FF	60.00
100	50.00
101 thru 104	@35.00
105 O:JSA, March, 1987	35.00
106	30.00
107	30.00
108 O:Johnny Thunder	85.00
109 thru 116	@30.00
117 CI,O:Super-Chief	50.00
118	30.00
119	25.00

ALL-STAR COMICS

58 RE,WW,R:JSA,I:Power Girl	7.50
59 RE,WW,Brain Wave	5.00
60 KG,WW,I:Vulcan	5.00
61 KG,WW,V:Vulcan	5.00
62 KG,WW,A:E-2 Superman	5.00
63 KG,WW,A:E-2 Superman, Solomon Grundy	5.00
64 WW,Shining Knight	4.00
65 KG,WW,E-2 Superman, Vandal Savage	4.00
66 JSon,BL,Injustice Society	3.50
67 JSon,BL	3.50
68 JSon,BL	3.50
69 JSon,BL,A:E-2 Superman, Starman,Dr.Mid-Nite	3.50
70 JSon,BL,Huntress	3.50
71 JSon,BL	3.50
72 JSon,A:Golden.Age Huntress	3.50
73 JSon	3.50
74 JSon	3.50

ALL STAR SQUADRON

1 RB,JOy,JSa,I:Degaton	1.75
2 RB,JOy,Robotman	1.00
3 RB,JOy,Robotman	1.00
4 RB,JOy,Robotman	1.00
5 RB/JOy,I:Firebrand(Dannette)	1.00
6 JOy,Hawkgirl	1.00
7 JOy,Hawkgirl	1.00
8 DH/JOy,A:Steel	1.00
9 DH/JOy,A:Steel	1.00
10 JOy,V:Binary Brotherhood	1.00
11 JOy,V:Binary Brotherhood	1.00
12 JOy,R:Dr.Hastor O:Hawkman	1.00
13 JOy,photo(c)	1.00
14 JOy,JLA crossover	1.00
15 JOy,JLA crossover	1.00
16 I&D:Nuclear	1.00
17 Trial of Robotman	1.00
18 V:Thor	1.00
19 V:Brainwave	1.00
20 JOy,V:Brainwave	1.00
21 JOy,I:Cyclotron (1st JOy Superman)	1.00
22 JOy,V:Deathbolt,Cyclotron	1.00
23 JOy,I:Amazing-Man	1.00
24 JOy,I:Brainwave,Jr..	4.50
25 JOy,I:Infinity Inc.	3.50
26 JOy,Infinity Inc.	3.00
27 Spectre	1.00
28 JOy,Spectre	1.00
29 JOy,retold story	1.00
30 V:Black Dragons	1.00
31 All-Star gathering	1.00
32 O:Freedom Fighters	1.00
33 Freedom Fighters,I:Tsunami	1.00
34 Freedom Fighters	1.00
35 RB,Shazam family	1.00
36 Shazam family	1.00
37 A:Shazam Family	1.00
38 V:The Real American	1.00
39 V:The Real American	1.00
40 D:The Real American	1.00
41 O:Starman	1.00
42 V:Tsunami,Kung	1.00
43 V:Tsunami,Kung	1.00
44 I:Night & Fog	1.00
45 I:Zyklon	1.00
46 V:Baron Blitzkrieg	1.00
47 TM,O:Dr.Fate	4.00
48 A:Blackhawk	1.00
49 A:Dr.Occult	1.00
50 Crisis	1.50
51 AA,Crisis	1.00
52 Crisis	1.00
53 Crisis,A:The Dummy	1.00
54 Crisis,V:The Dummy	1.00
55 Crisis,V:Anti-Monitor	1.00
56 Crisis	1.00
57 A:Dr.Occult	1.00
58 I:Mekanique	1.00
59 A:Mekanique,Spectre	1.00
60 Crisis 1942, conclusion	1.00
61 O:Liberty Belle	1.00
62 O:The Shining Knight	1.00
63 O:Robotman	1.00
64 WB/TD,V:Funny Face	1.00
65 DH/TD,O:J.Quick	1.00
66 TD,O:Tarantula	1.00
67 TD,Last Issue,O:JSA	1.00
Ann.#1 JOy,O:G.A.,Atom	1.25
Ann.#2 JOy,Infinity Inc.	1.50
Ann.#3 WB,JOy,KG,GP,DN	1.25

ALL STAR WESTERN
(see WEIRD WESTERN TALES)

AMBUSH BUG
June, 1985

1 KG,I:Cheeks	1.25
2 KG,	1.00
3 KG,	1.00
4 KG,September,1985	1.00
STOCKING STUFFER	
1 KG,R:Cheeks	1.25

AMBUSH BUG NOTHING SPECIAL

1 KG,A:Sandman,Death	3.00

AMERICA vs. JUSTICE SOCIETY
January, 1985

1 AA,R,Thomas Script	1.50
2 AA	1.25
3 AA	1.25
4 AA,April,1985	1.25

AMERICAN FREAK: A TALE OF THE UN-MEN
Vertigo

1 B:DLp,(s),VcL,R:Un-Men	2.25
2 VcL,A:Crassus	2.25
3 VcL,A:Scylla	2.25
4 VcL,A:Scylla	2.25
5 VcL,Final Issue	2.25

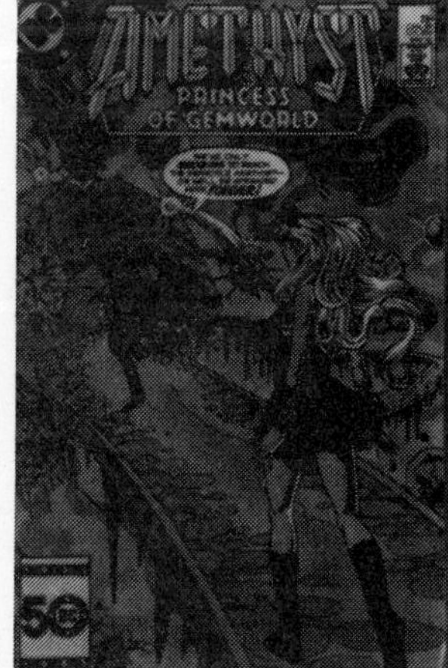

Amethyst #5 © DC Comics, Inc.

AMETHYST
[Limited series]
May, 1983

1 Origin	1.25
2 thru 7 EC	@1.00
8 EC,O:Gemworld	1.00
9 EC	1.00
10 EC	1.00
11 EC	1.00
12 EC,May, 1984	1.00
Spec.#1 KG	1.25

[Regular Series]
January, 1985

1 thru 12 EC . . . . @1.00
13 EC,Crisis,A:Dr.Fate 1.00
14 EC 1.00
15 EC,Castle Amethyst Destroyed 1.00
16 EC,August, 1986 . . . . 1.00
Spec.#1 EM, ... 1.25

[Mini Series]
November, 1987

1 EM 1.25
2 EM 1.25
3 EM 1.25
4 EM,O:Mordru,Feb., 1988 . . . . . 1.25

ANGEL & THE APE

1 Apes of Wrath Pt.#1 . . . . 1.00
2 Apes of Wrath Pt.#2, A:G.Gardner 1.00
3 Apes of Wrath Pt. #3, A: Inferior Five 1.00
4 Apes of Wrath Pt. #4, A: Inferior Five, final issue 1.00

ANIMA
Vertigo

1 R:Anima 2.00
2 V:Scarecrow 2.00
3 V:Scarecrow 2.00
4 A:Nameless one 2.00
5 CI,V:Arkana 1.75

ANIMAL-MAN

1 BB(c),B:GMo(s),ChT,DHz, B:Animal Rights,I:Dr.Myers . . 20.00
2 BB(c),ChT,DHz,A:Superman . . 14.00
3 BB(c),ChT,DHz,A:B'wana Beast 8.00
4 BB(c),ChT,DHz,V:B'wana Beast, E:Animal Rights 8.00
5 BB(c),ChT,DHz, I&D:Crafty Coyote 9.00
6 BB(c),ChT,DHz,A:Hawkman . . . 6.00
7 BB(c),ChT,DHz,D:Red Mask . . . 5.00
8 BB(c),ChT,DHz,V:Mirror Master 5.00
9 BB(c),DHz,TG,A:Martian Manhunter 5.00
10 BB(c),ChT,DHz,A:Vixen, B:O:Animal Man 5.00
11 BB(c),ChT,DHz,I:Hamed Ali, Tabu,A:Vixen 5.00
12 BB(c),D:Hamed Ali,A:Vixen, B'wanaBeast 4.50
13 BB(c),I:Dominic Mndawe,R:B'wana Beast,Apartheid 4.50
14 BB(c),TG,SeM,A:Future Animal Man,I:Lennox 4.50
15 BB(c),ChT,DHz,A:Dolphin 4.50
16 BB(c),ChT,DHz,A:JLA. 4.50
17 BB(c),ChT,DHz,A:Mirr.Master . 4.50
18 BB(c),ChT,DHz,A:Lennox 4.50
19 BB(c),ChT,DHz,D:Ellen, Cliff,Maxine 4.50
20 BB(c),ChT,DHz,I:Bug-Man . . . 4.50
21 BB(c),ChT,DHz,N&V:Bug-Man 4.50
22 BB(c),PCu,SeM,A:Rip Hunter . 4.50
23 BB(c),A:Phantom Stranger . . . 3.50
24 BB(c),V:Psycho Pirate 3.50
25 BB(c),ChT,MFm,I:Comic Book Limbo 3.50
26 BB(c),E:GMo(s),ChT,MFm, A:Grant Morrison 3.50
27 BB(c),B:PMi(s),ChT,MFm, ... 3.00
28 BB(c),ChT,MFm,I:Nowhere Man, I&D:Front Page 3.00
29 ChT,SDi,V:National Man 3.00
30 BB(c),ChT,MFm,V:Angel Mob . 3.00
31 BB(c),ChT,MFm, ... 3.00
32 BB(c),E:PMi(s),ChT,MFm, ... 3.00
33 BB(c),B:TV(s),SDi,A:Travis Cody 3.00
34 BB(c),SDi,Requiem 3.00
35 BB(c),SDi,V:Radioactive Dogs . 3.00
36 BB(c),SDi,A:Mr.Rainbow 3.00
37 BB(c),SDi,Animal/Lizard Man . 3.00
38 BB(c),SDi,A:Mr.Rainbow 2.50
39 BB(c),TMd,SDi,Wolfpack in San Diego 2.50
40 BB(c),SDi,War of the Gods x-over 2.50
41 BB(c),SDi,V:Star Labs Renegades,I:Winky 2.50
42 BB(c),SDi,V:Star Labs Renegades 2.50
43 BB(c),SDi,I:Tristess,A:Vixen . . 2.50
44 BB(c),SDi,A:Vixen 2.50
45 BB(c),StP,SDi,I:L.Decker 2.50
46 BB(c),SDi,I:Frank Baker 2.50
47 BB(c),SDi,I:Shining Man, (B'wana Beast) 2.50
48 BB(c),SDi,V:Antagon 2.50
49 BB(c),SDi,V:Antagon 2.50
50 BB(c),E:TV(s),SDi,I:Metaman . 3.50
51 BB(c),B:JaD(s),StP,B:Flesh and Blood 3.00
52 BB(c),StP,Homecoming 3.00
53 BB(c),StP,Flesh and Blood . . . 3.00
54 BB(c),StP,Flesh and Blood . . . 3.00
55 BB(c),StP,Flesh and Blood . . . 3.00
56 BB(c),StP,E:Flesh and Blood, Double-sized 5.00

Vertigo

57 BB(c),StP,B:Recreation, Ellen in NY 2.50
58 BB(c),StP,Wild Side 2.50
59 BB(c),RsB,GHi(i),Wild Town . . 2.50
60 RsB,GHi(i),Wild life 2.50
61 BB(c),StP,Tooth and Claw#1 . . 2.50
62 BB(c),StP,Tooth and Claw#2 . . 2.50
63 BB(c),V:Leviathan 2.50
64 DIB(c),WSm,DnS(i), Breath of God 2.50
65 RDB(c),WSm, Perfumed Garden 2.25
66 A:Kindred Spirit 2.25
67 StP,Mysterious Ways #1 . . . . . 2.25
68 StP,Mysterious Ways #2 . . . . . 2.25
69 Animal Man's Family 2.25
70 GgP(c),StP, ... 2.25
71 GgP(c),StP,Maxine Alive? 2.25
72 StP, ... 2.25
73 StP,Power Life Church 1.95
Ann.#1 BB(c),JaD,TS(i),RIB(i), Children Crusade,F:Maxine . . . 4.25
TPB Rep #1 thru 10 . . . . 19.95

AQUAMAN
January-February, 1962

1 NC,I:Quisp 375.00
2 NC,V:Captain Sykes 200.00
3 NC,Aquaman from Atlantis . . 125.00
4 NC,A:Quisp 90.00
5 NC,The Haunted Sea 85.00
6 NC,A:Quisp 70.00
7 NC,Sea Beasts of Atlantis . . . 70.00
8 NC,Plot to Steal the Seas 70.00
9 NC,V:King Neptune 70.00
10 NC,A:Quisp 70.00
11 I: Mera 56.00
12 NC,The Cosmic Gladiators . . 50.00
13 NC,Invasion of the Giant Reptiles 50.00
14 NC,AquamanSecretPowers . . 50.00
15 NC,Menace of the Man-Fish . 50.00
16 NC,Duel of the Sea Queens . 45.00
17 NC,Man Who Vanquished Aquaman 45.00
18 W:Aquaman & Mera 50.00
19 NC,Atlanteans for Sale 42.00
20 NC,Sea King's DoubleDoom . 42.00
21 NC,I:Fisherman 35.00
22 NC,The Trap of the Sinister Sea Nymphs 35.00
23 NC,I:Aquababy 35.00
24 NC,O:Black Manta 28.00
25 NC,Revolt of Aquaboy 28.00
26 NC,I:O.G.R.E. 28.00
27 NC,Battle of the Rival Aquamen' 28.00
28 NC,Hail Aquababy,King of Atlantis 28.00
29 I:Ocean Master 29.00
30 NC,C:JLA 22.00
31 NC,V:O.G.R.E. 22.00
32 NC,V:Tryton 22.00
33 NC,I:Aquagirl 40.00

Aquaman #61 © DC Comics, Inc.

34 NC,I:Aquabeast 25.00
35 I:Black Manta 25.00
36 NC,What Seeks the Awesome Threesome? 25.00
37 I:Scavenger 25.00
38 NC,I:Liquidator 25.00
39 NC,How to Kill a Sea King . . 25.00
40 JAp,Sorcerers from the Sea . 22.00
41 JAp,Quest for Mera #1 . . . . . 14.00
42 JAp,Quest for Mera #2 . . . . . 14.00
43 JAp,Quest for Mera #3 . . . . . 14.00
44 JAp,Quest for Mera #4 . . . . . 14.00
45 JAp,Quest for Mera #5 . . . . . 14.00
46 JAp,Quest for Mera concl. . . 14.00
47 JAp,Revolution in Atlantis #1 rep.Adventure #268 . . . . . . 12.00
48 JAp,Revolution in Atlantis #2 rep.Adventure #260 . . . . 17.00
49 JAp,As the Seas Die 10.00
50 JAp,NA,A:Deadman 25.00
51 JAp,NA,A:Deadman 25.00
52 JAp,NA,A:Deadman 25.00
53 JAp,Is California Sinking? 8.00
54 JAp,Crime Wave 8.00
55 JAp,Return of the Alien 8.00
56 JAp,I&O:Crusader (1970) 8.00
57 JAp,V:Black Manta (1977) . . . 8.00
58 JAp,O:Aquaman rtd 9.00
59 JAp,V:Scavenger 8.00
60 DN,V:Scavenger 8.00
61 DN,BMc,A:Batman 8.00
62 DN,A:Ocean Master 7.00
63 DN,V:Ocean Master, final issue 7.00

[2nd Series]

1 Poseidonis Under Attack, C:J'onn J'onzz,Blue Beetle . . . 2.25
2 V:Oumland 2.00
3 I:Iqula 2.00
4 V:Iqula,A:Queequeg 1.50
5 A:Aqualad,Titans,M.Manhunter, R:Manta 1.50
6 V: Manta 1.50
7 R:Mera 1.50
8 A:Batman,V:NKV Demon 1.50
9 Eco-Wars#1,A:Sea Devils 1.50
10 Eco-Wars#2,A:Sea Devils 1.50
11 V:Gigantic Dinosaur 1.50

12 A:laula 1.50
13 V:The Scavenger 1.50
14 V:The Scavenger 1.50

AQUAMAN
[Mini-Series]
February, 1986

1 V:Ocean Master 5.50
2 V:Ocean Master 3.00
3 V:Ocean Master 3.00
4 V:Ocean Master 3.00

[2nd Mini-Series]

1 CS,Atlantis Under Siege 3.00
2 CS,V:Invaders 1.75
3 CS,Mera turned Psychotic 1.50
4 CS,Poseidonis Under Siege . . . 1.50
5 CS,Last Stand,final issue 1.50
Spec#1 MPa,Legend o/Aquaman . 2.00

AQUAMAN:TIME & TIDE

1 PDd(s),O:Aquaman 2.00
2 PDd(s),O:Aquaman contd. 1.75
3 PDd(s),O:Aquaman contd. 1.75
4 PDd(s),O:Aquaman,final issue. . 1.75

ARAK
September, 1981

1 EC,O:Ara 1.50
2 EC 1.00
3 EC,I:Valda 1.00
4 thru 10 EC . . . . @1.00
11 EC,AA 1.00
12 EC,AA,I:Satyricus 1.00
13 thru 19 AA . . . . @1.00
20 AA,O:Angelica 1.00
21 AA 1.00
22 AA 1.00
23 AA 1.00
24 Double size 1.50
25 thru 30 . . . . @1.00
31 D Arak,becomes shaman 1.00
32 thru 48 . . . . @1.00
49 CI/TD 1.00
50 TD,November, 1985 . . . . 1.25
Ann.#1 . . . . 1.00

ARCANA: THE BOOKS OF MAGIC
Vertigo

Ann.#1 JBo(c),JNR(s),PrG,Children's
Crusade,R:Tim Hunter,
A:Free Country 4.50

ARION
November, 1982

1 JDu 1.50
2 JDu 1.00
3 JDu 1.00
4 JDu,O:Arion 1.00
5 JDu 1.00
6 JDu 1.00
7 thru 12 . . . . @1.00
13 JDu 1.00
14 JDu 1.00
15 JDu 1.00
16 thru 35, Oct. 1985 . . . . @1.00
Spec. 1.25

ARION THE IMMORTAL

1 RWi,R:Arion 1.75
2 RWi,V:Garffon 1.50
3 RWi,V:Garn Daanuth 1.50
4 RWi,V:Garn Daanuth 1.50
5 RWi,Darkworlet 1.50
6 RWi,MG,A:Power Girl 1.50

ARMAGEDDON 2001
May 1991

1 DJu,DG,I&O:Waverider 6.00
1a 2nd printing 2.50
1b 3rd printing (silver) 2.00
2 DJu,ATi,Monarch revealed as Hawk,
D:Dove,L:Capt Atom(JLE) 4.00
Spec.#1 MR 1.75

ARMAGEDDON 2001 ARMAGEDDON: THE ALIEN AGENDA

1 DJu,JOy,A:Monarch,Capt.Atom 1.75
2 V:Ancient Romans 1.25
3 JRu(i),The Old West 1.25
4 DG,GP,V:Nazi's,last issue 1.25

ARMAGEDDON: INFERNO

1 TMd,LMc,A:Creeper,Batman,
Firestorm 1.75
2 AAd,LMc,WS,I:Abraxis,A:Lobo . 1.50
3 AAd,WS,LMc,TMd,MN,R:Justice
Society 1.50
4 AAd,WS,LMc,TMd,MN,DG,
V:Abraxis,A:Justice Society . . . 1.50

ATARI FORCE
January, 1984

1 JL,I:TempestDart 1.50
2 JL 1.00
3 JL 1.00
4 RA/JL/JO 1.00
5 RA/JL/JO 1.00
6 thru 12 JL . . . . @1.00
13 KG 1.00
14 thru 20 EB . . . . @1.00
21 EB August, 1985 . . . . 1.00

ATLANTIS CHRONICLES

1 EM,Atlantis 50,000 years ago . 3.50
2 EM,Atlantis Sunk 3.25
3 EM,Twin Cities of Poseidonis
& Tritonis 3.25
4 EM,King Orin's Daughter
Cora Assumes Throne 3.25
5 EM,Orin vs. Shalako 3.25
6 EM,Contact with Surface
Dwellers 3.25
7 EM,Queen Atlanna gives Birth to
son(Aquaman)48 pg.final issue 3.25

ATOM, THE
June-July, 1962

1 MA,GK,I:Plant Master 650.00
2 MA,GK,V:Plant Master 250.00
3 MA,GK,I:Chronos 175.00
4 MA,GK,Snapper Carr 125.00
5 MA,GK 125.00
6 MA,GK, ... 90.00
7 MA,GK,1st Atom & Hawkman
team-up 200.00
8 MA,GK,A:JLA,V:Doctor Light . 75.00
9 MA,GK 75.00
10 MA,GK 75.00
11 MA,GK 56.00
12 MA,GK 56.00
13 MA,GK 56.00
14 MA,GK 56.00
15 MA,GK 56.00
16 MA,GK 40.00
17 MA,GK 40.00
18 MA,GK 40.00
19 MA,GK,A:Zatanna 40.00
20 MA,GK 40.00
21 MA,GK 28.00
22 MA,GK 28.00
23 MA,GK 28.00
24 MA,GK,V:Jason Woodrue . . . 28.00
25 MA,GK 28.00
26 GK 28.00
27 GK 28.00
28 GK 28.00
29 GK,A:E-2 Atom,Thinker. 90.00
30 GK 28.00
31 GK,A:Hawkman 25.00
32 GK 25.00
33 GK 25.00

Atom #33 © DC Comics, Inc.

34 GK,V:Big Head 25.00
35 GK 25.00
36 GK,A:Golden Age Atom 40.00
37 GK,I:Major Mynah 25.00
38 "Sinister stopover Earth"
Aug.-Sept., 1968 . . . . 25.00

Becomes:

ATOM & HAWKMAN
October-November, 1968

39 MA, V:Tekla 25.00
40 DD,JKu,MA 25.00
41 DD,JKu,MA 25.00
42 MA,V:Brama 25.00
43 MA,I:Gentleman Ghost 25.00
44 DD 25.00
45 DD, Oct.-Nov., 1969 . . . . 25.00

ATOM SPECIAL

1 SDi,V:Chronos 3.00

AVATAR

1 A:Midnight & Allies 8.00
2 Search for Tablets 6.00
3 V:Cyric, Myrkul, final issue . . . 6.00

BATGIRL

Spec.#1 V: Cormorant,I:Slash . . 10.00

BATMAN
Spring, 1940

1 I:Joker,Cat(Catwoman),V:Hugo
Strange 38,000.00
2 V:Joker/Catwoman team . 7,500.00
3 V:Catwoman 5,000.00
4 V:Joker 3,500.00
5 V:Joker 2,500.00
6 V:'Clock Maker' 1,800.00
7 V:Joker 1,800.00
8 V:Joker 1,800.00
9 V:Joker 1,800.00
10 V:Catwoman 1,800.00
11 V:Joker,Penguin 2,000.00
12 V:Joker 1,800.00
13 V:Joker 1,500.00
14 V:Penguin;Propaganda sty 1,600.00
15 V:Catwoman 1,500.00
16 I:Alfred,V:Joker 3,500.00
17 V:Penguin 1,000.00
18 V:Tweedledum &
Tweedledee 1,000.00

Batman #7 © DC Comics, Inc.

Batman #11 © DC Comics, Inc.

No.	Description	Price
19	V:Joker	1,000.00
20	V:Joker	1,000.00
21	V:Penguin	750.00
22	V:Catwoman,Cavalier	750.00
23	V:Joker	1,200.00
24	I:Carter Nichols, V:Tweedledum &Tweedledee	850.00
25	V:Joker/Penguin team	1,150.00
26	V:Cavalier	750.00
27	V:Penguin	750.00
28	V:Joker	800.00
29	V:Scuttler	750.00
30	V:Penguin,I:Ally Babble	750.00
31	I:Punch and Judy	600.00
32	O:Robin,V:Joker	650.00
33	V:Penguin,Jackall	700.00
34	A:Ally Babble	575.00
35	V:Catwoman	575.00
36	V:Penguin,A:King Arthur	600.00
37	V:Joker	750.00
38	V:Penguin	600.00
39	V:Catwoman,Christmas Story	575.00
40	V:Joker	750.00
41	V:Penguin	525.00
42	V:Catwoman	500.00
43	V:Penguin	500.00
44	V:Joker,A:Carter Nichols,Meets ancester Silas Wayne	750.00
45	V:Catwoman	500.00
46	V:Joker,A:Carter Nichols, Leonardo Da Vinci	450.00
47	O:Batman,V:Catwoman	1,500.00
48	V:Penguin, Bat-Cave story	525.00
49	I:Mad Hatter & Vicki Vale	700.00
50	V:Two-Face,A:Vicki Vale	500.00
51	V:Penguin	450.00
52	V:Joker	500.00
53	V:Joker	500.00
54	V:'The Treasure Hunter'	450.00
55	V:Joker	500.00
56	V:Penguin	450.00
57	V:Joker	500.00
58	V:Penguin	450.00
59	I:Deadshot	450.00
60	V:'Shark' Marlin	450.00
61	V:Penguin	575.00
62	O:Catwoman,I:Knight & Squire	600.00
63	V:Joker	375.00
64	V:Killer Moth	350.00
65	I:Wingman,V:Catwoman	400.00
66	V:Joker	400.00
67	V:Joker	400.00

No.	Description	Price
68	V:Two-Face,Alfred story	300.00
69	I:King of the Cats, A:Catwoman	400.00
70	V:Penguin	350.00
71	V:Mr. Cipher	350.00
72	'The Jungle Batman'	350.00
73	V:Joker,A:Vicki Vale	400.00
74	V:Joker	400.00
75	I:The Gorilla Boss	350.00
76	V:Penguin	375.00
77	'The Crime Predictor'	350.00
78	'The Manhunter from Mars'	350.00
79	A:Vicki Vale	350.00
80	V:Joker	350.00
81	V:Two-Face	350.00
82	'The Flying Batman'	300.00
83	V:'Fish' Frye	300.00
84	V:Catwoman	350.00
85	V:Joker	325.00
86	V:Joker	325.00
87	V:Joker	325.00
88	V:Mr. Mystery	325.00
89	I:Aunt Agatha	325.00
90	I:Batboy	275.00
91	V:Blinky Grosset	275.00
92	I:Ace, the Bat-Hound	275.00
93	'The Caveman Batman'	275.00
94	Alfred has Amnesia	275.00
95	'The Bat-Train'	275.00
96	'Batman's College Days'	275.00
97	V:Joker	275.00
98	A:Carter Nichols,Jules Verne	275.00
99	V:Penguin,A:Carter Nichols, Bat Masterson	275.00
100	'Great Batman Contest'	1,200.00
101	'The Great Batman Hunt'	250.00
102	V:Mayne Mallok	250.00
103	A:Ace, the Bat-Hound	250.00
104	V:Devoe	250.00
105	A:Batwoman	325.00
106	V:Keene Harper gang	250.00
107	V:Daredevils	250.00
108	Bat-cave story	250.00
109	'The 1,000 Inventions of Batman'	250.00
110	V:Joker	275.00
111		185.00
112	I:Signalman	185.00
113	I:Fatman	185.00
114		185.00
115		185.00
116		185.00
117		185.00

No.	Description	Price
118		185.00
119		185.00
120		185.00
121	I:Mr.Freeze	135.00
122		135.00
123	A:Joker	150.00
124	"Mystery Seed from Space"	135.00
125		135.00
126		135.00
127	A:Superman & Joker	190.00
128		135.00
129	O:Robin(Retold)	175.00
130		135.00
131	I:2nd Batman	100.00
132		100.00
133		100.00
134		100.00
135		100.00
136	A:Joker,Bat-Mite	150.00
137	V:Mr.Marvel,The Brand	100.00
138	A:Bat-Mite	100.00
139	I:Old Batgirl	100.00
140	A:Joker	100.00
141	V:Clockmaster	110.00
142	Batman robot story	100.00
143	A:Bathound	100.00
144	A:Joker,Bat-Mite,Bat-Girl	100.00

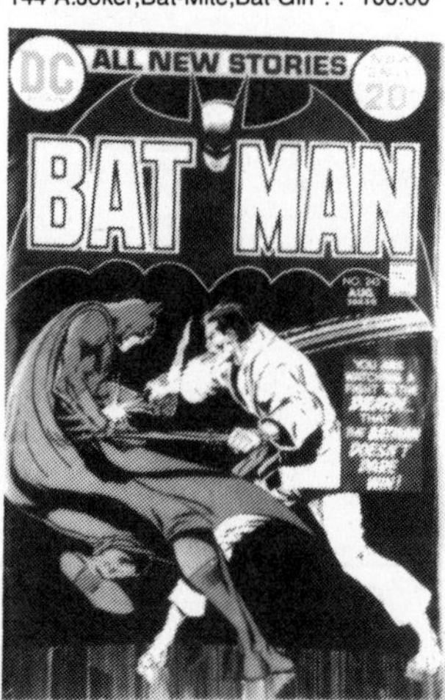

Batman #243 © DC Comics, Inc.

No.	Description	Price
145	V:Mr.50,Joker	125.00
146	A:Bat-Mite,Joker	80.00
147	Batman becomes Bat-Baby	75.00
148	A:Joker	125.00
149	V:Maestro	70.00
150	V:Biff Warner,Jack Pine	70.00
151	V:Harris Boys	50.00
152	A:Joker	60.00
153	Other Dimension story	55.00
154	V:Dr. Dorn	55.00
155	1st S.A. Penguin	225.00
156	V:Gorilla Gang	55.00
157	V:Mirror Man	55.00
158	A:Bathound,Bat-Mite	55.00
159	A:Joker,Clayface	70.00
160	V:Bart Cullen	55.00
161	A:Bat-Mite	55.00
162	F:Robin	55.00
163	A:Joker	65.00
164	CI,A:Mystery Analysts,new Batmobile	50.00
165	V:The Mutated Man	50.00
166	Escape story	50.00
167	V:Karabi & Hydra, the Crime Cartel	50.00
168	V:Mr. Mammoth	50.00

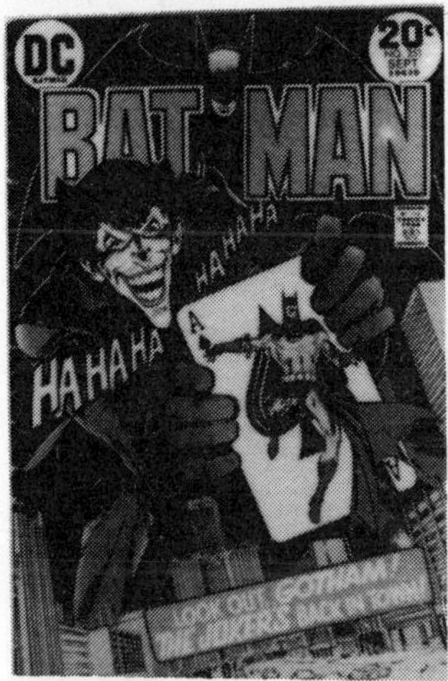

Batman #251 © DC Comics, Inc.

169 A:Penguin 95.00
170 V:Getaway Genius 50.00
171 CI,1st S.A. Riddler 325.00
172 V:Flower Gang 35.00
173 V:Elwood Pearson 35.00
174 V:Big Game Hunter 35.00
175 V:Eddie Repp 35.00
176 Giant rep.A:Joker,Catwom. . 50.00
177 BK,A:Elongated Man,Atom . 26.00
178 CI 26.00
179 CI,2nd Riddler(Silver) 80.00
180 BK,A:Death-Man 26.00
181 CI,I:Poison Ivy 30.00
182 A:Joker,(giant size rep). . . . 26.00
183 CI,A:Poison Ivy 26.00
184 CI,Mystery of the Missing
Manhunters 26.00
185 Giant rep. 35.00
186 A:Joker 35.00
187 Giant rep.A:Joker 35.00
188 CI,A:Eraser 16.00
189 CI,A:Scarecrow 16.00
190 CI,A:Penguin 22.00
191 CI,The Day Batman Soldout 16.00
192 CI,The Crystal ball that
betrayed Batman 16.00
193 Giant rep. 16.00
194 MSy,BK,A:Blockbuster,Mystery
Analysts of Gotham City 15.00
195 CI 15.00
196 BK,Psychic Super-Sleuth . . 15.00
197 MSy,A:Bat Girl,Catwoman . . 45.00
198 A:Joker,Penguin,Catwoman,
O:Batman rtd,(G-Size rep) . . 50.00
199 CI,'Peril o/t Poison Rings' . . 15.00
200 NA(c),O:rtd,A:Joker,Pengiun,
Scarecrow 130.00
201 A:Batman Villians 16.00
202 BU:Robin 14.00
203 NA(c),(giant size) 14.00
204 FR(s),IN,JG, ... 12.00
205 FR(s),IN,JG, ... 12.00
206 FR(s),IN,JG, ... 12.00
207 FR(s),IN,JG, ... 12.00
208 GK,new O:Batman,
A:Catwoman 17.00
209 FR(s),IN,JG, ... 12.00
210 A:Catwoman 14.00
211 FR(s),IN,JG, ... 12.00
212 FR(s),IN,JG, ... 12.00
213 RA,30th Anniv.Batman,new O:
Robin,rep.O:Alfred,Joker 35.00
214 IN,A:Batgirl 12.00
215 IN,DG 12.00
216 IN,DG,I:DaphnePennyworth 12.00
217 NA(c) 13.00
218 NA(c),giant 14.00
219 NA,IN,DG,Batman Xmas . . . 20.00
220 NA(c),IN 12.00
221 IN,DG 12.00
222 IN,Rock'n Roll story 20.00
223 NA(c),giant 14.00
224 NA(c) 10.00
225 NA(c),IN,DG 10.00
226 IN,DG I:10-Eyed Man 10.00
227 IN,DG,A:Daphne
Pennyworth 10.00
228 giant Deadly Traps rep. . . . 12.00
229 IN 10.00
230 NA(c),Robin 10.00
231 . . . . 10.00
232 DON(s),NA,DG,
I:Ras al Ghul 25.00
233 giant Bruce Wayne iss. 12.00
234 NA,DG,IN,1stS.A.Two-Face 75.00
235 CI,V:Spook 8.00
236 NA 8.00
237 NA 20.00
238 NA,JC,JKu,giant 10.00
239 NA,RB 8.00
240 NA(c),RB,giant,R-Ghul 8.00
241 IN,DG,RB,A:Kid Flash 8.00
242 RB,MK 8.00
243 NA,DG,Ras al Ghul 17.00
244 NA,Ras al Ghul 17.00
245 NA,IN,DG,FMc,Ras al Ghul . 17.00
246 . . . . 8.00
247 Deadly New Year 8.00
248 . . . . 8.00
249 'Citidel of Crime' 8.00
250 IN,DG 8.00
251 NA,V:Joker 35.00
252 . . . . 8.00
253 AN,DG,A:Shadow 8.00
254 NA,GK,B:100 page issues . . 11.00
255 GK,CI,NA,DG,I:CrazyQuilt . . 14.00
256 Catwoman 14.00
257 IN,DG,V:Penguin 15.00
258 IN,DG 9.00
259 GK,IN,DG,A:Shadow 9.00
260 IN,DG,Joker 16.00
261 CI,GK,E:100 page issues . . 10.00
262 A:Scarecrow 5.50
263 DG(i),A:Riddler 5.50
264 DON(s),DG,A:Devil Dayre . . . 5.50
265 RB,BWr 6.00
266 DG,Catwoman(old Costume) . 8.50
267 DG 5.50
268 DON(s),IN,TeB,V:Sheikh 5.50
269 A:Riddler 5.50
270 B:DvR(s) 5.50
271 IN,FMc 5.50
272 JL 5.50
273 V:Underworld Olympics/76 . . 5.50
274 . . . . 5.50
275 . . . . 5.50
276 . . . . 5.50
277 . . . . 5.50
278 . . . . 5.50
279 A:Riddler 5.50
280 . . . . 5.50
281 . . . . 5.50
282 . . . . 5.50
283 V:Camouflage 5.50
284 JA,R:Dr.Tzin Tzin 5.50
285 . . . . 5.00
286 V:Joker 5.00
287 BWi,MGr,Penguin 7.50
288 BWi,MGr,Penguin 7.50
289 MGr, V:Skull 5.00
290 MGr,V:Skull Dagger 5.00
291 B:Underworld Olympics #1,
A:Catwoman 7.00
292 A:Riddler 5.00
293 A:Superman & Luthor 5.00
294 E:DvR(s),E:Underworld
Olympics,A:Joker 6.50
295 GyC(s),MGo,JyS,V:Hamton . . 5.00
296 B:DvR(s),V:Scarecrow 5.00
297 RB,Mad Hatter 5.00
298 JCA,DG,V:Baxter Bains 5.00
299 DG 5.00
300 WS,DG,A:Batman E-2,
Robin E-2 . . . . 12.00
301 JCa,TeB, ... 4.25
302 JCa,DG,V:Human Dynamo . . 4.25
303 JCa,DG, ... 4.25
304 E:DvR(s),V:Spook 4.25
305 GyC,JCa,DeH,V:Thanatos . . . 5.50
306 JCa,DeH,DN,V:Black Spider . 5.00
307 B:LWn(s),JCa,DG,
I:Limehouse Jack 5.00
308 JCa,DG,V:Mr.Freeze 5.00
309 E:LWn(s),JCa,FMc,
V:Blockbuster 5.00
310 IN,DG,A:Gentleman Ghost . . 5.00
311 SEt,FMc,IN,Batgirl,
V:Dr.Phosphorus 5.00
312 WS,DG,Calenderman 5.00
313 IN,FMc,VTwo-Face 5.00
314 IN,FMc,V:Two-Face 5.00
315 IN,FMc,V:Kiteman 5.00
316 IN,FMc,F:Robin,
V:Crazy Quilt 5.00
317 IN,FMc,V:Riddler 5.00
318 IN,I:Fire Bug 5.00
319 JKu(c),IN,DG,A:Gentleman
Ghost,E:Catwoman 5.00
320 BWr(c) 4.25
321 DG,WS,A:Joker,Catwoman . . 8.00
322 V:Cap.Boomerang,Catwoman 5.00
323 IN,A:Catwoman 5.00
324 IN,A:Catwoman 5.00
325 . . . . 4.25
326 A:Catwoman 5.00
327 IN,A:Proffessor.Milo 4.25
328 A:Two-Face 4.25
329 IN,A:Two-Face 4.25
330 . . . . 4.25
331 DN,FMc,V:Electrocutioner . . . 4.25
332 IN,DN,Ras al Ghul.1st solo
Catwoman story 7.00
333 IN,DN,A:Catwoman,
Ras al Ghul 5.50
334 FMc,Ras al Ghul,Catwoman . 5.50
335 IN,FMc,Catwoman,Ras al
Ghul 5.50
336 JL,FMc,Loser Villains 5.00
337 DN,V:Snow Man 4.25
338 DN 4.25
339 A:Poison Ivy 4.25
340 GC,A:Mole 4.25
341 A:Man Bat 4.25
342 V:Man Bat 4.25
343 GC,KJ,I:The Dagger 4.25
344 GC,KJ,Poison Ivy 4.25
345 I:New Dr.Death,A:Catwoman . 5.00
346 DN,V:Two Face 4.25
347 . . . . 4.25
348 GC,KJ,Man-Bat,A:Catwoman 5.00
349 GC,AA,A:Catwoman 5.00
350 GC,TD,A:Catwoman 5.00
351 GC,TD,A:Catwoman 5.00
352 . . . . 4.25
353 JL,DN,DA,A:Joker 6.00
354 DN,AA,V:HugoStrange,A:
Catwoman 5.00
355 DN,AA:A:Catwoman 5.00
356 DG,DN,Hugo Strange 4.00
357 DN,AA,I:Jason Todd 6.00
358 A:King Croc 4.00
359 DG,O:King Croc,Joker 6.00
360 . . . . 4.00
361 DN,Man-Bat,I:HarveyBullock . 4.00
362 V:Riddler 4.00
363 V:Nocturna 4.00
364 DN,AA,J.Todd 1st full solo
story (cont'dDetective #531) . . 4.00
365 DN,AA,C:Joker 4.00
366 DN,AA,Joker,J.Todd in
Robin Costume 26.00
367 DN,AA,PoisonIvy 7.00
368 DN,AA,I:2nd Robin

(Jason Todd) 20.00
369 DN,AA,I:Dr.Fang,V:Deadshot 3.50
370 DN,AA 3.50
371 DN,AA,V:Catman 4.00
372 DN,AA,A:Dr.Fang 3.50
373 DN,AA,V:Scarecrow 3.50
374 GC,AA,V:Penguin 5.00
375 GC,AA,V:Dr.Freeze 3.50
376 DN,Halloween issue 3.50
377 DN,AA,V:Nocturna 3.50
378 V:Mad Hatter 3.50
379 V:Mad Hatter 3.50
380 AA,V:Nocturna 3.50
381 . . . . 3.50
382 A:Catwoman 4.50
383 . . . . 3.50
384 V:Calender Man 3.50
385 V:Calender Man 3.50
386 I:Black Mask 3.25
387 V:Black Mask 3.25
388 V:Capt.Boomerang & Mirror Master 3.25
389 V:Nocturna,Catwoman 4.00
390 V:Nocturna,Catwoman 4.00
391 V:Nocturna,Catwoman 4.00
392 A:Catwoman 4.00
393 PG,V:Cossack 3.25
394 PG,V:Cossack 3.25
395 V:Film Freak 3.25
396 V:Film Freak 3.25
397 V:Two-Face,Catwoman 4.00
398 V:Two-Face,Catwoman 4.00
399 HaE(s),Two-Face 3.50
400 BSz,AAd,GP,BB,A:Joker . . . 20.00
401 JBy(c),TVE,Legends, A:Magpie 3.25
402 JSn,Fake Batman 3.25
403 DCw,Batcave discovered . . . 3.25
404 DM,FM(s),B:Year 1,I:Modern Age Catwoman 15.00
405 FM,DM,Year 1 . . . . 8.00
406 FM,DM,Year 1 . . . . 8.00
407 FM,DM,E:Year 1 . . . . 8.00
408 CW,V:Joker, new O:Jason Todd 5.00
408a 2nd printing 1.00
409 DG,RA,V:Crime School 4.00
409a 2nd printing 1.00
410 DC,Jason Todd 4.00
411 DC,DH,V:Two Face 3.00
412 DC,DH,I:Mime 3.00
413 DC,DH 3.00
414 JAp,Slasher 3.00
415 JAp,Millenium Week #2 . . . . 3.00
416 JAp,1st Batman/Nightwing T.U. 3.00
417 JAp,B:10 Nights,I:KGBeast . 13.00
418 JAp,V:KGBeast 11.00
419 JAp,V:KGBeast 11.00
420 JAp,E:10 Nights,D:KGBeast 11.00
421 DG 3.50
422 MBr,V:Dumpster Slayer 3.00
423 TM(c),DC,Who is Batman . . . 4.00
424 MBr,Robin 3.00
425 MBr,Gordon Kidnapped 3.00
426 JAp,B:Death in the Family, V:Joker 12.00
427 JAp,V:Joker 9.00
428 JAp,D:2nd Robin 10.00
429 JAp,A:Superman, E:Death in the Family 6.00
430 JAp,JSn,V:Madman 5.00
431 JAp,Murder Investigation 2.50
432 JAp 2.50
433 JBy,JAp,Many Deaths of the Batman #1 . . . . 5.00
434 JBy,JAp,Many Deaths #2 . . . 4.00
435 JBy,Many Deaths #3 . . . . . . 4.00
436 PB,B:Year#3,A:Nightwing,I:Tim Drake as child 8.00
436a 2ndPrint(green DC logo) . . . 2.00
437 PB,year#3 . . . . 3.00
438 PB,year#3 . . . . 2.50
439 PB,year#3 . . . . 2.50
440 JAp,Lonely Place of Dying #1, A:Tim Drake (face not shown) . 4.00
441 JAp,Lonely Place Dying 4.00
442 JAp,I:3rd Robin(Tim Drake) . . 6.00
443 JAp,I:Crimesmith 2.00
444 JAp,V:Crimesmith 2.00
445 JAp,I:K.G.Beast Demon 2.00
446 JAp,V:K.G.Beast Demon 2.00

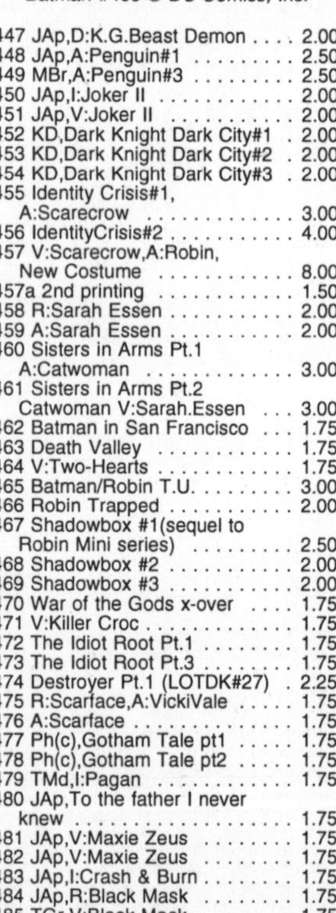

Batman #409 © DC Comics, Inc.

447 JAp,D:K.G.Beast Demon 2.00
448 JAp,A:Penguin#1 . . . . 2.50
449 MBr,A:Penguin#3 . . . . 2.50
450 JAp,I:Joker II 2.00
451 JAp,V:Joker II 2.00
452 KD,Dark Knight Dark City#1 . 2.00
453 KD,Dark Knight Dark City#2 . 2.00
454 KD,Dark Knight Dark City#3 . 2.00
455 Identity Crisis#1, A:Scarecrow 3.00
456 IdentityCrisis#2 . . . . 4.00
457 V:Scarecrow,A:Robin, New Costume 8.00
457a 2nd printing 1.50
458 R:Sarah Essen 2.00
459 A:Sarah Essen 2.00
460 Sisters in Arms Pt.1 A:Catwoman 3.00
461 Sisters in Arms Pt.2 Catwoman V:Sarah.Essen . . . 3.00
462 Batman in San Francisco . . . 1.75
463 Death Valley 1.75
464 V:Two-Hearts 1.75
465 Batman/Robin T.U. 3.00
466 Robin Trapped 2.00
467 Shadowbox #1(sequel to Robin Mini series) 2.50
468 Shadowbox #2 . . . . 2.00
469 Shadowbox #3 . . . . 2.00
470 War of the Gods x-over 1.75
471 V:Killer Croc 1.75
472 The Idiot Root Pt.1 . . . . 1.75
473 The Idiot Root Pt.3 . . . . 1.75
474 Destroyer Pt.1 (LOTDK#27) . 2.25
475 R:Scarface,A:VickiVale 1.75
476 A:Scarface 1.75
477 Ph(c),Gotham Tale pt1 . . . . . 1.75
478 Ph(c),Gotham Tale pt2 . . . . . 1.75
479 TMd,I:Pagan 1.75
480 JAp,To the father I never knew 1.75
481 JAp,V:Maxie Zeus 1.75
482 JAp,V:Maxie Zeus 1.75
483 JAp,I:Crash & Burn 1.75
484 JAp,R:Black Mask 1.75
485 TGr,V:Black Mask 1.75

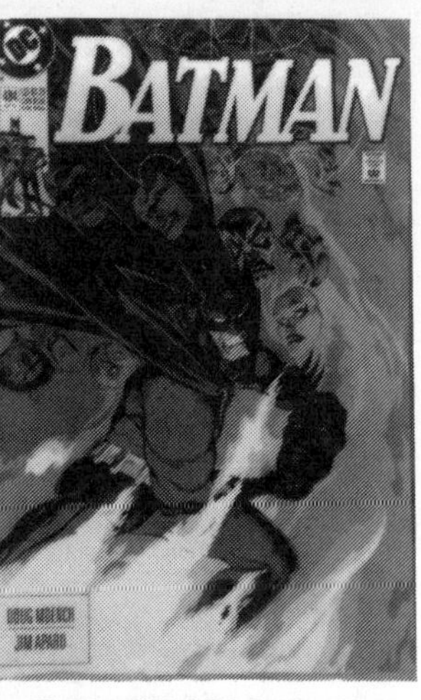

Batman #484 © DC Comics, Inc.

486 JAp,I:Metalhead 1.75
487 JAp,V:Headhunter 1.75
488 JAp,N:Azrael 10.00
489 JAp,Bane vs Killer Croc, I:Azrael as Batman 13.00
489a 2nd Printing 1.25
490 JAp,Bane vs.Riddler 6.00
490a 2nd Printing 1.75
490b 3rd Printing 1.25
491 JAp,V:Joker,A:Bane 4.00
491a 2nd Printing 1.25
492 B:DgM(s),NB,Knightfall#1,V:Mad Hatter,A:Bane 5.50
492a Platinum Ed. 65.00
492b 2nd Printing 1.25
493 NB,Knightfall,#3,Mr.Zsasz . . . 4.00
494 JAp,TMd,Knightfall #5,A:Bane, V:Cornelius,Stirk,Joker 3.00
495 NB,Knightfall#7,V:Poison Ivy,A:Bane 2.50
496 JAp,JRu,Knightfall#9,V:Joker, Scarecrow,A:Bane 2.50
497 JAp,DG,Knightfall#11,V:Bane, Batman gets back broken 7.00
497a 2nd Printing 1.50
498 JAp,JRu,Knightfall#15,A:Bane, Catwoman,Azrael Becomes Batman 2.00
499 JAp,SHa,Knightfall#17, A:Bane,Catwoman 2.00
500 JQ(c),JAp,MM,Die Cut(c), Direct Market,Knightfall#19, V:Bane,N:Batman 5.00
500a KJo(c),Newstand Ed. 3.50
501 MM,I:Mekros 1.75
502 MM,V:Mekros 1.75
503 MM,V:Catwoman 1.75
504 MM,V:Catwoman 1.75
505 MM,V:Canibal 1.75
506 KJo(c),MM,A:Ballistic 1.75
507 KJo(c),MM,A:Ballistic 1.75
508 KJo(c),MM,V:Abattior 1.75
509 KJo(c),MM,KnightsEnd#1, A:Shiva, ... 2.50
Ann.#1 CS 250.00
Ann.#2 . . . . 135.00
Ann.#3 A:Joker 100.00
Ann.#4 . . . . 50.00
Ann.#5 . . . . 45.00
Ann.#6 . . . . 40.00
Ann.#7 . . . . 35.00
Ann.#8 TVE,A:Ras al Ghul 8.00
Ann.#9 JOy,AN,PS 7.00

Ann.#10 DCw,DG,V:HugoStrange 7.00
Ann.#11 JBy(c),AMo(s),V:Penguin 8.00
Ann.#12 RA,V:Killer 5.00
Ann.#13 A:Two-Face 4.00
Ann.#14 O:Two-Face 3.00
Ann.#15 Armageddon Pt.3 6.00
Ann.#15a 2nd printing(silver) 2.50
Ann.#16 SK(c),Eclipso,V:Joker 3.00
Ann.#17 EB,Bloodline#8, I.Decimator 3.00
Ann.#18 Elseworld Story 3.25

Batman Annual #2 © DC Comics, Inc.

PF Batman Returns:Movie Adaption, SE,JL, 6.00
Newsstand Format 4.00
Spec.#1 MGo,I:Wrath 4.00
TPB,Many Deaths o/t Batman; rep.#'s 433-435 3.95
TPB,Death in the Family;reprints Batman#426-429 6.50
2nd printing 4.00
3rd printing 4.00
TPB Batman:Gothic,rep.Legends of the Dark Knight#6-10 12.95
TPB Knightfall rep #1-11 12.95
TPB Knightfall rep #12-19 12.95
TPB Prey,rep.Legends of the Dark Knight#11-15 12.95
TPB Venom 9.95
TPB Year One FM(s), 12.95
TPB Year Two 9.95
Batman Archives Vol.3 39.95
Greatest Batman Stories Ever Told:
HC 60.00
SC 16.00
Batman JOy,Movie adaptation 3.00
Perfect Bound 6.00
Batman:Arkham Asylum,DMc 28.00
Batman:Blind Justice 7.50
Batman:The Blue,The Grey,and The Bat;JL (Elseworlds) 5.95
Batman:Bride of the Demon,TGr, V:Ra's Al Ghul 21.00
Batman:Dark Joker KJo 26.00
Batman/Houdini:The Devil's Workshop 6.50
Batman:Digital Justice 26.00
Batman:Full Circle AD,A:Reaper 7.00
Batman Gallery,collection of past (c),posters,pin-ups,JQ(c) 4.00
Batman:Holy Terror 6.50
Batman:Gotham By Gaslight,MMi, V:Jack the Ripper 6.00
Batman:In Darkest Knight MiB(s),JBi 5.50
Batman/Judge Dredd:Judgement on Gotham,SBs,V:Scarecrow,Judge Death 8.00
Batman:The Killing Joke,BB, AMo(s),O:Joker,Batgirl paralyzed 18.00
2nd thru 6th Printings @5.00
Batman:Master of the Future,EB, Sequel to Goth by Gaslight 6.00
Batman:Night Cries,SHa 30.00
Batman/Dracula:Red Rain KJo,MJ, Batman becomes Vampire, HC,Elseworlds Story 50.00
SC 12.00
Batman:Seduction of the Gun, V:Illegal Gun Control 3.00
Batman:Son o/t Demon,JBi,HC 55.00
SC 17.00
2nd thru 4th Printings @8.95
Two-Face Strikes Twice#1 5.25
Two-Face Strikes Twice#2 5.25
Batman:Vengeance of Bane, GN,I:Bane 30.00
2nd Printing 5.00
Batman:Year One Rep.Batman #404-#407 14.00
2nd Printing 9.95
3rd Printing 9.95

BATMAN ADVENTURES
(Based on TV cartoon series)

1 MeP,V:Penguin 9.00
2 MeP,V:Catwoman 6.00
3 MeP,V:Joker 5.00
4 MeP,V:Scarecrow 4.00
5 MeP,V:Scarecrow 4.00
6 MeP,A:Robin 4.00
7 MeP,V:Killer Croc,w/card 10.00
8 MeP,Larceny my Sweet 3.00
9 MeP,V:Two Face 3.00
10 MeP,V:Riddler 3.00
11 MeP,V:Man-Bat 2.50
12 MeP,F:Batgirl 2.50
13 MeP,V:Talia 2.50
14 MeP,F:Robin 2.00
15 MeP,F:Commissioner Gordon 2.00
16 MeP,V:Joker 2.00
17 MeP,V:Talia 2.00
18 MeP,R:Batgirl 1.75
19 MeP,V:Scarecrow 1.75
20 MeP,V:Mastermind,Mr.Nice, Perfessor 1.75
21 MeP,V:Man-Bat,Tygrus 1.75
22 MeP,V:Two-Face 1.50
Spec. Mad Love 3.95
TPB Collected Adventures #1 5.95
TPB Collected Adventures #2 5.95

BATMAN & OUTSIDERS
August, 1983

1 B:MiB(s),JAp,O:Outsiders, O:Geo Force 3.50
2 JAp,V:Baron Bedlam 2.50
3 JAp,V:Agent Orange 2.00
4 JAp,V:Fearsome Five 2.00
5 JAp,A:New Teen Titans 2.50
6 JAp,V:Cryonic Man 1.50
7 JAp,V:Cryonic Man 1.50
8 JAp,A:Phantom Stranger 1.50
9 JAp,I:Master of Disaster 1.50
10 JAp,A:Master of Disaster 1.50
11 JAp,V:Takeo 1.50
12 JAp,DG,O:Katana 1.50
13 JAp,Day,O:Batman 1.50
14 BWg,Olympics,V:Maxi Zeus 1.50
15 TVE,Olympics,V:Maxi Zeus 1.50
16 JAp,L:Halo 1.50
17 JAp,V:Ahk-Ton 1.50
18 JAp,V:Ahk-Ton 1.50
19 JAp,A:Superman 1.50
20 JAp,V:Syonide,R:Halo 1.50
21 TVE,JeM,Solo Stories 1.50
22 AD,O:Halo,I:Aurakles 1.50
23 AD,O:Halo,V:Aurakles 1.50
24 AD,C:Kobra 1.50
25 AD,V:Kobra 1.50
26 AD, 1.50
27 AD,V:Kobra 1.50
28 AD,I:Lia Briggs(Looker) 1.50
29 AD,V:Metamorpho 1.50
30 AD,C:Looker 1.50
31 AD,I&J:Looker 1.50
32 AD,L:Batman, 1.50
Ann.#1 JA N:Geo-Force, I:Force of July 1.75
Ann.#2 V:Tremayne,W:Metamorpho & Sapphire Stagg 1.50
Becomes:

ADVENTURES OF THE OUTSIDERS
May, 1986

33 AD,V:Baron Bedlam 1.50
34 AD,Masters of Disaster 1.50
35 AD,V:Adolph Hitler 1.50
36 AD,A:Masters of Disaster 1.50
37 1.50
38 1.50
39 thru 47 JAp,reprints Outsiders #1-#9 @1.50

BATMAN: THE CULT

1 JSn,BWr,V:Deacon Blackfire 10.00
2 JSn,BWr,V:Deacon Blackfire 7.00
3 JSn,BWr,V:Deacon Blackfire 6.00
4 JSn,BWr,V:Deacon Blackfire 6.00

BATMAN: THE DARK KNIGHT RETURNS

1 FM,KJ,V:Two-Face 36.00
1a 2nd printing 7.00
1b 3rd printing 5.00
2 FM,KJ,V:Sons of the Batman 17.00
2a 2nd printing 4.00
2b 3rd printing 2.50
3 FM,KJ,D:Joker 9.00
3a 2nd printing 3.00
4 FM,KJ,Batman vs.Superman, A:Green Arrow,D:Alfred 7.50
HC 60.00
Paperback book 20.00
Warner paperback 17.00
HC,sign/num. 350.00
2nd-8th printing 12.95

BATMAN: A DEATH IN THE FAMILY

1 rep. Batman #426-429 8.00
1a 2nd printing 5.00
1b 3rd printing 4.00

BATMAN FAMILY
September-October, 1975

1 MGr,NA(rep.) Batgirl & Robin begins,giant 7.50
2 V:Clue Master 4.50
3 Batgirl & Robin reveal ID 5.00
4 4.50
5 4.50
6 Joker Daughter 6.00
7 CS,A:Sportsmaster, G.A.Huntress 3.50
8 First solo Robin story, C:Joker's Daughter 3.00
9 Joker's Daughter 5.50
10 R:B'woman,1st solo Batgirl sty 4.00
11 MR,Man-Bat begins 5.00
12 MR 5.00
13 MR,DN,BWi 5.00
14 HC/JRu,Man-Bat 4.00
15 MGo,Man-Bat 3.00
16 MGo,Man-Bat 3.00
17 JA,DH,MG,Batman, B:Huntress A:Demon,MK(c),A:Catwoman 6.00
18 MGo,JSon,BL,Huntress,BM 3.00
19 MGo,JSon,BL,Huntress,BM 3.00

20 MGo,JSon,DH,A:Ragman, ElongatedMan, Oct.-Nov.,1978 4.00

BATMAN: GOTHAM NIGHTS

1 Gotham City Mini-series 1.75
2 Lives of Gotham Citizens 1.50
3 Lives of Gotham Citizens 1.50
4 Lives of Gotham Citizens 1.50

BATMAN: LEGENDS OF THE DARK KNIGHT

1 EH,Shaman of Gotham Pt.#1, Yellow(c) 7.00
1a Blue,Orange or Pink(c) 7.00
2 EH,Shaman of Gotham Pt2 . . . 5.00
3 EH,Shaman of Gotham Pt3 . . . 4.00
4 EH,Shaman of Gotham Pt4 . . . 4.00
5 EH,Shaman of Gotham Pt5 . . . 4.00
6 KJ,Gothic Pt1 . . . . 4.50
7 KJ,Gothic Pt2 . . . . 4.00
8 KJ,Gothic Pt3 . . . . 4.00
9 KJ,Gothic Pt4 . . . . 4.00

Batman: Legends of the Dark Knight #36 © DC Comics, Inc.

10 KJ,Gothic Pt#5 . . . . 4.00
11 PG,TA,Prey Pt#1 . . . . 4.00
12 PG,TA,Prey Pt2 . . . . 4.00
13 PG,TA,Prey Pt3 . . . . 4.00
14 PG,TA,Prey Pt4 . . . . 4.00
15 PG,TA,Prey Pt5 . . . . 4.00
16 TVE,Venom Pt 1 . . . . 15.00
17 TVE,JL,Venom Pt2 . . . . 12.00
18 TVE,JL,Venom Pt3 . . . . 12.00
19 TVE,JL,Venom Pt4 . . . . 12.00
20 TVE,JL,Venom Pt5 . . . . 12.00
21 BS,Faith Pt.1 . . . . 2.50
22 BS,Faith Pt.2 . . . . 2.50
23 BS,Faith Pt.3 . . . . 2.50
24 GK,Flyer Pt.1 . . . . 2.50
25 GK,Flyer Pt.2 . . . . 2.50
26 GK,Flyer Pt.3 . . . . 2.50
27 Destroyer Pt.2 (Batman#474) . 3.00
28 MWg,Faces Pt.1,V:Two-Face . 4.00
29 MWg,Faces Pt 2,V:Two-Face . 4.00
30 MWg,Faces Pt.3,V:Two-Face . 4.00
31 BA,Family 2.50
32 Blades Pt 1 . . . . 2.50
33 Blades Pt 2 . . . . 2.50
34 Blades Pt 3 . . . . 2.50
35 BHa,Destiny Part 1 . . . . 2.50
36 BHa,Destiny Part 2 . . . . 2.50
37 I:Mercy,V:The Cossack 2.50
38 KON,R:Bat-Mite 2.50
39 BT,Mask#1 . . . . 2.50
40 BT,Mask#2 . . . . 2.50
41 Sunset 2.25
42 CR,Hothouse #1 . . . . 2.25
43 CR,Hothouse #2,V:Poison Ivy . 2.25
44 SMc,Turf #1 . . . . 2.25
45 Turf#2 . . . . 2.25
46 RH,A:Catwoman,V:Catman . . . 2.50
47 RH,A:Catwoman,V:Catman . . . 2.50
48 RH,A:Catwoman,V:Catman . . . 2.50
49 RH,A:Catwoman,V:Catman . . . 2.50
50 BBl,JLe,KN,KM,WS,MZ,BB, V:Joker 8.00
51 JKu,A:Ragman 2.25
52 Tao #1,V:Dragon 2.25
53 Tao #2,V:Dragon 2.25
54 MMi 2.00
55 B:Watchtower 2.00
56 CDi(s),V:Battle Guards 2.00
57 CDi(s),E:Watchtower 2.00
58 Storm 2.00
59 DON(s),RoW,B:Qarry 2.00
60 RoW,V:Asp 2.00
61 RoW,V:Asp 2.00
62 RoW,KnightsEnd#4,A:Shiva, Nightwing 1.75
Ann.#1 JAp,KG,DSp,TL,JRu, MGo,JQ,'Duel',C:Joker 5.50
Ann.#2 MN,LMc,W:Gordn&Essen . 4.00
Ann.#3 MM,I:Cardinal Sin 3.75
Ann.#4 JSon(c),Elseworlds Story . 3.50
Collected Legends of the Dark Knight BB(c),rep.#32-34,38,42-43 . . 12.95
TPB Shaman rep #1-5 . . . . 12.95

BATMAN: MASK OF THE PHANTASM

1 Movie Adapt. 5.25
1a Newstand Ed. 3.25

BATMAN RECORD COMIC

1966

1 . . . . 1.00

BATMAN: RUN, RIDDLER RUN

1 MBg,Batman V:Riddler 5.50
2 MBg,Batman V:Riddler 5.25
3 MBg,V:Perfect Securities 5.25

BATMAN: SHADOW OF THE BAT

1 NB,Last Arkham Part 1 . . . . . . 3.50
1a Collector set,w/posters,pop-up 5.50
2 NB,Last Arkham Part 2 . . . . . . 3.00
3 NB,Last Arkham Part 3 . . . . . . 3.00
4 NB,Last Arkham Part 4 . . . . . . 3.00
5 NB,A:Black Spider 2.50
6 NB,I:Chancer 2.50
7 Misfits Part 1 . . . . 2.50
8 Misfits Part 2 . . . . 2.50
9 Misfits Part 3 . . . . 2.50
10 MC,V:Mad Thane of Gotham . 2.00
11 V:Kadaver 2.00
12 V:Kadaver,A:Human Flea 2.00
13 NB,'The Nobody' 2.00
14 NB,Gotham Freaks#1 . . . . 2.00
15 NB,Gotham Freaks#2 . . . . 2.00
16 BBl,MM,A:Anarchy,Scarecrow . 2.00
17 BBl,V:Scarecrow 2.00
18 BBl,A:Anarchy,Scarecrow 2.00
19 BBl,Knightquest:The Crusade Pt.2, V:Gotham criminals 2.00
20 VGi,Knightquest:The Crusade, V:Tally Man 2.00
21 BBl,Knightquest:The Search, V:Mr.Asp 2.00
22 BBl,Knightquest:The Search, In London 2.00
23 BBl,Knightquest:The Search . . 2.00
24 BBl,Knightquest:The Crusade . 2.00
25 BSf(c),BBl,Knightquest: Crusade, A:Joe Public,V:Corrosive Man . 2.00
26 BSf(c),BBl,Knightquest: Crusade, V:Clayface 2.00
27 BSf(c),BBl,Knightquest: Crusade, I:Clayface Baby 2.00
28 BSf(c),BBl, ... 2.00
29 BSf(c),BBl,KnightsEnd#2, A:Nightwing 2.95
Ann.#1 TVE,DG,Bloodlines#3, I:Joe Public 3.75

BATMAN: SWORD OF AZRAEL

1 JQ,KN,I:Azrael 25.00
2 JQ,KN,A:Azrael 20.00
3 JQ,KN,V:Biis,A:Azrael 23.00
4 JQ,KN,V:Biis,A:Azrael 20.00
TPB rep.#1-4 . . . . 13.00
TPB Platinum 50.00

BATMAN/ GREEN ARROW: THE POISON TOMORROW

1 MN,JRu,V:Poison Ivy 6.25

BATMAN/GRENDEL: DEVIL'S MASQUE & DEVIL'S RIDDLE

1 MWg,Batman meets Grendel . . 5.25
2 MWg,Batman Vs. Grendel 5.25

BATMAN/JUDGE DREDD: VENDETTA IN GOTHAM

1 AIG(s),V:Ventriliquist 5.25

BATMAN/SPAWN: WAR DEVIL

1 DgM,CDi,AIG(s),KJ,V:Croatoan 5.50

BATMAN vs. PREDATOR

1 NKu,AKu,inc.8 trading cards (Prestige) 9.00
1a Newsstand 5.00
2 NKu,AKu,Inc. pinups (prestige) 7.00
2a Newsstand 4.00
3 NKu,AKu,conclusion,inc. 8 trading cards (Prestige) 7.00
3a Newsstand 4.00
TPB,rep.#1-3 . . . . 5.95

BATTLE CLASSICS

September-October, 1978

1 JKu, reprints 1.50

BEAUTIFUL STORIES FOR UGLY CHILDREN

Piranha Press

1 thru 11 . . . . @2.00
12 thru 14 . . . . @2.50
15 Blood Day 2.50
16 thru 23 . . . . @2.50

BEOWOLF

April-May, 1975

1 thru 5 . . . . @1.00
6 February-March, 1976 . . . . . . 1.00

BEST OF THE BRAVE & THE BOLD

1 JL(c),NA,rep B&B #85. . . . . . . 2.50
2 JL(c),NA,rep.B&B #81 . . . . 2.50
3 JL(c),NA,rep.B&B #82 . . . . 2.50
4 JL(c),NA,rep.B&B #80 . . . . 2.50
5 JL(c),NA,rep.B&B #93 . . . . 2.50
6 JL(c),NA,rep.B&B #83 . . . . 2.50

BEWARE THE CREEPER
May-June, 1968

1 . . . . 12.00
2 . . . . 7.50
3 . . . . 7.50
4 . . . . 7.50
5 . . . . 7.50
6 March-April, 1969 . . . . 7.50

BIG ALL-AMERICAN COMIC BOOK
December, 1944

1 JKu 3,000.00

BIG BOOK OF FUN COMICS
Spring , 1936

1 . . . . 5,200.00

BLACK CANARY

1 TVE/DG,New Wings Pt.1 . . . . . 2.25
2 TVE/DG,New Wings Pt.2 . . . . . 2.00
3 TVE/DG,New Wings Pt.3 . . . . . 2.00
4 TVE/DG,New Wings Pt.4,Conc 2.00

[Regular series]

1 TVE,Hero Worship Pt.1 . . . . . . 2.25
2 TVE,Hero Worship Pt.2 . . . . . . 2.00
3 TVE,Hero Worship Pt.3 . . . . . . 2.00
4 TVE,V:Whorrsman 2.00
5 . . . . 2.00
6 Blynde Woman's Bluff 2.00
7 TVE,V:Maniacal Killer 2.00
8 . . . . 1.75
9 A:Huntress 1.75
10 TVE,A:Nightwing,Huntress . . . 1.75
11 TVE,A:Nightwing 1.75
12 final issue 1.75

BLACK CONDOR

1 I&O:Black Condor 3.00
2 V:Sky Pirate 2.00
3 V:Sky Pirate 2.00
4 V:The Shark 1.50
5 V:Mind Force 1.50
6 V:Mind Force 1.50
7 Forest Fire 1.50
8 MG,In Jail 1.50
9 A:The Ray 1.50
10 . . . . 1.25
11 O:Black Condor 1.25

BLACKHAWK
Prev: Golden Age

108 DD,CCu,DD&CCu(c),The Threat from the Abyss A:Blaisie 322.00
109 DD,CCu,DD&CCu(c),The Avalance Kid 100.00
110 DD,CCu,DD&CCu(c),Mystery of Tigress Island 100.00
111 DD,CCu,DD&CCu(c),Menace of the Machines 100.00
112 DD,CCu,DD(c),The Doomed Dog Fight 100.00
113 DD,CCu,CCu(c),Volunteers of Doom 100.00
114 DD,CCu,DD&CCu(c),Gladiators of Blackhawk Island 100.00
115 DD,CCu,DD&CCu(c),The Tyrant's Return 100.00
116 DD,CCu,DD&CCu(c),Prisoners of the Black Island 100.00
117 DD,CCu,DD&CCu(c),Menace of the Dragon Boat 100.00
118 DD,CCu,DD&SMo(c),FF,The Bandit With 1,000 Nets 110.00
119 DD,CCu,DD&SMo(c), V:Chief Blackhawk 70.00
120 DD,CCu,DD&SMo(c),The Challenge of the Wizard 70.00
121 DD,CCu,DD&CCu(c),Secret Weapon of the Archer 70.00
122 DD,CCu,DD&CCu(c),The Movie That Backfired 70.00
123 DD,CCu,DD&CCu(c),The Underseas Gold Fort 70.00
124 DD,CCu,DD&CCu(c),Thieves With A Thousand Faces 70.00
125 DD,CCu,DD&CCu(c),Secrets o/t Blackhawk Time Capsule . 70.00
126 DD,CCu,DD&CCu(c),Secret of the Glass Fort 70.00
127 DD,CCu,DD&CCu(c),Blackie-The Winged Sky Fighter 70.00
128 DD,CCu,DD&CCu(c),The Vengeful Bowman 70.00
129 DD,CCu,DD&CCu(c),The Cavemen From 3,000 B.C. . . 70.00
130 DD,CCu,DD&SMo(c),The Mystery Missle From Space . 70.00
131 DD,CCu,DD&CCu(c),The Return of the Rocketeers . . . 50.00
132 DD,CCu,DD&CCu(c),Raid of the Rocketeers 50.00
133 DD,CCu,DD&CCu(c),Human Dynamo 50.00
134 DD,CC,DD&CC(c),The Sinister Snowman 50.00
135 DD,CCu,DD&CCu(c),The Underworld Supermarket . . . 50.00
136 DD,CCu,DD&CCu(c),The Menace of the Smoke-Master 50.00
137 DD,CCu,DD&CCu(c),The Weapons That Backfired 50.00
138 DD,CCu,DD&SMo(c),The Menace of the Blob 50.00
139 DD,CCu,DD&CCu(c),The Secret Blackhawk 50.00
140 DD,CCu,DD&CCu(c),The Space Age Marauders 50.00
141 DD,CCu,DD&CCu(c),Crimes of the Captive Masterminds . . 40.00
142 DD,CCu,DD&CCu(c),Alien Blackhawk Chief 40.00
143 DD,SMo,DD&CCu(c),Lady Blackhawk's Rival 40.00
144 DD,CCu,DD&CCu(c),The Underworld Sportsmen 40.00
145 DD,CCu,DD&CCu(c),The Deadly Lensman 40.00
146 DD,CCu,DD&CCu(c),The Fantastic Fables of Blackhawk 40.00
147 DD,SMo,DD&CCu(c),The Blackhawk Movie Queen 40.00
148 DD,CCu,DD&CCu(c),Four Dooms For The Blackhawks . 40.00
149 DD,CCu,DD&CCu(c),Masks of Doom 40.00
150 DD,CCu,DD&SMo(c), Blackhawk Mascot from Space 35.00
151 DD,CCu,DD&CCu(c),Lost City35.00
152 DD,CCu,DD&SMo(c),Noah's Ark From Space 35.00
153 DD,CCu,DD&SMo(c), Boomerang Master 35.00
154 DD,CCu,DD&SMo(c),The Beast Time Forgot 35.00
155 DD,CCu,DD&CCu(c),Killer Shark's Land Armada 35.00
156 DD,CCu,DD&SMo(c),Peril of the Plutonian Raider 35.00
157 DD,CCu,DD&SMo(c),Secret of the Blackhawk Sphinx 35.00
158 DD,CCu,DD&SMo(c),Bandit Birds From Space 35.00
159 DD,CCu,DD&SMo(c),Master of the Puppet Men 35.00
160 DD,CCu,DD&CCu(c),The Phantom Spy 35.00
161 DD,SMo,DD&SMo(c),Lady Blackhawk's Crime Chief . . . 35.00
162 DD,CCu,DD&CCu(c),The Invisible Blackhawk 35.00
163 DD,CCu,DD&SMo(c), Fisherman of Crime 35.00
164 DD,O:Blackhawk retold 28.00
165 DD,V:League of Anti Blackhawks 25.00
166 DD,A:Lady Blackhawk 25.00
167 DD,The Blackhawk Bandits . 15.00
168 DD,Blackhawk Time Travelers 15.00
169 DD,Sinister Hunts of Mr. Safari 15.00
170 DD,A:Lady Blackhawk,V:Killer Shark 15.00
171 DD,Secret of Alien Island . . 15.00
172 DD,Challenge of the GasMaster 15.00
173 DD,The Super Jungle Man . 15.00
174 DD,Andre's Impossible World 15.00
175 DD,The Creature with Blackhawk's Brain 15.00
176 DD,Stone Age Blackhawks . 15.00
177 DD,Town that time Forgot . . 15.00
178 DD,Return of the Scorpions 15.00
179 DD,Invisible Dr.Dunbar 15.00
180 DD,Son of Blackhawk 15.00
181 DD,I:Tom Thumb Blackhawk 10.00
182 DD,A:Lady Blackhawk 10.00
183 DD,V:Killer Shark 10.00
184 DD,Island of Super Monkeys 10.00
185 DD,Last 7 days of the Blackhawks 10.00
186 DD,A:Lady Blackhawk 10.00
187 DD,V:Porcupine 10.00
188 DD,A:Lady Blackhawk 10.00
189 DD:O:rtd 10.00
190 DD,FantasticHumanStarfish 10.00
191 DD,A:Lady Blackhawk 8.00
192 DD,V:King Condor 8.00
193 DD,The Jailer's Revenge . . . 8.00
194 DD,The Outlaw Blackhawk . . 8.00
195 DD,A:Tom Thumb Blackhawk 8.00
196 DD,Blackhawk WWII Combat Diary story 8.00
197 DD:new look 8.00
198 DD:O:rtd 10.00
199 DD,Attack with the Mummy Insects 8.00
200 DD,A:Lady Blackhawk, I:Queen Killer Shark 9.00
201 DD,Blackhawk Detached Diary Story,F:Hendrickson 8.00
202 DD,Combat Diary,F:Andre . . . 8.00
203 DD:O:Chop-Chop 9.00
204 DD,A:Queen Killer Shark . . . 8.00
205 DD,Combat Diary story 8.00
206 DD,Combat Diary, F:Olaf . . . 8.00
207 DD,Blackhawk Devil Dolls . . . 8.00
208 DD,Detached service diary F:Chuck 8.00
209 DD,V:King Condor 8.00
210 DD,Danger..Blackhawk Bait rep.Blackhawk #139. . . . . 8.00
211 DD,GC,Detached service diary 5.00
212 DD,Combat Diary, F:Chop-Chop 5.00
213 DD,Blackhawk goes Hollywood 5.00
214 DD,Team of Traitors 5.00
215 DD,Detached service diary F:Olaf 5.00
216 DD,A:Queen Killer Shark . . . 5.00
217 DD,Detached service diary F:Stanislaus 5.00
218 DD,7 against Planet Peril . . . 5.00
219 DD,El Blackhawk Peligroso . . 5.00
220 DD,The Revolt of the Assembled Man 5.00
221 DD,Detach service diary F:Hendrickson 4.50
222 DD,The Man from E=MC2 . . 4.50
223 DD,V:Mr.Quick CHange 4.50
224 DD,Combat Diary, F:Stanislaus 4.50
225 DD,A:Queen Killer Shark . . . 4.50
226 DD,Secret Monster of Blackhawk Island 4.50

227 DD,Detached Service diary F:Chop-Chop 4.50
228 DD (1st art on JLA characters) Blackhawks become super-heroes, Junk-Heap heroes #1(C:JLA) . 4.50
229 DD,Junk-Heap Heroes #2 (C:JLA) 4.50
230 DD,Junk-Heap Heroes concl. (C:JLA) 4.50
231 DD,A:Lady Blackhawk 4.50
232 DD,A:Lady Blackhawk 4.50
233 DD,Too Late,The Leaper . . . 4.50
234 DD,The Terrible Twins 4.50
235 DD,A Coffin for a Blackhawk 4.50
236 DD,Melt,Mutant, Melt 4.50
237 DD,Magnificent 7 Assassins . 4.50
238 DD,Walking Booby-Traps . . . 4.50
239 DD,The Killer That Time Forgot 4.50
240 DD,He Who Must Die 4.50
241 DD,A Blackhawk a Day 4.50
242 Blackhawks back in blue & black costumes 4.50
243 Mission Incredible (1968) . . . 4.50
244 GE,new costumes,Blackhawks become mercenaries (1976) . . 2.00
245 GE,Death's Double Deal 2.00
246 RE,GE,Death's Deadly Dawn 2.00
247 RE,AM,Operation:Over Kill . . 2.00
248 JSh,Vengeance is Mine!.. Sayeth the Cyborg 2.00
249 RE,GE,V:Sky-Skull 2.00
250 RE,GE,FS,D:Chuck(1977) . . . 2.00
251 DSp,Back to WWII(1982) . . . 2.00
252 thru 258 DSp . . . . @2.00
259 . . . . 2.00
260 HC,ATh 2.00
261 thru 271 DSp . . . . @2.00
272 . . . . 2.00
273 and 274 DSp . . . . @2.00

[2nd Series]

1 HC Mini-series,Blackhawk accused of communism 4.50
2 HC,visits Soviet Union 3.50
3 HC,Atom Bomb threat to N.Y. . 3.50

[3rd Series]

1 All in color for a Crime pt.1 I:The Real Lady Blackhawk . . 1.50
2 All in color for a Crime pt.2 . . . 1.50
3 Agent Rescue Attempt in Rome 1.50
4 Blackhawk's girlfriend murdered 1.50
5 I:Circus Organization 1.50
6 Blackhawks on false mission . . 1.50
7 V:Circus,A:Suicide Squad, rep. 1st Blackhawk story 2.50
8 Project: Assimilation 1.50
9 V:Grundfest 1.50
10 Blackhawks Attacked 1.50
11 Master plan revealed 1.50
12 Raid on BlackhawkAirwaysHQ 1.75
13 Team Member Accused of . . . 1.75
14 Blackhawk test pilots 1.75
15 Plans for independence 1.75
16 Independence, final issue 1.75
Ann.#1 Hawks in Albania 2.95
Spec.#1 Assassination of JFK to Saigon,1975 . . . . 3.50

BLACK HOOD

Impact

1 O:Black Hood 1.25
2 Nick Cray becomes Black Hood 1.00
3 New Year's Eve,A:Creeptures . 1.00
4 Nate Cray become Black Hood, Dr.M.Harvey becomes Ozone . 1.00
5 E:Nate Cray as Black Hood V:Ozone 1.00
6 New Black Hood 1.00
7 History of Seaside City 1.25
8 V:Hit Coffee 1.25
9 V:Hit Coffee 1.25
10 Slime of Your Life #1 . . . . 1.25
11 Slime of Your Life #2 . . . . 1.25
12 Final Issue 1.25
Ann#1 Earthquest,w/trading card . 2.50

BLACK LIGHTNING

April, 1977

1 TVE/FS,I&O:Black Lightning . . 1.50
2 TVE/FS,A:Talia 1.25
3 TVE,I:Tobias Whale 1.25
4 TVE,A:Jimmy Olsen 1.25
5 TVE,A:Superman 1.25
6 TVE,I:Syonide 1.25
7 TVE,V:Syonide 1.25
8 TVE,V:Tobias Whale 1.25
9 TVE,V:Annihilist 1.25
10 TVE,V:Trickster 1.25
11 TVE,The Ray back-up story, September-October, 1978 . . . . 1.25

BLACK MASK

1 I:Black Mask 4.95
2 V:Underworld 4.95
3 V:Valentine 4.95

BLACK ORCHID

1 DMc,O:Black Orchid, A:Batman,Luthor,Poison Ivy . 10.00
2 DMc,O:cont,Arkham Asylum . . 8.00
3 DMc,A:SwampThing,conc. 8.00
TPB rep. #1 thru #3 . . . . 19.95

Vertigo

1 DMc(c),B:DiF(s),JIT,SnW,I:Sherilyn Somers,I:Logos,F:Walt Brody . 2.50
1a Platinum Ed. 40.00
2 JIT,SnW,Uprooting,V:Logos . . . 2.25
3 JIT,SnW,Tainted Zone, V:Fungus 2.25
4 JIT,SnW,I:Nick & Orthia 2.25
5 DMc(c),JIT,SnW, A:Swamp Thing 2.25
6 JIT,BMc(i),God in the Cage . . . 2.25
7 JIT,RGu,SnW, Upon the Threshold 2.25
8 DMc(c),RGu,A:Silent People . . 2.25
9 DMc(c),RGu, ... 2.25
10 DMc(c),RGu, ... 2.25
11 DMc(c),RGu,In Tennessee . . . 1.95
Ann.#1 DMc(c),DiF(s),GyA,JnM,F:Suzy, Childrens Crusade,BU:retells Adventure Comics#430 . . . . . . 4.25

BLASTERS SPECIAL

1 A:Snapper Carr, Spider Guild . 2.00

BLOODBATH

1 A:Superman 3.75
2 A:New Heroes 3.75

BLOOD SYNDICATE

(Milestone)

1 I:Blood Syndicate,Rob Chaplick, Dir.Mark.Ed.,w/B puzzle piece, Skybox card,Poster 4.00
1a Newstand Ed. 1.75
2 I:Boogieman,Tech-9 Vs. Holocaust 1.75
3 V:S.Y.S.T.E.M.,I:Mom,D:Tech-9 1.75
4 V:S.Y.S.T.E.M. 1.75
5 I:John Wing,Kwai,Demon Fox . 1.75
6 V:John Wing 1.75
7 I:Edmund,Cornelia 1.75
8 V:Demon Fox 1.75
9 O:Blood Syndicate,I:Templo . . . 1.75
10 WS(c),Ccs,Shadow War,I:Iota, Sideshow,Rainsaw,Slag,Ash, Bad Betty,Oro 1.75
11 IV(s),Ccs,A:Aquamaria 1.75
12 IV(s),Ccs,V:Dinosaur 1.75
13 IV(s),Ccs,B:Roach War, ... 1.75
14 IV(s),Ccs,V:Roaches 1.75
15 IV(s),Ccs,E:Roach War, ... 1.75
16 IV(s),Ccs,Worlds Collide#6, A:Superman 1.50

Blood Syndicate #1 © DC Comics, Inc.

BLUE BEETLE

June, 1986

1 O:Blue Beetle 2.00
2 V:Fire Fist 1.00
3 V:Madmen 1.00
4 V:Doctor Alchemy 1.00
5 A:Question 1.00
6 V:Question 1.00
7 A:Question 1.00
8 A:Chronos 1.00
9 A:Chronos 1.00
10 Legends, V:Chronos 1.00
11 A:New Teen Titans 1.00
12 A:New Teen Titans 1.00
13 A:New Teen Titans 1.00
14 Pago Island,I:Catalyst 1.00
15 RA:V:Carapax 1.00
16 RA,Chicago Murders 1.00
17 R:Dan Garrett/Blue Beetle . . . 1.00
18 D:Dan Garrett 1.00
19 RA,R:Dr. Cyber 1.00
20 RA,Millennium,A:JLI 1.00
21 RA,A:Mr.Miracle, Millennium tie in 1.00
22 RA,Prehistoric Chicago 1.00
23 DH,V:The Madmen 1.00
24 DH,final issue 1.00

BLUE DEVIL

June, 1984

1 O:Blue Devil 2.50
2 . . . . 1.50
3 A:Superman 1.50
4 A:JLA 1.50
5 . . . . 1.50
6 EC,I:Bolt 1.00
7 KG 1.00
8 GV 1.00
9 thru 16 . . . . @1.00
17 Crisis 1.25
18 Crisis 1.25
19 . . . . 1.00
20 RM,Halloween 1.00
21 RM,I:Roadmaster 1.00
22 RM,A:Jorj & Lehni 1.00
23 A:Jorj & Lehni 1.00
24 V:Blue Devil Toys 1.00
25 Mary Frances Cassidy 1.00
26 Special Baseball issue 1.00
27 Godfrey Goose 1.00
28 real live fan guest star 1.00
29 . . . . 1.00

30 Double sized 1.25
31 BSz,V:Seraph,December,1986 1.25
Ann.#1 . . . . 1.50

BOMBA, THE JUNGLE BOY

September-October, 1967

1 CI,MA,I:Bomba 15.00
2 thru 6 . . . . @10.00
7 September-October, 1968 . . 10.00

BOOKS OF MAGIC

1 B:NGa(s),JBo,F:Phantom Stranger, A:J.Constantine,Tim Hunter, Doctor Occult,Mister E 18.00
2 SHp,F:J.Constantine,A:Spectre, Dr.Fate,Demon,Zatanna 14.00
3 CV,F:Doctor Occult, A:Sandman 12.00
4 E:NGa(s),PuJ,F:Mr.E,A:Death . 11.00
TPB rep.#1-4 . . . . 19.95

[Regular Series]
Vertigo

1 MkB,B:Bindings,R:Tim Hunter . . 2.25
2 CV(c),MkB,V:Manticore 2.25
3 CV(c),MkB,E:Bindings, ... 1.95

BOOSTER GOLD

February, 1986

1 DJ,V:Blackguard 3.00
2 DJ,V:Minddancer 2.50
3 DJ,V:Minddancer 2.00
4 DJ,V:Minddancer 1.50
5 DJ,V:Fascinator 1.50
6 DJ,A:Superman 1.00
7 DJ,A:Superman 1.00
8 DJ,A:Braniac 5,Cham.Boy, Ultra Boy Pt.1 . . . . 1.25
9 DJ,A:Braniac 5,Cham.Boy, Ultra Boy Pt.2 . . . . 1.25
10 DJ,V:1000 . . . . 1.00
11 DJ,V:Shockwave 1.00
12 DJ,Booster Weakening 1.00
13 DJ,I:Rip Hunter(modern) 1.00
14 DJ,Rip Hunter 1.00
15 DJ,Rip Hunter 1.00
16 DJ,Boosters new company . . . 1.00
17 DJ,A:Cheshire & Hawk 1.00
18 DJ,V:Broderick 1.00
19 DJ,V:Rainbow Raider 1.00
20 DJ,V:Rainbow Raider 1.00
21 DJ,Goldstar captured by aliens 1.00
22 DJ,A:J.L.I.,D:Goldstar 1.00
23 DJ,A:Superman & Luthor 1.25
24 DJ,Millenium 1.00
25 DJ,last issue 1.00

BOY COMMANDOS

Winter, 1942-43

1 S&K,O:Liberty Belle;Sandman & Newsboy Legion 2,000.00
2 S&K 750.00
3 S&K 500.00
4 and 5 . . . . @350.00
6 S&K 225.00
7 S&K 225.00
8 S&K 225.00
9 . . . . 225.00
10 S&K 225.00
11 Infinity(c) 225.00
12 thru 16 . . . . @125.00
17 Science Fiction(c) 135.00
18 thru 20 . . . . @125.00
21 . . . . 90.00
22 . . . . 90.00
23 S&K,S&K,(c) 100.00
24 thru 25 . . . . @90.00
26 Science Fiction(c) 100.00
27 . . . . 85.00
28 . . . . 85.00
29 S&K story 90.00
30 Baseball Storm 90.00
31 . . . . 85.00
32 A:Dale Evans(c) 90.00
33 . . . . 85.00
34 I:Wolf 85.00
35 . . . . 85.00
36 November-December, 1949 120.00

Brave and the Bold #72
© DC Comics, Inc.

BRAVE AND THE BOLD

August-September, 1955

1 JKu,RH,IN,I:VikingPrince,Golden Gladiator,Silent Knight . . . 1,500.00
2 F:Viking Prince 700.00
3 F:Viking Prince 400.00
4 F:Viking Prince 400.00
5 B:Robin Hood 450.00
6 JKu,F:Robin Hood,E:Golden Gladiator 300.00
7 JKu,F:Robin Hood 300.00
8 JKu,F:Robin Hood 300.00
9 JKu,F:Robin Hood 300.00
10 JKu,F:Robin Hood 300.00
11 JKu,F:Viking Prince 190.00
12 JKu,F:Viking Prince 190.00
13 JKu,F:Viking Prince 190.00
14 JKu,F:Viking Prince 190.00
15 JKu,F:Viking Prince 190.00
16 JKu,F:Viking Prince 175.00
17 JKu,F:Viking Prince 175.00
18 JKu,F:Viking Prince 175.00
19 JKu,F:Viking Prince 175.00
20 JKu,F:Viking Prince 175.00
21 JKu,F:Viking Prince 175.00
22 JKu,F:Viking Prince 175.00
23 JKu,O:Viking Prince 225.00
24 JKu,E:Viking Prince,Silent Knight 175.00
25 RA,I&B:Suicide Squad 225.00
26 F:Suicide Squad 160.00
27 Creature of Ghost Lake . . . 160.00
28 I:Justice League of America,O:Snapper Carr . . 3,000.00
29 F:Justice League 1,300.00
30 F:Justice League 1,200.00
31 F:Cave Carson 135.00
32 F:Cave Carson 110.00
33 F:Cave Carson 110.00
34 JKu,I&O:S.A. Hawkman . . 1,200.00
35 JKu:F:Hawkman 375.00
36 JKu:F:Hawkman 375.00
37 F:Suicide Squad 140.00
38 F:Suicide Squad 120.00
39 F:Suicide Squad 120.00
40 JKu,F:Cave Carson 80.00
41 F:Cave Carson 80.00
42 JKu,F:Hawkman 200.00
43 JKu,O:Hawkman 230.00
44 JKu,F:Hawkman 200.00
45 CI,F:Strange Sports 35.00
46 CI,F:Strange Sports 35.00
47 CI,F:Strange Sports 35.00
48 CI,F:Strange Sports 35.00
49 CI,F:Strange Sports 35.00
50 F:GreenArrow & JonnJ'onzz . 95.00
51 F:Aquaman & Hawkman 50.00
52 JKu,F:Sgt.Rock 60.00
53 ATh,F:Atom & Flash 35.00
54 I&O:Teen Titans 225.00
55 F:Metal Man & Atom 30.00
56 F:Flash & J'onn J'onzz 30.00
57 I&O:Metamorpho 100.00
58 F:Metamorpho 45.00
59 F:Batman & Green Lantern . . 70.00
60 A:Teen Titans,I:Wonder Girl . 70.00
61 MA,O:Starman,BlackCanary . 60.00
62 MA,O:Starman,BlackCanary . 60.00
63 F:Supergirl&WonderWoman . 20.00
64 F:Batman,V:Eclipso 60.00
65 DG,FMc,F:Flash & Doom Patrol 20.00
66 F:Metamorpho & Metal Men . 20.00
67 CI,F:Batman & Flash 30.00
68 F:Batman,Metamorpho,Joker, Riddler,Penguin 55.00
69 F:Batman & Green Lantern . . 20.00
70 F:Batman & Hawkman 20.00
71 F:Batman & Green Arrow . . . 20.00
72 CI,F:Spectre & Flash 20.00
73 F:Aquaman & Atom 20.00
74 B:Batman T.U.,A:Metal Men . 20.00
75 F:Spectre 20.00
76 F:Plastic Man 20.00
77 F:Atom 20.00
78 F:Wonder Woman 20.00
79 NA,F:Deadman 28.00
80 NA,DG,F:Creeper 25.00
81 NA,F:Flash 25.00
82 NA,F:Aquaman,O:Ocean Master 25.00
83 NA,F:Teen Titans 36.00
84 NA,F:Sgt.Rock 25.00
85 NA,F:Green Arrow 25.00
86 NA,F:Deadman 25.00
87 F:Wonder Woman 12.00
88 F:Wildcat 12.00
89 RA,F:Phantom Stranger 12.00
90 F:Adam Strange 12.00
91 F:Black Canary 12.00
92 F:Bat Squad 12.00
93 NA,House of Mystery 23.00
94 NC,F:Teen Titans 12.00
95 F:Plastic Man 9.00
96 F:Sgt.Rock 9.00
97 NC(i),F:Wildcat 9.00
98 JAp,F:Phantom Stranger 9.00
99 NC,F:Flash 9.00
100 NA,F:Green Arrow 25.00
101 JA,F:Metamorpho 5.00
102 NA,JA,F:Teen Titans 6.00
103 FMc,F:Metal Men 5.00
104 JAp,F:Deadman 5.00
105 JAp,F:Wonder Woman 5.00
106 JAp,F:Green Arrow 5.00
107 JAp,F:Black Canary 5.00
108 JAp,F:Sgt.Rock 5.00
109 JAp,F:Demon 5.00
110 JAp,F:Wildcat 5.00
111 JAp,F:Joker 12.50
112 JAp,F:Mr.Miracle. 7.50
113 JAp,F:Metal Men 7.50
114 JAp,F:Aquaman 7.50
115 JAp,O:Viking Prince 7.50
116 JAp,F:Spectre 7.50
117 JAp,F:Sgt.Rock 7.50
118 JAp,F:Wildcat,V:Joker 11.00
119 JAp,F:Man-Bat 4.00
120 JAp,F:Kamandi 4.00
121 JAp,F:Metal Men 4.00

122 JAp,F:Swamp Thing 4.00
123 JAp,F:Plastic Man 4.00
124 JAp,F:Sgt.Rock 4.00
125 JAp,F:Flash 4.00
126 JAp,F:Aquaman 4.00
127 JAp,F:Wildcat 4.00
128 JAp,F:Mr.Miracle 4.00
129 F:Green Arrow,V:Joker 11.00
130 F:Green Arrow,V:Joker 11.00
131 JAp,F:WonderWoman,
A:Catwoman 5.00
132 JAp,F:King Fu Foom 4.00
133 JAp,F:Deadman 4.00
134 JAp,F:Green Lantern 4.00
135 JAp,F:Metal Men 4.00
136 JAp,F:Metal Men,Green Arr. . 4.00
137 F:Demon 4.00
138 JAp,F:Mr.Miracle 4.00
139 JAp,F:Hawkman 4.00
140 JAp,F:Wonder Woman. 4.00
141 JAp,F:Bl.Canary,A:Joker . . . 10.00
142 JAp,F:Aquaman 3.00
143 O:Human Target 3.25
144 JAp,F:Green Arrow 3.25
145 JAp,F:Phantom Stranger 3.00
146 JAp,F:E-2 Batman 3.00

Brave and the Bold #200
© DC Comics, Inc.

147 JAp,A:Supergirl 3.00
148 JSon,JAp,F:Plastic Man 3.00
149 JAp,F:Teen Titans 3.50
150 JAp,F:Superman 3.00
151 JAp,F:Flash 3.50
152 JAp,F:Atom 3.00
153 DN,F:Red Tornado 3.00
154 JAp,F:Metamorpho 3.00
155 JAp,F:Green Lantern 3.00
156 DN,F:Dr.Fate 3.00
157 JAp,F:Kamandi 3.00
158 JAp,F:Wonder Woman 3.00
159 JAp,A:Ras al Ghul 3.00
160 JAp,F:Supergirl 3.00
161 JAp,F:Adam Strange 3.00
162 JAp,F:Sgt.Rock 3.00
163 DG,F:Black Lightning 3.00
164 JL,F:Hawkman 3.00
165 DN,F:Man-bat 3.00
166 DG,TA,DSp,F:Black Canary
A:Penguin,I:Nemesis 3.00
167 DC,DA,F:Blackhawk 3.00
168 JAp,DSp,F:Green Arrow 3.25
169 JAp,DSp,F:Zatanna 3.00
170 JA,F:Nemesis 3.00
171 JL,DSp,V:Scalphunter 3.00
172 CI,F:Firestorm 3.00
173 JAp,F:Guardians 3.00
174 JAp,F:Green Lantern 3.00
175 JAp,A:Lois Lane 3.00
176 JAp,F:Swamp Thing 3.00
177 JAp,F:Elongated Man 3.00
178 JAp,F:Creeper 3.00
179 EC,F:Legion o/Superheroes . 3.00
180 JAp,F:Spectre,Nemesis 3.00
181 JAp,F:Hawk & Dove 3.00
182 JAp,F:E-2 Robin 3.00
183 CI,V:Riddler 3.00
184 JAp,A:Catwoman 4.00
185 F:Green Arrow 3.25
186 JAp,F:Hawkman 3.00
187 JAp,F:Metal Men 3.00
188 JAp,F:Rose & Thorn 3.00
189 JAp,A:Thorn 3.00
190 JAp,F:Adam Strange 3.00
191 JAp,V:Joker,Penguin 7.50
192 JAp,F:Superboy 3.00
193 JAp,D:Nemesis 3.00
194 CI,F:Flash 3.00
195 JA,I:Vampire 3.00
196 JAp,F:Ragman 3.00
197 JSon,W:Earth II Batman &
Catwoman 4.00
198 F:Karate Kid 3.00
199 RA,F:Spectre 3.00
200 DGb,JAp,A:Earth-2 Batman,I:
Outsiders (GeoForce,Katana,Halo),
E:Batman T.U.,final issue . . . 12.00

[Limited Series]

1 SAP,Green Arrow/Butcher T.U. . 2.00
2 SAP,A:Black Canary,Question . 2.00
3 SAP,Green Arrow/Butcher 2.00
4 SAP,GA on Trial;A:Black
Canary 2.00
5 SAP,V:Native Canadians,I.R.A. . 2.00

BREATHTAKER

1 I:Breathtaker(Chase Darrow) . . 6.00
2 Chase Darrow captured 6.00
3 O:Breathtaker 6.00
4 V:The Man, final issue 4.95

BROTHER POWER, THE GEEK

September-October, 1968

1 . . . . 35.00
2 November-December, 1968 . 25.00

BUGS BUNNY

1 A:Bugs,Daffy,Search for Fudd
Statues 1.00
2 Search for Statues cont.
V:WitchHazel 1.00
3 Bugs&Co.in outer space, final . 1.50

BUTCHER, THE

1 MB,I:John Butcher 5.00
2 MB,in San Francisco 3.50
3 MB,V:Corporation 3.00
4 MB,A:Green Arrow 2.50
5 MB,A:Corvus,final issue 2.25

BUZZY

Winter, 1944

1 . . . . 165.00
2 . . . . 75.00
3 thru 5 . . . . @40.00
6 thru 10 . . . . @35.00
11 thru 15 . . . . @25.00
16 thru 25 . . . . @25.00
26 thru 35 . . . . @20.00
36 thru 45 . . . . @15.00
46 thru 76 . . . . @15.00
77 October, 1958 . . . . 15.00

CAMELOT 3000

December, 1982

1 BB,O:Arthur,Merlin 4.00
2 BB,A:Morgan LeFay 3.25
3 BB,J:New Knights 3.25
4 BB,V:McAllister 3.25
5 BB,O:Morgan Le Fay 3.25
6 BB,TA,W:Arthur 3.25
7 BB,TA,R:Isolde 3.25
8 BB,TA,D:Sir Kay 3.25
9 BB,TA,L:Sir Percival 3.25
10 BB,TA,V:Morgan Le Fay 3.25
11 BB,TA,V:Morgan Le Fay 3.25
12 BB,TA,D:Arthur 3.25

CAPTAIN ACTION

{Based on toy}
October-November, 1968

1 WW,I:Captain Action,Action
Boy,A:Superman 45.00
2 GK,WW, V:Krellik 30.00
3 GK,I:Dr.Evil 27.00
4 GK,A:Dr.Evil 22.00
5 GK,WW,A:Matthew Blackwell,
last issue 35.00

CAPTAIN ATOM

March, 1987

1 PB,O:Captain Atom 3.00
2 PB,C:Batman 2.00
3 PB,O:Captain Atom 1.75
4 PB,A:Firestorm 1.75
5 PB,A:Firestorm 1.75
6 PB,Dr.Spectro 1.75
7 R:Plastique 1.75
8 PB,Capt.Atom/Plastique 1.75
9 V:Bolt 1.75
10 PB,A:JLI 2.00
11 PB,A:Firestorm 1.50
12 PB,I:Major Force 1.50
13 PB,Christmas issue 1.50
14 PB,A:Nightshade 1.50
15 PB,Dr.Spectro, Major Force . . 1.50
16 PB,A:JLI,V:Red Tornado 1.75
17 V:Red Tornado;A:Swamp
Thing,JLI 1.75
18 PB,A:Major Force 1.50
19 PB,Drug War 1.50
20 FMc,BlueBeetle 1.50
21 PB,A:Plastique,Nightshade . . . 1.50
22 PB,A:MaxLord,Nightshade,
Plastique 1.50
23 PB,V:The Ghost 1.50
24 PB,Invasion X-over 1.50
25 PB,Invvasion X-over 1.50
26 A:JLA,Top Secret Pt.1 . . . . . . 1.75
27 A:JLA,Top Secret Pt.2 . . . . . . 1.75
28 V:Ghost, Top Secret Pt.3 . . . . 1.50
29 RT,Captain Atom cleared
(new direction) 1.50
30 Janus Directive #11,V:Black
Manta 1.50
31 RT,Capt.Atom's Powers,
A:Rocket Red 1.50
32 Loses Powers 1.50
33 A:Batman 2.00
34 C:JLE 1.50
35 RT,Secret o/t Silver Shield,
A:Major Force 1.50
36 RT,Las Vegas Battle,A:Major
Force 1.50
37 I:New Atomic Skull 1.25
38 RT,A:Red Tornado,
Black Racer 1.25
39 RT,A:Red Tornado 1.25
40 RT,V:Kobra 1.25
41 RT,A:Black Racer,
Red Tornado 1.25
42 RT,A:Phantom Stranger,Red
Tornado,Black Racer,
Death from Sandman 1.25
43 RT,V:Nekron 1.25
44 RT,V:Plastique 1.25
45 RT,A:The Ghost,I:Ironfire 1.25
46 RT,A:Superman 1.25
47 RT,A:SupermanV:Ghost 1.25
48 RT,R:Red Tornado 1.25

49 RT,Plastique on trial 1.25
50 RT,V:The Ghost,DoubleSize . . 2.00
51 RT 1.00
52 RT,Terror on RTE.91' 1.00
53 RT,A:Aquaman 1.00
54 RT,A:Rasputin,Shadowstorm . . 1.00
55 RT,Inside Quantum Field 1.00
56 RT,Quantum Field cont. 1.00
57 RT,V:ShadowStorm, Quantum.Field 1.00
Ann.#1 I:Maj.Force 1.50
Ann.#2 A:RocketRed,Maj.Force . . 1.50

CAPTAIN CARROT
March, 1982

1 RA,A:Superman,Starro 1.25
2 AA 1.00
3 thru 19 . . . . @1.00
20 A:Changeling,November, 1983 1.00

CAPTAIN STORM
May-June, 1964

1 IN(c),Killer Hunt 14.00
2 IN(c),First Shot-Last Shot 8.00
3 JKu,Death of a PT Boat 8.00
4 IN(c),First Command-Last Command 8.00
5 IN(c), Killer Torpedo 8.00
6 JKu,IN(c),Medals For An Ocean 8.00
7 IN(c),A Bullet For The General 8.00
8 IN(c),Death of A Sub 8.00
9 IN(c),Sink That Flattop 8.00
10 IN(c),Only The Last Man Lives 8.00
11 IN(c),Ride a Hot Torpedo 8.00
12 JKu(c),T.N.T. Tea Party Abroad PT 47 . . . . 8.00
13 JKu,Yankee Banzai 8.00
14 RH(c),Sink Capt. Storm 8.00
15 IN(c),My Enemy-My Friend . . . 8.00
16 IN(c),Battle of the Stinging Mosquito 8.00
17 IN(c),First Shot for a Dead Man 8.00
18 March-April, 1967 . . . . 8.00

CATWOMAN
[Limited Series]

1 O:Catwoman 14.00
2 Catwoman'sSister kidnapped . 10.00
3 Battle 8.00
4 Final,V:Batman 8.00

[Regular Series]

1 B:JDy(s),JBa,DG,A:Bane 4.00
2 JBa,DG,A:Bane 2.00
3 JBa,DG,at Santa Prisca 2.00
4 JBa,DG,Bane's Secret 2.00
5 JBa,V:Ninjas 2.00
6 JBa,A:Batman 1.75
7 JBa,A:Batman 1.75
8 JBa,V:Zephyr 1.75
9 JBa,V:Zephyr 1.75
10 JBa,V:Arms Dealer 1.75
11 JBa, ... 1.75
12 JBa,Knights End #6,A:Batman 1.50
Ann.#1 Elseworlds Story,A:Ra's Al Ghul, ... 2.95

CATWOMAN DEFIANT

1 TGr,DG,V:Mr.Handsome 6.00

CENTURIONS
June, 1987

1 DH,V:Doc Terror 1.00
2 DH,O:Centurions 1.00
3 DH,V:Doc Terror 1.00
4 DH,September, 1987 . . . . 1.00

CHAIN GANG WAR

1 I:Chain Gang 2.50
2 V:8-Ball 1.75
3 C:Deathstroke 1.75
C:Deathstroke 1.75
5 Embossed(c),A:Deathstroke . . . 2.50
6 A:Deathstroke,Batman 1.75
7 V:Crooked Man 1.75
8 B:Crooked Man 1.75
9 V:Crooked Man 1.75
10 A:Deathstroke,C:Batman 1.75
11 A:Batman, ... 1.75
12 E:Crooked Man,D:Chain Gang, Final Issue 1.75

CHALLENGERS OF THE UNKNOWN
April-May, 1958

1 JK&JK(c),The Man Who Tampered With Infinity . . . 1,500.00
2 JK&JK(c),The Monster Maker 600.00
3 JK&JK(c),The Secret of the Sorcerer's Mirror 450.00
4 JK,WW,JK(c),The Wizard of Time 400.00
5 JK,WW&JK(c),The Riddle of the Star-Stone 400.00
6 JK,WW,JK(c),Captives of the Space Circus 375.00
7 JK,WW,JK(c),The Isle of No Return 375.00
8 JK,WW,JK&WW(c),The Prisoners of the Robot Planet 375.00
9 The Plot To Destroy Earth . 200.00
10 The Four Faces of Doom . . 200.00
11 The Creatures From The Forbidden World 125.00
12 The Three Clues To Sorcery 125.00
13 The Prisoner of the Tiny Space Ball 125.00
14 O: Multi Man 135.00
15 The Lady Giant and the Beast125.00
16 Prisoners of the Mirage World100.00
17 The Secret of the Space Capsules 100.00
18 The Menace of Mystery Island100.00
19 The Alien Who Stole a Planet 100.00
20 Multi-Man Strikes Back . . . 100.00
21 Weird World That Didn't Exist 100.00
22 The Thing In Challenger Mountain 90.00
23 The Island In The Sky 55.00
24 The Challengers Die At Dawn 55.00
25 Captives of the Alien Hunter . 55.00
26 Death Crowns The Challenge King 55.00
27 Master of the Volcano Men . . 55.00
28 The Riddle of the Faceless Man 55.00
29 Four Roads to Doomsday . . . 55.00
30 Multi-Man...Villain Turned Hero 55.00
31 O:Challengers 65.00
32 One Challenger Must Die . . . 30.00
33 Challengers Meet Their Master 30.00
34 Beachhead, USA 30.00
35 War Against The Moon Beast 30.00
36 Giant In Challenger Mountain 30.00
37 Triple Terror of Mr. Dimension 30.00
38 Menace the Challengers Made 30.00
39 Phantom of the Fair 30.00
40 Super-Powers of the Challengers 30.00
41 The Challenger Who Quit . . . 16.00
42 The League of Challenger-Haters 16.00
43 New look begins 16.00
44 The Curse of the Evil Eye . . . 16.00
45 Queen of the Challenger-Haters 16.00
46 Strange Schemes of the Gargoyle 16.00
47 The Sinister Sponge 16.00
48 A:Doom Patrol 20.00
49 Tyrant Who Owned the World 16.00
50 Final Hours for the Challengers 16.00
51 A:Sea Devil 16.00
52 Two Are Dead - Two To Go . 16.00
53 Who is the Traitor Among Us? 16.00
54 War of the Sub-Humans 16.00
55 D:Red Ryan 16.00
56 License To Kill 16.00
57 Kook And The Kilowatt Killer . 16.00
58 Live Till Tomorrow 16.00
59 Seekeenakee - The Petrified Giant 16.00
60 R:Red Ryan 8.00
61 Robot Hounds of Chang 8.00
62 Legion of the Weird 8.00
63 None Shall Escape the Walking Evil 8.00
64 JKu(c),Invitation to a Hanging . 7.00
65 The Devil's Circus 7.00
66 JKu(c),Rendezvous With Revenge 7.00
67 NA(c),The Dream Killers 7.00
68 NA(c),One of Us is a Madman 7.00
69 JKu(c),I:Corinna 7.00
70 NA(c),Scream of Yesterdays . 7.00
71 NC(c),When Evil Calls 7.00
72 NA(c),A Plague of Darkness . . 7.00
73 NC(c),Curse of the Killer Time Forgot 7.00
74 GT&NA(c),A:Deadman 8.00
75 JK(c),Ultivac Is Loose 5.00
76 JKu(c),The Traitorous Challenger 5.00
77 JK(c),Menace of the Ancient Vials 5.00
78 JK(c),The Island of No Return . 5.00
79 JKu(c),The Monster Maker . . . 5.00
80 NC(c),The Day The Earth Blew Up 5.00
81 MN&NA(c),Multi-Man's Master Plan 5.00
82 MN&NA(c),Swamp Thing 4.00
83 Seven Doorways to Destiny . . 4.00
84 To Save A Monster 4.00
85 The Creature From The End Of Time 4.00
86 The War At Time's End 4.00
87 July, 1978 . . . . 4.00

CHALLENGERS OF THE UNKNOWN

1 BB(c) In The Spotlight 1.50
2 . . . . 1.50
3 Challengers 'Split Up' 1.75
4 'Separate Ways' 1.75
5 Moffet 1.75
6 GK(c),Challengers reunited . . . 1.75
7 AAd(c),June pregnant 1.75
8 final issue 1.75

CHECKMATE
April, 1988

1 From Vigilante & Action Comics 3.75
2 Chicago Bombings cont. 2.50
3 V:Terrorist Right 2.00
4 V:Crime Lords Abroad,B.U.Story 'Training of a Knight' begins . . 2.00
5 Renegade nation of Quarac . . . 2.00
6 Secret Arms Deal 1.75
7 Checkmate Invades Quarac . . . 1.75
8 Consequences-Quarac Invasion 1.75
9 Checkmate's security in doubt . 1.75
10 V:Counterfeiting Ring 1.75
11 Invasion X-over 1.75
12 Invasion Aftermath extra 1.75
13 CommanderH.Stein's vacation 1.75
14 R:Blackthorn 1.75
15 Janus Directive #1 . . . . 1.75
16 Janus Directive #3 . . . . 1.75
17 Janus Directive #6 . . . . 1.75
18 Janus Directive #9 . . . . 1.75
19 Reorganization of Group 1.75
20 'Shadow of Bishop' A:Peacemaker, Pt.1 . . . . 1.75
21 Peacemaker behind Iron Curtain, Pt.2 . . . . 1.75
22 Mystery of Bishop Cont.,Pt.3 . . 1.75
23 European Scientists Suicides, Pt.4 . . . . 1.75
24 Bishop Mystery cont. Pt.5 . . . . 1.50

25 Bishop's Identity Revealed ... 1.50
26 Mazarin kidnaps H.Stein's kids 1.50
27 Stein rescue attempt,I:Cypher . 1.50
28 A:Cypher, Bishop-Robots 1.50
29 A:Cypher,Blackthorn 1.50
30 Irish Knight W.O'Donnell/British Knight L.Hawkins team-up ... 1.50
31 V:Cypher International 2.00
32 V:Cypher International 2.00
33 final issue (32 pages) 2.00

CHILDREN'S CRUSADE
Vertigo

1 NGa(s),CBa,MkB(i),F:Rowland, Payne (From Sandman) 4.75
2 NGa(s),AaK(s),JaD(s),PSj,A:Tim Hunter,Suzy,Maxine,final issue 4.50

CHRISTMAS WITH THE SUPER-HEROES

1 JBy(c) 2.95
2 PC,GM,JBy,NKu,DG A:Batman Superman,Deadman,(last Supergirl appearance) 2.95

CINDER & ASHE
March, 1988

1 JL,I:Cinder & Ashe 2.00
2 JL,Viet Nam Flashbacks 2.00
3 JL,Truth About Lacey revealed 2.00
4 JL,final issue, June, 1988 .... 2.00

CLASH

1 AKu,I:Joe McLash(b/w) 4.95
2 AKu,Panja-Rise to Power 4.95
3 AKu,V:Archons,conclusion 4.95

CLAW THE UNCONQUERED
May-June, 1975

1 .... 2.00
2 .... 1.50
3 Nudity panel 1.25
4 thru 7 .... @1.00
8 KG 1.00
9 KG/BL,Origin 1.00
10 KG 1.00
11 KG 1.00
12 KG/BL,Aug.-Sept., 1978 .... 1.00

COMET
Impact

1 TL,I&O:Comet I:Applejack, Victoria Johnson, Ben Lee 1.50
2 TL,A:Applejack,Lance Perry ... 1.25
3 TL,V:Anti-nuclear terrorists ... 1.25
4 TL,I&V:Black Hood,I:Inferno ... 1.25
5 V:Cyborg Soldier 1.25
6 TL,I:The Hangman 1.25
7 'Press Problems' 1.25
8 TL,Comet ID discovered 1.25
9 TL,'Bad Judgment' 1.25
10 Fly/Comet T.U.,V:Dolphus 1.25
11 V:Inferno 1.25
12 V:Inferno 1.25
13 O:Comet's Powers 1.25
14 O:Comet's Powers Part 2 .... 1.25
15 Rob finds his mother 1.25
16 V:Aliens 1.25
17 "Shocking Truth" 1.25
18 Last Issue 1.25
Ann.#1 Earthquest,w/trading card . 2.25

COMIC CAVALCADE
1942-3

1 Green Lantern, Flash, Wildcat, Wonder Woman, Black Pirate 3,000.00
2 ShM,B:Mutt & Jeff 1,000.00
3 ShM, B:HotHarrigan, Sorcerer 700.00
4 Gay Ghost, A:Scribby, A:Red Tornado 600.00
5 Green Lantern, Flash Wonder Woman 600.00
6 Flash, Wonder Woman Green Lantern 500.00
7 A:Red Tornado, E:Scribby .. 500.00
8 Flash, Wonder Woman Green Lantern 500.00
9 Flash, Wonder Woman Green Lantern 500.00
10 Flash, Wonder Woman Green Lantern 500.00
11 Flash, Wonder Woman Green Lantern 450.00
12 E:Red, White & Blue 450.00
13 A:Solomon Grundy 700.00
14 Flash, Wonder Woman, Green Lantern 450.00
15 B:Johnny Peril 450.00
16 thru 21 Flash, Wonder Woman, Green Lantern . @450.00
22 A:Atom 450.00
23 A:Atom 450.00
24 A:Solomon Grundy 500.00
25 A:Black Canary 325.00
26 ATh, E:Mutt & Jeff 300.00
27 ATh,ATh(c) 300.00
28 ATh E:Flash, Wonder Woman Green Lantern 300.00
29 E:Johnny Peril 350.00
30 RG,B:Fox & Crow 200.00
31 thru 39 RG .... @100.00
40 RG,ShM 100.00
41 thru 49 RG,ShM .... @75.00
50 thru 62 RG,ShM .... @90.00
63 RG,ShM, July 1954 ...... 150.00

CONGO BILL
August-September, 1954

1 .... 450.00
2 .... 400.00
3 thru 7 Aug.-Sept.,1955 .. @350.00

CONGORILLA

1 R:Congo Bill 2.00
2 BB(c),V:Congo Bill 1.75
3 BB(c),V:Congo Bill 1.75

COOL WORLD

1 Prequel to Movie 1.75
2 Movie Adaption 1.75
3 Movie Adaption 1.75

COPS

1 PB,O:Cops,double-size 2.50
2 PB,V:Big Boss 1.50
3 PB,RT,V:Dr.Bad Vibes 1.25
4 BS,A:Sheriff Sundown 1.25
5 PB,Blitz the Robo-Dog 1.25
6 PB,A:Ms.Demeaner 1.25
7 PB,A:Tramplor 1.25
8 PB,V:BigBoss & Ally 1.25
9 PB,Cops Trapped 1.25
10 PB,Dr.Bad Vibes becomes Dr.Goodvibes 1.25
11 PB,V:Big Boss 1.25
12 PB,V:Dr.Badvibe's T.H.U.G.S . 1.25
13 Berserko/Ms.Demeanor marriage proposal 1.25
14 A:Buttons McBoom-Boom 1.25
15 Cops vs. Crooks, final issue .. 1.25

COSMIC BOY
December, 1986

1 KG,EC,Legends tie-in 2.00
2 KG,EC,'Is History Destiny' 1.25
3 KG,EC,'Past,Present,Future' .. 1.25
4 KG,EC,Legends 1.25

COSMIC ODYSSEY

1 MMi,A:Superman,Batman,John Stewart,Starfire,J'onnJ'onzz, NewGods,Demon,JSn story .. 6.00
2 MMi,'Disaster'(low dist) 6.50

Cosmic Odyssey #1 © DC Comics, Inc.

3 MMi,Return to New Genesis .. 5.00
4 MMi,A:Dr.Fate, final 4.00

CRIMSON AVENGER

1 Mini-series 1.00
2 V:Black Cross 1.00
3 'V:Killers of the Dark Cross' ... 1.00
4 'V:Dark Cross,final issue 1.00

CRISIS ON INFINITE EARTHS
April, 1985

1 B:MWn(s),GP,DG,I:Pariah,I&O:Alex Luthor,D:Crime Syndicate ... 10.00
2 GP,DG,V:Psycho Pirate, A:Joker,Batman 6.00
3 GP,DG,D:Losers 5.00
4 GP,D:Monitor,I:2nd Dr.Light ... 5.00
5 GP,JOy,I:Anti-Monitor 5.00
6 GP,JOy,I:2nd Wildcat,A:Fawcett, Quality & Charlton heroes 5.00
7 GP,JOy,DG,D:Supergirl 8.00
8 GP,JOy,D:1st Flash 12.00
9 GP,JOy,D:Aquagirl 5.00
10 GP,JOy,D:Psimon,A:Spectre .. 5.00
11 GP,JOy,D:Angle Man 6.00
12 E:MWn(s),GP,JOy,D:Huntress,Kole, Kid Flash becomes 2nd Flash, D:Earth 2 .... 8.00

CRUCIBLE
Impact

1 JQ,F:The Comet 1.25
2 JQ,A:Black Hood,Comet 1.50
3 JQ,Comet Vs.Black Hood 1.50
4 JQ,V:Tomorrow Men 1.50
5 JQ,Black Hod vs Shield 1.25
6 JQ,V:The Crucible 1.25

CRUSADERS
Impact

1 DJu(c),I:Crusaders,inc Trading cards 1.25
2 V:Kalathar 1.00
3 V:Kalathar 1.00
4 Crusaders form as group 1.00
5 V:Cyber-Punks 1.25
6 V:Cyborg Villains 1.25
7 F:Fireball 1.25
8 Last Issue 1.25

DALE EVANS COMICS
September-October, 1948

1 Ph(c),ATh,B:Sierra Smith . . . 400.00
2 Ph(c),ATh 200.00
3 ATh 150.00
4 thru 11 . . . . @150.00
12 thru 23 . . . . @75.00
24 July-August, 1952 . . . . 75.00

DAMAGE

1 I:Damage,V:Metallo 2.00
2 V:Symbolix 2.00
3 V:Troll 2.00
4 V:Troll 1.75

DANGER TRAIL
July-August, 1950

1 Cl,Ath,I:King For A Day 550.00
2 ATh 400.00
3 ATh 550.00
4 ATh 350.00
5 March-April, 1951 . . . . 350.00

DANGER TRAIL

1 thru 4 Cl,FMc,F:King Faraday V:Cobra 2.00

DARK MANSION OF FORBIDDEN LOVE, THE
September-October, 1971

1 . . . . 6.00
2 . . . . 3.50
3 . . . . 3.50
4 March-April, 1972 . . . . 3.50

Darkstars #2 © DC Comics, Inc.

DARKSTARS

1 TC(c),LSn,I:Darkstars 5.00
2 TC(c),LSn,F:Ferin Colos 3.00
3 LSn,J:Mo,Flint,V:Evil Star 3.00
4 TC,V:Evilstar 5.00
5 TC,A:Hawkman,Hawkwoman . . 4.00
6 TC,A:Hawkman 3.00
7 TC,V:K'llash 2.50
8 F:Ferris Colos 2.00
9 Colos vs K'lassh 2.00
10 V:Con Artists 2.00
11 TC,Trinity#4,A:Green Lantern, L.E.G.I.O.N. 2.00
12 TC(c),Trinity#7,A:Green Lantern, L.E.G.I.O.N. 2.00
13 TC(c),V:Alien Underworld 2.00
14 I:Annihilator 2.00
15 V:Annihilator 2.00
16 V:Annihilator 2.00
17 Murders 2.00
18 B:Eve of Destruction 2.00
19 A:Flash 2.00
20 E:Eve of Destruction 2.00
21 A:John Stewart,Donna Troy . . 2.00
22 A:Controllers 1.95

DC CHALLENGE
November, 1985

1 GC,Batman 4.00
2 Superman 1.50
3 Cl,Adam Strange 1.50
4 GK/KJ,Aquaman 1.50
5 DGb,Dr.Fate,Capt.Marvel 1.50
6 Dr. 13 . . . . 1.50
7 Gorilla Grodd 1.50
8 DG,Outsiders, New Gods 1.50
9 New Teen Titans,JLA 1.50
10 CS,New Teen Titans,JLA 1.50
11 KG,Outsiders 1.50
12 DCw,TMd,DSp,New Teen Titans, October, 1986 . . . . 2.50

DC COMICS PRESENTS
July-August, 1978
[all have Superman]

1 JL,DA,F:Flash 3.50
2 JL,DA,F:Flash 2.50
3 JL,F:Adam Strange 1.75
4 JL,F:Metal Men,A:Mr.IQ 1.75
5 MA,F:Aquaman 1.75
6 CS,F:Green Lantern 1.75
7 DD,F:Red Tornado 1.75
8 MA,F:Swamp Thing 1.75
9 JSon,JA,RH,F:Wonder Woman 1.75
10 JSon,JA,F:Sgt.Rock 1.75
11 JSon,F:Hawkman 1.75
12 RB,DG,F:Mr.Miracle 1.75
13 DD,DG,F:Legion 2.00
14 DD,DG,F:Superboy 1.50
15 JSon,F:Atom,C:Batman 1.50
16 JSon,F:Black Lightning 1.50
17 JL,F:Firestorm 1.50
18 DD,F:Zatanna 1.50
19 JSon,F:Batgirl 2.00
20 JL,F:Green Arrow 1.50
21 JSon,JSa,F:Elongated Man . . . 1.50
22 DD,FMc,F:Captain Comet 1.50
23 JSon,F:Dr.Fate 1.50
24 JL,F:Deadman 1.50
25 DD,FMc,F:Phantom Stranger . 1.50
26 GP,DG,JSn,I:New Teen Titans, Cyborg,Raven,Starfire A:Green Lantern 14.00
27 JSn,RT,I:Mongul 4.00
28 JSn,RT,GK,F:Mongul 3.00
29 JSn,RT,AS,F:Spectre 2.00
30 CS,AS,F:Black Canary 1.50
31 JL,DG,AS,F:Robin 1.50
32 KS,AS,F:Wonder Woman 1.50
33 RB,DG,AS,F:Captain Marvel . . 1.50
34 RB,DG,F:Marvel Family 1.50
35 CS,GK,F:Man-bat 1.50
36 JSn,F:Starman 2.00
37 JSn,AS,F:Hawkgirl 1.50
38 GP(c),DH,AS,DG,D:Crimson Avenger,F:Flash 1.25
39 JSon,AS,F:Plastic Man, Toyman 1.25
40 IN,FMc,AS,F:Metamorpho 1.25
41 JL,FMc,GC,RT,I:New Wonder Woman,A:Joker 3.00
42 IN,FMc,F:Unknown Soldier . . . 1.25
43 BB(c),CS,F:Legion 1.25
44 IN,FMc,F:Dial H for Hero 3.00
45 RB,F:Firestorm 1.25
46 AS,I:Global Guardians 1.25
47 CS,I:Masters of Universe. 1.25
48 GK(c),AA,IN,FMc,F:Aquaman . 1.25
49 RB,F:Captain Marvel 1.25
50 KS,CS,F:Clark Kent 1.25
51 AS,FMc,CS,F:Atom,Masters of the Universe 1.25
52 KG,F:Doom Patrol, I:Ambush Bug 2.00
53 CS,TD,RA,DG,I:Atari Force . . . 1.25
54 DN,DA,F:Gr.Arrow,Bl.Canary . 1.25
55 AS,F:Air Wave,A:Superboy . . . 1.25
56 GK(c),F:Power Girl 1.25
57 AS,FMc,F:Atomic Knights 1.25
58 GK(c),AS,F:Robin,Elongated Man 1.25
59 KG,KS,F:Ambush Bug 1.25
60 GK(c),IN,TD,F:Guardians 1.25
61 GP,F:Omac 1.25
62 GK(c),IN,F:Freedom Fighters . 1.25
63 AS,EC,F:Amethyst 1.25
64 GK(c),AS,FMc,F:Kamandi 1.25
65 GM,F:Madame Xanadu 1.25
66 JKu,F:Demon 1.25
67 CS,MA,F:Santa Claus 1.25
68 GK(c),CS,MA,F:Vixen 1.25
69 IN,DJ,F:Blackhawk 1.25
70 AS,TD,F:Metal Men 1.25
71 CS,F:Bizarro 1.25
72 AS,DG,F:Phant.Stranger,Joker 3.50
73 Cl,F:Flash 1.25
74 AS,RT,F:Hawkman 1.25
75 TMd,F:Arion 1.25
76 EB,F:Wonder Woman 1.25
77 CS,F:Forgotten Heroes 3.50
78 CS,F:Forgotten Villains 3.50
79 CS,AW,F:Legion 1.25
80 CS,F:Clark Kent 1.25
81 KG,BO,F:Ambush Bug 1.25
82 KJ,F:Adam Strange 1.25
83 IN,F:Batman/Outsiders. 1.25
84 JK,ATh,MA,F:Challengers 1.25
85 RV,AW,AMo(s), F:Swamp Thing 4.00
86 Crisis,F:Supergirl 1.25
87 CS,AW,Crisis,I:Earth Prime Superboy 1.50
88 KG,Crisis,F:Creeper 1.25
89 MMi(c),AS,F:Omega Men 1.25
90 DCw,F:Firestorm,Capt.Atom . . 1.25
91 CS,F:Captain Comet 1.25
92 CS,F:Vigilante 1.25
93 JSn(c),AS,KS,F:Elastic Four . . 1.25
94 GP(c),TMd,DH,Crisis,F:Lady Quark,Pariah,Harbinger 1.25
95 MA(i),F:Hawkman 1.25
96 JSon,KS,F:Blue Devil 1.25
97 RV,F:Phantom Zone Villians, final issue,double-sized 1.50
Ann.#1,RB,F:Earth 2 Superman . . 1.50
Ann.#2 GK(c),KP,I:Superwoman . 1.25
Ann.#3 GK,F:Captain Marvel 1.25
Ann.#4 EB,JOy,F:Superwoman . . 1.25

DC/MARVEL CROSSOVER CLASSICS

TPB, rep all x-overs 17.95

DC GRAPHIC NOVEL
November, 1983

1 JL,Star Raiders 6.00
2 Warlords 6.00
3 EC,Medusa Chain 6.00
4 JK,Hunger Dogs 6.00
5 Me and Joe Priest 7.00
6 Space Clusters 7.00

DC S.F. GRAPHIC NOVEL

1 KG,Hell on Earth 6.00
2 Nightwings 6.00
3 Frost and Fire 6.00
4 Merchants of Venus 6.00
5 Metalzoic 6.00
6 MR,Demon-Glass Hand 6.00
7 Sandkings 6.00

DC SPECIAL
October-December, 1968
[All reprint]

1 CI,F:Flash,Batman,Adam Strange, (#1 thru #21 reps) 8.00
2 F:Teen Titans 5.00
3 GA,F:Black Canary 5.00
4 Mystery 5.00
5 JKu,F:Viking Prince/Sgt.Rock 5.00
6 Wild Frontier 5.00
7 F:Strange Sports 5.00
8 Wanted 5.00
9 5.00
10 LAW 5.00
11 NA,BWr,F:Monsters 5.00
12 JKu,F:Viking Prince 5.00
13 F:Strange Sports 5.00
14 Wanted,F:Penguin/Joker 6.00
15 GA,F:Plastic Man 6.00
16 F:Super Heroes & Gorillas 3.50
17 F:Green Lantern 3.50
18 Earth Shaking Stories 3.50
19 F:War Against Gianta 3.50
20 Green Lantern 3.50
21 F:War Against Monsters 3.50
22 Three Musketeers 3.50
23 Three Musketeers 3.50
24 Three Musketeers 3.50
25 Three Musketeers 3.50
26 F:Enemy Ace(rep) 3.50
27 RB,JR,F:Captain Comet 3.50
28 DN,DA,Earth disasters 3.50
29 JSon,BL,O:JSA 4.00

DC SPECIAL SERIES
September, 1977

1 MN,DD,IN,FMc,JSon,JA,BMc, JRu,F:Batman,Flash,Green Lantern,Atom,Aquaman 5.00
2 BWr(c),BWr,F:Swamp Thing rep. 4.00
3 JKu(c),F:Sgt.Rock 3.00
4 AN,RT,Unexpected Annual 3.00
5 CS,F:Superman 3.25
6 BMc(i),Secret Society Vs.JLA 3.00
7 AN,F:Ghosts 3.00
8 RE,DG,F:Brave&Bold,Deadman 3.50
9 SD,RH,DAy,F:Wonder Woman 3.00
10 JSon,MN,DN,TA,Secret Origins, O:Dr.Fate 3.00
11 JL,KS,MA,IN,WW,AS,F:Flash 3.50
12 MK(c),RT,RH,TS,Secrets of Haunted House 3.00
13 JKu(c),RT,SBi,RE,F:Sgt.Rock 3.00
14 BWr(c),F:Swamp Thing rep. 3.50
15 MN,JRu,MR,DG,MGo, F:Batman 4.50
16 RH,D:Jonah Hex 3.25
17 F:Swamp Thing rep. 3.50
18 JK(c),digest,F:Sgt.Rock rep. 3.00
19 digest,Secret Origins O:Wonder Woman 3.50
20 BWr(c),F:Swamp Thing rep. 3.50
21 FM,JL,DG,RT,DA,F:Batman, Legion 18.00
22 JKu(c),F:G.I.Combat 3.25
23 digest size,F:Flash 3.25
24 F:Worlds Finest 3.25
25 F:Superman II,Photo Album 3.50
26 RA,F:Superman's Fortress 4.00
27 JL,DG,F:Batman vs.Hulk 7.50

DC SUPERSTARS

1 F:Teen Titans rep. 4.00
2 F:DC Super Stars/Space 1.50
3 CS,F:Superman,Legion 2.50
4 DC,MA,F:Super Stars/Space 1.50
5 CI,F:Flash rep. 1.50
6 MA,F:Super Stars/Space 1.50
7 F:Aquaman rep. 1.50
8 CI,MA,F:Adam Strange 4.00
9 F:Superman rep. 1.50
10 DD,FMc,F:Superhero Baseball Special,A:Joker 5.50
11 GM,Magic 1.50
12 CS,MA,F:Superboy 1.50
13 SA 1.50
14 RB,BL,JA,JRu,Secret Origins 1.50
15 JKu(c),RB,RT(i),War Heroes 1.50
16 DN,BL,I:Star Hunters 1.50
17 JSon,MGr,BL,I&O:Huntress,O:Gr. Arrow,D:EarthII Catwoman 3.50
18 RT,DG,BL,F:Deadman,Phantom Stranger 2.50

DC UNIVERSE: TRINITY

1 TC,GeH,BKi,F:Darkstars,Green Lantern,L.E.G.I.O.N.,V:Triarch 3.50
2 BKi,SHa,F:Darkstars,Green Lantern, L.E.G.I.O.N.,V:Triarch 3.50

DEADMAN
May, 1985

1 CI,NA,rep 5.00
2 NA,rep. 5.00
3 NA,rep. 3.00
4 NA,rep. 3.00
5 NA,rep. 2.50
6 NA,rep. 2.50
7 NA,rep.November, 1985. 2.50

[Mini-Series]
March, 1986

1 JL,A:Batman 3.00
2 JL,V:Sensei,A:Batman 2.50
3 JL,D:Sensei 2.00
4 JL,V:Jonah, final issue 2.00

DEADMAN:EXORCISM
[Limited-Series]

1 KJo,A:Phantom Stranger 5.25
2 KJo,A:Phantom Stranger 5.25

DEADMAN: LOVE AFTER DEATH

1 KJo,Circus of Monsters 4.25
2 KJo,Circus of Monsters 4.25

DEATH:THE HIGH COST OF LIVING
Vertigo

1 B:NGa(s),CBa,MBu(i),Death becomes Human,A:Hettie 6.00
1a Platinum Ed. 85.00
2 CBa,MBu(i),V:Eremite,A:Hettie 5.00
3 E:NGa(s),CBa,MBu(i),V:Eremite, A:Hettie 4.50
3a Error Copy 6.00
HC 19.95
TPB w/Tori Amos Intro 12.95

DEADSHOT

1 LMc,From Suicide Squad 1.25
2 LMc,Search for Son 1.00
3 LMc,V:Pantha 1.00
4 LMc,final issue 1.00

DEATH GALLERY
Vertigo

1 DMc(c),NGa Death Sketch, Various Pinups 3.50

DEATHSTROKE: THE TERMINATOR

1 MZ(c),(from New Teen Titans) SE,I:2nd Ravager 5.50
1a Second Printing,Gold 3.00
2 MZ(c),SE,Quraci Agents 3.00
3 SE,V:Ravager 3.00
4 SE,D:2ndRavager(Jackel) 3.00
5 Winter Green Rescue Attempt 3.00
6 MZ(c),SE,B:City of Assassins, A:Batman 3.00
7 MZ(c),SE,A:Batman 2.50
8 MZ(c),SE,A:Batman 2.00
9 MZ(c),SE,E:City of Assassins, A:Batman;I:2nd Vigilante 2.00
10 MZ(c),ANi,GP,A:2nd Vigilante 2.00
11 MZ(c),ANi,GP,A:2nd Vigilante 2.00
12 MGo,Short Stories re:Slade 2.00
13 SE,V:Gr.Lant.,Flash,Aquaman 2.00
14 ANi,Total Chaos#1,A:New Titans, Team Titans,V:Nightwing 2.00
15 ANi,Total Chaos#4,A:New Titans, Team Titans,I:Sweet Lili 2.00
16 ANi,Total Chaos#7 2.00
17 SE,Titans Sell-Out #2 A:Brotherhood of Evil 2.00
18 SE,V:Cheshire,R:Speedy 2.00
19 SE,V:Broth.of Evil,A:Speedy 2.00
20 SE,MZ(c),V:Checkmate 2.00
21 SE,MZ(c),A:Checkmate 2.00
22 MZ(c),Quality of Mercy#1 2.00
23 MZ(c),Quality of Mercy#2 2.00
24 MZ(c),V:The Black Dome 2.00
25 MZ(c),V:The Black Dome 2.00
26 MZ(c),SE,in Kenya 2.00
27 MZ(c),SE,B:World Tour, in Germany 2.00
28 MZ(c),SE,in France 2.00
29 KM(c),SE,in Hong Kong 2.00
30 SE,A:Vigilante 2.00
31 SE,in Milwaukie 2.00
32 SE,in Africa 2.00
33 SE,I:Fleur de Lis 2.00
34 SE,E:World Tour 2.00
35 V:Mercenaries 2.00
36 V:British General 2.00
37 V:Assassin 2.00
38 A:Vigilante, 1.95
Ann.#1 Eclipso,A:Vigilante 3.75
Ann.#2 SE,I:Gunfire 3.50
TPB Full Circle rep#1-4, New Titans#70 12.95

DEMOLITION MAN

1 thru 4 Movie Adapt 1.75

Demon #7 © DC Comics, Inc.

DEMON
[1st Regular Series]

1 JK,I:Demon 30.00
2 JK 20.00
3 JK 15.00
4 JK 15.00
5 JK 15.00
6 JK 12.00
7 JK 12.00
8 JK 12.00

9 JK 12.00
10 JK 10.00
11 JK 10.00
12 JK 10.00
13 JK 10.00
14 thru 16 JK @10.00

[Limited Series]

1 MWg,B:Jason Blood's Case 5.00
2 MWg,Fight to Save Gotham 3.00
3 MWg,Fight to Save Gotham 2.50
4 MWg,final issue 2.50

[2nd Regular Series]

1 VS,A:Etrigan (32 pages) 4.00
2 VS,V:TheCrone 2.50
3 VS,A:Batman 2.25
4 VS,A:Batman 2.25
5 VS,ThePit 2.25
6 VS,In Hell 2.25
7 VS,Etrigan-King of Hell 2.25
8 VS,Klarion the Witch Boy 2.25
9 VS,Jason Leaves Gotham 2.25
10 VS,A:PhantomStranger 2.25
11 VS,A:Klarion,C:Lobo 3.00
12 VS,Etrigan Vs. Lobo 2.50
13 VS,Etrigan Vs. Lobo 2.50
14 VS,V:Odd Squad,A:Lobo 2.50
15 VS,Etrigan Vs.Lobo 2.50
16 VS,Etrigan & Jason Blood switch bodies 2.00
17 VS, War of the Gods x-over 2.00
18 VS,V:Wotan,A:Scape Goat 2.00
19 VS,O:Demon,Demon/Lobo pin-up 3.50
20 VS,V:Golden Knight 2.00
21 VS,Etrigan/Jason, A:Lobo,Glenda 2.00
22 MWg,V:Mojo & Hayden 2.25
23 VS,A:Robin 2.00
24 VS,A:Robin 2.00
25 VS,V:Gideon Ryme 2.00
26 VS,B:America Rules 2.00
27 VS,A:Superman 2.00
28 VS,A:Superman 2.00
29 VS,E:America Rules 2.00
30 R:Asteroth 2.00
31 VS(c),A:Lobo 2.00
32 VS(c),A:Lobo,W.Woman 2.00
33 VS(c),A:Lobo,V:Asteroth 2.00
34 A:Lobo 2.00
35 A:Lobo,V:Belial 2.00
36 A:Lobo,V:Belial 2.00
37 A:Lobo,Morax 2.00
38 A:Lobo,Morax 2.00
39 A:Lobo 2.00
40 New Direction,B:GEn(s) 5.00
41 V:Mad Bishop 2.50
42 V:Demons 2.25
43 A:Hitman 2.00
44 V:Gotho-Demon,A:Hitman 2.00
45 V:Gotho-Demon,A:Hitman 2.00
46 R:Haunted Tank 2.00
47 V:Zombie Nazis 2.00
48 A:Haunted Tank,V:Zombie Nazis 2.00
49 b:Demon's Son,A:Joe Gun 1.95
Ann.#1 Eclipso,V:Klarion 3.25
Ann.#2 I:Hitman 3.75

DETECTIVE COMICS

March, 1937

1 I:Slam Bradley 32,500.00
2 JoS 10,000.00
3 JoS 6,000.00
4 JoS 3,000.00
5 JoS 3,000.00
6 JoS 2,000.00
7 JoS 2,000.00
8 JoS,Mr. Chang(c) 2,200.00
9 JoS 2,000.00
10 2,000.00
11 1,700.00
12 1,700.00
13 1,700.00
14 1,700.00
15 1,700.00
16 1,700.00
17 I:Fu Manchu 1,700.00
18 Fu Manchu(c) 2,200.00
19 1,700.00
20 I:Crimson Avenger 2,500.00
21 1,400.00
22 1,750.00
23 1,100.00
24 1,100.00
25 1,100.00
26 1,200.00
27 BK,I:Batman 95,000.00
28 BK,V:Frenchy Blake 8,000.00
29 BK,,I:Doctor Death 14,000.00
30 BK,V:Dr. Death 3,500.00
31 BK,I:Monk 13,000.00
32 BK,V:Monk 3,000.00
33 O:Batman,V:Scarlet Horde 18,000.00
34 V:Due D'Orterre 3,000.00
35 V:Sheldon Lenox 4,500.00
36 I:Hugo Strange 3,600.00
37 V:Count Grutt, last Batman solo 3,000.00

Detective Comics #7
© DC Comics, Inc.

Detective Comics #11
© DC Comics, Inc.

38 I:Robin, the Boy Wonder 20,000.00
39 V:Green Dragon 2,500.00
40 I:Clayface (Basil Karlo) 3,000.00
41 V:Graves 1,500.00
42 V:Pierre Antal 1,200.00
43 V:Harliss Greer 1,200.00
44 Robin Dream Story 1,200.00
45 V:Joker 1,700.00
46 V:Hugo Strange 1,000.00
47 Meets Harvey Midas 1,000.00
48 Meets Henry Lewis 1,000.00
49 V:Clayface 1,000.00
50 V:Three Devils 1,000.00
51 V:Mindy Gang 800.00
52 V:Loo Chung 800.00
53 V:Toothy Hare gang 800.00
54 V:Hook Morgan 800.00
55 V:Dr. Death 800.00
56 V:Mad Mack 800.00
57 Meet Richard Sneed 800.00
58 I:Penguin 2,300.00
59 V:Penguin 1,100.00
60 V:Joker,I:Air Wave 1,000.00
61 The Three Racketeers 700.00
62 V:Joker 1,200.00
63 I:Mr. Baffle 800.00
64 I:Boy Commandos,V:Joker 2,200.00
65 Meet Tom Bolton 1,000.00
66 I:Two-Face 1,500.00
67 V:Penguin 1,000.00
68 V:Two-Face 750.00
69 V:Joker 900.00
70 Meet the Amazing Carlo 600.00
71 V:Joker 700.00
72 V:Larry the Judge 600.00
73 V:Scarecrow 600.00
74 I:Tweedledum & Tweedledee 600.00
75 V:Robber Baron 600.00
76 V:Joker 900.00
77 V:Dr. Matthew Thorne 600.00
78 V:Baron Von Luger 600.00
79 'Destiny's' Auction 600.00
80 V:Two-Face 700.00
81 I:Cavalier 550.00
82 V:Blackee Blondeen 550.00
83 V:Dr. Goodwin 600.00
84 V:Ivan Krafft 550.00
85 V:Joker 700.00
86 V:Gentleman Jim Jewell 500.00
87 V:Penguin 550.00
88 V:Big Hearted John 500.00
89 V:Cavalier 500.00
90 V:Capt. Ben 500.00
91 V:Joker 600.00
92 V:Braing Bulow 450.00
93 V:'Tiger' Ragland 450.00
94 V:Lefty Goran 450.00
95 V:The Blaze 450.00
96 F:Alfred 450.00
97 V:Nick Petri 450.00
98 Meets Casper Thurbridge 450.00
99 V:Penguin 600.00
100 V:Digger 610.00
101 V:Joe Bart 400.00
102 V:Joker 600.00
103 Meet Dean Gray 450.00
104 V:Fat Frank gang 450.00
105 V:Simon Gurlan 450.00
106 V:Todd Torrey 450.00
107 V:Bugs Scarpis 450.00
108 Meet Ed Gregory 450.00
109 V:Joker 600.00
110 V:Prof. Moriarty 400.00
111 'Coaltown, USA' 400.00
112 'Case Without A Crime' 400.00
113 V:Blackhand 400.00
114 V:Joker 600.00
115 V:Basil Grimes 400.00

116 A:Carter Nichols, Robin Hood 400.00
117 'Steeplejack's Slowdown' . 400.00
118 V:Joker 600.00
119 V:Wiley Derek 400.00
120 V:Penguin 475.00
121 F:Commissioner Gordon . . 400.00
122 V:Catwoman 400.00
123 V:Shiner 400.00
124 V:Joker 500.00
125 V:Thinker 400.00
126 V:Penguin 400.00
127 V:Dr. Agar 400.00
128 V:Joker 500.00
129 V:Diamond Dan mob 400.00
130 . . . . 400.00
131 V:'Trigger Joe' 325.00
132 V:Human Key 325.00
133 Meets Arthur Loom 325.00
134 V:Penguin 350.00
135 A:Baron Frankenstein, Carter Nichols 325.00
136 A:Carter Nichols 325.00
137 V:Joker 425.00
138 V:Joker,O:Robotman 600.00
139 V:Nick Bailey 325.00
140 I:Riddler 1,600.00
141 V:'Blackie' Nason 350.00
142 V:Riddler 500.00
143 V:Pied Piper 350.00
144 A:Kay Kyser (radio personality) 350.00
145 V:Yellow Mask mob 350.00
146 V:J.J. Jason 350.00
147 V:Tiger Shark 350.00
148 V:Prof. Zero 350.00
149 V:Joker 450.00
150 V:Dr. Paul Visio 375.00
151 I&O:Pow Wow Smith 375.00
152 V:Goblin 375.00
153 V:Slits Danton 375.00
154 V:Hatch Marlin 375.00
155 A:Vicki Vale 375.00
156 'The Batmobile of 1950' . . 375.00
157 V:Bart Gillis 350.00
158 V:Dr. Doom 350.00
159 V:T. Worthington Chubb . . 350.00
160 V:Globe-Trotter 350.00
161 V:Bill Waters 375.00
162 Batman on railroad 375.00
163 V:Slippery Jim Elgin 375.00
164 Bat-signal story 375.00
165 'The Strange Costumes of Batman' 375.00
166 Meets John Gillen 375.00
167 A:Carter Nichols, Cleopatra 375.00
168 O:Joker 3,000.00
169 V:'Squint' Tolmar 375.00
170 Batman teams with Navy and Coast Guard 375.00
171 V:Penguin 500.00
172 V:Paul Gregorian 375.00
173 V:Killer Moth 375.00
174 V:Dagger 375.00
175 V:Kangaroo Kiley 375.00
176 V:Mr. Velvet 375.00
177 Bat-Cave story 275.00
178 V:Baron Swane 275.00
179 'Mayor Bruce Wayne' 275.00
180 V:Joker 300.00
181 V:Human Magnet 300.00
182 V:Maestro Dorn 300.00
183 V:John Cook 300.00
184 I:Firefly(Garfield Lynns) . . . 300.00
185 'Secret's of Batman's Utility Belt' 300.00
186 'The Flying Bat-Cave' 300.00
187 V:Two-Face 300.00
188 V:William Milden 300.00
189 V:Styx 300.00
190 Meets Dr. Sampson, O:Batman 400.00
191 V:Executioner 275.00
192 V: Nails Riley 275.00
193 V:Joker 275.00
194 V:Sammy Sabre 275.00
195 Meets Hugo Marmon 275.00
196 V:Frank Lumardi 275.00
197 V:Wrecker 275.00
198 Batman in Scotland 275.00
199 V:Jack Baker 275.00
200 V:Brand Keldon 400.00
201 Meet Human Target 275.00
202 V:Jolly Roger 275.00
203 V:Catwoman 300.00
204 V:Odo Neral 275.00
205 O:Bat-Cave 375.00
206 V:Trapper 250.00
207 Meets Merko the Great . . 250.00
208 V:Groff 250.00
209 V:Inventor 250.00
210 V:'Brain' Hobson 250.00
211 V:Catwoman 250.00
212 Meets Jonathan Bard 250.00
213 V:Mirror-Man 350.00
214 'The Batman Encyclopedia' 225.00
215 I:Ranger, Legionairy, Gaucho & Musketeer,A:Knight & Squire (See World's Finest 89) . . . 225.00
216 A:Brane Taylor 225.00
217 Meets Barney Barrows . . . 225.00
218 V:Dr. Richard Marston . . . 225.00
219 V:Marty Mantee 225.00
220 A:Roger Bacon, historical scientist/philosopher 225.00
221 V:Paul King 225.00
222 V:'Big Jim' Jarrell 225.00
223 V:'Blast' Varner 225.00
224 . . . . 225.00
225 I&O:Martian Manhunter (J'onn J'onzz) 3,600.00
226 O:Robin's costume, A:J'onn J'onzz 800.00
227 A:Roy Raymond, J'onn J'onzz 300.00
228 A:Roy Raymond, J'onnJ'onz 300.00
229 A:Roy Raymond, J'onnJ'onz 300.00
230 A:Martian Manhunter,I:Mad Hatter 340.00
231 A:Batman,Jr.,Roy Raymond J'onn J'onzz 200.00
232 A:J'onn J'onzz 175.00
233 I&O:Batwoman 750.00
234 V:Jay Caird 175.00
235 O:Batman's Costume 340.00
236 V:Wallace Walby 210.00
237 F:Robin 175.00
238 V:Checkmate(villain) 175.00
239 Batman robot story 175.00
240 V:Burt Weaver 175.00
241 The Rainbow Batman 175.00
242 Batcave story 140.00
243 V:Jay Vanney 140.00
244 O:Batarang 140.00
245 F:Comm.Gordon 140.00
246 . . . . 140.00
247 I:Professor Milo 140.00
248 . . . . 140.00
249 V:Collector 140.00
250 V:John Stannor 140.00
251 V:Brand Ballard 140.00
252 Batman in a movie 140.00
253 I:Terrible Trio 140.00
254 A:Bathound 140.00
255 V:Fingers Nolan 140.00
256 Batman outer-space story . 140.00
257 Batman sci-fi story 150.00
258 Batman robot story 140.00
259 I:Calendar Man 140.00
260 Batman outer space story . 140.00
261 I:Dr. Double X 110.00
262 V:Jackal-Head 110.00
263 V:The Professor 110.00
264 . . . . 110.00
265 O:Batman retold 175.00
266 V:Astro 100.00
267 I&O:Bat-Mite 125.00
268 V:"Big Joe" Foster 110.00

Detective Comics #400
© DC Comics, Inc.

269 V:Director 110.00
270 Batman sci-fi story 110.00
271 V:Crimson Knight,O:Martian Manhunter(retold) 90.00
272 V:Crystal Creature 75.00
273 A:Dragon Society 90.00
274 V:Nails Lewin 75.00
275 A:Zebra-Man 75.00
276 A:Batmite 75.00
277 Batman Monster story 75.00
278 A:Professor Simms 75.00
279 Batman robot story 75.00
280 A:Atomic Man 75.00
281 Batman robot story 65.00
282 Batman sci-fi story 65.00
283 V:Phantom of Gotham City . 65.00
284 V:Hal Durgan 65.00
285 V:Harbin 65.00
286 A:Batwoman 65.00
287 A:Bathound 65.00
288 V:Multicreature 65.00
289 A:Bat-Mite 65.00
290 Batman's robot story 65.00
291 Batman sci-fi story 65.00
292 Last Roy Raymond 65.00
293 A:Aquaman,J'onnJ'onzz . . . 65.00
294 V:Elemental Men, A:Aquaman 65.00
295 A:Aquaman 65.00
296 A:Aquaman 65.00
297 A:Aquaman 65.00
298 I:Clayface(Matt Hagen) . . . 100.00
299 Batman sci-fi stories 60.00
300 I:Mr.Polka-dot,E:Aquaman . . 65.00
301 A:J'onnJ'onzz 45.00
302 A:J'onnJ'onnz 40.00
303 A:J'onnJ'onnz 40.00
304 A:Clayface,J'onnJ'onz 40.00
305 Batman sci-fi story 40.00
306 A:J'onnJ'onnz 40.00
307 A:J'onnJ'onnz 40.00
308 A:J'onnJ'onnz 40.00
309 A:J'onnJ'onnz 40.00
310 A:Bat-Mite,J'onnJ'onnz 40.00
311 I:Cat-Man,Zook 45.00
312 A:Clayface,J'onnJ'onnz 35.00
313 A:J'onnJ'onnz 35.00
314 A:J'onnJ'onnz 35.00
315 I:Jungle Man 38.00
316 A:Dr.DoubleX,J'onnJ'onz . . . 35.00
317 A:J'onnJ'onnz 35.00

318 A:Cat-Man,J'onnJ'onnz 35.00
319 A:J'onnJ'onnz 35.00
320 A:Vicki Vale 35.00
321 I:Terrible Trio 38.00
322 A:J'onnJ'onnz 35.00
323 I:Zodiac Master, A:J'onn J'onnz 35.00

Detective Comics #455
© DC Comics, Inc.

324 A:Mad Hatter,J'onnJ'onnz .. 35.00
325 A:Cat-Man,J'onnJ'onnz 35.00
326 Batman sci-fi story 35.00
327 CI,25th ann,symbol change . 52.00
328 D:Alfred,I:WayneFoundation 55.00
329 A:Elongated Man 26.00
330 "Fallen Idol of Gotham" 26.00
331 A:Elongated Man 26.00
332 A:Joker 27.00
333 A:Gorla 22.00
334 .... 22.00
335 .... 22.00
336 .... 22.00
337 "Deep Freeze Menace 22.00
338 .... 22.00
339 .... 22.00
340 .... 22.00
341 A:Joker 27.00
342 .... 22.00
343 BK,CI,Elongated Man 16.00
344 .... 16.00
345 CI,I:Blockbuster 16.00
346 .... 16.00
347 CI,Elongated Man 16.00
348 Elongated Man 16.00
349 BK(c),CI,Blockbuster 16.00
350 Elongated Man 16.00
351 CI,A:Elongated Man, I:Cluemaster 16.00
352 BK,Elongated Man 16.00
353 .... 16.00
354 BK,Elongated Man,I:Dr. Tzin-Tzin 16.00
355 CI,Elongated Man 16.00
356 BK,Outsider,Alfred 16.00
357 .... 16.00
358 BK,Elongated Man 16.00
359 I:new Batgirl 25.00
360 .... 16.00
361 CI 16.00
362 CI,Elongated Man 16.00
363 CI,Elongated Man 16.00
364 BK,Elongated Man 16.00
365 A:Joker 30.00
366 Elongated Man 16.00
367 Elongated Man 16.00
368 BK,Elongated Man 16.00
369 CA,Elongated Man, Catwoman 35.00
370 BK,Elongated Man 16.00
371 BK,Elongated Man 12.00
372 BK,Elongated Man 12.00
373 BK,Elongated Man 12.00
374 BK,Elongated Man 12.00
375 CI,Elongated Man 12.00
376 .... 12.00
377 MA,Elongated Man, V:Riddler 12.00
378 Elongated Man 12.00
379 CI,Elongated Man 12.00
380 Elongated Man 12.00
381 GaF,Marital Bliss Miss 12.00
382 FR(s),BbB,JoG,GaF(s),SGe 12.00
383 FR(s),BbB,JoG,GaF(s),SGe 12.00
384 FR(s),BbB,JoG,GaF(s),SGe, BU:Batgirl 12.00
385 E:FR(s),BbB,JoG,NA(c),GK,MA, MkF,BU:Batgirl 12.00
386 BbK,MkF,BbB,JoG, BU:Batgirl 12.00
387 RA,rep.Detective #27 ..... 35.00
388 JBr(s),BbB,JoG, GK,MA,FR(s) 15.00
389 FR(s),BbB,JoG,GK,MA, ... 11.00
390 FR(s),BbB,JoG,GK,MA, A:Masquerader 11.00
391 FR(s),NA(c),BbB, JoG,GK,MA, ... 11.00
392 FR(s),BbB,JoG,I:Jason Bard 11.00
393 FR(s),BbB,JoG,GK,MA 11.00
394 FR(s),BbB,JoG,GK,MA 11.00
395 FR(s),NA,DG,GK,MA 15.00
396 FR(s),BbB,JoG,GK,MA 11.00
397 DON(s),NA,DG,GK,MA 15.00
398 FR(s),BbB,JoG,GK,ViC 11.00
399 NA(c),DON(s),BbB,JoG, GK,ViC,Robin 12.00

Detective Comics #532
© DC Comics, Inc.

400 FR(s),NA,DG,GK,I:Man-Bat . 30.00
401 NA(c),FR(s),JoG, BbB,JoG,GK,ViC 10.00
402 FR(s),NA,DG,V:Man-Bat ... 15.00
403 FR(s),BbB,JoG,NA(c),GK,ViC, BU:Robin 11.00
404 NA,GC,GK,A:Enemy Ace .. 15.00
405 IN,GK,I:League of Assassins . 9.00
406 DON(s),BbB,FrG 9.00
407 FR(s),NA,DG,V:Man-bat ... 15.00
408 MWn(s),LWn(s),NA,DG, V:DrTzin Tzin 15.00
409 B:FR(s),BbB,FrG,DH,DG 9.00
410 DON(s),FR(s),NA,DG,DH, .. 15.00
411 NA(c),DON(s),BbB,DG,DH . 10.00
412 NA(c),BbB,DG,DH 10.00
413 NA(c),BbB,DG,DH 10.00
414 DON(s),IN,DG,DH 9.00
415 BbB,DG,DH 9.00
416 DH 9.00
417 BbB,DG,DH,BU:Batgirl 9.00
418 DON(s),DH,IN,DG,A:Creeper 9.00
419 DON(s),DH 9.00
420 DH 9.00
421 DON(s),BbB,DG,DH,A:Batgirl 8.00
422 BbB,DG,DH,Batgirl 8.00
423 BbB,DG,DH, ... 8.00
424 BbB,DG,DH,Batgirl 8.00
425 BWr(c),DON(s),IN,DG,DH, .. 9.00
426 LWn(s),DG,A:Elongated Man 8.00
427 IN,DG,DH,BU:Batgirl 8.00
428 BbB,DG,ENB(s),DD,JoG, BU:Hawkman 8.00
429 DG,JoG,V:Man-Bat 8.00
430 BbB,NC,ENS(s),DG, A:Elongated Man 8.00
431 DON(s),IN,MA, ... 8.00
432 MA,A:Atom 8.00
433 DD,DG,MA 8.00
434 IN,DG,ENB(s),RB,DG 8.00
435 E:FR(s),DG,IN 8.00
436 MA,(i),DG,A:Elongated Man . 8.00
437 JA,WS,I:Manhunter 17.00
438 JA,WS,Manhunter 14.00
439 DG,WS,O:Manhunter,Kid Eternity rep. 12.50
440 JAp,WS 12.50
441 HC,WS 12.50
442 ATh,WS 12.50
443 WS,D:Manhunter 15.00
444 JAp,B:Bat-Murderer, A:Ra's Al Ghul 8.00
445 JAp,MGr,A:Talia 8.00
446 JAp,last giant 8.00
447 DG(i),A:Creeper 7.50
448 DG(i),E:Bat-Murderer, A:Creeper,Ra's Al Ghul 7.50
449 'Midnight Rustler in Gotham' . 8.00
450 WS 9.00
451 thru 454 .... @7.50
455 MGr,A:Hawkman,V:Vampire . 7.00
456 V:Ulysses Vulcan 7.00
457 O:Batman rtd 10.00
458 A:Man Bat 7.00
459 A:Man Bat 7.00
460 .... 7.00
461 V:Capt.Stingaree 7.00
462 V:Capt.Stingaree,A:Flash ... 7.00
463 MGr,Atom,I:Calc.,Bl.Spider .. 7.00
464 MGr,TA,BlackCanary 7.00
465 TA,Elongated Man 7.00
466 MR,TA,V:Signalman 12.00
467 MR,TA 12.00
468 MR,TA,A:JLA 12.00
469 WS,I:Dr.Phosphorus 7.00
470 WS,AM,V:Dr.Phosphorus ... 7.00
471 MR,TA,A:Hugo Strange ... 12.00
472 MR,TA,A:Hugo Strange ... 12.00
473 MR,TA,R:Deadshot 12.00
474 MR,TA,A:Penguin, N:Deadshot 13.50
475 MR,TA,A:Joker 20.00
476 MR,TA,A:Joker 20.00
477 MR,DG,rep.NA 12.00
478 MR,DG,I:3rd Clayface 12.00
479 MR,DG,A:3rd Clayface 12.00
480 DN,MA 8.00
481 JSt,CR,DN,DA,MR, A:ManBat 10.00
482 HC,MGo,DG,A:Demon 7.00
483 DN,DA,SD,A:Demon, 40 Anniv. 9.00
484 DN,DA,Demon,O:1st Robin .. 6.00

485 DN,DA,D:Batwoman,A:Demon
A:Ras al Ghul 5.00
486 DN,DA,DG,I:Odd Man,
V:Scarecrow 5.00
487 DN,DA,A:Ras Al Ghul 5.00
488 DN,V:Spook,Catwoman 6.50
489 IN,DH,DN,DA,Ras Al Ghul . . 5.00
490 DN,DA,PB,FMc,A:Black
Lightning;A:Ras Al Ghul 5.00
491 DN,DA,PB,FMc,A:Black
Lightning;V:Maxie Zeus 5.00
492 DN,DA,A:Penguin 6.50
493 DN,DA,A:Riddler 5.00
494 DN,DA,V:Crime Doctor 5.00
495 DN,DA,V:Crime Doctor 5.00
496 DN,DA,A:Clayface I 5.00
497 DN,DA 5.00
498 DN,DA,V:Blockbuster 5.00
499 DN,DA,V:Blockbuster 5.00
500 DG,CI,WS,TY,JKu,Dead-
man,Hawkman,Robin 10.00
501 DN,DA 5.00
502 DN,DA 5.00
503 DN,DA,Batgirl,Robin,
V:Scarecrow 5.00
504 DN,DA,Joker 7.00
505 DN,DA 5.00
506 DN,DA 5.00
507 DN,DA 5.00
508 DN,DA,V:Catwoman 7.00
509 DN,DA,V:Catman,Catwoman . 7.00
510 DN,DA,V:Madhatter 5.00
511 DN,DA,I:Mirage 5.00
512 GC,45th Anniv. 5.00
513 V:Two-Face 5.00
514 . . . . 5.00
515 . . . . 5.00
516 . . . . 5.00
517 . . . . 5.00
518 V:Deadshot 5.00
519 . . . . 5.00
520 A:Hugo Strange,Catwoman . . 6.00
521 IN,TVE,A:Catwoman,B:BU:Green
Arrow 6.50
522 D:Snowman 5.00
523 V:Solomon Grundy 5.00
524 2nd A:J.Todd 6.00
525 J.Todd 5.00
526 DN,AA,A:Joker,Catwoman
500th A:Batman 15.00
527 V:Man Bat 4.00
528 Green Arrow,Ozone 4.00
529 I:Night Slayer,Nocturna 4.00
530 V:Nocturna 4.00
531 GC,AA,Chimera,J.Todd (see
Batman #364) 4.00
532 GC,Joker 7.00
533 . . . . 4.00
534 GC,A:Gr.Arrow,V:PoisonIvy . . 4.00
535 GC,A:Gr.Arrow,V:Crazy Quitt
2nd A:New Robin 6.00
536 GC,A:Gr.Arrow,V:Deadshot . . 4.00
537 GC,A:Gr.Arrow, ... 4.00
538 GC,A:Gr.Arrow,V:Catman . . . 4.00
539 GC,A:Gr.Arrow, ... 4.00
540 GC,A:Gr.Arrow,V:Scarecrow . 4.00
541 GC,A:Gr.Arrow,V:Penguin . . . 5.50
542 GC,A:Gr.Arrow 4.00
543 GC,A:Gr.Arrow,V:Nightslayer . 4.00
544 GC,A:Gr.Arrow,V:Nightslayer
Nocturna 4.00
545 . . . . 4.00
546 . . . . 4.00
547 . . . . 4.00
548 PB 4.00
549 PB,KJ,AMo(s),Gr.Arrow 4.50
550 KJ,AMo(s),Gr.Arrow 4.50
551 PB,V:Calendar Man 4.00
552 V:Black Mask 4.00
553 V:Black Mask 4.00
554 KJ,N:Black Canary 4.00
555 GC,DD,GreenArrow 4.00
556 GC,Gr.Arrow,V:Nightslayer . . 4.00
557 V:Nightslayer 4.00
558 GC,Green Arrow 4.00
559 GC,Green Arrow 4.00
560 GC,A:Green Arrow 4.00

Detective Comics #639
© DC Comics, Inc.

561 . . . . 4.00
562 GC,V:Film Freak 4.00
563 V:Two Face 4.00
564 V:Two Face 4.00
565 GC,A:Catwoman 5.50
566 GC,Joker 7.00
567 GC,HarlanEllison 5.00
568 KJ,Legends tie-in,A:Penguin . 5.50
569 AD,V:Joker 9.00
570 AD,EvilCatwoman,A:Joker . . . 9.00
571 AD,V:Scarecrow 5.00
572 AD,CI,A:Elongated Man,Sherlock
Holmes,SlamBradley,50thAnn . 8.00
573 AD,V:Mad Hatter 5.00
574 AD,End old J.Todd/Robin sty 5.00
575 AD,Year 2,Pt.1,I:Reaper . . . 16.00
576 TM,AA,Yr.2,Pt.2,R:JoeChill . 13.00
577 TM,AA,Yr.2,Pt.3,V:Reaper . . 13.00
578 TM,AA,Yr.2,Pt.4,D:JoeChill . 13.00
579 I:NewCrimeDoctor 3.00
580 V:Two Face 3.00
581 V:Two Face 3.00
582 Millenium X-over 3.00
583 I:Ventriloquist 3.00
584 V:Ventriloquist 3.00
585 I:Rat Catcher 3.00
586 V:Rat Catcher 3.00
587 NB,V:Corrosive Man 3.00
588 NB,V:Corrosive Man 3.00
589 Bonus Book #5 . . . . 4.00
590 NB,V:Hassan 3.00
591 NB,V:Rollo 3.00
592 V:Psychic Vampire 3.00
593 NB,V:Stirh 3.00
594 NB,A:Mr.Potato 3.00
595 IN,bonus book #11 . . . . 3.00
596 V:Sladek 3.00
597 V:Sladek 3.00
598 DCw,BSz,Blind Justice #1 . . . 8.00
599 DCw,BSz,Blind Justice #2 . . . 4.00
600 DCw,BSz,Blind Justice #3,
50th Anniv.(double size) 5.00
601 NB,I:Tulpa 3.00
602 NB,A:Jason Blood 2.50
603 NB,A:Demon 2.50
604 NB,MudPack #1,V:Clayface,
poster insert 2.50
605 NB,MudPack #2,V:Clayface . 2.50
606 NB,MudPack #3,V:Clayface . 2.50
607 NB,MudPack #4,V:Clayface,
poster insert 2.50
608 NB,I:Anarky 2.00
609 NB,V:Anarky 2.00
610 NB,V:Penguin 3.00
611 NB,V:Catwoman,Catman . . . 3.00
612 NB,A:Vicki Vale 1.75
613 Search for Poisoner 1.75
614 V:Street Demons 1.75
615 NB,Return Penguin #2 (see
Batman #448-449) 2.75
616 NB, ... 1.75
617 A:Joker 1.75
618 NB,DG,A:Tim Drake 1.75
619 NB,V:Moneyspider 1.75
620 NB,V:Obeah,Man 1.75
621 NB,SM,Obeah,Man 1.75
622 Demon Within Pt #1 . . . . 2.00
623 Demon Within Pt #2 . . . . 2.00

Detective Comics #644
© DC Comics, Inc.

624 Demon Within Pt #3 . . . . 2.00
625 JAp,I:Abattior 1.75
626 JAp,A:Electrocutioner 1.75
627 600th issue w/Batman,rep.
Detective #27 . . . . 4.00
628 JAp,A:Abattoir 1.75
629 JAp,'The Hungry Grass' 1.75
630 JAp,I:Stiletto 1.75
631 JAp,V:Neo-Nazi Gangs 1.75
632 JAp,V:Creature 1.75
633 TMd,Fake Batman? 1.75
634 'The Third Man' 1.75
635 Video Game Pt.#1 . . . . 1.75
636 Video Game Pt.#2 . . . . 1.75
637 Video Game Pt.#3 . . . . 1.75
638 JAp,Walking Time Bomb 1.75
639 JAp,The Idiot Root Pt.2 . . . . . 1.75
640 JAp,The Idiot Root Pt.4 . . . . . 1.75
641 JAp,Destroyer Pt.3
(see LOTDK#27) 2.00
642 JAp,Faces Pt.2 . . . . 1.75
643 JAp,'Librarian of Souls' 1.75
644 TL,Electric City Pt.1
A:Electrocutioner 1.75
645 TL,Electric City Pt.2 . . . . 1.75
646 TL,Electric City Pt.3 . . . . 1.75
647 TL,V:Cluemaster 1.75
648 MWg(c),TL,V:Cluemaster . . . 1.75
649 MWg(c),TL,V:Cluemaster . . . 1.75
650 TL,A:Harold,Ace 1.75
651 TL,'A Bullet for Bullock' 1.75
652 GN,R:Huntress 1.75

653 GN,A:Huntress 1.75
654 MN,The General Pt.1 . . . . . . 1.75
655 MN,The General Pt.2 . . . . . . 1.75
656 MN,The General Pt.3,C:Bane 5.00
657 MN,A:Azrael,I:Cypher 10.00
658 MN,A:Azrael 8.00
659 MN,Knightfall#2, V:Ventriloquist,A:Bane 7.50
660 Knightfall#4,Bane Vs. Killer Croc 4.50
661 GN,Knightfall#6,V:Firefly, Joker,A:Bane 3.50
662 GN,Knightfall#8,V:Firefly, Joker,A:Huntress,Bane 3.00
663 GN,Knightfall#10,V:Trogg, Zombie,Bird,A:Bane 3.00
664 GN,Knightfall#12,A:Azrael . . . 3.00
665 GN,Knightfall#16,A:Azrael . . . 3.00
666 GN,SHa,A:Azrael,Trogg, Zombie,Bird 2.00
667 GN,SHa,Knightquest:Crusade, V:Trigger Twins, ... 1.75
668 GN,SHa,Knightquest:Crusade, Robin locked out of Batcave . . 1.75
669 GN,SHa,Knightquest:Crusade, V:Trigger Twins 1.75
670 GN,SHa,Knightquest:Crusade, F:Rene Montoya 1.75
671 GN,SHa,V:Joker 1.75
672 KJ(c),GN,SHa,Knightquest: Crusade,V:Joker 1.75
673 KJ(c),GN,SHa,Knightquest: Crusade,V:Joker 1.75
674 KJ(c),GN,SHa,Knightquest: Crusade 1.75
675 Foil(c),KJ(c),GN,SHa,Knightquest: Crusade,V:Gunhawk 3.25
675a Newsstand Ed. 1.75
676 KJ(c),GN,SHa,KnightsEnd#3, A:Nightwing 2.50
Ann.#1 KJ,TD,A:Question,Talia, V:Penguin 6.00
Ann.#2 VS,A:Harvey Harris 6.00
Ann.#3 DJu,DG,Batman in Japan . 2.50
Ann.#4 Armageddon Pt.10 . . . . . . 3.00
Ann.#5 SK(c),TMd,Eclipso,V:The Ventriloquist,Joker 3.00
Ann.#6 JBa,I:Geist 2.75
Ann.#7 Elseworlds Story 3.25

DOC SAVAGE
November, 1985

1 AKu/NKu,D:Orig. Doc Savage . 3.00
2 AKu/NKu,V:Nazi's 2.50
3 AKu/NKu,V:Nazi's 2.50
4 AKu/NKu,V:Heinz 2.50

[2nd Series]

1 'Five in the Sky'(painted cov.) . 3.00
2 Chip Lost in Himalayas 2.25
3 Doc declares war on USSR 2.25
4 DocSavage/Russian team-up . . 2.25
5 V:The Erisians 2.25
6 U.S.,USSR,China Alliance vs. Erisians 2.25
7 Mind Molder Pt.1, I:Pat Savage 2.25
8 . . . . 2.25
9 In Hidalgo 2.25
10 V:Forces of the Golden God . . 2.25
11 Sunlight Rising Pt.1 . . . . 2.25
12 Sunlight Rising Pt.2 . . . . 2.25
13 Sunlight Rising Pt.3 . . . . 2.25
14 Sunlight Rising Pt.4 . . . . 2.25
15 SeaBaron #1 . . . . 2.25
16 EB,Shadow & Doc Savage . . . 2.25
17 EB,Shadow & Doc Savage . . . 2.25
18 EB,Shadow/DocSavage conc. . 2.25
19 All new 1930's story 2.25
20 V:Airlord & his Black Zepplin . . 2.25
21 Airlord (30's story conc.) 2.25
22 Doc Savages Past Pt.1 . . . . . . 2.25
23 Doc Savages Past Pt.2 . . . . . . 2.25
24 Doc Savages Past Pt.3 (final) . 2.25
Ann.#1 1956 Olympic Games . . 4.50

DOCTOR FATE
July, 1987

1 KG,V:Lords of Chaos 2.75
2 KG,New Dr. Fate 2.25
3 KG,A:JLI 2.25
4 KG,V:Lords of Chaos Champion 2.25

[2nd Series]

1 New Dr.Fate,V:Demons 3.00
2 A:Andrew Bennett(I,Vampire) . . 2.50
3 A:Andrew Bennett(I,Vampire) . . 2.00
4 V:I,Vampire 2.00
5 Dr.Fate & I,Vampire in Europe . 2.00
6 A:Petey 1.75
7 Petey returns home dimension . 1.75
8 Linda become Dr.Fate again . . 1.75
9 Eric's Mother's Ghost, A:Deadman 1.75
10 Death of Innocence Pt.1 . . . . . 1.75
11 Return of Darkseid, Death of Innocence Pt.2 . . . . 1.75
12 Two Dr.Fates Vs.Darkseid, Death of Innocence Pt.3 . . . . . 1.75
13 Linda in the Astral Realm, Death of Innocence Pt.4 . . . . . 1.75
14 Kent & Petey vs. Wotan 1.75
15 V:Wotan,A:JLI 2.00
16 Flashback-novice Dr.Fate 1.50
17 Eric's Journey thru afterlife . . . 1.50
18 Search for Eric 1.50
19 A:Dr.Benjamine Stoner, Lords of Chaos, Phantom Stranger, Search for Eric continued 1.50
20 V:Lords of Chaos,Dr.Stoner, A:Phantom Stranger 1.50
21 V:Chaos,A:PhantomStranger . . 1.50
22 A:Chaos and Order 1.50
23 Spirits of Kent & Inza Nelson . 1.50
24 L:Dr.Fate Characters 1.50
25 I:New Dr. Fate 1.50
26 Dr.Fate vs. Orig.Dr.Fate 1.50
27 New York Crime 1.50
28 'Diabolism' 1.50
29 Kent Nelson 1.50
30 'Resurrection' 1.50
31 'Resurrection' contd. 1.50
32 War of the Gods x-over 1.75
33 War of the Gods x-over 1.75
34 A:T'Gilian 1.75
35 Kent Nelson in N.Y. 1.75
36 Search For Inza,A:Shat-Ru . . . 1.75
37 Fate Helmet Powers revealed . 1.75
38 'The Spirit Motor,'Flashback . . 1.75
39 U.S.Senate Hearing 1.75
40 A:Wonder Woman 1.75
41 O:Chaos and Order,last issue . 1.75
Ann.#1 TS,R:Eric's dead mother . 2.95

DOOM FORCE

Spec.#1 MMi(c),RCa,WS,PCu,KSy, I:Doom Force 2.75

DOOM PATROL
[1st series]
(see MY GREATEST ADVENTURE)

DOOM PATROL
[2nd Regular Series]
October, 1987

1 SLi,R:Doom Patrol,plus Who's Who background of team, I:Kalki . . . 3.00
2 SLi,V:Kalki 1.50
3 SLi,I:Lodestone 1.50
4 SLi,I:Karma 1.50
5 SLi,R:Chief 1.50
6 B:PuK(s),EL,GyM(i), I:Scott Fischer 2.00
7 EL,GyM(i),V:Shrapnel 1.75
8 EL,GyM(i),V:Shrapnel 1.75
9 E:PuK(s),EL,GyM(i),V:Garguax, & Bonus Book 1.75
10 EL,A:Superman 2.00
11 EL,R:Garguax 1.75
12 EL,A:Garguax 1.75

Doom Patrol #1 © DC Comics, Inc.

13 EL,A:Power Girl 1.75
14 EL,A:Power Girl 1.75
15 EL,Animal-Veg-.Mineral Man . . 1.75
16 V:GenImmotus,Animal-Veg.- Mineral Man 1.50
17 D:Celsius,A:Aquaman & Sea Devils, Invasion tie-in 4.00
18 Invasion 1.50
19 B:GMo(s),New Direction, I:Crazy Jane 15.00
20 I:Rebis(new Negative-Being), A:CrazyJane,Scissormen . . . 10.00
21 V:Scissormen 7.00
22 City of Bone,V:Scissormen . . . 7.00
23 A:RedJack,Lodestone kidnap . 7.00
24 V:Red Jack 7.00
25 Secrets of New Doom Patrol . . 7.00
26 I:Brotherhood of Dada 5.00
27 V:Brotherhood of Dada 5.00
28 Trapped in nightmare,V:Dada . 5.00
29 Trapped in painting, A:Superman 4.00
30 SBs(c),V:Brotherhood of Dada 4.00
31 SBs(c),A:The Pale Police 4.00
32 SBs(c),V:Cult of Unwritten Book 4.00
33 SBs(c),V:Cult,A:Anti-God the DeCreator 3.00
34 SBs(c),Robotman vs. his brain, R:The Brain & Mr.Mallah 3.00
35 SBs(c),A:Men from N.O.W.H.E.R.E. 3.00
36 SBs(c),V:Men from N.O.W.H.E.R.E. 3.25
37 SBs(c),Rhea Jones Story 2.50
38 SBs(c),V:Aliens 2.50
39 SBs(c),V:Aliens 2.50
40 SBs(c),Aliens 2.50
41 SBS(c),Aliens 2.50
42 O:Flex Mentallo 2.50
43 SBs(c),V:N.O.W.H.E.R.E. 2.50
44 SBs(c),V:N.O.W.H.E.R.E. 2.50
45 . . . . 2.50
46 SBs(c),RCa,MkK,A:Crazy Jane, Dr.Silence 2.50
47 Scarlet Harlot (Crazy Jane) . . . 2.50
48 V:Mr.Evans 2.50
49 TTg(c),RCa,MGb,I:Mr.Nobody . 2.50
50 SBs(c),V:Brotherhood of Dada & bonus artists portfolio 3.00
51 SBs(c),Mr.Nobody Runs for President 2.50
52 SBs(c),Mr.Nobody saga conc . 2.50

53 SBs(c),Parody Issue,A:Phantom Stranger,Hellblazer,Mr.E 2.50
54 Rebis'Transformation 2.50
55 SBs(c),V:Crazy Jane, Candle Maker 2.50
56 SBs(c),RCa,V:Candle Maker . . 2.50
57 SBs(c),RCa,V:Candle Maker, O:Team,Double-sized 5.50
58 SBs(c),V:Candle Maker 2.25
59 TTg(c),RCa,SnW(i),A:Candlemaker D:Larry Trainor 2.25
60 JHw(c),RCa,SnW(i), V:Candlemaker,A:Magnus 2.25
61 TTg(c),RCa,SnW(i),A:Magnus D:Candlemaker 2.25
62 DFg(c),RCa,SnW(i), V:Nanomachines 2.25
63 E:GMo(s),RCa,R:Crazy Jane, V:Keysmiths,BU:Sliding from the Wreckage 2.25

Vertigo

64 BB(c),B:RaP(s),RCa,SnW(i), B:Sliding from the Wreckage, R:Niles Caulder 2.25
65 TTg(c),RCa,SnW(i),Nannos . . . 2.25
66 RCa,E:Sliding from the Wreckage 2.25
67 TTg(c),LiM,GHi(i),New HQ,I:Charlie, George,Marion,V:Wild Girl 2.25
68 TTg(c),LiM,GHi(i),I:Indentity Addict 2.25
69 TTg(c),LiM,GHi(i),V:Identity Addict 2.25
70 TTg(c),SEa,TS(i),I:Coagula, V:Codpiece 2.25
71 TTg(c),LiM,TS(i),Fox & Crow . . 2.25
72 TTg(c),LiM,TS(i),Fox vs Crow . 2.25
73 LiM,GPi(i),Head's Nightmare . . 2.25
74 LiM,TS(i),Bootleg Steele 2.25
75 BB(c),TMK,Teiresias Wars#1, Double size 2.25
76 Teiresias Wars#2 . . . . 2.25
77 BB(c),TMK,N:Cliff, ... 2.25
78 BB(c),V:Tower of Babel 2.25
79 BB(c),E:Teiresias Wars 2.25
80 V:Yapping Dogs 1.95
Ann.#1 A:Lex Luthor 2.00
Ann.#2 RaP(s),MkW,Children's Crusade,F:Dorothy,A:Maxine . . 4.25
Doom Patrol/Suicide Squad #1 EL, D:Mr.104,Thinker,Psi,Weasel . 2.50
TPB Crawling From the Wreckage, SBs(c),rep.#19-25, ... 19.95

DOORWAY TO NIGHTMARE

January-February, 1978

1 I:Madame Xanadu 1.00
2 . . . . 1.00
3 . . . . 1.00
4 JCr 1.00
5 September-October, 1978 . . . 1.00

DOUBLE ACTION COMICS

January, 1940

2 Pre-Hero DC 7,000.00

DRAGONLANCE

1 Krynn's Companion's advent. . 11.00
2 Vandar&Riva vs.Riba's brother 8.00
3 V:Takhesis,Queen of Darkness 6.00
4 V:Lord Soth & Kitiara 5.00
5 V:Queen of Darkness 5.00
6 Gnatch vs. Kalthanan 5.00
7 Raistlin's Evil contd. 5.00
8 Raistlin's Evil concl. 5.00
9 Journey to land o/t Minotaurs A:Tanis, Kitiara 5.00
10 Blood Sea,'Arena of Istar' 4.00
11 Cataclysm of Krynn Revealed 'Arena of Istar' contd. 4.00
12 Horak vs.Koraf, Arena contd. . 4.00
13 Test of High Sorcery #1 . . . . . 5.50
14 Test of High Sorcery #2 . . . . . 5.50
15 Test of High Sorcery #3 . . . . . 4.00
16 Test of High Sorcery #4 . . . . . 4.00
17 Winter'sKnight:DragonkillPt.1 . 3.00
18 Winter'sKnight:DragonkillPt.1 . 3.00
19 Winter'sKnight:DragonkillPt.1 . 3.00
20 Winter'sKnight:DragonkillPt.1 . 3.00
21 Move to New World 2.50
22 Taladas Pt.1,A:Myrella 2.50
23 Taladas Pt.2,Riva vs. Dragon . 2.00
24 Taladas Pt.3,V:Minotaur Lord . 2.00
25 Taladas Pt.4,V:Axantheas 2.00
26 Rune Discovery,V:Agents of Eristem 2.00
27 V:Agents of Eristem 2.00
28 Riva continued. 2.00
29 Riva continued 2.00
30 Dwarf War Pt #1 . . . . 1.75
31 Dwarf War Pt #2 . . . . 1.75
32 Dwarf War Pt #3 . . . . 1.75
33 Dwarf War Pt #4 . . . . 1.75
34 conc., last issue 1.75
Ann.#1 Myrella o/t Robed Wizards 2.95

DYNAMIC CLASSICS

Sept-October 1978

1 Rep Det. 395 & 438 . . . . 3.00

ECLIPSO

1 BS,MPn,V:South American Drug Dealers 2.50

Eclipso #2 © DC Comics, Inc.

2 BS,MPn,A:Bruce Gordon 2.00
3 BS,MPn,R:Amanda Waller 2.00
4 BS,A:Creeper,Cave Carson . . . 3.25
5 A:Creeper,Cave Carson 3.00
6 LMc,V:Bruce Gordon 3.00
7 London,1891 . . . . 4.50
8 A:Sherlock Holmes 1.50
9 I:Johnny Peril 1.50
10 CDo,V:Darkseid 1.50
11 A:Creeper,Peacemaker,Steel . 1.50
12 V:Shadow Fighters 1.50
13 D:Manhunter,Commander Steel, Major Victory,Peacemaker, Wildcat,Dr.Midnight,Creeper . . 1.75
14 A:JLA 1.50
15 A:Amanda Waller 1.50
16 V:US Army 1.50
17 A:Amanda Waller,Martian Manhunter,Wonder Woman,Flash, Bloodwynd,Booster Gold 1.75
18 A:Spectre,JLA,final issue 2.00
Ann.#1 I:Prism 2.50

ECLIPSO: THE DARKNESS WITHIN

1 BS,Direct w/purple diamond, A:Superman,Creeper 4.00
1a BS,Newstand w/out diamond . 3.00
2 BS,MPn,DC heroes V:Eclipso, D:Starman 3.00

80 PAGE GIANTS

August, 1964

1 Superman 120.00
2 Jimmy Olsen 70.00
3 Lois Lane 40.00
4 Golden Age-Flash 30.00
5 Batman 45.00
6 Superman 35.00
7 JKu&JKu(c),Sgt. Rock's Prize Battle Tales 30.00
8 Secret Origins,O:JLA,Aquaman, Robin,Atom, Superman . . . 100.00
9 Flash 35.00
10 Superboy 32.00
11 Superman,A:Lex Luthor 35.00
12 Batman 40.00
13 Jimmy Olsen 30.00
14 Lois Lane 30.00
15 Superman & Batman 50.00
16 JLA #39 . . . . 75.00
17 Batman #176 . . . . 40.00
18 Superman #183 . . . . 18.00
19 Our Army at War #164 . . . . . 10.00
20 Action #334 . . . . 16.00
21 Flash #160 . . . . 30.00
22 Superboy #129 . . . . 7.00
23 Superman #187 . . . . 13.00
24 Batman #182 . . . . 26.00
25 Jimmy Olsen #95 . . . . 10.00
26 Lois Lane #68 . . . . 10.00
27 Batman #185 . . . . 35.00
28 World's Finest #161 . . . . 11.00
29 JLA #48 . . . . 16.00
30 Batman #187 . . . . 35.00
31 Superman #193 . . . . 13.00
32 Our Army at War #177 . . . . . . 8.00
33 Action #347 . . . . 11.00
34 Flash #169 . . . . 30.00
35 Superboy #138 . . . . 6.00
36 Superman #197 . . . . 12.00
37 Batman #193 . . . . 16.00
38 Jimmy Olsen #104 . . . . 5.00
39 Lois Lane #77 . . . . 6.00
40 World's Finest #170 . . . . 10.00
41 JLA #58 . . . . 12.00
42 Superman #202 . . . . 12.00
43 Batman #198 . . . . 24.00
44 Our Army at War #190 . . . . . . 5.00
45 Action #360 . . . . 8.00
46 Flash #178 . . . . 18.00
47 Superboy #147 . . . . 7.00
48 Superman #207 . . . . 12.00
49 Batman #203 . . . . 14.00
50 Jimmy Olsen #113 . . . . 5.00
51 Lois Lane #86 . . . . 6.00
52 World's Finest #179 . . . . 6.00
53 JLA #67 . . . . 8.00
54 Superman #212 . . . . 12.00
55 Batman #208 . . . . 13.00
56 Our Army at War #203 . . . . . . 5.00
57 Action #373 . . . . 8.00
58 Flash #187 . . . . 13.00
59 Superboy #156 . . . . 6.00
60 Superman #217 . . . . 10.00
61 Batman #213 . . . . 35.00
62 Jimmy Olsen #122 . . . . 5.00
63 Lois Lane #95 . . . . 5.00
64 World's Finest #188 . . . . 6.00
65 JLA #76 . . . . 7.00
66 Superman #222 . . . . 10.00
67 Batman #218 . . . . 13.00
68 Our Army at War #216 . . . . . . 5.00

69 Adventure #390 . . . . 6.00
70 Flash #196 . . . . 12.00
71 Superboy #165 . . . . 6.00
72 Superman #227 . . . . 10.00
73 Batman #223 . . . . 14.00
74 Jimmy Olsen #131 . . . . 5.00
75 Lois Lane #104 . . . . 4.00
76 World's Finest #197 . . . . 5.00
77 JLA #85 . . . . 6.00
78 Superman #232 . . . . 10.00
79 Batman #228 . . . . 12.00
80 Our Army at War #229 . . . . . . 5.00
81 Adventure #403 . . . . 6.00
82 Flash #205 . . . . 9.00
83 Superboy #174 . . . . 5.00
84 Superman #239 . . . . 10.00
85 Batman #233 . . . . 12.00
86 Jimmy Olsen #140 . . . . 5.00
87 Lois Lane #113 . . . . 4.00
88 World's Finest #206 . . . . 5.00
89 JLA #93 . . . . 6.00

EL DIABLO

1 I:El Diablo, double-size 2.50
2 V:Crime Lord Benny Contreras 2.00
3 'Day of the Dead' Celebration . 2.00
4 Storm #1 . . . . 2.25
5 Storm #2 . . . . 2.25
6 Storm #3 . . . . 2.25
7 Storm #4 . . . . 2.25
8 V:Car-Theft Ring 2.00
9 V:Crime Lord of Dos Rios 2.00
10 The Franchise #1 . . . . 2.00
11 The Franchise #2 . . . . 2.00
12 A:Greg Sanders (golden age) . 2.00
13 The River #1 . . . . 2.00
14 The River #2 . . . . 2.00
15 The River #3 . . . . 2.00
16 Final Issue 2.00

ELECTRIC WARRIOR

1 SF series,I:Electric Warriors . . . 2.50
2 'Bloodstalker Mode' 2.00
3 Rogue Warrior vs. Z-Primes . . 2.00
4 Primmies vs. Electric Warriors . 2.00
5 Lek 0-03 Rebels 2.00
6 Lek 0-03 vs. Masters 1.75
7 Lek'sFate,Derek Two-Shadows 1.75
8 Derek Two-Shadows Betrayed . 1.75
9 Fate of Derek Two-Shadows . . 1.75
10 Two-Shadows as one 1.75
11 Rebellion 1.75
12 Rebellion continued 1.75
13 V:Prime One 1.75
14 Mutants Join Rebellion 1.75
15 Invaders Arrival 1.75
16 Unified Warriors vs. Invaders . 1.75
17 V:Terrans, O:Electric Warriors . 1.75
18 Origin continued, final issue . . 1.75

ELONGATED MAN

1 A:Copperhead 1.00
2 Modora,A:Flash,I:Sonar 1.00
3 A:Flash,V:Wurst Gang 1.00

ELVIRA

1 DSp,BB(c) 3.25
2 thru 9 . . . . @1.00
10 . . . . 2.00
11 DSt(c)Find Cain 2.50

ENIGMA
Vertigo

1 B:PrM(s),DFg,I:Enigma,Michael Smith,V:The Head 3.75
2 DFg,I:The Truth 3.25
3 DFg,V:The Truth,I:Envelope Girl, Titus Bird 3.25
4 DFg,D:The Truth,I:Interior League 3.25
5 DFg,I:Enigma's Mother 3.00
6 DFg,V:Envelope Girl 3.00
7 DFg,V:Enigma's Mother,D:Envelope Girl,O:Enigma 3.00
8 E:PrM(s),DFg,final issue 3.00

EXTREMIST
Vertigo

1 B:PrM(s),TMK,I:The Order, Extremist(Judy Tanner) 2.50
1a Platinum Ed. 50.00
2 TMK,D:Extremist(Jack Tanner) 2.25
3 TMK,V:Patrick 2.25
4 E:PrM(s),TMK,D:Tony Murphy . 2.25

FIGHTING AMERICAN

1 GrL,R:Fighting American 1.75
2 GrL,Media Circus 1.75
3 GrL,I&V:Gross Nation Product, Def Iffit 1.75
4 GrL,V:Gross Nation Product, Def Iffit 1.75
5 GrL,PhorOptor 1.75
6 Final Issue 1.50

FIRESTORM
March, 1978

1 AM,JRu,I&O:Firestorm 4.00
2 AM,BMc,A:Superman 2.50
3 AM,I:Killer Froat 2.50
4 AM,BMc,I:Hyena 2.50
5 AM,BMc,Hyena 2.50

FIRESTORM, THE NUCLEAR MAN
(see FURY OF FIRESTORM)

FIRST ISSUE SPECIAL
April, 1975

1 JK,Atlas 3.00
2 Green Team 2.50
3 Metamorpho 2.50
4 Lady Cop 2.50
5 JK,Manhunter 2.75
6 JK,Dingbats 2.50
7 SD,Creeper 2.50
8 MGr,Warlord 15.00
9 WS,Dr.Fate 3.00
10 Outsiders(not Batman team) . . 2.50
11 NR,AM Code:Assassin 2.50
12 new Starman 2.50
13 return of New Gods 3.50

FLASH COMICS
January, 1940

1 SMo,SMo(c),O:Flash,Hawkman,The Whip & Johnny Thunder,B:Cliff Cornwall,Minute Movies . 25,000.00
2 B:Rod Rain 3,000.00
3 SMo,SMo(c),B:The King . . 2,400.00
4 SMo,SMo(c),F:The Whip . 2,000.00
5 SMo,SMo(c),F:The King . . 1,800.00
6 F:Flash 2,100.00
7 Hawkman(c) 1,300.00
8 Male bondage(c) 1,200.00
9 Hawkman(c) 1,100.00
10 SMo,SMo(c),Flash(c) 1,200.00
11 SMo,SMo(c) 900.00
12 SMo,SMo(c),B:Les Watts . . 900.00
13 SMo,SMo(c) 750.00
14 SMo,SMo(c) 750.00
15 SMo,SMo(c) 750.00
16 SMo,SMo(c) 750.00
17 SMo,SMo(c),E:Cliff Cornwall 750.00
18 SMo,SMo(c) 750.00
19 SMo,SMo(c) 750.00
20 SMo,SMo(c) 750.00
21 SMo(c) 650.00
22 SMo,SMo(c) 650.00
23 SMo,SMo(c) 650.00
24 SMo,SMo(c),Flash V:Spider-Men of Mars,A:Hawkgirl . . . 950.00
25 SMo,SMo(c) 575.00
26 SMo,SMo(c) 575.00
27 SMo,SMo(c) 575.00
28 SMo,SMo(c),Flash goes to Hollywood 575.00
29 SMo,SMo(c) 575.00
30 SMo,SMo(c),Flash in'Adventure of the Curiosity Ray!' 575.00
31 SMo,SMo(c),Hawkman(c) . . 525.00
32 SMo,SM(c),Flash in'Adventure of the Fictious Villians' 500.00
33 SMo,SMo(c) 500.00

Flash Comics #11 © DC Comics, Inc.

34 SMo,SMo(c),Flash in 'The Robbers of the Round Table' 500.00
35 SMo,SMo(c) 500.00
36 SMo,SMo(c),Flash in'The Mystery of the Doll Who Walks Like A Man' 500.00
37 SMo,SMo(c) 500.00
38 SMo,SMo(c) 500.00
39 SMo,SMo(c) 500.00
40 SMo,SMo(c),Flash in 'The Man Who Could Read Man's Souls!' 500.00
41 SMo,SMo(c) 450.00
42 SMo,SMo(c),Flash V:The Gangsters Baby! 450.00
43 SMo,SMo(c) 450.00
44 SMo,SMo(c),Flash V:The Liars Club 450.00
45 SMo,SMo(c),F:Hawkman,Big Butch Makes Hall of Fame . 450.00
46 SMo,SMo(c) 450.00
47 SMo,SMo(c),Hawkman in 'Crime Canned for the Duration' . . . 450.00
48 SMo,SMo(c) 450.00
49 SMo,SMo(c) 450.00
50 SMo,SMo(c),Hawkman in 'Tale o/t 1,000 Dollar Bill' . . 450.00
51 SMo,SMo(c) 400.00
52 SMo,SMo(c),Flash in 'Case of the Machine that Thinks Like A Man' 400.00
53 SMo,SMo(c),Hawkman in 'Simple Simon Met the Hawkman' 400.00
54 SMo,SMo(c),Flash in 'Mysterious Bottle from the Sea' 400.00
55 SMo,SMo(c),Hawkman in 'The Riddle of the Stolen Statuette! 3 . . . . 400.00
56 SMo,SMo(c) 400.00
57 SMo,SMo(c),Hawkman in 'Adventure of the Gangster and the Ghost' 400.00
58 SMo,SMo(c),'Merman meets

the Flash' . . . 400.00
59 SMo,SMo(c),Hawkman V:Pied Piper . . . 400.00
60 SMo,SMo(c),Flash V:The Wind Master . . . 400.00
61 SMo,SMo(c),Hawkman V:The Beanstalk . . . 400.00
62 JKu,Flash in 'High Jinks on the Rinks' . . . 425.00
63 JKu(c),Hawkman in 'The Tale of the Mystic Urn' . . . 375.00
64 . . . 375.00
65 JKu(c),Hawkman in 'Return of the Simple Simon' . . . 375.00
66 . . . 375.00
67 JKu(c) . . . 375.00
68 Flash in 'The Radio that Ran Wild' . . . 375.00
69 . . . 375.00
70 JKu(c) . . . 375.00
71 JKu(c),Hawkman in 'Battle of the Birdmen' . . . 375.00
72 JKu . . . 375.00
73 JKu(c) . . . 375.00
74 JKu(c) . . . 375.00
75 JKu(c),Hawkman in 'Magic at the Mardi Gras' . . . 375.00
76 A:Worry Wart . . . 375.00
77 Hawkman in 'The Case of the Curious Casket' . . . 375.00
78 . . . 375.00
79 Hawkman in 'The Battle of the Birds' . . . 375.00
80 Flash in 'The Story of the Boy Genius' . . . 375.00
81 JKu(c),Hawkman's Voyage to Venus . . . 375.00
82 A:Walter Jordan . . . 375.00
83 JKu,JKu(c),Hawkman in 'Destined for Disaster' . . . 375.00
84 Flash V:'The Changeling' . . 375.00
85 JKu,JKu(c),Hawkman in Hollywood . . . 375.00
86 JKu,1st Black Canary,Flash V:Stone Age Menace . . . 1,100.00
87 Hawkman meets the Foil . . 500.00
88 JKu,Flash in 'The Case of the Vanished Year!' . . . 500.00
89 I:The Thorn . . . 500.00
90 Flash in 'Nine Empty Uniforms' . . . 500.00
91 Hawkman V:The Phantom Menace . . . 600.00
92 1st full-length Black Canary story . . . 950.00
93 Flash V:Violin of Villainy . . . 600.00
94 JKu(c) . . . 600.00
95 . . . 600.00
96 . . . 600.00
97 Flash in 'The Dream that Didn't Vanish' . . . 600.00
98 JKu(c),Hawkman in 'Crime Costume!' . . . 600.00
99 Flash in 'The Star Prize of the Year' . . . 600.00
100 Hawkman in 'The Human -Fly Bandits!' . . . 1,100.00
101 . . . 900.00
102 Hawkman in 'The Flying Darkness' . . . 900.00
103 . . . 1,100.00
104 JKu,Hawkman in 'Flaming Darkness' February, 1949 . 2,200.00

FLASH

February-March, 1959

105 CI,O:Flash,I:Mirror Master . . . 3,000.00
106 CI,I&O:Gorilla Grodd, O:Pied Piper . . . 750.00
107 CI,A:Grodd . . . 450.00
108 CI,A:Grodd . . . 450.00
109 CI,A:Mirror Master . . . 325.00
110 CI,MA,I:Kid Flash, Weather Wizard . . . 675.00
111 CI,A:Kid Flash,The Invasion Of the Cloud Creatures . . . 190.00
112 CI,I&O:Elongated Man, A:Kid Flash . . . 225.00
113 CI,I&O:Trickster . . . 215.00
114 CI,A:Captain Cold . . . 160.00
115 CI,A:Grodd . . . 110.00
116 CI,A:Kid Flash,The Man Who Stole Central City . . . 110.00
117 CI,MA,I:Capt.Boomerang . 150.00
118 CI,MA . . . 110.00
119 CI,W:Elongated Man . . . 110.00
120 CI,A:Kid Flash,Land of Golden Giants . . . 110.00
121 CI,A:Trickster . . . 82.00
122 CI,I&O:The Top . . . 82.00
123 I:Earth 2,R:G.A.Flash . . . 625.00
124 CI,A:Capt.Boomerang . . . 77.00
125 CI,A:Kid Flash,The Conquerors of Time . . . 70.00
126 CI,A:Mirror Master . . . 70.00
127 CI,A:Grodd . . . 70.00
128 CI,O:Abra Kadabra . . . 70.00
129 CI,A:Capt.Cold,Trickster,A:Gold. Age Flash,C:JLA (flashback) 160.00

Flash Comics #204 © DC Comics, Inc.

Age Flash,C:JLA(flashback) 140.00
130 CI,A:Mirror Master, Weather Wizard . . . 70.00
131 CI,A:Green Lantern . . . 70.00
132 CI,A:Daphne Dean . . . 70.00
133 CI,A:Abra Kadabra . . . 70.00
134 CI,A:Captain Cold . . . 70.00
135 CI,N:Kid Flash . . . 70.00
136 CI,A:Mirror Master . . . 70.00
137 CI,Vandal Savage,R:JSA, A:G.A.Flash . . . 275.00
138 CI,A:Pied Piper . . . 66.00
139 CI,I&O:Prof.Zoom(Reverse Flash) . . . 100.00
140 CI,O:Heat Wave . . . 66.00
141 CI,A:Top . . . 45.00
142 CI,A:Trickster . . . 45.00
143 CI,A:Green Lantern . . . 45.00
144 CI,A:Man Missile,Kid Flash . 45.00
145 CI,A:Weather Wizard . . . 45.00
146 CI,A:Mirror Master . . . 43.00
147 CI,A:Mr.Element,A:Reverse Flash . . . 43.00
148 CI,A:Capt.Boomerang . . . 43.00
149 CI,A:Abra Kadabra . . . 43.00
150 CI,A:Captain Cold . . . 43.00
151 CI,A:Earth II Flash, The Shade . . . 67.00
152 CI,V:Trickster . . . 35.00
153 CI,A:Mr.Element,Rev.Flash . 35.00
154 CI,The Day Flash Ran Away with Himself . . . 35.00
155 CI,A:MirrorMaster,Capt.Cold,Top Capt. Boomerang,Grodd . . . 35.00
156 CI,A:Kid Flash,The Super Hero who Betrayed the World . . . 35.00
157 CI,A:Doralla Kon,The Top . . 35.00
158 CI,V:The Breakaway Bandit A:The Justice League . . . 35.00
159 CI,A:Kid Flash . . . 35.00
160 CI,giant . . . 46.00
161 CI,A:Mirror Master . . . 30.00
162 CI,Who Haunts the Corridor of Chills . . . 30.00
163 CI,A:Abra kadabra . . . 30.00
164 CI,V:Pied Piper,A:KidFLash . 30.00
165 CI,W:Flash,Iris West . . . 35.00
166 CI,A:Captain Cold . . . 30.00
167 CI,O:Flash,I:Mopee . . . 30.00
168 CI,A:Green Lantern . . . 30.00
169 CI,O:Flash rtd,giant . . . 45.00
170 CI,A:Abra Kadabra, G.A.Flash . . . 30.00
171 CI,A:Dexter Myles,Justice League,Atom;V:Dr Light . . . 24.00
172 CI,A:Grodd . . . 24.00
173 CI,A:Kid Flash,EarthII Flash V:Golden Man . . . 24.00
174 CI,A:Mirror Master,Top Captain Cold . . . 24.00
175 2nd Superman/Flash race, C:Justice League o/America . 90.00
176 giant-size . . . 24.00
177 RA,V:The Trickster . . . 24.00
178 CI,(giant size) . . . 32.00
179 RA,Fact or Fiction . . . 24.00
180 RA,V:Baron Katana . . . 24.00
181 RA,V;Baron Katana . . . 12.00
182 A:Abra Kadabra . . . 12.00
183 RA,V:The Frog . . . 12.00
184 RA,V:Dr Yom . . . 12.00
185 RA,Threat of the High Rise Buildings . . . 12.00
186 RA,A:Sargon . . . 12.00
187 CI,AbraKadabra,giant . . . 23.00
188 A:Mirror Master . . . 12.00
189 JKu(c),RA,A:Kid Flash . . . 12.00
190 JKu(c),RA,A:Dexter Myles . . 12.00
191 JKu(c),RA,A:Green Lantern . 12.00
192 RA;V:Captain Vulcan . . . 12.00
193 A:Captain Cold . . . 12.00
194 . . . 12.00
195 GK,MA . . . 12.00
196 CI,giant . . . 23.00
197 GK . . . 12.00
198 GK . . . 12.00
199 GK . . . 12.00
200 IN,MA . . . 14.00
201 IN,MA,A:G.A. Flash . . . 7.50
202 IN,MA,A:Kid Flash . . . 7.50
203 IN . . . 7.50
204 . . . 7.50
205 giant . . . 12.00
206 A:Mirror Master . . . 7.50
207 . . . 7.50
208 . . . 7.50
209 A:Capt.Boomerang,Grodd Trickster . . . 7.50
210 CI . . . 7.50
211 O:Flash . . . 10.00
212 A:Abra Kadabra . . . 7.50
213 CI . . . 7.50
214 CI,rep.Showcase #37 (O:Metal Men),giant size. . . . 12.00
215 IN,FMc,rep.Showcase #14 . 14.00
216 A:Mr.Element . . . 7.50
217 NA,A:Gr.Lant,Gr.Arrow . . . 13.00
218 NA,A:Gr.Lant,Gr.Arrow . . . 13.00
219 NA,L:Greeen Arrow . . . 13.00
220 IN,DG,A:KidFlash,Gr.Lantern . 7.50
221 IN . . . 7.50

222 IN 7.50
223 DG,Green Lantern 7.50
224 IN,DG,A:Green Lantern 7.50
225 IN,DG,A:Gr.Lant,Rev.Flash . . 8.50
226 NA,A:Capt. Cold 10.00
227 IN,FMc,DG,Capt.Boomerang,
Green Lantern 7.50
228 IN 7.50
229 IN,FMc,A:Green Arrow,
V:Rag Doll (giant size) 9.00
230 A:VandalSavage,Dr.Alchemy . 7.50
231 FMc 7.50
232 giant 9.00
233 giant 9.00
234 V:Reverse Flash 5.00
235 . . . . 4.00
236 MGr 4.00
237 IN,FMc,MGr,A:Prof Zoom,
Green Lantern 4.50
238 MGr 4.00
239 . . . . 4.00
240 MGr 4.00
241 A:Mirror Master 4.00
242 MGr,D:Top 4.00
243 IN,FMc,MGr,TA,O:Top,
A:Green Lantern 4.00
244 IN,FMc,A:Rogue's Gallery . . . 4.00
245 IN,FMc,DD,TA,I:PlantMaster . 4.00
246 IN,FMc,DD,TA,I:PlantMaster . 4.00
247 . . . . 4.00
248 FMc,IN,I:Master 4.00
249 FMc,IN,V:Master 4.00
250 IN,FMc,I:Golden Glider 4.00
251 FMc,IN,V:Golden Glider 3.50
252 FMc,IN,I:Molder 3.50
253 FMc,IN,V:Molder 3.50
254 FMc 3.50
255 FMc,A:MirrorMaster 3.50
256 FMc,V:Top 3.50
257 FMc,A:Green Glider 3.50
258 FMc,A:Black Hand 3.50
259 FMc,IN 3.50
260 FMc,IN 3.50
261 FMc,IN,V:Golden Glider 3.50
262 FMc,IN,V:Golden Glider 3.50
263 FMc,IN,V:Golden Glider 3.50
264 FMc,IN,V:Golden Glider 3.50
265 FMc,IN 3.50
266 FMc,IN,V:Heat Wave 3.50
267 FMc,IN,V:Heat Wave 3.50
268 FMc,IN,A:E2 Flash 3.50
269 FMc,IN,A:Kid Flash 3.50
270 FMc,IN,V:Clown 3.50
271 RB,V:Clown 3.50
272 RB,V:Clown 3.50
273 RB 3.50
274 RB 3.50
275 AS,D:Iris West,PCP story . . . 4.00
276 AS,A:JLA 3.50
277 AS,FMc,A:JLA,
V:MirrorMaster 3.50
278 A:Captain.Boomerang
& Heatwave 3.50
279 A:Captain.Boomerang
& Heatwave 3.50
280 DH 3.50
281 DH,V:Reverse Flash 4.00
282 DH,V:Reverse Flash 4.00
283 DH,V:Reverse Flash 4.00
284 DH,Flash's life story
I:Limbo Lord 3.50
285 DH,V:Trickster 3.50
286 DH,I:Rainbow Raider 3.50
287 DH,V:Dr.Alchemy 3.50
288 DH,V:Dr.Alchemy 3.50
289 DH,GP,1st GP DC art; V:Dr.
Alchemy;B:B.U.Firestorm 6.00
290 GP 3.00
291 GP,DH,V:Sabretooth 3.00
292 GP,DH,V:Mirror Master 3.00
293 GP,DH,V:Pied Piper 3.00
294 GP,DH,V:Grodd 3.00
295 CI,JSn,V:Grodd 3.00
296 JSn,A:Elongated Man 3.00
297 CI,A:Captain Cold 3.00
298 CI,V:Shade,Rainbowraider . . 3.00
299 CI,V:Shade,Rainbowraider . . 3.00
300 A:New Teen Titans 5.00
301 CI,A:Firestorm 3.00
302 CI,V:Golden Glider 3.00
303 CI,V:Golden Glider 3.00
304 CI,PB,I:Col.Computron;E:B.U.
Firestorm 3.00
305 KG,CI,A:G.A.Flash,B:Dr.Fate . 4.00
306 CI,KG,V:Mirror Master 4.00
307 CI,KG,V:Pied Piper 3.00
308 CI,KG 3.00

Flash Comics #309 © DC Comics, Inc.

309 CI,KG 4.00
310 CI,KG,V:Capt.Boomerang . . . 3.00
311 CI,KG,V:Capt.Boomerang . . . 3.00
312 CI,A:Heatwave 3.00
313 KG,A:Psylon,E:Dr.Fate 3.00
314 CI,I:Eradicator 3.00
315 CI,V:Gold Face 3.00
316 CI,V:Gold Face 3.00
317 CI,V:Gold Face 3.00
318 CI,DGb,V:Eradicator;B:
B.U.Creeper 3.00
319 CI,DGb,V:Eradicator 3.00
320 CI,V:Eradicator 3.00
321 CI,D:Eradicator 3.00
322 CI,V:Reverse Flash 3.00
323 CI,V:Reverse Flash;E:
B.U.Creeper 3.00
324 CI,D:Reverse Flash 4.00
325 CI,A:Rogues Gallery 3.00
326 CI,A:Weather Wizard 3.00
327 CI,A:JLA,G.Grodd 3.00
328 CI 3.00
329 CI,A:J.L.A.,G.Grodd 3.00
330 CI,FMc,V:G.Grodd 3.00
331 CI,FMc,V:G.Grodd 3.00
332 CI,FMc,V:Rainbow Raider . . . 3.00
333 CI,FMc,V:Pied Piper 3.00
334 CI,FMc,V:Pied Piper 3.00
335 CI,FMc,V:Pied Piper 3.00
336 CI,FMc,V:Pied Piper 3.00
337 CI,FMc,V:Pied Piper 3.00
338 CI,FMc,I:Big Sir 3.00
339 CI,FMc,A:Big Sir 3.00
340 CI,FMc,Trial,A:Big Sir 3.00
341 CI,FMc,Trial,A:Big Sir 3.00
342 CI,FMc,Trial,V:RogueGallery . 3.00
343 CI,FMc,Trial,A:GoldFace 3.00
344 CI,O:Kid Flash,Trial 3.00
345 CI,A:Kid Flash,Trial 3.00
346 CI,FMc,Trial,V:AbraKadabra . 3.00
347 CI,FMc,Trial,V:AbraKadabra . 3.00
348 CI,FMc,Trial,V:AbraKadabra . 3.00
349 CI,FMc,Trial,V:AbraKadabra . 3.00
350 CI,FMc,Trial,V:AbraKadabra . 7.00
Ann.#1 O:ElongatedMan,
G.Grodd 280.00

FLASH
[2nd Series]
October, 1985

1 JG,Legends,C:Vandal Savage 10.00
2 JG,V:Vandal Savage 6.00
3 JG,I:Kilgore 4.00
4 JG,A:Cyborg 4.00
5 JG,V:Speed Demon 4.00
6 JG,V:Speed Demon 4.00
7 JG,V:Red Trinity 4.00
8 JG,V:BlueTrinity,Millenium 4.00
9 JG,I:Chunk,Millenium 4.00
10 V:Chunk,Chunks World 3.00
11 Return to Earth 3.00
12 Velocity 9 . . . . 3.00
13 Vandal Savage,V:Velocity 9
Adicts 3.00
14 V:Vandal Savage 3.00
15 A:Velocity 9 Junkies 3.00
16 C:V.Savage,SpeedMcGeePt.1 . 3.00
17 GLa,Speed McGee Pt.2 . . . . . 3.00
18 GLa,SpeedMcGeePt.3,
V:V.Savage 2.25
19 JM:+bonus book,R:Rogue
Gallery,O:Blue/Red Trinity 2.25
20 A:Durlan 2.25
21 A:Manhunter,Invasion x-over . . 2.25
22 A:Manhunter,Invasion x-over . . 2.25
23 V:Abrakadabra 2.25
24 GLa,FlashRegainsSpeed,
A:L.Lane 2.25
25 GLa,Search for Flash 2.25
26 GLa,I:Porcupine Man 2.25
27 GLa,Porcupine Man as Flash . 2.25
28 GLa,A:Golden Glider,
Capt.Cold 2.25
29 A:New Phantom Lady 2.25
30 GLa,Turtle Saga Pt.1 . . . . 2.25
31 GLa,Turtle Saga Pt.2 . . . . 2.00
32 GLa,Turtle Saga Pt.3,
R:G.A.Turtle 2.00
33 GLa,Turtle Saga Pt.4 . . . . 2.00
34 GLa,Turtle Saga Pt.5 . . . . 2.00
35 GLa,Turtle Saga Pt.6,
D:G.A.Turtle 2.00
36 GLa,V:Cult 2.00
37 GLa,V:Cult 2.00
38 GLa,V:Cult 2.00
39 GLa,V:Cult 2.00
40 GLa,A:Dr.Alchemy 2.00
41 GLa,A:Dr.Alchemy 2.00
42 GLa,MechanicalTroubles 2.00
43 GLa,V:Kilgore 2.00
44 GLa,V:Velocity 2.00
45 V:Gorilla Grod 2.00
46 V:Gorilla Grod 2.00
47 V:Gorilla Grod 2.00
48 . . . . 2.00
49 A:Vandal Savage 2.00
50 N:Flash (double sz)V:Savage . 4.00
51 I:Proletariat 2.00
52 I.R.S. Mission 1.75
53 A:Superman,Race to Save
Jimmy Olsen 1.75
54 Terrorist Airline Attack 1.75
55 War of the Gods x-over 1.75
56 The Way of a Will Pt.1 . . . . . . 1.75
57 The Way of a Will Pt.2 . . . . . . 1.75
58 Meta Gene-activated Homeless 1.75
59 The Last Resort 1.75
60 Love Song of the Chunk 1.75
61 Wally's Mother's Wedding Day 1.75
62 GLa,Year 1, Pt1 . . . . 2.25
63 GLa,Year 1, Pt2 . . . . 1.75
64 GLa,Year 1, Pt3 . . . . 1.75
65 GLa,Year 1, Pt4 . . . . 1.75
66 A:Aq'man,V:Marine Marauder . 1.75
67 GLa,V:Abra Kadabra 1.75

68 GLa,V:Abra Kadabra 1.75
69 GLa,Gorilla Warfare#2 . . . . . . 1.75
70 Gorilla Warfare#4 . . . . 1.75
71 GLa,V:Dr.Alchemy 1.75
72 GLa,V:Dr.Alchemy,C:Barry Allen 1.75
73 GLa,Xmas Issue,R:Barry Allen 2.25
74 GLa,A:Barry Allen? 2.25
75 GLa,A:Reverse Flash,V:Mob Violence 2.00
76 GLa,A:Reverse Flash 2.00
77 GLa,G.A.Flash vs Reverse Flash 2.00
78 GLa,V:Reverse Flash 2.00
79 GLa,V:Reverse Flash,48 pgs. . 3.00
80 AD(c),V:Frances Kane 2.75
80a Newstand Ed 1.75
81 AD(c) 1.75
82 AD(c),A:Nightwing 1.75
83 AD(c),A:Nightwing,Starfire 1.75
84 AD(c),I:Razer 1.75
85 AD(c),V:Razer 1.75
86 AD(c),A:Argus 1.75
86 V:Santa Claus 1.75
87 Chrisma issue 1.75
88 . . . . 1.75
89 On Trial 1.75
90 On Trial#2 . . . . 1.75
91 Out of Time 1.75
92 I:3rd Flash 1.50
Ann.#1 JG,The Deathtouch 4.00
Ann.#2 A:Wally's Father 3.00
Ann.#3 Roots 2.50
Ann.#4 Armageddon Pt7 . . . . 2.50
Ann.#5 TC(1st Full Work),Eclipso, V:Rogue's Gallery 10.00
Ann.#6 Bloodlines#4,I:Argus 2.75
Spec #1,IN,DG,CI,50th Anniv., Three Flash's 4.50
T.V. Spec.#1,JS,w/episode guide . 4.25

FLASH GORDON

1 DJu,I:New Flash Gordon 2.50
2 DJu,A:Lion-Men,Shark-Men . . . 2.00
3 DJu,V:Shark-Men 1.50
4 DJu,Dale Kidnapped by Voltan 1.50
5 DJu,Alliance Against Ming 1.50
6 DJu,Arctic City 1.50
7 DJu,Alliance vs. Ming 1.50
8 DJu,Alliance vs. Ming 1.50
9 DJu,V:Ming, final issue 1.50

FLY

Impact

1 I&O:Fly I:Arachnus,Chromium . 1.50
2 V:Chromium 1.25
3 O:Arachnus, I:Lt.Walker Odell . 1.00
4 A:Black Hood, V:Arachnus 1.00
5 V:Arachnus 1.00
6 I:Blackjack 1.00
7 Oceanworld,V:Dolphus 1.00
8 A:Comet,Dolphus 1.00
9 Teenage Suicide 1.00
10 V:General Mechanix 1.00
11 Suicide Issue 1.25
12 V:Agent from WEB 1.25
13 I:Tremor 1.25
14 V:Domino 1.25
15 V:Domino 1.25
16 V:Arachnus 1.25
17 Final Issue 1.25
Ann.#1 Earthquest,w/trading card . 2.25

FORBIDDEN TALES OF DARK MANSION

May-June, 1972

5 thru 14 . . . . @1.50
15 February-March, 1974 . . . . . . 1.50

FOREVER PEOPLE

1 Return of Forever People 1.75
2 'Return of Earth of Yesterday' . 1.25
3 A:Mark Moonrider 1.25
4 The Dark controlls M.Moonrider 1.25
5 R:MotherBox,Infinity Man 1.25
6 Donny's Fate, final issue 1.25

FORGOTTEN REALMS

1 A:RealmsMaster,PriamAgrivar . 8.00
2 Mystic Hand of Vaprak, A:Ogre Mage 6.00
3 Mystic Hand of Vaprak contd. . 5.50
4 Ogre Mage vs.Omen the Wizard 5.50
5 Dragon Reach #1 . . . . 5.50
6 Dragon Reach #2 . . . . 4.50
7 Dragon Reach #3 . . . . 3.50
8 Dragon Reach #4 . . . . 3.00
9 V:Giant Squid 2.50
10 'Head Cheese' 2.50
11 Triangles #1 . . . . 2.50
12 Triangles #2 . . . . 2.50
13 Triangles #3 . . . . 2.50
14 A:Lich Viranton the Mage 2.00
15 Avatar Comics tie-in 2.00
16 Mad Gods and Paladins Pt.1 . 2.00
17 Mad Gods and Paladins Pt.2 . 2.00
18 Mad Gods and Paladins Pt.3 . 2.00
19 Mad Gods and Paladins Pt.4 . 2.00
20 Realms Master Crew captured 2.00
21 Catewere Tribe 2.00
22 V:The Akri 1.75
23 A:Sandusk the Leprechaun . . . 1.75
24 'Everybody wants to rule the realms' 1.75
25 The Wake, final issue 1.75
Ann.#1 V:Advanced D&D crew . . 2.95

FOUR STAR BATTLE TALES

February-March, 1973

1 thru 5, Nov.-Dec.,1973 . . . . @1.50

FOUR STAR SPECTACULAR

March-April, 1976

1 . . . . 1.50
2 thru 6 . . . . @1.25

FOX AND THE CROW

December-January, 1951

1 . . . . 600.00
2 . . . . 300.00
3 . . . . 175.00
4 . . . . 175.00
5 . . . . 165.00
6 thru 10 . . . . @125.00
11 thru 20 . . . . @100.00
21 thru 40 . . . . @100.00
41 thru 60 . . . . @40.00
61 thru 80 . . . . @30.00
81 thru 94 . . . . @20.00
95 . . . . 25.00
96 thru 99 . . . . @10.00
100 . . . . 14.00
101 thru 108 . . . . @10.00

Becomes:

STANLEY & HIS MONSTER

109 thru 112 Oct.Nov.,1968 . . @10.00

FREEDOM FIGHTERS

March-April, 1976

1 Freedom Fighters go to Earth 1 1.50
2 . . . . 1.00
3 . . . . 1.00
4 . . . . 1.00
5 A:Wonder Woman 1.00
6 thru 9 . . . . @1.00
10 O:Doll Man 1.00
11 O:Ray 1.00
12 O:Firebrand 1.00
13 O:Black Condor 1.00
14 A:Batgirl 1.00
15 O:Phantom Lady 1.00

FROM BEYOND THE UNKNOWN

October-November, 1969

1 JKu,CI 70.00
2 MA(c),CI,ATh 18.00
3 NA(c),CI 15.00
4 MA(c),CI, ... 15.00
5 MA(c),CI 15.00
6 NA(c),I:Glen Merrit 18.00
7 CI,JKu(c) 15.00
8 NA(c),CI 18.00
9 NA(c),CI 18.00
10 MA(c),CI 15.00
11 MA(c),CI 12.00
12 JKu(c),CI 15.00
13 JKu(c),CI,WW 20.00
14 JKu(c),CI 15.00
15 MA(c),CI 12.00
16 MA(c),CI 12.00
17 MA(c),CI 12.00
18 MK(c),CI 10.00
19 MK(c),CI 10.00
20 . . . . 10.00
21 . . . . 10.00
22 MA(c) 12.00
23 CI,Space Museum 10.00
24 CI 10.00

FUNNY STOCKING STUFFER

March, 1985

1 . . . . 1.00

FUNNY STUFF

Summer, 1944

1 B:3 Mousketeer Terrific Whatzit 500.00
2 . . . . 250.00
3 . . . . 150.00
4 . . . . 140.00
5 . . . . 140.00
6 thru 10 . . . . @85.00
11 thru 20 . . . . @50.00
21 . . . . 40.00
22 C:Superman 140.00
23 thru 30 . . . . @40.00
31 thru 78 . . . . @30.00
79 July-August, 1954 . . . . 30.00

FURY OF FIRESTORM

June, 1982

1 PB,I:Black Bison 3.50
2 PB,V:Black Bison 2.00
3 PB,V:Pied Piper, Killer Frost . . 1.50
4 PB,A:JLA,Killer Frost 1.50
5 PB,V:Pied Piper 1.25
6 V:Pied Piper 1.25
7 I:Plastique 1.25
8 V:Typhoon 1.25
9 V:Typhoon 1.25
10 V:Hyena 1.25
11 V:Hyena 1.25
12 PB,V:Hyena 1.25
13 . . . . 1.25
14 PB,I:Enforcer,A:Multiplex 1.25
15 V:Multiplex 1.25
16 V:Multiplex 1.25
17 I:2000 Committee,Firehawk . . . 1.00
18 I:Tokamak,A:Multiplex 1.25
19 GC,V:Goldenrod 1.25
20 A:Killer Frost 1.25
21 D:Killer Frost 1.00
22 O:Firestorm 1.00
23 I:Bug & Byte 1.00
24 I:Blue Devil,Bug & Byte 2.50
25 I:Silver Deer 1.00
26 V:Black Bison 1.00
27 V:Black Bison 1.00
28 I:Slipknot 1.00
29 I:2000 C'tee,I:Breathtaker 1.00
30 V:2000 Committee 1.00
31 V:2000 Committee 1.00
32 Phantom Stranger 1.00

Fury of Firestorm #77
© DC Comics, Inc.

33 A:Plastique 1.00
34 I:Killer Frost 2 .... 1.00
35 V:K.Frost/Plastique,I:Weasel .. 1.00
36 V:Killer Frost & Plastique 1.00
37 .... 1.00
38 V:Weasel 1.00
39 V:Weasel 1.00
40 .... 1.00
41 Crisis 1.00
42 Crisis,A:Firehawk 1.00
43 V:Typhoon 1.00
44 V:Typhoon 1.00
45 V:Multiplex 1.00
46 A:Blue Devil 1.00
47 A:Blue Devil 1.00
48 I:Moonbow 1.00
49 V:Moonbow 1.00
50 W:Ed Raymond 1.50
51 A:King Crusher 1.00
52 A:King Crusher 1.00
53 V:Steel Shadow 1.00
54 I:Lava 1.00
55 Legends,V:World's
Luckiest Man 1.00
56 Legends,A:Hawk 1.00
57 .... 1.00
58 I:Parasite II 1.00
59 .... 1.00
60 Secret behind Hugo's accident 1.00
61 V:Typhoon 1.00
61a Superman Logo 60.00
62 A:Russian 'Firestorm' 1.00
63 A:Capt.Atom 1.00
64 A:Suicide Squad 1.00
Ann.#1 EC,A:Firehawk,
V:Tokamak 1.50
Ann.#2 .... 1.00
Ann.#3 .... 1.00
Ann.#4 KG,CS,GC,DG 1.00
Ann.#5 JLI,Suicide Squad
I:New Firestorm 1.50

Becomes:

FIRESTORM, THE NUCLEAR MAN

November, 1987

65 A:New Firestorm 1.00
66 A:Green Lantern 1.00
67 .... 1.00
68 .... 1.00
69 V:Zuggernaut,Stalnivolk USA . 1.00
70 V:Flying Dutchman 1.00
71 Trapped in the Timestream ... 1.00
72 V:Zuggernaut 1.00
73 V:Stalnivolk & Zuggernaut 1.00
74 Quest for Martin Stein 1.00
75 Return of Martin Stein 1.00
76 Firestorm & Firehawk
vs Brimstone 1.00
77 Firestorm & Firehawk in Africa 1.00
78 'Exile From Eden' Pt.1 ...... 1.00
79 'Exile From Eden' Pt.2 ...... 1.00
80 A:Power Girl,Starman,Invasion
x-over 1.00
81 A:Soyuz,Invasion aftermath ... 1.00
82 Invasion Aftermath 1.00
83 V:Svarozhich 1.00
84 .... 1.00
85 Soul of Fire,N:Firestorm 1.00
86 TMd,Janus Directive #7 ..... 1.00
87 TMd 1.00
88 TMd,E:Air Wave B:Maser 1.00
89 TMd,V:Firehawk,Vandermeer
Steel 1.00
90 TMd,Elemental War #1 ...... 1.00
91 TMd,Elemental War #2 ...... 1.00
92 TMd,Elemental War #3 ...... 1.00
93 TMd 1.00
94 TMd,A:Killer Frost 1.00
95 TMd,V:Captains of Industry ... 1.00
96 TMd,A:Shango,African God &
Obatala,Lord o/t White Cloth .. 1.00
97 TMd,A:Obatala,V:Shango 1.00
98 TMd,A:Masar 1.00
99 TMd,A:Brimstone,PlasmaGiant 1.00
100 TMd,AM,V:Brimstone (Firestorm
back-up story) final issue 3.25

GAMMARAUDERS

1 I:Animal-Warrior Bioborgs 1.50
2 V:The Slugnoids 1.50
3 V:Slugnoids,I:Squawk the
Penguinoid 1.50
4 V:Slugnoids 1.50
5 V:Bioborg/Podnoid 1.50
6 Slash vs.Sassin,A:RadicalDebs 1.50
7 Jok findsSword that was broken 2.00
8 Jok's search for KirkwardDerby 2.00
9 Jok the Congressman 2.00
10 The Big Nada, final issue 2.00

GANG BUSTERS

December-January, 1947-48

1 .... 400.00
2 .... 200.00
3 thru 8 .... @125.00
9 Ph(c) 135.00
10 Ph(c) 135.00
11 thru 13 Ph(c) .... @100.00
14 Ph(c),FF 175.00
15 thru 16 .... @70.00
17 .... 160.00
18 thru 20 .... @60.00
21 thru 25 .... @50.00
26 JK 45.00
27 thru 40 .... @40.00
41 thru 44 .... @35.00
45 Comics Code 35.00
46 thru 50 .... 35.00
51 MD 38.00
52 thru 66 .... @38.00
67 December-January, 1958-59 . 38.00

GHOSTS

September-October, 1971

1 JAp,NC(c),Death's Bridegroom! 12.00
2 WW,NC(c),Mission
Supernatural 10.00
3 TD,NC(c),Death is my Mother . 6.00
4 GT,NC(c),The Crimson Claw . 6.00
5 NC(c),Death, The Pale
Horseman 6.00
6 NC(c),A Specter Poured
The Potion 4.00
7 MK(c),Death's Finger Points .. 4.00
8 NC(c),The Cadaver In
The Clock 4.00
9 AA,NC(c),The Last Ride
Of Rosie The Wrecker 4.00
10 NC(c),A Specter Stalks Saigon 4.00
11 NC(c),The Devils Lake 4.00
12 NC(c),The Macabre Mummy
Of Takhem-Ahtem 4.00
13 NC(c),Hell Is One Mile High .. 4.00
14 NC(c),The Bride Wore
A Shroud 4.00
15 AA,NC(c),The Ghost That
Wouldn't Die 4.00
16 NC(c),Death's Grinning Face . 4.00
17 NC(c),Death Held the
Lantern High 4.00
18 AA,NC(c),Graveyard of
Vengeance 4.00
19 AA,NC(c),The Dead Live On .. 4.00
20 NC(c),The Haunting Hussar
Of West Point 4.00
21 NC(c),The Ghost In The
Devil's Chair 3.50
22 NC(c),The Haunted Horns
Of Death 3.50
23 NC(c),Dead Is My Darling! ... 3.50
24 AA,NC(c),You Too, Will Die .. 3.50
25 AA,NC(c),Three Skulls On
The Zambezi 3.50
26 DP,NC(c),The Freaky Phantom
Of Watkins Glen 3.50
27 NC(c),Conversation With
A Corpse 3.50
28 DP,NC(c),Flight Of The
Lost Phantom 3.50
29 NC(c),The Haunted Lady
Of Death 3.50
30 NC(c),The Fangs of
the Phantom 3.50
31 NC(c),Blood On The Moon ... 3.50
32 NC(c),Phantom Laughed Last . 3.50
33 NC(c),The Hangman of
Haunted Island 3.50
34 NC(c),Wrath of the Ghost Apes 3.50
35 NC(c),Feud with a Phantom .. 3.50
36 NC(c),The Boy Who Returned
From The Gave 3.50
37 LD(c),Fear On Ice 3.50
38 LD(c),Specter In The Surf 3.50
39 LD(c),The Haunting Hitchhicker 3.50
40 LD(c),The Nightmare That
Haunted The World 3.50
41 LD(c),Ship of Specters 3.50
42 LD(c),The Spectral Sentries .. 3.50
43 LD(c),3 Corpses On A Rope .. 3.50
44 LD(c),The Case of the
Murdering Specters 3.50
45 LD(c),Bray of the
Phantom Beast 3.50
46 LD(c),The World's Most
Famous Phantom 3.50
47 LD(c),Wrath of the
Restless Specters 3.50
48 DP,LD(c),The Phantom Head . 3.50
49 The Ghost in the Cellar 3.50
50 Home Is Where The Grave Is 3.50
51 The Ghost Who Would Not Die 3.50
52 LD(c),The Thunderhead
Phantom 3.50
53 LD(c),Whose Spirit Invades Me 3.50
54 LD(c),The Deadly Dreams
Of Ernie Caruso 3.50
55 LD(c),The House That Was
Built For Haunting 3.50
56 LD(c),The Triumph Of The
Teen-Age Phantom 3.50
57 LD(c),The Flaming Phantoms
of Oradour 3.50
58 LD(c),The Corpse in the Closet 3.50
59 LD(c),That Demon Within Me . 3.50
60 LD(c),The Spectral Smile
of Death 3.50
61 LD(c),When Will I Die Again .. 3.00
62 LD(c),The Phantom Hoaxer! .. 3.00
63 LD(c),The Burning Bride 3.00
64 LD(c),Dead Men Do Tell Tales 3.00

65 LD(c),The Imprisoned Phantom 3.00
66 LD(c),Conversation With A Corpse 3.00
67 LD(c),The Spectral Sword 3.00
68 LD(c),The Phantom of the Class of '76 . . . . 3.00
69 LD(c),The Haunted Gondola . . 3.00
70 LD(c),Haunted Honeymoon . . 3.00
71 LD(c),The Ghost Nobody Knew 3.00
72 LD(c),The Ghost of Washington Monument 3.00
73 LD(c),The Specter Of The Haunted Highway 3.00
74 LD(c),The Gem That Haunted the World! 3.00
75 LD(c),The Legend Of The Lottie Lowry 3.00
76 LD(c),Two Ghosts of Death Row 3.00
77 LD(c),Ghost, Where Do You Hide? 3.00
78 LD(c),The World's Most Famous Phantom 3.00
79 LD(c),Lure of the Specter 3.00
80 JO(c),The Winged Specter . . 3.00
81 LD(c),Unburied Phantom 3.00
82 LD(c),The Ghost Who Wouldn't Die 3.00
83 LD(c),Escape From the Haunt of the Amazon Specter 3.00
84 LD(c),Torment of the Phantom Face 3.00
85 LD(c),The Fiery Phantom of Faracutin 3.00
86 LD(c),The Ghostly Garden . . . 3.00
87 LD(c),The Phantom Freak 3.00
88 LD(c),Harem In Hell 3.00
89 JKu(c),Came The Specter Shrouded In Seaweed 3.00
90 The Ghost Galleon 3.00
91 LD(c),The Haunted Wheelchair 3.00
92 DH(c),Double Vision 3.00
93 MK(c),The Flaming Phantoms of Nightmare Alley 3.00
94 LD(c),Great Caesar's Ghost . . 3.00
95 All The Stage Is A Haunt 3.00
96 DH(c),Dread of the Deadly Domestic 3.00
97 JAp(c),A Very Special Spirit A:Spectre 8.00
98 JAp(c),The Death of a Ghost A:Spectre 8.00
99 EC(c),Till Death Do Us Join A:Spectre 8.00
100 EC&DG(c),The Phantom's Final Debt 2.00
101 MK(c),The Haunted Hospital . 2.00
102 RB&DG(c),The Fine Art Of Haunting 2.00
103 RB&DG(c),Visions and Vengeance 2.00
104 LD(c),The First Ghost 2.00
105 JKu(c) 2.00
106 JKu(c) 2.00
107 JKu(c) 2.00
108 JKu(c) 2.00
109 EC(c) 2.00
110 EC&DG(c) 2.00
111 JKu(c) 2.00
112 May, 1982 . . . . 2.00

G.I. COMBAT

January, 1957

Prev: Golden Age

44 RH,JKu,The Eagle and the Wolves 250.00
45 RH,JKu,Fireworks Hill 125.00
46 JKu,The Long Walk To Wansan 80.00
47 RH, The Walking Weapon . . 80.00
48 No Fence For A Jet 80.00
49 Frying Pan Seat 80.00
50 Foxhole Pilot 80.00
51 RH,The Walking Grenade . . . 55.00

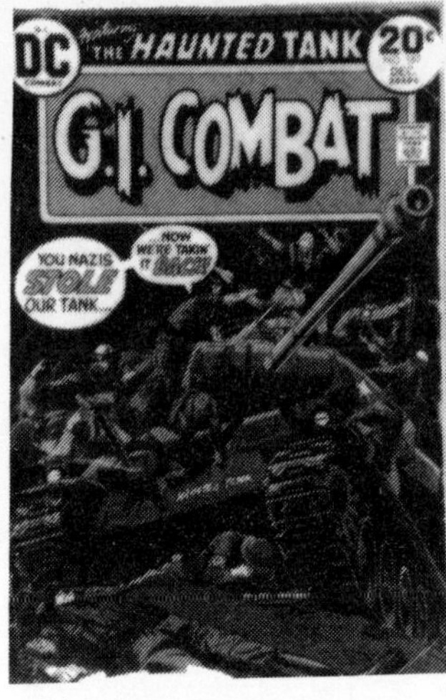

G.I. Combat #167 © DC Comics, Inc.

52 Jku,JKu(c),Call For A Tank . . 55.00
53 JKu,The Paper Trap 55.00
54 RH,JKu,Sky Tank 55.00
55 Call For A Gunner 55.00
56 JKu,JKu(c),The D.I.-And the Sand Fleas 55.00
57 RH,Live Wire For Easy 55.00
58 JKu(c),Flying Saddle 55.00
59 JKu,Hot Corner 55.00
60 RH,Bazooka Crossroads . . 55.00
61 JKu(c),The Big Run 35.00
62 RH,JKu,Drop An Inch 35.00
63 MD,JKu(c),Last Stand 35.00
64 MD,RH,JKu,JKu(c),The Silent Jet 35.00
65 JKu,Battle Parade 35.00
66 MD,The Eagle of Easy Company 35.00
67 JKu(c),I:Tank Killer 50.00
68 JKu,RH,The Rock 35.00
69 JKu,RH,The Steel Ribbon . . . 35.00
70 JKu,Bull's-Eye Bridge 35.00
71 MD,JKu(c),Last Stand 40.00
72 MD,JKu(c),Ground Fire 40.00
73 RH,JKu(c),Window War 40.00
74 RH,A Flag For Joey 40.00
75 RH,Dogtag Hill 40.00
76 MD,RH,JKu,Bazooka For A Mouse 40.00
77 RH,JKu,H-Hour For A Gunner 40.00
78 MD,RH,JKu(c),Who Cares About The Infantry 40.00
79 JKu,RH,Big Gun-Little Gun . . 40.00
80 JKu,RH(c),Flying Horsemen . 40.00
81 Jump For Glory 35.00
82 IN,Get Off My Back 35.00
83 Too Tired To Fight 40.00
84 JKu(c),Dog Company Is Holding 35.00
85 IN,JKu(c),The T.N.T. Trio . . . 35.00
86 JKu,RH(c),Not Return 35.00
87 RH(c),I:Haunted Tank 100.00
88 RH,JKu(c),Haunted Tank Vs. Ghost Tank 35.00
89 JA,RH,IN,Tank With Wings . . 35.00
90 JA,IN,RH,Tank Raiders . . . 35.00
91 IN,RH,The Tank and the Turtle 25.00
92 JA,IN,The Tank of Doom . . . 25.00
93 RH(c),JA,No-Return Mission . 25.00
94 IN,RH(c),Haunted Tank Vs. The Killer Tank 25.00
95 JA,RH(c),The Ghost of the Haunted Tank 25.00
96 JA,RH(c),The Lonesome Tank 25.00
97 IN,RH(c),The Decoy Tank . . . 25.00
98 JA,RH(c),Trap of Dragon's Teeth 25.00
99 JA,JKu,RH(c),Battle of the Thirsty Tanks 25.00
100 JA,JKu,Return of the Ghost Tank 25.00
101 JA,The Haunted Tank Vs. Attila's Battle Tiger 20.00
102 JKu(c),Haunted Tank Battle Window 20.00
103 JKu,JA,RH(c),Rabbit Punch For A Tiger 20.00
104 JA,JKu,RH(c),Blind Man's Radar 20.00
105 JA,JKu(c),Time Bomb Tank . 20.00
106 JA,JKu(c),Two-Sided War . . 20.00
107 JKu(c),The Ghost Pipers . . . 20.00
108 JKu(c),The Wounded Won't Wait,I:Sgt.Rock 22.00
109 JKu(c),Battle of the Tank Graveyard 20.00
110 IN,JKu(c),Choose Your War 20.00
111 JA,JKu(c),Death Trap 20.00
112 JA,JKu(c),Ghost Ace 15.00
113 JKu,RH(c),Tank Fight In Death Town 15.00
114 JA,RH(c),O:Haunted Tank . . 50.00
115 JA,RH(c),Medals For Mayhem15.00
116 IN,JA,JKu(c),Battle Cry For A Dead Man 15.00
117 JA,RH,JKu(c),Tank In The Ice Box 15.00
118 IN,JA,RH(c),My Buddy-My Enemy 15.00
119 IN,RH(c),Target For A Firing Squad 15.00
120 IN,JA,RH(c),Pull ATiger'sTail 15.00
121 RH(c),Battle of Two Wars . . 15.00
122 JA,JKu(c),Who Dies Next? . . 15.00
123 IN,RH(c),The Target of Terror 15.00
124 IN,RH(c),Scratch That Tank 15.00
125 RH(c),Stay Alive-Until Dark . 15.00
126 JA,RH(c),Tank Umbrella . . . 15.00
127 JA,JKu(c),Mission-Sudden Death 15.00
128 RH(c),The Ghost of the Haunted Tank 15.00
129 JA,RH(c),Hold That Town For A Dead Man 15.00
130 RH(c),Battle of the Generals 15.00
131 JKu&RH(c),Devil For Dinner 15.00
132 JA,JKu(c),The Executioner . 15.00
133 JKu(c),Operation:Death Trap 15.00
134 MD,JKu(c),Desert Holocaust 15.00
135 GE,JKu(c),Death is the Joker 15.00
136 JKu(c),Kill Now-Pay Later . . 15.00
137 JKu(c),We Can't See 15.00
138 JKu(c),I:The Losers 18.00
139 JKu(c),Corner of Hell 15.00
140 RH,MD,JKu(c),The LastTank 15.00
141 MD,JKu(c),Let Me Live.. Let Me Die 5.00
142 RH,JKu(c),Checkpoint-Death . 5.00
143 RH,JKu(c),The Iron Horseman 5.00
144 RH,MD,JKu(c),Every Man A Fort 5.00
145 MD,JKu(c),Sand,Sun and Death 5.00
146 JKu(c),Move the World 5.00
147 JKu(c),Rebel Tank 5.00
148 IN,JKu(c),The Gold-Plated General 5.00
149 JKu(c),Leave The Fighting To Us 5.00
150 JKu(c),The Death of the Haunted Tank 5.00
151 JKu(c),A Strong Right Arm . . 5.00
152 JKu(c),Decoy Tank 5.00
153 JKu(c),The Armored Ark 5.00
154 JKu(c),Battle Prize 5.00
155 JKu(c),The Long Journey . . . 5.00
156 JKu(c),Beyond Hell 5.00
157 JKu(c),The Fountain 5.00

158 What Price War 5.00
159 JKu(c),Mission Dead End . . . 5.00
160 JKu(c),Battle Ghost 5.00
161 JKu(c),The Day of the Goth . 5.00
162 JKu(c),The Final Victor 5.00
163 A Crew Divided 5.00
164 Siren Song 5.00
165 JKu(c),Truce,Pathfinder 5.00
166 Enemy From Yesterday 5.00
167 JKu(c),The Finish Line 5.00
168 NA(c),The Breaking Point . . . 5.00
169 WS(c),The Death of the Haunted Tank 5.00
170 Chain of Vengeance 5.00
171 JKu(c),The Man Who Killed Jeb Stuart 5.00
172 RH(c),At The Mercy of My Foes 5.00
173 JKu(c),The Final Crash 5.00
174 JKu(c),Vow To A Dead Foe . 5.00
175 JKu(c),The Captive Tank . . . 5.00
176 JKu(c),A Star Can Cry 5.00
177 JKu(c),The Tank That Missed D-Day 5.00
178 JKu(c),A Tank Is Born 5.00
179 JKu(c),One Last Charge 5.00
180 JKu(c),The Saints Go Riding On 5.00
181 JKu(c),The Kidnapped Tank . 5.00
182 JKu(c),Combat Clock 5.00
183 JKu(c),6 Stallions To Hell- And Back 5.00
184 JKu(c),Battlefield Bundle 5.00
185 JKu(c),No Taps For A Tank . 5.00
186 JKu(c),Souvenir From A Headhunter 5.00
187 JKu(c),The General Died Twice 5.00
188 The Devil's Pipers 5.00
189 The Gunner is a Gorilla 5.00
190 The Tiger and The Terrier . . 5.00
191 Decoy For Death 5.00
192 The General Has Two Faces 5.00
193 JKu(c),The War That Had To Wait 5.00
194 GE(c),Blitzkrieg Brain 5.00
195 JKu(c),The War That Time Forgot 5.00
196 JKu(c),Dead Men Patrol 5.00
197 JKu(c),Battle Ark 5.00
198 JKu(c),The Devil Rides A Panzer 5.00
199 JKu(c),A Medal From A Ghost 5.00
200 JKu(c),The Tank That Died . 5.00
201 NA&RH(c),The Rocking Chair Soldiers 3.50
202 NA&RH(c),Walking Wounded Don't Cry 3.50
203 JKu(c),To Trap A Tiger 3.50
204 JKu(c),A Winter In Hell 3.50
205 JKu(c),A Gift From The Emperor 3.50
206 JKu(c),A Tomb For A Tank . . 3.50
207 JKu(c),Foxhole for a Sherman 3.50
208 JKu(c),Sink That Tank 3.50
209 JKu(c),Ring Of Blood 3.50
210 JKu(c),Tankers Also Bleed . 3.50
211 JKu(c),A Nice Day For Killing 3.50
212 JKu(c),Clay Pigeon Crew . . . 3.50
213 JKu(c),Back Door To War . . . 3.50
214 JKu(c),The Tanker Who Couldn't Die 3.50
215 JKu(c),Last Stand For Losers 3.50
216 JKu(c),Ghost Squadron 3.50
217 JKu(c), The Pigeon Spies . . . 3.50
218 JKu(c), 48 Hours to Die 3.50
219 thru 288 . . . . @3.50

GILGAMESH II

1 JSn,O:Gilgamesh 5.00
2 JSn,V:Nightshadow 4.50
3 JSn,V:Robotic Ninja 4.50
4 JSn,final issue 3.95

GOLDEN AGE
Elseworld

1 PS,F:JSA,All-Star Squadron . . 7.00
2 PS,I:Dynaman 6.00
3 PS,IR:Mr. Terrific is Ultra-Humanite 6.00
4 PS,D:Dynaman,Mr. Terrific, . . . 5.50

GREATEST BATMAN STORIES EVER TOLD

1 HC 60.00
1a SC 16.00

GREATEST JOKER STORIES EVER TOLD

1 HC 45.00
1a SC 16.00

GREATEST SUPERMAN STORIES EVER TOLD

1 HC 75.00
1a SC 15.95

GREEN ARROW
[Limited Series]

1 TVE,DG,O:Green Arrow 5.00
2 TVE,DG,A:Vertigo 3.50
3 TVE,DG,A:Vertigo 3.50
4 TVE,DG,A:Black Canary 3.50

GREEN ARROW

1 EH,DG,V:Muncie 10.00
2 EH,DG,V:Muncie 6.00
3 EH,DG,FMc,V:Fyres 4.50
4 EH,DG,FMc,V:Fryes 4.50
5 EH,DG,FMc,Gauntlet 4.50
6 EH,DG,FMc,Gauntlet 4.50
7 EB,DG,A:Black Canary 4.50
8 DG,Alaska 4.00
9 EH,DG,FMc,R:Shado 4.00
10 EH,DG,FMc,A:Shado 4.00
11 EH,DG,FMc,A:Shado 4.00
12 EH,DG,FMc,A:Shado 3.00
13 DJu,DG,FMc,Moving Target . . 3.00
14 EH,DG,FMc 3.00
15 EH,DG,FMc,Seattle And Die . . 3.00
16 EH,DG,FMc,Seattle And Die . . 3.00
17 DJu,DG,FMc,The Horse Man . 2.50
18 DJu,DG,FMc,The Horse Man . 2.50
19 EH,DG,FMc,A:Hal Jordan 2.50
20 EH,DG,FMc,A:Hal Jordan 2.50
21 DJu,DG,B:Blood of Dragon, A:Shado 2.50
22 DJu,DG,A:Shado 2.50
23 DJu,DG,A:Shado 2.50
24 DJu,DG,E:Blood of Dragon . . . 2.50
25 TVE,Witch Hunt #1 . . . . 2.25
26 Witch Hunt #2 . . . . 2.25
27 DJu,DG,FMc,R:Warlord 2.25
28 DJu,DG,FMc,A:Warlord 2.25
29 DJu,DG,FMc,Coyote Tears . . . 2.25
30 DJu,DG,FMc,Coyote Tears . . . 2.25
31 FMc,V:Drug Dealers 2.25
32 FMc,V:Drug Dealers 2.25
33 DJu,FMc,Psychology Issue . . . 2.25
34 DJu,DG,A:Fryes,Arrested 2.25
35 B:Black Arrow Saga,A:Shade . 2.25
36 Black Arrow Saga,A:Shade . . . 2.25
37 Black Arrow Saga,A:Shade . . . 2.25
38 E:Black Arrow Saga,A:Shade . . 2.25
39 DCw,Leaves Seattle 2.25
40 MGr,Spirit Quest,A: Indian Shaman 2.25
41 DCw,I.R.A. 2.25
42 DCw,I.R.A 2.25
43 DCw,I.R.A. 2.25
44 DCw,Rock'n'Runes Pt#1 . . . . . 2.25
45 Rock'n'Runes Pt#2 . . . . 2.25
46 DCw,Africa 2.25
47 DCw,V:Trappers 2.25
48 DCw,V:Trappers 2.25
49 V:Trappers 2.25
50 MGr(c),50th Anniv.,R:Seattle . . 3.00
51 Tanetti's Murder Pt#1 . . . . 2.00
52 Tanetti's Murder Pt#2 . . . . 2.00
53 The List Pt.#1,A:Fyres 2.00
54 The List Pt.#2,A:Fyres 2.00
55 Longbow Hunters tie-in 2.00
56 A:Lt. Cameron 2.00
57 And Not A Drop to Drink Pt#1 . 2.00
58 And Not A Drop to Drink Pt#2 . 2.00
59 Predator Pt1 . . . . 2.00
60 Predator Pt 2 . . . . 2.00
61 FS,F:Draft Dodgers 2.00
62 FS 2.00
63 FS,B:Hunt for Red Dragon . . . 2.00
64 FS,Hunt for Red Dragon 2.00
65 MGr(c),Hunt for Red Dragon . . 2.00
66 MGr(c),E:Hunt for Red Dragon 2.00
67 MGr(c),FS,V:Rockband Killer . 2.00
68 MGr(c),FS,BumRap 2.00
69 MGr(c),Reunion Tour #1 . . . . . 2.00
70 Reunion Tour #2 . . . . 2.00
71 Wild in the Streets #1 . . . . 2.00
72 MGr(c),Wild in the Streets#2 . . 2.00
73 MGr(c),F:Vietnam Vet 2.00
74 SAP,MGr(c),V:Sniper 2.00
75 MGr(c),A:Speedy Shado, Black Canary 3.00
76 MGr(c),R:Eddie Fyers 2.00
77 MGr(c),A:Eddie Fyers 2.00
78 MGr(c),V:CIA 2.00
79 MGr(c),V:CIA 2.00
80 MGr(c),E:MGr(s),V:CIA 2.00
81 B:CDi(s),JAp,V:Shrapnel, Nuklon 2.00
82 JAp,I:Rival 2.00
83 JAp,V:Yakuza 2.00
84 E:CDi(s),,JAp,In Las Vegas . . . 2.00
85 AIG(s),JAp,A:Deathstroke 2.00
86 DgM(s),JAp,A:Catwoman 2.00
87 JAp,V:Factory Owner 2.00
88 JAp,A:M.Manhunter,Bl.Beetle . 1.95
Ann.#1 A:Question,FablesII 3.50
Ann.#2 EH,DG,FMc,A:Question . . 3.00
Ann.#3 A:Question 2.50
Ann.#4 'The Black Alchemist' 3.25
Ann.#5 TVE,FS,Eclipso,Batman . . 3.25
Ann.#6 JBa(c),I:Hook 3.50

GREEN ARROW LONGBOW HUNTERS
August, 1987

1 MGr,N:GreenArrow,I:Shado . . 12.00
1a 2nd printing 3.00
2 MGr,'Shadow' Revealed 7.00
2a 2nd printing 3.00
3 MGr,Tracking Snow 7.00
TPB, rep #1-#3 . . . . 12.95

GREEN ARROW: THE WONDER YEARS

1 MGr,GM,B:New O:Green Arrow 2.50
2 MGr,GM,I:Brianna Stone 2.00
3 MGr,GM,A:Brianna Stone 2.00
4 MGr,GM,Conclusion 2.00

GREEN LANTERN
Autumn, 1941

1 O:Green Lantern, V:Master of Light, Arson in the Slums 14,000.00
2 V:Baldy,Tycoon's Legacy . 3,200.00
3 . . . . 2,200.00
4 Doiby and Green Lantern join the Army 1,700.00
5 V:Nazis and Black Prophet,A:General Prophet 1,200.00
6 V:Nordo & Hordes of War Hungy Henchmen,Exhile of Exiles, A:Shiloh 1,000.00
7 The Wizard of Odds 950.00
8 The Lady and Her Jewels, A:Hop Harrigan 950.00
9 V:The Whistler, The School for Vandals 850.00

Green Lantern #3 © DC Comics, Inc.

Green Lantern #10 © DC Comics, Inc.

10 V:Vandal Savage,The Man Who Wanted the World,O:Vandal Savage 850.00
11 The Distardly Designs of Doiby Dickles' Pals 750.00
12 O:The Gambler 750.00
13 A:Angela Van Enters 750.00
14 Case of the Crooked Cook . 750.00
15 V:Albert Zero, One...Two... Three...Stop Thinking 750.00
16 V:The Lizard 750.00
17 V:Kid Triangle, Reward for Green Lantern 750.00
18 V:The Dandy,The Connoisseur of crime,X-mas(c) 800.00
19 V:Harpies, Sing a Song of Disaster A:Fate 700.00
20 A:Gambler 700.00
21 V:The Woodman,The Good Humor Man 650.00
22 A:Dapper Dan Crocker 650.00
23 Doiby Dickles Movie Ajax Pictures 650.00
24 A:Mike Mattson, Once A Cop 650.00
25 The Diamond Magnet 650.00
26 The Scourge of the Sea . . . 650.00
27 V:Sky Pirate 650.00
28 The Tricks of the Sports Master 650.00
29 Meets the Challange of the Harlequin 650.00
30 I:Streak the Wonder Dog . . 650.00
31 The Terror of the Talismans 500.00
32 The Case of the Astonishing Juggler 500.00
33 Crime goes West 500.00
34 Streak meets the Princess . 500.00
35 V:The Three-in-One Criminal 500.00
36 The Mystery of the Missing Messanger 700.00
37 A:Sargon 700.00
38 Double Play,May-June, 1949 700.00

GREEN LANTERN

1 GK,O:Green Lantern 1,700.00
2 GK,I:Qward,Pieface 600.00
3 GK,V:Qward 350.00
4 GK,Secret of GL Mask 300.00
5 GK,I:Hector Hammond 300.00
6 GK,I:Tomar-Re 300.00
7 GK,I&O:Sinestro 200.00
8 GK,1st Story in 5700 A.D. . . 200.00
9 GK,A:Sinestro 200.00
10 GK,O:Green Lantern's Oath 200.00
11 GK,V:Sinestro 140.00
12 GK,Sinestro,I:Dr.Polaris . . . 140.00
13 GK,A:Flash,Sinestro 150.00
14 GK,I&O:Sonar,1st Jordan Brothers story 130.00
15 GK,Zero Hour story 135.00
16 GK,MA,I:Star Saphire, O:Abin Sur 125.00
17 GK,V:Sinestro 125.00
18 GK 125.00
19 GK,A:Sonar 125.00
20 GK,A:Flash 125.00
21 GK,O:Dr.Polaris 100.00
22 GK,A:Hector Hammond,Jordan Brothers story 100.00
23 GK,I:Tattooed Man 100.00
24 GK,O:Shark 100.00
25 GK,V:Sonar,HectorHammond 100.00
26 GK,A:Star Sapphire 100.00
27 GK 100.00
28 GK,I:Goldface 100.00
29 GK,I:Black Hand 120.00
30 GK,I:Katma Tui 100.00
31 GK,Jordan brothers story . . . 75.00
32 GK 75.00
33 GK,V:Dr. Light 75.00
34 GK,V:Hector Hammond 75.00
35 GK,I:Aerialist 75.00
36 GK 75.00
37 GK,I:Evil Star 75.00
38 GK,A:Tomar-Re 75.00
39 GK,V:Black Hand 75.00
40 GK,O:Guardians,A:Golden Age Green Lantern 400.00
41 GK,A:Star Sapphire 50.00
42 GK,A:Zatanna 50.00
43 GK,A:Major Disaster 50.00
44 GK,A:Evil Star 50.00
45 GK,I:Prince Peril,A:Golden Age Green Lantern 80.00
46 GK,V:Dr.Polaris 50.00
47 GK,5700 A.D. V:Dr.Polaris . . 50.00
48 GK,I:Goldface 50.00
49 GK,I:Dazzler 50.00
50 GK,V:Thraxon the Powerful . . 50.00
51 GK,Green Lantern's Evil Alter-ego 30.00
52 GK,A:Golden Age Green Lantern Sinestro 40.00
53 GK,CI,Jordon brothers story . 30.00
54 GK,Menace in the Iron Lung . 30.00
55 GK,Cosmic Enemy #1 . . . . . 30.00
56 GK 30.00
57 GK,V:Major Disaster 30.00
58 GK,Perils of the Powerless Green Lantern 30.00
59 GK,I:Guy Gardner(imaginary story) 175.00
60 GK,I:Lamplighter 20.00
61 GK,A:Gold.Age Gr.Lantern . . 25.00
62 Steel Small,Rob Big 20.00
63 NA(c),This is the Way the World Ends 20.00
64 MSy,We Vow Death to Green Lantern 20.00
65 MSy,Dry up and Die 20.00
66 MSy,5700 AD story 20.00
67 DD,The First Green Lantern . 20.00
68 GK,I Wonder where the Yellow Went? 20.00
69 GK,WW,If Earth Fails the Test.. It Means War 20.00
70 GK,A Funny Thing Happened on the way to Earth 20.00
71 GK,DD,MA,Jordan brothers . 15.00
72 GK,Phantom o/t SpaceOpera 15.00
73 GK,MA,A:Star Sapphire, Sinestro 15.00
74 GK,MA,A:Star Sapphire, Sinestro 15.00
75 GK,Qward 15.00
76 NA,Gr.Lantern & Gr.Arrow team-up begins 125.00
77 NA,Journey to Desolation . . . 50.00
78 NA,A:Black Canary,A Kind of Loving..A Way to Death 50.00
79 NA,DA,A:Black Canary,Ulysses Star is Still Alive 40.00
80 NA,DG,Even an Immortal can die 40.00
81 NA,DG,A:Black Canary,Death be my Destiny 27.00
82 NA,DG,A:Black Canary, V:Sinestro,(BWr 1 page) 27.00
83 NA,DG,A:BlackCanary,Gr.Lantern reveals I.D. to Carol Ferris . . 27.00
84 NA,BWr,V:Black Hand 27.00
85 NA,Speedy on Drugs Pt.1, rep.Green Lantern #1 . . . . . . 40.00
86 NA,DG,Speedy on Drugs Pt.2, ATh(rep)Golden Age G.L. . . . 40.00
87 NA,DG,I:John Stewart, 2nd Guy Gardner app. 31.00
88 all reprints. 10.00
89 NA,And Through Him Save the World 25.00
90 MGr,New Gr.Lantern rings . . . 6.00
91 MGr,V:Sinestro 5.00
92 MGr,V:Sinestro 5.00
93 MGr,TA,War Against the World Builders 4.00
94 MGr,TA,DG,Green Arrow Assassin Pt.1 . . . . 4.00
95 MGr,Gr.Arrow Assassin Pt.2 . . 4.00
96 MGr,A:Katma Tui 4.00
97 MGr,V:Mocker 4.00
98 MGr,V:Mocker 4.00
99 MGr,V:Mocker 4.00
100 MGr,AS,I:Air Wave 6.00
101 MGr,A:Green Arrow 5.50
102 AS,A:Green Arrow 4.50
103 AS,Earth-Asylum for an Alien 3.50
104 AS,A:Air Wave 5.00
105 AS,Thunder Doom 5.00
106 MGr,Panic..In High Places & Low 5.00
107 AS,Green Lantern Corp.story 5.00
108 MGr,BU:G.A.Green Lantern, V:Replikon 6.00
109 MGr,Replicon#2,GA.GL.#2 . . 5.00
110 MGr,GA.GL.#3 . . . . 5.00
111 AS,O:Green Lantern, A:G.A.Green Lantern 6.00
112 AS,O&A:G.A. Green Lantern . 7.00
113 AS,Christmas story 4.00
114 AS,I:Crumbler 4.00
115 AS,V:Crumbler 4.00

116 Guy Gardner as Gr.Lantern . 18.00
117 JSon,I:KariLimbo,V:Prof.Ojo . 4.00
118 AS,V:Prof.Ojo 4.00
119 AS,G.L.& G.A.solo storys . . . 3.50
120 DH,A:Kari,V:El Espectro 3.50
121 DH,V:El Espectro 3.50
122 DH,A:Guy Gardner,Superman 6.00
123 JSon,DG,E:Green Lantern/Green Arrow T.U.,A:G.Gardner, V:Sinestro 6.50
124 JSon,V:Sinestro 3.50
125 JSon,FMc,V:Sinestro 3.50
126 JSon,FMc,V:Shark 3.50
127 JSon,FMc,V:Goldface 3.50
128 JSon,V:Goldface 3.50
129 JSon,V:Star Sapphire 3.50
130 JSon,FMc,A:Sonar,B:Tales of the Green Lantern Corps 3.00
131 JSon,AS,V:Evil Star 3.00
132 JSon,AS,E:Tales of GL Corps B:B.U.Adam Strange 3.00
133 JSon,V:Dr.Polaris 2.50
134 JSon,V:Dr.Polaris 2.50
135 JSon,V:Dr.Polaris 2.50
136 JSon,A:Space Ranger, Adam Strange 2.50
137 JSon,CI,MA,I:Citadel,A:Space Ranger,A.Strange 2.50
138 JSon,A&O:Eclipso 4.00
139 JSon,V:Eclipso 3.00
140 JSon,I:Congressman Block Adam Strange 2.50
141 JSon,I:OmegaMen 6.00
142 JSon,A:OmegaMen 4.00
143 JSon,A:OmegaMen 4.00
144 JSon,D:Tattooed Man,Adam Strange 2.50
145 JSon,V:Goldface 2.50
146 JSon,CI,V:Goldface E:B.U.Adam Strange 2.50
147 JSon,CI,V:Goldface 2.50
148 JSon,DN,DA,V:Quardians . . . 2.50
149 JSon,A:GL.Corps 2.50
150 JSon,anniversary 3.50
151 JSon,GL.Exiled in space 2.50
152 JSon,CI,GL Exile #2 . . . . 2.50
153 JSon,CI,Gr.Lantern Exile #3 . 2.50
154 JSon,Gr.Lantern Exile #4 . . . 2.50
155 JSon,Gr.Lantern Exile #5 . . . 2.50
156 GK,Gr.Lantern Exile #6 . . . . . 2.50
157 KP,IN,Gr.Lantern Exile #7 . . . 2.50
158 KP,IN,Gr.Lantern Exile #8 . . . 2.50
159 KP,Gr.Lantern Exile #9 . . . . . 2.50
160 KP,Gr.Lantern Exile #10 . . . . 2.50
161 KP,A:Omega Men,Exile #11 . 2.50
162 KP,Gr.Lantern Exile #12 . . . . 2.50
163 KP,Gr.Lantern Exile #13 . . . . 2.50
164 KP,A:Myrwhidden,Exile #14 . 2.50
165 KP,A:John Stewart & Gr.Arrow Green Lantern Exile #15 . . . . . 2.00
166 GT,FMc,DGi,Exile #16 . . . . . 2.00
167 GT,FMc,G.L.Exile #17 . . . . . 2.00
168 GT,FMc,G.L. Exile #18 . . . . . 2.00
169 Green Lantern Exile #19 . . . 2.00
170 GT,MSy,GreenLanternCorps 2.00
171 ATh,TA,DGb,Green Lantern Exile #20 . . . . 2.00
172 DGb,E:Gr.Lant.Exile 2.00
173 DGb,I:Javelin,A:Congressman Bloch 2.00
174 DGb,V:Javelin 2.00
175 DGb,A:Flash 2.25
176 DGb,V:The Shark 2.00
177 DGb,rep. Gr.Lant #128 . . . . . 2.00
178 DGb,A:Monitor,V:Demolition Team 2.00
179 DGb,I:Predator 2.00
180 DGb,A:JLA 2.00
181 DGi,Hal Jordan quits as GL . 2.75
182 DGi,John Stewart taks over V:Major Disaster 2.50
183 DGi,V:Major Disaster 2.50
184 DGb,Rep. Gr.Lant. #59 . . . . . 3.50
185 DGi,DH,V:Eclipso 4.00
186 DGi,V:Eclipso 4.00
187 BWi,John Stewart meets Katma Tui 2.25
188 JSon,C:GrArrow,V:Sonar,John Stewart reveals I.D. to world . . 3.50
189 JSon,V:Sonar 2.00
190 JSon,A:Green Arrow/Black Canary,Guy Gardner 2.00
191 JSon,IR:Predator is Star Sapphire 2.00
192 JSon,O:Star Sapphire 2.00
193 JSon,V:Replikon, A:G.Gardner 2.50
194 JSon,Crisis,R:G.Gardner 6.00
195 JSon,Guy Gardner as Green Lantern,develops attitude . . . 13.00
196 JSon,V:Shark,Hal Jordan regains ring 4.00
197 JSon,V:Shark,Sonar, Goldface 3.50
198 JSon,D:Tomar-Re,Hal returns as Green Lantern,(double size) . . 3.00
199 JSon,V:Star Sapphire 2.00
200 JSon,final Gr.Lantern issue . . 2.50

Becomes:

GREEN LANTERN CORPS

201 JSon,I:NewGr.LantCorps,V:Star Sapphire, Sonar, Dr.Polaris . . . 1.75
202 JSon,set up headquarters . . . 1.75
203 JSon,tribute to Disney 1.75
204 JSon,Arisia reaches puberty . 1.75
205 JSon,V:Black Hand 1.75
206 JSon,V:Black Hand 1.75
207 JSon, Legneds crossover . . . 1.75
208 JSon,I:Rocket Red Brigade, Green Lanterns in Russia#1 . . 1.75
209 JSon,In Russia #2 . . . . 1.75
210 JSon,In Russia #3 . . . . 1.75
211 JSon,John Stewart proposes to Katma Tui 1.50
212 JSon,W:J.Stewart&KatmaTui . 1.50
213 Json,For Want of a Male 1.50
214 IG,5700 A.D. Story 1.50
215 IG,Salaak and Chip quit 1.50
216 IG,V:Carl 1.50
217 JSon,V:Sinestro 1.50
218 BWg,V:Sinestro 1.50
219 BWg,V:Sinestro 1.50
220 JSon,Millenium 1.50
221 JSon,Millenium 1.50
222 JSon,V:Sinestro 1.50
223 GK,V:Sinestro 1.50
224 GK,V:Sinestro 2.00
Ann.#1 GK 2.00
Ann.#2 JSa,BWg,S:AnM 2.50
Ann.#3 JBy,JL,JR 2.00
Spec.#1 A:Superman 2.00
Spec.#2 MBr,RT,V:Seeker 2.00
TPB rep.#84-87,89,Flash #217-219 . . . . 12.95
TPB rep. reprints of #1-7 . . . . 8.95

GREEN LANTERN
[2nd Regular Series]

1 PB,A:Hal Jordan,John Stuart, Guy Gardner 5.00
2 PB,A:Tattooed Man 3.00
3 PB,Jordan vs.Gardner 4.00
4 PB,Vanishing Cities 2.00
5 PB Return to OA 2.00
6 PB 3GL'sCaptive 2.00
7 PB R:Guardians 2.00
8 PB R:Guardians 2.00
9 JSon,G.Gardner Pt1 . . . . 3.00
10 JSon,G.Gardner Pt2 . . . . 3.00
11 JSon,G.Gardner Pt3 . . . . 3.00
12 JSon,G.Gardner Pt4 . . . . 3.00
13 Jordan,Gardner,Stuart(giant) . . 2.50
14 PB,Mosaic Pt.1 . . . . 2.00
15 RT,Mosaic Pt.2 . . . . 2.00
16 MBr,RT,Mosaic Pt.3 . . . . 2.00
17 MBr,RT,Mosaic Pt.4 . . . . 2.00
18 JSon,JRu,G.Gardner, A:Goldface 2.00

Green Lantern (2nd Series) #7
© DC Comics, Inc.

19 MBr,PB,JSon,A:All Four G.L.'s, O:Alan Scott,A:Doiby Dickles (D.Size-50th Ann.Iss.) 3.00
20 PB,RT,Hal Jordan G.L. Corp story begins, A:Flicker 1.50
21 PB,RT,G.L. Corp. Pt 2, V:Flicker 1.50
22 PB,RT,G.L. Corp. Pt.3, R:Star Sapphire 1.50
23 PB,RT,V:Star Sapphire, A:John Stuart 1.50
24 PB,RT,V:Star Sapphire 1.50
25 MBr,JSon,RT,Hal Vs.Guy, A:JLA 2.75
26 MBr,RT,V:Evil Star,Starlings 1.50
27 MBr,V:Evil Star,Starlings 1.50
28 MBr,V:Evil Star,Starlings 1.50
29 MBr,RT,R:Olivia Reynolds . . . 1.50
30 MBr,RT,Gorilla Warfare#1 . . . . 1.50
31 MBr,RT,Gorilla Warfare#3 . . . . 1.50
32 RT(i),A:Floro,Arisia 1.50
33 MBr,RT,Third Law#1, A;New Guardians 1.50
34 MBr,RT,Third Law#2,I:Entropy 1.50
35 MBr,RT,Third Law#3,V;Entropy 1.50
36 V:Dr.Light 1.50
37 MBg,RT,A:Guy Gardner 1.50
38 MBr,RT,A:Adam Strange 1.50
39 MBr,RT,A:Adam Strange 1.50
40 RT(i),A:Darkstar, V:Reverse Flash 1.75
41 MBr,RT,V:Predator, C:Deathstroke 1.50
42 MBr,RT,V:Predator, Deathstroke 1.50
43 RT(i),A:Itty 1.50
44 RT(i),Trinity#2,A:L.E.G.I.O.N . . 1.75
45 GeH,Trinity#5,A:L.E.G.I.O.N., Darkstars 1.75
46 MBr,A:All Supermen, V:Mongul 13.00
47 A:Green Arrow 5.00
48 KM(c),B:Emerald Twilight,I:Kyle Rayner (Last Green Lantern) . 11.00
49 KM(c),GJ(s),A:Sinestro 9.00
50 KM(c),GJ(s),D:Sinestro,Kiliwog, Guardians,I:Last Green Lantern (in Costume) 9.00
51 V:Ohm,A:Mongul 3.00
52 V:Mongul 1.75
53 A:Superman,V:Mongul 1.75

Ann.#1 Eclipso,V:Star Sapphire . . 2.75
Ann.#2 Bloodlines#7,I:Nightblade . 2.50

GREEN LANTERN CORPS QUARTERLY

1 DAb,JSon,FH,PG,MBr,F:Alan Scott G'nort 3.00
2 DAb,JSon,PG,AG,Alan Scott . . 2.75
3 DAb,RT,F:Alan Scott,G'Nort . . 2.75
4 TA,AG(i),F:H.Jordan,G'Nort . . . 2.75
5 F:Alan Scott,I:Adam 2.75
6 JBa,TC,F:Alan Scott 3.25
7 Halloween Issue 3.25
8 GeH,SHa,final issue 3.25

GREEN LANTERN: EMERALD DAWN

[1st Limited Series]

1 MBr,RT,I:Mod.Age.Gr.Lantern . . 8.00
2 MBr,RT,I:Legion (not group) . . . 6.00
3 MBr,RT,V:Legion 4.00
4 MBr,RT,A:Green Lantern Corps 3.50
5 MBr,RT,V:Legion 3.00
6 MBr,RT,V:Legion 3.00
TPB rep#1-6 . . . . 5.50

[2nd Limited Series]

1 MBr,A:Sinestro,Guy Gardner . . . 2.50
2 MBr,RT,V:Alien Aliance 1.50
3 MBr,RT,Sinestro's Home Planet 1.50
4 MBr,RT,Korugar Revolt 1.50
5 MBr,RT,A:G.Gardner 1.50
6 MBr,RT,Trial of Sinestro 1.50

GREEN LANTERN: GANTHET'S TALE

1 JBy,O:Guardians 7.00

GREEN LANTERN/ GREEN ARROW

1 NA rep. 5.00
2 NA,DG rep. 4.00
3 NA,DG rep. 4.00
4 NA,DG rep. 4.00
5 NA,DG rep. 4.00
6 NA,DG rep. 4.00
7 NA,DG rep. 4.00
TPB Roadback 8.95

GREEN LANTERN: MOSAIC

1 F:John Stewart 2.00
2 D:Ch'p 1.75
3 V:Sinestro 1.50
4 F:The Children on Oa 1.50
5 V:Hal Jordan 1.50
6 A:Kilowog 1.50
7 V:Alien Faction 1.50
8 V:Ethereal Creatures 1.50
9 Christmas issue 1.50
10 V:Guardians 1.50
11 R:Ch'p 1.50
12 V:KKK 1.50
13 V:KKK,Racism 1.50
14 A:Salaak,Ch'p 1.50
15 A:Katma Tui,Ch'p 1.50
16 LMc,A:JLA,Green Lantern 1.50
17 A:JLA 1.50
18 final issue 1.50

GREGORY III

Bookshelf Ed. 4.95
Platinum Ed. 30.00

GRIFFIN

1 I:Matt Williams as Griffin 5.50
2 V:Carson 5.25
3 A:Mary Wayne 5.25
4 A:Mary Wayne 5.25
5 Face to Face with Himself 5.25
6 Final Issue 5.25

GUNFIRE

1 B:LWn(s),StE,I:Ricochet 2.00
2 StE,V:Ricochet 2.00
3 StE,I:Purge 1.75

GUY GARDNER

1 JSon,A:JLA,JLE 2.00
2 JSon,A:Kilowog 1.50
3 JSon,V:Big,Ugly Alien 1.50
4 JSon,G.Gardner vs Ice 1.50
5 JSon,A:Hal Jordan,V:Goldface . 1.50
6 JSon,A:Hal Jordan,V:Goldface . 1.50
7 JSon,V:Goldface 1.50
8 JSon,V:Lobo 1.50
9 JSon,Boodikka 1.50
10 JSon,V:Boodikka 1.50
11 JSon,B:Year One 1.50
12 JSon,V:Batman,Flash,Green Lantern 1.50
13 JSon,Year One#3 . . . . 1.50
14 JSon,E:Year One 1.50
15 V:Bad Guy Gardner 1.50
16 B:CDi(s),MaT,V:Guy's Brother . 1.75
Becomes:

GUY GARDNER: WARRIOR

17 V:Militia 2.00
18 B:Emerald Fallout,N:Guy Gardner, V:Militia 8.00
19 A:G.A.Green Lantern,V:Militia . 4.00
20 A:JLA,Darkstars, ... 2.00
21 E:Emerald Fallout,V:H.Jordan . 2.00
22 I:Dementor 1.50

GUY GARDNER: REBORN

1 JSon,JRu,V:Goldface,C:Lobo . . 6.00
2 JSon,JRu,A:Lobo,V:Weaponers of Qward 5.50
3 JSon,JRu,A:Lobo,N:G.Gardner V:Qwardians 5.50

HACKER FILES

1 TS,Soft Wars#1,I:Jack Marshall 2.25
2 TS,Soft Wars#2 . . . . 1.95
3 TS,Soft Wars#3 . . . . 1.95
4 TS,Soft Wars#4 . . . . 1.95
5 TS,A:Oracle(Batgirl) 1.95
6 TS,A:Oracle,Green Lantern . . . 1.95
7 TS,V:Digitronix 1.95
8 TS,V:Digitronix 1.95
9 TS,V:Digitronix 1.75
10 V:Digitronix 1.95
11 TS,A:JLE 1.95
12 TS,V:Digitronix,final issue 1.95

HAMMERLOCKE

1 I:Hammerlocke 2.50
2 V:Tharn the Iron Spider 1.75
3 V:Tharn the Iron Spider 1.75
4 O:Hammerlocke 1.75
5 V:Sahara Skyhawk 1.75
6 V:Tharn the Iron Spider 1.75
7 V:Tharn 1.75
8 CSp,V:Iron Spider 1.75

HARDWARE

(Milestone)

1 DCw,I:Hardware,Edwin Alva,Reprise, Dir.Mark.Ed.,w/A puzzle piece, Skybox Card,Poster, ... 6.00
1a NewsstandEd. 2.00
1b Platinum Ed. 65.00
2 DCw,V:Repirise,I:Barraki Young 2.00
3 DCw,O:EDwin Alva, I:S.Y.S.T.E.M. 2.00
4 DCw,V:S.Y.S.T.E.M. 2.00
5 DCw,I:Deathwish 2.00
6 DCw,V:Deathwish 1.75
7 DCw,O:Deathwish 1.75
8 DCw(c),O:Hardware 1.75
9 DCw(c),I:Technique 1.75
10 DCw(c),I:Harm,Transit 1.75
11 WS(c),DCw,Shadow War, I:Iron Butterfly,Dharma 1.75
12 RB,V:Harm 1.75
13 DCw,A:Reprise 1.75
14 DCw, ... 1.75
15 DCw(c),HuR,V:Alva 1.75
16 Die-Cut(c),JBy(c),DCw, N:Hardware 4.25
16a Newsstand ED. 2.25
17 Worlds Collide#2,A:Steel 1.50

HAWK & DOVE

[1st Regular Series]

August 1968

1 SD 40.00
2 SD 25.00
3 GK 25.00
4 GK 25.00
5 GK,C:Teen Titans 28.00
6 GK 25.00

[Limited Series]

1 RLd,I:New Dove 6.00
2 RLd,V:Kestrel 5.00
3 RLd,V:Kestrel 4.50
4 RLd,V:Kestrel 4.50
5 RLd,V:Kestrel,O:New Dove . . . 4.50
TPB rep #1-5 . . . . 9.95

[2nd Regular Series]

1 A:Superman,Green Lantern Hawkman 2.00
2 V:Aztec Goddess 1.75
3 V:Aztec Goddess 1.75
4 I:The Untouchables 1.50
5 I:Sudden Death, A:1st Dove's Ghost 1.50
6 A:Barter,Secrets o/Hawk&Dove 1.25
7 A:Barter,V:Count St.Germain . . 1.25
8 V:Count St.Germain 1.25
9 A:Copperhead 1.25
10 V:Gauntlet & Andromeda 1.25
11 A:New Titans,V:M.A.C., Andromeda Gauntlet 1.25
12 A:New Titans,V:Scarab 1.50
13 1960's,I:Shellshock 1.25
14 Prelue to O:Hawk & Dove, V:Kestrel 1.25
15 O:Hawk & Dove begins 1.25
16 HawkV:Dove,V:Lord of Chaos . 1.25
17 V:Lords-Order & Chaos 1.25
18 The Creeper #1 . . . . 1.25
19 The Creeper #2 . . . . 1.25
20 KM,DG,Christmas Story 1.50
21 Dove 1.25
22 V:Sudden Death 1.25
23 A:Velv.Tiger,SuddenDeath . . . 1.25
24 A:Velv.Tiger,SuddenDeath . . . 1.25
25 Recap 1st 2 yrs.(48 pg) 2.00
26 Dove's past 1.50
27 The Hunt for Hawk 1.50
28 War of the Gods,A:Wildebeest A:Uncle Sam,final issue, double size 2.00
Ann.#1 In Hell 2.00
Ann.#2 CS,KGa,ArmageddonPt.5 . 2.00

HAWKMAN

April-May, 1964

[1st Regular Series]

1 MA,V:Chac 400.00
2 MA,V:Tralls 175.00
3 MA,V:Sky Raiders 100.00
4 MA,I&O:Zatanna 110.00
5 MA 100.00
6 MA 65.00
7 MA,V:I.Q. 65.00
8 MA 65.00
9 MA,V:Matter Master 65.00
10 MA,V:Caw 65.00
11 MA 45.00
12 MA 45.00
13 MA 45.00
14 GaF,MA,V:Caw 45.00
15 GaF,MA,V:Makkar 45.00
16 GaF,MA,V:Ruthvol 45.00

17 GaF,MA,V:Raven 45.00
18 GaF,MA,A:Adam Strange . . . 34.00
19 GaF,MA,A:Adam Strange . . . 34.00
20 GaF,MA,V:Lionmane 32.00
21 GaF,MA,V:Lionmane 32.00
22 V:Falcon 32.00
23 V:Dr.Malevolo 32.00
24 Robot Raiders from Planet Midnight 32.00
25 DD,V:Medusa,G.A.Hawkman 32.00
26 RdM,CCu,DD, ... 32.00
27 DD,JKu(c),V:Yeti 32.00

[2nd Regular Series]

1 DH,A:Shadow Thief 3.00
2 DH,V:Shadow Thief 2.00
3 DH,V:Shadow Thief 1.50
4 DH A:Zatanna 1.50
5 DH,V:Lionmane 1.50
6 DH,V:Gentleman Ghost, Lionmane 1.50
7 DH,Honor Wings 1.50
8 DH,Shadow War contd. 1.50
9 DH,Shadow War contd. 1.50
10 JBy(c),D:Hyatis Corp 1.50
11 End of Shadow War 1.25
12 Hawks on Thanagar 1.25
13 DH,Murder Case 1.25
14 DH,Mystery o/Haunted Masks . 1.25
15 DH,Murderer Revealed 1.25
16 DH,Hawkwoman lost 1.25
17 EH,DH,final issue 1.25
TPB rep.Brave & Bold apps. . . . 19.95

[3rd Regular Series]

1 B:JOs(s),JD,R:Hawkman, V:Deadline 4.50
2 JD,A:Gr.Lantern,V:Meta-Tech . 2.50
3 JD,I:Airstryke 2.25
4 JD,RM 2.00
5 JD(c),V:Count Viper 2.00
6 JD(c),A:Eradicator 2.00
7 JD(c),PuK(s),LMc,B:King of the Netherworld 2.00
8 LMc,E:King of the Netherworld . 2.00
9 BML(s), ... 2.00
10 I:Badblood 2.00
11 V:Badblood 1.75
Ann.#1 JD,I:Mongrel 3.75

Hawkworld #25 © DC Comics, Inc.

HAWKWORLD

1 TT,Hawkman, Origin retold . . . 8.00
2 TT,Katar tried for treason 6.00
3 TT,Hawkgirl's debut 6.00

[1st Regular Series]

1 GN,Byth on Earth,R:Kanjar Ro . 4.00
2 GN,Katar & Shayera in Chicago 3.00
3 GN,V:Chicago Crime 2.00
4 GN,Byth's Control Tightens . . . 2.00
5 GN,Return of Shadow Thief . . . 2.00
6 GN,Stolen Thanagarian Ship . . 2.00
7 GN,V:Byth 2.00
8 GN,Hawkman vs. Hawkwoman 2.00
9 GN,Hawkwoman in Prison 2.00
10 Shayera returns to Thanagar . 2.00
11 GN,Blackhawk,Express 2.00
12 GN,Princess Treska 2.00
13 TMd,A:Firehawk,V:Marauder . . 2.00
14 GN,Shayera's Father 2.00
15 GN,War of the Gods X-over . . 2.00
16 GN War of the Gods X-over . . 2.00
17 GN,Train Terrorists 2.00
18 GN,V:Atilla 2.00
19 GN,V:Atilla 2.00
20 V:Smir'Beau 2.00
21 GN,Thanagar Part 1, A:J.S.A. Hawkman 2.00
22 GN,Thanagar Part 2 . . . . 2.00
23 GN,Thanagar Part 3 . . . . 2.00
24 GN,Thanagar Part 4 . . . . 2.00
25 GN,Thanagar Part 5 . . . . 2.00
26 GN,V:Attilla battle armor 2.00
27 JD,B:Flight's End 2.00
28 JD,Flight's End #2 . . . . 2.00
29 TT(c),JDu,Flight's End #3 . . . . 2.00
30 TT,Flight's End #4 . . . . 2.00
31 TT,Flight's End #5 . . . . 2.00
32 TT,V:Count Viper,final issue . . 2.50
Ann.#1 A:Flash 4.50
Ann.#2 Armageddon Pt.6 . . . . . . 4.00
Ann.#2a reprint (Silver) 3.50
Ann.#3 Eclipso tie-in 3.25

HEART OF THE BEAST

GNv SeP, ... 19.95

Heckler #1 © DC Comics, Inc.

HECKLER

1 KG,MJ,I:The Heckler 1.25
2 KG,MJ,V:The Generic Man . . . 1.25
3 KG,MJ,V:Cosmic Clown 1.25
4 KG,V:Bushwacker 1.25
5 KG,Theater Date 1.25
6 KG,I:Lex Concord 1.25
7 KG,V:Cuttin'Edge 1.25

HELLBLAZER

January, 1988

1 B:JaD(s),JRy, F:John Constantine 30.00
2 JRy,I:Papa Midnight 23.00
3 JRy,I:Blathoxi 16.00
4 JRy,I:Resurrection Crusade, Gemma 14.00
5 JRy,F:Pyramid of Fear 14.00
6 JRy,V:Resurrection Crusade, I:Nergal 14.00
7 JRy,V:Resurrection Crusade, I:Richie Simpson 10.00
8 JRy,AA,Constantine receives demon blood,V:Nergal 10.00
9 JRy,A:Swamp Thing 10.00
10 JRy,V:Nergal 10.00
11 MBu,Newcastle Incident Pt.1 . . 8.00
12 JRy,D:Nergal 8.00
13 JRy,John has a Nightmare . . . 7.00
14 JRy,B:The Fear Machine, I:Mercury,Marj,Eddie 6.00
15 JRy,Shepard's Warning. 5.00
16 JRy,Rough Justice 5.00
17 MkH,I:Mr. Wester 5.00
18 JRy,R:Zed 5.00
19 JRy,I:Simon Hughes 5.00
20 JRy,F:Mr.Webster 5.00
21 JRy,I:Jallakuntilliokan 5.00
22 JRy,E:The Fear Machine. 5.00
23 I&D:Jerry O'Flynn 4.00
24 E:JaD(s),I:Sammy Morris 4.00
25 GMo(s),DvL,Early Warning . . . 4.00
26 GMo(s), ... 4.00
27 NGa(s),DMc,Hold Me 10.00
28 B:JaD(s),RnT,KeW,F:S.Morris . 5.00
29 RnT,KeW,V:Sammy Morris . . . 4.00
30 RnT,KeW,D:Sammy Morris . . . 4.00
31 E:JaD(s),SeP,Constantine's Father's Funeral 4.00
32 DiF(s),StP,I&D:Drummond . . . 3.50
33 B:JaD(s),MPn,I:Pat McDonell . 3.50
34 SeP,R:Mercury,Marj 3.50
35 SeP,Constantine's Past 3.50
36 Future Death,(preview of World Without End) 3.50
37 Journey to England's Secret Mystics 3.50
38 Constantine's Journey contd. . 3.50
39 Journey to Discovery 3.50
40 DMc,I:2nd Kid Eternity 7.00
41 B:GEn(s),WSm,MPn,Dangerous Habits 8.00
42 Dangerous Habits 7.00
43 I:Chantinelle 7.00
44 Dangerous Habits 7.00
45 Dangerous Habits 7.00
46 Dangerous Habits epilogue, I:Kit(John's girlfriend) 7.00
47 SnW(i),Pub Where I Was Born 4.00
48 Love Kills 4.00
49 X-mas issue,Lord o/t Dance . . 4.00
50 WSm,Remarkable Lives,A:Lord of Vampires (48pgs) 5.00
51 JnS,SeP,Laundromat-Possession 3.50
52 thru 55 GF(c),WSm, Royal Blood . . . . @3.50
56 GF(c),B:GEn(s),DvL, V:Danny Drake 3.00
57 GF(c),SDi,Mortal Clay#1, V:Dr. Amis 3.00
58 GF(c),SDi,Mortal Clay#2, V:Dr. Amis 3.00
59 GF(c),WSm,MkB(i),KDM,B:Guys & Dolls 3.00
60 GF(c),WSm,MkB(i),F:Tali, Chantinelle 3.00
61 GF(c),WSm,MkB(i),E:Guys & Dolls, V:First of the Fallen 3.00
62 GF(c),SDi,End of the Line, I:Gemma,AIDS storyline insert w/ Death 3.00

Vertigo

63 GF(c),SDi,C:Swamp Thing,Zatanna Phantom Stranger 2.50
64 GF(c),SDi,B:Fear & Loathing, A:Gabriel (Racism) 2.75
65 GF(c),SDi,D:Dez 2.50
66 GF(c),SDi,E:Fear and Loathing 2.50
67 GF(c),SDi,Kit leaves John 2.50
68 GF(c),SDi,F:Lord of Vampires, Darius,Mary 2.50
69 GF(c),SDi,D:Lord of Vampires . 2.25
70 GF(c),SDi,Kit in Ireland 2.25
71 GF(c),SDi,A:WWII Fighter Pilot 2.25
72 GF(c),SDi,B:Damnation's Flame,A:Papa Midnight 2.25
73 GF(c),SDi,Nightmare NY, A:JFK 2.25
74 GF(c),SDi,I:Cedella,A:JFK 2.25
75 GF(c),SDi,E:Damnation's Flame 2.25
76 GF(c),SDi,R:Brendan 2.25
77 Returns to England 2.25
78 GF(c),SDi,B:Rake at the Gates of Hell 2.25
79 GF(c),SDi,In Hell 1.95
Ann.#1 JaD(s),BT,Raven Scar . . . 7.00
Spec.#1 GF(c),GEn(s),SDi,John Constantine's teenage years . . 4.50
TPB Original Sins,rep.#1-9 . . . . 19.95
TPB Dangerous Habits, rep.#41-46 . . . . 14.95

HERCULES UNBOUND
October-November, 1975

1 thru 11 . . . . @1.00
12 August-September, 1977 . . . . 1.00

HEROES AGAINST HUNGER

1 NA,DG,JBy,CS,AA,BWr,BS, Superman,Batman 3.50

HERO HOTLINE

1 thru 6, Mini-series . . . . @1.75

HEX
September, 1985

1 MT,I:Hex 4.50
2 MT 2.00
3 MT,V:Conglomerate 2.00
4 MT,V:Conglomerate 2.00
5 MT,A:Chainsaw Killer 2.00
6 MT,V:Conglomerate 2.00
7 MT,Tries to Return to own era . 2.00
8 MT,The Future 2.50
9 MT,Future Killer Cyborgs 1.50
10 MT,V:Death Cult 1.50
11 MT,V:The Batman 2.50
12 MT,A:Batman,V:Terminators . . 2.50
13 MT,I:New Supergroup 2.50
14 MT,A:The Dogs of War 1.50
15 KG,V:Chainsaw Killer 1.50
16 KG,V:Dogs of War 1.50
17 KG,Hex/Dogs of War T.U. V:XXGG 1.50
18 KGr,Confronting the Past,final Issue, ... 1.50

HISTORY OF DC UNIVERSE
September, 1986

1 GP, From start to WWII 4.00
2 GP, From WWII to present . . . 4.00

HITCHHIKER'S GUIDE TO THE GALAXY

1 Based on the book 7.00
2 Based on the book 6.50
3 Based on the book 6.50

HOPALONG CASSIDY
February, 1954

86 GC,Ph(c):William Boyd & Topper, 'The Secret o/t Tattooed Burro' 175.00
87 GC,Ph(c),'The Tenderfoot Outlaw' 100.00
88 Ph(c),GC,'15 Robbers of Rimfire Ridge' 75.00
89 GC,Ph(c),'One-Day Boom Town' 75.00
90 GC,Ph(c),'Cowboy Clown Robberies' 50.00
91 GC,Ph(c),'The Riddle of the Roaring R Ranch' 55.00
92 GC,Ph(c),'The Sky-Riding Outlaws' 55.00
93 GC,Ph(c),'The Silver Badge of Courage' 55.00
94 GC,Ph(c),'Mystery of the Masquerading Lion' 55.00
95 GC,Ph(c),'Showdown at the Post-Hole Bank' 55.00
96 GC,Ph(c),'Knights of the Range' 55.00
97 GC,Ph(c),'The Mystery of the Three-Eyed Cowboy' 55.00
98 GC,Ph(c),'Hopalong's Unlucky Day' 55.00
99 GC,Ph(c),'Partners in Peril' . . 55.00
100 GC,Ph(c),'The Secrets of a Sheriff' 75.00
101 GC,Ph(c),'Way Out West Where The East Begins' 45.00
102 GC,Ph(c),'Secret of the Buffalo Hat' 45.00
103 GC,Ph(c),'The Train-Rustlers of Avalance Valley' 45.00
104 GC,Ph(c),'Secret of the Surrendering Outlaws' 45.00
105 GC,Ph(c),'Three Signs to Danger' 45.00
106 GC,Ph(c),'The Secret of the Stolen Signature' 45.00

Hopalong Cassidy #90
© DC Comics, Inc.

107 GC,Ph(c),'The Mystery Trail to Stagecoach Town' 45.00
108 GC,Ph(c),'The Mystery Stage From Burro Bend' 45.00
109 GC,'The Big Gun on Saddletop Mountain' 45.00
110 GC,'The Dangerous Stunts of Hopalong Cassidy' 35.00
111 GC,'Sheriff Cassidy's Mystery Clue' 35.00
112 GC,'Treasure Trail to Thunderbolt Ridge 35.00
113 GC,'The Shadow of the Toy Soldier 35.00
114 GC,'Ambush at Natural Bridge' 35.00
115 GC,'The Empty-Handed Robberies' 35.00
116 GC,'Mystery of the Vanishing Cabin' 35.00
117 GC,'School for Sheriffs' 35.00
118 GC,'The Hero of Comanche Ridge' 35.00
119 GC,'The Dream Sheriff of Twin Rivers' 35.00
120 GC,'Salute to a Star-Wearer' 35.00
121 GC,'The Secret of the Golden Caravan' 35.00
122 GC,'The Rocking Horse Bandits' 35.00
123 GK,'Mystery of the One-Dollar Bank Robbery' . . 35.00
124 GK,'Mystery of the Double-X Brand' 35.00
125 GK,'Hopalong Cassidy's Secret Brother' 35.00
126 GK,'Trail of the Telltale Clues' 35.00
127 GK,'Hopalong Cassidy's Golden Riddle' 35.00
128 GK,'The House That Hated Outlaws' 35.00
129 GK,'Hopalong Cassidy's Indian Sign' 35.00
130 GK,'The Return of the Canine Sheriff' 35.00
131 GK&GK(c),'The Amazing Sheriff of Double Creek' 35.00
132 GK,'Track of the Invisible Indians' 35.00
133 GK,'The Golden Trail to Danger' 35.00
134 GK,'Case of the Three Crack-Shots' 35.00
135 GK,May-June, 1959 . . . . . . 35.00

HOT WHEELS
March-April, 1970

1 ATh 25.00
2 thru 5 ATh . . . . @20.00
6 NA 30.00

HOUSE OF MYSTERY
December-January, 1952

1 I Fell In Love With A Monster 950.00
2 The Mark of X 400.00
3 . . . . 300.00
4 The Man With the Evil Eye . 250.00
5 The Man With the Strangler Hands! 250.00
6 The Monster in Clay! 200.00
7 Nine Lives of Alger Denham! 200.00
8 . . . . 200.00
9 . . . . 200.00
10 The Wishes of Doom 200.00
11 Deadly Game of G-H-O-S-T 175.00
12 The Devil's Chessboard . . . 175.00
13 The Theater Of A Thousand Thrills! 175.00
14 . . . . 175.00
15 The Man Who Could Change the World 175.00
16 Dead Men Tell No Tales! . . 150.00
17 . . . . 150.00
18 . . . . 150.00
19 . . . . 150.00
20 The Beast Of Bristol 150.00
21 Man Who Could See Death 150.00
22 The Phantom's Return 150.00
23 . . . . 150.00
24 Kill The Black Cat 150.00
25 The Man With Three Eyes! . 150.00
26 . . . . 100.00
27 Fate Held Four Aces! 100.00
28 The Wings Of Mr. Milo! 100.00
29 . . . . 100.00

30 . . . . 100.00
31 The Incredible Illusions! . . . 100.00
32 Pied Piper of the Sea 100.00
33 Mr. Misfortune! 100.00
34 The Hundred Year Duel . . . 100.00
35 . . . . 100.00

House of Mystery #26
© DC Comics, Inc.

36 The Treasure of Montezuma! 75.00
37 MD,The Statue That Came to Life 75.00
38 The Voyage Of No Return . . 75.00
39 . . . . 75.00
40 The Coins That Came To Life 75.00
41 The Impossible Tricks! 75.00
42 The Stranger From Out There 75.00
43 . . . . 75.00
44 The Secret Of Hill 14 . . . . . . 75.00
45 . . . . 75.00
46 The Bird of Fate 75.00
47 The Robot Named Think 75.00
48 The Man Marooned On Earth 75.00
49 The Mysterious Mr. Omen . . 75.00
50 . . . . 60.00
51 Man Who Stole Teardrops . . 60.00
52 The Man With The Golden Shoes 60.00
53 The Man Who Hated Mirrors . 60.00
54 The Woman Who Lived Twice 60.00
55 I Turned Back Time 60.00
56 The Thing In The Black Box . 60.00
57 The Untamed 60.00
58 . . . . 60.00
59 The Tomb Of Ramfis 60.00
60 The Prisoner On Canvas . . . 60.00
61 JK,Superstition Day 60.00
62 The Haunting Scarecrow . . . 40.00
63 JK,The Lady and The Creature 40.00
64 The Golden Doom 40.00
65 JK,The Magic Lantern 40.00
66 JK,Sinister Shadow 40.00
67 The Wizard Of Water 40.00
68 The Book That Bewitched . . . 40.00
69 The Miniature Disasters 40.00
70 JK,The Man With Nine Lives . 40.00
71 The Menace o/t Mole Man . . 40.00
72 JK,Dark Journey 40.00
73 Museum That Came to Life . . 42.00
74 Museum That Came To Life . 42.00
75 Assignment Unknown! 42.00
76 JK,Prisoners Of The Tiny Universe 45.00
77 The Eyes That Went Berserk 45.00
78 JK(c),The 13th Hour 45.00
79 JK(c),The Fantastic Sky Puzzle 45.00
80 Man With Countless Faces! . 40.00
81 The Man Who Made Utopia . 40.00
82 The Riddle of the Earth's Second Moon 40.00
83 The Mystery of the Martian Eye 40.00
84 JK,BK,The 100-Century Doom 45.00
85 JK(c),Earth's Strangest Salesman 40.00
86 The Baffling Bargains 40.00
87 The Human Diamond 40.00
88 Return of the Animal Man . . . 40.00
89 The Cosmic Plant! 40.00
90 The Invasion Of the Energy Creatures! 40.00
91 DD&SMo(c),The Riddle of the Alien Satellite 40.00
92 DD(c),Menace of the Golden Globule 40.00
93 NC(c),I Fought The Molten Monster 40.00
94 DD&SMo(c),The Creature In Echo Lake 40.00
95 The Wizard's Gift 40.00
96 The Amazing 70-Ton Man . . 40.00
97 The Alien Who Change History 40.00
98 DD&SMo(c),The Midnight Creature 40.00
99 The Secret of the Leopard God 40.00
100 The Beast Beneath Earth . . 40.00
101 The Magnificent Monster . . . 35.00
102 Cellmate to a Monster 35.00
103 Hail the Conquering Aliens . 35.00
104 I was the Seeing-Eye Man . 35.00
105 Case of the Creature X-14 . 35.00
106 Invaders from the Doomed Dimension 35.00
107 Captives o/t Alien Fisherman 35.00
108 RMo,Four Faces of Frank Forbes 35.00
109 ATh,JKu,Secret of the Hybrid Creatures 35.00
110 Beast Who Stalked Through Time 35.00
111 Operation Beast Slayer 35.00
112 Menace of Craven's Creatures 35.00
113 RMo,Prisoners of Beast Asteroid 35.00
114 The Movies from Nowhere . 35.00
115 Prisoner o/t Golden Mask . . 35.00
116 RMo,Return of the Barsfo Beast 35.00
117 Menace of the Fire Furies . . 25.00
118 RMo,Secret o/SuperGorillas 25.00
119 Deadly Gift from the Stars . . 25.00
120 ATh,Catman of KarynPeale . 25.00
121 RMo,Beam that Transformed Men 25.00
122 Menace fo the Alien Hero . . 25.00
123 RMo,Lure o/t Decoy Creature 25.00
124 Secret of Mr. Doom 25.00
125 Fantastic Camera Creature . 25.00
126 The Human Totem Poles . . 25.00
127 RMo,Cosmic Game o/Doom 25.00
128 NC,The Sorcerer's Snares . 25.00
129 Man in the Nuclear Trap . . . 25.00
130 The Alien Creature Hunt . . . 25.00
131 Vengeance o/t GeyserGod . 20.00
132 MMe,Beware My Invisible Master 20.00
133 MMe,Captive Queen of Beast Island 20.00
134 MMe,Secret Prisoner of Darkmore Dungeon 20.00
135 MMe,Alien Body Thief 20.00
136 MMe,Secret o/t StolenFace . 20.00
137 MMe,Tunnel to Disaster . . . 20.00
138 MMe,Creature Must Die . . . 20.00
139 MMe,Creatures of Vengeful Eye 20.00
140 I&Only app.:Astro 20.00
141 MMe,The Alien Gladiator . . 20.00
142 MMe,The Wax Demons . . . 20.00
143 J'onn J'onzz begins 200.00
144 J'onn J'onzz on Weird World of Gilgana 100.00
145 J'onn J'onzz app 75.00
146 BP,J'onn J'onzz 75.00
147 J'onn J'onzz 75.00
148 J'onn J'onzz 75.00
149 ATh,J'onn J'onzz 75.00
150 MMe,J'onn J'onzz 75.00
151 J'onn J'onzz 75.00
152 MMe,J'onn J'onzz 75.00
153 J'onn J'onzz 75.00
154 J'onn J'onzz 75.00
155 J'onn J'onzz 75.00
156 JM,I:Dial H for Hero (Giantboy Cometeer,Mole)J.J'onzz sty . 80.00
157 JM,Dial H for Hero (Human Bullet,Super Charge,Radar Sonar Man) J'onn J'onnzz sty 75.00
158 JM,Dial H for Hero (Quake MasterSquid)J'onn J'onzz sty 75.00
159 JM,Dial H for Hero (Human Starfish,Hypno Man,Mighty Moppet) J'onn J'onzz sty . . . 75.00
160 JM,Dial H for Hero (King Kandy A:Plastic Man,I:Marco Xavier (J'onn J'onzz new secret I.D.) 100.00
161 JM,Dial H for Hero (Magneto, Hornet Man,Shadow Man) . . 40.00
162 JM,Dial H for Hero (Mr.Echo, Future Man) J'onnJ'onzz sty . 40.00
163 JM,Dial H for Hero(Castor&Pollux, King Coil) J'onnJ'onzz sty . . . 40.00
164 JM,Dial H for Hero (Super Nova Zip Tide) J'onnJ'onzz sty . . . 40.00
165 JM,Dial H for Hero (Whoozis, Whatsis,Howzis) J'onn J'onzz story 40.00
166 JM,Dial H for Hero (Yankee Doodle Kid,Chief Mighty Arrow) J'onn J'onzz sty 40.00
167 JM,Dial H for Hero (Balloon Boy, Muscle Man,Radar Sonar Man) J'onn J'onzz sty 40.00
168 JM,Dial H for Hero (Thunderbolt, Mole,Cometeer,Hoopster) J'onn J'onzz sty 40.00
169 JM,I:Gem Girl in Dial H for Hero,J'onnJ'onzz sty 40.00
170 JM,Dial H for Hero (Baron BuzzSaw,Don Juan,Sphinx Man) J'onn J'onzz sty 40.00
171 JM,Dial H for Hero (King Viking Whirl-I-Gig) J'onnJ'onzz sty . . 40.00
172 JM,Dial H for Hero 40.00
173 E:Dial H for Hero,F:J'onn Jonzz 40.00
174 New direction,SA pg.13 . . . 12.00
175 I:Cain 12.00
176 SA,Cain's Game Room 12.00
177 Curse of the Car 12.00
178 NA,The Game 15.00
179 BWr,NA,JO,Widow'sWalk . . 45.00
180 GK,WW,BWr,SA,Room 13 . 12.00
181 BWr,The Siren of Satan . . . 12.00
182 ATh,The Devil's Doorway . . 12.00
183 BWr,WW(i),DeadCanKill . . . 14.00
184 ATh,GK,WW,Eye o/Basilisk . 12.00
185 AW,The Beautiful Beast . . . 14.00
186 BWr,NA,Nightmare 14.00
187 ATh,Mask of the Red Fox . . . 7.00
188 TD,BWr,House of Madness . 12.00
189 WW(i),Eyes of the Cat 6.00
190 ATh,Fright 9.00
191 BWr,TD,Christmas Story,. . . . 7.50
192 JAp,GM,DH,Garnener of Eden 5.00
193 BWr 11.00
194 ATh,NR,RH(rep),JK(rep)

Born Loser 8.00
195 NR,BWr,ThingsOld..Things Forgotten 12.00
196 GM,GK,ATh(rep)A Girl & Her Dog 4.00
197 DD,NR,House of Horrors . . . 4.00
198 MSy,NC,Day of the Demon . . 4.00
199 WW,RB,Sno'Fun 5.00
200 MK,TD,The Beast's Revenge 4.00
201 JAp,The Demon Within 4.00
202 MSy,GC(rep),SA,The Poster Plague,John Prentice? 4.00
203 NR,Tower of Prey 4.00
204 BWr,AN,All in the Family 9.00
205 The Coffin Creature 4.00
206 MSy,TP,The Burning 4.00
207 JSn,The Spell 9.00
208 Creator of Evil 4.00
209 AA,JAp,Tomorrow I Hang . . . 8.00
210 The Immortal 4.00
211 NR,Deliver Us From Evil 7.50
212 MA,AN,Ever After 4.00
213 AN,Back from the Realm of the Damned 7.50
214 NR,The Shaggy Dog 7.50
215 The Man Who Wanted Power over Women 4.00
216 TD,Look into My Eyes & Kill . 4.00
217 NR,AA,Swamp God 7.50
218 FT,An Ice Place to Visit 4.00
219 AA,NR,Pledge to Satan 4.00
220 AA,AN,They Hunt Butterflies Don't They? 4.00

House of Mystery #221

© DC Comics, Inc.

221 FT,BWr,MK,He Who Laughs Last 8.00
222 AA,Night of the Teddy Bear . 4.00
223 Demon From the Deep 4.00
224 FR,AA,SheerFear,B:100pg . 11.00
225 AA,FT,AN,See No Evil 5.00
226 AA,FR,NR,SA,Monster in House Tour of House of Mystery 7.50
227 NR,AA,The Carriage Man . . . 5.00
228 FR,NA(i),The Rebel 6.00
229 NR,Nightmare Castle, last 100 page 6.00
230 Experiment In Fear 4.00
231 Cold,Cold Heart 6.00
232 Last Tango in Hell 4.00
233 FR,Cake! 4.00
234 AM,Lafferty's Luck 4.00
235 NR,Wings of Black Death . . . 4.00
236 SD,NA(i)Death Played a Sideshow 7.50
237 FT,Night of the Chameleon . . 4.00
238 . . . . 4.00
239 Day of the Witch 4.00
240 The Murderer 4.00
241 FR,NR,DeathPulls theStrings 4.00
242 FR,The Balloon Vendor 4.00
243 Brother Bear 4.00
244 FT,Kronos..Zagros-Eborak . . 4.00
245 AN,Check the J.C.Demon Catalogue Under...Death 4.00
246 DeathVault of Eskimo Kings . 4.00
247 SD,Death Rides the Waves . . 4.00
248 NightJamieGaveUp theGhost 4.00
249 Hit Parade of Death 4.00
250 AN,Voyage to Hell 4.00
251 WW,AA,theCollector,68 pgs . 5.00
252 DP,RT,AA,FR,AN,ManKillers . 5.00
253 TD,AN,GK,KJ,Beware the Demon Child 3.50
254 SD,AN,MR,TheDevil's Place . 4.00
255 RE,GM,SometimesLeopards . 7.50
256 DAy,AN,Museum of Murders . 7.50
257 RE,MGo,TD(i),MBr,Xmas iss. 3.00
258 SD,RB,BMc,DG(i),The Demon and His Boy 3.00
259 RE,RT,MGo,DN,BL,'Hair Today, Gone Tomorrow,last giant 3.50
260 Go to Hades 3.00
261 The Husker 3.00
262 FreedFrom Infernos of Hell . . 3.00
263 JCr,Is There Vengeance After Death? 3.00
264 Halloween Issue 3.00
265 The Perfect Host 3.00
266 The Demon Blade 3.00
267 A Strange Way to Die 3.00
269 Blood on the Grooves 3.00
270 JSh,JRu,JBi,Black Moss 3.00
271 TS,HellHound of Brackenmoor 3.00
272 DN,DA,theSorcerer's Castle . 3.00
273 The Rites of Inheritance 3.00
274 MR,JBi,Hell Park 3.00
275 JCr,'Final Installment' 3.00
276 SD,MN,'Epode' 3.00
277 HC,AMi,'Limited Engagement' 3.00
278 'TV or Not TV' 3.00
279 AS,Trial by Fury 3.00
280 VMK,DAy,Hungry Jaws of Death 3.00
281 Now Dying in this Corner . . . 3.00
282 JSw,DG,Superman/Radio Shack ins 3.00
283 RT,AN'Kill Me Gently' 3.00
284 KG,King and the Dragon 3.00
285 Cold Storage 3.00
286 Long Arm of the Law 3.00
287 NR,AS,BL,Legend o/t Lost . . 3.00
288 DSp,Piper at Gates of Hell . . 3.00
289 Brother Bobby's Home for Wayward Girls & Boys 3.00
290 TS,I:I..Vampire 3.00
291 TS,DAy,I..Vampire #2 . . . . . . 3.00
292 TS,MS,TD,RE,DSp,Wendigo . 3.00
293 GT,TS,A:I..Vampire #3 . . . . . 3.00
294 CI,TY,GT,TD,The Darkness . 3.00
295 TS,TVE,JCr,I..Vampire #4 . . . 3.00
296 CI,BH,Night Women 3.00
297 TS,DCw,TD,I..Vampire #5 . . . 3.00
298 TS,'Stalker on a Starless Night' 3.00
299 TS,DSp,I..Vampire #6 . . . . . . 3.00
300 GK,DA,JSon,JCr,DSp,Anniv. . 3.00
301 JDu,TVE,KG,TY '...Virginia' . . 3.00
302 TS,NR,DSp,I..Vampire #7 . . . 3.00
303 TS,DSp,I..Vampire #8 . . . . . . 3.00
304 EC,RE,I..Vampire #9 . . . . . . 3.00
305 TVE,EC,I..Vampire #10 . . . . . 3.00
306 TS,TD,I..Vampire #11, A:Jack the Ripper 3.00
307 TS,I..Vampire #12 . . . . 3.00
308 TS,MT,NR,I..Vampire #13 . . . 3.00
309 TS,I..Vampire #14 . . . . 3.00
310 TS(i),I..Vampire #15 . . . . 3.00
311 I..Vampire #16 . . . . 3.00
312 TS(i),I..Vampire #17 . . . . 3.00
313 TS(i),CI,I..Vampire #18 . . . . . 3.00
314 TS,I..Vampire #19 . . . . 3.00
315 TS(i),TY,I..Vampire #20 . . . . 3.00
316 TS(i),GT,TVE,I..Vampire #21 . 3.00
317 TS(i),I..Vampire #22 . . . . 3.00
318 TS(i),I..Vampire #23 . . . . 3.00
319 TS,JOy,I..Vampire conc. 3.00
320 GM,Project: Inferior 3.00
321 final issue 3.00

HOUSE OF SECRETS

November-December, 1956

1 MD,JM,The Hand of Doom . 600.00
2 JPr,RMo,NC,Mask of Fear . . 300.00
3 JM,JK,MMe,The Three Prophecies 225.00
4 JM,JK,MMe,Master of Unknown 150.00
5 MMe,The Man Who Hated Fear 100.00
6 NC,MMe,Experiment 1000 . . 100.00
7 RMo,Island o/t Enchantress . 100.00
8 JK,RMo,The Electrified Man 100.00
9 JM,JSt,The Jigsaw Creatures 90.00
10 JSt,NC,I was a Prisoner of the Sea 90.00

House of Secrets #20

© DC Comics, Inc.

11 KJ(c),NC,The Man who couldn't stop growing 90.00
12 JK,The Hole in the Sky 100.00
13 The Face in the Mist 75.00
14 MMe,The Man who Stole Air . 75.00
15 The Creature in the Camera . 75.00
16 NC,We matched wits with a Gorilla genius 60.00
17 DW,Lady in the Moon 60.00
18 MMe,The Fantastic Typewriter 60.00
19 MMe,NC,Lair of the Dragonfly 60.00
20 Incredible FireballCreatures . 60.00
21 Girl from 50,000 Fathoms . . . 60.00
22 MMe,Thing from Beyond 60.00
23 MMe,I&O:Mark Merlin 75.00
24 NC,Mark Merlin story 40.00
25 MMe,Mark Merlin story 40.00
26 NC,MMe, Mark Merlin story . 40.00
27 MMe,Mark Merlin 40.00

28 MME,Mark Merlin 40.00
29 NC,MMe,Mark Merlin 40.00
30 JKu,MMe,Mark Merlin 40.00
31 DD,MMe,RH,Mark Merlin . . . 35.00
32 MMe,Mark Merlin 35.00
33 MMe,Mark Merlin 35.00
34 MMe,Mark Merlin 35.00
35 MMe,Mark Merlin 35.00
36 MMe,Mark Merlin 35.00
37 MMe,Mark Merlin 35.00
38 MMe,Mark Merlin 35.00
39 JKu,MMe,Mark Merlin 35.00
40 NC,MMe,Mark Merlin 35.00
41 MMe,Mark Merlin 35.00
42 MMe,Mark Merlin 35.00
43 RMo,MMe,CI,Mark Merlin . . . 35.00
44 MMe,Mark Merlin 35.00
45 MMe,Mark Merlin 35.00
46 MMe,Mark Merlin 35.00
47 MMe,Mark Merlin 35.00
48 ATh,MMe,Mark Merlin 40.00
49 MMe,Mark Merlin 35.00
50 MMe,Mark Merlin 40.00
51 MMe,Mark Merlin 30.00
52 MMe,Mark Merlin 30.00
53 CI,Mark Merlin 30.00
54 RMo,MMe,Mark Merlin 30.00
55 MMe,Mark Merlin 30.00
56 MMe,Mark Merlin 30.00
57 MMe,Mark Merlin 30.00
58 MMe,O:Mark Merlin 30.00
59 MMe,Mark Merlin 30.00
60 MMe,Mark Merlin 30.00
61 I:Eclipso,A:Mark Merlin 150.00
62 MMe,Eclipso,Mark Merlin . . . 75.00
63 GC,ATh,Eclipso,Mark Merlin . 50.00
64 MMe,ATh,M Merlin,Eclipso . . 50.00
65 MMe,ATh,M Merlin,Eclipso . . 50.00
66 MMe,ATh,M Merlin,Eclipso . . 75.00
67 MMe,ATh,M Merlin,Eclipso . . 35.00
68 MMe,Mark Merlin,Eclipso . . . 35.00
69 MMe,Mark Merlin,Eclipso . . . 35.00
70 MMe,Mark Merlin,Eclipso . . . 35.00
71 MMe,Mark Merlin,Eclipso . . . 35.00
72 MMe,Mark Merlin,Eclipso . . . 35.00
73 MMe,D:Mark Merlin,I:Prince Ra-Man; Eclipso 35.00
74 MMe,Prince Ra-Man,Eclipso . 35.00
75 MMe,Prince Ra-Man,Eclipso . 35.00
76 MMe,Prince Ra-Man,Eclipso . 35.00
77 MMe,Prince Ra-Man,Eclipso . 35.00
78 MMe,Prince Ra-Man,Eclipso . 35.00
79 MMe,Prince Ra-Man,Eclipso . 35.00
80 MMe,Prince Ra-Man,Eclipso . 35.00
81 I:Abel, new mystery format Don't Move It 10.00
82 DD,NA,One & only, fully guaranteed super-permanent 100% . . 8.00
83 ATh,The Stuff that Dreams are Made of 8.00
84 DD,If I had but world enough and time 8.00
85 DH,GK,NA,Second Chance . . . 8.00
86 GT,GM,Strain 8.00
87 DD,DG,RA,MK,The Coming of Ghaglan 8.00
88 DD,The Morning Ghost 8.00
89 GM,DH,Where Dead MenWalk 8.00
90 GT,RB,NA,GM,The Symbionts 10.00
91 WW,MA,The Eagle's Talon . . . 8.00
92 BWr,TD(i),I:Swamp Thing (Alex Olson) 400.00
93 JAp,TD,ATh(rep.)Lonely in Death 6.50
94 TD,ATh(rep.)Hyde.and go Seek 6.50
95 DH,NR,The Bride of Death . . . 4.00
96 DD,JAb,WW, the Monster 8.00
97 JAp,Divide and Murder 4.00
98 MK,ATh(rep),Born Losers 4.50
99 NR,TD(i),Beyond His Imagination 4.00
100 TP,TD,AA,Rest in Peace 4.00
101 AN,Small Invasion 3.00
102 NR,A Lonely Monstrosity 3.00

House of Secrets #43
© DC Comics, Inc.

103 AN,Village on Edge o/Forever 5.00
104 NR,AA,GT,Ghosts Don't Bother Me...But... . . . . 3.00
105 JAp,AA,An Axe to Grind 3.00
106 AN,AA,This Will Kill You 5.00
107 AA,The Night of the Nebbish . 5.00
108 A New Kid on the Block 3.00
109 AA,AN...And in Death, there is no Escape 3.00
110 Safes Have Secrets, Too . . . 2.50
111 TD,Hair-I-Kari 2.50
112 Case of the Demon Spawn . . 2.50
113 MSy,NC,NR,Spawns of Satan 2.50
114 FBe,Night Game 2.50
115 AA,AN,Nobody Hurts My Brother 2.50
116 NR,Like Father,Like Son 2.50
117 AA,AN,Revenge for the Deadly Dummy 2.50
118 GE,Very Last Picture Show . . 2.50
119 A Carnival of Dwarves 2.50
120 TD,AA,The Lion's Share 2.50
121 Ms.Vampire Killer 2.50
122 AA,Requiem for Igor 2.50
123 ATh,A Connecticut Ice Cream Man in King Arthur's Court . . . 3.00
124 Last of the Frankensteins . . . 2.50
125 AA,FR,Instant Re-Kill 2.50
126 AN,On Borrowed Time 2.50
127 MSy,A Test of Innocence . . . 2.50
128 AN,Freak Out! 2.50
129 Almost Human 2.50
130 All Dolled Up! 2.50
131 AN,Point of No Return 2.50
132 Killer Instinct 2.50
133 Portraits of Death 2.50
134 NR,Inheritance of Blood 2.50
135 The Vegitable Garden 3.50
136 Last Voyage of Lady Luck . . . 2.00
137 The Harder They Fall 2.00
138 Where Dreams are Born 3.50
139 SD,NR,A Real Crazy Kid . . . 2.00
140 NR,O:Patchwork Man 2.50
141 You Can't Beat the Devil 3.00
142 Playmate 2.00
143 The Evil Side 2.00
144 The Vampire of Broadway . . . 2.25
145 Operation wasSuccessful,But 2.00
146 Snake's Alive 2.00
147 AN,The See-Through Thief . . 2.00
148 SD,Sorcerer's Apprentice . . . 2.00
149 The Evil One 2.00
150 A:PhantomStranger & Dr.13 . 2.25
151 MGo,Nightmare 2.50
152 Sister Witch 2.00
153 VM,AN,Don't Look Now 2.00
154 JL,Last issue 2.00

HUMAN TARGET SPECIAL

1 DG(i),Prequel to T.V. Series . . 2.00

HUNTRESS, THE

1 JSon/DG 2.00
2 JSon,Search for Family's Murderer 2.00
3 JSon,A:La Bruja 1.50
4 JSon,Little Italy/Chinatown Gangs 1.50
5 JSon,V:Doctor Mandragora . . . 1.50
6 JSon,Huntress'secrets revealed 1.50
7 JSon,V:Serial Killer 1.50
8 JSon,V:Serial Killer 1.50
9 JSon,V:Serial Killer 1.50
10 JSon,Nuclear Terrorists in NY . 1.50
11 JSon,V:Wyvern,Nuclear Terrorists contd. 1.50
12 JSon,V:Nuclear Terrorists cont 1.50
13 JSon,Violence in NY 1.50
14 JSon,Violence contd.,New Mob boss 1.50
15 JSon,I:Waterfront Warrior 1.50
16 JSon,Secret of Waterfront Warrior revealed 1.50
17 JSon,Batman+Huntress#1 . . . 1.25
18 JSon,Batman+Huntress#2 . . . 1.25
19 JSon,Batman+Huntress#3,final issue 1.25

HUNTRESS
[Limited Series]

1 CDi(s),MN,V:Redzone 1.75
2 MN,V:Redzone 1.50

ICON
Milestone

1 Direct Market Ed.,MBr,MG,I:Icon, Rocket,S.H.R.E.D.,w/poster, card,C puzzle piece 3.25
1a Newsstand Ed. 2.00
2 MBr,MG,I:Payback 1.75
3 MBr,MG,V:Payback 1.75
4 MBr,MG,Teen Pregnancy Issue 1.75
5 MBr,MG,V:Blood Syndicate 1.75
6 MBr,MG,V:Blood Syndicate 1.75
7 MBr,MG, ... 1.75
8 MBr,MG,O:Icon 1.75
9 WS(c),MBr,MG,Shadow War, I:Donner,Blitzen, ... 1.75
10 MBr,MG,V:Holocaust 1.75
11 MBr,Hero Worship 1.75
12 Sanctimony 1.75
13 MBr,Rocket & Static T.U. 1.75
14 JBy(c), ... 1.75
15 Worlds Collide#4,A:Superboy . 1.75

IMMORTAL DR. FATE

1 WS,KG,rep. 1.75
2 KG,rep. 1.25
3 KG,rep. 1.25

IMPACT WINTER SPECIAL
Impact

1 CI/MR/TL,A:All Impact Heros, President Kidnapped 2.50

INFERIOR FIVE
March-April, 1967

1 MSy 40.00

2 MSy,A:Plastic Man 20.00
3 . . . . 14.00
4 . . . . 14.00
5 . . . . 14.00
6 thru 9 . . . . @10.00
10 A:Superman 10.00
11 JO 12.00
12 JO 12.00

Infinity, Inc. #4 © DC Comics, Inc.

INFINITY, INC.
March, 1984

1 JOy,O:Infinity Inc. 4.00
2 JOy,End of Origin 3.00
3 JOy,O:Jade 2.50
4 JOy,V:JSA 2.50
5 JOy,V:JSA 2.50
6 JOy,V:JSA 2.50
7 JOy,V:JSA 2.50
8 JOy,V:Ultra Humanite 2.50
9 JOy,V:Ultra Humanite 2.50
10 JOy,V:Ultra Humanite 2.00
11 DN,GT,O:Infinity Inc. 2.00
12 Infinity Unmasks,I:Yolanda Montez (New Wildcat) 2.00
13 DN,V:Rose & Thorn 2.00
14 1st TM DC art,V:Chroma 4.00
15 TM,V:Chroma 3.00
16 TM,I:Helix (Mr. Bones) 3.00
17 TM,V:Helix 3.00
18 TM,Crisis 3.00
19 TM,JSA,JLA x-over, I:Mekanique 3.00
20 TM,Crisis 3.00
21 TM,Crisis,I:HourmanII, Dr.Midnight 3.00
22 TM,Crisis 3.00
23 TM,Crisis 3.00
24 TM,Crisis 3.00
25 TM,Crisis,JSA 3.00
26 TM,V:Carcharo 3.00
27 TM,V:Carcharo 3.00
28 TM,V:Carcharo 3.00
29 TM,V:Helix 3.00
30 TM,Mourning of JSA 3.00
31 TM,V:Psycho Pirate 3.00
32 TM,V:Psycho Pirate 3.00
33 TM,O:Obsidian 3.00
34 TM,A: Global Guardians 3.00
35 TM,V:Infinitors 3.00
36 TM,V:Injustice Unl. 3.00
37 TM,TD,O:Northwind 3.00
38 Helix on Trial 1.75

Infinity, Inc. #15 © DC Comics, Inc.

39 O:Solomon Grundy 1.75
40 V:Thunderbolt 1.75
41 Jonni Thunder 1.75
42 TD,V:Hastor,L:Fury 1.75
43 TD,V:Hastor,Silver Scarab . . . 1.75
44 TD,D:Silver Scarab 1.75
45 MGu,A:New Teen Titans, V:Ultra-Humanite 1.75
46 TD,Millenium,V:Floronic Man . . 1.75
47 TD,Millenium,V:Harlequin 1.75
48 TD,O:Nuklon 1.75
49 Silver Scarab becomes Sandman 2.00
50 TD,V:The Wizard,O:Sandman . 3.00
51 W:Fury & Sandman,D:Skyman 1.75
52 V:Helix 1.75
53 V:Justice Unlimited,last issue . 1.75
Ann.#1 TM,V:Thorn 4.00
Ann.#2 V:Degaton,x-over Young All-Stars Annual #1 . . . . 2.00
Spec.#1 TD,A:Outsiders,V:Psycho Pirate 1.50

INVASION!

1 TM,I:Vril Dox,Dominators (20th century) 4.50
2 TM,KG,DG,I:L.E.G.I.O.N. 4.00
3 BS,DG,I:Blasters 3.50
Daily Planet-Invasion! 16p 2.00

IRONWOLF

1 HC,rep. 2.00

IRONWOLF: FIRES OF THE REVOLUTION

Hardcov.GN MMi,CR,R:Ironwolf . 29.95

ISIS
October-November, 1976

1 RE/WW 5.00
2 MN 1.00
3 thru 6 . . . . @1.00
7 O:Isis 1.00
8 December-January, 1977-78 . . 1.00

IT'S GAMETIME
September-October, 1955

1 . . . . 400.00
2 . . . . 350.00
3 . . . . 350.00
4 March-April, 1956 . . . . 350.00

JACKIE GLEASON AND THE HONEYMOONERS
June-July, 1956

1 Based on TV show 450.00
2 . . . . 350.00
3 . . . . 300.00
4 . . . . 300.00
5 . . . . 300.00
6 . . . . 300.00
7 . . . . 300.00
8 . . . . 300.00
9 . . . . 300.00
10 . . . . 300.00
11 . . . . 300.00
12 April-May, 1958 . . . . 350.00

JAGUAR
Impact

1 I&O:Jaguar I: Timon De Guzman, Maxx 13,Prof.Ruiz, Luiza Timmerman 1.00
2 Development of Powers 1.00
3 A:Maxx-13 . . . . 1.00
4 A:Black Hood 1.00
5 V:Void,The Living Black Hole . . 1.00
6 'The Doomster,'A:Maxx-13 . . . . 1.00
7 Jaguar Secret Discovered, V:Void 1.00
8 V:Aryan League 1.00
9 I:Moonlighter(w/trading cards) . 1.00
10 V:Invisible Terror 1.25
11 Defending Comedienne 1.25
12 V:The Bodyguard 1.25
13 V:Purge 1.25
14 'Frightmare in Rio',last iss. . . . 1.25
Ann.#1 Earthquest,w/trading card . 2.50

JEMM, SON OF SATURN
September, 1984

1 GC/KJ mini-series 1.50
2 GC 1.00
3 GC,Origin 1.00
4 A:Superman 1.00
5 thru 12 GC, Aug. 1985 . . . . @1.00

JIMMY WAKELY
September-October, 1949

1 Ph(c),ATh,The Cowboy Swordsman 450.00
2 Ph(c),ATh,The Prize Pony . . 275.00
3 Ph(c),ATh,The Return of Tulsa Tom 275.00
4 Ph(c),ATh,FF,HK,Where's There'sSmokeThere'sGunfire 300.00
5 ATh,The Return of the Conquistadores 225.00
6 ATh,Two Lives of Jimmy Wakely 225.00
7 The Secret of Hairpin Canyon 225.00
8 ATh,The Lost City of Blue Valley 225.00
9 ATh,The Return of the Western Firebrands 200.00
10 ATh,Secret of Lantikin's Light 200.00
11 ATh,Trail o/a Thousand Hoofs200.00
12 ATh,JKU,The King of Sierra Valley 200.00
13 ATh,The Raiders of Treasure Mountain 200.00
14 ATh(c),JKu,The Badmen of Roaring Flame Valley . . . 200.00
15 GK(c),Tommyguns on the Range 200.00
16 GK(c),The Bad Luck Boots . 175.00
17 GK(c),Terror atThunderBasin 175.00
18 July-August, 1952 . . . . 200.00

JOHNNY THUNDER
February-March, 1973

1 ATh 5.00
2 GK,MD 4.00
3 ATh,GK,MD,July-August, 1973 4.00

 All comics prices listed are for *Near Mint* condition.

JOKER

1 IN,DG,A:TwoFace 23.00
2 IN,JL WillieTheWeeper 13.00
3 JL,A:Creeper 12.00
4 JL,A:GreenArrow 10.00
5 10.00
6 V:Sherlock Holmes 10.00
7 IN,A:Luthor 10.00
8 10.00
9 A:Catwoman 12.00
Greatest Joker Stories Ever Told:
1 HC 45.00
1a SC 16.00

JONAH HEX

March-April, 1977

1 'Vengeance For A Fallen Gladiator' 45.00
2 'The Lair of the Parrot' 20.00
3 'The Fugitive' 15.00
4 'The Day of Chameleon' 15.00
5 'Welcome to Paradise' 15.00
6 'The Lawman' 11.00
7 'Son of the Apache' 11.00
8 O:Jonah Hex 10.00
9 BWr(c) 10.00
10 GM(c),'Violence at Vera Cruz' 10.00
11 'The Holdout' 8.00
12 JS(c) 8.00
13 'The Railroad Blaster' 8.00
14 'The Sin Killer' 8.00
15 'Saw Dust and Slow Death' 8.00
16 'The Wyandott Verdict!' 6.00
17 6.00
18 6.00
19 'The Duke of Zarkania!' 6.00
20 'Phantom Stage to William Bend' 6.00
21 'The Buryin'!' 6.00
22 'Requiem For A Pack Rat' 6.00
23 'The Massacre of the Celestials!' 6.00
24 'Minister of the Lord' 6.00
25 'The Widow Maker' 6.00
26 'Death Race to Cholera Bend!' 5.00
27 'The Wooden Six Gun!' 5.00
28 'Night of the Savage' 5.00
29 'The Innocent' 5.00
30 O:Jonah Hex 7.50
31 A:Arbee Stoneham 5.00
32 A:Arbee Stoneham 5.00
33 'The Crusador' 5.00
34 'Christmas in an Outlaw Town' 5.00
35 'The Fort Charlotte Brigade' 5.00
36 'Return to Fort Charlotte' 5.00
37 DAy,A:Stonewall Jackson 5.00
38 5.00
39 'The Vow of a Samurai!' 5.00
40 DAy 5.00
41 DAy,'Two for the Hangman!' 5.00
42 'Wanted for Murder' 5.00
43 JKu(c) 5.00
44 JKu(c),DAy 5.00
45 DAy,Jonah gets married 5.00
46 JKu(c),DAy 5.00
47 DAy,'Doom Rides the Sundown Town' 5.00
48 DAy,A:El Diablo 5.00
49 DAy 5.00
50 DAy,'The Hunter' 5.00
51 DAy,'The Comforter' 4.00
52 DAy,'Rescue!' 4.00
53 DAy 4.00
54 4.00
55 'Trail of Blood' 4.00
56 DAy,'The Asylum' 4.00
57 B:El Diablo backup story 4.00
58 DAy,'The Treasure of Catfish Pond' 4.00
59 DAy,'Night of the White Lotus' 4.00
60 DAy,'Domain of the Warlord' 4.00
61 DAy,'In the Lair of the Manchus!'4.00
62 DAy,'The Belly of the Malay Tiger!' 4.00
63 DAy 4.00
64 DAy,'The Pearl!' 4.00
65 DAy,'The Vendetta!' 4.00
66 DAy'Requiem for a Coward' 4.00
67 DAy,'Deadman's Hand!' 4.00
68 DAy,'Gunfight at Gravesboro!' 4.00
69 DAy,'The Gauntlet!' 4.00
70 DAy 4.00
71 DAy,'The Masquerades' 4.00
72 DAy,'Tarantula' 4.00
73 DAy,Jonah in a wheel chair 4.00
74 DAy,A:Railroad Bill 4.00
75 DAy,JAp,A:Railroad Bill 4.00
76 DAy,Jonah goes to Jail 3.00
77 DAy,'Over the Wall' 3.00
78 DAy,Me Ling returns 3.00
79 DAy,'Duel in the Sand' 3.00
80 A:Turnbull 3.00
81 DAy 3.00
82 DAy 3.00
83 thru 89 DAy @3.00
90 thru 92 @3.00
92 August, 1985 3.00

JONAH HEX AND OTHER WESTERN TALES

September-October, 1979

1 2.00
2 NA,ATh,SA,GK 3.00
3 January-February, 1980 1.75

JONAH HEX: TWO-GUN MOJO

Vertigo

1 B:JLd(s),TT,SG(i),R:Jonah Hex, I:Slow Go Smith 7.00
1a Platinum Ed. 75.00
2 TT,SG(i),D:Slow Go Smith,I:Doc Williams,Wild Bill Hickok 5.00
3 TT,SG(i),Jonah captured 4.50
4 TT,SG(i),O:Doc Williams 4.50
5 TT,SG(i),V::Doc Williams 4.50

JONNI THUNDER

February, 1985

1 DG,origin issue 1.00
2 DG 1.00
3 DG 1.00

JUSTICE, INC.

May-June, 1975

1 AMc,JKu(c),O:Avenger 3.00
2 JK 1.00
3 JK 1.00
4 JK,JKu(c),November-December, 1975 1.00

[Mini-Series]

1 PerfectBound 'Trust & Betrayal' 3.95
2 PerfectBound 3.95

JUSTICE LEAGUE AMERICA

(see JUSTICE LEAGUE INTERNATIONAL)

JUSTICE LEAGUE EUROPE

1 BS,A:Wonder Woman 4.50
2 BS,Search for Nazi-Killer 3.00
3 BS,A:Jack O'Lantern, Queen Bee 2.50
4 BS,V:Queen Bee 2.50
5 JRu,BS,Metamorpho's Baby, A:Sapphire Starr 2.50
6 BS,V:Injustice League 2.00
7 BS,Teasdale Imperative#2, A:JLA 2.00
8 BS,Teasdale Imperative#4, A:JLA 2.00
9 BS,ANi,A:Superman 2.00
10 BS,V:Crimson Fox 1.75
11 BS,C:DocMagnus&Metal Men 1.75
12 BS,A:Metal Men 1.75
13 BS,V:One-Eyed Cat, contd from JLA #37 1.75
14 I:VCR 1.75
15 BS,B:Extremists Vector saga, V:One-Eyed Cat,A:BlueJay 1.75
16 BS,A:Rocket Reds, Blue Jay 1.75
17 BS,JLI in Another Dimension 1.50
18 BS,Extremists Homeworld 1.50
19 BS,E:Extremist Vector Saga 1.50
20 MR,I:Beefeater,V:Kilowog 1.50
21 MR,JRu,New JLE embassy in London,A:Kilowog 1.50
22 MR,JLE's Cat stolen 1.50
23 BS,O:Crimson Fox 1.50
24 BS,Worms in London 1.50
25 BS,V:Worms 1.50
26 BS,V:Starro 1.50
27 BS,JLE V:JLE,A:JLA,V:Starro 1.50
28 BS, JLE V:JLE,A:J'onnJ'onzz, V:Starro 1.75
29 BS,Breakdowns #2,V:Global Guardians 2.00
30 Breakdowns#4,V:J.O'Lantern 1.50
31 Breakdowns #6,War of the Gods tie-in 1.50
32 Breakdowns #8,A:Chief(Doom Patrol) 1.50
33 Breakdowns #10,Lobo vs. Despero 1.50
34 Breakdowns #12,Lobo vs.Despero 1.50
35 Breakdowns #14,V:Extremists, D:Silver Sorceress 1.50
36 Breakdowns #16,All Quit 1.50
37 B:New JLE,I:Deconstructo 1.75
38 V:Deconstructo,A:Batman 1.50
39 V:Deconstructo,A:Batman 1.50
40 J:Hal Jordan,A:Metamorpho 1.50
41 A:Metamorpho,Wond.Woman 1.50
42 A:Wonder Woman,V:Echidna 1.50
43 V:Amos Fortune 1.50
44 V:Amos Fortune 1.50
45 Red Winter#1,V:Rocket Reds 1.50

Justice League Europe #42
© DC Comics, Inc.

46 Red Winter#2 1.50
47 Red Winter#3,V:Sonar 1.50
48 Red Winter#4,V:Sonar 1.50
49 Red Winter #5,V:Sonar 1.50
50 Red Winter#6,Double-sized, V:Sonar,J:Metamorpho 3.25

Ann.#1 A:Global Guardians 2.00
Ann.#2 MR,CS,ArmageddonPt.7 3.00
Ann.#3 RT(i),Eclipso tie-in 2.75
Justice League Spectacular JLE(c) New Direction 1.50

Becomes: Justice League International [2nd Series]

JUSTICE LEAGUE INTERNATIONAL [1st Series]

1 KM,TA,New Team,I:Max. Lord 11.00
2 KM,AG,A:BlueJay & Silver Sorceress 7.50
3 KM,AG,J:Booster Gold, V:Rocket Lords 6.00
3a Superman Logo 140.00
4 KM,AG,V:Royal Flush 4.00
5 KM,AG,A:The Creeper 3.00
6 KM,AG,A:The Creeper 3.00
7 KM,AG,L:Dr.Fate,Capt.Marvel, J:Rocket Red,Capt.Atom (Double size) 3.00
8 KM,AG,KG,Move to Paris Embassy, I:C.Cobert,B.U.Glob.Guardians. 2.50
9 KM,AG,KG,Millenium,Rocket Red-Traitor 2.50
10 KG,KM,AG,A:G.L.Corps, Superman,I:G'Nort 2.50
11 KM,AG,V:Construct,C:Metron 2.50
12 KG,KM,AG,O:Max Lord 2.50
13 KG,AG,A:Suicide Squad 2.50
14 SL,AG,J:Fire&Ice,L:Ron, I:Manga Kahn 2.50
15 SL,AG,V:Magna Kahn 2.00
16 KM,AG,I:Queen Bee 2.00
17 KM,AG,V:Queen Bee 2.00
18 KM,AG,MPn,A:Lobo,Guy Gardner (bonus book) 4.00
19 KM,JRu,A:Lobo vs.Guy Gardner, J:Hawkman & Hawkwoman 3.00
20 KM,JRu(i),A:Lobo,G.Gardner 2.00
21 KM,JRu(i),A:Lobo vs.Guy Gardner 2.00
22 KM,JRu,Imskian Soldiers 2.00
23 KM,JRu,I:Injustice League 2.00
24 KM,JRu,DoubleSize + Bonus Bk#13,I:JusticeLeagueEurope 3.00
25 KM(c),JRu(i),Vampire story 2.00
Ann.#1 BWg,DG,CR 2.00
Ann.#2 BWg,JRu,A:Joker 3.00
Ann.#3 KM(c),JRu,JLI Embassies 2.50
Spec.#1 Mr.Miracle 2.00
Spec.#2,The Huntress 2.95
TPB new beginning,rep #1-#7 12.95
TPB The Secret Gospel of Maxwell Lord Rep. #8-#12, Ann.#1 12.95

Becomes:

JUSTICE LEAGUE AMERICA

26 KM(c),JRu(i),Possessed Blue Beetle 2.50
27 KM(c),JRu,DG(i),'Exorcist', (c)tribute 2.00
28 KM(c),JRu(i), A:Black Hand 2.00
29 KM(c),JRu(i),V:Mega-Death 2.00
30 KM(c),BWg,JRu,J:Huntress, D:Mega-Death 2.00
31 ANi,AH,JRu,Teasdale Imperative #1,N:Fire,Ice,A:JLE 3.00
32 ANi,AH,Teasdale Imperative #3, A:JLE 3.00
33 ANi,AH,Guy Gardner vs. Kilowog 2.50
34 ANi,AH,'Club JLI,'A:Aquaman 2.50
35 ANi,JRu,AH,A:Aquaman 2.50
36 Gnort vs. Scarlet Skier 1.75
37 ANi,AH,L:Booster Gold 1.75
38 JRu,AH,R:Desparo,D:Steel 1.75
39 JRu,AH,V:Desparo,D:Mr.Miracle, Robot 1.75
40 AH,Mr.Miracle Funeral 1.75
41 MMc,MaxForce 1.75
42 MMc,J:L-Ron 1.75
43 AH,KG,The Man Who Knew Too Much #1 1.75
44 AH,Man Knew Too Much #2 1.75
45 AH,MJ,JRu,Guy & Ice's 2nd date 1.75
46 Glory Bound #1,I:Gen.Glory 1.75
47 Glory Bound #2,J:Gen.Glory 1.75
48 Glory Bound #3,V:DosUberbot 1.75
49 Glory Bound #4 1.75
50 Glory Bound #5 (double size) 2.00
51 JRu,AH,V:BlackHand, R:Booster Gold 1.75
52 TVE,Blue Beetle Vs. Guy Gardner A:Batman 1.75
53 Breakdowns #1, A:JLE 2.00
54 Breakdowns #3, A:JLE 2.00
55 Breakdowns #5,V:Global Guardians 2.00
56 Breakdowns #7, U.N. revokes JLA charter 1.75
57 Breakdowns #9,A:Lobo, V:Despero 1.75
58 BS,Breakdowns #11,Lobo Vs.Despero 1.75
59 BS,Breakdowns #13, V:Extremists 1.75
60 KM,TA,Breakdowns #15, End of J.L.A.. 1.75
61 DJu,I:Weapons Master,B:New JLA Line-up,I:Bloodwynd 3.00
62 DJu,V:Weapons Master 2.00
63 DJu,V:Starbreaker 2.00
64 DJu,V:Starbreaker 2.00
65 DJu,V:Starbreaker 2.00
66 DJu,Superman V:Guy Gardner 2.00
67 DJu,Bloodwynd mystery 2.00
68 DJu,V:Alien Land Baron 2.00
69 DJu, Doomsday Part 1-A 16.00
69a 2nd printing 2.00
70 DJu,Funeral for a Friend#1 10.00
70a 2nd printing 2.00
71 DJu,J:Agent Liberty,Black Condor, The Ray,Wonder Woman 6.00
71a Newsstand ed., 4.00
71b 2nd Printing 1.50
72 DJu,A:Green Arrow,Black Canary,Atom,B:Destiny's Hand 5.00
73 DJu,Destiny's Hand #2 4.00
74 DJu,Destiny's Hand #3 3.00
75 DJu,E:Destiny's Hand #4,Martian Manhunter as Bloodwynd 2.00
76 DJu,Blood Secrets#1, V:Weaponmaster 1.50
77 DJu,Blood Secrets#2, V:Weaponmaster 1.50
78 MC,V:The Extremists 1.50
79 MC,V:The Extremists 1.50
80 KWe,N:Booster Gold 1.50
81 KWe,A:Captain Atom 1.50
82 KWe,A:Captain Atom 1.50
83 KWe,V:Guy Gardner 1.50
84 KWe,A:Ice 1.75
85 KWe,V:Frost Giants 1.75
86 B:Cults of the Machine 1.75
87 N:Booster Gold 1.75
88 E:Cults of the Machine 1.75
89 Judgement Day#1, V:Overmaster 1.75
90 Judgement Day#4, 1.50
Ann.#4 KM(c),I:JL Antartica 3.00
Ann.#5 MR,KM,DJu,Armageddon 4.00
Ann.#5a 2nd Printing,silver 2.00
Ann.#6 DC,Eclipso 2.75
Ann.#7 I:Terrorsmith 2.75
Ann.#8 Elseworlds Story 2.95
Justice League Spectacular DJu, JLA(c) New Direction 2.00

JUSTICE LEAGUE INTERNATIONAL [2nd Regular Series]

Prev: Justice League Europe

51 Aztec Cult 1.50
52 V:Aztec Cult 1.50
53 R:Fox's Husband 1.50
54 RoR,I:Creator 1.50
55 RoR,A:Creator 1.50
56 RoR,V:Terrorists 1.50
57 RoR,V:Terrorists 1.50
58 RoR,V:Aliens 1.50
59 RoR,A:Guy Gardner 1.50
60 GJ(s),RoR, 1.75
61 GJ(s),V:Godfrey 1.75
62 GJ(s),N:Metamorpho,V:Godfrey 1.75
63 GJ(s),In Africa 1.75
64 GJ(s),V:Cadre 1.75
65 Judgement Day#3, V:Overmaster 1.75
66 Judgement Day#6, V:Overmaster 1.50
Ann.#4 Bloodlines#9,I:Lionheart 2.75
Ann.#5 3.25
Ann.#6 Elseworlds Story 2.95

JUSTICE LEAGUE INTERNATIONAL QUARTERLY

1 I:Conglomerate 5.00
2 MJ(i),R:Mr.Nebula 3.50
3 V:Extremists,C:Original JLA 3.50
4 KM(c),MR,CR,A:Injustice League. 2.95
5 KM(c),Superhero Attacks 2.95
6 EB,Elongated Man,B.U.Global Guardians,Powergirl,B.Beetle 2.95
7 EB,DH,MR.Global Guardians 2.95
8 2.95
9 DC,F:Power Girl,Booster Gold 3.50
10 F:Flash,Fire & Ice 3.50
11 F:JL Women 3.50
12 F:Conglomerate 3.50
13 V:Ultraa 3.50
14 MMi(c),PuK(s),F:Captain Atom, Blue Beetle,Nightshade, Thunderbolt 3.75
15 F:Praxis 3.50

Justice League of America #11
© DC Comics, Inc.

JUSTICE LEAGUE OF AMERICA

October-November, 1960

1 MSy,I&O:Despero 2,400.00
2 MSy,A:Merlin 600.00

3 MSy,I&O:Kanjar Ro 500.00
4 MSy,J:Green Arrow 350.00
5 MSy,I&O:Dr.Destiny 275.00
6 MSy,Prof. Fortune 200.00
7 MSy,Cosmic Fun-House . . . 200.00
8 MSy,For Sale-Justice League 200.00
9 MSy,O:JLA 350.00
10 MSy,I:Felix Faust 200.00
11 MSy,A:Felix Faust 150.00
12 MSy,I&O:Dr Light 160.00
13 MSy,A:Speedy 150.00
14 MSy,J:Atom 150.00
15 MSy,V:Untouchable Aliens . 150.00
16 MSy,I:Maestro 110.00
17 MSy,A:Tornado Tyrant 110.00
18 MSy,V:Terrane,Ocana 110.00
19 MSy,A:Dr.Destiny 110.00
20 MSy,V:Metal Being 110.00
21 MSy,R:JSA,1st S.A Hourman, Dr.Fate 250.00
22 MSy,R:JSA 225.00
23 MSy,I:Queen Bee 55.00
24 MSy,A:Adam Strange 55.00
25 MSy,I:Draad,the Conqueror . . 55.00
26 MSy,A:Despero 55.00
27 MSy,V:I,A:Amazo 55.00
28 MSy,I:Headmaster Mind, A:Robin 55.00
29 MSy,I:Crime Syndicate,A:JSA, 1st S.A. Starman 65.00
30 MSy,V:Crime Syndicate, A:JSA 65.00
31 MSy,J:Hawkman 40.00
32 MSy,I&O:Brain Storm 31.00
33 MSy,I:Endless One 28.00
34 MSy,A:Dr.Destiny,Joker 35.00
35 MSy,A:Three Demons 28.00
36 MSy,A:Brain Storm, Handicap story 28.00
37 MSy,A:JSA,x-over, 1st S.A.Mr.Terrific 75.00
38 MSy,A:JSA,Mr.Terrific 50.00
39 Giant 32.00
40 MSy,A:Shark,Penguin 28.00
41 MSy,I:Key 28.00
42 MSy,A:Metamorpho 17.00
43 MSy,I:Royal Flush Gang 17.00
44 MSy,A:Unimaginable 17.00
45 MSy,I:Shaggy Man 17.00
46 MSy,A:JSA,Blockbuster,Solomon Grundy,1st S.A.Sandman . . . 60.00
47 MSy,A:JSA,Blockbuster, Solomon Grundy 30.00
48 Giant 26.00
49 MSy,A:Felix Faust 14.00
50 MSy,A:Robin 14.00
51 MSy,A:Zatanna,Elong.Man . . 14.00
52 MSy,A:Robin,Lord of Time . . 14.00
53 MSy,A:Hawkgirl 14.00
54 MSy,A:Royal Flush Gang . . . 14.00
55 MSy,A:JSA,E-2 Robin 35.00
56 MSy,A:JSA,E-2 Robin 25.00
57 MSy,Brotherhood 14.00
58 Reprint(giant size). 14.00
59 MSy,V:Impossibles 14.00
60 MSy,A:Queen Bee,Batgirl . . . 14.00
61 MSy,A:Lex Luthor,Penguin . . 14.00
62 MSy,V:Bulleters 9.00
63 MSy,A:Key 9.00
64 DD,I:Red Tornado,A:JSA . . . 12.00
65 DD,A:JSA 12.00
66 DD,A:Demmy Gog 9.00
67 MSy,Giant reprints 9.00
68 DD,V:Choas Maker 10.00
69 DD,L:Wonder Woman 8.00
70 DD,A:Creeper 8.00
71 DD,L:J'onn J'onnz 8.00
72 DD,A:Hawkgirl 8.00
73 DD,A:JSA 10.00
74 DD,D:Larry Lance,A:JSA . . . 10.00
75 DD,J:Black Canary 9.00
76 Giant,MA,two page pin-up 7.00
77 DD,A:Joker,L:Snapper Carr . . . 8.00
78 DD,R:Vigilante 5.00
79 DD,A:Vigilante 5.00

Justice League of America #30
© DC Comics, Inc.

80 DD,A:Tomar-Re,Guardians . . . 5.00
81 DD,V:Jest-Master 5.00
82 DD,A:JSA 7.50
83 DD,A:JSA,Spectre 7.50
84 DD,Devil in Paradise 5.00
85 Giant reprint 6.00
86 DD,V:Zapper 5.00
87 DD,A:Zatanna,I:Silver Sorceress,Blue Jay 5.00
88 DD,A:Mera 5.00
89 DD,A:Harlequin Ellis, (i.e. Harlan Ellison) 5.00
90 CI(c),MA(ci),DD,V:Pale People 5.00
91 DD,A:JSA,V:Solomon Grundy . 5.00
92 DD,A:JSA,V:Solomon Grundy . 7.00
93 DD:A:JSA,(giant size) 7.00
94 DD,NA,O:Sandman,rep. Adventure #40 . . . . 23.00
95 DD,rep.More Fun Comics #67, All American Comics #25 . . . . 5.00
96 DD,I:Starbreaker 5.00
97 DD,MS,O:JLA 6.00
98 DD,A:Sargon,Gold.Age reps . . 4.00
99 DD,G.A. reps.. . . . . 4.00
100 DD,A:JSA,Metamorpho, R:7 Soldiers of Victory 8.00
101 DD,A:JSA,7 Soldiers 7.00
102 DD,DG,A:JSA,7 Soldiers D:Red Tornado 7.00
103 DD,DG,Halloween issue, A:Phantom Stranger 4.00
104 DD,DG,A:Shaggy Man, Hector Hammond 4.00
105 DD,DG,J:ElongatedMan 4.00
106 DD,DG,J:RedTornado 4.00
107 DD,DG,I:Freedom Fighters, A:JSA 7.50
108 DD,DG,A:JSA, Freedom Fighters 7.00
109 DD,DG,L:Hawkman 4.00
110 DD,DG,A:John Stewart, Phantom Stranger 4.00
111 DD,DG,I:Injustice Gang 4.00
112 DD,DG,A:Amazo 4.00
113 DD,DG,A:JSA 6.00
114 DD,DG,A:SnapperCarr 4.00
115 DD,FMc,A:J'onnJ'onnz 4.00
116 DD,FMc,I:Golden Eagle 5.00
117 DD,FMc,R:Hawkman 3.50
118 DD,FMc 3.50
119 DD,FMc,A:Hawkgirl 3.50
120 DD,FMc,A:Adam Strange . . . 3.50
121 DD,FMc,W:Adam Strange . . . 3.50
122 DD,FMc,JLA casebook story V:Dr.Light 3.50
123 DD,FMc,A:JSA 5.50
124 DD,FMc,A: JSA 5.50
125 DD,FMc,A:Two-Face 3.50
126 DD,FMc,A:Two-Face 3.50
127 DD,FMc,V:Anarchist 3.50
128 DD,FMc,J:W.Woman 3.50
129 DD,FMC,D:RedTornado 3.00
130 DD,FMc,O:JLASatellite 3.00
131 DD,FMc,V:Queen Bee,Sonar . 3.00
132 DD,FMc,A:Supergirl 3.00
133 DD,FMc,A:Supergirl 3.00
134 DD,FMc,A:Supergirl 3.00
135 DD,FMc,A:Squad.of Justice . . 3.00
136 DD,FMc,A:E-2Joker 3.50
137 DD,FMc,Superman vs. Capt. Marvel 4.00
138 NA(c),DD,FMc,A:Adam Strange 3.00
139 NA(c),DD,FMc,A:AdamStrange, Phantom Stranger,doub.size . . 3.50
140 DD,FMc,Manhunters 3.00
141 DD,FMc,Manhunters 3.00
142 DD,FMc,F:Aquaman,Atom, Elongated Man 3.00
143 DD,FMc,V:Injustice Gang . . . 3.50
144 DD,FMc,O:JLA 3.00
145 DD,FMc,A:Phant.Stranger . . . 3.00
146 J:Red Tornado,Hawkgirl 3.00
147 DD,FMc,A:Legion 3.00
148 DD,FMc,A:Legion 3.00
149 DD,FMc,A:Dr.Light 3.00
150 DD,FMc,A:Dr.Light 3.00
151 DD,FMc,A:Amos Fortune 2.50
152 DD,FMc 2.50
153 GT,FMc,I:Ultraa 2.50
154 MK(c),DD,FMc 2.50
155 DD,FMc 2.50
156 DD,FMc 2.50
157 DD,FMc,W:Atom 2.50
158 DD,FMc,A:Ultraa 2.50
159 DD,FMc,A:JSA,Jonah Hex, Enemy Ace 3.00
160 DD,FMc,A:JSA,Jonah Hex, Enemy Ace 3.00
161 DD,FMc,J:Zatanna 2.50
162 DD,FMc 2.50
163 DD,FMc,V:Mad Maestro 2.50
164 DD,FMc,V:Mad Maestro 2.50
165 DD,FMc 2.50
166 DD,FMc,V:Secret Society . . . 2.50
167 DD,FMc,V:Secret Society . . . 2.50
168 DD,FMc,V:Secret Society . . . 2.50
169 DD,FMc,A:Ultraa 2.50
170 DD,FMc,A:Ultraa 2.50
171 DD,FMc,A:JSA,D:Mr.Terrific . 2.50
172 DD,FMc,A:JSA,D:Mr.Terrific . 2.50
173 DD,FMc,A:Black Lightning . . . 2.50
174 DD,FMc,A:Black Lightning . . . 2.50
175 DD,FMc,V:Dr.Destiny 2.50
176 DD,FMc,V:Dr.Destiny 2.00
177 DD,FMc,V:Desparo 2.00
178 JSn(c),DD,FMc,V:Desparo . . 2.00
179 JSn(c),DD,FMc,J:Firestorm . . 2.50
180 JSn(c),DD,FMc,V:Satin Satan 2.00
181 DD,FMc,L:Gr.Arrow,V:Star . . 3.50
182 DD,FMc,A:Green Arrow, V:Felix Faust 3.00
183 JSn(c),DD,FMc,A:JSA, NewGods 3.00
184 GP,FMc,A:JSA,NewGods . . . 3.00
185 JSn(c),GP,FMc,A:JSA, New Gods 3.00
186 FMc,GP,V:Shaggy Man 2.00
187 DH,FMc,N:Zatanna 2.00
188 DH,FMc,V:Proteus 2.00
189 BB(c),RB,FMc,V:Starro 2.00
190 BB(c),RB,LMa,V:Starro 2.00
191 RB,V:Amazo 2.00
192 GP,O:Red Tornado 2.00
193 GP,RB,JOy,I:AllStarSquad . . 2.50
194 GP,V:Amos Fortune 2.00

195 GP,A:JSA,V:Secret Society . . 3.00
196 GP,RT,A:JSA,V:Secret Soc. . 3.00
197 GP,RT,KP,A:JSA,V:Secret Society 3.00
198 DH,BBr,A:J.Hex,BatLash 2.00
199 GP(c),DH,BBr,A:Jonah Hex, BatLash 2.00
200 GP,DG,BB (1st Batman),PB,TA, BBr,GK,CI,JAp,JKu,Anniv.,A:Adam Strange,Phantom Stranger, J:Green Arrow 4.50
201 GP(c),DH,A:Ultraa 2.00
202 GP(c),DH,BBr,JLA in Space . 2.00
203 GP(c),DH,RT,V:Royal Flush Gang 2.00
204 GP(c),DH,RT,V:R.FlushGang 2.00
205 GP(c),DH,RT,V:R.FlushGang 2.00
206 DH,RT,A:Demons 3 . . . . 2.00

Justice League of America #207
© DC Comics, Inc.

207 GP(c),DH,RT,A:All Star Squadron,JSA 2.50
208 GP(c),DH,RT,A:All Star Squadron,JSA 2.50
209 GP(c),DH,RT,A:All Star Squadron,JSA 2.50
210 RB,RT,JLA casebook #1 . . . . 2.00
211 RB,RT,JLA casebook #2 . . . . 2.00
212 GP(c),RB,PCu,RT,c.book #3 . 2.00
213 GP(c),DH,RT 2.00
214 GP(c),DH,RT,I:Siren Sist.h'd . 2.00
215 GP(c),DH,RT 2.00
216 DH 2.00
217 GP(c),RT(i) 2.00
218 RT(i),A:Prof.Ivo 2.00
219 GP(c),RT(i),A:JSA 2.25
220 GP(c),RT,O:Bl.Canary,A:JSA 2.25
221 Beasts #1 . . . . 2.00
222 RT(i),Beasts #2 . . . . 2.00
223 RT(i),Beasts #3 . . . . 2.00
224 DG(i),V:Paragon 2.00
225 V:Hellrazor 2.00
226 FMc(i),V:Hellrazor 2.00
227 V:Hellrazor,I:Lord Claw 2.00
228 GT,AN,R:J'onnJonzz,War of the Worlds Pt.1 . . . . 2.00
229 War of the Worlds Pt.2 . . . . . 2.00
230 War of the Worlds conc. 2.00
231 RB(i),A:JSA,Supergirl 2.25
232 A:JSA Supergirl 2.25
233 New JLA takes over book, B:Rebirth,F:Vibe 2.00
234 F:Vixen 2.00
235 F:Steel 2.00
236 E:Rebirth,F:Gypsy 2.00
237 A:Superman,Flash,WWoman . 2.00
238 A:Superman,Flash,WWoman . 2.00
239 V:Ox 2.00
240 MSy,TMd 2.00
241 GT,V:Amazo 2.00
242 GT,V:Amazo,Mask(Toy tie-in) insert 2.00
243 GT,L:Aquaman,V:Amazo 2.00
244 JSon,Crisis,A:InfinityInc,JSA . 2.00
245 LMc,Crisis,N:Steel 2.00
246 LMc,JLA leaves Detroit 2.00
247 LMc,JLA returns to old HQ . . 2.00
248 LMc,F:J'onn J'onzz 2.00
249 LMc,Lead-in to Anniv. 2.00
250 LMc,Anniv.,A:Superman, Green Lantern,Green Arrow, Black Canary,R:Batman 2.75
251 LMc,V:Despero 1.75
252 LMc,V:Despero,N:Elongated Man 1.75
253 LMc,V:Despero 1.75
254 LMc,V:Despero 1.75
255 LMc,O:Gypsy 1.75
256 LMc,Gypsy 1.75
257 LMc,A:Adam,L:Zatanna 1.75
258 LMc,Legends x-over,D:Vibe . 1.75
259 LMc,Legends x-over 1.75
260 LMc,Legends x-over,D:Steel . 1.75
261 LMc,Legends,final issue 4.00
Ann.#1 DG(i),A:Sandman 3.00
Ann.#2 I:NewJLA 2.00
Ann.#3 MG(i),Crisis 2.00

JUSTICE LEAGUE TASK FORCE

1 F:Mart.Manhunter,Nightwing, Aquaman,Flash,Gr.Lantern . . . 2.00
2 V:Count Glass,Blitz 1.75
3 V:Blitz,Count Glass 1.75
4 DG,F:Gypsy,A:Lady Shiva 1.75
5 JAl,Knightquest:Crusade,F:Bronze Tiger,Green Arrow,Gypsy 2.00
6 JAl,Knightquest:Search,F:Bronze Tiger,Green Arrow,Gypsy 1.75
7 PDd(s),F:Maxima,Wonder Woman, Dolphin,Gypsy,Vixen,V:Luta . . 1.75
8 PDd(s),SaV,V:Amazons 1.75
9 GrL,V:Wildman 1.75
10 Purification Plague#1 . . . . . . 1.75
11 Purification Plague#2 . . . . . . 1.75
12 Purification Plague#3 . . . . . . 1.75
13 Jugdement Day#2, V:Overmaster 1.75
14 Jugdement Day#5, V:Overmaster 1.50

JUSTICE SOCIETY OF AMERICA

[Limited Series]

1 B:Veng.From Stars,A:Flash . . . 2.00
2 A:BlackCanary,V:Solomon Grundy, C:G.A.Green Lantern. 1.50
3 A:G.A.Green Lantern,Black Canary, V:Sol.Grundy 1.50
4 A:G.A.Hawkman,C:G.A.Flash . . 1.50
5 A:G.A.Hawkman,Flash 1.50
6 FMc(i),A:Bl.Canary,G.A.Gr.Lantern, V:Sol.Grundy,V.Savage 1.50
7 JSA united,V:Vandal Savage . . 1.50
8 E:Veng.FromStar,V:V.Savage, Solomon Grundy, ... 1.50
Spec.#1 DR,MG,End of JSA 2.00

[Regular Series]

1 V:The New Order 1.75
2 V:Ultra Gen 1.50
3 R:Ultra-Humanite 1.50
4 V:Ultra-Humanite 1.50
5 V:Ultra-Humanite 1.50
6 F:Johnny Thunderbolt 1.50
7 ..Or give me Liberty 1.50
8 Pyramid Scheme 1.50
9 V:Kulak 1.50
10 V:Kulak,final issue 1.50

KAMANDI, THE LAST BOY ON EARTH

October-November, 1972

1 JK,O:Kamandi 16.00
2 JK 10.00
3 JK 8.00
4 JK,I:Prince Tuftan 7.00
5 thru 10 JK . . . . @7.00
11 thru 28 JK . . . . @3.00
29 A:Superman 3.00
30 JK 3.00
31 thru 57 . . . . @3.00
58 A:Karate Kid 3.00
59 JSn,A:Omac, Sept.-Oct,1978 . 3.50

KAMANDI: AT EARTH'S END

1 R:Kamandi 2.00
2 V:Kingpin,Big Q 2.00
3 A:Sleeper Zom,Saphira 2.00
4 A:Superman 2.00
5 A:Superman,V:Ben Boxer 2.00
6 final issue 2.00

KARATE KID

March-April, 1976

1 I:Iris Jacobs,A:Legion 1.50
2 A:Major Disaster 1.00
3 . . . . 1.00
4 . . . . 1.00
5 . . . . 1.00
6 thru 10 . . . . @1.00
11 A:Superboy/Legion 1.00
12 A:Superboy/Legion 1.00
13 A:Superboy/Legion 1.00
14 A:Robin 1.00
15 July-August, 1978 . . . . 1.00

KID ETERNITY

1 O:Kid Eternity 7.00
2 A:Mr.Keeper 5.50
3 True Origin revealed,final iss. . 5.50

KID ETERNITY

1 thru 3 GMo(s),DFg,O:Kid Eternity,rtd 4.95

Vertigo

1 B:ANo(s),SeP,R:Kid Eternity, A:Mdm.Blavatsky,Hemlock . . . 2.75
2 SeP,A:Sigmund Freud,Carl Jung, A:Malocchio 2.50
3 SeP,A:Malocchio,I:Dr.Pathos . . 2.25
4 SeP,A:Neal Cassady 2.25
5 SeP,In Cyberspace 2.25
6 SeP,A:Dr.Pathos,Marilyn Monroe 2.25
7 SeP,I:Infinity 2.25
8 SeP,In Insane Asylum 2.25
9 SeP,Asylum,A:Dr.Pathos 2.25
10 SeP,Small Wages 2.25
11 ANi(s),I:Slap 2.25
12 SeP,A:Slap 2.25
13 SeP,Date in Hell#1 . . . . 2.25
14 SeP,Date in Hell#2 . . . . 2.25

KISSYFUR

1 . . . . 2.00

KOBALT

Milestone

1 JBy(c),I:Kobalt,Richard Page . . 2.25
2 . . . . 1.75

KOBRA

1 JK,I:Kobra & Jason Burr 2.00
2 I:Solaris 1.50
3 KG/DG,TA,V:Solaris 1.75

4 V:Servitor 1.00
5 RB/FMc,,A:Jonny Double 1.00
6 MN/JRu,A:Jonny Double 1.00
7 MN/JRu,A:Jonny Double last iss 1.00

KONG THE UNTAMED
June-July, 1975

1 thru 4 . . . . @1.00
5 February-March, 1976 . . . . 1.00

KRYPTON CHRONICLES

1 CS,A:Superman 1.25
2 CS,A:Black Flame 1.00
3 CS,O:Name of Kal-El 1.00

LAST ONE
Vertigo

1 B:JMD(s),DSw,I:Myrwann,Patrick Maguire's Story 3.25
2 DSw,Pat's Addiction to Drugs . 3.00
3 DSw,Pat goes into Coma 3.00
4 DSw,In Victorian age 3.00
5 DSw,Myrwann Memories 3.00
6 E:JMD(s),DSw,final Issue 3.00

LEADING COMICS
Winter, 1941-42

1 O:Seven Soldiers of Victory, B:Crimson Avenger,Green Arrow & Speedy,Shining Knight, A:The Dummy 2,000.00
2 MMe,V:Black Star 700.00
3 V:Dr. Doome 550.00
4 'Seven Steps to Conquest', V:The Sixth Sense 450.00
5 'The Miracles that Money Couldn't Buy' 450.00
6 'The Treasure that Time Forgot' 400.00
7 The Wizard of Wisstark . . . 400.00
8 Seven Soldiers Go back through the Centuries 400.00
9 V:Mr. X,'Chameleon of Crime' 400.00
10 King of the Hundred Isles . . 400.00
11 'The Hard Luck Hat!' 300.00
12 'The Million Dollar Challenge!' 300.00
13 'The Trophies of Crime' . . . 300.00
14 Bandits from the Book' 300.00
15 (fa) 90.00
16 thru 22 (fa) . . . . @45.00
23 (fa),I:Peter Porkchops 100.00
24 thru 30 (fa) . . . . @45.00
31 (fa) 30.00
32 (fa) 30.00
33 (fa) 50.00
34 thru 40 (fa) . . . . @30.00
41 (fa),February-March, 1950 . . 30.00

LEAVE IT TO BINKY
February-March, 1948

1 . . . . 175.00
2 . . . . 70.00
3 . . . . 60.00
4 . . . . 60.00
5 thru 14 . . . . @30.00
15 SM,Scribbly 40.00
16 thru 60 . . . . @15.00
61 thru 71 . . . . @7.50

LEGEND OF THE SHIELD
Impact

1 I:Shield,V:Mann-X,I:Big Daddy, Lt.Devon Hall,Arvell Hauser,Mary Masterson-Higgins 1.50
2 Shield in Middle East 1.00
3 Shield Goes A.W.O.L. 1.00
4 Hunt for Shield 1.00
5 A:Shield's Partner Dusty 1.00
6 O:Shield, V:The Jewels 1.00
7 Shield/Fly team-up 1.00
8 V:Weapon 1.00
9 Father Vs. Son 1.00
10 Arvell Hauser 1.00
11 inc,Trading cards 1.00
12 . . . . 1.25
13 Shield court martialed 1.25
14 Mike Barnes becomes Shield . 1.25
15 Shield becomes a Crusader . . 1.25
16 V:Soviets,final issue 1.25
Ann.#1 Earthquest,w/trading card . 2.25

LEGEND OF WONDER WOMAN

1 Return of Atomia 1.00
2 A:Queens Solalia & Leila 1.00
3 Escape from Atomia 1.00
4 conclusion 1.00

Legends #5 © DC Comics, Inc.

LEGENDS

1 JBy,V:Darkseid 3.50
2 JBy,A:Superman 2.50
3 JBy,I:Suicide Squad 2.50
4 JBy,V:Darkseid 2.50
5 JBy,A:Dr. Fate 2.50
6 JBy,I:Justice League 7.50
TPB rep#1-6 JBy(c) 9.95

LEGENDS OF THE DARK KNIGHT
(see BATMAN)

LEGENDS OF THE WORLD FINEST

1 WS(s),DIB,V:Silver Banshee,Blaze, Tullus,Foil(c), ... 5.25
2 WS(s),DIB,V:Silver Banshee,Blaze, Tullus,Foil(c), ... 5.25
3 WS(s),DIB,V:Silver Banshee,Blaze, Tullus,Foil(c), ... 5.25

L.E.G.I.O.N. '89-94

1 BKi,V:Computer Tyrants 4.00
2 BKi,V:Computer Tyrants 3.00
3 BKi,V:Computer Tyrants, A:Lobo 4.00
4 BKi,V: Lobo 4.00
5 BKi,J:Lobo(in the rest of the series),V:Konis-Biz 3.00
6 BKi,V:Konis-Biz 3.00
7 BKi,Stealth vs. Dox 3.00
8 BKi,R:Dox 3.00
9 BKi,J:Phase (Phantom Girl) . . . 2.50
10 BKi,Stealth vs Lobo 2.50
11 BKi,V:Mr.Stoorr 2.50
12 BKi,V:Emerald Eye 2.50
13 BKi,V:Emerald Eye 2.50
14 BKi,V:Pirates 2.50
15 BKi,V:Emerald Eye 2.50
16 BKi,J:LarGand 2.50
17 BKi,V:Dragon-Ro 2.50
18 BKi,V:Dragon-Ro 2.50
19 V:Lydea,L:Stealth 2.50
20 Aftermath 2.50
21 D:Lyrissa Mallor,V:Mr.Starr . . . 2.50
22 V:Mr.Starr 2.50
23 O:R.J.Brande(double sized) . . 3.50
24 BKi,V:Khunds 2.50
25 BKi,V:Khunds 2.50
26 BKi,V:Khunds 2.50
27 BKi,J:Lydea Mallor 2.50
28 KG,Birth of Stealth's Babies . . 2.50
29 BKi,J:Capt.Comet,Marij'n Bek . 2.50
30 BKi,R:Stealth 2.50
31 Lobo vs.Capt.Marvel 3.50
32 V:Space Biker Gang 2.00
33 A:Ice-Man 2.00
34 MPn,V:Ice Man 2.00
35 Legion Disbanded 2.00
36 Dox proposes to Ignea 2.00
37 V:Intergalactic Ninjas 2.00
38 BKi,Lobo V:Ice Man 2.00
39 BKi,D:G'odd,V:G'oddSquad . . . 2.00
40 BKi,V:Kyaltic Space Station . . 2.00
41 BKi,A:Stealth'sBaby 2.00
42 BKi,V:Yeltsin-Beta 2.00
43 BKi,V:Yeltsin-Beta 2.00
44 V:Yeltsin-Beta,C:Gr.Lantern . . 2.00
45 . . . . 2.00
46 BKi,A:Hal Jordan 2.00
47 BKi,Lobo vs Hal Jordan 2.00
48 BKi,R:Ig'nea 2.00
49 BKi,V:Ig'nea 2.00
50 BKi,V:Ig'nea,A:Legion'67 . . . . 3.75
51 F:Lobo,Telepath 2.00
52 BKi,V:Cyborg Skull of Darius . . 2.00
53 BKi,V:Shadow Creature 2.00
54 BKi,V:Shadow Creature 2.00
55 BKi,V:Shadow Beast 2.00
56 BKi,A:Masked Avenger 2.00
57 BKi,Trinity,V:Green Lantern . . . 2.00
58 BKi,Trinity#6,A:Green Lantern, Darkstar 2.00
59 F:Phase 2.00
60 V:Phantom Riders 2.00
61 Little Party 2.00
62 A:R.E.C.R.U.I.T.S. 2.00
63 A:Superman 2.00
64 BKi(c),V:Mr.B 2.00
65 BKi(c),V:Brain Bandit 2.00
66 Stealth and Dox name child . . 2.00
67 F:Telepath 2.00
68 . . . . 1.75
Ann.#1 A:Superman,V:Brainiac . . 5.50
Ann.#2 Armageddon 2001 . . . . 3.50
Ann.#3 Eclipso tie-in 3.25
Ann.#4 SHa(i),I:Pax 3.75

LEGION OF SUPER-HEROES
[Reprint Series]

1 rep. Tommy Tomorrow 10.00
2 rep. Tommy Tomorrow 6.00
3 rep. Tommy Tomorrow 6.00
4 rep. Tommy Tomorrow 6.00

[1st Regular Series]
Prev: SUPERBOY (& LEGION)

259 JSon,L:Superboy 5.00
260 RE,I:Circus of Death 3.50
261 RE,V:Circus of Death 3.00
262 JSh,V:Engineer 3.00
263 V:Dagon the Avenger 3.00
264 V:Dagon the Avenger 3.00
265 JSn,DG,Superman/Radio Shack insert 3.00

266 R:Bouncing Boy,Duo Damsel 2.50
267 SD,V:Kantuu 2.50
268 SD,BWi,V:Dr.Mayavale 2.50
269 V:Fatal Five 2.50
270 V:Fatal Five 2.50
271 V:Tharok (Dark Man) 2.50
272 CI,SD,O:J:Blok, I:New
Dial 'H' for Hero 2.50
273 V:Stargrave 2.50
274 SD,V:Captain Frake 2.50
275 V:Captain Frake 2.50
276 SD,V:Mordru 2.50
277 A:Reflecto(Superboy) 2.50
278 A:Reflecto(Superboy) 2.50
279 A:Reflecto(Superboy) 2.50
280 R:Superboy 2.50
281 SD,V:Time Trapper 2.50
282 V:Time Trapper 2.50
283 O:Wildfire 2.50
284 PB,V:Organleggor 2.50
285 PB,KG(1st Legion)V:Khunds . 4.00
286 PB,KG,V:Khunds 3.00
287 KG,V:Kharlak 5.00
288 KG,V:Kharlak 3.00
289 KG,Stranded 3.00

Legion of Super-Heroes Ann. #1
© DC Comics, Inc.

290 KG,B:Great Darkness Saga,
J:Invisible Kid II 3.00
291 KG,V:Darkseid's Minions 2.00
292 KG,V:Darkseid's Minions 2.00
293 KG,Daxam destroyed 2.00
294 KG,E:Great Darkness Saga,
V:Darkseid,A:Auron,Superboy . 2.00
295 KG,A:Green Lantern Corps . . 1.75
296 KG,D:Cosmic Boys family . . . 1.75
297 KG,O:Legion,A:Cosmic Boy . 1.75
298 KG,EC,I:Amethyst 1.75
299 KG,R:Invisible Kid I 1.75
300 KG,CS,JSon,DC,KS,DG 2.00
301 KG,R:Chameleon Boy 1.75
302 KG,A:Chameleon Boy 1.75
303 KG,V:Fatal Five 1.75
304 KG,V:Fatal Five 1.75
305 KG,V:Micro Lad 1.75
306 KG,CS,RT,O:Star Boy 1.75
307 KG,GT,Omen 1.75
308 KG,V:Omen 1.75
309 KG,V:Omen 1.75
310 KG,V:Omen 1.75
311 KG,GC,New Headquarters . . 1.75
312 KG,V:Khunds 1.75
313 KG,V:Khunds 1.75

Ann.#1 IT,KG,I:Invisible Kid 3.50
Ann.#2 DGb,W:Karate Kid and
Princess Projectra 2.00
Ann.#3 CS,RT,A:Darkseid 2.00
Ann.#4 reprint 2.00
Ann.#5 reprint 1.50
Legion Archives Vol 1 HC 39.95
Legion Archives Vol 2 HC 39.95
Legion Archives Vol 3 HC 39.95
Legion Archives Vol 4 HC 39.95

Becomes:

TALES OF LEGION OF SUPER HEROES

LEGION OF SUPER-HEROES

[3rd Regular Series]

1 KG,V:Legion of Super-Villians . 3.50
2 KG,V:Legion of Super-Villians . 2.50
3 KG,V:Legion of Super-Villians . 2.50
4 KG,D:Karate Kid 2.50
5 KG,D:Nemesis Kid 2.50

Legion of Super-Heroes #13
© DC Comics, Inc.

6 JO,F:Lightning Lass 2.25
7 SLi,A:Controller 2.25
8 SLi,V:Controller 2.25
9 Sli,V:Sklarians 2.25
10 V:Khunds 2.25
11 EC,KG,L:Orig 3 members 2.00
12 SLi,EC,A:Superboy 2.00
13 SLi,V:Lythyls,F:TimberWolf . . . 2.00
14 SLi,J:Sensor Girl (Princess
Projectra),Quislet,Tellus,Polar
Boy,Magnetic Kid 2.00
15 GLa,V:Dr. Regulus 2.00
16 SLi,Crisis tie-in,F:Braniac5 . . . 2.00
17 GLa,O:Legion 2.00
18 GLa,Crisis tie-in,V:InfiniteMan . 2.00
19 GLa,V:Controller 2.00
20 GLa,V:Tyr 2.00
21 GLa,V:Emerald Empress 1.75
22 GLa,V:Restorer,A:Universo . . . 1.75
23 SLi,GLa,A:Superboy,
Jonah Hex 1.75
24 GLa,NBi,A:Fatal Five 1.75
25 GLa,V:FatalFive, ... 1.75
26 GLa,V:FatalFive,O:SensorGirl . 1.75
27 GLa,GC,A:Mordru 1.75
28 GLa,L:StarBoy 1.75
29 GLa,V:Starfinger 1.75
30 GLa,A:Universo 1.75

31 GLa,A:Ferro Lad,Karate Kid . . 1.75
32 GLa,V:Universo,I:Atmos 1.75
33 GLa,V:Universo 1.75
34 GLa,V:Universo 1.75
35 GLa,V:Universo,R:Saturn Girl . 1.75
36 GLa,R:Cosmic Boy 1.75
37 GLa,V:Universo,I:Superboy
(Earth Prime) 11.00
38 GLa,V:TimeTrapper,
D:Superboy 11.00
39 CS,RT,O:Colossal Boy 1.75
40 GLa,I:New Starfinger 1.75
41 GLa,V:Starfinger 1.75
42 GLa,Millenium,V:Laurel Kent . 1.75
43 GLa,Millenium,V:Laurel Kent . . 1.75
44 GLa,O:Quislet 1.75
45 GLa,CS,MGr,DC,30th Ann. . . . 3.50
46 GLa,Conspiracy 1.75
47 GLa,PB,V:Starfinger 1.75
48 GLa,Conspiracy,A:Starfinger . . 1.75
49 PB,Conspiracy,A:Starfinger . . . 1.75
50 KG,V:Time Trapper,A:Infinite
Man,E:Conspiracy 3.00
51 KG,V:Gorak,L:Brainiac5 . . . . 1.75
52 KG,V:Gil'Dishpan 1.75
53 KG,V:Gil'Dishpan 1.75
54 KG,V:Gorak 1.75
55 KG,EC,JL,EL,N:Legion 1.75
56 EB,V:Inquisitor 1.75
57 KG,V:Emerald Empress 1.75
58 KG,V:Emerald Empress 1.75
59 KG,MBr,F:Invisible Kid 1.75
60 KG,B:Magic Wars 1.75
61 KG,Magic Wars 1.75
62 KG,D:Magnetic Lad 1.75
63 KG,E:Magic Wars #4,final iss. . 1.75
Ann.#1 KG,Murder Mystery 2.50
Ann.#2 KG,CS,O:Validus,
A:Darkseid 3.00
Ann.#3 GLa,I:2nd Karate Kid 2.50
Ann.#4 BKi,V:Starfinger 2.50
Ann #5 I:2nd Legion Sub.Heroes . 2.50

[4th Regular Series]

1 KG,R:Cosmic Boy, Chameleon 4.00
2 KG,R:Ultra Boy,I:Kono 3.00
3 KG,D:Block,V:Roxxas 2.50
4 KG,V:Time Trapper 2.50
5 KG,V:Mordru,A:Glorith 2.50
6 KG,I:Laurel Gand,2.50
7 KG,V:Mordru 2.25
8 KG,O:Legion 2.25
9 KG,O:Laurel Gand 2.25

LEGION OF SUBSTITUTE HEROES

Spec.#1 KG 1.25

LEGIONNAIRES

1 CSp,V:Mano and the Hand,Bagged
w/card 3.50
1a w/out card 2.50
2 CSp,V:Mano 2.00
3 CSp,I:2nd Emerald Empress . . 2.00
4 CSp,R:Fatal Five 2.00
5 CSp,V:Fatal Five 2.00
6 CSp,V:Fatal Five 1.75
7 AH,V:Devil Fish 1.75
8 CDo,F:Brainiac 5 . . . . 1.75
9 CSp,A:Kid Quantum 1.75
10 CSp,A:Kono,I:2nd Kid Pyscho . 1.75
11 CSp,J:2nd Kid Pyscho 1.75
12 CSp,A:2nd Kid Pyscho 1.75
13 FFo,V:Grimbor 1.75
14 V:Grimbor 1.75
15 V:Grimbor 1.75
16 In Time 1.50
Ann.#1 Elseworlds Story 2.95

LEGIONAIRRES THREE

1 EC,V:Time Trapper 1.25
2 EC,V:Time Trapper 1.00
3 EC,V:Time Trapper 1.00
4 EC,V:Time Trapper 1.00

LIMITED COLLECTORS EDITION
Summer, 1973

21 Shazam ... 10.00
22 Tarzan ... 7.00
23 House of Mystery ... 7.00
24 Rudolph, the Red-nosed Reindeer ... 4.00
25 NA,NA(c),Batman ... 10.00
27 Shazam ... 7.00
29 Tarzan ... 4.00
31 NA,O:Superman ... 8.00
32 Ghosts ... 4.00
33 Rudolph ... 3.00
34 X-Mas with Superheroes ... 5.00
35 Shazam ... 5.00
36 The Bible ... 4.00
37 Batman ... 10.00
38 Superman ... 8.00
39 Secret Origins ... 8.00
40 Dick Tracy ... 4.00
41 ATh,Super Friends ... 6.00
42 Rudolph ... 3.00
43 X-mas with Super-Heroes ... 4.00
44 NA,Batman ... 10.00
45 Secret Origins-Super Villians ... 3.00
46 ATh,JLA ... 5.00
47 Superman ... 4.00
48 Superman-Flash Race ... 4.00
49 Superboy & Legion of Super-Heroes ... 4.00
50 Rudolph ... 3.00
51 NA,NA(c),Batman ... 10.00
52 NA,NA(c),The Best of DC ... 6.00
57 Welcome Back Kotter ... 3.00
59 NA,BWr,Batman,1978 ... 12.00

LITTLE SHOP OF HORRORS

1 GC ... 2.50

Lobo #3 © DC Comics, Inc.

LOBO
[1st Limited Series]

1 SBs,Last Czarnian #1 ... 8.00
1a 2nd Printing ... 3.00
2 SBs,Last Czarnian #2 ... 5.00
3 SBs,Last Czarnian #3 ... 4.00
4 SBs,Last Czarnian #4 ... 4.00
Ann.#1 Bloodlines#1,I:Layla ... 3.75
Lobo Paramilitary X-Mas SBs ... 5.50
Lobo:Blazing Chain of Love,DCw ... 2.00
TPB Last Czarnian,rep.#1-4 ... 9.95
TPB Lobo's Greatest Hits ... 12.95

[Regular Series]

1 VS,Foil(c),V:Dead Boys ... 3.25
2 VS, ... 2.00
3 VS, ... 2.00
4 VS,Quigly Affair ... 2.00
5 V:Bludhound ... 2.00
6 I:Bim Simms ... 2.00
7 A:Losers ... 1.75
Ann.#1 Elseworlds Story ... 3.50

LOBO'S BACK

1 SBs,w/3(c) inside,V:Loo ... 4.50
1a 2nd printing ... 1.50
2 SBs,Lobo becomes a woman ... 4.00
3 V:Heaven ... 2.50
4 V:Heaven ... 2.50
TPB rep #1-4 ... 9.95

LOBO: A CONTRACT ON GAWD

1 AIG(s),KD, ... 2.00
2 AIG(s),KD,A:Dave ... 2.00
3 AIG(s),KD, ... 1.75
4 AIG(s),KD,Final Issue ... 1.75

LOBO CONVENTION SPECIAL

1 Lobo at Comic Convention ... 2.00

LOBO'S BACK

1 SBs,w/3(c) inside,V:Loo ... 4.50
1a 2nd printing ... 1.50
2 SBs,Lobo becomes a woman ... 2.50
3 SBs,V:Heaven ... 2.50
4 SBs,V:Heaven ... 2.50

LOBO: INFANTICIDE

1 KG,V:Su,Lobo Bastards ... 2.00
2 Lobo at Boot Camp ... 1.75
3 KG,Lobo Vs.his offspring ... 1.75
4 KG,V:Lobo Bastards ... 1.75

LOBO: PORTRAIT OF A VICTIM

1 VS,I:John Doe ... 2.00

LOBO: UNAMERICAN GLADIATORS

1 CK,V:Satan's Brothers ... 2.00
2 CK,V:Jonny Caesar ... 2.00
3 CK,MMi(c),V:Satan Brothers ... 2.00
4 CK,MMi(c),V:Jonny Caeser ... 2.00

LOBOCOP

1 StG(s), ... 2.25

LOIS AND CLARK: THE NEW ADVENTURES OF SUPERMAN

TPB ... 9.95

LOIS LANE
August, 1986

1 GM ... 1.50
2 GM ... 1.50

LOONEY TUNES MAG.

1 thru 6 ... @1.95

LOONEY TUNES

1 Warner Bros. cartoons ... 1.75
2 Warner Bros. cartoons ... 1.75
3 Warner Bros. cartoons ... 1.75
4 Warner Bros. cartoons ... 1.50

LORDS OF THE ULTRAREALM

1 PB ... 3.50
2 PB ... 2.00
3 thru 6 PB ... @1.50
Spec.#1 PB,DG,Oneshot ... 2.25

LOSERS SPECIAL

1 Crisis,D:Losers ... 1.25

MADAME XANADU

1 MR/BB ... 2.00

MAN-BAT

1 SD,AM,A:Batman ... 12.00
2 V:The Ten-Eyed Man ... 8.50
Reprint NA(c) ... 4.00

MAN-BAT vs. BATMAN

1 NA,DG,reprint ... 4.00

MANHUNTER

1 from Millenium-Suicide Squad ... 1.50
2 in Tokyo,A:Dumas ... 1.25
3 The Yakuza,V:Dumas ... 1.25
4 Secrets Revealed-Manhunter, Dumas & Olivia ... 1.25
5 A:Silvia Kandery ... 1.25
6 A:Argent,contd.Suicide Squad Annual #1 ... 1.25
7 Vlatavia, V:Count Vertigo ... 1.25
8 FS,A:Flash,Invasion x-over ... 1.25
9 FS,Invasion Aftermath extra (contd from Flash #22) ... 1.25
10 Salvage Pt.1 ... 1.25
11 Salvage Pt.2 ... 1.25
12 ... 1.25
13 ... 1.25
14 Janus Directive #5 ... 1.25
15 I:Mirage ... 1.25
16 V:Outlaw ... 1.25
17 In Gotham,A:Batman ... 1.50
18 Saints & Sinners Pt.1,R:Dumas 1.25
19 Saints & Sinners Pt.2,V:Dumas 1.25
20 Saints & Sinners Pt.3,V:Dumas 1.25
21 Saints & Sinners Pt.4, A:Manhunter Grandmaster ... 1.25
22 Saints & Sinners Pt.5, A:Manhunter Grandmaster ... 1.25
23 Saints & Sinners Pt.6,V:Dumas 1.25
24 DG,Showdown, final issue ... 1.25

MAN OF STEEL

1 JBy,DG,I:Modern Superman ... 4.50
1 2nd edition ... 3.00
2 JBy,DG,R:Lois Lane ... 3.00
3 JBy,DG,A:Batman ... 3.00
4 JBy,DG,V:Lex Luther ... 3.00
5 JBy,DG,I:Modern Bizarro ... 3.00
6 JBy,DG,A:Lana Lang ... 3.00
TBP rep. Man of Steel ... 12.95

MANY LOVES OF DOBIE GILLIS
May-June, 1960

1 ... 150.00
2 ... 75.00
3 and 4 ... @65.00
5 thru 9 ... @40.00
10 thru 25 ... @28.00
26 October, 1964 ... 28.00

MARTIAN MANHUNTER

1 A:JLI ... 1.75
2 A:JLI,V:Death God ... 1.50
3 V:Death God,A:Dr.Erdel ... 1.50
4 A:JLI,final issue ... 1.50

[Mini-Series]

1 EB,American Secrets #1 ... 5.25
2 EB,American Secrets #2 ... 4.95
3 EB,American Secrets #3 ... 4.95

MASK
December, 1985
1 HC(c),TV tie-in,I:Mask Team . . 2.00
2 HC(c),In Egypt,V:Venom 1.75
3 HC(c),'Anarchy in the U.K.' . . . 1.75
4 HC(c),V:Venom, final issue, March, 1986 . . . . 1.00

[2nd Series]
February, 1987
1 CS/KS,reg.series 1.25
2 CS/KS,V:Venom 1.00
3 CS/KS,V:Venom 1.00
4 CS/KS,V:Venom 1.00
5 CS/KS,Mask operatives hostage 1.00
6 CS/KS,I:Jacana 1.00
7 CS/KS,Mask gone bad? 1.00
8 CS/KS,Matt Trakker,V:Venom . 1.00
9 CS/KS,V:Venom, last issue, October, 1987 . . . . 1.00

MASTERS OF THE UNIVERSE
May, 1986
1 GT,AA,O:He-Man 1.50
2 GT,AA,V:Skeletor 1.25
3 GT,V:Skeletor 1.25

MASTERWORKS SERIES OF GREAT COMIC BOOK ARTISTS
May, 1983
1 . . . . 2.50
2 . . . . 2.50
3 December, 1983 . . . . 2.50

'MAZING MAN
January, 1986
1 I:Maze 1.00
2 . . . . 1.00
3 . . . . 1.00
4 . . . . 1.00
5 . . . . 1.00
6 Shea Stadium 1.00
7 Shea Stadium 1.00
8 Cat-Sitting 1.00
9 Bank Hold-up 1.00
10 . . . . 1.00
11 Jones Beach 1.00
12 FM(c),last issue, Dec., 1986 . . 1.00
Spec.#1 . . . . 2.25
Spec.#2 . . . . 2.25
Spec.#3 KB/TM 2.25

MEN OF WAR
August, 1977
1 I:Gravedigger,Code Name: Gravedigger,I:Enemy Ace 1.50
2 JKu(c),The Five-Walled War . . 1.00
3 JKu(c),The Suicide Strategem 1.00
4 JKu(c),Trail by Fire 1.00
5 JKu(c),Valley of the Shadow . . 1.00
6 JKu(c),A Choice of Deaths . . . 1.00
7 JKu(c),Milkrun 1.00
8 JKu(c),Death-Stroke 1.00
9 JKu(c),Gravedigger-R.I.P. 1.00
10 JKu(c),Crossroads 1.00
11 JKu(c),Berkstaten 1.00
12 JKu(c),Where Is Gravedigger? 1.00
13 JKu(c),Project Gravedigger - Plus One 1.00
14 JKu(c),The Swirling Sands of Death 1.00
15 JKu(c),The Man With the Opened Eye 1.00
16 JKu(c),Hide and Seek The Spy 1.00
17 JKu(c),The River of Death . . . 1.00
18 JKu(c),The Amiens Assault . . . 1.00
19 JKu(c),An Angel Named Marie 1.00
20 JKu(c),Cry:Jerico 1.00
21 JKu(c),Home-Is Where The Hell Is 1.00
22 JKu(c),Blackout On The Boardwalk 1.00
23 JKu(c),Mission: Six Feet Under 1.00
24 JKu&DG(c),The Presidential Peril 1.00
25 GE(c),Save the President 1.00
26 March, 1980 . . . . 1.00

MERCY
Vertigo
Graphic Novel I:Mercy 8.00

METAL MEN
April-May, 1965
[1st Regular Series]
1 RA,I:Missile Men 350.00
2 RA,Robot of Terror 135.00
3 RA,Moon's Invisible Army 80.00
4 RA,Bracelet of Doomed Hero . 80.00
5 RA,Menace of the Mammoth Robots 80.00
6 RA,I:Gas Gang 55.00
7 RA,V:Solar Brain 55.00
8 RA,Playground of Terror 55.00
9 RA,A:Billy 55.00
10 RA,A:Gas Gang 55.00
11 RA,The Floating Furies 40.00
12 RA,A:Missle Men 40.00
13 RA,I:Nameless 40.00
14 RA,A:Chemo 40.00
15 RA,V:B.O.L.T.S. 40.00
16 RA,Robots for Sale 40.00
17 JKu(c),RA,V:Bl.Widow Robot 40.00
18 JKu(c),RA 40.00
19 RA,V:Man-Horse of Hades . . 40.00
20 RA,V:Dr.Yes 40.00
21 RA,C:Batman & Robin,Flash Wonder Woman 28.00
22 RA,A:Chemo 28.00
23 RA,A:Sizzler 28.00
24 RA,V:Balloonman 28.00
25 RA,V:Chemo 28.00
26 RA,V:Metal Mods 28.00
27 RA,O:Metal Men,rtd 46.00
28 RA 28.00
29 RA,V:Robot Eater 28.00
30 RA,GK,in the Forbidden Zone 28.00
31 RA,GK, ... 23.00
32 RA,Robot Amazon Blues . . . 18.00
33 MS,The Hunted Metal Men . . 18.00
34 MS 18.00
35 MS 18.00
36 MS,The Cruel Clowns 18.00
37 MS,To walk among Men 18.00
38 MS 18.00
39 MS,Beauty of the Beast 18.00
40 MS 18.00
41 MS 18.00
42 RA,reprint 10.00
43 RA,reprint 10.00
44 RA,reprint,V:Missile Men 10.00
45 WS 10.00
46 WS,V:Chemo 10.00
47 WS,V:Plutonium Man 10.00
48 WS,A:Eclipso 15.00
49 WS,A:Eclipso 15.00
50 WS,JSa 10.00
51 JSn,V:Vox 10.00
52 JSn,V:Brain Children 10.00
53 JA(c),V:Brain Children 10.00
54 JSn,A:Green Lantern 10.00
55 JSn,A:Green Lantern 10.00
56 JSn,V:Inheritor 10.00

[Limited Series]
1 DJu,BBr,Foil(c) 8.00
2 DJu,BBr,O:Metal Men 5.00
3 DJu,BBr,V:Missile Men 3.50
4 DJu,BBr,final issue 3.00

METAMORPHO
July-August, 1965
[Regular Series]
1 A:Kurt Vornok 85.00
2 Terror from the Telstar 45.00

Metamorpho #11 © DC Comics, Inc.

3 Who stole the USA 45.00
4 V:Cha-Cha Chaves 28.00
5 V:Bulark 28.00
6 . . . . 28.00
7 thru 9 . . . . @20.00
10 I:Element Girl 24.00
11 thru 17 March-April, 1968 . @15.00

[Limited Series]
1 GN,V:The Orb of Ra 1.75
2 GN,A:Metamorpho's Son 1.75
3 GN,V:Elemental Man 1.75
4 GN,final Issue 1.75

MILLENIUM
January, 1988
1 JSa,IG 2.50
2 JSa,IG 1.75
3 JSa,IG 1.75
4 JSa,IG 1.75
5 JSa,IG 1.75
6 JSa,IG 1.75
7 JSa,IG 1.75
8 JSa,IG,I:New Guardians 1.75

MISTER E
1 (From Books of Magic) 1.75
2 A:The Shadower 1.75
3 A:The Shadower 1.75
4 A:Tim Hunter, Dr. Fate, Phantom Stranger, final issue 1.75

MISTER MIRACLE
1 JK,I:Mr.Miracle 16.00
2 JK,I:Granny Goodness 10.00
3 JK,'Paraniod Pill' 9.00
4 JK,I:Barda 8.00
5 JK,I:Vermin Vundabar 8.00
6 JK,I:Female Furies 8.00
7 JK,V:Kanto 8.00
8 JK,V:Lump 8.00
9 JK,O:Mr.Miracle,C:Darkseid . . . 7.00
10 JK,A:Female Furies 6.00
11 JK,V:Doctor Bedlum 6.00
12 JK 6.00
13 JK 6.00
14 JK 6.00
15 JK,O:Shilo Norman 6.00
16 JK 6.00
17 JK 6.00
18 JK,W:Mr.Miracle & Barda 6.00
19 MR,NA,DG,TA,JRu,AM 6.00
20 MR 4.00

21 MR 4.00
22 MR 4.00
23 MG 4.00
24 MG,RH 4.00
25 MG,RH 4.00
Spec.#1 SR 2.50

[2nd Series]

1 IG 2.50
2 IG 1.75
3 IG,A:Highfather,Forever People 1.50
4 IG,A:The Dark,Forever People . 1.50
5 IG,V:TheDark,A:ForeverPeople 1.50
6 A:G.L. Gnort 1.25
7 A:Blue Beetle,Booster Gold . . . 1.25
8 RM,A:Blue Beetle,Booster Gold 1.25
9 I:Maxi-Man 1.25
10 V:Maxi-Man 1.25
11 . . . . 1.25
12 . . . . 1.25
13 Manga Khan Saga begins, A:L-Ron,A:Lobo 3.00
14 A:Lobo 3.00
15 Manga Khan contd 1.25
16 MangaKhan cont.,JLA#39tie-in 1.25
17 On Apokolips,A:Darkseid 1.25
18 On Apokolips 1.25
19 Return to Earth, contd from JLA#42 . . . . 1.25
20 IG,Oberon 1.25
21 Return of Shilo 1.25
22 New Mr Miracle revealed 1.25
23 Secrets of the 2 Mr. Miracles revealed, A:Mother Box 1.25
24 . . . . 1.25
25 . . . . 1.25
26 Monster Party Pt#1 . . . . 1.25
27 Monster Party Pt#2, A:Justice League 1.25
28 final issue 1.25

MR. DISTRICT ATTORNEY

January-February, 1948

1 The Innocent Forger 500.00
2 The Richest Man In Prison . 200.00
3 The Honest Convicts 150.00
4 The Merchant of Death 150.00
5 The Booby-Trap Killer 150.00
6 The D.A. Meets Scotland Yard125.00
7 The People vs. Killer Kane . 125.00
8 The Rise and Fall of 'Lucky' Lynn 125.00
9 The Case of the Living Counterfeit 125.00
10 The D.A. Takes a Vacation . 100.00
11 The Game That Has No Winners 100.00
12 Fake Accident Racket 100.00
13 The Execution of Caesar Larsen 100.00
14 The Innocent Man In Murderers' Row 100.00
15 Prison Train 100.00
16 The Wire Tap Crimes 100.00
17 The Bachelor of Crime 100.00
18 The Case of the Twelve O'Clock Killer 100.00
19 The Four King's Of Crime . . 100.00
20 You Catch a Killer 100.00
21 I Was A Killer's Bodyguard . . 75.00
22 The Marksman of Crime 75.00
23 Diary of a Criminal 75.00
24 The Killer In The Iron Mask . . 75.00
25 I Hired My Killer 75.00
26 The Case of the Wanted Criminals 75.00
27 The Case of the Secret Six . . 75.00
28 Beware the Bogus Beggars . 75.00
29 The Crimes of Mr. Jumbo . . . 75.00
30 Man of a Thousand Faces . . 75.00
31 The Hot Money Gang 75.00
32 The Case o/t Bad Luck Clues 75.00
33 A Crime Is Born 75.00
34 The Amazing Crimes of Mr. X 75.00
35 This Crime For Hire 75.00
36 The Chameleon of Crime . . . 75.00
37 Miss Miller's Big Case 75.00
38 The Puzzle Shop For Crime . 75.00
39 Man Who Killed Daredevils . . 75.00
40 The Human Vultures 75.00
41 The Great Token Take 75.00
42 Super-Market Sleuth 75.00
43 Hotel Detective 75.00
44 S.S. Justice,B:Comics Code . 50.00
45 Miss Miller, Widow 50.00
46 Mr. District Attorney, Public Defender 50.00
47 The Missing Persons Racket . 50.00
48 Manhunt With the Mounties . 50.00
49 The TV Dragnet 50.00
50 The Case of Frank Bragan, Little Shot 50.00
51 The Big Heist 50.00
52 Crooked Wheels of Fortune . 50.00
53 The Courtroom Patrol 50.00
54 The Underworld Spy Squad . 50.00
55 The Flying Saucer Mystery . . 50.00
56 The Underworld Oracle 50.00
57 The Underworld Employment Agency 50.00
58 The Great Bomb Scare 50.00
59 Great Underworld Spy Plot . . 50.00
60 The D.A.'s TV Rival 50.00
61 SMo(c),Architect of Crime . . . 50.00
62 A-Bombs For Sale 50.00
63 The Flying Prison 50.00
64 SMo(c),The Underworld Treasure Hunt 50.00
65 SMo(c),World Wide Dragnet . 50.00
66 SMo(c),The Secret of the D.A.'s Diary 50.00
67 January-February, 1959 . . . . 50.00

MODESTY BLAISE

1 DG,V:Gabriel 4.95
2 DG,V:Gabriel 4.95

MORE FUN COMICS

(See: NEW FUN COMICS)

MOVIE COMICS

April, 1939

1 'Gunga Din' 1,600.00
2 Stagecoach 1,000.00
3 East Side of Heaven 800.00
4 Captain Fury,B:Oregon Trail 750.00
5 Man in the Iron Mask 750.00
6 September, 1939 . . . . 850.00

MS. TREE QUARTERLY

1 MGr,A:Batman 3.50
2 A:Butcher 2.95
3 A:Butcher 2.95
4 'Paper Midnight' 3.95
5 Murder/Rape Investigation 3.95
6 Gothic House 3.95
7 . . . . 3.95
8 CI,FMc,Ms Tree Pregnant(c), B.U. King Faraday 3.95
9 Child Kidnapped 3.95

MUTT AND JEFF

1939

1 . . . . 800.00
2 . . . . 400.00
3 . . . . 300.00
4 and 5 . . . . @250.00
6 thru 10 . . . . @130.00
11 thru 20 . . . . @110.00
21 thru 30 . . . . @67.00
31 thru 50 . . . . @35.00
51 thru 70 . . . . @30.00
71 thru 80 . . . . @25.00
81 thru 99 . . . . @20.00
100 . . . . 25.00
101 thru 103 . . . . @20.00
104 thru 148 . . . . @15.00

MY GREATEST ADVENTURE

January-February, 1955

1 LSt,I Was King Of Danger Island 800.00
2 My Million Dollar Dive 400.00
3 I Found Captain Kidd's Treasure 250.00
4 I Had A Date With Doom . . . 250.00
5 I Escaped From Castle Morte 225.00
6 I Had To Spend A Million . . 200.00
7 I Was A Prisoner On Island X 175.00
8 The Day They Stole My Face 175.00
9 I Walked Through The Doors of Destiny 175.00
10 We Found A World Of Tiny Cavemen 175.00
11 LSt(c),My Friend, Madcap Manning 150.00
12 MMe(c),I Hunted Big Game in Outer Space 150.00
13 LSt(c),I Hunted Goliath The Robot 150.00
14 LSt,I Had the Midas Touch of Gold 150.00
15 JK, I Hunted the Worlds Wildest Animals 150.00
16 JK,I Died a Thousand Times 150.00
17 JK,I Doomed the World . . . 150.00
18 JK(c),We Discovered The Edge of the World 150.00
19 I Caught Earth's Strangest Criminal 150.00
20 JK,I Was Big-Game on Neptune 150.00
21 JK,We Were Doomed By The Metal-Eating Monster . . 150.00
22 I Was Trapped In The Magic Mountains 125.00
23 I Was A Captive In Space Prison 125.00
24 NC(c),I Was The Robinson Crusoe of Space 125.00
25 I Led Earth's Strangest Safari! 125.00
26 NC(c),We Battled The Sand Creature 125.00
27 I Was the Earth's First Exile 125.00
28 I Stalked the Camouflage Creatures 150.00
29 I Tracked the Forbidden Powers 125.00
30 We Cruised Into the Supernatural! 125.00
31 I Was A Modern Hercules . . . 75.00
32 We Were Trapped In A Freak Valley! 75.00
33 I Was Pursued by the Elements 75.00
34 DD,We Unleashed The Cloud Creatures 75.00
35 I Solved the Mystery of Volcano Valley 75.00
36 I Was Bewitched By Lady Doom 75.00
37 DD&SMo(c),I Hunted the Legendary Creatures! 75.00
38 DD&SMo(c),I Was the Slave of the Dream-Master 75.00
39 DD&SMo(c),We were Trapped in the Valley of no Return . . . 75.00
40 We Battled the Storm Creature 75.00
41 DD&SMo(c),I Was Tried by a Robot Court 45.00
42 DD&SMo(c),My Brother Was a Robot 45.00
43 DD&SMo(c),I Fought the Sonar Creatures 45.00
44 DD&SMo(c),We Fought the Beasts of Petrified Island . . . 45.00
45 DD&SMo(c),We Battled the Black Narwahl 45.00
46 DD&SMo(c),We Were Prisoners of the Sundial of Doom 45.00

My Greatest Adventure #3
© DC Comics, Inc.

47 We Became Partners of the Beast Brigade 45.00
48 DD&SMo(c),I Was Marooned On Earth 45.00
49 DD&SMo(c),I Was An Ally Of A Criminal Creature 45.00
50 DD&SMo(c),I Fought the Idol King 45.00
51 DD&SMo(c),We Unleashed the Demon of the Dungeon . . 40.00
52 DD&SMo(c),I Was A Stand-In For an Alien 40.00
53 DD&SMo(c),I, Creature Slayer 40.00
54 I Was Cursed With an Alien Pal 40.00
55 DD&SMo(c),I Beacame The Wonder-Man of Space 40.00
56 DD&SMo(c),My Brother-The Alien 40.00
57 DD&SMo(c),Don't Touch Me Or You'll Die 40.00
58 DD&SMo(c),ATh,I was Trapped in the Land of L'Oz 45.00
59 DD&SMo(c),Listen Earth-I Am Still Alive 45.00
60 DD&SMo(c),ATh,I Lived in Two Worlds 45.00
61 DD&SMo(c),ATh,I Battled For the Doom-Stone 45.00
62 DD&SMo(c),I Fought For An Alien Enemy 22.00
63 DD&SMo(c),We Braved the Trail of the Ancient Warrior . . 22.00
64 DD&SMo(c),They Crowned My Fiance Their King! 22.00
65 DD&SMo(c),I Lost the Life or Death Secret 22.00
66 DD&SMo(c),I Dueled with the Super Spirits 22.00
67 I Protected the Idols of Idoro! 22.00
68 DD&SMo(c),My Deadly Island of Space 22.00
69 DD&SMo(c),I Was A Courier From the Past 22.00
70 DD&SMo(c),We Tracked the Fabled Fish-Man! 22.00
71 We Dared to open the Door of Danger Dungeon 22.00
72 The Haunted Beach 22.00
73 I Defeiller Mountain 22.00
74 GC(c),We Were Challenged By The River Spirit 22.00
75 GC(c),Castaway Cave-Men of 1950 . . . . 22.00
76 MMe(c),We Battled the Micro-Monster 22.00
77 ATh,We Found the Super-Tribes of Tomorrow 25.00
78 Destination-'Dead Man's Alley' 22.00
79 Countdown in Dinosaur Valley 22.00
80 BP,I:Doom Patrol 300.00
81 BP,ATh,I:Dr. Janus 125.00
82 BP,F:Doom Patrol 125.00
83 BP,F:Doom Patrol 125.00
84 BP,V:General Immortus . . . 125.00
85 BP,ATh,F:Doom Patrol 125.00

Becomes:

DOOM PATROL

March, 1964

86 BP,I:Brogherhood of Evil 82.00
87 BP,O:Negative Man 55.00
88 BP,O:Chief 50.00
89 BP,I:Animal-Veg.-MineralMan 50.00
90 BP,A:Brotherhood of Evil . . . 50.00
91 BP,I:Manto, Gargvax 50.00
92 BP,I:Dr.Tymc, A:Mento 50.00
93 BP,A:Brotherhood of Evil . . . 50.00
94 BP,I:Dr.Radich, The Claw . . . 50.00
95 BP,A:Animal-Vegetable -Mineral Man 50.00
96 BP,A:General Immortus, Brotherhood of Evil 46.00
97 BP,A:General Immortus, Brotherhood of Evil 46.00
98 BP,I:Mr.103 . . . . 46.00
99 I:Beast Boy 50.00
100 BP,O:Beast Boy,Robotman . 53.00
101 BP,A:Beast Boy 28.00
102 BP,A:Beast Boy,Challengers of the Unknown 27.00
103 BP,A:Beast Boy 27.00
104 BP,W:Elasti-Girl,Mento, C:JLA,Teen Titans 27.00
105 BP,A:Beast Boy 27.00
106 BP,O:Negative Man 27.00
107 BP,A:Beast Boy, I:Dr.Death . 27.00
108 BP,A:Brotherhood of Evil . . 27.00
109 BP,I:Mandred 27.00
110 BP,A:Garguax,Mandred, Brotherhood of Evil 25.00
111 BP,I:Zarox-13,A:Brotherhood of Evil 25.00
112 BP,O:Beast Boy,Madame Rouge 25.00
113 BP,A:Beast Boy,Mento 25.00
114 BP,A:Beast Boy 25.00
115 BP,A:Beast Boy 25.00
116 BP,A:Madame Rouge 25.00
117 BP,I:Black Vulture 25.00
118 BP,A:Beast Boy 25.00
119 BP,A:Madam Rouge 25.00
120 I:Wrecker 25.00
121 JO,D:Doom Patrol 65.00
122 rep.Doom Patrol #89 . . . . . . 5.00
123 rep.Doom Patrol #95 . . . . . . 5.00
124 rep.Doom Patrol #90 . . . . . . 5.00

MY NAME IS CHAOS

1 JRy,Song Laid Waste to Earth . 4.95
2 JRy,Colonization of Mars 4.95
3 JRy,Search for Eternal Beings . 4.95
4 JRy,final issue 4.95

MYSTERY IN SPACE

April-May, 1951

1 Cl&FrG(c),FF,B:Knights of the Galaxy,Nine Worlds to Conquer 1,700.00
2 Cl(c),MA,A:Knights of the Galaxy, Jesse James-Highwayman of Space 700.00
3 Cl(c),A:Knights of the Galaxy, Duel of the Planets 600.00
4 Cl(c),S&K,MA,A:Knights of the Galaxy, Master of Doom . . 450.00
5 Cl(c),A:Knights of the Galaxy, Outcast of the Lost World . 450.00
6 Cl(c),A:Knights of the Galaxy, The Day the World Melted . 400.00
7 GK(c),ATh,A:Knights of the Galaxy, Challenge o/t Robot Knight 400.00
8 MA,It's a Women's World . . 400.00
9 MA(c),The Seven Wonders of Space 400.00
10 MA(c),The Last Time I Saw Earth 400.00
11 GK(c),Unknown Spaceman . 275.00
12 MA,The Sword in the Sky . . 275.00
13 MA(c),MD,Signboard in Space 275.00
14 MA,GK(c),Hollywood in Space 275.00
15 MA(c),Doom from Station X 275.00
16 MA(c),Honeymoon in Space 250.00
17 MA(c),The Last Mile of Space 250.00
18 MA(c),GK,Chain Gang of Space 250.00
19 MA(c),The Great Space-Train Robbery 275.00

Mystery in Space #20
© DC Comics, Inc.

20 MA(c),The Man in the Martian Mask 200.00
21 MA(c),Interplanetary Merry- Go-Round 200.00
22 MA(c),The Square Earth . . . 200.00
23 MA(c),Monkey-Rocket to Mars 200.00
24 MA(c),A:Space Cabby, Hitchhiker of Space 200.00
25 MA(c),Station Mars on the Air 200.00
26 GK(c),Earth is the Target . . 150.00
27 The Human Fishbowl 150.00
28 The Radio Planet 150.00
29 GK(c),Space-Enemy Number One 150.00
30 GK(c),The Impossible World Named Earth 150.00
31 GK(c),The Day the Earth Split in Two 150.00
32 GK(c),Riddle of the Vanishing Earthmen 150.00
33 The Wooden World War . . . 150.00
34 GK(c),The Man Who Moved the World 150.00
35 The Counterfeit Earth 150.00
36 GK(c),Secret of the

All comics prices listed are for *Near Mint* condition.

Moon Sphinx 150.00
37 GK(c),Secret of the Masked Martians 150.00
38 GK(c),The Canals of Earth . 150.00
39 GK(c),Sorcerers of Space . . 150.00
40 GK(c),Riddle of the Runaway Earth 150.00
41 GK(c),The Miser of Space . 135.00
42 GK(c),The Secret of the Skyscraper Spaceship 135.00
43 GK(c),Invaders From the Space Satellites 135.00
44 GK(c),Amazing Space Flight of North America 135.00
45 GK(c),MA,Flying Saucers Over Mars 135.00
46 GK(c),MA,Mystery of the Moon Sniper 135.00
47 GK(c),MA,Interplanetary Tug of War 135.00
48 GK(c),MA,Secret of the Scarecrow World 135.00
49 GK(c),The Sky-High Man . . 135.00
50 GK(c),The Runaway Space-Train 135.00
51 GK(c),MABattle of the Moon Monsters 135.00
52 GK(c),MSy,Mirror Menace of Mars 135.00
53 GK(c),B:Adam Strange stories, Menace o/t Robot Raiders 1,200.00
54 GK(c),Invaders of the Underground World 300.00
55 GK(c),The Beast From the Runaway World 175.00
56 GK(c),The Menace of the Super-Atom 125.00
57 GK(c),Mystery of the Giant Footsteps 125.00
58 GK(c),Chariot in in the Sky . 125.00
59 GK(c),The Duel of the Two Adam Stranges 125.00
60 GK(c),The Attack of the Tentacle World 125.00
61 CI&MA(c),Threat of the Tornado Tyrant 75.00
62 CI&MA(c),The Beast with the Sizzling Blue Eyes 75.00
63 The Weapon that Swallowed Men 75.00
64 The Radioactive Menace . . . 75.00
65 Mechanical Masters of Rann . 75.00
66 Space-Island of Peril 75.00
67 Challenge of the Giant Fireflies 75.00
68 CI&MA(c),Fadeaway Doom . . 75.00
69 CI&MA(c),Menace of the Aqua-Ray Weapon 75.00
70 CI&MA(c),Vengeance of the Dust Devil 75.00
71 CI&MA(c),The Challenge of the Crystal Conquerors 75.00
72 The Multiple Menace Weapon 60.00
73 CI&MA(c),The Invisible Invaders of Rann 60.00
74 CI&MA(c),The Spaceman Who Fought Himself 60.00
75 CI&MA(c),The Planet That Came to a Standstill 175.00
76 CI&MA(c),Challenge of the Rival Starman 60.00
77 CI&MA(c),Ray-Gun in the Sky 60.00
78 CI&MA(c),Shadow People of the Eclipse 60.00
79 CI&MA(c),The Metal Conqueror of Rann 60.00
80 CI&MA(c),The Deadly Shadows of Adam Strange . . 60.00
81 CI&MA(c),The Cloud-Creature That Menaced Two Worlds . . 30.00
82 CI&MA(c),World War on Earth and Rann 30.00
83 CI&MA(c),The Emotion-Master of Space 30.00
84 CI&MA(c),The Powerless Weapons of Adam Strange . . 30.00
85 CI&MA(c),Riddle of the Runaway Rockets 30.00
86 CI&MA(c),Attack of the Underworld Giants 30.00
87 MA(c),The Super-Brain of Adam Strange,B:Hawkman . 150.00
88 CI&MA(c),The Robot Wraith of Rann 125.00
89 MA(c),Siren o/t Space Ark . . 125.00
90 CI&MA(c),Planets and Peril, E:Hawkman 125.00
91 CI&MA(c),Puzzle of the Perilous Prisons 20.00
92 DD&SMo(c),The Alien Invasion From Earth,B:Space Ranger . 20.00

Mystery in Space #28
© DC Comics, Inc.

93 DD&SMo(c),The Convict Twins of Space 20.00
94 DD&SMo(c),The Adam Strange Story 20.00
95 The Hydra-Head From Outer Space 20.00
96 The Coins That Doomed Two Planets 20.00
97 The Day Adam Strange Vanished 20.00
98 The Wizard of the Cosmos . . 20.00
99 DD&SMo(c),The World-Destroyer From Space 20.00
100 DD&SMo(c),GK,The Death of Alanna 20.00
101 GK(c),The Valley of 1,000 Dooms 20.00
102 GK,The Robot World of Rann 20.00
103 The Billion-Dollar Time-Capsule(Space Ranger),I:Ultra the Multi-Agent 20.00
104 thru 109 . . . . @10.00
110 Sept. 1966 . . . . 10.00
111 JAp,SD,MR,DSp,Sept. 1980 10.00
112 JAp,TS,JKu(c) 10.00
113 JKu(c),MGo 10.00
114 JKu(c),JCr,SD,DSp 10.00
115 JKu(c),SD,GT,BB 10.00
116 JSn(c),JCr,SD 10.00
117 DN,GT,March, 1981 . . . . . . 10.00

MYSTERY PLAY
Vertigo

HC GMo(s),JMu, ... 19.95

NATHANIEL DUSK
February, 1984

1 GC(p) 1.50
2 thru 4 GC(p), May 1984 . . . @1.25

NATHANIEL DUSK II
October, 1985

1 thru 4 GC,January, 1986 . . . @2.00

NAZZ, THE

1 Michael'sBook 5.50
2 Johnny'sBook 4.95
3 Search for Michael Nazareth . . 4.95
4 V:Retaliators,final issue 4.95

NEW ADVENTURES OF SUPERBOY
(See: SUPERBOY)

NEW BOOK OF COMICS
1937

1 Dr.Occult 9,500.00
2 Dr.Occult 6,500.00

NEW COMICS
1935

1 . . . . 10,000.00
2 . . . . 5,000.00
3 thru 6 . . . . @3,500.00
7 thru 11 . . . . @3,000.00

Becomes:

NEW ADVENTURE COMICS
January, 1937

12 S&S 3,000.00
13 thru 20 . . . . @2,500.00
21 . . . . 2,500.00
22 thru 31 . . . . @2,200.00

Becomes:

ADVENTURE COMICS

More Fun Comics #32
© DC Comics, Inc.

NEW FUN COMICS
February, 1935

1 B:Oswald the Rabbit, Jack Woods 30,000.00
2 . . . . 10,000.00
3 . . . . 6,000.00
4 . . . . 6,000.00

5 . . . . 6,000.00
6 S&S,B:Dr.Occult, Henri Duval 10,000.00

Becomes:

MORE FUN COMICS

7 S&S,WK 3,600.00
8 S&S,WK 2,800.00
9 S&S,E:Henri Duval 2,800.00
10 S&S 1,800.00
11 S&S,B:Calling all Girls . . . 1,800.00
12 S&S 1,500.00
13 S&S 1,500.00
14 S&S,Color,Dr.Occult 7,000.00
15 S&S 2,500.00
16 S&S,Christmas(c) 2,500.00
17 S&S 2,000.00
18 S&S 1,000.00
19 S&S 1,000.00
20 HcK,S&S 1,000.00
21 S&S 750.00
22 S&S 750.00
23 S&S 750.00
24 S&S 750.00
25 S&S 650.00
26 S&S 650.00
27 S&S 650.00
28 S&S 650.00
29 S&S 650.00
30 S&S 650.00
31 S&S 650.00

More Fun Comics #38
© DC Comics, Inc.

32 S&S,E:Dr. Occult 650.00
33 . . . . 650.00
34 . . . . 650.00
35 . . . . 650.00
36 B:Masked Ranger 600.00
37 thru 40 . . . . @600.00
41 E:Masked Ranger 500.00
42 thru 50 . . . . @500.00
51 I:The Spectre 2,200.00
52 O:The Spectre Pt.1, E:Wing Brady 25,000.00
53 O:The Spectre Pt.2, B:Capt.Desmo 18,000.00
54 E:King Carter,Spectre(c) . . 5,000.00
55 I:Dr.Fate,E:Bulldog Martin, Spectre(c) 7,500.00
56 B:Congo Bill,Dr.Fate(c) . . . 1,800.00
57 Spectre(c) 1,800.00
58 Spectre(c) 1,800.00
59 A:Spectre 2,500.00
60 Spectre(c) 1,600.00
61 Spectre(c) 1,500.00
62 Spectre(c) 1,500.00
63 Spectre(c),E:St.Bob Neal . 1,500.00
64 Spectre(c),B:Lance Larkin . 1,500.00
65 Spectre(c) 1,500.00
66 Spectre(c) 1,500.00
67 Spectre(c),O:Dr. Fate, E:Congo Bill,Biff Bronson . 4,000.00
68 Dr.Fate(c),B:Clip Carson . . 1,200.00
69 Dr.Fate(c) 1,200.00
70 Dr.Fate(c),E:Lance Larkin . 1,200.00
71 Dr.Fate(c),I:Johnny Quick . 3,400.00
72 Dr. Fate has Smaller Helmet, E:Sgt. Carey,Sgt.O'Malley . 1,000.00
73 Dr.Fate(c),I:Aquaman,Green Arrow,Speedy 5,200.00
74 Dr.Fate(c),A:Aquaman . . . 1,200.00
75 Dr.Fate(c) 1,000.00
76 Dr.Fate(c),MMe,E:Clip Carson, B:Johnny Quick 1,000.00
77 MMe,Green Arrow(c) 1,000.00
78 MMe,Green Arrow(c) 1,000.00
79 MMe,Green Arrow(c) 1,000.00
80 MMe,Green Arrow(c) 1,000.00
81 MMe,Green Arrow(c) 700.00
82 MMe,Green Arrow(c) 700.00
83 MMe,Green Arrow(c) 700.00
84 MMe,Green Arrow(c) 700.00
85 MMe,Green Arrow(c) 700.00
86 MMe 700.00
87 MMe,E:Radio Squad 700.00
88 MMe,Green Arrow(c) 700.00
89 MMe,O:Gr.Arrow&Speedy . . 800.00
90 MMe,Green Arrow(c) 700.00
91 MMe,Green Arrow(c) 500.00
92 MMe,Green Arrow(c) 500.00
93 MMe,B:Dover & Clover 500.00
94 MMe,Green Arrow(c) 500.00
95 MMe,Green Arrow(c) 500.00
96 MMe,Green Arrow(c) 500.00
97 MMe,JKu,E:Johnny Quick . . 500.00
98 E:Dr. Fate 500.00
99 Green Arrow(c) 500.00
100 . . . . 650.00
101 O&I:Superboy, E:The Spectre 4,800.00
102 A:Superboy 800.00
103 A:Superboy 700.00
104 Superboy(c) 450.00
105 Superboy(c) 450.00
106 . . . . 450.00
107 E:Superboy 450.00
108 A:Genius Jones,'Genius Meets Genius' 100.00
109 A:Genius Jones, The Disappearing Deposits 100.00
110 A:Genius Jones, Birds, Brains and Burglary 100.00
111 A:Genius Jones, Jeepers Creepers 100.00
112 A:Genius Jones, The Tell-Tale Tornado 100.00
113 A:Genius Jones, Clocks and Shocks 100.00
114 A:Genius Jones, The Milky Way 100.00
115 A:Genius Jones,Foolish Questions 100.00
116 A:Genius Jones,Palette For Plunder 100.00
117 A:Genius Jones,Battle of the Pretzel Benders 100.00
118 A:Genius Jones,The Sinister Siren 100.00
119 A:Genius Jones,A Perpetual Jackpot 100.00
120 A:Genius Jones,The Man in the Moon 100.00
121 A:Genius Jones,The Mayor Goes Haywire 75.00
122 A:Genius Jones,When Thug-Hood Was In Floor 75.00
123 A:Genius Jones,Hi Diddle Diddle, the Cat and the Fiddle 75.00

More Fun Comics #107
© DC Comics, Inc.

124 A:Genius Jones, The Zany Zoo 75.00
125 Genius Jones, Impossible But True 475.00
126 A:Genius Jones,The Case of the Gravy Spots 75.00
127 November-December, 1947 150.00

NEW GODS, THE
February-March, 1971

1 JK,I:Orion 25.00
2 JK 19.00
3 JK 16.50
4 JK,O:Manhunter, rep. 14.00
5 JK,I:Fastbak & Black Racer . . 14.00
6 JK 14.00
7 JK,O:Orion 14.00
8 JK 14.00
9 JK,I:Forager 14.00
10 JK 14.00
11 JK 14.00
12 DN,DA,R:New Gods 5.00
13 DN,DA 5.00
14 DN,DA 5.00
15 RB,BMc 5.00
16 DN,DA 5.00
17 DN,DA 5.00
18 DN,DA 5.00

NEW GODS
(Reprints)

1 JK reprint 2.25
2 JK reprint 2.00
3 JK reprint 2.00
4 JK reprint 2.00
5 JK reprint 2.00
6 JK rep.+NewMaterial 2.00

NEW GODS
[2nd Series]

1 From Cosmic Odyssey 2.00
2 A:Orion of New Genesis 1.50
3 A:Orion 1.50
4 Renegade Apokolyptian Insect Colony 1.50
5 Orion vs. Forager 1.50
6 A:Eve Donner, Darkseid 1.50
7 Bloodline #1 . . . . 1.50
8 Bloodline #2 . . . . 1.50
9 Bloodline #3 . . . . 1.50

All comics prices listed are for *Near Mint* condition.

10 Bloodline #4 . . . . 1.50
11 Bloodline #5 . . . . 1.50
12 Bloodlines #6 . . . . 1.50
13 Back on Earth 1.50
14 I:Reflektor 1.50
15 V:Serial Killer 1.50
16 A:Fastbak & Metron 1.50
17 A:Darkseid, Metron 1.50
18 A:YugaKhan,Darkseid, Moniters 1.50
19 V:Yuga Khan 1.50
20 Darkseid Dethroned, V:Yuga Khan 1.50
21 A:Orion 1.50
22 A:Metron 1.50
23 A:Forever People 1.50
24 A:Forever People 1.50
25 The Pact #1,R:Infinity Man . . . 1.50
26 The Pact #2 . . . . 1.50
27 Asault on Apokolips,Pact#3 . . . 1.50
28 Pact #4, final issue 1.50

NEW GUARDIANS

1 JSon,from Millenium series . . . 2.50
2 JSon,Colombian Drug Cartel . . 1.75
3 JSon,in South Africa, V:Janwillem's Army 1.25
4 JSon,V:Neo-Nazi Skinheads in California 1.25
5 JSon,Tegra Kidnapped 1.25
6 JSon, In China, Invasion x-over 1.25
7 JSon, Guardians Return Home 1.25
8 JSon, V:Janwillem 1.25
9 JSon, A:Tome Kalmaku, V:Janwillem 1.25
10 JSon, A:Tome Kalmaku 1.25
11 PB,Janwillem's secret 1.25
12 PB,New Guardians Future revealed, final issue 1.25

NEW TEEN TITANS

November, 1980

1 GP,RT,V:Gordanians (see DC Comics Presents #26 . . . . . . 14.00
2 GP,RT,I:Deathstroke the Terminator, I&D:Ravager . . . 18.00
3 GP,I:Fearsome Five 7.00
4 GP,RT,A:JLA,O:Starfire 8.00
5 CS,RT,O:Raven,I:Trigon 7.00
6 GP,V:Trigon,O:Raven 5.00
7 GP,RT,O:Cyborg 6.00
8 GP,RT,A Day in the Life 5.00
9 GP,RT,A:Terminator, V:Puppeteer 6.00
10 GP,RT,A:Terminator 9.00
11 GP,RT,V:Hyperion 3.50
12 GP,RT,V:Titans of Myth 3.50
13 GP,RT,R:Robotman 3.00
14 GP,RT,I:New Brotherhood of Evil,V:Zahl and Rouge 3.00
15 GP,RT,D:Madame Rouge 3.00
16 GP,RT,I:Captain Carrot 3.00
17 GP,RT,I:Frances Kane 3.00
18 GP,RT,A:Orig.Starfire 3.00
19 GP,RT,A:Hawkman 3.00
20 GP,RT,V:Disruptor 3.00
21 GP,RT,GC,I:Brother Blood, Night Force 3.00
22 GP,RT,V:Brother Blood 2.50
23 GP,RT,I:Blackfire 2.50
24 GP,RT,A:Omega Men,I:X-hal . 2.50
25 GP,RT,A:Omega Men 2.50
26 GP,RT,I:Terra,Runaway #1 . . . 2.50
27 GP,RT,A:Speedy,Runaway #2 2.50
28 GP,RT,V:Terra 3.50
29 GP,RT,V:Broth.of Evil 2.00
30 GP,RT,V:Broth.of Evil,J:Terra . 2.00
31 GP,RT,V:Broth.of Evil 1.50
32 GP,RT,I:Thunder & Lightning . 1.50
33 GP,I:Trident 1.50
34 GP,V:The Terminator 3.00
35 KP,RT,V:Mark Wright 1.50
36 KP,RT,A:Thunder & Lightning . 1.50
37 GP,RT,A:Batman/Outsiders(x-over BATO#5),V:Fearsome Five . . . 2.00

New Teen Titans #24
© DC Comics, Inc.

38 GP,O:Wonder Girl 1.50
39 GP,Grayson quits as Robin . . . 5.00
40 GP,A:Brother Blood 1.50
Ann.#1 GP,RT,Blackfire 3.50
Ann.#2 GP,I:Vigilante 3.00
Ann.#3 GP,DG,D:Terra,A:Deathstroke V:The H.I.V.E. 3.50
Ann.#4 rep.Direct Ann.#1 . . . . . . 1.25
TPB Judas Contract rep.#39-44, Ann.#3,new GP(c) 14.95

[Special Issues]

Keebler:GP,DG,Drugs 3.00
Beverage:Drugs,RA 3.00
IBM:Drugs 4.00

Becomes:

TALES OF THE TEEN TITANS

41 GP,A:Brother Blood 1.75
42 GP,DG,V:Deathstroke 7.00
43 GP,DG,V:Deathstroke 7.00
44 GP,DG,I:Nightwing,O:Deathstroke Joe Wilson becomes Jericho . 12.00
45 GP,A:Aqualad,V:The H.I.V.E. . 1.50
46 GP,A:Aqualad,V:The H.I.V.E. . 1.50
47 GP,A:Aqualad,V:The H.I.V.E. . 1.50
48 SR,V:The Recombatants 1.50
49 GP,CI,V:Dr.Light,A:Flash 1.50
50 GP/DG W:Wonder Girl & Terry Long,C:Batman, Wonder Woman 2.50
51 RB,A:Cheshire 1.50
52 RB,A:Cheshire 1.50
53 RB,I:Ariel,A:Terminator 2.50
54 RB,A:Terminator 2.50
55 A:Terminator 2.50
56 A:Fearsome Five 1.50
57 A:Fearsome Five 1.50
58 E:MWn(s),A:Fearsome Five . . 1.50
59 rep. DC presennts #26 . . . . . . 1.00
60 thru 91 rep. . . . . @1.00

[Limited Series]

1 GP,O:Cyborg 2.00
2 GP,O:Raven 2.00
3 GD,O:Changling 2.00
4 GP/EC,O:Starfire 2.00

NEW TEEN TITANS

[Direct sales series]

August, 1984

1 B:MWn(s),GP,L:Raven 5.00
2 GP,D:Azareth,A:Trigon 3.50
3 GP,V:Raven 3.00
4 GP,V:Trigon,Raven 3.00
5 GP,D:Trigon,Raven disappears 3.00
6 GP,A:Superman,Batman 2.50
7 JL,V:Titans of Myth 2.50
8 JL,V:Titans of Myth 2.50
9 JL,V:Titans of Myth,I:Kole 2.50
10 JL,O:Kole 2.50
11 JL,O:Kole 2.50
12 JL,Ghost story 2.50
13 EB,Crisis 2.25
14 EB,Crisis 2.25
15 EB,A:Raven 2.25
16 EB,A:OmegaMen 2.25
17 EB,V:Blackfire 2.25
18 E:MWn(s),EB,V:Blackfire 2.25
19 EB,V:Mento 2.25
20 GP(c),EB,V:Cheshire,J.Todd . . 2.25
21 GP(c),EB,V:Cheshire,J.Todd . . 2.25
22 GP(c),EB,V:Blackfire,Mento, Brother Blood 2.25
23 GP(c),V:Blackfire 2.25
24 CB,V:Hybrid 2.25
25 EB,RT,V:Hybrid,Mento,A:Flash 2.25
26 KGa,V:Mento 2.25
27 KGa,Church of Br.Blood 2.00
28 EB,RT,V:Brother Blood,A:Flash 2.00
29 EB,RT,V:Brother Blood, A:Flash,Robin 2.00
30 EB,Batman,Superman 2.25
31 EB,RT,V:Brother Blood,A:Flash Batman,Robin,Gr.Lantern Corps Superman 2.00
32 EB,RT,Murder Weekend 2.00
33 EB,V:Terrorists 2.00
34 EB,RT,V:Mento,Hybird 2.00
35 PB,RT,V:Arthur & Eve 2.00
36 EB,RT,I:Wildebeest 2.50
37 EB,RT,V:Wildebeest 2.00
38 EB,RT,A:Infinity 2.00
39 EB,RT,F:Raven 2.00
40 EB,RT,V:Gentleman Ghost . . . 2.00
41 EB,V:Wildebeest,A:Puppeteer, Trident,Wildebeest 2.00
42 EB,RT,V:Puppeteer,Gizmo, Trident,Wildebeest 2.00
43 CS,RT,V:Phobia 2.00
44 RT,V:Godiva 2.00
45 EB,RT,A:Dial H for Hero 2.00
46 EB,RT,A:Dial H for Hero 2.00
47 O:Titans,C:Wildebeest 2.00
48 EB,RT,A:Red Star 2.00
49 EB,RT,A:Red Star 2.00
Ann.#1 A:Superman,V:Brainiac . . 2.50
Ann.#2 JBy,JL,O:Brother Blood . . 3.00
Ann.#3 I:Danny Chase 2.50
Ann.#4 V:Godiva 2.50

Becomes:

NEW TITANS

50 B:MWn(s),GP,BMc,B:Who is Wonder Girl? 5.00
51 GP,BMc 3.00
52 GP,BMc 3.00
53 GP,RT 3.00
54 GP,RT,E:Who is Wonder Girl? 3.00
55 GP,RT,I:Troia 3.00
56 MBr,RT,Tale of Middle Titans . 2.50
57 GP,BMc,V:Wildebeast 2.50
58 GP,TG,BMc,V:Wildebeast 2.50
59 GP,TG,BMc,V:Wildebeast 2.50
60 GP,TG,BMc,3rd A:Tim Drake (Face Revealed),Batman 5.00
61 GP,TG,BMc,A:Tim Drake, Batman 5.00
62 TG,AV,A:Deathstroke 4.00
63 TG,AV,A:Deathstroke 4.00
64 TG,AV,A:Deathstroke 4.00
65 TG,AV,A:Deathstroke,Tim Drake, Batman 4.00

66 TG,AV,V:Eric Forrester 2.50
67 TG,AV,V:Eric Forrester 2.50
68 SE,V:Royal Flush Gang 2.50
69 SE,V:Royal Flush Gang 2.50
70 SE,A:Deathstroke 4.00
71 TG,AV,B:Deathstroke,
B:Titans Hunt 7.00

New Titans #72 © DC Comics, Inc.

72 TG,AV,D:Golden Eagle 5.00
73 TG,AV,I:Phantasm 5.00
74 TG,AV,I:Pantha 4.00
75 TG,AV,IR:Jericho/Wildebeest . 4.00
76 TG,AV,V:Wildebeests 3.00
77 TG,AV,A:Red Star,N:Cyborg . . 3.00
78 TG,AV,V:Cyborg 3.00
79 TG,AV,I:Team Titans 4.00
80 KGa,PC,A:Team Titans 3.00
81 CS,AV,War of the Gods 3.00
82 TG,AV,V:Wildebeests 3.00
83 TG,AV,D:Jericho 3.50
84 TG,AV,E:Titans Hunt 3.00
85 TG,AV,I:Baby Wildebeest 2.50
86 CS,AV,E:Deathstroke. 2.50
87 TG,AV,A:Team Titans 2.50
88 TG,AV,CS,V:Team Titans 2.50
89 JBr,I:Lord Chaos 2.50
90 TG,AV,Total Chaos#2,A:Team
Titans,D'stroke,V:Lord Chaos . 2.00
91 TG,AV,Total Chaos#5,A:Team
Titans,D'stroke,V:Lord Chaos . 2.00
92 E:MWn(s),TG,AV,Total Chaos#8,
A:Team Titans,V:Lord Chaos . 2.00
93 TG,AV,Titans Sell-Out#3 . . . . . 2.00
94 PJ,F:Red Star & Cyborg 2.00
95 PJ,Red Star gains new powers 2.00
96 PJ,I:Solar Flare,
V:Konstantine 2.00
97 TG,AV,B:The Darkening,R:Speedy
V:Brotherhood of Evil 2.00
98 TG,AV,V:Brotherhood of Evil . . 2.00
99 TG,AV,I:Arsenal (Speedy) 2.00
100 TG,AV,W:Nightwing&Starfire,
V:Deathwing,Raven,A:Flash,Team
Titans,Hologram(c) 4.00
101 AV(i),L:Nightwing 2.00
102 AV(i),A:Prester John 2.00
103 AV(i),V:Bro. of Evil 2.00
104 Terminus #1 . . . . 2.00
105 Terminus #2 . . . . 2.00
106 Terminus #3 . . . . 2.00
107 Terminus #4 . . . . 2.00
108 A:Supergirl,Flash 2.00
109 F:Starfire 2.00
110 A:Flash,Serg.Steele 2.00
111 A:Checkmate 2.00
112 A:Checkmate 2.00
Ann.#5 V:Children of the Sun . . . 4.00
Ann.#6 CS,F:Starfire 4.00
Ann.#7 Armageddon 2001,I:Future
Teen Titans 6.00
Ann.#8 PJ,Eclipso,V:Deathstroke . 3.75
Ann.#9 Bloodlines#5,I:Anima 3.75
Ann.#10 Elseworlds story 3.75

NEW TITANS SELL-OUT SPECIAL

1 SE,AV,AH,I:Teeny Titans,
w/Nightwing poster 3.75

New York World's Fair Comics #2(nn) © DC Comics, Inc.

NEW YORK WORLD'S FAIR

1 1939 . . . . 12,000.00
2 1940 . . . . 7,000.00

NIGHT FORCE

August, 1982

1 GC,1:Night Force 1.25
2 thru 13 GC . . . . @1.00
14 GC,September,1983 . . . . 1.00

NUTSY SQUIRREL

September-October, 1954

61 SM 40.00
62 thru 71 . . . . @25.00
72 November, 1957 . . . . 25.00

OMAC

September-October, 1974

1 JK,I&O:Omac 10.00
2 JK,I:Mr.Big 8.00
3 JK,100,000 foes 8.00
4 JK,V:Kafka 8.00
5 JK,New Bodies for Old 8.00
6 JK,The Body Bank 8.00
7 JK,The Ocean Stealers 8.00
8 JK,Last issue 8.00

[2nd Series]

1 JBy,B&W prestige 5.00
2 JBy,The Great Depression era . 4.50
3 JBy,'To Kill Adolf Hitler' 4.50
4 JBy,D:Mr.Big 4.50

OMEGA MEN

December, 1982

1 KG,V:Citadel 2.50

Omega Men #5 © DC Comics, Inc.

2 KG,O:Broot 2.00
3 KG,I:Lobo 8.00
4 KG,D:Demonia,I:Felicity 1.50
5 KG,V:Lobo 5.00
6 KG,V:Citadel,D:Gepsen 2.00
7 O:Citadel,L:Auron 2.00
8 R:Nimbus,I:H.Hokum 2.00
9 V:HarryHokum,A:Lobo 5.00
10 A:Lobo (First Full Story) 7.00
11 V:Blackfire 1.50
12 R:Broots Wife 1.50
13 A:Broots Wife 1.50
14 Karna 1.50
15 Primus Goes Mad 1.50
16 Spotlight Issue 1.50
17 V:Psions 1.50
18 V:Psions 1.50
19 V:Psions,C:Lobo 3.00
20 V:Psions,A:Lobo 5.00
21 Spotlight Issue 1.25
22 Nimbus 1.25
23 Nimbus 1.25
24 Okaara 1.25
25 Kalista 1.25
26 V:Spiderguild 1.25
27 V:Psions 1.25
28 V:Psions 1.25
29 V:Psions 1.25
30 R:Primus,I:Artin 1.25
31 Crisis tie-in 1.25
32 Felicity 1.25
33 Regufe World 1.25
34 A:New Teen Titans 1.25
35 A:New Teen Titans 1.25
36 Last Days of Broot 1.25
37 V:Spiderguild,A:Lobo 4.00
38 A:Tweener Network 1.25
Ann.#1 KG,R:Harpis 2.25
Ann.#2 KG,O:Primus 2.25

OUR ARMY AT WAR

August, 1952

1 CI(c),Dig Your Foxhole Deep 750.00
2 CI(c),Champ 400.00
3 GK(c),No Exit 300.00
4 IN(c),Last Man 300.00
5 IN(c),T.N.T. Bouquet 250.00
6 IN(c),Battle Flag 250.00
7 IN(c),Dive Bomber 250.00
8 IN(c),One Man Army 250.00
9 GC(c),Undersea Raider 250.00
10 IN(c),Soldiers on the

High Wire 250.00
11 IN(c),Scratch One Meatball . 250.00
12 IN(c),The Big Drop 200.00
13 BK(c),Ghost Ace 200.00
14 Drummer of Waterloo 200.00
15 IN(c),Thunder in the Skies . 200.00
16 IN(c),A Million To One Shot 200.00
17 IN(c),The White Death 200.00
18 IN(c),Frontier Fighter 200.00
19 IN(c),The Big Ditch 200.00
20 IN(c),Abandon Ship 200.00
21 IN(c),Dairy of a Flattop 150.00
22 JGr(c),Ranger Raid 150.00
23 IN(c),Jungle Navy 150.00
24 IN(c),Suprise Landing 150.00
25 JGr(c),Take 'Er Down 150.00
26 JGr(c),Sky Duel 150.00
27 IN(c),Diary of a Frogman . . 150.00
28 JGr(c),Detour-War 150.00
29 IN(c),Grounded Fighter 150.00
30 JGr(c),Torpedo Raft 150.00
31 IN(c),Howitzer Hill 150.00
32 JGr(c),Battle Mirror 125.00
33 JGr(c),Fighting Gunner 125.00
34 JGr(c),Point-Blank War 125.00
35 JGr(c),Frontline Tackle 125.00
36 JGr(c),Foxhole Mascot 125.00
37 JGr(c),Walking Battle Pin . . 125.00
38 JGr(c),Floating Pillbox 125.00
39 JGr(c),Trench Trap 125.00
40 RH(c),Tank Hunter 125.00
41 JGr(c),Jungle Target 125.00
42 IN(c),Shadow Targets 100.00
43 JGr(c),A Bridge For Billy . . . 100.00
44 JGr(c),Thunder In The Desert 100.00
45 JGr(c),Diary of a Fighter Pilot 100.00
46 JGr(c),Prize Package 100.00
47 JGr(c),Flying Jeep 100.00
48 JGr(c),Front Seat 100.00
49 JKu(c),Landing Postponed . 100.00
50 JGr(c),Mop-Up Squad . . . 100.00
51 JGr(c),Battle Tag 75.00
52 JGr(c),Pony Express Pilot . . . 75.00
53 JGr(c),One Ringside-For War 75.00
54 JKu(c),No-Man Secret 75.00
55 JGr(c),No Rest For A Raider . 75.00
56 JKu(c),You're Next 75.00
57 JGr(c),Ten-Minute Break 75.00
58 JKu(c),The Fighting Snow Bird 75.00
59 JGr(c),The Mustang Had
My Number 75.00
60 JGr(c),Ranger Raid 75.00
61 JGr(c),A Pigeon For Easy Co. 85.00
62 JKu(c),Trigger Man 85.00
63 JGr(c),The Big Toss 85.00
64 JKu(c),Tank Rider 85.00
65 JGr(c),Scramble-War Upstairs 85.00
66 RH(c),Gunner Wanted 85.00
67 JKu(c),Boiling Point 85.00
68 JKu(c),End of the Line 85.00
69 JGr(c),Combat Cage 85.00
70 JGr(c),Torpedo Tank 85.00
71 JGr(c),Flying Mosquitoes . . . 85.00
72 JGr(c),No. 1 Pigeon 85.00
73 JKu(c),Shooting Gallery 85.00
74 JGr(c),Ace Without Guns . . . 85.00
75 JGr(c),Blind Night Fighter . . . 85.00
76 JKu(c),Clipped Hellcat 85.00
77 JGr(c),Jets Don't Dream 85.00
78 IN(c),Battle Nurse 85.00
79 JGr(c),What's the Price
of a B-17? 85.00
80 JGr(c),The Sparrow And
The...Hawk 85.00
81 JGr(c),Sgt. Rock in The
Rock of Easy Co. 950.00
82 JGr(c),Gun Jockey 200.00
83 JGr(c),B:Sgt.Rock Stories,
The Rock and the Wall 400.00
84 JKu(c),Laughter On
Snakehead Hill 125.00
85 JGr(c),Ice Cream Soldier . . 150.00
86 RH(c),Tank 711 . . . . 125.00
87 RH(c),Calling Easy Co. 125.00
88 JKu(c),The Hard Way 125.00

Our Army at War #8 © DC Comics, Inc.

89 RH(c),No Shoot From Easy 125.00
90 JKu(c),3 Stripes Hill 125.00
91 JGr(c),No Answer from Sarge 125.00
92 JGr(c),Luck of Easy 85.00
93 JGr(c),Deliver One Airfield . . 85.00
94 JKu(c),Target-Easy Company 85.00
95 JKu(c),Battle Of The Stripes . 85.00
96 JGr(c),Last Stand For Easy . . 85.00
97 JKu(c),What Makes A
Sergeant Run? 85.00
98 JKu(c),Soldiers Never Die . . . 85.00
99 JKu(c),Easy's Hardest Battle . 85.00
100 JKu(c),No Exit For Easy . . . 85.00
101 JKu(c),End Of Easy 50.00
102 JKu(c),The Big Star 50.00
103 RH(c),Easy's Had It 50.00
104 JKu(c),A New Kind Of War . 50.00
105 JKu(c),T.N.T. Birthday 50.00
106 JKu(c),Meet Lt. Rock 50.00
107 JKu(c),Doom Over Easy . . . 50.00
108 JGr(c),Unknown Sergeant . . 50.00
109 JKu(c),Roll Call For Heroes . 50.00
110 JKu(c),That's An Order . . . 50.00
111 JKu(c),What's The Price
Of A Dog Tag 50.00
112 JKu(c),Battle Shadow 50.00
113 JKu(c),Eyes Of A
Blind Gunner 50.00
114 JKu(c),Killer Sergeant 50.00
115 JKu(c),Rock's Battle Family . 50.00
116 JKu(c),S.O.S. Sgt. Rock . . . 50.00
117 JKu(c),Snafu Squad 45.00
118 RH(c),The Tank Vs. The
Tin Soldier 45.00
119 JKu(c),A Bazooka For
Babyface 45.00
120 JGr(c),Battle Tags
For Easy Co. 25.00
121 JKu(c),New Boy In Easy . . . 25.00
122 JKu(c),Battle of the
Pajama Commandoes 25.00
123 JGr(c),Battle Brass Ring . . . 25.00
124 JKu(c),Target-Sgt. Rock . . . 25.00
125 JKu(c),Hold-At All Costs . . . 25.00
126 RH(c),The End Of
Easy Company 25.00
127 JKu(c),4 Faces of Sgt. Rock 25.00
128 JKu(c),O:Sgt. Rock 125.00
129 JKu(c),Heroes Need Cowards 25.00
130 JKu(c),No Hill For Easy . . 25.00
131 JKu(c),One Pair of
Dogtags For Sale 25.00
132 JKu(c),Young Soldiers
Never Cry 25.00
133 JKu(c),Yesterday's Hero . . 25.00
134 JKu(c),The T.N.T. Book . . 25.00
135 JKu(c),Battlefield Double . . . 25.00
136 JKu(c),Make Me A Hero . . . 25.00
137 JKu(c),Too Many Sergeants 25.00
138 JKu(c),Easy's Lost Sparrow 25.00
139 JKu(c),A Firing Squad
For Easy 25.00
140 JKu(c),Brass Sergeant . . . 25.00
141 JKu(c),Dead Man's Trigger . 25.00
142 JKu(c),Easy's New Topkick . 25.00
143 JKu(c),Easy's T.N.T. Crop . . 25.00
144 JKu(c),The Sparrow And
The Tiger 25.00
145 JKu(c),A Feather For
Little Sure Shot 25.00
146 JKu(c),The Fighting Guns
For Easy 25.00
147 JKu(c),Book One:Generals
Don't Die 25.00
148 JKu(c),Book Two:Generals
Don't Die:Generals Are
Sergeants With Stars 25.00
149 JKu(c),Surrender Ticket . . . 25.00
150 JKu(c),Flytrap Hill 25.00
151 JKu(c),War Party,
I:Enemy Ace 125.00
152 Jku(c),Last Man-Last Shot . 30.00
153 JKu(c),Easy's Last Stand . . 25.00
154 JKu(c),Boobytrap Mascot . . 25.00
155 JKu(c),No Stripes For Me . . 25.00
156 JKu(c),The Human Tank Trap 25.00
157 JKu(c),Nothin's Ever
Lost In War 25.00
158 JKu(c),Iron Major-Rock
Sergeant 25.00
159 JKu(c),The Blind Gun 25.00
160 JKu(c),What's The Color
Of Your Blood 25.00
161 JKu(c),Dead End
For A Dogface 25.00
162 JKu(c),The Price and
The Sergeant 25.00
163 JKu(c),Kill Me-Kill Me 25.00
164 JKu(c),No Exit For Easy,
reprint from #100 . . . . 25.00
165 JKu(c),The Return of the
Iron Major 15.00
166 JKu(c),Half A Sergeant 15.00
167 JKu(c),Kill One-Save One . . 15.00
168 JKu(c),I Knew The
Unknown Soldier 15.00
169 JKu(c),Nazi On My Back . . . 15.00
170 JKu(c),Buzzard Bait Hill . . 15.00
171 JKu(c),The Sergeant Must Die 15.00
172 JKu(c),A Slug For A Sergeant 15.00
173 JKu(c),Easy's Hardest Battle,
reprint from #99 . . . . 15.00
174 JKu(c),One Kill Too Many . . 15.00
175 JKu(c),T.N.T. Letter 15.00
176 JKu(c),Give Me Your Stripes 15.00
177 JKu(c),Target-Easy Company,
reprint from #94 . . . . 15.00
178 JKu(c),Only One Medal
For Easy 15.00
179 JKu(c),A Penny Jackie
Johnson 15.00
180 JKu(c),You Can't
Kill A General 15.00
181 RH(c),Monday's Coward-
Tuesday's Hero 15.00
182 NA,RH(c),The Desert Rats
of Easy 18.00
183 NA,JKu(c),Sergeants Don't
Stay Dead 18.00
184 JKu(c),Candidate For A
Firing Squad 15.00
185 JKu(c),Battle Flag For A G.I. 15.00
186 NA,JKu(c),3 Stripes Hill
reprint from #90 . . . . 18.00
187 JKu(c),Shadow of a Sergeant 10.00
188 JKu(c),Death Comes for Easy 10.00
189 JKu(c),The Mission Was
Murder 10.00

190 JKu(c),What Make's A Sergeant Run?, reprint from #97 . . . . 10.00
191 JKu(c),Death Flies High, A:Johnny Cloud 10.00
192 JKu(c),A Firing Squad For A Sergeant 10.00
193 JKu(c),Blood In the Desert . 10.00
194 JKu(c),A Time For Vengeance10.00
195 JKu(c),Dead Town 10.00
196 JKu(c),Stop The War-I Want To Get Off 10.00
197 JKu(c),Last Exit For Easy . . 10.00
198 JKu(c),Plugged Nickel 10.00
199 JKu(c),Nazi Ghost Wolf 10.00
200 JKu(c),The Troubadour . . . 15.00
201 JKu(c),The Graffiti Writer . . 10.00
202 JKu(c),The Sarge Is Dead . . . 6.00
203 JKu(c),Easy's Had It, reprint from # 103 . . . . 6.00
204 JKu(c) 6.00
205 JKu(c) 6.00
206 JKu(c),There's A War On . . . 6.00
207 JKu(c),A Sparrow's Prayer . . 6.00
208 JKu(c),A Piece of Rag...And A Hank of Hair 6.00
209 JKu(c),I'm Still Alive 6.00
210 JKu(c),I'm Kilroy 5.00
211 JKu(c),The Treasure of St. Daniel 5.00
212 JKu(c),The Quiet War 5.00
213 JKu(c),A Letter For Bulldozer 5.00
214 JKu(c),Where Are You? 5.00
215 JKu(c),Pied Piper of Peril . . . 5.00
216 JKu(c),Doom Over Easy, reprint from # 107 . . . . 5.00
217 JKu(c),Surprise Party 5.00
218 JKu(c),Medic! 6.00
219 JKu(c),Yesterday's Hero 5.00
220 JKu(c),Stone-Age War 5.00
221 JKu(c),Hang-Up 5.00
222 JKu(c),Dig In, Easy 5.00
223 JKu(c),On Time 5.00
224 JKu(c),One For The Money . . 5.00
225 JKu(c),Face Front 5.00
226 JKu(c),Death Stop 5.00
227 JKu(c),Traitor's Blood 5.00
228 JKu(c),It's A Dirty War 5.00
229 JKu(c),The Battle of the Sergeants, reprint from #128 . . 6.00
230 JKu(c),Home Is The Hunter 5.00
231 JKu(c),My Brother's Keeper . 5.00
232 JKu(c),3 Men In A Tub 5.00
233 JKu(c),Head Count 5.00
234 JKu(c),Summer In Salerno . . 5.00
235 JKu(c),Pressure Point 5.00
236 JKu(c),Face The Devil 5.00
237 JKu(c),Nobody Cares 5.00
238 JKu(c),I Kid You Not 5.00
239 JKu(c),The Soldier 5.00
240 JKu(c),NA 8.00
241 JKu(c),War Story 5.00
242 JKu(c),Infantry 5.00
243 JKu(c),24 Hour Pass 5.00
244 JKu(c),Easy's First Tiger 5.00
245 JKu(c),The Prisoner 5.00
246 JKu(c),Naked Combat 5.00
247 JKu(c),The Vision 5.00
248 JKu(c),The Firing Squad 5.00
249 JKu(c),The Luck of Easy,WW 8.00
250 JKu(c),90 Day Wonder 5.00
251 JKu(c),The Iron Major 5.00
252 JKu(c),The Iron Hand 5.00
253 JKu(c),Rock and Iron 5.00
254 JKu(c),The Town 5.00
255 JKu(c),What's It Like 5.00
256 JKu(c),School For Sergeants . 5.00
257 JKu(c),The Castaway 5.00
258 JKu(c),The Survivors 5.00
259 JKu(c),Lost Paradise 5.00
260 JKu(c),Hell's Island 5.00
261 JKu(c),The Medal That Nobody Wanted 5.00
262 JKu(c),The Return 5.00
263 JKu(c),The Cage 5.00
264 JKu(c),The Hunt 5.00
265 JKu(c),The Brother 5.00
266 JKu(c),The Evacuees 5.00
267 JKu(c),A Bakers Dozen 5.00
268 JKu(c),The Elite 5.00
269 JKu(c) 5.00
270 JKu(c),Spawn of the Devil . . 5.00
271 JKu(c),Brittle Harvest 5.00
272 JKu(c),The Bloody Flag 5.00
273 JKu(c),The Arena 5.00
274 JKu(c),Home Is The Hero . . . 5.00
275 JKu(c),Graveyard Battlefield . 5.00
276 JKu(c),A Bullet For Rock 5.00
277 JKu(c),Gashouse Gang 5.00
278 JKu(c),Rearguard Action 5.00
279 JKu(c),Mined City 5.00
280 JKu(c),Mercy Mission 5.00
281 JKu(c),Dead Man's Eyes 5.00
282 JKu(c),Pieces of Time 5.00
283 JKu(c),Dropouts 5.00
284 JKu(c),Linkup 5.00
285 JKu(c),Bring Him Back 5.00
286 JKu(c),Firebird 5.00
287 JKu(c),The Fifth Dimension . . 5.00
288 JKu(c),Defend-Or Destroy . . . 5.00
289 JKu(c),The Line 5.00
290 JKu(c),Super-Soldiers 5.00
291 JKu(c),Death Squad 5.00
292 JKu(c),A Lesson In Blood . . . 5.00
293 JKu(c),It Figures 5.00
294 JKu(c),Coffin For Easy 5.00
295 JKu(c),The Devil in Paradise . 5.00
296 JKu(c),Combat Soldier 5.00
297 JKu(c),Percentages 5.00
298 JKu(c),Return to Chartres . . . 5.00
299 JKu(c),Three Soldiers 5.00
300 JKu(c),300th Hill 5.00
301 JKu(c),The Farm 5.00

Becomes:

SGT. ROCK

302 JKu(c),Anzio-The Bloodbath, part I 8.00
303 JKu(c),Anzio, part II 6.00
304 JKu(c),Anzio, part III 6.00
305 JKu(c),Dead Man's Trigger, reprint from #141 . . . . 6.00
306 JKu(c),The Last Soldier 6.00
307 JKu(c),I'm Easy 6.00
308 JKu(c),One Short Step 6.00
309 JKu(c),Battle Clowns 6.00
310 JKu(c),Hitler's Wolf Children 6.00
311 JKu(c),The Sergeant and the Lady 6.00
312 JKu(c),No Name Hill 6.00
313 JKu(c),A Jeep For Joey 6.00
314 JKu(c),Gimme Sky 6.00
315 JKu(c),Combat Antenna 6.00
316 JKu(c),Another Hill... . . . . . . 6.00
317 JKu(c),Hell's Oven 6.00
318 JKu(c),Stone-Age War 6.00
319 JKu(c),To Kill a Sergeant . . . 6.00
320 JKu(c),Never Salute a Sergeant 6.00
321 JKu(c),It's Murder Out Here . 5.00
322 JKu(c),The Killer 5.00
323 JKu(c),Monday's Hero 5.00
324 JKu(c),Ghost of a Tank 5.00
325 JKu(c),Future Kill, part I 5.00
326 JKu(c),Future Kill, part II 5.00
327 JKu(c),Death Express 5.00
328 JKu(c),Waiting For Rock 5.00
329 JKu(c),Dead Heat 5.00
330 JKu(c),G.I. Trophy 5.00
331 JKu(c),The Sons of War 5.00
332 JKu(c),Pyramid of Death 5.00
333 JKu(c),Ask The Dead 5.00
334 JKu(c),What's Holding Up The War 5.00
335 JKu(c),Killer Compass 5.00
336 JKu(c),The Red Maple Leaf . 5.00
337 JKu(c),A Bridge Called Charlie 5.00
338 JKu(c),No Escape From the Front 5.00
339 JKu(c),I Was Here Before . . 5.00
340 JKu(c),How To Win A War . 5.00
341 JKu(c),High-Flyer 5.00
342 JKu(c),The 6 sides of Sgt. Rock 5.00
343 thru 350 . . . . @5.00
351 thru 422 . . . . @2.00

OUR FIGHTING FORCES

October-November, 1954

1 IN,JGr(c),Human Booby Trap 500.00
2 RH,IN,IN(c),Mile-Long Step 250.00
3 RA,JKu(c),Winter Ambush . 200.00
4 RA,JGr(c),The Hot Seat . . . 150.00
5 IN,RA,JGr(c),The Iron Punch 150.00
6 IN,RA,JGr(c),The Sitting Tank 125.00
7 RA,JKu,JGr(c),Battle Fist . . 125.00

Our Fighting Forces #8
© DC Comics, Inc.

8 IN,RA,JGr(c),No War For A Gunner 125.00
9 JKu,RH,JGr(c),Crash-Landing At Dawn 125.00
10 WW,RA,JGr(c),Grenade Pitcher 150.00
11 JKu,JGr(c),Diary of a Sub . . 100.00
12 IN,JKu,JGr(c),Jump Seat . . 100.00
13 RA,JGr(c),Beach Party 100.00
14 JA,RA,IN,JGr(c),Unseen War 100.00
15 RH,JKu,JGr(c),Target For A Lame Duck 100.00
16 RH,JGr(c),Night Fighter . . . 100.00
17 RA,JGr(c),Anchored Frogman 100.00
18 RH,JKu,JGr(c),Cockpit Seat 100.00
19 RA,JKu(c),Straighten ThatLine100.00
20 RA,MD,JGr(c),The Floating Pilot 100.00
21 RA,JKu(c),The Bouncing Baby of Company B 65.00
22 JKu,RA,JGr(c),3 Doorways To War 65.00
23 RA,IN,JA,JGr(c),Tin Fish Pilot 65.00
24 RA,RH,JGr(c),Frogman Duel . 65.00
25 RA,JKu(c),Dead End 65.00
26 IN,RH,JKu(c),Tag Day 65.00
27 MD,RA,JKu(c),TNT Escort . . 65.00
28 RH,MD,JKu(c),All Quiet at C.P.65.00
29 JKu,JKu(c),Listen To A Jet . . 65.00
30 IN,RA,JKu(c),Fort For A Gunner 65.00
31 MD,RA,JKu(c),Silent Sub . . . 55.00
32 RH,MD,RH(c),PaperWorkWar 55.00
33 RH,JKu,JKu(c),Frogman In A Net 55.00

All comics prices listed are for *Near Mint* condition.

34 JA,JGr,JKu(c),Calling U-217 55.00
35 JA,JGr,JKu(c),Mask of a Frogman 55.00
36 MD,JA,JKu(c),Steel Soldier 55.00
37 JA,JGr,JGr(c),Frogman In A Bottle 55.00
38 RH,RA,JA,JGr(c),Sub Sinker 55.00
39 JA,RH,RH(c),Last Torpedo 55.00
40 JGr,JA,JKu,JKu(c),The Silent Ones 55.00
41 JGr,RH,JA,JKu(c),Battle Mustang 75.00
42 RH,MD,JGr(c),Sorry-Wrong Hill 45.00
43 MD,JKu,JGr(c),Inside Battle 25.00
44 MD,RH,RA,JGr(c),Big Job For Baker 45.00
45 RH,RA,JGr(c),B:Gunner and Sarge, Mop-Up Squad 175.00
46 RH,RA,JGr(c),Gunner's Squad 45.00
47 RH,JKu(c),TNT Birthday 45.00
48 JA,RH,JGr(c),A Statue For Sarge 45.00
49 MD,RH,JGr(c),Blind Gunner 45.00
50 JA,RH,JGr(c),I:Pooch,My Pal, The Pooch 45.00
51 RA,JA,RH(c),Underwater Gunner 25.00
52 MD,JKu,JKu(c),The Gunner and the Nurse 25.00
53 JA,RA,JGr(c),An Egg For Sarge 25.00
54 25.00
55 MD,RH,JGr(c),The Last Patrol 25.00
56 RH,RA,JGr(c),Bridge of Bullets 25.00
57 JA,IN,JGr(c),A Tank For Sarge 25.00
58 JA,JGr(c),Return of the Pooch 25.00
59 RH,JA,JGr(c),Pooch-Patrol Leader 25.00
60 RH,JA,JGr(c),Tank Target 25.00
61 JA,JGr(c),Pass to Peril 25.00
62 JA,JGr(c),The Flying Pooch 25.00
63 JA,RH,JGr(c),Pooch-Tank Hunter 25.00
64 JK,RH,JGr(c),A Lifeline For Sarge 25.00
65 IN,JA,JGr(c),Dogtag Patrol 25.00
66 JKu,JA,JGr(c),Trail of the Ghost Bomber 25.00
67 IN,JA,JGr(c),Purple Heart For Pooch 25.00
68 JA,JGr(c),Col. Hakawa's Birthday Party 25.00
69 JA,JKu,JGr(c), Destination Doom 25.00
70 JA,JKu(c),The Last Holdout 25.00
71 JA,JGr(c),End of the Marines 20.00
72 JA,JGr(c),Four-Footed Spy 15.00
73 IN,JGr(c),The Hero Maker 15.00
74 IN,JGr(c),Three On A T.N.T. Bull's-Eye 15.00
75 JKu(c),Purple Heart Patrol 15.00
76 JKu(c),The T.N.T. Seat 15.00
77 JKu(c),No Foxhole-No Home 15.00
78 JGr(c),The Last Medal 15.00
79 JA,JGr(c),Backs to the Sea 15.00
80 JA,JGr(c),Don't Come Back 15.00
81 JA,JGr(c),Battle of the Mud Marines 15.00
82 JA,JGr(c),Battle of the Empty Helmets 15.00
83 RA,JKu(c),Any Marine Can Do It 15.00
84 JA,JKu(c),The Gun of Shame 15.00
85 Ja,JKu(c),The TNT Pin-Points 15.00
86 JKu(c),3 Faces of Combat 15.00
87 JKu(c),Battle o/t Boobytraps 15.00
88 GC,JKu(c),Devil Dog Patrol 15.00
89 JKu(c),TNT Toothache 15.00
90 JKu(c),Stop the War 15.00
91 JKu(c),The Human Shooting Gallery 8.00
92 JA,JKu(c),The Bomb That Stopped The War 8.00
93 IN,JKu(c),The Human Sharks 8.00
94 RH(c),E:Gunner,Sarge & Pooch, The Human Blockbusters 8.00
95 GC,RH(c),B:The Fighting Devil Dog, Lt. Rock, The Fighting Devil Dog 8.00
96 JA,RH(c),Battle of Fire 8.00
97 IN(c),Invitation To A Firing Squad 8.00
98 IN(c),E:The Fighting Devil Dog, Death Wore A Grin 8.00
99 JA,JKu(c),B:Capt. Hunter, No Mercy in Vietnam 8.00
100 GC,IN(c),Death Also Stalks the Hunter 6.00
101 JA,RH(c),Killer of Vietnam 6.00
102 RH,JKu(c),Cold Steel For A Hot War 6.00
103 JKu(c),The Tunnels of Death 6.00
104 JKu(c),Night Raid In Vietnam 6.00
105 JKu(c),Blood Loyality 6.00
106 IN(c),Trail By Fury 6.00
107 IN(c),Raid Of The Hellcats 6.00
108 IN(c),Kill The Wolf Pack 6.00
109 IN(c),Burn, Raiders, Burn 6.00
110 IN(c),Mountains Full of Death 6.00
111 IN(c),Train of Terror 6.00
112 IN(c),What's In It For The Hellcats? 6.00
113 IN(c),Operation-Survival 6.00
114 JKu(c),No Loot For The Hellcats 6.00
115 JKu(c),Death In The Desert 6.00
116 JKu(c),Peril From the Casbah 6.00
117 JKu(c),Colder Than Death 6.00
118 JKu(c),Hell Underwater 6.00
119 JKu(c),Bedlam In Berlin 6.00
120 JKu(c),Devil In The Dark 6.00
121 JKu(c),Take My Place 6.00
122 JKu(c),24 Hours To Die 6.00
123 JKu(c),B:Born Losers,No Medals No Graves 6.00
124 JKu(c),Losers Take All 6.00
125 Daughters of Death 6.00
126 JKu(c),Lost Town 6.00
127 JKu(c),Angels Over Hell's Corner 6.00
128 JKu(c),7 11 War 6.00
129 JKu(c),Ride The Nightmare 6.00
130 JKu(c),Nameless Target 6.00
131 JKu(c),Half A Man 6.00
132 JKu(c),Pooch, The Winner 6.00
133 JKu(c),Heads or Tails 6.00
134 JKu(c),The Real Losers 6.00
135 JKu(c),Death Picks A Loser 6.00
136 JKu(c),Decoy For Death 6.00
137 JKu(c),God Of The Losers 6.00
138 JKu(c),The Targets 6.00
139 JKu(c),The Pirate 6.00
140 JKu(c),Lost...One Loser 6.00
141 JKu(c),Bad Penny, The 6.00
142 JKu(c), 1/2 A Man 6.00
143 JKu(c),Diamonds Are For Never 6.00
144 JKu(c),The Lost Mission 6.00
145 JKu(c),A Flag For Losers 6.00
146 JKu(c),The Forever Walk 6.00
147 NA(c),The Glory Road 6.00
148 JKu(c),The Last Charge 6.00
149 FT(c),A Bullet For A Traitor 6.00
150 JKu(c),Mark Our Graves 6.00
151 JKu(c),Kill Me With Wagner 6.00
152 JK(c),A Small Place In Hell 6.00
153 JK(c),Big Max 6.00
154 JK(c),Bushido,Live By The Code, Die By The Code 6.00
155 JK(c),The Partisans 6.00
156 JK(c),Good-Bye Broadway 6.00
157 JK(c),Panama Fattie 6.00
158 JK(c),Bombing Out On The Panama Canal 6.00
159 JK(c),Mile-A-Minute Jones 6.00
160 JKu(c),Ivan 6.00
161 JKu(c),The Major's Dream 6.00
162 Gung-Ho 6.00
163 JKu(c),The Unmarked Graves 6.00
164 JKu(c),A Town Full Of Losers 6.00
165 LD(c),The Rowboat Fleet 6.00
166 LD(c),Sword of Flame 6.00
167 LD(c),A Front Seat In Hell 6.00
168 LD(c),A Cold Day To Die 6.00
169 JKu(c),Welcome Home-And Die 6.00
170 JKu(c),A Bullet For The General 6.00
171 JKu(c),A Long Day... A Long War 6.00
172 JKu(c),The Two-Headed Spy 6.00
173 JKu(c),An Appointment With A Direct Hit 6.00
174 JKu(c),Winner Takes-Death 6.00
175 JKu(c),Death Warrant 6.00
176 JKu(c),The Loser Is A Teen-Ager 6.00
177 JKu(c),This Loser Must Die 6.00
178 JKu(c),Last Drop For Losers 6.00
179 JKu(c),The Last Loser 6.00
180 JKu(c),Hot Seat In A Cold War 6.00
181 JKu(c),Sept.-Oct., 1978 6.00

OUTCASTS
October, 1987

1 2.00
2 thru 10 @1.75
11 final issue 1.75

OUTLAWS

1 LMc,I:Hood 1.95
2 LMc,O:Hood 1.95
3 LMc,V:Evil King 1.95
4 LMc,V:Lord Conductor 1.95
5 LMc,Archery contest 1.95
6 LMc,Raid on King's Castle 1.95
7 LMc,Refuge, V:Lord Conductor 1.95

OUTSIDERS
November, 1985

[1st Regular Series]

1 JAp,I:Looker 3.50
2 JAp,V:Nuclear Family 2.50
3 JAp,V:Force of July 2.00
4 JAp,V:Force of July 2.00
5 JAp,Christmas Issue 2.00
6 JAp,V:Duke of Oil 2.00
7 JAp,V:Duke of Oil 2.00
8 JAp,Japan 2.00
9 JAp/SD/JOp,BlkLightning 2.00
10 JAp,I:Peoples Heroes 2.00
11 JAp,Imprisoned in death camp 1.75
12 JAp,Imprisoned in death camp 1.75
13 JAp,desert island 1.75
14 JAp,Looker/murder story 1.75
15 DJu,V:Bio-hazard 1.75
16 Halo vs.Firefly 1.75
17 JAp,J:Batman 1.75
18 JAp,BB,V:Eclipso 2.00
19 JAp,V:Windfall 1.75
20 JAp,Masters of Disaster 1.75
21 JAp,V:Kobra,I:Clayface IV 1.75
22 JAp,V:Strike Force Kobra 1.75
23 Return of People's Heroes 1.75
24 TVE,JAp,V:Skull,A:Duke of Oil 1.75
25 JAp,V:Skull 1.75
26 JAp,in Markovia 1.75
27 EL,Millenium 1.75
28 EL,Millenium,final issue 1.75
Ann.#1,KN,V:Skull,A:Batman 2.50
Spec.#1,A:Infinity,Inc 1.75

[2nd Regular Series]

1 Alpha,TC(c),B:MiB(s),PaP, I:Technocrat,Faust,Wylde 3.50
1a Omega,TC(c),PaP,V:Vampires 3.50
2 PaP,V:Sanction 2.00
3 PaP,V:Eradicator 2.00
4 PaP,A:Eradicator 2.00
5 PaP,V:Atomic Knight,A:Jihad 2.00
6 PaP,V:Jihad 2.00
7 PaP,C:Batman 2.00

8 PaP,V:Batman,I:Halo 2.00
9 PaP,V:Batman 1.75

PEACEMAKER
January, 1988

1 A:Dr.Tzin-Tzin 1.25
2 . . . . 1.25
3 . . . . 1.25
4 . . . . 1.25

PENGUIN TRIUMPHANT

1 JSon,A:Batman,Wall Street . . . 6.00

PETER CANNON: THUNDERBOLT

1 thru 6 MC . . . . @1.50
7 MC,'Battleground' 1.50
8 MC,Cairo Kidnapped 1.50
9 MC 1.50
10 MC,A:JLA 1.50
11 MC,V:Havoc,A:Checkmate . . . 1.50
12 MC,final Issue 1.25

PETER PANDA
August-September, 1953

1 . . . . 165.00
2 . . . . 95.00
3 thru 9 . . . . @60.00
10 August-September, 1958 . . . 60.00

PETER PORKCHOPS
November-December, 1949

1 . . . . 175.00
2 . . . . 105.00
3 thru 10 . . . . @80.00
11 thru 30 . . . . @40.00
31 thru 61 . . . . @20.00
62 October-December, 1960 . . . 20.00

PHANTOM, THE
October, 1987

1 JO,A:Modern Phantom,13th Phantom 2.00
2 JO,Murder Trial in Manhattan . 1.50
3 JO,A:Chessman 1.50
4 JO,V:Chessman,final issue . . . 1.50

PHANTOM, THE

1 LMc,V:Gun Runners 2.50
2 LMc,V:Gun Runners 2.00
3 LMc,V:Drug Smugglers 1.75
4 LMc,In America,A:Diana Palner 1.75
5 LMc,Racial Riots 1.50
6 LMc,in Africa,Toxic Waste Problem 1.50
7 LMc,'Gold Rush' 1.50
8 LMc,'Train Surfing' 1.50
9 LMc,'The Slave Trade' 1.50
10 LMc,Famine in Khagana 1.50
11 LMc,Phantom/Diana Wedding proposal 1.50
12 LMc,Phantom framed for murder 1.50
13 W:Phantom & Diana Palner C:Mandrake last issue 1.50

PHANTOM STRANGER
August-September, 1952

1 . . . . 950.00
2 . . . . 600.00
3 thru 6, June-July, 1953 . . @500.00

PHANTOM STRANGER
May-June, 1969

1 Cl rep.&new material 50.00
2 Cl rep.&new material 23.00
3 Cl rep.&new material 23.00
4 NA,I:Tala,1st All-new issue . . 30.00
5 MSy,MA,A:Dr.13 . . . . 18.00
6 MSy,A:Dr.13 . . . . 18.00

Phantom Stranger #33
© DC Comics, Inc.

7 JAp,V:Tala 18.00
8 JAp,A:Dr.13 . . . . 18.00
9 JAp,A:Dr.13 . . . . 18.00
10 JAp,I:Tannarak 18.00
11 JAp,V:Tannarak 14.00
12 JAp,TD,Dr.13 solo story 14.00
13 JAp,TD,Dr.13 solo 14.00
14 JAp,TD,Dr.13 solo 14.00
15 JAp,ATh(rep),TD,Iron Messiah 9.00
16 JAp,TD,MMes(rep)Dr.13 solo . 9.00
17 JAp,I:Cassandra Craft 9.00
18 TD,Dr.13 solo 9.00
19 JAp,TD,Dr.13 solo 9.00
20 JAp,'And A Child Shall Lead Them' 9.00
21 JAp,TD,Dr.13 solo 6.00
22 JAp,TD,I:Dark Circle 6.00
23 JAp,MK,I:Spawn-Frankenstein . 6.00
24 JAp,MA,Spawn Frankenstein . 6.50
25 JAp,MA,Spawn Frankenstein . 6.00
26 JAp,A:Frankenstein 6.00
27 V:Dr. Zorn 6.00
28 BU:Spawn of Frankenstein . . . 6.00
29 V:Dr.Zorn 6.00
30 E:Spawn of Frankenstein 6.00
31 B:BU:Black Orchid 7.00
32 NR,BU:Black Orchid 7.00
33 MGr,A:Deadman 6.50
34 BU:Black Orchid 7.00
35 BU:Black Orchid 7.00
36 BU:Black Orchid 7.00
37 BU:Black Orchid 7.00
38 BU:Black Orchid 7.00
39 thru 41 A:Deadman . . . . . . @6.00

PHANTOM STRANGER
October, 1987

1 MMi,CR,V:Eclipso 3.00
2 MMi,CR,V:Eclipso 2.25
3 MMi,CR,V:Eclipso 2.25
4 MMi,CR,V:Eclipso, Jan. 1988 . . 2.25

PHANTOM ZONE, THE
January, 1982

1 GD/TD,A:Jax-Ur 1.25
2 GC/TD,A:JLA 1.00
3 GC/TD,A:Mon-El 1.00
4 GC/TD 1.00

PICTURE STORIES FROM THE BIBLE
Autumn, 1942-43

1 thru 4 Old Testament . . . @125.00
1 thru 3 New Testament . . . @150.00

PLASTIC MAN
[1st Series]
November-December, 1966

1 GK,I:Dr.Drome(1966 series begins) 40.00
2 V:The Spider 19.00
3 V:Whed 18.00
4 V:Dr.Dome 18.00
5 1,001 Plassassins 18.00
6 V:Dr.Dome 10.00
7 O:Plastic Man Jr.,A:Original Plastic Man,Woozy Winks . . . 10.00
8 V:The Weasel 10.00
9 V:Joe the Killer Pro 10.00
10 V:Doll Maker(series ends) . . . 10.00
11 (1976 series begins) 3.00
12 I:Carrot-Man 3.00
13 A:Robby Reed 3.00
14 V:Meat By-Product & Sludge . . 3.00
15 I:Snuffer,V:Carrot-Man 3.00
16 V:Kolonel Kool 3.00
17 O:Plastic Man 3.50
18 V:Professor Klean 3.00
19 I&Only App.Marty Meeker 3.00
20 V:Snooping Sneetches October-November, 1977 . . . . 3.00

PLASTIC MAN

1 Mini-series,Origin retold 1.25
2 V:The Ooze Brothers 1.25
3 In Los Angeles 1.25
4 End-series,A:Superman 1.25

PLOP!
September-October, 1973

1 SA-AA,GE,ShM 5.00
2 AA,SA 4.00
3 AA,SA 4.00
4 BW,SA 4.00
5 MA,MSy,SA 4.00
6 MSy,SA 4.00
7 SA 3.50
8 SA 3.50
9 SA 3.50
10 SA 3.50
11 ATh,SA 4.00
12 SA 3.50
13 WW(c),SA 5.00
14 WW,SA 5.00
15 WW(c),SA 5.00
16 SD,WW,SA 5.00
17 SA 3.50
18 SD,WW,SA 5.00
19 WW,SA 5.00
20 SA,WW 5.00
21 JO,WW 5.00
22 JO,WW,BW 5.00
23 BW,WW 3.00
24 SA,WW,November-December, 1976 . . . . 2.00

POWER GIRL

1 mini-series 1.00
2 A:The Weaver, mongo Krebs . . 1.00
3 V:The Weaver 1.00
4 V:Weaver, final issue 1.00

POWER OF SHAZAM

HC JOy(a&s),O:Captain Marvel . 22.00

POWER OF THE ATOM

1 1st Issue, Origin retold 1.00
2 Return of Powers 1.00
3 I:Strobe 1.00
4 A:Hawkman+bonus book #8 . . 1.00
5 DT,A:Elongated Man 1.00

6 JBy,V:Chronos 1.00
7 GN,Invasion,V:Khunds,Chronos 1.00
8 GN,Invasion,V:Chronos 1.00
9 GN,A:Justice League 1.00
10 GN,I:Humbug 1.00
11 GN,V:Paul Hoben 1.00
12 GN,V:Edg the Destroyer 1.00
13 GN,Blood Stream Journey . . . 1.00
14 GN,V:Humbug 1.00
15 GN,V:Humbug 1.00
16 GN,V:The CIA 1.00
17 GN,V:The Sting 1.00
18 GN,V:The CIA, last issue 1.00

PREZ
August-September, 1973

1 I:Prez (from Sandman #54) . . . 15.00
2 thru 4 F:Prez 11.00

PRINCE
Piranha Press

1 DCw,KW,based on rock star . 10.00
1a Second printing 2.50
1b 3rd printing 2.00

PRISONER, THE

1 Based on TV series 5.00
2 'By Hook or by Crook' 5.00
3 'Confrontation' 5.00
4 'Departure' final issue 5.00

PSYCHO

1 I:Psycho 5.25
2 Sonya Rescue 4.95
3 'Psycho against the World' . . . 4.95

QUESTION, THE
February, 1987

1 DCw,R:Question,I:Myra,A:Shiva 3.50
2 DCw,A:Batman,Shiva 2.00
3 DCw,I:Mayor Firman 2.00
4 DCw,V:Hatch 2.00
5 DCw,Hub City fall Apart 2.00
6 DCw,Abuse story 2.00
7 DCw,V:Mr.Volk 2.00
8 DCw,I:Mikado 2.00
9 DCw,O:Rodor 2.00
10 DCw,O:Rodor cont. 2.00
11 DCw,Transformation 2.00
12 DCw,Poisoned Ground 2.00
13 DCw,V:The Spartans 2.00
14 DCw,V:The Spartans 2.00
15 DCw,The Klan in Hub City . . . 2.00
16 DCw,'Butch Cassidy & Sundance Kid' 2.00
17 DCw,A:Green Arrow 2.50
18 DCw,A:Green Arrow 2.50
19 DCw,V:Terrorists 2.00
20 DCw,Travelling Circus 2.00
21 DCw,V:Junior Musto 2.00
22 DCw,Election Night 2.00
23 DCw,Election Night contd 2.00
24 DCw,Election Night contd 2.00
25 DCw,Myra Critically Ill 2.00
26 A:Riddler 2.00
27 DCw 2.00
28 DCw,A:Lady Shiva 2.00
29 DCw,V:Lady Shiva 2.00
30 DCw,A:Lady Shiva 2.00
31 DCw,Hub City Chaos contd . . 2.00
32 DCw,Identity Crisis 2.00
33 DCw,Identity Crisis contd 2.00
34 DCw,Identity Crisis contd 2.00
35 DCw,Fate of Hub City 2.00
36 DCw,final issue (contd.G.A.Ann#3 Question Quarterly #1) 2.00
Ann.#1 DCw,A:Batman,G.A. 3.00
Ann.#2 A:Green Arrow 4.00

QUESTION QUARTERLY

1 DCw 4.50
2 DCw 3.95
3 DCw(c) Film 2.95

4 DCw,MM,'Waiting for Phil' 2.95
5 DCw,MMi,MM,last issue 2.95

RAGMAN
[1st Limited Series]

1 I&O:Ragman 5.00
2 I:Opal 3.50
3 V:Mr. Big 3.00
4 JKu(1st interior on character) . . 3.00
5 JKu,O:Ragman,final issue 3.00

[2nd Limited Series]

1 PB,O:Ragman 4.00
2 PB,O:Ragman Powers 3.50
3 PB,Original Ragman 2.75
4 PB,Gang War 2.75
5 PB,V:Golem 2.75
6 PB,V:Golem,A:Batman 2.75
7 PB,V:Golem,A:Batman 2.75
8 PB,V:Golem,A:Batman 2.75

RAGMAN: CRY OF THE DEAD

1 JKu(c),R:Ragman 2.00
2 JKu(c),A:Marinette 2.00
3 JKu(c),V:Marinette 2.00
4 JKu(c),Exorcism 2.00
5 JKu(c),V:Marinette 2.00
6 JKu(c),final issue 2.00

THE RAY
[Limited Series]

1 JQ,ANi,I&O:Ray(Ray Torril) . . 20.00
2 JQ,ANi,I:G.A. Ray 16.00
3 JQ,ANi,A:G.A. Ray 14.00
4 JQ,ANi,V:Dr.Polaris 12.00
5 JQ,ANi,V:Dr.Polaris 12.00
6 JQ,ANi,C:Lobo,final issue . . . 12.00
TPB In A Blaze of Power 9.95

[Regular Series]

1 JQ(c),RPr,V:Brinestone, A:Superboy 3.50
1a Newsstand Ed. 1.75
2 RPr,V:Brinestone,A:Superboy . 1.75
3 RPr,I:Deathmasque 1.75

Real Fact Comics #5
© DC Comics, Inc.

REAL FACT COMICS
March-April, 1946

1 S&K,Harry Houdini story . . . 275.00
2 S&K, Rin-Tin-Tin story 175.00
3 H.G. Wells story 125.00
4 Jimmy Stewart story,B:Just Imagine 175.00
5 Batman & Robin(c) 950.00
6 O:Tommy Tomorrow 650.00
7 'The Flying White House' . . . 85.00
8 VF,A:Tommy Tomorrow 325.00
9 S&K,Glen Miller story 150.00
10 'The Vigilante' by MMe 150.00
11 EK,'How the G-Men Capture Public Enemies!' 90.00
12 'How G-Men are Trained' . . . 90.00
13 Dale Evans story 300.00
14 Will Rogers story,'Diary of Death' 80.00
15 A:The Master Magician-Thurston 85.00
16 A:Four Reno Brothers, T.Tommorrow 275.00
17'I Guard an Armored Car' 75.00
18 'The Mystery Man of Tombstone' 75.00
19 'The Weapon that Won the West' 75.00
20 JKu 85.00
21 JKu,July-August, 1949 . . . . . 85.00

REAL SCREEN COMICS
Spring, 1945

1 B:Fox & the Crow,Flippity & Flop 550.00
2 (fa) 300.00
3 (fa) 150.00
4 thru 7 (fa) . . . . @140.00
8 thru 11 (fa) . . . . @100.00
12 thru 20 (fa) . . . . @80.00
21 thru 30 (fa) . . . . @60.00
31 thru 40 (fa) . . . . @40.00
41 thru 128 (fa) . . . . @30.00

Becomes:

TV SCREEN CARTOONS

129 thru 137 . . . . @40.00
138 January-February, 1961 . . . 40.00

RED TORNADO

1 Cl/FMc 1.00
2 Cl/FMc,A:Superman 1.00
3 Cl/FMc 1.00
4 Cl/FMc 1.00

RICHARD DRAGON, KUNG FU FIGHTER
April-May, 1975

1 O:Richard Dragon 1.50
2 JSn/AM 1.50
3 JK 1.00
4 thru 8 RE/WW . . . . @1.00
9 RE 1.00
10 thru 17 RE . . . . @1.00
18 November-December, 1977 . . 1.00

RIMA, THE JUNGLE GIRL
April-May, 1974

1 NR,I:Rima,O:Pt. 1 . . . . 2.00
2 NR,O:Pt.2 . . . . 1.50
3 NR,O:Pt.3 . . . . 1.00
4 NR,O:Pt.4 . . . . 1.00
5 NR 1.00
6 NR 1.00
7 April-May, 1975 . . . . 1.00

RING, THE

1 GK,Opera Adaption 12.00
2 GK,Sigfried's Father's Sword . . 7.00
3 GK,to save Brunhilde 6.00
4 GK, final issue 6.00
TPB rep.#1 thru #4 . . . . 19.95

RIP HUNTER, TIME MASTER
March-April, 1961

1 . . . . 350.00
2 . . . . 175.00
3 . . . . 125.00
4 . . . . 100.00

5 . . . . 100.00
6 Ath 75.00
7 Ath 75.00
8 thru 15 . . . . @60.00
16 thru 20 . . . . @45.00
21 thru 28 . . . . @35.00
29 November-December, 1965 . 35.00

Robin (1st Limited Series) #1
© DC Comics, Inc.

ROBIN
[1st Limited Series]

1 TL,BB(c),Trial Pt1(&Poster) . . . 7.00
1a 2nd printing 3.00
1b 3rd printing 1.50
2 TL,BB(c) Trial Pt 2 . . . . 3.50
2a 2nd printing 1.50
3 TL,BB(c) Trial Pt 3 . . . . 2.00
4 TL,Trial Pt 4 . . . . 2.00
5 TL,Final issue,A:Batman 2.00
TPB BB(c),rep.#1-5,Batman# 455-457 . . . . 7.95

[2nd Limited Series]

1 Direct,Hologram(c)Joker face . . 2.00
1a (c)Joker straightjacket 2.00
1b (c)Joker standing 2.00
1c (c)Batman 2.00
1d Newsstand(no hologram) 1.00
1e collectors set,extra holo. . . . 12.00
2 Direct,Hologram(c) Robin/Joker Knife 1.50
2a (c)Joker/Robin-Dartboard 1.50
2b (c)Robin/Joker-Hammer 1.50
2c Newsstand(no hologram) 1.00
2d collectors set,extra holo. 8.00
3 Direct,Holo(c)Robin standing . . 1.50
3a (c)Robin swinging 1.50
3b Newsstand(no hologram) 1.50
3c collectors set,extra holo. 6.00
4 Direct,Hologram, ... 1.50
4a Newsstand (no hologram) . . . 1.00
4b collectors set,extra holo. 4.00
Collectors set (#1 thru #4) 30.00

[3rd Limited Series]

1 TL,A:Huntress,Collector's Ed. movable(c),poster 3.00
1a MZ(c),Newsstand Ed. 1.50
2 TL,V:KGBeast,A:Huntress 2.75
2a MZ(c),Newsstand Ed 1.50
3 TL,V:KGBeast,A:Huntress 2.75
3a MZ(c),newsstand Ed. 1.50
4 TL,V:KGBeast,A:Huntress 2.75
4a MZ(c),newsstand Ed. 1.50
5 TL,V:KGBeast,A:Huntress 2.75
5a MZ(c),newsstand Ed. 1.50
6 TL,V:KGBeast,King Snake, A:Huntress. 2.75
6a MZ(c),Newsstand Ed. 1.50

[Regular Series]

1 B:CDi(s),TG,SHa,V:Speedboyz 4.00
1a Newstand Ed. 2.00
2 TG,V:Speedboyz 2.00
3 TG,V:Cluemaster, Electrocutioner 1.75
4 TG,V:Cluemaster,Czonk, Electrocutioner 1.75
5 TG,V:Cluemaster,Czonk, Electrocutioner 1.75
6 TG,A:Huntress 1.75
7 TG,R:Robin's Father 1.75
8 TG,KnightsEnd#5,A:Shiva 1.50
TPB A Hero Reborn,JAp,TL, ... 4.95
TPB Tragedy and Triumph, TL,NBy, ... 9.95
Ann.#1 TL,Eclipso tie-in,V:Anarky 3.00
Ann.#2 KD,JL,Bloodlines#10, I:Razorsharp 2.75

ROBIN 3000

1 CR,Elseworlds,V:Skulpt 5.25
2 CR,Elseworlds,V:Skulpt 5.25

ROBIN HOOD TALES
January-February, 1957

7 . . . . 120.00
8 thru 13 . . . . @120.00
4 March-April, 1958 . . . . 120.00

ROBOTECH DEFENDERS

1 MA,mini-series 3.50
2 MA 3.00

ROGAN GOSH
Vertigo

1 PF PrM(s) (From Revolver) . . . 7.25

RONIN
July, 1983

1 FM,1:Billy 7.00
2 FM,I:Casey 5.00
3 FM,V:Agat 5.00
4 FM,V:Agat 5.00
5 FM,V:Agat 6.00
6 FM,D:Billy 8.00
Paperback, FM inc. Gatefold . . . 12.00

ROOTS OF THE SWAMP THING
July, 1986

1 BWr,rep.SwampThing#1 . . 3.00
2 BWr,rep.SwampThing#3 . . 3.00
3 BWr,rep.SwampThing#5 . . 3.00
4 BWr,rep.SwampThing#7 . . 3.00
5 BWr,rep.SwampThing#9
, H.O.S. #92, final issue 3.00

RUDOLPH THE RED -NOSED REINDEER
December, 1950

1950 . . . . 50.00
1951 thru 1954 . . . . @35.00
1955 thru 1962 Winter . . . . . @20.00

SAGA OF RAS AL GHUL

1 NA,DG,reprints 5.00
2 rep. 4.00
3 rep.Batman #242ó 4.00
4 rep.Batman #244õ, Detective #410 . . . . 4.00
TPB reps. 17.95

SAGA OF THE SWAMP THING
May, 1982

1 JmP(s),TY,DSp,O:Swamp Thing, BU:PhantomStranger 4.00
2 Ph(c),TY,DSp,I:Grasp 2.00
3 TY,DSp,V:Vampires 2.00
4 TY,TD,V:Demon 2.00
5 TY, ... 2.00
6 TY,I:General Sunderland 2.00
7 TY, ... 2.00
8 TY, ... 2.00
9 TY, ... 2.00
10 TY, ... 2.00
11 TY,I:Golem 2.00
12 LWn(s),TY 2.00
13 TY,D:Grasp 2.00
14 A:Phantom Stranger 2.00
15 . . . . 2.00
16 SBi,JTo, ... 2.00
17 I:Matthew Cable 4.00
18 JmP(s),LWn(s),SBi,JTo,BWr, R:Arcane 2.00
19 JmP(s),SBi,JTo,V:Arcane 2.00
20 B:AMo(s),Day,JTo(i),D:Arcane (Original incarnation) 30.00
21 SBi,JTo,O:Swamp Thing,I:Floronic Man,D:General Sunderland . . 28.00
22 SBi,JTo,O:Floronic Man 15.00
23 SBi,JTo,V:Floronic Man 15.00
24 SBi,JTo,V:Floronic Man,A:JLA, In Arkham 15.00
25 SBi,A:Jason Blood,I:Kamara . 12.00
26 SBi,A:Demon, D:Matthew Cable 12.00
27 SBi,D:Kamara,A:Demon 8.00
28 SwM,Burial of Alec Holland . . . 8.00
29 SBi,JTo,R:Arcane 8.00
30 SBi,AA,D:Abby,C:Joker, V:Arcane 10.00
31 RV,JTo,D:Arcane 7.00
32 SwM,Tribute to WK Pogo strip 7.00
33 rep.H.O.S.#92,A:Cain & Abel . 7.00
34 SBi,JTo,Swamp Thing & Abby Fall in Love 11.00
35 SBi,JTo,Nukeface Pt.1 . . . . . . 5.00
36 SBi,JTo,Nukeface Pt.2 . . . . . . 5.00
37 RV,JTo,I:John Constantine, American Gothic Pt.1 . . . . . . 34.00
38 SnW,JTo,V:Water-Vampires (Pt.1) A:J.Constantine 14.00
39 SBi,JTo,V:Water-Vampires (Pt.2) A:J.Constantine 10.00
40 SBi,JTo,C:J.Constantine, The Curse 8.00
41 SBi,AA,Voodoo Zombies #1 . . 4.00
42 SBi,JTo,RoR, Voodoo Zombies #2 . . . . 4.00
43 SnW,RoR,Windfall, I:Chester Williams 4.00
44 SBi,JTo,RoR,V:Serial Killer, C:Batman,Constantine,Mento . 6.00
45 SnW,AA,Ghost Dance 4.00
Ann.#1 MT,TD,Movie Adaption . . 2.00
Ann.#2 AMo(s),E:Arcane,A:Deadman, Phantom Stranger,Spectre, Demon,Resurrection of Abby . 10.00
Ann.#3 AMo(s),Ape issue 4.00
TPB rep.#21-#27 . . . . 12.95
TPB rep.#28-34,Ann.#2 . . . . 14.95
Becomes:

SWAMP THING

46 B:AMo(s) cont'd,SBi,JTo,Crisis, A:John Constantine,Phantom Stranger 4.00
47 SBi,Parliment of Trees,Full origin,A:Constantine 4.00
48 SBi,JTo,V:Brujeria, A:Constantine. 4.00
49 SBi,AA,A:Constantine,Demon,Ph. Stranger,Spectre,Deadman . . . 4.00
50 SBi,RV,JTo,concl.American Gothic,D:Zatara&Sargon, Double Size 7.00

All comics prices listed are for *Near Mint* condition.

51 RV,AA,L:Constantine 4.00
52 RV,AA,Arkham Asylum,A:Flor. Man,Lex Luthor,C:Joker, 2-Face,Batman 5.50
53 JTo,V:Batman,Swamp Thing Banished to Space 5.00
54 JTo script,RV,AA,C:Batman . . 3.00
55 RV,AA,JTo,A:Batman,. 3.00
56 RV,AA,My Blue Heaven 3.00
57 RV,AA,A:Adam Strange 3.00
58 RV,AA,A:Adam Strange,GC, Spectre preview 3.00
59 JTo,RV,AA,D:Patchwork Man . 3.00

Direct Sales Only

60 JTo,Loving the Alien 3.00
61 RV,AA,All Flesh is Grass G.L.Corps X-over 3.00
62 RV(&script),AA,Wavelength, A:Metron,Darkseid 3.00
63 RV,AA,Loose Ends(reprise) . . 3.00
64 E:AMo(s),SBi,TY,RV,AA, Return of the Good Gumbo . . . 3.00
65 RV,JTo,A:Constantine 3.50
66 RV,Elemental Energy 2.50
67 RV,V:Solomon Grundy, Hellblazer preview 5.00
68 RV,O:Swamp Thing 2.50
69 RV,O:Swamp Thing 2.50
70 RV,AA,Quest for SwampThing 2.50
71 RV,AA,Fear of Flying 2.50
72 RV,AA,Creation 2.50
73 RV,AA,A:John Constantine . . . 3.00
74 RV,AA,Abbys Secret 2.50
75 RV,AA,Plant Elementals 2.50
76 RV,AA,A:John Constantine . . . 3.00
77 TMd,AA,A:John Constantine . . 3.00
78 TMd,AA,Phantom Pregnancy . 2.50
79 RV,AA,A:Superman,Luthor . . . 2.50
80 RV,AA,V:Aliends 2.50
81 RV,AA,Invasion x-over 2.50
82 RV,AA,A:Sgt.Rock & Easy Co. 2.50
83 RV,AA,A:Enemy Ace 2.50
84 RV,AA,A:Sandman 6.00
85 RV,TY,Time Travel contd. 2.50
86 RV,TY,A:Tomahawk 2.50
87 RV,TY,Camelot,A:Demon 2.50
88 RV,TY,A:Demon,Golden Gladiator 2.50
89 MM,AA,The Dinosaur Age . . . 2.50
90 BP,AA,Birth of Abbys Child (Tefe) 2.75
91 PB,AA,Abbys Child (New Elemental) 2.50
92 PB,AA,Ghosts of the Bayou . . 2.50
93 PB,AA,New Power 2.50
94 PB,AA,Ax-Murderer 2.50
95 PB,AA,Toxic Waste Dumpers . 2.50
96 PB,AA,Tefes Powers 2.50
97 PB,AA,Tefe,V:Nergal, A:Arcane 2.50
98 PB,AA,Tefe,in Hell 2.50
99 PB,AA,Tefe,A:Mantago, John Constantine 3.00
100 PB,AA,V:Angels of Eden, (48 pages) 3.50
101 AA,A:Tefe 2.50
102 V:Mantagos Zombies,inc. prev. of Worlds Without End 2.50
103 Green vs. Grey 2.50
104 Quest for Elementals Pt.1 . . . 2.50
105 Quest for Elementals Pt.2 . . . 2.50
106 Quest for Elementals Pt.3 . . . 2.50
107 Quest for Elementals Pt.4 . . . 2.50
108 Quest for Elementals Pt.5 . . . 2.50
109 Quest for Elementals Pt.6 . . . 2.50
110 TMd,A:Father Tocsin 2.50
111 V:Ghostly Zydeco Musician . . 2.50
112 TMd,B:Swamp Thing for Governor 2.50
113 E:Swamp Thing for Governor 2.50
114 TMd,Hellblazer 2.75
115 TMd,A:Hellblazer,V:Dark Conrad 2.75
116 From Body of Swamp Thing . 2.25
117 JD,The Lord of Misrule, Mardi Gras 2.25
118 A Childs Garden,A:Matthew the Raven 2.25
119 A:Les Perdu 2.25
120 F:Lady Jane 2.25
121 V:Sunderland Corporation . . . 2.25
122 I:The Needleman 2.25
123 V:The Needleman 2.25
124 In Central America 2.25
125 V:Anton Arcane,20th Anniv. . 3.75
126 Mescalito 2.25
127 Project Proteus #1 . . . . 2.25
128 Project proteus #2 . . . . 2.25

Vertigo

129 CV(c),B:NyC(s),SEa,KDM(i), Sw.Thing's Deterioration 2.25
130 CV(c),SEa,KDM(i),A:John Constantine,V:Doctor Polygon . 2.25
131 CV(c),SEa,KDM(i),I:Swamp Thing's,Doppleganger, F:The Folk 2.25
132 CV(c),SEa,KDM(i), V:Doppleganger 2.25
133 CV(c),SEa,KDM(i),R:General Sunderland,V:Thunder Petal . . 2.25
134 CV(c),SEa,KDM(i),Abby Leaves, C:John Constantine 2.25
135 CV(c),SEa,KDM(i),A:J.Constantine, Swamp Thing Lady Jane meld 2.25
136 CV(c),RsB,KDM(i),A:Lady Jane, Dr.Polygon,John Constantine . 2.25
137 CV(c),E:NyC(s),RsB,KDM(i), IR:Sunderland is Anton Arcane, A:J.Constantine 2.25
138 CV(c),DiF(s),RGu,KDM,B:Mind Fields 2.25
139 CV(c),DiF(s),RGu,KDM,A:Black Orchid,In Swamp Thing's mind, cont'd fr.Black Orchid #5 . . . . . 2.25
140 B:Bad Gumbo 2.50
140a Platinum Ed. 45.00
141 A:Abigail Arcane 2.25
142 Bad Gumbo#3 . . . . 2.25
143 E:Bad Gumbo 2.25
144 In New York City 1.95
Ann.#4 PB/AA,A:Batman 2.75
Ann.#5 A:BrotherPower Geek . . . 3.25
Ann.#6 Houma 3.50
Ann.#7 CV(c),NyC(s),MBu(i),Childrens Crusade,F:Tefe,A:Maxine,BU: Beautyand the Beast 4.25

SANDMAN

[1st Regular Series]

1 JK,I&O:Sandman,I:General Electric 8.50
2 V:Dr.Spider 5.00
3 Brain that Blanked out the Bronx 5.00
4 JK,Panic in the Dream Stream . 5.00
5 JK,Invasion of the Frog Men . . 5.00
6 JK,WW,V:Dr.Spider 6.00

[2nd Regular Series]

1 B:NGa(s),SK,I:2nd Sandman . 70.00
2 SK,A:Cain,Abel 45.00
3 SK,A:John Constantine 40.00
4 SK,A:Demon 35.00
5 SK,A:Mr.Miracle,J'onnJ'onzz . 29.00
6 V:Doctor Destiny 24.00
7 V:Doctor Destiny 21.00
8 Sound of her wings,F:Death . 50.00
8a Guest Ed.Pin Up Covr 225.00
9 Tales in the Sand,Doll's House prologue 20.00
10 B:Doll's House,A:Desire & Despair,I:Brut & Glob 18.00
11 MovingIn,A:2ndS-man 18.00
12 Play House,D;2ndS'man 18.00
13 Men of Good Fortune,A:Death, Lady Constantine 18.00
14 Collectors,D:Corinthian 19.00
15 Into' Night,DreamVortex 17.00
16 E:Doll's House,Lost Hearts . . 17.00
17 Calliope 13.00

Sandman (1st Regular Series) #1
© DC Comics, Inc.

18 Dream of a 1000 Cats 13.00
19 Midsummer Nights Dream . . 15.00
19a error copy 75.00
20 Strange Death Element Girl, A:Death 13.00
21 Family Reunion,B:Season of Mists 18.00
22 Season of Mists,I:Daniel Hall 20.00
23 Season of Mists 13.00
24 Season of Mists 13.00
25 Season of Mists 13.00
26 Season of Mists 11.00
27 E:Season of Mists 11.00
28 Ownership of Hell 11.00
29 A:Lady J.Constantine 7.00
30 Ancient Rome;A:Death,Desire . 8.00
31 Ancient Rome Pt.#2 . . . . 7.00
32 B:The Game of You 8.00
33 The Game of You 7.00
34 The Game of You 6.00
35 The Game of You 6.00
36 The Game of You,48pgs 7.00
37 The Game of You,Epilogue . . . 6.00
38 Convergence 5.00
39 Convergence,A:Marco Polo . . . 5.00
40 Convergence,A:Cain,Abel,Eve, Matthew the Raven 5.00
41 JIT,VcL,(i),B:Brief Lives, F:Endless 6.00
42 JIT,VcL,(i),F:Delirium,Dream . . 5.00
43 JIT,VcL,(i),A:Death,Etain 5.00
44 JIT,VcL,(i),R:Corinthian, Destruction 4.50
45 JIT,VcL,(i),F:Tiffany, Ishtar(Belli) 4.50
46 JIT,VcL,(i),F:Morpheus/Bast,A:AIDS insert story,F:Death 4.50

Vertigo

47 JIT,VcL,(i),A:Endless 3.00
48 JIT,VcL,(i),L:Destruction 3.00
49 JIT,VcL,(i),E:Brief Lives, F:Orpheus 3.00
50 DMc(c),CR,Tales of Baghdad, pin-upsby TM,DMc,MK 4.00
50a Gold Ed. 70.00
51 BT,MBu(i),B:Inn at the end of the World,Gaheris' tale 3.00
52 BT,MBu(i),JWk,Cluracan's Story 3.00
53 BT,DG,MBu(i),MZi,Hob's Leviathan 3.00

54 BT,MiA,MBu(i),R:Prez 3.00
55 SAp,VcL,BT,MBu(i),F:Klaproth, Cerements's Story 3.00
56 BT,MBu(i),DG(i),SLi(i),GyA,TyH(i), E:Inn at the end of the World, C:Endless 3.00
57 MaH,B:Kindly Ones,Inc.American Freak Preview 2.50
58 A:Lucifer 2.50
59 R:Fury 2.50
60 Kindly Ones#4 . . . . 2.50
61 Kindly Ones#5 . . . . 2.25
62 Murder 1.95
TPB Dream Country,Rep.#17-20 15.00
TPB The Dolls House,Rep.#8-16 15.00
Fables and Reflections,HC,rep. . 29.95
TPB Preludes & Nocturnes, Rep.#1-8 . . . . 15.00
Season of Mists,HC,rep.#21-28 . 40.00
Season of Mists,SC 19.95
Spec.BT,Glow in the Dark(c),The Legend of Orpheus, (inc. Portrait Gallery) 6.00
A Game of You,HC,rep.#32-37 . 32.00
TPB Sandman:A Game of You . 19.95
TPB Fables & Reflections 19.95

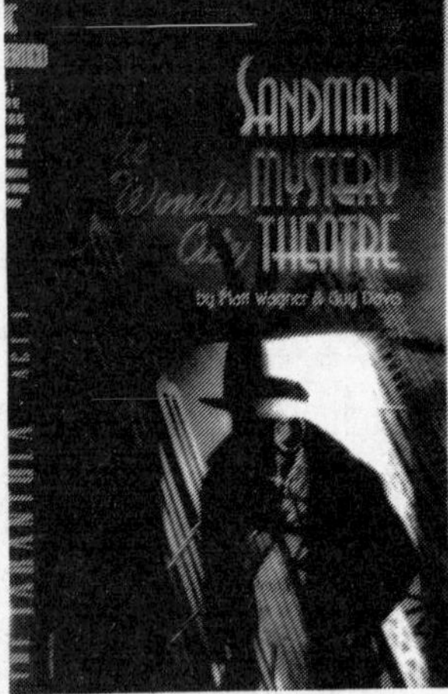

Sandman Mystery Theatre #1
© DC Comics, Inc.

SANDMAN MYSTERY THEATRE
Vertigo

1 B:MWg(s),GyD,R:G.A.Sandman, B:Tarantula,I:Mr.Belmont, Dian Belmont 3.50
2 GyD,V:Tarantula 3.00
3 GyD,V:Tarantula 2.50
4 GyD,E:Tarantula 2.50
5 JWk,B:The Face 2.25
6 JWk,The Face #2 . . . . 2.25
7 JWk,The Face #3 . . . . 2.25
8 JWk,E:The Face 2.25
9 RGT,B:The Brute,I:Rocket Ramsey 2.25
10 RGT,The Brute#2 . . . . 2.25
11 RGT,The Brute#3 . . . . 2.25
12 RGT,E:The Brute 2.25
13 GyD,B:The Vamp 2.25
14 GyD,The Vamp#2 . . . . 2.25
15 GyD,The Vamp#3 . . . . 2.25
16 GyD,E:The Vamp 1.95

SCARAB
Vertigo

1 GF(c),B:JnS(s),SEa,MkB(i), R&O:Scarab,V:Halaku-umid . . 2.25
2 GF(c),SEa,MkB(i),A:Phantom Stranger 2.25
3 GF(c),SEa,MkB(i),in North Carolina 2.25
4 GF(c),SEa,MkB(i),V:Rathoroch . 2.25
5 GF(c),SEa,MkB(i), ... 2.25
6 GF(c),SEa,MkB(i),V:Gloryboys . 2.25
7 GF(c),SEa,MkB(i),V:Scientists . 2.25
8 GF(c),SEa,MkB(i),Final Issue . . 2.25

SCARLETT

1 I:Scarlett,Blood o/t Innocent . . . 2.00
2 Blood of the Innocent cont. . . . 1.75
3 Blood of the Innocent cont. . . . 1.75
4 V:The Nomads 1.75
5 GM,O:Nomads 1.75
6 thru 8 GM,Blood of the Damned 1.75
9 GM,V:Undead 1.75
10 B:Blood of the City 1.75
11 I:Afterburn 1.75
12 V:Sligoth 1.75
13 V:Gearsman 1.75
14 final issue 1.75

SCRIBBLY
August-September, 1948

1 SM 600.00
2 . . . . 400.00
3 thru 5 . . . . @300.00
6 thru 10 . . . . @250.00
11 thru 15, Dec-Jan.1951-2 . @200.00

SEA DEVILS
September-October, 1961

1 RH 350.00
2 RH 150.00
3 thru 5 RH . . . . @100.00
6 thru 10 RH . . . . @50.00
11 . . . . 35.00
12 . . . . 35.00
13 JKu,GC,RA 35.00
14 thru 20 . . . . @35.00
21 I:Capt X,Man Fish 25.00
22 thru 35, May-June, 1967 . . @25.00

SEBASTIAN O
Vertigo

1 GMo(s),SY,I:Sebastian O,A:Lord Lavender,Roaring Boys 2.50
2 GMo(s),SY,V:Roaring Boys, Assassins,A:Abbe, ... 2.50
3 GMo(s),SY,D:Lord Lavender . . 2.50

SECRET HEARTS
September-October, 1949

1 'Make Believe Sweetheart' . 250.00
2 ATh,'Love Is Not A Dream' . 125.00
3 'Sing Me A Love Song' 110.00
4 ATh 110.00
5 ATh 110.00
6 . . . . 110.00
7 . . . . 110.00
8 . . . . 75.00
9 . . . . 75.00
10 thru 20 . . . . @70.00
21 thru 26 . . . . @50.00
27 B:Comics Code 35.00
28 thru 30 . . . . @35.00
31 thru 70 . . . . @25.00
71 thru 110 . . . . @20.00
111 thru 120 . . . . @15.00
121 thru 150 . . . . @5.00
151 thru 153, July 1971 . . . . . . @3.00

SECRET ORIGINS
February-March, 1973

1 O:Superman,Batman,Ghost, Flash 8.00
2 O:Green Lantern,Atom, Supergirl 5.00
3 O:Wonder Woman,Wildcat . . . 4.00
4 O:Vigilante by MMe 4.00
5 O:The Spectre 3.00
6 O:Blackhawk,Legion of Super Heroes 3.00
7 O:Robin, Aquaman,October-November, 1974 . . . . 3.00

SECRET ORIGINS
April, 1986

1 JOy,WB,F:Superman 4.00
2 GK,F:Blue Beetle 3.50
3 JBi,F:Captain Marvel 3.00
4 GT,F:Firestorm 2.75
5 GC,F:Crimson Aventer 3.00
6 DG,MR,F:Batman 5.00
7 F:Sandman,Guy Gardner 3.00
8 MA,F:Shadow Lass,Dollman . . . 2.50
9 GT,F:Skyman,Flash 2.50
10 JL,JO,JA,F:Phantom Stranger . 2.25
11 LMc,TD,F:Hawkman,Powergirl 2.00
12 F:Challengers of the Unknown I:G.A. Fury 2.00
13 EL,F:Nightwing 3.00
14 F:Suicide Squad 2.25
15 KMo,DG,F:Deadman,Spectre . 2.25
16 AKu,F:Hourman,Warlord 2.00
17 KGi,F:Green Lantern 2.25
18 . . . . 2.00
19 JM(c),MA 2.00
20 RL,DG,F:Batgirl 3.00
21 GM,MA,F:Jonah Hex 2.00
22 F:Manhunter,Millenium tie-in . . 2.00
23 F:Manhunter,Millenium tie-in . . 2.00
24 F:Dr.Fate,Blue Devil 2.00
25 F:The Legion 2.00
26 F:Black Lightning 2.00
27 F:Zatanna,Zatara 1.75
28 RLd,GK,F:Nightshade,Midnight 1.75
29 F:Atom,Red Tornado 1.75
30 F:Elongated Man 1.75
31 F:Justice Society of America. . 1.75
32 F:Justice League America. . . . 3.00
33 F:Justice League Inter.. . . . . . 2.00
34 F:Justice League Inter. 2.00
35 KSu,F:Justice League Inter. . . 2.00
36 F:Green Lantern 3.00
37 F:Legion of Subst. Heroes . . . 1.75
38 F:Green Arrow,Speedy 2.00
39 F:Batman,Animal Man 4.00
40 F:Gorilla City 1.75
41 F:Flash Villains 2.50
42 DC,F:Phantom Girl 1.75
43 TVE,TT,F:Hawk & Dove 1.75
44 F:Batman,Clayface tie-in 3.00
45 F:Blackhawk,El Diablo 1.75
46 CS,F:All Headquarters 1.75
47 CS,F:The Legion 1.75
48 KG,F:Ambush Bug 1.75
49 F: The Cadmus Project 2.50
50 GP,CI,DG,F:Batman,Robin, Flash,Black Canary 5.00
Ann.#1 JBy,F:Doom Patrol 3.00
Ann.#2 CI,MA,F:Flash 2.00
Ann.#3 F:The Teen Titans 3.00
Spec.#1 SK,PB,DG,F:Batman's worst Villians,A:Penguin 4.00
TPB DG,New Origin Batman 4.50

SECRET SOCIETY OF SUPER-VILLAINS
May-June, 1976

1 A:Capt.Boomerang, Grodd, Sinestro 2.50
2 R:Capt.Comet,A:Green Lantern 2.50
3 A:Mantis, Darkseid 2.00
4 A:Kalibak,Darkseid,Gr.Lantern . 2.00
5 RB,D:Manhunter,A:JLA 2.00
6 RB/BL,A:Black Canary 1.50
7 RB/BL,A:Hawkgirl,Lex Luthor . . 1.50
8 RB/BL,A:Kid Flash 1.50
9 RB/BMc,A:Kid Flash, Creeper . 1.50

10 DAy/JAb,A:Creeper 1.25
11 JO,N:Wizard 1.25
12 BMc,A:Blockbuster 1.25
13 A:Crime Syndicate of America 1.00
14 A:Crime Syndicate of America 1.00
15 A:G.A.Atom, Dr. Mid Nite 1.25

SECRETS OF HAUNTED HOUSE

April-May, 1975

1 LD(c),Dead Heat 2.00
2 ECh(c),A Dead Man 1.50
3 ECh(c),Pathway To Purgatory 1.50
4 LD(c),The Face of Death 1.50
5 BWr(c),Gunslinger! 1.50
6 JAp(c),Deadly Allegiance 1.50
7 JAp(c),It'll Grow On You 1.50
8 MK(c),Raising The Devil 1.00
9 LD(c),The Man Who Didn't Believe in Ghosts 1.00
10 MK(c),Ask Me No Questions 1.00
11 MK(c),Picasso Fever! 1.00
12 JO&DG(c),Yorick's Skull 1.00
13 JO&DG(c),The Cry of the Warewolf 1.00
14 MK(c),Selina 1.00
15 LD(c),Over Your Own Dead Body 1.00
16 MK(c),Water, Water Every Fear 1.00
17 LD(c),Papa Don 1.00
18 LD(c),No Sleep For The Dying 1.00
19 LD(c),The Manner of Execution 1.00
20 JO(c),The Talisman of the Serpent 1.00
21 LD(c),The Death's Head Scorpion 1.00
22 LD(c),See How They Die 1.00
23 LD(c),The Creeping Red Death 1.00
24 LD(c),Second Chance To Die 1.00
25 LD(c),The Man Who Cheated Destiny 1.00
26 MR(c),Elevator to Eternity 1.00
27 DH(c),Souls For the Master 1.00
28 DH(c),Demon Rum 1.00
29 MK(c),Duel of Darkness 1.00
30 JO(c),For the Love of Arlo 1.00
31 I:Mister E 2.00
32 The Legend of the Tiger's Paw 1.00
33 In The Attic Dwells Dark Seth 1.00
34 Double Your Pleasure 1.00
35 Deathwing, Lord of Darkness 1.00
36 RB&DG(c),Sister Sinister 1.00
37 RB&DG(c),The Third Wish Is Death 1.00
38 RB&DG(c),Slaves of Satan 1.00
39 RB&DG(c),The Witch-Hounds of Salem 1.00
40 RB&DG(c),The Were-Witch of Boston 1.00
41 JKu(c),House at Devil's Tail 1.00
42 JKu(c),Mystic Murder 1.00
43 JO(c),Mother of Invention 1.00
44 BWr(c),Halloween God 1.00
45 EC&JO(c),Star-Trakker 1.00
46 March, 1982 1.00

SINISTER HOUSE OF SECRET LOVE

October-November, 1971

1 1.50
2 JJ(c) 1.50
3 ATh 1.00
4 April-May, 1972 1.00

Becomes:

SECRETS OF SINISTER HOUSE

June-July, 1972

5 2.00
6 1.00
7 NR 1.00
8 1.00
9 1.00
10 NA(i) 4.00
11 1.00
12 1.00
13 1.00
14 1.00
15 1.00
16 1.00
17 DBa 1.00
18 June-July, 1974 1.00

SECRETS OF THE LEGION OF SUPER-HEROES

January, 1981

1 O:Legion 1.50
2 O:Brainaic 5 1.00
3 March, 1981,O:Karate Kid 1.00

Sensation Comics #16
© DC Comics, Inc.

SENSATION COMICS

January, 1942

1 I:Wonder Woman,Wildcat 5,500.00
2 I:Etta Candy & the Holiday Girls, Dr. Poison 1,800.00
3 Diana Price joins Military Intelligence 900.00
4 I:Baroness PaulaVonGunther 750.00
5 V:Axis Spies 600.00
6 Wonder Woman receives magic lasso,V:Baroness Gunther 600.00
7 V:Baroness Gunther 500.00
8 Meets Gloria Bullfinch 500.00
9 A:The Real Diana Prince 500.00
10 V:Ishti 500.00
11 I:Queen Desira 500.00
12 V:Baroness Gunther 400.00
13 V:Olga,Hitler(c) 400.00
14 400.00
15 V:Simon Slikery 400.00
16 V:Karl Schultz 400.00
17 V:Princess Yasmini 400.00
18 V:Quito 400.00
19 Wonder Woman goes berserk 400.00
20 V:Stoffer 400.00
21 V:American Adolf 325.00
22 V:Cheetah 325.00
23 'War Laugh Mania' 325.00
24 I:Wonder Woman's mental radio 325.00
25 325.00
26 A:Queen Hippolyte 325.00
27 V:Ely Close 325.00
28 V:Mayor Prude 325.00
29 V:Mimi Mendez 325.00
30 V:Anton Unreal 325.00
31 'Grow Down Land' 275.00
32 V:Crime Chief 275.00
33 Meets Percy Pringle 275.00
34 I:Sargon 300.00
35 V:Sontag Henya in Atlantis 225.00
36 V:Bedwin Footh 225.00
37 A:Mala((1st app. All-Star #8) 225.00
38 V:The Gyp 225.00
39 V:Nero 225.00
40 I:Countess Draska Nishki 225.00
41 V:Creeper Jackson 175.00
42 V:Countess Nishki 175.00
43 Meets Joel Heyday 175.00
44 V:Lt. Sturm 175.00
45 V:Jose Perez 175.00
46 V:Lawbreakers Protective League 175.00
47 V:Unknown 175.00
48 V:Topso and Teena 175.00
49 V:Zavia 175.00
50 V:'Ears' Fellock 175.00
51 V:Boss Brekel 150.00
52 Meets Prof. Toxino 150.00
53 V:Wanta Wynn 150.00
54 V:Dr. Fiendo 150.00
55 V:Bughumans 150.00
56 V:Dr. Novel 150.00
57 V:Syonide 150.00
58 Meets Olive Norton 150.00
59 V:Snow Man 150.00
60 V:Bifton Jones 150.00

Sensation Comics #103
© DC Comics, Inc.

61 V:Bluff Robust 150.00
62 V:Black Robert of Dogwood 150.00
63 V:Prof. Vibrate 150.00
64 V:Cloudmen 150.00
65 V:Lim Slait 150.00
66 V:Slick Skeener 150.00
67 V:Daredevil Dix 150.00
68 'Secret of the Menacing Octopus' 150.00
69 V:Darcy Wells 150.00
70 Unconquerable Woman of Cocha Bamba 150.00
71 V:Queen Flaming 150.00
72 V:Blue Seal Gang 150.00
73 Wonder Woman time travel story. 150.00

74 V:Spug Spangle 150.00
75 V:Shark 150.00
76 V:King Diamond 150.00
77 V:Boss Brekel 150.00
78 V:Furiosa 150.00
79 Meets Leila and Solala 150.00
80 V:Don Enrago 150.00
81 V:Dr. Frenzi 125.00
82 V:King Lunar 125.00
83 V:Prowd 125.00
84 V:Duke Daxo 125.00
85 Meets Leslie M. Gresham . . 125.00
86 'Secret of the Amazing Bracelets' 125.00
87 In Twin Peaks(in Old West) 125.00
88 Wonder Woman in Holywood 125.00
89 V:Abacus Rackeett gang . . 125.00
90 'The Secret of the Modern Sphinx' 125.00
91 . . . . 125.00
92 V:Duke of Deceptions 125.00
93 V:Talbot 125.00
94 . . . . 125.00
95 . . . . 125.00
96 . . . . 150.00
97 . . . . 150.00
98 'Strange Mission' 150.00
99 I:Astra 150.00
100 . . . . 175.00
101 'Battle for the Atom World' 150.00
102 'Queen of the South Seas' 150.00
103 V:Robot Archers 150.00
104 'The End of Paradise Island' 150.00
105 'Secret of the Giant Forest' 150.00
106 E:Wonder Woman 150.00
107 ATh,Mystery issue 250.00
108 ATh,I:Johnny Peril 225.00
109 Ath,A:Johnny Peril 250.00

Becomes:

SENSATION MYSTERY

110 B:Johnny Peril 150.00
111 'Spectre in the Flame' 125.00
112 'Death has 5 Guesses' . . . 125.00
113 . . . . 125.00
114 GC,'The Haunted Diamond' 125.00
115 'The Phantom Castle' 125.00
116 'The Toy Assassins', July-August, 1953 . . . . 125.00

SERGEANT BILKO

May-June, 1957

1 Based on TV show 400.00
2 . . . . 225.00
3 . . . . 200.00
4 . . . . 175.00
5 . . . . 175.00
6 thru 17 . . . . @150.00
18 March-April, 1960 . . . . 150.00

SERGEANT BILKO'S PVT. DOBERMAN

June-July, 1958

1 . . . . 225.00
2 . . . . 150.00
3 . . . . 100.00
4 . . . . 100.00
5 . . . . 100.00
6 thru 10 . . . . @75.00
11 February-March, 1960 . . . . . 75.00

SGT. ROCK

(See: OUR ARMY AT WAR)

SGT. ROCK SPECIAL

October, 1988

#1 rep.Our Army at War#162-3 . . 2.00
#2 rep.Brave & Bold #52 . . . . 2.00
#3 rep.Showcase #45 . . . . 2.00
#4 rep.Our Army at War#147-8 . . 2.00
#5 rep.Our Army at War#81&103 . 2.00
#6 rep.Our Army at War #160 . . . 2.00
#7 rep.Our Army at War #85 . . . . 2.00
#8 rep. 2.00
#9 . . . . 2.00
#10 thru #20 reprints. . . . . @2.00

Sgt. Rock Special #1
© DC Comics, Inc.

SGT. ROCK'S PRIZE BATTLE TALES

Winter, 1964

1 . . . . 125.00

SGT. ROCK SPECIAL

1 TT,MGo,JKu,CR,(new stories) . 2.95

SHADE

June-July, 1977

[1st Regular Series]

1 SD,I&O: Shade 4.00
2 SD,V:Form 2.50
3 SD,V:The Cloak 2.50
4 SD,Return to Meta-Zone 2.50
5 SD,V:Supreme Decider 2.50
6 SD,V:Khaos 2.50
7 SD,V:Dr.Z.Z. 2.50
8 SD,last issue 2.50

SHADE, THE CHANGING MAN

July, 1990

1 B:PrM(s),CBa,MPn,I:Kathy George, I&D:Troy Grezer 9.00
2 CBa,MPn,Who Shot JFK#1 . . . 5.50
3 CBa,MPn,Who Shot JFK#2 . . . 4.50
4 CBa,MPn,V:American Scream . 3.25
5 CBa,MPn,V:Hollywood Monsters 3.00
6 CBa,MPn,V:Ed Loot 3.00
7 CBa,MPn,I:Arnold Major 2.75
8 CBa,Mpn,I:Lenny 2.75
9 CBa,MPn,V:Arnold Major 2.75
10 CBa,MPn,Paranioa 2.75
11 CBa,MPn,R:Troy Grezer 2.50
12 CBa,MPn,V:Troy Grezer 2.50
13 CBa,MPn,I:Fish Priest 2.50
14 CBa,MPn,V:Godfather of Guilt . 2.50
15 CBa,MPn,I:Spirit 2.50
16 CBa,MPn,V:American Scream . 2.50
17 RkB(i),V:Rohug 2.50
18 MPn,E:American Scream 2.50
19 MPn,V:Dave Messiah Seeker . 2.50
20 JD,CBa,MPn,RkB,R:Roger . . . 2.50
21 MPn,The Road,A:Stringer 2.25
22 The Road,Childhood 2.25

Shade, The Changing Man #2
© DC Comics, Inc.

23 The Road 2.25
24 The Road 2.25
25 The Road 2.25
26 MPn(i),F:Lenny 2.25
27 MPn(i),Shade becomes female 2.25
28 MPn(i),Changing Woman#2 . . 2.25
29 MPn(i),Changing Woman#3 . . 2.25
30 Another Life 2.25
31 Ernest & Jim#1 . . . . 2.25
32 Ernest & Jim#2 . . . . 2.25

Vertigo

33 CBa,B:Birth Pains, ... 2.25
34 CBa,RkB(i),GID(i),A:Brian Juno, Garden of Pain 2.25
35 CBa,RkB(i),E:Birth Pains, V:Juno 2.25
36 CBa,PrG(i),RkB(i),B:Passion child, I:Miles Laimling 2.25
37 CBa,RkB(i),Shade/Kathy 2.25
38 CBa,RkB(i),Great American Novel 2.25
39 CBa,SEa,RkB(i),Pond Life . . . 2.25
40 PBd,at Hotel Shade 2.25
41 GID,Pandora's Story,Kathy is pregnant 2.25
42 CBa,RkB(i),SY,B:History Lesson, A:John Constantine 2.50
43 CBa,RkB(i),PBd,Trial of William Matthieson,A:J.Constantine . . . 2.50
44 CBa,RkB(i),E:History Lesson, D:William Matthieson,A:John Constantine 2.50
45 CBa,B:A Season in Hell 2.25
46 CBa(c),GID,Season in Hell#2 . 2.25
47 CBa(c),GID,A:Lenny 2.25
48 CBa(c),GID, ... 2.25
49 CBa(c),GID,Kathy's Past 1.95

SHADO, SONG OF THE DRAGON

1 GM(i),From G.A. Longbow Hunters 5.50
2 GM(i),V:Yakuza 4.95
3 GM(i),V:Yakuza 4.95
4 GM(i),V:Yakuza 4.95

All comics prices listed are for *Near Mint* condition.

SHADOW, THE
October-November, 1973
[1st Regular Series]

1 MK,The Doom Puzzle 27.00
2 MK,V:Freak Show Killer 17.00
3 MK,BWr 23.00
4 MK,Ninja Story 16.00
5 FR 11.00
6 MK 16.00
7 FR 10.00
8 FR 10.00
9 FR 10.00
10 . . . . 10.00
11 A:Avenger 10.00
12 . . . . 10.00

[Limited Series]

1 HC,R:Shadow 6.00
2 HC,O:Shadow 4.00
3 HC,V:Preston Mayrock 3.00
4 HC,V:Preston Mayrock 3.00
TPB rep. #1 thru #4 . . . . 12.95

[2nd Regular Series]

1 BSz,Shadows & Light Pt.#1 . . . 3.50
2 BSz,Shadows & Light Pt.#2 . . . 3.50
3 BSz,Shadows & Light Pt.#3 . . . 3.50
4 BSz,Shadows & Light Pt.#4 . . . 3.50
5 BSz,Shadows & Light Pt.#5 . . . 3.50
6 BSz,Shadows & Light Pt.#6 . . . 3.50
7 MR,KB,Harold Goes to Washington 2.00
8 KB,Seven Deadly Finns Pt#1 . . 2.00
9 KB,Seven Deadly Finns Pt#2 . . 2.00
10 KB,Seven Deadly Finns Pt#3 . 2.00
11 KB,Seven Deadly Finns Pt#4 . 2.00
12 KB,Seven Deadly Finns Pt#5 . 2.00
13 KB,Seven Deadly Finns Pt#6 . 2.00
14 KB,Body And Soul Pt.#1 . . . . . 2.00
15 KB,Body And Soul Pt.#2 . . . . . 2.00
16 KB,Body And Soul Pt.#3 . . . . . 2.00
17 KB,Body And Soul Pt.#4 . . . . . 2.00
18 KB,Body And Soul Pt.#5 . . . . . 2.00
19 KB,Body And Soul Pt.#6 . . . . . 2.00
Ann.#1 JO,AA,Shadows & Light prologue 3.00
Ann.#2 KB,Agents 2.50

SHADOW CABINET
Milestone

0 WS(c),3RL,Shadow War,Foil(c),A:All Milestone characters 3.00
1 JBy(c),3RW,I&D:Corpsickle . . . 2.00
2 3RW,V:Arcadian League 1.75

SHADOW OF BATMAN

1 reprints of Detective Comics . . 10.00
2 thru 4 . . . . @7.50

SHADOW OF THE BATMAN
December, 1985

1 WS,AM,MR,rep. 10.00
2 MR,TA,rep.A:Hugo Strange . . . 7.50
3 MR,TA,rep.A:Penguin 7.50
4 MR,TA,rep.A:Joker 8.50
5 MR,DG,rep. 7.50

SHADOW STRIKES!, THE
September, 1989

1 EB,Death's Head 3.00
2 EB,EB,PoliticalKiller,V:Rasputin 2.50
3 EB,V:Mad Monk,V:Rasputin . . . 2.00
4 EB,D:Mad Monk,V:Rasputin . . . 2.00
5 EB,Shadow & Doc Savage#1 . 2.00
6 Shadow & Doc Savage #3 . . . . 2.00
7 RM,A:Wunderkind,O:Shadow's Radio Show 2.00
8 EB,A:Shiwan Khan 2.00
9 Fireworks#2 . . . . 2.00
10 EB,Fireworks#3 . . . . 2.00
11 EB,O:Margo Lane 2.00
12 EB,V:Chicago Mob 2.00
13 EB,V:Chicago Mob 2.00
14 EB,V:Chicago Mob 2.00
15 EB,V:Chicago Mob 2.00
16 Assassins Pt 1 . . . . 2.00
17 Assassins Pt #2 . . . . 2.00
18 Shrevvie 2.00
19 NY,NJ Tunnel 2.00
20 Shadow+Margo Vs.Nazis 2.00
21 V:Shiwan Khan 2.00
22 V:Shiwan Khan 2.00
23 V:Shiwan Khan 2.00
24 Search for Margo Lane 2.00
25 In China 2.00
26 V:Shiwan Khan 2.00
27 V:Shiwan Khan,Margo Rescued 2.00
28 SL,In Hawaii 2.00
29 DSp,'Valhalla',V:Nazis 2.00
30 The Shadow Year One,Pt 1 . . 2.00
31 The Shadow Year One Pt2 . . . 2.00
Ann.#1 DSp 'Crimson Dreams' . . 4.25

SHADOW WAR OF HAWKMAN
May, 1985

1 AA,V:Thangarians 1.50
2 AA,V:Thangarians 1.25
3 AA,V:Thangarians,A:Aquaman, Elong.Man 1.25
4 AA,V:Thangarians 1.25
Spec.#1 V:Thangarians 1.25

Shazam! #1 © DC Comics, Inc.

SHAZAM!
February, 1973
[1st Regular Series]

1 B:DON(s),CCB,O:Capt.Marvel . 3.50
2 CCB,A:Mr.Mind 2.50
3 CCB,V:Shagg Naste 2.00
4 E:DON(s),CCB,V:Ibac 2.00
5 B:ESM(s),CCB,A:Leprechaun . 2.00
6 B:DON(s),CCB,Dr,Sivana 2.00
7 CCB,A:Capt Marvel Jr. 2.00
8 CCB,O:Marvel Family 2.00
9 E:DON(S)DC,CCB,A:Mr.Mind, Captain Marvel Jr. 2.00
10 ESM(s)CCB,BO 2.00
11 ViCKS,BO,rep. 2.00
12 BO,DG 2.00
13 BO,KS,A:Luthor 2.00
14 KS,A:Monster Society 2.00
15 KS,BO,Luther 2.00
16 KS,BO 2.00
17 KS,BO 2.00
18 KS,BO 2.00
19 KS,BO,Mary Marvel 2.00
20 KS,A:Marvel Family 2.00
21 reprint 2.00
22 reprint 2.00
23 reprint 2.00
24 reprint 2.00
25 KS,DG,I&O:Isis 2.00
26 KS 2.00
27 KS,A:KidEternity 2.50
28 KS 2.00
29 KS 2.00
30 KS 2.00
31 KS,A:MinuteMan 2.00
32 KS 2.00
33 KS 2.00
34 O:Capt.Marvel Jr. 2.00
35 DN,KS,A:Marvel Family 2.00

[Limited Series]

1 O:Shazam&Capt.Marvel 1.50
2 V:Black Adam 1.25
3 V:Black Adam 1.25
4 V:Black Adam 1.25

SHAZAM ARCHIVES

1 Rep.Whiz Comics#2-15 . . . . . 49.95

SHAZAM, THE NEW BEGINNING
April, 1987

1 O:Shazam & Capt.Marvel 1.50
2 V:Black Adam 1.25
3 V:Black Adam 1.25
4 V:Black Adam 1.25

SHERLOCK HOLMES
September-October, 1975

1 . . . . 1.00

SHOWCASE
March-April, 1956

1 F:Fire Fighters 1,850.00
2 JKu,F:Kings of Wild 600.00
3 F:Frogmen 525.00
4 CI,JKu,I&O:S.A. Flash (Barry Allen) 11,000.00
5 F:Manhunters 650.00
6 JK,I&O:Challengers of the Unknown 1,800.00
7 JK,F:Challengers 900.00
8 CI,F:Flash,I:Capt.Cold 4,000.00
9 F:Lois Lane 1,600.00
10 F:Lois Lane 1,100.00
11 JK(c),F:Challengers 800.00
12 JK(c),F:Challengers 800.00
13 CI,F:Flash,Mr.Element . . . 2,000.00
14 CI,F:Flash,Mr.Element . . . 2,000.00
15 I:Space Ranger 700.00
16 F:Space Ranger 400.00
17 GK(c),I:Adam Strange . . . 1000.00
18 GK(c),F:Adam Strange 510.00
19 GK(c),F:Adam Strange 510.00
20 I:Rip Hunter 500.00
21 F:Rip Hunter 250.00
22 GK,I&O:S.A. Green Lantern (Hal Jordan) 3,000.00
23 GK,F:Green Lantern 950.00
24 GK,F:Green Lantern 950.00
25 JKu,F:Rip Hunter 200.00
26 JKu,F:Rip Hunter 200.00
27 RH,I:Sea Devils 450.00
28 RH,F:Sea Devils 250.00
29 RH,F:Sea Devils 250.00
30 O:Aquaman 400.00
31 GK(c),F:Aquaman 240.00
32 F:Aquaman 240.00
33 F:Aquaman 240.00
34 GK,MA,I&O:S.A. Atom 900.00
35 GK,MA,F:Atom 500.00
36 GK,MA,F:Atom 400.00
37 RA,I:Metal Man 450.00
38 RA,F:Metal Man 350.00

39 RA,F:Metal Man 260.00
40 RA,F:Metal Man 235.00
41 F:Tommy Tomorrow 75.00
42 F:Tommy Tomorrow 75.00
43 F:Dr.No(James Bond 007) . 350.00
44 F:Tommy Tomorrow 55.00
45 JKu,O:Sgt.Rock 110.00
46 F:Tommy Tomorrow 40.00
47 F:Tommy Tomorrow 40.00
48 F:Cave Carson 28.00
49 F:Cave Carson 28.00
50 thru 51 MA,CI,F:I Spy . . . . @35.00
52 F:Cave Carson 28.00
53 JKu(c),RH,F:G.I.Joe 35.00
54 JKu(c),RH,F:G.I.Joe 35.00
55 MA,F:Dr.Fate,Spectre,1st S.A. Green Lantern,Solomon Grundy 200.00
56 MA,F:Dr.Fate 50.00
57 JKu,F:Enemy Ace 60.00
58 JKu,F:Enemy Ace 60.00
59 F:Teen Titans 75.00
60 MA,F:Spectre 140.00
61 MA,F:Spectre 70.00
62 JO,I:Inferior 5 . . . . 55.00
63 JO,F:Inferior 5 . . . . 29.00
64 MA,F:Spectre 75.00
65 F:Inferior 5 . . . . 29.00
66 I:B'wana Beast 13.00
67 F:B'wana Beast 13.00
68 I:Maniaks 13.00
69 F:Maniaks 13.00
70 I:Binky 13.00
71 F:Maniaks 13.00
72 JKu,ATh,F:Top Gun 13.00
73 SD,I&O:Creeper 65.00
74 I:Anthro 50.00
75 SD,I:Hawk & Dove 70.00
76 NC,I:Bat Lash 35.00
77 BO,I:Angel & Ape 35.00
78 I:Jonny Double 17.00
79 I:Dolphin 28.00
80 NA(c),F:Phantom Stranger . . 13.00
81 I:Windy & Willy 13.00

DC Showcase #31 © DC Comics, Inc.

82 I:Nightmaster 43.00
83 BWr,MK,F:Nightmaster 42.00
84 BWr,MK,F:Nightmaster 42.00
85 JKu,F:Firehair 12.00
86 JKu,F:Firehair 12.00
87 JKu,F:Firehair 12.00
88 F:Jason's Quest 6.00
89 F:Jason's Quest 6.00
90 thru 91 F:Manhunter . . . . . . @5.00
92 F:Manhunter 5.00
93 F:Manhunter 5.00
94 JA,JSon,I&O:2nd Doom Patrol 9.00
95 JA,JSon,F:2nd Doom Patrol . . 6.00
96 JA,JSon,F:2nd Doom Patrol . . 6.00
97 JO,JSon,O:Power Girl 5.00

DC Showcase #85 © DC Comics, Inc.

98 JSon,DG,Power Girl 5.00
99 JSon,DG,Power Girl 5.00
100 JSon,all star issue 6.00
101 JKu(c),AM,MA,Hawkman . . . 5.00
102 JKu(c),AM,MA,Hawkman . . . 5.00
103 JKu(c),AM,MA,Hawkman . . . 5.00
104 RE,OSS Spies 5.00

SHOWCASE' 93

1 AAd(c),EH,AV,F:Catwoman, Blue Devil,Cyborg 5.50
2 KM(c),EH,AV,F:Catwoman, Blue Devil,Cyborg 4.00
3 KM(c),EH,TC,F:Catwoman, Blue Devil,Flash 3.50
4 F:Catwoman,Blue Devil, Geo-Force 2.50
5 F:KD,DG,BHi,F:Robin,Blue Devil,Geo-Force, ... 2.50
6 MZ(c),KD,DG,F:Robin,Blue Devil,Deathstroke 2.50
7 BSz(c),KJ,Knightfall#13,F:Two-Face,Jade&Obsidian 5.00
8 KJ,Knightfall#14,F:Two-Face, Peacemaker,Fire and Ice 4.00
9 F:Huntress,Peacemaker,Shining Knight 2.50
10 BWg,SI,F:Huntress,Batman, Dr.Light,Peacemaker,Deathstroke, Katana,M.Manhunter 2.50
11 GP(c),F:Robin,Nightwing, Peacemaker,Deathstroke,Deadshot, Katana,Dr.Light,Won.Woman . 2.50
12 AD(c),BMc,F:Robin,Nightwing, Green Lantern,Creeper 2.50

SHOWCASE' 94

1 KN,F:Joker,Gunfire,Orion,Metro 2.25
2 KON(c),E:Joker,B:Blue Beetle . 2.25
3 MMi(c),B:Razorsharpe, ... 2.25
4 AlG(s),DG,F:Arkham Asylum inmates E:Razorsharpe,Blue Bettle, . . . 2.25
5 WS(c),CDi(s),PJ,B:Robin & Huntress, F:Bloodwynd,Loose Cannon . . 2.25
6 PJ,KK(s),F:Robin & Huntress . . 2.25
7 JaL(c),PDd(s),F:Comm. Gordon 2.25
8 AlG(s),O:Scarface,Ventriloquist, F:Monarch,1st Wildcat 1.95

SILVER AGE DC CLASSICS

Action #252(rep) 1.50
Adventure #247(rep) 1.50
Brave and Bold #28 (rep) 1.50
Detective #225 (rep) 1.50
Detective #327 (rep) 1.50
Green Lantern #76 (rep) 1.50
House of Secrets #92 (rep) 2.00
Showcase #4 (rep) 1.75
Showcase #22 (rep) 1.50
Sugar & Spike #99(1st printing) . . 1.50

SILVER BLADE

September, 1987

1 KJ,GC,maxi-series 1.50
2 thru 12 GC . . . . @1.50

SKIN GRAFT

Vertigo

1 B:JeP(s),WaP,I:John Oakes, A:Tattooed Man(Tarrant) 3.25
2 WaP,V:Assassins 3.00
3 WaP,In Kyoto,I:Mizoguchi Kenji . 3.00
4 E:JeP(s),WaP,V:Tarrant,Kenji . . 3.00

SKREEMER

May, 1989

1 . . . . 1.50
2 thru 6 . . . . @2.00

SKULL AND BONES

1 EH,I&O:Skull & Bones 4.95
2 EH,V:KGB 4.95
3 EH,V:KGB 4.95

SLASH MARAUD

November, 1987

1 PG 2.25
2 thru 10 PG . . . . @2.00

SONIC DISRUPTORS

1 thru 10 . . . . @1.75

SON OF AMBUSH BUG

July, 1986

1 thru 6 KG . . . . @1.00

SPANNER'S GALAXY

December, 1984

1 mini-series 1.50
2 thru 6 . . . . @1.00

SPECTRE, THE

November-December, 1967

1 MA,V:Captain Skull 80.00
2 NA,V:Dirk Rawley 65.00
3 NA,A:Wildcat 57.00
4 NA 57.00
5 NA 57.00
6 MA 30.00
7 MA,BU:Hourman 30.00
8 MA,Parchment of Power Perilous 30.00
9 BWr(2nd BWr Art) 35.00
10 MA 30.00

[2nd Regular Series]
April, 1987

1 GC,O:Spectre 3.50
2 GC,Cult of BRM 3.00
3 GC,Fashion Model Murders . . . 2.00
4 GC 2.00
5 GC,Spectre's Murderer 2.00
6 GC,Spectre/Corrigan separated 2.00
7 A:Zatanna,Wotan 2.00
8 A:Zatanna,Wotan 2.00
9 GM,Spectre's Revenge 2.00

10 GM,A:Batman,Millenium 2.25
11 GM,Millenium 2.00
12 GM,The Talisman Pt.1 . . . . . . 1.75
13 GM,The Talisman Pt.2 . . . . . . 1.75

Spectre (1st Series) #1
© DC Comics, Inc.

14 GM,The Talisman Pt.3 . . . . . . 1.75
15 GM,The Talisman Pt.4 . . . . . . 1.75
16 Jim Corrigan Accused 1.75
17 New Direction,'Final Destiny' . . 1.75
18 Search for Host Body 1.75
19 'Dead Again' 1.75
20 Corrigan Detective Agency . . . 1.75
21 A:Zoran 1.50
22 BS,Sea of Darkness,A:Zoran . 1.50
23 A:Lords of Order,
Invasion x-over 1.50
24 BWg,Ghosts i/t Machine#1 . . . 1.50
25 Ghosts in the Machine #2 . . . . 1.50
26 Ghosts in the Machine #3 . . . . 1.50
27 Ghosts in the Machine #4 . . . . 1.50
28 Ghosts in the Machine #5 . . . . 1.50
29 Ghosts in the Machine #6 . . . . 1.50
30 Possession 1.50
31 Spectre possessed, final issue 1.50
Ann.#1, A:Deadman 2.75

[3rd Regular Series]

1 B:JOs(s),TMd,R:Spectre,
Glow in the dark(c) 10.00
2 TMd,Murder Mystery 6.00
3 TMd,O:Spectre 5.00
4 TMd,O:Spectre 4.00
5 TMd,BB(c),V:Kidnappers 3.50
6 TMd,Spectre prevents evil 3.50
7 TMd 3.50
8 TMd,Glow in the dark(c) 5.00
9 TMd,MWg(c),V:The Reaver . . . 3.00
10 TMd,V:Michael 2.50
11 TMd,V:Azmodeus 2.50
12 V:Reaver 2.50
13 TMd,V:Count Vertigo,
Glow in the Dark(c), ... 3.00
14 JoP,A:Phantom Stranger, ... 2.00
15 TMd,A:Phantom Stranger,Demon,
Doctor Fate,John Constantine . 2.00
16 JAp,V:I.R.A. 2.00
17 TT(c),TMd,V:Eclipso 2.00
18 TMd,D:Eclipso 2.00
19 TMd,V:Hate 2.00
20 A:Lucien 1.75
TPB Punishment and Crimes 9.95

SPELLJAMMER
September, 1990

1 RogueShip#1 . . . . 3.00
2 RogueShip#2 . . . . 2.50
3 RogueShip#3 . . . . 2.00
4 RogueShip#4 . . . . 2.00
5 New Planet 1.75
6 Tember, Planet contd 1.75
7 Planet contd 1.75
8 conclusion 1.75
9 Meredith Possessed 1.75
10 Tie-in w/Dragonlance #33&34 . 1.75
11 Dwarf Citidel 1.75
12 Kirstig Vs. Meredith 1.75
13 Tember to the Rescue 1.75
14 Meredith's Son #1 . . . . 1.75
15 Meredith's Son #2 . . . . 1.75

STANLEY & HIS MONSTER
(see FOX AND THE CROW)

STANLEY & HIS MONSTER

1 R:Stanley 1.25
2 I:Demon Hunter 1.25
3 A:Ambrose Bierce 1.25
4 final issue 1.25

S.T.A.R. CORPS

1 A:Superman 2.00
2 I:Fusion,A:Rampage 1.75
3 I:Brainstorm 1.75
4 I:Ndoki 1.75
5 I:Trauma 1.75
6 I:Mindgame 1.75

STAR HUNTERS
October-November, 1977

1 DN&BL 1.00
2 LH&BL 1.00
3 MN&BL,D:Donovan Flint 1.00
4 thru 7 . . . . @1.00

STARMAN
October, 1988

1 TL,I&O:New Starman 3.00
2 TL,V:Serial Killer,C:Bolt 2.00
3 TL,V:Bolt 1.50
4 TL,V:Power Elite 1.50
5 TL,Invasion,A:PowerGirl,
Firestorm 1.50
6 TL,Invasion,A:G.L.,Atom 1.50
7 TL,Soul Searching Issue 1.50
8 TL,V:LadyQuark 1.50
9 TL,A:Batman,V:Blockbuster . . . 2.00
10 TL,A:Batman,V:Blockbuster . . . 2.00
11 TL,V:Power Elite 1.25
12 TL,V:Power Elite,A:Superman . 1.50
13 TL,V:Rampage 1.25
14 TL,A:A:Superman,V:Parasite . . 1.50
15 TL,V:Deadline 1.25
16 TL,O:Starman 1.25
17 TL,V:Dr.Polaris,A:PowerGirl . . 1.25
18 TL,V:Dr.Polaris,A:PowerGirl . . 1.25
19 TL,V:Artillery 1.25
20 TL,FireFighting 1.25
21 TL,Starman Quits 1.25
22 TL,V:Khunds 1.25
23 TL,A:Deadline 1.25
24 TL,A:Deadline 1.25
25 TL,V:Deadline 1.25
26 V:The Mist 1.25
27 V:The Mist 1.25
28 A:Superman 7.00
29 V:Plasmax 1.25
30 Seduction of Starman #1 . . . . 1.25
31 Seduction of Starman #2 . . . . 1.25
32 Seduction of Starman #3 . . . . 1.25
33 Seduction of Starman #4 . . . . 1.25
34 A:Batman 1.25
35 A:Valor,Mr.Nebula,ScarletSkier 1.25
36 A:Les Mille Yeux 1.25
37 A:Les Mille Yeux 1.25
38 War of the Gods X-over 1.25
39 V:Plasmax 1.25
40 V:Las Vegas 1.25
41 V:Maaldor 1.25
42 'Star Shadows'Pt.1,A:Eclipso . 3.00
43 'Star Shadows'Pt.2,A:Lobo,
Eclipso 2.50
44 'Star Shadows'Pt.3,A:Eclipso
V:Lobo 2.50
45 Star Shadows Pt 4, V:Eclipso . 2.50

STAR SPANGLED COMICS
October, 1941

1 O:Tarantula,B:Captain X of the
R.A.F.,Star Spangled Kid,
Armstrong of the Army . . . 2,000.00
2 V:Dr. Weerd 700.00
3 . . . . 450.00
4 V:The Needle 450.00
5 V:Dr. Weerd 450.00
6 E:Armstrong 300.00
7 S&K,O&1st app:The Guardian,
B:Robotman,The Newsboy
Legion, TNT 3,500.00
8 O:TNT & Dan the Dyna-Mite 1,000.00
9 . . . . 900.00
10 . . . . 900.00
11 . . . . 750.00
12 Newsboy Legion stories,
'Prevue of Peril!' 750.00
13 'Kill Dat Story!' 750.00
14 'The Meanest Man on Earth!' 750.00

Star Spangled Comics #7
© DC Comics, Inc.

15 'Playmates of Peril' 750.00
16 'Playboy of Suicide Slum!' . . 750.00
17 V:Rafferty Mob 750.00
18 O:Star Spangled Kid 900.00
19 E:Tarantula 700.00
20 B:Liberty Belle 750.00
21 . . . . 550.00
22 'Brains for Sale' 550.00
23 'Art for Scrapper's Sake' . . . 550.00
24 . . . . 550.00
25 'Victuals for Victory' 550.00
26 'Louie the Lug goes Literary' 550.00
27 'Turn on the Heat!' 550.00
28 'Poor Man's Rich Man' 550.00
29 'Cabbages and Comics' . . . 550.00
30 . . . . 275.00
31 'Questions Please!' 275.00
32 . . . . 275.00

33 ... 275.00
34 'From Rags to Run!' ... 275.00
35 'The Proud Poppas' ... 275.00
36 'Cowboy of Suicide Slum' .. 275.00
37 ... 275.00
38 ... 275.00
39 'Two Guardians are a Crowd' 275.00
40 ... 275.00
41 Back the 6th War Loan(c) .. 225.00
42 ... 225.00
43 American Red Cross(c) ... 225.00
44 ... 225.00
45 7th War Loan (c) ... 225.00
46 ... 225.00
47 ... 225.00
48 ... 225.00
49 ... 225.00
50 ... 225.00
51 A:Robot Robber ... 225.00
52 'Rehearsal for Crime' ... 225.00
53 'The Poet of Suicide Slum' . 225.00
54 'Dead-Shot Dade's Revenge' 225.00
55 'Gabby Strikes a Gusher' .. 225.00
56 'The Treasuer of Araby' ... 225.00
57 'Recruit for the Legion' ... 225.00
58 'Matadors of Suicide Slum' . 225.00
59 ... 225.00
60 ... 225.00
61 ... 225.00
62 'Prevue of Tomorrow' ... 225.00
63 ... 225.00
64 'Criminal Cruise' ... 225.00
65 B:Robin,(c) & stories ... 750.00
66 V:No Face ... 500.00
67 'The Castle of Doom ... 400.00
68 ... 400.00
69 'The Stolen Atom Bomb' ... 400.00
70 V:The Clock ... 400.00
71 'Perils of the Stone Age' ... 400.00
72 'Robin Crusoe' ... 400.00
73 V:The Black Magician ... 400.00
74 V:The Clock ... 400.00
75 The State vs. Robin ... 400.00
76 V:The Fence ... 400.00
77 'The Boy who Wanted Robin for Christmas' ... 400.00
78 "Rajah Robin' ... 400.00
79 'V:The Clock,'The Tick-Tock Crimes' ... 400.00
80 'The Boy Disc Jockey' ... 400.00
81 'The Seeing-Eye Dog Crimes' 300.00
82 'The Boy who Hated Robin' 300.00
83 'Who is Mr. Mystery',B:Captain Compass backup story ... 300.00
84 How can we Fight Juvenile Delinquency? ... 300.00
85 'Peril at the Pole' ... 300.00
86 ... 350.00
87 V:Sinister Knight ... 350.00
88 Robin Declares War on Batman, B:Batman app. ... 350.00
89 'Batman's Utility Belt?' ... 350.00
90 'Rancho Fear!' ... 350.00
91 'Cops 'n' Robbers?' ... 350.00
92 'Movie Hero No. 1?' ... 350.00
93 ... 350.00
94 'Underworld Playhouse' ... 350.00
95 'The Man with the Midas Touch', E:Robin(c),Batman story ... 350.00
96 B:Tomahawk(c) & stories .. 275.00
97 'The 4 Bold Warriors' ... 225.00
98 ... 225.00
99 'The Second Pocahontas' .. 225.00
100 'The Frontier Phantom' ... 250.00
101 Peril on the High Seas ... 175.00
102 ... 175.00
103 'Tomahawk's Death Duel!' . 175.00
104 'Race with Death!' ... 175.00
105 'The Unhappy Hunting Grounds' ... 175.00
106 'Traitor in the War Paint' .. 175.00
107 'The Brave who Hunted Tomahawk' ... 175.00
108 'The Ghost called Moccasin Foot!' ... 175.00
109 'The Land Pirates of Jolly Roger Hill!' ... 175.00
110 'Sally Raines Frontier Girl' 175.00
111 'The Death Map of Thunder Hill' ... 175.00
112 ... 200.00
113 FF,V:'The Black Cougar' .. 250.00
114 'Return of the Black Cougar' 250.00
115 'Journey of a Thousand Deaths' ... 250.00
116 'The Battle of Junction Fort' 250.00
117 'Siege?' ... 250.00
118 V:Outlaw Indians ... 175.00
119 'The Doomed Stockade?' . 175.00
120 'Revenge of Raven Heart!' 175.00
121 'Adventure in New York!' .. 175.00
122 'I:Ghost Breaker,(c)& stories 175.00
123 'The Dolls of Doom' ... 125.00
124 'Suicide Tower' ... 125.00
125 The Hermit's Ghost Dog!' . 125.00
126 'The Phantom of Paris!' .. 125.00
127 'The Supernatural Alibi!' .. 125.00
128 C:Batman,'The Girl who lived 5,000 Years!' ... 125.00
129 'The Human Orchids' ... 150.00

Star Spangled Comics #63
© DC Comics, Inc.

130 'The Haunted Town', July, 1952 ... 165.00

Becomes:

STAR SPANGLED WAR STORIES

August, 1952

131 CS&StK(c),I Was A Jap Prisoner of War ... 450.00
132 CS&StK(c),The G.I. With The Million-Dollar Arm ... 350.00
133 CS&StK(c),Mission-San Marino ... 325.00
3 CS&StK(c),Hundred-Mission Mitchell ... 200.00
4 CS&StK(c),The Hot Rod Tank 200.00
5 LSt(c),Jet Pilot ... 200.00
6 CS(c),Operation Davy Jones 200.00
7 CS(c),Rookie Ranger,The .. 150.00
8 CS(c),I Was A Holywood Soldier ... 150.00
9 CS&StK(c),Sad Sack Squad 150.00
10 CS,The G.I. & The Gambler 150.00
11 LSt(c),The Lucky Squad ... 135.00
12 CS(c),The Four Horseman of Barricade Hill ... 135.00
13 No Escape ... 135.00
14 LSt(c),Pitchfork Army ... 135.00
15 The Big Fish ... 135.00
16 The Yellow Ribbon ... 135.00
17 IN(c),Prize Target ... 135.00
18 IN(c),The Gladiator ... 135.00
19 IN(c),The Big Lift ... 135.00
20 JGr(c),The Battle of the Frogmen ... 135.00
21 JGr(c),Dead Man's Bridge .. 125.00
22 JGr(c),Death Hurdle ... 125.00
23 JGr(c),The Silent Frogman . 125.00
24 JGr(c),Death Slide ... 125.00
25 JGr(c),S.S. Liferaft ... 125.00
26 JGr(c),Bazooka Man ... 125.00
27 JGr(c),Taps for a Tail Gunner 125.00
28 JGr(c),Tank Duel ... 125.00
29 JGr(c),A Gun Called Slugger 125.00
30 JGr(c),The Thunderbolt Tank 125.00
31 IN(c),Tank Block ... 75.00
32 JGr(c),Bridge to Battle ... 75.00
33 JGr(c),Pocket War ... 75.00
34 JGr(c),Fighting...Snowbirds .. 75.00
35 JGr(c),Zero Hour ... 75.00
36 JGr(c),A G.I. Passed Here .. 75.00
37 JGr(c),A Handful of T.N.T. .. 75.00
38 RH(c),One-Man Army ... 75.00
39 JGr(c),Flying Cowboy ... 75.00
40 JGr(c),Desert Duel ... 75.00
41 IN(c),A Gunner's Hands ... 50.00
42 JGr(c),Sniper Alley ... 50.00
43 JGr(c),Top Kick Brother ... 50.00
44 JGr(c),Tank 711 Doesn't Answer ... 50.00
45 JGr(c),Flying Heels ... 50.00
46 JGr(c),Gunner's Seat ... 50.00
47 JGr(c),Sidekick ... 50.00
48 JGr(c),Battle Hills ... 50.00
49 JGr(c),Payload ... 50.00
50 JGr(c),Combat Dust ... 50.00
51 JGr(c),Battle Pigeon ... 45.00
52 JGr(c),Cannon-Man ... 45.00
53 JGr(c),Combat Close-Ups ... 45.00
54 JGr(c),Flying Exit ... 45.00
55 JKu(c),The Burning Desert .. 45.00
56 JKu(c),The Walking Sub ... 45.00
57 JGr(c),Call For a Frogman .. 45.00
58 JGr(c),MD,Waist Punch ... 45.00
59 JGr(c),Kick In The Door ... 45.00
60 JGr(c),Hotbox ... 45.00
61 JGr(c),MD,Tow Pilot ... 45.00
62 JGr(c),The Three GIs ... 45.00
63 JGr(c),Flying Range Rider .. 45.00
64 JGr(c),MD,Frogman Ambush . 45.00
65 JGr(c),JSe,Frogman Block .. 45.00
66 JGr(c),Flattop Pigeon ... 45.00
67 RH(c),MD,Ashcan Alley ... 45.00
68 JGr(c),The Long Step ... 45.00
69 JKu(c),Floating Tank, The' .. 45.00
70 JKu(c),No Medal For Frogman ... 40.00
71 JKu(c),Shooting Star ... 40.00
72 JGr(c),Silent Fish ... 40.00
73 JGr(c),MD,The Mouse & the Tiger ... 40.00
74 JGr(c),MD,Frogman Bait ... 40.00
75 JGr(c),MD,Paratroop Mousketeers ... 40.00
76 MD,JKu(c),Odd Man ... 40.00
77 MD,JKu(c),Room to Fight ... 40.00
78 MD,JGr(c),Fighting Wingman 40.00
79 MD,JKu(c),Zero Box ... 40.00
80 MD,JGr(c),Top Gunner ... 40.00
81 MD,RH(c),Khaki Mosquito ... 40.00
82 MD,JKu(c),Ground Flier ... 40.00
83 MD,JGr(c),Jet On My Shoulder ... 40.00
84 MD,IN(c),O:Mademoiselle Marie ... 100.00
85 IN(c),A Medal For Marie ... 75.00
86 JGr(c),A Medal For Marie ... 75.00
87 JGr(c),T.N.T. Spotlight ... 50.00
88 JGr(c),The Steel Trap ... 50.00
89 IN(c),Trail of the Terror ... 50.00
90 RA(c),Island of Armored Giants ... 225.00

91 JGr(c),The Train of Terror . . . 35.00
92 Last Battle of the Dinosaur Age . . . 75.00
93 Goliath of the Western Front . 35.00
94 JKu(c),The Frogman and the Dinosaur . . . 75.00
95 Guinea Pig Patrol,Dinosaurs . 75.00
96 Mission X,Dinosaur . . . 75.00
97 The Sub-Crusher, Dinosaur . 75.00
98 Island of Thunder, Dinosaur . 75.00
99 The Circus of Monsters, Dinosaur . . . 75.00
100 The Volcano of Monsters, Dinosaur . . . 125.00
101 The Robot and the Dinosaur 75.00
102 Punchboard War,Dinosaur . 75.00
103 Doom at Dinosaur Island, Dinosaur . . . 75.00
104 The Tree of Terror, Dinosaurs . . . 75.00
105 The War of Dinosaur Island 75.00
106 The Nightmare War, Dinosaurs . . . 75.00
107 Battle of the Dinosaur Aquarium . . . 75.00
108 Dinosaur D-Day . . . 75.00
109 The Last Soldiers . . . 75.00
110 thru 133 . . . @75.00
134 NA . . . 85.00
135 . . . 60.00
136 . . . 60.00
137 Dinosaur . . . 60.00
138 Enemy Ace . . . 50.00
139 . . . 35.00
140 . . . 35.00
141 . . . 35.00
142 . . . 15.00
143 . . . 15.00
144 NA,JKu . . . 20.00
145 . . . 15.00
146 . . . 15.00
147 . . . 15.00
148 . . . 15.00
149 . . . 15.00
150 JKu,Viking Prince . . . 15.00
151 I:Unknown Soldier . . . 30.00
152 . . . 10.00
153 . . . 10.00
154 O:Unknown Soldier . . . 20.00
155 . . . 10.00
156 I:Battle Album . . . 8.00
157 thru 160 . . . 6.00
161 E:Enemy Ace . . . 6.00
162 thru 170 . . . @10.00
171 thru 200 . . . @8.00
201 thru 204 . . . @2.50

Becomes:

UNKNOWN SOLDIER

April-May, 1977

205 thru 247 . . . @1.00
248 and 249 O:Unknown Soldier @1.25
250 . . . 1.00
251 B:Enemy Ace . . . 1.00
252 thru 268 . . . @1.00

STAR TREK

February, 1984

[1st Regular Series]

1 TS,The Wormhole Connection 15.00
2 TS,The Only Good Klingon . . . 8.00
3 TS,Errand of War . . . 7.00
4 TS,Deadly Allies . . . 7.00
5 TS,Mortal Gods . . . 7.00
6 TS,Who is Enigma? . . . 5.00
7 EB,O:Saavik . . . 5.00
8 TS,Blood Fever . . . 5.00
9 TS,Mirror Universe Saga #1 . . 5.00
10 TS,Mirror Universe Saga #2 . . 5.00
11 TS,Mirror Universe Saga #3 . . 5.00
12 TS,Mirror Universe Saga #4 . . 5.00
13 TS,Mirror Universe Saga #5 . . 4.00
14 TS,Mirror Universe Saga #6 . . 4.00
15 TS,Mirror Universe Saga #7 . . 4.00
16 TS,Mirror Universe Saga end . 4.00
17 TS,The D'Artagnan Three . . . 4.00
18 TS,Rest & Recreation . . . 4.00
19 DSp,W.Koenig story . . . 4.00
20 TS,Girl . . . 4.00
21 TS,Dreamworld . . . 4.00
22 TS,The Wolf #1 . . . 4.00
23 TS,The Wolf #2 . . . 3.50

Star Trek #1 © DC Comics, Inc.

24 TS,Double Blind #1 . . . 3.50
25 TS,Double Blind #2. . . . 3.50
26 TSV:Romulans . . . 3.50
27 TS,Day in the Life . . . 3.50
28 GM,The Last Word . . . 3.00
29 Trouble with Bearclaw . . . 3.00
30 CI,F:Uhura . . . 3.00
31 TS,Maggie's World . . . 3.00
32 TS,Judgment Day . . . 3.00
33 TS,20th Anniv. . . . 4.50
34 V:Romulans . . . 2.50
35 GM,Excelsior . . . 2.50
36 GM,StarTrek IV tie-in . . . 2.50
37 StarTrek IV tie-in . . . 2.50
38 AKu,The Argon Affair . . . 2.50
39 TS,A:Harry Mudd . . . 2.50
40 TS,A:Harry Mudd . . . 2.50
41 TS,V:Orions . . . 2.50
42 TS,The Corbomite Effect . . . 2.50
43 TS,Paradise Lost #1 . . . 2.50
44 TS,Paradise Lost #2 . . . 2.50
45 TS,Paradise Lost #3 . . . 2.50
46 TS,Getaway . . . 2.50
47 TS,Idol Threats . . . 2.50
48 TS,The Stars in Secret Influence . . . 2.50
49 TS,Aspiring to be Angels . . . 2.50
50 TS,Anniv. . . . 3.50
51 TS,Haunted Honeymoon . . . 2.50
52 TS,'Hell in a Hand Basket' . . . 2.50
53 'You're Dead,Jim' . . . 2.50
54 Old Loyalties . . . 2.50
55 TS,Finnegan's Wake . . . 2.50
56 GM,Took place during 5 year Mission . . . 2.50
Ann.#1 All Those Years Ago . . . 3.00
Ann.#2 DJw,The Final Voyage . . . 2.50
Ann.#3 CS,F:Scotty . . . 2.50
Star Trek III Adapt.TS . . . 2.50
Star Trek IV Adapt. TS . . . 2.50
StarTrek V Adapt. . . . 2.50

[2nd Regular Series]

October, 1989

1 The Return . . . 7.00
2 The Sentence . . . 4.00
3 Death Before Dishonor . . . 3.50
4 Reprocussions . . . 3.50
5 Fast Friends . . . 3.50
6 Cure All . . . 3.50
7 Not Sweeney! . . . 3.50
8 Going,Going . . . 3.00
9 ...Gone . . . 3.00
10 Trial of James Kirk #1 . . . 3.00
11 Trial of James Kirk #2 . . . 3.00
12 Trial of James Kirk #3 . . . 3.00
13 Return of Worthy #1 . . . 3.00
14 Return of Worthy #2 . . . 3.00
15 Return of Worthy #3 . . . 3.00
16 Worldsinger . . . 2.50
17 Partners? #1 . . . 2.50
18 Partners? #2 . . . 2.50
19 Once A Hero . . . 2.50
20 . . . 2.50
21 Kirk Trapped . . . 2.25
22 A:Harry Mudd . . . 2.25
23 The Nasgul,A:Harry Mudd . . . 2.25
24 25th Anniv.,A:Harry Mudd . . . 3.50
25 Starfleet Officers Reunion . . . 2.25
26 Pilkor 3 . . . 2.25
27 Kirk Betrayed . . . 2.25
28 V:Romulans . . . 2.25
29 Mediators . . . 2.25
30 Veritas #1 . . . 2.25
31 Veritas #2 . . . 2.25
32 Veritas #3 . . . 2.25
33 Veritas #4 . . . 2.25
34 JD,F:Kirk,Spock,McCoy . . . 2.25
35 Tabukan Syndrome#1 . . . 2.25
36 Tabukan Syndrome#2 . . . 2.25
37 Tabukan Syndrome#3 . . . 2.25
38 Tabukan Syndrome#4 . . . 2.25
39 Tabukan Syndrome#5 . . . 2.25
40 Tabukan Syndrome#6 . . . 2.25
41 Runaway . . . 2.25
42 Helping Hand . . . 2.25
43 V:Binzalans . . . 2.25
44 Acceptable Risk . . . 2.25
45 V:Trelane . . . 2.25
46 V:Captain Klaa . . . 2.25
47 F:Spock & Saavik . . . 2.25
48 The Neutral Zone . . . 2.25
49 weapon from Genesis . . . 2.25
50 "The Peacemaker" . . . 3.75
51 "The Price" . . . 2.00
52 V:Klingons . . . 2.00
53 Timecrime #1 . . . 2.00
54 Timecrime #2 . . . 2.00
55 Timecrime #3 . . . 2.00
56 Timecrime #4 . . . 2.00
57 Timecrime #5 . . . 2.00
58 F:Chekov . . . 2.00
59 Uprising . . . 2.00
60 Hostages . . . 2.00
61 On Talos IV . . . 2.25
62 V:Aliens . . . 1.95
Ann.#1 GM,sty by G.Takei(Sulu) . 4.00
Ann.#2 Kirks 1st Yr At Star Fleet Academy . . . 4.00
Ann #3 KD,F:Ambassador Sarek . 3.50
Ann.#4 F:Spock on Pike's ship . . 3.50
Spec.#1 PDd(s),BSz, . . . 3.75
Debt of Honor,AH,CCI(s),HC . . . 27.00
Debt of Honor SC . . . 14.95
Spec. 25th Anniv.. . . . 6.95
Star Trek VI,movie adapt(direct) . . 5.95
Star Trek VI,movie(newsstand) . . 2.95
TPB Best of Star Trek reps. . . . 19.95
TPB Who Killed Captain Kirk?, rep.Star Trek#49-55 . . . 16.95

STAR TREK: MODULA IMPERATIVE

1 Planet Modula . . . 6.00
2 Modula's Rebels . . . 4.50
3 Spock/McCoy rescue Attempt . 4.00
4 Rebel Victory . . . 4.00
TPB reprints both minis . . . 19.95

STAR TREK: NEXT GENERATION
February, 1988

1 based on TV series,Where No Man Has Gone Before 12.00
2 Spirit in the Sky 9.00
3 Factor Q 8.00
4 Q's Day 8.00
5 Q's Effects 8.00
6 Here Today 8.00

[2nd Regular Series]

1 Return to Raimon 10.00
2 Murder Most Foul 7.00
3 Derelict 6.00
4 The Hero Factor 6.00
5 Serafin's Survivors 5.00
6 Shadows in the Garden 5.00
7 The Pilot 4.00
8 The Battle Within 4.00
9 The Pay Off 4.00
10 The Noise of Justice 4.00
11 The Imposter 3.00
12 Whoever Fights Monsters 3.00
13 The Hand of the Assassin 3.00
14 Holiday on Ice 3.00
15 Prisoners of the Ferengi 2.50
16 I Have Heard the Mermaids Singing 2.50
17 The Weapon 2.50
18 MM,Forbidden Fruit 2.50
19 The Lesson 2.50
20 Lost Shuttle 2.50
21 Lost Shuttle cont. 2.50
22 Lost Shuttle cont. 2.50
23 Lost Shuttle cont. 2.50
24 Lost Shuttle conc. 2.50
25 Okona S.O.S. 2.50
26 Search for Okona 2.25
27 Worf,Data,Troi,Okona trapped on world 2.25
28 Worf/K'Ehleyr story 2.25
29 Rift,Pt.1 . . . . 2.25
30 Rift,Pt 2 . . . . 2.25
31 Rift conclusion 2.25
32 . . . . 2.25
33 R:Mischievous Q 2.25
34 V:Aliens,F:Mischievous Q 2.25
35 Way of the Warrior 2.25
36 Shore Leave in Shanzibar#1 . . 2.25
37 Shore Leave in Shanzibar#2 . . 2.25
38 Shore Leave in Shanzibar#3 . . 2.25
39 Divergence #1 . . . . 2.25
40 Divergence #2 . . . . 2.25
41 V:Strazzan Warships 2.25
42 V:Strazzans 2.25
43 V:Strazzans 2.25
44 Disrupted Lives 2.25
45 F:Enterprise Surgical Team . . . 2.25
46 Deadly Labyrinth 2.25
47 Worst of Both World's#1 . . . . . 2.25
48 Worst of Both World's#2 . . . . . 2.25
49 Worst of Both World's#3 . . . . . 2.25
50 Double Sized,V:Borg 3.75
51 V:Energy Beings 2.00
52 in the 1940's 2.00
53 F:Picard 2.00
54 F:Picard 2.00
55 Data on Trial 2.00
56 Abduction 2.00
57 Body Switch 2.00
58 Body Switch 2.00
59 B:Children in Chaos 2.00
60 Children in Chaos#2 . . . . 2.00
61 E:Children in Chaos 1.95
Ann.#1 A:Mischievous Q 3.50
Ann.#2 BP,V:Parasitic Creatures . 3.50
Ann.#3 . . . . 2.50
Ann.#4 MiB(s),F:Dr.Crusher 3.50
Spec.#1 . . . . 3.75
Star Trek N.G.:Sparticus 5.00

STAR TREK N.G.: MODULA IMPERATIVE

1 A:Spock,McCoy 6.00
2 Modula Overrun by Ferengi . . . 5.00
3 Picard,Spock,McCoy & Troi trapped 4.00
4 final issue 4.00

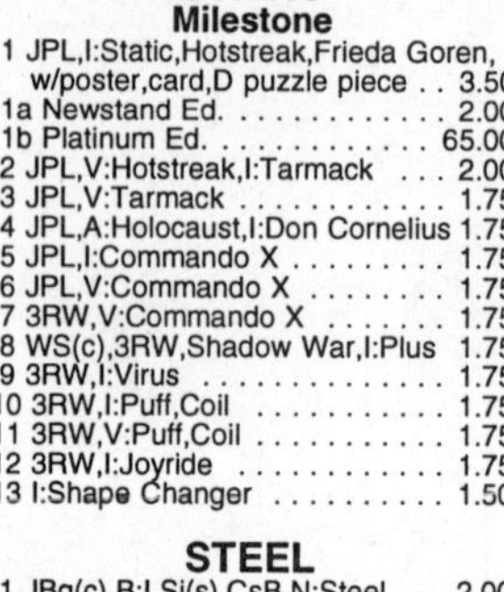

STATIC
Milestone

1 JPL,I:Static,Hotstreak,Frieda Goren, w/poster,card,D puzzle piece . . 3.50
1a Newstand Ed. 2.00
1b Platinum Ed. 65.00
2 JPL,V:Hotstreak,I:Tarmack . . . 2.00
3 JPL,V:Tarmack 1.75
4 JPL,A:Holocaust,I:Don Cornelius 1.75
5 JPL,I:Commando X 1.75
6 JPL,V:Commando X 1.75
7 3RW,V:Commando X 1.75
8 WS(c),3RW,Shadow War,I:Plus 1.75
9 3RW,I:Virus 1.75
10 3RW,I:Puff,Coil 1.75
11 3RW,V:Puff,Coil 1.75
12 3RW,I:Joyride 1.75
13 I:Shape Changer 1.50

STEEL

1 JBg(c),B:LSi(s),CsB,N:Steel . . . 2.00
2 JBg(c),CsB,V:Toastmaster 1.75
3 JBg(c),CsB,V:Amertek 1.75
4 JBg(c),CsB, ... 1.75
5 JBg(c),CsB,V:Sister's Attacker . 1.75
6 JBg(c),CsB,Worlds Collide#5, . 1.50
Ann.#1 Elseworlds story 2.95

STEEL, THE INDESTRUCTIBLE MAN
March, 1978

1 DH,I:Steel 1.00
2 DH 1.00
3 DH 1.00
4 DH 1.00
5 October-November, 1978 . . . . 1.00

STRANGE ADVENTURES
August-September, 1950

1 The Menace of the Green Nebula 1,700.00
2 S&K,JM(c),Doom From Planet X 750.00
3 The Metal World 500.00
4 BP,The Invaders From the Nth Dimension 450.00
5 The World Inside the Atom . 425.00
6 The Confessions of a Martian 425.00
7 The World of Giant Ants . . . 425.00
8 MA,ATh,Evolution Plus 425.00
9 MA,B:Captain Comet,The Origin of Captain Comet . . 950.00
10 MA,CI,The Air Bandits From Space 400.00
11 MA,CI,Day the Past Came Back 325.00
12 MA,CI,GK(c),The Girl From the Diamond Planet 325.00
13 MA,CI,GK(c),When the Earth was Kidnapped 325.00
14 MA,CI,GK(c),Destination Doom 325.00
15 MA,CI,GK(c),Captain Comet-Enemy of Earth 300.00
16 MA,CI,GK(c),The Ghost of Captain Comet 300.00
17 MA,CI,GK(c),Beware the Synthetic Men 300.00
18 CI,MA(c),World of Flying Men 300.00
19 CI,MA(c),Secret of the Twelve Eternals 300.00
20 CI,Slaves of the Sea Master 300.00
21 CI,MA(c),Eyes of the Other Worlds 225.00
22 CI,The Guardians of the

Strange Adventures #5
© DC Comics, Inc.

Clockwork Universe 225.00
23 CI,MA(c),The Brain Pirates of Planet X 225.00
24 CI,MA(c),Doomsday on Earth 225.00
25 CI,GK(c),The Day That Vanished 225.00
26 CI,Captain Vs. Miss Universe 225.00
27 CI,MA(c),The Counterfeit Captain Comet 225.00
28 CI,Devil's Island in Space . . 225.00
29 CI,The Time Capsule From 1,000,000 B.C. 225.00
30 CI,MA(c),Menace From the World of Make-Believe 200.00
31 CI,Lights Camera Action . . . 200.00
32 CI,MA(c),The Challenge of Man-Ape the Mighty 200.00
33 CI,MA(c),The Human Beehive 200.00
34 CI,MA(c) 200.00
35 CI,MA(c),Cosmic Chessboard 200.00
36 CI,MA(c),The Grab-Bag Planet 200.00
37 CI,MA(c),The Invaders From the Golden Atom 200.00
38 CI,MA(c),Seeing-Eye Humans 200.00
39 CI,MA(c),The Guilty Gorilla . 250.00
40 CI,MA(c),The Mind Monster . 180.00
41 CI,MA(c),The Beast From Out of Time 180.00
42 CI,MD,MA(c),The Planet of Ancient Children 180.00
43 CI,MD,MA(c),The Phantom Prize Fighter 180.00
44 CI,MA(c),The Planet That Plotted Murder 180.00
45 CI,MD,MA(c),Gorilla World . 180.00
46 CI,MA(c),E:Captain Comet Interplanetary War Base . . . 180.00
47 CI,MA(c),The Man Who Sold the Earth 180.00
48 CI,MA(c),Human Phantom . 180.00
49 CI,MA(c),The Invasion from Indiana 180.00
50 CI,MA(c),The World Wrecker 150.00
51 CI,MA(c),The Man Who Stole Air 150.00
52 CI,MA(c),Prisoner of the Parakeets 150.00
53 CI,MA(c),The Human Icicle . 150.00
54 CI,MA(c),The Electric Man . . 80.00
55 CI,MA(c),The Gorilla Who

Strange Adventures #17
© DC Comics, Inc.

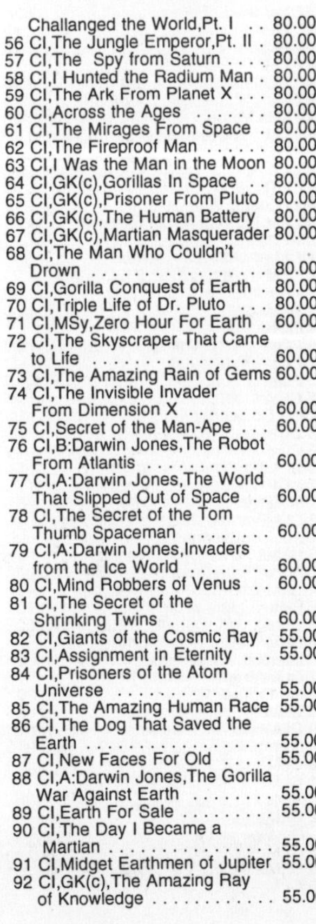

Challanged the World,Pt. I . . 80.00
56 CI,The Jungle Emperor,Pt. II . 80.00
57 CI,The Spy from Saturn 80.00
58 CI,I Hunted the Radium Man . 80.00
59 CI,The Ark From Planet X . . . 80.00
60 CI,Across the Ages 80.00
61 CI,The Mirages From Space . 80.00
62 CI,The Fireproof Man 80.00
63 CI,I Was the Man in the Moon 80.00
64 CI,GK(c),Gorillas In Space . . 80.00
65 CI,GK(c),Prisoner From Pluto 80.00
66 CI,GK(c),The Human Battery 80.00
67 CI,GK(c),Martian Masquerader 80.00
68 CI,The Man Who Couldn't Drown 80.00
69 CI,Gorilla Conquest of Earth . 80.00
70 CI,Triple Life of Dr. Pluto . . . 80.00
71 CI,MSy,Zero Hour For Earth . 60.00
72 CI,The Skyscraper That Came to Life 60.00
73 CI,The Amazing Rain of Gems 60.00
74 CI,The Invisible Invader From Dimension X 60.00
75 CI,Secret of the Man-Ape . . . 60.00
76 CI,B:Darwin Jones,The Robot From Atlantis 60.00
77 CI,A:Darwin Jones,The World That Slipped Out of Space . . 60.00
78 CI,The Secret of the Tom Thumb Spaceman 60.00
79 CI,A:Darwin Jones,Invaders from the Ice World 60.00
80 CI,Mind Robbers of Venus . . 60.00
81 CI,The Secret of the Shrinking Twins 60.00
82 CI,Giants of the Cosmic Ray . 55.00
83 CI,Assignment in Eternity . . . 55.00
84 CI,Prisoners of the Atom Universe 55.00
85 CI,The Amazing Human Race 55.00
86 CI,The Dog That Saved the Earth 55.00
87 CI,New Faces For Old 55.00
88 CI,A:Darwin Jones,The Gorilla War Against Earth 55.00
89 CI,Earth For Sale 55.00
90 CI,The Day I Became a Martian 55.00
91 CI,Midget Earthmen of Jupiter 55.00
92 CI,GK(c),The Amazing Ray of Knowledge 55.00

93 CI,GK(c),A:Darwin Jones, Space-Rescue By Proxy 55.00
94 MA,CI,GK(c),Fisherman of Space 55.00
95 CI,The World at my Doorstep 55.00
96 CI,MA(c),The Menace of Saturn's Rings 55.00
97 CI,MA(c),MSy,Secret of the Space-Giant 55.00
98 CI,GK(c),MSy,Attack on Fort Satellite 55.00
99 CI,MSy,GK(c),Big Jump Into Space 55.00
100 CI,MSy,The Amazing Trial of John (Gorilla) Doe 75.00
101 CI,MSy,GK(c),Giant From Beyond 40.00
102 MSy,GK(c),The Three Faces

Strange Adventures #235
© DC Comics, Inc.

of Barry Morrell 45.00
103 GK(c),The Man Who Harpooned Worlds 45.00
104 MSy,GK(c),World of Doomed Spacemen 45.00
105 MSy,GK(c),Fisherman From the Sea 45.00
106 MSy,CI,GK(c),Genie in the Flying Saucer 45.00
107 MSy,CI,GK(c),War of the Jovian Bubble-Men 45.00
108 MSy,CI,GK(c),The Human Pet of Gorilla Land 45.00
109 MSy,CI,GK(c),The Man Who Weighted 100 Tons 45.00
110 MSy,CI,GK(c),Hand From Beyond 45.00
111 MSy,CI,GK(c),Secret of the Last Earth-Man 40.00
112 MSy,CI,GK(c),Menace of the Size-Changing Spaceman 40.00
113 MSy,CI,GK(c),Deluge From Space 40.00
114 MSy,CI,GK(c),Secret of the Flying Buzz Saw 40.00
115 MSy,CI,GK(c),The Great Space-Tiger Hunt 40.00
116 MSy,CI,RH,GK(c),Invasion of the Water Warriors 40.00
117 MSy,CI,GK(c),I:Atomic Knights 350.00
118 MSy,CI,The Turtle-Men of Space 100.00
119 MSy,CI,MA(c),Raiders From the Giant World 70.00
120 MSy,CI,MA,Attack of the Oil Demons 125.00
121 MSy,CI,MA(c),Invasion of the Flying Reptiles 38.00
122 MSy,CI,MA(c),David and the Space-Goliath 38.00
123 MSy,CI,MA(c),Secret of the Rocket-Destroyer 38.00
124 MSy,CI,MA(c),The Face-Hunter From Saturn 38.00
125 MSy,CI,The Flying Gorilla Menace 38.00
126 MSy,CI,MA(c),Return of the Neanderthal Man 38.00
127 MSy,CI,MA(c),Menace From the Earth-Globe 38.00
128 MSy,CI,MA(c),The Man With the Electronic Brain . . . 38.00
129 MSy,CI,MA(c),The Giant Who Stole Mountains 38.00
130 MSy,CI,MA.War With the Giant Frogs 38.00
131 MSy,CI,MA(c),Emperor of the Earth 38.00
132 MSy,CI,MA(c),The Dreams of Doom 38.00
133 MSy,CI,MA(c),The Invisible Dinosaur 38.00
134 MSy,CI,MA(c), The Aliens Who Raided New York 38.00
135 MSy,CI,MA(c),Fishing Hole in the Sky 30.00
136 MSy,CI,MA(c),The Robot Who Lost Its Head 30.00
137 MSy,CI,MA(c),Parade of the Space-Toys 30.00
138 MSy,CI,MA(c),Secret of the Dinosaur Skeleton 30.00
139 MSy,CI,MA(c),Space-Roots of Evil 30.00
140 MSy,CI,MA(c),Prisoner of the Space-Patch 30.00
141 MSy,CI,MA(c),Battle Between the Two Earths 30.00
142 MSy,CI,MA(c),The Return of the Faceless Creature 30.00
143 MSy,CI,MA(c),The Face in the Atom-Bomb Cloud 30.00
144 MSy,CI,MA(c),A:Atomic Knights, When the Earth Blacked Out 30.00
145 MSy,CI,MA,The Man Who Lived Forever 30.00
146 MSy,CI,MA(c),Perilous Pet of Space 30.00
147 MSy,CI,MA(c),The Dawn-World Menace 30.00
148 MSy,CI,MA(c),Earth Hero, Number One 30.00
149 MSy,CI,MA(c),Raid of the Rogue Star 30.00
150 MSy,CI,MA(c),When Earth Turned into a Comet 30.00
151 MSy,CI,MA(c),Invasion Via Radio-Telescope 25.00
152 MSy,MA(c),The Martian Emperor of Earth 25.00
153 MSy,MA(c),Threat of the Faceless Creature 25.00
154 CI,MSy,MA,GK(c),Earth's Friendly Invaders 25.00
155 MSy,MA,GK(c),Prisoner of the Undersea World 25.00
156 MSy,CI,MA(c),The Man With the Head of Saturn . . . 25.00
157 MSy,CI,MA(c),Plight of the Human Cocoons 25.00
158 MSy,CI,MA(c),The Mind Masters of Space 25.00
159 MSy,CI,MA(c),The Maze of Time 25.00
160 MSy,CI,MA(c),A:Atomic Knights, Here Comes the

Wild Ones . . . 25.00
161 MSy,CI,MA(c),Earth's Frozen Heat Wave,E:Space Museum 20.00
162 CI,MA(c),Mystery of the 12 O'Clock Man . . . 18.00
163 MA(c),The Creature in the Black Light . . . 20.00
164 DD&SMo(c),I Became a Robot . . . 18.00
165 DD&SMo(c),I Broke the Supernatural Barrier . . . 18.00
166 DD&SMo(c),I Lived in Two Bodies . . . 18.00
167 JkS(c),The Team That Conqured Time . . . 18.00
168 JkS(c),I Hunted Toki the Terrible . . . 15.00
169 DD&SMo(c),The Prisoner of the Hour Glass . . . 15.00
170 DD&SMo(c),The Creature From Strange Adventures . . . 15.00
171 The Diary o/t 9-Planet Man? 15.00
172 DD&SMo(c),I Became the Juggernaut Man . . . 15.00
173 The Secret of the Fantasy Films . . . 15.00
174 JkS(c),The Ten Ton Man . . 15.00
175 Danger: This Town is Shrinking . . . 15.00
176 DD&SMo(c),The Case of the Cosmonik Quartet . . . 15.00
177 I Lived a Hundred Lives, O:Immortal Man . . . 20.00
178 JkS(c),The Runaway Comet 15.00
179 JkS(c),I Buried Myself Alive . 15.00
180 CI,I:Animal Man,'I Was the Man With Animal Powers . . 250.00
181 The Man of Two Worlds . . . 12.00
182 JkS(c),The Case of the Blonde Bombshell . . . 12.00
183 JM(c),The Plot to Destroy the Earth . . . 12.00
184 GK(c),A:Animal Man,The Return of the Man With Animal Powers . . . 135.00
185 JkS(c),Ilda-Gangsters Inc. . . 12.00
186 Beware the Gorilla Witch . . 12.00
187 JkS(c),O:The Enchantress . 20.00
188 SD,JkS(c),I Was the Four Seasons . . . 12.00
189 SD,JkS(c),The Way-Out Worlds of Bertram Tilley . . . 12.00
190 CI,A:Animal Man,A-Man-the Hero with Animal Powers . . 150.00
191 JkS(c),Beauty vs. the Beast 12.00
192 Freak Island . . . 12.00
193 The Villian Maker . . . 12.00
194 JkS(c),The Menace of the Super- Gloves . . . 12.00
195 JkS(c),Secret of the Three Earth Dooms,A:Animal Man . 12.00
196 JkS(c),Mystery of the Orbit Creatures . . . 12.00
197 The Hostile Hamlet . . . 10.00
198 JkS(c),Danger! Earth is Doomed . . . 10.00
199 Robots of the Round Table . 10.00
200 . . . 10.00
201 JkS,Animal Man . . . 50.00
202 . . . 10.00
203 . . . 10.00
204 . . . 10.00
205 CI,I&O:Deadman . . . 50.00
206 NA,MSy . . . 40.00
207 NA . . . 30.00
208 NA . . . 30.00
209 NA . . . 30.00
210 NA . . . 30.00
211 NA . . . 30.00
212 NA . . . 30.00
213 NA . . . 30.00
214 NA . . . 30.00
215 NA . . . 30.00
216 NA . . . 30.00
217 MA,MSy,A:Adam Strange . . 10.00
218 MA,CI,MSy . . . 8.00
219 CI,JKu . . . 8.00
220 CI,JKu . . . 8.00
221 CI . . . 8.00
222 MA,New Adam Strange . . . 10.00
223 MA,CI . . . 8.00
224 MA,CI . . . 8.00
225 MA,JKu . . . 8.00
226 MA,JKu,New Adam Strange 10.00
227 JKu . . . 10.00
228 NA(c) . . . 25.00
229 . . . 8.00
230 GM(c) . . . 8.00
231 E:Atomic Knights . . . 8.00
232 JKu . . . 6.00
233 JKu . . . 6.00
234 JKu . . . 6.00
235 NA(c) . . . 20.00
236 . . . 6.00
237 . . . 6.00
238 MK(c) . . . 6.00
239 . . . 6.00
240 MK(c) . . . 6.00
241 . . . 6.00
242 MA . . . 6.00
243 . . . 6.00
244 October-November, 1974 . . . 6.00

STREETS

1 Tenderloin . . . 4.95
2 Procurement . . . 4.95
3 . . . 4.95

SUGAR & SPIKE
April-May, 1956

1 SM . . . 650.00
2 SM . . . 350.00
3 SM . . . 275.00
4 SM . . . 230.00
5 SM . . . 230.00
6 thru 10 SM . . . @150.00
11 thru 20 SM . . . @125.00
21 thru 29 SM . . . @65.00
30 SM,A:Scribbly . . . 80.00
31 thru 50 SM . . . @65.00
51 thru 70 SM . . . @50.00
71 thru 79 SM . . . @20.00
80 SM,I:Bernie the Brain . . . 30.00
81 thru 97 SM . . . @20.00
98 SM,October-November, 1971 20.00

SUICIDE SQUAD
May, 1987

1 LMc,Legends,I:Jihad . . . 2.50
2 LMc,V:The Jihad . . . 2.00
3 LMc,V:Female Furies . . . 1.75
4 LMc,V:William Hell . . . 1.75
5 LM,A:Penguin . . . 2.50
6 LM,A:Penguin . . . 2.50
7 LMc,V:Peoples Hero . . . 1.50
8 LMc,O:SquadMembers . . . 1.50
9 LMc,Millenium . . . 1.50
10 LMc,A:Batman . . . 1.50
11 LMc,A:Vixen,Speedy . . . 1.50
12 LMc,Enchantress, V:Nightshade . . . 1.50
13 LMc,X-over,JLI#13 . . . 2.00
14 Nightshade Odyssey #1 . . . 1.50
15 Nightshade Odyssey #2 . . . 1.50
16 R:Shade . . . 3.00
17 LMc,V:The Jihad . . . 1.25
18 LMc,V:Jihad . . . 1.25
19 LMc,Personal Files 1988 . . . 1.25
20 LMc,V:Mirror Master . . . 1.25
21 LMc,bonus book #10 . . . 1.25
22 LMc,D:Senator Cray . . . 1.25
23 LMc,Invasion . . . 1.25
24 LMc,V:Guerillas . . . 1.25
25 L:Nightshade . . . 1.25
26 D:Rick Flag,Jihad . . . 1.25
27 Janus Directive #2 . . . 1.25
28 Janus Directive #4 . . . 1.25
29 Janus Directive #8 . . . 1.25
30 Janus Directive #10 . . . 1.25

Suicide Squad #1 © DC Comics, Inc.

31 Personal Files 1989 . . . 1.25
32 V:Female Furies . . . 1.25
33 GI,V:Female Furies . . . 1.25
34 GI,V:Granny Goodness . . . 1.25
35 LMc,GI,V:Female Furies . . . 1.25
36 GI,D:Original Dr.Light . . . 1.25
37 GI,A:Shade,The Changing Man,V:Loa . . . 1.50
38 LMc,GI,O:Bronze Tiger . . . 1.25
39 GI,D:Loa . . . 1.25
40 Phoenix Gambit #1,A:Batman Int. Poster . . . 1.50
41 Phoenix Gambit #2 . . . 1.25
42 Phoenix Gambit,A:Batman . . . 1.25
43 Phoenix Gambit,A:Batman . . . 1.25
44 I:New Atom,O:Captain Boomerang . . . 1.25
45 A:Kobra . . . 1.00
46 A:Kobra . . . 1.00
47 GI,A:Kobra,D:Ravan . . . 1.00
48 GI,New Thinker . . . 1.00
49 GI,New Thinker . . . 1.00
50 GI,50 Years of S.Squad . . . 2.00
51 A:Deadshot . . . 1.00
52 R:Docter Light . . . 1.00
53 GI,The Dragon's Horde #1 . . . 1.00
54 GI,The Dragon's Horde #2 . . . 1.00
55 GI,The Dragon's Horde #3 . . . 1.00
56 GI,The Dragon's Horde #4 . . . 1.00
57 GI,The Dragon's Horde conc. . 1.00
58 GI,War of the Gods x-over . . . 1.00
59 GI,A:Superman, Batman, Aquaman,A:Jihad, Hayoth . . . 1.25
60 GI,A:Superman,Batman, Aquaman,Jihad,The Hayoth . . 1.25
61 GI,A:Superman,Batman, Aquaman,V:Jihad . . . 1.25
62 GI,R:Ray Palmer,A:Batman Superman,Aquaman . . . 1.25
63 GI,I:Gvede, Lord of Death . . . 1.25
64 GI,A:Task Force X . . . 1.25
65 GI,Bronze Tiger . . . 1.25
66 GI,Final Iss.E:Suicide Squad . . 1.25
Ann.#1 GN,V:Argent,A:Manhunter 1.75

SUPERBOY
March 1949

1 Superman (c) . . . 4,000.00
2 'Superboy Day' . . . 1,000.00
3 . . . 750.00
4 The Oracle of Smallville . . . 600.00

5 Superboy meets Supergirl, Pre-*Adventure* #252 ...... 575.00
6 I:Humpty Dumpty,the Hobby Robber 450.00
7 WB,V:Humpty Dumpty 450.00
8 CS,I:Superbaby,V:Humpty Dumpty 425.00
9 V:Humpty Dumpty 380.00
10 CS,I:Lana Lang 425.00
11 CS,2nd Lang,V:Humpty Dumpty 350.00
12 CS,The Heroes Club 350.00
13 CS,Scout of Smallville 350.00
14 CS,I:Marsboy 350.00
15 CS,A:Superman 350.00
16 CS,A:Marsboy 250.00
17 CS,Superboy's Double 250.00
18 CS,Lana Lang-Hollywood Star 250.00
19 CS,The Death of Young Clark Kent 250.00
20 CS,The Ghost that Haunted Smallville 250.00
21 CS,Lana Lang-Magician ... 200.00

Superboy #19 © DC Comics, Inc.

22 CS,The New Clark Kent ... 200.00
23 CS,The Super Superboy ... 200.00
24 CS,The Super Fat Boy of Steel 200.00
25 CS,Cinderella of Smallville . 200.00
26 CS,A:Superbaby 200.00
27 CS,Clark Kent-Runaway. .. 210.00
28 CS,The Man Who Defeated Superboy 200.00
29 CS,The Puppet Superboy .. 200.00
30 CS,I:Tommy Tuttle 150.00
31 CS,The Amazing Elephant Boy From Smallville 150.00
32 CS,His Majesty King Superboy 150.00
33 CS,The Crazy Costumes of the Boy of Steel 150.00
34 CS,Hep Cats o/Smallville .. 150.00
35 CS,The Five Superboys ... 150.00
36 .... 150.00
37 CS,I:Thaddeus Lang 150.00
38 CS,Public Chimp #1 ...... 150.00
39 CS,Boy w/Superboy Powers 150.00
40 CS,The Magic Necklace ... 100.00
41 CS,Superboy Meets Superbrave 100.00
42 CS,Gaucho of Smallville ... 100.00
43 CS,Super-Farmer o/Smallville 100.00
44 The Amazing Adventure of Superboy's Costume 100.00
45 A Trap For Superboy 100.00
46 The Battle of Fort Smallville 100.00
47 CS,A:Superman 100.00
48 CS,Boy Without Super-Suit . 100.00
49 I:Metallo (Jor-El's Robot) .. 125.00
50 The Super-Giant of Smallville 100.00
51 I:Krypto 75.00
52 CS,The Powerboy from Earth 75.00
53 CS,A:Superman 75.00
54 CS,The Silent Superboy 75.00
55 CS,A:Jimmy Olson 75.00
56 CS,A:Krypto 75.00
57 CS,One-Man Baseball Team . 75.00
58 CS,The Great Kryptonite Mystery 75.00
59 CS,A:Superbaby 75.00
60 The 100,000 Cowboy 75.00
61 The School For Superboys .. 60.00
62 I:Gloria Kent 60.00
63 CS,The Two Boys of Steel .. 60.00
64 CS,A:Krypto 60.00
65 Superboy's Moonlight Spell .. 60.00
66 The Family with X-Ray Eyes . 60.00
67 I:Klax-Ar 60.00
68 O&I:Bizarro 375.00
69 How Superboy Learned To Fly 55.00
70 O:Superboy's Glasses 55.00
71 A:Superbaby 55.00
72 The Flying Girl of Smallville . 55.00
73 CS,A:Superbaby 55.00
74 A:Jor-El & Lara 55.00
75 A:Superbaby 55.00
76 I:Super Monkey 55.00
77 Superboy's Best Friend 55.00
78 O:Mr.Mzyzptik 100.00
79 A:Jar-El & Lara 55.00
80 Superboy meets Supergirl ... 90.00
81 The Weakling From Earth ... 45.00
82 A:Bizarro Krypto 45.00
83 I:Kryptonite Kid 45.00
84 A:William Tell 45.00
85 Secret of Mighty Boy 45.00
86 I:PeteRoss,A:Legion 100.00
87 I:Scarlet Jungle of Krypton .. 45.00
88 The Invader from Earth 45.00
89 I:Mon-El 175.00
90 A:Pete Ross 45.00
91 CS,Superboy in Civil War .. 45.00
92 CS,I:Destructo,A:Lex Luthor . 45.00
93 A:Legion 38.00
94 I:Superboy Revenge Squad, A:Pete Ross 23.00
95 Imaginary Story,The Super Family From Krypton 23.00
96 A:Pete Ross,Lex Luther 23.00
97 Krypto Story 20.00
98 Legion,I&O:Ultraboy 35.00
99 O: The Kryptonite Kid 20.00
100 I:Phantom Zone 135.00
101 The Handsome Hound of Steel 12.00
102 O:Scarlet Jungle of Krypton 12.00
103 CS,A:King Arthur,Jesse James Red Kryptonite 12.00
104 O:Phantom Zone 12.00
105 CS,'The Simpleton of Steel' 12.00
106 CS,A:Brainiac 12.00
107 CS,I:Superboy Club of Smallville 12.00
108 The Kent's First Super Son . 12.00
109 The Super Youth of Bronze . 12.00
110 A:Jor-El 12.00
111 Red Kryptonite Story 12.00
112 CS,A:Superbaby 12.00
113 'The Boyhood of Dad Kent' . 12.00
114 A:Phantom Zone, Mr.Mxyzptlk 12.00
115 A:Phantom Zone,Lex Luthor 12.00
116 'The Wolfboy of Smallville' . 12.00
117 A:Legion 12.00
118 CS,'The War Between Superboy and Krypto' 10.00
119 V:Android Double 9.00

120 A:Mr.Mxyzptlk 9.00
121 CS,A:Jor-El,Lex Luthor 8.00
122 Red Kryptonite Story 8.00
123 CS,The Curse of the Superboy Mummy 8.00
124 I:Insect Queen 8.00
125 O:Kid Psycho 8.00
126 O:Krypto 8.00
127 A:Insect Queen 8.00
128 A:Phantom Zone,Kryptonite Kid,Dev En 8.00
129 rep.A:Mon-El,SuperBaby ... 10.00
130 .... 5.00
131 A;Lex Luthor,Mr.Mxyzptlk,I: Space Canine Patrol Agents .. 5.00
132, CS,A:Space Canine Patrol Agents 5.00
133 A:Robin, repr. 5.00
134 'The Scoundrel of Steel' 5.00
135 A:Lex Luthor 5.00
136 A:Space Canine Agents 5.00
137 Mysterious Mighty Mites 5.00
138 giant, Superboy's Most Terrific Battles 10.00

Superboy #200 © DC Comics, Inc.

139 'The Samson of Smallville' .. 5.00
140 V:The Gambler 5.00
141 No Mercy for a Hero 5.00
142 A:Super Monkey 5.00
143 NA(c),'The Big Fall' 5.00
144 'Superboy's Stolen Identity' . 5.00
145 NA(c)Kents become young .. 5.00
146 NA(c),CS,'The Runaway' ... 5.00
147 giant O:Legion 10.00
148 NA(c),CS,C:PolarBoy 5.50
149 NA(c),A:Bonnie & Clyde 5.50
150 JAb,V:Mr.Cipher 5.50
151 NA(c),A:Kryptonite Kid 5.50
152 NA(c),WW, ... 5.50
153 NA(c),WW,A;Prof Mesmer ... 5.50
154 WW(i),A:Jor-El & Lara 'Blackout For Superboy' 5.50
155 NA(c),WW,'Revolt of the Teenage Robots' 5.50
156 giant 7.00
157 WW 5.50
158 WW,A:Jor-El & Lara 5.50
159 WW(i),A:Lex Luthor 5.50
160 WW,'I Chose Eternal Exile' .. 5.50
161 WW,'The Strange Death of Superboy' 5.50
162 A:Phantom Zone 4.00
163 NA(c),'Reform School Rebel' . 4.00
164 NA(c),'Your Death Will

Destroy Me' 4.00
165 giant 7.00
166 NA(c),A:Lex Luthor 4.00
167 NA(c),MA,A:Superbaby 4.00
168 NA(c),MA,Hitler 4.00
169 MA,A:Lex Luthor 3.00
170 MA,A:Genghis Khan 3.00
171 MA,A:Aquaboy 3.00
172 MA(i),GT,A:Legion, O:Lightning Lad,Yango 5.00
173 NA(c),GT,DG,O:CosmicBoy . 4.00
174 giant 6.00
175 NA(c),MA,Rejuvenation of Ma & Pa Kent 4.00
176 NA(c),MA,GT,WW,A:Legion . 4.00
177 MA,A:Lex Luthor 2.00
178 NA(c),MA,Legion Reprint . . . 3.00
179 MA,A:Lex Luthor 2.00
180 MA,O:Bouncing Boy 2.00
181 MA 2.00
182 MA,A:Bruce Wayne 2.00
183 MA,GT,CS(rep),A:Legion . . . 3.00
184 MA,WW,O:Dial H rep. 3.50
185 A:Legion 3.00
186 MA 2.00
187 MA 2.00
188 MA,DC,O:Karkan,A:Legn . . . 2.00
189 MA 2.00
190 MA,WW 2.50
191 MA,DC O:SunBoy retold 2.00
192 MA 2.00
193 MA,WW,N:Chameleon Boy, Shrinking Violet 2.50
194 MA 2.00
195 MA,WW,I:Wildfire, N:Phantom Girl 2.50
196 last Superboy solo 2.00
197 DC,Legion begins, New Costumes,I:Tyr 6.00
198 DC N:Element Lad, Princess Projects 3.00
199 DC,A:Tyr, Otto Orion 3.00
200 DC,M:Bouncing Boy & Duo Damsel 5.00
201 DC,Wildfire returns 3.00
202 N:Light Lass 3.00
203 MGr,D:Invisible Kid 3.00
204 MGr,A:Supergirl 3.00
205 MGr,CG,100 pages 3.00
206 MGr,A:Ferro Lad 3.00
207 MGr,O:Lightning Lad 3.00
208 MGr,CS,68pp,Legion of Super Villains 3.00
209 MGr,N:Karate Kid 3.00
210 MGr,O:Karate Kid 3.00
211 MGr 2.50
212 MGr,L:Matter Eater Lad 2.50
213 MGr,V:Benn Pares 2.50
214 MGr,V:Overseer 2.50
215 MGr,A:Emerald Empress . . . 2.50
216 MGr,I:Tyroc 2.50
217 MGr,I:Laurel Kent 2.50
218 J:Tyroc,A:Fatal Five 2.50
219 MGr,A:Fatal Five 2.50
220 MGi,BWi 2.50
221 MGr,BWi,I:Grimbor 2.50
222 MGr,BWi,MN,BL,A:Tyroc 2.50
223 MGr,BWi, ... 2.50
224 MGr,BWi,V:Pulsar Stargrave . 2.50
225 MGr(c),BWi,JSh,MN 2.50
226 MGr(c),MN,JSh,JA, I:Dawnstar 2.75
227 MGr(c),JSon,JA,V:Stargrave . 2.00
228 MGr(c),JSh,JA, D:Chemical King 2.50
229 MGr(c),JSh,JA,V:Deregon . . . 2.00
230 MGr(c),JSh,V:Sden 2.00
Becomes:

SUPERBOY & THE LEGION OF SUPER-HEROES

231 MGr(c),JSh,MN,JA,doub.size begins,V:Fatal Five 2.00
232 MGr(c),JSh,RE,JA,V: Dr.Regulus 2.00
233 MGr(c),JSh,BWi,MN,BL, I:Infinite Man 2.00
234 MGr(c),RE,JA,V:Composite Creature 2.00
235 MGr,GT 2.00
236 MGr(c),BMc,JSh,MN,JRu, V:Khunds 2.00
237 MGr(c),WS,JA 2.50
238 JSn(c),reprint 2.00
239 MGR(c),JSn,JRu,Ultra Boy accused 2.50
240 MGr(c),HC,BWi,JSh,BMc, O:Dawnstar;V:Grimbor 2.00
241 JSh,BMc,A:Ontir 2.00
242 JSh,BMc,E:Double Size . . . 2.00
243 MGr(c),JA,JSon 2.00
244 JSon,V:Dark Circle 2.00
245 MA,JSon,V:Mordu 2.00
246 MGr(c),JSon,DG,MA, V:Fatal Five 2.00
247 JSon,JA,anniv.issue. 2.00
248 JSon 2.00
249 JSon,JA 2.00
250 JSn,V:Omega 2.50
251 JSn,Brainiac 5 goes insane . . 2.50
252 JSon,V:Starburst bandits 2.00
253 JSon,I:Blok,League of Super Assassins 2.00
254 JSon,V:League of Super Assassins 2.00
255 JSon,A:Jor-El 2.00
256 JSon 2.00
257 SD,JSon,DA,V:Psycho Warrior 2.00
258 JSon,V:Psycho Warrior 2.00
Becomes:

Legion of Super Heroes
[2nd Series]

[NEW ADVENTURES OF] SUPERBOY
January, 1980

1 KS 1.50
2 KS 1.25
3 KS 1.25
4 KS 1.25
5 KS 1.25
6 KS 1.25
7 KS,JSa 1.25
8 thru 33 KS . . . . @1.25
34 KS,I:Yellow Peri 1.25
35 thru 44 KS . . . . @1.25
45 KS,I:Sunburst 1.25
46 KS,A:Sunburst 1.25
47 KS,A:Sunburst 1.25
48 KS 1.25
49 KS,A:Zatara 1.25
50 KS,KG,A:Legion 1.50
51 KS,FM(c)In Between Years . . . 1.00
52 KS 1.00
53 KS 1.00
54 KS 1.00

SUPERBOY
February, 1990

1 TV Tie-in,JM,photo(c) 1.00
2 JM,T.J.White Abducted 1.00
3 JM,'Fountain of Youth' 1.00
4 JM,'Big Man on Campus' 1.00
5 JM,Legion Homage 1.00
6 JM,Luthor 1.00
7 JM,Super Boy Arrested 1.00
8 JM,AAd(i),Bizarro 1.00
9 JM/CS,PhantomZone#1 . . . . . . 1.00
10 JM/CS,PhantomZone#2 . . . . . 1.00
11 CS 1.00
12 CS,X-Mas in Smallville 1.00
Becomes:

ADVENTURES OF SUPERBOY

13 A:Mr.Mxyzptlk 1.00
14 CS,A:Brimstone 1.00
15 CS,Legion Homage 1.00
16 CS,Into the Future 1.00
17 CS,A:Luthor 1.00
18 JM,'At the Movies' 1.00
19 JM,Blood Transfusion 1.00
20 JM,O:Nicknack,(G.Gottfried script) 1.00
21 V:Frost Monster 1.25

SUPERBOY
[2nd Series]

1 B:KK(s),TG,DHz,V:Sidearm . . . 2.50
2 TG,DHz,I:Knockout 2.00
3 TG,DHz,I:Scavenger 1.75
4 TG,DHz,MeP,I:Lock n' Load . . . 1.75
5 TG,DHz,I:Silver Sword 1.75
6 TG,DHz,Worlds Collide#3, C:Rocket 1.50

SUPER FRIENDS
November, 1976

1 ECh(c),JO,RE,'Fury o/t Superfoes',A:Penguin 2.50
2 RE,A:Penguin 1.50
3 RF(c),RF,A:JLA 1.50
4 RF,V:Riddler,I:Skyrocket 1.50
5 RF(c),RF,V:Greenback 1.50
6 RF(c),RF,A:Atom 1.50
7 RF(c),RF,I:Zan & Jana, A:Seraph 1.50
8 RF(c),RF,A:JLA 1.50
9 RF(c),RF,A:JLA,I:Iron Maiden . 1.50
10 RF(c),RF'TheMonkeyMenace' . 1.50
11 RF(c),RF 1.50
12 RF(c),RF,A:TNT 1.50
13 RF(c),RF 1.50
14 RF(c),RF 1.50
15 RF(c),RF, A:The Elementals . . 1.50
16 RF(c),RF,V:The Cvags 1.50
17 RF(c),RF,A:Queen Hippolyte . 1.50
18 KS(c),V:Tuantra,Time Trapper . 1.50
19 RF(c),RF,V:Menagerie Man . . 1.50
20 KS(c),KS,V:Frownin' Fritz 1.50
21 RF(c),RF,V:Evil Superfriends Doubles 1.50
22 RF(c),RF,V:Matador Mob 1.50
23 FR(c),RF,V:Mirror Master 1.50
24 RF(c),RF,V:Exorians 1.50
25 RF(c),RF,V:Overlord, A:Green Lantern, Mera 1.50
26 RF(c),RF,A:Johnny Jones 1.50
27 RF(c),RF,'The Spaceman Who Stole the Stars 1.50
28 RF(c),RF,A:Felix Faust 1.50
29 RF(c),RF,B.U.KS,'Scholar From the Stars 1.50
30 RF(c),RF,V:Grodd & Giganta . 1.50
31 RF(c),RF,A:Black Orchid 1.50
32 KS(c),KS,A:Scarecrow 1.50
33 RF(c),RF,V:Menagerie Man . . 1.50
34 RF(c)RF,'The Creature That Slept a Million Years' 1.50
35 RT,'Circus o/t Super Stars . . . 1.50
36 RF(c),RF,A:Plastic Man & Woozy 1.50
37 RF(c),RF,A:Supergirl; B.U. A:Jack O'Lantern 1.50
38 RF(c),RF,V:Grax; B.U. A:Serpah 1.50
39 RF(c),RF,A:Overlord; B.U. A:Wonder Twins 1.50
40 RF(c),RF,V:The Monacle; B.U. Jack O'Lantern 1.50
41 RF(c),RF,V:Toyman; B.U. A:Seraph 1.50
42 RT,A:Flora,V:Flame; B.U.Wonder Twins' Christmas Special 1.50
43 KS(c),RT,V:Futuro; B.U.JSon A:Plastic Man 1.50
44 KS(c),RT,'Peril o/t Forgotten Identities'; B.U.Jack O'Lantern . 1.50
45 KS(c),RT,A:Bushmaster, Godiva, Rising Sun, Olympian, Little Mermaid, Wild Huntsman;

B.U. Plastic Man,V: Sinestro .. 1.50
46 RT,V:The Conqueror;
B.U. BO,Seraph 1.50
47 KS(c),RT,A:Green Fury
August 1981 .... 1.50

SUPERGIRL
[1st Regular Series]
November, 1972

1 'Trail of the Madman';
Superfashions From Fans;
B:B.U. DG,Zatanna 2.50
2 BO(c)A:Prof.Allan,Bottle
City of Kandor 1.50
3 BO(c),'The Garden of Death' . 1.50
4 V:Super Scavanger 1.50
5 BO(c),A:Superman,V:Dax; B.U.
MA:Rep.Hawkman #4 ...... 1.50
6 BO(c),'Love & War' 1.50
7 BO(c),A:Zatanna 1.50
8 BO(c),A:Superman,Green Lantern
Hawkman 1.50
9 BO(c),V:Sharkman 1.50
10 A:Prey,V:Master Killer
September 1974 .... 1.50

[DARING NEW ADVENTURES OF] SUPERGIRL
[2nd Regular Series]
November 1982

1 CI,BO,I:Psi; B:B.U.Lois Lane .. 1.50
2 CI,BO,C:Decay 1.00
3 CI,BO,V:Decay,'Decay Day' ... 1.00
4 CI,BO,V:The Gang 1.00
5 CI,BO,V:The Gang 1.00
6 CI,BO,V:The Gang 1.00
7 CI,BO,V:The Gang 1.00
8 CI,BO,A:Doom Patrol 1.00
9 CI,BO,V:Reactron,
A:DoomPatrol 1.00
10 CI,BO,'Radiation Fever' 1.00
11 CI,BO,V:Chairman 1.00
12 CI,BO,V:Chairmann 1.00
13 CI,BO,N:Supergirl,A:Superman
V:Blackstarr 1.00

Becomes:

SUPERGIRL
December, 1983

14 GK(c),CI,BO,V:Blackstarr
A:Rabbi Nathan Zuber 1.25
15 CI,BO,V:Blackstarr,
A:Blackstarr's Mom 1.25
16 KG/BO(c),CI,BO,
A:Ambush Bug 1.25
17 CI/DG(c),CI,BO,V:Matrix
Prime 1.25
18 DG(c),CI,BO, V:Kraken 1.25
19 EB/BO(c),CI,BO,'Who Stole
Supergirl's Life' 1.25
20 CI,BO,C:JLA,Teen Titans:
Teh Parasite 1.50
21 EB/BO(c),EB,Kryptonite Man .. 1.25
22 EB(c),CI,BO,'I Have Seen the
Future & it is Me' 1.25
23 EB(c),CI,BO,'The Future
Begins Today'
September 1984 .... 1.25
#1 JL/DG(c),GM,Movie Adaption . 1.50
#1 AT,Honda give-away 1.50

[Limited Series]

1 KGa(c),B:RSt(s),JBr,O:Supergirl 2.00
2 KGa(c),JBr, ... 1.75
3 KGa(c),JBr,D:Clones 1.75
4 KGa(c),RSt(s),JBr,final Issue .. 1.75

SUPERGIRL/TEAM LUTHOR SPECIAL

1 JBr,F:Supergirl,Lex Luthor 4.00

SUPER HEROES BATTLE SUPER GORILLA
Winter, 1976

1 Superman Flash rep. 1.00

SUPERMAN
Summer 1939

1 JoS,O:Superman,reprints Action
#1-4 .... 70,000.00
2 JoS,I:George Taylor 5,500.00
3 JoS,V:Superintendent
Lyman 3,800.00
4 JoS,V:Lex Luthor 3,000.00
5 JoS,V:Lex Luthor 2,000.00
6 JoS,V:'Brute' Bashby 1,650.00
7 JoS,I:Perry White 1,700.00
8 JoS,V:Jackal 1,400.00
9 JoS,V:Joe Gatson 1,400.00
10 JoS,V:Lex Luthor 1,300.00
11 JoS,V:Rolf Zimba 1,200.00
12 JoS,V:Lex Luthor 1,200.00
13 JoS,I:Jimmy Olsen,V:Lex
Luthor,'The Archer' 1,200.00
14 JoS,I:Lightning Master ... 1,200.00
15 JoS,V:The Evolution King . 1,000.00
16 JoS,V:Mr. Sinus 900.00
17 JoS,V:Lex Luthor,Lois Lane first
suspects Clark is Superman 850.00
18 JoS,V:Lex Luthor 800.00
19 JoS,V:Funnyface,
1st Imaginary story 800.00
20 JoS,V:Puzzler,Leopard 800.00
21 JoS,V:Sir Gauntlet 700.00

Superman #6, © DC Comics, Inc.

22 JoS,V:Prankster 600.00
23 JoS,Propaganda story 600.00
24 V:Cobra King 750.00
25 Propaganda story 600.00
26 I:J.Wilbur Wolfingham,
A:Mercury 575.00
27 V:Toyman 575.00
28 V:J.Wilbur Wolfingham,
A:Hercules 575.00
29 V:Prankster 575.00
30 I&O:Mr. Mxyztplk 950.00
31 V:Lex Luthor 500.00
32 V:Toyman 500.00
33 V:Mr. Mxyztptlk 500.00
34 V:Lex Luthor 500.00
35 V:J.Wilbur Wolfingham 500.00
36 V:Mr. Mxyztptlk 500.00
37 V:Prankster,A:Sinbad 500.00
38 V:Lex Luthor 500.00
39 V:J.Wilbur Wolfingham 500.00
40 V:Mr. Mxyzptlk,A:Susie
Thompkins 500.00
41 V:Prankster 400.00
42 V:J.Wilbur Wolfingham 400.00
43 V:Lex Luthor 400.00
44 V:Toyman,A:Shakespeare .. 400.00
45 A:Hocus & Pocus,Lois Lane
as Superwoman 400.00
46 V:Mr. Mxyzptlk,Lex Luthor,
Superboy flashback 400.00
47 V:Toyman 400.00
48 V:Lex Luthor 400.00
49 V:Toyman 400.00
50 V:Prankster 400.00
51 V:Mr. Mxyzptlk 325.00
52 V:Prankster 325.00
53 WB,O:Superman 1,200.00
54 V:Wrecker 325.00
55 V:Prankster 350.00
56 V:Prankster 325.00
57 V:Lex Luthor 325.00
58 V:Tiny Trix 325.00
59 V:Mr.Mxyztptlk 325.00
60 V:Toyman 325.00
61 I:Kryptonite,V:Prankster ... 600.00
62 V:Mr.Mxyzptlk,A:Orson
Welles 300.00
63 V:Toyman 300.00
64 V:Prankster 300.00
65 V:Mala,Kizo and U-Ban ... 300.00
66 V:Prankster 300.00
67 A:Perry Como,I:Brane
Taylor 300.00
68 V:Lex Luthor 300.00
69 V:Prankster,A:Inspector
Erskine Hawkins 300.00
70 V:Prankster 300.00
71 V:Lex Luthor 275.00
72 V:Prankster 275.00
73 Flashback story 275.00
74 V:Lex Luthor 275.00
75 V:Prankster 275.00
76 A:Batman (Superman &
Batman revel each other's
identities) 850.00
77 A:Pocahontas 275.00
78 V:Kryptonian snagriff,
A:Lana Lang 275.00
79 V:Lex Luthor,A:Inspector
Erskine Hawkins 275.00
80 A:Halk Kar 275.00
81 V:Lex Luthor 275.00
82 V:Mr. Mxyzptlk 250.00
83 V:'The Brain' 250.00
84 Time-travel story 250.00
85 V:Lex Luthor 250.00
86 V:Mr.Mxyzptlk 250.00
87 WB,V:The Thing from
40,000 AD' 250.00
88 WB,V:Lex Luthor,Toyman,
Prankster team 275.00
89 V:Lex Luthor 250.00
90 V:Lex Luthor 225.00
91 'The Superman Stamp' 225.00
92 Goes back to 12th Century
England 225.00
93 V:'The Thinker' 225.00
94 'Clark Kent's Hillbilly Bride' . 225.00
95 A:Susie Thompkins 225.00
96 V:Mr. Mxyzptlk 200.00
97 'Superboy's Last Day In
Smallville' 200.00
98 'Clark Kent, Outlaw!' 200.00
99 V:Midnite gang 200.00
100 F:Superman-Substitute
Schoolteacher 1,000.00
101 A:Lex Luthor 175.00
102 I:Superman Stock
Company 175.00
103 A:Mr.Mxyzptlk 175.00
104 F:Clark Kent,Jailbird 175.00
105 A:Mr.Mxyzptlk 175.00
106 A:Lex Luthor 175.00
107 F:Superman In 30th century

(pre-Legion) 175.00
108 I:Perry White Jr. 175.00
109 I:Abner Hokum 175.00
110 A:Lex Luthor 175.00
111 Becomes Mysto the Great . 156.00
112 A:Lex Luthor 156.00
113 A:Jor-El 156.00
114 V:The Great Mento 156.00
115 V:The Organizer 156.00
116 Return to Smallville 156.00
117 A:Lex Luthor 156.00
118 F:Jimmy Olsen 156.00
119 A:Zoll Orr 156.00
120 V:Gadget Grim 156.00
121 I:XL-49 (Futureman) 120.00
122 In the White House 120.00
123 CS,pre-Supergirl tryout
A:Jor-El & Lara 125.00
124 F:Lois Lane 120.00
125 F:Superman College Story 120.00
126 F:Lois Lane 120.00
127 WB,I&O:Titano 120.00
128 V:Vard & Boka 120.00
129 WB,I&O:Lori Lemaris 120.00

Superman #236 © DC Comics, Inc.

130 A:Krypto,the Superdog . . . 120.00
131 A:Mr. Mxyzptlk 86.00
132 A:Batman & Robin 86.00
133 F:Superman Joins Army . . . 86.00
134 A:Supergirl & Krypto 86.00
135 A:Lori Lemaris,Mr.Mxyzptlk . 86.00
136 O:Discovery Kryptonite 86.00
137 CS,I:Super-Menace 86.00
138 A:Titano,Lori Lemaris 86.00
139 CS,O:Red Kryptonite 86.00
140 WB,I:Bizarro Jr,Bizarro
Supergirl,Blue Kryptonite. . . 100.00
141 I:Lyla Lerrol,A:Jor-EL
& Lara 62.00
142 WB,CS,A:Al Capone 62.00
143 WB,F:Bizarro meets
Frankenstein 62.00
144 O:Superboy's 1st Public
Appearance 62.00
145 F:April Fool's Issue 62.00
146 F:Superman's life story 85.00
147 CS,I:Adult Legion 80.00
148 CS,V:Mxyzptlk 62.00
149 CS:A:Luthor,C:JLA 75.00
150 CS,KS,V:Mxyzptlk 35.00
151 CS 30.00
152 A:Legion 32.00
153 CS 30.00
154 CS,V:Mzyzptlk 30.00
155 WB,CS,V:Cosmic Man 30.00
156 CS,A:Legion,Batman 30.00
157 CS,I:Gold kryptonite 35.00
158 CS,I:Nightwing&Flamebird . . 30.00
159 CS,Imaginary Tale
F:Lois Lane 30.00
160 CS,F:Perry White 30.00
161 D:Ma & Pa Kent 35.00
162 A:Legion 25.00
163 CS 24.00
164 CS,Luthor,I:Lexor 24.00
165 CS,A:Saturn Woman 24.00
166 CS 24.00
167 CS,I:Ardora,Brainiac 48.00
168 CS 24.00
169 Great DC Contest 24.00
170 CS,A:J.F.Kennedy,Luthor . . 24.00
171 CS,Mxyzptlk 24.00
172 CS,Luthor,Brainiac 24.00
173 CS,A:Batman 24.00
174 Mxyzptlk 24.00
175 CS,Luthor 24.00
176 CS,Green Kryptonite 24.00
177 Fortress of Solitude 24.00
178 CS, Red Kryptonite 24.00

Superman #259 © DC Comics, Inc.

179 CS,Clark Kent in Marines . . 24.00
180 CS 24.00
181 Superman 2965 . . . . 24.00
182 CS,Toyman 24.00
183 giant 24.00
184 Secrets of the Fortress 15.00
185 JM,Superman's Achilles
Heel 15.00
186 CS,The Two Ghosts of
Superman 15.00
187 giant 20.00
188 V:Zunial,The Murder Man . . 11.00
189 WB,The Mystery of Krypton's
Second Doom 15.00
190 WB,I:Amalak 15.00
191 The Prisoner of Demon 15.00
192 CS,Imaginary Story,
I:Superman Jr. 15.00
193 giant 18.00
194 CS,Imaginary,A:Supes Jr. . . 15.00
195 CS,V:Amalak 15.00
196 WB,reprint 15.00
197 giant 18.00
198 CS,F:The Real Clark Kent . . 15.00
199 CS,F:Superman/Flash race,
A:JLA 150.00
200 WB,A:Brainiac 15.00
201 CS,F:Clark Kent Abandons
Superman 9.00
202 A:Bizarro,(giant size) 13.00
203 F:When Superman Killed His
Friends 9.00
204 NA(c),RA,A:Lori Lemaris 9.00
205 NA(c),I:Black Zero 9.00
206 NA(c),F:The Day Superman
Became An Assistant 9.00
207 CS,F:The Case Of the
Collared Crimefighter 13.00
208 NA(c),CS 9.00
209 CS,F:The Clark Kent Monster 9.00
210 CS,F:Clark Kent's Last Rites . 8.00
211 CS,RA 9.00
212 giant 13.00
213 CS,JA,V:Luthor,C:Brainiac 5 9.00
214 NA(c),CS,JA,F:The Ghosts
That Haunted Superman 9.00
215 NA(c),CS,JA,V:Luthor,
Imaginary Story 9.00
216 JKu(c),RA,Superman in Nam 9.00
217 CS,A:Mr.Mxyzptlk 13.00
218 CS,JA,A:Mr.Mxyzptlk 9.00
219 CS,F:Clark Kent-Hero,
Superman Public Enemy 9.00
220 CS,A:Flash 9.00
221 CS,F:The Two Ton Superman 9.00
222 giant 13.00
223 CS,A:Supergirl 9.00
224 CS,Imaginary Story 9.00
225 CS,F:The Secret of the
Super Imposter 9.00
226 CS,F:When Superman Became
King Kong 9.00
227 Krypton,(giant) 13.00
228 CS,DA 9.00
229 WB,CS 9.00
230 CS,DA,Luthor 9.00
231 CS,DA,Luthor 9.00
232 F:Krypton,(giant) 13.00
233 CS,MA,I:Quarrum 9.00
234 NA(c),CS,MA, ... 9.00
235 CS,MA 9.00
236 CS,MA,DG,A:Green Arrow . . 9.00
237 NA(c),CS,MA, ... 9.00
238 CS,MA,GM 9.00
239 giant 13.00
240 CS,DG,MK,A:I-Ching 6.00
241 CS,MA,A:Wonder Woman . . . 4.50
242 CS,MA,A:Wonder Woman . . . 4.50
243 CS,MA 4.50
244 CS,MA 4.50
245 100 pg reprints 7.00
246 CS,MA,RB,I:S.T.A.R. Labs . . 3.50
247 CS,MA,Guardians o/Universe 3.50
248 CS,MA,A:Luthor,I:Galactic
Golem 3.50
249 CS,MA,DD,NA,I:Terra-Man . . 7.50
250 CS,MA,Terraman 3.50
251 CS,MA,RB 3.50
252 NA(c),rep.100pgs 7.00
253 CS,MA 3.50
254 CS,MA,NA 7.50
255 CS,MA,DG 3.00
256 CS,MA 3.00
257 CS,MA,DD,DG,A:Tomar-Re . 3.00
258 CS,MA,DC 3.00
259 CS,MA,A:Terra-Man 3.00
260 CS,DC,I:Valdemar 3.00
261 CS,MA,V:Star Sapphire 3.00
262 CS,MA 3.00
263 CS,MA,DD,FMc 3.00
264 DC,CS,I:SteveLombard 3.00
265 CS,MA 3.00
266 CS,MA,DD,V:Snowman 3.00
267 CS,MA,BO, ... 3.00
268 CS,BO,DD,MA,A:Batgirl 3.00
269 CS,MA 3.00
270 CS,MA,V:Valdemar 3.00
271 CS,BO,DG,V:Brainiac 3.00
272 100pg.reprints 5.00
273 CS,DG 2.50
274 CS 2.50
275 CS,DG,FMc 2.50
276 CS,BO,I&O:Captain Thunder . 2.50

All comics prices listed are for *Near Mint* condition.

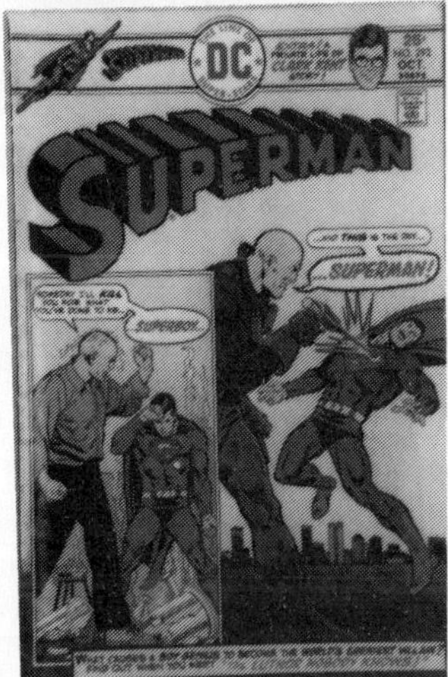

Superman #292 © DC Comics, Inc.

277 CS 2.50
278 CS,BO,Terraman,100page . . 5.00
279 CS,Batgirl,Batman 3.00
280 CS,BO 2.50
281 CS,BO,I:Vartox 2.50
282 CS,KS,N:Luthor 2.50
283 CS,BO,Mxyzptlk 2.50
284 CS,BO,100p reprint 5.00
285 CS,BO 2.50
286 CS,BO 2.50
287 CS,BO,R:Krypto 2.50
288 CS,BO 2.50
289 CS,BO,JL 2.50
290 CS,V:Mxyzptlk 2.50
291 CS,BO 2.50
292 CS,BO,AM,O:Luthor 2.50
293 CS,BO 2.50
294 CS,JL,A:Brain Storm 2.50
295 CS,BO 2.50
296 CS,BO,Identity Crisis #1 . . . . 2.50
297 CS,BO,Identity Crisis #2 . . . . 2.50
298 CS,BO,Identity Crisis #3 . . . . 2.50
299 CS,BO,Identity Crisis #4
A:Luthor,Brainiac,Bizarro 2.50
300 CS,BO,2001,anniversary 5.50
301 BO,JL,V:Solomon Grundy . . . 2.50
302 JL,BO,V:Luthor,A:Atom 2.50
303 CS,BO,I:Thunder&Lightning . 2.50
304 CS,BO,V:Parasite 2.50
305 CS,BO,V:Toyman 2.50
306 CS,BO,V:Bizarro 2.50
307 NA(c),JL,FS,A:Supergirl 2.50
308 NA(c),JL,FS,A:Supergirl 2.50
309 JL,FS,A:Supergirl 2.25
310 CS,V:Metallo 2.25
311 CS,FS,A:Flash 2.25
312 CS,FS,A:Supergirl 2.25
313 NA(c),CS,DA,A:Supergirl 2.25
314 NA(c),CS,DA,A:Gr.Lantern . . 2.25
315 CS,DA,V:Blackrock 2.25
316 CS,DA,V:Metallo 2.25
317 NA(c),CS,DA,V:Metallo 2.25
318 CS 2.00
319 CS,V:Solomon Grundy 2.00
320 CS,V:Solomon Grundy 2.00
321 CS,V:Parasite 2.00
322 CS,V:Solomon Grundy 2.00
323 CS,DA,I:Atomic Skull 2.00
324 CS,A:Atomic Skull 2.00
325 CS 2.00
326 CS,V:Blackrock 2.00
327 CS,KS,V:Kobra,C:JLA 2.00
328 CS,KS,V:Kobra 2.00
329 KS,CS 2.00
330 CS,F:glasses explained 2.00
331 CS,I:Master Jailer 2.00
332 CS,V:Master Jailer 2.00
333 CS,V:Bizarro 2.00
334 CS 2.00
335 CS,W:Mxyzptlk 2.00
336 CS,V:Rose And Thorn 2.00
337 CS,A:Brainiac,Bizarro 2.00
338 CS,F:Kandor enlarged 2.00
339 CS,I:N.R.G.X 2.00
340 CS,V:N.R.G.X 2.00
341 CS,F:Major Disaster 2.00
342 CS,V:Chemo 2.00
343 CS 2.00
344 CS,A:Phantom Stranger 2.00
345 CS,'When time ran backward' 2.00
346 CS,'Streak of Bad Luck' 2.00
347 JL 2.00
348 CS 2.00
349 CS,V:Mxyzptlk 2.00
350 CS,'Clark Kent's Vanishing
Classmate' 2.00
351 CS,JL,A:Mxyzptlk 2.00
352 CS,RB 2.00
353 CS,origin 2.00
354 CS,JSon,I:Superman 2020 . . 2.00
355 CS,JSon,F:Superman 2020 . . 2.00
356 CS,V:Vartox 2.00
357 CS,DCw,F:Superman 2020 . . 2.00
358 CS,DG,DCw 2.00
359 CS 2.00
360 CS,AS,F:World of Krypton . . . 2.00
361 CS,AS 2.00
362 CS,KS,DA 2.00
363 CS,RB,C:Luthor 2.00
364 GP(c),RB,AS 2.00
365 CS,KS 2.00
366 CS,KS 2.00
367 CS,GK,F:World of Krypton . . 2.00
368 CS,AS 2.00
369 RB,FMc,V:Parasite 2.00
370 CS,KS,FMc,A:Chemo 2.00
371 CS 2.00
372 CS,GK,F:Superman 2021 . . . 2.00
373 CS,V:Vartox 2.00
374 GK(c),CS,DA,KS,V:Vartox . . . 2.00
375 CS,DA,GK,V:Vartox 2.00
376 CS,DA,CI,BO,SupergirlPrev. . 1.75
377 GK(c),CS,V:Terra-Man 1.75
378 CS 1.75
379 CS,V:Bizarro 1.75
380 CS 1.75
381 GK(c),CS 1.75
382 GK(c),CS 1.75
383 CS 1.75
384 GK(c),CS 1.75
385 GK(c),CS,V:Luthor 1.75
386 GK(c),CS,V:Luthor 1.75
387 GK(c),CS 1.75
388 GK(c),CS 1.75
389 GK(c),CS 1.75
390 GK(c),CS,V:Vartox 1.75
391 GK(c),CS,V:Vartox 1.75
392 GK(c),CS,V:Vartox 1.75
393 IN,DG,V:Master Jailer 1.75
394 CS,V:Valdemar 1.75
395 CS,V:Valdemar 1.75
396 CS 1.75
397 EB,V:Kryptonite Man 1.75
398 CS,AS,DJ 1.75
399 CS,BO,EB 1.75
400 HC(c),FM,AW,JO,JSo,MR,
TA,WP,MK,KJ,giant 4.00
401 CS,BO,V:Luthor 1.75
402 CS,BO,WB 1.75
403 CS,BO,AS 1.75
404 CI,BO,V:Luthor 1.75
405 KS,KK,AS,F:Super-Batman . . 1.75
406 IN,AS,KK 1.75
407 IN,V:Mxyzptlk 1.75
408 CS,AW,JRu,F:Nuclear
Holocaust 1.75
409 CS,AW,KS 1.75
410 CS,AW,V:Luthor 1.75

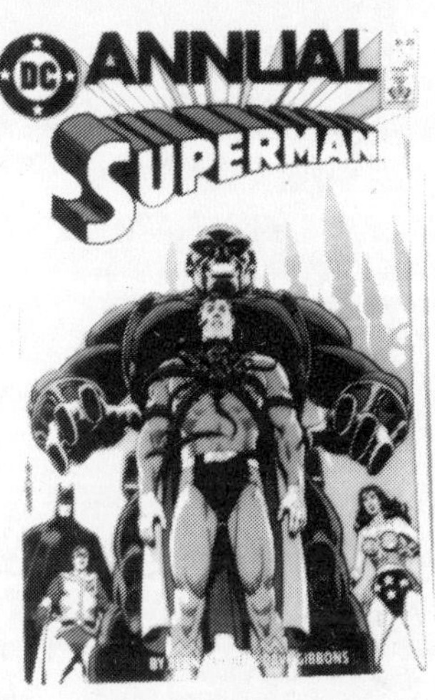

Superman Annual #11
© DC Comics, Inc.

411 CS,MA,F:End Earth-Prime . . 1.75
412 CS,AW,V:Luthor 1.75
413 CS,AW,V:Luthor 1.75
414 CS,AW,Crisis tie-in 2.00
415 CS,AW,Crisis,W:Super Girl . . 2.00
416 CS,AW,Luthor 1.75
417 CS,V:Martians 1.75
418 CS,V:Metallo 1.75
419 CS,V:Iago 1.75
420 CS,F:Nightmares 1.75
421 CS,V:Mxyzptlk 1.75
422 BB(c),CS,TY,LMa,V:Werewolf 1.75
423 AMo(s),CS,GP,F:Last
Superman 10.00
Ann.#1 I:Supergirl Rep 325.00
Ann.#2 I&O:Titano 200.00
Ann.#3 I:Legion 135.00
Ann.#4 O:Legion 110.00
Ann.#5 A:Krypton 85.00
Ann.#6 A:Legion 60.00
Ann.#7 O:Superman,Silver Anniv. 50.00
Ann.#8 F:Secret origins 35.00
Ann.#9 GK(c),ATh,TA,CS,
A:Batman 6.00
Ann.#10 CS,MA,F:Sword of
Superman 5.00
Ann.#11 AMo(s),DGb,A:Batman,
Robin,Wonder Woman 6.00
Ann.#12 BB(c),AS,A:Lex Luthor,
Last War Suit 3.00
Game Give-away 10.00
Giveaway CS,AT 2.00
Pizza Hut 1977 . . . . 5.00
Radio Shack 1980 JSw,DG 4.00
Radio Shack 1981 CS 3.00
Radio Shack 1982 CS 3.00
Spec.#1 GK 3.50
Spec.#2 GK,V:Brainiac 3.50
Spec.#3 IN,V:Amazo 3.50
Superman III Movie,CS 1.50
Superman IV Movie,DH,DG,FMc . 1.50

Becomes:

ADVENTURES OF SUPERMAN

424 JOy,I:Man O'War 3.00
425 JOy,Man O'War 2.50
426 JOy,Legends,V:Apokolips . . . 2.50
427 JOy,V:Qurac 2.50
428 JOy,V:Qurac,I:JerryWhite . . . 2.50
429 JOy,V:Concussion 2.50
430 JOy,V:Fearsome Five 2.50

431 JOy,A:Combattor 2.00
432 JOy,I:Jose Delgado 2.00
433 JOy,V:Lex Luthor 2.00
434 JOy,I:Gang Buster 2.50
435 JOy,A:Charger 2.00
436 JOy,Millenium x-over 2.00
437 JOy,Millenium X-over 2.00
438 JOy,N:Brainiac 2.50
439 JOy,R:Superman Robot 2.00
440 JOy,A:Batman,Wond.Woman 2.00
441 JOy,V:Mr.Mxyzptlk 2.00
442 JOy,V:Dreadnaught,A:JLI . . . 2.00
443 JOy,DHz,I:Husque 2.00
444 JOy,Supergirl SagaPt.2 . . . . . 2.00
445 JOy,V:Brainiac 2.00
446 JOy,A:Gangbuster,
A:Luthor's Old Costume 2.00
447 JOy,A:Gangbuster 2.00
448 JOy,I:Dubbilex,A:Gangbuster . 2.00
449 JOy,Invasion X-over 2.00
450 JOy,Invasion X-over 2.00
451 JOy,'Superman in Space' . . . 2.00
452 DJu,V:Wordbringer 2.00
453 JOy,DJu,A:Gangbuster 2.00
454 JOy,DJu,V:Mongul 2.50
455 DJu,ATb,A:Eradicator 3.50
456 DJu,ATb,V:Turmoil 2.00
457 DJu,V:Intergang 2.00
458 DJu,KJ,R:Elastic Lad
(Jimmy Olsen) 2.00
459 DJu,V:Eradicator 3.00
460 DJu,NKu,V:Eradicator 3.00
461 DJu,GP,V:Eradicator 3.00
462 DJu,ATb,Homeless
Christmas Story 2.00
463 DJu,ATb,Superman Races
Flash 3.00
464 DJu,ATb,Day of Krypton
Man #2,A:Lobo 3.50
465 DJu,ATb,Day of Krypton
Man #5,V:Draaga 3.00
466 DJu,DG,V:Team Excalibur
Astronauts,I:Hank Henshaw
(becomes Cyborg Superman) 12.50
467 DJu,ATb,A:Batman 2.50
468 DJu,ATb,Man Of Steel's
Journal,V:Hank Henshaw . . . 10.00
469 DJu,ATb,V:Dreadnaught 2.00
470 DJu,ATb,Soul Search #3,
D:Jerry White 2.00
471 CS,Sinbad Contract #2 . . . . . 2.00
472 DJu,ATb,Krisis of Krimson
Kryptonite #2 . . . . 3.00
473 DJu,ATb,A:Green Lantern,
Guy Gardner 2.00
474 DJu,ATb,Drunk Driving issue . 2.00
475 DJu,ATb,V:Kilgrave,Sleez . . . 2.00
476 DJu,BBr,Time & Time Again Pt.1,
A:Booster Gold,Legion 2.00
477 DJu,BBr,T & T Again Pt4,
A:Legion 2.00
478 DJu,BBr,T & T Again Pt7,
A:Legion,Linear Man 2.00
479 EH,Red Glass Trilogy#2 . . . . 2.00
480 JOy,DJu,BMc,TG,BBr,CS,
Revenge of the Krypton
Man Pt.#3 . . . . 3.00
481 1st TG Supes,DHz,V:Parasite 2.00
482 TG,DHz,V:Parasite 2.00
483 TG,DHz,V:Blindspot 2.00
484 TG,Blackout #1,V:Mr.Z 2.00
485 TG,DHz,Blackout #5,A:Mr.Z . 2.00
486 TG,V:Purge 2.00
487 TG,DHz,X-mas,A:Agent
Liberty 2.00
488 TG,Panic in the Sky Pt.3,
V:Brainiac. 3.00
489 TG,Panic in the Sky,Epiloge . 3.00
490 TG,A:Agent Liberty,Husque . . 1.75
491 TG,DHz,V:Cerberus,Metallo . 1.75
492 WS(c),V:Sons of Liberty,
A:Agent Liberty 1.75
493 TG,Blaze/Satanus War Pt.1 . 1.75
494 TG,DHz,I:Kismet 1.75
495 TG,DHz,A:Forever People,

Adventures of Superman #494
© DC Comics, Inc.

Darkseid 1.75
496 V:Mr.Mxyzptlk,C:Doomsday . . 6.00
496a 2nd printing 1.50
497 TG,Doomsday Part 3,A:Maxima,
Bloodwynd 12.00
497a 2nd printing 1.75
498 TG,Funeral for a Friend#1 . . . 5.00
498a 2nd Printing 1.25
499 TG,DHz,Funeral for a
Friend#5 . . . . 4.00
500 JOy(c),B:KK(s),TG,DJu,JBg,JG,
BBr,Bagged,Superman in limbo,
I:Four Supermen,Direct Sales . 3.50
500a Newsstand Ed. 3.00
500b Platinum Ed. 90.00
501 TG,Reign of Supermen#2,Direct
Sales,Die-Cut(c),Mini-poster
F:Superboy 2.50
501a Newstand Ed. 2.00
502 TG,A:Supergirl,V:Stinger 2.00
503 TG,Cyborg Superman Vs.
Superboy 2.50
504 TG,DHz,A:All Supermen,
V:Mongul 3.50
505 TG,DHz,Superman returns to
Metropolis,Holografx(c) 3.50
505a Newstand Ed. 2.00
506 TG,DHz,A:Guardian 1.75
507 Spilled Blood#1,V:Bloodsport 1.75
508 BKi,A:Challengers of the
Unknown 1.75
509 BKi,A:Auron 1.75
510 BKi,Bizarro's World#2,
V:Bizarro 1.75
511 BKi,A:Guardian 1.75
512 BKi,V:Parasite 1.75
513 BKi,Battle for Metropolis #4, . 1.75
514 BKi,Fall of Metropolis #4 . . . . 1.50
Ann.#1 JSn(c),DJu,I:Word Bringer 3.00
Ann.#2 CS/JBy,KGa/DG,BMc,
A:L.E.G.I.O.N.'90 (Lobo) 5.50
Ann.#3 BHi,JRu,DG,
Armageddon 2001. . . . . 3.00
Ann.#4 BMc,A:Lobo,Guy Gardner,
Eclipso tie-in 3.00
Ann.#5 TG,I:Sparx 2.75
Superman Archives HC rep 39.95

SUPERMAN'S BUDDY
1954

1 w/costume 1,000.00
1 w/out costume 400.00

SUPERMAN'S CHRISTMAS ADVENTURE

1 (1940) 600.00
2 (1944) 475.00

SUPERMAN AND THE GREAT CLEVELAND FIRE
1948

1 for Hospital Fund 400.00

SUPERMAN (miniature)
1942

1 Py-Co-Pay Tooth Powder
Give- Away 600.00
2 CS,Superman Time Capsule 400.00
3 CS,Duel in Space 250.00
4 CS,Super Show in Metropolis 250.00

SUPERMAN RECORD COMIC
1966

1 w/record 100.00
1 w/out record 35.00

SUPERMAN-TIM STORE PAMPHLETS
1942

Superman-Tim store Monthly
Membership Pamphlet, 16
pages of stories, games,
puzzles (1942), each 100.00
Superman-Tim store Monthly
Membership Pamphlet, 16
pages of stories, games,
puzzles (1943), each 100.00
Superman-Tim store Monthly
Membership Pamphlet, 16
pages of stories, games,
puzzles (1944), each 100.00
Superman-Tim store Monthly
Membership Pamphlet, 16
pages of stories, games,
puzzles (1945), each 100.00
Superman-Tim store Monthly
Membership Pamphlet, 14-16
pages of stories, games,
puzzles, 5"x8" color(c),
(1946), each 100.00
Superman-Tim stamp
album, 1946 . . . . 150.00
Superman-Tim store Monthly
Membership Pamphlet, 14-16
pages of stories, games,
puzzles, 5"x8" color(c),
(1947), each 100.00
Superman-Tim stamp album,
Superman story, 1947 . . . . 175.00
Superman-Tim store Monthly
Membership Pamphlet, 14-16
pages of stories, games,
puzzles, 5"x8" color(c),(1948),
each 100.00
Superman-Tim stamp
album, 1948 . . . . 125.00
Superman-Tim store Monthly
Membership Pamphlet, 14-16
pages of stories, games,
puzzles, 5"x8" color(c),
(1949), each 100.00
Superman-Tim store Monthly
Membership Pamphlet, 14-16
pages of stories, games,
puzzles, 5"x8" color(c)
(1950), each 100.00

SUPERMAN
[2nd Regular Series]
January, 1987

1 JBy,TA,I:Metallo 3.50
2 JBy,TA,V:Luthor 3.00

 All comics prices listed are for *Near Mint* condition.

Superman (2nd Regular Series) #65
© DC Comics, Inc.

3 JBy,TA,Legends tie-in 2.50
4 JBy,KK,V:Bloodsport 2.25
5 JBy,KK,V:Host 2.00
6 JBy,KK,V:Host 2.00
7 JBy,KK,V:Rampage 2.00
8 JBy,KK,A:Superboy,Legion 2.00
9 JBy,KK,V:Joker 3.50
10 JBy,KK,V:Rampage 2.00
11 JBy,KK,V:Mr.Mxyzptlk 2.00
12 JBy,KK,A:Lori Lemerias 2.00
13 JBy,KK,Millenium 2.00
14 JBy,KK,A:Green Lantern 2.00
15 JBy,KK,I:New Prankster 2.00
16 JBy,KK,A:Prankster 2.00
17 JBy,KK,O:Silver Banshee 2.00
18 MMi,KK,A:Hawkman 2.00
19 JBy,V:Skyhook 2.00
20 JBy,KK,A:Doom Patrol 2.50
21 JBy,A:Supergirl 2.00
22 JBy,A:Supergirl 2.00
23 MMi,CR,O:Silver Banshee ... 2.00
24 KGa,V:Rampage 2.00
25 KGa,V:Brainiac 2.00
26 KGa,BBr,V:Baron Sunday 2.00
27 KGa,BBr,V:Guardian 2.00
28 KGa,BBr,Supes Leaves Earth . 2.00
29 DJu,BBr,V:Word Bringer 2.00
30 KGa,DJu,A:Lex Luthor 2.00
31 DJu,PCu,V:Mxyzptlk 2.00
32 KGa,V:Mongul 2.00
33 KGa,A:Cleric 2.00
34 KGa,V:Skyhook 2.00
35 CS,KGa,A:Brainiac 2.00
36 JOy,V:Prankster 2.00
37 JOy,A:Guardian 2.00
38 JOy,Jimmy Olsen Vanished .. 2.00
39 JOy,KGa,V:Husque 2.00
40 JOy,V:Four Armed Terror 2.00
41 JOy,Day of Krypton Man #1, A:Lobo 3.50
42 JOy,Day of Krypton Man #4, V:Draaga 3.50
43 JOy,V:Krypton Man 2.00
44 JOy,A:Batman 2.00
45 JOy,F:Jimmy Olsen's Dairy ... 2.00
46 DJu,JOy,A:Jade,Obsidian, I:New Terra-Man 2.00
47 JOy,Soul Search #2,V:Blaze .. 2.00
48 CS,Sinbad Contract #1 ...... 2.00
49 JOy,Krisis of K.Kryptonite#1 .. 3.00
50 JBy,KGa,DJu,JOy,BBr,CS,Krisis of Krimson Kryptonite #4, Clark Proposes To Lois 6.00
50a 2nd printing 1.50
51 JOy,I:Mr.Z 1.75
52 KGa,V:Terra-Man 1.75
53 JOy,Superman reveals i.d.. ... 3.50
53a 2nd Printing 1.25
54 JOy,KK,Time & Time Again#3 . 1.75
55 JOy,KK,Time & Time Again#6 . 1.75
56 EH,KK,Red Glass Trilogy#1 .. 1.75
57 JOy,DJu,BBr,ATi,JBq,BMc,TG, Revenge o/t Krypton Man #2 .. 3.50
58 DJu,BBr,I:Bloodhounds 1.75
59 DJu,BBr,A:Linear Men 1.75
60 DJu,EB,I:Agent Liberty, V:Intergang 2.00
61 DJu,BBr,A:Waverider, V:Linear Men 1.75
62 DJu,BBr,Blackout #4,A:Mr.Z .. 1.75
63 DJu,A:Aquaman 1.75
64 JG,Christmas issue 1.75
65 DJu,Panic in the Sky#2, I:New Justice League 3.50
66 DJu,Panic in the Sky#6, V:Brainiac 4.00
67 DJu,Aftermath 1.75
68 DJu,V:Deathstroke 1.75
69 WS(c),DJu,A:Agent Liberty ... 1.75
70 DJu,BBr,A:Robin,V:Vampires . 1.75
71 DJu,Blaze/Satanus War 1.75
72 DJu,Crisis at Hand#2 .... 1.75
73 DJu,A:Waverider,V:Linear Men,C:Doomsday 6.00
73a 2nd printing 1.50
74 DJu,V:Doomsday,A:JLA 12.00
74a 2nd printing 1.75
75 DJu,V:Doomsday,D:Superman, Collectors Ed. 25.00
75a newstand Ed. 10.00
75b 2nd printing 6.00
75c 3rd printing 1.50
75d 4th Printing 1.25
75e Platinum Ed. 150.00
76 DJu,BBr,Funeral for Friend#4 . 4.00
77 DJu,BBr,Funeral for Friend#8 . 4.00
78 DJu,BBr,Reign of Supermen#3, Die-Cut(c),Mini poster,F:Cyborg Supes,A:Doomsday 2.50
78a Newsstand Ed. 2.00
79 DJu,BBr,Memorial Service for Clark 2.00
80 DJu,BBr,Coast City Blows up, V:Mongul 4.00
81 DJu,O:Cyborg Superman 3.50
82 DJu,Chromium(c),A:All Supermen, V:Cyborg Superman 5.00
82a Newstand Ed. 2.25
83 DJu,A:Batman 1.75
84 DJu,V:Toyman 1.75
85 DJu,V:Toyman 1.75
86 DJu,A:Sun Devils 1.75
87 DJu(c&s),SI,JRu,Bizzaro's World#1 R:Bizarro 1.75
88 DJu(c&s),SI,JRu,Bizzaro's World#5 D:Bizarro 1.75
89 DJu(c&s),V:Cadmus Project .. 1.75
90 DJu(c&s),Battle for Metropolis#3, ... 1.50
91 DJu(c&s),Fall of Metropolis#3 . 1.50
Ann.#1 RF,BBr,A:Titano 2.00
Ann.#2 RF,BBr,R:Newsboy Legion & Guardian 3.00
Ann.#3 DAb(1st Work),TA,DG, Armageddon 2001. .... 9.00
Ann.#3a 2nd printing(silver) 2.00
Ann.#4 Eclipso 2.75
Ann.#5 Bloodlines#6,DL,I:Myriad . 2.75
Ann.#6 Elseworlds Story 2.95
Earth Day 1991 KGa 5.50
Earth Stealers JBy,CS,JOy 2.95
Greatest Superman Stories Ever Told:
HC 75.00
SC 15.95
Legacy of Superman#1 WS,JG,F: Guardian,Waverider,Sinbad ... 4.00
Newstime-The Life and Death of the Man of Steel-Magazine, DJu,BBr,JOy,JG,JBg 3.25
Spec#1 WS,V:L.Luthor,'Sandman' 6.00
Speeding Bullets EB 8.00
Under a Yellow Sun KGa,EB, ... 5.95
TPB Panic in the Sky rep. Panic in the Sky 9.95
TPB Return of Superman rep.Reign of Superman 14.95
TPB World Without Superman ... 7.50

SUPERMAN, EARTH DAY 1991

1 KGa,Metropolis 'Clean-Up' 5.50

SUPERMAN/DOOMSDAY: HUNTER/PREY

1 DJu(a&s),BBr,R:Doomsday,R:Cyborg Superman,A:Darkseid 4.95
2 DJu(a&s),BBr,V:Doomsday,Cyborg Superman,A:Darkseid 4.95
3 DJu(a&s),BBr,V:Doomsday, ... 4.95

SUPERMAN FAMILY

Prev: Superman's Pal, Jimmy Olsen
April-May, 1974

164 KS,NC(c),Jimmy Olsen:'Death Bites with Fangs of Stone' ... 2.50
165 KS,NC(c),Supergirl:'Princess of the Golden Sun' 2.00
166 KS,NC(c),Lois Lane:'The Murdering Arm of Metropolis' . 2.00
167 KS,NC(c),Jimmy Olsen:'A Deep Death for Mr. Action' ... 2.00
168 NC(c),Supergirl:'The Girl with the See-Through Mind' .. 2.00
169 NC(c),Lois Lane:'Target of the Tarantula' 2.00
170 KS(c),Jimmy Olsen:'The Kid Who Adopted Jimmy Olsen' .. 2.00
171 ECh(c),Supergirl:'Cleopatra-Queen of America' 2.00
172 KS(c),Lois Lane:'The Cheat the Whole World Cheered' ... 2.00
173 KS(c),Jimmy Olsen:'Menace of the Micro-Monster' 2.00
174 KS(c),Supergirl:'Eyes of the Serpent' 2.00
175 KS(c),Lois Lane:'Fadeout For Lois' 2.00
176 KS(c),Jimmy Olsen:'Nashville, Super-Star' .. 2.00
177 KS(c),Supergirl:'Bride of the Stars' 1.50
178 KS(c),Lois Lane:'The Girl With the Heart of Steel' 1.50
179 KS(c),Jimmy Olsen:'I Scared Superman to Death' 1.50
180 KS,Supergirl:'The Secret of the Spell-Bound Supergirl' 1.50
181 ECh(c),Lois Lane:'The Secret Lois Lane Could Never Tell' .. 1.50
182 CS&NA(c),Jimmy Olsen: 'Death on Ice' 1.50
183 NA(c),Supergirl:'Shadows of Phantoms' 1.50
184 NA(c),Supergirl:'The Visitors From The Void' 1.50
185 NA(c),Jimmy Olsen: The Fantastic Fists and Fury Feet of Jimmy Olsen' 1.50
186 JL&DG(c),Jimmy Olsen: 'The Bug Lady' 1.50
187 JL(c),Jimmy Olsen:'The Dealers of Death' 1.50
188 JL&DG(c),Jimmy Olsen: 'Crisis in Kandor' 1.50
189 JL(c),Jimmy Olsen:'The Night of the Looter' 1.50
190 Jimmy Olsen:'Somebody Stole My Town' 1.50

191 Superboy:'The Incredible Shrinking Town' 1.50
192 RA&DG(c),Superboy:'This Town For Plunder' 1.50
193 RA&DG(c),Superboy:'Menace of the Mechanical Monster' . . . 1.50
194 MR,Superboy:'When the Sorcerer Strikes' 1.50
195 RA&DG(c),Superboy:'The Curse of the Un-Secret Identity' 1.50
196 JL&DG(c),Superboy:'The Shadow of Jor-El' 1.50
197 JL(c),Superboy:'Superboy's Split Personality' 1.50
198 JL(c),Superboy:'Challenge of the Green K-Tastrophe' 1.50
199 RA&DG(c),Supergirl:'The Case of Cape Caper' 1.50
200 RA&DG(c),Lois Lane: 'Unhappy Anniversary' 1.50
201 RA&DG(c),Supergirl:'The Face on Cloud 9' 1.50
202 RA&DG(c),Supergirl:'The Dynamic Duel' 1.50
203 RA&DG(c),Supergirl:'The Supergirl From Planet Earth' . . 1.50
204 RA&DG(c),Supergirl:'The Earth-quake Enchantment' . . . 1.50
205 RA&DG(c),Supergirl:'Magic Over Miami' 1.50
206 RA&DG(c),Supergirl:'Strangers at the Heart's Core' 1.50
207 RA&DG(c),Supergirl:'Look Homeward, Argonian' 1.50
208 RA&DG(c),Supergirl:'The Super-Switch to New York' . . . 1.50
209 Supergirl:'Strike Three-You're Out' 1.50
210 Supergirl:'The Spoil Sport of New York' 1.50
211 RA&DG(c):Supergirl:'The Man With the Explosive Mind' 1.50
212 RA&DG(c):Supergirl:'Payment on Demand' 1.50
213 thru 221 . . . . @1.50
222 September, 1982 . . . . 1.50

Superman: The Man of Steel #16

© DC Comics, Inc.

SUPERMAN: THE MAN OF STEEL

1 B:LSi(s),DJu,BMc,JOy,BBr,TG, Revenge o/t Krypton Man#1 . . 5.50
2 JBg,V:Cerberus 3.00
3 JBg,War of the Gods X-over . . 2.50
4 JBg,V:Angstrom 2.50
5 JBg,CS,V:Atomic Skull 2.50
6 JBg,Blackout#3,A:Mr.Z 2.50
7 JBg,V:Cerberus 2.50
8 KD,V:Jolt,Blockhouse 2.50
9 JBg,Panic in the Sky#1, V:Brainiac. 3.00
10 JBg,Panic in the Sky#5, D:Draaga 2.50
11 JBg,V:Flashpoint 2.00
12 JBg,V:Warwolves 2.00
13 JBg,V:Cerberus 2.00
14 JBg,A:Robin,V:Vampires 2.00
15 KG,KGa,Blaze/Satanus War . . 2.00
16 JBg,Crisis at Hand#1 . . . . 2.00
17 JBg,V:Underworld, C:Doomsday 7.00
17a 2nd printing 1.50
18 JBg,I:Doomsday,V: Underworld 12.00
18a 2nd printing 4.00
18b 3rd printing 2.00
19 JBg,Doomsday Part 5 . . . . . . 12.00
19a 2nd printing 2.00

Superman: The Man of Steel #17

© DC Comics, Inc.

20 JBg,Funeral for a Friend#3 . . . 4.00
21 JBg,Funeral for a Friend#7 . . . 4.00
22 JBg,Reign of Supermen#4,Direct Sales,Die-Cut(c),mini-poster, F:Man of Steel 2.50
22a Newsstand Ed. 1.75
23 JBg,V:Superboy 2.00
24 JBg,V:White Rabbit,A:Mongul . 2.00
25 JBg,A:Real Superman 5.00
26 JBg,A:All Supermen,V:Mongul, Cyborg Superman 2.50
27 JBg,A:Superboy,Lex Luthor . . . 2.00
28 JBg(c),A:Steel 1.75
29 LSi(s),JBg,Spilled Blood#3, V:Hi-Tech,Blood Thirst 1.75
30 LSi(s),JBg,V:Lobo,Vinyl(c) 3.00
30a Newstand Ed. 1.75
31 MBr,A:Guardian 1.75
32 MBr,Bizarro's World#4, V:Bizarro 1.75
33 MBr,V:Parasite 1.75
34 JBg,A:Lex Men,Dubbile Men . . 1.75
35 JBg,Worlds Collide#1, I:Fred Bentson 1.50
Ann.#1 Eclipso tie-in,A:Starman . . 2.75
Ann.#2 Bloodlines#2,I:Edge 2.75
Ann.#3 MBr,Elseworlds Story, . . . 2.95

SUPERMAN'S GIRL FRIEND, LOIS LANE

March-April, 1958

1 CS,KS 1,350.00
2 CS,KS 500.00
3 CS,KS,spanking panel shown 350.00
4 CS,KS 250.00
5 CS,KS 250.00
6 CS,KS 150.00
7 CS,KS 150.00
8 CS,KS 150.00
9 CS,KS, A:Pat Boone 150.00
10 CS,KS 150.00
11 CS,KS 85.00
12 CS,KS 85.00
13 CS,KS 85.00
14 KS,'Three Nights in the Fortress of Solitude' 85.00
15 KS,I:Van-Zee 85.00
16 KS, Lois' Signal-Watch 85.00
17 KS,CS,A:Brainiac 85.00
18 KS,A:Astounding Man 85.00
19 KS,'Superman of the Past' . . 85.00
20 KS,A:Superman 85.00
21 KS,A:Van-Zee 75.00
22 KS,A:Robin Hood 75.00
23 KS,A:Elastic Lass, Supergirl . 75.00
24 KS,A:Van-Zee, Bizarro 75.00
25 KS,'Lois Lane's Darkest Secret' 75.00
26 KS,A:Jor-El 75.00
27 KS,CS,A:Bizarro 75.00
28 KS,A:Luthor 75.00
29 CS,A:Aquaman,Batman,Green Arrow 75.00
30 KS,A:Krypto,Aquaman 65.00
31 KS,A:Lori Lemaris 65.00
32 KS,CS,A:Bizarro 65.00
33 KS,CS,A:Phantom Zone,Lori Lemaris, Mon-El 70.00

Superman's Girl Friend, Lois Lane #11

© DC Comics, Inc.

34 KS,A:Luthor,Supergirl 65.00
35 KS,CS,A:Supergirl 65.00
36 KS,CS,Red Kryptonite Story . 65.00
37 KS,CS,'The Forbidden Box' . 65.00
38 KS,CS,A:Prof.Potter, Supergirl 65.00
39 KS,CS,A:Supergirl,Jor-El, Krypto, Lori Lemaris 65.00

 All comics prices listed are for *Near Mint* condition.

40 KS,'Lois Lane, Hag!' 65.00
41 KS,CS,'The Devil and
Lois Lane' 65.00
42 KS,A:Lori Lemaris 50.00
43 KS,A:Luthor 50.00
44 KS,A:Lori Lemaris,Braniac,
Prof. Potter 50.00
45 KS,CS,'The Superman-Lois
Hit Record' 50.00
46 KS,A:Luthor 50.00
47 KS,'The Incredible Delusion' . 50.00
48 KS,A:Mr. Mxyzptlk 50.00
49 KS,The Unknown Superman . 50.00
50 KS,A:Legion 50.00
51 KS,A:Van-Zee & Lori Lemaris 30.00
52 KS,'Truce Between Lois
Lane and Lana Lang' 30.00
53 KS,A:Lydia Lawrence 30.00
54 KS,CS,'The Monster That
Loved Lois Lane' 30.00
55 KS,A:Superigrl 30.00
56 KS,'Lois Lane's
Super-Gamble!' 32.00
57 KS,'The Camera From
Outer Space' 30.00
58 KS,'The Captive Princess' . . . 30.00
59 KS,CS,A:Jor-El & Batman . . . 30.00
60 KS,'Get Lost,Superman!' 30.00
61 KS,A:Mxyzptlk 30.00
62 KS,A:Mxyzptlk 30.00
63 KS,'The Satanic Schemes
of S.K.U.L.' 30.00
64 KS,A:Luthor 20.00
65 KS,A:Luthor 20.00
66 KS,'They Call Me the Cat!' . . 20.00
67 KS,'The Bombshell of
the Boulevards' 20.00
68 . . . . 22.00
69 KS,Lois Lane's Last Chance . 20.00
70 KS,I:Silver Age Catwoman,
A:Batman,Robin,Penguin . . 100.00
71 KS,A:Catwoman,Batman,
Robin,Penguin 75.00
72 KS,CS,A:Ina Lemaris 8.00
73 KS,'The Dummy and
the Damsel!' 8.00
74 KS,A:Justice League & Bizarro
World,I:Bizarro Flash 18.00
75 KS,'The Lady Dictator' 8.00
76 KS,A:Hap-El 8.00
77 giant size 10.00
78 KS,Courtship,Kryptonian Style . 8.00
79 KS,B:NA(c) 5.00
80 KS,'Get Out of My Life,
Superman' 5.00
81 KS,'No Witnessesin
Outerspace' 5.00
82 GT,A:Brainiac&Justice League 5.00
83 GT,'Witch on Wheels' 5.00
84 GT,KS,'Who is Lois Lane?' . . . 5.00
85 GT,KS,A:Kandorians 5.00
86 giant size 7.00
87 GT,KS,A:Cor-Lar 5.00
88 GT,KS,'Through a Murderer's
Eyes' 5.00
89 CS,A:Batman & Batman Jr. . . . 6.00
90 GT,A:Dahr-nel 5.00
91 GT,A:Superlass 5.00
92 GT,A:Superhorse 5.00
93 GT,A:Wonder Woman 5.00
94 GT,KS,A:Jor 5.00
95 giant size 7.00
96 GT,A:Jor 4.00
97 GT,KS,A:Lori Lemaris,
Luma Lynai,Lyla Lerrol 4.00
98 GT,A:Phantom Zone 4.00
99 GT,KS,A:Batman 5.00
100 GT,A:Batman 5.00
101 GT,KS,'The Super-Reckless
Lois Lane' 4.00
102 GT,KS,When You're Dead,
You're Dead 4.00
103 GT,KS,A:Supergirl 4.00
104 giant size 7.00
105 RA,I&O:Rose & Thorn 4.50
106 WR,'I am Curious Black!' . . . 4.00
107 WR,The Snow-Woman Wept . 4.00
108 WR,The Spectre Suitor 4.00
109 WR,'I'll Never Fall
in Love Again' 4.00
110 WR,'Indian Death Charge!' . . 4.00
111 WR,A:Justice League 4.00
112 WR,KS,A:Lori Lemaris 3.00
113 giant size 7.00
114 WR,KS,A:Rose & Thorn 4.00
115 WR,A:The Black Racer 3.00
116 WR,A:Darkseid & Desaad . . . 3.00
117 WR,'S.O.S From Tomorrow!' . 3.00
118 WR,A:Darkseid & Desaad . . . 3.00
119 WR,A:Darkseid & Lucy Lane . 3.00
120 WR,'Who Killed Lucy Lane?' . 3.00
121 WR,A:The Thorn 3.00
122 WR,A:The Thorn 3.00
123 JRo,'Ten Deadly Division
of the 100' 3.00
124 JRo,'The Hunters' 3.00
125 JRo,'Death Rides Wheels!' . . 3.00
126 JRo,'The Brain Busters' 3.00
127 JRo,'Curse of the Flame' . . . 3.00
128 JRo,A:Batman & Aquaman . . 3.00
129 JRo,'Serpent in Paradise' . . . 3.00
130 JRo,'The Mental Murster' . . . 3.00
131 JRo,Superman–Marry Me!' . . 3.00
132 JRo,Zatanna B.U. 3.00
133 JRo,'The Lady is a Bomb' . . . 3.00
134 JRo,A:Kandor 3.00
135 JRo,'Amazing After-Life
of Lois Lane' 3.00
136 JRo,A:Wonder Woman 3.00
137 JRo,'The Stolen Subway'
Sept.-Oct.,1974 . . . . 4.00
Ann.#1 . . . . 70.00
Ann.#2 . . . . 45.00

SUPERMAN'S PAL, JIMMY OLSEN

September-October, 1954

1 CS,'The Boy of 100 Faces!' 1,600.00
2 CS,The Flying Jimmy Olsen 700.00
3 CS,'The Man Who Collected
Excitement 500.00

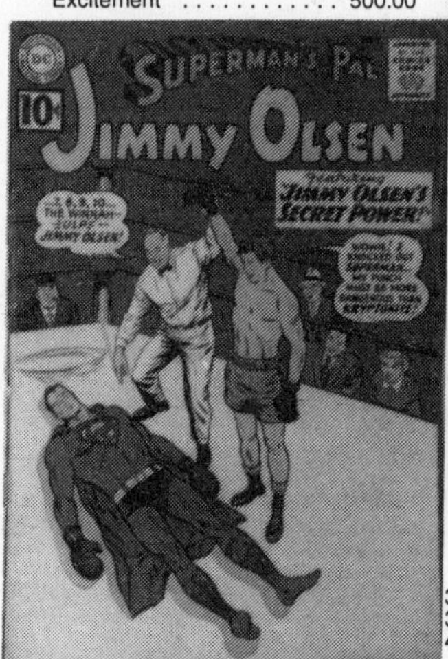

Superman's Pal, Jimmy Olsen #55

© DC Comics, Inc.

4 CS,'King For A Day!' 300.00
5 CS,'The Story of Superman's
Souvenirs 300.00
6 CS,Kryptonite story 275.00
7 CS,'The King of Marbles' . . 275.00

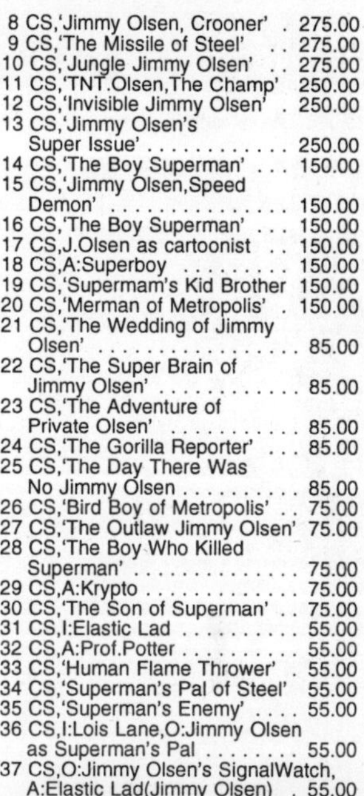

8 CS,'Jimmy Olsen, Crooner' . 275.00
9 CS,'The Missile of Steel' . . 275.00
10 CS,'Jungle Jimmy Olsen' . . 275.00
11 CS,'TNT.Olsen,The Champ' 250.00
12 CS,'Invisible Jimmy Olsen' . 250.00
13 CS,'Jimmy Olsen's
Super Issue' 250.00
14 CS,'The Boy Superman' . . . 150.00
15 CS,'Jimmy Olsen,Speed
Demon' 150.00
16 CS,'The Boy Superman' . . . 150.00
17 CS,J.Olsen as cartoonist . . 150.00
18 CS,A:Superboy 150.00
19 CS,'Supermam's Kid Brother 150.00
20 CS,'Merman of Metropolis' . 150.00
21 CS,'The Wedding of Jimmy
Olsen' 85.00
22 CS,'The Super Brain of
Jimmy Olsen' 85.00
23 CS,'The Adventure of
Private Olsen' 85.00
24 CS,'The Gorilla Reporter' . . . 85.00
25 CS,'The Day There Was
No Jimmy Olsen 85.00
26 CS,'Bird Boy of Metropolis' . . 75.00
27 CS,'The Outlaw Jimmy Olsen' 75.00
28 CS,'The Boy Who Killed
Superman' 75.00
29 CS,A:Krypto 75.00
30 CS,'The Son of Superman' . . 75.00
31 CS,I:Elastic Lad 55.00
32 CS,A:Prof.Potter 55.00
33 CS,'Human Flame Thrower' . 55.00
34 CS,'Superman's Pal of Steel' 55.00
35 CS,'Superman's Enemy' 55.00
36 CS,I:Lois Lane,O:Jimmy Olsen
as Superman's Pal 55.00
37 CS,O:Jimmy Olsen's SignalWatch,
A:Elastic Lad(Jimmy Olsen) . 55.00

Superman's Pal, Jimmy Olsen #107

© DC Comics, Inc.

38 CS,'Olsen's Super-Supper' . . 55.00
39 CS,'The Super-Lad of Space' 55.00
40 CS,A:Supergirl,Hank White
(Perry White's son) 55.00
41 CS,'The Human Octopus' . . . 40.00
42 CS,'Jimmy The Genie' 40.00
43 WB,CS,'Jimmy Olsen's Private
Monster' 40.00
44 CS,'Miss Jimmy Olsen' 40.00
45 CS,A:Kandor 40.00
46 CS,A:Supergirl,Elastic Lad . . 40.00
47 CS,'Monsters From Earth!' . . 40.00

48 CS,I:Superman Emergency Squad 40.00
49 CS,A:Congorilla & Congo Bill 40.00
50 CS,A:Supergirl,Krypto,Bizarro 40.00
51 CS,A:Supergirl 30.00
52 CS,A:Mr. Mxyzptlk, Miss Gzptlsnz 30.00
53 CS,A:Kandor,Lori Lemaris, Mr.Mxyztlk 30.00
54 CS,A:Elastic Lad 30.00
55 CS,A:Aquaman,Thor 30.00
56 KS,Imaginary story 30.00
57 KS,A:Supergirl,Imaginary story 15.00
58 CS,C:Batman 15.00
59 CS,A:Titano 15.00
60 CS,'The Fantastic Army of General Olsen' 15.00
61 CS,Prof. Potter 15.00
62 CS,A:Elastic Lad,Phantom Zone 15.00
63 CS,A:Supergirl,Kandor 16.00
64 CS,'Jimmy Olsen's Super-Romance 15.00
65 CS,A:Miss Gzptlsnz 15.00
66 CS,KS,A:Mr. Mxyzptlk 15.00
67 CS,'The Dummy That Haunted Jimmy Olsen' 15.00
68 CS,'The Helmet of Hate' 15.00
69 CS,A:Nightwing,Flamebird . . 15.00
70 A:Supergirl,Lori Lemaris, Element Lad 15.00
71 CS,A:Mr. Mxyzptlk 10.00
72 CS,A:Legion of Super-Heroes, Jimmy Olsen becomes honorary member 12.00
73 A:Kandor 12.00
74 CS,A:Mr. Mxyzptlk,Lex Luthor 10.00
75 CS,A:Supergirl 10.00
76 CS,A:Legion of Super-Heroes 10.00
77 CS,Jimmy Olsen becomes Colossal Boy, A:Titano 10.00
78 CS,A:Aqualad 10.00
79 CS,'The Red-Headed Beetle of 1,000 B.C.' 10.00
80 CS,A:Bizarro 10.00
81 CS,KS,A:Lori Lemaris,I&O only A:Mighty Eagle 10.00
82 CS,'The Unbeatable Jimmy Olsen' 10.00
83 CS,A:Kandor 10.00
84 CS,A:Titano 10.00
85 CS,C:Legion of Super-Heroes 12.00
86 CS,A:Congorilla,Braniac 6.00
87 A:Lex Luthor,Brainiac,Legion of Super-Villians 10.00
88 C:Legion of Super-Heroes . . . 7.50
89 I:Agent Double-Five,C:John F. Kennedy 6.00
90 CS,A:Mr. Mxyzptlk 6.00
91 CS,C:Batman & Robin 5.00
92 JM,A:Batman,Robin,Supergirl . 5.00
93 'The Batman-Superman of Earth-X!' 5.00
94 O:Insect Queen retold 5.00
95 Giant 11.00
96 I:Tempus 4.00
97 A:Fortress of Solitude 4.00
98 'The Bride of Jungle Jimmy' . . 4.00
99 A:Legion of Super-Heroes 4.00
100 A:Legion of Super-Heroes . . . 7.50
101 A:Jor-El and Lara 4.00
102 'Superman's Greatest Double Cross!' 4.00
103 'The Murder of Clark Kent!' . . 4.00
104 Giant 8.00
105 V:Tempus 3.50
106 CS,A:Legion of Super-Heroes 3.50
107 A:Krypto 3.50
108 CS,'The Midas of Metropolis' . 3.50
109 A:Lex Luthor 3.50
110 CS,'Jimmy Olsen's Blackest Deeds!' 3.50
111 . . . . 3.50
112 . . . . 3.50
113 V:Magnaman 5.00
114 'The Wrong Superman!' 3.50
115 A:Aquaman 3.50
116 A:Brainiac 3.50
117 'Planet of the Capes' 3.50
118 A:Lex Luthor 3.50
119 'Nine Lives Like a Cat!' 3.50
120 V:Climate King 3.50
121 thru 125 . . . . @3.50
126 CS,Riddle of Kryptonite Plus . 3.50
127 CS,Jimmy in Revolutionary War 3.50
128 I:Mark Olsen(Jimmy's Father) 3.50
129 MA,A:Mark Olsen 3.50
130 MA,A:Robin,Brainiac 3.50
131 . . . . 5.00
132 MA,When Olsen Sold out Superman 3.50
133 JK,B:New Newsboy Legion, I:Morgan Edge 8.00
134 JK,I:Darkseid 12.00
135 JK,I:New Guardian 7.50
136 JK,O:New Guardian, I:Dubbilex 6.00
137 JK,I:Four Armed Terror 5.00
138 JK,V:Four Armed Terror 5.00
139 JK,A:Don Rickles,I:Ugly Mannheim 5.00
140 . . . . 5.00
141 JK,A:Don Rickles,Lightray B:Newsboy Legion rep 5.00
142 JK,I:Count Dragorian 5.00
143 JK,V:Count Dragorian 5.00
144 JK,A Big Thing in a Deep Scottish Lake 5.00
145 JK,Brigadoon 5.00
146 JK,Homo Disastrous 5.00
147 JK,Superman on New Genesis,A:High Father, I:Victor Volcanium 5.00
148 JK,V:Victor Volcanium, E:Newsboy Legion rep 5.00
149 BO(i),The Unseen Enemy, B:Plastic Man rep 3.50
150 BO(i) A Bad Act to Follow . . . 3.50
151 BO(i),A:Green Lantern 3.50
152 MSy,BO,I:Real Morgan Edge 3.50
153 MSy,Murder in Metropolis . . . 3.50
154 KS,The Girl Who Was Made of Money 3.50
155 KS,Downfall of Judas Olsen . 3.50
156 KS,Last Jump for a Skyjacker 3.50
157 KS,Jimmy as Marco Polo . . . 3.50
158 KS,A:Lena Lawrence (Lucy Lane) 3.50
159 KS,Jimmy as Spartacus 3.50
160 KS,A:Lena Lawrence (Lucy Lane) 3.50
161 KS,V:Lucy Lane 3.50
162 KS,A:Lex Luthor 3.50
163 KS,Jimmy as Marco Polo February 1974 . . . . 3.50

SUPERMAN SPECTACULAR
1982

1 A:Luthor & Terra-Man 2.50

SUPERMAN, THE SECRET YEARS
February, 1985

1 CS,KS,FM(c) 1.50
2 CS,KS,FM(c) 1.25
3 CS,KS,FM(c) 1.25
4 CS,KS,FM(c), May 1985 . . . . . 1.25

SUPERMAN VS. AMAZING SPIDER-MAN
April, 1976

1 RA/DG,oversized 10.00
1a 2nd printing, signed 15.00

SUPERMAN WORKBOOK
1945

1 rep. Superman #14 . . . . 750.00

SUPER POWERS
July, 1984
[Kenner Action Figures]

1 A:Batman & Joker 1.75
2 A:Batman & Joker 1.25
3 A:Batman & Joker 1.00
4 A:Batman & Joker 1.00
5 JK(c),JK,A:Batman & Joker . . . 1.25

[2nd Series]

1 JK,'Seeds of Doom' 1.00
2 JK,'When Past & Present Meet' 1.00
3 JK,'Time Upon Time' 1.00
4 JK,There's No Place Like Rome 1.00
5 JK,'Once Upon a Tomorrow' . . 1.00
6 JK,'Darkkseid o/t Moon' 1.00

[3rd Series]

1 CI,'Threshold' 1.00
2 CI,'Escape' 1.00
3 CI,'Machinations' 75
4 CI,'A World Divided' 75

SUPER-TEAM FAMILY
October-November, 1975

1 rep. 1.00
2 Creeper/Wildcat 1.00
3 RE/WW,Flash & Hawkman . . . 1.00
4 . . . . 1.00
5 . . . . 1.00
6 . . . . 1.00
7 . . . . 1.00
8 JSh,Challengers 1.00
9 JSh,Challengers 1.00
10 JSh,Challengers 1.00
11 Supergirl,Flash,Atom 1.00
12 Green Lantern,Hawkman 1.00
13 Aquaman, Capt. Comet 1.00
14 Wonder Woman,Atom 1.00
15 Flash & New Gods, March-April, 1978 . . . . 1.00

SWAMP THING
[1st Regular Series]
October-November, 1972

1 B:LWn(s),BWr,O:Swamp Thing 55.00
2 BWr,I:Arcane 28.00
3 BWr,I:Patchwork Man 20.00
4 BWr 20.00
5 BWr 15.00
6 BWr 15.00
7 BWr,A:Batman 20.00
8 BWr,Lurker in Tunnel 13 . . . . 14.00
9 BWr 14.00
10 E:BWr,A;Arcane 14.00
11 thru 22 NR . . . . @6.00
23 NR,reverts to Dr.Holland 6.00
24 NR 6.00
TPB rep.#1-10,House of Secrets #92,Dark Genesis Saga 19.95

SWAMP THING
(see SAGA OF THE SWAMP THING)

SWORD OF SORCERY
February-March, 1973

1 MK(c),HC 10.00
2 BWv,NA,Hc 15.00
3 BWv,HC,MK,WS 10.00
4 HC,WS 5.00
5 November-December, 1973 . . 5.50

SWORD OF THE ATOM
September, 1983

1 GK 1.50
2 thru 4 GK . . . . @1.25
Spec.#1 GK 1.25
Spec.#2 GK 1.25
Spec.#3 PB 1.50

TAILGUNNER JO
September, 1988

1 . . . . 1.25
2 . . . . 1.25
3 . . . . 1.25
4 thru 6 . . . . @1.25

TALES OF THE GREEN LANTERN CORPS
May, 1981

1 JSon,FMc,O:Green Lantern . . . 1.50
2 JSon,FMc, ... 1.25
3 JSon,FMc, ... 1.25

TALES OF THE LEGION OF SUPER HEROES
August, 1984
(Previously: Legion of Super Heroes)

314 KG,V:Ontiir 1.50
315 KG(i),V:Dark Circle 1.50
316 KG(i),O:White Witch 1.50
317 KG(i),V:Dream Demon 1.50
318 KG(i),V:Persuader 1.50
319 KG(i),V:Persuader, A:Superboy 1.50
320 DJu,V:Magpie 1.50
321 DJu,Exile,V:Kol 1.50
322 DJu,Exile,V:Kol 1.50
323 DJu,Exile,V:Kol 1.50
324 DJu,EC,V:Dev-Em 1.50
325 DJu,V:Dark Circle 1.50
326 reprint of Baxter #1 . . . . 1.00
327 reprint of Baxter #2 . . . . 1.00
328 reprint of Baxter #3 . . . . 1.00
329 reprint of Baxter #4 . . . . 1.00
330 reprint of Baxter #5 . . . . 1.00
331 reprint of Baxter #6 . . . . 1.00
332 reprint of Baxter #7 . . . . 1.00
333 reprint of Baxter #8 . . . . 1.00
334 reprint of Baxter #9 . . . . 1.00
335 reprint of Baxter #10 . . . . 1.00
336 reprint of Baxter #11 . . . . 1.00
337 reprint of Baxter #12 . . . . 1.00
338 reprint of Baxter #13 . . . . 1.00
339 reprint of Baxter #14 . . . . 1.00
340 reprint of Baxter #15 . . . . 1.00
341 reprint of Baxter #16 . . . . 1.00
342 reprint of Baxter #17 . . . . 1.00
343 reprint of Baxter #19 . . . . 1.00
344 reprint of Baxter #19 . . . . 1.00
345 reprint of Baxter #20 . . . . 1.00
346 reprint of Baxter #21 . . . . 1.00
347 reprint of Baxter #22 . . . . 1.00
348 reprint of Baxter #23 . . . . 1.00
349 reprint of Baxter #24 . . . . 1.00
350 reprint of Baxter #25 . . . . 1.00
351 reprint of Baxter #26 . . . . 1.00
352 reprint of Baxter #27 . . . . 1.00
353 reprint of Baxter #28 . . . . 1.00
354 reprint of Baxter #29 . . . . 1.00
Ann.#4 rep. Baxter Ann.#1 . . . . . 1.00
Ann.#5 rep. Baxter Ann.#2 . . . . . 1.00

TALES OF THE NEW TEEN TITANS
June, 1982

1 GP, O:Cyborg 2.00
2 GP, O:Raven 2.00
3 GD, O:Changling 2.00
4 GP/EC,O:Starfire 2.00

TALES OF THE TEEN TITANS
(see NEW TEEN TITANS)

TALES OF THE UNEXPECTED
February-March, 1956

1 The Out-Of-The-World Club 750.00

Tales of the Unexpected #2
© DC Comics, Inc.

2 . . . . 400.00
3 . . . . 250.00
4 Seven Steps to the Unknown 250.00
5 . . . . 250.00
6 'The Girl in the Bottle' 175.00
7 NC(c),Pen That Never Lied 175.00
8 . . . . 175.00
9 LSt(c),The Amazing Cube . 175.00
10 MMe(c),The Strangest Show On Earth 175.00
11 LSt(c),Who Am I? 100.00
12 JK,Four Threads of Doom . . 100.00
13 JK(c),Weapons of Destiny . . 100.00
14 SMo(c),The Forbidden Game 90.00
15 JK,MMe,Three Wishes to Doom 100.00
16 JK,The Magic Hammer 100.00
17 JK,Who Is Mr. Ashtar? 100.00
18 JK(c),MMe,A Man Without A World 100.00
19 NC,Man From Two Worlds . . 90.00
20 NC(c),The Earth Gladiator . . 90.00
21 JK,The Living Phantoms 90.00
22 JK(c),The Man From Robot Island 90.00
23 JK,The Invitation From Mars! 90.00
24 LC,The Secret Of Planetoid Zero! 90.00
25 The Sorcerer's Asteroid! 90.00
26 MMe,The Frozem City 90.00
27 MMe,The Prison In Space . . 90.00
28 The Melting Planet 90.00
29 The Phantom Raider 90.00
30 The Jinxed Planet 90.00
31 RH,Keep Off Our Planet 75.00
32 Great Space Cruise Mystery . 75.00
33 The Man Of 1,000 Planets . . 75.00
34 Ambush In Outer Space 75.00
35 MMe,I Was A Space Refugee! 75.00
36 The Curse Of The Galactic Goodess 75.00
37 The Secret Prisoners Of Planet 13 . . . . 75.00
38 The Stunt Man Of Space . . . 75.00
39 The Creatures From The Space Globe 75.00
40 B:Space Ranger,The Last Days Of Planet Mars! 650.00
41 SMo(c),The Destroyers From The Stars! 250.00
42 The Secret Of The Martian Helmet 250.00
43 The Riddle Of The Burning Treasures,I:Space Ranger 500.00
44 DD&SMo(c),The Menace Of The Indian Aliens 150.00
45 DD&SMo(c),The Sheriff From Jupiter 150.00
46 DD&SMo(c),The Duplicate Doom! 150.00
47 DD(c),The Man Who Stole The Solar System 100.00
48 Bring 'Em Back Alive- From Space 100.00
49 RH,The Fantastic Lunar-Land 100.00
50 MA,King Barney The Ape . . 100.00
51 Planet Earth For Sale 90.00
52 Prisoner On Pluto 90.00
53 Interplanetary Trouble Shooter 90.00
54 The Ugly Sleeper Of Klanth, Dinosaur 100.00
55 The Interplanetary Creature Trainer 90.00
56 B:Spaceman At Work,Invaders From Earth 90.00
57 The Jungle Beasts Of Jupiter 90.00
58 The Boss Of The Saturnian Legion 90.00
59 The Man Who Won A World . 90.00
60 School For Space Sleuths . . 90.00
61 The Mystery Of The Mythical Monsters 75.00
62 The Menace Of The Red Snow Crystals 75.00
63 Death To Planet Earth 75.00
64 Boy Usurper Of Planet Zonn . 75.00
65 The Creature That Couldn't Exist 75.00
66 MMe,Trap Of The Space Convict 75.00
67 The Giant That Devoured A Village 75.00
68 Braggart From Planet Brax . . 40.00
69 Doom On Holiday Asteroid . . 40.00
70 The Hermit Of Planetoid X . . 40.00
71 Manhunt In Galaxy G-2! 40.00
72 The Creature Of 1,000 Dooms 40.00
73 The Convict Defenders Of Space! 40.00
74 Prison Camp On Asteroid X-3! 40.00
75 The Hobo Jungle Of Space . . 40.00
76 The Warrior Of Two Worlds! . 40.00
77 Dateline-Outer Space 40.00
78 The Siren Of Space 40.00
79 Big Show On Planet Earth! . . 40.00
80 The Creature Tamer! 40.00
81 His Alien Master! 40.00
82 Give Us Back Our Earth!, E:Space Ranger 40.00
83 DD&SMo(c),The Anti-Hex Merchant! 30.00
84 DD&SMo(c),The Menace Of The 50-Fathom Men 30.00
85 JkS(c),The Man Who Stole My Powers,B:Green Glob 30.00
86 DD&SMo(c),They'll Never Take Me Alive! 25.00
87 JkS(c),The Manhunt Through Two Worlds 25.00
88 DD&SMo(c),GK,The Fear Master 25.00
89 DD,SMo(c),Nightmare on Mars 25.00
90 JkS(c),The Hero Of 5,000 BC 25.00
91 JkS(c),The Prophetic Mirages, I:Automan 25.00
92 The Man Who Dared To Die! 25.00
93 JkS(c),Prisoners Of Hate Island 25.00
94 The Monster Mayor - USA . . 25.00
95 The Secret Of Chameleo-Man 25.00
96 Wanted For Murder...1966... 6966 . . . . 25.00
97 One Month To Die 25.00
98 Half-Man/Half Machine 25.00
99 JkS(c),Nuclear Super-Hero! . 25.00
100 Judy Blonde, Secret Agent! . 25.00

101 The Man in The Liquid Mask! 20.00
102 Bang!Bang! You're Dead .. 20.00
103 JA,ABC To Disaster 20.00
104 NA(c),Master Of The Voodoo Machine 20.00

Becomes:

UNEXPECTED, THE

February-March, 1968

105 The Night I Watched Myself Die 15.00
106 B:Johnny Peril,The Doorway Into Time 10.00
107 MD,JkS(c),The Whip Of Fear! 12.00
108 JkS(c),Journey To A Nightmare 10.00
109 JkS(c),Baptism By Starfire! . 10.00
110 NA(c),Death Town, U.S.A.! . 15.00
111 NC(c),Mission Into Eternity . 10.00
112 NA(c),The Brain Robbers! .. 15.00
113 NA(c),The Shriek Of Vengeance 15.00
114 NA(c),My Self-My Enemy! . 15.00
115 BWr,NA(c),Diary Of A Madman 15.00
116 NC(c),Express Train To Nowhere! 10.00
117 NC(c),Midnight Summons The Executioner! 10.00
118 NA(c),A:Judge Gallows,Play A Tune For Treachery 15.00
119 BWr,NC(c),Mirror,Mirror On The Wall 12.00
120 NC(c),Rambeau's Revenge . 10.00
121 BWr,NA(c),Daddy's Gone-A-Hunting 16.00
122 WW,DG(c),The Phantom Of The Woodstock Festival .. 12.00
123 NC(c),Death Watch! 10.00
124 NA(c),These Walls Shall Be Your Grave 15.00
125 NC(c),Screech Of Guilt! 8.00
126 ATh,NC(c),You Are Cordially Invited To Die! 10.00
127 GT,JK,ATh,NC(c),Follow The Piper To Your Grave 10.00
128 DW,BWr,NC(c),Where Only The Dead Are Free! 12.00
129 NC(c),Farewell To A Fading Star 8.00
130 NC(c),One False Step 8.00
131 NC(c),Run For Your Death! .. 8.00
132 MD,GT,NC(c),The Edge Of Madness 10.00
133 WW,JkS(c),A:Judge Gallows, Agnes Doesn't Haunt Here Anymore! 12.00
134 GT,NC(c),The Restless Dead 10.00
135 NC(c),Death, Come Walk With Me! 8.00
136 SMo,GT,NC(c),An Incident of Violence 10.00
137 WW,NC(c),Dark Vengeance! 12.00
138 WW,NC(c),Strange Secret of the Huan Shan Idol 12.00
139 GT,NC(c),The 2 Brains of Beast Bracken! 10.00
140 JkS(c),The Anatomy of Hate . 8.00
141 NC(c),Just What Did Eric See? 8.00
142 NC(c),Let The Dead Sleep! .. 8.00
143 NC(c),Fear is a Nameless Voice 8.00
144 NC(c),The Dark Pit of Dr. Hanley 8.00
145 NC(c),Grave of Glass 6.00
146 NC(c),The Monstrosity! 6.00
147 NC(c),The Daughter of Dr. Jekyll 6.00
148 NC(c),Baby Wants Me Dead! 6.00
149 NC(c),To Wake the Dead ... 6.00
150 NC(c),No One Escapes From Gallows Island 6.00
151 NC(c),Sorry, I'm Not Ready To Die! 6.00
152 GT,NC(c),Death Wears Many Faces 8.00
153 NC(c),Who's That Sleeping In My Grave? 6.00
154 NC(c),Murder By Madness .. 6.00
155 NC(c),Non-Stop Journey Into Fear 6.00
156 NC(c),A Lunatic Is Loose Among Us! 6.00
157 NC(c),The House of the Executioner 6.00
158 NC(c),Reserved for Madmen Only 6.00
159 NC(c),A Cry in the Night ... 6.00
160 NC(c),Death of an Exorcist .. 6.00
161 BWr,NC(c),Has Anyone Seen My Killer 10.00
162 JK,NC(c),I'll Bug You To Your Grave 7.00
163 DD,LD(c),Room For Dying .. 5.00
164 House of the Sinister Sands . 5.00
165 LD(c),Slayride in July 5.00
166 LD(c),The Evil Eyes of Night . 5.00
167 LD(c),Scared Stiff 5.00
168 LD(c),Freak Accident 5.00
169 LD(c),What Can Be Worse Than Dying? 5.00
170 LD(c),Flee To Your Grave ... 5.00
171 LD(c),I.O.U. One Corpse 5.00
172 LD(c),Strangler in Paradise .. 5.00
173 LD(c),What Scared Sally? ... 5.00
174 LD(c),Gauntlet of Fear 5.00
175 LD(c),The Haunted Mountain 5.00
176 JkS(c),Having A Wonderful Crime 5.00
177 ECh(c),Reward for the Wicked 5.00
178 LD(c),Fit To Kill! 5.00
179 LD(c),My Son, The Mortician . 5.00
180 GT,LD(c),The Loathsome Lodger of Nightmare Inn 7.00
181 LD(c),Hum of the Haunted .. 5.00
182 LD(c),Sorry, This Coffin is Occupied 5.00
183 LD(c),The Dead Don't Always Die 5.00
184 LD(c),Wheel of Misfortune! .. 5.00
185 LD(c),Monsters from a Thousand Fathoms 5.00
186 LD(c),To Catch a Corpse ... 5.00
187 LD(c),Mangled in Madness .. 5.00
188 LD(c),Verdict From The Grave 5.00
189 SD,LD(c),Escape From the Grave 6.00
190 LD(c),The Jigsaw Corpse ... 4.00
191 MR,JO(c),Night of the Voodoo Curse 6.00
192 LD(c),A Killer Cold & Clammy 4.00
193 DW,LD(c),Don't Monkey the Murder 4.00
194 LD(c),Have I Got a Ghoul For You 4.00
195 JCr,LD(c),Whose Face is at My Window 6.00
196 LD(c),The Fear of Number 13 4.00
197 LD(c),Last Laugh of a Corpse 4.00
198 JSn(c),Rage of the Phantom Brain 4.00
199 LD(c),Dracula's Daughter ... 4.00
200 GT,RA&DG(c),A:Johnny Peril, House on the Edge of Eternity 6.00
201 Do Unto Others 4.00
202 JO,LD(c),Death Trap 4.00
203 MK(c),Hang Down Your Head, Joe Mundy 4.00
204 DN,JKu(c),Twinkle, Twinkle Little Star 4.00
205 JkS,A:Johnny Peril,The Second Possession of Angela Lake .. 4.00
206 JkS,A:Johnny Peril,The Ultimate Assassin 4.00
207 JkS,A:Johnny Peril,Secret of the Second Star 4.00
208 JkS,A:Johnny Peril,Factory of Fear 4.00
209 JkS,Game for the Ghastly ... 4.00
210 Vampire of the Apes,Time Warp 4.00
211 A:Johnny Peril,The Temple of the 7 Stars 4.00
212 JkS,MK(c),A:Johnny Peril,The Adventure of the Angel's Smile 4.00
213 A:Johnny Peril,The Woman Who Died Forever 4.00
214 JKu(c),Slaughterhouse Arena 4.00
215 JKu(c),Is Someone Stalking Sandra 4.00
216 GP,JKu(c),Samurai Nightmare 4.00
217 ShM,DSp,EC(c),Dear Senator 4.00
218 KG,ECh&DG(c),I'll Remember You Yesterday 4.00
219 JKu(c),A Wild Tale 4.00
220 ShM,JKu(c),The Strange Guide 4.00
221 SD,ShM,JKu(c),Em the Energy Monster 4.00
222 KG,SD(c),May, 1982 .... 4.00

TALOS OF THE WILDERNESS

1 GK,special 2.00

TARZAN

April, 1972

(Previously published by Gold Key)

207 JKu,O:Tarzan Pt.1 .... 5.00
208 JKu,O:Tarzan Pt.2 .... 3.00
209 JKu,O:Tarzan Pt.3 .... 3.00
210 JKu,O:Tarzan Pt.4 .... 3.00
211 thru 257 .... @2.00
258 February, 1977 .... 2.00

TARZAN FAMILY

November-December, 1975

(Formerly: Korak, Son of Tarzan)

60 B:Korak 1.00
61 thru 66 Nov.-Dec.,1976 .... @1.00

TEAM TITANS

1 KM,Total Chaos#3,A:New Titans, Deathstroke,V:Lord Chaos, BU:KGa,Killowat 2.50
1a BU:AV(i),Mirage 2.50
1b BU:MN,GP,Nightrider 2.50
1c BU:AH,Redwing 2.50
1d BU:GP(i),Terra 2.50
2 KM,Total Chaos#6,A:New Titans, V:Chaos,C:Battalion ... 2.00
3 KM,Total Chaos#9,V:Lord Chaos, A:New Titans 2.00
4 KM,Titans Sell-Out#4, J:Battalion, Troia 2.00
5 KM,A:Battalion 2.00
6 ANi,A:Battalion 2.00
7 PJ,I:Nightwing of 2001 ...... 2.00
8 PJ,A:Raven 2.00
9 PJ,V:Bloodwing 2.00
10 PJ,V:Vampiric Creatures 2.00
11 PJ,F:Battalion 2.00
12 PJ,F:Battalion 2.00
13 PJ,New Direction 2.00
14 PJ,V:Clock King,Chronos,Calander Man,Time Commander 2.00
15 PJ, ... 2.00
16 PJ,F:Nightrider 2.00
17 PJ,A:Deathwing 2.00
18 IR:Leader 2.00
19 V:Leader 2.00
20 PJ,V:Lazarium 2.00
21 PJ,V:US Government 2.00
22 PJ,A:Chimera 1.95
Ann.#1 I:Chimera 3.50
Ann.#2 PJ,Elseworlds Story 3.75

TEEN BEAT

November-December, 1967

1 Monkees photo 17.00

Becomes:

TEEN BEAM

2 Monkees 14.00

Teen Titans (1st Series) #19
© DC Comics, Inc.

TEEN TITANS [1st Series]
January, 1966

1 NC,Titans join Peace Corps . 150.00
2 NC,I:Garn Akaru 70.00
3 NC,I:Ding Dong Daddy 40.00
4 NC,A:Speedy 40.00
5 NC,I:Ant 40.00
6 NC,A:Beast Boy 28.00
7 NC,I:Mad Mod 29.00
8 IN/JAb,I:Titans Copter 29.00
9 NC,A:Teen Titan Sweatshirts . 29.00
10 NC,I:Bat-Bike 29.00
11 IN/NC A:Speedy 26.00
12 NC,in Spaceville 21.00
13 NC,Christmas story 21.00
14 NC,I:Gargoyle 21.00
15 NC,I:Capt. Rumble 21.00
16 NC,I:Dimension X 21.00
17 NC,A:Mad Mod 21.00
18 NC,1:Starfire (Russian) 25.00
19 GK,WW,J:Speedy 21.00
20 NA,NC J:Joshua 23.00
21 NA,NC,A:Hawk,Dove 23.00
22 NA,NC,O:Wondergirl 23.00
23 GK,NC,N:Wondergirl 12.00
24 GK,NC 12.00
25 NC,I:Lilith,A:J.L.A 12.00
26 NC,I:Mal 14.00
27 NC 12.00
28 NC,A:Ocean Master 12.00
29 NC,A:Ocean Master 12.00
30 NC,A:Aquagirl 12.00
31 NC,GT,A:Hawk,Dove 12.00
32 NC,I:Gnarrk 9.00
33 GT,NS,A:Gnarrk 9.00
34 GT,NC 9.00
35 GT,NC,O:Mal 9.00
36 GT,NC,JAp,V:Hunchback 9.00
37 GT,NC 9.00
38 GT,NC 9.00
39 GT,NC,Rep.Hawk & Dove 9.00
40 NC,A:Aqualad 9.00
41 NC,DC,Lilith Mystery 9.00
42 NC 9.00
43 NC,Inherit the Howling Night . . 9.00
44 C:Flash 9.00
45 IN,V:Fiddler 9.00
46 IN,A:Fiddler 12.00
47 C:Two-Face 6.00
48 I:Bumblebee,Harlequin,
A:Two-Face 11.00
49 R:Mal As Guardian 6.00
50 DH,I:Teen Titans West 10.00
51 DH,A:Teen Titans West 6.00
52 DH,A:Teen Titans West 6.00
53 O:Teen Titans, A:JLA 8.00

TEEN TITANS SPOTLIGHT
August, 1986

1 DCw,DG,Starfire "Apartheid" . . 1.50
2 DCw,DG,Starfire Apartheid#2 . 1.00
3 RA,Jericho 1.00
4 RA,Jericho 1.00
5 RA,Jericho 1.00
6 RA,Jericho 1.00
7 JG,Hawk 1.50
8 JG,Hawk 1.00
9 Changeling 1.00
10 EL,Aqualad And Mento 1.50
11 JO,Brotherhood of Evil 1.00
12 EC,Wondergirl 1.00
13 Cyborg 1.00
14 1stNightwing/Batman
Team-up 2.50
15 EL,Omega Men 1.50
16 Thunder And Lightning 1.00
17 DH,Magennta 1.00
18 ATi,Aqualad,A:Aquaman 1.50
19 Starfire,A:Harbinger,Millenium
X-over 1.00
20 RT(i),Cyborg 1.00
21 DSp,Flashback sty w/orig.Teen
Titans 1.25

TEMPUS FUGITIVE
1990

1 KSy,Time Travel,I:Ray 27 . . . . 4.95
2 KSy,Viet Nam 4.95
3 KSy,World War I 4.95
4 KSy,final issue 4.95

3-D Batman © DC Comics, Inc.

3-D BATMAN
1953, 1966

1 rep.Batman #42 & #48 . . . . 700.00
1a A:Tommy Tomorrow (1966) 250.00

THRILLER
November, 1983

1 TVE 1.75
2 TVE,O:Thriller 1.50
3 TVE 1.50
4 TVE 1.50
5 TVE,DG,Elvis satire 1.50
6 TVE,Elvis satire 1.50
7 TVE 1.50
8 TVE 1.50
9 TVE 1.50
10 TVE 1.50
11 AN 1.50
12 AN 1.50

TIMBER WOLF

1 AG(i),V:Thrust 2.00
2 V:Captain Flag 1.50
3 AG(i),V:Creeper 1.50
4 AG(i),V:Captain Flag 1.50
5 AG(i),V:Dominators,Capt.Flag . 1.50

TIME MASTERS
February, 1990

1 ATi,O:Rip Hunter,A:JLA 2.50
2 ATi,A:Superman 2.00
3 ATi,A:Jonah Hex, Cave Carson 2.00
4 ATi,Animal Man #22 x-over . . . 2.00
5 ATi,A:Viking Prince 2.00
6 ATi,A:Dr.Fate 2.00
7 ATi,A:GrLantern,Arion 2.00
8 ATi,V:Vandal Savage 2.00

TITANS SELL-OUT SPECIAL

1 SE,AV,I:Teeny Titans,
w/Nightwing poster 3.75

TIME WARP
October-November, 1979

1 JAp,RB,SD,MK(c),DN,TS 15.00
2 DN,JO,TS,HC,SD,MK(c),GK . 10.00
3 DN,SD,MK(c),TS 10.00
4 MN,SD,MK(c),DN 10.00
5 DN,MK(c),July 1980 . . . . 1.00

TOMAHAWK
September-October, 1950

1 Prisoner Called Tomahawk . 700.00
2 FF(4pgs),Four Boys
Against the Frontier 350.00
3 Warpath 225.00
4 Tomahawk Wanted: Dead
or Alive 225.00
5 The Girl Who Was Chief . . . 225.00
6 Tomahawk-King of the Aztecs 175.00
7 Punishment of Tomahawk . 175.00
8 The King's Messenger 175.00
9 The Five Doomed Men 175.00
10 Frontied Sabotage 175.00
11 Girl Who Hated Tomahawk . 150.00
12 Man From Magic Mountain . 150.00
13 Dan Hunter's Rival 150.00
14 The Frontier Tinker 150.00
15 The Wild Men of
Wigwam Mountain 150.00
16 Treasure of the Angelique . . 150.00
17 Short-Cut to Danger 150.00
18 Bring In M'Sieur Pierre 150.00
19 The Lafayette Volunteers . . 150.00
20 NC(c),The Retreat of
Tomahawk 150.00
21 NC(c),The Terror of the
Wrathful Spirit 100.00
22 CS(c),Admiral Tomahawk . . 100.00
23 CS(c),The Indian Chief
From Oxford 100.00
24 NC(c),Adventure In the
Everglades 100.00
25 NC(c),The Star-Gazer of
Freemont 100.00
26 NC(c),Ten Wagons For
Tomahawk 100.00
27 NC(c),Frontier Outcast 100.00
28 I:Lord Shilling 125.00
29 The Conspiracy of Wounded
Bear 150.00
30 The King of the Thieves . . 100.00
31 NC(c),The Buffalo Brave
From Misty Mountain 75.00
32 NC(c),The Clocks That
Went to War 75.00
33 The Paleface Tribe 75.00
34 The Capture of General

Washington 75.00
35 Frontier Feud 75.00
36 NC(c),A Cannon for Fort Reckless 75.00
37 NC(c),The Feathered Warriors 75.00
38 The Frontier Zoo 75.00
39 The Redcoat Trickster 75.00
40 Fearless Fettle-Daredevil . . 75.00
41 The Captured Chieftain 75.00
42 The Prisoner Tribe 75.00
43 Tomahawk's Little Brother . . . 75.00
44 The Brave Named Tomahawk 75.00
45 The Last Days of Chief Tory . 75.00
46 The Chief With 1,000 Faces . 50.00
47 The Frontier Rain-Maker 50.00
48 Indian Twin Trouble 50.00
49 The Unknown Warrior 50.00
50 The Brave Who Was Jinxed . 50.00
51 General Tomahawk 50.00
52 Tom Thumb of the Frontier . . 50.00
53 The Four-Footed Renegade . 50.00
54 Mystery of the 13th Arrows . . 50.00
55 Prisoners of the Choctaw . . . 50.00
56 The Riddle of the Five Little Indians 50.00
57 The Strange Fight at Fort Bravo 75.00
58 Track of the Mask 35.00
59 The Mystery Prisoner of Lost Island 35.00
60 The Amazing Walking Fort . . 35.00
61 Tomahawk's Secret Weapons 35.00
62 Strongest Man in the World . 35.00
63 The Frontier Super Men 35.00
64 The Outcast Brave 35.00
65 Boy Who Wouldn't Be Chief . 35.00
66 DD&SMo(c),A Trap For Tomahawk 35.00
67 DD&SMo(c),Frontier Sorcerer 35.00
68 DD&SMo(c),Tomahawk's Strange Ally 35.00
69 DD&SMo(c),Tracker-King of the Wolves 35.00
70 DD&SMo(c),Three Tasks for Tomahawk 35.00
71 DD&SMo(c),The Boy Who Betrayed His Country 35.00
72 DD&SMo(c),The Frontier Pupil 35.00
73 DD&SMo(c),The Secret of the Indian Sorceress 35.00
74 DD&SMo(c),The Great Paleface Masquerade 35.00
75 DD&SMo(c),The Ghost of Lord Shilling 35.00
76 DD&SMo(c),The Totem-Pole Trail 35.00
77 DD&SMo(c),The Raids of the One-Man Tribe 35.00
78 DD&SMo(c),The Menace of the Mask 35.00
79 DD&SMo(c),Eagle Eye's Debt of Honor 35.00
80 DD&SMo(c),The Adventures of Tracker 25.00
81 The Strange Omens of the Indian Seer 25.00
82 The Son of the Tracker 25.00
83 B:Tomahawk Rangers,20 Against the Tribe 25.00
84 There's a Coward Among the Rangers 25.00
85 The Wispering War 25.00
86 Rangers vs. King Colossus . . 15.00
87 The Secrets of Sgt. Witch Doctor 15.00
88 The Rangers Who Held Back the Earth 15.00
89 The Terrible Tree-Man 15.00
90 The Prisoner In The Pit 15.00
91 The Tribe Below the Earth . . 15.00
92 The Petrified Sentry of Peaceful Valley 15.00
93 The Return of King Colosso . 15.00
94 Rip Van Ranger 15.00
95 The Tribe Beneath the Sea . . 15.00

Tomahawk #6 © DC Comics, Inc.

96 The Ranger Killers 15.00
97 The Prisoner Behind the Bull's-Eye 15.00
98 The Pied Piper Rangers 15.00
99 The Rangers vs. Chief Cobweb15.00
100 The Weird Water-Tomahawk 15.00
101 Tomahawk, Enemy Spy . . . 10.00
102 The Dragon Killers 10.00
103 The Frontier Frankenstein . . 10.00
104 The Fearful Freak of Dunham's Dungeon 10.00
105 The Attack of the Gator God 10.00
106 The Ghost of Tomahawk . . . 10.00
107 Double-Cross of the Gorilla Ranger 10.00
108 New Boss For the Rangers . 10.00
109 The Caveman Ranger 10.00
110 Tomahawk Must Die 10.00
111 Vengeance of the Devil-Dogs 6.00
112 The Rangers vs. Tomahawk . 6.00
113 The Mad Miser of Carlisle Castle 6.00
114 The Terrible Power of Chief Iron Hands 6.00
115 The Deadly Flaming Ranger . 6.00
116 NA(c),The Last Mile of Massacre Trail 6.00
117 NA(c),Rangers'Last Stand . . . 6.00
118 NA(c),Tomahawk, Guilty of Murder 6.00
119 NA(c),Bait For a Buzzard . . . 6.00
120 NC(c),The Coward Who Lived Forever 6.00
121 NA(c),To Kill a Ranger 6.00
122 IN(c),Must the Brave Die 6.00
123 NA(c),The Stallions of Death . 6.00
124 NA(c),The Valley of No Return 6.00
125 NA(c),A Chief's Feather For Little Bear 6.00
126 NA(c),The Baron of Gallows Hill 6.00
127 NA(c),The Devil is Waiting . . 6.00
128 NA(c),Rangers-Your 9 Lives For Mine 6.00
129 NA(c),Treachery at Thunder Ridge 6.00
130 NA(c),Deathwatch at Desolation Valley 6.00
131 JKu(c),B:Son of Tomahawk, Hang Him High 6.00
132 JKu(c),Small Eagle...Brother Hawk 3.00
133 JKu(c),Scalp Hunter 3.00
134 JKu(c),The Rusty Ranger . . . 3.00
135 JKu(c),Death on Ghost Mountain 3.00
136 JKu(c),A Piece of Sky 3.00
137 JKu(c),Night of the Knife 3.00
138 JKu(c),A Different Kind of Christmas 3.00
139 JKu(c),Death Council 3.00
140 Jku(c),The Rescue, May-June, 1972 . . . . 3.00

TOR

May-June, 1975

1 JKu,O:Tor 1.00
2 thru Tor reprint 6 . . . . @1.00

TOTAL RECALL

1 Movie Adaption 3.00

TSR WORLDS

TSR

1 I:SpellJammer 4.50

TV SCREEN CARTOONS

(see REAL SCREEN COMICS)

TWILIGHT

1 JL,Last Frontier 5.50
2 JL,K.SorensenVs.T.Tomorrow . 4.95
3 JL,K.SorensenVs.T.Tomorrow (Conclusion) 4.95

UNAUTHORIZED BIO OF LEX LUTHOR

1 EB 3.95

UNDERWORLD

December, 1987

1 EC,New Yorks Finest 1.00
2 EC,A:Black Racer 1.00
3 EC,V:Black Racer 1.00
4 EC,final issue 1.00

UNEXPECTED, THE

(see TALES OF THE UNEXPECTED)

UNKNOWN SOLDIER

(see STAR SPANGLED)

UNKNOWN SOLDIER

April, 1977

1 True Origin revealed,Viet Nam 1970 . . . . 1.50
2 Origin contd.,Iran 1977 . . . . . . 1.50
3 Origin contd.Afghanistan1982 . 1.50
4 Nicaragua 1.50
5 Nicaragua contd. 1.50
6 . . . . 1.50
7 Libia 1.50
8 Siberia, U.S.S.R. 1.75
9 North Korea 1952 . . . . 1.75
10 C.I.A. 1.75
11 C.I.A., Army Intelligence 1.75
12 final issue,Oct.1982 . . . . 1.75

UNTOLD LEGEND OF BATMAN

July, 1980

1 JA,JBy,(1st DC work)O:Batman 6.00
2 JA,O:Joker&Robin 4.50
3 JA,O:Batgirl 4.50

V

(TV Adaptation)

February, 1985

1 CI/TD 1.35
2 CI/TD 1.25
3 CI/TD 1.25

All comics prices listed are for *Near Mint* condition.

4 CI/TD 1.25
5 CI/TD 1.00
6 CI/TD 1.00
7 CI/TD 1.00
8 CI/TD 1.00
9 CI/TD 1.00
10 CI/TD 1.00
11 CI/TD 1.00
12 CI/TD 1.00
13 CI/TD 1.00
14 CI/TD 1.00
15 CI/TD 1.00
16 CI/TD 1.00
17 DG 1.00
18 DG 1.00

V FOR VENDETTA

September, 1988

1 Reps.Warrior Mag(U.K.),I:V,
A:M.Storm (Moore scripts) . . . 5.00
2 Murder Spree 3.50
3 Govt. Investigators close in . . . 3.00
4 T.V. Broadcast take-over 3.00
5 Govt.Corruption Expose 3.00
6 Evey in Prison 3.00
7 Evey released 2.50
8 Search for V,A:Finch 2.50
9 V:Finch 2.50
10 D:V 2.50
TPB 1990 . . . . 14.95

Valor #1 © DC Comics, Inc.

VALOR

1 N:Valor,A:Lex Luthor Jr 2.00
2 MBr,AG,V:Supergirl 1.50
3 MBr,AG,V:Lobo 1.50
4 MBr,AG,V:Lobo 1.50
5 MBr,A:Blasters 1.50
6 A:Blasters,V:Kanjar Ru 1.50
7 A:Blasters 1.50
8 AH(c),V:The Unimaginable . . . 1.50
9 AH(c),PCu,A:Darkstar 1.50
10 AH(c),V:Unimaginable 1.50
11 A:Legionnaires 1.50
12 AH(c),B:D.O.A. 4.00
13 AH(c),D:Valor's Mom 3.50
14 AH(c),A:JLA,Legionnaires 2.50
15 SI(c),D.O.A #4. . . . . 2.00
16 CDo,D.O.A #5. . . . . 2.00
17 CDo,LMc,D:Valor 1.75
18 A:Legionnaires 1.75
19 CDo,A:Legionnaires,V:Glorith . 1.75
20 CDo,A:Wave Rider 1.75
21 . . . . 1.50

VERTIGO JAM

1 GF(c),NGa(s),ANo(s),PrM(s),GEn(s),
JaD(s),KN,SDi,SEa,NyC(s),EiS,PhH,
KDM(i),SeP,MiA,RaP(s),MPn(i),
Vertigo Short Stories 4.50

VERTIGO PREVIEW

Preview of new Vertigo titles,
new Sandman story 1.75

VERTIGO VISIONS: DR. OCCULT

1 F:Dr. Occult 3.95

VERTIGO VISIONS: THE GEEK

1 RaP(s),MiA,V:Dr.Abuse 4.25

VERTIGO VISIONS: PHANTOM STRANGER

1 AaK(s),GyD,The Infernal House 3.75

VIGILANTE, THE

October, 1983

1 KP,DG,F:Adrian Chase 3.50
2 KP 3.00
3 KP,Cyborg 2.50
4 DN,V:Exterminator 2.50
5 KP 2.50
6 O:Vigilante 3.00
7 O:Vigilante 3.00
8 RA,V:Electrocutioner 2.50
9 RA,V:Electrocutioner 2.50
10 RA,DG,avenges J.J. 2.50
11 RA,V:Controller 2.00
12 GK,"Journal" 2.00
13 GK,"Locke Room Murder" 2.00
14 RA,V:Hammer 2.00
15 RA,V:Electrocutioner 2.00
16 RA 2.00
17 Moore 3.00
18 Moore 3.00
19 RA 2.00
20 A:Nightwing 2.50
21 A:Nightwing 2.50
22 . . . . 2.00
23 V:Electrocutioner 2.00
24 "Mother's Day" 2.00
25 RM,V:Police Torturers 2.00
26 V:Electrocutioner 2.00
27 V:Electrocutioner 2.00
28 New Vigilante 2.00
29 RM,New Vigilante 2.00
30 RM,D:Glitz Jefferson 2.00
31 RM,New York Violence 2.00
32 RM,New York Violence 2.00
33 RM,V:Rapist 2.00
34 . . . . 2.00
35 JBy(c),O:MadBomber 2.00
36 MGr(c),V:Peacemaker 2.25
37 MGr,RM,V:Peacemaker 2.25
38 MGr,PeaceMaker 2.25
39 White Slavery 2.00
40 HC(c),White Slavery 2.00
41 . . . . 2.00
42 A:Peacemaker,V:Terrorists . . . 2.00
43 V:PeaceMaker 2.00
44 DC,V:Qurac 2.00
45 I:Black Thorn 2.00
46 Viigilante in Jail 2.00
47 A:Batman 2.50
48 I:Homeless Avenger 2.00
49 . . . . 2.00
50 KSy(c)D:Vigilante 2.50
Ann.#1 . . . . 3.00
Ann.#2 V:Cannon 2.50

WANDERERS

June, 1988

1 I:New Team 1.25
2 V:The Performer 1.25
3 A:Legion of Superheroes 1.25
4 V:Controller Hunters 1.25
5 O:Wanderers 1.25
6 V:Terrorists 1.25
7 V:Medtorians 1.25
8 O:Psyche 1.25
9 O:Psyche 1.25
10 F:Quantum Queen 1.25
11 F:Quantum Queen 1.25
12 V:Aliens 1.25
13 V:Dinosaurs 1.25

WANTED: THE WORLD'S MOST DANGEROUS VILLIANS

July-August, 1972

1 rep. Batman,Green Lantern . . . 4.00
2 Batman/Joker/Penguin 5.00
3 . . . . 3.00
4 . . . . 3.00
5 . . . . 3.00
6 . . . . 3.00
7 . . . . 3.00
8 . . . . 3.00
9 . . . . 3.00

WARLORD

January, 1976

1 MGr,O:Warlord 16.00
2 MGr,I:Machiste 9.00
3 MGr,'War Gods of Skartaris' . . 7.00
4 MGr,'Duel of the Titans' 6.50
5 MGr,'The Secret of Skartaris' . . 6.50
6 MGr,I:Mariah,Stryker 6.00
7 MGr,O:Machiste 5.50
8 MGr,A:Skyra 5.50
9 MGr,N:Warlord 5.50
10 MGr,I:Ashiya 6.00
11 MGr,rep.1stIssue special#8 . . . 5.00
12 MGr,I:Aton 5.00
13 MGr,D:Stryker 5.00
14 MGr,V:Death 5.00
15 MGr,I:Joshua 5.00
16 MGr,I:Saaba 5.00
17 MGr,'Citadel of Death' 5.00
18 MGr,I:Shadow 5.00
19 MGr,'Wolves of the Steppes' . . 5.00
20 MGr,I:Joshua clone 5.00
21 MGr,D:Joshua clone,Shadow . 3.00
22 MGr'Beast in the Tower' 3.00
23 MGr,'Children of Ba'al' 3.00
24 MGr,I:ligia 3.00
25 MGr,I:Ahir 3.00
26 MGr,'The Challenge' 3.00
27 MGr,'Atlantis Dying' 3.00
28 MGr,I:Wizard World' 3.00
29 MGr,I:Mongo Ironhand' 3.00
30 MGr,C:Joshua 3.00
31 MGr,'Wing over Shamballah' . . 3.00
32 MGr,I:Shakira 3.00
33 MGr,Birds of Prey,
A:Shakira 3.00
34 MGr,Sword of the Sorceror,
I:Hellfire 3.00
35 MGr,C:Mike Grell 3.00
36 MGr,'Interlude' 3.00
37 MGr,JSn,I:Firewing,B:Omac . . 6.00
38 MGr,I:Jennifer,A:Omac 3.00
39 MGr,JSn,'Feast of Agravar' . . . 4.00
40 MGr,N:Warlord 3.00
41 MGr,A:Askir 2.50
42 MGr,JSn,A:Tara,Omac 3.50
43 MGr,JSn,'Berserk'A:Omac . . . 3.50
44 MGr,'The Gamble' 3.00
45 MGr,'Nightmare in Vista
Vision',A:Omac 3.00
46 MGr,D:Shakira 3.00
47 MGr,I:Mikola,E:Omac 3.00
48 MGr,EC,TY,I:Arak,Claw(B) . . . 3.00
49 MGr,TY,A:Shakira,E:Claw 2.50
50 MGr,'By Fire and Ice' 2.50
51 MGr,TY,rep.#1,
I(B):Dragonsword 1.50

52 MGr,TY,'Back in the U.S.S.R. . 2.50
53 MT,TY,'Sorcerer's Apprentice' . 1.50
54 MT,'Sorceress Supreme',
E:Dragonsword 1.50
55 MT,'Have a Nice Day' 1.50
56 MT,JD,I:Gregmore,(B:)Arion . . 1.50
57 MT,'The Two Faces of
Travis Morgan' 1.50
58 MT,O:Greamore 1.50
59 MGr,A:Joshua 2.00
60 JD,'Death Dual' 1.50
61 JD,A:Greamore 1.50
62 JD,TMd,A:Mikola,E:Arion 1.50
63 JD,RR,I(B):Barren Earth 1.50
64 DJu,RR'Elsewhere' 1.50
65 DJu,RR,A:Wizard World,
No Barren Earth 2.00
66 DJu'Wizard World',
No Barren Earth 2.00
67 DJu,RR,'The Mark' 1.50
68 DJu,RR 1.50
69 DJu,RR 1.50
70 DJu,'Outback' 1.50
71 DJu/DA,'The Journey Back'
No Barren Earth 1.50
72 DJu,DA,I:Scarhart,No Barren
Earth 1.50
73 DJ,DA,'Cry Plague' 1.50
74 DJu,No Barren Earth 1.50
75 DJu,'All Dreams Must Pass'
No Barren Earth 1.50
76 DJu,DA,RR,A:Sarga 1.50
77 DJu,DA,RR,Let My People Go 1.50
78 DJu,RR,'Doom's Mouth' 1.50
79 PB,RM,'Paradox',No Barren
Earth 1.50
80 DJu,DA,RR,'Future Trek' 1.50
81 DJu,DA,RR,'Thief's Magic' . . . 1.50
82 DJu,DA,RR,'Revolution' 1.50
83 DJu,RR,'All the President's
Men' 1.50
84 DJu,DA,RR,'Hail to the Chief' . 1.50
85 DJu,RR,'The Price of Change' 1.50
86 DJ,DA,No Barren Earth 1.50
87 DJu,RB,RR,I:Hawk 1.50
88 DJu,RB,RR,I:Patch,E:Barren
Earth 1.50
89 RB,I:Sabertooth 1.50
90 RB,'Demon's of the Past' 1.50
91 DJu,DA,I:Maddox,O:Warlord
O:Jennifer 1.25
92 NKu,'Evil in Ebony' 1.75
93 RR,A:Sabertooth 1.25
94 'Assassin's Prey' 1.25
95 AKu,'Dragon's Doom' 1.75
96 'Nightmare Prelude' 1.25
97 RB,A:Saaba,D:Scarhart 1.25
98 NKu,Crisis tie-in 1.75
99 NKu'Fire and Sword' 1.75
100 AKu,D:Greamore,Sabertooth . 2.00
101 MGr,'Temple of Demi-god' . . 1.50
102 I:Zuppara,Error-Machiste
with two hands 1.50
103 JBi,'Moon Beast' 1.50
104 RR,'Dragon Skinner' 1.25
105 RR,'Stallers of Skinner' 1.25
106 RR,I:Daimon 1.25
107 RR,'Bride of Yano' 1.25
108 RR,I:Mortella 1.25
109 RR,A:Mortella 1.25
110 RR,A:Skyra III 1.25
111 RR,'Tearing o/t Island Sea' . . 1.25
112 RR,'Obsession' 1.25
113 RR,'Through Fiends
Destroy Me' 1.25
114 RR,'Phenalegeno Dies' 1.25
115 RR,'Citadel of Fear' 1.25
116 RR,'Revenge of the Warlord' . 1.25
117 RR,A:Power Girl 1.25
118 RR,A:Power Girl 1.25
119 RR,A:Power Girl 1.25
120 ATb,A:Power Girl 1.50
121 ATb,A:Power Girl 1.50
122 ATb,A:Power Girl 1.50
123 JD,TMd,N:Warlord 1.25
124 JD,TMd,I:Scavenger 1.25
125 JD,TMd,D:Tara 1.25
126 JD,TMd,A:Machiste 1.25
127 JD,'The Last Dragon' 1.25
128 JD,I:Agife 1.25
129 JD,Vision of Quest 1.25
130 JD,A:Maddox 1.25
131 JD,RLd,'Vengeful Legacies . . 5.00
132 'A New Beginning' 1.25
133 JD,final issue (44pg) 2.00
Ann.#1 MGr,A:Shakira 3.00
Ann.#2 I:Krystovar 1.25
Ann.#3 DJu,'Full Circle' 1.25
Ann.#4 A:New Gods,
Legends tie-in 1.25
Ann.#5 AKu,Hellfire 1.75
TPB Warlord:Savage Empire,
Rep.#1-10,12,Special #8 . . . . 19.95

[Limited Series]

1 Travis Morgan retrospective . . . 1.75
2 Fate of T. Morgan revealed . . . 1.75
3 Return of Deimos 1.75
4 V:Deimos 1.75
5 MGr(c),Skartaros at War 1.75

WAR OF THE GODS

1 GP,A:Lobo,Misc.Heroes,Circe
(direct), ... 1.75
2 GP,A:Misc.Heroes,V:Circe,
w/poster 1.75
2a (Newsstand), ... 1.75
3 GP,A:Misc.Heroes,V:Circe,
w/poster 1.75
3a Newsstand 1.75
4 GP,A:Misc.Heroes,V:Circe,
w/poster 1.75
4a Newsstand 1.75

WASTELAND

December, 1987

1 Selection of Horror stories 1.75
2 . . . . 1.75
3 . . . . 1.75
4 . . . . 1.75
5 'The big crossover story' 1.75
6 . . . . 1.75
7 'Great St.Louis Electrical
Giraffe Caper' 1.75
8 'Dead Detective' 1.75
9 . . . . 1.75
10 TT,African Folk Tale 1.75
11 'Revenge o/t Swamp Creature' 1.75
12 JO,'After the Dead Detective' . 1.75
13 TT(c),JO 2.00
14 JO,RM,'Whistling Past the
Graveyard' 2.00
15 JO,RM 2.00
16 JO 2.00
17 JO 2.00
18 JO,RM,final issue 2.00

WATCHMEN

September, 1986

1 B:AMo,DGb,D:Comedian 7.50
2 DGb,Funeral for Comedian . . . 6.00
3 DGb,F:Dr.Manhattan 5.00
4 DGb,O:Dr.Manhattan 5.00
5 DGb,F:Rorschach 5.00
6 DGb,O:Rorschach 5.00
7 DGb,F:Nite Owl 5.00
8 DGb,F:Silk Spectre 5.00
9 DGb,O:Silk Spectre 5.00
10 DGb,A:Rorschach 5.00
11 DGb,O:Ozymandius 5.00
12 DGb,D:Rorsharch 5.00
TPB rep.#1-12 . . . . 14.95

WEB

Impact

1 I:Gunny, Bill Grady, Templar . . 1.25
2 O:The Web, I:Brew, Jump,
Sunshine Kid 1.00
3 Minions of Meridian, I:St.James 1.00

Watchmen #9 © DC Comics, Inc.

4 Agent Jump vs. UFO 1.00
5 Agent Buster/Fly team-up
V:Meridian 1.00
6 I:Posse,A:Templar 1.00
7 V:Meridian's Forces 1.00
8 R: Studs 1.00
9 Earthquest Pt 1 . . . . 2.50
10 V:Templar 1.25
11 V:Templar 1.25
12 "The Gauntlet",A:Shield 1.25
13 Frenzy#1 . . . . 1.25
14 Frenzy#2 . . . . 1.25
Ann.#1 Earthquest,w/trading card . 2.50

WEIRD, THE

April, 1988

1 BWr,A:JLI 4.00
2 BWr,A:JLI 3.00
3 BWr,V:Jason 3.00
4 final issue 2.50

WEIRD WAR TALES

September-October, 1971

1 JKu(c),JKu,RH,Fort which
Did Not Return 4.00
2 JKu,MD,Military Madness 2.00
3 JKu(c),RA,The Pool 2.00
4 JKu(c),Ghost of Two Wars . . . 2.00
5 JKu(c),RH,Slave 2.00
6 JKu(c),Pawns, The Sounds
of War 2.00
7 JKu(c),JKu,RH,Flying Blind . . . 2.00
8 NA(c),The Avenging Grave . . . 5.00
9 NC(c),The Promise 2.00
10 NC(c),Who is Haunting
the Haunted Chateau 2.00
11 NC(c),ShM,October 30, 1918:
The German Trenches, WWI . . 2.00
12 MK(c),God of Vengeance 2.00
13 LD(c),The Die-Hards 2.00
14 LD(c),ShM,The Ghost of
McBride's Woman 2.00
15 LD(c),Ace King Just Flew
In From Hell 2.00
16 LD(c),More Dead Than Alive . . 2.00
17 GE(c),Dead Man's Hands 2.00
18 GE(c),Captain Dracula 2.00
19 LD(c),The Platoon That
Wouldn't Die 1.50
20 LD(c),Operation Voodoo 1.50
21 LD(c),One Hour To Kill 1.50
22 LD(c),Wings of Death 1.50

23 LD(c),The Bird of Death 1.50
24 LD(c),The Invisible Enemy . . . 1.50
25 LD(c),Black Magic...White Death 1.50
26 LD(c),Jump Into Hell 1.50
27 LD(c),Survival of the Fittest 1.50
28 LD(c),Isle of Forgotten Warriors 1.50
29 LD(c),Breaking Point 1.50
30 LD(c),The Elements of Death . 1.50
31 LD(c),Death Waits Twice 1.50
32 LD(c),The Enemy, The Stars . . 1.50
33 LD(c),Pride of the Master Race 1.50
34 LD(c),The Common Enemy . . . 1.50
35 LD(c),The Invaders 1.50
36 JKu(c),Escape 1.50
37 LD(c),The Three Wars of Don Q 1.50
38 JKu(c),Born To Die 1.50
39 JKu(c),The Spoils of War 1.50
40 ECh(c),Back From The Dead . 1.50
41 JL(c), The Dead Draftees of Regiment Six 1.50
42 JKu(c),Old Soldiers Never Die 1.50
43 ECh(c),Bulletproof 1.50
44 JKu(c),ShM,The Emperor Weehawken 1.50
45 JKu(c),The Battle of Bloody Valley 1.50
46 Kill Or Be Killed 1.50
47 JKu(c),Bloodbath of the Toy Soldiers 1.50
48 JL(c),Ultimate Destiny 1.50
49 The Face Of The Enemy 1.50
50 ECh(c),-An Appointment With Destiny 1.50
51 JKu(c),Secret Weapon 1.50
52 JKu(c),The Devil Is A Souvenir Hunter 1.50
53 JAp(c), Deadly Dominoes 1.50
54 GM(c),Soldier of Satan 1.50
55 JKu(c),A Rebel Shall Rise From The Grave 1.50
56 AM(c),The Headless Courier . . 1.50
57 RT(c),Trial By Combat 1.50
58 JKu(c),Death Has A Hundred Eyes 1.50
59 The Old One 1.50
60 JKu(c),Night Flight 1.50
61 HC(c),Mind War 1.50
62 JKu(c),The Grubbers 1.50
63 JKu(c),Battleground 1.50
64 JKu(c),Deliver Me For D-Day . 1.50
65 JKu(c),The Last Cavalry Charge 1.50
66 JKu(c),The Iron Star 1.50
67 JKu(c),The Attack of the Undead 1.50
68 FM,JKu(c),The Life and Death of Charlie Golem 1.50
69 JKu(c),The Day After Doomsday 1.50
70 LD(c),The Blood Boat 1.50
71 LD(c),False Prophet 1.50
72 JKu(c),Death Camp 1.50
73 GE(c),The Curse of Zopyrus . . 1.50
74 GE(c),March of the Mammoth . 1.50
75 JKu(c),The Forgery 1.50
76 JKu(c),The Fire Bug 1.50
77 JKu(c),Triad 1.50
78 JKu(c),Indian War In Space . . 1.50
79 JKu(c),The Gods Themselves . 1.50
80 JKu(c),An Old Man's Profession 1.50
81 JKu(c),It Takes Brains To Be A Killer 1.50
82 GE(c),Funeral Fire 1.50
83 GE(c),Prison of the Mind 1.50
84 JKu(c),Devil's Due 1.50
85 thru 124 June 1983 . . . . . . @1.50

ALL STAR WESTERN

1 NA(c),CI, ... 12.00
2 NA(c),GM,B:Outlaw 5.00
3 NA(c),GK,O:El Diablo 4.00
4 NA(c),GK,JKu,GM, ... 4.00
5 NA(c),JAp,E:Outlaw 4.00
6 GK,B:Billy the Kid 4.00
7 . . . . 4.00
8 E:Billy the Kid 4.00
9 FF, ... 6.00
10 GM,I:Jonah Hex 110.00
11 GM,A:Jonah Hex 50.00

Becomes: **WEIRD WESTERN TALES**

June-July, 1972

12 NA,BWr,JKu, ... 6.00
13 . . . . 6.00
14 ATh, ... 3.00
15 NA(c),GK, ... 6.00
16 thru 28 . . . . @1.50
29 O:Jonah Hex 8.00
30 . . . . 1.50
31 thru 38 . . . . @1.50
39 I&O:Scalphunter 1.50
40 thru 70 . . . . @1.50

WEIRD WORLDS

August-September, 1971

1 JO,MA,John Carter 10.00
2 NA,JO(c),MA,BWr 15.00
3 MA,NA 12.00
4 MK(c),MK 5.00
5 MK(c),MK 5.00
6 MK(c),MK 5.00
7 John Carter ends 5.00
8 HC,I:Iron Wolf 4.00
9 HC 4.00
10 HC,Last issue 4.00

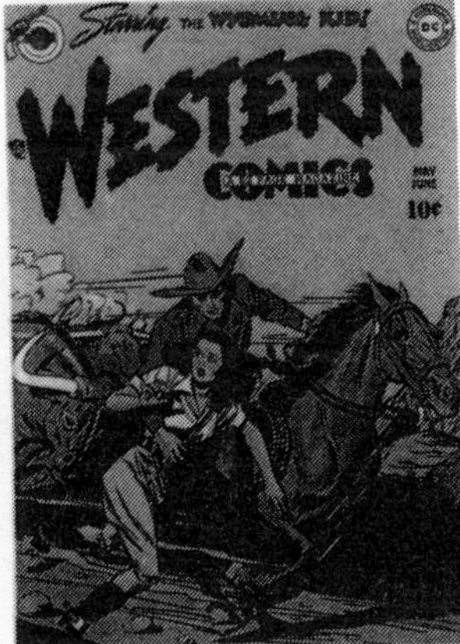

Western Comics #3 © DC Comics, Inc.

WESTERN COMICS

January-February, 1948

1 MMe,B:Vigilante,Podeo Rick, WyomingKid,CowboyMarshal 450.00
2 MMe,Vigilante vs. Dirk Bigger 225.00
3 MMe,Vigilante vs. Pecos Kid 175.00
4 MMe,Vigilante as Pecos Kid 175.00
5 I:Nighthawk 150.00
6 Wyoming Kid vs. 'The Murder Mustang' 125.00
7 Wyoming Kid in 'The Town That Was Never Robbed . . 125.00
8 O:Wyoming Kid 150.00
9 Wyoming Kid vs. Jack Slaughter 125.00
10 Nighthawk in 'Tunnel ofTerror' 125.00
11 Wyoming Kid vs. Mayor Brock 100.00
12 Wyoming Kid vs. Baldy Ryan 100.00
13 I:Running Eagle 100.00
14 Wyoming Kid in 'The Siege of Praire City 100.00
15 Nighthawk in 'Silver, Salt and Pepper 100.00
16 Wyoming Kid vs. Smilin' Jim 100.00
17 BP,Wyoming Kid vs. Prof. Penny 100.00
18 LSt on Nighthawk,WyomingKid in 'Challenge of the Chiefs' . 100.00

Western Comics #35
© DC Comics, Inc.

19 LSt,Nighthawk in 'The Invisible Rustlers 100.00
20 LSt,Nighthawk in 'The Mystery Mail From Defender Dip' 75.00
21 LSt,Nighthawk in 'Rattlesnake Hollow' 75.00
22 LSt,I:Jim Pegton 75.00
23 LSt,Nighthawk reveals ID to Jim 75.00
24 The $100,000 Impersonation . 75.00
25 V:Souix Invaders 75.00
26 The Storming of the Sante Fe Trail 75.00
27 The Looters of Lost Valley . . 75.00
28 The Thunder Creek Rebellion 75.00
29 Six Guns of the Wyoming Kid 75.00
30 V:Green Haired Killer 75.00
31 The Sky Riding Lawman 75.00
32 Death Rides the Stage Coach 75.00
33 . . . . 75.00
34 Prescription For Killers 75.00
35 The River of Rogues 75.00
36 Nighthawk(c),Duel in the Dark 55.00
37 The Death Dancer 65.00
38 Warpath in the Sky 65.00
39 Death to Fort Danger 65.00
40 Blind Man's Bluff 65.00
41 thru 60 . . . . @55.00
61 thru 85 . . . . @40.00

WHO'S WHO

1 . . . . 2.00
2 thru 9 . . . . @1.50
10 inc. 1.25
11 inc. Infinity Inc. 1.25
12 inc. Kamandi 1.25
13 inc. Legion of Super Heroes/ Villains 1.25
14 inc. 1.25
15 inc. Metal Men 1.25

16 inc. New Gods 1.25
17 inc. Outsiders 1.25
18 inc. Power Girl 1.25
19 inc. Robin 1.25
20 inc. 1.25
21 inc. The Spectre 1.25
22 inc. Superman 1.25
23 inc. Teen Titans 1.25
24 inc. Unknown Soldier 1.25
25 inc. 1.25
26 inc. 1.25

WHO'S WHO
(PACKET)

1 inc. Superman 6.00
1a 2nd printing 5.50
2 inc. Flash 5.50
2a 2nd printing 5.00
3 inc. Green Lantern 5.50
4 inc. Wonder Woman 5.50
5 inc. Batman. 5.50
6 inc. Hawkman 5.50
7 inc. Shade 5.50
8 inc. Lobo 6.00
9 inc. Legion of Super-Heroes 5.50
10 inc. Robin 5.50
11 inc. L.E.G.I.O.N. '91 5.50
12 inc. Aquaman 5.50
13 Villains issue, inc. Joker 6.00
14 inc. New Titans 5.50
15 inc. Doom Patrol 5.50
16 inc. Catwoman,final issue 5.00

WHO'S WHO UPDATE 93

1 F:Eclipso,Azrael 5.25

WHO'S WHO IN IMPACT

1 Shield 4.95
2 Black Hood 4.95

WHO'S WHO IN THE LEGION

1 History/Bio of Legionnaires 1.25
2 inc. Dream Girl 1.25
3 inc. Karate Kid 1.25
4 inc. Lightning Lad 1.25
5 inc. Phantom Girl 1.25
6 inc. Timber Wolf 1.25
7 wraparound(c) 1.25

WHO'S WHO IN STAR TREK

1 HC(c) 1.50
2 HC(c) 1.50

WHO'S WHO UPDATE '87

1 inc. Blue Beetle 1.50
2 inc. Catwoman 1.25
3 inc. Justice League 1.25
4 1.25
5 inc. Superboy 1.25

WHO'S WHO UPDATE '88

1 inc. Brainiac 1.25
2 inc. JusticeLeagueInternational 1.25
3 inc. Shado 1.25
4 inc. Zatanna 1.25

WHO'S WHO UPDATE '93

1 F:Eclipso,Azrael 4.95

WILD DOG
September, 1987

1 mini series DG(i),I:Wild Dog 1.00
2 DG(i),V:Terrorists 1.00
3 DG(i) 1.00
4 DG(i),O:Wild Dog, final issue 1.00
Spec.#1 2.50

WINDY & WILLY
May-June, 1969

1 thru 4 @1.00

WITCHCRAFT
Vertigo

1 CV(c),Three Witches from Sandman 3.25
2 F:Mildred 1.95

WONDER WOMAN
Summer, 1942

1 O:Wonder Woman,A:Paula Von Gunther 6,200.00
2 I:Earl of Greed,Duke of Deception and Lord Conquest, A:Mars 1,300.00
3 Paula Von Gunther reforms 850.00
4 A:Paula Von Gunther 650.00
5 I:Dr. Psycho,A:Mars 650.00
6 I:Cheetah 525.00
7 525.00
8 I:Queen Clea 525.00
9 I:Giganto 525.00
10 I:Duke Mephisto Saturno 525.00
11 I:Hypnoto 400.00
12 I:Queen Desira 400.00
13 V:King Rigor & the Seal Men 400.00

Wonder Woman #10
© DC Comics, Inc.

14 I:Gentleman Killer 400.00
15 I:Solo 400.00
16 I:King Pluto 400.00
17 Wonder Woman goes to Ancient Rome 400.00
18 V:Dr. Psycho 400.00
19 V:Blitz 400.00
20 V:Nifty and the Air Pirates 400.00
21 I:Queen Atomia 350.00
22 V:Saturno 350.00
23 V:Odin and the Valkyries 350.00
24 I:Mask 350.00
25 V:Purple Priestess 350.00
26 I:Queen Celerita 350.00
27 V:Pik Socket 350.00
28 V:Cheetah,Clea,Dr. Poison, Giganta,Hypnata,Snowman, Zara (Villainy,Inc.) 325.00
29 V:Paddy Gypso 325.00
30 'The Secret of the Limestone Caves' 325.00
31 V:Solo 250.00
32 V:Uvo 250.00
33 V:Inventa 250.00
34 V:Duke of Deception 250.00
35 'Jaxo,Master of Thoughts' 250.00
36 V:Lord Cruello 250.00
37 A:Circe 250.00
38 V:Brutex 250.00
39 'The Unmasking of Wonder Woman' 250.00
40 'Hollywood Goes To Paradise Island' 250.00
41 'Wonder Woman,Romance Editor' 200.00
42 V:General Vertigo 200.00
43 'The Amazing Spy Ring Mystery' 200.00
44 V:Master Destroyer 200.00
45 'The Amazon and the Leprachaun' 350.00
46 V:Prof. Turgo 200.00
47 V:Duke of Deception 200.00
48 V:Robot Woman 200.00
49 V:Boss 200.00
50 V:Gen. Voro 200.00
51 V:Garo 175.00
52 V:Stroggo 175.00
53 V:Crime Master of Time 175.00
54 A:Merlin 175.00
55 'The Chessmen of Doom' 175.00
56 V:Plotter Gang 175.00
57 V:Mole Men 175.00
58 V:Brain 175.00
59 V:Duke Dozan 175.00
60 A:Paula Von Gunther 175.00
61 'Earth's Last Hour' 125.00
62 V:Angles Andrews 125.00
63 V:Duke of Deception 125.00
64 V:Thought Master 125.00
65 V:Duke of Deception 125.00
66 V:Duke of Deception 125.00
67 'Confessions of a Spy' 125.00
68 'Landing of the Flying Saucers' 125.00
69 A:Johann Gutenberg,Chris. Columbus, Paul Revere and the Wright Brothers 125.00
70 I:Angle Man 125.00
71 'One-Woman Circus' 100.00
72 V:Mole Goldings 100.00
73 V:Prairie Pirates 100.00
74 'The Carnival of Peril' 100.00
75 V:Angler 100.00
76 100.00
77 V:Smokescreen gang 100.00
78 V:Angle Man 100.00
79 V:Spider 100.00
80 V:Machino 100.00
81 V:Duke of Deception, Angle Man 100.00
82 A:Robin Hood 100.00
83 'The Boy From Nowhere' 100.00
84 V:Duke of Deception, Angle Man 100.00
85 V:Capt. Virago 100.00
86 V:Snatcher 100.00
87 'The Day the Clocks Stopped' 100.00
88 V:Duke of Deception 100.00
89 'The Triple Heroine' 100.00
90 Wonder Woman on Jupiter 100.00
91 'The Interplanetary Olympics' 75.00
92 V:Angle Man 75.00
93 V:Duke of Deception 75.00
94 V:Duke of Deception, A:Robin Hood 75.00
95 O:Wonder Woman's tiara 85.00
96 V:Angle Man 75.00
97 'The Runaway Time Express' 75.00
98 75.00
99 V:Silicons 75.00
100 Anniversary Issue 85.00
101 V:Time Master 50.00
102 F:Steve Trevor 50.00
103 V:Gadget-Maker 50.00
104 A:Duke of Deception 50.00
105 O,I:Wonder Woman 250.00

106 W.Woman space adventure 50.00
107 Battles space cowboys 50.00
108 Honored by U.S. Post Off. . 50.00
109 V:Slicker 50.00
110 I:Princess 1003 .... 50.00
111 I:Prof. Menace 50.00
112 V:Chest of Monsters 40.00
113 A:Queen Mikra 40.00
114 V:Flying Saucers 40.00
115 A:Angle Man 40.00
116 A:Professor Andro 40.00
117 A:Etta Candy 40.00
118 A:Merman 40.00
119 A:Mer Boy 40.00
120 A:Hot & Cold Alien 40.00
121 A:Wonder Woman Family . . 25.00
122 I:Wonder Tot 25.00
123 A:Wonder Girl,Wonder Tot . 25.00
124 A:Wonder Girl,Wonder Tot . 25.00
125 WW-Battle Prize 25.00
126 I:Mr.Genie 25.00
127 Suprise Honeymoon 15.00
128 O:InvisiblePlane 15.00
129 A:WonderGirl,WonderTot . . 15.00
130 A:Angle Man 15.00
131 .... 8.00
132 V:Flying Saucer 8.00
133 A:Miss X 8.00
134 V:Image-Maker 8.00

156 V:Brain Pirate 7.00
157 A:Egg Fu,the First 7.00
158 A:Egg Fu,the First 7.00
159 Origin 8.00
160 A:Cheetah,Dr. Psycho 6.00
161 A:Angle Man 6.00
162 O:Diana Prince 6.00
163 A:Giganta 6.00
164 A:Angle Man 6.00
165 A:Paper Man,Dr.Psycho 6.00
166 A:Egg Fu,The Fifth 6.00
167 A:Crimson Centipede 6.00
168 RA,ME,V:Giganta 6.00
169 RA,ME,Crimson Centipede . . 6.00
170 RA,ME,V:Dr.Pyscho 6.00
171 A:Mouse Man 5.00
172 IN,A:Android Wonder Woman 5.00
173 A:Tonia 5.00
174 A:Angle Man 5.00
175 V:Evil Twin 5.00
176 A:Star Brothers 5.00
177 A:Super Girl 5.00
178 MSy,DG,I:New Wonder
Woman 5.00
179 D:Steve Trevor,I:Ching 4.00
180 MSy,DG,wears no costume
I:Tim Trench 4.00
181 MSy,DG,A:Dr.Cyber 3.00
182 MSy,DG 4.00

204 DH,BO,rewears costume 1.75
205 DH,BO 1.75
206 DH,O:Wonder Woman 2.50
207 RE 1.75
208 RE 1.75
209 RE 1.75
210 RE 1.75
211 RE,giant 3.00
212 CS,A:Superman,tries to
rejoin JLA 1.75
213 IN,A:Flash 1.75
214 CS,giant,A:Green Lantern . . . 3.00
215 A:Aquaman 1.50
216 A:Black Canary 1.50
217 DD,A:Green Arrow 2.00
218 KS,Red Tornado 1.50
219 CS,A:Elongated Man 1.50
220 DG,NA,A:Atom 2.00
221 CS,A:Hawkman 1.50
222 A:Batman 2.00
223 R:Steve Trevor 1.50
224 .... 1.50
225 .... 1.50
226 .... 1.50
227 .... 1.50
228 B:War stories 1.50
229 .... 1.50
230 V:Cheetah 1.50
231 .... 1.50

Wonder Woman #35
© DC Comics, Inc.

Wonder Woman #36
© DC Comics, Inc.

Wonder Woman #202
© DC Comics, Inc.

135 V:Multiple Man 8.00
136 V:Machine Men 8.00
137 V:Robot Wonder Woman . . . 8.00
138 V:Multiple Man 8.00
139 Amnesia revels Identity 8.00
140 A:Morpheus,Mr.Genie 8.00
141 A:Angle Man 8.00
142 A:Mirage Giants 8.00
143 A:Queen Hippolyte 8.00
144 I:Bird Boy 8.00
145 V:Phantom Sea Beast 8.00
146 $1,000 Dollar Stories 8.00
147 Wonder Girl becomes Bird Girl
and Fish Girl 8.00
148 A:Duke of Deception 8.00
149 Last Day of the Amazons . . . 8.00
150 V:Phantome Fish Bird 8.00
151 F:1st Full Wonder Girl story . 7.00
152 F:Wonder Girl 7.00
153 V:Duke of Deception 7.00
154 V:Boiling Man 7.00
155 I married a monster 7.00

183 MSy,DG,V:War 4.00
184 MSy,DG,A:Queen Hippolyte . 4.00
185 MSy,DG,V:Them 3.00
186 MSy,DG,I:Morgana 3.00
187 MSy,DG,A:Dr.Cyber 3.50
188 MSy,DG,A:Dr.Cyber 3.00
189 MSy,DG 3.00
190 MSy,DG 3.00
191 MSy,DG 3.00
192 MSy,DG 3.00
193 MSy,DG 3.00
194 MSy,DG 3.00
195 MSy,WW 3.50
196 MSy,DG,giant,Origin rep. . . . 4.50
197 MSy,DG 3.50
198 MSy,DG 3.50
199 JJ(c),DG 7.00
200 JJ(c),DG 7.00
201 DG,A:Catwoman 4.00
202 DG,A:Catwoman,I:Fafhrd
& the Gray Mouser 4.00
203 DG,Womens lib 2.00

232 MN,A:JSA 1.50
233 GM 1.50
234 .... 1.50
235 .... 1.50
236 .... 1.50
237 RB(c),O:Wonder Woman . . . 1.75
238 RB(c) 1.50
239 RB(c) 1.50
240 .... 1.50
241 JSon,DG,A:Spectre 1.50
242 .... 1.50
243 .... 1.50
244 .... 1.50
245 .... 1.50
246 .... 1.50
247 .... 1.50
248 D:Steve Trevor 1.50
249 A:Hawkgirl 1.50
250 I:Orana 1.50
251 O:Orana 1.50
252 .... 1.25
253 .... 1.25

254 . . . . 1.25
255 V:Bushmaster 1.25
256 V:Royal Flush Gang 1.25
257 . . . . 1.25
258 . . . . 1.25
259 . . . . 1.25
260 . . . . 1.25
261 . . . . 1.25
262 RE,A:Bushmaster 1.25
263 . . . . 1.25
264 . . . . 1.25
265 . . . . 1.25
266 . . . . 1.25
267 R:Animal Man 18.00
268 A:Animal Man 15.00
269 WW(i),Rebirth of Wonder
Woman Pt.1 . . . . 1.50
270 Rebirth Pt.2 . . . . 1.25
271 JSon,B:Huntress,Rebirth Pt.3 1.50
272 JSon 1.50
273 JSon,A:Angle Man 1.50
274 JSon,I:Cheetah II 1.25
275 JSon,V:Cheetah II 1.25
276 JSon,V:Kobra 1.25
277 JSon,V:Kobra 1.25
278 JSon,V:Kobra 1.25
279 JSon,A:Demon,Catwoman . . 2.50
280 JSon,A:Demon,Catwoman . . 2.50
281 JSon,Earth 2 Joker 2.50
282 JSon,Earth 2 Joker 2.50
283 Earth 2 Joker 2.50
284 . . . . 1.25
285 JSon,V:Red Dragon 1.25
286 . . . . 1.25
287 DH,RT,JSon,Teen Titans . . . 2.25
288 GC,RT,New Wonder Woman 1.25
289 GC,RT,JSon,New W.Woman . 1.25
290 GC,RT,JSon,New W.Woman . 1.25
291 GC,FMc,A:Zatanna 1.25
292 GC,FMc,RT,Supergirl 1.25

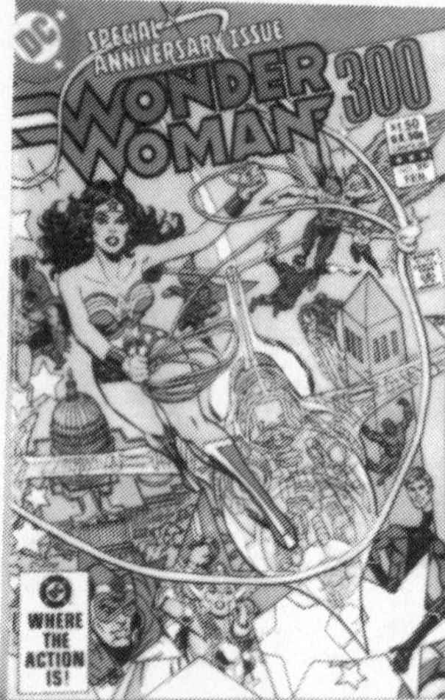

Wonder Woman #300
© DC Comics, Inc.

293 GC,FMc,Starfire,Raven 1.25
294 GC,FMc,JSon,V:Blockbuster . 1.25
295 GC,FMc,JSon,Huntress 1.25
296 GC,Fmc,JSon 1.25
297 MK(c),GC,FMc,JSon, ... 1.25
298 GC,FMc,JSon 1.25
299 GC,FMc,JSon 1.25
300 GC,FMc,RA,DG,KP,RB,KG
C:New Teen Titans 3.25
301 GC,FMc 1.25
302 GC,FMc,V:Artemis 1.25
303 GC,FMc,Huntress 1.25
304 GC,FMc,Huntress 1.25
305 GC,Huntress,I:Circe 1.25
306 DH,Huntress 1.25
307 DH,Huntress,Black Canary . . 1.25
308 DH,Huntress,Black Canary . . 1.25
309 DH,Huntress 1.25
310 DH,Huntress 1.25
311 DH,Huntress 1.25
312 DH,DSp,A:Gremlins 1.25
313 DH,V:Circe 1.25
314 DH,Huntress 1.25
315 DH,Huntress 1.25
316 DH,Huntress 1.25
317 DH,V:Cereberus 1.25
318 DH,V:Space Aliens 1.25
319 DH,V:Dr.Cyber 1.25
320 DH, ... 1.25
321 DH,Huntress 1.25
322 IN 1.25
323 DH,A:Cheetah, Angle Man . . 1.25
324 DH 1.25
325 DH 1.25
326 DH 1.25
327 DH,Crisis 1.25
328 DH,Crisis 1.25
329 DH,Crisis, giant 2.00

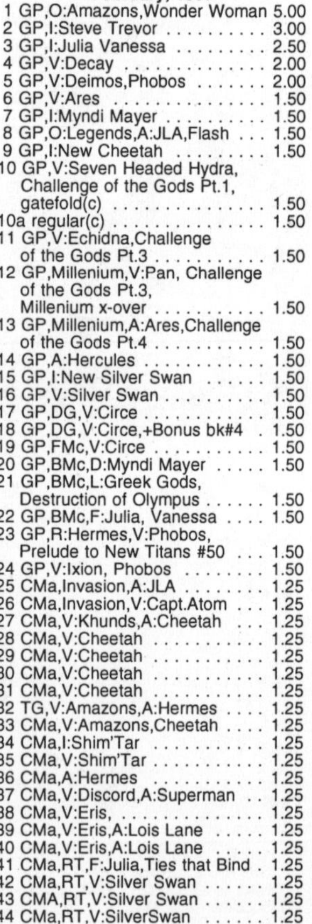

WONDER WOMAN
[2nd Regular Series]
February, 1987

1 GP,O:Amazons,Wonder Woman 5.00
2 GP,I:Steve Trevor 3.00
3 GP,I:Julia Vanessa 2.50
4 GP,V:Decay 2.00
5 GP,V:Deimos,Phobos 2.00
6 GP,V:Ares 1.50
7 GP,I:Myndi Mayer 1.50
8 GP,O:Legends,A:JLA,Flash . . . 1.50
9 GP,I:New Cheetah 1.50
10 GP,V:Seven Headed Hydra,
Challenge of the Gods Pt.1,
gatefold(c) 1.50
10a regular(c) 1.50
11 GP,V:Echidna,Challenge
of the Gods Pt.3 . . . . 1.50
12 GP,Millenium,V:Pan, Challenge
of the Gods Pt.3,
Millenium x-over 1.50
13 GP,Millenium,A:Ares,Challenge
of the Gods Pt.4 . . . . 1.50
14 GP,A:Hercules 1.50
15 GP,I:New Silver Swan 1.50
16 GP,V:Silver Swan 1.50
17 GP,DG,V:Circe 1.50
18 GP,DG,V:Circe,+Bonus bk#4 . 1.50
19 GP,FMc,V:Circe 1.50
20 GP,BMc,D:Myndi Mayer 1.50
21 GP,BMc,L:Greek Gods,
Destruction of Olympus 1.50
22 GP,BMc,F:Julia, Vanessa 1.50
23 GP,R:Hermes,V:Phobos,
Prelude to New Titans #50 . . . 1.50
24 GP,V:Ixion, Phobos 1.50
25 CMa,Invasion,A:JLA 1.25
26 CMa,Invasion,V:Capt.Atom . . . 1.25
27 CMa,V:Khunds,A:Cheetah . . . 1.25
28 CMa,V:Cheetah 1.25
29 CMa,V:Cheetah 1.25
30 CMa,V:Cheetah 1.25
31 CMa,V:Cheetah 1.25
32 TG,V:Amazons,A:Hermes 1.25
33 CMa,V:Amazons,Cheetah 1.25
34 CMa,I:Shim'Tar 1.25
35 CMa,V:Shim'Tar 1.25
36 CMa,A:Hermes 1.25
37 CMa,V:Discord,A:Superman . . 1.25
38 CMa,V:Eris, ... 1.25
39 CMa,V:Eris,A:Lois Lane 1.25
40 CMa,V:Eris,A:Lois Lane 1.25
41 CMa,RT,F:Julia,Ties that Bind . 1.25
42 CMa,RT,V:Silver Swan 1.25
43 CMA,RT,V:Silver Swan 1.25
44 CMa,RT,V:SilverSwan 1.25

Wonder Woman (2nd Regular Series) #1 © DC Comics, Inc.

45 CM,RT,Pandora's Box 1.25
46 RT,Suicide Issue,D:Lucy 1.50
47 RT,A:Troia 1.25
48 RTP,A:Troia 1.25
49 recap of 1st four years 1.25
50 RT,SA,BB,AH,CM,KN,PCR,MW
A:JLA,Superman 2.00
51 RT,V:Mercury 1.25
52 CM,KN,Shards,V:Dr.Psycho . . 1.25
53 RT,A:Pariah 1.25
54 RT,V:Dr.Psycho 1.25
55 RT,V:Dr.Psycho 1.25
56 RT,A:Comm.Gordon 1.25
57 RT,A:Clark Kent,Bruce Wayne 1.25
58 RT,War of the Gods,V:Atlas . . 2.00
59 RT,War of the Gods,
A:Batman Robin 2.00
60 RT,War of the Gods,
A:Batman, Lobo 2.00
61 RT,War of the Gods,V:Circe . . 2.00
62 War o/t Gods,Epilogue. 1.50
63 BB(c)A:Deathstroke,Cheetah . . 1.75
64 BB(c),Kidnapped Child 1.50
65 BB(c),PCu,V:Dr.Psycho 1.50
66 BB(c),PCu,Exodus In Space#1 1.50
67 BB(c),PCu,Exodus In Space#2 1.50
68 BB(c),PCu,Exodus In Space#3 1.50
69 PCu, Exodus In Space#4 . . . . 1.50
70 PCu,Exodus In Space#5 . . . . . 1.50
71 BB(c),DC,RT,Return fr.space . 1.50
72 BB(c),O:retold 1.75
73 BB(c),Diana gets a job 1.50
74 BB(c),V:White Magician 1.50
75 BB(c),A:The White Magician . . 1.50
76 BB(c),A:Doctor Fate 1.50
77 BB(c) 1.50
78 BB(c),A:Flash 1.50
79 BB(c),V:Mayfly,A:Flash 1.50
80 BB(c),V:Ares Buchanan 1.50
81 BB(c),V:Ares Buchanan 1.50
82 BB(c),V:Ares Buchanan 1.50
83 BB(c),V:Ares Buchanan 1.50
84 BB(c),V:Ares Buchanan 1.75
85 BB(c), ... 1.75
86 BB(c),Turning Point 1.75
87 BB(c),No Quarter,NoSanctuary 1.75
88 BB(c),A:Superman 1.50
Ann.#1,GP,AAd,RA,BB,JBo,JL,CS
Tales of Paradise Island 2.00
Ann.#2 CM,F:Mayer Agency 2.50
Ann.#3 Eclipso tie-in 2.50

Spec #1 A:Deathstroke,Cheetah . 2.25

WORLD OF KRYPTON

July, 1979

1 HC/MA.O:Jor-El 1.50
2 HC/MA,A:Superman 1.00
3 HC 1.00

[2nd Series]

1 MMi,John Byrne script 1.00
2 MMi,John Byrne script 1.00
3 MMi,John Byrne script 1.00
4 MMi,A:Superman 1.00

WORLD OF METROPOLIS

1988

1 DG(i),O:Perry White 1.00
2 DG(i),O:Lois Lane 1.00
3 DG(i),Clark Kent 1.00
4 DG(i),O:Jimmy Olsen 1.00

WORLD OF SMALLVILLE

1988

1 KS/AA,Secrets of Ma&Pa Kent 1.25
2 KS/AA,'Stolen Moments' 1.25
3 KS/AA,Lana Lang/Manhunter . . 1.25
4 KS/AA,final issue 1.25

WORLDS COLLIDE

1 MBr(c),3RW,CsB,Ccs,DCw, TG,A:Blood Syndicate,Icon, Hardware,Static,Superboy, Superman,Steel,Vinyl Cling(c) . 3.95
1a Newsstand Ed. 2.50

WORLD'S BEST COMICS

Spring, 1941

1 Superman vs. the Rainmaker, Batman vs. Wright 7,200.00

Becomes:

WORLD'S FINEST COMICS

2 Superman V:'The Unknown X', Batman V:Ambrose Taylor 2,200.00
3 I&O:Scarecrow 1,700.00

World's Finest Comics #14
© DC Comics, Inc.

4 Superman V:Dan Brandon, Batman V:Ghost Gang . . . 1,300.00
5 Superman V:Lemuel P.Potts, Batman V:Brains Kelly . . . 1,300.00
6 Superman V:Metalo,Batman meets Scoop Scanlon 1,000.00
7 Superman V:Jenkins,Batman V:Snow Man Bandits 1,000.00
8 Superman:'Talent Unlimited' Batman V:Little Nap Boyd, B:Boy Commandos 900.00
9 Superman:'One Second to Live',Batman V:Bramwell B. Bramwell 950.00
10 Superman V:The Insect Master, Batman reforms Oliver Hunt 750.00
11 Superman V:Charlie Frost, Batman V:Rob Calendar . . . 675.00
12 Superman V:Lynx,Batman: 'Alfred Gets His Man' 675.00
13 Superman V:Dice Dimant, Batman,V:Swami Pravhoz . . 675.00
14 Superman V:Al Bandar,Batman V:Jib Buckler 675.00
15 Superman V:Derby Bowser, Batman V:Mennekin 675.00
16 Superman:'Music for the Masses, Batman V:Nocky Johnson . . 675.00
17 Superman:'The Great Godini', Batman V:Dr.Dreemo 650.00
18 Superman:'The Junior Reporters, Batman V:Prof.Brane 600.00
19 A:The Joker 600.00
20 A:Toyman 600.00
21 Superman:'Swindle in Sweethearts!' 450.00
22 Batman V:Nails Finney 450.00
23 Superman:'The Colossus of Metropolis' 450.00
24 . . . . 450.00
25 Superman V:Ed Rook,Batman: 'The Famous First Crimes' . 450.00
26 'Confessions of Superman' . 450.00
27 'The Man Who Out-Supered Superman 450.00
28 A:Lex Luther,Batman V:Glass Man 450.00

World's Finest Comics #47
© DC Comics, Inc.

29 Superman:'The Books that couldn't be Bound' 450.00
30 Superman:'Sheriff Clark Kent', Batman V:Joe Coyne 450.00
31 'Superman's Super-Rival',Batman: 'Man with the X-Ray Eyes' . 400.00
32 Superman visits Ancient Egypt 400.00
33 'Superman Press, Inc.', Batman V:James Harmon . . 400.00
34 'The Un-Super Superman' . 400.00
35 Daddy Superman,A:Penguin 400.00
36 Lois Lane,Sleeping Beauty . 400.00
37 'The Superman Story',Batman V:T-Gun Jones 400.00
38 If There were No Superman 400.00
39 Superman V:Big Jim Martin, Batman V:J.J.Jason 400.00
40 Superman V:Check,Batman:'4 Killers Against Fate!' 400.00
41 I:Supermanium, E:Boy Commandos 320.00
42 Superman goes to Uranus, A:Marco Polo & Kubla Khan 300.00
43 A:J.Wilbur Wolfingham 300.00
44 Superman:'The Revolt of the Thought Machine' 300.00
45 Superman:'Lois Lane and Clark Kent,Private Detectives 300.00
46 Superman V:Mr. 7 . . . . 300.00
47 Superman:'The Girl Who Hated Reporters 300.00
48 A:Joker 300.00
49 Superman meets the Metropolis Shutterbug Society, A:Penguin 300.00
50 'Superman Super Wrecker' . 300.00
51 Superman:'The Amazing Talents of Lois Lane' 300.00
52 A:J.Wilbur Wolfingham 300.00
53 Superman V:Elias Toomey . 300.00
54 'The Superman Who Avoided Danger!' 300.00
55 A:Penguin 300.00
56 Superman V:Dr.Vallin,Batman V:Big Dan Hooker 300.00
57 'The Artificial Superman' . . . 300.00
58 Superman V:Mr.Fenton 300.00
59 A:Lex Luthor,Joker 300.00
60 A:J.Wilbur Wolfingham 300.00
61 A:Joker,'Superman's Blackout' 250.00
62 A:Lex Luthor 250.00
63 Superman:'Clark Kent, Gangster' 250.00
64 Superman:'The Death of Lois Lane,Batman:'Bruce Wayne... Amateur Detective' 250.00
65 'The Confessions of Superman', Batman V:The Blaster 250.00
66 'Superman,Ex-Crimebuster; Batman V:Brass Haley 250.00
67 Superman:'Metropolis-Crime Center!' 250.00
68 Batman V:The Crimesmith . 250.00
69 A:Jor-El,Batman V:Tom Becket 250.00
70 'The Two Faces of Superman', Batman:'Crime Consultant' . 250.00
71 B:Superman/Batman team-ups 550.00
72 V:Heavy Weapon gang 350.00
73 V:Fang 350.00
74 'The Contest of Heroes' . . . 300.00
75 V:The Purple Mask Mob . . . 300.00
76 'When Gotham City Challenged Metropolis 225.00
77 V:Prof.Pender 225.00
78 V:Varrel mob 225.00
79 A:Aladdin 225.00
80 V:Mole 225.00
81 Meet Ka Thar from future . . 175.00
82 A:Three Musketeers 175.00
83 'The Case of the Mother Goose Mystery' 175.00
84 V:Thad Linnis gang 175.00
85 Meet Princess Varina 175.00
86 V:Henry Bartle 175.00
87 V:Elton Craig 175.00
88 1st team-up Luthor & Joker 185.00
89 I:Club of Heroes 175.00
90 A:Batwoman 175.00
91 V:Rohtul,descendent of Lex Luthor 125.00

92 Ist & only A:Skyboy 125.00
93 V:Victor Danning 125.00
94 O:Superman/Batman team,
A:Lex Luthor 350.00
95 'Battle o/t Super Heroes' . . . 100.00
96 'Super-Foes from Planet X' 100.00
97 V:Condor Gang 100.00
98 I:Moonman 100.00
99 JK,V:Carl Verril 100.00
100 A:Kandor, Lex Luthor 225.00
101 A:Atom Master 100.00
102 V:Jo-Jo Groff gang,
B:Tommy Tomorrow 100.00
103 'The Secrets of the
Sorcerer's Treasure 100.00
104 A:Lex Luthor 100.00
105 V:Khalex 100.00
106 V:Duplicate Man 100.00
107 'The Secret of the Time
Creature' 100.00
108 'The Star Creatures' 100.00
109 V:Fangan 100.00
110 'The Alien Who Doomed
Robin!' 100.00
111 V:Floyd Frisby 100.00
112 . . . . 100.00
113 1st Bat-Mite/Mr.Mxyzptlk
team-up 100.00
114 'Captives o/t Space Globes' 100.00
115 The Curse That Doomed
Superman 60.00
116 V:Vance Collins 60.00
117 A:Batwoman,Lex Luthor . . . 60.00
118 V:Vath-Gar 60.00

World's Finest Comics #144
© DC Comics, Inc.

119 V:General Grambly 60.00
120 V:Faceless Creature 60.00
121 I:Miss Arrowette 60.00
122 V:Klor 30.00
123 A:Bat-Mite & Mr. Mxyzptlk . . 30.00
124 V:Hroguth,E:Tommy
Tomorrow 30.00
125 V:Jundy,B:Aquaman 30.00
126 A:Lex Luthor 30.00
127 V:Zerno 30.00
128 V:Moose Morans 30.00
129 Joker/Luthor T.U. 40.00
130 . . . . 25.00
131 V:Octopus 25.00
132 V:Denny Kale,Shorty Biggs . 25.00
133 . . . . 25.00
134 V:Band of Super-Villians . . . 25.00
135 V:The Future Man 25.00
136 The Batman Nobody
Remembered 25.00
137 A:Lex Luthor 25.00
138 V:General Grote 25.00
139 V:Sphinx Gang,E:Aquaman . 25.00
140 CS,V:Clayface 25.00
141 CS,A:Jimmy Olsen 25.00
142 CS,O:Composite Man 25.00
143 CS,A:Kandor,I:Mailbag 20.00
144 CS,A:Clayface,Brainiac 20.00
145 CS,Prison for Heroes 20.00
146 CS,Batman,Son of Krypton . 20.00
147 CS,A:Jimmy Olsen 20.00
148 CS,A:Lex Luthor,Clayface . . 20.00
149 CS,The Game of the
Secret Identities 20.00
150 CS,V:Rokk and Sorban 15.00
151 CS,A:Krypto,BU:Congorilla . 12.00
152 CS,A:The Colossal Kids,Bat-
mite,V:Mr.Mxyzptlk 12.00
153 CS,V:Lex Luthor 12.00
154 CS,The Sons of Batman &
Superman(Imaginary) 12.00
155 CS,The 1000th Exploit of
Batman & Superman 12.00
156 CS,I:BizarroBatman,V:Joker 55.00
157 CS,The Abominable Brats
(Imaginary story) 12.00
158 CS,V:Brainiac 12.00
159 CS,A:Many Major villians,I:Jim
Gordon as Anti-Batman & Perry
White as Anti-Superman 12.00
160 V:Dr Zodiac. 12.00
161 CS,80 page giant 15.00
162 V:The Jousting Master 10.00
163 CS,The Court of No Hope . . 10.00
164 CS,I:Genia,V:Brainiac 10.00
165 CS,The Crown of Crime . . . 10.00
166 CS,V:Muto & Joker 12.00
167 CS,The New Superman &
Batman(Imaginary) V:Luthor . 10.00
168 CS,R:Composite Superman 10.00
169 The Supergirl/Batgirl Plot;
V:Batmite,Mr.Mxyzptlk 11.00
170 80 page giant,reprint 10.00
171 CS,V:The Executioners 7.00
172 CS,Superman & Batman
Brothers (Imaginary) 7.00
173 CS,The Jekyll-Hyde Heroes . 7.00
174 CS,Secrets of the Double
Death Wish 7.00
175 NA(1st Batman),C:Flash . . . 12.00
176 NA,A:Supergirl & Batgirl . . . 10.00
177 V:Joker & Luthor 9.00
178 CS,The Has-Been Superman 5.00
179 CS,giant 6.00
180 RA,ME,Supermans Perfect
Crime 5.00
181 RA,ME 5.00
182 RA,ME,The Mad Manhunter . 5.00
183 RA,ME,Supermans Crimes
of the Ages 5.00
184 RA,ME,A:JLA,Robin 5.00
185 CS,The Galactic Gamblers . . 5.00
186 RA,ME,The Bat Witch 5.00
187 RA,ME,Demon Superman . . . 5.00
188 giant,reprint 6.00
189 RA,ME,V:Lex Luthor 6.00
190 RA,V:Lex Luthor 4.00
191 RA,A:Jor-El,Lara 4.00
192 RA,The Prison of No Escape 4.00
193 The Breaking of Batman
and Superman 4.00
194 RA,ME,Inside the Mafia 4.00
195 RA,ME,Dig Now-Die Later . . . 4.00
196 CS,The Kryptonite Express,
E:Batman 4.00
197 giant 5.00
198 DD,B:Superman T.U.,
A:Flash 45.00
199 DD,Superman & Flash race 45.00
200 NA(c),DD,Prisoners of the
Immortal World; A:Robin 3.00
201 NA(c),DD,A Prize of Peril,
A:Green Lantern,Dr. Fate. 3.00
202 NA(c),DD,Vengeance of the
Tomb Thing,A:Batman 3.00
203 NA(c),DD,Who's Minding the
Earth,A:Quamar 3.00
204 NA(c),DD,Journey to the
End of Hope,A:Wonder Woman 3.00
205 NA(c),DD,The Computer that
Captured a Town,Frazetta Ad,
A:Teen Titans 5.00
206 DD,giant reprint 5.00
207 DD,Superman,A:Batman,
V:Dr.Light 3.00
208 NA(c),DD,A:Dr Fate 3.00
209 NA(c),DD,A:Green Arrow,
Hawkman,I&V:The Temper . . 3.00
210 NA(c),DD,A:Batman 3.00
211 NA(c),DD,A:Batman 3.00
212 CS(c),And So My World
Begins,A:Martian Manhunter . . 3.00
213 DD,Peril in a Very Small
Place,A:The Atom 3.00
214 DD,A:Vigilante 3.00
215 DD,Saga of the Super Sons
(Imaginary story) 3.00
216 DD,R:Super Sons,Little Town
with a Big Secret 3.00
217 DD,MA,Heroes with
Dirty Hands 3.00
218 DD,DC,A:Batman,
BU:Metamorpho 3.00
219 DD,Prisoner of Rogues Rock;
A:Batman 3.00
220 DD,MA,Let No Man Write My
Epitaph,BU:Metamorpho 3.00
221 DD,Cry Not For My Forsaken
Son; R:Super Sons 3.00
222 DD,Evil In Paradise 3.00
223 DD,giant,A:Deadman,Aquaman
Robotman 4.00
224 DD,giant,A:Super Sons,
Metamorpho,Johnny Quick . . . 4.00
225 giant,A:Rip Hunter,Vigilante,
Black Canary,Robin 4.00
226 A:Sandman,Metamorpho,
Deadman,Martian Manhunter . 5.00
227 MGr,BWi,A:The Demonic Duo,
Vigilante,Rip Hunter,Deadman,
I:Stargrave 4.00
228 ATh,A:Super Sons,Aquaman,
Robin,Vigilante 4.00
229 I:Powerman,A:Metamorpho . . 2.50
230 A:Super-Sons,Deadman,
Aquaman 4.00
231 A:Green Arrow,Flash 2.50
232 DD,The Dream Bomb 2.50
233 A:Super-Sons 2.50
234 CS,Family That Fled Earth . . 2.50
235 DD,V:Sagitaurus 2.50
236 DD,A:The Atom 2.50
237 Intruder from a Dead World . . 2.50
238 DD,V:Luthor,A:Super-Sons. . . 2.50
239 CS,A:Gold(from Metal Men) . 2.50
240 DD,A:Kandor 2.50
241 Make Way For a New World . 2.50
242 EC,A:Super-Sons 2.50
243 CS,AM,A:Robin 2.50
244 NA(c),JL,MA,MN,TA,giant
B:Green Arrow 3.00
245 NA(C),CS,MA,MN,TA,
GM,JSh,BWi,giant 3.00
246 NA(c),KS,MA,MN,TA,GM,
DH,A:JLA 3.00
247 KS,GM,giant 3.00
248 KS,GM,DG,TVE,A:Sgt.Rock . 3.00
249 KS,SD,TVE,A:Phantom
Stranger,B:Creeper 5.00
250 GT,SD,Superman,Batman,
Wonder Woman,Green Arrow,
Black Canary,team-up 3.00
251 GT,SD,JBi,BL,TVE,RE,
JA,A:Poison Ivy,Speedy,
I:CountVertigo 3.00
252 GT,TVE,SD,JA,giant 3.00
253 KS,DN,TVE,SD,B:Shazam . . 3.00

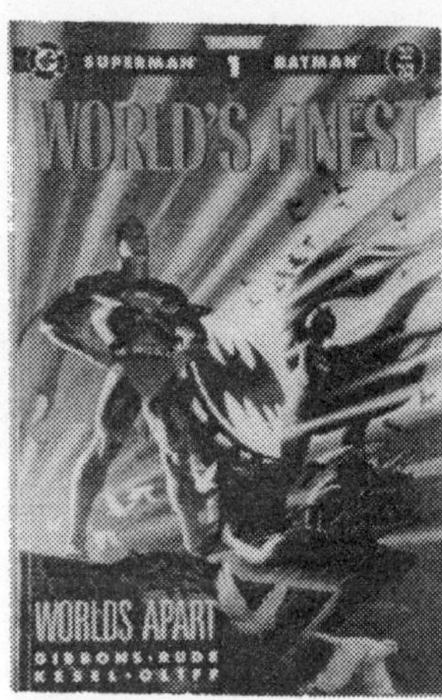
World's Finest (Ltd. Series) #1
© DC Comics, Inc.

World's Finest (Ltd. Series) #2
© DC Comics, Inc.

254 GT,DN,TVE,SD,giant 3.00
255 JL,DA,TVE,SD,DN,KS, E:Creeper 3.00
256 MA,DN,KS,DD,Hawkman,Black Lightning,giant 3.00
257 DD,FMc,DN,KS,GT,RB, RT,giant 3.00
258 NA(c),RB,JL,DG,DN,KS,RT, giant 3.00
259 RB,DG,MR,MN,DN,KS 3.00
260 RB,DG,MN,DN 2.50
261 RB,DG,AS,RT,EB,DN, A:Penguin, Terra Man 4.00
262 DG,DN,DA,JSon,RT, Aquaman 2.50
263 RB,DG,DN,TVE,JSh,Aquaman, Adam Strange 2.50
264 RB,DG,TVE,DN,Aquaman 2.50
265 RB,DN,RE,TVE, ... 2.50
266 RB,TVE,DN 2.50
267 RB,DG,TVE,AS,DN, A:Challengers of the Unknown 2.50
268 DN,TVE,BBr,RT,AS 2.50
269 RB,FMc,TVE,BBr,AS,DN,DA . 2.50
270 NA(c),RB,RT,TVE,AS, DN,LMa 2.50
271 GP(c),RB,FMc,O:Superman/ Batman T.U. 2.75
272 RB,DN,TVE,BBr,AS 2.50
273 TVE,LMa,JSon,AS,DN,DA, A:Plastic Man 2.50
274 TVE,LMa,BBr,GC,AS,DN, Green Arrow 2.50
275 RB,FMc,TVE,LMa,DSp,AS, DN,DA,A:Mr.Freeze 2.50
276 GP(c),RB,TVE,LMa,DSp,CI, DN,DA 2.50
277 GP(c),RT,TVE,DSp,AS,DN, DH,V:Dr.Double X 2.50
278 GP(c),RB,TVE,LMa,DSp,DN . 2.50
279 KP,TVE,LMa,AS,DN, B:Kid Eternity 2.50
280 RB,TVE,LMa,AS,DN 2.50
281 GK(c),IN,TVE,LMa,AS,DN ... 2.50
282 IN,FMc,GK,CI,last giant E:Kid Eternity 2.50
283 GT,FMc,GK 2.25
284 GT,DSp,A:Legion,E:G.Arrow . 2.50
285 FM(c),RB,A:Zatanna 2.25
286 RB,A:Flash 2.50
287 TVE,A:Flash 2.50
288 A:JLA 2.25
289 GK(c),Kryll way of Dying 2.25
290 TD(i),I:Stalagron 2.25
291 WS(c),TD(i),V:Stalagron 2.25
292 thru 294 ...... @2.25
295 FMc(i) 2.25
296 RA 2.25
297 GC,V:Pantheon 2.25
298 V:Pantheon 2.25
299 GC,V:Pantheon 2.25
300 RA,GP,KJ,MT,FMc,A:JLA ... 2.25
301 Rampage 2.25
302 DM,NA(rep) 2.25
303 Plague 2.25
304 SLi,O:Null&Void 2.25
305 TVE,V:Null&Void 2.25
306 SLi,I:Swordfish & Barracuda . 2.25
307 TVE,V:Null&Void 2.25
308 GT,Night and Day 2.25
309 MT,AA,V:Quantum 2.25
310 I:Sonik 2.25
311 A:Monitor 2.25
312 AA,I:Network 2.25
313 AA(i),V:Network 2.25
314 AA(i),V:Executrix 2.25
315 V:Cathode 2.25
316 LSn,I:Cheapjack 2.25
317 LSn,V:Cheapjack 2.25
318 AA(i),A:Sonik 2.25
319 AA(i),I:REM 2.25
320 AA(i),V:REM 2.25
321 AA,V:Chronos 2.25
322 KG,The Search 2.25
323 AA(i),final issue 2.25

WORLD'S FINEST
[Limited Series]

1 SR,KK,Worlds Apart 8.00
2 SR,KK,Worlds Collide 6.00
3 SR,KK,Worlds At War 6.00
TPB rep.#1-3 ...... 19.95

WORLD'S GREATEST SUPER-HEROES
1977

1 A:Batman,Robin 2.50

WORLD WITHOUT END
1990

1 The Host, I:Brother Bones 5.00
2 A:Brother Bones 3.50
3 ...... 3.50
4 House of Fams 2.50
5 Female Fury 2.50
6 conclusion 2.50

WRATH OF THE SPECTRE
May, 1988

1 JAp,rep.AdventureCom.#431-3 2.50
2 JAp,rep.AdventureCom.#434-6 2.50
3 JAp,rep.AdventureCom.#437-40 2.50
4 JAp,reps.,final issue 2.50

YOUNG ALL STARS
June, 1987

1 I:IronMunro&FlyingFox,D:TNT . 4.50
2 V:Axis Amerika 2.50
3 V:Axis Amerika 2.00
4 I:The Tigress 1.50
5 I:Dyna-mite,O:Iron Munro 1.50
6 ...... 1.50
7 Baseball Game,A:Tigress 1.25
8 Millenium 1.25
9 Millenium 1.25
10 Hugo Danner 1.25
11 'Birth of Iron Munro' 1.25
12 'Secret of Hugo Danner' 1.25
13 'V:Deathbolt,Ultra-Humanite .. 1.25
14 Fury+Ultra Humanite 1.25
15 IronMunro At high school 1.25
16 Ozyan Inheritance 1.25
17 Ozyan Inheritance 1.25
18 Ozyan Inheritance 1.25
19 Ozyan 1.50
20 O:Flying Fox 1.50
21 Atom & Evil#1 ...... 1.50
22 Atom & Evil#2 ...... 1.50
23 Atom & Evil#3 ...... 1.50
24 Atom & Evil#4 ...... 1.50
25 ...... 1.50
26 End of the All Stars? 1.75
27 'Sons of Dawn' begins 1.75
28 Search for Hugo Danner 1.75
29 A:Hugo Danner 1.75
30 V:Sons of Dawn 1.75
31 V:Sons of Dawn,last issue ... 1.75
Ann.#1 MG,V:Mekanique 2.25

YOUNG LOVE
September-October, 1963

39 ...... 8.00
40 thru 50 ...... @5.00
51 thru 70 ...... @4.00
71 thru 80 ...... @3.00
81 thru 126 ...... @1.50

XOMBI
Milestone

0 WS(c),DCw,Shadow War,Foil(c), I:Xombi,Twilight 2.50
1 JBy(c),B:Silent Cathedrals 2.00

ZATANNA
1987

1 R:Zatanna 2.25
2 N:Zatanna 2.25
3 Come Together 2.25
4 V:Xaos 2.25

The World's Greatest Comic Magazine!

By Phil Mateer

The World's Greatest Comic Magazine begins with the cover, which may be the most-parodied cover in comics (along with the Superman-hoisting-the-car shot from *Action* #1). The reader takes in the huge green monster first, a typical Jack Kirby behemoth erupting from the pavement, and then scans the four figures arrayed against it.

Then the eye travels to the left, up to the monster's upraised arm to its hand, which is gripping a woman who is partially transparent. Her dialogue focuses attention on the flaming man in the center and then on the lumpy orange thing underneath him, seen only from behind, and finally to the strangely elongated figure on the lower right. Only then does the reader have time to study the title and cover blurb: "The FANTASTIC FOUR featuring, 'The Thing!' 'Mr. Fantastic!' 'Human Torch!' 'Invisible Girl!' together for the first time in one mighty magazine!"

On the inside splash page, that title appears again in large smoky letters floating in the air over a busy city street. A crowd gasps and points. "Look," they seem to be saying. "Up in the sky!" And then the story begins.

In that first issue, after a seven-page sequence introducing each of the members and their powers, the book recaps how they began: scientist Reed Richards wants to beat the Russkies into space and browbeats test pilot Ben Grimm into piloting their experimental rocket ship on an unauthorized flight into space. Sue Storm, Reed's fiancee, and her brother Johnny come along because uh, well, because four of them are necessary to justify the title, apparently.

The ship, unshielded, passes through a band of "cosmic rays" and heads back to earth. Ben manages to get them down in one piece, but the rays have changed them. Sue turns invisible, then reappears. Ben blames Reed, and as they start to fight Ben changes, becoming incredibly powerful (but monstrous). Reed ducks out of Ben's way, his body elongating like a rubber band, and Johnny bursts into flames and finds that he can fly.

After they calm down, they assess their situation, and all four have the same thought: "We've changed! All of us! We're *more* than just human!" Reed starts to talk about their responsibilities, but Ben cuts him off: "You don't have to make a speech, big shot! We understand! We've gotta *use* that power to help mankind, right?"

Johnny is the first to extend his hand: "I'm calling myself The Human Torch, and I'm with you all the way!" Reed puts his hand on top, then Sue and Reed says, "There's only

one still missing, Ben!" The lumpy orange paw, with its four fingers, dwarfs the others. "I ain't Ben anymore. I'm what Sue called me-The Thing!!"

And that's only the first thirteen pages! The F.F. still have to discover Monster Isle and fight the Mole Man-but the image that lingers is of those four clasped hands, supporting and enfolding one another.

Origins

In the real world, it began with a golf game. In early 1961, Martin Goodman, Marvel's then publisher, had been playing with one of his counterparts at DC Comics and listening to his competitor brag about the success of DC's revival of the Justice League. Costumed heroes were getting hot again, the man had said. Goodman, who had watched Marvel limp along on the edge of bankruptcy for years, producing Western comics, romances, comedy, and monster/horror books, went back to the office determined to milk the new trend.

Goodman tapped Stan Lee, a longtime staffer, for the job of producing some sort of super team book for Marvel; it's likely that Goodman, like most publishers, wanted it to be as close to the successful Justice League as possible, in both concept and story.

It wasn't. Lee turned to Jack Kirby, who had recently left DC and linked up with Marvel after failing to find work elsewhere, and gave him a treatment for the new title in mid-1961. That treatment, partially reprinted in *Fantastic Four* #358, thirty years later, is Lee's synopsis of the first half of *F.F.* #1, including the introduction of the main characters and their origins.

It's an interesting document-for example, the original concept of Sue was of a woman permanently invisible, who could only be seen by her clothing, like H. G. Wells' Invisible Man. The Torch had apparently given the Comics Code Authority fits-Lee mentions that he can never burn people or even shoot fireballs at them; he can only burn through objects. The really fascinating characterization is of The Thing-he's even more monstrous as a character, mentally and physically. Ben Grimm is only in the group because he wants to take Sue away from Reed, and he couldn't care less about helping mankind!

The Magic Collaboration

That little two-page treatment is fascinating in other ways, too. First, it seems to establish Lee as the originator of the concept, something that the two creators have often disputed. Second, it shows just how much Kirby did bring to that first issue: The art that came from the treatment dramatized and enhanced the skeletal summary, making it bolder and more visually striking, and smoothing over some of the plot points while creating or highlighting others. Kirby obviously did more than just sit down and draw what Lee had written.

Who created the Fantastic Four, Lee or Kirby? Neither. It was a collaboration; their talents happened to come together in the right place, at the right time, and something was born that could only have come from a combination of their skills-something marvelous. Like another famous collaboration taking place at the same time, as John Lennon and Paul McCartney struggled to express a new sound in the dark, smoky nightclubs of Hamburg, Germany, the F.F. was a group effort.

The Fantastic Four and the Beatles had something else in common-they were born of a sense of desperation, of the energy of creation that comes from taking one last chance, with nothing left to lose. Marvel was on the edge of bankruptcy; there was nothing stopping

Lee and Kirby from throwing everything but the kitchen sink into a last-ditch attempt to be different, to take old concepts and make them new again.

The parts themselves weren't that new. The four main characters were familiar pulp stereotypes-the noble scientist, the muscular tough guy with the soft heart, the young hot-head, the girlfriend. Kirby, who had recently created *Challengers of the Unknown* for DC, visualized the F.F. much the same way. (There's a panel in the first issue, as the four stumble out of their downed rocket in their purple jumpsuits, just before their powers appear, where they could *be* the Challengers. It's almost as if it were a 1961 imaginary story: What if the Challengers of the Unknown got superpowers?)

A Family Affair

Much has been made of the way Lee and Kirby "humanized" the superhero, by having the F.F. bicker among themselves and show human frailties. But that first issue's central image of clasped hands is the real key to the F.F.'s popularity: they're a family, a rough-and-tumble but ultimately solid bulwark against the outside world. They have built-in stresses, like any family. Reed's all intellect, can be stubborn, and is a little too quick to give orders to suit the others; Johnny hates to be treated like a kid and is rebellious because of it; Sue gets upset if she's patronized or underestimated; Ben has to live with his tragic deformity and blames Reed, who feels guilty in return. At bottom, though, none of it matters. They come together for one another, and, while they may fight among themselves, woe to the outsider who tries to break them up.

To the adolescent readers who made *The Fantastic Four* so successful, it must have been comforting. Here was a family just like most of their own-fighting and sniping at one another, but ultimately loving one another, too. If your own parents were arguing or if you and your siblings bickered like The Torch and The Thing, it was nice to think that everyone would pull together if the outside world threatened, and that the family unit would survive no matter what-just like the F.F.!

The End of the F.F.?

Given this unifying theme of family (a concept that Lee and Kirby emphasized constantly and that every other creator on the book has dealt with), it's ironic that the F.F. has generated so much attention in the past year by seeming to break up. Issue #381 (October 1993) featured the "death" of Reed Richards at the hands of a "dying" Dr. Doom, and the surviving cast members have all faced problems and undergone personality change. Rumors of the book's cancellation and its replacement with a new title, *Fantastic Force*, have generated considerable controversy, and Marvel has fueled it by hinting that most of the cast will "die" at the end of the current storyline, sometime in the late summer or fall of 1994.

Would they actually kill Reed Richards and Dr. Doom for good? Is this, finally, the end of the Fantastic Four?

Well, it could be but it's not very likely. Even if Marvel's current management was sincere in saying that the characters were dead/deceased/demised or joined the choir invisible/etc., there would be nothing to stop a new Marvel management in, say, ten years from bringing them back. (Look at Jean Grey/Phoenix, who was specifically killed off by an editor, never to return, but who returned fewer than seven years later.)

There's certainly no economic reason for Marvel to cancel the book. Quite the opposite, in fact. Spring 1994 circulation figures showed sales of about 220,000 per issue, on

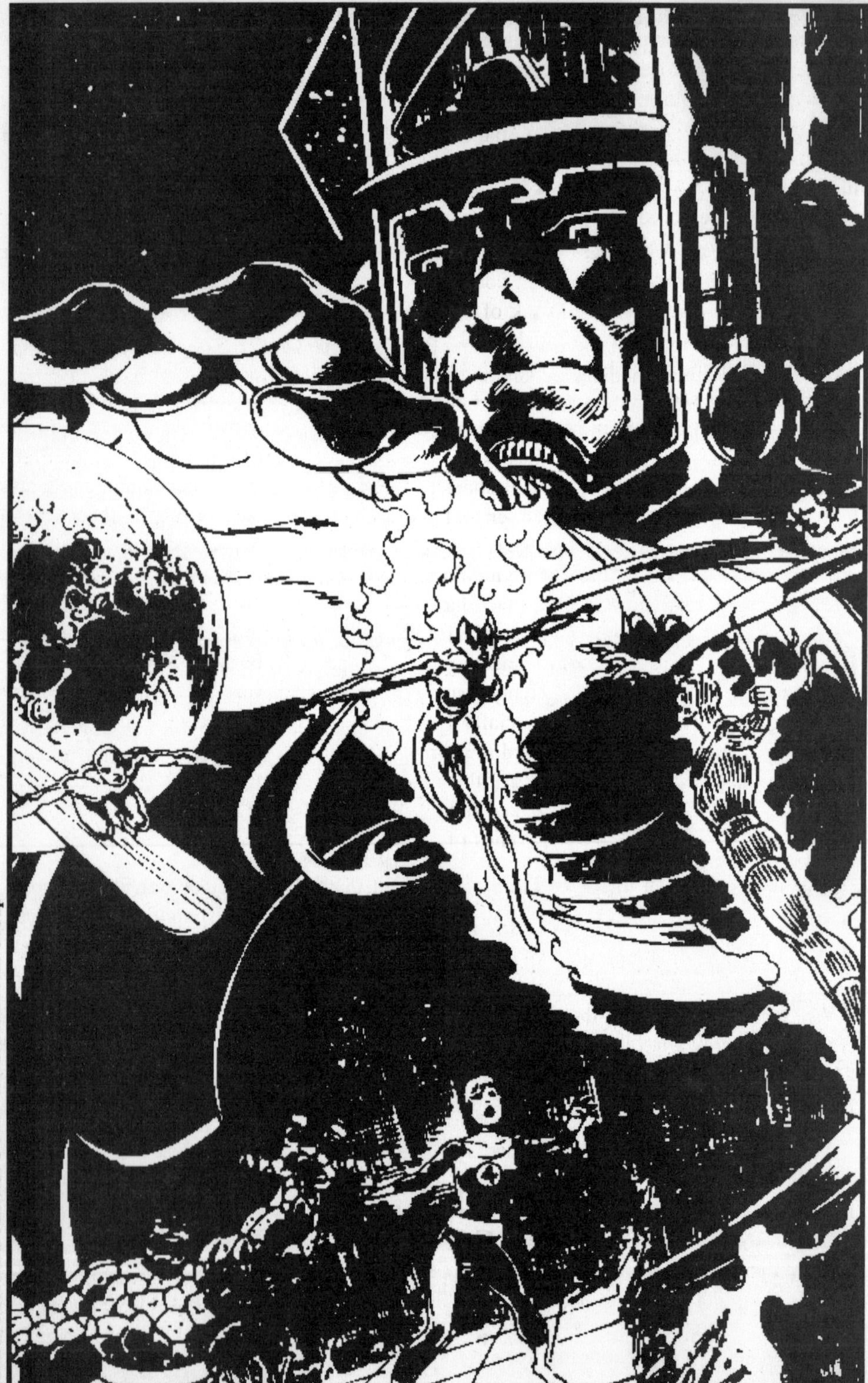

the high end of the book's average for the previous five years and very healthy for any book in today's market. (Marvel's average circulation per title is probably around 110,000, so sales on F.F. are not the problem.)

Besides, there's at least one F.F. movie on the horizon, featuring the original characters; also there's an F.F. cartoon as half of *Marvel Action Hour*, slated for TV syndication in the fall of 1994, featuring the original characters. The F.F. aren't exactly Superman, but Marvel as a corporation does have quite a bit of merchandizing potential wrapped up in them. Heck, the stockholders would end up voting to revive the group!

All of these are good reasons, but there's one better-the F.F. are too much a part of Marvel's history; they're family. Tom Defalco, Marvel's current editor-in-chief and the F.F.'s writer for the last three years, counts Stan Lee as a major influence on his writing, and he has mastered the Lee knack of seeming to change the characters and keeping a book interesting without violating the underlying mythology and basic concepts that made it successful in the first place.

In fact, in his second issue as writer, #357, Defalco eliminated a longtime plot development by having the "Alicia Masters" who had married Johnny turn out to be one of the shape-shifting alien Skrulls instead. This allowed a return of the "real" Alicia as Ben's love interest and reinstated a crucial character relationship-the innocent blind sculptress who *can't* see Ben as a monster and senses his inner nobility. She's beauty to his beast and leavens his tragedy. Defalco's change showed that he understood the relationship was a cornerstone of the F.F.'s character dynamics.

Defalco and artist Paul Ryan, in fact, have done more than thirty consecutive issues of the F.F., a record topped only by Lee and Kirby themselves in the 1960s and by writer/artist John Byrne in the 1980s. (Ralph Macchio, the book's editor, has been on board for more than seven years, or more than eighty issues.) Despite their track record, all three have been the subject of criticism, especially from old-time fans, that they're "ruining" the comic because they don't understand the characters!

A rereading of the last few years of the title indicates little evidence of this. Most plot or character developments that looked out of place at the time have eventually been explained, and the characterization comes off as much more subtle (and justifiable) than it might have seemed at first.

The intense fan reaction to rumors of the book's demise, and changes/deaths of its characters, is a tribute to *The Fantastic Four's* place in comics history and to the effect its themes have had on generations of readers. They're fond of the book and react to threats to its characters much as they'd react to someone threatening their own families.

They can relax, though-the F.F. *is* a family, and the available evidence indicates that its creators do know what they're doing. Readers should be able to look forward to an issue #400 in 1995 and to many more after that, and (eventually) to seeing Reed, Sue, Ben, and Johnny bickering and bonding as always, just them against the world.

That's how it is with family.

THE FANTASTIC FOUR: A COLLECTOR'S GUIDE

There are two problems with collecting a title of almost four hundred issues-it's hard to get all of them, and the early ones cost more than your car! What follows isn't meant as a guide to speculators or investors but as a look at the better buys (and the most essential stories) of the F.F.'s run.

The Early Years

(Issues #1-30)

All of these are available as part of the Marvel Masterworks series, so you can own a piece of comics history without ransoming your firstborn. Nuff said!

These issues, especially toward the end, show Lee and Kirby using increasingly sophisticated plot and art (Lee's subplots and Kirby's photo collages, for example) as they gain confidence in the book and its possibilities.

The World's Greatest Comic Magazine

(Issues #31-50)

The key sequence here is issues #38-50, which are Lee and Kirby at their best. (In Good to Very Good condition, most of these are available for around $15, and they're essential reading if you want to know what all the fuss over the F.F. was about.) These twelve issues represent the most astonishing year's run of any comic series; they've never been matched for sustained creative power.

In #38, the F.F. lose their powers and in #39-40 have to fight Dr. Doom, with only guest-star Daredevil to help them. In #40, Reed changes a now-human Ben back into The Thing, and in a remarkable seven-page sequence the enraged and embittered Thing goes after Dr. Doom, wades through every weapon and trap thrown at him, and crushes Doom's armor, wrists, and spirit. Then, he quits the F.F.

Issues #41-43 are a fight against an evil Thing (courtesy of the Frightful Four's "ID machine") and lead into Reed and Sue's wedding in *F.F. Annual* #3, which features just about every character in the Marvel Universe, including Lee and Kirby. Issues #44-47 introduce the Inhumans, Johnny's longtime girlfriend Crystal, the Great Refuge and all this leads up to the introduction of the Silver Surfer and Galactus, in issues #48-50, is the topper to Lee and Kirby's remarkable year. It wraps Lee's sense of humanity and heroism (and tragedy) and Kirby's sense of power and cosmic scale (and again, somehow, humanity) into one seamless whole.

After the Top, Where Do You Go?

(Issues #51-102)

After the galactic scale of #48-50, some smaller stories were in order- issue #51, "This Man-This Monster" is a self-contained story of what it means to be The Thing and of the responsibilities that go with power.

Issues #51-53 introduce the Black Panther, and then the ante gets upped again for issues #57-60, where Dr. Doom steals the Surfer's power and tries to conquer the world with it. In #61-62, the F.F. enter the negative zone for the first time, and #66-67 featured the origin of Him, who later becomes Warlock.

It's common for critics to pinpoint the period after #67 as the beginning of the F.F.'s decline, but "decline" is misleading. It's true that few new characters or concepts are created after Him, but any issue from #68-102 has Lee's scripting and Kirby's art, and that's enough to recommend it.

Having established a huge cast of characters and concepts, Lee and Kirby seem content to tell stories within those parameters. Failure to constantly top yourself isn't necessarily the same as declining!

These later issues are relatively cheap-VG copies run around $5 and deserve to be read.

The Thing © Marvel Entertainment Group

Of them, issues #84-87 offer a good Dr. Doom story (with an unusual, for comics, ending) while #90-93 have The Thing kidnapped by Skrulls and taken to fight in their alien arena (the Skrulls, as shape shifters, have all chosen to look like American gangsters, or Edward G. Robinson, and nobody could draw Depression-era gangsters like Kirby). Similarly, #94 introduces Agatha Harkness, and Kirby has a lot of fun with the witchy mood of the story.

Post-Kirby

(Issues #103-125)

There are many reasons why Kirby left with issue #102, but the biggest was surely that he and Lee had been on the book for almost nine years straight, and they were tired of it. They'd hung every change on the concept they could and were repeating themselves. Lee stayed for two more years, mostly with artist John Buscema, and the stories, while certainly readable, also show a winding-down of the book's creative energy.

Post-Lee: Enter Roy Thomas

(Issues #126-181)

Issue #126, the first Roy Thomas edited book, has an announcement on the letters page about Lee's leaving, and also has the first cover parody of *F.F.* #1. Thomas edited (and wrote most issues of) the book for almost five years in the early 1970s, and he kept things moving briskly. Sales declined, however (as they did on most of Marvel's books during this period), falling from 276,000 in 1972 to just under 200,000 in 1977. Most issues from this era are priced at $3 to $4 in nice shape; the best are probably the ones with George Perez art: #164-167; #170-172; #176-178. This whole later sequence involves the reintroduction of Marvel Boy (later Quasar), the Hulk, The Thing becoming Ben Grimm (and his substitution in the group by Luke Cage), Galactus, and the Impossible Man, and it's a good representation of the pleasures of the Roy Thomas reign.

Doctor Doom © Marvel Entertainment Group

A State of Transition

(Issues #182-231)

Marvel itself was going through a number of editorial changes during the mid to late 1970s, and this probably affected the book. By 1979, circulation had dropped to its lowest point ever, 178,000. The Len Wein/George Perez issues, #184-188 and #191-192, are worth a look, especially at only $2 to $3 each in nice condition. Issues #209-214, by Marv Wolfman and John Byrne, involve the F.F. getting zapped by a Skrull aging ray, and their gradual slide into old age and death (no, they didn't really die this time, either). These issues are the high point of this run, and the Byrne art, which significantly increased sales, set's the stage for the next transition.

The Byrne Era

(Issues #232-293)

John Byrne was the writer and artist of all the issues during this period, and these are the absolute bargain of the whole *F.F.* run-Very Fine copies of most of them are only about $3, and are often discounted. At sixty-one and a half issues, Byrne's run on the book is the longest since Lee/Kirby and the best at recalling their imaginative plot twists, effective characterization, and evocative art.

Englehart

(Issues #294-333)

It's tough to follow a long, admired run on a title, and for some reason the Steve Englehart authored stories never caught on with fans-in the last two years of his tenure, circulation dipped below 200,000 for only the second time in the book's history. Issues #318-319, with the Molecule Man and the only appearance (and origin story) of the Beyonder since the Secret Wars II series, are the most interesting.

Simonized

(Issues #334-354)

Writer/artist Walt Simonson, brought onto the book to zap up the sales figures, did just that. Except for issues #347-349, which have guest art by Art Adams, these books list for under $2, and they're imaginative fun (#337, the first with Simonson art, starts a time-travel story with Iron Man and Thor guesting and dialogue from Reed like "I'm turning on the redundancy existentialators. Hold tight! This is going to be rough!"). Issues #345-346 have the F.F. lost and powerless on an island occupied by dinosaurs and the U.S. Army, and Simonson's love for drawing dinosaurs is obvious. Issues #350 and 352 feature Dr. Doom, with a Reed/Doom time battle in #352 that jumps back and forth among the pages-a clever idea that's executed flawlessly.

Defalco/Ryan

(Issues #355-Present)

These have already been covered. Too soon to tell yet, but it *is* the third-longest sustained creative team in the F.F.'s history, and it's been worth reading. Issue #358, the 30th anniversary issue, sports both Marvel's first die-cut cover (which doesn't make it interesting) and Lee's original 1961 synopsis for *F.F.* #1 (which does).

Issue #381, with the "deaths" of Reed Richards and Dr. Doom, is up to the $5 to $10 range, but if Reed and Doom come back by #400 it won't hold its value.

For $10.00, you'd be better off buying a cruddy copy of one of the classic Lee/Kirby issues, and some junk food, and curling up to relive the F.F.'s classic years. You won't be sorry.

ACTION FORCE
March, 1987

1 U.K. G.I. Joe Series 1.50
2 thru 39 . . . . @1.00
40 1988 . . . . 1.00

ACTUAL CONFESSIONS
See: LOVE ADVENTURES

ACTUAL ROMANCES
October, 1949

1 . . . . 35.00
2 Photo Cover 20.00

ADVENTURE INTO MYSTERY
Atlas
May, 1956

1 BEv(c),Future Tense 150.00
2 Man on the 13th Floor 70.00
3 Next Stop Eternity 60.00
4 AW, The Hex 70.00
5 BEv,The People Who Weren't 60.00
6 The Wax Man 60.00
7 May, 1957 . . . . 60.00

ADVENTURES INTO TERROR
See: JOKER COMICS

ADVENTURES INTO WEIRD WORLDS
January, 1952

1 RH,GT,The Walking Death . 200.00
2 The Thing In the Bottle . . . 125.00
3 The Thing That Waited 85.00
4 BEv,RH,The Village Graveyard 85.00
5 BEv,I Crawl Thru Graves . . . 85.00
6 The Ghost Still Walks 85.00
7 Monsters In Disguise 85.00
8 Nightmares 85.00
9 Do Not Feed 85.00

Adventures into Weird Worlds #27
© Marvel Entertainment Group

10 BEv,Down In The Cellar . . . 100.00
11 Phantom 75.00
12 Lost In the Graveyard 75.00
13 Where Dead Men Walk 75.00
14 A Shriek In the Night 75.00
15 Terror In Our Town 75.00
16 The Kiss of Death 75.00
17 RH,He Walks With A Ghost . 75.00
18 Ivan & Petroff 75.00
19 It Happened One Night 75.00
20 The Doubting Thomas 75.00
21 What Happened In the Cave . 85.00
22 RH,The Vampire's Partner . . 60.00
23 The Kiss of Death 60.00
24 Halfway Home 60.00
25 BEv,JSt,The Mad Mamba . . . 60.00
26 Good-Bye Earth 60.00
27 The Dwarf of Horror Moor . . 125.00
28 DW,Monsters From the Grave 75.00
29 Bone Dry 45.00
30 JSt,The Impatient Ghost; June, 1954 . . . . 45.00

ADVENTURES OF CAPTAIN AMERICA
September, 1991

1 KM,JRu,O:Capt. America 5.75
2 KM,KWe,TA,O:Capt.America . . 5.50
3 KM,KWe,JRu,D:Lt.Col.Fletcher 5.50
4 KWe,JRu,V:Red Skull 5.50

ADVENTURES OF CYCLOPS & PHOENIX

1 SLo(s),GeH,AV,O:Cable 3.50
2 SLo(s),GeH,AV,O:Cable 3.25
3 SLo(s),GeH,AV,O:Cable 2.95

ADVENTURES OF HOMER GHOST
Atlas
June, 1957

1 . . . . 25.00
2 August, 1957 . . . . 20.00

ADVENTURES OF PINKY LEE
Atlas
July, 1955

1 . . . . 125.00
2 . . . . 65.00
3 . . . . 54.00
4 . . . . 54.00
5 . . . . 54.00

ADVENTURES ON THE PLANET OF THE APES
October, 1975

1 GT,Planet of the Apes Movie Adaptation 3.50
2 GT,Humans Captured 3.00
3 GT,Man Hunt 3.00
4 GT,Trial By Fear 3.00
5 GT, Fury in the Forbidden Zone 3.00
6 GT,The Forbidden Zone,Cont'd 2.50
7 AA,Man Hunt Cont'd 2.50
8 AA,Brent & Nova Enslaved . . . 2.50
9 AA,Mankind's Demise 2.50
10 AA,When Falls the Lawgiver . . 2.50
11 AA,The Final Chapter; December, 1976 . . . . 2.50

AIRTIGHT GARAGE
Epic

1 thru 4 rep.Moebius GNv . . . . @2.50

AKIRA
Epic
September, 1988

1 The Highway,I:Kaneda,Tetsuo, Koy,Ryu,Colonel,Takaski . . . 22.00
1a 2nd printing 4.50
2 Pursuit,I:Number27,(Masaru) . 14.00
2a 2nd printing 4.50
3 Number 41,V:Clown Gang . . . 10.00
4 King of Clowns,V:Colonel . . . 10.00
5 Cycle Wars,V:Clown Gang . . . 9.00
6 D:Yamagota 8.00
7 Prisoners and Players,I:Miyok . 8.00
8 Weapon of Vengeance 8.00
9 Stalkers 8.00
10 The Awakening 8.00
11 Akira Rising 7.00
12 Enter Sakaki 7.00
13 Desperation 7.00
14 Caught in the Middle 7.00
15 Psychic Duel 7.00
16 Akira Unleashed 7.00
17 Emperor of Chaos 5.50
18 Amid the Ruins 5.50
19 To Save the Children 5.50
20 Revelations 5.50
21 . . . . 5.00
22 . . . . 5.00
23 . . . . 5.00
24 Clown Gang 5.00
25 Search For Kay 5.00
26 Juvenile A Project 5.00
27 Kay and Kaneda 5.00
28 Tetsuo 4.50
29 Tetsuo 4.50
30 Tetsuo,Kay,Kaneda 4.50
31 D:Kaori,Kaneda,Vs.Tetsuo . . . 4.50
32 Tetsuo'sForces vs.U.S.Forces . 4.50
33 Tetsuo V:Kaneda 4.50
34 . . . . 4.50
35 . . . . 4.50
TPB Akira:Reprints#1-#3 . . . . . . 13.95
TPB Akira:Reprints#4-#6 . . . . . . 14.95
TPB Akira:Reprints#7-#9 . . . . . . 14.95
TPB Akira:Reprints#10-#12 . . . . 14.95
TPB Akira:Reprints#13-#15 . . . . 14.95

ALF
Star
March, 1988

1 Photo Cover 2.00
1a 2nd printing 1.00
2 Alf Causes trouble 1.50
3 More adventures 1.50
4 Willie on Melmac 1.50
5 I:Alf's evil twin 1.50
6 Photo Cover 1.50
7 Pygm-Alien 1.50
8 Ochmoneks' Garage 1.25
9 Alf's Independence Day 1.25
10 Alf goes to College 1.25
11 Halloween special 1.00
12 Alf loses memory 1.00
13 Racetrack of my Tears 1.00
14 Night of the Living Bread 1.25
15 Alf on the Road 1.00
16 More Adventures 1.00
17 Future vision 1.00
18 More Adventures 1.00
19 The Alf-strologer 1.00
20 Alf the Baby Sitter pt.1 . . . . . . 1.00
21 Alf the Baby Sitter pt.2 . . . . . . 1.00
22 X-Men parody 1.00
23 Alf visits Australia 1.00
24 Rhonda visits Earth 1.00
25 More Adventures 1.00
26 Alf gets a job 1.00
27 Alf lost 1.00
28 Alf's Amnesia 1.00
29 Alf/Brian reporters 1.00
30 Shakespeare Baby 1.00
31 Alf's Summer Camp 1.00
32 Arnold Schwarzemeimac 1.00
33 Dungeons & Dragons Spoof . . 1.00
34 Alf-Red & Alf-Blue(2 Alfs) 1.00
35 Gone with the Wind 1.00
36 More Adventures 1.00
37 Melmacian Gothic 1.00
38 Boundtree Hunters 1.00
39 Pizarro Alf 1.00
40 A:Zoreo 1.00
41 TV 1.00
42 V:Alf 1.00
43 House Break-in 1.00
44 A:Fantastic Fur 1.00

All comics prices listed are for *Near Mint* condition.

45 Melmenopaus 1.00
46 Goes to Center of Earth 1.00
47 Meteor Bye-Products Pt.1 . . . . 1.00
48 Meteor Bye-Products Pt.2 . . . . 1.00
49 1st Rhonda solo story 1.00
50 Final Issue, giant size 1.75
Ann.#1 Evol.War 3.00
Ann.#2 . . . . 1.75
Spring Spec.#1 . . . . 1.75
Holiday Spec.#2 . . . . 2.00

ALIEN LEGION
Epic
April, 1984

1 FC,TA,I:Sarigar,Montroc 4.50
2 FC,TA,CP,V:Harkilons 3.00
3 FC,TA,CW,V:Kroyzo 2.75
4 FC,TA,CW,F:Skob 2.25
5 FC,CW,D:Skob 2.25
6 FC,CW,WPo,V:Harkilons 2.25

Alien Legion #7
© Marvel Entertainment Group

7 CW,WPo,I:Lora 2.00
8 CW,WPo,V:Harkilons 2.00
9 CW,V:Harkilons 2.00
10 CW,LSn,V:Harkilons 2.00
11 CW,LSn,V:Harkilons 2.00
12 LSn,A:Aob-Sin 2.00
13 LSn,F:Montroc 2.00
14 LSn,V:Cordar 2.00
15 LSn,V:Alphor,Betro,&Gamoid . 2.00
16 LSn,J:Tomaro 2.00
17 LSn,Durge on Drugs 2.00
18 LSn,V:Dun 2.00
19 LSn,A:GalarcyScientist 2.00
20 LSn,L:Skilene 2.00

[2nd Series]

1 LSn,I:Guy Montroc 2.00
2 LSn,V:Quallians 1.50
3 LSn,Hellscope 1.50
4 LSn,V:Harkillons 1.50
5 LSn,F:JuggerGrimrod 1.50
6 LSn,F:JuggerGrimrod 1.50
7 LSn,A:Guy Montroc 1.50
8 LSn,I:Nakhira 1.50
9 LSn,V:Harkilons 1.50
10 LSn,V:Harkilons 1.50
11 LSn,V:Harkilons 1.50
12 LSn,Tamara Pregnant 1.50
13 LSn,V:MomojianKndrel 1.50
14 LSn,J:Saravil 1.50
15 LSn,J:Spellik 1.50
16 LSn,D:Jugger's Father 1.50
17 LSn,O:JuggerGrimrod 1.50
18 LSn,O:JuggerGrimrod 1.50

ALIEN LEGION: ON THE EDGE
Epic

1 LSn,V:B'Be No N'ngth 5.50
2 LSn,V:B'Be No N'ngth 4.50
3 LSn,V:B'Be No N'ngth 4.50

ALIEN LEGION TENANTS OF HELL
Epic

1 LSn,Nomad Squad On
Combine IV 4.50
2 LSn,L:Torie Montroc,I:Stagg . . 4.50
Alien Legion: Slaughterworld 9.95

ALL-SELECT COMICS
Fall, 1943
Timely (Daring Comics)

1 B:Capt.America,Sub-Mariner,
Human Torch;WWII 2,500.00
2 A:Red Skull,V:Axis Powers 1,000.00
3 B:Whizzer,V:Axis 650.00
4 V: Axis 500.00
5 E:Sub-Mariner,V:Axis 500.00
6 A:The Destroyer,V:Axis . . . 450.00
7 E:Whizzer,V:Axis 450.00
8 V:Axis Powers 450.00
9 V:Axis Powers 450.00
10 E:Capt.America,Human Torch;
A:The Destroyer 450.00
11 I:Blonde Phantom,A:Miss
America 750.00

Becomes:

BLONDE PHANTOM

12 B:Miss America;The Devil's
Playground 650.00
13 B:Sub-Mariner;Horror In
Hollywood 400.00
14 E:Miss America;Horror At
Haunetd Castle 300.00

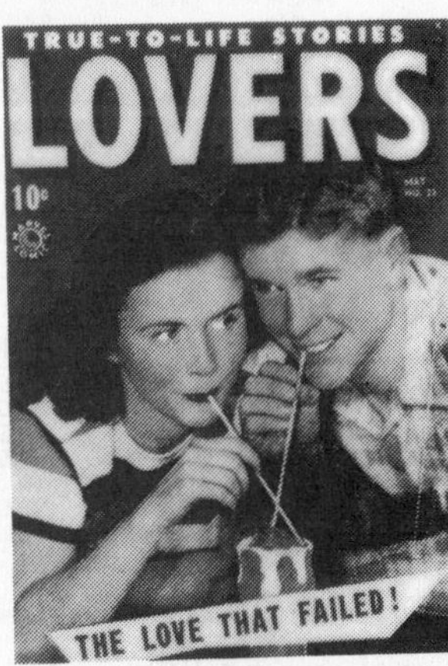

Lovers #23
© Marvel Entertainment Group

15 The Man Who Deserved
To Die 300.00
16 A:Capt.America,Bucky;
Modeled For Murder 400.00
17 Torture & Rescue 275.00
18 Jealously,Hate & Cruelty . . . 275.00

19 Killer In the Hospital 275.00
20 Blonde Phantom's Big Fall 275.00
21 Murder At the Carnival 275.00
22 V: Crime Bosses 275.00

Becomes:

LOVERS

23 Love Stories 50.00
24 My Dearly Beloved 25.00
25 The Man I Love 30.00
26 thru 29 . . . . @15.00
30 . . . . 30.00
31 thru 36 . . . . @15.00
37 . . . . 34.00
38 . . . . 34.00
39 . . . . 14.00
40 . . . . 14.00
41 . . . . 14.00
42 thru 65 . . . . @14.00
66 . . . . 12.00
67 ATh 30.00
68 thru 85 . . . . @12.00
86 August, 1957 . . . . 12.00

ALL SURPRISE
Timely
Fall, 1943

1 (fa),F:Super Rabbit,Gandy,
Sourpuss 110.00
2 . . . . 50.00
3 . . . . 35.00
4 thru 10 . . . . @35.00
11 HK 50.00
12 Winter, 1946 . . . . 35.00

ALL-TRUE CRIME
See: OFFICIAL TRUE CRIME CASES

ALL WINNERS COMICS
Summer, 1941

1 S&K,BEv,B:Capt.America & Bucky,
Human Torch & Toro,Sub-Mariner
A:The Angel,Black Marvel 6,000.00
2 S&K,B:Destroyer,Whizzer . 1,700.00

All Winners #10
© Marvel Entertainment Group

3 BEv,Bucky & Toro Captured 1,100.00
4 BEv,Battle For Victory
For America 1,400.00
5 V:Nazi Invasion Fleet 750.00
6 V:Axis Powers,A:
Black Avenger 850.00

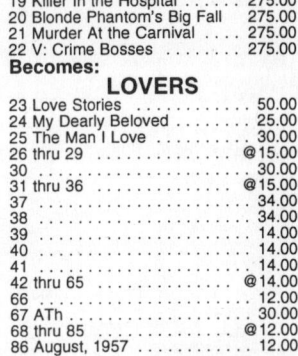

7 V:Axis Powers 650.00
8 V:Axis Powers 650.00
9 V:Nazi Submarine Fleet ... 650.00
10 V:Nazi Submarine Fleet ... 650.00
11 V: Nazis 450.00
12 A:Red Skull,E:Destroyer; Jap P.O.W. Camp 500.00
13 V:Japanese Fleet 450.00
14 V:Japanese Fleet 450.00
15 Japanese Supply Train 450.00
16 In Alaska V:Gangsters 450.00
17 V:Gansters;Atomic Research Department 450.00
18 V:Robbers;Internal Revenue Department 450.00
19 I:All Winners Squad, Fall, 1946 .... 1,100.00
21 A:All-Winners Squad;Riddle of the Demented Dwarf ... 1,000.00

Becomes:

ALL TEEN COMICS

20 F:Georgie,Willie, Mitzi,Patsy Walker 40.00

Becomes:

TEEN COMICS

21 A:George,Willie,Mitzi, Patsy Walker 48.00
22 A:George,Willie,Margie, Patsy Walker 30.00
23 A:Patsy Walker,Cindy,George 30.00
24 .... 45.00
25 .... 30.00
26 .... 40.00
27 .... 30.00
28 .... 45.00
29 .... 30.00
30 .... 45.00
31 thru 34 .... @30.00
35 May, 1950 .... 30.00

Becomes:

JOURNEY INTO UNKNOWN WORLDS

Atlas

36(1) RH,End of the Earth .. 800.00
37(2) BEv,GC,When Worlds Collide 400.00
38(3) GT,Land of Missing Men 350.00
4 MS,RH,Train to Nowhere ... 250.00
5 MS,Trapped in Space 250.00
6 GC,RH,World Below the Atlantic 250.00
7 BW,RH,House That Wasn't . 400.00
8 RH,The Stone Thing 225.00
9 MS,JSt,The People Who Couldn't Exist 250.00
10 THe Undertaker 225.00
11 BEv,Frankie Was Afraid ... 200.00
12 The Last Voice You Hear .. 200.00
13 The Witch Woman 125.00
14 BW,BEv,CondemnedBuilding 300.00
15 They Crawl By Night 300.00
16 Scared to Death 125.00
17 BEv,GC,RH,The Ice Monster Cometh 125.00
18 The Broth Needs Somebody 150.00
19 GC,The Long Wait 150.00
20 GC,RH,The Race That Vanished 125.00
21 thru 25 .... @100.00
26 thru 35 .... @75.00
36 thru 44 .... @65.00
45 AW,SD 75.00
46 .... 50.00
47 .... 50.00
48 GW 50.00
49 .... 50.00
50 JDa,RC 75.00
51 WW,SD,JSe 75.00
52 .... 50.00
53 RC,BP 70.00
54 AT,BP 65.00
55 AW,RC,BEv 70.00
56 BEv 65.00
57 JO 55.00
58 MO 55.00
59 AW,August, 1957 .... 70.00

ALL WINNERS COMICS

[2nd Series]
August, 1948

1 F:Blonde Phantom,A:Capt.America Sub-Mariner,Human Torch . 750.00

Becomes:

ALL WESTERN WINNERS

2 B,I&O:Black Rider,B:Two-Gun Kid, Kid-Colt 275.00
3 Black Rider V: Satan 175.00
4 Black Rider Unmasked 175.00

Becomes:

WESTERN WINNERS

5 I Challenge the Army 175.00
6 The Mountain Mystery 150.00
7 Ph(c) Randolph Scott 150.00

Becomes:

BLACK RIDER

8 Ph(c),B:Black Rider;Valley of Giants 250.00
9 Wrath of the Redskin 125.00
10 O:Black Rider 150.00
11 Redmen on the Warpath 75.00
12 GT,The Town That Vanished 75.00
13 The Terrified Tribe 75.00
14 The Tyrant of Texas 75.00
15 Revolt of the Redskins 60.00
16 thru 18 .... @60.00
19 SSh,GT,A:Two-Gun Kid 60.00
20 GT 75.00
21 SSh,GT,A:Two-Gun Kid 65.00
22 SSh,A:Two-Gun Kid 65.00
23 SSh,A:Two-Gun Kid 65.00
24 SSh,JSt 65.00
25 SSh,JSt,A:Arrowhead 65.00
26 SSh,A:Kid-Colt 65.00
27 SSh,A:Kid-Colt 70.00

Becomes:

WESTERN TALES OF BLACK RIDER

28 JSe,D:Spider 80.00
29 .... 60.00
30 .... 60.00
31 .... 60.00

Becomes:

GUNSMOKE WESTERN

32 F:Kid Colt,Billy Buckskin 60.00
33 .... 57.00
34 .... 28.00
35 .... 57.00
36 .... 57.00
37 .... 30.00
38 .... 23.00
39 .... 23.00
40 .... 40.00
41 thru 43 .... @20.00
44 .... 23.00
45 .... 23.00
46 thru 55 .... @20.00
56 .... 23.00
57 thru 76 .... @18.00
77 July, 1963 .... 16.00

ALPHA FLIGHT

August, 1983

1 JBy,I:Puck,Marrina,Tundra 6.00
2 JBy,I:Master,Vindicator Becomes Guardian,B:O:Marrina 3.00
3 JBy,O:Master,A:Namor,Invisible Girl, ... 2.50
4 JBy,A:Namor,Invisible Girl, E:O:Marrina,A:Master 2.50
5 JBy,B:O:Shaman,F:Puck 2.50
6 JBy,E:O:Shaman,I:Kolomag ... 2.50
7 JBy,B:O:Snowbird,I:Delphine Courtney & Deadly Ernest 2.50
8 JBy,E:O:Snowbird,O:Deadly Ernest,I:Nemesis 2.50
9 JBy,O:Aurora,A:Wolverine, Super Skrull 3.50
10 JBy,O:Northstar,V:SuperSkrull . 3.00
11 JBy,I:Omega Flight,Wild Child O:Sasquatch 2.50
12 JBy,D:Guardian,V:Omega Flight 3.00
13 JBy,C:Wolverine,Nightmare .. 10.00
14 JBy,V:Genocide 2.00
15 JBy,R:Master 2.00
16 JBy,BWi,V:Master,C:Wolverine I:Madison Jeffries 3.00
17 JBy,BWi,A:Wolverine,X-Men .. 8.00
18 JBy,BWi,J:Heather,I:Ranaq ... 2.00
19 JBy,I:Talisman,V:Ranaq 2.00
20 JBy,I:Gilded Lily,N:Aurora 2.00
21 JBy,BWi,O:Gilded Lily,Diablo . 2.00
22 JBy,BWi,I:Pink Pearl 2.00
23 JBy,BWi,D:Sasquatch, I:Tanaraq 2.00
24 JBy,BWi,V:Great Beasts,J:Box 2.50
25 JBy,BWi,V:Omega Flight I:Dark Guardian 2.00
26 JBy,BWi,A:Omega Flight,Dark Guardian 2.00
27 JBy,V:Omega Flight 2.00
28 JBy,Secret Wars II,V:Omega Flight,D:Dark Guardian 2.00
29 MMi,V:Hulk,A:Box 2.00
30 MMi,I&O:Scramble,R:Deadly Ernest 2.00
31 MMi,D:Deadly Ernest, O:Nemesis 2.00
32 MMi(c),JBg,O:Puck,I:2nd Vindicator 2.00
33 MMi(c),SB,X-Men,I:Deathstrike 6.00
34 MMi(c),SB,Wolverine,V: Deathstrike 7.00
35 DR,R:Shaman 2.00
36 MMi(c),DR,A:Dr.Strange 2.00
37 DR,O:Pestilence,N:Aurora 2.00
38 DR,A:Namor,V:Pestilence 2.00
39 MMi(c),DR,WPo,A:Avengers .. 2.50
40 DR,WPo,W:Namor & Marrina . 2.50
41 DR,WPo,I:Purple Girl, J:Madison Jeffries 2.50
42 DR,WPo,I:Auctioneer,J:Purple Girl, A: Beta Flight 2.50
43 DR,WPo,V:Mesmero,Sentinels 2.50
44 DR,WPo,D:Snowbird, A:Pestilence 2.50
45 JBr,WPo,R:Sasquatch, L:Shaman 2.50
46 JBr,WPo,I:2nd Box 2.50
47 MMi,WPo,TA,Vindicator solo . 2.50
48 SL(i),I:Omega 2.50
49 JBr,WPo,I:Manikin,D:Omega .. 2.50
50 WS(c),JBr,WPo,L:Northstar,Puck, Aurora,A:Loki,Double size 2.75
51 JLe(1st Marv),WPo(i),V:Cody . 8.00
52 JBr,WPo(i),I:Bedlam, A:Wolverine 6.00
53 JLe,WPo(i),I:Derangers,Goblyn D&V:Bedlam,A:Wolverine 8.00
54 WPo(i),O&J:Goblyn 2.00
55 JLe,TD,V:Tundra 4.00
56 JLe,TD,V:Bedlamites 4.00
57 JLe,TD,V:Crystals, C:Dreamqueen 4.00
58 JLe,AM,V:Dreamqueen 4.00
59 JLe,AM,I:Jade Dragon,R:Puck . 4.00
60 JLe,AM,V:J.Dragon,D.Queen . 4.00
61 JLe,AM,on Trial (1st JLe X-Men) 4.00
62 JLe,AM,V:Purple Man 4.00
63 MG,V:U.S.Air Force 2.00
64 JLe,AM,V:Great Beasts 4.00
65 JLe(c),AM(i),Dream Issue 2.00
66 JLe(c),I:China Force 2.00
67 JLe(c),O:Dream Queen 2.00
68 JLe(c),V:Dream Queen 2.00
69 JLe(c),V:Dream Queen 2.00
70 MM(i),V:Dream Queen 2.00

71 MM(i),I:Sorcerer 2.00
72 V:Sorcerer 2.00
73 MM(i),V:Sorcerer 2.00
74 MM(i),Alternate Earth 2.00
75 JLe(c),MMi(i),Double Size 2.50
76 MM(i),V:Sorcerer. 2.00
77 MM(i),V:Kingpin 2.00
78 MM(i),A:Dr.Strange,Master 2.00
79 MM(i),AofV,V:Scorpion,Nekra 2.00
80 MM(i),AofV,V:Scorpion,Nekra 2.00
81 JBy(c),MM(i),B:R:Northstar 2.00
82 JBy(c),MM(i),E:R:Northstar 2.00
83 JSh 2.00
84 MM(i),Northstar 2.00
85 MM(i) 2.00
86 MBa,MM,V:Sorcerer 2.00
87 JLe(c),MM(i),A:Wolverine 7.00
88 JLe(c),MM(i),A:Wolverine 5.00
89 JLe(c),MM(i),R:Guardian,A: Wolverine 5.00
90 JLe(c),MM(i),A:Wolverine 5.00
91 MM(i),A:Dr.Doom 2.00
92 Guardian vs.Vindicator 2.00
93 MM(i),A:Fant.Four,I:Headlok 2.00
94 MM(i),V:Fant.Four,Headlok 2.00
95 MM(i),Lifelines 2.00
96 MM(i),A:Master 2.00
97 B:Final Option,A:Her 2.00
98 A:Avengers 2.00
99 A:Avengers 2.00
100 JBr,TMo,DR,LMa,E:Final Option A:Galactus,Avengers,D: Guardian,G-Size 2.50
101 TMo,Final Option Epilogue, A:Dr.Strange,Avengers 2.00
102 TMo,I:Weapon Omega, 2.00
103 TMo,V:Diablo,U.S.Agent 2.00
104 TMo,N:Alpha Flight,Weapon Omega is Wild Child 2.00
105 TMo,V:Pink Pearl 2.00
106 MPa,Aids issue,Northstar acknowledges homosexuality 6.00
106a 2nd printing 3.00
107 A:X-Factor,V:Autopsy 2.50
108 A:Soviet Super Soldiers 2.00
109 V:Peoples Protectorate 2.00
110 PB,Infinity War,I:2nd Omega Flight,A:Wolverine 2.00
111 PB,Infinity War,V:Omega Flight,A:Wolverine 2.00
112 PB,Infinity War,V:Master 2.00
113 V:Mauler 2.00
114 A:Weapon X 2.00
115 PB,I:Wyre,A:Weapon X 2.00
116 PB,I:Rok,V:Wyre 2.00
117 PB,V:Wyre 2.00
118 PB,V:Thunderball 2.00
119 PB,V:Wrecking Crew 2.00
120 PB,10th Anniv.,V:Hardliners, w/poster 2.50
121 PCu,V:Brass Bishop,A:Spider-Man,Wolverine,C:X-Men 2.00
122 PB,BKi,Inf.Crusade 2.00
123 PB,BKi,Infinity Crusade 2.00
124 PB,BKi,Infinity Crusade 2.00
125 PB,V:Carcass 2.00
126 V:Carcass 2.00
127 SFu(s),Infinity Crusade 2.00
128 B:No Future 2.00
129 C:Omega Flight 2.00
130 E:No Future,last issue, Double Sized 2.50
Ann.#1 LSn,V:Diablo,Gilded Lily 2.25
Ann.#2 JBr,BMc 1.75
Spec.#1 PB,A:Wolverine, O:First Team,V:Egghead 3.75
Spec.#1 Newsstand ver.of #97 1.50
Spec.#2 Newsstand ver.of #98 1.50
Spec.#3 Newsstand ver.of #99 1.50
Spec.#4 Newsstand ver.of #100 2.00

AMAZING ADVENTURES

June, 1961

1 JK,SD,O&B:Dr.Droom;Torr 750.00
2 JK,SD,This is Manoo 300.00
3 JK,SD,Trapped in the Twilight World 300.00
4 JK,SD, I Am X 300.00
5 JK,SD, Monsteroso 300.00
6 JK,SD,E:Dr.Droom; Sserpo 300.00

Becomes:

AMAZING ADULT FANTASY

December, 1961

7 SD,Last Man on Earth 400.00
8 SD,The Coming of the Krills 350.00
9 SD,The Terror of Tim Boo Ba 300.00
10 SD,Those Who Change 300.00
11 SD,In Human Form 300.00
12 SD,Living Statues 300.00

Amazing Adult Fantasy #11

© Marvel Entertainment Group

13 SD,At the Stroke of Midnight 300.00
14 SD,Beware of the Giants 350.00

Becomes:

AMAZING FANTASY

August, 1962

15 JK(c),SD,I&O:Spider-Man, I:Aunt May, Flash Thompson, Burglar, I&D:Uncle Ben 16,000.00

AMAZING ADVENTURES

August, 1970

[1st Regular Series]

1 JK,JB,B:Inhumans,Bl.Widow 17.00
2 JK,JB,A:Fantastic Four 11.00
3 JK,GC,BEv,V:Mandarin 10.00
4 JK,GC,BEv,V:Mandarin 10.00
5 NA,TP,DH,BEv,V:Astrologer 12.00
6 NA,DH,SB,V:Maximus 10.00
7 NA,DH,BEv 10.00
8 NA,DH,BEv,E:Black Widow, A:Thor,(see Avengers #95) 10.00
9 MSy,BEv,V:Magneto 12.00
10 GK(c),MSy,V:Magneto, E:Inhumans 12.00
11 GK(c),TS,B:O:New Beast, A:X-Men 20.00
12 GK(c),TS,MP,A:Iron Man 13.00
13 JR(c),TS,V:New Br'hood Evil Mutants,I:Buzz Baxter(Mad Dog) 13.00
14 GK(c),TS,JM,V:Quasimodo 13.00
15 JSn(c),TS,A:X-Men,V:Griffin 13.00
16 JSn(c),FMc(i),V:Juggernaut 13.00
17 JSn,A:X-Men,E:Beast 13.00
18 HC,NA,B:Killraven 12.00
19 HC,Sirens on 7th Avenues 5.00
20 Coming of the Warlords 5.00
21 Cry Killraven 5.00
22 thru 23 Killraven. @5.00
24 New Year Nightmare-2019AD 5.00
25 RB,V:Skar 5.00
26 GC,V:Ptson-Rage Vigilante 5.00
27 CR,JSn,V:Death Breeders 5.00
28 JSn,CR,V:Death Breeders 5.00
29 thru 33 CR,Killraven. @5.00
34 CR,D:Hawk 5.00
35 KG,Killraven Continued. 5.00
36 CR,Killraven Continued. 5.00

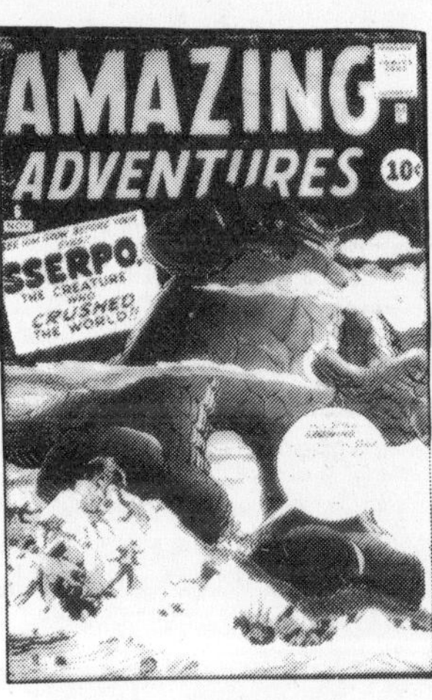

Amazing Adventures #6

© Marvel Entertainment Group

37 CR,O:Old Skull 5.00
38 CR,Killraven Continued. 5.00
39 CR,E:Killraven 5.00

[2nd Regular Series]

1 rep.X-Men#1,38,Professor X 6.00
2 rep.X-Men#1,39,O:Cyclops 5.00
3 rep.X-Men#2,40,O:Cyclops 5.00
4 rep.X-Men#2,41,O:Cyclops 5.00
5 rep.X-Men#3,42,O:Cyclops 5.00
6 JBy(c),rep.X-Men#3,43,Cyclops 5.00
7 rep.X-Men#4,44,O:Iceman 5.00
8 rep.X-Men#4,45,O:Iceman 5.00
9 JBy(c),X-Men#5,46,O:Iceman 5.00
10 rep.X-Men#5,47,O:Iceman 5.00
11 rep.X-Men#6,48,Beast 5.00
12 rep.X-Men#6,Str.Tales#168 5.00
13 rep.X-Men #7 5.00
14 rep.X-Men #8 5.00

AMAZING COMICS

Timely Comics

Fall, 1944

1 F:Young Allies,Destroyer, Whizzer, Sergeant Dix 575.00

Becomes:

COMPLETE COMICS

2 F:Young Allies,Destroyer,Whizzer Sergeant Dix; Winter'44-5 475.00

AMAZING DETECTIVE CASES

Atlas

November, 1950

3 Detective/Horror Stories 100.00
4 Death of a Big Shot 50.00
5 50.00
6 Danger in the City 50.00

7 . . . . 40.00
8 . . . . 40.00
9 GC, The Man Who Wasn't . . 40.00
10 GT 40.00
11 The Black Shadow 60.00
12 MS,BK, Harrigan's Wake . . . 60.00
13 BEv,JSt, ... 85.00
14 Hands Off; September, 1952 . 60.00

AMAZING HIGH ADVENTURE

August, 1984

1 BSz,JSo,JS 3.00
2 PS,AW,BSz,TA,MMi,BBl,CP,CW 2.50
3 MMi,VM,JS 2.50
4 JBo,JS,SBi 2.50
5 JBo; October, 1986 . . . . 2.50

AMAZING SPIDER-MAN

March, 1963

1 JK(c),SED,I:Chameleon,J.Jonah & John Jameson,A:F.Four . 14,000.00
2 SD,I:Vulture,Tinkerer C:Mysterio(disguised) 2,800.00
3 SD,I&O:Dr.Octopus 1,600.00
4 SD,I&O:Sandman,I:Betty Brant,Liz Allen 950.00
5 SD,V:Dr.Doom,C:Fant.Four . . 850.00
6 SD,I&O:Lizard,The Connors . . 950.00
7 SD,V:Vulture 600.00

Amazing Spider-Man #4
© Marvel Entertainment Group

8 SD,JK,I:Big Brain,V:Human Torch,A:Fantastic Four 600.00
9 SD,I&O:Electro 625.00
10 SD,I:Enforcers,Big Man . . . 550.00
11 SD,V:Dr.Octopus, D:Bennett Brant 400.00
12 SD,V:Dr.Octopus 400.00
13 SD,I:Mysterio 450.00
14 SD,I:Green Goblin, V:Enforcers, Hulk 1,300.00
15 SD,I:Kraven,A:Chameleon . 400.00
16 SD,A:Daredevil, V:Ringmaster 300.00
17 SD,2nd A:Green Goblin, A:Human Torch 400.00
18 SD,V:Sandman,Enforcers, C:Avengers,F.F.,Daredevil . 275.00
19 SD,V:Sandman,I:Ned Leeds A:Human Torch 250.00
20 SD,I&O:Scorpion 280.00
21 SD,A:Beetle,Human Torch . 200.00
22 SD,V:The Clown,Masters of Menace 175.00
23 SD,V:Gr.Goblin(3rd App.) . . 250.00
24 SD,V:Mysterio 150.00
25 SD,I:Spider Slayer,Spencer Smythe,C:Mary Jane 170.00
26 SD,I:CrimeMaster,V:Green Goblin 200.00
27 SD,V:CrimeMaster, Green Goblin 175.00
28 SD,I:Molten Man,Peter Parker Graduates High School,rare in near-mint condition 275.00
29 SD,V:Scorpion 135.00
30 SD,I:Cat Burglar 135.00
31 SD,I:Gwen Stacy,Harry Osborn Prof.Warren,V:Dr.Octopus . . 175.00
32 SD,V:Dr.Octopus 100.00
33 SD,V:Dr.Octopus 100.00
34 SD,V:Kraven 100.00
35 SD,V:Molten Man 100.00
36 SD,I:The Looter 100.00
37 SD,V:Professor Stromm, I:Norman Osborn 135.00
38 SD,V:Joe Smith(Boxer) 100.00
39 JR,IR:Green Goblin is Norman Osborn 175.00
40 JR,O:Green Goblin 200.00
41 JR,I:Rhino,C:Mary Jane 90.00
42 JR,V:John Jameson,I:Mary Jane (Face Revealed) 100.00
43 JR,O:Rhino 76.00
44 JR,V:Lizard(2nd App.) 76.00
45 JR,V:Lizard 76.00
46 JR,I&O:Shocker 80.00
47 JR,V:Kraven 76.00
48 JR,I:Fake Vulture,A:Vulture . . 76.00
49 JR,V:Fake Vulture,Kraven . . . 76.00
50 JR,I:Kingpin,Spidey Quits, C:Johnny Carson 250.00
51 JR,V:Kingpin 100.00
52 JR,V:Kingpin,I:Robbie Robertson,D:Fred Foswell . . . 65.00
53 JR,V:Dr.Octopus 60.00
54 JR,V:Dr.Octopus 55.00
55 JR,V:Dr.Octopus 55.00
56 JR,V:Dr.Octopus,I:Capt.Stacy 55.00
57 JR,DH,A:Kazar 55.00
58 JR,DH,V:Spencer Smythe, Spider Slayer 55.00
59 JR,DH,V:Kingpin 60.00
60 JR,DH,V:Kingpin 60.00
61 JR,DH,V:Kingpin 60.00
62 JR,DH,V:Medusa 48.00
63 JR,DH,V:1st & 2nd Vulture 48.00
64 JR,DH,V:Vulture 48.00
65 JR,JM,V:Prisoners 48.00
66 JR,DH,V:Mysterio 48.00
67 JR,JM,V:Mysterio,I:Randy Robertson 48.00
68 JR,JM,V:Kingpin 50.00
69 JR,JM,V:Kingpin 50.00
70 JR,JM,V:Kingpin 50.00
71 JR,JM,V:Quicksilver,C:Scarlet Witch,Toad,A:Kingpin 45.00
72 JR,JB,JM,V:Shocker 40.00
73 JR,JB,JM,I:Man Mountain Marko, Silvermane 40.00
74 JR,JM,V:Silvermane 36.00
75 JR,JM,V:Silvermane,A:Lizard 36.00
76 JR,JM,V:Lizard,A:H.Torch . . . 36.00
77 JR,JM,V:Lizard,A:H.Torch . . . 36.00
78 JR,JM,I&O:Prowler 40.00
79 JR,JM,V:Prowler 35.00
80 JR,JB,JM,V:Chameleon 35.00
81 JR,JB,JM,I:Kangaroo 35.00
82 JR,JM,V:Electro 35.00
83 JR,I:Richard Fisk(as Schemer), Vanessa(Kingpin's wife) V:Kingpin 38.00
84 JR,JB,JM,V:Schemer,Kingpin 35.00
85 JR,JB,JM,V:Schemer,Kingpin 35.00
86 JR,JM,V:Black Widow, C:Iron Man, Hawkeye 32.00
87 JR,JM,Reveals ID to his friends,changes mind 32.00
88 JR,JM,V:Dr.Octopus 32.00
89 GK,JR,V:Dr.Octopus 32.00
90 GK,JR,V:Dr.Octopus D:Capt.Stacy 40.00
91 GK,JR,I:Bullit 32.00
92 GK,JR,V:Bullit,A:Iceman 32.00
93 JR,V:Prowler 32.00
94 JR,SB,V:Beetle,O:Sp-M 50.00
95 JR,SB,London,V:Terrorists . . 32.00
96 GK,JR,A:Green Goblin,Drug Mention,No Comic Code 75.00
97 GK,V:Green Goblin,Drugs . . . 75.00
98 GK,V:Green Goblin,Drugs . . . 75.00
99 GK,Prison Riot,A:Carson . . . 32.00

Amazing Spider-Man #47
© Marvel Entertainment Group

100 JR(c),GK,Spidey gets four arms from serum 130.00
101 JR(c),GK,I:Morbius,the Living Vampire,A:Lizard . . . 175.00
101a Reprint,Metallic ink 2.50
102 JR(c),GK,O:Morbius, V:Lizard 135.00
103 GK,V:Kraven,A:Kazar 25.00
104 GK,V:Kraven,A:Kazar 25.00
105 GK,V:Spenser Smythe, Spider Slayer 25.00
106 JR,V:Spenser Smythe, Spider Slayer 25.00
107 JR,V:Spenser Smythe, Spider Slayer 25.00
108 JR,R:Flash Thompson, I:Sha-Shan,V:Vietnamese . . . 25.00
109 JR,A:Dr.Strange, V:Vietnamese 25.00
110 JR,I:The Gibbon 25.00
111 JR,V:The Gibbon,Kraven . . 25.00
112 JR,Spidey gets an Ulcer . . . 25.00
113 JSn,JR,I:Hammerhead V:Dr.Octopus 27.00
114 JSn,JR,V:Hammerhead,Dr. Octopus,I:Jonas Harrow 27.00
115 JR,V:Hammerhead, Dr.Octopus 25.00
116 JR,JM,V:The Smasher 23.00
117 JR,JM,V:Smasher,Disruptor 23.00
118 JR,JM,V:Smasher,Disruptor 23.00
119 JR,A:Hulk 36.00
120 GK,JR,V:Hulk 36.00
121 GK,JR,V:Green Goblin

D:Gwen Stacy,Drugs 115.00
122 GK,JR,D:Green Goblin ... 130.00
123 GK,JR,A:Powerman 21.00
124 GK,JR,I:Man-Wolf 23.00
125 RA,JR,O:Man-Wolf 22.00
126 JM(c),RA,JM,V:Kangaroo, A: Human Torch 21.00
127 JR(c),RA,V:3rd Vulture, A:Human Torch 21.00
128 JR(c),RA,V:3rd Vulture 21.00
129 K&R(c),RA,I:Punisher, Jackal 300.00
129a reprint,Marv.Milestone 2.95
130 JR(c),RA,V:Hammerhead, Dr.Octopus,I:Spider-Mobile .. 16.00
131 GK(c),RA,V:Hammerhead, Dr.Octopus 16.00
132 GK(c),JR,V:Molten Man ... 15.00
133 JR(c),RA,V:Molten Man ... 15.00
134 JR(c),RA,I:Tarantula,C: Punisher(2nd App.) 28.00
135 JR(c),RA,V:Tarantula, A:Punisher 67.00
136 JR(c),RA,I:2nd Gr.Goblin .. 50.00
137 GK(c),RA,V:Green Goblin .. 38.00
138 K&R(c),RA,I:Mindworm 14.00
139 K&R(c),RA,I:Grizzly,V:Jackal 14.00
140 GK(c),RA,I:Gloria Grant, V:Grizzly,Jackal 14.00
141 JR(c),RA,V:Mysterio 14.00
142 JR(c),RA,V:Mysterio 14.00
143 K&R(c),RA,I:Cyclone 14.00
144 K&R(c),RA,V:Cyclone 14.00
145 K&R(c),RA,V:Scorpion 14.00
146 RA,JR,V:Scorpion 14.00
147 JR(c),RA,V:Tarantula 14.00
148 GK(c),RA,V:Tarantula,IR:Jackal is Prof.Warren 16.00
149 K&R(c),RA,D:Jackal 16.00

Amazing Spider-Man #71
© Marvel Entertainment Group

150 GK(c),RA,V:SpenserSmythe 14.00
151 RA,JR,V:Shocker 14.00
152 K&R(c),RA,V:Shocker 14.00
153 K&R(c),RA,V:Paine 14.00
154 JR(c),SB,V:Sandman 14.00
155 JR(c),SB,V:Computer 14.00
156 JR(c),RA,I:Mirage,W:Ned Leeds & Betty Brant 15.00
157 JR(c),RA,V:Dr.Octopus 14.00
158 JR(c),RA,V:Dr.Octopus 14.00
159 JR(c),RA,V:Dr.Octopus 14.00
160 K&R(c),RA,V:Tinkerer 14.00
161 K&R(c),RA,A:Nightcrawler, C:Punisher 18.00
162 JR(c),RA,Nightcrawler, Punisher,I:Jigsaw 28.00
163 JR(c),RA,Kingpin 11.00
164 JR(c),RA,Kingpin 11.00
165 JR(c),RA,Lizard 11.00
166 JR(c),RA,Lizard 11.00
167 JR(c),RA,V:Spiderslayer, I:Will-o-the Wisp 11.00
168 JR(c),KP,V:Will-o-the Wisp . 11.00
169 RA,V:Dr.Faustas 11.00
170 RA,V:Dr.Faustas 11.00
171 RA,A:Nova 12.00
172 RA,V:Molten Man 11.00
173 JR(c),RA,JM,V:Molten Man . 11.00
174 RA,TD,JM,A:Punisher 20.00
175 RA,JM,A:Punisher,D:Hitman 20.00
176 RA,TD,V:Green Goblin 16.00
177 RA,V:Green Goblin 16.00
178 RA,JM,V:Green Goblin 16.00
179 RA,V:Green Goblin 16.00
180 RA,IR&V:Green Goblin is Bart Hamilton) 16.00
181 GK(c),SB,O:Spider-Man.. .. 10.00
182 RA,A:Rocket Racer 9.00
183 RA,BMc,V:Rocket Racer 9.00
184 RA,V:White Tiger 9.00
185 RA,V:White Tiger 9.00
186 KP,A:Chameleon,Spidey cleared by police of charges .. 9.00
187 JSn,BMc,A:Captain America,V:Electro 10.00
188 KP,A:Jigsaw 9.00
189 JBy,JM,A:Man-Wolf 10.00
190 JBy,JM,A:Man-Wolf 10.00
191 KP,V:Spiderslayer 8.00
192 KP,JM,V:The Fly 8.00
193 KP,JM,V:The Fly 8.00
194 KP,I:Black Cat 10.00
195 KP,AM,JM,O:Black Cat 9.00
196 AM,JM,D:Aunt May,A:Kingpin 8.00
197 KP,JM,V:Kingpin 8.00
198 SB,JM,V:Mysterio 8.00
199 SB,JM,V:Mysterio 8.00
200 JR(c),KP,JM,D:Burglar,Aunt May alive,O:Spider-Man 27.00
201 KP,JM,A:Punisher 25.00
202 KP,JM,A:Punisher 25.00
203 FM(c),KP,A:Dazzler 9.00
204 JR2(c),KP,V:Black Cat 8.00
205 KP,JM,V:Black Cat 8.00
206 JBy,GD,V:Jonas Harrow ... 10.00
207 JM,V:Mesmero 8.00
208 JR2,AM,BBr,V:Fusion(1stJR2 SpM art),I:Lance Bannon ... 11.00
209 KJ,BMc,JRu,BWi,AM, I:Calypso, V:Kraven 9.00
210 JR2,JSt,I:Madame Web 7.50
211 JR2,JM,A:Sub-mariner 7.50
212 JR2,JM,I:Hydro-Man 7.50
213 JR2,JM,V:Wizard 7.50
214 JR2,JM,V:Frightful Four, A: Namor,Llyra 7.50
215 JR2,JM,V:Frightful Four, A: Namor,Llyra 7.50
216 JR2,JM,A:Madame Web 7.50
217 JR2,JM,V:Sandman, Hydro-Man 7.50
218 FM(c),JR2,JM,AM,V:Sandman Hydro-Man 7.50
219 FM(c),LMc,JM,V:Grey Gargoyle,A:Matt Murdock 7.50
220 BMc,A:Moon Knight 7.50
221 JM(i),A:Ramrod 7.00
222 WS(c),BH,JM,I:SpeedDemon 7.00
223 JR2,AM,A:Red Ghost 7.00
224 JR2,V:Vulture 7.00
225 JR2,BWi,V:Foolkiller 7.00
226 JR2,JM,A:Black Cat 7.00
227 JR2,JM,A:Black Cat 7.00
228 RL,Murder Mystery 7.00
229 JR2,JM,V:Juggernaut 8.50
230 JR2,JM,V:Juggernaut 8.50
231 JR2,AM,V:Cobra 7.00
232 JR2,JM,V:Mr.Hyde 7.00
233 JR2,JM,V:Tarantula 7.00
234 JR2,DGr,V:Tarantula 7.00
235 JR2,V:Tarantula,C:Deathlok O:Will-o-the Wisp 7.00
236 JR2,D:Tarantula 7.00
237 BH,A:Stilt Man 7.00
238 JR2,JR,I:Hobgoblin (inc. Tattoo transfer) 70.00
238a w/out Tattoo 30.00
239 JR2,V:Hobgoblin 40.00
240 JR2,BL,Vulture 6.00
241 JR2,O:Vulture 6.00
242 JR2,Mad Thinker 6.00
243 JR2,Peter Quits School 6.00
244 JR2,KJ,V:Hobgoblin 12.00
245 JR2,V:Hobgoblin 17.00
246 JR2,DGr,Daydreams issue .. 6.00
247 JR2,JR,V:Thunderball 6.00
248 JR2,BBr,RF,TA,V:Thunderball, Kid who Collects Spider-Man . 6.00
249 JR2,DGr,V:Hobgoblin, A:Kingpin 14.00
250 JR2,KJ,V:Hobgoblin 14.00
251 RF,KJ,V:Hobgoblin,Spidey Leaves for Secret Wars 15.00
252 RF,BBr,returns from Secret Wars,N:Spider-Man 23.00
253 RL,I:Rose 10.00
254 RL,JRu,V:Jack O'Lantern ... 7.00
255 RF,JRu,Red Ghost 6.50

Amazing Spider-Man #229
© Marvel Entertainment Group

256 RF,JRu,I:Puma,A:Black Cat . 8.00
257 RF,JRu,V:Puma, A:Hobgoblin 10.00
258 RF,JRu,A:Black Cat,Fant.Four, Hobgoblin,V:Black Costume . 15.00
259 RF,JRu,A:Hobgoblin,O: Mary Jane 16.00
260 RF,JRu,BBr,V:Hobgoblin ... 12.00
261 CV(c),RF,JRu,V:Hobgoblin . 12.00
262 Ph(c),BL,Spidey Unmasked .. 8.00
263 RF,BBr,I:Spider-Kid 5.00
264 Paty,V:Red Nine 5.00
265 RF,JRu,V:Black Fox, I:Silver Sable 15.00
265a 2nd printing 1.50
266 RF,JRu,I:Misfits,Toad 5.00
267 BMc,PDd(s),A:Human Torch . 5.00
268 JBy(c),RF,JRu,Secret WarsII . 5.00
269 RF,JRu,V:Firelord 5.00
270 RF,BMc,V:Firelord,

A:Avengers,I:Kate Cushing . . . 5.00
271 RF,JRu,A:Crusher Hogan, V:Manslaughter 5.00
272 SB,KB,I&O:Slyde 5.00
273 RF,JRu,Secret Wars II, A:Puma 5.00
274 TMo,JR,Secret Wars II, Beyonder V:Mephisto,A:1st Ghost Rider 10.00
275 RF,JRu,V:Hobgoblin,O:Spidey (From Amaz.Fantasy#15) . . . 13.00
276 RF,BBr,V:Hobgoblin 10.00
277 RF,BL,CV,A:Daredevil, Kingpin 8.00
278 A:Hobgoblin,V:Scourge, D:Wraith 6.00
279 RL,A:Jack O'Lantern, 2nd A:Silver Sable 7.00
280 RF,BBr,V:Sinister Syndicate, A:Silver Sable,Hobgoblin, Jack O'Lantern 6.00
281 RF,BBr,V:Sinister Syndicate, A:Silver Sable,Hobgoblin, Jack O'Lantern 11.00
282 RL,BL,A:X-Factor 5.50
283 RF,BL,V:Titania,Absorbing Man,C:Mongoose 6.50
284 RF,BBr,JRu,B:Gang War, A: Punisher,Hobgoblin 13.00
285 MZ(c),A:Punisher,Hobgoblin 18.00
286 ANi(i),V:Hobgoblin,A:Rose . 10.00
287 EL,ANi,A:Daredevl,Hobgoblin 8.00
288 E:Gang War,A:Punisher, Falcon,Hobgoblin,Daredevil, Black Cat, Kingpin 9.00
289 TMo,IR:Hobgoblin is Ned Leeds, I:2nd Hobgoblin (Jack O' Lantern) 20.00
290 JR2,Peter Proposes 8.00
291 JR2,V:Spiderslayer 8.00
292 AS,V:Spiderslayer,Mary Jane Accepts proposal 8.00
293 MZ,BMc,V:Kraven 12.00
294 MZ,BMc,D:Kraven 12.00
295 BSz(c),KB(i),Mad Dog Pt.#2 . 8.00
296 JBy(c),AS,V:Dr.Octopus 7.00
297 AS,V:Dr.Octopus 7.00
298 TM,BMc,V:Chance,C:Venom (not in costume) 40.00
299 TM,BMc,V:Chance,I:Venom 30.00
300 TM,O:Venom 70.00
301 TM,A:Silver Sable 18.00
302 TM,V:Nero,A:Silver Sable . . 18.00
303 TM,A:Silver Sable,Sandman 18.00
304 TM,JRu,V:Black Fox,Prowler I:Jonathan Caesar 16.00
305 TM,JRu,V:BlackFox,Prowler 16.00
306 TM,V:Humbug,Chameleon . 13.00
307 TM,O:Chameleon 13.00
308 TM,V:Taskmaster,J.Caesar . 13.00
309 TM,I:Styx & Stone 13.00
310 TM,V:Killershrike 13.00
311 TM,Inferno,V:Mysterio 13.00
312 TM,Inferno,Hobgoblin V: Green Goblin 16.00
313 TM,Inferno,V:Lizard 14.00
314 TM,X-mas issue,V:J.Caesar 14.00
315 TM,V:Venom,Hydro-Man . . . 20.00
316 TM,V:Venom 20.00
317 TM,V:Venom,A:Thing 20.00
318 TM,V:Scorpion 10.00
319 TM,V:Scorpion,Rhino 10.00
320 TM,B:Assassin Nation Plot A:Paladin,Silver Sable 10.00
321 TM,A:Paladin,Silver Sable . . . 8.00
322 TM,A:Silver Sable,Paladin . . . 8.00
323 TM,A:Silver Sable,Paladin, Captain America 8.00
324 TM(c),EL,AG,V:Sabretooth,A: Capt.America,Silver Sable . . . 17.00
325 TM,E:Assassin Nation Plot, V:Red Skull,Captain America, Silver Sable 8.00
326 V:Graviton,A of V. 5.00
327 EL,AG,V:Magneto,A of V. . . . 6.00
328 TM,V:Hulk,A of V. 12.00
329 EL,V:Tri-Sentinel 6.00
330 EL,A:Punisher,Black Cat 6.00
331 EL,A:Punisher,C:Venom 8.00
332 EL,V:Venom,Styx & Stone . 12.00
333 EL,V:Venom,Styx & Stone . 12.00
334 EL,B:Sinister Six,A:Iron Man . 6.00
335 EL,TA,A:Captain America . . . 6.00
336 EL,D:Nathan Lubensky, A:Dr.Strange,Chance 5.00
337 WS(c),EL,TA,A:Nova 5.00
338 EL,A:Jonathan Caesar 5.00
339 EL,JR,E:Sinister Six,A:Thor D:Jonathan Caesar 5.00
340 EL,V:Femme Fatales 4.00
341 EL,V:Tarantula,Powers Lost . 4.00
342 EL,A:Blackcat,V:Scorpion . . . 4.00
343 EL,Powers Restored, C:Cardiac,V:Chameleon 4.00
344 EL,V:Rhino,I:Cardiac,Cletus Kassady(Carnage),A:Venom . 10.00
345 MBa,V:Boomerang,C:Venom, A:Cletus Kassady(infected w/ Venom-Spawn) 15.00
346 EL,V:Venom 10.00
347 EL,V:Venom 10.00
348 EL,A:Avengers 4.00
349 EL,A:Black Fox 4.00
350 EL,V:Doctor Doom,Black Fox 5.00
351 MBa,A:Nova,V:Tri-Sentinal . . 5.00
352 MBa,A:Nova,V:Tri-Sentinal . . 4.00
353 MBa,B:Round Robin:The Side Kick's Revenge,A:Punisher, Nova,Moon Knight,Darkhawk . 4.00
354 MBa,A:Nova,Punisher, Darkhawk,Moon Knight 4.00
355 MBa,A:Nova,Punisher, Darkhawk,Moon Knight 4.00
356 MBa,A:Moon Knight, Punisher,Nova 4.00
357 MBa,A:Moon Knight, Punisher,Darkhawk,Nova 4.00
358 MBa,E:Round Robin:The Side Kick's Revenge,A:Darkhawk, Moon Knight,Punisher,Nova, Gatefold(c) 4.00
359 CMa,A:Cardiac,C:Cletus Kasady (Carnage) 6.00
360 CMa,V:Cardiac,C:Carnage . . 7.00
361 MBa,I:Carnage 18.00
361a 2nd printing 3.00
362 MBa,V:Carnage,Venom . . . 12.00
362a 2nd printing 3.00
363 MBa,V:Carnage,Venom, . . . 10.00
364 MBa,V:Shocker 3.00
365 MBa,JR,V:Lizard,30th Anniv., Hologram(c),w/poster,Prev.of Spider-Man 2099 by RL 6.00
366 JBi,A:Red Skull,Taskmaster . 3.00
367 JBi,A:Red Skull,Taskmaster . 3.00
368 MBa,B:Invasion of the Spider Slayers #1,BU:Jonah Jameson 2.50
369 MBa,V:Electro,BU:Gr.Goblin . 2.50
370 MBa,V:Scorpion,BU:A.May . . 2.00
371 MBa,V:Spider-Slayer, BU:Black Cat 2.50
372 MBa,V:Spider-Slayer 2.50
373 MBa,V:Sp.-Slayer,BU:Venom 3.00
374 MBa,V:Venom 3.00
375 MBa,V:Venom,30th Anniv.,Holo graphx(c) 5.00
376 V:Styx&Stone,A:Cardiac 2.00
377 V:Cardiac,O:Styx&Stone 2.00
378 MBa,Total Carnage#3,V:Shriek, Carnage,A:Venom,Cloak 2.00
379 MBa,Total Carnage#7, V:Carnage,A:Venom 2.00
380 MBa,Maximum Carnage#11 . 2.00
381 MBa,V:Dr.Samson,A:Hulk . . . 1.75
382 MBa,V:Hulk,A:Dr.Samson . . . 1.75
383 MBa,V:Jury 1.75
384 MBa,AM,V:Jury 1.75
385 B:DvM(s),MBa,RyE,V:Jury . . 1.50
386 MBa,RyE,B:Lifetheft,V:Vulture 1.50
387 MBa,RyE,V:Vulture 1.50
388 Blue Foil(c),MBa,RyE,RLm,TP, E:Lifetheft,D:Peter's Synthetic Parents,BU:Venom,Cardiac, Chance, ... 3.50
388a Newsstand Ed. 2.50
389 MBa,RyE,E:Pursuit, V:Chameleon, ... 1.75
390 MBa,RyE,B:Shrieking, A:Shriek,w/cel 2.95
390a Nesstand Ed. 1.50
391 MBa,RyE,V:Shriek,Carrion . . 1.50
Ann.#1 SD,I:Sinister Six 300.00
Ann.#2 SD,A:Dr.Strange 130.00
Ann.#3 JR,DH,A:Avengers 70.00
Ann.#4 A:H.Torch,V:Mysterio, Wizard 70.00
Ann.#5 JR(c),A:Red Skull,I:Peter Parker's Parents 80.00
Ann.#6 JR(c),Rep.Ann.#1,Fant. Four Ann.#1,SpM #8 . . . . . . 21.00
Ann.#7 JR(c),Rep.#1,#2,#38 . . . 21.00
Ann.#8 Rep.#46,#50 . . . . 21.00
Ann.#9 JR(c),Rep.Spec.SpM #2 . 23.00
Ann.#10 JR(c),GK,V:Human Fly . 12.00
Ann.#11 GK(c),DP,JM,JR2,AM, . 12.00
Ann.#12 JBy(c),KP,Rep.#119, #120 . . . . 10.00
Ann.#13 JBy,TA,V:Dr.Octopus . . 12.00
Ann.#14 FM,TP,A:Dr.Strange, V:Dr.Doom,Dormammu 13.00
Ann.#15 FM,KJ,BL,Punisher . . . 22.00
Ann.#16 JR2,JR,I:New Captain Marvel,A:Thing 9.00
Ann.#17 EH,JM,V:Kingpin 7.00
Ann.#18 RF,BL,JG,V:Scorpion . . . 7.00
Ann.#19 JR(c),MW,V:Spiderslayer 7.00
Ann.#20 BWi(i),V:Iron Man 2020 . 7.00
Ann.#21 JR(c),PR,W:SpM,direct 16.00
Ann.#21a W:SpM,news stand . . 15.00
Ann.#22 JR(c),MBa(1stSpM),SD, JG,RLm,TD,Evolutionary War, I:Speedball,New Men 9.00
Ann.#23 JBy(c),RLd,MBa,RF, AtlantisAttacks#4,A:She-Hulk . 9.00
Ann.#24 GK,SD,MZ,DGr, A:Ant Man 5.00
Ann.#25 EL(c),SB,PCu,SD, Vibranium Vendetta#1,Venom . 6.00
Ann.#26 Hero Killers#1,A:New Warriors,BU:Venom,Solo 6.00
Ann.#27 TL,I:Annex,w/card 3.50
Ann.#28 SBt(s),V:Carnage,BU:Cloak & Dagger,Rhino 3.25
G-Size Superheroes #1 GK, A:Morbius,Man-Wolf 55.00
G-Size #1 JR(c),RA,DH, A:Dracula 25.00
G-Size #2 K&R(c),RA,AM, A:Master of Kung Fu 18.00
G-Size #3 GK(c),RA,DocSavage 18.00
G-Size #4 GK(c),RA,Punisher . . 80.00
G-Size #5 GK(c),RA,V:Magnum . 15.00
G-Size #6 Rep.Ann.#4 . . . . 10.00
GNv Fear Itself RA,A:S.Sable . . 12.95
GNv Spirits of the Earth CV,Scotland, V:Hellfire Club 25.00
TPB Assassination Plot, rep.#320-325 . . . . 14.95
TPB Carnage,rep.#361-363 . . . . . 6.95
TPB Cosmic Adventures rep. Amaz.SpM #327-329,Web #59 61,Spec.SpM #158-160 . . . . 19.95
TPB Kraven's Last Hunt, Reps. AS #293,294,Web.#31,32,P.Parker #131,132,SC 15.95
HC 19.95
TPB Origin of the Hobgoblin rep.#238, 239,244,245,249-251 . . . . . . 14.95
TPB Saga of the Alien Costume,reps. #252-259 . . . . 9.95
TPB Spider-Man Vs. Venom,reps. A.SpM#298-300,315-317 . . . 10.00
TPB Venom Returns rep.Amaz.SpM. #331-333,344-347 . . . . 12.95
TPB The Wedding,Reps.A.S.

#290-292,Ann#21 . . . . 12.95
Nothing Can Stop the Juggernaut, reps.#229,230 . . . . 3.95
Sensational Spider-Man,reps. Ann.#14,15; 4.95
Skating on Thin Ice(Canadian) . 15.00
Skating on Thin Ice(US) 1.50
Soul of the Hunter MZ,BMc, R:Kraven 7.00
Unicef:Trial of Venom, A:Daredevil,V:Venom 50.00

See Also:
PETER PARKER;
SPECTACULAR SPIDER-MAN;
WEB OF SPIDER-MAN

SPIDER-MAN INDEX
April, 1985

1 . . . . 3.00
2 . . . . 2.50
3 . . . . 2.50
4 . . . . 2.00
5 A:Punisher 2.50
6 . . . . 2.00
7 . . . . 2.00
8 . . . . 2.00
9 . . . . 2.00

AMERICAN TAIL II
December, 1991

1 movie adaption 1.00
2 movie adaption 1.00

ANIMAX
Star Comics
December, 1986

1 Based on Toy Line 1.00
2 . . . . 1.00
3 . . . . 1.00
4 June, 1987 . . . . 1.00

ANNIE
(Treasury Edition)
October, 1982

1 Movie Adaptation 1.25
2 November, 1982 . . . . 1.25

ANNIE OAKLEY
Atlas
Spring, 1948

1 A:Hedy Devine 225.00
2 CCB,I:Lana,A:Hedy Devine . 125.00
3 . . . . 100.00
4 . . . . 100.00
5 . . . . 60.00
6 . . . . 50.00
7 . . . . 50.00
8 . . . . 50.00
9 AW, ... 50.00
10 . . . . 45.00
11 June, 1956 . . . . 45.00

A-1

1 The Edge 5.95
2 Cheeky,Wee Budgie Boy 5.95
3 King Leon 5.95
4 King Leon 5.95

ARIZONA KID
Atlas
March, 1951

1 RH,Coming of the Arizons Kid 100.00
2 RH,Code of the Gunman . . . 45.00
3 RH(c) 42.00
4 . . . . 42.00
5 . . . . 40.00
6 January, 1952 . . . . 40.00

ARRGH!
December, 1974
Satire

1 Vampire Rats 3.75
2 . . . . 2.00
3 Beauty And the Big Foot 2.00
4 The Night Gawker 2.00
5 September, 1975 . . . . 2.00

ARROWHEAD
April, 1954

1 Indian Warrior Stories 65.00
2 . . . . 45.00
3 . . . . 45.00
4 November, 1954 . . . . 45.00

ASTONISHING
See: MARVEL BOY

ASTONISHING TALES
August, 1970

1 BEv(c),JK,WW,KaZar,Dr.Doom 20.00
2 JK,WW,Ka-Zar,Dr.Doom 12.00
3 BWS,WW,Ka-Zar,Dr.Doom . . 18.00
4 BWS,WW,Ka-Zar,Dr.Doom . . 18.00
5 BWS,GT,Ka-Zar,Dr.Doom . . . 18.00
6 BWS,BEv,GT,I:Bobbi Morse . 18.00
7 HT,GC,Ka-Zar,Dr.Doom 10.00
8 HT,TS,GT,GC,TP,Ka-Zar 10.00
9 GK(c),JB,Ka-Zar,Dr.Doom 7.00
10 GK(c),BWS,SB,Ka-Zar 10.00
11 GK,O:Kazar 7.00
12 JB,DA,NA,V:Man Thing 8.00
13 JB,RB,DA,V:Man Thing 3.00
14 GK(c),rep. Kazar 3.00
15 GK,TS,Kazar 3.00
16 RB,AM,A:Kazar 3.00
17 DA,V:Gemini 3.00
18 JR(c),DA,A:Kazar 3.00
19 JR(c),DA,JSn,JA,I:Victorious . . 3.00
20 JR(c),A:Kazar 3.00
21 RTs(s),DAy,B:It 3.00
22 RTs(s),DAy,V:Granitor 3.00

Astonishing Tales #30
© Marvel Entertainment Group

23 RTs(s),DAy,A:Fin Fang Foom . 3.00
24 RTs(s),DAy,E:It 3.00
25 RB(a&s),B:I&O:Deathlok, GP(1st art) 60.00
26 RB(a&s),I:Warwolf 25.00
27 RB(a&s),V:Warwolf 20.00
28 RB(a&s),V:Warwolf 20.00
29 rep.Marv.Super Heroes #18 . 35.00
30 RB(a&s),KP, ... 20.00
31 RB(a&s),BW,KP,V:Ryker . . . 20.00
32 RB(a&s),KP,V:Ryker 16.00
33 RB(a&s),KJ,I:Hellinger 16.00
34 RB(a&s),KJ,V:Ryker 16.00
35 RB(a&s),KJ, I:Doomsday-Mech 16.00
36 RB(a&s),KP,E:Deathlok, I:Godwulf 20.00

A-TEAM
March, 1984

1 . . . . 1.00
2 . . . . 1.00
3 May, 1984 . . . . 1.00

ATOMIC AGE
Epic
November, 1990

1 AW 4.50
2 AW 4.50
3 AW,February, 1991 . . . . 4.50

AVENGERS
September, 1963

1 JK,O:Avengers,V:Loki 2,000.00
1a rep.Marvel Milestone 2.95
2 JK,V:Space Phantom 570.00
3 JK,V:Hulk,Sub-Mariner 400.00
4 JK,R&J:Captain America . . . 800.00
5 JK,L:Hulk,V:Lava Men 230.00
6 JK,I:Masters of Evil 180.00
7 JK,V:Baron Zemo, Enchantress 180.00
8 JK,I:Kang 190.00
9 JK(c),DH,I&D:Wonder Man . 215.00
10 JK(c),DH,I:Immortus 175.00
11 JK(c),DH,A:Spider-Man, V:Kang 140.00
12 JK(c),DH,V:Moleman, Red Ghost 90.00
13 JK(c),DH,I:Count Nefaria . . . 95.00
14 JK,DH,V:Count Nefaria 90.00
15 JK,DH,D:Baron Zemo 80.00
16 JK,J:Hawkeye,Scarlet Witch, Quicksilver 80.00
16a Marvel Milestone 2.95

Avengers #8
© Marvel Entertainment Group

17 JK(c),DH,V:Mole Man,A:Hulk 75.00
18 JK(c),DH,V:The Commisar . . 75.00
19 JK(c),DH,I&O:Swordsman, O:Hawkeye 80.00
20 JK(c),DH,WW,V:Swordsman, Mandarin 50.00

21 JK(c),DH,WW,V:Power Man (not L.Cage),Enchantress . . . 50.00
22 JK(c),DH,WW,V:Power Man . 50.00
23 JK(c),DH,JR,V:Kang 40.00
24 JK(c),DH,JR,V:Kang 40.00
25 JK(c),DH,V:Dr.Doom 40.00
26 DH,V:Attuma 40.00
27 DH,V:Attuma,Beetle 40.00
28 JK(c),DH,I:1st Goliath, I:Collector 42.00
29 DH,V:Power Man,Swordsman 40.00
30 JK(c),DH,V:Swordsman 40.00
31 DH,V:Keeper of the Flame . . 40.00
32 DH,I:Bill Foster 30.00
33 DH,V:Sons of the Serpent A:Bill Foster 30.00
34 DH,V:Living Laser 30.00
35 DH,V:Mandarin 30.00
36 DH,V:The Ultroids 30.00
37 GK(c),DH,V:Ultroids 30.00
38 GK(c),DH,V:Enchantress, Ares,J:Hercules 30.00
39 DH,V:Mad Thinker 30.00
40 DH,V:Sub-Mariner 30.00
41 JB,V:Dragon Man,Diablo 20.00
42 JB,V:Dragon Man,Diablo 20.00
43 JB,V:Red Guardian 20.00
44 JB,V:Red Guardian, O:Black.Widow 20.00
45 JB,V:Super Adoptoid 20.00
46 JB,V:Whirlwind 20.00
47 JB,GT,V:Magneto 25.00
48 GT,I&O:New Black Knight . . . 25.00
49 JB,V:Magneto 25.00
50 JB,V:Typhon 20.00
51 JB,GT,R:Iron Man,Thor V:Collector 20.00
52 JB,J:Black Panther, I:Grim Reaper 22.00
53 JB,GT,A:X-Men; x-over X-Men #45 . . . . 30.00
54 JB,GT,V:Masters of Evil I:Crimson Cowl(Ultron) 19.00
55 JB,I:Ultron,V:Masters of Evil . 16.00
56 JB,D:Bucky retold, V:Baron Zemo 16.00
57 JB,I:Vision,V:Ultron 50.00
58 JB,O&J:Vision 33.00
59 JB,I:Yellowjacket 20.00
60 JB,W:Yellowjacket & Wasp . . 18.00
61 JB,A:Dr.Strange,x-over Dr. Strange #178 . . . . 17.00
62 JB,I:Man-Ape,A:Dr.Strange . . 17.00
63 GC,I&O:2nd Goliath(Hawkeye) V:Egghead 16.00
64 GC,V:Egghead,O:Hawkeye . . 16.00
65 GC,V:Swordsman,Egghead . . 16.00
66 BWS,I:Ultron 6,Adamantium . 17.00
67 BWS,V:Ultron 6 . . . . 17.00
68 SB,V:Ultron 13.00
69 SB,I:Nighthawk,Grandmaster, Squadron Supreme, V:Kang . 15.00
70 SB,O:Squadron Supreme V:Kang 13.00
71 SB,I:Invaders,V:Kang 20.00
72 SB,A:Captain Marvel, I:Zodiac 13.00
73 HT(i),V:Sons of Serpent 13.00
74 JB,TP,V:Sons of Serpent, IR:Black Panther on TV 13.00
75 JB,TP,I:Arkon 14.00
76 JB,TP,V:Arkon 13.00
77 JB,TP,V:Split-Second Squad . 13.00
78 SB,TP,V:Lethal Legion 13.00
79 JB,TP,V:Lethal Legion 13.00
80 JB,TP,I&O:Red Wolf 14.00
81 JB,TP,A:Red Wolf 13.00
82 JB,TP,V:Ares,A:Daredevil . . . 13.00
83 JB,TP,I:Valkyrie, V:Masters of Evil 14.00
84 JB,TP,V:Enchantress,Arkon . 13.00
85 JB,V:Squadron Supreme . . . 13.00
86 JB,JM,A:Squad Supreme . . . 13.00
87 SB(i),O:Black Panther, V: A.I.M. 24.00
88 SB,JM,V:Psyklop,A:Hulk, Professor.X 13.00
89 SB,B:Kree/Skrull War 13.00
90 SB,V:Sentry #459,Ronan, Skrulls 13.00
91 SB,V:Sentry #459,Ronan, Skrulls 13.00
92 SB,V:Super Skrull,Ronan, . . . 14.00
93 NA,TP,V:Super-Skrull,G-Size 50.00
94 NA,JB,TP,V:Super-Skrull, I:Mandroids 35.00
95 NA,TP,V:Maximus,Skrulls, A:Inhumans,O:Black Bolt . . . 35.00
96 NA,TP,V:Skrulls,Ronan 35.00
97 GK&BEv(c),JB,TP,E:Kree-Skrull War,V:Annihilus,Ronan,Skrulls, A:G.A. Heroes 17.00
98 BWS,SB,V:Ares,R:Hercules, R&N:Hawkeye 20.00
99 BWS,TS,V:Ares 20.00
101 RB,DA,A:Watcher 9.00
102 RB,JSt,V:Grim Reaper, Sentinels 9.00
103 RB,JSt,V:Sentinels 9.00
104 RB,JSt,V:Sentinels 9.00
105 JB,JM,V:Savage Land Mutates; A:Black Panther 9.00
106 GT,DC,RB,V:Space Phantom 9.00
107 GT,DC,JSn,V:Space Phantom, Grim Reaper 11.00
108 DH,DC,JSt,V:Space Phantom,Grim Reaper 9.00
109 DH,FMc,V:Champion, L:Hawkeye 9.00
110 DH,V:Magneto,A:X-Men . . . 17.00
111 DH,J:Bl.Widow,A:Daredevil, X-Men,V:Magneto 17.00
112 DH,I:Mantis,V:Lion-God, L:Black Widow 10.00

Avengers #103

© Marvel Entertainment Group

113 FBe(i),V:The Living Bombs . . 8.00
114 JR(c),V:Lion-God,J:Mantis, Swordsman 7.50
115 JR(c),A:Defenders,V:Loki, Dormammu 10.00
116 JR(c),A:Defenders,S.Surfer V:Loki,Dormammu 10.00
117 JR(c),FMc(i),A:Defenders,Silv. Surfer,V:Loki,Dormammu . . . 10.00
118 JR(c),A:Defenders,S.Surfer V:Loki,Dormammu 10.00
119 JR(c),DH(i),V:Collector 7.00
120 JSn(c),DH(i),V:Zodiac 7.00
121 JR&JSn(c),JB,DH,V:Zodiac . . 7.00
122 K&R(c),V:Zodiac 7.00
123 JR(c),DH(i),O:Mantis 7.00
124 JR(c),JB,DC,V:Kree,O:Mantis 7.00
125 JR(c),JB,DC,V:Thanos 12.00
126 DC(i),V:Klaw,Solarr 7.00
127 GK(c),SB,JSon,A:Inhumans, V:Ultron,Maximus 7.00
128 K&R(c),SB,JSon,V:Kang 7.00
129 SB,JSon,V:Kang 7.00
130 GK(c),SB,JSon,V:Slasher, Titanic Three 7.00
131 GK(c),SB,JSon,V:Kang, Legion of the Unliving 6.00
132 SB,JSon,Kang,Legion of the Unliving 6.00
133 GK(c),SB,JSon,O:Vision 6.00
134 K&R(c),SB,JSon,O:Vision . . 6.00
135 JSn&JR(c),GT,O:Mantis, Vision,C:Thanos 7.50
136 K&R(c),rep Amazing Adv#12 . 6.00
137 JR(c),GT,J:Beast, Moondragon 7.50
138 GK(c),GT,V:Toad 6.00
139 K&R(c),GT,V:Whirlwind 6.00
140 K&R(c),GT,V:Whirlwind 6.00
141 GK(c),GP,V:Squad.Sinister . . 5.00
142 K&R(c),GP,V:Squadron Sinister,Kang 5.00
143 GK(c),GP,V:Squadron Sinister,Kang 5.00
144 GP,GK(c),V:Squad.Sinister, O&J:Hellcat,O:Buzz Baxter . . . 5.00
145 GK(c),DH,V:Assassin 5.00
146 GK(c),DH,KP,V:Assassin . . . 5.00
147 GP,V:Squadron Supreme . . . 5.00
148 JK(c),GP,V:Squad.Supreme . 5.00
149 GP,V:Orka 5.00
150 GP,JK,rep.Avengers #16 . . . . 5.00
151 GP,new line-up, R:Wonder Man 4.50
152 JB,JSt,I:New Black Talon . . . 5.00
153 JB,JSt,V:L.Laser,Whizzer . . . 4.50
154 GP,V:Attuma 4.50
155 SB,V:Dr.Doom,Attuma 4.50
156 SB,I:Tyrak,V:Attuma 4.50
157 DH,V:Stone Black Knight . . . 4.50
158 JK(c),SB,I&O:Graviton, ... 4.50
159 JK(c),SB,V:Graviton, ... 4.50
160 GP,V:Grim Reaper 4.50
161 GP,V:Ultron,A:Ant-Man 4.50
162 GP,V:Ultron,I:Jocasta 4.50
163 GT,A:Champions,V:Typhon . . 4.50
164 JBy,V:Lethal Legion 5.50
165 JBy,V:Count Nefario 5.50
166 JBy,V:Count Nefario 5.50
167 GP,A:Guardians,A:Nighthawk, Korvac,V:Porcupine 4.00
168 GP,A:Guardians,V:Korvac, I:Gyrich 4.00
169 SB,I:Eternity Man 4.00
170 GP,R:Jocasta,C:Ultron, A:Guardians 4.00
171 GP,V:Ultron,A:Guardians, Ms Marvel 4.00
172 SB,KJ,V:Tyrak 4.00
173 SB,V:Collector 4.00
174 GP(c),V:Collector 4.00
175 V&O:Korvac,A:Guardians . . . 4.00
176 V:Korvac,A:Guardians 4.00
177 DC(c),D:Korvac,A:Guardians . 4.00
178 CI,V:Manipulator 4.00
179 JM,AG,V:Stinger,Bloodhawk . 4.00
180 JM,V:Monolith,Stinger, D:Bloodhawk 4.00
181 JBy,GD,I:Scott Lang 5.50
182 JBy,KJ,V:Maximoff 4.50
183 JBy,KJ,J:Ms.Marvel 4.50
184 JBy,KJ,J:Falcon, V:Absorbing Man 4.50
185 JBy,DGr,O:Quicksilver & Scarlet Witch,I:Bova,V:Modred 4.50
186 JBy,DGr,V:Modred,Chthon . . 4.50
187 JBy,DGr,V:Chthon,Modred . . 4.50

All comics prices listed are for *Near Mint* condition.

188 JBy,DGr,V:The Elements . . . 4.50
189 JBy,DGr,V:Deathbird 4.50
190 JBy,DGr,V:Grey Gargoyle,
A:Daredevil 4.50
191 JBy,DGr,V:Grey Gargoyle,
A:Daredevil 4.50
192 I:Inferno 3.00
193 FM(c),SB,DGr,O:Inferno 3.00
194 GP,JRu,J:Wonder Man 3.00
195 GP,JRu,A:Antman,
I&C:Taskmaster 4.00
196 GP,JA,A:Antman,
V:Taskmaster, ... 4.00
197 CI,JAb,V:Red Ronin 3.00
198 GP,DGr,V:Red Ronan 3.00
199 GP,DGr,V:Red Ronan 3.00
200 GP,DGr,V:Marcus,
L:Ms.Marvel 4.00
201 GP,DGr,F:Jarvis 3.00
202 GP,V:Ultron 3.00
203 CI,V:Crawlers,F:Wonderman . 2.50
204 DN,DGr,V:Yellow Claw 2.50
205 DGr,V:Yellow Claw 2.50
206 GC,DGr,V:Pyron 2.50
207 GC,DGr,V:Shadowlord 2.50
208 GC,DGr,V:Berserker 2.50
209 DGr,A:Mr.Fantastic,V:Skrull . . 2.50
210 GC,DGr,V:Weathermen 2.50
211 GC,DGr,Moon Knight,J:Tigra . 2.50
212 DGr,V:Elfqueen 2.50
213 BH,DGr,L:Yellowjacket 2.50
214 BH,DGr,V:Gh.Rider,A:Angel . 5.50
215 DGr,A:Silver Surfer,
V:Molecule Man 3.00
216 DGr,A:Silver Surfer,
V:Molecule Man 3.00
217 BH,DGr,V:Egghead,
R:Yellowjacket,Wasp 2.50
218 DP,V:M.Hardy 2.50
219 BH,A:Moondragon,Drax 3.50
220 BH,DGr,D:Drax,V:MnDragon . 3.50
221 J:She Hulk 2.50
222 V:Masters of Evil 2.50
223 A:Antman 2.50
224 AM,A:Antman 2.50
225 A:Black Knight 2.50
226 A:Black Knight 2.50
227 J:2nd Captain Marvel,
O:Avengers 2.50

Avengers Ann. #22

© Marvel Entertainment Group

228 V:Masters of Evil 2.50
229 JSt,V:Masters of Evil 2.50
230 A:Cap.Marvel,L:Yellowjacket . 2.50
231 AM,JSi,J:2nd Captain Marvel,
Starfox 2.50
232 AM,JSi 2.50
233 JBy,V:Annihilus 2.50
234 AM,JSi,O:ScarletWitch 2.50
235 AM,JSi,V:Wizard 2.50
236 AM,JSi,A:SpM,V:Lava Men . . 2.50
237 AM,JSi,A:SpM,V:Lava Men . . 2.50
238 AM,JSi,V:Moonstone,
O:Blackout 2.50
239 AM,JSi,A:David Letterman . . 2.50
240 AM,JSi,A:Dr.Strange 2.50
241 AM,JSi,V:Morgan LeFey 2.50
242 AM,JSi,Secret Wars 2.50
243 AM,JSi,Secret Wars 2.50
244 AM,JSi,V:Dire Wraiths 2.50
245 AM,JSi,V:Dire Wraiths 2.50
246 AM,JSi,V:Eternals 2.50
247 AM,JSi,A:Eternals,V:Deviants 2.50
248 AM,JSi,A:Eternals,V:Deviants 2.50
249 AM,JSi,A:Maelstrom 2.50
250 AM,JSi,A:W.C.A.
V:Maelstrom 3.00
251 BH,JSi,A:Paladin 2.50
252 BH,JSi,J:Hercules
V:Blood Brothers 2.50
253 BH,JSi,J:Black Knight 2.50
254 BH,JSi,A:W.C.A. 2.50
255 TP,p(c),JB,Legacy of
Thanos/Santuary II 2.50
256 JB,TP,A:Kazar 2.50
257 JB,TP,D:Savage Land,
I:Nebula 3.00
258 JB,TP,A:SpM,Firelord,Nebula 2.50
259 JB,TP,V:Nebula 2.50
260 JB,TP,SecretWarsII,
IR:Nebula is Thanos' Grand
daughter 2.50
261 JB,TP,Secret Wars II 2.50
262 JB,TP,J:Submariner 2.50
263 JB,TP,X-Factor tie-in,
Rebirth,Marvel Girl Pt.1 . . . . . . 5.00
264 JB,TP,I:2nd Yellow Jacket . . . 2.50
265 JB,TP,Secret Wars II 2.50
266 JB,TP,Secret Wars II,A:
Silver Surfer 2.50
267 JB,TP,V:Kang 2.50
268 JB,TP,V:Kang 2.50
269 JB,TP,V:Kang,A:Immortus . . . 2.50
270 JB,TP,V:Moonstone 2.50
271 JB,TP,V:Masters of Evil 2.50
272 JB,TP,A:Alpha Flight 2.50
273 thru 277 JB,TP,V:Masters of
Evil . . . . @2.50
278 JB,TP,V:Tyrok,J:Dr.Druid . . . 2.50
279 JB,TP,new leader 2.50
280 BH,KB,O:Jarvis 2.50
281 JB,TP,V:Olympian Gods 2.50
282 JB,TP,V:Cerberus 2.50
283 JB,TP,V:Olympian Gods 2.50
284 JB,TP,V:Olympian Gods 2.50
285 JB,TP,V:Zeus 2.50
286 JB,TP,V:Fixer 2.50
287 JB,TP,V:Fixer 2.50
288 JB,TP,V:Sentry 459 . . . . 2.50
289 JB,TP,J:Marrina 2.50
290 JB,TP,V:Adaptoid 2.50
291 JB,TP,V:Marrina 2.50
292 JB,TP,V:Leviathon 2.50
293 JB,TP,V:Leviathon 2.50
294 thru 297 JB,TP,V:Nebula . @2.50
298 JB,TP,Inferno,Edwin Jarvis . . 2.50
299 JB,TP,Inferno,V:Orphan
Maker,R:Gilgemesh 2.50
300 JB,TP,WS,Inferno,V:Kang,
O:Avengers,J:Gilgemesh,
Mr.Fantastic,Invis.Woman 3.50
301 BH,DH,A:SuperNova 2.25
302 RB,TP,V:SuperNova,
A:Quasar 2.25
303 RB,TP,V:SuperNova,A:FF . . . 2.00
304 RB,TP,V:U-Foes,Puma 2.00
305 PR,TP,V:Lava Men 2.25
306 PR,TP,O:Lava Men 2.00
307 PR,TP,V:Lava Men 2.00
308 PR,TP,A:Eternals,J:Sersi . . . 2.00
309 PR,TP,V:Blastaar 2.00
310 PR,TP,V:Blastaar 2.00
311 PR,TP,Acts of Veng.,V:Loki . . 3.00
312 PR,TP,Acts of Vengeance,
V:Freedom Force 3.00
313 PR,TP,Acts of Vengeance,
V:Mandarin,Wizard 3.00
314 PR,TP,J:Sersi,A:Spider-Man,
V:Nebula 4.50
315 PR,TP,A:SpM,V:Nebula 3.00
316 PR,TP,J:Spider-Man 3.00
317 PR,TP,A:SpM,V:Nebula 3.00
318 PR,TP,A:SpM,V:Nebula 3.00
319 PR,B:Crossing Line 2.00
320 PR,TP,A:Alpha Flight 2.00
321 PR,Crossing Line#3 . . . . 2.00
322 PR,TP,Crossing Line#4 . . . . . 2.00
323 PR,TP,Crossing Line#5 . . . . . 2.00
324 PR,TP,E:Crossing Line 2.00
325 V:MotherSuperior,
Machinesmith 2.00
326 TP,I:Rage 5.00
327 TP,V:Monsters 2.00
328 TP,O:Rage 4.00
329 TP,J:Sandman,Rage 2.75
330 TP,V:Tetrarch of Entropy . . . 2.00
331 TP,J:Rage,Sandman 2.00
332 TP,V:Dr.Doom 2.00
333 HT,V:Dr.Doom 2.00
334 NKu,TP,B:Collector,
A:Inhumans 2.00
335 RLm(c),SEp,TP,V:Thane
Ector,A:Collector, ... 1.75
336 RLm(c),SEp,TP 1.75
337 RLm(c),SEp,TP,V:ThaneEctor 1.75
338 RLm(c),SEp,TP,A:Beast, ... 1.75
339 RLm(c),SEp,TP,E:Collector . . 1.75
340 RLm(c),F:Capt.Amer.,Wasp . . 1.75
341 SEp,TP,A:New Warriors,V:Sons
of Serpents 1.75
342 SEP,TP,A:New Warriors,
V:Hatemonger 1.75
343 SEp,TP,J:Crystal,C&I:2nd
Swordsman,Magdalene 2.00
344 SEp,TP,I:Proctor 3.00
345 SEp,TP,Oper. Galactic Storm
Pt.5,V:Kree,Shiar 1.75
346 SEp,TP,Oper. Galactic Storm
Pt.12,I:Star Force 1.75
347 SEp,TP,Oper. Galactic Storm
Pt.19,D:Kree Race,Conclusion 2.00
348 SEp,TP,F:Vision 1.75
349 SEp,TP,V:Ares 1.75
350 SEp,TP,rep.Avengers#53,A:Prof.
X,Cyclops,V:StarJammers 3.00
351 KWe,V:Star Jammers 1.75
352 V:Grim Reaper 1.75
353 V:Grim Reaper 1.75
354 V:Grim Reaper 1.75
355 BHs(s),SEp,I:Gatherers,
Coal Tiger 2.00
356 B:BHs(s),SEp,TP,A:Bl.Panther
D:Coal Tiger 1.75
357 SEp,TP,A:Watcher 1.75
358 SEp,TP,V:Arkon 1.75
359 SEp,TP,A:Arkon 1.75
360 SEp,TP,V:Proctor,double-size,
bronze foil(c) 6.00
361 SEp,I:Alternate Vision 2.00
362 SEp,TP,V:Proctor 2.00
363 SEp,TP,V:Proctor,D:Alternate
Vision,C:Deathcry,Silver Foil(c),
30th Anniv., ... 4.50
364 SEp,TP,I:Deathcry,V:Kree . . . 1.75
365 SEp,TP,V:Kree 1.75
366 SEp,TP,V:Kree,N:Dr.Pym,Gold
Foil(c) 4.50
367 F:Vision 1.75
368 SEp,TP,Bloodties#1,
A:X-Men 4.00
369 SEp,TP,E:BHs(s),Bloodties#5,
D:Cortez,V:Exodus,Platinum
Foil(c) 3.50

370 SEp(c),TP(c),GI,V:Deviants, A:Kro,I:Delta Force 1.75
371 GM,TP,V:Deviants,A:Kro 1.75
372 B:BHs(s),SEp,TP,I:2nd Gatherers,A:Proctor 1.75
373 SEp,TP,I:Alternate Jocasta, V:Sersi 1.75
374 SEp,TP,O&IR:Proctor is Alternate Black Knight 1.75
375 SEp,TP,Double Sized,D:Proctor, L:Sersi,Black Knight 2.50
Ann.#1 DH,V:Mandarin, Masters of Evil 38.00
Ann.#2 DH,JB,V:Scar.Centurion . 15.00
Ann.#3 rep.#4,T.ofSusp.#66-68 . 16.00
Ann.#4 rep.#5,#6 . . . . 7.50
Ann.#5 JK(c),rep.#8,#11 . . . . 7.50
Ann.#6 GP,HT,V:Laser,Nuklo, Whirlwind 6.00
Ann.#7 JSn,JRu,V:Thanos,A:Captain Marvel,D:Warlock(2nd) 34.00
Ann.#8 GP,V:Dr.Spectrum 6.00
Ann.#9 DN,V:Arsenal 5.00
Ann.#10 MGo,A:X-Men,Spid.Woman, I:Rogue,V:Br.o/Evil Mutants . . . 8.50
Ann.#11 DP,V:Defenders 5.00
Ann.#12 JG,V:Inhumans,Maximus 4.00
Ann.#13 JBy,V:Armin Zola 4.00
Ann.#14 JBy,KB,V:Skrulls 4.00
Ann.#15 SD,KJ,V:Freedom Force 4.00
Ann.#16 RF,BH,TP,JR2,BSz,KP,AW, MR,BL,BWi,JG,KN,A:Silver Surfer,Rebirth Grandmaster . . 4.50
Ann.#17 MBr,MG,Evol.Wars,J:2nd Yellow Jacket 4.00
Ann.#18 MBa,MG,Atlan.Attack#8, J:Quasar 3.00
Ann.#19 HT,Terminus Factor 2.50
Ann.#20 Subterran.Odyssey#1 . . . 2.50
Ann.#21 Citizen Kang#4 . . . . 2.50
Ann.#22 I:Bloodwraith,w/card 3.25
G-Size#1 JR(c),RB,DA,I:Nuklo . . . 6.00
G-Size#2 JR(c),DC,O:Kang, D:Swordsman,O:Rama-Tut . . . 5.00
G-Size#3 GK(c),DC,V:Kang,Legion of the Unliving 5.00
G-Size#4 K&R(c),DH,W:Scarlet Witch &Vision,O:Mantis,Moondragon . 5.00
G-Size#5 rep,Annual #1. . . . . 3.00
GNv Death Trap:The Vault RLm, A:Venom 20.00
TPB Greatest Battles of the Avengers 15.95
TPB Korvac Saga,rep.#167-177 . 12.95

AVENGERS INDEX

Index 1 . . . . 1.25
Index 7 #132-#154 . . . . 2.95
Index 8 #150-#174 . . . . 2.95

AVENGERS LOG

1 GP(c),History of the Avengers . 2.25

AVENGERS SPOTLIGHT

August, 1989
Formerly: Solo Avengers

21 AM,DH,TMo,JRu,Hawkeye, Starfox 1.00
22 AM,DH,Hawkeye,O:Swordsman 1.00
23 AM,DH,KD,Hawkeye,Vision . . . 1.00
24 AM,DH,Hawkeye,O:Espirita . . . 1.00
25 AM,TMo,Hawkeye,Rick Jones . 1.00
26 A of V,Hawkeye,Iron Man 2.00
27 A of V,AM,DH,DT,Hawkeye, Avengers 1.00
28 A of V,AM,DH,DT,Hawkeye, Wonder Man,Wasp 1.00
29 A of V,DT,Hawkeye,Iron Man . 1.00
30 AM,DH,Hawkeye,New Costume 1.00
31 AM,DH,KW,Hawkeye,US.Agent 1.00
32 AM,KW,Hawkeye,U.S.Agent . . 1.00
33 AM,DH,KW,Hawkeye,US.Agent 1.00
34 AM,DH,KW,SLi(c),Hawkeye U.S.Agent 1.00
35 JV,Gilgamesh 1.00
36 AM,DH,Hawkeye 1.00
37 BH,Dr.Druid 1.00
38 JBr,Tigra 1.00
39 GCo,Black Knight 1.00
40 Vision,Last Issue 1.00

AVENGERS STRIKEFILE

1 BHa(s),Avengers Pin-ups 2.00

AVENGERS: THE TERMINATRIX OBJECTIVE

1 B:MGu(s),MG,Holografx(c), V:Terminatrix 2.75
2 MG,V:Terminatrix,A:Kangs 2.00
3 MG,V:Terminatrix,A:Kangs 2.00
4 MG,Last issue 2.00

AVENGERS WEST COAST

September, 1989
Prev: West Coast Avengers

47 JBy,V:J.Random 2.50
48 JBy,V:J.Random 2.50
49 JBy,V:J.Random,W.Man 2.50
50 JBy,R:G.A.Human Torch 2.50
51 JBy,R:Iron Man 2.50
52 JBy,V:MasterPandmonum 2.50
53 JBy,Acts ofVeng.,V:U-Foes . . . 2.50
54 JBy,Acts ofVeng.,V:MoleMan . 2.50
55 JBy,Acts ofVeng.finale,V:Loki Magneto kidnaps Sc.Witch . . . 3.00
56 JBy,V:Magneto 3.00
57 JBy,V:Magneto 3.00
58 V:Vibro, ... 2.00
59 TMo,V:Hydro-Man,A:Immortus 2.00
60 PR,V:Immortus, ... 2.00
61 PR,V:Immortus 2.00
62 V:Immortus 2.00
63 PR,I:Living Lightning 2.00
64 F:G.A. Human Torch 2.00
65 PR,V:Ultron,Grim Reaper 2.00
66 PR,V:Ultron,Grim Reaper 2.00
67 PR,V:Ultron,Grim Reaper 2.00
68 PR,V:Ultron 2.00
69 PR,USAgent vs Hawkeye, I:Pacific Overlords 3.00
70 DR,V:Pacific Overlords 1.50
71 DR,V:Pacific Overlords 1.50
72 DR,V:Pacific Overlords 1.50
73 DR,V:Pacific Overlords 1.50
74 DR,J:Living Lightning,Spider Woman,V:Pacific Overlords. . . 1.50
75 HT,A:F.F,V:Arkon,double 2.00
76 DR,Night Shift,I:Man-Demon . . 1.50
77 DR,A:Satannish & Nightshift . . 1.50
78 DR,V:Satannish & Nightshift . . 1.50
79 DR,A:Dr.Strange,V:Satannish . 1.50
80 DR,Galactic Storm Pt.2 . . . . . . 1.50
81 DR,Galactic Storm Pt.9 . . . . . . 1.50
82 DR,Galactic Storm Pt.16 A:Lilandra 1.50
83 V:Hyena 1.50
84 DR,I:Deathweb,A:SpM, O:Spider-Woman 1.75
85 DR,A:SpM,V:Death Web 1.50
86 DR,A:SpM,V:Death Web 1.50
87 DR,A:Wolverine,V:Bogatyri . . . 1.75
88 DR,A:Wolverine,V:Bogatyri . . . 1.75
89 DR,V:Ultron 1.50
90 DR,A:Vision,V:Ultron 1.50
91 DR,V:Ultron,I:War Toy 1.50
92 DR,V:Goliath(Power Man) 1.50
93 DR,V:Doctor Demonicus 1.50
94 DR,J:War Machine 1.75
95 DR,A:Darkhawk,V:Doctor Demonicus 1.50
96 DR,Inf.Crusade 1.50
97 ACe,Inf.Crusade,V:Power Platoon 1.50
98 DR,I:4th Lethal Legion 1.50
99 DR,V:4th Lethal Legion 1.50
100 DR,D:Mockingbird,V:4th Lethal Legion,Red Foil(c) 4.50
101 DR,Bloodties#3,V:Exodus . . . 4.00
102 DR,L:Iron Man,Spider-Woman, US Agent,Scarlet Witch,War Machine,last issue 3.50
Ann.#4 JBy,TA,MBa,Atlan.Attacks #12,V:Seven Brides of Set . . . 4.00
Ann.#5 Terminus Factor 3.50
Ann.#6 Subterranean Odyssey#5 . 2.50
Ann.#7 Assault on Armor City#4 . 2.25
Ann.#8 DR,I:Raptor w/card 3.25

BALDER THE BRAVE

November, 1985

1 WS,SB,V:Frost Giants 1.50
2 WS,SB,V:Frost Giants 1.25
3 WS,SB,V:Frost Giants 1.25
4 WS,SB,V:Frost Giants;Feb,1986 1.25

BARBARIANS, THE

Atlas
June, 1975

1 O: Andrax,A: Iron Jaw 1.75

BARBIE

January, 1991

1 with Credit Card 3.00
2 . . . . 1.50
3 . . . . 1.25
4 Ice Skating 1.25
5 Sea Cruise 1.25
6 Sun Runner Story 1.25
7 Travel issue 1.25
8 TV Commercial 1.25
9 Music Tour Van 1.25
10 Barbie in Italy 1.25
11 Haunted Castles 1.25
12 Monkey Bandit 1.25
13 MW,A:Skipper,Ken 1.25
14 Country Fair 1.25
15 Barbie in Egypt Pt.1 . . . . 1.25
16 Barbie in Egypt Pt.2 . . . . 1.25
17 Weightwatchers/Art issue 1.25
18 V:heavy Metal Band 1.25
19 A:Surfer Pal 1.25
20 Skipper at Special Olympics . . 1.25
21 I:Whitney,female fire fighter . . . 1.25
22 Barbie in Greece 1.25
23 thru 27 . . . . @1.25
28 Valentine's Day Issue 1.25
29 Skipper babysits 1.25
30 Cowgirls on the Range 1.25
31 Rest and Relaxation 1.25
32 A:Dandy the Gorilla 1.25
33 thru 41 . . . . @1.25
42 . . . . 1.50

BARBIE FASHION

January, 1991

1 thru 28 . . . . @1.00

BATTLE

Atlas
March, 1951

1 They called Him a Coward . . 70.00
2 The War Department Secrets 34.00
3 The Beast of the Bataan . . . 26.00
4 I:Buck Private O'Toole 26.00
5 Death Trap Of Gen. Wu. . . . 26.00
6 RH 26.00
7 Enemy Sniper 26.00
8 A Time to Die 26.00
9 RH 28.00
10 . . . . 26.00
11 thru 20 . . . . @17.00
21 . . . . 31.00
22 . . . . 17.00
23 . . . . 31.00
24 . . . . 17.00
25 . . . . 17.00
26 JR 18.00
27 . . . . 17.00
28 JSe 17.00
29 . . . . 17.00
30 . . . . 17.00

31 RH 19.00
32 JSe,GT 17.00
33 GC,JSe,JSt 17.00
34 JSe 17.00
35 . . . . 17.00
36 BEv 19.00
37 RA,JSt 20.00
38 . . . . 15.00
39 . . . . 15.00
40 . . . . 15.00
41 . . . . 18.00
42 thru 46 . . . . @15.00
47 JO 15.00
48 . . . . 15.00
49 . . . . 15.00
50 BEv 16.00
51 . . . . 15.00
52 GWb 15.00
53 . . . . 15.00
54 . . . . 15.00
55 GC 30.00
56 . . . . 15.00
57 . . . . 15.00
58 . . . . 18.00
59 . . . . 15.00
60 A:Combat Kelly 15.00
61 A:Combat Kelly 15.00
62 A:Combat Kelly 15.00
63 . . . . 26.00
64 . . . . 26.00
65 . . . . 26.00
66 JSe,JK 32.00
67 JSe,JK 32.00
68 JSe,JK 24.00
69 RH,JSe,JK 24.00
70 BEv,SD; June, 1960 . . . . . . 24.00

BATTLE ACTION
Atlas
February, 1952

1 . . . . 70.00
2 . . . . 30.00
3 . . . . 23.00
4 . . . . 23.00
5 . . . . 20.00
6 . . . . 23.00
7 . . . . 23.00
8 . . . . 30.00
9 . . . . 23.00
10 . . . . 23.00
11 thru 15 . . . . @18.00
16 thru 26 . . . . @15.00
27 . . . . 19.00
28 . . . . 15.00
29 . . . . 15.00
30 August, 1957 . . . . 19.00

BATTLE BRADY
See: MEN IN ACTION

BATTLEFIELD
Atlas
April, 1952

1 RH, Slaughter on Suicide Ridge 60.00
2 . . . . 27.00
3 Ambush Patrol 27.00
4 . . . . 27.00
5 Into the Jaws of Death 27.00
6 thru 10 . . . . @16.00
11 GC,May, 1953 . . . . 16.00

BATTLEFRONT
Atlas
June, 1952

1 RH(c),Operation Killer 78.00
2 . . . . 42.00
3 Spearhead 33.00
4 Death Trap of General Chun . 33.00
5 Terror of the Tank Men 28.00
6 A:Combat Kelly 28.00
7 A:Combat Kelly 28.00
8 A:Combat Kelly 28.00
9 A:Combat Kelly 28.00
10 A:Combat Kelly 28.00
11 thru 20 . . . . @16.00
21 thru 39 . . . . @13.00
40 AW 30.00
15 . . . . 13.00
16 AW 30.00
43 thru 48 August,1957 . . . . . @13.00

BATTLEGROUND
Atlas
September, 1954

1 . . . . 64.00
2 JKz 35.00
3 thru 8 . . . . @23.00
9 . . . . 30.00
10 . . . . 20.00
11 . . . . 30.00
12 . . . . 15.00
13 . . . . 30.00
14 . . . . 25.00
15 . . . . 15.00
16 . . . . 15.00
17 . . . . 15.00
18 . . . . 30.00
19 . . . . 15.00
20 August, 1957 . . . . 15.00

BATTLESTAR GALACTICA
March, 1979

1 EC,B:TV Adaptation; Annihalation 3.50
2 EC,Exodus 2.50
3 EC,Deathtrap 2.50
4 WS,Dogfight 2.50
5 WS,E:TV Adaptation;Ambush . 2.50
6 Nightmare 2.50
7 Commander Adama Trapped . 2.50
8 Last Stand 2.50
9 Space Mimic 2.50
10 This Planet Hungers 2.50
11 WS,Starbbuck's Dilemma 2.00
12 WS,Memory Ends 2.00
13 WS,All Out Attack 2.00
14 Radiation Threat 2.00
15 Ship of Crawling Death 2.00
16 . . . . 2.00
17 Animal on the Loose 2.00
18 Battle For the Forbidden Fruit . 2.00
19 Starbuck's Back 2.00
20 Duel to the Death 2.00
21 To Slay a Monster..To Deatroy a World 2.00
22 WS,A Love Story? 2.00
23 December, 1981 . . . . 2.00

BEAUTY AND THE BEAST
January, 1985

1 DP,Beast & Dazzler,direct 4.00
1a DP,Beast & Dazzler,UPC 2.00
2 DP,Beast & Dazzler 2.00
3 DP,Beast & Dazzler 2.00
4 DP,Beast & Dazzler 2.00

BEST WESTERN
June, 1949

58 A:KidColt,BlackRider,Two-Gun Kid;Million DollarTrainRobbery 85.00
59 A:BlackRider,KidColt,Two-Gun Kid;The Black Rider Strikes . . 75.00

Becomes:

WESTERN OUTLAWS & SHERIFFS

60 PH(c),Hawk Gaither 85.00
61 Ph(c),Pepper Lawson 65.00
62 Murder at Roaring House Bridge 65.00
63 thru 65 . . . . @65.00
66 . . . . 40.00
67 . . . . 60.00
68 thru 72 . . . . @40.00
73 June, 1952 . . . . 35.00

BEAVIS & BUTT-HEAD

1 Based on the MTV Show 8.00
1a 2nd Printing 2.25
2 Dead from the Neck up 2.75
3 Break out at Burger World 2.50
4 Tattoo Parlor 1.95
5 Field Day 1.95

BEWARE
March, 1973

1 Reprints 4.50
2 thru 8 . . . . @2.50

Becomes:

TOMB OF DARKNESS

9 Reprints 2.00
10 thru 22 . . . . @1.00
23 November, 1976 . . . . 2.00

BIKER MICE FROM MARS

1 I:Biker Mice 1.50
2 thru 3 . . . . 1.50

BILL & TED'S BOGUS JOURNEY
November, 1991

1 Movie Adaption 3.25

BILL & TED'S EXCELLENT COMICS
December, 1991

1 From Movie; Wedding Reception 1.25
2 Death Takes a Vacation 1.25
3 'Daze in the Lives' 1.25
4 Station Plague 1.25
5 Bill & Ted on Trial 1.25
6 Time Trial 1.25
7 Time Trial, Concl 1.25
8 History Final 1.25
9 I:Morty(new Death) 1.25
10 'Hyperworld' 1.25
11 Lincoln assassination 1.25
12 Last issue 1.25

BILLY BUCKSKIN WESTERN
Atlas
November, 1955

1 MD,Tales of the Wild Frontier 70.00
2 MD,Ambush 45.00
3 MD,AW, Thieves in the Night 45.00

Becomes:

2-GUN KID

4 SD,A: Apache Kid 60.00

Becomes:

TWO-GUN WESTERN

5 B:Apache Kid,Doc Holiday, Kid Colt Outlaw 55.00
6 . . . . 30.00
7 . . . . 30.00
8 RC 40.00
9 AW 40.00
10 . . . . 30.00
11 AW 40.00
12 September, 1957,RC 40.00

BIZARRE ADVENTURES
See: MARVEL PREVIEW

BLACK AXE

1 JR2(c),A:Death's Head II 2.00
2 JR2(2),A:Sunfire,V:The Hand . . 2.00
3 A:Death's Head II,V:Mesphisto . 2.00
4 in ancient Egypt 2.00
5 KJ(c),In Wakanda 2.00
6 KJ(c),A:Black Panther 2.00
7 KJ(c),A:Black Panther 1.75

BLACK DRAGON
Epic
May 1985

1 JBo 6.00
2 JBo 4.00
3 JBo 3.00
4 JBo 3.00
5 JBo 3.00
6 JBo 3.00

BLACK GOLIATH
February, 1976

1 GT,O:Black Goliath,Cont's From Powerman #24 6.00
2 GT,V:Warhawk 4.00
3 GT,D:Atom-Smasher 4.00
4 KP,V:Stilt-Man 4.00
5 D:Mortag, November, 1976 4.00

BLACK KNIGHT, THE
Atlas
May, 1955

1 O: Crusader;The Black Knight Rides 450.00
2 Siege on Camelot 350.00
3 Blacknight Unmasked 275.00
4 Betrayed 275.00
5 SSh,The Invincible Tartar; April, 1956 275.00

BLACK KNIGHT
June, 1990

1 TD,R:Original Black Knight 2.00
2 TD,A:Dreadknight 1.75
3 RB,A:Dr.Strange 1.75
4 RB,TD,A:Dr Strange, Valkyrie Sept. 1990 1.75

Black Panther #10
© Marvel Entertainment Group

BLACK PANTHER
[1st Series]
January, 1977

1 JK,V:Collectors 10.00
2 JK,V:Six Million Year Man 6.00
3 JK,V:Ogar 5.00
4 JK,V:Collectors 5.00
5 JK,V:Yeti 5.00
6 JK,V:Ronin 5.00
7 JK,V:Mister Little 5.00
8 JK,D:Black Panther 5.00
9 JK,V:Jakarra 5.00
10 JK,V:Jakarra 5.00
11 JK,V:Kilber the Cruel 4.00
12 JK,V:Kilber the Cruel 4.00
13 JK,V:Kilber the Cruel 4.00
14 JK,A:Avengers,V:Klaw 4.00
15 JK,A:Avengers,V:Klaw, May 1979 4.00

BLACK PANTHER
July 1988

1 Mini-series,I:Panther Spirit 5.50
2 V:Supremacists 3.00
3 A:Malaika 2.50
4 V:Panther Spirit, Oct.,1988 2.00

BLACK PANTHER: PANTHER'S PREY
May, 1991

1 DT,A:W'Kabi,V:Solomon Prey 6.50
2 DT,V:Solomon Prey 6.00
3 DT,V:Solomon Prey 6.00
4 DT,V:Solomon Prey 6.00

BLACK RIDER
See: ALL WINNERS COMICS

BLACK RIDER RIDES AGAIN
Atlas
September, 1957

1 JK,Treachery at Hangman's Ridge 120.00

BLACKWULF

1 AMe,Embossied(c),I:Mammoth, Touchstone,Toxin,D:Pelops, V:Tantalus, 2.50

BLACKSTONE, THE MAGICIAN
May, 1948

2 B:Blonde Phantom 300.00
3 200.00
4 September, 1948,Bondage(c) 200.00

BLADE RUNNER
October, 1982

1 AW, Movie Adaption 1.50
2 AW, 1.50

BLAZE
[Limited Series]

1 HMe(s),RoW,A:Clara Menninger 2.00
2 HMe(s),RoW,I:Initiate 2.00
3 HMe(s),RoW, 2.00
4 HMe(s),RoW,D:Initiate,Last issue 2.00

BLAZE CARSON
September, 1948

1 SSh(c),Fight,Lawman or Crawl 125.00
2 Guns Roar on Boot Hill 75.00
3 A:Tex Morgan 85.00
4 A:Two-Gun Kid 75.00
5 A:Tex Taylor 75.00

Becomes:

REX HART

6 CCB,Ph(c),B:Rex Hart, A:Black Rider 120.00
7 Ph(c),Mystery at Bar-2 Ranch 100.00
8 Ph(c),The Hombre Who Killed His Friends 100.00

Becomes:

WHIP WILSON

9 Ph(c),B:Whip Wilson,O:Bullet; Duel to the Death 300.00
10 Ph(c),Wanted for Murder 200.00
11 Ph(c) 200.00

Becomes:

GUNHAWK, THE

12 The Redskin's Revenge 75.00
13 GT,The Man Who Murdered Gunhawk 60.00
14 60.00
15 60.00
16 60.00
17 60.00
18 December, 1951 60.00

BLAZE, THE WONDER COLLIE
October, 1949

2 Ph(c),Blaze-Son of Fury 125.00
3 Ph(c), Lonely Boy;Feb.,1950 100.00

BLONDE PHANTOM
See: ALL-SELECT COMICS

BLOOD
February, 1988

1 6.00
2 5.00
3 5.00
4 April, 1988 5.00

BLOODLINES
Epic

1 F:Kathy Grant-Peace Corps 5.95

BLOODSEED

1 LSh,I:Bloodseed 2.25
2 LSh,V:Female Bloodseed 2.25

BOOK OF THE DEAD

1 thru 4 Horror rep 2.00

BOZZ CHRONICLES, THE
Epic
December, 1985

1 thru 5 @1.75
6 May, 1986 1.75

BRATS BIZARRE
Epic

1 3.25
2 2.50

BRUTE FORCE
August, 1990

1 JD/JSt 1.00
2 1.00
3 1.00
4 November, 1990 1.00

BUCK DUCK
Atlas
June, 1953

1 (fa)stories 36.00
2 21.00
3 21.00
4 December, 1953 21.00

BUCKAROO BANZAI
December, 1984

1 Movie Adaption 2.00
2 Conclusion, February, 1985 2.00

BULLWINKLE & ROCKY
Star
November, 1987

1 EC&AM,Based on 1960's TV Series 3.00
2 EC&AM, 2.00
3 EC&AM,Rumpled Mudluck Thyme Mag 2.00
4 EC&AM,Boris and Natasha 2.00
5 EC&AM, 2.00
6 EC&AM,Wassamatta Me 2.00
7 EC&AM,Politics,Moose V:Boris 2.00

All comics prices listed are for *Near Mint* condition.

8 EC&AM,Superhero, March,1989 2.00
9 EC 2.00

BULLWINKLE & ROCKY COLLECTION

TPB, AM,early stories 4.95

Cable #1
© Marvel Entertainment Group

CABLE

[Limited Series]

1 JR2,DGr,V:Mutant Liberation Front,A:Weapon X 7.00
2 JR2,DGr,V:Stryfe,O:Weapon X . 5.00

[Regular Series]

1 B:FaN(s),ATi,O:Cable,V:New Canaanites,A:Stryfe,foil(c) 5.00
2 ATi,V:Stryfe 2.50
3 ATi,A:Six Pack 2.25
4 ATi,A:Six Pack 2.25
5 DaR,V:Sinsear 2.25
6 DT,A:Tyler,Zero,Askani, Mr.Sinister,C:X-Men 2.25
7 V:Tyler,A:Askani,X-Men,Domino 2.25
8 O:Cable,V:Tyler,A:X-Men,Cable is Nathan Summers 2.25
9 MCW,B:Killing Field,A:Excalibur, V:Omega Red 2.25
10 MCW,A:Acolytes,Omega Red . 2.25
11 MCW,,E:Killing Field,D:Katu . . 2.25
12 SLo(s),B:Fear & Loathing, V:Senyaka 2.25
13 V:D'Spayre 2.00
TPB Cable,rep.New Mutants #87-94 . . . . 15.95

CADILLACS & DINOSAURS

Epic
November, 1990

1 Rep.Xenozoic Tales 3.00
2 Rep.Xenozoic Tales 2.50
3 Rep.Xenozoic Tales 2.50
4 Rep.Xenozoic Tales 2.50
5 Rep.Xenozoic Tales 2.50
6 Rep.Xenozoic Tales, April,1991 2.50

CAGE

1 DT,R:Luke Cage,I:Hardcore, . . 1.75
2 DT,V:Hammer 1.50
3 DT,A:Punisher,V:Untouchables 1.50
4 DT,A:Punisher,V:Untouchables 1.50
5 DT,I:New Power Man 1.50
6 DT,V:New Power Man 1.50
7 DT,A:Avengers West Coast . . . 1.50
8 DT,V:Steele,Wonder Man 1.50
9 V:Rhino,A:Hulk 1.50
10 DT,V:Hulk,Rhino 1.50
11 DT,V:Rapidfire 1.50
12 A:Iron Fist,double size 2.00
13 V:The Thinker 1.50
14 PCu,I:Coldfire 1.50
15 DT,For Love Nor Money#2, A:Silver Sable,Terror 1.50
16 DT,For Love Nor Money#5, A:Silver Sable,Terror 1.50
17 DT,Infinty Crusade 1.50
18 A:Dred,V:Creed 1.50
19 A:Dakota North 1.50
20 Last issue 1.50

CAMP CANDY

May, 1990

1 thru 6, Oct. 1990 . . . . @1.00

CAPTAIN AMERICA COMICS

Timely/Atlas
May, 1941

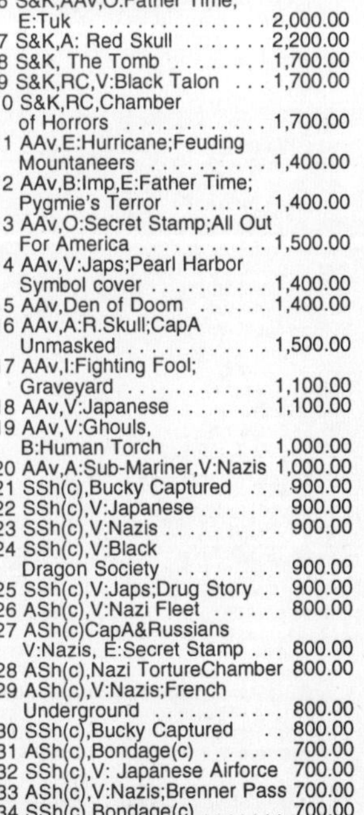

1 S&K,Hitler(c),I&O:Capt.America & Bucky,A:Red Skull,B:Hurricane, Tuk the Caveboy 35,000.00
2 S&K,RC,AAv,Hitler(c), I:Circular Shield;Trapped in the Nazi Stronghold . . . 5,500.00
3 S&K,RC,AAv,Stan Lee's 1st Text, A:Red Skull,Bondage(c) . . 4,000.00
4 S&K,AAv,Horror Hospital . 2,500.00
5 S&K,AAv,Ringmaster's Wheel of Death 2,400.00
6 S&K,AAv,O:Father Time, E:Tuk 2,000.00
7 S&K,A: Red Skull 2,200.00
8 S&K, The Tomb 1,700.00
9 S&K,RC,V:Black Talon . . . 1,700.00
10 S&K,RC,Chamber of Horrors 1,700.00
11 AAv,E:Hurricane;Feuding Mountaneers 1,400.00
12 AAv,B:Imp,E:Father Time; Pygmie's Terror 1,400.00
13 AAv,O:Secret Stamp;All Out For America 1,500.00
14 AAv,V:Japs;Pearl Harbor Symbol cover 1,400.00
15 AAv,Den of Doom 1,400.00
16 AAv,A:R.Skull;CapA Unmasked 1,500.00
17 AAv,I:Fighting Fool; Graveyard 1,100.00
18 AAv,V:Japanese 1,100.00
19 AAv,V:Ghouls, B:Human Torch 1,000.00
20 AAv,A:Sub-Mariner,V:Nazis 1,000.00
21 SSh(c),Bucky Captured . . . 900.00
22 SSh(c),V:Japanese 900.00
23 SSh(c),V:Nazis 900.00
24 SSh(c),V:Black Dragon Society 900.00
25 SSh(c),V:Japs;Drug Story . . 900.00
26 ASh(c),V:Nazi Fleet 800.00
27 ASh(c)CapA&Russians V:Nazis, E:Secret Stamp . . . 800.00
28 ASh(c),Nazi TortureChamber 800.00
29 ASh(c),V:Nazis;French Underground 800.00
30 SSh(c),Bucky Captured . . 800.00
31 ASh(c),Bondage(c) 700.00
32 SSh(c),V: Japanese Airforce 700.00
33 ASh(c),V:Nazis;Brenner Pass 700.00
34 SSh(c),Bondage(c) 700.00
35 SSh(c),CapA in Japan 700.00
36 SSh(c),V:Nazis;Hitler(c) . . . 800.00
37 ASh(c),CapA in Berlin, A:Red Skull 700.00
38 ASh(c),V:Japs;Bondage(c) . 700.00
39 ASh(c),V:Japs;Boulder Dam 700.00
40 SSh(c),V:Japs;Ammo Depot 700.00
41 ASh(c),FinalJapaneseWar(c) 600.00
42 ASh(c),V:Bank Robbers . . . 600.00
43 ASh(c),V:Gangsters 600.00
44 ASh(c),V:Gangsters 600.00
45 ASh(c),V:Bank Robbers . . . 600.00
46 ASh(c),Holocaust(c) 600.00
47 ASh(c),Final Nazi War(c) . . 600.00

Captain America #113
© Marvel Entertainment Group

48 ASh(c),V:Robbers 550.00
49 ASh(c),V:Sabatuers 575.00
50 ASh(c),V:Gorilla Gang . . . 575.00
51 ASh(c),V:Gangsters 550.00
52 ASh(c),V:Atom Bomb Thieves 550.00
53 ASh(c),V:Burglars 550.00
54 ASh(c),TV Studio, V:Gangsters 550.00
55 V:Counterfeiters 550.00
56 SSh(c),V:Art Theives 550.00
57 Symbolic CapA(c) 550.00
58 ASh(c),V:Bank Robbers . . . 550.00
59 SSh(c)O:CapA Retold;Private Life of Captain America . . 1,100.00
60 V:The Human Fly 550.00
61 SSh(c),V:Red Skull; Bondage(c) 900.00
62 SSh(c),Kingdom of Terror . . 550.00
63 SSh(c),I&O:Asbestos Lady; The Parrot Strikes 600.00
64 Diamonds Spell Doom 550.00
65 When Friends Turn Foes . . 550.00
66 O:Golden Girl;Bucky Shot . . 700.00
67 E:Toro(in Human Torch); Golden Girl Team-Up 550.00
68 A:Golden Girl;Riddle of the Living Dolls 550.00
69 Weird Tales of the Wee Males, A:Sun Girl 550.00
70 A:Golden Girl,Sub-Mariner, Namora;Worlds at War 550.00
71 A:Golden Girl; Trapped 550.00
72 Murder in the Mind 550.00
73 The Outcast of Time 550.00
74 A:Red Skull;Capt.America's Weird Tales 1,100.00
75 Thing in the Chest 550.00
76 JR(c),CapA CommieSmasher 550.00
77 CapA Commie Smasher . . . 400.00
78 JR(c),V:Communists; September, 1954 . . . . 400.00

CAPTAIN AMERICA

Prev: Tales of Suspense
April, 1968

100 JK,A:Avengers 325.00
101 JK,I:4th Sleeper 90.00
102 JK,V:Red Skull,4th Sleeper . 45.00
103 JK,V:Red Skull 45.00
104 JK,DA,JSo,V:Red Skull 45.00
105 JK,DA,A:Batroc 45.00

Captain America #135
© Marvel Entertainment Group

106 JK,Cap.Goes Wild 45.00
107 JK,Red Skull 45.00
108 JK,Trapster 45.00
109 JK,O:Captain America 50.00
110 JSo,JSt,A:Hulk,Rick Jones in Bucky Costume 60.00
111 JSo,JSt,I:Man Killer 55.00
112 JK,GT,Album 30.00
113 JSo,TP,Avengers, D:Madame Hydra 55.00
114 JR,SB,C:Avengers 20.00
115 JB,SB,A:Red Skull 20.00
116 GC,JSt,A:Avengers 20.00
117 JR(c),GC,JSt,I:Falcon 35.00
118 JR(c),GC,JSt,A:Falcon 18.00
119 GC,JSt,O:Falcon 18.00
120 GC,JSt,A:Falcon 18.00
121 GC,JSt,V:Man Brute 18.00
122 GC,JSt,Scorpion 15.00
123 GC,JSt,A:NickFury, V:Suprema 15.00
124 GC,JSt,I:Cyborg 15.00
125 GC,Mandarin 15.00
126 JK&BEv(c),GC,A:Falcon ... 15.00
127 GC,WW,A:Nick Fury 15.00
128 GC,V:Satan's Angels 15.00
129 GC,Red Skull 15.00
130 GC,I:Batroc 17.00
131 GC,V:Hood 13.00
132 GC,A:Bucky Barnes 13.00
133 GC,O:Modok,B:Capt.America/ Falcon Partnership 13.00
134 GC,V:Stone Face 13.00
135 JR(c),GC,TP,A:Nick Fury .. 13.00
136 GC,BEv,V:Tyrannus 13.00
137 GC,BEv,A:Spider-Man 15.00
138 JR,A:Spider-Man 14.00
139 JR,Falcon solo 10.00
140 JR,O:Grey Gargoyle 10.00
141 JR,JSt,V:Grey Gargoyle ... 10.00
142 JR,JSt,Nick Fury 10.00
143 JR,Red Skull 9.00
144 GM,JR,N:Falcon,V:Hydra ... 9.00
145 GK,JR,V:Hydra 9.00
146 JR(c),SB,V:Hydra 8.00
147 GK(c),SB,V:Hydra 8.00
148 SB,JR,Red Skull 8.00
149 GK(c),SB,JM,V:Batroc 8.00
150 K&R(c),SB,V:The Stranger .. 8.00
151 SB,V:Mr.Hyde 8.00
152 SB,V:Scorpion,Mr.Hyde 8.00
153 SB,JM,V:50's Cap 8.00
154 SB,V:50's Cap 8.00
155 SB,FMc,O:50's Cap 8.00
156 SB,FMc,V:50's Cap 8.00
157 SB,I:The Viper 8.00
158 SB,V:The Viper 7.00
159 SB,V:PlantMan,Porcupine ... 7.00
160 SB,FMc,V:Solarr 7.00
161 SB,V:Dr.Faustus 7.00
162 JSn(c),SB,V:Dr.Faustus 7.00
163 SB,I:Serpent Squad 8.00
164 JR(c),I:Nightshade 8.00
165 SB,FMc,V:Yellow Claw 7.00
166 SB,FMc,V:Yellow Claw 7.00
167 SB,V:Yellow Claw 7.00
168 SB,I&O:Phoenix (2nd Baron Zemo) 8.00
169 SB,FMc,C:Black Panther 7.00
170 K&R(c),SB,C:Black Panther . 7.00
171 JR(c),SB,A:Black Panther ... 7.00
172 GK(c),SB,C:X-Men 12.00
173 GK(c),SB,A:X-Men 14.00
174 GK(c),SB,A:X-Men 14.00
175 SB,A:X-Men 14.00
176 JR(c),SB,O:Capt.America .. 10.00
177 JR(c),SB,A:Lucifer,Beast 6.00
178 SB,A:Lucifer 6.00
179 SB,A:Hawkeye 6.00
180 GK(c),SB,I:1st Nomad(Cap) . 8.00
181 GK(c),SB,I&O:New Cap 7.00
182 FR,Madam Hydra 7.00
183 GK(c),FR,R:Cap,D:New Cap . 8.00
184 K&R(c),HT,A:Red Skull 6.00
185 GK(c),SB,FR,V:Red Skull ... 6.00
186 GK(c),FR,O:Falcon 7.00
187 K&R(c),FR,V:Druid 5.50
188 GK(c),SB,V:Druid 5.50
189 GK(c),FR,V:Nightshade 5.50
190 GK(c),FR,A:Nightshade 5.50
191 FR,A:Stilt Man,N.Fury 5.50
192 JR(c),FR,A:Dr.Faustus 5.50
193 JR(c),JK,'Mad Bomb' 5.50
194 JK,I:Gen.Heshin 5.50
195 JK,1984 .... 5.50
196 thru 199 JK,Madbomb .... @5.50
200 JK,Madbomb 7.00
201 JK,Epilogue 5.00
202 JK,Night People 5.00
203 JK,Night People 5.00
204 JK,I:Argon 5.00
205 JK,V:Argon 5.00
206 JK,I:Swine 5.00
207 JK,V:Swine 5.00
208 JK,I:Arnim Zola,D:Swine 5.00
209 JK,O:Arnim Zola,I:Primus ... 5.00
210 JK,A:Red Skull 5.00
211 JK,A:Red Skull 5.00
212 JK,A:Red Skull 5.00
213 JK,I:Night Flyer 5.00
214 JK,D:Night Flyer 5.00
215 GT,Redwing 5.00
216 Reprint,JK 5.00
217 JB, I:Quasar(Marvel Boy) I:Vamp 6.00
218 SB,A:Iron Man 5.00
219 SB,JSt,V:TheCorporation ... 5.00
220 SB,D:L.Dekker 5.00
221 SB,Ameridroid 5.00
222 SB,I:Animus(Vamp) 5.00
223 SB,Animus 5.00
224 MZ,V:Animus 5.00
225 SB,A:Nick Fury 5.00
226 SB,A:Nick Fury 5.00
227 SB,A:Nick Fury 5.00
228 SB,Constrictor 5.00
229 SB,R:SuperAgents of Shield . 5.00
230 SB,A:Hulk 5.00
231 SB,DP,A:Grand Director 5.00
232 SB,DP,V:Grand Director 5.00
233 SB,DP,D:Sharon Carter 5.00
234 SB,DP,A:Daredevil 5.50
235 SB,FM,A:Daredevil 5.50
236 SB,V:Dr.Faustus 5.00
237 SB,'From the Ashes' 5.00
238 SB,V:Hawk Riders 5.00
239 JBy(c),SB,V:Hawk Riders ... 5.00
240 SB,V:A Guy Named Joe 5.00
241 A:Punisher 55.00
242 JSt,A:Avengers 4.00
243 GP(c),RB,V:Adonis 4.00
244 TS,'A Monster Berserk' 4.00
245 CI,JRn,Nazi Hunter 4.00
246 GP(c),JBi,V:Joe 4.00
247 JBy,V:BaronStrucker 5.50
248 JBy,JRu,Dragon Man 5.50
249 JBy,O:Machinesmith, A:Air-Walker 5.50
250 JBy,Cap for Pres 5.50

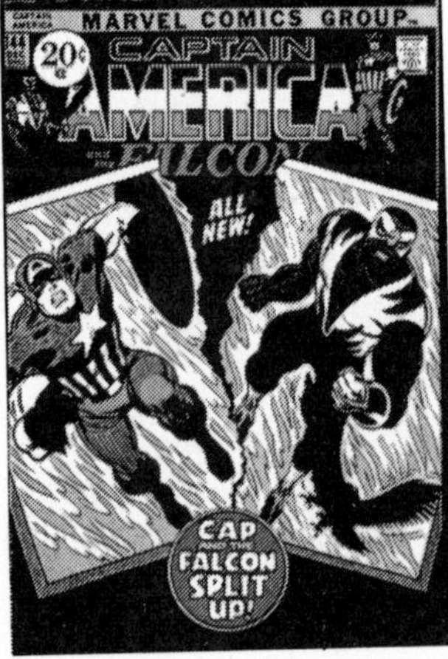

Captain America #144
© Marvel Entertainment Group

251 JBy,V:Mr.Hyde 5.50
252 JBy,V:Batrok 5.50
253 JBy,V:Baron Blood 5.50
254 JBy,D:B.Blood,UnionJack,I:3rd Union Jack 5.50
255 JBy,40th Anniv.,O:Cap 5.50
256 GC,V:Demon Druid 3.50
257 A:Hulk 3.50
258 MZ,V:Blockbuster 3.50
259 MZ,V:Dr. Octopus 3.50
260 AM,In Jail 3.50
261 MZ,A:Nomad 4.00
262 MZ,V:Ameridroid 3.50
263 MZ,V:Red Skull 3.50
264 MZ,X-Men 5.00
265 MZ,A:Spider-Man,N.Fury 4.00
266 MZ,A:Spider-Man 4.00
267 MZ,V:Everyman 3.50
268 MZ,A:Defenders(x-over from Def.#106) 3.50
269 MZ,A:Team America 3.50
270 MZ,V:Tess-One 3.50
271 MZ,V:Mr.X 3.50
272 MZ,I:Vermin 4.50
273 MZ,A:Nick Fury 3.00
274 MZ,D:SamSawyer 3.00
275 MZ,V:Neo-Nazis 3.00
276 MZ,V:Baron Zemo 3.00
277 MZ,V:Baron Zemo 3.00
278 MZ,V:Baron Zemo 3.00
279 MZ,V:Primus 3.00

280 MZ,V:Scarecrow 3.00
281 MZ,A:Spider Woman,
R:'50's Bucky 3.00
282 MZ,I:2nd Nomad 6.00
282a (second primting) 1.75
283 MZ,A:Viper 3.00
284 SB,Nomad 3.00
285 MZ,V:Porcupine 3.00
286 MZ,V:Deathlok 7.00
287 MZ,V:Deathlok 7.00
288 MZ,V:Deathlok,D:Hellinger . . 7.00
289 MZ,A:Red Skull 3.00
290 JBy(c),RF,A:Falcon 3.00
291 JBy(c),HT,V:Tumbler 3.00
292 I&O:Black Crow 3.00
293 V:Mother Superior 3.00
294 R:Nomad 3.00
295 V:Sisters of Sin 3.00
296 V:Baron Zemo 3.00
297 O:Red Skull 3.00
298 V:Red Skull 3.00
299 V:Red Skull 3.00
300 D:Red Skull 4.50
301 PNe,A:Avengers 2.50
302 PNe,I:Machete,V:Batroc 2.50
303 PNe,V:Batroc 2.50
304 PNe,V:Stane Armor 2.50
305 PNe,A:Capt.Britain,V:Modred 2.75
306 PNe,A:Capt.Britain,V:Modred 2.75
307 PNe,I:Madcap 2.50
308 PNe,I:Armadillo,
Secret WarsII 2.50
309 PNe,V:Madcap 2.50
310 PNe,V:Serpent Society,I:Cotton
Mouth,Diamondback 3.50
311 PNe,V:Awesome Android . . . 2.50
312 PNe,I:Flag Smasher 2.50
313 PNe,D:Modok 2.50
314 PNe,A:Nighthawk 2.50
315 PNe,V:Serpent Society 2.50
316 PNe,A:Hawkeye 2.50
317 PNe,I:Death-Throws 2.50
318 PNe,V&D:Blue Streak 2.50
319 PNe,V:Scourge,D:Vamp 2.50
320 PNe,V:Scourge 2.50
321 PNe,V:Flagsmasher,
I:Ultimatum 2.50
322 PNe,V:Flagsmasher 2.50
323 PNe,I:Super Patriot
(US Agent) 5.00
324 PNe,V:Whirlwind,Trapster . . . 2.50
325 I:Slug,A:Nomad 2.50
326 V:Dr.Faustus 2.50
327 MZ(c)V:SuperPatriot 4.00
328 MZ(c),I:Demolition Man 2.50
329 MZ(c),A:Demolition Man 2.50
330 A:Night Shift,Shroud 2.50
331 A:Night Shift,Shroud 2.50
332 BMc,Rogers resigns 10.00
333 B:John Walker Becomes
6th Captain America 8.00
334 I:4th Bucky 6.00
335 V:Watchdogs 5.00
336 A:Falcon 3.50
337 TMo,I:The Captain 3.50
338 KD,AM,V:Professor Power . . 3.50
339 KD,TD,Fall of Mutants,
V:Famine 3.50
340 KD,AM,A:Iron Man, ... 3.00
341 KD,AM,I:Battlestar,A:Viper . . 2.50
342 KD,AM,A:D-Man,Falcon,
Nomad,Viper 2.50
343 KD,AM,A:D-Man,Falcon,
Nomad 2.50
344 KD,AM,A:D-Man,Nomad 3.00
345 KD,AM,V:Watchdogs 2.50
346 KD,AM,V:Resistants 2.50
347 KD,AM,V:RWinger&LWinger . 2.50
348 KD,AM,V:Flag Smasher 2.50
349 KD,AM,V:Flag Smasher 2.50
350 KD,AM,doub-size,Rogers Ret.
as Captain Am,V:Red Skull,
E:6th Cap 4.50
351 KD,AM,A:Nick Fury 2.50
352 KD,AM,I:Supreme Soviets . . . 2.50
353 KD,AM,V:Supreme Soviets . . 2.50
354 KD,AM,I:USAgent,
V:Machinesmith 4.00
355 RB,AM,A:Falcon,Battlestar . . 2.50
356 AM,V:Sisters of Sin 2.50
357 KD,AM,V:Sisters of Sin
Baron Zemo,Batroc 2.50
358 KD,B:Blood Stone Hunt 2.50
359 KD,V:Zemo,C:Crossbones . . 2.00
360 KD,I:Crossbones 2.75
361 KD,V:Zemo,Batroc 2.00
362 KD,V:Zemo,Crossbones 2.00
363 KD,E:Blood Stone Hunt,
V:Crossbones,C:Wolverine . . . 2.00
364 KD,V:Crossbones 2.00
365 KD,Acts of Vengeance,
V:SubMariner,Red Skull 2.00
366 1st RLm Capt.Amer.,Acts of
Vengeance,V:Controller 2.50
367 KD,Acts of Vengeance,
Magneto Vs. Red Skull 3.00
368 RLm,V:Machinesmith 2.00
369 RLm,I:Skeleton Crew 2.00
370 RLm,V:Skeleton Crew 2.00
371 RLm,V:Trump,Poundcakes . . 2.00
372 RLm,B:Streets of Poison,
Cap on Drugs,C:Bullseye 2.50
373 RLm,V:Bullseye,A:Bl.Widow . 2.00
374 RLm,V:Bullseye,A:Daredevil . 2.00
375 RLm,V:Daredevil 2.00
376 RLm,A:Daredevil 2.00
377 RLm,V:Crossbones,Bullseye . 2.00
378 RLm,E:Streets of Poison,Red
Skull vs Kingpin,V:Crossbones 2.00
379 RLm(c),V:Serpent Society . . . 2.00
380 RLm,V:Serpent Society 2.00
381 RLm,V:Serpent Society 2.00
382 RLm,V:Serpent Society 2.00
383 RLm(c),RLm,50th Anniv.
64Pages 4.50
384 RLm,A:Jack Frost 2.00
385 RLm,A:USAgent 2.00
386 RLm,Cap./USAgent T.U. 1.75
387 B:Superia Strategem 1.75
388 A:Paladin 1.75
389 Superia Strategem #3 . . . . . . 1.75
390 Superia Strategem #4 . . . . . . 1.75
391 Superia Strategem #5 . . . . . . 1.75
392 E:Superia Strategem 1.75
393 V:Captain Germany 1.50
394 A:Red Skull,Diamondback . . . 1.50
395 A:Red Skull,Crossbones 1.50
396 I:2nd Jack O'Lantern 1.75
397 V:Red Skull,X-Bones,Viper . . 1.50
398 Operation:Galactic Storm
Pt.1,V:Warstar 1.75
399 Operation Galactic Storm
Pt.8,V:Kree Empire 1.50
400 Operation Galactic Storm
Pt.15,BU:rep.Avengers #4 . . . . 3.50
401 R:D-Man,A:Avengers 1.50
402 RLe,B:Man & Wolf,
A:Wolverine 2.00
403 RLe,A:Wolverine 1.75
404 RLe,A:Wolverine 1.75
405 RLe,A:Wolverine 1.75
406 RLe,A:Wolverine 1.75
407 RLe,A:Wolverine,Cable 1.75
408 RLe,E:Man & Wolf 1.75
409 RLe,V:Skeleton Crew 1.50
410 RLe,V:Crossbones,Skel.Crew 1.50
411 RLe,V:Snapdragon 1.50
412 RLe,V:Batroc,A:Shang-Chi . . 1.50
413 A:Shang-Chi,V:Superia 1.50
414 RLe,A:Kazar,Black Panther . . 1.50
415 Rle,A:Black Panther,Kazar . . 1.50
416 RLe,Savage Land Mutates,
A:Black.Panther,Kazar 1.50
417 RLe,A:Black Panther,Kazar,
V:AIM 1.50
418 RLe,V:Night People 1.50
419 RLe,V:Viper 1.50
420 RLe,I:2nd Blazing Skull,
A:Nightshift 1.50
421 RLe,V:Nomad 1.50
422 RLe,I:Blistik 1.50
423 RTs(s),MCW,V:Namor 1.50
424 MGv(s),A:Sidewinder 1.50
425 B:MGu(s),DHv,Embossed(c),I:2nd
Super Patriot,Dead Ringer . . . 3.25
426 DHv,A:Super Patriot,Dead Ringer,
V:Resistants 1.50
427 DHv,V:Super Patriot,Dead
Ringer 1.75
428 DHv,I:Americop 1.75
429 DHv,V:Kono 1.50

Captain America Ann. #8
© Marvel Entertainment Group

Ann.#1 rep. 14.00
Ann.#2 rep. 11.00
Ann.#3 JK, ... 5.00
Ann.#4 JK,V:Magneto,I:Mutant
Force 10.00
Ann.#5 'Deathwatcher' 4.00
Ann.#6 A:Contemplator 4.00
Ann.#7 O:Shaper of Worlds 4.00
Ann.#8 MZ,A:Wolverine 48.00
Ann.#9 MBa,SD,Terminus Factor
#1,N:Nomad 4.50
Ann.#10 MM,Baron Strucker Pt.3
(see Punisher Ann.#4) 2.50
Ann.#11 Citizen Kang#1 . . . . 2.50
Ann.#12 I:Bantam,w/card 3.25
Ann.#13 RTs(s),MCW, ... 3.25
Drug Wars PDd(s),SaV,A:New
Warriors 2.00
G-Size#1 GK(c),rep.O:Cap.Amer. 12.00
HC vol.Slipcase Rep.#1
thru #10 (From 1940's) 75.00
Medusa Effect RTs(s),MCW,RB,
V:Master Man 2.95
Movie Adapt 2.00
Spec.#1 Rep.Cap.A #110,#111 . . 2.00
Spec.#2 Rep.Cap.A.#113
& Strange Tales #169 . . . . 2.00
TPB Bloodstone Hunt,rep.
#357-364 . . . . 15.95
TPB War and Remembrance,
rep #247-255 . . . . 12.95

CAPTAIN CONFEDERACY

Epic

November, 1991

1 I:Capt.Confederacy,Kid Dixie . . 2.25
2 Meeting of Superhero Reps . . . 2.25
3 Framed for Murder 2.25
4 Superhero conference,final iss. 2.25

CAPTAIN JUSTICE
March, 1988

1 Based on TV Series 1.00
2 April, 1988 . . . . 1.00

CAPTAIN MARVEL
May, 1968

1 GC,O:retold,V:Sentry#459 . . . 95.00
2 GC,V:Super Skrull 27.00
3 GC,V:Super Skrull 20.00
4 GC,Sub-Mariner 20.00
5 DH,I:Metazoid 20.00
6 DH,I:Solam 12.00
7 JR(c),DH,V:Quasimodo 12.00
8 DH,I:Cuberex 12.00

Captain Marvel #5
© Marvel Entertainment Group

9 DH,D:Cuberex 12.00
10 DH,V:Number 1 . . . . 11.00
11 BWS(c),I:Z0 . . . . 11.00
12 K&R(c),I:Man-Slayer 8.00
13 FS,V:Man-Slayer 8.00
14 FS,Iron Man 8.00
15 TS,DA,Z0 . . . . 7.50
16 DH,Ronan 7.50
17 GK,DA,O:R.Jones ret,N:Capt. Marvel 8.50
18 GK,JB,DA,I:Mandroid 7.50
19 GK,DA,Master.of.MM 7.50
20 GK,DA,I:Rat Pack 7.50
21 GK,DA,Hulk 7.50
22 GK(c),WB,V:Megaton 7.50
23 GK(c),WB,FMc,V:Megaton . . . 7.50
24 GK(c),WB,ECh,I:L.Mynde 7.50
25 1st JSn,Cap.Marvel,Cosmic Cube Saga Begins 30.00
26 JSn,DC,Thanos(2ndApp.) A:Thing 40.00
27 JSn,V:Thanos,A:Mentor, Starfox, I:Death 28.00
28 JSn,DGr,Thanos Vs.Drax, A:Avengers 27.00
29 JSn,AM,O:Zeus,C:Thanos I:Eon,O:Mentor 14.00
30 JSn,AM,Controller,C:Thanos . 14.00
31 JSn,AM,Avengers, Thanos,Drax,Mentor 18.00
32 JSn,AM,DGr,O:Drax, Moondragon,A:Thanos 18.00
33 JSn,KJ,E:Cosmic Cube Saga 1st D:Thanos 34.00
34 JSn,JA,V:Nitro(leads to his Death) 8.00
35 GK(c),AA,Ant Man 4.00
36 AM,Watcher,Rep.CM#1 . . . . . 6.00
37 AM,KJ,Nimrod 4.00
38 AM,KJ,Watcher 4.00
39 AM,KJ,Watcher 4.00
40 AM,AMc,Watcher 4.00
41 AM,BWr,CR,BMc,TA,Kree 4.50
42 AM,V:Stranger,C:Drax 4.00
43 AM,V:Drax 4.50
44 GK(c),AM,V:Drax 4.50
45 AM,I:Rambu 4.00
46 AM,TA,D:Fawn 4.00
47 AM,TA,A:Human Torch 4.00
48 AM,TA,I:Chetah 4.00
49 AM,V:Ronan,A:Cheetah 4.00
50 AM,TA,Avengers, V:Super Adaptiod 4.00
51 AM,TA,V:Mercurio,4-D Man . . 4.00
52 AM,TA,V:Phae-dor 4.00
53 AM,TA,A:Inhumans 4.00

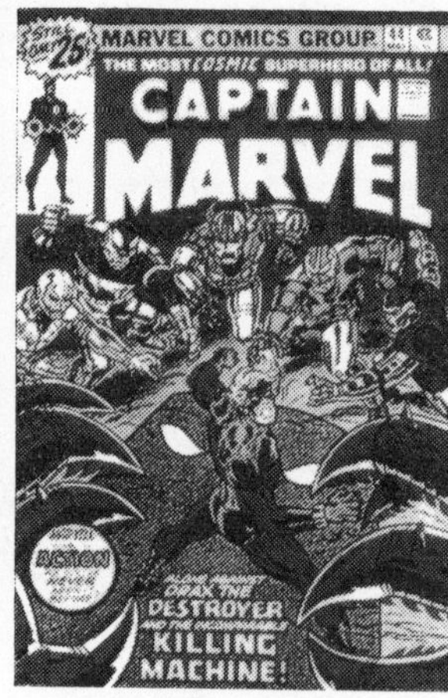

Captain Marvel #44
© Marvel Entertainment Group

54 PB,V:Nitro 4.00
55 PB,V:Death-grip 4.00
56 PB,V:Death-grip 4.00
57 PB,V:Thor,A;Thanos 8.00
58 PB,Drax/Titan 4.00
59 PB,Drax/Titan,I:Stellarax 4.00
60 PB,Drax/Titan 4.00
61 PB,V:Chaos 4.00
62 PB,V:Stellarax 4.00
G-Size #1 reprints 8.00

CAPTAIN MARVEL

1 MBr,I:Powerkeg,V:Moonstone (1989) 3.00
1 DyM(s),MBr,V:Skinhead(1993) . 2.00

CAPTAIN PLANET
October, 1991

1 I&O:Captain Planet 1.00
2 V:Dr.Blights' Smog Monster . . . 1.00
3 V:Looten Plunder 1.00
4 'Pollutionland' 1.25
5 V:Duke Nukem 1.25
6 A:Capt.Pollution,Eco-Villains . . 1.25
7 thru 9 . . . . @1.25
10 V:Litterbug 1.25
11 BHi,V:Greedly 1.25
12 V:Looten Plunder,last issue . . . 1.25

CAPT. SAVAGE & HIS LEATHERNECK RAIDERS
January, 1968

1 SSh(c),C:Sgt Fury;The Last Bansai 13.50
2 SSh(c),O:Hydra;Return of Baron Strucker 6.00
3 SSh,Two Against Hydra 6.00
4 SSh,V:Hydra;The Fateful Finale 6.00
5 SSh,The Invincible Enemy . . . 6.00
6 Mission;Save a Howler 6.00
7 SSh,Objective:Ben Grimm . . . 6.50
8 Mission:Foul Ball 6.00

Becomes:

CAPT. SAVAGE & HIS BATTLEFIELD RAIDERS

9 . . . . 6.00
10 To the Last Man 5.00
11 A:Sergeant Fury 5.00
12 V:The Japanese 3.75
13 The Junk Heap Juggernauts . . 5.00
14 Savage's First Mission 5.00
15 Within the Temple Waits Death 5.00
16 V:The Axis Powers 5.00
17 V:The Axis Powers 5.00
18 V:The Axis Powers 5.00
19 March, 1970 . . . . 5.00

CARE BEARS
Star
November, 1985

1 . . . . 1.50
2 thru 14 . . . . @1.00

Marvel

15 thru 20 . . . . @1.00

CARTOON KIDS
Atlas
1957

1 A:Dexter the Demon,Little Zelda,Willie,Wise Guy 25.00

CAR WARRIORS
Epic
1990

1 Based on Roll Playing Game . . 2.25
2 Big Race Preparations 2.25
3 Ft.Delorean-Lansing Race begin 2.25
4 Race End, Final issue 2.25

CASEY–CRIME PHOTOGRAPHER
August, 1949

1 Ph(c),Girl on the Docks 80.00
2 Ph(c),Staats Cotsworth 50.00
3 Ph(c),He Walked With Danger 50.00
4 Ph(c),Lend Me Your Life . . . 50.00

Becomes:

TWO GUN WESTERN
[1st Series]

5 JB,B,I&O:Apache Kid 120.00
6 The Outcast 75.00
7 Human Sacrifice 75.00
8 JR,DW,A:Kid Colt,Texas Kid, Doc Holiday 75.00
9 A:Kid Colt,Marshall"Frosty" Bennet Texas Kid 75.00
10 . . . . 75.00
11 thru 13 . . . . @60.00
14 June, 1952 . . . . 60.00

CAT, THE
November, 1972

1 JM,I&O:The Cat 12.00
2 JM,V:The Owl 9.00
3 BEv,V:Kraken 9.00
4 JSn,V:Man-Bull;June, 1973 . . . 9.00

CHAMBER OF CHILLS
November, 1972

1 SSh,A Dragon Stalks By

All comics prices listed are for *Near Mint* condition.

Night,(H.Ellison Adapt.) 5.00
2 FB,BEv,SD,Monster From the Mound,(RE Howard Adapt.) . . 3.00
3 FB,BEv,SD, Thing on the Roof 3.00
4 FB,BEv,SD, Opener of the Crypt,(J.Jakes,E.A.Poe Adapt) 3.00
5 FB,BEv,SD, Devils Dowry 3.00
6 FB,BEv,SD, Mud Monster 3.00
7 thru 24 FB,BEv,SD . . . . . . @3.00
25 FB,BEv,SD November, 1976 . . 3.00

CHAMBER OF DARKNESS

October, 1969

1 JB, Tales of Maddening Magic 35.00
2 NA(script),Enter the Red Death 13.00
3 JK,BWS,JB, Something Lurks on Shadow Mountain 15.00
4 BWS,JK Monster Man Came Walking 42.00
5 JK,SD, And Fear Shall Follow (Lovecraft Adapt.) 7.00
6 SD 7.00
7 SD,JK,BWr, Night of the Gargoyle 20.00
8 DA,BEv, Beast that Walks Like a Man Special, 5 Tales of Maddening Magic,Jan. 1972 . 7.00

Becomes:

MONSTERS ON THE PROWL

9 SAD,BWS,Monster Stories Inc,Gorgilla 5.50
10 JK,Roc 3.00
11 JK,A Titan Walks the Land . . . 3.00
12 HT,JK,Gomdulla The Living Pharoah 3.00
13 HT,JK,Tragg 3.00
14 JK,SD,Return of the Titan 3.00
15 FrG,JK,The Thing Called It . . . 3.00
16 JSe,SD,JK, Serpent God of Lost Swamp,A:King Kull 3.00
17 JK,SD,The Coming of Colossus 3.00
18 JK,SD,Bruttu 3.00
19 JK,SD,Creature From the Black Bog 3.00
20 JK,SD,Oog Lives Again 3.00
21 JK,SD,A Martian Stalks the City 3.00
22 JK,SD,Monster Runs Amok . . . 2.50
23 JK,The Return of Grogg 2.50
24 JK,SD, Magnetor 2.50
25 JK,Colossus Lives Again 2.50
26 JK,SD,The Two Headed Thing 2.50
27 JK,Sserpo 2.50
28 JK,The Coming of Monsteroso 2.50
29 JK,SD Monster at my Window . 2.50
30 JK,Diablo Demon from the 5th Dimension, October, 1974 . . 2.50

CHAMPIONS

June, 1986

1 GK(c),DH,I&O:Champions . . . 20.00
2 DH,O:Champions 14.00
3 GT,Assault on Olympus 13.00
4 GT,'Murder at Malibu' 12.00
5 DH,I:Rampage 12.00
6 JK(c),GT,V:Rampage 12.00
7 GT,O:Black Widow,I:Darkstar . 12.00
8 BH,O:Black Widow 12.00
9 BH,BL,V:Crimson Dynamo . . . 12.00
10 BH,BL,V:Crimson Dynamo . . 12.00
11 JBy,A:Black Goliath,Hawkeye 13.00
12 JBy,BL,V:Stranger 13.00
13 JBy,BL,V:Kamo Tharn 13.00
14 JBy,I:Swarm 13.00
15 JBy,V:Swarm 13.00
16 BH,A:Magneto,Dr.Doom, Beast 12.00
17 GT,JBy,V:Sentinels,last issue 13.00

CHILDREN OF THE VOYAGE

1 F:Sam Wantling 3.25

Champions #1

© Marvel Entertainment Group

2 Counterfeit Man 2.25
3 V:Voyager 2.25
4 Last Issue 2.25

CHILI

May, 1969

1 . . . . 18.00
2 . . . . 10.00
3 . . . . 9.00
4 . . . . 9.00
5 . . . . 9.00
6 thru 15 . . . . @7.00
16 thru 20 . . . . @6.00
21 thru 25 . . . . @5.00
26 December, 1973 . . . . 5.00
Spec.#1,1971 . . . . 10.00

CHUCK NORRIS

Star

January, 1987

1 SD 1.00
2 . . . . 1.00
3 . . . . 1.00
4 . . . . 1.00
5 September, 1987 . . . . 1.00

CINDY COMICS

See: KRAZY COMICS

CLASSIC CONAN

See: CONAN SAGA

CLASSIC X-MEN

See: X-MEN

CLIVE BARKER'S BOOK OF THE DAMNED

Epic

November, 1991

1 JBo,Hellraiser companion 4.95
2 MPa,Hellraiser Companion 4.95

CLIVE BARKER'S HELLRAISER

Epic

1 BWr,DSp 12.00
2 . . . . 8.00
3 . . . . 6.50
4 . . . . 6.25
5 . . . . 6.25
6 . . . . 6.25
7 The Devil's Brigade #1 . . . . . . 6.25
8 The Devil's Brigade #2&3 . . . . 6.25
9 The Devil's Brigade #4&5 . . . . 6.25
10 The Devil's Brigade #6&7 foil Cover 5.50
11 The Devil's Brigade #8&9 . . . . 4.50
12 The Devil's Brigade #10-12 . . . 4.50
13 MMi,RH,Devil's Brigade #13 . . 4.50
14 The Devil's Brigade #14 . . . . . 4.95
15 The Devil's Brigade #15 . . . . . 4.95
16 E:Devil's Brigade 4.95
17 BHa,DR,The Harrowing 4.95
18 O:Harrowers 4.95
19 A:Harrowers 4.95
20 NGa(s),DMc,Last Laugh 4.95

CLOAK & DAGGER

(Limited Series)

October, 1983

1 RL,TA,I:Det.O'Reilly, Father Delgado 2.50
2 RL,TA,V:Duane Hellman 2.00
3 RL,TA,V:Street Gang 2.00
4 RL,TA,O:Cloak & Dagger, ... 2.00

CLOAK & DAGGER

[1st Regular Series]

July 1985

1 RL,Pornography 2.00
2 RL,Dagger's mother 1.50
3 RL,A:Spider-Man 2.00
4 RL,Secret Wars II 1.50
5 RL,I:Mayhem 1.25
6 RL,A:Mayhem 1.25
7 RL,A:Mayhem 1.25
8 TA, Drugs 1.50
9 AAd,TA,A:Mayhem 3.00
10 BBl,TA,V:Dr. Doom 1.25
11 BBl,TA,Last Issue 1.25

[Mutant Misadventures of] CLOAK & DAGGER

[2nd Regular Series]

October, 1988

1 CR(i),A:X-Factor 3.00
2 CR(i),C:X-Factor,V:Gromitz . . . 2.50
3 SW(i),JLe(c),A:Gromitz 2.00
4 TA(i),Inferno,R:Mayhem 2.00
5 TA(i),R:Mayhem 2.00
6 TA(i),A:Mayhem 1.75
7 A:Crimson Daffodil,V:Ecstacy . . 1.75
8 Acts of Vengeance prelude . . . 1.75
9 Acts of Vengeance 2.00
10 Acts of Vengeance,"X-Force" name used,Dr.Doom 2.50
11 . . . . 1.50
12 A:Dr.Doom 1.50
13 A:Dr.Doom 1.50
14 RL 1.50
15 RL 1.50
16 RL,A:Spider-Man 2.50
17 A:Spider-Man, ... 2.50
18 Inf.Gauntlet X-over, A:Spider-Man, Ghost Rider . . . 3.00
19 O:Cloak & Dagger,final issue . 2.50

CODENAME:GENETIX

1 PGa,A:Wolverine 2.00
2 PGa,V:Prime EvilA:Wolverine . 2.00
3 . . . . 2.00
4 A:Wolverine,Kazar 2.00

CODE NAME: SPITFIRE

See: SPITFIRE AND THE TROUBLESHOOTERS

COMBAT
Atlas
June, 1952

1 War Stories, Bare Bayonets . 75.00
2 Break Thru,(Dedicated to US Infantry) 35.00
3 . . . . 25.00
4 . . . . 40.00
5 thru 10 . . . . @25.00
11 April, 1953 . . . . 25.00

COMBAT CASEY
See: WAR COMBAT

COMBAT KELLY AND THE DEADLY DOZEN
Atlas
November, 1951

1 RH,Korean war stories 100.00
2 Big Push 50.00
3 The Volunteer 30.00
4 V:Communists 30.00
5 OW,V:Communists 30.00
6 V:Communists 30.00
7 V: Communists 30.00
8 Death to the Reds 30.00
9 . . . . 30.00
10 . . . . 30.00
11 . . . . 25.00
12 thru 16 . . . . @25.00
17 A:Combat Casey 35.00
18 A:Battle Brady 15.00
19 V:Communists 15.00
20 V:Communists 15.00
21 Transvestite Cover 30.00
22 thru 40 . . . . @15.00
41 thru 44 August, 1957 . . . . @15.00

COMBAT KELLY
June, 1972

1 JM, Stop the Luftwaffe 3.00
2 The Big Breakout 2.00
3 O:Combat Kelly 2.00
4 Mutiny,A:Sgt.Fury and the Howling Commandoes 2.00
5 Escape or Die 2.00
6 The Fortress of Doom 2.00
7 Nun Hostage,V:Nazis 2.00
8 V:Nazis 2.00
9 October, 1973 . . . . 2.00

COMET MAN
February, 1987

1 BSz(c),I:Comet Man 1.50
2 BSz(c),A:Mr.Fantastic 1.00
3 BSz(c),A:Hulk 1.00
4 BSz(c),A:Fantastic Four 1.00
5 BSz(c),A:Fantastic Four 1.00
6 BSz(c),Last issue, July,1987 . . 1.00

COMIX BOOK
(black & white magazine)
1974

1 . . . . 7.50
2 . . . . 4.50
3 . . . . 5.00
4 . . . . 3.75
5 1976 . . . . 3.75

COMMANDO ADVENTURES
Atlas
June, 1957

1 Seek, Find and Destroy 35.00
2 MD, Hit 'em and Hit 'em Hard, August,1957 . . . . 30.00

COMPLETE COMICS
See: AMAZING COMICS

COMPLETE MYSTERY
August, 1948

1 Seven Dead Men 175.00
2 Jigsaw of Doom 125.00
3 Fear in the Night 125.00
4 A Squealer Dies Fast 125.00

Becomes:

TRUE COMPLETE MYSTERY

5 Rice Mancini, The Deadly Dude 110.00
6 Ph(c),The Frame-up that Failed 90.00
7 Ph(c),Caught 90.00
8 Ph(c),The Downfall of Mr. Anderson, October, 1949 . . . 90.00

CONAN THE BARBARIAN
October, 1979

1 BWS/DA,O:Conan,A:Kull . . . 225.00
2 BWS/SB,Lair o/t Beast-Men . . 90.00
3 BWS,SB,Grey God Passes . 165.00
4 BWS,SB,Tower o/t Elephant . 60.00
5 BWS,Zukala's Daughter 60.00
6 BWS,SB,Devil Wings Over Shadizar 37.00
7 BWS,SB,DA,C:Thoth-Amon, I:Set 37.00
8 BWS,TS,TP,Keepers o/t Crypt 37.00
9 BWS,SB,Garden of Fear 37.00
10 BWS,SB,JSe,Beware Wrath of Anu;BU:Kull 45.00
11 BWS,SB,Talons of Thak 45.00

Conan the Barbarian #14

© Marvel Entertainment Group

12 BWS,GK,Dweller in the Dark, Blood of the Dragon B.U. . . . 28.00
13 BWS,SB,Web o/t Spider-God 28.00
14 BWS,SB,Green Empress of Melnibone 40.00
15 BWS,SB 40.00
16 BWS,Frost Giant's Daughter . 25.00
17 GK,Gods of Bal-Sagoth, A:Fafnir 13.00
18 GK,DA,Thing in the Temple, A:Fafnir 13.00
19 BWS,DA,Hawks from the Sea 25.00
20 BWS,DA,Black Hound of Vengeance,A:Fafnir 25.00
21 BWS,CR,VM,DA,SB, Monster of the Monoliths 20.00
22 BWS,DA,rep.Conan #1 . . . . . 24.00
23 BWS,DA,Shadow of the Vulture,I:Red Sonja 30.00
24 BWS,Song of Red Sonja . . . 26.00
25 JB,SB,JSe,Mirrors of Kharam Akkad,A:Kull 12.00
26 JB,Hour of the Griffin 7.00
27 JB,Blood of Bel-Hissar 6.00
28 JB,Moon of Zembabwei 6.00
29 JB,Two Against Turan 6.00
30 JB,The Hand of Nergal 6.00
31 JB,Shadow in the Tomb 4.00
32 JB,Flame Winds of Lost Khitai 4.00
33 JB,Death & 7 Wizards 4.00
34 JB,Temptress in the Tower of Flame 4.00
35 JB,Hell-Spawn of Kara-Shehr . 4.00
36 JB,Beware of Hyrkanians bearing Gifts 4.00
37 NA,Curse of the Golden Skull . 8.00
38 JB,Warrior & Were-Woman . . . 3.50
39 JB,Dragon from the Inland Sea 3.50
40 RB,Fiend from Forgotten City . 3.50
41 JB,Garden of Death & Life . . . 3.50
42 JB,Night of the Gargoyle 3.50
43 JB,Tower o/Blood,A:RedSonja 3.50
44 JB,Flame&Fiend,A:RedSonja . 5.00
45 JB,Last Ballad of Laza-Lanti . . 5.00
46 JB,JSt,Curse of the Conjurer . . 3.50
47 JB,DA,Goblins in the Moonlight 3.50
48 JB,DG,DA,Rats Dance at Ravengard,BU:Red Sonja 3.50
49 JB,DG,Wolf-Woman 3.50
50 JB,DG,Dweller in the Pool . . . 3.50
51 JB,DG,Man Born of Demon . . 3.00
52 JB,TP,Altar and the Scorpion . 3.00
53 JB,FS,Brothers of the Blade . . 3.00
54 JB,TP,Oracle of Ophir 3.00
55 JB,TP,Shadow on the Land . . 3.00
56 JB,High Tower in the Mist 3.00
57 MP,Incident in Argos 3.00
58 JB,Queen o/tBlackCoast, 2nd A:Belit 4.00
59 JB,Ballad of Belit,O:Belit 3.00
60 JB,Riders o/t River Dragons . . 3.00
61 JB,She-Pirate,I:Amra 2.50
62 JB,Lord of the Lions,O:Amra . . 2.50
63 JB,Death Among Ruins, V&D:Amra 2.50
64 JSon,AM,rep.Savage Tales#5 . 2.50
65 JB,Fiend o/tFeatheredSerpent . 2.50
66 JB,Daggers & Death Gods, C:Red Sonja 2.50
67 JB,Talons of the Man-Tiger, A:Red Sonja 2.50
68 JB,Of Once & Future Kings, V:KingKull,A:Belit,Red Sonja . . 2.50
69 VM,Demon Out of the Deep . . 2.50
70 JB,City in the Storm 2.50
71 JB,Secret of Ashtoreth 2.50
72 JB,Vengeance in Asgalun 2.50
73 JB,..In the Well of Skelos 2.50
74 JB,Battle at the Black Walls C:Thoth-Amon 2.50
75 JB,Hawk-Riders of Harakht . . . 2.50
76 JB,Swordless in Stygia 2.50
77 JB,When Giants Walk the Earth 2.50
78 JB,rep.Savage Sword #1, A:Red Sonja 2.50
79 HC,Lost Valley of Iskander . . . 2.50
80 HC,Trial By Combat 2.50
81 HC,The Eye of the Serpent . . . 2.00
82 HC,The Sorceress o/t Swamp . 2.00
83 HC,The Dance of the Skull . . . 2.00
84 JB,Two Against the Hawk-City, I:Zula 2.00
85 JB,Of Swordsmen & Sorcerers, O:Zulu 2.00
86 JB,Devourer of the Dead 2.00
87 TD, rep. Savage Sword #3. . . . 2.00
88 JB,Queen and the Corsairs . . . 2.00
89 JB,Sword & the Serpent, A:Thoth-Amon 2.00

All comics prices listed are for *Near Mint* condition.

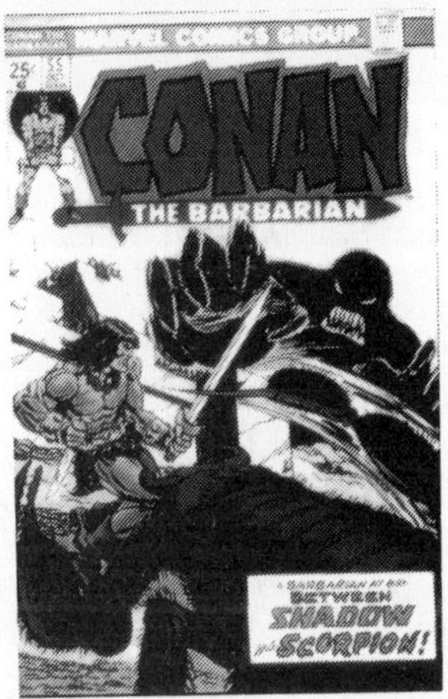

Conan the Barbarian #55
© Marvel Entertainment Group

90 JB,Diadem of the Giant-Kings . 2.00
91 JB,Savage Doings in Shem . . 2.00
92 JB,The Thing in the Crypt 2.00
93 JB,Of Rage & Revenge 2.00
94 JB,BeastKing ofAbombi,L:Zulu 2.00
95 JB,The Return of Amra 2.00
96 JB,Long Night of Fang & Talon Pt.1 . . . . 2.00
97 JB,Long Night of Fang & Talon Pt.2 . . . . 2.00
98 JB,Sea-Woman 2.00
99 JB,Devil Crabs o/t Dark Cliffs . 2.00
100 JB,Death on the Black Coast, D:Belit (double size) 3.50
101 JB,The Devil has many Legs . 1.75
102 JB,The Men Who Drink Blood 1.75
103 JB,Bride of the Vampire 1.75
104 JB,The Vale of Lost Women . 1.75
105 JB,Whispering Shadows 1.75
106 JB,Chaos in Kush 1.75
107 JB,Demon of the Night 1.75
108 JB,Moon-Eaters of Darfar . . . 1.75
109 JB,Sons o/t Bear God 1.75
110 JB,Beward t/Bear o/Heaven . 1.75
111 JB,Cimmerian Against a City . 1.75
112 JB,Buryat Besieged 1.75
113 JB,A Devil in the Family 1.75
114 JB,The Shadow of the Beast . 1.75
115 JB,A War of Wizards, A:Red Sonja Double size 10th Anniv. (L:Roy Thomas script) 2.50
116 JB,NA,Crawler in the Mist . . . 1.75
117 JB,Corridor of Mullah-Kajar . . 1.75
118 JB,Valley of Forever Night . . 1.75
119 JB,Voice of One Long Gone . 1.75
120 JB,The Hand of Erlik 1.75
121 JB,BMc,Price of Perfection . . 1.75
122 JB,BMc,The City Where Time Stood Still 1.75
123 JB,BMc,Horror Beneath the Hills 1.75
124 JB,BMc,the Eternity War 1.75
125 JB,BMc,the Witches ofNexxx . 1.75
126 JB,BMc,Blood Red Eye of Truth 1.75
127 GK,Snow Haired Woman of the Wastes 1.75
128 GK,And Life Sprang Forth From These 1.75
129 GK,The Creation Quest 1.75
130 GK,The Quest Ends 1.75
131 GK,The Ring of Rhax 1.75
132 GK,Games of Gharn 1.75
133 GK,The Witch of Widnsor . . . 1.75
134 GK,A Hitch in Time 1.75
135 MS,JRu,The Forest o/t Night . 1.75
136 JB,The River of Death 1.75
137 AA,Titans Gambit 1.75
138 VM,Isle of the Dead 1.75
139 VM,In the Lair of the Damned 1.75
140 JB,Spider Isle 1.75
141 JB,The Web Tightens 1.75
142 JB,The Maze,the Man, the Monster 1.75
143 JB,Life Among the Dead 1.75
144 JB,The Blade & the Beast . . . 1.75
145 Son of Cimmeria 1.75
146 JB,Night o/t Three Sisters . . . 1.75
147 JB,Tower of Mitra 1.75
148 JB,The Plague of Forlek 1.75
149 JB,Deathmark 1.75
150 JB,Tower of Flame 1.75
151 JB,Vale of Death 1.50
152 JB,Dark Blade of Jergal Zadh 1.50
153 JB,Bird Men of Akah Ma'at . . 1.50
154 JB,the Man-Bats of Ur-Xanarrh 1.50
155 JB,SL,The Anger of Conan . . 1.50
156 JB,The Curse 1.50
157 JB,The Wizard 1.50
158 JB,Night of the Wolf 1.50

Conan the Barbarian #83
© Marvel Entertainment Group

159 JB,Cauldron of the Doomed . 1.50
160 Veil of Darkness 1.50
161 JB,House of Skulls,A:Fafnir . . 1.50
162 JB,Destroyer in the Flame, A:Fafnir 1.50
163 JB,Cavern of the Vines of Doom,A:Fafnir 1.50
164 The Jeweled Sword of Tem . 1.50
165 JB,V:Nadine 1.50
166 JB,GI,Blood o/t Titan,A:Fafnir 1.50
167 JB,Creature From Time's Dawn,A:Fafnir 1.50
168 JB,Bird Woman & the Beast . 1.50
169 JB,Tomb of the Scarlet Mage 1.50
170 JB,Dominion of the Dead, A&D:Fafnir 1.50
171 JB,Barbarian Death Song . . . 1.50
172 JB,Reavers in Borderland . . . 1.50
173 JB,Honor Among Thieves . . . 1.50
174 JB,V:Tetra 1.50
175 JB,V:Spectre ofDeath 1.50
176 JB,Argos Rain 1.50
177 JB,V:Nostume 1.50
178 JB,A:Tetra,Well of Souls 1.50
179 JB,End of all there is,A:Kiev . 1.50
180 JBV:AnitRenrut 1.50
181 JB,V:KingMaddoc II 1.50
182 JB,V:King of Shem 1.50
183 JB,V:Imhotep 1.50
184 JB,V:Madoc 1.50
185 JB,R:Tetra 1.50
186 JB,The Crimson Brotherhood 1.50
187 JB,V:Council of Seven 1.50
188 JB,V:Devourer-Souls 1.50
189 JB,V:Devourer-Souls 1.50
190 JB,Devourer-Souls 1.50
191 Deliverance 1.50
192 JB,V:TheKeeper 1.50
193 Devourer-Souls 1.50
194 V:Devourer-Souls 1.50
195 Blood of Ages 1.50
196 V:Beast 1.50
197 A:Red Sonja 1.50
198 A:Red Sonja 1.50
199 O:Kaleb 1.50
200 JB,D.sizeV:Dev-Souls 2.00
201 NKu,GI,Thulsa Doom 1.50
202 . . . . 1.50
203 V:Thulsa Doom 1.50
204 VS,GI,A:Red Sonja,I:Strakkus 1.50
205 A:Red Sonja 1.50
206 VS,GI,Heku trilogy Pt.1 . . . . . 1.50
207 VS,GI,Heku Pt.2,O:Kote 1.50
208 VS,GI,Heku Pt.3 . . . . 1.50
209 VS,GI,Heku epilogue 1.50
210 VS,GI,V:Sevante 1.50
211 VS,GI,V:Sevante 1.50
212 EC,GI 1.50
213 V:Ghamud Assassins 1.50
214 AA 1.50
215 VS,AA,Conan Enslaved 1.50
216 V:Blade of Zed 1.50
217 JLe(c),V:Blade of Zed 1.50
218 JLe(c),V:Picts 1.50
219 JLe(c),V:Forgotten Beasts . . . 1.50
220 Conan the Pirate 1.50
221 Conan the Pirate 1.50
222 AA,DP,Revenge 1.50
223 AA,Religious Cult 1.50
224 AA,Cannibalism 1.50
225 AA,Conan Blinded 1.50
226 AA,Quest for Mystic Jewel . . 1.50
227 AA,Mystic Jewel Pt.2 . . . . . . 1.50
228 AA,Cannibalism Pt.1 . . . . 1.50
229 AA,Cannibalism Pt.2 . . . . 1.50
230 FS,SDr,Citadel Pt.1 . . . . 1.50
231 FS,DP,Citadel Pt.2 . . . . 1.50
232 RLm,Birth of Conan 3.00
233 RLm,DA,B:Conan as youth . 2.00
234 RLm,DA 2.00
235 RLm,DA 2.00
236 RLm,DA 2.00
237 DA,V:Jormma 1.50
238 DA,D:Conan 1.50
239 Conan Possessed 1.50
240 Conan Possessed 1.50
241 TM(c),R:RoyThomasScript . . 3.50
242 JLe(c),A:Red Sonja 2.50
243 WPo(c),V:Zukala, ... 2.00
244 A:Red Sonja,Zula 1.50
245 A:Red Sonja,V:King of Vampires 1.50
246 A:Red Sonja,V:MistMonster . . 1.50
247 A:Red Sonja,Zula 1.50
248 V:Zulu 1.50
249 A:Red Sonja,Zula 1.50
250 A:RedSonja,Zula,V:Zug double size. 2.00
251 Cimmeria,V:Shumu Gorath . . 1.50
252 ECh 1.50
253 ECh,V:Kulan-Goth(X-Men Villain) 1.50
254 ECh,V:Shuma-Gorath (Dr. Strange Villain) 1.50

Conan the Barbarian #84
© Marvel Entertainment Group

255 ECh,V:Shuma-Gorath 1.50
256 ECh,D:Nemedia's King 1.50
257 ECh,V:Queen Vammator 1.50
258 AA(i),A:Kulan Gath 1.50
259 V:Shuma-Gorath 1.50
260 AA(i),V:Queen Vammatar . . . 1.50
261 V:Cult of the Death Goddess . 1.50
262 V:The Panther 1.50
263 V:Malaq 1.50
264 V:Kralic 1.50
265 V:Karlik 1.50
266 Conan the Renegade(adapt) . 1.50
267 adaption of Tor 1.50
268 adaption of Tor 1.50
269 V:Agohoth,Prince Borin 1.50
270 Devourer of the Dead 1.50
271 V:Devourer of Souls 1.50
272 V:Devourer 1.50
273 V:Purple Lotus 1.50
274 V:She-Bat 1.50
275 RTs(s),Last Issue cont. in Savage Sword of Conan 6.00
Giant#1 GK,TS,Hour of the Dragon, inc.rep.Conan#3, I:Belit 8.00
Giant#2 GK,TS,Conan Bound, inc. rep Conan #5 . . . . 5.00
Giant#3 GK,TS,To Tarantia & the Tower,inc.rep.Conan#6 . 5.00
Giant#4,GK,FS,Swords of the South,inc.rep.Conan #7 . . . . . 5.00
Giant#5 rep.Conan #14,#15 & Back-up story #12 . . . . 5.00
KingSz.#1 rep.Conan #2,#4 . . . . 10.00
Ann.#2 BWS,Phoenix on the Sword A:Thoth-Amon 4.00
Ann.#3 JB,HC,Mountain of the Moon God, B.U.Kull story . 2.00
Ann.#4 JB,Return of the Conqueror,A:Zenobia 2.00
Ann.#5 JB,W:Conan/Zenobia 2.00
Ann.#6 GK,King of the Forgotten People 2.00
Ann.#7 JB,Red Shadows & Black Kraken 1.50
Ann.#8 VM,Dark Night of the White Queen 1.50
Ann.#9 . . . . 1.50
Ann.#10 Scorched Earth (Conan #176 x-over) 1.50
Ann.#11 . . . . 1.50

Conan-Barbarian Movie Spec.#1 . 1.25
Conan-Destroyer Movie Spec.#1 . 1.25
Red Nails Special Ed.BWS 4.00
Conan the Rogue, JB,V:Romm . . 9.95

CLASSIC CONAN
June, 1987

1 BWS,rep. 2.00
2 BWS,rep. 2.00
3 BWS,rep. 2.00

Becomes:

CONAN SAGA

4 rep. 2.00
5 rep. 2.00
6 rep. 2.00
7 rep. 2.00
8 rep. 2.00
9 rep. 2.00
10 rep. 2.00
11 rep. 2.00
12 rep. 2.00
13 rep. 2.00
14 rep.Savage Sword #5 . . . . . . 2.00
15 rep.Savage Sword #7 . . . . . . 2.00
16 rep.Savage Sword #12 . . . . . . 2.00
17 rep.Savage Sword 2.00
18 rep.Savage Sword 2.00
19 rep.Savage Sword #28 . . . . . . 2.00
20 rep.Savage Sword #25 . . . . . . 2.00
21 rep.Savage Sword 2.00
22 rep.Giant Size Conan #1&2 . . 2.00
23 rep.Hour of the Dragon 2.00
24 rep.Hour of the Dragon 2.00
25 rep.Savage Sword 2.00
26 rep.Savage Sword #11 . . . . . . 2.00
27 rep.Savage Sword #15 . . . . . . 2.00
28 rep.Savage Sword #16 . . . . . . 2.25
29 rep.Savage Sword #17 . . . . . . 2.25
30 rep.Savage Sword #18 . . . . . . 2.25
31 rep.Savage Sword #19 . . . . . . 2.25
32 rep.Savage Sword #5 . . . . . . 2.25
33 rep.Savage Sword #5 . . . . . . 2.25
34 rep.Savage Sword # 2.25
35 rep.Savage Sword #32 . . . . . . 2.25
36 rep.Savage Sword #12 . . . . . . 2.25
37 rep.Savage Sword #34 . . . . . . 2.25
38 rep.Conan #94_ 2.25
39 rep.Conan #96a 2.25
40 rep.Savage Sword #26 . . . . . . 2.25
41 rep.Savage Sword #27 . . . . . . 2.25
42 rep.Savage Sword #40 . . . . . . 2.25
43 rep.Savage Sword #41 . . . . . . 2.25
44 rep.Savage Sword #42 . . . . . . 2.25
45 rep.Savage Sword #43 . . . . . . 2.25
46 rep.Savage Sword #15 . . . . . . 2.25
47 rep.Savage Sword #22 . . . . . . 2.25
48 rep.Savage Sword #23 . . . . . . 2.25
49 rep.Sav.Sword Super Spec#2 . 2.25
50 rep.Conan #58 . . . . 2.25
51 rep.Conan #59< 2.25
52 rep.Conan #61 . . . . 2.25
53 thru 63 rep.Savage Sword . @2.25

CONAN CLASSICS

1 rep. Conan #1 . . . . 1.50
2 rep. Conan #2 . . . . 1.50

KING CONAN
March, 1980

1 JB/ECh,I:Conn,V:Thoth-Amon . 4.00
2 JB,Black Sphinx of Nebthu . . . 2.00
3 JB,Dragon Wings Over Zembabwei 2.00
4 JB,V:Thoth-Amon 2.00
5 JB,The Sorcerer in the Realm of Madness 2.00
6 JB,The Lady's Name Is..Trouble 2.00
7 PS,JB 2.50
8 A:Queen Reclaimed 2.50
9 JB,V:Medusa Monster 2.00
10 V:Sea Monster 2.00
11 V:Giant Totem Monster 1.50
12 V:Monster 1.50
13 V:Monster 1.50
14 V:Demon 1.50
15 V:Sea Monster 1.50
16 Conan Into Battle 1.50
17 A:Conn 1.50
18 King of the Freaks? 1.50
19 MK(c),Skull & X-Bones cover . 1.50

Becomes:

CONAN THE KING

20 MS,The Prince is Dead 1.50
21 MS,Shadows 1.50
22 GI/MS,The Black Dragons,Prince Conan II back-up story begins . 1.50
23 MS/GI,Ordeal 1.50
24 GI/MS,Fragments:AWitch'sTale 1.50
25 MS/GI,Daggers 1.50
26 MS/GI,PrinceConanII B.U.ends 1.25
27 MS/GI,A Death in Stygia 1.25
28 MS/GI,Call of the Wild, A:Red Sonja 1.25
29 MS,The Sleeping Lion 1.25
30 GI,Revenge on the Black River 1.25
31 GI,Force of Arms 1.25
32 GI,Juggernaut 1.25
33 . . . . 1.25
34 . . . . 1.25
35 . . . . 1.25
36 . . . . 1.25
37 AW,Sack of Belverus 1.25
38 MM,A:Taurus,Leora 1.25
39 The Tower 1.25
40 . . . . 1.25
41 V:Leora 1.25
42 Thee Armada,A:Conn 1.25
43 . . . . 1.25
44 . . . . 1.25
45 V:Caliastros 1.25
46 V:Caliastros 1.25
47 TD,V:Caliastros 1.25
48 . . . . 1.25
49 . . . . 1.25
50 GI,50th Anniversary issue 1.25
51 GI,Death of Prince Conn 1.25
52 GI,Prince Conn story contd . . . 1.25
53 GI,A:Thoth-Amon 1.25
54 GI,V:Thoth-Amon 1.25
55 GI,Sorcerers Ring,final issue . . 1.50

CONEHEADS

1 Based SNL 1.75

CONTEST OF CHAMPIONS
June, 1982

1 JR2,Grandmaster vs. Mistress Death, A:Alpha Flight 8.00
2 JR2,Grandmaster vs. Mistress Death, A:X-Men 6.00
3 JR2,D:Grandmaster, Rebirth Collector, A:X-Men 6.00

COPS: THE JOB

1 MGo(c),V:Serial killer 1.50
2 MGo(c) 1.25
3 MGo(c),V:Eviscerator 1.25
4 MGo(c),D:Eviscerator,Nick 1.25

COSMIC POWERS

1 RMz(s),RLm,JP,F:Thanos 2.75
2 RMz(s),JMr,F:Terrax 2.75
3 RMz(s),F:Jack of Hearts 2.50
4 RMz(s),RLm,F:Legacy 2.50
5 RMz(s),F:Morg 2.50

COUNT DUCKULA
Star
November, 1988

1 O:CountDuckula,B:DangerMouse1.25
2 A:Danger Mouse 1.00
3 thru 15 . . . . @1.00

COWBOY ACTION
See: WESTERN THRILLERS

COWBOY ROMANCES
October, 1949
1 Ph(c),Outlaw and the Lady . 125.00
2 Ph(c),William Holden/Mona Freeman,Streets of Laredo .. 75.00
3 Phc,Romance in Roaring Valley 50.00
Becomes:
YOUNG MEN
4 A Kid Names Shorty 75.00
5 Jaws of Death 50.00
6 Man-Size 50.00
7 The Last Laugh 50.00
8 Adventure stories continued .. 50.00
9 Draft Dodging story 50.00
10 US Draft Story 50.00
11 Adventure stories continued . 40.00
12 B:On the Battlefield, inc.Spearhead 40.00
13 RH,Break-through 40.00
14 RH,Fox Hole 40.00
15 Battlefield stories cont, ... 40.00
16 Sniper Patrol 40.00
17 Battlefield stories cont, ... 40.00
18 BEv,Warlord 40.00
19 BEv 40.00
20 BEv,E:On the Battlefield ... 40.00
21 B:Flash Foster and his High Gear Hot Shots 40.00
22 Screaming Tires 40.00
23 E:Flash Foster and his High Gear Hot Shots 40.00
24 BEv,B:Capt. America,Human Torch,Sub-Mariner,O:Capt. America,Red Skull 450.00
25 BEv,JR, Human Torch,Capt America,Sub-Mariner 350.00
26 BEv,Human Torch, Capt. America,Sub Mariner 350.00
27 Bev, Human Torch/Toro V:Hypnotist 350.00
28 E:Human Torch, Capt America, Sub Mariner,June, 1954 ... 350.00

COWGIRL ROMANCES
See: DARING MYSTERY

COYOTE
Epic
June, 1983
1 SL, ... 2.50
2 SL 2.00
3 BG 1.50
4 SL 1.50
5 SL 1.50
6 SL 1.50
7 SL,SD 1.50
8 SL 1.50
9 SL,SD 1.50
10 SL 1.50
11 FS,1st TM art,O:Slash 4.00
12 TM 3.00
13 TM 3.00
14 FS,TM,A:Badger 3.50
15 SL 1.50
16 SL,A:Reagan,Gorbachev 1.50

CRASH RYAN
Epic
October, 1984
1 War Story 1.75
2 Doomsday 1.50
3 Fortress Japan 1.50
4 January, 1985 .... 1.50

CRAZY
Atlas
December, 1953
1 BEv,satire, Frank N.Steins Castle 100.00
2 BEv,Beast from 1000 Fathoms 75.00
3 Bev,Madame Knockwurst's Whacks Museum 65.00
4 BEv,I Love Lucy satire 65.00
5 BEv,Censorship satire 65.00
6 BEv,satire 65.00
7 BEv,satire,July, 1954 ...... 65.00

CRAZY
February, 1973
1 Not Brand Echh reps, ... Forbushman 4.50
2 Big,Batty Love and Hisses issue 3.00
3 Stupor-Man,A:Fantastical Four, June 1973 .... 3.00

CRAZY
(Black and white magazine)
October, 1973
1 Satire,parody 3.50
2 .... 2.00
3 thru 81 .... @1.50
82 X-Men(c) 1.50
83 thru 93 .... @1.00

CREATURES ON THE LOOSE
See: TOWER OF SHADOWS

CRIME CAN'T WIN
See: KRAZY COMICS

CRIME FIGHTERS
April, 1948
1 Police Stories 90.00
2 Jewelry robbery 45.00
3 The Nine who were Doomed . 45.00
4 Human Beast at Bay 35.00
5 V:Gangsters 35.00
6 Pickpockets 35.00
7 True Cases, Crime Can't Win 35.00
8 True Cases, Crime Can't Win 35.00
9 Ph(c),It Happened at Night .. 35.00
10 Ph(c),Killer at Large, November, 1949 .... 35.00
Atlas
11 V:Gangsters,September, 1954 35.00
12 V:Gangsters 35.00
13 Clay Pidgeon January, 1955 . 35.00

CRITICAL MASS
Epic
January, 1990
1 KS,GM,BSzF:ShadowlineSaga . 4.95
2 .... 4.95
3 GM,SDr,JRy 4.95
4 .... 4.95
5 JZ 4.95
6 .... 4.95
7 July, 1990 .... 4.95

CROSSOVER CLASSICS
TPB Marvel and D.C. GP(c),reprints both Spider-Man/Superman,the Batman/Hulk and the X-Men/New Teen Titans Battles 17.95

CRYPT OF SHADOWS
January, 1973
1 BW,RH,Midnight on Black Mountain 5.50
2 Monster at the Door 2.50
3 Dead Man's Hand 2.50
4 Cl,Secret in the Vault 2.50
5 JM,The Graveyard Ghoul 2.50
6 BEv,Don't Bury Me Deep 2.50
7 JSt,The Haunting of Bluebeard 2.50
8 How Deep my Grave 2.50
9 Beyond Death 2.50
10 A Scream in the Dark 2.50
11 The Ghouls in my Grave 2.00
12 Behind the Locked Door 2.00
13 SD,Back From the Dead 2.00
14 The Thing that Creeps 2.00
15 My Coffin is Crowded 2.00
16 .... 2.00
17 In the Hands of Shandu 2.00
18 SD,Face of Fear 2.00
19 SD,Colossus that Challenged the World 2.00
20 A Monster walks Among Us .. 2.00
21 SD,Death Will Be Mine, November 1975 .... 2.00

CUPID
December, 1949
1 Ph(c),Cora Dod's Amazing Decision 60.00
2 Ph(c),Betty Page, Mar. 1950 125.00

CURSE OF THE WEIRD
1 thru 4 SD,rep. 50's Sci-Fi 1.50

CYBERSPACE 3000
1 A:Dark Angel,Galactus,V:Badoon, Glow in the dark(c) 3.25
2 SeT,A:Galactus,Dark Angel ... 2.00
3 SeT,A:Galactus,Keeper 2.00
4 SeT,A:Keeper 2.00
5 SeT,A:Keeper 2.00
6 SeT,A:Warlock 2.00
7 SeT,I:Gamble 2.00
8 SeT,A:Warlock 1.75

DAKOTA NORTH
1986
1 (Now in Cage) 1.50
2 .... 1.25
3 .... 1.25
4 .... 1.25
5 February, 1987 .... 1.25

DAMAGE CONTROL
May, 1989
1 EC/BWi;A:Spider-Man 3.00
2 EC/BWi;A:Fant.Four 2.00
3 EC/BWi;A:Iron Man 2.00
4 EC/BWi;A:X-Men 2.00
[2nd Series]
1 EC,A:Capt.America&Thor 3.00
2 EC,A:Punisher 2.50
3 EC 2.00
4 EC,Punisher 2.00
[3rd Series]
1 Clean-up Crew Returns 1.50
2 A:Hulk,New Warriors 1.50
3 A:Avengers W.C.,Wonder Man, Silver Surfer 1.50
4 A:SilverSurfer & others 1.50

DANCES WITH DEMONS
1 CAd 2.95
2 CAd,V:Manitou 1.95
3 CAd,V:Manitou 1.95
4 CAd,last issue 1.95

DAREDEVIL
April, 1964
1 B:StL(s),JK(c),BEv, I&O:Daredevil,I:Karen Page, Foggy Nelson 1,300.00
2 JK(c),JO,V:Electro 425.00
3 JK(c),JO,I&O:The Owl 250.00
4 JK(c),JO,I&O:Killgrave 185.00
5 JK(c),WW,V:Masked Matador 175.00
6 WW,I&O Original Mr. Fear .. 125.00
7 WW,I:Red Costume,V:Namor 150.00
8 WW,I&O:Stiltman 110.00
9 WW(i),Killers Castle 100.00
10 WW(i),V:Catman 100.00
11 WW(i),R:Cat 80.00
12 JK,JR,2nd A:Kazar 75.00
13 JK,JR,O:Ka-Zar 75.00
14 JR,If This Be Justice 75.00
15 JR,A:Ox 75.00

Daredevil #163
© Marvel Entertainment Group

16 JR,A:Spider-Man,
I:Masked Marauder 85.00
17 JR,A:Spider-Man 85.00
18 DON(s),JR,I:Gladiator 60.00
19 JR,V:Gladiator 60.00
20 JR(c),GC,V:Owl 50.00
21 GC,BEv,V:Owl 35.00
22 GC,V:Tri-man 35.00
23 GC,V:Tri-man 35.00
24 GC,A:Ka-Zar 35.00
25 GC,V:Leapfrog 30.00
26 GC,V:Stiltman 30.00
27 GC,Spider-Man 32.00
28 GC,V:Aliens 30.00
29 GC,V:The Boss 30.00
30 BEv(c),GC,A:Thor 30.00
31 GC,V:Cobra 28.00
32 GC,V:Cobra 28.00
33 GC,V:Beetle 28.00
34 BEv(c),GC,O:Beetle 28.00
35 BEv(c),GC,A:Susan Richards 28.00
36 GC,A:FF 28.00
37 GC,V:Dr.Doom 28.00
38 GC,A:FF 28.00
39 GC,GT,V:Unholy Three 28.00
40 GC,V:Unholy Three 28.00
41 GC,D:Mike Murdock 30.00
42 GC,DA,I:Jester 28.00
43 JK(c),GC,A:Capt.America . . . 24.00
44 JSo(c),GC,V:Jester 20.00
45 GC,V:Jester 20.00
46 GC,V:Jester 20.00
47 GC,'Brother Take My Hand' . 20.00
48 GC,V:Stiltman 20.00
49 GC,V:Robot,I:Starr Saxon . . . 20.00
50 JR(c),BWS,JCr,V:Robot 25.00
51 B:RTs(s),BWS,V:Robot 25.00
52 BWS,JCr,A:Black Panther . . . 25.00
53 GC,O:Daredevil. 27.00
54 GC,V:Mr.Fear,A:Spidey 20.00
55 GC,V:Mr.Fear 16.00
56 GC,V:Death Head 16.00
57 GC,V:Death Head 16.00
58 GC,V:Stunt Master 15.00
59 GC,V:Torpedo 15.00
60 GC,V:Crime Wave 15.00
61 GC,V:Cobra 15.00
62 GC,O:Night Hawk 15.00
63 GC,V:Gladiator 15.00
64 GC,A:Stuntmaster 15.00
65 GC,V:BrotherBrimstone 15.00
66 GC,V:BrotherBrimstone 15.00
67 BEv(c),GC,Stiltman 15.00
68 AC,V:Kragg Blackmailer,
a:Bl.Panther,DD'sID Rev. . . . 15.00
69 E:RTs(s),GC,V:Thunderbolts,
A:Bl.Panther(DD's ID Rev) . . 15.00
70 GC,V:Terrorists 15.00
71 RTs(s),GC,V:Terrorists 15.00
72 GyC(s),GC,Tagak,V:Quother . 12.00
73 GC,V:Zodiac 12.00
74 B:GyC(s),GC,I:Smasher 12.00
75 GC,V:El Condor 12.00
76 GC,TP,V:El Condor 12.00
77 GC,TP,V:Manbull 12.00
78 GC,TP,V:Manbull 12.00
79 GC,TP,V:Manbull 12.00
80 GK(c),GC,TP,V:Owl 12.00
81 GK(c),GC,JA,A:Black Widow . 12.00
82 GK(c),GC,JA,V:Scorpion 12.00
83 JR(c),BWS,BEv,V:Mr.Hyde . . 14.00
84 GK(c),GC,Assassin 10.00
85 GK(c),GC,A:Black Widow . . . 10.00
86 GC,TP,V:Ox 10.00
87 GC,TP,V:Electro 10.00
88 GK(c),GC,TP,O:Black Widow 10.00
89 GC,TP,A:Black Widow 10.00
90 E:StL(s),GK(c),GC,TP,V:Ox . 10.00
91 GK(c),GC,TP,I:Mr. Fear III . . 10.00
92 GK(c),GC,TP,A:BlackPanther 10.00
93 GK(c),GC,TP,A:Black Widow 10.00
94 GK(c),GC,TP,V:Damon Dran . 10.00
95 GK(c),GC,TP,V:Manbull 10.00
96 GK(c),GC,ECh,V:Manbull . . . 10.00
97 GK(c),V:Dark Messiah 10.00
98 E:GyC(s),GC,ECh,V:Dark
Messiah 10.00
99 B:SvG(s),JR(c),V:Hawkeye . . 10.00
100 GC,V:Angar the Screamer . 25.00
101 RB,A:Angar the Screamer . . . 9.00
102 A:Black Widow 7.00
103 JR(c),DH,A:Spider-Man 7.00
104 GK(c),DH,V:Kraven 7.00
105 DH,JSn,DP,C:Thanos 12.00
106 JR(c),DH,A:Black Widow 7.00
107 JSn(c),JB(i),A:Capt.Marvel . . 7.00
108 K&R(c),PG(i),V:Beetle 7.00
109 GK(c),DH(i),V:Beetle 7.00
110 JR(c),GC,A:Thing,O:Nekra . . 7.00
111 JM(i),I:Silver Samurai 8.50
112 GK(c),GC,V:Mandrill 7.00
113 JR(c),V:Gladiator 7.00
114 GK(c),I:Death Stalker 7.00
115 V:Death Stalker 6.00
116 GK(c),GC,V:Owl 6.00
117 E:SvG(s),K&R(c),V:Owl 6.00
118 JR(c),DH,I:Blackwing 6.00
119 GK(c),DH(i),V:Crusher 6.00
120 GK(c),V:Hydra,I:El Jaguar . . . 6.00
121 GK(c),A:Shield 5.00
122 GK(c),V:Blackwing 5.00
123 V:Silvermane,I:Jackhammer . 5.00
124 B:MWn(s),GK(c),GC,KJ,
I:Copperhead 5.00
125 GK(c),KJ(i),V:Copperhead . . . 5.00
126 GK(c),KJ(i),D: 2nd Torpedo . . 5.00
127 GK(c),KJ(i),V:3rd Torpedo . . . 5.00
128 GK(c),KJ(i),V:Death Stalker . . 5.00
129 KJ(i),V:Man Bull 5.00
130 KJ(i),V:Brother Zed 5.00
131 KJ(i),I&O:2nd Bullseye 24.00
132 KJ(i),V:Bullseye 6.00
133 JM(i),GK(c),V:Jester 4.00
134 JM(i),V:Chamelon 4.00
135 JM(i),V:Jester 4.00
136 JB,JM,V:Jester 4.00
137 JB,V:Jester 4.00
138 JBy,A:Ghost Rider 15.00
139 SB,V:A Bomber 4.00
140 SB,V:Gladiator 4.00
141 GC,Bullseye 4.00
142 GC,V:Cobra 4.00
143 E:MWn(s),GC,V:Cobra 4.00
144 GT,V:Manbull 4.00
145 GT,V:Owl 4.00
146 GC,V:Bullseye 5.00

Daredevil #181
© Marvel Entertainment Group

147 GC,V:Killgrave 3.50
148 GC,V:Deathstalker 3.50
149 KI,V:Smasher 3.50
150 GC,KJ,I:Paladin 4.50
151 GC,Daredevil Unmasked 3.50
152 KJ,V:Paladin 3.50
153 GC,V:Cobra 3.50
154 GC,V:Mr. Hyde 3.50
155 V:Avengers 3.50
156 GC,V:Death Stalker 3.50
157 GC,V:Death Stalker 3.50
158 FM,V:Death Stalker 56.00
159 FM,V:Bullseye 30.00
160 FM,Bullseye 20.00
161 FM,V:Bullseye 20.00
162 SD,JRu,'Requiem' 5.00
163 FM,V:Hulk,I:Ben Urich 16.00
164 FM,KJ,A:Avengers 16.00
165 FM,KJ,V:Dr.Octopus 16.00
166 FM,KJ,V:Gladiator 16.00
167 FM,KJ,V:Mauler 16.00
168 FM,KJ,I&O:Elektra 50.00
169 FM,KJ,V:Bullseye 17.00
170 FM,KJ,V:Bullseye 17.00
171 FM,KJ,V:Kingpin 10.00
172 FM,KJ,V:Bullseye 10.00
173 FM,KJ,V:Gliadator 10.00
174 FM,KJ,A:Gladiator 10.00
175 FM,KJ,A:Elektra,V:Hand . . . 23.00
176 FM,KJ,A:Elektra 17.00
177 FM,KJ,A:Stick 10.00
178 FM,KJ,A:PowerMan&I.Fist . . 10.00
179 FM,KJ,V:Elektra 15.00
180 FM,KJ,V:Kingpin 10.00
181 FM,KJ,V:Bullseye,D:Elektra,
A:Punisher 18.00
182 FM,KJ,A:Punisher 9.00
183 FM,KJ,V:PunisherDrug 9.00
184 FM,KJ,V:PunisherDrug 9.00
185 FM,KJ,V:King Pin 7.00
186 FM,KJ,V:Stiltman 7.00
187 FM,KJ,A:Stick 7.00
188 FM,KJ,A:Black Widow 7.00
189 FM,KJ,A:Stick,A:BlackWidow . 7.00
190 FM,KJ,R:Elektra 15.00
191 FM,TA,A:Bullseye 7.00
192 KJ,V:Kingpin 4.00
193 KJ,Betsy 4.00
194 KJ,V:Kingpin 4.00
195 KJ,Tarkington Brown 4.00
196 KJ,A:Wolverine 3.00

Daredevil #257
© Marvel Entertainment Group

197 V:Bullseye 3.00
198 V:Dark Wind 3.00
199 V:Dark Wind 3.00
200 JBy(c),V:Bullseye 3.50
201 JBy(c),A:Black Widow 2.50
202 I:Micah Synn 2.50
203 JBy(c),I:Trump 2.50
204 BSz(c),V:Micah Synn 2.50
205 I:Gael 2.50
206 V:Micah Synn 2.50
207 BSz(c),A:Black Widow 2.50
208 Harlan Ellison 2.75
209 Harlan Ellison 2.75
210 DM,V:Micah Synn 2.50
211 DM,V:Micah Synn 2.50
212 DM,V:Micah Synn 2.50
213 DM,V:Micah Synn 2.50
214 DM,V:Micah Synn 2.50
215 DM,A:Two-Gun Kid 2.50
216 DM,V:Gael 2.50
217 BS(c),V:Gael 2.50
218 KP,V:Jester 2.50
219 FM,JB 3.00
220 DM,D:Heather Glenn 2.50
221 DM,Venice 2.50
222 DM,A:Black Widow 2.50
223 DM,Secret Wars II 2.50
224 DM,V:Sunturion 2.50
225 DM,V:Vulture 2.50
226 FM(plot),V:Gladiator 3.00
227 FM,Kingpin,Kar.Page 8.00
228 FM,DM,V:Kingpin 5.00
229 FM,Kingpin,Turk 5.00
230 R:Matt's Mother 5.00
231 FM,DM,V:Kingpin 5.00
232 FM,V:Kingpin,Nuke 5.00
233 FM,Kingpin,Nuke,Cpt Am. 5.00
234 SD,KJ,V:Madcap 2.00
235 SD,KJ,V:Mr. Hyde 2.00
236 BWS,A:Black Widow 5.00
237 AW(i),V:Klaw 2.00
238 SB,SL,AAd(c)V:Sabretooth . . 9.00
239 AAd(c),AW,GI(i),V:Rotgut . . . 2.00
240 AW,V:Rotgut 2.00
241 MZ(c),TM,V:Trixter 4.00
242 KP,V:Caviar Killer 2.00
243 AW,V:Nameless One 2.00
244 TD(i),V:Nameless One 2.00
245 TD(i),A:Black Panther 2.00
246 TD(i),V:Chance 2.00
247 KG,A:Black Widow 2.00
248 RL,AW,A:Wolverine,
V:Bushwhacker 11.00
249 RL,AW,V:Wolverine,
Bushwhacker 10.00
250 JR2,AW,I:Bullet 3.50
251 JR2,AW,V:Bullet 3.00
252 JR2,AW,Fall o/Mutants 4.50
253 JR2,AW,V:Kingpin 3.00
254 JR2,AW,I:Typhoid Mary . . . 15.00
255 JR2,AW,A:Kingpin,TMary . . . 8.00
256 JR2,AW,A:Kingpin,TMary . . . 8.00
257 JR2,AW,A:Punisher 13.00
258 RLm,V:Bengal 3.50
259 JR2,AW,V:TyphoidMary 5.00
260 JR2,AW,V:T.Mary,K.pin 5.00
261 JR2,AW,HumanTorch 2.50
262 JR2,AW,Inferno 2.50
263 JR2,AW,Inferno 2.50
264 SD,AW,MM,V:The Owl 2.50
265 JR2,AW,Inferno 2.50
266 JR2,AW,V:Mephisto 2.50
267 JR2,AW,V:Bullet 2.50
268 JR2,AW,V:TheMob 2.50
269 JR2,AW,V:Pyro&Blob 2.50
270 JR2,AW,A:Spider-Man,
I:Blackheart 3.00
271 JR2,AW,I:Number9 . . . . 2.50
272 JR2,AW,I:Shotgun 3.00
273 JR2,AW,V:Shotgun 2.50
274 JR2,AW,V:Inhumans 2.50
275 JR2,AW,ActsOfVen.,V:Ultron . 2.50
276 JR2,AW,ActsOfVen.,V:Ultorn . 2.50
277 RL,AW,Vivian's Story 1.75
278 JR2,AW,V:Blackheart,
A:Inhumans 2.50
279 JR2,AW,V:Mephisto,
A:Inhumans 2.50
280 JR2,AW,V:Mephisto,
A:Inhumans 2.50
281 JR2,AW,V:Mephisto,
A:Inhumans 2.50
282 JR2,AW,V:Mephisto,
A:Silver Surfer, Inhumans 2.50
283 MBa,AW,A:Captain America 2.00
284 LW,AW,R:Bullseye 1.75
285 LW,AW,B:Bullseye
become DD#1 . . . . 1.75
286 LW,AW,GCa,Fake
Daredevil #2 . . . . 1.75
287 LW,AW,Fake Daredevil #3 . . 1.75
288 LW,AW,A:Kingpin 1.75
289 LW,AW,A:Kingpin 1.75
290 LW,AW,E:Fake Daredevil . . . 1.75
291 LW,AW,V:Bullet 1.75
292 LW,A:Punisher,V:Tombstone . 2.50
293 LW,A:Punisher,V:Tombstone . 2.00
294 LW,V:The Hand. 1.75
295 LW,V:The Hand,
A:GhostRider. 1.75
296 LW,AW,V:The Hand 1.75
297 B:DGC(s),LW,AW,B:Last Rites,
V:Typhoid Mary,A:Kingpin 3.00
298 LW,AW,A:Nick Fury,Kingpin . 2.50
299 LW,AW,A:Nick Fury,Kingpin . 2.50
300 LW,AW,E:Last Rites, ... 4.50
301 V:The Owl 1.75
302 V:The Owl 1.75
303 V:The Owl. 1.75
304 AW,Non-action issue 1.75
305 AW,A:Spider-Man 1.75
306 AW,A:Spider-Man 1.75
307 1st SMc DD,Dead Man's Hand #1,
A:Nomad 3.00
308 SMc,Dead Man's Hand #5,
A:Punisher,V:Silvermane 2.00
309 SMc,Dead Man's Hand#7,
A:Nomad,Punisher 2.00
310 SMc,Inf.War,V:Calipso 2.00
311 SMc,V:Calypso 2.00
312 Firefighting issue 1.75
313 SMc,V:Pyromaniac 2.00
314 SMc,V:Mr.Fear,I:Shock 2.00
315 SMc,V:Mr.Fear 2.00
316 Goes Underground 1.75
317 SMc,Comedy Issue 2.00

Daredevil #309
© Marvel Entertainment Group

318 SMc,V:Taskmaster 2.00
319 SMc,Fall from Grace Prologue,
A:Silver Sable,Garrett,Hand . 25.00
319a 2nd Printing 10.00
320 SMc,B:Fall from Grace,
V:Crippler,S.Sable,A:Stone . . 20.00
321 SMc,N:Daredevil,A:Venom,
Garret, V:Hellspawn,Glow
in the Dark(c) 14.00
321a Newsstand Ed. 7.00
322 SMc,A:Venom,Garret,Siege . . 7.00
323 SMc,V:Venom,A:Siege,Garret,
I:Erynys 5.00
324 SMc,A:Garret,R:Elektra,
A:Stone, Morbius 3.50
325 SMc,E:Fall from Grace, A:Garret,
Siege,Elektra,Morbius,V:Hand,
D:Hellspawn,Double size 5.00
326 SMc,B:Tree of Knowledge,
I:Killobyte,A:Capt.America 2.00
327 E:DGC(s),SMc,A:Capt.Amer. . 1.75
328 GtW(s),V:Wirehead,A:Captain
America,S.Sable,Wild Pack . . . 1.75
329 B:DGC(s),SMc,A:Captain
America, S.Sable,Iron Fist 1.75
330 SMc,A:Gambit 1.50
Ann.#1 GC 30.00
Ann.#2 reprints. 10.00
Ann.#3 reprints 10.00
Ann.#4 (1976)GT,A:Black
Panther,Namor 6.00
Ann.#5 (1989)MBa,JLe,JR2,KJ,WPo,
AM,Atlan.Attacks,A:Spid.Man . 5.00
Ann.#6 TS,Lifeform#2,A:Typhoid
Mary 2.75
Ann.#7 JG,JBr,Von Strucker
Gambit Pt.1,A:Nick Fury 2.50
Ann.#8 Sys.Bytes#2,A:Deathlok . . 2.75
Ann.#9 MPa,I:Devourer,w/card,tie-in
to "Fall From Grace" 5.00
Ann.#10 I:Ghostmaker,A:Shang
Chi, Elektra 2.95
G-Size #1 GK(c),reprints 15.00
TPB Born Again,rep.#227-#233 . 10.95
TPB Fall of the Kingpin,
rep.#297-300 . . . . 15.95
TPB Gangwar,Reprints
#169-#172,#180 . . . . 12.95
TPB Marked for Death,reps#159-
161,163,164 . . . . 9.95
Daredevil/Punisher:Child's Play

reprints#182-#184 . . . . 7.00

DAREDEVIL: THE MAN WITHOUT FEAR

1 B:FM(s),JR2,AW,O:Daredevil,A:Stick, D:Daredevil's Father 9.00
2 JR2,AW,A:Stick,Stone,Elektra . . 7.00
3 JR2,AW,A:Elektra,Kingpin 6.00
4 JR2,AW,A:Kingpin,I:Mickey 5.00
5 JR2,AW,A:Mickey,Last Issue . . 4.50

DARING MYSTERY COMICS

Timely
January, 1940

1 ASh(c),JSm,O:Fiery Mask, A:Monako John Steele,Doc Doyle, Flash FosterBarney Mullen, Sea Rover, Bondage (c) . 9,000.00
2 ASh(c),JSm,O:Phantom Bullet A:Zephyr Jones & K4,Laughing Mask Mr.E,B:Trojak 3,000.00
3 ASh(c),JSm,A:Phantom Reporter,Marvex,Breeze Barton, B:Purple Mask . . . 2,000.00
4 ASh(c),A:G-Man Ace,K4,Monako, Marvex,E:Purple Mask, B:Whirlwind Carter 1,300.00
5 JSm,B:Falcon,A:Fiery Mask,K4, Little Hercules,Bondage(c) 1,250.00
6 S&K,O:Marvel Boy,A:Fiery Mask, Flying Fame,Dynaman, Stuporman,E:Trojak 1,600.00
7 S&K,O:Blue Diamond,A:The Fin, Challenger,Captain Daring, Silver Scorpion,Thunderer . 1,500.00
8 S&K,O:Citizen V,A:Thunderer, Fin Silver Scorpion,Captain Daring Blue Diamond 1,200.00

Becomes:

DARING COMICS

9 ASh(c),B:Human Torch,Toro, Sub Mariner 450.00
10 ASh(c),A;The Angel 350.00
11 ASh(c),A:The Destroyer . . . 350.00
12 E:Human Torch,Toro,Sub-Mariner, Fall, 1945 . . . . 350.00

Becomes:

JEANIE COMICS

13 B:Jeanie,Queen of the Teens Mitzi,Willie 70.00
14 Baseball(c) 40.00
15 Schoolbus(c) 40.00
16 Swimsuit(c) 56.00
17 HK,Fancy dress party(c), Hey Look 37.00
18 HK,Jeanie'sDate(c),Hey Look 37.00
19 Ice-Boat(c),Hey Look 37.00
20 Jukebox(c) 30.00
21 . . . . 30.00
22 HK,Hey Look 37.00
23 . . . . 30.00
24 . . . . 30.00
25 . . . . 30.00
26 . . . . 30.00
27 E:Jeanie,Queen of Teens . . . 30.00

Becomes:

COWGIRL ROMANCES

28 Ph(c),Mona Freeman/MacDonald Carey,Copper Canyon 95.00

DARK ANGEL

See: HELL'S ANGEL

DARK CRYSTAL

April, 1983

1 movie adaption 1.00
2 movie adaption,May 1983 . . . . 1.00

DARK GUARD

1 A:All UK Heroes 2.95
2 A:All UK Heroes 1.75
3 V:Leader,MyS-Tech 1.75
4 V:MyS-Tech 1.75

Darkhawk #20
© Marvel Entertainment Group

DARKHAWK

March, 1991

1 MM,I&O:Darkhawk, A:Hobgoblin 10.00
2 MM,A:SpiderMan,V:Hobgoblin . 8.00
3 MM,A:SpiderMan,V:Hobgoblin . 6.00
4 MM,I:Savage Steel 5.00
5 MM,I:Portal 4.00
6 MM,A:Cap.Am,D.D.,Portal, V:U-Foes 4.00
7 MM,I:Lodestone 3.00
8 MM,V:Lodestone 3.00
9 MM,A:Punisher,V:Savage Steel 4.00
10 MM,A&N:Tombstone 2.50
11 MM,V:Tombstone 2.50
12 MM,V:Tombstone,R:Dark Hawks'Father 2.50
13 MM,V:Venom 6.00
14 MM,V:Venom,D:Dark Hawks Father 5.00
15 MM,Heart of the Hawk,concl . . 2.00
16 MM,V:Terrorists 2.00
17 MM,I:Peristrike Force 2.00
18 MM,V:Mindwolf 2.00
19 MM,R:Portal,A:Spider-Man,V:The Brotherhood of Evil Mutants . . 2.00
20 MM,A:Spider-Man,Sleepwalker, V:Brotherhood of Evil Mutants . 2.00
21 MM,B:Return to Forever 1.75
22 MM,A:Ghost Rider 1.75
23 MM,I:Evilhawk 1.75
24 V:Evilhawk 1.50
25 MM,O:Darkhawk,V:Evilhawk, Holo-graphx(c) 4.00
26 A:New Warriors 1.50
27 A:New Warriors,V:Zarrko 1.50
28 A:New Warriors,Zarrko 1.50
29 A:New Warriors 1.50
30 I:Purity 1.50
31 Infinity Crusade 1.50
32 R:Savage Steel 1.50
33 I:Cuda 1.50
34 V:Cuda 1.50
35 DFr(s),V:Venom 1.50
36 DFr(s),V:Scokers,A:Venom . . . 1.50
37 DFr(s),V:Venom 1.50
38 DFr(s),N:Darkhawk 1.50
39 DFr(s), ... 1.50
40 DFr(s), ... 1.75
Ann.#1 MM,Assault on ArmorCity . 3.25
Ann.#2 GC,AW,I:Dreamkiller, w/Trading card 3.25
Ann.#3 I:Damek 2.95

DARKHOLD

1 RCa,I:Redeemers,Polybagged w/poster,A:Gh.Rider,Blaze . . . 3.25
2 RCa,R:Modred 2.50
3 A:Modred,Scarlet Witch 2.00
4 V:Sabretooth,N'Garai 2.00
5 A:Punisher, Ghost Rider 2.00
6 RCa,V:Dr.Strange 2.00
7 A:Dr.Strange,V:Japanese Army 2.00
8 Betrayal #1 . . . . 2.00
9 Diabolique 2.00
10 V:Darkholders 2.00
11 Midnight Massacre#3,D:Modred, Vicki 2.50
12 V:Chthon 2.00
13 V:Missing Link 2.00
14 Vicki's Secret revealed 2.00
15 Siege of Darkness Pt.#4 . . . . . 2.00
16 Siege of Darkness Pt.#12 . . . . 2.00

DARK MAN MOVIE ADAPTION

September, 1990

1 BH/MT/TD 2.25
2 BH/TD 1.50
3 BH/TD,final issue 1.50

DARKMAN

September, 1990

1 JS,R:Darkman 3.95
2 JS,V:Witchfinder 2.95
3 JS,Witchfinder 2.95
4 JS,V:Dr.West 2.95
5 JS,Durant 2.95
6 JS,V:Durant 2.95

DATE WITH MILLIE

Atlas
October, 1956
[1st Series]

1 . . . . 100.00
2 . . . . 50.00
3 thru 7 . . . . @40.00

[2nd Series]
October, 1959

1 . . . . 50.00
2 thru 7 . . . . @30.00

Becomes:

LIFE WITH MILLIE

8 . . . . 30.00
9 . . . . 23.00
10 . . . . 23.00
11 thru 20 . . . . @19.00

Becomes:

MODELING WITH MILLIE

21 . . . . 30.00
22 thru 53 . . . . @17.00
54 June, 1967 . . . . 17.00

DATE WITH PATSY

September, 1957

1 A:Patsy Walker 35.00

DAZZLER

March, 1981

1 AA,JR2,A:X-Men,Spm, O:Dazzler 4.00
2 WS,JR2,AA,X-Men,A:SpM 2.50
3 JR2,Dr.Doom 1.50
4 FS,Dr.Doom 1.25
5 FS,I:Blue Shield 1.25
6 FS,Hulk 1.25
7 FS,Hulk 1.25

All comics prices listed are for *Near Mint* condition.

Dazzler #42
© Marvel Entertainment Group

8 FS,Quasar 1.25
9 FS,D:Klaw 1.25
10 FS,Galactus 1.25
11 FS,Galactus 1.25
12 FS,The Light That Failed 1.25
13 FS,V:Grapplers 1.25
14 FS,She Hulk 1.25
15 FS,BSz,Spider Women 1.25
16 FS,BSz,Enchantress 1.25
17 FS,Angel,V:Doc Octopus 1.50
18 FS,BSz,A:Fantastic Four,Angel, V:Absorbing Man 1.50
19 FS,Blue Bolt,V:Absorbing Man 1.25
20 FS,V:Jazz and Horn 1.25
21 FS,A:Avengers,F.F.,C:X-Men, (double size) 1.25
22 FS,V:Rogue,Mystique 2.00
23 FS,V:Rogue,A:Powerman, Iron Fist 2.00
24 FS,V:Rogue,A:Powerman, Iron Fist 1.75
25 FS,'The Jagged Edge' 1.25
26 FS,Lois London 1.25
27 FS,Fugitive 1.25
28 FS,V:Rogue 2.00
29 FS,Roman Nekoboh 1.25
30 FS,Moves to California 1.25
31 FS,The Last Wave 1.25
32 FS,A:Inhumans 1.25
33 Chiller 1.25
34 FS,Disappearance 1.25
35 FS,V:Racine Ramjets 1.25
36 JBy(c),FS,V:Tatterdemalion . . . 1.25
37 JBy(c),FS 1.25
38 PC,JG,X-Men 6.00
39 PC,JG,Caught in the grip of death 1.25
40 PC,JG,Secret Wars II 1.75
41 PC,JG,A:Beast 1.25
42 PC,JG,A:Beast,last issue 2.00

DEADLIEST HEROES OF KUNG FU
(magazine)
Summer, 1975

1 . . . . 3.50

DEADLY FOES OF SPIDERMAN
May, 1991

1 AM,KGa,V:Sinister Syndicate . . 5.00
2 AM,Boomerang on Trial 3.50
3 AM,Deadly Foes Split 3.50
4 AM,Conclusion 3.50

DEADLY HANDS OF KUNG FU
April, 1974

1 NA(c),JSa,JSon,O:Sons of the Tiger, B:Shang-Chi, Bruce Lee Pin-up 4.00
2 NA(c),JSa 2.50
3 NA(c),JSon,A:Sons of the Tiger 2.50
4 NA(Bruce Lee)(c),JSon,Bruce Lee biography 4.00
5 . . . . 3.00
6 GP,JSon,A:Sons of the Tiger . 3.00
7 GP,JSon,A:Sons of the Tiger . 3.00
8 GP,JSon,A:Sons of the Tiger . . 3.00
9 GP,JSon,A:Sons of the Tiger . 3.00
10 GP,JSon,A:Sons of the Tiger . 3.00
11 NA(c),GP,JSon,A:Sons of the Tiger 3.00
12 NA(c),GP,JSon,A:Sons of the Tiger 3.00
13 GP,JSon,A:Sons of the Tiger . 3.00
14 NA(c),GP,JSon,A:Sons of the Tiger 3.00
15 JSa,Annual #1 . . . . 5.00
16 JSon,A:Sons of the Tiger 2.00
17 NA9c),JSon,KG,A:Sons of the Tiger 2.00
18 JSon,A:Sons of the Tiger 2.00
19 JSon,I:White Tiger 2.00
20 GP,O:White Tiger 3.00
21 . . . . 2.00
22 KG 2.00
23 GK 2.00
24 KG 2.00
25 . . . . 2.00
26 . . . . 2.00
27 . . . . 2.00
28 JSon,O:Jack of Hearts 4.00
29 . . . . 2.00
30 . . . . 2.00
31 JSon 2.00
32 MR,JSon 2.00
33 MR,February, 1977 . . . . 2.00
Special Album Edition,NA, Summer 1974 . . . . 3.00

DEAD OF NIGHT
December, 1973

1 JSt,Horror reprints,A Haunted House is not a Home 3.00
2 BEv(c),House that Fear Built . 1.75
3 They Lurk Below 1.75
4 Warewolf Beware 1.75
5 Deep Down 1.75
6 Jack the Ripper 1.75
7 SD,The Thirteenth Floor 1.75
8 Midnight Brings Dark Madness 1.75
9 Deathride 1.75
10 SD,I Dream of Doom 1.75
11 GK/BWr(c),I:Scarecrow, Fires of Rebirth,Fires of Death August, 1975 . . . . 1.75

DEADPOOL

1 B:FaN(s),JMd,MFm(i),V:Slayback, Nyko 7.00
2 JMd,MFm(i),V:Black Tom Cassidy, Juggernaut 5.50
3 JMd,MFm(i),I:Comcast,Makeshift, Rive,A:Slayback 4.50
4 E:FaN(s),JMd,MFm(i),A:Slayback, Kane 4.00

DEATH³

1 I:Death Metal,Death Wreck . . . 2.95
2 V:Ghost Rider 1.75
3 A:Hulk,Cable,Storm,Thing 1.75
4 Last issue 1.75

DEATHLOK
July, 1990
[Limited Series]

1 JC,SW,I:Michael Colins (2nd Deathlok) 10.00
2 JC,SW,V:Wajler 8.00
3 DCw,SW,V:Cyberants 7.00
4 DCw,SW,V:Sunfire,final issue . 7.00

[Regular Series]

1 DCw,MM,V:Warwolf 4.00
2 DCw,MM,A:Dr.Doom,Machine Man, Forge 3.25
3 DCw,MM,V:Dr.Doom, A:Mr.Fantastic 3.00
4 DCw,MM,A:X-Men,F.F.,Vision, O:Mechadoom 3.00
5 DCw,MM,V:Mechadoom, A:X-Men,Fantastic Four 3.00
6 DCw,MM,A:Punisher, V:Silvermane 2.50
7 DCw,MM,A:Punisher, V:Silvermane 2.50
8 A:Main Frame,Ben Jacobs 2.00
9 DCw,MM,A:Ghost Rider, V:Nightmare 2.50
10 DCw,MM,A:GhR,V:Nightmare . 2.50
11 DCw,MM,V:Moses Magnum . . 2.00
12 DCw,MM,Biohazard Agenda . . 2.00
13 DCw,MM,Biohazard Agenda . . 2.00
14 DCw,MM,Biohazard Agenda . . 2.00
15 DCw,MM,Biohazard Agenda . . 2.00
16 DCw,MM,Inf.War,V:Evilok 2.00
17 WMc,MM,B:Cyberwar 2.00
18 WMc,A:Silver Sable 2.00
18a Newstand Ed. 1.75
19 SMc,Cyberwar#3 . . . . 2.00
20 SMc,Cyberwar#4 . . . . 2.00
21 E:Cyberwar,A:Cold Blood Nick Fury 2.00
22 V:Moses Magnum, A:Black Panther 2.00
23 A:Bl.Panther,V:Phreak,Stroke . 2.00
24 V:MosesMagnum,A:Bl.Panther 2.00
25 WMc,V:MosesMagnum,A:Black Panther,holo-grafx(c) 3.25
26 V:Hobogoblin 2.00
27 R:Siege 2.00
28 Infinty Crusade 2.00
29 Inner Fears 2.00
30 KHd,V:Hydra 2.00
31 GWt(s),KoK,B:Cyberstrike, R:1st Deathlok 2.00
32 GWt(s),KoK,A:Siege 2.00
33 GWt(s),KoK,V:Justice Peace . . 2.00
34 GWt(s),KoK,E:Cyberstrike,V:Justice Peace,final issue 2.00
Ann.#1 JG,I:Timestream 2.75
Ann.#2 I:Tracer,w/card 2.95

DEATHLOK SPECIAL

1 Rep.MiniSeries 4.00
2 Rep.MiniSeries 2.50
3 Rep.MiniSeries 2.50
4 Rep.MiniSeries, final issue 2.50

DEATH METAL

1 JRe,I:Argon,C:Alpha Flight 1.95
2 JRe,V:Alpha Flight 1.95
3 JRe,I:Soulslug 1.95
4 Re,Last Issue 1.95

DEATH METAL VS. GENETIX

1 PaD,w/card 2.95
2 PaD,w/card 2.95

DEATH'S HEAD
December, 1988

1 V:Backbreaker 20.00
2 A:Dragons Claws 12.00
3 . . . . 8.00
4 V:Plague Dog 6.00
5 V:Big Shot 6.00

6 V:Big Shot 6.00
7 6.00
8 6.00
9 A:Fantastic Four 7.00
10 A:Iron Man 7.00
TPB Reprints#1-#10 12.95

DEATH'S HEAD
[Limited Series]

1 A:'Old' Death's Head 1.95

DEATH'S HEAD II
March, 1992

[Limited Series]

1 LSh,I:2nd Death's Head, D:1st Death's Head 10.00
1a 2nd printing,Silver 3.50
2 LSh,A:Fantastic Four 7.00
2a 2nd printing,Silver 3.00
3 LSh,I:Tuck 5.00
4 LSh,A:Wolverine,Spider-Man, Punisher 4.00

[Regular Series]

1 LSh,A:X-Men,I:Wraithchilde 3.00
2 LSh,A:X-Men 2.25
3 LSh,A:X-Men,V:Raptors 2.25
4 LSh,A:X-Men,V:Wraithchilde 2.25
5 V:UnDeath's Head II, A:Warheads 2.25
6 R:Tuck,V:Major Oak 2.25
7 V:Major Oak 2.25
8 V:Wizard Methinx 2.25
9 BHi,V:Cybernetic Centaurs 2.25
10 DBw,A:Necker 2.25
11 SCy,R:Charnel 2.25
12 DAn(s),SvL,V:Charnel 2.25
13 SvL,A:Liger 2.25
14 SvL,Brain Dead Cold,Blue Foil(c) 3.25
15 SvL,V:Duplicates 2.25
16 2.25
Spec. Gold Ed. LSh(a&s) 3.95

DEATH'S HEAD II/DIE CUT

1 I:Die Cut 3.25
2 O:Die Cut 1.75

DEATH'S HEAD II/ KILLPOWER:BATTLETIDE
[1st Limited Series]

1 GSr,A:Wolverine 2.50
2 thru 4 GSr,A:Wolverine @2.00

[2nd Limited Series]

1 A:Hulk 3.25
2 V:Hulk 1.75
3 A:Hulk 1.75
4 last issue 1.75

DEATH-WRECK

1 A:Death's Head II 1.95
2 V:Gangsters 1.95
3 A:Dr.Necker 1.95
4 last issue 1.95

DEEP, THE
November, 1977

1 CI,Movie Adaption 2.00

DEFENDERS
August, 1972

1 SB,I&D:Necrodames 70.00
2 SB,V:Calizuma 40.00
3 GK(c),SB,JM,V:UndyingOne 30.00
4 SB,FMc,Bl.Knight,V:Valkyrie 30.00
5 SB,FMc,D:Omegatron 30.00
6 SB,FMc,V:Cyrus Black 23.00
7 SB,FBe,A:Hawkeye 23.00
8 SB,FBe,Avengers,SilverSurfer 23.00
9 SB,FMc,Avengers 23.00
10 SB,FBe,Thor vs. Hulk 30.00
11 SB,FBe,A:Avengers 18.00
12 SB,JA,Xemnu 14.00
13 GK(c),SB,KJ,J:Night Hawk 14.00
14 SB,DGr,O:Hyperion 14.00
15 SB,KJ,A:Professor X,V:Magneto, Savage Land Mutates 23.00
16 GK(c),SB,Professor X,V:Magneto, Savage Land Mutates 23.00
17 SB,DGr,Power Man 10.00
18 GK(c),SB,DGr,A:Power Man 10.00
19 GK(c),SB,KJ,A:Power Man 10.00
20 K&R(c),SB,A:Thing 10.00
21 GK(c),SB,O:Valkyrie 8.00
22 GK(c),SB,V:Sons o/t Serpent 8.00
23 GK(c),SB,A:Yellow Jacket 8.00
24 GK(c),SB,BMc,A:Daredevil 8.00
25 GK(c),SB,JA,A:Daredevil 8.00
26 K&R(c),SB,A:Guardians 13.00
27 K&R(c),SB,A:Guardians C:Starhawk 13.00
28 K&R(c),SB,A:Guardians I:Starhawk 14.00

Defenders #11
© Marvel Entertainment Group

29 K&R(c),SB,A:Guardians 13.00
30 JA(i),A:Wong 6.00
31 GK(c),SB,JM,Nighthawk 6.00
32 GK(c),SB,JM,O:Nighthawk 6.00
33 GK(c),SB,JM,V:Headmen 6.00
34 SB,JM,V:Nebulon 6.00
35 GK(c),SB,KJ,I:Red Guardian 6.00
36 GK(c),SB,KJ,A:Red Guardian 6.00
37 GK(c),SB,KJ,J:Luke Cage 6.00
38 SB,KJ,V:Nebulon 6.00
39 SB,KJ,V:Felicia 6.00
40 SB,KJ,V:Assassin 6.00
41 KG,KJ,Nighthawk 6.00
42 KG,KJ,V:Rhino 6.00
43 KG,KJ,Cobalt Man,Egghead 6.00
44 KG,KJ,J:Hellcat,V:Red Rajah 6.00
45 KG,KJ,Valkyrie V:Hulk 6.00
46 KG,KJ,L:DrStrange,LukeCage 6.00
47 KG,KJ,Moon Knight 6.00
48 KG,A:Wonder Man 6.00
49 KG,O:Scorpio 6.00
50 KG,Zodiac,D:Scorpio 6.00
51 KG,Moon Knight 6.00
52 KG,Hulk,V:Sub Mariner 6.00
53 KG,DC,MG,TA,C&I:Lunatik 5.00
54 MG,Nigh Fury 5.00
55 CI,O:Red Guardian 5.00
56 CI,KJ,Hellcat,V:Lunatik 5.00
57 DC,Ms.Marvel 5.00
58 Return of Dr.Strange 5.00
59 I:Belathauzer 5.00
60 V:Vera Gemini 5.00
61 Spider-Man,A:Lunatik 6.00
62 Hercules,C:Polaris 5.00
63 Mutli Heroes 5.00
64 Mutli Heroes 5.00
65 Red Guardian 5.00
66 JB,Valkyrie I 5.00
67 Valkryie II 5.00
68 HT,When Falls the Mountain 5.00
69 HT,A:The Anything Man 5.00
70 HT,A:Lunatik 5.00
71 HT,O:Lunatik 5.00
72 HT,V:Lunatik 5.00
73 HT,Foolkiller,V:WizardKing 6.00
74 HT,Foolkiller,L:Nighthawk 6.00
75 HT,Foolkiller 5.00
76 HT,O:Omega 3.00
77 HT,Moon Dragon 3.00
78 HT,Yellow Jacket 3.00
79 HT,Tunnel World 3.00
80 HT,DGr,Nighthawk 3.00
81 HT,Tunnel World 3.00
82 DP,JSt,Tunnel World 3.00
83 DP,JSt,Tunnel World 3.00
84 DP,JSt,Black Panther 3.00
85 DP,JSt,Black Panther 3.00
86 DP,JSt,Black Panther 3.00
87 DP,JSt,V:Mutant Force 3.00
88 DP,JSt,Matt Mardock 3.00
89 DP,JSt,D:Hellcat's Mother, O:Mad-Dog 3.00
90 DP,JSt,Daredevil 3.00
91 DP,JSt,Daredevil 3.00
92 DP,JSt,A:Eternity, Son of Satan 4.00
93 DP,JSt,Son of Satan 4.00
94 DP,JSt,I:Gargoyle 3.00
95 DP,JSt,V:Dracula,O:Gargoyle 3.00
96 DP,JSt,Ghost Rider 4.50
97 DP,JSt,False Messiah 3.00
98 DP,JSt,A:Man Thing 3.00
99 DP,JSt,Conflict 3.00
100 DP,JSt,DoubleSize,V:Satan 4.00
101 DP,JSt,Silver Surfer 3.00
102 DP,JSt,Nighthawk 3.00
103 DP,JSt,I:Null 3.00
104 DP,JSt,Devilslayer,J:Beast 3.00
105 DP,JSt,V:Satan 3.00
106 DP,Daredevil,D:Nighthawk 3.00
107 DP,JSt,Enchantress,A:D.D. 3.00
108 DP,A:Enchantress 3.00
109 DP,A:Spider-Man 3.50
110 DP,A:Devilslayer 3.00
111 DP,A:Hellcat 3.00
112 DP,A:SquadronSupreme 3.00
113 DP,A:SquadronSupreme 3.00
114 DP,A:SquadronSupreme 3.00
115 DP,A:Submariner 3.00
116 DP,Gargoyle 3.00
117 DP,Valkyrie 3.00
118 DP,V:Miracleman 3.00
119 DP,V:Miracleman 3.00
120 DP,V:Miracleman 3.00
121 DP,V:Miracleman 3.00
122 DP,A:Iceman 3.00
123 DP,I:Cloud,V:Secret Empire 3.00
124 DP,V:Elf 3.00
125 DP,New Line-up:Gargoyle,Moon dragon,Valkyrie,Iceman,Beast, Angel,W:Son of Satan & Hellcat I:Mad Dog 5.00
126 DP,A:Nick Fury 3.00
127 DP,V:Professor Power 3.00
128 DP,V:Professor Power 3.00
129 DP,V:Professor Power,New Mutants X-over 3.00
130 DP,V:Professor Power 3.00
131 DP,V:Walrus,A:Frogman 3.00
132 DP,V:Spore Monster 3.00
133 DP,V:Spore Monster 3.00
134 DP,I:Manslaughter 3.00
135 DP,V:Blowtorch Brand 3.00
136 DP,V:Gargoyle 3.00
137 DP,V:Gargoyle 3.00
138 DP,O:Moondragon 3.00

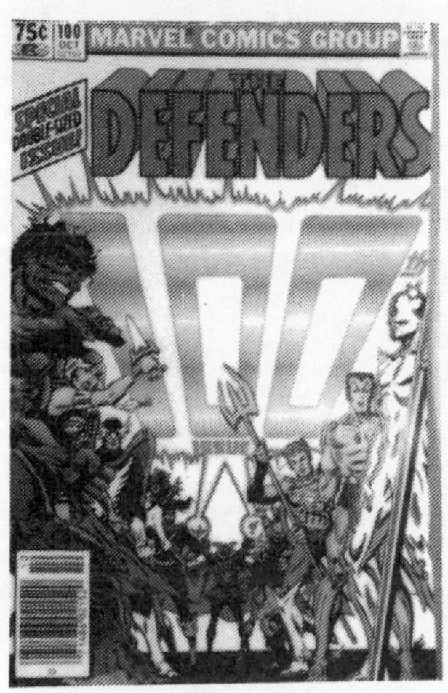

Defenders #100

© Marvel Entertainment Group

139 DP,A:Red Wolf,V:Trolls 3.00
140 DP,V:Asgardian Trolls 3.00
141 DP,All Flesh is Grass 3.00
142 DP,V:M.O.N.S.T.E.R. 3.00
143 DP,I:Andromeda,Runner 3.00
144 DP,V:Moondragon 3.00
145 DP,V:Moondragon 3.00
146 DP,Cloud 3.00
147 DP,A:Andromeda,I:Interloper . 3.00
148 DP,A:Nick Fury 3.00
149 DP,V:Manslaughter,O:Cloud . 3.00
150 DP,O:Cloud,double-size 3.50
151 DP,A:Interloper 3.00
152 DP,Secret Wars II,D:Moondragon,Valkyrie,Gargoyle 4.00
Giant#1 GK(c),JSn,AM,O:Hulk . . 12.00
Giant#2 GK,KJ,Son of Satan 8.00
Giant#3 JSn,DA,JM,DN,A:D.D.. . . 6.00
Giant#4 GK(c),DH,A:YellowJack . 6.00
Giant#5 K&R(c),DH,A:Guardians . 6.00
Ann.#1 SB,KJ 6.00

DEFENDERS OF DYNATRON CITY

1 FC,I:Defenders of Dynatron City (from video game & TV ser.) . . 1.25
2 FC,O:Defender of D.City 1.25
3 FC,A:Dr Mayhem 1.25
4 FC 1.25
5 FC,V:Intelligent Fleas 1.25
6 FC,V:Dr.Mayhem 1.25

DEFENDERS OF THE EARTH

January, 1987

1 AS,Flash Gordon & Mandrake . 1.00
2 AS,Flash Gordon & Mandrake . 1.00
3 AS,O:Phantom 1.00
4 AS,O:Mandrake,September,1984 1.00

DELLA VISION

Atlas
April, 1955

1 The Television Queen 70.00
2 . . . . 50.00
3 . . . . 50.00
Becomes:

PATTY POWERS

4 . . . . 35.00

5 . . . . 22.00
6 . . . . 22.00
7 October, 1956 . . . . 22.00

DENNIS THE MENACE

November, 1981

1 . . . . 1.25
2 thru 12 . . . . @1.00
13 November, 1982 . . . . 1.00

DESTROYER, THE

November 1989

1 Black & White Mag. 3.50
2 thru 9 . . . . @2.25
10 June 1990 . . . . 2.25
TPB rep. B/w mag(color) 9.95

THE DESTROYER: TERROR

December, 1991

1 V:Nuihc 1.95
2 V:Nuihc 1.95
3 GM,V:Nuihc 1.95
4 DC,'The Last Dinosaur' 1.95

DEVIL DINOSAUR

April, 1978

1 JK,I:Devil Dinosaur,Moon Boy . 3.50
2 JK,War With the Spider God . . 2.00
3 JK,Giant 2.00
4 JK,Objects From the Sky 2.00
5 JK,The Kingdom of the Ants . . 2.00
6 JK.The Fall 2.00
7 JK,Prisoner of the Demon Tree 2.00
8 JK,V:Dino Riders 2.00
9 JK,Lizards That Stand, December,1978 . . . . 2.00

DEVIL-DOG DUGAN

Atlas
July, 1956

1 War Stories 40.00
2 . . . . 30.00
3 . . . . 20.00
Becomes:

TALE OF THE MARINES

4 BP,War Stories 20.00
Becomes:

MARINES AT WAR

5 War Stories 15.00
6 . . . . 15.00
7 The Big Push,August, 1957 . 15.00

DEXTER THE DEMON

See: MELVIN THE MONSTER

DIE-CUT

1 A:Beast 2.50
2 V:X-Beast 1.75
3 A:Beast,Prof.X 1.75
4 V:Red Skull 1.75

DIE-CUT VS. G-FORCE

1 SFr(s),LSh(c),I:G-Force 2.75
2 SFr(s),LSh(c),Last issue 2.75

DIGITEK

1 DPw,I:Digitek,C:Deathlok 2.25
2 DPw,A:Deathlok,V:Bacillicons . 2.25
3 DPw,A:Deathlok,V:Bacillicons . 2.25
4 DPw,V:Bacillicons 2.25

DINO RIDERS

February, 1989

1 Based on Toys 1.00
2 . . . . 1.00
3 May, 1989 . . . . 1.00

DINOSAURS: A CELEBRATION

Epic

Horns and Heavy Armor 4.95
Bone-Heads and Duck-Bills 4.95
Terrible Claws and Tyrants 4.95
Egg Stealers and Earth Shakers . 4.95

DOC SAVAGE

October, 1972

1 JM,Pulp Adapts,Death Eighty Stories High 8.50
2 JSo(c),The Feathered Serpent Strikes 6.00
3 JSo(c),Silver Death's Head . . . 6.00
4 JSo(c),The Hell Diver 5.00
5 GK(c),Night of the Monsters . . 5.00
6 JSo(c),Where Giants Walk 5.00
7 JSo(c),Brand of the Werewolfs . 5.00
8 In the Lair of the Werewolf January, 1974 . . . . 5.00
Giant#1 thru #2 Reprints 4.50

DOC SAVAGE

August, 1975
(black & white magazine)

1 JB,Ph(c),Ron Ely 5.75
2 JB 3.25
3 JB 3.25
4 . . . . 3.25
5 thru 7 . . . . @3.25
8 Spring 1977 . . . . 3.25

DOCTOR WHO

October, 1984

1 BBC TV Series,UK reprints, Return of the Daleks 4.50
2 Star Beast 3.00
3 Transformation 3.00
4 A:K-9,Daleks 3.00
5 V:Time Witch,Colin Baker interview 3.00
6 B:Ancient Claw saga 3.00
7 . . . . 3.00
8 The Collector 3.00
9 The Life Bringer 3.00
10 This is your Life 3.00
11 The Deal 3.00
12 End of the Line 3.00
13 V:The Cybermen 3.00
14 Clash of the Neutron Knight . . 3.00
15 B:Peter Davison-Dr. Who 3.00
16 Into the Realm of Satan, ... 3.00
17 Peter Davison Interview 3.00
18 A:Four Dr.Who's 3.00
19 A:The Sontarans 3.00
20 The Stockbridge Horror 3.00
21 The Stockbridge Horror 3.00
22 The Stockbridge Horror 3.00
23 The Unearthly Child, August 1984 . . . . 3.00

DOPEY DUCK COMICS

Timely
Fall, 1945

1 A:Casper Cat,Krazy Krow . . . 75.00
2 A:Casper Cat,Krazy Krow . . . 72.00
Becomes:

WACKY DUCK

3 Paperchase(c) 65.00
4 Wacky Duck(c) 90.00
5 Duck & Devil(c) 57.00
6 Cliffhanger(c) 57.00
1 Baketball(c) 40.00
2 Traffic Light(c) 40.00
Becomes: JUSTICE COMICS

DR. STRANGE

[1st Series]
Prev: Strange Tales
June, 1968

169 DA,O:Dr.Strange 96.00
170 DA,A:Ancient One 40.00
171 TP,DA,V:Dormammu 38.00

172 GC,TP,V:Dormammu 38.00
173 GC,TP,V:Dormammu 38.00
174 GC,TP,I:Satannish 38.00
175 GC,TP,I:Asmodeus 38.00
176 GC,TP,V:Asmodeus 38.00
177 GC,TP,D:Asmodeus,
N:Dr.Strange 38.00
178 GC,TP,A:Black Knight 38.00
179 BWS(c),rep.AmazSpM
Ann.#2 . . . . 38.00

Dr. Strange #179
© Marvel Entertainment Group

180 GC,TP,V:Nightmare 38.00
181 FB(c),GC,TP,I:Demons of
Despair 38.00
182 GC,TP,V:Juggernaut 39.00
183 BEv(c),GC,TP,
I:Undying Ones 36.00

[2nd Regular Series]

1 FB,DG,I:Silver Dagger 35.00
2 FB,DG,I:Soul Eater 20.00
3 FB,A:Dormammu 12.00
4 FB,DG,V:Death 8.00
5 FB,DG,A:Silver Dagger 8.00
6 FB(c),GC,KJ,A:Umar,I:Gaea . . 6.00
7 GC,JR,A:Dormammu 6.00
8 GK(c),GC,TP,O:Clea 6.00
9 GK(c),GC,A:Dormammu,O:Clea 6.00
10 B:MWn(s),GK(c),GC,A:Eternity 6.00
11 JR(c),GC,TP,A:Eternity 6.00
12 GC,TP,A:Eternity 6.00
13 GC,TP,A:Eternity 6.00
14 GC,TP,A:Dracula 7.00
15 GC,TP,A:Devil 6.00
16 GC,TP,A:Devil 6.00
17 GC,TP,A:Styggro 6.00
18 GC,A:Styggro 6.00
19 GC,AA,I:Xander 6.00
20 A:Xander 6.00
21 DA,O:Dr.Strange 4.00
22 I:Apalla 4.00
23 E:MWn(s),JSn,A:Wormworld . . 4.00
24 JSn,A:Apalla,I:Visamajoris . . . 4.00
25 AM,V:Dr.Strange Yet 4.00
26 JSn,A:The Ancient One 4.00
27 TS,A:Stygyro,Sphinx 3.50
28 TS,A:Ghost Rider,
V:In-Betweener 5.00
29 TS,A:Nighthawk 3.50
30 I:Dweller 3.50
31 TS,A:Sub Mariner 3.50
32 A:Sub Mariner 3.50
33 TS,A:The Dreamweaver 3.50
34 TS,A:Nightmare,D:CyrusBlack . 3.50

Doctor Strange #24
© Marvel Entertainment Group

35 TS,V:Dweller,I:Ludi 3.50
36 Thunder of the Soul 3.50
37 Fear,the Final Victor 3.50
38 GC,DG,A:Baron Mordo 3.50
39 GC,DG,A:Baron Mordo 3.50
40 GC,A:Asrael 3.50
41 GC,A:Man Thing 3.00
42 GC,A:Black Mirror 3.00
43 V:Shadow Queen 3.00
44 GC,A:Princess Shialmar 3.00
45 GC,A:Demon in the Dark 3.00
46 FM,A:Sibylis 3.00
47 MR,TA,I:Ikonn 3.00
48 MR,TA,Brother Voodoo 3.00
49 MR,TA,A:Baron Mordo 3.00
50 MR,TA,A:Baron Mordo 3.00
51 MR,TA,A:Sgt. Fury,
V:Baron Mordo 3.00
52 MR,TA,A:Nightmare 2.50
53 MR,TA,A:Nightmare,Fantastic
Four,V:Rama-Tut 2.50
54 PS,V:Tiboro 2.50
55 MGo,TA,V:Madness 2.50
56 PS,TA,O:Dr.Strange 4.00
57 KN,TA,A:Dr.Doom 2.50
58 DGr,TA,V:Dracula 2.50
59 DGr,TA,V:Dracula 2.50
60 DGr,TA,Scarlet Witch 2.50
61 DGr,TA,V:Dracula 2.50
62 SL,V:Dracula 2.50
63 CP,V:Topaz 2.50
64 TSa,'Art Rage' 2.50
65 PS,Charlatan 2.50
66 PS,'The Cosen One' 2.50
67 SL,A:Jessica Drew,Shroud . . . 2.50
68 PS,A:Black Knight 2.00
69 PS,A:Black Knight 2.00
70 BBl,V:Umar 2.00
71 DGr,O:Dormammu 2.00
72 PS,V:Umar 2.00
73 PS,V:Umar 2.00
74 MBg,Secret Wars II 2.00
75 A:Fantastic Four 2.00
76 A:Fantastic Four 2.00
77 A:Topaz 2.00
78 A:Cloak,I:Ecstacy 3.00
79 A:Morganna 2.00
80 A:Morganna,C:Rintah 2.00
81 V:Urthona,I:Rintah 2.00
Ann.#1 CR,'Doomworld' 4.50
G-Size#1 K&R(c),reps Strange
Tales#164-#168 . . . . 6.00

[3rd Regular Series]

1 V:Dorammu 8.50
2 V:Dorammu 5.00
3 I:Dragon Force 3.00
4 EL(c),A:Dragon Force 3.00
5 JG,V:Baron Mordo 5.00
6 JG,I:Mephista 4.00
7 JG,V:Agamotto,Mephisto 3.00
8 JG,V:Mephisto & Satanish 3.00
9 JG,O:Dr.Strange 3.00
10 JG,V:Morbius 5.00
11 JG,A of V,V:Hobgoblin,
C:Morbius 6.00
12 JG,A of V,V:Enchantress 2.75
13 JG,A of V,V:Arkon 2.75
14 JG,B:Vampiric Verses,
A:Morbius 3.50
15 JG,A:Morbius,Amy Grant(C) . . 5.00
16 JG,A:Morbius,Brother Voodoo . 3.50
17 JV,TD,A:Morbius,Br.Voodoo . . 3.50
18 JG,E:Vampiric Verses,A:Morbius,
Brother Voodoo,R:Varnae 3.50
19 GC,A:Azrael 2.50
20 JG,TD,A:Morbius,V:Zom 3.50
21 JG,TD,B:Dark Wars,
R:Dormammu 2.50
22 JG,TD,LW,V:Dormammu 2.50
23 JG,LW,V:Dormammu 2.50
24 JG,E:Dark Wars,V:Dormammu 2.50
25 RLm,A:Red Wolf, Black Crow . 2.50
26 GI,V:Werewolf By Night 2.50
27 GI,V:Werewolf By Night 2.50
28 X-over G.R.#12,V:Zodiac 4.00
29 A:Baron Blood 2.50
30 Topaz' Fate 2.50
31 TD,Inf.Gauntlet,A:Silver Surfer 3.00
32 Inf.Gauntlet,A:Warlock,Silver
Surfer,V:Silver Dagger 2.50
33 Inf.Gauntlet,V:Thanos,
Zota,A:Pip 2.50
34 Inf.Gauntlet,V:Dr.Doom,
A:Pip,Scartlet Witch 2.50
35 Inf.Gauntlet,A:Thor,Pip,
Scarlet Witch 2.50
36 Inf.Gauntlet,A:Warlock(leads
into Warlock&Inf.Watch#1) . . . 3.00
37 GI,V:Frankensurfer 2.00
38 GI,Great Fear #1 . . . . 2.00
39 GI,Great Fear #2 . . . . 2.00
40 GI,Great Fear #3,A:Daredevil . 2.00
41 GI,A:Wolverine 3.00
42 GI,Infinity War,V:Galactus,A:
Silver Surfer 2.25
43 GI,Infinity War,Galactus Vs.
Agamotto,A:Silver Surfer 2.00
44 GI,Infinity War,V:Juggernaut . . 2.00
45 GI,Inf.War,O:Doctor Strange . . 2.00
46 GI,Inf.War,R:old costume 2.00
47 GI,Inf.War,V:doppleganger . . . 2.00
48 GI,V:The Vishanti 2.00
49 GI,R:Dormammu 2.00
50 GI,A:Hulk,G.R,Silver Surfer,
V:Dormammu(leads into Secret
Defenders)holo-grafx(c) 4.25
51 GI,V:Religious Cult 2.00
52 GI,A:Morbius 2.00
53 GI,Closes Mansion,L:Wong . . . 2.00
54 GI,Infinity Crusade 2.00
55 GI,Inf.Crusade 2.00
56 GI,Inf.Crusade 2.00
57 A:Kyllian,Urthona 2.00
58 V:Urthona 2.00
59 GI,V:Iskelior 2.00
60 B:DQ(s),Siege of
Darkness Pt.#7 . . . . 4.00
61 Siege of Darkness Pt.#15 . . . . 3.25
62 V:Dr.Doom 2.25
63 JJ(c),V:Morbius 2.00
64 MvR,V:Namor 2.00
65 MvR,V:Namor,Vengeance 2.25
66 A:Wong 1.95
Ann #2 Return of Defenders,Pt4 . 5.00
Ann #3 GI,I:Killiam,w/card 3.25
Ann.#4 V:Salome 2.95

Doctor Strange #50
© Marvel Entertainment Group

GNv Triumph and Torment MBg,
F:Dr. Strange & Dr.Doom 9.95
HC 14.95

DR. STRANGE CLASSICS
March, 1984
1 SD,Reprints 1.00
2 .... 1.00
3 .... 1.00
4 June, 1984 .... 1.00

DR. STRANGE VS. DRACULA
1 rep. MWn(s),GC 2.00

DR. STRANGE/ G.R. SPECIAL
1 Newsstand vers. of Dr.Str.#28 . 6.00

DR. ZERO
Epic
April, 1988
1 BSz,DCw,I:Dr.Zero 2.00
2 BSz,DCw 1.50
3 BSz,DCw 1.50
4 thru 6 .... @1.50
7 DSp 1.50
8 End series, August, 1989 .... 1.50

DOLLY DILL
1945
1 Newsstand 70.00

DOOM 2099
1 PB,I:Doom 2099,V:Tiger Wylde,
foil(c) 5.00
2 I:Rook Seven 2.50
3 PB,V:Tiger Wylde 2.00
4 PB,V:Tiger Wylde 1.75
5 PB,I:Fever 1.75
6 I:Duke Stratosphear 1.75
7 PB,I:Paloma,V:Duke,Fever Haze 1.75
8 PB,C:Ravage 1.75
9 EC,V:Jack the Ripper 1.75
10 PB,w/Poster 1.75
11 PB,I:Thandaza 1.75
12 PB,V:Thandaza 1.75
13 PB(c),JFm(s),V:Necrotek 1.75
14 RLm(c),PB,Fall o/t Hammer#4 . 1.75
15 PB,I:Radian 1.75
16 EC(a&s), ... 1.75
17 PB,V:Radian,w/card 1.75
18 PB, ... 1.50
19 PB,C:Bloodhawk 1.50

DOUBLE DRAGON
July, 1991
1 I:Billy&Jimmy Lee 1.00
2 Dragon Statue Stolen,V:Stelth . 1.00
3 Billy Vs. Jimmy 1.00
4 Dragon Force out of control ... 1.00
5 V:Stealth 1.00
6 V:Nightfall, final issue 1.00

D.P. 7
November, 1986
1 O:DP7 .... 1.00
2 V:Headhunter 1.00
3 RT,Headhunters 1.00
4 RT,V:Wompus 1.00
5 RT,Exorcist 1.00
6 RT,I:The Sweat Shop 1.00
7 RT,V:Clinic 1.00
8 RT,V:Clinic 1.00
9 RT,AW,I:New Paranormals ... 1.00
10 RT,I:Mysterious People 1.00
11 AW(i)V:Regulator 1.00
12 O:Randy 1.00
13 O:Charly 1.00
14 AW 1.00
15 .... 1.00
16 V:BlackPower 1.00
17 .... 1.00
18 Pitt tie-in 1.00
19 .... 1.25
20 Spitfire 1.25
21 .... 1.25
22 .... 1.25
23 A:PsiForce 1.25
24 A:Mastodon 1.25
25 V:Famileech 1.50
26 V:Famileech 1.50
27 The Pitt 1.50
28 V:The Candidate 1.25
29 Deadweight 1.50
30 V:Para-troop 1.25
31 A:Chrome 1.50
32 I:The Cure,last issue,
June 1989 .... 1.50
Ann.#1,I:Witness 1.00

DRACULA LIVES
1973
(black & white magazine)
1 .... 7.50
2 O:Dracula 6.50
3 .... 5.00
4 MP 4.00
5 thru 12 .... @3.00
13 July, 1975 .... 3.00

DRAFT, THE
1988
1 Sequel to The Pit 3.75

DRAGON LINES
[1st Limited Series]
1 RLm,V:Terrorist on Moon,
Embossed(c) 3.00
2 RLm,V:Kuei Emperor 2.25
3 RLm,V:Spirit Boxer 2.25
4 RLm,K:Kuei Emperor 2.25

[Regular Series]
1 B:PQ(s),RLm,I:Tao 2.50
2 RLm, ... 2.50

DRAGONSLAYER
October, 1981
1 Movie adapt. 1.25
2 Movie adapt,November, 1981 . 1.25

DRAGON STRIKE
1 Based on TSR Game 1.50

DRAGON'S TEETH/ DRAGON'S CLAWS
July, 1988
1 GSr,I:Mercy Dragon,
Scavenger,Digit Steel 1.75
2 GSr,V:Evil Dead 1.50
3 GSr,Go Home 1.50
4 GSr 1.50
5 GSr,I:Death's Head 18.00
6 thru 10 GSr .... @1.75

DREADLANDS
Epic
1 Post-Apocalyptic Mini-series .. 3.95
2 Trapped in Prehistoric Past ... 3.95
3 V:Alien Time Travelers 3.95
4 Final Issue 3.95

DREADSTAR
Epic
November, 1982
1 JSn,I:Lord Papal 4.00
2 JSn,O:Willow 3.00
3 JSn,V:Lord Papal 2.50
4 JSn,I:Z 2.50
5 JSn,V:Teutun 2.50
6 JSn,BWr,Interstellar Toybox ... 2.50
7 JSn,BWr,V:Dr.Mezlo 2.50
8 JSn,V:Z 2.50
9 JSn,V:Z 2.50
10 JSn,V:Z 2.50
11 JSn,O:Lord Papal 2.25
12 JSn,I:Dr.Delphi 2.25
13 JSn,V:Infra Red & Ultra Violet . 2.25
14 JSn,V:Lord Papal 2.25
15 JSn,new powers 2.25
16 JSn,V:Lord Papal 2.00
17 JSn,V:Willows father 2.00
18 JSn,V:Dr.Mezlo 2.00
19 JSn,V:Dr Mezlo 2.00
20 JSn,D:Oedi 2.00
21 JSn,D:Dr.Delphi 2.00
22 JSn,V:Lord Papal 2.00
23 JSn,V:Lord Papal 2.00
24 JSn,JS,V:Lord Papal 2.00
25 JSn,V:Lord Papal 2.00
26 JSn,R:Oedi 2.00
Ann.#1 JSn,The Price 2.50
See OTHER PUB. section

DREADSTAR & COMPANY
July, 1985
1 JSo,reprint 1.25
2 JSo,rep. 1.00
3 JSo,rep. 1.00
4 JSo,rep. 1.00
5 JSo,rep,December, 1985. .... 1.00

DROIDS
Star
April, 1986
1 JR 3.00
2 AW 3.00
3 JR/AW 3.00
4 AW 3.00
5 AW 3.00
6 EC/AW,A:Luke Skywalker 3.00
7 EC/AW,A:Luke Skywalker 3.00
8 EC/AW,A:Luke Skywalker 3.00

DUNE
April, 1985
1 Movie Adapt,Rep. Marvel
Super Spec,BSz 1.50
2 Movie Adapt,BSz 1.50
3 Movie Adapt,BSz,June, 1985 . 1.50

DYNOMUTT
November, 1977
1 Based on TV series 1.00
2 thru 5 @1.00
6 September, 1978 1.00

ECTOKID
Razorline
1 I:Dex Mungo,BU:Hokum & Hex 2.75
2 O:Dex 2.00
3 I:Ectosphere 2.00
4 I:Brothers Augustine 2.00
5 A:Saint Sinner 2.00
6 Highway 61 Revisited 2.00
7 2.00
8 V:Ice Augustine 1.75
9 Love is like a Bullet 1.95

ELECTRIC UNDERTOW
December, 1989
1 MBa,Strike Force 3.95
2 MBa, Will Deguchis 3.95
3 MBa, Alien Invaders 3.95
4 MBa,Attack on Beijing 3.95
5 MBa, Morituri defeated,March, 1990 3.95

ELEKTRA: ASSASSIN
August, 1986
1 FM,BSz,V:Shield 10.00
2 FM,BSz,I:Garrett 8.00
3 FM,BSz,V:Shield,A:Garrett 7.00
4 FM,BSz,V:Shield,A:Garrett 7.00
5 FM,BSz,I:Chastity,A:Garrett 7.00
6 FM,BSz,A:Nick Fury,Garrett 7.00
7 FM,BSz,V:Ken Wind,A:Garrett 7.00
8 FM,BSz,V:Ken Wind,A:Garrett 9.00
TPB Rep #1-8 12.95

ELEKTRA LIVES AGAIN
Graphic Novel FM,R:Elektra,A:Matt Murdock,V:The Hand 35.00

ELEKTRA: SAGA
February, 1984
1 FM,rep.Daredevil 7.00
2 FM,rep.Daredevil 7.00
3 FM,rep.Daredevil 7.00
4 FM,rep.Daredevil 7.00
TPB Reprints#1-#4 16.95

ELFQUEST
August, 1985
1 WP,reprints 6.00
2 WP 4.00
3 WP 4.00
4 WP 4.00
5 WP 4.00
6 WP,Young Cutter V:Mad Coil 4.00
7 WP,Young Cutter V:Mad Coil 3.00
8 WP 3.00
9 WP 3.00
10 WP,A:Cutter, Skywise 3.00
11 WP,I:Two Edge 3.00
12 WP,The Mysterious Forest 3.00
13 WP,The Forest, A:Leetah 3.00
14 WP,A:The Bone Woman 3.00
15 WP,The Forest, continued 3.00
16 WP,Forbidden Grove 2.50
17 WP,Blue Mountain 2.50
18 WP,Secrets 2.50
19 WP,Twisted Gifts 2.50
20 WP,Twisted Gifts 2.50
21 WP 2.50
22 WP,A:Winnowill 2.50
23 WP,Blue Mountain,A:Winnowill 2.50
24 WP,The Quest Usurped 2.50
25 WP,Northern Wastelands 2.50
26 WP,Rayeks Story 2.50
27 WP,Battle Preparations 2.50
28 WP,Elves vs. Trolls 2.50
29 WP,Battle Beneath Blue Mountain 2.00
30 WP 2.00
31 WP 2.00
32 WP,Conclusion, March 1988 2.00

ELSEWHERE PRINCE
Epic
May, 1990
1 thru 5 @2.00
6 October, 1990 2.00

ELVIRA
October, 1988
Spec.Black & White,Movie Adapt 2.00

EPIC
1 Wildcards,Hellraiser 4.95
2 Nightbreed,Wildcards 4.95
3 DBw,MFm,Alien Legion, 4.95
4 Stalkers,Metropol,Wildcards 4.95

EPIC GRAPHIC NOVEL
Moebius 1: Upon a Star 10.00
Moebius 2: Arzach 10.00
Moebius 3: Airtight Garage 10.00
Moebius 4: Long Tomorrow 10.00
Moebius 5: 10.00
Moebius 6: Pharadonesia 10.00
Last of Dragons 7.00
The Incal 1 Moebius 11.00
The Incal 2 Moebius 11.00
The Incal 3 Moebius 11.00
JBo,Someplace Strange 7.00
MZ,Punisher 16.95

EPIC ILLUSTRATED
Spring, 1980
1 Black and White/Color Mag. 6.00
2 thru 10 @4.50
11 thru 15 @3.50
16 4.00
17 thru 20 @3.00
21 thru 25 @3.00
26 thru 34, March, 1986 @5.50

EPIC LITE
Epic
November, 1991
One-shot short stories 3.95

ETERNALS
[1st Series]
July, 1976
1 JK,I:Ikaris 4.50
2 JK,I:Ajak 3.50
3 JK,I:Sersi 5.00
4 JK,Night of the Demons 2.50
5 JK,I:Makarri,Zuras Thena,Domo 2.50
6 JK,Gods & Men at City College 2.50
7 JK,V:Celestials 2.50
8 JK,I:Karkas, Reject 2.50
9 JK,I:Sprite,Reject vs. Karkas 2.50
10 JK,V:Celestials 2.50
11 JK,I:Kingo Sunen 2.50
12 JK,I:Uni-Mind 2.50
13 JK,I:FOrgottenOne(Gilgamesh) 2.50
14 JK,V:Hulk 2.50
15 JK,V:Hulk 2.50
16 JK,I:Dromedan 2.50
17 JK,I:Sigmar 2.50
18 JK,I:Nerve Beast 2.50
19 JK,Secret o/t Pyramid 2.50
Ann.#1 JK,V:Timekillers 3.00

ETERNALS, THE
[2nd Series]
October, 1985
1 SB,I:Cybele 1.25
2 SB,V:Deviants 1.00
3 SB,V:Deviants 1.00
4 SB,V:Deviants 1.00
5 SB,V:Deviants 1.00
6 SB,V:Deviants 1.00

Eternals #1
© Marvel Entertainment Group

7 SB,V:Deviants 1.00
8 WS,SB,V:Deviants 1.00
9 WS,SB,V:Deviants 1.00
10 WS,SB,V:Deviants 1.00
11 WS,KP,V:Deviants 1.00
12 WS,KP,V:Deviants 1.25

ETERNALS: HEROD FACTOR
November, 1991
1 MT/BMc,A:Sersi (giant size) 2.50

EVERYMAN
Epic
One Shot.Supernatural Story (Animated Cel Artwork) 4.50

EWOKS
Star
June 1985
1 Based on TV Series 3.00
2 2.50
3 2.50
4 A:Foonars 2.50
5 Wicket vs. Ice Demon. 2.50
6 Mount Sorrow, A:Teebo 2.50
7 A:Logray,V:Morag 2.50
8 2.50
9 Lost in Time 2.50
10 Lost in Time 1.00
11 Kneesaa Shrunk,A:Fleebogs 1.00
12 1.00
13 1.00
14 Teebo- King for a Day 1.00
15 September,1987 1.00

EXCALIBUR
April, 1988
1 AD,Special,O:Excalibur, V:Technet 13.00
1a 2nd Printing 5.00
1b 3rd Printing 4.50
2 AAd,Mojo Mayhem,A:X-Babies 6.00
3 Air Apparent Spec.RLm,KJ,JG,TP, RL,EL,JRu,A:Coldblood 5.25

[Regular Series]
1 B:CCl(s),AD,V:Warwolves, I:Widget 12.00
2 AD,V:Warwolves,I:Kylun 8.00

3 AD,V:Juggernaut 5.00
4 AD,V:Arcade,Crazy Gang 4.00
5 AD,V:Arcade 4.00
6 AD,Inferno,I:Alistaire Stuart . . . 4.00
7 AD,Inferno 4.00
8 RLm,JRu,A:New Mutants 4.00
9 AD,I:Nazi-Excalibur 4.00
10 MR,V:Nazi-Excalibur 4.00
11 MR,V:Nazi-Excalibur 4.00
12 AD,Fairy Tale Dimension 4.00
13 AD,The Prince,N.Capt.Britian . 4.00
14 AD,Too Many Heroes 3.50
15 AD,I:US James Braddock 3.50
16 AD,V:Anjulie 3.50
17 AD,C:Prof.X,Starjammers 3.50
18 DJ,DA,V:Jamie Braddock 3.50
19 RL,TA,AM,V:Jamie Braddock . 3.50
20 RLm,JRu,V:Demon Druid 3.50
21 I:Crusader X 3.00
22 V:Crusader X 3.00
23 AD,V:Magik 3.00
24 AD,Return Home,C:Galactus . . 3.00
25 E:CCl(s),AM,A:Galactus,Death, Watcher 3.00
26 RLm,JRu,V:Mastermind 3.00
27 BWS,BSz,A:Nth Man 4.00
28 BBl,Night at Bar 2.50
29 JRu,V:Nightmare,A:PowerPack 2.50
30 DR,AM,A:Doctor Strange 2.50
31 DR,AM,V:Son of Krakoa 2.50
32 V:Mesmero 2.50
33 V:Mesmero 2.50
34 V:Mesmero 2.50
35 AM,Missing Child 2.50
36 AM,V:Silv.Sable,Sandman . . . 2.50
37 A:Avengers W.C.,Dr.Doom . . . 2.50
38 A:Avengers W.C.,Dr.Doom . . . 2.50
39 A:Avengers W.C.,Dr.Doom . . . 2.50
40 O:Excalibur,Trial-Lockheed . . . 2.50
41 V:Warwolves,C:Cable 3.50
42 AD,Team Broken Up 5.00
43 AD,Nightcrawler,V:Capt.Brit . . 3.00
44 AD,Capt.Britain On Trial 3.00
45 AD,I:N-Men, ... 3.00
46 AD,Return of Kylun,C:Cerise . . 3.00
47 AD,I:Cerise 3.00
48 AD,A:Anti-Phoenix 3.00
49 AD,MFm,V:Necrom,R:Merlyn . 3.00
50 AD,Phoenix,V:Necrom,Merlyn . 4.00
51 V:Giant Dinosaurs 2.00
52 O:Phoenix,A:Prof X,MarvGirl . . 2.00
53 A:Spider-Man,V:The Litter 2.00
54 AD,MFm,V:Crazy Gang 2.50
55 AD,MFm,A:Psylocke 2.50
56 AD,MFm,A:Psylocke, V:Saturyne,Jamie Braddock . . 2.50
57 A:X-Men,Alchemy,V:Trolls 2.75
58 A:X-Men,Alchemy,V:Trolls 2.75
59 A:Avengers 2.00
60 A:Avengers 2.00
61 AD,MFm,Phoenix Vs.Galactus 2.25
62 AD,MFm,A:Galactus 2.25
63 AD,MFm,V:Warpies 2.25
64 AD,MFm,V:RCX,R:Rachel 2.25
65 AD,MFm,R:Dark Phoenix 2.25
66 AD,MFm,V:Ahab,Sentinels, O:Widget 2.25
67 AD,MFm,V:Ahab,Sentinels . . . 2.25
68 V:Starjammers 2.00
69 A:Starjammers 2.00
70 A:Starjammers 2.00
71 DaR,Hologram(c),N:Excalibur . 5.00
72 KeL,V:Siena Blaze 2.00
73 TSr,V:Siena Blaze 2.00
74 InC,A:Mr.Sinster,Siena Blaze . 2.00
75 SLo(s),KeL,I:Daytripper(Amanda Sefton),Britannic(Capt.Britain), BU:Nightcrawler 3.50
75a Newstand Ed. 2.25
76 KeL,V:D'spayre 2.00
77 KeL,R:Doug Ramsey 2.00
78 A:Zero,Doug Ramsey 1.95
79 A:Zero,Doug Ramsey 1.95
Ann.#1 I:Khaos,w/card 3.25
Spec #1 The Possession 4.00
Spec #2 RLm,DT,JG,RL, A:Original X-Men 2.75

FAFHRD AND THE GRAY MOUSER

Epic
October, 1990

1 MMi 5.00
2 & 3 MMi . . . . @5.00
4 MMi, February 1991 . . . . 5.00

FAITHFUL

November, 1949

1 Ph(c),I Take This Man 35.00
2 Ph(c),Love Thief,Feb.,1950 . . 35.00

Falcon #4

© Marvel Entertainment Group

FALCON

November, 1983

1 PS,V:Nemesis 2.00
2 V:Sentinels 1.50
3 V:Electro 1.50
4 A:Capt.America, February, 1984 1.50

FALLEN ANGELS

April, 1987

1 KGa,TP,A:Sunspot,Warlock . . . 4.00
2 KGa,TP,I:Gomi,Fallen Angels . 3.00
3 KGa,TP,A:X-Factor 3.00
4 KGa,TP,A:Moon Boy, Devil Dinosaur 3.00
5 JSon,D:Angel,Don 3.00
6 JSon,Coconut Grove 2.50
7 KGa,Captured in CoconutGrove 2.50
8 KGa,L:Sunspot,Warlock 2.50

FANTASTIC FOUR

November, 1961

1 JK,I&O:Mr.Fantastic,Thing Invisible Girl,Human Torch Mole Man 11,000.00
2 JK,I:Skrulls 2,400.00
3 JK,I:Miracleman 1,300.00
4 JK,R:Submariner 1,700.00
5 JK,JSt,I&O:Doctor Doom . . 1,900.00
6 JK,V:Doctor Doom 1,000.00
7 JK,I:Kurrgo 600.00
8 JK,I:Alicia Masters,I&O: Puppet Master 600.00
9 JK,V:Submariner 550.00
10 JK,V:Doctor Doom,I:Ovoids . 550.00
11 JK,I:Impossible Man 400.00
12 JK,V:Hulk 500.00

Fantastic Four #47

© Marvel Entertainment Group

13 JK,SD,I&O:Red Ghost, I:Watcher 350.00
14 JK,SD,V:Submariner 250.00
15 JK,I:Mad Thinker 250.00
16 JK,V:Doctor Doom 250.00
17 JK,V:Doctor Doom 250.00
18 JK,I:Super Skrull 250.00
19 JK,I&O:Rama Tut 250.00
20 JK,I:Molecule Man 250.00
21 JK,I:Hate Monger 175.00
22 JK,V:Mole Man 175.00
23 JK,V:Doctor Doom 175.00
24 JK,I:Infant Terrible 175.00
25 JK,Thing vs.Hulk 300.00
26 JK,V:Hulk,A:Avengers 300.00
27 JK,A:Doctor Strange 130.00
28 JK,1st X-Men x-over 165.00
29 JK,V:Red Ghost 120.00
30 JK,I&O:Diablo 120.00
31 JK,V:Mole Man 100.00
32 JK,V:Superskrull 100.00
33 JK,I:Attuma 100.00
34 JK,I:Gideon 100.00
35 JK,I:Dragon Man,A:Diablo . . 100.00
36 JK,I:Medusa,Frightful Four . 100.00
37 JK,V:Skrulls 90.00
38 JK,V:Frightful Four,I:Trapster 90.00
39 JK,WW,A:Daredevil 90.00
40 JK,A:Daredevil,Dr.Doom 90.00
41 JK,V:Fright.Four,A:Medusa . . 76.00
42 JK,V:Frightful Four 76.00
43 JK,V:Frightful Four 76.00
44 JK,JSt,I:Gorgon, V:Dragon Man 80.00
45 JK,JSt,I:Inhumans(Black Bolt,Triton Lockjaw,Crystal,Karnak) 90.00
46 JK,JSt,V:Seeker 74.00
47 JK,JSt,I:Maximus,Attilan, Alpha Primitives 60.00
48 JK,JSt,I:Silver Surfer, C:Galactus 675.00
49 JK,JSt,A:Silver Surfer, V:Galactus 200.00
50 JK,JSt,V:Galactus,Silver Surfer,I:Wyatt Wingfoot 250.00
51 JK,JSt,I:Negative Zone 50.00
52 JK,JSt,I:Black Panther 110.00
53 JK,JSt,I:Klaw,Vibranium 50.00

54 JK,JSt,I:Prester John 45.00
55 JK,JSt,A:Silver Surfer 70.00
56 JK,JSt,O:Klaw,A:Inhumans, C:Silver Surfer 58.00
57 JK,JSt,V:Doc Doom, A:Silver Surfer. 58.00
58 JK,JSt,V:Doc Doom, A:Silver Surfer. 58.00
59 JK,JSt,V:Doc Doom, A:Silver Surfer. 58.00
60 JK,JSt,V:Doc Doom, A:Silver Surfer. 58.00
61 JK,JSt,V:Sandman, A:Silver Surfer 58.00
62 JK,JSt,I:Blastaar 40.00
63 JK,JSt,V:Blastaar 38.00
64 JK,JSt,I:The Kree,Sentry 38.00
65 JK,JSt,I:Ronan,Supreme Intelligence 43.00
66 JK,JSt,O:Him,A:Crystal 82.00
67 JK,JSt,I:Him 95.00
68 JK,JSt,V:Mad Thinker 38.00
69 JK,JSt,V:Mad Thinker 35.00
70 JK,JSt,V:Mad Thinker 35.00
71 JK,JSt,V:Mad Thinker 35.00
72 JK,JSt,A:Watcher,S.Surfer . . 50.00
73 JK,JSt,A:SpM,DD,Thor 30.00

Fantastic Four #100
© Marvel Entertainment Group

74 JK,JSt,A:Silver Surfer 45.00
75 JK,JSt,A:Silver Surfer 45.00
76 JK,JSt,V:Psycho Man,S.Surf . 40.00
77 JK,JSt,V:Galactus,S.Surfer . . 40.00
78 JK,JSt,V:Wizard 27.00
79 JK,JSt,A:Crystall,V:Mad Thinker 27.00
80 JK,JSt,A:Crystal 27.00
81 JK,JSt,J:Crystal,V:Wizard . . . 27.00
82 JK,JSt,V:Maximus 27.00
83 JK,JSt,V:Maximus 27.00
84 JK,JSt,V:Doctor Doom 23.00
85 JK,JSt,V:Doctor Doom 23.00
86 JK,JSt,V:Doctor Doom 23.00
87 JK,JSt,V:Doctor Doom 23.00
88 JK,JSt,V:Mole Man 23.00
89 JK,JSt,V:Mole Man 23.00
90 JK,JSt,V:Skrulls 19.00
91 JK,JSt,V:Skrulls,I:Torgo 19.00
92 JK,JSt,V:Torgo,Skrulls 19.00
93 JK,V:Torgo,Skrulls 19.00
94 JK,JSt,I:Agatha Harkness . . . 19.00
95 JK,JSt,I:Monocle 20.00
96 JK,JSt,V:Mad Thinker 19.00
97 JK,JSt,V:Monster from Lost Lagoon 19.00
98 JK,JSt,V:Kree Sentry 19.00
99 JK,JSt,A:Inhumans 19.00
100 JK,JSt,V:Puppetmaster 70.00
101 JK,JSt,V:Maggia 16.00
102 JK,JSt,V:Magneto 18.00
103 JR,V:Magneto 18.00
104 JR,V:Magneto 18.00
105 JR,L:Crystal 12.00
106 JR,JSt,'Monster's Secret' . . 12.00
107 JB,JSt,V:Annihilus 12.00
108 JK,JB,JR,JSt, V:Annihilus . . 12.00
109 JB,JSt,V:Annihilus 12.00
110 JB,JSt,V:Annihilus 12.00
111 JB,JSt,A:Hulk 12.00
112 JB,JSt,Thing vs. Hulk 32.00
113 JB,JSt,I:Overmind 10.00
114 JR(c),JB,V:Overmind 8.00
115 JR(c),JB,JSt,I:Eternals 10.00
116 JB,JSt,O:Stranger 10.00
117 JB,JSt,V:Diablo 8.00
118 JR(c),JB,JM,V:Diablo 8.00
119 JB,JSt,V:Klaw 8.00
120 JB,JSt,I:Gabriel(Airwalker) (Robot) 8.00
121 JB,JSt,V:Silver Surfer,D: Gabriel Destroyer 15.00
122 JR(c),JB,JSt,V:Galactus, A:Silver Surfer 15.00
123 JB,JSt,V:Galactus, A:Silver Surfer 14.00
124 JB,JSt,V:Monster 7.00
125 E:StL(s),JB,JSt,V:Monster . . . 7.00
126 B:RTs(s),JB,JSt, O:FF,MoleMan 7.00
127 JB,JSt,V:Mole Man 7.00
128 JB,JSt,V:Mole Man 10.00
129 JB,JSt,I:Thundra, V:Frightful Four 7.00
130 JSo(c),JB,JSt,V:Frightful Four 6.00
131 JSo(c),JB,JSt,V:QuickSilver . . 6.00
132 JB,JSt,J:Medusa 6.00
133 JSt(i),V:Thundra 6.00
134 JB,JSt,V:Dragon Man 6.00
135 JB,JSt,V:Gideon 6.00
136 JB,JSt,A:Shaper 6.00
137 JB,JSt,A:Shaper 6.00
138 JB,JSt,O:Miracle Man 6.00
139 JB,V:Miracle Man 6.00
140 JB,JSt,O:Annihilus 6.00
141 JR(c),JB,JSt,V:Annihilus 6.00
142 RB,JSt,A:Doc Doom 6.00
143 GK(c),RB,V:Doc Doom 6.00
144 RB,JSt,V:Doc Doom 6.00
145 JSt&GK(c),RA,I:Ternak 6.00
146 RA,JSt,V:Ternak 6.00
147 RB,JSt,V:Subby 6.00
148 RB,JSt,V:Frightful Four 6.00
149 RB,JSt,V:Sub-Mariner. 6.00
150 GK(c),RB,JSt,W:Crystal & Quicksilver,V:Ultron 7.00
151 RB,JSt,O:Thundra 5.00
152 JR(c),RB,JM,A:Thundra 5.00
153 GK(c),RB,JSt,A:Thundra 5.00
154 GK(c),rep.Str.Tales #127 . . . 5.00
155 RB,JSt,A:Surfer 8.00
156 RB,JSt,A:Surfer,V:Doom 8.00
157 RB,JSt,A:Surfer 8.00
158 RB,JSt,V:Xemu 5.00
159 RB,JSt,V:Xemu 5.00
160 K&R(c),JB,V:Arkon 4.50
161 RB,JSt,V:Arkon 4.50
162 RB,DA,JSt,V:Arkon 4.50
163 RB,JSt,V:Arkon 4.50
164 JK(c),GP,JSt,V:Crusader,R: Marvel Boy,I:Frankie Raye . . . 4.50
165 GP,JSt,O:Crusader, O&D:Marvel Boy 4.50
166 GP,V:Hulk 7.50
167 JK(c),GP,JSt,V:Hulk 7.50
168 RB,JSt,J:Luke Cage 5.00
169 RB,JSt,V:Puppetmaster 5.00
170 GP,JSt,L:Luke Cage 5.00
171 JK(c),RB,GP,JSt,I:Gor 4.00

Fantastic Four #170
© Marvel Entertainment Group

172 JK(c),GP,JSt,V:Destroyer . . . 4.00
173 JB,JSt,V:Galactus,O:Heralds . 4.00
174 JB,V:Galactus 4.00
175 JB,A:High Evolutionary 4.00
176 GP,JSt,V:Impossible Man . . . 4.00
177 JP,JS,A:Frightful Four I:Texas Twister,Capt.Ultra 3.50
178 GP,V:Frightful Four,Brute . . . 3.50
179 JSt,V:Annihilus 3.50
180 reprint #101 . . . . 3.50
181 E:RTs(s),JSt,V:Brute, Annihilus 3.50
182 SB,JSt,V:Brute,Annihilus 3.50
183 SB,JSt,V:Brute,Annihilus 3.50
184 GP,JSt,V:Eliminator 3.50
185 GP,JSt,V:Nich.Scratch 3.50
186 GP,JSi,I:Salem's Seven 3.50
187 GP,JSt,V:Klaw,Molecule Man 3.50
188 GP,JSt,V:Molecule Man 3.50
189 reprint FF Annual #4 . . . . . . 3.50
190 SB,O:Fantastic Four 3.50
191 GP,JSt,V:Plunderer, Team Breaks Up 3.50
192 GP,JSt,V:Texas Twister 3.50
193 KP,JSt,V:Darkoth,Diablo 3.50
194 KP,V:Darkoth,Diablo 3.50
195 KP,A:Sub-Mariner 3.50
196 KP,V:Invincible Man (Reed), A:Dr.Doom,Team Reunited . . . 3.50
197 KP,JSt,Red Ghost 3.50
198 KP,JSt,V:Doc Doom 3.50
199 KP,JSt,V:Doc Doom 3.50
200 KP,JSt,V:Doc Doom 6.00
201 KP,JSt,FF's Machinery 3.00
202 KP,JSt,V:Quasimodo 3.00
203 KP,JSt,V:Mutant 3.00
204 KP,JSt,V:Skrulls 3.00
205 KP,JSt,V:Skrulls 3.00
206 KP,JSt,V:Skrulls,A:Nova 3.00
207 SB,JSt,V:Monocle,A:SpM . . . 4.00
208 SB,V:Sphinx,A:Nova 2.50
209 JBy,JSt,I:Herbie,A:Nova 5.00
210 JBy,JS,A:Galactus 4.00
211 JBy,JS,I:Terrax,A:Galactus . . 4.50
212 JBy,JSt,V:Galactus,Sphinx . . 4.00
213 JBy,JSt,V:Terrax,Galactus Sphinx 4.00
214 JBy,JSt,V:Skrull 4.00
215 JBy,JSt,V:Blastaar 4.00
216 JBy,V:Blastaar 4.00
217 JBy,JSt,A:Dazzler 4.50

218 JBy,JSt,V:FrightfulFour, A:Spider-Man 4.00
219 BSz,JSt,A:Sub-Mariner 3.00
220 JBy,JSt,A:Vindicator 3.50
221 JBy,JSt,V:Vindicator 3.50
222 BSz,JSt,V:Nicholas Scratch . . 2.75
223 BSz,JSt,V:Salem's Seven . . . 2.75
224 BSz,A:Thor 2.75
225 BSz,A:Thor 2.75
226 BSz,A:Shogun 2.75
227 BSz,JSt,V:Ego-Spawn 2.75
228 BSz,JSt,V:Ego-Spawn 2.75
229 BSz,JSt,I:Firefrost,Ebon Seeker 3.00
230 BSz,JSt,A:Avengers, O:Firefrost & Ebon Seeker . . . 2.75
231 BSz,JSt,V:Stygorr 2.75
232 JBy,New Direction,V:Diablo . . 5.00
233 JBy,V:Hammerhead 3.50
234 JBy,V:Ego 3.50
235 JBy,O:Ego 3.50
236 JBy,V:Dr.Doom,A:Puppet Master, 20th Anniv. 4.50
237 JBy,V:Solons 3.50

Fantastic Four #286
© Marvel Entertainment Group

238 JBy,O:Frankie Raye, new Torch 3.50
239 JBy,I:Aunt Petunia, Uncle Jake 3.50
240 JBy,A:Inhumans,b:Luna 3.50
241 JBy,A:Black Panther 3.50
242 JBy,A:Daredevil,Thor,Iron Man Spider-Man,V:Terrax 3.50
243 JBy,A:Daredevil,Dr.Strange, Spider-Man,Avengers,V:Galactus, Terrax 4.00
244 JBy,A:Avengers,Dr.Strange, Galactus, Frankie Raye Becomes Nova 4.50
245 JBy,V:Franklin Richards 3.50
246 JBy,V:Dr.Doom, A:Puppet Master 3.50
247 JBy,A:Dr.Doom,I:Kristoff, D:Zorba 3.50
248 JBy,A:Inhumans 3.50
249 JBy,V:Gladiator 3.50
250 JBy,A:Capt.America,SpM V:Gladiator 4.00
251 JBy,A:Annihilus 3.00
252 JBy,1st sideways issue,V: Ootah,A:Annihilus,w/tattoo . . . 4.50
252a w/o tattoo 2.00
253 JBy,V:Kestorans,A:Annihilus . 3.00
254 JBy,V:Mantracora, A:She-Hulk,Wasp 3.00
255 JBy,A:Daredevil,Annihilus, V:Mantracora 3.00
256 JBy,A:Avengers,Galactus, V:Annihilus,New Costumes . . . 3.00
257 JBy,A:Galactus,Death,Nova, Scarlet Witch 3.50
258 JBy,A:Dr.Doom,D:Hauptmann 3.00
259 JBy,V:Terrax,Dr.Doom, C:Silver Silver 3.00
260 JBy,V:Terrax, Dr.Doom, A:Silver Surfer,Sub-Mariner . . . 5.00
261 JBy,A:Sub-Mariner,Marrina, Silver Surfer,Sc.Witch,Lilandra 5.00
262 JBy,O:Galactus,A:Odin, (J.Byrne in story) 3.50
263 JBy,V:Messiah,A:Mole Man . . 3.00
264 JBy,V:Messiah,A:Mole Man . . 3.00
265 JBy,A:Trapster,Avengers, J:She-Hulk,Secret Wars 4.50
266 KGa,JBy,A:Hulk,Sasquatch, V:Karisma 3.00
267 JBy,A:Hulk,Sasquatch,Morbius, V:Dr.Octopus,Sue miscarries . . 4.00
268 JBy,V:Doom's Mask 3.00
269 JBy,R:Wyatt Wingfoot, I:Terminus 3.00
270 JBy,V:Terminus 3.00
271 JBy,V:Gormuu 3.00
272 JBy,I:Warlord (Nathaniel Richards) 3.00
273 JBy,V:Warlord 3.00
274 JBy,AG,cont.from Thing#19, A:Sp.M's Black Costume 3.00
275 JBy,AG,V:T.J.Vance 3.00
276 JBy,JOy,V:Mephisto, A:Dr.Strange 3.00
277 JBy,JOy,V:Mephisto, A:Dr.Strange,R:Thing 3.00
278 JBy,JOy,O:Dr.Doom,A:Kristoff (as Doom) 3.00
279 JBy,JOy,V:Dr.Doom(Kristoff), I:New Hate-Monger 3.00
280 JBy,JOy,I:Malice, V:Hate-Monger 3.00
281 JBy,JOy,A:Daredevil,V:Hate Monger,Malice 3.00
282 JBy,JOy,A:Power Pack,Psycho Man,Secret Wars II 3.00
283 JBy,JOy,V:Psycho-Man 3.00
284 JBy,JOy,V:Psycho-Man 3.00
285 JBy,JOy,Secret Wars II A:Beyonder 3.00
286 JBy,TA,R:Jean Grey, A:Hercules Capt.America 4.50
287 JBy,JSt,A:Wasp,V:Dr.Doom . 3.00
288 JBy,JSt,V:Dr.Doom,Secret Wars II 3.00
289 JBy,AG,D:Basilisk,V:Blastaar, R:Annihilus 3.00
290 JBy,AG,V:Annihilus 3.00
291 JBy,CR,A:Nick Fury 3.00
292 JBy,AG,A:Nick Fury,V:Hitler . . 3.00
293 JBy,AG,A:Avengers.W.C. . . . 3.00
294 JOy,AG,V:FutureCentralCity . 2.25
295 JOy,AG,V:Fut.Central City . . . 2.25
296 BWS,KGa,RF,BWi,AM,KJ,JB, SL,MS,JRu,JOy,JSt,25th Anniv.,V:MoleMan 4.00
297 JB,SB,V:Umbra-Sprite 2.25
298 JB,SB,V:Umbra-Sprite 2.25
299 JB,SB,She-Hulk,V:Thing, A:Spider-Man,L:She-Hulk 2.50
300 JB,SB,W:Torch & Fake Alicia (Lyja),A:Puppet-Master,Wizard, Mad Thinker,Dr.Doom 3.00
301 JB,SB,V:Wizard,MadThinker . 2.25
302 JB,SB,V:Project Survival 2.25
303 JB,RT,A:Thundra,V:Machus . 2.25
304 JB,JSt,V:Quicksilver, A:Kristoff 2.25
305 JB,JSt,V:Quicksilver, J:Crystal,A:Dr.Doom 2.25
306 JB,JSt,A:Capt.America, J:Ms.Marvel,V:Diablo 2.25
307 JB,JSt,L:Reed&Sue,V:Diablo . 2.25
308 JB,JSt,I:Fasaud 2.25
309 JB,JSt,V:Fasaud 2.25
310 KP,JSt,V:Fasaud,N:Thing & Ms.Marvel 2.25
311 KP,JSt,A:Black Panther, Dr.Doom,V:THRob 2.25
312 KP,JSt,A:Black Panther, Dr.Doom,X-Factor 2.25
313 SB,JSt,V:Lava Men, A:Moleman 2.00
314 KP,JSt,V:Belasco 2.00
315 KP,JSt,V:Mast.Pandem. 2.00
316 KP,JSt,A:CometMan 2.00
317 KP,JSt,L:Crystal 2.00
318 KP,JSt,V:Dr.Doom 2.00
319 KP,JSt,G-Size,O:Beyonder . . 2.25
320 KP,JSt,Hulk vs Thing 2.50
321 RLm,RT,A:She-Hulk 2.00
322 KP,JSt,Inferno,V:Graviton . . . 2.00
323 KP,JSt,RT,Inferno A:Mantis . . 2.00
324 KP,JSt,RT,A:Mantis 2.00
325 RB,RT,A:Silver Surfer, D:Mantis 2.50
326 KP,RT,I:New Frightful Four . . 2.00
327 KP,RT,V:Frightful Four 2.00
328 KP,RT,V:Frightful Four 2.00
329 RB,RT,V:Mole Man 2.00
330 RB,RT,V:Dr.Doom 2.00
331 RB,RT,V:Ultron 2.00
332 RB,RT,V:Aron 2.00
333 RB,RT,V:Aron,Frightful Four . 2.00
334 RB,Acts of Vengeance 2.00
335 RB,RT,Acts of Vengeance . . 2.00
336 RLm,Acts of Vengeance, . . . 2.00
337 WS,A:Thor,Iron Man, B:Timestream saga 5.00
338 WS,V:Deathshead,A:Thor, Iron Man 3.00
339 WS,V:Gladiator 2.50
340 WS,V:Black Celestial 2.50
341 WS,A:Thor,Iron Man 2.50
342 A:Rusty,C:Spider-Man 2.50
343 WS,V:Stalin 2.50
344 WS,V:Stalin 2.50
345 WS,V:Dinosaurs 2.50
346 WS,V:Dinosaurs 2.50
347 AAd,ATi(i)A:Spider-Man, GhostRider,Wolverine,Hulk . . . 7.00
347a 2nd printing 4.50
348 AAd,ATi(i)A:Spider-Man, GhostRider,Wolverine,Hulk . . . 5.50
348a 2nd printing 4.00
349 AAd,ATi(i),AM(i)A:Spider-Man, Wolverine,GhostRider,Hulk, C:Punisher 5.50
350 WS,Am(i),R:Ben Grimm as Thing,(48p) 3.25
351 MBa,Kubic 2.50
352 WS,Reed Vs.Dr.Doom 2.50
353 WS,E:Timestream Saga, A:Avengers, ... 2.50
354 WS,Secrets of the Time Variance Authority 2.50
355 AM,V:Wrecking Crew 2.00
356 B:TDF(s),PR,A:New Warriors, V:Puppet Master 2.00
357 PR,V:Mad Thinker, Puppetmaster, ... 2.00
358 PR,AAd,30th Anniv.,1st Marv. Die Cut(c),D:Lyja,V:Paibok,BU: Dr.Doom 5.00
359 PR,I:Devos the Devastator . . 2.00
360 PR,V:Dreadface 2.00
361 PR,V:Dr.Doom,X-masIssue . . 2.00
362 PR,A:Spider-Man, I:WildBlood 2.00
363 PR,I:Occulus,A:Devos 1.75
364 PR,V:Occulus 1.75
365 PR,V:Occulus 1.75
366 PR,Infinity War,R:Lyja 1.75
367 PR,Inf.War,A:Wolverine 1.75
368 PR,V:Infinity War X-Men 1.75

369 PR,Inf.War,R:Malice,
A:Thanos 1.75
370 PR,Inf.War,V:Mr.Fantastic
Doppleganger 1.75
371 PR,V:Lyja,foil(c) 6.00
371a 2nd Printing 3.00
372 PR,A:Spider-Man,Silver
Sable 1.75
373 PR,V:Aron,Silver sable 1.75
374 PR,V:Secret Defenders 2.00
375 V:Dr.Doom,A:Inhumans,Lyja,
Holo-Grafix(c) 4.50
376 PR,A:Nathan Richards,V:Paibok,
Devos,w/Dirt Magazine 3.25
376a w/out Dirt Magazine 1.50
377 PR,V:Paibok,Devos,Klaw,
I:Huntara 1.75
378 PR,A:Sandman,SpM,DD 1.75
379 PR,V:Ms.Marvel 1.75
380 PR,A:Dr.Doom,V:Hunger 2.00
381 PR,D:Dr.Doom,Mr.Fantastic,
V:Hunger 10.00
382 PR,V:Paibok,Devos,Huntara . 4.00
383 PR,V:Paibok,Devos,Huntara . 2.00
384 PR,A:Ant-Man,V:Franklin
Richards 1.50
385 PR,A:Triton,Tiger Shark,
Starblast#7 . . . . 1.50
386 PR,Starblast#11,A:Namor,Triton,
b:Johnny & Lyja child 1.50
387 Die-Cut & Foil (c),PR,N:Invisible
Woman,J:Ant-Man,A:Namor . . 3.25
387a Newsstand Ed. 1.50
388 PR,I:Dark Raider,V:FF,
Avengers,w/cards 1.50
Ann.#1 JK,SD,I:Atlantis,Dorma,
Krang,V:Namor,O:FF 360.00
Ann.#2 JK,JSt,O:Dr.Doom 220.00
Ann.#3 JK,W:Reed and Sue . . 130.00
Ann.#4 JK,JSt,I:Quasimodo 50.00
Ann.#5 JK,JSt,A:Inhumans,Silver
Surfer,Black Panther,
I:Psycho Man 100.00
Ann.#6 JK,JSt,I:Annihilus,
Franklin Richards 40.00
Ann.#7 JK(c),reprints 23.00
Ann.#8 JR(c),reprints 12.00
Ann.#9 JK(c),reprints. 12.00
Ann.#10 reprints Ann.#3 . . . . . . 12.00
Ann.#11 JK(c),JB,A:The Invaders . 8.00
Ann.#12 A:The Invaders 7.00
Ann.#13 V:The Mole Man 7.00
Ann.#14 GP,V:Salem's Seven . . . 7.00
Ann.#15 GP,V:Dr.Doom,Skrulls . . 5.00
Ann.#16 V:Dragonlord 5.00
Ann.#17 JBy,V:Skrulls 5.00
Ann.#18 KGa,V:Skrulls,W:Black
Bolt and Medusa,A:Inhumans . 5.00
Ann.#19 JBy,V:Skrulls 5.00
Ann.#20 TD(i),V:Dr.Doom 4.00
Ann.#21 JG,JSt,Evol.Wars 4.00
Ann.#22 RB,Atlantis Attacks,
A:Avengers 4.00
Ann.#23 JG,GCa,Days of Future
Present #1 . . . . 5.00
Ann.#24 JG,AM,Korvac Quest #1,
A:Guardians of the Galaxy . . . 3.00
Ann.#25 Citizen Kang #3 . . . . 2.50
Ann.#26 HT,I:Wildstreak,
V:Dreadface,w/card 3.25
Ann.#27 MGu,V:Justice Peace . . . 2.95
G-Size#1 RB,Thing/Hulk 15.00
G-Size#2 K&R(c),JB,Time to Kill . 9.00
G-Size#3 RB,JSt,Four Horseman . 9.00
G-Size#4 JB,JSt,I:Madrox 10.00
G-Size#5 JK(c),V:Psycho Man,
Molecule Man 7.00
G-Size#6 V:Annihilus 7.00
Spec.#1 Rep.Ann.#1 JBy(c) 2.00
TPB Rep.#347-349 . . . . 5.95
TPB Trial of Galactus,reprints
#242-244,#257-262 . . . . 9.95
Fantastic Four Roast,FH,MG,FM,JB,
MA,TA 5.00

FANTASTIC FOUR ROAST

1 FH/MG/FM/JB/MA/TA,May,1982 5.00

FANTASTIC FOUR UNLIMITED

1 HT,A:Bl.Panther,V:Klaw 4.50
2 HT,JQ(c),A:Inhumans 4.25
3 HT,V:Blastaar,Annihilus 4.25
4 RTs(s),HT,V:Mole Man,A:Hulk . 4.25
5 RTs(s),HT,V:Frightful Four 4.25
6 RTs(s),HT,V:Namor 3.95

FANTASTIC FOUR vs. X-MEN

February, 1987

1 JBg,TA,V:Dr.Doom 5.00
2 JBg,TA,V:Dr.Doom 3.50
3 JBg,TA,V:Dr.Doom 3.50
4 JBg,TA,V:Dr.Doom, June 1987 3.50
TPB Reprints Mini-series 12.95

FANTASTIC WORLD OF HANNA-BARBERA

December, 1977

1 . . . . 1.00
2 . . . . 1.00
3 June, 1978 . . . . 1.00

Fantasy Masterpieces #9
© Marvel Entertainment Group

FANTASY MASTERPIECES

February, 1966

1 JK/DH/SD,reprints 40.00
2 JK,SD,DH,Fin Fang Foom . . . 14.00
3 GC,DH,JK,SD,Capt.A rep. . . . 13.00
4 JK,Capt.America rep. 13.00
5 JK,Capt.America rep. 13.00
6 JK,Capt.America rep. 13.00
7 SD,Sub Mariner rep. 13.00
8 H.Torch & Sub M.rep. 15.00
9 SD,MF,O:Human Torch Rep . 15.00
10 rep.All Winners #19 . . . . 12.00
11 JK,(rep),O:Toro 12.00

FANTASY MASTERPIECES [Volume 2]

December, 1979

1 JB,JSt,Silver Surfer rep. 6.00
2 JB,JSt,Silver Surfer rep. 6.00
3 JB,JSt,Silver Surfer rep. 6.00
4 JB,JSt,Silver Surfer rep. 6.00
5 JB,JSt,Silver Surfer rep. 6.00
6 JB,JSt,Silver Surfer rep. 6.00
7 JB,JSt,Silver Surfer rep. 6.00
8 JB/JSn,Warlock rep.Strange
Tales #178 . . . . 5.00
9 JB,JSn,rep.StrangeTales#179 . 5.00
10 JB,JSn,rep.StrangeTales#180 . 5.00
11 JB,JSn,rep.StrangeTales#181 . 5.00
12 JB,JSn,rep.Warlock #9 . . . . . . 5.00
13 JB,JSn,rep.Warlock #10 . . . . . 5.00
14 JB,JSn,rep.Warlock #11 . . . . . 5.00

FAREWELL TO WEAPONS

1 DirtBag,W/Nirvana Tape 3.50

FEAR

November, 1970

1 1950's Monster rep. B:I Found
Monstrum,The Dweller
in the Black Swamp 9.00
2 X The Thing That Lived 5.00
3 Zzutak, The Thing That
Shouldn't Exist 5.00
4 I Turned Into a Martian 5.00
5 I Am the Gorilla Man 4.00
6 The Midnight Monster 4.00
7 I Dream of Doom 4.00
8 It Crawls By Night! 4.00
9 Dead Man's Escape 4.00

Fear #3
© Marvel Entertainment Group

10 GM,B:Man-Thing 9.00
11 RB,I:Jennifer Kale,Thog 5.00
12 JSn,RB 5.00
13 VM,Where World's Collide . . . 3.00
14 VM,Plague o/t Demon Cult . . . 3.00
15 VM,Lord o/t Dark Domain 3.00
16 VM,ManThing in Everglades . . 3.00
17 VM,I:Wundarr(Aquarian) 3.00
18 VM 3.00
19 VM,FMc,I:Howard the Duck,
E:Man-Thing 12.00
20 PG,B:Morbius 40.00
21 GK,V:Uncanny Caretaker . . . 23.00
22 RB,V:Cat-Demond 20.00
23 1st CR art,A World He
Never Made 20.00
24 CR,V:Blade 20.00
25 You Always Kill the One
You Love 17.00
26 V:Uncanny Caretaker 17.00
27 V:Simon Stroud 17.00

 All comics prices listed are for *Near Mint* condition.

28 Doorway Down into Hell 17.00
29 Death has a Thousand Eyes . 17.00
30 Bloody Sacrifice 17.00
31 last issue,December 1975 . . . 17.00

FEUD
Epic

1 I:Skids,Stokes,Kite 2.50
2 V:Grunts,Skide,Stockers 2.25
3 . . . . 2.25
4 . . . . 2.25

FIGHT MAN

1 I:Fight Man 2.00

FIRESTAR
March, 1986

1 MW,SL,O:Firestar,A:X-Men, New Mutants 5.00
2 MW,BWI,A:New Mutants 7.00
3 AAd&BSz(c),MW,SL, A:White Queen 3.50
4 MW,SL,V:White Queen 3.50

FISH POLICE

1 V:S.Q.U.I.D,Hook 1.25
2 V:Hook 1.25
3 V:Hook 1.25
4 V:Hook 1.25
5 V:Goldie Prawn 1.25
6 Shark Bait #1 . . . . 1.25

FLINTSTONE KIDS
Star Comics
August, 1987

1 thru 10 . . . . @1.00
11 April, 1989 . . . . 1.00

FLINTSTONES
October, 1977

1 From TV Series 1.50
2 . . . . 1.25
3 . . . . 1.25
4 A:Jetsons 1.25
5 . . . . 1.25
6 . . . . 1.25
7 February, 1979 . . . . 1.25

FOOLKILLER
October, 1990

1 I:Kurt Gerhardt (Foolkiller III) 4.00
2 O:Foolkiller I & II 3.00
3 Old Costume 2.50
4 N:Foolkiller 2.50
5 Body Count 2.50
6 Fools Paradise 2.50
7 Who the Fools Are 2.50
8 Sane Must Inherit Earth,A:SpM 3.00
9 D:Darren Waite 2.00
10 New Identity, July 1991 . . . . . 2.00

FOORFUR
Star Comics
August, 1987

1 thru 6 . . . . @1.00

FORCE WORKS

1 TmT,Pop-up(c),I:Century,V:Kree, N:US Agent 3.95

FOR YOUR EYES ONLY

1 HC,James Bond rep. 2.00
2 HC,James Bond rep. 2.00

FRAGGLE ROCK

1 thru 8 . . . . @1.00

[Volume 2]
April, 1988

1 thru 5 . . . . @1.00
6 September, 1988 . . . . 1.00

FRANCIS, BROTHER OF THE UNIVERSE
(one shot) 1980

1 . . . . 2.50

FRANKENSTEIN
See: MONSTER OF FRANKENSTEIN

FRED HEMBECK DESTROYS THE MARVEL UNIVERSE

1 . . . . 2.00

FRIGHT
June, 1975

1 . . . . 1.50

FRONTIER WESTERN
February, 1956

1 RH, ... 85.00
2 AW,GT 65.00
3 MD 65.00
4 MD 40.00
5 RC 50.00
6 AW, ... 60.00
7 JR 30.00
8 RC 30.00
9 . . . . 30.00
10 August, 1957 . . . . 30.00

FUNNY FROLICS
Summer, 1945

1 (fa) 86.00
2 . . . . 46.00
3 . . . . 38.00
4 . . . . 38.00
5 HK 45.00

FURY

1 MCW,O:Fury,A:S.A. Heroes . . . 3.25

GAMBIT

1 HMe(c),LW,KJ,Embossed(c),D:Henri LeBeau,V:Assassin's Guild . . . 6.50
1a Gold Ed. 30.00
2 LW,KJ,C:Gideon,A:Rogue 5.00
3 LW,KJ,A:Candra,Rogue, D:Gambit's Father 4.50
4 LW,KJ,A:Candra,Rogue,D:Tithe Collector 4.00

GARGOYLE
June, 1985

1 BWr(c),from 'Defenders' 2.00
2 . . . . 1.50
3 . . . . 1.50
4 . . . . 1.50

GENERIC COMIC

1 . . . . 1.50

GENETIX

1 B:ALa(s),w/cards 2.75
2 I:Tektos 2.00
3 V:Tektos 1.75
4 thru 5 PGa,V:MyS-Tech 1.75
6 V:Tektos 1.95

GENE DOGS

1 I:Gene DOGS,w/cards 2.75
2 V:Genetix 2.00
3 V:Hurricane 2.00
4 last issue 1.75

GEORGIE COMICS
Spring, 1945

1 Georgie stories begin 85.00
2 Pet Shop (c) 42.00
3 Georgie/Judy(c) 30.00
4 Wedding Dress(c) 30.00
5 Monty/Policeman(c) 30.00
6 Classroom(c) 30.00
7 Fishing(c) 40.00
8 Soda Jerk(c) 30.00
9 Georgie/Judy(c),HK,Hey Look 40.00
10 Georgie/Girls(c),HK,Hey Look 40.00
11 Table Tennis(c),A:Margie,Millie 25.00
12 Camping(c) 25.00
13 Life Guard(c),HK,Hey Look . . 35.00
14 Classroom(c),HK,Hey Look . . 40.00
15 Winter Sports(c) 20.00
16 . . . . 20.00
17 HK,Hey Look 20.00
18 . . . . 20.00
19 Baseball(c) 20.00
20 Title change to Georgie & Judy Comics 20.00
21 Title change to Georgie & Judy Comics 15.00
22 Georgie comics 15.00
23 . . . . 15.00
24 . . . . 15.00
25 . . . . 34.00
26 . . . . 15.00
27 . . . . 15.00
28 . . . . 15.00
29 . . . . 28.00
30 thru 38 . . . . @15.00
39 October, 1952 . . . . 15.00

GETALONG GANG
May, 1985

1 thru 5 . . . . @1.00
6 March, 1986 . . . . 1.00

GHOST RIDER
[1st Regular Series]
September, 1973

1 GK,JSt,C:Son of Satan 90.00
2 GK,I:Son of Satan,A:Witch Woman 50.00
3 JR,D:Big Daddy Dawson, new Cycle 30.00
4 GK,A:Dude Jensen 30.00
5 GK,JR,I:Roulette 30.00
6 JR,O:Ghost Rider 17.00
7 JR,A:Stunt Master 17.00
8 GK,A:Satan,I:Inferno 15.00
9 GK,TP,O:Johnny Blaze 18.00
10 JSt,A:Hulk 18.00
11 GK,KJ,SB,A:Hulk 13.00
12 GK,KJ,FR,A:Phantom Eagle . 12.00
13 GK,JS,GT,A:Trapster 12.00
14 GT,A:The Orb 12.00
15 SB,O:The Orb 12.00
16 DC,GT,Blood in the Water . . 12.00
17 RB,FR,I:Challenger 12.00
18 RB,FR,A:Challenger,Sp.M. . . . 13.00
19 GK,FR,A:Challenger 12.00
20 GK,KJ,JBy,A:Daredevil 25.00
21 A:Gladiator,D:Eel 9.00
22 AM,DH,KP,JR,A:Enforcer 9.00
23 JK,DH,DN,I:Water Wiz. 9.00
24 GK,DC,DH,A:Enforcer 9.00
25 GK,DH,A:Stunt Master 9.00
26 GK,DP,A:Dr. Druid 9.00
27 SB,DP,A:Hawkeye 9.00
28 DP,A:The Orb 9.00
29 RB,DP,A:Dormammu 9.00
30 DP,A:Dr.Strange 10.00
31 FR,DP,BL,A:Bounty Hunt. 7.00
32 KP,BL,DP,A:Bounty Hunt. 7.00
33 DP,I:Dark Riders 7.00
34 DP,C:Cyclops 7.00
35 JSn,AM,A:Death 8.00
36 DP,Drug Mention 7.00
37 DP,I:Dick Varden 6.00
38 DP,A:Death Cult 6.00
39 DP,A:Death Cult 6.00
40 DP,I:Nuclear Man 6.00
41 DP,A:Jackal Gang 6.00
42 DP,A:Jackal Gang 6.00
43 CI:Crimson Mage 6.00

Ghost Rider #1

© Marvel Entertainment Group

44 JAb,CI,A:Crimson Mage 6.00
45 DP,I:Flagg Fargo 6.00
46 DP,A:Flagg Fargo 6.00
47 AM,DP 6.00
48 BMc,DP 6.00
49 DP,I:The Manitou 6.00
50 DP,A:Night Rider 9.00
51 AM,PD,A:Cycle Gang 5.00
52 AM,DP 5.00
53 DP,I:Lord Asmodeus 5.00
54 DP,A:The Orb 5.00
55 DP,A:Werewolf By Night 5.50
56 DP,A:Moondark,I:Night Rider . 5.00
57 AM,DP,I:The Apparition 5.00
58 DP,FM,A:Water Wizard 5.00
59 V:Water Wizard,Moon Dark . . . 5.00
60 DP,HT,A:Black Juju 5.00
61 A:Arabian Knight 5.00
62 KJ,A:Arabian Knight 5.00
63 LMc,A:The Orb 5.00
64 BA,V:Azmodeus 5.00
65 A:Fowler 5.00
66 BL,A:Clothilde 5.00
67 DP,A:Sally Stantop 5.00
68 O:Ghost Rider 7.00
69 . . . . 5.00
70 I:Jeremy 5.00
71 DP,I:Adam Henderson 5.00
72 A:Circus of Crime 5.00
73 A:Circus of Crime 5.00
74 A:Centurions 5.00
75 I:Steel Wind 5.50
76 DP,A:Mephisto,I:Saturnine . . . 5.00
77 O:Ghost Rider's Dream 7.00
78 A:Nightmare 5.00
79 A:Man Cycles 5.00
80 A:Centurions 5.00
81 D:Ghost Rider 11.00

[2nd Regular Series]

1 JS,MT,I:2nd Ghost Rider, Deathwatch 25.00
1a 2nd printing 8.00
2 JS,MT,I:Blackout 16.00
3 JS,MT,A:Kingpin,V:Blackout, Deathwatch 13.00
4 JS,MT,V:Mr.Hyde 20.00
5 JLe(c),JS,MT,A:Punisher 15.00
5a rep.Gold 8.00
6 JS,MT,A:Punisher 10.00
7 MT,V:Scarecrow 8.00
8 JS,MT,V:H.E.A.R.T 8.00
9 JS,MT,A:Morlocks,X-Factor . . . 6.00
10 JS,MT,V:Zodiac 6.00
11 LSn,MT,V:Nightmare, A:Dr.Strange 5.00
12 JS,MT,A:Dr.Strange 5.00
13 MT,V:Snow Blind,R:J.Blaze . . . 6.00
14 MT,Blaze Vs.Ghost Rider. 6.00
15 MT,A:Blaze,V:Blackout Glow in Dark(c) 10.00
15a 2nd printing (gold) 5.00
16 MT,A:Blaze,Spider-Man, V:Hobgoblin 5.00
17 MT,A:Spider-Man,Blaze, V:Hobgoblin 5.00
18 MT,V:Reverend Styge 3.00
19 MT,A:Mephisto 3.00
20 MT(i),O:Zodiac 3.00
21 MT(i),V:Snowblind, A:Deathwatch 3.00
22 MT,A:Deathwatch,Ninjas 3.00
23 MT,I:Hag & Troll,A:Deathwatch 3.00
24 MT,V:Deathwatch,D:Snowblind, C:Johnny Blaze 3.00
25 V:Blackout (w/Center spread pop-up) 5.00
26 A:X-Men,V:The Brood 4.00
27 A:X-Men,V:The Brood 4.00
28 NKu,JKu,Rise of the Midnight Sons#1,V:Lilith,w/poster 4.50
29 NKu,JKu,A:Wolverine,Beast . . 3.00
30 NKu,JKu,V:Nightmare 2.50
31 NKu,JKu,Rise o/t Midnight Sons#6, A:Dr.Strange,Morbius, Nightstalkers,Redeemers, V:Lilith,w/poster 3.50
32 BBi,A:Dr.Strange 2.25
33 BBI,AW,V:Madcap (inc.Superman tribute on letters page) 2.25
34 BBI,V:Deathwatchs' ninja 2.00
35 BBI,AW,A:Heart Attack 2.00
36 BBI,V:Mr.Hyde,A:Daredevil . . . 2.00
37 BBI,A:Archangel,V:HeartAttack 2.00
38 MM,V:Scarecrow 2.00
39 V:Vengeance 2.00
40 Midnight Massacre#2, D:Demogblin 2.50
41 Road to Vengeance#1 . . . . . . 2.00
42 Road to Vengeance#2 . . . . . . 2.00
43 Road to Vengeance#3 . . . . . . 2.00
44 Siege of Darkness Pt.#2 . . . . . 2.00
45 Siege of Darkness Pt.#10 . . . . 2.00
46 HMe(s),New Beginning 2.00
47 HMe(s),RG, ... 2.00
48 HMe(s),RG,A:Spider-Man 2.00
49 HMe(s),RG,A:Hulk,w/card 2.25
50 Red Foil(c),AKu,SMc,A:Blaze, R:2nd Ghost Rider 2.95
50a Newsstand Ed. 2.50
51 SvL, ... 1.95
Ann.#1 I:Night Terror,w/card 3.25
TPB Midnight Sons,rep.GhR#28,31, Morbius#1,Darkhold#1,Spirirts of Vengeance#1,Nightstalkers#1 19.95
TPB Resurrected rep.#1-#7 . . . . 12.95
Poster Book 4.95

GHOST RIDER AND BLAZE: SPIRITS OF VENGEANCE

1 AKu,polybagged w/poster,V:Lilith, Rise of the Midnight Sons#2 . . 4.50
2 AKu,V:Steel Wind 2.50
3 AKu,CW,V:The Lilin 2.00
4 AKu,V:Hag & Troll,C:Venom . . 3.00
5 AKu,BR,Spirits of Venom#2, A:Venom,Spidey,Hobgoblin . . . 5.00
6 AKu,Spirits of Venom#4,A:Venom, Spider-Man,Hobgoblin 3.50
7 AKu,V:Steel Vengeance 2.00
8 V:Mephisto 2.00
9 I:Brimstone 2.00
10 AKu,V:Vengeance 2.00
11 V:Human Spider Creature 2.00
12 AKu,BR,Vengeance,glow in the dark(c) 3.25
13 AKu,Midnight Massacre#5 . . . 2.50
14 Missing Link#2 . . . . 2.00
15 Missing Link#3 . . . . 2.00
16 V:Zarathos,Lilith 2.00
17 HMe(s),Siege/Darkness Pt#8 . 2.00
18 HMe(s),Siege/Darkness Pt#13 2.00
19 HMe(s),HMz,V:Vampire 2.00
20 HMe(s),A:Steel Wind 2.00
21 HMe(s),HMz,V:Werewolves . . . 2.00
22 HMe(s),HMz,V:Cardiac 2.25
23 HMe(s),HMz,A:Steel Wind . . . 1.95

GHOST RIDER/CAPTAIN AMERICA: FEAR

1 GN, AW, V:Scarecrow 6.25

GHOST RIDER 2099

1 Holografx(c),LKa,CBa,MBu,I:Ghost Rider 2099,w/card 2.75
1a Newsstand Ed. 1.75
2 LKa,CBa,MBu, ... 1.50
3 LKa,CBa,MBu,Search & Destroy 1.50

G.I. JOE

June, 1982

1 HT,BMc,Baxter paper 5.00
2 DP,JAb,North Pole 6.00
3 HT,JAb,Trojan Robot 3.00
4 HT,JAb,Wingfield 3.00
5 DP,Central Park 3.00
6 HT,V:Cobra 3.00
7 HT,Walls of Death 3.00

G.I. Joe #44

© Marvel Entertainment Group

8 HT,Sea Strike 3.00
9 The Diplomat 3.00
10 Springfield 3.00
11 Alaska Pipeline 3.00
12 V:Snake Eyes 3.50
13 Rio Lindo 3.00
14 V:Destro 3.00
15 A:Red Eye 3.00
16 V:Cobra 3.00
17 Loose Ends 3.00
18 V:Destro 3.00
19 D:General Kwinn 3.00
20 JBy(c),GI,Clutch 3.00
21 SL(i),Silent Interlude 3.00
22 V:Destro 3.00
23 I:Duke 2.00
24 RH,I:Storm Shadow 3.00

25 FS,I:Zartan 3.00
26 SL(i),O:Snake Eyes 3.50
27 FS,O:Snake Eyes 3.00
28 Swampfire 3.00
29 FS,V:Destro 3.00
30 JBy(c),FS,V:Dreddnoks 3.00
31 V:Destro 2.00
32 FS,V:Dreddnoks 2.50
33 FS,Celebration 2.00
34 Shakedown 2.00
35 JBy(c),MBr,V:Dreddnoks 2.00
36 MBr,Shipwar 2.00
2a to 36a 2nd printings . . . . . @1.00
37 FS,Twin Brothers,I:Flint 2.00
38 V:Destro 2.00
39 Jungle 2.00
40 Hydrofoil 2.00
41 . . . . 2.00
42 A:Stormshadow 2.00
43 Death Issue,New Joe 2.00
44 V:Cobra 2.00
45 V:Cobra 2.00
46 V:Cobra 2.00
47 V:Cobra,D:Stormshadow 2.00
48 V:Cobra 2.00
49 V:Cobra,I:Serpentor 2.00
50 I:G.I.Joe Missions,R:S'shadow 2.25
51 V:Cobra Emperor 1.50
52 V:Stormshadow 1.50
53 Hawk V:Cobra 1.50
54 V:Destro 1.50
55 The Pit 1.50
56 V:Serpentor 1.50
57 V:Destro 1.50
58 V:Cobra 1.50
59 Armor 1.50
60 TM,I:Zanzibar 2.50
61 MR,D:Cobra Commander 1.25
62 Trial 1.25
63 A:GI Joe Snow Job 1.25
64 V:Baroness 1.25
65 V:Cobra 1.25
66 Stalker Rescued 1.25
67 . . . . 1.25
68 I:Battleforce 2000 . . . . 1.25
69 TSa 1.25
70 V:Destro 1.25
71 thru 74 . . . . @1.25
75 MR 1.25
76 D:Serpentor 1.25
77 MR,V:Cobra 1.25
78 V:Cobra 1.25
79 MR,V:Dreadnoks 1.25
80 V:Cobra 1.25
81 MR,V:Dreadnoks 1.00
82 MR,V:Cobra 1.00
83 I:RoadPig 1.00
84 MR,O:Zartan 1.00
85 Storm Shadow,Vs.Zartan 1.00
86 MR,25th Anniv. 1.00
87 TSa,V:Cobra 1.00
88 TSa,V:Python Patrol 1.00
89 MBr,V:Road Pig 1.00
90 MBr,R:Red Ninjas 1.00
91 TSa,V:Red Ninjas,D:Blind Masters 1.00
92 MBr,V:Cobra Condor 1.00
93 MBr,V:Baroness 1.00
94 MBr,A:Snake Eyes 1.00
95 MBr,A:Snake Eyes 1.00
96 MBr,A:Snake Eyes 1.00
97 . . . . 1.00
98 MBr,R:Cobra Commander 1.00
99 HT 1.00
100 MBr 1.50
101 MBr 1.00
102 MBr 1.00
103 MBr,A:Snake Eyes 1.00
104 MBr,A:Snake Eyes 1.00
105 MBr,A:Snake Eyes 1.00
106 MBr,StormShadowStalker . . . 1.00
107 . . . . 1.00
108 I:G.I.Joe Dossiers 1.00
109 Death Issue 1.00
110 Mid-East Crisis 1.00
111 A:Team Ninjas 1.00
112 A:Team Ninjas 1.00
113 V:Cobra 1.00
114 V:Cobra 1.00
115 Story Concl.Dusty Dossier . . 1.00
116 Destro:Search&Destroy #1 . . 1.00
117 Destro:Search&Destroy #2 . . 1.00
118 Destro:Search&Destroy #3 . . 1.00
119 HT,Android Dopplegangers . . 1.00
120 V:Red Ninjas,Slice & Dice . . . 1.00
121 V:Slice & Dice 1.25
122 V:Slice & Dice 1.25
123 I:Eco-Warriors,A:Big Man . . . 1.25
124 V:Headman 1.25
125 V:Headhunters 1.25
126 R:Firefly 1.25
127 R:Original G.I.Joe 1.25
128 V:Firefly 1.25
129 V:Cobra Commander 1.25
130 V:Cobra Commander 1.25
131 V:Cobra Commander 1.25
132 V:Cobra 1.25
133 V:Cobra 1.25
134 V:Red Ninjas, Firefly, Hostilities 1.25
135 V:Cobra Ninja w/card 1.75
136 w/Trading Card 1.75
137 V:Night Creepers,w/card 1.75
138 V:Night Creepers,w/card 1.75
139 R:Transformers,V:Cobra 1.25
140 A:Transformers 1.25
141 A:Transformers 1.25
142 A:Transformers 1.25
143 F:Scarlet 1.25
144 O:Snake Eyes 1.25
145 V:Cobra 1.25
146 F:Star Brigade 1.25
147 F:Star Brigade 1.25
148 F:Star Brigade 1.25
149 . . . . 1.25
150 Cobra Commander vs. Snake Eyes 2.00

G.I. JOE EUROPEAN MISSIONS
June, 1988

1 British rep. 1.25
2 . . . . 1.50
3 . . . . 1.50
4 . . . . 1.50
5 thru 15 . . . . @1.75

G.I. JOE SPECIAL MISSIONS
October, 1986

1 HT,New G.I. Joe 1.75
2 HT 1.50
3 HT 1.50
4 HT 1.50
5 HT 1.50
6 HT,Iron Curtain 1.50
7 HT 1.50
8 HT 1.50
9 HT 1.50
10 thru 21 HT . . . . @1.00
22 . . . . 1.00
23 HT 1.00
24 . . . . 1.00
25 HT 1.00
26 HT 1.00
27 . . . . 1.00
28 HT,final 1.00

G.I. JOE VS. TRANSFORMERS

1 HT,mini-series 1.75
2 HT,Cobra 1.50
3 HT,Cobra,Deceptions 1.00
4 HT,Cobra,Deceptions 1.00

G.I. JOE UNIVERSE

1 Biographies rep.#1 . . . . 2.50
2 . . . . 2.00
3 MZ(c) 2.00
4 . . . . 1.25

G.I. JOE YEARBOOK

1 Biographies 2.50
2 MG 2.00
3 MZ(c) 2.00
4 . . . . 2.00

G.I. TALES
See: SERGEANT BARNEY BARKER

GIRL COMICS
Atlas
November, 1949

1 Ph(c),True love stories,I Could Escape From Love 90.00
2 Ph(c),JKu,Blind Date 50.00
3 BEv,Ph(c),Liz Taylor 75.00
4 PH(c),Borrowed Love 35.00
5 Love stories 35.00
6 same 35.00
7 same 35.00
8 same 35.00
9 same 35.00
10 The Deadly Double-Cross . . . 35.00
11 Love stories 35.00
12 BK,The Dark Hallway 45.00
Becomes:

GIRL CONFESSIONS

13 . . . . 45.00
14 . . . . 30.00
15 . . . . 30.00
16 BEv 35.00
17 BEv 35.00
18 BEv 35.00
19 . . . . 25.00
20 . . . . 25.00
21 thru 34 . . . . @17.00
35 August, 1954 . . . . 17.00

GIRLS LIFE
Atlas
January, 1954

1 . . . . 40.00
2 . . . . 22.00
3 . . . . 15.00
4 . . . . 15.00
5 . . . . 15.00
6 November, 1954 . . . . 15.00

GODZILLA
August, 1977

1 HT,JM,Based on Movie Series 7.50
2 HT,FrG,GT,Seattle Under Seige 5.00
3 HT,TD,A;Champions 3.50
4 TS,TD,V;Batragon 3.50
5 TS,KJ,Isle of the Living Demons 5.00
6 HT,A Monster Enslaved 5.00
7 V:Red Ronin 5.00
8 V:Red Ronin 5.00
9 Las Gamble in Las Vegas . . . 5.00
10 V:Yetrigar 5.00
11 V;Red Ronin,Yetrigar 3.50
12 Star Sinister 3.50
13 V:Mega-Monster 3.50
14 V:Super-Beasts 3.50
15 Stampede 3.50
16 Jaws of Fear 3.50
17 Godzilla Shrunk 3.50
18 Battle Beneath Eighth Avenue . 3.50
19 Panic on the Pier 3.50
20 A;Fantastic Four 4.00
21 V;Devil Dinosaur 3.50
22 V:Devil Dinosaur 3.50
23 A;Avengers 4.00
24 July, 1979 . . . . 3.50

Godzilla #23
© Marvel Entertainment Group

GROO CHRONICLES
Epic
1989

1 SA 8.00
2 SA 4.00
3 SA 4.00
4 SA 4.00
5 SA 4.00
6 SA 3.50

GROO, THE WANDERER
(see Pacific, Eclipse)
Epic

1 SA,I:Minstrel 16.00
2 SA,A:Minstrel 10.00
3 SA,Medallions 7.00
4 SA,Airship 6.00
5 SA,Slavers 6.00
6 SA,The Eye of the Kabala 5.00
7 SA,A:Sage 5.00
8 SA,A:Taranto 6.00
9 SA,A:Sage 5.00
10 SA,I:Arcadio 5.00
11 SA,A:Arcadio 5.00
12 SA,Groo Meets the Thespians 4.00
13 SA,A:Sage 4.00
14 SA 4.00
15 SA,Monks 4.00
16 SA,A:Taranto 4.00
17 SA,Pirannas 4.00
18 SA,I:Groo Ella 4.00
19 SA,A:Groo Ella 3.00
20 SA,A:Groo Ella 3.00
21 SA,I:Arba,Dakarba 3.00
22 SA,Ambassador 3.00
23 SA,I:Pal,Drumm 3.00
24 SA,Arcadio's 3.00
25 SA,Taranto 3.00
26 SA,A:Arba,Taranto 3.00
27 SA,A:Minstrel,Sage 3.00
28 SA 3.00
29 SA,I:Ruferto 4.00
30 SA,A:Ruferto 3.00
31 SA,A:Pal,Drumm 2.00
32 SA,C:Sage 2.00
33 SA,Pirates 2.00
34 SA,Wizard's amulet 2.00
35 SA,A:Everybody 2.00
36 SA,A:Everybody 2.00
37 SA,A:Ruferto 2.00
38 SA,Dognappers 2.00
39 SA,A:Pal,Drumm 2.00
40 SA 2.00
41 SA,I:Granny Groo 2.00
42 SA,A:Granny Groo 2.00
43 SA,A:Granny Groo 2.00
44 SA,A:Ruferto 2.00
45 SA 2.00
46 SA,New Clothes 2.00
47 SA,A:Everybody 2.00
48 SA,A:Ruferto 2.00
49 SA,C:Chakaal 2.00
50 SA,double size 3.00
51 SA,A:Chakaal 2.00
52 SA,A:Chakaal 2.00
53 SA,A:Chakaal 2.00
54 SA,A:Ahak 2.00
55 SA,A:Ruferto 2.00
56 SA,A:Minstrael 2.00
57 SA,A:Ruferto 2.00
58 SA,A:Idol 2.00
59 SA 2.00
60 SA,A:Ruferto 2.00
61 SA,A:Horse 2.00
62 SA,A:Horse 1.75
63 SA,A:Drumm 1.75
64 SA,A:Artist 1.75
65 SA 1.75
66 SA 1.75
67 SA 1.75
68 SA 1.75
69 SA 1.75
70 SA 1.50
71 SA 1.50
72 SA 1.50
73 SA,Amnesia Pt1 . . . . . 1.50
74 SA,Amnesia Pt2 . . . . . 1.50
75 SA,Memory Returns 1.50
76 SA 1.50
77 SA 1.50
78 SA,R:Weaver,Scribe 1.50
79 SA,Groo the Assassin 1.50
80 SA,I:Thaiis Pt.1 . . . . . 1.50
81 SA,Thaiis Pt.2 . . . . . 1.50
82 SA,Thaiis Pt.3 . . . . . 1.50
83 SA,Thaiis Pt.4 . . . . . 1.50
84 SA,Thaiis Conclusion 1.50
85 SA,Groo turns invisible 1.50
86 SA,Invisible Groo 1.50
87 SA,Groo's Army 1.50
88 SA,V:Cattlemen,B.U. Sage . . . 2.50
89 SA,New Deluxe Format 2.25
90 SA,Worlds 1st Lawyers 2.25
91 SA,Bonus Pages 2.25
92 SA,Groo Becomes Kid Groo . . 2.25
93 SA,Groo destroys glacier 2.25
94 SA 2.25
95 SA,Endangered Species 2.25
96 SA,Wager of the Gods#1 . . . . 2.25
97 SA,Wager of the Gods#2 . . . . 2.25
98 SA,Wager of the Gods#3 . . . . 2.25
99 SA,E:Wager of the Gods 2.25
100 SA,Groo gets extra IQ points 2.75
101 SA,Groo loses intelligence . . 2.25
102 SA,F:Newly literate Groo 2.25
103 SA,General Monk 2.25
104 SA,F:Oso,Ruferto 2.25
105 SA,V:Minotaurs 2.25
106 SA,B:Man of the People 2.25
107 SA,Man of the People#2 . . . . 2.25
108 SA,Man of the People#3 . . . . 2.25
109 SA,E:Man of the People 2.25
110 SA,Mummies 2.25
111 SA,The Man who Killed Groo 2.25
112 SA,Rufferto Avenged 2.25
113 SA, ... 2.25
GNv Death of Groo 8.00
GNv 2nd print 8.00
TPB Groo Carnival 8.95

GROOVY
March, 1968

1 Monkeys,Ringo Starr,Photos . 50.00
2 Cartoons,Gags,Jokes 30.00
3 July, 1968 . . . . . 30.00

Guardians of the Galaxy #1
© Marvel Entertainment Group

GUARDIANS OF THE GALAXY
June, 1990

1 B:JV(a&s),I:Taserface,R:Aleta 10.00
2 MZ(c),JV,V:Stark,C:Firelord . . . 6.00
3 JV,V:Stark,I:Force,C:Firelord . . 5.00
4 JV,V:Stark,A:Force,Firelord . . . 4.00
5 JV,TM(c),V:Force,I:Mainframe (Vision) 4.00
6 JV,V:Force,Vance Possesses Capt.America Shield 4.00
7 GP(c),JV,I:Malevolence, O:Starhawk 4.50
8 SLi(c),JV,V:Yondu,C:Rancor . . 5.00
9 RLd(c),JV,I:Replica,Rancor . . . 6.00
10 JLe(c),JV,V:Rancor,The Nine I&C:Overkill(Taserface) 5.00
11 BWi(c),JV,V:Rancor,I:Phoenix . 5.00
12 ATb(c),JV,V:Overkill A:Firelord 3.00
13 JV,A:Ghost Rider,Force, Malevolence 7.00
14 JS(c),JV,A:Ghost Rider,Force, Malevolence 7.00
15 JSn(c),JV,I:Protege,V:Force . . 3.00
16 JV,V:Force,A:Protege, Malevolence,L:Vance Astro . . . 3.25
17 JV,V:Punishers(Street Army), L:Martinex,N:Charlie-27, ... 3.00
18 JV,V:Punishers,I&C:Talon,A: Crazy Nate 4.00
19 JV,V:Punishers,A:Talon 3.00
20 JV,I:Major Victory (Vance Astro) J:Talon & Krugarr 3.00
21 JV,V:Rancor 2.50
22 JV,V:Rancor 2.50
23 MT,V:Rancor,C:Silver Surfer . . 2.50
24 JV,A:Silver Surfer 3.50
25 JV, Prismatic Foil(c) V:Galactus,A:SilverSurfer 5.00
25a 2nd printing,Silver 2.50
26 JV,O:Guardians(retold) 2.00
27 JV,Infinity War,O:Talon, A:Inhumans 2.00
28 JV,Inf.War,V:Various Villians . . 2.00
29 HT,Inf.War,V:Various Villians . 2.00
30 KWe,A:Captain America 2.00
31 KWe,V:Badoon,A:Capt.A. 1.75
32 KWe,V:Badoon Gladiator 1.75

33 KWe,A:Dr.Strange,R:Aleta . . . 1.50
34 KWe,J:Yellowjacket II 1.50
35 KWe,A:Galatic Guardians, V:Bubonicus 1.50
36 KWe,A:Galatic Guardians, V:Dormammu 1.50
37 KWe,V:Dormammu,A:Galatic Guardians 1.50
38 KWe,N:Y.jacket,A:Beyonder . . 1.50
39 KWe,Rancor Vs. Dr.Doom,Holografx(c) 3.25
40 KWe,V:Loki,Composite 1.50
41 KWe,V:Loki,A:Thor 1.50
42 KWe,I:Woden 1.50
43 KWe,A:Woden,V:Loki 1.50
44 KWe,R:Yondu 1.50
45 KWe,O:Starhawk 1.50
46 KWe,N:Major Victory 1.50
47 KWe,A:Beyonder,Protoge, Overkill 1.50
48 KWe,V:Overkill 1.75
49 KWe,A:Celestial 1.75
50 Foil(c),R:Yondu,Starhawk separated,BU:O:Guardians 2.95
Ann.#1 Korvac Quest #4,I:Krugarr 3.00
Ann.#2 HT,I:Galactic Guardians, System Bytes #4 . . . . 3.00
Ann.#3 CDo,I:Irish Wolfhound, w/Trading card 3.25
TPB rep #1 thru #6 . . . . 12.95

GUNHAWK, THE
See: BLAZE CARSON

GUNHAWKS
October, 1972

1 SSh,B:Reno Jones & Kid Cassidy Two Rode Together . . 4.00
2 Ride out for Revenge 2.75
3 Indian Massacre 2.75
4 Trial by Ordeal 2.75
5 The Reverend Mr. Graves 2.75
6 E:Reno Jones & Kid Cassidy D:Kid Cassidy 2.75
7 A Gunhawks Last Stand A;Reno Jones, October, 1973 2.75

GUNRUNNER

1 I:Gunrunner,w/trading cards . . . 2.95
2 A:Ghost Rider 2.00
3 V:Cynodd 2.00
4 . . . . 2.00
5 A:Enhanced 2.00

GUNSLINGER
See: TEX DAWSON, GUNSLINGER

GUNSMOKE WESTERN
See: ALL WINNERS COMICS

HARROWERS

1 MSt(s),GC,F:Pinhead 3.25
2 GC,AW(i), ... 2.75
3 GC,AW(i), ... 2.75
4 GC,AW(i), ... 2.75
5 GC,AW(i),Devil's Pawn#1 . . . . 2.75
6 GC,AW(i),Devil's Pawn#2 . . . . 2.75

HARVEY
October, 1970

1 . . . . 6.00
2 thru 5 . . . . @4.00
6 December, 1972 . . . . 4.00

HAVOK & WOLVERINE
Epic
March, 1988

1 JMu,KW,V:KGB,Dr.Neutron . . . 7.00
2 JMu,KW,V:KGB,Dr.Neutron . . . 5.00
3 JMu,KW,V:Meltdown 5.00
4 JMu,KW,V:Meltdown,Oct.1989 . 5.00

TPB rep.#1-4 . . . . 16.95

Hawkeye Limited Series #4
© Marvel Entertainment Group

HAWKEYE
September, 1983
[1st Limited Series]

1 A:Mockingbird 3.00
2 I:Silencer 2.50
3 I:Bombshell,Oddball 2.00
4 V:Crossfire,W:Hawkeye & Mockingbird, (Dec. 1983) 2.00

[2nd Limited Series]

1 B:CDi(s),ScK,V:Trickshot, I:Javelynn,Rover 2.00
2 ScK,V:Viper 2.00
3 ScK,A:War Machine,N:Hawkeye, V:Secret Empire 2.00
4 E:CDi(s),ScK,V:Trickshot,Viper, Javelynn 2.00

HEADMASTERS
STAR
July, 1987

1 FS,Transformers 1.25
2 . . . . 1.00
3 . . . . 1.00
4 January, 1988 75

HEARTS OF DARKNESS

One Shot JR2/KJ,F:G.R.,Punisher, Wolverine,V:Blackheart,(double Gatefold Cover) 5.50

HEATHCLIFF
Star
April, 1985

1 thru 16 . . . . @1.00
17 Masked Moocher 1.00
18 thru 49 . . . . @1.00
50 Double-size 1.00
51 thru 55 . . . . @1.00

HEATHCLIFF'S FUNHOUSE
Star
May, 1987

1 thru 9 . . . . @1.00
10 1988 . . . . 1.00

HEAVY HITTERS

Ann.#1 . . . . 4.00

HEDY DEVINE COMICS
August, 1947

22 I:Hedy Devine 50.00
23 BW,Beauty and the Beach, HK,Hey Look 56.00
24 High Jinx in Hollywood, HK, Hey Look 56.00
25 Hedy/Bull(c),HK,Hey Look . . . 60.00
26 Skating(c),HK,Giggles&Grins . 40.00
27 Hedy at Show(c),HK,Hey Look 56.00
28 Hedy/Charlie(c),HK,Hey Look 56.00
29 Tennis(c),HK,Hey Look 56.00
30 . . . . 56.00
31 thru 34 . . . . @25.00
35 thru 49 . . . . @25.00
50 September, 1952 . . . . 25.00

HEDY WOLFE
Atlas
August, 1957

1 Patsy Walker's Rival 35.00

HELLHOUND

1 Hellhound on my Trial 2.50
2 Love in Vain 2.50
3 Last Fair Deal Gone Down 2.25

HELLRAISER
See: CLIVE BARKER'S HELLRAISER

HELLRAISER III HELL ON EARTH

1 Movie Adaptation,(prestige) . . . 4.95
1a Movie Adapt.(magazine) 2.95

HELLSTORM

1 R:Daimon Hellstrom, Parchment(c) 4.00
2 A:Dr.Strange,Gargoyle 3.00
3 O:Hellstorm. 2.75
4 V:Ghost Rider 2.75
5 MB, ... 2.50
6 MB,V:Dead Daughter 2.50
7 A:Armaziel 2.50
8 Hell is where the heart is 2.25
9 LKa(s),Highway to Heaven . . . 2.25
10 LKa(s),Heaven's Gate 2.25
11 LKa(s),PrG,Life in Hell 2.25
12 Red Miracles 2.25
13 Red Miracles Sidewalking 2.25
14 Red Miracles Murder is Easy . 2.25
15 Cigarette Dawn 2.00

HELL'S ANGEL

1 GSr,A:X-Men,O:Hell's Angel . . 3.00
2 GSr,A:X-Men,V:Psycho Warriors 2.50
3 GSr,A:X-Men,V:MyS-Tech 2.00
4 GSr,A:X-Men,V:MyS-Tech 2.00
5 GSr,A:X-Men,V:MyS-Tech 2.00
6 Gfr,A:X-Men,V:MyS-Tech 2.00
7 DMn,A:Psylocke,V:MyS-Tech . . 2.00

Becomes:

DARK ANGEL

8 DMn,A:Psylocke 2.00
9 A:Punisher 2.00
10 MyS-Tech Wars tie-in 2.00
11 A:X-Men,MyS-Tech wars tie-in 2.00
12 A:X-Men 2.00
13 A:X-Men,Death's Head II 2.00
14 Afthermath#2 . . . . 1.75
15 Afthermath#3 . . . . 1.75
16 SvL,E:Afthermath,last issue . . 1.75

HERCULES PRINCE OF POWER
September, 1982

1 BL,I:Recorder 3.00
2 BL,I:Layana Sweetwater 2.00

Hell's Angel #4
© Marvel Entertainment Group

3 BL,V:The Brothers,C:Galactus . 2.00
4 BL,A:Galactus 2.00

[2nd Series]
March, 1984
1 BL,I:Skyypi 2.50
2 BL,A:Red Wolf 1.50
3 BL,A:Starfox 1.50
4 BL,D:Zeus, June, 1984 . . . . . . 1.50

HERO
May, 1990
1 . . . . 2.50
2 . . . . 2.00
3 . . . . 1.50
4 RH 1.50
5 RH 1.50
6 October, 1990 . . . . 1.50

HERO FOR HIRE
June, 1972
1 GT,JR,I&O:Power Man 36.00
2 GT,A:Diamond Back 15.00
3 GT,I:Mace 12.00
4 V:Phantom of 42nd St. 12.00
5 GT,A:Black Mariah 12.00
6 V:Assassin 7.00
7 GT,Nuclear Bomb issue 7.00
8 GT,A:Dr.Doom 7.00
9 GT,A:Dr.Doom,Fant.Four 7.00
10 GT,A:Dr.Death,Fant.Four 7.00
11 GT,A:Dr.Death 6.00
12 GT,C:Spider-Man 6.00
13 A:Lion Fang 6.00
14 V:Big Ben 6.00
15 Cage Goes Wild 6.00
16 O:Stilletto,D:Rackham 6.00
Becomes: POWER MAN

HEROES FOR HOPE
1 TA/JBy/HC/RCo/BWr,A:XMen . 6.00

HOKUM & HEX
Razorline
1 BU:Saint Sinner 2.75
2 I:Analyzer 2.00
3 I:Wrath 2.00
4 I:Z-Man 2.00
5 V:Hyperkind 2.00
6 B:Bloodshed 2.00
7 V:Bloodshed 2.00
8 V:Bloodshed 2.00
9 E:Bloodshed,final issue 2.25

HOLIDAY COMICS
January, 1951
1 LbC(c),Christmas(c) 100.00
2 LbC(c),Easter Parade(c) . . . 100.00
3 LbC(c),4th of July(c) 80.00
4 LbC(c),Summer Vacation . . . 65.00
5 LbC(c),Christmas(c) 70.00
6 LbC(c),Birthday(c) 80.00
7 LbC(c),Rodeo (c) 65.00
8 LbC(c),Christmas(c)
October, 1952 . . . . 65.00

HOLLYWOOD SUPERSTARS
Epic
November, 1990
1 DSp 2.00
2 thru 4 DSp . . . . @2.25
5 DSp, March, 1991 . . . . 2.25

HOMER, THE HAPPY GHOST
March, 1955
1 . . . . 45.00
2 . . . . 25.00
3 . . . . 16.00
4 thru 15 . . . . @16.00
16 thru 22 . . . . @14.00

[2nd Series]
November, 1969
1 . . . . 8.00
2 thru 5 . . . . @7.50

HOOK
1 JRy,GM,movie adaption 1.00
2 JRy,Return to Never Land 1.00
3 Peter Pans Magic 1.00
4 conclusion 1.00
Hook Super Spec.#1 . . . . 2.95

HORRORS, THE
January, 1953
11 LbC(c),The Spirit of War 90.00
12 LbC(c),Under Fire 75.00
13 LbC(c),Terror Castle 75.00
14 LbC(c),Underworld Terror . . . 75.00
15 LbC(c),The Mad Bandit,
April, 1954 . . . . 75.00

HOUSE II
1 1987, Movie Adapt 2.00

HOWARD THE DUCK
January, 1976
1 FB,SL,A:SpiderMan,I:Beverly . . 7.00
2 FB,V:TurnipMan&Kidney Lady . 2.00
3 JB,Learns Quack Fu 1.50
4 GC,V:Winky Man 1.50
5 GC,Becomes Wrestler 1.50
6 GC,V:Gingerbread Man 1.50
7 GC,V:Gingerbread Man 1.50
8 GC,A:Dr.Strange,ran for Pres. . 1.50
9 GC,V:Le Beaver 1.00
10 GC,A:Spider-Man 2.00
11 GC,V:Kidney Lady 1.00
12 GC,I:Kiss 4.00
13 GC,A:Kiss 4.00
14 GC,Howard as Son of Satan . . 2.00
15 GC,A:Dr.Strange,A:Dr.Bong . . 1.00
16 GC,DC,JB,DG,TA,
V:Incredible Creator 1.00
17 GC,D:Dr.Bong 1.00
18 GC,Howard the Human #1 . . . 1.00
19 GC,Howard the Human #2 . . . 1.00
20 GC,V:Sudd 1.00
21 GC,V:Soofi 1.00
22 A:ManThing,StarWars Parody . 1.00
23 A:ManThing,StarWars Parody . 1.00
24 GC,NightAfter..SavedUniverse 1.00

Howard the Duck #7
© Marvel Entertainment Group

25 GC,V:Circus of Crime 1.00
26 GC,V:Circus of Crime 1.00
27 GC,V:Circus of Crime 1.00
28 GC,Cooking With Gas 1.00
29 Duck-Itis Poster Child 1978 . . . 1.00
30 Iron Duck,V:Dr. Bong 1.00
31 Iron Duck,V:Dr. Bong 1.00
32 V:Gopher 1.00
33 BB(c),The Material Duck 1.00
Ann.#1, V:Caliph of Bagmom 1.00

HOWARD THE DUCK MAGAZINE
October, 1979
(black & white)
1 . . . . 2.50
2 . . . . 1.50
3 . . . . 1.50
4 Beatles,Elvis,Kiss 5.00
5 . . . . 1.50
6 . . . . 1.50
7 . . . . 2.00
8 . . . . 1.50
9 March, 1981 . . . . 1.50

HUGGA BUNCH
Star Comics
October, 1986
1 . . . . 1.25
2 thru 5 . . . . @1.00
6 August, 1987 . . . . 1.00

HUMAN FLY
July, 1987
1 I&O:Human Fly,A:Spider-Man . 5.00
2 A:Ghost Rider 7.50
3 DC,JSt(c),DP,'Fortress of Fear' 1.75
4 JB/TA(c),'David Drier' 1.75
5 V:Makik 1.75
6 Fear in Funland 1.75
7 ME,Fury in the Wind 1.75
8 V:White Tiger 1.75
9 JB/TA(c),ME,V:Copperhead,A:
White Tiger,Daredevil 1.75
10 ME,Dark as a Dungeon 1.75
11 ME,A:Daredevil 1.75
12 ME,Suicide Sky-Dive 1.75
13 BLb/BMc(c),FS,V:Carl Braden . 1.75
14 BLb/BMc(c),SL,Fear Over
Fifth Avenue 1.75

Human Fly #3
© Marvel Entertainment Group

15 BLb/BMc(c),War in the Washington Monument 1.75
16 BLb/BMc(c),V:Blaze Kendall 1.75
17 BLb,DP,Murder on the Midway 1.75
18 V:Harmony Whyte 1.75
19 BL(c),V:Jacopo Belbo March, 1979 1.75

RED RAVEN COMICS
Timely Comics
August, 1940

1 JK,O:Red Raven,I:Magar,A:Comet Pierce & Mercury,Human Top, Eternal Brain 7,000.00

Becomes:

HUMAN TORCH
Fall, 1940

2 (#1)ASh(c),BEv,B:Sub-Mariner A:Fiery Mask,Falcon,Mantor, Microman 10,000.00
3 (#2)Ash(c),BEv,V:Sub-Mariner,Bondage(c) 2,400.00
4 (#3)ASh(c),BEv,O:Patriot 1,800.00
5 (#4)V:Nazis,A:Patriot,Angel crossover 1,300.00
5a(#5)ASh(c),V:Sub-Mariner 1,800.00
6 ASh(c),Doom Dungeon 800.00
7 ASh(c),V:Japanese 800.00
8 ASh(c),BW,V:Sub-Mariner 1,350.00
9 ASh(c),V:General Rommel 800.00
10 ASh(c),BW,V:Sub-Mariner 900.00
11 ASh(c),Nazi Oil Refinery 600.00
12 ASh(c),V:Japanese, Bondage(c) 600.00
13 ASh(c),V:Japanese, Bondage(c) 600.00
14 ASh(c),V:Nazis 600.00
15 ASh(c),Toro Trapped 600.00
16 ASh(c),V:Japanese 500.00
17 ASh(c),V:Japanese 500.00
18 ASh(c),V:Japanese, MacArthurs HQ 500.00
19 ASh(c),Bondage(c) 500.00
20 ASh(c),Last War Issue 500.00
21 ASh(c),V:Organized Crime 500.00
22 ASh(c),V:Smugglers 500.00
23 ASh(c),V:Giant Robot 500.00
24 V:Mobsters 500.00
25 The Masked Monster 500.00
26 Her Diary of Terror 500.00

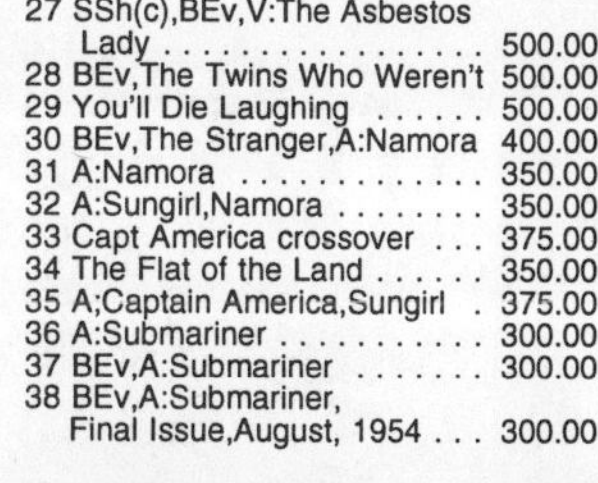
27 SSh(c),BEv,V:The Asbestos Lady 500.00
28 BEv,The Twins Who Weren't 500.00
29 You'll Die Laughing 500.00
30 BEv,The Stranger,A:Namora 400.00
31 A:Namora 350.00
32 A:Sungirl,Namora 350.00
33 Capt America crossover 375.00
34 The Flat of the Land 350.00
35 A;Captain America,Sungirl 375.00
36 A:Submariner 300.00
37 BEv,A:Submariner 300.00
38 BEv,A:Submariner, Final Issue,August, 1954 300.00

Human Torch #3
© Marvel Entertainment Group

HUMAN TORCH
September, 1974

1 JK,rep.StrangeTales #101 6.00
2 rep.Strange Tales #102 4.00
3 rep.Strange Tales #103 4.00
4 rep.Strange Tales #104 4.00
5 rep.Strange Tales #105 4.00
6 rep.Strange Tales #106 4.00
7 rep.Strange Tales #107 4.00
8 rep.Strange Tales #108 4.00

HYPERKIND
Razorline

1 I:Hyperkind,BU:EctoKid 2.75
2 I:Bliss 2.00
3 V:Living Void 2.00
4 FBk(s),I:Paragon John 2.00
5 V:Paragon John 2.00
6 Vetus Unleashed 2.00
7 2.00
8 I:Tempest 2.00
9 I:Lazurex,w/card 2.25

ICEMAN
December, 1984

1 DP,mini-series 2.00
2 DP,V:Kali 1.50
3 DP,A;Original X-Men,Defenders Champions 1.50
4 DP,Oblivion,June, 1985 1.50

IDEAL
Timely
July, 1948

1 Antony and Cleopatra 175.00
2 The Corpses of Dr.Sacotti 150.00
3 Joan of Arc 125.00
4 Richard the Lionhearted A:The Witness 200.00
5 Phc,Love and Romance 70.00

Becomes:

LOVE ROMANCES

6 Phc,I Loved a Scoundrel 38.00
7 30.00
8 34.00
9 thru 20 @19.00
21 33.00
22 19.00
23 19.00
24 33.00
25 30.00
26 thru 34 @16.00
35 16.00
36 30.00
37 16.00
38 30.00
39 16.00
40 thru 44 @16.00
45 19.00
46 15.00
47 15.00
48 10.00
49 29.00
50 10.00
51 10.00
52 10.00
53 29.00
54 10.00
55 10.00
56 10.00
57 19.00
58 thru 74 @10.00
75 18.00
76 10.00
77 10.00
78 18.00
79 10.00
80 10.00
81 10.00
82 JK(c) 18.00
83 10.00
84 JK 20.00
85 23.00
86 thru 95 @8.00
96 JK 18.00
97 10.00
98 JK 30.00
99 JK 18.00
100 10.00
101 10.00
102 10.00
103 10.00
104 10.00
105 JK 18.00
106 JKJuly, 1963 18.00

IDEAL COMICS
Timely
Fall, 1944

1 B:Super Rabbit,Giant Super Rabbit V:Axis(c) 80.00
2 Super Rabbit at Fair(c) 56.00
3 Beach Party(c) 45.00
4 How to Catch Robbers 45.00

Becomes:

WILLIE COMICS

5 B:Willie,George,Margie,Nellie Football(c) 58.00
6 Record Player(c) 30.00
7 Soda Fountain(c),HK,Hey Look 42.00
8 Fancy Dress(c) 30.00
9 30.00
10 HK,Hey Look 40.00
11 HK,Hey Look 40.00
12 25.00
13 35.00
14 thru 18 @24.00
19 35.00

20 Li'L Willie Comics 24.00
21 Li'L Willie Comics 24.00
22 . . . . 24.00
23 May, 1950 . . . . 24.00

IDOL
Epic

1 I:Idol 2.95
2 Phantom o/t Set 2.95
3 Conclusion 2.95

IMMORTALIS

1 A:Dr.Strange 1.95
2 A:Dr.Strange 1.95
3 A:Dr.Strange,V:Vampires 1.95

IMPOSSIBLE MAN SUMMER VACATION

1 GCa,DP 2.50
2 . . . . 2.00

INCAL, THE
Epic
November, 1988

1 Moebius,Adult 2.50
2 Moebius,Adult 2.00
3 Moebius,Adult, January, 1989 . 2.00

INCOMPLETE DEATH'S HEAD

1 thru 10 rep.Death's Head #1
thru #10 . . . . @2.00
11 rep.Death's Head #11 . . . . 1.75

INCREDIBLE HULK
May, 1962

1 JK,I:Hulk(Grey Skin),Rick Jones,
Thunderbolt Ross,Betty Ross,
Gremlin,Gamma Base . . . 6,000.00
2 JK,SD,O:Hulk,(Green skin) 1,500.00
3 JK,O:rtd.,I:Ring Master,
Circus of Crime 1,000.00
4 JK,V:Mongu 800.00
5 JK,I:General Fang 800.00
6 SD,I:Metal Master 1,400.00
See: **Tales to Astonish #57-#101**
April, 1968
102 MSe,GT,O:Retold 175.00
103 MSe,I:Space Parasite 90.00
104 MSe,O&N:Rhino 75.00
105 MSe,GT,I:Missing Link 55.00
106 MSe,HT,GT 50.00
107 HT,V:Mandarin 50.00
108 HT,JMe,A:Nick Fury 50.00
109 HT,JMe,A:Ka-Zar 50.00
110 HT,JMe,A:Ka-Zar 50.00
111 HT,DA,I:Galaxy Master 25.00
112 HT,DA,O:Galaxy Master . . . 25.00
113 HT,DA,V:Sandman 25.00
114 HT,DA 25.00
115 HT,DA,A:Leader 25.00
116 HT,DA,V:Super Humanoid . 25.00
117 HT,DA,A:Leader 25.00
118 HT,V:Sub-Mariner 25.00
119 HT,V:Maximus 16.00
120 HT,V:Maximus 16.00
121 HT,I:The Glob 16.00
122 HT,V:Thing 20.00
123 HT,V:Leader 16.00
124 HT,SB,V:Rhino,Leader 16.00
125 HT,V:Absorbing Man 16.00
126 HT,A:Dr.Strange 16.00
127 HT,Moleman vs.Tyrannus
I:Mogol 10.00
128 HT,A:Avengers 10.00
129 HT,V:Glob 10.00
130 HT,Banner Vs Hulk 10.00
131 HT,A:Iron Man 9.00
132 HT,JSe,V:Hydra 9.00
133 HT,JSe,I:Draxon 9.00
134 HT,SB,I:Golem 9.00
135 HT,SB,V:Kang 9.00

Incredible Hulk #107
© Marvel Entertainment Group

Incredible Hulk #316
© Marvel Entertainment Group

136 HT,SB,I:Xeron 9.00
137 HT,V:Abomination 9.00
138 HT,V:Sandman 9.00
139 HT,V:Leader 9.00
140 HT,V:Psyklop 9.00
141 HT,JSe,I&O:Doc Samson . . 10.00
142 HT,JSe,V:Valkyrie,A:Doc
Samson 7.50
143 DA,JSe,V:Dr.Doom 7.50
144 DA,JSe,V:Dr.Doom 7.50
145 HT,JSe,O:Retold 9.00
146 HT,JSe,Leader 6.00
147 HT,JSe,Doc Samson loses
Powers 6.00
148 HT,JSe,I:Fialan 6.00
149 HT,JSe,I:Inheritor 6.00
150 HT,JSe,I:Viking,A:Havoc 6.50
151 HT,JSe,C:Ant Man 6.00
152 HT,DA,Many Cameos 6.00
153 HT,JSe,C:Capt.America 6.00
154 HT,JSe,A:Ant Man,
V:Chameleon 6.00
155 HT,JSe,I:Shaper of Worlds . . 6.00
156 HT,V:Hulk 6.00
157 HT,I:Omnivac,Rhino 6.00
158 HT,C:Warlock,V:Rhino 6.00
159 HT,V:Abomination,Rhino 6.00
160 HT,V:Tiger Shark 6.00
161 HT,V:Beast 8.00
162 HT,I:Wendigo I 9.50
163 HT,I:Gremlin 6.00
164 HT,I:Capt.Omen 6.00
165 HT,I:Aquon 6.00
166 HT,I:Zzzax 6.00
167 HT,JAb,V:Modok 6.00
168 HT,JAb,I:Harpy 6.00
169 HT,JAb,I:Bi-Beast 6.00
170 HT,JAb,V:Volcano 6.00
171 HT,JAb,A:Abomination,Rhino 6.00
172 HT,JAb,X:X-Men 7.00
173 HT,V:Cobolt Man 6.00
174 HT,V:Cobolt Man 6.00
175 JAb,V:Inhumans 6.00
176 HT,JAb,A:Man-Beast,C:Warlock
Crisis on Counter-Earth 11.00
177 HT,JAb,D:Warlock 15.00
178 HT,JAb,Warlock Lives 15.00
179 HT,JAb, ... 6.00
180 HT,JAb,I:Wolverine
V:Wendigo I 110.00
181 HT,JAb,A:Wolverine (1st
Full Story),V:Wendigo II . . . 350.00
182 HT,JAb,I&D:Crackajack
Jackson,C:Wolverine 60.00
183 HT,V:Zzzaz 5.00
184 HT,V:Living Shadow 5.00
185 HT,V:General Ross 5.00
186 HT,I:Devastator 5.00
187 HT,JSt,V:Gremlin 5.00
188 HT,JSt,I:Droog 5.00
189 HT,JSt,I:Datrine 5.00
190 HT,MSe,Toadman 5.00
191 HT,JSt,Toadman,I:Glorian . . . 5.00
192 HT,V:The Lurker 5.00
193 HT,JSt,Doc.Samson regains
Powers 5.00
194 SB,JSt,V:Locust 5.00
195 SB,JSt,V:Abomination 5.00
196 SB,JSt,V:Army 5.00
197 BWr(c),SB,JSt,A:Man-Thing . 5.00
198 SB,JSt,A:Man-Thing 5.00
199 SB,JSt,V:Shield,Doc Samson 5.00
200 SB,JSt,Multi,Hulk in Glenn
Talbots Brain 33.00
201 SB,JSt,V:Fake Conan 4.00
202 SB,JSt,A:Jarella 4.00
203 SB,JSt,A:Jarella 4.00
204 SB,JStI:Kronus 4.00
205 SB,JSt,D:Jarella 4.00
206 SB,JSt,C:Dr.Strange 4.00
207 SB,JSt,A:Dr.Strange 4.00
208 SB,JSt,V:Absorbing Man 4.00
209 SB,JSt,V:Absorbing Man 4.00
210 SB,A:Dr.Druid,O:Merlin II . . . 4.00
211 SB,A:Dr.Druid 4.00
212 SB,I:Constrictor 4.50
213 SB,TP,I:Quintronic Man 4.00
214 SB,Jack of Hearts 4.00
215 SB,V:Bi-Beast 3.50
216 SB,Gen.Ross 3.50
217 SB,I:Stilts,A:Ringmaster 3.50
218 SB,KP,Doc Samson versus
Rhino 3.50
219 SB,V:Capt.Barravuda 3.50
220 SB,Robinson Crusoe 3.50
221 SB,AA,A:Sting Ray 3.50
222 JSn,AA,Cavern of Bones . . . 3.50
223 SB,V:Leader 3.50
224 SB,V:The Leader 3.50
225 SB,V:Leader,A:Doc Samson . 3.50
226 SB,JSt,A:Doc Samson 3.50
227 SB,JK,A:Doc Samson 3.50

All comics prices listed are for *Near Mint* condition.

Incredible Hulk #340
© Marvel Entertainment Group

228 SB,BMc,I:Moonstone,V:Doc Samson . . . 3.50
229 SB,O:Moonstone,V:Doc Samson . . . 3.50
230 JM,BL,A:Bug Thing . . . 3.50
231 SB,I:Fred Sloan . . . 3.50
232 SB,A:Capt.America . . . 3.50
233 SB,A:Marvel Man . . . 3.50
234 SB,Marvel Man Changes name to Quasar . . . 3.50
235 SB,A:Machine Man . . . 3.50
236 SB,A:Machine Man . . . 3.50
237 SB,A:Machine Man . . . 3.50
238 SB,JAb,Jimmy Carter . . . 3.50
239 SB,I:Gold Bug . . . 3.50
240 SB,Eldorado . . . 3.50
241 SB,A:Tyrannus . . . 3.00
242 SB,Eldorado . . . 3.00
243 SB,A:Gammernon . . . 3.00
244 SB,A:It . . . 3.00
245 SB,A:Super Mandroid . . . 3.00
246 SB,V:Capt.Marvel . . . 3.00
247 SB,A:Bat Dragon . . . 3.00
248 SB,V:Gardener . . . 3.00
249 SD,R:Jack Frost . . . 3.00
250 SB,A:Silver Surfer . . . 12.00
251 MG,A:3-D Man . . . 3.00
252 SB,A:Woodgod . . . 3.00
253 SB,A:Woodgod . . . 3.00
254 SB,I:U-Foes . . . 3.00
255 SB,V:Thor . . . 3.00
256 SB,I&O:Sabra . . . 3.00
257 SB,I&O:Arabian Knight . . . 3.00
258 I:Soviet Super Soldiers . . . 3.00
259 SB,A:Soviet Super-Soldiers O:Darkstar . . . 3.00
260 SB,Sugata . . . 3.00
261 SB,V:Absorbing Man . . . 3.00
262 SB,I:Glazer . . . 3.00
263 SB,Avalanche . . . 3.00
264 SB,A:Corruptor . . . 3.00
265 SB,I:Rangers . . . 3.50
266 SB,V:High Evolutionary . . . 2.50
267 SB,V:Rainbow,O:Glorian . . . 2.50
268 SB,I:Pariah . . . 2.50
269 SB,I:Bereet . . . 2.50
270 SB,A:Abomination . . . 2.50
271 SB,I:Rocket Raccoon, 20th Anniv. . . . 2.50
272 SB,C:X-Men,I:Wendigo III . . . 4.00
273 SB,A:Alpha Flight . . . 4.00
274 SB,Beroct . . . 2.50
275 SB,JSt,I:Megalith . . . 2.50
276 SB,JSt,V:U-Foes . . . 2.50
277 SB,JSt,U-Foes . . . 2.50
278 SB,JSt,C:X-Men, Avengers,Fantastic Four . . . 2.50
279 SB,JSt,C:X-Men, Avengers,Fantastic Four . . . 2.50
280 SB,JSt,Jack Daw . . . 2.50
281 SB,JSt,Trapped in Space . . . 2.50
282 SB,JSt,A:She Hulk . . . 2.50
283 SB,JSt,A:Avengers . . . 2.50
284 SB,JSt,A:Avengers . . . 2.50
285 SB,JSt,Northwind,V:Zzzax . . . 2.50
286 SB,JSt,V:Soldier . . . 2.50
287 SB,JSt,V:Soldier . . . 2.50
288 SB,JSt,V:Abomination . . . 2.50
289 SB,JSt,V:Modok . . . 2.50
290 SB,JSt,V:Modok . . . 2.50
291 SB,JSt,V:Thunderbolt Ross . . . 2.50
292 SB,JSt,V:Dragon Man . . . 2.50
293 SB,V:Nightmare . . . 2.50
294 SB,V:Boomerang . . . 2.50
295 SB,V:Boomerang . . . 2.50
296 SB,A:Rom . . . 2.50
297 SB,V:Nightmare . . . 2.50
298 KN(c),SB,V:Nightmare . . . 2.50
299 SB,A:Shield . . . 2.50
300 SB,A:Spider-Man,Avengers Doctor Strange . . . 6.00
301 SB,Crossroads . . . 2.50
302 SB,Crossroads . . . 2.50
303 SB,V:The Knights . . . 2.50
304 SB,V:U-Foes . . . 2.50
305 SB,V:U-Foes . . . 2.50
306 SB,V:Klaatu . . . 2.50
307 SB,V:Klaatu . . . 2.50
308 SB,V:Puffball Collective . . . 2.50
309 SB,V:Goblin & Glow . . . 2.50
310 Crossroads . . . 2.50
311 Crossroads . . . 2.50
312 Secret Wars II,O:Bruce . . . 3.50
313 A:Alpha Flight . . . 2.50
314 JBy,V:Doc Samson . . . 6.00
315 JBy,A:Doc Samson,Banner & Hulk Separated . . . 3.00
316 JBy,A:Avengers,N:Doc Samson . . . 3.00
317 JBy,I:Hulkbusters,A:Doc Samson . . . 3.00
318 JBy,A:Doc Samson . . . 3.00
319 JBy,W:Bruce & Betty . . . 5.00
320 AM,A:Doc Samson . . . 2.50
321 AM,A:Avengers . . . 2.50
322 AM,A:Avengers . . . 2.50
323 AM,A:Avengers . . . 2.50
324 AM,R:Grey Hulk(1st since #1), A:Doc Samson . . . 11.00
325 AM,Rick Jones as Hulk . . . 3.50
326 A:Rick Jones,New Hulk . . . 6.00
327 AM,F:General Ross . . . 2.50
328 AM,1st PDd(s),Outcasts . . . 10.00
329 AM,V:Enigma . . . 5.00
330 1st TM Hulk,D:T-bolt Ross . 30.00
331 TM,V:Leader . . . 23.00
332 TM,V:Leader . . . 15.00
333 TM,V:Leader . . . 15.00
334 TM,I:Half-life . . . 15.00
335 HorrorIssue . . . 5.00
336 TM,A:X-Factor . . . 15.00
337 TM,A:X-Factor, A:Doc Samson . . . 15.00
338 TM,I:Mercy,V:Shield . . . 15.00
339 TM,A:RickJones . . . 15.00
340 TM,Hulk vs Wolverine . . . 50.00
341 TM,V:Man Bull . . . 11.00
342 TM,V:Leader . . . 11.00
343 TM,V:Leader . . . 11.00
344 TM,V:Leader . . . 11.00
345 TM,V:Leader,Double-Size . . 13.00
346 TM,EL,L:Rick Jones . . . 7.00
347 In Las Vegas,I:Marlo Chandler, V:Absorbing Man . . . 5.00
348 V:Absorbing Man . . . 4.00
349 A:Spider-Man . . . 4.50
350 Hulk vs Thing,A:Beast V:Dr.Doom . . . 5.00
351 R:Jarella's World . . . 4.00
352 V:Inquisitor . . . 4.00
353 R:Bruce Banner . . . 4.00
354 V:Maggia . . . 4.00
355 V:Glorian . . . 4.00
356 V:Glorian,Cloot . . . 4.00
357 V:Glorian,Cloot . . . 4.00
358 V:Glorian,Cloot . . . 4.00
359 JBy(c),C:Wolverine(illusion) . . 5.00
360 V:Nightmare & Dyspare . . . 4.00
361 A:Iron Man,V:Maggia . . . 4.00
362 V:Werewolf By Night . . . 4.00
363 Acts of Vengeance . . . 4.00
364 A:Abomination,B:Countdown . 4.00
365 A:Fantastic Four . . . 4.00
366 A:Leader,I:Riot Squad . . . 4.00
367 1st DK Hulk,I:Madman(Leader's brother),E:Countdown . . . 23.00
368 SK,V:Mr.Hyde . . . 18.00
369 DK,V:Freedom Force . . . 12.00
370 DK,R:Original Defenders . . . 12.00
371 DK,BMc,A:Orig.Defenders . . 10.00
372 DK,R:Green Hulk . . . 20.00
373 DK,Green Hulk & Grey Hulk 10.00
374 DK,BMc,Skrulls, R:Rick Jones . . . 10.00
375 DK,BMc,V:Super Skrull . . . 10.00
376 DK,BMc,Green Hulk,Grey Hulk & Banner fight . . . 12.00
377 DK,BMc,New Green Hulk, combination of green,grey, and Bruce Banner,A:Ringmaster . 22.00
377a 2nd printing (gold) . . . 8.50
378 V:Rhino,Christmas Issue . . . 4.00
379 DK,MFm,I:Pantheon . . . 10.00
380 A:Nick Fury,D:Crazy-8 . . . 4.00
381 DK,MFm,Hulk J:Pantheon . . . 6.00
382 DK,MFm,A:Pantheon . . . 6.00
383 DK,MFm,Infinity Gauntlet . . . 6.00
384 DK,MFm,Infinity Gauntlet . . . 6.00
385 DK,MFm,Infinity Gauntlet . . . 6.00
386 DK,MFm,V:Sabra,A:Achilles . 5.00
387 DK,MFm,V:Sabra,A:Achilles . 5.00
388 DK,MFm,I:Speed Freak,Jim Wilson,revealed to have AIDS . 5.00
389 1st Comic art By Gary Barker (Garfield),A:Man-Thing,Glob . . 4.00
390 DK,MFm,B:War & Pieces, C:X-Factor . . . 5.00
391 DK,MFm,V:X-Factor . . . 5.00
392 DK,MFm,E:War & Pieces, A:X:Factor . . . 5.00
393 DK,MFm,R:Igor,A:Soviet Super Soldiers,30th Anniv.,Green foil(c) . . . 10.00
393a 2nd printing,Silver . . . 2.50
394 MFm(i),F:Atalanta,I:Trauma . . 3.00
395 DK,MFm,A:Punisher, I:Mr.Frost . . . 4.00
396 DK,MFm,A:Punisher, V:Mr.Frost . . . 4.00
397 DK,MFm,B:Ghost of the Past,V:U-Foes,A:Leader . . . 4.00
398 DK,MFm,D:Marlo,V:Leader . . 4.00
399 JD,A:FF,Dr.Strange . . . 3.00
400 JD,MFm,E:Ghost of the Past, V:Leader,1st Holo-grafx(c),1st GFr Hulk(pin-up) . . . 6.50
400a 2nd Printing . . . 2.50
401 JDu,O:Agememnon . . . 2.00
402 JDu,V:Juggernaut . . . 2.00
403 GFr,V:Red Skull,A:Avengers . 5.00
404 GFr,V:Red Skull,Juggernaut, A:Avengers . . . 3.50
405 GFr,Ajax Vs. Achilles . . . 2.75
406 GFr,V:Captain America . . . 2.00
407 GFr,I:Piecemeal,A:Madman, B:O:Ulysses . . . 2.00
408 GFr,V:Madman,Piecemeal, D:Perseus,A:Motormouth, Killpower . . . 1.75
409 GFr,A:Motormouth,Killpower, V:Madman . . . 1.75

410 GFr,A:Nick Fury,S.H.I.E.L.D., Margo agrees to marry Rick . . 1.75
411 GFr,V:Nick Fury,S.H.I.E.L.D. . 1.75
412 PaP,V:Bi-Beast,A:She-Hulk . . 1.75
413 GFr,CaS,B:Troyjan War, I:Cassiopea,Armageddon, V:Trauma 1.50
414 GFr,CaS,V:Trauma,C:S.Surfer 1.50
415 GFr,CaS,V:Trauma,A:Silver Surfer,Starjammers 1.50
416 GFr,CaS,E:Troyjan War,D:Trauma, A:S.Surfer,Starjammers 1.50
417 GFr,CaS,Rick's/Marlo's Bachelor/ Bachelorette Party 1.75
418 GFr,CaS,W:Rick & Marlo, A:Various Marvel persons, Die Cut(c) 2.50
418a Newsstand Ed. 1.50
419 CaS,V:Talos 1.50
Ann.#1,A:Inhumans 56.00
Ann.#2 rep.O:Hulk,A:Leader . . . 35.00
Ann.#3 rep.A:Leader 10.00
Ann.#4 IR:Hulk/Banner 8.00
Ann.#5 V:Xemnu,Diablo 6.00
Ann.#6 HT,A:Dr.Strange,I:Paragon (Her) 4.00
Ann.#7 JBy,BL,A:Angel,Iceman A:Doc Samson 7.00
Ann.#8 Alpha Flight 6.00
Ann.#9 Checkmate 3.00
Ann.#10,A:Captain Universe 3.00
Ann.#11 RB,JSt,A:Spider-Man, Avengers,V:Unis 4.00
Ann.#12 . . . . 3.00
Ann.#13 . . . . 3.00
Ann.#14 JBy,SB 3.00
Ann.#15 V:Abomitation 3.00
Ann.#16 HT,Life Form #3, A:Mercy 3.00
Ann.#17 Subterran.Odyssey #2 . . 3.00
Ann #18 KM,TA,TC(1st Work),Return of the Defenders,Part 1 . . . . . . 7.00
Ann.#19 I:Lazarus,w/card 3.25
G-Size #1 rep.Greatest Foes . . . 10.00
TPB Ground Zero rep.#340-345 . 12.95

INCREDIBLE HULK: FUTURE IMPERFECT

1 GP,V:Maestro 12.00
2 GP,V:Maestro 10.00

INCREDIBLE HULK vs. WOLVERINE

October, 1986

1 HT,rep #181 B:,V:Wolverine. . 14.00

INCOMPLETE DEATH'S HEAD

1 rep.Death's Head #1 . . . . 2.00
2 rep.Death's Head #2 . . . . 2.00
3 rep.Death's Head #3 . . . . 2.00
4 rep.Death's Head #4 . . . . 1.75

[Further Adventures of] INDIANA JONES

January, 1983

1 JBy/TA 2.00
2 JBy/TA 1.50
3 . . . . 1.50
4 KGa 1.50
5 KGa 1.50
6 HC/TA 1.50
7 thru 24 KGa . . . . @1.50
25 SD,What Lurks Within the Tomb 1.50
26 SD 1.50
27 SD 1.50
28 SD 1.50
29 SD 1.50
30 SD 1.50
31 SD,The Summit Meeting 1.50
32 SD,Fly the Friendly Skies 1.50
33 SD 1.50
34 SD, March, 1986 . . . . 1.50

INDIANA JONES AND THE LAST CRUSADE

1 B&W,Mag.,movie adapt, 1989. . 2.95

[Mini-Series]

1 Rep,Movie adapt, 1989. . . . . . 1.25
2 Rep,Movie adapt. 1.25
3 Rep,Movie adapt 1.25
4 Rep,Movie adapt. 1.25

INDIANA JONES AND THE TEMPLE OF DOOM

1 Movie adapt, 1984 . . . . 1.25
2 Movie adapt 1.25
3 Movie adapt 1.25

INFINITY CRUSADE

1 RLm,AM,I:Goddess,A:Marvel Heroes,foil(c) 4.00
2 RLm,AM,V:Goddess 3.00
3 RLm,AM,V:Goddess,Mephisto . 3.00
4 RLm,AM,V:Goddess,A:Magnus 3.00
5 RLm,AM,V:Goddess 3.00
6 RLm,AM,V:Goddess 3.00

Infinity Gauntlet #3

© Marvel Entertainment Group

INFINITY GAUNTLET

July, 1991

1 GP,O:Infinity Gauntlet 12.00
2 GP,JRu,2ndRebirth:Warlock . . 8.00
3 GP,JRu,I:Terraxia 6.00
4 GP,JRu,RLm,V:Thanos 6.00
5 JRu,RLm,V:Thanos,D:Terraxia . 8.00
6 RLm,JRu,V:Nebula 8.00
TPB rep. #1 thru 6 . . . . 24.95

INFINITY WAR

1 RLm,AM,R:Magus,Thanos 6.00
2 RLm,AM,V:Magus,A:Everyone . 4.00
3 RLm,AM,V:Magus,A:Everyone . 3.50
4 RLm,AM,Magus gets Gauntlet . 3.50
5 RLm,AM,V:Magus 3.50
6 RLm,AM,V:Magus 3.50

INHUMANOIDS

Star

January, 1987

1 Hasbro Toy 1.00
2 O:Inhumanoids 1.00
3 V:D'Compose 1.00
4 A:Sandra Shore, July, 1987 . . . 1.00

INHUMANS

October, 1975

1 GP,V:Blastaar 4.00
2 GP,V:Blastaar 2.50
3 GP,I:Kree S 2.00
4 GK,Maximus 2.00
5 GK,V:Maximus 2.00
6 GK,Maximus 2.00
7 GK,DP,I:Skornn 2.00
8 GP,DP,Skornn 2.00
9 reprint,V:Mor-Tog 2.00
10 KP,D:Warkon 2.00
11 KP,JM,I:Pursuer 2.00
12 KP,Hulk 2.00
Spec#1(The Untold Saga), O:Inhumans 2.00

INHUMANS: THE UNTOLD SAGA

1 . . . . 1.50

INTERFACE

Epic

December, 1989

1 ESP 2.50
2 thru 7 . . . . @2.00
8 . . . . 2.25

INVADERS

August, 1975

1 FR,JR(c),A:Invaders, A:Mastermind 10.00
2 FR,JR(c)I:Brain Drain 8.00
3 FR,JR(c),I:U-Man 7.00
4 FR,O&V:U-Man 6.00
5 RB,JM,V:Red Skull 6.00
6 FR,V:Liberty Legion 6.00
7 FR,I:Baron Blood, 1st Union Jack 6.00
8 FR,FS,J:Union Jack 6.00
9 FR,FS,O:Baron Blood 6.00
10 FR,FS,rep.Captain America Comics#22 . . . . 6.00
11 FR,FS,I:Blue Bullet 5.00
12 FR,FS,I:Spitfire 5.00
13 FR,FS,GK(c),I:Golem, Half Face 5.00
14 FR,FS,JK(c),I:Crusaders 5.00
15 FR,FS,JK(c),V:Crusaders 5.00
16 FR,JK(c),V:Master Man 5.00
17 FR,FS,GK(c),I:Warrior Woman 5.00
18 FR,FS,GK(c),R:1st Destroyer . 5.00
19 FR,FS,V:Adolph Hitler 5.00
20 FR,FS,GK(c),I&J:2nd Union Jack BU:rep.Marvel Comics #1 . . . . 7.50
21 FR,FS,GK(c),BU:rep.Marvel Mystery #10 . . . . 5.50
22 FR,FS,GK(c),O:Toro 3.00
23 FR,FS,GK(c),I:Scarlet Scarab . 3.00
24 FR,FS,GK(c),rep.Marvel Mystery #17 . . . . 4.00
25 FR,FS,GK(c),V:Scarlet Scarab 3.00
26 FR,FS,GK(c),V:Axis Agent . . . 3.00
27 FR,FS,GK(c),V:Axis Agent . . . 3.00
28 FR,FS,I:2nd Human Top, Golden Girl,Kid Commandos . . 3.00
29 FR,FS,I:Teutonic Knight 3.00
30 FR,FS,V:Teutonic Knight 3.00
31 FR,FS,V:Frankenstein 3.00
32 FR,FS,JK(c),A:Thor 4.50
33 FR,FS,JK(c),A:Thor 4.50
34 FR,FS,V:Master Man 3.00
35 FR,FS,I:Iron Cross 3.00
36 FR,FS,O:Iron Cross 3.00
37 FR,FS,V:Iron Cross 3.00
38 FR,FS,V:Lady Lotus 3.00
39 FR,FS,O:Lady Lotus 3.00
40 FR,FS,V:Baron Blood 3.00
41 E:RTs(s)FR,FS,V:Super Axis, double-size 4.00
Ann.#1 A:Avengers,R:Shark 5.00
G-Size#1 FR,rep.Submariner#1 . . 5.00

[Limited Series]

1 R:Invaders 2.00
2 V:Battle Axis 2.00
3 R:Original Vison (1950's) 2.00
4 V:The Axis 2.00

IRON FIST
November, 1975

1 JBy,A:Iron Man 35.00
2 JBy,V:H'rythl 20.00
3 JBy,KP,KJ,V:Ravager 16.00
4 JBy,V:Radion 16.00
5 JBy,V:Scimitar 16.00
6 JBy,O:Misty Knight 12.50
7 JBy,V:Khimbala Bey 12.50
8 JBy,V:Chaka 12.50
9 JBy,V:Chaka 12.50
10 JBy,DGr,A:Chaka 12.50
11 JBy,V:Wrecking Crew 12.50
12 JBy,DGr,V:Captain America . 12.50
13 JBy,A:Boomerang 12.50
14 JBy,I:Sabretooth 195.00
14a reprint,Marv.Milestone 4.00
15 JBy,A&N:Wolverine,A:X-Men September 1977 . . . . 45.00

IRONJAW
Atlas
January, 1975

1 NA(c),MSy 2.00
2 NA(c) 1.50
3 . . . . 1.25
4 July, 1975 O:IronJaw 1.25

Iron Man #11
© Marvel Entertainment Group

IRON MAN
May, 1968

1 B:StL,AGw(s),JCr,GC, I:Mordius 375.00
2 JCr,I:Demolisher 125.00
3 JCr,V:The Freak 95.00
4 JCr,A:Unicorn 75.00
5 JCr,GT,I:Cerebos 65.00
6 JCr,GT,V:Crusher 75.00
7 JCr,GT,V:Gladiator 50.00
8 JCr,GT,O:Whitney Frost 45.00
9 JCr,GT,A:Mandarin 42.00
10 JCr,GT,V:Mandarin 42.00
11 JCr,GT,V:Mandarin 35.00
12 JCr,GT,I:Controller 35.00
13 JCr,GT,A:Nick Fury 35.00
14 JCr,V:Night Phantom 35.00
15 JCr,GT,A:Red Ghost 32.00
16 JCr,GT,V:Unicorn 27.00
17 JCr,GT,I:Madam Masque, Midas 29.00
18 JCr,GT,V:Madame Masque . . 27.00
19 JCr,GT,V:Madame Masque . . 27.00
20 JCr,I:Charlie Gray 27.00
21 JCr,I:Eddie 20.00
22 JCr,D:Janice Cord 20.00
23 JCr,I:Mercenary 22.00
24 JCr,GT,V:Madame Masque . . 20.00
25 JCr,A:Sub-Mariner 24.00
26 JCr,DH,J:Val-Larr 20.00
27 JCr,DH,I:Firebrand 20.00
28 E:AGw(s),JCr,DH, V:Controller 20.00
29 B:StL,AyB(s),DH,V:Myrmidon 22.00
30 DH,I:Monster Master 22.00
31 DH,I:Mastermind 18.00
32 GT,I:Mechanoid 17.00
33 DH,I:Spy Master 17.00
34 DH,A:Spy Master 17.00

Iron Man #78
© Marvel Entertainment Group

35 DH,A:Daredevil,Spymaster . . 17.00
36 E:AyB(s),DH,I:RamRod 17.00
37 DH,A:Ramrod 17.00
38 GT,Jonah 17.00
39 HT,I:White Dragon 15.00
40 GT,A:White Dragon 15.00
41 GT,JM,I:Slasher 15.00
42 GT,I:Mikas 15.00
43 GT,JM,A:Mikas,I:Guardsmen 15.00
44 GT,A:Capt.America 15.00
45 GT,A:Guardsman 15.00
46 GT,D:Guardsman 15.00
47 BS,JM,O:Iron Man 22.00
48 GT,V:Firebrand 14.00
49 GT,V:Adaptoid 14.00
50 B:RTs(s),GT,V:Prin.Python . . 14.00
51 GT,C:Capt.America 14.00
52 GT,I:Raga 14.00
53 GT,JSn,I:BlackLama 12.00
54 GT,BEv,Sub-Mariner,I:Madame MacEvil (Moondragon) 14.00
55 JSn,I:Destroyer,Thanos,Mentor Starfox(Eros),Blood Bros. . . 110.00
55a reprint,Marv.Milestone 2.95
56 JSn,I:Fangor 25.00
57 GT,R:Mandarin 10.00
58 GT,V:Mandarin 10.00
59 GT,A:Firebrand 10.00
60 GT,C:Daredevil 10.00
61 GT,Marauder 10.00
62 whiplash 10.00
63 GT,A:Dr.Spectrum 10.00
64 GT,I:Rokk 10.00
65 GT,O:Dr.Spectrum 10.00
66 GT,V:Thor 10.00
67 GT,V:Freak 10.00
68 GT,O:Iron Man 12.00
69 GT,V:Mandarin 8.00
70 GT,A:Sunfire 8.00
71 GT,V:Yellow Claw 7.00
72 E:RTs(s),GT,V:Black Lama . . . 7.00
73 B:LWn(s),KP,JM,V:Titanic Three 7.00
74 KP,V:Modok 7.00
75 V:Black Lama 7.00
76 Rep,A:Hulk 7.00
77 V:Thinker 7.00
78 GT,V:Viet Cong 7.00
79 GT,I:Quasar(not Current one) . 7.00
80 JK(c),O:Black Lama 7.00
81 A:Black Lama 6.00
82 MSe,A:Red Ghost 6.00

Iron Man #128
© Marvel Entertainment Group

83 E:LWn(s),HT,MSe,Red Ghost . 6.00
84 HT,A:Dr.Ritter 6.00
85 HT,MSe,A:Freak 6.00
86 B:MWn(s),GT,I:Blizzard 7.00
87 GT,V:Blizzard 6.00
88 E:MWn(s),GT, V:Blood Brothers 6.00
89 GT,A:D.D.,Blood Bros. 6.00
90 JK(c),GT,Controller,A:Thanos . 7.50
91 GT,BL,A:Controller 6.00
92 JK(c),GT,V:Melter 6.00
93 JK(c),HT,V:Kraken 6.00
94 JK(c),HT,V:Kraken 6.00
95 JK(c),GT,PP,V:Ultimo 6.00
96 GT,DP,V:Ultimo 6.00
97 GT,DP,I:Guardsman II 6.00
98 GT,DP,A:Sunfire 6.00
99 GT,V:Mandarin 6.00
100 JSn(c),GT,V:Mandarin 14.00
101 GT,I:Dread Knight 5.00
102 GT,O:Dread Knight 5.00
103 GT,V:Jack of Hearts 5.00
104 GT,V:Midas 5.00
105 GT,V:Midas 5.00
106 GT,V:Midas 5.00
107 KP,V:Midas 5.00
108 CI,A:Growing Man 5.00
109 JBy(c),CI,V:Van Guard 5.00

110 KP,I:C.Arcturus 5.00
111 KP,O:Rigellians 5.00
112 AA,KP,V:Punisher from Beyond 5.00
113 KP,HT,V:Unicorn,Spymaster . 5.50
114 KG,I:Arsenal 5.00
115 JR2,O:Unicorn,V:Ani-men . . . 5.00
116 JR2,BL,V:MadameMasque . . 5.00
117 BL,JR2,1st Romita Jr 6.00
118 JBy,BL,A:Nick Fury 7.00
119 BL,JR2,Alcholic Plot 6.00
120 JR2,BL,A:Sub-Mariner, I:Rhodey(becomes War Machine), Justin Hammer 12.00
121 BL,JR2,A:Submariner 4.00
122 DC,CI,BL,O:Iron Man 4.00
123 BL,JR2,V:Blizzard 4.00
124 BL,JR2,A:Capt.America 4.00
125 BL,JR2,A:Ant-Man 4.00
126 BL,JR2,V:Hammer 4.00
127 BL,JR2,Battlefield 4.00
128 BL,JR2,Alcohol 5.00
129 SB,A:Dread Night 3.50
130 BL,V:Digital Devil 3.50
131 BL,V:Hulk 3.50
132 BL,V:Hulk 3.50
133 BL,A:Hulk,Ant-Man 3.50
134 BL,V:Titanium Man 3.50
135 BL,V:Titanium Man 3.50
136 V:Endotherm 3.50
137 BL,Fights oil rig fire 3.50
138 BL,Dreadnought,Spymaster . . 3.50
139 BL,Dreadnought,Spymaster . . 3.50
140 BL,V:Force 3.50
141 BL,JR2,V:Force 3.50
142 BL,JR2,Space Armor 3.50
143 BL,JR2,V:Sunturion 3.50
144 BL,JR2,Sunturion,O:Rhodey . 3.50
145 BL,JR2,A:Raiders 3.50
146 BL,JR2,I:Black Lash 3.50
147 BL,JR2,V:Black Lash 3.00
148 BL,JR2,V:Terrorists 3.00
149 BL,JR2,V:Dr.Doom 3.00
150 BL,JR2,V:Dr.Doom,Dble 4.00
151 TA,BL,A:Antman 2.50
152 BL,JR2,New Armor 2.50
153 BL,JR2,V:Living Laser 2.50
154 BL,JR2,V:Unicorn 2.50
155 JR2,V:Back-Getters 2.50
156 JR2,I:Mauler 3.00
157 V:Spores 2.50
158 CI,AM,Iron Man Drowning . . . 2.50
159 PS,V:Diablo 2.50
160 SD,V:Serpent'sSquad 2.50
161 A:Moon Knight 2.50
162 V:Space Ships 2.50
163 V:Chessmen 2.50
164 LMc,A:Bishop 2.50
165 LMc,Meltdown 2.50
166 LMc,V:Melter 2.25
167 LMc,Alcholic Issue 2.25
168 LMc,A:Machine Man 2.25
169 LMc,B:Rhodey as 2nd Ironman 8.00
170 LMc,2nd Ironman 7.00
171 LMc,2nd Ironman 3.00
172 LMc,V:Firebrand 3.00
173 LMc,Stane International 3.00
174 LMc,Alcoholism 3.00
175 LMc,Alcoholism 2.75
176 LMc,Alcoholism 2.75
177 LMc,Alcoholism 2.75
178 LMc,V:Wizard 2.75
179 LMc,V:Mandarin 2.50
180 LMc,V:Mandarin 2.50
181 LMc,V:Mandarin 2.50
182 LMc,Secret Wars 2.50
183 LMc,Turning Point 2.50
184 LMc,Moves to California 2.50
185 LMc,V:Zodiac Field 2.50
186 LMc,I:Vibro 2.50
187 LMc,V:Vibro 2.50
188 LMc,I:New Brother's Grimm . 2.50
189 LMc,I:Termite 3.00
190 LMc,O:Termite,A:Scar.Witch . 2.50

Iron Man #232
© Marvel Entertainment Group

191 LMc,New Grey Armor 2.50
192 LMc,V:Iron Man(Tony Stark) . 2.50
193 LMc,V:Dr.Demonicus 2.50
194 LMc,I:Scourge,A:West Coast Avengers 2.50
195 LMc,A:Shaman 2.50
196 LMc,V:Dr.Demonicus 2.50
197 LMc,Secret Wars II 2.50
198 SB,V:Circuit Breaker 2.00
199 LMc,E:Rhodey as 2nd Ironman, V:Obadiah Stone 2.50
200 LMc,D:Obadiah Stone 5.00
201 MBr,V:Madam Masque 2.00
202 A:Kazar 2.00
203 MBr,A:Hank Pym 2.00
204 MBr,V:Madame Masque 2.00
205 MBr,V:A.I.M. 2.00
206 MBr,V:Goliath 2.00
207 MBr,When t/Sky Rains Fire . . 2.00
208 MBr,V:A.I.M. 2.00
209 V:Living Laser 2.00
210 MBr,V:Morgan Le Fey 2.00
211 AS,V:Living Laser 2.00
212 DT,V:Iron Monger 2.00
213 A:Dominic Fortune 2.00
214 A:Spider-Woman 2.00
215 BL,AIM 2.00
216 BL,MBr,D:Clymenstra 2.00
217 BL,MRr,V:Hammer 2.00
218 BL,MBr,Titanic 2.00
219 BL,V:The Ghost 2.00
220 BL,MBr,V:The Ghost, D:Spymaster 2.00
221 BL,MBr,V:The Ghost 2.00
222 BL,MBr,R:Abrogast 2.00
223 BL,MBr,V:Blizzard,Beetle . . . 2.00
224 BL,V:Justin Hammer,Force . . 2.00
225 BL,MBr,B:Armor Wars 6.00
226 BL,MBr,V:Stingray 4.50
227 BL,MBr,V:Mandroids, ... 4.00
228 BL,MBr,V:Guardsmen 4.00
229 BL,D:Titanium Man 4.00
230 V:Firepower, ... 4.00
231 V:Firepower,N:Iron Man 4.00
232 BWS,Nightmares,E:Armor Wars 4.50
233 JG,BL,A:AntMan 2.00
234 JG,BL,A:Spider-Man 3.00
235 JG,BL,V:Grey Gargoyle 1.50
236 JG,BL,V:Grey Gargoyle 1.50
237 JG,BL,V:SDI Monster 1.50
238 JG,BL,V:Rhino,D:M.Masque . 1.50
239 JG,BL,R:Ghost 1.50
240 JG,BL,V:Ghost 1.50
241 BL,V:Mandarin 1.50
242 BL,BWS,V:Mandarin 3.00
243 BL,BWS,Stark Paralyzed . . . 3.00
244 BL,V:Fixer,A:Force(D.Size) . . 4.00
245 BL(c),V:Dreadnaughts 1.50
246 BL,HT,V:A.I.M.,Maggia 1.50
247 BL,A:Hulk 2.00
248 BL,Tony Stark Cured 2.00
249 BL,V:Dr.Doom 1.50
250 BL,V:Dr.Doom,A of V 2.00
251 HT,AM,V:Wrecker,A of V . . . 1.50
252 HT,AM,V:Chemistro,A of V . . 1.50
253 BL,V:Slagmire 1.50
254 BL,V:Spymaster 1.50
255 HT,V:Devestator I:2nd Spymaster 1.50
256 JR2,V:Space Station 1.50
257 V:Samurai Steel 1.50
258 JR2,BWi,B:Armor Wars II,V: Titanium Man 2.25
259 JR2,BWi,V:Titanium Man 2.00
260 JR2,BWi,V:Living Laser 2.00
261 JR2,BWi,A:Mandarin 1.75
262 JR2,BWi,A:Mandarin 1.75
263 JR2,BWi,A:Wonderman, V:Living Laser 1.75
264 JR2,BWi,A:Mandarin 1.75
265 JR2,BWi,V:Dewitt 1.50
266 JR2,BWi,E:Armor Wars II . . . 1.50
267 PR,BWi,B:New O:Iron Man, Mandarin,V:Vibro 1.75
268 PR,BWi,E:New O:Iron Man. . 1.50
269 PR,BWi,A:Black Widow 1.50
270 PR,BWi,V:Fin Fang Foom . . . 1.50
271 PR,BWi,V:Fin Fang Foom . . . 1.50
272 PR,BWi,O:Mandarin 1.50
273 PR,BWi,V:Mandarin 1.50
274 MBr,BWi,V:Mandarin 1.50
275 PR,BWi,A:Mandarin,Fin Fang Foom (Double size) 2.00
276 PR,BWi,A:Black Widow 1.50
277 PR,BWi,A:Black Widow 1.50
278 BWi,Galactic Storm Pt.6 A:Capt.America,V:Shatterax . . 1.50
279 BWi,Galactic Storm Pt.13, V:Ronan,A:Avengers 1.50
280 KHd,V:The Stark 1.50
281 KHd,I&V:Masters of Silence, C:War Machine Armor 3.50
282 KHd,I:War Machine Armor, V:Masters of Silence 3.50
283 KHd,V:Masters of Silence . . . 2.50
284 KHd,Stark put under Cryogenic Freeze,B:Rhodey as Iron Man . 3.00
285 KHd,BWi(i),Tony's Funeral . . 2.00
286 KHd,V:Avengers West Coast . 1.75
287 KHd,I:New Atom Smasher . . 1.75
288 KHd,30th Anniv.,V:Atom Smasher,foil(c) 4.50
289 KHd,V:Living Laser, R:Tony Stark 1.50
290 KHd,30th Anniv.,N:Iron Man, Gold foil(c) 4.50
291 KHd,E:Rhodey as Iron Man, Becomes War Machine 2.00
292 KHd,Tony reveals he is alive . 1.50
293 KHd,V:Controller 1.50
294 KHd,Infinity Crusade 1.50
295 KHd,Infinity Crusade 1.50
296 KHd,V:Modam,A:Omega Red 1.50
297 KHd,V:Modam,Omega Red . . 1.50
298 KHd(c),I:Earth Mover 1.50
299 KHd(c),R:Ultimo 1.50
300 KHd,TMo,N:Iron Man,I:Iron Legion, Foil(c),A:W.Machine,V:Ultimo . 4.25
300a Newstand Ed. 2.75
301 KHd,B:Crash and Burn, A:Deathlok,C:Venom 1.50
302 KHd,V:Venom 1.75
303 KHd,V:New Warriors, C:Thundrstrike 1.75
304 KHd,C:Hulk,V:New Warriors,

Thundrstrike,N:Iron Man 1.75
305 KHd,V:Hulk, ... 1.50
G-Size #1 Reprints 8.00
Ann.#1 rep.Iron Man #25 . . . . . . 20.00
Ann.#2 rep.Iron Man #6 . . . . 10.00
Ann.#3 SB,Manthing 6.00
Ann.#4 DP,GT,V:Modok,
A:Champions 4.00
Ann.#5 JBr,A:Black Panther 2.50
Ann.#6 A:Eternals,V:Brother
Tode 2.50
Ann.#7 LMc,A:West Coast
Avengers, I:New Goliath 2.50
Ann.#8 A:X-Factor 3.00
Ann.#9 V:Stratosfire,A:Sunturion . 2.50
Ann.#10 PS,BL,Atlantis Attacks #2
A:Sub-Mariner 3.00
Ann.#11 SD,Terminus Factor #2 . 2.00
Ann.#12 Subterran.Odyssey #4 . . 2.00
Ann.#13 GC,AW,Assault on Armor
City,A:Darkhawk 2.50
Ann.#14 TMo,I:Face Theif,w/card,
BU:War Machine 3.25
TPB Armor Wars rep.#225-#232 12.95
TPB Many Armors of Iron Man . 15.95
TPB Power of Iron Man 9.95
Iron Manual BSz(c),guide to Iron
Man's technology 2.00

IRON MAN & SUBMARINER

1 GC,April, 1968 . . . . 225.00

IRON MANUAL

1 BSz(c),Guide to Iron Man's
technology 1.75

ISLAND OF DR. MOREAU

October, 1977

1 GK(c),movie adapt 2.00

IT'S A DUCK'S LIFE

February, 1950

1 F;Buck Duck,Super Rabbit . . 56.00
2 . . . . 30.00
3 thru 10 . . . . @20.00
11 February, 1952 . . . . 20.00

JACK OF HEARTS

January, 1984

1 Mini series 1.50
2 O:Jack of Hearts 1.00
3 . . . . 1.00
4 Final issue,April 1984 . . . . 1.00

JAMES BOND JR.

1 I&O:JamesBondJr.(TVseries) . . 1.00
2 Adventures Contd. 1.25
3 V:Goldfinger,Odd Job 1.25
4 thru 6 . . . . @1.25
V:Scumlord 1.25
8 V:Goldfinger,Walter D.Plank . . 1.25
9 V:Dr.No in Switzerland 1.25
10 V:Robot,Dr.DeRange 1.25
11 V:S.C.U.M. 1.25
12 V:Goldfinger,Jaws 1.25

JANN OF THE JUNGLE

See: JUNGLE TALES

JEANIE COMICS

See: DARING MYSTERY

JIHAD

Epic

1 Cenobites vs. Nightbreed 4.50
2 E:Cenobites vs. Nightbreed . . . 4.50

JOHN CARTER, WARLORD OF MARS

June, 1977

1 GK,DC,O:John Carter,Created
by Edgar Rice Burroughs 2.00
2 GK/DC(c),GK,RN, White Apes
of Mars 1.50
3 GK,RN,Requiem for a Warlord . 1.50
4 GK,RN, Raiding Party 1.50
5 GK,RN,Giant Battle Issue 1.50
6 GK/DC(c),GK,Alone Against a
World 1.50
7 GK,TS,Showdown 1.50
8 GK,RN,Beast With Touch of
Stone 1.50
9 GK,RN,Giant Battle Issue 1.50
10 GK,The Death of Barsoom? . . 1.50
11 RN,O:Dejah Thoris 1.00
12 RN,City of the Dead 1.00
13 RN,March of the Dead 1.00
14 RN,The Day Helium Died 1.00
15 RN,GK,Prince of Helium
Returns 1.00
16 RN,John Carters Dilemna 1.00
17 BL,What Price Victory 5.00
18 FM,Tars Tarkas Battles Alone . 1.00
19 RN(c),War With the Wing Men 1.00
20 RN(c),Battle at the Bottom
of the World 1.00
21 RN(c),The Claws of the Banth 1.00
22 RN(c),The Canyon of Death . . 1.00
23 Murder on Mars 1.00
24 GP/TA(c),Betrayal 1.00
25 Inferno 1.00
26 Death Cries the Guild of
Assassins 1.00
27 Death Marathon 1.00
28 Guardians of the Lost
City October, 1979 . . . . 2.00
Ann.#1 RN(c),GK,Battle
story 1.50
Ann.#2 RN(c),GK,Outnumbered 1.00
Ann.#3 RN(c),GK,Battle
story 1.50

JOKER COMICS

Timely

April, 1942

1 BW,I&B:Powerhouse Pepper,
A:Stuporman 1,000.00
2 BW,I:Tessie the Typist 400.00
3 BW,A:Tessie the Typist,
Squat Car Squad 275.00
4 BW,Squat Car (c) 275.00
5 BW,same 275.00
6 BW, ... 175.00
7 BW 175.00
8 BW 175.00
9 BW 175.00
10 BW,Shooting Gallery (c) . . . 175.00
11 BW 150.00
12 BW 150.00
13 BW 150.00
14 BW 150.00
15 BW 150.00
16 BW 150.00
17 BW 150.00
18 BW 150.00
19 BW 150.00
20 BW 150.00
21 BW 125.00
22 BW 125.00
23 BW,HK,'Hey Look' 135.00
24 BW,HK,'Laff Favorites' 125.00
25 BW,HK,same 125.00
26 BW,HK,same 125.00
27 BW 125.00
28 . . . . 30.00
29 BW 125.00
30 BW 125.00
31 BW 100.00
32 B:Millie,Hedy 30.00
33 HK 45.00
34 . . . . 30.00
35 HK 45.00
36 HK 45.00
37 . . . . 30.00
38 . . . . 30.00
39 . . . . 30.00
40 . . . . 30.00
41 A:Nellie the Nurse 30.00
42 I:Patty Pin-up 45.00

Becomes:

ADVENTURES INTO TERROR

43(1)AH,B:Horror Stories 200.00
44(2)AH,'Won't You Step Into
My Palor' 150.00
3 GC,'I Stalk By Night' 100.00
4 DR,'The Torture Room' . . . 100.00
5 GC,DR,'The Hitchhicker' . . . 125.00
6 RH,'The Dark Room' 80.00
7 GT(c),BW,'Where Monsters
Dwell' 250.00
8 JSt,'Enter... the Lizard' 80.00
9 RH(c),JSt,'The Dark
Dungeon' 90.00
10 'When the Vampire Calls' . . . 90.00
11 JSt,'Dead Man's Escape' . . . 60.00
12 BK,'The Man Who Cried
Ghost' 90.00
13 BEv(c),'The Hands of Death' . 60.00
14 GC,'The Hands' 60.00
15 'Trapped by the Tarantula' . . 60.00
16 RH(c),'Her Name Is Death' . . 60.00
17 'I Die Too Often',Bondage(c) . . 60.00
18 'He's Trying To Kill Me' 60.00
19 'The Girl Who Couldn't Die' . . 60.00
20 . . . . 60.00
21 . . . . 50.00
22 . . . . 50.00
23 . . . . 50.00
24 MF,GC 70.00
25 thru 30 . . . . @50.00
31 May, 1954 . . . . 50.00

Journey Into Mystery #14
© Marvel Entertainment Group

JOURNEY INTO MYSTERY

June, 1952

1 RH(c),B:Mystery/Horror
stories 1,400.00
2 'Don't Look' 600.00
3 'I Didn't See Anything' 450.00
4 RH,BEv(c),'I'm Drowning,'
severed hand (c) 450.00
5 RH,BEv(c),'Fright' 250.00
6 BEv(c),'Till Death Do
Us Part' 250.00
7 BEv(c),'Ghost Guard' 250.00

8 'He Who Hesitates' 250.00
9 BEv(c),'I Made A Monster' . 250.00
10 'The Assassin of Paris' 250.00
11 RH,GT,'Meet the Dead' . . . 200.00
12 'A Night At Dragmoor Castle' 200.00
13 'The Living and the Dead' . . 200.00
14 DAy,RH,'The Man Who Owned A World' 200.00
15 RH(c),'Till Death Do Us Part' 200.00
16 DW,'Vampire Tale' 200.00
17 SC,'Midnight On Black Mountain' 200.00
18 'He Wouldn't Stay Dead' . . . 200.00
19 JF,'The Little Things' 200.00
20 BEv,BP,'After Man, What' . . 200.00
21 JKu,'The Man With No Past' 225.00
22 'Haunted House' 200.00
23 GC,'Gone, But Not Forgotten' 150.00
24 'The Locked Drawer' 150.00
25 'The Man Who Lost Himself' 150.00
26 'The Man From Out There' . 150.00
27 'BP,JSe,'Masterpiece' 150.00
28 'The Survivor' 150.00
29 'Three Frightened People' . . 150.00
30 JO,'The Lady Who Vanished' 150.00
31 'The Man Who Had No Fear' 150.00
32 'Elevator In The Sky' 150.00
33 SD,AW,'There'll Be Some Changes Made' 175.00
34 BP,BK,'The Of The Mystic Ring' 150.00
35 LC,JF,'Turn Back The Clock' 150.00
36 'I, The Pharaoh' 150.00
37 BEv(c),'The Volcano' 150.00
38 SD,'Those Who Vanish' . . . 150.00
39 BEv(c),DAy,WW,'The Forbidden Room' 150.00
40 BEv(c),JF,'The Strange Secret Of Henry Hill' 150.00
41 BEv(c),GM,RC,'I Switched Bodies' 125.00
42 BEv(c),GM,'What Was Farley's Other Face 125.00
43 AW,'Ghost Ship' 125.00
44 thru 50 SD,JK . . . . @125.00
51 thru 55 SD,JK . . . . @125.00
56 thru 61 SD,JK . . . . @125.00
62 SD,JK,I:Xemnu 175.00
63 thru 68 SD,JK . . . . @100.00
69 thru 82 . . . . @100.00
83 JK,SD,I&O:Thor 3,000.00
84 JK,SD,DH,I:Executioner . . . 750.00
85 JK,SD,I:Loki,Heimdall,Balder, Tyr,Odin,Asgard 350.00
86 JK,SD,DH,V:Tomorrow Man 250.00
87 JK,SD,V:Communists 175.00
88 JK,SD,V:Loki 175.00
89 JK,SD,O:Thor(rep) 200.00
90 SD,I:Carbon Copy 125.00
91 JSt,SD,I:Sandu 100.00
92 JSt,SD,V:Loki,I:Frigga 100.00
93 DAy,JK,SD,I:Radioactive Man 125.00
94 JSt,SD,V:Loki 100.00
95 JSt,SD,I:Duplicator 100.00
96 JSt,SD,I:Merlin II 100.00
97 JK,I:Lava Man,O:Odin 120.00
98 DH,JK,I&O:Cobra 82.00
99 DH,JK,I:Mr.Hyde,Surtur 82.00
100 DH,JK,V:Mr.Hyde 82.00
101 JK,V:Tomorrow Man 55.00
102 JK,I:Sif,Hela 60.00
103 JK,I:Enchantress, Executioner 60.00
104 JK,Giants 55.00
105 JK,V:Hyde,Cobra 55.00
106 JK,O:Balder 55.00
107 JK,I:Grey Gargoyle,Karnilla . 60.00
108 JK,A:Dr.Strange 55.00
109 JK,V:Magneto 70.00
110 JK,V:Hyde,Cobra,Loki 50.00
111 JK,V:Hyde,Cobra,Loki 50.00
112 JK,V:Hulk,O:Loki 105.00
113 JK,V:Grey Gargoyle 52.00
114 JK,I&O:Absorbing Man 45.00
115 JK,O:Loki,V:Absorbing Man . 53.00
116 JK,V:Loki,C:Daredevil 45.00
117 JK,V:Loki 45.00
118 JK,I:Destroyer 45.00
119 JK,V:Destroyer,I:Hogun, Fandrall,Volstagg 45.00
120 JK,A:Avengers,Absorbing Man 45.00
121 JK,V:Absorbing Man 45.00
122 JK,V:Absorbing Man 45.00
123 JK,V:Absorbing Man 45.00
124 JK,A:Hercules 45.00
125 JK,A;Hercules 45.00
Annual #1, JK,I:Hercules 100.00

Becomes: THOR

JOURNEY INTO MYSTERY
[2nd series]
October, 1972

1 GK,TP,MP,'Dig Me No Grave' . 8.00
2 GK,'Jack the Ripper' 4.00
3 JSn,TP,'Shambler From the Stars' 4.00
4 GC,DA,'Haunter of the Dark', H.P. Lovecraft adaptation 4.00
5 RB,FrG,'Shadow From the Steeple',R. Bloch adaptation . 4.00
6 Mystery Stories 3.00
7 thru 19 . . . . @3.00

JOURNEY INTO UNKNOWN WORLDS
See: ALL WINNERS COMICS

JUNGLE ACTION
Atlas
October, 1954

1 JMn,JMn(c),B:Leopard Girl . 145.00
2 JMn,JMn(c) 120.00
3 JMn,JMn(c) 100.00
4 JMn,JMn(c) 100.00
5 JMn,JMn(c) 100.00
6 JMn,JMn(c),August, 1955 . . 100.00

JUNGLE ACTION
October, 1972

1 JB(c),Lorna,Tharn,Jann reprints 8.50
2 GK(c),same 4.50
3 JSn(c),same 4.50
4 GK(c),same 4.50
5 JR(c),JB,B:Black Panther, V:Man-Ape 7.50
6 RB/FrG(c),RB,V:Kill-Monger . . 4.50
7 RB/KJ(c),RB,V:Venomn 4.50
8 RB/KJ(c),RB,GK, O:Black Panther 4.50
9 GK/KJ(c),RB,V:Baron Macabre 4.50
10 GK/FrG(c),V:King Cadaver . . . 4.50
11 GK(c),V:Baron Macabre,Lord Karnaj 4.50
12 RB/KJ(c),V:Kill Monger 4.00
13 GK/JK(c),V:White Gorilla, Sombre 4.00
14 GK(c),V:Prehistoric Monsters 4.00
15 GK(c),V:Prehistoric Monsters 4.00
16 GK(c),V:Venomm 4.00
17 GK(c),V:Kill Monger 4.00
18 JKu(c),V:Madame Slay 4.00
19 GK(c),V:KKK,'Sacrifice of Blood' 4.00
20 V:KKK,'Slaughter In The Streets' 4.00
21 V:KKK,'Cross Of Fire, Cross Of Death' 3.50
22 JB(c),V:KKK,Soul Stranger . . . 3.50
23 JBy(c),V:KKK 3.50
24 GK(c),I:Wind Eagle, November, 1976 . . . . 3.50

JUNGLE TALES
Atlas
September, 1954

1 B:Jann of the Jungle,Cliff Mason,Waku 97.00
2 GT,Jann Stories cont. 75.00
3 Cliff Mason,White Hunter, Waku Unknown Jungle 75.00
4 Cliff Mason,Waku,Unknown Jungle 75.00
5 RH(c),SSh,Cliff Mason,Waku, Unknown Jungle 75.00
6 DH,SSh,Cliff Mason,Waku, Unknown Jungle 75.00
7 DH,SSh,Cliff Mason,Waku, Unknown Jungle 75.00

Becomes:

JANN OF THE JUNGLE

8 SH,SSh,'The Jungle Outlaw' . 95.00
9 'With Fang and Talons' 45.00
10 AW,'The Jackal's Lair' 55.00
11 'Bottonless Pit' 45.00
12 'The Lost Safari' 45.00
13 'When the Trap Closed' 45.00
14 V:Hunters 45.00
15 BEv(c),DH,V:Hunters 45.00
16 BEv(c),AW,'Jungle Vengeance' 70.00
17 BEv(c),DH,AW,June, 1957 . . 70.00

JUSTICE
November, 1986

1 I:Justice 1.25
2 . . . . 1.00
3 Yakuza Assassin 1.00
4 thru 8 . . . . @1.00
9 KG 1.00
10 thru 18 . . . . @1.00
19 thru 31 . . . . @1.25
32 Last issue,A:Joker 1.50

JUSTICE COMICS
Atlas
Fall, 1947

7(1) B:FBI in Action,'Mystery of White Death' 100.00
8(2),HK,'Crime is For Suckers' . 65.00
9(3),FBI Raid 60.00
4 Bank Robbery 60.00
5 Subway(c) 45.00
6 E:FBI In Action 45.00
7 Symbolic(c) 45.00
8 Funeral(c) 45.00
9 B:'True Cases Proving Crime Can't Win' 45.00
10 Ph(c),Bank Hold Up 45.00
11 Ph(c),Behind Bars 45.00
12 Ph(c),The Crime of Martin Blaine 35.00
13 Ph(c),The Cautiouc Crook . . . 45.00
14 Ph(c) 45.00
15 Ph(c) 40.00
16 F:"Ears"Karpik-Mobster 30.00
17 'The Ragged Stranger' 30.00
18 'Criss-Cross' 30.00
19 'Death Of A Spy' 30.00
20 'Miami Mob' 30.00
21 'Trap' 30.00
22 'The Big Break' 30.00
23 thru 51 . . . . @28.00
52 'Flare Up' 28.00

Becomes:

TALES OF JUSTICE
May 1955

53 BEv,'Keeper Of The Keys' . . 65.00
54 thru 57 . . . . @45.00
58 BK 50.00
59 BK 50.00
60 thru 63 . . . . @35.00
64 RC,DW,JSe 45.00

65 RC 45.00
66 JO,AT 45.00
67 DW,August, 1957 . . . . 45.00

KATHY
Atlas
October, 1959

1 'Teenage Tornado' 30.00
2 . . . . 17.00
3 thru 15 . . . . @10.00
16 thru 26 . . . . @6.00
27 February, 1964 . . . . 6.00

KA-ZAR
[1st Series]
January, 1974

1 O:Savage Land 3.50
2 DH,JA,A:Shanna The She-Devil 2.50

Ka-Zar #16

© Marvel Entertainment Group

3 DH,V:Man-God,A:El Tigre 2.50
4 DH,V:Man-God 2.50
5 DH,D:El-Tigre 2.50
6 JB/AA,V:Bahemoth 2.00
7 JB/BMc'Revenge of the River-Gods' 2.00
8 JB/AA,'Volcano of Molten Death' 2.00
9 JB,'Man Who Hunted Dinosaur' 2.00
10 JB,'Dark City of Death' 2.00
11 DH/FS,'Devil-God of Sylitha' . . 1.50
12 RH,'Wizard of Forgotten Death' 1.50
13 V:Lizard Men 1.50
14 JAb,V:Klaw 1.50
15 VM,V:Klaw,'Hellbird' 1.50
16 VM,V:Klaw 1.50
17 VM,V:Klaw 1.50
18 VM,V:Klaw,Makrum 1.50
19 VM,V:Klaw,Raknor the Slayer . 1.50
20 VM,V:Klaw,'Fortress of Fear' . . 1.50

[2nd Series]

1 BA,O:Ka-Zar 2.00
2 thru 7 BA . . . . @1.50
8 BA,Kazar Father 1.50
9 BA 1.50
10 BA,Direct D 1.50
11 BA/GK,Zabu 1.50
12 BA,Panel Missing 1.50
12a Scarce Reprint 2.00
13 BA 2.00
14 BA/GK,Zabu 1.50

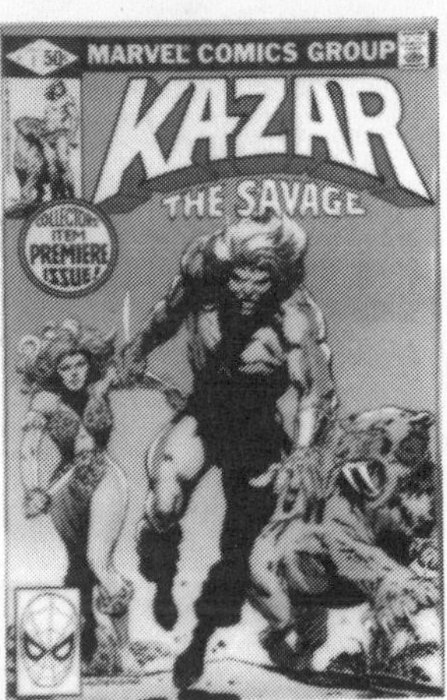

Ka-Zar #1 [2nd Series]

© Marvel Entertainment Group

15 BA 1.50
16 . . . . 1.50
17 Detective 1.50
18 . . . . 1.50
19 . . . . 1.50
20 A:Spiderman 2.00
21 . . . . 2.00
22 A:Spiderman 2.00
23 A:Spiderman 2.00
24 A:Spiderman 2.00
25 A:Spiderman 2.00
26 A:Spiderman 2.00
27 A:Buth 1.50
28 Pangea 1.50
29 W:Kazar & Shanna, Doub.Size 2.00
30 V:Pterons 1.50
31 PangeaWarII 1.50
32 V:Plunderer 1.50
33 V:Plunderer 1.50
34 Last Issue Doub.Size 2.00

[1970 Reprints Series]
August, 1970

1 X-Men ID 14.00
2 Daredevil 12, 13 . . . . 10.00
3 DDH,Spiderman,March, 1971 10.00

KELLYS, THE
See: KID KOMICS

KENT BLAKE OF THE SECRET SERVICE
May, 1951

1 U.S. Govt. Secret Agent stories,Bondage cover 64.00
2 JSt,Drug issue,'Man with out A Face 42.00
3 'Trapped By The Chinese Reds' 27.00
4 Secret Service Stories 27.00
5 RH(c),'Condemned To Death' 27.00
6 Cases from Kent Blake files 27.00
7 RH(c),Behind Enemy Lines . . 27.00
8 V:Communists 27.00
9 thru 13 . . . . @27.00
14 July, 1953 . . . . 27.00

KICKERS INC.
November, 1986

1 SB,O:Kickers 1.25
2 SB 1.00
3 RF,Witches 1.00
4 RF,FIST 1.00
5 RF,A:D.P.7 . . . . 1.00
6 RF 1.00
7 RF 1.00
8 RF 1.00
9 . . . . 1.00
10 TD 1.00
11 . . . . 1.00
12 October, 1987 . . . . 1.00

KID & PLAY

1 Based on Rap Group 1.25
2 Drug Issue 1.25
3 At your Friends Expense 1.25
4 . . . . 1.25
5 . . . . 1.25
6 Record Contract 1.25
7 Fraternity Pledging 1.25
8 Kid and Cindy become an item 1.25
9 C:Marvel Heroes 1.25

KID COLT OUTLAW
Atlas
August, 1948

1 B:Kid Colt,A:Two-Gun Kid . 450.00
2 'Gun-Fighter and the Girl' . . 225.00
3 'Colt-Quick Killers For Hire' 150.00

Kid Colt Outlaw #114

© Marvel Entertainment Group

4 'Wanted',A:Tex Taylor 150.00
5 'Mystery of the Missssing Mine',A:Blaze Carson 150.00
6 A:Tex Taylor,'Valley of the Warewolf' 125.00
7 B:Nimo the Lion 125.00
8 . . . . 125.00
9 . . . . 135.00
10 'The Whip Strikes',E:Nimo the Lion' 135.00
11 O:Kid Colt 150.00
12 . . . . 80.00
13 DRi 80.00
14 . . . . 80.00
15 'Gun Whipped in Shotgun City' 80.00
16 . . . . 80.00
17 . . . . 80.00
18 DRi 80.00
19 . . . . 60.00
20 'The Outlaw' 60.00
21 thru 30 . . . . @60.00

31 .... 55.00
32 .... 55.00
33 thru 45 A:Black Rider .... @40.00
46 RH(c) 35.00
47 DW 35.00
48 RH(c),JKu 38.00
49 .... 35.00
50 .... 35.00
51 thru 56 .... @30.00
57 AW 38.00
58 AW 38.00
59 AW 38.00
60 AW 38.00
61 .... 20.00
62 .... 20.00
63 .... 20.00
64 .... 25.00
65 .... 25.00
66 thru 78 .... @20.00
79 Origin Retold 25.00
80 thru 86 .... @20.00
87 JDa(reprint) 25.00
88 AW 30.00
89 AW,Matt Slade 30.00
90 thru 99 .... @12.00
100 .... 19.00
101 .... 14.00
102 .... 10.00
103 'The Great Train Robbery' 10.00
104 JKu(c),DH,'Trail of Kid Colt' 10.00
105 DH,V:Dakota Dixon 10.00
106 JKu(c),'The Circus of Crime' 10.00
107 .... 10.00
108 BEv 10.00
109 DAy,V:The Barracuda 10.00
110 GC,V:Iron Mask 10.00
111 JKu(c),V:Sam Hawk, The Man Hunter 10.00
112 JKu(c),V:Mr. Brown 10.00
113 JKu(c),GC,V:Bull Barton 10.00
114 JKu(c),Return of Iron Mask 10.00
115 JKu(c),V:The Scorpion 10.00
116 JKu(c),GC,V:Dr. Danger & Invisible Gunman 10.00
117 JKu(c),GC,V:The Fatman & His Boomerang 10.00
118 V:Scorpion,Bull Barton, Dr. Danger 10.00
119 DAy(c),JK,V:Bassett The Badman 10.00
120 'Cragsons Ride Again' 10.00
121 A:Rawhide Kid,Iron Mask 7.50
122 V:Rattler Ruxton 7.50
123 V:Ringo Barker 7.50
124 A:Phantom Raider 7.50
125 A:Two-Gun Kid 7.50
126 V:Wes Hardin 6.00
127 thru 129 .... @6.00
130 O:Kid Colt 6.00
131 thru 150 .... @6.00
151 thru 200 reprints .... @4.00
201 thru 228 reprints .... @2.00
229 April, 1979 .... 2.00

KID FROM DODGE CITY

Atlas
July, 1957

1 .... 40.00
2 September, 1957 .... 21.00

KID FROM TEXAS

Atlas
June, 1957

1 .... 45.00
2 August, 1957 .... 25.00

KID KOMICS

Timely
February, 1943

1 SSh(c),BW,O:Captain Wonder & Tim Mulrooney I:Whitewash, Knuckles,Trixie Trouble, Pinto Pete Subbie 1,500.00
2 AsH(c),F:Captain Wonder Subbie, B:Young Allies, B:Red Hawk,Tommy Tyme 700.00
3 ASh(c),A:The Vision & Daredevils 500.00
4 ASh(c),B:Destroyer,A:Sub-Mariner, E:Red Hawk,Tommy Tyme 450.00
5 ASh(c),V:Nazis 350.00
6 ASh(c),V:Japanese 350.00
7 ASh(c),B;Whizzer 350.00
8 ASh(c),V:Train Robbers 350.00
9 ASh(c),V:Elves 350.00
10 ASh(c),E:Young Allies, The Destoyer,The Whizzer 350.00

Becomes:

KID MOVIE KOMICS

11 F:Silly Seal,Ziggy Pig HK,Hey Look 150.00

Rusty #14
© Marvel Entertainment Group

Becomes:

RUSTY COMICS

12 F:Rusty,A:Mitzi 70.00
13 Do not Disturb(c) 42.00
14 Beach(c),BW,HK,Hey Look 67.00
15 Picnic(c),HK,Hey Look 56.00
16 Juniors Grades,HK,HeyLook 56.00
17 John in Trouble,HK,HeyLook 56.00
18 John Fired 30.00
19 Fridge raid(c),HK 30.00
20 And Her Family,HK 57.00
21 And Her Family,HK 90.00
22 .... 90.00

Becomes:

KELLYS, THE

23 F:The Kelly Family(Pop, Mom,Mike,Pat & Goliath) 52.00
24 Mike's Date,A;Margie 34.00
25 Wrestling(c) 34.00

Becomes:

SPY CASES

26(#1) Spy stories 100.00
27(#2) BEv,Bondage(c) 60.00
28(#3) Sabotage,A:Douglas Grant Secret Agent 60.00
4 The Secret Invasion 40.00
5 The Vengeance of Comrade de Casto 40.00
6 A:Secret Agent Doug Grant 40.00
7 GT,A:Doug Grant 40.00

Spy Cases #9
© Marvel Entertainment Group

8 Atom Bomb(c),Frozen Horror 50.00
9 Undeclared War 40.00
10 Battlefield Adventures 35.00
11 Battlefield Adventures 30.00
12 Battlefield Adventures 30.00
13 Battlefield Adventures 30.00
14 Battlefield Adventures 30.00
15 Doug Grant 30.00
16 Doug Grant 30.00
17 Doug Grant 30.00
18 Contact in Ankara 30.00
19 Final Issue,October, 1953 .... 30.00

KID SLADE GUNFIGHTER

See: MATT SLADE

KILLPOWER: THE EARLY YEARS

1 B:MiB,Goes on Rampage 3.25
2 thru 3 O:Killpower 2.00
4 E:MiB,last issue 2.00

KING ARTHUR & THE KNIGHTS OF JUSTICE

1 Based on Cartoon 1.25
2 Based on Cartoon 1.25
3 Based on Cartoon 1.25

KING CONAN:

See: CONAN THE KING

KITTY PRIDE & WOLVERINE

November, 1984

1 AM,V:Ogun 8.00
2 AM,V:Ogun 6.00
3 AM,V:Ogun 5.00
4 AM,V:Ogun 5.00
5 AM,V:Ogun 5.50
6 AM,D:Ogun, April, 1985 .... 5.50

KNIGHTS OF PENDRAGON

July, 1990
[1st Regular Series]

1 GEr 2.75
2 thru 7 .... @2.25

8 inc.SBi Poster 2.25
9 V:Bane Fisherman 2.25
10 Cap.Britain/Union Jack 2.25
11 A:Iron Man 2.25
12 A:Iron Man,Union Jack 2.25
13 O:Pendragon 2.25
14 A:Mr.Fantastic,Invisible Woman Black Panther 2.25
15 BlackPanther/Union Jack T.U. . 2.25
16 A:Black Panther 2.25
17 D:Albion, Union Jack, A:Black Panther 2.25
18 A:Iron Man,Black Panther 2.25

[2nd Regular Series]

1 GEr,A:Iron Man,R:Knights of Pendragon,V:MyS-TECH 2.25
2 A:Iron Man,Black Knight 2.00
3 PGa,A:Iron Man,Black Knight . . 2.00
4 Gawain Vs. Bane 2.00
5 JRe,V:Magpie 2.00
6 A:Spider-Man 2.00
7 A:Spider-Man,V:Warheads 2.00
8 JRe,A:Spider-Man 2.00
9 A:Spider-Man,Warheads 2.00
10 V:Baron Blood 2.00
11 . . . . 2.00
12 MyS-TECH Wars,V:Skire 2.00
13 A:Death's Head II 2.00
14 A:Death's Head II 2.00
15 D:Adam,A:Death's Head II . . . 2.00

KRAZY KOMICS
Timely
July, 1942

1 B:Ziggy Pig,Silly Seal 200.00
2 Toughy Tomcat(c) 115.00
3 Toughy Tomcat/Bunny(c) . . . 62.00
4 Toughy Tomcat/Ziggy(c) 62.00
5 Ziggy/Buzz Saw(c) 62.00
6 Toughy/Cannon(c) 62.00
7 Cigar Store Indian(c) 62.00
8 Toughy/Hammock(c) 62.00
9 Hitler(c) 62.00
10 Newspaper(c) 80.00
11 Canoe(c) 44.00
12 Circus(c) 75.00
13 Pirate Treasure(c) 44.00
14 Fishing(c) 44.00
15 Ski-Jump(c) 45.00
16 Airplane(c) 33.00
17 Street corner(c) 33.00
18 Mallet/Bell(c) 33.00
19 Bicycle(c) 33.00
20 Ziggy(c) 33.00
21 Toughy's date(c) 33.00
22 Crystal Ball(c) 33.00
23 Sharks in bathtub(c) 33.00
24 Baseball(c) 33.00
25 HK,Krazy Krow(c) 48.00
26 Super Rabbit(c) 33.00

Becomes:

CINDY COMICS

27 HK,B:Margie,Oscar 75.00
28 HK,Snow sled(c) 50.00
29 . . . . 50.00
30 . . . . 50.00
31 HK 50.00
32 . . . . 30.00
33 A;Georgie 30.00
34 thru 40 . . . . @30.00

Becomes:

CRIME CAN'T WIN

41 Crime stories 90.00
42 . . . . 45.00
43 GT,Horror story 60.00
4 thru 11 . . . . @35.00
12 September, 1953 . . . . 35.00

KRAZY KOMICS
Timely
[2nd Series]
August, 1948

1 BW,HK,B:Eustice Hayseed . 225.00
2 BW,O:Powerhouse Pepper November, 1948 . . . . 150.00

KRAZY KROW
Summer, 1945

1 B:Krazy Krow 92.00
2 . . . . 55.00
3 Winter, 1945-46 . . . . 55.00

Kree-Skrull War #1
© Marvel Entertainment Group

KREE-SKULL WAR
September, 1983

1 JB,NA,reprints 5.00
2 JB,NA,October, 1983 . . . . 5.00

KRULL
November, 1983

1 Ph(c),BBI,movie adapt 1.00
2 BBI,reprint,Marvel Super Special,December, 1983 . . . . . 1.00

KULL
[1st Series]
June, 1971

1 MSe,RA,WW,A King Comes Riding,O:Kull 10.00
2 MSe,JSe,Shadow Kingdom . . . 5.00
3 MSe,JSe,Death Dance of Thulsa Doom 5.00
4 MSe,JSe,Night o/t Red Slayers 3.00
5 MSe,JSe,Kingdom By the Sea . 3.00
6 MSe,JSe,Lurker Beneath the Sea 2.00
7 MSe,JSe,Delcardes'Cat, A:Thulsa Doom 2.00
8 MSe,JSe,Wolfshead 2.00
9 MSe,JSe,The Scorpion God . . 2.00
10 MSe,Swords o/t White Queen . 2.00
11 MP,King Kull Must Die, O:Kull cont.,A:Thulsa Doom 2.00
12 MP,SB,Moon of Blood,V:Thulsa Doom,B:SD,B.U.stories 2.00
13 MP,AM,Torches From Hell, V:Thulsa Doom 2.00
14 MP,JA,The Black Belfry, A:Thulsa Doom 2.00
15 MP,Wings o/t Night-Beast, E:SD,B.U.stories 2.00
16 EH,Tiger in the Moon, A:Thulsa Doom 2.00
17 AA,EH,Thing from Emerald Darkness 2.00
18 EH,AA,Keeper of Flame & Frost 2.00
19 EH,AA,The Crystal Menace . . 2.00
20 EH,AA,Hell Beneath Atlantis . . 2.00
21 City of the Crawling Dead 1.75
22 Talons of the Devil-Birds 1.75
23 Demon Shade 1.75
24 Screams in the Dark 1.75
25 A Lizard's Throne 1.75
26 Into Death's Dimension 1.75
27 The World Within 1.75
28 Creature and the Crown, A:Thulsa Doom 1.75
29 To Sit the Topaz Throne, V:Thulsa Doom, final issue . . . 1.75

[2nd Series]

1 JB,Brule 2.50
2 Misareenia 2.00

[3rd Series]
May, 1983

1 JB,BWi,DG,Iraina 1.50
2 JB,Battle to the Death 1.25
3 JB 1.00
4 JB 1.00
5 JB 1.00
6 JB 1.00
7 JB,Masquerade Death 1.00
8 JB 1.00
9 JB 1.00
10 JB,June, 1985 . . . . 1.00

KULL AND THE BARBARIANS
May, 1975

1 NA,GK,reprint Kull #1 . . . . 5.00
2 BBI,reprint,December, 1983 . . . 2.00
3 NA,HC,,O:Red Sonja 3.00

LABRYNTH
May, 1986

1 Movie adapt 2.00
2 . . . . 1.50
3 January, 1987 . . . . 1.50

LAFF-A-LYMPICS
March, 1978

1 F;Hanna Barbera 2.00
2 thru 5 . . . . @1.50
6 thru 13, March 1979 . . . . . . @1.00

LANA
August, 1948

1 F:Lana Lane The Show Girl, A:Rusty,B:Millie 75.00
2 HK,Hey Look,A:Rusty 50.00
3 Show(c),B:Nellie 30.00
4 Ship(c) 30.00
5 Audition(c) 30.00
6 Stop sign(c) 30.00
7 Beach(c) 30.00

Becomes:

LITTLE LANA

8 Little Lana(c) 26.00
9 Final Issue,March, 1950 . . . . 26.00

LANCE BARNES: POST NUKE DICK

1 I:Lance Barnes 2.50
2 Cigarettes 2.50
3 Warring Mall Tribe 2.50
4 V:Ex-bankers,last issue 2.50

LAST AMERICAN
Epic
December, 1990

1 . . . . 3.50
2 . . . . 3.00
3 . . . . 2.50
4 Final issue, March, 1991. . . . . 2.25

LAST STARFIGHTER, THE
October, 1984

1 JG(c),BBI,Movie adapt 1.00
2 Movie adapt 1.00
3 BBI,December, 1984 . . . . 1.00

LAWBREAKERS ALWAYS LOSE!
Spring, 1948

1 Partial Ph(c),Adam and Eve, HK,Giggles and Grins 125.00
2 FBI V:Fur Theives 60.00
3 . . . . 50.00
4 Asylum(c) 50.00
5 . . . . 50.00
6 Pawnbroker(c) 55.00
7 Crime at Midnight 125.00
8 Prison Break 40.00
9 Ph(c),He Prowled at Night . . 40.00
10 Phc(c),I Met My Murderer October, 1949 . . . . 40.00

LAWDOG

1 B:CDi(s),FH,I:Lawdog 2.50
2 FH,V:Vocal-yokel Cultist 2.25
3 FH,Manical Nazis 2.25
4 FH,V:Zombies 2.25
5 thru 6 FH . . . . @2.25
7 FH,V:Zombies 2.25
8 FH,w/card 2.25
9 FH,w/card 2.25
10 last issue, w/card 2.25

LAWDOG & GRIMROD: TERROR AT THE CROSSROADS

1 . . . . 3.50

LEGION OF MONSTERS
September, 1975
(black & white magazine)

1 NA(c),GM,I&O:Legion of Monsters,O:Manphibian 30.00

LEGION OF NIGHT
October, 1991

1 WPo/SW,A:Fin Fang Foom . . . 5.50
2 WPo,V:Fin Fang Foom 5.50

LETHAL FOES OF SPIDERMAN

1 B:DFr(s),SMc,R:Stegron 2.00
2 SMc,A:Stegron 2.00
3 SMc,V:Spider-Man 2.00
4 E:DFr(s),SMc,Last Issue 2.00

LIFE OF CAPTAIN MARVEL
August, 1985

1 rep.Iron Man #55, Capt.Marvel #25,26 . . . . 9.00
2 rep.Capt.Marvel#26-28 . . . . . . 6.50
3 rep.Capt.Marvel#28-30 Marvel Feature #12 . . . . 6.00
4 rep.Marvel Feature #12,Capt. Marvel #31,32,Daredevil#105 . 6.00
5 rep.Capt.Marvel #32-#34 . . . . . 6.00

LIFE OF CHRIST

1 Birth of Christ 2.99
2 MW,The Easter Story 2.99

LIFE OF POPE JOHN-PAUL II

1 JSt, January, 1983 . . . . 5.00
1a Special reprint 3.00

LIFE WITH MILLIE
See: DATE WITH MILLIE

Life of Captain Marvel #3
© Marvel Entertainment Group

LIGHT AND DARKNESS WAR
Epic
October, 1988

1 . . . . 4.00
2 . . . . 3.00
3 thru 6 December, 1989 . . . @2.50

LINDA CARTER, STUDENT NURSE
Atlas
September, 1961

1 . . . . 24.00
2 thru 9, January, 1963 . . . . @15.00

LI'L KIDS
August, 1970

1 . . . . 7.50
2 thru 11 . . . . @4.50
12 June, 1973 . . . . 4.50

LI'L PALS
September, 1972

1 . . . . 2.50
2 thru 5, May, 1973 . . . . @2.50

LITTLE ASPRIN
July, 1949

1 HK,A;Oscar 66.00
2 HK 38.00
3 December, 1949 . . . . 20.00

LITTLE LANA
See: LANA

LITTLE LENNY
June, 1949

1 . . . . 40.00
2 . . . . 22.00
3 November, 1949 . . . . 22.00

LITTLE LIZZIE
June, 1949

1 Roller Skating(c) 44.00
2 Soda(c) 25.00
3 Movies(c) 25.00
4 Lizzie(c) 25.00
5 Lizzie/Swing(c) April,1950 . . . 25.00

[2nd Series]
September, 1953

1 . . . . 30.00
2 . . . . 20.00
3 January, 1954 . . . . 20.00

LOGAN'S RUN
January, 1977

1 GP,From Movie 4.00
2 GP,Cathedral Kill 2.50
3 GP,Lair of Laser Death 2.50
4 GP,Dread Sanctuary 2.50
5 GP,End Run 2.50
6 MZ,B.U.Thanos/Drax 23.00
7 TS,Cathedral Prime 2.50

LONGSHOT
September, 1985

1 AAd,WPo(i),BA,I:Longshot . . . 22.00
2 AAd,WPo(i),I:RicoshetRita . . . 17.00
3 AAd,WPo(i),I:Mojo,Spiral 15.00
4 AAd,WPo(i),A:Spider-Man . . . 16.00
5 AAd,WPo(i),A:Dr. Strange . . . 15.00
6 AAd,WPo(i),A:Dr. Strange . . . 18.00
TPB Reprints #1-#6 . . . . 16.95

LORNA, THE JUNGLE GIRL
Atlas
July, 1953

1 Terrors of the Jungle,O:Lorna 135.00
2 Headhunter's Strike I:Greg Knight 65.00
3 . . . . 50.00
4 . . . . 50.00
5 . . . . 50.00
6 RH(c),GT 40.00
7 RH(c) 40.00
8 Jungle Queen Strikes Again . 40.00
9 . . . . 40.00
10 White Fang 40.00
11 Death From the Skies 40.00
12 Day of Doom 30.00
13 thru 17 . . . . @30.00
18 AW(c) 45.00
19 thru 25 . . . . @30.00
26 August, 1957 . . . . 30.00

LOVE ADVENTURES
Atlas
October, 1949

1 Ph(c) 60.00
2 Ph(c),Tyrone Power/Gene Tierney 55.00
3 thru 12 . . . . @26.00

Becomes:

ACTUAL CONFESSIONS

13 . . . . 16.00
14 December, 1952 . . . . 16.00

LOVE DRAMAS
October, 1949

1 Ph(c),JKa 75.00
2 January, 1950 . . . . 50.00

LOVE ROMANCES
See: IDEAL

LOVERS
See: ALL-SELECT COMICS

LOVE SECRETS
October, 1949

1 . . . . 50.00
2 January, 1950 . . . . 35.00

MACHINE MAN
April, 1978

1 JK,From 2001 . . . . 5.00
2 JK 3.00
3 JK,V:Ten-For,The Mean

Machine Man #10
© Marvel Entertainment Group

Machine 3.00
4 JK,V;Ten-For,Battle on A Busy Street 3.00
5 JK,V;Ten-For,Day of the Non-Hero 2.50
6 JK,V;Ten-For 2.50
7 JK,With A Nation Against Him . 2.50
8 JK,Escape:Impossible 2.50
9 JK,In Final Battle 2.50
10 SD,Birth of A Super-Hero 2.50
11 SD,V;Binary Bug 2.50
12 SD,"Where walk the Gods" . . . 2.50
13 SD,Xanadu 2.50
14 SD,V:Machine Man 2.50
15 SD,A:Thing,Human Torch 2.50
16 SD,I:Baron Brimstone And the Satan Squad 2.50
17 SD,Madam Menace 2.50
18 A:Alpha Flight 6.50
19 I:Jack o'Lantern 20.00

MACHINE MAN
[Limited-Series]
October, 1984

1 HT,BWS,V:Baintronics 5.00
2 HT,BWS,C:Iron Man of 2020 . . 5.00
3 HT,BWS,I:Iron Man of 2020 . . . 6.00
4 HT,BWS,V:Iron Man of 2020 . . 4.50
TPB rep.#1-4 . . . . 5.95

MAD ABOUT MILLIE
April, 1969

1 . . . . 23.00
2 thru 16 . . . . @12.50
17 December, 1970 . . . . 12.50
Ann.#1 . . . . 10.00

MADBALLS
Star
September, 1986

1 Based on Toys 1.25
2 thru 9 . . . . @1.00
10 June, 1988 . . . . 1.00

MAD DOG

1 from Bob TV Show 1.50
2 V:Trans World Trust Corp. 1.25
3 V:Cigarette Criminals 1.25
4 V:Dogs of War 1.25
5 thru 6 . . . . @1.95

MAGIK
December, 1983

1 JB,TP,F:Storm and Illyana 4.00
2 JB,TP,A:Belasco,Sym 3.50
3 TP,A:New Mutants,Belasco . . . 3.50
4 TP,V:Belasco,A:Sym 3.50

MAGNETO

0 JD,JBo,rep. origin stories. . . . 10.00

MAN COMICS
Atlas
December, 1949

1 GT,Revenge 80.00
2 GT,Fury in his Fists 40.00
3 Mantrap 35.00
4 The Fallen Hero 35.00
5 Laugh,Fool,Laugh 35.00
6 Black Hate 25.00
7 The Killer 25.00
8 BEv,An Eye For an Eye 30.00
9 B:War Issues,Here Comes Sergeant Smith 22.00
10 Korean Communism 22.00
11 RH,Cannon Fodder 22.00
12 The Black Hate 22.00
13 GC,RH,Beach Head 22.00
14 GT,No Prisoners 35.00
15 . . . . 20.00
16 . . . . 16.00
17 RH 16.00
18 thru 20 . . . . @16.00
21 GC 16.00
22 BEv,BK,JSt 50.00
23 thru 26 . . . . @16.00
27 E:War Issues 16.00
28 Where Mummies Prowl, Sept., 1953 . . . . 16.00

MAN FROM ATLANTIS
February, 1978

1 TS,From TV Series,O:Mark Harris 1.50
2 FR,FS,The Bermuda Triangle Trap 1.25
3 FR,FS,Undersea Shadow 1.25
4 FR,FS,Beware the Killer Spores 1.25
5 FR,FS,The Ray of the Red Death 1.25
6 FR,FS,Bait for the Behemoth . 1.25
7 FR,FS,Behold the Land Forgotten, August, 1978 . . . . 1.25

MAN-THING
[1st Series]
January, 1974

1 FB,JM,A:Howard the Duck . . . 17.00
2 VM,ST,Hell Hath No Fury . . . 10.00
3 VM,JA,I:Original Foolkiller 9.00
4 VM,JA,O&D:Foolkiller 7.00
5 MP,Night o/t Laughing Dead . . 4.00
6 MP,V:Soul-Slayers,Drug Issue . 4.00
7 MP,A Monster Stalks Swamp . . 4.00
8 MP,Man Into Monster 4.00
9 MP,Deathwatch 4.00
10 MP,Nobody Dies Forever 4.00
11 MP,Dance to the Murder 4.00
12 KJ,Death-Cry of a Dead Man . 4.00
13 TS,V:Captain Fate 4.00
14 AA,V:Captain Fate 4.00
15 A Candle for Saint Cloud 4.00
16 JB,TP,Death of a Legend 4.00
17 JM,Book Burns in Citrusville . . 4.00
18 JM,Chaos on the Campus . . . 4.00
19 JM,FS,I:Scavenger 4.00
20 JM,A:Spider-Man,Daredevil., Shang-Chi,Thing 4.50
21 JM,O:Scavenger,Man Thing . . 4.00
22 JM,C:Howard the Duck 4.00

Giant-Sized

1 MP,SD,JK,Rep.The Glob 6.00
2 JB,KJ,The Monster Runs Wild . 4.00
3 AA,A World He Never Made . . 4.00
4 FS,EH,inc.H.Duck vs.Gorko . . . 4.00
5 DA,EH,inc.H.Duck vs.Vampire . 6.00

MAN-THING
[2nd Series]
November, 1979

1 JM,BWi 2.00
2 BWi,JM,Himalayan Nightmare . 1.50
3 BWi.JM,V:Snowman 1.50
4 BWi,DP,V:Mordo,A:Dr Strange . 1.50
5 DP,BWi,This Girl is Terrified . . 1.50
6 DP,BWi,Fraternity Rites 1.00
7 BWi,DP Return of Captain Fate 1.00
8 BWi,DP,V:Captain Fate 1.00
9 BWi(c),Save the Life of My Own Child 1.00
10 BWi,DP,Swampfire 1.00
11 Final issue, July, 1981 . . . . . . 1.00

MARINES AT WAR
See: DEVIL-DOG DUGAN

MARINES IN ACTION
Atlas
June, 1955

1 B:Rock Murdock,Boot Camp Brady 35.00
2 thru 13 . . . . @16.00
14 September, 1957 . . . . 16.00

MARINES IN BATTLE
Atlas
August, 1954

1 RH,B:Iron Mike McGraw 60.00
2 . . . . 30.00
3 thru 6 . . . . @25.00
7 . . . . 35.00
8 . . . . 25.00
9 . . . . 25.00
10 . . . . 25.00
11 thru 16 . . . . @20.00
17 . . . . 35.00
18 thru 22 . . . . @20.00
23 . . . . 35.00
24 . . . . 20.00
25 September, 1958 . . . . 25.00

MARSHALL LAW
Epic
October, 1987

1 . . . . 4.50
2 . . . . 3.00
3 . . . . 2.50
4 . . . . 2.50
5 . . . . 2.25
6 May, 1989 . . . . 1.95

MARVEL ACTION UNIVERSE
TV Tie-in
January, 1989

1 Rep.Spider-Man & Friends . . . 2.50

MARVEL ADVENTURES
STARRING DAREDEVIL
December, 1975

1 Rep,Daredevil #22 . . . . 2.00
2 thru 5, Rep,Daredevil #23-26 @1.25
6 DD #27 October, 1976 . . . . . . 1.25

MARVEL & DC PRESENTS
November, 1982

1 WS,TA,X-Men & Titans,A:Darkseid, Deathstroke(3rd App.), ... 18.00

MARVEL BOY
December, 1950

1 RH,O:Marvel Boy,Lost World 450.00

2 BEv,The Zero Hour 400.00

Becomes:

ASTONISHING

3 BEv,Marvel Boy,V:Mr Death 400.00
4 BEv,Stan Lee,The Screaming Tomb 300.00
5 BEv,Horro in the Caves of Doom 300.00
6 BEv,My Coffin is Waiting E:Marvel Boy 300.00
7 JR,Nightmare 100.00
8 RH,Behind the Wall 100.00
9 RH(c),The Little Black Box . 100.00
10 BEv,Walking Dead 100.00
11 BF,JSt.Mr Mordeau 85.00
12 GC,BEv,Horror Show 85.00
13 BK,MSy,Ghouls Gold 85.00
14 BK,The Long Jump Down .. 85.00
15 BEv(c),Grounds for Death ... 75.00
16 BEv(c),DAy,SSh,Don't Make a Ghoul of Yourself 85.00
17 Who Was the Wilmach Werewolf? 75.00
18 BEv(c),JR,Vampire at my Window 100.00
19 BK,Back From the Grave ... 85.00
20 GC,Mystery at Midnight ... 75.00
21 Manhunter 60.00
22 RH(c),Man Against Werewolf 60.00
23 The Woman in Black 65.00
24 JR,The Stone Face 60.00
25 RC,I Married a Zombie 70.00
26 RH(c),I Died Too Often 55.00
27 .... 55.00
28 No Evidence 55.00
29 BEv(c),GC,Decapitation(c) .. 55.00
30 Tentacled eyeball story 90.00
31 .... 50.00
32 A Vampire Takes a Wife 50.00
33 SMo 50.00
34 Transformation 50.00
35 .... 50.00
36 Pithecanthrope Giant 50.00
37 BEv,Poor Pierre 50.00
38 The Man Who Didn't Belong . 40.00
39 .... 40.00
40 .... 40.00
41 .... 40.00
42 .... 40.00
43 .... 40.00
44 RC 50.00
45 BK 50.00
46 .... 40.00
47 BK 50.00
48 .... 40.00
49 .... 40.00
50 .... 40.00
51 .... 40.00
52 .... 40.00
53 .... 45.00
54 .... 45.00
55 .... 55.00
56 .... 40.00
57 .... 60.00
58 .... 35.00
59 .... 35.00
60 .... 55.00
61 .... 35.00
62 .... 38.00
63 August, 1957 .... 38.00

MARVEL CHILLERS

October, 1975

1 GK(c),I:Mordred the Mystic ... 4.00
2 E:Mordred 2.50
3 HC/BWr(c),B:Tigra,The Were Woman 2.50
4 V:Kraven The Hunter 2.50
5 V:Rat Pack,A:Red Wolf 2.50
6 RB(c),JBy,V:Red Wolf 2.50
7 JK(c),GT,V:Super Skrull E:Tigra,October, 1976 ..... 2.50

MARVEL CHRISTMAS SPECIAL

1 DC/AAd/KJ/SB/RLm,A:Ghost Rider X-Men,Spider-Man 2.25

MARVEL CLASSICS COMICS

1976

1 GK/DA(c),B:Reprints from Pendulum Illustrated Comics Dr.Jekyll & Mr. Hyde 5.00
2 GK(c),AN,Time Machine 3.50
3 GK/KJ(c) The Hunchback of Notre Dame 3.50
4 GK/DA(c),20,000 Leagues– Beneath the Sea 3.50
5 GK(c),RN,Black Beauty 3.50
6 GK(c),Gullivers Travels 3.50
7 GK(c),Tom Sawyer 3.50
8 GK(c),AN,Moby Dick 3.50
9 GK(c),NR,Dracula 3.50
10 GK(c),Red Badge of Courage . 3.50
11 GK(c),Mysterious Island 3.50
12 GK/DA(c),AN,Three Musketeers 3.50
13 GK(c),Last of the Mohicans ... 3.50
14 GK(c),War of the Worlds 3.50
15 GK(c),Treasure Island 3.50
16 GK(c),Ivanhoe 3.00
17 JB/ECh(c),The Count of Monte Cristo 3.00
18 ECh(c),The Odsyssey 3.00
19 JB(c),Robinson Crusoe 3.00
20 Frankenstein 3.00
21 GK(c),Master of the World .. 3.00
22 GK(c),Food of the Gods 3.00
23 Moonstone 3.00
24 GK/RN(c),She 3.00
25 The Invisible Man 3.00
26 JB(c),The Illiad 3.00
27 Kidnapped 3.00
28 MGo(1st art) The Pit and the Pendulum 10.00
29 The Prisoner of Zenda 3.00
30 The Arabian Nights 3.00
31 The First Men in the Moon ... 3.00
32 GK(c),White Fang 3.00
33 The Prince and the Pauper ... 3.00
34 AA,Robin Hood 3.00
35 FBe,Alice in Wonderland 3.00
36 A Christmas Carol December, 1978 .... 3.00

MARVEL COLLECTORS ITEM CLASSICS

February, 1965

1 SD,JK,reprint FF #2 .... 46.00
2 SD,JK,reprint FF #3 .... 25.00
3 SD,JK,reprint FF #4 .... 25.00
4 SD,JK,reprint FF #7 .... 25.00
5 SD,JK,reprint FF #8 .... 12.00
6 SD,JK,reprint FF #9 .... 12.00
7 SD,JK,reprint FF #13 ...... 12.00
8 SD,JK,reprint FF #10 ...... 12.00
9 SD,JK,reprint FF #14 ...... 12.00
10 SD,JK,reprint FF #15 ...... 12.00
11 SD,JK,reprint FF #16 ...... 10.00
12 SD,JK,reprint FF #17 ...... 10.00
13 SD,JK,reprint FF #18 ...... 10.00
14 SD,JK,reprint FF #20 ...... 10.00
15 SD,JK,reprint FF #21 ...... 10.00
16 SD,JK,reprint FF #22 ...... 10.00
17 SD,JK,reprint FF #23 ...... 10.00
18 SD,JK,reprint FF #24 ...... 10.00
19 SD,JK,reprint FF #27 ...... 10.00
20 SD,JK,reprint FF #28 ...... 10.00
21 SD,JK,reprint FF #29 ...... 10.00
22 SD,JK,reprint FF #30 ...... 10.00

Becomes:

MARVEL'S GREATEST COMICS

23 SD,JK,reprint FF#31 .... 4.00
24 SD,JK,reprint FF#32 .... 4.00
25 SD,JK,reprint FF#33 .... 4.00
26 SD,JK,reprint FF#34 .... 4.00
27 SD,JK,reprint FF#35 .... 4.00
28 SD,JK,reprint FF#36 .... 4.00
29 JK,reprint FF#37 .... 4.00
30 JK,reprint FF#38 .... 4.00
31 JK,reprint FF#40 .... 4.00
32 JK,reprint FF#42 .... 4.00
33 JK,reprint FF#44 .... 4.00
34 JK,reprint FF#47 .... 4.00
35 JK,reprint FF#48 .... 8.50
36 JK,reprint FF#49 .... 7.00
37 JK,reprint FF#50 .... 7.00
38 JK,reprint FF#51 .... 3.00
39 JK,reprint FF#52 .... 3.00
40 JK,reprint FF#53 .... 3.00
41 JK,reprint FF#54 .... 3.00
42 JK,reprint FF#55 .... 3.00
43 JK,reprint FF#56 .... 3.00
44 JK,reprint FF#61 .... 3.00
45 JK,reprint FF#62 .... 3.00
46 JK,reprint FF#63 .... 3.00
47 JK,reprint FF#64 .... 3.00
48 JK,reprint FF#65 .... 3.00
49 JK,reprint FF#66 .... 6.00
50 JK,reprint FF#67 .... 6.00
51 thru 75 JK,reprint FF ..... @1.75
76 thru 82 JK,reprint FF ..... @1.25
83 thru 95 Reprint FF .... @1.25
96 Reprint FF#, January, 1981 . 1.25

MARVEL COMICS

October-November, 1939

1 FP(c),BEv,CBu,O:Sub-Mariner I&B:The Angel,A:Human Torch, Kazar,Jungle Terror, B:The Masked Raider .. 80,000.00

Becomes:

MARVEL MYSTERY COMICS

2 CSM(c),BEv,CBu,PGn, B:American, Ace,Human Torch,Sub-Mariner,Kazar 10,000.00

Marvel Mystery Comics #10
© Marvel Entertainment Group

3 ASh(c),BEv,CBu,PGn, E:American Ace 4,500.00
4 ASh(c),BEv,CBu,PGn, I&B:Electro,The Ferret, Mystery Detective 3,500.00
5 ASh(c),BEv,CBu,PGn, Human Torch(c) 8,000.00

6 ASh(c),BEv,CBu,PGn, Anglel(c) 2,400.00
7 ASh(c),BEv,CBu,PGn, Bondage(c) 2,300.00
8 ASh(c),BEv,CBu,PGn,Human TorchV:Sub-Mariner 2,500.00
9 ASh(c),BEv,CBu,PGn,Human Torch V:Sub-Mariner(c) . . 7,000.00
10 ASh(c),BEv,CBu,PGn,B:Terry Vance Boy Detective 2,000.00
11 ASh(c),BEv,CBu,PGn, Human Torch V:Nazis(c) . . 1,600.00
12 ASh(c),BEv,CBu, PGn,Angel(c) 1,500.00
13 ASh(c),BEv,CBu,PGn,S&K, I&B:The Vision 1,700.00
14 ASh(c),BEv,CBu,PGn,S&K, Sub-Mariner V:Nazis 1,000.00
15 ASh(c),BEv,CBu,PGn,S&K, Sub-Mariner(c) 1,000.00
16 ASh(c),BEv,CBu,PGn,S&K, HumanTorch/NaziAirbase(c)1,000.00
17 ASh(c),BEv,CBu,PGn,S&K Human Torch/Sub-Mariner 1,100.00
18 ASh(c),BEv,CBu,PGn,S&K, Human Torch & Toro(c) . . . 950.00
19 ASh(c),BEv,CBu,PGn,S&K, O:Toro,E:Electro 900.00
20 ASh(c),BEv,CBu,PGn,S&K, O:The Angel 1,000.00
21 ASh(c),BEv,CBu,PGn,S&K, I&B:The Patriot 900.00
22 ASh(c),BEv,CBu,PGn,S&K, Toro/Bomb(c) 750.00
23 ASh(c),BEv,CBu,PGn,S&K, O:Vision,E:The Angel 750.00
24 ASh(c),BEv,CBu,S&K, Human Torch(c) 750.00
25 ASh(c),BEv,CBu,S&K,Nazi(c) 750.00
26 ASh(c),BEv,CBu,S&K, Sub-Mariner(c) 650.00
27 ASh(c),BEv,CBu, S&K,E:Kazar 650.00
28 ASh(c),BEv,CBu,S&K,Bondage (c),B:Jimmy Jupiter 650.00
29 ASh(c),BEv,CBu,Bondage(c) 650.00
30 BEv,CBu,Pearl Harbor(c) . 650.00
31 BEv,CBu,HUman Torch(c) . 650.00
32 CBu,I:The Boboes 650.00
33 ASHc(c),CBu,Japanese(c) . 650.00
34 ASh(c),CBu,V:Hitler 750.00
35 ASh(c),Beach Assault(c) . . . 650.00
36 ASh(c),Nazi Invasion of New York(c) 650.00
37 SSh(c),Nazi(c) 650.00
38 SSh(c),Battlefield(c) 650.00
39 ASh(c),Nazis/U.S(c) 650.00
40 ASh(c),Zeppelin(c) 650.00
41 ASh(c),JapaneseCommand(c) 550.00
42 ASh(c),Japanese Sub(c) . . . 550.00
43 ASh(c),Destroyed Bridge(c) . 550.00
44 ASh(c),Nazi Super Plane(c) 550.00
45 ASh(c),Nazi(c) 550.00
46 ASh(c),Hitler Bondage(c) . . 550.00
47 ASh(c),Ruhr Valley Dam(c) . 550.00
48 ASh(c),E:Jimmy Jupiter, Vision,Allied Invasion(c) . . . 550.00
49 SSh(c),O:Miss America, Bondage(c) 700.00
50 ASh(c),Bondage(c),Miss Patriot 550.00
51 ASh(c),Nazi Torture(c) 500.00
52 ASh(c),Bondage(c) 500.00
53 ASh(c),Bondage(c) 500.00
54 ASh(c),Bondage(c) 500.00
55 ASh(c),Bondage(c) 500.00
56 ASh(c),Bondage(c) 500.00
57 ASh(c),Torture/Bondage(c) . 500.00
58 ASH(c),Torture(c) 500.00
59 ASh(c),Testing Room(c) . . . 500.00
60 ASh(c),Japanese Gun(c) . 500.00
61 Torturer Chamber(c) 500.00
62 ASh(c),Violent(c) 500.00
63 ASh(c),NaziHighCommand(c) 500.00
64 ASh(c),Last Nazi(c) 500.00
65 ASh(c),Bondage(c) 500.00
66 ASh(c),Last Japanese(c) . . . 500.00
67 ASh(c),Treasury raid(c) 450.00
68 ASh(c),Torture Chamber(c) . 450.00
69 ASh(c),Torture Chamber(c) . 450.00
70 Cops & Robbers(c) 450.00
71 ASh(c),Egyptian(c) 450.00
72 Police(c) 450.00
73 Werewolf Headlines(c) 450.00
74 ASh(c),Robbery(c),E:The Patriot 450.00
75 Tavern(c),B:Young Allies . . 450.00
76 ASh(c),Shoot-out(c),B:Miss America 450.00
77 Human Torch/Sub-Mariner(c) 450.00
78 Safe Robbery(c) 450.00
79 Super Villians(c),E:The Angel 425.00
80 I:Capt America(in Marvel) . 600.00
81 Mystery o/t Crimson Terror . 500.00
82 I:Sub-Mariner/Namora Team-up O:Namora,A:Capt America . 800.00
83 The Photo Phantom,E;Young Allies 400.00
84 BEv,B:The Blonde Phantom 600.00
85 BEv,A:Blonde Phantom, E;Miss America 400.00
86 BEv,Blonde Phantom ID Revealed,E:Bucky 450.00

Marvel Mystery Comics #77
© Marvel Entertainment Group

87 BEv,I:Capt America/Golden Girl Team-up 500.00
88 BEv,E:Toro 450.00
89 BEv,I:Human Torch/Sun Girl Team-up 500.00
90 BEv,Giant of the Mountains 500.00
91 BEv,I:Venus,E:Blonde Phantom,Sub-Mariner 500.00
92 BEv,How the Human Torch was Born,D:Professor Horton,I:The Witness,A:Capt America . . . 800.00
92a Marvel #33(c)rare,reprints 4,000.00

Becomes:

MARVEL TALES

August, 1949

93 The Ghoul Strikes 550.00
94 BEv,The Haunted Love 400.00
95 The Living Death 300.00
96 MSy,The Monster Returns . 300.00
97 DRi,MSy,The Wooden Horror 300.00
98 BEv,BK,MSy,The Curse of the Black Cat 300.00
99 DRi,The Secret of the Wax Museum 300.00
100 The Eyes of Doom 300.00
101 The Man Who Died Twice . 300.00
102 BW,A Witch Among Us . . . 400.00
103 RA,A Touch of Death 275.00
104 RH(c),BW,BEv,The Thing in the Mirror 375.00
105 RH(c),GC,JSt,The Spider . 250.00
106 RH(c),BK,BEv,In The Dead of the Night 250.00
107 GC,OW,BK,The Thing in the Sewer 250.00
108 RH(c),BEv,JR,Horror in the Moonlight 150.00
109 BEv(c),A Sight for Sore Eyes150.00
110 RH,SSh,A Coffin for Carlos 150.00
111 BEv,Horror Under the Earth 150.00
112 The House That Death Built 150.00
113 RH,Terror Tale 150.00
114 BEv(c),GT,JM,2 for Zombie 150.00
115 The Man With No Face . . . 150.00
116 JSt 150.00
117 BEv(c),GK,Terror in the North 150.00
118 RH,DBr,GC,A World Goes Mad 150.00
119 RH,They Gave Him A Grave 150.00
120 GC,Graveyard(c) 150.00
121 GC,Graveyard(c) 150.00
122 JKu,Missing One Body . . . 150.00
123 No Way Out 150.00
124 He Waits at the Tombstone 150.00
125 JF,Horror House 150.00
126 DW,It Came From Nowhere 100.00
127 BEv(c),GC,MD,Gone is the Gargoyle 100.00
128 Emily,Flying Saucer(c) . . . 100.00
129 You Can't Touch Bottom . 100.00
130 RH(c),JF,The Giant Killer . 100.00
131 GC,BEv,Five Fingers 100.00
132 . . . . 75.00
133 . . . . 75.00
134 BK,JKu,Flying Saucer(c) . . . 90.00
135 thru 141 . . . . @75.00
142 . . . . 75.00
143 . . . . 75.00
144 . . . . 80.00
145 . . . . 75.00
146 . . . . 50.00
147 . . . . 75.00
148 . . . . 50.00
149 . . . . 50.00
150 . . . . 50.00
151 . . . . 50.00
152 . . . . 75.00
153 . . . . 85.00
154 . . . . 50.00
155 . . . . 50.00
156 . . . . 50.00
157 . . . . 75.00
158 . . . . 50.00
159 August, 1957 . . . . 75.00

MARVEL COMICS PRESENTS

September, 1988

1 WS(c),B:Wolverine(JB,KJ),Master of Kung Fu(TS),Man-Thing(TGr,DC) F:Silver Surfer(AM) 12.00
2 F:The Captain(AM) 7.50
3 JR2(c),F:The Thing(AM) 6.00
4 F:Thor(AM) 6.00
5 F:Daredevil(DT,MG) 6.00
6 F:Hulk 5.00
7 F:Submariner(SD) 5.00
8 CV(c),E:Master of Kung Fu,F: Iron Man(JS) 5.00
9 F:Cloak,El Aquila 5.00
10 E:Wolverine,B:Colossus(RL,CR), F:Machine Man(SD,DC) 5.00
11 F:Ant-Man(BL),Slag(RWi) 3.00
12 E:Man-Thing,F:Hercules(DH), Namorita(FS) 3.00

Marvel Comics Presents #44
© Marvel Entertainment Group

13 B:Black Panther(GC,TP),F: Shanna,Mr.Fantastic & Invisible Woman 3.00
14 F:Nomad(CP),Speedball(SD) . 3.00
15 F:Marvel Girl(DT,MG),Red Wolf(JS) 3.00
16 F:Kazar(JM),Longshot(AA) . . . 3.00
17 E:Colossus,B:Cyclops(RLm), F:Watcher(TS) 4.00
18 F:She-Hulk(JBy,BWi),Willie Lumpkin(JSt) 3.00
19 RLd(c)B:Dr.Strange(MBg), I:Damage Control(EC,AW) . . . 3.00
20 E:Dr.Strange,F:Clea(RLm) . . . 3.00
21 F:Thing,Paladin(RWi,DA) 3.00
22 F:Starfox(DC),Wolfsbane & Mirage 3.00
23 F:Falcon(DC),Wheels(RWi) . . . 3.00
24 E:Cyclops,B:Havok(RB,JRu), F:Shamrock(DJ,DA) 3.00
25 F:Ursa Major,I:Nth Man 4.00
26 B&I:Coldblood(PG),F:Hulk 2.50
27 F:American Eagle(RWi) 2.50
28 F:Triton(JS) 2.50
29 F:Quasar(PR) 2.50
30 F:Leir(TMo) 2.50
31 EL,E:Havok,B:Excalibur (EL,TA) 4.00
32 TM(c),F:Sunfire(DH,DC) 3.00
33 F:Namor(JLe) 4.00
34 F:Captain America(JsP) 3.00
35 E:Coldblood,F:Her(EL,AG) . . . 4.00
36 BSz(c),F:Hellcat(JBr) 4.00
37 E:Bl.Panther,F:Devil-Slayer . . . 3.00
38 E:Excalibur,B:Wonderman(JS), Wolverine(JB),F:Hulk(MR,DA) . 4.50
39 F:Hercules(BL),Spider-Man . . . 3.50
40 F:Hercules(BL),Overmind(DH) . 3.50
41 F:Daughters of the Dragon(DA), Union Jack(KD) 3.50
42 F:Iron Man(MBa),Siryn(LSn) . . 3.50
43 F:Iron Man(MBa),Siryn(LSn) . . 3.50
44 F:Puma(BWi),Dr.Strange 3.50
45 E:Wonderman,F:Hulk(HT), Shooting Star 3.50
46 RLd(c),B:Devil-Slayer,F:Namor, Aquarian 3.50
47 JBy(c),E:Wolverine,F:Captain America,Arabian Knight(DP) . . 3.50
48 B:Wolverine&Spider-Man(EL), F:Wasp,Storm&Dr.Doom 5.00
49 E:Devil-Slayer,F:Daredevil(RWi), Gladiator(DH) 4.00
50 E:Wolverine&Spider-Man,B:Comet Man(KJo),F:Captain Ultra(DJ), Silver Surfer(JkS) 5.00
51 B:Wolverine(RLd),F:Iron Man (MBr,DH),Le Peregrine 3.25
52 F:Rick Jones,Hulk(RWi,TMo) . 3.25
53 E:Wolverine,Comet Man,F: Silver Sable&Black Widow (RLd,BWi),B:Stingray 3.75
54 B:Wolverine&Hulk(DR), Werewolf,F:Shroud(SD,BWi) . . 5.00
55 F:Collective Man(GLa) 4.50
56 E:Stingray,F:Speedball(SD) . . . 4.50
57 DK(c),B:Submariner(MC,MFm), Black Cat(JRu) 4.50
58 F:Iron Man(SD) 4.50
59 E:Submariner,Werewolf, F:Punisher 4.50
60 B:Poison,Scarlet Witch, F:Captain America(TL) 4.50
61 E:Wolverine&Hulk, F:Dr.Strange 4.50
62 F:Wolverine(PR),Deathlok(JG) 4.00
63 F:Wolverine(PR),E:Scarlet Witch,Thor(DH) 4.00
64 B:Wolverine&Ghost Rider(MT), Fantastic Four(TMo),F:Blade . . 4.00
65 F:Starfox(ECh) 3.50
66 F:Volstagg 3.50
67 E:Poison,F:Spider-Man(MG) . . 3.50
68 B:Shanna(PG),E:Fantastic Four F:Lockjaw(JA,AM) 3.50
69 B:Daredevil(DT),F:Silver Surfer 3.50
70 F:BlackWidow&Darkstar(AM) . 3.50
71 E:Wolverine&Ghost Rider,F: Warlock(New Mutants)(SMc) . . 3.50
72 B:Weapon X(BWS),E:Daredevil, F:Red Wolf(JS) 7.00
73 F:Black Knight(DC), Namor(JM) 5.00
74 F:Constrictor(SMc),Iceman & Human Torch(JSon,DA) 5.00
75 F:Meggan & Shadowcat, Dr.Doom(DC) 5.00
76 F:Death's Head(BHi,MFm), A:Woodgod(DC) 5.00
77 E:Shanna,B:Sgt.Fury&Dracula (TL,JRu),F:Namor 4.00
78 F:Iron Man(KSy),Hulk&Selene . 4.00
79 E:Sgt.Fury&Dracula,F:Dr.Strange, Sunspot(JBy) 4.00
80 F:Daughters of the Dragon,Mister Fantastic(DJ),Captain America (SD,TA) 4.00
81 F:Captain America(SD,TA), Daredevil(MR,AW),Ant-Man . . 3.50
82 B:Firestar(DT),F:Iron Man(SL), Power Man 3.50
83 F:Hawkeye,Hum.Torch(SD,EL) 3.00
84 E:Weapon X 3.00
85 B:Wolverine(SK),Beast(RLd,JaL-1st Work),F:Speedball(RWi), I:Cyber 8.00
86 F:PaladinE:RLd on Beast 5.00
87 E:Firestar,F:Shroud(RWi) 4.00
88 F:Solo,Volcana(BWi) 4.00
89 F:Spitfire(JSn),Mojo(JMa) 4.00
90 B:Ghost Rider & Cable,F: Nightmare 4.50
91 F:Impossible Man 3.50
92 E:Wolverine,Beast, F:Northstar(JMa) 3.50
93 SK(c),B:Wolverine,Nova, F:Daredevil 3.00
94 F:Gabriel 3.00
95 SK(c),E:Wolverine,F:Hulk 3.00
96 B:Wolverine(TT),E:Nova, F:Speedball 3.00
97 F:Chameleon,Two-Gun Kid, E:Ghost Rider/Cable 3.00
98 E:Wolverine,F:Ghost Rider, Werewolf by Night 2.50
99 F:Wolverine,Ghost Rider, Mary Jane,Captain America. . . 2.50
100 SK,F:Ghost Rider,Wolverine, Dr.Doom,Nightmare 3.00
101 SK(c),B:Ghost Rider&Doctor Strange,Young Gods,Wolverine &Nightcrawler,F:Bar With No Name 2.00
102 RL,GC,AW,F:Speedball 2.00
103 RL,GC,AW,F:Puck 2.00
104 RL,GC,AW,F:Lockheed 2.00
105 RL,GC,AW,F:Nightmare 2.00
106 RL,GC,AW,F:Gabriel,E:Ghost Rider&Dr.Strange 2.00
107 GC,AW,TS,B:Ghost Rider& Werewolf 2.00
108 GC,AW,TS,SMc,E:Wolverine& Nightcrawler,B:Thanos 2.00
109 SLi,TS,SMc,B:Wolverine& Typhoid Mary,E:Young Gods . . 2.00
110 SLi,SMc,F:Nightcrawler 2.00
111 SK(c),SLi,RWi,F:Dr.Strange, E:Thanos 2.00
112 SK(c),SLi,F:Pip,Wonder Man, E:Ghost Rider&Werewolf 2.00
113 SK(c),SLi,B:Giant Man, Ghost Rider&Iron Fist 1.75
114 SK(c),SLi,F:Arabian Knight . . 1.75
115 SK(c),SLi,F:Cloak&Dagger . . 1.75
116 SK(c),SLi,E:Wolverine & Typhoid Mary 1.75
117 SK,PR,B:Wolverine&Venom, I:Ravage 2099 . . . . 4.00
118 SK,PB,RWi,E:Giant Man, I:Doom 2099 . . . . 3.00
119 SK,GC,B:Constrictor,E:Ghost Rider&Iron Fist,F:Wonder Man 3.00
120 SK,GC,E:Constrictor,B:Ghost Rider/Cloak & Dagger, F:Spider-Man 2.50
121 SK,GC,F:Mirage,Andromeda . 2.50
122 SK(c),GK,E:Wolverine&Venom, Ghost Rider&Cloak&Dagger,F: Speedball&Rage,Two-Gun Kid 2.50
123 SK(c),DJ,SLi,B:Wolverine&Lynx, Ghost Rider&Typhoid Mary, She-Hulk,F:Master Man 1.75
124 SK(c),DJ,MBa,SLi,F:Solo . . . 1.75
125 SLi,SMc,DJ,B:Iron Fist 1.75
126 SLi,DJ,E:She-Hulk 1.75
127 SLi,DJ,DP,F:Speedball 1.75
128 SLi,DJ,RWi,F:American Eagle 1.75
129 SLi,DJ,F:Ant Man 1.75
130 DJ.SLi,RWi,E:Wolverine&Lynx, Ghost Rider&Typhoid Mary,Iron Fist,F:American Eagle 1.75
131 MFm,B:Wolverine,Ghost Rider& Cage,Iron Fist&Sabretooth, F:Shadowcat 1.75
132 KM(c),F:Iron Man 1.75
133 F:Cloak & Dagger 1.75
134 SLi,F:Vance Astro 1.75
135 SLi,F:Daredevil 1.75
136 B:Gh.Rider&Masters of Silence, F:Iron Fist,Daredevil 1.75
137 F:Ant Man 1.75
138 B:Wolverine,Spellbound 1.75
139 F:Foreigner 1.75
140 F:Captain Universe 1.75
141 BCe(s),F:Iron Fist 1.75
142 E:Gh.Rider&Masters of Silence, F:Mr.Fantastic 1.75
143 Siege of Darkness Pt.#3, B:Werewolf,Scarlet Witch, E:Spellbound 2.00
144 Siege of Darkness Pt.#6, B:Morbius 2.00
145 Siege of Darkness Pt.#11 . . . 2.00
146 Siege of Darkness Pt.#14 . . . 1.75
147 B:Vengeance,F:Falcon,Masters of Silence,American Eagle 1.75
148 E:Vengeance,F:Capt.Universe, Black Panther 1.75
149 F:Daughter o/t Dragon,Namor, Vengeance,Starjammers 1.75
150 ANo(s),SLi,F:Typhoid Mary,DD,

Vengeance,Wolverine 1.75
151 ANo(s),F:Typhoid Mary,DD, Vengeance 1.75
152 CDi(s),PR,B:Vengeance,Wolverine, War Machine,Moon Knight ... 1.75
153 CDi(s),A:Vengeance,Wolverine, War Machine,Moon Knight ... 1.75
154 CDi(s),E:Vengeance,Wolverine, War Machine,Moon Knight ... 1.75
155 CDi(s),B:Vengeance,Wolverine, War Machine,Kymaera 1.75
156 B:Shang Chi,F:Destroyer ... 1.50
157 F:Nick Fury 1.50
158 AD,I:Clan Destine,E:Kymaera, Shang Chi,Vengeance 1.50
TPB Ghost Rider & Cable,rep #90-97 .... 3.95
TPB Save the Tyger,rep.Wolverine story from #1-10 .... 3.95

MARVEL COMICS SUPER SPECIAL
[Magazine, 1977]

1 JB,WS,Kiss,Features &Photos 65.00
2 JB,Conan(1978) 5.00
3 WS,Close Encounters 4.00
4 GP,KJ,Beatles story 12.00

Becomes:

MARVEL SUPER SPECIAL

5 Kiss 1978 .... 35.00
6 GC,Jaws II 3.00
7 Does Not Exist
8 Battlestar Galactica(Tabloid) .. 3.00
9 Conan 4.00
10 GC,Starlord 3.00
11 JB,RN,Weirdworld, ... 3.00
12 JB,Weirdworld, ... 3.00
13 JB,Weirdworld, ... 3.00
14 GC,Meteor,adapt 3.00
15 Star Trek 6.00
15a Star Trek 9.00
16 AW,B:Movie Adapts,Empire Strikes Back 7.00
17 Xanadu 2.00
18 HC(c),JB,Raiders of the Lost Ark 2.00
19 HC,For Your Eyes Only 5.00
20 Dragonslayer 2.50
21 JB,Conan 1.00
22 JSo(c),AW,Bladerunner 2.00
23 Annie 2.00
24 Dark Crystal 2.00
25 Rock and Rule 2.00
26 Octopussy 2.50
27 AW,Return of the Jedi 6.00
28 PH(c),Krull 2.00
29 DSp,Tarzan of the Apes 2.00
30 Indiana Jones and the Temple of Doom 2.50
31 The Last Star Fighter 2.00
32 Muppets Take Manhattan 2.00
33 Buckaroo Banzai 2.00
34 GM,Sheena 2.00
35 JB,Conan The Destroyer 2.00
36 Dune 2.00
37 2010 .... 2.00
38 Red Sonja 2.00
39 Santa Claus 2.00
40 JB,Labrynth 2.00
41 Howard the Duck,Nov.,1986 .. 2.00

MARVEL DOUBLE FEATURE
December, 1973

1 JK,GC,B:Tales of Suspense Reprints,Capt America, Iron-Man 5.00
2 JK,GC ,A:Nick Fury 2.50
3 JK,GC 2.50
4 JK,GC,Cosmic Cube 2.50
5 JK,GC,V:Red Skull 2.50
6 JK,GC,V:Adaptoid 2.50
7 JK,GC,V:Tumbler 2.50
8 JK,GC,V:Super Adaptoid 2.50
9 GC,V:Batroc 2.50
10 GC 2.50
11 GC,Capt.America Wanted 2.50
12 GC,V:Powerman,Swordsman . 2.50
13 GC,A:Bucky 2.50
14 GC,V:Red Skull 2.50
15 GK,GC,V:Red Skull 2.50
16 GC,V;Assassin 2.50
17 JK,GC,V:Aim,Iron Man & Sub-Mariner #1 .... 4.00
18 JK,GC,V:Modok,Iron Man #1 .. 5.00
19 JK,GC,E:Capt.America 5.00
20 JK(c) 2.50
21 Capt.America,Black Panther March, 1977 .... 2.50

MARVEL FANFARE
March, 1972

1 MG,TA,PS,F:Spider-Man, Daredevil,Angel 13.00
2 MG,SM,FF,TVe,F:SpM,Ka-Zar 10.00
3 DC,F:X-Men 8.00
4 PS,TA,MG,F:X-Men,Deathlok .. 8.00
5 MR,F:Dr.Strange 4.00
6 F:Spider-Man,Scarlet Witch ... 4.50
7 F:Hulk/Daredevil 3.00
8 CI,TA,GK,F:Dr.Strange 3.00
9 GM,F:Man Thing 3.00
10 GP,B:Black Widow 3.50
11 GP,D:M.Corcoran 3.50
12 GP,V:Snapdragon 3.50
13 GP,E:B.Widow,V:Snapdragon . 3.50
14 F:Fantastic Four,Vision 2.75
15 BWS,F:Thing,Human Torch .. 3.00

Marvel Fanfare #23
© Marvel Entertainment Group

16 DC,JSt,F:Skywolf 2.50
17 DC,JSt,F:Skywolf 2.50
18 FM,JRu,F:Captain America ... 3.00
19 RL,F:Cloak and Dagger 2.50
20 JSn,F:Thing&Dr.Strange 2.50
21 JSn,F:Thing And Hulk 2.50
22 KSy,F:Iron Man 2.50
23 KSy,F:Iron Man 2.50
24 F:Weird World 3.00
25 F:Weird World 2.50
26 F:Weird World 2.50
27 F:Daredevil 2.50
28 KSy,F:Alpha Flight 2.50
29 JBy,F:Hulk 3.00
30 BA,AW,F:Moon Knight 2.50
31 KGa,F:Capt.America,

Marvel Fanfare #15
© Marvel Entertainment Group

Yellow Claw 2.50
32 KGa,PS,F:Capt.America, Yellow Claw 2.50
33 JBr,F:X-Men 7.00
34 CV,F:Warriors Three 2.50
35 CV,F:Warriors Three 2.50
36 CV,F:Warriors Three 2.50
37 CV,F:Warriors Three 2.50
38 F:Captain America 2.50
39 JSon,F:Hawkeye,Moon Knight . 2.50
40 DM,F:Angel,Storm,Mystique .. 3.00
41 DGb,F:Dr.Strange 2.50
42 F:Spider-Man 4.00
43 F:Sub-Mariner,Human Torch .. 2.50
44 KSy,F:Iron Man vs.Dr.Doom .. 2.50
45 All Pin-up Issue,WS,AAd,MZ, JOy,BSz,KJ,HC,PS,JBy 4.00
46 F:Fantastic Four 2.50
47 MG,F:Spider-Man,Hulk 3.00
48 KGa,F:She-Hulk 2.50
49 F:Dr.Strange 2.50
50 JSon,JRu,F:Angel 3.00
51 JB,JA,GC,AW,F:Silver Surfer . 4.00
52 F:Fantastic Four 2.50
53 GC,AW,F:Bl.Knight,Dr.Strange 2.50
54 F:Black Knight,Wolverine 3.50
55 F:Powerpack,Wolverine 3.50
56 CI,DH,F:Shanna t/She-Devil .. 2.25
57 BBl,AM,F:Shanna,Cap.Marvel . 2.25
58 BBl,F:Shanna,Vision/Sc.Witch . 2.25
59 BBl,F:Shanna,Hellcat 2.25
60 PS,F:Daredevil,Capt.Marvel .. 2.25

MARVEL FEATURE
[1st Regular Series]
December, 1971

1 RA,BE,NA,I&O:Defenders & Omegatron 75.00
2 BEv,F:The Defenders 38.00
3 BEv,F:The Defenders 38.00
4 F:Antman 15.00
5 F:Antman 10.00
6 F:Antman 8.00
7 CR,F:Antman 8.00
8 JSc,CR,F:Antman,O:Wasp 8.00
9 CR,F:Antman 8.00
10 CR,F:Antman 8.00
11 JSn,JSt,F:Thing & Hulk 15.00
12 JSn,JSt,F:Thing,Iron Man, Thanos,Blood Brothers 12.00

[2nd Regular Series]

(All issues feature Red Sonja)
1 DG,The Temple of Abomination 3.50
2 FT,Blood of the Hunter 2.00
3 FT,Balek Lives 2.00
4 FT,Eyes of the Gorgon 2.00
5 FT,The Bear God Walks 2.00
6 FT,C:Conan,Belit 2.00
7 FT,V:Conan,A:Belit,Conan#68 . . 2.00

MARVEL FRONTIER COMICS SPECIAL

1 All Frontier Characters 3.25

MARVEL FUMETTI BOOK

April, 1984
1 NA(c),Stan Lee, All photos . . . 1.25

MARVEL GRAPHIC NOVEL

1982
1 JSn,D:Captain Marvel,A:Most Marvel Characters 35.00
1a 2nd printing 10.00
1b 3rd-5th printing 7.00
2 F:Elric,Dreaming City 12.00
2a 2nd printing 7.00
3 JSn,F:Dreadstar 12.00
3a 2nd-3rd printing 7.00
4 BMc,I:New Mutants,Cannonball Sunspot,Psyche,Wolfsbane . . 24.00
4a 2nd printing 10.00
4b 3rd-4th printing 8.00
5 BA,F:X-Men 17.00
5a 2nd printing 9.00
5b 3rd-5th printing 7.00
6 WS,F:Starslammers 10.00
6a 2nd printing 7.00
7 CR,F:Killraven 7.00
8 RWi,AG,F:Super Boxers 9.00
8a 2nd printing 7.00
9 DC,F:Futurians 10.00
9a 2nd printing 7.00
10 RV,F:Heartburst 8.00
10a 2nd printing 6.00
11 VM,F:Void Indigo 12.00
12 F:Dazzler the Movie 11.00
12a 2nd printing 6.00
13 MK,F:Starstruck 7.00
14 JG,F:SwordsofSwashbucklers . 6.00
15 CV,F:Raven Banner 6.00
16 GLa,F:Alladin Effect 6.00
17 MS,F:Living Monolith 7.00
18 JBy,F:She-Hulk 10.00
18 later printings 8.95
19 F:Conan 6.00
20 F:Greenberg the Vampire 6.00
21 JBo,F:Marada the She-wolf . . 6.00
22 BWr,Hooky,F:Spider-Man . . . 12.00
23 DGr,F:Dr.Strange 6.00
24 FM,BSz,F:Daredevil 10.00
25 F:Dracula 8.00
26 FC,TA,F:Alien Legion 6.00
27 BH,F:Avengers 6.00
28 JSe,F:Conan the Reaver 6.50
29 BWr,F:Thing & Hulk 8.00
30 F:A Sailor's Story 6.00
31 F:Wolf Pack 6.00
32 SA,F:Death of Groo 10.00
33 F:Thor 6.00
34 AW,F:Cloak & Dagger 6.00
35 MK/RH,F:The Shadow 13.00
36 F:Willow movie adaption 7.00
37 BL,F:Hercules 7.00
38 JB,F:Silver Surfer 16.00
39 F:Iron Man,Crash 14.50
40 JZ,F:The Punisher 20.00
41 F:Roger Rabbit 7.00
42 F:Conan of the Isles 9.00
43 EC,F:Ax 6.00
44 BJ,F:Arena 6.00
45 JRy,F:Dr.Who 9.00
46 TD,F:Kull 7.00
47 GM,F:Dreamwalker 7.00
48 F:Sailor's Storm II 7.00
49 MBd,F:Dr.Strange&Dr.Doom . 18.00
50 F:Spider-Man,Parallel Lives . . 9.00
51 F:Punisher,Intruder 15.00
52 DSp,F:Roger Rabbit 9.00
53 PG,F:Conan 6.95
54 HC,F:Wolverine & Nick Fury . 17.00

MARVEL HOLIDAY SPECIAL

1 StG(s),PDd(s),SLo(s),RLm,PB, . 3.25

MARVEL MASTERPIECES COLLECTION

1 Joe Jusko Masterpiece Cards . . 3.25
2 F:Wolverine,Thanos,Apocalypse 3.25
3 F:Gambit,Venom,Hulk 3.25
4 F:Wolverine Vs. Sabretooth . . . 3.25

MARVEL MILESTONE EDITION

1 X-Men #1 rep. 2.95
2 Fantastic Four #1, Rep. 2.95
3 Amazing Fantasy #15 rep. 2.95
4 Incredible Hulk #1 . . . . 2.95
5 Amazing Spider-Man #1 . . . . . 2.95

MARVEL MINI-BOOKS

1966
(black & white)
1 F:Capt America,Spider-Man,Hulk Thor,Sgt.Fury 10.00
2 thru 6 same . . . . @10.00

MARVEL MOVIE PREMIERE

1975
(black & white magazine)
1 Land That Time Forgot, Burroughs adapt 5.00

MARVEL MOVIE SHOWCASE FEATURING STAR WARS

November, 1982
1 Rep,Stars Wars #1-6 . . . . 4.00
2 December, 1982 . . . . 4.00

MARVEL MOVIE SPOTLIGHT FEATURING RAIDERS OF THE LOST ARK

November, 1982
1 Rep,Raiders of Lost Ark#1-3 . . 3.00

MARVEL MYSTERY COMICS

See: MARVEL COMICS

MARVEL NO-PRIZE BOOK

January, 1983
1 MGo(c),Stan Lee as Dr Doom(c) 3.00

MARVEL PREMIERE

April, 1972
1 GK,O:Warlock,Receives Soul Gem, Creation of Counter Earth . . . 50.00
2 GK,JK,F:Warlock 35.00
3 BWS,F:Dr.Strange 37.00
4 FB,BWS,F:Dr.Strange 15.00
5 MP,CR,F:Dr.Strange,I:Sligguth 10.00
6 MP,FB,F:Dr.Strange 10.00
7 MP,CR,F:Dr.Strange,I:Dagoth 10.00
8 JSn,F:Dr.Strange 10.00
9 NA,FB,F:Dr.Strange 10.00
10 FB,F:Dr.Strange, D:Ancient One 11.00
11 NA,FB,F:Dr.Strange,I:Shuma 10.00
12 NA,FB,F:Dr.Strange 10.00
13 NA,FB,F:Dr.Strange 10.00
14 NA,FB,F:Dr.Strange 10.00
15 GK,DG,I&O:Iron Fist Pt.1 . . . 65.00
16 DG,O:Iron Fist Pt.2,V:Scythe . 24.00
17 DG,'Citadel on the Edge of Vengeance' 15.00
18 DG,V:Triple Irons 15.00
19 DG,A:Ninja 13.00
20 I:Misty Knight 13.00
21 V:Living Goddess 13.00
22 V:Ninja 13.00

Marvel Premiere #24
© Marvel Entertainment Group

23 PB,V:Warhawk 13.00
24 PB,V:Monstroid 13.00
25 1st JBy,AMc,E:Iron Fist 20.00
26 JK,GT,F:Hercules 3.00
27 F:Satana 3.00
28 F:Legion Of Monsters,A:Ghost Rider,Morbius,Werewolf. 45.00
29 JK,I:Liberty Legion, O:Red Raven 2.50
30 JK,F:Liberty Legion 2.50
31 JK,I:Woodgod 2.50
32 HC,F:Monark 2.50
33 HC,F:Solomon Kane 2.50
34 HC,F:Solomon Kane 2.50
35 I&O:Silver Age 3-D Man 2.50
36 F:3-D Man 2.50
37 F:3-D Man 2.50
38 AN,MP,I:Weird World 3.00
39 AM,I:Torpedo(1st solo) 2.50
40 AM,F:Torpedo 2.50
41 TS,F:Seeker 3000 . . . . 2.50
42 F:Tigra 2.50
43 F:Paladin 2.50
44 KG,F:Jack of Hearts(1stSolo) . 2.50
45 GP,F:Manwolf 3.00
46 GP,F:Manwolf 3.00
47 JBy,I:2nd Antman(Scott Lang) . 5.00
48 JBy,F:2nd Antman 4.00
49 F:The Falcon 2.50
50 TS,TA,F:Alice Cooper 7.50
51 JBi,F:Black Panther,V:Klan . . . 2.50
52 JBi,F:B.Panther,V:Klan 2.50
53 JBi,F:B.Panther,V:Klan 2.50
54 GD,TD,I:Hammer 2.50
55 JSt,F:Wonderman(1st solo) . . . 3.50
56 HC,TA,F:Dominic Fortune 2.50
57 WS(c),I:Dr.Who 3.50
58 TA(c),FM,F:Dr.Who 2.50
59 F:Dr.Who 2.50
60 WS(c),DGb,F:Dr.Who 2.50
61 TS,F:Starlord 2.50

MARVEL PRESENTS
December, 1985

1 BMc,F:Bloodstone 7.50
2 BMc,O:Bloodstone 6.00
3 AM,B:Guardians/Galaxy 30.00
4 AM,I:Nikki 17.00
5 AM,'Planet o/t Absurd' 17.00
6 AM,V:Karanada 17.00
7 AM,'Embrace the Void' 17.00
8 AM,JB,JSt,reprint.S.Surfer#2 . 20.00
9 AM,O:Starhawk 17.00
10 AM,O:Starhawk 17.00
11 AM,D:Starhawk's Children . . 17.00
12 AM,E:Guardians o/t Galaxy . 17.00

MARVEL PREVIEW
February, 1975
(black & white magazine)

1 NA,AN,Man Gods From
Beyond the Stars 5.00
2 GM(c),O:Punisher 200.00
3 GM(c),Blade the Vampire Slayer 3.00
4 GM(c),I&O:Starlord 4.00
5 Sherlock Holmes 3.00
6 Sherlock Holmes 3.00
7 KG,Satana,A:Sword in the Star 4.00
8 GM,MP,Legion of Monsters . 12.00
9 Man-God,O:Starhawk 3.00
10 JSn,Thor the Mighty 4.00
11 JBy,I:Starlord 6.00
12 MK,Haunt of Horror 3.50
13 JSn(c),Starhawk 5.00
14 JSn(c),Starhawk 5.00
15 MK(c),Starhawk 3.50
16 GC,Detectives 3.00
17 GK,Black Mask 3.00
18 GC,Starlord 3.00
19 Kull 3.00
20 HC,NA,GP,Bizarre Adventures 5.00
21 SD,Moonlight 5.00
22 JB,King Arthur 3.00
23 JB,GC,FM,Bizarre Adventures . 5.00
24 Debut Paradox 3.00

Becomes:

BIZARRE ADVENTURES

25 MG,TA,MR,Lethal Ladies 3.00
26 JB(c),King Kull 3.00
27 JB,AA,GP,Phoenix,A:Ice-Man . 7.50
28 MG,TA,FM,NA,The Unlikely
Heroes,Elektra 5.00
29 JB,WS,Horror 3.50
30 JB,Tomorrow 3.00
31 JBy,After the Violence Stops . . 3.50
32 Gods 3.00
33 Ph(c),Horror 3.00
34 PS,Christmas Spec,Son of Santa
Howard the Duck,Feb.,1983 . . 4.00

MARVEL PREVIEW 1993

Preview of 1993 . . . . 3.95

MARVEL SAGA
December, 1985

1 JBy,Fantastic Four,Wolv. 2.50
2 Hulk 1.50
3 Spider-Man 2.50
4 X-Men 2.50
5 Thor 1.50
6 Fantastic Four 1.50
7 Avengers 1.50
8 X-Men 2.00
9 Angel 1.50
10 X-Men 2.00
11 X-Men 2.00
12 O:Capt. America 1.50
13 O:Daredevil,Elektra 1.50
14 O:Green Goblin 2.00
15 Avengers 1.50
16 Daredevil,X-Men 2.00
17 Kazar,X-Men 2.00
18 Hawkeye-Quicksilver 1.50
19 SpM,Thor,Daredevil 2.00
20 Daredevil,Giant Man 1.50
21 FF,V:Frightful Four 1.50
22 Wedding 1.50
23 and 24 . . . . @1.50
25 O:Silver Surfer,Dec.,1987 . . . . 2.25

MARVEL SPECTACULAR
August, 1973

1 JK,rep Thor #128 . . . . 2.50
2 JK,rep Thor #129 . . . . 2.00
3 JK,rep Thor #130 . . . . 2.00
4 JK,rep Thor #133 . . . . 2.00
5 JK,rep Thor #134 . . . . 2.00
6 JK,rep Thor #135 . . . . 1.75
7 JK,rep Thor #136 . . . . 1.75
8 JK,rep Thor #137 . . . . 1.75
9 JK,rep Thor #138 . . . . 1.75
10 JK,rep Thor #139 . . . . 1.75
11 JK,rep Thor #140 . . . . 1.75
12 JK,rep Thor #141 . . . . 1.75
13 JK,rep Thor #142 . . . . 1.75
14 JK,rep Thor #143 . . . . 1.75
15 JK,rep Thor #144 . . . . 1.75
16 JK,rep Thor #145 . . . . 1.75
17 JK,rep Thor #146 . . . . 1.75
18 JK,rep Thor #147 . . . . 1.75
19 JK,rep Thor#148,Nov.,1975 . . 1.75

MARVEL SPOTLIGHT
November, 1971
[1st Regular Series]

1 NA(c)WW,F:Red Wolf 25.00
2 MP,BEv,NA,I&O:Werewolf . . . 50.00
3 MP,F:Werewolf 30.00
4 SD,MP,F:Werewolf 25.00
5 SD,MP,I&O:Ghost Rider . . . 150.00
6 MP,TS,F:Ghost Rider 60.00
7 MP,TS,F:Ghost Rider 60.00
8 JM,MB,F:Ghost Rider 60.00
9 TA,F:Ghost Rider 50.00
10 SD,JM,F:Ghost Rider 50.00
11 SD,F:Ghost Rider 50.00
12 SD,2nd A:Son of Satan 60.00
13 F:Son of Satan 28.00
14 JM,F:Son of Satan,I:Ikthalon . 28.00
15 JM,F:S of S,I:Baphomet 20.00
16 JM,F:Son of Satan 20.00
17 JM,F:Son of Satan 15.00
18 F:Son of Satan,I:Allatou 15.00
19 F:Son of Satan 15.00
20 F:Son of Satan 15.00
21 F:Son of Satan 15.00
22 F:Son of Satan,Ghost Rider . 20.00
23 F:Son of Satan 15.00
24 JM,F:Son of Satan 15.00
25 GT,F:Sinbad 4.00
26 F:The Scarecrow 4.00
27 F:The Sub-Mariner 4.00
28 F:Moon Knight(1st full solo) . 12.00
29 F:Moon Knight 10.00
30 JSt,JB,F:Warriors Three 4.00
31 HC,JSn,F:Nick Fury 4.00
32 I:Spiderwoman,Jessica Drew . 9.00
33 F:Deathlok,I:Devilslayer 8.00

MARVEL SPOTLIGHT
[2nd Regualar Series]
July, 1979

1 PB,F:Captain Marvel 2.50
1a No'1' on Cover 4.00
2 FM(c),F:Captain Marvel,A:Eon . 2.00
3 PB,F:Captain Marvel 2.00
4 PB,F:Captain Marvel 2.00
5 FM(c),SD,F:Dragon Lord 2.00
6 F:Star Lord 2.00
7 FM(c),F:StarLord 2.00
8 FM,F:Captain Marvel 2.50
9 FM(c),SD,F:Captain Universe . 2.00
10 SD,F:Captain Universe 2.00
11 SD,F:Captain Universe 2.00

MARVEL SUPER ACTION
(One-Shot)
January, 1976

1 TD,GE,FS,MP,HC,F:Punisher,
Weirdworld,Dominic Fortune,
I:Huntress(Mockingbird) . . . 100.00

MARVEL SUPER ACTION
May, 1977

1 JK,reprint,Capt.America #100 . 3.50
2 JK,reprint,Capt.America #101 . 2.00
3 JK,reprint,Capt.America #102 . 2.00
4 BEv,RH,reprint,Marvel Boy #1 . 2.00
5 JK,reprint,Capt.America #103 . 2.00
6 JK,reprint,Capt.America #104 . 2.00
7 JK,reprint,Capt.America #105 . 2.00
8 JK,reprint,Capt.America #106 . 2.00
9 JK,reprint,Capt.America #107 . 2.00
10 JK,reprint,Capt.America #108 . 2.00
11 JK,reprint,Capt.America #109 . 2.00
12 JSo,reprint,Capt.America #110 2.00
13 JSo,reprint,Capt.America #111 2.00
14 JB,reprint,Avengers #55 . . . . . 2.00
15 JB,reprint,Avengers #56 . . . . . 2.00
16 Reprint,Avengers,annual #2 . . 2.00
17 Reprint,Avengers # 2.00
18 JB(c),reprint,Avengers #57 . . . 2.00
19 JB(c),reprint,Avengers #58 . . . 2.00
20 JB(c),reprint,Avengers #59 . . . 2.00
21 Reprint,Avengers #60 . . . . 1.50
22 JB(c),reprint,Avengers #61 . . . 1.50
23 Reprint,Avengers #63 . . . . 1.50
24 Reprint,Avengers #64 . . . . 1.50
25 Reprint,Avengers #65 . . . . 1.50
26 Reprint,Avengers #66 . . . . 1.50
27 BWS,Reprint,Avengers #67 . . . 1.50
28 BWS,Reprint,Avengers #68 . . . 1.50
29 Reprint,Avengers #69 . . . . 1.50
30 Reprint,Avengers #70 . . . . 1.50
31 Reprint,Avengers #71 . . . . 1.50
32 Reprint,Avengers #72 . . . . 1.50
33 Reprint,Avengers #73 . . . . 1.50
34 Reprint,Avengers #74 . . . . 1.50
35 JB(c),Reprint,Avengers #75 . . 1.50
36 JB(c),Reprint,Avengers #75 . . 1.50
37 JB(c),Reprint,Avengers #76
November, 1981 . . . . 1.50

MARVEL SUPERHEROES
October, 1966
(One-Shot)

1 Rep. D.D. #1, Avengers #2,
Marvel Mystery #8 . . . . 70.00

MARVEL SUPERHEROES
[1st Regular Series]
(Prev.: Fantasy Masterpieces)

1 Rep. D.D.#1,Avengers #2,
Marvel Mystery #8,one-shot . 75.00
12 GC,I&O:Captain Marvel . . . 125.00
13 GC,2nd A:Captain Marvel . . . 65.00
14 F:Spider-Man 110.00
15 GC,F:Medusa 25.00
16 I:Phantom Eagle 25.00
17 O:Black Knight 25.00
18 GC,I:Guardians o/t Galaxy . . 70.00
19 F:Kazar 25.00
20 F:Dr.Doom,Diablo 25.00
21 thru 31 reprints . . . . @12.00
32 thru 55 rep. Hulk/Submariner
from Tales to Astonish . . . . @2.00
56 reprints Hulk #102 . . . . 3.50
57 thru 105 reps.Hulk issues . . @1.50

MARVEL SUPERHEROES
May, 1990
[2nd Regular Series]

1 RLm,F:Hercules,Moon Knight,
Magik,Bl.Panther,Speedball . . . 4.00
2 . . . . 3.50
3 F:Captain America,Hulk,Wasp . 4.50
4 AD,F:SpM,N.Fury,D.D.,Speedball
Wond.Man,Spitfire,Bl.Knight . . 3.50
5 F:Thor,Thing,Speedball,
Dr.Strange 3.50

6 RB,SD,F:X-Men,Power Pack,
Speedball,Sabra 3.00
7 RB,F:X-Men,Cloak & Dagger . . 2.75
8 F:X-Men,Iron Man,Namor 2.50
9 F:Avengers W.C,Thor,Iron Man 3.00
10 DH,F:Namor,Fantastic Four,
Ms.Marvel#24 . . . . 3.50
11 F:Namor,Ms.Marvel#25 . . . . . . 3.00
12 F:Dr.Strange,Falcon,Iron Man . 3.00
13 F:Iron Man 2.75
14 BMc,RWi,,F:Iron Man,
Speedball, Dr.Strange 2.75
15 KP,DH,F:Thor,Iron Man,Hulk . . 2.75
Holiday Spec.#1 AAd,DC,JRu,F:FF,
X-Men,Spider-Man,Punisher . . 3.25
Holiday Spec.#2 AAd(c),SK,MGo,
RLm,SLi,F:Hulk,Wolverine,
Thanos,Spider-Man 3.25
Fall Spec.RB,A:X-Men,Shroud,
Marvel Boy,Cloak & Dagger . . 2.25

MARVEL SUPER SPECIAL
See: MARVEL COMICS

MARVEL TAILS
November, 1983

1 ST,Peter Porker 2.00

MARVEL TALES
1964

1 All reprints,O:Spider-Man . . . 250.00
2 rep.Avengers #1,X-Men #1,
Hulk #3 . . . . 75.00
3 rep.Amaz.SpM.#6 . . . . 40.00
4 thru 7 rep.Amaz.SpM.#7-10 @20.00
8 rep.Amaz.SpM.#13 . . . . 18.00
9 rep.Amaz.SpM.#14 . . . . 24.00
10-12 rep.Amaz.SpM.#15-#17 @18.00
13 rep.Amaz.SpM.#18
Rep.1950's Marvel Boy 15.00
14 thru 16 rep.Amaz.SpM.#19-#21
Reps.Marvel Boy . . . . @7.50
17 thru 22 rep.Amaz.SpM.
#22-#27 . . . . @5.50
23 thru 27 rep.Amaz.SpM.
#30-#34 . . . . @5.50
28 rep.Amaz.SpM.#35&36 . . . . . . 5.00

Marvel Tales #15

© Marvel Entertainment Group

29 rep.Amaz.SpM.#39&40 . . . . . . 5.00
30 rep.Amaz.SpM.#58&41 . . . . . . 5.00
31 rep.Amaz.SpM.#42 . . . . 5.00
32 rep.Amaz.SpM.#43&44 . . . . . . 5.00
33 rep.Amaz.SpM.#45&47 . . . . . . 5.00
34 rep.Amaz.SpM.#48 . . . . 4.00
35 rep.Amaz.SpM.#49 . . . . 4.00
36 thru 41 rep.
Amaz.SpM#51-#56 . . . . @4.00
42 thru 53 rep.
Amaz.SpM#59-#70 . . . . @4.00
54 thru 80 rep.
Amaz.SpM#73-#99 . . . . @4.00
81 rep.Amaz.SpM.#103 . . . . 4.00
82 rep.Amaz.SpM.#103-4 . . . . . . 4.50
83 thru 97 rep.
Amaz.SpM#104-#118 . . . . . @4.00
98 rep.Amaz.SpM.#121 . . . . 5.00
99 rep.Amaz.SpM.#122 . . . . 4.50
100 rep.Amaz.SpM.#123,BU:Two
Gun Kid,Giant-Size 3.50
101 thru 105 rep.Amaz.
SpM.#124-#128 . . . . @3.00
106 rep.Amaz.SpM.#129,
(I:Punisher) 12.00
107 thur 110 rep.Amaz.
SpM.#130-133 . . . . @2.00
111 Amaz.SpM#134,A:Punisher . . 6.00
112 Amaz.SpM#135,A:Punisher . . 5.00
113 thru 136 rep.Amaz.Spider
Man #136-#159 . . . . @2.00
137 rep.Amaz.Fantasy#15 . . . . . . 7.00
138 rep.Amaz.SpM.#1 . . . . 7.00
139 thru 149 rep.
AmazSpM#2-#12 . . . . @2.00
150 rep.AmazSpM Ann#1 . . . . . . 2.00
151 rep.AmazSpM#13 . . . . 2.00
152 rep.AmazSpM#14 . . . . 4.00
153 thru 190
rep.AmazSpM#15-52 . . . . . @2.00
191 rep. #96-98 . . . . 2.25
192 rep. #121-122 . . . . 2.25
193 thru 198 rep.Marv.Team
Up#59-64 . . . . @2.00
199 . . . . 2.00
200 rep. SpM Annual 14 . . . . 2.00
201 thru 206 rep.Marv.
Team Up#65-70 . . . . @2.00
207 . . . . 2.00
208 . . . . 2.00
209 MZ(c),rep.SpM#129,Punisher 7.00
210 MZ(c),rep.SpM#134 . . . . 5.00
211 MZ(c),rep.SpM#135 . . . . 5.00
212 MZ(c),rep.Giant-Size#4 . . . . . 5.00
213 MZ(c),rep.Giant-Size#4 . . . . . 5.00
214 MZ(c),rep.SpM#161 . . . . 5.00
215 MZ(c),rep.SpM#162 . . . . 3.00
216 MZ(c),rep.SpM#174 . . . . 3.00
217 MZ(c),rep.SpM#175 . . . . 3.00
218 MZ(c),rep.SpM#201 . . . . 3.00
219 MZ(c),rep.SpM#202 . . . . 3.00
220 MZ(c),rep.Spec.SpM #81 . . . 3.00
221 MZ(c),rep.Spec.SpM #82 . . . 3.00
222 MZ(c),rep.Spec.SpM #83 . . . 2.00
223 thru 227 TM(c),rep.
SpM #88-92 . . . . @2.25
228 TM(c),rep.Spec.SpM.#17 . . . 2.00
229 TM(c),rep.Spec.SpM.#18 . . . 2.00
230 TM(c),rep.SpM #203 . . . . 2.00
231 TM(c),rep.Team-Up#108 . . . . 2.00
232 TM(c),rep. 2.00
233 TM(c),rep. X-Men 2.00
234 TM(c),rep. X-Men 2.00
235 TM(c),rep. X-Men 2.00
236 TM(c),rep. X-Men 2.00
237 TM(c),rep. 2.00
238 TM(c),rep. 2.00
239 TM(c),rep.SpM,Beast 2.00
240 rep.SpM,Beast,MTU#90 . . . . 1.50
241 rep.MTU#124 . . . . 1.50
242 rep.MTU#89,Nightcrawler . . . 1.50
243 rep.MTU#117,SpM,Wolverine 1.50
244 MR(c),rep. 1.50
245 MR(c),rep. 1.50
246 MR(c),rep. 1.50
247 MR(c),rep.MTU Annual #6 . . . 1.50
248 MR(c),rep. 1.50
249 MR(c),rep.MTU #14 . . . . 1.50
250 MR(c),rep.MTU #100 . . . . . . 1.50
251 rep.Amaz.SpM.#100 . . . . 1.50
252 rep.Amaz.SpM.#101 . . . . 3.50
253 rep.Amaz.SpM.#102 . . . . 3.00
254 rep.MTU #15,inc.2 Ghost
Rider pin-ups by JaL 3.00
255 SK(c),rep.MTU #58,
BU:Ghost Rider 1.75
256 rep. MTU 1.50
257 rep.Amaz.SpM.#238 . . . . 1.50
258 rep.Amaz.SpM.#239 . . . . 1.50
259 thru 261 rep.Amaz.SpM.#249
thru 251 . . . . 1.50
262 rep Marvel Team-Up #53 . . . 1.25
263 rep Marvel Team-Up #54 . . . 1.25
264 rep.B:Amaz.SpM.Ann.#5 . . . 1.25
265 rep.E:Amaz.SpM.Ann.#5 . . . 1.25
266 thru 274 rep.Amaz.SpM#252
thru #260 . . . . @1.25
275 rep.Amaz.SpM#261 . . . . 1.25
276 rep.Amaz.SpM#263 . . . . 1.25
277 rep.Amaz.SpM#265 . . . . 1.25
278 thru 282 rep.Amaz.SpM#268
thru 272 . . . . 1.25
283 rep.Amaz.SpM#273 . . . . 1.25
284 rep.Amaz.SpM#275 . . . . 1.25
285 rep.Amaz.SpM#276 . . . . 1.25
286 rep.Amaz.SpM#277 . . . . 1.25
287 rep.Amaz.SpM#278 . . . . 1.25

MARVEL TALES
See: MARVEL COMICS

MARVEL TEAM-UP
March, 1972

(Spider-Man in all,unless *)
1 RA,F:Hum.Torch,V:Sandman . 65.00
2 RA,F:Hum.Torch,V:Sandman . 30.00
3 F:Human Torch,V:Morbius . . . 55.00
4 GK,F:X-Men,A:Morbius 60.00
5 GK,F:Vision 11.00
6 GK,F:Thing,O:Puppet Master,
V:Mad Thinker 11.00
7 RA,F:Thor 11.00
8 JM,F:The Cat 11.00
9 RA,F:Iron Man 11.00
10 JM,F:Human Torch 11.00

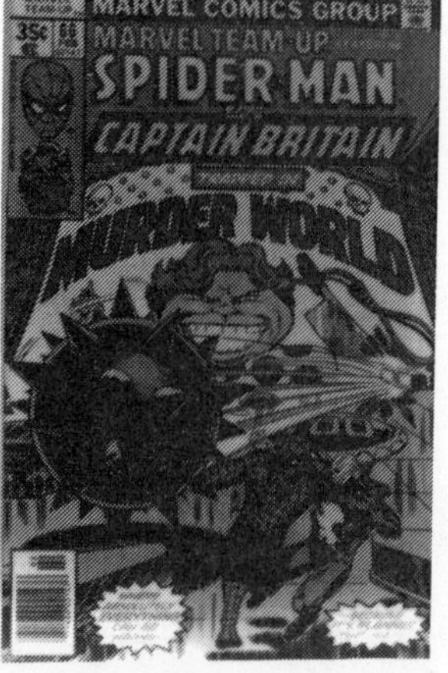

Marvel Team-Up #66

© Marvel Entertainment Group

11 JM,F:The Inhumans 9.00
12 RA,F:Werewolf 11.00
13 GK,F:Captain America 9.00
14 GK,F:Sub-Mariner 9.00

15 RA,F:Ghostrider 17.00
16 GK,JM,F:Captain Marvel 8.00
17 GK,F:Mr.Fantastic,
A:Capt.Marvel 8.00
18 *F:Hulk,Human Torch 8.00
19 SB,F:Ka-Zar 8.00
20 SB,F:Black Panther 9.00
21 SB,F:Dr.Strange 6.00
22 SB,F:Hawkeye 6.00
23 *F:Human Torch,Iceman,
C:Spider-Man,X-Men 7.00
24 JM,F:Brother Voodoo 6.00
25 JM,F:Daredevil 6.00
26 *F:H.Torch,Thor,V:Lavamen . . 6.00
27 JM,F:The Hulk 6.00
28 JM,F:Hercules 6.00
29 *F:Human Torch,Iron Man 6.00
30 JM,F:The Falcon 7.00
31 JM,F:Iron Fist 7.00
32 *F:Hum.Torch,Son of Satan . . 5.00
33 SB,F:Nighthawk 5.00
34 SB,F:Valkyrie 5.00
35 SB,*F:H.Torch,Dr.Strange 5.00
36 SB,F:Frankenstein 6.00
37 SB,F:Man-Wolf 6.00
38 SB,F:Beast 5.00
39 SB,F:H.Torch,I:Jean Dewolff . . 5.00
40 SB,F:Sons of the Tiger 5.00
41 SB,F:Scarlet Witch 5.00
42 SB,F:Scarlet Witch,Vision 5.00
43 SB,F:Dr.Doom 5.00
44 SB,F:Moon Dragon 5.00
45 SB,F:Killraven 5.00
46 SB,F:Deathlok 8.00
47 F:The Thing 5.00
48 SB,F:Iron Man,I:Wraith 5.00
49 SB,F:Iron Man 5.00
50 SB,F:Dr.Strange 5.00
51 SB,F:Iron Man 3.00
52 SB,F:Captain America 3.00
53 1st JBy New X-Men,F:Hulk . . 15.00
54 JBy,F:Hulk,V:Woodgod 6.00
55 JBy,F:Warlock,I:Gardener 8.00
56 SB,F:Daredevil 3.00
57 SB,F:Black Widow 3.00
58 SB,F:Ghost Rider,V:Trapster . . 7.00
59 JBy,F:Yellowjacket,V:Equinox . 5.00
60 JBy,F:Wasp,V:Equinox 5.00
61 JBy,F:Human Torch 5.00
62 JBy,F:Ms.Marvel 5.00
63 JBy,F:Iron Fist 5.50
64 JBy,F:Daughters o/t Dragon . . 5.00
65 JBy,I:Captain Britain(U.S.)
I:Arcade 7.50
66 JBy,F:Captain Britain 6.50
67 JBy,F:Tigra,V:Kraven 5.00
68 JBy,F:Man-Thing,I:D'Spayre . . 5.00
69 JBy,F:Havok 6.00
70 JBy,F:Thor 5.00
71 F:The Falcon,V:Plantman 4.00
72 F:Iron Man 4.00
73 F:Daredevil 4.00
74 BH,F:Not ready for prime time
players(Saturday Night Live) . . 5.00
75 JBy,F:Power Man 4.00
76 HC,F:Dr.Strange 4.00
77 HC,F:Ms.Marvel 4.00
78 DP,F:Wonderman 4.00
79 JBy,TA,F:Red Sonja 5.00
80 SpM,F:Dr.Strange,Clea 4.00
81 F:Satana 4.00
82 SB,F:Black Widow 4.00
83 SB,F:Nick Fury 4.00
84 SB,F:Master of Kung Fu 4.00
85 SB,F:Bl.Widow,Nick Fury 4.00
86 BMc,F:Guardians o/t Galaxy . . 5.00
87 GC,F:Black Panther 3.50
88 SB,F:Invisible Girl 3.50
89 RB,F:Nightcrawler 4.50
90 BMc,F:The Beast 3.50
91 F:Ghost Rider 6.00
92 Cl,F:Hawkeye,I:Mr.Fear IV . . . 3.50
93 Cl,F:Werewolf
I:Tatterdemalion (named) 5.00
94 MZ,F:Shroud 3.50
95 I:Mockingbird(Huntress) 4.00
96 F:Howard the Duck 3.50
97 *F:Hulk,Spiderwoman 3.50

Marvel Team-Up #25

© Marvel Entertainment Group

98 F:Black Widow 3.50
99 F:Machine Man 3.50
100 FM,JBy,F:F.F.,I:Karma,
BU:Storm & Bl.Panther 12.00
101 F:Nighthawk 3.00
102 F:Doc Samson,Rhino 3.00
103 F:Antman 3.00
104 *F:Hulk,Ka-zar 3.00
105 *F:Powerman,Iron Fist,Hulk . . 3.00
106 HT,F:Captain America 3.00
107 HT,F:She-Hulk 3.00
108 HT,F:Paladin 3.00
109 HT,F:Dazzler 3.00
110 HT,F:Iron Man 3.00
111 HT,F:Devil Slayer 3.00
112 HT,F:King Kull 3.00
113 HT,F:Quasar,V:Lightmaster . . 3.00
114 HT,F:Falcon 3.00
115 HT,F:Thor 3.00
116 HT,F:Valkyrie 3.00
117 HT,F:Wolv,V:Prof Power . . . 10.00
118 HT,F:Professor X 4.00
119 KGa,F:Gargoyle 3.00
120 KGa,F:Dominic Fortune 3.00
121 KGa,F:Human Torch,I:Leap
Frog(Frog Man) 3.00
122 KGa,F:Man-Thing 3.00
123 KGa,F:Daredevil 3.00
124 KGa,F:Beast 3.50
125 KGa,F:Tigra 3.00
126 BH,F:Hulk 3.00
127 KGa,F:Watcher,X-mas issue . 3.00
128 Ph(c)KGa,F:Capt.America. . . 3.00
129 KGa,F:The Vision 3.00
130 KGa,F:The Scarlet Witch . . . 3.00
131 KGa,F:Leap Frog 3.00
132 KGa,F:Mr.Fantastic 3.00
133 KGa,F:Fantastic Four 3.00
134 F:Jack of Hearts 3.00
135 F:Kitty Pryde 3.00
136 F:Wonder Man 3.00
137 *F:Aunt May & F.Richards . . . 3.00
138 F:Sandman,I:New Enforcers . 3.00
139 F:Sandman,Nick Fury 3.00
140 F:Black Widow 3.00
141 SpM(2nd App Black Costume)
F:Daredevil 4.00
142 F:Captain Marvel(2nd one) . . 3.00
143 F:Starfox 3.00
144 F:M.Knight,V:WhiteDragon . . 3.00
145 F:Iron Man 3.00
146 F:Nomad 3.50
147 F:Human Torch 3.00
148 F:Thor 3.00
149 F:Cannonball 3.50
150 F:X-Men,V:Juggernaut 5.50
Ann.#1 SB,F:New X-Men 16.00
Ann.#2 F:The Hulk 5.00
Ann.#3 F:Hulk,PowerMan 4.00
Ann.#4 F:Daredevil,Moon Knight . 3.00
Ann.#5 F:Thing,Scarlet Witch,
Quasar,Dr.Strange 3.00
Ann.#6 F:New Mutants,Cloak &
Dagger(cont.New Mutants#22) 4.00
Ann.#7 F:Alpha Flight 3.00

MARVEL TEAM-UP INDEX

January, 1986

1 thru 6 . . . . @1.75

MARVEL
Treasury Edition

September, 1974

1 SD,Spider-Man,I:Contemplator . 7.00
2 JK,F:Fant.Four,Silver Surfer . . . 6.00
3 F:Thor 3.50
4 BWS,F:Conan 4.50
5 O:Hulk 4.00
6 GC,FB,SD,F:Dr.Strange 3.50
7 JB,JK,F:The Avengers 4.50
8 F:X-Mas stories 5.00
9 F:Super-Hero Team-Up 3.50
10 F:Thor 3.50
11 F:Fantastic Four 3.50
12 F:Howard the Duck 3.50
13 F:X-Mas stories 3.50
14 F:Spider-Man 4.00
15 BWS,F:Conan,Red Sonja 4.50
16 F:Defenders 3.00
17 F:The Hulk 3.00
18 F:Spider Man,X-Men 5.00
19 F:Conan 4.50
20 F:Hulk 2.50
21 F:Fantastic Four 2.50
22 F:Spider-Man 3.50
23 F:Conan 3.00
24 F:The Hulk 2.50
25 F:Spider-Man,Hulk 3.00
26 GP,F:Hulk,Wolv.,Hercules . . . 10.00
27 HT,F:Hulk,Spider-Man 3.50
28 JB,JSt,F:SpM/Superman 6.00

MARVEL TREASURY OF OZ

1975

(oversized)

1 JB,movie adapt 4.00

MARVEL TREASURY SPECIAL

1 Vol. I Spiderman,1974 . . . . . . 4.00
2 Vol. II Capt. America,1976 . . . 3.50

MARVEL TWO-IN-ONE

January, 1974

(Thing in all, unless *)

1 GK,F:Man-Thing 20.00
2 GK,JSt,F:Namor,Namorita . . . 10.00
3 F:Daredevil 10.00
4 F:Capt.America,Namorita 10.00
5 F:Guardians of the Galaxy . . . 17.00
6 F:Dr.Strange 15.00
7 F:Valkyrie 6.00
8 F:Ghost Rider 12.00
9 F:Thor 6.00
10 KJ,F:Black Widow 6.00
11 F:Golem 4.00
12 F:Iron Man 4.00
13 F:Power Man 4.00
14 F:Son of Satan 8.00
15 F:Morbius 12.00

16 F:Ka-zar 4.00
17 F:Spider-Man 4.50
18 F:Spider-Man 4.50

Marvel Two-In-One #7
© Marvel Entertainment Group

19 F:Tigra 4.00
20 F:The Liberty Legion 4.00
21 F:Doc Savage 3.50
22 F:Thor,Human Torch 3.50
23 F:Thor,Human Torch 3.50
24 SB,F:Black Goliath 3.50
25 F:Iron Fist 4.00
26 F:Nick Fury 3.00
27 F:Deathlok 7.00
28 F:Sub-Mariner 3.00
29 F:Master of Kung Fu 3.00
30 JB,F:Spiderwoman 5.00
31 F:Spiderwoman 3.00
32 F:Invisible girl 3.00
33 F:Modred the Mystic 3.00
34 F:Nighthawk,C:Deathlok 4.00
35 F:Skull the Slayer 3.00
36 F:Mr.Fantastic 3.00
37 F:Matt Murdock 3.00
38 F:Daredevil 3.00
39 F:The Vision 3.00
40 F:Black Panther 3.00
41 F:Brother Voodoo 3.00
42 F:Captain America 3.00
43 JBy,F:Man-Thing 5.00
44 GD,F:Hercules 3.00
45 GD,F:Captain Marvel 4.50
46 F:The Hulk 5.00
47 GD,F:Yancy Street Gang,
I:Machinesmith 3.00
48 F:Jack of Hearts 3.00
49 GD,F:Dr.Strange 3.00
50 JBy,JS,F:Thing & Thing 4.00
51 FM,BMc,F:Wonderman,Nick
Fury, Ms.Marvel 5.00
52 F:Moon Knight,I:Crossfire 3.00
53 JBy,JS,F:Quasar,C:Deathlok . . 4.00
54 JBy,JS,D:Deathlok,
I:Grapplers 10.00
55 JBy,JS,I:New Giant Man 3.00
56 GP,GD,F:Thundra 2.50
57 GP,GD,F:Wundarr 2.50
58 GP,GD,I:Aquarian,A:Quasar . . 2.50
59 F:Human Torch 2.50
60 GP,GD,F:Impossible Man,
I:Impossible Woman 2.50
61 GD,F:Starhawk,I&O:Her 3.00
62 GD,F:Moondragon 3.00
63 GD,F:Warlock 3.00
64 DP,GD,F:Stingray,
I:Serpent Squad 2.50
65 GP,GD,F:Triton 2.50
66 GD,F:Scarlet Witch,
V:Arcade 2.50
67 F:Hyperion,Thundra 2.50
68 F:Angel,V:Arcade 2.50
69 GD,F:Guardians o/t Galaxy . . . 5.00
70 F:The Inhumans 2.50
71 F:Mr.Fantastic,I:Deathurge,
Maelstrom 2.50
72 F:Stingray 2.50
73 F:Quasar 2.50
74 F:Puppet Master,Modred 2.50
75 F:The Avengers,O:Blastaar . . . 2.50
76 F:Iceman,O:Ringmaster 2.50
77 F:Man-Thing 2.50
78 F:Wonder Man 2.50
79 F:Blue Diamond,I:Star Dancer . 2.50
80 F:Ghost Rider 5.00
81 F:Sub-Mariner 2.00
82 F:Captain America 2.00
83 F:Sasquatch 3.00
84 F:Alpha Flight 3.00
85 F:Giant-Man 2.00
86 O:Sandman 2.25
87 F:Ant-Man 2.00
88 F:She-Hulk 2.00
89 F:Human Torch 2.00
90 F:Spider-Man 2.25
91 V:Sphinx 2.00
92 F:Jocasta,V:Ultron 2.00
93 F:Machine Man,D:Jocasta 2.25
94 F:Power Man,Iron Fist 2.00
95 F:Living Mummy 2.00
96 F:Sandman,C:Marvel Heroes . 2.00
97 F:Iron Man 2.00

Marvel Two-In-One #4
© Marvel Entertainment Group

98 F:Franklin Richards 2.00
99 JBy(c),F:Rom 2.00
100 F:Ben Grimm 2.50
Ann.#1 SB,F:Liberty Legion 5.00
Ann.#2 JSn,2nd D:Thanos,A:Spider
Man,Avengers,Capt.Marvel,
I:Lord Chaos,Master Order . . 35.00
Ann.#3 F:Nova 4.00
Ann.#4 F:Black Bolt 3.50
Ann.#5 F:Hulk,V:Pluto 3.00
Ann.#6 I:American Eagle 3.00
Ann.#7 I:Champion,A:Hulk,Thor,
DocSamson,Colossus,Sasquatch,
WonderMan 3.50

OFFICIAL HANDBOOK OF THE MARVEL UNIVERSE

January, 1983

1 Abomination-Avengers'
Quintet 7.50
2 BaronMordo-Collect.Man 6.00
3 Collector-Dracula 5.00
4 Dragon Man-Gypsy Moth 5.00
5 Hangman-Juggernaut 5.00
6 K-L 5.00
7 Mandarin-Mystique 4.00
8 Na,oria-Pyro 4.00
9 Quasar to She-Hulk 4.00
10 Shiar-Sub-Mariner 4.00
11 Subteraneans-Ursa Major 4.00
12 Valkyrie-Zzzax 4.00
13 Book of the Dead 4.00
14 Book of the Dead 4.00
15 Weaponry 4.00

[2nd Series]

1 Abomination-Batroc 5.00
2 Beast-Clea 4.00
3 Cloak & D.-Dr.Strange 4.00
4 Dr.Strange-Galactus 4.00
5 Gardener-Hulk 4.00
6 Human Torch-Ka-Zar 3.25
7 Kraven-Magneto 3.25
8 Magneto-Moleman 3.25
9 Moleman-Owl 3.25
10 . . . . 3.25
11 . . . . 2.50
12 S-T 2.50
13 . . . . 2.50
14 V-Z 2.50
15 . . . . 2.50
16 Book of the Dead 2.50
17 Handbook of the Dead,inc.
JLe illus. 2.50
18 . . . . 2.50
19 . . . . 2.50
20 Inc.RLd illus. 2.50

Marvel Universe Update

1 thru 8 . . . . @1.75

Marvel Universe Packet

1 inc. Spider-Man 5.50
2 inc. Captain America 4.50
3 inc. Ghost Rider 5.00
4 inc. Wolverine 4.50
5 inc. Punisher 4.25
6 inc. She-Hulk 3.95
7 inc. Daredevil 3.95
8 inc. Hulk 3.95
9 inc. Moon Knight 3.95
10 inc. Captain Britain 3.95
11 inc. Storm 3.95
12 inc. Silver Surfer 3.95
13 inc. Ice Man 4.50
14 inc. Thor 4.50
15 thru 22 . . . . @4.50
23 inc. Cage 4.50
24 inc. Iron Fist 4.50
25 inc.Deadpool,Night Thrasher . . 4.50
26 inc. Wonderman 4.95
27 inc.Beta Ray Bill,Pip 4.95
28 inc.X-Men 4.95
29 inc.Carnage 4.95
30 thru 36 . . . . @4.95

MARVEL X-MEN COLLECTION

1 thru 3 JL from the 1st series
X-Men Cards 3.25

MARVELS

1 B:KBk(s),AxR,I:Phil Sheldon,
A:G.A.Heroes,Human Torch Vs
Namor 14.00
2 AxR,A:S.A.Avengers,FF,X-Men 11.00
3 AxR,FF vs Galactus 9.00
4 AxR,Final issue 7.50

All comics prices listed are for *Near Mint* condition.

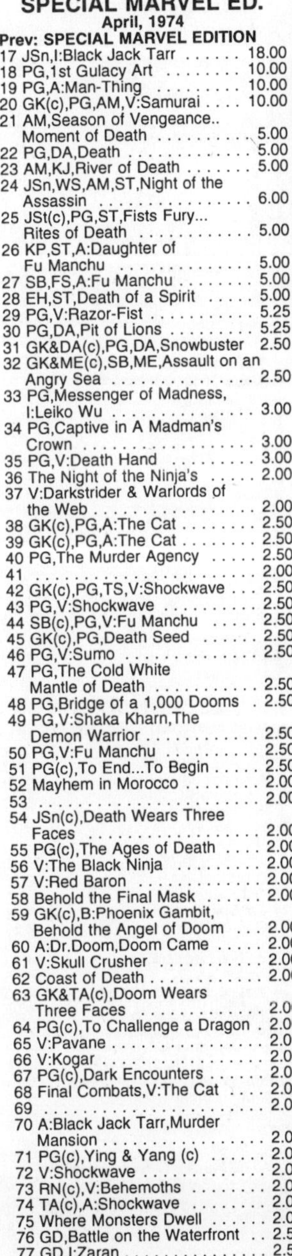

MARVIN MOUSE
Atlas
September, 1957

1 BEv,F:Marvin Mouse 28.00

MASTER OF KUNG FU, SPECIAL MARVEL ED.
April, 1974
Prev: SPECIAL MARVEL EDITION

17 JSn,I:Black Jack Tarr 18.00
18 PG,1st Gulacy Art 10.00
19 PG,A:Man-Thing 10.00
20 GK(c),PG,AM,V:Samurai 10.00
21 AM,Season of Vengeance.. Moment of Death 5.00
22 PG,DA,Death 5.00
23 AM,KJ,River of Death 5.00
24 JSn,WS,AM,ST,Night of the Assassin 6.00
25 JSt(c),PG,ST,Fists Fury... Rites of Death 5.00
26 KP,ST,A:Daughter of Fu Manchu 5.00
27 SB,FS,A:Fu Manchu 5.00
28 EH,ST,Death of a Spirit 5.00
29 PG,V:Razor-Fist 5.25
30 PG,DA,Pit of Lions 5.25
31 GK&DA(c),PG,DA,Snowbuster 2.50
32 GK&ME(c),SB,ME,Assault on an Angry Sea 2.50
33 PG,Messenger of Madness, I:Leiko Wu 3.00
34 PG,Captive in A Madman's Crown 3.00
35 PG,V:Death Hand 3.00
36 The Night of the Ninja's 2.00
37 V:Darkstrider & Warlords of the Web 2.00
38 GK(c),PG,A:The Cat 2.50
39 GK(c),PG,A:The Cat 2.50
40 PG,The Murder Agency 2.50
41 . . . . 2.00
42 GK(c),PG,TS,V:Shockwave . . . 2.50
43 PG,V:Shockwave 2.50
44 SB(c),PG,V:Fu Manchu 2.50
45 GK(c),PG,Death Seed 2.50
46 PG,V:Sumo 2.50
47 PG,The Cold White Mantle of Death 2.50
48 PG,Bridge of a 1,000 Dooms . 2.50
49 PG,V:Shaka Kharn,The Demon Warrior 2.50
50 PG,V:Fu Manchu 2.50
51 PG(c),To End...To Begin 2.50
52 Mayhem in Morocco 2.00
53 . . . . 2.00
54 JSn(c),Death Wears Three Faces 2.00
55 PG(c),The Ages of Death 2.00
56 V:The Black Ninja 2.00
57 V:Red Baron 2.00
58 Behold the Final Mask 2.00
59 GK(c),B:Phoenix Gambit, Behold the Angel of Doom . . . 2.00
60 A:Dr.Doom,Doom Came 2.00
61 V:Skull Crusher 2.00
62 Coast of Death 2.00
63 GK&TA(c),Doom Wears Three Faces 2.00
64 PG(c),To Challenge a Dragon . 2.00
65 V:Pavane 2.00
66 V:Kogar 2.00
67 PG(c),Dark Encounters 2.00
68 Final Combats,V:The Cat 2.00
69 . . . . 2.00
70 A:Black Jack Tarr,Murder Mansion 2.00
71 PG(c),Ying & Yang (c) 2.00
72 V:Shockwave 2.00
73 RN(c),V:Behemoths 2.00
74 TA(c),A:Shockwave 2.00
75 Where Monsters Dwell 2.00
76 GD,Battle on the Waterfront . . 2.50
77 GD,I:Zaran 2.50

Master of Kung Fu #100
© Marvel Entertainment Group

78 GD,Moving Targets 2.50
79 GD,This Side of Death 2.50
80 GD,V:Leopard Men 2.50
81 GD,V:Leopard Men 2.50
82 GD,Flight into Fear 2.50
83 GD, ... 2.50
84 GD,V:Fu Manchu 2.50
85 GD,V:Fu Manchu 2.50
86 GD,V:Fu Manchu 2.50
87 GD,V:Zaran, ... 2.50
88 GD,V:Fu Manchu 2.50
89 GD,D:Fu Manchu 2.50
90 MZ,Death in Chinatown 2.50
91 GD,Gang War,drugs 2.75
92 GD,Shadows of the Past 2.50
93 GD,Cult of Death 2.50
94 GD,V:Agent Synergon 2.50
95 GD,Raid 2.50
96 GD,I:Rufus Carter 2.50
97 GD,V:Kung Fu's Dark Side . . . 2.50
98 GD,Fight to the Finish 2.50
99 GD,Death Boat 2.50
100 GD,Doublesize 3.00
101 GD,Not Smoke,Nor Beads, Nor Blood 2.00
102 GD,Assassins,1st GD(p) 3.00
103 GD,V:Assassins 2.50
104 GD,Fight without Reason, C:Cerberus 2.50
105 GD,I:Razor Fist 2.50
106 GD,C:Velcro 2.50
107 GD,A:Sata 2.50
108 GD 2.50
109 GD,Death is a Dark Agent . . 2.50
110 GD,Perilous Reign 2.50
111 GD 2.50
112 GD(c),Commit and Destroy . . 2.00
113 GD(c),V:Panthers 2.00
114 Fantasy o/t Autumn Moon . . . 2.25
115 GD 2.50
116 GD 2.50
117 GD,Devil Deeds Done in Darkness 2.50
118 GD,D:Fu Manchu,double 2.50
119 GD 2.50
120 GD,Dweller o/t Dark Stream . 2.50
121 Death in the City of Lights' . . 2.00
122 . . . . 2.00
123 V:Ninjas 2.00
124 . . . . 2.00
125 . . . . 2.00
Giant#1,CR,PG 3.00
Giant#2 PG,V:Yellow Claw 2.00
Giant#3 . . . . 2.00
Giant#4 JK,V:Yellow Claw 2.00
Spec.#1 Bleeding Black 2.95

MASTER OF KUNG FU: BLEEDING BLACK

1 V:ShadowHand,1991 . . . . 2.95

MASTERS OF TERROR
July, 1975

1 GM(c),FB,BWS,JSn,NA 3.00
2 JSn(c),GK,VM,September, 1975 2.00

MASTERS OF THE UNIVERSE
Star
May, 1986

1 I:Hordak 1.50
2 thru 11 . . . . @1.00
12 March, 1988 . . . . 1.00
Movie #1 GT 2.00

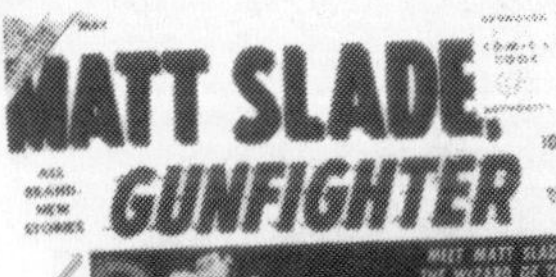

Matt Slade, Gunfighter #1
© Marvel Entertainment Group

MATT SLADE, GUNFIGHTER
Atlas
May, 1956

1 AW,AT,F:Matt Slade,Crimson Avenger 80.00
2 AW,A:Crimson Avenger 50.00
3 A:Crimson Avenger 35.00
4 A:Crimson Avenger 35.00

Becomes:

KID SLADE GUNFIGHTER

5 F:Kid Slade 40.00
6 . . . . 21.00
7 AW,Duel in the Night 45.00
8 July, 1957 . . . . 21.00

MELVIN THE MONSTER
Atlas
July, 1956

1 . . . . 46.00
2 thru 6 . . . . @34.00

Becomes:

DEXTER THE DEMON
September, 1957

7 . . . . 18.00

MEMORIES
Epic
1 Space Adventures 2.50

MENACE
Atlas
May, 1953
1 RH,BEv,GT,One Head Too Many 225.00
2 RH,BEv,GT,JSt,Burton's Blood150.00
3 BEv,RH,JR,The Werewolf . . 100.00
4 BEv,RH,The Four Armed Man 100.00
5 BEv,RH,GC,GT,I&O:Zombie 175.00
6 BEv,RH,JR,The Graymoor Ghost 100.00
7 JSt,RH,Fresh out of Flesh . . 75.00
8 RH,The Lizard Man 75.00
9 BEv,The Walking Dead 85.00
10 RH(c),Half Man,Half... . . . . . . 75.00
11 JKz,JR,Locked In,May, 1954 . 75.00

MEN IN ACTION
Atlas
April, 1952
1 Sweating it Out 55.00
2 US Infantry stories 30.00
3 RH 20.00
4 War stories 20.00
5 Squad Charge 20.00
6 War stories 20.00
7 RH(c),BK,No Risk Too Great 40.00
8 JRo(c),They Strike By Night . 20.00
9 SSh(c),Rangers Strike Back . 20.00
Becomes:

BATTLE BRADY
10 SSh(c),F:Battle Brady 45.00
11 SSh(c) 28.00
12 SSh(c),Death to the Reds . . . 20.00
13 . . . . 20.00
14 Final Issue,June, 1953 . . . . . 20.00

MEN'S ADVENTURES
See: TRUE WESTERN

MEPHISTO vs. FOUR HEROES
April, 1987
1 JB,BWi,A:Fantastic Four 2.50
2 JB,BWi,A:X-Factor 2.25
3 JB,AM,A:X-Men 2.25
4 JB,BWi,A:Avengers,July, 1987 . 2.00

MERC
November, 1986
1 GM,O:Mark Hazard 1.50
2 GM 1.00
3 M,Arab Terrorists 1.00
4 GM 1.00
5 GM 1.00
6 GM 1.00
7 GM 1.00
8 GM 1.00
9 NKu/AKu 1.00
10 . . . . 1.00
11 . . . . 1.00
12 October, 1987 . . . . 1.00
Ann.#1 D:Merc 1.25

METEOR MAN
1 R:Meteor Man 1.25
2 V:GhostStrike,Malefactor,Simon 1.25
3 A:Spider-Man 1.25
4 A:Night Thrasher 1.25

METROPOL
Epic
1 Ted McKeever 2.95
2 . . . . 2.95
3 . . . . 2.95
4 . . . . 2.95
5 . . . . 2.95
6 . . . . 2.95
7 . . . . 2.95
8 Return of Eddy Current 2.95
9 'Wings of Silence' 2.95
10 'Rotting Metal,Rusted Flesh' . . 2.95
11 'Diagram of the Heart' 2.95

METROPOL A.D.
Epic
1 R:The Angels 3.50
2 V:Demons 3.50
3 V:Nuclear Arsenal 3.50

MICRONAUTS
[1st Series]
January, 1979
1 MGo,JRu,O:Micronauts 3.00
2 MGo,JRu,Earth 2.50
3 MGo,JRu 2.00

Micronauts #58

© Marvel Entertainment Group

4 MGo 2.00
5 MGo,V:Prometheus 2.00
6 MGo 2.00
7 MGo,A:Man Thing 2.00
8 MGo,BMc,I:Capt. Univ. 2.50
9 MGo,I:Cilicia 2.00
10 MGo 2.00
11 MGo 2.00
12 MGo 2.00
13 HC,F:Bug 1.50
14 HC,V:Wartstaff 1.50
15 HC,AM,A:Fantastic Four 1.50
16 HC,AM,A:Fantastic Four 1.50
17 HC,AM,A:Fantastic Four 1.50
18 HC,Haunted House Issue 1.50
19 PB,V:Odd John 1.50
20 PB,A:Antman 1.50
21 PB,I:Microverse 1.50
22 PB 1.50
23 PB,V:Molecule Man 1.50
24 MGo,V:Computrex 1.50
25 PB,A:Mentallo 1.50
26 PB,A:Baronkarza 1.25
27 PB,V:Hydra,A:Shield 1.25
28 PB,V:Hydra,A:Shield 1.25
29 PB,Doc Samson 1.25
30 PB,A:Shield 1.25
31 PB,A:Dr.Strange 1.25
32 PB,A:Dr.Strange 1.25
33 PB,A:Devil of Tropica 1.25
34 PB,A:Dr.Strange 1.25
35 O:Microverse 1.50
36 KG,Dr.Strange 1.50
37 KG,Nightcrawler 3.50
38 GK,1st direct 2.50
39 SD 1.75
40 GK,A:FF 1.75
41 GK,Dr.Doom 1.25
42 GK 1.25
43 . . . . 1.25
44 . . . . 1.25
45 Arcade 1.25
46 . . . . 1.25
47 . . . . 1.25
48 JG 2.00
49 JG,V:BaronKarza 1.50
50 JG,V:BaronKarza 1.50
51 JG 1.50
52 JG 1.50
53 JG,V:Untouchables 1.50
54 JG,V:Tribunal 1.50
55 JG,V:KarzaWorld 1.50
56 JG,Kaliklak 1.50
57 JG,V:BaronKarza 1.50
58 JG,V:BaronKarza 1.50
59 JG,V:TheMakers 1.50
Ann.#1,SD 2.00
#2 SD 1.50

[2nd Series]
1 V:The Makers 1.50
2 AAd(c),V:The Makers 1.50
3 Huntarr'sEgg 1.00
4 V:The Makers 1.00
5 The Spiral Path 1.00
6 L:Bug 1.00
7 Acroyear 1.00
8 V:Scion 1.00
9 R:Devil 1.00
10 V:Enigma Force 1.00
11 V:Scion 1.00
12 V:Scion 1.00
13 V:Dark Armada 1.00
14 V:Keys of the Zodiac 1.00
15 O:Marionette 1.00
16 Secret Wars II 1.50
17 V:Scion 1.00
18 Acroyear 1.00
19 R:Baron Karza 1.00
20 Last Issue 1.25

MICRONAUTS (Special Edition)
December, 1983
1 MGo/JRu,rep. 2.00
2 MGo/JRu,rep. 2.00
3 Rep.MG/JRu 2.00
4 Rep.MG/JRu 2.00
5 Rep.MG/JRu,April, 1984 . . . . . 2.00

MIDNIGHT MEN
1 HC,I:Midnight Men 2.75
2 HC,J:Barnett 2.25
3 HC,Pasternak is Midnight Man . 2.25
4 HC,Last issue 2.25

MIDNIGHT SONS UNLIMITED
1 JQ,JBi,MT(c),A:Midnight Sons . 4.25
2 BSz(c),F:Midnight Sons 4.25
3 JR2(c),JS,A:SpiderMan 4.25
4 Siege of Darkness #17,D:2nd Ghost Rider 4.25
5 DQ(s),F:Mordred,Vengeance, Morbius,Werewolf,Blaze, I:Wildpride 4.25
6 DQ(s),F:Dr.Strange 3.95

MIGHTY MARVEL WESTERN
October, 1968
1 JK,All reprints,B:Rawhide Kid Kid Colt,Two-Gun Kids 7.50

2 JK,DAy,Beware of the Barker Brothers 5.00
3 HT(c),JK,DAy,Walking Death . . 5.00
4 HT(c),DAy 5.00
5 HT(c),DAy,Ambush 5.00
6 HT(c),DAy Doom in the Desert 5.00
7 DAy,V:Murderous Masquerader 5.00
8 HT(c),DAy,Rustler's on the Range 5.00
9 JSe(c),JK,DAy,V:Dr Danger . . 5.00
10 OW,DH,Cougar 5.00
11 V:The Enforcers 2.00
12 JK,V:Blackjack Bordon 2.00
13 V:Grizzly 2.00
14 JK.V:The Enforcers 2.00
15 Massacre at Medicine Bend . . 2.00
16 JK,Mine of Death 2.00
17 Ambush at Blacksnake Mesa . 2.00
18 Six-Gun Thunderer 2.00
19 Reprints cont 2.00
20 same 2.00
21 same 1.50
22 . . . . 1.50
23 same 1.50
24 JDa,E:Kid Colt 1.50
25 B:Matt Slade 1.50
26 thru 31 Reprints . . . . @1.50
32 JK,AW,Ringo Kid #23 . . . . 1.25
33 thru 36 Reprints . . . . @1.25
37 JK,AW Two-Gun #51 . . . . 1.25
38 thru 45 Reprints . . . . @1.25
46 same,September, 1976 . . . . . . 1.25

MIGHTY MOUSE
Fall, 1946
[1st Series]

1 Terytoons Presents 650.00
2 . . . . 350.00
3 . . . . 250.00
4 Summer, 1947 . . . . 250.00

MIGHTY MOUSE
October, 1990

1 EC,Dark Mite Returns 3.00
2 EC,V:The Glove 2.00
3 EC/JBr(c)Prince Say More 1.50
4 EC/GP(c)Alt.Universe #1 . . . . . 1.50
5 EC,Alt.Universe #2 . . . . 1.50
6 'Ferment',A:MacFurline' 1.50
7 EC,V:Viral Worm 1.25
8 EC,BAT-BAT:Year One, O:Bug Wonder 1.25
9 EC,BAT-BAT:Year One, V:Smoker 1.25
10 'Night o/t Rating Lunatics' 1.25

MILLIE THE MODEL
Winter, 1945

1 O:Millie the Model, Bowling(c) 300.00
2 Totem Pole(c) 200.00
3 Anti-Noise(c) 125.00
4 Bathing Suit(c) 125.00
5 Blame it on Fame 125.00
6 Beauty and the Beast 125.00
7 Bathing Suit(c) 125.00
8 Fancy Dress(c),HK,Hey Look 125.00
9 Paris(c),BW 135.00
10 Jewelry(c),HK,Hey Look . . . 125.00
11 HK,Giggles and Grins 75.00
12 A;Rusty,Hedy Devine 50.00
13 A;Hedy Devine,HK,Hey Look 60.00
14 HK,Hey Look 60.00
15 HK,Hey Look 40.00
16 . . . . 60.00
17 thru 20 . . . . @40.00
21 thru 30 . . . . @40.00
31 thru 75 . . . . @30.00
76 thru 99 . . . . @20.00
100 . . . . 22.00
101 thru 126 . . . . @15.00
127 Millie/Clicker 20.00
128 A:Scarlet Mayfair 15.00
129 The Truth about Agnes 15.00

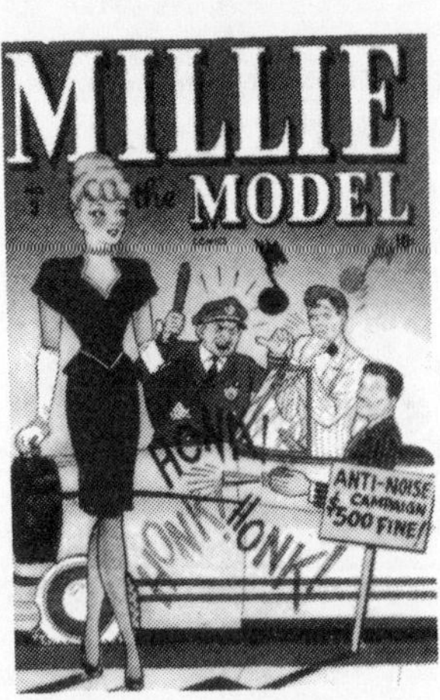

Millie the Model #3
© Marvel Entertainment Group

130 thru 153 . . . . @15.00
154 B:New Millie 15.00
155 thru 206 . . . . @15.00
207 December, 1973 . . . . 15.00
Ann.#1 How Millie Became a Model 125.00
Ann.#2 Millies Guide to the world of Modeling 75.00
Ann.#3 Many Lives of Millie 50.00
Ann.#4 Many Lives of Millie 30.00

MISS AMERICA COMICS
1944

1 Miss America(c),pin-ups . . . 600.00

MISS AMERICA MAGAZINE
November, 1944

2 Ph(c),Miss America costume I;Patsy Walker,Buzz Baxter, Hedy Wolfe 600.00
3 Ph(c),A:Patsy Walker,Miss America 300.00
4 Ph(c),Betty Page,A:Patsy Walker,Miss America 300.00
5 Ph(c),A:Patsy Walker,Miss America 300.00
6 Ph(c),A:Patsy Walker 50.00
7 Patsy Walker stories 25.00
8 same 25.00
9 same 25.00
10 same 25.00
11 same 25.00
12 same 25.00
13 thru 18 . . . . @25.00
21 . . . . 35.00
22 thru 45 . . . . @20.00
46 thru 92 . . . . @15.00
93 November, 1958 . . . . 15.00

MISS FURY COMICS
Timely
Winter, 1942-43

1 Newspaper strip reprints, ASh(c) O:Miss Fury 1,600.00
2 V:Nazis(c) 750.00
3 Hitler/Nazi Flag(c) 600.00
4 ASh(c),Japanese(c) 500.00
5 ASh(c),Gangster(c) 500.00
6 Gangster(c) 500.00
7 Gangster(c) 500.00
8 Atom-Bomb Secrets(c) Winter, 1946 . . . . 500.00

MISTY
Star
December, 1985

1 F:Millie the Models Niece 1.50
2 thru 5 . . . . @1.00
6 May, 1986 . . . . 1.00

MITZI COMICS
Timely
Spring, 1948

1 HK:Hey Look,Giggles and Grins 75.00

Becomes:

MITZI'S BOYFRIEND

2 F:Chip,Mitzi/Chip(c) 33.00
3 Chips adventures 25.00
4 thru 7 same . . . . @25.00

Becomes:

MITZI'S ROMANCES

8 Mitzi/Chip(c) 32.00
9 . . . . 25.00
10 December, 1949 . . . . 25.00

MODELING WITH MILLIE
See: DATE WITH MILLIE

MOEBIUS
Epic
October, 1987

1 . . . . 12.00
2 . . . . 12.00
3 . . . . 15.00
4 . . . . 12.00
5 . . . . 12.00
6 1988 . . . . 12.00

MOLLY MANTON'S ROMANCES
September, 1949

1 Ph(c),Dare Not Marry 46.00
2 Ph(c),Romances of 35.00

Becomes:

ROMANTIC AFFAIRS

3 Ph(c) 27.00

MONSTER OF FRANKENSTEIN
January, 1973

1 MP,Frankenstein's Monster . . 18.00
2 MP,Bride of the Monster 9.00
3 MP,Revenge 9.00
4 MP,Monster's Death 9.00
5 MP,The Monster Walks Among Us 9.00

Becomes:

FRANKENSTEIN

6 MP,Last of the Frankensteins . 5.00
7 JB,The Fiend and the Fury . . . 5.00
8 JB,A:Dracula 10.00
9 JB,A:Dracula 10.00
10 JB,Death Strikes Frankenstein 5.00
11 Carnage at Castle Frankenstein 3.75
12 Frankenstein's Monster today . 3.75
13 Undying Fiend 3.75
14 Fury of the Night Creature . . . 3.75
15 Trapped in a Nightmare 3.75
16 The Brute and the Berserker . . 3.75
17 Phoenix Aflame 3.75
18 Children of the Damned September, 1975 . . . . 3.75

MONSTERS ON THE PROWL
See: CHAMBER OF DARKNESS

MONSTERS UNLEASHED
July, 1973

1 GM(c),GC,DW,Black&White Mag 6.00
2 JB,FB,BEv,B:Frankenstein . . . 8.00
3 NA(c),GK,GM,GT,B:Man-Thing 4.00
4 JB,GC,BK,I:Satana 4.00
5 JB 5.00
6 MP 4.00
7 AW 4.00
8 GP,NA 4.00
9 A:Wendigo 5.00
10 O:Tigra 4.00
11 FB(C),April, 1975 . . . . 4.00
Ann.#1 GK 4.00

MOON KNIGHT
[1st Regular Series]
November, 1980

1 BSz,O:Moon Knight 6.00
2 BSz,V:Slasher 3.50
3 BSz,V:Midnight Man 3.00
4 BSz,V:Committee of 5 . . . . 3.00
5 BSz,V:Red Hunter 3.00
6 BSz,V:White Angels 3.00
7 BSz,V:Moon Kings 3.00
8 BSz,V:Moon Kings, Drug 2.75
9 BSz,V:Midnight Man 2.75
10 BSz,V:Midnight Man 2.75
11 BSz,V:Creed (Angel Dust) . . . 2.75
12 BSz,V:Morpheus 2.50
13 BSz,A:Daredevil & Jester 2.50
14 BSz,V:Stained Glass Scarlet . . 2.50
15 FM(c),BSz,1st Direct 4.00
16 V:Blacksmith 2.50
17 BSz,V:Master Sniper 2.50
18 BSz,V:Slayers Elite 2.50
19 BSz,V:Arsenal 2.50
20 BSz,V:Arsenal 2.50
21 A:Bother Voodoo 2.25
22 BSz,V:Morpheus 2.25
23 BSz,V:Morpheus 2.25
24 BSz,V:Stained Glass Scarlet . . 2.25
25 BSz,Black Specter 2.25
26 KP,V:Cabbie Killer 2.00
27 A:Kingpin 2.00
28 BSz,"Spirits in the Sands" 2.00
29 BSz,V:Werewolf 3.00
30 BSz,V:Werewolf 3.00
31 TA,V:Savage Studs 2.00
32 KN,Druid Walsh 2.00
33 KN,V:Druid Walsh 2.00
34 KN,Marc Spector 2.00
35 KN,X-Men,FF,V:The Fly
DoubleSized 3.00
36 A:Dr.Strange 2.00
37 V:Zohar 2.00
38 V:Zohar 2.00

[2nd Regular Series]

1 O:Moon Knight,DoubleSize . . . 2.50
2 Yucatan 2.00
3 V:Morpheus 2.00
4 A:Countess 2.00
5 V:Lt.Flint 2.00
6 GI,LastIssue 2.00

[3rd Regular Series]

1 V:Bushmaster 5.00
2 A:Spider-Man 4.00
3 V:Bushmaster 2.50
4 RH,A:Midnight,Black Cat 2.50
5 V:Midnight,BlackCat 2.50
6 A:BrotherVoodoo 2.50
7 A:BrotherVoodoo 2.50
8 TP,A:Punisher,A of V 6.50
9 TP,A:Punisher,A of V 6.50
10 V:Killer Shrike,A of V 2.00
11 TP,V:Arsenal 2.00
12 TP,V:Bushman,A:Arsenal 2.00
13 TP,V:Bushman 2.00
14 TP,V:Bushman 2.00
15 TP,Trial o/Marc Spector #1,A:
Silv.Sable,Sandman,Paladin . . 3.00
16 TP,Trial o/Marc Spector #2,A:
Silv.Sable,Sandman,Paladin . . 3.00
17 TP,Trial o/Marc Spector #3 . . . 3.00
18 TP,Trial o/Marc Spector #4 . . . 3.00
19 RLd(c),TP,SpM,Punisher 5.50
20 TP,A:Spider-Man,Punisher . . . 4.00
21 TP,Spider-Man,Punisher 4.00
22 I:Harbinger 2.00
23 Confrontation 2.00
24 A:Midnight 2.00
25 MBa,TP,A:Ghost Rider 3.25
26 BSz(c),TP,B:Scarlet Redemption
V:Stained Glass Scarlet 2.00
27 TP,V:Stained Glass Scarlet . . . 2.00
28 TP,V:Stained Glass Scarlet . . . 2.00
29 TP,V:Stained Glass Scarlet . . . 2.00
30 TP,V:Stained Glass Scarlet . . . 2.00
31 TP,E:Scarlet Redemption,
A:Hobgoblin 2.50
32 TP,V:Hobgoblin,SpM(in Black) 4.50
33 TP,V:Hobgoblin,A:Spider-Man . 4.00
34 V:Killer Shrike 1.75
35 TP,Return of Randall Spector
Pt.1,A:Punisher 2.00
36 TP,A:Punisher,Randall 2.00
37 TP,A:Punisher,Randall 2.00
38 TP,A:Punisher,Randall 2.00
39 TP,N:Moon Knight,A:Dr.Doom . 2.00
40 TP,V:Dr.Doom 2.00
41 TP,Infinity War,I:Moonshade . . 2.00
42 TP,Infinity War,V:Moonshade . 2.00
43 TP(i),Infinity War 2.00
44 Inf.War,A:Dr.Strange.FF 2.00
45 V:Demogoblin 2.00
46 V:Demogoblin 2.00
47 Legacy Quest Scenario 2.00
48 I:Deadzone 2.00
49 V:Deadzone 2.00
50 A:Avengers,I:Hellbent,
Die-cut(c) 3.50
51 A:Gambit,V:Hellbent 2.00
52 A:Gambit,Werewolf 2.00
53 "Pang" 2.00
54 . . . . 2.00
55 SPa,V:Sunstreak 28.00
56 SPa,V:Seth 23.00
57 SPa,Inf.Crusade 17.00
58 SPa(c),A:Hellbent 2.00
59 SPa(c), ... 2.00
60 E:TKa(s),SPa,D:Moonknight . . 6.00
Spec.#1 ANi,A:Shang-Chi 2.50

MOON KNIGHT
(Special Edition)
November, 1983

1 BSz,reprints 2.00
2 BSz,reprints 2.00
3 BSz,reprints,January, 1984 . . . 2.00

MOONSHADOW
Epic
May, 1985

1 JMu,O:Moonshadow 6.00
2 JMu,Into Space 4.00
3 JMu,The Looney Bin 3.50
4 JMu,Fights Ira 3.50
5 JMu,Prisoner 3.50
6 JMu,Hero of War 3.50
7 JMu,UnkshussFamily 3.50
8 JMu,Social Outcast 3.50
9 JMu,Search For Ira 3.50
10 JMu,Internat.House of T 3.50
11 JMu,UnkshussFamily 3.50
12 JMu,UnkshussFamily,Feb.1987 3.50

MONSTER MENACE

1 thru 4 SD,rep. 1.25

MORBIUS

1 V:Lilith,Lilin,A:Blaze,Gh.Rider,
Rise o/t Midnight Sons #3,
polybagged w/poster 4.00
2 V:Simon Stroud 2.50
3 A:Spider-Man 2.00
4 I:Dr.Paine,C:Spider-Man 2.00
5 V:Basilisk,(inc Superman tribute
on letters page) 2.00
6 V:Basilisk 2.00
7 V:Vic Slaughter 2.00
8 V:Nightmare 2.00
9 V:Nightmare 2.00
10 Two Tales 2.00
11 A:Nightstalkers 2.00
12 Midnight Massacre#4 . . . . . . 2.50
13 R:Martine,A:Lilith 2.00
14 RoW,V:Nightmare,A:Werewolf . 2.00
15 A:Ghost Rider,Werewolf 2.00
16 GWt(s),Siege of Darkness#5 . . 2.00
17 GWt(s),Siege of Darkness#17 . 2.00
18 GWt(s),A:Deathlok 2.00
19 GWt(s),A:Deathlok 2.00
20 GWt(s),I:Bloodthirst 2.00
21 B:Dance of the Hunter,A:SpM . 1.95
22 A:Spider-Man 1.95
23 E:Dance of the Hunter,A:SpM . 1.95

Morbius #2
© Marvel Entertainment Group

MORBIUS REVISITED

1 WMc,rep.Fear#20 . . . . 1.95
2 WMc,rep.Fear#28 . . . . 1.95
3 WMc,rep.Fear#29 . . . . 1.95
4 WMc,rep.Fear#30 . . . . 1.95
5 WMc,rep.Fear#31 . . . . 1.95

MORT THE DEAD TEENAGER

1 LHa(s),I:Mort 1.75
2 thru 3 LHa(s), ... 1.75
4 LHa(s),last issue 1.75

MOTHER TERESA
1984

1 Mother Teresa Story 2.00

MOTOR MOUTH

1 GFr,A:Nick Fury,I:Motor
Mouth,Killpower 4.00
2 GFr,A:Nick Fury, ... 2.50
3 GFr,V:Killpower,A:Punisher . . . 2.50
4 GFr,A:Nick Fury,Warheads,
Hell's Angel,O:Killpower 2.50
5 GFr,A:Excalibur,Archangel 2.50
6 GFr,A:Cable,Punisher 2.50
7 EP,A:Cable,Nick Fury 2.00
8 JFr,A:Cable,Nick Fury 2.00
9 JFr,A:Cable,N.Fury,V:Harpies . 2.00
10 V:Red Sonja 2.00

11 V:Zachary Sorrow 2.00
12 A:Death's Head II 2.00
13 A:Death's Head II 2.00

MS. MARVEL
January, 1977

1 JB,O:Ms Marvel 5.00

Ms. Marvel #14

© Marvel Entertainment Group

2 JB,JSt,V:Scorpion 4.00
3 JB,JSt,V:Doomsday Man 3.00
4 JM,JSt,V:Destructor 3.00
5 JM,JSt,A:V:Vision 3.00
6 JM,JSt,V:Grotesk 3.00
7 JM,JSt,V:Modok 3.00
8 JM,JSt,V:Grotesk 3.00
9 KP,JSt,I:Deathbird 5.00
10 JB,TP,V:Deathbird,Modok 3.00
11 V:Elementals 2.00
12 V;Hecate 2.00
13 Bedlam in Boston 2.00
14 V:Steeplejack 2.00
15 V:Tigershark 2.00
16 V:Tigershark,A:Beast 2.00
17 . . . . 2.00
18 I:Mystique,A;Avengers 6.50
19 A:Captain Marvel 3.00
20 V:Lethal Lizards,N:Ms.Marvel 2.00
21 V:Lethal Lizards 2.00
22 V:Deathbirds 2.00
23 The Woman who Fell to Earth
April, 1979 . . . . 2.00

MUPPET BABIES
Star
August, 1984

1 thru 10 . . . . @1.00
11 thru 20 . . . . @1.00
21 thru 25 July, 1989 . . . . . . @1.00

MUPPETS TAKE MANHATTAN

1 movie adapt,November, 1984 . 1.00
2 movie adapt 1.00
3 movie adapt,January, 1985 . . . 1.00

MUTATIS
Epic

1 I:Mutatis 2.25
2 O:Mutatis 2.25
3 A:Mutatis 2.25

MY DIARY
December, 1949

1 Ph(c),The Man I Love 48.00
2 Ph(c),I Was Anybody's Girl
March, 1950 . . . . 45.00

MY LOVE
July, 1949

1 Ph(c),One Heart to Give 45.00
2 Ph(c),Hate in My Heart 30.00
3 Ph(c), ... 30.00
4 Ph(c),Betty Page, April, 1950 115.00

MY LOVE
September, 1969

1 Love story reprints 7.50
2 thru 9 . . . . @4.00
10 . . . . 5.00
11 thru 38 . . . . @3.00
39 March, 1976 . . . . 3.00

MY ROMANCE
September, 1948

1 Romance Stories 45.00
2 . . . . 27.00
3 . . . . 27.00

Becomes:

MY OWN ROMANCE

4 Romance Stories Continue . . 47.00
5 thru 10 . . . . @25.00
11 thru 20 . . . . @18.00
21 thru 50 . . . . @15.00
51 thru 54 . . . . @11.00
55 . . . . 30.00
56 thru 60 . . . . @11.00
61 thru 70 . . . . @6.00
71 . . . . 55.00
72 thru 76 . . . . @10.00

Becomes:

TEENAGE ROMANCE

77 Romance Stories Continue . . 10.00
78 thru 85 . . . . @10.00
86 March, 1962 . . . . 10.00

MYS-TECH WARS

1 BHi,A:FF,X-Men,Avengers 2.00
2 A:FF,X-Men,X-Force 2.00
3 BHi,A:X-Men,X-Force 2.00
4 A:Death's Head II 2.00

MYSTERY TALES
Atlas
March, 1952

1 GC,Horror Strikes at Midnight 350.00
2 BK,BEv,OW,The Corpse
is Mine 175.00
3 RH,GC,JM, The Vampire
Strikes 125.00
4 Funeral of Horror 125.00
5 Blackout at Midnight 125.00
6 . . . . 125.00
7 JRo,The Ghost Hunter 125.00
8 BEv 125.00
9 BEv(c),the Man in the Morgue 125.00
10 BEV(c),GT,What Happened
to Harry 125.00
11 BEv(c) 100.00
12 GT,MF 100.00
13 . . . . 90.00
14 BEv(c),GT 90.00
15 RH(c),EK 90.00
16 . . . . 90.00
17 RH(c) 90.00
18 AW,DAy,GC 100.00
19 . . . . 90.00
20 Electric Chair 90.00
21 JF,MF,Decapitation 100.00
22 JF,MF 100.00
23 thru 27 . . . . @75.00
28 . . . . 60.00
29 thru 32 . . . . @65.00
33 BEv 55.00
34 . . . . 55.00
35 BEv 55.00
36 . . . . 65.00
37 DW 55.00
38 . . . . 55.00
39 BK 65.00
40 . . . . 65.00
41 thru 43 . . . . @55.00
44 AW 75.00
45 SD 70.00
46 RC,SD,JP 75.00
47 DAy 70.00
48 . . . . 55.00
49 GM,AT 40.00
50 JO,AW 75.00
51 DAy 75.00
52 . . . . 50.00
53 . . . . 50.00
54 RC,August, 1957 . . . . 60.00

MYSTICAL TALES
Atlas
June, 1956

1 BEv,BP,JO,Say the Magical
Words 165.00
2 BEv(c),JO,Black Blob 75.00
3 BEv(c),RC,Four Doors To . . . 85.00

Mystical Tales #1

© Marvel Entertainment Group

4 BEv(c).The Condemned 75.00
5 AW,Meeting at Midnight 80.00
6 BK,AT,He Hides in the Tower 65.00
7 BEv,JF,JO,AT,FBe,The
Haunted Tower 70.00
8 BK,SC, Stone Walls Can't
Stop Him,August, 1957 . . . . 75.00

MYSTIC COMICS
Timely
March, 1940
[1st Series]

1 ASh(c),O:The Blue Blaze,Dynamic
Man,Flexo,B:Dakor the Magician
A:Zephyr Jones,3X's,Deep Sea
Demon,Bondage(c) 7,200.00
2 ASh(c),B:The Invisible Man
Mastermind, ... 1,800.00
3 ASh(c),O:Hercules 1,500.00
4 ASh(c),O:Thin Man,Black Widow
E:Hercules,Blue Blazes,Dynamic
Man,Flexo,Invisible Man . . 1,600.00
5 ASh(c)O:The Black Marvel,
Blazing Skull,Super Slave

Terror,Sub-Earth Man . . . 1,600.00
6 ASh(c),O:The Challenger, B:The Destroyer 1,500.00
7 S&K(c),B:The Witness,O:Davey and the Demon,E;The Black Widow,Hitler(c) 1,300.00
8 Bondage(c) 1,000.00
9 MSy,DRi,,Hitler/Bondage(c) 1,000.00
10 E:Challenger,Terror 1,000.00

[2nd Series]
October, 1944

1 B:The Angel,Human Torch, Destroyer,Terry Vance, Tommy Tyme,Bondage(c) . 850.00
2 E:Human Torch,Terry Vance,Bondage(c) 500.00
3 E:The Angel,Tommy Tyme Bondage(c) 450.00
4 ASh(c),A:Young Allies Winter, 1944-45 . . . . 400.00

MYSTIC
[3rd Series]
March, 1951

1 MSy,Strange Tree 300.00
2 MSy,Dark Dungeon 200.00
3 GC,Jaws of Creeping Death 150.00
4 BW,MSy,The Den of the Devil Bird 275.00
5 MSy,Face 100.00
6 BW,She Wouldn't Stay Dead 275.00
7 GC,Untold Horror waits in the Tomb 100.00
8 DAy(c),BEv,GK,A Monster Among Us 100.00
9 BEv 100.00
10 GC 100.00
11 JR,The Black Gloves 75.00
12 GC 75.00
13 In the Dark 75.00
14 The Corpse and I 75.00
15 GT,JR,House of Horror 75.00
16 A Scream in the Dark 75.00
17 BEv,Behold the Vampire 75.00
18 BEv(c),The Russian Devil . . . 75.00
19 Swamp Girl 75.00
20 RH(c) 75.00
21 BEv(c),GC 65.00
22 RH(c) 65.00
23 RH(c),RA,Chilling Tales 65.00
24 GK,How Many Times Can You Die 65.00
25 RH(c),RA,E.C.Swipe 65.00
26 Severed Head(c) 75.00
27 Who Walks with a Zombie . . 70.00
28 DW,Not Enough Dead 70.00
29 SMo,The Unseen 70.00
30 RH(c),DW 70.00
31 SC,JKz 70.00
32 The Survivor 70.00
33 thru 36 . . . . @70.00
37 thru 51 . . . . @60.00
52 . . . . 75.00
53 thru 57 . . . . @60.00
58 thru 60 . . . . @65.00
61 . . . . 60.00

'NAM, THE
December, 1986

1 MGo,Vietnam War 5.50
1a 2nd printing 1.50
2 MGo,Dust Off 3.00
3 MGo,Three Day Pass 2.00
4 MGo,TV newscrew 2.00
5 MGo,Top Sgt. 2.00
6 MGo,Monsoon 2.00
7 MGo,Cedar Falls 2.00
8 MGo,5th to the 1st 2.00
9 MGo,ActionIssue 2.00
10 MGo,Saigon 2.00
11 MGo,Christmas 1.75
12 MGo,AgentOrange 1.75
13 MGo 1.75
14 . . . . 1.75

The 'Nam #1
© Marvel Entertainment Group

15 ReturningVets 1.75
16 . . . . 1.75
17 Vietcong 1.75
18 . . . . 1.75
19 . . . . 1.75
20 . . . . 1.75
21 . . . . 1.75
22 Thanksgiving 1.75
23 XmasTruce of'67 . . . . 1.75
24 TetOffensive 1.75
25 TetOffensive-KheSanh 1.75
26 HomefrontIssue 1.75
27 Candle in the Wind 1.75
28 Borderline 1.75
29 PeaceTalks 1.75
30 TheBunker 1.75
31 Fire and Ice 1.75
32 Nam in America 1.75
33 SpecialistDaniels 1.75
34 OperationPhoenix 1.75
35 Xmas-BobHope 1.75
36 RacialTension 1.75
37 Colorblind 1.75
38 Minefields 1.75
39 . . . . 1.75
40 . . . . 1.75
41 ,A:Thor,Iron Man, Cap.Am . . . 1.75
42 . . . . 1.75
43 . . . . 1.75
44 SDr 1.75
45 . . . . 1.75
46 . . . . 1.75
47 TD 1.75
48 TD 1.75
49 Donut Dolly #1 . . . . 1.75
50 HT,Donut Dolly #2 DoubSz . . . 1.75
51 HT,Donut Dolly #3 . . . . 1.75
52 Frank Castle(Punisher)#1 . . . . 6.00
52a 2nd printing 2.00
53 Punisher #2 . . . . 4.00
54 Death of Joe Hallen #1 . . . . . . 1.75
55 TD,Death of Joe Hallen #2 . . . 1.50
56 TD,Death of Joe Hallen #3 . . . 1.50
57 TD,Death of Joe Hallen #4 . . . 1.50
58 TD,Death of Joe Hallen #5 . . . 1.50
59 P.O.W. Story #1 . . . . 1.50
60 P.O.W. Story #2 . . . . 1.50
61 P.O.W. Story #3 . . . . 1.50
62 Speed & Ice Pt.1 . . . . 1.50
63 Speed & Ice Pt.2 . . . . 1.50
64 Speed & Ice Pt.3 . . . . 1.50
65 Speed & Ice Pt.4 . . . . 1.75
66 RH,Speed & Ice Pt.5 . . . . 1.75
67 A:Punisher 2.00
68 A:Punisher 2.00
69 A:Punisher 2.00
70 Don Lomax writes 1.75
71 Vietnamese Point of View 1.75
72 The trials of war 1.75
73 War on the Homefront 1.75
74 Seige at An Loc 1.75
75 My Lai Massacre 2.25
76 R:Rob Little 1.75
77 Stateside 1.75
78 . . . . 1.75
79 Beginning of the End#1 . . . . . 1.75
80 MGo(c),'68 Tet Offensive 1.75
81 MGo(c),TET Offensive ends . . 1.75
82 TET Offensive 1.75
83 thru 84 Last issue 1.75

'NAM MAGAZINE, THE
August, 1988
(black & white)

1 Reprints 3.00
2 thru 9 . . . . @2.50
10 May, 1989 . . . . 2.50

NAMORA
Fall, 1948

1 BEv,DR 560.00
2 BEv,A:Sub-Mariner,Blonde Phantom 480.00
3 BEv,A:Sub-Mariner,Dec.,1948 430.00

NAMOR THE SUB-MARINER
April, 1990

1 JBy,BWi,I:Desmond & Phoebe Marrs 7.00
2 JBy,BWi,V:Griffin 4.00
3 JBy,BWi,V:Griffin 3.50
4 JBy,A:Reed & Sue Richards, Tony Stark 3.00
5 JBy,A:FF,IronMan,C:Speedball 3.00
6 JBy,V:Sluj 3.00
7 JBy,V:Sluj 3.00
8 JBy,V:Headhunter,R:D.Rand . . 3.00
9 JBy,V:Headhunter 3.00
10 JBy,V:Master Man,Warrior Woman 3.00
11 JBy,V:Mast.Man,War.Woman . 3.00
12 JBy,R:Invaders,Spitfire 3.00
13 JBy,Namor on Trial,A:Fantastic Four,Captain America,Thor . . . 3.00
14 JBy,R:Lady Dorma,A:Kazar Griffin 3.00
15 JBy,A:Iron Fist 3.00
16 JBy,A:Punisher,V:Iron Fist . . . 2.50
17 JBy,V:Super Skrull(Iron Fist) . . 2.50
18 JBy,V:SuperSkrull,A:Punisher . 2.50
19 JBy,V:Super Skrull,D:D.Marrs . 2.50
20 JBy,Search for Iron Fist, O:Namorita 2.50
21 JBy,Visit to K'un Lun 2.50
22 JBy,Fate of Iron Fist, C:Wolverine 2.50
23 JBy,BWi,Iron Fist Contd., C:Wolverine 2.50
24 JBy,BWi,V:Wolverine 3.00
25 JBy,BWi,V:Master Khan 2.50
26 JaL,BWi,Search For Namor . 18.00
27 JaL,BWi,V:Namorita 13.00
28 JaL,BWi,A:Iron Fist 10.00
29 JaL,BWi,After explosion 8.00
30 JaL,A:Doctor Doom 6.00
31 JaL,V:Doctor Doom 6.00
32 JaL,V:Doctor Doom, Namor regains memory 5.00
33 JaL,V:Master Khan 4.00
34 JaL,R:Atlantis 4.00
35 JaL,V:Tiger Shark 3.00
36 JaL,I:Suma-Ket,A:Tiger Shark . 3.00
37 JaL,Blue Holo-Grafix,Altantean Civil War,N:Namor 4.50

38 JaL,O:Suma-Ket 2.50
39 A:Tigershark,V:Suma-Ket 1.50
40 V:Suma-Ket 1.50
41 V:War Machine 1.50
42 MCW,A:Stingray,V:Dorcas . . . 1.50
43 MCW,V:Orka,Dorcas 1.50
44 I:Albatross 1.50
45 GI,A:Sunfire,V:Attuma 1.50
46 GI, ... 1.50
47 GI,Starblast #2 . . . . 1.50
48 GI,Starblast #9,A:FF 1.50
49 GI,A:Ms. Marrs 1.50
50 GI,Holo-grafx(c),A:FF 3.25
50a Newsstand Ed. 2.00
51 AaL, ... 1.75
52 GI,I:Sea Leopard 1.50
Ann.#1 Subterran.Odyssey #3 . . . 2.00
Ann.#2 Return o/Defenders Pt.3 . 4.00
Ann.#3 I:Assassin,A:Iron Fist,
w/Trading card 3.25
Ann.#4 V:Hydra 2.95

NAVY ACTION
August, 1954

1 US Navy War Stories 60.00
2 Navy(c) 30.00
3 thru 17 . . . . @20.00
18 August, 1957 . . . . 20.00

NAVY COMBAT
Atlas
June, 1955

1 DH,B;Torpedo Taylor 65.00
2 DH 30.00
3 DH 25.00
4 DH 25.00
5 DH 25.00
6 A:Battleship Burke 25.00
7 thru 10 . . . . @25.00
11 MD 20.00
12 RC 35.00
13 . . . . 20.00
14 . . . . 25.00
15 . . . . 20.00
16 . . . . 20.00
17 AW 35.00
18 . . . . 20.00
19 . . . . 20.00
20 October, 1958 . . . . 20.00

NAVY TALES
Atlas
January, 1957

1 BEv(c),BP,Torpedoes 55.00
2 AW,RC,One Hour to Live . . . 50.00
3 JSe(c) 40.00
4 JSe(c),GC,JSt,RC,July, 1957 40.00

NELLIE THE NURSE
Atlas
1945

1 Beach(c) 160.00
2 Nellie's Date(c) 85.00
3 Swimming Pool(c) 55.00
4 Roller Coaster(c) 55.00
5 Hospital(c),HK,Hey Look 60.00
6 Bedside Manner(c) 40.00
7 Comic book(c)A:Georgie . . . 40.00
8 Hospital(c),A:Georgie 40.00
9 BW,Nellie/Swing(c)A:Millie . . 55.00
10 Bathing Suit(c),A:Millie 40.00
11 HK,Hey Look 60.00
12 HK,Giggles 'n' Grins 40.00
13 HK 35.00
14 HK 60.00
15 HK 60.00
16 HK 60.00
17 HK.A:Annie Oakley 35.00
18 HK 55.00
19 . . . . 35.00
20 . . . . 35.00
21 . . . . 30.00
22 . . . . 30.00
23 . . . . 30.00
24 . . . . 30.00
25 . . . . 30.00
26 . . . . 30.00
27 . . . . 30.00
28 HK,Rusty Reprint 32.00
29 thru 35 . . . . @25.00
36 October, 1952 . . . . 25.00

NEW ADVENTURES OF CHOLLY & FLYTRAP
Epic

1 . . . . 4.95
2 . . . . 3.95
3 . . . . 3.95

NEW MUTANTS, THE
March, 1983

1 BMc,MG,O:New Mutants 13.00
2 BMc,MG,V:Sentinels 8.00
2a Ltd.Test Cover 75c 55.00
3 BMc,MG,V:Brood Alien 6.50

New Mutants #34
© Marvel Entertainment Group

4 SB,BMc,A:Peter Bristow 6.00
5 SB,BMc,A:Dark Rider 6.00
6 SB,AG,V:Viper 6.00
7 SB,BMc,V:Axe 6.00
8 SB,BMc,I:Amara Aquilla 6.00
9 SB,TMd,I:Selene 5.00
10 SB,BMc,C:Magma 5.00
11 SB,TMd,I:Magma 5.00
12 SB,TMd,J:Magma 5.00
13 SB,TMd,I:Cypher(Doug Ramsey)
A:Kitty Pryde,Lilandra 6.00
14 SB,TMd,J:Magik,A:X-Men 5.00
15 SB,TMd,Mass.Academy 4.00
16 SB,TMd,V:Hellions,I:Warpath
I:Jetstream 8.00
17 SB,TMd,V:Hellions,A:Warpath . 5.00
18 BSz,V:Demon Bear,I:New
Warlock,Magus 7.50
19 BSz,V:Demon Bear 4.00
20 BSz,V:Demon Bear 4.00
21 BSz,O&J:Warlock,doub.sz . . 10.00
22 BSz,A:X-Men 4.50
23 BSz,Sunspot,Cloak & Dagger . 4.00
24 BSz,A:Cloak & Dagger 4.00
25 BSz,A:Cloak & Dagger 4.00
26 BSz,I:Legion(Prof.X's son) . . . 4.50
27 BSz,V:Legion 4.00
28 BSz,O:Legion 4.00

New Mutants #35
© Marvel Entertainment Group

29 BSz,V:Gladiators,I:Guido
(Strong Guy) 5.00
30 BSz,A:Dazzler 4.00
31 BSz,A:Shadowcat 4.00
32 SL,V:Karma 3.50
33 SL,V:Karma 3.50
34 SL,V:Amahl Farouk 3.50
35 BSz,J:Magneto 4.00
36 BSz,A:Beyonder 3.50
37 BSz,D:New Mutants 3.50
38 BSz,A:Hellions 3.50
39 BSz,A:White Queen 3.50
40 JG,KB,V:Avengers 3.50
41 JG,TA,Mirage 3.50
42 JG,KB,A:Dazzler 3.50
43 SP,V:Empath,A:Warpath 3.50
44 JG,V:Legion 3.50
45 JG,A:Larry Bodine 3.50
46 JG,KB,Mutant Massacre 5.00
47 JG,KB,V:Magnus 3.50
48 JG,CR,Future 3.50
49 VM,Future 3.50
50 JG,V:Magus,R:Prof.X 4.00
51 KN,A:Star Jammers 3.50
52 RL,DGr,Limbo 3.50
53 RL,TA,V:Hellions 3.50
54 SB,TA,N:New Mutants 3.50
55 BBl,TA,V:Aliens 3.00
56 JBr,TA,V:Hellions,A:Warpath . . 3.00
57 BBl,TA,I&J:Bird-Boy 3.00
58 BBl,TA,Bird-Boy 4.00
59 BBl,TA,Fall of Mutants,
V:Dr.Animus 5.00
60 BBl,TA,F.of M.,D:Cypher 5.50
61 BBl,TA,Fall of Mutants 5.00
62 JMu,A:Magma,Hellions 3.00
63 BHa,JRu,Magik 3.50
64 BBl,TA,R:Cypher 3.00
65 BBl,TA,V:FreedomForce 3.00
66 BBl,TA,V:Forge 3.00
67 BBl,I:Gosamyr 3.00
68 BBl,V:Gosamyr 3.00
69 BBl,AW,I:Spyder 3.00
70 TSh,AM,V:Spyder 3.00
71 BBl,AW,V:N'Astirh 3.50
72 BBl,A,Inferno 3.50
73 BBl,W,A:Colossus 3.50
74 BBl,W,A:X-Terminators 3.00
75 JBy,Mc,Black King,
V:Magneto 3.50
76 RB,TP,J:X-Terminators 3.00

77 RB,V:Mirage 3.00
78 RL,AW,V:FreedomForce 3.00
79 BBl,AW,V:Hela 3.00
80 BBl,AW,Asgard 3.00
81 LW,TSh,JRu,A:Hercules 3.00
82 BBl,AW,Asgard 3.00
83 BBl,Asgard 3.00
84 TSh,AM,A:QueenUla 3.00
85 RLd&TMc(c),BBl,V:Mirage . . . 3.00
86 RLd,BWi,V:Vulture,C:Cable . . 15.00
87 RLd,BWi,I:Mutant Liberation Front,Cable 55.00
87a 2nd Printing 2.00
88 RLd,2nd Cable,V:Freedom Force 20.00
89 RLd,V:Freedom Force 14.00
90 RLd,A:Caliban,V:Sabretooth . 10.00
91 RLd,A:Caliban,Masque, V:Sabretooth 10.00
92 RLd(c),BH,V:Skrulls 5.00
93 RLd,A:Wolverine,Sunfire, V:Mutant Liberation Front . . . 14.00
94 RLd,A:Wolverine,Sunfire, V:Mutant Liberation Front . . . 12.00
95 RLd,Extinction Agenda,V:Hodge A:X-Men,X-Factor,D:Warlock . 10.00
95a 2nd printing(gold) 5.00
96 RLd,ATb,JRu,Extinction Agenda V:Hodge,A:X-Men,X-Factor . . . 8.00
97 E:LSi(s),RLd(c),JRu,Extinction Agenda,V:Hodge 8.00
98 FaN(s),RLd,I:Deadpool,Domino, Gideon,L:Rictor 16.00
99 FaN(s),RLd,I:Feral,Shatterstar, L:Sunspot,J:Warpath 12.00
100 FaN(s),RLd,J:Feral,Shatterstar, I:X-Force,V:Masque,Imperial Protectorate,A:MLF 10.00
100a 2nd Printing(Gold) 8.00
100b 3rd Printing(Silver) 3.50

New Mutants Annual #11

© Marvel Entertainment Group

Ann.#1 BMc,TP,L.Cheney 7.00
Ann.#2 AD,V:Mojo,I:Psylocke,Meggan (American App.) 7.00
Ann.#3 AD,PN,V:Impossible Man . 3.00
Ann.#4 JBr,BMc,Evol.Wars 6.00
Ann.#5 RLd,JBg,MBa,KWi,Atlantis Attacks,A:Namorita,I:Surf 9.00
Ann.#6 RLd(c),Days o/Future Present V:FranklinRichards,(Pin-ups) . . 6.00
Ann.#7 JRu,RLd,Kings of Pain, I:Piecemeal & Harness, Pin-ups X-Force 5.00
Spec #1,AAd,TA,Asgard War 6.00
Summer Spec.#1 BBl,Megapolis . 3.50
TPB Demon Bear,rep.#18-21 . . . . 8.95

NEW MUTANTS: DEMON BEAR

CCl/BSz,Rep.DemonBear 8.95

NEW WARRIORS

July, 1990

1 MBa,AW,V:Terrax, O:New Warriors 23.00
1a Gold rep. 4.50
2 MBa,AW,I:Midnight's Fire, I:Silhouette 16.00
3 MBa,LMa,V:Mad Thinker 12.00
4 MBa,LMa,I:Psionex 10.00
5 MBa,LMa,V:Star Thief, C:White Queen 9.00
6 MBa,LMa,V:StarThief,A: Inhumans 6.00
7 MBa,LMa,V:Bengal,C:Punisher 7.00
8 MBa,LMa,V:Punisher,Force of Nature 9.00
9 MBa,LMa,V:Punisher,Bengal, Force of Nature 6.00
10 MBa,LMa,V:Hellions,White Queen,I:New Sphinx 5.00
11 MBa,LMa(i),V:Sphinx,B:Forever Yesterday 4.00
12 MBa,LMa(i),V:Sphinx 4.00
13 MBa,LMa(i),V:Sphinx,E:Forever Yesterday 4.00
14 MBa,LMa(i),A:Namor, Darkhawk 3.00
15 MBa,LMa(i),V:Psionex,R:Terrax, N:Nova 3.00
16 MBa,LMa(i),A:Psionex, V:Terrax 3.00
17 MBa,LMa(i),A:Silver Surfer,Fant. Four,V:Terrax,I:Left Hand 3.00
18 MBa,LMa(i),O:Night Thrasher . 2.50
19 MBa,LMa(i),V:Gideon 2.50
20 MBa,LMa(i),V:Clan Yashida, Marvel Boy kills his father 2.50
21 MBa,LMa(i),I:Folding Circle . . . 2.50
22 MBa,LMa(i),A:Darkhawk,Rage . 2.50
23 MBa,LMa(i),V:Folding Circle . . 2.50
24 LMa(i),V:Folding Circle 2.50
25 MBa,LMa(i),Die-Cut(c),Marvel Boy found guilty of murder,D:Tai, O:Folding Circle 5.00
26 DaR,LMa(i),V:Guardsmen 2.00
27 DaR,LMa(i),Inf.War,Speedball Vs. his doppelganger,N:Rage 2.00
28 DaR,LMa(i),I:Turbo,Cardinal . . 2.00
29 DaR,LMa(i),V:Trans-Sabal . . . 2.00
30 DaR,LMa(i),V:Trans Sabal . . . 2.00
31 DaR,LMa(i)A:Cannonball,Warpath, Magma,O&N:Firestar 2.00
32 DaR,LMa(i),B:Forces of Darkness, Forces of Light,A:Spider-Man, Archangel,Dr.Strange 1.75
33 DaR,LMa(i),A:Cloak & Dagger, Turbo,Darkhawk 1.75
34 DaR,LMa(i),A:Avengers,SpM, Thing,Torch,Darkhawk, C:Darkling 1.75
35 DaR,LMa(i),A:Turbo 1.75
36 DaR,LMa(i),A:Turbo 1.75
37 F:Marvel Boy,V:Wizard 1.75
38 DaR,LMa(i),D:Rage's granny, V:Poison Memories 1.75
39 DaR,LMa(i),L:Namorita 1.50
40 DaR,LMa(i),B:Starlost, V:Supernova 2.50
40a Newsstand Ed. 1.50
41 DaR,LMa(i),V:Supernova 1.50
42 DaR,LMa(i),E:Starlost,N:Nova, V:Supernova 1.50
43 DaR,LMa(i),N&I:Justice (Marvel Boy) 1.50
44 Ph(c),DaR,LMa(i),N&I:Kymaera (Namorita) 1.50
45 DaR,LMa(i),Child's Play#2, N:Silhouette,Speedball, V:Upstarts 1.50
46 DaR,LMa(i),Child's Play#4, V:Upstarts 1.50
47 DaR,LMa(i),Time & Time Again #1, A:Sphinx,I:Powerpax 1.75
48 DaR,LMa(i),Time & Time Again #4, J:Cloak&Dagger,Darkhawk,Turbo, Powerpax,Bandit 1.50
Ann.#1 MBa,A:X-Force,V:Harness, Piecemeal,Kings of Pain #2 . . 5.00
Ann.#2 Hero Killers #4,V:Sphinx . 2.75
Ann.#3 LMa(i),E:Forces of Light, Forces of Darkness,I:Darkling w/card 3.25
Ann.#4 DaR(s),V:Psionex 3.25
TPB New Beginnings rep.Thor #411, 412,New Warriors #1-#4 . . . . 12.95

NFL SUPERPRO

1 . . . . 8.00
Spec.#1 reprints 2.00

(Regular Series)
October, 1991

1 A:Spider-Man,I:Sanzionaire . . . 2.50
2 V:Quickkick 1.25
3 I:Instant Replay 1.00
4 V:Sanction 1.00
5 A:Real NFL Player 1.25
6 Racism Iss.,recalled by Marvel . 6.00
7 thru 11 . . . . @1.25
12 V:Nefarious forces of evil 1.25

NICK FURY, AGENT OF S.H.I.E.L.D.

June, 1968

[1st Regular Series]

1 JSo/JSt,I:Scorpio 42.00
2 JSo,A:Centaurius 25.00

Nick Fury #1

© Marvel Entertainment Group

3 JSo,DA,V:Hell Hounds 21.00
4 FS,O:Nick Fury 20.00
5 JSo,V:Scorpio 25.00
6 FS,"Doom must Fall" 11.00
7 FS,V:S.H.I.E.L.D. 11.00
8 FS,Hate Monger 7.00
9 FS,Hate Monger 7.00
10 FS,JCr,Hate Monger 7.00
11 BS(c),FS,Hate Monger 7.00

12 BS 9.00
13 . . . . 6.00
14 . . . . 5.00
15 I:Bullseye 24.00
16 JK,rep. 4.00
17 JK,rep. 4.00
18 JK,rep. 4.00

[Limited Series]

1 JSo,rep. 2.50
2 JSo,rep. 2.00

[2nd Regular Series]

1 BH,I:New Shield,V:Death's Head(not British hero) 3.50
2 KP,V:Death's Head 2.00
3 KP,V:Death's Head 1.50
4 KP,V:Death's Head 1.50
5 KP,V:Death's Head 1.50
6 KP,V:Death's Head 1.50
7 KP,Chaos Serpent #1 . . . . 1.50
8 KP,Chaos Serpent #2 . . . . 1.50
9 KP,Chaos Serpent #3 . . . . 1.50
10 KP,Chaos Serpent ends, A:Capt.America 1.50
11 D:Murdo MacKay 1.50
12 Hydra Affair #1 . . . . 1.50
13 Hydra Affair #2 . . . . 1.50
14 Hydra Affair #3 . . . . 1.50
15 Apogee of Disaster #1 . . . . . . 1.50
16 Apogee of Disaster #2 . . . . . . 1.50
17 Apogee of Disaster #3 . . . . . . 1.50
18 Apogee of Disaster #4 . . . . . . 1.50
19 Apogee of Disaster #5 . . . . . . 1.50
20 JG,A:Red Skull 2.50
21 JG,R:Baron Strucker 2.00
22 JG,A:Baron Strucker,R:Hydra . 2.00
23 JG,V:Hydra 2.00
24 A:Capt.Am,Thing,V:Mandarin . 1.75
25 JG,Shield Vs. Hydra 2.00
26 JG,A:Baron Strucker, C:Wolverine 2.50
27 JG,V:Hydra,A:Wolverine 2.50
28 V:Hydra,A:Wolverine 2.50
29 V:Hydra,A:Wolverine 2.50
30 R:Leviathan,A:Deathlok 2.00
31 A:Deathlok,V:Leviathan 2.00
32 V:Leviathan 2.00
33 Super-Powered Agents 2.00
34 A:Bridge(X-Force),V:Balance of Terror 2.00
35 A:Cage,V:Constrictor 2.00
36 . . . . 2.00
37 . . . . 2.00
38 Cold War of Nick Fury #1 . . . . 2.00
39 Cold War of Nick Fury #2 . . . . 2.00
40 Cold War of Nick Fury #3 . . . . 2.00
41 Cold War of Nick Fury #4 . . . . 2.00
42 I:Strike Force Shield 2.00
43 R:Clay Quatermain 2.00
44 A:Captain America 2.00
45 A:Bridge 2.00
46 V:Gideon,Hydra 2.00
47 V:Baron Strucker,last issue . . . 2.00

NICK FURY, VERSUS S.H.I.E.L.D.

June, 1988

1 JSo(c),D:Quartermail 12.00
2 BSz(c),Into The Depths 15.00
3 Uneasy Allies 8.00
4 V:Hydra 6.00
5 V:Hydra 6.00
6 V:Hydra, December, 1988 . . . 6.00
TPB Reprints #1-#6 . . . . 15.95

NIGHTBREED

Epic
April, 1990

1 . . . . 5.50
2 . . . . 3.50
3 . . . . 3.00
4 . . . . 2.50
5 JG 2.50
6 BBl,Blasphemers Pt.1 . . . . 2.50
7 JG,Blasphemers Pt.2 . . . . 2.50
8 BBl,MM,Blasphemers Pt.3 . . . . 2.50
9 BBl,Blasphemers Pt.4 . . . . 2.50
10 BBl,Blasphemers Pt.5 . . . . . . 2.50
11 South America Pt.1 . . . . 2.25
12 South America Pt.2 . . . . 2.25
13 Emissaries o/Algernon Kinder . 2.25
14 Rawhead Rex Story 2.25
15 Rawhead Rex 2.25
16 Rawhead Rex 2.25
17 KN(i),V:Werewolves 2.25
18 V:Werewolves 2.25
19 V:Werewolves 2.25
20 Trapped in the Forest 2.25
21 V:Ozymandias 2.50
22 V:Ozymandias 2.50
23 F:Peloquin 2.50
24 Search for New Midian 2.50
25 Search for New Midian 2.50
Nightbreed:Genesis, Rep.#1-#4 . . 9.95

NIGHTCAT

1 DCw,I&O:Night Cat 4.50

NIGHTCRAWLER

November, 1985

1 DC,A;Bamfs 5.00
2 DC 3.00
3 DC,A:Other Dimensional X-Men 3.00
4 DC,A:Lockheed,V:Dark Bamf February, 1986 . . . . 3.00

NIGHTMARE ON ELM STREET

October, 1989

1 RB/TD/AA.,Movie adapt 3.00
2 AA,Movie adapt,Dec., 1989 . . . 2.25

NIGHTMASK

November, 1986

1 O:Night Mask 1.25
2 V:Gnome 1.00
3 V:Mistress Twilight 1.00
4 EC,D:Mistress Twilight 1.00
5 EC,Nightmare 1.00
6 EC 1.00
7 EC 1.00
8 EC 1.00
9 . . . . 1.00
10 Lucian 1.00
11 and 12, Oct. 1987 . . . . @1.00

NIGHT NURSE

November, 1972

1 The Making of a Nurse 4.00
2 Moment of Truth 2.50
3 . . . . 2.00
4 Final Issue,May, 1973 . . . . . . 2.00

NIGHT RIDER

October, 1974

1 Reprint Ghost Rider #1 . . . . . . 5.00
2 Reprint Ghost Rider #2 . . . . . . 2.00
3 Reprint Ghost Rider #3 . . . . . . 2.00
4 Reprint Ghost Rider #4 . . . . . . 2.00
5 Reprint Ghost Rider #5 . . . . . . 2.00
6 Reprint Ghost Rider #6 August, 1975 . . . . 2.00

NIGHTSTALKERS

1 TP(i),Rise o/t Midnight Sons#5 A:GR,J.Blaze,I:Meatmarket, polybagged w/poster 3.00
2 TP(i),V:Hydra 2.50
3 TP(i),V:Dead on Arrival 2.00
4 TP(i),V:Hydra 2.00
5 TP(i),A:Punisher 1.75
6 TP(i),A:Punisher 2.00
7 TP(i),A:Ghost Rider 2.00
8 Hannibal King vs Morbius 2.00
9 MPa,A:Morbius 2.00
10 Midnight Massacre#1,D:Johnny Blaze,Hannibal King 2.50
11 O:Blade 2.00
12 V:Vampires 2.00
13 V:Vampires 2.00
14 Wld,Siege of Darkness#1 . . . . 2.00
15 Wld,Siege of Darkness#9 . . . . 2.00
16 V:Dreadnought 2.00
17 F:Blade 2.00
18 D:Hannibal King,Frank Drake, last issue 2.00

Night Thrasher #1
© Marvel Entertainment Group

NIGHT THRASHER

[Limited Series]

1 B:FaN(s),DHv,N:Night Thrasher, V:Bengal 2.50
2 DHv,I:Tantrium 2.25
3 DHv,V:Gideon 2.25
4 E:FaN(s),DHv,A:Silhoutte 2.25

[Regular Series]

1 B:FaN(s),MBa,JS,V:Poison Memories 3.25
2 JS,V:Concrete Dragons 2.00
3 JS(c),I:Aardwolf,A:Folding Circle 2.00
4 JS(c),V:Aardwolf,I:Air Force . . . 2.00
5 JS,V:Air Force 2.00
6 Face Value,A:Rage 2.00
7 DdB,V:Bandit 2.00
8 DdB,V:Bandit 2.00
9 DdB,A:Tantrum 2.00
10 DdB,A:Iron Man,w/card 2.25
11 DdB,Time & Time Again #2 . . 2.25
12 DdB,Time & Time Again #5 . . 1.95

NOMAD

November, 1990
[Limited Series]

1 A:Capt America 4.00
2 A:Capt.America 3.00
3 A:Capt.America 2.50
4 A:Capt.America, final issue, February 1989 . . . . 2.50

NOMAD

[Regular Series]

1 R:Nomad(Gatetfold(c),map) . . . 4.00
2 V:Road Kill Club 2.50
3 V:U.S.Agent 3.00
4 DeadMan's Hand#2,V:Deadpool 2.50
5 DeadMan's Hand#4,V:Punisher 2.00
6 DeadMan's Hand#8,A:Punisher,

Daredevil 2.00
7 Inf War,V:Gambit Doppleganger 2.00
8 L.A.Riots 2.00
9 I:Ebbtide 2.00
10 A:Red Wolf 2.00
11 in Albuquerque 2.00
12 In Texas 2.00
13 AIDS issue 2.00
14 Hidden in View 2.00
15 Hidden in View 2.00
16 A:Gambit 2.00
17 Bucky Kidnapped 2.00
18 A:Captain America,Slug 2.00
19 FaN(s),Faustus Affair 2.00
20 A:Six Pack 2.00
21 A:Man-Thing 2.00
22 B:American Dreamers,V:Zaran 2.00
23 American Dreamers#2 . . . . . . 2.00
24 American Dreamers#3 . . . . . . 2.00
25 E:American Dreamers,
Final Issue 2.00

NORTHSTAR

1 SFr,DoC,V:Weapon:P.R.I.M.E. . 2.00
2 SFr,DoC,V:Arcade 2.00
3 SFr,DoC,V:Arcade 1.75

NOT BRAND ECHH

August, 1967

1 JK(c),BEv,Forbush Man(c) . . 30.00
2 MSe,FrG,Spidey-Man,Gnat-Man
& Rotten 15.00
3 MSe(C),JK,FrG,O:Charlie
America 15.00
4 GC,JTg,TS,Scaredevil,
ECHHs-Men 15.00
5 JK,TS,GC,I&O:Forbush Man . 15.00
6 MSe(c),GC,TS,W:Human Torch 15.00
7 MSe(c),GC,TS,O:Fantastical
Four,Stupor Man 15.00
8 MSe(c),GC,TS,C:Beatles . . . 17.00
9 Bulk V:Sunk-Mariner 17.00
10 JK,The Worst of... . . . . 17.00
11 King Konk 17.00
12 Frankenstein,A:Revengers . . 17.00
13 Stamp Out Trading Cards(c) . 17.00

NOTHING CAN STOP THE JUGGERNAUT

1989

1 JR2,rep.SpM#229æ 3.95

NOVA

September, 1976

[1st Regular Series]

1 B:MWn(s),JB,JSt,I&O:Nova . . . 15.00
2 JB,JSt,I:Condor,Powerhouse . . . 8.00
3 JB,JSt,I:Diamondhead 6.00
4 SB,TP,A:Thor,I:Corruptor 6.00
5 SB,V:Earthshaker 6.00
6 SB,V:Condor,Powerhouse,
Diamondhead,I:Sphinx 6.00
7 SB,War in Space,O:Sphinx 6.00
8 V:Megaman 6.00
9 V:Megaman 6.00
10 V:Condor,Powerhouse,
Diamond-head Sphinx 6.00
11 V:Sphinx 4.50
12 A:Spider-Man 5.00
13 I:Crimebuster,A:Sandman 4.50
14 A:Sandman 4.00
15 CI,C:Spider-Man, Hulk 4.00
16 CI,A:Yellow Claw 4.00
17 A:Yellow Claw 3.50
18 A:Yellow Claw, Nick Fury 3.50
19 CI,TP,I:Blackout 3.50
20 What is Project X? 3.50
21 JB,BMc,JRu 3.50
22 CI,I:Comet 3.50
23 CI,V:Dr.Sun 3.50
24 CI,I:New Champions,V:Sphinx . 3.50
25 E:MWn(s),CI,A:Champions,
V:Sphinx 3.50

[2nd Regular Series]

1 B:FaN(s),ChM,V:Gladiator,Foil
Embossed(c) 3.25
2 ChM,V:Tail Hook Rape 2.00
3 ChM,A:Spider-Man,Corruptor . . 2.00
4 ChM,I:NovaO:O 2.00
5 ChM,R:Condor,w/card 2.25
6 ChM,Time & Time Again #3 . . . 2.25
7 ChM,Time & Time Again #6 . . . 1.95

Nth MAN

August, 1989

1 . . . . 2.00
2 thru 7 . . . . @1.00
8 DK 2.00
9 thru 15 . . . . @1.00
16 final issue,September, 1990 . . 1.00

OBNOXIO THE CLOWN

April, 1983

1 X-Men 2.00

OFFCASTES

1 I:Offcastes 2.50
2 V:Kaoro 1.95
3 Last Issue 1.95

OFFICIAL INDEX TO FANTASTIC FOUR

December, 1986

1 . . . . 1.50
2 thru 10 . . . . @1.25

OFFICIAL MARVEL INDEX TO THE X-MEN

1 . . . . 2.25
2 . . . . 1.95
3 . . . . 1.95

OFFICIAL TRUE CRIME CASES

Fall, 1947

24 (1)SSh(c),The Grinning Killer 100.00
25 (2)She Made Me a Killer,HK . 85.00

Becomes:

ALL-TRUE CRIME

26 SSh(c),The True Story of Wilbur
Underhill 85.00
27 Electric Chair(c),Robert Mais . 70.00
28 Cops V:Gangsters(c) 25.00
29 Cops V:Gangsters(c) 25.00
30 He Picked a Murderous Mind 25.00
31 Hitchiking Thugs(c) 25.00
32 Jewel Thieves(c) 25.00
33 The True Story of Dinton
Phillips 25.00
34 Case of the Killers Revenge . 25.00
35 Ph(c),Date with Danger 25.00
36 Ph(c) 25.00
37 Ph(c),Story of Robert Marone 25.00
38 Murder Weapon,Nick Maxim . 25.00
39 Story of Vince Vanderee 25.00
40 . . . . 25.00
41 Lou "Lucky" Raven 25.00
42 BK,Baby Face Nelson 35.00
43 Doc Channing Paulson 25.00
44 Murder in the Big House 25.00
45 While the City Sleeps 25.00
46 . . . . 25.00
47 Gangster Terry Craig 25.00
48 GT,They Vanish By Night . . . 25.00
49 BK,Squeeze Play 35.00
50 Shoot to Kill 25.00
51 Panic in the Big House 25.00
52 Prison Break, Sept., 1952 . . . 25.00

OLYMPIANS

Epic

July, 1991

1 Spoof Series 3.95
2 Conclusion 3.95

OMEGA THE UNKNOWN

March, 1976

1 JM,I:Omega 4.25
2 JM,A:Hulk 2.50
3 JM,A:Electro 2.00
4 JM,V:Yellow Claw 2.00
5 JM,V:The Wrench 2.00
6 JM,V:Blockbuster 2.00
7 JM,V:Blockbuster 2.00
8 JM,C:New Foolkiller,V:Nitro . . . 6.00
9 JM,A:New Foolkiller,
D:Blockbuster 7.50
10 JM,D:Omega the Unknown . . . 2.00

ONE, THE

Epic

July, 1985

1 thru 5 . . . . @1.75
6 February, 1986 . . . . 1.75

ONYX OVERLORD

Epic

1 JBi,Sequel to Airtight Garage . . 3.00
2 JBi,The Joule 2.75
3 JBi,V:Overlord 2.75
4 V:Starbilliard 2.75

OPEN SPACE

December, 1989

1 . . . . 6.00
2 . . . . 5.25
3 . . . . 5.25
4 August, 1990,last issue 5.25

ORIGINAL GHOST RIDER

1 MT(c),rep Marvel Spotlight#5 . . 2.25
2 rep.Marvel Spotlight#6 . . . . 2.00
3 rep.Marvel Spotlight#7 . . . . 2.00
4 JQ(c),rep.Marvel Spotlight#8 . . 2.00
5 KM(c),rep.Marvel spotlight#9 . . 2.00
6 rep.Marvel Spotlight#10 . . . . . 2.00
7 rep.Marvel Spotlight#11 . . . . . 2.00
8 rep.Ghost Rider#1 . . . . 2.00
9 rep.Ghost Rider#2 . . . . 2.00
10 rep.Marvel Spotlight#12 . . . . 2.00
11 rep.Ghost Rider#3 . . . . 2.00
12 rep.Ghost Rider#4 . . . . 2.00
13 rep.Ghost Rider#38 . . . . 2.00
14 th 18 rep.Ghost Rider#6-10 . @1.75
19 rep.Ghost Rider#11 . . . . 1.75
20 rep.Ghost Rider#12 . . . . 1.75

ORIGINAL GHOST RIDER RIDES AGAIN

July, 1991

1 rep.GR#68+#69(O:JohnnyBlaze) 3.00
2 rep.G.R. #70,#71 . . . . 2.00
3 rep.G.R. #72,#73 . . . . 2.00
4 rep.G.R. #74,#75 . . . . 2.00
5 rep.G.R. #76,#77 . . . . 2.00
6 rep.G.R. #78,#79 . . . . 2.00
7 rep.G.R. #80,#81 . . . . 2.00

OUR LOVE

September, 1949

1 Ph(c),The Guilt of Nancy Crane 55.00
2 Ph(c),My Kisses Were Cheap 35.00

Becomes:

TRUE SECRETS

3 Love Stories,continued 50.00
4 . . . . 24.00
5 . . . . 24.00
6 BEv 30.00
7 . . . . 24.00
8 . . . . 24.00
9 . . . . 24.00
10 . . . . 24.00
11 thru 21 . . . . @18.00
22 BEv 30.00
23 thru 39 . . . . @12.00
40 September, 1956 . . . . 12.00

All comics prices listed are for *Near Mint* condition.

OUR LOVE STORY
October, 1969

1 . . . . 7.50
2 . . . . 5.00
3 . . . . 5.00
4 . . . . 5.00
5 JSo 15.00
6 thru 13 . . . . @5.00
14 Gary Friedrich &Tarpe Mills . . 7.50
15 thru 37 . . . . @2.00
38 February, 1976 . . . . 2.00

OUTLAW FIGHTERS
Atlas
August, 1954

1 GT,Western Tales 55.00
2 GT 35.00
3 . . . . 35.00
4 A;Patch Hawk 35.00
5 RH, Final Issue,April, 1955 . . 35.00

OUTLAW KID
Atlas
September, 1954

1 SSh,DW,B&O:Outlaw Kid,A;Black Rider 120.00
2 DW,A:Black Rider 55.00
3 DW,AW,GWb 50.00
4 DW(c),Death Rattle 35.00
5 . . . . 35.00
6 . . . . 35.00
7 . . . . 35.00
8 AW,DW 45.00
9 . . . . 35.00
10 . . . . 45.00
11 thru 17 . . . . @25.00
18 AW 40.00
19 September, 1957 . . . . 25.00

[2nd series]
August, 1970

1 JSe(c),DW,Jo,Showdown,rep . 5.00
2 DW,One Kid Too Many 5.00
3 HT(c),DW,Six Gun Double Cross 3.00
4 DW 2.00
5 DW 2.00
6 DW 2.00
7 HT(c),DW,Treachery on the Trail 2.00
8 HT(c),DW,RC,Six Gun Pay Off 2.00
9 JSe(c),DW,GWb,The Kids Last Stand 3.00
10 GK(c),DAy,NewO:Outlaw Kid . 1.50
11 GK(c),Thunder Along the Big Iron 1.50
12 The Man Called Bounty Hawk . 1.50
13 The Last Rebel 1.50
14 The Kid Gunslingers of Calibre City 1.50
15 GK(c),V:Madman of Monster Mountain 1.50
16 The End of the Trail 1.50
17 thru 29 . . . . @1.50
30 October, 1975 . . . . 1.50

PARAGON

1 I:Paragon,Nightfire 5.00

PATSY & HEDY
Atlas
February, 1952

1 B:Patsy Walker&Hedy Wolfe . 75.00
2 Skating(c) 35.00
3 Boyfriend Trouble 30.00
4 Swimsuit(c) 30.00
5 Patsy's Date(c) 30.00
6 Swimsuit/Picnic(c) 30.00
7 Double-Date(c) 30.00
8 The Dance 30.00
9 . . . . 30.00
10 . . . . 30.00
11 thru 25 . . . . @20.00
26 thru 50 . . . . @15.00
51 thru 60 . . . . @10.00
61 thru 109 . . . . @6.00
110 February, 1967 . . . . 6.00

PATSY & HER PALS
May, 1953

1 MWs(c),F:Patsay Walker . . . 60.00
2 MWs(c),Swimsuit(c) 30.00
3 MWs(c),Classroom(c) 22.00
4 MWs(c),Golfcourse(c) 22.00
5 MWs(c).Patsy/Buzz(c) 22.00
6 thru 10 . . . . @22.00
11 thru 28 . . . . @15.00
29 August, 1957 . . . . 15.00

PATSY WALKER
1945

1 F:Patsy Walker Adventures 250.00
2 Patsy/Car(c) 125.00
3 Skating(c) 75.00
4 Perfume(c) 75.00
5 Archery Lesson(c) 75.00
6 Bus(c) 75.00
7 Charity Drive(c) 75.00
8 Organ Driver Monkey(c) 75.00
9 Date(c) 75.00
10 Skating(c),Wedding Bells . . . 75.00
11 Date with a Dream 50.00
12 Love in Bloom,Artist(c) 50.00
13 Swimsuit(c),There Goes My Heart;HK,Hey Look 60.00
14 An Affair of the Heart, HK,Hey Look 60.00
15 Dance(c) 50.00
16 Skating(c) 50.00
17 Patsy's Diary(c),HK,Hey Look 60.00
18 Autograph(c) 50.00
19 HK,Hey Look 60.00
20 HK,Hey Look 60.00
21 HK,Hey Look 60.00

Patsy and Her Pals #3
© Marvel Entertainment Group

22 HK,Hey Look 60.00
23 . . . . 40.00
24 . . . . 40.00
25 HK,Rusty 65.00
26 . . . . 30.00
27 . . . . 30.00
28 . . . . 30.00
29 . . . . 30.00
30 HK,Egghead Double 45.00
31 . . . . 30.00
32 thru 57 . . . . @20.00
58 thru 99 . . . . @15.00
100 . . . . 15.00
101 thru 123 . . . . @8.00
124 December, 1965 . . . . 8.00
Fashion Parade #1 . . . . 40.00

PETER PARKER, THE SPECTACULAR SPIDER-MAN
December, 1976

1 SB,V:Tarantula 50.00
2 SB,V:Kraven,Tarantula 23.00
3 SB,I:Lightmaster 15.00
4 SB,V:Vulture,Hitman 15.00
5 SB,V:Hitman,Vulture 15.00
6 SB,V:Morbius,rep.M.T.U.#3 . . 20.00
7 SB,V:Morbius,A:Human Torch 25.00
8 SB,V:Morbius 25.00
9 SB,I:White Tiger 10.00
10 SB,A:White Tiger 10.00
11 JM,V:Medusa 9.00
12 SB,V:Brother Power 9.00
13 SB,V:Brother Power 9.00
14 SB,V:Brother Power 9.00
15 SB,V:Brother Power 9.00
16 SB,V:The Beetle 9.00
17 SB,A:Angel & Iceman Champions disbanded 12.00
18 SB,A:Angel & Iceman 12.00
19 SB,V:The Enforcers 9.00
20 SB,V:Lightmaster 9.00
21 JM,V:Scorpion 9.00
22 MZ,A:Moon Knight,V:Cyclone . 9.00
23 A:Moon Knight,V:Cyclone 9.00
24 FS,A:Hypno-Hustler 6.00
25 JM,FS,I:Carrion 7.00

Peter Parker #25
© Marvel Entertainment Group

26 JM,A:Daredevil,V:Carrion 6.50
27 DC,FM,I:Miller Daredevil, V:Carrion 30.00
28 FM,A:Daredevil,V:Carrion . . 25.00
29 JM,FS,V:Carrion 5.50
30 JM,FS,V:Carrion 5.50
31 JM,FS,D:Carrion 5.50
32 BL,JM,FS,V:Iguana 5.50
33 JM,FS,O:Iguana 5.50
34 JM,FS,V:Iguana,Lizard 5.50
35 V:Mutant Mindworm 5.50
36 JM,V:Swarm 5.50
37 DC,MN,V:Swarm 5.50
38 SB,V:Morbius 8.00

39 JM,JR2,V:Schizoid Man 5.50
40 FS,V:Schizoid Man 5.50
41 JM,V:Meteor Man,A:GiantMan . 5.00
42 JM,A:Fant.Four,V:Frightful 4 . . 5.00
43 JBy(c),MZ,V:The Ringer,
V:Belladonna 5.00
44 JM,V:The Vulture 5.00
45 MSe,V:The Vulture 5.00
46 FM(c),MZ,V:Cobra 5.00
47 MSe,A:Prowler II 5.00
48 MSe,A:Prowler II 5.00
49 MSe,I:Smuggler 5.00
50 JR2,JM,V:Mysterio 5.00
51 MSe&FM(c),V:Mysterio 5.00
52 FM(c),D:White Tiger 5.00
53 JM,FS,V:Terrible Tinkerer 5.00
54 FM,WS,MSe,V:Silver Samurai . 5.00
55 LMc,JM,V:Nitro 5.00
56 FM,JM,V:Jack-o-lantern 13.00
57 JM,V:Will-o-the Wisp 5.00
58 JBy,V:Ringer,A:Beetle 6.00
59 JM,V:Beetle 5.00
60 JM&FM(c),O:Spider-Man,
V:Beetle 5.50
61 JM,V:Moonstone 4.50
62 JM,V:Goldbug 4.50
63 JM,V:Molten Man 4.50
64 JM,I:Cloak&Dagger 12.00
65 BH,JM,V:Kraven,Calypso 4.50
66 JM,V:Electro 4.00
67 AMb,V:Boomerang 4.00
68 LMc,JM,V:Robot of Mendell
Stromm 4.00
69 AM,A:Cloak & Dagger 9.00
70 A:Cloak & Dagger 8.00
71 JM,Gun Control issue 4.00
72 AM,V:Dr.Octopus 4.00
73 AM,JM,V:Dr.Octopus,A:Owl . . 4.00
74 AM,JM,V:Dr.Octopus,R:Bl.Cat . 4.00
75 AM,JM,V:Owl,Dr.Octopus 4.50

Peter Parker #40
© Marvel Entertainment Group

76 AM,Black Cat on deathbed . . . 3.50
77 AM,V:Gladiator,Dr.Octopus . . . 3.50
78 AM,V:Dr.Octopus,C:Punisher . 3.50
79 AM,V:Dr.Octopus,A:Punisher . 4.00
80 AM,F:J.Jonah Jameson 3.50
81 A:Punisher 10.00
82 A:Punisher 10.00
83 A:Punisher 10.00
84 AM,F:Black Cat 3.50
85 AM,O:Hobgoblin powers
(Ned Leeds) 24.00
86 FH,V:Fly 3.50
87 AM,Reveals I.D.to Black Cat . . 3.50
88 AM,V:Cobra,Mr.Hyde 3.50
89 AM,Secret Wars,A:Kingpin . . . 3.50
90 AM,Secret Wars 4.00
91 AM,V:Blob 3.50
92 AM,I:Answer 3.50
93 AM,V:Answer 3.50
94 AM,A:Cloak & Dagger,V:
Silver Mane 3.50
95 AM,A:Cloak & Dagger,V:
Silvermane 3.50
96 AM,A:Cloak & Dagger,V:
Silvermane 3.50
97 HT,JM,A:Black Cat 3.50
98 HT,JM,I:Spot 3.50
99 HT,JM,V:Spot 3.50
100 AM,V:Kingpin,C:Bl.Costume . 5.00
101 JBy(c),AM,V:Killer Shrike . . . 3.00
102 JBy(c),AM,V:Backlash 3.00
103 AM,V:Blaze;Not John Blaze . 3.00
104 JBy(c),AM,V:Rocket Racer . . 3.00
105 AM,A:Wasp 3.00
106 AM,A:Wasp 3.00
107 RB,D:Jean DeWolf,I:SinEater 5.00
108 RB,A:Daredevil,V:Sin-Eater . . 4.00
109 RB,A:Daredevil,V:Sin-Eater . . 4.00
110 RB,A:Daredevil,V:Sin-Eater . . 4.00
111 RB,Secret Wars II 3.00
112 RB,A:Santa Claus,Black Cat . 3.00
113 RB,Burglars,A:Black Cat 3.00
114 BMc,V:Lock Picker 3.00
115 BMc,A:Black Cat,Dr.Strange,
I:Foreigner 3.50
116 A:Dr.Strange,Foreigner,Black
Cat,Sabretooth 12.00
117 DT,C:Sabretooth,A:Foreigner,
Black Cat,Dr.Strange 5.00
118 MZ,D:Alexander,V:SHIELD . . 3.00
119 RB,BMc,V:Sabretooth,
A:Foreigner,Black Cat 12.00

Peter Parker #116
© Marvel Entertainment Group

A:Foreigner,Black Cat 6.00
120 KG 3.00
121 RB,BMc,V:Mauler 3.00
122 V:Mauler 3.00
123 V:Foreigner,Black Cat 3.00
124 V:Dr.Octopus 3.00
125 V:Wr.Crew,A:Spiderwoman . . 3.00
126 JM,A:Sp.woman,V:Wrecker . . 3.00
127 AM,V:Lizard 3.00
128 C:DDevil,A:Bl.Cat,Foreigner . 3.50
129 A:Black Cat,V:Foreigner 3.00
130 A:Hobgoblin 6.00
131 MZ,BMc,V:Kraven 12.00
132 MZ,BMc,V:Kraven 12.00
133 BSz(c),Mad Dog Pt.3 . . . . . . 8.00
Ann.#1 RB,JM,V:Dr.Octopus 5.00
Ann.#2 JM,I&O:Rapier 4.50
Ann.#3 JM,V:Manwolf 4.50
Ann.#4 AM,O:Aunt May,A:Bl.Cat . 5.00
Ann.#5 I:Ace,Joy Mercado 4.50
Ann.#6 V:Ace 4.50
Ann.#7 Honeymoon iss,A:Puma . . 4.50
Becomes:
SPECTACULAR SPIDER-MAN

PETER PORKER
Star
May, 1985

1 Parody 2.50
2 . . . . 1.50
3 . . . . 1.50
4 . . . . 1.50
5 V:Senior Simians 1.50
6 A Blitz in Time 1.50
7 . . . . 1.50
8 Kimono My House 1.25
9 Uncouth my Tooth 1.25
10 Lost Temple of the Golden
Retriever 1.25
11 Dog Dame Afternoon 1.25
12 The Gouda,Bad & Ugly 1.25
13 Halloween issue 1.25
14 Heavy Metal Issue 1.25
15 . . . . 1.25
16 Porker Fried Rice,Final Issue 1.25
17 September, 1987 . . . . 1.25

PETER, THE LITTLE PEST
November, 1969

1 F:Peter 6.00
2 Rep,Dexter & Melvin 5.00
3 Rep,Dexter & Melvin 5.00
4 Rep,Dexter & Melvin,
May, 1970 . . . . 5.00

PHOENIX (UNTOLD STORY)
April, 1984

1 JBy,O:Phoenix (R.Summers) . 12.00

PILGRIM'S PROGRESS

1 adapts John Bunyans novel . . 10.00

PINHEAD

1 Red Foil(c),from Hellraiser 2.95
2 DGC(s),V:Cenobites 2.50
3 DGC(s),V:Cenobites 2.50
4 DGC(s),V:Cenobites 2.50
5 DGC(s),Devil in Disguise 2.50
6 DGC(s), ... 2.50

PINHEAD VS. MARSHALL LAW

1 KON,In Hell 2.95
2 KON 2.95

PINOCHIO & THE EMPEROR OF THE NIGHT
March, 1988

1 Movie adapt 1.25

PIRATES OF DARK WATERS
November, 1991

1 based on T.V. series 1.00
2 Search for 13 Treasures 1.00
3 V:Albino Warriors,Konk 1.00
4 A:Monkey Birds 1.25
5 Tula Steals 1st Treasuer 1.25
6 thru 9 . . . . @1.25

PITT, THE
March, 1988

1 SB,SDr,A:Spitfire ... 4.50

PLANET OF THE APES
August, 1974
(black & white magazine)

1 MP ... 6.00
2 MP ... 4.00
3 ... 3.00
4 ... 5.00
5 ... 5.00
6 thru 10 ... @2.50
11 thru 20 ... @2.00
21 thru 28 ... @1.50
29 February, 1977 ... 1.50

PLANET TERRY
Star
April, 1985

1 thru 11 ... @1.00
12 March, 1986 ... 1.00

PLASMER

1 A:Captain America ... 3.50
2 A:Captain Britain,Black Knight .. 2.25
3 A:Captain Britain ... 2.25
4 A:Captain Britain ... 1.95

PLASTIC FORKS
Epic
1990

1 ... 5.50
2 thru 5 ... @5.25

POLICE ACADEMY
November, 1989

1 Based on TV Cartoon ... 1.25
2 ... 1.00
3 ... 1.00
4 ... 1.00
5 ... 1.00
6 February, 1990 ... 1.00

POLICE ACTION
January, 1954

1 JF,GC,Riot Squad ... 80.00
2 JF,Over the Wall ... 40.00
3 ... 30.00
4 DAy ... 30.00
5 DAy ... 30.00
6 ... 30.00
7 BPNovember, 1954 ... 30.00

POLICE BADGE
See: SPY THRILLERS

POPPLES
Star
December, 1986

1 Based on Toys ... 1.00
2 ... 1.00
3 ... 1.00
4 ... 1.00
5 August, 1987 ... 1.00

POWDERED TOAST-MAN

Spec. F:Powder Toast-Man ... 3.25

POWERHOUSE PEPPER COMICS
1943

1 BW,Movie Auditions(c) ... 650.00
2 BW,Dinner(c) ... 400.00
3 BW,Boxing Ring(c) ... 350.00
4 BW,Subway(c) ... 350.00
5 BW, Bankrobbers(c), November, 1948 ... 400.00

POWER LINE
Epic
May, 1988

1 BMc(i) ... 2.25
2 Aw(i) ... 2.00
3 A:Dr Zero ... 2.00
4 ... 2.00
5 thru 7 GM ... @2.00
8 GM September, 1989 ... 2.00

POWER MAN
Prev: Hero for Hire
February, 1974

17 GT,A:Iron Man ... 12.00
18 GT,V:Steeplejack ... 7.50
19 GT,V:Cottonmouth ... 7.50
20 GT,Heroin Story ... 7.50
21 V:Original Power Man ... 5.00
22 V:Stiletto & Discus ... 5.00
23 V:Security City ... 5.00
24 GT,I:BlackGoliath(BillFoster) .. 5.00
25 A:Circus of Crime ... 5.00
26 GT,V:Night Shocker ... 5.00
27 GP,AMc,V:Man Called X ... 5.00
28 V:Cockroach ... 5.00
29 V:Mr.Fish ... 5.00
30 RB,KJ,KP,I:Piranha ... 5.00
31 SB,NA(i),V:Piranha ... 5.00
32 JSt,FR,A:Wildfire ... 3.50
33 FR,A:Spear ... 3.50
34 FR,A:Spear,Mangler ... 3.50
35 DA,A:Spear,Mangler ... 3.50
36 V:Chemistro ... 3.50
37 V:Chemistro ... 3.50
38 V:Chemistro ... 3.50
39 KJ,V:Chemistro,Baron ... 3.50
40 V:Baron ... 3.50
41 TP,V:Thunderbolt,Goldbug ... 3.50
42 V:Thunderbolt,Goldbug ... 3.50
43 AN,V:Mace ... 3.50
44 TP,A:Mace ... 3.50
45 JSn,A:Mace ... 4.00
46 GT,I:Zzzax(recreated) ... 3.50
47 BS,A:Zzzax ... 4.00
48 JBy,A:Iron Fist ... 5.00
49 JBy,A:Iron Fist ... 5.00

Becomes:

POWER MAN & IRON FIST

50 JBy,I:Team-up with Iron Fist .. 6.00
51 MZ,Night on the Town ... 2.50
52 MZ,V:Death Machines ... 2.50
53 SB,O:Nightshade ... 2.50
54 TR,O:Iron Fist ... 3.50
55 Chaos at the Coliseum ... 2.50
56 Mayhem in the Museum ... 2.50
57 X-Men,V:Living Monolith ... 7.00
58 1st El Aguila(Drug) ... 2.00
59 BL(c),TVE,V:Big Apple Bomber ... 1.75
60 BL(c),V:Terrorists ... 1.75
61 BL(c),V:The Maggia ... 1.75
62 BL(c),KGa,V:Man Mountain D:Thunerbolt ... 1.75
63 BL(c),Cage Fights Fire ... 1.75
64 DGr&BL(c),V:Suetre,Muertre .. 1.75
65 BL(c),A:El Aquila, ... 1.75
66 FM(c),Sabretooth(2nd App.) . 60.00
67 V:Bushmaster ... 1.75
68 FM(c),V:Athur Nagan ... 2.00
69 V:Soldier ... 2.00
70 FM(c)V:El Supremo ... 1.75
71 FM(c),I:Montenegro ... 1.75
72 FM(c),V:Chako ... 1.75
73 FM(c),V:Rom ... 1.75
74 FM(c),V:Ninja ... 1.75
75 KGa,O:IronFist ... 2.50
76 KGa,V:Warhawk ... 2.50
77 KGa,A:Daredevil ... 2.50
78 KGa,A:El Aguila,Sabretooth (Slasher)(3rd App.) ... 32.00
79 V:Dredlox ... 1.75
80 KJ(c),V:Montenegro ... 1.75
81 V:Black Tiger ... 1.75

Power Man and Iron Fist #77
© Marvel Entertainment Group

82 V:Black Tiger ... 1.75
83 V:Warhawk ... 1.75
84 V:Constrictor,A:Sabertooth (4th App.) ... 10.00
85 KP,V:Mole Man ... 1.75
86 A:Moon Knight ... 1.75
87 A:Moon Knight ... 1.75
88 V:Scimtar ... 1.75
89 V:Terrorists ... 1.75
90 V:Unus BS(c) ... 1.75
91 "Paths and Angles" ... 1.75
92 V:Hammeread,I:New Eel ... 1.75
93 A:Chemistro ... 1.75
94 V:Chemistro ... 1.75
95 Danny Rand ... 1.75
96 V,Chemistro ... 1.75
97 K'unlun,A:Fera ... 1.75
98 V:Shades & Commanche ... 1.75
99 R:Daught.of Dragon ... 1.75
100 O:K'unlun,DoubleSize ... 1.75
101 A:Karnak ... 1.75
102 V:Doombringer ... 1.75
103 O:Doombringer ... 1.75
104 V:Dr.Octopus,Lizard ... 1.75
105 F:Crime Buster ... 1.75
106 Luke Gets Shot ... 1.75
107 JBy(c),Terror issue ... 1.75
108 V:Inhuman Monster ... 1.75
109 V:The Reaper ... 1.75
110 V:Nightshade,Eel ... 1.75
111 I:Captain Hero ... 1.75
112 JBy(c),V:Control7 ... 1.75
113 JBy(c),A:Capt.Hero ... 1.75
114 JBy(c),V:Control7 ... 1.75
115 JBy(c),V:Stanley ... 1.75
116 JBy(c),V:Stanley ... 1.75
117 R:K'unlun ... 1.75
118 A:Colleen Wing ... 1.75
119 A:Daught.of Dragon ... 1.75
120 V:Chiantang ... 1.75
121 Secret Wars II ... 1.75
122 V:Dragonkin ... 1.75
123 V:Race Killer ... 1.75
124 V:Yellowclaw ... 1.75
125 MBr,LastIssue;D:Iron Fist ... 3.00
Giant#1 reprints ... 4.00
Ann.#1 Earth Shock ... 5.00

POWER PACHYDERMS
September, 1989

1 Elephant Superheroes ... 1.50

POWER PACK
August, 1984

1 JBr,BWi,I&O:Power Pack, I:Snarks 4.00
2 JBr,BWi,V:Snarks 2.50
3 JBr,BWi,V:Snarks 2.00
4 JBr,BWi,V:Snarks 2.00
5 JBr,BWi,V:Bogeyman 2.00
6 JBr,BWi,A:Spider-Man 2.00
7 JBr,BWi,A:Cloak & Dagger . . . 2.00
8 JBr,BWi,A:Cloak & Dagger . . . 2.00
9 BA,BWi,A:Marrina 1.50

Power Pack #2
© Marvel Entertainment Group

10 BA,BWi,A:Marrina 1.50
11 JBr,BWi,V:Morlocks 2.00
12 JBr,BWi,A:X-Men,V:Morlocks . 4.00
13 BA,BWi,Baseball issue 1.50
14 JBr,BWi,V:Bogeyman 1.50
15 JBr,BWi,A:Beta Ray Bill 1.50
16 JBr,BWi,I&O:Kofi,J:Tattletale (Franklin Richards) 2.00
17 JBr,BWi,V:Snarks 1.50
18 BA,SW,Secret Wars II, V:Kurse 2.00
19 BA,SW,Doub.size,Wolverine . 11.00
20 BMc,A:NewMutants 1.50
21 BA,TA,C:Spider-Man 1.50
22 JBg,BWi,V:Snarks 1.50
23 JBg,BWi,V:Snarks,C:FF 1.50
24 JBg,BWi,V:Snarks,C:Cloak . . . 2.00
25 JBg,BWi,A:FF,V:Snarks 1.25
26 JBg,BWi,A:Cloak & Dagger . . . 1.25
27 JBg,AG,A:Wolverine,X-Factor, V:Sabretooth 14.00
28 A:Fantastic Four,Hercules 1.25
29 JBg,DGr,A:SpM,V:Hobgoblin . . 2.00
30 VM,Crack 1.25
31 JBg,I:Trash 1.25
32 JBg,V:Trash 1.25
33 JBg,A:Sunspot,Warlock, C:Spider-Man 1.75
34 TD,V:Madcap 1.25
35 JBg,A:X-Factor,D:Plague 1.75
36 JBg,V:Master Mold 1.25
37 SDr(i),I:Light-Tracker 1.25
38 SDr(i),V:Molecula 1.25
39 V:Bogeyman 1.25
40 A:New Mutants,V:Bogeyman . . 1.75
41 SDr(i),V:The Gunrunners 1.25
42 JBg,SDr,Inferno,V:Bogeyman . 2.00
43 JBg,SDr,AW,Inferno, V:Bogeyman 2.00
44 JBr,Inferno,A:New Mutants . . . 2.25
45 JBr,End battle w/Bogeyman . . 1.50
46 WPo,A:Punisher,Dakota North 6.00
47 JBg,I:Bossko 1.50
48 JBg,Toxic Waste #1 . . . . 1.50
49 JBg,JSh,Toxic Waste #2 . . . . . 1.50
50 AW(i),V:Snarks 1.50
51 GM,I:Numinus 1.50
52 AW(i),V:Snarks,A:Numinus . . . 1.50
53 EC,A of V,A:Typhoid Mary . . . 1.50
54 JBg,V:Mad Thinker 1.50
55 DSp,V:Mysterio 1.50
56 TMo,A:Fant.Four,Nova 1.50
57 TMo,A:Nova,V:Star Stalker . . . 1.50
58 TMo,A:Galactus,Mr.Fantastic . 1.50
59 TMo,V:Ringmaster 1.50
60 TMo,V:Puppetmaster 1.50
61 TMo,V:Red Ghost & Apes 1.50
62 V:Red Ghost & Apes (last issue) 1.75
Holiday Spec.JBr,Small Changes . 2.25

PRINCE NAMOR, THE SUB-MARINER
September, 1984

1 I:Dragonrider, Dara 2.50
2 I:Proteus 1.50
3 . . . . 1.25
4 December, 1984 . . . . 1.25

PRIVATE EYE
Atlas
January, 1951

1 . . . . 80.00
2 . . . . 50.00
3 GT 50.00
4 . . . . 35.00
5 . . . . 35.00
6 JSt 35.00
7 . . . . 35.00
8 March, 1952 . . . . 35.00

PSI FORCE
November, 1986

1 MT,O:PSI Force 1.25
2 MT 1.00
3 MT,CIA 1.00
4 MT,J:Network 1.00
5 MT 1.00
6 MT(c) 1.00
7 MT(c) 1.00
8 MT 1.00
9 MT(c) 1.00
10 PSI Hawk 1.00
11 . . . . 1.00
12 MT(c) 1.00
13 . . . . 1.00
14 AW 1.00
15 . . . . 1.00
16 RLm 1.25
17 RLm 1.25
18 RLm 1.25
19 RLm 1.25
20 RLm,V:Medusa Web;Rodstvow 1.50
21 RLm 1.50
22 RLm,A:Nightmask 1.50
23 A:D.P.7 . . . . 1.50
24 . . . . 1.50
25 . . . . 1.25
26 . . . . 1.25
27 thru 31 . . . . @1.50
32 June, 1989 . . . . 1.50
Ann.#1 . . . . 1.25

PSYCHONAUTS
Epic

1 thru 4 War in the Future 4.95

PUNISHER
January, 1986
[Limited Series]

1 MZ,Circle of Blood,double size 40.00
2 MZ,Back to the War 20.00

Punisher Limited Series #1
© Marvel Entertainment Group

3 MZ,V:The Right 15.00
4 MZ,V:The Right 12.00
5 V:Jigsaw,end Mini-Series 12.00

[Regular Series]

1 KJ,V:Wilfred Sobel,Drugs 22.00
2 KJ,V:General Trahn,Bolivia . . . 12.00
3 KJ,V:Colonel Fryer 8.00
4 KJ,I:The Rev,Microchip Jr. 8.00
5 KJ,V:The Rev 8.00
6 DR,KN,V:The Rosettis 8.00
7 DR,V:Ahmad,D:Rose 8.00
8 WPo,SW(1st Punisher), V:Sigo & Roky 12.00
9 WPo,SW,D:MicrochipJr,V:Sigo . 9.00
10 WPo,SW,A:Daredevil (x-over w/Daredevil #257) 15.00
11 WPo,SW,O:Punisher 7.00
12 WPo,SW,V:Gary Saunders . . . 7.00
13 WPo,SW,V:Lydia Spoto 7.00
14 WPo,SW,I:McDowell,Brooks . . 7.00
15 WPo,SW,V:Kingpin 6.00
16 WPo,SW,V:Kingpin 5.00
17 WPo,SW,V:Kingpin 5.00
18 WPo,SW,V:Kingpin,C:X-Men . . 5.00
19 LSn,In Australia 4.00
20 WPo(c),In Las Vegas 4.00
21 EL,SW,Boxing Issue 4.00
22 EL,SW,I:Saracen 4.00
23 EL,SW,V:Scully 4.00
24 EL,SW,A:Shadowmasters 4.00
25 EL,AW,A:Shadowmasters 4.00
26 RH,Oper.Whistle Blower#1 . . . 3.00
27 RH,Oper.Whistle Blower#2 . . . 3.00
28 BR,A:Dr.Doom,A of Veng. 3.00
29 BR,A:Dr.Doom,A of Veng. 3.00
30 BR,V:Geltrate 3.00
31 BR,V:Bikers #1 . . . . 3.00
32 BR,V:Bikers #2 . . . . 3.00
33 BR,V:The Reavers 3.00
34 BR,V:The Reavers 3.00
35 BR,MF,Jigsaw Puzzle #1 . . . . 3.00
36 MT,MF,Jigsaw Puzzle #2 . . . . 2.50
37 MT,Jigsaw Puzzle #3 . . . . 2.50
38 BR,MF,Jigsaw Puzzle #4 . . . . 2.50
39 JSh,Jigsaw Puzzle #5 . . . . . . 2.50
40 BR,JSh,Jigsaw Puzzle #6 . . . . 2.50
41 BR,TD,V:Terrorists 2.50
42 MT,V:Corrupt Mili. School 3.00
43 BR,Border Run 2.00
44 Flag Burner 2.00
45 One Way Fare 2.00

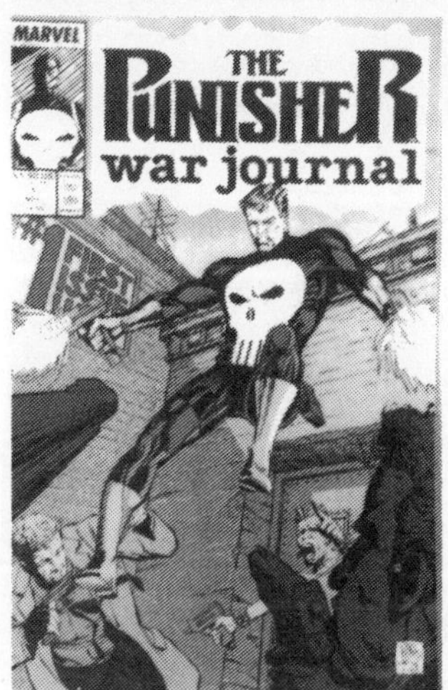

Punisher War Journal #1
© Marvel Entertainment Group

46 HH,Cold Cache 2.00
47 HH,Middle East #1 . . . . 2.00
48 HH,Mid.East #2,V:Saracen . . . 2.00
49 HH,Punisher Hunted 2.00
50 HH,MGo(c),I:Yo Yo Ng 3.00
51 Chinese Mafia 2.00
52 Baby Snatchers 2.00
53 thru 57 HH,in Prison . . . . . . @3.00
58 V:Kingpin's Gang,A:Micro 3.00
59 MT(c),V:Kingpin 2.00
60 VM,AW,Black Punisher,
A:Luke Cage 2.00
61 VM,A:Luke Cage 2.00
62 VM,AW,A:Luke Cage 1.50
63 MT(c),VM,V:Thieves 1.50
64 Eurohit #1 . . . . 1.50
65 thru 70 Eurohit . . . . @1.50
71 AW(i) 1.50
72 AW(i) 1.50
73 AW(i),Police Action #1 . . . . . . 1.50
74 AW(i),Police Action #2 . . . . . . 1.50
75 AW(i),Police Action #3,foil(c),
double size 3.25
76 LSn,in Hawaii 1.50
77 VM,Survive#1 . . . . 1.50
78 VM,Survive#2 . . . . 1.50
79 VM,Survive#3 . . . . 1.50
80 Goes to Church 1.50
81 V:Crooked Cops 1.50
82 B:Firefight 1.50
83 Firefight#2 . . . . 1.50
84 E:Firefight 1.50
85 Suicide Run 2.00
86 Suicide Run#3,Foil(c), ... 3.25
87 Suicide Run#6 . . . . 1.50
88 LSh(c),Suicide Run#9 . . . . 1.50
89 . . . . 1.75
90 Hammered 1.75
91 Silk Noose 1.50
92 Razor's Edge 1.50
Ann.#1 MT,A:Eliminators,
Evolutionary War. 8.00
Ann.#2 JLe,Atlantis Attacks #5,
A:Moon Knight 5.00
Ann.#3 LS,MT,Lifeform #1 . . . . . . 4.00
Ann.#4 Baron Strucker Pt.2
(see D.D.Annual #7) 3.00
Ann.#5 System Bytes #1 . . . . 2.50
Ann.#6 I:Eradikator,w/card 3.25
GNv 8.00
Summer Spec #1 VM,MT 3.50
Summer Spec #2 SBs(c) 2.50
Summer Spec #3 V:Carjackers . . 2.50
Summer Spec #4 . . . . 2.95
Punisher:No Escape A:USAgent,
Paladin 6.00
Movie Spec.BA 5.95
Punisher: The Prize 5.50
Punisher:Bloodlines DC 6.25
Punisher:Blood on the Moors . . . 16.95
Punisher:G-Force 5.25
Punisher:Origin of Mirco Chip #1,
O:Mirco Chip 2.00
Punisher:Origin of Mirco Chip #2
V:The Professor 2.00
Classic Punisher rep early
B/w magazines 7.00
Punisher:Back To School Spec.
#1 JRy,short stories 3.25
#2 BSz 2.95
Punisher:Die Hard in the Big
Easy Mardi Gras 5.25
Holiday Spec.#1 V:Young
Mob Capo 3.25
Holiday Spec #2 . . . . 2.95
Punisher:Ghosts o/t Innocent#1
TGr, V:Kingpin's Dead Men . . . 5.95
Punisher:Ghosts o/t Innocent#2
TGr, V:Kingpin,Snake 5.95

PUNISHER/CAP. AMERICA: BLOOD AND GLORY

1 thru 3 KJ,V:Drug Dealers . . . @6.25

PUNISHER ARMORY

July, 1990

1 JLe(c) 6.00
2 JLe(c) 3.00
3 . . . . 2.50
4 thru 6 . . . . @2.25
7 thru 9 . . . . @2.00

CLASSIC PUNISHER

1 TDz 4.95

PUNISHER/DAREDEVIL

1 Rep.Daredevil 6.00

PUNISHER MAGAZINE

October, 1989

1 MZ,rep.,Punisher #1 . . . . 2.50
2 MZ,rep 2.25
3 thru 13 KJ,rep. . . . . @2.25
14 rep. PWJ #1 . . . . 2.25
15 rep. PWJ 2.25
16 rep.,1990 . . . . 2.25

PUNISHER MOVIE COMIC

November, 1989

1 Movie adapt 1.50
2 Movie adapt 1.50
3 Movie adapt,December, 1989 . 1.50

PUNISHER MOVIE SPECIAL

1 Movie Adapt.BA,1989 . . . . 5.95

PUNISHER: NO ESCAPE

OneShot A:USAgent,Paladin,1990 5.50

PUNISHER P.O.V.

July, 1991

1 BWr,Punisher/Nick Fury 6.00
2 BWr,A:Nick Fury,Kingpin 5.50
3 BWr,V:Mutant Monster,
A:Vampire Slayer 5.25
4 BWr,A:Nick Fury 5.25

PUNISHER: THE PRIZE

1 1990 . . . . 4.95

PUNISHER 2099

1 TMo,Jake Gallows family Killed,
foil(c) 5.00
2 TMo,I:Fearmaster,Kron,Multi
Factor 3.00
3 TMo,V:Frightening Cult 2.25
4 TMo,V:Cyber Nostra 1.75
5 TMo,V:Cyber Nostra,Fearmaster 1.75
6 TMo,V:Multi-Factor 1.75
7 TMo,Love and Bullets#1 . . . . . 1.75
8 TMo,Love and Bullets#2 . . . . . 1.75
9 TMo,Love and Bullets#3 . . . . . 1.75
10 TMo,I:Jigsaw 1.50
11 TMo,V:Jigsaw 1.50
12 TMo,A:Spider-Man 2099 . . . . . 1.50
13 TMo,Fall of the Hammer#5 . . . 1.50
14 WSm, ... 1.50
15 TMo,V:Fearmaster,
I:Public Enemy 1.50
16 TMo,V:Fearmaster,
Public Enemy 1.75
17 TMo,V:Public Enemy 1.50

PUNISHER WAR JOURNAL

November, 1988

1 CP,JLe,O:Punisher 12.00
2 CP,JLe,A:Daredevil 10.00
4 CP,JLeV:The Sniper 8.00
5 CP,JLe,V:The Sniper 8.00
6 CP,JLe,A:Wolverine 14.00
7 CP,JLe,A:Wolverine 10.00
8 JLe,I:Shadowmasters 8.00
9 JLe,A:Black Widow 5.00
10 JLe,V:Sniper 5.00
11 JLe,Shock Treatment 5.00
12 JLe,AM,V:Bushwacker 5.00
13 JLe(c),V:Bushwacker 4.00
14 JLe(c),DR,RH,A:Spider-Man . . 5.00
15 JLe(c),DR,RH,A:Spider-Man . . 5.00
16 MT(i),Texas Massacre 3.25
17 JLe,AM,Hawaii 4.00
18 JLe,AM,Kahuna,Hawaii 4.00
19 JLe,AM,Traume in Paradise . . 4.00
20 AM 3.25
21 TSm,AM 3.00
22 TSm,AM,Ruins #1 . . . . 3.00
23 TSm,AM,Ruins #2 . . . . 3.00
24 . . . . 3.00
25 MT 3.50
26 MT,A:Saracen 3.50
27 MT,A:Saracen 3.50
28 MT 3.50
29 MT,A:Ghostrider 3.50
30 MT,A:Ghostrider 3.50
31 NKu,Kamchatkan
Konspiracy#1 . . . . 3.00
32 Kamchatkan Konspiracy #2 . . . 2.25
33 Kamchatkan Konspiracy #3 . . . 2.25
34 V:Psycho 2.25
35 Movie Stuntman 2.25
36 Radio Talk Show #1 . . . . 2.25
37 Radio Talk Show #2 . . . . 2.25
38 . . . . 2.25
39 DGr,V:Serial Killer 2.25
40 MWg 2.00
41 Armageddon Express 2.00
42 Mob run-out 2.00
43 JR2(c) 2.00
44 Organ Donor Crimes 2.00
45 Dead Man's Hand #3,V:Viper . 2.25
46 Dead Man's Hand #6,V:Chainsaw
and the Praetorians 2.00
47 Dead Man's Hand #7,A:Nomad,
D.D,V:Hydra,Secret Empire . . . 2.00
48 B:Payback 2.00
49 JR2(c),V:Corrupt Cop 2.00
50 MT,V:Highjackers,I:Punisher
2099 . . . . 3.50
51 E:Payback 2.00
52 A:Ice(from The'Nam) 2.00
53 A:Ice(from the Nam) 2.00
54 Hyper#1 . . . . 2.00
55 Hyper#2 . . . . 2.00

56 Hyper#3 . . . . 2.00
57 & 58 A:Ghost Rider,Daredevil @2.00
59 F:Max the Dog 2.00
60 CDi(s),F:Max the Dog 2.00
61 CDi(s),Suicide Run#1,Foil(c) . . 3.25
62 CDi(s),Suicide Run#4 . . . . 2.00
63 CDi(s),Suicide Run#7 . . . . 2.00
64 CDi(s),Suicide Run#10 . . . . . . 3.25
64a Newsstand Ed. 2.50
65 B:Pariah 2.00
66 A:Captain America 1.95
TPB reprints #6,7 . . . . 4.95

Punisher War Zone #1

© Marvel Entertainment Group

PUNISHER WAR ZONE

1 JR2,KJ,Punisher As Johnny Tower
Die-Cut Bullet Hole(c) 5.50
2 JR2,KJ,Mafia Career 4.00
3 JR2,KJ,Punisher/Mafia,contd . . 3.50
4 JR2,KJ,Cover gets Blown 3.00
5 JR2,KJ,A:Shotgun 3.00
6 JR2,KJ,A:Shotgun 3.00
7 JR2,V:Rapist in Central Park . . 2.00
8 JR2,V:Rapist in Central Park . . 2.00
9 JR2,V:Magnificent Seven 2.00
10 JR2,V:Magnificent Seven 2.00
11 JR2,MM,V:Magnificent Seven . 2.00
12 Punisher Married 2.00
13 Self-Realization 2.00
14 Psychoville#3 . . . . 2.00
15 Psychoville#4 . . . . 2.00
16 Psychoville#5 . . . . 2.00
17 Industrial Esponiage 2.00
18 Jerico Syndrome#2 . . . . 2.00
19 Jerico Syndrome#3 . . . . 2.00
20 B:2 Mean 2 Die 2.00
21 2 Mean 2 Die#2 . . . . 2.00
22 A:Tyger Tyger 2.00
23 Suicide Run#2,Foil(c) 3.25
24 Suicide Run#5, ... 2.00
25 Suicide Run#8, ... 2.50
26 CDi(s),JB,Pirates 2.00
27 CDi(s),JB, ... 1.95
28 CDi(s),JB,Sweet Revenge 1.95
29 CDi(s),JB,The Swine 1.95
Ann.#1 Jb,MGo,(c),I:Phalanx,
w/Trading card 3.25

PUSSYCAT
October, 1968
(black & white magazine)

1 BEv,BWa,WW 125.00

QUASAR
October, 1989

1 O:Quasar 4.00
2 V:Deathurge,A:Eon 2.50
3 A:Human Torch,V:The Angler . 2.00
4 Acts of Vengeance,A:Aquarian . 2.00
5 A of Veng,V:Absorbing Man . . . 2.00
6 V:Klaw,Living Laser,Venom,
Red Ghost 6.00
7 MM,A:Cosmic SpM,V:Terminus 4.00
8 MM,A:New Mutants,BlueShield 2.00
9 MM,A:Modam 2.00
10 MM,A:Dr.Minerva 2.00
11 MM,A:Excalibur,A:Modred 2.00
12 MM,A:Makhari,Blood Bros. . . . 1.75
13 JLe(c)MM,J.into Mystery #1 . . 1.75
14 TM(c)MM,J.into Mystery #2 . . . 2.00
15 MM,Journey into Mystery #3 . . 1.75
16 MM,Double sized 2.25
17 MM,Race,A:Makkari,Whizzer,
Quicksilver,Capt.Marv,Super
Sabre,Barry Allen Spoof 2.50
18 GCa,N:Quasar 1.75
19 GCa,B:Cosmos in Collision,
C:Thanos 2.50
20 GCa,A:Fantastic Four 2.50
21 GCa,V:Jack of Hearts 2.50
22 GCa,D:Quasar,A:Ghost Rider . 2.50
23 GCa,A:Ghost Rider 2.50
24 GCa,A:Thanos,Galactus,
D:Maelstrom 2.50
25 GCa,A:Eternity & Infinity,N:Quasar,
E:Cosmos Collision 2.50
26 GCa,Inf.Gauntlet,A:Thanos . . . 3.00
27 GCa,Infinity Gauntlet,I:Epoch . 2.50
28 GCa,A:Moondragon,Her,
X-Men 2.00
29 GCa,A:Moondragon,Her 1.50
30 GCa,What If? tie-in 1.50
31 GCa,R:New Universe 1.50
32 GCa,Op.GalacticStorm Pt.3 . . 1.50
33 GCa,Op.GalacticStorm Pt.10 . . 1.50
34 GCa,Op.GalacticStorm Pt 17 . 1.50
35 GCa,Binary V:Her 1.50
36 GCa,V:Soul Eater 1.50
37 GCa,V:Soul Eater 1.50
38 GCa,Inf.War,V:Warlock 1.50
39 SLi,Inf.War,V:Deathurge 1.50
40 SLi,Inf.War,V:Deathurge 1.50
41 R:Marvel Boy 1.50
42 V:Blue Marvel 1.50
43 V:Blue Marvel 1.50
44 V:Quagmire 1.50
45 V:Quagmire,Antibody 1.50
46 Neutron,Presence 1.50
47 1st Full Thunderstrike Story . . 1.50
48 A:Thunderstrike 1.50
49 Kalya Vs. Kismet 1.50
50 A:Man-Thing,Prism(c) 3.25
51 V:Angler,A:S.Supreme 1.50
52 V:Geometer 1.50
53 . . . . 1.50
54 MGu(s),Starblast #2 . . . . 1.50
55 MGu(s),A:Stranger 1.50
56 MGu(s),Starblast #10 . . . . 1.50
57 MGu(s),A:Kismet 1.50
58 . . . . 1.25
59 A:Thanos,Starfox 1.25

QUESTPROBE
August, 1984

1 JR,A:Hulk,I:Chief Examiner . . . 2.00
2 AM,JM,A:Spider-Man 1.75
3 JSt,A:Thing & Torch 1.50

QUICK-TRIGGER WESTERN
See: WESTERN THRILLERS

RAIDERS OF THE LOST ARK
September, 1981

1 JB/KJ,movie adaption 2.00
2 JB/KJ, ... 1.75
3 JB/KJ,November,1981 . . . . 1.75

RAVAGE 2099

1 PR,I:Ravage 2.50
2 PR,V:Deathstryk 2.00
3 PR,V:Mutroids 2.00
4 PR,V:Mutroids 1.50
5 PR,Hellrock 1.50
6 PR,N:Ravage 1.50
7 PR,new Powers 1.50
8 V:Deathstryke 1.50
9 PR,N:Ravage 1.50
10 V:Alchemax 1.50
11 A:Avatarr 1.50
12 Ravage Transforms 1.50
13 V:Fearmaster 1.50
14 V:Punisher 2099 . . . . 1.50
15 Fall of the Hammer #2 . . . . . . 1.50
16 I:Throwback 1.50
17 GtM,V:Throwback,O:X-11 . . . . 1.50
18 GtM,w/card 1.75
19 GtM, ... 1.75
20 GtM,V:Hunter 1.50

RAWHIDE KID
Atlas
March, 1955

1 B:Rawhide Kid & Randy,
A:Wyatt Earp 400.00
2 Shoot-out(c) 175.00
3 V:Hustler 100.00
4 Rh(c) 100.00
5 GC 100.00
6 Six-Gun Lesson 75.00
7 AW 75.00
8 . . . . 75.00
9 . . . . 75.00
10 thru 16 . . . . @60.00
17 JK,O:Rawhide Kid 60.00
18 thru 20 . . . . @50.00
21 . . . . 40.00
22 . . . . 40.00
23 JK,O:Rawhide Kid Retold . . . 85.00
24 thru 30 . . . . @40.00
31 JK,DAy,No Law in Mesa 35.00
32 JK,DAy,Beware of the
Parker Brothers 35.00
33 JK(c),JDa,V:Jesse James . . . 40.00
34 JDa,JK,V:Mister Lightning . . . 40.00
35 JK(c),GC,JDa,I&D:The Raven 40.00
36 DAy,A Prisoner in
Outlaw Town 35.00
37 JK(c),DAy,GC,V:The Rattler . 35.00
38 DAy.V:The Red Raven 35.00
39 DAy 35.00
40 JK(c),DAy,A:Two Gun Kid . . 35.00
41 JK(c),The Tyrant of
Tombstone Valley 35.00
42 JK 35.00
43 JK 35.00
44 JK(c),V:The Masked Maverick 35.00
45 JK(c),O:Rawhide Kid Retold . 40.00
46 JK(c),ATh 30.00
47 JK(c),The Riverboat Raiders . 25.00
48 GC,V:Marko the Manhunter . 20.00
49 The Masquerader 20.00
50 A;Kid Colt,V:Masquerader . . 20.00
51 DAy,Trapped in the
Valley of Doom 20.00
52 DAy,Revenge at
Rustler's Roost 20.00
53 Guns of the Wild North 20.00
54 DH,BEv,The Last Showdown 20.00
55 . . . . 20.00
56 DH,JTgV:The Peacemaker . . 20.00
57 V:The Scorpion 20.00
58 DAy 20.00
59 V:Drako 20.00
60 DAy,HT,Massacre at Medicine
Bend 20.00
61 DAy,TS,A:Wild Bill Hickok . . . 15.00
62 Gun Town,V:Drako 15.00
63 Shootout at Mesa City 15.00

64 HT,Duel of the Desparadoes . 15.00
65 JTg,HT,BE 15.00
66 JTg,BEv,Death of a Gunfighter 15.00
67 Hostage of Hungry Hills 15.00
68 JB,V:The Cougar 15.00
69 JTg,The Executioner 15.00
70 JTg,The Night of the Betrayers 12.00
71 JTg,The Last Warrior 12.00
72 JTg,The Menace of Mystery Valley 12.00
73 JTg,The Manhunt 12.00
74 JTg,The Apaches Attack 12.00
75 JTg,The Man Who Killed The Kid 12.00
76 JTg,V:The Lynx 12.00
77 JTg,The Reckoning 12.00
78 JTg 12.00
79 JTg,AW,The Legion of the Lost 12.00
80 Fall of a Hero 12.00
81 thru 85 . . . . @12.00
86 JK,O:Rawhide Kid retold 13.00
87 thru 99 . . . . @7.00
100 O:Rawhide Kid retold 10.00
101 thru 135 . . . . @6.50
126 thru 150 . . . . @6.00
151 May, 1979 . . . . 6.00

RAWHIDE KID
August, 1985

1 JSe,mini-series 1.50
2 . . . . 1.25
3 . . . . 1.25
4 . . . . 1.25

RAZORLINE FIRST CUT
Razorline

1 Intro Razorline 1.00

REAL EXPERIENCES
See: TESSIE THE TYPIST

RED RAVEN
See: HUMAN TORCH

Red Sonja #1

© Marvel Entertainment Group

RED SONJA
[1st Series]
January, 1977

1 FT,O:Red Sonja,'Blood of the Unicorn' 3.50
2 FT,'Demon of the Maze' 2.50
3 FT,'The Games of Gita' 2.00
4 FT,'The Lake of the Unknown' . 2.00
5 FT,'Master of the Bells' 2.00
6 FT,'The Singing Tower' 1.25
7 FT,'Throne of Blood' 1.25
8 FT,Vengeance o/t Golden Circle 1.25
9 FT,'Chariot o/t Fire-Stallions' . . 1.25
10 FT,Red Lace Pt.1 . . . . 1.25
11 FT,Red Lace Pt.2 . . . . 1.25
12 JB/JRu,'Ashes & Emblems' . . . 1.25
13 JB/AM,'Shall Skranos Fall' . . . 1.25
14 SB/AM,'Evening on the Border' 1.25
15 JB/TD,'Tomb of 3 Dead Kings' May, 1979 . . . . 1.25

[2nd Series]
February, 1983

1 TD,GC 1.25
2 GC, March,1983 . . . . 1.00

[3rd Series]
August, 1983

1 . . . . 1.25
2 . . . . 1.25
3 thru 13 . . . . @1.25
1 movie adaption, 1985 . . . . 1.25
2 movie adaption, 1985 . . . . 1.25

RED WARRIOR
Atlas
January, 1951

1 GT,Indian Tales 75.00
2 GT(c),The Trail of the Outcast 50.00
3 The Great Spirit Speaks 40.00
4 O:White Wing 40.00
5 . . . . 40.00
6 Final Issue,December, 1951 . 40.00

RED WOLF
May, 1972

1 SSh(c),GK,JSe,F:Red Wolf & Lobo 5.50
2 GK(c),SSh,Day of the Dynamite Doom 3.00
3 SSh,War of the Wolf Brothers . 3.00
4 SSh,V:Man-Bear 3.00
5 GK(c),SSh 3.00
6 SSh,JA,V;Devil Rider 3.00
7 SSh,JA,Echoes from a Golden Grave 3.00
8 SSh,Hell on Wheels 3.00
9 DAy,To Die Again,O:Lobo September, 1973 . . . . 3.00

REN AND STIMPY SHOW

1 Polybagged w/Air Fowlers, Ren(c) 30.00
1a Stimpy(c) 30.00
1b 2nd Printing 6.00
1c 3rd Printing 2.00
2 Frankenstimpy 24.00
2a 2nd Printing 2.00
3 Christmas issue 20.00
3a 2nd Printing 2.00
4 Where's Stimpy? 15.00
5 Teacher Bingo 10.00
6 A:SpM,V:Powdered Toast Man 8.00
7 F:Offical Yak Shaving Day . . . 6.00
8 F:Bun Boy Burger Bunny 5.00
9 Untamed World 4.00
10 Bug Out 3.00
11 Ren's Peaceful Place 3.00
12 Teacher Bingo 3.00
13 Halloween issue 2.50
14 Mars needs Vecro 2.50
15 Christmas Spec. 2.25
16 . . . . 2.25
17 This Year's Model 2.25
18 U.S. Ohhhhh No! 2.25
19 Minimalist issue 2.25
20 F:Muddy Mudskipper 1.95
TPB Running Joke,rep.#1-4,w/new material 12.95

RETURN OF THE JEDI

1 AW,movie adapt 3.00
2 AW,movie adapt 3.00
3 AW,movie adapt 3.00
4 AW,movie adapt 3.00

REX HART
See: BLAZE CARSON

RINGO KID
January, 1970
[2nd Series]

1 AW,Reprints 3.00
2 JSe,Man Trap 2.00
3 JR,the Man From the Panhandle 1.50
4 HT(c),The Golden Spur 2.00
5 JMn,Ambush 2.00
6 Capture or Death 2.00
7 HT(c),JSe,JA,Terrible Treasure of Vista Del Oro 2.00
8 The End of the Trail 2.00
9 JSe,Mystery of the Black Sunset 2.00
10 Bad day at Black Creek 2.00
11 Bullet for a Bandit 1.50
12 A Badge to Die For 1.50
13 DW,Hostage at Fort Cheyenne 1.50
14 Showdown in the Silver Cartwheel 1.50
15 Fang,Claw, and Six-Gun 1.50
16 Battle of Cattleman's Bank . . . 1.50
17 Gundown at the Hacienda . . . 1.50
18 . . . . 1.50
19 Thunder From the West 1.50
20 AW 1.50
21 thru 29 . . . . @1.50
30 November, 1973 . . . . 1.50

RINGO KID WESTERN
Atlas
August, 1954

1 JSt,O:Ringo Kid,B:Ringo Kid 150.00
2 I&O:Arab,A:Black Rider 75.00
3 . . . . 50.00
4 . . . . 50.00
5 . . . . 50.00
6 . . . . 55.00
7 . . . . 55.00
8 JSe 55.00
9 . . . . 30.00
10 JSe(c),AW 40.00
11 JSe(c) 30.00
12 JO 30.00
13 AW 40.00
14 thru 20 . . . . @30.00
21 September, 1957 . . . . 30.00

ROBOCOP
March, 1990

1 LS,I:Nixcops 9.00
2 LS,V:Nixcops 5.00
3 LS 3.50
4 LS 3.00
5 LS,WarzonePt1 . . . . 3.00
6 LS,WarzonePt2 . . . . 3.00
7 LS 2.50
8 LS,V:Gang-5 . . . . 2.50
9 LS,V:Vigilantes 2.50
10 LS 2.50
11 HT 2.50
12 LS,Robocop Army #1 . . . . 2.00
13 LS,Robocop Army #2 . . . . 2.00
14 LS,Robocop Army #3 . . . . 2.00
15 LS,Robocop Army #4 . . . . 2.00
16 TV take over 2.00
17 LS,V:The Wraith 2.00
18 LS,Mindbomb #1 . . . . 2.00
19 LS,Mindbomb #2 . . . . 2.00
20 In Detroit 2.00
21 LS,Beyond the Law Pt.1 . . . . . 2.00
22 LS,Beyond the Law Pt.2 . . . . . 2.00
23 LS,Beyond the Law Pt.3,final . 2.00
Robocop Movie Adapt 4.95

Robocop II Movie Adapt 4.95

ROBOCOP II
August, 1990

1 MBa,rep.Movie Adapt 2.00
2 MBa,rep.Movie Adapt 1.50
3 MBa,rep.Movie Adapt 1.50

ROBOTIX
February, 1986

1 Based on toys 1.00

ROCKET RACCOON
May, 1985

1 MM 1.50
2 MM 1.50
3 MM 1.50
4 MM,August, 1985 . . . . 1.50

ROCKO'S MODERN LIFE

1 . . . . 1.95
2 . . . . 1.95

ROM
December, 1979

1 SB,I&O:Rom 3.00
2 FM(c),SB,V:Dire Wraiths 2.50
3 FM(c),SB,I:Firefall 2.50
4 SB,A:Firefall 2.00

Rom #47

© Marvel Entertainment Group

5 SB,A:Dr.Strange 2.00
6 SB,V:Black Nebula 1.50
7 SB,V:Dark Nebula 1.50
8 SB,V:Dire Wraiths 1.50
9 SB,V:Serpentyne 1.50
10 SB,V:U.S.Air Force 1.50
11 SB,V:Dire Wraiths 1.50
12 SB,A:Jack O' Hearts 1.75
13 SB,V:Plunderer 1.25
14 SB,V:Mad Thinker 1.25
15 SB,W:Brandy and Dire Wraith . 1.25
16 SB,V:Watchwraith 1.25
17 SB,A:X-Men 3.00
18 SB,A:X-Men 3.00
19 SB,JSt,C:X-Men 1.50
20 SB,JSt,A:Starshine 1.25
21 SB,JSt,A:Torpedo 1.25
22 SB,JSt,A:Torpedo 1.25
23 SB,JSt,A:Powerman,Iron Fist. . 1.25
24 SB,JSt,A:Nova 1.25
25 SB,JSt,Double-Sized 1.50
26 SB,JSt,V:Galactus 1.00
27 SB,JSt,V:Galactus 1.00
28 SB,JSt,D:Starshine 1.00
29 SB,Down in the Mines 1.00
30 SB,JSt,A:Torpedo 1.00
31 SB,JSt,V:Evil Mutants,Rogue . 2.00
32 SB,JSt,V:Evil Mutants 2.00
33 SB,V:Sybil 1.00
34 SB,A:Sub-Mariner 1.00
35 SB,A:Sub-Mariner 1.00
36 SB,V:Scarecrow 1.00
37 SB,A:Starshine 1.00
38 SB,A:Master of Kung Fu 1.00
39 SB,A:Master of Kung Fu 1.00
40 SB,A:Torpedo 1.00
41 SB,A:Dr.Strange 1.00
42 SB,A:Dr.Strange 1.00
43 SB,Rom Becomes Human . . . 1.00
44 SB,A:Starshine,O:Gremlin 1.00
45 SB,V:Soviet Super Soldiers . . . 1.00
46 SB,V:Direwraiths 1.00
47 SB,New Look for Wraiths 1.00
48 SB,V:Dire Wraiths 1.00
49 SB,V:Dire Wraiths 1.00
50 SB,D:Torpedo,V:Skrulls 1.25
51 SB,F:Starshine 1.00
52 BSz(c),SB,V:Dire Wraiths 1.00
53 SB,BSz,V:Dire Wraiths 1.00
54 V:Dire Wraiths 1.00
55 V:Dire Wraihs 1.00
56 A:Alpha Flight 2.00
57 A:Alpha Flight 2.00
58 JG(c),A:Antman 1.00
59 SD,BL,V:Microbe Menace 1.00
60 SD,TP,V:Dire Wraiths 1.00
61 SD,V:Wraith-Realm 1.00
62 SD,A:Forge 1.25
63 SD,V:Dire Wraiths 1.00
64 SD,V:Dire Wraiths 1.00
65 SD,A:X-Men,Avengers 1.25
66 SD,Rom leaves Earth 1.25
67 SD,V:Scorpion 1.00
68 BSz(c)SD,Man & Machine . . . 1.00
69 SD,V:Ego 1.00
70 SD 1.00
71 SD,V:Raak 1.00
72 SD,Secret Wars II 1.25
73 SD,JSt 1.00
74 SD,JBy,Code of Honor 1.00
75 SD,CR,Doublesize,last issue . . 1.50
Ann.#1 PB,A:Stardust 1.50
Ann.#2 I:Knights of Galador 1.25
Ann.#3 A:New Mutants 2.00
Ann.#4 V:Gladiator 1.25

ROMANCE DIARY
December, 1949

1 . . . . 55.00
2 March, 1950 . . . . 55.00

ROMANCES OF THE WEST
November, 1949

1 Ph(c),Calamity Jane,
Sam Bass 100.00
2 March, 1950 . . . . 65.00

ROMANCE TALES
October, 1949
(no #1 thru 6)

7 . . . . 50.00
8 . . . . 35.00
9 March, 1950 . . . . 30.00

ROMANTIC AFFAIRS
See: MOLLY MANTON'S ROMANCES

ROYAL ROY
Star
May, 1985

1 thru 5 . . . . @1.00
6 March, 1986 . . . . 1.00

RUGGED ACTION
Atlas
December, 1954

1 Man-Eater 50.00
2 JSe,DAy.Manta-Ray 30.00
3 DAy 30.00
4 . . . . 30.00

Becomes:

STRANGE STORIES OF SUSPENSE

5 RH,The Little Black Box . . . 150.00
6 BEv,The Illusion 75.00
7 JSe(c),BEv,Old John's House 85.00
8 AW,BP,TYhumbs Down 85.00
9 BEv(c),Nightmare 75.00
10 RC,MME,AT 85.00
11 . . . . 65.00
12 . . . . 65.00
13 . . . . 60.00
14 AW 65.00
15 BK 60.00
16 August, 1957 . . . . 60.00

RUSTY COMICS
See: KID KOMICS

SABRETOOTH
[Limited Series]

1 B:LHa(s),MT,A:Wolverine 7.50
2 MT,A:Mystique,C:Wolverine . . . 6.00
3 MT,A:Mystique,Wolverine 5.50
4 E:LHa(s),MT,D:Birdy 5.00

SABRETOOTH CLASSICS

1 rep. Power Man/Iron Fist #66 . . 1.75
2 rep. Power Man/Iron Fist #78 . . 1.50
3 rep. Power Man/Iron Fist #84 . . 1.50

SACHS & VIOLENS
Epic

1 GP,PDd(s) 5.00
2 GP,PDd(s),V:Killer 3.25
3 GP,PDd(s),V:White Slavers . . . 2.25

SAGA OF CRYSTAR
May, 1983

1 O:Crystar 2.25
2 A:Ika 1.25
3 A:Dr.Strange 1.50
4 . . . . 1.25
5 . . . . 1.25
6 A:Nightcrawler 2.00
7 I:Malachon 1.25
8 . . . . 1.25
9 . . . . 1.25
10 Chaos 1.25
11 Alpha Flight,February, 1985 . . 2.00

SAGA OF ORIGINAL HUMAN TORCH

1 RB,O:Original Human Torch . . 3.00
2 RB,A:Toro 2.50
3 RB,V:Adolph Hitler 2.50
4 RB,Torch vs. Toro 2.50

ST. GEORGE
Epic
June, 1988

1 KJ,Shadow Line 1.25
2 KJ,I:Shrek 1.25
3 KJ 1.50
4 KJ 1.50
5 . . . . 1.50
6 . . . . 1.50
7 DSp 1.50
8 October, 1989 . . . . 1.50

SAINT SINNER
Razorline

1 I:Phillip Fetter 2.75

2 F:Phillip Fetter 2.00
3 in Vertesque 2.00
4 . . . . 2.00
5 Arcadia 2.00
6 . . . . 2.00
7 The Child Stealer 2.00

SAM & MAX GO TO THE MOON

1 Dirtbag Special,w/Nirvana Tape 4.00

[Regular Series]

1 MMi,AAd,F:Skull Boy 3.25
2 AAd,MMi 2.95
3 . . . . 2.95

SAMURAI CAT

Epic

1 I:MiaowaraTomokato 2.25
2 I:Con-Ed,V:Thpaghetti-Thoth . . 2.25
3 EmpireStateStrikesBack 2.25

SAVAGE COMBAT TALES

February, 1975

1 F:Sgt Strykers Death Squad . . 1.25
2 ATh,A:Warhawk 1.25
3 July, 1975 . . . . 1.25

SAVAGE SWORD OF CONAN

August, 1974
(black & white magazine)

1 BWS,JB,NA,GK,O:Blackmark, 3rdA:Red Sonja,Boris(c) 75.00
2 NA(c),HC,GK,'Black Colossus,' B.U.King Kull;B.U.Blackmark . 35.00
3 JB,BWS,GK,'At The Mountain of the Moon God;B.U.s: Kull;Blackmark 30.00
4 JB,RCo,GKIron Shadows in the Moon B.U.Blackmark,Boris(c) 15.00
5 JB,A WitchShall beBorn,Boris(c)15.00
6 AN,'Sleeper 'Neath the Sands' 12.50
7 JB,Citadel at the Center of Time Boris(c) 12.50
8 inc.GK,'Corsairs against Stygia 12.50
9 Curse of the Cat-Goddess, Boris(c),B.U.King Kull 12.50
10 JB,'Sacred Serpent of Set' Boris(c) 10.00
11 JB,'The Abode of the Damned' 10.00
12 JB,Haunters of Castle Crimson Boris(c) 10.00
13 GK,The Thing in the Temple, B.U. Solomon Kane 10.00
14 NA,Shadow of Zamboula, B.U.Solomon Kane 10.00
15 JB,Boris(c),'Devil in Iron' 10.00
16 JB,BWS,People of the Black Circle,B.U.Bran Mak Morn . . . 10.00
17 JB,'On to Yimsha!, B.U.Bran Mak Morn 10.00
18 JB,'The Battle of the Towers' B.U. Solomon Kane 10.00
19 JB,'Vengeance in Vendhya' B.U. Solomon Kane 10.00
20 JB,'The Slithering Shadow' B.U. Solomon Kane 10.00
21 JB,'Horror in the Red Tower' . 10.00
22 JB,'Pool o/t Black One' B.U. Solomon Kane 10.00
23 JB,FT,'Torrent of Doom' B.U. Solomon Kane 10.00
24 JB,BWS,'Tower of the Elephant'B.U.Cimmeria 10.00
25 DG,SG,Jewels of Gwahlur, B.U.Solomon Kane. 10.00
26 JB/TD,Beyond the Black River, B.U.Solomon Kane 8.00
27 JB/TD,Children of Jhebbal Sag 8.00
28 JB/AA,Blood of the Gods 8.00
29 ECh,FT,Child of Sorcery, B.U. Red Sonja 8.00
30 FB,The Scarlet Citadel 8.00
31 JB/TD,The Flaming Knife Pt.1 . 8.00
32 JB/TD,Ghouls of Yanaldar Pt.2 8.00
33 GC,Curse of the Monolith, B.U.Solomon Kane 8.00
34 CI/AA,MP,Lair o/t Ice Worm;B.U. Solomon Kane,B.U.King Kull . . 8.00
35 ECh,Black Tears 8.00
36 JB,AA,Hawks over Shem 8.00
37 SB,Sons of the White Wolf B.U. Solomon Kane 8.00
38 JB/TD,The Road of the Eagles 8.00
39 SB/TD,The Legions of the Dead, B.U.Solomon Kane concl. 8.00
40 JB/TD,A Dream of Blood 8.00
41 JB/TD,Quest for the Cobra Crown A:Thoth-Amon,B.U.Sol.Kane . . 8.00
42 JB/TD,Devil-Tree of Gamburu, A:Thoth-Amon,B.U.Sol.Kane . . 8.00
43 JB/TD,King Thoth-Amon, B.U.King Kull 8.00
44 SB/TD,The Star of Khorala . . . 8.00
45 JB/TD,The Gem in the Tower, B.U. Red Sonja 8.00
46 EC/TD,Moon of Blood, B.U. Hyborian Tale 8.00

Savage Sword of Conan
© Marvel Entertainment Group

47 GK/JB/JRu,Treasure of Tranicos C:Thoth-Amon 8.00
48 JB/KJ,A Wind Blows from Stygia C:Thoth-Amon 8.00
49 JB/TD,When Madness Wears the Crown, B.U.Hyborian Tale 6.00
50 JB/TD,Swords Across the Alimane 6.00
51 JB/TD,Satyrs' Blood 6.00
52 JB/TD,Conan the Liberator . . . 6.00
53 JB,The Sorcerer and the Soul, B.U. Solomon Kane 6.00
54 JB,The Stalker Amid the Sands, B.U. Solomon Kane 6.00
55 JB,Black Lotus & Yellow Death B.U. King Kull 6.00
56 JB/TD,The Sword of Skelos . . 6.00
57 JB/TD,Zamboula 6.00
58 JB/TD,KGa,For the Throne of Zamboula,B.U.OlgerdVladislav 6.00
59 AA,ECh,City ofSkulls,B.U.Gault 6.00
60 JB,The Ivory Goddess 6.00
61 JB,Wizard Fiend of Zingara . . . 6.00
62 JB/ECh,Temple of the Tiger, B.U. Solomon Kane 6.00
63 JB/ECh,TP/BMc,GK,Moat of Blood I:Chane of the Elder Earth . . . 6.00
64 JB/ECh,GK,Children of Rhan, B.U. Chane 6.00
65 GK,JB,Fangs of the Serpent, B.U. Bront 6.00
66 thru 75 . . . . @6.00
76 thru 80 . . . . @5.00
81 JB/ECh,Palace of Pleasure, B.U. Bront 5.00
82 AA,BWS,Devil in the Dark.Pt.1 B.U.repConan#24,Swamp Gas 5.00
83 AA,MW,NA,ECh,Devil in the Dark Pt.2,B.U. Red Sonja,Sol.Kane . 5.00
84 VM,Darksome Demon of Rabba Than 5.00
85 GK,Daughter of the God King . 5.00
86 GK,Revenge of the Sorcerer . . 5.00
87 . . . . 5.00
88 JB,Isle of the Hunter 5.00
89 AA,MW,Gamesman of Asgalun, B.U. Rite of Blood 5.00
90 JB,Devourer of Souls 5.00
91 JB,VM,Forest of Friends, B.U. The Beast,The Chain . . . 5.00
92 JB,The Jeweled Bird 5.00
93 JB/ECh,WorldBeyond the Mists 5.00
94 thru 101 . . . . @5.00
102 GD,B.U.Bran Mac Morn 4.00
103 GD,White Tiger of Vendhya, B.U. Bran Mac Morn 4.00
104 . . . . 4.00
105 . . . . 4.00
106 Feud of Blood 4.00
107 thru 118 . . . . @4.00
119 ECh,A:Conan's Sister 4.00
120 Star of Thama-Zhu 4.00
121 . . . . 4.00
122 . . . . 4.00
123 ECh,Secret of the GreatStone 4.00
124 ECh,Secret of the Stone 4.00
125 Altar of the Goat God 4.00
126 The Mercenary 4.00
127 Reunion in Scarlet,Return of Valeria 4.00
128 . . . . 4.00
129 . . . . 4.00
130 Reavers of the Steppes 4.00
131 GI,Autumn of the Witch 4.00
132 ECh,Masters o/t Broadsword . 4.00
133 . . . . 4.00
134 Conan the Pirate 4.00
135 Conan the Pirate 4.00
136 NKu,Stranded on DesertIsland 4.00
137 ECh,The Lost Legion 4.00
138 ECh,Clan o/t Lizard God 4.00
139 ECh,A:Valeria 4.00
140 ECh,The Ghost's Revenge . . 4.00
141 ECh 4.00
142 ECh,V:Warlord 4.00
143 ECh 4.00
144 ECh 4.00
145 ECh 4.00
146 ECh 4.00
147 ECh 4.00
148 BMc 4.00
149 TGr,BMc,Conan Enslaved . . . 4.00
150 ECh 4.00
151 ECh 4.00
152 ECh,Valley Beyond the Stars 4.00
153 Blood on the Sand,Pt.1 . . . . . 4.00
154 Blood on the Sand,Pt.2 . . . . . 4.00
155 ECh,V:Vampires 4.00
156 V:Corinthian Army 4.00
157 V:Hyborians 4.00
158 ECh,The Talisman-Gem 4.00
159 Conan Enslaved 4.00
160 . . . . 4.00
161 V:Magician/Monsters 4.00
162 AW,Horned God,B.U.Sol.Kane 3.00
163 V:Picts 3.00
164 Conan's Revenge 3.00
165 B.U. King Kull 3.00
166 ECh,Conan in New World,Pt.1 3.00
167 ECh,Conan in New World,Pt.2 3.00
168 ECh,Conan in New

World,concl 3.00
169 . . . . 3.00
170 AW,A:Red Sonja,Valeria
B.U. Solomon Kane 3.00
171 TD,Conan Youth Story 2.50
172 JS,JRu,Haunted Swamp,
B.U.King Kull,Valeria,
Red Sonja 2.50
173 ECh,Under Siege 2.50
174 AA,Red Stones of
Rantha Karn 2.50
175 The Demonslayer Sword 2.50
176 FH,TT,V:Wizard,B.U. Witch
Queen,Dagon,Ghouls 2.50
177 LMc,TD,ECh,Conan the Prey,
B.U.King Conan,Red Sonja . . . 2.50
178 AA,The Dinosaur God 2.50
179 ECh,A:Red Sonja,Valeria,
B.U.Conan 2.50
180 ECh,Sky-God Bardisattva,
B.U. King Kull 2.50
181 TD,Conan the Pagan God?,
B.U. Voodoo Tribe 2.50
182 RB/RT,V:Killer Ants 2.50
183 ECh,V:Kah-Tah-Dhen,
B.U.King Kull 2.50
184 AA,Return of Sennan 2.50
185 The Ring of Molub 2.50
186 AW,A:Thulsa Doom 2.50
187 ECh,A:Conan's Brother? 2.50
188 V:Kharban the Sorcerer 2.50
189 A:Search Zukala for Gem . . . 2.50
190 JB/TD,Skull on the Seas Pt.1 2.25
191 JB/ECh,Skull on the Seas Pt.2
Thulsa Doom Vs.Thoth-Amon . 2.25
192 JB/ECh,Skull on the Seas Pt.3
B.U. King Kull 2.25
193 JB/ECh,Skull on the Seas concl.
V:Thulsa Doom & Thoth-Amon 2.25
194 JB/ECh,Wanted for Murder,
B.U. Li-Zya 2.25
195 JB/ECh,V:Yamatains,
Giant Tortoise 2.25
196 JB/ECh,Treasure of the Stygian
Prince-Toth-Mekri,A:Valeria . . . 2.25
Ann.#1 SB,BWS,inc.'Beware the
Wrath of Anu',B.U. King
Kull Vs.Thulsa Doom 2.25

SAVAGE TALES
May, 1971
(black & white magazine)

1 GM,BWS,JR,I&O:Man-Thing,
B:Conan,Femizons,A:Kazar 100.00
2 GM,FB,BWS,AW,BWr,A:King
Kull rep,Creatures on
the Loose #10 . . . . 40.00
3 FB,BWS,AW,JSo 25.00
4 NA(c),E:Conan 16.00
5 JSn,JB,B:Brak the Barbarian 16.00
6 NA(c),JB,AW,B:Kazar 8.00
7 GM,NA 6.00
8 JB,A:Shanna,E:Brak 5.00
9 MK,A:Shanna 5.00
10 RH,NA,AW,A:Shanna 5.00
11 RH 5.00
12 Summer, 1975 . . . . 5.00
Ann.#1 GM,GK,BWS,O:Kazar . . . 6.00

SAVAGE TALES
November, 1985
(black & white magazine)

1 MGo,I:The 'Nam 2.00
2 MGo 4.00
3 MGo 4.00
4 MGo 4.00
5 MGo 4.00
6 MGo 3.00
7 MGo 3.00
8 MGo 3.00
9 MGo,March, 1987 . . . . 3.00

SCARLET WITCH

1 ALa(s),DAn(s),JH,I:Gargan,
C:Master Pandemonium 2.00
2 C:Avengers West Coast 2.00
3 A:Avengers West Coast 2.00
4 V:Lore,last issue 2.00

SCOOBY-DOO
October, 1977

1 B:DynoMutt 1.50
2 thru 8 . . . . @1.00
9 February, 1979 . . . . 1.00

SECRET DEFENDERS

1 F:Dr.Strange(in all),Spider
Woman,Nomad,Darkhawk,
Wolverine,V:Macabre 3.25
2 F:Spider Woman,Nomad,Darkhawk,
Wolverine,V:Macabre 2.50
3 F:Spider Woman,Nomad,Darkhawk,
Wolverine,V:Macabre 2.00
4 F:Namorita,Punisher,
Sleepwalker,V:Roadkill 2.00
5 F:Naromita,Punisher,
Sleepwalker, V:Roadkill 2.00
6 F:Spider-Man,Scarlet Witch,Captain
America,V:Suicide Pack 2.00
7 F:Captain America,Scarlet Witch,
Spider-Man 2.00
8 F:Captain America,Scarlet Witch,
Spider-Man 2.00
9 F:War Machine,Thunderstrike,
Silver Surfer 2.00
10 F:War Machine,Thunderstrike,
Silver Surfer 2.00
11 TGb,F:Hulk,Nova,Northstar . . . 2.00
12 RMz(s),TGb,F:Thanos 2.75
13 RMz(s),TGb,F:Thanos,Super Skrull,
Rhino,Nitro,Titanium Man 2.00
14 RMz(s),TGb,F:Thanos,Super Skrull,
Rhino,Nitro,Titanium Man,
A:Silver Surfer 2.00
15 F:Dr.Druid,Cage,Deadpool . . . 2.25
16 F:Dr.Druid,Cage,Deadpool . . . 1.95

SECRET WARS
May, 1984

1 MZ,A:X-Men,Fant.Four,Avengers,
Hulk,SpM in All,I:Beyonder . . . 4.50
2 MZ,V:Magneto 3.50
3 MZ,I:Titania & Volcana 2.50
4 BL,V:Molecule Man 2.50
5 BL,F:X-Men 2.50
6 MZ,V:Doctor Doom 2.00
7 MZ,I:New Spiderwoman 3.00
8 MZ,I:Alien Black Costume
(for Spider-Man) 20.00
9 MZ,V:Galactus 2.00
10 MZ,V:Dr.Doom 2.00
11 MZ,V:Dr.Doom 2.00
12 MZ,Beyonder Vs. Dr.Doom . . . 2.50
TPB rep #1-#12 . . . . 19.95

SECRET WARS II
July, 1985

1 AM,SL,A:X-Men,New Mutants . 2.00
2 AM,SL,A:Fantastic Four 1.50
3 AM,SL,A:Daredevil 1.50
4 AM,I:Kurse 1.50
5 AM,SL,I:Boom Boom 5.00
6 AM,SL,A:Mephisto 1.50
7 AM,SL,A:Thing 1.50
8 AM,SL,A:Hulk 1.50
9 AM,SL,A:Everyone,double-size 2.00

SECTAURS
June, 1985

1 Based on toys 1.50
2 thru 10 1986 . . . . @1.00

SEMPER FI
December, 1988

1 JSe 2.00
2 JSe 1.50
3 JSe 1.50
4 JSe 1.50
5 JSe 1.50
6 . . . . 1.50
7 . . . . 1.00
8 . . . . 1.00
9 August, 1989,final issue 1.00

SENSATIONAL SPIDERMAN

1 KM/TP/KJ,Rep. 5.95

SERGEANT BARNEY BARKER
August, 1956

1 JSe,Comedy 65.00
2 JSe,Army Inspection(c) 45.00
3 JSe,Tank(c) 45.00
Becomes:

G.I. TALES

4 JSe,At Grips with the Enemy 30.00
5 . . . . 20.00
6 JO,BP,GWb, July, 1957 . . . . 25.00

SGT. FURY & HIS HOWLING COMMANDOS
May, 1963

1 Seven Against the Nazis . . 650.00
2 JK,Seven Doomed Men . . . 225.00
3 JK,Midnight on Massacre
Mountain 125.00
4 JK,V:Lord Ha-Ha,D:Junior
Juniper 125.00
5 JK,V:Baron Strucker 125.00
6 JK,The Fangs of the Fox . . . 75.00
7 JK,Fury Court Martial 75.00
8 JK,V:Dr Zemo,I:Percival
Pinkerton 75.00
9 DAy,V:Hitler 75.00

Sgt. Fury #23
© Marvel Entertainment Group

10 DAy,On to Okinwawa,I:Capt.
Savage 75.00
11 DAy,V:Capt Flint 40.00
12 DAy,Howler deserts 40.00
13 DAy,JK,A;Capt.America . . . 110.00
14 DAy,V:Baron Strucker 40.00
15 DAy,SD,Too Small to Fight
Too Young to Die 40.00
16 DAy,In The Desert a Fortress
Stands 40.00
17 DAy,While the Jungle Sleeps 40.00

18 DAy,Killed in Action 40.00
19 DAy,An Eye for an Eye 40.00
20 DAy,V:the Blitz Squad 40.00
21 DAy,To Free a Hostage 30.00
22 DAy,V:Bull McGiveney 30.00
23 DAy,The Man who Failed . . . 30.00
24 DAy,When the Howlers Hit the Home Front 30.00
25 DAy,Every Man my Enemy . . 30.00
26 DAy,Dum Dum Does it the Hard Way 30.00
27 DAy,O:Fury's Eyepatch 30.00
28 DAy,Not a Man Shall Remain Alive 30.00
29 DAy,V:Baron Strucker 30.00
30 DAy,Incident in Italy 30.00
31 Day,Into the Jaws of Death . . 20.00
32 DAy,A Traitor in Our Midst . . 20.00
33 DAy,The Grandeur That was Greece 20.00

Sgt. Fury #64
© Marvel Entertainment Group

34 DAy,O:Howling Commandoes 20.00
35 DAy,Berlin Breakout,J:Eric Koenig 20.00
36 DAy,My Brother My Enemy . . 20.00
37 DAy,In the Desert to Die 20.00
38 This Ones For Dino 20.00
39 Into the Fortress of Fear 20.00
40 That France Might be Free . 20.00
41 V:The Blitzers 20.00
42 Three Were AWOL 20.00
43 Scourge of the Sahara,A:Bob Hope,Glen Miller 20.00
44 JSe,The Howlers First Mission 20.00
45 JSe,I:The War Lover 20.00
46 JSe,They Also Serve 20.00
47 Tea and Sabotage 20.00
48 A:Blitz Squad 20.00
49 On to Tarawa 20.00
50 The Invasion Begins 20.00
51 The Assassin 20.00
52 Triumph at Treblinka 20.00
53 To the Bastions of Bavaria . . 20.00
54 Izzy Shoots the Works 20.00
55 Cry of Battle, Kiss of Death . . 15.00
56 Gabriel Blow Your Horn 15.00
57 TS,The Informer 15.00
58 Second Front 15.00
59 D-Day for Dum Dum 15.00
60 Authorised Personnel Only . 15.00
61 The Big Breakout 15.00
62 The Basic Training of Fury . . 15.00
63 V:Nazi Tanks 15.00
64 The Peacemonger,A:Capt Savage 15.00
65 Eric Koenig,Traitor 15.00
66 Liberty Rides the Underground 15.00
67 With a Little Help From My Friends 15.00
68 Welcome Home Soldier 15.00
69 While the City Sleeps 15.00
70 The Missouri Marauders . . . 15.00
71 Burn,Bridge,Burn 15.00
72 Battle in the Sahara 15.00
73 Rampage on the Russian Front 15.00
74 Each Man Alone 15.00
75 The Deserter 12.00
76 He Fought the Red Baron . . . 12.00
77 A Traitor's Trap,A:Eric Koenig 12.00
78 Escape or Die 12.00
79 Death in the High Castle 12.00
80 To Free a Hostage 12.00
81 The All American 12.00
82 Howlers Hit The Home Front,rep 12.00
83 Dum DumV:Man-Mountain McCoy 12.00
84 The Devil's Disciple 12.00
85 Fury V:The Howlers 12.00
86 Germ Warfare 12.00
87 Dum Dum does it...rep 12.00
88 Save General Patton 12.00
89 O:Fury's eyepatch,rep 12.00
90 The Chain That Binds 12.00
91 Not A Man...rep 10.00
92 Some Die Slowly 10.00
93 A Traitor...rep 10.00
94 GK(c),Who'll Stop the Bombs 10.00
95 7 Doomed Men, rep 10.00
96 GK(c),Dum-Dum Sees it Through 10.00
97 Till the Last Man Shall Fail . . 10.00
98 A:Deadly Dozen 10.00
99 Guerillas in Greece 10.00
100 When a Howler Falls 10.00
101 Pearl Harbor 7.00
102 Death For A Dollar 7.00
103 Berlin Breakout 7.00
104 The Tanks Are Coming 7.00
105 My Brother,My Enemy 7.00
106 Death on the Rhine 7.00
107 Death-Duel in the Desert . . . 7.00
108 Slaughter From the Skies . . . 7.00
109 This Ones For Dino,rep 7.00
110 JSe(c),The Reserve 7.00
111 V:Colonel Klaw 7.00
112 V:Baron Strucker 7.00
113 That France Might Be Free,rep 7.00
114 Jungle Bust Out 7.00
115 V:Baron Strucker 7.00
116 End of the Road 7.00
117 Blitz Over Britain 7.00
118 War Machine 7.00
118 War Machine 7.00
119 They Strike by Machine 7.00
120 Trapped in the Compound of Death 7.00
121 An Eye for an Eye 5.00
122 A;The Blitz Squad 5.00
123 To Free a Hostage 5.00
124 A:Bull McGiveney 5.00
125 The Man Who Failed 5.00
126 When the Howlers Hit Home.. 5.00
127 Everyman My Enemy,rep . . . 5.00
128 Dum Dum does it...rep 5.00
129 O:Fury's Eyepatch 5.00
130 A:Baron Strucker 5.00
131 Armageddon 5.00
132 Incident in Italy 5.00
133 thru 140 . . . . @5.00
141 thru 150 . . . . @5.00
151 thru 160 . . . . @4.00
161 thru 166 . . . . @4.00
167 December, 1981 . . . . 4.00
Ann.#1 Korea #4,#5 . . . . 80.00
Ann.#2 This was D-Day 40.00
Ann.#3 Vietnam 25.00
Ann.#4 Battle of the Bulge 15.00
Ann.#5 Desert Fox 7.50
Ann.#6 Blaze of Battle 7.50
Ann.#7 Armageddon 7.50

SEVEN BLOCK
Epic
1990

1 . . . . 2.50

SHADOWMASTERS
October, 1989

1 RH 11.00
2 . . . . 7.00
3 . . . . 6.00
4 January, 1990 . . . . 5.00

SHADOWRIDERS

1 I:Shadowriders,A:Cable,GR . . . 2.00
2 A:Ghost Rider 2.00
3 A:Cable 2.00
4 A:Cable 2.00

SHANNA, THE SHE-DEVIL
December, 1972

1 GT,F:Shanna 7.50
2 RA,The Dungeon of Doom . . . 5.00
3 RA,The Hour of the Bull 3.00
4 RA,Mandrill 3.00
5 JR(c),RA,V:Nekra, Aug., 1973 3.00

SHEENA
December, 1984

1 Movie Adapt 1.00
2 February, 1985 . . . . 1.00

SHE-HULK
February, 1980
[1st Regular Series]

1 JB,BWi,I&O:She-Hulk 4.00
2 BWi,D:She-Hulk's best friend . . 2.50
3 BWi,Wanted for Murder 2.50
4 BWi,V:Her Father 2.50
5 BWi,V:Silver Serpent 2.50
6 A:Iron Man 2.00
7 BWi,A:Manthing 2.00
8 BWi,A:Manthing 2.00
9 BWi,Identity Crisis 2.00
10 V:The Word 2.00
11 BWi,V:Dr.Morbius 2.00
12 V:Gemini 2.00
13 V:Man-Wolf 1.50
14 V:Hellcat 1.50
15 V:Lady Kills 1.50
16 She Hulk Goes Berserk 1.50
17 V:Man-Elephant 1.50
18 V:Grappler 1.50
19 V:Her Father 1.50
20 A:Zapper 1.50
21 V:Seeker 1.50
22 V:Radius 1.50
23 V:Radius 1.50
24 V:Zapper 1.50
25 Double-sized,last issue 2.00

[2nd Regular Series]

1 JBy,V:Ringmaster 4.00
2 JBy 2.75
3 JBy,A:Spider-Man 2.25
4 JBy,I:Blond Phantom 2.25
5 JBy 2.25
6 JBy,A:U.S.1,Razorback 2.25
7 JBy,A:U.S.1,Razarback 2.25
8 JBy,A:Saint Nicholas 2.25
9 AM(i) 2.00
10 AM(i) 2.00
11 . . . . 2.00
12 . . . . 2.00
13 SK(c) 2.00
14 MT(c),A:Howard the Duck 2.00
15 SK(c) 2.00

16 SK(c) 2.00
17 SK(c),V:Dr.Angst 2.00
18 SK(c) 2.00
19 SK(c),V:Nosferata 2.00
20 SK(c),Darkham Asylum 2.00
21 SK(c),V:Blonde Phantom 2.00
22 SK(c),V:Blonde Phantom,A:All Winners Squad 2.00
23 V:Blonde Phantom 2.00
24 V:Deaths'Head 4.00
25 A:Hercules,Thor 2.00
26 A:Excalibur 2.00
27 Cartoons in N.Y. 2.00
28 Game Hunter Stalks She-Hulk 2.00
29 A:Wolv.,Hulk,SpM,Venom 2.50
30 MZ(c),A:Silver Surfer,Thor Human Torch 2.25
31 JBy,V:Spragg the Living Hill . . 2.50
32 JBy,A:Moleman,V:Spragg 2.00
33 JBy,A:Moleman,V:Spragg 2.00
34 JBy,Returns to New York 2.00
35 JBy,V:X-Humed Men 2.00
36 JBy,X-mas issue (#8 tie-in) . . . 2.00
37 JBy,V:Living Eraser 2.00
38 JBy,V:Mahkizmo 2.00
39 JBy,V:Mahkizmo 2.00
40 JBy,V:Spraggs,Xemnu 2.00
41 JBy,V:Xemnu 2.00
42 JBy,V:USArcher 2.00
43 JBy,V:Xemnu 2.00
44 JBy,R:Rocket Raccoon 2.00
45 JBy,A:Razorback 2.00
46 JBy,A:Rocket Raccoon 2.00
47 V:D'Bari 2.00
48 JBy,A:Rocket Raccoon 2.00
49 V:Skrulls,D'Bari 2.00
50 JBy,WS,TA,DGb,AH,HC, D:She-Hulk 4.00
51 TMo,V:Savage She-Hulk 2.00
52 D:She-Hulk,A:Thing,Mr.Fantastic, I:Rumbler,V:Titania 2.00
53 AH(c),A:Zapper 2.00
54 MGo(c),A:Wonder Man 2.00
55 V:Rumbler 2.00
56 A:War Zone 2.00
57 A:Hulk 2.00
58 V:Electro 2.00
59 V:Various Villains 2.00
60 last issue 2.00

SHE HULK: CEREMONY

1 JBr/SDr 4.50
2 JBr/FS 4.50

SHIELD

February, 1973

1 . . . . 5.00
2 . . . . 3.00
3 . . . . 3.00
4 . . . . 3.00
5 October, 1973 . . . . 3.00

SHOGUN WARRIORS

February, 1979

1 HT,DGr,F:Raydeen, Combatra, Dangard Ace 4.00
2 HT,DGr,V:Elementals of Evil . . 2.50
3 AM(c),HT,DGr,V:Elementals of Evil 2.50
4 HT,DGr,'Menace of the Mech Monsters' 2.50
5 HT,DGr,'Into The Lair of Demons' 2.50
6 HT,ME 2.00
7 HT,ME 2.00
8 HT,ME 2.00
9 'War Beneath The Waves' . . . 2.00
10 'Five Heads of Doom' 2.00
11 TA(c) 2.00
12 WS(c) 2.00
13 'Demons on the Moon' 2.00
14 V:Dr. Demonicus 2.00
15 . . . . 2.00
16 . . . . 2.00
17 . . . . 2.00
18 . . . . 2.00
19 A:Fantastic Four 2.50
20 September, 1980 . . . . 2.00

SHROUD

Limited Series

1 B:MiB(s),MCW,A:Spider-Man, V:Scorpion 2.00
2 MCW,A:Spider-Man,V:Scorpion . 2.00
3 MCW,I:Kali 2.00
4 MCW,Final Issue 2.00

SILVERHAWKS

August, 1987

1 thru 5 . . . . @1.00
6 June, 1988 . . . . 1.00

Silver Sable #2

© Marvel Entertainment Group

SILVER SABLE

1 Foil stamped(c),A:Sandman, Spider-Man 4.00
2 I:Gattling 2.00
3 V:Gattling,Foreigner 1.75
4 Infinity War,V:Doctor Doom . . . 1.75
5 Infinity War,V:Doctor Doom . . . 1.50
6 A:Deathlok 1.50
7 A:Deathlok 1.50
8 V:Hydra 1.50
9 O:Silver Sable 1.50
10 A:Punisher,Leviathan 1.50
11 Cyber Warriors,Hydra 1.50
12 V:Cyberwarriorss,R:Sandman . 1.50
13 For Love Nor Money#3, A:Cage,Terror 1.50
14 For Love Nor Money#6, A:Cage,Terror 1.50
15 V:Viper,A:Captain America . . . 1.50
16 SBt,Infinty Crusade 1.50
17 Infinity Crusade 1.50
18 A:Venom 1.50
19 Siege of Darkness x-over 1.50
20 GWt(s),StB,BU:Sandman,Fin . . 1.50
21 Gang War 1.50
22 . . . . 1.50
23 GWt(s),A:Deadpool,Daredevil, BU:Sandman 1.50
24 GWt(s),BU:Crippler,w/card . . . 1.75
25 V:Hydra 2.00
26 F:Sandman 1.50

SILVER SURFER

[1st Series]

August, 1968

1 B:StL(s),JB,JSr,GC,O:Silver Surfer, O:Watcher,I:Shala Bal 350.00
2 JB,JSr,GC,A:Watcher 150.00
3 JB,JSr,GC,I:Mephisto 125.00
4 JB,A:Thor,low distribution scarce 350.00
5 JB,A:Fant.Four,V:Stranger . . . 80.00
6 JB,FB,A:Watcher 90.00
7 JB,A:Watcher,I:Frankenstein's Monster 80.00
8 JB,DA,A:Mephisto,I:Ghost 60.00
9 JB,DA,A:Mephisto,A:Ghost . . . 60.00
10 JB,DA,South America 60.00
11 JB,DA 50.00
12 JB,DA,V:The Abomination . . . 50.00
13 JB,DA,V:Doomsday Man . . . 50.00
14 JB,DA,A:Spider-Man 70.00
15 JB,DA,A:Human Torch 50.00
16 JB,V:Mephisto 50.00
17 JB,V:Mephisto 50.00
18 E:StL(s),JK,V:Inhumans 50.00

[2nd Regular Series]

1 JBy,TP,Direct Only,V:Mephisto 15.00

[3rd Regular Series]

1 MR,JRu,A:Fantastic Four, Galactus,V:Champion 14.00
2 MR,A:Shalla Bal,V:Skrulls 9.00
3 MR,V:Collector & Runner 8.00
4 MR,JRu,A:Elders,I:Obliterator . . 7.00
5 MR,JRu,V:Obliterator 6.00
6 MR,JRu,O:Obliterator,A:Kree, Skrulls 6.00
7 MR,JRu,V:Supremor,Elders/ Soul Gems 5.00
8 MR,JRu,V:Supremor 5.00
9 MR,Elders Vs.Galactus 5.00
10 MR,A:Galactus,Eternity 5.00
11 JSon,JRu,V:Reptyl 4.50
12 MR,JRu,V:Reptyl,A:Nova 4.50
13 JSon,DC,V:Ronan 4.50
14 JSon,JRu,V:Skrull Surfer 4.50
15 RLm,JRu,A:Fantastic Four . . 12.00
16 RLm,Inbetweener possesses Soul Gem,A:Fantastic Four . . . 6.00
17 RLm,A:Inbetweener,Galactus, Fantastic Four,D:Trader, Possessor,Astronomer 5.00
18 RLm,Galactus V:Inbetweener . 5.00
19 RLm,MR,V:Firelord 4.50
20 RLm,A:Superskrull,Galactus . . 4.50
21 MR,DC,V:Obliterator 4.50
22 RLm,V:Ego 4.50
23 RLm,V:Dragon 4.50
24 RLm,V:G.I.G.O. 4.50
25 RLm,V:Ronan,Kree Skrull War 4.50
26 RLm,V:Nenora 4.50
27 RLm,V:Stranger 4.50
28 RLm,D:Super Skrull,V:Reptyl . 4.50
29 RLm,V:Midnight Sun 4.50
30 RLm,V:Midnight Sun 4.50
31 RLm,O:Living Tribunal & Stranger (double size) 5.50
32 RF,JSt,A:Mephisto 4.50
33 Rlm,V:Impossible Man 4.50
34 RLm,(1stJSn),2nd R:Thanos . 16.00
35 RLm,A:Thanos,R:Drax 16.00
36 RLm,V:Impossible Man,A:Warlock Capt.Marvel,C:Thanos 8.50
37 RLm,V:Drax,A:Mentor 6.00
38 RLm,V:Thanos(continued in Thanos Quest) 10.00
39 JSh,V:Algol 3.50
40 RLm,V:Dynamo City 4.00
41 RLm,V:Dynamo City,A:Thanos 5.00
42 RLm,V:Dynamo City,A:Drax . . 4.00
43 RLm,V:DynamoCity 4.00
44 RLm,R:Thanos,Drax, O:Inf.Gems 5.50
45 RLm,Thanos vs. Mephisto . . . 8.00
46 RLm,R:Warlock,A:Thanos . . . 12.00
47 RLm,Warlock V:Drax,

A:Thanos 10.00
48 RLm,A:Galactus,Thanos 6.00
49 RLm,V:Thanos Monster 5.00
50 RLm,Silver Stamp(D.size),
V:Thanos Monster 10.00
50a 2nd printing 4.00
50b 3rd printing 2.50
51 RLm,Infinity Gauntlet x-over 4.00
52 RLm,Infinity Gauntlet x-over 3.00
53 RLm,Infinity Gauntlet x-over 2.50
54 RLm,I.Gauntlet x-over,V:Rhino 2.50
55 RLm,I.Gauntlet x-over,Universe
According to Thanos pt.1 2.50
56 RLm,I.Gauntlet x-over,Universe
According to Thanos pt.2 2.50
57 RLm,Infinity Gauntlet x-over 2.50
58 RLm(c),Infinity Gauntlet x-over,
A:Hulk,Namor,Dr.Strange 2.50
59 RLm(c),TR,Infinity Gauntlet,
Thanos V:Silver Surfer 2.50
60 RLm,V:Midnight Sun,
A:Inhumans 2.00
61 RLm,I:Collection.Agency 2.00
62 RLm,O:Collection Agency 2.00
63 RLm,A:Captain Marvel 2.00
64 RLm,V:Dark Silver Surfer 2.00
65 RLm,R:Reptyl,I:Princess
Alaisa 2.00
66 RLm,I:Avatar,Love & Hate 2.00
67 RLm(c),KWe,Inf.War,V:Galactus
A:DrStrange 2.00
68 RLm(c),KWe,Inf.War,O:Nova 2.00
69 RLm(c),KWe,Infinity War,
A:Galactus 2.00
70 RLm(c),Herald War#1,I:Morg 2.00
71 RLm(c),Herald War#2,V:Morg 2.00
72 RLm(c),Herald War#3,R:Nova 2.00

Silver Surfer #65

© Marvel Entertainment Group

73 RLm,R:Airwalker 2.00
74 RLm,V:Terrax 2.00
75 RLm,E:Herald Ordeal,V:Morg,
D:Nova 6.00
76 RLm,A:Jack of Hearts 1.50
77 RLm,A:Jack of Hearts 1.50
78 RLm,R:Morg,V:Nebula 1.50
79 RLm,V:Captain Atlas 1.50
80 RLm,I:Ganymede,Terrax
Vs.Morg 1.50
81 RLm,O:GanymedeI:Tyrant 1.50
82 RLm,V:Tyrant,double sized 2.50
83 Infinity Crusade 1.50
84 RLm(c),Inf.Crusade 1.50
85 RLm(c),Infinity Crusade 1.50
86 RLm(c), Blood & Thunder Pt#2
V:Thor,A:Beta Ray Bill 1.50
87 RLm(c),Blood & Thunder Pt#7 1.50
88 RLm(c),Blood & Thunder Pt#10 1.50
89 RLm(c),CDo,C:Legacy 1.50
90 RLm(c),A:Legacy,C:Avatar 1.50
91 RLm 1.50
92 RLm,V:Avatar 1.75
93 V:Human Torch 1.50
Ann.#1 RLm,JSon,Evolution War 7.00
Ann.#2 RLm,Atlantis Attacks 5.00
Ann.#3 RLm,Lifeform #4 4.00
Ann.#4 RLm,Korvac Quest #3,A:
Guardians of Galaxy 3.00
Ann.#5 RLm,Ret.o/Defenders #3 2.50
Ann.#6 RLm(c),I:Legacy,w/card 3.75
GNv The Enslavers,KP 16.95
GNv Homecoming,
A:Moondragon 12.95
TPB Rebirth of Thanos,reprints
#34-38 12.95

SILVER SURFER
Epic
December, 1988

1 Moebius,V:Galactus 3.00
2 Moebius,V:Galactus 3.00
Graphic Novel 14.95

SILVER SURFER THE ENSLAVERS

1 KP 16.95

SILVER SURFER VS. DRACULA

1 rep,MWn(s),GC,TP 1.75

SILVER SURFER/ WARLOCK: RESURRECTION

1 JSn,V:Mephisto,Death 3.50
2 JSn,TA,V:Death 3.00
3 JSn,TA,V:Mephisto 3.00
4 JSn,TA,V:Mephisto 3.00

SISTERHOOD OF STEEL
Epic
December, 1984

1 I:Sisterhood 2.00
2 2.00
3 2.00
4 thru 8 @1.50

SIX FROM SIRIUS
Epic
July, 1984

1 PG,limited series 3.00
2 PG 2.00
3 PG 2.00
4 PG 2.00

SIX FROM SIRIUS II
Epic
February, 1986

1 PG 1.75

SIX-GUN WESTERN
Atlas
January, 1957

1 JSe(c),RC,JR,'Kid Yukon
Gunslinger' 85.00
2 SSh,AW,DAy,JO,'His Guns
Hang Low' 65.00
3 AW,BP,DAy 65.00
4 JSe(c),JR,GWb 40.00

SKULL, THE SLAYER
August, 1975

1 GK(c),O:Skull the Slayer 2.50
2 GK(c),'Man Against Gods' 1.50
3 'Trapped in the Tower
of Time' 1.50
4 'Peril of the Pyramids',
A:Black Knight 1.50
5 A:Black Knight 1.50
6 'The Savage Sea' 1.50
7 'Dungeon of Blood' 1.50
8 JK(c),November, 1976 1.50

SLAPSTICK

1 TA(i),I:Slapstick 1.50
2 TA(i),A:Spider-Man,V:Overkill 1.25
3 V:Dr.Denton 1.25
4 A:GR,DD,FF,Cap.America 1.25

SLEDGE HAMMER
February, 1988

1 1.25
2 March, 1988 1.00

SLEEPWALKER
June, 1991

1 BBl,I:Rick Sheridan,C:8-Ball 3.50
2 BBl,V:8-Ball 2.50
3 BBl,A:Avengers,X-Men,X-Factor,
FF,I:Cobweb,O:Sleepwalker 2.00
4 RL,I:Bookworm 2.00
5 BBl,A:SpM,K.Pin,V:Ringleader 2.00
6 BBl,A:SpM,Inf.Gauntlet x-over 2.00
7 BBl,Infinity Gauntlet x-over,
V:Chain Gang 2.00
8 BBl,A:Deathlok 1.50
9 BBl,I:Lullabye 1.50
10 BBl,MM,I:Dream-Team 1.50
11 BBl,V:Ghost Rider 1.50
12 JQ,A:Nightmare 2.50
13 BBl,MM,I:Spectra 1.50
14 BBl,MM,V:Spectra 1.50
15 BBl,MM,I:Thought Police 1.50
16 BBl,MM,A:Mr.Fantastic,Thing 1.50
17 BBl,A:Spider-Man,Darkhawk,
V:Brotherhood o/Evil Mutants 1.50
18 JQ(c),Inf.War,A:Prof.X 1.50
19 V:Cobweb,w/pop out Halloween
Mask 2.00
20 V:Chain Gang,Cobweb 1.50
21 V:Hobgoblin 1.50
22 V:Hobgoblin,8-Ball 1.50
23 V:Cobweb,Chain Gang 1.50
24 Mindfield#6 1.50
25 O:Sleepwalker,Holo-grafx(c) 3.50
26 V:Mindspawn 1.50
27 A:Avengers 1.50
28 I:Psyko 1.50
29 DG,V:Psyko 1.50
30 V:Psyko 1.50
31 DG(ci),A:Spectra 1.50
32 V:Psyko 1.50
33 V:Mindspawn,Last issue 1.50
Holiday Spec.#1 JQ(c) 2.25

SLEEZE BROTHERS
August, 1989

1 Private Eyes 1.75
2 thru 6 @1.75

SMURFS
December, 1982

1 1.00
2 1.00
3 1.00
Treasury Edition 2.50

SOLARMAN
January, 1989

1 JM 1.25
2 MZ/NR,A:Dr.Doom, May, 1990 1.25

SOLO AVENGERS
December, 1987

1 MBr,JRu,JLe,AW,Hawkeye; Mockingbird 6.00
2 MBr,JRu,KD,BMc,Hawkeye; Capt.Marvel 1.50
3 MBr,JRu,BH,SDr,Hawkeye; Moon Knight 1.50
4 RLm,JRu,PR,BL,Hawkeye; Black Knight 2.00
5 MBr,JRu,JRy,Hawkeye; Scarlet Witch 1.50
6 MBr,JRu,TGr,Hawkeye;Falcon . 1.25
7 MBr,JG,BL,Hawkeye;Bl.Widow . 1.25
8 MBr,Hawkeye;Dr.Pym 1.25
9 MBr,JBr,SDr,Hawkeye;Hellcat . 1.25
10 MBr,LW,Hawkeye;Dr.Druid . . . 1.25
11 MBr,JG,BL,Hawkeye;Hercules . 1.00
12 RLm,SDr,Hawkeye; New Yellow Jacket 2.00
13 RLm,JG,Hawkeye;WonderMan 2.00
14 AM,AD,JRu,Hawkeye;She-Hulk 1.00
15 AM,Hawkeye;Wasp 1.00
16 AM,DP,JA,Hawkeye; Moondragon 1.00
17 AM,DH,DC,Hawkeye; Sub-Mariner 1.00
18 RW,DH,Hawkeye;Moondragon 1.00
19 RW,DH,Hawkeye,BlackPanther 1.00
20 RW,DH,Hawkeye;Moondragon 1.00

Becomes:
AVENGERS SPOTLIGHT

SOLOMON KANE
September, 1985

1 F:Solomon Kane 1.50
2 . . . . 1.00
3 BBl,'Blades of the Brotherhood' 1.00
4 MMi 1.00
5 'Hills of the Dead' 1.00
6 . . . . 1.00

SON OF SATAN
December, 1975

1 GK(c),JM,F:Daimon Hellstrom 23.00
2 Demon War,O:Possessor . . . 16.00
3 . . . . 12.00
4 The Faces of Fear 12.00
5 V:Mind Star 12.00
6 A World Gone Mad 12.00
7 Mirror of Judgement 12.00
8 RH,To End in Nightmare February, 1977 . . . . 12.00

SOVIET SUPER SOLDIERS

1 AMe,JS,I:Redmont 4 . . . . 2.00

SPACEMAN
Atlas
September, 1953

1 BEv(c),F:Speed Carter and the Space Sentinals 300.00
2 JMn,'Trapped in Space' . . . 200.00
3 BEv(c),JMn,V:Ice Monster . 150.00
4 JMn 150.00
5 GT 150.00
6 JMn,'The Thing From Outer Space',October, 1954 . . . . 150.00

SPACE SQUADRON
Atlas
June, 1951

1 F:Capt. Jet Dixon,Blast,Dawn, Revere,Rusty Blake 350.00
2 GT(c), ... 300.00
3 'Planet of Madness',GT 200.00
4 . . . . 200.00
5 . . . . 200.00

Becomes:
SPACE WORLDS

6 'Midnight Horror', April, 1952 . . . . 190.00

SPECIAL COLLECTOR'S EDITION
December, 1975

1 Kung-Fu,Iron Fist 6.00

SPECIAL MARVEL EDITION
January, 1971

1 JK,B:Thor,B:Reprints 6.00
2 JK,V:Absorbing Man 5.00
3 JK,'While a Universe Trembles' 5.00
4 JK,'Hammer and the Holocaust', E:Thor 5.00
5 JSe(c),JK,DAy,B:Sgt. Fury . . . 5.00
6 HT(c),DAy,'Death Ray of Dr. Zemo' 4.00
7 DAy,V:Baron Strucker 4.00
8 JSe(c),DAy'On To Okinawa' . . 4.00
9 DAy,'Crackdown of Captain Flint 4.00
10 DAy 4.00
11 JK,DAy,A:Captaim America & Bucky 4.00
12 DAy,V:Baron Strucker 4.00
13 JK/DAy(c),DAy,SD,'Too Small to Fight, Too Young To Die' . . 4.00
14 DAy,E:Reprints,Sgt. Fury 4.00
15 JSn,AM,I:Shang-Chi & Master of Kung Fu,I&O:Nayland Smith, Dr. Petrie 35.00
16 JSn,AM,I&O:Midnight 25.00
KingSz.Ann.#1 A:Iron Fist 7.00

Becomes:
MASTER OF KUNG FU

SPECTACULAR SPIDER-MAN
July, 1968
(magazine)

1 . . . . 65.00
2 V:Green Goblin,Nov.1968 . . 110.00

Space Squadron #4
© Marvel Entertainment Group

SPECTACULAR SPIDER-MAN
December, 1976

Prev: Peter Parker

134 SB,A:Sin-Eater,V:Electro 4.50
135 SB,A:Sin-Eater,V:Electro 3.00
136 SB,D:Sin-Eater,V:Electro 3.00
137 SB,I:Tarantula II 3.00
138 SB,A:Capt.A.,V:TarantulaII . . 3.00
139 SB,O:Tombstone 4.00
140 SB,A:Punisher,V:Tombstone . 5.00
141 SB,A:Punisher,V:Tombstone 11.00
142 SB,A:Punisher,V:Tombstone . 8.00
143 SB,A:Punisher,D:Persuader, I:Lobo Brothers. 8.00
144 SB,V:Boomerang 3.00
145 SB,A:Boomerang 3.00
146 SB,R:Green Goblin 5.00
147 SB,V:Hobgoblin (Demonic Power) 21.00
148 SB,Inferno 3.00
149 SB,V:Carrion II 3.00
150 SB,A:Tombstone,Trial J.Robertson 3.00
151 SB,V:Tombstone 3.00
152 SB,O:Lobo Bros.,A:Punisher, Tombstone 4.00
153 SB,V:Hammerhead,A: Tombstone 2.50
154 SB,V:Lobo Bros.,Puma 2.50
155 SB,V,Tombstone 2.50
156 SB,V:Banjo,A:Tombstone . . . 2.50
157 SB,V:Shocker,Electro, A:Tombstone 2.50
158 SB,Super Spider Spec., I:Cosmic Spider-Man 14.00
159 Cosmic Powers,V:Brothers Grimm 9.00
160 SB,A:Hydro Man,Shocker, Rhino,Dr.Doom 8.00
161 SB,V:Hobgoblin,Hammerhead, Tombstone 3.00
162 SB,V:Hobgoblin,Carrion II . . . 3.00
163 SB,V:Hobgoblin,D:Carrion II . 3.00
164 SB,V:Beetle 2.75
165 SB,SDr,D:Arranger,I:Knight & Fogg 2.50
166 SB,O:Knight & Fogg 2.50
167 SB,D:Knight & Fogg 2.50
168 SB,A:Kingpin,Puma, Avengers 2.50
169 SB,I:Outlaws,A:R.Racer, Prowler,Puma,Sandman 2.50
170 SB,A:Avengers,Outlaws 2.50
171 SB,V:Puma 2.50
172 SB,V:Puma 2.50
173 SB,V:Puma 2.50
174 SB,A:Dr.Octopus 2.50
175 SB,A:Dr.Octopus 2.50
176 SB,I:Karona 2.50
177 SB,V:Karona,A:Mr.Fantastic . 2.50
178 SB,B:Child Within,V:Green Goblin, A:Vermin 3.50
179 SB,V:Green Goblin,Vermin . . 3.00
180 SB,V:Green Goblin,Vermin . . 3.00
181 thru 183 SB,V:Gr.Goblin . . @3.00
184 SB,E:Child Within,V:Green Goblin 3.00
185 SB,A:Frogman,White Rabbit . 2.00
186 SB,B:FuneralArrangements V:Vulture 2.00
187 SB,V:Vulture 2.00
188 SB,E:Funeral Arrangements V:Vulture 2.00
189 SB,30th Ann.,Hologram(c), V:Green Goblin 11.00
189a Gold 2nd printing 3.25
190 SB,V:Rhino,Harry Osborn . . . 2.00
191 thru 193 SB,Eye o/t Puma @1.75
194 SB,Death of Vermin#1 . . . . . 1.75
195 SB,Death of Vermin#2 . . . . . 1.75
195a Dirtbag Spec,w/Dirt#2 tape . 2.50
196 SB,Death of Vermin#3 . . . . . 1.75
197 SB,A:X-Men,V:Prof.Power . . . 1.75
198 SB,A:X-Men,V:Prof.Power . . . 1.75
199 SB,A:X-Men,Green Goblin . . 2.00
200 SB,V:Green Goblin,D:Harry Osborn,Holografx(c) 7.00
201 SB,Total Carnage,V:Carnage, Shriek,A:Black Cat,Venom . . . 1.75

202 SB,Total Carnage#9,A:Venom, V:Carnage 1.75
203 SB,Maximum Carnage#13 . . 1.50
204 SB,A:Tombstone 1.50
205 StG(s),SB,V:Tombstone, A:Black Cat 1.50
206 SB,V:Tombstone 1.50
207 SB,A:The Shroud 1.50
208 SB,A:The Shroud 1.50
209 StB,SB,I:Dead Aim, BU:Black Cat 1.50
210 StB,SB,V:Dead Aim, BU:Black Cat 1.50
211 Pursuit#2,V:Tracer 1.50
212 . . . . 1.50
213 ANo(s),V:Typhiod Mary,w/cel 2.95
213a Newsstand Ed. 1.50
Ann.#8 MBa,RLm,TD,Evolutionary Wars,O:Gwen Stacy Clone . . . 4.00
Ann.#9 DR,MG,DJu,MBa,Atlantis Attacks 4.00
Ann.#10 SLi(c),RB,MM,TM,RA . . . 6.00
Ann.#11 EL(c),RWi,Vib.Vendetta . 2.50
Ann.#12 Hero Killers#2,A:New Warriors,BU:Venom 4.50
Ann.#13 I:Noctune,w/Card 3.25

SPEEDBALL
September, 1988

1 SD,JG,O:Speedball 2.00
2 SD,JG,V:Sticker,Graffiti Gorillas 1.50
3 SD,V:Leaper Logan 1.25
4 SD,DA,Ghost Springdale High . 1.25
5 SD,V:Basher 1.25
6 SD,V:Bug-Eyed Voice 1.25
7 SD,V:Harlequin Hit Man 1.25
8 SD,V:Bonehead Gang 1.25
9 SD,V:Nathan Boder 1.25
10 SD,V:Mutated Pigs,Killer Chickens, last issue 1.25

SPELLBOUND
Atlas
March, 1952

1 'Step into my Coffin' 275.00
2 BEv,RH,'Horror Story', A:Edgar A. Poe 150.00
3 RH(c),OW 125.00
4 RH,Decapitation story 125.00
5 BEv,JM,'Its in the Bag' 125.00
6 BK,'The Man Who Couldn't be Killed' 125.00
7 BEv,JMn,'Don't Close the Door' 100.00
8 BEv(c),RH,JSt,DAy, 'The Operation' 100.00
9 BEv(c),RH,'The Death of Agatha Slurl' 100.00
10 JMn(c),BEv,RH,'The Living Mummy' 100.00
11 'The Empty Coffin' 75.00
12 RH,'My Friend the Ghost' . . . 75.00
13 JM,'The Dead Men' 75.00
14 BEv(c),RH,JMn,'Close Shave' 75.00
15 'Get Out of my Graveyard' . . 75.00
16 RH,BEv,JF,JSt,'Behind the Door' 75.00
17 BEv(c),GC,BK,'Goodbye Forever' 85.00
18 BEv(c),JM 75.00
19 BEv(c),BP,'Witch Doctor' . . . 75.00
20 RH(c),BP 75.00
21 RH(c) 60.00
22 . . . . 60.00
23 . . . . 60.00
24 JMn(c),JR 50.00
25 JO,'Look into my Eyes' 50.00
26 JR,'The Things in the Box' . . 50.00
27 JMn,JR,'Trap in the Mirage' . 50.00
28 BEv 50.00
29 JSe(c),SD 65.00
30 BEv(c) 50.00
31 . . . . 50.00
32 BP,'Almost Human' 50.00
33 AT 50.00
34 June, 1957 . . . . 50.00

SPELLBOUND
January, 1988

1 . . . . 1.50
2 . . . . 1.50
3 . . . . 1.50
4 A:New Mutants 2.00
5 . . . . 1.50
6 double-size 2.25

SPIDER-MAN
August, 1990

1 TM Purple Web(c),V:Lizard, A:Calypso,B:Torment 5.00
1a Silver Web(c) 7.00
1b Bag,Purple Web 10.00
1c Bag,Silver Web 20.00
1d 2nd print,Gold(c) 5.00
1e 2nd print Gold UPC(rare) . . . 40.00
1f Platinum Ed. 250.00
2 TM,V:Lizard,A:Calypso 6.00
3 TM,V:Lizard,A:Calypso 5.00
4 TM,V:Lizard,A:Calypso 5.00

Spider-Man #3

© Marvel Entertainment Group

5 TM,V:Lizard,A:Calypso, E:Torment 5.00
6 TM,A:Ghost Rider,V:Hobgoblin 6.00
7 TM,A:Ghost Rider,V:Hobgoblin 6.00
8 TM,B:Perceptions,A:Wolverine I:Wendigo IV 5.00
9 TM,A:Wolverine,Wendigo 4.00
10 TM,RLd,SW,JLe(i),A:Wolv. . . . 4.00
11 TM,A:Wolverine,Wendigo. 4.00
12 TM,E:Perceptions,A:Wolv.. . . . 4.00
13 TM,V:Morbius,R:Black Cost. . . 6.00
14 TM,V:Morbius,A:Black Cost. . . 5.00
15 EL,A:Beast 3.00
16 TM,RLd,A:X-Force,V:Juggernaut, Black Tom,cont.in X-Force#4 . 3.50
17 RL,AW,A:Thanos,Death 3.50
18 EL,B:Return of the Sinister Six, A:Hulk 3.00
19 EL,A:Hulk,Deathlok 2.50
20 EL,A:Nova 2.50
21 EL,A:Hulk,Deathlok,Solo 2.50
22 EL,A:Ghost Rider,Hulk 2.50
23 EL,E:Return of the Sinister Six, A:Hulk,G.Rider,Deathlok,FF . . 2.50
24 Infinity War,V:Hobgoblin, Demogoblin 2.25
25 CMa,A:Excalibur,V:Arcade . . . 2.25
26 RF,MBa,Hologram(c),30th Anniv. I:New Burglar 5.00
27 MR,Handgun issue 2.25
28 MR,Handgun issue 2.25
29 CMa,Ret.to Mad Dog Ward#1 . 2.25
30 CMa,Ret.to Mad Dog Ward#2 . 2.25
31 CMa,Ret.to Mad Dog Ward#3 . 2.25
32 BMc,A:Punisher,V:Master of Vengeance 2.25
33 BMc,A:Punisher,V:Master of Vengeance. 2.25
34 BMc,A:Punisher,V:Master of Vengeance 2.25
35 TL,Total Carnage#4,V:Carnage, Shriek,A:Venom,Black Cat . . . 2.25
36 TL,Total Carnage#8,V:Carnage, A:Venom,Morbius 2.25
37 TL,Total Carnage#12, V:Carnage 2.00
38 thru 40 KJ,V:Electro 2.00
41 TKa(s),JaL,I:Platoon, A:Iron Fist 2.00
42 TKa(s),JaL,V:Platoon, A:Iron Fist 2.00
43 TKa(s),JaL,V:Platoon, A:Iron Fist 2.00
44 HMe(s),TL,V:Hobgoblin 2.25
45 HMe(s),TL,SHa,Pursuit#1, V:Chameleon 2.00
46 HMe(s),TL,V:Hobgoblin,w/cel . 3.25
46a Newsstand Ed. 1.75
47 TL,SHa,V:Demogoblin 1.95
48 TL,SHa,V:Hobgoblin, D:Demogoblin 1.95
TPB Torment Rep.#1-#5 . . . . . . 12.95

SPIDER-MAN & AMAZING FRIENDS
December, 1981

1 DSp,A:Iceman,I:Firestar 5.50

SPIDER-MAN CLASSICS

1 rep.Amazing Fantasy#15 . . . . . 1.75
2 thru 11 rep.Amaz.SpM#1-#10 @1.75
12 rep.Amaz.SpM#11 . . . . 1.50
13 rep.Amaz.SpM#12 . . . . 1.50
14 rep.Amaz.SpM#13 . . . . 1.50
15 rep.Amaz.SpM#14,w/cel 3.25
15a Newsstand Ed. 1.50

SPIDER-MAN COMICS MAGAZINE
January, 1987

1 . . . . 2.50
2 thru 12 . . . . @1.50
13 1988 . . . . 1.50

SPIDER-MAN: MUTANT AGENDA

0 thru 2 Paste in Book . . . . . . @1.50
3 Paste in Book 1.50

SPIDER-MAN/PUNISHER/ SABERTOOTH: DESIGNER GENES

1 SMc,Foil(c) 9.50

SPIDER-MAN SAGA
November, 1991

1 SLi(c),History from Amazing Fantasy #15-Amaz.SpM#100 . 3.25
2 SLi(c),Amaz.SpM#101-#175 . . 3.25
3 Amaz.SpM#176-#238 . . . . 3.25
4 Amaz.SpM #239-#300 . . . . 3.25

SPIDER-MAN 2099

1 RL,AW,I:Spider-Man 2099 . . . . 6.00
2 RL,AW,O:Spider-Man 2099 . . . 3.50
3 RL,AW,V:Venture 2.50
4 RL,AW,I:Specialist,

A:Doom 2099 2.00
5 RL,AW,V:Specialist 2.00
6 RL,AW,I:New Vulture 2.00
7 RL,AW,Vulture of 2099 1.75
8 RL,AW,V:New Vulture 1.75
9 KJo,V:Alchemax 1.75
10 RL,AW,O:Wellvale Home 1.75
11 RL,AW,V:S.I.E.G.E. 1.75
12 RL,AW,w/poster 1.75
13 RL,AW,V:Thanatos 1.75
14 PDd(s),RL(c),TGb,Downtown 1.75
15 PDd(s),RL,I:Thor 2099, Heimdall 2099 1.75
16 PDd(s),RL,Fall of the Hammer#1 1.75
17 PDd(s),RL,V:Bloodsword 1.75
18 PDd(s),RLm,V:Lyla 1.75
19 PDd(s),RL,w/card 1.75
20 PDd(s),RL,Crash & Burn 1.75
21 V:Gangs 1.50

SPIDER-MAN UNLIMITED

1 RLm,Maximun Carnage#1,I:Shriek, R:Carnage 5.00
2 RLm,Maximum Carnage#14 4.50
3 RLm,O:Doctor Octopus 4.50
4 RLm,V:Mystrerio,Rhino 4.25
5 RLm,A:Human Torch, I:Steel Spider 4.25

SPIDER-MAN VS. DRACULA

1 rep. 1.75

SPIDER-MAN vs. VENOM

1990

1 TM(c) 8.95

SPIDER-MAN vs. WOLVERINE

1990

1 MBr,AW,D:Ned Leeds(the original Hobgoblin),V:Charlie 35.00
1a reprint 5.00

SPIDER-MAN & X-FACTOR: SHADOW GAMES

1 PB,I:Shadowforce 2.25
2 PB,V:Shadowforce 1.95

SPIDER-WOMAN

April, 1978

1 CI,TD,O:Spiderwoman 6.00
2 CI,TD,I:Morgan Le Fey 2.00
3 CI,TD,I:Brother's Grimm 2.00
4 CI,TD,V:Hangman 2.00
5 CI,TD,Nightmares 2.00
6 CI,A:Werewolf By Night 2.00
7 CI,SL,AG,V:Magnus 2.00
8 CI,AG,"Man who would not die" 2.00
9 CI,AG,A:Needle,Magnus 2.00
10 CI,AG,I:Gypsy Moth 2.00
11 CI,AG,V:Brothers Grimm 1.50
12 CI,AG,V:Brothers Grimm 1.50
13 CI,AG,A:Shroud 1.50
14 BSz(c),CI,AG,A:Shroud 1.50
15 BSz(c),CI,AG,A:Shroud 1.50
16 BSz(c),CI,AG,V:Nekra 1.50
17 CI,Deathplunge 1.50
18 CI,A:Flesh 1.50
19 CI,A:Werewolf By Night, V:Enforcer 1.75
20 FS,A:Spider-Man 1.50
21 FS,A:Bounty Hunter 1.50
22 FS,A:Killer Clown 1.50
23 TVE,V:The Gamesmen 1.50
24 TVE,V:The Gamesmen 1.50
25 SL,Two Spiderwomen 1.50
26 JBy(c),SL,V:White Gardenia 1.50
27 BSz(c),JBi,A:Enforcer 1.50
28 BSz(c),SL,A:Enforcer,Spidey 1.50

Sports Action #2

© Marvel Entertainment Group

29 JR2(c),ECh,FS,A:Enforcer, Spider-Man 1.50
30 FM(c),SL,JM,I:Dr.Karl Malus 1.50
31 FM(c),SL,JM,A:Hornet 1.50
32 FM(c),SL,JM,A:Werewolf 1.75
33 SL,V:Yesterday's Villian 1.50
34 SL,AM,V:Hammer and Anvil 1.50
35 SL,AG,V:Angar the Screamer 1.50
36 SL,Spiderwoman Shot 1.50
37 SL,TA,BWi,AM,FS,A:X-Men,I: Siryn,V:Black Tom 3.50
38 SL,BWi,A:X-Men,Siryn 3.00
39 SL,BWi,Shadows 1.50
40 SL,BWi,V:The Flying Tiger 1.50
41 SL,BWi,V:Morgan LeFay 1.50
42 SL,BWi,V:Silver Samurai 1.50
43 SL,V:Silver Samurai 1.50
44 SL,V:Morgan LeFay 1.50
45 SL,Spider-Man Thief Cover 1.50
46 SL,V:Mandroids,A:Kingpin 1.50
47 V:Daddy Longlegs 1.50
48 O:Gypsy Moth 1.50
49 A:Tigra 1.50
50 PH(c),D:Spiderwoman 3.50

[Limited Series]

1 V:Therak 2.00
2 O:Spider-Woman 2.00
3 V:Deathweb 2.00
4 V:Deathweb,Last issue 2.00

SPIDEY SUPER STORIES

October, 1974

1 Younger reader's series in association with the Electric Company,O:Spider-Man 4.00
2 A:Kraven 3.00
3 A:Ringleader 3.00
4 A:Medusa 3.00
5 A:Shocker 3.00
6 A:Iceman 3.00
7 A:Lizard, Vanisher 3.00
8 A:Dr. Octopus 3.00
9 A:Dr. Doom 3.00
10 A:Green Goblin 3.25
11 A:Dr. Octopus 3.00
12 A:The Cat,V:The Owl 3.00
13 A:Falcon 3.00
14 A:Shanna 3.00
15 A:Storm 3.25
16 2.50
17 A:Captain America 2.50
18 A:Kingpin 2.50
19 A:Silver Surfer,Dr. Doom 3.25
20 A;Human Torch,Invisible Girl 2.50
21 A:Dr. Octopus 2.50
22 A:Ms. Marvel,The Beetle 2.50
23 A:Green Goblin 3.00
24 A:Thundra 2.50
25 A:Dr. Doom 2.50
26 A:Sandman 2.50
27 A:Thor,Loki 2.50
28 A:Medusa 2.50
29 A:Kingpin 2.50
30 A:Kang 2.50
31 A:Moondragon,Dr. Doom 2.50
32 A:Spider-Woman,Dr. Octopus 2.50
33 2.50
34 A:Sub-Mariner 2.50
35 2.50
36 A:Lizard 2.50
37 A:White Tiger 2.50
38 A:Fantastic Four 2.50
39 A:Hellcat,Thanos 6.00
40 A:Hawkeye 2.00
41 A:Nova,Dr. Octopus 2.00
42 A:Kingpin 2.00
43 A:Daredevil,Ringmaster 2.00
44 A:Vision 2.00
45 A:Silver Surfer,Dr. Doom 3.25
46 A:Mysterio 2.00
47 A:Spider-Woman,Stilt-Man 2.00
48 A:Green Goblin 2.25
49 Spidey for President 2.00
50 A:She-Hulk 2.00
51 2.00
52 2.00
53 A:Dr. Doom 2.00
54 'Attack of the Bird-Man' 2.00
55 A:Kingpin 2.00
56 A:Captain Britain, Jack O'Lantern 3.00
57 March, 1982 2.00

SPITFIRE AND THE TROUBLESHOOTERS

October, 1986

1 HT/JSt 1.00
2 HT 1.00
3 HT,Macs Armor 1.00
4 TM/BMc(Early TM work) 5.00
5 HT/TD,A:StarBrand 1.00
6 HT,Trial 1.00
7 HT 1.00
8 HT,New Armor 1.00
9 1.00

Becomes:

CODE NAME: SPITFIRE

10 MR/TD 1.00
11 1.00
12 1.00
13 1.00

SPOOF

October, 1970

1 MSe 3.00
2 MSe,'Brawl in the Family' 2.00
3 MSe,Richard Nixon cover 2.00
4 MSe,'Blechhula' 2.00
5 MSe,May, 1973 4.00

SPORT STARS

November, 1949

1 The Life of Knute Rockne 200.00

Becomes:

SPORTS ACTION

2 BP(c),The Life of George Gipp 200.00
3 BEv,Hack Wilson 125.00
4 Art Houtteman 100.00
5 Nile Kinnick 100.00
6 Warren Gun 100.00
7 Jim Konstanty 100.00
8 Ralph Kiner 100.00
9 Ed "Strangler" Lewis 100.00

10 JMn,'The Yella-Belly' 100.00
11 'The Killers' 100.00
12 'Man Behind the Mask' 125.00
13 Lew Andrews 125.00
14 MWs,Ken Roper,
September, 1952 .... 100.00

SPOTLIGHT
September, 1978

1 F:Huckleberry Hound, Yogi Bear 1.25
2 Quick Draw McDraw 1.00
3 The Jetsons 1.00
4 Magilla Gorilla, March, 1979 .. 1.00

SPY CASES
See: KID KOMICS

SPY FIGHTERS
March, 1951

1 GT 100.00
2 GT 50.00
3 .... 40.00
4 thru 13 .... @35.00
14 thru 15 July, 1953 ...... @40.00

SPYKE
Epic

1 BR,I:Spyke 2.75
2 V:Conita 2.75
3 thru 4 BR .... @1.95

SPY THRILLERS
Atlas
November, 1954

1 'The Tickling Death' 75.00
2 V:Communists 40.00
3 .... 30.00
4 .... 30.00

Becomes:

POLICE BADGE

5 September, 1955 .... 30.00

SQUADRON SUPREME
September, 1985

1 BH,L:Nighthawk 3.00
2 BH,F:Nuke,A:Scarlet Centurion 2.00
3 BH,D:Nuke 2.00
4 BH,L:Archer 1.50
5 BH,L:Amphibian 1.50
6 PR,J:Institute of Evil 1.50
7 JB,JG,V:Hyperion 1.50
8 BH,V:Hyperion 1.50
9 BSz(c),PR,D:Tom Thumb 1.50
10 PR,V:Quagmire 1.50
11 PR,V:Redeemers 1.50
12 PR,D:Nighthawk,Foxfire,
Black Archer 2.00

STALKERS
Epic
April, 1990

1 MT 1.50
2 MT 1.50
3 MT 1.50
4 MT 1.50
5 MT 1.50
6 VM,MT 1.50
7 VM,MT 1.50
8 VM,MT 1.50
9 VM 1.50
10 VM 1.50
11 VM 1.50
12 VM, 1991 .... 1.50

STARBLAST

1 MGu(s),HT,After the Starbrand . 2.25
2 MGu(s),HT,After the Starbrand . 2.00
3 MGu(s),HT,After the Starbrand . 2.00
4 MGu(s),HT,Final Issue 2.00

STARBRAND
October, 1986

1 JR2,O:Starbrand 1.50
2 JR2/AW 1.00
3 JR2/AW 1.00
4 JR2/AW 1.00
5 JR2/AW 1.00
6 JR2/AW 1.00
7 JR2/AW 1.00
8 JR2/AW 1.00
9 KG/BWi,A:Nightmask 1.00
10 .... 1.00
11 JR2,TP 1.00
12 JR2,TP,X-Men X-over 1.25
13 JR2,TP 1.25
14 JR2,TP 1.25
15 & 16 .... @1.25
17 JBy,TP,New Starbrand 1.50
18 JBy/TP 1.50
19 JBy/TP 1.50
Ann.#1 .... 1.25

STAR COMICS MAGAZINE
December, 1986
(digest size)

1 F:Heathcliff,Muppet Babies,
Ewoks 1.50
2 thru 13 1988 .... @1.50

STAR-LORD, SPECIAL EDITION
February, 1982

1 JBy reprints 6.00

STARRIORS
August, 1984

1 .... 1.50
2 .... 1.25
3 .... 1.25
4 February, 1982 .... 1.25

STARSTRUCK
March, 1985

1 MK 2.00
2 MK 1.75
3 thru 8 MK, Feb. 1986 ..... @1.50

STAR TREK
April, 1980

1 DC,KJ,rep.1st movie Adapt .. 6.00
2 DC,KJ,rep.1st movie Adapt ... 5.00
3 DC,KJ,rep.1st movie Adapt ... 4.00
4 DC,KJ,The Weirdest Voyage .. 4.00
5 DC,KJ,Dr.McCoy..Killer 4.00
6 DC,KJ,A:Ambassador Phlu ... 4.00
7 MN,KJ,Kirk/Spock(c) 4.00
8 DC(p),F:Spock 4.00
9 DC,FS,Trapped in a Web of
Ghostly Vengeance 4.00
10 KJ(i),Spock the Barbarian 4.00
11 TP(i),Like A Woman Scorned . 4.00
12 TP(i),Trapped in a Starship
Gone Mad 4.00
13 TP(i),A:Barbara McCoy 4.00
14 LM,GD,We Are Dying,
Egypt,Dying 4.00
15 GK,The Quality of Mercy 4.00
16 LM,There's no Space
like Gnomes 4.00
17 EH,TP,The Long Nights Dawn 4.00
18 A Thousand Deaths,last iss .. 4.00

STAR WARS
July, 1977

1 HC,30 Cent,movie adaption. . 22.00
1a HC,35 Cent(square Box). . . 340.00
2 HC,movie adaptation 10.00
3 HC,movie adaptation 10.00
4 HC,SL,movie adapt.(low dist.) 13.00
5 HC,SL,movie adaptation 10.00
6 HC,DSt,E:movie adaption ... 10.00

Star Trek #16
© Marvel Entertainment Group

7 HC,FS,F:Luke&Chewbacca ... 7.00
8 HC,TD,Eight against a World .. 7.00
9 HC,TP,V:Cloud Riders 7.00
10 HC,TP,Behemoth fr.Below ... 7.00
11 CI,TP,Fate o/Luke Skywalker . 5.00
12 TA,CI,Doomworld 5.00
13 TA,JBy,CI,Deadly Reunion ... 5.00
14 TA,CI 5.00
15 CI,V:Crimson Jack 5.00
16 WS,V:The Hunter 5.00
17 Crucible, Low Dist. 6.00
18 CI,Empire Strikes(Low Dist). . . 6.00
19 CI,Ultimate Gamble(Low Dist) . 6.00
20 CI,Death Game(Scarce) 6.00
21 TA,CI,Shadow of a Dark
Lord(Scarce) 6.00
22 CI,Han Solo vs.Chewbacca ... 5.00
23 CI,Flight Into Fury 5.00
24 CI,Ben Kenobi Story 5.00
25 CI,Siege at Yavin 5.00
26 CI,Doom Mission 4.00
27 CI,V:The Hunter 4.00
28 CI,Cavern o/t Crawling Death . 4.00
29 CI,Dark Encounter 4.00
30 CI,A Princess Alone 4.00
31 CI,Return to Tatooine 4.00
32 CI,The Jawa Express 4.00
33 CI,GD,V:Baron Tagge 4.00
34 CI,Thunder in the Stars 4.00
35 CI,V:Darth Vader 4.00
36 CI,V:Darth Vader 4.00
37 CI,V:Darth Vader 4.00
38 TA,MG,Riders in the Void 4.00
39 AW,B:Empire Strikes Back ... 6.00
40 AW,Battleground Hoth 5.00
41 AW,Imperial Pursuit 5.00
42 AW,Bounty Hunters 5.00
43 AW,Betrayal at Bespin 5.00
44 AW,E:Empire Strikes Back ... 5.00
45 CI,GD,Death Probe 4.00
46 DI,TP,V:Dreamnaut Devourer . 4.00
47 CI,GD,Droid World 4.00
48 CI,Leia vs.Darth Vader 4.00
49 SW,TP,The Last Jedi 4.00
50 WS,AW,TP,G-Size issue 5.00
51 WS,TP,Resurrection of Evil ... 3.00
52 WS,TP 3.00
53 CI,WS 3.00
54 CI,WS 3.00
55 thru 66 WS,TP .... @3.00
67 TP 3.00

68 GD,TP 3.00
69 GD,TP 3.00
70 A:Han Solo 3.00
71 A:Han Solo 2.50
72 . . . . 2.50
73 Secret of Planet Lansbane . . . 2.50
74 thru 91 . . . . @2.50
92 BSz(c) 2.50
93 thru 97 . . . . @2.50
98 AW 2.50
99 . . . . 2.50
100 Painted(c),double-size 3.50
101 BSz 2.50
102 KRo's Back 2.50
103 thru 106 . . . . @2.50
107 WPo(i),last issue 3.00
Ann.#1 WS(c),V:Winged Warlords 5.00
Ann.#2 RN 4.00
Ann.#3 RN,Darth Vader(c) 4.00

STEELGRIP STARKEY

Epic
July, 1986

1 . . . . 1.75
2 . . . . 1.75
3 . . . . 1.75
4 . . . . 1.75
5 . . . . 1.75
6 June, 1987 . . . . 1.75

STEELTOWN ROCKERS

April, 1990

1 SL 1.50
2 SL 1.50
3 SL 1.50
4 SL 1.50
5 SL 1.50
6 SL,September, 1990 . . . . 1.50

STRANGE COMBAT TALES

1 thru 2 . . . . 2.75
3 Tiger by the Tail 2.50
4 Midnight Crusade 2.50

STRANGE STORIES OF SUSPENSE

See: RUGGED ACTION

STRANGE TALES

June, 1951
[1st Regular Series]

1 'The Room' 1,600.00
2 'Trapped In A Tomb' 600.00
3 JMn,'Man Who Never Was' 450.00
4 BEv,'Terror in the Morgue' . 500.00
5 'A Room Without A Door' . . 500.00
6 RH(c),'The Ugly Man' 300.00
7 'Who Stands Alone' 300.00
8 BEv(c),'Something in the Fog' 300.00
9 'Drink Deep Vampire' 300.00
10 BK,'Hidden Head' 300.00
11 BEv(c),GC,'O'Malley's Friend' 200.00
12 'Graveyard At Midnight' . . . 200.00
13 BEv(c),'Death Makes A Deal' 200.00
14 GT,'Horrible Herman' 200.00
15 BK,'Don't Look Down' 200.00
16 Decapitation cover 200.00
17 DBr,JRo,'Death Feud' 200.00
18 'Witch Hunt' 200.00
19 RH(c),'The Rag Doll' 200.00
20 RH(c),GC,SMo,'Lost World' . 200.00
21 BEv 150.00
22 BK,JF 150.00
23 'The Strangest Tale in the World' 150.00
24 'The Thing in the Coffin' . . . 150.00
25 . . . . 150.00
26 . . . . 150.00
27 JF,'The Garden of Death' . . 150.00
28 'Come into my Coffin' 150.00
29 'Witch-Craft' 150.00

Strange Tales #106
© Marvel Entertainment Group

Strange Tales #41
© Marvel Entertainment Group

30 'The Thing in the Box' 150.00
31 'The Man Who Played with Blocks' 150.00
32 . . . . 150.00
33 JMn(c),'Step Lively Please' . 150.00
34 'Flesh and Blood' 125.00
35 'The Man in the Bottle' 125.00
36 . . . . 125.00
37 'Out of the Storm' 125.00
38 . . . . 125.00
39 'Karnoff's Plan' 125.00
40 BEv,'The Man Who Caught a Mermaid' 125.00
41 BEv,'Riddle of the Skull' . . . 135.00
42 DW,BEv,JMn,'Faceless One' 135.00
43 JF,'The Mysterious Machine' 125.00
44 . . . . 125.00
45 JKa,'Land of the Vanishing Men' 135.00
46 thru 57 . . . . @90.00
58 AW 100.00
59 BK 125.00
60 . . . . 85.00
61 BK 125.00
62 . . . . 85.00
63 . . . . 125.00
64 AW 100.00
65 . . . . 85.00
66 . . . . 85.00
67 thru 78 . . . . @100.00
79 SD,JK,Dr.Strange Prototype 105.00
80 thru 83 SD,JK . . . . @90.00
84 SD,JK,Magneto Prototype . . 125.00
85 SD,JK 100.00
86 SD,JK,'I Who Created Mechano' 100.00
87 SD,JK,'Return of Grogg' . . . 100.00
88 SD,JK,'Zzutak' 100.00
89 SD,JK,'Fin Fang Foom' 275.00
90 SD,JK,'Orrgo the Unconquerable' 90.00
91 SD,JK,'The Sacrifice' 90.00
92 SD,JK,'The Thing That Waits For Me' 90.00
93 SD,JK,'The Wax People' 90.00
94 SD,JK,'Pildorr the Plunderer' . 90.00
95 SD,JK,'Two-Headed Thing' . . 90.00
96 SD,JK,'I Dream of Doom' . . . 90.00
97 SD,JK,'When A Planet Dies' 250.00
98 SD,JK,'No Human Can Beat Me' 100.00
99 SD,JK,'Mister Morgan's Monster' 100.00
100 SD,JK,'I Was Trapped in the Crazy Maze' 100.00
101 B:StL(s),SD,JK, B:Human Torch 600.00
102 SD,JK,I:Wizard 250.00
103 SD,JK,I:Zemu 200.00
104 SD,JK,I:The Trapster 200.00
105 SD,JK,V:Wizard 200.00
106 SD,A:Fantastic Four 120.00
107 SD,V:Sub-Mariner 145.00
108 SD,JK,A:FF,I:The Painter . 120.00
109 SD,JK,I:Sorcerer 120.00
110 SD,I&B:Dr.Strange, Nightmare 700.00
111 SD,I:Asbestos, Baron Mordo 200.00
112 SD,I:The Eel 80.00
113 SD,I:Plant Man 80.00
114 SD,JK,A:Captain America . 200.00
115 SD,O:Dr.Strange 290.00
116 SD,V:Thing 65.00
117 SD,V:The Eel 55.00
118 SD,V:The Wizard 55.00
119 SD,C:Spider-Man 75.00
120 SD,1st Iceman/Torch T.U. . . 60.00
121 SD,V:Plantman 40.00
122 SD,V:Dr.Doom 35.00
123 SD,A:Thor,I:Beetle 35.00
124 SD,I:Zota 35.00
125 SD,V:Sub-Mariner 35.00
126 SD,I:Dormammu,Clea 45.00
127 SD,V:Dormammu 32.00
128 SD,I:Demon 30.00
129 SD,I:Tiboro 30.00
130 SD,C:Beatles 35.00
131 SD,I:Dr.Vega 30.00
132 SD,I:Orini 30.00
133 SD,I:Shazana 30.00
134 SD,E:Torch,I:Merlin 30.00
135 SD,JK:I:Shield & Hydra B:Nick Fury 60.00
136 SD,JK,V:Dormammu 20.00
137 SD,JK,A:Ancient One 22.00
138 SD,JK,I:Eternity 22.00
139 SD,JK,V:Dormammu 20.00
140 SD,JK,V:Dormammu 20.00
141 SD,JK,I:Fixer,Mentallo 23.00
142 SD,JK,I:THEM,V:Hydra 20.00
143 SD,JK,V:Hydra 20.00

Strange Tales #81

© Marvel Entertainment Group

144 SD,JK,V:Druid,I:Jasper Sitwell 20.00
145 SD,JK,I:Mr.Rasputin 20.00
146 SD,JK,V:Dormammu,I:AIM . 20.00
147 BEv,JK,F:Wong 20.00
148 BEv,JK,O:Ancient One 27.00
149 BEv,JK,V:Kaluu 20.00
150 BEv,JK,JB(1st Marvel Art) I:Baron Strucker,Umar 20.00
151 JK,JSo(1st Marvel Art), I:Umar 35.00
152 BEv,JK,JSo,V:Umar 18.00
153 JK,JSo,MSe,V:Hydra 18.00
154 JSo,MSe,I:Dreadnought . . . 18.00
155 JSo,MSe,A:L.B.Johnson . . . 18.00
156 JSo,MSe,I:Zom 18.00
157 JSo,MSe,A:Zom,C:Living Tribunal 18.00
158 JSo,MSe,A:Zom,I:Living Tribunal(full story) 19.00
159 JSo,MSe,O:Nick Fury,A:Capt. America,I:Val Fontaine 30.00
160 JSo,MSe,A:Captain America I:Jimmy Woo. 20.00
161 JSo,I:Yellow Claw 20.00
162 JSo,DA,A:Captain America. . 18.00
163 JSo,DA,V:Yellow Claw 18.00
164 JSo,DA,V:Yellow Claw 18.00
165 JSo,DA,V:Yellow Claw 18.00
166 DA,GT,JSo,A:AncientOne . . 18.00
167 JSo,DA,V:Doctor Doom . . . 30.00
168 JSo,DA,E:Doctor Strange,Nick Fury,V:Yandroth 18.00
169 JSo,I&O:Brother Voodoo 5.00
170 JSo,O:Brother Voodoo 5.00
171 GC,V:Baron Samed 4.00
172 GC,DG,V:Dark Lord 4.00
173 GC,DG,I:Black Talon 4.00
174 JB,JM,O:Golem 4.00
175 SD,R:Torr 4.00
176 F:Golem 4.00
177 FB,F:Golem 4.00
178 JSn,B&O:Warlock,I:Magus . 26.00
179 JSn,I:Pip,I&D:Capt.Autolycus 20.00
180 JSn,I:Gamora,Kray-tor 20.00
181 JSn,E:Warlock 20.00
182 SD,GK,rep Str.Tales #123,124 . . . . 3.00
183 SD,rep Str.Tales #130,131 . . 3.00
184 SD,rep Str.Tales #132,133 . . 3.00
185 SD,rep Str.Tales #134,135 . . 3.00
186 SD,rep Str.Tales #136,137 . . 3.00
187 SD,rep Str.Tales #138,139 . . 3.00
188 SD,rep Str.Tales #140,141 . . 3.00
Ann.#1 V:Grottu,Diablo 260.00
Ann.#2 A:Spider-Man 300.00

[2nd Regular Series]

1 BBl,CW,B:Cloak&Dagger,Dr. Strange,V:Lord of Light 1.50
2 BBl,CW,V:Lord of Light,Demon 1.25
3 BBl,AW,CW,A:Nightmare,Khat . 1.25
4 BBl,CW,V:Nightmare 1.25
5 BBl,V:Rodent,A:Defenders 1.25
6 BBl,BWi,V:Erlik Khan, A:Defenders 1.25
7 V:Nightmare,A:Defenders 1.25
8 BBl,BWi,V:Kaluu 1.25
9 BBl,BWi,A:Dazzler,I:Mr.Jip, V:Kaluu 1.25
10 BBl,BWi,RCa,A:Black Cat, V:Mr.Jip,Kaluu 1.25
11 RCa,BWi,V:Mr.Jip,Kaluu 1.25
12 WPo,BWi,A:Punisher,V:Mr.Jip . 2.50
13 JBr,BWi,RCa,Punisher, Power Pack 2.00
14 JBr,BWi,RCa,Punisher,P.Pack 2.00
15 RCa,BMc,A:Mayhem 1.25
16 RCa,BWi,V:Mr.Jip 1.25
17 RCa,BWi,V:Night 1.25
18 RCa,KN,A:X-Factor',V:Night . . 1.50
19 MMi(c),EL,TA,RCa,A:Thing . . . 1.25

STRANGE TALES OF THE UNUSUAL

December, 1955

1 JMn(c),BP,DH,JR,'Man Lost' 175.00
2 BEv,'Man Afraid' 85.00
3 AW,'The Invaders' 100.00
4 'The Long Wait' 60.00
5 RC,SD,'The Threat' 80.00
6 BEv 65.00
7 JK,JO 75.00
8 . . . . 65.00
9 BEv(c),BK 75.00
10 GM,AT 60.00
11 BEv(c),August, 1957 . . . . 60.00

STRANGE WORLDS

December, 1958

1 JK,SD 350.00
2 SD 200.00
3 JK 150.00
4 AW 150.00
5 SD 125.00

STRAWBERRY SHORTCAKE

Star

June, 1985

1 . . . . 1.25
2 . . . . 1.00
3 . . . . 1.00
4 . . . . 1.00
5 . . . . 1.00
6 . . . . 1.00
7 April, 1986 . . . . 1.00

STRAY TOASTERS

Epic

January, 1988

1 BSz 5.00
2 BSz 4.50
3 BSz 4.00
4 BSz,End mini-series 4.00

STRIKEFORCE MORITURI

December, 1986

1 BA,SW,WPo(1st pencils- 3 pages),I:Blackwatch 3.25
2 BA,SW,V:The Horde 1.50
3 BA,SW,V:The Horde 1.50
4 BA,SW,WPo,V:The Horde 2.00
5 BA,SW,V:The Horde 1.50
6 BA,SW,V:The Horde 1.25
7 BA,SW,V:The Horde 1.25
8 BA,SW,V:The Horde 1.25
9 BA,SW,V:THe Horde 1.25
10 WPo,(1st pencils-full story), SW,R:Black Watch,O:Horde . . 4.00
11 BA,SW,V:The Horde 1.25
12 BA,SW,D:Jelene 1.25
13 BA,SW,Old V:NewTeam 1.25
14 BA,AW,V:The Horde 1.25
15 BA,AW,V:The Horde 1.25
16 WPo,SW,V:The Horde 3.00
17 WPo(c),SW,V:The Horde 1.25
18 BA,SW,V:Hammersmith 1.25
19 BA,SW,V:THe Horde,D:Pilar . . 1.25
20 BA,SW,V:The Horde 1.25
21 MMi(c),TD(i),V:The Horde 1.25
22 TD(i),V:The Horde 1.25
23 MBa,VM,V:The Horde 1.50
24 VM(i),I:Vax,V:The Horde 1.75
25 TD(i),V:The Horde 1.75
26 MBa,VM,V:The Horde 1.75
27 MBa,VM,O:MorituriMaster 1.75
28 MBa,V:The Tiger 1.75
29 MBa,V:Zakir Shastri 1.75
30 MBa,V:Andre Lamont,The Wind 1.75
31 MBa(c),V:The Wind,last issue . 1.75

STRYFE'S STRIKE FILE

1 LSn,NKu,GCa,BP,C:Siena Blaze,Holocaust 4.00
1a 2nd Printing 1.75

Sub-Mariner #69

© Marvel Entertainment Group

SUB-MARINER

May, 1968

1 JB,O:Sub-Mariner 150.00
2 JB,A:Triton 48.00
3 JB,A:Triton 25.00
4 JB,V:Attuma 25.00
5 JB,I&O:Tiger Shark 30.00
6 JB,DA,V:Tiger Shark 25.00
7 JB,I:Ikthon 25.00
8 JB,V:Thing 28.00
9 MSe,DA,A:Lady Dorma 25.00
10 GC,DA,O:Lemuria 25.00
11 GC,V:Capt.Barracuda 17.00
12 MSe,I:Lyna 17.00
13 MSe,JS,A:Lady Dorma 17.00
14 MSe,V:Fake Human Torch . . 36.00
15 MSe,V:Dragon Man 17.00

16 MSe,I:Nekaret,Thakos 12.00
17 MSe,I:Stalker,Kormok 12.00
18 MSe,A:Triton 12.00
19 MSe,I:Stingray 14.00
20 JB,V:Dr.Doom 12.00
21 MSe,D:Lord Seth 12.00
22 MSe,A:Dr.Strange 12.00
23 MSe,I:Orka 9.00
24 JB,JM,V:Tiger Shark 9.00
25 SB,JM,O:Atlantis 9.00
26 SB,A:Red Raven 9.00
27 SB,I:Commander Kraken ... 10.00
28 SB,V:Brutivae 9.00
29 SB,V:Hercules 8.00
30 SB,A:Captain Marvel 10.00
31 SB,A:Triton 8.00
32 SB,JM,I&O:Llyra 8.00
33 SB,JM,I:Namora 9.00
34 SB,JM,AK,1st Defenders ... 18.00
35 SB,JM,A:Silver Surfer 17.00
36 BWr,SB,W:Lady Dorma 9.00
37 RA,D:Lady Dorma 8.00
38 RA,JSe,O:Rec,I:Thakorr,Fen .. 8.00
39 RA,JM,V:Llyra 8.00
40 GC,I:Turalla,A:Spidey 10.00
41 GT,V:Rock 6.00
42 GT,JM,V:House Named Death 6.00
43 GC,V:Tunal 6.00
44 MSe,JM,V:Human Torch 7.00
45 MSe,JM,V:Tiger Shark 6.00
46 GC,D:Namor's Father 6.00
47 GC,A:Stingray,V:Dr.Doom 6.00
48 GC,V:Dr.Doom 6.00

Sub-Mariner #40

© Marvel Entertainment Group

49 GC,V:Dr.Doom 6.00
50 BEv,I:Namorita 9.00
51 BEv,O:Namorita,C:Namora ... 7.00
52 GK,V:Sunfire 6.00
53 BEv,V:Sunfire 6.00
54 BEv,AW,V:Sunfire,I:Lorvex ... 6.00
55 BEv,V:Torg 6.00
56 DA,I:Coral 6.00
57 BEv,I:Venus 6.00
58 BEv,I:Tamara 6.00
59 BEv,V:Tamara 6.00
60 BEv,V:Tamara 6.00
61 BEv,JM,V:Dr.Hydro 6.00
62 HC,JSt,I:Tales of Atlantis. 6.00
63 HC,JSt,V:Dr.Hydro,I:Arkus ... 6.00
64 HC,JSe,I:Maddox 6.00
65 DH,DP,V:She-Devil,inc.BEv
Eulogy Pin-up 6.00
66 DH,V:Orka,I:Raman 6.00
67 DH,A:FF,V:Triton,N:Namor
I&O:Force 6.00
68 DH,O:Force 6.00
69 GT,V:Spider-Man 7.00
70 GT,I:Piranha 6.00
71 GT,V:Piranha 6.00
72 DA,V:Slime/Thing 6.00

[Limited Series]

1 RB,BMc,Namor's Birth 2.50
2 RB,BMc,Namor Kills Humans .. 2.00
3 RB,BMc,V:Surface Dwellers ... 2.00
4 RB,BMc,V:Human Torch 2.00
5 RB,BMc,A:Invaders 2.00
6 RB,BMc,V:Destiny 2.00
7 RB,BMc,A:Fantastic Four 2.00
8 RB,BMc,A:Hulk,Avengers 2.00
9 RB,BMc,A:X-Men,Magneto 2.00
10 RB,BMc,V:Thing 2.00
11 RB,BMc,A:Namorita,
Defenders 2.00
12 RB,BMc,A:Dr.Doom,
AlphaFlight 2.00

(SAGA OF THE) SUB-MARINER

[Mini-Series]

November, 1988

1 RB,BMc,Namor's Birth 2.50
2 RB,BMc,Namor Kills Humans . 1.50
3 RB,BMc,V:Surface Dwellers ... 1.50
4 RB,BMc,V:Human Torch 1.50
5 RB,BMc,A:Invaders 1.50
6 RB,BMc,V:Destiny 1.50
7 RB,BMc,A:Fantastic Four 1.50
8 RB,BMc,A:Hulk,Avengers 1.50
9 RB,BMc,A:X-Men,Magneto ... 2.00
10 RB,BMc,V:Thing 1.50
11 RB,BMc,A:Namorita,Defenders 1.50
12 RB,BMc,A:Dr.Doom,Alp.Flight . 1.50

SUB-MARINER COMICS

Timely

Spring, 1941

1 ASh(c),BEv,PGn,B:Sub-
Mariner, The Angel 8,000.00
2 ASh(c),BEv,Nazi
Submarine (c) 2,200.00
3 ASh(c),BEv 1,600.00
4 ASh(c),BEv,BW 1,300.00
5 .... 1,000.00
6 ASh(c) 750.00
7 .... 750.00
8 ASh(c) 750.00
9 ASh(c),BW 750.00
10 ASh(c) 750.00
11 ASh(c) 500.00
12 ASh(c) 500.00
13 ASh(c) 500.00
14 ASh(c) 500.00
15 ASh(c) 500.00
16 ASh(c) 500.00
17 ASh(c) 500.00
18 ASh(c) 500.00
19 .... 500.00
20 ASh(c) 500.00
21 SSh(c),BEv 400.00
22 SSh(c),BEv 400.00
23 SSh(c),BEv 400.00
24 MSy(c),BEv,A:Namora,
bondage cover 400.00
25 MSy(c),HK,B:The Blonde
Phantom, A:Namora,
bondage(c) 500.00
26 BEv,A:Namora 400.00
27 DRi(c),BEv,A:Namora 400.00
28 DRi(c),BEv,A:Namora 400.00
29 BEv,A:Namora,Human Torch 400.00
30 DRi(c),BEv,'Slaves Under
the Sea' 400.00
31 BEv,'The Man Who Grew',
A:Capt. America,E:Blonde
Phantom 400.00
32 BEv,O:Sub-Mariner 800.00
33 BEv,O:Sub-Mariner,A:Human
Torch,B:Namora 400.00
34 BEv,A:Human Torch,bondage
cover 350.00
35 BEv,A:Human Torch 350.00
36 BEv 350.00
37 JMn(c),BEv 350.00
38 SSh(c),BEv,JMn 400.00
39 JMn(c),BEv 350.00
40 JMn(c),BEv 350.00
41 JMn(c),BEv 350.00
42 BEv,October, 1955 .... 400.00

SUBURBAN JERSEY NINJA SHE-DEVILS

1 I:Ninja She-Devils 1.50

SUPERNATURAL THRILLERS

December, 1972

1 JSo(c),JSe,FrG,IT! 1.50
2 VM,DA,The Invisible Man 1.50
3 GK,The Valley of the Worm .. 1.25
4 Dr. Jekyll and Mr. Hyde 1.25
5 RB,The Living Mummy 1.25
6 GT,JA,The Headless Horseman 1.25
7 VM,B:The Living Mummy,'
Back From The Tomb' 1.25
8 VM,'He Stalks Two Worlds' .. 1.25
9 GK/AM(c),VM,DA,'Pyramid of
the Watery Doom' 1.25
10 VM,'A Choice of Dooms' 1.25
11 VM,'When Strikes the ASP' ... 1.25
12 VM,KJ,'The War That Shook
the World' 1.25
13 VM,DGr,'The Tomb of the
Stalking Dead' 1.25
14 VM,AMc,'All These Deadly
Pawns' 1.25
15 TS, E:The Living Mummy,'Night
of Armageddon',October, 1975 1.25

SUPER SOLDIERS

1 I:Super Soldier,A:USAgent 2.75
2 A:USAgent 2.00
3 A:USAgent 2.00
4 A:USAgent,Avengers 2.00
5 A:Captain America,AWC 2.00
6 O:Super Soldiers 2.00
7 in Savage Land 2.00

SUPER-VILLAIN CLASSICS

May, 1983

1 O:Galactus 3.50

SUPER-VILLAIN TEAM-UP

August, 1975

1 GT/BEv(c),B:Dr.Doom/Sub-
Mariner,A:Attuma,Tiger Shark 6.00
2 SB,A:Tiger Shark, Attuma 4.00
3 EH(c),JA,V:Attuma 4.00
4 HT,JM,Dr.Doom vs. Namor ... 4.00
5 RB/JSt(c),HT,DP,A:Fantastic
Four,I:Shroud 4.00
6 HT,JA,A:Shroud,Fantastic Four 3.00
7 RB/KJ(c),HT,O:Shroud 3.00
8 KG,V:Ringmaster 3.00
9 ST,A:Avengers,Iron Man 3.00
10 BH,DP,A:Capt.America,
V:Attuma,Red Skull 3.00
11 DC/JSt(c),BH,DP,B:Dr. Doom,
Red Skull,A:Capt. America ... 3.00
12 DC/AM(c),BH,DP,Dr.Doom vs.
Red Skull 3.00
13 KG,DP,Namor vs. Krang 3.00
14 JBy/TA(c),BH,DP,V:Magneto,
X-over with Champions #15 .. 5.00
15 GT,ME,A:Red Skull 3.00
16 CI,A:Dr. Doom 3.00
17 KP(c),Red Skull Vs.Hatemonger

All comics prices listed are for *Near Mint* condition.

June 1976 . . . . 3.00
Giant#1 F:Namor, Dr.Doom 3.00
Giant#2 F:Namor, Dr.Doom 3.00

SUSPENSE
Atlas
December, 1949

1 BP,Ph(c),Sidney Greenstreet/ Peter Lorne (Maltese Falcon) 275.00
2 Ph(c),Dennis O'Keefe/Gale Storm (Abandoned) 150.00
3 B:Horror stories,'The Black Pit' 150.00
4 'Thing In Black' 100.00
5 BEv,GT,RH,BK,DBr,'Hangman's House' 110.00
6 BEv,GT,PAM,RH,'Madness of Scott Mannion' 100.00
7 DBr,GT,DR,'Murder' 100.00
8 GC,DRi,RH,'Don't Open the Door' 100.00
9 GC,DRi,'Back From The Dead'100.00
10 JMn(c),WIP,RH,'Trapped In Time' 100.00
11 MSy,'The Suitcase' 85.00
12 GT,'Dark Road' 85.00
13 JMn(c),'Strange Man', bondage cover 85.00
14 RH,'Death And Doctor Parker' 85.00
15 JMn(c),OW,'The Machine' . . . 85.00
16 OW,'Horror Backstage' 85.00
17 'Night Of Terror' 85.00
18 BK,'The Cozy Coffin' 100.00
19 BEv,RH 85.00
20 . . . . 85.00
21 BEv(c) 85.00
22 BEv(c),BK,OW 85.00
23 BEv 85.00
24 RH,GT 100.00
25 'I Died At Midnight' 100.00
26 BEv(c) 75.00
27 DBr 80.00
28 BEv 65.00
29 JMn,BF,JRo,April, 1953 . . . . 65.00

SWORDS OF THE SWASHBUCKLERS

1 JG,Adult theme 2.25
2 JG 1.75
3 JG 1.75
4 JG 1.50
5 JG 1.50
6 JG 1.50
7 JG 1.50
8 . . . . 1.50
9 . . . . 1.50
10 . . . . 1.50
11 . . . . 1.50
12 June, 1987 . . . . 1.50

TALE OF THE MARINES
See: DEVIL-DOG DUGAN

TALES OF ASGARD
October, 1968

1 . . . . 35.00
Vol.2 #1 Feb,1984 . . . . 2.00

TALES OF G.I. JOE
January, 1988

1 reprints,#1 . . . . 2.00
2 #2 . . . . 1.50
3 #3 . . . . 1.50
4 #4 . . . . 1.50
5 #5 . . . . 1.50
6 #6 . . . . 1.50
7 rep. #7 - #16 . . . . 1.50

TALES OF JUSTICE
See: JUSTICE COMICS

TALES OF SUSPENSE
January, 1959

1 DH(c),AW,'The Unknown Emptiness' 1,100.00
2 SK,'Robot in Hiding' 500.00
3 SD,JK,'The Aliens Who Captured Earth' 400.00
4 JK,AW,'One Of Us Is A Martian' 450.00
5 JF,'Trapped in the Tunnel To Nowhere' 275.00
6 JK(c),'Howl in the Swamp' . 275.00
7 SD,JK,'The Molten Man-Thing'275.00
8 BEv,'Monstro' 275.00
9 JK(c),JF,'Diablo' 275.00
10 RH,'I Bought Cyclops Back To Life' 275.00
11 JK(c),'I Created Sporr' 200.00
12 RC,'Gorkill The Living Demon'200.00
13 'Elektro' 200.00
14 JK(c),'I Created Colossus' . . 200.00
15 JK/DAy(c),'Behold...Goom' . 200.00
16 JK/DAy(c),'The Thing Called Metallo' 250.00
17 JK/DAy(c),'Goo Gam, Son of Goom' 200.00
18 JK/DAy(c),'Kraa the Inhuman' 200.00
19 JK,DAy,SD,'The Green Thing' 200.00
20 JK,DAy,SD,'Colossus Lives Again' 200.00
21 JK/DAy(c),SD,'This Is Klagg' 150.00
22 JK/DAy(c),SD,'Beware Of Bruttu' 150.00
23 JK,DAy,SD,'The Creature in the Black Bog' 150.00
24 JK,DAy,SD,'Insect Man' . . . 150.00
25 JK,DAy,SD,'The Death of Monstrollo' 150.00
26 JK,DAy,SD,'The Thing That Crawled By Night' 150.00
27 JK,DAy,SD,'When Oog Lives Again' 150.00
28 JK,DAy,SD,'Back From the Dead' 150.00
29 JK,DAy,SD,DH,'The Martian Who Stole A City' 125.00
30 JK,DAy,SD,DH,'The Haunted Roller Coaster' 125.00
31 JK,DAy,SD,DH,'The Monster in the Iron Mask' 125.00
32 JK,DAy,SD,DH,'The Man in the Bee-Hive' 125.00
33 JK,DAy,SD,DH,'Chamber of Fear' 125.00
34 JK,DAy,SD,DH,'Inside The Blue Glass Bottle' 125.00
35 JK,DAy,SD,DH,'The Challenge of Zarkorr' 125.00
36 SD,'Meet Mr. Meek' 125.00
37 DH,SD,'Hagg' 125.00
38 'The Teenager who ruled the World 125.00
39 JK,O&I:Iron Man 2,700.00
39a rep.#39,Marvel Milestone . . . 2.95
40 JK,C:Iron Man 1,100.00
41 JK 475.00
42 DH,SD,I:Red Pharoah 230.00
43 JK,DH,I:Kala,A:Iron Man . . . 230.00
44 DH,SD,V:Mad Pharoah 230.00
45 DH,V:Jack Frost 230.00
46 DH,CR,I:Crimson Dynamo . 130.00
47 SD,V:Melter 130.00
48 SD,N:Iron Man 175.00
49 SD,A:Angel 110.00
50 DH,I:Manderin 80.00
51 DH,I:Scarecrow 70.00
52 DH,I:Black Widow 105.00
53 DH,O:Watcher 80.00
54 DH,V:Mandarin 50.00
55 DH,V:Mandarin 50.00
56 DH,I:Unicorn 50.00
57 DH,I&O:Hawkeye 120.00
58 DH,B:Captain America 190.00
59 DH,1st S.A. Solo Captain America, I:Jarvis 210.00
60 DH,JK,V:Assassins 80.00
61 DH,JK,V:Mandarin 50.00
62 DH,JK,O:Mandarin 50.00
63 JK,O:Captain America 140.00
64 DH,JK,A:Black Widow, Hawkeye 50.00
65 DH,JK,I:Red Skull 80.00
66 DH,JK,O:Red Skull 78.00
67 DH,JK,V:Adolph Hitler 35.00
68 DH,JK,V:Red Skull 35.00
69 DH,JK,I:Titanium Man 37.00
70 DH,JK,V:Titanium Man 35.00
71 DH,JK,WW,V:Titanium Man . 32.00
72 DH,JK,V:The Sleeper 32.00
73 JK,GT,A:Black Knight 32.00
74 JK,GT,V:The Sleeper 32.00
75 JK,I:Batroc,Sharon Carter . . . 35.00
76 JR,V:Mandarin 32.00
77 JK,JR,V:Ultimo,I:Peggy Carter 32.00
78 GC,JK,V:Ultimo 32.00
79 GC,JK,V:Red Skull, I:Cosmic Cube 45.00
80 GC,JK,V:Red Skull 50.00
81 GC,JK,V:Red Skull 37.00
82 GC,JK,V:The Adaptoid 37.00
83 GC,JK,V:The Adaptoid 37.00
84 GC,JK,V:Mandarin 37.00
85 GC,JK,V:Batroc 37.00
86 GC,JK,V:Mandarin 37.00
87 GC,V:Mole Man 37.00
88 JK,GC,V:Power Man 37.00
89 JK,GC,V:Red Skull 37.00
90 JK,GC,V:Red Skull 37.00
91 GC,JK,V:Crusher 37.00
92 GC,JK,A:Nick Fury 37.00
93 GC,JK,V:Titanium Man 37.00
94 GC,JK,I:Modok 39.00
95 GC,JK,V:Grey Gargoyle,IR:Cap. America 37.00
96 GC,JK,V:Grey Gargoyle 37.00
97 GC,JK,I:Whiplash, A:Black Panther 37.00
98 GC,JK,I:Whitney Frost A:Black Panther 37.00
99 GC,JK,A:Black Panther 60.00

Becomes:
CAPTAIN AMERICA

TALES OF THE ZOMBIE
August, 1973
(black & white magazine)

1 Reprint Menace #5,O:Zombie 18.00
2 GC,GT 10.00
3 . . . . 10.00
4 'Live and Let Die' 10.00
5 BH 10.00
6 . . . . 10.00
7 thru 9 AA . . . . @10.00
10 March, 1975 . . . . 10.00

TALES TO ASTONISH
[1st Series]
January, 1959

1 JDa,'Ninth Wonder o/t World'1,000.00
2 SD,'Capture A Martian' 500.00
3 SD,JK,'The Giant From Outer Space' 350.00
4 SD,JK,'The Day The Martians Struck' 350.00
5 SD,AW,'The Things on Easter Island' 350.00
6 SD,JK,'Invasion of the Stone Men' 300.00
7 SD,JK,'The Thing on Bald Mountain' 250.00
8 SD,JK,'Mummex, King of the Mummies' 250.00
9 JK(c),SD,'Droom, the Living Lizard' 250.00
10 JK,SD,'Titano' 250.00
11 JK,SD,'Monstrom, the Dweller in the Black Swamp' 200.00

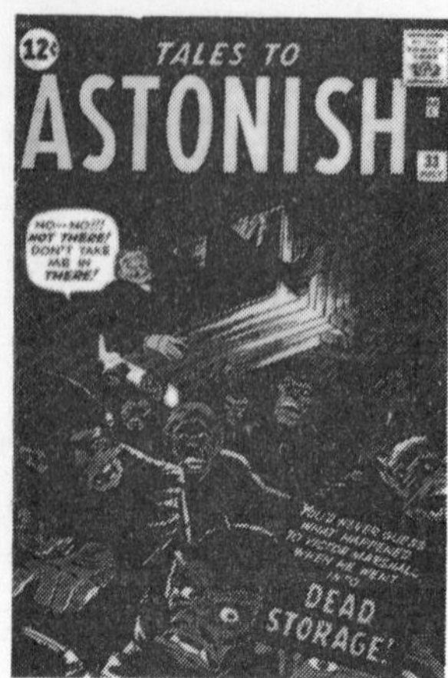

Tales to Astonish #33
© Marvel Entertainment Group

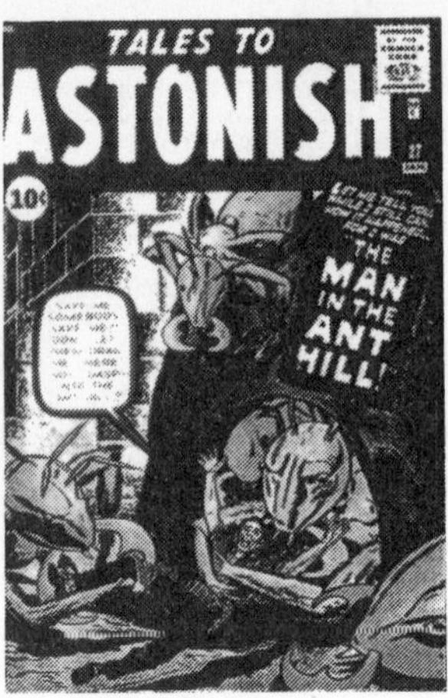

Tales to Astonish #27
© Marvel Entertainment Group

Tales to Astonish #51
© Marvel Entertainment Group

12 JK/DAy(c),SD,'Gorgilla' 200.00
13 JK,SD,'Groot, the Monster From Planet X' 200.00
14 JK,SD,'Krang' 200.00
15 JK/DAy,'The Blip' 200.00
16 JK,SD,'Thorr' 200.00
17 JK,SD,'Vandoom' 200.00
18 JK,SD,'Gorgilla Strikes Again' 200.00
19 JK,SD,'Rommbu' 200.00
20 JK,SD,'X, The Thing That Lived' 200.00
21 JK,SD,'Trull the Inhuman' . . 150.00
22 JK,SD,'The Crawling Creature' 150.00
23 JK,SD,'Moomba is Here' . . . 150.00
24 JK,SD,'The Abominable Snowman' 150.00
25 JK,SD,'The Creature From Krogarr' 150.00
26 JK,SD,'Four-Armed Things' . 150.00
27 StL(s),SD,JK,I:Antman . . . 2,500.00
28 JK,SD,I Am the Gorilla Man 125.00
29 JK,SD,When the Space Beasts Attack 125.00
30 JK,SD,Thing From the Hidden Swamp 125.00
31 JK,SD,The Mummy's Secret 125.00
32 JK,SD,Quicksand 125.00
33 JK,SD,Dead Storage 125.00
34 JK,SD,Monster at Window . 125.00
35 StL(s),JK,SD, B:Ant Man(2nd App.) 1,200.00
36 JK,SD,V:Comrade X 450.00
37 JK,SD,V:The Protector 225.00
38 JK,SD,Betrayed By t/nts . . . 225.00
39 JK,DH,V:Scarlet Beetle 225.00
40 JK,SD,DH,The Day Ant-Man Failed 225.00
41 DH,St,SD,V:Kulla 150.00
42 DH,JSe,SD,Voice of Doom . 150.00
43 DH,SD,Master of Time 150.00
44 JK,SD,I&O:Wasp 175.00
45 DH,SD,V:Egghead 125.00
46 DH,SD,I:Cyclops(robot) 125.00
47 DH,SD,V:Trago 125.00
48 DH,SD,I:Porcupine 125.00
49 JK,DH,AM,Ant-Man Becomes Giant-Man 150.00
50 JK,SD,I&O:Human Top 75.00
51 JK,V:Human Top 75.00
52 I&O:Black Knight 75.00
53 DH,V:Porcupine 75.00
54 DH,I:El Toro 75.00
55 V:Human Top 75.00
56 V:The Magician 75.00
57 A:Spider-Man 100.00
58 V:Colossus(not X-Men one) . 75.00
59 V:Hulk,Black Knight 100.00
60 SD,B:Hulk,Giant Man 200.00
61 SD,I:Glenn Talbot, V:Egghead 100.00
62 I:Leader,N:Wasp 100.00
63 SD,O:Leader(1st full story) . 100.00
64 SD,V:Leader 100.00
65 DH,SD,N:Giant-Man,. 100.00
66 JK,SD,V:Leader,Chameleon . 75.00
67 JK,SD,I:Kanga Khan 75.00
68 JK,N:Human Top,V:Leader . . 75.00
69 JK,V:Human Top,Leader, E:Giant-Man 75.00

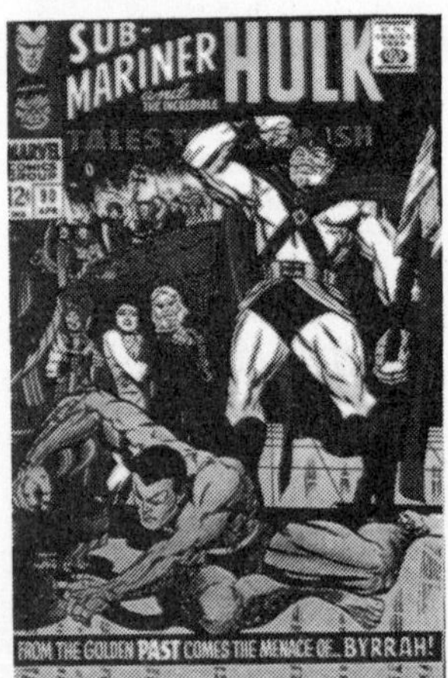

Tales to Astonish #90
© Marvel Entertainment Group

70 JK,B:Sub-Mariner/Hulk,I: Neptune 80.00
71 JK,V:Leader,I:Vashti 56.00
72 JK,V:Leader 56.00
73 JK,V:Leader,A:Watcher 56.00
74 JK,V:Leader,A:Watcher 56.00
75 JK,A:Watcher 56.00
76 JK,Atlantis 56.00
77 JK,V:Executioner 56.00
78 GC,JK,Prince and the Puppet 56.00
79 JK,Hulk vs.Hercules 56.00
80 GC,JK,Moleman vs Tyrannus 56.00
81 GC,JK,I:Boomerang,Secret Empire, Moleman vs Tyrannus 56.00
82 GC,JK,V:Iron Man 60.00
83 JK,V:Boomerang 50.00
84 GC,JK,Like a Beast at Bay . . 50.00
85 GC,JB,Missile & the Monster 50.00
86 JB,V:Warlord Krang 50.00
87 BEv,IR:Hulk 50.00
88 BEv,GK,V:Boomerang 50.00
89 BEv,GK,V:Stranger 50.00
90 JK,I:Abomination 50.00
91 BEv,DA,V:Abomination 50.00
92 MSe,C:Silver Surfer x-over . 62.00
93 MSe,Silver Surver x-over . . . 60.00
94 BEv,MSe,V:Dragorr,High Evolutionary. 50.00
95 BEv,MSe,V:High Evolutionary 50.00
96 MSe,Skull Island,High Evol. . 50.00
97 MSe,C:Kazar,X-Men 55.00
98 DA,MSe,I:Legion of the Living Lightning,I:Seth 50.00
99 DA,MSe,V:Legion of the Living Lighting 50.00
100 MSe,DA,Hulk v.SubMariner . 60.00
101 MSe,GC,V:Loki 70.00

Becomes: INCREDIBLE HULK

TALES TO ASTONISH
[2nd Series]
December, 1979

1 JB,rep.Sub-Mariner#1 . . . . 1.75
2 JB,rep.Sub-Mariner#2 . . . . 1.25
3 JB,rep.Sub-Mariner#3 . . . . 1.25
4 JB,rep.Sub-Mariner#4 . . . . 1.25
5 JB,rep.Sub-Mariner#5 . . . . 1.25
6 JB,rep.Sub-Mariner#6 . . . . 1.25
7 JB,rep.Sub-Mariner#7 . . . . 1.25
8 JB,rep.Sub-Mariner#8 . . . . 1.25
9 JB,rep.Sub-Mariner#9 . . . . 1.25

 All comics prices listed are for *Near Mint* condition.

Tales to Astonish #94
© Marvel Entertainment Group

10 JB,rep.Sub-Mariner#10 . . . . . . 1.25
11 JB,rep.Sub-Mariner#11 . . . . . . 1.25
12 JB,rep.Sub-Mariner#12 . . . . . . 1.25
13 JB,rep.Sub-Mariner#13 . . . . . . 1.25
14 JB,rep.Sub-Mariner#14 . . . . . . 1.25

TARZAN
June, 1977

1 JB,Edgar Rice Burroughs Adapt 1.50
2 JB,O:Tarzan 1.25
3 JB,'The Alter of the Flaming God',I:LA 1.25
4 JB,TD,V:Leopards 1.25
5 JB,TD,'Vengeance',A:LA 1.25
6 JB,TD,'Rage of Tantor,A:LA . . 1.25
7 JB,TD,'Tarzan Rescues The Moon' 1.00
8 JB,'Battle For The Jewel Of Opar' 1.00
9 JB,'Histah, the Serpent' 1.00
10 JB,'The Deadly Peril of Jane Clayton' 1.00
11 JB 1.00
12 JB,'Fangs of Death' 1.00
13 JB,'Lion-God' 1.00
14 JB,'The Fury of Fang and Claw' 1.00
15 JB,'Sword of the Slaver' 1.00
16 JB,'Death Rides the Jungle Winds' 1.00
17 JB,'The Entrance to the Earths Core' 1.00
18 JB,'Corsairs of the Earths Core' 1.00
19 'Pursuit' 1.00
20 'Blood Bond' 1.00
21 'Dark and Bloody Sky' 1.00
22 JM,RN,'War In Pellucidar' 1.00
23 'To the Death' 1.00
24 'The Jungle Lord Returns' 1.00
25 RB(c),V:Poachers 1.00
26 RB(c),'Caged' 1.00
27 RB(c),'Chaos in the Caberet' . . 1.00
28 'A Savage Against A City' 1.00
29 October, 1979 . . . . 1.00
Ann.#1 JB 1.50
Ann.#2 'Drums of the Death-Dancers' 1.25
Ann.#3 'Ant-Men and the She-Devils 1.25

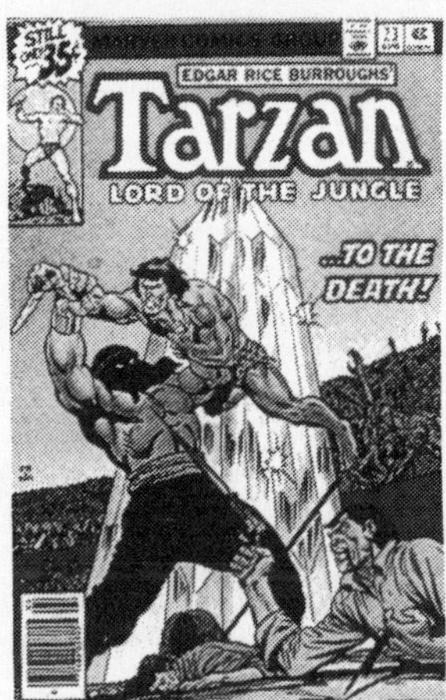

Tarzan #23
© Marvel Entertainment Group

TARZAN OF THE APES
July, 1984

1 (movie adapt.) 1.25
2 . . . . 1.25

TEAM AMERICA
June, 1982

1 O:Team America 2.50
2 V:Marauder 1.25
3 LMc,V:Mr.Mayhem 1.25
4 Lmc,V:Arcade Assassins 1.25
5 A:Marauder 1.25
6 A:R.U. Ready 1.25
7 LMc,V:Emperor of Texas 1.25
8 DP,V:Hydra 1.25
9 A:Iron Man 1.25
10 V:Minister Ashe 1.00
11 A:Marauder,V:GhostRider 5.50
12 DP,Marauder unmasked, May, 1983 . . . . 2.50

TEAM HELIX

1 A:Wolverine 2.00
2 A:Wolverine 2.00

TEEN COMICS
See: ALL WINNERS COMICS

TEENAGE ROMANCE
See: MY ROMANCE

TERMINATOR 2
September, 1991

1 KJ,movie adaption 1.25
2 KJ,movie adaption 1.25
3 KJ,movie adaption 1.25
Terminator II (bookshelf format) . . 4.95
Terminator II (B&W mag. size) . . . 2.25

TERRARISTS
Epic

1 thru 4 w/card 2.50

TERROR INC.

1 JZ,I:Hellfire 3.00
2 JZ,I:Bezeel,Hellfire 2.50
3 JZ,A:Hellfire 2.00
4 JZ,A:Hellfire,V:Barbatos 2.00
5 JZ,V:Hellfire,A:Dr Strange 2.00
6 JZ,MT,A:Punisher 2.00
7 JZ,V:Punisher 2.00
8 Christmas issue 2.00
9 JZ,V:Wolverine 2.25
10 V:Wolverine 2.25
11 A:Silver Sable,Cage 2.00
12 For Love Nor Money#4,A:Cage, Silver Sable 2.00
13 Inf.Crusade,A:Gh.Rider 2.00

TESSIE THE TYPIST
Timely
Summer, 1944

1 BW,'Doc Rockblock' 265.00
2 BW,'Powerhouse Pepper' . . 175.00
3 Football cover 50.00
4 BW 100.00
5 BW 100.00
6 BW,HK,'Hey Look' 100.00
7 BW 100.00
8 BW 100.00
9 BW,HK,'Powerhouse Pepper' 125.00
10 BW,A:Rusty 125.00
11 BW,A:Rusty 125.00
12 BW,HK 125.00
13 BW,A:Millie The Model,Rusty 110.00
14 BW 80.00
15 HK,A:Millie,Rusty 80.00
16 HK 55.00
17 HK,A:Millie, Rusty 55.00
18 HK 55.00
19 Annie Oakley story 45.00
20 . . . . 40.00
21 A:Lana, Millie 40.00
22 . . . . 40.00
23 . . . . 40.00

Becomes:

TINY TESSIE

24 . . . . 35.00

Becomes:

REAL EXPERIENCES

25 Ph(c),January, 1950 . . . . 25.00

TEXAS KID
Atlas
January, 1951

1 GT,JMn,O:Texas Kid 100.00
2 JMn 50.00
3 JMn,'Man Who Didn't Exist' . 35.00
4 JMn 35.00
5 JMn 35.00
6 JMn 35.00
7 JMn 35.00
8 JMn 35.00
9 JMn 35.00
10 JMn,July, 1952 . . . . 35.00

TEX DAWSON, GUNSLINGER
January, 1973

1 JSo(c) 2.00

Becomes:

GUNSLINGER

2 . . . . 1.25
3 June, 1973 . . . . 1.25

TEX MORGAN
August, 1948

1 . . . . 125.00
2 'Boot Hill Welcome For A Bad Man' 75.00
3 . . . . 60.00
4 'Trapped in the Outlaws Den', A:Arizona Annie 60.00
5 'Valley of Missing Cowboys' . 60.00
6 'Never Say Murder', A:Tex Taylor 60.00
7 CCB,Ph(c),'Captain Tootsie', A:Tex Taylor 70.00
8 Ph(c),'Terror Of Rimrock Valley', A:Diablo 70.00

9 Ph(c),'Death to Tex Taylor' February, 1950 .... 70.00

TEX TAYLOR
September, 1948

1 'Boot Hill Showdown' 125.00
2 'When Two-Gun Terror Rides the Range' 75.00
3 'Thundering Hooves and Blazing Guns' 70.00
4 Ph(c),'Draw or Die Cowpoke' 75.00
5 Ph(c),'The Juggler of Yellow Valley',A:Blaze Carson 75.00
6 Ph(c),'Mystery of Howling Gap' 70.00
7 Ph(c),'Trapped in Times' Lost Land',A:Diablo 95.00
8 Ph(c),'The Mystery of Devil-Tree Plateau',A:Diablo 95.00
9 Ph(c),'Guns Along the Border', A:Nimo,March, 1950 ...... 95.00

THANOS QUEST
1990

1 JSn,RLm,V:Elders, for Soul Gems 20.00
1a 2nd printing 5.50
2 JSn,RLm,O:SoulGems,I: Infinity Gauntlet (story cont.in SilverSurfer #44) 16.00
2a 2nd printing 5.50

THING, THE
July, 1983

1 JBy,O:Thing 2.50
2 JBy,Woman from past 1.50
3 JBy,A:Inhumans 1.25
4 JBy,A:Lockjaw 1.25
5 JBy,A:Spider-Man,She-Hulk ... 1.50
6 JBy,V:Puppet Master 1.25
7 JBy,V:Goody Two Shoes 1.25
8 JBy,V:Egyptian Curse 1.25
9 JBy,F:Alicia Masters 1.25
10 JBy,Secret Wars 1.25

Thing #27
© Marvel Entertainment Group

11 JBy,B:Rocky Grimm 1.25
12 JBy,F:Rocky Grimm 1.25
13 JBy,F:Rocky Grimm 1.25
14 F:Rocky Grimm 1.25
15 F:Rocky Grimm 1.25
16 F:Rocky Grimm 1.25
17 F:Rocky Grimm 1.25
18 F:Rocky Grimm 1.25
19 F:Rocky Grimm 1.25
20 F:Rocky Grimm 1.25
21 V:Ultron 1.25
22 V:Ultron 1.25
23 R:Thing to Earth,A:Fant.Four . 1.25
24 V:Rhino,A:Miracle Man 1.25
25 V:Shamrock 1.25
26 A:Vance Astro 1.50
27 I:Sharon Ventura 1.25
28 A:Vance Astro 1.25
29 A:Vance Astro 1.25
30 Secret Wars II,A:Vance Astro . 1.25
31 A:Vance Astro 1.25
32 A:Vance Astro 1.25
33 A:Vance Astro,I:NewGrapplers 1.25
34 V:Titania,Sphinx 1.25
35 I:New Ms.Marvel,PowerBroker 1.25
36 Last Issue,A:She-Hulk 1.25

[Mini-Series]

1 rep.Marvel Two-in-One #50 ... 1.75
2 rep Marvel Two-in-One,V:GR .. 1.75
3 rep Marvel Two-in-One #51 ... 1.25
4 rep Marvel Two-in-One #43 ... 1.25

THOR, THE MIGHTY
Prev: Journey Into Mystery
March, 1966

126 JK,V:Hercules 86.00
127 JK,I:Pluto,Volla 40.00
128 JK,V:Pluto,A:Hercules 40.00
129 JK,V:Pluto,I:Ares 40.00
130 JK,V:Pluto,A:Hercules 40.00
131 JK,I:Colonizers 40.00
132 JK,A:Colonizers,I:Ego 40.00
133 JK,A:Colonizers,A:Ego 40.00
134 JK,I:High Evolutionary, Man-Beast 50.00
135 JK,O:High Evolutionary 45.00
136 JK,F:Odin 40.00
137 JK,I:Ulik 45.00
138 JK,V:Ulik,A:Sif 40.00
139 JK,V:Ulik 40.00
140 JK,V:Growing Man 40.00
141 JK,V:Replicus 28.00
142 JK,V:Super Skrull 28.00
143 JK,BEv,V:Talisman 28.00
144 JK,V:Talisman 28.00
145 JK,V:Ringmaster 28.00
146 JK,O:Inhumans Part 1 .... 30.00
147 JK,O:Inhumans Part 2 .... 30.00

The Mighty Thor #148
© Marvel Entertainment Group

148 JK,I:Wrecker,O:Black Bolt .. 30.00
149 JK,O:Black Bolt,Medusa ... 28.00
150 JK,A:Triton 28.00
151 JK,V:Destroyer 28.00
152 JK,V:Destroyer 28.00
153 JK,F:Dr.Blake 28.00
154 JK,I:Mangog 28.00
155 JK,V:Mangog 28.00
156 JK,V:Mangog 28.00
157 JK,D:Mangog 28.00
158 JK,O:Don Blake Part 1 .... 60.00
159 JK,O:Don Blake Part 2 .... 28.00
160 JK,I:Travrians 28.00
161 JK,Shall a God Prevail 23.00
162 JK,O:Galactus 35.00
163 JK,I:Mutates,A:Pluto 23.00
164 JK,A:Pluto,V:Greek Gods .. 23.00
165 JK,V:Him/Warlock 45.00
166 JK,V:Him/Warlock 40.00
167 JK,F:Sif 23.00
168 JK,O:Galactus 35.00
169 JK,O:Galactus 35.00
170 JK,BEv,V:Thermal Man 21.00
171 JK,BEv,V:Wrecker 21.00
172 JK,BEv,V:Ulik 21.00
173 JK,BEv,V:Ulik,Ringmaster .. 21.00
174 JK,BEv,V:Crypto-Man 21.00
175 JK,Fall of Asgard,V:Surtur .. 21.00
176 JK,V:Surtur 21.00
177 JK,I:Igon,V:Surtur 21.00
178 JK,C:Silver Surfer 24.00
179 JK,MSe,C:Galactus 21.00
180 NA,JSi,V:Loki 15.00
181 NA,JSi,V:Loki 15.00
182 JB,V:Dr.Doom 7.50
183 JB,V:Dr.Doom 7.50
184 JB,I:The Guardian 7.50
185 JB,JSt,V:Silent One 7.50
186 JB,JSt,V:Hela 7.50
187 JB,JSt,V:Odin 7.50
188 JB,JM,F:Odin 7.50
189 JB,JSt,V:Hela 7.50
190 JB,I:Durok 7.50
191 JB,JSt,V:Loki 7.50
192 JB 7.50
193 JB,SB,V:Silver Surfer 50.00
194 JB,SB,V:Loki 7.50
195 JB,JR,V:Mangog 7.50
196 JB,NR,V:Kartag 7.50
197 JB,V:Mangog 7.50
198 JB,V:Pluto 7.50
199 JB,V:Pluto,Hela 7.50
200 JB,Ragnarok 10.00
201 JB,JM,Odin resurrected. 6.00
202 JB,V:Ego-Prime 6.00
203 JB,V:Ego-Prime 6.00
204 JB,JM,Demon from t/Depths . 6.00
205 JB,V:Mephisto 6.00
206 JB,V:Absorbing Man 5.00
207 JB,V:Absorbing Man 5.00
208 JB,V:Mercurio 5.00
209 JB,I:Druid 5.00
210 JB,DP,I:Ulla,V:Ulik 5.00
211 JB,DP,V:Ulik 4.00
212 JB,JSt,V:Sssthgar 4.00
213 JB,DP,I:Gregor 4.00
214 SB,JM,V:Dark Nebula 4.00
215 JB,JM,J:Xorr 4.00
216 JB,JM,V:4D-Man 4.00
217 JB,SB,I:Krista,V:Odin 4.00
218 JB,JM,A:Colonizers 4.00
219 JB,I:Protector 4.00
220 JB,V:Avalon 4.00
221 JB,V:Olympus 4.00
222 JB,JSe,A:Hercules,V:Pluto .. 4.00
223 JB,A:Hercules,V:Pluto 4.00
224 JB,V:Destroyer 4.00
225 JB,JSi,I:Fire Lord 10.00
226 JB,A:Watcher,Galactus 4.00
227 JB,JSi,V:Ego 4.00
228 JB,JSi,A:Galactus,D:Ego 4.00
229 JB,JSi,A:Hercules,I:Dweller .. 4.00
230 JB,A:Hercules 4.00
231 JB,DG,V:Armak 4.00
232 JB,JSi,A:Firelord 4.00

The Mighty Thor
© Marvel Entertainment Group

233 JB,Asgard Invades Earth . . . 4.00
234 JB,V:Loki 4.00
235 JB,JSi,I:Possessor
(Kamo Tharnn) 4.00
236 JB,JSi,V:Absorbing Man 3.50
237 JB,JSi,V:Ulik 3.50
238 JB,JSi,V:Ulik 3.50
239 JB,JSi,V:Ulik 3.50
240 SB,KJ,V:Seth 3.50
241 JB,JGi,I:Geb 3.50
242 JB,JSi,V:Servitor 3.50
243 JB,JSt,V:Servitor 3.50
244 JB,JSt,V:Servitor 3.50
245 JB,JSt,V:Servitor 3.50
246 JB,JSt,A:Firelord 3.50
247 JB,JSt,A:Firelord 3.50
248 JB,V:Storm Giant 3.50
249 JB,V:Odin 3.50
250 JB,D:Igron,V:Mangog 3.50
251 JB,A:Sif 3.50
252 JB,V:Ulik 3.50
253 JB,I:Trogg 3.50
254 JK,O:Dr.Blake rep 3.50
255 Stone Men of Saturn Rep. . . 3.50
256 JB,I:Sporr 3.50
257 JK,JB,I:Fee-Lon 3.50
258 JK,JB,V:Grey Gargoyle 3.50
259 JB,A:Spider-Man 4.00
260 WS,I:Doomsday Star 4.00
261 WS,I:Soul Survivors 3.00
262 WS,Odin Found,I:Odin Force 3.00
263 WS,V:Loki 3.00
264 WS,V:Loki 3.00
265 WS,V:Destroyer 3.00
266 WS,Odin Quest 3.00
267 WS,F:Odin 3.00
268 WS,V:Damocles 3.00
269 WS,V:Stilt-Man 3.00
270 WS,V:Blastaar 3.00
271 Avengers,Iron Man x-over . . 3.00
272 JB,Day the Thunder Failed . . 3.00
273 JB,V:Midgard Serpent 3.00
274 JB,D:Balder,I:Hermod,Hoder . 3.00
275 JB,V:Loki,I:Sigyn 3.00
276 JB,Trial of Loki 2.50
277 JB,V:Fake Thor 2.50
278 JB,V:Fake Thor 2.50
279 A:Pluto,V:Ulik 2.50
280 V:Hyperion 2.50
281 O:Space Phantom 2.50
282 V:Immortus,I:Tempus 2.50
283 JB,V:Celestials 2.50
284 JB,V:Gammenon 2.50
285 JB,R:Karkas 2.50
286 KP,KRo,D:Kro,I:Dragona 2.50
287 KP,2nd App & O:Forgotten
One(Hero) 2.50
288 KP,V:Forgotten One 2.50
289 KP,V:Destroyer 2.50
290 I:Red Bull(Toro Rojo) 2.50
291 KP,A:Eternals,Zeus 2.50
292 KP,V:Odin 2.50
293 KP,Door to Minds Eye 2.50
294 KP,O:Odin & Asgard,I:Frey . . 2.50
295 KP,I:Fafnir,V:Storm Giants. . . 2.50
296 KP,D:Siegmund 2.50
297 KP,V:Sword of Siegfried 2.50
298 KP,V:Dragon(Fafnir) 2.50
299 KP,A:Valkyrie,I:Hagen 2.50
300 KP,giant,O:Odin & Destroyer,
Rindgold Ring Quest ends,D:Uni-
Mind,I:Mother Earth 5.00
301 KP,O:Mother Earth,V:Apollo . 2.00
302 KP,V:Locus 2.00
303 Whatever Gods There Be . . . 2.00

The Mighty Thor #121
© Marvel Entertainment Group

304 KP,V:Wrecker 2.00
305 KP,R:Gabriel(Air Walker) . . . 2.00
306 KP,O&V:Firelord,O:AirWalker 2.00
307 KP,I:Dream Demon 2.00
308 KP,V:Snow Giants 2.00
309 V:Bomnardiers 2.00
310 KP,V:Mephisto 2.00
311 KP,GD,A:Valkyrie 2.00
312 KP,V:Tyr 2.00
313 KP,Thor Trial 2.00
314 KP,A:Drax,Moondragon 2.00
315 KP,O:Bi-Beast 2.00
316 KP,A:Iron Man,Man Thing,
V:Man-Beast 2.00
317 KP,V:Man-Beast 2.00
318 GK,V:Fafnir 2.00
319 KP,I&D:Zaniac 2.00
320 KP,V:Rimthursar 2.50
321 I:Menagerie 2.00
322 V:Heimdall 2.00
323 V:Death 2.00
324 V:Graviton 2.00
325 JM,O:Darkoth,V:Mephisto . . . 2.50
326 I:New Scarlet Scarab 2.50
327 V:Loki & Tyr 2.00
328 I:Megatak 2.50
329 HT,V:Hrungnir 2.00
330 BH,I:Crusader 2.00
331 Threshold of Death 2.00
332 V:Dracula 2.50
333 BH,V:Dracula 2.50
334 Quest For Rune Staff 2.00
335 V:Possessor 2.00
336 A:Captain Ultra 2.50
337 WS,I:Beta Ray Bill,A:Surtur . . 8.00
338 WS,O:Beta Ray Bill,I:Lorelei . 4.50
339 WS,V:Beta Ray Bill 3.00
340 WS,A:Beta Ray Bill 2.50
341 WS,V:Fafnir 2.25
342 WS,V:Fafnir,I:Eilif 2.25
343 WS,V:Fafnir 2.25
344 WS,Balder Vs.Loki,I:Malekith . 2.25
345 WS,V:Malekith 2.25
346 WS,V:Malekith 2.25
347 WS,V:Malekith,I:Algrim
(Kurse) 2.25
348 WS,V:Malekith 2.25
349 WS,R:Beta Ray Bill,O:Odin,
I&O:Vili & Ve(Odin's brothers) . 2.25
350 WS,V:Surtur 2.25
351 WS,V:Surtur 2.25
352 WS,V:Surtur 2.25
353 WS,V:Surtur,D:Odin 2.25
354 WS,V:Hela 2.25
355 WS,SB,A:Thor's Great
Grandfather 2.25
356 BL,BG,V:Hercules 2.25
357 WS,A:Beta Ray Bill 2.25
358 WS,A:Beta Ray Bill 2.25
359 WS,V:Loki 2.25
360 thru 362 WS,V:Hela . . . . . @2.25
363 WS,Secret Wars II,V:Kurse . . 2.50
364 WS,I:Thunder Frog 2.25
365 WS,A:Thunder Frog 2.25
366 WS,A:Thunder Frog 2.25
367 WS,D:Malekith,A:Kurse 2.25
368 WS,F:Balder t/Brave,Kurse . . 2.25
369 WS,F:Balder the Brave 2.25
370 JB,V:Loki 2.25
371 SB,I:Justice Peace,V:Zaniac . 2.25
372 SB,V:Justice Peace 2.25
373 SB,A:X-Factor,(Mut.Mass) . . . 5.00
374 WS,SB,A:X-Factor,(Mut.Mass)
A:Sabretooth 6.00
375 WS,SB,N:Thor(Exoskeleton) . 2.25
376 WS,SB,V:Absorbing Man . . . 2.25
377 WS,SB,N:Thor,A:Ice Man . . . 2.25
378 WS,SB,V:Frost Giants 2.25
379 WS,V:Midgard Serpent 2.25
380 WS,V:Midgard Serpent 2.25
381 WE,SB,A:Avengers 2.50
382 WS,SB,V:Frost Giants,Loki . . 2.50
383 BBr,Secret Wars story 2.50
384 RF,BBr,I:Future Thor(Dargo) . 4.00
385 EL,V:Hulk 2.00
386 RF,BBr,I:Leir 2.00
387 RF,BBr,V:Celestials 2.00
388 RF,BBr,V:Celestials 2.00
389 RF,BBr,V:Celestials 2.00
390 RF,BBr,A:Avengers,V:Seth . . 2.00
391 RF,BBr,I:Mongoose,Eric
Masterson,A:Spiderman 8.00
392 RF,I:Quicksand 2.00
393 RF,BBr,V:Quicksand,A:DD . . 2.00
394 RF,BBr,V:Earth Force 2.00
395 RF,V:Earth Force 2.00
396 RF,A:Black Knight 2.00
397 RF,A:Loki 2.00
398 RF,DH,R:Odin,V:Seth 2.00
399 RF,RT,R:Surtur,V:Seth 2.00
400 RF,JSt,CV,V:Surtur,Seth 4.00
401 V:Loki 2.00
402 RF,JSt,V:Quicksand 2.00
403 RF,JSt,V:Executioner 2.00
404 RF,JSt,TD,V:Annihilus 2.00
405 RF,JSt,TD,V:Annihilus 2.00
406 RF,JSt,TD,V:Wundagore 2.00
407 RF,JSt,R:Hercules,High Evol. 2.00
408 RF,JSt,I:Eric Masterson/Thor
V:Mongoose 3.50
409 RF,JSt,V:Dr.Doom 2.00
410 RF,JSt,V:Dr.Doom,She-Hulk . 2.00

411 RF,JSt,C:New Warriors V:Juggernaut,A of V 12.00
412 RF,JSt,I:New Warriors V:Juggernaut,A of V 20.00
413 RF,JSt,A:Dr.Strange 1.75
414 RF,JSt,V:Ulik 1.75
415 HT,O:Thor 1.75
416 RF,JSt,A:Hercules 1.75
417 RF,JSt,A:High Evolutionary . . 1.75
418 RF,JSt,V:Wrecking Crew 1.75
419 RF,JSt,B:Black Galaxy Saga,I:Stellaris 1.75
420 RF,JSt,A:Avengers,V:Stellaris 1.75
421 RF,JSt,V:Stellaris 1.75
422 RF,JSt,V:High Evol.,Nobilus . 1.75
423 RF,JSt,A:High Evol.,Celestials Count Tagar 1.75
424 RF,JSt,V:Celestials,E:Black Galaxy Saga 1.75
425 RF,AM,V:Surtur,Ymir 1.75
426 RF,JSt,HT,O:Earth Force . . . 1.50
427 RF,JSt,A:Excalibur 1.50
428 RF,JSt,A:Excalibur 1.50
429 RF,JSt,A:Ghost Rider 2.00
430 RF,AM,A:Mephisto,Gh.Rider . 1.75
431 HT,AM,V:Ulik,Loki 1.75
432 RF,D:Loki,Thor Banished,Eric Masterson becomes 2nd Thor . 6.00
433 RF,V:Ulik 3.00
434 RF,AM,V:Warriors Three 2.00
435 RF,AM,V:Annihilus 1.75
436 RF,AM,V:Titania,Absorbing Man,A:Hercules 1.50
437 RF,AM,V:Quasar 1.50
438 RF,JSt,A:Future Thor(Dargo) . 1.50
439 RF,JSt,A:Drago 1.50
440 RF,AM,I:Thor Corps 1.50
441 RF,AM,Celestials vs.Ego 1.50
442 RF,AM,Don Blake,Beta Ray Bill,Mephisto 1.50
443 RF,AM,A:Dr.Strange,Silver Surfer,V:Mephisto 1.50
444 RF,AM,Special X-mas tale . . 1.50
445 AM,Galactic Storm Pt.7 V:Gladiator 1.50
446 AM,Galactic Storm Pt 14 A:Avengers 1.50
447 RF,AM,V:Absorbing Man A:Spider-Man 1.50
448 RF,AM,V:Titania,A:SpM 1.50
449 RF,AM,V:Ulik 1.50
450 RF,AM,V:Heimdall,A:Code Blue Double-Sized,Gatefold(c),rep. Journey Into Mystery#87 . . . . . 3.25
451 RF,AM,I:Bloodaxe 1.50
452 RF,AM,V:Bloodaxe 1.50
453 RF,AM,V:Mephisto 1.50
454 RF,AM,V:Mephisto,Loki, Karnilla 1.50
455 AM(i),V:Loki,Karnilla,R:Odin, A:Dr.Strange 1.50
456 RF,AM,V:Bloodaxe 1.50
457 RF,AM,R:1st Thor 1.50
458 RF,AM,Thor vs Eric 1.50
459 RF,AM,C&I:Thunderstrike(Eric Masterson) 2.00
460 I:New Valkyrie 1.50
461 V:Beta Ray Bill 1.50
462 A:New Valkyrie 1.50
463 Infinity Crusade 1.50
464 Inf.Crusade,V:Loki 1.50
465 Infinity Crusade 1.50
466 Infinity Crusade 1.50
467 Infinity Crusade 1.50
468 RMz(s),Blood & Thunder#1 . . 1.50
469 RMz(s),Blood & Thunder#5 . . 1.50
470 MCW,Blood & Thunder#9 . . . 1.50
471 MCW,E:Blood & Thunder . . . 1.50
472 B:RTs(s),MCW,I:Godling,C:High Evolutionary 1.50
473 MCW,V:Godling,High Evolutionary I&C:Karnivore(Man-Beast) 1.75
474 MCW,C:High Evolutionary . . . 1.50
475 MCW,Foil(c),A:Donald Blake, N:Thor 2.50
475a Nesstand Ed. 2.00
Ann.#2 JK,V:Destroyer 45.00
Ann.#3 JK,rep,Grey Gargoyle. . . . 9.00
Ann.#4 JK,rep,TheLivingPlanet. . . 8.00
Ann.#5 JK,JB,Hercules,O:Odin . . 7.00
Ann.#6 JK,JB,A:Guardians of the Galaxy,V:Korvac 8.00
Ann.#7 WS,Eternals 7.00
Ann.#8 JB,V:Zeus 5.00
Ann.#9 LMc,Dormammu 3.50
Ann.#10 O:Chthon,Gaea,A:Pluto . 3.50
Ann.#11 O:Odin 3.50
Ann.#12 BH,I:Vidar(Odin's son) . . 3.50
Ann.#13 JB,V:Mephisto 3.00
Ann.#14 AM,DH,Atlantis Attacks . 3.00
Ann.#15 HT,Terminus Factor #3 . 2.50
Ann.#16 Korvac Quest Pt.2, Guardians of Galaxy 2.50
Ann.#17 Citizen Kang#2 . . . . 2.50
Ann.#18 TGr,I:The Flame,w/card . 3.25
G-Size.#1 Battles,A:Hercules 5.00
TPB Alone Against the Celestials, rep.Thor#387-389 . . . . 5.95
TPB Ballad of Beta Ray Bill,rep. Thor#337-340 . . . . 8.95

THOR CORPS
[Limited Series]

1 TDF(s),PO,V:Demonstaff 2.00
2 TDF(s),PO,A:Invaders 2.00
3 TDF(s),PO,A:Spider-Man 2099 . 2.00
4 TDF(s),PO,Last Issue 2.00

THREE MUSKETEERS

1 thru 2 movie adapt. 1.25

THUNDERCATS
Star
December, 1985

1 JM,TV tie-in 3.00
1a 2nd printing 1.00
2 JM,A:Berbils,V:Mumm-Ra 2.00
3 . . . . 1.50
4 JM,I:Lynxana 1.50
5 JM 1.50
6 JM 1.50
7 Return to Thundera 1.50
8 V:Monkiang 1.50
9 V:Pekmen 1.00
10 . . . . 1.00
11 I:The Molemen 1.00
12 'The Protectors' 1.00
13 EC/AW,V:Safari Joe 1.00
14 V:Snaf 1.00
15 JM,A:Spidera 1.00
16 'Time Capsula' 1.00
17 . . . . 1.00
18 EC/AW,'Doom Gaze' 1.00
19 . . . . 1.00
20 EC/AW 1.00
21 JM,A:Hercules Baby 1.00
22 I:Devious Duploids 1.00
23 V:Devious Duploids 1.00
24 June, 1988 . . . . 1.00

THUNDERSTRIKE

1 B:TDF(s),RF,Holografx(c), V:Bloodaxe,I:Car Jack 3.25
2 RF,V:Juggernaut 1.50
3 RF,I:Sangre 1.50
4 RF,A:Spider-Man,I:Pandora . . . 1.50
5 RF,A:Spider-Man,V:Pandora . . . 1.50
6 RF,I:Blackwulf,Bristle,Schizo,Lord Lucian,A:SpM,Code:Blue,Stellaris, V:SHIELD,Pandora,C:Tantalus 1.50
7 KP,V:Tantalus,D:Jackson 1.75
8 RF,I&V:Officer ZERO 1.75
9 RF,V:Bloodaxe 1.50

TIMESPIRITS
Epic
January, 1985

1 TY 2.00
2 . . . . 1.75
3 . . . . 1.75
4 AW 1.50
5 . . . . 1.50
6 . . . . 1.50
7 . . . . 1.50
8 March, 1986 . . . . 1.50

TINY TESSIE
See: TESSIE THE TYPIST

TOMB OF DARKNESS
See: BEWARE

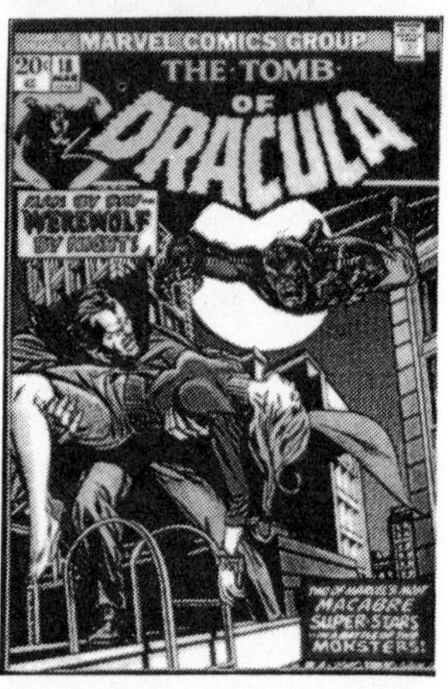

Tomb of Dracula #18
© Marvel Entertainment Group

TOMB OF DRACULA
April, 1972

1 GC,Night of the Vampire 60.00
2 GC,Who Stole My Coffin? . . . 30.00
3 GC,TP,I:Rachel Van Helsing . 20.00
4 GC,TP,Bride of Dracula! 20.00
5 GC,TP,To Slay A Vampire . . . 20.00
6 GC,TP,Monster of the Moors . 15.00
7 GC,TP,Child is Slayer o/t Man 15.00
8 GC(p),The Hell-Crawlers 15.00
9 The Fire Cross 15.00
10 GC,I:Blade Vampire Slayer . . 22.00
11 GC,TP,Master of the Undead Strikes Again! 11.00
12 GC,TP,House that Screams . 11.00
13 GC,TP,O:Blade 16.00
14 GC,TP,Vampire has Risen from the Grave 11.00
15 GC,TP,Stay Dead 11.00
16 GC,TP,Back from the Grave . 11.00
17 GC,TP,A Vampire Rides This Train! 11.00
18 GC,TP,A:Werewolf By Night . 12.00
19 GC,TP,Snowbound in Hell . . 11.00
20 GC,TP,ManhuntForAVampire 11.00
21 GC,TP,A:Blade 12.00
22 GC,TP,V:Gorna 9.00
23 GC,TP,Shadow over Haunted Castle 9.00
24 GC,TP,I am your Death 9.00
25 GC,TP,Blood Stalker of Count Dracula 9.00
26 GC,TP,A Vampire Stalks the Night 9.00
27 GC,TP,..And the Moon Spews Death! 9.00

28 GC,TP,Five came to Kill a Vampire' 9.00
29 GC,TP,Vampire goes Mad? . . 9.00

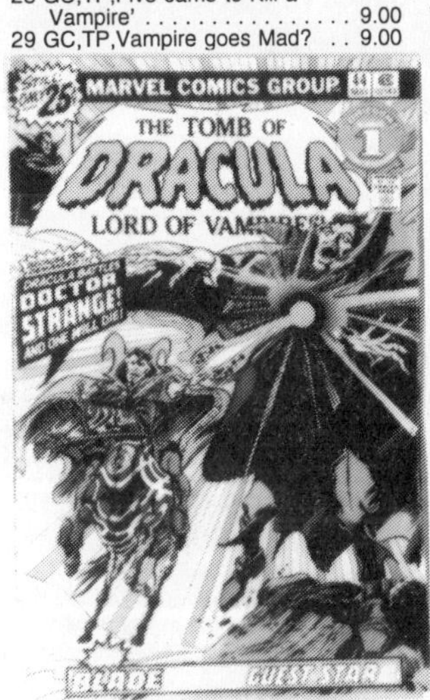

Tomb of Dracula #44
© Marvel Entertainment Group

30 GC,TP,A:Blade 9.00
31 GC,TP,Child of Blood 9.00
32 GC,TP,The Vampire Walks Among Us 9.00
33 GC,TP,Blood on My Hands . . . 9.00
34 GC,TP,Bloody Showdown 9.00
35 GC,TP,A:Brother Voodoo 9.00
36 GC,TP,Dracula in America . . . 9.00
37 GC,TP,The Vampire Walks Among Us 5.00
38 GC,TP,Bloodlust for a Dying Vampire 9.00
39 GC,TP,Final Death of Dracula . 9.00
40 GC,TP,Triumph of Dr.Sun 9.00
41 GC,TP,A:Blade 8.00
42 GC,TP,V:Dr.Sun 7.00
43 GC,TP,A:NewYear'sNightmare 7.00
44 GC,TP,A:Dr.Strange 7.00
45 GC,TP,A:Hannibal King 8.00
46 GC,TP,W:Dracula & Domini . . 7.00
47 GC,TP,Death-Bites 7.00
48 GC,TP,A:Hannibal King 8.00
49 GC,TP,A:Robin Hood, Frankenstein's Monster 7.00
50 GC,TP,A:Silver Surfer 12.00
51 GC,TP,A:Blade 7.50
52 GC,TP,V:Demon 6.00
53 GC,TP,A:Hannibal King,Blade . 7.50
54 GC,TP,Twas the Night Before Christmas 6.00
55 GC,TP,Requiem for a Vampire 6.00
56 GC,TP,A:Harold H. Harold . . . 6.00
57 GC,TP,The Forever Man 6.00
58 GC,TP,A:Blade 7.00
59 GC,TP,The Last Traitor 6.00
60 GC,TP,The Wrath of Dracula . 6.00
61 GC,TP,Resurrection 6.00
62 GC,TP,What Lurks Beneath . . 6.00
63 GC,TP,A:Janus 6.00
64 GC,TP,A:Satan 6.00
65 GC,TP,Where No Vampire Has Gone Before 6.00
66 GC,TP,Marked for Death 6.00
67 GC,TP,A:Lilith 6.00
68 GC,TP,Dracula turns Human . . 6.00
69 GC,TP,Cross of Fire 6.00
70 GC,TP,double size,last issue . 7.50
Savage Return of Dracula. rep. Tomb of Dracula #1,#2 . . . . . . 2.00
Wedding of Dracula. rep.Tomb of Dracula #30,#45,#46 . . . . . . 2.00
Requiem for Dracula. rep.Tomb of Dracula #69,70 . . . . 2.00

TOMB OF DRACULA
[Mini-Series]
November, 1991

1 GC,AW,Day of Blood 6.00
2 GC,AW,Dracula in DC 5.50
3 GC,AW,A:Blade 5.50
4 GC,AW,D:Dracula 5.50

TOMB OF DRACULA
November, 1979
(black & white magazine)

1 . . . . 3.50
2 SD 5.00
3 FM 5.00
4 . . . . 3.00
5 . . . . 3.00
6 September, 1980 . . . . 3.00

TOMORROW KNIGHTS
Epic
June, 1990

1 . . . . 1.95
2 . . . . 1.50
3 . . . . 1.50
4 Origin 1.50
5 . . . . 2.25
6 . . . . 2.25

TOP DOG
Star Comics
April, 1985

1 . . . . 1.25
2 thru 14, June 1987 . . . . @1.00

TOR

1 JKu,R:Tor,Magazine Format . . . 6.25
2 JKu 6.25
3 JKu,V:The Iduard Ring 6.25

TOUGH KID SQUAD COMICS
Timely
March, 1942

1 O:The Human Top,Tough Kid Squad,A:The Flying Flame, V:Doctor Klutch 4,500.00

TOWER OF SHADOWS
September, 1969

1 JR(c),JSo,JCr,'At The Stroke of Midnight' 15.00
2 JR(c),DH,DA,NA,'The Hungry One' 8.00
3 GC,BWs,GT,'Midnight in the Wax Museum' 9.00
4 DH,'Within The Witching Circle' 6.00
5 DA,BWS,WW,'Demon That Stalks Hollywood' 7.00
6 WW,SD,'Pray For the Man in the Rat-Hole 8.00
7 BWS,WW,'Titano' 8.00
8 WW,SD,'Demons of Dragon-Henge' 7.00
9 BWr(c),TP,Lovecraft story 5.50
Becomes:

CREATURES ON THE LOOSE
March, 1971

10 BWr,A:King Kull 32.00
11 DAy,rep Moomba is Here 4.00
12 JK,'I Was Captured By Korilla' 4.00
13 RC,'The Creature From Krogarr' 4.00
14 MSe,'Dead Storage' 4.00
15 SD,'Spragg the Living Mountain' 2.25

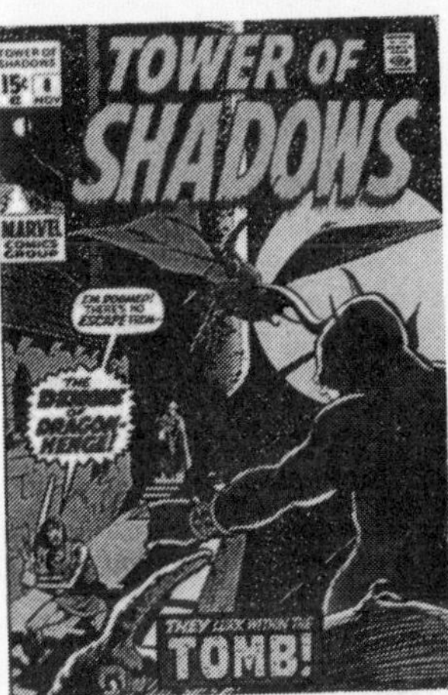

Tower of Shadows #8
© Marvel Entertainment Group

16 GK,BEv,GK,B&O:Gullivar Jones, Warrior of Mars 4.00
17 GK,'Slaves o/t Spider Swarm' . 2.25
18 RA,'The Fury of Phra' 4.00
19 WB,JM,GK,'Red Barbarian of Mars' 4.00
20 GK(c),GM,SD,'The Monster... And the Maiden 4.00
21 JSo(c),GM,'Two Worlds To Win',E:Guilliver 4.00
22 JSo(c),SD,VM,B:Thongor, Warrior of Lost Lemuria 4.00
23 VM,'The Man-Monster Strikes' 4.00
24 VM,'Attack of the Lizard-Hawks' 2.25
25 VM,GK(c),'Wizard of Lemuria' . 4.00
26 VM,'Doom of the Serpent Gods' 1.75
27 VM,SD,'Demons Dwell in the Crypts of Yamath' 3.50
28 SD,'The Hordes of Hell' 3.50
29 GK(c),'Day of the Dragon Wings', E:Thongor,Warrior of Lost Lemuria 3.50
30 B:Man-Wolf,'Full Moon, Dark Fear' 3.50
31 GT,'The Beast Within' 3.50
32 GT,V:Kraven the Hunter 3.50
33 GK(c),GP,'The Name of the Game is Death' 3.50
34 GP,'Nightflight to Fear' 3.50
35 GK(c),GP 3.50
36 GK(c),GP,'Murder by Moonlight' 1.75
37 GP,September, 1975 . . . . 3.50

TOXIC AVENGER
March, 1991

1 VM(i)I&O:Toxic Avenger 2.25
2 VM(i) 1.75
3 VM(i)'Night of LivingH.bodies . . 1.50
4 Legend of Sludgeface 1.50
5 I:Biohazard 1.50
6 V:Biohazard 1.50
7 'Sewer of Souviaki' 1.50
8 'Sewer of Souviaki' conc. 1.50
9 Abducted by Aliens 1.50
10 'Die,Yuppie Scum' Pt.1 . . . . . . 1.50

TOXIC CRUSADERS

1 F:Toxic Avengers & Crusaders 1.50
2 SK(c),V:Custard-Thing 1.25
3 SK(c),V:Custard-Thing 1.25
4 V:Giant Mutant Rats 1.25

Creatures on the Loose #13
© Marvel Entertainment Group

Transformers #8
© Marvel Entertainment Group

5 V:Dr.Killemoff 1.25
6 V:Dr.Killemoff 1.25
7 F:Yvonne 1.25
8 V:Psycho 1.25

(2nd Series)

1 . . . . 1.25
2 . . . . 1.25

TRANSFORMERS

September, 1984

[1st Regular Series]

1 FS,Toy Comic 3.00
2 FS,OptimusPrime V:Megatron . 2.00
3 FS.A:Spider-Man 2.00
4 MT(c),FS 1.50
5 Transformers Dead? 1.50
6 Autobots vs.Decepticons 1.50
7 KB,V:Megatron 1.50
8 KB,A:Dinobots 1.50
9 MM,A:Circuit Breaker 1.50
10 Dawn of the Devastator 1.50
11 HT 1.50
12 HT,V:Shockwave 1.50
13 DP,Return of Megatron 1.50
14 DP,V:Decepticons 1.50
15 DP 1.50
16 KN,A:Bumblebee 1.50
17 DP,I:New Transformers Pt.1 . . 1.50
18 DP,I:New Transformers Pt.2 . . 1.50
19 DP,I:Omega Supreme 1.50
20 HT,Skid vs.Ravage 1.50
21 DP,I:Aerialbots 1.25
22 DP,I:Stuntacons(Menasor) . . . 1.25
23 DP,Return of Circuit Breaker . . 1.25
24 DP,D:Optimus Prime 1.25
25 DP,Decpticons (full story) 1.25
26 DP 1.25
27 DP,V:Head Hunter 1.25
28 DP 1.25
29 DP,I:Scraplets, Triplechangers 1.25
30 DP,V:Scraplets 1.25
31 DP,Humans vs. Decepticons . . 1.25
32 DP,'Autobots for Sale' 1.25
33 DP,Autobots vs.Decepticons . . 1.25
34 V:Sky Lynx 1.25
35 JRy,I:UK.version Transformers 1.25
36 . . . . 1.00
37 . . . . 1.00
38 . . . . 1.00
39 . . . . 1.00
40 Autobots' New Leader 1.00
41 . . . . 1.00
42 Return of Optimus Prime 1.00
43 Optimus Prime,Goldbug 1.00
44 FF,Return of Circuit Breaker . . 1.00
45 V:The Jammers 1.00
46 I:New Transformers 1.00
47 B:Underbase saga,I:Seacons . 1.00
48 Optimus Prime/Megatron
(past story) 1.00
49 Underbase saga Contd. 1.00
50 E:Underbase saga,I:New
Characters 1.00
51 I:Pretender Decepticon Beasts 1.00
52 I:Mecannibles Pt.1 . . . . 1.00
53 Mecannibles Pt.2 . . . . 1.00
54 I:Micromasters 1.00
55 MG 1.00
56 Return of Megatron 1.00
57 Optimus Prime vs.Scraponok . 1.00
58 V:Megatron 1.00
59 A:Megatron,D:Ratchet 1.00
60 Battle on Cybertron 1.00
61 O:Transformers 1.00
62 B:Matrix Quest Pt.1 . . . . 1.00
63 . . . . 1.00
64 I:The Klud 1.00
65 GSr 1.00
66 E:Matrix Quest Pt.5 . . . . 1.00
67 V:Unicorn,Also Alternative
World 1.00
68 I:Neoknights 1.00
69 Fate of Ratchet & Megatron
revealed 1.00
70 Megatron/Ratchet fused
together 1.00
71 Autobots Surrender to
Decepticons 1.00
72 Decepticon Civil War,
I:Gravitron 1.00
73 I:Unicron,A:Neoknights 1.00
74 A:Unicron&Brothers of Chaos . 1.00
75 V:Thunderwing & Dark Matrix . 1.00
76 Aftermath of War 1.00
77 Unholy Alliance 1.00
78 Galvatron vs.Megatron 1.00
79 Decepticons Invade Earth 1.00
80 Return of Optimus Prime,final . 1.00

[2nd Regular Series]

1 Split Foil(c),A:Dinobots 3.50
2 A:G.I.Joe,Cobra 2.00
3 . . . . 2.00
4 MaG,V:Jhiaxus 2.00
5 . . . . 2.00
6 V:Megatron 2.00
7 V:Darkwing 2.00
8 V:Darkwing 1.75
9 . . . . 1.75

TRANSFORMERS COMICS MAGAZINE

October, 1986

1 Digest Size 1.50
2 thru 10 . . . . @1.50
11 1988 . . . . 1.50

TRANSFORMERS, THE MOVIE

December, 1986

1 Animated Movie adapt 1.25
2 Animated Movie adapt 1.25
3 Animated Movie adapt,February,
1987 . . . . 1.25

TRANSFORMERS UNIVERSE

December, 1986

1 . . . . 1.25
2 . . . . 1.25
3 . . . . 1.25
4 March, 1987 . . . . 1.25

TRANSMUTATION OF IKE GARAUDA

Epic

1 JSh,I:IkeGaruda 3.95
2 JSh,conclusion 3.95

TROUBLE WITH GIRLS

1 BBl,AW,R:Lester Girls 2.75
2 BBl,AW,V:Lizard Lady 2.25
3 BBl,AW,V:Lizard Lady 2.25
4 BBl,AW,last issue 2.25

TRUE COMPLETE MYSTERY

See: COMPLETE MYSTERY

TRUE SECRETS

See: OUR LOVE

TRUE WESTERN

December, 1949

1 Ph(c),Billy the Kid 75.00
2 Ph(c),Alan Ladd,Badmen vs.
Lawmen 82.00

Becomes:

TRUE ADVENTURES

3 BP,MSy,Boss of Black Devil . 60.00

Becomes:

MEN'S ADVENTURES

4 He Called me a Coward 75.00
5 Brother Act 45.00
6 Heat of Battle 35.00
7 The Walking Death 35.00
8 RH,Journey Into Death 35.00
9 Bullets,Blades and Death . . . 23.00
10 BEv,The Education of Thomas
Dillon 23.00
11 Death of A Soldier 23.00
12 Firing Squad 23.00
13 RH(c),The Three Stripes 23.00
14 GC,BEv,Steel Coffin 23.00
15 JMn(c) 23.00
16 . . . . 23.00
17 . . . . 23.00
18 . . . . 23.00
19 JRo 23.00
20 RH(c) 23.00
21 BEv(c),JSt,The Eye of Man . . 30.00
22 BEv,JR,Mark of the Witch . . . 30.00
23 BEv(c),RC,The Wrong Body . 38.00

24 RH,JMn,GT,Torture Master .. 30.00
25 SSh(c),Who Shrinks My Head 30.00
26 Midnight in the Morgue 30.00
27 CBu(c),A:Capt.America,Human Torch,Sub-Mariner 300.00
28 BEv,A:Capt.America,Human Torch, Sub-Mariner,July, 1954 .... 300.00

TRY-OUT WINNER BOOK
March, 1988

1 Spiderman vs. Doc Octopus . 15.00

TV STARS
August, 1978

1 A:Great Grape Ape 1.25
2 .... 1.00
3 .... 1.00
4 A:Top Cat,February, 1979 ... 1.00

2-GUN KID
See: BILLY BUCKSKIN

TWO-GUN KID
Atlas
March, 1948

1 B:Two-Gun Kid,The Sheriff . 475.00
2 Killers of Outlaw City 225.00
3 RH,A:Annie Oakley 175.00
4 RH,A:Black Rider 175.00

Two-Gun Kid #83
© Marvel Entertainment Group

5 .... 200.00
6 .... 150.00
7 RH,Brand of a Killer 150.00
8 The Secret of the Castle of Slaves 150.00
9 JSe,Trapped in Hidden Valley A:Black Rider 150.00
10 JK(c),The Horrible Hermit of Hidden Mesa 150.00
11 JMn(c),GT,A:Black Rider .. 100.00
12 JMn(c),GT,A:Black Rider .. 100.00
13 thru 24 .... @75.00
25 AW 75.00
26 .... 70.00
27 .... 70.00
28 .... 70.00
29 .... 70.00
30 AW 75.00
31 thru 44 .... 50.00
45 .... 55.00
46 .... 55.00
47 .... 35.00
48 .... 40.00
49 .... 30.00
50 .... 30.00
51 .... 40.00
52 thru 59 .... @20.00
60 DAy,New O:Two Gun Kid .. 20.00
61 JK,DAy,The Killer and The Kid 20.00
62 JK,DAy,At the Mercy of Moose Morgan 20.00
63 DAy,The Guns of Wild Bill Taggert 10.00
64 DAy,Trapped by Grizzly Gordon 10.00
65 DAy,Nothing Can Save Fort Henry 10.00
66 DAy,Ringo's Raiders 10.00
67 DAy,The Fangs of the Fox .. 10.00
68 DAy,The Purple Phantom ... 10.00
69 DAy,Badman Called Goliath . 10.00
70 DAy,Hurricane 10.00
71 DAy,V:Jesse James 10.00
72 DAy,V:Geronimo 10.00
73 Guns of the Galloway Gang . 10.00
74 Dakota Thompson 10.00
75 JK,Remember the Alamo ... 10.00
76 JK,Trapped on the Doom ... 10.00
77 JK,V:The Panther 10.00
78 V:Jesse James 10.00
79 The River Rats 10.00
80 V:The Billy Kid 10.00
81 The Hidden Gun 4.00
82 BEv,Here Comes the Conchos 4.00
83 Durango,Two-Gun Kid Unmasked 4.00
84 Gunslammer 4.00
85 Fury at Falcon Flats, A:Rawhide Kids 4.00
86 V:Cole Younger 4.00
87 OW,The Sidewinder and the Stallion 4.00
88 thru 100 .... @4.00
101 .... 4.00
102 thru 135 .... @2.00
136 April, 1977 .... 2.00

TWO GUN WESTERN
See: CASEY–CRIME PHOTOGRAPHER

TWO-GUN WESTERN
See: BILLY BUCKSKIN

2001: A SPACE ODYSSEY
October, 1976

1 JK,FRg,Based on Movie 3.00

2001: A SPACE ODYSSEY
December, 1976

1 JK,Based on Movie 2.50
2 JK,Vira the She-Demon 1.25
3 JK,Marak the Merciless 1.25
4 JK,Wheels of Death 1.25
5 JK,Norton of New York 1.25
6 JK,Immortality ...Death 1.25
7 JK,The New Seed 1.25
8 JK,Capture of X-51,I&O:Mr. Machine(Machine-Man) 4.00
9 JK,A:Mr Machine 1.25
10 Hotline to Hades,A:Mr Machine September, 1977 .... 1.25

2010
April, 1985

1 TP,movie adapt 1.00
2 TP,movie adapt,May, 1985 ... 1.00

2099 UNLIMITED

1 DT,I:Hulk 2099,A:Spider-Man 2099, I:Mutagen 4.50
2 DT,F:Hulk 2099,Spider-Man 2099, I:R-Gang 4.25
3 GJ(s),JJB,F:Hulk & SpM 2099 . 4.25
4 PR(c),GJ(s),JJB,I:Metalscream 2099,Lachryma 2099 .... 4.25
5 GJ(s),I:Vulx,F:Hazarrd 2099 ... 3.95

UNCANNY TALES
Atlas
June, 1952

1 RH,While the City Sleeps .. 325.00
2 JMn,BEv 175.00
3 Escape to What 150.00
4 JMn,Nobody's Fool 150.00
5 Fear 150.00
6 He Lurks in the Shadows .. 150.00
7 BEv,Kill,Clown,Kill 125.00
8 JMn,Bring Back My Face ... 125.00
9 RC,The Executioner 125.00
10 RH(c),JR,The Man Who Came Back To Life 125.00
11 GC,The Man Who Changed 100.00
12 BP,BEv,Bertha Gets Buried 100.00
13 RH,Scared Out of His Skin . 100.00
14 RH,The Victims of Vonntor . 100.00
15 JSt,The Man Who Saw Death 100.00
16 JMn,GC,Zombie at Large .. 100.00
17 GC,I Live With Corpses ... 100.00
18 JF,BP,Clock Face(c) 100.00
19 DBr,RKr,The Man Who Died Again 100.00
20 DBr,Ted's Head 100.00
21 thru 27 .... @80.00
28 .... 90.00
29 thru 41 .... @60.00
42 .... 65.00
43 thru 49 .... @55.00
50 .... 60.00
51 .... 65.00
52 .... 55.00
53 .... 55.00
54 .... 65.00
55 .... 55.00
56 September, 1957 .... 65.00

UNCANNY TALES FROM THE GRAVE
December, 1973

1 RC,Room of no Return 3.00
2 DAy,Out of the Swamp 1.75
3 No Way Out 1.75
4 JR,SD,Vampire 1.75
5 GK,GT,Don't Go in the Cellar . 1.75
6 JR,SD,The Last Kkrul 1.75
7 RH,SD,Never Dance With a Vampire 1.75
8 SD,Escape Into Hell 1.75
9 JA,The Nightmare Men 1.75
10 SD,DH,Beware the Power of Khan 1.75
11 SD,JF,RH,Dead Don't Sleep .. 1.75
12 SD,Final Issue,October, 1975 . 1.75

UNKNOWN WORLDS OF SCIENCE FICTION
January, 1975
(black & white magazine)

1 AW,RKr,AT,FF,GC 4.00
2 FB,GP 3.25
3 GM,AN,GP,GC 3.25
4 .... 3.25
5 GM,NC,GC 3.25
6 FB,AN,GC,November, 1975 .. 3.25
Spec.#1 AN,NR,JB 3.50

U.S.A. COMICS
Timely
August, 1941

1 S&K(c),BW,Bondage(c),The Defender(c) 5,000.00
2 S&K(c),BW,Capt Terror(c) . 1,700.00
3 S&K(c),Capt Terror(c) 1,400.00
4 .... 1,100.00
5 Hitler(c),O:American Avenger 900.00
6 ASh(c),Capt.America(c) ... 1,100.00
7 BW,O:Marvel Boy 900.00
8 Capt.America (c) 750.00

9 Bondage(c), Capt America . . 750.00
10 SSh(c),Bondage(c), Capt. America 750.00
11 SSh(c),Bondage(c), Capt. America 600.00
12 ASh(c),Capt America 600.00
13 ASh(c),Capt America 600.00
14 Capt America 450.00
15 Capt America 450.00
16 ASh(c),Bondage(c), Capt America 450.00
17 Bondage(c),Capt America . . 450.00

U.S. 1
May, 1983

1 AM(c),HT,Trucking Down the Highway 1.25
2 HT,Midnight 1.00
3 FS,ME,Rhyme of the Ancient Highwayman 1.00
4 FS,ME 1.00
5 FS,ME,Facing The Maze 1.00
6 FS,ME 1.00
7 FS,ME 1.00
8 FS,ME 1.00
9 FS,ME,Iron Mike-King of the Bike 1.00
10 FS,ME 1.00
11 FS,ME 1.00
12 FS,ME,Final Issue,Oct.,1984 . . 1.00

UNTAMED

1 I:Griffen Palmer 2.75
2 V:Kosansui 2.25
3 V:Kosansui 2.25

U.S. AGENT

1 V:Scourge,O:U.S.Agent 2.00
2 thru 3 V:Scourge . . . . @2.00
4 last issue 2.00

VAMPIRE TALES
August, 1973
(black & white magazine)

1 BEv,B:Morbius the Living Vampire 15.00
2 JSo,I:Satana 6.00
3 A:Satana 10.00
4 GK 10.00
5 GK,O:Morbius The Living Vampire 15.00
6 AA,I:Lilith 10.00
7 HC,PG 10.00
8 AA,A:Blade The Vampire Slayer 10.00
9 RH,AA 10.00
10 . . . . 10.00
11 June, 1975 . . . . 10.00
Ann.#1 . . . . 10.50

VAULT OF EVIL
February, 1973

1 B:1950's reps,Come Midnight, Come Monster 5.00
2 The Hour of the Witch 3.00
3 The Woman Who Wasn't 3.00
4 Face that Follows 3.00
5 Ghost 3.00
6 The Thing at the Window 3.00
7 Monsters 3.00
8 The Vampire is my Brother . . . 3.00
9 Giant Killer 3.00
10 The Lurkers in the Caves 3.00
11 Two Feasts For a Vampire . . . 3.00
12 Midnight in the Haunted Mansion 3.00
13 Hot as the Devil 3.00
14 Midnight in the Haunted Manor 3.00
15 Don't Shake Hands with the Devil 3.00
16 A Grave Honeymoon 3.00
17 Grave Undertaking 3.00
18 The Deadly Edge 3.00

Vault of Evil #8
© Marvel Entertainment Group

19 Vengeance of Ahman Ra 3.00
20 . . . . 3.00
21 Victim of Valotorr 3.00
22 . . . . 3.00
23 The Black Magician Lives Again,November, 1975 . . 1.25

VENOM

1 MBa,A:Spider-Man.holo-grafx(c) 8.00
1a Gold Ed.. . . . . 75.00
1b Black Ed.. . . . . 350.00
2 MBa,A:Spider-Man 6.00
3 MBa,Families of Venom's victims 5.00
4 RLm,A:Spider-Man,V:Life Foundation 4.50
5 RLm,V:Five Symbiotes,A:SpM . 4.50
6 RLm,V:Spider-Man 4.50
Venom:Deathtrap:The Vault RLm, A:Avengers,Freedom Froce . . . 6.95

VENOM: ENEMY WITHIN

1 BMc,Glow-in-the-dark(C), A:Demogoblin,Morbius 3.25
2 BMc,A:Demogoblin,Morbius . . . 3.25
3 BMc,V:Demogoblin,A:Morbius . 3.25

VENOM: FUNERAL PYRE

1 TL,JRu,A:Punisher 4.00
2 TL,JRu,AM,V:Gangs 3.50
3 TL,JRu,Last issue 3.50

VENOM: THE MACE

1 Embossed(c),CP(s),LSh,I:Mace . 3.25
2 CP(s),LSh,V:Mace 2.95

VENOM: THE MADNESS

1 B:ANi(s),KJo,V:Juggernaut 3.50
2 KJo,V:Juggernaut 3.25
3 E:ANi(s),KJo,V:Juggernaut 3.25

VENUS
Atlas
August, 1948

1 B:Venus,Hedy Devine,HK,Hey Look 525.00
2 Venus(c) 325.00
3 Carnival(c) 275.00
4 Cupid(c).HK,Hey Look 300.00

5 Serenade(c) 300.00
6 Wrath of a Goddess,A:Loki . 250.00
7 The Romance That Could Not Be 250.00
8 The Love Trap 250.00
9 Whom the Gods Destroy . . 250.00
10 B:Scince Fiction/Horror, Trapped On the Moon 250.00
11 The End of the World 300.00
12 GC,The Lost World 250.00
13 BEv,King of the Living Dead 350.00
14 BEv,The Fountain of Death . 350.00
15 BEv,The Empty Grave 350.00
16 BEv,Where Gargoyles Dwell 350.00
17 BEv,Tower of Death, Bondage(c) 350.00
18 BEv,Terror in the Tunnel . . . 350.00
19 BEv,THe Kiss Of Death . . . 350.00

VERY BEST OF MARVEL COMICS

One Shot reps Marvel Artists Favorite Stories 12.95

VIDEO JACK
November, 1987

1 KGi,O:Video Jack 2.50
2 KGi 2.00
3 KGi 1.75
4 KGi 1.75
5 KGi 1.75
6 KGi,NA,BWr,AW 1.25

VISION & SCARLET WITCH
[1st Series]
November, 1982

1 RL,V:Halloween 2.00
2 RL,V:Isbisa,D:Whizzer 1.50
3 RL,A:Wonderman,V:GrimReaper 1.50
4 RL,A:Magneto,Inhumans 1.50

[2nd Series]

1 V:Grim Reaper 2.00
2 V:Lethal Legion,D:Grim Reaper 1.75
3 V:Salem's Seven 1.75
4 I:Glamor & Illusion 1.75
5 A:Glamor & Illusion 1.75
6 A:Magneto 1.75
7 V:Toad 1.75
8 A:Powerman 1.75
9 V:Enchantress 1.75
10 A:Inhumans 1.75
11 A:Spider-Man 1.75
12 Birth of V&S's Child 1.25

VISIONARIES
Star
November, 1987

1 thru 5 . . . . @1.00
6 September, 1988 . . . . 1.00

VOID INDIGO
Epic
November, 1984

1 VM,Epic Comics 2.00
2 VM,Epic Comics,March, 1985 . 2.00

WACKY DUCK
See: DOPEY DUCK

WALLY THE WIZARD
Star
April, 1985

1 . . . . 1.25
2 thru 11 . . . . @1.00
12 March, 1986 . . . . 1.00

WAR, THE
1989

1 Sequel to The Draft & The Pit . 3.50
2 . . . . 3.50

3 3.50
4 1990 3.50

WAR ACTION
Atlas
April, 1952

1 JMn,RH,War Stories, Six Dead Men 75.00
2 31.00
3 Invasion in Korea 25.00
4 thru 10 @25.00
11 40.00
12 40.00
13 BK 40.00
14 Rangers Strike,June, 1953 25.00

WAR ADVENTURES
Atlas
January, 1952

1 GT,Battle Fatigue 75.00
2 The Story of a Slaughter 30.00
3 JRo 25.00
4 RH(c) 25.00
5 RH,Violent(c) 25.00
6 Stand or Die 25.00
7 JMn(c) 25.00
8 BK 40.00
9 RH(c) 20.00
10 JRo(c),Attack at Dawn 20.00
11 Red Trap 20.00
12 20.00
13 RH(c),The Commies Strike February, 1953 20.00

WAR COMBAT
Atlas
March, 1952

1 JMn,Death of a Platoon Leader 55.00
2 30.00
3 JMn(c) 20.00
4 JMn(c) 20.00
5 THe Red Hordes 20.00

Becomes:

COMBAT CASEY

6 BEv,Combat Casey cont 40.00
7 30.00
8 JMn(c) 22.00
9 20.00
10 RH(c) 30.00
11 15.00
12 15.00
13 thru 19 @30.00
20 15.00
21 thru 33 @12.00
34 July, 1957 12.00

WAR COMICS
Atlas
December, 1950

1 You Only Die Twice 100.00
2 Infantry's War 50.00
3 35.00
4 GC,The General Said Nuts 35.00
5 35.00
6 The Deadly Decision of General Kwang 35.00
7 RH 35.00
8 RH,No Survivors 35.00
9 RH 35.00
10 35.00
11 thru 21 @25.00
22 45.00
23 thru 37 @20.00
38 JKu 35.00
39 20.00
40 20.00
41 20.00
42 20.00
43 AT 30.00
44 20.00
45 20.00
46 RC 35.00
47 20.00
48 20.00
49 September, 1957 30.00

WARHEADS

1 GEr,I:Warheads,A:Wolverine, 2.25
2 GEr,V:Nick Fury 2.00
3 DTy,A:Iron Man 2.00
4 SCy,A:X-Force 2.00
5 A:X-Force,C:Deaths'Head II 2.00
6 SCy,A:Death's Head II 2.00
7 SCy,A:Death's Head II,S.Surfer 2.00
8 SCy,V:Mephisto 2.00
9 SCy,V:Mephisto 2.00
10 JCz,V:Mephisto 2.00
11 A:Death's Head II 2.00
12 V:Mechanix 2.00
13 Xenophiles Reptiles 2.00
14 last issue 2.00

WARHEADS: BLACK DAWN

1 A:Gh.Rider,Morbius 3.25
2 V:Dracula 2.00

WAR IS HELL
January, 1973

1 B:Reprints,Decision at Dawn 2.00
2 Anytime,Anyplace,War is Hell 1.50
3 Retreat or Die 1.50
4 Live Grenade 1.50
5 Trapped Platoon 1.50
6 We Die at Dawn 1.50
7 While the Jungle Sleeps,A:Sgt Fury 1.50
8 Killed in Action,A;Sgt Fury 1.50
9 B:Supernatural,War Stories 1.50
10 Death is a 30 Ton Tank 1.50
11 1.50
12 1.50
13 1.50
14 1.50
15 October, 1975 1.50

WARLOCK
[1st Regular Series]
August, 1972

1 GK,I:Counter Earth,A:High Evolutionary 39.00
2 JB,TS,V:Man Beast 20.00
3 GK,TS,V:Apollo 13.00
4 JK,TS,V:Triax 12.00
5 GK,TS,V:Dr.Doom 12.00
6 TS(i),O:Brute 12.00
7 TS(i),V:Brute,D:Dr.Doom 12.00
8 TS(i),R:Man-Beast(cont in Hulk #176) 12.00
9 JSn,1st'Rebirth'Thanos,O:Magnus, N:Warlock,I:In-Betweener 24.00
10 JSn,SL,O:Thanos,V:Magus, A:In-Betweener 43.00
11 JSn,SL,D:Magus,A:Thanos, In-Betweener 37.00
12 JSn,SL,O:Pip,V:Pro-Boscis A:Starfox 18.00
13 JSn,SL,I&O:Star-Thief 18.00
14 JSn,SL,V:Star-Thief 18.00
15 JSn,A:Thanos,V:Soul-Gem 35.00

[2nd Regular Series]

1 JSn,rep.Strange Tales #178-180 Baxter Paper 11.00
2 JSn,rep.Strange Tales #180 & Warlock #9 10.00
3 JSn,rep.Warlock #10-#12 10.00
4 JSn,rep.Warlock #13-#15 10.00
5 JSn,rep.Warlock #15 10.00
6 JSn,rep. 10.00

WARLOCK
(Limited Series)

1 Rep.Warlock Series 3.50
2 Rep.Warlock Series 3.00
3 Rep.Warlock Series 3.00
4 Rep.Warlock Series 3.00
5 Rep.Warlock Series 3.00
6 Rep.Warlock Series 3.00

Warlock & the Infinity Watch
© Marvel Entertainment Group

WARLOCK AND THE INFINITY WATCH

1 AMe,Trial of the Gods(from Infinity Gauntlet) 4.50
2 AMe,I:Infinity Watch(Gamora,Pip, Moondragon,Drax & 1 other) 3.50
3 RL,TA,A:High Evolutionary, Nobilus,I:Omega 3.00
4 RL,TA,V:Omega 2.50
5 AMe,TA,V:Omega 2.50
6 AMe,V:Omega(Man-Beast) 2.50
7 TR,TA,V:Mole Man,A:Thanos 2.50
8 TR,TA,Infinity War,A:Thanos 2.25
9 AMe,TA,Inf.War,O:Gamora 2.00
10 AMe,Inf.War,Thanos vs Doppleganger 2.50
11 O:Pip,Gamora,Drax,M'dragon 2.00
12 TR,Drax Vs.Hulk 2.00
13 TR,Drax vs Hulk 2.00
14 AMe,V:United Nations 2.00
15 AMe,Magnus,Him 2.00
16 TGr,I:Count Abyss 2.00
17 TGr,I:Maxam 2.00
18 AMe,Inf.Crusade,N:Pip 2.00
19 TGr,A:Hulk,Wolverine,Infinity Crusade 2.00
20 AMe,Inf.Crusade 2.00
21 V:Thor 2.00
22 AMe,Infinity Crusade 2.00
23 JSn(s),TGb,Blood & Thunder#4 2.00
24 JSn(s),TGb,V:Geirrodur 2.00
25 JSn(s),AMe,Die-Cut(c),Blood & Thunder #12 3.25
26 A:Avengers 2.00
27 TGb,V:Avengers 2.00
28 TGb,V:Man-Beast 2.00
29 A:Maya 1.95
30 PO, 1.95

WARLOCK CHRONICLES

1 TR,F:Adam Warlock,holo-grafx(c), I:Darklore,Meer'lyn 3.25
2 TR,Infinity Crusade,Thanos revealed to have the Reality Gem 2.25
3 TR,A:Mephisto 2.25
4 TR,A:Magnus 2.25

5 TR(c),Inf.Crusade 2.25
6 TR,Blood & Thunder Pt.#3 2.25
7 TR,Blood & Thunder Pt.#7 2.25
8 TR,Blood & Thunder Pt.#11 2.25

WAR MACHINE

1 GG,Foil Embossed(c),B:LKa&StB, O:War Machine,V:Cable, C:Deathlok 3.25
1a Newstand Ed. 2.25
2 GG,V:Cable,Deathlok,w/card 1.75
3 GG,V:Cable,Deathlok 1.75
4 GG,C:Force Works 1.50

WAR MAN
Epic

1 thru 2 CDi(s) 2.50

WEAVEWORLD
Epic

1 MM, Clive Barker adaptation 4.95
2 MM,'Into the Weave' 4.95
3 MM 4.95

Web of Spider-Man #79
© Marvel Entertainment Group

WEB OF SPIDER-MAN
April, 1985

1 JM,V:New Costume 30.00
2 JM,V:Vulture 10.00
3 JM,V:Vulture 8.00
4 JM,JBy,V:Dr.Octopus 7.00
5 JM,JBy,V:Dr.Octopus 7.00
6 MZ,BL,JM,Secret Wars II 7.00
7 SB,A:Hulk,V:Nightmare, C:Wolverine 7.00
8 V:Smithville Thunder 7.00
9 V:Smithville Thunder 7.00
10 JM,A:Dominic Fortune, V:Shocker 7.00
11 BMc,V:Thugs 7.00
12 BMc,SB,V:Thugs 7.00
13 BMc,V:J.JonahJameson 7.00
14 KB,V:Black Fox 7.00
15 V:Black Fox,I:Chance 8.00
16 MS,KB,V:Magma 5.00
17 MS,V:Magma 5.00
18 MS,KB,Where is Spider-Man? 8.00
19 MS,BMc,I:Solo,Humbug 6.00
20 MS,V:Terrorists 5.00
21 V:Fake Spider-Man 5.00
22 MS,V:Terrorists 5.00
23 V:Slyde 5.00
24 SB,V:Vulture,Hobgoblin 6.00
25 V:Aliens 5.00
26 V:Thugs 5.00
27 V:Headhunter 5.00
28 BL,V:Thugs 5.00
29 A:Wolverine,2nd App:New Hobgoblin 24.00
30 KB,O:Rose,C:Daredevil,Capt. America,Wolverine,Punisher 16.00
31 MZ,BMc,V:Kraven 13.00

Web of Spider-Man #93
© Marvel Entertainment Group

32 MZ,BMc,V:Kraven 12.00
33 BSz(c),SL,V:Kingpin,Mad Dog Ward Pt.#1 5.00
34 SB,A:Watcher 4.00
35 AS,V:Living Brain 4.00
36 AS,V:Phreak Out,I:Tombstone 6.00
37 V:Slasher 4.00
38 AS,A:Tombstone,V:Hobgoblin 6.00
39 AS,V:Looter(Meteor Man) 4.00
40 AS,V:Cult of Love 4.00
41 AS,V:Cult of Love 4.00
42 AS,V:Cult of Love 4.00
43 AS,V:Cult of Love 4.00
44 AS,V:Warzone,A:Hulk 3.00
45 AS,V:Vulture 3.00
46 A:Dr.Pym,V:Nekra 3.00
47 AS,V:Hobgoblin 5.00
48 AS,O:New Hobgoblin's Demonic Power 17.00
49 VM,V:Drugs 3.00
50 AS,V:Chameleon(double size) 5.00
51 MBa,V:Chameleon,Lobo Bros. 4.00
52 FS,JR,O:J.Jonah Jameson V:Chameleon 4.00
53 MBa,V:Lobo Bros.,C:Punisher A:Chameleon 4.50
54 AS,V:Chameleon,V:Lobo Bros. 4.00
55 AS,V:Chameleon,Hammerhead, V:Lobo Bros. 4.00
56 AS,I&O:Skin Head, A:Rocket Racer 3.50
57 AS,D:SkinHead, A:Rocket Racer 3.00
58 AS,V:Grizzly 3.00
59 AS,Acts of Vengeance,V:Titania A:Puma,Cosmic Spider-Man 7.50
60 AS,A of V,V:Goliath 4.50
61 AS,A of V,V:Dragon Man 4.00
62 AS,V:Molten Man 3.00
63 AS,V:Mister Fear 3.00
64 AS,V:Graviton,Titania,Trapster 3.00
65 AS,V:Goliath,Trapster,Graviton 3.00
66 AS,V:Tombstone,A:G.Goblin 4.00
67 AS,A:Gr.Goblin,V:Tombstone 4.00
68 AS,A:Gr.Goblin,V:Tombstone 3.50
69 AS,V:Hulk 3.00
70 AS,I:The Spider/Hulk 3.00
71 A:Silver Sable 2.50
72 AM,A:Silver Sable 2.50
73 AS,A:Human Torch, Colossus,Namor 2.50
74 AS,I:Spark,V:Bora 2.50
75 AS,C:New Warriors 2.50
76 AS,Spidey in Ice 2.50
77 AS,V:Firebrand,Inheritor 2.50
78 AS,A:Firebrand,Cloak&Dagger 2.50
79 AS,V:Silvermane 2.50
80 AS,V:Silvermane 2.50
81 I:Bloodshed 2.25
82 V:Man Mountain Marko 2.25
83 V:A.I.M. Supersuit 2.25
84 AS,B:Name of the Rose 3.00
85 AS,Name of the Rose 2.50
86 AS,I:Demogoblin 2.50
87 AS,I:Praetorian Guard 2.50
88 AS,Name of the Rose 2.50
89 AS,E:Name of the Rose, I:Bloodrose 2.50
90 AS,30th Ann.,w/hologram, polybagged,V:Mysterio 5.00
90a Gold 2nd printing 3.25
91 AS,V:Whisper And Pulse 2.00
92 AS,V:Foreigner 2.00
93 AS,BMc,V:Hobgoblin,A:Moon Knight,Foreigner 2.00
94 AS,V:Hobgoblin,A:MoonKnight 2.00
95 AS,Spirits of Venom#1,A:Venom, J.Blaze,GR,V:Hag & Troll 5.00
96 AS,Spirits of Venom#3, A:G.R, J.Blaze,Venom,Hobgoblin 4.00
97 AS,I:Dr.Trench,V:Bloodrose 1.75
98 AS,V:Bloodrose,Foreigner 1.75
99 I:Night Watch,V:New Enforcer 1.75
100 AS,JRu,V:Enforcers,Bloodrose, Kingpin(Alfredo),I:Spider Armor, O:Night Watch,Holografx(c) 5.00

Web of Spider-Man #50
© Marvel Entertainment Group

101 AS,Total Carnage,V:Carnage, Shriek,A:Cloak and Dagger, Venom 1.75
102 Total Carnage#6,V:Carnage, A:Venom,Morbius 1.75

103 AS,Maximum Carnage#10,
V:Carnage 1.50
104 AS,Infinity Crusade 1.50
105 AS,Infinity Crusade 1.50
106 AS,Infinity Crusade 1.50
107 AS,A:Sandman,Quicksand . . 1.50
108 B:TKa(s),AS,I:Sandstorm,
BU:Cardiac 1.50
109 AS,V:Shocker,A:Night Thrasher,
BU:D:Calypso 1.50
110 AS,I:Warrant,A:Lizard 1.50
111 AS,V:Warrant,Lizard 1.50
112 AS,Pursuit#3,V:Chameleon,
w/card 1.75
113 AS,A:Gambit,Black Cat,w/cel . 3.25
113a Newsstand Ed. 1.75
Ann.#1 V:Future Max 5.00
Ann.#2 AAd,MMi,A:Warlock 8.00
Ann.#3 AS,DP,JRu,JM,BL 4.50
Ann.#4 AS,TM,RLm,Evolutionary
Wars,A:Man Thing,V:Slug 5.00
Ann.#5 AS,SD,JS,Atlantis
Attacks,A:Fantastic Four 3.50
Ann.#6 SD,JBr,SB,A:Punisher . . . 4.50
Ann.#7 Vibranium Vendetta #3 . . 2.50
Ann.#8 Hero Killers#3,A:New
Warriors,BU:Venom,Black Cat . 3.00
Ann.#9 CMa,I:Cadre,w/card 3.25
Ann.#10 V:Shriek 2.95

WEIRD WONDERTALES

December, 1973

1 B:Reprints 5.00
2 I Was Kidnapped by a Flying
Saucer 2.50
3 The Thing in the Bog 2.50
4 It Lurks Behind the Wall 2.50
5 . . . . 2.50
6 The Man Who Owned a Ghost 2.50
7 The Apes That Walked
like Men 2.50
8 Reap A Deadly Harvest 2.50
9 The Murder Mirror 2.50
10 Mister Morgans Monster 2.50
11 Slaughter in Shrangri-La 2.50
12 The Stars Scream Murder 2.50
13 The Totem Strikes 2.50
14 Witching Circle 2.50
15 . . . . 2.50
16 The Shark 2.50
17 Creature From Krogarr 2.50
18 Krang 2.50
19 A:Dr Druid 2.50
20 The Madness 2.50
21 A:Dr Druid 2.50
22 The World Below,May, 1975 . . 2.50

WEREWOLF BY NIGHT

September, 1972

1 MP(cont from Marvel Spotlight)
FullMoonRise..WerewolfKill . . 34.00
2 MP,Like a Wild Beast at Bay . 20.00
3 MP,Mystery of the Mad Monk 10.00
4 MP,The Danger Game 10.00
5 MP,A Life for a Death 10.00
6 MP,Carnival of Fear 8.00
7 MP,JM,Ritual of Blood 8.00
8 MP,Krogg,Lurker from Beyond . 8.00
9 TS,V:Tatterdemalion 8.00
10 TS,bondage cover 8.00
11 GK,TS,Full Moon..Fear Moon . 6.00
12 GK,Cry Monster 6.00
13 MP,ManMonsterCalledTaboo . 6.00
14 MP,Lo,the Monster Strikes . . . 6.00
15 MP,(new)O:Werewolf,
V:Dracula 7.00
16 MP,TS,A:Hunchback of Notre
Dame 6.00
17 Behold the Behemoth 6.00
18 War of the Werewolves 6.00
19 V:Dracula 7.00
20 The Monster Breaks Free 6.00
21 GK(c),To Cure a Werewolf . . . 4.50
22 GK(c),Face of a Friend 4.50
23 Silver Bullet for a Werewolf . . . 4.50
24 GK(c),V:The Brute 4.50
25 GK(c),Eclipse of Evil 4.50
26 GK(c),A Crusade of Murder . . 4.50
27 GK(c),Scourge o/t Soul-Beast . 4.50
28 GK(c),V:Dr.Glitternight 4.50
29 GK(c),V:Dr.Glitternight 4.50
30 GK(c),Red Slash across
Midnight 4.50
31 Death in White 4.50
32 I&O:Moon Knight 48.00
33 Were-Beast..Moon Knight
A:Moon Knight(2nd App) 26.00
34 GK(c),TS,House of Evil..House
of Death 3.50
35 TS,JS,BWi,Jack Russell vs.
Werewolf 4.00
36 Images of Death 3.50
37 BWr(c),BW,A:Moon Knight,
Hangman,Dr.Glitternight 8.50
38 . . . . 3.50
39 V:Brother Voodoo 3.50
40 A:Brother Voodoo,V:Dr.
Glitternight 3.50
41 V:Fire Eyes 3.50
42 A:IronMan,Birth of a Monster . 3.50
43 Tri-Animal Lives,A:Iron Man . . 3.50
Giant#2,SD,A:Frankenstein
Monster (reprint) 3.00
Giant#3 GK(c),Transylvania 3.50
Giant#4 GK(c),A:Morbius 12.00
Giant#5 GK(c),Peril of
Paingloss 2.50

West Coast Avengers #1
© Marvel Entertainment Group

WEST COAST AVENGERS

[Limited Series]
September, 1984

1 BH,A:Shroud,J:Hawkeye,IronMan,
WonderMan,Mockingbird,Tigra 8.00
2 BH,V:Blank 5.00
3 BH,V:Graviton 5.00
4 BH,V:Graviton 5.00

[Regular Series]

1 AM,JSt,V:Lethal Legion 6.00
2 AM,JSt,V:Lethal Legion 4.00
3 AM,JSt,V:Kraven 3.00
4 AM,JSt,A:Firebird,Thing,I:Master
Pandemonium 3.00
5 AM,JSt,A:Werewolf,Thing 3.00
6 AM,KB,A:Thing 3.00
7 AM,JSt,V:Ultron 3.00
8 AM,JSt,V:Rangers,A:Thing . . . 3.00
9 AM,JSt,V:Master Pandemonium 3.00
10 AM,JSt,V:Headlok,Griffen 3.00
11 AM,JSt,A:Nick Fury 2.50
12 AM,JSt,V:Graviton 2.50
13 AM,JSt,V:Graviton 2.50
14 AM,JSt,V:Pandemonium 2.50
15 AM,JSt,A:Hellcat 2.50
16 AM,JSt,V:Tiger Shark,
Whirlwind 2.50
17 AM,JSt,V:Dominus' Minions . . 2.50
18 AM,JSt,V:The Wild West 2.50
19 AM,JSt,A:Two Gun Kid 2.50
20 AM,JSt,A:Rawhide Kid 2.50
21 AM,JSt,A:Dr.Pym,Moon Knight 2.50
22 AM,JSt,A:Fant.Four,Dr.Strange,
Night Rider 2.00
23 AM,RT,A:Phantom Rider 2.00
24 AM,V:Dominus 2.00
25 AM,V:Abomination 2.00
26 AM,V:Zodiac 2.00
27 AM,V:Zodiac 1.75
28 AM,V:Zodiac 1.75
29 AM,V:Taurus,A:Shroud 1.75
30 AM,C:Composite Avenger 1.75
31 AM,V:Arkon 1.75
32 AM,TD,V:Yetrigar,J:Wasp 1.75
33 AM,O:Ant-Man,Wasp;
V:Madam X,El Toro 1.75
34 AM,V:Quicksilver,J:Vision &
Scarlet Witch 1.75
35 AM,V:Dr.Doom,Quicksilver . . . 1.75
36 AM,V:The Voice 1.75
37 V:The Voice,A:Mantis 1.75
38 AM,TMo,V:Defiler 1.75
39 AM,V:Swordsman 1.75
40 AM,MGu,V:NightShift,
A:Shroud 1.75
41 TMo,I:New Phantom Rider,
L:Moon Knight 1.75
42 JBy,Visionquest#1,V:Ultron . . . 3.50
43 JBy,Visionquest#2, ... 2.50
44 JBy,Visionquest#3,J:USAgent . 2.00
45 JBy,Visionquest#4,
I:New Vision 2.50
46 JBy,I:Great Lakes Avengers . . 2.00
Ann. #1 MBr,GI,V:Zodiak 2.25
Ann. #2 AM,A:SilverSurfer,V:Death,
Collector,R:Grandmaster 2.00
Ann. #3 AM,RLm,TD,Evolutionary
Wars,R:Giant Man 3.50

Becomes:
AVENGERS WEST COAST

WESTERN GUNFIGHTERS

August, 1970
[2nd series]

1 JK,JB,DAy,B:Ghost Rider
A:Fort Rango,The Renegades
Gunhawk 6.00
2 HT(c),DAy,JMn,O:Nightwind,
V:Tarantula 3.50
3 DAy,V:Hurricane(reprint) 3.50
4 HT(c),DAy,TS,B:Gunhawk,
Apache Kid,A;Renegades . . . 3.50
5 DAy,FrG,A:Renegades 3.50
6 HT(c),DAy,SSh,Death of
Ghost Rider 4.00
7 HT(c),DAy,SSh,,O:Ghost Rider
retold,E:Ghost Rider,Gunhawk 5.00
8 DAy,SSh,B:Black Rider,Outlaw
Kid(rep) 3.00
9 DW,Revenge rides the Range . 3.00
10 JK,JMn,O:Black Rider,B:Matt
Slade,E:Outlaw Kid 3.00
11 JK,Duel at Dawn 3.00
12 JMn,O:Matt Slade 3.00
13 Save the Gold Coast Expires . 3.00
14 JSo(c),Outlaw Town 3.00
15 E:Matt Slade,Showdown in
Outlaw Canyon 3.00
16 B:Kid Colt,Shoot-out in Silver
City 3.00
17 thru 20 . . . . @3.00

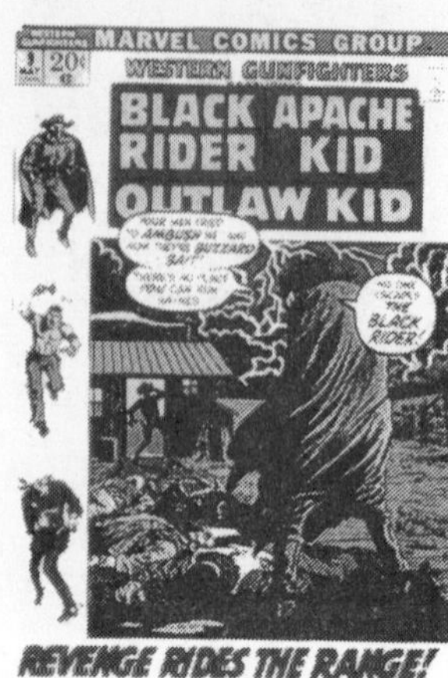

Western Gunfighters #9
© Marvel Entertainment Group

21 thru 24 . . . . @2.50
25 . . . . 2.50
26 F:Kid Colt,Gun-Slinger,Apache Kid 2.50
27 thru 32 . . . . @2.50
33 November, 1975 . . . . 2.50

WESTERN KID
December, 1954
[1st Series]

1 JR,B:Western Kid,O:Western Kid (Tex Dawson) 85.00
2 JMn,JR,Western Adventure . . 40.00
3 JMn(c),JR,Gunfight(c) 35.00
4 JMn(c),JR,The Badlands . . . 35.00
5 JR 35.00
6 JR 35.00
7 JR 35.00
8 JR 35.00
9 JR,AW 45.00
10 JR,AW,Man in the Middle . . . 45.00
11 . . . . 25.00
12 . . . . 25.00
13 . . . . 25.00
14 . . . . 25.00
15 . . . . 25.00
16 . . . . 25.00
17 August, 1957 . . . . 25.00

WESTERN KID
December, 1971
[2nd Series]

1 Reprints 4.00
2 . . . . 3.00
3 . . . . 3.00
4 . . . . 3.00
5 August, 1972 . . . . 3.00

WESTERN OUTLAWS
Atlas
February, 1954

1 JMn(c),RH,BP,The Greenville Gallows,Hanging(c) 100.00
2 . . . . 50.00
3 thru 10 . . . . @40.00
11 AW 45.00
12 . . . . 30.00
13 MB 35.00
14 AW 45.00
15 AT,GT 40.00
16 BP 30.00
17 . . . . 35.00
18 . . . . 30.00
19 . . . . 40.00
20 . . . . 35.00
21 August, 1957 . . . . 35.00

WESTERN OUTLAWS & SHERIFFS
See: BEST WESTERN

WESTERN TALES OF BLACK RIDER
See: ALL WINNERS COMICS

WESTERN TEAM-UP
November, 1973

1 Rawhide Kid/Dakota Kid 2.00

WESTERN THRILLERS
November, 1954

1 JMn,Western tales 70.00
2 . . . . 35.00
3 . . . . 35.00
4 . . . . 35.00

Becomes:

COWBOY ACTION

5 JMn(c),The Prairie Kid 45.00
6 . . . . 30.00
7 . . . . 30.00
9 . . . . 30.00
10 . . . . 30.00
11 MN,AW,Ther Manhunter March, 1956 . . . . 45.00

Becomes:

QUICK-TRIGGER WESTERN

12 Bill Larson Strikes 55.00
13 The Man From Cheyenne . . . 60.00
14 BEv,RH(c) 50.00
15 AT 40.00
16 JK 35.00
17 GT 35.00
18 GM 35.00
19 JSe 30.00

WESTERN WINNERS
See: ALL WINNERS COMICS

WHAT IF?
[1st Regular Series]
February, 1977

1 Spider-Man joined Fant.Four . 18.00
2 GK(c),Hulk had Banner brain . 11.00
3 GK,KJ,F:Avengers 7.00
4 GK(c),F:Invaders 7.00
5 F:Captain America 7.00
6 F:Fantastic Four 7.00
7 GK(c),F:Spider-Man 7.00
8 GK(c),F:Daredevil 5.50
9 JK(c),F:Avengers of the '50s . . 6.00
10 JB,F:Thor 5.00
11 JK,F:FantasticFour 4.00
12 F:Hulk 4.00
13 JB,Conan Alive Today 6.00
14 F:Sgt. Fury 5.00
15 CI,F:Nova 5.00
16 F:Master of Kung Fu 5.00
17 CI,F:Ghost Rider 9.00
18 TS,F:Dr.Strange 4.00
19 PB,F:Spider-Man 5.00
20 F:Avengers 4.00
21 GC,F:Sub-Mariner 4.00
22 F:Dr.Doom 4.00
23 JB,F:Hulk 4.00
24 GK,RB,Gwen Stacy had lived . 5.00
25 F:Thor,Avengers,O:Mentor . . 4.00
26 JBy(c),F:Captain America . . . 4.00
27 FM(c),Phoenix hadn't died . . 12.00
28 FM,F:Daredevil,Ghost Rider. . 12.00
29 MG(c),F:Avengers 4.00

What If? #9
© Marvel Entertainment Group

30 RB,F:Spider-Man 5.00
31 Wolverine killed the Hulk . . . 16.00
32 Avengers lost to Korvac 3.50
33 BL,Dazzler herald of Galactus . 3.50
34 FH,FM,JBy,BSz:Humor issue . 3.50
35 FM,Elektra had lived 6.00
36 JBy,Fant.Four had no powers . 3.00
37 F:Thing,Beast,Silver Surfer . . . 3.50
38 F:Daredevil,Captain America . . 3.00
39 Thor had fought Conan 3.00
40 F:Dr.Strange 3.00
41 F:Sub-Mariner 3.50
42 F:Fantastic Four 3.00
43 F:Conan 3.00
44 F:Captain America 3.00
45 F:Hulk,Berserk 3.50
46 Uncle Ben had lived 5.00
47 F:Thor,Loki 3.00
Spec.#1 F:Iron Man,Avengers . . . 4.00
Best of What IF? rep.#1,#24, #27,#28 . . . . 12.95

[2nd Regular Series]

1 RWi,MG,The Avengers had lost the Evolutionary War 5.50
2 GCa,Daredevil Killed Kingpin, A:Hobgoblin, The Rose 4.00
3 Capt.America Hadn't Given Up Costume,A:Avengers 3.50
4 MBa,Spider-Man kept Black Costume,A:Avengers,Hulk 4.50
5 Vision Destroyed Avengers, A:Wonder Man 3.50
6 RLm,X-Men Lost Inferno, A:Dr.Strange 6.00
7 RLd,Wolverine Joined Shield, A:Nick Fury,Black Widow 7.00
8 Iron Man Lost The Armor Wars, A:Ant Man 3.50
9 RB,New X-Men Died 5.00
10 MZ(c),BMc,Punisher's Family Didn't Die,A:Kingpin 5.00
11 TM(c),JV,SM,Fant.Four had the Same Powers,A:Nick Fury . . . 3.50
12 JV,X-Men Stayed in Asgard, A:Thor,Hela 3.00
13 JLe(c),Prof.X Became Juggernaut,A:X-Men 3.00
14 RLm(c),Capt.Marvel didn't die A:Silver Surfer 2.50
15 GCa,Fant.Four Lost Trial of Galactus,A:Gladiator 2.25

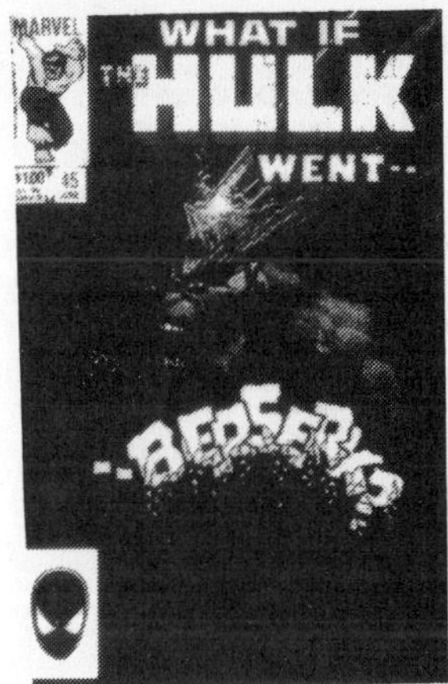

What If? #45
© Marvel Entertainment Group

16 Wolverine Battled Conan, A:X-Men,Red Sonja . . . 5.00
17 Kraven Killed Spider-Man, A:Daredevil,Captain America . . . 2.50
18 LMc,Fant.Four fought Dr.Doom before they gained powers . . . 2.25
19 RW,Vision took over Earth, A:Avengers,Dr.Doom . . . 2.25
20 Spider-Man didn't marry Mary Jane,A:Venom,Kraven . . . 3.00
21 Spider-Man married Black Cat, A:Vulture,Silver Sable . . . 2.50
22 RLm,Silver Surfer didn't escape Earth,A:F.F,Mephisto,Thanos . 3.00
23 New X-Men never existed, A:Eric the Red,Lilandra . . . 2.50
24 Wolverine Became Lord of Vampires,A:Punisher . . . 3.50
25 Marvel Heroes lost Atlantis Attacks,double size . . . 3.25
26 LMc,Punisher Killed Daredevil, A:Spider-Man . . . 2.50
27 Submariner Joined Fantastic Four,A:Dr. Doom . . . 2.00
28 RW,Capt.America led Army of Super-Soldiers,A:Submariner . 2.00
29 RW,Capt.America formed the Avengers . . . 2.00
30 Inv.Woman's 2nd Child had lived,A:Fantastic Four . . . 2.00
31 Spider-Man/Captain Universe Powers . . . 2.00
32 Phoenix Rose Again Pt.1 . . . 2.00
33 Phoenix Rose Again Pt.2 . . . 2.00
34 Humor Issue . . . 1.75
35 B:Time Quake,F.F. vs.Dr. Doom & Annihilus . . . 1.75
36 Cosmic Avengers,V:Guardians of the Galaxy . . . 1.75
37 X-Vampires,V:Dormammu . . . 1.75
38 Thor was prisoner of Set . . . 1.50
39 E:Time Quake,Watcher saved the Universe . . . 1.50
40 Storm remained A thief? . . . 1.50
41 JV,Avengers fought Galactus . 2.00
42 KWe,Spidey kept extra arms . . 1.75
43 Wolverine married Mariko . . . 1.75
44 Punisher possessedby Venom 1.75
45 Barbara Ketch became G.R. . . 1.50
46 Cable Killed Prof.X,Cyclops & Jean Grey . . . 1.75
47 Magneto took over USA . . . 1.75
48 Daredevil Saved Nuke . . . 1.50
49 Silver Surfer had Inf.Gauntlet? 1.50
50 Hulk killed Wolverine . . . 4.00
51 PCu,Punisher is Capt.America 1.50
52 BHi,Wolverine led Alpha Flight 1.50
53 F:Iron Man,Hulk . . . 1.50
54 F:Death's Head . . . 1.50
55 LKa(s),Avengers lose G.Storm 1.50
56 Avengers lose G.Storm#2 . . . 1.50
57 Punisher a member of SHIELD 1.50
58 Punisher kills SpM . . . 1.50
59 Wolverine lead Alpha Flight . . 1.50
60 RoR,Scott & Jean's Wedding . 1.50
61 Spider-Man's Parents . . . 1.95
62 Woverine vs Weapon X . . . 1.95
63 F:War Machine,Iron Man . . . 1.95

WHAT THE -?!
[Parodies]
August, 1988

1 . . . 6.00
2 JBy,JOy,AW, . . . 4.00
3 TM, . . . 5.00
4 . . . 4.00
5 EL,JLe,WPo,Wolverine . . . 5.00
6 Wolverine,Punisher . . . 4.00
7 . . . 2.50
8 DK . . . 2.50
9 . . . 1.75
10 JBy,X-Men,Dr.Doom, Cap. America . . . 1.75
11 DK,RLd(part) . . . 2.00
12 Conan, F.F.,Wolverine. . . . 1.50
13 Silver Burper,F.F.,Wolverine. . . 1.50
14 Spittle-Man . . . 1.50
15 Capt Ultra,Wolverine . . . 1.50
16 Ant Man,Watcher . . . 1.25
17 Wulverean/Pulverizer,Hoagg/ Spider-Ham,SleepGawker,F.F. 1.25
18 . . . 1.25
19 . . . 1.25
20 Infinity Wart Crossover . . . 1.25
21 Weapon XX,Toast Rider . . . 1.25
22 F:Echs Farce . . . 1.25
23 . . . 1.25
24 Halloween issue . . . 1.25
25 . . . 1.25
26 Spider-Ham 2099 . . . 1.25
Summer Spec. . . . 2.50

WHERE CREATURES ROAM
July, 1970

1 JK,SD,DAy,B:Reprints The Brute That Walks . . . 4.50
2 JK,SD,Midnight/Monster . . . 2.25
3 JK,SD,DAy,Thorg . . . 2.25
4 JK,SD,Vandoom . . . 2.25
5 JK,SD,Gorgilla . . . 2.25
6 JK,SD,Zog . . . 2.25
7 SD . . . 2.25
8 The Mummy's Secret,E:Reprints September, 1971 . . . 2.25

WHERE MONSTERS DWELL
January, 1970

1 B:Reprints,Cyclops . . . 5.00
2 Sporr . . . 3.50
3 Grottu . . . 3.50
4 . . . 3.50
5 Taboo . . . 3.50
6 Groot . . . 3.50
7 Rommbu . . . 3.50
8 The Four-Armed Men . . . 3.50
9 Bumbu . . . 3.50
10 Monster That Walks Like A Man . . . 3.50
11 Gruto . . . 3.00
12 Orogo . . . 3.00
13 The Thing That Crawl . . . 3.00
14 The Green Thing . . . 3.00
15 Kraa- The Inhuman . . . 3.00
16 Beware the Son Of Goom . . . 3.00
17 The Hidden Vampires . . . 3.00
18 The Mask of Morghum . . . 3.00
19 The Insect Man . . . 3.00
20 Klagg . . . 3.00
21 Fin Fang Foom . . . 3.00
22 Elektro . . . 3.00
23 The Monster Waits For Me . . . 3.00
24 The Things on Easter Island . . 3.00
25 The Ruler of the Earth . . . 3.00
26 . . . 3.00
27 . . . 3.00
28 Droom,The Living Lizard . . . 3.00
29 thru 37 Reprints . . . @3.00
38 Reprints,October, 1975 . . . 3.00

WHIP WILSON
See: BLAZE CARSON

WILD
Atlas
February, 1954

1 BEv,JMn,Charlie Chan Parody . . . 100.00
2 BEv,RH,JMn,Witches(c) . . . 70.00
3 CBu(c),BEv,RH,JMn, . . . 50.00
4 GC,Didja Ever See a Cannon Brawl . . . 50.00
5 RH,JMn,August, 1954 . . . 50.00

WILD CARDS
Epic
September, 1990

1 JG . . . 5.50
2 JG,V:Jokers . . . 4.50
3 A:Turtle . . . 4.50

WILD THING

1 A:Virtual Reality Venom and Carnage . . . 3.00
2 A:VR Venom and Carnage . . . 2.00
3 A:Shield . . . 2.00
4 . . . 2.00
5 Virtual Reality Gangs . . . 2.00
6 Virtual Reality Villians . . . 2.00
7 V:Trask . . . 1.75

WILD WEST
Spring, 1948

1 SSh(c),B:Two Gun Kids,Tex Taylor,Arizona Annie . . . 125.00
2 SSh(c),CCb, Captain Tootsie 100.00

Becomes:

WILD WESTERN

3 SSh(c),B:Tex Morgan,Two Gun Kid,Tex Taylor,Arizona Annie 140.00
4 Rh,SSh,CCB,Capt. Tootsie. A:Kid Colt,E:Arizona Annie . 100.00
5 RH,CCB,Captain Tootsie A;Black Rider,Blaze Carson 125.00
6 A:Blaze Carson,Kid Colt . . . 75.00
7 . . . 75.00
8 RH . . . 75.00
9 Ph(c),B:Black Rider . . . 100.00
10 Ph(c) . . . 125.00
11 . . . 75.00
12 . . . 60.00
13 . . . 60.00
14 . . . 60.00
15 . . . 65.00
16 thru 20 . . . @55.00
21 thru 29 . . . @50.00
30 JKa . . . 55.00
31 thru 40 . . . @35.00
41 thru 47 . . . @25.00
48 . . . 35.00
49 thru 53 . . . @25.00
54 AW . . . 45.00
55 AW . . . 45.00
56 . . . 25.00
57 September, 1957 . . . 25.00

William Shatner's Tek World #1
© Marvel Entertainment Group

WILLIAM SHATNER'S TEK WORLD

1 LS,Novel adapt. 2.25
2 LS,Novel adapt.cont. 2.00
3 LS,Novel adapt.cont. 2.00
4 LS,Novel adapt.cont. 2.00
5 LS,Novel adapt.concludes 2.00
6 LS,V:TekLords 2.00
7 E:The Angel 2.00
8 thru 9 . . . . @2.00
10 . . . . 2.00
11 thru 15 . . . . 2.00
16 thru 17 . . . . 2.00
18 . . . . 2.00
19 Sims of the Father#1 . . . . . . 1.75
20 Sims of the Father#2 . . . . . . 1.75
21 Who aren't in Heaven 1.75
22 Father and Guns 1.75

WILLIE COMICS
See: IDEAL COMICS

WILLOW
August, 1988

1 Movie adapt. 1.00
2 Movie adapt. 1.00
3 Movie adapt,October, 1988. . . . 1.00

WITNESS, THE
September, 1948

1 . . . . 450.00

WOLFPACK
August, 1988

1 I:Wolfpack 1.00
2 thru 11 . . . . @1.00
12 July, 1988 . . . . 1.00

WOLVERINE
September, 1982
[Limited Series]

1 B:CCl(s),FM,JRu,A:Mariko,
I:Shingen 37.00
2 FM,JRu,A:Mariko,I:Yukio 30.00
3 FM,JRu,A:Mariko,Yukio 30.00
4 B:CCl(s),FM,JRu,A:Mariko,
D:Shingen 32.00

[Regular Series]

1 JB,AW,V:Banipur 30.00
2 JB,KJ,V:Silver Samurai 17.00
3 JB,AW,V:Silver Samurai 12.00
4 JB,AW,I:Roughouse,
Bloodsport 10.00
5 JB,AW,V:Roughouse,
Bloodsport 10.00
6 JB,AW,V:Roughouse,
Bloodsport 10.00
7 JB,A:Hulk 9.00
8 JB,A:Hulk 9.00
9 GC,Old Wolverine Story 9.00
10 JB,BSz,V:Sabretooth
(1st battle) 32.00
11 JB,BSz,B:Gehenna Stone 7.00
12 JB,BSz,Gehenna Stone 7.00
13 JB,BSz,Gehenna Stone 7.00
14 JB,BSz,Gehenna Stone 7.00
15 JB,BSz,Gehenna Stone 7.00
16 JB,BSz,E:Gehenna Stone 7.00
17 JBy,KJ,V:Roughouse 6.00
18 JBy,KJ,V:Roughouse 5.00
19 JBy,KJ,A of V,I:La Bandera . . . 5.00
20 JBy,KJ,A of V,V:Tigershark . . . 5.00
21 JBy,KJ,V:Geist 5.00
22 JBy,KJ,V:Geist,Spore 5.00
23 JBy,KJ,V:Geist,Spore 5.00
24 GC,'Snow Blind' 4.50
25 JB,O:Wolverine(part) 5.00
26 KJ,Return to Japan 4.50
27 thru 30 Lazarus Project 4.50
31 MS,DGr,A:Prince o'Mandripoor 4.50
32 MS,DGr,V:Ninjas 4.50
33 MS,Wolverine in Japan 4.50
34 MS,DGr,Wolverine in Canada . 4.50
35 MS,DGr,A:Puck 4.50
36 MS,DGr,A:Puck,Lady D'strike . 4.50
37 MS,DGr,V:Lady Deathstrike . . 4.50
38 MS,DGr,A:Storm,I:Elsie Dee . . 4.50
39 MS,DGr,Wolverine Vs. Clone . 4.50
40 MS,DGr,Wolverine Vs. Clone . 4.50

Wolverine #7
© Marvel Entertainment Group

41 MS,DGr,R:Sabretooth,
A:Cable 12.00
41a 2nd printing 2.25
42 MS,DGr,A:Sabretooth,Cable . . 8.00
42a 2nd printing 2.00
43 MS,DGr,A:Sabretooth,C:Cable 5.00
44 LSn,DGr 4.00
45 MS,DGr,A:Sabretooth 5.00
46 MS,DGr,A:Sabretooth 4.50
47 V:Tracy 4.00
48 LHa(s),MS,DGr,B:Shiva
Scenario 4.00
49 LHa(s),MS,DGr, ... 4.00
50 LHa(s),MS,DGr,A:X-Men,Nick Fury,
I:Shiva,Slash-Die Cut(c) 7.50
51 MS,DGr,A:Mystique,X-Men . . . 3.50
52 MS,DGr,A:Mystique,V:Spiral . . 3.50
53 MS,A:Mystique,V:Spiral,Mojo . 3.50
54 A:Shatterstar 3.50
55 MS,V:Cylla,A:Gambit,Sunfire . . 3.50
56 MS,A:Gambit,Sunfire,V:Hand,
Hydra 3.50
57 MS,D:Lady Mariko,A:Gambit . . 4.00
58 A:Terror 3.00
59 A:Terror 3.00
60 Sabretooth vs.Shiva,
I:John Wraith 3.50
61 MT,History of Wolverine and
Sabretooth,A:John Wraith 3.50
62 MT,A:Sabretooth,Silver Fox . . 3.00
63 MT,V:Ferro,D:Silver Fox 3.00
64 MPa,V:Ferro,Sabretooth 3.00
65 MT,A:Professor X 3.00
66 MT,A:X-Men 3.00
67 MT,A:X-Men 3.00
68 MT,V:Epsilon Red 3.00
69 DT,A:Rogue,V:Sauron,tie-in to
X-Men#300 . . . . 2.75
70 DT,Sauron,A:Rogue,Jubilee . . 2.75
71 DT,V:Sauron,Brain Child,A:Rogue,
Jubilee 2.75
72 thru 73 DT,V:Sentinels . . . . @2.75
74 ANi,V:Sentinels 2.50
75 AKu,Hologram(c),Wolv. has Bone
Claws,leaves X-Men 7.00
76 DT(c),B:LHa(s),A:Deathstrike,
Vindicator,C:Puck 2.25
77 AKu,A:Vindicator,Puck,V:Lady
Deathstrike 2.25
78 AKu,V:Cylla,Bloodscream 2.00
79 AKu,V:Cyber,I:Zoe Culloden . . 2.00
80 IaC,V:Cyber, ... 2.00
81 IaC,V:Cyber,A:Excalibur 2.25
82 AKu,BMc,A:Yukio,Silver
Samurai 1.95
83 AKu,A:Alpha Flight 1.95
TPB Wolverine rep Marvel Comics
Presents #1-#10 . . . . 2.95
Jungle Adventure MMi,(Deluxe) . . 5.50
Bloodlust (one shot),AD
V:Siberian Were-Creatures . . . 6.00
Global Jeapordy,PDd(s) 2.95
Rahne of Terror, C:Cable 8.00
GNv Bloody ChoicesJB,A:N.Fury 12.95
Inner Fury,BSz,V:Nanotech
Machines 6.25

WOLVERINE & PUNISHER: DAMAGING EVIDENCE

1 B:CP(s),GEr,A:Kingpin 2.25
2 GEr,A:Kingpin,Sniper 2.25
3 GEr,Last issue 2.25

WOLVERINE SAGA
September, 1989

1 RLd(c), ... 6.50
2 . . . . 5.00
3 . . . . 5.00
4 December, 1989 . . . . 5.00

WONDER DUCK
September, 1949

1 Whale(c) 50.00
2 . . . . 33.00
3 March, 1950 . . . . 33.00

WONDERMAN
March, 1986

1 KGa,one-shot special 3.00

WONDER MAN
September, 1991

1 B:GJ(s),JJ,V:Goliath 2.25

2 JJ,A:West Coast Avengers . . . 1.50
3 JJ,V:Abominatrix,I:Spider 1.50
4 JJ,I:Splice,A:Spider 1.50
5 JJ,A:Beast,V:Rampage 1.50
6 JJ,A:Beast,V:Rampage 1.50
7 JJ,Galactic Storm Pt.4,
A:Hulk & Rich Jones 1.50
8 JJ,GalacticStorm Pt.11,A:Vision 1.50
9 JJ,GalacticStorm Pt 18,A:Vision 1.50
10 JJ,V:Khmer Rouge 1.50
11 V:Angkor 1.50
12 V:Angkor 1.50
13 Infinity War 1.50
14 Infinity War,V:Warlock 1.50
15 Inf.War,V:Doppleganger 1.50
16 JJ,I:Armed Response,
A:Avengers West Coast 1.50
17 JJ,A:Avengers West Coast . . . 1.50
18 V:Avengers West Coast 1.50
19 . . . . 1.50
20 V:Splice,Rampage 1.50
21 V:Splice,Rampage 1.50
22 JJ,V:Realm of Death 1.50
23 JJ,A:Grim Reaper,Mephisto . . 1.50
24 JJ,V:Grim Reaper,Goliath 1.50
25 JJ,N:Wonder Man,D:Grim Reaper,
V:Mephisto 3.25
26 A:Hulk,C:Furor,Plan Master . . . 1.50
27 A:Hulk 1.50
28 RoR,A:Spider-Man 1.50
29 RoR,A:Spider-Man 1.50
Spec.#1 (1985),KGa 3.00
Ann.#1 System Bytes #3 . . . . 2.25
Ann.#2 I:Hit-Maker,w/card 2.95

WORLD CHAMPIONSHIP WRESTLING

1 F:Lex Luger,Sting 1.50
2 . . . . 1.25
3 . . . . 1.25
4 Luger Vs El Gigante 1.25
5 Rick Rude Vs. Sting 1.25
6 F:Dangerous Alliance,R.Rude . 1.25
7 F:Steiner Brothers 1.25
8 F:Sting,Dangerous Alliance . . . 1.25
9 Bunkhouse Brawl 1.25
10 Halloween Havoc 1.25
11 Sting vs Grapplers 1.25
12 F:Ron Simmons 1.25

WORLD OF FANTASY
Atlas
May, 1956

1 The Secret of the Mountain . 175.00
2 AW,Inside the Tunnel 100.00
3 DAy,SC, The Man in the Cave 75.00
4 BEv(c),Back to the Lost City . 60.00
5 BEv(c),BP,In the Swamp 60.00
6 BEv(c),The Strange Wife of
Henry Johnson 60.00
7 BEv(c),GM,Man in Grey 60.00
8 GM,JO,MF,The Secret of the
Black Cloud 75.00
9 BEv,BK 65.00
10 . . . . 50.00
11 AT 60.00
12 BEv(c) 50.00
13 BEv,JO 50.00
14 JMn(c),GM,JO 50.00
15 JK(c) 50.00
16 AW,SD,JK 75.00
17 JK(c),SD 70.00
18 JK(c) 70.00
19 JK(c),SD,August, 1959 . . . . . 70.00

WORLD OF MYSTERY
Atlas
June, 1956

1 BEv(c),AT,JO,The Long Wait 175.00
2 BEv(c),The Man From
Nowhere 60.00
3 SD,AT,JDa, The Bugs 75.00
4 SD(c),BP,What Happened in the
Basement 85.00
5 JO,She Stands in the Shadows 60.00
6 AW,SD,Sinking Man 90.00
7 Pick A Door July, 1957 . . . . . 60.00

WORLD OF SUSPENSE
Atlas
April, 1956

1 JO,BEv,A Stranger Among Us 150.00
2 SD,When Walks the Scarecrow 75.00
3 AW,The Man Who Couldn't
Be Touched 85.00
4 Something is in This House . 60.00
5 BEv,DH,JO 60.00
6 BEv(c),BP 60.00
7 AW,The Face 75.00
8 The Prisoner of the Ghost Ship 60.00

WORLDS UNKNOWN
May, 1973

1 GK,AT,The Coming of the
Martians,Reprints 3.00
2 GK,TS,A Gun For A Dinosaur . 2.00
3 The Day the Earth Stood
Still 2.00
4 JB,Arena 2.00
5 DA,JM,Black Destroyer 2.00
6 GK(c),The Thing Called It 2.00
7 GT,The Golden Voyage of
Sinbad,Part 1 . . . . 2.00
8 The Golden Voyage of
Sinbad,Part 2, August, 1974 . 2.00

WULF THE BARBARIAN
February, 1975

1 O:Wulf 2.00
2 NA,I:Berithe The Swordsman . 1.50
3 . . . . 1.50
4 September, 1975 . . . . 1.50

WYATT EARP
Atlas
November, 1955

1 JMn,F:Wyatt Earp 100.00
2 AW,Saloon(c) 60.00
3 JMn(c),The Showdown,
A:Black Bart 50.00
4 Ph(c),Hugh O'Brian,JSe,
India Sundown 50.00
5 Ph(c),Hugh O'Brian,DW,
Gun Wild Fever 50.00
6 . . . . 50.00
7 AW 60.00
8 . . . . 50.00
9 and 10 . . . . @50.00
11 . . . . 60.00
12 AW 50.00
13 thru 20 . . . . @35.00
21 JDa(c) 30.00
22 thru 29 . . . . @25.00
30 Reprints 2.50
31 thru 33 Reprints . . . . @1.25
34 June, 1973 . . . . 1.25

X-FACTOR
February, 1986

1 WS(c),JG,BL,JRu,I:X-Factor,
Rusty 16.00
2 JG,BL,I:Tower 8.00
3 JG,BL,V:Tower 7.00
4 KP,JRu,V:Frenzy 5.00
5 JG,JRu,I:Alliance of Evil,
C:Apocalypse 7.00
6 JG,BMc,I:Apocalypse 9.00
7 JG,JRu,V:Morlocks,I:Skids 3.50
8 MS,JRu,V:Freedom Force 3.50
9 JRu(i),V:Freedom Force
(Mutant Massacre) 7.00
10 WS,BWi,V:Marauders(Mut.Mass),
A:Sabretooth 8.00
11 WS,BWi,A:Thor(Mutant Mass) . 5.00
12 MS,BWi,V:Vanisher 4.00
13 WS,DGr.V:Mastermold 4.00
14 WS,BWi,V:Mastermold 4.00
15 WS,BWi,D:Angel 5.00
16 DM,JRu,V:Masque 4.00
17 WS,BWi,I:Rictor 6.00
18 WS,BWi,V:Apocalypse 4.00
19 WS,BWi,V:Horsemen of
Apocalypse 4.00
20 JBr,A:X-Terminators 3.00
21 WS,BWi,V:The Right 3.00
22 SB,BWi,V:The Right 3.00
23 WS,BWi,C:Archangel 5.00
24 WS,BWi,Fall of Mutants,
I:Archangel 15.00
25 WS,BWi,Fall of Mutants 5.00
26 WS,BWi,Fall of Mutants,
N:X-Factor 5.00
27 WS,BWi,Christmas Issue 3.50
28 WS,BWi,V:Ship 3.00
29 WS,BWi,V:Infectia 3.00
30 WS,BWi,V:Infectia,Free.Force . 3.00
31 WS,BWi,V:Infectia,Free.Force . 3.00
32 SLi,A:Avengers 3.00
33 WS,BWi,V:Tower & Frenzy,
R:Furry Beast 3.00
34 WS,BWi,I:Nanny,
Orphan Maker 3.00
35 JRu(i),WS(c),V:Nanny,
Orphan Maker 3.00
36 WS,BWi,Inferno,V:Nastirh 3.50
37 WS,BWi,Inferno,V:Gob.Queen . 3.50
38 WS,AM,Inferno,A:X-Men,D:
MadelynePryor(GoblinQueen) . 3.50
39 WS,AM,Inferno,A:X-Men,
V:Mr.Sinister 3.50
40 RLd,AM,O:Nanny,Orphan Maker
1st Liefeld Marvel work 14.00
41 AAd,AM,I:Alchemy 3.50
42 AAd,AM,A:Alchemy 3.50
43 PS,AM,V:Celestials 3.00
44 PS,AM,V:Rejects 2.50
45 PS,AM,V:Rask 2.50
46 PS,AM,V:Rejects 2.50
47 KD,AM,V:Father 2.50
48 thru 49 PS,AM,V:Rejects 2.50
50 RLd&TM(c),RB,AM,A:Prof.X
(double sized),BU:Apocalypse . 5.00
51 AM,V:Sabretooth,Caliban 7.00
52 RLd(c),AM,V:Sabretooth,
Caliban 6.00
53 AM,V:Sabretooth,Caliban 6.00
54 MS,AM,A:Colossus,I:Crimson . 2.00
55 MMi(c),CDo,AM,V:Mesmero . . 2.00
56 AM,V:Crimson 2.00
57 NKu,V:Crimson 2.00
58 JBg,AM,V:Crimson 2.00
59 AM,V:Press Gang 2.00
60 JBg,AM,X-Tinction Agenda#3 . 8.00
60a 2nd printing(gold) 7.00
61 JBg,AM,X-Tinction Agenda#6 . 6.50
62 JBg,AM,JLe(c),E:X-Agenda . . . 7.50
63 WPo,I:Cyberpunks 16.00
64 WPo,ATb,V:Cyberpunks 10.00
65 WPo,ATb,V:Apocalypse 7.00
66 WPo,ATb,I:Askani,
V:Apocalypse 7.00
67 WPo,ATb,V:Apocalypse,I:Shinobi
Shaw,D:Sebastian Shaw 7.00
68 WPo,ATb,JLe(c),V:Apocalypse,
L:Nathan,(taken into future) . . 12.00
69 WPo,V:Shadow King 5.00
70 MMi(c),JRu,Last old team 3.50
71 LSn,AM,New Team 6.00
71a 2nd printing 1.50
72 LSn,AM,Who shot Madrox
revealed 4.00
73 LSn,AM,Mob Chaos in D.C.. . . 3.00
74 LSn,AM,I:Slab 2.75
75 LSn,AM,I:Nasty Boys(doub.sz) 3.25
76 LSn,AM,A:Hulk,Pantheon 2.50
77 LSn,AM,V:Mutant Lib. Front. . . 2.25
78 LSn,AM,V:Mutant Lib. Front . . 2.25
79 LSn,AM,V:Helle's Belles 2.25
80 LSn,AM,V:Helle's Belles,
C:Cyber 2.25
81 LSn,AM,V:Helle's Belles,Cyber 2.25

82 JQ(c),LSn,V:Brotherhood of Evil Mutants,I:X-iles 2.25
83 MPa,A:X-Force,X-iles 2.25
84 JaL,X-Cutioners Song #2, V:X-Force,A:X-Men 7.00
85 JaL,X-Cutioners Song #6, Wolv.& Bishop,V:Cable 9.00
86 JaL,AM,X-Cutioner's Song#10, A:X-Men,X-Force,V:Stryfe 7.00
87 JQ,X-Cutioners Song Aftermath 3.00
88 JQ,AM,V:2nd Genegineer, I:Random 3.00
89 JQ,V:Mutates,Genosha 2.00
90 JQ,AM,Genosha vs. Aznia . . . 2.00
91 AM,V:Armageddon 1.75
92 JQ,AM,V:Fabian Cortez, Acolytes,hologram(c) 6.00
93 Magneto Protocols 1.75
94 PR,J:Forge 1.75
95 B:JMD(s),AM,Polaris Vs. Random 1.50
96 A:Random 1.50
97 JD,I:Haven,A:Random 1.50
98 GLz,A:Haven,A:Random 1.50
99 JD,A:Haven,Wolfsbane returns to human 1.50
100 JD,Red Foil(c),V:Haven, D:Madrox 3.25
100a Newstand Ed. 2.00
101 JD,AM,Aftermath 1.50
102 JD,AM,V:Crimson Commando, Avalanche 1.50
103 JD,AM,A:Malice 1.50
104 JD,AM,V:Malice, C:Mr. Sinister 1.50
Spec #1 JG,Prisoner of Love 5.00
Ann.#1 BL,BBr,V:CrimsonDynamo 5.00
Ann.#2 TGr,JRu,A:Inhumans 4.00
Ann.#3 WS(c),AM,JRu,PC,TD, Evolutionary War 3.50
Ann.#4 JBy,WS,JRu,MBa,Atlantis Attacks,BU:Doom & Magneto . 3.50
Ann.#5 JBg,AM,DR,GI,Days of Future Present,A:Fant.Four,V:Ahab . . 4.00
Ann.#6 Flesh Tears Saga Pt.4, A:X-Force, New Warriors 4.00
Ann #7 JQ,JRu,Shattershot Pt.3 . 4.00
Ann.#8 I:Charon,w/card 3.25
Ann.#9 JMD(s),MtB,V:Prof.Power, A:Prof.X,O:Haven 3.25

X-FORCE
August, 1991
(bagged, white on black graphic)

1 RLd,V:Stryfe,Mutant Liberation Front,with X-Force Card 6.00
1a with Shatterstar Card 4.50
1b with Deadpool Card 4.50
1c with Sunspot & Gideon Card . 4.50
1d with Cable Card 7.50
1e Unbagged Copy 1.75
1f 2nd Printing 1.75
2 RLd,I:New Weapon X,V: Deadpool 4.50
3 RLd,C:Spider-Man, V:Juggernaut,Black Tom 4.00
4 RLd,SpM/X-Force team-up, V:Juggernaut(cont.from SpM#16) Sideways format 3.50
5 RLd,A:Brotherhood Evil Mutants 3.00
6 RLd,V:Bro'hood Evil Mutants . . 2.50
7 RLd,V:Bro'hood Evil Mutants . . 2.50
8 MMi,O:Cable(Part) 3.00
9 RLd,D:Sauron,Masque 2.50
10 MPa,V:Mutant Liberation Front 2.00
11 MPa,Deadpool Vs Domino . . . 2.00
12 MPa,A:Weapon Prime,Gideon . 2.00
13 MPa,V:Weapon Prime 2.00
14 TSr,V:Weapon Prime,Krule . . . 2.00
15 GCa,V:Krule,Deadpool 2.00
16 GCa,X-Cutioners Song #4, X-Factor V:X-Force 3.00
17 GCa,X-Cutioners Song#8,

X-Force #1
© Marvel Entertainment Group

Apocalypse V:Stryfe 3.00
18 GCa,X-Cutioners Song#12, Cable vs Stryfe 3.00
19 GCa,X-Cutioners Song Aftermath,N:X-Force 1.75
20 GCa,O:Graymalkin 1.75
21 GCa,V:War Machine,SHIELD . 1.75
22 GCa,V:Externals 1.50
23 GCa,V:Saul,Gigeon,A:Six Pack 1.50
24 GCa,A:Six Pack,A:Deadpool . . 1.50
25 GCa,A:Mageneto,Exodus, R:Cable 6.00
26 GCa(c),MtB,I:Reignfire 1.50
27 GCa(c),MtB,V:Reignfire,MLF, I:Moonstar,Locus 1.50
28 MtB,V:Reignfire,MLF 1.50
29 MtB,V:Arcade,C:X-Treme 1.50
30 TnD,V:Arcade,A:X-Treme 1.50
31 F:Siryn 1.50
32 Child's Play#1,A:New Warriors 1.50
33 Child's Play#3,A:New Warriors, V:Upstarts 1.50
34 F:Rictor,Domino,Cable 1.75
35 TnD,R:Nimrod 1.50
Ann.#1 Shattershot Pt1 . . . . 2.75
Ann.#2 JaL,LSn,I:X-Treme,w/card 3.25

X-FORCE & SPIDER-MAN: SABOTAGE

TPB rep.X-Force #3 & #4 and Spider-Man #16 . . . . 6.95

X-MEN
September, 1963

1 JK,O:X-Men,I:Professor X,Beast Cyclops,Marvel Girl,Iceman Angel,Magneto 3,600.00
2 JK,I:Vanisher 1,300.00
3 JK,I:Blob 550.00
4 JK,I:Quicksilver,Scarlet Witch Mastermind,Toad 600.00
5 JK,V:Broth. of Evil Mutants . 400.00
6 JK,V:Sub-Mariner 300.00
7 JK,V:Broth. of Evil Mutants, Blob 250.00
8 JK,I:Unus,1st Ice covered Iceman 250.00
9 JK,A:Avengers,I:Lucifer 250.00
10 JK,I:Modern Kazar 250.00
11 JK,I:Stranger 200.00
12 JK,O:Prof.X,I:Juggernaut . . 225.00
13 JK,JSt,V:Juggernaut 175.00

X-Men #137
© Marvel Entertainment Group

14 JK,I:Sentinels 175.00
15 JK,O:Beast,V:Sentinels 175.00
16 JK,V:Mastermold,Sentinels . 175.00
17 JK,V:Magneto 125.00
18 V:Magneto 125.00
19 I:Mimic 125.00
20 V:Lucifer 125.00
21 V:Lucifer,Dominus 100.00
22 V:Maggia 100.00
23 V:Maggia 100.00
24 I:Locust(Prof.Hopper) 100.00
25 JK,I:El Tigre 100.00
26 V:El Tigre 85.00
27 C:Fant.Four,V:Puppet Master 85.00
28 I:Banshee 100.00
29 V:Super-Apaptoid 80.00
30 JK,I:The Warlock 80.00
31 JK,I:Cobalt Man 67.00
32 V:Juggernaut 67.00
33 GK,A:Dr.Strange,Juggernaut . 67.00
34 V:Tyrannus,Mole Man 67.00
35 JK,A:Spider-Man,Banshee . . 75.00
36 V:Mekano 58.00
37 DH,V:Blob,Unus 58.00
38 DH,A:Banshee,O:Cyclops . . . 65.00
39 DH,GT,A:Banshee,V:Mutant Master,O:Cyclops 58.00
40 DH,GT,V:Frankenstein, O:Cyclops 58.00
41 DH,GT,I:Grotesk,O:Cyclops . 50.00
42 DH,GT,JB,V:Grotesk, O:Cyclops,D:Prof.X 50.00
43 GT,JB,V:Magneto,Quicksilver, Scarlet Witch,C:Avengers . . . 54.00
44 V:Magneto,Quicksilver,Sc.Witch, R:Red Raven,O:Iceman 54.00
45 PH,JB,V:Magneto,Quicksilver, Scarlet Witch,O:Iceman 54.00
46 DH,V:Juggernaut,O:Iceman . . 50.00
47 DH,I:Maha Yogi 50.00
48 DH,JR,V:Quasimodo 50.00
49 JSo,DH,C:Magneto,I:Polaris, Mesmero,O:Beast 60.00
50 JSo,V:Magneto,O:Beast 55.00
51 JSo,V:Magneto,Polaris, Erik the Red,O:Beast 55.00
52 DH,MSe,JSt,O:Lorna Dane V:Magneto,O:Beast 50.00
53 1st BWS,O:Beast 65.00

54 BWS,DH,I:Havok,O:Angel . . . 70.00
55 BWS,DH,O:Havok,Angel 60.00
56 NA,V:LivingMonolith,O:Angel . 56.00
57 NA,V:Sentinels,A:Havok 56.00
58 NA,A:Havoc,V:Sentinels 56.00
59 NA,V:Sentinels,A:Havoc 56.00

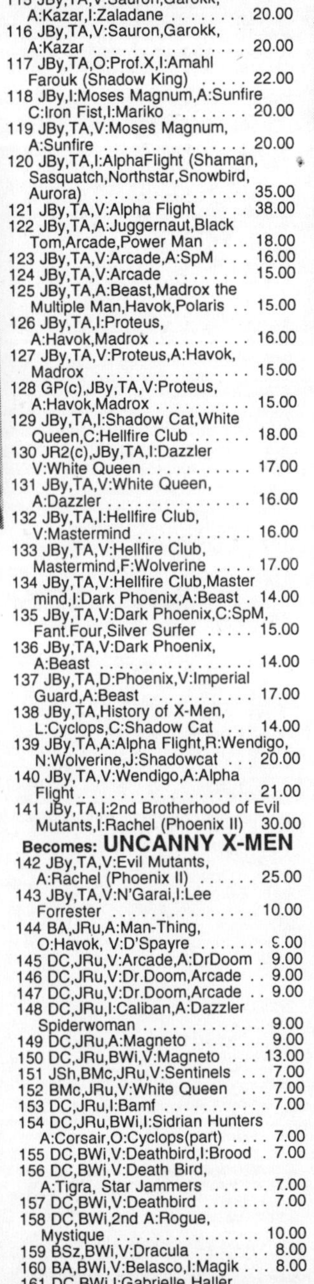

X-Men #138

© Marvel Entertainment Group

60 NA,I:Sauron 60.00
61 NA,V:Sauron 56.00
62 NA,A:Kazar,Sauron,Magneto . 56.00
63 A:Ka-Zar,V:Magneto 56.00
64 DH,A:Havok,I:Sunfire 47.00
65 NA,MSe,A:Havok,Shield,
Return of Prof.X 56.00
66 SB,MSe,V:Hulk,A:Havok 40.00
67 rep.X-Men #12,#13 . . . . 25.00
68 rep.X-Men #14,#15 . . . . 25.00
69 rep.X-Men #16,#19 . . . . 25.00
70 rep.X-Men #17,#18 . . . . 25.00
71 rep.X-Men #20 . . . . 25.00
72 rep.X-Men #21,#24 . . . . 25.00
73 thru 93 rep.X-Men #25-45 . @25.00
94 GK(c),B:CCl(s),DC,BMc,B:2nd
X-Men,V:Count Nefaria 275.00
95 GK(c),DC,V:Count Nefaria,
Ani-Men,D:Thunderbird 75.00
96 DC,I:Moira McTaggert,
Kierrok 56.00
97 DC,V:Havok,Polaris,Eric
the Red,I:Lilandra 45.00
98 DC,V:Sentinels,Stephen Lang 45.00
99 DC,V:Sentinels,S.Lang 46.00
100 DC,V:Stephen Lang 46.00
101 DC,I:Phoenix,Black Tom,
A:Juggernaut 42.00
102 DC,O:Storm,V:Juggernaut,
Black Tom 30.00
103 DC,V:Juggernaut,Bl.Tom . . . 28.00
104 DC,V:Magneto,I:Star
Jammers,A:Lilandra 25.00
105 DC,BL,V:Firelord 25.00
106 DC,TS,V:Firelord 25.00
107 DC,DGr,I:Imperial Guard,Star
Jammers,Gladiator,Corsair . . 27.00
108 JBy,TA,A:Star Jammers,
C:Fantastic Four,Avengers. . . 42.00
109 JBy,TA,I:Vindicator 35.00
110 TD,DC,V:Warhawk 21.00
111 JBy,TA,V:Mesmero,A:Beast,
Magneto 20.00
112 GP(c),JBy,TA,V:Magneto,
A:Beast 25.00
113 JBy,TA,V:Magneto,A:Beast . 25.00
114 JBy,TA,A:Beast,R:Sauron . . 25.00
115 JBy,TA,V:Sauron,Garokk,
A:Kazar,I:Zaladane 20.00
116 JBy,TA,V:Sauron,Garokk,
A:Kazar 20.00
117 JBy,TA,O:Prof.X,I:Amahl
Farouk (Shadow King) 22.00
118 JBy,I:Moses Magnum,A:Sunfire
C:Iron Fist,I:Mariko 20.00
119 JBy,TA,V:Moses Magnum,
A:Sunfire 20.00
120 JBy,TA,I:AlphaFlight (Shaman,
Sasquatch,Northstar,Snowbird,
Aurora) 35.00
121 JBy,TA,V:Alpha Flight 38.00
122 JBy,TA,A:Juggernaut,Black
Tom,Arcade,Power Man 18.00
123 JBy,TA,V:Arcade,A:SpM . . . 16.00
124 JBy,TA,V:Arcade 15.00
125 JBy,TA,A:Beast,Madrox the
Multiple Man,Havok,Polaris . . 15.00
126 JBy,TA,I:Proteus,
A:Havok,Madrox 16.00
127 JBy,TA,V:Proteus,A:Havok,
Madrox 15.00
128 GP(c),JBy,TA,V:Proteus,
A:Havok,Madrox 15.00
129 JBy,TA,I:Shadow Cat,White
Queen,C:Hellfire Club 18.00
130 JR2(c),JBy,TA,I:Dazzler
V:White Queen 17.00
131 JBy,TA,V:White Queen,
A:Dazzler 16.00
132 JBy,TA,I:Hellfire Club,
V:Mastermind 16.00
133 JBy,TA,V:Hellfire Club,
Mastermind,F:Wolverine 17.00
134 JBy,TA,V:Hellfire Club,Master
mind,I:Dark Phoenix,A:Beast . 14.00
135 JBy,TA,V:Dark Phoenix,C:SpM,
Fant.Four,Silver Surfer 15.00
136 JBy,TA,V:Dark Phoenix,
A:Beast 14.00
137 JBy,TA,D:Phoenix,V:Imperial
Guard,A:Beast 17.00
138 JBy,TA,History of X-Men,
L:Cyclops,C:Shadow Cat . . . 14.00
139 JBy,TA,A:Alpha Flight,R:Wendigo,
N:Wolverine,J:Shadowcat . . . 20.00
140 JBy,TA,V:Wendigo,A:Alpha
Flight 21.00
141 JBy,TA,I:2nd Brotherhood of Evil
Mutants,I:Rachel (Phoenix II) 30.00

Becomes: UNCANNY X-MEN

142 JBy,TA,V:Evil Mutants,
A:Rachel (Phoenix II) 25.00
143 JBy,TA,V:N'Garai,I:Lee
Forrester 10.00
144 BA,JRu,A:Man-Thing,
O:Havok, V:D'Spayre 9.00
145 DC,JRu,V:Arcade,A:DrDoom . 9.00
146 DC,JRu,V:Dr.Doom,Arcade . . 9.00
147 DC,JRu,V:Dr.Doom,Arcade . . 9.00
148 DC,JRu,I:Caliban,A:Dazzler
Spiderwoman 9.00
149 DC,JRu,A:Magneto 9.00
150 DC,JRu,BWi,V:Magneto . . . 13.00
151 JSh,BMc,JRu,V:Sentinels . . . 7.00
152 BMc,JRu,V:White Queen . . . 7.00
153 DC,JRu,I:Bamf 7.00
154 DC,JRu,BWi,I:Sidrian Hunters
A:Corsair,O:Cyclops(part) 7.00
155 DC,BWi,V:Deathbird,I:Brood . 7.00
156 DC,BWi,V:Death Bird,
A:Tigra, Star Jammers 7.00
157 DC,BWi,V:Deathbird 7.00
158 DC,BWi,2nd A:Rogue,
Mystique 10.00
159 BSz,BWi,V:Dracula 8.00
160 BA,BWi,V:Belasco,I:Magik . . . 8.00
161 DC,BWi,I:Gabrielle Haller,
O:Magneto,Professor X 10.00
162 DC,BWi,V:Brood 10.00

Uncanny X-Men #151

© Marvel Entertainment Group

163 DC,BWi,V:Brood 7.00
164 DC,BWi,V:Brood,I:Binary 7.00
165 PS,BWi,V:Brood 8.00
166 PS,BWi,V:Brood,A:Binary,
I:Lockheed 8.00
167 PS,BWi,V:Brood,A:N.Mutants 8.00
168 PS,BWi,I:Madelyne Pryor . . . 7.00
169 PS,BWi,I:Morlocks 7.00
170 PS,BWi,A:Angel,V:Morlocks . 7.00
171 WS,BWi,J:Rogue,V:Binary . 11.00
172 PS,BWi,V:Viper,Silver
Samurai, ... 9.00
173 PS,BWi,V:Viper,Silver
Samurai, ... 8.00
174 PS,BWi,A:Mastermind 7.00
175 PS,JR2,BWi,W:Cyclops and
Madelyne,V:Mastermind 8.00
176 JR2,BWi,I:Val Cooper 7.00
177 JR2,JR,V:Brotherhood of
Evil Mutants 6.00
178 JR2,BWi,BBr,V:Brotherhood
of Evil Mutants 6.00
179 JR2,DGr,V:Morlocks 6.00
180 JR2,DGr,BWi,Secret Wars . . 6.00
181 JR2,DGr,A:Sunfire 6.00
182 JR2,DGr,V:S.H.I.E.L.D. 6.00
183 JR2,DGr,V:Juggernaut 6.00
184 JR2,DGr,V:Selene,I:Forge . . . 7.00
185 JR2,DGr,V:Shield,U.S.
Govt.,Storm loses powers 6.00
186 BWS,TA,Lifedeath,
V:Dire Wraiths 7.00
187 JR2,DGr,V:Dire Wraiths 6.00
188 JR2,DGr,V:Dire Wraiths 6.00
189 JR2,SL,V:Selene,A:Magma . . 6.00
190 JR2,DGr,V:Kulan Gath,A:SpM,
Avengers,New Mutants 6.00
191 JR2,DGr,A:Avengers,Spider-Man,
New Mutants,I:Nimrod 6.00
192 JR2,DGr,V:Magus 6.00
193 JR2,DGr,V:Hellions,I:Firestar
Warpath,20th Anniv. 8.00
194 JR2,DGr,SL,V:Nimrod 6.00
195 BSz(c),JR2,DGr,A:Power
Pack,V:Morlocks 6.00
196 JR2,DGr,J:Magneto 7.00
197 JR2,DGr,V:Arcade 6.00
198 BWS,F:Storm,'Lifedeath II' . . 6.00
199 JR2,DGr,I:Freedom Force,
Rachel becomes 2nd Phoenix . 6.00
200 JR2,DGr,A:Magneto,I:Fenris 10.00

X-Men #171
© Marvel Entertainment Group

201 RL,WPo(i),I:Nathan Christopher (Cyclops son) . . . 20.00
202 JR2,AW,Secret Wars II 5.00
203 JR2,AW,Secret Wars II 5.00
204 JBr,WPo,V:Arcade 6.00
205 BWS,A:Lady Deathstrike . . . 18.00
206 JR2,DGr,V:Freedom Force . . 5.00
207 JR2,DGr,V:Selene 5.00
208 JR2,DGr,V:Nimrod, A:Hellfire Club 5.00
209 JR2,CR,V:Nimrod,A:Spiral . . . 5.00
210 JR2,DGr,I:Marauders, (Mutant Massacre) 20.00
211 JR2,BBl,AW,V:Marauders, (Mutant Massacre) 20.00
212 RL,DGr,V:Sabretooth, (Mutant Massacre) 35.00
213 AD,V:Sabretooth (Mut.Mass) 35.00
214 BWS,BWi,V:Malice,A:Dazzler 6.00
215 AD,DGr,I:Stonewall,Super Sabre,Crimson Commando . . . 5.00
216 BWS(c),JG,DGr,V:Stonewall . 5.00
217 WS(c),JG,SL,V:Juggernaut . . 5.00
218 AAD(c),MS,DGr,V:Juggernaut 5.00
219 BBl,DGr,V:Marauders,Polaris becomes Malice,A:Sabertooth . 7.00
220 MS,DGr,A:Naze 5.00
221 MS,DGr,I:Mr.Sinister, V:Maruaders 10.00
222 MS,DGr,V:Marauders,Eye Killers,A:Sabertooth 17.00
223 KGa,DGr,A:Freedom Force . . 5.00
224 MS,DGr,V:Adversary 5.00
225 MS,DGr,Fall of Mutants I:1st US App Roma 9.00
226 MS,DGr,Fall of Mutants 9.00
227 MS,DGr,Fall of Mutants 9.00
228 RL,TA,A:OZ Chase 5.00
229 MS,DGr,I:Reavers,Gateway . 5.00
230 RL,DGr,Xmas Issue 5.00
231 RL,DGr,V:Limbo 5.00
232 MS,DGr,V:Brood 5.00
233 MS,DGr,V:Brood 5.00
234 MS,JRu,V:Brood 5.00
235 RL,CR,V:Magistrates 5.00
236 MS,DGr,V:Magistrates 5.00
237 RL,TA,V:Magistrates 5.00
238 MS,DGr,V:Magistrates 5.00
239 MS,DGr,Inferno,A:Mr.Sinister 5.50
240 MS,DGr,Inferno,V:Marauders 6.00
241 MS,DGr,Inferno,O:Madeline Pryor,V:Marauders 6.00
242 MS,DGr,Inferno,D:N'Astirh, A:X-Factor,Double-sized 6.00
243 MS,Inferno,A:X-Factor. 6.00
244 MS,DGr,I:Jubilee 10.00
245 RLd,DGr,Invasion Parody . . . 5.00
246 MS,DGr,V:Mastermold, A:Nimrod 5.00
247 MS,DGr,V:Mastermold 5.00
248 JLe(1st X-Men Art),DGr, V:Nanny & Orphan Maker . . . 30.00
248a 2nd printing 2.00
249 MS,DGr,C:Zaladane, V:Savage Land Mutates. 5.00
250 MS,SL,I:Zaladane. 5.00
251 MS,DGr,V:Reavers 5.00
252 JLe,BSz(c),RL,SW,V:Reavers 5.00
253 MS,SL,V:Amahl Farouk 5.00
254 JLe(c),MS,DGr,V:Reavers . . . 5.00
255 MS,DGr,V:Reavers,D:Destiny 5.00
256 JLe,SW,Acts of Vengeance, V:Manderin,A:Psylocke 12.00
257 JLe,JRu,AofV,V:Manderin . . 12.00
258 JLe,SW,AofV,V:Manderin . . 13.50
259 MS,DGr,V:Magistrates, ... 4.50
260 JLe(c),MS,DGr,A:Dazzler . . . 4.50
261 JLe(c),MS,DGr,V:Hardcase & Harriers 4.50
262 KD,JRu,V:Masque,Morlocks . 4.50
263 JRu(i),O:Forge,V:Morlocks . . 4.50
264 JLe(c),MC,JRu,V:Magistrate . 4.50
265 JRu(i),V:Shadowking 4.50
266 NKu(c),MC,JRu,I:Gambit . . . 38.00
267 JLe,WPo,SW,V:Shadowking 16.00
268 JLe,SW,A:Captain America, Black Widow,V:The Hand, Baron Strucker 22.00
269 JLe,ATi,Rogue V:Ms.Marvel . 9.00
270 JLe,ATi,SW,X-Tinction Agenda #1, A:Cable,New Mutants . . . 13.00
270a 2nd printing(Gold) 4.50
271 JLe,SW,X-Tinction Agenda #4,A:Cable,New Mutants 10.00
272 JLe,SW,X-Tinction Agenda #7,A:Cable,New Mutants 10.00
273 JLe,WPo,JBy,KJ,RL,MS,MGo, LSn,SW,A:Cable,N.Mutants . . . 8.50
274 JLe,SW,V:Zaladane,A:Magneto, Nick Fury,Kazar 6.00
275 JLe,SW,R:Professor X,A:Star Jammers,Imperial Guard 12.00
275a 2nd Printing (Gold) 3.00
276 JLe,SW,V:Skrulls,Shi'ar 6.00
277 JLe,SW,V:Skrulls,Shi'ar 6.00
278 PS,Professor X Returns to Earth,V:Shadowking 4.50
279 NKu,SW,V:Shadowking 4.50
280 E:CCl(s),NKu,A:X-Factor, D:Shadowking,Prof.X Crippled . 4.50
281 WPo,ATi,new team (From X-Men #1),D:Pierce,Hellions,V:Sentinels, I:Trevor Fitzroy,Upstarts 6.00
281a 2nd printing,red(c) 1.25
282 WPo,ATi,V:Fitzroy,C:Bishop . 8.00
282a 2nd printing,gold(c) of #281 inside 1.25
283 WPo,ATi,I:Bishop,Malcolm, Randall 11.00
284 WPo,ATi,SOS from USSR. . . 3.50
285 WPo,I:Mikhail(Colossus' brother from Russia) 3.00
286 JLe,WPo,ATi,A:Mikhail 3.00
287 JR2,O:Bishop, D:Malcolm,Randall 4.50
288 NKu,BSz,A:Bishop 3.00
289 WPo,ATi,Forge proposes to Storm 3.00
290 WPo,SW,V:Cyberpunks, L:Forge 3.00
291 TR,V:Morlocks 2.50
292 TR,V:Morlocks 2.50
293 TR,D:Morlocks,Mikhail 2.50
294 BP,TA,X-Cutioner's Song#1, Stryfe shoots Prof X,A:X-Force, X-Factor,polybag.w/ProfX card 4.50
295 BP,TA,X-Cutioners Song #5, V:Apocalypse 3.00
296 BP,TA,X-Cutioners Song #9, A:X-Force,X-Factor,V:Stryfe . . 3.00
297 BP,X-Cutioners Song Aftermath 2.00
298 BP,TA,V:Acolytes 2.00
299 BP,A:Forge,Acolytes,I:Graydon Creed (Sabretooth's son) 2.00
300 JR2,DGr,BP,V:Acolytes,A:Forge, Nightcrawler,Holografx(c) 6.50

Uncanny X-Men #200
© Marvel Entertainment Group

301 JR2,DGr,I:Sienna Blaze, V:Fitzroy 2.00
302 JR2,V:Fitzroy 2.00
303 JR2,V:Upstarts,D:Illyana 2.00
304 JR2,JaL,PS,L:Colossus, V:Magneto,Holo-grafx(c) 5.00
305 JD,F:Rogue,Bishop 2.00
306 JR2,V:Hodge 2.00
307 JR2,Bloodties#4,A:Avengers, V:Exodus,Cortez 2.00
308 JR2,Scott & Jean announce impending marriage 1.75
309 JR2,O:Professor X & Amelia . 1.75
310 JR2,DG,A:Cable,V:X-Cutioner, w/card 2.25
311 JR2,DG,AV,V:Sabretooth, C:Phalanx 1.75
312 JMd,DG,A:Yukio,I:Phalanx, w/card 1.75
313 JMd,DG,V:Phalanx 1.75
314 LW,BSz,R:White Quen 1.50
Ann.#1 rep.#9,#11 . . . . 45.00
Ann.#2 rep.#22,#23 . . . . 35.00
Ann.#3 GK(c),GP,TA,A:Arkon . . 18.00
Ann.#4 JR2,BMc,A:Dr.Strange . . 12.00
Ann.#5 BA,BMc,A:F.F. 10.00
Ann.#6 BSz,BWi,Dracula 11.00
Ann.#7 MGo,TMd,BWi,TA,BBr,BA,JRu, BBl,SL,AM,V:Impossible Man . 8.00
Ann.#8 SL,Kitty's story 8.00
Ann.#9 AAd,AG,MMi,Asgard,V:Loki, Enchantress,A:New Mutants . 13.00
Ann.#10 AAd,TA,V:Mojo, J:Longshot,A:New Mutants . . 13.00
Ann.#11 AD,V:Horde,A:CaptBrit . . 6.00
Ann.#12 AAd,BWi,RLm,TD,Evol. War,V:Terminus,Savage Land . 6.00
Ann.#13 MBa,JRu,Atlantis Attacks 5.00
Ann.#14 AAd,DGr,BWi,AM,ATi, V:Ahab,A:X-Factor, ... 10.00

Ann.#15,TR,JRu,MMi(c),Flesh Tears, Pt.3,A:X-Force,New Warriors . . 4.50
Ann.#16 JaL,JRu,Shattershot Part.2 . . . . 8.00
Ann.#17 JPe,MFm,I:X-Cutioner, D:Mastermind,w/card 4.00
Ann.#18 JR2,V:Caliban, BU:Bishop 2.95
G-Size #1,GK,DC,I:New X-Men (Colossus,Storm,Nightcrawler, Thunderbird,3rd A:Wolv.) . . 250.00
G-Size #2,rep.#57-59 . . . . 40.00
TPB Dark Phoenix Saga 12.95
TPB Day of Future Present 14.95
TPB Days of Future Past 4.95
TPB From the Ashes 16.95
TPB X-Tinction Agenda 19.95
X-Men Survival Guide to the Manison NKu(c) 6.95

X-MEN
[2nd Regular Series]
October, 1991

1 A(c);Storm,Beast,B:CCl(s),JLe,SW I:Fabian Cortez,Acolytes, V:Magneto 2.50
1 B(c);Colossus,Psylocke 2.50
1 C(c);Cyclops,Wolverine 2.50
1 D(c);Magneto 2.50
1 E(c);Gatefold w/pin-ups 5.00
2 JLe,SW,V:Magneto Contd. 5.00
3 E:CCl(s),JLe,SW,V:Magneto . . 4.00
4 JBy(s),JLe,SW,I:Omega Red, V:Hand 6.00
5 B:SLo(s),JLe,SW,V:Hand, Omega Red,I:Maverick 5.00
6 thru 7 JLe,SW,V:Omega Red,Hand, Sabretooth . . . . @4.00
8 JLe,SW,Bishop vs. Gambit . . . 3.50
9 JLe,SW,A:Ghost Rider,V:Brood 3.50
10 JLe,SW,MT,Longshot Vs. Mojo, BU:Maverick 3.50
11 E:SLo(s)JLe,MT,V:Mojo, BU:Maverick 3.50
12 B:FaN(s),ATb,BWi,I:Hazard . . . 2.50
13 ATb,BWi,V:Hazard 2.50
14 NKu,X-Cutioners Song#3,A:X-Fact. X-Force,V:Four Horsemen . . . 3.00
15 NKu,X-Cutioners Song #7, V:Mutant Liberation Front 3.00
16 NKu,MPn,X-Cutioners Song #11, A:X-Force,X-Factor,V:Dark Riders, Apocalypse Vs.Archangel,IR:Stryfe is Nathan Summers 3.00
17 NKu,MPn,R:Illyana,A:Darkstar . 2.50
18 NKu,MPn,R:Omega Red,V:Soul Skinner 2.50
19 NKu,MPn,V:Soul Skinner, Omega Red 2.50
20 NKu,MPn,J.Grey vs Psylocke . 2.00
21 NKu,V:Silver Samurai,Shinobi . 2.00
22 BPe,V:Silver Samurai,Shinobi . 2.00
23 NKu,MPn,V:Dark Riders, Mr.Sinister 2.00
24 NKu,BSz,A Day in the Life . . . 2.00
25 NKu,Hologram(c),V:Magneto,Wolv.'s Adamantium skel. pulled out . . 7.00
26 NKu,Bloodties#2,A:Avengers, I:Unforgiven 2.25
27 RiB,I:Threnody 2.00
28 NKu,MRy,F:Sabretooth 2.50
29 NKu,MRy,V:Shinobi 2.00
30 NKu,MRy,W:Cyclops&Jean Grey, w/card 3.75
31 NKu,MRy,A:Spiral,Matsuo, D:Kwannon 1.50
32 NKu,MRy,A:Spiral,Matsuo 1.50
33 NKu,MRy,F:Gambit & Sabretooth 1.50
34 NKu,MRy,A:Riptide 1.50
Ann.#1 JLe,Shattershot Pt.1, I:Mojo II 3.00
Ann.#2 I:Empyrean,w/card 3.25

X-MEN ADVENTURES
[1st Season]

1 V:Sentinals, Based on TV Cartoon 4.00
2 V:Sentinals,D:Morph 3.00
3 V:Magneto,A:Sabretooth 2.00
4 V:Magneto 2.00
5 V:Morlocks 2.00
6 V:Sabretooth 2.00
7 V:Cable,Genosha,Sentinels . . . 1.75
8 A:Colossus,A:Juggernaut 1.75
9 I:Colussus(on cartoon), V:Juggernaut 1.75
10 A:Angel,V:Mystique 1.75
11 I:Archangel(on cartoon) 1.75
12 V:Horsemen of Apocalypse . . . 1.75
13 RMc(s),I:Bishop(on cartoon) . . 1.75
14 V:Brotherhood of Evil Mutants . 1.75

[2nd Season]

1 R:Morph,I:Mr. Sinister (on cartoon) 1.50
2 I:Nasty Boys (on cartoon) 1.50
3 I:Shadow King (on cartoon) . . . 1.50
4 I:Omega Red (on cartoon) 1.50
5 I:Alpha Flight (on cartoon) 1.25
6 F:Gambit 1.25

X-MEN/ALPHA FLIGHT
January, 1986

1 PS,BWi,V:Loki 5.00
2 PS,BWi,V:Loki 4.00

X-MEN/ ANIMATION SPECIAL

TV Screenplay Adapt 10.95

X-MEN AT STATE FAIR

1 KGa,Dallas Times Herald . . . 25.00

X-MEN CLASSICS
December, 1983

1 NA,rep. 3.50
2 NA,rep. 3.50
3 NA,rep. 3.50

X-MEN: EARLY YEARS

1 rep. X-Men (first series) #1 . . . 1.75
2 rep. X-Men (first series) #2 . . . 1.50
3 rep. X-Men (first series) #3 . . . 1.50

CLASSIC X-MEN
September, 1986

1 AAd(c),JBo,New stories, rep. giant size X-Men 1 . . . . 10.00
2 rep.#94,JBo/AAd(c),BU: Storm & Marvel Girl 6.00
3 rep.#95,JBo/AAd(c),BU: I:Thunderbird II 5.00
4 rep.#96,JBo/AAd(c),BU: Wolverine & N.Crawler 4.50
5 rep.#97,JBo/AAd(c),BU: Colossus 4.00
6 rep.#98,JBo/AAd(c),BU: JeanGrey,I:Seb.Shaw 4.00
7 rep.#99,JBo/AAd(c),BU: HellfireClub,W.Queen 4.00
8 rep.#100,JBo/AAd(c),BU: O:Jean Grey/Phoenix 4.00
9 rep.#101,JBo/AAd(c),BU: Nightcrawler 4.00
10 rep.#102,JBo/AAd(c),BU: Wolverine,A:Sabretooth 10.00
11 rep.#103,JBo/BL(c),BU:Storm . 3.50
12 rep.#104,JBo/AAd(c),BU: O:Magneto 4.00
13 rep.#105,JBo/AAd(c),BU: JeanGrey & Misty Knight 3.50
14 rep.#107,JBo/AAd(c),BU: Lilandra 3.50
15 rep.#108,JBo/AAd(c),BU: O:Starjammers 3.50
16 rep.#109,JBo/AAd(c),BU: Banshee 3.50
17 rep.#111,JBo/TA(c),BU: Mesmero 6.50
18 rep.#112,JBo/AAd(c),BU: Phoenix 3.00
19 rep.#113,JBo/AAd(c),BU: Magnetoo 3.00
20 rep.#114,JBo/AAd(c), BU:Storm 3.00
21 rep.#115,JBo/AAd(c), BU:Colossus. 2.75
22 rep.#116,JBo/AAd(c), BU:Storm 2.75
23 rep.#117,JBo/KGa(c),BU: Nightcrawler 2.75
24 rep.#118,JBo/KGa(c),BU: Phoenix 2.75
25 rep.#119,JBo/KGa(c),BU:Wolv. 3.00
26 rep.#120,JBo/KGa(c),BU:Wolv. 5.50
27 rep.#121,JBo/KD(c),BU: Wolverine & Phoenix 3.00
28 rep.#122,JBo/KD(c),BU:X-Men 2.50
29 rep.#123,JBo/KD(c),BU: Colossus 2.50
30 rep.#124,JBo/SLi(c),BU: O:Arcade 2.25
31 rep.#125,JBo/SLi(c),BU: Professor.X 2.25
32 rep.#126,JBo/SLi(c),BU: Wolverine. 3.00
33 rep.#127,JBo/SLi(c),BU: Havok 2.25
34 rep.#128,JBo/SLi(c),BU: W.Queen,M.Mind 2.25
35 rep.#129,JBo/SLi(c),BU: K.Pryde 2.25
36 rep.#130,MBr/SLi(c),BU: Banshee & Moira 2.25
37 rep.#131,RL/SLi(c),BU: Dazzler 2.25
38 rep.#132,KB/SLi(c),BU: Dazzler 2.25
39 rep.#133,2nd JLe X-Men/SLi(c), BU:Storm 8.00
40 rep.#134,SLi(c),BU:N.Crawler . 2.00
41 rep.#135,SLi(c),BU: Mr. Sinister,Cyclops 2.00
42 rep.#136,SLi(c),BU: Mr. Sinister,Cyclops 2.00
43 rep.#137,JBy(c),BU: Phoenix,Death 2.50

X-Men Classics #1

© Marvel Entertainment Group

Classic X-Men #6
© Marvel Entertainment Group

Becomes:
X-MEN CLASSICS
44 rep.#138,KD/SLi(c) 2.00
45 thru 49 rep.#139-145,SLi(c) @2.00
50 thru 69 rep.#146-165 . . . . . @1.50
70 rep.#166 . . . . 1.75
71 thru 74 rep.#167-170 . . . . . @1.50
75 thru 81 rep.#171-177 . . . . . @1.25
82 rep.#178 . . . . 1.25

X-MEN: DAYS OF FUTURE PAST
1 Rep. X-Men #141-142 . . . . 4.00

X-MEN: DAYS OF FUTURE PRESENT
1 MMi(c),Rep.F.F.Ann.#23,X-Men Ann.#14,X-Factor Ann.#5, New Mutant Ann.#10 . . . . . . 14.95

X-MEN INDEX
1 . . . . 2.95
2 . . . . 2.95
3 . . . . 2.95
4 . . . . 2.95
5 . . . . 2.95
6 . . . . 2.95
7 . . . . 2.95

X-MEN/MICRONAUTS
January, 1984
1 JG,BWi,Limited Series 3.50
2 JG,BWi,KJo,V:Baron Karza . . . 2.50
3 JG,BWi,V:Baron Karza 2.50
4 JG,BWi,V:Baron Karza,Apr.1984 2.50

X-MEN SPOTLIGHT ON STARJAMMERS
1990
1 DC,F:Starjammers,A:Prof.X . . . 5.00
2 DC,F:Starjammers,A:Prof.X . . . 5.00

X-MEN 2099
1 B:JFM(s),RLm,JP,I:X-Men 2099 4.00
1a Gold Ed. 40.00
2 RLm,JP,V:Rat Pack 2.00
3 RLm,JP,D:Serpentina 1.75
4 RLm,JP,I:Theatre of Pain 1.75
5 RLm,JP,Fall of the Hammer#3 . 1.75
6 RLm,JP,I:Freakshow 1.50
7 RLm,JP,V:Freakshow 1.50
8 RLm(c),JS3,JP,N;Metalhead, I:2nd X-Men 2099 . . . . 1.50
9 RLm,JP,V:2nd X-Men 2099 . . . 1.50
10 RLm,JP,A:La Lunatica 1.50

X-MEN UNLIMITED
1 CBa,BP,O:Siena Blaze 7.00
2 JD,O:Magneto 6.00
3 FaN(s),BSz(c),MMK,Sabretooth joins X-Men,A:Maverick 6.50
4 SLo(s),RiB,O:Nightcrawler,Rogue, Mystique,IR:Mystique is Nightcrawler's mother 5.50
5 JFM(s),LSh,After Shi'ar/ Kree War 3.95

X-MEN VS. AVENGERS
April, 1987
1 MS,JRu,V:Soviet SuperSoldiers 4.00
2 MS,JRu,V:Sov.Super Soldiers . 3.00
3 MS,JRu,V:Sov.Super Soldiers . 3.00
4 KP,JRu,BMc,AW,AM,V:Magneto July 1987 . . . . 3.00
TPB 12.95

X-MEN VS. DRACULA
1 rep. X-Men Ann.#6 . . . . 2.00

X-MEN: X-TINCTION AGENDA
TPB,rep.X-Men #270-272,X-Factor #60-62,New Mutants #95-97 19.95

X-TERMINATORS
October, 1988
1 JBg,AW,AM,I:N'astirh 4.00
2 JBg,AM,V:N'astirh 2.50
3 JBg,AM,V:N'astirh 2.50
4 JBg,AM,A:New Mutants, Jan.-1989 . . . . 2.50

YOGI BEAR
November, 1977
1 A:Flintstones 1.25
2 . . . . 1.25
3 . . . . 1.25
4 . . . . 1.25
5 . . . . 1.25
6 . . . . 1.25
7 . . . . 1.25
8 . . . . 1.25
9 March, 1979 . . . . 1.25

YOUNG ALLIES COMICS
Timely
Summer, 1941
1 S&K,Hitler(c),I&O:Young Allies 1st meeting Capt. America & Human Torch,A:Red Skull 4,500.00
2 S&K,A;Capt America,Human Torch 1,200.00
3 Remember Pearl Harbor(c) . 900.00
4 A;Capt. America,Torch,Red Skull ASh(c),Horror In Hollywood A:Capt America,Torch 1,000.00
5 ASh(c) 500.00
6 ASh(c) 400.00
7 ASh(c) 400.00
8 ASh(c) 400.00
9 ASh(c),Axis leaders(c),B:Tommy Type 400.00
10 ASh(c) 400.00
11 ASh(c) 300.00
12 ASh(c) 300.00
13 ASh(c) 300.00
14 . . . . 300.00
15 ASh(c) 300.00
16 ASh(c) 300.00
17 ASh(c) 300.00

Young Allies #15
© Marvel Entertainment Group

18 ASh(c) 300.00
19 ASh(c),E:Tommy Type 300.00
20 October, 1946 . . . . 300.00

YOUNG HEARTS
November, 1949
1 . . . . 37.50
2 February, 1950 . . . . 22.00

YOUNG MEN
See: COWBOY ROMANCES

YUPPIES FROM HELL
1989
1 Satire 2.95
2 . . . . 2.95
3 . . . . 2.95

ZORRO
Marvel United Kingdom
1990
1 Don Diego 1.00
2 thru 12 . . . . @1.00

DC'S THE GOLDEN AGE

Fans of DC's The Golden Age *miniseries may be interested to learn that the heroes of the four-book series were once "real" heroes of the Golden Age of comics and indeed had lengthy runs in various popular books of that era. CVA enlisted the help of renowned Golden Age expert Ron Goulart to explore the murky depths of the comic book origins of these recycled heroes.*

By Ron Goulart

In an attempt to follow in the footsteps of *Watchmen,* James Robinson and Paul Smith's *The Golden Age* offers a batch of mostly lesser known comic book characters from more than half a century ago. These once, innocent and altruistic superhero crime fighters were humanized and given flaws, foibles, and a wide range of vices to work with in the post-World War II era they found themselves in.

The central character in the four books is Tex Thompson. He appears to be a Fascist

and a rabble-rouser this time around but was a simple, clean-cut hero in his initial run. He was there at the very start of the original Golden Age and he appeared in the lineup of the first issue of *Action Comics,* the magazine that introduced Superman in the spring of 1938.

In those days, he spelled his last name Thomson, without the p, and to avoid confusion we'll refer to him from now on simply as Tex. Tex's adventures were written and drawn by Bernard Baily, best known as the original artist on *The Spectre*. Tex, at the outset, was a blond, mustached world traveler. He was so eager for action that he ran ads in the newspapers, "I want adventure-what can you offer? I will go anyplace that holds a promise of excitement."

On his thrill-seeking peregrinations, Tex was accompanied by his plump, bald sidekick, Bob Daley. Tex and Bob had some bizarre adventures in their first years, even encountering zombies at one point.

The recurrent villain was a sinister fellow known as the Gorrah, who had a single eye in the middle of his forehead. With *Action* #33 (February 1941), Tex became Mr. America. He decked himself out in a red, white, and blue version of a Revolutionary War outfit and put on a domino mask and a black pigtail wig. His weapon of choice was a bullwhip and he swore "to wipe out saboteurs and fifth columnists."

A few issues later, Daley became Fatman, with an improvised costume that included a lamp shade as a helmet. One speculates that Robinson and Smith faced one of their biggest problems when they translated this obvious comic-relief buffoon into a serious character who'd fit into their "noire" take on the waning years of the Golden Age. Wisely, they made little reference to this phase of Daley's career.

Starting with *Action* #52 (September 1942), Tex changed his name to Americommando. He ditched Bob eventually and worked in such locales as occupied Europe, helping partisans fight against "the Fascist hordes." He was last seen in *Action* #74 (July 1944).

Another Baily creation who appears in the miniseries is The Hour-Man, who made his debut in *Adventure Comics* #48 (March 1940) and was the first true superhero to appear in that title. He set up shop with no advance notice and his origin was summed up in a single caption-"Rex Tyler, a young chemist, discovers MIRACLO, a powerful chemical that transforms him from a meek, mild scientist to the underworld's most formidable foe. With Miraclo, he has for ONE HOUR the power of chained lightning and speed almost as swift as thought. But unless he performs his deeds of strength and daring within one hour, the effects of Miraclo wear off and the Hour-Man becomes his former, meek self."

Tyler's nickname was "Tick-Tock." Like Tex, he solicited adventure by way of newspaper ads aimed at getting him clients for his altruism. His ad read, "The oppressed: Young man, anxious to help the oppressed, offers services free to all who need him. Apply Box 28, post office." A bit brighter than his time-limit colleagues, such as the original Blue Beetle, Hour-Man had enough sense to know that if he took a second dose of Miraclo, he'd get another sixty minutes of superpowers.

He began life as a star, alternating *Adventure* covers with the slouch-hatted Sandman, through #60 (March 1941). But then he was upstaged, first by Starman and then by the upgraded Sandman, as produced by Joe Simon and Jack Kirby. Time ran out on The Hour-Man with #83 (February 1943).

Another important character in *The Golden Age* is Liberty Belle. Created by writer Don Cameron and artist Chuck Winter, she began life as a backup feature in *Boy Commandos* #1 in the winter of 1942. After two issues with Simon and Kirby's kid gang, she became a regular in *Star Spangled Comics,* commencing with issue #20 (May 1943). In

A HOMEFRONT KEPT CLEAN AND SAFE BY BRIGHTLY GARBED GODS.
MEN OF POWERS. SUPER POWERS.
OF FLIGHT.
OF SPEED.
OF STRENGTH.

every-day life she was Libby Belle Lawrence, "top-ranking girl athlete, world-famous newspaper columnist and radio commentator." It's possible her civilian identity was modeled in part on the then-well-known newspaperwoman, Dorothy Thompson.

After returning from Europe, where she'd witnessed and reported on Nazi terror, Libby decided to do even more for America. She became Liberty Belle to fight spies and saboteurs. Her costume consisted of a blue long-sleeved sport shirt, yellow riding breeches, and brown boots. Instead of a mask, she simply let down her long blonde hair and wore it in the peekaboo fashion made popular by the movie star Veronica Lake.

When her services were needed, a call to the kindly old caretaker was in order. He would then ring the Liberty Bell, setting up a sympathetic vibration in the tiny metal replica of Libby wore as a pin, letting her know she was wanted. She, in turn, would phone the caretaker in Philadelphia and learn what her next assignment was to be. (Today, of course, a good beeper would eliminate a lot of this circumlocution.) Liberty Belle survived the Second World War and left *Star Spangled* after #68 (May 1947).

Starman © DC Comics

The original Atom was introduced in *All-American Comics* #19 (October 1940) as the Mighty Atom, a name possibly borrowed from that of a real-life, and diminutive, strongman of the day. The Atom is redheaded Al Pratt, who stands just over five feet tall. His school chums would "constantly kid him about his small size" and nicknamed him the Atom.

Vowing to do something about his ninety-seven-pound-weakling status, Pratt underwent physical fitness training with a down-on-his-luck trainer he met. He was turned into a muscleman, one who "now has a tremendous strength that is unbelievable in one so small." He adopted a secret costumed identity as the Atom and began a career of crime fighting. Since nobody treated his civilian self with any respect even after he became the Atom, Pratt was one of the more anguished heroes of the 1940s.

Johnny Quick debuted in *More Fun Comics* #71 (September 1941). A crowded comic book at times, *More Fun* housed such heroes as The Spectre, Dr. Fate, the Green Arrow, Aquaman, and, eventually, Superboy. Never quite a star, and featured only on three covers, Johnny Quick was, nevertheless, an interesting character. Although an imitation of the more popular Flash (he got his super speed by reciting a magic formula), his adventures were nicely drawn and usually well written.

The gifted Mort Meskin drew the feature in its early years, and later on artists such as Don Barry took over. His civilian identity was that of Johnny Chambers, "ace newsreel cameraman," and his sidekick was his assistant, redheaded Tubby Watts. Johnny Quick flourished in *More Fun* until early in 1946 and was then relocated to *Adventure Comics,* where he remained until late in 1954.

Perhaps the most radically changed character in the new series was Robotman, who became a violent, thick-witted bully, much different than his original incarnation. He first appeared in *Star Spangled Comics* #7 (June 1942). Jerry Siegel, much influenced by pulp magazine science fiction robotics, created the character. Paul Cassidy and other members of the Superman shop handled the early artwork. According to the origin story, Robotman had been a regular human being, "rich, young Professor Robert Crane."

While working on a new robot with his assistant in his "palatial laboratory-residence," he was fatally shot by burglars. His quick-thinking associate removed his brain and plopped it into the skull of the robot. Thus was born Robotman, who at first looked quite a bit like the Tin Man of Oz. In order to function in a world that believed him dead, Crane adopted the alias Paul Dennis and fashioned synthetic skin to wear over his metallic face and hands. He then began a dual-identity life, passing as a human until it was time to fight crime as Robotman.

The character's finest hour came in the autumn of 1943, when Jimmy Thompson took over the feature. A newspaper veteran, Thompson achieved just the right mix of the humorous and the straight in his drawing, a blend that suited the not-quite-serious exploits of the metallic sleuth. In *Star Spangled* #29, Thompson introduced Robbie the Robotdog. Built by Robotman, the mechanical hound was initially polite and sedate, but after a hiatus of a few issues, Robbie came back in slightly altered form. Besides having acquired a shaggy-dog suit to wear for a disguise, he had a new personality. Feisty and vain, he now read Sherlock Holmes and assured his metal master he was a crack investigator himself.

Once Thompson had his basic team, he went on to produce a long series of attractive-looking and entertaining yarns. He drew the character throughout his run in *Star Spangled,* which ended with #82 (July 1948), and stuck with Robotman when he moved into *Detective Comics* as of #138 (August 1948). Thompson left the job in 1949. Among the later artists was Joe Certa. Otto Binder, who'd written about a robot named Adam Link in the *Amazing Stories* pulp in the late 1940s, contributed scripts in that same time period. Robotman ended the first phase of his career in 1953. In 1963, an entirely different Robotman became a member of the Doom Patrol.

One of the characters who played a fairly important part in *The Golden Age* was not from the DC stable at all! Captain Triumph came from *Crack Comics,* where he was first seen in #27 (January 1943). This was one of the Quality line (which included *Police Comics,* home of Plastic Man and the Spirit, and *Military Comics,* where Blackhawk held forth) published by E. M. "Busy" Arnold. When Arnold went out of business in the 1950s, DC licensed some of his features.

The Captain was just about the only superhero ostensibly created by an established newspaper comic-strip artist. Alfred Andriola was between strips when he did his stint with Triumph. His *Charlie Chan* had ended in May of 1942, and his *Kerry Drake* wouldn't get rolling until the fall of 1943. Andriola filled in the time by drawing the *Dan Dunn* strip during its final days and turned out six episodes of Captain Triumph.

The captain was actually two people, twin brothers named Michael and Lance Gallant. Michael was killed in an explosion rigged by saboteurs. His spirit, however, came back and offered the surviving twin the opportunity of becoming a superhero. "I can make you invisible! You shall fly through space in seconds! Nothing physical will harm you! All you need to do, Lance, is rub the birthmark on your wrist. Whenever you rub it, I will enter

Hourman and Robotman © DC Comics

your body and you will become *Captain Triumph!*" Apparently, it never occurred to either of the brothers to use the family name and call their joint self Captain Gallant.

At any rate, Lance accepted the proposition, delivered amidst much thunder and lightning. He rubbed his wrist and became Captain Triumph, his costume a red T-shirt and spotless white riding breeches. Andriola was an artist who always had a great deal of help with his work and it's impossible now to determine who actually did the writing and drawing on the early Captain Triumph adventures. They were, though, quite handsomely done. Other artists who drew the feature were Marv Leav and Reed Crandall. Alex Kotzky contributed several handsome renderings of the captain for *Crack* covers.

Other Quality characters who play roles in *The Golden Age* are the Ray, Dolman, Miss America, the Black Condor and, briefly seen, Stormy Foster and Hercules.

Dan Dunbar, who was transformed into Dynaman in the miniseries, was originally the junior partner in the team of TNT and Dan the Dyna-mite. Not an especially successful dynamic duo, they appeared in *Star Spangled* from #7 (April 1942) through #23 (August 1943). Nobody mentions TNT's real name in *The Golden Age* since it was Tex N. Thomas, too close to Tex Thompson and likely to cause reader confusion.

This Tex was a "popular physical-training and science instructor" at a big city high school and Dan was his star pupil. When crime reared its head, they shook hands and the rings they wore pressed together, "releasing positive and negative elements of secret power they have discovered!" On top of which, "their outer clothing, treated with a special chemical, explodes through spontaneous combustion and out of the smoke and flame of the blast charges the eighth wonder of the world the human dynamos of atomic force." Editor-writer Mort Weisinger created the team and the chief artist was Louis Cazeneuve.

Among the other venerable heroes who appear in the books are the original Green Lantern, a man who needs no introduction; Manhunter, based on the Simon and Kirby version of the hero that appeared in *Adventure* from 1942 to 1944; Johnny Thunder, possessor of a magic thunderbolt that granted his wishes and a long time resident of *Flash Comics* and member of the Justice Society of America; Starman, who for a brief while was the leading man in *Adventure;* Mr. Terrific, from *Sensation Comics;* and Tarantula, from *Star Spangled.* These last two were drawn back then by Hal Sharp, who frequently ghosted the Flash. Briefly glimpsed are such once-thriving characters as Uncle Sam, Dr. Midnite, Sargon the Sorcerer, the Phantom Lady, the Guardian, and Wildcat.

Jack Kirby:

The King of Comics

By Ron Goulart

His real name was Jacob Kurtzberg, and he was born in 1917 on New York's Lower East Side. It was a rough place to grow up, and Kirby, a lifelong movie buff, called it "Edward G. Robinson territory." One of the positive things the place gave him was "a fierce drive to get out of it." His earliest escapes were fantasy ones, aided by the movies and the adventure novels that he devoured (Edgar Rice Burroughs and H. G. Wells were his favorites).

Kirby began drawing during his childhood and sketched his first cartoons for the weekly newsletter of a club for the underprivileged. In 1935, he was hired by the Fleischer animation studios, then located on Broadway in Manhattan, and worked on the *Popeye* cartoons.

"The pay was steady, the work was lousy," he recalled. "You sat at a table surrounded by rows and rows of other tables, three hundred people. I thought of my father's garment shop and my art school, I thought of Chester Gould breaking the mold with *Dick Tracy,* and my idol Milton Caniff with *Terry and the Pirates*. I got impatient."

By 1937, his impatience had taken him to a shoestring syndicate called Lincoln Features, run by a third-rate cartoonist named H. T. Elmo. This outfit supplied strips and panels to several hundred small-town weekly newspapers. Kirby turned out political cartoons, true-fact panels, and an assortment of comic strips.

Some were drawn in an imitation Alex Raymond fashion, others in a rough version of the later Kirby style. Among them were the adventure strips *Detective Riley*, *Cyclone Burke*, and *The Black Buccaneer* and the humor strips *Socko the Seadog* and *Abdul Jones*. They were drawn in daily strip format, even though they ran only once a week. To a couple of the features, he signed the name Jack Curtiss.

Kirby's earliest comic book work appeared in *Jumbo Comics* in the summer of 1938. Originally a tabloid-size publication, this Fiction House title was packaged by the shop run by Jerry Iger and Will Eisner. Kirby drew *The Count of Monte Cristo*, *The Diary of Dr. Hayward*, and *Wilton of the West*.

At about the same time he drew a strip entitled *The Lone Rider*, for Robert Farrell's low-budget Associated Features Syndicate. It was obviously inspired by the successful radio hero, the Lone Ranger, and the young artist used the somewhat dashing pen name of Lance Kirby. In 1940, he combined two of his earlier aliases and used Jack Kirby from then on.

From the late 1930s on, Kirby concentrated on comic books since the pay was better.

JACK
KIRBY-

He drew one more comic strip in 1940, however, doing a daily *Blue Beetle* for several months. The Beetle was a leading character in the Fox line of comic books, for whom the young Kirby briefly turned out such back-of-the-book features as *Wing Turner* and *Cosmic Carson.*

While his earliest comic book work was done alone, Kirby's best-known features of the 1940s were in collaboration with Joe Simon, an editor-artist he'd first met over at the Fox offices. The team usually worked with Kirby penciling and Simon inking, or at least supervising the inking when the work load got too heavy. Simon, Kirby's senior by two years, also handled the business end of things.

They first worked together on the Blue Bolt, a superhero who flashed into view in the first issue of, appropriately enough, *Blue Bolt* (January 1940). Simon had created the blue-clad hero and drew the origin story himself. Kirby came aboard as penciler with the second issue. Even then Kirby's work was energetic, hyperactive, and unlike anything else in comics. He and Simon left the feature after the tenth issue of the magazine.

Branching out, the team began to appear, often only briefly, all over the growing comic book field. They came up with the origin story of the crimson-costumed crime fighter Mr. Scarlet for *Wow Comics,* produced two episodes in the career of the costumed hero the Black Owl for *Prize Comics,* created Marvel Boy for *Daring Comics*, and drew exactly one story about this Timely superteen.

For Timely's more successful *Marvel Mystery Comics*, they crafted the Vision, who began in #13 (November 1940). This unearthly crusader appeared out of smoke to do battle with werewolves, witches, devil worshipers, and similar supernatural antagonists. All of these stories were filled with Kirby's cinematic staging and bang-up action.

Kirby had realized quite early in his career that he was working in a medium that differed from that of the newspaper strip, that he wasn't telling stories in small daily doses. He almost always had from eight to twelve pages and plenty of room. He began breaking up his pages in new ways, introducing dynamic layouts and sometimes tossing in a splash panel that stretched across two pages. And he always emphasized action. "I had to compete with the movie camera," he said. "I tore my characters out of the panels. I made them jump all over the page."

Among the other characters the duo worked on were Captain Daring, Mercury, and the original Captain Marvel. Substituting for C. C. Beck, they produced the first issue of *Captain Marvel Adventures* in a somewhat uncharacteristic cartoony style. Late in 1940, Simon and Kirby came up with one of the most successful comic book characters ever - Captain America. The greatest superpatriot of them all, Cap made his debut in *Captain America* #1 (cover dated March 1941). Up until that time, the only characters who got comic books of their own first had to have a successful tryout elsewhere-Superman in *Action Comics,* Batman in *Detective Comics*, and the Human Torch in *Marvel.*

"Captain America was created for a time that needed noble figures," Kirby once explained. "We weren't at war yet, but everyone knew it was coming. That's why Captain America was born; America needed a superpatriot."

As to their hero's appearance, Kirby said, "Drape the flag on anything and it looks good. We gave him a chain-mail shirt and a shield, like a modern-day crusader." Cap and his young sidekick, Bucky, teamed up against the "vicious elements who seek to overthrow the U.S. government!" Chief among those vicious elements was the Red Skull, a Nazi agent who wore a crimson death's-head mask and was to Captain America and Bucky what the Joker was to Batman and Robin.

When not battling enemies of democracy, the star-spangled team ran into some rather spooky foes, including a phantom hound, Oriental zombies, the Hunchback of Hollywood, the Black Talon, and the Black Witch. As comics historian Mike Barson has pointed out, these early horror tales were "a crazy combination of 1930s movies, pulps, and detective fiction."

For the initial issue of *Captain America*, Simon and Kirby, with considerable help from their crew of assistants, produced four adventures of Cap and Bucky. For good measure, they also did an adventure of Tuk the Cave Boy and Hurricane (who had been known as Mercury during his single appearance in the only issue of Timely's *Red Raven Comics*). The two of them only stuck with their super patriot for ten issues before they were lured over to the DC stable.

It was for Detective Comics, Inc., that Simon and Kirby did some of their most impressive work of the Golden Age. They took over the established Sandman with #72 of *Adventure Comics* (March 1942) and rejuvenated him into a star character. Making use of the flamboyant splash panels and lively layouts Kirby had perfected for Captain America helped push the character to the top. Emphasizing the Sandman's association with sleep, they concocted stories that made use of dreams and nightmares. Also for *Adventure,* Simon and Kirby converted the plainclothes Manhunter into a red-costumed hero. They did some striking work on the feature and even drew the former backup character on three covers.

For *Detective Comics*, Batman's home base, they created their most popular kid gang, the Boy Commandos. The group first appeared in #64 (June 1942). Unlike many of the boy heroes of World War II, they were directly involved in combat overseas and fought against the Axis forces in both Europe and the Pacific. Originally numbering four teenagers, the gang was international in makeup and consisted of Alfy from England, Jan from Holland, Andre from France, and Brooklyn from America. Their mentor was Captain Rip Carter, the leader of "an outfit of tough commandos," and the boys were described as "company mascots."

Carrying on with the usual lively and audacious layouts, Kirby did a vigorous job in penciling the feature. He and Simon mixed action, some humor, and even a touch of fantasy into their stories (managing to get in their war yarns such elements as the predictions of Nostradamus, Egyptian mummies, and ghosts!). Simon and Kirby went into the service themselves and abandoned the boys in 1943 but returned to them for a spell just after the end of World War II.

Combining two of their favorite themes, the team came up with the Newsboy Legion for DC's *Star Spangled Comics*. Starting with #7 (April 1942) of the faltering title, the new Simon-Kirby feature introduced a gang of feisty and courageous street kids who lived in Suicide Slum. They tangled with sundry hoods and saboteurs, looked after by a moonlighting beat cop who dressed up in a blue-and-gold uniform and called himself the Guardian. Kirby, aided by Simon, also turned out every *Star Spangled* cover from #7 through #40.

After the war, the two resumed their association. For Harvey, they did *Stuntman,* the first issue of which appeared in the spring of 1946. The second and final issue showed up two months later. This was another costumed-hero feature, handsomely drawn and displaying more humor than Simon and Kirby had hitherto used. They also used some impressive double-page splash panels.

Simon has said, "Kirby and I thought we did some of our best on the comic books we provided for Harvey." Unfortunately, the immediate postwar years were not a good time for costumed crime fighters. Furthermore, there was a glut of new titles. "Bundles were refused, unopened," explained Simon. The Simon and Kirby titles were cancelled. Even less successful was another kid-gang title, *The Boy Explorers*, which lasted just one issue.

Joe Simon, fortunately, had a few other ideas. One of them turned out to be the most successful venture he and Kirby worked on together. While he was serving in the Coast Guard, Simon "felt there should be an adult comic" since so many "adults, the officers and the men and the people at that point in time were reading kid comic books."

Simon drew up some sample title pages and a sample cover he called *Young Romance*. The reason he picked love for the first adult category was simple: "It was about the only thing that hadn't been done." When Kirby saw the stuff, he "loved the idea." The two men wrote, drew, and packaged an issue and took it to the Prize Group, the publishers of *Prize Comics*, *Headline Comics*, and *Frankenstein*. The first issue of *Young Romance* came out in the autumn of 1947 and, since Simon and Kirby were the first comic book creators to get a percentage of the profits, they did extremely well. That first issue, with a cover showing an eternal triangle unfolding in the studio of a handsome artist, sold out a run of 500,000 copies.

The circulation soon jumped to one million per issue, as did their companion title, *Young Love,* which came along at the end of 1948. "The things made millions," recalled Simon, and prompted a new comic book genre that inspired dozens of rival titles over the next decade. Kirby's romance style was still impressive, but it was toned down from what he'd been doing on the short-lived Stuntman adventures. Still, he drew in a realistic fashion; a more dynamic version of the sort of thing Ken Ernst was doing on the soap opera newspaper strip, *Mary Worth.*

Also drawn in a realistic, though rougher and tougher, style were the true-crime titles the team began to turn out. While the superheroes began to fade away in the immediate postwar years, titles such as *Crime Does Not Pay* began to blossom. In the forefront of those producing such material were Simon and Kirby.

They first renovated *Headline Comics*, taking a comic book full of clean-cut kid heroes and turning it into a crime book chock full of gangsters and murders. They also contributed fact-crime stories to *Clue Comics*. (That Hillman magazine became *Real Clue* with the June 1947 issue.)

Simon has admitted that although *Headline* was inspired by the earlier *Crime Does Not Pay,* "We had our own style, we didn't copy them." He maintained, "We didn't agree with certain things they did. We didn't care for violence and sex." Be that as it may, Kirby penciled some pretty strong pages, rich with bullet-ridden bodies and spilled blood. Subsequently, he and Simon, with a staff that included Mort Meskin, Bill Draut, and Marv Stein, also brought forth *Justice Traps the Guilty* and *Police Trap*.

Kirby and his longtime partner did one final kid gang in 1950 and 1951. This was a historical Western titled *Boys' Ranch*, published by Harvey and making it through just six issues. Meskin helped out on this one, too. In 1954, the Simon-Kirby collaboration introduced another super patriotic hero.

The first issue of *Fighting American*, published by the Prize Group, had a cover date of April-May 1954. Partnered with a kid sidekick named Speedboy, Fighting American rounded up gangsters, ghouls, and Communist spies. As the feature progressed, its tone lightened and became almost self-spoofing, introducing Communist villains such as Rhode Island Red and Poison Ivan. The title expired after seven issues.

Starting back in 1950, the duo (again with an assist from the gifted Mort Meskin), had also begun dabbling in horror. For the Prize folks they did *Black Magic*, which purported to offer "True Amazing Accounts" of voodoo, ghosts, and demons.

The team split up in the mid-1950s, although they worked together again briefly for

Archie in 1959 to create a new version of the Shield called *The Double Life of Private Strong*, a feeble imitation of Captain America and *The Fly*.

On his own, Kirby next worked for both DC and Marvel. He drew *The Yellow Claw*, *The Black Rider*, and *The Green Arrow*. In 1957, he created *The Challengers of the Unknown*. The first important hero team to emerge in the Silver Age, they possessed no special powers and had to rely on their wits and diversified abilities to wage their campaign against odd and unusual villainy. The Challengers debuted in DC's *Showcase* #6 (February 1957), moving into their own magazine the next year. Kirby, restless, abandoned them after the eighth issue. On his last five issues, Wally Wood served as his inker.

Returning to Marvel, Kirby then went through his monster phase. Teaming with Stan Lee, he rendered a multitude of stories dealing with huge alien entities with names like Moomba, Xom, Grottu, and Fing Fang Foom. These immense and mean-minded creatures flourished in such titles as *Tales to Astonish* and *Journey into Mystery*.

Then in 1961, Kirby made his first contribution to what would eventually be called the Silver Age. According to Stan Lee, Marvel got back into the superhero business when publisher Martin Goodman "mentioned that he had noticed one of the titles published by National Comics [which is what DC was calling itself at the time] seemed to be selling better than most. It was a book called *The Justice League of America* and was composed of a team of superheroes. Well, we didn't need a house to fall on us."

Lee agreed to come up with a new Marvel team of heroes. "Characters I could personally relate to," he explained. "They'd be flesh and blood, they'd have faults and foibles, they'd be fallible and feisty." Naturally enough, he picked Kirby to work on the new project. The result was the Fantastic Four. It turned out to be the cornerstone of the entire Marvel Comic's empire. The magazine had a continuing influence and, in the opinion of historian Gerard Jones, "Nearly all modern superhero comics have drawn and continue to draw upon the first eighty or so issues of *Fantastic Four* for inspiration and material." Kirby remained with the Fantastic Four for nearly a decade.

Definitely on a roll, Kirby and Lee next invented the Hulk, an appealing combination of Mr. Hyde, the Frankenstein monster, the Wolf Man, and the Jolly Green Giant. Then came Thor, a hammer-tossing character who mixed superheroics with Norse mythology. In 1963, it was another new hero group, X-Men. An important and influential bunch, they were the first team of mutants to show up in the Marvel universe.

Also that year, the Kirby-Lee team introduced "the war mag for people who hate war mags," *Sgt. Fury and His Howling Commandoes*. Nick Fury was, as Lee described him, "a hard-as-nails, two-fisted, tough-talking, fast-moving, cigar-chomping, lusty, gutsy, brawling leader of men" and was a far cry from Rip Carter, who had shepherded the kinder, gentler Boy Commandos.

In 1965, Fury began leading a double life, when Marvel introduced a new Nick Fury title devoted to his later work as an agent of S.H.I.E.L.D. A secret intelligence agency, whose initials stood for Supreme Headquarters International Espionage Law Enforcement Division, S.H.I.E.L.D. was inspired by the popular television show, *The Man From U.N.C.L.E.* As Lee put it, "We were going to out-Bond Bond and out-UNCLE U.N.C.L.E." Late in 1966, Jim Steranko became Kirby's inker, and a few issues later, he took over as both artist and writer on the book.

There was a great deal of migration on the part of artists and writers in the 1970s, mostly consisting of moving back and forth between Marvel and DC. Kirby returned to DC in 1970. "I was living here in California," Kirby recalled, and Carmine Infantino, then editorial director for DC, was visiting the state and got in touch with him. "To make

Orion and Darkseid © DC Comics

it short, they wanted me to save *Superman*. I said, 'Well, I wasn't too happy with what was happening at Marvel. I thought maybe this was the time to change.' But I said, 'I don't want to take work away from the guys who have been doing it for years. I'll take that book *Jimmy Olsen*. I'll take the one that has no sales and I'll do my own books, titles of my own.' So I turned *Jimmy Olsen* into something different."

Kirby enlivened *Jimmy Olsen* by bringing back an old Simon and Kirby creation, the Newsboy Legion. He plunked Jimmy, the Legion, and the Guardian into weird and wild adventures with vampires, werewolves, and, once, Don Rickles.

Kirby followed that with his own complex New Gods, Fourth World concept, an epic drama that unfolded in no less than three separate titles, *Mr.Miracle*, *Forever People*, and *New Gods*. Kirby penciled and wrote these titles, creating an enormous mythology of his own, made up of bits and pieces of myths and popular culture that had influenced his work over the years. The complex saga involved new gods, New Genesis, the Astro-Force, and beings named Darkseid, Orion, Lightray, and Metron. Kirby blended his wall-banger style with dialogue worthy of an Elizabethan tragedy-"FIEND OF THE PITS! No being of New Genesis ever spawned one like YOU!!" and "HAHAHAH-I smell the seeds of FEAR sprouting in your stone heart, Kalibak!"

Kirby's grandiose new titles had power and plenty of operatic splendor, but all were canceled within a couple years of their debuts. Because he had a five-year contract with DC, he came up with other books. These included *The Demon*, which lasted from 1972 to early 1974, and *Kamandi the Last Boy on Earth*.

In *The Comic Book Heroes*, Will Jacobs and Gerard Jones described the latter comic as "a twist on *Planet of the Apes*, about a human boy in a post-nuclear-war future in which other animals have gained intelligence and reduced mankind to slavery. It was allowed to become repetitious when Kirby settled for a long series of talking animals (including even talking snails)." *Kamandi* held on until 1978, but Kirby had long since left it. He also came up with *Omac* (One Man Army Corps), another science fiction effort in a futuristic setting. That failed, too.

For Kirby, the 1970s were years of decline. "Kirby's art took a slow but steady turn for the worse," commented Jacobs and Jones. "At the same time, his scripting, always unusual, began to take a swing toward the oblique and confusing." His art became almost a parody of the classic Kirby style. Human figures became impossibly muscle-bound and stiff, faces grew uninvitingly harsh and angular. Even his flair for movement and action seemed to lock into a repetitious pattern. When his contract ran out in 1975, Kirby left DC.

In recent years, Kirby worked in animation, drew for independent publishers on such titles as *Captain Victory* and *Destroyer Duck*, and even made a brief return to DC for another go-round with his Fourth World series.

In 1993, Kirby invented yet another universe, the Secret City Saga for Topps. He drew most of the covers, and the interior stuff was provided by such writers and artists as Roy Thomas, Gerry Conway, Don Heck, John Severin, and Dick Ayers. The series, which included comic books titled *Bombast*, *Captain Glory*, *Night Glider*, and *Satan's Six*, was not a hit.

Anyone who knows comics will no doubt agree with what *The Encyclopedia of American Comics* said about Kirby–"Next to Superman, Kirby is probably the most important figure in the history of comic books."

A-1 COMICS
Magazine Enterprises
1944

N# A:Kerry Drake,Johnny Devildog & Streamer Kelly . 150.00
1 A:Dotty Driple,Mr. EX,Bush Berry and Lew Loyal 90.00
2 A:Texas Slim & Dirty Dalton, The Corsair,Teddy Rich,Dotty Dripple,IncaDinca,TommyTinker Little Mexico and Tugboat . . . 50.00
3 same 30.00
4 same 30.00
5 same 30.00
6 same 28.00
7 same 25.00

A-1 Comics #8
© Magazine Enterprises

8 same 25.00
9 Texas Slim Issue 28.00
10 Same characters as issues 2-8 . . . . 25.00
11 Teena 40.00
12 Teena 30.00
13 JCr,Guns of Fact and Fiction, narcotics & junkies featured 130.00
14 Tim Holt WesternAdventures 325.00
15 Teena 30.00
16 Vacation Comics 28.00
17 Jim Holt #2, E:A-1 on cover 190.00
18 Jimmy Durante, Ph(c) 150.00
19 Tim Holt #3 . . . . 150.00
20 Jimmy Durante Ph(c) 100.00
21 OW,Joan of Arc movie adapt. 125.00
22 Dick Powell (1949) 120.00
23 Cowboys N' Indians #6 . . . . . 35.00
24 FF(c),LbC,Trail Colt #2 . . . . 250.00
25 Fibber McGee & Molly (1949) 40.00
26 LbC, Trail Colt #2 . . . . 185.00
27 Ghost Rider#1,O:GhostRider 350.00
28 Christmas (Koko & Kola) . . . 20.00
29 FF(c), Ghost Rider #2 . . . . . 325.00
30 BP, Jet Powers #1 . . . . 165.00
31 FF,Ghost Rider#3,O:Ghost Rider 300.00
32 AW,GE,Jet Powers #2 . . . . 115.00
33 Muggsy Mouse #2 . . . . 30.00
34 FF(c),Ghost Rider #4 . . . . . 300.00
35 AW,Jet Powers 190.00
36 Muggsy Mouse 35.00
37 FF(c),Ghost Rider 310.00
38 AW,WW,Jet Powers 190.00
39 Muggsy Mouse 20.00
40 Dogface Dooley 28.00
41 Cowboys N' Indians 22.00
42 BP,Best of the West 225.00
43 Dogface Dooley 20.00
44 Ghost Rider 125.00
45 American Air Forces 25.00
46 Best of the West 100.00
47 FF,Thunda 635.00
48 Cowboys N' Indians 22.00
49 Dogface Dooley 15.00
50 BP,Danger Is Their Busines65 50.00
51 Ghost Rider 125.00
52 Best of the West 100.00
53 Dogface Dooley 15.00
54 BP,American Air Forces 25.00
55 BP,U.S. Marines 25.00
56 BP,Thunda 100.00
57 Ghost Rider 110.00
58 American Air Forces 25.00
59 Best of the West 100.00
60 The U.S. Marines 25.00
61 Space Ace 240.00
62 Starr Flagg 200.00
63 Manhunt 150.00
64 Dogface Dooley 15.00
65 BP,American Air Forces 25.00
66 Best of the West 100.00
67 American Air Forces 25.00
68 U.S. Marines 25.00
69 Ghost Rider 120.00
70 Best of the West 75.00
71 Ghost Rider 110.00
72 U.S. Marines 25.00
73 BP,Thunda 75.00
74 BP,American Air Forces 20.00
75 Ghost Rider 100.00
76 Best of the West 75.00
77 Manhunt 110.00
78 BP,Thunda 80.00
79 American Air Forces 28.00
80 Ghost Rider 100.00
81 Best of the West 75.00
82 BP,Cave Girl 200.00
83 BP,Thunda 75.00
84 Ghost Rider 100.00
85 Best of the West 75.00
86 BP,Thunda 70.00
87 Best of the West 75.00
88 Bobby Benson's B-Bar-B . . . 45.00
89 BP,Home Run,Stan Musial . 135.00
90 Red Hawk 60.00
91 BP,American Air Forces 20.00
92 Dream Book of Romance . . . 30.00
93 BP,Great Western 100.00
94 FF,White Indian 150.00
95 BP,Muggsy Mouse 15.00
96 BP,Cave Girl 175.00
97 Best of the West 70.00
98 Undercover Girl 175.00
99 Muggsy Mouse 12.00
100 Badmen of the West 125.00
101 FF,White Indian 135.00
101(a) FG, Dream Book of Romance, Marlon Brando . . 90.00
103 BP,Best of the West 75.00
104 FF,White Indian 125.00
105 Great Western 60.00
106 Dream Book of Love 40.00
107 Hot Dog 25.00
108 BP,BC,Red Fox 75.00
109 Dream Book of Romance . . 25.00
110 Dream Book of Romance . . 25.00
111 I'm a Cop 65.00
112 Ghost Rider 90.00
113 BP,Great Western 60.00
114 Dream Book of Love 40.00
115 Hot Dog 18.00
116 BP,Cave Girl 155.00
117 White Indian 55.00
118 BP(c),Undercover Girl 175.00
119 Straight Arrow's Fury 75.00
120 Badmen of the West 75.00
121 Mysteries of the Scotland Yard 75.00
122 Black Phantom 185.00
123 Dream Book of Love 25.00
124 Hot Dog 18.00
125 BP,Cave Girl 155.00
126 BP,I'm a Cop 75.00
127 BP,Great Western 60.00
128 BP,I'm a Cop 65.00
129 The Avenger 175.00
130 BP,Strongman 95.00
131 BP,The Avenger 125.00
132 Strongman 80.00
133 BP,The Avenger 125.00
134 Strongman 75.00
135 White Indian 50.00
136 Hot Dog 15.00
137 BP,Africa 125.00
138 BP,Avenger 125.00
139 BP,Strongman, 1955 . . . . . 85.00

ABBIE AN' SLATS
United Features Syndicate
March, 1948

1 RvB(c) 100.00
2 RvB(c) 75.00
3 RvB(c) 55.00
4 August, 1948 . . . . 45.00
N# 1940,Earlier Issue 200.00
N# 165.00

ABBOTT AND COSTELLO
St. John Publishing Co.
February, 1948

1 PP(c), Waltz Time 275.00
2 Jungle Girl and Snake cover 125.00
3 Outer Space cover 85.00
4 MD, Circus cover 60.00
5 MD,Bull Fighting cover 60.00
6 MD,Harem cover 60.00
7 MD,Opera cover 60.00
8 MD,Pirates cover 60.00
9 MD,Polar Bear cover 60.00
10 MD,PP(c),Son of Sinbad tale 125.00
11 MD 55.00
12 PP(c) 50.00
13 Fire fighters cover 50.00
14 Bomb cover 50.00
15 Bubble Bath cover 50.00
16 thru 29 MD . . . . @50.00
30 thru 39 MD . . . . @40.00
40 MD,September, 1956 . . . . . . 40.00

Ace Comics #24 © David McKay Publ.

ACE COMICS
David McKay Publications
April, 1937

1 JM, F:Katzenjammer Kids . 1,600.00
2 JM, A:Blondie 500.00
3 JM, A:Believe It Or Not . . . 350.00
4 JM, F:Katzenjammer Kids . . 325.00

5 JM, A:Believe It Or Not . . . 290.00
6 JM, A:Blondie 275.00
7 JM, A:Believe It Or Not . . . 270.00
8 JM, A:Jungle Jim 265.00
9 JM, A:Blondie 270.00
10 JM, F:Katzenjammer Kids . . 250.00
11 I:The Phantom series 325.00
12 A:Blondie, Jungle Jim 225.00
13 A:Ripley's Believe It Or Not . 190.00
14 A:Blondie, Jungle Jim 190.00
15 A:Blondie 185.00
16 F:Katzenjammer Kids 185.00
17 A:Blondie 185.00
18 A:Ripley's Believe It Or N8t . 185.00
19 F:Katzenjammer Kids 175.00
20 A:Jungle Jim 175.00
21 A:Blondie 160.00
22 A:Jungle Jim 150.00
23 F:Katzenjammer Kids 150.00
24 A:Blondie 150.00
25 . . . . 150.00
26 O:Prince Valiant 500.00
27 thru 36 . . . . @135.00
37 Krazy Kat Ends 100.00
38 thru 49 . . . . @90.00
50 thru 59 . . . . @85.00
60 thru 69 . . . . @80.00
70 thru 79 . . . . @75.00
80 thru 89 . . . . @70.00
90 thru 99 . . . . @55.00
100 . . . . 65.00
101 thru 109 . . . . @55.00
110 thru 119 . . . . @52.00
120 thru 143 . . . . @50.00
144 Beginning of Phantom covers 80.00
145 thru 150 . . . . @70.00
151 October-November, 1949 . . 75.00

ACES HIGH
E.C. Comics
March-April, 1955

1 GE(c) 200.00
2 GE(c) 125.00
3 GE(c) 100.00
4 GE(c) 100.00
5 GE(c)Nov.-Dec., 1955 . . . . . 100.00

ADVENTURES INTO DARKNESS
Standard Publications
August, 1952

5 JK(c) 100.00
6 GT, JK 75.00
7 JK(c) 75.00
8 ATh 85.00
9 JK 75.00
10 JK,ATh,MSy 65.00
11 JK,ATh,MSy 65.00
12 JK,ATh,MYs 65.00
13 Cannibalism feature 75.00
14 . . . . 65.00

ADVENTURES INTO THE UNKNOWN!
American Comics Group
Fall 1948

1 FG, Haunted House cover . 675.00
2 Haunted Island cover 325.00
3 AF, Sarcophagus cover . . . 350.00
4 Monsters cover 200.00
5 Monsters cover 200.00
6 Giant Hands cover 150.00
7 Skeleton Pirate cover 135.00
8 Horror 125.00
9 Snow Monster 125.00
10 Red Bats 125.00
11 Death Shadow 125.00
12 OW(c) 100.00
13 OW(c),Dinosaur 110.00
14 OW(c),Cave 110.00
15 Red Demons 110.00
16 . . . . 100.00
17 OW(c),The Thing Type 120.00

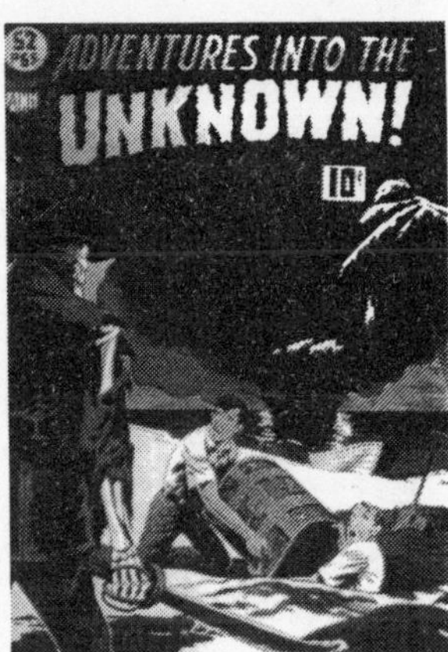

Adventures Into the Unknown! #7
© American Comics Group

18 OW(c),Wolves 110.00
19 OW(c),Graveyard 100.00
20 OW(c),Graveyard 100.00
21 Bats and Dracula 100.00
22 Death 100.00
23 Bats 90.00
24 . . . . 90.00
25 . . . . 90.00
26 . . . . 90.00
27 AW 135.00
28 thru 39 . . . . @80.00
40 thru 49 . . . . @75.00
50 . . . . 75.00
51 Lazarus 125.00
52 Lazarus 120.00
53 . . . . 120.00
54 . . . . 120.00
55 . . . . 120.00
56 Lazarus 120.00
57 . . . . 120.00
58 Lazurus 120.00
59 . . . . 80.00
60-61 . . . . 60.00
62 thru 69 . . . . @60.00
70 thru 79 . . . . @35.00
80 thru 89 . . . . @30.00
90 thru 99 . . . . @35.00
100 . . . . 30.00
101 thru 115 . . . . @25.00
116 AW,AT 20.00
117 thru 120 . . . . @20.00
121 thru 152 . . . . @15.00
153 A:Magic Agent 15.00
154 O:Nemesis 12.00
155 . . . . 12.00
156 A:Magic Agent 15.00
157 thru 173 . . . . @10.00
174 August, 1967 . . . . 10.00

ADVENTURES IN WONDERLAND
Lev Gleason Publications
April, 1955

1 . . . . 35.00
2 . . . . 25.00
3 . . . . 20.00
4 . . . . 20.00
5 . . . . 25.00

ADVENTURES OF MIGHTY MOUSE
St. John Publishing Co.
November, 1951

1 Mighty Mouse Adventures . 125.00
2 Menace of the Deep 100.00
3 Storm Clouds of Mystery . . . 75.00
4 Thought Control Machine . . . 50.00

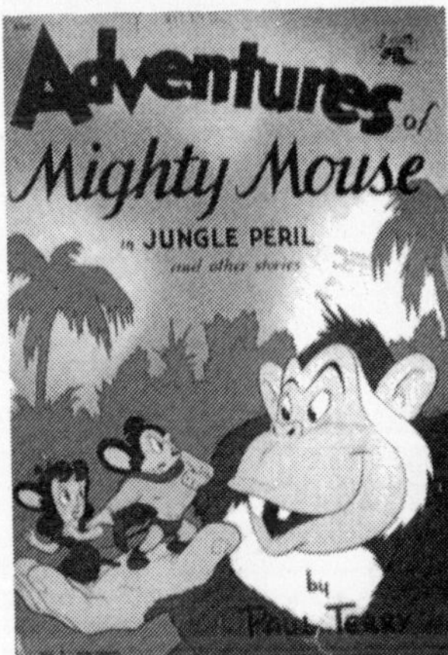

Adventures of Mighty Mouse #5
© St. John Publishing Co.

5 Jungle Peril 50.00
6 'The Vine of Destruction' 50.00
7 Space Ship(c) 50.00
8 Charging Alien(c) 50.00
9 Meteor(c) 45.00
10 Revolt at the Zoo" 45.00
11 Jungle(c) 45.00
12 A:Freezing Terror 45.00
13 A:Visitor from Outer Space . . 45.00
14 V:Cat 40.00
15 . . . . 40.00
16 . . . . 40.00
17 . . . . 40.00
18 May, 1955 . . . . 40.00

AGGIE MACK
Four Star Comics/ Superior Comics
January, 1948

1 AF,HR(c) 120.00
2 JK(c) 60.00
3 AF,JK(c) 50.00
4 AF 75.00
5 AF,JK(c) 55.00
6 AF,JK(c) 50.00
7 AF,Burt Lancaster on cover . 55.00
8 AF,JK(c), August 1949 . . . . . 50.00

BILL BARNES, AMERICA'S AIR ACE
Street and Smith Publications
July, 1940

1 (Bill Barnes Comics) 375.00
2 Second Battle Valley Forge . 245.00
3 A:Aviation Cadets 185.00
4 Shotdown(c) 175.00
5 A:Air Warden, Danny Hawk 170.00
6 A:Danny Hawk,RocketRodney 150.00
7 How to defeat the Japanese 150.00
8 Ghost Ship 150.00
9 Flying Tigers, John Wayne . 155.00
10 I:Roane Waring 150.00
11 Flying Tigers 150.00
12 War Workers 150.00

Becomes:

AIR ACE

2-1 Invades Germany 100.00

2-2 Jungle Warfare 65.00
2-3 A:The Four Musketeers . . . 55.00
2-4 A:Russell Swann 55.00
2-5 A:The Four Musketeers . . . 55.00
2-6 Raft(c) 50.00
2-7 BP, What's New In Science 50.00
2-8 XP-59 . . . . 50.00
2-9 The Northrop P-61 . . . . 50.00
2-10 NCG-14 . . . . 45.00
2-11 Whip Lanch 45.00
2-12 PP(c) 45.00
3-1 . . . . 40.00
3-2 Atom and It's Future 40.00
3-3 Flying in the Future 40.00
3-4 How Fast Can We Fly 40.00
3-5 REv(c) 40.00
3-6 V:Wolves 40.00
3-7 BP(c), Vortex of Atom Bo90 75.00
3-8 February-March, 1947 . . . . 32.00

AIRBOY
(see AIR FIGHTERS COMICS)

AIR FIGHTERS COMICS
Hillman Periodicals
November, 1941

1 I:BlackCommander (only App) 1,000.00
2 O:Airboy A:Sky Wolf 1,500.00
3 O:Sky Wolf and Heap 800.00
4 A:Black Angel, Iron Ace . . . 500.00
5 A:Sky Wolf and Iron Ace . . 450.00
6 Airboy's Bird Plane 400.00
7 Airboy battles Kultur 335.00
8 A:Skinny McGinty 325.00

Air Fighters Comics #9 © Hillman Periodicals

9 A:Black Prince, Hatchet Man 320.00
10 I:The Stinger 315.00
11 Kida(c) 310.00
12 A:Misery 310.00
2-1 A:Flying Dutchman 300.00
2-2 I:Valkyrie 350.00
2-3 Story Panels cover 300.00
2-4 V:Japanese 300.00
2-5 Air Boy in Tokyo 300.00
2-6 'Dance of Death' 300.00
2-7 A:Valkyrie 300.00
2-8 Airboy Battles Japanese . . 300.00
2-9 Airboy Battles Japanese . . 300.00
2-10 O:Skywolf 340.00
Becomes:

AIRBOY

2-11 . . . . 300.00
2-12 A:Valykrie 225.00
3-1 . . . . 175.00
3-2 . . . . 150.00
3-3 Never published
3-4 I:The Heap 150.00
3-5 Airboy 130.00
3-6 A:Valykrie 130.00
3-7 AMc,Witch Hunt 130.00
3-8 A:Condor 125.00
3-9 O:The Heap 155.00
3-10 . . . . 125.00
3-11 . . . . 125.00
3-12 Airboy missing 175.00
4-1 Elephant in chains cover . 160.00
4-2 I:Rackman 95.00
4-3 Airboy profits on name . . 100.00
4-4 S&K 125.00
4-5 S&K,The American Miracle 135.00
4-6 S&K,A:Heap and Flying Fool 135.00
4-7 S&K 135.00
4-8 S&K,Girlfriend captured . . 135.00
4-9 S&K,Airboy in quick sand . 135.00
4-10 S&K,A:Valkyrie 135.00
4-11 S&K,A:Frenchy 135.00
4-12 FBe 120.00
5-1 LSt 75.00
5-2 I:Wild Horse of Calabra . . . 75.00
5-3 . . . . 75.00
5-4 CI 75.00
5-5 Skull on cover 75.00
5-6 . . . . 75.00
5-7 . . . . 75.00
5-8 Bondage Cover 85.00

Airboy #64 (6/5) © Hillman Periodicals

5-9 Zoi,Row 75.00
5-10 A:Valykrie,O:The Heap . . . 85.00
5-11 Airboy vs. The Rats 75.00
5-12 BK,Rat Army captures Airboy 75.00
6-1 . . . . 75.00
6-2 . . . . 75.00
6-3 . . . . 75.00
6-4 Airboy boxes 80.00
6-5 A:The Ice People 75.00
6-6 . . . . 75.00
6-7 Airboy vs. Chemical Giant . 75.00
6-8 O:The Heap 85.00
6-9 . . . . 75.00
6-10 . . . . 75.00
6-11 . . . . 75.00
6-12 . . . . 75.00
7-1 . . . . 70.00
7-2 BP 70.00
7-3 BP 70.00
7-4 I:Monsters of the Ice 70.00
7-5 V:Monsters of the Ice 70.00
7-6 . . . . 70.00
7-7 Mystery of the Sargasso Sea 70.00
7-8 A:Centaur 70.00
7-9 I:Men of the StarlightRobot . 70.00
7-10 O:The Heap 70.00
7-11 . . . . 70.00
7-12 Airboy visits India 70.00
8-1 BP,A:Outcast and Polo Bandits 65.00
8-2 BP,Suicide Dive cover 65.00
8-3 I:The Living Fuse 65.00
8-4 A:Death Merchants of the Air 70.00
8-5 A:Great Plane from Nowhere 65.00
8-6 . . . . 65.00
8-7 . . . . 65.00
8-8 . . . . 65.00
8-9 . . . . 65.00
8-10 A:Mystery Walkers 65.00
8-11 . . . . 65.00
8-12 . . . . 70.00
9-1 . . . . 65.00
9-2 A:Valykrie 60.00
9-3 A:Heap (cover) 60.00
9-4 A:Water Beast, Frog Headed Riders 65.00
9-5 A:Heap vs.Man of Moonlight 60.00
9-6 Heap cover 60.00
9-7 Heap cover 60.00
9-8 Heap cover 65.00
9-9 . . . . 65.00
9-10 Space cover 65.00
9-11 . . . . 60.00
9-12 Heap cover 60.00
10-1 Heap cover 60.00
10-2 Ships on Space 60.00
10-3 . . . . 60.00
10-4 May, 1953 . . . . 60.00

AL CAPP'S DOG PATCH COMICS
Toby Press
June, 1949

1 . . . . 150.00
2 A:Daisy 110.00
3 . . . . 100.00
4 December, 1949 . . . . 100.00

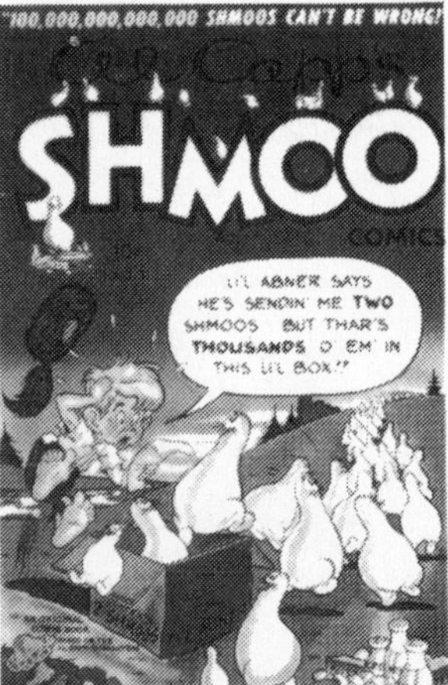

Al Capp's Shmoo #1 © Toby Press

AL CAPP'S SHMOO
Toby Press
July, 1949

1 100 Trillion Schmoos 200.00

2 Super Shmoo(c) 150.00
3 . . . . 150.00
4 . . . . 140.00
5 April, 1950 . . . . 140.00

AL CAPP'S WOLF GAL
Toby Press
1951

1 Pin-Up 200.00
2 1952 . . . . 175.00

ALL-FAMOUS CRIME
Star Publications
May, 1951

8 LbC(c) 75.00
9 LbC(c) 85.00
10 LbC(c) 60.00
4 LbC(c) 60.00
5 LbC(c) 60.00

Becomes:

ALL-FAMOUS POLICE CASES

6 LbC(c) 75.00
7 LbC(c) 65.00
8 LbC(c) 60.00
9 LbC(c) 55.00
10 thru 15 LbC(c) . . . . @50.00
16 September, 1954 . . . . 60.00

ALL GOOD COMICS
R. W. Voight/Fox Publ. /St. John Publ.

1 1944 . . . . 85.00
1 1946 . . . . 65.00
N# 1949 . . . . 350.00

ALL GREAT COMICS
(see DAGGER, DESERT HAWK)

ALL HERO COMICS
Fawcett Publications
March, 1943

1 A:Capt. Marvel Jr.,Capt. Midnight,Ibis, Golden Arrow and Spy Smasher 750.00

All Humor Comics #14
© Comic Favorites, Inc./Quality Comics

ALL HUMOR COMICS
Comic Favorites, Inc. (Quality Comics)
Spring 1946

1 . . . . 100.00
2 PG 50.00
3 I:Kelly Poole 25.00
4 thru 7 . . . . @25.00
8 PG 25.00
9 . . . . 25.00
10 . . . . 25.00
11 thru 17 . . . . @18.00

ALL LOVE ROMANCES
(see SCREAM COMICS)

ALL NEGRO COMICS

1 . . . . 1,000.00

ALL-NEW COMICS
Family Comics (Harvey Publ.)
January, 1943

1 A:Steve Case, Johnny Rebel I:Detective Shane 600.00
2 JKu,O:Scarlet Phantom 325.00

All New Short Story Comics #3
© Family Comics/Harvey Publications

3 . . . . 250.00
4 AdH 225.00
5 Flash Gordon 250.00
6 I:Boy Heroes and Red Blazer 250.00
7 JKu,AS(c),A:Black Cat & Zebra 250.00
8 JKu,A:Shock Gibson 250.00
9 JKu,A:Black Cat 250.00
10 JKu,A:Zebra 225.00
11 A:Man in Black, Girl Commandos 225.00
12 JKu 225.00
13 Stuntman by S&K, A:Green Hornet&cover 250.00
14 A:Green Hornet 225.00
15 Smaller size, Distributed by Mail, March-April, 1947 . 300.00

ALL TOP COMICS
William H. Wise Co.
1944

N# 132pgs.,A:Capt. V,Red Robbins 140.00

ALL TOP COMICS
Fox Features Syndicate
Spring 1946

1 A:Cosmo Cat, Flash Rabbit 135.00
2 . . . . 60.00
3 . . . . 45.00
4 . . . . 45.00
5 . . . . 45.00
6 . . . . 45.00
7 . . . . 45.00
7a 85.00
8 JKa(c),Blue Beetle 1st app . 650.00
9 JKa(c),A:Rulah 375.00
10 JKa(c),A:Rulah 400.00
11 A:Rulah,Blue Beetle 300.00
12 A:Rulah,Jo Jo,Blue Beetle . 300.00
13 A:Rulah 275.00
14 A:Rulah,Blue Beetle 350.00
15 A:Rulah 275.00
16 A:Rulah,Blue Beetle 300.00
17 A:Rulah,Blue Beetle 300.00
18 A:Dagar,Jo Jo 225.00

Green Publ.

6 1957 . . . . 20.00
6 1958 . . . . 20.00
6 1959 . . . . 20.00
6 1959 . . . . 20.00
6 Supermouse cover 20.00

ALLEY OOP
Argo Publications
November, 1955

1 . . . . 80.00
2 . . . . 55.00
3 March, 1956 . . . . 55.00

AMAZING GHOST STORIES
(See: WEIRD HORRORS)

AMAZING-MAN COMICS
Centaur Publications
September, 1939

5 BEv,O:Amazing Man . . . 11,000.00
6 BEv,B:The Shark 2,500.00
7 BEv,I:Magician From Mars 1,400.00
8 BEv 1,200.00
9 BEv 1,200.00
10 BEv 900.00
11 BEv,I:Zardi 800.00
12 SG(c) 800.00
13 SG(c) 800.00
14 B:Reef Kinkaid, Dr. Hypo . . 600.00
15 A:Zardi 500.00
16 Mighty Man's powers revealed 550.00
17 A:Dr. Hypo 500.00
18 BLb(a),SG(c) 500.00
19 BLb(a),SG(c) 500.00
20 BLb(a),SG(c) 500.00
21 O:Dash Dartwell 450.00
22 A:Silver Streak, The Voice . 450.00
23 I&O:Tommy the Amazing Kid 500.00
24 B:King of Darkness,Blue Lady450.00
25 A:Meteor Marvin 800.00
26 A:Meteor Marvin,Electric Ray February, 1942 . . . . 600.00

AMAZING WILLIE MAYS
Famous Funnies
1954

1 Willie Mays(c) 450.00

AMERICA'S BEST COMICS
Nedor/Better/Standard Publications
February 1942

1 B:Black Terror, Captain Future, The Liberator, Doc Strange 700.00
2 O:American Eagle 350.00
3 B:Pyroman 275.00
4 A:Doc Strange, Jimmy Cole 225.00
5 A:Lone Eagle, Capt. Future 195.00
6 A:American Crusader 175.00
7 A:Hitler,Hirohito 175.00
8 The Liberator ends 150.00

9 ASh(c) 160.00
10 ASh(c) 125.00
11 ASh(c) 125.00
12 Red Cross cover 125.00
13 . . . . 125.00
14 Last American Eagle app . . 125.00
15 ASh(c) 110.00
16 ASh(c) 115.00
17 Doc Strange carries football 110.00
18 Bondage cover 110.00
19 ASh(c) 110.00
20 vs. the Black Market 100.00
21 Infinity cover 100.00
22 A:Captain Future 100.00
23 B:Miss Masque 135.00
24 Bondage cover 120.00
25 A:Sea Eagle 100.00
26 A:The Phantom Detective . . 135.00
27 ASh(c) 125.00
28 A:Commando Cubs, Black Terror 125.00
29 A:Doc Strange 125.00
30 ASh(c) 125.00
31 July, 1949 . . . . 125.00

AMERICA'S BIGGEST COMICS BOOK
William H. Wise
1944

1 196 pgs. A:Grim Reaper, Zudo, Silver Knight, Thunderhoof, Jocko and Socko,Barnaby Beep,Commando Cubs 225.00

AMERICA'S GREATEST COMICS
Fawcett Publications
Fall 1941

1 MRa(c),A:Capt. Marvel, Bulletman,Spy Smasher and Minute Man 1,250.00
2 . . . . 625.00
3 . . . . 400.00
4 B:Commando Yank 375.00
5 Capt.Marvel in "Lost Lighting" 375.00
6 Capt.Marvel fires Machine Gun 300.00
7 A:Balbo the Boy Magician . 275.00
8 A:Capt.Marvel Jr.,Golden Arrow Summer 1943 . . . . . 300.00

AMERICA IN ACTION
Dell Publishing Co.
1942

1 . . . . 80.00

ANDY COMICS
(see SCREAM COMICS)

ANGEL
Dell Publishing Co.
August, 1954

(1) *see Dell Four Color #576*
2 . . . . 10.00
3 thru 16 . . . . @8.00

ANIMAL COMICS
Dell Publishing Co.
1942

1 WK,Pogo 700.00
2 Uncle Wiggily(c),A:Pogo . . . 300.00
3 Muggin's Mouse(c),A:Pogo . 225.00
4 Uncle Wiggily(c) 225.00
5 Uncle Wiggily(c) 200.00
6 Uncle Wiggily 125.00
7 Uncle Wiggily 125.00
8 Pogo 150.00
9 War Bonds(c),A:Pogo 165.00
10 Pogo 125.00
11 Pogo 125.00
12 Pogo 125.00
13 Pogo 125.00
14 Pogo 125.00
15 Pogo 125.00

Animal Comics #17 © Dell Publ. Co.

16 Uncle Wiggily 80.00
17 Pogo(c) 125.00
18 Pogo(c) 75.00
19 Pogo(c) 75.00
20 Pogo 75.00
21 Pogo(c) 100.00
22 Pogo 75.00
23 Pogo 75.00
24 Pogo(c) 100.00
25 Pogo(c) 100.00
26 Pogo(c) 100.00
27 Pogo(c) 50.00
28 Pogo(c) 50.00
29 Pogo(c) 50.00
30 Pogo(c) 50.00

ANIMAL FABLES
E.C. Comics
July-August 1946

1 B:Korky Kangaroo,Freddy Firefly Petey Pig and Danny Demon 225.00
2 B:Aesop Fables 150.00
3 . . . . 125.00
4 . . . . 125.00
5 Firefly vs. Red Ants 125.00
6 . . . . 125.00
7 O:Moon Girls,Nov.-Dec.1947 375.00

ANIMAL FAIR
Fawcett Publications
March 1946

1 B:Captain Marvel Bunny, Sir Spot 125.00
2 A:Droopy, Colonel Walrus . . 60.00
3 . . . . 35.00
4 A:Kid Gloves, Cub Reporter . 35.00
5 . . . . 35.00
6 . . . . 35.00
7 . . . . 35.00
8 . . . . 25.00
9 . . . . 25.00
10 . . . . 25.00
11 February 1947 . . . . 25.00

ANNIE OKLEY & TAGG
Dell Publishing Co.
1953

(1) *see Dell Four Color #438*
(2) *see Dell Four Color #481*
(3) *see Dell Four Color #575*
4 . . . . 50.00
5 . . . . 50.00
6 . . . . 50.00
7 . . . . 50.00

Animal Fair #2 © Fawcett Publications

8 . . . . 50.00
9 . . . . 50.00
10 . . . . 50.00
11 thru 18 . . . . @40.00

ARCHIE COMICS
MLJ Magazines
Winter, 1942-43

1 I:Jughead & Veronica 7,500.00
2 . . . . 1,500.00
3 . . . . 1,000.00
4 . . . . 700.00
5 . . . . 700.00
6 . . . . 450.00
7 . . . . 400.00
8 . . . . 400.00
9 . . . . 400.00
10 . . . . 400.00
11 . . . . 400.00
12 . . . . 275.00
13 . . . . 275.00
14 . . . . 275.00
15 . . . . 275.00
16 . . . . 250.00
17 . . . . 250.00
18 . . . . 250.00
19 . . . . 250.00

Archie Publications

20 . . . . 250.00
21 . . . . 225.00
22 thru 31 . . . . @135.00
32 thru 42 . . . . @90.00
43 thru 50 . . . . @75.00
51 thru 60 . . . . @50.00
61 thru 70 . . . . @40.00
71 thru 80 . . . . @30.00
81 thru 99 . . . . @25.00
100 . . . . 35.00
101 . . . . 25.00
102 thru 115 . . . . @15.00
116 thru 130 . . . . @12.00
131 thru 145 . . . . @10.00
146 thru 160 . . . . @7.50
161 thru 180 . . . . @5.00
181 thru 200 . . . . @4.00
201 thru 250 . . . . @3.00
251 thru 280 . . . . @2.00
281 thru 389 . . . . @1.50

ARCHIE'S GIANT SERIES MAGAZINE

Archie Publications
1954

1	600.00

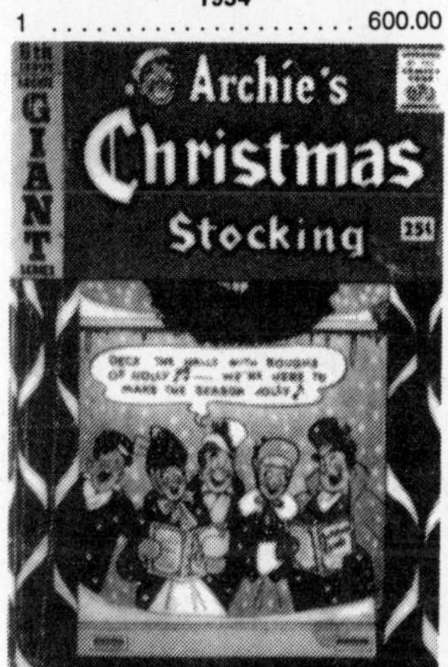

Archie #6 © Archie Publications

2	350.00
3	225.00
4	200.00
5	200.00
6	150.00
7	150.00
8	150.00
9	150.00
10	150.00
11 thru 20	@125.00
21 thru 29	@100.00
30 thru 35	@30.00
136 thru 141	@30.00
142	32.00
143 thru 160	@12.00
161 thru 199	@8.00
200	5.00
201 thru 250	@2.50
251 thru 299	@1.50
300 thru 500	@1.00

ARCHIE'S GIRLS BETTY AND VERONICA

Archie Publications
1950

1	750.00
2	375.00
3	225.00
4	175.00
5	170.00
6	160.00
7	160.00
8	160.00
9	160.00
10	160.00
11 thru 15	@125.00
16 thru 20	@100.00
21	90.00
22 thru 29	@85.00
30 thru 40	@60.00
41 thru 50	@50.00
51 thru 60	@40.00
61 thru 70	@35.00
71 thru 80	@30.00
81 thru 90	@25.00
91 thru 99	@20.00
100	25.00
101 thru 120	@15.00
121 thru 140	@10.00
141 thru 160	@7.00
161 thru 180	@3.00
181 thru 199	@2.00
200	3.00
201 thru 220	@2.00
221 thru 240	@1.50
241 thru 347	@1.00

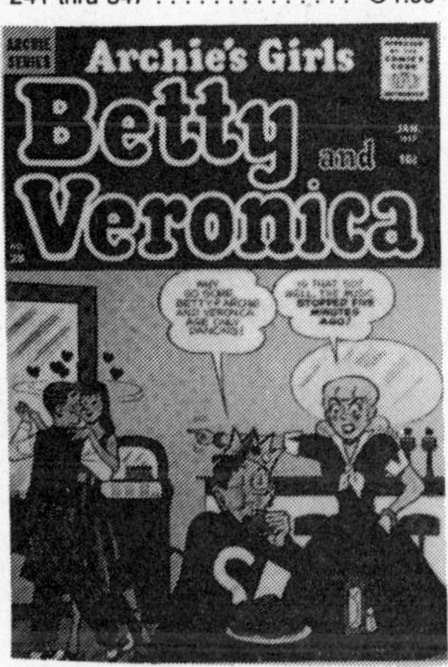

Archie's Girls Betty and Veronica #27 © Archie Publications

ARCHIE'S JOKE BOOK MAGAZINE

Archie Publications
1953

1	400.00
2	225.00
3	160.00
15 thru 19	@125.00
20 thru 25	@100.00
26 thru 35	@75.00
36 thru 40	@50.00
41	125.00
42 thru 48	@50.00
49 thru 60	@20.00
61 thru 70	@15.00
71 thru 80	@10.00
81 thru 100	@5.00
101 thru 200	@2.50
201 thru 288	@1.00

ARCHIE'S MECHANICS

Archie Publications
September, 1954

1	500.00
2	350.00
3	250.00

ARCHIE'S PAL, JUGHEAD

Archie Publications
1949

1	600.00
2	300.00
3	200.00
4	175.00
5	175.00
6	150.00
7	125.00
8	125.00
9	125.00
10	125.00
11 thru 15	@100.00
16 thru 20	@85.00
21 thru 30	@65.00
31 thru 39	@50.00
40 thru 50	@35.00
51 thru 60	@30.00
61 thru 70	@25.00
71 thru 80	@20.00
81 thru 99	@15.00
100	17.00
101 thru 126	@10.00

Archie's Pals 'n' Gals © Archie Publications

ARCHIE'S PALS 'N' GALS

Archie Publications
1952 thru 53

1	400.00
2	225.00
3	150.00
4	135.00
5	135.00
6	80.00
7	80.00
8 thru 10	@75.00
11 thru 15	@50.00
16 thru 20	@35.00
21 thru 30	@20.00
31 thru 40	@20.00
41 thru 50	@12.00
51 thru 60	@10.00
61 thru 70	@7.00
71 thru 80	@5.00
81 thru 99	@2.50
100	3.00
101 thru 120	@2.00
121 thru 160	@1.50
161 thru 224	@1.00

ARCHIE'S RIVAL REGGIE

Archie Publications
1950

1	400.00
2	225.00
3	175.00
4	150.00
5	150.00
6	125.00
7 thru 10	@100.00
11 thru 13	@75.00
14 thru 15	@65.00
16 August, 1954	70.00

ARMY & NAVY COMICS

(see SUPERSNIPE COMICS)

Archie's Rival Reggie #3
© Archie Publications

ARROW, THE
Centaur Publications
October 1940

1 B:Arrow 1,000.00
2 BLB(c) 600.00
3 O:Dash Dartwell,Human Meteor, Rainbow, Bondage cover, October, 1941 . . . . . 550.00

ATOMAN
Spark Publications
February 1946

1 JRo,MMe,O:Atoman,A:Kid Crusaders 250.00
2 JRo,MMe 175.00

ATOMIC COMICS
Green Publishing Co.
January, 1946

1 S&S,A:Radio Squad, Barry O'Neal 525.00
2 MB,A:Inspector Dayton, Kid Kane 275.00
3 MB,A:Zero Ghost Detective 175.00
4 JKa(c), July-August, 1946 . . 150.00

ATOMIC COMICS
Daniels Publications
1946 (Reprints)

1 A:Rocketman,Yankee Boy, Bondage cover,rep. 125.00

ATOMIC MOUSE
Capital Stories/ Charlton Comics
March, 1953

1 AFa,O:Atomic Mouse 120.00
2 AFa,Ice Cream cover 65.00
3 AFa,Genie and Magic Carpet cover 40.00
4 AFa 40.00
5 AFa,A:Timmy the Timid Ghost 40.00
6 thru 10 Funny Animal . . . . @35.00
11 thru 14 Funny Animal . . . . @20.00
15 A:Happy the Marvel Bunny . . 25.00
16 Funny Animal,Giant 27.00
17 thru 30 Funny Animal . . . . @20.00
31 thru 36 Funny Animal . . . . @15.00
37 A:Atom the Cat 15.00
38 thru 40 Funny Animal . . . . @12.00
41 thru 53 Funny Animal . . . . @10.00
54 June, 1963 . . . . 10.00

ATOMIC THUNDER BOLT, THE
Regor Company
February, 1946

1 I:Atomic Thunderbolt, Mr. Murdo 225.00

AVIATION AND MODEL BUILDING (see TRUE AVIATION PICTURE STORIES)

AVON ONE-SHOTS
Avon Periodicals
1949-1953
{Listed in Alphabetical Order}

1 Atomic Spy Cases 150.00

Attack on Planet Mars
© Avon Periodicals

N# WW,Attack on Planet Mars . 450.00
1 Batchelor's Diary 135.00
1 Badmen of the West 150.00
N# Badmen of Tombstone 75.00
1 Behind Prison Bars 140.00
2 Betty and Her Steady 35.00
N# Blackhawk Indian Tomahawk War 75.00
1 Blazing Sixguns 75.00
1 Butch Cassidy 80.00
N# Chief Crazy Horse 100.00
N# FF,Chief Victorio's Apache Massacre 250.00
N# City of the Living Dead 225.00
1 Complete Romance 150.00
N# Custer's Last Fight 75.00
1 Dalton Boys 70.00
N# Davy Crockett 70.00
N# The Dead Who Walk 225.00
1 Diary of Horror,Bondage(c) . 175.00
N# WW,An Earth Man on Venus 650.00
1 Eerie, bondage (c) 500.00
1 Escape from Devil's Island . 150.00
N# Fighting Daniel Boone 75.00
N# For a Night of Love 125.00
1 WW,Flying Saucers 340.00
N# Flying Saucers. 320.00
1 Going Steady with Betty 60.00
N# Hooded Menace 250.00
N# King of the Badmen of Deadwood 80.00
1 King Solomon's Mines 175.00
N# Kit Carson & the Blackfeet Warriors 50.00
N# Last of the Comanches 75.00
N# Masked Bandit 75.00
1 WW,Mask of Dr. Fu Manchu 500.00
N# Night of Mystery 150.00
1 Outlaws of the Wild West . . 150.00
1 Out of this World 325.00
N# Pancho Villa 125.00
1 Phantom Witch Doctor 185.00
1 Pixie Puzzle Rocket to Adventureland 50.00
1 Prison Riot,drugs 125.00
N# Red Mountain Featuring Quantrell's Raiders 125.00
N# Reform School Girl 550.00
1 Robotmen of the Lost Planet 550.00
N# WW(c),Rocket to the Moon 550.00
N# JKu,Secret Diary of Eerie Adventures 700.00
1 Sheriff Bob Dixon's Chuck Wagon 65.00
1 Sideshow 135.00
1 JKu,Sparkling Love 80.00
N# Speedy Rabbit 35.00
1 Teddy Roosevelt & His Rough Riders 100.00
N# The Underworld Story 125.00
N# The Unknown Man 130.00
1 War Dogs of the U.S. Army . . 75.00
N# White Chief of the Pawnee Indians 65.00
N# Women to Love 150.00

BABE
Prize/Headline Feature
June-July 1948

1 BRo,A;Boddy Rogers 75.00
2 BRo,same 50.00
3 Bro,same 40.00
4 thru 9 BRo,same . . . . @35.00

BABE RUTH SPORTS COMICS
Harvey Publications
April, 1949

1 BP 300.00
2 BP 200.00
3 BP,Joe Dimaggio(c) 185.00
4 BP,Bob Feller(c) 150.00
5 thru 8,BP . . . . @150.00
9 BP, Stan Musial(c) 125.00
11 February, 1951 . . . . 100.00

BANNER COMICS
Ace Magazines
September, 1941

3 B:Captain Courageous, Lone Warrior 500.00
4 JM(c),Flag(c) 350.00
5 . . . . 325.00

Becomes:

CAPTAIN COURAGEOUS COMICS

6 I:The Sword 325.00

BARNYARD COMICS
Animated Cartoons
June, 1944

1 (fa) 90.00
2 (fa) 45.00
3 (fa) 30.00
4 (fa) 30.00
5 (fa) 30.00
6 thru 12 (fa) . . . . @25.00
13 FF(ti) 30.00
14 FF(ti) 30.00
15 FF(ti) 30.00
16 . . . . 35.00
17 FF(ti) 30.00
18 FF,FF(ti) 75.00
19 FF,FF(ti) 75.00
20 FF,FF(ti) 75.00
21 FF(ti) 30.00
22 FF,FF(ti) 75.00

23 FF(ti) 30.00
24 FF,FF(ti) 75.00
25 FF,FF(ti) 75.00
26 FF(ti) 30.00
27 FF(ti) 30.00
28 . . . . 20.00
29 FF(ti) 30.00
30 . . . . 20.00
31 . . . . 20.00

Becomes:

DIZZY DUCK

32 thru 39 . . . . @15.00

BASEBALL COMICS
Will Eisner Productions
Spring, 1949

1 A:Rube Rocky 500.00

BASEBALL HEROS
Fawcett Publications
1952

N# Babe Ruth cover 500.00

BASEBALL THRILLS
Ziff-Davis Publ. Co.
Summer 1951

10 Bob Feller Predicts Pennant Winners 275.00
2 BP, Yogi Berra story 200.00
3 EK, Joe DiMaggio story, Summer 1952 . . . . 250.00

BATTLEFIELD ACTION
(see DYNAMITE)

BEANY & CECIL
Dell Publishing Co.
January, 1952

1 . . . . 100.00
2 . . . . 75.00
3 . . . . 75.00
4 . . . . 75.00
5 . . . . 75.00

BEN BOWIE & HIS MOUNTAIN MEN
Dell Publishing Co.
1952

(1) *see Dell Four Color #443*
(2 thru 6) *see Dell Four Color*
7 . . . . 15.00
8 thru 10 . . . . @15.00
11 I:Yellow Hair 17.00
12 . . . . 12.00
13 . . . . 12.00
14 . . . . 12.00
15 . . . . 12.00
16 . . . . 12.00
17 . . . . 12.00

BEST COMICS
Better Publications
November, 1939

1 B:Red Mask 375.00
2 A:Red Mask, Silly Willie 225.00
3 A:Red Mask 225.00
4 Cannibalism story, February, 1940 . . . . 250.00

BEWARE
(see CAPTAIN SCIENCE)

BIG CHIEF WAHOO
Eastern Color Printing
July, 1942

1 . . . . 250.00
2 BWa(c),Three Ring Circus . 125.00
3 BWa(c) 75.00
4 BWa(c) 75.00
5 BWa(c),Wild West Rodeo . . . 75.00
6 A:Minnie-Ha-Cha 50.00
7 . . . . 50.00
8 . . . . 50.00
9 . . . . 50.00
10 . . . . 50.00
11 thru 22 . . . . @20.00
23 1943 . . . . 20.00

BIG SHOT COMICS
Columbia Comics Group
May, 1940

1 MBI,OW,Skyman,B:The Face, Joe Palooka, Rocky Ryan . . 800.00
2 MBi,OW,Marvelo cover 375.00
3 MBi,Skyman cover 275.00
4 MBi,OW,Joe Palooka cover 250.00
5 MBi,Joe Palooka cover 250.00
6 MBi,Joe Palooka cover 250.00
7 MBi,Elect Joe Palooka and Skyman 200.00
8 MBi,Joe Palooka and Skyman dress as Santa 200.00
9 MBi,Skyman 210.00
10 MBi,Skyman 210.00
11 MBi 175.00
12 MBi,OW 175.00
13 MBi,OW 175.00
14 MBi,OW,O:Sparky Watts . . . 175.00
15 MBi,OW,O:The Cloak 200.00
16 MBi,OW 150.00
17 MBi(c),OW 150.00
18 MBi,OW 150.00
19 MBi,OW,The Face cover . . . 160.00
20 MBi,OW,OW(c),Skyman cov. 160.00
21 MBi,OW,A:Raja the Arabian Knight 90.00
22 MBi,OW,Joe Palooka cover . 90.00
23 MBi,OW,Sparky Watts cover . 80.00
24 MBi,OW,Uncle Sam cover . . 90.00

Big Shot #55 © Columbia Comics

25 MBi,OW,Sparky Watts cover . 80.00
26 MBi,OW,Devildog cover 90.00
27 MBi,OW,Skyman cover 100.00
28 MBi,OW,Hitler cover 130.00
29 MBi,OW,I:Captain Yank . . . 100.00
30 MBi,OW,Santa cover 80.00
31 MBi,OW,Sparky Watts cover . 70.00
32 MBi,OW,B:Vic Jordan newspaper reps 80.00
33 MBi,OW,Sparky Watts cover . 60.00
34 MBi,OW 70.00
35 MBi,OW 70.00
36 MBi,OW,Sparky Watts cover . 60.00
37 MBi,OW 70.00
38 MBi,Uncle Slap Happy cover . 75.00
39 MBi,Uncle Slap Happy cover . 75.00
40 MBi,Joe Palooka Happy cover 75.00
41 MBi,Joe Palooka 65.00
42 MBi,Joe Palooka parachutes . 65.00
43 MBi,V:Hitler 75.00
44 MBi,Slap Happy cover 65.00
45 MBi,Slap Happy cover 65.00
46 MBi,Uncle Sam cover,V:Hitler 75.00
47 MBi,Uncle Slap Happy cover . 65.00
48 MBi 65.00
49 MBi 60.00
50 MBi,O:The Face 60.00
51 MBi 50.00
52 MBi,E:Vic Jordan (Hitler cov) newspaper reps 75.00
53 MBi,Uncle Slap Happy cover . 50.00
54 MBi,Uncle Slap Happy cover . 50.00
55 MBi,Happy Easter cover 50.00
56 MBi 50.00
57 MBi 50.00
58 MBi 50.00
59 MBi,Slap Happy 50.00
60 MBi,Joe Palooka 50.00
61 MBi 45.00
62 MBi 45.00
63 MBi 45.00
64 MBi,Slap Happy 35.00
65 MBi,Slap Happy 35.00
66 MBi,Slap Happy 35.00
67 MBi 35.00
68 MBi,Joe Palooka 35.00
69 MBi 35.00
70 MBi,OW,Joe Palooka cover . 35.00
71 MBi,OW 38.00
72 MBi,OW 38.00
73 MBi,OW,The Face cover 38.00
74 MBi,OW 38.00
75 MBi,OW,Polar Bear swim club cover 38.00
76 thru 80 MBi,OW . . . . @35.00
81 thru 84 MBi,OW . . . . @28.00
85 MBi,OW,Dixie Dugan cover . . 28.00
86 thru 95 MBi,OW . . . . @25.00
96 MBi,OW,X-Mas cover 25.00
97 thru 99 MBi,OW . . . . @25.00
100 MBi,OW,Special issue 30.00
101 thru 103 MBi,OW . . . . . . @25.00
104 MBi, August, 1949 . . . . 25.00

BIG-3
Fox Features Syndicate
Fall 1940

1 B:Blue Beetle,Flame,Samson 800.00
2 A:Blue Beetle,Flame,Samson 350.00
3 same 300.00
4 same 275.00
5 same 270.00
6 E:Samson, bondage cover . 265.00
7 A:V-Man, January, 1942 . . . 250.00

BILL BARNES, AMERICA'S AIR ACE
(see AIR ACE)

BILL BOYD WESTERN
Fawcett Publications
February, 1950

1 B:Bill Boyd, MidnitePh(c) . . . 250.00
2 P(c) 150.00
3 B:Ph(c) 125.00
4 . . . . 100.00
5 . . . . 100.00
6 . . . . 100.00
7 . . . . 75.00
8 . . . . 75.00
9 . . . . 75.00
10 . . . . 75.00
11 . . . . 70.00
12 . . . . 70.00
13 . . . . 70.00
14 . . . . 70.00
15 . . . . 65.00
16 . . . . 65.00
17 . . . . 65.00

18 . . . . 65.00
19 . . . . 65.00
20 . . . . 65.00
21 . . . . 65.00
22 E:Ph(c) 65.00
23 June, 1952 . . . . 75.00

BILL STERN'S SPORTS BOOK
Approved Comics
Spring-Summer, 1951

1 Ewell Blackwell 95.00
2 . . . . 75.00
2-2 EK Giant 100.00

BILLY THE KID ADVENTURE MAGAZINE
Toby Press
October, 1950

1 AW,FF,AW(c),FF(c) 175.00
2 Photo cover 50.00
3 AW,FF 160.00
4 . . . . 30.00
5 . . . . 30.00
6 Photo cover 30.00
7 Photo cover 30.00
8 . . . . 30.00
9 HK Pot-Shot Pete 60.00

Billy the Kid #10 © Toby Press

10 . . . . 30.00
11 . . . . 30.00
12 . . . . 30.00
13 HK 35.00
14 AW,FF 50.00
15 thru 21 . . . . @25.00
22 AW,FF 30.00
23 thru 29 . . . . @22.00
30 1955 . . . . 25.00

BINGO COMICS
Howard Publications
1945

1 . . . . 125.00

BLACK CAT COMICS
Harvey Publications (Home Comics)
June-July, 1946

1 JKu 250.00
2 JKu,JSm(c) 150.00
3 JSm(c) 125.00
4 B:Red Demon 125.00
5 S&K 150.00
6 S&K,A:Scarlet Arrow,
O:Red Demon 150.00
7 S&K 160.00
8 S&K,B:Kerry Drake 125.00
9 S&K,O:Stuntman 160.00
10 JK,JSm 100.00
11 . . . . 100.00
12 "Ghost Town Terror" 100.00
13 thru 16 LEI . . . . @100.00
17 A:Mary Worth, Invisible
Scarlet 100.00
18 LEI 100.00
19 LEI 100.00
20 A:Invisible Scarlet 100.00
21 LEI 90.00
22 LEI 90.00
23 LEI 90.00
24 LEI 90.00
25 LEI 90.00
26 LEI 90.00
27 X-Mas issue 100.00
28 I:Kit,A:Crimson Raider 100.00
29 Black Cat bondage cover . . 110.00

Becomes:

BLACK CAT MYSTERY

30 RP,Black Cat(c) 85.00
31 RP 50.00
32 BP,RP,Bondage cover 65.00
33 BP,RP,Electrocution cover . . 60.00
34 BP,RP 50.00
35 BP,RP,OK 75.00
36 RP 100.00
37 RP 50.00
38 RP 50.00
39 RP 100.00
40 RP 50.00
41 . . . . 55.00
42 . . . . 55.00
43 BP 55.00
44 BP,HN,JkS,Oil Burning cover 65.00
45 BP,HN,Classic cover 120.00
46 BP,HN 60.00
47 BP,HN 60.00
48 BP,HN 60.00
49 BP,HN 60.00
50 BP,Rotting Face 100.00
51 BP,HN,MMe 60.00
52 BP 45.00
53 BP 45.00

Becomes:

BLACK CAT WESTERN

54 A:Black Cat & Story 65.00
55 A:Black Cat 50.00
56 same 50.00

Becomes:

BLACK CAT MYSTIC

58 JK,Starts Comic Code 65.00
59 KB 60.00
60 JK 60.00
61 HN 50.00
62 . . . . 40.00
63 JK 40.00
64 JK 55.00
65 April, 1963 . . . . 55.00

BLACK DIAMOND WESTERN
(see DESPERADO)

UNCLE SAM QUARTERLY
Quality Comics Group
Fall, 1941

1 BE,LF(c),JCo 1,200.00
2 LG(c),BE 550.00
3 GT,GT(c) 450.00
4 GT,GF(c) 350.00
5 RC,GT 300.00
6 thru 8 GT . . . . @275.00

Becomes:

BLACKHAWK
Comic Magazines
Winter, 1944

9 Bait for a Death Trap 1,500.00
10 RC 600.00
11 RC 400.00
12 Flies to thrilling adventure . . 375.00
13 Blackhawk Stalks Danger . . 375.00
14 BWa 350.00
15 Patrols the Universe 350.00
16 RC,BWa,Huddles for Action 325.00
17 BWa,Prepares for Action . . 325.00

Blackhawk #12 © Comic Magazines

18 RC,RC(c),BWa,One for All
and All for One 300.00
19 RC,RC(c),BWa,Calls
for Action 300.00
20 RC,RC(c),BWa,Smashes
Rugoth the ruthless God . . . 300.00
21 BWa,Battles Destiny
Written n Blood 250.00
22 RC,RC(c),BWa,Fear battles
Death and Destruction 250.00
23 RC,RC(c),BWa,Batters
Down Oppression 250.00
24 RC,RC(c),BWa 250.00
25 RC,RC(c),BWa,V:The Evil
of Mung 250.00
26 RC,RC(c),V:Menace of a
Sunken World 225.00
27 BWa,Destroys a War-Mad
Munitions Magnate 225.00
28 BWa,Defies Destruction in the
Battle of the Test Tube 225.00
29 BWa,Tale of the Basilisk
Supreme Chief 225.00
30 BWa,RC,RC(c),The Menace
of the Meteors 225.00
31 BWa,RC,RC(c),JCo,Treachery
among the Blackhawks 185.00
32 BWa,RC,RC(c),A:Delya,
Flying Fish 185.00
33 RC,RC(c),BWa,
A:The Mockers 185.00
34 BWa,A:Tana,Mavis 185.00
35 BWa,I:Atlo,Strongest Man
on Earth 185.00
36 RC,RC(c),BWa,V:Tarya . . . 175.00
37 RC,RC(c),BWa,V:Sari,The
Rajah of Ramastan 175.00
38 BWa 175.00
39 RC,RC(c),BWa,V:Lilith 175.00
40 RC,RC(c),BWa,Valley of
Yesterday 175.00
41 RC,RC(c),BWa 135.00
42 RC,RC(c),BWa,
V:Iron Emperor 135.00
43 RC,RC(c),BWa,Terror
from the Catacombs 135.00
44 RC,RC(c),BWa,The King

of Winds 135.00
45 BWa,The Island of Death . . 135.00
46 RC,RC(c),BWa,V:DeathPatrol 135.00
47 RC,RC(c),BWa,War! 135.00
48 RC,RC(c),BWa,A:Hawks of Horror,Port of Missing Ships 135.00
49 RC,RC(c),BWa,A:Valkyrie, Waters of Terrible Peace . . 135.00
50 RC,RC(c),BWa,I:Killer Shark, Flying Octopus 150.00
51 BWa,V:The Whip, Whip of Nontelon 125.00
52 RC,RC(c),BWa,Traitor in the Ranks 125.00
53 RC,RC(c),BWa,V:Golden Mummy 125.00
54 RC,RC(c),BWa,V:Dr. Deroski, Circles of Suicide 125.00
55 RC,RC(c),BWa,V:Rocketmen 125.00
56 RC,RC(c),BWa,V:The Instructor, School for Sabotage 125.00
57 RC,RC(c),BWa,Paralyzed City of Armored Men 125.00
58 RC,RC(c),BWa,V:King Cobra, The Spider of Delanza 125.00
59 BWa,V:Sea Devil 125.00
60 RC,RC(c),BWa,V:Dr. Mole and His Devils Squadron 125.00
61 V:John Smith, Stalin's Ambassador of Murder 110.00
62 V:General X, Return of Genghis Kahn 110.00
63 RC,RC(c),The Flying Buzz-Saws 110.00
64 RC,RC(c),V:Zoltan Korvas, Legion of the Damned 110.00
65 Olaf as a Prisoner in Dungeon of Fear 110.00
66 RC,RC(c),V:The Red Executioner, Crawler 110.00
67 RC,RC(c),V:Future Fuehrer . 110.00
68 V:Killers of the Kremlin 100.00
69 V:King of the Iron Men, Conference of the Dictators . 100.00
70 V:Killer Shark 100.00
71 V:Von Tepp, The Man Who could Defeat Blackhawk O:Blackhawk 135.00
72 V:Death Legion 100.00
73 V:Hangman,The Tyrannical Freaks 100.00
74 Plan of Death 100.00
75 V:The Mad Doctor Baroc, The Z Bomb Menace 100.00
76 The King of Blackhawk Island 100.00
77 V:The Fiendish Electronic Brain 100.00
78 V:The Killer Vulture, Phantom Raider 100.00
79 V:Herman Goering, The Human Bomb 100.00
80 V:Fang, the Merciless, Dr. Death 100.00
81 A:Killer Shark, The Sea Monsters of Killer Shark . . . 100.00
82 V:Sabo Teur, the Ruthless Commie Agent 100.00
83 I:Hammmer & Sickle, V:Madam Double Cross 100.00
84 V:Death Eye,Dr. Genius, The Dreaded Brain Beam . . 100.00
85 V:The Fiendish Impersonator 100.00
86 V:The Human Torpedoes . . 100.00
87 A:Red Agent Sovietta,V:Sea Wolf, Le Sabre,Comics Code 80.00
88 V:Thunder the Indestructible, The Phantom Sniper 80.00
89 V:The Super Communists . . . 80.00
90 V:The Storm King, Villainess who smashed the Blackhawk team 80.00
91 Treason in the Underground . 80.00
92 V:The World Traitor 80.00
93 V:Garg the Destroyer, O:Blackhawk 95.00
94 V:Black Widow, Darkk the Destroyer 80.00
95 V:Madam Fury, Queen of the Pirates 80.00
96 Doom in the Deep 80.00
97 Revolt of the Slave Workers . 80.00
98 Temple of Doom 80.00
99 The War That Never Ended . 80.00
100 The Delphian Machine 85.00
101 Satan's Paymaster 80.00
102 The Doom Cloud 80.00
103 The Super Race 80.00
104 The Jet Menace 80.00
105 The Red Kamikaze Terror . 80.00
106 The Flying Tank Platoon . . 80.00
107 The Winged Menace 80.00

(Please see DC Listings)

BLACK HOOD

(see LAUGH COMICS)

BLACK TERROR

Better Publications/ Standard

Winter, 1942-43

1 Bombing cover 750.00
2 V:Arabs,Bondage(c) 360.00
3 V:Nazis,Bondage(c) 275.00
4 V:Sub Nazis 225.00
5 V:Japanese 225.00
6 Air Battle 170.00
7 Air Battle,V:Japanese, A:Ghost 170.00
8 V:Nazis 170.00
9 V:Japanese,Bondage(c) . . . 180.00
10 V:Nazis 170.00
11 thru 16 . . . . @150.00
17 Bondage(c) 165.00
18 ASh 150.00
19 ASh 150.00
20 ASh 150.00
21 ASh 165.00
22 FF,ASh 150.00
23 ASh 150.00
24 Bondgae(c) 165.00
25 ASh 150.00
26 GT,ASh 150.00
27 MME,GT,ASh 150.00

BLAZING COMICS

Enwil Associates/Rural Home

June, 1944

1 B:Green Turtle, Red Hawk, Black Buccaneer 250.00
2 Green Turtle cover 150.00
3 Green Turtle cover 145.00
4 Green Turtle cover 145.00
5 March, 1945 . . . . 145.00
5a Black Buccaneer(c),1955 . . . 50.00
6 Indian-Japanese(c), 1955 . . . 50.00

BLONDIE COMICS

David McKay

Spring, 1947

1 . . . . 125.00
2 . . . . 55.00
3 . . . . 50.00
4 . . . . 50.00
5 . . . . 50.00
6 thru 10 . . . . @30.00
11 thru 15 . . . . @20.00

Harvey Publications

16 . . . . 25.00
17 thru 20 . . . . @15.00
21 thru 30 . . . . @12.00
31 thru 50 . . . . @10.00
51 thru 80 . . . . @7.50
81 thru 99 . . . . @6.00
100 . . . . 7.50
101 thru 124 . . . . @6.00
125 Giant 7.00
126 thru 135 . . . . @6.00
136 thru 140 . . . . @5.00
141 thru 163 . . . . @7.00

King Publications

164 thru 167 . . . . @7.00
168 thru 174 . . . . @3.00

Charlton Comics

175 thru 200 . . . . @2.00
201 thru 220 . . . . @1.50

BLUE BEETLE, THE

Fox Features Syndicate/ Holyoke Publ.

Winter 1939

1 O:Blue Beetle,A:Master Magician 2,000.00
2 . . . . 600.00
3 JSm(c) 450.00
4 Mentions marijuana 300.00
5 A:Zanzibar the Magician . . . 300.00
6 B:Dynamite Thor, O:Blue Beetle 300.00
7 A:Dynamo 275.00
8 E:Thor,A:Dynamo 275.00
9 A:Black Bird,Gorilla 275.00
10 A:Black Bird, bondage cover 275.00
11 A:Gladiator 250.00
12 A:Black Fury 250.00
13 B:V-Man 275.00

Blue Beetle #25

© Fox Features Syndicate

14 JKu,I:Sparky 275.00
15 JKu 275.00
16 . . . . 225.00
17 A:Mimic 200.00
18 E:V-Man,A:Red Knight 200.00
19 JKu,A:Dascomb Dinsmore . 250.00
20 I&O:The Flying Tiger Squadron 250.00
21 . . . . 150.00
22 A:Ali-Baba 150.00
23 A:Jimmy DooLittle 150.00
24 I:The Halo 150.00
25 . . . . 150.00
26 General Patton story 175.00
27 A:Tamoa 135.00
28 . . . . 125.00
29 . . . . 125.00
30 L:Holyoke 125.00
31 F:Fox 110.00
32 Hitler cover 135.00
33 Fight for Freedom 100.00
34 A:Black Terror,Menace of K-4 80.00
35 . . . . 80.00
36 The Runaway House 80.00
37 Inside the House 80.00
38 Revolt of the Zombies 80.00

39 80.00
40 80.00
41 A:O'Brine Twins 75.00
42 75.00
43 75.00
44 75.00
45 75.00
46 A:Puppeteer 90.00
47 JKa,V:Junior Crime Club 400.00
48 JKa,A:Black Lace 325.00
49 JKa 325.00
50 JKa,The Ambitious Bride 300.00
51 JKa, Shady Lady 275.00
52 JKa(c),Bondage cover 400.00
53 JKa,A:Jack "Legs" Diamond,Bondage(c) 300.00
54 JKa,The Vanishing Nude 550.00
55 JKa 275.00
56 JKa,Tri-State Terror 275.00
57 JKa,The Feagle Bros. 275.00
58 50.00
59 50.00
60 August, 1960 50.00

BLUE BEETLE

(see THING!, THE)

BLUE BOLT

Funnies, Inc./Novelty Press/ Premium Service Co

June, 1940

1 JSm,PG,O:Blue Bolt 1,200.00
2 JSm 650.00
3 S&K,A:Space Hawk 450.00
4 PG 450.00
5 BEv,B:Sub Zero 400.00
6 JK,JSm 400.00

Blue Bolt #7

© Funnies, Inc./Novelty Press

7 S&K,BEv 450.00
8 S&K(c) 400.00
9 400.00
10 S&K(c) 400.00
11 BEv(c) 225.00
12 225.00
2-1 BEv(c),PG,O:Dick Cole & V:Simba 150.00
2-2 BEv(c),PG 125.00
2-3 PG,Cole vs Simba 100.00
2-4 BD 100.00
2-5 I:Freezum 100.00
2-6 O:Sgt.Spook, Dick Cole 75.00
2-7 BD 75.00
2-8 BD 75.00
2-9 JW 75.00
2-10 JW 75.00
2-11 JW 75.00
2-12 E:Twister 75.00
3-1 A:115th Infantry 50.00
3-2 A:Phantom Sub 50.00
3-3 50.00
3-4 JW(c) 35.00
3-5 Jor 35.00
3-6 Jor 35.00
3-7 X-Mas cover 35.00
3-8 35.00
3-9 A:Phantom Sub 35.00
3-10 DBa 35.00
3-11 April Fools cover 35.00
3-12 35.00
4-1 Hitler,Tojo,Mussolini cover 65.00
4-2 Liberty Bell cover 30.00
4-3 What are You Doing for Your Country 30.00
4-4 I Fly for Vengence 30.00
4-5 TFH(c) 30.00
4-6 HcK 30.00
4-7 JWi(c) 30.00
4-8 E:Sub Zero 30.00
4-9 30.00
4-10 30.00
4-11 30.00
4-12 30.00
5-1 thru 5-12 @20.00
6-1 20.00
6-2 War Bonds (c) 30.00
6-3 20.00
6-4 Racist(c) 35.00
6-5 Soccer cover 22.00
6-6 thru 6-12 @20.00
7-1 thru 7-12 @20.00
8-1 Baseball cover 25.00
8-2 JHa 18.00
8-3 JHe 18.00
8-4 JHa 18.00
8-5 JHe 18.00
8-6 JDo 18.00
8-7 LbC(c). 20.00
8-8 18.00
8-9 AMc(c) 18.00
8-10 18.00
8-11 Basketball cover 20.00
8-12 18.00
9-1 AMc,Baseball cover 22.00
9-2 AMc 18.00
9-3 18.00
9-4 JHe 18.00
9-5 JHe 18.00
9-6 LbC(c),Football cover 22.00
9-7 JHe 20.00
9-8 Hockey cover 25.00
9-9 LbC(c),3-D effect 22.00
9-10 20.00
9-11 20.00
9-12 20.00
10-1 Baseball cover,3-D effect 25.00
10-2 3-D effect 22.00

Star Publications

102 LbC(c),Cameleon 120.00
103 LbC(c),same 100.00
104 LbC(c),same 100.00
105 LbC(c),O:Blue Bolt Space, Drug Story 250.00
106 S&K,LbC(c),A;Space Hawk 200.00
107 S&K,LbC(c),A;Space Hawk 200.00
108 S&K,LbC(c),A:Blue Bolt 200.00
109 BW,LbC(c) 200.00
110 B:Horror covers,A:Target 200.00
111 Weird Tales of Horror, A:Red Rocket 150.00
112 JyD,WiP 175.00
113 BW,JyD,A:Space Hawk 150.00
114 LbC(c),JyD 150.00
115 LbC(c),JyD,A:Sgt.Spook 200.00
116 LbC(c),JyD,A:Jungle Joe 150.00
117 LbC(c),A:Blue Bolt, Jo-Jo 150.00
118 WW,LbC(c),A:White Spirit 200.00
119 LbC(c) 150.00

Becomes:

GHOSTLY WEIRD STORIES

Star Publications

September, 1953

120 LbC,A:Jo-Jo 135.00
121 LbC,A:Jo-Jo 110.00
122 LbC,A:The Mask 110.00
123 LbC,A:Jo-Jo 110.00
124 LbC, September, 1954 110.00

BLUE CIRCLE COMICS

Enwil Associates/Rural Home

June, 1944

1 B:Blue Circle,O:Steel Fist 120.00
2 80.00
3 Hitler parody cover 100.00
4 55.00
5 E:Steel Fist,A:Driftwood Davey 55.00
6 45.00

BLUE RIBBON COMICS

MLJ Magazines

November, 1939

1 JCo,B:Dan Hastings, Richy-Amazing Boy 1,400.00
2 JCo,B:Bob Phantom, Silver Fox 550.00
3 JCo,A:Phantom,Silver Fox 450.00
4 O:Fox,Ty Gor,B:Doc Strong, Hercules 500.00
5 Gattling Gun cover 300.00
6 Amazing Boy Richy cover 275.00
7 A:Fox cover,Corporal Collins V:Nazis 275.00
8 E:Hercules 275.00
9 O&I:Mr. Justice 1,000.00
10 Mr. Justice cover 450.00
11 SCp(c) 450.00
12 E:Doc Strong 450.00
13 B:Inferno 450.00
14 A:Inferno 400.00
15 A:Inferno,E:Green Falcon 400.00
16 O:Captain Flag 750.00
17 Captain Flag V:Black Hand 450.00
18 Captain Flag-Black Hand 400.00
19 Captain Flag cover 375.00
20 Captain Flag V:Nazis cover 375.00
21 Captain Flag V:Death 350.00
22 Circus Cover, March, 1942 350.00

BLUE RIBBON COMICS

St. John Publications

February, 1949

1 Heckle & Jeckle 40.00
2 MB(c),Diary Secrets 55.00
3 MB,MB(c),Heckle & Jeckle 35.00
4 Teen-age Diary Secrets 55.00
5 MB,Teen-age Diary Secrets 65.00
6 Dinky Duck 12.00

BO

Charlton Comics

June, 1955

1 35.00
2 30.00
3 October, 1955 30.00

BOB COLT

Fawcett Publications

November, 1950

1 B:Bob Colt,Buck Skin 250.00
2 Death Round Train 150.00
3 Mysterious Black Knight of the Prairie 125.00
4 Death Goes Downstream 125.00
5 The Mesa of Mystery 125.00
6 The Mysterious Visitors 125.00
7 Dragon of Disaster 100.00
8 Redman's Revenge 100.00
9 Hidden Hacienda 100.00
10 Fiend from Vulture

Mountain 100.00

BOLD STORIES
Kirby Publishing Co.
March, 1950

1 WW,Near nudity cover 400.00
2 GI,Cobra's Kiss 300.00
3 WW,Orge of Paris,July, 1950 350.00
4 Case of the Winking Buddha 125.00
5 It Rhymes with Lust 125.00
6 Candid Tales, April 1950 . . . 125.00

BOMBER COMICS
Elliot Publishing Co.
March, 1944

1 B:Wonder Boy,Kismet, Eagle Evans 200.00
2 Wonder Boy cover 150.00
3 Wonder Boy-Kismet cover . 150.00
4 Hitler,Tojo, Mussolini cover . 175.00

BOOK OF ALL COMICS
William H. Wise
1945

1 A:Green Mask,Puppeteer . . 200.00

BOOK OF COMICS, THE
William H. Wise
1945

N# A:Captain V 200.00

BOY COMICS
Comic House, Inc.
(Lev Gleason Publ.)
April, 1942

3 O:Crimebuster,Bombshell,Young Robin, B:Yankee Longago, Swoop Storm 1,400.00
4 Hitler,Tojo,Mussolini cover . 550.00
5 Crimebuster saves day cover 400.00
6 O:Iron Jaw & Death of Son, B:Little Dynamite 950.00
7 Hitler,Tojo,Mussolini cover . 350.00

Boy Comics #8 © Lev Gleason Publ.

8 D:Iron Jaw 400.00
9 I:He-She 350.00
10 Iron Jaw returns 500.00
11 Iron Jaw falls in love 250.00
12 Crimebuster V:Japanese . . . 250.00
13 V:New,more terrible Iron Jaw 250.00
14 V:Iron Jaw 250.00
15 I:Rodent,D:Iron Jaw 275.00
16 Crimebuster V:Knight 180.00
17 Flag cover,Crimebuster V:Moth 185.00
18 Smashed car cover 175.00
19 Express train cover 175.00
20 Coffin cover 175.00
21 Boxing cover 125.00
22 Under Sea cover 125.00
23 Golf cover 125.00
24 County insane asylum cover 125.00
25 52 pgs 125.00
26 68 pgs 125.00
27 Express train cover 135.00
28 E:Yankee Longago 135.00
29 Prison break cover 135.00
30 O:Crimebuster,Murder cover 165.00
31 68 pgs 125.00
32 E:Young Robin Hood 125.00
33 . . . . 125.00
34 Suicide cover & story 85.00
35 . . . . 75.00
36 . . . . 75.00
37 . . . . 75.00
38 . . . . 75.00
39 E:Little Dynamite 75.00
40 . . . . 75.00
41 thru 50 . . . . @65.00
51 thru 56 . . . . @55.00
57 B:Dilly Duncan 60.00
58 . . . . 55.00
59 . . . . 55.00
60 Iron Jaw returns 75.00
61 O:Iron Jaw,Crimebuster 80.00
62 A:Iron Jaw 75.00
63 thru 70 . . . . @60.00
71 E:Dilly Duncan 60.00
72 . . . . 60.00
73 . . . . 60.00
74 thru 79 . . . . @50.00
80 I:Rocky X 50.00
81 thru 88 . . . . @50.00
89 A:The Claw 55.00
90 same 55.00
91 same 55.00
92 same 55.00
93 The Claw(c),A:Rocky X 60.00
94 . . . . 40.00
95 . . . . 40.00
96 . . . . 40.00
97 . . . . 40.00
98 A:Rocky X 50.00
99 . . . . 40.00
100 . . . . 50.00
101 thru 118 . . . . @50.00
119 March, 1956 . . . . 50.00

BOY EXPLORERS
(see TERRY AND THE PIRATES)

BRENDA STARR
Fourstar-Superior
1947

1 (13) 350.00
2 (14) JKa Bondage(c) 375.00
3 . . . . 300.00
4 JKa Bondage(c) 325.00
5 . . . . 275.00
6 . . . . 275.00
7 . . . . 275.00
8 . . . . 275.00
9 . . . . 275.00
10 . . . . 275.00
11 . . . . 300.00
12 . . . . 300.00

BRENDA STARR
Four Star Comics Corp.
September, 1947

13 . . . . 375.00
14 Bondage cover 385.00
2-3 . . . . 300.00
2-4 Operating table cover 350.00
2-5 Swimsuit cover 275.00
2-6 . . . . 275.00
2-7 . . . . 275.00
2-8 Cosmetic cover 275.00
2-9 Giant Starr cover 275.00
2-10 Wedding cover 275.00
2-11 . . . . 275.00
2-12 . . . . 275.00
13 . . . . 175.00
14 . . . . 175.00
15 August, 1949 . . . . 175.00

BRICK BRADFORD
Best Books
(Standard Comics)
July, 1949

5 . . . . 85.00
6 Robot cover 65.00
7 AS 60.00
8 . . . . 60.00

BROADWAY ROMANCES
Quality Comics Group
January, 1950

1 PG,BWa&(c) 175.00

Brenda Starr #14

© Four Star Comics Corp.

2 BWa,Glittering Desire 100.00
3 BL,Stole My Love 45.00
4 Enslaved by My Past 50.00
5 Flame of Passion,Sept.,1950 . 50.00

BRONCHO BILL
Visual Editions
(Standard Comics)
January, 1948

5 . . . . 55.00
6 AS(c) 35.00
7 AS(c) 28.00
8 ASh 28.00
9 AS(c) 28.00
10 AS(c) 28.00
11 AS(c) 22.00
12 AS(c) 22.00
13 AS(c) 22.00
14 ASh 22.00
15 ASh 22.00
16 AS(c) 22.00

BRUCE GENTRY
Four Star Publ./
Visual Editions/
Superior
January, 1948

1 B:Ray Bailey reprints 200.00

2 Plane crash cover 150.00
3 E:Ray Bailey reprints 135.00
4 Tiger attack cover 100.00
5 . . . . 100.00
6 Help message cover 100.00
7 . . . . 100.00
8 End of Marriage cover, July, 1949 . . . . 100.00

BUCCANEERS
(see KID ETERNITY)

BUCK JONES
Dell Publishing Co.
October, 1950

1 . . . . 120.00
2 . . . . 55.00
3 . . . . 40.00
4 . . . . 40.00
5 . . . . 40.00
6 . . . . 40.00
7 and 8 . . . . @40.00

Buck Rogers #3 © Eastern Color Printing

BUCK ROGERS
Eastern Color Printing
Winter 1940

1 Partial Painted(c) 1,350.00
2 . . . . 800.00
3 Living Corpse from Crimson Coffin 700.00
4 One man army of greased lightning 600.00
5 Sky Roads 650.00
6 September, 1943 . . . . 650.00

Toby Press

100 Flying Saucers 150.00
101 . . . . 125.00
9 . . . . 125.00

BUG MOVIES
Dell Publishing Co.
1931

1 . . . . 110.00

BUGS BUNNY
DELL GIANT EDITIONS
Dell Publishing Co.
Christmas

1 Christmas Funnies (1950) . . 250.00
2 Christmas Funnies (1951) . . 175.00
3 Christmas Funnies (1952) . . 150.00
4 Christmas Funnies (1953) . . 150.00
5 Christmas Funnies (1954) . . 150.00
6 Christmas Party (1955) 125.00
7 Christmas Party (1956) 135.00
8 Christmas Funnies (1957) . . 135.00
9 Christmas Funnies (1958) . . 135.00
1 County Fair (1957) 175.00

Halloween

1 Halloween Parade (1953) . . 175.00
2 Halloween Parade (1954) . . 150.00
3 Trick 'N' Treat Halloween Fun (1955) 160.00
4 Trick 'N' Treat Halloween Fun (1956) 155.00

Vacation

1 Vacation Funnies (1951) . . . 250.00
2 Vacation Funnies (1952) . . . 225.00
3 Vacation Funnies (1953) . . . 175.00
4 Vacation Funnies (1954) . . . 150.00
5 Vacation Funnies (1955) . . . 150.00
6 Vacation Funnies (1956) . . . 135.00
7 Vacation Funnies (1957) . . . 135.00
8 Vacation Funnies (1958) . . . 135.00
9 Vacation Funnies (1959) . . . 135.00

Bugs Bunny #8 © Dell Publishing Co.

BUGS BUNNY
Dell Publishing Co.
1942
see Four Color for early years

28 thru 30 . . . . @20.00
31 thru 50 . . . . @15.00
51 thru 70 . . . . @12.00
71 thru 85 . . . . @10.00
86 Giant-Show Time 50.00
87 thru 100 . . . . @7.00
101 thru 120 . . . . @5.00
121 thru 140 . . . . @4.00
141 thru 190 . . . . @3.00
191 thru 245 . . . . @2.00

BULLETMAN
Fawcett Publications
Summer, 1941

1 I:Bulletman & Bulletgirl . . . 1,700.00
2 MRa(c) 800.00
3 MRa(c) 550.00
4 V:Headless Horror, Guillotine cover 500.00
5 Riddle of Dr. Riddle 450.00
6 V:Japanese 400.00
7 V:Revenge Syndicate 375.00
8 V:Mr. Ego 350.00
9 V:Canine Criminals 350.00
10 I:Bullet Dog 375.00

Bulletman #7 © Fawcett Publications

11 V:Fiendish Fiddler 325.00
12 . . . . 300.00
13 . . . . 300.00
14 V:Death the Comedian 300.00
15 V:Professor D 300.00
16 VanishingElephant,Fall 1946 300.00

BUSTER CRABBE
Lev Gleason Pub.
1953

1 Ph(c) 100.00
2 ATh 125.00
3 ATh 125.00
4 F. Gordon(c) 100.00

BUSTER CRABBE
Famous Funnies
November, 1951

1 The Arrow of Death 180.00
2 AW&GE(c) 200.00
3 AW&GE(c) 225.00
4 FF(c) 250.00
5 AW,FF,FF,(c) 700.00
6 Sharks cover 60.00
7 FF 60.00
8 Gorilla cover 60.00
9 FF 60.00
10 . . . . 60.00
11 Snakes cover 50.00
12 September, 1953 . . . . 50.00

BUZ SAWYER
Standard Comics
June, 1948

1 . . . . 120.00
2 I:Sweeney 75.00
3 . . . . 50.00
4 . . . . 50.00
5 June, 1949 . . . . 50.00

CALLING ALL BOYS
Parents Magazine Institute
January, 1946

1 Skiing 50.00
2 . . . . 30.00
3 Peril Out Post 25.00
4 Model Airplane 25.00
5 Fishing 25.00
6 Swimming 25.00
7 Baseball 25.00
8 School 25.00
9 The Miracle Quarterback . . . 25.00
10 Gary Cooper cover 30.00
11 Rin-Tin-Tin cover 25.00

12 Bob Hope cover 40.00
13 Bing Cosby cover 30.00
14 J. Edgar Hoover cover 25.00
15 Tex Granger cover 18.00
16 . . . . 18.00
17 Tex Granger cover, May, 1948 18.00

Becomes:

TEX GRANGER

18 Bandits of the Badlands 55.00
19 The Seven Secret Cities 45.00
20 Davey Crockett's Last Fight . 35.00
21 Canyon Ambush 35.00
22 V:Hooded Terror 35.00
23 V:Billy the Kid 35.00
24 A:Hector, September, 1949 . . 40.00

CALLING ALL GIRLS
Parent Magazine Press, Inc.
September, 1941

1 . . . . 65.00
2 Virginia Weidler cover 30.00
3 Shirley Temple cover 50.00
4 Darla Hood cover 25.00
5 Gloria Hood cover 25.00
6 . . . . 18.00
7 . . . . 18.00
8 . . . . 18.00
9 Flag cover 20.00
10 . . . . 18.00
11 thru 20 . . . . @15.00
21 thru 39 . . . . @10.00
40 Liz Taylor 45.00
41 . . . . 7.00
42 . . . . 7.00
43 October, 1945 . . . . 7.00

CALLING ALL KIDS
Quality Comics, Inc.
December/January, 1946

1 Funny Animal stories 30.00
2 . . . . 18.00
3 . . . . 12.00
4 . . . . 10.00
5 . . . . 10.00
6 . . . . 10.00
7 . . . . 10.00
8 . . . . 10.00
9 . . . . 10.00
10 . . . . 10.00
11 thru 25 . . . . @6.00
26 August, 1949 . . . . 6.00

CAMERA COMICS
U.S. Camera Publishing Corp.
July-September, 1944

1 Airfighter,Grey Comet 100.00
2 How to Set Up a Darkroom . 60.00
3 Linda Lens V:Nazi cover 70.00
4 Linda Lens cover 50.00
5 Diving cover 50.00
6 Jim Lane cover 50.00
7 Linda Lens cover 50.00
8 Linda Lens cover 50.00
9 Summer, 1946 . . . . 50.00

CAMP COMICS
Dell Publishing Co.
February, 1942

1 Ph(c),WK,A:Bugs Bunny . . . 300.00
2 Ph(c),WK,A:Bugs Bunny . . . 250.00
3 Ph(c),Wk 300.00

CAPTAIN AERO COMICS
Holyoke Publishing Co.
December, 1941

1 B:Flag-Man&Solar,Master of Magic Captain Aero, Captain Stone 550.00
2 A:Pals of Freedom 325.00
3 JKu,B:Alias X,A:Pals of Freedom 325.00
4 JKu,O:Gargoyle, Parachute jump 325.00
5 JKu 275.00
6 JKu,Flagman,A:Miss Victory 275.00
7 Alias X 175.00
8 O:Red Cross,A:Miss Victory 175.00
9 A:Miss Victory,Alias X 150.00
10 A:Miss Victory,Red Cross . . 100.00
11 A:Miss Victory 75.00
12 same 75.00
13 same 75.00
14 same 75.00
15 AS(c),A:Miss Liberty 75.00
16 AS(c),Leather Face 60.00
17 LbC(c) 60.00
21 LbC(c) 75.00
22 LbC(c),I:Mighty Mite 75.00
23 LbC(c) 75.00
24 American Planes Dive Bombs Japan 80.00
25 LbC(c),Science Fiction(c) . . 100.00
26 LbC(c) 85.00

CAPTAIN BATTLE
New Friday Publ./ Magazine Press
Summer, 1941

1 B:Captain Battle,O:Blackout 550.00
2 Pirate Ship cover 400.00
3 Dungeon cover 325.00
4 . . . . 250.00
5 V:Japanese, Summer, 1943 225.00

CAPTAIN BATTLE, Jr.
Comic House
Fall, 1943

1 Claw V:Ghost, A:Sniffer . . . 450.00
2 Man who didn't believe in Ghosts 375.00

CAPTAIN COURAGEOUS
(see BANNER COMICS)

CAPTAIN EASY
Standard Comics
1939

N# Swash Buckler 400.00
10 . . . . 50.00
11 . . . . 35.00
12 . . . . 35.00
13 ASh(c) 35.00
14 . . . . 35.00
15 . . . . 35.00
16 ASh(c) 35.00
17 September, 1949 . . . . 35.00

CAPTAIN FEARLESS COMICS
Helnit Publishing Co.
August, 1941

1 O:Mr. Miracle,Alias X,Captain Fearless Citizen Smith, A:Miss Victory 375.00
2 A:Border Patrol, September, 1941 . . . . 235.00

CAPTAIN FLASH
Sterling Comics
November, 1954

1 O:Captain Flash 150.00
2 V:Black Knight 90.00
3 Beasts from 1,000,000 BC . . 90.00
4 Flying Saucer Invasion 90.00

CAPTAIN FLEET
Approved Comics
Fall, 1952

1 Storm and Mutiny ...Typhoon 75.00

CAPTAIN FLIGHT COMICS
Four Star Publications
March, 1944

N# B:Captain Flight,Ace Reynolds Dash theAvenger,Professor X 140.00
2 . . . . 70.00
3 . . . . 60.00
4 B:Rock Raymond Salutes America's Wartime Heroines . 65.00
5 Bondage cover,B:Red Rocket A:The Grenade 85.00
6 Girl tied at the stake 65.00
7 Dog Fight cover 60.00
8 B:Yankee Girl,A:Torpedoman 110.00
9 Dog Fight cover 100.00
10 Bondage cover 120.00
11 LBc(c),Future(c), Feb-March, 1947 . . . . 100.00

CAPTAIN GALLANT
Charlton Comics
1955

1 Ph(c),Buster Crabbe 55.00
2 and 3 . . . . @45.00
4 September, 1956 . . . . 45.00

CAPTAIN JET
Four Star Publ.
May, 1952

1 Factory bombing cover 75.00
2 Parachute jump cover 50.00
3 Tank bombing cover 30.00
4 Parachute cover 30.00
5 . . . . 30.00

CAPTAIN KIDD
(see ALL GREAT COMICS)

CAPTAIN MARVEL ADVENTURES
Fawcett Publications
Spring, 1941

N# JK, B:Captain Marvel & Sivana 15,000.00
2 GT,JK(c),Billy Batson (c) . . 2,200.00
3 JK(c),Thunderbolt (c) 1,400.00
4 Shazam(c) 900.00
5 V:Nazis 650.00
6 Solomon, Hercules, Atlas, Zeus, Achilles & Mercury cover . . 500.00
7 Ghost of the White Room . . 425.00
8 Forward America 425.00
9 A:Ibac the Monster, Nippo the Nipponese, Relm of the Subconscious 425.00
10 V:Japanese 425.00
11 V:Japanese and Nazis 375.00
12 Joins the Army 375.00
13 V:Diamond-Eyed Idol of Doom 375.00
14 Nippo meets his Nemesis . . 375.00
15 Big "Paste the Axis" contest 375.00
16 Uncle Sam cover, Paste the Axis 375.00
17 P(c), Paste the Axis 350.00
18 P(c), O:Mary Marvel 600.00
19 Mary Marvel & Santa cover . 350.00
20 Mark of the Black Swastika 2,000.00
21 Hitler cover 2,000.00
22 B:Mr. Mind serial, Shipyard Sabotage 450.00
23 A:Steamboat 300.00
24 Minneapolis Mystery 300.00
25 Sinister Faces cover 300.00
26 Flag cover 300.00
27 Joins Navy 250.00
28 Uncle Sam cover 275.00
29 Battle at the China Wall . . . 225.00
30 Modern Robinson Crusoe . . 225.00
31 Fights his own Conscience . 225.00
32 V:Mole Men, Dallas 225.00
33 Mt. Rushmore parody cover, Omaha 200.00
34 Oklahoma City 200.00
35 O:Radar the International

Captain Marvel #17
© Fawcett Publications

Policeman, Indianapolis 175.00
36 Missing face contest, St. Louis 175.00
37 V:Block Busting Bubbles, Cincinnati 175.00
38 V:Chattanooga Ghost, Rock Garden City 175.00
39 V:Mr. Mind's Death Ray, Pittsburgh 175.00
40 V:Ghost of the Tower, Boston 175.00
41 Runs for President, Dayton 160.00
42 Christmas special, St. Paul 160.00
43 V:Mr. Mind,I:Uncle Marvel, Chicago 160.00
44 OtherWorlds,Washington,D.C. 160.00
45 V:Blood Bank Robbers 160.00
46 E: Mr. Mind Serial, Tall Stories of Jonah Joggins 160.00
47 160.00
48 Signs Autographs cover 150.00
49 V: An Unknown Killer 150.00
50 Twisted Powers 150.00
51 Last of the Batsons 125.00
52 O&I:Sivana Jr.,V:Giant Earth Dreamer 150.00
53 Gets promoted 125.00
54 Marooned in the Future, Kansas City 150.00
55 Endless String, Columbus 125.00
56 Goes Crazy, Mobile 125.00
57 A:Haunted Girl, Rochester 125.00
58 V:Sivana 125.00
59 125.00
60 Man who made Earthquakes 125.00
61 I&V: Oggar, the Worlds Mightiest Immortal 150.00
62 The Great Harness Race 125.00
63 Stuntman 125.00
64 125.00
65 V:Invaders from Outer Space 125.00
66 Atomic War cover 150.00
67 Hartford 125.00
68 Scenes from the Past, Baltimore 125.00
69 Gets Knighted 125.00
70 Horror in the Box 125.00
71 Wheel of Death 125.00
72 125.00
73 Becomes a Petrophile 125.00
74 Who is the 13th Guest 125.00
75 V:Astonishing Yeast Menace 125.00
76 A:Atom Ambassador 125.00
77 The Secret Life 125.00
78 O:Mr. Tawny 150.00
79 O:Atom,A:World's Worst Actor 175.00
80 Twice told story 200.00
81 A:Mr. Atom 100.00
82 A:Mr. Tawny 100.00
83 Indian Chief 100.00
84 V:Surrealist Imp 100.00
85 Freedom Train 125.00
86 A:Mr. Tawny 100.00
87 V:Electron Thief 100.00
88 Billy Batson's Boyhood 100.00
89 V:Sivana 100.00
90 A:Mr. Tawny 100.00
91 A:Chameleon Stone 90.00
92 The Land of Limbo 90.00
93 Book of all Knowledge 90.00
94 Battle of Electricity 90.00
95 The Great Ice Cap 90.00
96 V:Automatic Weapon 90.00
97 Wiped Out 90.00
98 United Worlds 90.00
99 Rain of Terror 90.00
100 V:Sivana,Plot against the Universe 200.00
101 Invisibility Trap 90.00
102 Magic Mix-up 90.00
103 Ice Covered World of 1,000,000 AD 90.00
104 Mr. Tawny's Masquerade 90.00
105 The Dog Catcher 90.00
106 V:Menace of the Moon 90.00
107 V:Space Hunter 90.00
108 V:Terrible Termites 90.00
109 The Invention Inventor 90.00
110 V:Sivana 90.00
111 The Eighth Sea 90.00
112 90.00
113 Captain Marvel's Feud 90.00
114 V:The Ogre 90.00
115 90.00
116 Flying Saucer 100.00
117 60.00
118 V:Weird Water Man 85.00
119 85.00
120 85.00
121 85.00
122 85.00
123 85.00
124 V:Discarded Instincts 85.00
125 V:Ancient Villain 85.00
126 85.00
127 85.00
128 85.00
129 85.00
130 85.00
131 85.00
132 V:Flood 85.00
133 85.00
134 85.00
135 Perplexing Past Puzzle 85.00
136 85.00
137 85.00
138 V:Haunted Horror 85.00
139 85.00
140 Hand of Horror 85.00
141 Horror 100.00
142 85.00
143 Great Stone Face on the Moon 85.00
144 85.00
145 85.00
146 85.00
147 85.00
148 V:The World 85.00
149 85.00
150 Captains Marvel's Wedding, November, 1953 150.00

CAPTAIN MARVEL JR.
Fawcett Publications
November, 1952

1 O:Captain Marvel, Jr., A:Capt. Nazi 1,700.00
2 O:Capt.Nippon,V:Capt. Nazi 800.00

Captain Marvel Jr. #12
© Fawcett Publications

3 Parade to Excitement 550.00
4 V:Invisible Nazi 500.00
5 V:Capt. Nazi 450.00
6 Adventure of Sabbac 400.00
7 City under the Sea 400.00
8 Dangerous Double 350.00
9 Independence cover 350.00
10 Hitler cover 400.00
11 300.00
12 Scuttles the Axis Isle in the Sky 300.00
13 V:The Axis,Hitler,cover 250.00
14 X-Mas cover, Santa wears Capt. Marvel uniform 325.00
15 250.00
16 A:Capt. Marvel, Sivana, Pogo 250.00
17 Meets his Future self 250.00
18 V:Birds of Doom 250.00
19 A:Capt. Nazi & Capt. Nippon 275.00
20 Goes on the Warpath 250.00
21 Buy War Stamps 200.00
22 Rides World's oldest steamboat 200.00
23 200.00
24 V:Weather Man 200.00
25 Flag cover 200.00
26 Happy New Year 200.00
27 Jungle Thrills 200.00
28 V:Sivana's Crumbling Crimes 200.00
29 Blazes a Wilderness Trail 200.00
30 200.00
31 150.00
32 Keeper of the Lonely Rock 150.00
33 150.00
34/35 I&O:Sivana Jr. 150.00
36 Underworld Tournament 150.00
37 FreddyFreeman'sNews-stand 150.00
38 A:Arabian Knight 150.00
39 V:Sivana Jr., Headline Stealer 150.00
40 Faces Grave Situation 150.00
41 I:The Acrobat 100.00
42 V:Sivana Jr. 100.00
43 V:Beasts on Broadway 100.00
44 Key to the Mystery 100.00
45 A:Icy Fingers 100.00
46 100.00
47 V:Giant of the Beanstalk 100.00
48 Whale of a Fish Story 100.00
49 V:Dream Recorder 100.00
50 Wanted: Freddy Freeman 100.00
51 The Island Riddle 80.00
52 A:Flying Postman 80.00
53 Atomic Bomb on the Loose 125.00

54 V:Man with 100 Heads 80.00
55 Pyramid of Eternity 80.00
56 Blue Boy's Black Eye 80.00
57 Magic Ladder 80.00
58 Amazing Mirror Maze 80.00
59 . . . . 80.00
60 V:Space Menace 80.00
61 V:Himself 75.00
62 . . . . 75.00
63 V:Witch of Winter 75.00
64 thru 70 . . . . @75.00
71 thru 74 . . . . @70.00
75 V:Outlaw of Crooked Creek . 70.00
76 thru 85 . . . . @70.00
86 Defenders of time 70.00
87 thru 89 . . . . @70.00
90 The Magic Trunk 30.00
91 thru 99 . . . . @65.00
100 V:Sivana Jr 70.00
101 thru 106 . . . . @65.00
107 The Horror Dimension 65.00
108 thru 118 . . . . @65.00
119 Condemned to Die, June, 1953 . . . . 65.00

CAPTAIN MIDNIGHT
Fawcett Publications
September, 1942

1 O:Captain Midnight, Capt. Marvel cover 1,200.00
2 Smashes Jap Juggernaut . . 600.00
3 Battles the Phantom Bomber 425.00
4 Grapples the Gremlins 400.00
5 Double Trouble in Tokyo . . 400.00
6 Blasts the Black Mikado . . . 325.00
7 Newspaper headline cover . 325.00
8 Flying Torpedoes Berlin-Bound 325.00
9 MRa(c), Subs in Mississippi 325.00
10 MRa(c), Flag cover 325.00
11 MRa(c), Murder in Mexico . . 250.00

Captain Midnight #1
© Fawcett Publications

12 V:Sinister Angels 250.00
13 Non-stop Flight around the World 250.00
14 V:King of the Villains 250.00
15 V:Kimberley Killer 250.00
16 Hitler's Fortress Breached . . 250.00
17 MRa(c), Hello Adolf 225.00
18 Death from the Skies 225.00
19 Hour of Doom for the Axis . 225.00
20 Brain and Brawn against Axis 225.00
21 Trades with Japanese 200.00
22 Plea for War Stamps 200.00
23 Japanese Prison cover 200.00
24 Rising Sun Flag cover 225.00
25 Amusement Park Murder . . 200.00
26 Hotel of Horror 200.00
27 Death Knell for Tyranny . . . 200.00
28 Gliderchuting to Glory 200.00
29 Bomb over Nippon 200.00
30 . . . . 200.00
31 . . . . 150.00
32 . . . . 150.00
33 V:Shark 150.00
34 . . . . 150.00
35 thru 40 . . . . @135.00
41 thru 50 . . . . @125.00
51 thru 63 . . . . @125.00
64 V:XOG, Ruler of Saturn . . . 125.00
65 . . . . 125.00
66 V:XOG 125.00
67 Fall, 1948 . . . . 125.00

Becomes:

SWEET HEART

68 Robert Mitchum 65.00
69 thru 118 . . . . @20.00
111 Ronald Reagan story 30.00
119 Marilyn Monroe 150.00
120 Atomic Bomb story . . . . . . @35.00
121 . . . . 15.00
122 1954 . . . . 12.00

CAPTAIN SCIENCE
Youthful Magazines
November, 1950

1 WW,O:Captain Science, V:Monster God of Rogor . . . 450.00
2 WW,V:Cat Men of Phoebus, Space Pirates 225.00
3 Ghosts from the Underworld 275.00
4 WW,Vampires 275.00
5 WW,V:Shark Pirates of Pisces 275.00
6 WW,V:Invisible Tyrants, bondage cover 400.00
7 WW,Bondage cover, December, 1951 . . . . 400.00

Becomes:

FANTASTIC

8 Isle of Madness 145.00
9 Octopus cover 90.00

Becomes:

BEWARE

10 SHn,Doll of Death 150.00
11 SHn,Horror Head 125.00
12 SHn,Body Snatchers 125.00

Becomes:

CHILLING TALES

13 MF,Screaming Skull 200.00
14 SHn,Smell of Death 125.00
15 SHn,Curse of the Tomb . . . 150.00
16 HcK,Mark of the Beast Bondage(c) 125.00
17 MFc(c),Wandering Willie, Oct.,1953 . . . . 150.00

CAPTAIN STEVE SAVAGE
[1st Series]
Avon Periodicals
1950

N# WW 250.00
2 EK(c),The Death Gamble . . 100.00
3 EK(c),Crash Landing in Manchuria 35.00
4 EK(c),V:Red Raiders from Siang-Po 35.00
5 EK(c),Rockets of Death 35.00
6 Operation Destruction 30.00
7 EK(c),Flight to Kill 30.00
8 EK(c),V:Red Mystery Jet . . . 30.00
9 EK(c) 30.00
10 . . . . 30.00
11 EK(c) 35.00
12 WW 70.00
13 . . . . 40.00

[2nd Series]
September/October, 1954

5 . . . . 35.00
6 WW 50.00
7 thru 13 . . . . @20.00

CAPTAIN VIDEO
Fawcett Publications
February, 1951

1 GE,Ph(c) 400.00
2 Time when Men could not Walk 325.00
3 GE,Indestructible Antagonist 275.00
4 GE,School of Spies 275.00
5 GE,Missiles of Doom, Photo cover 275.00
6 GE,Island of Conquerors, Photo cover; Dec. 1951 . . . 275.00

CASPER, THE FRIENDLY GHOST
St. John Publishing
September, 1949

1 O:Baby Huey 550.00
2 . . . . 350.00
3 . . . . 300.00
4 . . . . 250.00
5 . . . . 250.00

Harvey Publications

7 . . . . 200.00
8 thru 9 . . . . @100.00
10 I:Spooky 150.00
11 A:Spooky 100.00
12 thru 18 . . . . @75.00
19 I:Nightmare 85.00
20 I:Wendy the Witch 85.00
21 thru 30 . . . . @50.00
31 thru 40 . . . . @40.00
41 thru 50 . . . . @30.00
51 thru 60 . . . . @25.00
61 thru 69 . . . . @20.00
70 July, 1958 . . . . 22.00

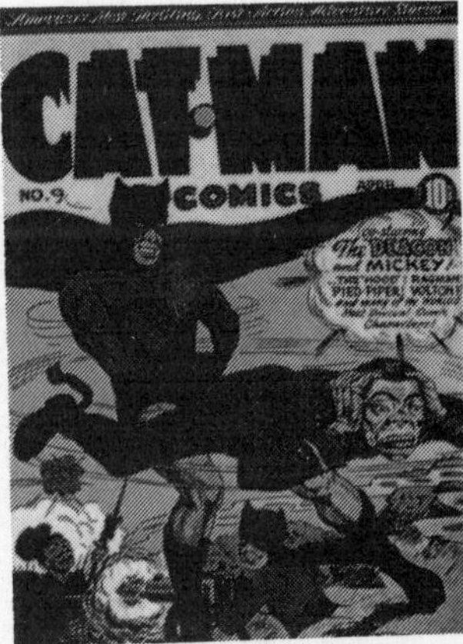

Cat Man Comics #9
© Helnit Publ. Co./Holyoke Publ. Co.

CAT MAN COMICS
Helnit Publ. Co./ Holyoke Publ. Co./ Continental Magazine
May, 1941

1 O:Deacon&Sidekick Mickey, Dr. Diamond & Ragman,A:Black Widow, B:Blaze Baylor 800.00
2 Ragman 400.00
3 B:Pied Piper 300.00
4 CQ 275.00

5 I&O: The Kitten 250.00
6 CQ 225.00
7 CQ 225.00
8 JKa, I:Volton 325.00
9 JKa 250.00
10 JKa,O:Blackout,
B:Phantom Falcon 225.00
11 JKa,DRi,BF 235.00
12 175.00
13 175.00
14 CQ 175.00
15 Rajah of Destruction 175.00
16 Bye-Bye Axis 200.00
17 Buy Bonds and Stamps 175.00
18 Buy Bonds and Stamps 175.00
19 CQ,Hitler,Tojo and
Mussolini cover 200.00
20 CQ,Hitler,Tojo and
Mussolini cover 200.00
21 CQ 175.00
22 CQ 175.00
23 CQ 175.00
N# V:Japanese,Bondage(c) 185.00
N# V:Demon 175.00
N# A:Leather Face 175.00
27 LbC(c),Flag cover,O:Kitten 200.00
28 LbC(c),Horror cover 225.00
29 LbC(c),BF 225.00
30 LbC(c),Bondage(c) 235.00
31 LbC(c) 225.00
32 August, 1946 225.00

CHALLENGER, THE
Interfaith Publications
1945

N# O:The Challenger Club 165.00
2 JKa 150.00
3 JKa 150.00
4 JKa,BF 150.00

CHAMBER OF CHILLS
Harvey Publications/ Witches Tales
June, 1951

21 200.00
22 100.00

Chamber of Chills #23
© Harvey Publications

23 Eyes Ripped Out 100.00
24 Bondage cover 110.00
5 Shrunken Skull,
Operation Monster 120.00
6 Seven Skulls of Magondi 100.00
7 Pit of the Damned 100.00
8 Formula for Death 100.00
9 Bondage cover 75.00
10 Cave of Death 75.00
11 Curse of Morgan Kilgane 60.00
12 Swamp Monster 60.00
13 The Lost Race 85.00
14 Down to Death 35.00
15 Nightmare of Doom 75.00
16 Cycle of Horror 75.00
17 Amnesia 75.00
18 Hair cut-Atom Bomb 85.00
19 Happy Anniversary 75.00
20 Shock is Struck 75.00
21 BP,Nose for News 85.00
22 Is Death the End? 75.00
23 BP,Heartline 75.00
24 BP,Bondage(c) 85.00
25 40.00
26 HN,Captains Return 40.00

Becomes:

CHAMBER OF CLUES

27 BP,A:Kerry Drake 50.00
28 A:Kerry Drake 30.00

CHAMPION COMICS
Worth Publishing Co.
December, 1939

2 B:Champ, Blazing Scarab, Neptina,
Liberty Lads, Jingleman 575.00
3 300.00
4 Bailout(c) 275.00
5 Jungleman(c) 275.00
6 MNe 275.00
7 MNe,Human Meteor 350.00
8 275.00
9 275.00
10 Bondage cover 325.00

Becomes:

CHAMP COMICS

11 Human Meteor 350.00
12 Human Heteor 300.00
13 Dragon's Teeth 275.00
14 Liberty Lads 275.00
15 Liberty Lads 275.00
16 Liberty Lads 275.00
17 Liberty Lads 275.00
18 Liberty Lads 275.00
19 A:The Wasp 250.00
20 A:The Green Ghost 275.00
21 250.00
22 A:White Mask 275.00
23 Flag cover 275.00
24 thru 29 @250.00

CHARLIE McCARTHY
Dell Publishing Co.
November, 1947

1 120.00
2 45.00
3 45.00
1 45.00
2 45.00
3 45.00
4 45.00
5 45.00
6 45.00
7 45.00
8 45.00
9 45.00

CHIEF, THE
Dell Publishing Co.
August, 1950

(1) *see Dell Four Color #290*
2 30.00

CHILLING TALES
(see CAPTAIN SCIENCE)

CHUCKLE THE GIGGLY BOOK OF COMIC ANIMALS
R. B. Leffing Well Co.
1944

1 125.00

CINEMA COMICS HERALD
Paramount/Universal/RKO/ 20th Century Fox
Giveaways 1941-43

N# Mr. Bug Goes to Town 40.00
N# Bedtime Story 40.00
N# Lady for a Night,J.Wayne 45.00
N# Reap the Wild Wind 40.00
N# Thunderbirds 40.00
N# They All Kissed Me 40.00
N# Bombardier 40.00
N# Crash Dive 40.00
N# Arabian Nights 40.00

CIRCUS THE COMIC RIOT
Globe Syndicate
June, 1938

1 BKa,WE,BW 2,200.00
2 BKa,WE,BW 1,250.00
3 BKa,WE,BW, August, 1938 1,250.00

CISCO KID, THE
Dell Publishing Co.

(1) *See Dell Four Color #292*
2 January, 1951 150.00
3 75.00
4 75.00
5 75.00
6 thru 10 @60.00
11 thru 20 @50.00

Cisco Kid #4 © Dell Publishing Co.

21 thru 36 @40.00
37 thru 41 Ph(c)'s @75.00

CLAIRE VOYANT
Leader Publ./Visual Ed./ Pentagon Publ.
1946-47

N# 250.00
2 JKa(c) 225.00
3 Case of the Kidnapped Bride 225.00
4 Bondage cover 235.00

CLOAK AND DAGGER
Approved Comics (Ziff-Davis)
Fall, 1952

1 NS(c),Al Kennedy of the Secret

All comics prices listed are for *Near Mint* condition.

Service 90.00

Clue Comics #14 (2/2)
© Hillman Periodicals

CLUE COMICS
Hillman Periodicals
January, 1943

1 O:Boy King,Nightmare,Micro-Face, Twilight,Zippo. 475.00
2 .... 250.00
3 Boy King V:The Crane 225.00
4 V:The Crane 200.00
5 V:The Crane 175.00
6 Hells Kitchen 125.00
7 V:Dr. Plasma,Torture(c) ... 150.00
8 RP,A:The Gold Mummy King 125.00
9 I:Paris 125.00
10 O:Gun Master 125.00
11 A:Gun Master 90.00
12 O:Rackman 125.00
2-1 S&K,O:Nightro,A:Iron Lady 150.00
2-2 S&K,Bondage(c) 165.00
2-3 S&K 125.00

Becomes:

REAL CLUE CRIME STORIES

2-4 DBw,S&K,True Story of Ma Barker 190.00
2-5 S&K, Newface surgery cover 150.00
2-6 S&K, Breakout cover 135.00
2-7 S&K, Stick up cover 135.00
2-8 Kidnapping cover 35.00
2-9 DBa,Boxing fix cover 35.00
2-10 DBa,Murder cover 35.00
2-11 Attempted bank robbery cover 35.00
2-12 Murder cover 35.00
3-1 thru 3-12 .... @25.00
4-1 thru 4-12 .... @45.00
5-1 thru 5-12 .... @25.00
6-1 thru 6-12 .... @25.00
6-10 Bondage(c) 45.00
7-1 thru 7-12 .... @20.00
8-1 thru 8-4 .... @20.00
8-5 May, 1953 .... 20.00

C-M-O COMICS
Comic Corp. of America (Centaur)
May, 1942

1 Invisible Terror 400.00
2 Super Ann 300.00

COCOMALT BIG BOOK OF COMICS
Harry A. Chesler
1938

1 BoW,PGn,FG,JCo,(Give away) Little Nemo 950.00

COLOSSUS COMICS
Sun Publications
March, 1940

1 A:Colossus 1,400.00

COLUMBIA COMICS
William H. Wise Co.
1944

1 Joe Palooka,Charlie Chan . 150.00

COMICS, THE
Dell Publishing Co.
March, 1937

1 I:Tom Mix & Arizona Kid ... 800.00
2 A:Tom Mix & Tom Beaty ... 400.00
3 A:Alley Oop 350.00
4 same 350.00
5 same 350.00
6 thru 11 same .... @350.00

COMICS ON PARADE
United Features Syndicate
April, 1938

1 B:Tarzan,Captain and the Kids, Little Mary, Mixup,Abbie & Slats, Broncho Bill,Li'l Abner ... 1,450.00
2 Circus Parade of all 600.00
3 .... 600.00
4 On Rocket 350.00
5 All at the Store 350.00
6 All at Picnic 250.00
7 Li'l Abner(c) 250.00
8 same 250.00

Comics on Parade #9
© United Features Syndicate

9 same 250.00
10 same 250.00
11 same 225.00
12 same 225.00
13 same 225.00
14 Abbie n' Slats (c) 225.00
15 Li'l Abner(c) 225.00
16 Abbie n' Slats(c) 225.00
17 Tarzan,Abbie n' Slats(c) ... 225.00
18 Li'l Abner(c) 225.00
19 same 225.00
20 same 225.00
21 Li'l Abner(c) 175.00
22 Tail Spin Tommy(c) 175.00
23 Abbie n' Slats(c) 175.00
24 Tail Spin Tommy(c) 175.00
25 Li'l Abner(c) 175.00
26 Abbie n' Slats(c) 175.00
27 Li'l Abner(c) 175.00
28 Tail Spin Tommy(c) 175.00
29 Abbie n' Slats(c) 175.00
30 Li'l Abner(c) 150.00
31 The Captain & the Kids(c) .. 125.00
32 Nancy and Fritzi Ritz(c) 80.00
33 Li'l Abner(c) 125.00
34 The Captain & the Kids(c) ... 90.00
35 Nancy and Fritzi Ritz(c) 70.00
36 Li'l Abner(c) 100.00
37 The Captain & the Kids(c) ... 75.00
38 Nancy and Fritzi Ritz(c) 60.00
39 Li'l Abner(c) 100.00
40 The Captain & the Kids(c) ... 75.00
41 Nancy and Fritzi Ritz(c) 55.00
42 Li'l Abner(c) 90.00
43 The Captain & the Kids(c) ... 75.00
44 Nancy and Fritzi Ritz(c) 50.00
45 Li'l Abner(c) 75.00
46 The Captain & the Kids(c) ... 60.00
47 Nancy and Fritzi Ritz(c) 50.00
48 Li'l Abner(c) 75.00
49 The Captain & the Kids(c) ... 60.00
50 Nancy and Fritzi Ritz(c) 50.00
51 Li'l Abner(c) 65.00
52 The Captain & the Kids(c) ... 45.00
53 Nancy and Fritzi Ritz(c) 40.00
54 Li'l Abner(c) 65.00
55 Nancy and Fritzi Ritz(c) 45.00
56 The Captain & the Kids(c) ... 45.00
57 Nancy and Fritzi Ritz(c) 40.00
58 Li'l Abner(c) 65.00
59 The Captain & the Kids(c) ... 40.00
60 Nancy and Fritzi Ritz(c) 35.00
61 thru 76 same .... @35.00
77 Nancy & Sluggo(c) 25.00
78 thru 103 same .... @25.00
104 same, February, 1955 ..... 25.00

COMPLETE BOOK OF COMICS AND FUNNIES
William H. Wise & Co.
1945

1 Wonderman-Magnet 230.00

CONFESSIONS OF LOVE
Artful Publications
April, 1950

1 .... 100.00
2 July, 1950 .... 70.00

CONFESSIONS OF LOVE
Star Publications
July, 1952

11 AW,LbC(c)Intimate Secrets of Daring Romance 45.00
12 AW,LbC(c),I Couldn't Say No 45.00
13 AW,LbC(c),Heart Break ... 45.00
14 AW,LbC(c),My Fateful Love 25.00
4 JyD,AW,LbC(c),The Longing Heart 25.00
5 AW,LbC(c),I Wanted Love ... 25.00
6 AW,LbC(c),My Jealous Heart . 25.00

Becomes:

CONFESSIONS OF ROMANCE

7 LbC(c)Too Good 40.00
8 AW,LbC(c),I Lied About Love 25.00
9 WW,AW,LbC(c),I Paid Love's Price 60.00
10 JyD,AW,LbC(c),My Heart Cries for Love 30.00
11 JyD,AW,LbC(c),Intimate Confessions, November, 1954 30.00

CONFESSIONS OF LOVELORN
(see LOVELORN)

CONQUEROR COMICS
Albrecht Publications
Winter, 1945

1 . . . . 80.00

CONTACT COMICS
Aviation Press
July, 1944

N# LbC(c),B:Black Venus, Golden Eagle 200.00
2 LbC(c),Peace Jet 150.00
3 LbC(c),LbC,E:Flamingo . . . 125.00
4 LbC(c),LbC 125.00
5 LbC(c),A:Phantom Flyer . . . 150.00
6 LbC(c),HK 175.00
7 LbC(c),Flying Tigers 100.00
8 LbC(c),Peace Jet 100.00
9 LbC(c),LbC,A:Marine Flyers 100.00
10 LbC(c),A:Bombers of the AAF 100.00
11 LbC(c),HK,AF,Salutes Naval Aviation 175.00
12 LbC(c),A:Sky Rangers, Air Kids, May, 1946 . . . . 125.00

COO COO COMICS
Nedor/Animated Cartoons (Standard)
October, 1942

1 O&I:Super Mouse 125.00
2 . . . . 55.00
3 . . . . 35.00
4 . . . . 35.00
5 . . . . 35.00
6 . . . . 30.00
7 thru 10 . . . . @30.00
11 thru 33 . . . . @25.00
34 thru 40 FF illustration . . . . @35.00
41 FF 75.00
42 FF 75.00
43 FF illustration 45.00
44 FF illustration 45.00
45 FF illustration 45.00
46 FF illustration 45.00
47 FF 75.00
48 FF illustration 35.00
49 FF illustration 35.00
50 FF illustration 35.00
51 thru 61 . . . . @15.00
62 April, 1952 . . . . 15.00

"COOKIE"
Michel Publ./Regis Publ. (American Comics Group)
April, 1946

1 . . . . 90.00
2 . . . . 50.00
3 . . . . 35.00
4 . . . . 35.00
5 . . . . 35.00
6 thru 20 . . . . @25.00
21 thru 30 . . . . @20.00
31 thru 54 . . . . @15.00
55 August, 1955 . . . . 15.00

COSMO CAT
Fox Features Syndicate
July/August, 1946

1 . . . . 100.00
2 . . . . 50.00
3 O:Cosmo Cat 65.00
4 thru 10 . . . . @35.00

COURAGE COMICS
J. Edward Slavin
1945

1 . . . . 45.00
2 Boxing cover 45.00
77 Naval rescue, PT99 cover . . 45.00

COWBOY COMICS
(see STAR RANGER)

COWBOYS 'N' INJUNS
Compix (M.E. Enterprises)
1946-47

1 Funny Animal Western 40.00
2 thru 8 . . . . @25.00

COWBOY WESTERN COMICS/HEROES
(see YELLOWJACKET COMICS)

COWGIRL ROMANCES
Fiction House Magazine
1952

1 The Range of Singing Guns 150.00
2 The Lady of Lawless Range . 80.00
3 Daughter of the Devil's Band 70.00
4 Bride Wore Buckskin 65.00
5 Taming of Lone-Star Lou . . . 60.00
6 Rose of Mustang Mesa 55.00
7 Nobody Loves a Gun Man . . 55.00
8 Wild Beauty 55.00
9 Gun-Feud Sweethearts 55.00
10 JKa,AW,No Girl of Stampede Valley 60.00
11 Love is Where You Find It . . 55.00
12 December, 1952 . . . . 55.00

COW PUNCHER
Avon Periodicals/ Realistic Publ.
January, 1947

1 JKu 175.00
2 JKu,JKa(c),Bondage cover . 150.00
3 AU(c) 100.00
4 . . . . 100.00
5 . . . . 100.00
6 WJo(c),Drug story 100.00
7 . . . . 100.00
1 JKu 125.00

CRACK COMICS
Comic Magazines (Quality Comics Group)
May, 1940

1 LF,O:Black Condor,Madame Fatal, Red Torpedo, Rock Bradden, Space Legion, B:The Clock,Wizard Wells . 2,000.00
2 Black Condor cover 900.00
3 The Clock cover 650.00
4 Black Condor cover 550.00
5 LF,The Clock cover 500.00
6 PG,Black Condor cover . . . 450.00
7 Clock cover 450.00
8 Black Condor cover 450.00
9 Clock cover 450.00
10 Black Condor cover 450.00
11 LF,PG,Clock cover 400.00
12 LF,PG,Black Condor cover . 400.00
13 LF,PG,Clock cover 400.00
14 AMc,LF,PG,Clack Condor(c) 400.00
15 AMc,LF,PG,Clock cover . . . 400.00
16 AMc,LF,PG,Black Condor(c) 400.00
17 FG,AMc,LF,PG,Clock cover 400.00
18 AMc,LF,PG,Black Condor(c) 400.00
19 AMc,LF,PG,Clock cover . . . 400.00
20 AMc,LF,PG,Black Condor(c) 400.00
21 AMc,LF,PG,same 300.00
22 LF,PG,same 300.00
23 AMc,LF,PG,same 300.00
24 AMc,LF,PG,same 300.00
25 AMc,same 190.00
26 AMc,same 190.00
27 AMc,I&O:Captain Triumph . 450.00

Crack Comics #32
© Quality Comics Group

28 Captain Triumph cover 200.00
29 A:Spade the Ruthless 200.00
30 I:Biff 175.00
31 Helps Spade Dig His Own Grave 100.00
32 Newspaper cover 100.00
33 V:Men of Darkness 100.00
34 . . . . 100.00
35 V:The Man Who Conquered Flame 100.00
36 Good Neighbor Tour 100.00
37 V:The Tyrant of Toar Valley 100.00
38 Castle of Shadows 100.00
39 V:Crime over the City 100.00
40 Thrilling Murder Mystery . . . 75.00
41 . . . . 75.00
42 All that Glitters is Not Gold . . 75.00
43 Smashes the Evil Spell of Silent 75.00
44 V:Silver Tip 75.00
45 V:King-The Jack of all Trades 75.00
46 V:Mr. Weary 75.00
47 V:Hypnotic Eyes Khor 75.00
48 Murder in the Sky 75.00
49 . . . . 75.00
50 A Key to Trouble 75.00
51 V:Werewolf 75.00
52 V:Porcupine 75.00
53 V:Man Who Robbed the Dead 75.00
54 Shoulders the Troubles of the World 75.00
55 Brain against Brawn 75.00
56 Gossip leads to Murder 75.00
57 V:Sitok - Green God of Evil . . 75.00
58 V:Targets 75.00
59 A Cargo of Mystery 75.00
60 Trouble is no Picnic 75.00
61 V:Mr. Pointer-Finger of Fear . 75.00
62 V:The Vanishing Vandals . . . 75.00

Becomes:

CRACK WESTERN

63 PG, I&O:Two-Gun Lil, B:Frontier Marshal,Arizona Ames, ... 120.00
64 RC,Arizona AmesV:Two-Legged Coyote 90.00
65 RC,Ames Tramples on Trouble 90.00
66 Arizona Ames Arizona Raines, Tim Holt,Ph(c) 75.00
67 RC, Ph(c) 85.00
68 . . . . 75.00
69 RC 75.00
70 O&I:Whip and Diablo 80.00
71 RC(c) 85.00
72 RC,Tim Holt,Ph(c) 72.00

73 Tim Holt,Ph(c) ... 55.00
74 RC(c) ... 60.00
75 RC(c) ... 60.00
76 RC(c),Stage Coach to Oblivion 60.00
77 RC(c),Comanche Terror ... 60.00
78 RC(c),Killers of Laurel Ridge . 60.00
79 RC(c),Fires of Revenge ... 60.00
80 RC(c),Mexican Massacre ... 60.00
81 RC(c),Secrets of Terror Canyon ... 60.00
82 The Killer with a Thousand Faces ... 40.00
83 Battlesnake Pete's Revenge . 40.00
84 PG(c),Revolt at Broke Creek May,1951 ... 40.00

CRACKAJACK FUNNIES
Dell Publishing Co.
June, 1938

1 AMc,A:Dan Dunn,The Nebbs, Don Winslow ... 1,000.00
2 AMc,same ... 500.00
3 AMc,same ... 350.00
4 AMc,same ... 250.00
5 AMc,Naked Women(c) ... 275.00
6 AMc,same ... 200.00
7 AMc,same ... 200.00
8 AMc,same ... 200.00
9 AMc,A:Red Ryder ... 300.00
10 AMc,A:Red Ryder ... 200.00
11 AMc,A:Red Ryder ... 190.00
12 AMc,A:Red Ryder ... 190.00
13 AMc,A:Red Ryder ... 190.00
14 AMc,A:Red Ryder ... 190.00
15 AMc,A:Tarzan ... 225.00
16 AMc ... 125.00

Crackajack Funnies #12
© Dell Publishing Co.

17 AMc ... 125.00
18 AMc ... 125.00
19 AMc ... 125.00
20 AMc ... 125.00
21 AMc ... 125.00
22 AMc ... 125.00
23 AMc ... 125.00
24 AMc ... 125.00
25 AMc,I:The Owl ... 325.00
26 AMc ... 250.00
27 AMc ... 250.00
28 AMc,A:The Owl ... 250.00
29 AMc,A:Ellery Queen ... 250.00
30 AMc,A:Tarzan ... 250.00
31 AMc,A:Tarzan ... 250.00
32 AMc,O:Owl Girl ... 275.00
33 AMc,A:Tarzan ... 200.00
34 AMc,same ... 200.00
35 AMc,same ... 200.00
36 AMc,same ... 200.00
37 AMc ... 150.00
38 AMc ... 150.00
39 AMc,I:Andy Panada ... 225.00
40 AMc,A:Owl(c) ... 150.00
41 AMc ... 150.00
42 AMc ... 150.00
43 AMc,A:Owl(c) ... 150.00

CRASH COMICS
Tem Publishing Co.
May, 1940

1 S&K,O:Strongman, B:Blue Streak, Perfect Human, Shangra . . 1,100.00
2 S&K ... 600.00
3 S&K ... 400.00
4 S&K,O&I:Catman ... 700.00
5 S&K, November, 1940 ... 400.00

CRIME AND PUNISHMENT
Lev Gleason Publications
April, 1948

1 CBi(c),Mr.Crime(c) ... 125.00
2 CBi(c) ... 65.00
3 CBi(c),BF ... 60.00
4 CBi(c),BF ... 40.00
5 CBi(c) ... 40.00
6 thru 10 CBi(c) ... @35.00
11 thru 15 CBi(c) ... @30.00
16 thru 27 CBi(c) ... @25.00
28 thru 38 ... @20.00
39 Drug issue ... 35.00
40 thru 44 ... @20.00

Crime and Punishment #6
© Lev Gleason Publications

45 Drug issue ... 30.00
46 thru 73 ... @15.00
66 ATh ... 175.00
67 Drug Storm ... 130.00
68 ATh(c) ... 100.00
69 Drug issue ... 30.00
74 August, 1955 ... 12.00

CRIME DETECTIVE COMICS
Hillman Publications
March-April, 1948

1 BFc(c),A:Invisible 6 ... 100.00
2 Jewel Robbery cover ... 40.00
3 Stolen cash cover ... 32.00
4 Crime Boss Murder cover ... 32.00
5 BK,Maestro cover ... 32.00
6 AMc,Gorilla cover ... 30.00
7 GMc,Wedding cover ... 30.00
8 ... 30.00
9 Safe Robbery cover (a classic) ... 140.00
10 ... 35.00
11 BP ... 35.00
12 BK ... 35.00
2-1 Bluebird captured ... 38.00
2-2 ... 25.00
2-3 ... 25.00
2-4 BK ... 35.00
2-5 ... 25.00
2-6 ... 25.00
2-7 BK,GMc ... 35.00
2-8 ... 25.00
2-9 ... 25.00
2-10 ... 25.00
2-11 ... 25.00
2-12 ... 25.00
3-1 Drug Story ... 25.00
3-2 thru 3-7 ... @24.00
3-8 May/June, 1953 ... 20.00

CRIME DOES NOT PAY
(see SILVER STREAK COMICS)

CRIME ILLUSTRATED
E.C. Comics
November-December, 1955

1 Grl,RC,GE,JO ... 75.00
2 Grl,RC,JCr,JDa,JO ... 60.00

CRIME MUST STOP
Hillman Periodicals
October, 1952

1 BK ... 275.00

CRIME MYSTERIES
Ribage Publishing Corp.
May, 1952

1 Transvestism,Bondage(c) . . 225.00
2 A:Manhunter, Lance Storm, Drug ... 150.00
3 FF-one page, A:Dr. Foo ... 100.00
4 A:Queenie Star, Bondage Star 175.00
5 Claws of the Green Girl ... 85.00
6 ... 85.00
7 Sons of Satan ... 85.00
8 Death Stalks the Crown, Bondage(c) ... 80.00
9 You are the Murderer ... 75.00
10 The Hoax of the Death ... 75.00
11 The Strangler ... 65.00
12 Bondage(c) ... 75.00
13 AT,6 lives for one ... 90.00
14 Painted in Blood ... 65.00
15 Feast of the Dead,Acid Face 125.00

Becomes:

SECRET MYSTERIES

16 Hiding Place,Horror ... 90.00
17 The Deadly Diamond,Horror . 55.00
18 Horror ... 60.00
19 Horror,July, 1955 ... 60.00

CRIMES ON THE WATERFRONT
(see FAMOUS GANGSTERS)

INTERNATIONAL COMICS
E.C. Publ. Co.
Spring, 1947

1 KS,I:Manhattan's Files ... 425.00
2 KS,A: Van Manhattan & Madelon ... 300.00
3 KS,same ... 250.00
4 KS,same ... 250.00
5 I:International Crime-Busting Patrol ... 250.00

Becomes:

INTERNATIONAL CRIME PATROL

6 A:Moon Girl & The Prince . . 400.00

Becomes:

CRIME PATROL

7 SMo,A:Capt. Crime Jr.,Field Marshall of Murder 350.00
8 JCr,State Prison cover 300.00
9 AF,JCr,Bank Robbery 300.00
10 AF,JCr,Wanted:James Dore 300.00
11 AF,JCr 300.00
12 AF,Grl,JCr,Interrogation(c) . 300.00
13 AF,JCr 300.00
14 AF,JCr,Smugglers cover . . . 300.00
15 AF,JCr,Crypt of Terror . . . 1,500.00
16 AF,JCr,Crypt of Terror . . . 1,250.00

Becomes:

CRYPT OF TERROR

E.C. Comics
April, 1950

17 JCr&(c),AF,'Werewolf Strikes Again' 1,800.00
18 JCr&(c),AF,WW,HK 'The Living Corpse' 1,500.00
19 JCr&(c),AF,Grl, 'Voodoo Drums' 1,500.00

Becomes:

TALES FROM THE CRYPT

October, 1950

20 JCr&(c),AF,GI,JKa 'Day of Death' 1,000.00
21 AF&(c),WW,HK,GI,'Cooper Dies in the Electric Chair . 800.00
22 AF, JCr(c) 800.00
23 AF&(c),JCr,JDa,Grl 'Locked in a Mauseleum' . . 500.00
24 AF(c),WW,JDa,JCr,Grl 'Danger...Quicksand' 500.00

Tales from the Crypt #23
© E.C. Comics

25 AF(c),WW,JDa,JKa,Grl 'Mataud Waxworks' 500.00
26 WW(c),JDa,Grl, 'Scared Graveyard' 400.00
27 JKa, WW(c), Guillotine cover 400.00
28 AF(c),JDa,JKa,Grl,JO 'Buried Alive' 400.00
29 JDa&(c),JKa,Grl,JO 'Coffin Burier' 400.00
30 JDa&(c),JO,JKa,Grl 'Underwater Death' 400.00
31 JDa&(c),JKa,Grl,AW 'Hand Chopper' 500.00
32 JDa&(c),GE,Grl,'Woman Crushed by Elephant' 300.00
33 JDa&(c),GE,JKa,Grl,'Lower Berth',O:Crypt Keeper 550.00
34 JDa&(c),JKa,GE,Grl,'Jack the Ripper,'Ray Bradbury adapt. 300.00
35 JDa&(c),JKa,JO,Grl, 'Werewolf' 300.00
36 JDa&(c),JKa,GE,Grl, Ray Bradbury adaptation 300.00
37 JDa(c),JO,BE 300.00
38 JDa(c),BE,RC,Grl,'Axe Man' 300.00
39 JDa&(c),JKa,JO,Grl,'Children in the Graveyard' 300.00
40 JDa&(c),GE,BK,Grl, 'Underwater Monster' 300.00
41 JDa&(c),JKa,GE,Grl, 'Knife Thrower' 250.00
42 JDa(c),JO,Vampire cover . . 250.00
43 JDa(c),JO,GE 250.00
44 JO,RC,Guillotine cover 250.00
45 JDa&(c),JKa,BK,GI,'Rat Takes Over His Life' 250.00
46 JDa&(c),GE,JO,GI,'Werewolf man being hunted,Feb.1955 350.00

CRIME REPORTER

St. John Publishing Co.
August, 1948

1 Death Makes a Deadline . . 175.00
2 GT,MB(c),Matinee Murders . 300.00
3 GT,MB(c),December, 1948 . 150.00

CRIMES BY WOMEN

Fox Features Syndicate
June, 1948

1 Bonnie Parker 500.00
2 Vicious Female 250.00
3 Prison break cover 240.00
4 Murder cover 225.00
5 . . . . 225.00
6 Girl Fight cover 250.00
7 . . . . 225.00
8 . . . . 225.00
9 . . . . 225.00
10 . . . . 225.00
11 . . . . 225.00
12 . . . . 225.00
13 ACME jewelry robbery cover 225.00
14 Prison break cover 225.00
15 August, 1951 . . . . 225.00

CRIME SMASHER

Fawcett Publications
Summer, 1948

1 The Unlucky Rabbit's Foot . 200.00

CRIME SMASHERS

Ribage Publishing Corp.
October, 1950

1 Girl Rape 300.00
2 JKu,A:Sally the Sleuth, Dan Turner, Girl Friday, Rat Hale 125.00
3 MFa 110.00
4 Zak(c) 110.00
5 WW 175.00
6 . . . . 80.00
7 Bondage cover,Drugs 120.00
8 . . . . 80.00
9 Bondage cover 80.00
10 . . . . 80.00
11 . . . . 80.00
12 . . . . 80.00
13 . . . . 80.00
14 . . . . 80.00
15 . . . . 80.00

CRIME SUSPENSTORIES

L.L. Publishing Co.
(E.C. Comics)
October-November, 1950

1a JCr,Grl 600.00
1 JCr,WW,Grl 500.00
2 JCr,JKa,Grl 350.00
3 JCr,WW,Grl 300.00
4 JCr,Gln,Grl,JDa 275.00
5 JCr,JKa,Grl,JDa 225.00
6 JCr,JDa,Grl 175.00
7 JCr,Grl 175.00
8 JCr,Grl 175.00
9 JCr,Grl 175.00
10 JCr,Grl 175.00
11 JCr,Grl 125.00
12 JCr,Grl 125.00
13 JCr,AW 150.00
14 JCr 125.00
15 JCr 125.00
16 JCr,AW 150.00
17 JCr,FF,AW, Ray Bradbury . 175.00
18 JCr,RC,BE 125.00
19 JCr,RC,GE,AF(c) 125.00
20 RC,JCr, Hanging cover . . . 150.00
21 JCr 85.00
22 RC,JO,JCr(c), Severed head cover 100.00
23 JKa,RC,GE 100.00
24 BK,RC,JO 80.00
25 JKa,(c),RC 80.00
26 JKa,(c),RC,JO 80.00
27 JKa,(c),GE,Grl,March, 1955 . 80.00

CRIMINALS ON THE RUN

Premium Group of Comics
August, 1948

4-1 LbC(c) 75.00
4-2 LbC(c), A:Young King Cole 60.00
4-3 LbC(c), Rip Roaring Action in Alps 60.00
4-4 LbC(c), Shark cover 60.00
4-5 AMc 60.00
4-6 LbC 50.00
4-7 LbC 50.00
5-1 LbC 150.00
5-2 LbC 50.00
10 LbC 65.00

Becomes:

CRIME-FIGHTING DETECTIVE

11 LbC, Brodie Gang Captured . 45.00
12 LbC(c), Jail Break Genius . . 35.00
13 . . . . 35.00
14 LbC(c), A Night of Horror . . . 50.00
15 LbC(c) 35.00
16 LbC(c), Wanton Murder 35.00
17 LbC(c), The Framer was Framed 35.00
18 LbC(c), A Web of Evil 35.00
19 LbC(c), Lesson of the Law . . 35.00

Becomes:

SHOCK DETECTIVE CASE

20 LbC(c), The Strangler 55.00
21 LbC(c), Death Ride 55.00

Becomes:

SPOOK DETECTIVE CASES

22 Headless Horror 120.00

Becomes:

SPOOK SUSPENSE AND MYSTERY

23 LbC,Weird Picture of Murder . 75.00
24 LbC(c),Mummy's Case 85.00
25 LbC(c),Horror Beyond Door . 70.00
26 LbC(c),JyD,Face of Death . . . 70.00
27 LbC(c),Ship of the Dead 70.00
28 LbC(c),JyD,Creeping Death . 70.00
29 LbC(c),Solo for Death 70.00
30 LbC(c),JyD,Nightmare, Oct.,1954 . . . . 70.00

Spook Suspense and Mystery #25
© Premium Group

CROWN COMICS
Golfing/McCombs Publ.
Winter 1944

1 . . . . 250.00
2 MB,I:Mickey Magic 125.00
3 MB,Jungle adventure cover 125.00
4 MB(c) 150.00
5 MB(c),Jungle adventure cover 150.00
6 MB(c),Jungle adventure cover 150.00
7 JKa,AF,MB(c),Race Car driving cover 150.00
8 MB 135.00
9 . . . . 85.00
10 Plane crash cover 85.00
11 LSt 75.00
12 LSt 75.00
13 LSt 75.00
14 . . . . 95.00
15 FBe 75.00
16 FBe,Jungle adventure(c) 75.00
17 FBe 75.00
18 FBe 75.00
19 BP,July, 1949 . . . . 75.00

CRUSADER FROM MARS
Approved Publ. (Ziff-Davis)
January-March, 1952

1 Mission Thru Space, Death in the Sai 350.00
2 Beachhead on Saturn's Ring, Bondage(c),Fall, 1952 . . . . . 300.00

CRYIN' LION, THE
William H. Wise Co.
Fall, 1944

1 . . . . 75.00
2 . . . . 45.00
3 Spring, 1945 . . . . 45.00

CRYPT OF TERROR
(see CRIME PATROL)

CYCLONE COMICS
Bibara Publ. Co.
June, 1940

1 O:Tornado Tom 475.00
2 . . . . 275.00
3 . . . . 200.00
4 Voltron 200.00
5 A:Mr. Q,October, 1940 . . . . 200.00

ALL GREAT COMICS
Fox Features Syndicate
October, 1947

12 A:Brenda Starr 225.00
13 JKa,O:Dagger, Desert Hawk 175.00

Becomes:

DAGAR, DESERT HAWK

14 JKa,Monster of Mura 250.00
15 JKa,Curse of the Lost Pharaoh 200.00
16 JKa,Wretched Antmen 150.00
19 Pyramid Doom 150.00
20 JKa(c),The Ghost of Fate . 150.00
21 . . . . 175.00
22 . . . . 150.00
23 Bondage cover 165.00

Becomes:

CAPTAIN KIDD

24 Blackbeard the Pirate 60.00
25 Sorceress of the Deep 60.00

Becomes:

MY SECRET STORY

26 He Wanted More Than Love . 45.00
27 My Husband Hated Me 32.00
28 I Become a Marked Women . 32.00
29 My Forbidden Rapture, April, 1950 . . . . 32.00

DAFFY
Dell Publishing Co.
March, 1953

(1) *see Dell Four Color #457*
(2) *see Dell Four Color #536*
(3) *see Dell Four Color #615*
4 thru 7 . . . . @18.00
8 thru 11 . . . . @15.00
12 thru 17 . . . . @12.00

Becomes:

DAFFY DUCK

18 . . . . 12.00
19 . . . . 12.00
20 . . . . 12.00
21 thru 30 . . . . @8.00

Gold Key

31 thru 40 . . . . @7.00
41 thru 59 . . . . @5.00
60 B&A:Road Runner 3.00
61 thru 90 same . . . . @3.00
91 thru 127 . . . . @2.00

Whitman

128 thru 145 . . . . @2.00

DAGWOOD
Harvey Publications
September, 1950

1 . . . . 65.00
2 . . . . 35.00
3 thru 10 . . . . @25.00
11 thru 20 . . . . @20.00
21 thru 30 . . . . @15.00
31 thru 50 . . . . @10.00
51 thru 70 . . . . @8.00
71 thru 109 . . . . @7.00
110 thru 140 . . . . @5.00

DANGER AND ADVENTURE
(see THIS MAGAZINE IS HAUNTED)

DANGER IS OUR BUSINESS
Toby Press/ I.W. Enterprises
1953

1 AW,FF,Men who Defy Death for a Living 250.00
2 Death Crowds the Cockpit . . 50.00
3 Killer Mountain 40.00
4 . . . . 40.00

5 thru 9 . . . . @35.00
10 June, 1955 . . . . 35.00

DAREDEVIL COMICS
Lev Gleason Publications
July, 1941

1 Daredevil Battles Hitler, A:Silver Streak, Lance Hale, Dickey Dean, Cloud Curtis,V:The Claw, O:Hitler 4,500.00
2 I:The Pioneer, Champion of American,B:London,Pat Patriot,Pirate Prince 2,000.00
3 CBi(c),O:Thirteen 1,000.00
4 CBi(c),Death is the Refere . . 750.00
5 CBi(c),I:Sniffer&Jinx, Claw V:Ghost,Lottery of Doom . . . 700.00

Daredevil #33
© Lev Gleason Publications

6 CBi(c) 600.00
7 CBi(c), What Ghastly Sight Lies within the Mysterious Trunk . 500.00
8 V:Nazis cover, E:Nightro . . 450.00
9 V:Double 450.00
10 America will Remember Pearl Harbor 450.00
11 Bondage cover, E:Pat Patriot, London 425.00
12 BW,CBi(c), O:The Law 650.00
13 BW,I:Little Wise Guys 650.00
14 BW,CBi(c) 350.00
15 BW,CBi(c), D:Meatball 475.00
16 BW,CBi(c) 300.00
17 BW,CBi(c), Into the Valley of Death 300.00
18 BW,CBi(c), O:Daredevil, double length story 650.00
19 BW,CBi(c), Buried Alive . . . 275.00
20 BW,CBi(c), Boxing cover . . 275.00
21 CBi(c), Can Little Wise Guys Survive Blast of Dynamite? . 450.00
22 CBi(c) 175.00
23 CBi(c), I:Pshyco 175.00
24 CBi(c), Punch and Judy Murders 175.00
25 CBi(c), baseball cover 225.00
26 CBi(c) 175.00
27 CBi(c), Bondage cover 225.00
28 CBi(c) 175.00
29 CBi(c) 175.00
30 CBi(c), Ann Hubbard White 1922-1943 . . . . 175.00
31 CBi(c), D:The Claw 400.00
32 V:Blackmarketeers 150.00
33 CBi(c) 150.00
34 CBi(c) 150.00

35 B:Two Daredevil stories
every issue 135.00
36 CBi(c) 135.00
37 CBi(c) 135.00
38 CBi(c), O:Daredevil 225.00
39 CBi(c) 125.00
40 CBi(c) 125.00
41 thru 50 CBi(c) . . . . @100.00
51 CBi(c) 80.00
52 CBi(c),Football cover 80.00
53 thru 57 . . . . @80.00
58 Football cover 80.00
59 . . . . 80.00
60 . . . . 80.00
61 thru 68 . . . . @80.00
69 E:Daredevil 80.00
70 . . . . 60.00
71 thru 78 . . . . @55.00
79 B:Daredevil 65.00
80 . . . . 60.00
81 . . . . 40.00
82 . . . . 40.00
83 thru 99 . . . . @40.00
100 . . . . 45.00
101 thru 133 . . . . @35.00
134 September, 1956 . . . . 35.00

DARING CONFESSIONS
(see YOUTHFUL HEART)

DARING LOVE
(see YOUTHFUL ROMANCES)

DARK MYSTERIES
Merit Publications
June-July, 1951

1 WW, WW(c), Curse of the
Sea Witch 325.00
2 WW, WW(c), Vampire Fangs
of Doom 250.00
3 Terror of the Unwilling
Witch 100.00
4 Corpse that Came Alive . . . 100.00
5 Horror of the Ghostly Crew . . 85.00
6 If the Noose Fits Wear It! . . . 85.00
7 Terror of the Cards of Death . 85.00
8 Terror of the Ghostly Trail . . 85.00
9 Witch's Feast at Dawn 85.00
10 Terror of the Burning Witch . 120.00
11 The River of Blood 75.00
12 Horror of the Talking Dead . . 75.00
13 Terror of the Hungry Cats . . . 75.00
14 Horror of the Fingers of Doom 80.00
15 Terror of the Vampires Teeth 75.00
16 Horror of the Walking Dead . 75.00
17 Terror of the Mask of Death . 75.00
18 Terror of the Burning Corpse 75.00
19 The Rack of Terror 100.00
20 Burning Executioner 90.00
21 The Sinister Secret 60.00
22 The Hand of Destiny 60.00
23 The Mardenburg Curse 50.00
24 Give A Man enough Rope,
July, 1955 . . . . 50.00

DAVY CROCKETT
Avon Periodicals
1951

1 . . . . 90.00

DEAD END CRIME STORIES
Kirby Publishing Co.
April, 1949

N# BP 225.00

DEAD-EYE WESTERN COMICS
Hillman Periodicals
November-December, 1948

1 BK 80.00
2 . . . . 45.00
3 . . . . 45.00
4 thru 12 . . . . @25.00
2-1 . . . . 20.00
2-2 . . . . 20.00
2-3 . . . . 35.00
2-4 . . . . 35.00
2-5 thru 2-12 . . . . @20.00
3-1 . . . . 20.00

DEADWOOD GULCH
Dell Publishing Co.
1931

1 . . . . 120.00

DEAR BEATRICE FAIRFAX
Best Books
(Standard Comics)
November, 1950

5 . . . . 40.00
6 thru 9 . . . . @25.00

DEAR LONELY HEART
Artful Publications
March, 1951

5 . . . . 75.00
6 . . . . 35.00
7 MB,Jungle Girl 75.00
8 . . . . 30.00
9 . . . . 30.00

DEAR LONELY HEARTS
Comic Media
August, 1953

1 Six Months to Live 38.00
2 Date Hungry, Price of Passion 22.00
3 thru 8 . . . . @22.00

DEARLY BELOVED
Approved Comics
(Ziff-Davis)
Fall, 1952

1 Ph(c) 75.00

DEBBIE DEAN, CAREER GIRL
Civil Service Publishing
April, 1945

1 . . . . 75.00
2 . . . . 70.00

DELL GIANT EDITIONS
Dell Publishing Co.
1953-58

Abe Lincoln Life Story 90.00
Cadet Gray of West Point 75.00
Golden West Rodeo Treasury . 100.00
Life Stories of
American Presidents 75.00
Lone Ranger Golden West . . . 250.00
Lone Ranger Movie Story 450.00
Lone Ranger Western
Treasury('53) 250.00
Lone Ranger Western
Treasury('54) 150.00
Moses & Ten Commandments . . 75.00
Nancy & Sluggo Travel Time . . 100.00
Pogo Parade 350.00
Raggedy Ann & Andy 250.00
Santa Claus Funnies 150.00
Tarzan's Jungle Annual #1 . . . 150.00
Tarzan's Jungle Annual #2 . . . 100.00
Tarzan's Jungle Annual #3 . . . 100.00
Tarzan's Jungle Annual #4 . . . 100.00
Tarzan's Jungle Annual #5 . . . 100.00
Tarzan's Jungle Annual #6 . . . 100.00
Tarzan's Jungle Annual #7 . . . 100.00
Treasury of Dogs 75.00
Treasury of Horses 75.00
Universal Presents-Dracula-
The Mummy & Other Stories 200.00
Western Roundup #1 . . . . 300.00
Western Roundup #2 . . . . 200.00
Western Roundup #3 . . . . 150.00
Western Roundup #4 thru #5 @150.00
Western Roundup #6 thru #10 @140.00
Western Roundup #11 thru #17@135.00
Western Roundup #18 . . . . . . 125.00
Western Roundup #19 thru #25 125.00
Woody Woodpecker Back
to School #1 . . . . 125.00
Woody Woodpecker Back
to School #2 . . . . 100.00
Woody Woodpecker Back
to School #3 . . . . 85.00
Woody Woodpecker Back
to School #4 . . . . 85.00
Woody Woodpecker County
Fair #5 . . . . 85.00
Woody Woodpecker Back
to School #6 . . . . 80.00
Woody Woodpecker County
Fair #2 . . . . 75.00

Also See:
Bugs Bunny
Marge's Little Lulu
Tom and Jerry, &
Walt Disney Dell Giant Editions

DELL GIANT COMICS
Dell Publishing Co.
September 1959

21 M.G.M. Tom & Jerry
Picnic Time 175.00
22 W.Disney's Huey, Dewey & Louie
Back to School (Oct 1959) . 100.00
23 Marge's Little Lulu &
Tubby Halloween Fun 175.00
24 Woody Woodpeckers
Family Fun 120.00
25 Tarzan's Jungle World 160.00
26 W.Disney's Christmas
Parade,CB 250.00
27 W.Disney's Man in
Space (1960) 150.00
28 Bugs Bunny's Winter Fun . . 150.00
29 Marge's Little Lulu &
Tubby in Hawaii 200.00

Dell Giant #22 © Dell Publishing Co.

30 W.Disney's DisneylandU.S.A. 150.00
31 Huckleberry Hound
Summer Fun 200.00
32 Bugs Bunny Beach Party . . . 85.00
33 W.Disney's Daisy Duck &
Uncle Scrooge Picnic Time . 150.00
34 Nancy&SluggoSummerCamp 100.00
35 W.Disney's Huey, Dewey &

Louie Back to School 100.00
36 Marge's Little Lulu & Witch Hazel Halloween Fun 200.00
37 Tarzan, King of the Jungle . 150.00
38 W.Disney's Uncle Donald and his Nephews Family Fun . . . 95.00
39 W.Disney's Merry Christmas . 95.00
40 Woody Woodpecker Christmas Parade 85.00
41 Yogi Bear's Winter Sports . . 200.00
42 Marge's Little Lulu & Tubby in Australia 185.00

Dell Giant #43 © Dell Publishing Co.

43 Mighty Mouse in OuterSpace 300.00
44 Around the World with Huckleberry & His Friends . 200.00
45 Nancy&SluggoSummerCamp 90.00
46 Bugs Bunny Beach Party . . . 80.00
47 W.Disney's Mickey and Donald in Vacationland 120.00
48 The Flintstones #1 (Bedrock Bedlam) 250.00
49 W.Disney's Huey, Dewey & Louie Back to School 85.00
50 Marge's Little Lulu & Witch Hazel Trick 'N' Treat . 200.00
51 Tarzan, King of the Jungle . 125.00
52 W.Disney's Uncle Donald & his Nephews Dude Ranch . . 80.00
53 W.Disney's Donald Duck Merry Christmas 75.00
54 Woody Woodpecker Christmas Party 100.00
55 W.Disney's Daisy Duck & Uncle Scrooge Show Boat (1961) . 225.00

DELL JUNIOR TREASURY
Dell Publishing Co.
June, 1955

1 Alice in Wonderland 75.00
2 Aladdin 65.00
3 Gulliver's Travels 50.00
4 Adventures of Mr. Frog 55.00
5 Wizard of Oz 60.00
6 Heidi 65.00
7 Santa & the Angel 65.00
8 Raggedy Ann 65.00
9 Clementina the Flying Pig . . . 60.00
10 Adventures of Tom Sawyer . . 60.00

DENNIS THE MENACE
Visual Editions/Literary Ent. (Standard, Pines)
August, 1953

1 . . . . 250.00

Dennis the Menace #1
© Visual Editions

2 . . . . 150.00
3 . . . . 75.00
4 . . . . 75.00
5 thru 10 . . . . @65.00
11 thru 20 . . . . @50.00
21 thru 30 . . . . @30.00
31 thru 40 . . . . @20.00
41 thru 50 . . . . @18.00
51 thru 60 . . . . @15.00
61 thru 70 . . . . @10.00
71 thru 90 . . . . @7.00
91 thru 140 . . . . @3.50
141 thru 166 . . . . @3.00

DESPERADO
Lev Gleason Publications
June, 1948

1 CBi(c) 65.00
2 CBi(c) 35.00
3 CBi(c) 30.00
4 CBi(c) 25.00
5 CBi(c) 25.00
6 CBi(c) 25.00
7 CBi(c) 25.00
8 CBi(c) 25.00

Becomes:

BLACK DIAMOND WESTERN

9 CBi(c) 90.00
10 CBi(c) 50.00
11 CBi(c) 35.00
12 CBi(c) 35.00
13 CBi(c) 35.00
14 CBi(c) 35.00
15 CBi(c) 35.00
16 thru 28 BW,Big Bang Buster @50.00
29 thru 40 . . . . @25.00
41 thru 52 . . . . @20.00
53 3-D 60.00
54 3-D 50.00
55 thru 60 . . . . @25.00

DETECTIVE EYE
Centaur Publications
November, 1940

1 B:Air Man, The Eye Sees, A:Masked Marvel 900.00
2 O:Don Rance, Mysticape, December, 1940 . . . . 650.00

DETECTIVE PICTURE STORIES
Comics Magazine Co.
December, 1936

1 The Phantom Killer 1,500.00
2 . . . . 600.00
3 . . . . 500.00
4 WE, Muss Em Up 500.00
5 Trouble, April, 1937 . . . . 475.00

DEXTER COMICS
Dearfield Publications
Summer, 1948

1 . . . . 35.00
2 . . . . 25.00
3 . . . . 15.00
4 . . . . 15.00
5 July, 1949 . . . . 15.00

DIARY CONFESSIONS
(see TENDER ROMANCE)

DIARY LOVES
Comic Magazines
(Quality Comics Group)
September, 1949

1 BWa 85.00
2 BWa 70.00
3 . . . . 28.00
4 RC 40.00
5 . . . . 20.00
6 . . . . 20.00
7 . . . . 20.00
8 BWa 60.00
9 BWa 60.00
10 BWa 60.00
11 . . . . 20.00
12 . . . . 20.00
13 . . . . 20.00
14 . . . . 20.00
15 BWa 45.00
16 BWa 45.00
17 . . . . 20.00
18 . . . . 20.00
19 . . . . 20.00
20 . . . . 20.00
21 BWa 35.00
22 thru 31 . . . . @15.00

Becomes:

G.I. SWEETHEARTS

32 Love Under Fire 25.00
33 . . . . 25.00
34 . . . . 25.00
35 . . . . 25.00
36 Lend Lease Love Affair 25.00
37 thru 45 . . . . @25.00

Becomes:

GIRLS IN LOVE

46 Somewhere I'll Find You 30.00
47 thru 56 . . . . @20.00
57 MB,MB(c), Can Love Really Change Him, Dec., 1956 . . . . 40.00

DIARY SECRETS
(see TEEN-AGE DIARY SECRETS)

DICK COLE
Curtis Publ./ Star Publications
December-January, 1949

1 LbC,LbC(c),CS,All sports cover 85.00
2 LbC 50.00
3 LbC, LbC(c) 40.00
4 LbC, LbC(c),Rowing cover . . 40.00
5 LbC,LbC(c) 40.00
6 LbC,LbC(c), Rodeo cover . . . 35.00
7 LbC,LbC(c) 35.00
8 LbC,LbC(c), Football cover . . 35.00
9 LbC,LbC(c), Basketball cover 35.00
10 Joe Louis 55.00

Becomes:

SPORTS THRILLS

11 Ted Williams & Ty Cobb . . . 250.00
12 LbC, Joe Dimaggio & Phil Rizzuto, Boxing cover 100.00
13 LbC(c),Basketball cover 65.00
14 LbC(c),Baseball cover 50.00
15 LbC(c),Baseball cover, November, 1951 . . . . 50.00

DICKIE DARE
Eastern Color Printing Co.
1941

1 BEv(c) 200.00
2 . . . . 125.00
3 . . . . 125.00
4 1942 . . . . 135.00

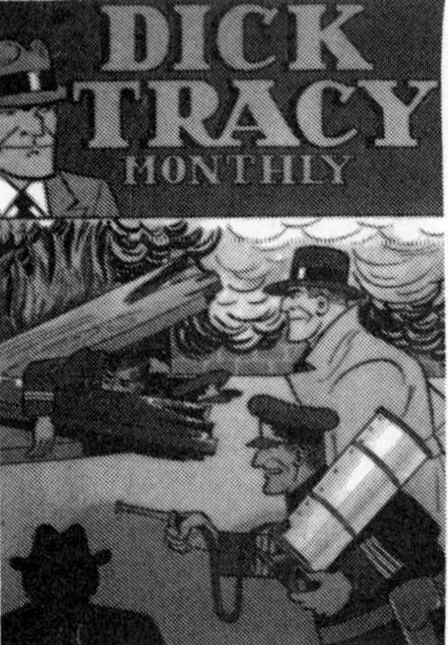

Dick Tracy Monthly #2
© Dell Publishing Co.

DICK TRACY MONTHLY
Dell Publishing Co.
January, 1948

1 ChG,Dick Tracy & the Mad Doctor' 350.00
2 ChG,A:MarySteele,BorisArson 200.00
3 ChG,A:Spaldoni,Big Boy . . . 200.00
4 ChG,A:Alderman Zeld 160.00
5 ChG,A:Spaldoni,Mrs.Spaldoni 160.00
6 ChG,A:Steve the Tramp . . . 160.00
7 ChG,A:Boris Arson,Mary Steele 160.00
8 ChG,A:Boris & Zora Arson . 160.00
9 ChG,A:Chief Yellowpony . . 160.00
10 ChG,A:Cutie Diamond 160.00
11 ChG,A:Toby Townly, Bookie Joe 125.00
12 ChG,A:Toby Townly, Bookie Joe 125.00
13 ChG,A:Toby Townly, Blake . 135.00
14 ChG,A:Mayor Waite Wright . 125.00
15 ChG,A:Bowman Basil 125.00
16 ChG,A:Maw,'Muscle' & 'Cut' Famon 125.00
17 ChG,A:Jim Trailer, Mary Steele 125.00
18 ChG,A:Lips Manlis, Anthel Jones 125.00
19 'Golden Heart Mystery' 150.00
20 'Black Cat Mystery' 150.00
21 'Tracy Meets Number One' . 150.00
22 'Tracy and the Alibi Maker' . 125.00
23 'Dick Tracy Meets Jukebox' 125.00
24 'Dick Tracy and Bubbles' . . 125.00
Becomes:

DICK TRACY COMICS MONTHLY
Harvey

25 ChG,A:Flattop 150.00
26 ChG,A:Vitamin Flintheart . . 125.00
27 ChG,'Flattop Escapes Prision' 125.00
28 ChG,'Case o/t Torture Chamber' 135.00
29 ChG,A:Brow,Gravel Gertie . 125.00
30 ChG,'Blackmail Racket' . . . 125.00
31 ChG,A:Snowflake Falls 100.00
32 ChG,A:Shaky,Snowflake Falls 100.00
33 ChG,'Strange Case of Measles' 125.00
34 ChG,A:Measles,Paprika . . . 100.00
35 ChG,'Case of Stolen $50,000' 100.00
36 ChG,'Case of the Runaway Blonde' 125.00
37 ChG,'Case of Stolen Money' 100.00
38 ChG,A:Breathless Mahoney 100.00
39 ChG,A:Itchy,B.O.Pleanty . . . 100.00
40 ChG,'Case of Atomic Killer' . 100.00
41 ChG,Pt.1'Murder by Mail' . . . 80.00
42 ChG,Pt.2'Murder by Mail' . . . 80.00
43 ChG,'Case of the Underworld Brat' 80.00
44 ChG,'Case of the Mouthwash Murder' 80.00
45 ChG,'Case of the Evil Eyes' . 80.00
46 ChG,'Case of the Camera Killers' 80.00
47 ChG,'Case of the Bloodthirsty Blonde' 80.00
48 ChG,'Case of the Murderous Minstrel' 80.00
49 ChG,Pt.1'Killer Who Returned From the Dead 80.00

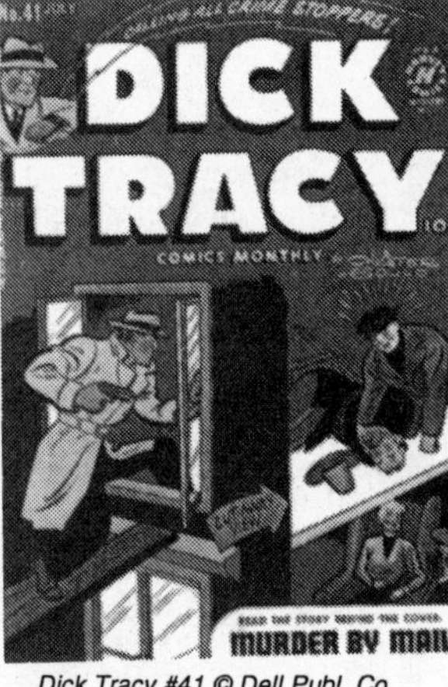

Dick Tracy #41 © Dell Publ. Co.

50 ChG,Pt.2'Killer Who Returned From the Dead' . . . 80.00
51 ChG,'Case of the High Tension Hijackers' 75.00
52 ChG,'Case of the Pipe-Stem Killer 75.00
53 ChG,Pt.1'Dick Tracy Meets the Murderous Midget' 75.00
54 ChG,Pt.2'Dick Tracy Meets the Murderous Midget' 75.00
55 ChG,Pt.3'Dick Tracy Meets the Murderous Midget' 75.00
56 ChG,'Case of the Teleguard Terror' 75.00
57 ChG,Pt.1'Case of the Ice Cold Killer' 100.00
58 ChG,Pt.2'Case of the Ice Cold Killer' 75.00
59 ChG,Pt.1'Case of the Million Dollar Murder' 75.00
60 ChG,Pt.2'Case of the Million Dollar Murder' 60.00
61 ChG,'Case of the Murderers Mask' 60.00
62 ChG,Pt.1'Case of the White Rat Robbers' 60.00
63 ChG,Pt.2'Case of the White Rat Robbers' 60.00
64 ChG,Pt.1'Case of the Interrupted Honeymoon' 60.00
65 ChG,Pt.2'Case of the Interrupted Honeymoon' 60.00
66 ChG,Pt.1'Case of the Killer's Revenge' 60.00
67 ChG,Pt.2'Case of the Killer's Revenge' 60.00
68 ChG,Pt.1'Case of the TV Terror' 60.00
69 ChG,Pt.2'Case of the TV Terror' 60.00
70 ChG,Pt.3'Case of the TV Terror' 60.00
71 ChG,A:Mrs. Forchune,Opal . . 60.00
72 ChG,A:Empty Wiliams,Bonny 60.00
73 ChG,A:Bonny Braids 60.00
74 ChG,A:Mr. & Mrs. Fortson Knox 60.00
75 ChG,A:Crewy Lou, Sphinx . . 60.00
76 ChG,A:Diet Smith,Brainerd . . 60.00
77 ChG,A:Crewy Lou, Bonny Braids 60.00
78 ChG,A:Spinner Records 60.00
79 ChG,A:Model Jones, Larry Jones 60.00
80 ChG,A:Tonsils,Dot View 60.00
81 ChG,A:Edward Moppet,Tonsils 60.00
82 ChG,A:Dot View,Mr. Crime . . 60.00
83 ChG,A:Rifle Ruby,Newsuit Nan 60.00
84 ChG,A:Mr. Crime,Newsuit Nan 60.00
85 ChG,A:Newsuit Nan, Mrs.Lava 60.00
86 ChG,A:Mr. Crime, Odds Zonn 60.00
87 ChG,A:Odds Zonn,Wingy . . . 60.00
88 ChG,A:Odds Zonn,Wingy . . . 60.00
89 ChG,Pt.1'Canhead' 60.00
90 ChG,Pt.2'Canhead' 60.00
91 ChG,Pt.3'Canhead' 60.00
92 ChG,Pt.4'Canhead' 60.00
93 ChG,Pt.5'Canhead' 60.00
94 ChG,Pt.6'Canhead' 60.00
95 ChG,A:Mrs. Green,Dewdrop . 60.00
96 ChG,A:Dewdrop,Sticks 60.00
97 ChG,A:Dewdrop,Sticks 60.00
98 ChG,A:Open-Mind Monty, Sticks 60.00
99 ChG,A:Open-Mind Monty, Sticks 70.00
100 ChG,A:Half-Pint,Dewdrop . . 75.00
101 ChG,A:Open-Mind Monty . . 60.00
102 ChG,A:Rainbow Reiley,Wingy 60.00
103 ChG,A:Happy,Rughead 60.00
104 ChG,A:Rainbow Reiley,Happy 60.00
105 ChG,A:Happy,Rughead 60.00
106 ChG,A:Fence,Corny,Happy . 60.00
107 ChG,A:Rainbow Reiley 60.00
108 ChG,A:Rughead,Corny,Fence 60.00
109 ChG,A:Rughead,Mimi,Herky 60.00
110 ChG,A:Vitamin Flintheart . . . 60.00
111 ChG,A:Shoulders,Roach . . . 60.00
112 ChG,A:Brilliant,Diet Smith . . 60.00
113 ChG,A:Snowflake Falls 60.00
114 ChG,A:'Sketch'Paree, ... 60.00
115 ChG,A:Rod & Nylon Hoze . . 60.00
116 ChG,A:Empty Williams 60.00
117 ChG,A:Spinner Records . . . 60.00
118 ChG,A:Sleet 60.00
119 ChG,A:Coffyhead 60.00
120 ChG,'Case Against Mumbles Quartet' 50.00
121 ChG,'Case of the Wild Boys' 50.00
122 ChG,'Case of the Poisoned Pellet' 50.00
123 ChG,'Case of the Deadly Treasure Hunt' 50.00

124 ChG,'Case of Oodles Hears Only Evil 50.00
125 ChG,'Case of the Desparate Widow' 50.00
126 ChG,'Case of Oodles' Hideout' 50.00
127 ChG,'Case Against Joe Period' 50.00
128 ChG,'Case Against Juvenile Delinquent' 50.00
129 ChG,'Case of Son of Flattop' 50.00
130 ChG,'Case of Great Gang Roundup' 50.00
131 ChG,'Strange Case of Flattop's Conscience' 55.00
132 ChG,'Case of Flattop's Big Show' 55.00
133 ChG,'Dick Tracy Follows Trail of Jewel Thief Gang' 50.00
134 ChG,'Last Stand of Jewel Thieves' 50.00
135 ChG,'Case of the Rooftop Sniper' 50.00
136 ChG,'Mystery of the Iron Room' 50.00
137 ChG,'Law Versus Dick Tracy' 50.00
138 ChG,'Mystery of Mary X' . . . 50.00
139 ChG,'Yogee the Merciless' . 50.00
140 ChG,'The Tunnel Trap' 50.00
141 ChG,'Case of Wormy & His Deadly Wagon 50.00
142 ChG,'Case of the Killer's Revenge' 50.00
143 ChG,'Strange Case of Measles' 50.00
144 ChG,'Strange Case of Shoulders' 50.00
145 ChG,'Case of the Feindish Photo-graphers';April, 1961 . . 50.00

DIME COMICS
Newsbook Publ. Corp.
1945

1 LbC,A:Silver Streak 125.00

DING DONG
Compix
(Magazine Enterprises)
1947

1 (fa) 50.00
2 (fa) 30.00
3 thru 5 (fa) . . . . @25.00

DINKY DUCK
St. John Publ. Co./Pines
November, 1951

1 . . . . 30.00
2 . . . . 20.00
3 thru 10 . . . . @15.00
11 thru 15 . . . . @10.00
16 thru 18 . . . . @7.00
19 Summer, 1958 . . . . 7.00

DIXIE DUGAN
Columbia Publ./
Publication Enterprises
July, 1942

1 Boxing cover,Joe Palooka . . 150.00
2 . . . . 75.00
3 . . . . 60.00
4 . . . . 45.00
5 . . . . 45.00
6 thru 12 . . . . @28.00
13 1949 . . . . 28.00

DIZZY DAMES
B&M Distribution Co.
(American Comics)
September-October, 1952

1 . . . . 45.00
2 . . . . 30.00
3 thru 6 July-Aug., 1953 . . . @20.00

DIZZY DON COMICS
Howard Publications/
Dizzy Dean Ent.
1943

1 B&W interior 45.00
2 B&W Interior 20.00
3 B&W Interior 15.00
4 B&W Interior 15.00
5 thru 21 . . . . @15.00
22 October, 1946 . . . . 40.00
1a 30.00
2a 30.00
3a 30.00

DIZZY DUCK
(see BARNYARD COMICS)

DOC CARTER V.D. COMICS
Health Publ. Inst.
1949

N# 125.00
N# 100.00

DOC SAVAGE COMICS
Street & Smith Publications
May, 1940

1 B:Doc Savage, Capt. Fury, Danny Garrett, Mark Mallory, Whisperer, Capt. Death, Treasure Island, A: The Magician . . 1,600.00
2 O:Ajax,The Sun Man,E:The Whisperer 600.00
3 Artic Ice Wastes 500.00
4 E:Treasure Island, Saves U.S. Navy 450.00

Doc Savage Comics #5
© Street & Smith Publications

5 O:Astron, the Crocodile Queen, Sacred Ruby 350.00
6 E: Capt. Fury, O:Red Falcon, Murderous Peace Clan . . . 275.00
7 V:Zoombas 275.00
8 Finds the Long Lost Treasure 275.00
9 Smashes Japan's Secret Oil Supply 275.00
10 O:Thunder Bolt, The Living Dead A:Lord Manhattan . . . 275.00
11 V:Giants of Destruction 225.00
12 Saves Merchant Fleet from Complete Destruction 225.00
2-1 The Living Evil 225.00
2-2 V:Beggar King 225.00
2-3 . . . . 225.00
2-4 Fight to Death 225.00
2-5 Saves Panama Canal from Blood Raider 225.00
2-6 . . . . 225.00
2-7 V:Black Knight 225.00
2-8 October, 1943 . . . . 225.00

DR. ANTHONY KING HOLLYWOOD LOVE DOCTOR
Harvey, Publ.
1952

1 . . . . 50.00
2 . . . . 30.00
3 . . . . 30.00
4 BP,May, 1954 . . . . 30.00

DOLL MAN
Comic Favorites
(Quality Comics Group)
Fall, 1941

1 RC,B:Doll Man & Justine Wright 1,000.00
2 B:Dragon 600.00
3 Five stories 425.00
4 Dolls of Death, Wanted: The Doll Man 400.00
5 Four stories 300.00
6 Buy War Stamps cover . . . 225.00
7 Four stories 225.00
8 BWa,Three stories,A:Torchy 275.00
9 . . . . 200.00
10 V:Murder Marionettes, Grim, The Good Sport 150.00
11 Shocks Crime Square in the Eye 150.00
12 . . . . 150.00
13 Blows Crime Sky High 150.00

Doll Man #45 © Quality Comics Group

14 Spotlight on Comics 150.00
15 Faces Danger 150.00
16 . . . . 150.00
17 Deals out Punishment for Crime 150.00
18 Redskins Scalp Crime 150.00
19 Fitted for a Cement Coffin . . 150.00
20 Destroys the Black Heart of Nemo Black 150.00
21 Problem of a Poison Pistol . 125.00
22 V:Tom Thumb 125.00
23 V:Minstrel, musician of menace 125.00
24 V:Elixir of Youth 125.00
25 V:Thrawn, Lord of Lightning 125.00
26 V:Sultan of Satarr &

Wonderous Runt 125.00
27 Space Conquest 125.00
28 V:The Flame 125.00
29 V:Queen MAB 125.00
30 V:Lord Damion 125.00
31 I:Elmo, the Wonder Dog . . . 110.00
32 A:Jeb Rivers 110.00
33 . . . . 110.00
34 . . . . 110.00
35 Prophet of Doom 110.00
36 Death Trap in the Deep . . . 110.00
37 V:The Skull,B:Doll Girl, Bondage(c) 150.00
38 The Cult of Death 100.00
39 V:The Death Drug 120.00
40 Giants of Crime 80.00
41 The Headless Horseman . . . 80.00
42 Tale of the Mind Monster . . . 80.00
43 The Thing that Kills 80.00
44 V:Radioactive Man 80.00
45 What was in the Doom Box? . 80.00
46 Monster from Tomorrow 80.00
47 V:Mad Hypnotist, October, 1953 . . . . 80.00

FAMOUS GANG, BOOK OF COMICS
Firestone Tire & Rubber Co.
1942

N# 600.00

Becomes:

DONALD AND MICKEY MERRY CHRISTMAS

N# (2),CB 450.00
N# (3),CB 425.00
N# (4),CB 550.00
N# (5),CB 400.00
N# (6),CB 350.00
N# (7),CB 325.00
N# (8),CB 400.00

DONALD AND MICKEY
Firestone

Donald & Mickey Merry Xmas(1943) 450.00
Donald & Mickey Merry Xmas(1944) 400.00
Donald & Mickey Merry Xmas(1945) 525.00
Donald & Mickey Merry Xmas(1946) 400.00
Donald & Mickey Merry Xmas(1947) 350.00
Donald & Mickey Merry Xmas(1948) 325.00
Donald & Mickey Merry Xmas(1949) 375.00

DONALD DUCK
Whitman

W.Disney's Donald Duck ('35) 1,000.00
W.Disney's Donald Duck ('36) . 600.00
W.Disney's Donald Duck ('38) 2,000.00

DONALD DUCK GIVEAWAYS

Donald Duck Surprise Party (Icy Frost Ice Cream 1948)WK . 900.00
Donald Duck (Xmas Giveaway 1944) 350.00
Donald Duck Tells About Kites (P.G.&E., Florida 1954) . . . 2,000.00
Donald Duck Tells About Kites (S.C.Edison 1954) 1,800.00
Donald Duck and the Boys (Whitman 1948) 125.00
Donald Ducks Atom Bomb (Cherrios 1947) 275.00

Donald Duck #62
© Dell Publishing Co.

(WALT DISNEY'S) DONALD DUCK
Dell Publishing Co.
November 1952

(#1-#25) See Dell Four Color
26 CB;"Trick or Treat" (1952) . . 225.00
27 CB(c);"Flying Horse"('53) . . . 45.00
28 CB(c); Robert the Robot 45.00
29 CB(c) 45.00
30 CB(c) 40.00
31 thru 39 . . . . @30.00
40 thru 44 . . . . @25.00
45 CB 70.00
46 CB; "Secret of Hondorica" . . . 75.00
47 thru 51 . . . . @22.00
52 CB; "Lost Peg-Leg Mine" . . . 70.00
53 . . . . 20.00
54 CB; "Forbidden Valley" 75.00
55 thru 59 . . . . @20.00
60 CB; "Donald Duck & the Titanic Ants" 70.00
61 thru 67 . . . . @15.00
68 CB 30.00
69 thru 78 . . . . @15.00
79 CB (1 page) 18.00
80 . . . . 15.00
81 CB (1 page) 18.00
82 . . . . 15.00
83 . . . . 15.00
84 . . . . 15.00

See: Independent Color Listings

DON FORTUNE MAGAZINE
Don Fortune Publ. Co.
August, 1946

1 CCB 90.00
2 CCB 60.00
3 CCB,Bondage(c) 40.00
4 CCB 40.00
5 CCB 40.00
6 CCB, January, 1947 . . . . 40.00

DON NEWCOMBE
Fawcett Publications
1950

1 Baseball Star 250.00

DON WINSLOW OF THE NAVY
Fawcett Publ./ Charlton Comics
February, 1943

1 Captain Marvel cover 500.00
2 Nips the Nipponese in the Solomons 250.00
3 Single-Handed invasion of the Philippines 200.00
4 Undermines the Nazis! 150.00
5 Stolen Battleship Mystery . . 150.00
6 War Stamps for Victory cover 150.00
7 Coast Guard 125.00
8 U.S. Marines 125.00
9 Fighting Marines 125.00
10 Fighting Seabees 125.00
11 . . . . 75.00
12 Tuned for Death 75.00
13 Hirohito's Hospitality 80.00
14 Catapults against the Axis . . 80.00
15 Fighting Merchant Marine . . . 70.00
16 V:The Most Diabolical Villain of all Time 70.00
17 Buy War Stamps cover 70.00
18 The First Underwater Convoy 65.00
19 Bonape Excersion 65.00
20 The Nazi Prison Ship 65.00
21 Prisoner of the Nazis 50.00

Don Winslow of the Navy #6
© Fawcett Publications

22 Suicide Football 50.00
23 Peril on the High Seas 50.00
24 Adventures on the High Seas 50.00
25 Shanghaied Red Cross Ship . 50.00
26 V:The Scorpion 50.00
27 Buy War Stamps 50.00
28 . . . . 50.00
29 Invitation to Trouble 50.00
30 . . . . 50.00
31 Man or Myth? 45.00
32 Return of the Renegade 45.00
33 Service Ribbons 45.00
34 Log Book 45.00
35 . . . . 45.00
36 . . . . 45.00
37 V: Sea Serpent 45.00
38 Climbs Mt. Everest 45.00
39 Scorpion's Death Ledger . . . 45.00
40 Kick Off! 50.00
41 Rides the Skis! 40.00
42 Amazon Island 40.00
43 Ghastly Doll Murder Case . . . 40.00
44 The Scorpions Web 40.00
45 V:Highwaymen of the Seas . . 40.00

46 Renegades Jailbreak 40.00
47 The Artic Expedition 40.00
48 Maelstrom of the Deep 40.00
49 The Vanishing Ship! 40.00
50 V:The Snake 40.00
51 A:Singapore Sal 35.00
52 Ghost of the Fishing Ships . . 35.00
53 . . . . 35.00
54 . . . . 35.00
55 . . . . 35.00
56 Far East 35.00
57 A:Singapore Sal 35.00
58 . . . . 35.00
59 . . . . 35.00
60 . . . . 35.00
61 . . . . 35.00
62 . . . . 35.00
63 . . . . 35.00
64 MB 50.00
65 Ph(c) 45.00
66 Ph(c) 45.00
67 Ph(c) 45.00
68 Ph(c) 45.00
69 Ph(c), Jaws of Destruction . . 45.00
70 . . . . 35.00
71 . . . . 35.00
72 . . . . 35.00
73 September, 1955 . . . . 35.00

DOPEY DUCK
Non-Pareil Publ. Corp.
Fall, 1945

1 A:Krazy Krow,Casper Cat . . . 75.00
2 same 70.00

Becomes:

WACKY DUCK

3 . . . . 55.00
4 . . . . 40.00
5 . . . . 40.00
6 Summer, 1947 . . . . 40.00

DOROTHY LAMOUR
(see JUNGLE LIL)

DOTTY DRIPPLE
Magazine Enterprises/ Harvey Publications
1946

1 . . . . 30.00
2 . . . . 15.00
3 thru 10 . . . . @10.00
11 thru 20 . . . . @7.00
21 thru 23 . . . . @5.00
24 June, 1952 . . . . 5.00

Becomes:

HORACE & DOTTY DRIPPLE

25 thru 42 . . . . @6.00
43 October, 1955 . . . . 6.00

DOUBLE COMICS
Elliot Publications

1 ('40),Masked Marvel 1,000.00
2 ('41),Tornado Tim 750.00
3 ('42) 600.00
4 ('43) 500.00
5 ('44) 500.00

DOUBLE UP
Elliot Publications
1941

1 . . . . 425.00

DOWN WITH CRIME
Fawcett Publications
November, 1951

1 A:Desarro 100.00
2 BP, A:Scanlon Gang 60.00
3 H-is for Heroin 55.00
4 BP, A:Desarro 50.00
5 No Jail Can Hold Me 55.00
6 The Puncture-Proof Assassin 40.00
7 The Payoff, November, 1952 40.00

DUDLEY
Prize Publications
November-December, 1952

1 . . . . 70.00
2 . . . . 40.00
3 March-April, 1950 . . . . 35.00

DUMBO WEEKLY
The Walt Disney Co.
1942

1 Gas giveaways 175.00
2 thru 16 . . . . @85.00

DURANGO KID
Magazine Enterprises
October-November, 1949

1 FF, Charles Starrett photo cover B:Durango Kid & Raider . . 400.00
2 FF, Charles Starrett Ph(c) . . 250.00
3 FF, Charles Starrett Ph(c) . 225.00
4 FF, Charles Starrett Ph(c), Two-Timing Guns 200.00
5 FF, Charles Starrett Ph(c), Tracks Across the Trail . . . 200.00
6 FF 125.00
7 FF,Atomic(c) 135.00
8 FF 125.00
9 FF 125.00
10 FF 125.00
11 FF 100.00
12 FF 100.00
13 FF 100.00
14 FF 100.00
15 FF 100.00
16 FF 100.00
17 O:Durango Kid 120.00
18 FMe,DAy(c) 55.00
19 FMe,FG 50.00
20 FMe,FG 50.00
21 FMe,FG 50.00
22 FMe,FG 55.00
23 FMe,FG,I:Red Scorpion 55.00
24 thru 30 FMe,FG . . . . @55.00
31 FMe,FG 55.00
32 thru 40 FG . . . . @50.00
41 FG,October, 1941 . . . . 60.00

DYNAMIC COMICS
Dynamic Publications
(Harry 'A' Chesler)
October, 1941

1 EK,O:Major Victory, Dynamic Man, Hale the Magician, A:Black Cobra 600.00
2 O:Dynamic Boy & Lady Satan,I:Green Knight, Lance Cooper 300.00
3 GT 250.00
8 Horror cover 250.00
9 MRa,GT,B:Mr.E 275.00
10 . . . . 200.00
11 GT 175.00
12 GT 175.00
13 GT 175.00
14 . . . . 150.00
15 . . . . 150.00
16 GT,Bondage(c),Marijuana . . 175.00
17 . . . . 225.00
18 Ric 150.00
19 A:Dynamic Man 100.00
20 same,Nude Woman 135.00
21 same 100.00
22 same 100.00
23 A:Yankee Girl,1.0948 . . . . . 100.00

DYNAMITE
Comic Media/Allen Hardy Publ.
May, 1953

1 DH(c),A:Danger#6 . . . . 80.00
2 . . . . 45.00
3 PAM,PAM(c),B:Johnny Dynamite,Drug 55.00
4 PAM,PAM(c),Prostitution 75.00
5 PAM,PAM(c) 35.00
6 PAM,PAM(c) 35.00
7 PAM,PAM(c) 35.00
8 PAM,PAM(c) 35.00
9 PAM,PAM(c) 35.00

Becomes:

JOHNNY DYNAMITE
Charlton Comics

10 PAM(c) 30.00
11 . . . . 30.00
12 . . . . 30.00

Becomes:

FOREIGN INTRIGUES

13 A:Johnny Dynamite 25.00
14 same 20.00
15 same 20.00

Becomes:

BATTLEFIELD ACTION

16 . . . . 20.00
17 . . . . 10.00
18 . . . . 10.00
19 . . . . 10.00
20 . . . . 10.00
21 thru 30 . . . . @7.00
31 thru 70 . . . . @3.00
71 thru 84 October 1984 . . . . . @1.00

EAGLE, THE
Fox Features Syndicate
July, 1941

1 B:The Eagle,A:Rex Dexter of Mars 700.00
2 B:Spider Queen 425.00
3 B:Joe Spook 350.00
4 January, 1942 . . . . 325.00

EAGLE
Rural Home Publ.
February-March, 1945

1 LbC 90.00
2 LbC,April-May, 1945 . . . . . . 75.00

EAT RIGHT TO WORK AND WIN
Swift Co.
1942

N# Flash Gordon,Popeye . . . 175.00

EDDIE STANKY
Fawcett Publications
1951

N# New York Giants 150.00

EERIE
Avon Periodicals
May-June, 1951

1 JKa,Horror from the Pit, Bondage(c) 400.00
2 WW,WW(c), Chamber of Death 250.00
3 WW,WW(c),JKa,JO Monster of the Storm 250.00
4 WW(c),Phantom of Reality . 225.00
5 WW(c), Operation Horror . . 225.00
6 Devil Keeps a Date 100.00
7 WW(c),JKa,JO,Blood for the Vampire 175.00
8 EK, Song of the Undead . . 100.00
9 JKa, Hands of Death 120.00
10 Castle of Terror 100.00
11 Anatomical Monster 85.00
12 Dracula 120.00
13 . . . . 100.00
14 Master of the Dead 100.00
15 . . . . 60.00
16 WW, Chamber of Death 75.00
17 WW(c),JO,JKa,August-

September,1954 . . . . 100.00

Eerie #5 © Avon Periodicals

EERIE ADVENTURES
Approved Comics
(Ziff-Davis)
Winter, 1951

1 BP,JKa,Bondage 125.00

EGBERT
Arnold Publications/
Comic Magazine
Spring, 1946

1 I:Egbert & The Count 90.00
2 . . . . 50.00
3 . . . . 25.00
4 . . . . 25.00
5 . . . . 25.00
6 thru 10 . . . . @25.00
11 thru 17 . . . . @20.00
18 1950 . . . . 20.00

EH!
Charlton Comics
December, 1953

1 DAy(c),DG 125.00
2 DAy(c) 80.00
3 DAy(c) 70.00
4 DAy(c) 70.00
5 DAy(c) 70.00
6 DAy(c) 70.00
7 DAy(c),November, 1954 . . . . 70.00

EL BOMBO COMICS
Frances M. McQueeny
1945

1 . . . . 50.00

ELLERY QUEEN
Superior Comics
May, 1949

1 LbC(c),JKa,Horror 200.00
2 . . . . 125.00
3 Drug issue 135.00
4 The Crooked Mile,
November, 1949 . . . . 125.00

ELLERY QUEEN
Approved Comics
(Ziff-Davis)
January-March, 1952

1 NS(c),The Corpse the Killed 200.00
2 NS,Killer's Revenge,
Summer, 1952 . . . . 175.00

ELSIE THE COW
D.S. Publishing Co.
October-November, 1949

1 P(c) 150.00
2 Bondage(c) 175.00
3 July-August, 1950 . . . . 150.00

ENCHANTING LOVE
Kirby Publishing Co.
October, 1949

1 Branded Guilty, Ph(c) 45.00
2 Ph(c),BP 28.00
3 Ph(c),Utter Defeat was our
Victory; Jan.-Feb., 1950 . . . . 20.00

ETTA KETT
Best Books, Inc.
(Standard Comics)
December, 1948

11 . . . . 45.00
12 . . . . 30.00
13 . . . . 30.00
14 September, 1949 . . . . 30.00

ERNIE COMICS
(see SCREAM COMICS)

Exciting Comics #3
© Better Publ./Visual Editions

EXCITING COMICS
Better Publ./Visual Editions
(Standard Comics)
April, 1940

1 O:Mask, Jim Hatfield,
Dan Williams 750.00
2 B:Sphinx 400.00
3 V;Robot 250.00
4 V:Sea Monster 225.00
5 V:Gargoyle 225.00
6 . . . . 175.00
7 AS(c) 175.00
8 . . . . 175.00
9 O:Black Terror & Tim,
Bondage(c) 950.00
10 A:Black Terror 300.00
11 same 275.00
12 Bondage(c) 275.00
13 Bondage(c) 275.00
14 O:Sphinx 200.00
15 O:Liberator 225.00
16 Black Terror 150.00
17 same 150.00
18 same 150.00
19 same 150.00
20 E:Mask,Bondage(c) 150.00
21 A:Liberator 160.00
22 O:The Eaglet,
B:American Eagle 165.00
23 Black Terror,B:American
Eagle 125.00
24 Black Terror 125.00
25 Bondage(c) 135.00
26 ASh(c) 125.00
27 ASh(c) 125.00
28 ASh(c) 150.00
29 ASh(c) 150.00
30 ASh(c),Bondage(c) 175.00
31 ASh(c) 150.00
32 ASh(c) 150.00
33 ASh(c) 150.00
34 ASh(c) 150.00
35 ASh(c),E:Liberator 150.00
36 ASh(c) 150.00
37 ASh(c) 150.00
38 ASh(c) 150.00
39 ASh(c)O:Kara, Jungle
Princess 165.00
40 ASh(c) 150.00
41 ASh(c) 150.00
42 ASh(c),B:Scarab 165.00
43 ASh(c) 150.00
44 ASh(c) 150.00
45 ASh(c),V:Robot 150.00
46 ASh(c) 150.00
47 ASh(c) 150.00
48 ASh(c) 150.00
49 ASh(c),E:Kara &
American Eagle 150.00
50 ASh(c),E:American Eagle . 150.00
51 ASh(c),B:Miss Masque 200.00
52 ASh(c),Miss Masque 150.00
53 ASh(c),Miss Masque 150.00
54 ASh(c),E:Miss Masque 150.00
55 ASh(c),O&B:Judy o/t Jungle 200.00
56 ASh(c) 175.00
57 ASh(c) 175.00
58 ASh(c) 175.00
59 ASh(c),FF,Bondage(c) 200.00
60 ASh(c),The Mystery Rider . 150.00
61 ASh(c) 150.00
62 ASh(c) 150.00
63 thru 65 ASh(c) . . . . @150.00
66 . . . . 100.00
67 GT 110.00
68 . . . . 100.00
69 September, 1949 . . . . 100.00

EXCITING ROMANCES
Fawcett Publications
1949

1 Ph(c) 55.00
2 thru 3 . . . . @30.00
4 Ph(c) 35.00
5 thru 14 . . . . @25.00

EXOTIC ROMANCE
(see TRUE WAR ROMANCES)

EXPLORER JOE
Approved Comics
(Ziff-Davis)
Winter, 1951

1 NS,The Fire Opal
of Madagscar 55.00
2 BK, October-November, 1952 75.00

EXPOSED
D.S. Publishing Co.
March-April, 1948

1 Corpses Cash and Carry . . 125.00
2 Giggling Killer 90.00
3 One Bloody Night 40.00
4 JO,Deadly Dummy 40.00
5 Body on the Beach 40.00

 All comics prices listed are for *Near Mint* condition.

6 Grl,The Secret in the Snow 160.00
7 The Gypsy Baron,
July-August, 1949 150.00

EXTRA
Magazine Enterprises
1947

1 250.00

EXTRA!
E.C. Comics
March-April, 1955

1 JCr,RC,JSe 90.00
2 JCr,RC,JSe 60.00
3 JCr,RC,JSe 60.00
4 JCr,RC,JSe 60.00
5 November-December, 1955 60.00

FACE, THE
Publication Enterprises (Columbia Comics)
1942

1 MBi(c),The Face 400.00
2 MBi(c) 275.00

Becomes:

TONY TRENT

3 MBi,A:The Face 65.00
4 1949 55.00

FAIRY TALE PARADE
Dell Publishing Co.
1942

1 WK,Giant 750.00
2 WK,Flying Horse 500.00
3 WK 350.00
4 WK 300.00
5 WK 300.00
6 WK 250.00
7 WK 250.00
8 WK 250.00
9 WK 250.00

FAMOUS COMICS
Zain-Eppy Publ.

N# Joe Palooka 275.00

FAMOUS CRIMES
Fox Features Syndicate
June, 1948

1 Cold Blooded Killer 175.00
2 Near Nudity cover 135.00
3 Crime Never Pays 165.00
4 65.00
5 65.00
6 65.00
7 Drug issue 135.00
8 thru 19 @50.00
20 August, 1951 40.00
51 1952 35.00

FAMOUS FAIRY TALES
K.K. Publication Co.
1942

N# WK, Giveaway 325.00
N# WK, Giveaway 250.00
N# WK, Giveaway 250.00

FAMOUS FEATURE STORIES
Dell Publishing Co.
1938

1 A:Tarzan, Terry and the Pirates
Dick Tracy,Smilin' Jack 475.00

FAMOUS FUNNIES
Eastern Color Printing Co.
1933

N# A Carnival of Comics 6,500.00
N# February, 1934,
1st 10¢ comic 15,000.00
1 July, 1934 11,000.00
2 2,500.00
3 B:Buck Rogers 3,000.00
4 Football cover 800.00

Famous Funnies #22
© Eastern Color Printing Co.

5 600.00
6 550.00
7 550.00
8 550.00
9 550.00
10 550.00
11 Four pages of Buck Rogers 450.00
12 Four pages of Buck Rogers 450.00
13 350.00
14 325.00
15 Football cover 325.00
16 325.00
17 Christmas cover 275.00
18 Four pages of Buck Rogers 400.00
19 325.00
20 300.00
21 Baseball 325.00
22 Buck Rogers 275.00
23 260.00
24 B: War on Crime 250.00
25 250.00
26 250.00
27 G-Men cover 250.00
28 250.00
29 250.00
30 250.00
31 200.00
32 200.00
33 A:Baby Face Nelson &
John Dillinger 200.00
34 200.00
35 Buck Rogers 200.00
36 200.00
37 200.00
38 Portrait,Buck Rogers 185.00
39 200.00
40 200.00
41 thru 50 @135.00
51 thru 57 @125.00
58 Baseball cover 125.00
59 125.00
60 125.00
61 100.00
62 100.00
63 100.00
64 100.00
65 JK 100.00
66 100.00
67 100.00
68 JK 100.00
69 100.00
70 100.00
71 BEv 80.00
72 BEv,B:Speed Spaulding 80.00
73 BEv 80.00
74 BEv 80.00
75 BEv 80.00
76 BEv 80.00
77 BEv,Merry Christmas cover 80.00
78 BEv 80.00
79 BEv 80.00
80 BEv,Buck Rogers 80.00
81 O:Invisible Scarlet O'Neil 70.00
82 Buck Rogers cover 80.00
83 Dickie Dare 70.00
84 Scotty Smith 70.00
85 Eagle Scout,Roy Rogers 70.00
86 Moon Monsters 70.00
87 Scarlet O'Neil 70.00
88 70.00
89 O:Fearless Flint 70.00
90 Bondage cover 75.00
91 60.00
92 60.00
93 60.00
94 War Bonds 70.00
95 Invisible Scarlet O'Neil 65.00
96 65.00
97 War Bonds Promo 65.00
98 65.00
99 65.00
100 Anniversary issue 65.00
101 thru 110 @50.00
111 thru 130 @40.00
131 thru 150 @30.00
151 thru 162 @25.00
163 Valentine's Day cover 30.00
164 25.00
165 25.00
166 25.00
167 25.00
168 25.00
169 AW 50.00
170 AW 50.00
171 thru 190 @25.00
191 thru 203 @20.00
204 War cover 20.00
205 thru 208 @20.00
209 FF(c),Buck Rogers 275.00
210 FF(c),Buck Rogers 275.00
211 FF(c),Buck Rogers 275.00
212 FF(c),Buck Rogers 275.00
213 FF(c),Buck Rogers 275.00
214 FF(c),Buck Rogers 275.00
215 FF(c),Buck Rogers 275.00
216 FF(c),Buck Rogers 275.00
217 22.00
218 July, 1955 22.00

FAMOUS GANG, BOOK OF COMICS
(see DONALD AND MICKEY MERRY CHRISTMAS)

FAMOUS GANGSTERS
Avon Periodicals
April, 1951

1 Al Capone, Dillinger,
Luciano & Shultz 155.00
2 WW(c),Dillinger Machine-
Gun Killer 165.00
3 Lucky Luciano & Murder Inc. 165.00

Becomes:

CRIME ON THE WATERFRONT

4 Underworld Gangsters who
Control the Shipment of Drugs!,
May, 1952 125.00

FAMOUS STARS
Ziff-Davis Publ. Co.
August, 1950

1 OW,Shelley Winter,Susan Peters & Shirley Temple 150.00
2 BEv,Betty Hutton, Bing Crosby100.00
3 OW,Judy Garland, Alan Ladd 100.00
4 RC,Jolson, Bob Mitchum . . . 90.00
5 BK,Elizabeth Taylor, Esther Williams 125.00
6 Gene Kelly, Spring, 1952 . . . 90.00

FAMOUS STORIES
Dell Publishing Co.
1942

1 Treasure Island 150.00
2 Tom Sawyer 150.00

FAMOUS WESTERN BADMEN
(see REDSKIN)

FANTASTIC
(see CAPTAIN SCIENCE)

FANTASTIC COMICS
Fox Features Syndicate
December, 1939

1 LFc(c),I&O:Samson,B:Star Dust, Super Wizard, Space Smith & Capt. Kid 1,500.00
2 BP,LFc(c),Samson destroyed the Battery and Routed the Foe 750.00
3 BP,LF(c),Slays the Iron Monster 550.00

Fantastic #3 © Fox Features Syndicate

4 GT,LFc(c),Demolishes the Closing Torture Walls 500.00
5 GT,LFc(c),Crumbles the Mighty War Machine 500.00
6 JSm(c),Bondage(c) 450.00
7 JSm(c) 450.00
8 GT,Destroys the Mask of Fire,Bondage(c) 450.00
9 Mighty Muscles saved the Drowning Girl 450.00
10 I&O:David 350.00
11 Wrecks the Torture Machine to save his fellow American . 250.00
12 Heaved the Huge Ship high into the Air 250.00
13 . . . . 250.00
14 . . . . 250.00
15 . . . . 250.00
16 E:Stardust 250.00
17 . . . . 250.00
18 I:Black Fury & Chuck 300.00
19 . . . . 250.00
20 . . . . 250.00
21 B&I: The Banshee,Hitler(c) . 300.00
22 . . . . 300.00
23 O:The Gladiator, Nov., 1941 300.00

FARGO KID
(see JUSTICE TRAPS OF THE GUILTY)

FAST FICTION
Seaboard Publ./ Famous Author Illustrated
October, 1949

1 Scarlet Pimpernel 200.00
2 HcK,Captain Blood 175.00
3 She 250.00
4 The 39 Steps 165.00
5 HcK,Beau Geste 165.00

Becomes:

STORIES BY FAMOUS AUTHORS ILLUSTRATED

1a Scarlet Pimpernel 190.00
2a Captain Blood 180.00
3a She 225.00
4a The 39 Steps 125.00
5a Beau Geste 135.00
6 HcK,MacBeth 150.00
7 HcK,Window 125.00
8 HcK,Hamlet 150.00
9 Nicholas Nickleby 135.00
10 HcK,Romeo & Juliet 135.00
11 GS,Ben Hur 145.00
12 GS,La Svengali 145.00
13 HcK,Scaramouche 145.00

FAWCETT FUNNY ANIMALS
Fawcett Publications
December, 1942

1 I:Hoppy the Marvel, Captain Marvel cover 350.00
2 X-Mas Issue 175.00
3 Spirit of '43 . . . . 120.00
4 and 5 . . . . @120.00
6 Buy War Bonds and Stamps . 80.00
7 . . . . 80.00
8 Flag cover 75.00
9 and 10 . . . . @70.00
11 thru 20 . . . . @50.00
21 thru 30 . . . . @30.00
31 thru 40 . . . . @25.00
41 thru 83 . . . . @20.00

Charlton Comics

84 . . . . 25.00
85 thru 91 Feb. 1956 . . . . . . @20.00

FAWCETT MOVIE COMICS
Fawcett Publications
1949

N# Dakota Lil 220.00
N#a Copper Canyon 200.00
N# Destination the Moon 500.00
N# Montana 150.00
N# Pioneer Marshal 150.00
N# Powder River Rustlers . . . 175.00
N# Singing Guns 160.00
7 Gunmen of Abilene 175.00
8 King of the Bull Whip 275.00
9 BP,The Old Frontier 160.00
10 The Missourians 160.00
11 The Thundering Trail 225.00
12 Rustlers on Horseback 165.00
13 Warpath 125.00
14 Last Outpost,RonaldReagan 300.00
15 The Man from Planet-X . . 1,100.00
16 10 Tall Men 100.00

Fawcett Movie Comic #14
© Fawcett Publications

17 Rose Cimarron 55.00
18 The Brigand 65.00
19 Carbine Williams 75.00
20 Ivan hoe, December, 1952 . 125.00

FEATURE BOOKS
David McKay Publications
May, 1937

N# Dick Tracy 4,000.00
N# Popeye 4,000.00
1 Zane Grey's King of the Royal Mounted 500.00
2 Popeye 500.00
3 Popeye and the "Jeep" 450.00
4 Dick Tracy 750.00
5 Popeye and his Poppa 400.00
6 Dick Tracy 600.00
7 Little Orphan Annie 700.00
8 Secret Agent X-9 . . . . 250.00
9 Tracy & the Famon Boys . . . 600.00
10 Popeye & Susan 400.00
11 Annie Rooney 200.00
12 Blondie 400.00
13 Inspector Wade 125.00
14 Popeye in Wild Oats 500.00
15 Barney Baxter in the Air . . . 175.00
16 Red Eagle 100.00
17 Gang Busters 275.00
18 Mandrake the Magician . . . 265.00
19 Mandrake 265.00
20 The Phantom 475.00
21 Lone Ranger 450.00
22 The Phantom 400.00
23 Mandrake in Teibe Castle . . 275.00
24 Lone Ranger 450.00
25 Flash Gordon on the Planet Mongo 500.00
26 Prince Valiant 600.00
27 Blondie 100.00
28 Blondie and Dagwood 90.00
29 Blondie at the Home Sweet Home 90.00
30 Katzenjammer Kids 100.00
31 Blondie Keeps the Home Fires Burning 85.00
32 Katzenjammer Kids 90.00
33 Romance of Flying 70.00
34 Blondie Home is Our Castle . 80.00
35 Katzenjammer Kids 90.00
36 Blondie on the Home Front . . 85.00
37 Katzenjammer Kids 85.00
38 Blondie the ModelHomemaker 75.00
39 The Phantom 300.00
40 Blondie 75.00

All comics prices listed are for *Near Mint* condition.

41 Katzenjammer Kids 80.00
42 Blondie in Home-Spun Yarns 75.00
43 Blondie Home-Cooked Scraps 75.00
44 Katzenjammer Kids in Monkey Business 75.00
45 Blondie in Home of the Free and the Brave 70.00
46 Mandrake in Fire World . . . 200.00
47 Blondie in Eaten out of House and Home 70.00
48 The Maltese Falcon 400.00
49 Perry Mason - The Case of the Lucky Legs 125.00
50 The Shoplifters Shoe, P. Mason 125.00
51 Rip Kirby - Mystery of the Mangler 200.00
52 Mandrake in the Land of X . 200.00
53 Phantom in Safari Suspense 250.00
54 Rip Kirby - Case of the Master Menace 190.00
55 Mandrake in 5-numbers Treasue Hunt 200.00
56 Phantom Destroys the Sky Band 250.00
57 Phantom in the Blue Gang, 1948 . . . . 250.00

FEATURE FUNNIES
Harry A. Chesler Publ./ Comic Favorites
October, 1937

1 RuG,RuG(c),A:Joe Palooka, Mickey Finn, Bungles, Dixie Dugan, Big Top, Strange as It Seems, Off the Record . 1,350.00
2 A: The Hawk 600.00
3 WE,Joe Palooka,The Clock . 450.00
4 RuG,WE,RuG(c),Joe Palooka 300.00
5 WE, Joe Palooka drawing . 300.00

Feature Funnies #6

© Harry A. Chesler Publications

6 WE, Joe Palooka cover . . . 300.00
7 WE,LLe, Gallant Knight story by Vernon Henkel 275.00
8 WE 250.00
9 WE, Joe Palooka story 275.00
10 WE,Micky Finn(c) 250.00
11 WE,LLe,The Bungles(c) . . . 250.00
12 WE, Joe Palooka(c) 275.00
13 WE,LLe, World Series(c) . . 300.00
14 WE,Ned Brant(c) 225.00
15 WE,Joe Palooka(c) 250.00
16 Mickey Finn(c) 225.00
17 WE 225.00
18 Joe Palooka cover 250.00
19 WE,LLe,Mickey Finn(c) 225.00
20 WE,LLe 225.00

Becomes:

FEATURE COMICS

21 Joe Palooka(c) 275.00
22 LLe(c),Mickey Finn(c) 200.00
23 B:Charlie Chan 225.00
24 AAr,Joe Palooka(c) 200.00
25 AAr,The Clock(c) 200.00
26 AAr,The Bundles(c) 200.00
27 WE,AAr,I:Doll Man 1,650.00
28 LF,AAr,The Clock(c) 675.00
29 LF,AAr,The Clock(c) 500.00
30 LF,AAr,Doll Man(c) 500.00
31 LF,AAr,Mickey Finn(c) 325.00
32 PGv,LF,GFx,Doll Man(c) . . . 275.00
33 PGv,LF,GFx,Bundles(c) . . . 250.00
34 PGv,LF,GFx,Doll Man(c) . . . 275.00
35 PGv,LF,GFx,Bundles(c) . . . 250.00
36 PGv,LF,GFx,Doll Man(c) . . . 275.00
37 PGv,LF,GFx,Bundles(c) . . . 250.00
38 PGv,GFx,Doll Man(c) 225.00
39 PGv,GFx,Bundles(c) 200.00
40 PGv,GFx,WE(c),Doll Man(c) 225.00
41 PGv,GFx,WE(c),Bundles(c) . 200.00
42 GFx,Doll Man(c) 150.00
43 RC,GFx,Bundles(c) 125.00
44 RC,GFx,Doll Man(c) 200.00
45 RC,GFx,Bundles(c) 125.00
46 RC,PGv,GFx,Doll Man(c) . . 150.00
47 RC,GFx,Bundles(c) 125.00
48 RC,GFx,Doll Man(c) 150.00
49 RC,GFx,Bundles(c) 125.00
50 RC,GFx,Doll Man(c) 150.00
51 RC,GFx,Bundles(c) 125.00
52 RC,GFx,Doll Man(c) 125.00
53 RC,GFx,Bundles(c) 100.00
54 RC,GFx,Doll Man(c) 125.00
55 RC,GFx,Bundles(c) 100.00
56 RC,GFx,Doll Man(c) 125.00
57 RC,GFx,Bundles(c) 100.00
58 RC,GFx,Doll Man cover . . . 125.00
59 RC,GFx,Mickey Finn(c) 100.00
60 RC,GFx,Doll Man(c) 125.00
61 RC,GFx,Bundles(c) 100.00
62 RC,GFx,Doll Man(c) 110.00
63 RC,GFx,Bundles(c) 100.00
64 BP,GFx,Doll Man(c) 110.00
65 BP,GFx(c),Bundles(c) 100.00
66 BP,GFx,Doll Man(c) 110.00
67 BP 100.00
68 BP,Doll Man vs.BeardedLady 110.00
69 BP,GFx(c),Devil cover 100.00
70 BP,Doll Man(c) 110.00
71 BP,GFx(c) 90.00
72 BP,Doll Man(c) 90.00
73 BP,GFx(c),Bundles(c) 80.00
74 Doll Man(c) 90.00
75 GFx(c) 75.00
76 GFx(c) 75.00
77 Doll Man cover until #140 . . . 80.00
78 Knows no Fear but the Knife Does 75.00
79 Little Luck God 75.00
80 . . . . 75.00
81 Wanted for Murder 65.00
82 V:Shawunkas the Shaman . . 60.00
83 V:Mechanical Man 60.00
84 V:Masked Rider, Death Goes to the Rodeo 60.00
85 V:King of Beasts 60.00
86 Is He A Killer? 60.00
87 The Maze of Murder 60.00
88 V:The Phantom Killer 60.00
89 Crook's Goose 60.00
90 V:Whispering Corpse 60.00
91 V:The Undertaker 60.00
92 V:The Image 60.00
93 . . . . 60.00
94 V:The Undertaker 60.00
95 Flatten's the Peacock's Pride 60.00
96 Doll Man Proves Justice is Blind 60.00
97 V:Peacock 60.00
98 V:Master Diablo 60.00
99 On the Warpath Again! 60.00
100 Crushes the City of Crime . . 75.00
101 Land of the Midget Men! . . . 45.00
102 The Angle 45.00
103 V:The Queen of Ants 45.00
104 V:The Botanist 45.00
105 Dream of Death 45.00
106 V:The Sword Fish 45.00
107 Hand of Horror! 45.00
108 V:Cateye 45.00
109 V:The Brain 45.00
110 V:Fat Cat 45.00
111 V:The Undertaker 45.00
112 I:Mr. Curio & His Miniatures 45.00
113 V:Highwayman 45.00
114 V:Tom Thumb 45.00
115 V:The Sphinx 45.00
116 V:Elbows 45.00
117 Polka Dot on the Spot 45.00
118 thru 143 . . . . @45.00
144 May, 1950 . . . . 45.00

FEDERAL MEN COMICS
Gerard Publ. Co.
1942

2 S&S,Spanking 175.00

FELIX THE CAT
Dell Publishing Co.
Feb.-March 1948

1 . . . . 175.00
2 . . . . 90.00

Felix the Cat #5 © Dell Publishing Co

3 . . . . 65.00
4 . . . . 65.00
5 . . . . 65.00
6 . . . . 50.00
7 . . . . 50.00
8 . . . . 50.00
9 . . . . 50.00
10 . . . . 50.00
11 thru 19 . . . . @45.00

Toby Press

20 thru 30 . . . . @75.00
31 . . . . 25.00
32 . . . . 60.00
33 . . . . 60.00
34 . . . . 25.00
35 . . . . 25.00
36 thru 59 . . . . @60.00
60 . . . . 55.00
61 . . . . 55.00

Harvey

62 thru 80 .... @18.00
81 thru 99 .... @15.00
100 .... 20.00
101 thru 118 .... @12.00
Spec., 100 pgs, 1952 .... 150.00
Summer Ann., 100 pgs. 1953 . 125.00
Winter Ann.,#2 100 pgs, 1954. . 100.00

FERDINAND THE BULL
Dell Publishing Co.
1938

1 .... 100.00

FIGHT AGAINST CRIME
Story Comics
May, 1951

1 Scorpion of Crime Inspector "Brains" Carroway 135.00
2 Ganglands Double Cross ... 60.00
3 Killer Dolan's Double Cross . 50.00
4 Hopped Up Killers - The Con's Slaughter,Drug issue . 65.00
5 Horror of the Avenging Corpse 50.00
6 Terror of the Crazy Killer ... 45.00
7 .... 45.00
8 Killer with the Two-bladed Knife 45.00
9 Rats Die by Gas,Horror 100.00
10 Horror of the Con's Revenge 100.00
11 Case of the Crazy Killer ... 100.00
12 Horror,Drug issue 110.00
13 The Bloodless Killer 100.00
14 Electric Chair cover 110.00
15 .... 100.00
16 RA,Bondage(c) 110.00
17 Knife in Neck(c) 110.00
18 Attempted hanging cover .. 100.00
19 Bondage(c) 110.00
20 Severed Head cover 175.00
21 .... 90.00

Becomes:

FIGHT AGAINST THE GUILTY

22 RA,Electric Chair 100.00
23 March, 1955 .... 60.00

Fight Comics #14
© Fiction House Magazines

FIGHT COMICS
Fight Comics Inc.
(Fiction House Magazines)
January, 1940

1 LF,GT,WE(c),O:Spy Fighter 1,000.00
2 GT,WE(c),Joe Lewis 500.00
3 WE(c),GT,B:Rip Regan, The Powerman 450.00
4 GT,LF(c) 300.00
5 WE(c) 300.00
6 GT,BP(c) 250.00
7 GT,BP(c),Powerman-Blood Money 250.00
8 GT,Chip Collins-Lair of the Vulture 250.00
9 GT,Chip Collins-Prey of the War Eagle 250.00
10 GT,Wolves of the Yukon ... 250.00
11 .... 225.00
12 RA,Powerman-Monster of Madness 225.00
13 Shark Broodie-Legion of Satan 225.00
14 Shark Broodie-Lagoon of Death 225.00
15 Super-American-Hordes of the Secret Dicator 300.00
16 B:Capt.Fight,SwastikaPlague 300.00
17 Super-American-Blaster of the Pig-Boat Pirates 275.00
18 Shark Broodie-Plague of the Yellow Devils 275.00
19 E:Capt. Fight 275.00
20 .... 200.00
21 Rip Carson-Hell's Sky-Riders 150.00
22 Rip Carson-Sky Devil's Mission 150.00
23 Rip Carson-Angels of Vengeance 150.00
24 Baynonets for the Banzai Breed! Bondage(c) 125.00
25 Rip Carson-Samurai Showdown 125.00
26 Rip Carson-Fury of the Sky-Brigade 125.00
27 War-Loot for the Mikado, Bondage(c) 125.00
28 Rip Carson 125.00
29 Rip Carson-Charge of the Lost Region 125.00
30 Rip Carson-Jeep-Raiders of the Torture Jungle 125.00
31 Gangway for the Gyrenes, Decapitation cover 150.00
32 Vengeance of the Hun-Hunters,Bondage(c) 125.00
33 B:Tiger Girl 100.00
34 Bondage(c) 125.00
35 MB 100.00
36 MB 100.00
37 MB 100.00
38 MB,Bondage(c) 125.00
39 MB,Senorita Rio-Slave Brand of the Spider Cult 100.00
40 MB,Bondage cover 125.00
41 MB,Bondage cover 125.00
42 MB 100.00
43 MB,Senorita Rio-The Fire-Brides o/t Lost Atlantis,Bondage(c) 125.00
44 MB,R:Capt. Fight 100.00
45 MB,Tonight Don Diablo Rides 100.00
46 MB 100.00
47 MB,SenoritaRio-Horror's Hacienda 100.00
48 MB 100.00
49 MB,JKa,B:Tiger Girl(c) 100.00
50 MB 100.00
51 MB,O:Tiger Girl 175.00
52 MB,Winged Demons of Doom 85.00
53 MB,Shadowland Shrine 85.00
54 MB,Flee the Cobra Fury 85.00
55 MB,Jungle Juggernaut 85.00
56 MB 85.00
57 MB,Jewels of Jeopardy 85.00
58 MB 85.00
59 MB,Vampires of CrystalCavern 85.00
60 MB,Kraal of Deadly Diamonds 85.00
61 MB,Seekers of the Sphinx, O:Tiger Girl 120.00
62 MB,Graveyard if the Tree Tribe 75.00
63 MB 75.00
64 MB,DawnBeast from Karama-Zan! 75.00
65 Beware the Congo Girl 75.00
66 Man or Ape! 70.00
67 Head-Hunters of Taboo Trek . 70.00
68 Fangs of Dr. Voodoo 70.00
69 Cage of the Congo Fury 70.00
70 Kraal of Traitor Tusks 70.00
71 Captives for the Golden Crocodile 70.00
72 Land of the Lost Safaris 70.00
73 War-Gods of the Jungle 70.00
74 Advengers of the Jungle 70.00
75 Perils of Momba-Kzar 70.00
76 Kraal of Zombi-Zaro 70.00
77 Slave-Queen of the Ape Man 70.00
78 Great Congo Diamond Robbery 75.00
79 A:Space Rangers 75.00
80 .... 60.00
81 E:Tiger Girl(c) 60.00
82 RipCarson-CommandoStrike . 60.00
83 NobodyLoves a Minesweeper 60.00
84 Rip Carson-Suicide Patrol ... 60.00
85 .... 60.00
86 GE,Tigerman,Summer,1954 . 75.00

FIGHTING AMERICAN
Headline Publications
(Prize)
April-May, 1954

1 S&K,O:Fighting American & Speedboy 800.00
2 S&K,S&K(c) 400.00
3 S&K,S&K(c) 350.00
4 S&K,S&K(c) 350.00
5 S&K,S&K(c) 350.00
6 S&K,S&K(c),O:Fighting American 300.00
7 S&K,S&K(c), April-May, 1955 275.00

FIGHTING DAVY CROCKETT
(see KIT CARSON)

FIGHTING INDIANS OF THE WILD WEST
Avon Periodicals
March, 1952

1 EK,EL,Geronimo, Crazy Horse, Chief Victorio 75.00
2 EK,Same, November, 1952 . 45.00

FIGHTING LEATHERNECKS
Toby Press
February, 1952

1 JkS,Duke's Diary 65.00
2 .... 50.00
3 .... 45.00
4 .... 45.00
5 .... 40.00
6 December, 1952 .... 30.00

FIGHTIN' TEXAN
(see TEXAN, THE)

FIGHTING YANK
Nedor Publ./Better Publ.
(Standard Comics)
September, 1942

1 B:Fighting Yank, A:Wonder Man, Mystico, Bondage cover ... 750.00
2 JaB 350.00
3 .... 250.00
4 AS(c) 200.00
5 AS(c) 165.00
6 AS(c) 165.00
7 AS(c),A:Fighting Yank 150.00
8 AS(c) 150.00

Fighting Yank #20 © Standard Comics

9 AS(c) 150.00
10 AS(c) 150.00
11 AS(c), A:Grim Reaper, Nazis bomb Washington cover . . . 125.00
12 AS(c), Hirohito bondage cover 150.00
13 AS(c) 125.00
14 AS(c) 125.00
15 AS(c) 125.00
16 AS(c) 125.00
17 AS(c) 125.00
18 AS(c), A:American Eagle . . 125.00
19 AS(c) 125.00
20 AS(c) 125.00
21 AS(c) A:Kara,Jungle Princess 150.00
22 AS(c) A:Miss Masque-cover story 200.00
23 AS(c) Klu Klux Klan parody cover 150.00
24 A:Miss Masque 140.00
25 JRo,MMe,A:Cavalier 165.00
26 JRo,MMe,A:Cavalier 140.00
27 JRo,MMe,A:Cavalier 140.00
28 JRo,MMe,AW,A:Cavalier . . . 145.00
29 JRo,MMe,August, 1949 . . . 135.00

FILM STAR ROMANCES
Star Publications
January-February, 1950

1 LbC(c), Rudy Valentino story 175.00
2 Liz Taylor & Robert Taylor, photo cover 200.00
3 May-June, 1950, photo cover 150.00

FIREHAIR COMICS
Flying Stories, Inc.
(Fiction House Magazine)
Winter, 1948

1 I:Firehair, Riders on the Pony Express 250.00
2 Bride of the Outlaw Guns . . 125.00
3 Kiss of the Six-Gun Siren! . 100.00
4 . . . . 100.00
5 . . . . 100.00
6 . . . . 90.00
7 War Drums at Buffalo Bend . 90.00
8 Raid on the Red Arrows 90.00
9 French Flags and Tomahawks 90.00
10 Slave Maiden of the Crees . . 90.00
11 Wolves of the Overland Trail,Spring, 1952 . . . . 90.00

FLAME, THE
Fox Feature Syndicate
Summer, 1940

1 LF,O:The Flame 1,300.00
2 GT,LF 600.00
3 BP 400.00
4 . . . . 350.00
5 GT 350.00
6 GT 350.00
7 A:The Yank 350.00
8 The Finger of the Frozen Death!, January, 1942 . . . . 350.00

FLAMING LOVE
Comic Magazines
(Quality Comics Group)
December, 1949

1 BWa,BWa(c),The Temptress I Feared in His Arms 175.00
2 Torrid Tales of Turbulent Passion 75.00
3 BWa,RC,My Heart's at Sea 125.00
4 One Women who made a Mockery of Love, Ph(c) 65.00
5 Bridge of Longing, Ph(c) 65.00
6 Men both Loved & Feared Me, October, 1950 . . . . 65.00

Flash Gordon #2 © Harvey Publications

FLASH GORDON
Harvey Publications
October, 1950

1 AR,Bondage(c) 175.00
2 AR 150.00
3 AR Bondage(c) 165.00
4 AR, April, 1951 . . . . 150.00

FLIP
Harvey Publications
April, 1954

1 HN 110.00
2 HN,BP,June, 1954 . . . . 100.00

FLY BOY
Approved Comics
(Ziff-Davis)
Spring, 1952

1 NS(c),Angels without Wings . 75.00
2 NS(c),Flyboy's Flame-Out, October-November, 1952 . . . 50.00

THE FLYING A'S RANGE RIDER
Dell Publishing Co.
June-August, 1953

(1) = *Dell Four Color #404*
2 Ph(c) all 40.00
3 . . . . 35.00
4 . . . . 35.00
5 . . . . 35.00
6 . . . . 35.00
7 . . . . 35.00
8 . . . . 35.00
9 . . . . 35.00
10 . . . . 35.00
11 . . . . 30.00
12 . . . . 30.00
13 . . . . 30.00
14 . . . . 30.00
15 . . . . 30.00
16 . . . . 30.00
17 ATh 40.00
18 thru 24 . . . . @30.00

FOODINI
Continental Publications
March, 1950

1 . . . . 75.00
2 . . . . 40.00
3 . . . . 35.00
4 August, 1950 . . . . 35.00

FOOTBALL THRILLS
Approved Comics
(Ziff-Davis)
Fall-Winter, 1952

1 BP,NS(c),Red Grange story 150.00
2 NS(c),Bronko Nagurski, Spring,1952 . . . . 125.00

FORBIDDEN LOVE
Comic Magazine
(Quality Comics Group)
March, 1950

1 RC,Ph(c),Heartbreak Road . 400.00
2 Ph(c),I loved a Gigolo 175.00
3 Kissless Bride 175.00
4 BWa,Brimstone Kisses, September, 1950 . . . . 250.00

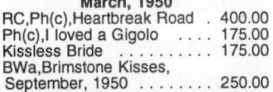

Forbidden Worlds #11
© American Comics Group

FORBIDDEN WORLDS
American Comics Group
July-August, 1951

1 AW,FF 675.00
2 . . . . 350.00
3 AW,WW,JD 375.00
4 Werewolf cover 165.00

5 AW 275.00
6 AW,King Kong cover 235.00
7 125.00
8 125.00
9 Atomic Bomb 150.00
10 JyD 110.00
11 The Mummy's Treasure 85.00
12 Chest of Death 85.00
13 Invasion from Hades 85.00
14 Million-Year Monster 85.00
15 The Vampire Cat 85.00
16 The Doll 85.00
17 85.00
18 The Mummy 85.00
19 Pirate and the Voodoo Queen 85.00
20 Terror Island 85.00
21 The Ant Master 65.00
22 The Cursed Casket 65.00
23 Nightmare for Two 65.00
24 65.00
25 Hallahan's Head 65.00
26 The Champ 65.00
27 SMo,The Thing with the Golden Hair 65.00
28 Portrait of Carlotta 65.00
29 The Frogman 65.00
30 The Things on the Beach 65.00
31 SMo,The Circle of the Doomed 60.00
32 The Invasion of the Dead Things 60.00
33 60.00
34 Atomic Bomb 70.00
35 Comics Code 55.00
36 thru 62 @35.00
63 AW 45.00
64 30.00
65 30.00
66 30.00
67 30.00
68 OW(c) 30.00
69 AW 45.00
70 30.00
71 30.00
72 OW,I:Herbie 150.00
73 30.00
74 30.00
75 JB 30.00
76 AW 40.00
77 30.00
78 AW,OW(c) 40.00
79 thru 85 JB @30.00
86 Flying Saucer 35.00
87 30.00
88 30.00
89 30.00
90 30.00
91 30.00
92 30.00
93 30.00
94 OW(c),A:Herbie 50.00
95 20.00
96 AW 35.00
97 thru 115 @20.00
116 OW(c)A:Herbie 25.00
117 20.00
118 20.00
119 20.00
120 20.00
121 20.00
122 20.00
123 20.00
124 20.00
125 I:O:Magic Man 25.00
126 A:Magic Man 15.00
127 same 15.00
128 same 15.00
129 same 15.00
130 same 15.00
131 same 15.00
132 same 15.00
133 I:O:Dragona 10.00
134 A:Magic Man 15.00
135 A:Magic Man 15.00
136 A:Nemesis 15.00
137 A:Magic Man 15.00
138 A:Magic Man 15.00
139 A:Magic Man 15.00
140 SD,A:Mark Midnight 18.00
141 thru 145 @12.00

FOREIGN INTRIGUES
(see DYNAMITE)

FOUR COLOR
Dell Publishing Co.
1939

N# Dick Tracy 4,000.00
N# Don Winslow of the Navy 900.00
N# Myra North 600.00
4 Disney'sDonaldDuck(1940) 6,000.00
5 Smilin' Jack 500.00
6 Dick Tracy 1,000.00
7 Gang Busters 250.00
8 Dick Tracy 575.00
9 Terry and the Pirates 475.00
10 Smilin' Jack 425.00
11 Smitty 275.00
12 Little Orphan Annie 375.00
13 Walt Disney's Reluctant Dragon (1941) 900.00
14 Moon Mullins 250.00
15 Tillie the Toiler 250.00
16 W.Disney's Mickey Mouse Outwits the Phantom Blob (1941) 5,500.00
17 W.Disney's Dumbo the Flying Elephant (1941) 1,000.00
18 Jiggs and Maggie 275.00
19 Barney Google and Snuffy Smith 275.00
20 Tiny Tim 225.00

Flash Gordon
© Harvey Publications

21 Dick Tracy 500.00
22 Don Winslow 250.00
23 Gang Busters 200.00
24 Captain Easy 225.00
25 Popeye 465.00

[Second Series]

1 Little Joe 350.00
2 Harold Teen 200.00
3 Alley Oop 350.00
4 Smilin' Jack 325.00
5 Raggedy Ann and Andy 350.00
6 Smitty 150.00
7 Smokey Stover 250.00
8 Tillie the Toiler 150.00
9 Donald Duck finds Pirate Gold! 5,500.00
10 Flash Gordon 500.00
11 Wash Tubs 225.00
12 Bambi 325.00
13 Mr. District Attorney 200.00
14 Smilin' Jack 250.00
15 Felix the Cat 450.00
16 Porky Pig 350.00
17 Popeye 350.00
18 Little Orphan Annie's Junior Commandos 300.00
19 W.Disney's Thumper meets the Seven Dwarfs 350.00
20 Barney Baxter 150.00
21 Oswald the Rabbit 250.00
22 Tillie the Toiler 110.00
23 Raggedy Ann and Andy 275.00
24 Gang Busters 200.00
25 Andy Panda 300.00
26 Popeye 325.00
27 Mickey Mouse and the Seven Colored Terror 500.00
28 Wash Tubbs 140.00
29 CB,Donald Duck and the Mummy's Ring 4,500.00
30 Bambi's Children 350.00
31 Moon Mullins 150.00
32 Smitty 150.00
33 Bugs Bunny 400.00
34 Dick Tracy 325.00
35 Smokey Stover 125.00
36 Smilin' Jack 175.00
37 Bringing Up Father 125.00
38 Roy Rogers 600.00
39 Oswald the Rabbit 175.00
40 Barney Google and Snuffy Smith 125.00
41 Mother Goose 175.00
42 Tiny Tim 110.00
43 Popeye 225.00
44 Terry and the Pirates 300.00
45 Raggedy Ann 225.00
46 Felix the Cat and the Haunted House 275.00
47 Gene Autry 300.00
48 CB,Porky Pig of the Mounties 600.00
49 W.Disney's Snow White and the Seven Dwarfs 300.00
50 WK,Fairy Tale Parade 200.00
51 Bugs Bunny Finds the Lost Treasure 250.00
52 Little Orphan Annie 225.00
53 Wash Tubbs 100.00
54 Andy Panda 150.00
55 Tillie the Toiler 75.00
56 Dick Tracy 250.00
57 Gene Autry 260.00
58 Smilin' Jack 175.00
59 WK,Mother Goose 150.00
60 Tiny Folks Funnies 75.00
61 Santa Claus Funnies 150.00
62 CB,Donald Duck in Frozen Gold 1,200.00
63 Roy Rogers-photo cover 350.00
64 Smokey Stover 75.00
65 Smitty 75.00
66 Gene Autry 250.00
67 Oswald the Rabbit 90.00
68 WK,Mother Goose 150.00
69 WK,Fairy Tale Parade 175.00
70 Popeye and Wimpy 175.00
71 WK,Walt Disney's Three Caballeros 600.00
72 Raggedy Ann 175.00
73 The Grumps 75.00
74 Marge's Little Lulu 750.00
75 Gene Autry and the Wildcat 225.00
76 Little Orphan Annie 175.00
77 Felix the Cat 250.00
78 Porky Pig & the Bandit Twins 150.00
79 Mickey Mouse in the Riddle of the Red Hat 550.00
80 Smilin' Jack 125.00
81 Moon Mullins 75.00
82 Lone Ranger 275.00
83 Gene Autry in Outlaw Trail 250.00
84 Flash Gordon 300.00
85 Andy Panda and the

Mad Dog Mystery 100.00
86 Roy Rogers-photo cover . . 250.00
87 WK,Fairy Tale Parade 150.00
88 Bugs Bunny 125.00
89 Tillie the Toiler 60.00
90 WK,Christmas with
Mother Goose 135.00
91 WK,Santa Claus Funnies . . 135.00
92 WK,W.Disney's Pinocchio . . 250.00
93 Gene Autry 175.00
94 Winnie Winkle 75.00
95 Roy Rogers,Ph(c) 225.00
96 Dick Tracy 165.00
97 Marge's Little Lulu 400.00
98 Lone Ranger 250.00
99 Smitty 60.00
100 Gene Autry Comics-photo
cover 175.00
101 Terry and the Pirates 160.00
102 WK,Oswald the Rabbit . . . 110.00
103 WK,Easter with
Mother Goose 135.00
104 WK,Fairy Tale Parade . . . 135.00
105 WK,Albert the Aligator . . . 550.00
106 Tillie the Toiler 50.00
107 Little Orphan Annie 150.00
108 Donald Duck in the
Terror of the River 900.00
109 Roy Rogers Comics 175.00
110 Marge's Little Lulu 275.00
111 Captain Easy 75.00
112 Porky Pig's Adventure in
Gopher Gulch 80.00
113 Popeye 100.00
114 WK,Fairy Tale Parade . . . 125.00
115 Marge's Little Lulu 260.00
116 Mickey Mouse and the
House of Many Mysteries . . 175.00
117 Roy Rogers Comics,
Ph(c) 125.00
118 Lone Ranger 250.00
119 Felix the Cat 225.00
120 Marge's Little Lulu 225.00
121 Fairy Tale Parade 50.00
122 Henry 65.00
123 Bugs Bunny's Dangerous
Venture 95.00
124 Roy Rogers Comics,Ph(c) . 125.00
125 Lone Ranger 165.00
126 WK,Christmas with
Mother Goose 120.00
127 Popeye 100.00
128 WK,Santa Claus Funnies . 125.00
129 W.Disney's Uncle Remus
and his tales of Brer Rabbit . 150.00
130 Andy Panda 50.00
131 Marge's Little Lulu 235.00
132 Tillie the Toiler 50.00
133 Dick Tracy 135.00
134 Tarzan and the Devil Ogre 450.00
135 Felix the Cat 150.00
136 Lone Ranger 150.00
137 Roy Rogers Comics 135.00
138 Smitty 50.00
139 Marge's Little Lulu 225.00
140 WK,Easter with
Mother Goose 120.00
141 Mickey Mouse and the
Submarine Pirates 150.00
142 Bugs Bunny and the
Haunted Mountain 90.00
143 Oswald the Rabbit & the
Prehistoric Egg 40.00
144 Poy Rogers Comics,Ph(c) . 125.00
145 Popeye 100.00
146 Marge's Little Lulu 225.00
147 W.Disney's Donald Duck
in Volcano Valley 600.00
148 WK,Albert the Aligator
and Pogo Possum 450.00
149 Smilin' Jack 70.00
150 Tillie the Toiler 40.00
151 Lone Ranger 125.00
152 Little Orphan Annie 100.00
153 Roy Rogers Comics 100.00

Dell Four Color #151
© Dell Publishing Co.

Dell Four Color #162
© Dell Publishing Co.

154 Andy Panda 50.00
155 Henry 40.00
156 Porky Pig and the Phantom 60.00
157 W.Disney's Mickey Mouse
and the Beanstalk 150.00
158 Marge's Little Lulu 225.00
159 CB,W.Disney's Donald Duck
in the Ghost of the Grotto . . 550.00
160 Roy Rogers Comics,Ph(c) . 100.00
161 Tarzan and the Fires
of Tohr 375.00
162 Felix the Cat 120.00
163 Dick Tracy 120.00
164 Bugs Bunny Finds the
Frozen Kingdom 90.00
165 Marge's Little Lulu 225.00
166 Roy Rogers Comics,Ph(c) . 100.00
167 Lone Ranger 125.00
168 Popeye 90.00
169 Woody Woodpecker,Drug . 120.00
170 W.Disney's Mickey Mouse
on Spook's Island 150.00
171 Charlie McCarthy 90.00
172 WK,Christmas with
Mother Goose 110.00
173 Flash Gordon 110.00
174 Winnie Winkle 40.00
175 WK,Santa Claus Funnies . 120.00
176 Tillie the Toiler 40.00
177 Roy Rogers Comics,Ph(c) . 100.00
178 CB,W.Disney's Donald Duck
Christmas on Bear Mountain 600.00
179 WK,Uncle Wiggily 120.00
180 Ozark the Ike 50.00
181 W.Disney's Mickey Mouse
in Jungle Magic 135.00
182 Porky Pig in Never-
Never Land 55.00
183 Oswald the Rabbit 40.00
184 Tillie the Toiler 40.00
185 WK,Easter with
Mother Goose 120.00
186 W.Disney's Bambi 95.00
187 Bugs Bunny and the
Dreadful Bunny 75.00
188 Woody Woodpecker 50.00
189 W.Disney's Donald Duck in
The Old Castle's Secret . . . 550.00
190 Flash Gordon 110.00
191 Porky Pig to the Rescue . . . 50.00
192 WK,The Brownies 110.00
193 Tom and Jerry 95.00
194 W.Disney's Mickey Mouse
in the World Under the Sea . 140.00
195 Tillie the Toiler 30.00
196 Charlie McCarthy in The
Haunted Hide-Out 75.00
197 Spirit of the Border 65.00
198 Andy Panda 40.00
199 W.Disney's Donald Duck in
Sheriff of Bullet Valley 550.00
200 Bugs Bunny, Super Sleuth . 75.00
201 WK,Christmas with
Mother Goose 110.00
202 Woody Woodpecker 45.00
203 CB,W.Disney's Donald Duck in
The Golden Christmas Tree 400.00
204 Flash Gordon 80.00
205 WK,Santa Claus Funnies . 110.00
206 Little Orphan Funnies 50.00
207 King of the Royal Mounted 100.00
208 W.Disney's Brer Rabbit
Does It Again 80.00
209 Harold Teen 25.00
210 Tippe and Cap Stubbs 22.00
211 Little Beaver 30.00
212 Dr. Bobbs 20.00
213 Tillie the Toiler 30.00
214 W.Disney's Mickey Mouse
and his Sky Adventure 100.00
215 Sparkle Plenty 70.00
216 Andy Panda and the
Police Pup 25.00
217 Bugs Bunny in Court Jester 75.00
218 W.Disney's 3 Little Pigs . . . 65.00
219 Swee'pea 50.00
220 WK,Easter with
Mother Goose 110.00
221 WK,Uncle Wiggly 90.00
222 West of the Pecos 45.00
223 CB,W.Disney's Donald Duck in
Lost in the Andes 500.00
224 Little Iodine 40.00
225 Oswald the Rabbit 25.00
226 Porky Pig and Spoofy 40.00
227 W.Disney's Seven Dwarfs . . 80.00
228 The Mark of Zorro 165.00
229 Smokey Stover 25.00
230 Sunset Press 40.00
231 W.Disney's Mickey Mouse
and the Rajah's Treasure . . 100.00
232 Woody Woodpecker 30.00
233 Bugs Bunny 70.00
234 W.Disney's Dumbo in Sky
Voyage 60.00
235 Tiny Tim 30.00
236 Heritage of the Desert 40.00
237 Tillie the Toiler 30.00

238 CB,W.Disney's Donald Duck
in Voodoo Hoodoo 400.00
239 Adventure Bound 25.00
240 Andy Panda 25.00
241 Porky Pig 40.00
242 Tippie and Cap Stubbs 20.00
243 W.Disney's Thumper
Follows His Nose 60.00
244 WK,The Brownies 85.00
245 Dick's Adventures in
Dreamland 25.00
246 Thunder Mountain 30.00
247 Flash Gordon 75.00
248 W.Disney's Mickey Mouse
and the Black Sorcerer 100.00
249 Woody Woodpecker 30.00
250 Bugs Bunny in
Diamond Daze 70.00
251 Hubert at Camp Moonbeam 25.00
252 W.Disney's Pinocchio 75.00
253 WK,Christmas with
Mother Goose 100.00
254 WK,Santa Claus Funnies . 110.00
255 The Ranger 30.00
256 CB,W.Disney's Donald Duck in
Luck of the North 300.00
257 Little Iodine 30.00
258 Andy Panda and the
Ballon Race 25.00
259 Santa and the Angel 30.00
260 Porky Pig, Hero of the
Wild West 40.00
261 W.Disney's Mickey Mouse
and the Missing Key 100.00
262 Raggedy Ann and Andy ... 35.00
263 CB,W.Disney's Donald Duck in
Land of the Totem Poles ... 300.00
264 Woody Woodpecker in
the Magic Lantern 30.00
265 King of the Royal Mountain . 65.00
266 Bugs Bunny on the Isle of
Hercules 70.00
267 Little Beaver 20.00
268 W.Disney's Mickey Mouse's
Surprise Visitor 100.00
269 Johnny Mack Brown,Ph(c) 150.00
270 Drift Fence 30.00
271 Porky Pig 35.00
272 W.Disney's Cinderella 55.00
273 Oswald the Rabbit 25.00
274 Bugs Bunny 65.00
275 CB,W.Disney's Donald Duck
in Ancient Persia 290.00
276 Uncle Wiggly 35.00
277 PorkyPig in DesertAdventure 40.00
278 Bill Elliot Comics,Ph(c) 90.00
279 W.Disney's Mickey Mouse &
Pluto Battle the Giant Ants . 100.00
280 Andy Panda in the Isle
of the Mechanical Men 25.00
281 Bugs Bunny in The Great
Circus Mystery 40.00
282 CB,W.Disney's Donald Duck in
The Pixilated Parrot 300.00
283 King of the Royal Mounted . 70.00
284 Porky Pig in the Kingdom
of Nowhere 40.00
285 Bozo the Clown 100.00
286 W.Disney's Mickey Mouse
and the Uninvited Guest 90.00
287 Gene Autry's Champion in the
Ghost Of Black Mountain,Ph(c) 60.00
288 Woody Woodpecker 30.00
289 Bugs Bunny in'Indian Trouble'60.00
290 The Chief 30.00
291 CB,W.Disney's Donald Duck in
The Magic Hourglass 300.00
292 The Cisco Kid Comics ... 100.00
293 WK,The Brownies 100.00
294 Little Beaver 30.00
295 Porky Pig in President Pig . 35.00
296 W.Disney's Mickey Mouse
Private Eye for Hire 90.00
297 Andy Panda in The
Haunted Inn 25.00

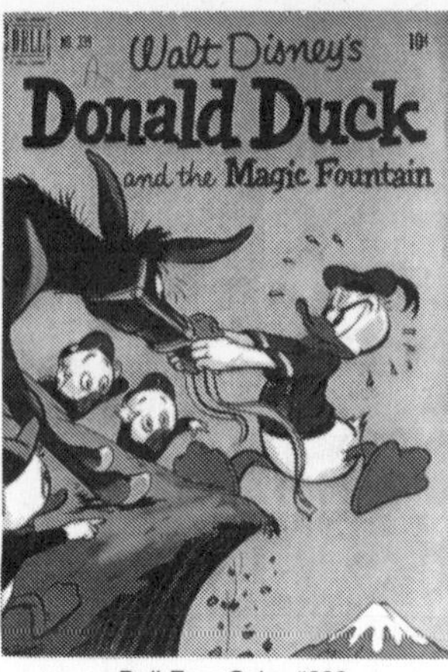

Dell Four Color #339
© Dell Publishing Co.

Dell Four Color #408
© Dell Publishing Co.

298 Bugs Bunny in Sheik
for a Day 60.00
299 Buck Jones & the Iron Trail . 90.00
300 CB,W.Disney's Donald Duck in
Big-Top Bedlam 300.00
301 The Mysterious Rider 30.00
302 Santa Claus Funnies 20.00
303 Porky Pig in The Land of
the Monstrous Flies 25.00
304 W.Disney's Mickey Mouse
in Tom-Tom Island 75.00
305 Woody Woodpecker 20.00
306 Raggedy Ann 25.00
307 Bugs Bunny in Lumber
Jack Rabbit 50.00
308 CB,W.Disney's Donald Duck in
Dangerous Disguise 250.00
309 Dollface and Her Gang 25.00
310 King of the Rotal Mounted . 40.00
311 Porky Pig in Midget Horses
of Hidden Valley 25.00
312 Tonto 75.00
313 W.Disney's Mickey Mouse in
the Mystery of the Double-
Cross Ranch 70.00
314 Ambush 30.00
315 Oswald Rabbit 15.00
316 Rex Allen,Ph(c) 120.00
317 Bugs Bunny in Hare Today
Gone Tomorrow 40.00
318 CB,W.Disney's Donald Duck in
No Such Varmint 250.00
319 Gene Autry's Champion ... 25.00
320 Uncle Wiggly 25.00
321 Little Scouts 10.00
322 Porky Pig in Roaring Rockies 30.00
323 Susie Q. Smith 15.00
324 I Met a Handsome Cowboy . 45.00
325 W.Disney's Mickey Mouse
in the Haunted Castle 75.00
326 Andy Panda 20.00
327 Bugs Bunny and the
Rajah's Treasure 40.00
328 CB,W.Disney's Donald Duck
in Old California 275.00
329 Roy Roger's Trigger,Ph(c) . . 65.00
330 Porky Pig meets the
Bristled Bruiser 25.00
331 Disney's Alice in
Wonderland 60.00
332 Little Beaver 20.00
333 Wilderness Trek 30.00
334 W.Disney's Mickey Mouse
and Yukon Gold 75.00
335 Francis the Famous
Talking Mule 30.00
336 Woody Woodpecker 20.00
337 The Brownies 25.00
338 Bugs Bunny and the
Rocking Horse Thieves 40.00
339 W.Disney's Donald Duck
and the Magic Fountain 55.00
340 King of the Royal Mountain 50.00
341 W.Disney's Unbirthday Party
with Alice in Wonderland 90.00
342 Porky Pig the Lucky
Peppermint Mine 25.00
343 W.Disney's Mickey Mouse in
Ruby Eye of Homar-Guy-Am . 75.00
344 Sergeant Preston from
Challenge of the Yukon 75.00
345 Andy Panda in Scotland Yard 25.00
346 Hideout 30.00
347 Bugs Bunny the Frigid Hare 40.00
348 CB,W.Disney's Donald Duck
The Crocodile Collector 75.00
349 Uncle Wiggly 25.00
350 Woody Woodpecker 20.00
351 Porky Pig and the Grand
Canyon Giant 20.00
352 W.Disney's Mickey Mouse
Mystery of Painted Valley ... 60.00
353 CB(c),W.Disney'sDuckAlbum 40.00
354 Raggedy Ann & Andy 25.00
355 Bugs Bunny Hot-Rod Hair . . 40.00
356 CB(c),W.Disney's Donald
Duck in Rags to Riches 75.00
357 Comeback 25.00
358 Andy Panada 20.00
359 Frosty the Snowman 25.00
360 Porky Pig in Tree Fortune . 20.00
361 Santa Claus Funnies 20.00
362 W.Disney's Mickey Mouse &
the Smuggled Diamonds 60.00
363 King of the Royal Mounted . 35.00
364 Woody Woodpecker 20.00
365 The Brownies 20.00
366 Bugs Bunny Uncle
Buckskin Comes to Town ... 40.00
367 CB,W.Disney's Donald Duck in
A Christmas for Shacktown . 225.00
368 Bob Clampett's
Beany and Cecil 165.00
369 Lone Ranger's Famous
Horse Hi-Yo Silver 55.00
370 Porky Pig in Trouble
in the Big Trees 20.00
371 W.Disney's Mickey Mouse

the Inca Idol Case 55.00
372 Riders of the Purple Sage . . 25.00
373 Sergeant Preston 45.00
374 Woody Woodpecker 20.00
375 John Carter of Mars 175.00
376 Bugs Bunny 40.00
377 Susie Q. Smith 15.00
378 Tom Corbett, Space Cadet 125.00
379 W.Disney's Donald Duck in
Southern Hospitality 60.00
380 Raggedy Ann & Andy 25.00
381 Marge's Tubby 100.00
382 W.Disney's Show White and
the Seven Dwarfs 50.00
383 Andy Panda 15.00
384 King of the Royal Mountain . 35.00
385 Porky Pig 20.00
386 CB,W.Disney's Uncle Scrooge
in Only A Poor Old Man . . . 650.00
387 W.Disney's Mickey Mouse
in High Tibet 65.00
388 Oswald the Rabbit 20.00
389 Andy Hardy Comics 20.00
390 Woody Woodpecker 20.00
391 Uncle Wiggly 20.00
392 Hi-Yo Silver 25.00
393 Bugs Bunny 40.00
394 CB(c),W.Disney's Donald Duck
in Malayalaya 75.00
395 Forlorn River 25.00
396 Tales of the Texas Rangers,
Ph(c) 65.00
397 Sergeant Preston o/t Yukon 45.00
398 The Brownies 20.00
399 Porky Pig in the Lost
Gold Mine 25.00

Dell Four Color #454
© Dell Publishing Co.

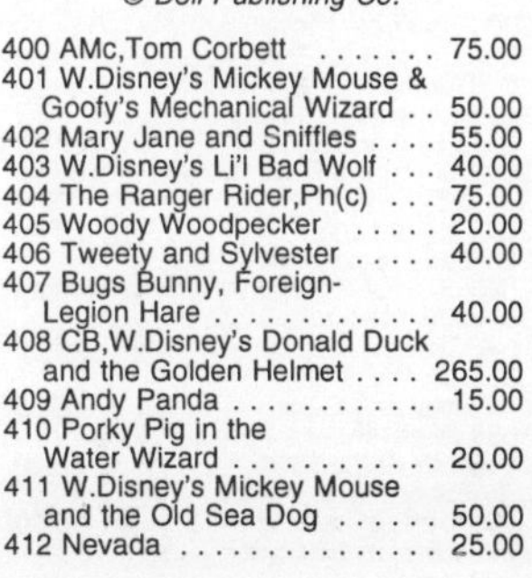

400 AMc,Tom Corbett 75.00
401 W.Disney's Mickey Mouse &
Goofy's Mechanical Wizard . . 50.00
402 Mary Jane and Sniffles 55.00
403 W.Disney's Li'l Bad Wolf . . . 40.00
404 The Ranger Rider,Ph(c) . . . 75.00
405 Woody Woodpecker 20.00
406 Tweety and Sylvester 40.00
407 Bugs Bunny, Foreign-
Legion Hare 40.00
408 CB,W.Disney's Donald Duck
and the Golden Helmet 265.00
409 Andy Panda 15.00
410 Porky Pig in the
Water Wizard 20.00
411 W.Disney's Mickey Mouse
and the Old Sea Dog 50.00
412 Nevada 25.00

413 Disney's Robin Hood(movie),
Ph(c) 50.00
414 Bob Clampett's Beany
and Cecil 125.00
415 Rootie Kazootie 75.00
416 Woody Woodpecker 20.00
417 Double Trouble with Goober 15.00
418 Rusty Riley 30.00
419 Sergeant Preston 35.00
420 Bugs Bunny 25.00
421 AMc,Tom Corbett 75.00
422 CB,W.Disney's Donald Duck
and the Gilded Man 260.00
423 Rhubarb 15.00
424 Flash Gordon 60.00
425 Zorro 100.00
426 Porky Pig 20.00
427 W.Disney's Mickey Mouse &
the Wonderful Whizzix 50.00
428 Uncle Wiggily 20.00
429 W.Disney's Pluto in
Why Dogs Leave Home 40.00
430 Marge's Tubby 55.00
431 Woody Woodpecker 20.00
432 Bugs Bunny and the
Rabbit Olympics 40.00
433 Wildfire 25.00
434 Rin Tin Tin,Ph(c) 140.00
435 Frosty the Snowman 20.00
436 The Brownies 20.00
437 John Carter of Mars 125.00
438 W.Disney's Annie
Oakley (TV) 75.00
439 Little Hiawatha 20.00
440 Black Beauty 20.00
441 Fearless Fagan 15.00

Dell Four Color #462
© Dell Publishing Co.

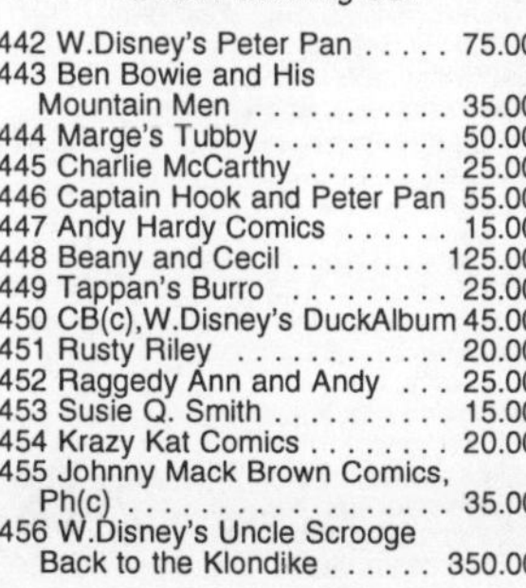

442 W.Disney's Peter Pan 75.00
443 Ben Bowie and His
Mountain Men 35.00
444 Marge's Tubby 50.00
445 Charlie McCarthy 25.00
446 Captain Hook and Peter Pan 55.00
447 Andy Hardy Comics 15.00
448 Beany and Cecil 125.00
449 Tappan's Burro 25.00
450 CB(c),W.Disney's DuckAlbum 45.00
451 Rusty Riley 20.00
452 Raggedy Ann and Andy . . . 25.00
453 Susie Q. Smith 15.00
454 Krazy Kat Comics 20.00
455 Johnny Mack Brown Comics,
Ph(c) 35.00
456 W.Disney's Uncle Scrooge
Back to the Klondike 350.00

457 Daffy 20.00
458 Oswald the Rabbit 15.00
459 Rootie Kazootie 50.00
460 Buck Jones 35.00
461 Marge's Tubby 50.00
462 Little Scouts 10.00
463 Petunia 15.00
464 Bozo 65.00
465 Francis the Talking Mule . . . 10.00
466 Rhubarb, the Millionaire Cat 10.00
467 Desert Gold 25.00
468 W.Disney's Goofy 50.00
469 Beettle Bailey 50.00
470 Elmer Fudd 15.00
471 Double Trouble with Goober 10.00
472 Wild Bill Elliot,Ph(c) 40.00
473 W.Disney's Li'l Bad Wolf . . . 30.00
474 Mary Jane and Sniffles 50.00
475 M.G.M.'s the Two
Mouseketeers 25.00
476 Rin Tin Tin,Ph(c) 40.00
477 Bob Clampett's Beany and
Cecil 125.00
478 Charlie McCarthy 25.00
479 Queen o/t West Dale Evans 100.00
480 Andy Hardy Comics 15.00
481 Annie Oakley and Tagg . . . 45.00
482 Brownies 20.00
483 Little Beaver 20.00
484 River Feud 25.00
485 The Little People 25.00
486 Rusty Riley 20.00
487 Mowgli, the Jungle Book . . . 20.00
488 John Carter of Mars 125.00
489 Tweety and Sylvester 15.00
490 Jungle Jim 22.00

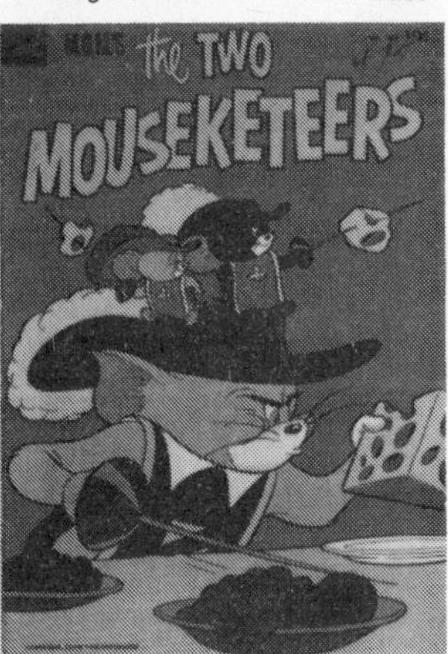

Dell Four Color #475
© Dell Publishing Co.

491 EK,Silvertip 35.00
492 W.Disney's Duck Album . . . 25.00
493 Johnny Mack Brown,Ph(c) . 25.00
494 The Little King 50.00
495 CB, W.Disney's Uncle
Scrooge 275.00
496 The Green Hornet 200.00
497 Zorro, (Sword of) 100.00
498 Bugs Bunny's Album 30.00
499 M.G.M.'s Spike and Tyke . . 15.00
500 Buck Jones 30.00
501 Francis the Famous
Talking Mule 20.00
502 Rootie Kazootie 40.00
503 Uncle Wiggily 20.00
504 Krazy Kat 25.00
505 W.Disney's the Sword and
the Rose (TV),Ph(c) 40.00

506 The Little Scouts 10.00
507 Oswald the Rabbit 15.00
508 Bozo 60.00
509 W.Disney's Pluto 35.00
510 Son of Black Beauty 20.00
511 EK,Outlaw Trail 30.00
512 Flash Gordon 35.00
513 Ben Bowie and His Mountain Men 22.00
514 Frosty the Snowman 20.00
515 Andy Hardy 15.00
516 Double Trouble With Goober 10.00
517 Walt Disney's Chip 'N' Dale 30.00
518 Rivets 15.00
519 Steve Canyon 55.00
520 Wild Bill Elliot,Ph(c) 40.00
521 Beetle Bailey 25.00
522 The Brownies 15.00
523 Rin Tin Tin,Ph(c) 55.00
524 Tweety and Sylvester 15.00
525 Santa Claus Funnies 20.00
526 Napoleon 15.00
527 Charlie McCarthy 20.00
528 Queen o/t West Dale Evans, Ph(c) 60.00
529 Little Beaver 20.00
530 Bob Clampett's Beany and Cecil 100.00
531 W.Disney's Duck Album 25.00
532 The Rustlers 25.00
533 Raggedy Ann and Andy 25.00
534 EK,Western Marshal 30.00
535 I Love Lucy,Ph(c) 265.00
536 Daffy 20.00
537 Stormy, the Thoroughbred 20.00
538 EK,The Mask of Zorro 100.00
539 Ben and Me 20.00
540 Knights of the Round Table, Ph(c) 35.00
541 Johnny Mack Brown,Ph(c) 25.00
542 Super Circus Featuring Mary Hartline 25.00
543 Uncle Wiggly 20.00
544 W.Disney's Rob Roy(Movie), Ph(c) 55.00
545 The Wonderful Adventures of Pinocchio 30.00
546 Buck Jones 30.00
547 Francis the Famous Talking Mule 20.00
548 Krazy Kat 20.00
549 Oswald the Rabbit 15.00
550 The Little Scouts 10.00
551 Bozo 50.00
552 Beetle Bailey 25.00
553 Susie Q. Smith 15.00
554 Rusty Riley 20.00
555 Range War 25.00
556 Double Trouble with Goober 10.00
557 Ben Bowie and His Mountain Men 20.00
558 Elmer Fudd 15.00
559 I Love Lucy,Ph(c) 175.00
560 W.Disney's Duck Album 30.00
561 Mr. Magoo 65.00
562 W.Disney's Goofy 30.00
563 Rhubarb, the Millionaire Cat 10.00
564 W.Disney's Li'l Bad Wolf 20.00
565 Jungle Jim 20.00
566 Son of Black Beauty 15.00
567 BF,Prince Valiant,Ph(c) 100.00
568 Gypsy Cat 18.00
569 Priscilla's Pop 12.00
570 Bob Clampett's Beany and Cecil 65.00
571 Charlie McCarthy 20.00
572 EK,Silvertip 30.00
573 The Little People 20.00
574 The Hand of Zorro 90.00
575 Annie and Oakley and Tagg, Ph(c) 45.00
576 Angel 10.00
577 M.G.M.'s Spike and Tyke 10.00
578 Steve Canyon 30.00
579 Francis the Talking Mule 20.00

Dell Four Color #565
© Dell Publishing Co.

580 Six Gun Ranch 20.00
581 Chip 'N' Dale 15.00
582 Mowgli, the Jungle Book 20.00
583 The Lost Wagon Train 25.00
584 Johnny Mack Brown,Ph(c) 30.00
585 Bugs Bunny's Album 25.00
586 W.Disney's Duck Album 30.00
587 The Little Scouts 8.00
588 MB,King Richard and the Crusaders,Ph(c) 70.00
589 Buck Jones 30.00
590 Hansel and Gretel 30.00
591 EK,Western Marshal 30.00
592 Super Circus 25.00
593 Oswald the Rabbit 10.00
594 Bozo 55.00
595 Pluto 20.00
596 Turok, Son of Stone 400.00
597 The Little King 25.00
598 Captain Davy Jones 15.00
599 Ben Bowie and His Mountain Men 20.00
600 Daisy Duck's Diary 30.00
601 Frosty the Snowman 18.00
602 Mr. Magoo and the Gerald McBoing-Boing 65.00
603 M.G.M.'s The Two Mouseketeers 20.00
604 Shadow on the Trail 25.00
605 The Brownies 20.00
606 Sir Lancelot 50.00
607 Santa Claus Funnies 20.00
608 EK,Silver Tip 30.00
609 The Littlest Outlaw,Ph(c) 25.00
610 Drum Beat,Ph(c) 65.00
611 W.Disney's Duck Album 30.00
612 Little Beaver 15.00
613 EK,Western Marshal 30.00
614 W.Disney's 20,000 Leagues Under the Sea (Movie) 40.00
615 Daffy 15.00
616 To The Last Man 25.00
617 The Quest of Zorro 95.00
618 Johnny Mack Brown,Ph(c) 25.00
619 Krazy Kat 15.00
620 Mowgli, Jungle Book 20.00
621 Francis the Famous Talking Mule 20.00
622 Beetle Bailey 25.00
623 Oswald the Rabbit 10.00
624 Treasure Island,Ph(c) 25.00
625 Beaver Valley 15.00
626 Ben Bowie and His Mountain Men 20.00
627 Goofy 20.00
628 Elmer Fudd 15.00
629 Lady & The Tramp with Jock 20.00
630 Priscilla's Pop 15.00
631 W.Disney's Davy Crockett Indian Fighter (TV),Ph(c) 55.00
632 Fighting Caravans 25.00
633 The Little People 20.00
634 Lady and the Tramp Album 18.00
635 Bob Clampett's Beany and Cecil 100.00
636 Chip 'N' Dale 15.00
637 EK,Silvertip 30.00
638 M.G.M.'s Spike and Tyke 10.00
639 W.Disney's Davy Crockett at the Alamo (TV),Ph(c) 50.00
640 EK,Western Marshal 30.00
641 Steve Canyon 30.00
642 M.G.M.'s The Two Mouseketeers 12.00
643 Wild Bill Elliott,Ph(c) 30.00
644 Sir Walter Raleigh,Ph(c) 40.00
645 Johnny Mack Brown,Ph(c) 25.00
646 Dotty Dripple and Taffy 15.00
647 Bugs Bunny's Album 20.00
648 Jace Pearson of the Texas Rangers,Ph(c) 35.00
649 Duck Album 20.00
650 BF,Prince Valiant 35.00
651 EK,King Colt 25.00
652 Buck Jones 22.00
653 Smokey the Bear 35.00
654 Pluto 20.00
655 Francis the Famous Talking Mule 20.00
656 Turok, Son of Stone 225.00
657 Ben Bowie and His Mountain Men 20.00
658 Goofy 20.00
659 Daisy Duck's Diary 15.00
660 Little Beaver 10.00
661 Frosty the Snowman 15.00
662 Zoo Parade 25.00
663 Winky Dink 35.00
664 W.Disney's Davy Crockett in the Great Keelboat Race (TV),Ph(c) 40.00
665 The African Lion 20.00
666 Santa Claus Funnies 15.00
667 EK,Silvertip and the Stolen Stallion 30.00
668 W.Disney's Dumbo 50.00
668a W.Disney's Dumbo 50.00
669 W.Disney's Robin Hood (Movie),Ph(c) 35.00
669 Robin Hood 20.00
670 M.G.M.'s Mouse Musketeers 10.00
671 W.Disney's Davey Crockett and the River Pirates(TV), Ph(c) 50.00
672 Quentin Durward,Ph(c) 40.00
673 Buffalo Bill Jr.,Ph(c) 45.00
674 The Little Rascals 50.00
675 EK,Steve Donovan,Ph(c) 35.00
676 Will-Yum! 25.00
677 Little King 25.00
678 The Last Hunt,Ph(c) 35.00
679 Gunsmoke 85.00
680 Out Our Way with the Worry Wart 10.00
681 Forever, Darling,Ph(c) 75.00
682 When Knighthood Was in Flower,Ph(c) 25.00
683 Hi and Lois 10.00
684 SB,Helen of Troy,Ph(c) 75.00
685 Johnny Mack Brown,Ph(c) 25.00
686 Duck Album 20.00
687 The Indian Fighter,Ph(c) 30.00
688 SB,Alexander the Great, Ph(c) 45.00
689 Elmer Fudd 10.00
690 The Conqueror, John Wayne Ph(c) 100.00
691 Dotty Dripple and Taffy 10.00
692 The Little People 15.00

 All comics prices listed are for *Near Mint* condition.

693 W.Disney's Brer Rabbit
Song of the South 35.00
694 Super Circus,Ph(c) 25.00
695 Little Beaver 10.00
696 Krazy Kat 15.00
697 Oswald the Rabbit 10.00
698 Francis the Famous
Talking Mule 20.00
699 BA,Prince Valiant 35.00
700 Water Birds and the
Olympic Elk 20.00
701 Jimmy Cricket 30.00
702 The Goofy Success Story . . 20.00
703 Scamp 20.00
704 Priscilla's Pop 10.00
705 Brave Eagle,Ph(c) 25.00
706 Bongo and Lumpjaw 12.00
707 Corky and White Shadow,
Ph(c) 20.00
708 Smokey the Bear 20.00
709 The Searchers,John
Wayne Ph(c) 225.00
710 Francis the Famous
Talking Mule 10.00
711 M.G.M.'s Mouse Musketeers 10.00
712 The Great Locomotive
Chase, Ph(c) 30.00
713 The Animal World 30.00
714 W.Disney's Spin
& Marty (TV) 60.00
715 Timmy 10.00
716 Man in Space 35.00
717 Moby Dick,Ph(c) 55.00
718 Dotty Dripple and Taffy 15.00
719 BF,Prince Valiant 35.00
720 Gunsmoke,Ph(c) 40.00
721 Captain Kangaroo,Ph(c) . . 110.00
722 Johnny Mack Brown,Ph(c) . 25.00
723 EK,Santiago 65.00
724 Bugs Bunny's Album 25.00
725 Elmer Fudd 10.00
726 Duck Album 15.00
727 The Nature of Things 25.00
728 M.G.M.'s Mouse Musketeers 10.00
729 Bob Son of Battle 15.00
730 Smokey Stover 15.00
731 EK,Silvertip and The
Fighting Four 30.00
732 Zorro, (the Challenge of) . . . 85.00
733 Buck Rogers 25.00
734 Cheyenne,C.Walker Ph(c) . . 70.00
735 Crusader Rabbit 175.00
736 Pluto 15.00
737 Steve Canyon 30.00
738 Westward Ho, the Wagons,
Ph(c) 25.00
739 MD,Bounty Guns 20.00
740 Chilly Willy 15.00
741 The Fastest Gun Alive,Ph(c) 35.00
742 Buffalo Bill Jr.,Ph(c) 50.00
743 Daisy Duck's Diary 15.00
744 Little Beaver 10.00
745 Francis the Famous
Talking Mule 20.00
746 Dotty Dripple and Taffy 10.00
747 Goofy 20.00
748 Frosty the Snowman 15.00
749 Secrets of Life,Ph(c) 30.00
750 The Great Cat 30.00
751 Our Miss Brooks,Ph(c) 40.00
752 Mandrake, the Magician . . . 60.00
753 Walt Scott's Little People . . 15.00
754 Smokey the Bear 25.00
755 The Littlest Snowman 20.00
756 Santa Claus Funnies 15.00
757 The True Story of
Jesse James,Ph(c) 65.00
758 Bear Country 20.00
759 Circus Boy,Ph(c) 75.00
760 W.Disney's Hardy Boys(TV) 65.00
761 Howdy Doody 70.00
762 SB,The Sharkfighters,Ph(c) . 75.00
763 GrandmaDuck'sFarmFriends 25.00
764 M.G.M.'s Mouse Musketeers 10.00
765 Will-Yum! 10.00

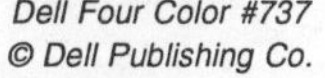

Dell Four Color #737
© Dell Publishing Co.

Dell Four Color #788
© Dell Publishing Co.

766 Buffalo Bill,Ph(c) 25.00
767 Spin and Marty 30.00
768 EK,Steve Donovan, Western
Marshal,Ph(c) 35.00
769 Gunsmoke 40.00
770 Brave Eagle,Ph(c) 15.00
771 MD,Brand of Empire 20.00
772 Cheyenne,C.Walker Ph(c) . . 50.00
773 The Brave One,Ph(c) 20.00
774 Hi and Lois 8.00
775 SB,Sir Lancelot and
Brian,Ph(c) 65.00
776 Johnny Mack Brown,Ph(c) . 25.00
777 Scamp 15.00
778 The Little Rascals 20.00
779 Lee Hunter, Indian Fighter . 25.00
780 Captain Kangaroo,Ph(c) . . 100.00
781 Fury,Ph(c) 50.00
782 Duck Album 18.00
783 Elmer Fudd 10.00
784 Around the World in 80
Days,Ph(c) 45.00
785 Circus Boys,Ph(c) 65.00
786 Cinderella 15.00
787 Little Hiawatha 15.00
788 BF,Prince Valiant 35.00
789 EK,Silvertip-Valley Thieves . 30.00
790 ATh,The Wings of Eagles,
J.Wayne Ph(c) 125.00
791 The 77th Bengal Lancers,
Ph(c) 45.00
792 Oswald the Rabbit 10.00
793 Morty Meekle 15.00
794 SB,The Count of Monte
Cristo 55.00
795 Jiminy Cricket 20.00
796 Ludwig Bemelman's
Madeleine and Genevieve . . . 20.00
797 Gunsmoke,Ph(c) 40.00
798 Buffalo Bill,Ph(c) 25.00
799 Priscilla's Pop 10.00
800 The Buccaneers,Ph(c) 40.00
801 Dotty Dripple and Taffy . . . 10.00
802 Goofy 20.00
803 Cheyenne,C.Walker Ph(c) . . 35.00
804 Steve Canyon 30.00
805 Crusader Rabbit 100.00
806 Scamp 15.00
807 MB,Savage Range 20.00
808 Spin and Marty,Ph(c) 30.00
809 The Little People 15.00
810 Francis the Famous
Talking Mule 20.00
811 Howdy Doody 50.00

812 The Big Land,A.Ladd Ph(c) . 60.00
813 Circus Boy,Ph(c) 65.00
814 Covered Wagon,A:Mickey
Mouse 25.00
815 Dragoon Wells Massacre . . 35.00
816 Brave Eagle,Ph(c) 15.00
817 Little Beaver 15.00
818 Smokey the Bear 20.00
819 Mickey Mouse in Magicland 18.00
820 The Oklahoman,Ph(c) 45.00
821 Wringle Wrangle,Ph(c) 40.00
822 ATh,W.Disney's Paul Revere's
Ride (TV) 60.00
823 Timmy 15.00
824 The Pride and the Passion,
Ph(c) 60.00
825 The Little Rascals 25.00
826 Spin and Marty and Annette,
Ph(c) 75.00
827 Smokey Stover 15.00
828 Buffalo Bill, Jr,Ph(c). 25.00
829 Tales of the Pony Express,
Ph(c) 25.00
830 The Hardy Boys,Ph(c) 55.00
831 No Sleep 'Til Dawn,Ph(c) . . 35.00
832 Lolly and Pepper 15.00
833 Scamp 15.00
834 Johnny Mack Brown,Ph(c) . 30.00
835 Silvertip- The Fake Rider . . 20.00
836 Man in Fight 25.00
837 All-American Athlete
Cotton Woods 25.00
838 Bugs Bunny's Life
Story Album 30.00
839 The Vigilantes 35.00
840 Duck Album 15.00
841 Elmer Fudd 8.00
842 The Nature of Things 25.00
843 The First Americans 25.00
844 Gunsmoke,Ph(c) 40.00
845 ATh,The Land Unknown . . 100.00
846 ATh,Gun Glory 90.00
847 Perri 30.00
848 Marauder's Moon 30.00
849 BF,Prince Valiant 30.00
850 Buck Jones 20.00
851 The Story of Mankind,
V.Price Ph(c) 30.00
852 Chilly Willy 10.00
853 Pluto 15.00
854 Hunchback of Notre Dame,
Ph(c) 85.00
855 Broken Arrow,Ph(c) 25.00
856 Buffalo Bill, Jr.,Ph(c) 25.00

857 The Goofy Adventure Story . 20.00
858 Daisy Duck's Diary 15.00
859 Topper and Neil 12.00
860 Wyatt Earp,Ph(c) 80.00
861 Frosty the Snowman 15.00
862 Truth About Mother Goose . 25.00
863 Francis the Famous Talking Mule 20.00
864 The Littlest Snowman 15.00
865 Andy Burnett,Ph(c) 40.00
866 Mars and Beyond 25.00
867 Santa Claus Funnies 15.00
868 The Little People 15.00
869 Old Yeller,Ph(c) 25.00
870 Little Beaver 12.00
871 Curly Kayoe 15.00
872 Captain Kangaroo,Ph(c) . . . 75.00
873 Grandma Duck's Farm Friends 15.00
874 Old Ironsides 20.00
875 Trumpets West 15.00
876 Tales of Wells Fargo,Ph(c) . 50.00
877 ATh,Frontier Doctor,Ph(c) . . 70.00
878 Peanuts 100.00
879 Brave Eagle,Ph(c) 15.00
880 MD,Steve Donovan,Ph(c) . . 25.00
881 The Captain and the Kids . . 15.00
882 ATh,W.Disney Presents Zorro 75.00
883 The Little Rascals 35.00
884 Hawkeye and the Last of the Mohicans,Ph(c) 30.00
885 Fury,Ph(c) 30.00
886 Bongo and Lumpjaw 15.00
887 The Hardy Boys,Ph(c) 45.00
888 Elmer Fudd 8.00
889 ATh,W.Disney's Clint & Mac(TV),Ph(c) 65.00
890 Wyatt Earp,Ph(c) 35.00
891 Light in the Forest, C.Parker Ph(c) 25.00
892 Maverick,J.Garner Ph(c) . . 120.00
893 Jim Bowie,Ph(c) 30.00
894 Oswald the Rabbit 8.00
895 Wagon Train,Ph(c) 65.00
896 Adventures of Tinker Bell . . 25.00
897 Jiminy Cricket 20.00
898 EK,Silvertip 30.00
899 Goofy 20.00
900 BF,Prince Valiant 35.00
901 Little Hiawatha 15.00
902 Will-Yum! 10.00
903 Dotty Dripple and Taffy 10.00
904 Lee Hunter, Indian Fighter . 20.00
905 W.Disney's Annette (TV), Ph(c) 120.00
906 Francis the Famous Talking Mule 20.00
907 Ath,Sugarfoot,Ph(c) 80.00
908 The Little People and the Giant 15.00
909 Smitty 15.00
910 ATh,The Vikings, K.Douglas Ph(c) 75.00
911 The Gray Ghost,Ph(c) 50.00
912 Leave it to Beaver,Ph(c) . . 125.00
913 The Left-Handed Gun, Paul Newman Ph(c) 65.00
914 ATh,No Time for Sergeants, Ph(c) 60.00
915 Casey Jones,Ph(c) 30.00
916 Red Ryder Ranch Comics . . 15.00
917 The Life of Riley,Ph(c) 75.00
918 Beep Beep, the Roadrunner 60.00
919 Boots and Saddles,Ph(c) . . 50.00
920 Ath,Zorro,Ph(c) 75.00
921 Wyatt Earp.Ph(c) 40.00
922 Johnny Mack Brown,Ph(c) . 35.00
923 Timmy 8.00
924 Colt .45,Ph(c) 52.00
925 Last of the Fast Guns,Ph(c) 35.00
926 Peter Pan 20.00
927 SB,Top Gun 20.00
928 Sea Hunt,L.Bridges Ph(c) . . 75.00
929 Brave Eagle,Ph(c) 15.00
930 Maverick,J. Garner Ph(c) . . 65.00
931 Have Gun, Will Travel,Ph(c) 75.00
932 Smokey the Bear 20.00
933 ATh,W.Disney's Zorro 60.00
934 Restless Gun 65.00
935 King of the Royal Mounted . 25.00
936 The Little Rascals 20.00
937 Ruff and Ready 45.00
938 Elmer Fudd 8.00
939 Steve Canyon 27.00
940 Lolly and Pepper 10.00
941 Pluto 15.00
942 Pony Express 18.00
943 White Wilderness 20.00
944 SB,7th Voyage of Sinbad . . 85.00
945 Maverick,J.Garner Ph(c) . . . 60.00
946 The Big Country,Ph(c) 30.00
947 Broken Arrow,Ph(c) 25.00
948 Daisy Duck's Diary 15.00
949 High Adventure,Ph(c) 30.00
950 Frosty the Snowman 15.00
951 ATh,Lennon Sisters Life Story,Ph(c) 110.00
952 Goofy 15.00
953 Francis the Famous Talking Mule 20.00
954 Man in Space 35.00
955 Hi and Lois 8.00
956 Ricky Nelson,Ph(c) 170.00
957 Buffalo Bee 35.00
958 Santa Claus Funnies 15.00
959 Christmas Stories 15.00
960 ATh,W.Disney's Zorro 85.00
961 Jace Pearson's Tales of Texas Rangers,Ph(c) 30.00
962 Maverick,J.Garner Ph(c) . . . 65.00
963 Johnny Mack Brown,Ph(c) . 30.00
964 The Hardy Boys,Ph(c) 40.00
965 GrandmaDuck'sFarmFriends 15.00
966 Tonka,Ph(c) 25.00
967 Chilly Willy 8.00
968 Tales of Wells Fargo,Ph(c) . 45.00
969 Peanuts 60.00
970 Lawman,Ph(c) 60.00
971 Wagon Train,Ph(c) 40.00
972 Tom Thumb 55.00
973 SleepingBeauty & the Prince 35.00
974 The Little Rascals 20.00
975 Fury,Ph(c) 35.00
976 ATh,W.Disney's Zorro,Ph(c) 75.00
977 Elmer Fudd 8.00
978 Lolly and Pepper 10.00
979 Oswald the Rabbit 8.00
980 Maverick,J.Garner Ph(c) . . . 65.00
981 Ruff and Ready 25.00
982 The New Adventures of Tinker Bell 25.00
983 Have Gun, Will Travel,Ph(c) 45.00
984 Sleeping Beauty's Fairy Godmothers 35.00
985 Shaggy Dog,Ph(c) 25.00
986 Restless Gun,Ph(c) 45.00
987 Goofy 15.00
988 Little Hiawatha 15.00
989 Jimmy Cricket 15.00
990 Huckleberry Hound 40.00
991 Francis the Famous Talking Mule 20.00
992 ATh,Sugarfoot,Ph(c) 85.00
993 Jim Bowie,Ph(c) 30.00
994 Sea HuntL.Bridges Ph(c) . . 45.00
995 Donald Duck Album 15.00
996 Nevada 25.00
997 Walt Disney Presents,Ph(c) . 35.00
998 Ricky Nelson,Ph(c) 160.00
999 Leave It To Beaver,Ph(c) . 125.00
1000 The Gray Ghost,Ph(c) 50.00
1001 Lowell Thomas' High Adventure,Ph(c) 30.00
1002 Buffalo Bee 25.00
1003 ATh,W.Disney's Zorro,Ph(c) 65.00
1004 Colt .45,Ph(c) 40.00
1005 Maverick,J.Garner Ph(c) . . 65.00
1006 SB,Hercules 65.00
1007 John Paul Jones,Ph(c) . . . 30.00
1008 Beep, Beep, the Road Runner 25.00
1009 CB,The Rifleman,Ph(c) . 120.00
1010 Grandma Duck's Farm Friends 75.00
1011 Buckskin,Ph(c) 45.00
1012 Last Train from Gun Hill,Ph(c) 55.00
1013 Bat Masterson,Ph(c) 65.00
1014 ATh,The Lennon Sisters, Ph(c) 110.00
1015 Peanuts 65.00
1016 Smokey the Bear 10.00
1017 Chilly Willy 8.00
1018 Rio Bravo,J.Wayne Ph(c) 175.00
1019 Wagoon Train,Ph(c) 40.00
1020 Jungle 15.00
1021 Jace Pearson's Tales of the Texas Rangers,Ph(c) . . . 30.00
1022 Timmy 10.00
1023 Tales of Wells Fargo,Ph(c) 45.00
1024 ATh,Darby O'Gill and the Little People,Ph(c) 50.00
1025 CB,W.Disney's Vacation in Disneyland 65.00
1026 Spin and Marty,Ph(c) 35.00
1027 The Texan,Ph(c) 35.00
1028 Rawhide, Clint Eastwood Ph(c) 175.00
1029 Boots and Saddles,Ph(c) . . 30.00
1030 Spanky and Alfalfa, the Little Rascals 20.00
1031 Fury,Ph(c) 35.00
1032 Elmer Fudd 8.00
1033 Steve Canyon,Ph(c) 25.00
1034 Nancy and Sluggo Summer Camp 15.00
1035 Lawman,Ph(c) 35.00
1036 The Big Circus,Ph(c) 25.00
1037 Zorro,Ph(c) 75.00
1038 Ruff and Ready 25.00
1039 Pluto 15.00
1040 Quick Draw McGraw 55.00
1041 ATh,Sea Hunt, L.Bridges Ph(c) 65.00
1042 The Three Chipmunks . . . 15.00
1043 The Three Stooges,Ph(c) 145.00
1044 Have Gun, Will Travel,Ph(c) 45.00
1045 Restless Gun,Ph(c) 45.00
1046 Beep Beep, the Road Runner 25.00
1047 CB,W.Disney's GyroGearloose 80.00
1048 The Horse Soldiers J.Wayne Ph(c) 125.00

Dell Four Color #976
© Dell Publishing Co.

1049 Don't Give Up the Ship
J.Lewis Ph(c) 35.00
1050 Huckleberry Hound 25.00
1051 Donald in Mathmagic Land 35.00
1052 RsM,Ben-Hur 65.00
1053 Goofy 20.00
1054 Huckleberry Hound
Winter Fun 25.00
1055 CB,Daisy Duck's Diary . . . 50.00
1056 Yellowstone Kelly,
C.Walker Ph(c) 30.00
1057 Mickey Mouse Album 20.00
1058 Colt .45,Ph(c) 30.00
1059 Sugarfoot 45.00
1060 Journey to the Center of the
Earth, P.Boone Ph(c) 80.00
1061 Buffalo Bill 30.00
1062 Christmas Stories 15.00
1063 Santa Claus Funnies 15.00
1064 Bugs Bunny's Merry
Christmas 25.00
1065 Frosty the Snowman 15.00
1066 ATh,77 Sunset Strip,Ph(c) . 80.00
1067 Yogi Bear 65.00
1068 Francis the Famous
Talking Mule 20.00
1069 ATh,The FBI Story,Ph(c) . . 65.00
1070 Soloman and Sheba,Ph(c) 55.00
1071 ATh,The Real McCoys,Ph(c) 85.00
1072 Blythe 20.00
1073 CB,Grandma Duck's Farm
Friends 65.00
1074 Chilly Willy 10.00
1075 Tales of Wells Fargo,Ph(c) 40.00
1076 MSy,The Rebel,Ph(c) 75.00
1077 SB,The Deputy,
H.Fonda Ph(c) 85.00
1078 The Three Stooges,Ph(c) . 65.00
1079 The Little Rascals 25.00
1080 Fury,Ph(c) 35.00
1081 Elmer Fudd 12.00
1082 Spin and Marty 30.00
1083 Men into Space,Ph(c) 40.00
1084 Speedy Gonzales 20.00
1085 ATh,The Time Machine . . 100.00
1086 Lolly and Pepper 10.00
1087 Peter Gunn,Ph(c) 65.00
1088 A Dog of Flanders,Ph(c) . . 20.00
1089 Restless Gun,Ph(c) 50.00
1090 Francis the Famous
Talking Mule 20.00
1091 Jacky's Diary 20.00
1092 Toby Tyler,Ph(c) 20.00
1093 MacKenzie's Raiders,Ph(c) 35.00
1094 Goofy 15.00
1095 CB,W.Disney's
GyroGearloose 75.00
1096 The Texan,Ph(c) 40.00
1097 Rawhide,C.Eastwood Ph(c) 125.00
1098 Sugarfoot,Ph(c) 50.00
1099 CB(c),Donald Duck Album . 20.00
1100 W.Disney's Annette's
Life Story (TV),Ph(c) 125.00
1101 Robert Louis Stevenson's
Kidnapped,Ph(c) 30.00
1102 Wanted: Dead or Alive,
Ph(c) 100.00
1103 Leave It To Beaver,Ph(c) 125.00
1104 Yogi Bear Goes to College 30.00
1105 ATh,Gale Storm,Ph(c) . . . 100.00
1106 ATh,77 Sunset Strip,Ph(c) . 65.00
1107 Buckskin,Ph(c) 35.00
1108 The Troubleshooters,Ph(c) 30.00
1109 This Is Your Life, Donald
Duck,O:Donald Duck 150.00
1110 Bonanza,Ph(c) 220.00
1111 Shotgun Slade 35.00
1112 Pixie and Dixie
and Mr. Jinks 35.00
1113 Tales of Wells Fargo,Ph(c) 40.00
1114 Huckleberry Finn,Ph(c) . . . 25.00
1115 Ricky Nelson,Ph(c) 125.00
1116 Boots and Saddles,Ph(c) . . 30.00
1117 Boy and the Pirate,Ph(c) . . 35.00
1118 Sword and the Dragon,Ph(c) 40.00
1119 Smokey and the Bear
Nature Stories 20.00
1120 Dinosaurus,Ph(c) 50.00
1121 RC,GE,Hercules Unchained 65.00
1122 Chilly Willy 10.00
1123 Tombstone Territory,Ph(c) . 45.00
1124 Whirlybirds,Ph(c) 40.00
1125 GK,RH,Laramie,Ph(c) 60.00
1126 Sundance,Ph(c) 55.00
1127 The Three Stooges,Ph(c) . 65.00
1128 Rocky and His Friends . . 200.00
1129 Pollyanna,H.Mills Ph(c) . . . 60.00
1130 SB,The Deputy,
H.Fonda Ph(c) 65.00
1131 Elmer Fudd 10.00
1132 Space Mouse 20.00
1133 Fury,Ph(c) 35.00
1134 ATh,Real McCoys,Ph(c) . . 75.00
1135 M.G.M.'s Mouse Musketeers 8.00
1136 Jungle Cat,Ph(c) 30.00
1137 The Little Rascals 20.00
1138 The Rebel,Ph(c) 60.00
1139 SB,Spartacus,Ph(c) 75.00
1140 Donald Duck Album 20.00
1141 Huckleberry Hound for
President 30.00
1142 Johnny Ringo,Ph(c) 50.00
1143 Pluto 20.00
1144 The Story of Ruth,Ph(c) . . 70.00
1145 GK,The Lost World,Ph(c) . 85.00
1146 Restless Gun,Ph(c) 40.00
1147 Sugarfoot,Ph(c) 50.00
1148 I aim at the Stars,Ph(c) . . . 35.00
1149 Goofy 15.00
1150 CB,Daisy Duck's Diary . . . 50.00
1151 Mickey Mouse Album 18.00
1152 Rocky and His Friends . . 165.00
1153 Frosty the Snowman 15.00
1154 Santa Claus Funnies 15.00
1155 North to Alaska 100.00
1156 Walt Disney Swiss
Family Robinson 30.00
1157 Master of the World 30.00
1158 Three Worlds of Gulliver . . 30.00
1159 ATh,77 Sunset Strip 60.00
1160 Rawhide 135.00
1161 Grandma Duck's
Farm Friends 60.00
1162 Yogi Bera joins the Marines 40.00
1163 Daniel Boone 30.00
1164 Wanted: Dead or Alive . . . 70.00
1165 Ellery Queen 75.00
1166 Rocky and His Friends . . 160.00
1167 Tales of Wells Fargo,Ph(c) 40.00
1168 The Detectives,
R.Taylor Ph(c) 60.00
1169 New Adventures of
Sherlock Holmes 125.00
1170 The Three Stooges,Ph(c) . 65.00
1171 Elmer Fudd 10.00
1172 Fury,Ph(c) 35.00
1173 The Twilight Zone 150.00
1174 The Little Rascals 25.00
1175 M.G.M.'s Mouse Musketeers 10.00
1176 Dondi,Ph(c) 25.00
1177 Chilly Willy 10.00
1178 Ten Who Dared 20.00
1179 The Swamp Fox,
L.Nielson Ph(c) 35.00
1180 The Danny Thomas Show 100.00
1181 Texas John Slaughter,Ph(c) 20.00
1182 Donald Duck Album 20.00
1183 101 Dalmatians 35.00
1184 CB,W.Disney's
Gyro Gearloose 75.00
1185 Sweetie Pie 15.00
1186 JDa,Yak Yak 50.00
1187 The Three Stooges,Ph(c) . 50.00
1188 Atlantis the Lost
Continent,Ph(c) 65.00
1189 Greyfriars Bobby,Ph(c) . . . 30.00
1190 CB(c),Donald and
the Wheel 30.00
1191 Leave It to Beaver,Ph(c) . 125.00
1192 Rocky Nelson,Ph(c) 130.00

Dell Four Color #1184
© Dell Publishing Co.

1193 The Real McCoys,Ph(c) . . 55.00
1194 Pepe,Ph(c) 30.00
1195 National Velvet,Ph(c) 25.00
1196 Pixie and Dixie
and Mr. Jinks 20.00
1197 The Aquanauts,Ph(c) 35.00
1198 Donald in Mathmagic Land 35.00
1199 Absent-Minded Professor,
Ph(c) 30.00
1200 Hennessey,Ph(c) 35.00
1201 Goofy 20.00
1202 Rawhide,C.Eastwood Ph(c) 135.00
1203 Pinocchio 20.00
1204 Scamp 15.00
1205 David Goliath,Ph(c) 30.00
1206 Lolly and Pepper 10.00
1207 MSy,The Rebel,Ph(c) 65.00
1208 Rocky and His Friends . . 135.00
1209 Sugarfoot,Ph(c) 50.00
1210 The Parent Trap,
H.Mills Ph(c) 65.00
1211 RsM,77 Sunset Strip,Ph(c) 50.00
1212 Chilly Willy 10.00
1213 Mysterious Island,Ph(c) . . . 55.00
1214 Smokey the Bear 20.00
1215 Tales of Wells Fargo,Ph(c) 40.00
1216 Whirlybirds,Ph(c) 45.00
1218 Fury,Ph(c) 35.00
1219 The Detectives,
R Taylor Ph(c) 45.00
1220 Gunslinger,Ph(c) 40.00
1221 Bonanza,Ph(c) 125.00
1222 Elmer Fudd 10.00
1223 GK,Laramie,Ph(c) 40.00
1224 The Little Rascals 25.00
1225 The Deputy,H.Fonda Ph(c) 60.00
1226 Nikki, Wild Dog of the North 15.00
1227 Morgan the Pirate,Ph(c) . . 50.00
1229 Thief of Bagdad,Ph(c) 65.00
1230 Voyage to the Bottom
of the Sea,Ph(c) 50.00
1231 Danger Man,Ph(c) 50.00
1232 On the Double 20.00
1233 Tammy Tell Me True 30.00
1234 The Phantom Planet 45.00
1235 Mister Magoo 55.00
1236 King of Kings,Ph(c) 60.00
1237 ATh,The Untouchables,
Ph(c) 110.00
1238 Deputy Dawg 75.00
1239 CB(c),Donald Duck Album . 25.00
1240 The Detectives,
R.Taylor Ph(c) 40.00
1241 Sweetie Pies 15.00

1242 King Leonardo and
His Short Subjects 100.00
1243 Ellery Queen 35.00
1244 Space Mouse 20.00
1245 New Adventures of
Sherlock Holmes 125.00
1246 Mickey Mouse Album 25.00
1247 Daisy Duck's Diary 25.00
1248 Pluto 25.00
1249 The Danny Thomas Show,
Ph(c) 120.00
1250 Four Horseman of the
Apocalypse,Ph(c) 45.00
1251 Everything's Ducky 25.00
1252 The Andy Griffith Show,
Ph(c) 190.00
1253 Spaceman 45.00
1254 "Diver Dan" 35.00
1255 The Wonders of Aladdin .. 30.00
1256 Kona, Monarch of
Monster Isle 30.00
1257 Car 54, Where Are You?,
Ph(c) 50.00
1258 GE,The Frogmen 35.00
1259 El Cid,Ph(c) 40.00
1260 The Horsemasters,Ph(c) . 45.00
1261 Rawhide,C.Eastwood Ph(c) 135.00
1262 The Rebel,Ph(c) 65.00
1263 RsM,77 Sinset Strip,Ph(c) . 50.00
1264 Pixie & Dixie & Mr.Jinks .. 20.00
1265 The Real McCoys,Ph(c) .. 55.00
1266 M.G.M.'s Spike and Tyke . 10.00
1267 CB,GyroGearloose 50.00
1268 Oswald the Rabbit 10.00
1269 Rawhide,C.Eastwood Ph(c) 135.00
1270 Bullwinkle and Rocky ... 110.00
1271 Yogi Bear Birthday Party .. 30.00
1272 Frosty the Snowman 15.00
1273 Hans Brinker,Ph(c) 25.00
1274 Santa Claus Funnies 15.00
1275 Rocky and His Friends .. 100.00
1276 Dondi 20.00
1278 King Leonardo and
His Short Subjects 100.00
1279 Grandma Duck's Farm
Friends 20.00
1280 Hennessey,Ph(c) 35.00
1281 Chilly Willy 10.00
1282 Babes in Toyland,Ph(c) ... 65.00
1283 Bonanza,Ph(c) 125.00
1284 RH,Laramie,Ph(c) 50.00
1285 Leave It to Beaver,Ph(c) . 125.00
1286 The Untouchables,Ph(c) . 100.00
1287 Man from Wells Fargo,Ph(c) 30.00
1288 RC,GE,The Twilight Zone . 85.00
1289 Ellery Queen 40.00
1290 M.G.M.'s Mouse
Musketeers 10.00
1291 RsM,77 Sunset Strip,Ph(c) 50.00
1293 Elmer Fudd 10.00
1294 Ripcord 35.00
1295 Mr. Ed, the Talking Horse,
Ph(c) 50.00
1296 Fury,Ph(c) 35.00
1297 Spanky, Alfalfa and the
Little Rascals 20.00
1298 The Hathaways,Ph(c) 25.00
1299 Deputy Dawg 50.00
1300 The Comancheros 125.00
1301 Adventures in Paradise .. 25.00
1302 JohnnyJason,TeenReporter 20.00
1303 Lad: A Dog,Ph(c) 20.00
1304 Nellie the Nurse 40.00
1305 Mister Magoo 55.00
1306 Target: The Corruptors,
Ph(c) 20.00
1307 Margie 20.00
1308 Tales of the Wizard of Oz . 60.00
1309 BK,87th Precinct,Ph(c) ... 60.00
1310 Huck and Yogi Winter
Sports 20.00
1311 Rocky and His Friends .. 100.00
1312 National Velvet,Ph(c) 20.00
1313 Moon Pilot.Ph(c) 30.00
1328 GE,The Underwater
City,Ph(c) 40.00
1330 GK,Brain Boy 35.00
1332 Bachelor Father 45.00
1333 Short Ribs 25.00
1335 Aggie Mack 20.00
1336 On Stage 25.00
1337 Dr. Kildare,Ph(c) 35.00
1341 The Andy Griffith Show,
Ph(c) 185.00
1348 JDa,Yak Yak 50.00
1349 Yogi Berra Visits the U.N. . 40.00
1350 Commanche,Ph(c) 20.00
1354 Calvin and the Colonel ... 35.00

FOUR FAVORITES
Ace Magazines
September, 1941

1 B:Vulcan, Lash Lighting, Magno
the Magnetic Man, Raven,
Flag cover,Hitler 550.00
2 A: Black Ace 275.00
3 E:Vulcan 250.00
4 E:Raven,B:Unknown Soldiers 250.00
5 B:Captain Courageous 200.00
6 A: The Flag, B: Mr. Risk ... 200.00
7 JM 175.00
8 .... 175.00
9 RP,HK 175.00
10 HK 200.00
11 HK,LbC,UnKnown Soldier .. 250.00
12 LbC 120.00
13 LbC 100.00
14 Fer 100.00
15 Fer 100.00
16 Bondage(c) 120.00
17 Magno Lighting 100.00
18 Magno Lighting 100.00

4 Favorites #19 © Ace Magazines

19 RP,RP(c) 100.00
20 RP,RP(c) 100.00
21 RP,RP(c) 75.00
22 RP(c) 75.00
23 RP(c) 75.00
24 RP(c) 75.00
25 RP(c) 75.00
26 RP(c) 75.00
27 RP(c) 65.00
28 .... 60.00
29 .... 60.00
30 .... 60.00
31 .... 60.00
32 .... 60.00

Frankenstein #10
© Crestwood/Prize Publications

FRANKENSTEIN COMICS
Crestwood Publications
(Prize Publ.)
Summer, 1945

1 B:Frankenstein,DBr,DBr(c) . 400.00
2 DBr,DBr(c) 200.00
3 DBr,DBr(c) 175.00
4 DBr,DBr(c) 175.00
5 DBr,DBr(c) 175.00
6 DBr,DBr(c),S&K 150.00
7 DBr,DBr(c),S&K 150.00
8 DBr,DBr(c),S&K 150.00
9 DBr,DBr(c),S&K 150.00
10 DBr,DBr(c),S&K 150.00
11 DBr,DBr(c)A:Boris Karloff .. 125.00
12 DBr,DBr(c) 125.00
13 DBr,DBr(c). 125.00
14 DBr,DBr(c) 125.00
15 DBr,DBr(c) 125.00
16 DBr,DBr(c) 125.00
17 DBr,DBr(c) 125.00
18 B:Horror 135.00
19 .... 85.00
3-4 .... 75.00
3-5 .... 75.00
3-6 .... 75.00
4-1 thru 4-6 .... @75.00
5-1 thru 5-4 .... @75.00
5-5 October-November, 1954 .. 75.00

FRISKY FABLES
Novelty Press/Premium Group
Spring, 1945

1 AFa 75.00
2 AFa 40.00
3 AFa 35.00
4 AFa 28.00
5 AFa 28.00
6 AFa 28.00
7 AFa,Flag (c) 30.00
2-1 AFa,Rainbow(c) 25.00
2-2 AFa 20.00
2-3 AFa 18.00
2-4 AFa 18.00
2-5 AFa 18.00
2-6 AFa 18.00
2-7 AFa 18.00
2-8 AFa,Halloween (c) 20.00
2-9 AFa,Thanksgiving(c) 15.00
2-10 AFa,Christman cover 18.00
2-11 AFa 20.00
2-12 AFa,Valentines Day cover . 15.00

3-1 AFa 12.00
3-2 AFa 12.00
3-3 AFa 15.00
3-4 AFa 12.00
3-5 AFa 12.00
3-6 AFa 12.00
3-7 AFa 12.00
3-8 AFa,Turkey (c) 12.00
3-9 AFa 12.00
3-10 AFa 12.00
3-11 AFa,1948(c) 12.00
3-12 AFa 12.00
4-1 thru 4-7 AFa . . . . @12.00
5-1 AFa 12.00
5-2 AFa 12.00
5-3 . . . . 12.00
5-4 Star Publications 12.00
39 LbC(c) 50.00
40 LbC(c) 50.00
41 LbC(c) 50.00
42 LbC(c) 50.00
43 LbC(c) 20.00

Becomes:

FRISKY ANIMALS
Star Publications

44 LbC 75.00
45 LbC 110.00
46 LbC,Baseball 60.00
47 LbC 60.00
48 LbC 60.00
49 LbC 60.00
50 LbC 60.00
51 LbC(c) 60.00
52 LbC(c) 75.00
53 LbC(c) 55.00
54 LbC(c),Supercat(c) 55.00
55 LbC(c),same 55.00
56 LbC(c),same 55.00
57 LbC(c),same 55.00
58 LbC(c),same,July, 1954 . . . . 55.00

FRITZI RITZ
United Features Syndicate/ St. John Publications
Fall, 1948

N# Special issue 75.00
2 . . . . 35.00
3 . . . . 30.00
4 thru 7 . . . . @25.00
6 A:Abbie & Slats 27.00
8 thru 10 . . . . @18.00
11 1958 . . . . 18.00

FROGMAN COMICS
Hillman Periodicals
January-February, 1952

1 . . . . 65.00
2 . . . . 35.00
3 . . . . 35.00
4 MMe 22.00
5 BK,AT 35.00
6 thru 10 . . . . @20.00
11 May, 1953 . . . . 20.00

FRONTIER ROMANCES
Avon Periodicals
November-December, 1949

1 She Learned to Ride and Shoot, and Kissing Came Natural . 250.00
2 Bronc-Busters Sweetheart, January-February, 1950 . . . 200.00

FRONTLINE COMBAT
Tiny Tot Publications (E.C. Comics)
July-August, 1951

1 HK(c),WW, JSe,JDa,Hanhung Changjn cover 500.00
2 HK(c),WW,Tank Battle cover 350.00
3 HK(c),WW,Naval Battleship fire cover 300.00
4 HK(c),WW, Bazooka cover . 250.00
5 HK(c),JSe 225.00
6 HK(c),WW,JSe 200.00
7 HK(c),WW,JSe,Document of the Action at Iwo Jima 200.00
8 HK(c),WW,ATh 200.00
9 HK(c),WW,JSe,Civil War iss. 200.00
10 GE,HK(c),WW, Crying Child cover 250.00
11 GE 175.00
12 GE,Air Force issue 175.00
13 JSe,GE,WW(c), Bi-Planes cover 175.00
14 JKu,GE,WW(c) 175.00
15 JSe,GE,WW(c), Jan., 1954 175.00

FRONT PAGE COMIC BOOK
Front Page Comics
1945

1 JKu,BP,BF(c),I:Man in Black 175.00

FUGITIVES FROM JUSTICE
St. John Publishing Co.
February, 1952

1 . . . . 85.00
2 MB, Killer Boomerang 75.00
3 GT 75.00
4 . . . . 35.00
5 Bondage cover, October, 1952 45.00

FUNNIES, THE
(1ST SERIES)
Dell Publishing Co.
1929-30

1 B:Foxy Grandpa, Sniffy . . . 400.00
2 thru 21 . . . . @175.00
N#(22) 150.00
N#(23) thru (36) . . . . @100.00

Funnies #6 © Dell Publishing Co.

FUNNIES, THE
(2ND SERIES)
Dell Publishing Co.
October, 1936

1 Tailspin Tommy,Mutt & Jeff, Capt. Easy,D.Dixon 1,200.00
2 Scribbly 600.00
3 . . . . 500.00
4 Christmas issue 375.00
5 . . . . 350.00
6 thru 22 . . . . @300.00
23 thru 29 . . . . @200.00
30 B:John Carter of Mars 600.00
31 inc. Dick Tracy 350.00
32 . . . . 350.00
33 . . . . 350.00
34 . . . . 350.00
35 John Carter (c) 350.00
36 John Carter (c) 350.00
37 John Carter (c) 350.00
38 Rex King of the Deep (c) . . 350.00
39 Rex King (c) 350.00
40 John Carter (c) 350.00
41 Sky Ranger (c) 350.00
42 Rex King (c) 350.00
43 Rex King (c) 350.00
44 Rex King (c) 350.00
45 I&O:Phantasmo:Master of the World 275.00
46 Phantasmo (c) 275.00
47 Phantasmo (c) 200.00
48 Phantasmo (c) 200.00
49 Phantasmo (c) 200.00
50 Phantasmo (c) 200.00
51 Phantasmo (c) 200.00
52 Phantasmo (c) 200.00
53 Phantasmo (c) 200.00
54 Phantasmo (c) 200.00
55 Phantasmo (c) 200.00
56 Phantasmo (c) E:John Carter 200.00
57 I&O:Captain Midnight 600.00
58 Captain Midnight (c) 200.00
59 Captain Midnight (c) 200.00
60 Captain Midnight (c) 200.00
61 Captain Midnight (c) 220.00
62 Captain Midnight (c) 200.00
63 Captain Midnight (c) 200.00
64 B: Woody Woodpecker 200.00

Becomes:

NEW FUNNIES
Dell Publishing Co.
July, 1942

65 Andy Panda, Ragady Ann & Andy, Peter Rabbit 400.00

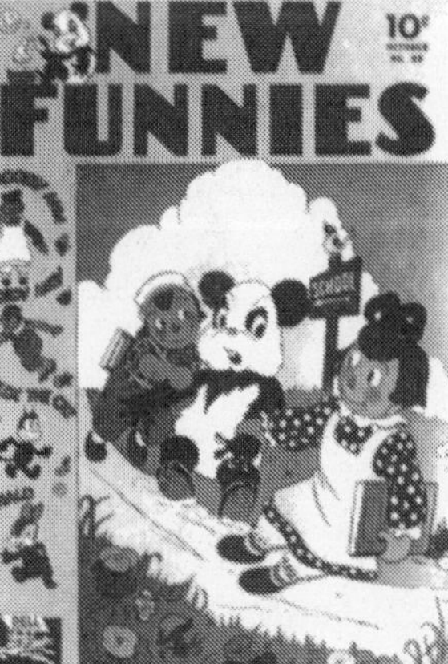

New Funnies #68 © Dell Publishing Co.

66 same 200.00
67 Felix the Cat 200.00
68 . . . . 200.00
69 WK, The Brownies 200.00
70 . . . . 200.00
71 . . . . 150.00
72 WK 150.00
73 . . . . 150.00
74 . . . . 150.00
75 WK,Brownies 150.00
76 CB,Andy Panda, Woody Woodpecker 500.00
77 same 150.00

78 Andy Panda 150.00
79 . . . . 100.00
80 . . . . 100.00
81 . . . . 100.00
82 WK,Brownies 125.00
83 WK,Brownies 125.00
84 WK,Brownies 100.00
85 WK,Brownies 125.00
86 . . . . 65.00
87 Woody Woodpecker 60.00
88 same 60.00
89 same 60.00
90 same 60.00
91 thru 99 . . . . @45.00
100 . . . . 50.00
101 thru 110 . . . . @25.00
111 thru 118 . . . . @20.00
119 Christmas 22.00
120 thru 142 . . . . @20.00
143 Christmas cover 25.00
144 thru 149 . . . . @15.00
150 thru 154 . . . . @10.00
155 Christmas cover 12.00
156 thru 167 . . . . @10.00
168 Christmas cover 12.00
169 thru 181 . . . . @10.00
182 I&O:Knothead & Splinter . . . 10.00
183 thru 200 . . . . @10.00
201 thru 240 . . . . @7.00
241 thru 288 . . . . @6.00

FUNNY BOOK
Funny Book Publ. Corp.
(Parents Magazine)
December, 1952

1 Alec, the Funny Bunny, Alice in Wonderland 75.00
2 Gulliver in Giant-Land 40.00
3 . . . . 28.00
4 Adventures of Robin Hood . . 25.00
5 . . . . 25.00
6 . . . . 25.00
7 . . . . 25.00
8 . . . . 25.00
9 . . . . 25.00

FUNNY FILMS
Best Syndicated Features
(American Comics Group)
September-October, 1949

1 B:Puss An' Boots, Blunderbunny 90.00
2 . . . . 45.00
3 . . . . 32.00
4 . . . . 30.00
5 . . . . 30.00
6 . . . . 30.00
7 . . . . 30.00
8 . . . . 30.00
9 . . . . 30.00
10 . . . . 30.00
11 thru 20 . . . . @20.00
21 thru 28 . . . . @18.00
29 May-June, 1954 . . . . 18.00

FUNNY FUNNIES
Nedor Publ. Co.
April, 1943

1 Funny Animals 100.00

FUNNYMAN
Magazine Enterprises of Canada
December, 1947

1 S&K,S&K(c) 165.00
2 S&K,S&K(c) 135.00
3 S&K,S&K(c) 100.00
4 S&K,S&K(c) 100.00
5 S&K,S&K(c) 100.00
6 S&K,S&K(c), August, 1948 . 100.00

FUTURE COMICS
David McKay Publications
June, 1940

1 Lone Ranger,Phantom . . . 1,200.00
2 Lone Ranger 650.00
3 Lone Ranger 475.00
4 Lone Ranger,Sept., 1940 . . 450.00

FUTURE WORLD COMICS
George W. Dougherty
Summer, 1946

1 . . . . 150.00
2 Fall, 1946 . . . . 125.00

GABBY HAYES WESTERN
Fawcett Publ./Charlton Comics
November, 1948

1 Ph(c) 250.00
2 Ph(c) 135.00
3 The Rage of the Purple Sage, Ph(c) 90.00
4 Ph(c) 90.00
5 Ph(c) 85.00
6 Ph(c) 85.00
7 Ph(c) 75.00
8 Ph(c) 75.00
9 Ph(c),V:The Kangaroo Crook 75.00
10 Ph(c) 75.00
11 Ph(c), Chariot Race 75.00
12 V:Beaver Ben, The Biting Bandit, Ph(c) 65.00
13 thru 15 . . . . @65.00
16 . . . . 50.00
17 . . . . 50.00
18 thru 20 . . . . @50.00
21 thru 51 . . . . @35.00
51 thru 59 December, 1954 . . @20.00

GANGSTERS AND GUN MOLLS
Realistic Comics
(Avon)
September, 1951

1 WW,A:Big Jim Colosimo, Evelyn Ellis 225.00
2 JKa, A:Bonnie Parker, The Kissing Bandit 165.00
3 EK, A:Juanita Perez, Crimes Homicide Squad 125.00
4 A:Mara Hite, Elkins Boys, June, 1952 . . . . 125.00

GANGSTERS CAN'T WIN
D.S. Publishing Co.
February-March, 1948

1 Shot Cop cover 125.00
2 A:Eddie Bentz 65.00
3 Twin Trouble Trigger Man . . 70.00
4 Suicide on SoundStageSeven 70.00
5 Trail of Terror 70.00
6 Mystery at the Circus 70.00
7 Talisman Trail 35.00
8 . . . . 35.00
9 Suprise at Buoy 13, June-July, 1949 . . . . 35.00

GANG WORLD
Literary Enterprises
(Standard Comics)
October, 1952

5 Bondage cover 75.00
6 Mob Payoff, January, 1953 . . 45.00

GASOLINE ALLEY
Star Publications
October, 1950

1 . . . . 125.00
2 LBc 75.00
3 LBc(c), April, 1950 . . . . 100.00

GEM COMICS
Spotlight Publ.
April, 1945

1 A:Steve Strong,Bondage(c) 125.00

Gene Autry #9 © Fawcett Publications

GENE AUTRY COMICS
Fawcett Publications
January, 1942

1 The Mark of Cloven Hoof . 2,200.00
2 . . . . 575.00
3 Secret of the Aztec Treasure 400.00
4 . . . . 375.00
5 Mystery of PaintRockCanyon 375.00
6 Outlaw Round-up 350.00
7 Border Bullets 350.00
8 Blazing Guns 325.00
9 Range Robbers 325.00
10 Fightin' Buckaroo, Danger's Trail, Sept., 1943 . . . . 325.00
11 . . . . 350.00
12 . . . . 325.00

GENE AUTRY COMICS
Dell Publishing Co.
May/June 1946

1 . . . . 325.00
2 Ph(c) 175.00
3 Ph(c) 135.00
4 Ph(c),I:Flap Jack 135.00
5 Ph(c), all 125.00
6 thru 10 . . . . @100.00
11 thru 19 . . . . @75.00
20 . . . . 80.00
21 thru 29 . . . . @55.00
30 thru 40, B:Giants . . . . . . @60.00
41 thru 56 E:Giants . . . . @50.00
57 . . . . 30.00
58 Christmas cover 35.00
59 thru 66 . . . . @30.00
67 thru 80, B:Giant . . . . @35.00
81 thru 90, E:Giant . . . . @25.00
91 thru 93 . . . . @20.00
94 Christmas cover 22.00
95 thru 99 . . . . @20.00
100 . . . . 25.00
101 thru 111 . . . . @20.00
112 thru 121 . . . . @15.00

GENE AUTRY'S CHAMPION
Dell Publishing Co.

August, 1950
(1) *see Dell Four Color #287*
(2) *see Dell Four Color #319*
3 thru 19 . . . . @15.00

GEORGE PAL'S PUPPETOON'S
Fawcett Publications
December, 1945
1 Captain Marvel (c) 250.00
2 . . . . 125.00
3 . . . . 85.00
4 thru 17 . . . . @75.00
18 December, 1947 . . . . 75.00

GERALD McBOING-BOING AND THE NEARSIGHTED MR. MAGOO
Dell Publishing Co.
August-October, 1952
1 . . . . 50.00
2 . . . . 40.00
3 . . . . 40.00
4 . . . . 40.00
5 . . . . 40.00

GERONIMO
Avon Periodicals
1950
1 Massacre at San Pedro Pass 85.00
2 EK(c), Murderous Battle at Kiskayah 50.00
3 EK(c) 50.00
4 EK(c),Apache Death Trap, February, 1952 . . . . 50.00

GET LOST
Mikeross Publications
February-March, 1954
1 . . . . 120.00
2 . . . . 75.00
3 June-July, 1954 . . . . 65.00

GHOST
Fiction House Magazine
Winter, 1951
1 The Banshee Bells 325.00
2 I Woke In Terror 150.00
3 The Haunted Hand of X . . . 125.00

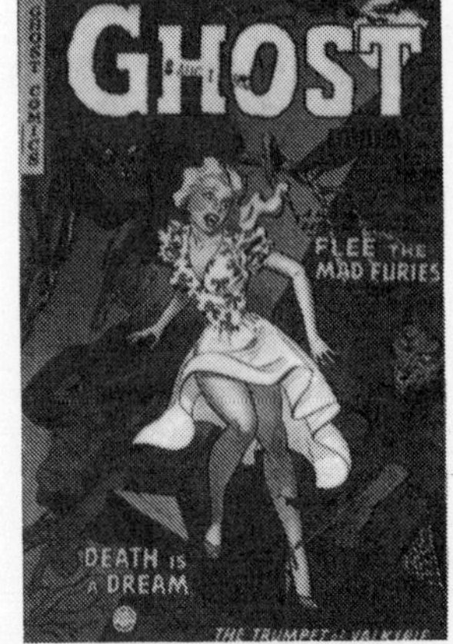

Ghost Comics #4
© Fiction House Magazine

4 Flee the Mad Furies 125.00
5 The Hex of Ruby Eye 125.00
6 The Sleepers in the Crypt . . 150.00
7 When Dead Rogues Ride . . 150.00
8 Curse of the Mist-Thing . . . 150.00
9 It Crawls by Night,Bondage(c) 165.00
10 Halfway to Hades 125.00
11 GE, The Witch's Doll, Summer, 1954 . . . . 150.00

GHOST BREAKERS
Street & Smith Publications
September, 1948
1 BP,BP(c), A:Dr. Neff 175.00
2 BP,BP(c), Breaks the Voodoo Hoodoo,December, 1948 . . 150.00

GHOSTLY WEIRD STORIES
(see BLUE BOLT)

GIANT BOY BOOK OF COMICS
Newsbook Publ.
(Lev Gleason)
1945
1 A:Crime Buster & Young Robin Hood 500.00

GIANT COMICS EDITION
St. John Publ.
1948
1 Mighty Mouse 275.00
2 Abbie and Slats 125.00
3 Terry Toons 200.00
4 Crime Comics 300.00
5 MB, Police Case Book 275.00
6 MB,MB(c), Western Picture Story 275.00
7 May not exist
8 The Adventures of Mighty Mouse 200.00
9 JKu,MB,Romance & Confession Stories,Ph(c) 250.00
10 Terry Toons 200.00
11 MB,MB(c),JKu,Western Picture Stories 225.00
12 MB,MB(c),Diary Secrets, Prostitute 400.00
13 MB,JKu, Romances 225.00
14 Mighty Mouse Album 225.00
15 MB(c),Romance 225.00
16 Little Audrey 200.00
N#, Mighty Mouse Album 200.00

GIANT COMICS EDITION
United Features Syndicate
1945
1 A:Abbie & Slats, Jim Hardy, Ella Cinders,Iron Vic 200.00
2 Elmo, Jim Hardy, Abbie & Slats, 1945 . . . . 175.00

G.I. COMBAT
Quality Comics Group
October, 1952
1 RC(c), Beyond the Call of Duty 275.00
2 RC(c), Operation Massacre 125.00
3 An Indestructible Marine . . . 120.00
4 Bridge to Blood Hill 120.00
5 Hell Breaks loose on Suicide Hill 120.00
6 Beachhead Inferno 100.00
7 Fire Power Assault 90.00
8 RC(c),Death-trap Hill 90.00
9 Devil Riders 90.00
10 RC(c), Two-Ton Booby Trap . 50.00
11 Hell's Heroes 45.00
12 Hand Grenade Hero 45.00
13 Commando Assault 45.00
14 Spear Head Assault 45.00
15 Vengeance Assault 45.00

G.I. Combat #2
© Quality Comics Group

16 Trapped Under Fire 40.00
17 Attack on Death Mountain . . . 40.00
18 Red Battle Ground 40.00
19 Death on Helicopter Hill 40.00
20 Doomed Legion-Death Trap . 40.00
21 Red Sneak Attack 38.00
22 Vengeance Raid 38.00
23 No Grandstand in Hell 38.00
24 Operation Steel Trap,Comics Code 38.00
25 Charge of the CommieBrigade 35.00
26 Red Guerrilla Trap 35.00

G.I. Combat #25
© Quality Comics Group

27 Trapped Behind Commie Lines 35.00
28 Atomic Battleground 35.00
29 Patrol Ambush 35.00
30 Operation Booby Trap 35.00
31 Human Fly on Heartbreak Hill 35.00
32 Atomic Rocket Assault 70.00
33 Bridge to Oblivion 35.00
34 RC,Desperate Mission 45.00
35 Doom Patrol 35.00
36 Fire Power Assault 35.00
37 Attack at Dawn 35.00

38 Get That Tank 35.00
39 Mystery of No Man's Land .. 35.00
40 Maneuver Battleground 35.00
41 Trumpet of Doom 35.00
42 March of Doom 35.00
43 Operation Showdown 35.00
See DC Comics for 44-120

GIFT COMICS
Fawcett Publications
March, 1942

1 A:Captain Marvel, Bulletman, Golden Arrow,Ibis, the Invincible, Spy Smasher .. 1,200.00
2 .... 900.00
3 .... 600.00
4 A:Marvel Family, 1949 .... 450.00

GIGGLE COMICS
Creston Publ./ American Comics Group
October, 1943

1 (fa)same 175.00
2 KHu 90.00
3 KHu 55.00
4 KHu 50.00
5 KHu 50.00
6 KHu 45.00
7 KHu 45.00
8 KHu 45.00
9 I:Super Katt 50.00
10 KHu 45.00
11 thru 20 KHu .... @30.00
21 thru 30 KHu .... @25.00
31 thru 40 KHu .... @20.00
41 thru 94 KHu .... @18.00
95 A:Spencer Spook 20.00
96 KHu 18.00
97 KHu 18.00
98 KHu 18.00
99 KHu 18.00
100 and 101 March-April,1955 @18.00

G.I. JANE
Stanhall Publ.
May, 1953

1 .... 55.00
2 thru 6 .... @25.00
7 thru 9 .... @20.00
10 December, 1954 .... 18.00

G.I. JOE
Ziff-Davis Publication Co.
1950

10 NS(c),Red Devils of Korea, V:Seoul City Lou 55.00
11 NS(c),The Guerrilla's Lair ... 35.00
12 NS(c) 35.00
13 NS(c),Attack at Dawn 35.00
14 NS(c),Temple of Terror, A:Peanuts the Great 30.00
2-6 It's a Foot Soldiers Job, I:Frankie of the Pump 30.00
2-7 BP,NS(c),The Rout at Sugar Creek 30.00
8 BP,NS(c),Waldo'sSqueezeBox 30.00
9 NS(c),Dear John 30.00
10 NS(c),Joe Flies the Payroll . 30.00
11 NS(c),For the Love of Benny . 30.00
12 NS(c),Patch work Quilt 30.00
13 NS(c) 30.00
14 NS(c),The Wedding Ring ... 30.00
15 The Lacrosse Whoopee 30.00
16 Mamie's Mortar 30.00
17 A Time for Waiting 30.00
18 Giant 80.00
19 Old Army Game..Buck Passer 25.00
20 General Confusion 25.00
21 Save 'Im for Brooklyn 25.00
22 Portrait of a Lady 25.00
23 Take Care of My Little Wagon 25.00
24 Operation 'Operation' 25.00
25 The Two-Leaf Clover 25.00
26 NS(c),Nobody Flies Alone Mud & Wings 25.00
27 "Dear Son...Come Home" ... 25.00
28 They Alway's Come Back Bondage cover 25.00
29 What a Picnic 22.00
30 NS(c),The One-Sleeved Kimono 22.00
31 NS(c),Get a Horse 20.00
32 thru 47 .... @20.00
48 Atom Bomb 25.00
49 thru 51 June, 1957 ...... @20.00

GINGER
Close-Up Publ. (Archie Publications)
January, 1951

1 GFs 75.00
2 .... 40.00
3 .... 30.00
4 .... 30.00
5 .... 25.00
6 .... 25.00
7 thru 9 .... @35.00
10 A:Katy Keene,Summer,1954 . 40.00

GIRLS IN LOVE
Fawcett Publications
May, 1950

1 .... 40.00
2 Ph(c),July, 1950 .... 35.00

GIRLS IN LOVE
(see DIARY LOVES)

G.I. SWEETHEARTS
(see DIARY LOVES)

G.I. WAR BRIDES
Superior Publ. Ltd.
April, 1954

1 .... 25.00
2 .... 12.00
3 thru 7 .... @10.00
8 June, 1955 .... 10.00

GOING STEADY
(see TEEN-AGE TEMPTATIONS)

GOLDEN ARROW
Fawcett Publications
Spring, 1942

1 B:Golden Arrow 175.00
2 .... 75.00
3 .... 60.00
4 .... 50.00
5 Spring, 1947 .... 50.00
6 BK 60.00
6a 1944 Well Known Comics (Giveaway) 65.00

GOLDEN LAD
Spark Publications
July, 1945

1 MMe,MMe(c),A:Kid Wizards, Swift Arrow,B:Golden Ladd 350.00
2 MMe,MMe(c) 175.00
3 MMe,MMe(c) 175.00
4 MMe,MMe(c), The Menace of the Minstrel 175.00
5 MMe,MMe(c),O:Golden Girl, June, 1946 .... 175.00

GOLDEN WEST LOVE
Kirby Publishing Co.
September-October, 1949

1 BP,I Rode Heartbreak Hill, Ph(c) 75.00
2 BP 60.00

Golden Lad #5 © Spark Publications

3 BP,Ph(c) 60.00
4 BP,April, 1950 .... 60.00

GOLD MEDAL COMICS
Cambridge House
1945

N# Captain Truth 125.00

GOOFY COMICS
Nedor Publ. Co./ Animated Cartoons (Standard Comics)
June, 1943

1 (fa) 125.00
2 .... 65.00
3 VP 45.00
4 VP 35.00
5 VP 35.00
6 thru 10 VP .... @35.00
11 thru 15 .... @30.00
15 thru 19 .... @25.00
20 thru 35 FF .... @40.00
36 thru 48 .... @25.00

GREAT AMERICAN COMICS PRESENTS– THE SECRET VOICE
4 Star Publ.
1944

1 Hitler,Secret Weapon 100.00

GREAT COMICS
Novak Publ. Co.
1945

1 LbC(c) 90.00

GREAT COMICS
Great Comics Publications
November, 1941

1 I:The Great Zorro 500.00
2 .... 300.00
3 The Lost City, January, 1942 550.00

GREAT LOVER ROMANCES
Toby Press
March, 1951

1 Jon Juan,A:Dr. King 65.00
2 Hollywood Girl 35.00
3 Love in a Taxi 20.00
4 The Experimental Kiss 20.00

All comics prices listed are for *Near Mint* condition.

5 After the Honeymoon 20.00
6 HK,The Kid Sister Falls in Love 35.00
7 Man Crazy 20.00
8 Stand-in Boyfriend 20.00
9 The Cheat 20.00
10 Heart Breaker 20.00
11 .... 20.00
12 .... 20.00
13 Powerhouse of Deciet 20.00
14 .... 20.00
15 Ph(c),Still Undecided, Liz Taylor 40.00
16 thru 21 .... @20.00
22 May, 1955 .... 20.00

GREEN GIANT COMICS
Pelican Publications
1941

1 Black Arrow, Dr. Nerod O:Colossus 5,500.00

GREEN HORNET COMICS
Helnit Publ. Co./ Family Comics (Harvey Publ.)
December, 1940

1 B:Green Hornet,P(c) 1,500.00
2 .... 700.00
3 BWh(c) 550.00
4 BWh(c) 450.00
5 BWh(c) 450.00
6 .... 450.00
7 BP, O:Zebra, B:Robin Hood & Spirit of 76 ...... 400.00
8 BP,Bondage cover 350.00
9 BP, Behind the Cover 325.00
10 BP 300.00
11 Who is Mr. Q? 300.00
12 BP,A:Mr.Q 275.00
13 Hitler cover 225.00
14 BP,Spirit of 76-Twinkle Twins, Bondage(c) 225.00

Green Hornet #12
© Helnit Publ./Family Comics

15 ASh(c),Nazi Ghost Ship ... 200.00
16 BP,Prisoner of War 200.00
17 BP,ASh(c),Nazis' Last Stand 200.00
18 BP,ASh(c),Jap's Treacherous Plot,Bondage cover 225.00
19 BP,ASh(c),Clash with the Rampaging Japs 200.00
20 BP,ASh(c),Tojo's Propaganda Hoax 225.00
21 BP,ASh(c),Unwelcome Cargo 200.00
22 ASh(c),Rendezvous with Jap Saboteurs 200.00
23 BF,ASh(c),Jap's Diabolical Plot #B2978 .... 200.00
24 BF,Science Fiction cover .. 225.00
25 thru 29 .... @200.00
30 BP,JKu 200.00
31 BP,JKu 225.00
32 BP,JKu 175.00
33 BP,JKu 175.00
34 BP,JKu 175.00
35 BP,JKu 175.00
36 BP,JKu,Bondage cover 175.00
37 BP,JKu 175.00
38 BP,JKu 175.00
39 S&K 175.00
40 thru 45 .... @150.00
46 Drug 160.00
47 September, 1949 .... 150.00

GREEN LAMA
Spark Publications/Prize Publ.
December, 1944

1 I:Green Lama, Lt. Hercules & Boy Champions 600.00
2 MRa,Forward to Victory in 1945 .... 450.00
3 MRa,The Riddles of Toys .. 325.00
4 MRa,Dive Bombs Japan ... 325.00
5 MRa,MRa(c),Fights for the Four Freedoms 325.00
6 MRa,Smashes a Plot against America 325.00
7 MRa,Merry X-Mas 325.00
8 MRa,Smashes Toy Master of Crime, March, 1946 .... 325.00

GREEN MASK, THE
Fox Features Syndicate
Summer, 1940

1 O:Green Mask & Domino . 1,000.00
2 A:Zanzibar 500.00
3 BP 325.00

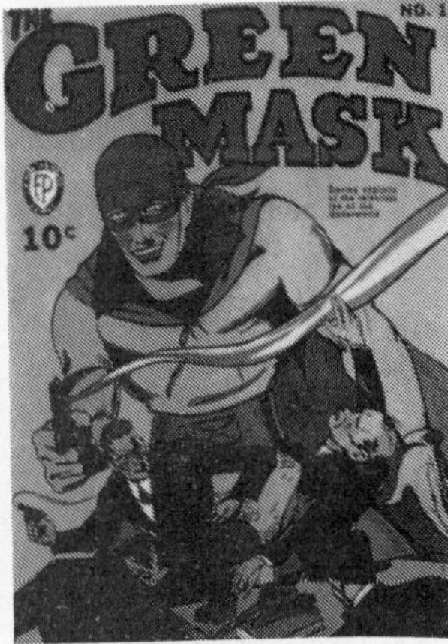

Green Mask #1
© Fox Features Syndicate

4 B:Navy Jones 250.00
5 .... 225.00
6 B:Nightbird,E:Navy Jones, Bondage cover 200.00
7 B:Timothy Smith & The Tumbler 150.00
8 JSs 150.00
9 E:Nightbird, Death Wields a Scalpel! 150.00
10 .... 125.00
11 The Banshee of Dead Man's Hill 125.00
2-1 Election of Skulls 100.00
2-2 Pigeons of Death 85.00
2-3 Wandering Gold Brick 80.00
2-4 Time on His Hands 80.00
2-5 JFe,SFd 80.00
2-6 Adventure of the Disappearing Trains, Oct.-Nov., 1946 ..... 80.00

GUMPS, THE
Dell Publishing Co.
1945

1 .... 75.00
2 .... 50.00
3 .... 40.00
4 .... 40.00
5 .... 40.00

GUNS AGAINST GANGSTERS
Curtis Publ./Novelty Press
September-October, 1948

1 LbC,LbC(c),B:Toni Gayle .. 125.00
2 LbC,LbC(c) 75.00
3 LbC,LbC(c) 65.00
4 LbC,LbC(c) 65.00
5 LbC,LbC(c) 65.00
6 LbC,LbC(c),Shark 65.00
2-1 LbC,LbC(c), September-October, 1949 .. 65.00

GUNSMOKE
Western Comics, Inc.
April-May, 1949

1 GRi,GRi(c),Gunsmoke & Masked Marvel,Bondage cover 200.00
2 GRi,GRi(c) 120.00
3 GRi,GRi(c) 120.00
4 GRi(c),Bondage(c) 80.00
5 GRi(c) 80.00
6 thru 10 .... @50.00
11 thru 15 .... @35.00
16 January, 1952 .... 35.00

HA HA COMICS
Creston Publ. (American Comics Group)
October, 1943

1 Funny Animal, all 150.00
2 .... 75.00
3 .... 55.00
4 .... 55.00
5 .... 55.00
6 thru 10 .... @40.00
11 .... 30.00
12 thru 15 KHu .... @30.00
16 thru 20 KHu .... @28.00
21 thru 30 KHu .... @25.00
31 thru 101 .... @20.00
102 February-March, 1955 .... 20.00

MISTER RISK
Humor Publ. (Ace Magazines)
October, 1950

1 (7) B:Mr. Risk 30.00
2 .... 25.00

Becomes:

MEN AGAINST CRIME

3 A:Mr. Risk, Case of the Carnival Killer 38.00
4 Murder-And the Crowd Roars 20.00
5 .... 20.00
6 .... 20.00
7 Get Them! 20.00

Becomes:

HAND OF FATE
Ace Magazines

8 .... 175.00

9 LC 80.00
10 LC 75.00
11 Genie(c) 55.00
12 55.00
13 Hanging(c) 55.00
14 55.00
15 55.00
16 50.00
17 50.00
18 50.00
19 Drug issue,Quicksand(c) 65.00
20 50.00
21 Drug issue 70.00
22 50.00
23 Graveyard(c) 50.00
24 LC,Electric Chair 90.00
25 November, 1954 45.00
25a December, 1954 50.00

HANGMAN COMICS
(see LAUGH COMICS)

HAP HAZARD COMICS
A.A. Wyn/Red Seal Publ./ Readers Research
Summer, 1944

1 Funny Teen 60.00
2 Dog Show 30.00
3 Sgr, 28.00
4 Sgr, 28.00
5 thru 10 Sgr, @20.00
11 thru 13 Sgr, @15.00
14 AF(c) 35.00
15 thru 24 @15.00

Becomes:

REAL LOVE

25 Dangerous Dates 45.00
26 20.00
27 LbC(c), Revenge Conquest 32.00
28 thru 40 @15.00
41 thru 66 @12.00
67 Comics code 10.00
68 thru 76, Nov. 1956 @10.00

HAPPY COMICS
Nedor Publications/ Animated Cartoons (Standard Comics)
August, 1943

1 Funny Animal in all 125.00
2 75.00
3 45.00
4 40.00
5 thru 10 @40.00
11 thru 20 @35.00
21 thru 30 @30.00
31 and 32 @50.00
33 FF 125.00
34 thru 37 FF @50.00
38 thru 40 @20.00

Becomes:

HAPPY RABBIT

41 Funny Animal in all 25.00
42 thru 50 @15.00

Becomes:

HARVEY COMIC HITS

51 Phantom 125.00
52 Steve Canyon's Air Power 65.00
53 Mandrake 110.00
54 Tim Tyler's Tales of Jungle Terror 65.00
55 Love Stories of Mary Worth 30.00
56 Phantom, Bondage cover 125.00
57 Kidnap Racket 110.00
58 Girls in White 25.00
59 Tales of the Invisible 60.00
60 Paramount Animated Comics 165.00
61 Casper the Friendly Ghost 165.00
62 Paramount Animated Comics, April, 1953 75.00

HAPPY HOULIHANS
(see SADDLE JUSTICE)

HAUNTED THRILLS
Four Star Publ. (Ajax/Farrell)
June, 1952

1 Ellery Queen 150.00
2 LbC,Ellery Queen 85.00
3 Drug Story 75.00
4 Ghouls Castle 65.00
5 Fatal Scapel 65.00
6 Pit of Horror 55.00
7 Trail to a Tomb 55.00
8 Vanishing Skull 55.00
9 Madness of Terror 55.00
10 55.00
11 Nazi Concentration Camp 75.00
12 RWb 55.00
13 45.00
14 RWb 50.00
15 The Devil Collects 40.00
16 40.00
17 Mirror of Madness 40.00
18 No Place to Go, November December, 1954 45.00

HAUNT OF FEAR
Fables Publ. (E.C. Comics)
May-June, 1950

15 JCr,JCr(c),AF,WW 1,600.00
16 JCr,JCr(c),AF,WW 750.00
17 JCr,JCr(c),AF,WW,O:Crypt of Terror,Vault of Horror & Haunt of Fear 750.00
4 AF(c),WW,JDa 600.00
5 JCr,JCr(c),WW,JDa,Eye Injury 500.00
6 JCr,JCr(c),WW,JDa 325.00
7 JCr,JCr(c),WW,JDa 325.00
8 AF(c),JKa,JDa, Shrunken Head 325.00
9 AF(c),JCr,JDa 325.00
10 AF(c),Grl,JDa 300.00
11 JKa,Grl,JDa 275.00
12 JCr,Grl,JDa 275.00
13 Grl,JDa 275.00
14 Grl,Grl(c),JDa,O:Old Witch 325.00
15 JDa 275.00

Haunt of Fear #16 © E.C. Comics

16 GRi(c),JDa,Ray Bradbury adaptation 275.00
17 JDa,Grl(c),Classic Ghastly (c) 275.00
18 JDa,Grl(c),JKa,Ray Bradbury adaptation 300.00
19 JDa,Guillotine (c), Bondage cover 300.00
20 RC,JDa,Grl,Grl(c) 250.00
21 JDa,Grl,Grl(c) 200.00
22 same 200.00
23 same 200.00
22 same 200.00
23 same 200.00
24 same 200.00
25 same 200.00
26 RC,same 250.00
27 same, Cannibalism 225.00
28 December, 1954 225.00

HAWK, THE
Approved Comics (Ziff-Davis)
Winter, 1951

1 MA,The Law of the Colt,P(c) 100.00
2 JKu,Iron Caravan of the Mojave, P(c) 55.00
3 Leverett's Last Stand,P(c) 50.00
4 Killer's Town,P(c) 40.00
5 35.00
6 35.00
7 35.00
8 MB(c),Dry River Rampage 40.00
9 MB,MB(c),JKu 45.00
10 MB(c) 40.00
11 MB(c) 40.00
12 MB,MB(c), May, 1955 40.00

HEADLINE COMICS
American Boys Comics/ Headline Publ. (Prize Publ.)
February, 1943

1 B:Jr. Rangers 225.00
2 JaB,JaB(c) 90.00
3 JaB,JaB(c) 75.00
4 75.00
5 HcK 75.00
6 HcK 75.00
7 HcK,Jr. Rangers 75.00
8 HcK,Hitler cover 125.00
9 HcK 75.00
10 HcK,Hitler story,Wizard(c) 125.00
11 40.00
12 HcK,Heroes of Yesterday 40.00
13 HcK,A:Blue Streak 45.00
14 HcK,A:Blue Streak 45.00
15 HcK,A:Blue Streak 45.00
16 HcK,O:Atomic Man 125.00
17 Atomic Man(c) 55.00
18 Atomic Man(c) 55.00
19 S&K,Atomic Man(c) 125.00
20 Atomic Man(c) 55.00
21 E:Atomic Man 55.00
22 HcK 25.00
23 S&K,S&K(c),Valentines Day Massacre 100.00
24 S&K,S&K(c),You can't Forget a Killer 100.00
25 S&K,S&K(c),CrimeNeverPays 75.00
26 S&K,S&K(c),CrimeNeverPays 75.00
27 S&K,S&K(c),CrimeNeverPays 75.00
28 S&K,S&K(c),CrimeNeverPays 75.00
29 S&K,S&K(c),CrimeNeverPays 75.00
30 S&K,S&K(c),CrimeNeverPays 75.00
31 S&K,S&K(c),CrimeNeverPays 75.00
32 S&K,S&K(c),CrimeNeverPays 75.00
33 S&K,S&K(c),Police and FBI heroes 75.00
34 S&K,S&K(c),same 75.00
35 S&K,S&K(c),same 75.00
36 S&K,S&K(c),same,Ph(c) 75.00
37 S&K,S&K(c),MvS,same,Ph(c) 35.00
38 S&K,S&K(c),same,Ph(c) 20.00
39 S&K,S&K(c),same,Ph(c) 20.00
40 S&K,S&K(c),Ph(c)Violent Crime 20.00
41 Ph(c),J.Edgar Hoover(c) 20.00

42 Ph(c) 15.00
43 Ph(c) 15.00
44 MMe,MvS,WE,S&K 35.00
45 JK 18.00
46 . . . . . 15.00
47 . . . . . 15.00
48 . . . . . 15.00
49 MMe 15.00
50 . . . . . 15.00
51 JK 18.00
52 . . . . . 15.00
53 . . . . . 15.00
54 . . . . . 15.00
55 . . . . . 15.00
56 S&K 28.00
57 . . . . . 15.00
58 . . . . . 15.00
59 . . . . . 15.00
60 MvS(c) 15.00
61 MMe,MvS(c) 15.00
62 MMe,MMe(c) 15.00
63 MMe,MMe(c) 15.00
64 MMe,MMe(c) 15.00
65 MMe,MMe(c) 15.00
66 MMe,MMe(c) 15.00
67 MMe,MMe(c) 15.00
68 MMe,MMe(c) 15.00
69 MMe,MMe(c) 15.00
70 MMe,MMe(c) 15.00
71 MMe,MMe(c) 15.00
72 MMe,MMe(c) 15.00
73 MMe,MMe(c) 15.00
74 MMe,MMe(c) 15.00
75 MMe,MMe(c) 15.00
76 MMe,MMe(c) 15.00
77 MMe,MMe(c),October, 1956 . 15.00

HEART THROBS
Comics Magazines (Quality)
August, 1949

1 BWa(c),PG,Spoiled Brat . . . 200.00
2 BWa(c),PG,Siren of the Tropics 140.00
3 PG 45.00
4 BWa(c),Greed Turned Me into a Scheming Vixen,Ph(c) 60.00
5 Ph(c) 25.00
6 BWa 60.00
7 . . . . . 25.00
8 BWa 60.00
9 I Hated Men,Ph(c) 40.00
10 BWa,My Secret Fears 50.00
11 . . . . . 18.00
12 . . . . . 15.00
13 . . . . . 18.00
14 BWa 18.00
15 My Right to Happiness,Ph(c) . 45.00
16 . . . . . 16.00
17 . . . . . 16.00
18 . . . . . 16.00
19 . . . . . 16.00
20 . . . . . 16.00
21 BWa 35.00
22 BWa 30.00
23 BWa 30.00
24 thru 30 . . . . . @15.00
31 thru 33 . . . . . @15.00
34 thru 39 . . . . . @15.00
40 BWa 25.00
41 . . . . . 15.00
42 . . . . . 15.00
43 . . . . . 15.00
44 . . . . . 15.00
45 . . . . . 15.00

BECOMES A DC COMIC (Please see DC listings)

HECKLE AND JECKLE
St. John Publ./Pines
November, 1951

1 Blue Ribbon Comics 165.00
2 Blue Ribbon Comics 100.00
3 . . . . . 75.00
4 . . . . . 60.00
5 . . . . . 60.00
6 . . . . . 60.00
7 . . . . . 55.00
8 . . . . . 50.00

Heckle and Jeckle #9
© St. John Publications

9 . . . . . 50.00
10 . . . . . 50.00
11 thru 15 . . . . . @35.00
16 thru 20 . . . . . @30.00
21 thru 33 . . . . . @22.00
34 June, 1959 . . . . . 22.00

HELLO PAL COMICS
Harvey Publications
January, 1943

1 B:Rocketman & Rocket Girl, Mickey Rooney cover, Ph(c) all 350.00
2 Charlie McCarthy cover 225.00
3 Bob Hope cover, May, 1943 275.00

HENRY
Dell Publishing Co.
October, 1946

1 . . . . . 60.00
2 . . . . . 25.00
3 thru 10 . . . . . @20.00
11 thru 20 . . . . . @15.00
21 thru 30 . . . . . @10.00
31 thru 40 . . . . . @9.00
41 thru 50 . . . . . @8.00
51 thru 65 . . . . . @7.00

HENRY ALDRICH COMICS
Dell Publishing Co.
August-September, 1950

1 . . . . . 60.00
2 . . . . . 30.00
3 . . . . . 25.00
4 . . . . . 25.00
5 . . . . . 25.00
6 thru 10 . . . . . @22.00
11 thru 22 . . . . . @16.00

HEROIC COMICS
Eastern Color Printing Co./ Famous Funnies
August, 1940

1 BEv,BEv(c),O:Hydroman,Purple Zombie, B:Man of India . . . 600.00
2 BEv,BEv(c),B:Hydroman covers 300.00

Heroic Comics #3
© Eastern Color Printing

3 BEv,BEv(c) 275.00
4 BEv,BEv(c) 250.00
5 BEv,BEv(c) 200.00
6 BEv,BEv(c) 200.00
7 BEv,BEv(c),O:Man O'Metal . 225.00
8 BEv,BEv(c) 150.00
9 BEv 150.00
10 BEv 150.00
11 BEv,E:Hydroman covers . . . 125.00
12 BEv,B&O:Music Master 150.00
13 BEv,RC,LF 125.00
14 BEv 150.00
15 BEv,I:Downbeat 150.00
16 BEv,CCB(c),A:Lieut Nininger, Major Heidger,Lieut Welch,B:P(c) 100.00
17 BEv,A:JohnJames Powers,Hewitt T.Wheless, Irving Strobing . 100.00
18 HcK,BEv,Pass the Ammunition 100.00
19 HcK,BEv,A:Barney Ross . . . 100.00
20 HcK,BEv 90.00
21 HcK,BEv 65.00
22 HcK,BEv,Howard Gilmore . . . 65.00
23 HcK,BEv 65.00
24 HcK,BEv 65.00
25 HcK,BEv 65.00
26 HcK,BEv 65.00
27 HcK,BEv 65.00
28 HcK,BEv,E:Man O'Metal 65.00
29 HcK,BEv,E:Hydroman 65.00
30 BEv 60.00
31 BEv,CCB,Capt. Tootsie 25.00
32 ATh,CCB,WWII(c), Capt. Tootsie 35.00
33 ATh, ... 35.00
34 WWII(c) 20.00
35 Ath,B:Rescue(c) 35.00
36 HcK,ATh 35.00
37 same 35.00
38 ATh 35.00
39 HcK,ATh 35.00
40 ATh,Boxing 35.00
41 Grl(c),ATh 35.00
42 ATh 35.00
43 ATh 30.00
44 HcK,ATh 30.00
45 HcK 30.00
46 HcK 30.00
47 HcK 30.00
48 HcK 30.00
49 HcK 30.00
50 HcK 30.00
51 HcK,ATh,AW 32.00

52 HcK,AW 32.00
53 HcK 30.00
54 . . . . 18.00
55 ATh 18.00
56 ATh(c) 28.00
57 ATh(c) 25.00
58 ATh(c) 25.00
59 ATh(c) 25.00
60 ATh(c) 25.00
61 BEv(c) 20.00
62 BEv(c) 20.00
63 BEv(c) 20.00
64 GE,BEv(c) 22.00
65 HcK(c),FF,ATh,AW,GE 50.00
66 HcK(c),FF 35.00
67 HcK(c),FF,Korean War(c) . . . 35.00
68 HcK(c),Korean War(c) 35.00
69 HcK(c),FF 40.00
70 HcK(c),FF,B:Korean War(c) . 35.00
71 HcK(c),FF 35.00
72 HcK(c),FF 40.00
73 HcK(c),FF 35.00
74 HcK(c) 35.00
75 HcK(c),FF 35.00
76 HcK,HcK(c) 12.00
77 same 12.00
78 same 12.00
79 same 12.00
80 same 12.00
81 FF,HcK(c) 15.00
82 FF,HcK(c) 15.00
83 FF,HcK(c) 15.00
84 HcK(c) 15.00
85 HcK(c) 15.00
86 FF,HcK(c) 20.00
87 FF,HcK(c) 20.00
88 HcK(c),E:Korean War covers 12.00
89 HcK(c) 12.00
90 HcK(c) 12.00
91 HcK(c) 12.00
92 HcK(c) 12.00
93 HcK(c) 12.00
94 HcK(c) 12.00
95 HcK(c) 12.00
96 HcK(c) 12.00
97 HcK(c),E:P(c),June, 1955 . . . 12.00

HICKORY
Comic Magazine
(Quality Comics Group)
October, 1949

1 ASa, ... 70.00
2 ASa, ... 35.00
3 ASa, ... 25.00
4 ASa, ... 25.00
5 ASa, ... 25.00
6 ASa,August, 1950 . . . . 25.00

HI-HO COMICS
Four Star Publications
1946

1 LbC(c) 90.00
2 LbC(c) 55.00
3 1946 . . . . 50.00

HI-JINX
B & I Publ. Co.
(American Comics Group)
July-August, 1947

1 (fa) all 65.00
2 . . . . 42.00
3 . . . . 40.00
4 thru 7 . . . . @38.00
N# 75.00

HI-LITE COMICS
E.R. Ross Publ.
Fall, 1945

1 . . . . 65.00

HIT COMICS
Comics Magazine
(Quality Comics Group)
July, 1940

1 LF(c),O:Neon,Hercules,I:The Red Bee, B:Bob & Swab, Blaze Barton Strange Twins,X-5 Super Agent Casey Jones,Jack & Jill . . 2,000.00
2 GT,LF(c),B:Old Witch 850.00
3 GT,LF(c),E:Casey Jones . . 700.00
4 GT,LF(c),B:Super Agent & Betty Bates,E:X-5 . . . . 600.00
5 GT,LF(c),B:Red Bee cover . 875.00
6 GT,LF(c) 550.00
7 GT,LF(c),E:Red Bee cover . 575.00
8 GT,LF(c),B:Neon cover . . . 500.00
9 JCo,LF(c),E:Neon cover . . . 500.00
10 JCo,RC,LF(c),B:Hercules(c) 500.00
11 JCo,RC,LF(c),A:Hercules . . 475.00
12 JCo,RC,LF(c),A:Hercules . . 475.00
13 JCo,RC,LF(c),A:Hercules . . 475.00
14 JCo,RC,LF(c),A:Hercules . . 475.00
15 JCo,RC,A:Hercules 450.00
16 JCo,RC,LF(c),A:Hercules . . 450.00
17 JCo,RC,LF(c),E:Hercules(c) 450.00
18 JCo,RC,RC(c),O:Stormy Foster,B:Ghost of Flanders . 500.00
19 JCo,RC(c),B:StormyFoster(c) 450.00
20 JCo,RC(c),A:Stormy Foster . 450.00
21 JCo,RC(c) 400.00
22 JCo 400.00
23 JCo,RC,RC(c) 375.00
24 JCo,E:Stormy Foster cover . 375.00
25 JCo,RP,O:Kid Eternity 500.00
26 JCo,RP,A:Black Hawk 400.00
27 JCo,RP,B:Kid Eternity covers 250.00
28 JCo,RP,A:Her Highness . . . 250.00
29 JCo,RP 250.00
30 JCo,RP,HK,V:Julius Caesar and his Legion of Warriors . 200.00
31 JCo,RP 200.00
32 JCo,RP,V:Merlin the Wizard 125.00
33 JCo,RP 100.00
34 JCo,RP,E:Stormy Foster . . . 100.00
35 JCo,Kid Eternity accused of Murder 100.00
36 JCo,The Witch's Curse 100.00
37 JCo,V:Mr. Silence 100.00

Hit Comics #38
© Quality Comics Group

38 JCo 100.00
39 JCo,Runaway River Boat . . 100.00
40 PG,V:Monster from the Past 100.00
41 PG,Did Kid Eternity Lose His Power? 75.00
42 PG,Kid Eternity Loses Killer Cronson 75.00
43 JCo,PG,V:Modern Bluebeard 75.00
44 JCo,PG,Trips up the Shoe . . 75.00
45 JCo,PG,Pancho Villa against Don Pablo 75.00
46 JCo,V:Mr. Hardeel 75.00
47 A Polished Diamond can be Rough on Rats 75.00
48 EhH,A Treasure Chest of Trouble 75.00
49 EhH,V:Monsters from the Mirror 75.00
50 EhH,Heads for Trouble 75.00
51 EhH,Enters the Forgotten World 65.00
52 EhH,Heroes out of the Past . 65.00
53 EhH,V:Mr. Puny 65.00
54 V:Ghost Town Killer 65.00
55 V:The Brute 65.00
56 V:Big Odds 60.00
57 Solves the Picture in a Frame 60.00
58 Destroys Oppression! 60.00
59 Battles Tomorrow's Crimes Today! 60.00
60 E:Kid Eternity covers, V:The Mummy 60.00
61 RC,RC(c),I:Jeb Rivers 75.00
62 RC(c) 65.00
63 RC(c),A:Jeb Rivers 75.00
64 RC,A:Jeb Rivers 75.00
65 Bondage cover,RC,July, 1950 80.00

HOLIDAY COMICS
Fawcett Publ.
November, 1942

1 Captain Marvel (c) 800.00

HOLIDAY COMICS
Star Publ.
January, 1951

1 LbC(c),(fa),Christmas cover . 120.00
2 LbC(c),Parade(c) 130.00
3 LbC(c),July 4th(c) 70.00
4 LbC(c),Vacation(c) 70.00
5 LbC(c),Christmas(c) 70.00
6 LbC(c),Birthday(c) 70.00
7 LbC(c) 65.00
8 LbC(c),Christmas(c) 70.00

HOLLYWOOD COMICS
New Age Publishers
Winter, 1944

1 (fa) 80.00

HOLLYWOOD CONFESSIONS
St. John Publ. Co.
October, 1949

1 JKu,JKu(c) 120.00
2 JKu,JKu(c), December, 1949 100.00

HOLLYWOOD DIARY
Comics Magazine
(Quality Comics)
December, 1949

1 . . . . 80.00
2 Photo cover 50.00
3 Photo cover 40.00
4 . . . . 40.00
5 Photo cover, August, 1950 . . 40.00

HOLLYWOOD FILM STORIES
Feature Publications
(Prize)
April, 1950

1 June Allison,Ph(c) 75.00
2 Lizabeth Scott,Ph(c) 55.00
3 Barbara Stanwick,Ph(c) 55.00
4 Beth Hutton, August, 1950 . . 55.00

HOLLYWOOD SECRETS
Comics Magazine
(Quality Comics Group)
November, 1949

1 BWa,BWa(c) 160.00
2 BWa,BWa(c),RC 100.00
3 Ph(c) 45.00
4 Ph(c),May, 1950 . . . . 45.00
5 Ph(c) 45.00
6 Ph(c) 45.00

HOLYOKE ONE-SHOT
Tem Publ.
(Holyoke Publ. Co.)
1944

1 Grit Grady 55.00
2 Rusty Dugan 50.00
3 JK,Miss Victory,O:Cat Woman 130.00
4 Mr. Miracle 55.00
5 U.S. Border Patrol 50.00
6 Capt. Fearless 50.00
7 Strong Man 55.00
8 Blue Streak 50.00
9 S&K, Citizen Smith 80.00
10 S&K, Capt. Stone 75.00

HONEYMOON ROMANCE
Artful Publications
(Digest Size)
April, 1950

1 . . . . 165.00
2 July, 1950 . . . . 150.00

HOODED HORSEMAN
(see OUT OF THE NIGHT)

HOPALONG CASSIDY
Fawcett Publications
February, 1943

1 B:Hopalong Cassidy & Topper,
Captain Marvel cover 1,500.00
2 . . . . 400.00
3 Blazing Trails 225.00
4 5-full length story 200.00
5 Death in the Saddle, Ph(c) . 175.00
6 . . . . 150.00
7 . . . . 150.00
8 Phantom Stage Coach 150.00
9 The Last Stockade 150.00
10 4-spine tingling adventures . 150.00
11 Desperate Jetters! Ph(c) . . . 135.00
12 The Mysterious Message . . 135.00
13 The Human Target, Ph(c) . . 125.00
14 Land of the Lawless, Ph(c) . 125.00
15 Death holds the Reins, Ph(c) 125.00
16 Webfoot's Revenge, Ph(c) . 125.00
17 The Hangman's Noose, Ph(c) 125.00
18 The Ghost of Dude Ranch,
Ph(c) 125.00
19 A:William Boyd,Ph(c) 125.00
20 The Notorious Nellie Blaine!,
B:P(c) 100.00
21 V:Arizona Kid 100.00
22 V:Arizona Kid 100.00
23 Hayride Horror 100.00
24 Twin River Giant 100.00
25 On the Trails of the Wild
and Wooly West 100.00
26 thru 30 . . . . @90.00
31 52 pages 50.00
32 36 pages 40.00
33 thru 35, 52 pages . . . . @50.00
36 36 pages 42.00
37 thru 40, 52 pages . . . . @50.00
40 36 pages 42.00
41 E:P(c) 40.00
42 B:Ph(c) 50.00
43 . . . . 50.00
44 . . . . 40.00
45 . . . . 50.00
46 thru 51 . . . . @40.00
52 . . . . 35.00
53 . . . . 40.00
54 . . . . 40.00
55 . . . . 35.00
56 . . . . 40.00
57 . . . . 40.00
58 thru 70 . . . . @35.00
71 thru 84 . . . . @25.00
85 E:Ph(c),January, 1954 . . . . . 25.00
(Please see DC listings)

Hoppy the Marvel Bunny #3
© Fawcett Publications

HOPPY THE MARVEL BUNNY
Fawcett Publications
December, 1945

1 A:Marvel Bunny 150.00
2 . . . . 65.00
3 . . . . 50.00
4 . . . . 50.00
5 . . . . 50.00
6 thru 14 . . . . @40.00
15 September, 1947 . . . . 40.00

HORRIFIC
Artful/Comic Media/
Harwell Publ./Mystery
September, 1952

1 Conductor in Flames(c) 125.00
2 Human Puppets(c) 60.00
3 DH(c),Bullet hole in
head(c) 100.00
4 DH(c),head on a stick (c) . . . 65.00
5 DH(c) 90.00
6 DH(c),Jack the Ripper 55.00
7 DH(c),Shrunken Skulls 55.00
8 DH(c),I:The Teller 65.00
9 DH(c),Claws of Horror, Wolves
of Midnight 45.00
10 DH(c),The Teller-four
eerie tales of Horror 45.00
11 DH(c),A:Gary Ghoul,Freddie,
Demon,Victor Vampire,
Walter Werewolf 35.00
12 DH(c),A:Gary Ghoul,Freddie
Demon,Victor Vampire,
Walter Werewolf 35.00
13 DH(c),A:Gary Ghoul,Freddie
Demom,Victor Vampire,
Walter Werewolf 35.00
Becomes:

TERRIFIC COMICS

14 . . . . 90.00
15 . . . . 60.00
16 B:Wonderboy 70.00
Becomes:

WONDERBOY

17 The Enemy's Enemy 125.00
18 Success is No Accident,
July, 1955 . . . . 110.00

HORROR FROM THE TOMB
(see MYSTERIOUS STORIES)

HORRORS, THE
Star Publications
January, 1953

11 LbC(c),JyD,of War 90.00
12 LbC(c),of War 85.00
13 LbC(c),of Mystery 75.00
14 LbC(c),of the Underworld . . . 85.00
15 LbC(c),of the Underworld,
April, 1954 . . . . 85.00

HORSE FEATHER COMICS
Lev Gleason Publications
November, 1947

1 BW 100.00
2 . . . . 45.00
3 . . . . 35.00
4 Summer, 1948 . . . . 35.00

HOT ROD AND SPEEDWAY COMICS
Hillman Periodicals
February-March, 1952

1 . . . . 90.00
2 BK 75.00
3 . . . . 30.00
4 . . . . 30.00
5 April-May, 1953 . . . . 30.00

HOT ROD COMICS
Fawcett Publications
February, 1952

N# BP,BP(c),F:Clint Curtis . . . 125.00
2 BP,BP(c),Safety comes in First 75.00
3 BP,BP(c),The Racing Game . 50.00
4 BP,BP(c),Bonneville National
Championships 50.00
5 BP,BP(c), ... 50.00
6 BP,BP(c),Race to Death,
February,1953 . . . . 50.00

HOT ROD KING
Approved Comics
(Ziff-Davis)
Fall, 1952

1 P(c) 120.00

HOWDY DOODY
Dell Publishing Co.
January, 1950

1 Ph(c) 400.00
2 Ph(c) 150.00
3 Ph(c) 100.00
4 Ph(c) 100.00
5 Ph(c) 100.00
6 P(c) 90.00
7 . . . . 75.00
8 . . . . 75.00
9 . . . . 75.00
10 . . . . 75.00
11 . . . . 60.00
12 . . . . 60.00
13 Christmas (c) 60.00
14 thru 20 . . . . @60.00
21 thru 38 . . . . @50.00

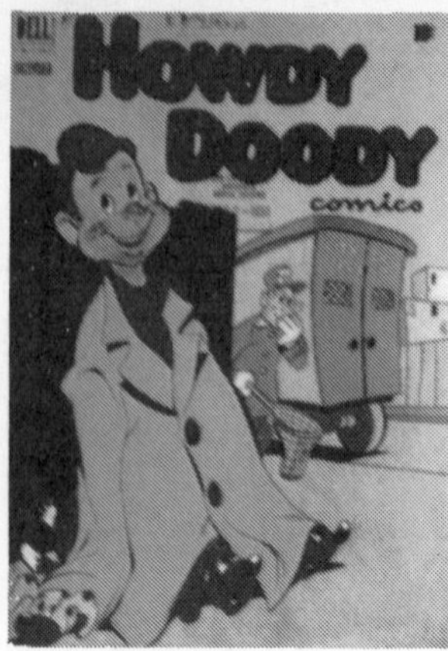

Howdy Doody Comics #12
© Dell Publishing Co.

HOW STALIN HOPES WE WILL DESTROY AMERICA
Pictorial News
1951

N# (Giveaway) 300.00

HUMBUG
Harvey Kurtzman
1957

1 JDa,WW,WE,End of the World125.00
2 JDa,WE,Radiator 75.00
3 JDa,WE 55.00
4 JDa,WE,Queen Victoria(c) . . . 50.00
5 JDa,WE 50.00
6 JDa,WE 50.00
7 JDa,WE,Sputnik(c) 60.00
8 JDa,WE,Elvis/George Washington(c) 55.00
9 JDa,WE 50.00
10 JDa,Magazine 50.00
11 JDw,WE,HK,Magazine 50.00

HUMDINGER
Novelty Press/ Premium Service
May-June, 1946

1 B:Jerkwater Line,Dink, Mickey Starlight 100.00
2 . . . . 45.00
3 . . . . 35.00
4 . . . . 35.00
5 . . . . 35.00
6 . . . . 35.00
2-1 . . . . 30.00
2-2 July-August, 1947 . . . . 30.00

HUMPHREY COMICS
Harvey Publications
October, 1948

1 BP,Joe Palooka 70.00
2 BP 35.00
3 BP 30.00
4 BP,A:Boy Heroes 40.00
5 BP 25.00
6 BP 25.00
7 BP,A:Little Dot 25.00
8 BP,O:Humphrey 30.00
9 BP 15.00
10 BP 15.00
11 thru 21 . . . . @15.00

22 April, 1952 . . . . 15.00

HYPER MYSTERY COMICS
Hyper Publications
May, 1940

1 B:Hyper 700.00
2 June, 1940 . . . . 500.00

IBIS, THE INVINCIBLE
Fawcett Publications
January, 1942

1 MRa(c),O:Ibis 800.00
2 Bondage cover 450.00
3 BW 325.00
4 BW,A:Mystic Snake People 275.00
5 BW,Bondage cover,The Devil's Ibistick 300.00
6 BW, The Book of Evil, Spring, 1948 . . . . 275.00

IDEAL ROMANCE
(see TENDER ROMANCE)

IF THE DEVIL WOULD TALK
Catechetical Guild
1950

N# Rare 500.00
N#, 1958 Very Rare 450.00

ILLUSTRATED STORIES OF THE OPERA
B. Bailey Publ. Co.
1943

N# Faust 300.00
N# Aida 275.00
N# Carman 300.00
N# Rigoletto 300.00

I LOVED
(see ZOOT COMICS)

I LOVE LUCY COMICS
Dell Publishing Co.
February, 1954

(1) *see Dell Four Color #535*
(2) *see Dell Four Color #559*
3 Lucile Ball Ph(c) all 275.00
4 . . . . 100.00
5 . . . . 100.00
6 thru 10 . . . . @85.00
11 thru 20 . . . . @75.00
21 thru 35 . . . . @60.00

IMPACT
E.C. Comics
March-April, 1955

1 RC,GE,BK,Grl 125.00
2 RC,JDu,Grl,BK,JO 100.00
3 JO,RC,JDU,Grl,JKa,BK 80.00
4 RC,JO,JDa,GE,Grl,BK 80.00
5 November-December, 1955 . 80.00

INCREDIBLE SCIENCE FANTASY
(see WEIRD SCIENCE)

INCREDIBLE SCIENCE FICTION
E.C. Comics
July-August, 1955

30 . . . . 225.00
31 . . . . 250.00
32 January-February, 1956 . . . 250.00
33 . . . . 225.00

INDIAN CHIEF
Dell Publishing Co.
July-September, 1951

3 P(c) all 25.00
4 . . . . 15.00
5 . . . . 15.00
6 A:White Eagle 15.00
7 . . . . 15.00
8 . . . . 15.00
9 . . . . 15.00
10 . . . . 15.00
11 . . . . 15.00
12 I:White Eagle 25.00
13 thru 29 . . . . @10.00
30 SB 15.00
31 SB 15.00
32 SB 15.00
33 SB 15.00

INDIAN FIGHTER
Youthful Magazines
May, 1950

1 Revenge of Chief Crazy Horse 55.00
2 Bondage cover 35.00
3 . . . . 20.00
4 Cheyenne Warpath 20.00
5 . . . . 20.00
6 Davy Crockett in Death Stalks the Alamo 20.00
7 Tom Horn-Bloodshed at Massacre Valley 20.00
8 Tales of Wild Bill Hickory, January, 1952 . . . . 20.00

INDIANS
Wings Publ. Co. (Fiction House)
Spring, 1950

1 B:Long Bow, Manzar, White Indian & Orphan 125.00
2 B:Starlight 65.00
3 Longbow(c) 50.00
4 Longbow(c) 50.00
5 Manzar(c) 50.00
6 Captive of the Semecas 40.00
7 Longbow(c) 40.00
8 A:Long Bow 40.00
9 A:Long Bow 40.00
10 Manzar(c) 40.00
11 thru 16 . . . . @30.00
17 Spring, 1953,Longbow(c) . . . 30.00

Indians on the Warpath #1
© St. John Publishing Co.

INDIANS ON THE WARPATH
St. John Publ. Co.
1950

N# MB(c) 140.00

INFORMER, THE
Feature Television Productions
April, 1954

1 MSy,The Greatest Social Menace of our Time! 45.00
2 MSy 28.00
3 MSy 25.00
4 MSy 25.00
5 December, 1954 . . . . 25.00

IN LOVE
Mainline/Charlton Comics
August, 1954

1 S&K,Bride of the Star 120.00
2 S&K,Marilyn's Men 75.00
3 S&K 50.00
4 S&K,Comics Code 30.00
5 S&K(c) 30.00
6 . . . . 15.00

Becomes:

I LOVE YOU

7 JK(c),BP 50.00
8 . . . . 15.00
9 . . . . 15.00
10 . . . . 15.00
11 thru 16 . . . . @10.00
17 . . . . 12.00
18 . . . . 9.00
19 . . . . 9.00
20 . . . . 9.00
21 thru 50 . . . . @6.00
51 thru 59 . . . . @4.00
60 Elvis 75.00
61 thru 100 . . . . @3.00
101 thru 130 . . . . @2.00

INTERNATIONAL COMICS
(see CRIME PATROL)

INTERNATIONAL CRIME PATROL
(see CRIME PATROL)

INTIMATE CONFESSIONS
Fawcett Publ./ Realistic Comics
1951

1a P(c) all, Unmarried Bride . 400.00
1 EK,EK(c),Days of Temptation... Nights of Desire 150.00
2 Doomed to Silence 100.00
3 EK(c), The Only Man For Me 60.00
3a Robert Briffault 60.00
4 EK(c),Tormented Love 75.00
5 Her Secret Sin 75.00
6 Reckless Pick-up 75.00
7 A Love Like Ours,Spanking . 100.00
8 Fatal Woman, March, 1953 . 75.00

INTIMATE LOVE
Standard Magazines
January, 1950

5 Wings on My Heart,Ph(c) . . . 30.00
6 WE,JSe,Ph(c) 35.00
7 WE,JSe,Ph(c),I Toyed with Love 35.00
8 WE,JSe,Ph(c) 35.00
9 Ph(c) 25.00
10 Ph(c),My Hopeless Heart . . . 35.00
11 thru 18 . . . . @10.00
19 ATh 35.00
20 . . . . 10.00
21 ATh 35.00
22 ATh 35.00
23 ATh 10.00
24 ATh 35.00
25 ATh 10.00
26 ATh 35.00
27 ATh 10.00
28 ATh,August, 1954 . . . . 10.00

INTIMATE SECRETS OF ROMANCE
Star Publications
September, 1953

1 LbC(c) 50.00
2 LbC(c) 45.00

INVISIBLE SCARLET O'NEIL
Harvey Publications
December, 1950

1 . . . . 75.00
2 . . . . 55.00
3 April, 1951 . . . . 50.00

IT REALLY HAPPENED
William H. Wise/ Visual Editions
1945

1 Benjamin Franklin, Kit Carson 95.00
2 The Terrible Tiddlers 50.00
3 Maid of the Margiris 35.00
4 Chaplain Albert J. Hoffman . . 30.00
5 AS(c),Monarchs of the Sea,Lou Gehrig, Amelia Earhart 80.00
6 AS(c),Ernie Pyle 30.00
7 FG,Teddy Roosevelt,Jefferson Davis, Story of the Helicopter 30.00
8 FG,Man O' War,Roy Rogers . 90.00
9 AS(c),The Story of Old Ironsides 30.00
10 AS(c),Honus Wagner, The Story of Mark Twain 75.00
11 AS(c),MB,Queen of the Spanish Main, October, 1947 . . . . 50.00

JACK ARMSTRONG
Parents' Institute
November, 1947

1 Artic Mystery 125.00
2 Den of the Golden Dragon . . 75.00
3 Lost Valley of Ice 60.00
4 Land of the Leopard Men . . . 60.00
5 Fight against Racketeers of the Ring 60.00
6 . . . . 50.00
7 Baffling Mystery on the Diamond 50.00
8 . . . . 50.00
9 Mystery of the Midgets 50.00
10 Secret Cargo 50.00
11 . . . . 45.00
12 Madman's Island 45.00
13 September, 1949 . . . . 45.00

JACE PEARSON OF THE TEXAS RANGERS
Dell Publishing Co.
May, 1952

(1) *see Dell Four Color #396*
2 Ph(c),Joel McRae 40.00
3 Ph(c),Joel McRae 40.00
4 Ph(c),Joel McRae 40.00
5 Ph(c),Joel McRae 40.00
6 Ph(c),Joel McRae 40.00
7 Ph(c),Joel McRae 40.00
8 Ph(c),Joel McRae 40.00
9 Ph(c),Joel McRae 40.00
(10) *see Dell Four Color #648*

Becomes:

TALES OF JACE PEARSON OF THE TEXAS RANGERS

11 . . . . 30.00
12 . . . . 30.00
13 . . . . 30.00
14 . . . . 30.00
15 ATh 40.00
16 ATh 40.00
17 . . . . 30.00
18 . . . . 30.00
19 . . . . 30.00
20 . . . . 30.00

JACKIE GLEASON
St. John Publishing Co.
September, 1955

1 Ph(c) 400.00
2 . . . . 300.00
3 . . . . 250.00
4 December, 1955 . . . . 225.00

Jackie Robinson #6
© Fawcett Publications

JACKIE ROBINSON
Fawcett Publications
May, 1950

N# Ph(c) all issues 500.00
2 . . . . 300.00
3 thru 5 . . . . @250.00
6 May, 1952 . . . . 250.00

JACK IN THE BOX
(see YELLOW JACKET COMICS)

JACKPOT COMICS
MLJ Magazines
Spring, 1941

1 CBi(c),B:Black Hood,Mr.Justice, Steel Sterling,Sgt.Boyle . . 1,150.00
2 SCp(c), ... 550.00
3 Bondage cover 500.00
4 First Archie 1,200.00
5 Hitler(c) 550.00
6 Son of the Skull v:Black Hood, Bondage(c) 500.00
7 Bondage (c) 500.00
8 Sal(c), ... 475.00
9 Sal(c), ... 525.00

Becomes:

JOLLY JINGLES

10 Super Duck,(fa) 175.00
11 Super Duck 80.00

12 Hitler parody cover,A:Woody Woodpecker 65.00
13 Super Duck 45.00
14 Super Duck 45.00
15 Super Duck 45.00
16 December, 1944 . . . . 45.00

JACK THE GIANT KILLER
Bimfort & Co.
August-September, 1953

1 HcK,HcK(c) 100.00

JAMBOREE
Round Publishing Co.
February, 1946

1 . . . . 90.00
2 March, 1946 . . . . 55.00

JANE ARDEN
St. John Publ. Co.
March, 1948

1 . . . . 100.00
2 June, 1948 . . . . 60.00

JEEP COMICS
R.B. Leffingwell & Co.
Winter, 1944

1 B;Captain Power 125.00
2 . . . . 75.00
3 LbC(c),March-April, 1948 . . . 75.00

JEFF JORDAN, U.S. AGENT
D.S. Publ. Co.
December, 1947

1 . . . . 55.00

JESSE JAMES
Avon Periodicals/ Realistic Publ.
August, 1950

1 JKu,The San Antonio Stage Robbery 100.00
2 JKu,The Daring Liberty Bank Robbery 75.00
3 JKu,The California Stagecoach Robberies 65.00
4 EK(c),Deadliest Deed! 25.00

Jesse James #5 © Avon Publications

5 JKu,WW,Great Prison Break . 65.00
6 JKu,Wanted Dead or Alive . . 65.00
7 JKu,Six-Gun Slaughter at San Romano! 55.00
8 EK,Daring Train Robbery! . . . 40.00
9 EK 25.00
10 thru 14 {Do not exist}
15 . . . . 40.00
16 . . . . 25.00
17 . . . . 15.00
18 JKu 18.00
19 JKu 18.00
20 AW,FF,A:Chief Vic,Kit West . 75.00
21 . . . . 15.00
22 . . . . 12.00
23 . . . . 12.00
24 EK,B:New McCarty 15.00
25 EK 15.00
26 EK 15.00
27 EK,E:New McCarty 15.00
28 . . . . 15.00
29 August, 1956 . . . . 15.00

JEST
Harry 'A' Chesler
1944

10 J. Rebel,Yankee Boy 65.00
11 1944,Little Nemo 70.00

JET ACES
Real Adventure Publ. Co. (Fiction House)
1952

1 Set 'em up in MIG Alley 55.00
2 Kiss-Off for Moscow Molly . . 30.00
3 Red Task Force Sighted 30.00
4 Death-Date at 40,000, 1953 . 30.00

JET FIGHTERS
Standard Magazines
November, 1953

5 ATh,Korean War Stories 50.00
6 Circus Pilot 20.00
7 ATh, Iron Curtains for Ivan, March, 1953 . . . . 45.00

JETTA OF THE 21st CENTURY
Standard Comics
December, 1952

5 Teen Stories 110.00
6 . . . . 45.00
7 April, 1953 . . . . 45.00

JIGGS AND MAGGIE
Best Books (Standard)/ Harvey Publ.
June, 1949

11 . . . . 60.00
12 thru 21 . . . . @30.00
22 thru 26 . . . . @22.00
27 February-March, 1954 . . . . . 22.00

JIM HARDY
Spotlight Publ.
1944

N# Dynamite Jim,Mirror Man . 225.00

JIM RAY'S AVIATION SKETCH BOOK
Vital Publishers
February, 1946

1 Radar, the Invisible eye . . . 135.00
2 Gen.Hap Arnold, May, 1946 125.00

JINGLE JANGLE COMICS
Eastern Color Printing Co.
February, 1942

1 B:Benny Bear,Pie Face Prince, Jingle Jangle Tales,Hortense 200.00
2 GCn 100.00
3 GCn 90.00
4 GCn,Pie Face cover 90.00
5 GCn,B:Pie Face 90.00
6 GCn, ... 80.00
7 . . . . 65.00
8 . . . . 65.00
9 . . . . 65.00
10 . . . . 65.00
11 thru 15 E:Pie Face . . . . . . @50.00
16 thru 20 . . . . @45.00
21 thru 25 . . . . @35.00
26 thru 30 . . . . @30.00
31 thru 41 . . . . @20.00
42 December, 1949 . . . . 20.00

JING PALS
Victory Publ. Corp.
February, 1946

1 Johnny Rabbit 50.00
2 . . . . 30.00
3 . . . . 30.00
4 August, 1948 . . . . 30.00

JOE COLLEGE
Hillman Periodicals
Fall, 1949

1 BP,DPr 40.00
2 BP, Winter, 1949 . . . . 30.00

JOE LOUIS
Fawcett Periodicals
September, 1950

1 Ph(c),Life Story 350.00
2 Ph(c),November, 1950 . . . . 250.00

JOE PALOOKA
Publication Enterprises (Columbia Comics Group)
1943

1 Lost in the Desert 375.00
2 Hitler cover 250.00
3 KO's the Nazis! 175.00
4 Eiffel tower cover, 1944 . . . 150.00

Joe Palooka #1 © Columbia Comics

JOE PALOOKA
Harvey Publications
November, 1954

1 Joe Tells How he became World Champ 300.00
2 Skiing cover 150.00
3 . . . . 75.00
4 Welcome Home Pals! 75.00
5 S&K,The Great Carnival Murder Mystery 125.00

6 Classic Joe Palooka (c) 80.00
7 BP,V:Grumpopski 75.00
8 BP,Mystery of the Ghost Ship 60.00
9 Drooten Island Mystery 60.00
10 BP 55.00
11 . . . . 50.00
12 BP,Boxing Course 50.00
13 . . . . 45.00
14 BP,Palooka's Toughest Fight 45.00
15 BP,O:Humphrey 75.00
16 BP,A:Humphrey 45.00
17 BP,A:Humphrey 45.00
18 . . . . 45.00
19 BP,Freedom Train(c) 50.00
20 Punch Out(c) 45.00
21 . . . . 35.00
22 V:Assassin 35.00
23 Big Bathing Beauty Issue . . . 35.00
24 . . . . 35.00
25 . . . . 35.00
26 BP,Big Prize Fight Robberies 35.00
27 BP,Mystery of Bal
Eagle Cabin 35.00
28 BP,Fights out West 35.00
29 BP,Joe Busts Crime
Wide Open 35.00
30 BP,V:Hoodlums 30.00
31 BP 30.00
32 BP,Fight Palooka was sure
to Lose 30.00
33 BP,Joe finds Ann 30.00
34 BP,How to Box like a Champ 30.00
35 BP,More Adventures of Little
Max 30.00
36 BP 30.00
37 BP,Joe as a Boy 30.00
38 BP 30.00
39 BP,Original Hillbillies with
Big Leviticus 30.00
40 BP,Joe's Toughest Fight . . . 30.00
41 BP,Humphrey's Grudge Fight 30.00
42 BP 30.00
43 BP 30.00
44 BP,M:Ann Howe 35.00
45 BP 25.00
46 Champ of Champs 25.00
47 BreathtakingUnderwaterBattle 25.00
48 BP,Exciting Indian Adventure 25.00
49 BP 25.00
50 BP,Bondage(c) 25.00
51 BP 25.00
52 BP,V:Balonki 25.00
53 BP 25.00
54 V:Bad Man Trigger McGehee 25.00
55 . . . . 25.00
56 Foul Play on the High Seas . 25.00
57 Curtains for the Champ 25.00
58 V:The Man-Eating Swamp
Terror 25.00
59 The Enemy Attacks 25.00
60 Joe Fights Escaped Convict . 25.00
61 . . . . 20.00
62 S&K 30.00
63 thru 68 . . . . @20.00
69 A Package from Home 20.00
70 BP 20.00
71 . . . . 20.00
72 . . . . 20.00
73 BP 20.00
74 thru 117 . . . . @20.00
118 March, 1961 . . . . 20.00
Giant 1 Body Building 65.00
Giant 2 Fights His Way Back . . 125.00
Giant 3 Visits Lost City 60.00
Giant 4 All in Family 65.00

JOE YANK
Visual Editions
(Standard Comics)
March, 1952

5 ATh,WE,Korean Jackpot! . . . 65.00
6 Bacon and Bullets,
G.I.Renegade 45.00
7 Two-Man War,A:Sgt. Glamour 18.00
8 ATh(c),Miss Foxhole of 1952, 30.00
9 G.I.'s and Dolls,Colonel Blood 15.00
10 A Good Way to Die,
A:General Joe 15.00
11 . . . . 15.00
12 RA 15.00
13 . . . . 15.00
14 . . . . 15.00
15 . . . . 15.00
16 July, 1954 . . . . 15.00

JOHN HIX SCRAPBOOK
Eastern Color Printing Co.
1937

1 Strange as It Seems 175.00
2 Strange as It Seems 150.00

JOHNNY DANGER
Toby Press
August, 1954

1 Ph(c),Private Detective 75.00

JOHNNY DYNAMITE
(see DYNAMITE)

JOHNNY HAZARD
Best Books
(Standard Comics)
August, 1948

5 FR 75.00
6 FR,FR(c) 55.00
7 FR(c) 50.00
8 FR,FR(c), May, 1949 . . . . . . 40.00

JOHNNY LAW, SKY RANGER
Good Comics (Lev Gleason)
April, 1955

1 . . . . 30.00
2 . . . . 20.00
3 . . . . 20.00
4 November, 1955 . . . . 20.00

JOHN WAYNE ADVENTURE COMICS
Toby Press
Winter, 1949

1 Ph(c),The Mysterious Valley
of Violence 500.00
2 AW,FF,Ph(c) 425.00
3 AW,FF,Flying Sheriff 425.00
4 AW,FF,Double-Danger,Ph(c) 425.00
5 Volcano of Death,Ph(c) . . . 400.00
6 AW,FF,Caravan of Doom,
Ph(c) 375.00
7 AW,FF,Ph(c) 325.00
8 AW,FF,Duel of Death,Ph(c) 350.00
9 Ghost Guns,Ph(c) 300.00
10 Dangerous Journey,Ph(c) . . 200.00
11 Manhunt!,Ph(c) 200.00
12 HK,Joins the Marines,Ph(c) . 210.00
13 V:Frank Stacy 175.00
14 Operation Peeping John . . . 175.00
15 Bridge Head 200.00
16 AW,FF,Golden Double-Cross 200.00
17 Murderer's Music 200.00
18 AW,FF,Larson's Folly 225.00
19 . . . . 150.00
20 Whale Cover 150.00
21 . . . . 150.00
22 Flash Flood! 150.00
23 Death on Two Wheels 150.00
24 Desert 150.00
25 AW,FF,Hondo!,Ph(c) 225.00
26 Ph(c) 175.00
27 Ph(c) 175.00
28 Dead Man's Boots! 175.00
29 AW,FF,Ph(c),Crash in
California Desert 225.00
30 The Wild One, Ph(c) 175.00
31 AW,FF,May, 1955 . . . . 200.00

JO-JO COMICS
Fox Features Syndicate
Spring, 1946

N# (fa) 50.00
2 (fa) 25.00
3 (fa) 25.00
4 (fa) 25.00
5 (fa) 25.00
6 (fa) 25.00
7 B:Jo-Jo Congo King 200.00
8 (7)B:Tanee,V:The
Giant Queen 150.00
9 (8)The Mountain of Skulls . . 150.00
10 (9)Death of the Fanged Lady 135.00
11 (10) 125.00
12 (11)Bondage(c),
Water Warriors 125.00
13 (12) Jade Juggernaut 125.00
14 The Leopards of Learda . . . 125.00
15 The Flaming Fiend 125.00
16 Golden Gorilla,bondage(c) . 135.00
17 Stark-Mad Thespian,
bondage(c) 135.00
18 The Death Traveler 125.00
19 Gladiator of Gore 125.00
20 . . . . 125.00
21 . . . . 125.00
22 . . . . 125.00
23 . . . . 125.00
24 . . . . 125.00
25 Bondage(c) 165.00
26 . . . . 125.00
27 . . . . 125.00
28 . . . . 125.00
29 July, 1949 . . . . 135.00

JOURNEY INTO FEAR
Superior Publications
May, 1951

1 MB,Preview of Chaos 200.00
2 Debt to the Devil 135.00
3 Midnight Prowler 110.00

Journey into Fear #15
© Superior Publications

4 Invisible Terror 100.00
5 Devil Cat 80.00
6 Partners in Blood 80.00
7 The Werewolf Lurks 80.00
8 Bells of the Damned 80.00
9 Masked Death 80.00
10 Gallery of the Dead 80.00
11 Beast of Bedlam 65.00
12 No Rest for the Dead 65.00

13 Cult of the Dead 65.00
14 Jury of the Undead 65.00
15 Corpse in Make-up 75.00
16 Death by Invitation 60.00
17 Deadline for Death 60.00
18 Here's to Horror 60.00
19 This Body is Mine! 60.00
20 Masters of the Dead 60.00
21 Horror in the Clock,
September, 1954 . . . . 60.00

JUDO JOE
Jay-Jay Corp.
August, 1952

1 Drug 35.00
2 . . . . 25.00
3 Drug, December, 1953 . . . . . 25.00

JUDY CANOVA
Fox Features Syndicate
May, 1950

23 (1)WW,WW(c) 85.00
24 (2)WW,WW(c) 80.00
3 JO,WW,WW(c)
September, 1950 . . . . 100.00

JUKE BOX
Famous Funnies
March, 1948

1 ATh(c),Spike Jones 250.00
2 Dinah Shore,Transvestitism 150.00
3 Vic Damone 100.00
4 Jimmy Durante 100.00
5 . . . . 90.00
6 January, 1949,Desi Arnaz . 125.00

JUMBO COMICS
Real Adventure Publ. Co. (Fiction House)
September, 1938

1 LF,BKa,JK,WE,WE(c),B:Sheena
Queen of the Jungle,The Hawk
The Hunchback 9,500.00
2 LF,JK,WE,BKa,BP,
O:Sheena 3,000.00

Jumbo Comics #45

© Real Adventure Publ./Fiction House

3 JK,WE,WE(c),BP,LF,BKa . 2,400.00
4 WE,WE(c),MMe,LF,BKa,
O:The Hawk 2,200.00
5 WE,WE(c),BP,BKa 1,500.00
6 WE,WE(c),BP,BKa 1,300.00
7 WE,BKa,BP 1,200.00
8 LF(c),BP,BKa,World of
Tommorow 1,200.00
9 LF(c),BP 1,300.00
10 WE,LF(c),BKa,Regular size
issues begin 600.00
11 LF(c),WE&BP,War of the
Emerald Gas 550.00
12 WE(c),WE&BP,Hawk in Buccaneer
Vengeance,Bondage(c) 600.00
13 WE(c),BP,Sheena in The
Thundering Herds 550.00
14 WE(c),LF,BP,Hawk in Siege
of Thunder Isle,B:Lightning . 700.00
15 BP(c),BP,Sheena(c) 400.00
16 BP(c),BP,The Lightning
Strikes Twice 450.00
17 BP(c), all Sheena covers
and lead stories 400.00
18 BP 375.00
19 BP(c),BKa,Warriors of
the Bush 375.00
20 BP,BKa,Spoilers of
the Wild 375.00
21 BP,BKa,Prey of the
Giant Killers 300.00
22 BP,BKa,Victims of the
Super-Ape,O:Hawk 325.00
23 BP,BKa,Swamp of the
Green Terror 325.00
24 BP,BKa,Curse of the Black
Venom 325.00
25 BP,BKa,Bait for the Beast . . 300.00
26 BP,BKa,Tiger-Man Terror . . 300.00
27 BP,BKa,Sabre-Tooth Terror 300.00
28 BKa,RWd,The Devil of
the Congo 300.00
29 BKa,RWd,Elephant-Scourge 300.00
30 BKa,RWd,Slashing Fangs . 300.00
31 BKa,RWd,Voodoo Treasure
of Black Slave Lake 275.00
32 BKa,RWd,AB,Captives of
the Gorilla-Men 275.00
33 BKa,RWd,AB,Stampede
Tusks 275.00
34 BKa,RWd,AB,Claws of the
Devil-Cat 275.00
35 BKa,RWd,AB,Hostage of the
Devil Apes 275.00
36 BKa,RWd,AB,Voodoo Flames 275.00
37 BKa,RWd,AB,Congo Terror . 275.00
38 BKa,RWd,ABDeath-Trap of
the River Demons 275.00
39 BKa,RWd,AB,Cannibal Bait . 275.00
40 BKa,RWd,AB,
Assagai Poison 275.00
41 BKa,RWd,AB,Killer's Kraal,
Bondage(c) 200.00
42 BKa,RWd,AB,Plague of
Spotted Killers 200.00
43 BKa,RWd,AB,Beasts of the
Devil Queen 200.00
44 BKa,RWd,AB,Blood-Cult of
K'Douma 200.00
45 BKa,RWd,AB,Fanged
Keeper of the Fire-Gem . . . 200.00
46 BKa,RWd,AB,Lair of the
Armored Monsters 200.00
47 BKa,RWd,AB,The Bantu
Blood-Monster 200.00
48 BKa,RWd,AB,Red Meat for
the Cat-Pack 200.00
49 BKa,RWd,AB,Empire of the
Hairy Ones 200.00
50 BKa,RWd,AB,Eyrie of the
Leopard Birds 200.00
51 BKa,RWd.AB,Monsters with
Wings 175.00
52 BKa,RWd,AB,Man-Eaters
Paradise 175.00
53 RWd,AB,Slaves of the
Blood Moon 175.00
54 RWd,AB,Congo Kill 175.00
55 RWd,AB,Bait for the Silver
King Cat 175.00
56 RWd,AB,Sabre Monsters of
the Aba-Zanzi,Bondage(c) . . 175.00
57 RWd,AB,Arena of Beasts . . 175.00
58 RWd,AB,Sky-Atlas of the
Thunder-Birds 175.00
59 RWd,AB,Kraal of Shrunken
Heads 175.00
60 RWd,AB,Land of the
Stalking Death 150.00
61 RWd,AB,King-Beast of
the Masai 150.00
62 RWd,AB,Valley of Golden
Death 150.00
63 RWd,AB,The Dwarf Makers 150.00
64 RWd,The Slave-Brand of Ibn
Ben Satan,Male Bondage . . 150.00
65 RWd,The Man-Eaters of
Linpopo 150.00
66 RWd,Valley of Monsters . . . 150.00
67 RWd,Land of Feathered Evil 150.00
68 RWd,Spear of Blood Ju-Ju . 150.00
69 RWd,AB,MB,Slaves for the
White Sheik 150.00
70 RWd,AB,MB,The Rogue
Beast's Prey 150.00
71 RWd,AB,MB,The Serpent-
God Speaks 125.00
72 RWd,AB,MB,Curse of the
Half-Dead 125.00
73 RWd,AB,MB,War Apes of
the T'Kanis 125.00
74 RWd,AB,MB,Drums of the
Voodoo God 125.00
75 RWd,AB,MB,Terror Trail of
the Devil's Horn 125.00
76 RWd,AB,MB,Fire Gems of
Skull Valley 125.00
77 RWd,AB,MB,Blood Dragons
from Fire Valley 125.00
78 RWd,AB,MB,Veldt of the
Vampire Apes 125.00
79 RWd,AB,MB,Dancing
Skeletons 125.00
80 RWd,AB,MB,Banshee Cats 125.00
81 RWd,MB,AB,JKa,Heads for
King' Hondo's Harem 110.00
82 RWd,MB,AB,JKa,Ghost Riders
of the Golden Tuskers 110.00
83 RWd,MB,AB,JKa,Charge of
the Condo Juggernauts 110.00
84 RWd,MB,AB,JKa,Valley of
the Whispering Fangs 110.00
85 RWd,MB,AB,JKa,Red Tusks
of Zulu-Za'an 110.00
86 RWd,MB,AB,JKa,Witch-Maiden
of the Burning Blade 110.00
87 RWd,AB,MB,JKa,Sargasso of
Lost Safaris 110.00
88 RWd,AB,MB,JKa,Kill-Quest
of the Ju-Ju Tusks 110.00
89 RWd,AB,MB,JKa,Ghost Slaves
of Bwana Rojo 110.00
90 RWd,AB,MB,JKa,Death Kraal
of the Mastadons 110.00
91 RWd,AB,MB,JKa,Spoor of
the Sabre-Horn Tiger 100.00
92 RWd,MB,JKa,Pied Piper
of the Congo 100.00
93 RWd,MB,JKa,The Beasts
that Dawn Begot 100.00
94 RWd,MB,JKa,Wheel of a
Thousand Deaths 100.00
95 RWd,MB,JKa,Flame Dance
of the Ju-Ju Witch 100.00
96 RWd,MB,JKa,Ghost Safari . 100.00
97 RWd,MB,JKa,Banshee Wail
of the Undead,Bondage(c) . 100.00
98 RWd,MB,JKa,Seekers of
the Terror Fangs 100.00
99 RWd,MB,JKa,Shrine of
the Seven Souls 100.00
100 RWd,MB,Slave Brand
of Hassan Bey 135.00
101 RWd,MB,Quest of the
Two-Face Ju Ju 100.00
102 RWd,MB,Viper Gods of
Vengeance Veldt 90.00

103 RWd,MB,Blood for the Idol of Blades 90.00
104 RWd,MB,Valley of Eternal Sleep 90.00
105 RWd,MB,Man Cubs from Momba-Zu 90.00
106 RWd,MB,The River of No-Return 90.00
107 RWd,MB,Vandals of the Veldt 90.00
108 RWd,MB,The Orphan of Vengeance Vale 90.00
109 RWd,MB,The Pygmy's Hiss is Poison 90.00
110 RWd,MB,Death Guards the Congo Keep 90.00
111 RWd,MB,Beware of the Witch-Man's Brew 90.00
112 RWd,MB,The Blood-Mask from G'Shinis Grave 85.00
113 RWd,MB,The Mask's of Zombi-Zan 85.00
114 RWd,MB 85.00
115 RWd,MB,Svengali of the Apes 85.00
116 RWd,MB,The Vessel of Marbel Monsters 85.00
117 RWd,MB,Lair of the Half-Man King 85.00
118 RWd,MB,Quest of the Congo Dwarflings 85.00
119 RWd,MB,King Crocodile's Domain 85.00
120 RWd,MB,The Beast-Pack Howls the Moon 85.00
121 RWd,MB,The Kraal of Evil Ivory 85.00
122 RWd,MB,Castaways of the Congo 85.00
123 RWd,MB, ... 85.00
124 RWd,MB,The Voodoo Beasts of Changra-Lo 85.00
125 RWd,MB,JKa(c),The Beast-Pack Strikes at Dawn 85.00
126 RWd,MB,JKa(c),Lair of the Swamp Beast 85.00
127 RWd,MB,JKa(c),The Phantom of Lost Lagoon 85.00
128 RWd,MB,JKa(c),Mad Mistress of the Congo-Tuskers 85.00
129 RWd,MB,JKa(c),Slaves of King Simbas Kraal 85.00
130 RWd,MB,JKa(c),Quest of the Pharaoh's Idol 85.00
131 RWd,JKa(c),Congo Giants at Bay 80.00
132 RWd,JKa(c),The Doom of the Devil's Gorge 80.00
133 RWd,JKa(c),Blaze the Pitfall Trail 80.00
134 RWd,JKa(c),Catacombs of the Jackal-Men 80.00
135 RWd,JKa(c),The 40 Thieves of Ankar-Lo 80.00
136 RWd,JKa(c),The Perils of Paradise Lost 80.00
137 RWd,JKa(c),The Kraal of Missing Men 80.00
138 RWd,JKa(c),The Panthers of Kajo-Kazar 80.00
139 RWd,JKa(c),Stampede of the Congo Lancers 80.00
140 RWd,JKa(c),The Moon Beasts from Vulture Valley . . 80.00
141 RWd,JKa(c),B:Long Bow . . 100.00
142 RWd,JKa(c),Man-Eaters of N'Gamba 100.00
143 RWd,JKa(c),The Curse of the Cannibal Drum 100.00
144 RWd,JKa(c),The Secrets of Killers Cave 100.00
145 RWd,JKa(c),Killers of the Crypt 100.00
146 RWd,JKa(c),Sinbad of the Lost Lagoon 100.00
147 RWd,JKa(c),The Wizard of Gorilla Glade 100.00
148 RWd,JKa(c),Derelict of the Slave King 100.00
149 RWd,JKa(c),Lash Lord of the Elephants 90.00
150 RWd,JKa(c),Queen of the Pharaoh's Idol 75.00
151 RWd,The Voodoo Claws of Doomsday Trek 75.00
152 RWd,Red Blades of Africa . 75.00
153 RWd,Lost Legions of the Nile 75.00
154 RWd,The Track of the Black Devil 75.00
155 RWd,The Ghosts of Blow- Gun Trail 75.00
156 RWd,The Slave-Runners of Bambaru 75.00
157 RWd,Cave of the Golden Skull 75.00
158 RWd,Gun Trek to Panther Valley 75.00
159 RWd,A:Space Scout 75.00
160 RWd,Savage Cargo, E:Sheena covers 75.00
161 RWd,Dawns of the Pit 75.00
162 RWd,Hangman's Haunt . . . 75.00
163 RWd,Cagliostro Cursed Thee 75.00
164 RWd,Death Bars the Door . 75.00
165 RWd,Day off from a Corpse 75.00
166 RWd,The Gallows Bird 75.00
167 RWd,Cult of the Clawmen, March, 1953 . . . . 75.00

JUNGLE COMICS
Glen Kel Publ./Fiction House
January, 1940

1 HcK,DBr,LF(c),O:The White Panther,Kaanga,Tabu, B:The Jungle Boy,Camilla, all Kaanga covers & stories . . 1,500.00
2 HcK,DBr,WE(c),B:Fantomah 650.00
3 HcK,DBr,GT,The Crocodiles of Death River 575.00
4 HcK,DBr,Wambi in Thundering Herds 550.00
5 WE(c),GT,HcK,DBr,Empire of the Ape Men 450.00
6 WE(c),GT,DBr,HcK,Tigress of the Deep Jungle Swamp 375.00
7 BP(c),DBr,GT,HcK,Live Sacrifice,Bondage(c) 350.00
8 BP(c),GT,HcK,Safari into Shadowland 350.00
9 GT,HcK,Captive of the Voodoo Master 350.00
10 GT,HcK,BP,Lair of the Renegade Killer 350.00
11 GT,HcK,V:Beasts of Africa's Ancient Primieval Swamp Land 250.00
12 GT,HcK,The Devil's Death-Trap 250.00
13 GT(c),GT,HcK,Stalker of the Beasts 275.00
14 HcK,Vengeance of the Gorilla Hordes 250.00
15 HcK,Terror of the Voodoo Cauldron 250.00
16 HcK,Caveman Killers 250.00
17 HcK,Valley of the Killer-Birds 250.00
18 HcK,Trap of the Tawny Killer, Bondage(c) 275.00
19 HcK,Revolt of the Man-Apes 250.00
20 HcK,One-offering to Ju-Ju Demon 250.00
21 HcK,Monster of the Dismal Swamp, Bondage(c) 225.00
22 HcK,Lair o/t Winged Fiend . 200.00
23 HcK,Man-Eater Jaws 200.00
24 HcK,Battle of the Beasts . . . 200.00
25 HcK,Kaghis the Blood God, Bondage(c) 225.00
26 HcK,Gorillas of the Witch-Queen 200.00

Jungle Comics #55
© Glen Kel. Publ./Fiction House

27 HcK,Spore o/t Gold-Raiders 200.00
28 HcK,Vengeance of the Flame God, Bondage(c) 225.00
29 HcK,Juggernaut of Doom . . 200.00
30 HcK,Claws o/t Black Terror 200.00
31 HcK,Land of Shrunken Skulls 175.00
32 HcK,Curse of the King-Beast 175.00
33 HcK,Scaly Guardians of Massacre Pool,Bondage(c) . 190.00
34 HcK,Bait of the Spotted Fury,Bondage(c) 190.00
35 HcK,Stampede of the Slave-Masters 175.00
36 HcK,GT,The Flame-Death of Ju Ju Mountain 175.00
37 HcK,GT,Scaly Sentinel of Taboo Swamp 175.00
38 HcK,GT,Duel of the Congo Destroyers 175.00
39 HcK,Land of Laughing Bones 175.00
40 HcK,Killer Plague 175.00
41 Hck,The King Ape Feeds at Dawn 150.00
42 Hck,RC,Master of the Moon-Beasts 165.00
43 HcK,The White Shiek 150.00
44 HcK,Monster of the Boiling Pool 150.00
45 HcK,The Bone-Grinders of B'Zambi, Bondage(c) 165.00
46 HcK,Blood Raiders of Tree Trail 135.00
47 HcK,GT,Monsters of the Man Pool, Bondage(c) 150.00
48 HcK,GT,Strangest Congo Adventure 135.00
49 HcK,GT,Lair of the King -Serpent 135.00
50 HcK,GT,Juggernaut of the Bush 135.00
51 HcK,GT,The Golden Lion of Genghis Kahn 125.00
52 HcK,Feast for the River Devils, Bondage(c) 150.00
53 HcK,GT,Slaves for Horrors Harem 150.00
54 HcK,GT,Blood Bride of the Crocodile 125.00
55 HcK,GT,The Tree Devil . . . 125.00
56 HcK,Bride for the Rainmaker Raj 125.00
57 HcK,Fire Gems of T'ulaki . . 125.00
58 HcK,Land of the

Cannibal God 125.00
59 HcK,Dwellers of the Mist Bondage(c) 150.00
60 HcK,Bush Devil's Spoor . . . 125.00
61 HcK,Curse of the Blood Madness 125.00
62 Bondage(c) 135.00
63 HcK,Fire-Birds for the Cliff Dwellers 110.00
64 Valley of the Ju-Ju Idols . . . 110.00
65 Shrine of the Seven Ju Jus, Bondage(c) 125.00
66 Spoor of the Purple Skulls . 110.00
67 Devil Beasts of the Golden Temple 110.00
68 Satan's Safari 110.00
69 Brides for the Serpent King . 110.00
70 Brides for the King Beast, Bondage(c) 125.00
71 Congo Prey,Bondage(c) . . . 125.00
72 Blood-Brand o/t Veldt Cats . 100.00
73 The Killer of M'omba Raj, Bondage(c) 125.00
74 AgF,GoldenJaws,Bondage(c) 125.00
75 AgF,Congo Kill 100.00
76 AgF,Blood Thrist of the Golden Tusk 100.00
77 AgF,The Golden Gourds Shriek Blood,Bondage(c) . . 125.00
78 AgF,Bondage(c) 125.00
79 AgF,Death has a Thousand Fangs 100.00
80 AgF,Salome of the Devil-Cats Bondage(c) 125.00
81 AgF,Colossus of the Congo 100.00
82 AgF,Blood Jewels of the Fire-Bird 100.00
83 AgF,Vampire Veldt, Bondage(c) 125.00
84 AgF,Blood Spoor of the Faceless Monster 100.00
85 AgF,Brides for the Man-Apes Bondage(c) 125.00
86 AgF,Firegems of L'hama Lost, Bondage(c) 120.00
87 AgF,Horror Kraal of the Legless One,Bondage(c) . . . 100.00
88 AgF,Beyond the Ju-Ju Mists 110.00
89 AgF,Blood-Moon over the Whispering Veldt 90.00
90 AgF,The Skulls for the Altar of Doom,Bondage(c) . 110.00
91 AgF,Monsters from the Mist Lands, Bondage(c) 110.00
92 AgF,Vendetta of the Tree Tribes 90.00
93 AgF,Witch Queen of the Hairy Ones 90.00
94 AgF,Terror Raid of the Congo Caesar 90.00
95 Agf,Flame-Tongues of the Sky Gods 90.00
96 Agf,Phantom Guardians of the Enchanted Lake,Bondage(c) . 85.00
97 AgF,Wizard of the Whirling Doom,Bondage(c) 100.00
98 AgF,Ten Tusks of Zulu Ivory 125.00
99 AgF,Cannibal Caravan, Bondage(c) 100.00
100 AgF,Hate has a Thousand Claws 100.00
101 AgF,The Blade of Buddha, Bondage(c) 100.00
102 AgF,Queen of the Amazon Lancers 85.00
103 AgF,The Phantoms of Lost Lagoon 85.00
104 AgF 85.00
105 AgF,The Red Witch of Ubangi-Shan 85.00
106 AgF,Bondage(c) 100.00
107 Banshee Valley 100.00
108 HcK,Merchants of Murder . 100.00
109 HcK,Caravan of the Golden Bones 85.00
110 HcK,Raid of the Fire-Fangs 85.00
111 HcK,The Trek of the Terror-Paws 85.00
112 HcK,Morass of the Mammoths 85.00
113 HcK,Two-Tusked Terror . . . 85.00
114 HcK,Mad Jackals Hunt by Night 85.00
115 HcK,Treasure Trove in Vulture Sky 85.00
116 HcK,The Banshees of Voodoo Veldt 85.00
117 HcK,The Fangs of the Hooded Scorpion 85.00
118 HcK,The Muffled Drums of Doom 85.00
119 HcK,Fury of the Golden Doom 85.00
120 HcK,Killer King Domain . . . 85.00
121 HcK,Wolves of the Desert Night 85.00
122 HcK,The Veldt of Phantom Fangs 85.00
123 HcK,The Ark of the Mist-Maids 85.00
124 HcK,The Trail of the Pharaoh's Eye 85.00
125 HcK,Skulls for Sale on Dismal River 85.00
126 HcK,Safari Sinister 100.00
127 Hck,Bondage(c) 85.00
128 HcK,Dawn-Men of the Congo 85.00
129 Hck,The Captives of Crocodile Swamp 85.00
130 Hck,Phantoms of the Congo 85.00
131 HcK,Treasure-Tomb of the Ape-King 85.00
132 HcK,Bondage(c) 100.00
133 HcK,Scourge of the Sudan Bondage(c) 100.00
134 HcK,The Black Avengers of Kaffir Pass 80.00
135 Hck 80.00
136 HcK,The Death Kraals of Kongola 80.00
137 BWg(c),HcK,The Safari of Golden Ghosts 80.00
138 BWg(c),HcK,Track of the Black Terror Bondage(c) 80.00
139 BWg(c)Hck,Captain Kidd of the Congo 80.00
140 BWg(c),HcK,The Monsters of Kilmanjaro 80.00
141 BWg(c)HcK,The Death Hunt of the Man Cubs 80.00
142 BWg(c),Hck,Sheba of the Terror Claws,Bondage(c) . . 100.00
143 BWg(c)Hck,The Moon of Devil Drums 100.00
144 BWg(c)Hck,Quest of the Dragon's Claw 100.00
145 BWg(c)Hck,Spawn of the Devil's Moon 100.00
146 BWg(c),HcK,Orphans of the Congo 100.00
147 BWG(c),HcK,The Treasure of Tembo Wanculu 100.00
148 BWg(c),HcK,Caged Beasts of Plunder-Men,Bondage(c) . 100.00
149 BWg(c),HcK 80.00
150 BWg(c),HcK,Rhino Rampage, Bondage(c) 100.00
151 BWg(c),HcK 80.00
152 BWg(c),HcK,The Rogue of Kopje Kull 80.00
153 BWg(c),HcK,The Wild Men of N'Gara 80.00
154 BWg(c),HcK,The Fire Wizard 80.00
155 BWg(c),HcK,Swamp of the Shrieking Dead 80.00
156 BWg(c),HcK 80.00
157 BWg(c),HcK 80.00
158 BWg(c),HcK,A:Sheena 80.00
159 BWg(c),HcK,The Blow-Gun Kill 80.00
160 BWg,HcK,King Fang 80.00
161 BWg(c),HcK,The Barbarizi Man-Eaters 80.00
162 BWg(c) 80.00
163 BWg(c),Jackals at the Kill, Summer,1954 . . . . 80.00

JUNGLE JIM
Best Books
(Standard Comics)
January, 1949

11 . . . . 35.00
12 Mystery Island 20.00
13 Flowers of Peril 20.00
14 . . . . 20.00
15 . . . . 20.00
16 . . . . 20.00
17 . . . . 20.00
18 . . . . 20.00
19 . . . . 20.00
20 1951 . . . . 20.00

JUNGLE JIM
Dell Publishing Co.
August, 1953

(1) *see Dell Four Color #490*
(1) *see Dell Four Color #565*
3 P(c) all 20.00
4 . . . . 20.00
5 . . . . 20.00
6 . . . . 15.00
7 . . . . 15.00
8 . . . . 15.00
9 . . . . 15.00
10 . . . . 15.00
11 . . . . 15.00
12 . . . . 15.00
13 'Mystery Island' 15.00
14 'Flowers of Peril' 15.00
15 thru 20 . . . . @15.00

JUNGLE JO
Hero Books
(Fox Features Syndicate)
March, 1950

N# 150.00
1 Mystery of Doc Jungle 175.00
2 . . . . 125.00
3 The Secret of Youth, September, 1950 . . . . 100.00

JUNGLE LIL
Hero Books
(Fox Features Syndicate)
April, 1950

1 Betrayer of the Kombe Dead 125.00

Becomes:

DOROTHY LAMOUR

2 WW,Ph(c)The Lost Safari . . 100.00
3 WW,Ph(c), August, 1950 . . . 90.00

JUNGLE THRILLS
(see TERRORS OF THE JUNGLE)

JUNIE PROM
Dearfield Publishing Co.
Winter, 1947

1 Teenage Stories 50.00
2 . . . . 25.00
3 . . . . 20.00
4 . . . . 20.00
5 . . . . 20.00
6 June, 1949 . . . . 20.00

JUNIOR COMICS
Fox Features Syndicate
September, 1947

9 AF,AF(c) ,Teenage Stories . 300.00
10 AF,AF(c) 250.00
11 AF,AF(c) 250.00

12 AF,AF(c) 250.00
13 AF,AF(c) 250.00
14 AF,AF(c) 250.00
15 AF,AF(c) 250.00
16 AF,AF(c),July,1948 . . . . 250.00

JUNIOR HOOP COMICS
Stanmor Publications
January, 1952

1 . . . . 40.00
2 . . . . 20.00
3 July, 1952 . . . . 20.00

JUSTICE TRAPS OF THE GUILTY
Headline Publications (Prize)
October-November, 1947

2-1 S&K,S&K(c),Electric chair cover 225.00
2 S&K,S&K(c) 125.00
3 S&K,S&K(c) 110.00
4 S&K,S&K(c),True Confession of a Girl Gangleader 100.00
5 S&K,S&K(c) 100.00
6 S&K,S&K(c) 100.00
7 S&K,S&K(c) 100.00
8 S&K,S&K(c) 100.00
9 S&K,S&K(c) 90.00
10 S&K,S&K(c) 100.00
11 S&K,S&K(c) 50.00
12 . . . . 25.00
13 . . . . 35.00
14 . . . . 25.00
15 . . . . 25.00
16 . . . . 25.00
17 . . . . 35.00
18 S&K,S&K(c) 50.00
19 S&K,S&K(c) 50.00
20 . . . . 22.00
21 S&K 35.00
22 S&K(c) 25.00
23 S&K(c) 25.00
24 . . . . 15.00
25 . . . . 20.00
26 . . . . 15.00
27 S&K(c) 25.00
28 . . . . 15.00
29 . . . . 15.00
30 S&K 35.00
31 thru 50 . . . . @15.00
51 thru 57 . . . . @14.00
58 Drug 75.00
59 thru 92 . . . . @12.00

Becomes:

FARGO KID
Headline Publications (Prize)

93 AW,JSe,O:Kid Fargo 75.00
94 JSe 50.00
95 June-July, 1958,JSe 50.00

KA'A'NGA COMICS
Glen-Kel Publ. (Fiction House)
Spring, 1949

1 Phantoms of the Congo . . . 275.00
2 V:The Jungle Octopus 150.00
3 . . . . 120.00
4 The Wizard Apes of Inkosi-Khan 100.00
5 . . . . 75.00
6 Captive of the Devil Apes . . . 60.00
7 GT,Beast-Men of Mombassa 65.00
8 The Congo Kill-Cry 60.00
9 . . . . 60.00
10 Stampede for Congo Gold . . 60.00
11 Claws of the Roaring Congo . 50.00
12 Bondage(c) 55.00
13 Death Web of the Amazons . 50.00
14 Slave Galley of the Lost Nile Bondage(c) 60.00
15 Crocodile Moon,Bondage(c) . 60.00
16 Valley of Devil-Dwarfs 60.00
17 Tembu of the Elephants 40.00
18 The Red Claw of Vengeance 40.00
19 The Devil-Devil Trail 40.00
20 The Cult of the Killer Claws, Summer, 1954 . . . . 40.00

KASCO COMICS
Kasco Grainfeed (Giveaway)
1945

1 BWo 85.00
2 1949,BWo 75.00

KATHY
Standard Comics
September, 1949

1 Teen-Age Stories 40.00
2 ASh 22.00
3 thru 6 . . . . @15.00
7 thru 17 . . . . @12.00

KATY KEENE
Archie Publications/Close-Up Radio Comics
1949

1 BWo 600.00
2 BWo 300.00
3 BWo 275.00
4 BWo 275.00
5 BWo 250.00
6 BWo 225.00
7 BWo 225.00
8 thru 12 BWo . . . . @200.00
13 thru 20 BWo . . . . @175.00
21 thru 29 BWo . . . . @150.00
30 thru 38 BWo . . . . @125.00
39 thru 62 BWo . . . . @100.00

KEEN DETECTIVE FUNNIES
Centaur Publications
July, 1938

1-8 B:The Clock, ... 800.00
1-9 WE 500.00
1-10 . . . . 400.00
1-11 Dean Denton 400.00
2-1 The Eye Sees 325.00
2-2 JCo 325.00
2-3 TNT 325.00
2-4 Gabby Flynn 325.00
5 . . . . 350.00
6 . . . . 325.00
7 Masked Marvel 550.00
8 PGn,Gabby Flynn,Nudity Expanded 16 pages 375.00
9 Dean Denton 325.00
10 . . . . 325.00
11 BEv,Sidekick 300.00
12 Masked Marvel(c) 400.00
3-1 Masked Marvel(c) 350.00
3-2 Masked Marvel(c) 350.00
3-3 BEv 300.00
16 BEv 500.00
17 JSm 350.00
18 The Eye Sees,Bondage(c) . 375.00
19 LFe 350.00
20 BEv,The Eye Sees 350.00
21 Masked Marvel(c) 335.00
22 Masked Marvel(c) 335.00
23 B:Airman 400.00
24 Airman 400.00

KEEN KOMICS
Centaur Publications
May, 1939

1 Teenage Stories 500.00
2 PGn,JaB,CBu 300.00
3 JCo 300.00

Keen Komics #3 (2/3)
© Centaur Publications

KEEN TEENS
Life's Romances Publ./Leader/ Magazine Enterprises
1945

N# P(c) 100.00
N# Ph(c),Van Johnson 75.00
3 Ph(c), ... 35.00
4 Ph(c),Glenn Ford 35.00
5 Ph(c),Perry Como 35.00
6 . . . . 35.00

Ken Maynard Western #3
© Fawcett Publications

KEN MAYNARD WESTERN
Fawcett Publications
September, 1950

1 B:Ken Maynard & Tarzan (horse) The Outlaw Treasure Trail 325.00
2 Invasion of the Badmen . . . 200.00
3 Pied Piper of the West 150.00
4 Outlaw Hoax 150.00
5 Mystery of Badman City . . . 150.00

6 Redwood Robbery 150.00
7 Seven Wonders of the West 150.00
8 Mighty Mountain Menace, Feb.,1952 . . . . 150.00

KEN SHANNON
Quality Comics Group
October, 1951

1 RC, Evil Eye of Count Ducrie 150.00
2 RC, Cut Rate Corpses 100.00
3 RC, Corpse that Wouldn't Sleep 85.00
4 RC, Stone Hatchet Murder . . 75.00
5 RC, Case of the Carney Killer 75.00

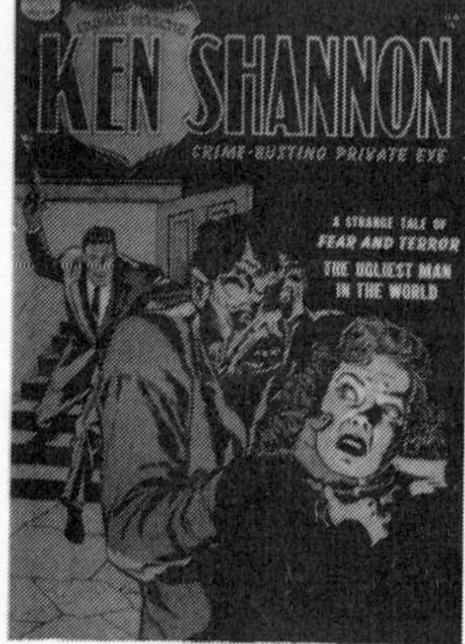

Ken Shannon #6
© Quality Comics Group

6 Weird Vampire Mob 50.00
7 RC,Ugliest Man in the World 65.00
8 Chinatown Murders,Drug 75.00
9 RC, Necklace of Blood 65.00
10 RC, Shadow of the Chair, Apr. 1953 . . . . 65.00

KERRY DRAKE DETECTIVE CASES
Life's Romances/M.E./ Harvey Publ.
1944

1 . . . . 125.00
2 A:The Faceless Horror 75.00
3 . . . . 65.00
4 A:Squirrel, Dr. Zero, Caresse 65.00
5 Bondage cover 75.00
6 A:Stitches 35.00
7 A:Shuteye 40.00
8 Bondage cover 40.00
9 Drug 65.00
10 BP,A:Meatball,Drug 65.00
11 BP,I:Kid Gloves 35.00
12 BP 35.00
13 BP,A:Torso 30.00
14 BP,Bullseye Murder Syndicate 30.00
15 BP,Fake Mystic Racket 30.00
16 BP,A:Vixen 25.00
17 BP,Case of the $50,000 Robbery 25.00
18 BP,A:Vixen 25.00
19 BP,Case of the Dope Smugglers 30.00
20 BP,Secret Treasury Agent . . 25.00
21 BP,Murder on Record 20.00
22 BP,Death Rides the Air Waves 20.00
23 BP,Blackmailer's Secret Weapon 20.00
24 Blackmailer's Trap 20.00
25 Pretty Boy Killer 20.00
26 . . . . 20.00
27 . . . . 20.00
28 BP 20.00
29 BP 20.00
30 Mystery Mine,Bondage(c) . . 25.00
31 . . . . 20.00
32 . . . . 20.00
33 August, 1952 . . . . 20.00

KEWPIES
Will Eisner Publications
Spring, 1949

1 . . . . 250.00

KEY COMICS
Consolidated Magazines
January, 1944

1 B:The Key, Will-O-The-Wisp 150.00
2 . . . . 85.00
3 . . . . 75.00
4 O:John Quincy,B:The Atom . 80.00
5 HoK,August, 1946 . . . . 75.00

KID COWBOY
Approved Comics/ St. John Publ. Co.
1950

1 B:Lucy Belle & Red Feather . 65.00
2 Six-Gun Justice 35.00
3 Shadow on Hangman's Bridge 30.00
4 Red Feather V:Eagle of Doom 25.00
5 Killers on the Rampage 25.00
6 The Stovepipe Hat 25.00
7 Ghost Town of Twin Buttes . 25.00
8 Thundering Hoofs 25.00
9 Terror on the Salt Flats 25.00
10 Valley of Death 25.00
11 Vanished Herds,Bondage(c) . 35.00
12 . . . . 25.00
13 . . . . 25.00
14 1954 . . . . 25.00

KIDDIE KARNIVAL
Approved Comics
1952

N# 150.00

KID ETERNITY
Comics Magazine (Quality Comics Group)
Spring, 1946

1 . . . . 325.00
2 . . . . 200.00
3 Follow Him Out of This World 225.00
4 Great Heroes of the Past . . 100.00
5 Don't Kid with Crime 100.00
6 Busy Battling Crime 90.00
7 Protects the World 90.00
8 Fly to the Rescue 90.00
9 Swoop Down on Crime 90.00
10 Golden Touch from Mr. Midas 90.00
11 Aid the Living by Calling the Dead 70.00
12 Finds Death 70.00
13 Invades General Poschka . . . 70.00
14 Battles Double 70.00
15 A: Master Man 70.00
16 Balance Scales of Justice . . . 65.00
17 A:Baron Roxx 65.00
18 A:Man with Two Faces 65.00

Becomes:

BUCCANEERS

19 RC,Sword Fight(c) 250.00
20 RC,Treasure Chest 200.00
21 RC,Death Trap 225.00
22 A:Lady Dolores,Snuff, Bondage(c) 150.00
23 RC,V:Treasure Hungry Plunderers of the Sea 200.00
24 A:Adam Peril,Black Roger, Eric Falcon 125.00

Kid Eternity #15
© Comics Magazine/Quality Comics

25 V:Clews 125.00
26 V:Admiral Blood 125.00
27 RC,RC(c)May, 1951 . . . . . . 200.00

KID ZOO COMICS
Street & Smith Publications
July, 1948

1 (fa) 100.00

KILLERS, THE
Magazine Enterprises
1947

1 LbC(c),Thou Shall Not Kill . 450.00
2 Grl,OW,Assassins Mad Slayers of the East,Hanging(c),Drug 450.00

KILROYS, THE
B&L Publishing Co./ American Comics
June-July, 1947

1 Three Girls in Love(c) 125.00
2 Flat Tire(c) 60.00
3 Right to Swear(c) 45.00
4 Kissing Booth(c) 45.00
5 Skiing(c) 45.00
6 Prom(c) 30.00
7 To School 30.00
8 . . . . 30.00
9 . . . . 30.00
10 B:Solid Jackson solo 30.00
11 . . . . 25.00
12 Life Guard(c) 25.00
13 thru 21 . . . . @25.00
22 thru 30 . . . . @20.00
31 thru 40 . . . . @18.00
41 thru 47 . . . . @15.00
48 3-D effect 100.00
49 3-D effect 100.00
50 thru 54, July 1954 . . . . . . @15.00

KING COMICS
David McKay Publications
April, 1936

1 AR,EC,B:Popeye,Flash Gordon.B: Henry,Mandrake 5,000.00
2 AR,EC,Flash Gordon 1,500.00
3 AR,EC,Flash Gordon 1,000.00
4 AR,EC,Flash Gordon 750.00
5 AR,EC,Flash Gordon 550.00
6 AR,EC,Flash Gordon 400.00
7 AR,EC,King Royal Mounties 375.00
8 AR,EC,Thanksgiving(c) . . . 350.00

King Comics #43
© David McKay Publications

9 AR,EC,Christmas(c) 350.00
10 AR,EC,Flash Gordon 350.00
11 AR,EC,Flash Gordon 325.00
12 AR,EC,Flash Gordon 325.00
13 AR,EC,Flash Gordon 325.00
14 AR,EC,Flash Gordon 325.00
15 AR,EC,Flash Gordon 325.00
16 AR,EC,Flash Gordon 325.00
17 AR,EC,Flash Gordon 300.00
18 AR,EC,Flash Gordon 300.00
19 AR,EC,Flash Gordon 300.00
20 AR,EC,Football(c) 300.00
21 AR,EC,Flash Gordon 250.00
22 AR,EC,Flash Gordon 250.00
23 AR,EC,Flash Gordon 250.00
24 AR,EC,Flash Gordon 250.00
25 AR,EC,Flash Gordon 250.00
26 AR,EC,Flash Gordon 225.00
27 AR,EC,Flash Gordon 225.00
28 AR,EC,Flash Gordon 225.00
29 AR,EC,Flash Gordon 225.00
30 AR,EC,Flash Gordon 225.00
31 AR,EC,Flash Gordon 225.00
32 AR,EC,Flash Gordon 225.00
33 AR,EC,Skiing(c) 225.00
34 AR,Ping Pong(c) 200.00
35 AR,Flash Gordon 200.00
36 AR,Flash Gordon 200.00
37 AR,Flash Gordon 200.00
38 AR,Flash Gordon 200.00
39 AR,Baseball(c) 200.00
40 AR,Flash Gordon 200.00
41 AR,Flash Gordon 175.00
42 AR,Flash Gordon 175.00
43 AR,Flash Gordon 175.00
44 AR,Golf(c) 175.00
45 AR,Flash Gordon 175.00
46 AR,B:Little Lulu 175.00
47 AR,Flash Gordon 175.00
48 AR,Flash Gordon 175.00
49 AR,Weather Vane 175.00
50 AR,B:Love Ranger 175.00
51 AR,Flash Gordon 175.00
52 AR,Flash Gordon 150.00
53 AR,Flash Gordon 150.00
54 AR,Flash Gordon 150.00
55 AR,Magic Carpet 150.00
56 AR,Flash Gordon 150.00
57 AR,Cows Over Moon(c) . . . 150.00
58 AR,Flash Gordon 150.00
59 AR,Flash Gordon 150.00
60 AR,Flash Gordon 150.00
61 AR,B:Phantom,Baseball(c) . 150.00
62 AR,Flash Gordon 150.00
63 AR,Flash Gordon 125.00
64 AR,Flash Gordon 125.00
65 AR,Flash Gordon 125.00
66 AR,Flash Gordon 125.00
67 AR,Sweet Pea 125.00
68 AR,Flash Gordon 125.00
69 AR,Flash Gordon 125.00
70 AR,Flash Gordon 125.00
71 AR,Flash Gordon 125.00
72 AR,Flash Gordon 100.00
73 AR,Flash Gordon 100.00
74 AR,Flash Gordon 100.00
75 AR,Flash Godron 100.00
76 AR,Flag(c) 125.00
77 AR,Flash Gordon 100.00
78 AR,Popeye,Olive Oil(c) 100.00
79 AR,Sweet Pea 100.00
80 AR,Wimpy(c) 100.00
81 AR,B:Blondie(c) 100.00
82 thru 91 AR . . . . @80.00
92 thru 98 AR . . . . @75.00
99 AR,Olive Oil(c) 80.00
100 . . . . 100.00
101 thru 116 AR . . . . @75.00
117 O:Phantom 60.00
118 Flash Gordon 75.00
119 Flash Gordon 60.00
120 Wimpy(c) 60.00
121 thru 140 . . . . @60.00
141 Flash Gordon 55.00
142 Flash Gordon 55.00
143 Flash Gordon 55.00
144 Flash Gordon 55.00
145 Prince Valiant 50.00
146 Prince Valiant 50.00
147 Prince Valiant 50.00
148 thru 154 . . . . @40.00
155 E:Flash Gordon 40.00
156 Baseball(c) 40.00
157 thru 159 . . . . @30.00

KING OF THE ROYAL MOUNTED
Dell Publishing Co.
December, 1948

(1) *see Dell Four Color #207*
(2) *see Dell Four Color #265*
(3) *see Dell Four Color #283*
(4) *see Dell Four Color #310*
(5) *see Dell Four Color #340*
(6) *see Dell Four Color #363*
(7) *see Dell Four Color #384*
8 . . . . 40.00
9 . . . . 40.00
10 . . . . 40.00
11 thru 28 . . . . @30.00

KIT CARSON
Avon Periodicals
1950

N# EK(c) 65.00
2 EK(c),Kit Carson's Revenge, Doom Trail 40.00
3 EK(c),V:Comanche Raiders . 35.00
4 . . . . 30.00
5 EK(c),Trail of Doom 30.00
6 EK(c) 30.00
7 EK(c) 35.00
8 EK(c) 30.00

Becomes:

FIGHTING DAVY CROCKETT

9 EK(c),October/Nov., 1955 . . . 35.00

KOKO AND KOLA
Compix/Magazine Enterprises
Fall, 1946

1 (fa) 40.00
2 X-Mas Issue 20.00
3 . . . . 15.00
4 . . . . 15.00
5 . . . . 15.00
6 May, 1947 . . . . 15.00

KO KOMICS
Gerona Publications
October, 1945

1 . . . . 250.00

KOMIK PAGES
Harry 'A' Chestler
April, 1945

1 JK,Duke of Darkness 200.00

KRAZY KAT COMICS
Dell Publishing Co.
May-June, 1951

1 . . . . 50.00
2 . . . . 35.00
3 . . . . 35.00
4 . . . . 35.00
5 . . . . 35.00

KRAZY LIFE
Fox Features Syndicate
1945

1 (fa) 55.00

LABOR IS A PARTNER
Catechetical Guild Educational Society
1949

1 . . . . 200.00

LAFFY-DAFFY COMICS
Rural Home Publ. Co.
February, 1945

1 (fa) 30.00
2 . . . . 30.00

LARGE FEATURE COMICS
Dell Publishing Co.
1939

1 Dick Tracy vs. the Blank . . . 900.00
2 Terry and the Pirates 475.00
3 Lone Ranger 475.00
4 Dick Tracy 500.00
5 Tarzan 750.00
6 Terry and the Pirates 400.00
7 Lone Ranger 500.00
8 Dick Tracy,Racket Buster . . 450.00
9 King of the Royal Mounted . 200.00
10 Gang Busters 300.00
11 Dick Tracy 450.00
12 Smilin'Jack 300.00
13 Dick Tracy 450.00
14 Smilin' Jack 300.00
15 Dick Tracy and the Kidnapped Princes 450.00
16 Donald Duck,1st Daisy. . . 1,750.00
17 Gang Busters 200.00
18 Phantasmo,Master of the World 150.00
19 W.Disney's Dumbo 1,400.00
20 Donald Duck 2,700.00
21 Private Buck 75.00
22 Nuts and Jolts 75.00
23 The Nebbs 100.00
24 Popeye in 'Thimble Theatre' 350.00
25 Smilin'Jack 300.00
26 Smitty 175.00
27 Terry and the Pirates 325.00
28 Grin and Bear It 75.00
29 Moon Mullins 150.00
30 Tillie the Toiler 150.00

[Series 2]

1 Peter Rabbit 275.00
2 Winnie Winkle 120.00
3 Dick Tracy 450.00
4 Tiny Tim 200.00
5 Toots and Casper 75.00
6 Terry and the Pirates 325.00

7 Pluto saves the Ship 500.00
8 Bugs Bunny 600.00
9 Bringing Up Father 100.00
10 Popeye 300.00
11 Barney Google&SnuffySmith 150.00
12 Private Buck 75.00
13 1001 Hours of Fun 75.00

LARRY DOBY, BASEBALL HERO
Fawcett Publications
1950

1 Ph(c),BW 400.00

LARS OF MARS
Ziff-Davis Publishing Co.
April-May, 1951

10 MA,'Terror from the Sky' . . . 300.00
11 GC 275.00

LASH LARUE WESTERN
Fawcett Publications
Summer, 1949

1 Ph(c),The Fatal Roundups . . 600.00
2 Ph(c),Perfect Hide Out 300.00
3 Ph(c),The Suspect 250.00
4 Ph(c),Death on Stage 250.00
5 Ph(c),Rustler's Haven 250.00
6 Ph(c) 225.00
7 Ph(c),Shadow of the Noose . 175.00
8 Ph(c),Double Deadline 175.00
9 Ph(c),Generals Last Stand . . 175.00
10 Ph(c) 175.00
11 Ph(c) 150.00
12 thru 20 Ph(c) . . . . @100.00
21 thru 29 Ph(c) . . . . @90.00
30 thru 46 Ph(c) . . . . @75.00
46 Ph(c),Lost Chance 75.00

LASSIE
(& SEVERAL SPECIAL ISSUES)
Dell Publishing Co.
October-December, 1950

1 Ph(c) all 100.00
2 . . . . 45.00
3 . . . . 28.00
4 . . . . 28.00
5 . . . . 28.00
6 . . . . 28.00
7 . . . . 28.00
8 . . . . 28.00
9 . . . . 28.00
10 . . . . 28.00
11 . . . . 20.00
12 Rocky Langford 22.00
13 . . . . 20.00
14 . . . . 20.00
15 I:Timbu 22.00
16 . . . . 20.00
17 . . . . 20.00
18 . . . . 20.00
19 . . . . 20.00
20 MB 25.00
21 MB 25.00
22 MB 25.00
23 thru 38 . . . . @15.00
39 I:Timmy 20.00
40 thru 62 . . . . @15.00
63 E:Timmy 10.00
64 thru 70 . . . . @9.00

LATEST COMICS
Spotlight Publ./ Palace Promotions
March, 1945

1 Funny Animal-Super Duper . . 60.00
2 . . . . 40.00

SPECIAL COMICS
MLJ Magazines
(Archie Publ.)
Winter, 1941

1 O:Boy Buddies & Hangman,
D:The Comet 1,000.00

Becomes:

HANGMAN COMICS

2 B:Hangman & Boy Buddies 800.00
3 V:Nazis cover,Bondage(c) . 425.00
4 V:Nazis cover 400.00
5 Bondage cover 400.00
6 . . . . 375.00
7 BF,Graveyard cover 375.00
8 BF 375.00

Becomes:

BLACK HOOD

9 BF 400.00
10 BF,A:Dusty, the
Boy Detective 250.00
11 Here lies the Black Hood . . 150.00
12 . . . . 150.00
13 EK(c) 150.00
14 EK(c) 150.00
15 EK 150.00
16 EK(c) 150.00
17 Bondage cover 150.00
18 . . . . 150.00
19 I.D. Revealed 200.00

Becomes:

LAUGH COMICS

20 BWo,B:Archie,Katy Keene . 400.00
21 BWo 200.00
22 BWo 200.00
23 Bwo 200.00
24 BWo,JK,Pipsy 200.00
25 BWo 200.00
26 BWo 125.00
27 BWo 125.00
28 BWo 125.00
29 BWo 125.00
30 BWo 125.00
31 thru 40 BWo . . . . @75.00
41 thru 50 BWo . . . . @55.00
51 thru 60 BWo . . . . @50.00
61 thru 80 BWo . . . . @25.00
81 thru 99 BWo . . . . @20.00
100 BWo 30.00
101 thru 126 BWo . . . . @15.00
127 A:Jaguar 20.00
128 A:The Fly 20.00
129 A:The Fly 20.00
130 A:Jaguar 20.00
131 A:Jaguar 20.00
132 A:The Fly 20.00
133 A:Jaguar 20.00
134 A:The Fly 20.00
135 A:Jaguar 20.00
136 A:Fly Girl 20.00
137 A:Fly Girl 20.00
138 A:The Fly 20.00
139 A:The Fly 20.00
140 A:Jaguar 20.00
141 A:Jaguar 20.00
142 thru 144 . . . . @20.00
145 A:Josie 15.00
146 thru 165 . . . . @8.00
166 Beatles cover 12.00
167 thru 220 . . . . @5.00
221 thru 250 . . . . @2.50
251 thru 300 . . . . @2.00
301 thru 400 . . . . @1.00

LAUGH COMIX
(see TOP-NOTCH COMICS)

LAUREL AND HARDY
St. John Publishing Co.
March, 1949

1 . . . . 350.00
2 . . . . 225.00
3 . . . . 175.00
26 Rep #1 . . . . 100.00
27 Rep #2 . . . . 100.00
28 Rep #3 . . . . 100.00

LAWBREAKERS
Law & Order Magazines (Charlton)
March, 1951

1 . . . . 125.00
2 . . . . 55.00
3 . . . . 40.00
4 Drug 55.00
5 . . . . 40.00
6 LM(c) 55.00
7 Drug 55.00
8 . . . . 40.00
9 StC(c) 40.00

Lawbreakers Suspense Stories #10
© Law & Order Magazines/Charlton

Becomes:

LAWBREAKERS SUSPENSE STORIES
January, 1953

10 StC(c) 85.00
11 LM(c),Negligee(c) 175.00
12 LM(c) 45.00
13 DG(c) 45.00
14 DG(c),Sharks 45.00
15 DG(c),Acid in Face(c) 150.00

Becomes:

STRANGE SUSPENSE STORIES

16 DG(c); January, 1954 . . . . . . 95.00
17 DG(c) 70.00
18 SD,SD(c) 135.00
19 SD,SD(c),Electric Chair . . . 175.00
20 SD,SD(c) 135.00
21 SD,SD(c) 65.00
22 SD,SD(c) 125.00

Becomes:

THIS IS SUSPENSE

23 WW; February, 1955
Comics Code 125.00
24 GE,DG(c) 60.00
25 DG(c) 40.00
26 DG(c) 40.00

Becomes:

STRANGE SUSPENSE STORIES

27 October, 1955 . . . . 40.00
28 . . . . 30.00
29 . . . . 30.00
30 . . . . 30.00
31 SD 75.00
32 SD 75.00

33 SD 75.00
34 SD 75.00
35 SD 75.00
36 SD 75.00
37 SD 75.00
38 .... 30.00
39 SD 70.00
40 SD 70.00
41 SD 70.00
42 .... 25.00
43 .... 25.00
44 .... 25.00
45 .... 25.00
46 .... 25.00
47 SD 60.00
48 SD 60.00
49 .... 25.00
50 SD 55.00
51 SD 55.00
52 SD 55.00
53 SD 55.00
54 thru 60 .... @15.00
61 thru 74 .... @10.00
75 SD,SD(c) 75.00
77 Oct 1965 .... 30.00

LAWBREAKERS ALWAYS LOSE
Crime Bureau Stories
Spring, 1948

1 HK; FBI Reward Poster Photo 125.00
2 .... 65.00
3 .... 50.00
4 Vampire 60.00
5 .... 40.00
6 Anti Wertham Edition 50.00
7 .... 125.00
8 .... 40.00
9 Ph(c) 40.00
10 Ph(c), October 1949 .... 40.00

LAW-CRIME
Essenkay Publications
April, 1948

1 LbC,LbC-(c);Raymond Hamilton Dies In The Chair 275.00
2 LbC,LbC-(c);Strangled Beauty Puzzles Police 200.00
3 LbC,LbC-(c);Lipstick Slayer Sought; August '43 .... 275.00

LEROY
Visual Editions
(Standard Comics)
November, 1949

1 FunniestTeenager of them All 25.00
2 .... 20.00
3 thru 6 .... @15.00

LET'S PRETEND
D.S. Publishing Company
May-June, 1950

1 From Radio Nursery Tales .. 75.00
2 .... 60.00
3 November, 1950 .... 55.00

MISS LIBERTY
Burten/Green Publishing
Circa 1944

1 Reprints-Shield,Wizard 200.00

Becomes:

LIBERTY COMICS

10 Reprints,Hangman 100.00
11 .... 75.00
12 Black Hood 75.00
14 .... 75.00
15 .... 50.00

LIBERTY GUARDS
Chicago Mail Order
(Comic Corp of America)
Circa 1942

1 PG(c),Liberty Scouts 175.00

Becomes:

LIBERTY SCOUTS
June, 1941

2 PG,PG(c)O:Fireman,Liberty Scouts 700.00
3 PG,PG(c) August,1941 O:Sentinel 550.00

LIFE STORY
Fawcett Publications
April, 1949

1 Ph(c) 60.00
2 Ph(c) 25.00
3 Ph(c) 22.00
4 Ph(c) 22.00
5 Ph(c) 22.00
6 Ph(c) 22.00
7 Ph(c) 20.00
8 Ph(c) 20.00
9 Ph(c) 20.00
10 Ph(c) 20.00
11 .... 18.00
12 .... 18.00
13 WW,Drug 75.00
14 thru 21 .... @18.00
22 Drug 25.00
23 thru 35 .... @18.00
36 Drug 22.00
37 thru 42 .... @15.00
43 GE 22.00
44 .... 15.00
45 1952 .... 15.00

LIFE WITH SNARKY PARKER
Fox Feature Syndicate
August, 1950

1 .... 125.00

LI'L ABNER
Harvey Publications
December, 1947

61 BP,BW,Sadie Hawkins Day . 200.00

Li'l Abner #80 © Harvey Publications

62 .... 125.00
63 .... 125.00
64 .... 125.00
65 BP 125.00
66 .... 90.00
67 .... 90.00
68 FearlessFosdick V:Any Face 100.00
69 .... 90.00
70 .... 90.00

Toby Press

71 .... 80.00
72 .... 75.00
73 .... 75.00
74 .... 75.00
75 HK 90.00
76 .... 75.00
77 HK 90.00
78 HK 90.00
79 HK 90.00
80 .... 55.00
81 .... 55.00
82 .... 55.00
83 Baseball 60.00
84 .... 55.00
85 .... 55.00
86 HK 90.00
87 .... 55.00
88 .... 55.00
89 .... 55.00
90 .... 55.00
91 Rep. #77 .... 60.00
92 .... 54.00
93 Rep. #71 .... 60.00
94 .... 55.00
95 Fearless Fosdick 75.00
96 .... 55.00
97 January, 1955 .... 55.00

LI'L GENIUS
Charlton Comics
1955

1 .... 35.00
2 .... 15.00
3 thru 15 .... @12.00
16 Giants 18.00
17 Giants 18.00
18 Giants,100 pages 22.00
19 thru 40 .... @8.00
41 thru 54 .... @5.00
55 1965 .... 5.00

LI'L PAN
Fox Features Syndicate
December-January, 1946-47

6 .... 35.00
7 .... 25.00
8 April-May, 1947 .... 25.00

LINDA
Ajax/Farrell
April-May, 1954

1 .... 75.00
2 Lingerie section 55.00
3 .... 40.00
4 October-November,1954 ... 40.00

Becomes:

PHANTOM LADY

5(1) MB,Dec-Jan'54-55 .... 325.00
2 Last Pre-Code Edition 275.00
3 Comics Code 200.00
4 Red Rocket,June, 1955 ... 200.00

LITTLE AUDREY
St. John Publ. Co./
Harvey Comics
April, 1948

1 .... 200.00
2 .... 100.00
3 thru 6 .... @75.00
7 thru 10 .... @40.00
11 thru 20 .... @25.00
21 thru 24 .... @18.00
25 B:Harvey Comics 55.00
26 A: Casper 25.00
27 A: Casper 25.00
28 A: Casper 25.00
29 thru 31 .... @20.00
32 A: Casper 25.00

33 A: Casper 25.00
34 A: Casper 25.00
35 A: Casper 25.00
36 thru 53 .... @12.00

Little Bit #2 © Jubilee Publishing Co.

LITTLE BIT
Jubilee Publishing Company
March, 1949

1 .... 20.00
2 June, 1949 .... 20.00

LITTLE DOT
Harvey Publications
September, 1953

1 I: Richie Rich & Little Lotta . 450.00
2 .... 250.00
3 .... 150.00
4 .... 125.00
5 O:Dots on Little Dot's Dress 135.00
6 1st Richie Rich(c) 135.00
7 .... 135.00
8 .... 65.00

Little Dot #1 © Harvey Publications

9 .... 65.00
10 .... 65.00
11 thru 20 .... @45.00
21 thru 30 .... @22.00
31 thru 38 .... @20.00
39 .... 50.00
40 thru 50 .... @12.00
51 thru 60 .... @10.00
61 thru 70 .... @8.00
71 thru 80 .... @6.00
81 thru 100 .... @5.00
101 thru 130 .... @3.00
131 thru 140 .... @3.00
141 thru 145, 52 pages ...... @3.50
146 thru 163 .... @1.00

LITTLE EVA
St. John Publishing Co.
May, 1952

1 .... 60.00
2 .... 30.00
3 .... 18.00
4 .... 18.00
5 thru 10 .... @12.00
11 thru 30 .... @10.00
31 November, 1956 .... 10.00

LITTLE GIANT COMICS
Centaur Publications
July, 1938

1 PG, B&W with Color(c) 275.00
2 B&W with Color(c) 225.00
3 B&W with Color(c) 250.00
4 B&W with Color(c) 250.00

LITTLE GIANT DETECTIVE FUNNIES
Centaur Publications
October, 1938

1 B&W 275.00
2 B&W 225.00
3 B&W 225.00
4 January 1939 .... 225.00

LITTLE GIANT MOVIE FUNNIES
Centaur Publications
August, 1938

1 Ed Wheelan-a 275.00
2 Ed Wheelan-a, Oct., 1938 . 225.00

LITTLE IKE
St. John Publishing Co.
April, 1953

1 .... 45.00
2 .... 22.00
3 .... 18.00
4 October, 1953 .... 18.00

LITTLE IODINE
Dell Publishing Co.
April, 1949

1 .... 65.00
2 .... 25.00
3 .... 25.00
4 .... 25.00
5 .... 25.00
6 thru 10 .... @15.00
11 thru 30 .... @12.00
31 thru 50 .... @9.00
51 thru 56 .... @7.00

LITTLE JACK FROST
Avon Periodicals
1951

1 .... 35.00

LITTLE MAX COMICS
Harvey Publications
October, 1949

1 I: Little Dot,Joe Palooka 80.00
2 A: Little Dot 45.00
3 A: Little Dot,Joe Palooka(c) . 30.00
4 .... 20.00
5 C: Little Dot 20.00
6 thru 10 .... @18.00
11 thru 22 .... @15.00
23 A: Little Dot 10.00
24 thru 37 .... @8.00
38 Rep. #20 .... 8.00
39 thru 72 .... @8.00
73 A: Richie Rich; Nov.'61 ...... 9.00

LITTLE MISS MUFFET
Best Books
(Standard Comics)
December, 1948

11 Strip Reprints 45.00
12 Strip Reprints 30.00
13 Strip Reprints; Mar.'49 ..... 30.00

LITTLE MISS SUNBEAM COMICS
Magazine Enterprises
June-July, 1950

1 .... 60.00
2 .... 30.00
3 .... 30.00
4 December-January, 1951 ... 30.00

LITTLE ORPHAN ANNIE
Dell Publishing Co.
1941

1 .... 100.00
2 .... 65.00
3 .... 65.00

Little Roquefort #2
© St. John's Publishing

LITTLE ROQUEFORT
St. John Publishing Co.
June,1952

1 .... 40.00
2 .... 20.00
3 thru 9 .... @15.00

Pines

10 Summer 1958 .... 18.00

LITTLE SCOUTS
Dell Publishing Co.
March, 1951

(1) *see Dell Four Color #321*
2 .... 10.00
3 .... 10.00
4 .... 10.00
5 .... 10.00

6 . . . . 10.00

LITTLEST SNOWMAN
Dell Publishing Co.
December, 1956

1 . . . . 20.00

LIVING BIBLE, THE
Living Bible Corp.
Autumn, 1945

1 LbC-(c) Life of Paul 125.00
2 LbC-(c) Joseph & His Brethern 75.00
3 LbC-(c) Chaplains At War . . 135.00

LONE EAGLE
Ajax/Farrell
April-May, 1954

1 . . . . 50.00
2 . . . . 30.00
3 Bondage(c) 35.00
4 October-November, 1954 . . . 30.00

LONE RANGER
Dell Publishing Co.
January-February 1948

1 B:Lone Ranger & Tonto
B:Strip Reprint 600.00
2 . . . . 250.00
3 . . . . 175.00
4 . . . . 175.00
5 . . . . 175.00
6 . . . . 150.00
7 . . . . 150.00
8 O:Retold 200.00
9 . . . . 140.00
10 . . . . 140.00
11 B:Young Hawk 100.00
12 thru 20 . . . . @100.00
21 . . . . 80.00
22 . . . . 80.00
23 O:Retold 125.00
24 thru 30 . . . . @75.00
31 (1st Mask Logo) 80.00
32 thru 36 . . . . @65.00
37 (E:Strip reprints) 65.00
38 thru 50 . . . . @50.00
51 thru 75 . . . . @45.00
76 thru 99 . . . . @37.00
100 . . . . 55.00
101 thru 111 . . . . @35.00
112 B:Clayton Moore Ph(c) . . . 125.00
113 thru 117 . . . . @65.00
118 O:Lone Ranger & Tonto
retold, Anniv. issue 125.00
119 thru 144 . . . . @60.00
145 final issue,May/July 1962 . . 60.00

THE LONE RANGER'S COMPANION TONTO
Dell Publishing Co.
January, 1951

(1) *see Dell Four Color #312*
2 P(c) all 50.00
3 . . . . 50.00
4 . . . . 28.00
5 . . . . 28.00
6 thru 10 . . . . @25.00
11 thru 20 . . . . @22.00
21 thru 25 . . . . @18.00
26 thru 33 . . . . @15.00

THE LONE RANGER'S FAMOUS HORSE HI-YO SILVER
Dell Publishing Co.
January, 1952

(1) *see Dell Four Color #369*
(1) *see Dell Four Color #392*
3 P(c) all 20.00
4 . . . . 20.00
5 . . . . 20.00
6 thru 10 . . . . @18.00
11 thru 36 . . . . @15.00

LONE RIDER
Farrell
(Superior Comics)
April, 1951

1 . . . . 80.00
2 I&O: Golden Arrow; 52 pgs. . 40.00
3 . . . . 35.00
4 . . . . 35.00
5 . . . . 35.00
6 E: Golden Arrow 40.00
7 G. Arrow Becomes Swift Arrow 45.00
8 O: Swift Arrow 55.00
9 thru 14 . . . . @25.00
15 O: Golden Arrow Rep. #2 . . . 30.00
16 thru 19 . . . . @20.00
20 . . . . 18.00
21 3-D (c) 65.00
22 . . . . 18.00
23 A: Apache Kid 20.00
24 . . . . 18.00
25 . . . . 18.00
26 July, 1955 . . . . 18.00

LONG BOW
Real Adventures Publ.
(Fiction House)
Winter, 1950

1 . . . . 75.00
2 . . . . 40.00
3 "Red Arrows Means War" . . . 35.00
4 "Trial of Tomahawk" 35.00
5 . . . . 35.00
6 "Rattlesnake Raiders" 30.00
7 . . . . 30.00
8 . . . . 30.00
9 Spring, 1953 . . . . 30.00

LOONEY TUNES AND MERRIE MELODIES
Dell Publishing Co.
1941

1 B:&1st Comic App.) Bugs Bunny
Daffy Duck,Elmer Fudd . . . 3,500.00
2 Bugs/Porky(c) 700.00
3 Bugs/Porky(c) B:WK,
Kandi the Cave 600.00
4 Bugs/Porky(c),WK 550.00
5 Bugs/Porky(c),WK,
A:Super Rabbit 450.00
6 Bugs/Porky/Elmer(c),E:WK,
Kandi the Cave 350.00
7 Bugs/Porky(c) 300.00
8 Bugs/Porky swimming(c),F:WK,
Kandi the Cave 350.00
9 Porky/Elmer car painted(c) . 375.00
10 Porky/Bugs/Elmer Parade(c) 275.00
11 Bugs/Porky(c),F:WK,
Kandi the Cave 275.00
12 Bugs/Porky rollerskating(c) . 250.00
13 Bugs/Porky(c) 250.00
14 Bugs/Porky(c) 250.00
15 Bugs/Porky X-Mas(c),F:WK
Kandi the Cave 275.00
16 Bugs/Porky ice-skating(c) . . 240.00
17 Bugs/Petunia Valentines(c) . 240.00
18 Sgt.Bugs Marine(c) 250.00
19 Bugs/Painting(c) 240.00
20 Bugs/Porky/ElmerWarBonds(c),
B:WK,Pat,Patsy&Pete 250.00
21 Bugs/Porky 4th July(c) 225.00
22 Porky(c) 225.00
23 Bugs/Porky Fishing(c) 225.00
24 Bugs/Porky Football(c) 225.00
25 Bugs/Porky/Petunia
Halloween(c),E:WK,Pat,
Patsy & Pete 225.00
26 Bugs Thanksgiving(c) 175.00
27 Bugs/Porky New Years(c) . . 175.00
28 Bugs/Porky Ice-Skating(c) . . 175.00
29 Bugs Valentine(c) 175.00
30 Bugs(c) 175.00
31 Bugs(c) 135.00

Looney Tunes & Merrie Melodies #32
© Dell Publ. Co.

32 Bugs/Porky Hot Dogs(c) . . . 135.00
33 Bugs/Porky War Bonds(c) . . 140.00
34 Bugs/Porky Fishing(c) 135.00
35 Bugs/Porky Swimming(c) . . 135.00
36 Bugs/Porky(c) 135.00
37 Bugs Halloween(c) 135.00
38 Bugs Thanksgiving(c) 135.00
39 Bugs X-Mas(c) 135.00
40 Bugs(c) 135.00
41 Bugs Washington's
Birthday(c) 100.00
42 Bugs Magician(c) 100.00
43 Bugs Dream(c) 100.00
44 Bugs/Porky(c) 100.00
45 Bugs War Bonds(c) 100.00
46 Bugs/Porky(c) 90.00
47 Bugs Beach(c) 90.00
48 Bugs/Porky Picnic(c) 90.00
49 Bugs(c) 90.00
50 Bugs(c) 90.00
51 thru 60 . . . . @60.00
61 thru 80 . . . . @40.00
81 thru 86 . . . . @25.00
87 Bugs X-Mas(c) 30.00
88 thru 99 . . . . @25.00
100 . . . . 35.00
101 thru 110 . . . . @22.00
111 thru 125 . . . . @20.00
126 thru 150 . . . . @18.00
151 thru 165 . . . . @15.00

Becomes:

LOONEY TUNES
August, 1955

166 thru 200 . . . . @10.00
201 thru 245 . . . . @8.00
246 final issue,Sept.1962 . . . . . . 8.00

LOST WORLD
Literacy Enterprises
(Standard Comics)
October, 1952

5 ATh, Alice in Terrorland . . . 150.00
6 ATh 125.00

LOVE AND MARRIAGE
Superior Comics Ltd.
March, 1952

1 . . . . 50.00
2 . . . . 25.00
3 thru 10 . . . . @20.00

11 thru 15 ... @20.00
16 September, 1954 ... 20.00

LOVE AT FIRST SIGHT
Periodical House
(Ace Magazines)
October, 1949

1 P(c) ... 55.00
2 P(c) ... 25.00
3 ... 15.00
4 P(c) ... 15.00
5 thru 10 ... @15.00
11 thru 33 ... @10.00
34 1st Edition Under Code ... 7.00
35 thru 41 ... @7.00
42 1956 ... 7.00

LOVE CONFESSIONS
Comics Magazine
(Quality Comics Group)
October, 1949

1 PG,BWa(c)& Some-a ... 150.00
2 PG ... 50.00
3 ... 30.00
4 RC ... 50.00
5 BWa ... 55.00
6 Ph(c) ... 15.00
7 Ph(c) Van Johnson ... 15.00
8 BWa ... 50.00
9 Ph(c)Jane Russell/Robert Mitchum ... 15.00
10 BWa ... 50.00
11 thru 18 Ph(c) ... @30.00
19 ... 15.00
20 BWa ... 50.00
21 ... 10.00
22 BWa ... 10.00
23 thru 28 ... @10.00
29 BWa ... 35.00
30 thru 38 ... @8.00
39 MB ... 15.00
40 ... 8.00
41 ... 8.00
42 ... 8.00
43 1st Edition Under Code ... 8.00
44 thru 46 ... @8.00
47 BWa(c) ... 20.00
48 thru 54 December, 1956 ... @8.00

LOVE DIARY
Our Publishing Co./Toytown
July, 1949

1 BK,Ph(c) ... 75.00
2 BK,Ph(c) ... 55.00
3 BK,Ph(c) ... 55.00
4 thru 9 Ph(c) ... @20.00
10 BEv, Ph(c) ... 25.00
11 thru 24 Ph(c) ... @15.00
25 ... 12.00
26 ... 12.00
27 Ph(c) ... 15.00
28 ... 12.00
29 Ph(c) ... 15.00
30 ... 12.00
31 JB(c) ... 12.00
32 thru 41 ... @12.00
42 MB(c) ... 12.00
43 thru 47 ... @12.00
48 1st Edition Under Code, Oct.'55 ... 12.00

LOVE DIARY
Quality Comics Group
September, 1949

1 BWa(c) ... 110.00

LOVE LESSONS
Harvey Publications
October, 1949

1 ... 50.00
2 ... 22.00
3 Ph(c) ... 18.00

4 ... 18.00
5 June, 1950 ... 18.00

LOVE LETTERS
Comic Magazines
(Quality Comics Group)
November, 1949

1 PG,BWa(c) ... 110.00
2 PG,BWa(c) ... 100.00
3 PG ... 60.00
4 BWa ... 80.00
5 ... 20.00
6 ... 20.00
7 ... 20.00
8 ... 20.00
9 Ph(c) of Robert Mitchum ... 30.00
10 ... 20.00
11 BWa ... 35.00
12 ... 15.00
13 ... 15.00
14 ... 15.00
15 ... 15.00
16 Ph(c) of Anthony Quinn ... 18.00
17 BWa, Ph(c) of Jane Russell ... 18.00
18 thru 30 ... @12.00
31 BWa ... 25.00

Becomes:

LOVE SECRETS

32 ... 32.00
33 ... 15.00
34 BWa ... 35.00
35 thru 39 ... @15.00
40 MB(c)1st Edition Under Code 25.00
41 thru 50 ... @12.00
50 MB ... 12.00
51 MB(c) ... 12.00
52 thru 56 ... @10.00

LOVELORN
Best Syndicated/Michel Publ.
(American Comics Group)
August-September, 1949

1 ... 60.00
2 ... 30.00
3 thru 10 ... @22.00
11 thru 17 ... @15.00
18 2pgs. MD-a ... 15.00
19 ... 12.00
20 ... 12.00
21 Prostitution Story ... 30.00
22 thru 50 ... @12.00
51 July, 1954 3-D ... 75.00

Becomes:

CONFESSIONS OF LOVELORN

52 3-D ... 100.00
53 ... 30.00
54 3-D ... 100.00
55 ... 20.00
56 Communist Story ... 35.00
57 Comics Code ... 15.00
58 thru 90 ... @15.00
91 AW ... 35.00
92 thru 105 ... @10.00
106 P(c) ... 10.00
107 P(c) ... 10.00
108 thru 114 ... @10.00

LOVE MEMORIES
Fawcett Publications
Autumn, 1949

1 Ph(c) ... 45.00
2 Ph(c) ... 25.00
3 Ph(c) ... 25.00
4 Ph(c) ... 25.00

LOVE MYSTERY
Fawcett Publications
June, 1950

1 GE, Ph(c) ... 100.00
2 GE, Ph(c) ... 75.00
3 GE & BP, Ph(c); October, 1950 75.00

Love Problems & Advice #1
© McCombs/Harvey Publ.

LOVE PROBLEMS AND ADVICE ILLUSTRATED
McCombs/Harvey Publications
Home Comics
June, 1949

1 BP ... 55.00
2 BP ... 30.00
3 ... 20.00
4 ... 20.00
5 L. Elias(c) ... 20.00
6 ... 18.00
7 BP ... 18.00
8 BP ... 18.00
9 BP ... 18.00
10 BP ... 18.00
11 BP ... 15.00
12 BP ... 15.00
13 BP ... 15.00
14 BP ... 15.00
15 ... 15.00
16 ... 15.00
17 thru 23 BP ... @15.00
24 BP, Rape Scene ... 20.00
25 BP ... 10.00
26 ... 10.00
27 ... 10.00
28 BP ... 10.00
29 BP ... 10.00
30 ... 10.00
31 ... 10.00
32 Comics Code ... 6.00
33 BP ... 6.00
34 ... 6.00
35 ... 6.00
36 ... 6.00
37 ... 6.00
38 S&K (c) ... 6.00
39 ... 6.00
40 BP ... 6.00
41 BP ... 6.00
42 ... 6.00
43 ... 6.00
44 March, 1957 ... 6.00

LOVERS LANE
Lev Gleason Publications
October, 1949

1 CBi (c),FG-a ... 45.00
2 P(c) ... 25.00
3 P(c) ... 18.00
4 P(c) ... 18.00
5 P(c) ... 18.00
6 GT,P(c), ... 18.00

7 P(c), 18.00
8 P(c), 18.00
9 P(c), 18.00
10 P(c) 18.00
11 thru 19 P(c) @15.00
20 Ph(c); FF 1 page Ad, 15.00
21 Ph(c) 9.00
22 Ph(c) 9.00
23 9.00
24 9.00
25 9.00
26 Ph(c) 9.00
27 Ph(c) 9.00
28 Ph(c) 9.00
29 thru 38 @9.00
39 Story Narrated by Frank Sinatra 25.00
40 9.00
41 June, 1954 9.00

LOVE SCANDALS
Comic Magazines (Quality Comics Group)
February, 1950

1 BW(c)&a 120.00
2 PG-a, Ph(c) 35.00
3 PG-a, Ph(c) 35.00
4 BWa(c)&a 18Pgs.; GFx-a 100.00
5 Ph(c), October, 1950 35.00

LOVE STORIES OF MARY WORTH
Harvey Publications
September, 1949

1 Newspaper Reprints 35.00
2 Newspaper Reprints 25.00
3 Newspaper Reprints 20.00
4 Newspaper Reprints, 20.00
5 May, 1950 20.00

LUCKY COMICS
Consolidated Magazines
January, 1944

1 Lucky Star 85.00
2 Henry C. Kiefer(c) 40.00
3 40.00
4 40.00
5 Summer, 1946,Devil(c) 40.00

LUCKY DUCK
Standard Comics (Literary Enterprises)
January, 1953

5 IS (c)&a 35.00
6 IS (c)&a 25.00
7 IS (c)&a 25.00
8 IS (c)&a, September, 1953 25.00

LUCKY FIGHTS IT THROUGH
Educational Comics
1949

N# HK-a, V.D. Prevention 1300.00

LUCKY "7" COMICS
Howard Publications
1944

1 Bondage(c) Pioneer 150.00

LUCKY STAR
Nationwide Publications
1950

1 JDa,B:52 pages western 65.00
2 JDa 40.00
3 JDa 40.00
4 JDa 35.00
5 JDa 35.00
6 JDa 35.00
7 JDa 35.00
8 thru 13 @25.00
14 1955,E:52 pages western 25.00

LUCY, THE REAL GONE GAL
St. John Publishing Co.
June, 1953

1 Negligee Panels,Teenage 65.00
2 35.00
3 MD-a 25.00
4 February, 1954 22.00

Becomes:

MEET MISS PEPPER
St. John Publishing Co.
April, 1954

5 JKu-a 100.00
6 JKu (c)&a, June,1954 90.00

MAD
E.C. Comics
October-November, 1952

1 JSe,HK(c),JDa,WW 3,000.00
2 JSe,JDa(c),JDa,WW 800.00
3 JSe,HK(c),JDa,WW 550.00
4 JSe,HK(c),JDa-Flob Was A Slob,JDa,WW 550.00
5 JSe,BE(c).JDa,WW 800.00
6 JSe,HK(c),Jda,WW 500.00
7 HK(c),JDa,WW 500.00
8 HK(c),JDa,WW 500.00
9 JSe,HK(c),JDa,WW 500.00
10 JSe,HK(c),JDa,WW 500.00
11 BW,BW(c),JDa,WW,Life(c) 500.00
12 BK,JDa,WW 400.00
13 HK(c),JDa,WW,Red(c) 400.00
14 RH,HK(c),JDa,WW, Mona Lisa(c) 400.00
15 JDa,WW,Alice in Wonderland(c) 400.00
16 HK(c),JDa,WW,Newspaper(c) 400.00
17 BK,BW,JDa,WW 400.00
18 HK(c),JDa,WW 400.00
19 JDa,WW,Racing Form(c) 300.00
20 JDa,WW,Composition(c) 300.00

Mad #7 © E.C. Comics

21 JDa,WW,1st A.E.Neuman(c) 300.00
22 BE,JDa,WW,Picasso(c) 300.00
23 Last Comic Format Edition, JDa,WW Think(c) 300.00
24 BK,WW, HK Logo & Border; 1st Magazine Format 600.00
25 WW, Al Jaffee Sterts As Reg. 225.00
26 BK,WW,WW(c) 175.00
27 WWa,RH,JDa(c) 175.00
28 WW,BE(c),RH Back(c) 150.00
29 JKa,BW,WW,WW(c); 1st Don Martin Artwork 150.00
30 BE,WW,RC; 1st A.E. Neuman(c) By Mingo 225.00
31 JDa,WW,BW,Mingo(c) 135.00
32 MD,JO 1st as reg.;Mingo(c); WW-Back(c) 125.00
33 WWa,Mingo(c);JO-Back(c) 125.00
34 WWa,Mingo(c);1st Berg as Reg. 100.00
35 WW,RC,Mingo Wraparound(c) 100.00
36 WW,BW,Mingo(c),JO,MD 75.00
37 WW,Mingo(c)JO,MD 75.00
38 WW,JO,MD 50.00
39 WW,JO,MD 50.00
40 WW,BW,JO,MD 50.00
41 WW,JO,MD 50.00
42 WW,JO,MD 50.00
43 WW,JO,MD 50.00
44 WW,JO,MD 50.00
45 WW,JO,MD 50.00
46 JO,MD 50.00
47 JO,MD 50.00
48 JO,MD 50.00
49 JO,MD 50.00
50 JO,MD 50.00
51 JO,MD 45.00
52 JO,MD 45.00
53 JO,MD 45.00
54 JO,MD 45.00
55 JO,MD 45.00
56 JO,MD 40.00
57 JO,MD 40.00
58 JO,MD 40.00
59 WW,JO,MD 45.00
60 JO,MD 40.00
61 JO,MD 35.00
62 JO,MD 35.00
63 JO,MD 35.00
64 JO,MD 35.00
65 JO,MD 35.00
66 JO,MD 30.00
67 JO,MD 30.00
68 Don Martin(c),JO,MD 30.00
69 JO,MD 30.00
70 JO,MD 30.00
71 JO,MD 30.00
72 JO,MD 30.00
73 JO,MD 30.00
74 JO,MD 30.00
75 Mingo(c),JO,MD 25.00
76 Mingo(c),SA,JO,MD 25.00
77 Mingo(c),SA,JO,MD 25.00
78 Mingo(c),SA,JO,MD 25.00
79 Mingo(c),SA,JO,MD 25.00
80 Mingo(c),SA,JO,MD 25.00
81 Mingo(c),SA,JO,MD 25.00
82 BW,Mingo(c),SA,JO,MD 25.00
83 Mingo(c),SA,JO,MD 25.00
84 Mingo(c),SA,JO,MD 25.00
85 Mingo(c)SA,JO,MD 25.00
86 Mingo(c);1st Fold-in Back(c), SA,JO,MD 25.00
87 Mingo(c),JO,MD 20.00
88 Mingo(c),JO,MD 20.00
89 WK,Mingo(c),JO,MD 25.00
90 Mingo(c); FF-Back(c),JO,MD 22.00
91 Mingo(c),JO,MD 20.00
92 Mingo(c),JO,MD 20.00
93 Mingo(c),JO,MD 20.00
94 Mingo(c),JO,MD 20.00
95 Mingo(c),JO,MD 20.00
96 Mingo(c),JO,MD 20.00
97 Mingo(c),JO,MD 20.00
98 Mingo(c),JO,MD 20.00
99 JDa,Mingo(c),JO,MD 22.00
100 Mingo(c),JO,MD 18.00
101 Infinity(c) by Mingo,JO,MD 18.00
102 Mingo(c)JO,MD 18.00
103 Mingo(c)JO,MD 18.00
104 Mingo(c)JO,MD 18.00
105 Mingo(c);Batman TV Spoof ,JO,MD 18.00
106 Mingo(c);FF-Back(c),JO,MD 20.00
107 Mingo(c),JO,MD 15.00
108 Mingo(c),JO,MD 15.00
109 Mingo(c),JO,MD 15.00
110 Mingo(c),JO,MD 15.00

111 Mingo(c),JO,MD 15.00
112 JO,MD 15.00
113 JO,MD 15.00
114 JO,MD 15.00
115 JO,MD 15.00
116 JO,MD 15.00
117 JO,MD 15.00
118 JO,MD 15.00
119 JO,MD 15.00
120 JO,MD 15.00
121 Beatles,JO,MD 20.00
122 MD & Mingo(c),JO,MD, Reagan 15.00
123 JO,MD 12.00
124 JO,MD 12.00
125 JO,MD 12.00
126 JO,MD 12.00
127 JO,MD 12.00
128 Last JO;MD. 12.00
129 MD 12.00
130 MD 12.00
131 MD 12.00
132 MD 12.00
133 MD 12.00
134 MD 12.00
135 JDa(c),MD 13.00
136 MD 12.00
137 BW,MD 12.00
138 MD 12.00
139 JDa(c),MD 13.00
140 thru 153 MD . . . . @10.00
154 Mineo(c),MD 10.00
155 . . . . 10.00
156 . . . . 10.00
157 . . . . 10.00
158 . . . . 10.00
159 . . . . 10.00
160 Mingo(c),JDa,AT 10.00
161 . . . . 9.00
162 Mingo(c),MD,AT 9.00
163 . . . . 9.00
164 Mingo,PaperMoon(c),AT, MD,SA 9.00
165 Don Martin(c),At,MD 9.00
166 . . . . 9.00
167 . . . . 9.00
168 Mingo(c),AT,MD 9.00
169 MD(c) 9.00
170 . . . . 9.00
171 Mingo(c) 8.00
172 Mingo(c) 8.00
173 JDa(c) 8.00
174 . . . . 8.00
175 . . . . 8.00
176 MD(c) 8.00
177 . . . . 8.00
178 JDa(c) 8.00
179 . . . . 8.00
180 Jaws(c),SA,MD,JDA,AT 8.00
181 G.Washington(c),JDa 8.00
182 . . . . 8.00
183 Mingo(c),AT,SA,MD 8.00
184 Mingo(c),Md,AT 8.00
185 . . . . 8.00
186 Star Trek Spoof 10.00
187 . . . . 8.00
188 . . . . 8.00
189 . . . . 8.00
190 . . . . 8.00
191 Clark(c),JDa,MD,AT 8.00
192 . . . . 8.00
193 Charlies Angels(c), Rickart,JDa,SA,MD 8.00
194 Rocky(c),Rickart,AT,MD 8.00
195 . . . . 8.00
196 Star Wars Spoof, Rickart,AT,JDa 15.00
197 . . . . 8.00
198 UPC(c),AT,MD 8.00
199 Jaffee(c),AT,JDa,SA,MD 8.00
200 Rickart(c),Close Encounters 10.00
201 Rickart(c),Sat.Night Fever . . 3.50
202 . . . . 3.50
203 Star Wars Spoof,Rickart(c) . . 5.00
204 Hulk TV Spoof,JawsII(c) 4.00
205 Rickart(c),Grease 3.00
206 Mingo,(c),AT,JDa,Md 3.00
207 Jones(c),Animal House(c) . . . 3.00
208 Superman Movie Spoof, Rickart(c) 4.00
209 Mingo(c),AT,MD 3.00
210 Mingo,Lawn Mower,AT, JDa,MD 3.00
211 Mingo(c) 3.00
212 Jda(c),AT,MD 4.00
213 JDa(c),SA,AT,JDa 4.00
214 . . . . 2.50
215 Jones(c),MD,AT,JDa 2.50
216 . . . . 2.50
217 Jaffee(c),For Pres,AT,MD . . . 2.50
218 Martin(c),AT,MD 2.50
219 thru 250 . . . . @2.50
251 thru 260 . . . . @2.50
261 thru 299 . . . . @2.00
300 thru 303 . . . . 5.00
304 thru 330 . . . . 2.00

MAGIC COMICS
David McKay Publications
August, 1939

1 Mandrake the Magician, Henry,Popeye,Blondie, Barney Baxter,Secret Agent X-9, Bunky,Henry on(c) . . 1,000.00
2 Henry on(c) 450.00
3 Henry on(c) 350.00
4 Henry on(c),Mandrake-Logo 300.00
5 Henry on(c),Mandrake-Logo 250.00
6 Henry on(c),Mandrake-Logo 225.00
7 Henry on(c),Mandrake-Logo 225.00
8 B:Inspector Wade,Tippie . . 200.00
9 Henry-Mandrake Interact(c) 200.00
10 Henry-Mandrake Interact(c) . 200.00
11 Henry-Mandrake Interact(c) . 175.00
12 Mandrake on(c) 175.00
13 Mandrake on(c) 175.00
14 Mandrake on(c) 175.00
15 Mandrake on(c) 175.00
16 Mandrake on(c) 175.00
17 B:Lone Ranger 200.00
18 Mandrake/Robot on(c) 175.00
19 Mandrake on(c) 175.00
20 Mandrake on(c) 150.00
21 Mandrake on(c) 150.00
22 Mandrake on(c) 150.00
23 Mandrake on(c) 150.00
24 Mandrake on(c) 150.00
25 B:Blondie; Mandrake in Logo for Duration 150.00
26 Blondie (c) 100.00
27 Blondie (c); High School Heroes 100.00
28 Blondie (c); High School Heroes 100.00
29 Blondie (c); High School Heroes 100.00
30 Blondie (c) 100.00
31 Blondie(c);High School Sports Page 85.00
32 Blondie (c);Secret Agent X-9 . 85.00
33 C. Knight's-Romance of Flying 85.00
34 ClaytonKnight's-War in the Air 85.00
35 Blondie (c) 85.00
36 July'42; Patriotic-(c) 90.00
37 Blondie (c) 85.00
38 ClaytonKnight's-Flying Tigers 85.00
39 Blondie (c) 85.00
40 Jimmie Doolittle Bombs Tokyo 85.00
41 How German Became British Censor 65.00
42 Joe Musial's-Dollar-a-Dither . 65.00
43 Clayton Knight's-War in the Air 65.00
44 Flying Fortress in Action 65.00
45 Clayton Knight's-Gremlins . . . 65.00
46 Adventures of Aladdin Jr. . . . 65.00
47 Secret Agent X-9 . . . . 65.00
48 General Arnold U.S.A.F. 65.00
49 Joe Musial's-Dollar-a-Dither . 65.00
50 The Lone Ranger 65.00

Magic Comics #8
© David McKay Publications

51 Joe Musial's-Dollar-a-Dither . 55.00
52 C. Knights-Heroes on Wings . 55.00
53 C. Knights-Heroes on Wings . 55.00
54 High School Heroes 55.00
55 Blondie (c) 60.00
56 High School Heroes 55.00
57 Joe Musial's-Dollar-a-Dither . 55.00
58 Private Breger Abroad 55.00
59 . . . . 55.00
60 . . . . 55.00
61 Joe Musial's-Dollar-a-Dither . 40.00
62 . . . . 40.00
63 B:Buz Sawyer, Naval Pilot . . 40.00
64 thru 70 . . . . @40.00
71 thru 80 . . . . @35.00
80 thru 90 . . . . @30.00
91 thru 99 . . . . @30.00
100 . . . . 35.00
101 thru 108 . . . . @25.00
108 Flash Gordon 35.00
109 Flash Gordon 35.00
110 thru 113 . . . . @25.00
114 The Lone Ranger 25.00
115 thru 119 . . . . @25.00
120 Secret Agent X-9 . . . . 30.00
121 Secret Agent X-9 . . . . 30.00
122 Secret Agent X-9 . . . . 30.00
123 Sec. Agent X-9;Nov-Dec.'49 30.00

MAJOR HOOPLE COMICS
Nedor Publications
1942

1 Mary Worth,Phantom Soldier; Buy War Bonds On(c) 175.00

MAJOR VICTORY COMICS
H. Clay Glover Svcs./ Harry A. Chestler
1944

1 O:Major Victory,I:Spider Woman 300.00
2 A: Dynamic Boy 200.00
3 A: Rocket Boy 200.00

MAN HUNT!
Magazine Enterprises
October, 1953

1 LbC,FG,OW(c);B:Red Fox, Undercover Girl, Space Ace 200.00
2 LbC,FG,OW(c);

Electrocution(c) 175.00
3 LbC,FG,OW,OW(c) 150.00
4 LbC,FG,OW,OW(c) 150.00
5 LbC,FG,OW,OW(c) 135.00
6 LbC,OW,OW(c) 135.00
7 LbC,OW; E:Space Ace 120.00
8 LbC,OW,FG(c);B:Trail Colt . 120.00
9 LbC,OW 120.00
10 LbC,OW,OW(c),Gwl 120.00
11 LbC,FF,OW;B:The Duke, Scotland Yard 175.00
12 LbC,OW 90.00
13 LbC,FF,OW;Rep.Trail Colt #1 175.00
14 LbC,OW;Bondage, Hypo-(c);1953 . . . . 135.00

MAN OF WAR
Comic Corp. of America (Centaur Publ.)
November, 1941

1 PG,PG(c);Flag(c);B:The Fire-Man,Man of War,The Sentinel, Liberty Guards,Vapoman . . 800.00
2 PG,PG(c);I: The Ferret 700.00

MAN O'MARS
Fiction House/ I.W. Enterprises
1953

1 MA, Space Rangers 200.00
1 MA, Rep. Space Rangers . . . 30.00

MARCH OF COMICS
K.K. Publications/ Western Publ.
1946
(All were Giveaways)

N# WK back(c),Goldilocks . . . 250.00
N# WK,How Santa got His Red Suit 250.00
N# WK,Our Gang 350.00
N# CB,Donald Duck; "Maharajah Donald" 6,000.00
5 Andy Panda 150.00
6 WK,Fairy Tales 200.00
7 Oswald the Lucky Rabbit . . 150.00
8 Mickey Mouse 500.00
9 Gloomey Bunny 75.00
10 Santa Claus 50.00
11 Santa Claus 35.00
12 Santa's Toys 50.00
13 Santa's Suprise 50.00
14 Santa's Kitchen 50.00
15 Hip-It-Ty Hop 75.00
16 Woody Woodpecker 150.00
17 Roy Rogers 175.00
18 Fairy Tales 90.00
19 Uncle Wiggily 75.00
20 CB,Donald Duck 2,800.00
21 Tom and Jerry 75.00
22 Andy Panda 65.00
23 Raggedy Ann and Andy . . . 100.00
24 Felix the Cat; By Otto Messmer 175.00
25 Gene Autrey 175.00
26 Our Gang 175.00
27 Mickey Mouse 300.00
28 Gene Autry 150.00
29 Easter 30.00
30 Santa 25.00
31 Santa 25.00
32 Does Not Exist
33 A Christmas Carol 25.00
34 Woody Woodpecker 75.00
35 Roy Rogers 160.00
36 Felix the Cat 150.00
37 Popeye 120.00
38 Oswald the Lucky Rabbit . . . 50.00
39 Gene Autry 150.00
40 Andy and Woody 50.00
41 CB,DonaldDuck,SouthSeas 2,000.00
42 Porky Pig 50.00
43 Henry 40.00
44 Bugs Bunny 75.00
45 Mickey Mouse 250.00
46 Tom and Jerry 70.00
47 Roy Rogers 135.00
48 Santa 20.00
49 Santa 20.00
50 Santa 20.00
51 Felix the Cat 120.00
52 Popeye 100.00
53 Oswald the Lucky Rabbit . . . 50.00
54 Gene Autrey 150.00
55 Andy and Woody 45.00
56 CB back(c),Donald Duck . . . 200.00
57 Porky Pig 45.00
58 Henry 30.00
59 Bugs Bunny 60.00
60 Mickey Mouse 150.00
61 Tom and Jerry 45.00
62 Roy Rogers 130.00
63 Santa 20.00
64 Santa 20.00
65 Jingle Bells 20.00
66 Popeye 85.00
67 Oswald the Lucky Rabbit . . . 30.00
68 Roy Rogers 130.00
69 Donald Duck 175.00
70 Tom and Jerry 35.00
71 Porky Pig 35.00
72 Krazy Kat 50.00
73 Roy Rogers 100.00
74 Mickey Mouse 135.00
75 Bugs Bunny 50.00
76 Andy and Woody 35.00
77 Roy Rogers 100.00
78 Gene Autrey; last regular sized issue 100.00
79 Andy Panda,5"x7" format . . . 25.00
80 Popeye 65.00
81 Oswald the Lucky Rabbit . . . 22.00
82 Tarzan 125.00
83 Bugs Bunny 30.00
84 Henry 20.00
85 Woody Woodpecker 22.00
86 Roy Rogers 80.00
87 Krazy Kat 25.00
88 Tom and Jerry 20.00
89 Porky Pig 20.00
90 Gene Autrey 80.00
91 Roy Rogers and Santa 80.00
92 Christmas w/Santa 15.00
93 Woody Woodpecker 20.00
94 Indian Chief 50.00
95 Oswald the Lucky Rabbit . . . 18.00
96 Popeye 55.00
97 Bugs Bunny 20.00
98 Tarzan,Lex Barker Ph(c) . . . 120.00
99 Porky Pig 20.00
100 Roy Rogers 75.00
101 Henry 15.00
102 Tom Corbet,P(c) 120.00
103 Tom and Jerry 15.00
104 Gene Autrey 75.00
105 Roy Rogers 75.00
106 Santa's Helpers 15.00
107 Not Published
108 Fun with Santa 15.00
109 Woody Woodpecker 18.00
110 Indian Chief 30.00
111 Oswald the Lucky Rabbit . . 15.00
112 Henry 12.00
113 Porky Pig 15.00
114 Tarzan,RsM 120.00
115 Bugs Bunny 25.00
116 Roy Rogers 65.00
117 Popeye 60.00
118 Flash Gordon, P(c) 110.00
119 Tom and Jerry 16.00
120 Gene Autrey 65.00
121 Roy Rogers 65.00
122 Santa's Suprise 12.00
123 Santa's Christmas Book . . . 12.00
124 Woody Woodpecker 15.00
125 Tarzan, Lex Barker Ph(c) . 100.00
126 Oswald the Lucky Rabbit . . 12.00
127 Indian Chief 20.00
128 Tom and Jerry 15.00
129 Henry 12.00
130 Porky Pig 12.00
131 Roy Rogers 65.00
132 Bugs Bunny 22.00
133 Flash Gordon,Ph(c) 80.00
134 Popeye 40.00
135 Gene Autrey 60.00
136 Roy Rogers 60.00
137 Gifts from Santa 10.00
138 Fun at Christmas 10.00
139 Woody Woodpecker 15.00
140 Indian Chief 25.00
141 Oswald the Lucky Rabbit . . 12.00
142 Flash Gordon 80.00
143 Porky Pig 15.00
144 RsM,Ph(c),Tarzan 100.00
145 Tom and Jerry 15.00
146 Roy Rogers,Ph(c) 60.00
147 Henry 10.00
148 Popeye 30.00
149 Bugs Bunny 20.00
150 Gene Autrey 60.00
151 Roy Rogers 60.00
152 The Night Before Christmas 10.00
153 Merry Christmas 10.00
154 Tom and Jerry 15.00
155 Tarzan,Ph(c) 100.00
156 Oswald the Lucky Rabbit . . 12.00
157 Popeye 25.00
158 Woody Woodpecker 15.00
159 Indian Chief 20.00
160 Bugs Bunny 15.00
161 Roy Rogers 50.00
162 Henry 10.00
163 Rin Tin Tin 32.00
164 Porky Pig 12.00
165 The Lone Ranger 50.00
166 Santa & His Reindeer 10.00
167 Roy Rogers and Santa 50.00
168 Santa Claus' Workshop . . . 10.00
169 Popeye 25.00
170 Indian Chief 25.00
171 Oswald the Lucky Rabbit . . 20.00
172 Tarzan 80.00
173 Tom and Jerry 10.00
174 The Lone Ranger 50.00
175 Porky Pig 12.00
176 Roy Rogers 45.00
177 Woody Woodpecker 12.00
178 Henry 10.00
179 Bugs Bunny 12.00
180 Rin Tin Tin 25.00
181 Happy Holiday 8.00
182 Happi Tim 10.00
183 Welcome Santa 8.00
184 Woody Woodpecker 12.00
185 Tarzan, Ph(c) 75.00
186 Oswald the Lucky Rabbit . . 10.00
187 Indian Chief 20.00
188 Bugs Bunny 18.00
189 Henry 9.00
190 Tom and Jerry 11.00
191 Roy Rogers 45.00
192 Porky Pig 11.00
193 The Lone Ranger 50.00
194 Popeye 25.00
195 Rin Tin Tin 30.00
196 Not Published
197 Santa is Coming 8.00
198 Santa's Helper 8.00
199 Huckleberry Hound 40.00
200 Fury 30.00
201 Bugs Bunny 15.00
202 Space Explorer 50.00
203 Woody Woodpecker 10.00
204 Tarzan 55.00
205 Mighty Mouse 30.00
206 Roy Rogers,Ph(c) 45.00
207 Tom and Jerry 10.00
208 The Lone Ranger,Ph(c) . . . 75.00
209 Porky Pig 10.00
210 Lassie 30.00
211 Not Published
212 Christmas Eve 8.00

213 Here Comes Santa 8.00
214 Huckleberry Hound 35.00
215 Hi Yo Silver 35.00
216 Rocky & His Friends 75.00
217 Lassie 20.00
218 Porky Pig 10.00
219 Journey to the Sun 30.00
220 Bugs Bunny 15.00
221 Roy and Dale,Ph(c) 40.00
222 Woody Woodpecker 10.00
223 Tarzan 55.00
224 Tom and Jerry 10.00
225 The Lone Ranger 40.00
226 Christmas Treasury 8.00
227 Not Published
228 Letters to Santa 8.00
229 The Flintstones 100.00
230 Lassie 20.00
231 Bugs Bunny 15.00
232 The Three Stooges 60.00
233 Bullwinkle 75.00
234 Smokey the Bear 20.00
235 Huckleberry Hound 35.00
236 Roy and Dale 30.00
237 Mighty Mouse 18.00
238 The Lone Ranger 40.00
239 Woody Woodpecker 10.00
240 Tarzan 45.00
241 Santa Claus Around the World 8.00
242 Santa Toyland 8.00
243 The Flintstones 100.00
244 Mr.Ed,Ph(c) 25.00
245 Bugs Bunny 15.00
246 Popeye 20.00
247 Mighty Mouse 20.00
248 The Three Stooges 55.00
249 Woody Woodpecker 10.00
250 Roy and Dale 30.00
251 Little Lulu & Witch Hazel . . 100.00
252 P(c),Tarzan 45.00
253 Yogi Bear 25.00
254 Lassie 20.00
255 Santa's Christmas List 8.00
256 Christmas Party 8.00
257 Mighty Mouse 20.00
258 The Sword in the Stone (Disney Version) 35.00
259 Bugs Bunny 15.00
260 Mr. Ed 20.00
261 Woody Woodpecker 10.00
262 Tarzan 45.00
263 Donald Duck 50.00
264 Popeye 20.00
265 Yogi Bear 20.00
266 Lassie 18.00
267 Little Lulu 90.00
268 The Three Stooges 45.00
269 A Jolly Christmas 8.00
270 Santa's Little Helpers 8.00
271 The Flintstones 75.00
272 Tarzan 45.00
273 Bugs Bunny 15.00
274 Popeye 20.00
275 Little Lulu 75.00
276 The Jetsons 100.00
277 Daffy Duck 12.00
278 Lassie 18.00
279 Yogi Bear 30.00
280 Ph(c),The Three Stooges . . 50.00
281 Tom & Jerry 10.00
282 Mr. Ed 20.00
283 Santa's Visit 7.00
284 Christmas Parade 7.00
285 Astro Boy 200.00
286 Tarzan 40.00
287 Bugs Bunny 12.00
288 Daffy Duck 8.00
289 The Flintstones 65.00
290 Ph(c), Mr. Ed. 18.00
291 Yogi Bear 25.00
292 Ph(c), The Three Stooges . . 45.00
293 Little Lulu 55.00
294 Popeye 20.00
295 Tom & Jerry 7.00
296 Lassie 15.00
297 Christmas Bells 7.00
298 Santa's Sleigh 7.00
299 The Flintstones 60.00
300 Tarzan 40.00
301 Bugs Bunny 12.00
302 Ph(c), Laurel & Hardy 30.00
303 Daffy Duck 7.00
304 Ph(c), The Three Stooges . . 45.00
305 Tom & Jerry 7.00
306 Ph(c), Daniel Boone 25.00
307 Little Lulu 45.00
308 Ph(c), Lassie 15.00
309 Yogi Bear 20.00
310 Ph(c) of Clayton Moore; The Lone Ranger 75.00
311 Santa's Show 6.00
312 Christmas Album 6.00
313 Daffy Duck 7.00
314 Laurel & Hardy 25.00
315 Bugs Bunny 12.00
316 The Three Stooges 35.00
317 The Flinstones 30.00
318 Tarzan 35.00
319 Yogi Bear 20.00
320 Space Family Robinson . . . 60.00
321 Tom & Jerry 7.00
322 The Lone Ranger 35.00
323 Little Lulu 30.00
324 Ph(c), Lassie 12.00
325 Fun With Santa 7.00
326 Christmas Story 7.00
327 The Flintstones 55.00
328 Space Family Robinson . . . 55.00
329 Bugs Bunny 12.00
330 The Jetsons 65.00
331 Daffy Duck 7.00
332 Tarzan 30.00
333 Tom & Jerry 7.00
334 Lassie 10.00
335 Little Lulu 25.00
336 The Three Stooges 40.00
337 Yogi Bear 20.00
338 The Lone Ranger 35.00
339 Not Published
340 Here Comes Santa 7.00
341 The Flintstones 55.00
342 Tarzan 30.00
343 Bugs Bunny 12.00
344 Yogi Bear 23.00
345 Tom & Jerry 7.00
346 Lassie 10.00
347 Daffy Duck 7.00
348 The Jetsons 55.00
349 Little Lulu 25.00
350 The Lone Ranger 30.00
351 Beep-Beep, The Road Runner 15.00
352 Space Family Robinson . . . 50.00
353 Beep-Beep, The Road Runner 15.00
354 Tarzan 25.00
355 Little Lulu 25.00
356 Scooby Doo, Where Are You 22.00
357 Daffy Duck & Porky Pig 7.00
358 Lassie 10.00
359 Baby Snoots 10.00
360 Ph(c), H.R. Pufnstuf 10.00
361 Tom & Jerry 7.00
362 Smokey the Bear 7.00
363 Bugs Bunny & Yosemite Sam 12.00
364 Ph(c), The Banana Splits . . . 7.00
365 Tom & Jerry 7.00
366 Tarzan 25.00
367 Bugs Bunny & Porky Pig . . . 12.00
368 Scooby Doo 20.00
369 Little Lulu 20.00
370 Ph(c), Lassie 10.00
371 Baby Snoots 7.00
372 Smokey The Bear 7.00
373 The Three Stooges 30.00
374 Wacky Witch 6.00
375 Beep-Beep & Daffy Duck . . . 6.00
376 The Pink Panther 15.00
377 Baby Snoots 7.00
378 Turok, Son of Stone 85.00
379 Heckle & Jeckle 5.00
380 Bugs Bunny & Yosemite Sam 10.00
381 Lassie 7.00
382 Scooby Doo 18.00
383 Smokey the Bear 5.00
384 The Pink Panther 12.00
385 Little Lulu 15.00
386 Wacky Witch 5.00
387 Beep-Beep & Daffy Duck . . . 5.00
388 Tom & Jerry 6.00
389 Little Lulu 15.00
390 The Pink Panther 12.00
391 Scooby Doo 18.00
392 Bugs Bunny & Yosemite Sam 10.00
393 Heckle & Jeckle 5.00
394 Lassie 7.00
395 Woodsy the Owl 5.00
396 Baby Snoots 5.00
397 Beep-Beep & Daffy Duck . . . 5.00
398 Wacky Witch 5.00
399 Turok, Son of Stone 65.00
400 Tom & Jerry 5.00
401 Baby Snoots 5.00
402 Daffy Duck 5.00
403 Bugs Bunny 5.00
404 Space Family Robinson . . . 40.00
405 Cracky 5.00
406 Little Lulu 15.00
407 Smokey the Bear 5.00
408 Turok, Son of Stone 45.00
409 The Pink Panther 10.00
410 Wacky Witch 5.00
411 Lassie 7.00
412 New Terrytoons 3.00
413 Daffy Duck 3.00
414 Space Family Robinson . . . 35.00
415 Bugs Bunny 7.00
416 The Road Runner 4.00
417 Little Lulu 15.00
418 The Pink Panther 10.00
419 Baby Snoots 3.00
420 Woody Woodpecker 3.00
421 Tweety & Sylvester 3.00
422 Wacky Witch 3.00
423 Little Monsters 3.00
424 Cracky 3.00
425 Daffy Duck 3.00
426 Underdog 18.00
427 Little Lulu 10.00
428 Bugs Bunny 3.00
429 The Pink Panther 5.00
430 The Road Runner 5.00
431 Baby Snoots 3.00
432 Lassie 5.00
433 Tweety & Sylvester 3.00
434 Wacky Witch 3.00
435 New Terrytoons 3.00
436 Cracky 3.00
437 Daffy Duck 3.00
438 Underdog 10.00
439 Little Lulu 10.00
440 Bugs Bunny 7.00
441 The Pink Panther 5.00
442 The Road Runner 5.00
443 Baby Snoots 3.00
444 Tom & Jerry 3.00
445 Tweety & Sylvester 3.00
446 Wacky Witch 2.00
447 Mighty Mouse 3.00
448 Cracky 2.00
449 The Pink Panther 3.00
450 Baby Snoots 3.00
451 Tom & Jerry 3.00
452 Bugs Bunny 5.00
453 Popeye 3.00
454 Woody Woodpecker 3.00
455 The Road Runner 3.00
456 Little Lulu 3.00
457 Tweety & Sylvester 3.00
458 Wacky Witch 2.00
459 Mighty Mouse 3.00
460 Daffy Duck 3.00
461 The Pink Panther 3.00
462 Baby Snoots 2.00

463 Tom & Jerry 3.00
464 Bugs Bunny 4.00
465 Popeye 3.00
466 Woody Woodpecker 3.00
467 Underdog 8.00
468 Little Lulu 4.00
469 Tweety & Sylvester 3.00
470 Wacky Witch 3.00
471 Mighty Mouse 3.00
472 Heckle & Jeckle 3.00
473 The Pink Panther 3.00
474 Baby Snoots 2.00
475 Little Lulu 3.00
476 Bugs Bunny 4.00
477 Popeye 3.00
478 Woody Woodpecker 3.00
479 Underdog 7.00
480 Tom & Jerry 8.00
481 Tweety & Sylvster 3.00
482 Wacky Witch 3.00
483 Mighty Mouse 3.00
484 Heckle & Jeckle 3.00
485 Baby Snoots 3.00
486 The Pink Panther 3.00
487 Bugs Bunny 4.00
488 April, 1982; Little Lulu 3.00

MARGE'S LITTLE LULU
Dell Publishing Co.

1 B:Lulu's Diary 450.00
2 I:Gloria,Miss Feeny 250.00
3 . . . . 200.00
4 . . . . 200.00
5 . . . . 200.00
6 . . . . 150.00
7 I:Annie,X-Mas Cover 150.00
8 . . . . 150.00
9 . . . . 150.00
10 . . . . 150.00
11 thru 18 . . . . @125.00
19 I:Wilbur 125.00
20 I:Mr.McNabbem 125.00
21 thru 25 . . . . @100.00
26 rep.Four Color#110 . . . . . . 100.00
27 . . . . 100.00
28 . . . . 100.00
29 . . . . 100.00
30 Christmas cover 100.00

Marge's Little Lulu #8
© Dell Publishing Co.

31 . . . . 70.00
32 . . . . 70.00
33 . . . . 70.00
34 . . . . 70.00
35 B:Mumday Story 70.00
36 . . . . 70.00
37 . . . . 70.00
38 . . . . 70.00
39 I:Witch Hazel 80.00
40 Halloween Cover 70.00
41 . . . . 65.00
42 Christmas Cover 65.00
43 Skiing Cover 65.00
44 Valentines Day Cover 65.00
45 2nd A:Witch Hazel 65.00
46 thru 60 . . . . @65.00
61 . . . . 50.00
62 . . . . 50.00
63 I:Chubby 50.00
64 . . . . 50.00
65 . . . . 50.00
66 . . . . 50.00
67 . . . . 50.00
68 I:Professor Cleff 50.00
69 thru 77 . . . . @50.00
78 Christmas Cover 50.00
79 . . . . 50.00
80 . . . . 50.00
81 thru 89 . . . . @35.00
90 Christmas Cover 35.00
91 thru 99 . . . . @35.00
100 . . . . 40.00
101 thru 122 . . . . @30.00
123 I:Fifi 30.00
124 thru 164 . . . . @25.00
165 giant sized 40.00
166 giant sized 40.00
167 . . . . 20.00
168 . . . . 20.00
169 . . . . 20.00
170 . . . . 12.00
171 . . . . 10.00
172 . . . . 15.00
173 . . . . 10.00
174 . . . . 10.00
175 . . . . 15.00
176 . . . . 15.00
177 . . . . 10.00
178 thru 196 . . . . @15.00
197 . . . . 10.00
198 . . . . 15.00
199 . . . . 15.00
200 . . . . 15.00
201 . . . . 6.00
202 . . . . 10.00
203 . . . . 6.00
204 . . . . 10.00
205 . . . . 10.00
206 . . . . 6.00

MARMADUKE MOUSE
Quality Comics Group
(Arnold Publications)
Spring, 1946

1 Funny Animal 65.00
2 Funny Animal 32.00
3 thru 8 Funny Animal . . . . . @25.00
9 Funny Animal 22.00
10 Funny Animal 22.00
11 thru 20 Funny Animal . . . . @20.00
21 thru 30 Funny Animal . . . . @18.00
31 thru 40 Funny Animal . . . . @15.00
41 thru 50 Funny Animal . . . . @12.00
51 thru 65 Funny Animal . . . . @10.00

MARTIN KANE
Hero Books
(Fox Features syndicate)
June, 1950

1 WW,WW-(c) 150.00
2 WW,JO, Auguat, 1950 . . . . 100.00

MARVEL FAMILY, THE
Fawcett Publications
December, 1945

1 O:Captain Marvel,Captain Marvel Jr., Mary Marvel,Uncle Marvel; V:Black Adam 800.00
2 . . . . 400.00
3 . . . . 300.00
4 The Witch's Tale 250.00
5 Civilization of a Prehistoric Race 225.00
6 . . . . 200.00
7 The Rock of Eternity 175.00
8 The Marvel Family Round Table 175.00
9 V: The Last Vikings 175.00
10 V: The Sivana Family 175.00
11 V: The Well of Evil 135.00
12 V: The Iron Horseman 135.00
13 . . . . 135.00
14 Captain Marvel Invalid 135.00
15 V: Mr. Triangle 125.00
16 World's Mightiest Quarrell . . 125.00

Marvel Family #18
© Fawcett Publications

17 . . . . 125.00
18 . . . . 125.00
19 V: The Monster Menace . . . 125.00
20 The Marvel Family Feud . . . 125.00
21 V: The Trio of Terror 100.00
22 V: The Triple Threat 100.00
23 March of Independence (c) . 110.00
24 V: The Fighting Xergos 100.00
25 Trial of the Marvel Family . . 100.00
26 V: Mr. Power 90.00
27 V: The Amoeba Men 90.00
28 . . . . 90.00
29 V: The Monarch of Money . . 90.00
30 A:World's Greatest Magician . 90.00
31 V:Sivana & The Great Hunger 80.00
32 The Marvel Family Goes Into Buisness 80.00
33 I: The Hermit Family 80.00
34 V: Sivana's Miniature Menace 80.00
35 V: The Berzerk Machines . . . 80.00
36 V: The Invaders From Infinity 80.00
37 V: The Earth Changer 80.00
38 V: Sivana's Instinct Exterminator Gun 80.00
39 The Legend of Atlantis 80.00
40 Seven Wonders of the Modern World 80.00
41 The Great Oxygen Theft 80.00
42 V: The Endless Menace 70.00
43 . . . . 70.00
44 V: The Rust That Menaced the World 70.00
45 The Hoax City 70.00
46 The Day Civilization Vanished 70.00
47 V: The Interplanetary Thieves 100.00
48 V: The Four Horsemen 70.00
49 ...Proves Human Hardness . . 70.00
50 The Speech Scrambler

Machine 70.00
51 The Living Statues 75.00
52 The School of Witches 65.00
53 V: The Man Who Changed
the World 65.00
54 . . . . 65.00
55 . . . . 65.00
56 The World's Mightiest Project 65.00
57 . . . . 65.00
58 The Triple Time Plot 65.00
59 . . . . 65.00
60 . . . . 65.00
61 . . . . 60.00
62 . . . . 60.00
63 V: The Pirate Planet 60.00
64 . . . . 60.00
65 . . . . 60.00
66 The Miracle Stone 60.00
67 . . . . 60.00
68 . . . . 60.00
69 V: The Menace of Old Age . . 60.00
70 V: The Crusade of Evil 60.00
71 . . . . 60.00
72 . . . . 60.00
73 . . . . 60.00
74 . . . . 60.00
75 The Great Space Struggle . . 60.00
76 . . . . 60.00
77 Anti-Communist 100.00
78 V: The Red Vulture 60.00
79 . . . . 60.00
80 . . . . 60.00
81 . . . . 60.00
82 . . . . 60.00
83 V: The Flying Skull 60.00
84 thru 87 . . . . @60.00
88 Jokes of Jeopardy 60.00
89 And Then There Were None;
January, 1954 . . . . 60.00

MARVELS OF SCIENCE
Charlton Comics
March, 1946

1 1st Charlton Book; Atomic
Bomb Story 100.00
2 . . . . 70.00
3 . . . . 70.00

Marvels of Science #1
© Charlton Comics

4 President Truman(c); Jun.'6 . 75.00

MARY MARVEL COMICS
Fawcett Publications/
Charlton Comics
December, 1945

1 Intro: Mary Marvel 600.00
2 . . . . 300.00
3 . . . . 250.00

Mary Marvel #19 © Fawcett
Publications/Charlton Comics

4 On a Leave of Absence . . . 225.00
5 Butterfly (c) 150.00
6 A:Freckles,Teenager of
Mischief 150.00
7 The Kingdom Undersea . . . 150.00
8 Holiday Special Issue 150.00
9 Air Race (c) 125.00
10 A: Freckles 125.00
11 A: The Sad Dryads 100.00
12 Red Cross Appeal on(c) . . . 100.00
13 Keep the Homefires Burning 100.00
14 Meets Ghosts (c) 100.00
15 A: Freckles 100.00
16 The Jukebox Menace 90.00
17 Aunt Agatha's Adventures . . . 90.00
18 . . . . 90.00
19 Witch (c) 90.00
20 . . . . 90.00
21 V: Dice Head 75.00
22 The Silver Slippers 75.00
23 The Pendulum Strikes 75.00
24 V: The Nightowl 75.00
25 A: Freckles 75.00
26 A: Freckles Dressed As Clown 75.00
27 The Floating Oceanliner 75.00
28 September, 1948 . . . . 75.00

Becomes:

MONTE HALE WESTERN

29 Ph(c),B:Monte Hale & His
Horse Pardner 250.00
30 Ph(c),B:Big Bow-Little
Arrow; CCB,Captain Tootsie 175.00
31 Ph(c),Giant 125.00
32 Ph(c),Giant 125.00
33 Ph(c),Giant 125.00
34 Ph(c),E:Big Bow-Little
Arrow;B:Gabby Hayes,Giant 125.00
35 Ph(c),Gabby Hayes, Giant . 125.00
36 Ph(c),Gabby Hayes, Giant . 125.00
37 Ph(c),Gabby Hayes 75.00
38 Ph(c),Gabby Hayes, Giant . 125.00
39 Ph(c);CCB, Captain Tootsie;
Gabby Hayes, Giant 125.00
40 Ph(c),Gabby Hayes, Giant . 125.00
41 Ph(c),Gabby Hayes 75.00
42 Ph(c),Gabby Hayes, Giant . . 90.00
43 Ph(c),Gabby Hayes, Giant . . 90.00
44 Ph(c),Gabby Hayes, Giant . . 90.00
45 Ph(c),Gabby Hayes 75.00
46 Ph(c),Gabby Hayes, Giant . . 75.00
47 Ph(c),A:Big Bow-Little Arrow;
Gabby Hayes, Giant 75.00
48 Ph(c),Gabby Hayes, Giant . . 75.00
49 Ph(c),Gabby Hayes 75.00
50 Ph(c),Gabby Hayes, Giant . . 75.00
51 Ph(c),Gabby Hayes, Giant . . 70.00
52 Ph(c),Gabby Hayes, Giant . . 70.00
53 Ph(c),A:Slim Pickens;
Gabby Hayes 50.00
54 Ph(c),Gabby Hayes, Giant . . 70.00
55 Ph(c),Gabby Hayes, Giant . . 70.00
56 Ph(c),Gabby Hayes, Giant . . 70.00
57 Ph(c),Gabby Hayes 50.00
58 Ph(c),Gabby Hayes, Giant . . 60.00
59 Ph(c),Gabby Hayes, Giant . . 60.00
60 thru 79 Ph(c),Gabby Hayes @45.00
80 Ph(c),E: Gabby Hayes 45.00
81 Ph(c) 45.00
82 Final Ph(c), Last Fawcett
Edition 45.00
83 1st Charlton Edition, R:G.
Hayes Back B&W Ph(c) 45.00
84 . . . . 45.00
85 . . . . 42.00
86 E: Gabby Hayes 42.00
87 . . . . 42.00
88 January, 1956 . . . . 42.00

MASK COMICS
Rural Home Publications
February-March, 1945

1 LbC,LbC-(c), Evil (c) 700.00
2 LbC-(c),A:Black Rider,The
Collector The Boy Magician;
Apr-May'45, Devil (c) 500.00

MASKED MARVEL
Centaur Publications
September, 1940

1 I: The Masked Marvel 800.00
2 PG, ... 600.00
3 December, 1940 . . . . 550.00

MASKED RANGER
Premier Magazines
April, 1954

1 FF,O&B:The Masked Ranger,
Streak the Horse,The
Crimson Avenger 175.00
2 . . . . 50.00
3 . . . . 50.00
4 B: Jessie James,Billy the Kid,
Wild Bill Hickock,
Jim Bowie's Life Story 60.00
5 . . . . 60.00
6 . . . . 60.00
7 . . . . 60.00
8 . . . . 60.00
9 AT,E:All Features; A:Wyatt
Earp August, 1955 . . . . 65.00

MASTER COMICS
Fawcett Publications
March, 1940
1-6 Oversized,7-Normal Format

1 O:Master Man;B:The Devil's Dagger,El
Carin-Master of Magic,Rick,O'Say,
Morton Murch,White Rajah,Shipwreck
Roberts, Frontier Marshall,
Mr. Clue, Streak Sloan . . . 3,500.00
2 Master Man (c) 1,000.00
3 Master Man (c) Bondage . . . 750.00
4 Master Man (c) 725.00
5 Master Man (c) 725.00
6 E: All Above Features 765.00
7 B:Bulletman,Zorro,The Mystery
Man, Lee Granger, Jungle
King,Buck Jones 1,300.00
8 B:The Red Gaucho,Captain
Venture, Planet Princess . . 650.00
9 Bulletman & Steam Roller . . 550.00
10 E: Lee Granger 550.00
11 O: Minute Man 1,300.00
12 Minute Man (c) 650.00

Master Comics #7
© Fawcett Publications

13 O: Bulletgirl; E: Red Gaucho 900.00
14 B: The Companions Three . 550.00
15 MRa, Bulletman & Girl (c) . . 550.00
16 MRa, Minute Man (c) 550.00
17 B:MRa on Bulletman 550.00
18 MRa, ... 550.00
19 MRa, Bulletman & Girl (c) . . 550.00
20 MRa,C:Cap.Marvel-Bulletman 550.00
21 MRa-(c),Capt. Marvel in Bulletman,I&O:CaptainNazi 2,500.00
22 MRa-(c),E:Mystery Man,Captain Venture; Bondage(c);Capt. Marvel Jr. X-Over In Bulletman; A:Capt. Nazi . . 2,400.00
23 MRa,MRa(c),B:Capt. Marvel Jr. V:Capt. Nazi . . . 1,300.00
24 MRa,MRa(c),Death By Radio 500.00
25 MRa,MRa(c),The Jap Invasion 500.00
26 MRa,MRa(c),Capt. Marvel Jr. Avenges Pearl Harbor 550.00
27 MRa.MRa(c),V For Victory(c) 550.00
28 MRa,MRa(c)Liberty Bell(c) . 550.00
29 MRa,MRa(c),Hitler & Hirohito(c) 550.00
30 MRa,MRa(c),Flag (c);Capt. Marvel Jr, V: Capt. Nazi . . . 500.00
31 MRa,MRa(c),E:Companions Three,Capt.Marvel Jr, V:Mad Dr. Macabre 350.00
32 MRa,MRa(c),E: Buck Jones; CMJr Strikes Terror Castle . 350.00
33 MRa,MRa(c),B:Balbo the Boy Magician, Hopalong Cassidy 350.00
34 MRa,MRa(c),Capt.Marvel Jr V: Capt.Nazi 350.00
35 MRa,MRa(c),CMJr Defies the Flame 350.00
36 MRa,MRa(c),Statue Of Liberty(c) 350.00
37 MRa,MRa(c),CMJr Blasts the Nazi Raiders 300.00
38 MRa,MRa(c),CMJr V: the Japs 300.00
39 MRa,MRa(c),CMJr Blasts Nazi Slave Ship 300.00
40 MRa,MRa(c),Flag (c) 300.00
41 MRa,MRa(c),Bulletman,Bulletgirl, CMJr X-Over In Minuteman . 350.00
42 MRa,MRa(c),CMJr V: Hitler's Dream Soldier 200.00
43 MRa(c),CMJr Battles For Stalingrad 200.00
44 MRa(c),CMJr In Crystal City of the Peculiar Penguins . . . 200.00
45 MRa(c), ... 200.00
46 MRa(c) 200.00
47 MRa(c),A:Hitler; E: Balbo . . 225.00
48 MRa(c),I:Bulletboy;Capt. Marvel A: in Minuteman . . . 250.00
49 MRa(c),E: Hopalong Cassidy, Minuteman 200.00
50 I&O: Radar,A:Capt. Marvel, B:Nyoka the Jungle Girl . . . 175.00
51 MRa(c),CMJr V: Japanese . 125.00
52 MRa(c),CMJr & Radar Pitch War Stamps on (c) 125.00
53 CMJR V: Dr. Sivana 125.00
54 MRa(c),Capt.Marvel Jr Your Pin-Up Buddy 125.00
55 . . . . 125.00
56 MRa(c) 100.00
57 CMJr V: Dr. Sivana 100.00
58 MRA,MRa(c), ... 100.00
59 MRa(c),A:The Upside Downies 110.00
60 MRa(c) 110.00
61 CMJr Meets Uncle Marvel . . 110.00
62 Uncle Sam on (c) 125.00
63 W/ Radar (c) 85.00
64 W/ Radar (c) 85.00
65 . . . . 85.00
66 CMJr & Secret Of the Sphinx 85.00
67 Knight (c) 85.00
68 CMJr in the Range of the Beasts 85.00
69 . . . . 85.00
70 . . . . 85.00
71 CMJr V:Man in the MetalMask 80.00
72 CMJr V: Sivana & The Whistle That Wouldn't Stop 80.00
73 CMJr V: The Ghost of Evil . . 80.00
74 CMJr & The Fountain of Age 80.00
75 CMJr V: The Zombie Master . 80.00
76 . . . . 80.00
77 Pirate Treasure (c) 80.00
78 CMJr in Death on the Scenic Railway 80.00
79 CMJr V: The Black Shroud . . 80.00
80 CMJr-The Land of Backwards 80.00
81 CMJr & The Voyage 'Round the Horn 75.00
82 CMJr,IN,Death at the Launching 75.00
83 . . . . 75.00
84 CMJr V: The Human Magnet 75.00
85 CMJr-Crime on the Campus 75.00
86 CMJr & The City of Machines 75.00
87 CMJr & The Root of Evil 75.00
88 CMJr V: The Wreckers; B: Hopalong Cassidy 75.00
89 . . . . 75.00
90 CMJr V: The Caveman 75.00
91 CMJr V: The Blockmen 70.00
92 CMJr V: The Space Slavers . 70.00
93 BK,CMJr,V:The Growing Giant 80.00
94 E: Hopalong Cassidy 70.00
95 B: Tom Mix; CMJr Meets the Skyhawk 70.00
96 CMJr Meets the Worlds Mightiest Horse 70.00
97 CMJr Faces the Doubting Thomas 70.00
98 KKK Type 70.00
99 Witch (c) 70.00
100 CMJr V: The Ghost Ship . . . 70.00
101 thru 105 . . . . @60.00
106 E: Bulletman 60.00
107 CMJr Faces the Disappearance of the Statue of Liberty 65.00
108 . . . . 50.00
109 . . . . 50.00
110 CMJr & The Hidden Death . 50.00
111 thru 122 . . . . @50.00
123 CMJr V: The Flying Desperado 50.00
124 . . . . 50.00
125 CMJr & The Bed of Mystery 50.00
126 thru 131 . . . . @50.00

Master Comics #95
© Fawcett Publications

132 V: Migs 55.00
133 E: Tom Mix; April, 1953 . . . 50.00

MD

E.C. Comics
April 1955-Jan. 1956

1 RC,GE,Grl,JO,JCr(c) 70.00
2 RC,GE,Grl,JO,JCr(c) 50.00
3 RC,GE,Grl,JO,JCr(c) 50.00
4 RC,GE,Grl,JO,JCr(c) 50.00
5 RC,GE,Grl,JO,JCr(c) 50.00

MEDAL OF HONOR COMICS

Stafford Publication
Spring, 1947

1 True Stories of Medal of Honor Recipants 50.00

My Life #10 © Fox Features Syndicate

MEET CORLISS ARCHER

Fox Features Syndicate
March, 1948

1 AF,AF(c), Teenage 250.00
2 AF(c) 200.00
3 . . . . 150.00

Becomes:

MY LIFE

4 JKa,AF, ... 175.00
5 JKa, ... 90.00
6 JKa,AF, ... 90.00
7 Watercolor&Ink Drawing on(c) 50.00
8 . . . . 35.00
9 . . . . 35.00
10 WW, July, 1950 . . . . 75.00

MEET MERTON
Toby Press
December, 1953

1 Dave Berg-a,Teen Stories . . . 30.00
2 Dave Berg-a 15.00
3 Dave Berg-a 12.00
4 Dave Berg-a; June, 1954 . . . 12.00

MEET THE NEW POST GAZETTE SUNDAY FUNNIES
Pitsberg Post Gazette

N# One Shot Insert F: Several Syndicated Characters in Stories Exclusive to This Edition . . . 550.00

MEL ALLEN SPORTS COMICS
Visual Editions
1949

1 GT 100.00
2 Lou Gehrig 90.00

MEN AGAINST CRIME
(see HAND OF FATE)

MERRY-GO-ROUND COMICS
LaSalle/Croyden/ Rotary Litho.
1944

1 LaSalle Publications Edition . 90.00
1a 1946, Croyden Edition 30.00
1b Sept-Oct.'47,Rotary Litho Ed. 40.00
2 . . . . 40.00

MERRY MOUSE
Avon Periodicals
June, 1953

1 (fa),F. Carin (c)&a 35.00
2 (fa),F. Carin (c)&a 20.00
3 (fa),F. Carin (c)&a 20.00
4 (fa),F. Carin (c)&a;Jan.'54 . . 20.00

METEOR COMICS
Croyden Publications
November, 1945

1 Captain Wizard & Baldy Bean 150.00

MICKEY FINN
Eastern Color/ Columbia Comics Group
1942

1 . . . . 175.00
2 . . . . 90.00
3 A: Charlie Chan 60.00
4 . . . . 40.00
5 thru 9 . . . . @25.00
10 thru 15 . . . . @20.00

(WALT DISNEY'S) MICKEY MOUSE
Dell Publishing Co.
December 1952
#1-#27 Dell Four Color

28 . . . . 25.00
29 . . . . 20.00
30 . . . . 20.00
31 . . . . 20.00
32 thru 34 . . . . @20.00
35 thru 50 . . . . @15.00
51 thru 73 . . . . @12.00
74 . . . . 15.00
75 thru 99 . . . . @12.00
100 thru 105 rep. . . . . @15.00
106 thru 120 . . . . @10.00
121 thru 130 . . . . @8.00
131 thru 146 . . . . @7.00
147 rep,Phantom Fires 10.00
148 rep. 10.00
149 thru 158 . . . . @6.00
159 rep. 10.00
160 thru 170 . . . . @5.00
171 thru 199 . . . . @2.50
200 rep. 3.00
201 thru 218 . . . . @2.50

See: Independent Color Comics

MICKEY MOUSE MAGAZINE
Kay Kamen

1 (1933) scarce 2,600.00
2 . . . . 850.00
3 thru 8 . . . . @750.00
9 . . . . 700.00

MICKEY MOUSE MAGAZINE
Kay Kamen

1 digest size (1933) 600.00
2 dairy give-away promo(1933) 250.00
3 dairy give-away promo(1934) 200.00
4 dairy give-away promo(1934) 200.00
5 dairy give-away promo(1934) 200.00
6 dairy give-away promo(1934) 200.00
7 dairy give-away promo(1934) 200.00
8 dairy give-away promo(1934) 200.00
9 dairy give-away promo(1934) 200.00
10 dairy give-awaypromo(1934) 200.00
11 dairy give-awaypromo(1934) 200.00
12 dairy give-awaypromo(1934) 200.00

Volume II

1 dairy give-away promo(1934) 165.00
2 dairy give-away promo(1934) 150.00
3 dairy give-away promo(1935) 150.00
4 dairy give-away promo(1935) 150.00
5 dairy give-away promo(1935) 150.00
6 dairy give-away promo(1935) 150.00
7 dairy give-away promo(1935) 150.00
8 dairy give-away promo(1935) 150.00
9 dairy give-away promo(1935) 150.00
10 dairy give-awaypromo(1935) 150.00
11 dairy give-awaypromo(1935) 150.00
12 dairy give-awaypromo(1935) 150.00

MICKEY MOUSE MAGAZINE
K.K. Pub./Westen Pub

1 (1935) 13¼"x10¼" 10,000.00
2 . . . . 1100.00
3 . . . . 600.00
4 . . . . 600.00
5 (1936) Donald Duck solo . . . 600.00
6 Donald Duck editor 600.00
7 . . . . 600.00
8 Donald Duck solo 600.00
9 . . . . 600.00
10 . . . . 600.00
11 Mickey Mouse, editor 550.00
12 . . . . 550.00

Volume II

1 . . . . 550.00
2 . . . . 550.00
3 Christmas issue, 100pg . . . 1,700.00
4 (1937) Roy Ranger adv.strip 500.00
5 Ted True strip 400.00
6 Mickey Mouse cut-outs 375.00
7 Mickey Mouse cut-outs 375.00
8 Mickey Mouse cut-outs 375.00
9 Mickey Mouse cut-outs 375.00
10 Full color 500.00
11 . . . . 400.00
12 Hiawatha 400.00

Mickey Mouse Magazine #9
© Kay Kamen

13 . . . . 400.00

Volume III

2 Big Bad Wolf (c) 375.00
3 First Snow White 750.00
4 (1938) Snow White 600.00
5 Snow White (c) 650.00
6 Snow White ends 500.00
7 7 Dwarfs Easter (c) 375.00
8 . . . . 350.00
9 Dopey(c) 350.00
10 Goofy(c) 350.00
11 Mickey Mouse Sheriff 350.00
12 A:Snow White 350.00

Volume IV

1 Practile Pig 350.00
2 I:Huey,Louis & Dewey(c) . . . 350.00
3 Ferdinand the Bull 350.00
4 (1939),B:Spotty 325.00
5 Pluto solo 350.00
7 Ugly Duckling 325.00
7a Goofy & Wilber 350.00
8 Big Bad Wolf(c) 350.00
9 The Pointer 350.00
10 July 4th 400.00
11 . . . . 300.00
12 Donald's Penguin 400.00

Volume V

1 Black Pete 400.00
2 Goofy(c) 550.00
3 Pinochio 600.00
4 (1940) 350.00
5 Jimmy Crickett(c) 375.00
6 Tugboat Mickey 375.00
7 Huey, Louis & Dewey(c) . . . 400.00
8 Figaro & Cleo 375.00
9 Donald(c),J.Crickett 450.00
10 July 4th 425.00
11 Mickey's Tailor 450.00
12 Change of format 3,000.00

{becomes:
Walt Disney Comics & Stories}

MICKEY MOUSE
Whitman

904 W.Disney's Mickey Mouse and his friends (1934) 800.00
948 Disney'sMickeyMouse('34) 750.00

MIDGET COMICS
St. John Publishing Co.
February, 1950

1 MB(c),Fighting Indian Stories 70.00
2 April, 1950;Tex West-Cowboy

Marshall 40.00

MIGHTY ATOM, THE
(see PIXIES)

MIGHTY MIDGET COMICS
Samuel E. Lowe & Co.
1942-43
4"x5" Format

1 Bulletman 60.00
2 Captain Marvel 60.00
3 Captain Marvel Jr. 55.00
4 Golden Arrow 50.00
5 Ibis the Invincible 60.00
6 Spy Smasher 60.00
7 Balbo, The Boy magician . . . 20.00
8 Bulletman 55.00
9 Commando Yank 35.00
10 Dr. Voltz, The Human Generator 30.00
11 Lance O'Casey 25.00
12 Leatherneck the Marine 25.00
13 Minute Man 40.00
14 Mister Q 25.00
15 Mr. Scarlet & Pinky 40.00
16 Pat Wilson & His Flying Fortress 25.00
17 Phantom Eagle 35.00
18 State Trooper Stops Crime . . 25.00
19 Tornado Tom 35.00

MIGHTY MOUSE
Fall, 1946
[1st Series]

1 Terytoons Presents 625.00
2 . . . . 300.00
3 . . . . 200.00
4 Summer, 1947 . . . . 200.00

MIGHTY MOUSE
St. John Publishing
August, 1947

5 . . . . 200.00
6 thru 10 . . . . @100.00
11 thru 20 . . . . @60.00
21 thru 25 . . . . @50.00
26 thru 30 . . . . @40.00
31 thru 34 . . . . @30.00
35 Flying Saucer 40.00
36 . . . . 35.00
37 . . . . 35.00
38 thru 45 Giant 100 pgs . . . . @90.00
46 thru 66 . . . . @25.00
67 P(c),. 25.00

Pines

68 thru 81 Funny Animal . . . . @25.00
82 Infinity (c) 25.00
83 June, 1959 . . . . 25.00

MIGHTY MOUSE ADVENTURE STORIES
St. John Publishing Co.
1953

N# 384 Pages,Rebound 275.00

MIKE BARNETT, MAN AGAINST CRIME
Fawcett Publications
December, 1951

1 The Mint of Dionysosi 70.00
2 Mystery of the Blue Madonna 40.00
3 Revenge Holds the Torch . . . 35.00
4 Special Delivery 35.00
5 Market For Morphine 45.00
6 October, 1952 . . . . 30.00

MILITARY COMICS
Comics Magazines
(Quality Comics Group)
August, 1941

1 JCo,CCu,FG,BP,WE(c),O:Blackhawk, Miss America, Death Patrol, Blue Tracer; B:X of the Underground, Yankee Eagle,Q-Boat, Shot & Shell, Archie Atkins, Loops & Banks 4,000.00
2 JCo,FG,BP,CCu,CCu(c),B: Secret War News 1,400.00
3 JCo,FG,BP,AMc,CCu,CCu(c), I&O:Chop Chop 1,200.00
4 FG,BP,AMc,CCu,CCu(c), . . 950.00
5 FG,BP,AMc,CCu,CCu(c), B: The Sniper 750.00
6 FG,BP,AMc,CCu,CCu(c) . . 600.00
7 FG,BP,AMc,CCu,CCu(c) E:Death Patrol 600.00
8 FG,BP,AMc,CCu,CCu(c) . . 600.00
9 FG,BP,AMc,CCu,CCu(c), B: The Phantom Clipper . . 600.00
10 FG,BP,CCu,AMc,WE(c) . . . 700.00
11 FG,BP,CCu,AMc, WE(c),Flag(c) 500.00
12 FG,BP,AMc,RC,RC(c) 650.00
13 FG,BP,AMc,RC,RC(c),E:X of the Underground 450.00
14 FG,AMc,RC,RC(c),B:Private Dogtag 450.00
15 FG,AMc,RC,RC(c), ... 450.00
16 FG,AMc,RC,RC(c),E:The Phantom Clipper,Blue Tracer 400.00
17 FG,AMc,RC,RC(c), B:P.T. Boat 400.00
18 FG,AMc,RC,RC(c), V: The Thunderer 400.00
19 FG,RC,RC(c), V:King Cobra 400.00
20 GFx,RC,RC(c), Death Patrol 400.00
21 FG,GFx 350.00
22 FG,GFx 350.00
23 FG,GFx 350.00
24 FG,GFx,V: Man-Heavy Glasses 350.00
25 FG,GFx,V: Wang The Tiger 350.00
26 FG,GFx,V: Skull 325.00
27 FG,JCo,R:The Death Patrol 325.00
28 FG,JCo, Dungeon of Doom . 325.00
29 FG,JCo,V: Xanukhara 325.00
30 FG,JCo,BWa,BWa(c),B.Hwk V: Dr. Koro 325.00
31 FG,JCo,BWa,E:Death Patrol; I: Captain Hitsu 325.00
32 JCo,A: Captain Hitsu 300.00
33 W/ Civil War Veteran 300.00
34 A: Eve Rice 300.00
35 Shipwreck Island 300.00
36 Cult of the Wailing Tiger . . . 300.00
37 Pass of Bloody Peace 300.00
38 B.Hwk Faces Bloody Death 300.00
39 A: Kwan Yin 300.00
40 V: Ratru 275.00
41 W/ Chop Chop (c) 275.00
42 V: Jap Mata Hari 275.00
43 . . . . 275.00

Becomes:

MODERN COMICS

44 Duel of Honor 300.00
45 V: Sakyo the Madman 200.00
46 RC, Soldiers of Fortune . . . 200.00
47 RC,PG,V:Count Hokoy 200.00
48 RC,PG,V:Pirates of Perool . 200.00
49 RC,PG,I:Fear,Lady Adventuress 200.00
50 RC,PG 200.00
51 RC,PG, Ancient City of Evil . 175.00
52 PG,BWa,V: The Vulture . . . 175.00
53 PG,BWa,B: Torchy 175.00
54 PG,RC,RC/CCu,BWa 165.00
55 PG,RC,RC/CCu,BWa 165.00
56 PG,RC/CCu,BWa 165.00
57 PG,RC/CCu,BWa 165.00
58 PG,RC,RC/CCu,BWa, V:The Grabber 165.00
59 PG,RC,RC/CCu,BWa 165.00
60 PG,RC/CCu,BWa,RC(c), V:Green Plague 165.00
61 PG,RC/CCu,BWa,RC(c) . . . 165.00
62 PG,RC/CCu,BWa,RC(c) . . . 165.00

Modern Comics #57
© Quality Comics Group

63 PG,RC/CCu,BWa,RC(c) . . . 155.00
64 PG,RC/CCu,BWa,RC(c) . . . 155.00
65 PG,RC/CCu,BWa,RC(c) . . . 155.00
66 PG,RC/CCu,BWa 155.00
67 PG,RC/CCu,BWa,RC(c) . . . 155.00
68 PG,RC/CCu,BWa,RC(c); I:Madame Butterfly 155.00
69 PG,RC/CCu,BWa,RC(c) . . . 155.00
70 PG,RC/CCu,BWa,RC(c) . . . 155.00
71 PG,RC/CCu,BWa,RC(c) . . . 155.00
72 PG,RC/CCu,BWa,RC(c) . . . 150.00
73 PG,RC/CCu,BWa,RC(c) . . . 150.00
74 PG,RC/CCu,BWa,RC(c) . . . 150.00
75 PG,RC/CCu,BWa,RC(c) . . . 150.00
76 PG,RC/CCu,BWa,RC(c) . . . 150.00
77 PG,RC/CCu,BWa,RC(c) . . . 150.00
78 PG,RC/CCu,BWa,JCo,RC(c) 150.00
79 PG,RC/CCu,BWa,JCo,RC(c) 150.00
80 PG,RC/CCu,BWa,JCo,RC(c) 150.00
81 PG,RC/CCu,BWa,JCo,RC(c) 150.00
82 PG,RC/CCu,BWa,JCo,RC(c) 150.00
83 PG,RC/CCu.BWa,JCo,RC(c); E: Private Dogtag 150.00
84 PG,RC/CCu,BWa,RC(c) . . . 150.00
85 PG,RC/CCu,BWa,RC(c) . . . 150.00
86 PG,RC/CCu,BWa,RC(c) . . . 150.00
87 PG,RC/CCu,BWa,RC(c) . . . 150.00
88 PG,RC/CCu,BWa,RC(c) . . . 150.00
89 PG,RC/CCu,BWa,RC(c) . . . 150.00
90 PG,RC/CCu,GFx,RC(c) . . . 150.00
91 RC/CCu,GFx,RC(c) 150.00
92 RC/CCu,GFx,RC(c) 150.00
93 RC/CCu,GFx,RC(c) 150.00
94 RC/CCu,GFx,RC(c) 150.00
95 RC/CCu,GFx,RC(c) 150.00
96 RC/CCu,GFx,RC/CCu(c) . . . 150.00
97 RC/CCu,GFx,RC/CCu(c) . . . 150.00
98 RC/CCu,GFx,RC/CCu(c) . . . 150.00
99 RC/CCu,GFx,JCo,RC/CCu(c) 150.00
100 GFx,JCo,RC/CCu(c) 150.00
101 GFx,JCo,RC/CCu(c) 150.00
102 GFx,JCo,WE,BWa, RC/CCu(c) 175.00

MILT GROSS FUNNIES
Milt Gross, Inc.
August, 1947

1 Gag Oriented Caricature 50.00
2 Gag Oriented Caricature . . . 45.00

MINUTE MAN
Fawcett Publications
Summer, 1941

1 V: The Nazis 750.00
2 V: The Mongol Horde 600.00
3 V: The Black Poet;Spr'42 . . 575.00

MIRACLE COMICS
Hillman Periodicals
February,1940

1 B:Sky Wizard,Master of Space, Dash Dixon,Man of Might,Dusty Doyle,Pinkie Parker, The Kid Cop,K-7 Secret Agent,Scorpion & Blandu,Jungle Queen . . . 800.00
2 . . . . 400.00
3 B:Bill Colt,The Ghost Rider . 350.00
4 A:The Veiled Prophet, Bullet Bob; Mar'41 . . . . 350.00

MISS CAIRO JONES
Croyden Publishers
1944

1 BO,Rep. Newspaper Strip . 125.00

MR. ANTHONY'S LOVE CLINIC
Hillman Periodicals
1945

1 Ph(c) 60.00
2 . . . . 35.00
3 . . . . 30.00
4 . . . . 30.00
5 Ph(c),Apr/May'50 . . . . 30.00

MR. MUSCLES
(see THING, THE)

MISTER MYSTERY
Media Publ./SPM Publ./ Aragon Publ.
September, 1951

1 HK,RA,Horror 250.00
2 RA,RA(c) 175.00
3 RA(c) 175.00
4 Bondage(c) 200.00
5 Lingerie(c) 200.00
6 Bondage(c) 200.00
7 BW,Bondage(c);The Brain Bats of Venus 400.00
8 Lingerie(c) 175.00
9 HN 150.00
10 . . . . 135.00
11 BW,Robot Woman 225.00
12 Flaming Object to Eye (c) . . 405.00
13 . . . . 100.00
14 . . . . 100.00
15 The Coffin & Medusa's Head 125.00
16 Bondage(c) 125.00
17 . . . . 100.00
18 BW,Bondage(c) 225.00

MISTER RISK
(see HAND OF FATE)

MISTER UNIVERSE
Mr. Publ./Media Publ./ Stanmore
July, 1951

1 . . . . 100.00
2 RA(c);Jungle That time Forgot 65.00
3 Marijuana Story 70.00
4 Mr. Universe Goes to War . . . 35.00
5 Mr. Universe Goes to War; April, 1952 . . . . 35.00

MODERN COMICS
(see MILITARY COMICS)

Mister Universe #1
© Mr. Publ./Media Publ.

MODERN LOVE
Tiny Tot Comics (E.C. Comics)
June-July, 1949

1 Stolen Romance 350.00
2 JcR,AF(c),I Craved Excitement 300.00
3 AF(c);Our Families Clashed 250.00
4 AF(c);I Was a B Girl 350.00
5 AF(c);Saved From Shame . 325.00
6 AF(c);The Love That Might Have Been 325.00
7 AF(c);They Won't Let Me Love Him 250.00
8 AF(c);Aug-Sept'50 . . . . 250.00

MOE & SHMOE COMICS
O.S. Publishing Co.
Spring, 1948

1 Gag Oriented Caricature . . . 35.00
2 Gag Oriented Caricature . . . 25.00

MOLLY O'DAY
Avon Periodicals
February, 1945

1 GT;The Enchanted Dagger . 275.00

MONKEYSHINES COMICS
Publ. Specialists/Ace/
Summer, 1944

1 (fa),Several Short Features . . 50.00
2 (fa),Same Format Throughout Entire Run 25.00
3 thru 16 Funny Animal . . . . @20.00

Ace

17 Funny Animal 20.00
18 thru 21 . . . . @15.00

Unity Publ.

22 (fa) 15.00
23 (fa) 15.00
24 (fa),AFa,AFa(c) 15.00
25 (fa) 15.00
26 (fa) 15.00
27 (fa),July, 1949 . . . . 15.00

MONSTER
Fiction House Magazines
1953

1 Dr. Drew 150.00
2 . . . . 125.00

MONSTER CRIME COMICS
Hillman Periodicals
October, 1952

1 52 Pgs,15 Cent Cover Price 400.00

MONTE HALL WESTERN
(see MARY MARVEL COMICS)

MONTY HALL OF THE U.S. MARINES
Toby Press
August, 1951

1 B:Monty Hall,Pin-Up Pete; (All Issues) 50.00
2 . . . . 30.00
3 thru 5 . . . . @25.00
6 . . . . 20.00
7 The Fireball Express 20.00
8 . . . . 20.00
9 . . . . 20.00
10 The Vial of Death 20.00
11 Monju Island Prison Break . . 20.00

MOON GIRL AND THE PRINCE
E.C. Comics
Autumn, 1947

1 JCr(c),O:Moon Girl 575.00
2 JCr(c),Battle of the Congo . 350.00
3 . . . . 300.00
4 V: A Vampire 325.00
5 1st E.C. Horror-Zombie Terror 600.00
6 . . . . 325.00
7 O:Star;The Fient Who Fights With Fire 325.00
8 True Crime Feature 300.00

Becomes:

A MOON, A GIRL ...ROMANCE

9 AF,Grl,AF(c),C:Moon Girl; Spanking Panels 475.00
10 AF,Grl,WW,AF(c),Suspicious of His Intentions 400.00
11 AF,Grl,WW,AF(c),Hearts Along the Ski Trail 400.00
12 AF,Grl,AF(c), March-April, 1950 . . . . 500.00

Mopsy #3 © St. John's Publishing Co.

MOPSY
St. John Publishing Co.
February, 1948

1 Paper Dolls Enclosed 100.00
2 . . . . 55.00
3 . . . . 50.00
4 Paper Dolls Enclosed 50.00
5 Paper Dolls Enclosed 50.00
6 Paper Dolls Enclosed 50.00
7 . . . . 40.00
8 Paper Dolls Enclosed;
Lingerie Panels 45.00
9 . . . . 40.00
10 . . . . 40.00
11 . . . . 30.00
12 . . . . 30.00
13 Paper Dolls Enclosed 35.00
14 thru 18 . . . . @30.00
19 Lingerie(c);Paper
Dolls Enclosed 35.00

MORTIE
Magazine Publishers
December, 1952

1 ...Mazie's Friend 30.00
2 . . . . 18.00
3 . . . . 15.00

MOTION PICTURE COMICS
Fawcett Publications
November, 1950

101 Ph(c),Monte Hale's-
Vanishing Westerner 225.00
102 Ph(c),Rocky Lane's-Code
of the Silver Sage 200.00
103 Ph(c),Rocky Lane's-Covered
Wagon Raid 200.00
104 BP,Ph(c),Rocky Lane's-
Vigilante Hideout 200.00
105 BP,Ph(c),Audie Murphy's-
Red Badge of Courage 250.00
106 Ph(c),George Montgomery's-
The Texas Rangers 200.00
107 Ph(c),Rocky Lane's-Frisco
Tornado 175.00
108 Ph(c),John Derek's-Mask
of the Avenger 125.00
109 Ph(c),Rocky Lane's-Rough
Rider of Durango 175.00
110 GE,Ph(c), When Worlds
Collide 600.00
111 Ph(c),Lash LaRue's-The
Vanishing Outpost 225.00
112 Ph(c),Jay Silverheels'-
Brave Warrior 125.00
113 KS,Ph(c),George Murphy's-
Walk East on Beacon 100.00
114 Ph(c),George Montgomery's-
Cripple Creek;Jan, 1953 . . . 100.00

MOTION PICTURES FUNNIES WEEKLY
1st Funnies Incorporated
1939

1 BEv,1st Sub-Mariner . . . 20,000.00
2 Cover Only 250.00
3 Cover Only 250.00
4 Cover Only 250.00

MOVIE CLASSICS
(NO #S)
Dell Publishing Co.
January, 1953

1 Around the World Under
the Sea 15.00
2 Bambi 15.00
3 Battle of the Buldge 15.00
4 Ph(c),Beach Blanket Bingo . . 30.00
5 Ph(c),Bon Voyage 15.00
6 Castilian 20.00
7 Cat 12.00
8 Cheyenne Autumn 30.00
9 Ph(c),Circus World,
John Wayne (c) 80.00
10 Ph(c),Countdown,J.Caan(c) . 25.00
11 Creature 35.00
12 Ph(c),David Ladd's Life Story 50.00
13 Ph(c),Die Monster Die 40.00
14 Dirty Dozen 35.00
15 Ph(c),Dr. Who & the Daleks 100.00
16 Dracula 35.00
17 El Dorado,J.WaynePh(c) . . . 100.00
18 Ensign Pulver 20.00
19 Frankenstein 35.00
20 Ph(c),Great Race 35.00
21 B.LancasterPh(c) 35.00
22 Hatari 60.00
23 Horizontal Lieutenant 20.00
24 Ph(c) Mr. Limpet 15.00
25 Jack the Giant Killer 55.00
26 Ph(c),Jason and the Argonauts 35.00
27 Lancelot & Guinevere 45.00
28 Lawrence 45.00
29 Lion of Sparta 15.00
30 Mad Monster Party 45.00
31 Magic Sword 40.00
32 Ph(c),Masque of the
Red Death 35.00
33 Maya 25.00
34 McHale's Navy 25.00
35 Ph(c) Merrills' Marauders . . . 20.00
36 Ph(c),Mouse on the Moon . . . 15.00
37 Mummy 35.00
38 Music Man 25.00
39 Ph(c),Naked Prey 40.00
40 Ph(c),Night of the Grizzly . . . 30.00
41 None but the Grave 40.00
42 Ph(c),Operation Bikini 25.00
43 Operation Cross Bold 25.00
44 Prince & the Pauper 25.00
45 Raven,V.Price(c) 40.00
46 Ring of Bright Water 30.00
47 Runaway 15.00
48 Ph(c),Santa Claus Conquers
the Martians 50.00
49 Ph(c),Six Black Horses 15.00
50 Sky Party 25.00
51 Smoky 15.00
52 Ph(c),Sons of Katie Elder . . 110.00
53 GE,Tales of Terror 25.00
54 Ph(c),3 Stooges meet
Hercules 50.00
55 Tomb of Legeia 20.00
56 Treasure Island 15.00
57 Twice Told Tales(V.Price) . . . 30.00
58 Two on a Guillotine 20.00
59 Valley of Gwangi 30.00
60 War Gods of the Deep 15.00
61 War Wagon (John Wayne) . . 75.00
62 Who's Minding the Mint 15.00
63 Wolfman 30.00
64 Ph(c),Zulu 25.00
65 . . . . 25.00

MOVIE COMICS
Fiction House Magazines
December, 1946

1 Big Town on(c) 250.00
2 MB,White Tie & Tails 200.00
3 MB,Andy Hardy Laugh Hit . 200.00
4 MB,Slave Girl 225.00

MOVIE LOVE
Famous Funnies Publications
February, 1950

1 Ph(c),Dick Powell(c) 60.00
2 Ph(c),Myrna Loy(c) 30.00
3 Ph(c),Cornell Wilde(c) 25.00
4 Ph(c),Paulette Goddard(c) . . 25.00
5 Ph(c),Joan Fontaine(c) 25.00
6 Ph(c),Ricardo Montalban(c) . 25.00
7 Ph(c),Fred Astaire(c) 30.00
8 AW,FF,Ph(c),Corinne
Calvert(c) 200.00
9 Ph(c),John Lund(c) 25.00
10 Ph(c),Mona Freeman(c) . . . 250.00
11 Ph(c),James Mason(c) 25.00
12 Ph(c),Jerry Lewis &
Dean Martin(c) 35.00
13 Ph(c),Ronald Reagan(c) . . . 125.00
14 Ph(c),Janet Leigh,Gene Kelly 35.00
15 Ph(c), ... 25.00
16 Ph(c),Angela Lansbury 50.00
17 FF,Ph(c),Leslie Caron 25.00
18 Ph(c),Cornel Wilde 25.00
19 Ph(c),John Derek 25.00
20 Ph(c),Debbie Reynolds 30.00
21 Ph(c),Patricia Medina 25.00
22 Ph(c),John Payne 25.00

MOVIE THRILLERS
Magazine Enterprises
1949

1 Ph(c),Burt Lancaster's-
Rope of Sand 185.00

MR. MUSCLES
(see THING!, THE)

MUGGY-DOO, BOY CAT
Stanhall Publications
July, 1953

1 . . . . 28.00
2 . . . . 15.00
3 . . . . 15.00
4 January, 1954 . . . . 15.00

MURDER, INCORPORATED
Fox Features Incorporated
January, 1948

1 For Adults Only-on(c) 175.00
2 For Adults Only-on(c);Male
Bondage(c),Electrocution sty 150.00
3 Dutch Schultz-Beast of Evil . 65.00
4 The Ray Hamilton Case,
Lingerie(c) 75.00
5 thru 8 . . . . @75.00
9 Bathrobe (c) 85.00
9a Lingerie (c) 95.00
10 . . . . 75.00
11 . . . . 65.00
12 . . . . 65.00
13 . . . . 75.00
14 Bill Hale-King o/t Murderers . 65.00
15 . . . . 65.00
16(5),Second Series 50.00
17(2) 50.00
18(3), Bondage(c) w/Lingerie,
August, 1951 . . . . 75.00

MURDEROUS GANGSTERS
Avon Periodicals/Realistic
July, 1951

1 WW,Pretty Boy Floyd,
Leggs Diamond 200.00
2 WW,Baby Face Nelson,Mad
Dog Esposito 150.00
3 P(c),Tony & Bud Fenner,
Jed Hawkins 125.00
4 EK(c),Murder By Needle-
Drug Story, June, 1952 . . . . 150.00

MUTINY
Aragon Magazines
October, 1954

1 AH(c),Stormy Tales of the
Seven Seas 75.00
2 AH(c) 45.00
3 Bondage(c),February, '55 . . . 50.00

MY CONFESSIONS
(see WESTERN TRUE CRIME)

MY DATE COMICS
Hillman Periodicals
July, 1944

1 S&K,S&K (c), Teenage 150.00
2 S&K,DB,S&K(c) 100.00
3 S&K,DB,S&K(c) 100.00
4 S&K,DB,S&K(c) 100.00

MY DESIRE
Fox Features Syndicate
October, 1949

1 Intimate Confessions 50.00
2 WW,They Called Me Wayward 50.00
3 I Hid My Lover 25.00
4 WW, April, 1950 . . . . 80.00

MY GREAT LOVE
Fox Features Syndicate
October, 1949

1 Reunion In a Shack 50.00
2 My Crazy Dreams 30.00
3 He Was Ashamed of Me . . . 25.00
4 My Two Wedding Rings;Apr'50 35.00

MY INTIMATE AFFAIR
Fox Features Syndicate
March, 1950

1 I Sold My Love 550.00
2 I Married a Jailbird;May'50 . . 30.00

MY LIFE
(see MEET CORLISS ARCHER)

MY LOVE AFFAIR
Fox Features Syndicate
July, 1949

1 Truck Driver's Sweetheart . . 55.00
2 My Dreadful Secret 35.00
3 WW,I'll Make Him Marry Me . 80.00
4 WW,They Called Me Wild . . . 80.00
5 WW,Beauty Was My Bait . . . 80.00
6 WW,The Man Downstairs . . . 80.00

My Love Affair #1
© Fox Features Syndicate

MY LOVE MEMORIES
(see WOMEN OUTLAWS)

MY LOVE LIFE
(see TEGRA, JUNGLE EMPRESS)

MY LOVE STORY
Fox Features Syndicate
September, 1949

1 Men Gave Me Jewels 55.00
2 He Dared Me 35.00
3 WW,I Made Love a Plaything 75.00
4 WW,I Tried to Be Good 75.00

MY PAST CONFESSIONS
(see WESTERN THRILLERS)

My Private Life #16
© Fox Features Syndicate

MY PRIVATE LIFE
Fox Features Syndicate
February, 1950

16 My Friendship Club Affair . . . 45.00
17 My Guilty Kisses;April'50 . . . 45.00

MY SECRET
Superior Comics
August, 1949

1 True Love Stories 55.00
2 I Was Guilty of Being a Cheating Wife 35.00
3 Was I His Second Love?; . . . 35.00

Becomes:

OUR SECRET

4 JKa,She Loves Me,She Loves Me Not; November, 1949 . . . 50.00
5 . . . . 35.00
6 . . . . 35.00
7 How Do You Fall In Love? . . . 38.00
8 His Kiss Tore At My Heart; June, 1950 . . . . 35.00

MY SECRET AFFAIR
Hero Books
(Fox Features Syndicate)
December, 1949

1 WW,SHn,My Stormy Love Affair 100.00
2 WW,I Loved a Weakling 65.00
3 WW, April, 1950 . . . . 85.00

MY SECRET LIFE
Fox Features Syndicate
July, 1949

22 WW,I Loved More Than Once 50.00
23 . . . . 75.00
24 Love Was a Habit 30.00
25 . . . . 30.00

Becomes:

ROMEO TUBBS

26 WW,That Lovable Teen-ager 75.00

MY SECRET LOVE
(see PHANTOM LADY)

MY SECRET MARRIAGE
Superior Comics
May, 1953

1 I Was a Cheat 50.00
2 . . . . 25.00
3 We Couldn't Wait 15.00
4 thru 23 . . . . @15.00
24 1956 . . . . 15.00

MY SECRET ROMANCE
Hero Books
(Fox Features Syndicate)
January, 1950

1 WW,They Called Me 'That' Woman 85.00
2 WW,They Called Me Cheap . 75.00

MYSTERIES WEIRD AND STRANGE
Superior Comics/ Dynamic Publ.
May, 1953

1 The Stolen Brain 150.00
2 The Screaming Room, Atomic Bomb 100.00
3 The Avenging Corpse 60.00
4 Ghost on the Gallows 60.00
5 Horror a la Mode 60.00
6 Howling Horror 60.00
7 Demon in Disguise 60.00
8 The Devil's Birthmark 60.00
9 . . . . 60.00
10 . . . . 75.00
11 . . . . 60.00

MYSTERIOUS ADVENTURES
Story Comics
March, 1951

1 Wild Terror of the Vampire Flag 175.00
2 Terror of the Ghoul's Corpse 100.00
3 Terror of the Witche's Curse . 75.00
4 The Little Coffin That Grew . . 75.00
5 LC,Curse of the Jungle, Bondage(c) 100.00
6 LC,Ghostly Terror in the Cave 70.00
7 LC,Terror of the Ghostly Castle 135.00
8 Terror of the Flowers of Deat 125.00
9 The Ghostly Ghouls- Extreme Violence 125.00
10 Extreme Violence 75.00
11 The Trap of Terror 125.00
12 SHn,Vultures of Death- Extreme Violence 125.00
13 Extreme Violence 125.00
14 Horror of the Flame Thrower Extreme Violence 125.00
15 DW,Ghoul Crazy 150.00
16 Chilling Tales of Horror 150.00
17 DW,Bride of the Dead 150.00
18 Extreme Violence 150.00
19 The Coffin 150.00
20 Horror o/t Avenging Corpse 150.00
21 Mother Ghoul's Nursery Tales, Bondage (c) 150.00
22 RA,Insane 75.00
23 RA,Extreme Violence 125.00
24 KS, ... 60.00
25 KS,August, 1955 . . . . 60.00

HORROR FROM THE TOMB
Premier Magazines
September, 1954

1 AT,GWb,The Corpse Returns 125.00

Becomes:

MYSTERIOUS STORIES

2 GWb(c),Eternal Life 125.00
3 GWb,The Witch Doctor 85.00
4 That's the Spirit 75.00
5 King Barbarossa 75.00
6 GWb,Strangers in the Night . . 85.00

Mysterious Stories #3
© Premier Magazines

7 KS,The Pipes of Pan;Dec'55 . 75.00

MYSTERIOUS TRAVELER COMICS
Trans-World Publications
November, 1948

1 BP,BP(c),Five Miles Down . 250.00

MYSTERY COMICS
William H. Wise & Co.
1944

1 AS(c),B:Brad Spencer-Wonderman, King of Futeria,The Magnet, Zudo-Jungle Boy,The Silver Knight 400.00
2 AS(c),Bondage (c) 250.00
3 AS(c),Robot(c),LanceLewis,B 225.00
4 AS(c),E:All Features, KKK Type(c) 225.00

MYSTERY MEN COMICS
Fox Features Syndicate
August, 1939

1 GT,DBr,LF(c),Bondage(c);I:Blue Beetle,Green Mask,Rex Dexter of Mars,Zanzibar,Lt.Drake,D-13 Secret Agent,Chen Chang, Wing Turner,Capt. Denny 1,650.00
2 GT,BP,DBr,LF(c), Rex Dexter (c) 750.00
3 LF(c) 650.00
4 LF(c),B:Captain Savage . . . 550.00
5 GT,BP,LF(c),Green Mask (c) 450.00
6 GT,BP 400.00
7 GT,BP,Bondage(c), Blue Beetle(c) 425.00
8 GT,BP,LF(c),Bondage(c), Blue Beetle 425.00
9 GT,BP,DBr(c),B:The Moth . . 350.00
10 GT,BP,JSm(c),A:Wing Turner; Bondage(c) 375.00

Mystery Men Comics #10
© Fox Features Syndicate

11 GT,BP,JSm(c),I:The Domino 270.00
12 GT,BP,JSm(c),BlueBeetle(c) 225.00
13 GT,I:The Lynx & Blackie . . . 275.00
14 GT,Male Bondage (c) 250.00
15 GT,Blue Beetle (c) 225.00
16 GT,Hypo(c),MaleBondage(c) 250.00
17 GT,BP,Blue Beetle (c) 225.00
18 GT,Blue Beetle (c) 225.00
19 GT,I&B:Miss X 275.00
20 GT,DBr,Blue Beetle (c) 225.00
21 GT,E:Miss X 225.00
22 GT,CCu(c),Blue Beetle (c) . 225.00
23 GT,Blue Beetle (c) 225.00
24 GT,BP,DBr, Blue Beetle (c) . 225.00
25 GT,Bondage(c); A:Private O'Hara 250.00
26 GT,Bondage(c);B:The Wraith 250.00
27 GT,Bondage(c),BlueBeetle(c) 250.00
28 GT,Bondage(c);Satan's Private Needlewoman 250.00
29 GT,Bondage(c),Blue Beetle (c) 250.00
30 Holiday of Death 225.00
31 Bondage(c);Feb'42 . . . . 250.00

MY STORY
(see ZAGO, JUNGLE PRINCE)

NATIONAL COMICS
Comics Magazines
(Quality Comics Group)
July, 1940

1 GT,HcK,LF(c),B:Uncle Sam,Wonder Boy,Merlin the Magician,Cyclone, Kid Patrol,Sally O'Neil-Policewoman, Pen Miller,Prop Powers, Paul Bunyan . . . 1,900.00
2 WE,GT,HcK,LF&RC(c) 900.00
3 GT,HcK,WE&RC(c) 700.00
4 GT,HcK,LF&RC(c),E:Cyclone; Torpedo Islands of Death . . 550.00
5 GT,LF&RC(c),B:Quicksilver; O:Uncle Sam 600.00
6 GT,LF&RC(c) 475.00
7 GT,LF&RC(c) 475.00
8 GT,LF&RC(c) 475.00
9 JCo,LF&RC(c) 475.00
10 RC,JCo,LF&RC(c) 475.00
11 RC,JCo,LF&RC(c) 475.00
12 RC,JCo,LF&RC(c) 350.00
13 RC,JCo,LF,LF&RC(c) 400.00
14 RC,JCo,LF,PG,LF&RC(c) . . 400.00
15 RC,JCo,LF,PG,LF&RC(c) . . 400.00
16 RC,JCo,LF,PG,LF&RC(c) . . 400.00
17 RC,JCo,LF,PG,LF&RC(c) . . 325.00
18 JCo,LF,PG,LF&RC(c), Pearl Harbor 400.00
19 JCo,LF,PG,RC(c),The Black Fog Mystery 325.00
20 JCo,LF,PG,LF&RC(c) 325.00
21 LF,JCo,PG,LF(c) 325.00
22 JCo,LF,PG,FG,GFx,LF(c), E:Jack & Jill,Pen Miller, Paul Bunyan 325.00
23 JCo,PG,FG,GFx,AMc,LF & GFx(c),B:The Unknown, Destroyer 171 . . . . 300.00
24 JCo,PG,RC,AMc,FG, GFx,RC(c) 250.00
25 AMc,RC,JCo,PG,FG, GFx,RC(c) 250.00
26 AMc,Jco,RC,PG,RC(c), E:Prop Powers,WonderBoy . 250.00
27 JCo,AMc 250.00
28 JCo,AMc 250.00
29 JCo,O:The Unknown;U.Sam V:Dr. Dirge 275.00
30 JCo,RC(c) 250.00
31 JCo,RC(c) 225.00
32 JCo,RC(c) 225.00
33 JCo,GFx,RC(c),B:Chic Carter; U.Sam V:Boss Spring 225.00
34 JCo,GFx,U.Sam V:Big John Fales 225.00
35 JCo,GFx,E:Kid Patrol 150.00
36 JCo 150.00
37 JCo,FG,A:The Vagabond . . 150.00
38 JCo,FG,Boat of the Dead . . 150.00

National Comics #54
© Comics Mag./Quality Comics Group

39 JCo,FG,Hitler(c);U.Sam V:The Black Market 175.00
40 JCo,FG,U.Sam V:The Syndicate of Crime 125.00
41 JCo,FG 125.00
42 JCo,FG,JCo(c),B:The Barker 100.00
43 JCo,FG,JCo(c) 100.00
44 JCo,FG 100.00
45 JCo,FG,E:Merlin the Magician 100.00
46 JCo,JCo(c),Murder is no Joke 100.00
47 JCo,JCo(c),E:Chic Carter . . 100.00
48 JCo,O:The Whistler 100.00
49 JCo,JCo(c),A Corpse for a Cannonball 100.00
50 JCo,JCo(c),V:Rocks Myzer 100.00
51 JCo,BWa,JCo(c), A:Sally O'Neil 150.00
52 JCo,A Carnival of Laughs . . . 80.00

53 PG,V:Scramolo 80.00
54 PG,V:Raz-Ma-Taz 80.00
55 JCo,AMc,V:The Hawk 80.00
56 GFx,JCo,AMc,V:The Grifter . . 80.00
57 GFX,JCo,AMc,V:Witch Doctor 80.00
58 GFz,JCo,AMc,Talking Animals 80.00
59 GFx,JCo,AMc,V:The Birdman 80.00
60 GFx,JCo,AMc,V:Big Ed Grew 80.00
61 GFx,AMc,Trouble Comes in Small Packages 50.00
62 GFx,AMc,V:Crocodile Man . . 50.00
63 GFx,AMc,V:Bearded Lady . . . 50.00
64 GFx,V:The Human Fly 50.00
65 GFx,GFx(c)V:The King 50.00
66 GFx,GFx(c)V:THe Man Who Hates the Circus 50.00
67 GFx,Gfx(c),A:Quicksilver; V:Ali Ben Riff Raff 50.00
68 GFx,GFx(c),V:Leo the LionMan50.00
69 GFx,Gfx(c),A:Percy the Powerful 50.00
70 GFx,GFx(c),Barker Tires of the Big Top 50.00
71 PG,GFx(c),V:SpellbinderSmith 50.00
72 PG,GFx(c),The Oldest Man in the World 50.00
73 PG,GFx(c),V:A CountrySlicker 50.00
74 PG,GFx(c),V:Snake Oil Sam . 50.00
75 PG,GFx(c),Barker Breakes the Bank at Monte Marlo;Nov'49 . 50.00

NEBBS, THE
Dell Publishing Co.
1941

1 rep. 60.00

NEGRO ROMANCES
Fawcett Publications
June, 1950

1 GE,Ph(c), Love's Decoy . . . 650.00
2 GE,Ph(c), A Tragic Vow . . . 500.00
3 GE,Ph(c), My Love Betrayed Me 500.00

Charlton Comics

4 Rep.FawcettEd.#2;May,1955 325.00

NEW ROMANCES
Standard Comics
May, 1951

5 Ph(c), The Blame I Bore 45.00
6 Ph(c), No Wife Was I 25.00
7 Ph(c), My Runaway Heart, Ray Miland 22.00
8 Ph(c) 22.00
9 Ph(c) 22.00
10 ATh,Ph(c) 50.00
11 ATh,Ph(c) of Elizabeth Taylor 65.00
12 Ph(c) 15.00
13 Ph(c) 15.00
14 ATh,Ph(c) 35.00
15 Ph(c) 15.00
16 ATh,Ph(c) 35.00
17 Ath, ... 35.00
18 and 19 . . . . @15.00
20 GT, ... 25.00
21 April, 1954 . . . . 15.00

NICKEL COMICS
Dell Publishing Co.
1938

1 Bobby & Chip 275.00

NICKEL COMICS
Fawcett Publications
May, 1940

1 JaB(c),O&I: Bulletman . . . 1,100.00
2 JaB(c), ... 500.00
3 JaB(c), ... 450.00
4 JaB(c), B: Red Gaucho . . . 400.00
5 CCB(c),Bondage(c) 350.00
6 and 7 CCB(c) . . . . @350.00
8 CCB(c),August 23, 1940, World's Fair 375.00

NIGHTMARE
(see WEIRD HORRORS)

NIGHTMARE
Ziff-Davis Publishing Co.

1 EK,GT,P(c),The Corpse That Wouldn't Stay Dead 200.00
2 EK,P(c),Vampire Mermaid . . 135.00

St. John Publishing Co.

3 EK,P(c),The Quivering Brain 125.00
4 P(c),1953 . . . . 100.00

NORTHWEST MOUNTIES
Jubilee Publications/
St. John Publ. Co.
October, 1948

1 MB,BLb(c),Rose of the Yukon 175.00
2 MB,BLb(c),A:Ventrilo 150.00
3 MB, Bondage(c) 170.00
4 MB(c),A:Blue Monk,July'49 . 165.00

NURSERY RHYMES
Ziff-Davis Publishing Co.
1950

1 How John Came Clean 75.00
2 The Old Woman Who Lived in a Shoe 50.00

NUTS!
Premere Comics Group
March, 1954

1 . . . . 125.00
2 . . . . 95.00
3 Mention of "Reefers" 100.00
4 . . . . 90.00
5 Captain Marvel Spoof;Nov.'54 90.00

NUTTY COMICS
Fawcett Publications
Winter, 1946

1 (fa),F:Capt. Kid,Richard Richard, Joe Miller...Among others . . 75.00

NYOKA THE JUNGLE GIRL
Fawcett Publications
Winter, 1945

1 Bondage(c);Partial Ph(c) of Kay Aldridge as Nyoka . . . 325.00
2 . . . . 200.00
3 . . . . 175.00
4 Bondage(c) 175.00
5 Barbacosi Madness; Bondage(c) 175.00
6 . . . . 150.00
7 North Pole Jungle;Bondage(c) 165.00
8 Bondage(c) 165.00
9 . . . . 150.00
10 . . . . 150.00
11 Danger! Death! in an Unexplored Jungle 90.00
12 . . . . 90.00
13 The Human Leopards 90.00
14 The Mad Witch Doctor; Bondage(c) 125.00
15 Sacred Goat of Kristan 80.00
16 BK,The Vultures of Kalahari . 90.00
17 BK 90.00
18 BK,The Art of Murder 90.00
19 The Elephant Battle 90.00
20 Explosive Volcano Action . . . 90.00
21 . . . . 65.00
22 The Weird Monsters 65.00
23 Danger in Duplicate 65.00
24 The Human Jaguar; Bondage(c) 80.00
25 Hand Colored Ph(c) 50.00
26 A Jungle Stampede 50.00
27 Adventure Laden 50.00
28 The Human Statues of the Jungle 50.00

Nyoka the Jungle Girl #5
© Fawcett Publications

29 Ph(c) 50.00
30 Ph(c) 50.00
31 thru 40 Ph(c) . . . . @40.00
41 thru 50 Ph(c) . . . . @30.00
51 thru 59 Ph(c) . . . . @25.00
60 Ph(c) 20.00
61 Ph(c),The Sacred Sword of the Jungle 20.00
62 & 63 Ph(c) . . . . @20.00
64 Ph(c), The Jungle Idol 20.00
65 Ph(c) 20.00
66 Ph(c) 20.00
67 Ph(c), The Sky Man 20.00
68 thru 74 Ph(c) . . . . @20.00
75 Ph(c), The Jungle Myth of Terror 20.00
76 Ph(c) 20.00
77 Ph(c),The Phantoms of the Elephant Graveyard;Jun'53 . . 20.00

OAKY DOAKS
Eastern Color Printing Co.
July, 1942

1 Humor Oriented 165.00

OH, BROTHER!
Stanhall Publications
January, 1953

1 Bill Williams-a 25.00
2 thru 5 . . . . @15.00

OK COMICS
United Features Syndicate
July, 1940

1 B:Pal Peyton,Little Giant, Phantom Knight,Sunset Smith,Teller Twins, Don Ramon, Jerrry Sly,Kip Jaxon, Leatherneck,Ulysses 350.00
2 October, 1940 . . . . 325.00

100 PAGES OF COMICS
Dell Publishing Co.
1937

101 Alley Oop,OG,Wash Tubbs, Tom Mix,Dan Dunn 700.00

ON THE AIR
NBC Network Comics
1947

1 Giveaway, no cover 140.00

ON THE SPOT
Fawcett Publications
Autumn, 1948

N# Bondage(c),PrettyBoyFloyd 150.00

Operation Peril #5
© American Comics Group/Michel Publ.

OPERATION PERIL
American Comics Group (Michel Publ.)
October-November, 1950

1 LSt,OW,OW(c),B:TyphoonTyler, DannyDanger,TimeTravellers 150.00
2 OW,OW(c) 85.00
3 OW,OW(c),Horror 80.00
4 OW,OW(c), Flying Saucers . . 80.00
5 OW,OW(c), Science Fiction . . 80.00
6 OW, Tyr. Rex 80.00
7 OW,OW(c) 75.00
8 OW,OW(c) 75.00
9 OW,OW(c) 75.00
10 OW,OW(c) 75.00
11 OW,OW(c), War 75.00
12 OW,OW(c),E:Time Travellers 75.00
13 OW,OW(c),War Stories 35.00
14 OW,OW(c),War Stories 35.00
15 OW,OW(c),War Stories 35.00
16 OW,OW(c),April-May,1953, War Stories 35.00

OUR FLAG COMICS
Ace Magazines
August, 1941

1 MA,JM,B:Capt.Victory,Unknown Soldier,The Three Cheers 1,000.00
2 JM,JM(c),O:The Flag 550.00
3 Tank Battle (c) 450.00
4 MA 450.00
5 I:Mr. Risk;April, 1942, Male Bondage 475.00

OUR GANG COMICS
Dell Publishing Co.
September-October, 1942

1 WK,Barney Bear, Tom & Jerry600.00
2 WK 250.00
3 WK,Benny Burro 200.00
4 WK 200.00
5 WK 200.00
6 WK 275.00
7 WK 150.00
8 WK,CB,Benny Burro 275.00
9 WK,CB,Benny Burro 225.00
10 WK,CB,Benny Burro 200.00
11 WK,I:Benny Bear 185.00
12 thru 20 WK . . . . @125.00
21 thru 29 WK . . . . @100.00
30 WK,Christmas(c) 75.00
31 thru 34 WK . . . . @75.00
35 WK,CB 75.00
36 WK,CB 75.00
37 thru 40 WK . . . . @75.00
41 thru 50 WK . . . . @20.00
51 thru 56 WK . . . . @15.00
57 . . . . 12.00
58 Our Gang 12.00
59 Our Gang 12.00

Becomes:

TOM AND JERRY
July, 1949

60 . . . . 45.00
61 . . . . 40.00
62 . . . . 25.00
63 . . . . 25.00
64 . . . . 25.00
65 . . . . 25.00
66 Christmas (c) 28.00
67 thru 70 . . . . @25.00
71 thru 76 . . . . @22.00
77 Christmas (c) 25.00
78 thru 80 . . . . @22.00
81 thru 89 . . . . @20.00
90 Christmas (c) 22.00
91 thru 99 . . . . @20.00
100 . . . . 25.00
101 thru 120 . . . . @15.00
121 thru 150 . . . . @12.00
151 thru 212 . . . . @10.00

OUR SECRET
(see MY SECRET)

OUTLAWS
D.S. Publishing Co.
February-March, 1948

1 HcK,Western Crime Stories 150.00
2 Grl,Doc Dawson's Dilema . . 150.00
3 Cougar City Cleanup 50.00
4 JO,Death Stakes A Claim . . . 60.00
5 RJ,RJ(c),Man Who Wanted Mexico 50.00
6 AMc,RJ,RJ(c),The Ghosts of

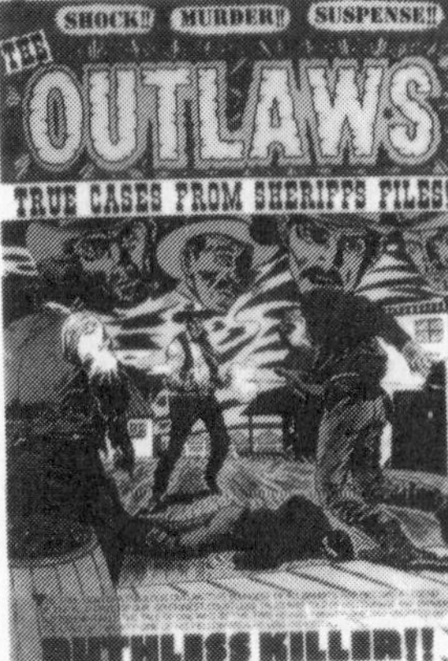

Outlaws #12 © D.S. Publishing Co.

Crackerbox Hill 50.00
7 Grl,Dynamite For Boss Cavitt 100.00
8 Grl,The Gun & the Pen . . . 100.00
9 FF,Shoot to Kill;June-July, 1949 . . . . 250.00

WHITE RIDER AND SUPER HORSE
Star Publications
September, 1950

1 LbC(c) 60.00
2 LbC(c) 30.00
3 LbC(c) 30.00
4 LbC(c) 35.00
5 LbC(c),Stampede of Hard Riding Thrills 35.00
6 LbC(c),Drums of the Sioux . . 35.00

Indian Warriors #7 © Star Publications

Becomes:

INDIAN WARRIORS

7 LbC(c),Winter on the Great Plains 40.00
8 LbC(c) 30.00

Becomes:

WESTERN CRIME CASES

9 LbC(c),The Card Sharp Killer 35.00

Becomes:

OUTLAWS, THE

10 LbC(c),Federated Express . . 35.00
11 LbC(c),Frontier Terror!!! 25.00
12 LbC(c),Ruthless Killer!!! 25.00
13 LbC(c),The Grim Avengers . . 25.00
14 AF,JKa,LbC(c),Trouble in Dark Canyon,April'54 . . . . . . 25.00

OUT OF THE NIGHT
American Comics Group/ Best Synd. Feature
February-March, 1952

1 AW 250.00
2 AW 200.00
3 . . . . 85.00
4 AW 200.00
5 . . . . 75.00
6 The Ghoul's Revenge 75.00
7 . . . . 75.00
8 The Frozen Ghost 75.00
9 Death Has Wings, Science Fiction 80.00
10 Ship of Death 75.00
11 . . . . 65.00
12 Music for the Dead 65.00
13 HN,From the Bottom of the Well 70.00
14 Out of the Screen 65.00
15 The Little Furry Thing 60.00
16 Nightmare From the Past . . . 60.00
17 The Terror of the Labyrinth . . 60.00

Becomes:

HOODED HORSEMAN

18 B: The Hooded Horseman . . 35.00
19 The Horseman's Strangest Adventure 70.00
20 OW,O:Johnny Injun 40.00
21 OW,OW(c) 30.00
22 OW 30.00
23 . . . . 30.00
24 . . . . 30.00
25 . . . . 30.00
26 O&I:Cowboy Sahib 40.00
27 January-February, 1953 . . . . 35.00

OUT OF THE SHADOWS
Visual Editions
(Standard Comics)
July, 1952

5 ATh,GT,The Shoremouth Horror 150.00
6 ATh,JKz,Salesman of Death 125.00
7 JK,Plant of Death 75.00
8 Mask of Death 60.00
9 RC,Till Death Do Us Part . . . 75.00
10 MS,We Vowed,Till Death Do Us Part 55.00
11 ATh,Fountain of Fear 75.00
12 ATh,Hand of Death 125.00
13 MS,The Cannibal 90.00
14 ATh,The Werewolf, August, 1954 . . . . 100.00

OXYDOL-DREFT
Giveaways
1950

The Set is More Valuable if the Original Envelope is Present

1 L'il Abner 75.00
2 Daisy Mae 75.00
3 Shmoo 80.00
4 AW&FF(c),John Wayne . . . 135.00
5 Archie 65.00
6 Terry Toons Comics 75.00

OZZIE AND BABS
Fawcett Publications
Winter, 1946

1 Humor Oriented, Teenage . . . 45.00
2 Humor Oriented 20.00
3 Humor Oriented 15.00
4 Humor Oriented 15.00
5 Humor Oriented 15.00
6 Humor Oriented 15.00
7 Humor Oriented 15.00
8 Humor Oriented 15.00
9 Humor Oriented 15.00
10 Humor Oriented 15.00
11 Humor Oriented 15.00
12 Humor Oriented 15.00
13 Humor Oriented;1949 . . . . . . 15.00

PAGEANT OF COMICS
St. John Publishing Co.
September, 1947

1 Rep. Mopsy 100.00
2 Rep. Jane Arden,Crime Reporter 100.00

PANHANDLE PETE AND JENNIFER
J. Charles Lave
Publishing Co.
July, 1951

1 (fa) 40.00
2 (fa) 30.00
3 (fa),November'51 . . . . 30.00

PANIC
Tiny Tot Publications
(E.C. Comics)
March, 1954

"Humor in a Jugular Vein"

1 BE,JKa,JO,JDa,AF(c) 175.00
2 BE,JO,WW,JDa,A:Bomb . . . 125.00
3 BE,JO,BW,WW,JDa,AF(c) . 110.00
4 BE,JO,WW,JDa,BW(c), Infinity(c) 110.00
5 BE,JO,WW,JDa,AF(c) 90.00
6 BE,JO,WW,JDa,Blank (c) . . . 90.00
7 BE,JO,WW,JDa 90.00
8 BE,JO,WW,JDa,Eye Chart (c) 90.00
9 BE,JO,WW,JDa,Ph(c), Confidential(c) 90.00
10 BE,JDa, Postal Package(c) . . 90.00
11 BE,WW,JDa,Wheaties parody as Weedies (c) 90.00
12 BE,WW,JDa,JDa(c); December-January 1955-56 110.00

PARAMOUNT ANIMATED COMICS
Family Publications
(Harvey Publ.)
June, 1953

1 (fa),B:Baby Herman & Katnip, Baby Huey,Buzzy the Crow 110.00
2 (fa) 60.00
3 (fa) 45.00
4 (fa) 45.00
5 (fa) 45.00
6 (fa) 45.00
7 (fa), Baby Huey (c) 90.00
8 (fa), Baby Huey (c) 35.00
9 (fa), Infinity(c),Baby Huey (c) . 35.00
10 thru 21 (fa),Baby Huey(c) . @25.00
22 (fa), July, 1956, Baby Huey (c) 25.00

PAROLE BREAKERS
Avon Periodicals/Realistic
December, 1951

1 P(c),Hellen Willis,Gun Crazed Gun Moll 175.00
2 JKu,P(c),Vinnie Sherwood, The Racket King 150.00
3 EK(c),John "Slicer" Berry, Hatchetman of Crime; July,1952 . . . . 125.00

PATCHES
Rural Home Publ./
Patches Publ.
March-April, 1945

1 LbC(c),Imagination In Bed(c) 125.00
2 Dance (c) 55.00
3 Rocking Horse (c) 50.00
4 Music Band (c) 50.00
5 LbC(c),A:Danny Kaye,Football 55.00
6 A: Jackie Kelk 45.00
7 A: Hopalong Cassidy 75.00
8 A: Smiley Burnettte 45.00
9 BK,A: Senator Claghorn 45.00
10 A: Jack Carson 45.00
11 A: Red Skeleton; Dec'47 . . . . 50.00

PAWNEE BILL
Story Comics
February, 1951

1 A:Bat Masterson,Wyatt Earp, Indian Massacre at Devil's Gulch 55.00
2 Blood in Coffin Canyon 35.00
3 LC,O:Golden Warrior,Fiery Arrows at Apache Pass; July'51 . . . . 35.00

PAY-OFF
D.S. Publishing Co.
July-August, 1948

1 . . . . 100.00
2 The Pennsylvania Blue-Beard 60.00
3 The Forgetful Forger 45.00
4 RJ(c),Lady and the Jewels . . 45.00
5 The Beautiful Embezzeler; March-April, 1949 . . . . 45.00

PEDRO
Fox Features Syndicate
January, 1950

1 WW,WW(c),Humor Oriented 150.00
2 August, 1950 . . . . 85.00

PENNY
Avon Publications
1947

1 The Slickest Chick of 'em All 55.00
2 . . . . 30.00
3 America's Teen-age Sweetheart 30.00
4 . . . . 30.00
5 . . . . 30.00
6 Perry Como Ph(c),September-October, 1949 . . . . 35.00

PEP COMICS
MJL Magazines/
Archie Publications
January, 1940

1 IN,JCo,MMe,IN(c),I:Shield, O:Comet,Queen of Diamonds, B:The Rocket,Press Guardian, Sergeant Boyle Chang,Bently of Scotland Yard 4,000.00
2 CBi,JCo,IN,IN(c),O:Rocket . . 900.00
3 JCo,IN,IN(c),Shield (c) 750.00
4 Cbi,JCo,MMe,IN,IN(c), C:Wizard(not Gareb) 600.00
5 Cbi,JCo,MMe,IN,IN(c), C:Wizard 575.00
6 IN,IN(c), Shield (c) 425.00
7 IN,IN(c),Bondage(c),Shield(c) 425.00
8 JCo,IN, Shield (c) 400.00
9 IN, Shield (c) 400.00
10 IN,IN(c), Shield (c) 400.00
11 MMe,IN,IN(c),I:Dusty ,Boy Detective 400.00
12 IN,IN(c),O:Fireball Bondage(c), E:Rocket,Queen of Diamonds 600.00
13 IN,IN(c),Bondage(c) 375.00
14 IN,IN(c) 375.00
15 IN,Bondage(c) 375.00
16 IN,O:Madam Satan 600.00

Pep Comics #42
© MJL Magazines/Archie Publ.

17 IN,IN(c),O:Hangman, D:Comet 1,150.00
18 IN,IN(c),Bondage(c) 375.00
19 IN 350.00
20 IN,IN(c),E:Fireball 350.00

21 IN,IN(c),Bondage(c), E: Madam Satan . . . 375.00
22 IN,IN(c)I:Archie, Jughead, Betty . . . 4,500.00
23 IN,IN(c) . . . 600.00
24 IN,IN(c) . . . 500.00
25 IN,IN(c) . . . 500.00
26 IN,IN(c),I:Veronica . . . 600.00
27 IN,IN(c),Bill of Rights (c) . . . 400.00
28 IN,IN(c), V:Capt. Swastika . . . 400.00
29 ASH (c) . . . 400.00
30 B:Capt.Commando . . . 400.00
31 Bondage(c) . . . 325.00
32 Bondage(c) . . . 325.00
33 . . . 300.00
34 Bondage(c) . . . 325.00
35 . . . 300.00
36 1st Archie(c) . . . 550.00
37 Bondage(c) . . . 275.00
38 ASH(c) . . . 250.00
39 ASH(c), Human Shield . . . 250.00
40 . . . 250.00
41 2nd Archie; I:Jughead . . . 275.00
42 F:Archie & Jughead . . . 250.00
43 F:Archie & Jughead . . . 250.00
44 . . . 250.00
45 . . . 250.00
46 . . . 200.00
47 E:Hangman,Infinity(c) . . . 200.00
48 B:Black Hood . . . 200.00
49 . . . 200.00
50 . . . 200.00
51 . . . 150.00
52 B:Suzie . . . 150.00
53 . . . 150.00
54 E:Captain Commando . . . 150.00
55 . . . 150.00
56 thru 58 . . . @125.00
59 E:Suzie . . . 125.00
60 B:Katy Keene . . . 125.00
61 . . . 100.00
62 I L'il Jinx . . . 100.00
63 . . . 100.00
64 . . . 100.00
65 E:Shield . . . 100.00
66 thru 71 . . . @75.00
72 thru 80 . . . @65.00
81 thru 90 . . . @50.00
91 thru 99 . . . @40.00
100 . . . 65.00
101 thru 110 . . . @35.00
111 thru 120 . . . @22.00
121 thru 130 . . . @20.00
131 thru 140 . . . @15.00
141 thru 150 . . . @12.00
151 thru 160,A:Super Heroes . . . @12.00
161 thru 200 . . . @6.00
201 thru 250 . . . @3.00
251 thru 300 . . . @2.00
301 thru 350 . . . @1.50
351 thru 411 . . . @1.00

PERFECT CRIME, THE
Cross Publications
October, 1949

1 BP,DW . . . 100.00
2 BP . . . 65.00
3 . . . 50.00
4 BP . . . 50.00
5 DW . . . 50.00
6 . . . 50.00
7 B:Steve Duncan . . . 50.00
8 Drug Story . . . 50.00
9 . . . 50.00
10 . . . 50.00
11 Bondage (c) . . . 65.00
12 . . . 40.00
13 . . . 40.00
14 Poisoning (c) . . . 40.00
15 "The Most Terrible Menace", Drug . . . 50.00
16 . . . 30.00
17 . . . 30.00
18 Drug (c) . . . 90.00
19 . . . 30.00
20 . . . 30.00
21 . . . 30.00
22 . . . 30.00
23 . . . 30.00

Perfect Crime #24
© Cross Publications

24 . . . 30.00
25 . . . 30.00
26 Drug w/ Hypodermic (c) . . . 110.00
27 . . . 30.00
28 . . . 30.00
29 . . . 30.00
30 E:Steve Duncan, Rope Strangulation (c) . . . 80.00
31 . . . 30.00
32 . . . 30.00
33 . . . 30.00

PERFECT LOVE
Approved Comics(Ziff-Davis)/ St. John Publ. Co.
August-September, 1951

1 (10),P(c),Our Kiss was a Prelude to Love Adrift . . . 75.00
2 . . . 50.00
3 P(c) . . . 30.00
4 . . . 30.00
5 . . . 30.00
6 . . . 30.00
7 . . . 30.00
8 EK . . . 35.00
9 EK,P(c) . . . 35.00
10 Ph(c), Dec '53 . . . 30.00

PERSONAL LOVE
Famous Funnies
January, 1950

1 Ph(c) Are You in Love . . . 75.00
2 Ph(c) Serenade for Suzette Mario Lanzo . . . 40.00
3 Ph(c) . . . 30.00
4 Ph(c) . . . 30.00
5 Ph(c) . . . 30.00
6 Ph(c) Be Mine Forever . . . 32.00
7 Ph(c) You'll Always Be Mine, Robert Walker . . . 32.00
8 EK,Ph(c),Esther Williams & Howard Keel . . . 38.00
9 EK,Ph(c),Debra Paget & Louis Jordan . . . 38.00
10 Ph(c),Loretta Young Joseph Cotton . . . 35.00
11 ATh, Ph(c),Gene Tierney & Glenn Ford . . . 55.00
12 Ph(c) Jane Greer & William Lundigan . . . 30.00
13 Ph(c) Debra Paget & Louis Jordan . . . 25.00
14 Ph(c) Kirk Douglas & Patrice Wymore . . . 40.00
15 Ph(c) Dale Robertson & Joanne Dru . . . 25.00
16 Ph(c) Take Back Your Love . 25.00
17 Ph(c) My Cruel Deception . . . 25.00
18 Ph(c) Gregory Peck & Susan Hayward . . . 35.00
19 Ph(c) Anthony Quinn . . . 35.00
20 Ph(c) The Couple in the Next Apartment, Bob Wagner 30.00
21 Ph(c) I'll Make You Care . . . 25.00
22 Ph(c) Doorway To Heartbreak 25.00
23 Ph(c) SaveMe from that Man 25.00

Personal Love #24 © Famous Funnies

24 FF, Ph(c) Tyrone Power . . . 200.00
25 FF, Ph(c) The Dark Light . . 200.00
26 Ph(c) Love Needs A Break . . 25.00
27 FF, Ph(c) Champ or Chump? 200.00
28 FF, Ph(c) A Past to Forget . 200.00
29 Ph(c) Charlton Heston . . . 35.00
30 Ph(c) The Lady is Lost . . . 25.00
31 Ph(c) Marlon Brando . . . 40.00
32 FF, Ph(c) The Torment, Kirk Douglas . . . 350.00
33 Ph(c) June ,1955 . . . 25.00

PETER COTTONTAIL
Key Publications
January, 1954

1 No 3-D (fa) . . . 40.00
1 Feb '54 3-D (fa) . . . 100.00
2 Rep of 3-D #1,not in 3-D . . . 30.00

PETER PAUL'S 4 IN 1 JUMBO COMIC BOOK
Capitol Stories
1953

1 F: Racket Squad in Action, Space Adventures,Crime & Justice,Space Western . . . 200.00

PETER PENNY AND HIS MAGIC DOLLAR
American Bakers Association
1947

1 History from Colonial America to the 1950's . . . 90.00
2 . . . 50.00

PETER RABBIT
Avon Periodicals
1947

1 H. Cady art 200.00
2 H. Cady art 175.00
3 H. Cady art 150.00
4 H. Cady art 150.00
5 H. Cady art 150.00
6 H. Cady art 150.00
7 thru 10 . . . . @30.00
11 . . . . 15.00

PHANTOM LADY
(see LINDA)

PHANTOM LADY
Fox Features Syndicate
August, 1947

13 MB,MB(c) Knights of the Crooked Cross 1,100.00
14 MB,MB(c) Scoundrels and Scandals 750.00
15 MB,MB(c) The Meanest Crook In the World 600.00
16 MB,MB(c) Claa Peete The Beautiful Beast, Negligee . . 600.00
17 MB.MB(c) The Soda Mint Killer, Bondage (c) 1,350.00
18 MB,MB(c) The Case of Irene Shroeder 550.00
19 MB,MB(c) The Case of the Murderous Model 550.00
20 MB,MB(c) Ace of Spades . . 500.00
21 MB,MB(c) 500.00
22 MB,JKa 500.00
23 MB,JKa Bondage (c) 550.00

Becomes:

MY LOVE SECRET

24 JKa, My Love Was For Sale . 75.00
25 Second Hand Love 40.00
26 WW I Wanted Both Men 80.00
27 I Was a Love Cheat 30.00
28 WW, I Gave Him Love 80.00
29 . . . . 30.00
30 Ph(c) 30.00

Phantom Lady #17
© Fox Features Syndicate

PHANTOM LADY
December-January, 1955
Ajax/Farrell Publ.

5 MB 350.00
1 . . . . 300.00
2 . . . . 250.00
3 June, 1955 . . . . 225.00

PHIL RIZZUTO
Fawcett Publications
1951

Ph(c) The Sensational Story of The American Leagues MVP 350.00

Pictorial Romances #8
© St. John's Publishing Co.

PICTORIAL CONFESSIONS
St. John Publishing Co.
September, 1949

1 MB,MB(c),I Threw Away My Reputation on a Worthless Love 100.00
2 MB,Ph(c) I Tried to be a Hollywood Glamour Girl 50.00
3 JKY,MB,MB(c),They Caught Me Cheating 75.00

Becomes:

PICTORIAL ROMANCES

4 Ph(c) MB, Trapped By Kisses I Couldn't Resist 100.00
5 MB,MB(c) 75.00
6 MB,MB(c) I Was Too Free With Boys 50.00
7 MB,MB(c) 50.00
8 MB,MB(c) I Made a Sinful Bargain 50.00
9 MB,MB(c) Dishonest Love . . . 50.00
10 MB,MB(c) I Was The Other Woman 50.00
11 MB,MB(c) The Worst Mistake A Wife Can Make . . . 55.00
12 MB,MB(c) Love Urchin 45.00
13 MB,MB(c) Temptations of a Hatcheck Girl 45.00
14 MB,MB(c) I Was A Gamblers Wife 45.00
15 MB,MB(c) Wife Without Pride or Principles 45.00
16 MB,MB(c) The Truth of My Affair With a Farm Boy 45.00
17 MB,MB(c) True Confessions of a Girl in Love 95.00
18 MB,MB(c) 95.00
20 MB,MB(c) 95.00
21 MB,MB(c) 35.00
22 MB,MB(c) 35.00
23 MB,MB(c) 35.00
24 MB,MB(c) March,1954 . . . . . 35.00

PICTORIAL LOVE STORIES
St. John Publishing Co.
October, 1952

1 MB,MB(c) I Lost My Head, My Heart and My Resistance . . . 90.00

PICTURE NEWS
299 Lafayette Street Corp.
January, 1946

1 Will The Atom Blow The World Apart 175.00
2 Meet America's 1st Girl Boxing Expert,Atomic Bomb 80.00
3 Hollywood's June Allison Shows You How to be Beautiful, Atomic Bomb 75.00
4 Amazing Marine Who Became King of 10,000 Voodoos, Atomic Bomb 80.00
5 G.I.Babies,Hank Greenberg . . 60.00
6 Joe Louis(c) 75.00
7 Lovely Lady, Englands Future Queen 70.00
8 Champion of them All 60.00
9 Bikini Atom Bomb, Joe DiMaggio 80.00
10 Dick Quick, Ace Reporter, Atomic Bomb January/February 1947 . . . . . 65.00

PICTURE STORIES FROM SCIENCE
Educational Comics
Spring, 1947

1 Understanding Air and Water 125.00
2 Fall '47 Amazing Discoveries About Food & Health 120.00

PICTURE STORIES FROM WORLD HISTORY
E.C. Comics
Spring, 1947

1 Ancient World to the Fall of Rome 120.00
2 Europes Struggle for Civilization 100.00

Pinhead and Foodini #4
© Fawcett Publications

PINHEAD AND FOODINI
Fawcett Publications

All comics prices listed are for *Near Mint* condition.

July, 1951

1 Ph(c) 150.00
2 Ph(c) 75.00
3 Ph(c) Too Many Pinheads ... 55.00
4 Foodini's Talking Camel
January, 1952 .... 55.00

PIN-UP PETE
Minoan Magazine Publishers
1952

1 Loves of a GI Casanova 85.00

PIONEER PICTURE STORIES
Street & Smith Publications
December, 1941

1 Red Warriors in Blackface .. 150.00
2 Life Story Of Errol Flynn 75.00
3 Success Stories of Brain
Muscle in Action 55.00
4 Legless Ace & Boy Commando
Raid Occupied France 55.00
5 How to Tell Uniform and
Rank of Any Navy Man 55.00
6 General Jimmy Doolittle 60.00
7 Life Story of Admiral Halsey . 60.00
8 Life Story of Timoshenko 55.00
9 Dec. '43,Man Who Conquered
The Wild Frozen North 55.00

PIRACY
E.C. Comics
October-November, 1954

1 WW,JDa,AW,WW(c),RC,AT 250.00
2 RC,JDa(c),WW,AW,AT 175.00
3 RC,GE, RC(c),Grl 150.00
4 RC,GE,RC(c),Grl 100.00
5 RC,GE,BK(c),Grl 100.00
6 JDa,RC,GE,BK(c),Grl 100.00
7 Oct Nov GE(c),RC,GE,Grl . 100.00

PIRATE COMICS
Hillman Periodicals
February-March, 1950

1 .... 125.00
2 .... 75.00
3 .... 65.00
4 Aug Sept 30 .... 60.00

PIXIES, THE
Magazine Enterprises
Winter, 1946

1 Mighty Atom 45.00
2 .... 25.00
3 .... 20.00
4 .... 20.00
5 .... 25.00

Becomes:

MIGHTY ATOM, THE

6 .... 25.00

PLANET COMICS
Love Romance Publ.
(Fiction House Magazines)
January, 1940

1 AB,DBR,HCk, Planet Comics,
WE&LF,O:Aura,B:Flint Baker,
Red Comet,Spurt Hammond,
Capt. Nelson Cole 6,200.00
2 HcK,LF(c) 2,000.00
3 WE(c),HcK 1,500.00
4 HcK,B:Gale Allan and
the Girl Squad 1,400.00
5 BP,HcK 1,250.00
6 BP,HcK,BP(c),The Ray
Pirates of Venus 1,300.00
7 BP,AB,HcK,BP(c) B:Buzz
Crandall Planet Payson .. 1,000.00
8 BP,AB HcK 1,000.00
9 BP,AB,GT,HcK,B:Don
Granville Cosmo Corrigan .. 975.00

Planet Comics #49
© Fiction House Magazines

10 BP,AB,GT HcK 975.00
11 HcK, B:Crash Parker 950.00
12 Dri,B:Star Fighter 950.00
13 Dri,B:Reef Ryan 800.00
14 Dri B:Norge Benson 750.00
15 B: Mars,God of War 1,500.00
16 Invasion From The Void ... 750.00
17 Warrior Maid of Mercury ... 750.00
18 Bondage(c) 775.00
19 Monsters of the Inner World 750.00
20 RP, Winged Man Eaters
of the Exile Star 750.00
21 RP,B:Lost World
Hunt Bowman 800.00
22 Inferno on the Fifth Moon .. 700.00
23 GT,Lizard Tyrant of
the Twilight World 650.00
24 GT,Grl Raiders From
The Red Moon 650.00
25 Grl,B:Norge Benson 650.00
26 Grl,B:The Space Rangers
Bondage(c) 700.00
27 Grl, The Fire Eaters of
Asteroid Z 550.00
28 Grl, Bondage (c) 600.00
29 Grl,Dragon Raiders of Aztla 550.00
30 GT,Grl City of Lost Souls .. 550.00
31 Grl,Fire Priests of Orbit X .. 550.00
32 Slaver's Planetoid 500.00
33 MA 500.00
34 MA,Bondage 550.00
35 MA B:Mysta of The Moon .. 500.00
36 MA Collosus of the
Blood Moon 500.00
37 MA, Behemoths of the
Purple Void 500.00
38 MA 450.00
39 MA. Death Webs Of Zenith 3 450.00
40 Chameleon Men from
Galaxy 9 .... 450.00
41 MA,Aaf,New O: Auro
Bondage (c) 500.00
42 MA,AaF,E:Gale Allan 450.00
43 MA,AaF Death Rays
From the Sun. 450.00
44 MA,Bbl,B:Futura 450.00
45 Ma,Bbl,Her Evilness
from Xanado 450.00
46 MA,Bbl,GE The Mecho-Men
From Mars 450.00
47 MA,Bbl,GE,The Great
Green Spawn 400.00
48 MA,GE 400.00
49 MA,GE, Werewolves From
Hydra Hell 400.00
50 MA,GE,The Things of Xeves 400.00
51 MA,GE, Mad Mute X-Adapts 350.00
52 GE,Mystery of the Time
Chamber 350.00
53 MB,GE,Bondage(c)
Dwarflings From Oceania .. 350.00
54 MB,GE,Robots From Inferno 350.00
55 MB,GE,Giants of the
Golden Atom 350.00
56 MB,GE,Grl 300.00
57 MB,GE,Grl 300.00
58 MB,GE,Grl 300.00
59 MB,GE,Grl,LSe 300.00
60 GE,Grl,Vassals of Volta ... 300.00
61 GE,Grl, The Brute in the
Bubble 225.00
62 GE,Musta,Moon Goddess .. 225.00
63 GE,Paradise or Inferno 225.00
64 GE,Monkeys From the Blue 225.00
65 The Lost World 225.00
66 The Plague of the
Locust Men 225.00
67 The Nymphs of Neptune ... 225.00
68 Synthoids of the 9th Moon . 225.00
69 The Mentalists of Mars 225.00
70 Cargo For Amazonia 225.00
71 Sandhogs of Mars 225.00
72 Last Ship to Paradise 225.00
73 The Martian Plague,
Winter 1953 .... 225.00

Plastic Man #44
© Comics Magazines/Quality Comics

PLASTIC MAN
Comics Magazines
(Quality Comics Group)
Summer, 1943

1 JCo,JCo(c)Game of Death . 1,600.00
2 JCo,JCo(c)The Gay Nineties
Nightmare 900.00
3 JCo,JCo(c) 550.00
4 JCo,JCo(c) 500.00
5 JCo,JCo(c) 400.00
6 JCo,JCo(c) 300.00
7 JCo,JCo(c) 300.00
8 JCo,JCo(c) 300.00
9 JCo,JCo(c) 300.00
10 JCo,JCo(c) 300.00
11 JCo,JCo(c) 250.00
12 JCo,JCo(c),V:Spadehead .. 250.00
13 JCo,JCo(c),V:Mr.Hazard ... 250.00
14 JCo,JCo(c),Words,Symbol
of Crime 250.00
15 JCo,JCo(c),V:BeauBrummel 250.00

16 JCo,JCo(c),Money Means Trouble 250.00
17 JCo,JCo(c),A:The Last Man on Earth 250.00
18 JCo,JCo(c),Goes Back to the Farm 250.00
19 JCo,JCo(c),V;Prehistoric Plunder 250.00
20 JCo,JCo(c),A:Sadly,Sadly . . 250.00
21 JCo,JCo(c),V:Crime Minded Mind Reader 225.00
22 JCo,JCo(c), Which Twin is the Phony 225.00
23 JCo,JCo(c),The Fountain of Age 225.00
24 JCo,JCo(c),The Black Box of Terror 225.00
25 JCo,JCo(c),A:Angus MacWhangus 225.00
26 JCo,JCo(c),On the Wrong Side of the Law? 225.00
27 JCo,JCo(c),V:The Leader . . 225.00
28 JCo,JCo(c),V:Shasta 225.00
29 JCo,JCo(c),V:Tricky Toledo . 225.00
30 JCo,JCo(c),V:Weightless Wiggins 225.00
31 JCo,JCo(c),V:Raka the Witch Doctor 175.00
32 JCo,JCo(c),V:Mr.Fission . . . 175.00
33 JCo,JCo(c),V:The Mad Professor 175.00
34 JCo,JCo(c),Smuggler'sHaven 175.00
35 JCo,JCo(c),V:The Hypnotist 175.00
36 JCo,JCo(c),The Uranium Underground 175.00
37 JCo,JCo(c),V:Gigantic Ants . 175.00
38 JCo,JCo(c),The Curse of Monk Mauley 175.00
39 JCo,JCo(c),The Stairway to Madness 175.00
40 JCo,JCo(c),The Ghoul of Ghost Swamp 175.00
41 JCo,JCo(c),The Beast with the Bloody Claws 150.00
42 JCo,JCo(c),The King of Thunderbolts 150.00
43 JCo,JCo(c),The Evil Terror . 150.00
44 JCo,JCo(c),The Magic Cup . 150.00
45 The Invisible Raiders 150.00
46 V:The Spider 150.00
47 The Fiend of a Thousand Faces 150.00
48 Killer Crossbones 150.00
49 JCo,The Weapon for Evil . . 150.00
50 V:Iron Fist 150.00
51 Incredible Sleep Weapon . . 125.00
52 V:Indestructible Wizard 135.00
53 V:Dazzia,Daughter of Darkness 135.00
54 V:Dr.Quomquat 135.00
55 The Man Below Zero 135.00
56 JCo, The Man Who Broke the Law of Gravity 135.00
57 The Chemist's Cauldron . . . 135.00
58 JCo,The Amazing Duplicating Machine 135.00
59 JCo,V:The Super Spy 135.00
60 The Man in the Fiery Disguise 125.00
61 V:King of the Thunderbolts . 125.00
62 V:The Smokeweapon 125.00
63 V:Reflecto 125.00
64 Nov'56 The Invisible Raiders 125.00

POCAHONTAS
Pocahontas Fuel Co.
October, 1941

N# 65.00
2 . . . . 50.00

POCKET COMICS
Harvey Publications
August, 1941

1 100 pages,O:Black Cat,Spirit of '76,Red Blazer Phantom Sphinx & Zebra,B:Phantom Ranger,British Agent #99, Spin Hawkins,Satan 450.00
2 . . . . 300.00
3 . . . . 200.00
4 Jan.'42,All Features End . . . 200.00

POGO POSSUM
Dell Publishing Co.

1 WK,A:Swamp Land Band . . 400.00
2 WK 225.00

Pogo Possum #5
© Dell Publishing Co.

3 WK 160.00
4 WK 160.00
5 WK 160.00
6 thru 10 WK . . . . @140.00
11 WK, Christmas cover . . . @125.00
12 thru 16 WK . . . . @125.00

POLICE COMICS
Comic Magazines (Quality Comics Group)
August, 1941

1 GFx,JCo,WE.PGn,RC,FG,AB, GFx(c),B&O:Plastic Man The Human Bomb,#711,I&B, Chic Canter,The Firebrand Mouthpiece,Phantom Lady The Sword 3,000.00
2 JCo,GFx,PGn,WE,RC,FG, GFx(c) 1,500.00
3 JCo,GFx,PGn,WE,RC,FG, GFx(c) 1,100.00
4 JCo,GFx,PGn,WE,RC,FG, GFx&WEC(c) 1,000.00
5 JCo,GFx,PGn,WE,RC,FG, GFx(c) 900.00
6 JCo,GFx,PGn,WE,RC,FG, GFx(c) 850.00
7 JCo,GFx,PGn,WE,RC,FG, GFx(c) 800.00
8 JCo,GFx,PGn,WE,RC,FG, GFx(c),B&O:Manhunter . . 1,000.00
9 JCo,GFx,PGn,WE,RC,FG, GFx(c) 750.00
10 JCo,GFx,PGn,WE,RC,FG, GFx(c) 750.00
11 JCo,GFx,PGn,WE,RC,FG, GFx(c),B:Rep:Rep.Spirit Strips 1,250.00
12 JCo,GFX,PGn,WE,FG,AB, RC(c) I:Ebony 750.00
13 JCo,GFx,PGn,WE,FG,AB,RC(c) E:Firebrand,I:Woozy Winks . 750.00
14 JCo,GFx,PGn,WE,Jku,GFX(c) 500.00
15 JCo,GFx,PGn,WE,Jku,GFX(c) E#711,B:Destiny 500.00
16 JCo,PGn,WE,JKu 500.00
17 JCo,PGn,WE,JKu,JCo(c) . . 500.00
18 JCo,PGn,WE,JCo(c) 500.00
19 JCo,PGn,WE,JCo(c) 500.00
20 JCo,PGn,WE,JCo(c),A:Jack Cole in Phantom Lady 500.00
21 JCo,PGn,WE,JCo(c) 400.00
22 JCo,PGn,WE,RP,JCo(c) The Eyes Have it 400.00
23 JCo,WE,RP,JCo(c),E:Phantom Lady 350.00
24 JCo,WE,HK,JCo(c),B:Flatfoot Burns 350.00
25 JCo,WE,HK,RP,JCo(c),The Bookstore Mysrery 350.00
26 JCo,WE,Hk,JCo,(c)E:Flatfoot Burns 350.00
27 JCo,WE,JCo(c) 350.00
28 JCo,WE,JCo(c) 350.00
29 JCo,WE,JCo(c) 350.00
30 JCo,WE,JCo(c),A Slippery Racket 350.00
31 JCo,WE,JCo(c),Is Plastic Man Washed Up? 250.00
32 JCo,WE,JCo(c),Fiesta Turns Into a Fracas 250.00
33 JCo,WE 250.00
34 JCo,WE,JCO(c) 250.00
35 JCo,WE,JCO(c) 250.00
36 JCo,WE,JCO(c),Rest In Peace 250.00
37 JCo,WE,PGn,JCo(c),Love Comes to Woozy 250.00
38 JCo,WE,PGn,JCo(c) 250.00
39 JCo,WE,PGn,JCo(c) 250.00

Police Comics #2
© Comics Magazine/Quality Comics

40 JCo,WE,PGn,JCo(c) 250.00
41 JCo,WE,PGn,JCo(c),E:Reps. of Spirit Strip 225.00
42 JCo,LF&WE,PGn,JCo(c), Woozy Cooks with Gas 225.00
43 JCo,LF&WE,PGn,JCo(c) . . . 225.00
44 JCo,PGn,LF,JCo(c) 200.00
45 JCo,PGn,LF,JCo(c) 200.00
46 JCo,PGn,LF,JCo(c) 200.00
47 JCo,PGn,LF,JCo(c), V:Dr.Slicer 200.00
48 JCo,PGn,LF,JCo(c),V:Big Beaver 200.00
49 JCo,PGn,LF,JCo(c),V:Thelma

Twittle 200.00
50 JCo,PGn,LF,JCo(c) 200.00
51 JCo,PGn,LF,JCo(c),V:The Granite Lady 150.00
52 JCo,PGn,LF,JCo(c) 150.00
53 JCo,PGn,LF,JCo(c), V:Dr.Erudite 150.00
54 JCo,PGn,LF,JCo(c) 150.00
55 JCo,PGn,LF,JCo(c),V:The Sleepy Eyes 150.00
56 JCo,PGn,LF,JCo(c),V:The Yes Man 150.00
57 JCo,PGn,LF,JCo(c), V:Mr.Misfit 150.00
58 JCo,PGn,LF,JCo(c),E:The Human Bomb 150.00
59 JCo,PGn,LF,JCo(c),A:Mr. Happiness 150.00
60 JCo,PGn,LF,JCo(c) 135.00
61 JCo,PGn,LF,JCo(c) 135.00
62 JCo,PGn,LF,JCo(c) 135.00
63 JCo,PGn,LF,JCo(c), V:The Crab 135.00
64 JCo,PGn,LF,HK,JCo(c) 135.00
65 JCo,PGn,LF,JCo(c) 135.00
66 JCo,PGn,LF,JCo(c) Love Can Mean Trouble 135.00
67 JCo,LF,JCo(c), V:The Gag Man 135.00
68 JCo,LF,JCo(c) 135.00
69 JCo,LF,JCo(c),V:Strecho 135.00
70 JCo,LF,JCo(c) 135.00
71 JCo,LF,JCo(c) 135.00
72 JCo,LF,JCo(c),V:Mr.Cat 135.00
73 JCo,LF,JCo(c) 135.00
74 JCo,LF,JCo(c),V:Prof.Dimwit 135.00
75 JCo,LF,JCo(c) 135.00
76 JCo,LF,JCo(c),V:Mr.Morbid 135.00
77 JCo,LF,JCo(c),V:Skull Face & Eloc 135.00
78 JCo,LF,JCo(c),A Hot Time In Dreamland 135.00
79 JCo,LF,JCo(c),V:Eaglebeak 135.00
80 JCo,LF,JCo(c),V:Penetro 135.00
81 JCo,LF,JCo(c),V:A Gorilla 135.00
82 JCo,LF,JCo(c) 135.00
83 JCo,LF,JCo(c) 135.00
84 JCo,LF,JCo(c) 135.00
85 JCo,LF,JCo(c),V:Lucky 7 135.00
86 JCo,LF,JCo(c),V:The Baker 135.00
87 JCo,LF,JCo(c) 135.00
88 JCo,LF,JCo(c),V:The Seen 135.00
89 JCo,JCo(c),V:The Vanishers 125.00
90 JCo,LF,JCo(c),V:Capt.Rivers 125.00
91 JCo,JCo(c),The Forest Primeval 135.00
92 JCo,LF,JCo(c),V:Closets Kennedy 135.00
93 JCo,JCo(c),V:The Twinning Terror 135.00
94 JCo,JCo(c),WE 175.00
95 JCo,JCo(c),WE,V:Scowls 175.00
96 JCo,JCo(c),WE,V:Black Widow 175.00
97 JCo,JCo(c),WE,V:The Mime 175.00
98 JCo,JCo(c),WE 175.00
99 JCo,JCo(c),WE 175.00
100 JCo,JCo(c) 200.00
101 JCo,JCo(c) 175.00
102 JCo,JCo(c),E:Plastic Man 175.00
103 JCo,LF,B&I:Ken Shannon; Bondage(c) 125.00
104 The Handsome of Homocide 75.00
105 Invisible Hands of Murder 75.00
106 Museum of Murder 75.00
107 Man with the ShrunkenHead 75.00
108 The Headless Horse Player 75.00
109 LF,Bondage(c),Blood on the Chinese Fan 85.00
110 Murder with a Bang 75.00
111 Diana the HomocidalHuntress 75.00
112 RC,The Corpse on the Sidewalk 75.00
113 RC,RC(c), The Dead Man with the Size 13 Shoe 75.00
114 The Terrifying Secret of the Black Bear 75.00
115 Don't Let Them Kill Me 75.00
116 Stage Was Set For Murder 75.00
117 Bullet Riddled Bookkeeper 75.00
118 Case of the Absent Corpse 75.00
119 A Fast & Bloody Buck 75.00
120 Death & The Derelict 75.00
121 Curse of the Clawed Killer 75.00
122 The Lonely Hearts Killer 75.00
123 Death Came Screaming 75.00
124 Masin Murder 75.00
125 Bondage(c),The Killer of King Arthur's Court 85.00
126 Hit & Run Murders 75.00
127 Oct'53,Death Drivers 75.00

POLICE LINE-UP
Avon Periodicals/ Realistic Comics
August, 1951

1 WW,P(c) 175.00
2 P(c),Drugs 150.00
3 JKu,EK,P(c) 85.00
4 July '52;EK 85.00

POLICE TRAP
Mainline/Charlton Comics
September, 1954

1 S&K(c) 90.00
2 S&K(c) 50.00
3 S&K(c) 50.00
4 S&K(c) 50.00
5 S&K,S&K(c) 85.00
6 S&K,S&K(c) 85.00

POLLY PIGTAILS
Parents' Magazine Institute
January, 1946

1 Ph(c) 55.00
2 Ph(c) 25.00
3 Ph(c) 20.00
4 Ph(c) 20.00
5 Ph(c) 20.00
6 Ph(c) 20.00
7 Ph(c) 15.00
8 15.00
9 15.00
10 15.00
11 thru 22 @10.00
22 Ph(c) 10.00
23 Ph(c) 10.00
34 thru 43 @10.00

POPEYE
Dell Publishing Co.
1948

1 250.00
2 150.00
3 'Welcome to Ghost Island' 125.00
4 125.00
5 125.00
6 125.00
7 125.00
8 125.00
9 125.00
10 125.00
11 100.00
12 100.00
13 100.00
14 100.00
15 100.00
16 100.00
17 100.00
18 100.00
19 100.00
20 100.00
21 thru 30 @75.00
31 thru 40 @65.00
41 thru 45 @50.00
46 O:Sweat Pea 65.00
47 thru 50 @45.00
51 thru 60 @35.00

Popeye #10 © King Features

61 thru 65 @25.00

POPULAR COMICS
Dell Publishing Co.
February, 1936

1 Dick Tracy, Little Orphan Annie 2,000.00
2 Terry Pirates 700.00
3 Terry,Annie,Dick Tracy 600.00
4 500.00
5 B:Tom Mix 500.00
6 400.00
7 400.00
8 400.00
9 400.00
10 Terry,Annie,Tracy 400.00
11 Terry,Annie,Tracy 300.00
12 Christmas(c) 300.00
13 Terry,Annie,Tracy 300.00
14 Terry,Annie,Tracy 300.00
15 same 300.00
16 same 300.00
17 same 300.00
18 same 300.00
19 same 300.00
20 same 300.00
21 same 250.00
22 same 250.00
23 same 250.00
24 same 250.00
25 same 250.00
26 same 250.00
27 E:Terry,Annie,Tracy 250.00
28 A:Gene Autry 200.00
29 200.00
30 200.00
31 A:Jim McCoy 200.00
32 A:Jim McCoy 200.00
33 200.00
34 200.00
35 Christmas(c),Tex Ritter 200.00
36 200.00
37 200.00
38 B:Gang Busters 225.00
39 225.00
40 225.00
41 225.00
42 225.00
43 255.00
44 165.00
45 Tarzan(c) 165.00
46 O:Martan,Marvel Man 225.00
47 150.00
48 150.00
49 150.00

Popular Comics #81
© Dell Publishing Co.

50 . . . . . 150.00
51 B&O:Voice 165.00
52 A:Voice 135.00
53 A:Voice 135.00
54 A:Voice 135.00
55 . . . . . 150.00
56 . . . . . 125.00
57 . . . . . 125.00
58 . . . . . 125.00
59 . . . . . 125.00
60 O:Prof. Supermind 125.00
61 . . . . . 100.00
62 . . . . . 100.00
63 B:Smilin' Jack 100.00
64 . . . . . 100.00
65 . . . . . 100.00
66 . . . . . 100.00
67 . . . . . 100.00
68 . . . . . 100.00
69 . . . . . 100.00
70 . . . . . 100.00
71 . . . . . 100.00
72 B:Owl,Terry & the Pirates . . 150.00
73 . . . . . 125.00
74 . . . . . 125.00
75 A:Owl 125.00
76 Captain Midnight 150.00
77 Captain Midnight 150.00
78 Captain Midnight 150.00
79 A:Owl 125.00
80 A:Owl 125.00
81 A:Owl 125.00
82 A:Owl 125.00
83 A:Owl 125.00
84 A:Owl 125.00
85 A:Owl 125.00
86 . . . . . 80.00
87 . . . . . 80.00
88 . . . . . 80.00
89 . . . . . 80.00
90 . . . . . 80.00
91 . . . . . 80.00
92 . . . . . 80.00
93 . . . . . 80.00
94 . . . . . 80.00
95 . . . . . 80.00
96 . . . . . 80.00
97 . . . . . 80.00
98 B:Felix Cat 85.00
99 . . . . . 80.00
100 . . . . . 100.00
101 thru 141 . . . . . 55.00
142 E:Terry & the Pirates 50.00
143 . . . . . 50.00
144 . . . . . 50.00
145 . . . . . 50.00

POPULAR ROMANCES
Better Publications
(Standard Comics)
December, 1949

5 B:Ph(c) 35.00
6 Ph(c) 20.00
7 RP 20.00
8 Ph(c) 20.00
9 Ph(c) 20.00
10 WW 35.00
11 thru 16 . . . . . @15.00
17 WE 20.00
18 thru 21 . . . . . @20.00
22 thru 27 ATh,Ph(c) . . . . . @40.00

Power Comics #3
© Holyoke/Narrative Publ.

SCHOOL DAY ROMANCES
Star Publications
November-December, 1949

1 LbC(c),Teen-Age 85.00
2 LbC(c) 50.00
3 LbC(c),Ph(c) 50.00
4 LbC(c),JyD,RonaldReagan . 125.00

Becomes:

POPULAR TEEN-AGERS

5 LbC(c),Toni Gay,
Eve Adams 95.00
6 LbC(c),Ginger Bunny,
Midge Martin 85.00
7 LbC(c) 85.00
8 LbC(c) 85.00
9 LbC(c) 45.00
10 LbC(c) 45.00
11 LbC(c) 35.00
12 LbC(c) 35.00
13 LbC(c),JyD 35.00
14 LbC,WW,Spanking 100.00
15 LbC(c),JyD 35.00
16 . . . . . 30.00
17 LbC(c),JyD 30.00
18 LbC(c) 30.00
19 LbC(c) 30.00
20 LbC(c),JyD 40.00
21 LbC(c),JyD 40.00
22 LbC(c) 25.00
23 LbC(c) 25.00

POWER COMICS
Holyoke/Narrative Publ.
1944

1 LbC(c) 365.00
2 B:Dr.Mephisto,Hitler(c) 375.00
3 LbC(c) 365.00
4 LbC(c) 300.00

PRIDE OF THE YANKEES
Magazine Enterprises
1949

1 N#,OW,Ph(c),The Life
of Lou Gehrig 425.00

PRISON BREAK
Avon Periodicals/Realistic
September, 1951

1 WW(c),WW 190.00
2 WW(c),WW,JKu 150.00
3 JD,JO 125.00
4 EK 100.00
5 EK,CI 100.00

PRIZE COMICS
Feature Publications
(Prize Publ.)
March, 1940

1 O&B:Power Nelson,Jupiter.
B:Ted O'Neil,Jaxon of
the Jungle,Bucky Brady,
Storm Curtis, Rocket(c) . . 1,000.00
2 B:The Owl 450.00
3 Power Nelson(c) 350.00
4 Power Nelson(c) 350.00
5 A:Dr.Dekkar 300.00
6 A:Dr.Dekkar 300.00
7 S&K,DBr,JK(c),O&B DR Frost,
Frankenstein,B:GreenLama,
Capt Gallant,Voodini
Twist Turner 800.00

Prize Comics #34
© Feature Publications

8 S&K,DBr 400.00
9 S&K,DBr,Black Owl(c) 400.00
10 DBr,Black Owl(c) 350.00
11 DBr,O:Bulldog Denny 325.00
12 DBr 325.00
13 DBR,O&B:Yank and
Doodle,Bondage(c) 350.00
14 DBr,Black Owl(c) 325.00
15 DBr,Black Owl(c) 325.00
16 DBr,JaB,B:Spike Mason . . . 325.00
17 DBr,Black Owl(c) 325.00
18 DBr,Black Owl(c) 325.00
19 DBr,Yank&Doodle(c) 325.00
20 DBr,Yank&Doodle(c) 325.00

21 DBr,JaB(c),Yank&Doodle(c) 250.00
22 DBr,Yank&Doodle(c) 250.00
23 DBr,Uncle Sam(c) 250.00
24 DBr,Abe Lincoln(c) 250.00
25 DBr,JaB,Yank&Doodle(c) 250.00
26 DBr,JaB,JaB(c),Liberty Bell(c) 250.00
27 DBr,Yank&Doodle(c) 150.00
28 DBr,Yank&Doodle(c) 125.00
29 DBr,JaB(c)Yank&Doodle(c) 125.00
30 DBr,Yank&Doodle(c) 150.00
31 DBr,Yank&Doodle(c) 125.00
32 DBr,Yank&Doodle(c) 125.00
33 DBr,Bondage(c),Yank & Doodle 150.00
34 DBr,O:Airmale;New Black Owl 150.00
35 DBr,B:Flying Fist & Bingo 100.00
36 DBr,Yank&Doodle(c) 100.00
37 DBr,I:Stampy,Hitler(c) 120.00
38 DBr,B.Owl,Yank&Doodle(c) 100.00
39 DBr,B.Owl,Yank&Doodle(c) 100.00
40 DBr,B.Owl,Yank&Doodle(c) 100.00
41 DBr,B.Owl,Yank&Doodle(c) 100.00
42 DBr,B.Owl,Yank&Doodle(c) 75.00
43 DBr,B.Owl,Yank&Doodle(c) 75.00
44 DBr, B&I:Boom Boom Brannigan 75.00
45 DBr 75.00
46 DBr 75.00
47 DBr 75.00
48 DBr,B:Prince Ra;Bondage(c) 90.00
49 DBr,Boom Boom(c) 60.00
50 DBr,Farnkenstein(c) 75.00
51 DBr 60.00
52 DBr, B:Sir Prize 60.00
53 DBr, The Man Who Could Read Features 70.00
54 DBr 60.00
55 DBr,Yank&Doodle(c) 60.00
56 DBr,Boom Boom (c) 60.00
57 DBr,Santa Claus(c) 60.00
58 DBr,The Poisoned Punch 60.00
59 DBr,Boom Boom(c) 60.00
60 DBr,Sir Prise(c) 60.00
61 DBr,The Man wih the Fighting Feet 60.00
62 DBr,Hck(c),Yank&Doodle(c) 60.00
63 DBr,S&K,S&K(c),Boom Boom(c) 75.00
64 DBr,Blackowl Retires 60.00
65 DBr,DBr(c),Frankenstein 65.00
66 DBr,DBr(c),Frankenstein 65.00
67 DBr,B:Brothers in Crime 60.00
68 DBr,RP(c) 60.00

Becomes:

PRIZE COMICS WESTERN

69 ACa(c),B:Dusty Ballew 80.00
70 ACa(c) 60.00
71 ACa(c) 60.00
72 ACa(c),JSe 60.00
73 ACa(c) 60.00
74 ACa(c) 60.00
75 JSe,S&K(c),6-Gun Showdown at Rattlesnake Gulch 65.00
76 Ph(c),Randolph Scott 75.00
77 Ph(c),JSe,Streets of Laredo,movie 60.00
78 Ph(c),JSe,HK,Bullet Code, movie 90.00
79 Ph(c),JSe,Stage to China, movie 90.00
80 Ph(c),Gunsmoke Justice 60.00
81 Ph(c),The Man Who Shot Billy The Kid 60.00
82 Ph(c),MBi,JSe&BE,Death Draws a Circle 60.00
83 JSe,S&K(c) 70.00
84 JSe 50.00
85 JSe,B:American Eagle 130.00
86 JSe 60.00
87 JSe&BE 60.00
88 JSe&BE 60.00
89 JSe&BE 60.00
90 JSe&Be 60.00
91 JSe&BE,JSe&BE(c) 60.00
92 JSe,JSe&BE(c) 60.00

Prize Comics Western #45 © Feature Publications

93 JSe,JSe&BE(c), 60.00
94 JSe&BE,JSe&BE(c) 60.00
95 JSe,JSe&BE(c) 60.00
96 JSe,JSe&BE,JSe&BE(c) 60.00
97 JSe,JSe&BE,JSeBE(c) 60.00
98 JSe&BE,JSe&BE(c) 60.00
99 JSe&BE,JSe&BE(c) 60.00
100 JSe,JSe(c) 75.00
101 JSe 60.00
102 JSe 60.00
103 JSe 60.00
104 JSe 60.00
105 JSe 60.00
106 JSe 50.00
107 JSe 50.00
108 JSe 70.00
109 JSe&AW 70.00
110 JSe&BE 65.00
111 JSe&BE 65.00
112 45.00
113 AW&JSe 75.00
114 MMe,B:The Drifter 35.00
115 MMe 35.00
116 MMe 35.00
117 MMe 35.00
118 MMe,E:The Drifter 35.00
119 Nov/Dec'56 35.00

PSYCHOANALYSIS
E.C. Comics
March-April, 1955

1 JKa,JKa(c) 90.00
2 JKa,JKa(c) 75.00
3 JKa,JKa(c) 75.00
4 JKa,JKa(c) Sept.-Oct. 1955 75.00

PUBLIC ENEMIES
D.S. Publishing Co.
1948

1 AMc 80.00
2 AMc 90.00
3 AMc 55.00
4 AMc 55.00
5 AMc 55.00
6 AMc 55.00
7 AMc,Eye Injury 65.00
8 55.00
9 50.00

PUNCH AND JUDY COMICS
Hillman Periodicals
1944

1 (fa) 75.00
2 40.00
3 30.00
4 thru 12 @30.00
2-1 25.00
2-2 JK 75.00
2-3 25.00
2-4 25.00
2-5 25.00
2-6 25.00
2-7 25.00
2-8 25.00
2-9 25.00
2-10 JK 75.00
2-11 JK 75.00
2-12 JK 75.00
3-1 JK 75.00
3-2 65.00
3-3 20.00
3-4 20.00
3-5 20.00
3-6 20.00
3-7 20.00
3-8 20.00
3-9 20.00

PUNCH COMICS
Harry 'A' Chesler
December, 1941

1 B:Mr.E,The Sky Chief,Hale the Magician,Kitty Kelly 500.00
2 A:Capt.Glory 250.00
3-8 Do Not Exist
9 B:Rocket Man & Rocket girl,Master Ken 200.00
10 JCo,A:Sky Chief 150.00
11 JCo,O:Master Key,A:Little Nemo 150.00
12 A:Rocket Boy,Capt.Glory 135.00
13 Ric(c) 135.00
14 GT 125.00

Punch Comics #11 © Harry 'A' Chesler

15 FSm(c) 125.00
16 125.00
17 125.00
18 FSm(c),Bondage(c),Drug 150.00
19 FSm(c) 125.00
20 Women semi-nude(c) 250.00
21 Drug 135.00
22 I:Baxter,Little Nemo 110.00
23 A:Little Nemo 110.00

PUPPET COMICS
Dougherty, Co.
Spring, 1946

1 Funny Animal 35.00
2 . . . . 30.00

PURPLE CLAW, THE
Minoan Publishing Co./ Toby Press
January, 1953

1 O:Purple Claw 125.00
2 . . . . 85.00
3 . . . . 85.00

PUZZLE FUN COMICS
George W. Dougherty Co.
Spring, 1946

1 PGn 125.00
2 . . . . 90.00

QUEEN OF THE WEST, DALE EVANS
Dell Publishing Co.
July, 1953

(1) *see Dell Four Color #479*
(1) *see Dell Four Color #528*
3 ATh, Ph(c) all 75.00
4 ATh,RsM 65.00
5 RsM 45.00
6 RsM 45.00
7 RsM 45.00
8 RsM 45.00
9 RsM 45.00
10 RsM 45.00
11 . . . . 32.00
12 RsM 40.00
13 RsM 40.00
14 RsM 40.00
15 RsM 40.00
16 RsM 40.00
17 RsM 40.00
18 RsM 40.00
19 . . . . 30.00
20 RsM 40.00
21 . . . . 30.00
22 RsM 40.00

RACKET SQUAD IN ACTION
Capitol Stories/ Charlton Comics
May-June, 1952

1 Carnival(c) 125.00
2 . . . . 60.00
3 Roulette 60.00
4 FFr(c) 60.00
5 Just off the Boat 75.00
6 The Kidnap Racket 55.00
7 . . . . 45.00
8 . . . . 45.00
9 2 Fisted fix 45.00
10 . . . . 45.00
11 SD,SD(c),Racing(c) 125.00
12 JoS,SD(c),Explosion(c) 200.00
13 JoS(c),The Notorious Modelling Agency Racket,Acid 60.00
14 DG(c),Drug 65.00
15 Photo Extortion Racket 35.00
16 thru 28 . . . . @35.00
29,March, 1958 . . . . 35.00

RAGGEDY ANN AND ANDY
Dell Publishing Co.
1942

1 Billy & Bonnie Bee 175.00
2 . . . . 85.00
3 DNo,B:Egbert Elephant 80.00
4 DNo,WK 100.00
5 DNo 75.00
6 DNo 75.00

Raggedy Ann + Andy #7
© Bobbs & Merrill Co.

7 Little Black Sambo 75.00
8 . . . . 75.00
9 . . . . 75.00
10 . . . . 75.00
11 . . . . 60.00
12 . . . . 60.00
13 . . . . 60.00
14 . . . . 60.00
15 . . . . 60.00
16 . . . . 60.00
17 . . . . 60.00
18 . . . . 60.00
19 . . . . 60.00
20 . . . . 60.00
21 Alice in Wonderland 65.00
22 thru 27 . . . . @40.00
28 WK 45.00
29 thru 39 . . . . @35.00

RALPH KINER HOME RUN KING
Fawcett Publications
1950

1 N#, Life Story of the Famous Pittsburgh Slugger . 350.00

RAMAR OF THE JUNGLE
Toby Press/ Charlton Comics
1954

1 Ph(c),TV Show 75.00
2 Ph(c) 55.00
3 . . . . 55.00
4 . . . . 55.00
5 Sept '56 . . . . 55.00

RANGE ROMANCES
Comics Magazines (Quality Comics)
December, 1949

1 PGn(c),PGn 125.00
2 RC(c),RC 150.00
3 RC,Ph(c) 90.00
4 RC,Ph(c) 75.00
5 RC,PGn,Ph(c) 75.00

RANGERS OF FREEDOM
Flying Stories, Inc. (Fiction House)
October, 1941

1 I:Ranger Girl & Rangers of Freedom;V:Super-Brain . . 900.00
2 V:Super -Brain 400.00
3 Bondage(c) The Headsman of Hate 325.00
4 Hawaiian Inferno 300.00
5 RP,V:Super-Brain 300.00
6 RP,Bondage(c);Bugles of the Damned 300.00
7 RP,Death to Tojo's Butchers 250.00

Becomes:

RANGERS COMICS

8 RP,B:US Rangers 250.00
9 GT,BLb,Commando Steel for Slant Eyes 250.00
10 BLb,Bondage (c) 275.00
11 Raiders of the Purple Death 225.00
12 A:Commando Rangers 225.00
13 GrI,B:Commando Ranger . . 225.00
14 GrI,Bondage(c) 225.00
15 GT,GrI,Bondage(c) 225.00
16 GrI,GT;Burma Raid 250.00
17 GT,GT,Bondage(c),Raiders of the Red Dawn 250.00
18 GT 250.00
19 GE,Blb,GT,Bondage(c) 200.00
20 GT 175.00
21 GT,Bondage(c) 200.00
22 GT,B&O:Firehair 175.00
23 GT,BLb,B:Kazanda 150.00
24 Bondage(c) 175.00
25 Bondage(c) 175.00
26 Angels From Hell 150.00
27 Bondage(c) 175.00
28 BLb,E:Kazanda;B&O Tiger Man 165.00
29 Bondage(c) 175.00
30 BLb,B:Crusoe Island 185.00
31 BLb,Bondage(c) 150.00
32 BLb 125.00
33 BLb,Drug 130.00
34 BLb 125.00
35 BLB,Bondage(c) 150.00
36 BLb,MB 125.00
37 BLb,Mb 125.00
38 BLb,MB,GE,Bondage(c) . . . 140.00
39 BLb,GE 100.00
40 BLb,GE,BLb(c) 100.00
41 BLb,GE 100.00
42 BLb,GE 100.00
43 BLb,GE 100.00
44 BLb,GE 100.00
45 BLb,GEI 100.00
46 BLb,GE 100.00
47 BLb,JGr 100.00
48 BLb,JGr 100.00
49 BLb,JGr 100.00
50 BLb,JGr,Bondage(c) 125.00
51 BLb,JGr 80.00
52 BLb,JGr,Bondage(c) 125.00
53 BLb,JGr,Prisoners of Devil Pass 80.00
54 JGr,When The Wild Commanches Ride 80.00
55 JGr,Massacre Guns at Pawnee Pass 80.00
56 JGr, Gun Smuggler of Apache Mesa 80.00
57 JGr,Redskins to the Rescue 80.00
58 JGr,Brides of the Buffalo Men 80.00
59 JGr,Plunder Portage 80.00
60 JGr, Buzzards of Bushwack Trail 80.00
61 BWh(c)Devil Smoke at Apache Basin 70.00
62 BWh(c)B:Cowboy Bob 70.00
63 BWh(c) 70.00
64 BWh(c)B:Suicide Smith 70.00
65 BWh(c):Wolves of the Overland Trail,Bondage(c) . . 70.00

66 BWh(c) 80.00
67 BWh(c)B:Space Rangers . . . 75.00
68 BWh(c);Cargo for Coje 75.00
69 BWh(c);Great Red Death Ray 75.00

REAL CLUE CRIME STORIES
(see CLUE COMICS)

REAL FUNNIES
Nedor Publishing Co.
January, 1943

1 (fa) 135.00
2 and 3 (fa) . . . . @65.00

REAL HEROES COMICS
Parents' Magazine Instituite
September, 1941

1 HcK,Franklin Roosevelt 150.00
2 J, Edgar Hoover 75.00
3 General Wavell 45.00
4 Chiang Kai Shek 45.00
5 Stonewall Jackson 65.00
6 Lou Gehrig 100.00
7 Chennault and his Flying Tigers 45.00
8 Admiral Nimitz 45.00
9 The Panda Man 35.00
10 Carl Akeley-Jungle Adventurer 35.00
11 Wild Jack Howard 32.00
12 General Robert L Eichelberger 30.00
13 HcK,Victory at Climback 30.00
14 Pete Gray 30.00
15 Alexander Mackenzie 30.00
16 Balto of Nome Oct '46 . . . . . 30.00

REAL LIFE STORY OF FESS PARKER
Dell Publishing Co.
1955

1 . . . . 65.00

REALISTIC ROMANCES
Avon Periodicals/ Realistic Comics
July-August, 1951

1 Ph(c) 90.00
2 Ph(c) 45.00
3 P(c) 30.00
4 P(c) 30.00
5 thru 14 . . . . @35.00
15 . . . . 25.00
16 Drug 50.00
17 . . . . 25.00

REAL LIFE COMICS
Visual Editions/Better/ Standard/Nedor
September, 1941

1 ASh(c),Lawrence of Arabia,Uncle Sam(c) 200.00
2 ASh(c),Liberty(c) 90.00
3 Adolph Hitler(c) 150.00
4 ASh(c)Robert Fulton, Charles DeGaulle 65.00
5 ASh(c)Alexander the Great . . 65.00
6 ASh(c)John Paul Jones,CDR . 55.00
7 ASh(c)Thomas Jefferson 55.00
8 Leonardo Da Vinci 55.00
9 US Coast Guard Issue 55.00
10 Sir Hubert Wilkens 55.00
11 Odyssey on a Raft 40.00
12 ImpossibleLeatherneck 40.00
13 ASh(c)The Eternal Yank 40.00
14 Sir Isaac Newton 40.00
15 William Tell 40.00
16 Marco Polo 40.00
17 Albert Einstein 40.00

Real Life Comics #12
© Visual Editions/Better/Standard

18 Ponce De Leon 40.00
19 The Fighting Seabees 40.00
20 Joseph Pulitzer 40.00
21 Admiral Farragut 35.00
22 Thomas Paine 35.00
23 Pedro Menendez 35.00
24 Babe Ruth 75.00
25 Marcus Whitman 30.00
26 Benvenuto Cellini 30.00
27 A Bomb Story 65.00
28 Robert Blake 30.00
29 Daniel DeFoe 30.00
30 Baron Robert Clive 30.00
31 Anthony Wayne 30.00
32 Frank Sinatra 35.00
33 Frederick Douglas 30.00
34 Paul Revere,Jimmy Stewart . 35.00
35 Rudyard Kipling 30.00
36 Story of the Automobile 30.00
37 Francis Manion 35.00
38 Richard Henry Dana 30.00
39 Samuel FB Morse 25.00
40 FG,ASh(c),Hans Christian Anderson 30.00
41 Abraham Lincoln,Jimmy Foxx 37.00
42 Joseph Conrad,Fred Allen . . 32.00
43 Louis Braille,O.W.Holmes . . . 30.00
44 Citizens of Tomorrow 30.00
45 ASh(c),Francois Villon 50.00
46 The Pony Express 50.00
47 ASh(c),Montezuma 30.00
48 . . . . 30.00
49 ASh(c),Gene Bearden, Baseball 35.00
50 FF,ASh(c),Lewis & Clark . . . 125.00
51 GE,ASh(c),Sam Houston . . . 75.00
52 GE,FF,ASh(c),JSe&BE Leif Erickson 135.00
53 JSe&BE,Henry Wells & William Fargo 50.00
54 GT,Alexander Graham Bell . . 50.00
55 ASh(c),JSe&BE, The James Brothers 50.00
56 JSe&BE 50.00
57 JSe&BE 50.00
58 JSe&BE,Jim Reaves 55.00
59 FF,JSe&BE,Battle Orphan Sept '52 . . . . 50.00

REAL LOVE
(see HAP HAZARD COMICS)

REAL WEST ROMANCES
Crestwood Publishing Co./ Prize Publ.
April-May, 1949

1 S&K,Ph(c) 90.00
2 Ph(c),Spanking 80.00
3 JSe,BE,Ph(c) 40.00
4 S&K,JSe,BE,Ph(c) 75.00
5 S&K,MMe,JSe,Audie Murphy Ph(c) 65.00
6 S&K,JSe,BE,Ph(c) 50.00

RECORD BOOK OF FAMOUS POLICE CASES
St. John Publishing Co.
1949

1 N#,JKu,MB(c) 200.00

RED ARROW
P.L. Publishing Co.
May,1951

1 Bondage(c) 45.00
2 . . . . 45.00
3 P(c) 35.00

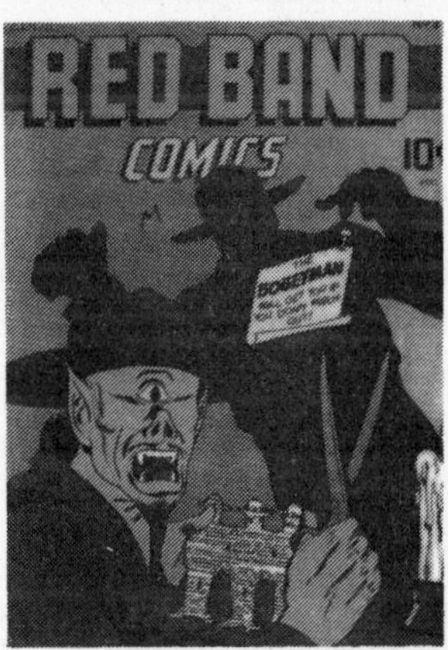

Red Band Comics #3
© Enwil Associates

RED BAND COMICS
Enwil Associates
November, 1944

1 The Bogeyman 150.00
2 O:Bogeyman,same(c)as#1 . . 125.00
3 A:Captain Wizard 110.00
4 May '45,Repof#3,Same(c) . . 110.00

RED CIRCLE COMICS
Enwil Associates (Rural Home Public)
January, 1945

1 B:Red Riot,The Prankster . . 150.00
2 LSt,A:The Judge 100.00
3 LSt,LSt(c) 75.00
4 LSt,LSt(c) covers of #4 stapled over other comics . . . 70.00

TRAIL BLAZERS
Street & Smith Publications
January, 1942

1 Wright Brothers 165.00
2 Benjamin Franklin,Dodgers . . 95.00
3 Red Barber,Yankees 100.00

4 Famous War song 75.00

Becomes:

RED DRAGON COMICS

5 JaB(c),B&O:Red Rover:
B:Capt.Jack Comkmando
Rex King&Jet,Minute Man . . 400.00
6 O:Red Dragon 350.00
7 The Curse of the
Boneless Men 250.00
8 China V:Japan 250.00
9 The Reducing Ray,Jan '44 . 250.00

November, 1947
(2nd Series)

1 B:Red Dragon 450.00
2 BP 350.00
3 BP,BP(c),I:Dr Neff 300.00
4 BP,BP(c) 400.00
5 BP,BP(c) 250.00
6 BP,BP(c) 250.00
7 BP,BP(c),May 49 . . . . 250.00

RED MASK
(see TIM HOLT)

RED RABBIT
Dearfield/
J. Charles Lave Publ. Co.
January, 1941

1 (fa) 55.00
2 . . . . 30.00
3 thru 10 . . . . @20.00
11 thru 22 . . . . @18.00

RED SEAL COMICS
Harry 'A' Chesler, Jr./Superior
October, 1945

14 GT,Bondage(c),Black Dwarf 250.00
15 GT,Torture 200.00
16 GT 250.00
17 GT,Lady Satan,Sky Chief . . 200.00
18 Lady Satan,Sky Chief 200.00
19 Lady Satan,Sky Chief 200.00
20 Lady Satan,Sky Chief 200.00
21 Lady Satan,Sky Chief 200.00
22 Rocketman 150.00

REDSKIN
Youthful Magazines
September, 1950

1 Redskin,Bondage(c) 65.00
2 Apache Dance of Death 45.00
3 Daniel Boone 30.00
4 Sitting Bull- Red Devil
of the Black Hills 30.00
5 . . . . 30.00
6 Geronimo- Terror of the
Desert,Bondage 45.00
7 Firebrand of the Sioux 30.00
8 . . . . 30.00
9 . . . . 30.00
10 Dead Man's Magic 30.00
11 . . . . 30.00
12 Quanah Parker,Bondage(c) . . 45.00

Becomes:

FAMOUS WESTERN BADMEN

13 Redskin- Last of the
Comanches 40.00
14 . . . . 25.00
15 The Dalton Boys Apr '52 . . . . 25.00

REMEMBER PEARL HARBOR
Street & Smith Publications
1942

1 N# JaB,Battle of the
Pacific,Uncle Sam(c) 250.00

RETURN OF THE OUTLAW
Minoan Publishing Co.
February, 1953

1 Billy The Kid 50.00
2 . . . . 30.00
3 thru 11 . . . . @20.00

REVEALING ROMANCES
A.A. Wyn
(Ace Magazines)
September, 1949

1 . . . . 30.00
2 . . . . 15.00
3 thru 6 . . . . @10.00

Rex Allen Comics #2 © Dell Publ. Co.

REX ALLEN COMICS
Dell Publishing Co.
February, 1951

(1) *see Dell Four Color #316*
2 Ph(c) all 60.00
3 thru 10 . . . . @45.00
11 thru 23 . . . . @35.00
24 ATh 40.00
25 thru 31 . . . . @35.00

REX DEXTER OF MARS
Fox Features Syndicate
Autumn, 1940

1 DBr,DBr(c) Battle of
Kooba 950.00

RIBTICKLER
Fox Features Syndicate
1945

1 . . . . 70.00
2 . . . . 35.00
3 Cosmo Cat 25.00
4 thru 6 . . . . @20.00
7 Cosmo Cat 22.00
8 thru 9 . . . . @20.00

RIN TIN TIN
Dell Publishing Co.
November, 1952

(1) *see Dell Four Color #434*
(1) *see Dell Four Color #476*
(1) *see Dell Four Color #523*
4 thru 10 Ph(c) all . . . . @50.00
11 thru 20 . . . . @70.00

ROCKET COMICS
Hillman Periodicals
March, 1940

1 O:Red Roberts;B:Rocket
Riley,Phantom Ranger,Steel
Shank,Buzzard Baynes,Lefty
Larson,The Defender,Man
with 1,000 Faces 1,000.00
2 500.00
3 May '40 E:All Features 600.00

ROCKET KELLY
Fox Features Syndicate
Autumn, 1945

N# 125.00
1 . . . . 125.00
2 A:The Puppeteer 90.00
3 . . . . 75.00
4 . . . . 75.00
5 Oct/Nov '46 . . . . 75.00
6 . . . . 75.00

ROCKETMAN
Ajax/Farrell Publications
June, 1952

1 Space Stories of the
Future 185.00

ROCKET SHIP X
Fox Features Syndicate
September, 1951

1 . . . . 350.00
2 N# Variant of Original 250.00

ROCKY LANE WESTERN
Fawcett/Charlton Comics
May, 1949

1 Ph(c)B:Rocky Lane,Slim
Pickins 550.00
2 Ph(c) 225.00
3 Ph(c) 160.00
4 Ph(c)CCB,Rail Riders
Rampage,F Capt Tootsie . . 150.00
5 Ph(c)The Missing
Stagecoaches 150.00
6 Ph(c)Ghost Town Showdown 125.00
7 Ph(c)The Border Revolt 135.00
8 Ph(c)The Sunset Feud 135.00
9 Ph(c)Hermit of the Hills 135.00
10 Ph(c)Badman's Reward . . . 125.00
11 Ph(c)Fool's Gold Fiasco . . . 100.00
12 Ph(c),CCB,Coyote Breed
F:Capt Tootsie,Giant 100.00
13 Ph(c),Giant 100.00
14 Ph(c) 80.00
15 Ph(c)B:Black Jacks
Hitching Post,Giant 85.00
16 Ph(c),Giant 75.00
17 Ph(c),Giant 75.00
18 Ph(c) 80.00
19 Ph(c),Giant 85.00
20 Ph(c)The Rodeo Rustler
E:Slim Pickens 85.00
21 Ph(c)B: Dee Dickens 75.00
22 Ph(c) 65.00
23 thru 30 . . . . @75.00
31 thru 40 . . . . @65.00
41 thru 55 . . . . @65.00
56 . . . . 60.00
57 thru 60 . . . . @55.00
61 thru 70 . . . . @45.00
71 thru 87 . . . . @40.00

ROD CAMERON WESTERN
Fawcett Publications
February, 1950

1 Ph(c) 350.00
2 Ph(c) 175.00
3 Ph(c),Seven Cities of Cipiola 150.00
4 Ph(c),Rip-Roaring Wild West 125.00
5 Ph(c),Six Gun Sabotage . . . 125.00
6 Ph(c),Medicine Bead Murders 125.00
7 Ph(c),Wagon Train Of Death 125.00
8 Ph(c),Bayou Badman 125.00

9 Ph(c),Rustlers Ruse 125.00
10 Ph(c),White Buffalo Trail . . . 125.00
11 Ph(c),Lead Poison 100.00
12 thru 19 Ph(c) . . . . @100.00
20 Phc(c),Great Army Hoax . . . 100.00

ROLY-POLY COMICS
Green Publishing Co.
1945

1 B:Red Rube&Steel Sterling . 175.00
6 A:Blue Cycle 90.00

Roly-Poly Comics #10
© Green Publishing

10 A:Red Rube 80.00
11 . . . . 75.00
12 . . . . 75.00
13 . . . . 75.00
14 A:Black Hood 75.00
15 A:Steel Fist;1946 . . . . 175.00

ROMANCE AND CONFESSION STORIES
St. John Publishing Co.
1949

1 MB(c),MB 200.00

ROMANTIC LOVE
Avon Periodicals/Realistic
September-October, 1949

1 P(c) 120.00
2 P(c) 60.00
3 P(c) 55.00
4 Ph(c) 55.00
5 P(c) 55.00
6 Ph(c),Drug,Thrill Crazy 80.00
7 P(c) 55.00
8 P(c) 55.00
9 EK,P(c) 65.00
10 thru 11 P(c) . . . . @50.00
12 EK 55.00
20 . . . . 50.00
21 . . . . 50.00
22 EK 60.00
23 EK 60.00

ROMANTIC MARRIAGE
Ziff-Davis/
St. John Publishing Co.
November-December, 1950

1 Ph(c),Selfish wife 85.00
2 P(c),Mother's Boy 45.00
3 P(c),Hen Peck House 40.00
4 P(c) 40.00
5 Ph(c) 40.00
6 Ph(c) 35.00
7 Ph(c) 35.00
8 P(c) 35.00
9 P(c) 35.00
10 P/PH(c) 75.00
11 . . . . 30.00
12 . . . . 30.00
13 Ph(c) 30.00
14 thru 20 . . . . @30.00
20 Ph(c) 30.00
21 . . . . 30.00
22 . . . . 30.00
23 MB 35.00
24 . . . . 30.00

ROMANTIC PICTURE NOVELETTES
Magazine Enterprises
1946

1 Mary Wothr adventure 75.00

ROMANTIC SECRETS
Fawcett Publ./Charlton Comics
September, 1949

1 Ph(c) 75.00
2 MSy(c) 35.00
3 MSy(c) 35.00
4 GE 45.00
5 BP 40.00
6 . . . . 22.00
7 BP 22.00
8 . . . . 22.00
9 GE 30.00
10 BP 25.00
11 . . . . 22.00
12 BP 25.00
13 . . . . 22.00
14 . . . . 22.00
15 . . . . 22.00
16 BP,MSy 25.00
17 BP 25.00
18 . . . . 20.00
19 . . . . 20.00
20 BP.MBi 25.00
21 . . . . 18.00
22 . . . . 18.00
23 . . . . 15.00
24 GE 35.00
25 MSy 15.00
26 BP,MSy 18.00
27 MSy 15.00
28 . . . . 15.00
29 BP 18.00
30 thru 32 . . . . @15.00
33 MSy 18.00
34 BP 18.00
35 . . . . 12.00
36 BP 18.00
37 BP 18.00
38 thru 52 . . . . @15.00

ROMANTIC STORY
Fawcett Publ./Charlton Comics
November, 1949

1 Ph(c) 75.00
2 Ph(c) 40.00
3 Ph(c) 30.00
4 Ph(c) 30.00
5 Ph(c) 30.00
6 Ph(c) 30.00
7 BP,Ph(c) 25.00
8 BP,Ph(c) 25.00
9 Ph(c) 22.00
10 Ph(c) 22.00
11 Ph(c) 22.00
12 Ph(c) 22.00
13 Ph(c) 22.00
14 Ph(c) 22.00
15 GE,Ph(c) 35.00
16 BP,Ph(c) 25.00
17 Ph(c) 20.00
18 Ph(c) 20.00
19 Ph(c) 20.00
20 BP,Ph(c) 22.00
22 ATh,Ph(c) 18.00

Charlton Comics

23 . . . . 15.00
24 Ph(c) 15.00
25 thru 29 . . . . @15.00
30 BP 20.00
31 thru 39 . . . . @15.00

ROMANTIC WESTERN
Fawcett Publications
Winter, 1949

1 Ph(c) 90.00
2 Ph(c),AW,AMc 100.00
3 Ph(c) 75.00

ROMEO TUBBS
(see MY SECRET LIFE)

ROUNDUP
D.S. Publishing Co.
July-August, 1948

1 HcK 100.00
2 Drug 75.00
3 . . . . 50.00
4 . . . . 50.00
5 Male Bondage 55.00

ROY CAMPANELLA, BASEBALL HERO
Fawcett Publications
1950

N# Ph(c),Life Story of the Battling Dodgers Catcher . . 400.00

Roy Campanella #1 (nn)
© Fawcett Publ.

ROY ROGERS
Dell Publishing Co.

1 photo (c) 400.00
2 . . . . 175.00
3 . . . . 160.00
4 . . . . 150.00
5 . . . . 10.00
6 thru 10 . . . . @125.00
11 thru 20 . . . . @75.00
21 thru 30 . . . . @65.00
31 thru 46 . . . . @50.00
47 thru 50 . . . . @40.00
51 thru 56 . . . . @35.00
57 Drug 45.00
58 thru 70 . . . . @35.00

71 thru 80 . . . . @30.00
81 thru 91 . . . . @25.00
Becomes:

ROY ROGERS AND TRIGGER

92 thru 99 . . . . @25.00
100 . . . . 40.00
101 thru 118 . . . . @25.00
119 thru 125 ATn . . . . @40.00
126 thru 131 . . . . @30.00
132 thru 144 RsM . . . . @35.00
145 . . . . 40.00

ROY ROGER'S TRIGGER
Dell Publishing Co.
May, 1951

(1) *see Dell Four Color #329*
2 Ph(c) 75.00
3 P(c) 20.00
4 P(c) 20.00
5 P(c) 20.00
6 thru 17 P(c) . . . . @12.00

RULAH, JUNGLE GODDESS
(see ZOOT COMICS)

SAARI, THE JUNGLE GODDESS
P.L. Publishing Co.
November, 1951

1 The Bantu Blood Curse . . . 200.00

SABU, ELEPHANT BOY
Fox Features Syndicate
June, 1950

1(30) WW,Ph(c) 125.00
2 JKa,Ph(c),August'50 . . . . 75.00

Saddle Justice #7

© Fables Publications/E.C. Comics

HAPPY HOULIHANS
Fables Publications
(E.C. Comics)
Autumn, 1947

1 O:Moon Girl 150.00
2 . . . . 135.00
Becomes:

SADDLE JUSTICE

3 HcK,JCr,AF 300.00
4 AF,JCr 275.00
5 AF,Grl,WI 250.00
6 AF,Grl 250.00
7 AF,Grl 250.00
8 AF,Grl,WI 250.00
Becomes:

SADDLE ROMANCES

9 Grl(c),Grl 300.00
10 AF(c),WW 325.00
11 AF(c),Grl 275.00

SAINT, THE
Avon Periodicals
August, 1947

1 JKa,JKa(c),Bondage(c) 350.00
2 . . . . 175.00
3 Rolled Stocking Leg(c) 150.00
4 MB(c) 125.00
5 Spanking Panel 200.00
6 B:Miss Fury 225.00
7 P(c),Detective Cases(c) 125.00
8 P(c),Detective Cases"(c) . . . 110.00
9 EK(c),The Notorious Murder Mob 110.00
10 WW,P(c),V:The Communist Menace 125.00
11 P(c),Wanted For Robbery . . . 75.00
12 P(c),The Blowpipe Murders March, 1952 . . . . 110.00

SAM HILL PRIVATE EYE
Close-Up Publications
1950

1 The Double Trouble Caper . . 75.00
2 . . . . 45.00
3 . . . . 40.00
4 Negligee panels 55.00
5 . . . . 35.00
6 . . . . 35.00
7 . . . . 35.00

SAMSON
Fox Features Syndicate
Autumn, 1940

1 BP,GT,A:Wing Turner 700.00
2 BP,A:Dr. Fung 350.00
3 JSh(c),A:Navy Jones 300.00
4 WE,B:Yarko 225.00
5 WE 225.00
6 WE,O:The Topper;Sept'41 . 225.00

SAMSON
Ajax Farrell Publ
(Four Star)
April, 1955

12 The Electric Curtain 125.00
13 Assignment Danger 90.00
14 The Red Raider;Aug'55 . . . . 85.00

SANDS OF THE SOUTH PACIFIC
Toby Press
January, 1953

1 2-Fisted Romantic Adventure 90.00

SCHOOL DAY ROMANCES
(see POPULAR TEEN-AGERS)

SCIENCE COMICS
Fox Features Syndicate
February, 1940

1 GT,LF(c),O&B:Electro,Perisphere Payne,The Eagle,Navy Jones; B:Marga,Cosmic Carson, Dr. Doom; Bondage(c) . . . 1,600.00
2 GT,LF(c) 800.00
3 GT,LF(c),Dynamo 625.00
4 JK,Cosmic Carson 625.00
5 Giant Comiscope Offer Eagle(c) 450.00
6 Dynamop(c) 450.00

Science Comics #3

© Fox Features Syndicate

7 Bondage(c),Dynamo 450.00
8 September, 1940 Eagle(c) . . 400.00

SCIENCE COMICS
Humor Publications
January, 1946

1 RP(c),Story of the A-Bomb . . 65.00
2 RP(c),How Museum Pieces Are Assembled 30.00
3 AF,RP(c),How Underwater Tunnels Are Made 65.00
4 RP(c),Behind the Scenes at A TV Broadcast 25.00
5 The Story of the World's Bridges; September, 1946 . . 30.00

SCIENCE COMICS
Ziff-Davis Publ. Co.
May, 1946

N# Used For A Mail Order Test Market 225.00

SCIENCE COMICS
Export Publication Enterprises
March, 1951

1 How to resurrect a dead rat . . 40.00

SCOOP COMICS
Harry 'A' Chesler Jr.
November, 1941

1 I&B:Rocketman&Rocketgirl;B:Dan Hastings;O&B:Master Key . 450.00
2 A:Rocketboy,Eye Injury 250.00
3 Partial rep. of #2 . . . . 225.00
4 thru 7 do not exist
8 1945 . . . . 150.00

SCREAM COMICS
Humor Publ./Current Books
(Ace Magazines)
Autumn, 1944

1 . . . . 60.00
2 . . . . 30.00
3 . . . . 25.00
4 thru 15 . . . . @25.00
16 I:Lily Belle 28.00
17 . . . . 20.00
18 Drug 35.00
19 . . . . 20.00
Becomes:

ANDY COMICS

20 Teenage 25.00
21 . . . . 25.00

Becomes:

ERNIE COMICS

22 Teenage 30.00
23 thru 25 . . . . @20.00

Becomes:

ALL LOVE ROMANCES

26 Ernie 25.00
27 LbC 32.00
28 thru 32 . . . . @15.00

(Capt. Silvers Log of...) SEA HOUND, THE

Avon Periodicals
1945

N# The Esmerelda's Treasure . 70.00
2 Adventures in Brazil 50.00
3 Louie the Llama 50.00
4 In Greed & Vengence; Jan-Feb, 1946 . . . . 50.00

SECRET LOVES

Comics Magazines (Quality Comics)
November, 1949

1 BWa(c) 100.00
2 BWa(c),Lingerie(c) 85.00
3 RC 60.00
4 . . . . 35.00
5 Boom Town Babe 40.00
6 . . . . 35.00

SECRET MYSTERIES (see CRIME MYSTERIES)

SELECT DETECTIVE

D.S. Publishing Co.
August-September, 1948

1 MB,Exciting New Mystery Cases 90.00
2 MB,AMc,Dead Men.... . . . . . . 70.00
3 Face in theFrame;Dec-Jan'48 60.00

SERGEANT PRESTON OF THE YUKON

Dell Publishing Co.
August, 1951

(1 thru 4) *see Dell Four Color #344; #373, 397, 419*
5 thru 10 P(c) . . . . @35.00
11 P(c) 30.00
12 P(c) 30.00
13 P(c),O:Sergeant Preston 35.00
14 thru 17 P(c) . . . . @30.00
18 P(c) 35.00
19 thru 29 Ph(c) . . . . @35.00

SEVEN SEAS COMICS

Universal Phoenix Features/ Leader Publ.
April, 1946

1 MB,RWb(c),B:South Sea Girl, Captain Cutlass 300.00
2 MB,RWb(c) 275.00
3 MB,AF,MB(c) 250.00
4 MB,MB(c) 250.00
5 MB,MB(c),Hangman's Noose 250.00
6 MB,MB(c);1947 . . . . 250.00

SHADOW COMICS

Street & Smith Publications
March, 1940

1-1 P(c),B:Shadow,Doc Savage, Bill Barnes,Nick Carter, Frank Merriwell,Iron Munro 3,000.00
1-2 P(c),B: The Avenger 1,200.00
1-3 P(c),A: Norgill the Magician 800.00
1-4 P(c),B:The Three

Seven Seas Comics #6 © Universal Phoenix Features/Leader Publ

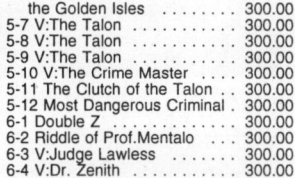

Musketeers 850.00
1-5 P(c),E: Doc Savage 850.00
1-6 A: Captain Fury 700.00
1-7 O&B: The Wasp 750.00
1-8 A:Doc Savage 550.00
1-9 A:Norgill the Magician . . . 550.00
1-10 O:Iron Ghost;B:The Dead End Kids 550.00
1-11 O:Hooded Wasp 600.00
1-12 Crime Does Not pay 500.00
2-1 . . . . 500.00
2-2 Shadow Becomes Invisible 500.00
2-3 O&B:supersnipe; F:Little Nemo 600.00
2-4 F:Little Nemo 500.00
2-5 V:The Ghost Faker 500.00
2-6 A:Blackstone the Magician 400.00
2-7 V:The White Dragon 400.00
2-8 A:Little Nemo 400.00
2-9 The Hand of Death 400.00
2-10 A:Beebo the WonderHorse 400.00
2-11 V:Devil Kyoti 400.00
2-12 V:Devil Kyoti 350.00
3-1 JaB(c),V:Devil Kyoti 350.00
3-2 Red Skeleton Life Story . . 350.00
3-3 V:Monstrodamus 350.00
3-4 V:Monstrodamus 350.00
3-5 V:Monstrodamus 350.00
3-6 V:Devil's of the Deep 350.00
3-7 V: Monstrodamus 350.00
3-8 E: The Wasp 350.00
3-9 The Stolen Lighthouse . . . 350.00
3-10 A:Doc Savage 350.00
3-11 P(c),V: Thade 350.00
3-12 V: Thade 350.00
4-1 Red Cross Appeal on (c) . 350.00
4-2 V:The Brain of Nippon . . . 350.00
4-3 Little Men in Space 350.00
4-4 ...Mystifies Berlin 350.00
4-5 ...Brings Terror to Tokio . . 350.00
4-6 V:The Tarantula 350.00
4-7 Crypt of the Seven Skulls . 350.00
4-8 V:the Indigo Mob 350.00
4-9 Ghost Guarded Treasure of the Haunted Glen 350.00
4-10 V:The Hydra 350.00
4-11 V:The Seven Sinners 350.00
4-12 Club Curio 300.00
5-1 A:Flatty Foote 300.00
5-2 Bells of Doom 300.00
5-3 The Circle of Death 300.00
5-4 The Empty Safe Riddle . . . 300.00
5-5 The Mighty Master Nomad . 300.00
5-6 ...Fights Piracy Among the Golden Isles 300.00
5-7 V:The Talon 300.00
5-8 V:The Talon 300.00
5-9 V:The Talon 300.00
5-10 V:The Crime Master 300.00
5-11 The Clutch of the Talon . . 300.00
5-12 Most Dangerous Criminal . 300.00
6-1 Double Z 300.00
6-2 Riddle of Prof.Mentalo . . . 300.00
6-3 V:Judge Lawless 300.00
6-4 V:Dr. Zenith 300.00

Shadow Comics #65 (6/5) © Street & Smith Publications

6-5 . . . . 300.00
6-6 ...Invades the Crucible of Death 300.00
6-7 Four Panel Cover 300.00
6-8 Crime Among the Aztecs . 300.00
6-9 I:Shadow Jr. 350.00
6-10 Devil's Passage 300.00
6-11 The Black Pagoda 300.00
6-12 BP,BP(c),Atomic Bomb Secrets Stolen 325.00
7-1 The Yellow Band 325.00
7-2 A:Shadow Jr. 325.00
7-3 BP,BP(c),Crime Under the Border 350.00
7-4 BP,BP(c),One Tree Island, Atomic Bomb 375.00
7-5 A:Shadow Jr. 325.00
7-6 BP,BP(c),The Sacred Sword of Sanjorojo 350.00
7-7 Crime K.O. 350.00
7-8 ...Raids Crime Harbor 350.00
7-9 BP.BP(c),Kilroy Was Here 350.00
7-10 BP,BP(c),The Riddle of the Flying Saucer 400.00
7-11 BP,BP(c),Crime Doesn't Pay 350.00
7-12 BP,BP(c)Back From the Grave 350.00
8-1 BP,BP(c),Curse of the Cat 350.00
8-2 BP,BP(c),Decay,Vermin & Murder in the Bayou 350.00
8-3 BP,BP(c),The Spider Boy . 350.00
8-4 BP,BP(c),Death Rises Out of the Sea 350.00
8-5 BP,BP(c),Jekyll-Hyde Murders 350.00
8-6 Secret of Valhalla Hall . . . 350.00
8-7 BP,BP(c),Shadow in Danger 350.00
8-8 BP,BP(c),...Solves a Twenty Year Old Crime . . . 350.00
8-9 BP,BP(c),3-D Effect(c) 350.00
8-10 BP,BP(c),Up&Down(c) . . . 350.00
8-11 BP,BP(c) 350.00

8-12 BP,BP(c),Arabs,Boat(c) . . 350.00
9-1 Airport(c) 350.00
9-2 BP,BP(c),Flying Cannon(c) 350.00
9-3 BP,BP(c),Shadow's Shadow 350.00
9-4 BP,BP(c) 350.00
9-5 Death in the Stars;Aug'49 . 350.00

SHARP COMICS
H.C. Blackerby
Winter, 1945

1 O:Planetarian(c) 200.00
2 O:The Pioneer 175.00

Sheena Queen of the Jungle #16
© Real Adventures/Fiction House

SHEENA, QUEEN OF THE JUNGLE
Real Adventures (Fiction House)
Spring, 1942

1 Blood Hunger 1,000.00
2 Black Orchid of Death 750.00
3 Harem Shackles 450.00
4 The Zebra Raiders 350.00
5 War of the Golden Apes . . . 275.00
6 . . . . 275.00
7 They Claw By Night 225.00
8 The Congo Colossus 225.00
9 and 10 . . . . @200.00
11 Red Fangs of the Tree Tribe 200.00
12 . . . . 175.00
13 Veldt o/t Voo Doo Lions . . . 175.00
14 The Hoo Doo Beasts of Mozambique 175.00
15 . . . . 175.00
16 Black Ivory 175.00
17 Great Congo Treasure Trek 175.00
18 Doom of the Elephant Drum Winter, 1952 . . . . 175.00

SHIELD-WIZARD COMICS
MLJ Magazines
Summer, 1940

1 IN,EA,O:Shield 1,500.00
2 O:Shield;I:Roy 655.00
3 Roy,Child Bondage(c) 450.00
4 Shield,Roy,Wizard 425.00
5 B:Dusty-Boy Dectective,Child Bondage 400.00
6 B:Roy the Super Boy,Child Bondage 350.00
7 Shield(c),Roy Bondage(c) . . 350.00
8 Bondage(c) 350.00
9 Shield/Roy(c) 325.00
10 Shield/Roy(c) 325.00
11 Shield/Roy(c) 325.00
12 Shield/Roy(c) 325.00
13 Bondage (c);Spring'44 . . . . 350.00

SHIP AHOY
Spotlight Publishers
November, 1944

1 LbC(c) 60.00

SHOCK DETECTIVE CASE
(see CRIMINALS ON THE RUN)

SHOCK DETECTIVE CASES
(see CRIMINALS ON THE RUN)

SHOCK SUSPENSTORIES
Tiny Tot Comics (E.C. Comics)
February-March, 1952

1 JDa,JKa,AF(c),ElectricChair . 650.00
2 WW,JDa,Grl,JKa,WW(c) . . . 350.00
3 WW,JDa,JKa,WW(c) 300.00
4 WW,JDa,JKa,WW(c) 300.00
5 WW,JDa,JKa,WW(c),Hanging 250.00
6 WW,AF,JKa,WW(c), Bondage(c) 300.00
7 JKa,WW,GE,AF(c),Face Melting 300.00
8 JKa,AF,AW,GE,WW,AF(c) . . 300.00
9 JKa,AF,RC,WW,AF(c) 300.00
10 JKa,WW,RC,JKa(c),Drug . . 300.00
11 JCr,JKa,WW,RC,JCr(c) 275.00
12 AF,JKa,WW,RC,AF(c)Drug(c) 300.00
13 JKa,WW,FF,JKa(c) 350.00
14 JKa,WW,BK,WW(c) 275.00
15 JKa,WW,RC,JDa(c) Strangulation 225.00
16 GE,RC,JKa,GE(c),Rape . . . 225.00
17 GE,RC,JKa,GE(c) 200.00
18 GE,RC,JKa,GE(c);Jan'55 . . 200.00

SHOCKING MYSTERY CASES
(see THRILLING CRIME CASES)

SILVER STREAK COMICS
Your Guide/New Friday/ Comic House/Newsbrook Publications/Lev Gleason
December, 1939

1 JCo,JCo(c),I&B:The Claw,Red Reeves Capt.Fearless;B:Mr. Midnight,Wasp;A:Spiritman 6,000.00
2 JSm,JCo,JSm(c) 1,600.00
3 JaB(c),I&O:Silver Streak; B:Dickie Dean,Lance Hale, Ace Powers,Bill Wayne, Planet Patrol 1,400.00
4 JCo,JaB(c)B:Sky Wolf; N:Silver Streak,I:Lance Hale's Sidekick-Jackie 750.00
5 JCo,JCo(c),Dickie Dean V:The Raging Flood 850.00
6 JCo,JaB,JCo(c),O&I:Daredevil [Blue & Yellow Costume]; R:The Claw 4,500.00
7 JCo,N: Daredevil 3,500.00
8 JCo,JCo(c) 1,100.00
9 JCo,BoW(c) 900.00
10 BoW,BoW(c) 700.00
11 DRi(c) I:Mercury 500.00
12 DRi(c) 450.00
13 JaB,JaB(c),O:Thun-Dohr . . . 450.00
14 JaB,JaB(c),A:Nazi Skull Men 450.00

Silver Streak #14
© Your Guide/New Friday

15 JaB,DBr,JaB(c), B:Bingham Boys 400.00
16 DBr,BoW(c) 400.00
17 DBr,JaB(c),E:Daredevil 400.00
18 DBr,JaB(c),B:The Saint 350.00
19 DBr,EA 250.00
20 BW,BEv,EA 250.00
21 BW,BEv 250.00

Becomes:

CRIME DOES NOT PAY

22(23) CBi(c),The Mad Musician & Tunes of Doom 1,000.00
23 CBi(c),John Dillinger-One Man Underworld 550.00
24 CBi(c),The Mystery of the Indian Dick 455.00
25 CBi(c),Dutch Shultz-King of the Underworld 250.00
26 CBi(c),Lucky Luciano-The Deadliest of Crime Rats . . . 250.00
27 CBi(c),Pretty Boy Floyd . . . 250.00
28 CBi(c), ... 250.00
29 CBi(c),Two-Gun Crowley-The Bad Kid with the Itchy Trigger Finger 225.00
30 CBi(c),"Monk"Eastman V:Thompson's Mob 225.00
31 CBi(c) The Million Dollar Bank Robbery 165.00
32 CBi(c),Seniorita of Sin . . . 165.00
33 CBi(c),Meat Cleaver Murder 165.00
34 CBi(c),Elevator Shaft 165.00
35 CBi(c),Case o/t MissingToe . 165.00
36 CBi(c) 150.00
37 CBi(c) 150.00
38 CBi(c) 150.00
39 FG,CBi(c) 150.00
40 FG,CBi(c) 150.00
41 FG,RP,CBi(c),The Cocksure Counterfeiter 100.00
42 FG,RP,CBi(c) 125.00
43 FG,RP,CBi(c) 75.00
44 FG,CBi(c),The Most Shot At Gangster 75.00
45 FG,CBi(c) 75.00
46 FG,CBi(c),ChildKidnapping(c) 80.00
47 FG,CBi(c),ElectricChair 125.00
48 FG,CBi(c) 75.00
49 FG,CBi(c) 75.00
50 FG,CBi(c) 75.00
51 FG,GT,CBi(c),1st Monthly Iss. 60.00
52 FG,GT,CBi(c) 60.00
53 FG,CBi(c) 60.00

54 FG,CBi(c) 60.00
55 FG,CBi(c) 60.00
56 FG,GT,CBi(c) 60.00
57 FG,CBi(c) 60.00
58 FG,CBi(c) 60.00
59 FG,Cbi(c) 60.00
60 FG,CBi(c) 60.00
61 FG,GT,CBi(c) 50.00
62 FG,CBi(c),Bondage(c) 65.00
63 FG,GT,CBi(c) 50.00
64 FG,GT,CBi(c) 50.00
65 FG,CBi(c) 50.00
66 FG,GT,CBi(c) 50.00
67 FG,GT,CBi(c) 50.00
68 FG,CBi(c) 50.00
69 FG,CBi(c) 50.00
70 FG,Cbi(c) 50.00
71 FG,CBi(c) 40.00
72 FG,CBi(c) 40.00
73 FG,CBi(c) 40.00
74 FG,CBi(c) 40.00
75 FG,CBi(c) 40.00
76 FG,CBI(c) 40.00
77 FG,CBi(c),The Electrified Safe 45.00
78 FG,CBi(c) 40.00
79 FG 40.00
80 FG 40.00
81 FG 40.00
82 FG 40.00
83 FG 40.00
84 FG 40.00
85 FG 40.00
86 FG 35.00
87 FG,P(c),The Rock-A-Bye Baby Murder 35.00
88 FG,P(c),Death Carries a Torch 35.00
89 FG,BF,BF P(c),The Escort Murder Case 35.00
90 FG,BF P(c),The Alhambra Club Murders 35.00
91 FG,AMc,BF P(c),Death Watches The Clock 35.00
92 BF,FG,BF P(c) 35.00
93 BF,FG,AMc,BF P(c) 35.00
94 BF,FG,BF P(c) 35.00
95 FG,AMc,BF P(c) 35.00
96 BF,FG,BF P(c),The Case of the Movie Star's Double 35.00
97 FG,BF P(c) 35.00
98 BF,FG,BF P(c),Bondage(c) 35.00
99 BF,FG,BF P(c) 35.00
100 FG,BF,AMc,P(c),The Case of the Jittery Patient 50.00
101 FG,BF,AMc,P(c) 30.00
102 FG,BF,AMc,BF P(c) 30.00
103 FG,BF,AMc,BF P(c) 30.00
104 thru 110 FG @30.00
111 thru 120 @30.00
121 thru 140 @320.00
141 JKu 25.00
142 JKu,CBi(c) 25.00
143 JKu,Comic Code 20.00
144 I Helped Capture"Fat Face" George Klinerz 15.00
145 RP,Double Barrelled Menace 15.00
146 BP,The Con & The Canary 15.00
147 JKu,BP,A Long Shoe On the Highway;July, 1955 20.00

SINGLE SERIES
United Features Syndicate
1938

1 Captain & The Kids 450.00
2 Bronco Bill 300.00
3 Ella Cinders 225.00
4 Li'l Abner 400.00
5 Fritzi Ritz 175.00
6 Jim Hardy 225.00
7 Frankie Doodle 175.00
8 Peter Pat 175.00
9 Strange As it Seems 175.00
10 Little Mary Mixup 150.00
11 Mr. & Mrs. Beans 150.00
12 Joe Jinx 125.00
13 Looy Dot Dope 125.00
14 Billy Make Believe 125.00
15 How It Began 125.00
16 Illustrated Gags 125.00
17 Danny Dingle 125.00
18 Li'l Abner 300.00
19 Broncho Bill 225.00
20 Tarzan 700.00
21 Ella Cinders 200.00
22 Iron Vic 150.00
23 Tailspin Tommy 175.00
24 Alice In Wonderland 225.00
25 Abbie an' Slats 175.00
26 Little Mary Mixup 150.00
27 Jim Hardy 150.00
28 Ella Cinders & Abbie AN' Slats 1942 175.00

SKELETON HAND
American Comics Group
September-October, 1952

1 175.00
2 The Were-Serpent of Karnak 125.00
3 Waters of Doom 100.00
4 Black Dust 100.00
5 The Rise & Fall of the Bogey Man 100.00
6 July-August, 1953 100.00

SKY BLAZERS
Hawley Publications
September, 1940

1 Flying Aces,Sky Pirates 225.00
2 November, 1940 200.00

SKYMAN
Columbia Comics Group
1941

1 OW,OW(c),O:Skyman,Face 450.00
2 OW,OW(c),Yankee Doodle 250.00
3 OW,OW(c) 175.00
4 OW,OW(c),Statue of Liberty(c) 1948 175.00

SKY PILOT
Ziff-Davis Publishing Co.
1950

10 NS P(c),Lumber Pirates 65.00
11 Ns P(c),The 2,00 Foot Drop; April-May, 1951 55.00

SKY ROCKET
Home Guide Publ.
(Harry 'A' Chesler)
1944

1 Alias the Dragon,Skyrocket 125.00

SKY SHERIFF
D.S. Publishing
Summer, 1948

1 I:Breeze Lawson & the Prowl Plane Patrol 65.00

SLAM BANG COMICS
Fawcett Publications
January, 1940

1 B:Diamond Jack,Mark Swift,LeeGranger,JungleKing 700.00
2 F:Jim Dolan Two-Fisted Crime Buster 350.00
3 A: Eric the Talking Lion 450.00
4 F: Hurricane Hansen-Sea Adventurer 300.00
5 300.00
6 I: Zoro the Mystery Man; Bondage(c) 350.00
7 Bondage(c);Sept., 1940 350.00

SLAPSTICK COMICS
Comic Magazine Distrib., Inc.
1945

N# Humorous Parody 100.00

SLAVE GIRL COMICS
Avon Periodicals
February, 1949

1 500.00
2 April, 1949 325.00

SLICK CHICK COMICS
Leader Enterprises, Inc.
1947

1 Teen-Aged Humor 65.00
2 Teen-Aged Humor 45.00
3 1947 45.00

SMASH COMICS
Comics Magazine, Inc.
(Quality Comics Group)
August, 1939

1 WE,O&B:Hugh Hazard, Bozo the Robot,Black X, Invisible Justice: B:Wings Wendall, Chic Carter 900.00
2 WE,A:Lone Star Rider 350.00
3 WE,B:Captain Cook,JohnLaw 250.00
4 WE,PGn,B:Flash Fulton 225.00
5 WE,PGn,Bozo Robot 225.00
6 WE,PGn,GFx,Black X(c) 225.00
7 WE,PGn,GFx,Wings Wendell(c) 200.00
8 WE,PGn,GFx,Bozo Robot 200.00
9 WE,PGn,GFx,Black X(c) 200.00
10 WE,PGn,GFx,Bozo robot(c) 200.00
11 WE,PGn,GFx,BP,Black X(c) 200.00
12 WE,PGn,GFx,BP,Bozo(c) 200.00
13 WE,PGn,GFx,AB,BP,B:Mango, Purple Trio,BlackX(c) 200.00
14 BP,LF,AB,PGn,I:The Ray 1,000.00
15 BP,LF,AB,PGn,The Ram(c) 500.00

Smash Comics #43
© Comics Magazine/Quality Comics

16 BP,LF,AB,PGn,Bozo(c) 500.00
17 BP,LF,AB,PGn,JCo, The Ram(c) 500.00
18 BP,LF,AB,JCo,PGn, B&O:Midnight 600.00
19 BP,LF,AB,JCo,PGn,Bozo(c) 350.00
20 BP,LF,AB,JCo,PGn, The Ram(c) 350.00
21 BP,LF,AB,JCo,PGn 350.00
22 BP,LF,AB,JCo,PGn, B:The Jester 350.00
23 BP,AB,JCo,RC,PGn, The Ram(c) 300.00
24 BP,AB,JCo,RC,PGn,A:Sword,

E:ChicCarter,
N:WingsWendall 300.00
25 AB,JCo,RC,PGn,O:Wildfire . 375.00
26 AB,JCo,RC,PGn,Bozo(c) . . 275.00
27 AB,JCo,RC,PGn,The Ram(c) 275.00
28 AB,JCo,RC,PGn,
1st Midnight (c) 275.00
29 AB,JCo,Rc,PGn,B;Midnight(c) 250.00
30 AB,JCo,PGn 250.00
31 AB,JCo,PGn 200.00
32 AB,JCo,PGn 200.00
33 AB,JCo,PGn,O:Marksman . . 275.00
34 AB,JCo,PGn 200.00
35 AB,JCo,RC,PGn 200.00
36 AB,JCo,RC,PGn,E:Midnight(c)250.00
37 AB,JCo,RC,PGn,Doc
Wacky becomes Fastest
Human on Earth 250.00
38 JCo,RC,PGn,B:Yankee Eagle 225.00
39 PGn,B:Midnight(c) 175.00
40 PGn,E:Ray 175.00
41 PGn 75.00
42 PGn,B:Lady Luck 85.00
43 PGn 100.00
44 PGn 85.00
45 PGn,E:Midnight(c) 85.00
46 RC,Twelve Hours to Live . . . 85.00
47 Wanted Midnight,
Dead or Alive 85.00
48 Midnight Meets the
Menace from Mars 85.00
49 PGn,FG,Mass of Muscle 85.00
50 I:Hyram the Hermit 85.00
51 A:Wild Bill Hiccup 75.00
52 PGn,FG,Did Ancient Rome Fall,
or was it Pushed? 75.00
53 Is ThereHonorAmongThieves 75.00
54 A:Smear-Faced Schmaltz . . . 75.00
55 Never Trouble Trouble until
Trouble Troubles You 75.00
56 The Laughing Killer 75.00
57 A Dummy that Turns Into
A Curse 75.00
58 . . . . 75.00
59 A Corpse that Comes Alive . . 75.00
60 The Swooner & the Trush . . . 75.00
61 . . . . 60.00
62 V:The Lorelet 60.00
63 PGn 60.00
64 PGn,In Search of King Zoris . 60.00
65 PGn,V:Cyanide Cindy 60.00
66 Under Circle's Spell 60.00
67 A Living Clue 60.00
68 JCo,Atomic Dice 60.00
69 JCo,V:Sir Nuts 60.00
70 . . . . 60.00
71 . . . . 55.00
72 JCo,Angela,the Beautiful
Bovine 55.00
73 . . . . 55.00
74 . . . . 55.00
75 The Revolution 55.00
76 Bowl Over Crime 55.00
77 Who is Lilli Dilli? 55.00
78 JCo,Win Over Crime 55.00
79 V:The Men From Mars 55.00
80 JCo,V:Big Hearted Bosco . . . 55.00
81 V:Willie the Kid 55.00
82 V:Woodland Boy 55.00
83 JCo,Quizmaster 55.00
84 A Date With Father Time . . . 55.00
85 JCo,A Singing Swindle 55.00

SMASH HITS SPORTS COMICS
Essankay Publications
January, 1949

1 LbC,LbC(c) 100.00

SMILEY BURNETTE WESTERN
Fawcett Publications
March, 1950

1 Ph(c),B:Red Eagle 375.00
2 Ph(c) 200.00
3 Ph(c) 200.00
4 Ph(c) 200.00

SMILIN' JACK
Dell Publishing Co.
1940

1 . . . . 75.00
2 . . . . 45.00
3 thru 8 . . . . @35.00

SMITTY
Dell Publishing Co.
1940

1 . . . . 65.00
2 . . . . 40.00
3 . . . . 25.00
4 thru 7 . . . . @20.00

SNAP
Harry 'A' Chesler Jr. Publications
1944

N# Humorous 75.00

SNAPPY COMICS
Cima Publications (Prize)
1945

1 A:Animale 110.00

SNIFFY THE PUP
Animated Cartoons (Standard Comics)
November, 1949

5 FF,Funny Animal 50.00
6 thru 9 Funny Animal . . . . . @20.00
10 thru 17 Funny Animal . . . . @15.00
18 September, 1953 . . . . 15.00

SOLDIER COMICS
Fawcett Publications
January, 1952

1 Fighting Yanks on Flaming
Battlefronts 50.00
2 Blazing Battles Exploding
with Combat 25.00
3 . . . . 25.00
4 A Blow for Freedom 20.00
5 Only The Dead Are Free . . . 20.00
6 Blood & Guts 15.00
7 The Phantom Sub 15.00
8 More Plasma! 15.00
9 Red Artillery 15.00
10 . . . . 15.00
11 September, 1953 . . . . 15.00

SOLDIERS OF FORTUNE
Creston Publications (American Comics Group)
February-March, 1952

1 OW(c),B:Ace Carter,
Crossbones, Lance Larson 125.00
2 OW(c) 75.00
3 OW(c) 60.00
4 . . . . 60.00
5 OW(c) 60.00
6 OW(c),OW,Bondage(c) 65.00
7 . . . . 60.00
8 OW 60.00
9 OW 60.00
10 OW 60.00
11 OW,Format Change to War . 25.00
12 . . . . 25.00
13 OW,February-March, 1953 . . 25.00

SON OF SINBAD
St. John Publishing Co.
February, 1950

1 JKu,JKu(c),The Curse of the
Caliph's Dancer 250.00

STEVE SAUNDERS SPECIAL AGENT
Parents Magazine/ Commended Comics
December, 1947

1 J. Edgar Hoover, Ph(c) 50.00
2 . . . . 25.00
3 thru 7 . . . . @20.00
8 September, 1949 . . . . 20.00

SPACE ACTION
Junior Books (Ace Magazines)
June, 1952

1 Invaders from a Lost Galaxy 350.00
2 The Silicon Monster from
Galaxy X 275.00
3 Attack on Ishtar,
October, 1952 . . . . 250.00

SPACE ADVENTURES
Capitol Stories/ Charlton Comics
July, 1952

1 AFa&LM(c) 250.00
2 . . . . 100.00
3 DG(c) 85.00
4 DG(c) 75.00
5 StC(c) 75.00
6 StC(c),Two Worlds 70.00
7 DG(c),Transformation 85.00
8 DG(c),All For Love 70.00
9 DG(c) 70.00
10 SD,SD(c) 200.00
11 SD,JoS 225.00
12 SD(c) 225.00
13 A:Blue Beetle 75.00
14 A:Blue Beetle 75.00
15 Ph(c) of Rocky Jones 75.00
16 BKa,A:Rocky Jones 100.00
17 A:Rocky Jones 75.00
18 A:Rocky Jones 75.00
19 . . . . 60.00
20 First Trip to the Moon 150.00
21 . . . . 65.00
22 Does Not Exist
23 SD,Space Trip to the Moon . 125.00
24 . . . . 85.00
25 Brontosaurus 85.00
26 SD,Flying Saucers 100.00
27 SD,Flying Saucers 100.00
28 Moon Trap 35.00
29 Captive From Space 35.00
30 Peril in the Sky 35.00
31 SD,SD(c),Enchanted Planet . 85.00
32 SD,SD(c),Last Ship from Earth 85.00
33 Galactic Scourge,
I&O:Captain Atom 235.00
34 SD,SD(c),A:Captain Atom . . . 90.00
35 thru 40 SD,SD(c),
A:Captain Atom . . . . @90.00
41 . . . . 20.00
42 SD,A:Captain Atom 20.00
43 . . . . 20.00
44 A:Mercury Man 20.00
45 A:Mercury Man 20.00
46 thru 58 . . . . @20.00
59 November, 1964 . . . . 20.00

SPACE BUSTERS
Ziff-Davis Publishing Co.
Spring, 1952

1 BK,NS(c),Ph(c),Charge of
the Battle Women 375.00
2 EK,BK,MA,NS(c),
Bondage(c),Ph(c) 325.00
3 Autumn, 1952 . . . . 300.00

SPACE COMICS
Avon Periodicals
March-April, 1954

4 (fa),F:Space Mouse 30.00

Space Comics #5 © Avon Publications

5 (fa),F:Space Mouse, May-June, 1954 . . . . 25.00

SPACE DETECTIVE
Avon Periodicals
July, 1951

1 WW,WW(c),Opium Smugglers of Venus 600.00
2 WW,WW(c),Batwomen of Mercury 300.00
3 EK(c),SeaNymphs ofNeptune 200.00
4 EK,Flame Women of Vulcan, Bondage(c) 275.00

SPACE MOUSE
Avon Periodicals
April, 1953

1 Funny Animal 45.00
2 Funny Animal 35.00
3 thru 5 Funny Animal . . . . . @20.00

SPACE PATROL
Approved Comics (Ziff-Davis)
Summer, 1952

1 BK,NS,Ph(c), The Lady of Diamonds 425.00
2 BK,NS,Ph(c),Slave King of Pluto,Oct.-Nov., 1952 . . . . 350.00

SPACE THRILLERS
Avon Periodicals
1954

N# Contents May Vary 600.00

SPACE WESTERN COMICS
(see YELLOWJACKET COMICS)

SPARKLER COMICS
United Features Syndicate
July, 1940

1 Jim Handy 225.00
2 Frankie Doodle,August, 1940 150.00

SPARKLER COMICS
United Features Syndicate
July, 1941

1 BHg,O:Sparkman;B:Tarzan,Captain & the Kids,Ella Cinders,Danny Dingle,Dynamite Dunn, Nancy, Abbie an' Slats, Frankie Doodle,Broncho Bill 850.00
2 BHg, The Case of Poisoned Fruit 375.00
3 BHg 325.00
4 BHg,Case of Sparkman & the Firefly 325.00
5 BHg,Sparkman,Natch 300.00
6 BHg,Case o/t Bronze Bees . 275.00
7 BHg,Case o/t Green Raiders 275.00
8 BHg,V:River Fiddler 275.00
9 BHg,N:Sparkman 275.00
10 BHg,B:Hap Hopper, Sparkman's ID revealed . . . 275.00
11 BHg,V:Japanese 225.00

Sparkler Comics #12
© United Features Syndicate

12 BHg,Another N:Sparkman . . 225.00
13 BHg,Hap Hopper Rides For Freedom 225.00
14 BHg,BHg(c),Tarzan V:Yellow Killer 250.00
15 BHg 225.00
16 BHg,Sparkman V:Japanese 225.00
17 BHg,Nancy(c) 225.00
18 BHg,Sparkman in Crete . . . 225.00
19 BHg,I&B:Race Riley ,Commandos 225.00
20 BHg,Nancy(c) 200.00
21 BHg,Tarzan(c) 200.00
22 BHg,Nancy(c) 175.00
23 BHg,Capt&Kids(c) 175.00
24 BHg,Nancy(c) 175.00
25 BHg,BHg(c),Tarzan(c) 225.00
26 BHg,Capt&Kids(c) 175.00
27 BHg,Nancy(c) 175.00
28 BHg,BHg(c),Tarzan(c) 225.00
29 BHg,Capt&Kids(c) 175.00
30 BHg,Nancy(c) 175.00
31 BHg,BHg(c),Tarzan(c) 225.00
32 BHg,Capt&Kids(c) 100.00
33 BHg,Nancy(c) 100.00
34 BHg,BHg(c),Tarzan(c) 200.00
35 BHg,Capt&Kids(c) 100.00
36 BHg,Nancy(c) 100.00
37 BHg,BHg(c),Tarzan(c) 200.00
38 BHg,Capt&Kids(c) 100.00
39 BHg,BHg(c),Tarzan(c) 200.00
40 BHg,Nancy(c) 100.00
41 BHg,Capt&Kids(c) 75.00
42 BHg,BHg,Tarzan(c) 150.00
43 BHg,Nancy(c) 75.00
44 BHg,Tarzan(c) 150.00
45 BHg,Capt&Kids(c) 75.00
46 BHg,Nancy(c) 75.00
47 BHg,Tarzan(c) 150.00
48 BHg,Nancy(c) 75.00
49 BHg,Capt&Kids(c) 75.00
50 BHg,BHg(c),Tarzan(c) 150.00
51 BHg,Capt&Kids(c) 75.00
52 BHg,Nancy(c) 75.00
53 BHg,BHg(c),Tarzan(c) 150.00
54 BHg,Capt&Kids(c) 65.00
55 BHg,Nancy(c) 65.00
56 BHg,Capt&Kids(c) 65.00
57 BHg,F:Li'l Abner 60.00
58 BHg,A:Fearless Fosdick 70.00
59 BHg,B:Li'l Abner 70.00
60 BHg,Nancy(c) 60.00
61 BHg,Capt&Kids(c) 60.00
62 BHg,Li'L Abner(c) 60.00
63 BHg,Capt&Kids(c) 60.00
64 BHg,Valentines (c) 60.00
65 BHg,Nancy(c) 60.00
66 BHg,Capt&Kids(c) 60.00
67 BHg,Nancy(c) 60.00
68 BHg, ... 60.00
69 BHg,B:Nancy (c) 60.00
70 BHg 60.00
71 thru 80 BHg . . . . @40.00
81 BHg,E:Nancy(c) 40.00
82 BHg 40.00
83 BHg,Tarzan(c) 30.00
84 BHg 30.00
85 BHg,E:Li'l Abner 30.00
86 BHg 30.00
87 BHg,Nancy(c) 30.00
88 thru 96 BHg . . . . @30.00
97 BHg,O:Lady Ruggles 50.00
98 BHg 30.00
99 BHg,Nancy(c) 30.00
100 BHg,Nancy(c) 45.00
101 thru 108 BHg . . . . @25.00
109 BHg,ATh 30.00
110 BHg 25.00
111 BHg 25.00
112 BHg 25.00
113 BHg,ATh 50.00
114 thru 120 BHg . . . . @25.00

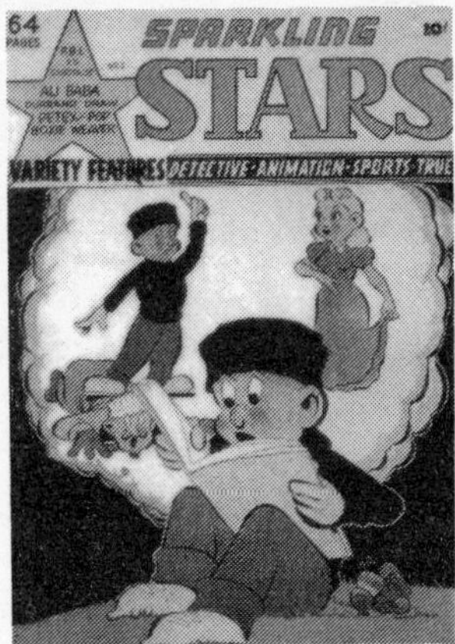

Sparkling Stars #2
© Holyoke Publishing

SPARKLING STARS
Holyoke Publishing Co.
June, 1944

1 B:Hell's Angels,Ali Baba,FBI,

Boxie Weaver,Petey & Pop . 80.00
2 . . . . 50.00
3 . . . . 35.00
4 thru 12 . . . . @30.00
13 O&I:Jungo, The Man-Beast . . 35.00
14 thru 19 . . . . @25.00
20 I:Fangs the Wolfboy 30.00
21 thru 28 . . . . @24.00
29 Bondage(c) 28.00
30 thru 32 . . . . @25.00
33 March, 1948 . . . . 25.00

SPARKMAN
Frances M. McQueeny
1944

1 O:Sparkman 200.00

SPARKY WATTS
Columbia Comics Group
1942

1 A:Skyman,Hitler(c) 185.00
2 . . . . 100.00
3 . . . . 75.00
4 O:Skyman 65.00
5 A:Skyman 50.00
6 thru 9 . . . . @35.00
10 1949 . . . . 35.00

SPECIAL COMICS
(see LAUGH COMICS)

SPECIAL EDITION COMICS
Fawcett Publications
August, 1940

1 CCB,CCB(c),F:Captain Marvel 6,000.00

Speed Comics #14
© Brookwood/Speed Publ./Harvey Publ.

SPEED COMICS
Brookwood/Speed Publ. Harvey Publications
October, 1939

1 BP,B&O:Shock Gibson,B:Spike Marlin,Biff Bannon 900.00
2 BP ,B:Shock Gibson(c) 450.00
3 BP,GT 275.00
4 BP 250.00
5 BP,DBr 250.00
6 BP,GT 200.00
7 GT,JKu,B:Mars Mason 200.00
8 JKu 175.00
9 JKu 175.00
10 JKu,E:Shock Gibson(c) 175.00
11 JKu,E:Mars Mason 175.00
12 B:The Wasp 250.00
13 I:Captain Freedom;B:Girls Commandos,Pat Parker . . . 300.00
14 Pocket sized format-100pgs. 250.00
15 Pocket size 250.00
16 JKu,Pocket size 250.00
17 O:Black Cat 350.00
18 B:Capt.Freedom,Bondage(c) 200.00
19 . . . . 190.00
20 . . . . 190.00
21 JKu(c) 190.00
22 JKu(c) 190.00
23 JKu(c),O:Girl Commandos . 235.00
24 . . . . 175.00
25 . . . . 175.00
26 Flag (c) 175.00
27 . . . . 175.00
28 E:Capt Freedom 175.00
29 Case o/t Black Marketeers . 175.00
30 POW Death Chambers 175.00
31 ASh(c),Nazi Thrashing(c) . . 150.00
32 ASh(c) 150.00
33 ASh(c) 150.00
34 ASh(c) 150.00
35 ASh(c),BlackCat'sDeathTrap 175.00
36 ASh(c) 150.00
37 RP(c) 150.00
38 RP(c),War Bond Plea with Iwo Jima flag allusion(c) 200.00
39 RP(c),B:Capt Freedom(c) . . 150.00
40 RP(c) 150.00
41 RP(c) 150.00
42 JKu,RP(c) 150.00
43 JKu,E:Capt Freedom(c) . . . 150.00
44 BP,JKu,Four Kids on a raft, January-February, 1947 . . . 150.00

SPEED SMITH THE HOT ROD KING
Ziff-Davis Publishing Co.
Spring, 1952

1 INS,Ph(c),A:Roscoe the Rascal 100.00

SPIRIT, THE
Will Eisner (Weekly Coverless Comic Book)
June, 1940

WE,O:SPirit 500.00
6/9/40 WE 250.00
6/16/40 WE,Black Queen . . 175.00
6/23/40 WE,Mr Mystic 150.00
6/30/40 WE 150.00
7/7/40 WE,Black Queen . . . 150.00
7/14/40 WE 100.00
7/21/40 WE 100.00
7/28/40 WE 100.00
8/4/40 WE 100.00
7/7/40-11/24/40,WE 70.00
12/1/40 WE,Ellen Spanking(c) 100.00
12/8/40-12/29/40 . . . . 60.00
1941 WE Each 50.00
3/16 WE I:Silk Satin 95.00
6/15 WE I Twilight 60.00
6/22 WE Hitler 60.00
1942 WE Each 40.00
2-1 . . . . 60.00
2-15 . . . . 45.00
2-23 . . . . 65.00
1943 WE Each,LF,WE scripts . . 30.00
1944 JCo,LF 15.00
1945 LF Each, ... 15.00
1946 WE Each 30.00
1/13 WE,O:The Spirit 50.00
1/20 WE,Satin 50.00
3/17 WE,I:Nylon 50.00
4/21 WE,I:Mr.Carrion 55.00
7/7 WE,I:Dulcet Tone&Skinny 50.00
10/6 WE,I:F:Gell 60.00
1947 WE Each 30.00
7/13.,WE,Hansel &Gretel . . . 45.00
7/20,WE,A:Bomb 50.00
9/28,WE,Flying Saucers 65.00
10/5,WE, Cinderella 32.00
12/7,WE,I:Power Puff 32.00
1948 WE Each 30.00
1/11,WE,Sparrow Fallon 35.00
1/25,WE,I:Last A Net 40.00
3/14,WE,A:Kretuama 35.00
4/4,WE,A:Wildrice 35.00
7/25,The Thing 60.00
8/22,Poe Tale,Horror 65.00
9/18, A:Lorelei 35.00
11/7,WE,A:Plaster of Paris . . 40.00
1949 WE Each 30.00
1/23 WE,I:Thorne 40.00
8/21 WE,I:Monica Veto 40.00
9/25 WE,A;Ice 40.00
12/4 WE,I:Flaxen 35.00
1950 WE Each 30.00
1/8 WE,I:Sand Saref 70.00
2/10, Horror Issue 35.00
1951 WE(Last WE 8/12/51) . @30.00
Non-Eisners . . . . @12.00
1952 Non-Eisners . . . . @12.00
7/27 WW,Denny Colt 350.00
8/3 WW,Moon 350.00
8/10 WW.Moon 350.00
8/17 WW,WE,Heart 300.00
8/24 WW,Rescue 300.00
8/31 WW,Last Man 300.00
9/7 WW,Man Moon 380.00
9/14 WE 80.00
9/21 WE Space 250.00
9/28 WE Moon 300.00
10/5 WE Last Story 125.00

SPIRIT, THE
Quality Comics Group/ Vital Publ.
1944

N# Wanted Dead or Alive! . . . 400.00
N# ...in Crime Doesn't Pay . . . 275.00
N# ...In Murder Runs Wild . . . 200.00
4 ...Flirts with Death 175.00
5 ...Wanted Dead or Alive . . . 150.00
6 ...Gives You Triple Value . . . 125.00
7 ...Rocks the Underworld . . . 125.00
8 . . . . 125.00
9 ...Throws Fear Into the Heart of Crime 125.00
10 ...Stalks Crime 125.00
11 ...America's Greatest Crime Buster 125.00
12 WE(c),...The Famous Outlaw Who Smashes Crime 200.00
13 WE(c),...and Ebony Cleans Out the Underworld;Bondage(c) . 200.00
14 WE(c) 200.00
15 WE(c),Bank Robber at Large 200.00
16 WE(c),The Caase of the Uncanny Cat 200.00
17 WE(c),The Organ Grinding Bank Robber 200.00
18 WE,WE(c),'The Bucket of Blood 250.00
19 WE,WE(c),'The Man Who Murdered the Spirit' 250.00
20 WE,WE(c),'The Vortex' 250.00
21 WE,WE(c),'P'Gell of Paris' . 250.00
22 WE(c),TheOctopus,Aug.1950 400.00

SPIRIT, THE
Fiction House Magazines
1952

1 Curse of Claymore Castle . 200.00
2 WE,WE(c),Who Says Crime Doesn't Pay 250.00
3 WE/JGr(c),League of Lions . 150.00
4 WE,WE&JGr(c),Last Prowl of Mr. Mephisto;Bondage (c) . 200.00
5 WE,WE(c),Ph(c)1954 . . . . . 250.00

SPIRITMAN
W. Eisner
1944

1 3 Spirit Sections from 1944 Bound Together 125.00
2 LF, 2 Spirit Sections from 1944 Bound Together 100.00

SPITFIRE COMICS
Harvey Publ.
August, 1941

1 MKd(c), 100pgs., Pocket size 275.00
2 100 pgs.,Pocket size, October, 1941 .... 250.00

Spook Comics #1 © Baily Publ.

SPOOK COMICS
Baily Publications
1946

1 A:Mr. Lucifer 125.00

SPOOK DETECTIVE CASES
(see CRIMINALS ON THE RUN)

SPOOKY
Harvey Publications
November, 1955

1 Funny Apparition 175.00
2 same 75.00
3 thru 10 same .... @35.00
11 thru 20 same .... @20.00
21 thru 30 same .... @15.00
31 thru 40 same .... @12.00
41 thru 70 same .... @7.00
71 thru 90 same .... @4.00
91 thru 120 same .... @3.00
121 thru 160 same .... @2.50
161 same,September, 1980 ..... 2.50

SPOOKY MYSTERIES
Your Guide Publishing Co.
1946

1 Rib-Tickling Horror 75.00

SPORT COMICS
(see TRUE SPORT PICTURE STORIES)

SPORTS THRILLS
(see DICK COLE)

SPOTLIGHT COMICS
Harry 'A' Chesler Jr. Publications
November, 1944

1 GT,GT(c),B:Veiled Avenger, Black Dwarf,Barry Kuda ... 300.00
2 .... 225.00
3 1945,Eye Injury 250.00

SPUNKY
Standard Comics
April, 1949

1 FF,Adventures of a Junior Cowboy 40.00
2 FF 25.00
3 .... 20.00
4 .... 20.00
5 .... 20.00
6 .... 20.00
7 November, 1951 .... 20.00

SPY AND COUNTER SPY
Best Syndicated Features (American Comics Group)
August-September, 1949

1 I&O:Jonathan Kent 125.00
2 .... 100.00

Becomes:

SPY HUNTERS

3 Jonathan Kent 85.00
4 J.Kent 60.00
5 J.Kent 60.00
6 J.Kent 60.00
7 OW(c),J.Kent 60.00
8 OW(c),J.Kent 60.00
9 OW(c),J.Kent 60.00
10 OW(c),J.Kent 60.00
11 .... 45.00
12 OW(c),MD 45.00
13 .... 40.00
14 .... 40.00
15 OW(c) 42.00
16 AW 75.00
17 .... 35.00
18 War (c) 35.00
19 .... 35.00
20 .... 35.00
21 B:War Content 35.00
22 .... 35.00
23 Torture 75.00
24 'BlackmailBrigade',July,1953 . 35.00

SPY SMASHER
Fawcett Publications
Autumn, 1941

1 B;Spy Smasher 1,500.00
2 Mra(c) 750.00
3 Bondage (c) 575.00
4 .... 525.00
5 Mra,Mt. Rushmore(c) 500.00
6 Mra,Mra(c),V:The Sharks of Steel 500.00
7 Mra 500.00
8 AB 400.00
9 AB,Hitler,Tojo, Mussolini(c) . 450.00
10 AB,Did Spy Smasher Kill Hitler? 450.00
11 AB,February, 1943 .... 400.00

SQUEEKS
Lev Gleason Publications
October, 1953

1 CBi(c),(fa) 30.00
2 CBi(c),(fa) 15.00
3 CBi(c),(fa) 12.00
4 (fa) 12.00
5 (fa),January, 1954 .... 12.00

STAMP COMICS
Youthful Magazines/Stamp Comics, Inc.
October, 1951

1 HcK,Birth of Liberty 175.00
2 HcK,RP,Battle of White Plains 100.00
3 HcK,DW,RP,Iwo Jima 75.00
4 HcK,DW,RP 75.00
5 HcK,Von Hindenberg disaster 85.00
6 HcK,The Immortal Chaplains 75.00
7 HcK,RKr,RP,B&O:Railroad . 100.00

Becomes:

THRILLING ADVENTURES IN STAMPS

8 HcK, 100 Pgs.,Jan.,1953 .. 250.00

Star Comics #14
© Comic Magazines/Ultem Publ.

STAR COMICS
Comic Magazines/Ultem Publ./Chesler Centaur Publications
February, 1937

1 B:Dan Hastings 800.00
2 .... 425.00
3 .... 350.00
4 WMc(c) 400.00
5 WMc(c),A:Little Nemo 400.00
6 CBi(c),FG 325.00
7 FG 275.00
8 BoW,BoW(c),FG,A:Little Nemo,Horror 350.00
9 FG,CBi(c) 275.00
10 FG,CBi(c),BoW,A:Impyk ... 425.00
11 FG,BoW,JCo 400.00
12 FG,BoW,B:Riders of the Golden West 300.00
13 FG,BoW 275.00
14 FG,GFx(c) 275.00
15 CBu,B:The Last Pirate 275.00
16 CBu,B:Phantom Rider 300.00
2-1 CBu,B:Phantom Rider(c) . 300.00
2-2 CBu,A:Diana Deane 275.00
2-3 GFx(c),CBu 250.00
2-4 CBu 250.00
2-5 CBu 225.00
2-6 CBu,E:Phanton Rider 225.00
2-7 CBu,August, 1939 ...... 250.00

STARLET O'HARA IN HOLLYWOOD
Standard Comics
December, 1948

1 The Terrific Tee-Age Comic 100.00
2 Her Romantic Adventures in Movie land 75.00

3 and 4, Sept., 1949 . . . . . . @50.00

STAR RANGER
Comics Magazines/Ultem/ Centaur Publ.
February, 1937

1 FG,I:Western Comic 1,000.00
2 . . . . 500.00
3 FG 400.00
4 . . . . 400.00
5 . . . . 300.00
6 FG 300.00
7 FG 275.00
8 GFx,FG,PGn,BoW 275.00
9 GFx,FG,PGn,BoW 275.00
10 JCo,GFx,FG,PGn,BoW 400.00
11 . . . . 350.00
12 JCo,JCo(c),FG,PGn 350.00

Becomes:

COWBOY COMICS

13 FG,PGn 500.00
14 FG,PGn 375.00

Becomes:

STAR RANGER FUNNIES

15 WE,PGn 500.00
2-1(16) JCo,JCo(c) 350.00
2-2(17) PGn,JCo,A:Night Hawk 325.00
2-3(18) JCo,FG 325.00
2-4(19) A:Kit Carson 325.00
2-5(20) October, 1939 . . . . . . 325.00

STARS AND STRIPES COMICS
Comic Corp of America (Centaur Publications)
May, 1941

2 PGn,PGn(c),'Called to Colors', The Shark,The Voice 1,000.00
3 PGn,PGn(c),O:Dr.Synthe . . 750.00
4 PGn,PGn(c),I:The Stars & Stripes 600.00
5 . . . . 500.00
6(5), December, 1941 . . . . . . 500.00

STAR STUDDED
Cambridge House
1945

N# 25 cents (c) price;128 pgs.; 32 F:stories 150.00
N# The Cadet,Hoot Gibson, Blue Beetle 125.00

STARTLING COMICS
Better Publ./Nedor Publ.
June, 1940

1 WE,LF,B&O:Captain Future, Mystico, Wonder Man; B:Masked Rider 800.00
2 Captain Future(c) 350.00
3 same 300.00
4 same 225.00
5 same 175.00
6 same 165.00
7 same 165.00
8 ASh(c) 165.00
9 Bondage(c) 190.00
10 O:Fighting Yank 900.00
11 Fighting Yank(c) 200.00
12 Hitler,Mussolini,Tojo cover . 225.00
13 JBi 200.00
14 JBi 200.00
15 Fighting Yank (c) 200.00
16 Bondage(c),O:FourComrades 225.00
17 Fighting Yank (c), E:Masked Rider 165.00
18 JBi,B&O:Pyroman 400.00
19 Pyroman(c) 175.00
20 Pyroman(c),B:Oracle 175.00
21 HcK,ASh(c)Bondage(c)O:Ape 175.00
22 HcK,ASh(c),Fighting Yank(c) 150.00
23 HcK,BEv,ASh(c),Pyroman(c) 150.00
24 HcK,BEv,ASh(c),Fighting Yank(c) 150.00
25 HcK,BEv,ASh(c),Pyroman(c) 150.00
26 BEv,ASh(c),Fighting Yank(c) 150.00

Startling Comics #27
© Better Publ./Nedor Publ.

27 BEv,ASh(c),Pyroman(c) . . . 150.00
28 BEv,ASh(c),Fighting Yank(c) 150.00
29 BEv,ASh(c),Pyroman(c) . . . 150.00
30 ASh(c),Fighting Yank(c) . . . 150.00
31 ASh(c),Pyroman(c) 150.00
32 ASh(c),Fighting Yank(c) . . . 150.00
33 ASh(c),Pyroman(c) 150.00
34 ASh(c),Fighting Yank(c), O:Scarab 165.00
35 ASh(c),Pyroman(c) 175.00
36 ASh(c),Fighting Yank(c) . . . 150.00
37 ASh(c),Bondage (c) 165.00
38 ASh(c),Bondage(c) 165.00
39 ASh(c),Pyroman(c) 165.00
40 ASh(c),E:Captain Future . . . 165.00
41 ASh(c),Pyroman(c) 165.00
42 ASh(c),Fighting Yank(c) . . . 165.00
43 ASh(c),Pyroman(c), E:Pyroman 165.00
44 GrI(c),Lance Lewis(c) 200.00
45 GrI(c),I:Tygra 200.00
46 GrI,GrI(c),Bondage(c) 225.00
47 ASh(c),Bondage(c) 200.00
48 ASh(c),Lance Lewis(c) 150.00
49 ASh(c),Bondage(c), E:Fighting Yank 175.00
50 ASh(c),Lance Lewis(c), Sea Eagle 150.00
51 ASh(c),Sea Eagle 150.00
52 ASh(c) 150.00
53 ASh(c),September, 1948 . . . 150.00

STARTLING TERROR TALES
Star Publications
May, 1952

10 WW,LbC(c),The Story Starts 225.00
11 LbC(c),The Ghost Spider of Death 150.00
12 LbC(c),White Hand Horror . . 65.00
13 JyD,LbC(c),Love From a Gorgor 65.00
14 LbC(c),Trapped by the Color of Blood 65.00
4 LbC(c),Crime at the Carnival 50.00
5 LbC(c),The Gruesome Demon of Terror 50.00
6 LbC(c),Footprints of Death . . 50.00

Startling Terror Tales #9
© Star Publications

7 LbC(c),The Case of the Strange Murder 65.00
8 RP,LbC(c),Phantom Brigade . 65.00
9 LbC(c),The Forbidden Tomb . 50.00
10 LbC(c),The Horrible Entity . . . 65.00
11 RP,LbC(c),The Law Will Win, July, 1954 . . . . 65.00

STEVE CANYON COMICS
Harvey Publications
February, 1948

1 MC,BP,O:Steve Canyon . . . 125.00
2 MC,BP 80.00
3 MC,BP,Canyon's Crew 75.00
4 MC,BP,Chase of Death 75.00
5 MC,BP,A:Happy Easter 75.00
6 MC,BP,A:Madame Lynx, December, 1948 . . . . 80.00

STEVE ROPER
Famous Funnies
April, 1948

1 Reprints newspaper strips . . 65.00
2 . . . . 35.00
3 thru 4 . . . . @25.00
5 December, 1948 . . . . 25.00

STORIES BY FAMOUS AUTHORS ILLUSTRATED
(see FAST FICTION)

STORY OF HARRY S. TRUMAN, THE
Democratic National Committee
1948

N# Giveaway-The Life of Our 33rd President 85.00

STRAIGHT ARROW
Magazine Enterprises
February-March, 1950

1 OW,B:Straight Arrow & his Horse Fury 250.00
2 BP,B&O:Red Hawk 125.00
3 BP,FF(c) 150.00
4 BP,Cave(c) 75.00
5 BP,StraightArrow'sGreatLeap 75.00
6 BP 60.00
7 BP,The Railroad Invades

Comanche Country 60.00
8 BP 60.00
9 BP 60.00
10 BP 60.00
11 BP,The Valley of Time 70.00
12 thru 19 BP @50.00
20 BP,Straight Arrow's Great War Shield 65.00
21 BP,O:Fury 75.00
22 BP,FF(c) 100.00
23 BP 45.00
24 BP,The Dragons of Doom 45.00
25 thru 27 BP @45.00
28 BP,Red Hawk 40.00
29 thru 35 BP @40.00
36 BP Drug 45.00
37 thru 38 BP @35.00
39 BP,The Canyon Beasts 30.00
40 BP,Secret of the Spanish Specters 30.00
41 and 42 BP @20.00
43 BP,I:Blaze 25.00
44 thru 53 BP @20.00
54 BP,March, 1956 20.00

STRANGE CONFESSIONS
Approved Publications (Ziff-Davis)
Spring, 1952

1 EK,Ph(c) 200.00
2 150.00
3 EK,Ph(c),Girls reformatory 150.00
4 Girls reformatory 150.00

STRANGE FANTASY
Farrell Publications/ Ajax Comics
August, 1952

(2)1 150.00
2 125.00
3 The Dancing Ghost 110.00
4 Demon in the Dungeon, A:Rocketman 100.00
5 Visiting Corpse 70.00
6 65.00
7 A:Madam Satan 100.00
8 A:Black Cat 75.00
9 S&K 85.00
10 75.00
11 Fearful Things Can Happen in a Lonely Place 75.00
12 The Undying Fiend 70.00
13 Terror in the Attic, Bondage(c) 100.00
14 Monster in the Building, October-November, 1954 70.00

UNKNOWN WORLD
Fawcett Publications
June, 1952

1 NS(c),Ph(c),Will You Venture to Meet the Unknown 175.00

Becomes:

STRANGE STORIES FROM ANOTHER WORLD

2 NS(c),Ph(c),Will You? Dare You 175.00
3 NS(c),Ph(c),The Dark Mirror 150.00
4 NS(c),Ph(c),Monsters of the Mind 150.00
5 NS(c),Ph(c),Dance of the Doomed February, 1953 150.00

STRANGE SUSPENSE STORIES
Fawcett Publications
June, 1952

1 BP,MSy,MBi 300.00
2 MBi,GE 200.00
3 MBi,GE(c) 175.00
4 BP 175.00
5 MBi(c),Voodoo(c) 175.00
6 BEv 75.00
7 BEv 85.00
8 AW 90.00
9 75.00
10 90.00
11 60.00
12 60.00
13 60.00
14 65.00
15 AW,BEv(c) 65.00

Charlton Comics

16 75.00
17 65.00
18 SD,SD(c) 135.00
19 SD,SD(c) 170.00
20 SD,SD(c) 125.00
21 75.00
22 SD(c) 100.00

Becomes:

THIS IS SUSPENSE!

23 WW 125.00
24 60.00
25 40.00
26 40.00

Becomes:

STRANGE SUSPENSE STORIES

27 40.00
28 30.00
29 30.00
30 30.00
31 SD(c) 85.00
32 SD 85.00
33 SD 85.00
34 SD,SD(c) 85.00
35 SD 85.00
36 SD,SD(c) 85.00
37 SD 90.00
38 85.00
39 SD 30.00
40 SD 85.00
41 SD 75.00
42 25.00
43 25.00
44 25.00
45 SD 65.00
46 25.00
47 SD 65.00
48 SD 65.00
49 25.00
50 SD 75.00
51 thru 53 SD @45.00
54 thru 60 @25.00
61 thru 74 @10.00
75 80.00
76 30.00
77 30.00

STRANGE SUSPENSE STORIES
(see LAWBREAKERS)

STRANGE TERRORS
St. John Publishing Co.
June, 1952

1 The Ghost of Castle Karloff, Bondage(c) 175.00
2 UnshackledFlight intoNowhere 100.00
3 JKu,Ph(c),The Ghost Who Ruled Crazy Heights 150.00
4 JKu,Ph(c),Terror from the Tombs 175.00
5 JKu,Ph(c),No Escaping the Pool of Death 125.00
6 LC,PAM,Bondage(c),Giant 175.00
7 JKu,JKu(c),Cat's Death,Giant 200.00

STRANGE WORLD OF YOUR DREAMS

Prize Group
August, 1952

1 S&K(c),What Do They Mean– Messages Rec'd in Sleep 275.00
2 MMe,S&K(c),Why did I Dream That I Was Being Married to a Man without a Face? 250.00
3 S&K(c) 225.00
4 MMe,S&K(c),The Story of a Man Who Dreamed a Murder that Happened 175.00

STRANGE WORLDS
Avon Periodicals
November, 1950

1 JKu,Spider God of Akka 425.00
2 WW,Dara of the Vikings 350.00
3 AW&FF,EK(c),WW,JO 750.00

Strange Worlds #4 © Avon Periodicals

4 JO,WW,WW(c),The Enchanted Dagger 350.00
5 WW,WW(c),JO,Bondage(c);Sirens of Space 300.00
6 EK,WW(c),JO,SC, Maid o/t Mist 250.00
7 EK, Sabotage on Space Station 1 165.00
8 JKu,EK,The Metal Murderer 165.00
9 The Radium Monsters 150.00
18 JKu 150.00
19 Astounding Super Science Fantasies 150.00
20 WW(c),Fighting War Stories 35.00
21 EK(c) 30.00
22 EK(c),Sept.-Oct., 1955 30.00

STRICTLY PRIVATE
Eastern Color Printing
July, 1942

1 You're in theArmyNow-Humor 125.00
2 F:Peter Plink, 1942 125.00

STUNTMAN COMICS
Harvey Publications
April-May, 1946

1 S&K,O:Stuntman 550.00
2 S&K,New Champ of Split-Second Action 375.00
3 S&K,Digest sized,Mail Order Only, B&W interior, October-November, 1946 500.00

SUGAR BOWL COMICS
Famous Funnies

May, 1948

1 ATh,ATh(c),The Newest in Teen Age! 80.00
2 . . . . 30.00
3 ATh 60.00
4 . . . . 30.00
5 January, 1949 . . . . 30.00

SUN FUN KOMIKS
Sun Publications
1939

1 F:Spineless Sam the Sweetheart 150.00

SUNNY, AMERICA'S SWEETHEART
Fox Features Syndicate
December, 1947

11 AF,AF(c) 270.00
12 AF,AF(c) 200.00
13 AF,AF(c) 200.00
14 AF,AF(c) 200.00

SUNSET CARSON
Charlton Comics
February, 1951

1 Painted, Ph(c);Wyoming Mail 600.00
2 Kit Carson-Pioneer 400.00
3 . . . . 300.00
4 Panhandle Trouble, August, 1951 . . . . 300.00

SUPER CIRCUS
Cross Publishing Co.
January, 1951

1 Partial Ph(c) 55.00
2 . . . . 40.00
3 . . . . 30.00
4 . . . . 30.00
5 1951 . . . . 30.00

SUPER COMICS
Dell Publishing Co.
May 1938

1 Dick Tracy,Terry and the Pirates,Smilin'Jack,Smokey Stover,Orphan Annie,etc. . 1,000.00
2 . . . . 450.00
3 . . . . 400.00
4 . . . . 375.00
5 Gumps(c) 325.00
6 . . . . 275.00
7 Smokey Stover(c) 275.00
8 Dick Tracy(c) 250.00
9 . . . . 250.00
10 Dick Tracy(c) 250.00
11 . . . . 225.00
12 . . . . 225.00
13 . . . . 225.00
14 . . . . 225.00
15 . . . . 225.00
16 Terry & the Pirates 200.00
17 Dick Tracy(c) 190.00
18 . . . . 190.00
19 . . . . 190.00
20 Smilin'Jack(c) 225.00
21 B:Magic Morro 175.00
22 Magic Morro(c) 190.00
23 all star(c) 165.00
24 Dick Tracy(c) 190.00
25 Magic Morro(c) 175.00
26 . . . . 190.00
27 Magic Morro(c) 175.00
28 Jim Ellis(c) 190.00
29 Smilin'Jack(c) 175.00
30 inc.The Sea Hawk 190.00
31 Dick Tracy(c) 150.00
32 Smilin' Jack(c) 165.00
33 Jim Ellis(c) 150.00
34 Magic Morro(c) 150.00
35 thru 40 Dick Tracy(c) . . . @150.00

Super Comics #14
© Dell Publishing Co.

41 B:Lightning Jim 135.00
42 thru 50 Dick Tracy(c) . . . @125.00
51 thru 54 Dick Tracy(c) . . . @100.00
55 . . . . 85.00
56 . . . . 85.00
57 Dick Tracy(c) 85.00
58 Smitty(c) 85.00
59 . . . . 85.00
60 Dick Tracy(c) 100.00
61 . . . . 75.00
62 Flag(c) 80.00
63 Dick Tracy(c) 80.00
64 Smitty(c) 75.00
65 Dick Tracy(c) 80.00
66 Dick Tracy(c) 80.00
67 Christmas(c) 80.00
68 Dick Tracy(c) 80.00
69 Dick Tracy(c) 80.00
70 Dick Tracy(c) 80.00
71 Dick Tracy(c) 70.00
72 Dick Tracy(c) 70.00
73 Smitty(c) 70.00
74 War Bond(c) 70.00
75 Dick Tracy(c) 70.00
76 Dick Tracy(c) 70.00
77 Dick Tracy(c) 70.00
78 Smitty(c) 55.00
79 Dick Tracy(c) 55.00
80 Smitty(c) 55.00
81 Dick Tracy(c) 55.00
82 Dick Tracy(c) 55.00
83 Smitty(c) 50.00
84 Dick Tracy(c) 55.00
85 Smitty(c) 50.00
86 All on cover 55.00
87 All on cover 55.00
88 Dick Tracy(c) 55.00
89 Smitty(c) 50.00
90 Dick Tracy(c) 55.00
91 Smitty(c) 50.00
92 Dick Tracy(c) 55.00
93 Dick Tracy(c) 55.00
94 Dick Tracy(c) 55.00
95 thru 99 . . . . @50.00
100 . . . . 65.00
101 thru 115 . . . . @40.00
116 Smokey Stover(c) 35.00
117 Gasoline Alley(c) 35.00
118 Smokey Stover(c) 35.00
119 Terry and the Pirates(c) . . . 40.00
120 . . . . 40.00
121 . . . . 40.00

SUPER-DOOPER COMICS
Able Manufacturing Co.
1946

1 A:Gangbuster 85.00
2 . . . . 50.00
3 & 4 . . . . @35.00
5 A:Captain Freedom,Shock Gibson 45.00
6 & 7 same . . . . @45.00
8 A:Shock Gibson, 1946 . . . . . 45.00

SUPER DUCK COMICS
MLJ Magazines/Close-Up (Archie Publ.)
Autumn, 1944

1 O:Super Duck 250.00
2 . . . . 125.00
3 I:Mr. Monster 90.00
4 & 5 . . . . @75.00
6 thru 10 . . . . @65.00

Super Duck #16
© MLJ Magazines/Archie Publ.

11 thru 20 . . . . @40.00
21 thru 40 . . . . @30.00
41 thru 60 . . . . @20.00
61 thru 94 . . . . @15.00

SUPER FUNNIES
Superior Comics Publishers
March, 1954

1 Dopey Duck 250.00
2 Out of the Booby-Hatch 45.00
3 F:Phantom Ranger 25.00
4 F:Phantom Ranger,Sept. 1954 25.00

SUPER MAGICIAN COMICS
Street & Smith Publications
May, 1941

1 B:The Mysterious Blackstone 200.00
2 V:Wild Tribes of Africa 150.00
3 V:Oriental Wizard 125.00
4 V:Quetzal Wizard,O:Transo . 100.00
5 A:The Moylan Sisters 100.00
6 JaB,JaB(c),The Eddie Cantor story 100.00
7 In the House of Skulls 125.00
8 A:Abbott & Costello 125.00
9 V:Duneen the Man-Ape . . . 100.00
10 V:Pirates o/t Sargasso Sea . 100.00
11 JaB(c),V:Fire Wizards 100.00
12 V:Baal 100.00

Super Magician #46 (4/10)
© Street & Smith Publications

2-1 A:The Shadow 175.00
2-2 In the Temple of the
10,00 Idols 70.00
2-3 Optical Illusion on (c)-
Turn Jap into Monkey 70.00
2-4 V:Cannibal Killers 70.00
2-5 V:The Pygmies of Lemuriai . 70.00
2-6 V;Pirates & Indians 70.00
2-7 Can Blackstone Catch the
Cannonball? 70.00
2-8 V:Marabout,B:Red Dragon . 70.00
2-9 . . . . 70.00
2-10 Pearl Dives Swallowed By
Sea Demons 70.00
2-11 Blackstone Invades
Pelican Islands 70.00
2-12 V:Bubbles of Death 70.00
3-1 . . . . 70.00
3-2 Bondage(c),Midsummers Eve 65.00
3-3 The Enchanted Garden . . . 65.00
3-4 Fabulous Aztec Treasure . . 65.00
3-5 A:Buffalo Bill 65.00
3-6 Magic Tricks to Mystify 65.00
3-7 V:Guy Fawkes 65.00
3-8 V:Hindu Spook Maker 65.00
3-9 . . . . 65.00
3-10 V:The Water Wizards 65.00
3-11 V:The Green Goliath 65.00
3-12 Lady in White 65.00
4-1 Cannibal of Crime 50.00
4-2 The Devil's Castle 50.00
4-3 V:Demons of Golden River . 50.00
4-4 V:Dr. Zero 50.00
4-5 Bondage(c) 55.00
4-6 V:A Terror Gang 50.00
4-7 . . . . 50.00
4-8 Mystery of the
Disappearing Horse 50.00
4-9 A Floating Light? 50.00
4-10 Levitation 50.00
4-11 Lost, Strange Land
of Shangri 50.00
4-12 I:Nigel Elliman 50.00
5-1 V:Voodoo Wizards of the
Everglades,Bondage (c) 55.00
5-2 Treasure of the Florida
Keys; Bondage (c) 50.00
5-3 Elliman Battles Triple Crime . 50.00
5-4 Can A Human Being Really
Become Invisible 50.00
5-5 Mystery of the Twin Pools . 50.00
5-6 A:Houdini 50.00
5-7 F:Red Dragon 50.00
5-8 F:Red Dragon,
Feb.-March, 1947 . . . . 50.00

SUPERMOUSE
Standard Comics/Pines
December, 1948

1 FF,(fa) 150.00
2 FF,(fa) 85.00
3 FF,(fa) 65.00
4 FF,(fa) 70.00
5 FF,(fa) 65.00
6 FF,(fa) 65.00
7 (fa) 25.00
8 (fa) 25.00
9 (fa) 25.00
10 (fa) 25.00
11 thru 20 (fa) . . . . @20.00
21 thru 44 (fa) . . . . @15.00
45 (fa),Autumn, 1958 . . . . 15.00

Super-Mystery Comics #23 (4/5)
© Periodical House/Ace Magazines

SUPER-MYSTERY COMICS
Periodical House (Ace Magazines)
July, 1940

1 B:Magno,Vulcan,Q-13,Flint
of the Mountes 800.00
2 Bondage (c) 400.00
3 JaB,B:Black Spider 350.00
4 O:Davy;A:Captain Gallant . . 275.00
5 JaB,JM(c),I&B:The Clown . . 275.00
6 JM,JM(c),V:The Clown 250.00
2-1 JM,JM(c),O:Buckskin,
Bondage(c) 250.00
2-2 JM,JM(c),V:The Clown . . . 200.00
2-3 JM,JM(c),V:The Clown . . . 200.00
2-4 JM,JM(c),V:The Nazis . . . 200.00
2-5 JM,JM(c),Bondage(c) 225.00
2-6 JM,JM(c),Bondage(c),
'Foreign Correspondent' . . . 225.00
3-1 B:Black Ace 250.00
3-2 A:Mr, Risk, Bondage(c) . . 275.00
3-3 HK,HK(c),I:Lancer;B:Dr.
Nemesis, The Sword 250.00
3-4 HK 250.00
3-5 HK,LbC,A:Mr. Risk 225.00
3-6 HK,LbC,A:Paul Revere Jr. 225.00
4-1 HK,LbC,A:Twin Must Die . 175.00
4-2 A:Mr. Risk 150.00
4-3 Mango out to Kill Davey! . 150.00
4-4 Danger Laughs at Mr. Risk 150.00
4-5 A:Mr. Risk 150.00
4-6 RP,A:Mr. Risk 150.00
5-1 RP 125.00
5-2 RP,RP(c),The Riddle of the
Swamp-Land Spirit 125.00
5-3 RP,RP(c),The Case of the
Whispering Death 125.00
5-4 RP,RP(c) 125.00
5-5 RP,Harry the Hack 125.00
5-6 . . . . 125.00
6-1 . . . . 100.00
6-2 RP,A:Mr. Risk 100.00
6-3 Bondage (c) 100.00
6-4 E:Mango;A:Mr. Risk 100.00
6-5 Bondage(c) 100.00
6-6 A:Mr. Risk 100.00
7-1 . . . . 100.00
7-2 KBa(c) 100.00
7-3 Bondage(c) 100.00
7-4 . . . . 100.00
7-5 . . . . 100.00
7-6 . . . . 100.00
8-1 The Riddle of the Rowboat . 90.00
8-2 Death Meets a Train 90.00
8-3 The Man Who Couldn't Die . 90.00
8-4 RP(c) 90.00
8-5 GT,MMe,Staged for Murder 90.00
8-6 Unlucky Seven,July, 1949 . . 90.00

ARMY AND NAVY COMICS
Street & Smith Publications
May, 1941

1 Hawaii is Calling You,Capt.
Fury,Nick Carter 275.00
2 Private Rock V;Hitler 150.00
3 The Fighting Fourth 100.00
4 The Fighting Irish 100.00
5 I:Super Snipe 250.00

Becomes:

SUPERSNIPE COMICS

6 A "Comic" With A Sense
of Humor 400.00
7 A:Wacky, Rex King 250.00
8 Axis Powers & Satan(c),
Hitler(c) 265.00
9 Hitler Voodoo Doll (c) 350.00
10 Lighting (c) 250.00
11 A:Little Nemo 250.00
12 Football(c) 250.00
2-1 B:Huck Finn 175.00
2-2 Battles Shark 175.00
2-3 Battles Dinosaur 175.00
2-4 Baseball(c) 175.00
2-5 Battles Dinosaur 175.00
2-6 A:Pochontas 175.00
2-7 A:Wing Woo Woo 175.00
2-8 A:Huck Finn 175.00
2-9 Dotty Loves Trouble 175.00
2-10 Assists Farm
Labor Shortage 175.00
2-11 Dotty & the Jelly Beans . . 175.00
2-12 Statue of Liberty 175.00
3-1 Ice Skating(c) 150.00
3-2 V:Pirates(c) 150.00
3-3 Baseball(c) 150.00
3-4 Jungle(c) 150.00
3-5 Learn Piglatin 150.00
3-6 Football Hero 150.00
3-7 Saves Girl From Grisley . . 150.00
3-8 Rides a Wild Horse 150.00
3-9 Powers Santa's Sleigh 150.00
3-10 Plays Basketball 150.00
3-11 Is A Baseball Pitcher 150.00
3-12 Flies with the Birds 150.00
4-1 Catches A Whale 100.00
4-2 Track & Field Athlete 100.00
4-3 Think Machine(c) 100.00
4-4 Alpine Skiier 100.00
4-5 Becomes a Boxer 100.00
4-6 Race Car Driver 100.00
4-7 Bomber(c) 100.00
4-8 Baseball Star 100.00
4-9 Football Hero 100.00
4-10 Christmas(c) 100.00
4-11 Artic Adventure 100.00
4-12 The Ghost Remover 100.00

5-1 August-September, 1949 . 100.00

SUPER SPY
Centaur Publications
October, 1940

1 O:Sparkler 750.00
2 November, 1940,A:Night Hawk, S.S. Swanson the Inner Circle, Drew Ghost,Tim Blain,Gentlemen of Misfortune,Duke Collins . . . 500.00

SUPER WESTERN COMICS
Youthful Magazines
August, 1950

1 BP,BP,(c),B;Buffalo Bill,Wyatt Earp,CalamityJane,SamSlade 55.00
2 thru 4 March, 1951 . . . . . @35.00

Superworld Comics #3
© Komos Publications

SUPERWORLD COMICS
Komos Publications
(Hugo Gernsback)
April, 1940

1 FP,FP(c),B:Military Powers, Buzz Allen,Smarty Artie, Alibi Alige 1,800.00
2 FP,FP(c),A:Mario 950.00
3 FP,FP(c),V:Vest Wearing Giant Grasshoppers 750.00

SUSPENSE COMICS
Et Es Go Mag. Inc.
(Continental Magazines)
December, 1945

1 LbC,Bondage(c),B:Grey Mask 600.00
2 DRi,I:The Mask 350.00
3 LbC,ASh(c),Bondage(c) . . . 600.00
4 LbC,LbC(c),Bondage(c) . . . 300.00
5 LbC,LbC(c) 300.00
6 LbC,LbC(c),The End of the Road 275.00
7 LbC,LbC(c) 275.00
8 LbC,LbC(c) 600.00
9 LbC,LbC(c) 275.00
10 RP,LbC,LbC(c) 275.00
11 RP,LbC,LbC(c),Satan(c) . . . 500.00
12 LbC,LbC(c),December, 1946 275.00

SUSPENSE DETECTIVE
Fawcett Publications
June, 1952

1 GE,MBi,MBi(c),Death Poised to Strike 175.00
2 GE,MSy 100.00
3 A Furtive Footstep 75.00
4 MBi,MSy,Bondage(c),A Blood Chilling Scream 65.00
5 MSy,MSy(c),MBi,A Hair-Trigger from Death, March, 1953 . . . 85.00

SUZIE COMICS
(see TOP-NOTCH COMICS)

SWEENEY
Standard Comics
June, 1949

4 Buzz Sawyer's Pal 45.00
5 September, 1949 . . . . 40.00

SWEETHEART DIARY
Fawcett
Winter, 1949

1 . . . . 75.00
2 . . . . 40.00
3 WW 75.00
4 WW 75.00
5 thru 10 . . . . @30.00
11 thru 14 . . . . @20.00

SWEETHEART DIARY
Charlton Comics
January 1953

32 . . . . 22.00
33 thru 40 . . . . @10.00
41 thru 65 . . . . @6.00

SWEET HEART
(see CAPTAIN MIDNIGHT)

SWEET LOVE
Harvey Publications
(Home Comics)
September, 1949

1 Ph(c) 35.00
2 Ph(c) 20.00
3 BP 20.00
4 Ph(c) 15.00
5 BP,JKa,Ph(c) 30.00

SWEET SIXTEEN
Parents' Magazine Group
August-September, 1946

1 Van Johnson story 100.00
2 Alan Ladd story 60.00
3 Rip Taylor 60.00
4 E:Taylor 60.00
5 Gregory Peck story (c) 50.00
6 Dick Hammes(c) 45.00
7 Ronald Reagan(c) 125.00
8 Shirley Jones(c) 45.00
9 William Holden(c) 45.00
10 James Stewart(c) 50.00
11 . . . . 45.00
12 Bob Cummings(c) 45.00
13 Robert Mitchum(c) 60.00

SWIFT ARROW
Farrell Publications(Ajax)
February-March, 1954

1 Lone Rider's Redskin Brother 60.00
2 . . . . 35.00
3 . . . . 30.00
4 . . . . 30.00
5 October-November, 1954 . . . 30.00

2nd Series
April, 1957

1 . . . . 30.00
2 B:Lone Rider 20.00
3 September, 1957 . . . . 20.00

TAFFY
Orbit Publications/Rural Home/
Taffy Publications
March-April, 1945

1 LbC(c),(fa),Bondage(c) 100.00
2 LbC(c),(fa) 60.00
3 (fa) 30.00
4 (fa) 25.00
5 LbC(c),A:Van Johnson 50.00
6 A:Perry Como 40.00
7 A:Dave Clark 45.00
8 A:Glen Ford 40.00
9 A:Lon McCallister 40.00
10 A:John Hodiak 40.00
11 A:Mickey Rooney 40.00
12 February, 1948 . . . . 40.00

Tailspin #1 (nn)
© Spotlight Publications

TAILSPIN
Spotlight Publications
November, 1944

N# LbC(c),A:Firebird 80.00

TALES FROM THE CRYPT
(see CRIME PATROL)

TALES FROM THE TOMB
(see Dell Giants)

TALES OF HORROR
Toby Press/Minoan Publ. Corp
June, 1952

1 Demons of the Underworld . 150.00
2 What was the Thing in the Pool?,Torture 125.00
3 The Big Snake 65.00
4 The Curse of King Kala! 65.00
5 Hand of Fate 65.00
6 The Fiend of Flame 65.00
7 Beast From The Deep 65.00
8 The Snake that Held A City Captive 65.00
9 It Came From the Bottom of the World 70.00
10 The Serpent Strikes 70.00
11 Death Flower? 70.00
12 Guaranteed to Make Your Hair Stand on End 75.00
13 Ghost with a Torch; October, 1954 . . . . 70.00

Tales of Horror #3
© Toby Press/Minoan Publ.

TALES OF TERROR
Toby Press
1952

1 Just A Bunch of Hokey Hogwash 75.00

TALES OF TERROR ANNUAL
E.C.
1951

N# AF 2,500.00
2 AF 1,100.00
3 . . . . 850.00

TALLY-HO COMICS
Baily Publishing Co.
December, 1944

N# FF,A:Snowman 200.00

TARGET COMICS
Funnnies Inc./Novelty Publ./ Premium Group/Curtis Circulation Co./Star Publications
February, 1940

1 BEv,JCo,CBu,JSm;B,O&I:Manowar, White Streak,Bull's-Eye;B:City Editor,High Grass Twins,T-Men, Rip Rory,Fantastic Feature Films, Calling 2-R 1,700.00
2 BEv,JSm,JCo,CBu,White Streak(c) 850.00
3 BEv,JSm,JCo,CBu 625.00
4 JSm,JCo 600.00
5 CBu,BW,O:White Streak . . 1,350.00
6 CBu,BW,White Streak(c) . . . 750.00
7 CBu,BW,BW(c),V:Planetoid Stories,Space Hawk(c) . . . 1,800.00
8 CBu,BW,White Shark(c) . . . 600.00
9 CBu,BW,White Shark(c) . . . 600.00
10 CBu,BW,JK(c),The Target(c) 850.00
11 BW,The Target(c) 750.00
12 BW,same 575.00
2-1 BW,CBu 400.00
2-2 BW,BoW(c) 400.00
2-3 BW,BoW(c),The Target(c) . 300.00
2-4 BW,B:Cadet 300.00
2-5 BW,BoW(c),The Target(c) . 275.00
2-6 BW,The Target(c) 275.00
2-7 BW,The Cadet(c) 275.00
2-8 BW,same 275.00
2-9 BW,The Target(c) 275.00
2-10 BW,same 350.00
2-11 BW,The Cadet(c) 275.00
2-12 BW,same 275.00
3-1 BW,same 250.00
3-2 BW 275.00
3-3 BW,The Target(c) 275.00
3-4 BW,The Cadet(c) 275.00
3-5 BW 275.00
3-6 BW,War Bonds(c) 275.00
3-7 BW 275.00
3-8 BW,War Bonds(c) 275.00
3-9 BW 275.00
3-10 BW 275.00
3-11 . . . . 65.00
3-12 . . . . 65.00
4-1 JJo(c) 50.00
4-2 ERy(c) 50.00
4-3 AVi 50.00
4-4 . . . . 50.00
4-5 APl(c),Statue of Liberty(c) . . 55.00
4-6 BW 50.00
4-7 AVi 50.00
4-8,Christmas(c) 50.00
4-9 . . . . 50.00
4-10 . . . . 50.00
4-11 . . . . 50.00
4-12 . . . . 50.00
5-1 . . . . 40.00
5-2 The Target 45.00
5-3 Savings Checkers(c) 40.00
5-4 War Bonds Ph(c) 40.00
5-5 thru 5-12 . . . . @40.00
6-1 The Target(c) 45.00
6-2 . . . . 40.00
6-3 Red Cross(c) 35.00
6-4 . . . . 35.00
6-5 Savings Bonds(c) 35.00
6-6 The Target(c) 40.00
6-7 The Cadet(c) 35.00
6-8 AFa 35.00
6-9 The Target(c) 40.00
6-10 . . . . 35.00
6-11 . . . . 35.00
6-12 . . . . 40.00
7-1 . . . . 35.00
7-2 Bondage(c) 40.00
7-3 The Target(c) 40.00
7-4 DRi,The Cadet(c) 35.00
7-5 . . . . 35.00
7-6 DRi(c) 35.00
7-7 The Cadet(c) 35.00
7-8 DRi(c) 35.00
7-9 The Cadet(c) 35.00
7-10 DRi,DRi(c) 35.00
7-11 . . . . 35.00
7-12 JH(c) 35.00
8-1 . . . . 35.00
8-2 DRi,DRi(c),BK 40.00
8-3 DRi,The Cadet(c) 35.00
8-4 DRi,DRi(c) 35.00
8-5 DRi,The Cadet(c) 35.00
8-6 DRi,DRi(c) 35.00
8-7 BK,DRi,DRi(c) 40.00
8-8 DRi,The Cadet(c) 35.00
8-9 DRi,The Cadet(c) 35.00
8-10 DRi,KBa,LbC(c) 75.00
8-11 DRi,The Cadet 35.00
8-12 DRi,The Cadet 35.00
9-1 DRi,LbC(c) 75.00
9-2 DRi 35.00
9-3 DRi,Bondage(c),The Cadet(c) 40.00
9-4 DRi,LbC(c) 75.00
9-5 DRi,Baseball(c) 35.00
9-6 DRi,LbC(c) 75.00
9-7 DRi 35.00
9-8 DRi,LbC(c) 75.00
9-9 DRi,Football(c) 35.00
9-10 DRi,LbC(c) 75.00
9-11,The Cadet 35.00
9-12 LbC(c),Gems(c) 75.00
10-1,The Cadet 35.00
10-2 LbC(c) 75.00
10-3 LbC(c) 75.00

Target #105 (10/3)
© Funnies Inc./Novelty Publ.

Becomes:

TARGET WESTERN ROMANCES
Star Publications
October-November, 1949

106 LbC(c),The Beauty Scar . . 140.00
107 LbC(c),The Brand Upon His Heart 110.00

Tarzan #20 © Dell Publishing Co.

TARZAN
Dell Publishing Co.
January-February 1948

1 V:White Savages of Vari . . 700.00
2 Captives of Thunder Valley . 400.00
3 Dwarfs of Didona 300.00
4 The Lone Hunter 300.00
5 The Men of Greed 300.00
6 Outlwas of Pal-ul-Don 250.00
7 Valley of the Monsters 250.00
8 The White Pygmies 250.00
9 The Men of A-Lur 250.00
10 Treasure of the Bolgani . . . 250.00

11 The Sable Lion 225.00
12 The Price of Peace 225.00
13 B:Lex Barker photo(c) 200.00
14 . . . . 200.00
15 . . . . 200.00
16 thru 20 . . . . @150.00
21 thru 30 . . . . @125.00
31 thru 54 E:L.Barker Ph(c) . . @75.00
55 thru 70 . . . . @55.00
71 thru 79 . . . . @35.00
80 thru 90 B:ScottGordonPh(c) @30.00
91 thru 99 . . . . @28.00
100 . . . . 40.00
101 thru 110 E:S.GordonPh(c) @25.00
111 thru 120 . . . . @20.00
121 thru 131 . . . . @15.00

TEEN-AGE DIARY SECRETS
St. John Publishing Co.
October, 1949

6 MB,PH(c) 75.00
7 MB,PH(c) 85.00
8 MB,PH(c) 75.00
9 MB,PH(c) 85.00

Becomes:

DIARY SECRETS

10 MB 65.00
11 MB 55.00
12 thru 19 MB . . . . @50.00
20 MB,JKu 55.00
21 thru 28 MB . . . . @30.00
29 MB,Comics Code 25.00
30 MB 25.00

TEEN-AGE ROMANCES
St. John Publishing Co.
January, 1949

1 MB(c),MB 150.00
2 MB(c),MB 85.00
3 MB(c),MB 90.00
4 Ph(c) 75.00
5 MB,Ph(c) 75.00
6 MB,Ph(c) 75.00
7 MB,Ph(c) 75.00
8 MB,Ph(c) 75.00
9 MB,MB(c),JKu 100.00
10 thru 27 MB,MB(c),JKu . . . @60.00
28 thru 30 . . . . @30.00
31 thru 34 MB(c) . . . . @30.00
35 thru 42 MB(c),MB . . . . . . @35.00
43 MB(c),MB,Comics Code 30.00
44 MB(c),MB 30.00
45 MB(c),MB 30.00

TEEN-AGE TEMPTATIONS
St. John Publishing Co.
October, 1952

1 MB(c),MB 150.00
2 MB(c),MB 60.00
3 MB(c),MB 80.00
4 MB(c),MB 80.00
5 MB(c),MB 80.00
6 MB(c),MB 80.00
7 MB(c),MB 80.00
8 MB(c),MB,Drug 90.00
9 MB(c),MB 75.00

Becomes:

GOING STEADY

10 MB(c),MB 65.00
11 MB(c),MB 50.00
12 MB(c),MB 50.00
13 MB(c),MB 50.00
14 MB(c),MB 50.00

TEENIE WEENIES, THE
Ziff-Davis Publishing Co.
1951

10 . . . . 85.00
11 . . . . 80.00

TEEN LIFE
(see YOUNG LIFE)

TEGRA, JUNGLE EMPRESS
(see ZEGRA, JUNGLE EMPRESS)

TELEVISION COMICS
Animated Cartoons
(Standard Comics)
February, 1950

5 Humorous Format,I:Willie Nilly 45.00
6 . . . . 35.00
7 . . . . 35.00
8 May, 1950 . . . . 35.00

TELEVISION PUPPET SHOW
Avon Periodicals
1950

1 F:Sparky Smith,Spotty, Cheeta, Speedy 80.00
2 November, 1950 . . . . 75.00

Tell it to the Marines #4 © Toby Press

TELL IT TO THE MARINES
Toby Press
March, 1952

1 I:Spike & Pat 80.00
2 A:Madame Cobra 55.00
3 Spike & Bat on a Commando Raid! 35.00
4 Veil Dancing(c) 40.00
5 . . . . 40.00
6 To Paris 35.00
7 Ph(c),The Chinese Bugle . . . 25.00
8 Ph(c),V:Communists in South Korea 25.00
9 Ph(c) 25.00
10 . . . . 25.00
11 . . . . 25.00
12 . . . . 25.00
13 John Wayne Ph(c) 50.00
14 Ph(c) 30.00
15 Ph(c),July, 1955 . . . . 30.00

TENDER ROMANCE
Key Publications
December, 1953

1 . . . . 65.00
2 . . . . 35.00

Becomes:

IDEAL ROMANCE

3 . . . . 35.00
4 thru 8 . . . . @20.00

Becomes:

DIARY CONFESSIONS

9 . . . . 25.00
10 . . . . 15.00

TERRIFIC COMICS
(see HORRIFIC)

TERRIFIC COMICS
Et Es Go Mag. Inc./ Continental Magazines
January, 1944

1 LbC,DRi(c),F:Kid Terrific Drug 575.00
2 LcC,ASh(c),B:Boomerang, 'Comics' McCormic 450.00
3 LbC,LbC(c) 350.00
4 LbC,RP(c) 450.00
5 LbC,BF,ASh(c),Bondage(c) . 400.00
6 LbC,LbC(c),BF,Nov.,1944 . . 400.00

TERROR ILLUSTRATED
E.C. Comics
November-December, 1955

1 JCr,GE,GrI,JO,RC(c) 75.00
2 Spring, 1956 . . . . 60.00

Terrors of the Jungle #6 © Star Publications

TERRIFYING TALES
Star Publications
January, 1953

11 LbC,LbC(c),'TyrantsofTerror' 200.00
12 LbC,LbC(c),'Bondage(c), 'Jungle Mystery' 150.00
13 LbC(c),Bondage(c),'The Death-Fire,Devil Head(c) . . . 200.00
14 LbC(c),Bondage(c),'The Weird Idol' 150.00
15 LbC(c),'The Grim Secret', April, 1954 . . . . 150.00

Becomes:

JUNGLE THRILLS
Star Publications
February, 1952

16 LbC(c),'Kingdom of Unseen Terror' 175.00

All comics prices listed are for *Near Mint* condition.

Becomes:

TERRORS OF THE JUNGLE

17 LbC(c),Bondage(c) 175.00
18 LbC(c),Strange Monsters 125.00
19 JyD,LbC(c),Bondage(c),The Golden Ghost Gorilla 125.00
20 JyD,LbC(c),The Creeping Scourge 125.00
21 LbC(c),Evil Eyes of Death! 150.00
4 JyD,LbC(c),Morass of Death 100.00
5 JyD,LbC(c),Bondage(c), Savage Train 125.00
6 JyD,LbC(c),Revolt of the Jungle Monsters 120.00
7 JyD,LbC(c) 100.00
8 JyD,LbC(c),Death's Grim Reflection 100.00
9 JyD,LbC(c),Doom to Evil-Doers 100.00
10 JyD,LbC(c),Black Magic, September, 1954 100.00

BOY EXPLORERS

1 S&K(c),S&K,The Cadet 600.00
2 S&K(c),S&K 750.00

Becomes:

TERRY AND THE PIRATES

3 S&K,MC(c),MC,Terry and Dragon Lady 200.00
4 S&K,MC(c),MC 125.00
5 S&K,MC(c),MC,BP, Chop-Chop(c) 75.00
6 S&K,.MC(c),MC 75.00
7 S&K,MC(c),MC,BP 75.00
8 S&K,MC(c),MC,BP 75.00
9 S&K,MC(c),MC,BP 75.00
10 S&K,MC(c),MC,BP 75.00
11 S&K,MC(c),MC,BP, A:Man in Black 60.00
12 S&K,MC(c),MC,BP 60.00
13 S&K,MC(c),MC,Belly Dancers 60.00
14 thru 20 S&K,MC(c),MC @50.00
22 thru 26 S&K,MC(c),MC @45.00
27 Charlton Comics 35.00
28 35.00

Terry-Toons #38

© Select/Timely/Marvel/St.Johns

TERRY-BEARS COMICS

St. John Publishing Co.

June, 1952

1 20.00
2 & 3 @15.00

TERRY-TOONS COMICS

Select,Timely,Marvel,St. Johns

1942

1 Paul Terry (fa) 650.00
2 320.00
3 thru 6 @250.00
7 Hitler,Hirohito,Mussolini(c) 165.00
8 thru 20 @100.00
21 thru 37 @75.00
38 I&(c):Mighty Mouse 750.00
39 Mighty Mouse 175.00
40 thru 49 All Mighty Mouse @85.00
50 I:Heckle & Jeckle 200.00
51 thru 60 @60.00
61 thru 70 @45.00
71 thru 86 @40.00

TEXAN, THE

St. John Publishing Co.

August, 1948

1 GT,F:Buckskin Belle,The Gay Buckaroo,Mustang Jack 80.00
2 GT 40.00
3 BLb(c) 35.00
4 MB,MB(c) 60.00
5 MB,MB(c),Mystery Rustlers of the Rio Grande 60.00
6 MB(c),Death Valley Double-Cross 50.00
7 MB,MB(c),Comanche Justice Strikes at Midnight 60.00
8 MB,MB(c),Scalp Hunters Hide their Tracks 60.00
9 MB(c),Ghost Terror of the Blackfeet 60.00
10 MB,MB(c),Treason Rides the Warpath 50.00
11 MB,MB(c),Hawk Knife 60.00
12 MB 60.00
13 MB,Doublecross at Devil's Den 60.00
14 MB,Ambush at Buffalo Trail 60.00
15 MB,Twirling Blades Tame Treachery 60.00

Becomes:

FIGHTIN' TEXAN

16 GT,Wanted Dead or Alive 45.00
17 LC,LC(c);Killers Trail, December, 1952 40.00

TEX FARRELL

D.S. Publishing Co.

March-April, 1948

1 Pride of the Wild West 75.00

TEX GRANGER

(see CALLING ALL BOYS)

TEX RITTER WESTERN

Fawcett Publications/ Charlton Comics

October, 1950

1 Ph(c),B:Tex Ritter, his Horse White Flash, his dog Fury, and his mom Nancy 400.00
2 Ph(c),Vanishing Varmints 200.00
3 Ph(c),Blazing Six-Guns 175.00
4 Ph(c),The Jaws of Terror 150.00
5 Ph(c),Bullet Trail 150.00
6 Ph(c),Killer Bait 150.00
7 Ph(c),Gunsmoke Revenge 125.00
8 Ph(c),Lawless Furnace Valley 125.00
9 Ph(c),The Spider's Web 125.00
10 Ph(c),The Ghost Town 125.00
11 Ph(c),Saddle Conquest 125.00
12 Ph(c),Prairie Inferno 75.00
13 Ph(c) 75.00
14 Ph(c) 75.00
15 Ph(c) 75.00
16 thru 19 Ph(c) @75.00
20 Ph(c),Stagecoach To Danger 75.00
21 75.00
22 Panic at Diamond B 60.00
23 A:Young Falcon 50.00
24 A:Young Falcon 50.00
25 A:Young Falcon 50.00
26 thru 38 @45.00
39 AW,AW(c) 45.00
40 thru 45 @40.00
46 May, 1959 40.00

THING!, THE

Song Hits/Capitol Stories/ Charlton Comics

February, 1952

1 Horror 350.00
2 Crazy King(c) 250.00
3 250.00
4 AFa(c),I Was A Zombie 200.00
5 LM(c),Severed Head(c) 225.00
6 175.00
7 Fingenail to Eye(c) 300.00
8 175.00
9 Severe 350.00
10 Devil(c) 175.00
11 SC,Cleaver 300.00
12 SD,SD(c),Neck Blood Sucking 375.00
13 SD,SD(c) 375.00
14 SD,SD(c) 375.00
15 SD,SD(c) 375.00
16 Eye Torture 250.00
17 BP,SD(c) 300.00

Becomes:

BLUE BEETLE

18 America's Fastest Moving Crusader Against Crime 75.00
19 JKa,Lightning Fast 85.00
20 JKa 85.00
21 The Invincible 60.00

Becomes:

MR. MUSCLES

22 World's Most Perfect Man 30.00
23 August, 1956 20.00

THIS IS SUSPENSE

(see LAWBREAKERS)

THIS IS WAR

Standard Comics

July, 1952

5 ATh,Show Them How To Die 70.00
6 ATh,Make Him A Soldier 60.00
7 One Man For Himself 20.00
8 Miracle on Massacre Hill 20.00
9 ATh,May, 1953 50.00

THIS IS SUSPENSE!

(see STRANGE SUSPENSE STORIES)

THIS MAGAZINE IS HAUNTED

Fawcett Publications/ Charlton Comics

October, 1951

1 MBi,F:Doctor Death 250.00
2 GE 175.00
3 MBi,Quest of the Vampire 85.00
4 BP,The Blind, The Doomed and the Dead 75.00
5 BP,GE,The Slithering Horror of Skontong Swamp! 175.00
6 Secret of the Walking Dead 75.00
7 The Man Who Saw Too Much 75.00
8 The House in the Web 75.00
9 The Witch of Tarlo 75.00
10 I Am Dr Death, Severed Head(c) 125.00
11 BP,Touch of Death 75.00
12 BP 75.00
13 BP,Severed Head(c) 125.00
14 BP,Horrors of the Damned 75.00

15 DG(c) 60.00
16 SD(c) 125.00
17 SD,SD(c) 175.00
18 SD,SD(c) 175.00
19 SD(c) 125.00
20 SMz(c) 75.00
21 SD(c) 125.00

Becomes:

DANGER AND ADVENTURE

22 The Viking King,F:Ibis the Invincible 50.00
23 F:Nyoka the Jungle Girl Comics Code 45.00
24 DG&AA(c) 35.00
25 thru 27 . . . . @30.00

Becomes:

ROBIN HOOD AND HIS MERRY MEN

28 . . . . 40.00
29 thru 37 . . . . @30.00
38 SD,August, 1958 . . . . 75.00

3-D-ELL

Dell Publishing Co.
1953

1 Rootie Kazootie 250.00
2 Rootie Kazootie 250.00
3 Flunkey Louise 225.00

THREE RING COMICS

Spotlight Publishers
March, 1945

1 Funny Animal 50.00

Three Stooges #5

© St. John's Publishing Co.

THREE STOOGES

Jubilee Publ.
February, 1949

1 JKu,Infinity(c) 575.00
2 JKu,On the Set of the 'The Gorilla Girl' 450.00

St. John Publishing Co.

1 JKu,'Bell Bent for Treasure, Sept., 1953 . . . . . 400.00
2 JKu 300.00
3 JKu,3D 300.00
4 JKu,Medical Mayhem 200.00
5 JKu,Shempador-Matador Supreme 200.00
6 JKu, ... 200.00
7 JKu,Ocotber, 1954 . . . . 200.00

THRILLING COMICS

Better Publ./Nedor/ Standard Comics
February, 1940

1 B&O:Doc Strange,B:Nickie Norton 800.00
2 B:Rio Kid,Woman in Red Pinocchio 350.00
3 B:Lone Eagle,The Ghost . . 300.00
4 Dr Strange(c) 225.00
5 Bondage(c) 200.00
6 Dr Strange(c) 200.00
7 Dr Strange(c) 200.00
8 V:Pirates 200.00
9 Bondage(c) 225.00
10 V:Nazis 225.00
11 ASh(c),V:Nazis 185.00
12 ASh(c) 165.00
13 ASh(c),Bondage(c) 200.00
14 ASh(c) 175.00
15 ASh(c),V:Nazis 175.00
16 Bondage(c) 185.00
17 Dr Strange(c) 175.00

Thrilling Comics #18

© Better Publ./Nedor/Standard Comics

18 Dr Strange(c) 175.00
19 I&O:American Crusader . . . 250.00
20 Bondage(c) 185.00
21 American Crusader(c) 150.00
22 Bondage(c) 175.00
23 American Crusader 150.00
24 I:Mike in Doc Strange 150.00
25 DR Strange(c) 150.00
26 Dr Strange(c) 150.00
27 Bondage(c) 175.00
28 Bondage(c) 175.00
29 E:Rio Kid;Bondage(c) 175.00
30 Bondage(c) 175.00
31 Dr Strange(c) 150.00
32 Dr Strange(c) 125.00
33 Dr Strange(c) 125.00
34 Dr Strange(c) 125.00
35 Dr Strange 125.00
36 ASh(c),B:Commando 135.00
37 BO,ASh(c) 125.00
38 ASh(c) 135.00
39 ASh(c),E:American Crusader 125.00
40 ASh(c) 125.00
41 ASh(c),F:American Crusader 135.00
42 ASh(c) 90.00
43 ASh(c) 90.00
44 ASh(c),Hitler(c) 100.00
45 EK,ASh(c) 100.00
46 ASh(c) 100.00
47 ASh(c) 90.00
48 EK,ASh(c) 90.00
49 ASh(c) 90.00
50 ASh(c) 90.00
51 ASh(c) 90.00
52 ASh(c),E:Th Ghost; Peto-Bondage(c) 100.00
53 ASh(c),B:Phantom Detective . 90.00
54 ASh(c),Bondage(c) 100.00
55 ASh(c),E:Lone Eagle 90.00
56 ASh(c),B:Princess Pantha . . 175.00
57 ASh(c) 150.00
58 ASh(c) 150.00
59 ASh(c) 150.00
60 ASh(c) 150.00
61 ASh(c),GRi,A:Lone Eagle . . 150.00
62 ASh(c) 150.00
63 ASh(c),GT 150.00
64 ASh(c) 150.00
65 ASh(c),E:Commando Cubs, Phantom Detective 150.00
66 ASh(c) 150.00
67 FF,ASh(c) 175.00
68 FF,ASh(c) 175.00
69 FF,ASh(c) 175.00
70 FF,ASh(c) 185.00
71 FF,ASh(c) 175.00
72 FF,ASh(c) 175.00
73 FF,ASh(c) 175.00
74 E:Princess Pantha; B:Buck Ranger 85.00
75 B:Western Front 50.00
76 . . . . 50.00
77 ASh(c) 50.00
78 Bondage(c) 55.00
79 BK 50.00
80 JSe,BE,April, 1951 . . . . 55.00

THRILLING CRIME CASES

Star Publications
June-July, 1950

41 LbC(c),The Unknowns 75.00
42 LbC(c),The Gunmaster 60.00
43 LbC,LbC(c),The Chameleon . 75.00
44 LbC(c),Sugar Bowl Murder . . 75.00
45 LbC(c),Maze of Murder 75.00

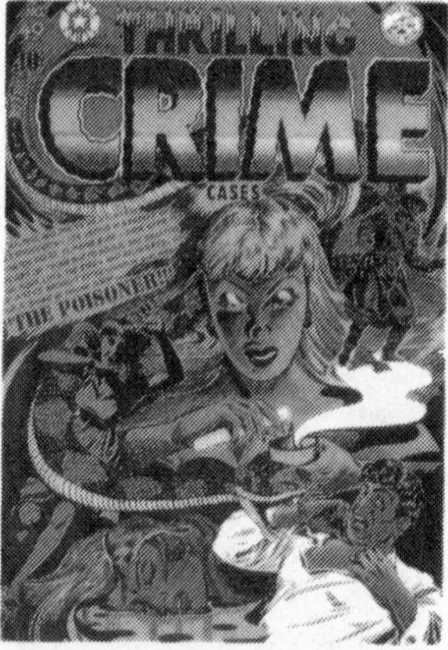

Thrilling Crime Cases #49

© Star Publications

46 LbC,LbC(c),Modern Communications 50.00
47 LbC(c),The Careless Killer . . 50.00
48 LbC(c),Road Black 50.00
49 LbC(c),The Poisoner 125.00

Becomes:

SHOCKING MYSTERY CASES

50 JyD,LbC(c),Dead Man's Revenge 150.00
51 JyD,LbC(c),A Murderer's Reward 75.00
52 LbC(c),The Carnival Killer . . . 65.00
53 LbC(c),The Long Shot of Evil 65.00
54 LbC(c),Double-Cross of Death 65.00
55 LbC(c),Return from Death . . 65.00
56 LbC(c),The Chase 100.00
57 LbC(c),Thrilling Cases 50.00
58 LbC(c),Killer at Large 65.00
59 LbC(c),Relentess Huntdown . 50.00
60 LbC(c),Lesson of the Law, October, 1954 . . . . 50.00

THRILLING ROMANCES
Standard Comics
December, 1949

5 Ph(c) 55.00
6 Ph(c) 25.00
7 Ph(c),JSe,BE 35.00
8 Ph(c) 25.00
9 Ph(c),GT 30.00
10 Ph(c),JSe,BE 30.00
11 Ph(c),JSe,BE 30.00
12 Ph(c),WW 45.00
13 Ph(c),JSe 25.00
14 Ph(c),Danny Kaye 18.00
15 Ph(c),Tony Martin,Ph(c) 18.00
16 Ph(c) 15.00
17 Ph(c) 15.00
18 Ph(c) 15.00
19 Ph(c) 15.00
20 Ph(c) 15.00
21 Ph(c) 15.00
22 Ph(c),ATn 35.00
23 Ph(c),ATn 35.00
24 Ph(c),ATn3 . . . . 35.00
25 Ph(c),ATn 35.00

THRILLING TRUE STORY OF THE BASEBALL GIANTS
Fawcett Publications
1952

N# Partial Ph(c),Famous Giants of the Past 450.00
2 Yankees Ph(c),Joe DiMaggio, Yogi Berra,Mickey Mantle, Casey Stengel 500.00

TICK TOCK TALES
Magazine Enterprises
January, 1946

1 (fa) Koko & Kola 65.00
2 (fa) Calender 35.00
3 thru 10 (fa) . . . . @25.00
11 thru 18 (fa) . . . . @20.00
19 (fa),Flag(c) 20.00
20 (fa) 20.00
21 (fa) 15.00
22 (fa) 15.00
23 (fa),Mugsy Mouse 15.00
24 thru 33 (fa) . . . . @15.00
34 (fa), 1951 . . . . 15.00

TIM HOLT
Magazine Enterprises
January-February, 1949

4 FBe,Ph(c) 150.00
5 FBe,Ph(c) 125.00
6 FBe,Ph(c),I:Calico Kid 150.00
7 FBe,Ph(c),Man-Killer Mustang 100.00
8 FBe,Ph(c) 100.00
9 FBe,DAy(c),TerribleTenderfoot 100.00
10 FBe,DAy(c),The Devil Horse 100.00
11 FBe,DAy(c),O&I:Ghost Rider 250.00
12 FBe,DAy(c),Battle at Bullock Gap 75.00
13 FBe,DAy(c),Ph(c) 75.00
14 FBe,DAy(c),Ph(c),The Honest Bandits 75.00
15 FBe,DAy,Ph(c) 75.00
16 FBe,DAy,Ph(c) 75.00
17 FBe,DAy,Ph(c) 250.00
18 FBe,DAy,Ph(c) 75.00
19 FBe,DAy,They Dig By Night . 60.00
20 FBe,DAy,O:Red Mask 90.00
21 FBe,DAy,FF(c) 225.00
22 FBe,DAy 55.00
23 FF,FBe,DAy 175.00
24 FBe,DAy,FBe(c) 55.00
25 FBe,DAy,FBe(c) 100.00
26 FBe,DAy,FBe(c) 50.00
27 FBe,DAy,FBe(c),V:Straw Man 50.00
28 FBe,DAy,FBe(c),Ph(c) 50.00
29 FBe,DAy,FBe,Ph(c), ... 50.00
30 FBe,DAy,FBe(c),Lady Doom & The Death Wheel 45.00
31 FBe,DAy,FBe(c) 45.00
32 FBe,DAy,FBe(c) 45.00
33 FBe,DAy,FBe(c) 45.00
34 FBe,DAy,FBe(c) 60.00
35 FBe,DAy,FBe(c) 60.00
36 FBe,DAy,FBe(c),Drugs 65.00
37 FBe,DAy,FBe(c) 65.00
38 FBe,DAy,FBe(c) 65.00
39 FBe,DAy,FBe(c),3D Effect . . 70.00
40 FBe,DAy,FBe(c) 70.00
41 FBe,DAy,FBe(c) 70.00

Becomes:

RED MASK

42 FBe,DAy,FBe(c),3D 120.00
43 FBe,DAy,FBe(c),3D 100.00
44 FBe,DAy,FBe(c),Death at Split Mesa,3D 90.00
45 FBe,DAy,FBe(c),V:False Red Mask 90.00
46 FBe,DAy,FBe(c) 90.00
47 FBe,DAy,FBe(c) 90.00
48 FBe,DAy,FBe(c),Comics Code 85.00
49 FBe,DAy,FBe(c) 85.00
50 FBe,DAy 85.00
51 FBe,DAy,The Magic of 'The Presto Kid' 85.00
52 FBe,DAy,O:Presto Kid 90.00
53 FBe,DAy 70.00
54 FBe,DAy,September, 1957 . . 90.00

TIM TYLER COWBOY
Standard Comics
November, 1948

11 . . . . 40.00
12 . . . . 30.00
13 The Doll Told the Secret 30.00
14 Danger at Devil's Acres 30.00
15 Secret Treasure 30.00
16 . . . . 30.00
17 . . . . 30.00
18 1950 . . . . 30.00

TINY TOTS COMICS
Dell Publishing Co.
1943

1 . . . . 250.00

TINY TOTS COMICS
E.C. Comics
March, 1946

N# Your First Comic Book B:Burton Geller(c) and art . . 175.00
2 . . . . 125.00
3 Celebrate the 4th 100.00
4 Go Back to School 120.00
5 Celebrate the Winter 100.00
6 Do Their Spring Gardening . . 90.00
7 On a Thrilling Ride 100.00
8 On a Summer Vacation . . . 100.00
9 On a Plane Ride 100.00
10 Merry X-Mas Tiny Tots E:Burton Geller(c)and art . . 100.00

Tip Top Comics #27
© United Features/St. John/Dell

TIP TOP COMICS
United Features,St. John,Dell
1930

1 HF,Li'l Abner 4,000.00
2 HF 900.00
3 HF,Tarzan(c) 800.00
4 HF,Li'l Abner(c) 550.00
5 HF,Capt&Kids(c) 475.00
6 HF 375.00
7 HF 375.00
8 HF,Li'l Abner(c) 375.00
9 HF,Tarzan(c) 400.00
10 HF,Li'L Abner(c) 375.00
11 HF,Tarzan(c) 325.00
12 HF,Li'l Abner 275.00
13 HF,Tarzan(c) 325.00
14 HF,Li'L Abner(c) 275.00
15 HF,Capt&kids(c) 275.00
16 HF,Tarzan(c) 325.00
17 HF,Li'L Abner(c) 275.00
18 HF,Tarzan(c) 325.00
19 HF,Football(c) 275.00
20 HF,Capt&Kids(c) 275.00
21 HF,Tarzan(c) 250.00
22 HF,Li'l Abner(c) 225.00
23 HF,Capt&Kids(c) 250.00
24 HF,Tarzan(c) 250.00
25 HF,Capt&Kids(c) 225.00
26 HF,Li'L Abner(c) 225.00
27 HF,Tarzan(c) 250.00
28 HF,Li'l Abner(c) 225.00
29 HF,Capt&Kids(c) 225.00
30 HF,Tarzan(c) 250.00
31 HFCapt&Kids(c) 225.00
32 HF Tarzan(c) 250.00
33 HF,Tarzan(c) 250.00
34 HF,Capt&Kids(c) 250.00
35 HF 225.00
36 HF,HK,Tarzan(c) 250.00
37 HF,Tarzan 250.00
38 HF 225.00
39 HF,Tarzan 250.00
40 HF 225.00
41 Tarzan(c) 225.00
42 . . . . 200.00
43 Tarzan(c) 250.00
44 HF 200.00
45 HF,Tarzan(c) 225.00
46 HF 200.00
47 HF,Tarzan(c) 225.00
48 HF 200.00
49 HF 175.00
50 HF,Tarzan(c) 200.00
51 . . . . 175.00

52 Tarzan(c) 190.00
53 . . . . 175.00
54 . . . . 225.00
55 . . . . 175.00
56 . . . . 175.00
57 BHg 225.00
58 . . . . 200.00
59 BHg 225.00
60 . . . . 175.00
61 BHg 225.00
62 BHg 225.00
63 thru 90 . . . . @90.00
91 thru 99 . . . . @65.00
100 . . . . 85.00
101 thru 150 . . . . @45.00
151 thru 188 . . . . @30.00
189 thru 225 . . . . @30.00

T-Man #23

© Comics Magazine/Quality Comics

T-MAN
Comics Magazines (Quality Comics Group)
September, 1951

1 JCo,Pete Trask-the Treasury Man 175.00
2 RC(c),The Girl with Death in Her Hands 90.00
3 RC,RC(c),Death Trap in Iran 85.00
4 RC,RC(c),Panama Peril 85.00
5 RC,RC(c),Violence in Venice 85.00
6 RC(c),The Man Who Could Be Hitler 80.00
7 RC(c),Mr. Murder & The Black Hand 80.00
8 RC(c),Red Ticket to Hell 80.00
9 RC(c),Trial By Terror 70.00
10 . . . . 70.00
11 The Voice of Russia 55.00
12 Terror in Tokyo 40.00
13 Mind Assassins 40.00
14 Trouble in Bavaria 40.00
15 The Traitor,Bondage(c) 40.00
16 Hunt For a Hatchetman 40.00
17 Red Triggerman 40.00
18 Death Rides the Rails 40.00
19 Death Ambush 40.00
20 The Fantastic H-Bomb Plot . . 60.00
21 The Return of Mussolini 40.00
22 Propaganda for Doom 35.00
23 Red Intrigue in Parid,H-Bomb 50.00
24 Red Sabotage 35.00
25 RC,The Ingenious Red Trap . 60.00
26 thru 37 . . . . @35.00
38 December, 1956 . . . . 35.00

TNT COMICS
Charles Publishing Co.
February, 1946

1 FBI story,YellowJacket 125.00

TODAY'S BRIDES
Ajax/Farrell Publishing Co.
November, 1955

1 . . . . 30.00
2 . . . . 18.00
3 . . . . 18.00
4 November, 1956 . . . . 18.00

TODAY'S ROMANCE
Standard Comics
March, 1952

5 . . . . 30.00
6 ATh 35.00
7 . . . . 15.00
8 . . . . 15.00

TOM AND JERRY
see DELL GIANT EDITIONS

Thrills of Tomorrow #17

© Harvey Publications

TOMB OF TERROR
Harvey Publications
June, 1952

1 BP,The Thing From the Center of the Earth 125.00
2 RP,The Quagmire Beast . . . 65.00
3 BP,RP,Caravan of the Doomed, Bondage(c) 75.00
4 RP,I'm Going to Kill You, Torture 65.00
5 RP 60.00
6 RP,Return From the Grave . . 60.00
7 RP,Shadow of Death 60.00
8 HN,The Hive 60.00
9 BP,HN,The Tunnel 60.00
10 BP,HN,The Trial 60.00
11 BP,HN,The Closet 60.00
12 BP,HN,Tale of Cain 85.00
13 BP,What Was Out There . . . 85.00
14 BP,SC,End Result 75.00
15 BP,HN,Break-up 125.00
16 BP,Going,Going,Gone 85.00
Becomes:

THRILLS OF TOMORROW

17 RP,BP,The World of Mr. Chatt 40.00
18 RP,BP,The Dead Awaken . . . 30.00
19 S&K,S&K(c),A:Stuntman . . . 150.00
20 S&K,S&K(c),A:Stuntman . . . 135.00

TOM CORBETT SPACE CADET
Prize Publications
May-June, 1955

1 . . . . 125.00
2 . . . . 100.00
3 September-October, 1955 . 100.00

TOM MIX
Ralston-Purina Co.
September, 1940

1 O:Tom Mix 1,300.00
2 . . . . 500.00
3 . . . . 350.00
4 thru 9 . . . . @350.00
Becomes:

TOM MIX COMMANDOS COMICS

10 . . . . 300.00
11 Invisible Invaders 300.00
12 Terrible Talons Of Tokyo . . 300.00

TOM MIX WESTERN
Fawcett Publications
January, 1948

1 Ph(c),Two-Fisted Adventures 57500.00
2 Ph(c),Hair-Triggered Action 250.00
3 Ph(c),Double Barreled Action 200.00
4 Ph(c),Cowpunching 200.00
5 Ph(c),Two Gun Action 200.00
6 CCB,Most Famous Cowboy 175.00
7 CCB,A Tattoo of Thrills . . . 175.00
8 EK,Ph(c),Gallant Guns 165.00
9 CCB,Song o/t Deadly Spurs 150.00
10 CCB,Crack Shot Western . . 150.00
11 CCB,EK(C),Triple Revenge . 150.00
12 King of the Cowboys 125.00
13 Ph(c),Leather Burns 125.00
14 Ph(c),Brand of Death 125.00
15 Ph(c),Masked Treachery . . . 125.00
16 Ph(c),Death Spurting Guns . 125.00
17 Ph(c),Trail of Doom 125.00
18 Ph(c),Reign of Terror 100.00
19 Hand Colored Ph(c) 110.00
20 Ph(c),CCB,F:Capt Tootsie . . 100.00
21 Ph(c) 100.00
22 Ph(c),The Human Beast . . . 100.00
23 Ph(c),Return of the Past . . . 100.00
24 Hand Colored Ph(c), The Lawless City 100.00
25 Hand Colored Ph(c), The Signed Death Warrant . 100.00
26 Hand Colored Ph(c), Dangerous Escape 100.00
27 Hand Colored Ph(c), Hero Without Glory 100.00
28 Ph(c),The Storm Kings 100.00
29 Hand Colored Ph(c),The Case of the Rustling Rose . 100.00
30 Ph(c),Disappearance in the Hills 100.00
31 Ph(c) 80.00
32 Hand Colored Ph(c), Mystery of Tremble Mountain 75.00
33 . . . . 75.00
34 . . . . 65.00
35 Partial Ph(c),The Hanging at Hollow Creek 75.00
36 Ph(c) 75.00
37 Ph(c) 75.00
38 Ph(c),36 pages 65.00
39 Ph(c) 75.00
40 Ph(c) 75.00
41 Ph(c) 70.00
42 Ph(c) 75.00
43 Ph(c) 50.00
44 Ph(c) 50.00
45 Partial Ph(c),The Secret

Letter 50.00
46 Ph(c) 50.00
47 Ph(c) 50.00
48 Ph(c) 50.00

Tom Mix Western #49
© Fawcett Publications

49 Partial Ph(c),Blind Date With Death 50.00
50 Ph(c) 50.00
51 Ph(c) 50.00
52 Ph(c) 50.00
53 Ph(c) 50.00
54 Ph(c) 50.00
55 Ph(c) 50.00
56 Partial Ph(c),Deadly Spurs . . 50.00
57 Ph(c)5 . . . . 50.00
58 Ph(c) 50.00
59 Ph(c) 50.00
60 Ph(c) 50.00
61 Partial Ph(c),Lost in the Night,May 1953 . . . . 60.00

TOMMY OF THE BIG TOP
King Features/ Standard Comics
1948

10 Thrilling Circus Adventures . . 30.00
11 . . . . 20.00
12 March, 1949 . . . . 20.00

TOM-TOM THE JUNGLE BOY
Magazine Enterprises
1946

1 (fa) 40.00
2 (fa) 30.00
3 Winter 1947,(fa),X-mas issue . 15.00
1 . . . . 15.00

TONTO
(See LONE RANGER'S COMPANION TONTO)

TONY TRENT
(see FACE, THE)

TOP FLIGHT COMICS
Four Star/St. John Publ. Co.
July, 1949

1 . . . . 50.00
1 Hector the Inspector 35.00

TOP LOVE STORIES
Star Publications
May, 1951

3 LbC(c) 65.00
4 LbC(c) 45.00
5 LbC(c) 45.00
6 LbC(c),WW 80.00
7 thru 16 LbC(c) . . . . @65.00
17 LbC(c),WW 45.00
18 LbC(c) 45.00
19 LbC(c),JyD 45.00

TOP-NOTCH COMICS
MLJ Magazines
December, 1939

1 JaB,JCo,B&O:The Wizard, B:Kandak,Swift of the Secret Service,The Westpointer, Mystic, Air Patrol,Scott Rand, Manhunter 2,100.00

Top-Notch Comics #15
© MLJ Magazines

2 JaB,JCo,B:Dick Storm, E:Mystic, B:Stacy Knight . . . 900.00
3 JaB,JCo,EA(c),E:Swift of the Secret Service,Scott Rand . 750.00
4 JCo,EA(c),MMe,O&I:Streak, Chandler 500.00
5 Ea(c),MMe,O&I:Galahad, B:Shanghai Sheridan 500.00
6 Ea(c),MMe,A:The Sheild . . . 450.00
7 Ea(c),MMe,N:The Wizard . . 500.00
8 E:Dick Sorm,B&O:Roy The Super Boy,The Firefly 600.00
9 O&I:Black Hood, B:Fran Frazier 1,700.00
10 . . . . 750.00
11 . . . . 375.00
12 . . . . 375.00
13 . . . . 375.00
14 Bondage(c) 400.00
15 MMe 375.00
16 . . . . 375.00
17 Bondage(c) 400.00
18 . . . . 375.00
19 Bondage(c) 400.00
20 . . . . 375.00
21 . . . . 300.00
22 . . . . 300.00
23 Bondage(c) 325.00
24 Black Hood Smashes Murder Ring 300.00
25 E:Bob Phantom 300.00
26 . . . . 300.00
27 E:The Firefly 300.00
28 B:Suzie,Pokey Okay, Gag Oriented 300.00
29 E:Kandak 300.00
30 . . . . 300.00
31 . . . . 200.00
32 . . . . 200.00
33 BWo,B:Dotty&Ditto 200.00
34 BWo 200.00

Suzie #63 © Archie Publications

35 BWo 200.00
36 BWo 200.00
37 thru 40 BWo . . . . @200.00
41 . . . . 200.00
42 BWo 200.00
43 . . . . 200.00
44 EW:Black Hood,I:Suzie 225.00
45 Suzie(c) 250.00

Becomes:

LAUGH COMIX

46 Suzie & Wilbur 100.00
47 Suzie & Wilbur 85.00
48 Suzie & Wilbur 85.00

Becomes:

SUZIE COMICS

49 B:Ginger 150.00
50 AFy(c) 90.00
51 AFy(c) 90.00
52 AFy(c) 90.00
53 AFy(c) 90.00
54 AFy(c) 100.00
55 AFy(c) 110.00
56 BWo,B;Katie Keene 65.00
57 thru 70 BWo . . . . @65.00
71 thru 79 BWo . . . . @55.00
80 thru 99 BWo . . . . @45.00
100 August, 1954, BWo 45.00

TOPS
Tops Mag. Inc. (Lev Gleason)
July, 1949

1 RC&BLb,GT,DBa,CBi(c),I'll Buy That Girl,Our Explosive Children 600.00
2 FG,BF,CBi(c),RC&BLb 575.00

TOPS COMICS
Consolidated Book Publishers
1944

2000 Don on the Farm 165.00
2001 The Jack of Spades V:The Hawkman 90.00
2002 Rip Raiders 65.00
2003 Red Birch 20.00

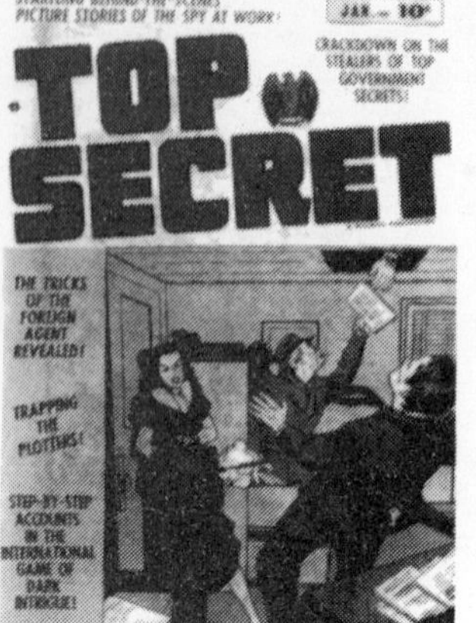

Top Secret #1 © Hillman Publ.

TOP SECRET
Hillman Publications
January, 1952

1 The Tricks of the Secret Agent Revealed 100.00

TOP SECRETS
Street & Smith Publications
November, 1947

1 BP,BP(c),Of the Men Who Guard the U.S. Mail 175.00
2 BP,BP(c),True Story of Jim the Penman 125.00
3 BP,BP(c),Crime Solved by Mental Telepathy 125.00
4 Highway Pirates 125.00
5 BP,BP(c),Can Music Kill . . . 125.00
6 BP,BP(c),The Clue of the Forgotten Film 125.00
7 BP,BP(c),Train For Sale . . . 150.00
8 BP,BP(c) 100.00
9 BP,BP(c) 100.00
10 BP,BP(c),July-August, 1949 100.00

TOPS IN ADVENTURE
Approved Comics (Ziff-Davis)
Autumn, 1952

1 BP,Crusaders From Mars . . 250.00

TOP SPOT COMICS
Top Spot Publishing Co.
1945

1 The Duke Of Darkness 150.00

TOPSY-TURVY
R.B. Leffingwell Publ.
April, 1945

1 I:Cookie 50.00

TOR
St. John Publishing Co.
September, 1953

1 JKu,JKu(c),O;Tor,One Million Years Ago 85.00
2 JKu,JKu(c),3-D Issue 75.00
3 JKu,JKu(c),ATh,historic Life . 80.00
4 JKu,JKu(c),ATh 80.00
5 JKu,JKu(c),ATh,October, 1954 80.00

TORCHY
Quality Comics Group
November, 1949

1 GFx,BWa(c),The Blonde Bombshell 700.00
2 GFx,GFx(c),Beauty at its' Best 300.00
3 GFX,GFx(c),You Can't Beat Nature 300.00
4 GFx,GFx(c),The Girl to Keep Your Eye On 400.00
5 BWa,GFx,BWa(c),At the Masquerade Party 450.00
6 September, 1950,BWa,GFx, BWa(c),The Libido Driven Boy Scout 500.00

TORMENTED, THE
Sterling Comics
July, 1954

1 Buried Alive 125.00
2 September, 1954,The Devils Circus 100.00

TOYLAND COMICS
Fiction House Magazines
January, 1947

1 Wizard of the Moon 125.00
2 Buddy Bruin & Stu Rabbit . . . 70.00
3 GT,The Candy Maker 75.00
4 July, 1947 . . . . 70.00

TOY TOWN COMICS
Toytown Publ./Orbit Publ.
February, 1945

1 LbC,LbC(c)(fa) 90.00
2 LbC,(fa) 50.00
3 LbC,LbC(c),(fa) 45.00
4 LbC,(fa) 45.00
5 LbC,(fa) 45.00
6 LbC,(fa) 45.00
7 LbC,(fa),May, 1947 . . . . 45.00

TRAIL BLAZERS
(see RED DRAGON COMICS)

Treasure Comics #3
© Prize Comics Group

TREASURE COMICS
Prize Comics Group
1943

1 S&K,Reprints of Prize Comics #7 through #11 . . . . 1,250.00

TREASURE COMICS
American Boys Comics (Prize Publications)
June-July, 1945

1 HcK,B:PaulBunyan,MarcoPolo 150.00
2 HcK,HcK(c),B:Arabian Knight, Gorilla King,Dr.Styx 75.00
3 HcK 55.00
4 HcK 55.00
5 HcK,JK 100.00
6 HcK,BK,HcK(c) 85.00
7 HcK,FF,HcK(c) 200.00
8 HcK,FF 200.00
9 HcK,DBa 55.00
10 JK,DBa,JK(c) 125.00
11 BK,HcK,DBa,The Weird Adventures of Mr. Bottle . . . 100.00
12 DBa,DBa(c),Autumn, 1947 . . 65.00

TREASURY OF COMICS
St. John Publishing Co.
1947

1 RvB,RvB(c),Abbie an' Slats 125.00
2 Jim Hardy 75.00
3 Bill Bimlin 75.00
4 RvB,RvB(c),Abbie an' Slats . 75.00
5 Jim Hardy,January, 1948 . . . 70.00

TRIPLE THREAT
Gerona Publications
Winter, 1945

1 F:King O'Leary,The Duke of Darkness,Beau Brummell . . . 75.00

TRUE AVIATION PICTURE STORIES
Parents' Institute/P.M.I.
August, 1942

1 How Jimmy Doolittle Bombed Tokyo 85.00
2 Knight of the Air Mail 45.00
3 The Amazing One-Man Air Force 40.00
4 Joe Foss America's No. 1 Air Force 40.00
5 Bombs over Germany 40.00
6 Flight Lt. Richard Hillary R.A.F. 40.00
7 "Fatty" Chow China's Sky Champ 40.00
8 Blitz over Burma 40.00
9 Off the Beam 40.00
10 "Pappy" Boyington 40.00
11 Ph(c) 40.00
12 . . . . 40.00
13 Ph(c),Flying Facts 40.00
14 . . . . 40.00
15 . . . . 40.00

Becomes:

AVIATION AND MODEL BUILDING

16 . . . . 45.00
17 February, 1947 . . . . 50.00

TRUE COMICS
True Comics/ Parents' Magazine Press
April, 1941

1 My Greatest Adventure-by Lowell Thomas 200.00
2 BEv,The Story of the Red Cross 100.00
3 Baseball Hall of Fame 125.00
4 Danger in the Artic 90.00
5 Father Duffy-the Fighting Chaplin 100.00
6 The Capture of Aquinaldo . . 100.00
7 JKa,Wilderness Adventures of George Washington 100.00
8 U.S. Army Wings 55.00
9 A Pig that Made History 55.00

10 Adrift on an Ice Pan 55.00
11 Gen. Douglas MacArthur . . . 60.00
12 Mackenzie-King of Cananda . 55.00
13 The Real Robinson Crusoe . . 60.00
14 Australia war base of the South Pacific 60.00

True Comics #15

© True Comics/Parents' Magazine

15 The Story of West Point 75.00
16 How Jimmy Doolittle Bombed Tokyo 70.00
17 The Ghost of Captain Blig, B.Feller 75.00
18 Battling Bill of the Merchant Marine 80.00
19 Secret Message Codes 45.00
20 The Story of India 40.00
21 Timoshenko the Blitz Buster . 45.00
22 Gen, Bernard L. Montgomery 40.00
23 The Story of Steel 40.00
24 Gen. Henri Giraud-Master of Escape 40.00
25 Medicine's Miracle Men 40.00
26 Hero of the Bismarck Sea . . . 40.00
27 Leathernecks have Landed . . 45.00
28 The Story of Radar 35.00
29 The Fighting Seabees 35.00
30 Dr. Norman Bethune-Blood Bank Founder 35.00
31 Our Good Neighbor Bolivia, Red Grange 45.00
32 Men against the Desert 30.00
33 Gen. Clark and his Fighting 5th 35.00
34 Angel of the Battlefield 30.00
35 Carlson's Marine Raiders 30.00
36 Canada's Sub-Busters 30.00
37 Commander of the Crocodile Fleet 30.00
38 Oregon Trailblazer 30.00
39 Saved by Sub 30.00
40 Sea Furies 30.00
41 Cavalcade of England 25.00
42 Gen. Jaques Le Clerc-Hero of Paris 25.00
43 Unsinkable Ship 30.00
44 El Senor Goofy 25.00
45 Tokyo Express 20.00
46 The Magnificent Runt 25.00
47 Atoms Unleashed, Atomic Bomb 55.00
48 Pirate Patriot 25.00
49 Smiking Fists 25.00
50 Lumber Pirates 25.00
51 Exercise Musk-Ox 25.00
52 King of the Buckeneers 25.00
53 Baseline Booby 25.00
54 Santa Fe Sailor 25.00
55 Sea Going Santa 25.00
56 End of a Terror 25.00
57 Newfangled Machines 25.00
58 Leonardo da Vinci-500 years too Soon 25.00
59 Pursuit of the Pirates 30.00
60 Emmett Kelly-The World's Funniest Clown 25.00
61 Peter Le Grand-Bold Buckaneer 25.00
62 Sutter's Gold 25.00
63 Outboard Outcome 25.00
64 Man-Eater at Large 25.00
65 The Story of Scotland Yard . . 25.00
66 Easy Guide to Football Formations 30.00

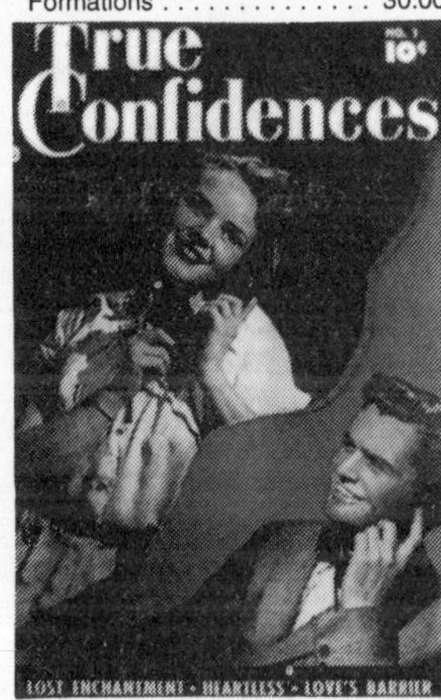

True Confidences #1

© Fawcett Publications

67 The Changing Zebra 25.00
68 Admiral Byrd 22.00
69 FBI Special Agent Steve Saunders 30.00
70 The Case of the Seven Hunted Men 25.00
71 Story of Joe DiMaggio 150.00
72 FBI 40.00
73 The 26 Mile Dash-Story of the Marathon 30.00
74 A Famous Coach's Special Football Tips 30.00
75 King of Reporters 30.00
76 The Story of a Buried Treasure 30.00
77 France's Greatest Detective . 30.00
78 Cagliostro-Master Rogue . . . 50.00
79 Ralph Bunche-Hero of Peace 30.00
80 Rocket Trip to the Moon . . . 150.00
81 Red Grange 150.00
82 Marie Celeste Ship of Mystery 100.00
83 Bullfighter from Brooklyn . . . 100.00
84 King of the Buckaneers, August, 1950 . . . . 100.00

TRUE CONFIDENCES
Fawcett Publications
Autumn, 1949

1 . . . . 75.00
2 & 3 . . . . @45.00
4 DP 45.00

TRUE CRIME COMICS
Magazine Village, Inc.
May, 1947

2 JCo(c),JCo(c),James Kent-Crook,Murderer,Escaped Convict; Drug 675.00
3 JCo,JCo(c),Benny Dickson-Killer;Drug 500.00
4 JCo,JCo(c),Little Jake-Big Shot 475.00
5 JCo(c),The Rat & the Blond Gun Moll;Drug 275.00
6 Joseph Metley-Swindler, Jailbird, Killer 125.00
2-1(7) ATh,WW,Ph(c),Phil Coppolla,September, 1949 . 400.00

TRUE LIFE SECRETS
Romantic Love Stories/ Charlton Comics
March-April, 1951

1 . . . . 60.00
2 . . . . 30.00
3 . . . . 25.00
4 . . . . 25.00
5 thru 20 . . . . @25.00
21 thru 25 . . . . @20.00
26 Comics Code 15.00
27 thru 29 . . . . @15.00

TRUE LIFE ROMANCES
Ajax/Farrell Publications
December, 1955

1 . . . . 45.00
2 . . . . 25.00
3 August, 1956 . . . . 30.00

TRUE LOVE PICTORIAL
St. John Publishing Co.
1952

1 Ph(c) 70.00
2 MB 35.00
3 MB(c),MB,JKu 150.00
4 MB(c),MB,JKu 150.00
5 MB(c),MB,JKu 150.00
6 MB(c) 60.00
7 MB(c) 60.00
8 MB(c) 50.00
9 MB(c) 40.00
10 MB(c),MB 50.00
11 MB(c),MB 50.00

True Movie #3 © Toby Press

TRUE MOVIE AND TELEVISION
Toby Press

August, 1950
1 Liz Taylor, Ph(c) 200.00
2 FF,Ph(c),John Wayne, L.Taylor 150.00
3 June Allyson,Ph(c) 150.00
4 Jane Powell,Ph(c),Jan.,1951 100.00

SPORT COMICS
Street & Smith Publications
October, 1940
1 F:Lou Gehrig 350.00
2 F:Gene Tunney 200.00
3 F:Phil Rizzuto 225.00
4 F:Frank Leahy 200.00

True Sport #8 © Street & Smith

Becomes:
TRUE SPORT PICTURE STORIES
5 Joe DiMaggio 250.00
6 Billy Confidence 100.00
7 Mel Ott 150.00
8 Lou Ambers 100.00
9 Pete Reiser 100.00
10 Frankie Sinkwich 100.00
11 Marty Serfo 80.00
12 JaB(c),Jack Dempsey 80.00
2-1 JaB(c),Willie Pep 75.00
2-2 JaB(c) 75.00
2-3 JaB(c),Carl Hubbell 85.00
2-4 Advs. in Football & Battle . 100.00
2-5 Don Hutson 75.00
2-6 Dixie Walker 100.00
2-7 Stan Musial 150.00
2-8 Famous Ring Champions of All Time 100.00
2-9 List of War Year Rookies . 150.00
2-10 Connie Mack 100.00
2-11 Winning Basketball Plays . . 75.00
2-12 Eddie Gottlieb 75.00
3-1 Bill Conn 85.00
3-2 The Philadelphia Athletics . . 70.00
3-3 Leo Durocher 100.00
3-4 Rudy Dusek 75.00
3-5 Ernie Pyle 75.00
3-6 Bowling with Ned Day 70.00
3-7 Return of the Mighty (Home from War);Joe DiMaggio(c) . 250.00
3-8 Conn V:Louis 200.00
3-9 Reuben Shark 75.00
3-10 BP,BP(c),Don "Dopey" Dillock 50.00
3-11 BP,BP(c),Death Scores a Touchdown 75.00
3-12 Red Sox V:Senators 70.00
4-1 Spring Training in Full Spring 75.00
4-2 BP,BP(c),How to Pitch 'Em Where They Can't Hit 'Em . . 35.00
4-3 BP,BP(c),1947 Super Stars 90.00
4-4 BP,BP(c),Get Ready for the Olympics 100.00
4-5 BP,BP,(c),Hugh Casey 75.00
4-6 BP,BP(c),Phantom Phil Hergesheimer 75.00
4-7 BP,BP(c),How to Bowl Better 35.00
4-8 Tips on the Big Fight 100.00
4-9 BP,BP(c),Bill McCahan 65.00
4-10 BP,BP(c),Great Football Plays 50.00
4-11 BP,BP(c),Football 50.00
4-12 BP,BP(c),Basketball 50.00
5-1 Satchel Paige 150.00
5-2 History of Boxing, July-August, 1949 . . . . 75.00

TRUE SWEETHEART SECRETS
Fawcett Publications
May, 1950
1 Ph(c) 60.00
2 WW 100.00
3 BD 40.00
4 BD 40.00
5 BD 40.00
6 thru 11 . . . . @35.00

True-To-Life Romances #12
© Star Publications

TRUE-TO-LIFE ROMANCES
Star Publications
November-December, 1949
3 LbC(c),GlennFord/JanetLeigh 55.00
4 LbC(c) 50.00
5 LbC(c) 50.00
6 LbC(c) 50.00
7 LbC(c) 50.00
8 LbC(c) 50.00
9 LbC(c) 50.00
10 LbC(c) 50.00
11 LbC(c) 45.00
12 LbC(c) 50.00
13 LbC(c),JyD 50.00
14 LbC(c),JyD 50.00
15 LbC(c),WW,JyD 75.00
16 LbC(c),WW,JyD 75.00
17 LbC(c),JyD 55.00
18 LbC(c),JyD 55.00
19 LbC(c),JyD 55.00
20 LbC(c),JyD 55.00
21 LbC(c),JyD 55.00
22 LbC(c) 40.00
23 LbC(c) 40.00

TRUE WAR ROMANCES
Comic Magazines, Inc.
(Quality Comics)
September, 1952
1 Ph(c) 65.00
2 . . . . 30.00
3 thru 10 . . . . @20.00
11 thru 20 . . . . @15.00
21 Comics Code 15.00
Becomes:
EXOTIC ROMANCES
22 . . . . 35.00
23 . . . . 20.00
24 . . . . 20.00
25 . . . . 20.00
26 . . . . 20.00
27 MB 35.00
28 MB 35.00
29 . . . . 20.00
30 MB 35.00
31 MB 35.00

TUROK, SON OF STONE
Dell Publishing Co.
December, 1954
(1) *see Dell Four Color #596*
(2) *see Dell Four Color #656*
3 . . . . 250.00
4 . . . . 225.00
5 . . . . 225.00
6 thru 10 . . . . @150.00
11 thru 20 . . . . @90.00
21 thru 29 . . . . @60.00
See Other Color section

TWEETY AND SYLVESTER
Dell Publishing Co.
June, 1952
(1) *see Dell Four Color #406*
(2) *see Dell Four Color #489*
(3) *see Dell Four Color #524*
4 thru 20 . . . . @15.00
21 thru 37 . . . . @8.00

TWINKLE COMICS
Spotlight Publications
May, 1945
1 Humor Format 70.00

TWO-FISTED TALES
Fables Publications
(E.C. Comics)
November-December, 1950
18 HK,JCr,WW,JSe,HK(c) 750.00
19 HK,JCr,WW,JSe,HK(c) 500.00
20 JDa,HK,WW,JSe,HK(c) 300.00
21 JDa,HK,WW,JSe,HK(c) 250.00
22 JDa,HK,WW,JSe,HK(c) 250.00
23 JDa,HK,WW,JSe,HK(c) 225.00
24 JDa,HK,WW,JSe,HK(c) 200.00
25 JDa,HK,WW,JSe,HK(c) 200.00
26 JDa,JSe,HK(c),Action at the Changing Reservoir . . . 150.00
27 JDa,JSe,HK(c) 150.00
28 JDa,JSe,HK(c) 150.00
29 JDa,JSe,HK(c) 200.00
30 JDa,JSe,JDa(c) 200.00
31 JDa,JSe,HK(c),Civil War Story 160.00
32 JDa,JKu,WW(c) 160.00
33 JDa,JKu,WW(c) 175.00
34 JDa,JSe,JDa(c) 160.00
35 JDa,JSe,JDa(c),Civil War Story 175.00
36 JDa,JSe,JSe(c),A Difference of Opinion 100.00
37 JSe,JSe(c),Bugles & Battle Cries 100.00

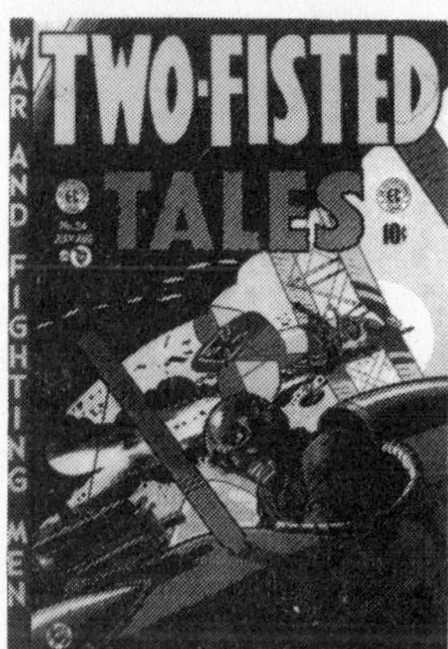

Two-Fisted Tales #34

© Fables Publ./E.C. Comics

38 JSe,JSe(c) 100.00
39 JSe,JSe(c) 100.00
40 JDa,JSe,GE,GE(c) 150.00
41 JSe,GE,JDa(c),March, 1955 100.00

UNCLE CHARLIE'S FABLES
Lev Gleason Publications
January, 1952

1 CBi(c),Ph(c) 55.00
2 BF,CBi(c),Ph(c) 30.00
3 CBi(c),Ph(c) 35.00
4 CBi(c),Ph(c) 35.00
5 CBi,Ph(c),September, 1952 . 30.00

UNCLE SAM
(see BLACKHAWK)

UNCLE SCROOGE
Dell Publishing Co.
March, 1952

(1) *see Dell Four Color #386*
(2) *see Dell Four Color #456*
(3) *see Dell Four Color #495*
4 . . . . 250.00
5 . . . . 200.00
6 . . . . 175.00
7 CB 135.00
8 . . . . 125.00
9 . . . . 125.00
10 . . . . 125.00
11 thru 20 . . . . @100.00
21 thru 30 . . . . @75.00
31 thru 39 . . . . @65.00
See Other Color section

UNDERWORLD
D.S. Publishing Co.
February-March, 1948

1 SMo(c),Violence 185.00
2 SMo(c),Electrocution 200.00
3 AMc,AMc(c),The Ancient Club 175.00
4 Grl,The Beer Baron Murder 150.00
5 Grl,The Postal Clue 90.00
6 The Polka Dot Gang 75.00
7 Mono-The Master 75.00
8 The Double Tenth 75.00
9 Thrilling Stories of the Fight Against Crime,June, 1953 . . 75.00

UNDERWORLD CRIME
Fawcett Publications
June, 1952

1 The Crime Army 150.00
2 Jailbreak 75.00
3 Microscope Murder 65.00
4 Death on the Docks 65.00
5 River of Blood 65.00
6 The Sky Pirates 65.00
7 Bondage & Torture(c) 150.00
8 . . . . 65.00
9 June, 1953 . . . . 65.00

UNITED COMICS
United Features Syndicate
1950

8 thru 26 Bushmiller(c), Fritzi Ritz . . . . @25.00

UNITED STATES FIGHTING AIR FORCE
Superior Comics, Ltd.
September, 1952

1 Coward's Courage 45.00
2 Clouds that Killed 25.00
3 Operation Decoy 15.00
4 thru 28 . . . . @15.00
29 October, 1959 . . . . 15.00

UNITED STATES MARINES
Wm. H. Wise/Magazine Ent/ Toby Press
1943

N# MBi,MBi(c),Hellcat out of Heaven 45.00
2 MBi,Drama of Wake Island . . 35.00
3 A Leatherneck Flame Thrower 30.00
4 MBi 30.00
5 BP 25.00
6 BP 25.00
7 BP 20.00
8 . . . . 20.00
9 . . . . 20.00
10 . . . . 20.00
11 1952 . . . . 20.00

UNKEPT PROMISE
Legion of Truth
1949

1 Anti:Alcoholic Drinking 50.00

UNKNOWN WORLDS
(see STRANGE STORIES FROM ANOTHER WORLD)

UNSEEN, THE
Visual Editions
(Standard Comics)
1952

5 ATh,The Hungry Lodger . . . 125.00
6 JKa,MSy,Bayou Vengeance . 90.00
7 JKz,MSy,Time is the Killer . . 90.00
8 JKz,MSy,The Vengance Vat . 90.00
9 JKz,MSy,Your Grave is Ready 90.00
10 JKz,MSy 90.00
11 JKz,MSy 90.00
12 ATh,GT,Till Death Do Us Part 100.00
13 . . . . 55.00
14 . . . . 55.00
15 ATh,The Curse of the Undead!, July, 1954 . . . . . . 100.00

UNTAMED LOVE
Comic Magazines
(Quality Comics Group)
January, 1950

1 BWa(c),PGn 120.00
2 Ph(c) 75.00
3 PGn 80.00
4 . . . . 75.00
5 PGn 80.00

Untamed Love #4

© Comic Magazines/Quality Comics

USA IS READY
Dell Publishing Co.
1941

1 Propaganda WWII 200.00

U.S. JONES
Fox Features Syndicate
November, 1941

1 Death Over the Airways . . . 600.00
2 January, 1942 . . . . 450.00

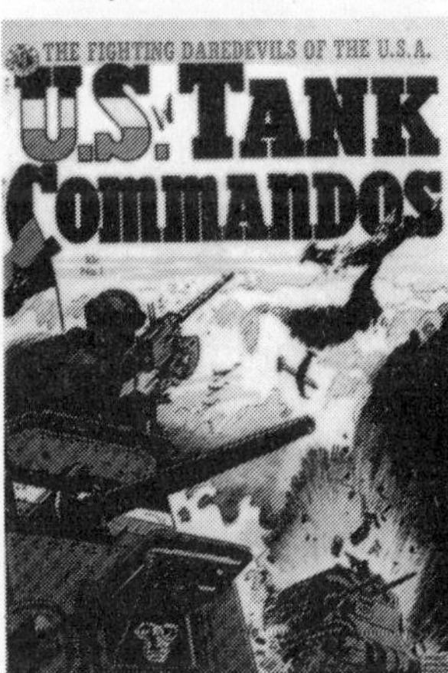

U.S. Tank Commandos #1

© Avon Periodicals

U.S. MARINES IN ACTION!
Avon Periodicals
August, 1952

1 On Land,Sea & in the Air . . . 35.00
2 The Killer Patrol 20.00
3 EK(c),Death Ridge, December, 1952 . . . . 22.00

U.S. TANK COMMANDOS
Avon Periodicals
June, 1952

1 EK(c),Fighting Daredevils of the USA 40.00
2 EK(c) 25.00
3 EK,EK(c),Robot Armanda . . . 25.00
4 EK,EK(c),March, 1953 . . . . . 25.00

VALOR
E.C. Comics
March, 1955

1 AW,AT,WW,WW(c),Grl,BK . 250.00
2 AW(c),AW,WWGrl,BK 200.00
3 AW,RC,BK,JOc(c) 150.00
4 WW(c),RC,Grl,BK,JO 150.00
5 WW(c),WW,AW,GE,Grl,BK . 125.00

VARIETY COMICS
Rural Home Publ./ Croyden Publ. Co.
1944

1 MvS,MvS(c),O:Capt, Valiant 100.00
2 MvS,MvS(c) 50.00
3 MvS,MvS(c) 45.00
4 . . . . 35.00
5 1946 . . . . 35.00

VAULT OF HORROR
(see WAR AGAINST CRIME)

V...COMICS
Fox Features Syndicate
January, 1942

1 V:V-Man 600.00
2 The Horror of the Dungeons, March, 1942 . . . 500.00

VERI BEST SURE SHOT COMICS
Holyoke Publishing Co.
1945

1 reprint Holyoke One-Shots . 175.00

VIC FLINT
St. John Publishing Co.
August, 1948

1 ...Crime Buster 60.00
2 . . . . 40.00
3 . . . . 35.00
4 . . . . 35.00
5 April, 1949 . . . . 35.00

VIC JORDAN
Civil Service Publications
April, 1945

1 Escape From a Nazi Prison . 70.00

VIC TORRY AND HIS FLYING SAUCER
Fawcett Publications
1950

1 Ph(c),Revealed at Last 300.00

VICTORY COMICS
Hillman Periodicals
August, 1941

1 BEv,BEv(c),F:TheConqueror 1,200.00
2 BEv,BEv(c) 600.00
3 The Conqueror(c) 400.00
4 December, 1941 . . . . 400.00

VIC VERITY MAGAZINE
Vic Verity Publications
1945

1 CCB,CCB(c),B:Vic Verity,Hot-Shot Galvan, Tom Travis . . . 80.00
2 CCB,CCB(c),Annual Classic

Victory Comics #4
© Hillman Periodicals

Dance Recital 45.00
3 CCB 40.00
4 CCB,I:Boomer Young;The Bee-U-TiFul Weekend 40.00
5 CCB,Championship Baseball Game 40.00
6 CCB,High School Hero 40.00
7 CCB,CCB(c),F:Rocket Rex . . 40.00

VOODOO
Four Star Publ./Farrell/ Ajax Comics
May, 1952

1 MB,South Sea Girl 200.00
2 MB 175.00
3 Face Stabbing 135.00
4 MB,Rendezvous 125.00
5 Ghoul For A Day,Nazi 85.00
6 The Weird Dead,Severed Head 90.00
7 Goodbye World 85.00
8 MB, Revenge 135.00
9 Will this thing Never Stew? . . 80.00
10 Land of Shadows & Screams 80.00
11 Human Harvest 75.00
12 The Wazen Taper 75.00
13 Bondage(c),Caskets to Fit Everybody 100.00
14 Death Judges the Beauty Contest 75.00
15 Loose their Heads 85.00
16 Fog Was Her Shroud 75.00
17 Apes Laughter,Electric Chair . 80.00
18 Astounding Fantasy 75.00
19 MB,Bondage(c); Destination Congo 100.00

Becomes:

VOODA

20 MB,MB(c),Echoes of an A-Bomb 120.00
21 MB,MB(c),Trek of Danger . . 100.00
22 MB,MB(c),The Sun Blew Away, August, 1955 . . . . . . 100.00

WACKY DUCK
(see DOPEY DUCK)

WALT DISNEY'S COMICS & STORIES
Dell Publishing Co.

N# 1943 dpt.store giveway . . . 350.00
N# 1945 X-mas giveaway 80.00

WALT DISNEY'S COMICS & STORIES
Dell Publishing Co.
October, 1940

1 (1940)FG,Donald Duck & Mickey Mouse 8,000.00
2 . . . . 3,000.00
3 . . . . 1,000.00
4 Christmas(c) 750.00
4a Promo issue 1,000.00
5 . . . . 600.00
6 . . . . 600.00

Walt Disney's Comics and Stories #2
© Dell Publ. Co.

7 . . . . 500.00
8 . . . . 475.00
9 . . . . 475.00
10 . . . . 450.00
11 . . . . 450.00
12 . . . . 500.00
13 . . . . 425.00
14 . . . . 450.00
15 3 Little Kittens 400.00
16 3 Little Pigs 375.00
17 The Ugly Ducklings 375.00
18 . . . . 350.00
19 . . . . 300.00
20 . . . . 300.00
21 . . . . 325.00
22 . . . . 290.00
23 . . . . 275.00
24 . . . . 275.00
25 . . . . 275.00
26 . . . . 275.00
27 . . . . 300.00
28 . . . . 275.00
29 . . . . 275.00
30 . . . . 275.00
31 CB; Donald Duck 1,750.00
32 CB 850.00
33 CB 600.00
34 CB;WK; Gremlins 500.00
35 CB;WK; Gremlins. 400.00
36 CB;WK; Gremlins 400.00
37 CB;WK; Gremlins 250.00
38 CB;WK; Gremlins 350.00
39 CB;WK; Gremlins 325.00
40 CB;WK; Gremlins 300.00
41 CB;WK; Gremlins 250.00
42 CB 250.00
43 CB 275.00
44 CB 275.00
45 CB 275.00
46 CB 275.00
47 CB 250.00

Walt Disney's Comics and Stories #18
© Dell Publ. Co.

48 CB 255.00
49 CB 250.00
50 CB 250.00
51 CB 225.00
52 CB; Li'l Bad Wolf begins . . . 225.00
53 CB 225.00
54 CB 225.00
55 CB 225.00
56 CB 225.00
57 CB 225.00
58 CB 225.00
59 CB 225.00
60 CB 225.00
61 CB; Dumbo 150.00
62 CB 150.00
63 CB; Pinocchio 150.00
64 CB; Pinocchio 150.00
65 CB; Pluto 150.00
66 CB 150.00
67 CB 150.00
68 CB 150.00
69 CB 150.00
70 CB 150.00
71 CB 125.00
72 CB 125.00
73 CB 125.00
74 CB 125.00
75 CB; Brer Rabbit 125.00
76 CB; Brer Rabbit 125.00
77 CB; Brer Rabbit 125.00
78 CB 125.00
79 CB 125.00
80 CB 125.00
81 CB 100.00
82 CB;Bongo 115.00
83 CB;Bongo 115.00
84 CB;Bongo 115.00
85 CB 115.00
86 CB;Goofy & Agnes 115.00
87 CB;Goofy & Agnes 100.00
88 CB;Goofy & Agnes, I:Gladstone Gander 125.00
89 CB;Goofy&Agnes,Chip'n'Dale 80.00
90 CB;Goofy & Agnes 80.00
91 CB 80.00
92 CB 80.00
93 CB 80.00
94 CB 80.00
95 . . . . 80.00
96 Little Toot 80.00
97 CB; Little Toot 80.00
98 CB; Uncle Scrooge 175.00
99 CB 75.00
100 CB 80.00
101 CB 75.00
102 CB 75.00
103 CB 60.00
104 . . . . 60.00
105 CB 75.00
106 CB 75.00
107 CB 75.00
108 . . . . 60.00
109 . . . . 60.00
110 CB 75.00
111 CB 75.00
112 CB; drugs 75.00
113 CB 75.00
114 CB 75.00
115 . . . . 30.00
116 . . . . 30.00
117 . . . . 30.00
118 . . . . 30.00
119 . . . . 30.00
120 . . . . 30.00
121 Grandma Duck begins 30.00
122 . . . . 30.00
123 . . . . 30.00
124 CB 50.00
125 CB;I:Junior Woodchucks . . . 75.00
126 CB 50.00
127 CB 50.00
128 CB 50.00
129 CB 50.00
130 CB 50.00
131 CB 50.00
132 CB A:Grandma Duck 50.00
133 CB 50.00
134 I:The Beagle Boys 85.00
135 CB 50.00
136 CB 50.00
137 CB 50.00
138 CB 50.00
139 CB 50.00
140 CB; I:Gyro Gearloose 80.00
141 CB 35.00
142 CB 35.00
143 CB; Little Hiawatha 35.00
144 CB; Little Hiawatha 35.00
145 CB; Little Hiawatha 35.00
146 CB; Little Hiawatha 35.00
147 CB; Little Hiawatha 35.00
148 CB; Little Hiawatha 35.00
149 CB; Little Hiawatha 35.00
150 CB; Little Hiawatha 35.00
151 CB; Little Hiawatha 35.00
152 thru 200 CB . . . . @25.00
201 CB 20.00
202 CB 20.00
203 CB 20.00
204 CB, Chip 'n' Dale & Scamp . 20.00
205 thru 240 CB . . . . @20.00
241 CB; Dumbo x-over 25.00
242 CB 25.00
243 CB 25.00
244 CB 25.00
245 CB 25.00
246 CB 25.00
247 thru 255 CB;GyroGearloose@25.00
256 thru 263 CB;Ludwig Von Drake & Gearloose . . . . . . @25.00

See: Independent Color Comics

WALT DISNEY ANNUALS

Walt Disney's Autumn Adventure . 4.00
Walt Disney's Holiday Parade . . . 3.50
Walt Disney's Spring Fever 3.25
Walt Disney's Summer Fun 3.25

WALT DISNEY DELL GIANT EDITIONS

Dell Publishing Co.

1 CB,W.Disney'sXmas Parade('49) 600.00
2 CB,W.Disney'sXmas Parade('50) 450.00
3 W.Disney'sXmas Parade('51) 100.00
4 W.Disney'sXmas Parade('52) . 90.00
5 W.Disney'sXmas Parade('53) . 90.00
6 W.Disney'sXmas Parade('54) . 90.00
7 W.Disney'sXmas Parade('55) . 90.00
8 CB,W.Disney'sXmas Parade('56) 200.00
9 CB,W.Disney'sXmas Parade('57) 250.00
1 CB,W.Disney's Christmas in Disneyland (1957) 200.00
1 CB,W.Disney's Disneyland Birthday Party (1958) 200.00
1 W.Disney's Donald and Mickey in Disneyland (1958) 125.00
1 W.Disney's Donald Duck Beach Party (1954) 125.00
2 W.Disney's Donald Duck Beach Party (1955) 90.00
3 W.Disney's Donald Duck Beach Party (1956) 80.00
4 W.Disney's Donald Duck Beach Party (1957) 80.00
5 W.Disney's Donald Duck Beach Party (1958) 80.00
6 W.Disney's Donald Duck Beach Party (1959) 80.00
1 W.Disney's Donald Duck Fun Book (1954) 450.00
2 W.Disney's Donald Duck Fun Book (1954) 400.00
1 W.Disney's Donald Duck in Disneyland (1955) 85.00
1 W.Disney's Huey, Dewey and Louie (1958) 100.00
1 W.Disney's DavyCrockett('55) 135.00
1 W.Disney's Lady and the Tramp (1955) 125.00
1 CB,W.Disney's Mickey Mouse Almanac (1957) 400.00
1 W.Disney's Mickey Mouse Birthday Party (1953) 375.00
1 W.Disney's Mickey Mouse Club Parade (1955) 325.00
1 W.Disney's Mickey Mouse in Fantasyland (1957) 150.00
1 W.Disney's Mickey Mouse in Frontierland (1956) 150.00
1 W.Disney's Summer Fun('58) 200.00
2 CB,W.Disney'sSummer Fun('59) 200.00
1 W.Disney's Peter Pan Treasure Chest (1953) 900.00
1 Disney Silly Symphonies('52) 250.00
2 Disney Silly Symphonies('53) 200.00
3 Disney Silly Symphonies('54) 200.00
4 Disney Silly Symphonies('54) 175.00
5 Disney Silly Symphonies('55) 175.00
6 Disney Silly Symphonies('56) 175.00
7 Disney Silly Symphonies('57) 250.00
8 Disney Silly Symphonies('58) 150.00
9 Disney Silly Symphonies('59) 150.00
1 Disney SleepingBeauty('59) . 300.00
1 CB,W.Disney's Uncle Scrooge Goes to Disneyland (1957) . 250.00
1 W.Disney's Vacation in Disneyland (1958) 100.00
1 CB,Disney'sVacation Parade('50) 1,000.00
2 Disney'sVacation Parade('51) 200.00
3 Disney'sVacation Parade('52) 100.00
4 Disney'sVacation Parade('53) 100.00
5 Disney'sVacation Parade('54) 100.00
6 Disney's Picnic Party (1955) 150.00
7 Disney's Picnic Party (1956) 150.00
8 CB,Disney's Picnic Party (1957) 175.00

DELL JUNIOR TREASURY

1 W.Disney's Alice in Wonderland (1955) 75.00

WALT DISNEY PRESENTS

Dell Publishing Co.

June-August, 1952

1 Ph(c), Four Color 40.00

2 Ph(c) 25.00
3 Ph(c) 25.00
4 Ph(c) 25.00
5 and 6 Ph(c) . . . . @25.00

WAMBI JUNGLE BOY
Fiction House Magazines
Spring, 1942

1 HcK,HcK(c),Vengence of the Beasts 350.00
2 HcK,HcK(c),Lair of the Killer Rajah 200.00
3 HcK,HcK(c) 150.00
4 HcK,HcK(c),The Valley of the Whispering Drums 100.00
5 HcK,HcK(c),Swampland Safari 75.00

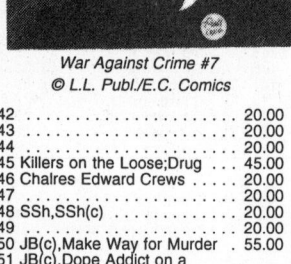

Wambi Jungle Boy #8
© Fiction House Magazines

6 Taming of the Tigress 65.00
7 Duel of the Congo Kings . . . 65.00
8 AB(c),Friend of the Animals . 65.00
9 Quest of the Devils Juju 65.00
10 Friend of the Animals 45.00
11 . . . . 45.00
12 Curse of the Jungle Jewels . . 45.00
13 New Adventures of Wambi . . 45.00
14 . . . . 45.00
15 The Leopard Legions 45.00
16 . . . . 45.00
17 Beware Bwana! 45.00
18 Ogg the Great Bull Ape, Winter, 1952 . . . . 45.00

WANTED COMICS
Toytown Comics/ Orbit Publications
September-October, 1947

9 Victor Everhart 75.00
10 Carlo Banone 45.00
11 Dwight Band 45.00
12 Ralph Roe 50.00
13 James Spencer;Drug 50.00
14 John "Jiggs" Sullivan;Drug . . 50.00
15 Harry Dunlap;Drug 30.00
16 Jack Parisi;Drug 30.00
17 Herber Ayers;Drug 30.00
18 Satans Cigarettes;Drug 100.00
19 Jackson Stringer 30.00
20 George Morgan 30.00
21 BK,Paul Wilson 35.00
22 . . . . 30.00
23 George Elmo Wells 20.00
24 BK,Bruce Cornett;Drug 40.00
25 Henry Anger 20.00
26 John Wormly 20.00
27 Death Always Knocks Twice . 20.00
28 Paul H. Payton 20.00
29 Hangmans Holiday 20.00
30 George Lee 20.00
31 M Consolo 20.00
32 William Davis 20.00
33 The Web of Davis 20.00
34 Dead End 20.00
35 Glen Roy Wright 25.00
36 SSh,SSh(c),Bernard Lee Thomas 20.00
37 SSh,SSh(c),Joseph M. Moore 20.00
38 SSh,SSh(c) 20.00
39 The Horror Weed;Drug 55.00
40 . . . . 20.00
41 . . . . 20.00

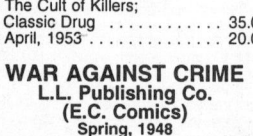

War Against Crime #7
© L.L. Publ./E.C. Comics

42 . . . . 20.00
43 . . . . 20.00
44 . . . . 20.00
45 Killers on the Loose;Drug . . . 45.00
46 Chalres Edward Crews 20.00
47 . . . . 20.00
48 SSh,SSh(c) 20.00
49 . . . . 20.00
50 JB(c),Make Way for Murder . 55.00
51 JB(c),Dope Addict on a Holiday of Murder;Drug 35.00
52 The Cult of Killers; Classic Drug 35.00
53 April, 1953 . . . . 20.00

WAR AGAINST CRIME
L.L. Publishing Co. (E.C. Comics)
Spring, 1948

1 Grl 400.00
2 Grl,Guilty of Murder 250.00
3 JCr(c) 250.00
4 AF,JCr(c) 225.00
5 JCr(c) 225.00
6 AF,JCr(c) 225.00
7 AF,JCr(c) 225.00
8 AF,JCr(c) 225.00
9 AF,JCr(c),The Kid 225.00
10 JCr(c),I:Vault Keeper . . . 1,500.00
11 JCr(c) 1,000.00

Becomes:

VAULT OF HORROR

12 AF,JCr,JCr(c),Wax Museum3,000.00
13 AF,WW,JCr(c),Grl,Drug . . . 800.00
14 AF,WW,JCr(c),Grl 750.00
15 AF,JCr,JCr(c),Grl,JKa 600.00
16 Grl,JKa,JCr,JCr(c) 550.00
17 JDa,Grl,JKa,JCr,JCr(c) 400.00
18 JDa,Grl,JKa,JCr,JCr(c) 400.00
19 JDa,Grl,JKa,JCr,JCr(c) 400.00
20 JDa,Grl,JKa,JCr,JCr(c) 275.00
21 JDa,Grl,JKa,JCr,JCr(c) 275.00
22 JDa,JKa,JCr,JCr(c) 275.00
23 JDa,Grl,JCr,JCr(c) 275.00
24 JDa,Grl,JO,JCr,JCr(c) 275.00
25 JDa,Grl,JKa,JCr,JCr(c) 275.00
26 JDa,Grl,JCr,JCr(c) 275.00
27 JDa,Grl,JCr,GE,JCr(c) 200.00
28 JDa,Grl,JCr,JCr(c) 200.00
29 JDa,Grl,JCr,JKa,JCr(c), JDa,Grl,JCr,JCr(c) Bradbury Adapt 200.00

Vault of Horror #18 © E.C. Comics

30 JDa,Grl,JCr,JCr(c) 200.00
31 JDa,Grl,JCr,JCr(c), Bradbury Adapt 175.00
32 JDa,Grl,JCr,JCr(c) 175.00
33 JDa,Grl,RC,JCr(c) 175.00
34 JDa,Grl,JCr,RC,JCr(c) 175.00
35 JDa,Grl,JCr,JCr(c) 175.00
36 JDa,Grl,JCr,BK,JCr(c),Drug 175.00
37 JDa,Grl,JCr,AW,JCr(c) Hanging 175.00
38 JDa,Grl,JCr,BK,JCr(c) 175.00
39 GRi,JCr,BK,RC,JCr(c) Bondage(c) 200.00
40 January, 1955, Grl,JCr,BK,JO JCr(c) 175.00

WAR BATTLES
Harvey Publications
February, 1952

1 BP,Devils of the Deep 45.00
2 BP,A Present From Benny . . 30.00
3 BP 20.00
4 . . . . 20.00
5 . . . . 20.00
6 HN 20.00
7 BP 25.00
8 . . . . 20.00
9 December, 1953 . . . . 20.00

WAR BIRDS
Fiction House Magazines
1952

1 Willie the Washout 75.00
2 Mystery MIGs of Kwanjamu . 45.00
3 thru 6 . . . . @40.00
7 Winter, 1953,Across the Wild Yalu 40.00

WAR COMICS
Dell Publishing Co.
May, 1940

1 AMc,Sky Hawk 300.00
2 O:Greg Gildam 150.00
3 100.00
4 O:Night Devils 125.00

WAR HEROES
Dell Publishing Co.
July-September, 1942

1 Gen. Douglas MacArthur (c) 125.00
2 65.00
3 50.00
4 A:Gremlins 100.00
5 45.00
6 thru 11 @40.00

WAR HEROES
Ace Magazines
May, 1952

1 Always Comin' 40.00
2 LC,The Last Red Tank 25.00
3 You Got it 20.00
4 A Red Patrol 20.00
5 Hustle it Up 20.00
6 LC,Hang on Pal 25.00
7 25.00
8 LC,April, 1953 25.00

WARPATH
Key Publications/ Stanmore
November, 1954

1 Red Men Raid 50.00
2 AH(c),Braves Battle 30.00
3 April, 1955 30.00

WARRIOR COMICS
H.C. Blackerby
1944

1 Ironman wing Brady 90.00

WAR SHIPS
Dell Publishing Co.
1942

1 AMc 75.00

WAR STORIES
Dell Publishing Co.
1942

5 O:The Whistler 135.00
6 A:Night Devils 100.00
7 A:Night Devils 100.00
8 A:Night Devils 100.00

WARTIME ROMANCES
St. John Publishing Co.
July, 1951

1 MB(c),MB 100.00
2 MB(c),MB 65.00
3 MB(c),MB 55.00
4 MB(c),MB 55.00
5 MB(c),MB 50.00
6 MB(c),MB 60.00
7 MB(c),MB 50.00
8 MB(c),MB 50.00
9 MB(c),MB 35.00
10 MB(c),MB 35.00
11 MB(c),MB 35.00
12 Mb(c),MB 35.00
13 MB(c) 30.00
14 MB(c) 30.00
15 MB(c) 30.00
16 MB(c),MB 30.00
17 MB(c) 30.00
18 MB(c),MB 30.00

WAR VICTORY COMICS
U.S. Treasury/War Victory/ Harvey Publ.
Summer, 1942

1 Savings Bond Promo with Top Syndicated Cartoonists, benefit USO 225.00

Becomes:

WAR VICTORY ADVENTURES

2 BP,2nd Front Comics 100.00
3 BP,F:Capt Cross of the Red Cross 90.00

Web of Evil #1
© Comic Magazines/Quality Comics

WEB OF EVIL
Comic Magazines, Inc. (Quality Comics Group)
November, 1952

1 Custodian of the Dead 250.00
2 JCo,Hangmans Horror 150.00
3 JCo 150.00
4 JCo,JCo(c),Monsters of the Mist 150.00
5 JCo,JCo(c),The Man who Died Twice,Electric Chair(c) 175.00
6 JCo,JCo(c),Orgy of Death 150.00
7 JCo,JCo(c),The Strangling Hands 150.00
8 JCo,Flaming Vengeance 125.00
9 JCo,The Monster in Flesh 125.00
10 JCo,Brain that Wouldn't Die 125.00
11 JCo,Buried Alive 125.00
12 Phantom Killer 60.00
13 Demon Inferno 60.00
14 RC(c),The Monster Genie 65.00
15 Crypts of Horror 60.00
16 Hamlet of Horror 60.00
17 Terror in Chinatown 65.00
18 Scared to Death,Acid Face 75.00
19 Demon of the Pit 60.00
20 Man Made Terror 60.00
21 December, 1954, Death's Ambush 60.00

WEB OF MYSTERY
A.A. Wyn Publ. (Ace Magazines)
February, 1951

1 MSy,Venom of the Vampires 175.00
2 MSy,Legacy of the Accursed 125.00
3 MSy,The Violin Curse 100.00
4 GC 100.00
5 100.00
6 LC 100.00
7 MSy 100.00
8 LC,LC(c),MSy,The Haunt of Death Lake 100.00
9 LC,LC(c) 100.00
10 100.00
11 MSy 100.00
12 LC 80.00
13 LC,LC(c) 80.00
14 MSy 80.00
15 80.00
16 80.00
17 LC,LC(c) 80.00
18 LC 80.00
19 LC 80.00
20 LC 80.00
21 MSy 80.00
22 80.00
23 80.00
24 LC 80.00
25 LC 80.00
26 80.00
27 LC 80.00
28 RP,1st Issue under Comics Code Authority 50.00
29 MSy,September, 1955 50.00

WEDDING BELLS
Quality Comics Group
February, 1954

1 OW 70.00
2 45.00
3 25.00
4 25.00
5 25.00
6 25.00
7 25.00
8 25.00
9 Comics Code 25.00
10 BWa 60.00
11 25.00
12 20.00
13 20.00
14 20.00
15 MB(c) 25.00
16 MB(c),MB 35.00
17 20.00
18 MB 25.00
19 MB 25.00

WEEKENDER, THE
Rucker Publishing Co.
September, 1945

3 125.00
4 100.00
2-1(5)JCo,WMc,January, 1946 145.00

WEIRD ADVENTURES
P.L. Publishing
May, 1951

1 MB,Missing Diamonds 175.00
2 Puppet Peril 150.00
3 Blood Vengeance, October 1951 150.00

WEIRD ADVENTURES
Approved Comics (Ziff-Davis)
July-August, 1951

10 P(c),Seeker from Beyond 150.00

WEIRD CHILLS
Key Publications
July, 1954

1 MBi(c),BW 250.00
2 Eye Torture(c) 240.00
3 Bondage(c),November, 1954 150.00

WEIRD COMICS
Fox Features Syndicate
April, 1940

1 LF(c),Bondage(c),B:Birdman,

Thor,Sorceress of Doom, BlastBennett,Typhon,Voodoo Man, Dr.Mortal 1,400.00
2 LF(c),Mummy(c) 650.00
3 JSm(c) 450.00
4 JSm(c) 450.00
5 Bondage(c),I:Dart,Ace;E:Thor 450.00
6 Dart & Ace(c) 425.00
7 Battle of Kooba 425.00

Weird Comics #8

© Fox Features Syndicate

8 B:Panther Woman,Dynamo, The Eagle 425.00
9 V:Pirates 350.00
10 A:Navy Jones 350.00
11 Dart & Ace(c) 300.00
12 Dart & Ace(c) 300.00
13 Dart & Ace(c) 300.00
14 The Rage(c) 300.00
15 Dart & Ace (c) 300.00
16 Flag,The Encore(c) 300.00
17 O:Black Rider 325.00
18 . . . . 300.00
19 . . . . 300.00
20 January, 1941,I'm The Master of Life and Death 300.00

WEIRD FANTASY
I.C. Publishing Co.
(E.C. Comics)
May-June, 1950

13(1)AF,HK,JKa,WW,AF(c), Roger Harvey's Brain 1,000.00
14(2)AF,HK,JKa,WW,AF(c), Cosmic Ray Brain Explosion 500.00
15(3)AF,HK,JKa,WW,AF(c),Your Destination is the Moon . . . 450.00
16(4)AF,HK,JKa,WW,AF(c) . . . 450.00
17(5)AF,HK,JKa,WW,AF(c),Not Made by Human Hands . . . 400.00
6 AF,HK,JKa,WW,AF(c) 300.00
7 AF,JKa,WW,AF(c) 300.00
8 AF,JKa,WW,AF(c) 300.00
9 AF,Jka,WW,JO,AF(c) 300.00
10 AF,Jka,WW,JO,AF(c) 350.00
11 AF,Jka,WW,JO,AF(c) 250.00
12 AF,Jka,WW,JO,AF(c) 250.00
13 AF,Jka,WW,JO,AF(c) 250.00
14 AF,JKa,WW,JO,AW&FF,AF(c)350.00
15 AF,JKa,JO,AW&RKr,AF(c), Bondage(c) 250.00
16 AF,JKa,JO,AW&RKr,AF(c) . 200.00
17 AF,JOP,JKa,AF(c),Bradbury 200.00
18 AF,JO,JKa,AF(c),Bradbury . 200.00
19 JO,JKa,JO(c),Bradbury 200.00
20 JO,JKa,FF,AF(c) 225.00
21 JO,JKa,AW&FF(c) 350.00
22 JO,JKa,JO(c),Nov.,1953 . . . 195.00

WEIRD HORRORS
St. John Publishing Co.
June, 1952

1 GT,Dungeon of the Doomed 175.00
2 Strangest Music Ever 100.00
3 PAM,Strange Fakir From the Orient 90.00
4 Murderers Knoll 90.00
5 Phantom Bowman 90.00
6 Monsters from Outer Space 165.00
7 LC,Deadly Double 175.00
8 JKu,JKu(c),Bloody Yesterday 125.00
9 JKu,JKu(c),Map Of Doom . . 125.00

Becomes:

NIGHTMARE

10 JKu(c),The Murderer's Mask 225.00
11 BK,Ph(c),Fangs of Death . . 175.00
12 JKu(c),The Forgotten Mask . 150.00
13 BP,Princess of the Sea 100.00

Becomes:

AMAZING GHOST STORIES

14 EK,MB(c), ... 125.00
15 BP 90.00
16 February, 1955, EK,JKu . . . 100.00

WEIRD MYSTERIES
Gilmore Publications
October, 1952

1 BW(c) 250.00
2 BWi 450.00
3 Severed Heads(c) 200.00
4 BW,Human headed ants(c) . 350.00
5 BW,Brains From Head(c) . . . 350.00
6 Severed Head(c) 250.00
7 Used in "Seduction" 300.00
8 The One That Got Away . . 200.00
9 Epitaph,Cyclops 200.00
10 The Ruby 150.00
11 Voodoo Dolls 150.00
12 September, 1954 . . . . 150.00

Weird Science #11 © E.C. Comics

WEIRD SCIENCE
E.C. Comics
1950

1 AF(c),AF,JKu,HK,WW 1,100.00
2 AF(c),AF,JKu,HK,WW,Flying Saucers(c) 600.00
3 AF(c),AF,JKu,HK 550.00
4 AF(c),AF,JKu,HK 550.00
5 AF(c),AF,JKu,HK,WW, Atomic Bomb(c) 400.00
6 AF(c),AF,JKu,HK 350.00
7 AF(c),AF,JKu,HK,Classic(c) . 400.00
8 AF(c),AF,JKu 350.00
9 WW(c),JKu,Classic(c) 400.00
10 WW(c),JKu,JO,Classic(c) . . 400.00
11 AF,JKu,Space war 275.00
12 WW(c),JKu,JO,Classic(c) . . 275.00
13 WW(c),JKu,JO, ... 300.00
14 WW(c),WW,JO 300.00
15 WW(c),WW,JO,GRi,AW, RKr,JKa 300.00
16 WW(c),WW,JO,AW,RKr,JKa 300.00
17 WW(c),WW,JO,AW,RKr,JKa 300.00
18 WW(c),WW,JO,AW,RKr, JKa,Atomic Bomb 250.00
19 WW(c),WW,JO,AW, FF,Horror(c) 400.00
20 WW(c),WW,JO,AW,FF,JKa . 400.00
21 WW(c),WW,JO,AW,FF,JKa . 400.00
22 WW(c),WW,JO,AW,FF 400.00

Becomes:

WEIRD SCIENCE FANTASY

23 WW(c),WW,AW,BK 200.00
24 WW,AW,BK,Classic(c) 225.00
25 WW,AW,BK,Classic(c) 250.00
26 AF(c),WW,RC, Flying Saucer(c) 200.00
27 WW(c),WW,RC 200.00
28 AF(c),WW 250.00
29 AF(c),WW,Classic(c) 400.00

Becomes:

INCREDIBLE SCIENCE FANTASY

30 WW,JDa(c),BK,AW,RKr,JO 250.00
31 WW,JDa(c),BK,AW,RKr . . . 300.00
32 JDa(c),BK,WW,JO 300.00
33 WW(c),BK,WW,JO 300.00

WEIRD TALES OF THE FUTURE
S.P.M. Publ./
Aragon Publications
March, 1952

1 RA 300.00
2 BW,BW(c) 500.00
3 BW,BW(c) 475.00
4 BW,BW(c) 300.00
5 BW,BW(c),Jumpin' Jupiter Lingerie(c) 525.00
6 Bondage(c) 250.00
7 BW,Devil(c) 300.00
8 July-August 1953 . . . . 200.00

WEIRD TERROR
Allen Hardy Associates
(Comic Media)
September, 1952

1 RP,DH,DH(c),Dungeon of the Doomed;Hitler 170.00
2 HcK(c),PAM 125.00
3 PAM,DH,DH(c) 100.00
4 PAM,DH,DH(c) 140.00
5 PAM,DH,RP,DH(c),Hanging(c)100.00
6 DH,RP,DH(c),Step into My Parlour 135.00
7 DH,PAM,DH(c),Blood o/t Bats 100.00
8 DH,RP,DH(c),Step into My Parlour 125.00
9 DH,PAM,DH(c),The Fleabite 100.00
10 DH,BP,RP,DH(c) 100.00
11 DH,DH(c),Satan's Love Call 125.00
12 DH,DH(c),King Whitey 85.00
13 DH,DH(c),September, 1954, Wings of Death 90.00

WEIRD THRILLERS
Approved Comics
(Ziff-Davis)
September-October, 1951

1 Ph(c),Monsters & The Model 240.00
2 AW,P(c),The Last Man 175.00
3 AW,P(c),Princess o/t Sea .. 150.00
4 AW,P(c),The Widows Lover . 165.00
5 BP,October, 1952,AW,P(c),
Wings of Death 150.00

WESTERN ACTION THRILLERS
Dell Publishing Co.
April, 1937

1 .... 500.00

WESTERN ADVENTURES COMICS
A.A. Wyn, Inc.
(Ace Magazines)
October, 1948

N#(1)Injun Gun Bait 125.00
N#(2)Cross-Draw Kid 65.00
N#(3)Outlaw Mesa 65.00
4 Sheriff 45.00
5 .... 45.00
6 Rip Roaring Adventure 45.00

Becomes:

WESTERN LOVE TRAILS

7 .... 65.00
8 Maverick Love 45.00
9 March, 1950 .... 40.00

WESTERN BANDIT TRAILS
St. John Publishing Co.
January, 1949

1 GT,MB(c) 100.00
2 GT,MB(c) 75.00
3 GT,MB,MB(c),Gingham Fury . 90.00

Western Crime-Busters #1
© Trojan Magazines

WESTERN CRIME-BUSTERS
Trojan Magazines
September, 1950

1 Gunslingin' Galoots 155.00
2 K-Bar Kate 90.00
3 Wilma West 90.00
4 Bob Dale 90.00
5 Six-Gun Smith 90.00
6 WW 185.00
7 WW,Wells Fargo Robbery . 185.00
8 .... 75.00
9 WW,Lariat Lucy 175.00
10 WW,April 1952;Tex Gordon 175.00

WESTERN CRIME CASES
(see WHITE RIDER)

WESTERNER, THE
Wanted Comics Group/
Toytown Publ.
June, 1948

14 F:Jack McCall 60.00
15 F:Bill Jamett 30.00
16 F:Tom McLowery 30.00
17 F:Black Bill Desmond 30.00
18 BK,F:Silver Dollar Dalton ... 50.00
19 MMe,F:Jess Meeton 30.00
20 .... 25.00
21 BK,MMe 50.00
22 BK,MMe 50.00
23 BK,MMe 50.00
24 BK,MMe 50.00
25 O,I,B:Calamity Jane 50.00
26 BK,F:The Widowmaker 65.00
27 .... 75.00
28 .... 20.00
29 .... 20.00
30 .... 20.00
31 .... 20.00
32 E:Calamity Jane 20.00
33 A:Quest 20.00
34 .... 20.00
35 SSh(c) 20.00
36 .... 20.00
37 Lobo-Wolf Boy 20.00
38 .... 20.00
39 .... 20.00
40 SSh(c) 20.00
41 December, 1951 .... 20.00

WESTERN FIGHTERS
Hillman Periodicals
April-May, 1948

1 S&K(c) 175.00
2 BF(c) 55.00
3 BF(c) 45.00
4 BK,BF 55.00
5 .... 35.00
6 .... 34.00
7 BK 55.00
8 .... 35.00
9 .... 35.00
10 BK 55.00
11 AMC&FF 160.00
2-1 BK 60.00
2-2 BP 40.00
2-3 thru 2-12 .... @20.00
3-1 thru 3-11 .... @20.00
3-12 BK 40.00
4-1 .... 20.00
4-2 BK 50.00
4-3 BK 50.00
4-4 BK 50.00
4-5 BK 50.00
4-6 BK 50.00
4-7 March-April 1953 .... 20.00

WESTERN FRONTIER
P.L. Publishers
(Approved Comics)
May, 1951

1 Flaming Vengeance 60.00
2 .... 35.00
3 Death Rides the Iron Horse . 25.00
4 .... 25.00
5 .... 25.00
6 .... 25.00
7 1952 .... 25.00

WESTERN HEARTS
Standard Magazine, Inc.
December, 1949

1 Ph(c),JSe 100.00
2 Ph(c),AW,FF 150.00
3 Ph(c) 45.00
4 Ph(c),JSe,BE 45.00
5 Ph(c),JSe,BE 45.00
6 Ph(c),JSe,BE 45.00
7 Ph(c),JSe,BE 45.00
8 Ph(c) 50.00
9 Ph(c),JSe,BE 65.00
10 Ph(c),JSe,BE 45.00

WESTERN LOVE
Feature Publications
(Prize Comics Group)
July-August, 1949

1 S&K 125.00
2 S&K 100.00
3 JSE,BE 75.00
4 JSE,BE 75.00
5 JSE,BE 75.00

WESTERN PICTURE STORIES
Comics Magazine Co.
February, 1937

Whirlwind Comics #2
© Nita Publications

1 WE,Treachery Trail,
1st Western 900.00
2 WE,Weapons of the West . 600.00
3 WE,Dragon Pass 450.00
4 June, 1937,CavemanCowboy 450.00

WESTERN THRILLERS
Fox Features Syndicate
August, 1948

1 .... 250.00
2 .... 90.00
3 GT,RH(c) 75.00
4 .... 90.00
5 .... 90.00
6 June, 1949 .... 75.00

Becomes:

MY PAST CONFESSIONS

7 .... 60.00
8 .... 40.00
9 .... 40.00
10 .... 40.00
11 .... 75.00
12 .... 20.00

WESTERN TRUE CRIME
Fox Features Syndicate
August, 1948

1 . . . . 125.00
2 . . . . 90.00
3 . . . . 50.00
4 JCr 125.00
5 . . . . 50.00
6 . . . . 50.00

Becomes:

MY CONFESSION

7 WW 100.00
8 WW,My Tarnished Reputation 90.00
9 I:Tormented Men 40.00
10 February, 1950,I Am Damaged Goods 40.00

WHACK
St. John Publishing Co.
December, 1953

1 Steve Crevice,Flush Jordan V:Bing(Crosby)The Merciful 175.00
2 . . . . 100.00
3 F:Little Awful Fannie 100.00

WHAM COMICS
Centaur Publications
November, 1940

1 PG,The Sparkler & His

Wham Comics #1 © Centaur Publ.

Disappearing Suit 750.00
2 December, 1940,PG,PG(C), Men Turn into Icicles 550.00

WHIRLWIND COMICS
Nita Publications
June, 1940

1 F:The Cyclone 500.00
2 A:Scoops Hanlon,Cyclone(c) 350.00
3 September, 1940,A:Magic Mandarin,Cyclone(c) 325.00

WHITE PRINCESS OF THE JUNGLE
Avon Periodicals
July, 1951

1 EK(c),Terror Fangs 225.00
2 EK,EK(c),Jungle Vengeance 175.00
3 EK,EK(c),The Blue Gorilla . 150.00
4 Fangs of the Swamp Beast 135.00
5 EK,Coils of the Tree Snake November, 1952 . . . . 135.00

White Princess of the Jungle #4
© Avon Periodicals

WHIZ COMICS
Fawcett Publications
February, 1940

1 O:Captain Marvel,B:Spy Smasher,Golden Arrow,Dan Dare, Scoop Smith,Ibis the Invincible, Sivana 45,000.00
2 . . . . 2,800.00
3 Make way for Captain Marvel 1,800.00
4 Captain Marvel Crashes Through 1,500.00
5 Captain Marvel Scores Again! 1,200.00
6 Circus of Death 900.00
7 B:Dr Voodoo,Squadron of Death 900.00
8 Saved by Captain Marvel! . 850.00
9 MRa,Captain Marvel on the Job 850.00
10 Battles the Winged Death . . 850.00
11 Hurray for Captain Marvel . . 650.00
12 Captain Marvel rides the Engine of Doom 650.00
13 Worlds Most Powerful Man! 600.00
14 Boomerangs the Torpedo . . 600.00
15 O:Sivana 750.00
16 . . . . 700.00
17 Knocks out a Tank 700.00
18 V:Spy Smasher 700.00
19 Crushes the Tiger Shark . . . 500.00
20 V:Sivana 500.00
21 O:Lt. Marvels 550.00
22 Mayan Temple 400.00
23 GT,A:Dr. Voodoo 400.00
24 . . . . 400.00
25 O&I:Captain Marvel Jr., Stops the Turbine of Death 1,700.00
26 . . . . 350.00
27 V:Death God of the Katonkas 325.00
28 V:Mad Dervish of Ank-Har . 325.00
29 Three Lt. Marvels (c), Pan American Olympics 325.00
30 . . . . 325.00
31 Douglass MacArthur&Spy Smasher(c) 275.00
32 Spy Smasher(c) 275.00
33 Spy Smasher(c) 300.00
34 Three Lt. Marvels (c) 250.00
35 Capt. Marvel and the Three Fates 275.00
36 Haunted Hallowe'en Hotel . . 225.00
37 Return of the Trolls 225.00
38 Grand Steeplechase 225.00

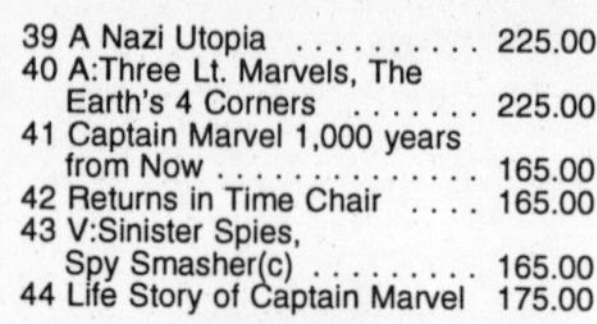

39 A Nazi Utopia 225.00
40 A:Three Lt. Marvels, The Earth's 4 Corners 225.00
41 Captain Marvel 1,000 years from Now 165.00
42 Returns in Time Chair 165.00
43 V:Sinister Spies, Spy Smasher(c) 165.00
44 Life Story of Captain Marvel 175.00

Whiz Comics #50
© Fawcett Publications

45 Cures His Critics 165.00
46 . . . . 165.00
47 Captain Marvel needs a Birthday 165.00
48 . . . . 165.00
49 Writes a Victory song 165.00
50 Captain Marvel's most embarrassing moment 165.00
51 Judges the Ugly-Beauty Contest 150.00
52 V:Sivana, Chooses His Birthday 150.00
53 Captain Marvel fights Billy Batson 150.00
54 Jack of all Trades 150.00
55 Family Tree 150.00
56 Tells what the Future Will Be 150.00
57 . . . . 150.00
58 . . . . 150.00
59 V:Sivana's Twin 150.00
60 Missing Person's Machine . 150.00
61 Gets a first name 125.00
62 Plays in a Band 125.00
63 Great Indian Rope Trick . . . 125.00
64 Suspected of Murder 125.00
65 Lamp of Diogenes 125.00
66 The Trial of Mr. Morris! 125.00
67 . . . . 125.00
68 Laugh Lotion, V:Sivana 125.00
69 Mission to Mercury 125.00
70 Climbs the World's Mightiest Mountain 125.00
71 Strange Magician 100.00
72 V:The Man of the Future . . . 100.00
73 In Ogre Land 100.00
74 Old Man River 100.00
75 The City Olympics 100.00
76 thru 81 . . . . @100.00
82 The Atomic Ship 100.00
83 Magic Locket 100.00
84 . . . . 100.00
85 The Clock of San Lojardo . . 100.00
86 V:Sinister Sivanas 100.00
87 The War on Olympia 100.00
88 The Wonderful Magic Carpet 100.00

89 Webs of Crime 100.00
90 . . . . 100.00
91 Infinity (c) 100.00
92 . . . . 100.00
93 Captain America become
a Hobo? 100.00
94 V:Sivana 100.00
95 Captain Marvel is grounded 100.00
96 The Battle Between Buildings 100.00
97 Visits Mirage City 100.00
98 . . . . 100.00
99 V:Menace in the Mountains . 100.00
100 . . . . 125.00
101 . . . . 75.00
102 A:Commando Yank 75.00
103 . . . . 75.00
104 . . . . 75.00
105 . . . . 75.00
106 A:Bulletman 75.00
107 The Great Experiment 85.00
108 thru 114 . . . . @75.00
115 The Marine Invasion 75.00
116 . . . . 75.00
117 V:Sivana 75.00
118 . . . . 75.00
119 . . . . 75.00
120 . . . . 75.00
121 . . . . 75.00
122 V:Sivana 75.00
123 . . . . 75.00
124 . . . . 75.00
125 Olympic Games of the Gods 75.00
126 . . . . 75.00
127 . . . . 75.00
128 . . . . 75.00
129 . . . . 75.00
130 . . . . 75.00
131 The Television Trap 75.00
132 thru 142 . . . . @75.00
143 Mystery of the Flying Studio 75.00
144 V:The Disaster Master 75.00
145 . . . . 57.00
146 . . . . 75.00
147 . . . . 75.00
148 . . . . 75.00
149 . . . . 75.00
150 V:Bug Bombs 75.00
151 . . . . 75.00
152 . . . . 75.00
153 V:The Death Horror 75.00
154 Horror Tale 75.00
155 V:Legend Horror 100.00

WHODUNIT?
D.S. Publishing Co.
August-September, 1948

1 MB,Weeping Widow 75.00
2 Diploma For Death 50.00
3 December-January, 1949 . . . 50.00

WHO IS NEXT?
Standard Comics
January, 1953

5 ATh,RA,Don't Let Me Kill . . 100.00

WILD BILL ELLIOT
Dell Publishing Co.
May, 1950

(1) *see Dell Four Color #278*
2 . . . . 45.00
3 thru 5 . . . . @35.00
6 thru 10 . . . . @35.00
(11-12) *see Four Color #472, 520*
13 thru 17 . . . . @30.00

WILD BILL HICKOK AND JINGLES
(see YELLOWJACKET COMICS)

WILBUR COMICS
MLJ Magazines
(Archie Publications)
Summer, 1944

1 F:Wilbur Wilkin-America's Song
of Fun 300.00
2 . . . . 150.00
3 . . . . 125.00
4 . . . . 100.00
5 I:Katy Keene 400.00
6 thru 10 . . . . @125.00
11 thru 20 . . . . @70.00
21 thru 30 . . . . @45.00
31 thru 40 . . . . @35.00
41 thru 50 . . . . @25.00
51 thru 89 . . . . @20.00
90 October, 1965 . . . . 20.00

WILD BILL HICKOK
Avon Periodicals
September-October, 1949

1 GRI(c),Frontier Fighter 100.00
2 Ph(c),Gambler's Guns 50.00
3 Ph(c),Great Stage Robbery . 25.00
4 Ph(c),Guerilla Gunmen 25.00
5 Ph(c),Return of the Renegade 25.00
6 EK,EK(c),Along the Apache
Trail 25.00
7 EK,EK(c)Outlaws of
Hell's Bend 25.00
8 Ph(c),The Border Outlaws . . 25.00
9 PH(c),Killers From Texas . . . 25.00
10 Ph(c) 25.00
11 EK,EK(c),The Hell Riders . . . 25.00
12 EK,EK(c),The Lost Gold MIne 30.00
13 EK,EK(c),Bloody Canyon
Massacre 30.00
14 . . . . 30.00
15 . . . . 20.00
16 JKa 25.00
17 thru 23 . . . . @20.00
24 EK,EK(c) 25.00
25 EK,EK(c) 25.00
26 EK,EK(c) 25.00
27 EK,EK(c) 25.00
28 EK,EK(c),May-June, 1956 . . . 25.00

Wild Boy of the Congo #15
© Approved/Ziff-Davis/St. Johns

WILD BOY OF THE CONGO
Approved(Ziff-Davis)/ St. John Publ. Co.
February-March, 1951

10(1)NS,PH(c),Bondage(c),The
Gorilla God 90.00
11(2)NS,Ph(c),Star of the Jungle 50.00
12(3)NS,Ph(c),Ice-Age Men 50.00
4 NS.Ph(c),Tyrant of the Jungle 55.00
5 NS,Ph(c),The White Robe
of Courage 40.00
6 NS,Ph(c) 40.00
7 MB,EK.Ph(c) 45.00
8 Ph(c),Man-Eater 40.00
9 Ph(c),Killer Leopard 40.00
10 . . . . 40.00
11 MB(c) 45.00
12 MB(c) 45.00
13 MB(c) 45.00
14 MB(c) 45.00
15 June, 1955 . . . . 35.00

WINGS COMICS
Wings Publ.
(Fiction House Magazines)
September, 1940

1 HcK,AB,GT,Ph(c),B:Skull Squad,
Clipper Kirk,Suicide Smith,
War Nurse,Phantom Falcons,
GreasemonkeyGriffin,Parachute
Patrol,Powder Burns 850.00
2 HCk,AB,GT,Bomber Patrol . 400.00
3 HcK,AB,GT 350.00
4 HcK,AB,GT,B:Spitfire Ace . . 300.00
5 HcK,AB,GT,Torpedo Patrol . 300.00
6 HcK,AB,GT,Bombs for Berlin 275.00
7 HcK,AB 275.00
8 HcK,AB,The Wings of Doom 275.00
9 Sky-Wolf 250.00
10 The Upside Down 250.00
11 . . . . 225.00
12 Fury of the fire Boards 225.00
13 Coffin Slugs For The
Luftwaffe 225.00
14 Stuka Buster 225.00
15 Boomerang Blitz 225.00
16 O:Capt.Wings 225.00
17 Skyway to Death 200.00
18 Horsemen of the Sky 200.00
19 Nazi Spy Trap 200.00
20 The One Eyed Devil 200.00
21 Chute Troop Tornado 175.00
22 TNT for Tokyo 175.00
23 RP,Battling Eagles of Bataan 175.00
24 RP,The Death of a Hero . . . 175.00
25 RP,Suicide Squeeze 175.00
26 Tojo's Eagle Trap 175.00
27 Blb,Mile High Gauntlet 175.00
28 Blb,Tail Gun Tornado 175.00
29 Blb,Buzzards from Berlin . . 175.00
30 Blb,Monsters of the
Stratosphere 150.00
31 BLb,Sea Hawks away 150.00
32 BLb,Sky Mammoth 150.00
33 BLb,Roll Call of the Yankee
Eagles 150.00
34 BLb,So Sorry,Mr Tojo 150.00
35 BLb,RWb,Hell's Lightning . . 150.00
36 RWb,The Crash-Master . . . 150.00
37 RWb,Sneak Blitz 150.00
38 RWb,Rescue Raid of the
Yank Eagle 150.00
39 RWb,Sky Hell/Pigboat Patrol 150.00
40 RWb,Luftwaffe Gamble 150.00
41 RWb,.50 Caliber Justice . . . 125.00
42 RWb,PanzerMeat forMosquito 125.00
43 RWb,Suicide Sentinels 125.00
44 RWb,Berlin Bombs Away . . 125.00
45 RWb,Hells Cargo 125.00
46 RWb,Sea-Hawk Patrol 125.00
47 RWb,Tojo's Tin Gibraltar . . . 125.00
48 RWb 125.00
49 RWb,Rockets Away 125.00
50 RWb,Mission For a Madman 125.00
51 RWb,Toll for a Typhoon . . . 100.00
52 MB,Madam Marauder 100.00
53 MB,Robot Death Over
Manhattan 100.00
54 MB,Juggernauts of Death . . 100.00
55 MB 100.00
56 MB,Sea Raiders Grave 100.00

Wings Comics #58
© Fiction House Magazines

57 MB,Yankee Warbirds over Tokyo 100.00
58 MB 100.00
59 MB,Prey of the Night Hawks 100.00
60 MB,E:Skull Squad, Hell's Eyes 100.00
61 MB,Raiders o/t Purple Dawn . 85.00
62 Twilight of the Gods 85.00
63 Hara Kiri Rides the Skyways . 85.00
64 Taps For Tokyo 85.00
65 AB,Warhawk for the Kill 85.00
66 AB,B:Ghost Patrol 85.00
67 AB 75.00
68 AB,ClipperKirkBecomesPhantom Falcon;O:Phantom Falcon . . . 75.00
69 AB,O:cont,Phantom Falcon . . 75.00
70 AB,N:Phantom Falcon; O:Final Phantom Falcon 75.00
71 Ghost Patrol becomes Ghost Squadron 70.00
72 V:Capt. Kamikaze 70.00
73 Hell & Stormoviks 70.00
74 BLb(c),Loot is What She Lived For 70.00
75 BLb(c),The Sky Hag 70.00
76 BLb(c),Temple of the Dead . . 70.00
77 BLb(c),Sky Express to Hell . . 70.00
78 BLb(c),Loot Queen of Satan's Skyway 70.00
79 BLb(c),Buzzards of Plunder Sky 70.00
80 BLb(c),Port of Missing Pilots . 70.00
81 BLb(c),Sky Trail of the Terror Tong 70.00
82 BLb(c),Bondage(c),Spider & The Fly Guy 75.00
83 BLb(c),GE,Deep Six For Capt. Wings 55.00
84 BLb(c),GE,Sky Sharks to the Kill 55.00
85 BLb(c),GE 55.00
86 BLb(c),GE,Moon Raiders . . . 55.00
87 BLb(c),GE 55.00
88 BLb(c),GE,Madmans Mission 55.00
89 BLb(c),GE,Bondage(c), Rockets Away 75.00
90 BLb(c),GE,Bondage(c),The Radar Rocketeers 75.00
91 BLb(c),GE,Bondage(c),V-9 for Vengeance 75.00
92 BLb(c),GE,Death's red Rocket 70.00
93 BLb(c),GE,Kidnap Cargo . . . 70.00
94 BLb(c),GE,Bondage(c),Ace of the A-Bomb Patrol 75.00
95 BLb(c),GE,The Ace of the Assassins 70.00
96 BLb(c),GE 70.00
97 BLb(c),GE,The Sky Octopus . 70.00
98 BLb(c),GE,The Witch Queen of Satan's Skyways 70.00
99 BLb(c),GE,The Spy Circus . . 70.00
100 BLb(c),GE,King of the Congo 75.00
101 BLb(c),GE,Trator of the Cockpit 70.00
102 BLb(c),GE,Doves of Doom . 70.00
103 BLb(c),GE 70.00
104 BLb(c),GE,Fireflies of Fury . 70.00
105 BLb(c),GE 70.00
106 BLb(c),GE,Six Aces & A Firing Squad 70.00
107 BLb(c),GE,Operation Satan . 70.00
108 BLb(c),GE,The Phantom of Berlin 70.00
109 GE,Vultures of Vengeance Sky 70.00
110 GE,The Red Ray Vortex . . . 70.00
111 GE,E:Jane Martin 60.00
112 The Flight of the Silver Saucers 65.00
113 Suicide Skyways 60.00
114 D-Day for Death Rays 60.00
115 Ace of Space 60.00
116 Jet Aces of Korea 60.00
117 Reap the Red Wind 60.00
118 Vengeance Flies Blind 60.00
119 The Whistling Death 60.00
120 Doomsday Mission 60.00
121 Ace of the Spyways 60.00
122 Last Kill Korea 60.00
123 The Cat & the Canaries . . . 60.00
124 Summer, 1954, Death Below Zero 60.00

WINNIE WINKLE
Dell Publishing Co.
1941

1 . . . . . 45.00
2 . . . . . 30.00
3 . . . . . 20.00
4 thru 7 . . . . . @20.00

WITCHCRAFT
Avon Periodicals
March-April, 1952

1 SC,JKu,Heritage of Horror . 275.00
2 SC,JKu,The Death Tattoo . . 200.00
3 EK,Better off Dead 150.00
4 Claws of the Cat, Boiling Humans 175.00
5 Ph(c),Where Zombies Walk 200.00
6 March, 1953 Mysteries of the Moaning Statue 150.00

WITCHES TALES
Harvey Publications
January, 1951

1 RP,Bondage(c),Weird Yarns of Unseen Terror 165.00
2 RP,We Dare You 75.00
3 RP,Bondage(c)Forest of Skeletons 55.00
4 BP 50.00
5 BP,Bondage(c),Share My Coffin 65.00
6 BP,Bondage(c),Servants of the Tomb 65.00
7 BP,Screaming City 65.00
8 Bondage(c) 70.00
9 Fatal Steps 50.00
10 BP,....,IT! 50.00
11 BP,Monster Maker 45.00
12 Bondage(c);The Web of the Spider 50.00
13 The Torture Jar 45.00
14 Transformation 60.00
15 Drooling Zombie 45.00
16 Revenge of a Witch 45.00

Witches Tales #15
© Harvey Publications

17 Dimension IV 65.00
18 HN,Bird of Prey 60.00
19 HN,The Pact 60.00
20 HN,Kiss & Tell 60.00
21 HN,The Invasion 60.00
22 HN,A Day of Panic 60.00
23 HN,The Wig Maker 60.00
24 HN,The Undertaker 60.00
25 What Happens at 8:30 PM? Severed Heads(c) 60.00
26 Up There 40.00
27 The Thing That Grew 40.00
28 Demon Flies 40.00

Becomes:

WITCHES WESTERN TALES

29 S&K,S&K(c),F:Davy Crockett 85.00
30 S&K.S&K(c) 85.00

Becomes:

WESTERN TALES

31 S&K,S&K(c),F:Davy Crockett 75.00
32 S&K,S&K(c) 75.00
33 S&K,S&K(c),July-Sept.,1956 . 75.00

WITH THE MARINES ON THE BATTLEFRONTS OF THE WORLD
Toby Press
June, 1953

1 Ph(c),Flaming Soul 150.00
2 Ph(c),March, 1954 . . . . . 35.00

WITTY COMICS
Irwin H. Rubin/Chicago Nite Life News
1945

1 . . . . . 75.00
2 1945 . . . . . 45.00
3 thru 7 . . . . . @35.00

WOMEN IN LOVE
Fox Features Synd./ Hero Books/ Ziff-Davis
August, 1949

1 . . . . . 250.00

WOMEN OUTLAWS
Fox Features Syndicate
July, 1948

1 .... 300.00
2 .... 250.00
3 .... 200.00
4 thru 8 .... @150.00

Becomes:

MY LOVE MEMORIES

9 .... 75.00
10 .... 35.00
11 .... 70.00
12 WW 75.00

WONDERBOY
(see HORRIFIC)

Wonder Comics #11
© Fox Features Syndicate

WONDER COMICS
Great Publ./Nedor/ Better Publications
May, 1944

1 SSh(c),B:Grim Reaper, Spectro Hitler(c) 400.00
2 ASh(c),O:Grim Reaper,B:Super Sleuths,Grim Reaper(c) 250.00
3 ASh(c),Grim Reaper(c) 200.00
4 ASh(c),Grim Reaper(c) 200.00
5 ASh(c),Grim Reaper(c) 200.00
6 ASh(c),Grim Reaper(c) 175.00
7 ASh(c),Grim Reaper(c) 175.00
8 ASh(c),E:Super Sleuths, Spectro 175.00
9 ASh(c),B:Wonderman 175.00
10 ASh(c),Wonderman(c) 200.00
11 Grl(c),B:Dick Devins 200.00
12 Grl(c),Bondage(c) 200.00
13 ASh(c),Bondage(c) 200.00
14 ASh(c),Bondage(c) E:Dick Devins 210.00
15 ASh(c),Bondage(c),B:Tara . 250.00
16 ASh(c),A:Spectro, E:Grim Reaper 175.00
17 FF,ASh(c),A:Super Sleuth .. 200.00
18 ASh(c),B:Silver Knight 175.00
19 ASh(c),FF 200.00
20 FF,October, 1948 .... 250.00

WONDERLAND COMICS
Feature Publications (Prize Comics Group)
Summer, 1945

1 (fa),B:Alex in Wonderland ... 50.00
2 .... 30.00
3 thru 8 .... @20.00
9 1947 .... 20.00

WONDER COMICS
Fox Features Syndicate
May, 1930

1 BKa,WE,WE(c),B:Wonderman, DR.Kung,K-51 .... 5,500.00
2 WE,BKa,LF(c),B:Yarko the Great,A:Spark Stevens ... 2,400.00

Becomes:

WONDERWORLD COMICS

3 WE,LF,BP,LF&WE,I:Flame 2,000.00
4 WE,LF,BP,LF(c) 750.00
5 WE,LF,BP,GT,LF(c),Flame . 600.00
6 WE,LF,BP,GT,LF(c),Flame . 600.00
7 WE,LF,BP,GT,LF(c),Flame . 600.00
8 WE,LF,BP,GT,LF(c),Flame . 600.00
9 WE,LF,BP,GT,LF(c),Flame . 600.00
10 WE,LF,BP,LF(c),Flame 600.00
11 WE,LF,BP,LF(c),O:Flame .. 750.00
12 BP,LF(c),Bondage(c),Flame 400.00
13 E:Dr Fung,Flame 375.00
14 JoS,Bondage(c),Flame 400.00
15 JoS&LF(c),Flame 400.00
16 Flame(c) 350.00
17 Flame(c) 350.00
18 Flame(c) 350.00
19 Male Bondage(c),Flame ... 375.00
20 Flame(c) 350.00
21 O:Black Club &Lion,Flame . 350.00
22 Flame(c) 350.00
23 Flame(c) 275.00
24 Flame(c) 275.00
25 A:Dr Fung,Flame 275.00
26 Flame(c) 275.00
27 Flame(c) 250.00
28 Bondage(c)I&O:US Jones, B:Lu-nar,Flame 350.00
29 Bondage(c),Flame 275.00
30 O:Flame(c),Flame 350.00
31 Bondage(c),Flame 275.00
32 Hitler(c),Flame 275.00
33 Male Bondage(c) January, 1942 .... 275.00

WORLD FAMOUS HEROES MAGAZINE
Comic Corp. of America (Centaur)
October, 1941

1 BLb,Paul Revere 550.00
2 BLb,Andrew Jackson,V: Dickinson 350.00
3 BLb,Juarez-Mexican patriot 250.00
4 BLb,Canadian Mounties ... 250.00

WORLD'S GREATEST STORIES
Jubilee Publications
January, 1949

1 F:Alice in Wonderland 120.00
2 F:Pinocchio 100.00

WORLD WAR III
Ace Periodicals
March, 1953

1 Atomic Bomb cover 325.00
2 May, 1953,The War That Will Never Happen 275.00

WOTALIFE COMICS
Fox Features Synd./ Green Publ.
August-September, 1946

3 (fa)B:L'il Pan,Cosmo Cat ... 35.00
4 .... 25.00
5 .... 20.00
6 .... 20.00
7 .... 20.00
8 .... 20.00
9 .... 20.00
10 .... 20.00
11 .... 20.00
12 July, 1947 .... 20.00

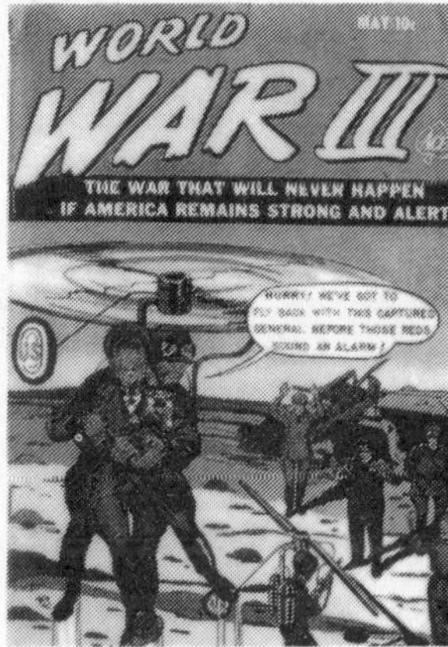

World War III #2 © Ace Periodicals

WOW COMICS
David McKay/Henle Publ.
July, 1936

1 WE,DBr(c),Fu Manchu, Buck Jones 1,400.00
2 WE,Little King 900.00
3 WE,WE(c) 900.00
4 WE,BKa,AR,DBr(c),Popeye, Flash Gordon,Nov.,1936 . 1,100.00

WOW COMICS
Fawcett Publications
Winter, 1940

N#(1)S&K,CCB(c),B&O:Mr Scarlett; B:Atom Blake,Jim Dolan,Rick O'Shay,Bondage(c) 10,000.00
2 B:Hunchback 850.00
3 V:Mummy Ray Gun 550.00
4 O:Pinky 550.00
5 F:Pinky the Whiz Kid 400.00
6 O:Phantom Eagle; B:Commando Yank 350.00
7 Spearhead of Invasion 325.00
8 All Three Heroes 325.00
9 A:Capt Marvel,Capt MarvelJr. Shazam,B:Mary Marvel 550.00
10 The Sinister Secret of Hotel Hideaway 275.00
11 .... 200.00
12 Rocketing adventures 200.00
13 Thrill Show 200.00
14 V:Mr Night 200.00
15 The Shazam Girl of America 175.00
16 Ride to the Moon 175.00
17 V:Mary Batson,Alter Ego Goes Berserk 175.00
18 I:Uncle Marvel,Infinity(c) V is For Victory 175.00
19 A Whirlwind Fantasy 175.00
20 Mary Marvel's Magic Carpet 175.00
21 Word That Shook the World 125.00
22 Come on Boys- Everybody Sing 125.00
23 Trapped by the Terror of the Future 125.00
24 Mary Marvel 125.00
25 Mary Marvel Crushes Crime 125.00
26 Smashing Star- Studded Stories 100.00
27 War Stamp Plea(c) 100.00
28 .... 100.00

29 .... 100.00
30 In Mirror Land 100.00

Wow Comics #31
© Fawcett Publications

31 Stars of Action 75.00
32 The Millinery Marauders 75.00
33 Mary Marvel(c) 75.00
34 A:Uncle Marvel 75.00
35 I:Freckles Marvel 75.00
36 Secret of the Buried City 75.00
37 7th War loan plea 75.00
38 Pictures That Came to Life 75.00
39 The Perilous Packages 75.00
40 The Quarrel of the Gnomes 75.00
41 Hazardous Adventures 60.00
42 .... 60.00
43 Curtain Time 60.00
44 Volcanic Adventure 60.00
45 .... 60.00
46 .... 60.00
47 .... 60.00
48 .... 60.00
49 .... 60.00
50 Mary Marvel/Commando Yank 60.00
51 .... 55.00
52 .... 55.00
53 Murder in the Tall Timbers 55.00
54 Flaming Adventure 55.00
55 Earthquake! 55.00
56 Sacred Pearls of Comatesh 55.00
57 .... 55.00
58 E:Mary Marvel;The Curse of the Keys 55.00
59 B:Ozzie the Hilarious Teenager 55.00
60 thru 64 .... @50.00
65 A:Tom Mix 55.00
66 A:Tom Mix 55.00
67 A:Tom Mix 55.00
68 A:Tom Mix 55.00
69 A:Tom Mix,Baseball 55.00

Becomes:

REAL WESTERN HERO

70 It's Round-up Time 200.00
71 CCB,P(c),A Rip Roaring Rodeo 125.00
72 w/Gabby Hayes 125.00
73 thru 75 .... @125.00

Becomes:

WESTERN HERO

76 Partial Ph(c)&P(c) 165.00
77 Partial Ph(c)&P(c) 90.00
78 Partial Ph(c)&P(c) 90.00
79 Partial Ph(c)&P(c), Shadow of Death 75.00
80 Partial Ph(c)&P(c) 90.00
81 CCB,Partial Ph(c)&P(c), F:Tootsie 90.00
82 Partial Ph(c)&P(c), A:Hopalong Cassidy 90.00
83 Partial Ph(c)&P(c) 90.00
84 Ph(c) 80.00
85 Ph(c) 75.00
86 Ph(c),The Case of the Extra Buddy, giant 80.00
87 Ph(c),The Strange Lands 80.00
88 Ph(c),A:Senor Diablo 80.00
89 Ph(c),The Hypnotist 80.00
90 Ph(c),The Menace of the Cougar, giant 75.00

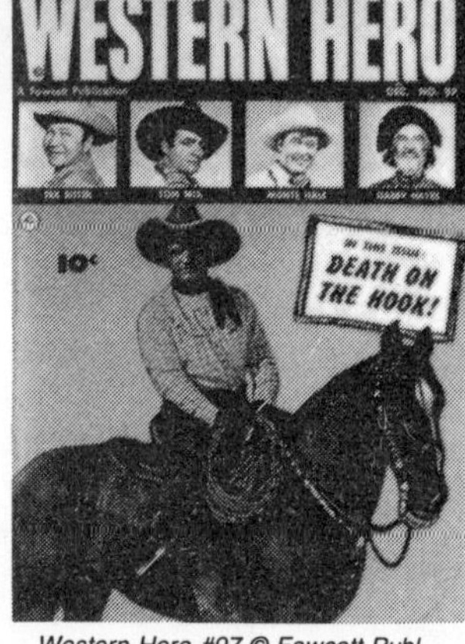

Western Hero #97 © Fawcett Publ.

91 Ph(c),Song of Death 75.00
92 Ph(c),The Fatal Hide-out, giant 75.00
93 Ph(c),Treachery at Triple T, giant 75.00
94 Ph(c),Bank Busters,giant 75.00
95 Ph(c),Rampaging River 65.00
96 Ph(c),Range Robbers,giant 75.00
97 Ph(c),Death on the Hook,giant 75.00
98 Ph(c),Web of Death,giant 75.00
99 Ph(c),The Hidden Evidence 65.00
100 Ph(c),A:Red Eagle,Giant 75.00
101 Ph(c) 75.00
102 thru 111 Ph(c) .... @65.00
112 Ph(c),March, 1952 .... 80.00

YANKEE COMICS
Chesler Publications
(Harry A. Chesler)
September, 1941

1 F:Yankee Doodle Jones 500.00
2 The Spirit of '41 .... 300.00
3 Yankee Doodle Jones 250.00
4 JCo,Yankee Doodle Jones March, 1942 .... 250.00

YELLOWJACKET COMICS
Levy Publ./Frank Comunale/ Charlton
September, 1944

1 O&B:Yellowjackets,B:Diana the Huntress 250.00
2 Rosita &The Filipino Kid 175.00
3 .... 150.00
4 Fall of the House of Usher 175.00
5 King of Beasts 150.00
6 .... 125.00
7 I:Diane Carter;The Lonely Guy 120.00
8 The Buzzing Bee Code 120.00
9 .... 120.00
10 Capt Grim V:The Salvage Pirates 120.00

Becomes:

JACK IN THE BOX

11 Funny Animal,Yellow Jacket 55.00
12 Funny Animal 25.00
13 BW,Funny Animal 80.00
14 thru 16 Funny Animal .... @30.00

Becomes:

COWBOY WESTERN COMICS

17 Annie Oakley,Jesse James 75.00
18 JO,JO(c) 50.00
19 JO,JO(c),Legends of Paul Bunyan 50.00
20 JO(c),Jesse James 35.00
21 Annie Oakley VisitsDryGulch 35.00
22 Story of the Texas Rangers 35.00
23 .... 35.00
24 Ph(c),F:James Craig 35.00
25 Ph(c),F:Sunset Carson 35.00
26 Ph(c) 65.00
27 Ph(c),Sunset Carson movie 150.00
28 Ph(c),Sunset Carson movie 100.00
29 Ph(c),Sunset Carson movie 100.00
30 Ph(c),Sunset Carson movie 150.00
31 Ph(c) 30.00
32 thru 34 Ph(c) .... @25.00
35 thru 37 Sunset Carson .... @75.00
38 .... 25.00
39 .... 25.00

Becomes:

SPACE WESTERN COMICS

40 Spurs Jackson,V:The Saucer Men 275.00
41 StC(c),Space Vigilantes 200.00
42 StC(c) 250.00
43 StC(c),Battle of Spacemans Gulch 200.00
44 StC(c),The Madman of Mars 200.00
45 StC(c),The Moon Bat 200.00

Becomes:

COWBOY WESTERN COMICS

46 .... 70.00

Becomes:

COWBOY WESTERN HEROES

47 .... 25.00
48 .... 25.00

Becomes:

COWBOY WESTERN

49 .... 25.00
50 F:Jesse James 20.00
51 thru 56 .... @20.00
58, giant 25.00
59 thru 66 .... @20.00
67 AW&AT 50.00

Becomes:

WILD BILL HICKOK AND JINGLES

68 AW 50.00
69 AW 35.00
70 AW 30.00
71 .... 20.00
72 .... 20.00
73 .... 20.00
74 1960 .... 20.00

YOGI BERRA
Fawcett
1957

1 Ph(c) 375.00

YOUNG BRIDES
Feature Publications (Prize Comics)
September-October, 1952

1 S&K,Ph(c) 100.00
2 S&K,Ph(c) 50.00
3 S&K,Ph(c) 45.00
4 S&K 45.00
5 S&K 45.00
6 S&K 45.00
2-1 S&K 40.00
2-2 S&K 25.00
2-3 S&K 35.00
2-4 S&K 35.00
2-5 S&K 35.00
2-6 S&K 35.00
2-7 S&K 35.00
2-8 S&K 20.00
2-9 S&K 20.00
2-10 S&K 35.00
2-11 S&K 35.00
2-12 S&K 35.00
3-1 . . . . 12.00
3-2 . . . . 10.00
3-3 . . . . 10.00
3-4 . . . . 10.00
3-5 . . . . 10.00
3-6 . . . . 10.00
4-1 . . . . 10.00
4-2 S&K 40.00
4-3 . . . . 10.00
4-4 S&K 35.00
4-5 . . . . 10.00

YOUNG EAGLE
Fawcett Publications/ Charlton Comics
December, 1950

1 Ph(c) 85.00
2 Ph(c),Mystery of Thunder Canyon 45.00
3 Ph(c),Death at Dawn 40.00
4 Ph(c) 40.00
5 Ph(c),The Golden Flood 40.00
6 Ph(c),The Nightmare Empire . 40.00
7 Ph(c),Vigilante Veangeance . 40.00
8 Ph(c),The Rogues Rodeo . . . 40.00
9 Ph(c),The Great Railroad Swindle 40.00
10 June, 1952, Ph(c),Thunder Rides the Trail,O:Thunder 25.00

YOUNG KING COLE
Novelty Press/Premium Svcs. Co.
Autumn, 1945

1-1 Detective Toni Gayle 100.00
1-2 . . . . 60.00
1-3 . . . . 55.00
1-4 . . . . 40.00
2-1 . . . . 40.00
2-2 . . . . 35.00
2-3 . . . . 35.00
2-4 . . . . 35.00
2-5 . . . . 35.00
2-6 . . . . 35.00
2-7 . . . . 35.00
3-1 . . . . 30.00
3-2 LbC 30.00
3-3 The Killer With The Hat . . . 25.00
3-4 The Fierce Tiger 25.00
3-5 AMc 25.00
3-6 . . . . 35.00
3-7 LbC(c),Case of the Devil's Twin 50.00
3-8 . . . . 40.00
3-9 The Crime Fighting King . . . 40.00
3-10 LbC(c) 40.00
3-11 LbC(c) 40.00
3-12 July, 1948,AMc(c) 25.00

Young King Cole #12 (3/1)
© Novelty Press/Premium Svcs. Co.

YOUNG LIFE
New Age Publications
Summer, 1945

1 Partial Ph(c),Louis Palma . . . 55.00
2 Partial Ph(c),Frank Sinatra . . . 60.00

Becomes:

TEEN LIFE

3 Partial Ph(c),Croon without Tricks,June Allyson(c) 45.00
4 Partial Ph(c),Atom Smasher Blueprints,Duke Ellington(c) . 40.00

Teen Life #5 © New Age Publications

5 Partial Ph(c), Build Your Own Pocket Radio, Jackie Robinson(c) 50.00

YOUNG LOVE
Feature Publ. (Prize Comics Group)
February-March, 1949

1 S&K,S&K(c) 175.00
2 S&K,Ph(c) 75.00
3 S&K,JSe,BE,Ph(c) 60.00
4 S&K,Ph(c) 40.00
5 S&K,Ph(c) 40.00
2-1 Ph(c) 60.00
2-2 Ph(c) 30.00
2-3 Ph(c) 30.00
2-4 Ph(c) 30.00
2-5 Ph(c) 30.00
2-6 S&K(c) 40.00
2-7 S&K(c),S&K 60.00
2-8 S&K 60.00
2-9 S&K(c),S&K 60.00
2-10 S&K(c),S&K 60.00
2-11 S&K(c),S&K 60.00
2-12 S&K(c),S&K 60.00
3-1 S&K(c),S&K 45.00
3-2 S&K(c),S&K 45.00
3-3 S&K(c),S&K 45.00
3-4 S&K(c),S&K 45.00
3-5 Ph(c) 35.00
3-6 BP,Ph(c) 35.00
3-7 Ph(c) 35.00
3-8 Ph(c) 35.00
3-9 MMe,Ph(c) 35.00
3-10 Ph(c) 35.00
3-11 Ph(c) 35.00
3-12 Ph(c) 35.00
4-1 S&K 35.00
4-2 Ph(c) 30.00
4-3 Ph(c) 30.00
4-4 Ph(c) 30.00
4-5 Ph(c) 30.00
4-6 S&K,Ph(c) 30.00
4-7 thru 4-12 Ph(c) . . . . @25.00
5-1 thru 5-12 Ph(c) . . . . @20.00
6-1 thru 6-9 . . . . @15.00
6-10 thru 6-12 . . . . @15.00
7-1 thru 7-7 . . . . @10.00
7-8 thru 7-11 . . . . @10.00
7-12 thru 8-5 . . . . @12.00
8-6 thru 8-12 . . . . @18.00

YOUNG ROMANCE COMICS
Feature Publ./Headline/ Prize Publ.
September-October, 1947

1 S&K(c),S&K 175.00
2 S&K(c),S&K 100.00
3 S&K(c),S&K 75.00
4 S&K(c),S&K 75.00
5 S&K(c),S&K 75.00
6 S&K(c),S&K 70.00
2-1 S&K(c),S&K 70.00
2-2 S&K(c),S&K 70.00
2-3 S&K(c),S&K 70.00
2-4 S&K(c),S&K 70.00
2-5 S&K(c),S&K 70.00
2-6 S&K(c),S&K 70.00
3-1 thru 3-12 S&K(c),S&K . . . @50.00
4-1 thru 4-12 S&K . . . . @40.00
5-1 ATh,S&K 45.00
2 . . . . 40.00
3 . . . . 40.00
5-4 thru 5-12 S&K . . . . @40.00
6-1 thru 6-3 . . . . @20.00

YOUR UNITED STATES
Lloyd Jacquet Studios
1946

1N# Teeming nation of Nations 135.00

YOUTHFUL HEART
Youthful Magazines
May, 1952

1 Frankie Lane(c) 100.00
2 Vic Damone 75.00
3 Johnnie Ray 75.00

Becomes:

DARING CONFESSIONS

4 DW,Tony Curtis 50.00
5 . . . . 35.00
6 DW 40.00
7 . . . . 35.00
8 DW 40.00

Youthful Romances #8

© Pix Parade/Ribage/Trojan

YOUTHFUL ROMANCES
Pix Parade/Ribage/ Trojan
August-September, 1949

1 . . . . 100.00
2 . . . . 55.00
3 Tex Beneke 45.00
4 . . . . 45.00
5 . . . . 30.00
6 . . . . 30.00
7 Tony Martin(c) 35.00
8 WW(c) 90.00
9 . . . . 30.00
10 . . . . 30.00
11 . . . . 30.00
12 . . . . 30.00
13 . . . . 30.00
14 . . . . 30.00

Becomes:

DARLING LOVE

15 WD 40.00
16 . . . . 30.00
17 DW,Ph(c) 30.00

ZAGO, JUNGLE PRINCE
Fox Features Syndicate
September, 1948

1 A:Blue Beetle 225.00
2 JKa 150.00
3 JKa 150.00
4 MB(c) 150.00

Becomes:

MY STORY

5 JKa,Too Young To Fall in Love 75.00
6 I Was A She-Wolf 35.00
7 I Lost My Reputation 35.00
8 My Words Condemned Me . . 35.00
9 WW,Wayward Bride 85.00
10 WW,March, 1950,Second Rate Girl 85.00
11 . . . . 35.00
12 . . . . 35.00

TEGRA, JUNGLE EMPRESS
Fox Features Syndicate
August, 1948

1 Blue Bettle,Rocket Kelly . . . 200.00

Becomes:

ZEGRA, JUNGLE EMPRESS

2 JKa 250.00
3 . . . . 200.00
4 . . . . 200.00
5 . . . . 200.00

Becomes:

MY LOVE LIFE

6 I Put A Price Tag On Love . . 65.00
7 An Old Man's Fancy 35.00
8 My Forbidden Affair 35.00
9 I Loved too Often 35.00
10 My Secret Torture 35.00
11 I Broke My Own Heart 35.00
12 I Was An Untamed Filly 35.00
13 I Can Never Marry You, August 1950 . . . . 30.00

ZIP COMICS
MLJ Magazines
February, 1940

1 MMe,O&B:Kalathar,The Scarlet Avenger,Steel Sterling,B:Mr Satan,Nevada Jones,War Eagle Captain Valor 1,600.00
2 MMe,CBi(c)B:Steel Sterling(c) 800.00
3 CBi,MMe,CBi(c) 600.00
4 CBi,MMe,CBi(c) 450.00
5 CBi,MMe,CBi(c) 450.00
6 CBi,MMe,CBi(c) 400.00
7 CBi,MMe,CBi(c) 375.00
8 CBi,MMe,CBi(c),Bondage(c) 400.00
9 CBi,MMe,CBi(c)E:Kalathar, Mr Satan;Bondage(c) 400.00
10 CBi,MMe,CBi(c),B:Inferno . . 450.00
11 CBi,MMe,CBi(c) 350.00
12 CBi,MMe,CBi(c),Bondage(c) 350.00
13 CBi,MMe,CBi(c)E:Inferno, Bondage(c),Woman in Electric Chair 350.00

Zip Comics #4

© MLJ Magazines/Archie Comics

14 CBi,MMe,CBi(c),Bondage(c) 350.00
15 CBi,MMe,CBi(c),Bondage(c) 350.00
16 CBi,MMe,CBi(c),Bondage(c) 350.00
17 CBi,CBI(c),E:Scarlet Avenger Bondage(c) 365.00
18 IN(c),B:Wilbur 350.00
19 IN(c),Steel Sterling(c) 325.00
20 IN(c),O&I:Black Jack Hitler(c) 500.00
21 IN(c),V:Nazis 300.00
22 IN(c) 300.00
23 IN(c),Flying Fortress 300.00
24 IN(c),China Town Exploit . . 300.00
25 IN(c),E:Nevada Jones 300.00
26 IN(c),B:Black Witch, E:Capt Valor 325.00
27 IN(c),I:Web,V:Japanese . . . 500.00
28 IN(C),O:Web,Bondage(c) . . 500.00
29 Steel Sterling & Web 275.00
30 V:Nazis 275.00
31 IN(c) 225.00
32 . . . . 250.00
33 Bondage(c) 265.00
34 I:Applejack;Bondage(c) 265.00
35 E:Zambini 250.00
36 I:Senor Banana 250.00
37 . . . . 250.00
38 E:Web 250.00
39 O&B:Red Rule 250.00
40 . . . . 200.00
41 . . . . 200.00
42 . . . . 200.00
43 . . . . 200.00
44 . . . . 200.00
45 E:Wilbur 200.00
46 . . . . 200.00
47 Crooks Can't Win, Summer, 1944 . . . . 200.00

ZIP-JET
St. John Publishing Co.
February, 1953

1 Rocketman 250.00
2 April,May, 1953, Assassin of the Airlanes 225.00

ZOOM COMICS
Carlton Publishing Co.
December, 1945

N# O:Captain Milksop 200.00

ZOOT COMICS
Fox Features Syndicate
Spring, 1946

N#(1)(fa) 75.00
2 A:Jaguar(fa) 70.00
3 (fa) 40.00
4 (fa) 40.00
5 (fa) 35.00
6 (fa) 35.00
7 B:Rulah 300.00
8 JKa(c),Fangs of Stone 250.00
9 JKa(c),Fangs of Black Fury 250.00
10 JKa(c),Inferno Land 250.00
11 JKa,The Purple Plague, Bondage(c) 275.00
12 JKa(c),The Thirsty Stone, Bondage(c) 275.00
13 Bloody Moon 200.00
14 Pearls of Pathos,Woman Carried off by Bird 250.00
15 Death Dancers 150.00
16 . . . . 150.00

Becomes:

RULAH, JUNGLE GODDESS

17 JKa(c),Wolf Doctor 375.00
18 JKa(c),Vampire Garden . . . 300.00
19 JKa(c) 250.00
20 . . . . 250.00
21 JKa(c) 250.00
22 JKa(c) 250.00
23 . . . . 210.00
24 . . . . 200.00
25 . . . . 200.00
26 . . . . 200.00
27 . . . . 210.00

Becomes:

I LOVED

28 . . . . 35.00
29 . . . . 25.00
30 . . . . 25.00
31 . . . . 25.00
32 My Poison Love, March, 1950 25.00

EXTREMELY MOTIVATED

By Jeff Juliard and Buddy Scalera

It's been almost four years now and Image Comics has failed to live up to the disastrous predictions of many of the industry's pundits. Despite an often bumpy ride during its first couple of years, this collection of high-profile artists and independent studios has settled into what looks like a stable groove.

As an integral part of the Image framework, Rob Liefeld's Extreme Studios has positioned Image for future success after a highly prosperous summer and to think that many industry experts said it would never last.

"I think what people need to realize is that Image has the strongest line average in the industry," says Matt Hawkins, Extreme's Marketing and Promotions Director. "For the number of books we put out, we sell, per book, almost double what any other company does in this industry. Granted there are other companies in the industry that have larger market share, but we're not about market share; we're about putting out good-quality books with quality stories. The fact that our books outsell every other company's in the industry should indicate the fact that we're succeeding in what we're trying to do."

Hawkins has been with Extreme Studios since meeting the studio's founder, Rob Liefeld, at a signing. Liefeld created Extreme Studios when he left Marvel (where he had been working on *New Mutants* #87-100 and *X-Force*) to form Image Comics.

"I think the studio system that Image has set up among the different owners is wonderful because they don't have that paranoia of when we hang up the phone are we going to screw with their careers behind their backs [or are] we going to make changes on their pages when they're not looking. Everything is right in the open," Liefeld said. "No dirty dealings. My studio is run very upright and honestly and we're staffed up to over forty people now. Sometimes I tell the young guys, 'Hey, man, if you have a disagreement with me, tell me.' I encourage them to kick down the doors as well. I respect that maybe you have to be confrontational to get your point across. At Marvel, I wasn't scared to use the position of strength that I had to get what I wanted. It was all about what I wanted, not what I deserved.

"I'm well aware that it got me a reputation for being difficult. Once you have that position of strength, if you don't use it, it was never any good to you anyway. So I said, I've got this tool I can negotiate with to get more say-so on the book, to up my page rate, to have some influence and some say-so with the people I get to work with. Heck, yeah, I was going to use that," Liefeld explained.

"There's a lot of people in the industry who are very complacent, very scared to confront the system. You know what? The creators run this business. Marvel and DC and all their corporate bull, they don't run this business. Neither does Image and any of the corporate bull that's crept into our organization. The creator is in control of his career and anytime can turn around and say, 'No, I don't want to do this,' and walk away and pick up another job. I always knew that I had that going for me," Liefeld added.

Extreme's first book was *Youngblood*, which was followed by *Zero*, *Brigade*, *Bloodstrike*, *Team Youngblood*, *Youngblood Strikefile*, *The NewMen*, *Supreme*, *Troll*, and a host of other titles. Despite an often spotty release schedule, these titles have done well, and Hawkins is quick to note that they are all among the top one hundred sellers.

In July of 1993, Liefeld took a six-month hiatus to explore new styles of writing and drawing. He also looked into options for animating *Youngblood* as a movie or television show.

"Sometimes you just get burned out and it was the first time that I had ever experienced total burnout. I had been doing this for seven years straight and was just badly in need of a break. I think Image really knocked the wind out of all our sails. You're going to see more Image creators going on hiatus in the next several months. We've all been doing this, some of us for the better part of a decade," Liefeld said.

"I never really took any vacations. A lot of people classify me as a workaholic. The work wasn't at the level that I was wanting to do it. I think there's a world of difference between being behind the eight ball and being in front of it, and I was definitely behind the eight ball. The decision was made, and I really needed the time to really get ahead. I started penciling in December and now I've got four issues [of *Youngblood*] in the can and that makes a world of difference. It's an unbelievable feeling, and I've never really been ahead," Liefeld added.

Liefeld's return, and the return of *Youngblood* with issue #6 in 1994, was a heavily promoted event. Hawkins noted that it marked a new direction for Extreme. "There was a lot of specu- lation about what it's going to be like," he says. "I think one of the things we've got going for us is low expectations. The book's going to change a lot of things."

"Sometimes you just get burned out and it was the first time that I had ever experienced total burnout. I had been doing this for seven years straight and was just badly in need of a break," Rob Liefeld said.

"When Rob and *Youngblood* came back, it was a hit in a big way," says Youngblood editor Eric Stephenson. "If people had a complaint about the first miniseries, it was that it was disjointed, without a clear focus. That's definitely not the case with this one. Rob was very focused and had a very clear idea of where he wanted to go with the book. I think it surprised a lot of people; the amount of attention he gave to the detail of each of the characters and all the little intrica- cies of the plot."

According to Stephenson, *Youngblood* #6 was a character-driven issue. Instead of the flashy combat scenes that Image books were known for, *Youngblood* #6 focused on each of the characters and who they are. There were also new members introduced with *Youngblood* and issue #7 saw Overkill returning for a grudge match with Badrock. This battle contin- ued over into *Team Youngblood*. According to Stephenson, this is a pattern that *Youngblood* fans will see frequently in the future. Stories will begin in *Youngblood*, continue in *Team Youngblood*, and then return to *Youngblood* for the conclusion.

"We've really tightened up the continuity between the two books," he explains, "because after all they are the same organization; they're just different branches. We're really going to drive that point home in the future."

A changing story line was only the tip of the iceberg for *Youngblood*. In true comic book hero form, *Youngblood* is poised to cross over into the mass market.

However, turning Youngblood into a cartoon is not something Liefeld and Extreme Studios take lightly. Liefeld pulled out of a deal with CBS over proposed changes to the characters and story.

"It was a done deal," explains Hawkins. "But once we started talking to them they started saying that you can't have a gun, you can't call it a gun, you can't point it at anybody, you can't use this character Riptide because she shows her thighs and it's too sexual. This was in preproduction, before we even had a signed contract! We thought that if this was preproduction, what would happen when there was a signed contract and they were actually heavily involved in the promoting of it as well. We didn't want to make a preschoolers show. We wanted to make a cutting-edge comic book show that was loyal to the comic book."

Liefeld added that the CBS network didn't provide him with the artistic freedom that he enjoys in the comic book market. "CBS was opposed to the whole violence issue. I didn't believe that I was going to be able to do the kind of show that I wanted to do. I don't want to do a show that was designed to sell toys. If you want to attach toys to it, that's fine. I want to do a show that's cool, that has great animation. My animation team was ready to go in September. CBS said that it was interested in September of last year. They said we'll have an answer in November. We were hoping to be working by November 1993. November, no answer. December, no answer. February was when I said bye-bye. At that point our lead time was massively eaten up," Liefeld said.

"Look at every comic project that CBS has touched in the last few years: *The Flash*, *Cadillacs and Dinosaurs*, and *The Fish Police*. All miserable failures. I think Jim Lee's WildC.A.T.S. is a great find for them. I hope that they are true to the book and allow Jim his say-so. Even though it wasn't an option for me, I'm rooting for Jim. It wasn't the place or the home I desired to be in," Liefeld added.

Despite the differences of opinions with the network executives, Extreme Studios continues to look for other mass-market ventures. Some future upcoming deals may include a *Youngblood* video game and a line of *Youngblood* trading cards from SkyBox. There are movie deals for some of Extreme's other characters as well. Liefeld has optioned *Dooms IV* to Steven Spielberg's company and has also made a deal with Tom Cruise's company, Cruise/Wagner, for *The Mark*. Hawkins explains that this is all part of an effort to make comics more accessible.

"We're really trying to do things to expand the genre. Big-budget films like *Batman* have actually expanded the market, and we're also trying to do things to bring in new readers; to make comics exciting, to make them fun and to really do things to grow our audiences."

According to Hawkins, growing audiences through mass marketing is easy for Liefeld's characters because he designs them with that market in mind.

"A lot of stuff that we do is very adaptable. One of Rob's major strengths is that when he creates characters, he thinks about it from a mass-marketing potential. A lot of the characters are very visual. They make great action figures, toys, and cartoons. When you have all that intermixed into a character, it's very usable. I think you're going to see an explosion of properties that the Image guys have created within the next ten years. They're

KODIAK! STOP CLOWNING AROUND AND PASS THE BALL!
SCREW THAT! FIRST I'M GONNA MAKE JERK-BOY HERE DISAPPEAR UP HIS OWN BUNT-HOLE!
OH, YEAH? A WIMP LIKE YOU IS GONNA-- OOOF!
THAT'S ENOUGH OF THAT, KODIAK-- NOBODY LIKES BULLIES!

going to be everywhere!"

With its characters poised to invade the market, Extreme Studios has not forgotten that its first mandate is to create comic books.

In an attempt to once again push the limits of the medium, Extreme published *Images of Tomorrow* during the summer of 1994. Several books, *Bloodstrike*, *Brigade*, *Supreme* and *Stormwatch*, all suddenly skipped ahead to issue #25, providing readers with a glimpse of the future. In some cases, that's fifteen issues ahead of where the stories were beforehand! When each of those books reach issue #24, it will skip #25 and go straight to #26. The upcoming issue #25 will fit seamlessly into each story line.

"Things were utterly and irrevocably changed in *Brigade* forever," Stephenson said. "People are going to think we've gone completely nuts. Also, Battlestone joined Youngblood again. He was sent to hunt Brigade down and put an end to their operation forever. This was the end of the story line. People will have to read #10-24 to find out how he got there."

The first thing readers noticed about *Bloodstrike* #25 is that the team is gone. "We kind of decided we have too many teams," says Hawkins. "Image has more teams than the NFL, the NBA, and the NHL combined. So we decided to make that book into a solo character called Bloodstrike. In the Extreme Prejudice crossover that was completed in the spring of 1994, we wiped out the entire team. The new character, Bloodstrike, appeared in issue #25 and then it dropped back to #11 and continued on with the beginning of that story, bringing it up to the twenty-fifth issue."

The Newmen, a team that sprung from the ashes of the Extreme Prejudice crossover last spring (1994), also provided interesting story lines for readers. In the second issue, they encountered a new villain named Girth. "He's someone I think the kids like," Stephenson said. "He wisecracks a lot, and he spends almost as much time talking as he does trying to kill his targets."

That story carried over into #3, and then in issue #4, Ripclaw from Cyberforce joined forces with the Newmen to fight a mystical being named Ikon. Stephenson says this villain was a departure for Extreme.

"He's a little bit different from all the other stuff we've done with Image in that his power isn't scientific or genetic. He's purely mystical in nature. It's not an innovative idea for comics in general, but it's not something we've dealt with a lot. I think Ripclaw is the closest thing Image has to it. He's an Indian and sort of in tune with mystical auras and stuff like that. The way the whole story line with Ripclaw and Ikon was resolved was really interesting. It wasn't resolved with a fight, instead they had to think their way through it."

Stephenson explains that there is quite a bit more in store for this team of unsuspecting do-gooders. "Basically, in the first five issues, we introduced the readers to the characters. People could choose who they liked and who they disliked in the book, and then we started rending their souls from them. We're going to really start beating up on them over the course of about a year, not just in terms of the kind of foes that they deal with but also the sort of emotional and interrelationship struggles they have."

From what Stephenson says, none of the Newmen will be spared. "There will be a love triangle between Dash, Byrd, and Reign that's going to have some real interesting ramifications and we're also going to deal with how Kodiak's abilities affect his mind. He's very feral in appearance and you'd think that would, at some point, start to affect his brain, too. Also, I always wanted to do something different with Exit. What if instead of just teleporting, he opens portals and goes places? We are going to deal with what it is that he passes through when he goes from one place to the next. If he gets stuck there, what happens? People are going to think we must really hate these characters, but, really, we

YAEP
+
RAPMUND

like them a lot! That's why we're doing all these mean things to them."

Changes also were in store for Prophet over the summer of 1994. *Prophet* #5, drawn by Stephen Platt, is the first issue in a story line that pits Kirby, Prophet's companion, against him. Kirby has been sent out to track Prophet down and bring him in.

"Prophet is sort of mixed up at this point," explained Stephenson. "He gets captured by the government, and they do some experimentation that causes him to flip out. He runs off into the Alaskan wilderness. There will be a four-part story in which Kirby has to track him down and bring him in. Ultimately, Kirby and Prophet will sort everything out, and that will take us into the next story arc."

Extreme also introduced a new character named Troll, and Jim Shooter wrote a story arc for *Youngblood*. "I said I had liked the stuff he, Shooter, had done over at Valiant, and I liked his *Legion of Super-Heroes* work as well. Honestly, those were my favorite stories as a kid. When he was writing the *Avengers*, that book to me was everything great about comic books. I just thought he was a great writer. He had great flair for dialogue, great plots, twists. I told him basically, 'To me, you wrote the definitive *Avengers*. I would love to get the definitive *Youngblood* out of you once I bring them back and tidy them up, and once I get to know them again.' And he said, 'I'd love to'", Liefeld said.

"There's not a whole lot of writers that I would be interested in writing with, just because I'm so spoiled and I can do whatever I want. If I want to do a whole issue about Badrock picking flowers in his garden, then so be it. I'm not restricted to doing what I don't want to do," Liefeld added.

One area of concern for Image fans has been the lateness of getting Image books on the shelves. Liefeld believes that these problems have finally been solved and all books will be on the comic book racks on time.

"The late books are a thing of the past. I'm angry that *Prophet* #5 took as long as it did to get out, but we were working with a new artist, Stephen Platt, whom I think was a little overwhelmed and felt the pressure of the expectations put on him. With the exception of Stephen, [Extreme] hasn't had a late book since December of 1993. *The Newmen*, *Team Youngblood*, *Brigade*, [and] *Bloodstrike*, those books have been coming out at a monthly clip, sometimes faster. We've actually gotten some books out early. There was so much that had gone wrong and it took so much to make it right. I remember when I left, I told the guys in the studio, 'This is your time. This is your time to make a name for yourself. This is your time to go out there and really hit some home runs. Get noticed. Get the books out on time.' I wanted to come back to a strong lineup and I think we have it now," Liefeld said.

Apart from the regular books, Extreme has also picked up the comic book and animation rights to the 1970s science fiction series *Battlestar Galactica*. With a plate this full, its hard to see Extreme Studios succumbing to the collapse that many industry people predicted for Image and its components.

"I think what people need to realize about Image is that a lot of what we do is stuff that the guys do because they think it's cool," says Hawkins. "They're not out there trying to make millions and millions of dollars. They're out there to put out really high-quality stories and really high-quality artwork. They want that kid that's in his bed under the covers with a flashlight to say `Oh man! This is awesome!' It's not about fifty-billion part crossovers with $3 cover prices and holograms and die-cuts. We're not out there to screw the kids out of their money. We're not beholden to any stockholders or any corporate executives. These guys are artists themselves. They control their own destinies, they do what they want to do, and they remain true to their art form."

New Men © Rob Liefeld

The best career move Liefeld ever made may have been taking time off and becoming once again extremely motivated to produce the best possible comic books. "I learned that being the big number one hotshot doesn't matter a lick in life. I think there was a race that I got caught up in, the hot books, hot artist, hot list. I was talking to another Image owner who is going to be leaving this summer. He was telling me the same thing, 'When you know you're leaving, it's the best feeling because none of that stuff matters anymore.' What I learned was that I needed to relax and step back," Liefeld said.

"The minute I stepped back and wasn't so caught up in the numbers game, the ratings game, the popularity game, the stuff that actually was important in the comics came back to me. I looked at my books and said, 'God! Why would I care about any of these characters?' I think there was a real period where we just introduced: `Hi, I'm Biff, the Superhero. I'm charging into a fight and read my adventures.' And that's all he did and that's a lot of what my books were doing at the time. It just helped me learn to put out the good books, make them the best you can. I've got a vision that I didn't have before. I'm very competitive by nature and have always been so. Now I'm very content.'

People look at the new *Youngblood* issues and comment on how different the tone of the book is, a lot more quiet, day-in-the-life stuff, characterization all over the place in terms of what are these characters doing after hours, what are their personal lives like, what are their motivations? Some of the characters seem very happy. Some of them seem very strange and weird, but no one is really angry or has a lot of rage. Some people have said, 'You don't have the rage your old work used to have.' Then they pointed out issues of *X-Force* and *Youngblood* where its people are screaming at each other for twenty-two pages. I was pretty frustrated at the time. That showed in the work. Now I'm very content and happy and I think that shows in the work. I think *Youngblood* is a very fun book as a result of it," Liefeld concluded.

ABBOTT AND COSTELLO
Charlton Comics
February, 1968
1 . . . . 25.00
2 thru 9 . . . . @12.00
10 thru 21 . . . . @9.50
22 August, 1971 . . . . 9.00

ABYSS, THE
Dark Horse
1 MK,Movie Adaption 2.50
2 MK 2.50

ACCIDENT MAN: THE DEATH TOUCH
Apocalypse
One Shot rep.Toxic #10-#16 . . . . 3.95

ADAM-12
Gold Key
December, 1973
1 . . . . 22.00
2 thru 9 . . . . @12.00
10 February, 1976 . . . . 12.00

ADAPTERS, THE
1 . . . . 2.00
2 . . . . 2.00

ADDAMS FAMILY
Gold Key
October, 1974
1 . . . . 40.00
2 . . . . 25.00
3 . . . . 20.00

ADLAI STEVENSON
Dell Publishing Co.
December, 1966
1 Political Life Story 25.00

ADVENTURES OF BARON MUNCHAUSEN
Now Comics
1 thru 4 Mini-Series . . . . @1.75

ADVENTURES OF CHRISSIE CLAWS
Hero Graphics
1 Trouble in Toyland 2.95

ADVENTURES OF FELIX THE CAT
Harvey
1 Short Stories 1.25

ADVENTURES OF KUNG FU PIG NINJA FLOUNDER AND 4-D MONKEY
1 thru 6 . . . . @1.80
7 thru 10 . . . . @2.00

ADVENTURES OF ROBIN HOOD
Gold Key
March, 1974
1 . . . . 6.00
2 thru 7, January 1975 . . . . @3.50

ADVENTURES OF THE FLY
Archie Publications/ Radio Comics
August, 1959
1 JSm/JK,O:Fly,I:SpiderSpry
A:Lancelot Strong/Shield . . 375.00
2 JSm/JK,DAy,AW 225.00
3 Jack Davis Art, O:Fly 175.00
4 V:Dazzler NA panel 100.00
5 A:Spider Spry 65.00
6 V:Moon Men 60.00
7 A:Black Hood 60.00
8 A:Lancelot Strong/Shield 60.00
9 A:Lancelot Strong/Shield
I:Cat Girl 60.00
10 A:Spider Spry 60.00
11 V:Rock Men 35.00
12 V:Brute Invaders 35.00
13 I:Kim Brand 40.00
14 I:Fly-Girl(Kim Brand) 50.00
15 A:Spider 35.00
16 A:Fly-Girl 35.00
17 A:Fly-Girl 35.00
18 A:Fly-Girl 35.00
19 A:Fly-Girl 35.00
20 O:Fly-Girl 38.00
21 A:Fly-Girl 25.00
22 A:Fly-Girl 25.00
23 A:Fly-Girl,Jaguar 25.00
24 A:Fly-Girl 25.00
25 A:Fly-Girl 25.00
26 A:Fly-Girl,Black Hood 25.00
27 A:Fly-Girl,Black Hood 25.00
28 A:Black Hood 25.00
29 A:Fly-Girl,Black Hood 25.00
30 A:Fly-Girl,R:Comet 30.00

ADVENTURES OF THE JAGUAR
Archie Publications/ Radio Comics
September, 1961
1 I:Ralph Hardy/Jaguar 125.00
2 10 cent cover 65.00
3 Last 10 cent cover 60.00
4 A:Cat-Girl 45.00
5 A:Cat-Girl 45.00
6 A:Cat-Girl 38.00
7 . . . . 30.00
8 . . . . 30.00
9 . . . . 30.00
10 . . . . 30.00
11 . . . . 30.00
12 A:Black Hood 30.00
13 A:Cat-Girl,A:Black Hood 30.00
14 A:Black Hood 30.00
15 V:Human Octopus,last issue
November, 1963 . . . . 25.00

ADVENTURES OF YOUNG DR. MASTERS
Archie Comics
August, 1964
1 . . . . 5.00
2 November, 1964 . . . . 5.00

AGAINST BLACKSHARD
Sirius Comics
1 3-D, August 1986 . . . . 2.25

AGE OF REPTILES
Dark Horse
1 DRd,Story on Dinosaurs 2.50
2 DRd,Story on Dinosaurs 2.50
3 DRd,Story on Dinosaurs 2.50
4 DRd,Story on Dinosaurs 2.50

AIR FIGHTERS, SGT. STRIKE SPECIAL
Eclipse
1 A:Airboy,Valkyrie 1.95

AIR WAR STORIES
Dell Publishing Co.
September-November, 1964
1 . . . . 15.00
2 . . . . 10.00
3 thru 8 . . . . @8.00

AIRBOY
Eclipse
1 TT/TY,D:Golden Age Airboy
O:New Airboy 3.25
2 TT/TY,I:Marisa,R:SkyWolf 2.25
3 A:The Heap 2.50
4 A:Misery 2.50
5 DSt(c),R:Valkyrie 4.00
6 R:Iron Ace,I:Marlene 3.00
7 PG(c), ... 2.50
8 FH/TT(c) 2.50
9 R:Flying Fool, Riot, O'Hara
Cocky, Judge & Turtle 1.75
10 I:Manic,D:Cocky, Judge
& Turtle 1.50
11 O:Birdie 1.50
12 R:Flying Fool 1.50

Airboy #9 © Eclipse Comics

13 I:New Bald Eagle 1.50
14 A:Sky Wolf, Iron Ace 1.50
15 A:Ku Klux Klan 1.50
16 D:Manic,A:Ku Klux Klan 1.50
17 A:HarryS.Truman,Misery 1.75
18 A:Gold.Age Black Angel 1.75
19 A:Gold.Age Rats 1.75
20 Rat storyline 1.75
21 I:Lester Mansfield (rel. of
Gold.Age Rackman), Artic
Deathzone #1 . . . . 1.75
22 DSp,Artic Deathzone #2 . . . . 1.75
23 A:Gold.Age Black Angle,
Artic Deathzone #3 . . . . 1.75
24 A: Heap 1.75
25 TY,I:Manure Man,A:Heap 1.50
26 R:Flying Dutchman 1.50
27 A:Iron Ace, Heap 1.50
28 A:Heap 1.50
29 . . . . 1.50
30 A:Iron Ace; Sky Wolf story 1.50
31 A:Valkyrie; Sky Wolf story 1.75
32 Hostage Virus, ... 1.75
33 DSp,SkyWolf sty,A:Sgt.Strike . 1.75
34 DSp,A:La Lupina 1.75
35 DSp,A:La Lupina, Sky Wolf . . . 1.75
36 . . . . 1.75
37 DSp 1.75
38 Cl, Heap story 1.75
39 Cl, Heap story 1.75
40 Cl, Heap story 1.75
41 V:Steel Fox, Golden Age rep.

O:Valkyrie 1.75
42 A:Rackman 1.95
43 Sky Wolf sty, A:Flying Fool . . . 1.95
44 A:Rackman 1.95
45 . . . . 1.95
46 EC,Airboy Diary #1 . . . . 1.95
47 EC,Airboy Diary #2 . . . . 1.95
48 EC,Airboy Diary #3 . . . . 1.95
49 EC,Airboy Diary #4 . . . . 1.95
50 AKu/NKu,double-size 3.95
Meets the Prowler Spec. 1.95
Mr. Monster Spec. 1.75
Vs Airmaidens Spec. 1.95

AIRMAIDENS SPECIAL
Eclipse Comics

1 A:Valkyrie 1.75

ALADDIN
Walt Disney

Prestige. Movie Adapt. 4.95

ALARMING ADVENTURES
Harvey Publications
October, 1962

1 AW,RC,JSe 40.00
2 AW,BP,RC,JSe 25.00
3 JSe,February, 1963 . . . . 25.00

ALARMING TALES
Harvey Publications
September, 1957

1 JK,JK(c) 75.00
2 JK,JK(c) 65.00
3 JK 45.00
4 JK,BP 45.00
5 JK,AW 50.00
6 JK,November, 1958 . . . . 40.00

ALIAS
Now Comics

1 . . . . 2.00
2 . . . . 1.75
3 . . . . 1.75
4 . . . . 1.75
5 . . . . 1.75

ALIAS: STORMFRONT
Now Comics

1 . . . . 1.75
2 . . . . 1.75

ALIEN ENCOUNTERS
Eclipse Comics

1 . . . . 3.50
2 . . . . 3.00
3 'I Shot the Last Martian' 3.00
4 . . . . 2.00
5 RCo,'Night of the Monkey' 2.00
6 'Now You See It,''Freefall' 2.00
7 . . . . 2.00
8 TY,'Take One Capsule Every
Million Years,M.Monroe(c) 2.75
9 The Conquered 2.00
10 . . . . 2.00
11 TT,'Old Soldiers' 2.00
12 'What A Relief,''Eyes
of the Sibyl' 2.00
13 GN,'The Light at the End' 2.00
14 JRy,GN,TL,RT,'Still born' 2.00

ALIEN TERROR
Eclipse
April, 1986

3-D #1 'Standard Procedure' 2.00

ALIEN 3
Dark Horse

1 Movie Adaptation 2.50
2 Movie Adapt.cont. 2.50
3 Movie Adapt.cont 2.50

Alien Worlds #2 © Pacific Comics

ALIEN WORLDS
Pacific

1 AW,VM,NR 4.00
2 DSt 3.50
3 . . . . 3.00
4 DSt(i) 3.00
5 thru 7 . . . . @3.00
3-D #1 AAd,DSt 5.50

Eclipse

8 AW 2.50
9 . . . . 2.50

ALIENS (II)
Dark Horse
[Mini-Series]

1 DB,Hicks,Newt hijack ship . . . 15.00
1a 2nd Printing 3.00
2 DB,Crazed general
training aliens 7.50
2a 2nd Printing 3.00
3 DB,HicksV:General Spears . . . 5.00
3a 2nd Printing 2.50
4 DB,Heroes reclaim earth
from aliens 5.00

ALIENS/PREDATOR: THE DEADLIEST OF SPECIES
Dark Horse

1 B:CCl(s),JG,F:Caryn Delacroix . 3.25
2 JG,V:Predator 2.75
3 JG,F:Caryn Delacroix 2.75
4 JG,V:Predator 2.75
5 JG,Roadtrip 2.75
6 JG,in Space Station 2.50

ALIENS VS. PREDATOR
Dark Horse

1 Duel to the Death 10.00
1a 2nd Printing 3.00
2 Dr. Revna missing 7.00
3 Predators attack Aliens 6.00
4 CW,F:Machiko & Predator 5.00
TPB Reprints series 19.95

ALIENS: COLONIAL MARINES
Dark Horse

1 I: Lt. Joseph Henry 3.00
2 I: Pvt. Carmen Vasquez 2.75
3 V:Aliens 2.75
4 F:Lt.Henry 2.75
5 V:Aliens 2.75
6 F:Herk Mondo 2.75
7 A:Beliveau 2.75
8 F:Lt.Joseph Henry 2.75
9 F:Lt.Joseph Henry 2.75

ALIENS: EARTH WAR
Dark Horse

1 SK,JBo(c),Renewal of
Alien's War 11.00
1a 2nd Printing 2.50
2 SK,JBo(c),To trap the Queen . . 9.00
3 SK,JBo(c) Stranded on
Alien's planet 7.00
4 SK,JBo(c),Resolution,final 7.00

ALIENS: GENOCIDE
Dark Horse

1 Aliens vs. Aliens 5.00
2 Alien Homeworld 4.00
3 Search for Alien Queen 4.00
4 Conclusion, inc. poster 4.00
Aliens:Genocide Collection
rep #1-#4 . . . . 13.95

Aliens: Hive #1 © Dark Horse

ALIENS: HIVE
Dark Horse

1 KJo,I:Stanislaw Mayakovsky . . 6.00
2 KJo,A:Norbert 4.00
3 KJo,A:Julie,Gill 4.00
4 KJo,A:Stan,Final 4.00

ALIENS: LABYRINTH
Dark Horse

1 F:Captured Alien 2.75
2 . . . . 2.75
3 O:Dr.Church 2.75
4 last issue 2.75

ALIENS: MUSIC OF THE SPEARS
Dark Horse

1 I:Damon Eddington 2.75
2 TBd(c),A:Damon Eddington . . . 2.75
3 TBd(c),A:Damon Eddington . . . 2.75
4 TBd(c),last issue 2.75

ALIENS: NEWT'S TALE
Dark Horse

1 How Newt Survived 5.50

2 JBo(c),Newt's point of view
on how 'Aliens' ended 4.95

ALIENS: ROGUE
Dark Horse

1 F:Mr.Kay 2.50
2 V:Aliens 2.50
3 V:Aliens 2.50
4 V:Alien King 2.50

ALIENS: SACRIFICE
Dark Horse

1 Rep.Aliens UK 4.95

ALIENS: SALVATION
Dark Horse

1 MMi,F:Selkirk 4.95

ALIENS: STRONGHOLD
Dark Horse

1 DoM 1.95

ALIENS: TRIBES
Dark Horse

1 Hard(c), Dave Dorman 24.95
TPB 11.95

ALL AMERICAN SPORTS
Charlton
October, 1967

1 . . . . 7.50

ALL HALLOWS EVE
Innovation

1 . . . . 4.95

ALLEY OOP
Dell Publishing Co.
December-February, 1962-63

1 . . . . 50.00
2 . . . . 45.00

ALPHA WAVE
Darkline

1 . . . . 1.75

ALTER EGO
First

1 . . . . 1.75
2 . . . . 1.50
3 . . . . 1.50
4 . . . . 1.25

ALVIN (& THE CHIPMUNKS)
Dell Publishing Co.
October-December, 1962

1 . . . . 50.00
2 . . . . 40.00
3 . . . . 30.00
4 thru 10 . . . . @25.00
11 thru 20 . . . . @20.00
21 thru 28 . . . . @18.00
1 Alvin for President & his pals
in Merry Christmas with
Clyde Crashcup & Leonardo . 15.00

AMAZING CHAN & THE CHAN CLAN
Gold Key
May, 1973

1 . . . . 7.50
2 . . . . 5.00
3 and 4 . . . . @5.00

AMAZON, THE
Comico

1 . . . . 1.95
2 . . . . 1.95
3 end mini-series 1.95

AMERICAN FLAGG
First

1 HC,I:American Flagg, Hard
Times Pt.1 . . . . 3.50
2 HC,Hard Times Pt.2 . . . . 2.75
3 HC,Hard Times Pt.3 . . . . 2.75
4 HC,Southern Comfort Pt.1 . . . . 2.75
5 HC,Southern Comfort Pt.2 . . . . 2.75
6 HC,Southern Comfort Pt.3 . . . . 2.75
7 HC,State o/t Union Pt.1 . . . . . . 2.50
8 HC,State o/t Union Pt.2 . . . . . . 2.50
9 HC,State o/t Union Pt.3 . . . . . . 2.50
10 HC,Solidarity-For Now Pt.1
I:Luthor Ironheart 2.50
11 HC,Solidarity-ForNowPt.2 . . . . 2.50
12 HC,Solidarity-ForNowPt.3 . . . . 2.50
13 HC 2.25
14 PB 2.25
15 HC,AmericanFlagg A Complete
story Pt.1 . . . . 2.25
16 HC,Complete Story Pt.2 . . . . . 2.00
17 HC,Complete Story Pt.3 . . . . . 2.00
18 HC,Complete Story Pt.4 . . . . . 2.00
19 HC,Bullets&BallotsPt.1 . . . . . . 2.00
20 HC,LSn,Bullets&BallotsPt.2 . . . 2.00
21 HC,LSn,Bullets&BallotsPt.3
Alan Moore sty. 2.00
22 HC,LSn,Bullets&BallotsPt.4
Alan Moore sty. 2.00
23 HC,LSn,England Swings Pt.1
Alan Moore sty. 2.00
24 HC,England Swings Pt.2,
Alan Moore sty. 2.00
25 HC,England Swings Pt.3,
Alan Moore sty. 2.00
26 HC,England Swings Pt.4,
Alan Moore sty. 2.00
27 Alan Moore sty. with Raul
the Cat 2.00
28 BWg 1.50
29 JSon 1.50
30 JSon 1.50
31 JSon,O:Bob Violence 1.50
32 JSon,A:Bob Violence 1.50
33 A:Bob Violence 1.50
34 A:Bob Violence 1.50
35 A:Bob Violence 1.50
36 A:Bob Violence 1.50
37 A:Bob Violence 1.50
38 New Direction 1.50
39 JSon,A:Bob Violence 1.50
40 A:Bob Violence 1.50
41 . . . . 1.50
42 F:Luther Ironheart 1.50
43 . . . . 1.50
44 . . . . 1.50
45 . . . . 1.50
46 PS 1.75
47 PS 1.75
48 PS 1.75
49 . . . . 1.75
50 HC,last issue 1.75
Special #1 HC,I:Time^{2} 2.50

American Flagg #1 © First Comics

AMERICAN, THE
Dark Horse

1 CMa,American joins a cult 2.50
2 CMa,V:"Feel-Good" cult 2.50
3 CMa,"ApeMask" cult 2.50
4 CMa,Final issue 2.50
ColorSpec.#1 . . . . 2.95

AMERICOMICS
AC Comics

1 GP(c),O:Shade 3.00
2 . . . . 2.00
3 Blue Beetle 2.00
4 O:Dragonfly 2.00
5 . . . . 1.75
6 . . . . 1.75
Spec.#1 Capt.Atom,BlueBeetle . . 1.50

ANOTHER CHANCE TO GET IT RIGHT
Dark Horse

1 . . . . 14.95

ANYTHING GOES
Fantagraphics

1 GK,FlamingCarot,Savage 3.50
2 S:AnM,JK,JSt,SK 3.50
3 DS,NA(c),A:Cerebus 3.00
4 . . . . 2.50
5 A:TMNTurtles 5.00
6 . . . . 2.00

APE NATION
Adventure Comics

1 Aliens land on Planet
of the Apes 4.00
2 General Ollo 3.00
3 V:Gen.Ollo,Danada 2.50
4 D:Danada 2.50

ARACHNAPHOBIA
Walt Disney

1 Movie Adapt 5.95
1a Newsstand 2.95

ARCHER & ARMSTRONG
Valiant

0 JiS(s),BWS,BL,I&O:Archer,
I:Armstrong,The Sect 6.00
0 Gold Ed.5 . . . . 50.00
1 FM(c),B:JiS(s),BWS,BL,Unity#3,
A:Eternal Warrior 5.00
2 WS(c),E:JiS(s),BWS,BL,Unity
#11,2nd A:Turok,A:X-O 6.00
3 B:BWS(a&s),BWi,V:Sect
in Rome 3.00
4 BWS,BWi,V:Sect in Rome 3.00
5 BWS,BWi,I:Andromeda 3.00
6 BWS,BWi,A:Andromeda,
V:Medoc 3.00
7 BWS,ANi,BWi,V:Sect in England 3.00
8 BWS,as Eternal Warrior #8,
Three Musketeers,I:Ivan 6.00
9 BCh,BWi,in Britain 3.00
10 BWS,A:Ivar 3.00
11 BWS,A:Solar,Ivar 3.00

 All comics prices listed are for *Near Mint* condition.

Archer & Armstrong #1 © Valiant

12 BWS,V:The Avenger 3.00
13 B:MBn(s),RgM,In Los Angeles 2.75
14 In Los Angeles 2.75
15 E:MBn(s),In Las Vegas,I:Duerst 2.75
16 V:Sect 2.75
17 B:MBn(s),In Florida 2.75
18 MV,in Heaven 2.75
19 MV,V:Mircobotic Cult,D:Duerst 2.75
20 MV,Chrismas Issue 2.75
21 MV,A:Shadowman,Master Darque 2.75
22 MV,A:Shadowman,Master Darque,w/card 2.75
23 MV, ... 2.75
24 MV, ... 2.75
25 MV,A:Eternal Warrior 2.50

ARCHIE
See Also: GOLDEN AGE SECTION

ARCHIE AND ME
Archie Publications
October, 1964

1 . . . . 120.00
2 . . . . 60.00
3 . . . . 25.00
4 . . . . 20.00
5 . . . . 20.00
6 thru 10 . . . . @15.00
11 thru 20 . . . . @5.00
21 thru 100 . . . . @3.00
101 thru 162 1987 . . . . @1.50

ARCHIE AS PURE HEART THE POWERFUL
Archie Publications
September, 1966

1 . . . . 50.00
2 . . . . 30.00
3 thru 6 . . . . @20.00

ARCHIE AT RIVERDALE HIGH
Archie Publications
August, 1972

1 . . . . 35.00
2 . . . . 15.00
3 . . . . 8.00
4 . . . . 6.00
5 . . . . 6.00
6 thru 10 . . . . @2.50
11 thru 114 . . . . @1.00

ARCHIE COMICS DIGEST
Archie Comics Digest
August, 1973

1 . . . . 35.00
2 . . . . 20.00
3 . . . . 9.00
4 . . . . 6.00
5 thru 10 . . . . @2.00
11 thru 88 . . . . @1.00

ARCHIE'S MADHOUSE
Archie Publications
September, 1959

1 . . . . 175.00
2 . . . . 85.00
3 . . . . 60.00
4 . . . . 60.00
5 . . . . 60.00
6 thru 10 . . . . @35.00
11 thru 16 . . . . @25.00
17 thru 21 . . . . @10.00
22 . . . . 40.00
23 thru 30 . . . . @10.00
31 thru 40 . . . . @3.50
41 thru 65 . . . . @1.00
66 February, 1969 . . . . 1.00

ARCHIE'S SUPERHERO SPECIAL DIGEST MAGAZINE
Archie Publications

1 JSm/SK,Rept.Double of Capt.Strong #1,FLy,Black Hood 1.20
2 GM,NA/DG,AMc,I:'70's Black Hood, Superhero rept. 2.00

ARCHIE'S TV LAUGH-OUT
Archie Publications
December, 1969

1 . . . . 30.00
2 . . . . 12.00
3 . . . . 6.00
4 . . . . 6.00
5 . . . . 6.00
6 thru 10 . . . . @2.00
11 thru 106 1986 . . . . @1.00

ARENA, THE
Alchemy

1 . . . . 1.00
2 . . . . 1.00

ARIANE & BLUEBEARD
Eclipse

Spec. CR 3.95

ARISTOKITTENS, THE
Gold Key
October, 1971

1 Disney 10.00
2 . . . . 5.00
3 . . . . 5.00
4 thru 9, Oct. 1975 . . . . @5.00

ARMAGEDDON FACTOR
AC Comics

1 Sentinels of Justice 1.95
2 . . . . 1.95

ARMOR
Continuity

1 TGr,NA,A:Silver Streak, Silver logo 7.00
1a 2nd printing,red logo 2.50
2 TGr,NA(c) 2.50
3 TGr,NA(c) 2.50
4 TGr,NA(c) 2.50

Armor #12 © Continuity Comics

5 BS,NA(c) 2.50
6 TVE,NA(c) 2.50
7 NA(c) 2.50
8 FS,NA(c) 2.50
9 FS,NA&KN(c) 2.50
10 FS,NA&KN(c) 2.50
11 SDr(i),KN(c) 2.50
12 KN(c) 2.50
13 NA(c),direct sales 2.50
14 KN(c), newsstand 2.50

[2nd Series]

1 V:Hellbender,Trading Card . . . 2.50

[3rd Series]

1 Deathwatch 2000 . . . . 4.00
2 thru 4 . . . . @2.50
5 thru 6 Rise of Magic . . . . . . @2.50

ARMORINES
Valiant

0 (from X-O #25),Card Stock (c), Diamond Distributors "Fall Fling" Retailer Meeting 15.00
0a Gold Ed. 25.00
1 JGz(s),JCf,B:White Death 2.50
2 JGz(s),JCf,E:White Death 2.50
3 JGz(s),JCf,V:Spider Aliens 2.25

ARMY ATTACK
Charlton
July, 1964

1 SG 7.00
2 SG 5.00
3 SG 4.00
4 . . . . 3.00
5 thru 47 . . . . @3.00

ARMY WAR HEROES
Charlton
December, 1963

1 . . . . 7.00
2 . . . . 3.00
3 thru 21 . . . . @3.00
22 GS,O&I:Iron Corporal 4.00
23 thru 38, June 1970 . . . . 3.00

ARROW
Malibu

1 V:Dr.Sheldon,A:Man O'War . . . 1.95

ART OF HOMAGE STUDIOS

Image
1 Various Pin-ups,All Homage Artists 4.95

ARTIC COMICS
1 . . . . 2.00

ASSASSIN, INC.
Solson
1 thru 4 . . . . @1.95

ASTRO BOY
Prev. Original Astro Boy
18 . . . . 1.75
19 . . . . 1.75
20 . . . . 1.75

ATLAS
Dark Horse
1 BZ,I:Atlas 2.75
2 BZ,V:Sh'en Chui 2.75

ATOM ANT
Gold Key
January, 1966
1 . . . . 50.00

ATOM-AGE COMBAT
Fago Magazines
November, 1958
1 . . . . 100.00
2 . . . . 60.00
3 March, 1959 . . . . 60.00

ATOMIC RABBIT
Charlton Comics
August, 1955
1 . . . . 90.00
2 . . . . 40.00
3 thru 10 . . . . @27.00
11 March, 1958 . . . . 35.00

Becomes:

ATOMIC BUNNY
12 . . . . 40.00
13 thru 18 . . . . @15.00
19 December, 1959 . . . . 15.00

AVENGERS, THE
Gold Key
November, 1968
1 . . . . 175.00

AXA
Eclipse
1 'Axa the Adopted' 1.75
2 . . . . 1.75

AXEL PRESSBUTTON
Eclipse
1 BB(c),Origin 1.75
2 . . . . 1.75
3 and 4 . . . . @1.75

AXIS ALPHA
Axis Comics
1 LSn,I:BEASTIES,Dethgrip, Shelter,W 2.75

AZ
Comico
1 . . . . 4.00
2 . . . . 2.25

AZTEC ACE
Eclipse
1 NR(i),I:AztecAce 4.00
2 NR(i) 3.50
3 NR(i) 3.00
4 NR(i) 3.00
5 NR(i) 3.00
6 NR(i) 3.00
7 NR(i) 3.00
8 NR(i) 3.00
9 NR(i) 3.00
10 NR(i) 2.00
11 . . . . 3.50
12 . . . . 2.50
13 . . . . 2.50
14 . . . . 2.50
15 F:Bridget 2.50

BABY HUEY, THE BABY GIANT
Harvey Publications
September, 1956
1 . . . . 200.00
2 . . . . 100.00
3 . . . . 60.00
4 . . . . 50.00
5 . . . . 50.00
6 thru 10 . . . . @27.00
11 thru 20 . . . . @15.00
21 thru 40 . . . . @12.00
41 thru 60 . . . . @6.00
61 thru 79 . . . . @3.00
80 . . . . 3.50
81 thru 95 . . . . @2.00
96 Giant size 4.00
97 Giant size 4.00
98 . . . . 2.00
99 October, 1980 . . . . 2.00

BABY HUEY AND PAPA
Harvey Publications
May, 1962
1 . . . . 100.00
2 . . . . 40.00
3 . . . . 20.00
4 . . . . 20.00
5 . . . . 20.00
6 . . . . 12.00
7 . . . . 12.00
8 . . . . 12.00
9 . . . . 12.00
10 . . . . 12.00
11 thru 20 . . . . @5.00
21 thru 33 . . . . @3.50
33 January, 1968 . . . . 3.50

BABY HUEY DUCKLAND
Harvey Publications
November, 1962
1 . . . . 60.00
2 . . . . 20.00
3 . . . . 20.00
4 . . . . 20.00
5 . . . . 20.00
6 thru 14 . . . . @10.00
15 November, 1966 . . . . 10.00

BACHELOR FATHER
Dell Publishing Co.
April-June, 1962
1 . . . . 45.00
2 . . . . 45.00

BACK TO THE FUTURE
Harvey
1 Chicago 1927 . . . . 1.25
2 Cretaceous Period 1.25
3 World War I 1.25

BAD COMPANY
Quality
1 thru 19 . . . . @1.50

BADGER
Capital
1 JBt,I:Badger,Ham,Daisy Yak,Yeti 7.00
2 JBt,I:Riley,A:YakYeti 5.00

Badger #3 © Capital Comics

3 JBt,O:Badger,Ham 4.00
4 JBt,A'Ham 4.00

First
5 BR,DruidTree Pt1 . . . . 3.50
6 BR,DruidTree Pt2 . . . . 3.00
7 BR,I:Wonktendonk,Lord Weterlackus 3.00
8 BR,V:Demon 3.00
9 BR,I:Connie,WOatesCbra 2.50
10 BR,A:Wonktendonk, I:Hodag Meldrum 2.50
11 BR,V:Hodag,L.W'lackus 2.50
12 BR,V:Hodag,L.W'lackus 2.50
13 BR,A:L.W'lakus,Clonezone, Judah 2.50
14 BR,I:HerbNg 2.50
15 BR,I:Wombat,JMoranlbob 2.50
16 BR,A:Yak,Yeti 2.50
17 JBt,I:Lamont 3.00
18 BR,I:SpudsGroganA:Cbra 2.50
19 BR,I:Senator1,ClZone 2.50
20 BR,Billionaire'sPicnic 2.50
21 BR,I&O:Phantom 2.50
22 BR,I:Dr.BuickRiviera 2.50
23 I:BobDobb,A:Yeti 2.50
24 BR,A:Riley 2.50
25 BR,I:Killdozer 2.50
26 BR,I:RoachWranger 2.50
27 BR,O:RoachWranger 2.50
28 BR,A:Yeti 2.50
29 A:Clonezone,C:GrimJack 2.50
30 BR,I:Dorgan 2.00
31 BR,I:HopLingSung 2.00
32 BR,D:Dorgan,HopLingSng . . . 2.00
33 RLm/AN,I:KidKang 5.00
34 RLm,I:Count Kohler 4.00
35 RLm,I:Count Kohler 4.00
36 RLm,V:Dire Wolf 4.00
37 AMe,A:Lamont 3.50
38 Animal Band 2.00
39 I:Buddy McBride 2.00
40 RLm,I:Sister Twyster 3.50
41 RLm,D:Sister Twyster 3.50
42 RLm,A:Paul Bunyan 3.50
43 RLm,V:Vampires 3.50
44 RLm,V:Vampires 3.50
45 RLm,V:Dr.Buick Riviera 3.50
46 RLm,V:Lort Weterlackus 3.50
47 RLm,Hmds.Sacr.BloodI 3.50
48 RLm,Hmds.Sacr.BloodII 3.50
49 RLm,TRoof off SuckerI 3.50
50 RLm,TRoof off SuckerII 5.00

51 RLm,V:Demon 3.00
52 TV,Tinku 4.00
53 TV,I:Shaza,Badass 4.00
54 TV,D:Shaza 4.00
55 I:Morris Myer 2.00
56 I:Dominance 2.00
57 A:KKang,V:L.W'lackus 2.00
58 A:Lamont,W'bat,V:SpudsJack . 2.00
59 Bad Art Issue 2.00
60 I:ChisumBros 2.25
61 V:ChismBros 2.00
62 I:Shanks 2.00
63 V:Shanks 2.00
64 A:Mavis Sykes 2.25
65 A:BruceLee 2.25
66 I:JoeNappleseed 2.25
67 Babysitting 2.25
68 V:GiantFoot 2.25
69 O:Mavis 2.25
70 BR:Klaus(last monthly) 2.25
Graphic Nov.BR,I:Mazis Sykes,D:Hodag 10.00
Badger Bedlam 4.95

BADGER GOES BERSERK
First

1 I:Larry,Jessie 5.00
2 MZ,V:Larry,Jessie 3.50
3 JBt/MZ,V:Larry,Jessie 3.00
4 JBt/MZ,V:Larry,Jessie 3.00

BAKER STREET

1 . . . . 3.00
2 . . . . 2.50

BALLAD OF HALO JONES
Quality

1 IG Alan Moore story 2.00
1a IG rep. 2.00
2 thru 12 . . . . @1.25

BAMM BAMM & PEBBLES FLINTSTONE
Gold Key
October, 1964

1 . . . . 30.00

BARB WIRE
Dark Horse-C.G.W.

1 Foil(c),I:Deathcard 2.25
2 DLw,I:Hurricane Max 2.00

BARBIE & KEN
Dell Publishing Co.
May-July, 1962

1 . . . . 140.00
2 . . . . 125.00
3 . . . . 125.00
4 . . . . 125.00
5 . . . . 125.00

BARNEY AND BETTY RUBBLE
Charlton Comics
January, 1973

1 . . . . 25.00
2 . . . . 10.00
3 . . . . 10.00
4 . . . . 10.00
5 . . . . 10.00
6 thru 10 . . . . @8.00
11 thru 22 . . . . @6.00
23 December, 1976 . . . . 6.00

BARRY M. GOLDWATER
Dell Publishing Co.
March, 1965

1 . . . . 20.00

BART-MAN
Bongo

1 Foil(c),I:Bart-Man 3.25
2 I:Penalizer 2.25

BASEBALL GREATS
Dark Horse

1 Jimmy Piersall story 3.25

BAT, THE
Adventure

1 R:The Bat,inspiration for Batman says Bob Kane 2.50

BATTLE FORCE
Blackthorne

1 . . . . 1.50
2 . . . . 1.50
3 . . . . 1.75

BATTLE OF THE PLANETS
Gold Key
June, 1979

1 TV Cartoon 3.50
2 . . . . 2.50
3 . . . . 2.50
4 . . . . 2.50
5 . . . . 2.50

Whitman

6 . . . . 1.50
7 thru 10 . . . . 1.50

BATTLETECH
Blackthorne

1 . . . . 1.50
2 . . . . 1.50
3 . . . . 1.50
4 . . . . 1.75
5 . . . . 1.75
6 . . . . 1.75

(Changed to Black & White)

1 3-D 2.50
2 3-D 2.50

BEAGLE BOYS, THE
Gold Key
November, 1964

1 . . . . 25.00
2 thru 5 . . . . @15.00
6 thru 10 . . . . @10.00
11 thru 20 . . . . @6.00
21 thru 46 . . . . @3.00
47 February, 1979 . . . . 3.00

BEANIE THE MEANIE
Fargo Publications
1958

1 thru 3 . . . . @15.00

B.E.A.S.T.I.E.S.
Axis Comics

1 JS(a&s),I:Beasties 1.95

THE BEATLES, LIFE STORY
Dell Publishing Co.
September-November, 1964

1 . . . . 400.00

BEAUTY AND THE BEAST
Innovation

1 From TV series 2.50
2 thru 3 From TV series 2.50
4 thru 5 Siege 2.50
6 Halloween 2.50

BEAUTY AND THE BEAST PORTRAIT OF LOVE
First

1 WP,TV tie in 12.00
2 . . . . 8.00
Book II:Night of Beauty 5.95

BEAUTY AND THE BEAST
Walt Disney

Movie adapt.(Prestige) 4.95
Movie adapt.(newsstand) 2.50

mini-series

1 Bewitched 1.50
2 Elsewhere 1.50
3 A:Catherine 2.50

BEDLAM
Eclipse

1 SBi,RV,reprint horror 1.75
2 SBi,RV,reprint horror 1.75

BEETLE BAILEY
Harvey

1 F:Mort Walker's B.Bailey 1.95
2 Beetle builds a bridge 1.25
3 thru 12 . . . . 1.25

BEETLEJUICE
Harvey

1 EC,'This is your lice' 2.00
Holiday Special #1 . . . . 1.25

BEN CASEY
Dell Publishing Co.
June-July, 1962

1 Ph(c) 25.00
2 Ph(c) 15.00
3 Ph(c) 15.00
4 Drug, Ph(c) 20.00
5 Ph(c) 15.00
6 Ph(c) 15.00
7 Ph(c) 15.00
8 Ph(c) 15.00
9 and 10 Ph(c) . . . . @15.00

Berni Wrightson #1 © Pacific Comics

BERNI WRIGHTSON MASTER OF THE MACABRE
Pacific

1 BWr 5.25

2 BWr 3.75
3 BWr 3.50
4 BWr 3.50

Eclipse

5 BWr 3.50

BEST FROM BOY'S LIFE
Gilberton Company
October, 1957

1 .... 45.00
2 .... 25.00
3 .... 20.00
4 LbC 30.00
5 .... 20.00

BEST OF DONALD DUCK & UNCLE SCROOGE
Gold Key
November, 1964

1 .... 42.00
2 September, 1967 .... 35.00

BEST OF DONALD DUCK
Gold Key
November, 1965

1 .... 40.00

BEST OF BUGS BUNNY
Gold Key
October, 1966

1 Both Giants 25.00
2 October, 1968 .... 20.00

BEST OF DENNIS THE MENACE, THE
Hallden/Fawcett Publ.
Summer, 1959

1 .... 35.00
2 thru 5 Spring, 1961 .... 20.00

BETTY AND ME
Archie Publications
August, 1965

1 .... 75.00
2 .... 40.00
3 .... 25.00
4 .... 25.00
5 .... 25.00
6 thru 10 .... @12.00
11 thru 30 .... @6.00
31 thru 50 .... @3.00
51 thru 55 .... @2.00
56 thru 163 .... @1.50
164 August, 1965 .... 1.50

BEVERLY HILLBILLYS
Dell Publishing Co.
April-June, 1963

1 Ph(c) 70.00
2 Ph(c) 30.00
3 Ph(c) 25.00
4 .... 15.00
5 .... 25.00
6 .... 25.00
7 .... 25.00
8 Ph(c) 25.00
9 Ph(c) 25.00
10 Ph(c) 25.00
11 Ph(c) 25.00
12 Ph(c) 25.00
13 Ph(c) 25.00
14 Ph(c) 25.00
15 .... 15.00
16 .... 15.00
17 Ph(c) 15.00
18 Ph(c) 15.00
19 Ph(c) 15.00
20 Ph(c) 15.00
21 Ph(c) 15.00

BEWITCHED
Dell Publishing Co.
April-June, 1965

1 .... 65.00
2 .... 30.00
3 Ph(c) 25.00
4 Ph(c) 25.00
5 Ph(c) 25.00
6 Ph(c) 25.00
7 Ph(c) 25.00
8 Ph(c) 25.00
9 Ph(c) 25.00
10 Ph(c) 25.00
11 Ph(c) 25.00
12 Ph(c) 25.00
13 Ph(c) 25.00
14 .... 15.00

BEYOND THE GRAVE
Charlton Comics
July, 1975

1 SD,TS(c),P(c) 5.00
2 thru 5 .... @2.00
6 thru 16 .... @1.50
17 October, 1984 .... 1.50

BIG
Dark Horse

1 Movie Adaption 2.00

BIG VALLEY, THE
Dell Publishing Co.
June, 1966

1 Ph(c) 30.00
2 .... 15.00
3 .... 15.00
4 .... 15.00
5 .... 15.00
6 .... 15.00

BILL BLACK'S FUN COMICS
AC Comics

1 Cpt.Paragon,B&W 2.50
2 B&W 2.25
3 B&W 2.25
4 Color 2.25

BILLY NGUYEN
Caliber

1 .... 2.50

BILLY THE KID
Charlton Publ. Co.
November, 1957

9 .... 40.00
10 .... 25.00
11 .... 22.00
12 .... 20.00
13 AW,AT 30.00
14 .... 20.00
15 AW,O:Billy the Kid 30.00
16 AW 30.00
17 .... 20.00
18 .... 20.00
19 .... 20.00
20 .... 30.00
21 .... 30.00
22 .... 30.00
23 .... 10.00
24 .... 30.00
25 JSe 30.00
26 JSe 30.00
27 .... 10.00
28 .... 10.00
29 .... 10.00
30 .... 10.00
31 thru 40 .... @7.00
41 thru 60 .... @5.00
61 thru 80 .... @2.00
81 thru 152 .... @1.00
153 March, 1983 .... 1.00

Bionic Woman #1 © Charlton Comics

BIONIC WOMAN, THE
Charlton

1 Oct, 1977, TV show adapt. .. 2.00
2 .... 1.50
3 .... 1.50
4 .... 1.50
5 .... 1.50

BIZARRE 3-D ZONE
Blackthorne

1 .... 2.50

[ORIGINAL] BLACK CAT

1 Reprints 2.00
2 MA(c) rep. 2.00
3 rep. 2.00

BLACK DIAMOND
AC Comics

1 Colt B..U. story 3.00
2 PG(c) 2.00
3 PG(c) 2.00
4 PG(c) 2.00
5 PG(c) 2.00

BLACK FURY
Charlton Comics
May, 1955

1 .... 25.00
2 .... 12.00
3 thru 15 .... @6.00
16 SD 30.00
17 SD 30.00
18 SD 30.00
19 and 20 .... @3.50
21 thru 30 .... @1.50
31 thru 56 .... @2.00
57 March-April, 1966 .... 2.00

BLACK HOOD
Archie Publications

1 ATh,GM,DW 1.00
2 ATh,DSp,A:Fox 1.00
3 ATh,GM 1.00

BLACK JACK
Charlton Comics
November, 1957

20 .... 30.00

21 . . . . . 15.00
22 . . . . . 25.00
23 AW,AT 30.00
24 SD 25.00
25 SD 25.00
26 SD 25.00
27 . . . . . 12.00
28 SD 25.00
29 . . . . . 10.00
30 November, 1959 . . . . . 10.00

BLACK PHANTOM
AC Comics

1 . . . . . 2.50
2 . . . . . 2.50

BLACK TERROR
Eclipse

1 . . . . . 3.95
2 . . . . . 3.95
3 . . . . . 4.95

BLACKBALL COMICS
Blackball Comics

1 KG,A:Trencher 3.25

BLANCHE GOES TO N.Y.
Dark Horse

1 Turn of the Century N.Y. 2.95

BLAST-OFF
Harvey Publications
October, 1965

1 JK,AW 25.00

BLAZING COMBAT
Warren Publishing Co.
October, 1965

1 FF(c) 75.00
2 FF(c) 20.00
3 FF(c) 15.00
4 FF(c),July 1966 . . . . . 15.00

BLOOD & ROSES
Sky Comics

1 I:Blood,Rose 2.75

BLOOD SWORD DYNASTY
Jademan

1 . . . . . 2.25
2 thru 6 . . . . . @1.50
7 . . . . . 1.95
8 . . . . . 1.95
9 . . . . . 1.95
10 thru 14 MB . . . . . @1.95
15 thru 18 MB . . . . . @1.25
19 Kim & Zeo Escape the Crips . . 1.25
20 Skeleton Executioners 1.25
21 Kim,Seeto 1.25
22 Infinite Wounded 1.25
23 Kim vs. Ask me not 1.25
24 . . . . . 1.25
25 . . . . . 1.25
26 V:Fiery Bird 1.25
27 A:Hero, Shou, Fiery Bird 1.25
28 Hero vs. Fiery Bird 1.25
29 . . . . . 1.25
30 . . . . . 1.25
31 V:Devil Child 1.25
32 . . . . . 1.25
33 . . . . . 1.25
34 . . . . . 1.25
35 Hero's ancestry 1.25
36 Hero & son in danger 1.25
37 A:Hell Clan,D:North Pole 1.25
38 Fiery Hawk Vs.Inf.Seeto 1.25
39 Hero vs.Infinite seeto 1.25
40 Kim Hung vs.Inf.Seeto 1.25

BLOOD SWORD
Jademan

1 . . . . . 3.25
2 . . . . . 2.50
3 thru 5 . . . . . @2.00
6 thru 9 . . . . . @1.75
10 thru 21 . . . . . @2.50
22 LW 1.95
23 LW,D:Poisonkiller 1.95
24 LW,A:Hero 1.95
25 . . . . . 1.95
26 . . . . . 1.95
27 . . . . . 1.95
28 V:DevilHeart 1.95
29 . . . . . 1.95
30 A:Purgatory 1.95
31 . . . . . 1.95
32 V:Mummy 1.95
33 V:Mummy 1.95
34 . . . . . 1.95
35 . . . . . 1.95
36 A:King Rat 1.95
37 . . . . . 1.95
38 Kim Hung in Danger 1.95
39 Masked Men to the Rescue . . 1.95
40 . . . . . 1.95
41 . . . . . 1.95
42 . . . . . 1.95
43 A:Russell School Pack 1.95
44 FirefoxV:Tyrant of Venom 1.95
45 A:Yuen Mo 1.95
46 V:Cannibal 2.50
47 . . . . . 1.95
48 A:Clairvoyant Assassin 1.95
49 Prophecy of Hero's fate 1.95
50 D:Poison Entity 1.95
51 . . . . . 1.95
52 Hero vs.Cannibal 1.95
53 Hero vs.Cannibal 1.95

BLOODFIRE
Lightning Comics

1 JZy(s),JJn 15.00
1a Platinum Ed. 50.00
1b B&W Promo Ed. Silver ink . . 35.00
1c B&W Promo Ed. Gold ink . 125.00
2 JZy(s),JJn,O:Bloodfire 12.00
3 JZy(s),JJn,I:Dreadwolf,
Judgement Day,Overthrow . . . 7.50
4 JZy(s),JJn,A:Dreadwolf, ... 5.00
5 JZy(s),JJn,I:Bloodstorm, w/card 3.50
6 SZ(s),TLw,V:Storman 3.50
7 SZ(s),TLw,A:Pres.Clinton 3.25
8 SZ(s),TLw,O:Prodigal 3.25
9 SZ(s),TLw,I:Prodigal
(in Costume) 3.25
10 SZ(s),TLw,B:Rampage,I:Thorpe 3.25

BLOODLORE
Brave New Worlds

1 Dreamweavers 1.95
2 A Blow to the Crown 1.95

BLOODSCENT
Comico

1 GC 2.00

BLOODSHOT
Valiant

0 KVH(a&s),DG(i),Chromium (c),
O:Bloodshot,A:Eternal Warrior . 3.50
0a Gold Ed.,w/Diamond "Fall Fling"
logo 25.00
1 BWS(c),B:KVH(s),DP,BWi,I:Carboni,
V:Mafia,1st Chromium(c) 7.00
2 DP,I:Durkins,V:Ax 3.50
3 DP,V:The Mob 3.00
4 DP,A:Eternal Warrior 2.50
5 DP,A:Eternal Warrior,Rai 2.50
6 DP,I:Ninjak (Not in Costume) . 10.00
7 DP,JDx,A:Ninjak (1st
appearance in costume) 7.00
8 DP,JDx,A:Geoff 2.50
9 DP,JDx,V:Slavery Ring 2.50
10 DP,JDx,V:Tunnel Rat 2.50
11 DP,JDx,V:Iwatsu 2.50
12 DP,JDx,Day Off 2.50
13 DP,JDx,V:Webnet 2.50
14 DP,JDx,V:Carboni 2.50
15 DP,JDx,V:Cinder 2.50
16 DP,JDx,w/Valiant Era Card . . . 2.50
17 DP,JDx,A:H.A.R.D.Corps 2.50
18 DP,KVH,After the Missile 2.50
19 DP,KVH,I:Uzzie the Clown . . . 2.25
Yearbook #1 KVH, ... 4.25

BLOODSTRIKE
Image

1 A:Brigade,Rub the Blood(c) . . . 3.50
2 V:Brigade,B:BU:Knight 2.50
3 B:ErS(s),ATi(c),V:Coldsnap . . . 2.25
4 ErS(s), ... 2.25
5 KG,A:Supreme, ... 2.25
6 KG(s),CAx,C&J:Chapel 2.25
7 KG,RHe,A:Badrock 2.25
8 RHe,A:Spawn 2.25
9 RHe,Extreme Prejudice #3, I:Extreme
Warrior,ATh,BU: Black & White 2.25

BLUE BEETLE
Charlton Comics
{1st S.A. Series}

1 O:Dan Garrett/BlueBeetle . . . 45.00
2 . . . . . 30.00
3 V:Mr.Thunderbolt 35.00
4 V:Praying Mantis Man 30.00
5 V:Red Knight 30.00
50 V:Scorpion(formerly Unusual
Tales) 35.00
51 V:Mentor 35.00
52 V:Magno 35.00
53 V:Praying Mantis Man 35.00
54 V:Eye of Horus 35.00

{2nd S.A. Series}

1 SD,I:Question 65.00
2 SD,O:TedKord,D:DanGarrett . 25.00
3 SD,I:Madmen,A:Question . . . 18.00
4 SD,A:Question 18.00
5 SD,VicSage(Question) app. in
Blue Beetle Story 18.00

BLUE BULLETEER
AC Comics

1 . . . . . 2.25

BLUE PHANTOM, THE
Dell Publishing Co.
June-August, 1962

1 . . . . . 20.00

BLUE RIBBON
Archie Publications

1 JK,AV,O:Fly rep. 1.50
2 TVe,Mr.Justice 1.50
3 EB/TD,O:Steel Sterling 1.50
4 . . . . . 1.00
5 S&K,Shield rep. 1.00
6 DAy/TD,Fox 1.00
7 TD,Fox 1.00
8 NA,GM,Blackhood 1.00
9 thru 11 . . . . . @1.00
12 SD,ThunderAgents 1.00
13 Thunderbunny 1.00
14 Web & Jaguar 1.00

BOLD ADVENTURE
Pacific

1 . . . . . 2.00
2 . . . . . 1.50
3 JSe 1.50

BOLT & STARFORCE
AC Comics

1 . . . . . 1.75
Bolt Special #1 . . . . . 1.50

BOMBAST
Topps

1 V:Savage Dragon,Trading Card . . . 3.25

BONANZA
Dell Publishing Co.
June-August, 1960

1 . . . 125.00
2 . . . 50.00
3 . . . 30.00
4 . . . 30.00
5 . . . 30.00
6 . . . 30.00
7 . . . 30.00
8 . . . 30.00
9 . . . 30.00
10 . . . 30.00
11 . . . 25.00
12 . . . 25.00
13 . . . 25.00
14 . . . 25.00
15 . . . 25.00
16 . . . 25.00
17 . . . 25.00
18 . . . 25.00
19 . . . 25.00
20 . . . 25.00
21 . . . 15.00
22 . . . 15.00
23 . . . 15.00
24 . . . 15.00
25 . . . 15.00
26 . . . 15.00
27 . . . 15.00
28 . . . 15.00
29 . . . 15.00
30 . . . 15.00
31 . . . 15.00
32 . . . 15.00
33 . . . 15.00
34 . . . 15.00
35 . . . 15.00
36 . . . 15.00
37 . . . 15.00

BORIS KARLOFF TALES OF MYSTERY
Gold Key
April, 1963

1 (Thriller) . . . 55.00
2 (Thriller) . . . 40.00
3 thru 8 . . . @20.00
9 WW . . . 30.00
10 . . . 20.00
11 AW,JO . . . 25.00
12 AT,AMc,JO . . . 20.00
13 . . . 15.00
14 . . . 15.00
15 RC,GE . . . 20.00
16 thru 20 . . . @15.00
21 JJ,Screaming Skull . . . 30.00
22 thru 50 . . . @10.00
51 thru 74 . . . @8.00
75 thru 96 . . . @5.00
97 February, 1980 . . . 5.00

BORIS THE BEAR
Color Classics
Dark Horse

1 thru 7 . . . @1.95

BOZO
Innovation

1 1950's reprint stories . . . 6.95

BOZO THE CLOWN
Blackthorne

1 3-D . . . 2.50
2 3-D . . . 2.50

BRADY BUNCH, THE
Dell Publishing Co.
February, 1970

1 . . . 30.00
2 . . . 30.00

BRAIN BOY
Dell Publishing Co.
April-June, 1962

1 . . . 45.00
2 . . . 30.00
3 . . . 25.00
4 . . . 25.00
5 . . . 25.00
6 . . . 25.00

BREAK-THRU
Malibu-Ultraverse

1 GJ(s),GP,AV(i),A:All Ultraverse Heroes . . . 2.75
2 GJ(s),GP,AV(i),A:All Ultraverse Heroes . . . 2.75

'BREED
Malibu-Bravura

1 JSn(a&s),Black (c),I:Stoner . . . 5.00
2 JSn(a&s),I:Rachel . . . 3.00
3 JSn(a&s),V:Rachel . . . 2.75
4 JSn(a&s),I:Stoner's Mom . . . 2.75
5 JSn(a&s),V:Rachel . . . 2.50

BRENDA LEE STORY, THE
Dell Publishing Co.
September, 1962

1 . . . 65.00

BRENDA STARR REPORTER
Dell Publishing Co.
October, 1963

1 . . . 125.00

BRIAN BOLLAND'S BLACK BOOK
Eclipse

1 BB . . . 2.50

BRIDES IN LOVE
Charlton Comics
August, 1956

1 . . . 25.00
2 . . . 10.00
3 thru 10 . . . @7.00
11 thru 30 . . . @3.50
31 thru 44 . . . @2.00
45 February, 1965 . . . 2.00

BRIGADE
Image
[1st Series]

1 RLd(s),MMy,I:Brigade . . . 5.00
1a Gold Ed. . . . 50.00
2 RLd(s),V:Genocide,w/coupon#4 4.00
2a w/o coupon . . . 2.00
3 V:Genocide . . . 2.50
4 CyP,Youngblood#5 flip . . . 2.50

[2nd Series]

0 RLd(s),ATi(c),JMs,NRd,I:Warcry, A:Emp,V:Youngblood . . . 2.25
1 V:Bloodstrike . . . 2.75
2 C:Coldsnap . . . 3.50
3 ErS(s),GP(c),MMy,NRd(i), V:Bloodstrike . . . 2.25
4 Rip(s),MMy,RHe,I:Roman, BU:Lethal . . . 2.25
5 Rip(s),MMy, . . . 2.25
6 Rip(s),MMy,I:Coral,BU:Hackers Tale . . . 2.25
7 Rip(s),MMy,V:Worlok . . . 2.25
8 ErS(s),MMy,Extreme Prejudice #2,BU:Black & White . . . 2.25
9 ErS(s),MMy,Extreme Prejudice #6,ATh,BU:Black & White . . . 2.25

Brigade #1 © Rob Liefeld

BUBBLE GUM CRISIS: GRAND MAL
Dark Horse

1 . . . 2.75
2 . . . 2.75
3 . . . 2.50

BUCK ROGERS
Gold Key
October, 1964

1 P(c) . . . 30.00
2 AMc,FBe,P(c),movie adapt . . . 3.00
3 AMc,FBe,P(c),movie adapt . . . 3.00
4 FBe,P(c) . . . 3.00
5 AMc,P(c) . . . 2.50
6 AMc,P(c) . . . 2.50

Whitman

7 thru 9 AMc,P(c) . . . @2.50
10 and 11 AMc,P(c) . . . @2.00
12 and 13 P(c) . . . 2.00
14 thru 16 . . . 2.00

BUCK ROGERS
TSR

1 thru 10 . . . @2.95

BUCKY O'HARE
Continuity

1 MGo . . . 2.75
2 . . . 2.00
3 . . . 2.00

BUFFALO BILL JR.
Dell Publishing Co.
January, 1956

1 . . . 50.00
2 . . . 30.00
3 . . . 30.00
4 . . . 30.00
5 . . . 30.00
6 . . . 30.00
7 thru 13 . . . @25.00

BUGGED-OUT ADVENTURES OF RALFY ROACH

Bugged Out Comics

1 I: Ralfy Roach 2.95

BULLWINKLE
Gold Key
November, 1962

1 Bullwinkle & Rocky 125.00
2 . . . . 85.00
3 thru 5 . . . . @30.00
6 and 7, rep. . . . . @20.00
8 thru 11 . . . . 30.00
12 rep. 15.00
13 and 14 . . . . @20.00
15 thru 19 . . . . @15.00
20 thru 24, rep. . . . . @8.00
25 . . . . 15.00

BULLWINKLE
Charlton Comics
July, 1970

1 . . . . 25.00
2 thru 7, July 1971 . . . . @15.00

BULLWINKLE & ROCKY
Eclipse

3-D 12.50

BULLWINKLE FOR PRESIDENT
Blackthorne

1 3-D Special 2.50

BURKE'S LAW
Dell Publishing Co.
January-February, 1964

1 . . . . 25.00
2 . . . . 15.00
3 . . . . 15.00

CADILLACS & DINOSAURS

1 Rep. from Xenozoic Tales
in 3-D 6.00

Topps

1 rep. Xenozoic Tales 2.95
2 rep. Xenozoic Tales 2.75
3 rep. Xenozoic Tales 2.25

CAGES
Tundra

1 DMc 14.00
2 DMc 11.00
3 DMc 7.50
4 DMc 7.50
5 thru 7 DMc 5.00

CAIN
Harris

1 B:DQ(s),I:Cain,Frenzy 5.00
2 BSz(c),HBk,V:Mortatira 3.25

CAIN'S HUNDRED
Dell Publishing Co.
May-July, 1962

1 . . . . 15.00
2 . . . . 12.00

CALIFORNIA RAISINS
Blackthorne

1 3-D 2.50
2 3-D 2.50
3 3-D 2.50
4 3-D 2.50
5 3-D,O:Calif.Raisins 2.50
6 thru 8 3-D . . . . @2.50

CALVIN & THE COLONEL
Dell Publishing Co.
April-June, 1962

1 . . . . 40.00
2 . . . . 30.00

CAP'N QUICK & FOOZLE
Eclipse

1 . . . . 2.00
2 and 3 . . . . @2.50

CAPT. ELECTRON
Brick Computers Inc.

1 . . . . 2.00
2 . . . . 2.25

CAPT. THUNDER & BLUE BOLT
Hero Graphics

1 I:Capt.Thunder & Paul Fremont 1.95
2 Paul becomes Blue Bolt 1.95
3 O:Capt.Thunder 1.95
4 V:Iguana Boys 1.95
5 V:Ian Shriver, in Scotland 1.95
6 V:Krakatoa 1.95
7 V:Krakatoa 1.95
8 A:Sparkplug (from League
of Champions) 1.95
9 A:Sparkplug 1.95
10 A:Sparkplug 1.95

CAPTAIN ATOM
See STRANGE SUSPENSE STORIES

CAPTAIN GLORY
Topps

1 A:Bombast,Night Glider,
Trading Card 3.25

CAPTAIN HARLOCK: FALL OF THE EMPIRE
Eternity

1 R:Captain Harlock 2.50
2 V:Tadashi 2.50
3 Bomb on the Arcadia 2.50
4 Final issue 2.50

CAPTAIN NICE
Gold Key
November, 1967

1 Ph(c) 35.00

CAPTAIN PARAGON
Americomics

1 thru 4 . . . . @2.00

CAPTAIN POWER
Continuity

1a NA,TVtie-in(direct sale) 2.00
1b NA,TVtie-in(newsstand) 2.00
2 NA 2.00

CAPTAIN STERN
Kitchen Sink Press

1 BWr,R:Captain Stern 5.25
2 BWr,Running Out of Time 4.95

CAPTAIN VENTURE & THE LAND BENEATH THE SEA
Gold Key
October, 1968

1 . . . . 35.00
2 . . . . 30.00

CAPTAIN VICTORY
Pacific

1 JK 2.00
2 JK 1.50

Captain Victory #1 © Pacific Comic

3 NA,JK,I:Ms.Mystic 1.75
4 JK 1.00
5 JK 1.00
6 JK,SD 1.00
7 thru 13 JK . . . . @1.00
Special #1 JK 1.50

CAR 54, WHERE ARE YOU?
Dell Publishing Co.
March-May, 1962

1 Ph(c) 40.00
2 thru 7 Ph(c) . . . . @25.00

CARCA JOU RENAISSANCE

1 and 2 . . . . @1.50

CAROLINE KENNEDY
Charlton Comics
1961

1 . . . . 50.00

CASPER ENCHANTED TALES
Harvey

1 short stories 1.25

CASPER
Harvey

1 collection of stories 1.00
2 thru 7 . . . . @1.00
8 . . . . 1.25

CASPER THE FRIENDLY GHOST
Blackthorne

1 3-D 2.50

CASPER & FRIENDS
Harvey

1 thru 4 . . . . @1.00
5 short stories, cont 1.25

CASPER GHOSTLAND
Harvey

1 short stories 1.25

CASPER'S GHOSTLAND
Harvey Publications
Winter, 1958-59

1 . . . . 100.00
2 . . . . 50.00
3 thru 10 . . . . @30.00
11 thru 20 . . . . @15.00
21 thru 40 . . . . @8.00
41 thru 61 . . . . @6.00
62 thru 77 . . . . @3.50
78 thru 97 . . . . @2.50
98 December, 1979 . . . . . 2.50

CAT TALES
Eternity

1 3-D 1.95

CATALYST: AGENTS OF CHANGE
Dark Horse-C.G.W.

1 JPn(c),V:US Army 2.25
2 JPn(c),I:Grenade 2.25
3 JPn(c),Rebel vs. Titan . . . 2.25
4 JPn(c),Titan vs. Grace . . . 2.00

CAVE GIRL
AC Comics

1 . . . . 2.95

CAVE KIDS
Gold Key
February, 1963

1 . . . . 20.00
2 . . . . 15.00
3 . . . . 15.00
4 . . . . 15.00
5 . . . . 15.00
6 . . . . 8.00
7 A:Pebbles & Bamm Bamm . . 10.00
8 thru 10 . . . . 8.00
11 thru 16 . . . . 8.00

CHAMPIONS
Eclipse

1 I:Flare,League of Champions Foxbat, Dr.Arcane 1.25
2 I:Dark Malice 1.50
3 I:Lady Arcane 1.25
4 O:Dark Malice 2.00
5 O:Flare 1.25
6 D:Giant Demonmaster 1.25

[New Series]
Hero

1 EL,I:Madame Synn,Galloping Galooper 5.00
2 I:Fat Man, Black Enchantress . 2.25
3 I:Sparkplug&Icicle,O:Flare . . . 2.25
4 I:Exo-Skeleton Man 2.25
5 A:Foxbat 2.25
6 I:Mechanon, C:Foxbat 1.95
7 A:Mechanon,J:Sparkplug,Icicle . 1.95
8 O:Foxbat 1.95
9 Flare #0 (Flare preview) . . . 1.95
10 Olympus Saga #1 . . . . . 1.95
11 Olympus Saga #2 . . . . . 1.95
12 Olympus Saga #3 . . . . . 1.95
Ann.#1 O:Giant & DarkMalice . . . 2.75
Ann.#2 . . . . 3.95

CHAMPIONS CLASSIC
Hero Graphics

1 GP(c),Rep.1st champions series 1.00

CHARLEMAGNE
Defiant

0 JiS(s),From Hero 2.00
1 JiS(s),I:Charles Smith 2.75
2 JiS(s),A:War Dancer 2.75
3 DGC(s),V:Dark Powers 2.50

CHARLIE CHAN
Dell Publishing Co.
October-December, 1965

1 . . . . 15.00
2 . . . . 10.00

CHARLTON BULLSEYE

Special #1 . . . . 2.00

CHEAP SHODDY ROBOT TOYS
Eclipse

1 A:Ronald Reagan 1.75

CHECKMATE
Gold Key
October, 1962

1 Ph(c) 25.00
2 Ph(c) 20.00

CHEMICAL MAN

1 . . . . 1.75

CHEYENNE
Dell Publishing Co.
October, 1956

1 Ph(c) all 85.00
2 . . . . 45.00
3 . . . . 45.00
4 . . . . 30.00
5 . . . . 30.00
6 . . . . 30.00
7 . . . . 30.00
8 . . . . 30.00
9 . . . . 30.00
10 . . . . 30.00
11 . . . . 30.00
12 . . . . 30.00
13 . . . . 25.00
14 . . . . 25.00
15 . . . . 25.00
16 . . . . 25.00
17 . . . . 25.00
18 . . . . 25.00
19 . . . . 25.00
20 . . . . 25.00
21 . . . . 25.00
22 . . . . 25.00
23 . . . . 25.00
24 . . . . 25.00
25 . . . . 25.00

CHEYENNE KID
(see WILD FRONTIER)

CHILD'S PLAY 2
Innovation

1 Movie Adapt Pt 1 . . . . . 2.50
2 Adapt Pt 2 . . . . 2.50
3 Adapt Pt 3 . . . . 2.50

CHILD'S PLAY 3
Innovation

1 Movie Adapt Pt 1 . . . . . 2.50
2 Movie Adapt Pt.2 . . . . . 2.50

CHILD'S PLAY: THE SERIES
Innovation

1 Chucky's Back 2.50
2 Straight Jacket Blues 2.50
3 M.A.R.K.E.D. 2.50
4 Chucky in Toys 4 You 2.50
5 Chucky in Hollywood 2.50

CHILDREN OF FIRE
Fantagor

1 RCo 2.00
2 RCo 2.00
3 RCo 2.00

CHIP 'N' DALE
Walt Disney

1 . . . . 3.50
2 . . . . 3.00
3 . . . . 2.50
4 . . . . 2.50
5 . . . . 2.50
6 . . . . 2.50
7 . . . . 2.50
8 Coast to Coast Pt 1 . . . . 2.00
9 Coast to Coast Pt 2 . . . . 2.00
10 Coast to Coast Pt 3 . . . . 2.00
11 Coast to Coast Pt 4 . . . . 2.00
12 'Showdown at Hoedown' . . . 1.75
13 Raining Cats & Dogs 1.75
14 'Cobra Kadabra' 1.75
15 I:Techno-Rats,WaspPatrol Fearless Frogs Pt.1 . . . . 1.75
16 A:Techno-Rats,WaspPatrol, Fearless Frogs Pt.2 . . . . 1.75
17 'For the Love of Cheese' . . . 1.75
18 'Ghastly Goat of Quiver Moore, Pt.1 . . . . 1.50

CHOO CHOO CHARLIE
Gold Key
December, 1969

1 . . . . 32.00

CHOPPER: EARTH, WIND, AND FIRE
Fleetway

1 F:Chopper 2.95

CHRISTMAS PARADE
Gladstone

1 GiantEdition 4.00
2 . . . . 3.50

CHROMA-TICK SPECIAL EDITION
New England Press

1 Rep.Tick#1,new stories . . . 3.95
2 Rep.Tick#2,new stories . . . 3.95
3 thru 8 Reps.& new stories . . @3.50

CHROME
Hot Comics

1 Machine Man 3.50
2 . . . . 2.00
3 . . . . 2.00
4 . . . . 2.00

CHROMIUM MAN
Triumphant Comics

0 Blue Logo 10.00
0 . . . . 2.50
1 I:Chromium Man,Mr.Death . . . 2.50
2 I:Prince Vandal 2.50
3 I:Candi,Breaker,Coil 2.50
4 JnR(s),AdP,Unleashed 2.50
5 JnR(s),AdP,Unleashed 2.50
6 JnR(s),B:Courier 2.50
7 JnR(s),Courier#2 . . . . . 2.50
8 JnR(s),Paradise 2.50

CHROMIUM MAN: VIOLENT PAST
Triumphant Comics

1 JnR(s), ... 2.50
2 JnR(s), ... 2.50

CHRONICLES OF CORUM
First

6 . . . . 2.25
7 thru 12 . . . . @2.00

CICERO'S CAT
Dell Publishing Co.

July-August, 1959

1 . . . . 15.00
2 . . . . 15.00

CIMMARON STRIP
Dell Publishing Co.
January, 1968

1 . . . . 18.00

Classic Star Wars #1
© Dark Horse Comics

CLASSIC STAR WARS
Dark Horse

1 AW,newspaper strip reps. 3.00
2 thru 10 AW,newspaper strip reps . . . . @2.75
11 thru 19 AW,newspaper strip rep . . . . @2.75
20 AW,newspaper strip reps., w/card 3.50
Volume #1 . . . . 15.99

CLASSICS ILLUSTRATED
See Also:
CLASSICS ILLUSTRATED SECTION

CLASSICS ILLUSTRATED
First

1 GW,The Raven 3.75
2 RG,Great Expectations 3.75
3 KB,Thru the Looking Glass . . . 3.75
4 BSz,Moby Dick 3.75
5 SG,TM,KE, Hamlet 3.75
6 PCr,JT, Scarlet Letter 3.75
7 DSp,Count of Monte Cristo . . . 3.75
8 Dr.Jekyll & Mr.Hyde 3.75
9 MP,Tom Sawyer 3.75
10 Call of the Wild 3.75
11 Rip Van Winkle 3.75
12 Dr. Moreau 3.75
13 Wuthering Heights 3.75
14 Fall of House of Usher 3.75
15 Gift of the Magi 3.75
16 A: Christmas Carol 3.75
17 Treasure Island 3.75
18 The Devils Dictionary 3.95
19 The Secret Agent 3.95
20 The Invisible Man 3.95
21 Cyrano de Bergerac 3.95
22 The Jungle Book 3.95
23 Swiss Family Robinson 3.95
24 Rime of Ancient Mariner 3.95
25 Ivanhoe 3.95
26 Aesop's Fables 3.95
27 The Jungle 3.95

CLIVE BARKER'S DREAD
Eclipse

Graphic Album 7.95

CLIVE BARKER'S TAPPING THE VEIN
Eclipse

1 . . . . 13.00
2 . . . . 8.50
3 . . . . 8.50
4 . . . . 8.50
5 inc."How Spoilers Breed" 8.50

CLYDE CRASHCUP
Dell Publishing Co.
August-October, 1963

1 . . . . 50.00
2 . . . . 35.00
3 thru 5 . . . . @35.00

COBALT 60
Innovation

1 reprints 4.95

COBALT BLUE
Innovation

Special #1 . . . . 1.95
Special #2 . . . . 1.95
1 and 2 . . . . @1.95

CODENAME: STRIKEFORCE
Spectrum

1 . . . . 1.00

CODENAME: STYKE FORCE
Image

1 MS(s),BPe,JRu(i), ... 2.25
2 MS(s),BPe,JRu(i), ... 2.25

Codename: Danger #4 © Lodestone

CODENAME: DANGER
Lodestone

1 RB/BMc,I:Makor 2.50
2 KB,I:Capt.Energy 2.00
3 PS/RB 1.50
4 PG 1.50

COLLECTOR'S DRACULA
Millennium

1 . . . . 4.25

COLORS IN BLACK
Dark Horse

1 B:Passion Play 2.95
2 Images 2.95
3 . . . . 2.95
4 Final issue 2.95

COLOSSAL SHOW, THE
Gold Key
October, 1969

1 . . . . 25.00

COLOUR OF MAGIC
Innovation

1 'Discworld' Adapt. 3.00
2 'The Sending of Eight' 2.50
3 'Lure of the Worm 2.50
4 final issue 2.50

COLT .45
Dell Publishing Co.
August, 1958

1 Ph(c) all 60.00
2 . . . . 40.00
3 . . . . 40.00
4 . . . . 40.00
5 . . . . 40.00
6 ATh 50.00
7 . . . . 40.00
8 . . . . 40.00
9 . . . . 40.00

COLT SPECIAL
AC Comics

1 . . . . 1.75
2 . . . . 1.75
3 . . . . 1.75

COMBAT
Dell Publishing Co.
October-November, 1961

1 SG 25.00
2 SG 15.00
3 SG 15.00
4 JFK cover, Story 2-D 20.00
5 SG 15.00
6 SG 10.00
7 SG 10.00
8 SG 10.00
9 SG 10.00
10 SG 10.00
11 SG 7.00
12 SG 7.00
13 SG 7.00
14 SG 7.00
15 SG 7.00
16 SG 7.00
17 SG 7.00
18 SG 7.00
19 SG 7.00
20 SG 7.00
21 SG 7.00
22 SG 7.00
23 SG 7.00
24 SG 7.00
25 SG 7.00
26 SG 7.00
27 SG 7.00
28 SG 5.00
29 SG 5.00
30 SG 5.00
31 SG 5.00

32 SG 5.00
33 SG 5.00
34 SG 5.00
35 SG 5.00
36 SG 5.00
37 thru 40 SG @5.00

COMET
Archie Publications
1 Cl,O:Comet 1.00
2 Cl,D:Hangman 1.00

COMIC ALBUM
Dell Publishing Co.
March-May, 1958
1 Donald Duck 35.00
2 Bugs Bunny 20.00
3 Donald Duck 30.00
4 Tom & Jerry 20.00
5 Woody Woodpecker 20.00
6 Bugs Bunny 20.00
7 Popeye 25.00
8 Tom & Jerry 20.00
9 Woody Woodpecker 20.00
10 Bugs Bunny 20.00
11 Popeye 25.00
12 Tom & Jerry 15.00
13 Woody Woodpecker 15.00
14 Bugs Bunny 15.00
15 Popeye 25.00
16 Flintstones 38.00
17 Space Mouse 22.00
18 3 Stooges,Ph(c) 50.00

COMICO X-MAS SPECIAL
Comico
1 SR/AW/DSt(c) 1.50

COMICS GREATEST WORLD (C.G.W.)
Dark Horse
(Arcadia)
1 B:MRi(s),FM(c),B:LW,B:O:Vortex, F:X,I:Seekers 3.00
1a White Ed. 50.00
1b Hologram(c) 25.00
2 JoP,I:Pit Bulls 1.50
3 AH,I:Ghost 1.50
4 I:Monster 1.50
TPB Arcadia 25.00
(Golden City)
1 B:BKs(s),JOy(c),I:Rebel, Amaz.Grace,V:WarMaker 1.25
1a Gold Ed. 25.00
2 I:Mecha 1.25
3 WS(c),I:Titan 1.25
4 E:BKs(s),GP(c),JD,I:Catalyst 1.25
TBP Golden City 25.00
(Steel Harbor)
1 B:CW(s),PG,I:Barb Wire, V:Ignition 1.25
2 MMi(c),TNa,I:Machine 1.25
3 CW(a&s),I:Wolf Gang 1.25
4 E:CW(s),VGi,I:Motorhead 1.25
TPB Steel Harbor 25.00
(Vortex)
1 B:RSd(s),LW,DoM,I:Division 13 1.25
2 I:Hero Zero 1.25
3 PC,I:King Tiger 1.25
4 B:RSd(s),E:MRi(s)BMc,E:LW, E:O:Vortex,C:Vortex 1.25
TPB Vortex 25.00
Sourcebook 10.00

COMIX INTERNATIONAL
Warren Magazines
July, 1974
1 35.00
2 WW,BW 20.00
3 8.00

4 RC 10.00
5 Spring, 1977 5.00

COMMANDER BATTLE AND HIS ATOMIC SUB
#20 3-D 2.50

COMMANDOSAURS
1 3.50

CONCRETE
Dark Horse
1 PC,ColorSpec. 3.50
EarthDay Spec. PC,Moebius 3.50

CONCRETE: FRAGILE CREATURE
Dark Horse
1 PC,'Rulers o/t Omniverse'Pt.1 3.50
2 PC,'Rulers o/t Omniverse'Pt.2 2.50
3 PC,'Rulers o/t Omniverse'Pt.3 2.50
4 PC,'Rulers o/t Omniverse'Pt.3 2.50

CORBEN SPECIAL
Pacific
1 RCo 1.75

CORMAC
Dark Horse
1 thru 3 @2.25

CORUM: THE BULL & THE SPEAR
First
1 thru 4 @1.95

COSMONEERS SPECIAL
1 1.95

COURTSHIP OF EDDIE'S FATHER
Dell Publishing Co.
January, 1970
1 Ph(c) 20.00
2 Ph(c) 18.00

COVER GIRL
1 1.95

COWBOY IN AFRICA
Gold Key
March, 1968
1 Chuck Conners,Ph(c) 20.00

CRACKED
Major Magazines
February-March, 1958
1 AW 100.00
2 40.00
3 thru 6 @30.00
7 thru 10 @18.00
11 thru 20 @10.00
21 thru 30 @7.00
31 thru 60 @3.00
61 thru 252 @2.50

CRAZYMAN
Continuity
[1st Series]
1 Embossed(c),NA/RT(i), O:Crazyman 6.00
2 NA/BB(c) 2.50
3 DBa,V:Terrorists 2.50
[2nd Series]
1 Die Cut(c) 2.50
2 thru 3 2.50
4 In Demon World 2.50

Crazyman #3 © Continuity Comics

CRIME MACHINE
Skywald Publications
February, 1971
1 8.00
2 6.00

CRIME SUSPENSE STORIES
Russ Cochran
1 Rep. C.S.S. #1 (1950) 1.75
2 Rep. C.S.S. 1.75
3 Rep. C.S.S. 1.75
4 thru 6 Rep. C.S.S 2.00
7 Rep. C.S.S 2.00

CRITICAL ERROR
Dark Horse
1 rep.Classic JBy story 2.75

CROSSFIRE
Eclipse
1 DSp 3.00
2 DSp 2.50
3 DSp 1.50
4 DSp 1.50
5 DSp 1.50
6 DSp 1.50
7 DSp 2.50
8 DSp 2.50
9 DSp 1.75
10 DSp 1.75
11 DSp 1.75
12 DSp,DSt(c),M.Monroe cover & story 2.50
13 DSp 1.75
14 DSp 1.75
15 DSp,O:Crossfire 1.75
16 DSp,'The Comedy Place' 1.75
17 DSp,'Comedy Place' Pt.2 1.75

CROSSFIRE & RAINBOW
Eclipse
1 DSp,V:Marx Brothers 1.75
2 DSp,PG(c),V:Marx Brothers 1.50
3 DSp,HC(c),A:Witness 1.50
4 DSp,DSt(c),'This Isn't Elvis' 3.50

CROSSROADS
First
1 Sable,Whisper 4.00

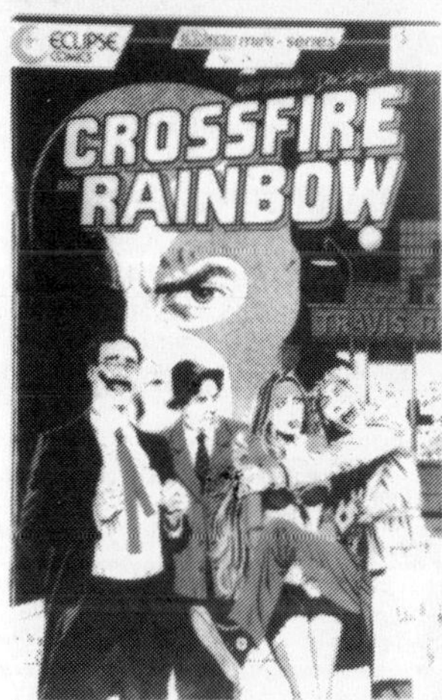

Crossfire & Rainbow #2
© Eclipse Comics

2 Sable,Badger ... 4.00
3 JSon,JAl,Badger/Luther Ironheart ... 4.00
4 Grimjack/Judah Macabee ... 4.00
5 LM,Grimjack/Dreadstar/Nexus ... 4.00

CRYING FREEMAN III
Viz

1 A:Dark Eyes,Oshu ... 6.00
2 A:Dark Eyes, V:Oshu ... 5.25
3 Freeman vs. Oshu ... 5.25
4 Freeman Defeated ... 5.25
5 Freeman clones, A:Nitta ... 5.25
6 V:Nitta ... 5.25
7 ... 4.95
8 ... 4.95
9 ... 4.95

CRYING FREEMAN IV
Viz

1 B:The Pomegranate ... 4.95
2 ... 2.75
3 ... 2.75
4 ... 2.75
5 thru 7 ... @2.75
8 E:The Pomegranate ... 2.75

[2nd Series]

1 The Festival ... 2.50

CYBERCRUSH: ROBOTS IN REVOLT
Fleetway

1 inc.Robo-Hunter,Ro-Busters ... 1.95

CYBERFORCE
Image

[Limited Series]

0 WS,O:Cyber Force ... 2.50
1 MS,I:Cyberforce,w/coupon #3 ... 8.00
1a w/o coupon ... 4.00
2 MS,V:C.O.P.S. ... 4.00
3 MS ... 2.50
4 MS,V:C.O.P.S,BU:Codename Styke Force. ... 2.50

[Regular Series]

1 EcS(s),MS,SW, ... 2.25
2 EcS(s),MS,SW,Killer Instinct #2, A:Warblade ... 2.25
3 EcS(s),MS,SW,Killer Instinct #4, A:WildC.A.T.S. ... 2.25

CYBERPUNK
Innovation

1 ... 1.95
2 ... 1.95
Bk 2,#1 ... 2.25
Bk 2,#2 ... 2.25

Cyberrad #6 © Continuity Comics

CYBERRAD
Continuity

1 NA layouts,I:Cyberran ... 3.00
2 NA l/o ... 2.50
3 NA l/o ... 2.50
4 NA l/o ... 2.50
5 NA l/o Glow in the Dark cov ... 5.00
6 NA l/o,Pullout poster ... 2.50
7 NA l/o,See-thru(c) ... 2.50

[2nd Series]

1 Hologram cover ... 2.00
2 NA(c),'The Disassembled Man' ... 2.00

[3rd Series]

1 Holo.(c),just say no ... 3.50

[4th Series]

1 Deathwatch 2000 Pt.8,w/ Trading card ... 2.50

DAGAR THE INVINCIBLE
Gold Key
October, 1972

1 O:Daggar;I:Villians Olstellon & Scorpio ... 15.00
2 ... 6.00
3 I:Graylon ... 5.00
4 ... 5.00
5 ... 5.00
6 1st Dark Gods story ... 4.00
7 ... 4.00
8 ... 4.00
9 ... 4.00
10 ... 4.00
11 thru 19 April, 1982 ... @2.00

DAI KAMIKAZE
Now

1 Speed Racer ... 7.00
1a 2nd printing ... 1.50
2 ... 2.00
3 ... 1.50
4 ... 1.50
5 ... 1.50
6 thru 12 ... @1.75

DAKTARI
Dell Publishing Co.
July, 1967

1 ... 20.00
2 ... 15.00
3 ... 15.00
4 ... 15.00

DALGODA
Fantagraphics

1 ... 3.50
2 KN,I:Grinwood'Daughter ... 3.00
3 KN ... 2.50
4 thru 8 ... @2.25

DANGER
Charlton Comics
June, 1955

12 ... 35.00
13 ... 25.00
14 ... 25.00

Becomes:

JIM BOWIE

15 ... 20.00
16 ... 10.00
17 ... 10.00
18 ... 10.00
19 April, 1957 ... 10.00

DANGER UNLIMITED
Dark Horse-Legend

1 JBy(a&s),KD,I:Danger Unlimited, B:BU:Torch of Liberty ... 2.50
2 JBy(a&s),KD,O:Danger Unlimited ... 2.25
3 JBy(a&s),KD,O:Torch of Liberty ... 2.25
4 JBy(a&s),KD,Final Issue ... 2.00

DANIEL BOONE
Gold Key
January, 1965

1 ... 50.00
2 thru 5 ... @30.00
6 thru 14 ... @20.00
15 April, 1969 ... 10.00

DANNY BLAZE
Charlton Comics
August, 1955

1 ... 35.00
2 ... 30.00

Becomes:

NATURE BOY

3 JB,O:Blue Beetle ... 125.00
4 ... 100.00
5 February, 1957 ... 85.00

DARE
Fantagraphics

1 F:Dan Dare ... 2.75
2 F:Dan Dare ... 2.75
3 F:Dan Dare ... 2.50
4 F:Dan Dare ... 2.50

DARE THE IMPOSSIBLE
Fleetway

1 DGb,rep.Dan Dare from 2000AD 1.95
2 DGb, Dare on Waterworld ... 1.95
3 DGb ... 1.95
4 DGb ... 1.95
5 DGb,"The Garden of Eden" ... 1.95
6 DGb ... 1.95
7 DGb,V:Deadly Primitives ... 1.95
8 DGb,The Doomsday Machine ... 1.95
9 thru 14 DGb ... @1.95

DARK, THE
Continüm

1 LSn(c),MBr,V:Futura ... 7.50

The Dark #3 © Continüm Comics

2 LSn,Shot by Futura 6.00
3 MBr,Dark has amnesia 4.00
4 GT(c),MBr,O:The Dark 4.00

[2nd Series]

1 BS(c),Red Foil(c), ... 20.00
1a BS(c),newstand ed. 5.00
1b BS(c),Blue foil 15.00
2 . . . . 4.00
3 BS(c),Foil(c), ... 15.00
4 GP(c),Foil(c),w/cards 12.00
Convention Book 1992 MBr,GP, MFm,MMi,VS,LSn,TV 10.00
Convention Book 1993 MBr,PC, ECh,BS,BWi,GP(c),Foil(c), . . 10.00

DARK ADVENTURES

1 . . . . 1.75
2 . . . . 1.75
3 . . . . 1.75

DARK DOMINION
Defiant

1 SD,I:Michael Alexander 2.75
2 LWn(s),SLi(i), ... 2.75
3 LWn(s),SLi(i), ... 2.75
4 LWn(s),B:Hoxhunt 2.75
5 LWn(s),I:Puritan,Judah 2.75
6 LWn(s),I:Lurk 2.75
7 LWn(s),V:Glimmer 2.75
8 LWn(s),V:Glimmer 2.50

DARK HORSE COMICS
Dark Horse

1 RL,CW,F:Predator,Robocop, I:Renegade,Time Cop,(double gatefold cover) 3.50
2 RL,CW,F:Predator,Robocop, Renegade,Time Cop 3.00
3 CW,F:Robocop,Time Cop,Aliens, Indiana Jones 3.00
4 F:Predator,Aliens,Ind.Jones . . . 2.75
5 F:Predator,E:Aliens 2.75
6 F:Robocop,Predator, E:Indiana Jones 2.75
7 F:Robocop,Predator,B:StarWars 6.00
8 B&I:X,Robocop 9.00
9 F:Robocop,E:Star Wars 6.00
10 E:X,B:Godzilla,Predator, James Bond 4.50
11 F:Godzilla,Predator,James Bond,B:Aliens 2.75
12 F:Predator 2.75
13 F:Predator,B:Thing 2.75
14 MiB(s),B:The Mark, ... 2.75
15 MiB(s),E:The Mark,B:Aliens . . 2.75
16 B:Predator,E:Thing,Aliens 2.75
17 B:Aliens,Star Wars:Droids 2.75
18 E:Predator, ... 2.75
19 RL(c),B:X,E:Star Wars:Droids, Aliens 2.75
20 B:Predator 2.75
21 F:Mecha 2.50

DARK SHADOWS
Gold Key
March, 1969

1 W/Poster,Ph(c) 185.00
2 Ph(c) 70.00
3 W/Poster,Ph(c) 85.00
4 thru 7,Ph(c) . . . . @60.00
8 thru 10 . . . . @50.00
11 thru 20 . . . . @35.00
21 thru 35 . . . . @30.00

Dark Shadows #2 © Innovation

DARK SHADOWS
Innovation

1 Based on 1990's TV series . . . 3.50
2 O:Victoria Winters 2.50
3 Barnabus Imprisoned 2.50
4 V: Redmond Swann 2.75

[2nd Series]

1 A:Nathan 2.75
2 thru 4 . . . . 2.75
Dark Shadows:Resurrected 15.95

DARKER IMAGE
Image

1 BML,BCi(s),RLd,SK,JLe,I:Blood Wulf,Deathblow,Maxx 3.00
1a Gold logo(c) 50.00
1b White(c) 30.00

DARKLON THE MYSTIC
Pacific

1 JSn 1.50

DARKWING DUCK
Walt Disney

1 I:Darkwing Duck 1.75
2 V:Taurus Bulba 1.75
3 'Fowl Play' 1.75
4 'End o/t beginning,'final issue . . 1.75

DARKWOOD
Aircel

1 thru 5 . . . . @2.00

DAUGHTERS OF TIME
3-D

1 I:Kris,Cori,Lhana 3.95

FRONTIER FIGHTER
Charlton Comics
August, 1955

1 . . . . 40.00
2 . . . . 20.00

Becomes:

DAVY CROCKETT

3 thru 7 . . . . @15.00
8 January, 1957 . . . . 10.00

Becomes:

KID MONTANA

9 . . . . 20.00
10 . . . . 9.00
11 . . . . 6.00
12 . . . . 6.00
13 . . . . 14.00
14 thru 20 . . . . @6.00
21 thru 35 . . . . @3.50
36 thru 49 . . . . @2.00
50 March, 1965 . . . . 2.00

DAZEY'S DIARY
Dell Publishing Co.
June-August, 1962

1 . . . . 25.00

DEAD CLOWN
Malibu

1 I:Force America 2.50
2 I:Sadistic Six 2.50
3 TMs(s),last issue 2.50

DEAD IN THE WEST
Dark Horse

1 TT(c), ... 3.95

DEAMON DREAMS
Pacific

1 . . . . 1.50
2 . . . . 1.50

DEAR NANCY PARKER
Gold Key
June, 1963

1 P(c) 18.00
2 P(c),September, 1963 . . . . . 15.00

DEATH RATTLE
Kitchen Sink

1 thru 5 . . . . @2.00

DEATHBLOW
Image

1 JLe,MN,I:Cybernary 2.75
2 JLe,BU:Cybernary 2.25

DEATHMATE
Valiant/Image

Preview (Advanced Comics) . . . 10.00
Preview (Previews) 10.00
Preview (Comic Defense Fund) . 15.00
Prologue BL,JLe,RLd,Solar meets Void 3.25
Prologue Gold 50.00
Blue SCh,HSn,F:Solar,Magnus, Battlestone,Livewire,Stronghold, Impact,Striker,Harbinger, Brigade,Supreme 5.25
Blue Gold Ed. 50.00

Yellow BCh,MLe,DP,F:Armstrong, H.A.R.D.C.A.T.S.,Ninjak,Zealot, Shadowman,Grifter,Ivar 5.25
Yellow Gold Ed. 50.00
Black JLe,MS,F:Warblade,Ripclaw, Turok,X-O Manowar 5.25
Black Gold Ed. 50.00
Red RLd,JMs, ... 5.25
Red Gold Ed 50.00
Epilogue 3.25
Epilogue Gold 50.00

DEFENDERS, THE
Dell Publishing Co.
September-November, 1962

1 .... 20.00
2 .... 18.00

DEMONIC TOYS
Eternity

1 Based on 1992 movie 2.50
2 thru 4 .... 2.50

DEN
Fantagor

1 thru 9 RCo .... @2.00
10 RCo,Last issue 2.00

DEN SAGA
Tundra/fantagor

1 RCo,O:Den begins 4.95

DEPUTY DAWG
Dell Publishing Co.
August, 1965

1 .... 45.00

DESTROYER DUCK
Eclipse

1 JK,AA,SA,I:Groo 12.00
2 JK,AA,Starling 1.50
3 thru 5 JK .... @1.50
6 thru 7 JK .... @2.00

Destroyer Duck #3 © Eclipse Comics

DESTROYER DUCK
Eclipse

1 JK,AA,SA,I:Groo 27.00
2 JK,AA,Starling 1.50
3 thru 5 JK .... @1.50
6 JK 2.00
7 JK 2.00

DETECTIVES, INC.
Eclipse

1 MR,rep.GraphicNovel 3.00
2 MR 2.25

[2nd Series]

1 GC,'A Terror of Dying Dreams' 2.50
2 GC 2.25
3 GC,'Cut to the Bone' 1.50

DEVIL KIDS STARRING HOT STUFF
Harvey Publications
July, 1962

1 .... 80.00
2 .... 40.00
3 thru 10 .... @20.00
11 thru 20 .... @15.00
21 thru 30 .... @10.00
31 thru 40 .... @7.00
41 thru 50 68 pgs. .... @7.00
51 thru 55 62 pgs. .... @5.00
56 thru 70 .... @3.00
71 thru 100 .... @2.00
101 thru 106 .... @1.00
107 October, 1981 .... 1.00

DICK TRACY

1 3-D 2.50

DICK TRACY: BIG CITY BLUES

1 Mini Series 3.95
2 Mini Series 5.95
3 Mini Series 5.95

DINO ISLAND
Mirage

1 thru 2 .... 2.75

DINOSAUR REX
Fantagraphics

1 thru 3 .... @2.00

DINOSAURS
Walt Disney

1 Citizen Robbie(From TV) 2.95

DINOSAURS ATTACK
Eclipse

1 HT,Based on Topps cards 3.50

DINOSAURS ATTACK
Eclipse

1 HT,Based on Topps cards 3.50

DINOSAURS FOR HIRE
Malibu

1 3-D rept. B&W 3.50

[2nd Series]

1 B:TMs(s),A:Reese,Archie, Lorenzo 3.00
2 BU:Dinosaurs 2099 .... 2.50
3 A:Ex-Mutants 2.50
4 V:Poacher,Revenue 2.50
5 .... 2.50
6 V:Samantha 2.50
7 V:Turret 2.50
8 Genesis#2 .... 2.50
9 Genesis#5 .... 2.50
10 Flip(c), ... 2.50
11 V:Tiny Lorenzo 2.50
12 I:Manhatten Bob 2.50
13 I:Lil' Billy Frankenstein 2.50

DISNEY ADVENTURES
Walt Disney

1 .... 2.75
2 .... 2.50
3 .... 2.25
4 .... 2.25
5 .... 2.25
6 .... 2.25
7 Joe Montana 2.25
8 Bronson Pinchot 2.25
9 Hulk Hogan 2.25
10 Mayim Bialik 2.25
11 .... 2.25
12 Monsters 2.25
13 A:Darkwing Duck (inc. work by DW) 2.25
14 inc. 'Big Top, Big Shot' 1.95
15 .... 1.95
16 inc.'Turnabout is Fowl Play' .. 1.95
17 inc.'Kitty Kat Kaper' 1.95
18 Kitty Kat Kaper 1.95
19 The Voice of Wisdom 1.95
20 thru 28 .... @1.95

DISNEY COLOSSAL COMICS COLLECTION
Walt Disney

1 inc.DuckTales, Chip'n'Dale ... 2.25
2 inc.Tailspin,Duck Tales 1.95
3 inc.Duck Tales 1.95
4 O:Darkwing Duck 1.95
5 Tailspin,Duck Tales 1.95
6 Darkwing Duck,Goofy 1.95
7 inc.Darkwing Duck.Goofy 1.95
8 inc.Little Mermaid 1.95
9 inc.Duck Tales 1.95

DISNEY COMICS IN 3-D
Walt Disney

1 .... 2.95

DISNEY COMICS SPEC: DONALD & SCROOGE

1 inc."Return to Xanadu" 8.95

DISNEYLAND BIRTHDAY PARTY
Gladstone

1 .... 6.00

DIVER DAN
Dell Publishing Co.
February-April, 1962

1 .... 30.00
2 .... 30.00

DNAgents #2 © Eclipse Comics

DNAGENTS
Eclipse

1 O:DNAgents 4.00
2 . . . . 3.00
3 . . . . 2.50
4 . . . . 2.50
5 . . . . 2.50
6 . . . . 2.50
7 . . . . 2.50
8 . . . . 2.50
9 DSp 2.50
10 . . . . 2.00
11 . . . . 2.00
12 . . . . 2.50
13 . . . . 2.00
14 . . . . 2.00
15 . . . . 2.50
16 . . . . 2.50
17 thru 21 . . . . @2.00
22 . . . . 1.75
23 . . . . 1.75
24 DSt(c) 1.75
25 . . . . 1.75

See also: NEW DNAGENTS

DO YOU BELIEVE IN NIGHTMARES?
St. John Publishing Co.
November, 1957

1 SD 125.00
2 DAy,January, 1958 . . . . 65.00

DOBER-MAN

1 . . . . 2.50

DOC SAVAGE
Millenium

1 V:Russians 2.50

DOC SAVAGE
Millenium

1 Monarch of Armageddon Pt.1 . 3.00
2 Monarch of Armageddon Pt.2 . 2.75
3 Monarch of Armageddon Pt.3 . 2.75

DOC SAVAGE: DEVIL'S THOUGHTS
Millenium

1 V:Hanoi Shan 2.50
2 V:Hanoi Shan 2.50
3 Final issue 2.50

DOC SAVAGE: MANUAL OF BRONZE
Millenium

1 Fact File 2.50

DOC SAVAGE: REPEL
Millenium

1 . . . . 2.50

DOCTOR BOOGIE
Media Arts

1 . . . . 1.75
2 . . . . 1.75

DOCTOR CHAOS
Triumphant Comics

1 JnR(s),I:Doctor Chaos 2.50
2 JnR(s), ... 2.50
3 JnR(s),B:Coming of the Cry,I:Cry 2.50
4 JnR(s),b:Ky'Li 2.50
5 JnR(s),E:Coming of the Cry,V:Cry 2.50

Doc Savage, Manual of Bronze
© Millenium

DOCTOR SOLAR MAN OF THE ATOM
Gold Key

1 BF,I:Dr. Solar 250.00
2 BF,I:Prof.Harbinger 100.00
3 BF,The Hidden Hands 60.00
4 BF,The Deadly Sea 60.00
5 BF,I:Dr.Solar in costume 60.00
6 FBe,I:Nuro 40.00
7 FBe,Vanishing Oceans 40.00
8 FBe,Thought Controller 40.00
9 FBe,Transivac The Energy Consuming Computer 40.00
10 FBe,The Sun Giant 40.00
11 FBe,V:Nuro 35.00
12 FBe,The Mystery of the Vanishing Silver 35.00
13 FBe,The Meteor from 100 Million BC 35.00
14 FBe,Solar's Midas Touch . . . 35.00
15 FBe O:Dr.Solar 45.00
16 FBe,V:Nuro 35.00
17 FBe,The Fatal Foe 35.00
18 FBe,The Mind Master 35.00
19 FBe,SolarV:Solar 35.00
20 AMc,Atomic Nightmares 35.00
21 AMc,Challenge from Outer Space 25.00
22 AMc,Nuro,I:King Cybernoid 25.00
23 AMc,A:King Cybernoid 25.00
24 EC,The Deadly Trio 25.00
25 EC,The Lost Dimension 25.00
26 EC,When Dimensions Collide 25.00
27 (1969) The Ladder to Mars 25.00
28 (1981),1 pg AMc,The Dome of Mystery 12.00
29 DSp,FBe,Magnus 12.00
30 DSp,FBe,Magnus 12.00

DOGHEAD
Tundra

1 Al Columbia,"Poster Child" . . . 4.95

DOGS OF WAR
Defiant

1 F:Shooter,Ironhead 2.75
2 . . . . 2.50

DOLLMAN
Eternity

1 Movie adapt. sequel 2.50
2 V:Sprug & Braindead Gang . . . 2.50
3 Toni Costa Kidnapped 2.50

DONALD DUCK ADVENTURES
Gladstone

1 CB,Jungle Hi-Jinks 5.00
2 CB,Dangerous Disquise 4.00
3 CB,Lost in the Andes 5.00
4 CB,Frozen Gold 4.00
5 Rosa Art 3.50
6 . . . . 2.50
7 . . . . 2.50
8 Rosa 3.50
9 . . . . 2.50
10 . . . . 2.50
11 . . . . 2.50
12 Giant size,Rosa 3.50
13 Rosa(c) 2.50
14 . . . . 3.00
15 CB 2.00
16 . . . . 2.00
17 . . . . 2.00
18 . . . . 2.00
19 . . . . 4.00
20 Giant size 4.00

DONALD DUCK ADVENTURES
Walt Disney

1 ROSA 5.00
2 . . . . 3.00
3 . . . . 2.50
4 . . . . 2.50
5 . . . . 2.50
6 . . . . 2.50
7 . . . . 2.00
8 . . . . 2.00
9 . . . . 2.00
10 'Run-Down Runner' 2.00
11 'Whats for Lunch-Supper' 2.00
12 'Head of Rama Putra' 2.00
13 'JustAHumble,BumblingDuck' . 2.00
14 'DayGladstonesLuckRanOut' . . 1.75
15 'A Tuft Luck Tale' 1.75
16 'Magica's Missin'Magic' 1.75
17 'Secret of Atlantis' 1.75
18 'Crocodile Donald' 1.75
19 'Not So Silent Service' 1.75
20 'Ghost of Kamikaze Ridge' . . . 1.50
21 'The Golden Christmas Tree' . 1.50
22 'The Master Landscapist' 1.50
23 'The Lost Peg Leg Mine' 1.50
24 'On Stolen Time' 1.50
25 Sense of Humor 1.50
26 Race to the South Seas 1.50
27 Nap in Nature 1.50
28 Olympic Tryout 1.50
29 rep.March of Comics#20 . . . . . 1.50
30 A:The Vikings 1.50
31 The Sobbing Serpent of Loch McDuck 1.50
32 It Was No Occident 1.50
33 Crazy Christmas on Bear Mountain 1.50
34 Sup.Snooper Strikes Again . . . 1.50

DONALD DUCK
Dell/Gold Key
December 1962

85 thru 97 . . . . 15.00
98 rep. #46 CB 15.00
99 . . . . 15.00
100 . . . . 10.00
101 . . . . 10.00
102 A:Super Goog 10.00
103 thru 111 . . . . @10.00
112 I:Moby Duck 10.00
113 thru 133 . . . . @10.00
134 CB rep. 10.00

 All comics prices listed are for *Near Mint* condition.

135 CB rep. 10.00
136 thru 156 . . . . @5.00
157 CB rep. 9.00
158 thru 163 . . . . @4.00
164 CB rep. 4.00
165 thru 216 . . . . @4.00

Whitman

217 . . . . 4.00
218 . . . . 4.00
219 CB rep. 4.00
220 thru 245 . . . . @4.00

Gladstone

246 CB,Gilded Man 12.00
247 CB 10.00
248 CB,Forbidden Valley 10.00
249 CB 10.00
250 CB,Pirate Gold 15.00
251 CB,Donald's Best Xmas 4.00
252 CB,Trail o/t Unicorn 4.00
253 CB 3.50
254 CB, in old Calif 7.00
255 CB 3.50
256 CB,Volcano Valley 3.50
257 CB,Forest Fire 4.00
258 CB 3.00
259 CB 3.00
260 CB 3.00
261 thru 266 CB . . . . @2.50
267 thru 277 CB . . . . @2.00
278 CB 4.00
279 CB 4.00

DONALD DUCK ALBUM
Dell Publishing Co.
May-July, 1959

1 CB(c) 20.00
2 . . . . 12.00

DOOMSDAY + 1
Charlton

1 JBy,JBy(c),P(c) 8.00
2 . . . . 6.00
3 JBy,JBy(c),P(c) 5.00
4 JBy,JBy(c),P(c),I:Lok 5.00
5 and 6 JBy,JBy(c),P(c) . . . . . @5.00
7 thru 12 JBy,JBy(c),P(c),rep . . . 2.00

DOOMSDAY SQUAD
Fantagraphics

1 rep. JBy 2.00
2 rep. JBy 2.00
3 rep. SS,A:Usagi Yojimbo 4.00
4 rep. JBy 2.00
5 thru 7, rep. JBy . . . . @2.00

DOUBLE DARE ADVENTURES
Harvey Publications

1 I:B-man,Glowing Gladiator, Magicmaster 22.00
2 AW/RC rep. A:B-Man,Glowing Gladiator, Magicmaster 17.00

DOUBLE LIFE OF PRIVATE STRONG
Archie Publications

1 JSm/JK,I:Lancelot Strong/Shield The Fly 275.00
2 JSm/JK,GT A:Fly 200.00

DR. KILDARE
Dell Publishing Co.
April-June, 1962

1 . . . . 40.00
2 . . . . 30.00
3 . . . . 30.00
4 . . . . 30.00
5 . . . . 30.00
6 . . . . 30.00
7 . . . . 30.00
8 . . . . 30.00
9 . . . . 30.00

DR. GIGGLES
Dark Horse

1 Horror movie adapt. 2.50
2 Movie adapt.contd. 2.50

DRACULA
Dell Publishing Co.
November, 1966

2 O:Dracula 25.00
3 . . . . 15.00
4 . . . . 15.00
6 . . . . 12.00
7 . . . . 10.00
8 . . . . 10.00

Dracula #2 © Topps Comics

DRACULA
Topps

1 MMi,Movie adaptation (trading cards in each issue) 6.00
1a Red Foil Logo 90.00
1b 2nd Print 2.95
2 MMi,Movie adapt.contd. 4.00
3 MMi,Movie adapt.contd. 4.00
4 MMi,Movie adapt.concludes . . . 4.00
Collected Album 13.95

DRACULA VS. ZORRO
Topps

1 DMg(s),TY,Black(c), ... 2.95
2 DMg(s),TY,w/Zorro #0 . . . . 2.95

DRACULA: VLAD THE IMPALER
Topps

1 EM,I:Vlad Dracua 3.25
1a Red Foil 90.00
2 EM 3.25

DRAGONCHIANG
Eclipse

1 TT 2.95

DRAGONFLIGHT
Eclipse

1 Anne McCaffrey novel adapt . . 4.95
2 novel adapt 4.95
3 novel adapt 4.95

DRAGONFLY
AC Comics

1 . . . . 3.50
2 . . . . 2.00
3 . . . . 2.00
4 thru 8 . . . . @1.75

DRAGONFORCE
Aircel

1 DK 7.50
2 thru 7 DK . . . . @5.00
8 thru 12 . . . . @5.00
13 . . . . 2.00

DRAGONRING
Aircel

1 . . . . 3.50
2 O:Dragonring 2.50
3 thru 15 . . . . @2.00

DREADSTAR
First

27 JSn,from Epic,traitor 2.50
28 JSn 2.25
29 JSn,V:Lord Papal 2.25
30 JSn,D:Lord Papal 2.25
31 JSn,I:The Power 2.25
32 JSn 2.25
33 . . . . 2.25
34 LM/VM,A:Malchek 2.25
35 LM/VM 2.25
36 LM/VM 2.25
37 LM/VM,A:Last Laugh 2.25
38 LM/VM 2.25
39 AMc,Crossroads tie-in 2.25
40 LM/VM 2.25
41 AMe 2.25
42 JSn,AMe,I:Pawns 2.25
43 JSn,AMe,Pawns Pt.2 . . . . 2.25
44 JSn,AMe,Pawns Pt.3 . . . . 2.25
45 JSn,AMe,Pawns Pt.4 . . . . 2.25
46 JSn,AMe,Pawns Pt.5 . . . . 2.25
47 JSn,AMe,Pawns Pt.6 . . . . 2.25
48 JSn,AMe,Pawns Pt.7 . . . . 2.25
49 JSn,AMe,Pawns Pt.8 . . . . 2.25
50 JSn,AMe,Pawns Pt.9 prestige format 4.25
51 JSn,AMe,Pawns Pt.10, Paladox epic begins 2.25
52 AMe 2.25
53 AMe,'Messing with Peoples Minds' 2.25
54 JSn,AMe,Pawns ends 2.25
55 AMe,I:Iron Angel 2.25
56 AME,A:Iron Angel 2.25
57 A:Iron Angel 2.25
58 A:Iron Angel 2.25
59 A:Iron Angel 2.25
60 AMe,Paladox epic ends 2.25
61 AME,A:Iron Angel 2.25
62 O:Dreadstar,I:Youngscuz 2.25
63 AMe,A:Youngscuz 2.25
64 AMe,A:Youngscuz 2.25

Malibu

1 JSn(c),PDd(s),EC, I:New Dreadstar 2.75
2 JSn(c),PDd(s),EC, ... 2.50

DREDD RULES
Fleetway

1 SBs(c),JBy,Prev.unpubl. in USA 5.00
2 inc.'Eldster Ninja Mud Wrestling Vigilantes' 3.50
3 inc.'That Sweet Stuff' 3.50
4 Our Man in Hondo City 3.50
5 . . . . 3.25
6 BKi,DBw 3.25
7 "Banana City" 3.25
8 "Over the Top" 3.25
9 "Shooting Match" 3.25
10 SBs,inc.Mega-City primer 3.25

11 SBs,Legend/Johnny Biker 3.25
12 SBs,Rock on Tommy Who ... 3.25
13 BMy,The Ballad of Toad McFarlane 3.25
14 thru 15 .... @3.25
16 A:Russians 3.25
17 F:Young Giant 3.25
18 F:Jonny Cool 2.95
19 V:Hunter's Club 2.95

DRIFT MARLO
Dell Publishing Co.
May-July, 1962

1 .... 18.00
2 .... 15.00

DRUG WARS
Pioneer

1 .... 1.95
2 .... 1.95
3 .... 1.95

DRUNKEN FIST
Jademan

1 .... 3.25
2 .... 2.50
3 .... 2.00
4 thru 9 .... @1.75
10 thru 27 .... @1.95
28 D:Mack 1.95
29 .... 1.95
30 .... 1.95
31 .... 1.95
32 Wong Mo-Gei vs.Swordsman . 1.95
33 Mo-Gei commits suicide 1.95
34 .... 1.95
35 .... 1.95
36 D:Fire Oak 1.95
37 Iron Law Kills Elephant-Man .. 1.95
38 A:Wayne Chan 1.95
39 D:Wayne Chan 1.95
40 D:Toro Yamamoto 1.95
41 Lord Algol vs. Ghing Mob 1.95
42 .... 1.95
43 D:Yamamoto,Swordsman in USA 1.95
44 'Cool Hand Wong' 1.95
45 'Black Cult Rising' 1.95
46 .... 1.95
47 .... 1.95
48 Evil Child 1.95
49 I:Hurricane Child 1.95
50 Lord Algol vs.Diabol.Ent. 1.95
51 F:Flying Thunder 1.95
52 Madcap vs.Yama 1.95
53 Swordsman vs.Catman 1.95

DUCK TALES
Gladstone

1 CB(r)I:LaunchpadMcQuck 4.50
2 CB(r) 3.00
3 .... 2.50
4 CB(r) 2.50
5 thru 11 .... @2.25
12 .... 4.00
13 .... 4.00

DUCK TALES
Walt Disney

1 .... 4.00
2 .... 2.50
3 .... 2.25
4 .... 2.25
5 Scrooges'Quest 2.25
6 Scrooges'Quest 2.00
7 Return to Duckburg 2.00
8 .... 2.00
9 7 Sojourns of Scrooge 2.00
10 Moon of Gold 2.00
11 Once & Future Warlock 2.00
12 Lost Beyond the MilkyWay ... 1.75
13 The Doomed of Sarras 1.75
14 Planet Blues 1.75
15 The Odyssey Ends 1.75
16 The Great Chase 1.75
17 Duck in Time Pt.1 .... 1.75
18 Duck in Time Pt.2 .... 1.75
19 Bail Out 1.75

DUDLEY DO-RIGHT
Charlton Comics
August, 1970

1 .... 40.00
2 thru 7 August 1971 ...... @30.00

DUNC & LOO
Dell Publishing Co.
October-December, 1961

1 .... 50.00
2 .... 40.00
3 .... 25.00
4 .... 25.00
5 .... 25.00
6 .... 25.00
7 .... 25.00
8 .... 25.00

DWIGHT D. EISENHOWER
Dell Publishing Co.
December, 1969

1 .... 20.00

DYNAMO
Tower Comics
August, 1966

1 WW,MSy,RC,SD,I:Andor ... 35.00
2 WW,DA,GT,MSy,Weed solo story A:Iron Maiden 25.00
3 WW,GT,Weed solo story, A:Iron Maiden 25.00
4 WW,DA,A:Iron Maiden, June, 1967 .... 25.00

DYNAMO JOE
First

1 .... 3.00
2 .... 2.00
3 thru 14 .... @1.50
Special #1 .... 1.25

EARLY DAYS OF SOUTHERN KNIGHTS

Vol. 2 Graphic Novel 5.00

EARTH 4
Continuity
[1st Series]

1 Deathwatch 2000 Pt.7,w/ Trading Card 2.50
2 Deathwatch 2000 .... 2.50
3 V:Hellbenders 2.50

[2nd Series]

1 WMc, ... 2.50
2 .... 2.50

EAST MEETS WEST
Innovation

1 .... 2.50
2 .... 2.50
3 .... 2.50

EBONY WARRIOR
Africa Rising

1 I:Ebony Warrior 1.95

ECHO OF FUTURE PAST
Continuity

1 NA,MGo,I:Bucky O'Hare, Frankenstein 4.00
2 NA,MGo,A:Bucky O'Hare, Dracula, Werewolf 3.50
3 NA,MGo,A:Bucky 3.50
4 NA,MGo,A:Bucky 3.50

Echo of Futurepast #4
© Continuity Comics

5 NA,MGo,A:Drawla&Bucky 3.50
6 Ath,B:Torpedo 3.50
7 ATh 3.50
8 Ath, ... 3.25
9 Ath,Last issue 3.25

ECLIPSE GRAPHIC NOVELS
Eclipse

1 Axa 7.00
2 MR,I Am Coyote 7.00
3 DSt,Rocketeer 10.00
3a hard cover 40.00
4 Silver Heels 9.00
4a hard cover 40.00
5 Sisterhood of Steel 10.00
6 Zorro in Old Calif. 8.00

ECLIPSE MONTHLY
Eclipse

1 SD,DW,I:Static&Rio 2.00
2 GC,DW 2.00
3 thru 8 DW .... @1.50
9 DW 1.75
10 DW 1.75

EDGE OF CHAOS
Pacific

1 GM 2.00
2 GM 2.00
3 GM 2.00

87th PRECINCT
Dell Publishing Co.
April-June, 1962

1 BK 75.00
2 .... 60.00

ELEMENTALS
Comico

1 BWg,I:Destroyers 9.00
2 BWg 5.00
3 BWg 5.00
4 BWg 4.50
5 BWg 4.00
6 BWg 3.00
7 BWg 2.00
8 BWg 2.00
9 BWg 2.00
10 BWg 2.00

Elementals #13 © Comico

11 BWg 1.50
12 BWg 1.50
13 thru 22 . . . . . @1.50
23 thru 29 . . . . . @1.75
Special #1 . . . . . 1.75
Special #2 . . . . . 1.95

[Second Series]

1 . . . . . 2.25
2 thru 4 . . . . . @1.95
5 thru 25 . . . . . @2.50
GN Death & Resurrection 12.95

ELFLORD
Aircel

1 Vol.II 3.50
2 . . . . . 2.50
3 thru 20 . . . . . @2.00
21 double size 4.95
22 thru 24 . . . . . @2.00
Special #1 . . . . . 2.00

ELFQUEST: WAVE DANCER
Warp

1 thru 2 . . . . . 3.25

ELFQUEST: BLOOD OF TEN CHIEFS
Warp

1 WP 2.25
2 WP 2.25
3 WP,B:Swift Spear 2.25

ELFQUEST: HIDDEN YEARS
Warp

1 WP 3.00
2 WP, w/coupon promo. 2.75
3 WP, w/coupon promo.Cont.sty. previewed in Harbinger#11 . . . 3.25
4 WP,w/coupon 2.50
5 WP,O:Skywise 2.50
6 WP,F:Timmain 2.50
7 F:Timmain 2.50
8 Daughter's Day 2.50
9 WP(s),Enemy Face 2.50
9 1/2 WP,JBy,Holiday Spec. 3.50
10 WP, ... 2.50
11 WP, ... 2.50
12 WP, ... 2.50

ELFQUEST: NEW BLOOD
Warp

1 JBy,artists try Elfquest 5.00
2 Barry Blair story 3.50
3 thru 5 . . . . . @2.50
6 thru 8 . . . . . 2.50
9 . . . . . 2.25
10 . . . . . 2.25
11 . . . . . 2.25
12 . . . . . 2.25
Summer Spec.1993 . . . . . 4.25

ELIMINATOR COLOR SPECIAL
Eternity

1 set in the future 2.95

Elric #1 © First Comics

ELRIC
Pacific

1 CR 4.00
2 CR 3.00
3 thru 6 CR . . . . . @2.50

ELRIC, BANE OF THE BLACK SWORD
First

1 Michael Moorcock adapt. 1.75
2 . . . . . 1.75
3 thru 5 . . . . . @1.95

ELRIC, SAILOR ON THE SEVEN SEAS

1 . . . . . 4.00
2 . . . . . 3.00
3 thru 7 . . . . . @2.00

ELRIC, SAILOR ON THE SEVEN SEAS
First

1 Michael Moorcock adapt. 4.00
2 . . . . . 3.00
3 thru 7 . . . . . @2.00

ELRIC–VANISHING TOWER
First

1 Michael Moorcock adapt. 2.50
2 thru 6 . . . . . @2.00

ELRIC, WEIRD OF THE WHITE WOLF
First

1 Michael Moorcock adapt. 3.00
2 . . . . . 2.00
3 . . . . . 2.00
4 . . . . . 2.00
5 . . . . . 2.00
Graphic Novel CR 7.00

E-MAN
Charlton Comics
October, 1973

1 JSon,O:E-Man 20.00
2 SD 8.00
3 . . . . . 8.00
4 SD 8.00
5 SD,Miss Liberty Bell 6.00
6 JBy 8.00
7 JBy 8.00
8 . . . . . 10.00
9 JBy 8.00
10 JBy,September, 1975 . . . . . 8.00

E-MAN
First

1 JSon,O:E-Man & Nova, A:Rog 2000, 1 pg. JBy 1.75
2 JSon,I:F-Men (X-Men satire) 1 page Mike Mist 1.25
3 JSon, V:F-Men 1.25
4 JSon,Michael Mauser solo 1.25
5 JSon,I:Psychobabbler,A:Omaha, The Cat Dancer 1.25
6 JSon,O:E-Man,V:Feeder 1.25
7 JSon,V:Feeder 1.25
8 JSon,V:HotWax,A:CuteyBunny . 1.25
9 JSon,I:Tyger Lili 1.25
10 JSon,O:Nova Kane pt.1 . . . . . 1.25
11 JSon,O:Nova Kane pt.2 . . . . . 1.25
12 JSon,A:Tyger Lili 1.25
13 JSon,V:Warp'sPrinceChaos . . 1.25
14 JSon,V:Randarr 1.25
15 JSon,V:Samuel Boar 1.25
16 JSon,V:Samuel Boar 1.25
17 JSon,'Smeltquest' satire 1.25
18 JSon,'Rosemary..& Time' 1.25
19 JSon, 'Hoodoo Blues' 1.25
20 JSon,A:Donald Duke 1.25
21 JSon,A:B-Team,(satire) 1.25
22 JSon,A:Teddy Q 1.25
23 JSon,A:TygerLili,B-Team 1.25
24 JSon,O:Michael Mauser 1.25
25 JSon,last issue 1.25
Spec #1 . . . . . 2.75

E-MAN
Comico

1 JSon 2.75
2 JSon 2.50
3 JSon 2.50

EMERGENCY
Charlton Comics
June, 1976

1 JSon(c),JBy 10.00
2 JSon 3.00
3 Thru 4 December, 1976 . . . . . 2.00

ENEMY
Dark Horse

1 MZ(c),StG(s),I:Enemy 2.75
2 MZ(c),StG(s),F:Heller 2.75
3 MZ(c),StG(s),A:Heller 2.50

ENSIGN O'TOOLE
Dell Publishing Co.
August-October, 1962

1 . . . . . 10.00
2 . . . . . 10.00

EPSILON WAVE
Independent

1 . . . . 3.00
2 . . . . 2.50
3 . . . . 2.25
4 . . . . 2.00

Elite Comics

5 thru 10 . . . . @2.00

ESPers #1 © Eclipse Comics

ESPERS
Eclipse

1 I:ESPers 2.00
2 JBo(c),V:Terrorists 1.50
3 V:Terrorists 1.50
4 Beirut 1.75
5 'The Liquidators' 1.75
6 V:Benito Giovanetti 1.75

ESPIONAGE
Dell Publishing Co.
May-July, 1964

1 . . . . 15.00
2 . . . . 15.00

ETERNAL WARRIOR
Valiant

1 FM(c),JDx,Unity #2,O:Eternal Warrior,Armstrong 6.00
1a Gold Ed. 50.00
1b Gold Foil Logo 60.00
2 WS(c),JDx,Unity #10,A:Solar, Harbinger,Eternal Warrior of 4001 . . . . 4.00
3 JDx,V:Armstrong,I:Astrea 3.00
4 JDx(i),I:Caldone, C:Bloodshot 10.00
5 JDx,I:Bloodshot,V:Iwatsu's Men 10.00
6 BWS,JDx,V:Master Darque . . . 3.00
7 BWS,V:Master Darque, D:Uncle Buck 3.00
8 BWS,as Archer & Armstrong #8 Three Musketeers,I:Ivar 6.00
9 MMo,JDx,B:Book of the Geomancer 3.00
10 JDx,E:Bk. o/t Geomancer 3.00
11 B:KVH(s),JDx(i), V:Neo-Nazis 3.00
12 JDx(i),V:Caldone 3.00
13 MMo,JDx(i),V:Caldone, A:Bloodshot 2.75
14 E:KVH(s),MMo,V:Caldone, A:Geoff 2.50
15 YG,A:Bloodshot,V:Tanaka 2.50
16 YG,A:Bloodshot 2.50
17 A:Master Darque 2.50
18 C:Doctor Mirage 2.50
19 KVH(s),TeH,A:Doctor Mirage . 2.50
20 KVH(s),Access Denied 2.50
21 KVH(s),TeH,V:Dr. Steiner 2.50
22 V:Master Darque,w/Valiant Era Card 2.50
23 KVH(s),TeH,Blind Fate 2.50
24 KVH(s),TeH,V:Immortal Enemy 2.50
25 MBn(s),A:Archer,Armstrong . . . 2.25
Yearbook 4.25

ETERNITY SMITH
Hero

1 . . . . 1.50
2 . . . . 1.50
3 . . . . 1.50
4 Knightshade solo 1.50
5 Knightshade solo 1.50
6 . . . . 1.50
7 . . . . 1.95
8 I:Indigo 1.95
9 A:Walter Koenig 1.95
10 . . . . 1.95

EUDAEMON
Dark Horse

1 Nel,I:New Eudaemon 3.00
2 Nel,V:Mordare 2.75
3 Nel,V:Mordare 2.75

EVA THE IMP
Red Top Comic/Decker
1957

1 . . . . 10.00
2 November, 1957 . . . . . . 9.00

EVANGELINE
Comico

1 . . . . 4.00
2 . . . . 3.00

Lodestone

1 . . . . 2.50
2 . . . . 2.50

First

1 . . . . 3.00
2 thru 9 . . . . @1.75
10 . . . . 1.95
11 . . . . 1.95
12 . . . . 1.95

EVERYTHING'S ARCHIE
Archie Publications
May, 1969

1 . . . . 35.00
2 . . . . 18.00
3 . . . . 10.00
4 . . . . 10.00
5 . . . . 10.00
6 . . . . 6.00
7 . . . . 6.00
8 thru 10 . . . . @6.00
11 thru 20 . . . . @3.00
21 thru 40 . . . . @1.50
41 thru 134 . . . . @1.00

EVIL DEAD III: ARMY OF DARKNESS
Dark Horse

1 JBo,Movie adaptation 2.50
2 JBo,Movie adaptation 2.50
3 JBo,Movie adaptation 2.50

EX-MUTANTS
Malibu

1 I&O:Ex-Mutants 2.25
2 V:El Motho,Beafcake,Brickhouse 2.25
3 A:Sliggo,Zygote 2.25
4 . . . . 2.25
5 Piper Kidnapped 1.95
6 A:Dr.Kildare 1.95
7 V:Dr.Kildare 1.95
8 O:Gelson 1.95
9 F:Dillion 1.95
10 F:Sluggtown 1.95
11 Man(s),Genesis#1,w/card 2.25
12 R0M(s),Genesis#4 . . . . . . 2.25
13 J:Gravestone,Arc 2.25
14 C:Eye 2.25
15 A:Arrow 2.50
16 A:Arrow,I:KillCorp 2.50
17 A:Arrow,V:KillCorp 2.50
18 A:Arrow,V:KillCorp 2.50

EXECUTIONER
Innovation

1 F:Mack Bolan 3.95
2 War against Mafia 2.75

EXEMPLARS

1 . . . . 1.95
2 . . . . 1.95

EXILES
Malibu-Ultraverse

1 TMs(s),PaP,I:Exiles 5.00
2 V:Kort 3.00
3 BWS,Mastodon,BU:Rune 3.50
4 V:Kort 2.75

EXTREME TOUR BOOK '94
Image

Tour Book 25.00

EXTREME ZERO
Image

0 RLd,CYp,ATi(i),I:Cybrid, Law&Order,Risk,Code 9, Lancers,Black Flag 2.75

FALCON, THE
Aircel

Spec. #1 . . . . 2.00

FAMILY AFFAIR
Gold Key
February, 1970

1 W/Poster,Ph(c) 25.00
2 . . . . 15.00
3 Ph(c) 15.00
4 Ph(c) 15.00

FAMOUS INDIAN TRIBES
Dell Publishing Co.
July-September, 1962

1 . . . . 12.00
2 . . . . 3.00

FANTASTIC VOYAGES OF SINBAD, THE
Gold Key
October, 1965

1 Ph(c) 20.00
2 June, 1967 . . . . 18.00

FASHION IN ACTION
Eclipse

Summer Special #1 . . . . 1.75
Winter Special #1 . . . . 2.00

FAT ALBERT
Gold Key
March, 1974

1 . . . . 4.00
2 . . . . 2.00

3 thru 10 @1.50
11 thru 28 @1.00
29 February, 1979 1.00

FATHOM
Comico
1 thru 3 From Elementals @2.50

FATMAN, THE HUMAN FLYING SAUCER
Lightning Comics
April, 1967
1 CCB,O:Fatman & Tin Man 45.00
2 CCB 30.00
3 CCB,(Scarce) 45.00

FAZE ONE
AC Comics
1 1.75

FAZE ONE FAZERS
AC Comics
1 5.00
2 3.00
3 2.00
4 thru 6 @1.75

FAZERS SKETCHBOOK
1 1.75

Fearbook #1 © Eclipse Comics

FEARBOOK
Eclipse
1 SBi,RV,'A Dead Ringer' 1.75

FELIX THE CAT
Harvey
1 thru 4 1.25
5 thru 7 1.50

FELIX'S NEPHEWS INKY & DINKY
Harvey Publications
September, 1957
1 45.00
2 thru 7 @20.00

FEMFORCE
AC Comics
1 O:Femforce 5.00
2 A:Captain Paragon 3.50
3 "Skin Game" 2.50
4 "Skin Game" 2.50
5 Back in the Past 2.50
6 EL,Back in the Past 2.50
7 HB,O:Captain Paragon 2.50
8 V:Shade 2.50
9 V:Dr.Rivits 2.50
10 V:Dr.Rivits 2.50
11 D:Haunted Horsemen 2.25
12 V:Dr.Rivits 2.25
13 V:She-Cat 2.25
14 V:Alizarin Crimson 2.25
15 V:Alizarin Crimson 2.25
16 thru 56 See Other Publishers Black & White
57 V:Goat God 2.75
58 I:New Sentinels 2.75
59 I:Paragon 2.75
60 V:Sentinels 2.75
61 F:Tara 2.75
62 V:Valkyra 2.75
63 I:Rayda 2.75
Spec.#1 1.50
Untold Origin Spec #1 4.95

FEMFORCE: UP CLOSE
AC Comics
1 F:Stardust 2.75
2 F:Stardust 2.75

FENRY
Raven Publications
1 6.95
1a Platinum Ed. 15.00

FERRET
Malibu
1 (From Protectors),DZ,V:Purple Dragon Tong,A:Iron Skull 2.25

[Regular Series]
1 thru 3 2.50
4 V:Toxin 2.50
4a Newstand Ed. 2.25
5 SEr,Genesis 2.25
6 SEr,Genesis crossover 2.25
7 V:Airman 2.25
8 I:Posse 2.25
9 DZ,R:Iron Skull,I:Deathsong 2.25
10 DZ 2.25

FIGHT THE ENEMY
Tower Comics
August, 1966
1 BV,Lucky 7 5.00
2 AMc 8.00
3 WW,AMc 4.00

FIGHTING AMERICAN
Harvey
1 SK,Rep Fighting American from 1950's 17.50

FIREARM
Malibu-Ultraverse
0 w/video 17.00
1 I:Firearm 3.00
2 BWS,A:Hardcase,BU:Rune 2.75
3 V:Sportsmen 2.25
4 HC,Break-Thru x-over 2.25
5 O:Prime 2.25
6 A:Prime 2.25
7 V:Killer 2.25
8 DIB(c), 2.25
9 at the Rose Bowl 1.95

FIRST ADVENTURES
First
1 thru 5 @1.25

FIRST GRAPHIC NOVELS
First
1 JBi,Beowolf 8.00
1a 2nd Printing 7.00
2 TT,Time Beavers 6.00
3 HC,American Flag Hard Times 12.00
4 Nexus,SR 8.00
5 Elric,CR 15.00
6 Enchanted Apples of Oz 6.00
7 Secret Island of Oz 8.00
8 HC,Time 2 28.00
9 TMNT 20.00
10 TMNT II 18.00
11 Sailor on the Sea 15.00
12 HC,American Flagg 12.00
13 Ice Ring 8.00
14 TMNT III 14.00
15 Hex Breaker 8.00
16 Forgotten Forest 9.00
17 Mazinger 9.00
18 TMNT IV 13.00
19 O;Nexus 8.00
20 American Flagg 12.00

1st FOLIO
Pacific
1 Joe Kubert School 1.50

FISH POLICE
Comico
Vol 2 #6 thru #15 rep. @2.50
Vol 2 #16 rep. 3.00
Vol 2 #17 rep.,AuA 3.00
1 Color Special 3.50

FITCH IN TIME
1 and 2 @1.50

FLARE
Hero
1 I:Darkon&Prof.Pomegranite 6.00
2 Blonde Bombshell,A:Galooper 3.25
3 I:Sky Marshall 3.00
Annual #1 4.50

[2nd Series]
1 A:Galloping Galooper 4.00
2 A:Lady Arcane 3.00
3 I:Britannia 3.00
4 A:Indigo 2.50
5 R:Eternity Smith,O:Die Kriegerin 3.95
6 I:Tigress 3.50
7 V:The Enemies 3.95
8 Morrigan Wars#4,A:Icicle Dragon 3.50
9 Morrigan Wars Pt.7 (B&W) 3.50

FLARE
Hero Graphics
1 I:Darkon&Prof.Pomegranite 6.00
2 Blonde Bombshell, A:Galooper 3.25
3 I:Sky Marshall 3.00
Annual #1 4.50

[2nd Series]
1 A:Galloping Galooper 4.00
2 A:Lady Arcane 3.00
3 I:Britannia 3.00
4 A:Indigo 3.00
5 R:Eternity Smith,O:Die Kriegerin 3.95
6 I:Tigress 3.50
7 V:The Enemies 3.95
8 Morrigan Wars#4,A:Icicle Dragon 3.50
9 Morrigan Wars Pt.7 (B&W) 3.50

FLARE ADVENTURES
Hero Graphics
1 thru 3 reprints 2.95

FLASH GORDON
Gold Key
June, 1965

1 . . . . 15.00

Flash Gordon #3 © King Comics

FLASH GORDON
King
Sept., 1966

1 AW,DH,A:Mandrake 20.00
1a Complimentary Army giveaway 15.00
2 FBe,A:Mandrake,R:Ming 15.00
3 RE 18.00
4 AW,B:Secret Agent X-9 . . . . . 20.00
5 AW 20.00
6 RC,On the Lost Continent of Mongo 20.00
7 MR, rep. 20.00
8 RC,JAp 20.00
9 AR,rep 25.00
10 AR,rep 25.00
11 RC 15.00

Charlton Sept. 1969

12 RC 20.00
13 JJ 15.00
14 thru 16 . . . . @15.00
17 Brick Bradford story 15.00
18 MK(1970) 15.00

Gold Key Oct.-Nov 1975

19 Flash returns to Mongo 4.00
20 thru 30 . . . . @3.00
31 thru 37 AW movie adapt . . . @1.50

FLAXEN
Dark Horse

1 Based on Model,w/poster 2.95

FLESH AND BONES
Fantagraphics

1 Moore 2.50
2 thru 4 Moore . . . . @2.00

FLINTSTONES
Harvey

1 . . . . 1.25
2 Romeo and Juliet 1.25

FLINTSTONES, THE
Dell Publishing Co.
November-December, 1961

#1 *see Dell Giant*
2 . . . . 60.00
3 . . . . 45.00
4 . . . . 45.00
5 and 6 . . . . @40.00

Gold Key

7 . . . . 40.00
8 A:Mr.& Mrs. J. Evil Scientists . 35.00
9 A:Mr.& Mrs. J. Evil Scientists 35.00
10 A:Mr.& Mrs. J. Evil Scientists 35.00
11 I:Pebbles 50.00
12 'The Too-Old Cowhand' 30.00
13 . . . . 30.00
14 . . . . 30.00
15 . . . . 30.00
16 I:Bamm-Bamm 40.00
17 . . . . 30.00
18 . . . . 30.00
19 . . . . 30.00
20 . . . . 30.00
21 . . . . 22.00
22 . . . . 22.00
23 . . . . 22.00
24 I:Gruesomes 25.00
25 . . . . 22.00
26 . . . . 22.00
27 . . . . 22.00
28 . . . . 22.00
29 . . . . 22.00
30 'Dude Ranch Roundup' 22.00
31 Christmas(c) 22.00
32 . . . . 20.00
33 A:Dracula & Frankenstein . . . 22.00
34 I:The Great Gazoo 30.00
35 . . . . 20.00
36 'The Man Called Flintstone' . . 20.00
37 thru 40 . . . . @20.00
41 thru 60 . . . . @16.00

FLINTSTONES, THE
Charlton Comics
November, 1970

1 . . . . 32.00
2 . . . . 15.00
3 thru 7 . . . . @12.00
8 . . . . 15.00
9 . . . . 12.00
10 . . . . 12.00
11 thru 20 . . . . @10.00
21 thru 50 . . . . @8.00

FLINTSTONES IN 3-D
Blackthorne

1 thru 5 . . . . @2.50

FLIPPER
Gold Key
April, 1966

1 Ph(c) 30.00
2 and 3 Ph(c) . . . . @20.00

FLY IN MY EYE EXPOSED
Eclipse

1 JJo(c),"Our Visitor" 4.95

FLY, THE
Archie Publications

1 JSn,A:Mr.Justice 1.25
2 thru 9 RB,SD . . . . @1.00

FLYING SAUCERS
Dell
April, 1967

1 . . . . 15.00
2 thru 5 . . . . 10.00

FLYMAN
Archie Publications
{Prev: Adventures of the Fly}

31 I:Shield (Bill Higgins), A:Comet, Black Hood 20.00
32 I:Mighty Crusaders 20.00
33 A:Mighty Crusaders, R:Hangman Wizard 20.00
34 MSy,A:Black Hood,Shield,Comet Shield back-up story begins . 15.00
35 O:Black Hood 15.00
36 O:Web,A:Hangman in Shield strip 15.00
37 A:Shield 15.00
38 A:Web 14.00
39 A:Steel Sterling 13.00

FOES
Ram Comics

1 TheMaster's Game 1.95
2 TheMaster's Game #2 . . . . 1.95

FORBIDDEN PLANET
Innovation

1 thru 4 Movie Adapt . . . . @2.50

Forbidden Planet #3 © Innovation

FORBIDDEN PLANET
Innovation

1 Movie Adapt 2.50
2 Movie adapt.contd. 2.50
3 Movie adapt.contd. 2.50

FORCE OF THE BUDDHA'S PALM
Jademan

1 . . . . 3.00
2 . . . . 2.25
3 thru 10 . . . . @1.75
11 thru 24 . . . . @1.95
25 V:Maskman 1.95
26 V:Maskman 1.95
27 A:SmilingDemon 1.95
28 Maskman v 10 Demons 1.95
29 Giant Bat 1.95
30 . . . . 1.95
31 . . . . 1.95
32 'White Crane Villa' 1.95
33 Devilito defeats White Crane & Giant Bat 1.95
34 Samsun Vs. Devilito 1.95
35 Samsun Vs.Devilito 1.95
36 Samson vs. Devilito 1.95
37 D:Galacial Moon 1.95
38 Persian Elders, Iron Boy 1.95
39 V:Mad Gen.,White Crane, Iron Boy 1.95
40 D:Heaven & Earth Elders 1.95

 All comics prices listed are for *Near Mint* condition.

41 thru 43 @1.95
44 D:White Crane 1.95
45 V:Iron Boy 1.95
46 thru 48 @1.95
49 Iron Boy vs Sainted Jade 1.95
50 Iron Boy & The Holy Blaze 1.95
51 D:Aquarius 1.95
52 V:Son o/t Gemini Lord 1.95
53 Nine Continent's return to full powers 1.95

4-D MONKEY

1 thru 3 @1.80

FRANK
Nemesis

1 thru 4 DGc(s),GgP 2.50

FRANK IN THE RIVER
Tundra

1 Avery/Jones style cartoons 2.95

FRANK MERRIWELL AT YALE
Charlton Comics
June, 1955

1 25.00
2 15.00
3 15.00
4 January, 1956 15.00

FRANKENSTEIN
Dell Publishing Co.
August-October, 1964

1 15.00
2 12.00
3 8.00
4 8.00

FREAK FORCE
Image

1 EL(s),KG 2.25
2 EL(s),KG 2.25
3 EL(s),KG 2.25
4 EL(s),KG,A:Vanguard 2.25

FREAKSHOW
Dark Horse

1 JBo,DMc,KB,"Wanda the Worm Woman","Lillie" 9.95

FREDDY
Dell Publishing Co.
May-July, 1963

1 7.00
2 and 3 @5.00

FREDDY'S DEAD

3-D 2.50
1 GN, Movie Adapt 6.95

FREDDY'S DEAD: THE FINAL NIGHTMARE
Innovation

1 Movie adaption, Pt.1 2.50
2 Movie adaption, Pt.2 2.50

FREEX
Malibu-Ultraverse

1 I:Freex 5.00
1a Ultra-Limited 50.00
1b Full Hologram (c) 75.00
2 L:Valerie,I:Rush 4.00
3 A:Rush 3.00
4 GJ(s),DdW,BWS,BU:Rune 2.75
5 GJ(s),V:Master of the Hunt 2.50
6 GJ(s),BH,Break Thru x-over, A:Night Man 2.25
7 BHr,MZ,O:Hardcase 2.25
8 BHr,V:Lost Angel 2.25
9 BHr,A:Old Man 2.25
10 BHr,V:Ms. Contrary 2.25
11 BHr,E:Origins 1.95

FRIDAY FOSTER
Dell Publishing Co.
October, 1972

1 12.00

[CASPER THE] FRIENDLY GHOST
Harvey Publications
August, 1958

1 150.00
2 75.00
3 thru 10 @35.00
11 thru 20 @25.00
21 thru 30 @12.00
31 thru 50 @8.00
51 thru 100 @6.00
101 thru 159 @3.00
160 thru 163 52 pgs. @2.00
164 thru 238 @1.00

FRIGHT NIGHT
Now

1 thru 22 @1.75

FRIGHT NIGHT
Now

1 Dracula,w/3-D Glasses 2.95

Fright Night II #1 © Now Comics

FRIGHT NIGHT II
Now

Movie Adaption 3.95

FRISKY ANIMALS ON PARADE
Ajax-Farrell Publ.
September, 1957

1 LbC(c) 60.00
2 20.00
3 LbC(c) 40.00

FROGMEN, THE
Dell Publishing Co.
February-April, 1962

1 GE,Ph(c) 40.00
2 GE,FF 50.00
3 GE,FF 50.00
4 20.00
5 ATh 30.00
6 20.00
7 20.00
8 20.00
9 20.00
10 20.00
11 20.00

FROM HERE TO INSANITY
Charlton Comics
February, 1955

8 60.00
9 40.00
10 SD(c) 75.00
11 JK 100.00
12 JK 100.00
3-1 175.00

F-TROOP
Dell Publishing Co.
August, 1966

1 Ph(c) 45.00
2 Ph(c) 25.00
3 Ph(c) 25.00
4 Ph(c) 25.00
5 Ph(c) 25.00
6 Ph(c) 25.00
7 Ph(c) 25.00

FUN-IN
Gold Key
February, 1970

1 18.00
2 thru 4 @8.00
5 8.00
6 9.00
7 thru 10 @5.00
11 thru 15 December 1974 @5.00

FUNKY PHANTOM
Gold Key
March, 1972

1 15.00
2 thru 5 @5.00
6 thru 12 @3.50
13 March, 1975 3.50

FUTURIANS
Lodestone

1 DC,I:Dr.Zeus 1.00
2 DC,I:MsMercury 1.00
3 DC 1.00
Eternity Graphic Novel, DC,Rep.+new material 9.95

GALLANT MEN, THE
Gold Key
October, 1963

1 RsM 12.00

GALLEGHER BOY REPORTER
Gold Key
May, 1965

1 10.00

GARRISON'S GORRILLAS
Dell Publishing Co.
January, 1968

1 Ph(c) 25.00
2 thru 5 Ph(c) @15.00

GASP!
American Comics Group
March, 1967

1 25.00
2 thru 4, Aug. 1967 @15.00

G-8 & BATTLE ACES
1 based on '40's pulp characters 3.00

GEN [13]
Image
1 JLe(s),BCi(s),I:Fairchild,Grunge, Freefall,Burnout 5.00
2 JLe(s),BCi(s), ... 4.00

GENESIS
Malibu
0 GP,w/Pog,F:Widowmaker, A:Arrow 3.50
0a Gold Ed. 25.00

GENTLE BEN
Dell Publishing Co.
February, 1968
1 Ph(c) 25.00
2 . . . . 15.00
3 thru 5 . . . . @15.00

GEORGE OF THE JUNGLE
Gold Key
February, 1969
1 . . . . 45.00
2 . . . . 35.00

GET SMART
Dell Publishing Co.
June, 1966
1 Ph(c) all 65.00
2 SD 50.00
3 SD 45.00
4 . . . . 40.00
5 . . . . 40.00
6 . . . . 40.00
7 . . . . 40.00
8 . . . . 40.00

GHOST BUSTERS II
Now
1 thru 3 Mini-series . . . . @1.95

GHOST STORIES
Dell Publishing Co.
September-November, 1962
1 . . . . 35.00
2 . . . . 20.00
3 . . . . 15.00
4 . . . . 15.00
5 . . . . 15.00
6 . . . . 15.00
7 . . . . 15.00
8 . . . . 15.00
9 . . . . 15.00
10 . . . . 15.00
11 . . . . 10.00
12 . . . . 10.00
13 . . . . 10.00
14 . . . . 10.00
15 . . . . 10.00
16 . . . . 10.00
17 . . . . 10.00
18 . . . . 10.00
19 . . . . 10.00
20 . . . . 10.00
21 . . . . 5.00
22 . . . . 5.00
23 . . . . 5.00
24 . . . . 5.00
25 . . . . 5.00
26 . . . . 5.00
27 . . . . 5.00
28 . . . . 5.00
29 . . . . 5.00
30 . . . . 5.00
31 . . . . 5.00
32 . . . . 5.00
33 . . . . 5.00
34 rep 5.00
35 rep 8.00
36 rep 5.00
37 rep 5.00

GIANT COMICS
Charlton Comics
Summer, 1957
1 A:Atomic Mouse,Hoppy 60.00
2 A:Atomic Mouse 40.00
3 . . . . 40.00

GIDGET
Dell Publishing Co.
April, 1966
1 Ph(c),Sally Field 45.00
2 Ph(c),Sally Field 40.00

GIFT, THE
First
Holiday Special 6.00

G.I. JOE 3-D
Blackthorne
1 . . . . 3.00
2 thru 5 . . . . @2.50
Annual #1 . . . . 2.50

GIL THORPE
Dell Publishing Co.
May-July, 1963
1 . . . . 15.00

GINGER FOX
Comico
1 thru 4 . . . . @1.75

G.I. RAMBOT
Wonder Color
1 thru 3 . . . . @1.95

G.I. ROBOT
Eternity
1 . . . . 1.80

GIRL FROM U.N.C.L.E.
Gold Key
January, 1967
1 'The Fatal Accidents Affair' . . 45.00
2 'The Kid Commandos Caper' . 25.00
3 'The Captain Kidd Affair' . . . 25.00
4 'One-Way Tourist Affair' 25.00
5 'The harem-Scarem Affair' . . . 25.00

GIVE ME LIBERTY
Dark Horse
1 FM/DGb 10.00
2 FM/DGb 8.00
3 FM/DGb 7.00
4 FM/DGb 7.00
TPB 16.00

GIVE ME LIBERTY
Dark Horse
1 FM/DGb 9.50
2 FM/DGb 7.50
3 FM/DGb 6.50
4 FM/DGb 6.00

GLOBAL FORCE
Silverline
1 thru 4 . . . . @1.95

GO-GO
Charlton Comics
June, 1966
1 Miss Bikini Luv 25.00
2 Beatles 35.00
3 Blooperman 15.00
4 . . . . 15.00
5 . . . . 10.00
6 JAp 15.00
7 . . . . 15.00
8 JAp 15.00
9 Ph(c),October, 1965 . . . . 15.00

GODS FOR HIRE
Hot Comics
1 thru 7 . . . . @1.75

GODZILLA COLOR SPECIAL
Dark Horse
1 AAd,R:Godzilla 4.00

GODZILLA COLORSPECIAL
Dark Horse
1 AAd,R:Godzilla,V:Gekido-Jin . . 3.00

GODZILLA vs BARKLEY
Dark Horse
1 MBn(s),JBt, ... 3.50

GOLDEN COMICS DIGEST
Gold Key
May, 1969
1 Tom & Jerry,Woody Woodpecker, Bugs Bunny . . . 12.00
2 Hanna-Barbera TV Fun Favorites 6.00
3 Tom & Jerry,Woody Woodpecker 4.00
4 Tarzan 15.00
5 Tom & Jerry,Woody Woodpecker, Bugs Bunny 3.00
6 Bugs Bunny 3.00
7 Hanna-Barbera TV Fun Favorites 5.00
8 Tom & Jerry,Woody Woodpecker, Bugs Bunny 3.00
9 Tarzan 12.00
10 Bugs Bunny 4.00
11 Hanna-Barbera TV Fun Favorites 4.00
12 Tom & Jerry,Bugs Bunny 4.00
13 Tom & Jerry 4.00
14 Bugs Bunny Fun Packed Funnies 4.00
15 Tom & Jerry,Woody Woodpecker, Bugs Bunny 4.00
16 Woody Woodpecker 4.00
17 Bugs Bunny 4.00
18 Tom & Jerry, ... 4.00
19 Little Lulu 15.00
20 Woody Woodpecker 4.00
21 Bugs Bunny Showtime 4.00
22 Tom & Jerry Winter Wingding . 4.00
23 Little Lulu & Tubby Fun Fling 14.00
24 Woody Woodpecker Fun Festival 4.00
25 Tom & Jerry 4.00
26 Bugs Bunny Halloween Hulla-Boo-Loo,Dr. Spektor article 4.00
27 Little Lulu & Tubby in Hawaii . 12.00
28 Tom & Jerry 4.00
29 Little Lulu & Tubby 12.00
30 Bugs Bunny Vacation Funni . . 4.00
31 Turk, Son of Stone 15.00
32 Woody Woodpecker Summer Fun 4.00
33 Little Lulu & Tubby Halloween Fun 12.00
34 Bugs Bunny Winter Funnies . . 4.00
35 Tom & Jerry Snowtime Funtime 4.00
36 Little Lulu & Her Friends 14.00
37 WoodyWoodpecker County Fair 4.00
38 The Pink Panter 4.00
39 Bugs Bunny Summer Fun 4.00
40 Little Lulu 15.00

41 Tom & Jerry Winter Carnival . . 3.00
42 Bugs Bunny 3.00
43 Little Lulu in Paris 14.00
44 Woody Woodpecker Family
Fun Festival 3.00
45 The Pink Panther 3.00
46 Little Lulu & Tubby 12.00
47 Bugs Bunny 3.00
48 The Lone Ranger,Jan., 1976 . . 5.00

GOLDEN PICTURE STORY BOOK
Racine Press (Western)
December, 1961

1 Huckleberry Hound 80.00
2 Yogi Bear 80.00
3 Babes In Toy Land 75.00
4 Walt Disney 80.00

GOMER PYLE
Gold Key
July, 1966

1 Ph(c) 45.00
2 . . . . 30.00
3 . . . . 30.00

GOOD GUYS
Defiant

1 JiS(s),I:Good Guys 3.75
2 JiS(s),V:Mulchmorg 3.25
3 V:Chasm 2.75
4 Seduction of the Innocent 3.25
5 I:Truc 2.75
6 A:Charlemagne 2.75
7 JiS(s),V:Scourge 2.50

GOOFY ADVENTURES
Walt Disney

1 . . . . 2.50
2 . . . . 2.00
3 thru 9 . . . . @1.75
10 Samurai 1.75
11 Goofis Khan 1.75
12 'Arizona Goof' Pt. 1 . . . . 1.75
13 'Arizona Goof' Pt. 2 . . . . 1.75
14 'Goofylution' 1.75
15 'Super Goof Vs.Cold Ray' 1.75
16 'Sheerluck Holmes' 1.50
17 GC,TP,'Tomb of Goofula' 1.50

GORGO
Charlton Comics
May, 1961

1 SD 150.00
2 SD,SD(c) 75.00
3 SD,SD(c) 55.00
4 SD(c) 45.00
5 thru 10 . . . . @45.00
11 . . . . 22.00
12 . . . . 10.00
13 thru 15 . . . . @22.00
16 SD 22.00
17 thru 22 . . . . @10.00
23 September, 1965 . . . . 10.00

GORGO'S REVENGE
Charlton Comics
1962

1 . . . . 30.00

Becomes:

RETURN OF GORGO, THE

2 . . . . 25.00
3 . . . . 25.00

GRATEFUL DEAD COMIX
Kitchen Sink

1 TT,inc.DireWolf(large format) . . 5.50
2 TT,inc.Jack Straw 4.95
3 TT,inc. Sugaree 4.95
4 TT,inc. Sugaree 4.95
5 TT,Uncle John's Band 4.95
6 TT,Eagle Mall #1 . . . . 4.95

GRAVESTONE
Malibu

1 D:Gravestone,V:Wisecrack . . . 2.25
1a Newsstand Ed. 1.95
2 A:Eternal Man, V:Night Plague . 2.25
2a Newsstand Ed. 1.95
3 Genesis Tie in,w/skycap 2.25
4 Genesis 2.25
5 V:Scythe 2.25
6 V:Jug 1.95
7 R:Bogg 2.25

GREAT AMERICAN WESTERN
AC Comics

1 . . . . 1.75
2 . . . . 2.95
3 . . . . 2.95
4 . . . . 3.50

GREAT EXPLOITS
Decker Publ./Red Top
October, 1957

91 BK 35.00

GREEN HORNET
Now

1 O:40's Green Hornet 21.00
1a 2nd Printing 4.00
2 O:60's Green Hornet 10.00
3 . . . . 5.00
4 . . . . 5.00
5 . . . . 5.00
6 . . . . 3.00
7 BSz(c),I:New Kato 3.00
8 . . . . 3.00
9 . . . . 2.50
10 . . . . 2.75
11 . . . . 2.25
12 . . . . 2.25
13 V:Ecoterrorists 2.25
14 V:Ecoterrorists 2.25
Spec #1 . . . . 2.50
Spec #2 . . . . 2.25

[2nd Series]

1 V:Johnny Dollar Pt.1 . . . . 2.25
2 V:Johnny Dollar Pt.2 . . . . 2.25
3 V:Johnny Dollar Pt.3 . . . . 2.25
4 V:Ex-Con/Politician 1.95
5 V:Ex-Con/Politician 1.95
6 Arkansas Vigilante 1.95
7 The Beast,Pt.1 . . . . 1.95
8 The Beast,Pt.2 . . . . 1.95
9 The Beast,Pt.3 . . . . 1.95
10 Green Hornet-prey 1.95
11 F:Crimson Wasp 1.95
12 Crimson Wasp/Johnny Dollar
Pt.1,polybagged w/Button 2.50
13 TD(i),Cr.Wasp/J.Dollar Pt.2 . . . 2.50
14 TD(i),Cr.Wasp/J.Dollar Pt.3 . . . 2.50
15 TD(i),Secondsight 1.95
Ann.#1 The Blue & the Green . . . 2.50

GREEN HORNET
Now
[2nd Series]

1 V:Johnny Dollar Pt.1 . . . . 2.25
2 V:Johnny Dollar Pt.2 . . . . 2.25
3 V:Johnny Dollar Pt.3 . . . . 2.25
4 V:Ex-Con/Politician 1.95
5 V:Ex-Con/Politician 1.95
6 Arkansas Vigilante 1.95
7 thru 9 The Beast . . . . @1.95
10 Green Hornet-prey 1.95
11 F:Crimson Wasp 1.95
12 Crimson Wasp/Johnny Dollar
Pt.1,polybagged w/Button 2.50
13 TD(i),Wasp/Dollar Pt.2 . . . . . . 2.50
14 TD(i),Wasp/Dollar Pt.3 . . . . . . 2.50
15 TD(i),Secondsight 1.95
16 A:Commissioner Hamiliton . . . 1.95
17 V:Gunslinger 1.95
18 V:Sister-Hood 1.95
19 V:Jewel Thief 1.95
20 F:Paul's Friend 1.95
21 V:Brick Arcade 1.95
22 V:Animal Testers 2.95

Green Hornet Ann. #1 © Now Comics

23 thru 25 Karate Wars . . . . . . @1.95
26 B:City under Siege 1.95
27 W/Card 1.95
28 V:Gangs 1.95
29 V:Gangs 1.95
30 thru 32 . . . . 1.95
Ann.#1 The Blue & the Green . . . 2.50
1993 Ann 2.95

GREEN HORNET, The
Gold Key
February, 1967

1 Bruce Lee,Ph(c) 125.00
2 Ph(c) 100.00
3 Ph(c) 100.00

GREEN HORNET: DARK TOMMORROW
Now

1 thru 3 Hornet Vs Kato . . . . . @2.50

GREEN HORNET: SOLITARY SENTINAL
Now

1 Strike Force 2.50
2 thru 3 . . . . 2.50

GREENHAVEN
Aircel

1 . . . . 3.00
2 . . . . 2.50
3 . . . . 2.00

GRENDEL
Comico

1 . . . . 6.00
1a 2nd printing 2.00
2 . . . . 5.00
3 . . . . 4.00
4 . . . . 3.00
5 . . . . 3.00

Grendel #30 © Comico

6 . . . . 3.00
7 MW 2.50
8 . . . . 2.50
9 . . . . 2.50
10 . . . . 2.50
11 . . . . 2.50
12 . . . . 2.50
13 KSy(c) 2.50
14 KSy(c) 2.50
15 KSy(c) 2.50
16 Mage 4.50
17 . . . . 3.00
18 . . . . 3.00
19 thru 32 . . . . @2.50
33 . . . . 3.50
34 thru 39 . . . . @2.50
40 . . . . 4.00

GRENDEL TALES: FOUR DEVILS, ONE HELL
Dark Horse

1 thru 5 MWg(c),F:Four Grendels 3.25
6 MWg(c),last issue 3.25

GRENDEL TALES: THE DEVIL IN OUR MIDST
Dark Horse

1 MWg(c), ... 2.95

GRENDEL TALES: THE DEVIL'S HAMMER
Dark Horse

1 MWg(a&s),I:Petrus Christus . . . 3.25
2 MWg(a&s),A:P.Christus 3.25
3 MWg(a&s),last issue 3.25

GRENDEL: DEVIL BY THE DEED
Dark Horse

1 MWg,RRa 3.95

GREYLORE
Sirius

1 thru 5 . . . . @2.00

GRIMJACK
First

1 TT Teenage suicide story 3.00
2 TT A:Munden's Bar 2.50
3 TT A:Munden's Bar 2.00
4 TT A:Munden's Bar 2.00
5 TT,JSon,A:Munden's Bar 2.00
6 TT,SR,A:Munden's Bar 2.00
7 TT,A:Munden's Bar 2.00
8 TT,A:Munden's Bar 2.00
9 TT 'My Sins Remembered' . . . 2.00
10 TT,JOy,A:Munden's Bar 2.00
11 TT,A:Munden'sBar 1.75
12 TT,A:Munden'sBar 1.75
13 TT,A:Munden'sBar 1.75
14 TT,A:Munden'sBar 1.75
15 TT,A:Munden'sBar 1.75
16 TT,A:Munden'sBar 1.75
17 TT,A:Munden'sBar 1.75
18 TT,A:Munden'sBar 1.75
19 TT,A:Munden'sBar 1.75
20 TT,A:Munden'sBar 1.75
21 TS,A:Munden's Bar 1.75
22 A:Munden's Bar 1.75
23 TS,A:Munden's Bar 1.75
24 PS,TT,rep.Starslayer10-11 . . . 1.75
25 TS,A:Munden's Bar 1.75
26 1st color TMNTurtles 10.00
27 TS,A:Munden's Bar 1.50
28 TS,A:Munden's Bar 1.50
29 A:Munden's Bar 1.50
30 A:Munden's Bar 1.50
31 A:Munden's Bar 1.50
32 A:Spook 1.50
33 JSon,Munden'sBarChristmas Tale 1.50
34 V:Spook 1.50
35 A:Munden's Bar 1.50
36 3rd Anniv.IssueD:Grimjack . . . 2.50
37 A:Munden's Bar 1.50
38 A:Munden's Bar 1.50
39 R.Grimjack 1.50
40 . . . . 1.75
41 'Weeping Bride' 1.75
42 'Hardball' 1.75
43 'Beneath the Surface' 1.75
44 Shadow Wars 1.75
45 Shadow Wars 1.75
46 Shadow Wars 1.75
47 Shadow Wars,A:EddyCurrent . 1.75
48 Shadow Wars 1.75
49 Shadow Wars 1.75
50 V:Dancer,ShadowWars ends . . 1.75
51 Crossroads tie-in,A:Judah Macabee 2.00
52 . . . . 2.00
53 Time Story 2.00
54 . . . . 2.50
55 FH 2.00
56 FH 2.00
57 FH 2.00
58 FH 2.00
59 FH 2.00
60 FH,Reunion Pt.1 . . . . 2.00
61 FH,Reunion Pt.2 . . . . 2.00
62 FH,Reunion Pt.3 . . . . 2.00
63 FH,A:Justice Drok 2.00
64 FH,O:Multiverse 2.00
65 FH 2.00
66 FH(c),Demon Wars Pt.1 . . . . . 2.00
67 FH(c),Demon Wars Pt.2 . . . . . 2.00
68 Demon Wars Pt.3 . . . . 2.00
69 Demon Wars Pt.4 . . . . 2.00
70 FH,I:Youngblood 2.00
71 FH,A:Youngblood 2.00
72 . . . . 2.00
73 FH(c) 2.00
74 FH(c) 2.00
75 FH,TS,V:The Major 2.00
76 FH,A:Youngblood 2.00
77 FH,A:Youngblood 2.25
78 . . . . 2.25
79 FH,Family Business #1 . . . . . 2.25
80 FH,Family Business #2 . . . . . 2.25
81 FH,Family Business #3 . . . . . 2.25

GRIMJACK CASEFILE
First

1 thru 5 rep. . . . . @1.95

GRIMM'S GHOST STORIES
Gold Key/Whitman
January, 1972

1 . . . . 7.00
2 . . . . 4.00
3 . . . . 4.00
4 . . . . 4.00
5 AW 5.00
6 . . . . 4.00
7 . . . . 4.00
8 AW 5.00
9 . . . . 3.00
10 . . . . 3.00
11 thru 16 . . . . @2.00
17 RC 4.00
18 thru 60, June 1982 . . . . @2.00

GROO
Pacific

1 SA,I:Sage,Taranto 20.00
2 SA,A:Sage 10.00
3 SA,C:Taranto 10.00
4 SA,C:Sage 7.50
5 SA,I:Ahax 7.50
6 SA,I:Gratic 7.50
7 SA,I:Chakaal 7.50
8 SA,A:Chakaal 7.50

Eclipse

Spec.#1 SA,O:Groo,rep Destroyer Duck #1 . . . . 23.00

GROUND ZERO

1 . . . . 1.35

GROUP LARUE
Innovation

1 . . . . 1.95
2 . . . . 1.95
3 . . . . 1.95

GULLIVER'S TRAVELS
Dell Publishing Co.
September-November, 1965

1 . . . . 20.00
2 and 3 . . . . @15.00

GUMBY
Comico

1 AAd,Summer Fun Special 5.00
1 AAd,Winter Fun Special 3.50

GUMBY IN 3-D

Special #1 . . . . 4.00
2 thru 7 . . . . @2.50

GUNSMOKE
Dell Publishing Co.
February, 1956

1 J.Arness Ph(c) all 90.00
2 . . . . 50.00
3 . . . . 50.00
4 . . . . 50.00
5 . . . . 50.00
6 . . . . 45.00
7 . . . . 45.00
8 . . . . 55.00
9 . . . . 55.00
10 AW,RC 60.00
11 . . . . 55.00
12 AW 60.00
13 . . . . 40.00
14 . . . . 40.00
15 . . . . 40.00
16 . . . . 40.00
17 . . . . 40.00
18 . . . . 40.00

19 .... 40.00
20 .... 40.00
21 .... 40.00
22 .... 40.00
23 .... 40.00
24 .... 40.00
25 .... 40.00
26 .... 40.00
27 .... 40.00

HALL OF FAME
J.C. Productions

1 WW,GK,ThunderAgents 1.00
2 WW,GK,ThunderAgents 1.00
3 WW,Thunder Agents 1.00

HALLOWE'EN HORROR
Eclipse

1 .... 1.50

HAMMER OF GOD: PENTATHLON
Dark Horse

1 MiB(s),NV 2.50

HAMMER OF GOD
First

1 thru 4 .... @1.95
Deluxe #1'Sword of Justice Bk#1' 4.95
Deluxe #2'Sword of Justice Bk#2' 4.95

HAMMER OF GOD: BUTCH
Dark Horse

1 MBn, ... 2.50

HAMSTER VICE

10 .... 2.00
3-D #1 .... 2.50

HAND OF FATE
Eclipse

1 I:Artemus Fate 1.75
2 F:Artemis & Alexis 2.00
3 Mystery & Suspense 2.00

HANNA-BARBERA BAND WAGON
Gold Key
October, 1962

1 .... 45.00
2 .... 40.00
3 April, 1963 .... 35.00

HANNA-BARBERA PARADE
Charlton Comics
September, 1971

1 .... 60.00
2 thru 10 December 1972 ... @30.00

HANNA-BARBERA SUPER TV HEROES
Gold Key
April, 1968

1 B:Birdman,Herculiods,Moby Dick, Young Samson & Goliath ... 90.00
2 .... 85.00
3 thru 7 October 1969 ..... @75.00

HARBINGER
Valiant

0 DL,O:Sting,V:Harada, from TPB (Blue Bird Ed.) ... 20.00
0 from coupons 110.00
1 DL,JDx,I:Sting,Torque, Zeppelin,Flamingo,Kris 60.00
1a w/o coupon 30.00
2 DL,JDx,V:Harbinger Foundation, I:Dr.Heyward 40.00
2a w/o coupon 20.00
3 DL,JDx,I:Ax,Rexo, V:Spider Aliens 30.00
3a w/o coupon 15.00
4 DL,JDx,V:Ax,I:Fort, Spikeman,Dog,Bazooka 35.00
4a w/o coupon 18.00
5 DL,JDx,I:Puff,Thumper, A:Solar,V:Harada 25.00
5a w/o coupon 13.00
6 DL,D:Torque,A:Solar, V:Harada,Eggbreakers 20.00
6a w/o coupon 10.00
7 DL,Torque's Funeral 12.00
8 FM(c),DL,JDx,Unity#8, A:Magnus,Eternal Warrior 4.00
9 WS(c),DL,Unity #16, A:Magnus,Armstrong,Rai, Archer,Eternal Warrior 4.00
10 DL,I:H.A.R.D.Corps, Daryl, Shetiqua 10.00
11 DL,V:H.A.R.D.Corps 5.00
12 DL,F:Zeppelin,A:Elfquest 3.00
13 Flamingo Vs. Rock 3.00
14 A:Magnus(Dream Sequence), C:Stronghold 5.00
15 I:Livewire,Stronghold 6.00
16 A:Livewire,Stronghold 3.00
17 HSn,I:Simon 3.00
18 HSn,I:Screen 3.00
19 HSn,I:Caliph 3.00
20 HSn,V:Caliph 3.00
21 I:Pete's Father 2.75
22 HSn,A:Archer & Armstrong ... 2.75
23 HSn,B:Twlight of the Eighth Day 2.75
24 HSn,V:Eggbreakers 2.75
25 HSn,V:Harada,E:Twlight of the Eighth Day 3.75
26 SCh,AdW,I:Jolt,Amazon, Mircowave,Anvil,Sonix 2.75
27 SCh,AdW,Chrismas issue 2.75
28 SCh,AdW,O:Sonix,J:Tyger ... 2.75
29 SCh,AdW,A:Livewire, Stronghold,w/card 2.75
30 SCh,AdW,A:Livewire, Stronghold 2.75
31 SCh,AdW,V:H.A.R.D.Corps ... 2.75
32 SCh,AdW,A:Eternal Warr 2.50
TPB w/#0,rep#1-4 .... 30.00
TPB 2nd Printing w/o #0 .... 9.95

Harbinger #6 © Valiant

HARBINGER FILES: HARADA
Valiant

1 BL,DC,O:Harada 2.75

HARD BOILED
Dark Horse

1 .... 7.50
2 .... 7.00
3 .... 7.00
TPB 14.95

HARDCASE
Malibu-Ultraverse

1 I:Hardcase,D:The Squad 5.00
1a Ultra-Limited 50.00
1b Full Hologram (c) 75.00
2 w/Stranger Trading Card 6.00
3 .... 3.00
4 A:Strangers 3.00
5 BWS,V:Hardwire,BU:Rune 3.00
6 V:Hardwire 2.75
7 ScB,Break-Thru x-over, I:Nanotech,A:Solution 2.25
8 GP,O:Solitare 2.25
9 B:O:Choice,I:Turf 2.25
10 O:Choice 2.25
11 ScB,V:Aladdin 2.25
12 AV,A:Choice 1.95

H.A.R.D. CORPS
Valiant

1 JLe(c),DL,BL,V:Harbinger Foundation, I:Flatline, D:Maniac 7.00
1a Gold Ed. 90.00
2 DL,BL,V:Harb.Foundation 4.00
3 DL,BL,J:Flatline 3.50
4 BL 3.50
5 BCh,BL(i),A:Bloodshot 4.00
5a Comic Defense System Ed. . 28.00
6 MLe,A:Spider Aliens 3.50
7 MLe,V:Spider Aliens, I:Hotshot . 4.00
8 MLe,V:Harada,J:Hotshot 3.00
9 MLe,V:Harada,A:Turok 2.75
10 MLe,A:Turok,V:Dinosaurs 2.50
11 YG,I:Otherman 2.50
12 MLe,V:Otherman 2.50
13 YG,D:Superstar 3.00
14 DvM(s),YG,V:Edie Simkus ... 2.50
15 DvM(s),YG,V:Edie Simkus ... 2.50
16 DvM(s),YG, ... 2.50
17 DvM(s),RLe,V:Armorines 2.50
18 DvM(s),RLe,V:Armorines, w/Valiant Era card 2.50
19 RLe,A:Harada 2.50
20 RLe,V:Harbingers 2.50
21 RLe,New Direction 2.25

HARDY BOYS, THE
Gold Key
April, 1970

1 .... 10.00
2 thru 4 .... @5.00

HARLEM GLOBTROTTERS
Gold Key
April, 1972

1 .... 8.00
2 thru 12, Jan. 1975 .... @3.00

HARLEY RIDER

1 GM,FS 2.00

HARSH REALM
Harris

1 JHi(s), ... 2.95

HARVEY HITS
Harvey Publications
September, 1957

1 The Phantom 150.00

2 Rags Rabbit 10.00
3 Richie Rich 450.00
4 Little Dot's Uncles 80.00
5 Stevie Mazie's Boy Friend . . 10.00
6 JK(c),BP,The Phantom 100.00
7 Wendy the Witch 75.00
8 Sad Sack's Army Life 25.00
9 Richie Rich's Golden Deeds 235.00
10 Little Lotta 60.00
11 Little Audrey Summer Fun . . 50.00
12 The Phantom 75.00
13 Little Dot's Uncles 40.00
14 Herman & Katnip 9.00
15 The Phantom 75.00
16 Wendy the Witch 45.00
17 Sad Sack's Army Life 15.00
18 Buzzy & the Crow 9.00
19 Little Audrey 25.00
20 Casper & Spooky 35.00
21 Wendy the Witch 30.00
22 Sad Sack's Army Life 15.00
23 Wendy the Witch 20.00
24 Little Dot's Uncles 26.00
25 Herman & Katnip 10.00
26 The Phantom 65.00
27 Wendy the Good Little Witch . 25.00
28 Sad Sack's Army Life 10.00
29 Harvey-Toon 18.00
30 Wendy the Witch 20.00
31 Herman & Katnip 5.00
32 Sad Sack's Army Life 10.00
33 Wendy the Witch 20.00
34 Harvey-Toon 10.00
35 Funday Funnies 5.00
36 The Phantom 50.00
37 Casper & Nightmare 14.00
38 Harvey-Toon 9.00
39 Sad Sack's Army Life 6.00
40 Funday Funnies 4.00
41 Herman & Katnip 4.00
42 Harvey-Toon 5.00
43 Sad Sack's Army Life 5.00
44 The Phantom 50.00
45 Casper & Nightmare 12.00
46 Harvey-Toon 5.00
47 Sad Sack's Army Life 3.50
48 The Phantom 50.00
49 Stumbo the Giant 50.00
50 Harvey-Toon 5.00
51 Sad Sack's Army Life 6.00
52 Casper & Nightmare 15.00
53 Harvey-Toons 5.00
54 Stumbo the Giant 25.00
55 Sad Sack's Army Life 4.00
56 Casper & Nightmare 12.00
57 Stumbo the Giant 25.00
58 Sad Sack's Army Life 4.00
59 Casper & Nightmare 12.00
60 Stumbo the Giant 25.00
61 Sad Sack's Army Life 4.00
62 Casper & Nightmare 12.00
63 Stumbo the Giant 22.00
64 Sad Sack's Army Life 4.00
65 Casper & Nightmare 9.00
66 Stumbo the Giant 22.00
67 Sad Sack's Army Life 4.00
68 Casper & Nightmare 9.00
69 Stumbo the Giant 22.00
70 Sad Sack's Army Life 4.00
71 Casper & Nightmare 3.00
72 Stumbo the Giant 22.00
73 Little Sad Sack 4.00
74 Sad Sack's Muttsy 4.00
75 Casper & Nightmare 7.00
76 Little Sad Sack 4.00
77 Sad Sack's Muttsy 4.00
78 Stumbo the Giant 20.00
79 Little Sad Sack 4.00
80 Sad Sack's Muttsy 4.00
81 Little Sad Sack 4.00
82 Sad Sack's Muttsy 4.00
83 Little Sad Sack 4.00
84 Sad Sack's Muttsy 4.00
85 Gabby Gob 4.00
86 G.I. Juniors 4.00
87 Sad Sack's Muttsy 4.00
88 Stumbo the Giant 20.00
89 Sad Sack's Muttsy 4.00
90 Gabby Goo 4.00
91 G.I. Juniors 4.00
92 Sad Sack's Muttsy 4.00
93 Sadie Sack 4.00
94 Gabby Goo 4.00
95 G.I. Juniors 4.00
96 Sad Sack's Muttsy 4.00
97 Gabby Goo 4.00
98 G.I. Juniors 4.00
99 Sad Sack's Muttsy 4.00
100 Gabby Goo 4.00
101 G.I. Juniors 4.00
102 Sad Sack's Muttsy 4.00
103 Gabby Goo 4.00
104 G.I. Juniors 4.00
105 Sad Sack's Muttsy 4.00
106 Gabby Goo 4.00
107 G.I. Juniors 4.00
108 Sad Sack's Muttsy 4.00
109 Gabby Goo 4.00
110 G.I. Juniors 4.00
111 Sad Sack's Muttsy 4.00
112 G.I. Juniors 4.00
113 Sad Sack's Muttsy 4.00
114 G.I. Juniors 4.00
115 Sad Sack's Muttsy 4.00
116 G.I. Juniors 4.00
117 Sad Sack's Muttsy 4.00
118 G.I. Juniors 4.00
119 Sad Sack's Muttsy 4.00
120 G.I. Juniors 4.00
121 Sad Sack's Muttsy 4.00
122 G.I. Juniors, November, 1967 4.00

HAUNT OF FEAR
Gladstone

1 EC Rep. H of F #17,WS#28 . . 3.00
2 EC Rep. H of F #5,WS #29 . . . 2.50

HAUNT OF FEAR
Russ Cochran

1 EC Rep. H of F #15 . . . . 1.50
2 EC Rep. H of F 1.50

HAUNT OF FEAR
Russ Cochran Publ.

1 EC Rep. H of F #14,WS#13 . . 2.25
2 EC Rep. H of F #18,WF#14 . . . 2.00
3 EC Rep. H of F #19,WF#18 . . . 2.00
4 EC Rep. H of F #16,WF#15 . . . 2.00
5 EC Rep. H of F #5,WF#22 . . . 2.00
6 EC Rep. H of F 2.00
7 EC Rep. H of F 2.00

HAVE GUN, WILL TRAVEL
Dell Publishing Co.
August, 1958

1 Richard Boone Ph(c) all 75.00
2 . . . . 50.00
3 . . . . 50.00
4 . . . . 35.00
5 . . . . 35.00
6 . . . . 35.00
7 . . . . 35.00
8 . . . . 35.00
9 . . . . 35.00
10 . . . . 35.00
11 . . . . 35.00
12 . . . . 35.00
13 . . . . 35.00
14 . . . . 35.00

HAWKMOON, COUNT BRASS
First

1 Michael Moorcock adapt. 1.95
2 . . . . 1.95
3 . . . . 1.95
4 . . . . 1.95

HAWKMOON JEWEL IN THE SKULL
First

1 Michael Moorcock adapt. 3.00
2 . . . . 2.50
3 . . . . 2.00
4 . . . . 2.00

Hawkmoon, Sword of the Dawn #2
© First Comics

HAWKMOON, MAD GOD'S AMULET
First

1 Michael Moorcock adapt. 2.00
2 . . . . 1.75
3 . . . . 1.75
4 . . . . 1.75

HAWKMOON, SWORD OF THE DAWN
First

1 Michael Moorcock adapt. 2.00
2 . . . . 1.75
3 . . . . 1.75
4 . . . . 1.75

HAWKMOON, THE RUNESTAFF
First

1 Michael Moorcock adapt. 2.00
2 . . . . 2.00
3 . . . . 1.95
4 . . . . 1.95

HEADMAN
Innovation

1 . . . . 2.50
2 . . . . 2.50

HEAVY METAL MONSTERS
3-D-Zone

1 w/3-D glasses 3.95

HECTOR HEATHCOTE
Gold Key
March, 1964

1 . . . . 30.00

All comics prices listed are for *Near Mint* condition.

HELLBOY: SEEDS OF DESTRUCTION

1 JBy,MMi,AAd,V:Vampire Frog, BU:Monkeyman & O'Brien . . . 2.75
2 MMi(c),JBy,AAd,BU:Monkeyman & O'Brien . . . 2.75
3 MMi(c),JBy,AAd,BU:Monkeyman & O'Brien . . . 2.50

HERBIE
American Comics Group
April-May, 1964

1 . . . 125.00
2 . . . 65.00
3 . . . 60.00
4 . . . 60.00
5 A:Beatles,Dean Martin, Frank Sinatra . . . 80.00
6 . . . 50.00
7 . . . 50.00
8 O:Fat Fury . . . 60.00
9 . . . 50.00
10 . . . 50.00
11 . . . 30.00
12 . . . 30.00
13 . . . 30.00
14 A:Nemesis,Magic Man . . . 30.00
15 thru 22 . . . @30.00
23 February, 1967 . . . 30.00

HERBIE
Dark Horse

1 JBy,reps.& new material . . . 2.50
2 Reps.& new material . . . 2.50

HERCULES
Charlton Comics
October, 1967

1 . . . 10.00
2 thru 7 . . . @5.00
8 scarce . . . 20.00
9 thru 13 Sept. 1969 . . . 4.00

HERO ALLIANCE END OF THE GOLDEN AGE
Innovation

1 RLm . . . 5.00
1A 2nd printing . . . 2.50
2 RLm . . . 4.00
3 RLm . . . 3.00

HERO ALLIANCE JUSTICE MACHINE

1 . . . 2.50

HERO ALLIANCE
Pied Piper

1 . . . 4.00
2 . . . 3.50
3 . . . 3.00
Graphic Novel . . . 10.00

Innovation

1 RLm,BS(c),R:HeroAlliance . . . 6.00
2 RLm,BS(c),Victor vs.Rage . . . 5.00
3 RLm,A:Stargrazers . . . 4.00
4 . . . 3.00
5 RLm(c) . . . 2.50
6 BS(c),RLm pin-up . . . 3.25
7 V:Magnetron . . . 2.50
8 I:Vector . . . 2.50
9 BS(c),V:Apostate . . . 2.50
10 A:Sentry . . . 2.25
11 . . . 2.25
12 I:Bombshell . . . 2.25
13 V:Bombshell . . . 2.25
14 Kris Solo Story . . . 2.25
15 JLA Parody Issue . . . 2.25
16 V:Sepulchre . . . 2.25
17 O:Victor,I&D:Misty . . . 2.25
Annual #1 PS,BS,RLm . . . 3.00

HERO ALLIANCE QUARTERLY
Innovation

1 Hero Alliance stories . . . 2.75
2 inc.'Girl Happy' . . . 2.75
3 inc.'Child Engagement' . . . 2.75
4 . . . 2.75

HERO ALLIANCE SPECIAL
Innovation

1 Hero Alliance update . . . 2.50

HI-SCHOOL ROMANCE DATE BOOK
Harvey Publications
November, 1962

1 BP . . . 18.00
2 . . . 8.00
3 March, 1963 . . . 8.00

HIGH CHAPPARAL
Gold Key
August, 1968

1 . . . 35.00

HIGH SCHOOL CONFIDENTIAL DIARY
Charlton Comics
June, 1960

1 . . . 15.00
2 thru 11 . . . @6.00

Becomes:

CONFIDENTIAL DIARY

12 . . . 5.00
13 thru 17 March, 1963 . . . @3.00

HILLBILLY COMICS
Charlton Comics
August, 1955

1 . . . 25.00
2 thru 4 July 1956 . . . @12.00

HIS NAME IS ROG... ROG 2000
A Plus Comics

1 . . . 1.75

THE HOBBIT
Eclipse

1 . . . 8.00
1a 2ndPrinting . . . 6.00
2 . . . 7.00
2a 2ndPrinting . . . 5.00
3 . . . 6.00

HOGAN'S HEROS
Dell Publishing Co.
June, 1966

1 Ph(c) . . . 40.00
2 Ph(c) . . . 25.00
3 JD,Ph(c) . . . 25.00
4 Ph(c) . . . 18.00
5 Ph(c) . . . 18.00
6 Ph(c) . . . 18.00
7 Ph(c) . . . 18.00
8 . . . 18.00
9 . . . 18.00

HOMAGE STUDIOS
Image

Swimsuit Spec.#1 JLe,WPo, MS . . . 2.25

HONEY WEST
Gold Key
September, 1966

1 . . . 75.00

Honeymooners #4 © Triad Publications

HONEYMOONERS
Lodestone

1 . . . 4.00
5 Mag. . . . 2.50

Triad
[2nd Series]

1 'They Know What They Like' . . 3.00
2 'The Life You Save' . . . 2.50
3 X-mas special,inc.Art Carney interview . . . 3.50
4 'In the Pink' . . . 3.00
5 'Bang, Zoom, To the Moon' . . . 2.00
6 'Everyone Needs a Hero' inc. Will Eisner interview . . . 2.00
7 . . . 2.00
8 . . . 2.00
9 Jack Davis(c) . . . 4.50
10 thru 13 . . . @2.00

HOT ROD RACERS
Charlton Comics
December, 1964

1 . . . 35.00
2 thru 5 . . . @20.00
6 thru 15 July 1967 . . . @15.00

HOT STUFF, THE LITTLE DEVIL
Harvey Publications
October, 1967

1 . . . 175.00
2 1st Stumbo the Giant . . . 100.00
3 thru 5 . . . @75.00
6 thru 10 . . . @50.00
11 thru 20 . . . @30.00
21 thru 40 . . . @20.00
41 thru 60 . . . @10.00
61 thru 100 . . . @5.00
101 thru 105 . . . @4.00
106 thru 112 52 pg Giants . . . @5.00
113 thru 172 . . . @2.00

HOT STUFF SIZZLERS
Harvey Publications
July, 1960

1 B:68 pgs . . . 75.00
2 thru 5 . . . @30.00
6 thru 10 . . . @15.00
11 thru 20 . . . @12.00
21 thru 30 . . . @10.00
31 thru 44 . . . @5.00
45 E:68 pgs . . . 4.00

46 thru 50 . . . . @3.00
51 thru 59 . . . . @2.50

HOTSHOTS

1 thru 4 . . . . @1.95

HOTSPUR
Eclipse

1 RT(i),I:Josef Quist 1.75
2 RT(i),Amulet of Kothique Stolen 1.75
3 RT(i),Curse of the SexGoddess 1.75

HOWARD CHAYKIN'S AMERICAN FLAGG!
First

1 thru 9 . . . . @1.75
10 thru 12 . . . . @1.95

H.P.LOVECRAFT'S CTHULHU
Millenium

1 I:Miskatonic Project,V:Mi-Go . . 2.50
2 Arkham, trading cards 2.50

HUCK & YOGI JAMBOREE
Dell Publishing Co.
March, 1961

1 . . . . 50.00

HUCKLEBERRY HOUND
Charlton
November, 1970

1 . . . . 15.00
2 thru 7 . . . . @7.50
3 Jan., 1972 . . . . 8.00

HUCKLEBERRY HOUND
Dell Publishing Co.
May-July, 1959

1 . . . . 50.00
2 . . . . 35.00
3 . . . . 35.00
4 . . . . 35.00
5 . . . . 35.00
6 . . . . 35.00
7 . . . . 35.00
8 . . . . 25.00
9 . . . . 25.00
10 . . . . 25.00
11 . . . . 20.00
12 . . . . 20.00
13 . . . . 20.00
14 . . . . 20.00
15 . . . . 20.00
16 . . . . 20.00
17 . . . . 20.00

Gold Key

18 Chuckleberry Tales 35.00
19 Chuckleberry Tales 35.00
20 Chuckleberry Tales 12.00
21 . . . . 12.00
22 . . . . 12.00
23 . . . . 12.00
24 . . . . 12.00
25 . . . . 12.00
26 . . . . 12.00
27 . . . . 12.00
28 . . . . 12.00
29 . . . . 12.00
30 . . . . 12.00
31 . . . . 10.00
32 . . . . 10.00
33 . . . . 10.00
34 . . . . 10.00
35 . . . . 10.00
36 . . . . 10.00
37 rep. 10.00
38 . . . . 10.00
39 . . . . 10.00
40 . . . . 10.00
41 . . . . 10.00
42 . . . . 10.00
43 . . . . 10.00

HUEY, DEWEY & LOUIE JUNIOR WOODCHUCKS
Gold Key
August, 1966

1 . . . . 30.00
2 thru 5 . . . . @20.00
6 thru 17 . . . . @15.00
18 . . . . 7.00
19 thru 25 . . . . @8.00
26 thru 30 . . . . @5.00
31 thru 57 . . . . @4.00
58 . . . . 5.00
59 . . . . 5.00
60 thru 80 . . . . @4.00
81 1984 . . . . 4.00

HYBRIDS
Continuity

0 Deathwatch 2000 prologue . . . 5.00
1 Deathwatch 2000 pt.4 . . . . 2.50
2 thru 3 . . . . 2.50
4 A:Valeria 2.50

I DREAM OF JEANNIE
Dell Publishing Co.
April, 1965

1 Ph(c),B.Eden 60.00
2 Ph(c),B.Eden 55.00

I SPY
Gold Key
August, 1966

1 Bill Cosby Ph(c) 125.00
2 Ph(c) 75.00
3 thru 4 AMc,Ph(c) . . . . @80.00
5 thru 6 Ph(c) Sept.1968 . . . @75.00

I'M DICKENS – HE'S FENSTER
Dell Publishing Co.
May-July, 1963

1 Ph(c) 25.00
2 Ph(c) 25.00

ICICLE
Hero Graphics

1 A:Flare,Lady Arcane,
V:Eraserhead 4.95

IMAGE ZERO
Image Comics

0 I:Troll,Deathtrap,Pin-ups,rep.
Savage Dragon #4,O:Stryker,
F:Shadowhawk 40.00

IMAGES OF SHADOWHAWK
Image

1 KG,V:Trencher 2.25

IMP

1 . . . . 2.25

INDIANA JONES AND THE ARMS OF GOLD
Dark Horse

1 In South America 2.75
2 In South America 2.75
3 V:Incan Gods 2.75

INDIANA JONES AND THE FATE OF ATLANTIS
Dark Horse

1 DBa,Search for S.Hapgood . . . 5.00
1a 2nd printing 3.00
2 DBa,Lost Dialogue of Plato . . . 3.00
3 Map Room of Atlantis 3.00
4 Atlantis, Last issue 3.00

Indiana Jones and the Fate of Atlantis #1 © Dark Horse Comics

INDIANA JONES: THUNDER IN THE ORIENT
Dark Horse

1 DBa(a&s),in Tripoli 2.75
2 DBa(a&s),Muzzad Ram 2.75
3 DBa(a&s),V:Sgt.Itaki 2.75
4 DBa(a&s),In Hindu Kush 2.75
5 DBa(a&s),V:Japanese Army . . 2.75
6 DBa(a&s),last issue 2.75

INTERVIEW WITH A VAMPIRE
Innovation

1 based on novel,preq.to
Vampire Chronicles 3.50
2 . . . . 3.00
3 Death & Betrayal 3.00
4 . . . . 3.00
5 D:Lestat 2.50
6 Transylvania Revelation 2.50
7 Louis & Claudia in Paris 2.50
8 thru 10 . . . . @2.50
11 . . . . 2.50

INTERVIEW WITH A VAMPIRE
Innovation

1 based on novel, preq. to
Vampire Chronicles 3.50
2 . . . . 3.00
3 Death & Betrayal 3.00
4 . . . . 3.00
5 D:Lestat 2.50
6 Transylvania Revelation 2.50
7 Louis & Claudia in Paris 2.50

INTIMATE
Charlton Comics
December, 1957

1 . . . . 8.00
2 and 3 . . . . @8.00

Becomes:

TEEN-AGE LOVE

4 . . . . 8.00
5 thru 9 . . . . @4.00

10 thru 35 ... @3.00
36 thru 96 ... @1.00

INTRUDER
TSR

1 thru 8 ... @2.95

INVADERS FROM HOME
Piranha Press

1 thru 6 ... @2.50

INVADERS, THE
Gold Key
October, 1967

1 Ph(c),DSp ... 45.00
2 Ph(c),DSp ... 30.00
3 Ph(c),DSp ... 30.00
4 Ph(c),DSp ... 30.00

INVINCIBLE FOUR OF KUNG FU & NINJA
Victory

1 ... 2.75
2 ... 2.50
3 ... 2.50
4 ... 1.80
5 thru 11 ... @2.00

IRON HORSE
Dell Publishing Co.
March, 1967

1 ... 12.00
2 ... 12.00

IRON MARSHAL
Jademan

1 ... 2.00
2 ... 1.75
3 ... 1.75
4 ... 1.75
5 ... 1.75
6 V:Bloody Duke ... 1.75
7 ... 1.75
8 ... 1.75
9 The Unicorn Sword ... 1.75
10 The Great Thor ... 1.75
11 A:Exterminator ... 1.75
12 Bloddy Duke vs. Exterminator . 1.75
13 Secret of Unicorn Supreme ... 1.75
14 A:The Great Thor ... 1.75
15 A:The Great Thor ... 1.75
16 V:Tienway Champ ... 1.75
17 thru 20 ... 1.75
21 Bloody Duke wounded ... 1.75
22 A:Great Thor ... 1.75
23 ... 1.75
24 ... 1.75
25 ... 1.75
26 Iron Marshal Betrayed ... 1.75
27 ... 1.75
28 ... 1.75
29 ... 1.75
30 ... 1.75

IRREGULARS, THE BATTLETECH Miniseries
Blackthorne

1 ... 1.75
2 ... 1.75
3 B&W ... 1.75

IRUKASHI

1 ... 1.75

IT! TERROR FROM BEYOND SPACE
Millenium

1 ... 2.50
2 ... 2.50

IT'S ABOUT TIME
Gold Key
January, 1967

1 Ph(c) ... 25.00

ITCHY & SCRATCHY
Bongo Comics

1 DaC(s), ... 2.25
2 DaC(s), ... 2.25

IVANHOE
Dell Publishing Co.
July-September, 1963

1 ... 25.00

JACK HUNTER
Blackthorne

1 ... 1.25
2 ... 1.25
3 ... 1.25

JADEMAN COLLECTION

1 ... 4.50
2 ... 3.00
3 ... 2.50
4 ... 2.50
5 ... 2.50

JADEMAN KUNG FU SPECIAL

1 I:Oriental Heroes, Blood Sword, Drunken Fist ... 5.00

JAKE TRASH
Aircel

1 thru 3 ... @2.00

JAMES BOND 007
Eclipse

1 MGr,PerfectBound ... 5.50
2 MGr ... 5.00
3 MGr,end series ... 5.00
Licence to Kill,Gr.Nov.MGr l/o ... 8.00

JAMES BOND 007: SERPENT'S TOOTH
Dark Horse

1 PG,V:Indigo ... 5.50
2 PG,V:Indigo ... 5.00
3 PG ... 5.25

JAMES BOND 007: SHATTERED HELIX
Dark Horse

1 V:Cerberus ... 2.50

JAMES BOND 007: A SILENT ARMAGEDDON
Dark Horse

1 V:Troy ... 3.25
2 V:Omega ... 3.25
3 V:Omega ... 3.25

JAM SPECIAL
Comico

1 ... 2.50

JASON GOES TO HELL
Topps

1 Movie adapt.,w/card ... 3.25
2 Movie adapt.,w/card ... 3.25

JET DREAM
Gold Key
June, 1968

1 ... 20.00

JETSONS, THE
Gold Key
January, 1963

1 ... 175.00
2 ... 100.00
3 thru 10 ... @75.00
11 thru 20 ... @50.00
21 thru 36 October 1970 ... @35.00

JETSONS, THE
Charlton Comics
November, 1970

1 ... 55.00
2 ... 31.00
3 thru 10 ... @20.00
11 thru 20 December 1973 .. @15.00

JEZEBEL JADE
Comico

1 AKu,A:Race Bannon ... 2.00
2 AKu ... 2.00
3 AKu ... 2.00

JIGSAW
Harvey Publications
September, 1966

1 ... 6.00
2 ... 3.50

J. N. Williamson's Masques #2
© Innovation

J. N. WILLIAMSON'S MASQUES
Innovation

1 TV,From horror anthology ... 4.95
2 Olivia(c) inc.Better Than One ... 4.95

JOHN BOLTON, HALLS OF HORROR
Eclipse

1 JBo ... 1.75
2 JBo ... 1.75

JOHN F. KENNEDY LIFE STORY
(WITH 2 REPRINTS)
Dell Publishing Co.
August-October, 1964

1 ... 35.00
2 ... 25.00

3 ... 25.00

JOHN LAW
Eclipse

1 WE ... 2.00

JOHNNY GAMBIT

1 ... 1.75

JOHNNY JASON TEEN REPORTER
Dell Publishing Co.
February-April, 1962

1 ... 10.00
2 ... 10.00

JOHNNY NEMO
Eclipse

1 I:Johnny Nemo ... 2.00
2 ... 2.00
3 F:Sindy Shade ... 2.50

JOHN STEELE SECRET AGENT
Gold Key
December, 1964

1 ... 65.00

JONNY DEMON
Dark Horse

1 SL(c),KBk,NV ... 2.50

JONNY QUEST
Gold Key
December, 1964

1 TV show ... 135.00

JONNY QUEST
Comico
June, 1986

1 DW,SR,A:Dr.Zin ... 4.50
2 WP/JSon,O:RaceBannon ... 3.50
3 DSt(c) ... 3.00
4 TY/AW,DSt(i) ... 2.50
5 DSt(c)A:JezebelJade ... 2.50
6 AKu ... 2.00
7 ... 2.00
8 KSy ... 2.00
9 MA ... 2.00
10 King Richard III ... 2.00
11 JSon,BSz(c) ... 1.50
12 DSp ... 1.50
12 DSp ... 1.50
13 CI ... 1.50
14 ... 1.50
15 thru 31 ... @1.75
Special #1 ... 1.75
Special #2 ... 1.75

JONNY QUEST CLASSICS
Comico

1 DW ... 2.00
2 DW,O:Hadji ... 2.00
3 DW ... 2.00

JON SABLE
First

1 MGr,A:President ... 4.50
2 MGr,Alcohol Issue ... 3.50
3 MGr,O:Jon Sable ... 3.00
4 MGr,O:Jon Sable ... 3.00
5 MGr,O:Jon Sable ... 3.00
6 MGr,O:Jon Sable ... 3.00
7 MGr,The Target ... 2.50
8 MGr,Nuclear Energy ... 2.50
9 MGr,Nuclear Energy ... 2.50
10 MGr,Tripitych ... 2.50
11 MGr,I:Maggie ... 2.50
12 MGr,Vietnam ... 2.50
13 MGr,Vietnam ... 2.50
14 MGr,East Germany ... 2.50
15 MGr,Nicaragua ... 2.50
16 MGr,A:Maggie ... 2.50
17 MGr,1984 Olympics ... 2.50
18 MGr,1984 Olympics ... 2.50
19 MGr,,The Widow ... 2.50
20 MGr,The Rookie ... 2.50
21 MGr,Africa ... 2.25
22 MGr,V:Sparrow ... 2.25
23 MGr,V:Sparrow ... 2.25
24 MGr,V:Sparrow ... 2.25
25 MGr,Shatter ... 3.00
26 MGr,Shatter ... 3.00
27 MGr,Shatter ... 3.00
28 MGr,Shatter ... 3.00
29 MGr,Shatter ... 3.00
30 MGr,Shatter ... 2.25

Jon Sable #33 © First Comics

31 MGr,Nicaragua ... 2.00
32 MGr,Nicaragua ... 2.00
33 MGr,SA,Leprechauns ... 2.25
34 MGr,Indians ... 2.00
35 MGr,Indians ... 2.00
36 MGr,Africa ... 2.00
37 MGr,Africa ... 2.00
38 MGr,Africa ... 2.00
39 MGr,Africa ... 2.00
40 MGr,1st Case ... 2.00
41 MGr,1st Case ... 2.00
42 MGr,V:Sparrow ... 2.00
43 MGr,V:Sparrow ... 2.00
44 Hard Way ... 2.00
45 Hard Way II ... 2.00
46 MM,The Tower pt.1 ... 2.00
47 MM,The Tower pt.2 ... 2.00
48 MM,Prince Charles ... 2.00
49 MM,Prince Charles ... 2.00
50 A:Maggie the Cat ... 2.00
51 Jon Sable,babysitter pt.1 ... 2.00
52 Jon Sable,babysitter pt.2 ... 2.00
53 MGr. ... 2.00
54 Jacklight pt.1 ... 2.00
55 Jacklight pt.2 ... 2.00
56 Jacklight pt.3 ... 2.00

JOSIE
Archie Publications
February, 1963

1 ... 100.00
2 ... 50.00
3 ... 25.00
4 ... 20.00
5 ... 25.00
6 thru 10 ... @15.00
11 thru 20 ... @12.00
21 thru 30 ... @7.00
31 thru 40 ... @5.00
41 thru 54 ... @4.00
55 thru 74 ... @2.00
75 thru 105 ... @1.00
106 October, 1962 ... 1.00

JUDGE COLT
Gold Key
October, 1969

1 ... 6.50
2 ... 4.50
3 ... 4.50
4 September, 1980 ... 4.50

Judge Dredd #29 © Eagle Comics

JUDGE DREDD
Eagle

1 BB,I:Judge Death(in USA) ... 13.00
2 BB(c),V:Perps ... 9.00
3 BB(c),V:Perps ... 7.00
4 BB(c),V:Perps ... 7.00
5 BB(c),V:Perps ... 7.00
6 BB(c),V:Perps ... 7.00
7 BB(c),V:Perps ... 7.00
8 BB(c),V:Perps ... 7.00
9 BB(c),V:Perps ... 7.00
10 BB(c),V:Perps ... 7.00
11 BB(c) ... 5.00
12 BB(c) ... 5.00
13 BB(c) ... 5.00
14 BB(c) ... 5.00
15 BB(c) ... 5.00
16 BB(c) ... 5.00
17 BB(c) ... 5.00
18 BB(c) ... 5.00
19 BB(c) ... 5.00
20 BB(c) ... 5.00
21 BB(c) ... 5.00
22 BB(c),V:Perps ... 3.00
23 BB(c),V:Perps ... 3.00
24 BB(c),V:Perps ... 3.00
25 BB(c),V:Perps ... 3.00
26 BB(c),V:Perps ... 3.00
27 BB(c),V:Perps ... 3.00
28 A:Judge Anderson,V:Megaman ... 2.75
29 A:Monty, the guinea pig ... 2.75
30 V:Perps ... 2.75
31 Destiny's Angel, Pt. 1 ... 2.75
32 Destiny's Angel, Pt. 2 ... 2.75
33 V:League of Fatties ... 2.75

34 V:Executioner 2.75

JUDGE DREDD
Quality

1 Cry of the Werewolf Pt.1 . . . . . 5.00
2 Cry of the Werewolf Pt.2 . . . . . 4.00
3 Anti-smoking 3.00
4 Wreckers 3.00
5 Highwayman 3.00
6 . . . . 2.50
7 . . . . 2.50
8 . . . . 2.50
9 . . . . 2.50
10 . . . . 2.50
11 . . . . 2.50
12 Starborn Thing, Pt.1 . . . . 2.50
13 Starborn Thing, Pt.2 . . . . 2.50
14 BB, V:50 foot woman 2.50
15 City of the Damned Pt.1 . . . . . 2.50
16 City of the Damned Pt.2 . . . . . 2.50
17 City of the Damned conc. 2.50
18 V:Mean Machine Angel 2.50
19 Dredd Angel 2.50
20 V:Perps 2.50
21 V:Perps 2.50
22/23 Booby Trap 2.50
24 Junk food fiasco 2.50
25/26 V:Perps 2.50
27 V:Perps 2.50
28 Dredd Syndrome 2.50
29 V:Perps 2.50
30 V:Perps 2.50
31 Hunt Pudge Dempsey's killer . 2.50
32 V:Mutated Sewer Alligator 2.50
33 V:Perps 2.50
34 V:Executioner 2.25
35 V:Shojan 2.25
36 V:Shojan 2.25
37 V:Perps 2.25
38 V:Perps 2.25
39 V:Perps 2.00
40 V:Perps 2.00
41 V:Perps 2.00
42 V:Perps 2.00
43 V:Perps 2.00
44 V:Perps 2.00
45 V:DNA Man 2.00
46 Genie lamp sty 2.00
47 V:Perps 2.00
48 Murder in Mega-City One 2.00
49 V:Perps 2.00
50 V:Perps 2.00
51 V:Perps 2.00
52 V:Perps 2.00
53 V:Perps 2.00
54 V:Perps 2.00
55 V:Perps 1.75
56 inc.JudgeDredd Postcards . . . 1.75
57 V:Perps 1.75
58 V:370lb Maniac 1.75
59 V:Perps 1.95
60 Social Misfit 1.95
61 V:Perps 1.95
62 . . . . 1.95
63 Mutants from the Badlands . . . 1.95
64 . . . . 1.95
65 . . . . 1.95
66 Wit and wisdom of Dredd 1.95
67 V:Otto Sump 1.95
68 V:Otto Sump 1.95
69 . . . . 1.95
70 Dinosaurs in Mega City 1 . . . . 1.95
71 . . . . 1.95
72 Pirates o/t Black Atlantic 1.95
73 . . . . 1.95
74 . . . . 1.95
75 . . . . 1.95
76 Diary of a Mad Citizen 1.95
TPB:Democracy Now 10.95
TPB:Rapture 12.95
Judge Dredd Special #1 . . . . 2.50

JUDGE DREDD: AMERICA
Fleetway

1 I:America 2.95

JUDGE DREDD: JUDGE CHILD QUEST
Eagle

1 . . . . 2.50
2 . . . . 2.50
3 . . . . 2.50
4 . . . . 2.50
5 . . . . 2.50

JUDGE DREDD'S CRIME FILE
Eagle

1 JBy 2.50
2 . . . . 2.50
3 . . . . 2.50
4 . . . . 2.50
5 . . . . 2.50
6 . . . . 2.50

Quality
(Prestige format)

1 A:Rogue Trooper 6.50
2 IG,V:Fatties, Energy Vampires & Super Fleas 5.95
3 Battles foes from dead A:Judge Anderson 5.95

JUDGE DREDD'S EARLY CASES
Eagle

1 Robot Wars, Pt.1 . . . . 2.50
2 Robot Wars, Pt.2 . . . . 2.50
3 V:Perps 2.50
4 IG, Judge Giant 2.50
5 V:Perps 2.50
6 V:Judge killing car Elvis 2.50

JUDGE DREDD'S HARDCASE PAPERS

1 V:The Tarantula 6.50
2 Junkies & Psychos 5.95
3 Crime Call Vid. Show 5.95
4 'Real Coffee',A:Johnny Alpha . . 5.95

JUDGE DREDD: THE MEGAZINE

1 Midnite's Children Pt.1 A:Chopper, Young Death 5.25
2 Midnite's Children Pt.2 . . . . . . 4.95

JUDGE PARKER
Argo
February, 1956

1 . . . . 20.00
2 . . . . 11.00

JUDGMENT DAY
Lightning Comics

1 B:JZy(s),KIK,V:Razorr,Rift, Nightmare 5.00
1a Gold Prism(c) 15.00
1b Purple Prism(c) 30.00
1c Misprint,Red Prism(c), Bloodfire Credits inside 40.00
1d Misprint,Gold Prism(c), Bloodfire Credits inside 40.00
1e Misprint,Green Prism(c), Bloodfire Credits inside 40.00
1f B&W Promo Ed. Gold ink . . . 12.50
1g B&W Promo Ed. Platinum Ed. 25.00
2 TLw,I:War Party,BU:Perg, w/card 3.50
3 ErP,O:X-Treme 3.25
4 ErP,In Hell 3.25
5 TLw,In Hell 3.25
6 TLw,I:Red Front,O:Salurio 3.25
7 O:Safeguard 3.25

JUDOMASTER
Charlton Comics

(Special War Series #4)
I:Judomaster 15.00
89 FMc,War stories begin 7.00
89 (90) FMc,A:Thunderbolt 6.00
91 FMc,DG,A:Sarge Steel 6.00
92 FMc,DG,A:Sarge Steel 6.00
93 FMc,DG,I:Tiger 6.00
94 FMc,DG,A:Sarge Steel 6.00
95 FMc,DG,A:Sarge Steel 5.00
96 FMc,DG,A:Sarge Steel 5.00
97 FMc,A:Sarge Steel 4.00
98 FMc,A:Sarge Steel 4.00

JUGHEAD AS CAPTAIN HERO
Archie Publications
October, 1966

1 . . . . 25.00
2 . . . . 15.00
3 thru 7 . . . . @10.00

JUGHEAD'S FANTASY
Archie Publications
August, 1960

1 . . . . 80.00
2 . . . . 60.00
3 . . . . 45.00

JUGHEAD'S JOKES
Archie Publications
August, 1967

1 . . . . 26.00
2 . . . . 14.00
3 thru 5 . . . . @7.00
6 thru 10 . . . . @5.00
11 thru 30 . . . . @2.00
31 thru 77 . . . . @1.00
78 September, 1982 . . . . 1.00

JUGHEAD WITH ARCHIE DIGEST
Archie Publications
March, 1974

1 . . . . 8.00
2 . . . . 4.00
3 thru 10 . . . . @2.00
11 thru 91 . . . . 1.00

JUNGLE COMICS
Blackthorne

1 DSt(c) 2.00
2 . . . . 2.00
3 . . . . 2.00

JUNGLE TALES OF TARZAN
Charlton Comics
December, 1964

1 . . . . 25.00
2 . . . . 20.00
3 . . . . 20.00
4 July, 1965 . . . . 20.00

JUNGLE WAR STORIES
Dell Publishing Co.
July-September, 1962

1 P(c) all 15.00
2 . . . . 8.00
3 . . . . 8.00
4 . . . . 8.00
5 . . . . 8.00
6 . . . . 8.00
7 . . . . 8.00
8 . . . . 8.00
9 . . . . 8.00
10 . . . . 8.00
11 . . . . 8.00

Becomes:

GUERRILLA WAR
12 . . . . 7.00
13 . . . . 7.00
14 . . . . 7.00

JUNIOR WOODCHUCKS
Walt Disney
1 CB,'Bubbleweight Champ' 1.50
2 CB,'Swamp of no Return' 1.50
3 'Rescue Run-Around' 1.50
4 'Cave Caper' 1.50

JURASSIC PARK
Topps
1 Movie Adapt.,w/card 6.00
1a Newsstand Ed. 4.00
2 Movie Adapt.,w/card 3.25
2a Newsstand Ed. 2.75
3 Movie Adapt.,w/card 3.25
3a Newsstand Ed. 2.75
4 Movie Adapt.,w/card 3.25
4a Newsstand Ed. 2.75

JURASSIC PARK: RAPTORS ATTACK
Topps
1 SEt(s), ... 2.75
2 SEt(s), ... 2.75

Justice Machine #2 © Comico

JUSTICE MACHINE
Comico
1 MGu 2.50
2 MGu 2.00
3 thru 14 MGu . . . . @1.50
15 thru 27 MGu . . . . @1.75
28 MGu 1.95
29 MGu,IW 1.95
Ann.#1:BWG,I:Elementals,
A: Thunder Agents 20.00
Ann.#1 . . . . 2.50
SummerSpectacular 1 . . . . 2.75
1 JBy(c) Mag size,B&W 30.00
2 MGu,Mag size,B&W 16.00
3 MGu,Mag size,B&W 10.00
4 MGu,Bluecobalt 8.00
5 MGu 7.00

MINI SERIES
1 thru 4 F:Elementals . . . . @1.95

JUSTICE MACHINE: CHIMERA CONSPIRACY

Millenium
1 AH,R&N:Justice Machine,
wraparound cover 2.50

JUST MARRIED
Charlton Comics
January, 1958
1 . . . . 25.00
2 . . . . 15.00
3 thru 10 . . . . @10.00
11 thru 30 . . . . @8.00
31 thru 113 . . . . @4.00
114 December, 1976 . . . . 4.00

KATO OF THE GREEN HORNET
Now
1 BA,1st Kato solo story 2.50
2 BA,Kato in China contd. 2.50
3 Kato in China contd 2.50
4 Final Issue 2.50

Kato II #1 © Now Comics

KATO II
Now
1 VM,JSh,A:Karthage 2.50
2 VM,JSh,V:Karthage 2.50
3 VM,JSh,V:Karthage 2.50

KATY KEENE FASHION BOOK MAGAZINE
Archie Publications
1955
1 . . . . 275.00
2 . . . . 175.00
3 thru 10 not published
11 thru 18 . . . . @125.00
19 . . . . 100.00
20 . . . . 90.00
21 . . . . 100.00
22 . . . . 100.00
23 Winter 1958-59 . . . . 100.00

KATY KEENE PINUP PARADE
Archie Publications
1955
1 . . . . 300.00
2 . . . . 175.00
3 . . . . 150.00
4 . . . . 150.00
5 . . . . 150.00
6 . . . . 125.00
7 . . . . 125.00
8 . . . . 125.00
9 . . . . 125.00
10 . . . . 125.00
11 . . . . 165.00
12 . . . . 125.00
13 . . . . 125.00
14 . . . . 125.00
15 September, 1961 . . . . 300.00

KELLY GREEN
Eclipse
1 SDr,O:Kelly Green 2.50
2 SDr,'One,Two,Three' 2.00
3 SDr,'Million Dollar Hit' 2.00
4 SDr,Rare 4.00

KELVIN MACE
Vortex
1 . . . . 6.50
1a 2nd printing 1.75
2 . . . . 4.00

KILLER INSTINCT TOUR BOOK
Image
1 All Homage Artist,I:Crusade . . . 5.00

KILLER TALES
Eclipse
1 . . . . 1.75

KING LEONARDO AND HIS SHORT SUBJECTS
Dell Publishing Co.
November-January, 1961-62
1 . . . . 75.00
2 . . . . 55.00
3 . . . . 55.00
4 . . . . 55.00

KING LOUIE & MOWGLI
Gold Key
May, 1968
1 . . . . 18.00

KING OF DIAMONDS
Dell Publishing Co.
July-September, 1962
1 Ph(c) 30.00

KINGS OF THE NIGHT
Dark Horse
1 . . . . 2.25
2 end Mini-Series 2.25

KIT KARTER
Dell Publishing Co.
May-July, 1962
1 . . . . 15.00

KNIGHTS OF THE ROUND TABLE
Dell Publishing Co.
November-January, 1963-4
1 P(c) 25.00

KOL MANIQUE RENAISSANCE
1 . . . . 1.50
2 . . . . 1.50

KONA
Dell Publishing Co.
February-April, 1962
1 P(c) all,SG 45.00
2 SG 20.00

3 SG 20.00
4 SG,B:Anak 20.00
5 SG 20.00
6 SG 20.00
7 SG 20.00
8 SG 20.00
9 SG 20.00
10 SG 20.00
11 SG 15.00
12 SG 15.00
13 SG 15.00
14 SG 15.00
15 SG 15.00
16 SG 15.00
17 SG 15.00
18 SG 15.00
19 SG 15.00
20 SG 15.00
21 SG 15.00

KONGA
Charlton Comics
1960

1 SD,DG(c) 200.00
2 DG(c) 100.00
3 SD 75.00
4 SD 75.00
5 SD 75.00
6 thru 15 SD @55.00
16 thru 22 @30.00
23 November, 1965 30.00

KONGA'S REVENGE
Charlton Comics

2 Summer, 1962 30.00
3 SD,Fall, 1964 40.00
1 December, 1968 17.00

KOOKIE
Dell Publishing Co.
February-April, 1962

1 55.00
2 50.00

KORAK, SON OF TARZAN
Gold Key
January, 1964

1 40.00
2 thru 11 @30.00
12 thru 21 @20.00
22 thru 30 @10.00
31 thru 40 @8.00
41 thru 44 @5.00
45 January, 1972 5.00

KULL IN 3-D
Blackthorne

1 2.50
2 2.50
3 2.50

KUNG FU & NINJA

1 1.80
2 1.80
3 1.80
4 1.80

LAD: A DOG
Dell Publishing Co.
1961

1 30.00
2 25.00

LADY ARCANE
Hero Graphics

1 A: Flare,BU:O:Giant 4.95
2 thru 3 2.95

LADY DEATH

1 BnP, 12.00
2 BnP, 8.00
3 BnP, 5.50

LARS OF MARS
Eclipse

1 3-D MA 2.50

LASER ERASER & PRESSBUTTON
Eclipse

1 GL,R:Laser Eraser 1.75
2 GL 1.75
3 GL,CK,'Tsultrine' 1.75
4 MC,'Death' 1.75
5 MC,JRy,'Gates of Hell' .95
6 'Corsairs of Illunium' .95
3-D#1 MC,GL(c),'Triple Cross' 1.50
9

LASH LARUE WESTERN
AC Comics

1 3.50
Annual 2.95

LAST OF THE VIKING HEROES
Genesis West

1 JK 4.00
2 JK 3.50
3 3.00
4 2.50
5A sexy cover 3.00
5B mild cover 2.50
6 2.50
7 AA(c) 3.50
8 2.25
9 Great Battle of Nidhogger 2.50
10 'Death Among the Heroes' 2.50
Summer Spec.#1 FF,JK 3.50
Summer Spec.#2 3.00
Summer Spec.#3,A:TMNT 2.50

LAUREL AND HARDY
Dell Publishing Co.
October, 1962

1 40.00
2 30.00
3 30.00
4 30.00

LAUREL & HARDY
Gold Key
January, 1967

1 25.00
2 October, 1967 25.00

LAWMAN
Dell Publishing Co.
February, 1959

1 Ph(c) all 65.00
2 40.00
3 ATh 45.00
4 30.00
5 30.00
6 30.00
7 30.00
8 30.00
9 30.00
10 30.00
11 30.00

LAW OF DREDD
Quality

1 V:Perps 3.00
2 BB,Lunar Olympics 2.50
3 BB,V:Judge Death 2.00
4 V:Father Earth 2.00
5 Cursed Earth 2.00
6 V:Perps 2.25
7 V:Perps 2.25

Fleetway

8 Blockmania 2.25
9 BB,DGi,Framed for murders 2.25
10 BB,Day the Law Died Pt.1 1.50
11 BB,Day the Law Died Pt.2 1.50
12 BB,V:Judge Cal 1.75
13 V:Judge Caligula 1.75
14 BB, V:Perps 1.75
15 Under investigation 1.75
16 V:Alien mercenary 1.75
17 thru 24 @1.75
25 Ugly Clinic 1.75
26 Judge Dredd & Gavel? 1.75
27 Cycles,Lunatics & Graffiti Guerillas 1.75
28 Cadet Training Mission 1.75
29 'Guinea Pig that changed the world 1.95
30 Meka-City,V:Robot 1.95
31 Iso-Block 666 1.95
32 Missing Game Show Hosts 1.95
33 League of Fatties, Final Issue 1.95

LAZARUS CHURCHYARD
Tundra

1 From UK Blast anthology 4.50
2 Goodnight Ladies 4.50

League of Champions
© Hero Graphics

LEAGUE OF CHAMPIONS
Hero Graphics
{Cont. from Champions #12}

1 Olympus Saga #4 2.95
2 Olympus Saga #5,O:Malice 2.95
3 Olympus Saga ends 2.95

LEATHERFACE
North Star

1 2.75
2 2.75
3 2.75

LEGACY
Majestic

1 I:Legacy 2.25

LEGEND OF CUSTER, THE
Dell Publishing Co.

January, 1968
1 Ph(c) 15.00

LEGEND OF SLEEPY HOLLOW
Tundra
One shot.BHa,W.Irving adapt. . . . 6.95

LEGENDS OF JESSE JAMES, THE
Gold Key
February, 1966
1 . . . . 20.00

LEGENDS OF NASCAR
Vortex
1 HT,Bill Eliott ($1.50 cover Price) 15,000 copies . . . . . . ±37.00
1a ($2.00 cover price) 45,000 copies . . . . ±10.00
1b 3rd pr., 80,000 copies 5.00
2 Richard Petty 4.50
3 Ken Schroder 3.50
4 Bob Alison 3.00
5 Bill Elliott 2.50
6 Jr. Johnson 2.50
7 Sterling Marlin 2.25
8 . . . . 2.00
9 Rusty Wallace 2.00

LEGENDS OF THE STARGRAZERS
Innovation
1 . . . . 1.95
2 . . . . 1.95
3 . . . . 1.95
4 . . . . 1.95
5 . . . . 1.95

LEJENTIA
1 . . . . 1.95
2 . . . . 2.25

LEMONADE KID
AC Comics
1 . . . . 2.50

LIBERTY PROJECT, THE
Eclipse
1 I:Liberty Project 2.50
2 . . . . 1.75
3 V:Silver City Wranglers 1.75
4 . . . . 1.75
5 . . . . 1.75
6 F:Cimarron,'Misery and Gin' . . 1.75
7 I:Menace 1.75
8 V:Savage 1.75

LIDSVILLE
Gold Key
October, 1972
1 . . . . 15.00
2 . . . . 7.00
3 and 4 . . . . @7.00
5 October, 1973 . . . . 7.00

LIEUTENANT, THE
Dell Publishing Co.
April-June, 1962
1 Ph(c) 15.00

LIFE & ADVENTURES OF SANTA CLAUS
Tundra
GN MP,L.Frank Baum adapt. . . . 24.95

LIFE IN HELL
Blackthorne
1 3-D 2.50

LIFE WITH ARCHIE
Archie Publications
September, 1958
1 . . . . 225.00
2 . . . . 100.00
3 . . . . 60.00
4 . . . . 60.00
5 . . . . 60.00
6 . . . . 30.00
7 . . . . 30.00
8 . . . . 30.00
9 . . . . 30.00
10 . . . . 30.00
11 thru 20 . . . . @20.00
21 thru 30 . . . . @15.00
31 thru 40 . . . . @10.00
41 . . . . 7.00
42 B:Pureheart 5.00
43 . . . . 5.00
44 . . . . 5.00
45 . . . . 5.00
46 O:Pureheart 15.00
47 thru 59 . . . . @3.50
60 thru 100 . . . . @2.50
101 thru 285 . . . . @1.00

THE LIGHT FANTASTIC
Innovation
1 Terry Pratchett adapt. 2.50
2 Adaptation continues 2.50
3 Adaptation continues 2.50
4 Adapt.conclusion 2.50

LIGHTNING COMICS PRESENTS
Lightning Comics
1 B&W Promo Ed. 3.50
1a B&W Promo Ed. Platinum . . 15.00
1b B&W Promo Ed. Gold 40.00

LINDA LARK
Dell Publishing Co.
October-December, 1961
1 . . . . 15.00
2 . . . . 8.00
3 . . . . 8.00
4 . . . . 8.00
5 . . . . 8.00
6 . . . . 8.00
7 . . . . 8.00
8 . . . . 8.00

LINUS, THE LIONHEARTED
Gold Key
September, 1965
1 . . . . 50.00

LIPPY THE LION AND HARDY HAR HAR
Gold Key
March, 1963
1 . . . . 50.00

LITA FORD
Malibu/Rock-It Comix
1 JBa, ... 3.95

LITTLE AMBROSE
Archie Publications
September, 1958
1 . . . . 75.00

LITTLE ARCHIE
Archie Publications
1956
1 . . . . 300.00
2 . . . . 150.00
3 . . . . 100.00
4 . . . . 100.00
5 . . . . 100.00
6 thru 10 . . . . @75.00
11 thru 20 . . . . @40.00
21 thru 30 . . . . @25.00
31 thru 40 . . . . @15.00
41 thru 60 . . . . @10.00
61 thru 80 . . . . @5.00
81 thru 100 . . . . @3.00
101 thru 180 . . . . @2.00

LITTLE ARCHIE MYSTERY
Archie Publications
May, 1963
1 . . . . 75.00
2 October, 1963 . . . . 40.00

LITTLE AUDREY & MELVIN
Harvey Publications
May, 1962
1 . . . . 50.00
2 thru 5 . . . . @20.00
6 thru 10 . . . . @15.00
11 thru 20 . . . . @10.00
21 thru 40 . . . . @7.00
41 thru 50 . . . . @5.00
51 thru 53 52 pgs Giant size . . @5.00
54 thru 60 . . . . @8.00
61 December, 1973 . . . . 6.00

LITTLE AUDREY TV FUNTIME
Harvey Publications
September, 1962
1 A:Richie Rich 35.00
2 same 20.00
3 same 15.00
4 . . . . 15.00
5 . . . . 15.00
6 thru 10 . . . . @6.00
11 thru 20 . . . . @5.00
21 thru 32 . . . . @3.50
33 October, 1971 . . . . 3.50

LITTLE DOT DOTLAND
Harvey Publications
July, 1962
1 . . . . 50.00
2 . . . . 25.00
3 . . . . 22.00
4 . . . . 18.00
5 . . . . 18.00
6 thru 10 . . . . @10.00
11 thru 20 . . . . @7.00
21 thru 50 . . . . @3.50
51 thru 60 . . . . @2.50
61 December, 1973 . . . . 2.50

LITTLE DOT'S UNCLES & AUNTS
Harvey Enterprises
October, 1961
1 . . . . 55.00
2 . . . . 30.00
3 . . . . 25.00
4 . . . . 15.00
5 . . . . 15.00
6 thru 10 . . . . @12.00
11 thru 20 . . . . @10.00
21 thru 40 . . . . @7.00
41 thru 51 . . . . @5.00
52 April, 1974 . . . . 5.00

LITTLE LOTTA
Harvey Publications
November, 1955
1 B:Richie Rich and Little Lotta 225.00
2 . . . . 125.00
3 . . . . 100.00

4 . . . . . . 60.00
5 . . . . . . 60.00
6 . . . . . . 45.00
7 . . . . . . 45.00
8 . . . . . . 45.00
9 . . . . . . 45.00
10 . . . . . . 45.00
11 thru 20 . . . . . . @30.00
21 thru 40 . . . . . . @20.00
41 thru 60 . . . . . . @15.00
61 thru 80 . . . . . . @7.00
81 thru 99 . . . . . . @5.00
100 thru 103 52 pgs . . . . . . @3.00
104 thru 120 . . . . . . @2.00
121 May, 1976 . . . . . . 2.00

LITTLE LOTTA FOODLAND
Harvey Publications
September, 1963

1 68 pgs 75.00
2 . . . . . . 40.00
3 . . . . . . 25.00
4 . . . . . . 14.00
5 . . . . . . 14.00
6 thru 10 . . . . . . @10.00
11 thru 20 . . . . . . @7.00
21 thru 26 . . . . . . @5.50
27 . . . . . . 4.50
28 . . . . . . 4.50
29 October, 1972 . . . . . . 3.50

LITTLE MERMAID
Walt Disney

1 based on movie 1.75
2 'Serpent Teen' 1.50
3 'Guppy Love' 1.50
4 . . . . . . 1.50

LITTLE MONSTERS, THE
Gold Key
November, 1964

1 . . . . . . 20.00
2 . . . . . . 10.00
3 thru 10 . . . . . . @7.00
11 thru 20 . . . . . . @3.00
21 thru 43 . . . . . . @2.00
44 February, 1978 . . . . . . 2.00

LITTLE MONSTERS
Now

1 thru 6 . . . . . . @1.75

LITTLE REDBIRDS

1 . . . . . . 2.50
2 . . . . . . 2.50
3 . . . . . . 2.50
4 . . . . . . 2.50

LITTLE SAD SACK
Harvey Publications
October, 1964

1 Richie Rich(c) 15.00
2 . . . . . . 5.00
3 . . . . . . 3.00
4 . . . . . . 3.00
5 . . . . . . 5.00
6 thru 19 Nov. 1967 . . . . . . @4.00

LITTLE STOOGES, THE
Gold Key
September, 1972

1 . . . . . . 10.00
2 . . . . . . 5.00
3 . . . . . . 5.00
4 . . . . . . 5.00
5 . . . . . . 5.00
6 . . . . . . 5.00
7 March, 1974 . . . . . . 5.00

LLOYD LLEWELLYN

1 . . . . . . 2.00

LOBO
Dell Publishing Co.
December,1965

1 . . . . . . 10.00
2 . . . . . . 8.00

LOCKE
Blackthorne

1 PO.Jones 1.75
2 TD 2.25
3 . . . . . . 1.25
4 . . . . . . 1.25
5 . . . . . . 1.25

LONE RANGER, THE
Gold Key
September, 1964

1 . . . . . . 30.00
2 . . . . . . 15.00
3 . . . . . . 10.00
4 . . . . . . 10.00
5 . . . . . . 10.00
6 . . . . . . 8.00
7 . . . . . . 8.00
8 . . . . . . 8.00
9 . . . . . . 8.00
10 . . . . . . 8.00
11 thru 18 . . . . . . @7.00
18 thru 27 . . . . . . @5.00
28 March, 1977 . . . . . . 5.00

Lost in Space #11 © Innovation

LOST IN SPACE
Innovatiom
{based on TV series}

1 O:Jupiter II Project 3.00
2 'Cavern of IdyllicSummersLost' 2.75
2a Special Edition 2.50
3 Do Not Go Gently into that Good Night',Bill Mumy script . . 2.50
4 'People are Strange' 2.50
5 The Perils of Penelope 2.50
6 Time Warp 2.50
7 thru 9 . . . . . . @2.50
10 inc.Afterthought 2.50
11 F:Judy Robinson 2.50
12 . . . . . . 2.95
13 Voyage/Bottom Soil 2.95
14 . . . . . . 2.50
15 . . . . . . 2.50
16 . . . . . . 2.50
Project Krell 2.50
Ann.#2 . . . . . . 2.95
Special- Seduction of the Innocent 2.50

LOST PLANET
Eclipse

1 BHa,I:Tyler FLynn 2.00
2 BHa,R:Amelia Earhart 1.75
3 BHa 1.25
4 BHa,'Devil's Eye' 1.25
5 BHa,A:Amelia Earhart 2.00
6 . . . . . . 2.00

LOVECRAFT
Adventure Comics

1 'The Lurking Fear' adapt. 2.95
2 Beyond the Wall of Sleep 2.95
3 . . . . . . 2.95
4 . . . . . . 2.95

LOVE DIARY
Charlton Comics
July, 1958

1 . . . . . . 30.00
2 . . . . . . 15.00
3 . . . . . . 10.00
4 . . . . . . 10.00
5 . . . . . . 7.00
6 . . . . . . 10.00
7 thru 10 . . . . . . @7.00
11 thru 15 . . . . . . @3.00
16 thru 20 . . . . . . @3.00
21 thru 40 . . . . . . @1.50
41 thru 101 . . . . . . @1.00
102 December, 1976 . . . . . . 1.00

LUCY SHOW, THE
Gold Key
June, 1963

1 Ph(c) 65.00
2 Ph(c) 45.00
3 . . . . . . 40.00
4 . . . . . . 40.00
5 . . . . . . 40.00

LUDWIG VON DRAKE
Dell Publishing Co.
November-December, 1961

1 . . . . . . 25.00
2 . . . . . . 15.00
3 . . . . . . 15.00
4 . . . . . . 15.00

LUGER
Eclipse

1 TY,I:Luger,mini-series 2.00
2 TY 1.75
3 TY,BHa,V:Sharks 1.75

LUNATIC

1 . . . . . . 1.75
2 . . . . . . 1.75

LUNATIC FRINGE
Innovation

1 . . . . . . 1.95
2 . . . . . . 1.75

LUNATIC FRINGE
Innovation

1 . . . . . . 1.75

LYNDON B. JOHNSON
Dell Publishing Co.
March, 1965

1 Ph(c) 15.00

M
Eclipse
1 thru 4 JMu 4.95

MACROSS
Comico
1 . . . . 12.00

Becomes:
Robotech, The Macross Saga

MAD FOLLIES
E.C. Comics
1963

(N#) 150.00
2 1964 . . . . 100.00
3 1965 . . . . 75.00
4 1966 . . . . 85.00
5 1967 . . . . 60.00
6 1968 . . . . 50.00
7 1969 . . . . 50.00

Madman #1 © Tundra

MADMAN
Tundra
1 . . . . 6.00
2 . . . . 5.00
3 . . . . 5.00

MADMAN ADVENTURES
Tundra
1 R & N:Madman 2.95
2 thru 3 . . . . 3.25

MAD SPECIAL
E.C. Publications, Inc.
Fall, 1970

1 . . . . 65.00
2 . . . . 40.00
3 . . . . 40.00
4 thru 8 . . . . @30.00
9 thru 13 . . . . @25.00
14 . . . . 15.00
15 . . . . 20.00
16 . . . . 15.00
17 . . . . 15.00
18 . . . . 18.00
19 thru 21 . . . . @18.00
22 thru 31 . . . . @8.00
32 . . . . 10.00
33 thru 58 . . . . @7.00

MAGE
Comico
1 MWg,I:Kevin Matchstick 13.00
2 MWg,I:Edsel 9.00
3 MWg,V:Umbra Sprite 5.00
4 MWg,V:Umbra Sprite 5.00
5 MWg,I:Sean (Spook) 5.00
6 MWg,Grendel begins 20.00
7 MWg,Grendel 9.00
8 MWg,Grendel 5.00
9 MWg,Grendel 4.00
10 MWg,Grendel,Styx 4.00
11 MWg,Grendel,Styx 3.00
12 MWg,D:Sean,Grendel 4.00
13 MWg,D:Edsel,Grendel 4.00
14 MWg,Grendel,O:Kevin 3.50
15 MWg,D:Umbra Sprite 5.00

MAGEBOOK
Comico
1 rep. Mage #1-4 . . . . 8.95
2 rep. Mage #5-8 . . . . 8.95

MAGIC FLUTE
Eclipse
1 CR 4.95

MAGILLA GORILLA
Gold Key
May, 1964

1 . . . . 25.00
2 thru 10 Dec. 1968 . . . . @15.00

MAGILLA GORILLA
Charlton Comics
November, 1970

1 . . . . 50.00
2 thru 5 . . . . @25.00

MAGNUS: ROBOT FIGHTER
Gold Key
February, 1963

1 RM,I:Magnus,Teeja,A-1, I&B:Capt.Johner&aliens . . . 250.00
2 RM,I:Sen.Zeremiah Clane . . 125.00
3 RM,I:Xyrkol 125.00
4 RM,I:Mekamn,Elzy 75.00
5 RM,The Immortal One 75.00
6 RM,I:Talpa 70.00
7 RM,I:Malev-6,ViXyrkol 85.00
8 RM,I:Outsiders(Chet, Horio, Toun, Malf) 70.00
9 RM, I:Madmot 70.00
10 RM,Mysterious Octo-Rob . . . 70.00
11 RM,I:Danae,Neo-Animals . . . 50.00
12 RM,The Volcano Makers . . . 50.00
13 RM,I:Dr Lazlo Noel 55.00
14 RM,The Monster Robs 50.00
15 RM,I:Mogul Radur 50.00
16 RM,I:Gophs 50.00
17 RM,I:Zypex 50.00
18 RM,I:V'ril Trent 50.00
19 RM,Fear Unlimited 50.00
20 RM,I:Bunda the Great 50.00
21 RM, Space Spectre 50.00
22 Rep. #1 . . . . 35.00
23 DSp,Mission Disaster 35.00
24 Pied Piper of North Am 35.00
25 The Micro Giants 35.00
26 The Venomous Vaper 35.00
27 Panic in Pacifica 35.00
28 Threats from the Depths . . . 35.00
29 Rep. #7 . . . . 16.00
30 Rep. #15 . . . . 16.00
31 Rep. #14 . . . . 16.00
32 Rep. #2 . . . . 16.00
33 Rep. #21 . . . . 16.00
34 Rep. #13 . . . . 16.00
35 Rep. #6 . . . . 16.00
36 Rep. #8 . . . . 16.00
37 Rep. #11 . . . . 16.00
38 Rep. #12 . . . . 16.00
39 Rep. #16 . . . . 16.00
40 Rep. #17 . . . . 16.00
41 Rep. #18 . . . . 16.00
42 Rep. #19 . . . . 16.00
43 Rep. #20 . . . . 16.00
44 Rep. #23 . . . . 16.00
45 Rep. #24 . . . . 16.00
46 Rep. #25 . . . . 16.00

Magnus: Robot Fighter #2
© Voyager Communications, Inc.

MAGNUS: ROBOT FIGHTER
Valiant
0 PCu,BL,"Emancipator",w/ BWS card 75.00
0a PCu,BL,w/o card 50.00
1 ANi,BL,B:Steel Nation 30.00
1a w/o coupon 15.00
2 ANi,BL,Steel Nation #2 . . . . . 25.00
2a w/o coupon 12.50
3 ANi,BL,Steel Nation #3 . . . . . 20.00
3a w/o coupon 10.00
4 ANi,BL,E:Steel Nation 16.00
4a w/o coupon 8.00
5 DL,BL(i),I:Rai(#1),V:Slagger Flipbook format 20.00
5a w/o coupon 10.00
6 DL,A:Solar,V:Grandmother A:Rai(#2) 15.00
6a w/o coupon 7.50
7 DL,EC,V:Rai(#3) 12.00
7a w/o coupon 6.00
8 DL,A:Rai(#4),Solar,X-O Armor.E:Flipbooks 12.00
8a w/o coupon 6.00
9 EC,V:Xyrkol,E-7 . . . . 7.00
10 V:Xyrkol 7.00
11 V:Xyrkol. 6.00
12 I:Turok,V:Dr. Noel, I:Asylum,40pgs 75.00
13 EC,Asylum Pt 1 . . . . 4.00
14 EC,Asylum Pt2 . . . . 4.00
15 FM(c),EC,Unity#4,I:Eternal Warrior of 4001,O:Unity 3.00
16 WS(c),EC,Unity#12,A:Solar, Archer,Armstrong,Harbinger, X-O,Rai,Eternal Warrior 3.00
17 JaB,V:Talpa 3.00
18 SD,R:Mekman,V:E-7 . . . . 3.00
19 SD,V:Mekmen 3.00
20 EC,Tale of Magnus' past 3.00
21 JaB,R:Malevalents,

Grandmother 5.00
21a Gold Ed. 60.00
22 JaB,D:Felina,V:Malevalents, Grandmother 4.00
23 V:Malevolents 3.00
24 V:Malevolents 3.00
25 N:Magnus,R:1-A,silver-foil (c) 4.00
26 I:Young Wolves 2.75
27 V:Dr.Lazlo Noel 2.75
28 V:The Malevs 2.50
29 JCf,A:Eternal Warrior 2.50
30 JCf,V:The Malevs 2.50
31 JCf,V:The Malevs 2.50
32 JCf,Battle for South Am 2.50
33 B:JOs(s),JCf,A:Ivar 2.50
34 JCf,Captured 2.50
35 JCf,V:Mekman 2.50
36 JCf,w/Valiant Era Card 2.50
37 JCf,A:Starwatchers 2.50
38 JCf, ... 2.50
39 JCf,F:Torque 2.25

MAKABRE
Apocalypse

1 Gangsters 3.95

MAN FROM PLANET X
Planet X Prod.

1 . . . . 3.00

MAN FROM U.N.C.L.E.
Gold Key
February, 1965

1 'The Explosive Affair' 100.00
2 'The Forthur Cookie Affair' . . . 65.00
3 'The Deadly Devices Affair' . . . 40.00
4 'The Rip Van Solo Affair' 40.00
5 'Ten Little Uncles Affair' 40.00
6 'The Three Blind Mice Affair' . 40.00
7 'The Pixilated Puzzle Affair' I:Jet Dream (back-up begins) 45.00
8 'The Floating People Affair' . . 40.00
9 'Spirit of St.Louis Affair' 40.00
10 'The Trojan Horse Affair' 40.00
11 'Three-Story Giant Affair' . . . 35.00
12 'Dead Man's Diary Affair' . . . 35.00
13 'The Flying Clowns Affair' . . . 35.00
14 'Great Brain Drain Affair' 35.00
15 'The Animal Agents Affair' . . . 35.00
16 'Instant Disaster Affair' 35.00
17 'The Deadly Visions Affair' . . 35.00
18 'The Alien Affair' 35.00
19 'Knight in Shining Armor Affair' 35.00
20 'Deep Freeze Affair' 35.00
21 rep. #10 . . . . 30.00
22 rep. #7 . . . . 30.00

MANIFEST DESTINY

1 . . . . 1.95

MANGLE TANGLE TALES
Innovation

1 . . . . 2.95

MAN IN BLACK
Harvey Publications
September, 1957

1 . . . . 75.00
2 . . . . 45.00
3 . . . . 45.00
4 March, 1958 . . . . 45.00

MAN OF WAR
Eclipse

1 . . . . 1.75
2 . . . . 1.75
3 . . . . 1.75

MARK, THE
Dark Horse

1 LSn 1.75
2 LSn 1.95
3 LSn 1.95
4 . . . . 1.95

THE MARK
Dark Horse

1 MiB(s),V:Archon 2.75
2 MiB(s),V:Archon 2.75
3 MiB(s),V:Archon,A:Pierce 2.75
4 MiB(s),last issue 2.75

MARKSMAN, THE
Hero

1 O:Marksman, Pt.#1 . . . . 1.95
2 O:Marksman, Pt.#2 . . . . 1.95
3 O:Marksman ends.I:Basilisk . . . 1.95
4 A:Flare 1.95
5 I:Radar,Sonar 1.95
Annual #1, A:Champions 1.95

Married with Children #1
© Now Comics

MARRIED WITH CHILDREN
Now

1 . . . . 6.00
1a 2nd printing 2.00
2 . . . . 4.00
3 . . . . 3.00
4 . . . . 2.50
5 . . . . 2.50
6 . . . . 2.00
7 . . . . 2.50

[2nd Series]

1 Peg-Host of Radio Show 2.25
2 The Bundy Invention 1.95
3 Psychodad,(photo cover) 1.95
4 Mother-In-Law,(photo cover) . . 1.95
5 Bundy the Crusader 1.95
6 Bundy J: The Order of the Mighty Warthog 1.95
7 Kelly the VJ 1.95
Flashback Spec. Peg and Al's first date 1.95
Kelly Bundy Spec.#1 . . . . 1.95
Kelly Bundy Spec.#2 . . . . 1.95
Kelly Bundy Spec.#3 . . . . 1.95
Quantum Quartet #1 . . . . 1.95
Flashback Spec.#3 . . . . 1.95
Spec.#4 . . . . 1.95
3-D Spec. 2.50
2099 Spec. 1.95

MARS
First

1 thru 12 . . . . @1.25

MARSHALL LAW: HATEFUL DEAD
Apocalypse

1 'Rise of the Zombies' 5.95

MARTIANS!!! IN 3-D

1 . . . . 2.00

MARY WORTH
ARGO
March, 1956

1 . . . . 30.00

MASK
Dark Horse

1 I:Lt.Kellaway Mask 15.00
2 V:Rapaz & Walter 10.00
3 O:Mask 7.50
4 final issue 7.50

MASK RETURNS
Dark Horse

1 inc.cut-out Mask 6.00
2 Mask's crime spree 4.00
3 thru 4 . . . . 4.00

MASKED MAN
Eclipse

1 . . . . 3.00
2 . . . . 2.00
3 . . . . 2.00
4 . . . . 2.00
5 . . . . 2.00
6 V:Roxie Lamada 2.00
7 . . . . 2.00
8 'Roxy' 1.75
9 W:Dick and Maggie 1.75
10 . . . . 2.00

MASTERWORK SERIES
Seagate DC

1 FFrep.DC,ShiningKnight 1.50
2 FFrep.DC,ShiningKnight 1.50
3 BWr,Horror DC rep. 1.50

MAVERICK
Dell Publishing Co.
April, 1958

1 Ph(c) all 100.00
2 Ph(c) 55.00
3 Ph(c) 55.00
4 Ph(c) 55.00
5 Ph(c) 55.00
6 Ph(c) 45.00
7 Ph(c) 45.00
8 Ph(c) 45.00
9 Ph(c) 45.00
10 Ph(c) 45.00
11 Ph(c) 45.00
12 Ph(c) 45.00
13 Ph(c) 45.00
14 Ph(c) 45.00
15 thru 19 Ph(c) 35.00

MAVERICK MARSHALL
Charlton Comics
November, 1958

1 . . . . 15.00
2 . . . . 10.00
3 . . . . 10.00
4 . . . . 10.00
5 . . . . 10.00

6 . . . . 10.00
7 May, 1960 . . . . 10.00

MAXIMORTAL
Tundra

1 RV,A:True-Man 4.50
2 Crack in the New World 4.25
3 RV,Secret of the Manhattan Project revealed 4.25
4 . . . . 4.25
5 A:True Man 3.25
6 A:El Guano 3.25

MAYA
Gold Key
March, 1968

1 . . . . 15.00

MAZE AGENCY
Comico

1 O:Maze Agency 3.00
2 . . . . 2.50
3 . . . . 2.50
4 . . . . 2.50
5 . . . . 2.50
6 . . . . 2.50
7 . . . . 2.75
8 . . . . 1.95
9 . . . . 1.95
10 . . . . 1.95
11 . . . . 1.95
12 . . . . 2.50
13 thru 15 . . . . @1.95
16 thru 23 . . . . @2.50
Spec #1 . . . . 2.75

McHALE'S NAVY
Dell Publishing Co.
May-July, 1963

1 Ph(c) 25.00
2 Ph(c) 20.00
3 Ph(c) 20.00

McKEEVER & THE COLONEL
Dell Publishing Co.
February-April, 1963

1 Ph(c) 35.00
2 Ph(c) 25.00
3 Ph(c) 25.00

MECHA
Dark Horse

1 thru 5 . . . . @1.75

MECHANICS
Fantagraphics

1 HB,rep.Love & Rockets 3.00
2 HB,rep.Love & Rockets 2.50
3 HB,rep.Love & Rockets 2.50

MEDIA STARR
Innovation

1 thru 3 . . . . @1.95

MEGALITH
Continuity

1 MT 6.00
2 MT 4.00
3 MT, Painted issue 2.50
4 NA,TVE 2.50
5 NA,TVE 2.50
6 MN 2.50
7 MN 2.50
8 . . . . 2.50
9 SDr(i) 2.50
10 . . . . 2.50

[2nd Series]

0 Deathwatch 2000 prologue . . . 5.00
1 Deathwatch 2000 Pt.5 . . . . 2.50

Megalith #3 © Continuity Comics

2 Deathwatch 2000 Pt.10 . . . . . . 2.50
3 . . . . 2.50
4 thru 5 Rise of Magic 2.50

MEGATON

1 . . . . 1.50

Entity Comics

Holiday Spec. w/card 2.95

MEGATON EXPLOSION

1 RLd,AMe,I:Youngblood preview 25.00

MEGATON MAN
Kitchen Sink

1 I:Megaton Man 6.00
2 . . . . 4.00
3 and 4 . . . . @3.00
5 . . . . 2.50
6 Border Worlds 2.50
7 Border Worlds 2.50
8 Border Worlds 2.50
9 Border Worlds 2.50
10 Last Issue 2.50

MELTING POT
Mirage

1 . . . . 3.50
2 . . . . 3.50

MELVIN MONSTER
Dell Publishing Co.
April-June, 1965

1 . . . . 100.00
2 . . . . 75.00
3 . . . . 75.00
4 . . . . 75.00
5 . . . . 75.00
6 . . . . 75.00
7 . . . . 75.00
8 . . . . 75.00
9 . . . . 75.00
10 . . . . 75.00

MEN FROM EARTH
Future Fun

1 based on Matt Mason toy 6.50

MERCHANTS OF DEATH
Eclipse

1 King's Castle, The Hero 3.50
2 King's Castle,Soldiers of Fortune 3.50
3 Ransom, Soldier of Fortune . . . 3.50
4 ATh(c),Ransom, Men o/t Legion 3.50
5 Ransom,New York City Blues . 3.50

MERLIN REALM
Blackthorne

1 3-D 2.50

META 4
First

1 IG 3.95
2 IG 2.25
3 IG/JSon,FinalMonthly 2.25

MICKEY & DONALD
Gladstone

1 1449 Firestone 8.00
2 . . . . 4.00
3 Man of Tomorrow 3.00
4 . . . . 2.50
5 . . . . 2.50
6 . . . . 2.50
7 . . . . 2.50
8 . . . . 2.50
9 . . . . 2.50
10 . . . . 2.00
11 . . . . 2.00
12 . . . . 2.00
13 . . . . 2.00
14 . . . . 2.00
15 . . . . 2.00
16 giant-size 2.50
17 . . . . 3.00
18 . . . . 4.00

MICKEY MANTLE COMICS
Magnum

1 JSt,Rise to Big Leagues 1.75

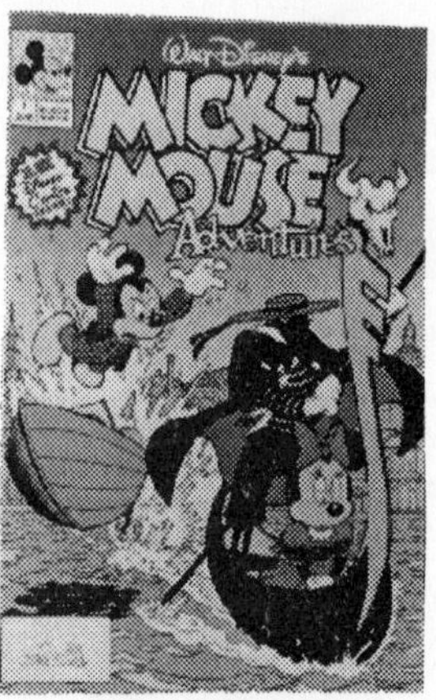

Mickey Mouse #1
© Walt Disney Comics

MICKEY MOUSE
Gladstone

219 FG,Seven Ghosts 6.00
220 FG,Seven Ghosts 7.00
221 FG,Seven Ghosts 7.00
222 FG,Editor in Grief 5.00
223 FG,Editor in Grief 4.00
224 FG,Crazy Crime Wave 3.00
225 FG,Crazy Crime Wave 3.00
226 FG,Captive Castaways 3.00

227 FG,Captive Castaways 3.00
228 FG,Captive Castaways 3.00
229 FG,Bat Bandit 3.00
230 FG,Bat Bandit 2.50
231 FG,Bobo the Elephant 2.50
232 FG,Bobo the Elephant 2.50
233 FG,Pirate Submarine 2.50
234 FG,Pirate Submarine 2.50
235 FG,Photo Racer 2.50
236 FG,Photo Racer 2.50
237 FG,Race for Riches 2.50
238 FG,Race for Riches 2.50
239 FG,Race for Riches 2.50
240 FG,March of Comics 2.50
241 FG 4.00
242 FG 2.50
243 FG 2.50
244 FG,60th Anniv 5.00
245 FG 2.25
245 FG 2.25
246 FG 2.25
247 FG 2.25
248 FG 2.25
249 FG 5.00
250 FG 2.25
251 FG 2.25
252 FG 2.25
253 FG 2.25
254 FG 2.25
255 FG 4.00
256 FG 4.00

MICKEY MOUSE
Walt Disney

1 .... 3.50
2 .... 3.00
3 .... 2.50
4 .... 2.50
5 .... 2.50
6 .... 2.00
7 Phantom Blot 2.00
8 Phantom Blot 2.00
9 .... 2.00
10 Sky Adventure 2.00
11 When Mouston Freezes Over . 2.00
12 Hail & Farewell 2.00
13 'What's Shakin'' 2.00
14 Mouseton,Eagle-Landing 2.00
15 'Lost Palace of Kashi' 2.00
16 'Scoundrels in Space' 2.00
17 'Sound of Blunder' Pt.1 ..... 1.75
18 'Sound of Blunder' Pt.2 ..... 1.75
19 50th Ann. Fantasia Celebration Sorcerer's Apprentice adapt .. 1.50

MICROBOTS, THE
Gold Key
December, 1971

1 .... 1.00

MIDNIGHT EYE: GOKU PRIVATE INVESTIGATOR
Viz

1 A.D. 2014: Tokyo city 5.25
2 V:Hakuryu,A:Yoko 4.95
3 A:Ryoko,Search for Ryu 4.95
4 Goku vs. Ryu 4.95
5 Leilah Abducted 4.95
6 Lisa's I.D. discovered 4.95

MIGHTY COMICS
(Prev: Flyman)

40 A:Web 12.00
41 A:Shield, Black Hood 10.00
42 A:Black Hood 10.00
43 A:Shield, Black Hood,Web ... 9.00
44 A:Black Hood, Steel Sterling Shield 9.00
45 Shield-Black Hood team-up O:Web 9.00
46 A:Steel Sterling, Black Hood, Web 9.00
47 A:Black Hood & Mr.Justice ... 9.00
48 A:Shield & Hangman 9.00
49 Steel Sterling-Black Hood team up, A:Fox 9.00

MIGHTY CRUSADERS
Red Circle
[1st Series]

1 O:Shield (Joe Higgins & Bill Higgins) 22.00
2 MSy,O:Comet 15.00
3 O:Fly-Man 12.50
4 A:Fireball,Jaguar,Web,Fox, Blackjack Hangman & more Golden Age Archie Heroes 15.00
5 I:Ultra-Men&TerrificThree 11.00

Archie Publications

6 V:Maestro,A:Steel Sterling ... 10.00
7 O:Fly-Girl,A:Steel Sterling ... 10.00

[2nd Series]

1 RB,R:Joe Higgins & Lancelot Strong as the SHIELD, Mighty Crusaders, A:Mr.Midnight 1.50
2 RB,V:Brain Emporer & Eterno . 1.50
3 RB,I:Darkling 1.50
4 DAy,TD 1.50
5 .... 1.00
6 DAy,TD,Shield 1.00
7 .... 1.00
8 .... 1.00
9 .... 1.00
10 .... 1.00
11 DAy,D:Gold Age Black Hood, I: Riot Squad, series based on toy lines 1.00
12 DAy,I:She-Fox 1.00
13 Last issue 1.00

MIGHTY HERCULES, THE
Gold Key
July, 1963

1 .... 35.00
2 .... 35.00

MIGHTY MOUSE
October, 1990

1 EC,Dark Mite Returns 3.00
2 EC,V:The Glove 2.00
3 EC/JBr(c)Prince Say More 1.50
4 EC/GP(c)Alt.Universe #1 ..... 1.50
5 EC,Alt.Universe #2 .... 1.50
6 'Ferment',A:MacFurline' 1.50
7 EC,V:Viral Worm 1.25
8 EC,BAT-BAT:Year One, O:Bug Wonder 1.25
9 EC,BAT-BAT:Year One, V:Smoker 1.25
10 'Night o/t Rating Lunatics' 1.25

MIGHTY MOUSE
Spotlight

1 FMc,PC(c) 1.50
2 FMc,CS(c) 1.50
1 Holiday Special 1.75

MIGHTY MUTANIMALS
Archie Publications
[Mini-Series]

1 Cont.from TMNT Adventures#19, A:Raphael, Man Ray, Leatherhead, Mondo Gecko,Deadman, Wingnut & Screwloose 1.25
2 V:Mr.Null,Malinga,Soul and Bean and the Malignoid Army 1.25
3 Alien Invasion help off, Raphael returns to Earth 1.25
4 "Days of Future Past" 1.25
5 "Into the Sun" 1.25
6 V:Null & 4 Horsemen Pt#2 .... 1.25
7 Jaws of Doom 1.50
Spec#1 rep. all #1-3 +SBi pin-ups 2.95

MIGHTY MUTANIMALS
Archie

1 Quest for Jagwar's Mother 1.25
2 V:Snake Eyes 1.25
3 .... 1.25
4 "Days of Future Past" 1.25
5 "Into the Sun" 1.25
6 V:Null & 4 Horsemen Pt#2 .... 1.25
7 Jaws of Doom 1.50

MIGHTY SAMSON
Gold Key
July, 1964

1 O:Mighty Samson 35.00
2 .... 15.00
3 .... 15.00
4 .... 15.00
5 .... 15.00
6 thru 10 .... @10.00
11 thru 20 .... @8.00
21 thru 31 .... @5.00
32 August, 1982 .... 5.00

MIKE GRELL'S SABLE
First

1 thru 8 rep. .... @1.75
9 .... 1.75
10 Triptych 1.75

MIKE SHAYNE PRIVATE EYE
Dell Publishing Co.
November-January, 1961-62

1 .... 15.00
2 .... 12.00
3 .... 12.00

MILLENNIUM INDEX
Eclipse

1 .... 2.00
2 .... 2.00

MILTON THE MONSTER & FEARLESS FLY
Gold Key
May, 1966

1 .... 50.00

MIRACLEMAN
Eclipse

1 R:Miracleman 3.25
2 AD,Moore,V:Kid Miracleman .. 2.25
3 AD,Moore,V:Big Ben 2.00
4 AD,Moore,R:Dr.Gargunza 2.00
5 AD,Moore,O:Miracleman 2.00
6 Moore,V:Miracledog, D:Evelyn Cream 2.00
7 Moore,D:Dr.Gargunza 2.00
8 Moore 2.00
9 RV,Moore,Birth of Miraclebaby . 2.50
10 JRy,RV,Moore 1.50
11 JTo,Moore,Book III, I:Miraclewoman 1.25
12 Moore 1.25
13 thru 19 .... @1.75
20 thru 23 .... @2.50
24 BWS(c),NGa(s), ... 2.95
3-D Special #1 .... 2.75
Graphic Album Book 1 .... 9.95
Graphic Album Book 2 .... 9.95
Graphic Album Book 3 .... 12.00

MIRACLEMAN APOCRYPHA
Eclipse

1 inc.'Rascal Prince' 2.50
2 Miracleman, Family Stories ... 2.50
3 .... 2.50

MIRACLEMAN FAMILY
Eclipse

1 British Rep.,A:Kid Miracleman . 1.95
2 Alan Moore scripts 1.95

MIRACLE SQUAD
Fantagraphics

1 Hollywood 30's 2.00
2 . . . . 2.00
3 . . . . 2.00
4 . . . . 2.00

MISS FURY
Adventure Comics

1 O:Cat Suit 2.50
2 Miss Fury impersonator 2.50
3 A:Three Miss Fury's 2.50
4 conclusion 2.50

MISSION IMPOSSIBLE
Dell Publishing Co.
May, 1967

1 Ph(c) 50.00
2 Ph(c) 35.00
3 Ph(c) 30.00
4 Ph(c) 30.00
5 Ph(c) 30.00

MISS PEACH
(& SPECIAL ISSUES)
Dell Publishing Co.
October-December, 1963

1 . . . . 50.00

MR. AND MRS. J. EVIL SCIENTIST
Gold Key
November, 1963

1 . . . . 40.00
2 . . . . 25.00
3 . . . . 25.00
4 . . . . 25.00

MORNINGSTAR

Special #1 . . . . 2.50

MR. JIGSAW

Special #1 . . . . 1.75

MR. MONSTER
Eclipse

1 I:Mr. Monster 9.00
2 DSt(c) 5.00
3 V:Dr. NoZone 3.50
4 . . . . 3.00
5 V:Flesh-eating Amoebo 3.00
6 KG,SD,reprints 3.00
7 . . . . 3.00
8 V:Monster in the Atomic
Telling Machine 3.00
9 V:Giant Clams 3.00
10 R:Dr.No Zone, 3-D 2.00

MR. MONSTER ATTACKS
Tundra

1 DGb,SK,short stories 4.25
2 SK,short stories cont. 4.25
3 DGb,last issue 4.25

MR. MONSTER SUPERDUPER SPECIAL
Eclipse

1 . . . . 2.50
2 . . . . 2.00
3 . . . . 2.00
4 . . . . 2.00
5 . . . . 2.00
6 . . . . 2.00

Mr. Monster © Eclipse Comics

Hi-Voltage Super Science 2.00
3-D Hi-Octane Horror,JKu,'Touch
of Death' reprint 1.75
True Crime #1 . . . . 1.75
True Crime #2 . . . . 1.75
True Crime 3-D #1 . . . . 2.00
Triple Treat 3.95

MR. MUSCLES
Charlton Comics
March, 1956

22 . . . . 25.00
23 August, 1956 . . . . 25.00

MR. MYSTIC
Eclipse

1 . . . . 2.00
2 . . . . 2.00
3 . . . . 2.00

MISTER X
Vortex

1 HB 8.00
2 HB 5.00
3 HB 3.50
4 HB 3.00
5 . . . . 3.00
6 thru 10 . . . . @2.50
11 thru 13 . . . . @2.00
14 . . . . 2.25

MONOLITH
Comico

1 from Elementals 2.50
2 'Seven Levels of Hell' 2.50
3 'Fugue and Variation' 2.50

MOD SQUAD
Dell Publishing Co.
January, 1969

1 . . . . 25.00
2 . . . . 15.00
3 . . . . 15.00
4 . . . . 15.00
5 thru 8 . . . . @15.00

MOD WHEELS
Gold Key
March, 1971

1 . . . . 10.00
2 thru 18 . . . . @5.00

19 January, 1976 . . . . 4.00

MONKEE'S, THE
Dell Publishing Co.
March, 1967

1 Ph(c) 75.00
2 Ph(c) 40.00
3 Ph(c) 40.00
4 Ph(c) 40.00
5 . . . . 30.00
6 Ph(c) 40.00
7 Ph(c) 40.00
8 . . . . 30.00
9 . . . . 30.00
10 Ph(c) 40.00
11 thru 17 . . . . 30.00

MOONWALKER IN 3-D
Blackthorne

1 thru 3 . . . . @2.50

MONROE'S, THE
Dell Publishing Co.
April, 1967

1 Ph(c) 15.00

MOTORBIKE PUPPIES
Dark Zulu Lies

1 I:Motorbike Puppies 2.50

MOVIE COMICS
Gold Key/Whitman
October, 1962

Alice in Wonderland 14.00
Aristocats 40.00
Bambi 1 . . . . 30.00
Bambi 2 . . . . 14.00
Beneath the Planet of the Apes . 35.00
Big Red 10.00
Blackbeard's Ghost 15.00
Buck Rogers Giant Movie Edition 15.00
Bullwhip Griffin 20.00
Captain Sinbad 45.00
Chitty, Chitty Bang Bang 30.00
Cinderella 15.00
Darby O'Gill & the Little People . 30.00
Dumbo 15.00
Emil & the Detectives 20.00
Escapade in Florence 40.00
Fall of the Roman Empire 25.00
Fantastic Voyage 35.00
55 Days at Peking 25.00
Fighting Prince of Donegal 20.00
First Men of the Moon 25.00
Gay Purr-ee 30.00
Gnome Mobile 20.00
Goodbye, Mr. Chips 20.00
Happiest Millionaire 15.00
Hey There, It's Yogi Bear 35.00
Horse Without a Head 15.00
How the West Was Won 30.00
In Search of the Castaways 40.00
Jungle Book, The 25.00
Kidnapped 15.00
King Kong 22.00
King Kong N# 6.00
Lady and the Tramp 15.00
Lady and the Tramp 1 . . . . 30.00
Lady and the Tramp 2 . . . . 10.00
Legend of Lobo, The 15.00
Lt. Robin Crusoe 15.00
Lion, The 15.00
Lord Jim 20.00
Love Bug, The 15.00
Mary Poppins 30.00
Mary Poppins 1 . . . . 50.00
McLintock 100.00
Merlin Jones as the Monkey's
Uncle 30.00
Miracle of the White Stallions . . 15.00
Misadventures of Merlin Jones . . 30.00
Moon-Spinners, The 40.00
Mutiny on the Bounty 25.00

Nikki, Wild Dog of the North 9.00
Old Yeller 15.00
One Hundred & One Dalmations 20.00
Peter Pan 1 .... 20.00
Peter Pan 2 .... 15.00
P.T. 109 .... 35.00
Rio Conchos 30.00
Robin Hood 15.00
Shaggy Dog & the Absent-Minded Professor 35.00
Snow White & the Seven Dwarfs 14.00
Snow White & the Seven Dwarfs 31.00
Son of Flubber 15.00
Summer Magic 45.00
Swiss Family Robinson 18.00
Sword in the Stone 35.00
That Darn Cat 40.00
Those Magnificent Men in Their Flying Machines 20.00
Three Stooges in Orbt 90.00
Tiger Walks, A 35.00
Toby Tyler 15.00
Treasure Island 15.00
20,000 Leagues Under the Sea . 15.00
Wonderful Adventures of Pinocchio 15.00
X, the Man with the X-Ray Eyes 50.00
Yellow Submarine 175.00

Ms. Mystic #9 © Pacific Comics

MS. MYSTIC
Pacific

1 NA,Origin 8.00
2 NA,Origin,I:Urth 4 .... 6.00

Continuity

1 NA,Origin rep. 2.00
2 NA,Origin,I:Urth 4 rep 2.00
3 NA,New material 2.00
4 TSh 2.00
5 DT 2.00
6 .... 2.00
7 .... 2.00
8 CH/Sdr,B:Love Story 2.00
9 DB 2.00
9a Newsstand(c) 2.00

[3rd Series]

1 O:Ms.Mystic 2.50
2 A:Hybrid 2.50

MADMAN COMICS
Dark Horse

1 MiA(s), ... 3.25

MAGNUS/NEXUS
Dark Horse/Valiant

1 MBn(s),SR, ... 3.25
2 MBn(s),SR, ... 3.25

MAN OF WAR
Malibu

1 thru 3 V:Lift 2.50
1a thru 5a Newsstand Ed. 1.95
4 w/poster 2.50
5 V:Killinger 2.50
6 KM,Genesis Crossover 2.50
7 DJu,Genesis Crossover 2.50
8 TMs(s),A:Rocket Ranger 2.25

MANTRA
Malibu-Ultraverse

1 AV,I:Mantra 4.00
1a Full Hologram (c) 75.00
2 AV,V:Warstrike 3.00
3 AV,V:Kismet Deadly 3.00
4 BWS,Mantra's marriage, BU:Rune 3.00
5 MiB(s),AV(i),V:Wiley Wolf 2.25
6 MiB(s),AV(i),Break Thru x-over 2.25
7 DJu,TA,A:Prime, O:Prototype 2.25
8 B:MiB(s),A:Warstrike 2.25
9 V:Iron Knight,Puppeteer 2.25
10 NBy(c),DaR,B:Archmage Quest, Flip Book(Ultraverse Premiere #2) 3.75
11 MiB(s),V:Boneyard 1.95

MARSHALL LAW: CAPE FEAR
Dark Horse

1 KON 2.95

MARSHALL LAW: SECRET TRIBUNAL
Dark Horse

1 KON, ... 2.95

MARTHA WASHINGTON GOES TO WAR
Dark Horse-Legends

1 FM(s),DGb, ... 2.95

MAVERICKS
Dagger

1 PuD,RkL,I:Mavericks 2.50
2 PuD,RkL, ... 2.50

MAXX
Image

1/2 SK,from Wizard 15.00
1 SK,I:The Maxx 2.25
1a glow in the dark(c) 50.00
2 SK,V:Mr.Gone 2.25
3 SK,V:Mr.Gone 2.25
4 SK, ... 2.25
5 SK, ... 2.25
6 SK, ... 1.95
7 SK,A:Pitt 1.95

MEGADETH
Malibu-Rock-it Comix

1 .... 4.25

METAL OF HONOR SPECIAL
Dark Horse

1 JKu, ... 2.50

METALLICA
Malibu-Rock-it Comix

1 .... 4.25

MEZZ GALACTIC TOUR
Dark Horse

1 MBn,MV, ... 2.50

MIGHTY MAGNOR
Malibu

1 thru 5 SA .... @1.95
6 SA 1.95

MONOLITH
Comico

1 from Elementals 2.50
2 Seven Levels of Hell 2.50
3 Fugue and Variation 2.50

MR. T AND THE T FORCE
Now

1 NA,R:Mr.T,V:Street Gangs 2.50
1a Gold Ed. 40.00
2 NA,V:Demons 2.25
3 NBy,w/card 2.25
4 NBy,In Urban America 2.25

MONSTER MASSACRE
Atomeka

1 SBs,DBr,DGb 8.50
1a Black Ed. 35.00

MOTORHEAD SPECIAL
Dark Horse

1 JLe(c),V:Mace Blitzkrieg 3.95

MS. TREE
Renegade

1 3-D 2.00

MS. VICTORY GOLDEN ANNIVERSARY
AC Comics

1 Ms.Victory celebration 5.00

MS. VICTORY SPECIAL
AC Comics

1 .... 1.75

MUMMY: RAMSES THE DAMNED
Millenium

1 Anne Rice Adapt. 5.00
2 JM,'Mummy in Mayfair' 3.75
3 JM 3.25
4 JM, To Egypt 3.00
5 JM'The Mummy's Hand' 2.50
6 JM 20th Century Egypt 2.50
7 JM,More Ramses Past Revealed2.50
8 JM,Hunt for Cleopatra 2.50
9 JM,Cleopatra's Wrath contd. .. 2.50
10 JM,Subterranian World 2.50

MUMMY ARCHIVES
Millenium

1.JM,Features,articles 2.50

MUNDEN'S BAR ANNUAL
First

1 BB,JOy,JSn,SR 2.95

MUNSTERS, THE
Gold Key
January, 1965

1 .... 150.00
2 .... 75.00
3 .... 55.00
4 .... 55.00
5 .... 55.00
6 thru 16 January 1968 .... @50.00

MUPPET BABIES
Harvey

1 Return of Muppet Babies 1.25

MUTANTS & MISFITS
Silverline

1 thru 4 . . . . @1.95

MY FAVORITE MARTIAN
Gold Key
January, 1964

1 . . . . 75.00
2 . . . . 40.00
3 thru 9 October, 1966 . . . . @40.00

MY LITTLE MARGIE
Charlton Comics
January, 1954

1 Ph(c) 150.00
2 Ph(c) 75.00
3 . . . . 40.00
4 . . . . 40.00
5 . . . . 40.00
6 . . . . 40.00
7 . . . . 40.00
8 . . . . 40.00
9 . . . . 45.00
10 . . . . 30.00
11 . . . . 15.00
12 . . . . 15.00
13 . . . . 30.00
14 thru 19 . . . . @25.00
20 . . . . 50.00
21 thru 35 . . . . @15.00
36 thru 53 . . . . @10.00
54 Beatles (c)November, 1965 . 100.00

MYSTERIES OF UNEXPLORED WORLDS/ SON OF VULCAN
Charlton Comics
August, 1956

1 . . . . 165.00
2 . . . . 55.00
3 . . . . 100.00
4 SD 110.00
5 SD,SD(c) 125.00
6 SD 125.00
7 . . . . 135.00
8 SD 125.00
9 SD 125.00
10 SD,SD(c) 135.00
11 SD,SD(c) 135.00
12 . . . . 75.00
13 thru 18 . . . . @20.00
19 SD(c) 50.00
20 . . . . 20.00
21 thru 24 SD . . . . @75.00
25 . . . . 15.00
26 SD 75.00
27 thru 30 . . . . @15.00
31 thru 45 . . . . @12.00
46 I:Son ofVulcan,Dr.Kong(1965) 15.00
47 V:King Midas 10.00
48 V:Captain Tuska 10.00

Becomes:

SON OF VULCAN

49 DC redesigns costume 6.00
50 V:Dr.Kong 5.00

MYSTERIOUS SUSPENSE

1 SD,A:Question 22.00

MYSTERY COMICS DIGEST
Gold Key
March, 1972

1 WW 8.00
2 WW 5.00
3 . . . . 3.00
4 Ripleys Believe It or Not 2.50
5 Boris Karloff 2.50
6 Twilight Zone 2.50
7 thru 20 . . . . @1.50
21 thru 26 Oct., 1975 . . . . @1.00

MYSTIC ISLE

1 . . . . 1.95

NANCY & SLUGGO
Dell Publishing Co.
September, 1957

146 B:Peanuts 20.00
147 . . . . 15.00
148 . . . . 15.00
149 . . . . 15.00
150 thru 161 . . . . 15.00
162 thru 165 . . . . 25.00
166 thru 176 A:OONA 30.00
177 thru 180 . . . . 25.00
181 thru 187 . . . . 12.00

NATIONAL VELVET
Dell Publishing Co.
May-July, 1961

1 Ph(c) 22.00
2 Ph(c) 20.00

NEAT STUFF
Fantagraphics

1 . . . . 4.50
2 . . . . 3.00
3 thru 5 . . . . @2.50
6 . . . . 2.25
7 . . . . 2.25

NECROPOLIS
Fleetway

1 SBs(c),CE,A:Dark Judges/ Sisters Of Death 2.95
2 . . . . 2.95
3 thru 9 . . . . @2.95

NECROSCOPE
Malibu

1 Novel adapt.(holo.cover) 3.25
1a 2nd printing 2.95
2 Adapt.continued 2.95

NEMESIS THE WARLOCK
Eagle

1 . . . . 2.00
2 thru 8 . . . . @1.50

NEW ADVENTURES OF FELIX THE CAT
Felix Comics,Inc

1 New stories 2.25
2 "The Magic Paint Brush" 2.25

NEW ADVENTURES OF PINNOCCIO
Dell Publishing Co.
October-December, 1962

1 . . . . 60.00
2 and 3 . . . . @50.00

NEW AMERICA
Eclipse

1 A:Scout 1.75
2 A:Scout 1.75
3 A:Roman Catholic Pope 1.75
4 A:Scout 1.75

NEW BREED
Pied Piper

1 . . . . 2.75
2 . . . . 2.25

NEW CHAMPIONS

1 . . . . 2.95
2 . . . . 2.95

NEW DNAGENTS
Eclipse

1 R:DNAgents 1.50
2 F:Tank 1.00
3 Repopulating the World 1.00
4 . . . . 1.00
5 'Last Place on Earth' 1.00
6 JOy(c),'Postscript' 1.00
7 V:Venimus 1.00
8 DSp,V:Venimus 1.00
9 V:Venimus,I:New Wave 1.00
10 I:New Airboy 1.00
11 Summer Fun Issue 1.25
12 V:Worm 1.25
13 EL,F:Tank 1.25
14 EL,Nudity,'Grounded' 1.25
15 thru 17 . . . . @1.25
3-D #1 . . . . 2.50

NEW JUSTICE MACHINE
Innovation

1 . . . . 1.95
2 . . . . 1.95
3 . . . . 2.50

NEWMEN
Image

1 JMs, ... 2.25
2 JMs,I:Girth 1.95
3 JMs,V:Girth,I:Ikonna 1.95

NEW ORLEANS SAINTS

1 Playoff season(football team) . 6.00

NEW STATESMEN
Fleetway

1 . . . . 4.50
2 thru 5 . . . . @3.95

NEWSTRALIA
Innovation

1 . . . . 1.75
2 . . . . 1.75
3 . . . . 1.95

NEW TERRYTOONS
Dell Publishing Co.
June-August, 1960

1 . . . . 25.00
2 thru 9 . . . . @15.00

NEW WAVE, THE
Eclipse

1 Error Pages 2.00
1a Correction 1.50
2 . . . . 1.00
3 'Space Station Called Hell' . . . 1.00
4 Birth of Megabyte 1.00
5 PG(c),O:Avalon 1.50
6 O:Megabyte 1.50
7 Avalon disappears 1.00
8 V:Heap,V:Druids 1.00
9 . . . . 1.00
10 V:Heap Team 1.00
11 . . . . 1.50
12 . . . . 1.50
13 V:Volunteers 1.50
14 1/3 issue 2.00

NEW WAVE vs. THE VOLUNTEERS
Eclipse

1 3-D,V:Volunteers 2.50
2 3-D,V:Volunteers 2.50

NEXT MAN
Comico
1 I&O:Next Man 2.50
2 . . . . . . 1.75
3 . . . . . . 1.75
4 . . . . . . 1.50
5 . . . . . . 1.50

Next Men #0 © Dark Horse Comics

NEXT MEN
Dark Horse
0 Rep Next Men from Dark Horse Presents 8.00
1 JBy,'Breakout'inc.trading card certificate 12.00
1a 2nd Printing Blue 3.00
2 JBy,World View 6.00
3 JBy,A:Sathanis 5.00
4 JBy,A:Sathanis 4.00
5 JBy,A:Sathanis 4.00
6 JBy,O:Senator Hilltop, Sathanis,Project Next Men . . . 3.50
7 JBy,I:M-4,Next Men Powers explained 3.50
8 JBy,I:Omega Project,A:M-4 . . . 3.00
9 JBy,A:Omega Project,A:M-4 . . 3.00
10 JBy,V:OmegaProject,A:M-4 . . . 3.00
11 JBy,V:OmegaProject,A:M-4 . . . 3.00
12 JBy,V:Dr.Jorgenson 3.00
13 JBy,Nathan vs Jack 3.00
14 JBy,I:Speedboy 2.75
15 JBy,in New York 2.75
16 JBy,Jasmine's Pregnant 2.75
17 FM(c),JBy,Arrested 2.75
18 JBy,On Trial 2.75
TPB rep.#1-6 . . . . . . 16.95
TPB Parallel Collection 16.95

NEXT MEN: FAITH
Dark Horse-Legends
1 JBy(a&s),V:Dr.Trogg, Blue Dahila 3.25
2 JBy,(a&s),F:Jack 2.75
3 MMi(c),JBy(a&s),I:Hellboy 3.50
4 JBy(a&s),Last issue 2.75

NEXT MEN: POWER
Dark Horse-Legends
1 JBy(a&s), ... 2.75
2 JBy(a&s), ... 2.75
3 JBy(a&s), ... 2.50

NEXT NEXUS
First
1 SR 1.95
2 SR 1.95
3 SR 1.95
4 SR 1.95

NEXUS
Capital
1 SR 7.00
2 SR,Origin 5.50
3 SR 5.00
4 SR 5.00
5 SR 5.00
6 SR,A:Badger,Trialogue Trilogy #1 . . . . . . 4.00

Nexus #8 © First Comics

First
7 SR,A:Badger,Trialogue Trilogy #2 . . . . . . 4.00
8 SR,A:Badger,Trialogue Trilogy #3 . . . . . . 4.00
9 SR,Teen Angel 2.50
10 SR,BWg,Talking Heads 2.00
11 SR,V:Clausius 2.00
12 SR,V:The Old General 2.00
13 SR,Sundra Peale solo 2.00
14 SR,A:Clonezone,Hilariator 2.00
15 SR,A:Clonezone 2.00
16 SR,A:Clonezone 2.00
17 Judah vs. Jacque,the Anvil . . . 2.00
18 SR,A:Clonezone 2.00
19 SR,A:Clonezone 2.00
20 SR,A:Clonezone 2.00
21 SR,A:Clonezone 2.00
22 KG,A:Badger 2.00
23 SR,A:Clonezone 2.00
24 SR,A:Clonezone 2.00
25 SR,A:Clonezone 2.00
26 SR,A:Clonezone 2.00
27 SR,A:Clonezone 2.00
28 MMi 2.00
29 A:Kreed & Sinclair 2.00
30 JL,C:Badger 2.50
31 Judah solo story 2.00
32 JG,Judah solo story 2.00
33 SR,A:Kreed & Sinclair 2.00
34 SR,Judah solo story 2.00
35 SR,Judah solo story 2.00
36 SR 2.00
37 PS 2.00
38 . . . . . . 2.00
39 SR, The Boom Search 2.00
40 SR 2.00
41 SR 2.00
42 SR,Bowl-Shaped world 2.00
43 PS 2.00
44 PS 2.00
45 SR,A:Badger Pt.1 . . . . . . 2.00
46 SR,A:Badger Pt.2 . . . . . . 2.00
47 SR,A:Badger Pt.3 . . . . . . 2.00
48 SR,A:Badger Pt.4 . . . . . . 2.00
49 PS,A:Badger Pt.5 . . . . . . 2.00
50 SF,double size,A:Badger Pt.6 Crossroads tie-in 3.50
51 PS 2.00
52 PS 2.00
53 PS 2.00
54 PS 2.00
55 PS 1.95
56 . . . . . . 1.95
57 AH 1.95
58 Sr,I:Stanislaus Korivitsky as Nexus 1.95
59 SR 1.95
60 SR 1.95
61 . . . . . . 1.95
62 . . . . . . 1.95
63 V:Elvonic Order 1.95
64 V:Elvonic Order 1.95
65 V:Elvonic Order 1.95
66 V:Elvonic Order 1.95
67 V:Elvonic Order 1.95
68 LM 1.95
69 . . . . . . 1.95
70 . . . . . . 1.95
71 V:Bad Brains 1.95
72 V:Renegade heads 1.95
73 Horatio returns to Ylum 1.95
74 Horatio vs. Stan 1.95
75 Horatio vs. Stan 1.95
76 . . . . . . 2.25
77 . . . . . . 2.25
78 O:Nexus,Nexus Files Pt#1 . . . 2.25
79 Nexus Files Pt#2 . . . . . . 2.25
80 Nexus.Files Pt#3,last iss. 2.25

NEXUS: ALIEN JUSTICE
Dark Horse
1 . . . . . . 4.25
2 . . . . . . 4.25

NEXUS LEGENDS
First
1 thru 13 rep.Nexus . . . . . . @1.50
14 rep.Nexus 1.75
15 rep.Nexus 1.75
16 rep.Nexus 1.75
17 rep.Nexus 1.75
18 rep.Nexus 1.95
19 rep.Nexus 1.95
20 SR,Sanctuary 1.95
21 SR 1.95
22 SR 1.95
23 SR 1.95

NEXUS THE LIBERATOR
Dark Horse
1 "Waking Dreams" 2.75
2 Civil War,D:Gigo 2.75
3 Civil War contd. 2.75
4 Last issue 2.75

NEXUS: THE ORIGIN
Dark Horse
1 SR,O:Nexus 4.50

NICK HOLIDAY
Argo
May, 1956
1 Strip reprints 30.00

NIGHT GLIDER
Topps
1 V:Bombast,C:Captain Glory, Trading Card 3.25

NIGHT MAN
Malibu-Ultraverse

1 I:Night Man 2.75
2 GeH,V:Mangle 2.25
3 SEt,GeH,A:Freex,Mangle 2.25
4 HC,I:Scrapyard,O:Firearm 2.25
5 SEt(s), ... 2.25
6 V:TNTNT 2.25
7 V:Nick 2.25
8 V:Werewolf 1.95

NIGHTMARE
Innovation

1 . . . . . 2.50

NIGHTMARE AND CASPER
Harvey Publications
August, 1963

1 . . . . . 40.00
2 . . . . . 20.00
3 . . . . . 20.00
4 . . . . . 20.00
5 . . . . . 20.00

Becomes:

CASPER AND NIGHTMARE

6 B:68 pgs 15.00
7 . . . . . 7.00
8 . . . . . 7.00
9 . . . . . 7.00
10 . . . . . 7.00
11 thru 20 . . . . . @3.50
21 thru 30 . . . . . @2.50
31 . . . . . 2.50
32 E:68 pgs 2.50
33 thru 45 . . . . . @2.00
46 August, 1974 . . . . . 2.00

NIGHTMARE ON ELM STREET
Blackthorne

1 3-D 2.50
2 3-D 2.50
3 3-D 2.50

NIGHTMARES ON ELM STREET
Innovation

1 Yours Truly, Freddy Krueger Pt.1 . . . . . 3.00
2 Yours Truly ,Freddy Krueger Pt.2 . . . . . 2.50
3 Loose Ends Pt.1,Return to Springwood 2.50
4 Loose Ends Pt 2 . . . . . 2.50
5 . . . . . 2.50
6 . . . . . 2.50

NIGHTMARES
Eclipse

1 . . . . . 2.50
2 . . . . . 2.00

NIGHT MUSIC
Eclipse

1 . . . . . 2.50
2 . . . . . 2.50
3 CR,JungleBear 3.00
4 Pelias&Melisande 2.00
5 Pelias 2.00
6 Salome 2.00
7 RedDog #1 . . . . . 2.00
Graphic Novel 8.00

NIGHTVEIL
AC Comics

1 . . . . . 3.50
2 . . . . . 2.50
3 . . . . . 2.25
4 . . . . . 2.25
5 . . . . . 2.25
6 . . . . . 1.75
7 . . . . . 1.75
Special #1 . . . . . 1.95

NIGHT WALKER
Fleetway

1 thru 2 . . . . . 2.95

NIGHTWOLF

1 . . . . . 1.75
2 . . . . . 1.75

9 LIVES OF FELIX
Harvey

1 thru 4 . . . . . @1.25

NINJA HIGH SCHOOL
Eternity

1 Reps.orig.N.H.S.in color 1.95
2 thru 13 reprints . . . . . @1.95

NINJA STAR

1 . . . . . 1.95

NINJAK
Valiant

1 B:MMo(s),JQ,JP,Chromium(c), I:Dr.Silk,Webnet 5.00
1a Gold Ed 35.00
2 JQ,JP,V:Dr.Silk,Webnet 3.00
3 JQ,JP,I:Seventh Dragon 2.50
4 MMo(a&s),V:Seventh Dragon,w/card 2.50
5 MMo(a&s),A:X-O Manowar . . . 2.50
6 MMo(a&s),A:X-O Manowar, V:Dr.Silk,Webnet 2.50
7 MMo(a&s),I:Rhaman 2.25

1963
Image

1 AnM(s),RV,DGb,I:Mystery, Inc. 2.50
1a Gold Ed. 50.00
2 RV,SBi,DGb,JV,I:The Fury 2.25
3 RV,SBi,I:U.S.A. 2.25
4 JV,SBi,I:N-Man, Johnny Beyond 2.25
5 JV,SBi,I:Horus 2.25
6 JV,SBi,I:Tommorrow Synicate, C:Shaft 2.25

NOID IN 3-D
Blackthorne

1 thru 3 . . . . . @2.50

NOMAN
Tower Comics
November, 1966

1 GK,OW 40.00
2 OW,A:Dynamo 30.00

NOSFERATU: PLAGUE OF TERROR
Millenium

1 I:Orlock 2.50
2 19th Century India,A:Sir W. Longsword 2.50
3 WWI/WWII to Viet Nam 2.50
4 O:Orlock,V:Longsword,conc. . . 2.50

NO TIME FOR SERGEANTS
Dell Publishing Co.
July, 1958

1 Ph(c) 25.00
2 Ph(c) 22.00
3 Ph(c) 22.00

NURSES, THE
Gold Key
April, 1963

1 . . . . . 20.00
2 . . . . . 15.00
3 . . . . . 15.00

NYOKA, JUNGLE GIRL
Charlton Comics
November, 1955

14 . . . . . 40.00
15 . . . . . 25.00
16 . . . . . 25.00
17 . . . . . 25.00
18 . . . . . 25.00
19 . . . . . 25.00
20 . . . . . 25.00
21 . . . . . 25.00
22 November, 1957 . . . . . 25.00

NYOKA, THE JUNGLE GIRL
AC Comics

1 . . . . . 1.95
2 . . . . . 1.95

OCCULT FILES OF DR. SPEKTOR
Gold Key
April, 1973

1 I:Lakot 10.00
2 thru 5 . . . . . 5.00
6 thru 10 . . . . . 3.50
11 I:Spertor as Werewolf 4.00
12 and 13 . . . . . 2.50
14 A:Dr. Solar 15.00
15 thru 24 . . . . . 2.50

Whitman

25 rep 2.00

O.G. WHIZ
Gold Key
February, 1971

1 . . . . . 60.00
2 . . . . . 35.00
3 . . . . . 25.00
4 . . . . . 25.00
5 . . . . . 25.00
6 . . . . . 25.00
7 . . . . . 8.00
8 . . . . . 8.00
9 . . . . . 8.00
10 . . . . . 8.00
11 January, 1979 . . . . . 8.00

O'MALLEY AND THE ALLEY CATS
Gold Key
April, 1971

1 . . . . . 15.00
2 thru 9 January, 1974 . . . . @10.00

OMEGA ELITE
Blackthorne

1 . . . . . 1.50
2 . . . . . 1.50

OMNI MEN
Blackthorne

1 . . . . . 1.25
2 . . . . . 1.25

ON A PALE HORSE
Innovation

1 Piers Anthony adapt 4.95
2 'Magician',I:Kronos 4.95
3 . . . . . 4.95
4 VV, ... 4.95

ONE-ARM SWORDSMAN

1 ... 2.95
2 ... 2.95
3 ... 2.75
4 ... 1.80
5 ... 1.80
6 ... 1.80
7 ... 1.80
8 ... 1.80
9 ... 2.00
10 ... 2.00
11 ... 2.00

ORBIT
Eclipse

1 DSt(c) ... 3.95
2 ... 3.95
3 ... 4.95

ORIENTAL HEROES
Jademan

1 ... 2.50
2 ... 2.00
3 thru 13 ... @1.50
14 thru 27 ... @1.95
28 V:Skeleton Secretary ... 1.95
29 Barbarian vs.Lone Kwoon ... 1.95
30 Barbarian vs.Lone Kwoon ... 1.95
31 SkeletonSecretaryUprisng ... 1.95
32 Uprising Continues ... 1.95
33 Jupiter Kills His Brother ... 1.95
34 Skeleton Sec. Suicide ... 1.95
35 Red Sect Vs. Global Cult ... 1.95
36 A:Tiger ... 1.95
37 Old Supreme ... 1.95
38 Tiger vs. 4 Hitmen ... 1.95
39 D:Infinite White, V:Red Sect. ... 1.95
40 The Golden Buddhha Temple ... 1.95
41 thru 43 ... 1.95
44 SilverChime rescue ... 1.95
45 Global Cult Battle ... 1.95
46 thru 48 ... @1.95
49 F:GoldDragon/SilverChime ... 1.95
50 Return to Global Cult ... 1.95
51 Gang Of Three Vs.White Beau & Lone Kwoon-Tin ... 1.95
52 Global Cult vs Red Sect ... 1.95
53 Global Cult vs.Red Sect ... 1.95

Original Astro Boy #1 © Now Comics

ORIGINAL ASTRO BOY
Now

1 KSy ... 3.00
2 KSy ... 2.00
3 KSy ... 2.00
4 KSy ... 2.00
5 KSy ... 2.00
6 thru 17 KSy ... @1.75

ORIGINAL DICK TRACY
Gladestone

1 rep.V:Mrs.Pruneface ... 1.95
2 rep.V:Influence ... 1.95
3 rep.V:TheMole ... 1.95
4 rep.V:ItchyOliver ... 1.95
5 rep.V:Shoulders ... 2.00

ORIGINAL E-MAN
First
{rep. Charlton stories}

1 JSon,O:E-Man & Nova ... 1.75
2 JSon,V:Battery,SamuelBoar ... 1.75
3 JSon,'City in the Sand' ... 1.75
4 JSon,A:Brain from Sirius ... 1.75
5 JSon,V:T.V. Man ... 1.75
6 JSon,I:Teddy Q ... 1.75
7 JSon,Vamfire ... 1.75

ORIGINAL SHIELD
ABC

1 DAy/TD,O:Shield ... 1.00
2 DAy,O:Dusty ... .75
3 DAy ... .75
4 DAy ... .75

ORIGIN OF THE DEFIANT UNIVERSE
Defiant

1 O:Defiant Characters ... 1.50

ORIGINS
Malibu-Ultraverse

1 O:Ultraverse Heroes ... 1.25

OUTBREED 999
Blackout Comics

1 ... 2.95

OUTCASTS

1 ... 1.25

OUTER LIMITS, THE
Dell Publishing Co.
January-March, 1964

1 P(c) ... 45.00
2 P(c) ... 25.00
3 P(c) ... 20.00
4 P(c) ... 20.00
5 P(c) ... 20.00
6 P(c) ... 20.00
7 P(c) ... 20.00
8 P(c) ... 20.00
9 P(c) ... 20.00
10 P(c) ... 20.00
11 thru 18 P(c) ... 15.00

OUT OF THE VORTEX
Dark Horse-C.G.W.

1 B:JOs(s),V:Seekers ... 2.25
2 MMi(c),DaW,A:Seekers ... 2.25
3 WS(c),E:JOs(s),DaW,A:Seeker, C:Hero Zero ... 2.25
4 DaW,A:Catalyst ... 2.25
5 V:Destroyers,A:Grace ... 2.25
6 V:Destroyers,A:Hero Zero ... 2.25
7 AAd(c),DaW,V:Destroyers, A:Mecha ... 2.25
8 DaW,A:Motorhead ... 2.00

OUTLAWS OF THE WEST
Charlton Comics
August, 1956

11 ... 40.00
12 ... 20.00
13 ... 20.00
14 Giant ... 25.00
15 ... 20.00
16 ... 20.00
17 ... 20.00
18 SD ... 50.00
19 ... 15.00
20 ... 15.00
21 thru 30 ... @10.00
31 thru 50 ... @5.00
51 thru 70 ... @3.00
71 thru 87 ... @2.00
88 April, 1980 ... 2.00

OUT OF THIS WORLD
Charlton Comics
August, 1956

1 ... 100.00
2 ... 50.00
3 SD ... 125.00
4 SD ... 125.00
5 SD ... 125.00
6 SD ... 125.00
7 SD,SD(c) ... 125.00
8 SD ... 100.00
9 SD ... 100.00
10 SD ... 100.00
11 SD ... 100.00
12 SD ... 100.00
13 ... 30.00
14 ... 30.00
15 ... 30.00
16 December, 1959 ... 100.00

OUTPOSTS
Blackthorne

1 ... 1.25
2 ... 1.25
3 ... 1.25
4 ... 1.25
5 ... 1.25
6 ... 1.25

OWL, THE
Gold Key
April, 1967

1 ... 25.00
2 April, 1968 ... 20.00

OZZY OSBORNE
Malibu-Rock-It Comix

1 w/guitar pick ... 3.95

PACIFIC PRESENTS
Pacific

1 DSt,Rocketeer,(3rd App.) ... 16.00
2 DSt,Rocketeer,(4th App.) ... 14.00
3 SD,I:Vanity ... 2.50
4 ... 2.00
5 ... 2.00

P.A.C.
Artifacts Inc

1 I:P.A.C. ... 1.95

PACT
Image

1 JV(s),WMc,I:Pact, C:Youngblood ... 2.25

PARADAX
Eclipes

1 ... 2.25

PARADIGM
Gauntlet

1 A:Predator ... 2.95

PARANOIA
Adventure Comics

1 (based on video game)'Clone1' 3.25
2 King-R-Thr-2 .... 2.95
3 R:Happy Jack,V:N3F 2.95
4 V:The Computer 2.95
5 V:The Computer 2.95
6 V:Lance-R-Lot,last issue 2.95

PARTRIDGE FAMILY, THE
Charlton Comics
March, 1971

1 .... 15.00
2 thru 4 .... @8.00
5 Summer Special 15.00
6 thru 21 .... @7.00
21 December, 1973 .... 7.00

PATHWAYS TO FANTASY
Pacific

1 BS,JJ art 3.00

PAT SAVAGE: WOMAN OF BRONZE
Millenium

1 F:Doc Savage's cousin 2.50

PEACEMAKER
Charlton

1 A:Fightin' 5 .... 5.00
2 A:Fightin' 5 .... 3.00
3 A:Fightin' 5 .... 3.00
4 O:Peacemaker,A:Fightin' 5 .... 4.00
5 A:Fightin' 5 .... 2.50

PEANUTS
Dell Publishing Co.
February, 1958

1 .... 85.00
2 .... 65.00
3 .... 65.00
4 .... 45.00
5 .... 30.00
6 .... 30.00
7 .... 30.00
8 .... 30.00
9 .... 30.00
10 .... 30.00
11 .... 30.00
12 .... 30.00
13 .... 30.00

PEANUTS
Gold Key
May, 1963

1 .... 50.00
2 thru 4 .... 30.00

PEBBLES & BAMM BAMM
Charlton Comics
January, 1972

1 .... 25.00
2 thru 10 .... @12.00
11 thru 35 .... @8.00
36 December, 1976 .... 8.00

PEBBLES FLINTSTONE
Gold Key
September, 1963

1 'A Chip off the old block' 55.00

PELLESTAR

1 .... 1.75

PERG
Lightning Comics

1 Glow in the dark(c),JS(c), B:JZy(s),KIK,I:Perg 3.75
1a Platinum Ed. 15.00
1b Gold Ed. 40.00
2 KIK,O:Perg 3.25
2a Platinum Ed. 10.00
3 Flip Book (c), ... 3.25
3a Platinum Ed 10.00
4 TLw,I:Helana 3.25
4a Platinum Ed 10.00
5 A:Helena 3.25
6 PIA,A:Helena 3.25

PERRY MASON MYSTERY MAGAZINE
Dell Publishing Co.
June-August, 1964

1 .... 20.00
2 Ray Burr Ph(c) 20.00

PETER PAN: RETURN TO NEVERNEVER LAND

1 Peter in Mass. 2.50
2 V:Tiger Lily 2.50

PETER POTAMUS
Gold Key
January, 1965

1 .... 50.00

PETTICOAT JUNCTION
Dell Publishing Co.
October-December, 1964

1 Ph(c) 50.00
2 Ph(c) 35.00
3 Ph(c) 35.00
4 .... 35.00
5 Ph(c) 35.00

The Phantom #19 © King Comics

PHANTOM, THE
Gold Key
November, 1962

1 RsM 75.00
2 B:King,Queen,Jacks 35.00
3 thru 10 .... @30.00
11 thru 17 .... @25.00

King

18 WW,B:Flash Gordon 30.00
19 .... 20.00
20 .... 20.00
21 thru 29 .... @20.00

Charlton Comics

30 thru 40 .... @15.00
41 thru 50 .... @10.00
46 I:Piranha 15.00
51 thru 70 .... @10.00
71 thru 73 .... @6.00
74 January, 1977 .... 6.00

PHANTOM
Wolf Publishing

1 Drug Runners 2.25
2 Mystery Child of the Sea 2.25
3 inc.feature pages on Phantom/Merchandise 2.25
4 TV Jungle Crime Buster 2.25
5 Castle Vacula-Transylvania 2.25
6 The Old West 2.25
7 Sercet of Colussus 2.75
8 Temple of the Sun God 2.75

PHANTOM BOLT, THE
Gold Key
October, 1964

1 .... 25.00
2 .... 15.00
3 .... 12.00
4 .... 12.00
5 .... 12.00
6 .... 12.00
7 November, 1966 .... 12.00

PHANTOM FORCE
Image

1 RLd,JK,w/card 2.75

PHAZE
Eclipse

1 BSz(c),Takes place in future 2.25
2 PG(c),V:The Pentagon 1.95
3 Schwieger Vs. Mammoth 1.95

PINK PANTHER, THE
Gold Key
April, 1971

1 .... 20.00
2 thru 10 .... @10.00
11 thru 30 .... @7.00
31 thru 60 .... @4.00
61 thru 4.00

PINOCCHIO

1 .... 1.50

PIRATE CORP.
Eternity

1 thru 5 .... @1.95

P.I.'S, THE
First

1 JSon,Ms.Tree,M Mauser 1.50
2 JSon,Ms.Tree,M Mauser 1.25
3 JSon,Ms.Tree,M Mauser 1.25

PITT
Image

1 DK,I:Pitt 4.00
2 DK,V:Quagg 2.25
3 .... 2.25
4 DK,V:Zoyvod 2.25

PLANET COMICS
Blackthorne

1 DSt(c) 2.00
2 .... 2.00
3 .... 2.00
4 .... 2.00

POLICE TRAP
Mainline
August-September, 1954

1 S&K(c) 100.00

 All comics prices listed are for *Near Mint* condition.

2 S&K(c) 60.00
3 S&K(c) 60.00
4 S&K(c) 60.00

Charlton Comics

5 S&K,S&K(c) 100.00
6 S&K,S&K(c) 100.00

Becomes:

PUBLIC DEFENDER IN ACTION

7 . . . . 40.00
8 . . . . 30.00
9 . . . . 30.00
10 thru 12, Oct. 1957 . . . . . . @30.00

POPEYE SPECIAL
Ocean

1 . . . . 1.75
2 . . . . 2.00

POWER AND GLORY
Malibu-Bravura

1a HC(a&s),I:American Powerhouse 3.50
1b HC(a&s),I:American Powerhouse 3.50
1c Blue Foil (c) 25.00
2 HC(a&s),O:American Powerhouse 2.75
3 HC(a&s), ... 2.50
4 HC(a&s), ... 2.50

POWER FACTOR
Pied Piper

1 . . . . 4.00
2 . . . . 3.00

POWER FACTOR
Innovation

1 thru 4 . . . . @2.25

PREDATOR
Dark Horse

1 CW,Mini Series 28.00
1a 2ndPrinting 12.00
1b 3rdPrinting 2.50
2 CW 14.00
2a 2ndPrinting 5.00
3 CW 10.00
3a 2ndPrinting 2.50
4 CW 7.00
4a 2ndPrinting 2.50

PREDATOR: BAD BLOOD
Dark Horse

1 CW,I:John Pulnick 2.75
2 CW,V:Predator 2.75
3 CW,V:Predator,C.I.A. 2.75

PREDATOR: BIG GAME
Dark Horse

1 Corp.Nakai Meets Predator . . . 4.50
2 Army Base Destroyed 3.50
3 Corp.Nakai Arrested 3.50
4 Nakai vs. Predator 3.50
TPB rep. #1-#4 . . . . 13.95

PREDATOR: BLOODY SANDS OF TIME
Dark Horse

1 DBa,CW,Predator in WWI 4.00
2 DBa,CW, WWII contd. 3.25

PREDATOR: COLD WAR
Dark Horse

1 Predator in Siberia 4.00
2 U.S. Elite Squad in Siberia . . . 3.25
3 U.S. vs. USSR commandos . . . 3.25
TPB 13.95

PREDATOR: RACE WAR
Dark Horse

0 F:Serial Killer 2.75
1 V:Serial Killer 2.75
2 D:Serial Killer 2.75
3 in Prison 2.75
4 Last Issue 2.75

PREDATOR 2
Dark Horse

1 DBy, Movie Adapt Pt1 . . . . 3.50
2 MBr, Movie Adapt. Pt2 . . . . . . 3.00

PREDATOR VS. MAGNUS
Valiant/Dark Horse

1 LW,A:Tekla 7.00
1a Platinum Ed. 25.00
2 LW,Magnus Vs. Predator 4.00

PRESSBUTTON
Eclipse
(see Axel Pressbutton)

5 . . . . 1.75
6 . . . . 1.75

PRIMAL
Dark Horse

1 Contd.from Primal:from the Cradle to the Grave 2.95
2 A:TJ Cyrus 2.50

PRIME
Malibu-Ultraverse

1 B:GJ(s),I:Prime 7.00
1a Ultra-Limited 50.00
1b Full Hologram (c) 100.00
2 V:Organism 8 . . . . 10.00
3 NBy,I:Prototype 6.00
4 NBy,V:Prototype 3.00
5 NBy,BWS,I:Maxi-Man, BU:Rune 3.00
6 NBy,A:Pres. Clinton 2.75
7 NBy,Break-Thru x-over 2.25
8 NBy,A:Mantra 2.25
9 NBy,Atomic Lies 2.25
10 NBy,A:Firearm,N:Prime 2.25
11 NBy, ... 2.25
12 NBy,(Ultraverse Premiere#3) 3.50

PRIMUS
Charlton Comics
February, 1972

1 . . . . 5.00
2 . . . . 5.00
3 thru 5 . . . . @5.00
6 thru 7 October, 1972 . . . . . @4.00

PRINCE VANDAL
Triumphant

1 JnR(s), ... 2.50
2 JnR(s), ... 2.50
3 JnR(s),ShG,I:Claire, V:Nicket 2.50
4 JnR(s),ShG,Game's End 2.50
5 JnR(s),ShG,The Sickness 2.50

PRISON SHIP

1 . . . . 1.75

PRIVATEERS
Vanguard Graphics

1 . . . . 1.50
2 . . . . 1.50

PROFESSIONAL: GOGOL 13
Viz

1 . . . . 4.95
2 and 3 . . . . @4.95

PROFESSOR OM
Innovation

1 . . . . 2.50

PROJECT A-KO
Malibu

1 Based on the Movie 2.95
2 Based on the Movie 2.95
3 Based on the Movie 2.95
4 Based on the Movie 2.95

PROPELLER MAN
Dark Horse

1 I:Propeller Man 2.95
2 O:Propeller Man 2.95
3 V:Manipulator 2.95
4 V:State Police 2.95
5 V:Manipulator 2.95
6 V:Thing 2.95
7 . . . . 2.95
8 Last issue 2.95

PROPHET
Image

1 RLd(s)DPs,O:Prophet 2.75
1a Gold Ed. 30.00
2 RLd(s),DPs,C:Bloodstrike 2.25
3 RLd(s),DPs,V:Bloodstrike, I:Judas 2.25
4 RLd(s),DPs,A:Judas 2.50
4a SPI(c),Limited Ed. 25.00
5 SPI 3.00

Protectors #1 © Malibu

PROTECTORS
Malibu

1 I:Protectors,inc.JBi poster (direct) 3.00
1a thru 12a Newsstand . . . . . @1.95
2 V:Mr.Monday,w/poster 2.50
3 V:Steel Army,w/poster 2.50
4 V:Steel Army 2.50
5 Die Cut(c),V:Mr.Monday 2.50
6 V:Mr.Monday 2.50
7 A:Thresher 2.50
8 V:Wisecrack 1.95
9 V:Wisecrack 2.50
10 I:Mantoka 2.50
11 A:Ms.Fury,V:Black Fury 2.50
12 A:Arrow 2.50
13 RAJ(s),Genesis#3 . . . . 2.25
14 RB(c),RAJ(s),Genesis#6 . . . . . 2.25
15 RAJ(s),J:Chalice 2.25

16 So Help Me God 2.25
17 L:Ferret 2.25
18 V:Regulators,BU:Mantako,
R:Mr. Monday 2.25
19 A:Gravestone,Arc 2.50
20 V:Nowhere Man 2.50
Protectors Handbook 2.50

PROTOTYPE
Malibu-Ultraverse

1 V:Ultra-Tech 3.00
2 I:Backstabber 3.00
3 LeS(s),DvA,JmP,BWS,
V:Ultra-Tech,BU:Rune 3.00
4 TMs(s),V:Wrath 2.25
5 TMs(s),A:Strangers,Break-
Thru x-over 2.25
6 TMs(s),Origins Month
C:Arena 2.25
7 TMs(s),V:Arena 2.25
8 TMs(s),V:Arena 2.25
9 Prototype Unplugged 2.25
10 TMs(s),V:Prototype 1.95

PROWLER
Eclipse

1 I:Prowler 1.75
2 GN,A:Original Prowler 1.75
3 GN 1.75
4 GN 1.75
5 GN, adaption of 'Vampire Bat' . 1.75
6 w/flexi-disk record 1.75

PROWLER IN 'WHITE ZOMBIE'
Eclipse

1 . . . . 1.75

PRUDENCE AND CAUTION

1 CCI(s), ... 3.25

PSYCHO
Innovation

1 Hitchcock movie adapt 2.50
2 continued 2.50
3 continued 2.50

PSYCHOBLAST
First

1 thru 9 . . . . @1.75

PUDGE PIG
Charlton Comics
September, 1958

1 . . . . 8.00
2 . . . . 8.00

PUMPKINHEAD
Dark Horse

1 Based on the movie 2.50

PUPPET MASTER
Eternity

1 Movie Adapt.Andre Toulon . . . 2.50
2 Puppets Protecting Diary 2.50
3 R:Andre Toulon 2.50
4 . . . . 2.50

PUPPET MASTER: CHILDREN OF THE PUPPET MASTER
Eternity

1 Killer Puppets on the loose . . . 2.50
2 concl. 2.50

QUANTUM LEAP
Innovation
{based on TV series}

1 1968 Memphis 3.50
1a Special Edition 2.50
2 Ohio 1962,'Freedom of the
Press' 3.00
3 1958 'The $50,000 Quest' 3.00
4 'Small Miracles' 2.50
5 . . . . 2.50
6 . . . . 2.50
7 Golf Pro,School Bus Driver . . . 2.50
8 1958,Bank Robber 2.50
9 NY 1969,Gay Rights 2.50
10 1960s' Stand-up Comic 2.50
11 1959,Dr.(LSD experiments) . . . 2.50
12 . . . . 2.50

Queen of the Damned #3 © Innovation

QUEEN OF THE DAMNED
Innovation

1 Anne Rice Adapt.'On the Road
to the Vampire Lestat' 3.50
2 Adapt. continued 2.50
3 The Devils Minion 2.50
4 Adapt.continued 2.50
5 Adapt.continued 2.50
6 Adapt.continued 2.50
7 Adapt.continued 2.50
8 Adapt.continued 2.50

QUICK-DRAW McGRAW
Charlton Comics
November, 1970

1 TV Animated Cartoon 35.00
2 . . . . 20.00
3 . . . . 20.00
4 . . . . 20.00
5 . . . . 20.00
6 . . . . 20.00
7 . . . . 20.00
8 January, 1972 . . . . 20.00

Q-UNIT
Harris

1 I:Q-Unit,w/card 3.25

RACE FOR THE MOON
Harvey Publications
March, 1958

1 BP 75.00
2 JK,AW,JK/AW(c) 150.00
3 JK,AW,JK/AW(c)
November, 1958 . . . . 150.00

RACE OF SCORPIONS
Dark Horse

Book 1 short stories 5.00
Book 2 . . . . 4.95
Book 3 . . . . 2.50
Book 4 Final issue 2.50

RACER-X
Now

Premire Special 5.00
1 . . . . 2.50
2 . . . . 2.50
3 . . . . 2.50
4 thru 11 . . . . @1.75

[2nd Series]

1 thru 10 . . . . @1.75

RACK & PAIN
Dark Horse

1 GCa(c),I:Rack,Pain 2.50
2 GCa(c),V:Web 2.50
3 GCa(c),V:Web 2.50
4 GCa(c),Final Issue 2.50

RADIOACTIVE MAN
Bongo

1 I:Radioactive Man 3.25

RAD PATROL

1 . . . . 1.95

RADRAX

1 . . . . 2.25
2 . . . . 2.25

RAEL
Eclipse

Vol 1 . . . . 6.95

RAGAMUFFINS
Eclipse

1 . . . . 3.00

Rai and the Future Force #9
© Voyager Communications

RAI
Valiant

0 DL,O:Bloodshot,I:2nd Rai,D:X-O,
Archer,Shadowman,F:all Valiant
heroes,bridges Valiant
Universe 1992-4001 . . . . 20.00

1 V:Grandmother 25.00
2 V:Icespike 20.00
3 V:Humanists,Makiko 45.00
4 V:Makiko,rarest Valiant 45.00
5 Rai leaves earth, C:Eternal Warrior 12.00
6 FM(c),Unity#7,V:Pierce 6.00
7 WS(c),Unity#15,V:Pierce, D:Rai,A:Magnus 7.00
8 Epilogue of Unity in 4001 5.00

Becomes:

RAI AND THE FUTURE FORCE

9 F:Rai,E.Warrior of 4001,Tekla, X-O Commander,Spylocke 2.50
9a Gold Ed. 40.00
10 Rai vs. Malev Emperor 2.50
11 SCh,V:Malevolents 2.50
12 V:Cyber Raiders 2.50
13 Spylocke Revealed 2.50
14 SCh,D:M'Ree 2.50
15 SCh,V:X-O 2.50
16 SCh,V:Malevs 2.50
17 2.50
18 JOs(s),Spk,V:Malevs 2.50
19 JCf,V:Malves 2.50
20 JOs(s),DR,V:Malves,Spylocke realed to be Spider Alien 2.50
21 DR,I:Starwatchers,b:Torque, w/card 2.50
22 DR,D:2nd Rai, A:Starwatchers 2.50
23 DR,A:Starwatchers, 2.50
24 DR,in Tibet 2.25
TPB #0-#4 11.95

RALPH SNART
Now
[Volume 3]

1 4.00
2 thru 10 @3.00
11 thru 21 @2.00
22 thru 26 @1.75
TPB 7.95

RALPH SNART ADVENTURES
Now

1 Inc trading cards 2.50
2 Inc trading cards 2.50
3 Inc trading cards 2.50
4 Inc trading cards 2.50
3-D Spec.#1 with 3-D glasses and trading cards 3.50

RAMAR OF THE JUNGLE
Toby Press
1954

1 Ph(c), John Hall 65.00

Charlton

2 50.00
3 50.00
4 50.00
5 Sept., 1956 50.00

RANGO
Dell Publishing Co.
August, 1967

1 Tim Conway Ph(c) 18.00

RANMA 1/2
Viz

1 I:Ranma 4.95
2 I:Upperclassmen Kuno 4.95
3 F:Upperclassmen Kuno 4.95
4 Confusion 2.75
5 A:Ryoga 2.95
6 Ryoga plots revenge 2.75
7 Conclusion 2.95

[2nd Series]

1 thru 4 @2.95

RAPTOR
Topps

1 SEt(s),w/ Zorro #0 3.25

RAT PATROL, THE
Dell Publishing Co.
March, 1967

1 Ph(c) 35.00
2 25.00
3 Ph(c) 20.00
4 Ph(c) 20.00
5 Ph(c) 20.00
6 Ph(c) 20.00

RAVEN
Renaissance Comics

1 I:Raven 2.50
2 V:Macallister 2.50

Ravens & Rainbows #1
© Pacific Comics

RAVENS AND RAINBOWS
Pacific

1 1.50

RAY BRADBURY CHRONICLES
Byron Press

1 short stories 10.00
2 short stories 10.00
3 short stories 10.00

Topps

1 w/Trading Card 3.25
2 w/Trading Card 3.25
3 w/Trading Card 3.25
4 thru 5 w/Trading Card 3.25

REAL GHOSTBUSTERS
Now

1 KSy(c) 4.50
2 thru 7 @2.50
8 thru 24 @1.75

[2nd Series]

1 Halloween Special 1.75
Ann. 3-D w/glasses & pinups 2.95

REAL WAR STORIES
Eclipse

1 BB 3.00
1a 2nd printing 1.50

RE-ANIMATOR
Adventure Comics

1 and 2 movie adaption @2.95

RE-ANIMATOR
Adventure

1 Prequel to Orig movie 2.50

RE-ANIMATOR: DAWN OF THE RE-ANIMATOR
Adventure

1 Prequel to movie 2.50
2 2.50
3 2.50
4 V:Erich Metler 2.50

RE-ANIMATOR: TALES OF HERBERT WEST
Adventure Comics

1 H.P.Lovecraft stories 4.95

REDBLADE
Dark Horse

1 V:Demons 2.50
2 V:Tull 2.50
3 Last Issue 2.50

RED DOG
Eclipse

1 CR,Mowgli 'Jungle Book' sty 2.00

RED HEAT

1 3-D 2.50

RED SONJA in 3-D
Blackthorne

1 2.50
2 2.50
3 2.50

REESE'S PIECES
Eclipse

1 reprint from Web of Horror 1.50
2 reprint from Web of Horror 1.50

REGGIE
Archie Publications
September, 1963

15 40.00
16 35.00
17 35.00
18 35.00

Becomes:

REGGIE AND ME

19 15.00
20 7.00
21 7.00
22 7.00
23 7.00
24 thru 40 @2.50
41 thru 125 @1.00
126 September, 1980 1.00

REGGIE'S WISE GUY JOKES
Archie Publications
April, 1968

1 15.00
2 6.00
3 6.00
4 6.00
5 2.50
6 2.50
7 2.50
8 2.50
9 2.50
10 2.50
11 thru 60, January 1982 @1.00

REPTILICUS
Charlton Comics
August, 1961

1 .... 80.00
2 .... 60.00

Becomes:

REPTISAURUS

3 .... 30.00
4 .... 25.00
5 .... 25.00
6 .... 25.00
7 .... 25.00
8 Summer, 1963 .... 25.00

RETURN OF KONGA, THE
Charlton Comics
1962

N# 30.00

RETURN OF MEGATON MAN
Kitchen Sink

1 .... 2.00
2 .... 2.00
3 .... 2.00

REVENGE OF THE PROWLER
Eclipse

1 GN,R:Prowler 1.75
2 GN,A:Fighting Devil Dogs with Flexi-Disk 2.50
3 GN,A:Devil Dogs 1.75
4 GN,V:Pirahna 1.75

REVENGERS
Continuity

1 NA,O:Megalith,I:Crazyman 5.50
2 NA,Megalith meets Armor & Silver Streak,Origin Revengers#1 .... 2.50
3 NA/NR,Origin Revengers #2 .... 2.50
4 NA,Origin Revengers #3 .... 2.50
5 NA,Origin Revengers #4 .... 2.50
6 I:Hybrids 3.00
Special #1 F:Hybrids 4.95

RIBIT
Comico

1 FT,Mini-series 1.95
2 FT,Mini-series 1.95
3 FT,Mini-series 1.95
4 FT,Mini-series 1.95

RICHIE RICH
Harvey Publications
November, 1960

1 .... 550.00
2 .... 300.00
3 .... 200.00
4 .... 200.00
5 .... 200.00
6 .... 100.00
7 .... 100.00
8 .... 100.00
9 .... 100.00
10 .... 100.00
11 thru 20 .... @45.00
21 thru 40 .... @30.00
41 thru 60 .... @20.00
61 thru 80 .... @15.00
81 thru 99 .... @7.00
100 .... 7.00
101 thru 111 .... @4.00
112 thru 116 52 pg Giants .... @6.00
117 thru 120 .... @5.00
121 thru 140 .... @4.00
141 thru 160 .... @3.00
161 thru 180 .... @2.00
181 thru 237 .... @1.00
238 .... 1.00

RICHIE RICH DOLLARS & CENTS
Harvey Publications
August, 1963

1 .... 100.00
2 .... 45.00
3 .... 20.00
4 .... 20.00
5 .... 20.00
6 .... 15.00
7 .... 15.00
8 .... 15.00
9 .... 15.00
10 .... 15.00
11 thru 20 .... @10.00
21 thru 30 .... @7.00
31 thru 43 .... @5.00
44 thru 60 .... @4.00
61 thru 70 .... @3.00
71 thruu 109 .... @1.00

RICHIE RICH MILLIONS
Harvey Publications
September, 1961

1 .... 100.00
2 .... 45.00
3 thru 10 .... @30.00
11 thru 20 .... @20.00
21 thru 30 .... @10.00
31 thru 48 .... @7.00
49 thru 60 .... @5.00
61 thru 64 .... @4.00
65 thru 74 .... @3.00
75 thru 94 .... @2.50
95 thru 112 .... @1.00
113 October, 1982 .... 1.00

RICHIE RICH SUCCESS STORIES
Harvey Publications
November, 1964

1 .... 85.00
2 .... 30.00
3 .... 30.00
4 .... 30.00
5 .... 30.00
6 .... 20.00
7 .... 20.00
8 .... 20.00
9 .... 20.00
10 .... 20.00
11 thru 30 .... @10.00
31 thru 38 .... @7.00
39 thru 55 .... @5.00
56 thru 66 .... @3.00
67 thru 104 .... @1.00
105 September, 1982 .... 1.00

RIO
Dark Horse

1 F:Doug Wildey art 2.95
2 F:Doug Wildey art 2.95

RIOT GEAR
Triumphant

1 JnR(s),I:Riot Gear 2.50
2 JnR(s),I:Rabin 2.50
3 JnR(s),I:Surzar 2.50
4 JnR(s),D:Captain Tich 2.50
5 JnR(s), ... 2.50
6 JnR(s), ... 2.50
7 JnR(s),Information Age 2.50
8 JnR(s), ... 2.50

RIOT GEAR: VIOLENT PAST
Triumphant

1 thru 2 .... 2.50

RIFLEMAN, THE
Dell Publishing Co.
July-September, 1959

1 Chuck Connors Ph(c) all 125.00
2 .... 75.00
3 ATh 65.00
4 .... 55.00
5 .... 55.00
6 ATh 75.00
7 .... 45.00
8 .... 45.00
9 .... 45.00
10 .... 45.00
11 .... 45.00
12 .... 45.00
13 .... 45.00
14 .... 45.00
15 .... 45.00
16 .... 45.00
17 .... 45.00
18 .... 45.00
19 .... 45.00
20 .... 45.00

R.I.P.
TSR

1 thru 8 .... @2.95

RIPLEY'S BELIEVE IT OR NOT!
Gold Key
April, 1967

4 Ph(c),AMc 35.00
5 GE,JJ 20.00
6 AMc 20.00
7 .... 15.00
8 .... 20.00
9 .... 15.00
10 GE 20.00
11 .... 10.00
12 .... 10.00
13 .... 10.00
14 .... 10.00
15 GE 12.00
16 .... 10.00
17 .... 10.00
18 .... 10.00
19 .... 10.00
20 .... 10.00
21 thru 30 .... @8.00
31 thru 38 .... @5.00
39 RC 6.00
40 thru 50 .... @5.00
51 thru 93 .... @2.00
94 February, 1980 .... 2.00

ROBIN HOOD
Eclipse

1 TT,Historically accurate series . 2.75
2 and 3 TT .... @2.75

ROBOCOP: MORTAL COILS
Dark Horse

1 V:Gangs 2.75
2 V:Gangs 2.75
3 V:Coffin,V:Gangs 2.75

ROBOCOP VERSUS TERMINATOR
Dark Horse

1 WS,w/Robocop cut-out 3.50
2 WS,w/Terminator cut-out 3.00
3 WS,w/cut-out 3.00
4 WS,Conclusion 3.00

ROBOCOP: PRIME SUSPECT
Dark Horse

1 Robocop framed 2.75

Robocop Versus Terminator #4
© Dark Horse Comics

2 thru 4 V:ZED-309s .... @2.50
Collected 13.95

ROBOCOP: ROULETTE
Dark Horse

1 V:ED-309s 2.75
2 I:Philo Drut 2.75
3 V:Stealthbot 2.75
4 last issue 2.75

ROBOCOP 3
Dark Horse

1 B:StG(s),Movie Adapt 2.75
2 V:Aliens,OCP 2.75
3 HNg,ANi(i) 2.75

ROBO HUNTER
Eagle

1 .... 1.50
2 thru 5 .... @1.00

ROBOTECH: GENESIS
Eternity

1 O:Robotech(trading cards) ... 2.95
1a Limited Edition,extra pages .. 5.95
2 thru 4 .... @2.50

ROBOTECH IN 3-D
Comico

1 .... 2.50

ROBOTECH MASTERS
Comico

1 .... 4.00
2 .... 3.00
3 Space Station Liberty 3.00
4 V:Bioroids 2.50
5 V:Flagship 2.50
6 'Prelude to Battle' 2.50
7 'The Trap' 2.50
8 F:Dana Sterling 2.50
9 'Star Dust' 2.50
10 V:Zor 2.50
11 A:De Ja Vu 2.00
12 2OR 2.00
13 .... 2.00
14 "Clone Chamber,"V:Zor 2.00
15 "Love Song" 2.00
16 V:General Emerson 2.00
17 "Mind Games" 2.00
18 "Dana in Wonderland" 2.00
19 .... 2.00
20 A:Zor,Musica 2.00
21 "Final Nightmare" 2.00
22 "The Invid Connection" 2.00
23 "Catastrophe," final issue 2.00

ROBOTECH, NEW GENERATION
Comico

1 .... 4.00
2 'The Lost City' 3.00
3 V:Yellow Dancer 3.00
4 A:Yellow Dancer 3.00
5 SK(i),A:Yellow Dancer 2.50
6 F:Rook Bartley 2.50
7 'Paper Hero' 2.00
8 .... 2.00
9 KSy,"The Genesis Pit" 2.00
10 V:The Invid 2.00
11 F:Scott Bernard 2.00
12 V:The Invid 2.00
13 V:The Invid 2.00
14 "Annie's Wedding" 2.00
15 "Seperate Ways" 2.00
16 "Metamorphosis" 2.00
17 "Midnight Sun" 2.00
18 .... 2.00
19 .... 2.00
20 "Birthday Blues" 2.00
21 "Hired Gun" 2.00
22 "The Big Apple" 2.00
23 Robotech Wars 2.00
24 Robotech Wars 2.00
25 V:Invid, last issue 2.00

ROBOTECH SPECIAL DANA'S STORY
Eclipse

1 .... 5.00

Robotech, the Macross Saga #3
© Comico

ROBOTECH, THE MACROSS SAGA
Comico
(formerly Macross)

2 .... 5.00
3 .... 4.00
4 .... 3.00
5 .... 2.50
6 J:Rick Hunter 2.50
7 V:Zentraedi 2.00
8 A:Rick Hunter 2.00
9 V:Zentraedi 2.00
10 "Blind Game" 2.00
11 V:Zentraedi 2.00
12 V:Zentraedi 2.00
13 V:Zentraedi 2.00
14 "Gloval's Reports" 2.00
15 V:Zentraedi 2.00
16 V:Zentraedi 2.00
17 V:Zentraedi 2.00
18 D:Roy Fokker 2.00
19 V:Khyron 2.00
20 V:Zentraedi 2.00
21 "A New Dawn" 2.00
22 V:Zentraedi 2.00
23 "Reckless" 2.00
24 HB,V:Zentraedi 2.00
25 "Wedding Bells" 2.00
26 "The Messenger" 2.00
27 "Force of Arms" 2.00
28 "Reconstruction Blues" 2.00
29 "Robotech Masters" 2.00
30 "Viva Miriya" 2.00
31 "Khyron's Revenge" 2.00
32 "Broken Heart" 2.00
33 "A Rainy Night" 2.00
34 'Private Time' 2.00
35 'Season's Greetings' 2.00
36 last issue 2.00
Graphic Novel #1 .... 6.00

ROBOTECH II: THE SENTINELS
Eternity

Swimsuit Spec.#1 .... 2.95

ROCK & ROLL Revolutionary
Prev: Black & White

15 Poison 3.50
16 Van Halen 1.95
17 Madonna 2.50
18 AliceCooper 1.95
19 Public Enemy, 2 Live Crew ... 2.50
20 Queensryche 1.95
21 Prince 1.95
22 AC/DC 1.95
23 Living Color 1.95
24 Anthrax 1.95
25 Z.Z.Top 2.50
26 Doors 2.50
27 Doors 2.50
28 Ozzy Osbourne 2.50
29 The Cure 2.50
30 .... 2.50
31 Vanilla Ice 2.50
32 Frank Zappa 2.50
33 Guns n' Roses 2.50
34 The Black Crowes 2.50
35 R.E.M. 2.50
36 Michael Jackson 2.50
37 Ice T 2.50
38 Rod Stewart 2.50
39 .... 2.50
40 N.W.A./Ice Cube 2.50
41 Paula Abdul 2.50
42 Metallica II 2.50
43 Guns 'N' Roses 2.50
44 Scorpions 2.50
45 Greatful Dead 2.50
46 Grateful Dead 2.50
47 Grateful Dead 2.50
48 (now b/w),Queen 2.50
49 Rush 2.50
50 Bob Dylan Pt.1 .... 2.50
51 Bob Dylan Pt.2 .... 2.50
52 Bob Dylan Pt.3 .... 2.50
53 Bruce Springsteen 2.50
54 U2 Pt.1 .... 2.50
55 U2 Pt.2 .... 2.50

ROCKETEER
Walt Disney

1 DSt(c)RH,MovieAdaptation . . . 7.00
Newsstand Version 3.25

ROCKETEER ADVENTURE MAGAZINE
Comico

1 DSt,MK,Rocketeer(6thApp.) . . 12.00
2 DSt,MK,Rocketeer(7thApp.) . . 10.00

ROCKETEER SPECIAL
Eclipse

1 DSt, Rocketeer(5th App.) 26.00

ROCKET MAN: KING OF THE ROCKET MEN
Innovation

1 Adapts movie series 2.50
2 Adapts movie series 2.50
3 Adapts movie series 2.50
4 Adapts movie series 2.50

ROCKET RANGER
Adventure Comics

1 Based on computer game . . . 2.95

ROCKMEEZ
Jzink Comics

1 I:Rockmeez,V:Pyrites 2.50
2 V:Pyrites,Silv.Embos.(c) 2.50

ROCKY HORROR PICTURE SHOW
Calibre/Tome

1 . . . . 8.50
1a 2nd printing 3.25
2 . . . . 3.50
3 'The Conclusion' 3.25
Rocky Horror Collection reps. . . . 4.95

ROG 2000
Pacific

1 One-Shot, JBy 2.00

ROGER RABBIT
Walt Disney

1 I:Rick Flint 4.50
2 . . . . 3.00
3 . . . . 2.50
4 . . . . 2.50
5 . . . . 2.50
6 . . . . 2.50
7 . . . . 2.50
8 . . . . 2.50
9 . . . . 2.50
10 'Tuned-in-toons' 2.50
11 'Who Framed Rick Flint' 2.00
12 'Somebunny to Love 2.00
13 'Honey,I Stink with Kids 2.00
14 'Who Fired Jessica Rabbit' . . . 1.75
15 'The Great Toon Detective' . . . 1.75
16 'See you later Aviator' 1.50
17 Flying Saucers over Toontown 1.50
18 'I Have Seen the Future' 1.50

ROGER RABBIT'S TOONTOWN
Walt Disney

1 (inc.Baby Herman,Jessica stories) 2.00
2 'Pre-Hysterical Roger' 1.75
3 'Lumberjack of tomorrow' 1.75
4 'The Longest Daze' 1.75

ROGUE TROOPER
Quality

1 thru 5 . . . . @1.00
6 . . . . 1.50

Roger Rabbit #1
© Walt Disney Comics

7 thru 21 . . . . @1.25
22/23 . . . . 1.50
24 . . . . 1.50
25/26 . . . . 1.50
27 thru 35 . . . . @1.50
36 . . . . 1.95
37 . . . . 1.95
38 thru 40 . . . . @1.50
41 thru 43 . . . . @1.75

ROGUE TROOPER: THE FINAL WARRIOR
Fleetway

1 RS,Golden Rebellion,pt 1 . . . . 2.95
2 thru 3 . . . . 2.95
4 "Saharan Ice-Belt War 2.95

ROMAN HOLIDAYS, THE
Gold Key
February, 1973

1 . . . . 15.00
2 . . . . 10.00
3 . . . . 10.00
4 November, 1973 . . . . 10.00

ROOM 222
Dell Publishing Co.
January, 1970

1 . . . . 25.00
2 . . . . 20.00
3 Drug 25.00
4 Ph(c) 20.00

ROY ROGERS WESTERN CLASSICS
AC Comics

1 . . . . 2.95
2 . . . . 2.95
3 . . . . 2.95
4 . . . . 3.95

RUFF AND READY
Dell Publishing Co.
September, 1958

1 . . . . 50.00
2 . . . . 30.00
3 . . . . 30.00
4 . . . . 25.00
5 . . . . 25.00
6 . . . . 25.00
7 . . . . 25.00
8 . . . . 25.00
9 . . . . 25.00
10 . . . . 25.00
11 . . . . 25.00
12 . . . . 25.00

RUN, BUDDY, RUN
Gold Key
June, 1967

1 . . . . 15.00

RUNE
Malibu-Ultraverse

1 BWS(a&s),from Ultraverse 2.50
2 CU(s),BWS,V:Aladdin 2.25
3 DaR,BWS,(Ultraverse Premiere #1),Flip book, ... 3.75
4 BWS,V:Twins 2.25
5 BWS, ... 1.95

RUST
Now

1 . . . . 4.00
2 . . . . 3.00
3 thru 11 . . . . @2.00
12 I:Terminator 10.00
13 thru 15 . . . . @1.75

[Volume 2]

1 thru 10 . . . . @1.75

RUST
Malibu

1 O:Rust 2.95
2 V:Marion Labs 2.95
3 I:Ashe Sapphire,5th Anniv. . . . 2.95
4 I:Rustmobile 2.95

SABLE
First

1 AIDS story 1.75
2 Sable in Iran 1.75
3 Pentathelon 1.75
4 . . . . 1.75
5 DCw,V:Tong Gangs 1.75
6 In Atlantic City 1.75
7 V:EnvironmentalTerrorists 1.75
8 In Argentina 1.95
9 In Kenya Pt.1 . . . . 1.95
10 In Kenya Pt.2 . . . . 1.95
11 Jon Sable bodyguard 1.95
12 In Cambodia Pt.1 . . . . 1.95
13 In Cambodia Pt.2 . . . . 1.95
14 Christmas story 1.95
15 A:Ted Koppel 1.95
16 Sable as 'B.B.Flemm' rev. 1.95
17 Turning point issue 1.95
18 Richard Rockwell(i) 1.95
19 A:Maggie the Cat 1.95
20 A:Gary Adler 1.95
21 Richard Rockwell(i) 1.95
22 A:Eden Kendall 1.95
23 TV cover 1.95
24 TV cover 1.95
25 TV cover 1.95
26 TV cover 1.95
27 . . . . 1.95
28 last issue 1.95

SABRE
Eclipse

1 PG 2.50
2 PG 3.00
3 thru 14 . . . . @2.00

SABRINA, THE TEENAGE WITCH
Archie Publications
April, 1971

1 . . . . 40.00
2 . . . . 15.00

3 . . . . . 7.00
4 . . . . . 7.00
5 . . . . . 7.00
6 thru 10 . . . . . @4.00
11 thru 20 . . . . . @2.00
21 thru 76 . . . . . @1.00
77 January, 1983 . . . . . 1.00

SAD SACK AND THE SARGE
Harvey Publications
September, 1957

1 . . . . . 80.00
2 . . . . . 35.00
3 thru 10 . . . . . @25.00
11 thru 20 . . . . . @15.00
21 thru 40 . . . . . @6.00
41 thru 50 . . . . . @5.00
51 thru 90 . . . . . @2.00
91 thru 96 52 pg Giants . . . . . @3.00
97 thru 154 . . . . . @1.00
155 June, 1982 . . . . . 1.00

SAD SACK'S ARMY LIFE
Harvey Publications
October, 1963

1 . . . . . 35.00
2 thru 10 . . . . . @20.00
11 thru 20 . . . . . @10.00
21 thru 30 . . . . . @7.00
31 thru 50 . . . . . @3.00
51 thru 60 . . . . . @2.00
61 May, 1976 . . . . . 2.00

SAD SACK'S FUNNY FRIENDS
Harvey Publications
December, 1955

1 . . . . . 55.00
2 thru 10 . . . . . @25.00
11 thru 20 . . . . . @15.00
21 thru 30 . . . . . @7.00
31 thru 40 . . . . . @3.00
41 thru 74 . . . . . @2.00
75 October, 1969 . . . . . 2.00

SAD SACK in 3-D
Blackthorne

1 and 2 . . . . . @2.50

SALOME
Eclipse

1 CR 2.00

SAM AND MAX, FREE-LANCE POLICE SPECIAL
Comico

1 . . . . . 2.75

SAM SLADE ROBO-HUNTER
Quality

1 . . . . . 1.00
2 . . . . . 1.00
3 Filby Case 1.00
4 . . . . . 1.00
5 . . . . . 1.00
6 Bax the Burner,Moore 1.00
7 . . . . . 1.00
8 thru 21 . . . . . @1.25
22/23 . . . . . 1.50
24 . . . . . 1.50
25/26 . . . . . 1.50
27 thru 33 . . . . . @1.50

SAMURAI
Eclipse

1 . . . . . 2.00
2 . . . . . 2.00
3 thru 5 . . . . . @2.00

SAMUREE
Continuity

1 NA,A:Revengers 2.00
2 A:Revengers 2.00
3 NA,A:Revengers 2.00
4 A:Revengers 2.00
5 BSz(c),A:Revengers 2.00
6 A:Revengers 2.00
7 . . . . . 2.00
8 Drug story 2.00
9 Drug story 2.00

[2nd Series]

1 thru 3 Rise of Magic 2.50

SANTANA
Malibu-Rock-it Comix

1 TT(c&s),TY, ... 3.95

SARGE STEEL/ SECRET AGENT

1 DG,I:SargeSteel & IvanChung . 5.00
2 DG,I:Werner Von Hess 2.50
3 DG,V:Smiling Skull 2.50
4 DG,V:Lynx 2.50
5 FMc,V:Ivan Chung 2.50
6 FMc,A:Judomaster 2.50
7 DG 2.50
8 V:Talon 2.50

Becomes:

SECRET AGENT

9 DG 3.50
10 DG,JAp,A:Tiffany Sinn 3.00

SATAN'S SIX
Topps

1 F:Satan's Six,w/Card 3.25
2 V:Kalazarr,w/Card 2.95
3 w/card 2.95

SATURDAY KNIGHTS
Hot

1 . . . . . 1.50
2 . . . . . 1.50
3 . . . . . 1.50
4 . . . . . 1.50

SAURAUS FAMILY
Blackthorne

1 3-D 2.00

SAVAGE DRAGON
Image

1 EL,I:Savage Dragon 10.00
2 EL,I:Superpatriot 6.00
3 EL,V:Bedrock,w'coupon#6 . . . . 6.00
3a EL,w/o coupon 2.25
Savage Dragon Versus Savage Megaton Man 1 EL,DSm,Dragon Vs.Megaton Man 2.50
Gold Ed. 30.00
TBP 9.95

[2nd Series]

1 EL,I:Freaks 2.75
2 EL,V:Teen.Mutant Ninja Turtles, Flip book Vanguard #0 . . . . . 3.50
3 EL,A:Freaks 2.25
4 EL,A:Freaks 2.25
5 EL,Might Man flip book 2.25
6 EL,A:Freaks 2.25
7 EL,Overlord 2.25
8 EL,V:Cutthroat,Hellrazor 2.25

SAVAGE DRAGON/ TEENAGE MUTANT NINJA TURLES CROSSOVER
Mirage

1 EL(s). 2.75

SAVED BY THE BELL
Harvey

1 based on TV series 1.25

SCAVENGERS
Quality

1 thru 7 . . . . . @1.25
8 thru 14 . . . . . @1.50

SCAVENGERS
Triumphant Comics

0 Fso(c),JnR(s), ... 2.50
0a "Free Copy" 2.50
0b Red Logo 2.50
1 JnR(s),I:Scavengers,Ximos, C:Doctor Chaos 2.50
1a 2nd Printing 2.50
2 JnR(s), ... 2.50
3 JnR(s),I:Lurok 2.50
4 JnR(s), ... 2.50
5 Fso(c),JnR(s),D:Jack Hanal . . . 2.50
6 JnR(s), ... 2.50
7 JnR(s),I:Zion 2.50
8 JnR(s),Nativity 2.50
9 JnR(s),The Challenge 2.50
10 JnR(s),Snowblind 2.50

SCION

1 and 2 . . . . . @2.00

SCOOBY DOO
Gold Key
March, 1970

1 . . . . . 30.00
2 . . . . . 20.00
3 . . . . . 15.00
4 . . . . . 15.00
5 . . . . . 15.00
6 . . . . . 12.00
7 . . . . . 12.00
8 . . . . . 12.00
9 . . . . . 12.00
10 . . . . . 12.00
11 thru 20 . . . . . @8.00
21 thru 29 . . . . . @5.00
30 February, 1975 . . . . . 5.00

SCOOBY DOO
Charlton Comics
April, 1975

1 . . . . . 15.00
2 . . . . . 6.00
3 . . . . . 6.00
4 . . . . . 6.00
5 . . . . . 6.00
6 . . . . . 4.00
7 . . . . . 4.00
8 . . . . . 4.00
9 . . . . . 4.00
10 . . . . . 4.00
11 December, 1976 . . . . . 4.00

SCORCHED EARTH
Tundra

1 Earth 2025,I:Dr.EliotGodwin . . . 3.50
2 Hunt for Eliot 2.95
3 Mystical Transformation 2.95

SCORPION CORP.
Dagger

1 PuD,JRI,CH, ... 2.75
2 PuD,JRI,CH,V:Victor Kyner . . . 2.75
3 PuD,BIH,V:Victor Kyner 2.75

SCORPIO ROSE
Eclipse

1 MR/TP,I:Dr.Orient 2.00
2 MR/TP 2.00

SCOUT
Eclipse
1 TT,I:Scout,Fash.In Action 6.00
2 TT,V:Buffalo Monster 3.00
3 TT,V:President Grail 2.50
4 TT,V:President Grail 2.50
5 TT,'Killin' Floor' 2.50
6 TT,V:President Grail 2.50
7 TT,TY,Rosanna's Diary 2.50
8 TT,TY 2.50
9 TT,TY,A:Airboy 2.50
10 TT,TY,I:Proj.Mountain Fire . . . 2.00
11 TT,FH,V:Rangers 2.00
12 TT,FH,'Me and the Devil' . . . 2.00
13 TT,FH,Monday:Eliminator 2.00
14 TT,FH,Monday:Eliminator 2.00
15 TT,FH,Monday:Eliminator 2.00
16 TT,3-D issue,F:Santana 2.00
17 TT,A:Beanworld 2.00
18 TT,FH,V:Lex Lucifer 2.00
19 TT,w/Record,V:Lex Lucifer . . . 3.00
20 TT,A:Monday:Eliminator 2.00
21 TT,A:Monday:Eliminator 1.75
22 TT,A:Swords of Texas 1.75
23 TT,A:Swords of Texas 1.75
24 TT,last Issue 1.75

Scout: War Shaman #1
© Eclipse Comics

SCOUT: WAR SHAMAN
Eclipse
1 TT,R:Scout (now a father) 2.25
2 TT,I:Redwire 1.95
3 TT,V:Atuma Yuma 1.95
4 TT,'Rollin' on the River' 1.95
5 TT,Hopi Katchina dieties 1.95
6 TT,Scout vs. Rosa Winter 1.95
7 TT,R:Redwire 1.95
8 TT,R:Beau LaDuke 1.95
9 TT,V:Doodyists 1.95
10 TT,TY,V:Redwire 1.95
11 TT,V:Redwire 1.95
12 TT,V:Snow Leopards 1.95
13 TT,F:Beau LaDuke 1.95
14 TT,V:Redwire 1.95
15 TT,V:Redwire 1.95
16 TT,'Wall of Death,'last issue . . 1.95

SEADRAGON
Elite
1 . . . . 3.00
1a 2nd printing 1.75
2 . . . . 2.00
3 . . . . 2.00
4 . . . . 2.00
5 thru 8 . . . . @1.75

SEA HUNT
Dell Publishing Co.
August, 1958
1 L.BridgesPh(c) all 75.00
2 . . . . 40.00
3 ATh 65.00
4 RsM 45.00
5 RsM 45.00
6 RsM 45.00
7 . . . . 40.00
8 RsM 45.00
9 RsM 45.00
10 RsM 45.00
11 RsM 45.00
12 . . . . 40.00
13 RsM 45.00

SEAQUEST
Nemesis
1 HC(c),DGC,KP,AA,Based on TV Show 2.50

SEBASTIAN
Walt Disney
1 From Little Mermaid 1.50
2 "While da Crab's Away" 1.50

SECOND LIFE OF DR. MIRAGE
Valiant
1 B:BL(s),BCh,V:Mast.Darque . . . 3.00
1a Gold Ed. 30.00
2 BCh,V:Master Darque 2.75
3 BCh 2.75
4 BCh,V:Bhrama 2.75
5 BCh,A:Shadowman,V:Master Darque 2.75
6 BCh,V:Dr.Eclipse 2.75
7 BCh,V:Dr.Eclipse,w/card 2.75
8 BCh, ... 2.75
9 BCh,A:Otherman 2.75
10 BCh,V:Otherman 2.50

SECRET AGENT
Gold Key
November, 1966
1 . . . . 75.00
2 . . . . 50.00

SECRET CITY SAGA
Topps
0 JK, ... 3.25
0 Gold Ed. 40.00
0 Red 25.00
1 thru 4 w/trading card 3.25

SECRET SQUIRREL
Gold Key
October, 1966
1 . . . . 50.00

SECRET WEAPONS
Valiant
1 JSP(a&s),BWi(i),I:Dr.Eclipse, A:Master Darque,A:Geoff, Livewire,Stronghold,Solar,X-O, Bloodshot,Shadowman 2.75
1a Gold Ed. 30.00
2 JSP(a&s),V:Master Darque, Dr.Eclipse 2.50
3 JSP(a&s),V:Speedshots 2.50
4 JSP(a&s),V:Scatterbrain 2.50
5 JSP(a&s),A:Ninjak 2.50
6 JPS(s),JPh(pl),TeH, V:Spider Aliens 2.50
7 JPS(s),V:Spider Aliens 2.50
8 JSP(a&pl),V:Harbingers 2.50
9 JSP(a&s),V:Webnet,w/card . . . 2.50
10 JSP(a&s),V:Webnet, w/card 2.50
11 PGr,New Line-up 2.75
12 PGr,A:Bloodshot 2.25

SEDUCTION OF THE INNOCENT
Eclipse
1 ATh,'Hanged by the Neck' reps. 2.50
2 . . . . 2.25
3 . . . . 2.00
4 ATh,NC,'World's Apart' 2.00
5 ATh,'The Phantom Ship' 2.00
6 ATh,RA,'Hands of Don Jose' . . 2.00
3-D #1 DSt(c) 2.25
3-D #2 ATh,MB,BWr,'Man Who Was Always on Time' 2.00

SEEKER: VENGEANCE
Sky Comics
1 JMt(s),I:Seeker 2.50

SENSEI
First
1 Mini-Series 2.75
2 . . . . 2.75
3 . . . . 2.75
4 . . . . 2.75

SENTINELS OF JUSTICE
AC Comics
1 Capt.Paragon 1.75
2 . . . . 1.75
3 . . . . 1.75
4 . . . . 1.75
5 . . . . 1.75
6 . . . . 1.75
7 . . . . 1.75

SENTRY: SPECIAL
Innovation
1 . . . . 2.75

SERAPHIM
Innovation
1 . . . . 2.50
2 . . . . 2.50

77 SUNSET STRIP
Dell Publishing Co.
January-March, 1960
1 Ph(c) 50.00
2 Ph(c),RsM 55.00

SEX WARRIORS
Dark Horse
1 I:Dakini 2.50
2 . . . . 2.50

SHADE SPECIAL
AC Comics
1 . . . . 1.50

SHADOW, THE
Archie Comics
August, 1964
1 . . . . 40.00
2 . . . . 30.00
3 . . . . 30.00
4 . . . . 30.00
5 . . . . 30.00
6 and 7 . . . . @25.00
8 September, 1965 . . . . 25.00

SHADOW COMICS
1 Guardians of Justice & The O-Force 1.50

THE SHADOW: IN THE COILS OF LEVIATHAN
Dark Horse

1 MK,V:Monster 3.25
2 MK, ... 3.25
3 MK,w/ GfD poster 3.25
4 MK,Final issue 3.25

SHADOWHAWK
Image

1 JV,I:Shadowhawk,Black Foil(c), Pin-up of The Others,w/ coupon#1 . . . . 10.00
1a w/o coupon 6.00
2 JV,V:Arsenal,A:Spawn, I:Infiniti 4.50
3 JV,V:Arsenal,w/glow-in-the-dark(c) 3.00
4 V:Savage Dragon 2.50
TPB rep.#1-4 . . . . 19.95

[2nd Series]

1 JV,Die Cut(c) 3.50
1a Gold Ed. 25.00
2 JV,Shadowhawk I.D. 4.00
2a Gold Ed. 30.00
3 Poster(c),JV,w/Ash Can 3.25

[3rd Series]

1 JV,CWf,V:Vortex,Hardedge, Red Foil(c) 2.25
1a Gold Ed. 20.00
2 JV,CWf,MA,I:Deadline, BU&I:US Male 2.25
3 JV(a&s),Shadowhawk has AIDS, V:Hardedge,Blackjak 2.25

Shadow Man #7
© Voyager Communications, Inc.

SHADOW MAN
Valiant

0 BH,TmR,Chromium (c),O:Maxim St.James,Shadowman 3.75
0a Newstand ed. 2.75
0b Gold Ed. 30.00
1 DL,JRu,I&O:Shadowman 25.00
2 DL,V:Serial Killer 20.00
3 V:Emil Sosa 15.00
4 DL,FM(c),Unity#6,A:Solar 6.00
5 DL,WS(c),Unity#14, A:Archer & Armstrong 5.00
6 SD,L:Lilora 4.00
7 DL,V:Creature 4.00
8 JDx(i),I:Master Darque 10.00
9 JDx(i),V:Darque's Minions 5.00
10 BH,I:Sandria 4.00
11 BH,N:Shadowman 4.00
12 BH,V:Master Darque 4.00
13 BH,V:Rev.Shadow Man 3.00
14 BH,JDx,V:Bikers 3.00
15 BH,JDx,V:JB,Fake Shadow Man,C:Turok 3.00
16 BH,JDx,I:Dr.Mirage, Carmen 8.00
17 BH,JDx,A:Archer and Armstrong 2.75
18 BH,JDx,A:Archer and Armstrong 2.75
19 BH,A:Aerosmith 3.00
20 BH,A:Master Darque, V:Shadowman's Father 2.75
21 BH,I:Maxim St.James (1895 Shadowman) 2.75
22 V:Master Darque 2.75
23 BH(a&s),A:Doctor Mirage, V:Master Darque 2.75
24 BH(a&s),V:H.A.T.E. 2.75
25 RgM,w/Valiant Era Trading Card 2.75
26 w/Valiant Era Trading Card . . . 2.75
27 BH,V:Drug Lord 2.75
28 BH,A:Master Darque 2.50
TPB rep.#1-3,6 . . . . 9.95

SHAMAN'S TEARS
Image

1 MGr,I:Shaman 4.00
1a Siver Prism Ed. 35.00
2 MGr,Poster(c) 3.50

SHANGHAI BREEZE

1 . . . . 1.75

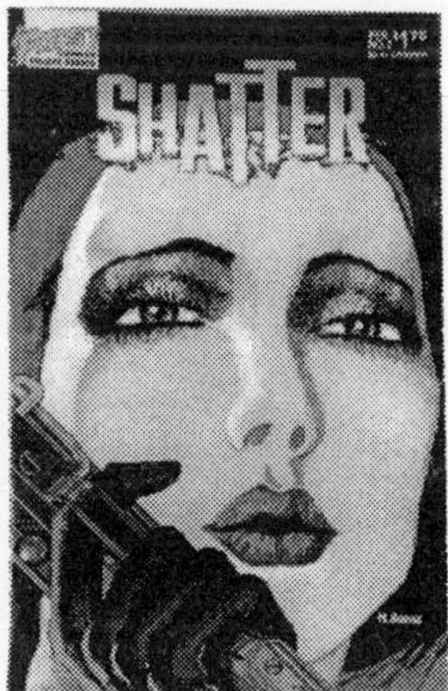

Shatter #2 © First Comics

SHATTER
First

1 . . . . 3.00
2 . . . . 2.50
3 . . . . 2.50
4 and 5 . . . . @2.00
6 thru 14 . . . . @1.75
Special #1 Computer Comic 5.00
#1a 2nd Printing 2.00

SHE-DEVILS ON WHEELS
Aircel

1 V:Man-Eaters 2.95
2 V:Man-Eaters 2.95
3 V:Man-Eaters 2.95

SHERIFF OF TOMBSTONE
Charlton Comics
November, 1958

1 AW,JSe 50.00
2 . . . . 30.00
3 thru 10 . . . . @20.00
11 thru 16 . . . . @20.00
17 September, 1961 . . . . 20.00

SHI
Crusade Comics

1 BiT,HMo,I:Shi 5.00

SHIELD

1 A:Steel Sterling 3.50
2 A:Steel Sterling 2.00
3 AN/EB,D:LancelotStrong 1.25

SHOCK SUSPENSE STORIES
Russ Cochran Press

1 reps.horror stories 1.50
2 inc.Kickback 1.50
3 thru 4 . . . . @2.00
5 thru 7 reps.horror stories 2.00
8 reps.horror stories 2.00

SHOOTING STARS

1 . . . . 2.50

SIEGEL & SHUSTER
Eclipse

1 . . . . 1.50
2 . . . . 1.75

SILENT MOBIUS
Viz

1 Katsumi 5.75
2 Katsumi vs. Spirit 5.25
3 Katsumi trapped within entity . . 4.95
4 Nami vs. Dragon 4.95
5 Kiddy vs. Wire 4.95
6 Search for Wire 4.95
GN 14.95

SILENT MOBIUS II
Viz

1 AMP Officers vs. Entities cont . 4.95
2 Entities in Amp H.Q. 4.95
3 V:Entity 4.95
4 The Esper Weapon 4.95
5 Last issue 4.95

SILENT MOBIUS III
Viz

1 F:Lebia/computer network 2.75
2 Lebia/computer link cont. 2.75
3 Lebia in danger 2.75
4 Return to Consciousness 2.75
5 Conclusion 2.75

SILVERBACK
Comico

1 thru 3 . . . . @2.50

SILVERHEELS
Pacific

1 . . . . 2.00
2 . . . . 1.50
3 . . . . 1.50

SILVER STAR
Pacific

1 JK 1.00
2 JK 1.00

3 JK 1.00
4 JK 1.00
5 JK 1.00
6 JK 1.00

SILVER STORM

1 . . . . 2.25
2 . . . . 1.95
3 . . . . 1.95
4 . . . . 1.95

SILVER STAR
Topps

1 w/Cards 2.95

SIMPSONS COMICS & STORIES
Welsh Publishing

1 . . . . 4.00
2 R:Sideshow Bob 2.25
3 Stolen Puma 2.25

Six Million Dollar Man #4
© Charlton Comics Group

SIX MILLION DOLLAR MAN, THE
Charlton

1 JSon,Lee Majors Ph(c) 3.00
2 NA(c),JSon,Ph(c) 3.00
3 Ph(c) 1.50
4 Ph(c) 1.50
5 Ph(c) 1.50
6 Ph(c) 1.50
7 Ph(c) 1.50
8 Ph(c) 1.50
9 Ph(c) 1.50

666: MARK OF THE BEAST
Fleetway

1 I:Fludd, BU:Wolfie Smith 1.95
2 thru 8. . . . . @1.95

SKATEMAN
Pacific

1 NA 1.50

SKY WOLF
Eclipse

1 V:Baron Von Tundra 1.75
2 TL,V:Baron Von Tundra 1.75
3 TL,cont. in Airboy #41 . . . . 1.75

SLAINE THE BERSERKER
Quality

1 thru 14 . . . . @1.25
15/16 . . . . 1.50
17 . . . . 1.50
18/19 . . . . 1.50
20 thru 28 . . . . @1.50

Becomes:

SLAINE THE KING

26 . . . . 1.50

SLAINE
Fleetway

1 thru 4 SBs,From 2000 AD . . @4.95

SLIMER
Now

1 . . . . 2.50
2 thru 15 . . . . @1.75
Becomes:

SLIMER & REAL GHOSTBUSTERS
Now

16 . . . . 1.75
17 . . . . 1.75
18 . . . . 1.75

SLUDGE
Malibu-Ultraverse

1 BWS,I:Sludge,BU:I:Rune 2.75
1a Ultra-Limited 50.00
2 AaL,I:Bloodstorm 2.25
3 AaL,V:River Men 2.25
4 AaL,Origins Month, V:Alligator 2.25
5 AaL,V:Garret Whale 2.25
6 AaL,A:Dragon Fang,Lord Pumpkin 2.25
7 V:Frank Hoag 2.25
8 AaL,V:Monsters 1.95

SNAGGLEPUSS
Gold Key
October, 1962

1 . . . . 35.00
2 . . . . 25.00
3 . . . . 25.00
4 September, 1963 . . . . 25.00

SNOOPER AND BLABBER DETECTIVES
Gold Key
November, 1962

1 . . . . 35.00
2 . . . . 25.00
3 May, 1963 . . . . 25.00

SNOW WHITE & SEVEN DWARVES GOLDEN ANNIV.
Gladstone

1 w/poster & stickers 24.00

SOLAR: MAN OF THE ATOM
Valiant

1 BWS,DP,BL,B:2nd Death B:Alpha & Omega 25.00
2 BWS,DP,BL,V:Dr Solar 18.00
3 BWS,DP,BL,V:Harada I:Harbinger Foundation 20.00
4 BWS,DP,BL,E:2nd Death V:Dr Solar 15.00

Solar: Man of the Atom #9
© Voyager Communications, Inc.

5 BWS,EC,V:Alien Armada 12.00
6 BWS,DP,SDr,V:Alien Armada X-O Armor 10.00
7 BWS,DP,SDr,V:Alien Armada X-O Armor 10.00
8 BWS,V:Dragon of Bangkok . . . 8.00
9 BWS,DP,SDr, V:Erica's Baby . . 8.00
10 BWS,DP,SDr,JDx,I:Eternal Warrior,E:Alpha&Omega 50.00
10a 2nd printing 6.00
11 SDr,A:Eternal Warrior, Prequel to Unity #0 . . . . 5.00
12 SDr,FM(c),Unity#9,O:Pierce, Albert 4.00
13 DP,SDr,WS(c),Unity#17, V:Pierce 4.00
14 DP,SDr,I:Bender (becomes Dr.Eclipse) 15.00
15 SD,V:Bender 6.00
16 Solar moves to California 3.00
17 SDr(i),V:X-O Manowar 3.00
18 SDr(i),A:X-Manowar 3.00
19 SDr(i),V:Videogame 3.00
20 SDr(i),Dawn of the Malevolence 3.00
21 SDr(i),Master Darque 3.00
22 SDr(i),V:Master Darque,A: Bender(Dr.Eclipse) 3.00
23 SDr(i),JQ(c),V:Master Darque,I:Solar War God 3.50
24 SDr(i),A:Solar War God 2.75
25 V:Dr.Eclpise 2.50
26 Phil and Gayle on vaction 2.50
27 in Austrialia 2.50
28 A:Solar War God 2.50
29 KVH(s),JP(i),Valiant Vision, A:Solar War God 3.00
30 KVH(s),JP,V:Energy Parasite 2.50
31 KVH(s),JP,Chrismas Issue . . . 2.50
32 KVH(s),JP,Parent's Night 2.50
33 KVH(s),PGr,JP,B:Solar the Destroyer,w/card 2.50
34 KVH(s),PGr,V:Spider Alien . . . 2.50
35 KVH(s),PGr,JP,E:Solar the Destroyer,Valiant Vision 2.50
36 KVH(s),PGr,JP,B:Revenge times two,V:Doctor Eclipse, Ravenus 2.25
TPB Alpha & Omega 9.95

SOLDIERS OF FREEDOM
Americomics
1 . . . . 1.75
2 . . . . 1.95

SOLITAIRE
Malibu-Ultraverse
1 w/card Ace of Clubs 2.75
1a w/card Ace of Diamonds 2.75
1b w/card Ace of Hearts 2.75
1c w/card Ace of Spades 2.75
1d Newsstand Ed. 2.25
2 GJ(s),JJ,Break-Thru x-over, V:Moon Man 2.25
3 Origins Month, I:Monkey-Woman 2.25
4 O:Solitaire 2.25
5 JJ,V:Djinn 2.25
6 JJ,V:Lone 1.95

SOLOMON KANE
Blackthorne
1 3-D Special 2.50
2 3-D Special 2.50
1 thru 4 . . . . @2.50

SOLUTION
Malibu-Ultraverse
1 DaR,I:Solution 3.00
2 DaR,BWS,V:Rex Mundi,Quatro, BU:Rune 3.00
3 DaR,A:Hardcase,Choice 2.50
4 DaR,Break-Thru x-over, A:Hardcase,Choice 2.50
5 F:Dropkick 2.25
6 B:O:Solution 2.25
7 KM,O:Solution 2.25
8 KM(c),E:O:Solution 2.25
9 F:Shadowmage 1.95

SOMERSET HOLMES
Pacific
1 BA,AW,I:Cliff Hanger & Somerset Holmes 2.50
2 thru 4 BA,AW . . . . . . @2.00
Eclipse
5 BA,AW 2.00
6 BA 2.00

SONG OF THE CID
Calibre/Tome
1 Story of El Cid 2.95
2 Story of El Cid concl. 2.95

SONIC THE HEDGEHOG
Archie
1 A:Mobius,V:Robotnik 1.50

SON OF MUTANT WORLD
Fantagor
1 BA 2.00
2 . . . . 2.00

SOULQUEST
Innovation
1 BA 3.95

SOUPY SALES COMIC BOOK
Archie Publications
1965
1 . . . . 75.00

SPACE ARK
AC Comics
1 . . . . 3.00
2 . . . . 2.00

SPACE FAMILY ROBINSON
Gold Key
December, 1962
1 DSp 150.00
2 . . . . 75.00
3 . . . . 45.00
4 . . . . 45.00
5 . . . . 45.00
6 B:Captain Venture 45.00
7 . . . . 45.00
8 . . . . 45.00
9 . . . . 45.00
10 . . . . 45.00
11 thru 20 . . . . @30.00
21 thru 36 October, 1969 . . . @25.00

SPACE GHOST
Gold Key
March, 1967
1 . . . . 6.00

Space Ghost #1 © Comico

SPACE GHOST
Comico
1 SR,V:Robot Master 3.50

SPACE MAN
Dell Publishing Co.
January-March, 1962
1 . . . . 50.00
2 . . . . 25.00
3 . . . . 25.00
4 . . . . 15.00
5 . . . . 15.00
6 . . . . 15.00
7 . . . . 15.00
8 . . . . 15.00
9 . . . . 15.00
10 . . . . 15.00

SPACE: 1999
A Plus Comics
1 GM,JBy 2.50

SPACE USAGI
Mirage
1 From TMNT 2.75
2 thru 3 From TMNT 2.75

SPACE WAR
Charlton Comics
October, 1959
1 . . . . 100.00
2 . . . . 50.00
3 . . . . 45.00
4 SD,SD(c) 90.00
5 SD,SD(c) 90.00
6 SD 85.00
7 . . . . 25.00
8 SD,SD(c) 85.00
9 . . . . 30.00
10 SD,SD(c) 85.00
11 . . . . 30.00
12 . . . . 30.00
13 . . . . 30.00
14 . . . . 30.00
15 . . . . 30.00
16 thru 27 . . . . @20.00
Becomes:

FIGHTIN' FIVE
28 SD,SD(c) 25.00
29 SD,SD(c) 25.00
30 SD,SD(c) 30.00
31 SD,SD(c) 30.00
32 . . . . 3.00
33 SD,SD(c) 30.00
34 Sd,SD(c) 30.00

Spawn #1 © Todd McFarlane

SPAWN
Image
1 TM,I:Spawn,w/GP,DK pinups 15.00
2 TM,V:The Violator 13.00
3 TM,V:The Violator 11.00
4 TM,V:The Violator, w/coupon #2 . . . . . . 13.00
4a w/o coupon 6.00
5 TM,O:Billy Kincaid 8.00
6 TM,I:Overt-Kill 7.00
7 TM,V:Overt-Kill 7.00
8 TM,AMo(s),F:Billy Kincaid . . . 4.00
9 NGa(s),TM,I:Angela 4.00
10 DS(s),TM,A:Cerebus 3.50
11 FM(s),TM 3.50
12 TM,Chapel killed Spawn 3.00
13 TM,A:Youngblood 3.00
14 TM,A:The Violator 2.75
15 TM 2.75
16 GCa,I:Anti-Spawn 2.50
17 GCa,V:Anti-Spawn 2.50
18 GCa,ATi,D:Anti-Spawn 2.50
TPB Capital Collection rep.#1-3 limited to 1200 . . . . . . 300.00

SPAWN/BATMAN
Image/DC

1 FM(s),TM, . . . 4.50

SPECTRUM COMICS PRESENTS
Spectrum

1 I:Survivors . . . 3.50

SPEED RACER
Now

1 . . . 3.50
1a 2nd printing . . . 1.50
2 thru 33 . . . @2.00
34 . . . 1.75
35 . . . 1.75
36 . . . 1.75
37 . . . 1.75
38 . . . 1.75
Special #1 . . . 2.50
#1 2nd printing . . . 1.75
Special #2 . . . 3.50
Classics, Vol #2 . . . 3.95
Classics, Vol #3 . . . 3.95

[2nd Series]

1 R:Speed Racer . . . 1.95
2 . . . 1.95
3 V:Giant Crab . . . 1.95
4 . . . 1.95
5 Racer-X . . . 1.95

Spellbinders #1 © Quality Comics

SPELLBINDERS
Quality

1 Nemesis the Warlock . . . 1.25
2 Nemesis the Warlock . . . 1.25
3 Nemesis the Warlock . . . 1.25
4 Nemesis the Warlock . . . 1.25
5 Nemesis the Warlock . . . 1.25
6 Nemesis the Warlock . . . 1.25
7 Nemesis the Warlock . . . 1.25
8 Nemesis the Warlock . . . 1.25
9 Nemesis the Warlock . . . 1.25
10 Nemesis the Warlock . . . 1.25
11 Nemesis the Warlock . . . 1.25

SPIDER
Eclipse

1 TT,'Blood Dance' . . . 7.00
2 TT,'Blood Mark' . . . 6.00
3 TT,The Spider Unmasked . . . 5.50

SPIDER: REIGN OF THE VAMPIRE KING
Eclipse

1 TT,I:Legion of Vermin . . . 5.25
2 thru 4 TT . . . @2.50

SPIDERFEMME
Personality

1 Rep. parody . . . 2.50

SPIRAL PATH
Eclipse

1 V:Tairngir . . . 1.75
2 V:King Artuk . . . 1.75

SPIRIT
Harvey
October, 1966

1 WE,O:Spirit . . . 35.00
2 WE,O:The Octopus . . . 35.00

SPLITTING IMAGE
Image

1 DSm,A:Marginal Seven . . . 2.25
2 DsM,A:Marginal Seven . . . 2.25

SPOOKY HAUNTED HOUSE
Harvey Publications
October, 1972

1 . . . 10.00
2 . . . 5.00
3 . . . 5.00
4 . . . 5.00
5 . . . 5.00
6 thru 10 . . . @2.50
11 thru 14 . . . @1.00
15 February, 1975 . . . 1.00

SPOOKY SPOOKTOWN
Harvey Publications
June, 1966

1 B:Casper,Spooky,68 pgs . . . 75.00
2 . . . 40.00
3 . . . 30.00
4 . . . 30.00
5 . . . 30.00
6 thru 10 . . . @18.00
11 thru 20 . . . @15.00
21 thru 30 . . . @15.00
31 thru 39 E:68 pgs . . . @4.50
40 thru 45 . . . @2.50
46 thru 65 . . . @1.00
66 December, 1976 . . . 1.00

SPYMAN

1 GT,JSo,1st prof work, I:Spyman . . . 15.00
2 DAy,JSo,V:Cyclops . . . 10.00
3 . . . 8.00

SQUALOR
First

1 . . . 2.75
2 . . . 2.75
3 . . . 2.75

STAINLESS STEEL RAT
Eagle

1 . . . 2.25
2 thru 6 . . . @1.50

STAN SHAW'S BEAUTY & THE BEAST
Dark Horse

1 Based on the book . . . 4.95

STAR BLAZERS
Comico

1 . . . 3.00
2 . . . 1.75
3 . . . 1.75
4 . . . 1.75

[2nd Series]

1 . . . 1.95
2 . . . 1.95
3 thru 5 . . . @2.50

STARFORCE SIX SPECIAL
AC Comics

1 . . . 1.50

STARLIGHT

1 . . . 1.95

STAR MASTERS
AC Comics

1 . . . 1.50

STAR REACH CLASSICS
Eclipse

1 JSn,NA(r) . . . 2.00
2 AN . . . 2.00
3 HC . . . 2.00
4 FB(r) . . . 2.00
5 . . . 2.00
6 . . . 2.00

STAR SLAMMERS
Malibu-Bravura

1 WS(a&s), . . . 2.50

STARSLAYER
Pacific

1 MGr,O:Starslayer . . . 3.00
2 MGr,DSt,I:Rocketeer . . . 27.00
3 DSt,MGr,A:Rocketeer(2ndApp.) 20.00
4 MGr,Baraka Kuhr . . . 2.00
5 MGr,SA,A:Groo . . . 17.00
6 MGr.conclusion story . . . 2.00

First

7 MGr layouts . . . 2.00
8 MGr layouts, MG . . . 1.50
9 MGr layouts, MG . . . 2.25
10 TT,MG,I:Grimjack . . . 4.00
11 TT,MG,A:Grimjack . . . 2.00
12 TT,MG,A:Grimjack . . . 2.00
13 TT,MG,A:Grimjack . . . 2.00
14 TT,A:Grimjack . . . 2.00
15 TT,A:Grimjack . . . 2.00
16 TT,A:Grimjack . . . 2.00
17 TT,A:Grimjack . . . 2.00
18 TT,Grimjack x-over . . . 2.00
19 TT,TS,A:Black Flame . . . 1.25
20 TT,TS,A:Black Flame . . . 1.25
21 TT,TS,A:Black Flame . . . 1.25
22 TT,TS,A:Black Flame . . . 1.25
23 TT,TS,A:Black Flame . . . 1.25
24 TT,TS,A:Black Flame . . . 1.25
25 TS,A:Black Flame . . . 1.25
26 TS,Black Flame full story . . . 1.25
27 A:Black Flame . . . 1.25
28 A:Black Flame . . . 1.25
29 TS,A:Black Flame . . . 1.25
30 TS,A:Black Flame . . . 1.25
31 2nd Anniversary Issue . . . 1.25
32 TS,A:Black Flame . . . 1.25
33 TS,A:Black Flame . . . 1.25
34 last issue . . . 1.25
Graphic Novel . . . 9.95

STAR TREK
Gold Key

1 Planet of No Return . . . 375.00
2 Devil's Isle of Space . . . 200.00
3 Invasion of City Builders . . . 175.00
4 Peril of Planet Quick Change 175.00

All comics prices listed are for *Near Mint* condition.

5 Ghost Planet 175.00
6 When Planets Collide 135.00
7 Voodoo Planet 125.00
8 Youth Trap 125.00
9 Legacy of Lazarus 125.00
10 Sceptre of the Sun 75.00
11 Brain Shockers 75.00
12 Flight of the Buccaneer 75.00
13 Dark Traveler 75.00
14 Enterprise Mutiny 75.00
15 Museum a/t End of Time . . . 75.00
16 Day of the Inquisitors 75.00
17 Cosmic Cavemen 75.00
18 The Hijacked Planet 75.00
19 The Haunted Asteroid 75.00
20 A World Gone Mad 75.00
21 The Mummies of Heitus VII . . 55.00
22 Siege in Superspace 50.00
23 Child's Play 50.00
24 The Trial of Capt. Kirk 50.00
25 Dwarf Planet 50.00
26 The Perfect Dream 50.00
27 Ice Journey 50.00
28 The Mimicking Menace 50.00
29 rep. Star Trek #1 . . . . 50.00
30 Death of a Star 30.00
31 'The Final Truth'. 30.00
32 'The Animal People' 30.00
33 'The Choice' 30.00
34 'The Psychocrystals' 30.00
35 rep. Star Trek #4 . . . . 30.00
36 'A Bomb in Time' 30.00
37 rep. Star Trek #5 . . . . 30.00
38 'One of our Captains is Missing' 30.00
39 'Prophet of Peace' 30.00
40 AMc,Furlough to Fury, A: Barbara McCoy 30.00
41 AMc,The Evictors 30.00
42 'World Against Time' 30.00
43 'World Beneath the Waves' . . 30.00
44 'Prince Traitor' 30.00
45 rep. Star Trek #7 . . . . 30.00
46 'Mr. Oracle' 30.00
47 AMc,'This Tree Bears Bitter Fruit' 30.00
48 AMc,Murder on Enterprise . . 30.00
49 AMc,'A Warp in Space' 30.00
50 AMc,'The Planet of No Life' . 30.00
51 AMc,DestinationAnnihilation6 20.00
52 AMc,'And A Child Shall Lead Them' 20.00
53 AMc,'What Fools..Mortals Be' 20.00
54 AMc,'Sport of Knaves' 20.00
55 AMc,A World Against Itself . 20.00
56 AMc,No Time Like The Past, A:Guardian of Forever 20.00
57 AMc,'Spore of the Devil' 20.00
58 AMc,'Brain Damaged Planet' . 20.00
59 AMc,'To Err is Vulcan' 20.00
60 AMc,'The Empire Man' 20.00
61 AMc,'Operation Con Game' . 20.00

STAR TREK: DEEP SPACE NINE
Malibu

1 Direct ed. 3.25
1a Photo(c). 3.00
2 w/skycap 2.75
3 Murder on DS9 . . . . 2.75
4 MiB(s),F:Bashir,Dax 2.75
5 MiB(s),V:Slaves 2.75
6 MiB(s),Three Stories 2.75
7 F:Kira 2.75
8 B:Requiem 2.75
9 E:Requiem 2.75
10 Descendants 2.50

STAR WARS: DARK EMPIRE
Dark Horse

1 CK,Destiny of a Jedi 25.00
1a 2nd Printing 5.00

Star Wars: Dark Empire #5
© Dark Horse Comics

1b Gold Ed. 50.00
2 CK,Destroyer of worlds, very low print run 30.00
2a 2nd Printing 5.00
2b Gold Ed. 50.00
3 CK,V:The Emperor 18.00
3a 2nd printing 4.00
3b Gold Ed. 50.00
4 CK,V:The Emperor 15.00
4a Gold Ed. 50.00
5 CK,V:The Emperor 13.00
5a Gold Ed. 50.00
6 CK,V:Emperor,last issue 12.00
6a Gold Ed. 50.00
TPB rep.#1-6 . . . . 19.95

STAR WARS: DROIDS
Dark Horse

1 F:C-3PO,R2-D2 . . . . 3.25
2 V:Thieves 2.50

STAR WARS: TALES OF THE JEDI
Dark Horse

1 RV,I:Ulic Qel-Droma 3.00
2 RV,A:Ulic Qel-Droma 2.75
3 RV,D:Andur 2.75
4 RV,A:Jabba the Hut 2.75
5 RV,last issue 2.75

STAR WARS IN 3-D
Blackthorne

1 thru 7 . . . . @2.50

STARWATCHERS
Valiant

1 MLe,DG,Chromium(c),Valiant Vision, ... 3.50

STARWOLVES: JUPITER RUN

1 . . . . 1.95

S.T.A.T.
Majestic

1 FdS(s),PhH,I:S.T.A.T. 2.50

STEALTH SQUAD
Petra Comics

1 I:Stealth Squad 2.50

STEED & MRS PEEL
Eclipse

1 IG,The Golden Game 4.95
2 IG,The Golden Game 4.95
3 IG,The Golden Game 4.95

STEEL CLAW
Quality

1 H:Ken Bulmer 1.25
2 . . . . 1.00
3 . . . . 1.00
4 . . . . 1.00

STEEL STERLING
Archie Publications
(formerly SHIELD)

4 EB 1.00
5 EB 1.00
6 EB 1.00
7 EB 1.00

STEVE ZODIAC & THE FIREBALL XL-5
Gold Key
January, 1964

1 . . . . 50.00

Sting of the Green Hornet #2
© Now Comics

STING OF THE GREEN HORNET
Now

1 Polybagged w/trading card . . . 2.75
2 inc.Full color poster 2.75
3 inc.Full color poster 2.75

STINGER

1 . . . . 1.75

STORMWATCH
Image

0 JSc(c),O:Stormwatch, V:Terrorists,w/card 2.50
1 JLe(c&s),ScC,TvS(i), I:Stormwatch 2.25
1a Gold Ed. 25.00
2 JLe(c&s),ScC,TvS(i),I:Cannon, Winter,Fahrenheit,Regent 2.25
3 JLe(c&s),ScC,TvS(i),V:Regent,

I:Backlash 2.25
4 V:Daemonites 2.25
5 SRf(s),BBh,V:Daemonites 2.25
6 BCi,ScC,TC,A:Mercs 2.25
7 BCi,ScC,TC,A:Mercs 2.25
8 BCi,ScC,TC,A:Mercs 2.25
9 BCi,I:Defile 2.25
25 BCi,A:Spartan 2.50
Sourcebok JLe(s),DT 2.75
Spec.#1 RMz(s),DT, 4.25

STRANGE DAYS
Eclipse

1 2.50
2 2.50
3 1.50

STRANGE SUSPENSE STORIES/ CAPTAIN ATOM
Charlton Comics

75 SD,O:CaptainAtom,1960Rep. 75.00
76 SD, Capt.Atom,1960Rep. 30.00
77 SD, Capt.Atom,1960Rep. 30.00

Becomes:

CAPTAIN ATOM
December, 1965

78 SD, new stories begin 65.00
79 SD,I:Dr.Spectro 40.00
80 SD 40.00
81 SD,V:Dr.Spectro 40.00
82 SD,I:Nightshade,Ghost 40.00

Captain Atom #89 © Charlton Comics

83 SD,I:Ted Kord/Blue Beetle 35.00
84 SD,N:Captain Atom 30.00
85 SD,A:Blue Beetle,I:Punch & Jewelee 30.00
86 SD,A:Ghost, Blue Beetle 30.00
87 SD,JAp,A:Nightshade 30.00
88 SD/FMc,JAp,A:Nightshade 30.00
89 SD/FMc,JAp,A:Nightshade, Ghost, last issue Dec.1967 30.00

STRANGERS
Malibu-Ultraverse

1 I:Strangers 5.00
1a Ultra-Limited 50.00
1b Full Hologram (c) 75.00
2 A:J.D.Hunt 5.00
3 I:TNTNT 3.50
4 A:Hardcase 3.00
5 BWS,BU:Rune 3.00
6 J:Yrial,I:Deathwish, 2.25
7 Break-Thru x-over 2.25
8 RHo,ANi,O:Solution 2.25
9 AV(i),I:Ulta Pirates 2.25
10 AV(i),V:Bastinado 2.25
11 in Alderson Disk 2.25
12 O:Yrial 1.95

STRAW MEN
Innovation

1 1.95
2 1.95

STREET FIGHTER
Ocean

1 1.75
2 1.75
3 1.75

STREET FIGHTER
Malibu

1 Based on Video Game 3.25

STRIKE!
Eclipse

1 TL,RT,I&O:New Strike 1.75
2 TL,RT 1.25
3 TL,RT 1.25
4 TL,RT,V:Renegade CIA Agents 1.25
5 TL,RT,V:Alien Bugs 1.25
6 TL,RT,'Legacy of the Lost' 1.75

STRIKER
Viz

1 thru 2 2.75

STRIKEFORCE AMERICA
Comico

1 SK(c),I:Strikeforce America 2.50

STRIKE! vs. SGT. STRIKE
Eclipse

Spec #1 TL,RT,'The Man' 1.95

STRONG MAN
AC Comics

1 2.95

STRONTIUM DOG
Eagle

1 1.50
2 1.25
3 1.25
4 1.25
5 1.25
6 1.25

Quality

7 1.25
8 1.25
9 1.25
10 1.25
11 1.25
12 1.25
13 1.25
14 1.25
15/16 1.50
17 1.50
18/19 1.50
20 thru 29 @1.50

STRONTIUM DOG
[2nd Series]

1 1.25

Quality

Special1 1.50

STUMBO THE GIANT
Blackthorne

1 3-D 2.50

STUMBO TINYTOWN
Harvey Publications
October, 1963

1 75.00
2 40.00
3 25.00
4 25.00
5 25.00
6 thru 12 @19.00
13 November, 1966 19.00

STUPID HEROES
Mirage

1 PeL(s), 2.75

STURM THE TROOPER

1 1.95
2 1.95
3 1.95

SUBSPECIES
Eternity

1 Movie Adaption 3.00
2 Movie Adaption 2.50
3 Movie Adaption 2.50
4 Movie Adaption 2.50

SUN RUNNERS
Pacific

1 2.50
2 2.00
3 2.00

Eclipse

4 2.00
5 2.00
6 'Sins of the Father' 1.75
7 'Dark Side of Mark Dancer' 1.75
Summer Special #1 1.75

SUNSET CARSON
AC Comics

1 Based on Cowboy Star 5.00

SUPER BOOK OF COMICS
Western Publishing Co.

N# Dick Tracy 225.00
1 Dick Tracy 190.00
2 Smitty,Magic Morro 36.00
3 30.00
4 Red Ryder,Magic Morro 30.00
5 Don Winslow,Magic Morro 30.00
5 Dom Winslow,Stratosphere Jim 30.00
5 Terry & the Pirates 70.00
6 Don Winslow 38.00
7 Little Orphan Annie 38.00
8 72.00
9 Terry & the Pirates 60.00

SUPER-BOOK OF COMICS
Western Publishing Co.
1944

1 Dick Tracy (Omar) 135.00
1 Dick Tracy (Hancock) 100.00
2 Bugs Bunny (Omar) 40.00
2 Bugs Bunny (Hancock) 30.00
3 Terry & the Pirates (Omar) 75.00
3 Terry & the Pirates (Hancock) 65.00
4 Andy Panda (Omar) 35.00
4 Andy Panda (Hancock) 30.00
5 Smokey Stover (Omar) 30.00
5 Smokey Stover (Hancock) 20.00
6 Porky Pig (Omar) 35.00
6 Porky Pig (Hancock) 30.00
7 Smilin' Jack (Omar) 40.00
7 Smilin' Jack (Hancock) 35.00
8 Oswald the Rabbit (Omar) 30.00
8 Oswald the Rabbit (Hancock) 20.00
9 Alley Oop (Omar) 80.00
9 Alley Oop (Hancock) 70.00

10 Elmer Fudd (Omar) 30.00
10 Elmer Fudd (Hancock) 20.00
11 Little Orphan Annie (Omar) .. 45.00
11 Little Orphan Amnie (Hancock) 35.00
12 Woody Woodpecker (Omar) . 35.00
12 WoodyWoodpecker(Hancock) 25.00
13 Dick Tracy (Omar) 80.00
13 Dick Tracy (Hancock) 75.00
14 Bugs Bunny (Omar) 30.00
14 Bugs Bunny (Hanock) 25.00
15 Andy Panda (Omar) 20.00
15 Andy Panda (Hancock) 15.00
16 Terry & the Pirates (Omar) .. 70.00
16 Terry & the Pirates (Hancock) 50.00
17 Smokey Stover (Omar) 30.00
17 Smokey Stover (Hancock) .. 30.00
18 Porky Pig (Omar) 25.00
18 Smokey Stover (Hancock) .. 20.00
19 Smilin' Jack (Omar) 35.00
N# Smilin' Jack (Hancock) 20.00
20 Oswald the Rabbit (Omar) .. 25.00
N# Oswald the Rabbit (Hancock) 15.00
21 Gasoline Alley (Omar) 45.00
N# Gasoline Alley (Hancock) ... 35.00
22 Elmer Fudd (Omar) 25.00
N# Elmer Fudd (Hancock) 30.00
23 Little Orphan Annie (Omar) .. 30.00
N# Little Orphan Annie (Hancock) 25.00
24 Woody Woodpecker (Omar) . 22.00
N# WoodyWoodpecker(Hancock) 18.00
25 Dick Tracy (Omar) 70.00
N# Dick Tracy (Hancock) 50.00
26 Bugs Bunny (Omar) 25.00
N# Bugs Bunny (Hancock) 20.00
27 Andy Panda (Omar) 20.00
27 Andy Panda (Hancock) 15.00
28 Terry & the Pirates (Omar) .. 70.00
28 Terry & the Pirates (Hancock) 50.00
29 Smokey Stover (Omar) 25.00
29 Smokey Stover (Hancock) .. 20.00
30 Porky Pig (Omar) 25.00
30 Porky Pig (Hancock) 20.00
N# Bugs Bunny (Hancock) 20.00

SUPER CAR
Gold Key
November, 1962

1 .... 150.00
2 .... 75.00
3 .... 75.00
4 August, 1963 .... 100.00

SUPERCOPS
Now

1 .... 1.75
2 .... 1.75
3 .... 1.75
4 .... 1.75

SUPER GOOF
Gold Key
October, 1965

1 .... 15.00
2 thru 10 .... @8.00
11 thru 20 .... @5.00
21 thru 30 .... @4.00
31 thru 73 .... @2.00
74 1982 .... 2.00

SUPER HEROES VERSUS SUPERVILLIANS
Archie Publications
July, 1966

1 A:Flyman,Black Hood,The Web, The Shield 40.00

SUPER MARIO BROS.

1 .... 1.95
2 .... 1.95
3 .... 1.95
4 .... 1.95

5 .... 1.95
6 .... 1.95
Spec #1 .... 1.95

SUPER-PATRIOT
Image

1 N:Super-Patriot 2.25
2 KN(i),O:Super-Patriot 2.25
3 A:Youngblood 2.25

SUPREME
Image

1 B:RLd(s&i),BrM, V:Youngblood 3.00
1a Gold Ed. 65.00
2 BrM,I:Heavy Mettle 2.50
3 thru 4 BrM 2.50
5 BrM(a&s),Clv(i),I:Thor, V:Chrome 2.50
6 BrM,Clv(i),I:Starguard, A:Thor,V:Chrome 2.50
7 Rip,ErS(s),SwM,A:Starguard, A:Thor, ... 2.50
8 Rip(s),SwM,V:Thor, ... 2.50
9 Rip&KtH(s),BrM,Clv(i), V:Thor 2.50
10 KrH(s),BrM,JRu(i), BU:I:Black & White 2.50
11 I:Newmen 2.50

SURGE
Eclipse

1 A:DNAgents 3.00
2 A:DNAgents 2.00
3 A:DNAgents 3.00
4 A:DNAgents 3.00

Survivors #3 © Spectrum Comics

SURVIVORS
Spectrum

1 Mag. size 5.00
2 .... 3.50
3 The Old One 2.50
4 .... 2.50

SURVIVORS
Fantagraphics

1 .... 2.50
2 .... 2.50
3 .... 2.50

SWORDS OF TEXAS
Eclipse

1 FH,New America 2.00
2 FH,V:Baja Badlands 1.75
3 FH,TY(c),V:Dogs of Danger ... 1.75
4 FH,V:Samurai Master 1.75

SYPHONS

1 .... 1.50
2 thru 7 .... @1.50

TAILSPIN
Walt Disney
[Mini-Series]

1 Take-off Pt.1 .... 2.75
2 Take-off Pt 2 .... 2.25
3 Take-off Pt 3,Khan Job 2.00
4 Take-off pt 4 .... 1.75

TAILSPIN
Walt Disney
[Reg.-Series]

1 Sky-Raker Pt.1 .... 2.50
2 Sky-Raker Pt.2 .... 2.00
3 Idiots Abroad 1.75
4 Contractual Desperation 1.75
5 The Oldman &the Sea Duck .. 1.75
6 F'reeze a Jolly Good Fellow .. 1.75

TALES CALCULATED TO DRIVE YOU BATS
Archie Publications
November, 1961

1 .... 45.00
2 .... 20.00
3 thru 6 Nov., 1962 .... @15.00

TALES FROM THE CRYPT
Gladstone

1 E.C.rep.AW/FF,GS 7.50
2 rep. 4.50
3 rep. 3.50
4 rep. 3.00
5 rep.TFTC #45 .... 3.00
6 rep.TFTC #42 .... 3.00

TALES FROM THE CRYPT
Russ Cochran Publ

1 rep. TFTC #31,CSS#12 ...... 2.75
2 rep. TFTC #34,CSS#15 ...... 2.50
3 rep. TFTC, CSS 2.50
4 rep. TFTC #43,CSS#18 ...... 2.50
5 rep. TFTC,CSS#23 .... 2.00

[2nd Series]

1 rep.horror stories 1.50
2 inc.The Maestro's Hand 1.50
3 thru 6 .... @2.00
7 thru 8 .... @2.00

TALES OF TERROR
Eclipse

1 .... 3.00
2 'Claustrophobia' 1.75
3 GM,'Eyes in the Darkness' ... 1.75
4 TT,TY,JBo(c),'The Slasher' ... 1.75
5 'Back Forty,''Shoe Button Eyes' 1.75
6 'Good Neighbors' 1.75
7 SBi,JBo,SK(i),'Video' 1.75
8 HB,'Revenant,''Food for Thought'1.75
9 .... 1.75
10 .... 2.00
11 TT,JBo(c),'Black Cullen' 2.00
12 JBo,FH,'Last of the Vampires' . 2.00
13 .... 2.00

TALES OF THE GREEN BERET

Dell Publishing Co.
January, 1967

1 SG 15.00
2 .... 10.00
3 .... 10.00
4 .... 10.00
5 .... 7.00

TALES OF THE GREEN HORNET
Now

1 NA(c),O:Green Hornet Pt.1 ... 3.00
2 O:Green Hornet Pt.2 .... 2.50
3 Gun Metal Green 1.95
4 Targets 1.95

TALES OF THE MYSTERIOUS TRAVELER
Charlton Comics
August, 1956

1 .... 200.00
2 SD 175.00
3 SD,SD(c) 175.00
4 SD,SD(c) 225.00
5 SD,SD(c) 225.00
6 SD,SD(c) 225.00
7 SD 175.00
8 SD 175.00
9 SD 175.00
10 SD,SD(c) 200.00
11 SD,SD(c) 200.00
12 .... 65.00
13 .... 65.00
14 (1985) 1.00
15 (1985) 1.00

TALES OF THE SUN RUNNERS
Sirius Comics

1 .... 1.50
2 .... 2.00
3 .... 2.00

TALESPIN
Walt Disney
(Mini-Series)

1 Take-off Pt.1 .... 2.75
2 Take-off Pt 2 .... 2.25
3 Take-off Pt 3,Khan Job 2.00
4 Take-off pt 4 .... 1.75

TALESPIN
Walt Disney
(Reg.-Series)

1 'Sky-Raker' Pt.1 .... 2.50
2 'Sky-Raker' Pt.2 .... 2.00
3 'Idiots Abroad' 1.75
4 'Contractual Desperation' 1.75
5 'The Oldman & the Sea Duck' . 1.75
6 'F'reeze a Jolly Good Fellow' .. 1.75

TANK GIRL
Dark Horse

1 thru 2 .... @2.50

TARGET AIRBOY
Eclipse

1 SK,A:Clint 1.95

TARZAN: THE BECKONING
Malibu

1 TY,I:The Spider Man 2.75
2 TY,Going back to Africa 2.50
3 thru 6 .... 2.50

TARZAN THE WARRIOR
Malibu

1 SBs(c),O:Tarzan 3.50
2 .... 2.75
3 .... 2.75
4 Wom'cha's Ship 2.75

Tarzan the Warrior #1
© Malibu Comics

TARZAN: LOVE, LIES, AND THE LOST CITY
Malibu

1 MWg&WS(s),Short Stories 3.95
2 The lost city of Opar 2.50
3 Final issue 2.50

TASMANIAN DEVIL & HIS TASTY FRIENDS
Gold Key
November, 1962

1 .... 70.00

TASTEE-FREEZ COMICS
Harvey Comics
1957

1 Little Dot 30.00
2 Rags Rabbit 15.00
3 Casper 25.00
4 Sad Sack 15.00
5 Mazie 15.00
6 Dick Tracy 30.00

TEAM ANARCHY
Anarchy

1 I:Team Anarchy 2.75
2 thru 3 .... 2.75
4 PuD,MaS,I:Primal 2.75

TEAM YANKEE
First

1 Adapted from Novel 1.95
2 .... 1.95
3 .... 1.95
4 thru 6 .... @1.95
Trade Paperback 12.95

TEAM YOUNGBLOOD
Image

1 B:ErS(s),ATi(c),CYp,NRD(i), I:Masada,Dutch,V:Giger 2.25
2 ATi(c),CYp,NRd(i),V:Giger 2.25
3 RLd(s),CYp,NRd(i),C:Spawn, V:Giger 2.25
4 ErS(s), ... 2.25
5 ErS(s),CNn,V:Lynx 2.25
6 ErS(s),N:Psi-Fire, BU:Black&White 2.25
7 ErS(s),CYp,ATh,Extreme Prejudice#1,I:Quantum, BU:Black & White 2.25
8 ErS(s),CYp,ATh,Extreme Prejudice#5,V:Quantum, BU:Black&White 2.25

TEEN-AGE CONFIDENTIAL CONFESSIONS
Charlton Comics
July, 1960

1 .... 9.00
2 thru 5 .... @5.00
6 thru 10 .... @3.00
11 thru 21 .... @2.00
22 1964 .... 2.00

TEENAGE HOTRODDERS
Charlton Comics
April, 1963

1 .... 22.00
2 thru 5 .... @12.00
6 thru 10 .... @7.00
11 thru 23 .... @5.00
24 .... 4.00

Becomes:

TOP ELIMINATOR

25 thru 29 .... @5.00

Becomes:

DRAG 'N' WHEELS

30 .... 6.00
31 thru 58 .... @4.00
59 May, 1973 .... 4.00

TEENAGE MUTANT NINJA TURTLES
First

1 .... 6.00
2 .... 4.50
Graphic Novel 17.00

TEENAGE MUTANT NINJA TURTLES
Archie
(From T.V. Series)

1 O:TMNT,April O'Neil,Shredder Krang 6.00
2 V:Shredder,O:Bebop & Rocksteady 4.00
3 V:Shredder & Krang 3.00

TEENAGE MUTANT NINJA TURTLES ADVENTURES
[2nd Series]

1 Shredder,Bebop,Rocksteady return to earth 5.00
2 I:Baxter Stockman 3.00
3 'Three Fragments' #1 .... 3.00
4 'Three Fragments' #2 .... 2.50
5 Original adventures begin, I:Man Ray 2.50
6 I:Leatherhead,Mary Bones 2.50
7 I:Cuddley the Cowlick; Inter-Galactic wrestling issue 2.50
8 I:Wingnut & Screwloose 2.00
9 I:Chameleon 2.00
10 I:Scumbug, Wyrm 2.00
11 I:Rat King & Sons of Silence; Krang returns to earth 2.00
12 Final Conflict #1, A:Leatherhead Wingnut,Screwloose,Trap, I:Malinga 2.00
13 Final Conflict #2 .... 2.00

14 Turtles go to Brazil;I:Jagwar Dreadman 2.00
15 I:Mr. Null 1.50
16 I&D:Bubbla,the Glubbab 1.50
17 Cap'n Mossback 1.25
18 'Man Who Sold World' 1.25
19 'Man Who Sold World' 1.25
20 V:Supersoldier,War.Dragon . . . 1.25
21 V:Vid Vicious 1.25
22 GC,Donatello captured 1.50
23 V:Krang,I:Slash,Belly Bomb . . 1.50
24 V:Krang 1.25
25 . . . . 1.50
26 I:T'Pau & Keeper 1.50
27 I:Nevermore,Nocturno&Hallocat 1.50
28 Turtle go to Spain, I:Nindar & Chein Klan 1.50
29 Warrior Dragon captured 1.50
30 TMNT/Fox Mutant Ninjara team-up 1.25
31 TMNT/Ninjara team-up cont . . 1.25
32 A:Sumo Wrestler Tatoo 1.25
33 The Karma of Katmandu 1.25
34 Search For Charlie Llama 1.25
35 . . . . 1.25
36 V:Shredder 1.25
37 V:Shredder 1.25
38 V:Null & 4 Horsemen Pt.1 . . . . 1.25
39 V:Null & 4 Horseman Pt.3 . . . . 1.25
40 1492,A:The Other 1.25
41 And Deliver us from Evil 1.25
42 Time Tripping Trilogy #1 . . . . 1.25
43 . . . . 1.25
44 . . . . 1.25
1990 Movie adapt(direct) 5.50
1990 Movie adapt(newsstand) . . . 2.50
1991 TMNT meet Archie 2.50
1991 Movie Adapt II 2.50
Spec.#2 Ghost of 13 Mile Island 2.50
Spec.#3 Night of the Monsterex . . 2.50
TMNT Universe 1.95

TEENAGE MUTANT NINJA TURTLES
Mirage

1 A:Casey Jones 3.00
2 JmL(a&s) 3.00

TEENAGE MUTANT NINJA TURTLES/ FLAMING CARROT
Mirage/Dark Horse

1 JmL 3.00
2 thru 3 JmL 3.00
4 JmL 3.00

TMNT PRESENTS: APRIL O'NEIL
Archie

1 A:Chien Khan,Vid Vicious 1.25
2 V:White Ninja,A:V.Vicious 1.25
3 V:Vhien Khan,concl. 1.25

TMNT: THE MALTESE TURTLE
Mirage

Spec. F:Raphael Detective 2.95

TMNT PRESENTS: DONATELLO

1 thru 2 . . . . @1.25

TMNT: APRIL O'NEIL THE MAY EAST SAGA
Archie

1 A:TMNT 1.25

TEENAGENTS
Topps

1 WS,AH,w/card 2.95
2 NV,w/card 2.95

TEEN CONFESSIONS
Charlton Comics
August, 1959

1 . . . . 30.00
2 . . . . 18.00
3 . . . . 12.00
4 . . . . 12.00
5 . . . . 12.00
6 . . . . 12.00
7 . . . . 12.00
8 . . . . 12.00
9 . . . . 12.00
10 . . . . 12.00
11 thru 30 . . . . @6.00
31 Beatles cover 35.00
32 thru 36 . . . . @2.00
37 Beatles cover,Fan Club story 35.00
38 thru 96 . . . . @2.00
97 November, 1976 . . . . 2.00

TEEN SECRET DIARY
Charlton Comics
October, 1959

1 . . . . 22.00
2 . . . . 15.00
3 . . . . 5.00
4 . . . . 5.00
5 . . . . 5.00
6 . . . . 5.00
7 . . . . 5.00
8 . . . . 5.00
9 . . . . 5.00
10 . . . . 5.00
11 June, 1961 . . . . 5.00

TENSE SUSPENSE
Fargo Publications
December, 1958

1 . . . . 30.00
2 February, 1959 . . . . 25.00

TERMINAL POINT
Dark Horse

1 thru 3 . . . . @2.50

TERMINATOR
Dark Horse

1 CW,Tempest 8.00
2 CW,Tempest 5.00
3 CW 4.00
4 CW 4.00

TERMINATOR
Now

1 . . . . 25.00
2 . . . . 12.00
3 . . . . 7.50
4 . . . . 5.00
5 . . . . 4.50
6 . . . . 4.00
7 . . . . 4.00
8 . . . . 4.00
9 . . . . 4.00
10 . . . . 4.00
11 . . . . 4.00
12 I:JohnConnor($1.75cov,dbl.sz) 4.00
13 . . . . 4.00
14 . . . . 4.00
15 . . . . 3.50
16 . . . . 3.50
17 . . . . 3.50
Spec. #1 . . . . 3.50

TERMINATOR: ALL MY FUTURES PAST
Now

1 Painted Art 4.00
2 Painted Art 4.00

TERMINATOR: THE BURNING EARTH

1 . . . . 8.00
2 . . . . 4.00
3 thru 5 . . . . @3.50

TERMINATOR: END GAME
Dark Horse

1 JG,Final Terminator series 3.00
2 JG,Cont.last Term.story 2.75
3 JG,(Conclusion of Dark Horse Terminator stories) 2.75

TERMINATOR: ENEMY WITHIN
Dark Horse

1 cont. from Sec.Objectives . . . 4.00
2 C890.L.threat contd. 3.00
3 Secrets of Cyberdyne 3.00
4 Conclusion 3.00
SC rep #1-4 . . . . 13.95

TERMINATOR: HUNTERS & KILLERS
Dark Horse

1 V:Russians 3.00
2 V:Russians 2.75
3 V:Russians 2.75

TERMINATOR: ONE SHOT
Dark Horse

1 MW,3-D const(c2,pop-up inside 7.00

TERMINATOR: SECONDARY OBJECTIVES
Dark Horse

1 cont. 1st DH mini-series 5.00
2 PG,A:New Female Terminator . 4.00
3 PG,Terminators in L.A.&Mexico 4.00
4 PG,Terminator vs Terminator concl. 4.00

TERMINATOR: THE BURNING EARTH
Now

1 . . . . 8.00
2 . . . . 4.00
3 . . . . 3.50
4 . . . . 3.50
5 . . . . 3.50

TERRAFORMERS
Wonder Comics

1 . . . . 1.00
2 . . . . 1.00
3 . . . . 1.00
4 . . . . 1.00

TERRANAUTS
Fantasy General

1 . . . . 1.75
2 . . . . 1.75

TESS

1 . . . . 1.95

TEXAS RANGERS IN ACTION
Charlton Comics
July, 1956

5 . . . . 30.00
6 . . . . 15.00
7 . . . . 15.00

Terraformers #1
© Wonder Color Comics

8 . . . . . 15.00
9 . . . . . 15.00
10 . . . . . 15.00
11 . . . . . 35.00
12 . . . . . 8.00
13 . . . . . 30.00
14 . . . . . 8.00
15 . . . . . 8.00
16 . . . . . 8.00
17 . . . . . 8.00
18 . . . . . 8.00
19 . . . . . 8.00
20 . . . . . 8.00
21 thru 30 . . . . . @6.00
31 thru 59 . . . . . @2.00
60 B:Riley's Rangers 3.00
61 thru 78 . . . . . @2.00
79 August, 1970 . . . . . 2.00

THAT WILKIN BOY
Archie Publications
January, 1969

1 . . . . . 15.00
2 . . . . . 7.00
3 . . . . . 7.00
4 . . . . . 7.00
5 . . . . . 7.00
6 . . . . . 7.00
7 . . . . . 7.00
8 . . . . . 7.00
9 . . . . . 7.00
10 . . . . . 7.00
11 thru 20 . . . . . @3.00
21 thru 26 E:Giant size . . . . . @2.00
27 thru 52 . . . . . @2.00

THING, THE
Darkhorse

1 JHi,From Movie 5.00
2 JHi,Final Issue 3.50

THING: COLD FEAR

1 R:Thing 3.00
2 . . . . . 2.75

THING FROM ANOTHER WORLD: CLIMATE OF FEAR
Dark Horse

1 Argentinian Military Base
(Bahiathetis) 2.75
2 Thing on Base 2.75
3 Thing/takeover 2.50
4 Conclusion 2.50
TPB 15.95

THING FROM ANOTHER WORLD: ETERNAL VOWS
Dark Horse

1 PG,I:Sgt. Rowan 2.75
2 PG 2.75
3 PG,in New Zealand 2.75
4 PG,Last issue 2.75

THIRD WORLD WAR
Fleet Way

1 HamburgerLady 2.50
2 . . . . . 2.50
3 The Killing Yields 2.50
4 thru 6 . . . . . @2.50

13: ASSASSIN
TSR

1 . . . . . 2.95
2 . . . . . 2.95
3 . . . . . 2.95
4 . . . . . 2.95
5 . . . . . 2.95
6 . . . . . 2.95
7 . . . . . 2.95

[Mini-series]

1 . . . . . 2.95

THOSE ANNOYING POST BROTHERS
Vortex

1 . . . . . 1.75
2 . . . . . 1.75
3 . . . . . 1.75
4 . . . . . 1.75
5 . . . . . 1.75
6 . . . . . 1.75

3-D ZONE PRESENTS
Renegade

1 L.B.Cole(c) 2.00
2 . . . . . 2.00
3 . . . . . 2.00
4 . . . . . 2.00
5 . . . . . 2.00
12 3-D Presidents 2.50
13 Flash Gordon 2.50
14 Tyranostar 2.50
15 Tyranostar 2.50
16 SpaceVixen 2.50

3-D ZONE - 3 DEMENTIA

15 . . . . . 2.50

THREE FACES OF GNATMAN

1 . . . . . 1.75

THREE STOOGES
Dell Publishing Co.
October-December, 1959

1 . . . . . 100.00
2 . . . . . 50.00
3 . . . . . 50.00
4 . . . . . 50.00
5 . . . . . 50.00
6 Ph(c),B:Prof. Putter 45.00
7 Ph(c) 45.00
8 Ph(c) 45.00
9 Ph(c) 45.00
10 Ph(c) 45.00
11 Ph(c) 40.00
12 Ph(c) 40.00
13 Ph(c) 40.00
14 Ph(c) 40.00
15 Ph(c) 45.00
16 Ph(c),E:Prof. Putter 45.00
17 Ph(c),B:Little Monsters 45.00
18 Ph(c) 40.00
19 Ph(c) 40.00
20 Ph(c) 40.00
21 Ph(c) 40.00
22 Ph(c),Movie Sleeve 45.00
23 Ph(c) 30.00
24 Ph(c) 30.00
25 Ph(c) 30.00
26 Ph(c) 30.00
27 Ph(c) 30.00
28 Ph(c) 30.00
29 Ph(c) 30.00
30 Ph(c) 30.00
31 Ph(c) 25.00
32 Ph(c) 25.00
33 Ph(c) 25.00
34 Ph(c) 25.00
35 Ph(c) 25.00
36 Ph(c) 25.00
37 Ph(c) 25.00
38 Ph(c) 25.00
39 Ph(c) 25.00
40 Ph(c) 25.00
41 Ph(c) 25.00
42 Ph(c) 25.00
43 Ph(c) 25.00
44 Ph(c) 25.00
45 Ph(c) 25.00
46 Ph(c) 25.00
47 Ph(c) 25.00
48 Ph(c) 25.00
49 Ph(c) 25.00
50 Ph(c) 25.00
51 . . . . . 20.00
52 Ph(c) 25.00
53 Ph(c) 25.00
54 Ph(c) 25.00
55 Ph(c) 25.00

THREE STOOGES 3-D
Eclipse

1 thru 3 reprints from 1953 . . . @2.50
4 reprints from 1953 . . . . . 3.50

THRILLING SCIENCE TALES
AC Comics

1 . . . . . 3.50

THRILLOGY
Pacific

1 . . . . . 1.50

THRILL-O-RAMA
Harvey Publications
October, 1965

1 A:Man in Black(Fate),DW,AW 10.00
2 AW,A:Pirana,I:Clawfang,
The Barbarian 10.00
3 A:Pirana, Fate, December, 1966 7.00

T.H.U.N.D.E.R. AGENTS
Archie Publications

1 WW,RC,GK,MSy,GT,I:Thunder
Agents,IronMaiden,Warlord . . 52.00
2 WW,MSy,D:Egghead 33.00
3 WW,DA,MSy,V:Warlords 24.00
4 WW,MSy,RC,I:Lightning 20.00
5 WW,RC,GK,MSy 20.00
6 WW,SD,MSy,I:Warp Wizard . . 15.00
7 WW,MSy,SD,D:Menthor 15.00
8 WW,MSy,GT,DA,I:Raven 15.00
9 OW,WW,MSy,A:Andor 12.00
10 WW,MSy,OW,A:Andor 12.00
11 WW,DA,MSy 10.00
12 SD,WW,MSy 9.00
13 WW,OW,A:Undersea Agent . 10.00
14 SD,WW,GK,N:Raven,A:Andor 10.00

T.H.U.N.D.E.R. Agents #7
© Archie Publications

15 WW,OW,GT,A:Andor 9.00
16 SD,GK,A:Andor 9.00
17 WW,OW,GT 8.00
18 SD,OW,RC 9.00
19 GT,I:Ghost 8.00
20 WW,RC,MSy,all reprints 5.00

T.H.U.N.D.E.R. AGENTS
J.C. Productions

1 MA,Centerfold 2.00
2 I:Vulcan 2.00

THUNDERBOLT
Charlton Comics

1 PAM,O:Thuderbolt 10.00
Prev: Son of Vulcan
51 PAM,V:Evila 5.00
52 PAM,V:Gore the Monster 3.50
53 PAM,V:The Tong 4.00
54 PAM,I:Sentinels 4.00
55 PAM,V:Sentinels 3.50
56 PAM,A:Sentinels 3.50
57 A:Sentinels 3.50
58 PAM,A:Sentinels 3.50
59 PAM,A:Sentinels 3.50
60 PAM,JAp,I:Prankster 4.00

TIGER GIRL
Gold Key
September, 1968

1 .... 25.00

TIME TUNNEL, THE
Gold Key
February, 1967

1 .... 35.00
2 .... 30.00

TIME TWISTERS
Quality

1 Alan Moore ser. 1.25
2 Alan Moore ser. 1.25
3 Alan Moore ser. 1.25
4 Alan Moore ser. 1.25
5 .... 1.25
6 Alan Moore ser. 1.25
7 Alan Moore ser. 1.25
8 .... 1.25
9 .... 1.25
10 .... 1.25
11 .... 1.25
12 .... 1.25
13 thru 21 .... @1.50

TIME 2

1 Graphic Novel 8.00

TIPPY'S FRIENDS GO-GO & ANIMAL
Tower Comics
June, 1966

1 .... 10.00
2 .... 4.50
3 .... 4.50
4 .... 4.50
5 .... 4.50
6 .... 4.50
7 .... 4.50
8 Beatles on cover & back 18.00
9 thru 14 .... @4.50
15 October, 1969 .... 4.50

TIPPY TEEN
Tower Comics
November, 1965

1 .... 8.00
2 thru 26 .... @3.50
27 February, 1970 .... 3.50

TITAN
Dark Horse

Spec.#1 BS(c),I:Inhibitors 3.95

TO DIE FOR

1 3-D 2.50

TOM MIX WESTERN
AC Comics

1 .... 2.95

TOMMY & THE MONSTERS

1 .... 2.00

TOM TERRIFIC!
Pines Comics
Summer, 1957

1 .... 120.00
2 .... 80.00
3 .... 80.00
4 .... 80.00
5 .... 80.00
6 Fall, 1958 .... 80.00

TOP CAT
Charlton Comics
November, 1970

1 .... 30.00
2 thru 10 .... @20.00
11 thru 19 .... @12.00
20 November, 1973 .... 12.00

TOR IN 3-D
Eclipse

1 JKu 3.00
1a B&W limited 100 sign 5.00
2 JKu 3.00

TOTAL ECLIPSE
Eclipse

1 BHa,BSz(c),A:Airboy,Skywolf .. 3.95
2 BHa,BSz(c),A:New Wave, Liberty Project 3.95
3 BHa,BSz(c),A:Scout,Ms.Tree .. 3.95
4 BHa,BSz(c),A:Miracleman, Prowler 3.95
5 BHa,BSz(c),A:Miracleman, Aztec Ace 3.95

TOTAL ECLIPSE, THE SERAPHIM OBJECTIVE
Eclipse

1 tie-in Total Eclipse #2 .... 1.95

TOTAL WAR
Gold Key
July, 1965

1 .... 35.00
2 .... 35.00
Becomes:
M.A.R.S. Patrol
3 WW 35.00
4 .... 20.00
5 .... 20.00
6 .... 20.00
7 .... 20.00
8 .... 20.00
9 .... 20.00
10 .... 20.00

Toy Boy #1 © Continuity Comics

TOY BOY
Continuity

1 NA.I&O:Toy Boy,A:Megalith ... 2.00
2 thru 6 TVE .... @2.00
7 MG 2.00

TRANCERS: THE ADVENTURES OF JACK DETH
Eternity

1 I:Jack Deth 2.50
2 A:Whistler, final issue 2.50

TRANSFORMERS

1 Robotics 1.50
2 .... 2.00
3 .... 2.50

TRANSFORMERS in 3-D
Blackthorne

1 .... 2.50
2 thru 5 .... @2.50

TRAVEL OF JAMIE McPHEETERS, THE
Gold Key
December, 1963

1 Kurt Russell 25.00

TREKKER
Dark Horse
1 . . . . 2.95

TRENCHER
Image
1 KG,I:Trencher 2.25
2 KG, ... 2.25
3 KG,V:Supreme 2.25
4 KG,V:Elvis 2.25

TRIBE
Image
1 TJn(s),LSn,I:The Tribe 2.50
1a Ivory(White) Editon 65.00
Axis Comics
2 TJn(s),LSn,V:Alex 2.25
3 TJn(s),LSn, ... 1.95

TROLL
Image
1 RLd(s),JMs,I:Evangeliste,
V:Katellan Command, ... 2.50

TROLL LORDS
Comico
Special #1 . . . . 1.75
1 . . . . 1.75
2 . . . . 1.75
3 . . . . 1.75
4 . . . . 2.50

TROUBLE WITH GIRLS
Comico
1 . . . . 3.00
2 . . . . 2.50
3 . . . . 2.50
4 . . . . 1.95

TRUE LOVE
Eclipse
1 ATh,NC,DSt(c),reprints 2.00
2 ATh,NC,BA(c),reprints 1.50

TUFF GHOSTS STARRING SPOOKY
Harvey Publications
July, 1962
1 . . . . 50.00
2 . . . . 30.00
3 . . . . 30.00
4 . . . . 30.00
5 . . . . 30.00
6 . . . . 20.00
7 . . . . 20.00
8 . . . . 20.00
9 . . . . 20.00
10 . . . . 20.00
11 thru 20 . . . . @10.00
21 thru 30 . . . . @7.00
31 thru 39 . . . . @3.00
40 thru 42 52 pg. Giants . . . . @3.00
43 October, 1972 . . . . 3.00

TUROK: DINOSAUR HUNTER
Valiant
1 BS,Chromium(c),O:Turok
retold,V:Monark 4.00
1a Gold Ed. 75.00
2 BS,V:Monark 2.75
3 BCh,V:Monark 2.75
4 TT(s),RgM,O:Turok 2.75
5 TT(s),RgM,V:Dinosaurs 2.75
6 TT(s),RgM,V:Longhunter 2.75
7 TT(a&s),B:People o/t Spider . . 2.75
8 TT(a&s),V:T-Rex 2.75
9 TT(a&s),E:People o/t Spider . . 2.75
10 MBn,RgM,A:Bile 2.75
11 MBn,RgM,V:Chun Yee,w/
ValiantEra card 2.75
12 MBn,RgM,V:Dinosaur 2.75
13 B:TT(c&s),RgM, ... 2.75
14 V:Dino-Pirate 2.50
Yearbook #1 MBn(s),DC,
V:Mon Ark 3.95

TUROK: SON OF STONE
Dell
1 I&O:Turok,Andar 375.00
2 . . . . 240.00
3 thru 5 . . . . @175.00
6 thru 10 . . . . @115.00
11 thru 16 . . . . @75.00
17 Prehistric Pygmies 75.00
18 thru 20 . . . . @75.00
21 thr 29 . . . . @45.00
Gold Key
30 . . . . 45.00
31 thru 40 . . . . @32.00
41 thru 50 . . . . @24.00
51 thru 60 . . . . @15.00
61 thru 75 . . . . @10.00
76 thru 91 . . . . @6.00
Whitman
92 thru 130 . . . . @5.00
Giant #1 . . . . 75.00

TURTLE SOUP
Millenium
1 Book 1, short stories 2.50
2 thru 4 . . . . 2.50

TV CASPER & COMPANY
Harvey Publications
August, 1963
1 B:68 pg. Giants 55.00
2 . . . . 30.00
3 . . . . 30.00
4 . . . . 30.00
5 . . . . 30.00
6 . . . . 25.00
7 . . . . 25.00
8 . . . . 25.00
9 . . . . 25.00
10 . . . . 25.00
11 thru 20 . . . . @7.00
21 thru 31 E:68 pg. Giants . . . @5.00
32 thru 45 . . . . @2.00
46 April, 1974 . . . . 2.00

TWEETY AND SYLVESTER
Gold Key
November, 1963
1 . . . . 14.00
2 thru 10 . . . . @7.00
11 thru 30 . . . . @4.00
31 thru 120 . . . . @2.00
121 July, 1984 . . . . 2.00

TWILIGHT AVENGER
Elite
1 . . . . 1.75
2 . . . . 1.75
3 . . . . 1.75
4 . . . . 1.75

TWILIGHT MAN
First
1 Mini-Series 2.75
2 Mini-Series 2.75
3 Mini-Series 2.75
4 Mini-Series 2.75

TWILIGHT ZONE
Now
1 NA,BSz(c) 8.00
1a 2nd printing Prestige
+Harlan Ellison sty 6.00

[Volume 2]
#1 'The Big Dry' (direct) 2.50
#1a Newsstand 1.95
2 'Blind Alley' 1.95
3 Extraterrestrial 1.95
4 The Mysterious Biker 1.95
5 Queen of the Void 1.95
6 Insecticide 1.95
7 The Outcasts,Ghost Horse . . . 1.95
8 Colonists on Alcor 1.95
9 Dirty Lyle's House of Fun
(3-D Holo) 2.95
10 Stairway to Heaven,Key to
Paradise 1.95
11 TD(i),Partial Recall 1.95
3-D Spec. 2.50
Ann. #1 . . . . 2.75

[Volume 3]
1 thru 2 . . . . 2.50

Twilight Zone #10 © Now Comics

TWILIGHT ZONE, THE
Dell Publishing Co.
March-May, 1961
1 RC,FF,GE,P(c) all 70.00
2 . . . . 45.00
3 ATh,MSy 30.00
4 ATh 30.00
5 . . . . 25.00
6 . . . . 25.00
7 . . . . 25.00
8 . . . . 25.00
9 ATh 30.00
10 . . . . 25.00
11 . . . . 25.00
12 AW 30.00
13 AW,RC,FBe,AMc 30.00
14 RC,JO,RC,AT 30.00
15 RC,JO 30.00
16 . . . . 20.00
17 . . . . 20.00
18 . . . . 20.00
19 JO 25.00
20 . . . . 20.00
21 RC 25.00
22 JO 25.00
23 JO 25.00
24 . . . . 20.00
25 GE,RC,ATh 20.00
26 RC,GE 20.00
27 GE 20.00
28 . . . . 15.00
29 . . . . 15.00
30 . . . . 15.00

31 . . . . 15.00
32 GE 20.00
33 . . . . 15.00
34 . . . . 15.00
35 . . . . 15.00
36 . . . . 15.00
37 . . . . 15.00
38 . . . . 15.00
39 WMc 15.00
40 . . . . 12.00
41 . . . . 12.00
42 . . . . 12.00
43 RC 15.00
44 . . . . 12.00
45 . . . . 12.00
46 . . . . 12.00
47 . . . . 12.00
48 . . . . 12.00
49 . . . . 12.00
50 FBe,WS 12.00
51 AW 15.00
52 . . . . 12.00
53 . . . . 12.00
54 . . . . 12.00
55 . . . . 12.00
56 . . . . 12.00
57 FBe 12.00
58 . . . . 12.00
59 FBe,AMc 15.00
60 . . . . 10.00
61 . . . . 10.00
62 . . . . 10.00
63 . . . . 10.00
64 . . . . 10.00
65 . . . . 10.00
66 . . . . 10.00
67 . . . . 10.00
68 . . . . 10.00
69 . . . . 10.00
70 . . . . 10.00
71 rep 8.00
72 . . . . 10.00
73 rep 8.00
74 . . . . 10.00
75 . . . . 10.00
76 . . . . 10.00
77 FBe 12.00
78 FBe,AMc 12.00
79 rep 8.00
80 FBe,AMc 12.00
81 . . . . 10.00
82 AMc 12.00
83 FBe,WS 12.00
84 FBe,AMc 12.00
85 . . . . 10.00
86 rep 8.00
87 thru 91 . . . . @10.00

TWISTED TALES
Pacific

1 RCo.AA 3.50
2 . . . . 2.00
3 . . . . 2.00
4 . . . . 2.00
5 . . . . 2.00
6 . . . . 2.00
7 . . . . 2.00
8 . . . . 2.00

Eclipse

9 . . . . 2.00
10 GM,BWr 2.00

TWISTED TALES OF BRUCE JONES
Eclipse

1 . . . . 2.00
2 . . . . 2.00
3 . . . . 2.00
4 . . . . 2.00

TWISTER
Harris

1 inc.Special newspaper/poster, and trading cards 2.95

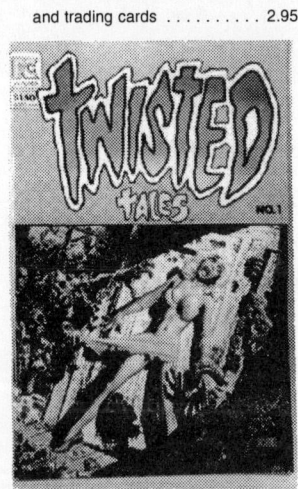

Twisted Tales #1 © Pacific Comics

TWO FISTED TALES
Russ Cochran

1 JSe,HK,WW,JCr,reps 1.50
2 Reps inc.War Story 1.50
3 rep. 1.50
4 thru 6 rep. 2.00
7 thru 8 rep. 2.00

Dark Horse

Spec. WW,WiS, ... 4.95

2000 A.D. Monthly #1 © Eagle Comics

2000 A.D. MONTHLY
Eagle

1 A:JudgeDredd 1.50
2 A:JudgeDredd 1.25
3 A:JudgeDredd 1.25
4 A:JudgeDredd 1.25
5 . . . . 1.25
6 . . . . 1.25

[2nd Series]

1 . . . . 1.25
2 . . . . 1.25
3 . . . . 1.25
4 . . . . 1.25
5 . . . . 1.25
6 . . . . 1.25

Quality

7 thru 27 . . . . @1.25
28/29 . . . . 1.50
30 . . . . 1.50
31/32 . . . . 1.50
33 . . . . 1.50
34 . . . . 1.50
35 . . . . 1.50
36 . . . . 1.50
37 . . . . 1.50

Becomes:

2000 A.D. SHOWCASE

38 . . . . 1.50
39 . . . . 1.50
40 . . . . 1.50
41 . . . . 1.50
42 . . . . 1.95
43 . . . . 1.95
44 . . . . 1.95
45 . . . . 1.95
46 . . . . 1.50
47 . . . . 1.75
48 . . . . 1.75
TPB:Killing Time 12.95

2112
Dark Horse

Graphic Novel, JBy,A:Next Men . 25.00

ULTRAMAN
Nemesis

1 EC,O:Ultraman 2.25
2 . . . . 2.50

ULTRAVERSE ORIGINS
Malibu-Ultraverse

1 O:Ultraverse Heroes 1.25

UNCLE SCROOGE
Dell/Gold Key

40 . . . . 60.00
41 . . . . 50.00
42 . . . . 50.00
43 . . . . 50.00
44 . . . . 50.00
45 . . . . 50.00
46 Lost Beneath the Sea 50.00
47 . . . . 50.00
48 . . . . 50.00
49 Loony Lunar Gold Rush 50.00
50 Rug Riders in the Sky 50.00
51 How Green Was my Lettuce . 45.00
52 Great Wig Mystery 45.00
53 Interplanetary Postman 45.00
54 Billion-Dollar Safari! 45.00
55 McDuck of Arabia 45.00
56 Mystery of the Ghost Town Railroad 45.00
57 Swamp of No Return 45.00
58 Giant Robot Robbers 45.00
59 North of the Yukon 45.00
60 Phantom of Notre Duck 45.00
61 So Far and No Safari 35.00
62 Queen of the Wild Dog Pack . 35.00
63 House of Haunts! 35.00
64 Treasure of Marco Polo! 35.00
65 Micro-Ducks from OuterSpace 35.00
66 Heedless Horseman 35.00
67 CB rep. 35.00
68 Hall of the Mermaid Queen! . 35.00
69 Cattle King! 35.00
70 CB,The Doom Diamond! 35.00
71 . . . . 30.00
72 CB rep. 30.00
73 CB rep. 30.00
74 thru 110 . . . . @20.00
111 thru 148 . . . . @12.00
149 . . . . 10.00

150 thru 168 . . . . @8.00
169 thru 173 . . . . @6.00

Whitman

174 thru 182 . . . . @6.00
183 thru 200 . . . . @5.00
201 thru 209 . . . . @4.00

Gladstone

210 CB 8.00
211 CB,Prize of Pizzaro 6.00
212 CB,city-golden roofs 6.00
213 CB,city-golden roofs 6.00
214 CB 6.00
215 CB, a cold bargain 4.00
216 CB 4.00
217 CB,7 cities of Cibola 5.00
218 CB 4.00
219 Don Rosa,Son of Sun 16.00
220 CB,Don Rosa 3.00
221 CB,A:BeagleBoys 3.00
222 CB,Mysterious Island 3.00
223 CB 3.00
224 CB,Rosa,Cash Flow 6.00
225 CB 2.50
226 CB,Rosa 4.00
227 CB 2.50
228 CB 2.50
229 CB 2.50
230 CB 5.00
231 CB,Rosa(c) 2.50
232 CB 2.50
233 CB 2.50
234 CB 2.50
235 Rosa 3.00
236 CB 2.50
237 CB 2.50
238 CB 2.50
239 CB 2.50
240 CB 2.50
241 CB,giant 5.00
242 CB,giant 4.00

Walt Disney

243 CB 3.50
244 . . . . 2.50
245 . . . . 2.50
246 . . . . 2.50
247 . . . . 2.50
248 . . . . 2.50
249 . . . . 2.50
250 . . . . 2.00
251 . . . . 2.00
252 . . . . 2.00
253 'Fab.Philosophers Stone 2.00
254 The Filling Station 2.00
255 The Flying Dutchman 2.00
256 CB,'Status Seeker' 1.75
257 'Coffee,Louie or Me' 1.75
258 CB,'Swamp of no return' 1.75
259 'The only way to travel' 1.75
260 The Waves Above,
The Gold Below 1.75
261 'Return to Zanadu' Pt.1 . . . . . 1.75
262 'Return to Zanadu' Pt.2 . . . . . 1.75
263 'Treasure Uncer Glass' 1.50
264 Snobs Club 1.50
265 CB,Ten Cent Valentine 1.50
266 The Money Ocean,Pt.1 . . . . . 1.50
267 The Money Ocean,Pt 2 . . . . . 1.50
268 CB,Island in the Sky 1.50
269 The Flowers 1.50
270 V:Magica DeSpell 1.50
271 The Secret o/t Stone 1.50
272 Canute The Brute's
Battle Axe 1.50
273 CB,Uncle Scrooge-Ghost . . . 1.50
274 CB,Hall of the Mermaid
Queen 1.50
275 CB,Christmas Cheers,inc.
D.Rosa centerspread 1.50
276 thru 278 . . . . @1.50
279 thru 280 . . . . @1.50
281 . . . . 1.50

UNCLE SCROOGE ADVENTURES

Gladstone

1 CB,McDuck of Arabia 6.00
2 translated from Danish 3.00
3 translated from Danish 3.00
4 CB 3.00
5 Rosa 3.00
6 CB 3.00
7 CB 3.00
8 CB 2.50
9 Rosa 3.00
10 CB 2.50
11 CB 2.25
12 CB 2.25
13 CB 2.25
14 Rosa 2.25
15 CB 2.25
16 CB 2.25
17 CB 2.25
18 CB 2.25
19 CB,Rosa(c) 2.25
20 CB,giant 4.00
21 CB,giant 4.00

UNCLE SCROOGE & DONALD DUCK

Gold Key

1 rep. 60.00

UNCLE SCROOGE GOES TO DISNEYLAND

Gladstone

1 CB,etc. 100pp 8.00

UNDERDOG

Spotlight

1 FMc,PC(c),The Eredicator 1.50
2 FMc,CS(c), Prisoner of Love/
The Return of Fearo 1.50

UNDERDOG

Charlton

July, 1970

1 Planet Zot 40.00
2 Simon Sez/The Molemen . . . 20.00
3 Whisler's Father 20.00
4 The Witch of Pycoon 20.00
5 The Snowmen 20.00
6 The Big Shrink 20.00
7 The Marbleheads 20.00
8 The Phoney Booths 20.00
9 Tin Man Alley 20.00
10 Be My Valentine (Jan. 1972) . 20.00

UNDERDOG

Gold Key

March, 1975

1 The Big Boom 20.00
2 The Sock Singer Caper 10.00
3 The Ice Cream Scream 8.00
4 . . . . 8.00
5 . . . . 8.00
6 Head in a Cloud 8.00
7 The Cosmic Canine 8.00
8 . . . . 8.00
9 . . . . 8.00
10 Bouble Trouble Gum 8.00
11 The Private Life of Shoeshine Boy
4.00
12 The Deadly Fist of Fingers . . . 4.00
13 . . . . 4.00
14 Shrink Shrank Shrunk 4.00
15 Polluter Palooka 4.00
16 The Soda Jerk 4.00
17 Flee For Your Life 4.00
18 Rain Rain Go Away...Okay . . . 4.00
19 Journey To the Center
of the Earth 4.00
20 The Six Million Dollar Dog . . . 4.00
21 Smell of Success 4.00
22 Antlers Away 4.00
23 Wedding Bells In Outer
Space (Feb.,1979) 4.00

UNDERDOG IN 3-D

Blackthorne

1 Wanted Dead or Alive 2.50

UNEARTHLY SPECTACULARS

1 DW,AT,I:Tiger Boy 5.00
2 WW,AW,GK,I:Earthman,Miracles,Inc.
A:Clawfang,TigerBoy 15.00
3 RC,AW,JO,A:Miracles,Inc. . . . 12.00

U.N. FORCE

Gauntlet Comics

0 BDC(s) 2.95
1 B:BDC(s),I:U.N.Force 2.95
2 O:Indigo 2.95
3 . . . . 2.95
4 A:Predator 2.95
5 B:Critial Mass 2.95

U.N. FORCE FILES

Gauntlet Comics

1 KP(c),F:Hunter Seeker,
Lotus 2.95

UNION

Image

1 MT,I:Union,A:Stormwatch 2.75
2 MT 2.75
3 MT 2.75
4 MT,Good Intentions 2.75

UNITY

Valiant

0 BWS,BL,Chapter#1,A:All
Valiant Heroes,V:Erica
Pierce 8.00
0a Red ed.,w/red logo 50.00
1 BWS,BL,Chapter#18,A:All
Valiant Heroes,D:Erica
Pierce 8.00
1a Gold logo 50.00
1b Platinum 60.00
TPB Previews Exclusive,Vol.I
Chap.#1-9 . . . . 25.00
TPB Previews Exclusive,Vol.II
Chap.#10-18 . . . . 25.00
TPB Chapters #1-4 . . . . 10.95

UNIVERSAL MONSTERS

Dark Horse

1 AAd,Creature From The Black
Lagoon 5.25
2 The Mummy 5.25

UNIVERSAL SOLDIER

Now

1 Based on Movie,Holo.(c) 2.75
2 Luc & Ronnie on the run from
UniSols 2.50
2a Photo cover 1.95
3 Photo(c) 1.95

UNKNOWN WORLDS OF FRANK BRUNNER

Eclipse

1 FB 2.50
2 FB 2.50

UNLEASHED!

Triumphant

0 JnR(s),I:Skyfire 2.50
1 JnR(s), ... 2.50

UNLV

1 Championship season (basketball
based on college team) 3.00

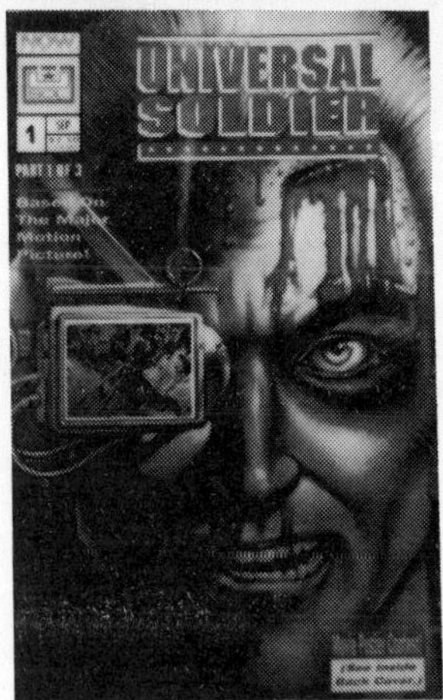

Universal Soldier #1 © Now Comics

UNTAMED LOVE

1 FF 2.00

UNUSUAL TALES
Charlton Comics
November, 1955

1 . . . . 120.00
2 . . . . 60.00
3 . . . . 35.00
4 . . . . 35.00
5 . . . . 35.00
6 SD,SD(c) 100.00
7 SD,SD(c) 100.00
8 SD,SD(c) 100.00
9 SD,SD(c) 120.00
10 SD,SD(c) 110.00
11 SD 110.00
12 SD 75.00
13 . . . . 30.00
14 SD 75.00
15 SD,SD(c) 80.00
16 . . . . 30.00
17 . . . . 30.00
18 . . . . 30.00
19 . . . . 30.00
20 . . . . 30.00
21 . . . . 20.00
22 SD 50.00
23 . . . . 20.00
24 . . . . 20.00
25 SD 50.00
26 SD 50.00
27 SD 50.00
28 . . . . 20.00
29 SD 50.00
30 thru 48 . . . . @15.00
49 March-April, 1965 . . . . 15.00

URI-ON

1 . . . . 1.50
2 . . . . 1.50

URTH 4
Continuity

1 TVE,NA(c) 2.00
2 TVE,NA 2.00
3 TVE,NA 2.00
4 NA,Last issue 2.00

USAGI YOJIMBO
Fantagraphics

1 SS,color Spec 5.00

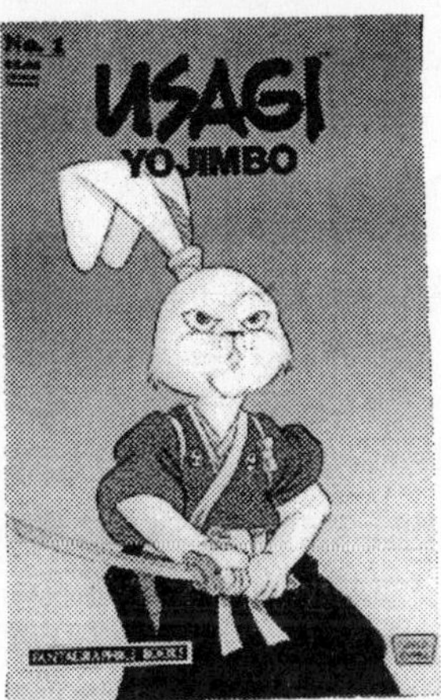

Usagi Yojimbo #1
© Fantagraphics Books

2 SS,color Spec. 5.00
3 SS,color Spec. 3.00

USAGI YOJIMBO
Mirage

1 thru 4 . . . . 3.00
5 thru 6 . . . . 3.00

VALERIA THE SHE BAT
Continuity

1 NA,I:Valeria 20.00
2 thru 4 . . . . . . [NOT RELEASED]
5 Rise of Magic 2.50

VALIANT ERA
Valiant

TPB rep.Magnus #12,Shadowman #8,Solar #10-11,Eternal Warrior#4-5 . . . . 13.95

VALIANT READER: GUIDE TO THE VALIANT UNIVERSE

1 O:Valiant Universe 1.00

VALIANT VISION STARTER KIT
Valiant

1 w/3-D Glasses 2.95
2 F:Starwatchers 2.95

VALKYRIE
Eclipse

1 PG,I:Steelfox,C:Airboy, Sky Wolf 3.00
2 PG,O:New Black Angel 2.50
3 PG 2.50

[2nd Series]

1 BA,V:Eurasian Slavers 1.95
2 BA,V:Cowgirl 1.95
3 BA,V:Cowgirl 1.95

VAMPIRE LESTAT
Innovation

1 Anne RiceAdap. 26.00
1a 2nd printing 5.00
1b 3rd printing 2.50
2 . . . . 13.00
2a 2nd printing 5.00
2b 3rd printing 2.50
3 . . . . 10.00
3a 2nd printing 2.50
4 . . . . 8.00
4a 2nd printing 2.50
5 . . . . 5.00
6 . . . . 3.50
7 . . . . 3.50
8 . . . . 3.50
9 scarce 4.00
9a 2nd Printing 2.50
10 . . . . 3.00
11 'Those Who Must Be Kept' . . . 2.50
12 conclusion 2.50
Vampire Companion #1 . . . . 4.00
Vampire Companion #2 (preview 'Interview With The Vampire' . . 2.50
Vampire Companion #3 . . . . 2.50
GN rep.#1-#12 (Innovation) 24.95
GN rep.#1-#12 (Ballantine) 25.00

VAMPIRELLA
Warren Publishing Co.
September, 1969

1 I:Vampirella 200.00
2 B:Amazonia 75.00
3 . . . . 250.00
4 . . . . 40.00
5 . . . . 40.00
6 . . . . 40.00
7 . . . . 40.00
8 . . . . 40.00
9 . . . . 45.00
10 . . . . 20.00
11 O& 1st app. Pendragon. 30.00
12 . . . . 25.00
13 . . . . 25.00
14 . . . . 25.00
15 . . . . 25.00
16 . . . . 20.00
17 B:Tomb of the Gods 20.00
18 . . . . 20.00
19 . . . . 25.00
20 thru 25 . . . . @20.00
26 . . . . 10.00
27 . . . . 12.00
28 thru 36 . . . . @10.00
37 . . . . 8.00
38 . . . . 7.00
39 . . . . 7.00
40 . . . . 7.00
41 . . . . 6.00
42 . . . . 6.00
43 . . . . 6.00
44 . . . . 6.00
45 . . . . 6.00
46 O:Vampirella 7.00
47 thru 100 . . . . @3.00
101 thru 111 . . . . @2.00
112 February, 1983 . . . . 2.00

VAMPIRELLA
Harris

1 V:Forces of Chaos, w/coupon for DSt poster 40.00
2 AH(c) 30.00
3 A:Dracula 15.00
4 A:Dracula 7.00

VANGUARD

1 . . . . 1.50

VANGUARD
Image

1 EL(s),BU:I:Vanguard 2.25
2 EL(s),Roxann, ... 2.25
3 AMe, ... 2.25
4 AMe, ... 2.25
5 AMe,V:Aliens 2.25
6 V:Bank Robber 1.95

VANGUARD ILLUSTRATED
Pacific

1 . . . . 1.50
2 DSt(c) 1.50
3 SR 1.50
4 SR 1.50
5 SR 1.50
6 GI 1.50
7 GE,I:Mr.Monster 6.00

VANITY
Pacific

1 . . . . 1.50
2 . . . . 1.50

Vault of Horror #1 © Gladstone

VAULT OF HORROR
Gladstone

1 Rep.GS,WW 5.00
2 Rep.VoH #27 & HoF #18 . . . . . 3.50
3 Rep.VoH #13 & HoF #22 . . . . . 3.00
4 Rep.VoH #23 & HoF #13 . . . . . 2.50
5 Rep.VoH #19 & HoF #5 . . . . . 2.50
6 Rep.VoH #32 & WF #6 . . . . . 2.50
7 Rep.VoH #26 & WS #7 . . . . . 2.50

VAULT OF HORROR
Russ Cochran Publ.

1 Rep.VoH #28 & WS #18 . . . . . 2.25
2 Rep.VoH #33 & WS #20 . . . . . 2.25
3 Rep.VoH #26 & WS #7 . . . . . 2.25
4 Rep.VoH #35 & WS #15 . . . . . 2.00
4 Rep.VoH #18 & WS #11 . . . . . 2.00
5 Rep.VoH #18 & WS #11 . . . . . 2.00

2nd Series

1 thru 7 Rep.VoH . . . . @1.50
8 . . . . 2.00

VECTOR
Now

1 . . . . 2.50
2 . . . . 1.75
3 . . . . 1.75
4 . . . . 1.75
5 . . . . 1.75

VEGAS KNIGHTS
Pioneer

1 . . . . 1.95
2 . . . . 1.95
3 . . . . 1.95

VENGEANCE OF VAMPIRELLA
Harris

1 Bzz 3.25
2 Bzz 2.95

VENTURE
AC Comics

1 . . . . 2.00
2 thru 4 . . . . @1.75

VIC FLINT
Argo Publ.
February, 1956

1 . . . . 35.00
2 . . . . 30.00

VILLAINS & VIGILANTES
Eclipse

1 A:Crusaders,Shadowman 2.00
2 A:Condor 2.00
3 V:Crushers 2.00
4 V:Crushers 2.00

VINTAGE MAGNUS ROBOT FIGHTER
Valiant

1 rep. Gold Key Magnus #22 (which is#1) 6.00
2 rep. Gold Key Magnus #3 . . . . 4.50
3 rep. Gold Key Magnus #13 . . . 3.50
4 rep. Gold Key Magnus #15 . . . 3.50

VIOLATOR
Image

1 AMo(s),BS,I:Admonisher 1.95

VIOLENT CASES
Tundra

1 20's Chicago 11.00

VIRGINIAN, THE
Gold Key
June, 1963

1 . . . . 30.00

VIRUS
Dark Horse

1 MP(c),F:The Wan Xuan & the crew of the Electra 2.50
2 MP(c),V:Captian Powell 2.50
3 MP(c),V:Virus 2.50
4 MP(c),Last issue 2.50

VOLTRON
Solson

1 TV tie-in 2.00
2 . . . . 1.50
3 . . . . 1.50

VORTEX
Vortex

1 Peter Hsu art 22.00
2 Mister X on cover 8.00
3 . . . . 5.00
4 . . . . 4.00
5 . . . . 3.00
6 thru 8 . . . . @3.00
9 thru 13 . . . . @1.75

VORTEX
Comico

1 from Elementals 2.50
2 . . . . 2.50

VOYAGE TO THE DEEP
Dell Publishing Co.
September-November, 1962

1 P(c) 35.00
2 P(c) 20.00
3 P(c) 20.00
4 P(c) 20.00

WACKY ADVENTURES OF CRACKY
Gold Key
December, 1972

1 . . . . 10.00
2 thru 11 . . . . @5.00
12 September, 1975 . . . . 3.00

WACKY WITCH
Gold Key
March, 1971

1 . . . . 18.00
2 . . . . 10.00
3 thru 20 . . . . @6.00
21 December, 1975 . . . . 4.00

WAGON TRAIN
Gold Key
January, 1964

1 . . . . 30.00
2 . . . . 20.00
3 . . . . 20.00
4 October, 1964 . . . . 20.00

WALLY
Gold Key
December, 1962

1 . . . . 18.00
2 . . . . 15.00
3 . . . . 15.00
4 September, 1963 . . . . 15.00

WALLY WOOD'S THUNDER AGENTS
Delux

1 GP,KG,DC,SD,InewMenth 3.00
2 GP,KG,DC,SD 2.50
3 KG,DC,SD 2.00
4 GP,KG,RB,DA 2.00
5 JOy,KG,A:CodenamDangr 2.00

WALT DISNEY ANNUALS

Walt Disney's Autumn Adventure . 4.00
Walt Disney's Holiday Parade #1 . 3.50
Walt Disney's Spring Fever 3.25
Walt Disney's Summer Fun 3.25
Walt Disney's Holiday Parade #2 . 3.25

WALT DISNEY'S AUTUMN ADVENTURE

1 Rep. CB 4.00

WALT DISNEY'S COMICS AND STORIES
Dell/ Gold Key

264 CB;VonDrake&Gearloose('62) 22.00
265 CB; Von Drake & Gearloose 22.00
266 CB; Von Drake & Gearloose 22.00
267 CB; Von Drake & Gearloose 22.00
268 CB; Von Drake & Gearloose 22.00
269 CB; Von Drake & Gearloose 22.00
270 CB; Von Drake & Gearloose 22.00
271 CB; Von Drake & Gearloose 22.00
272 CB; Von Drake & Gearloose 22.00
273 CB; Von Drake & Gearloose 22.00
274 CB; Von Drake & Gearloose 22.00
275 CB 22.00
276 CB 22.00
277 CB 22.00
278 CB 22.00
279 CB 22.00

280 CB 22.00
281 CB 22.00
282 CB 22.00
283 CB 22.00
284 . . . . . 22.00
285 . . . . . 22.00
286 CB 22.00
287 . . . . . 15.00
288 CB 15.00
289 CB 15.00
290 . . . . . 15.00
291 CB 15.00
292 CB 15.00
293 CB; Grandma Duck's Farm Friends 15.00
294 CB 15.00
295 . . . . . 15.00
296 . . . . . 15.00
297 CB; Gyro Gearloose 15.00
298 CB; Daisy Duck's Dairy 15.00
299 CB rep. 15.00
300 CB rep. 15.00
301 CB rep. 12.00
302 CB rep. 12.00
303 CB rep. 12.00
304 CB rep. 12.00
305 CB rep. Gyro Gearloose . . . 12.00
306 CB rep. 12.00
307 CB rep. 12.00
308 CB 12.00
309 CB 12.00
310 CB 12.00
311 CB 12.00
312 CB 12.00
313 thru 327 . . . . . @8.00
328 CB rep. 12.00
329 . . . . . 8.00
330 . . . . . 8.00
331 . . . . . 8.00
332 . . . . . 8.00
333 . . . . . 8.00
334 . . . . . 8.00
335 CB rep. 10.00
336 . . . . . 7.00
337 . . . . . 7.00
338 . . . . . 7.00
339 . . . . . 7.00
340 . . . . . 7.00
341 . . . . . 7.00
342 CB rep. 10.00
343 CB rep. 10.00
344 CB rep. 10.00
345 CB rep. 10.00
346 CB rep. 10.00
347 CB rep. 10.00
348 CB rep. 10.00
349 CB rep. 10.00
350 CB rep. 10.00
351 CB rep. with poster 12.00
351a CB rep. without poster . . . 10.00
352 CB rep. with poster12 . . . . . 12.00
352a CB rep. without poster . . . 10.00
353 CB rep. with poster 12.00
353a CB rep. without poster . . . 10.00
354 CB rep. with poster 12.00
354a CB rep. without poster . . . 10.00
355 CB rep. with poster 12.00
355a CB rep. without poster . . . 10.00
356 CB rep. with poster 12.00
356a CB rep. without poster . . . 10.00
357 CB rep. with poster 12.00
357a CB rep. without poster . . . 10.00
358 CB rep. with poster 12.00
358a CB rep. without poster . . . 10.00
359 CB rep. with poster 12.00
359a CB rep. without poster . . . 10.00
360 CB rep. with poster 12.00
360a CB rep. without poster . . . 10.00
361 thru 400 CB rep. . . . . . @10.00
401 thru 409 CB rep. . . . . . @7.00
410 CB rep. Annette Funichello . . 7.00
411 thru 429 CB rep. . . . . . @7.00
430 . . . . . 3.00
431 CB rep. 5.00
432 CB rep. 5.00
433 . . . . . 3.00
434 CB rep. 3.00
435 CB rep. 7.00
436 CB rep. 5.00
437 . . . . . 3.00
438 . . . . . 3.00
439 CB rep. 5.00
440 CB rep. 5.00
441 . . . . . 3.00
442 CB rep. 5.00
443 CB rep. 5.00
444 . . . . . 3.00
445 . . . . . 3.00
446 thru 465 CB rep. . . . . . @5.00
466 . . . . . 5.00
467 thru 473 CB rep. . . . . . @5.00

Whitman

474 thru 493 CB rep. . . . . . @4.00
494 CB rep.Uncle Scrooge 5.00
495 thru 505 CB rep. . . . . . @4.00
506 . . . . . 3.00
507 CB rep. 4.00
508 CB rep. 4.00
509 CB rep. 4.00
510 CB rep. 4.00

Gladstone

511 translation of Dutch 7.00
512 translation of Dutch 8.00
513 translation of Dutch 6.00
514 translation of Dutch 5.00
515 translation of Dutch 4.00
516 translation of Dutch 4.00
517 translation of Dutch 3.50
518 translation of Dutch 3.50
519 CB,Donald Duck 3.50
520 translation of Dutch 3.00
521 Walt Kelly 3.00
522 CB,WK,nephews 3.00
523 Rosa,Donald Duck 3.00
524 Rosa,Donald Duck 3.00
525 translation of Dutch 3.00
526 Rosa,Donald Duck 3.00
527 CB 3.00
528 Rosa,Donald Duck 3.00
529 CB 3.00
530 Rosa,Donald Duck 3.00
531 WK(c)Rosa,CB 3.00
532 CB 2.50
533 CB 2.50
534 CB 2.50
535 CB 2.50
536 CB 2.50
537 CB 2.25
538 CB 2.25
539 CB 2.25
540 CB 2.25
541 double-size,WK(c) 3.00
542 CB 5.00
543 CB,WK(c) 2.25
544 CB,WK(c) 2.25
545 CB 2.25
546 CB,WK,giant 4.00
547 CB,WK,giant 4.00

Walt Disney

548 CB,WK 2.75
549 CB, ... 2.25
550 CB,prev.unpub.story! 2.50
551 . . . . . 2.25
552 . . . . . 2.25
553 . . . . . 2.25
554 . . . . . 2.25
555 . . . . . 2.25
556 . . . . . 2.25
557 . . . . . 2.25
558 'Donald's Fix-it Shop' 2.25
559 'Bugs' 2.25
560 CB,April Fools Story 2.00
561 CB,Donald the 'Flipist' 2.00
562 CB,'3DirtyLittleDucks' 1.75
563 CB,'Donald Camping' 1.75
564 CB,'Dirk the Dinosaur' 1.75
565 CB,DonaldDuck,TruantOfficer 1.75
566 CB,'Will O' the Wisp' 1.75
567 CB,'Turkey Shoot' 1.75
568 CB,'AChristmas Eve Story' . . 1.50
569 CB, New Years Resolutions . 1.50
570 CB,Donald the Mailman +Poster 1.50
571 CB,'Atom Bomb' 2.95
572 CB, April Fools 1.50
573 TV Quiz Show 1.50
574 Pinnochio,64pgs 2.50
575 Olympic Torch Bearer, Li'l Bad Wolf,64 pgs. 2.95
576 . . . . . 1.50
577 A:Truant Officers,64 pgs. . . . 2.95
578 CB,Old Quacky Manor 1.50
579 CB,Turkey Hunt 1.50
580 CB,The Wise Little Red Hen, 64 page-Sunday page format . . . 2.95
581 CB,Duck Lake 1.50

WALT DISNEY COMICS DIGEST

Gold Key

June, 1968

[All done by Carl Banks]

1 Rep,Uncle Scrooge 23.00
2 . . . . . 13.00
3 . . . . . 13.00
4 . . . . . 13.00
5 . . . . . 15.00
6 . . . . . 7.00
7 . . . . . 7.00
8 . . . . . 7.00
9 . . . . . 7.00
10 . . . . . 7.00
11 . . . . . 7.00
12 . . . . . 7.00
13 . . . . . 7.00
14 . . . . . 5.00
15 . . . . . 5.00
16 rep.Don 10.00
17 . . . . . 6.00
18 . . . . . 6.00
19 . . . . . 6.00
20 . . . . . 6.00
21 . . . . . 7.00
22 . . . . . 7.00
23 . . . . . 7.00
24 . . . . . 7.00
25 . . . . . 7.00
26 . . . . . 7.00
27 . . . . . 7.00
28 . . . . . 7.00
29 . . . . . 7.00
30 . . . . . 7.00
31 . . . . . 7.00
32 . . . . . 4.00
33 . . . . . 7.00
34 rep.4Color#318 . . . . . 10.00
35 . . . . . 7.00
36 . . . . . 7.00
37 . . . . . 7.00
38 rep.Disneyland#1 . . . . . 7.00
39 . . . . . 5.00
40 . . . . . 4.00
41 . . . . . 3.00
42 . . . . . 4.00
43 . . . . . 4.00
44 . . . . . 15.00
45 . . . . . 3.00
46 . . . . . 4.00
47 . . . . . 3.00
48 . . . . . 3.00
49 . . . . . 3.00
50 . . . . . 4.00
51 rep.4Color 71 . . . . . 5.00
52 . . . . . 3.50
53 . . . . . 2.00
54 . . . . . 2.00
55 . . . . . 2.00
56 . . . . . 3.50
57 February, 1976 . . . . . 3.50

WALT DISNEY SHOWCASE
Gold Key

1 Boatniks (photo cover) 17.00
2 Moby Duck 10.00
3 Bongo & Lumpjaw 8.00
4 Pluto 8.00
5 $1,000,000 Duck (photo cover) 15.00
6 Bedknobs & Broomsticks 12.00
7 Pluto 8.00
8 Daisy & Donald 8.00
9 101 Dalmatians rep. 10.00
10 Napoleon & Samantha 12.00
11 Moby Duck rep. 7.00
12 Dumbo rep. 8.00
13 Pluto rep. 7.00
14 World's Greatest Athlete 12.00
15 3 Little Pigs rep. 12.00
16 Aristocats rep. 12.00
17 Mary Poppins rep. 12.00
18 Gyro Gearloose rep. 12.00
19 That Darn Cat rep. 12.00
20 Pluto rep. 8.00
21 Li'l Bad Wolf & 3 Little Pigs . . . 7.00
22 Unbirthday Party rep. 10.00
23 Pluto rep. 9.00
24 Herbie Rides Again rep. 8.00
25 Old Yeller rep. 8.00
26 Lt. Robin Crusoe USN rep. . . . 7.00
27 Island at the Top of the World . 7.00
28 Brer Rabbit, Bucky Bug rep. . . 8.00
29 Escape to Witch Mountain . . . 8.00
30 Magica De Spell rep. 15.00
31 Bambi rep. 8.00
32 Spin & Marty rep. 7.00
33 Pluto rep. 7.00
34 Paul Revere's Ride rep. 7.00
35 Goofy rep. 7.00
36 Peter Pan rep. 7.00
37 Tinker Bell & Jiminy Cricket rep. 7.00
38 Mickey & the Sleuth, Pt. 1 . . . 7.00
39 Mickey & the Sleuth, Pt. 2 . . . 7.00
40 The Rescuers 7.00
41 Herbie Goes to Monte Carlo . . 7.00
42 Mickey & the Sleuth 7.00
43 Pete's Dragon 8.00
44 Return From Witch Mountain & In Search of the Castaways . . 9.00
45 The Jungle Book rep. 9.00
46 The Cat From Outer Space . . . 7.00
47 Mickey Mouse Surprise Party . 8.00
48 The Wonderful Adventures of Pinocchio 7.00
49 North Avenue Irregulars; Zorro 7.00
50 Bedknobs & Broomsticks rep. . 6.00
51 101 Dalmatians 6.00
52 Unidentified Flying Oddball . . . 6.00
53 The Scarecrow 6.00
54 The Black Hole 6.00

WALT KELLY'S CHRISTMAS CLASSICS
Eclipse

1 . . . . 2.00

WALT KELLY'S SPRINGTIME TALES
Eclipse

1 . . . . 2.50

WAR DANCER
Defiant

1 B:JiS(s),I:Ahrq Tsolmec 2.75
2 I:Massakur 2.75
3 V:Massakur 2.75
4 JiS(s),A:Nudge 3.25

WARHAWKS
TSR

1 . . . . 2.95
2 . . . . 2.95
3 . . . . 2.95
4 . . . . 2.95
5 . . . . 2.95
6 . . . . 2.95
7 . . . . 2.95

WARHAWKS 2050
TSR

1 Pt.1 . . . . 2.95

WAR HEROES
Charlton Comics
February, 1963

1 . . . . 3.50
2 . . . . 2.00
3 . . . . 2.00
4 thru 10 . . . . @2.00
11 thru 26 . . . . @1.00
27 November, 1967 . . . . 1.00

WARMASTER

1 . . . . 3.95
2 . . . . 3.95

Warp Special #2 © First Comics

WARP
First

1 FB,JSon,I:Lord Cumulus & Prince Chaos, play adapt pt.1 . . . . . . 2.00
2 FB,SD,play adapt pt.2 . . . . 1.50
3 FB,SD,play adapt pt.3 . . . . 1.50
4 FB,SD,I:Xander,play pt.4 . . . . . 1.50
5 FB, play adapt pt.5 . . . . 1.50
6 FB/MG, play adapt pt.6 . . . . . . 1.50
7 FB/MG, play adapt pt.7 . . . . . . 1.50
8 FB/MG,BWg,play adapt pt.8 . . 1.25
9 FB/MG,BWg,play adapt conc. . 1.25
10 JBi/MG,BWg, Second Saga, I:Outrider 1.25
11 JBi/MG,A:Outrider 1.25
12 JBi/MG,A:Outrider 1.25
13 JBi/MG,A:Outrider 1.25
14 JBi/MG,A:Outrider 1.25
15 JBi/MG/BWg 1.25
16 BWg/MG,A:Outrider 1.25
17 JBi/MG,A:Outrider 1.25
18 JBi/MG,A:Outrider&Sargon . . . 1.25
19 MG,last issue 1.25
Special #1 HC,O:Chaos 1.50
Special #2 MS/MG,V:Ylem 1.50
Special #3 . . . . 1.50

WARSTRIKE
Malibu-Ultraverse

1 HNg,TA,in South America 1.95

WARRIORS OF PLASM
Defiant

1 JiS(s),DL,A:Lorca 3.25
2 JiS(s),DL,Sedition Agenda 3.25
3 JiS(s),DL,Sedition Agenda 3.25
4 JiS(s),DL,Sedition Agenda 3.25
5 JiS(s),B:Demon in Darkridge 2.75
6 JiS(s),Demon in Darkridge#2 . . . . 2.75
7 JiS(s),DL, ... 2.75
8 JiS(s),DL,40pages 3.00
9 JiS(s),LWn(s),DL,40pages 3.00
10 DL, ... 2.50
GN Home for the Holidays 5.95

WART AND THE WIZARD
Gold Key
February, 1964

1 . . . . 14.00

WAVE WARRIORS

1 . . . . 2.00
2 . . . . 2.00

WAXWORK in 3-D
Blackthorne

1 . . . . 2.50

WAYFARERS
Eternity

1 . . . . 1.80
2 . . . . 1.80

WEB OF HORROR
Major Magazines
December, 1969

1 JJ(c),Ph(c),BWr 25.00
2 JJ(c),Ph(c),BWr 20.00
3 April, 1970 . . . . 20.00

WEIRD FANTASY
Russ Cochran

1 Reps 1.50
2 Reps.inc.The Black Arts 1.50
3 thru 4 rep. . . . . @1.50
5 thru 7 rep. 2.00
8 . . . . 2.00

WEIRD SCIENCE
Gladstone

1 Rep. double size 5.00
2 Rep. #16 . . . . 3.50
3 Rep. #9 . . . . 3.50
4 Rep. 2.00

WEIRD SCIENCE FANTASY
Russ Cochran

1 Rep. W.S.F. #23 (1954) 1.50
2 Rep. Flying Saucer Invasion . . 1.50
3 Rep. 1.50
4 thru 6 Rep. 2.00
7 rep #29 . . . . 2.00
8 . . . . 2.00

WEIRD TALES ILLUSTRATED
Millenium

1 KJo,JBo,PCr,short stories 4.95

WENDY
Blackthorne

1 3-D 2.50

WENDY, THE GOOD LITTLE WITCH
Harvey Publications
August, 1960

1 55.00
2 26.00
3 21.00
4 21.00
5 21.00
6 16.00
7 16.00
8 16.00
9 16.00
10 16.00
11 thru 20 @11.00
21 thru 30 @6.00
31 thru 50 @3.50
51 thru 69 @2.50
70 thru 74 52 pg Giants @3.50
75 thru 92 @1.50
93 April, 1976 1.50

WENDY WITCH WORLD
Harvey Publications
October, 1961

1 35.00
2 17.00
3 17.00
4 17.00
5 17.00
6 11.00
7 11.00
8 11.00
9 11.00
10 11.00
11 thru 20 @7.00
21 thru 30 @3.50
31 thru 39 @2.50
40 thru 50 @1.50
51 thru 52 @1.00
53 September, 1974 1.00

WEREWOLF
Blackthorne

1 3-D 3.50

WHAM

1 1.75

WHISPER
Capital

1 MG(c) 10.00
2 8.00

First

1 2.50
2 2.00
3 2.00
4 1.50
5 1.50
6 thru 12 @1.25
13 thru 19 @1.75
20 O:Whisper 1.95
21 thru 26 @1.95
27 Ghost Dance #2 1.95
28 Ghost Dance #3 1.95
29 thru 37 @1.95
Special #1 4.00

WHITE FANG
Walt Disney

1 Movie Adapt. 5.95

WHITE TRASH
Tundra

1 I:Elvis & Dean 3.95
2 Trip to Las Vegas contd. 3.95
3 V:Purple Heart Brigade 3.95

WHODUNNIT
Eclipse

1 DSp,A:Jay Endicott 2.00
2 DSp,'Who Slew Kangaroo?' 2.00
3 DSp,'Who Offed Henry Croft' 2.00

WILD ANIMALS
Pacific

1 1.50

WILD BILL PECOS
AC Comics

1 3.50

WILDC.A.T.S.
Image

1 B:BCi(s),JLe,SW(i), I:WildC.A.T.S. 3.50
1a Gold Ed. 90.00
1b Gold and Signed 125.00
2 JLe,SW(i),V:Master Gnome, I:Wetworks,Prism foil(c), w/coupon#5 8.00
2a w/o coupon 4.00
3 RLd(c),JLe,SW(i), V:Youngblood 2.75
4 E:BCi(s),JLe,LSn,SW(i),w/card, A:Youngblood,BU:Tribe 2.75
4a w/red card 50.00
5 BCi(s),JLe,SW,I:Misery 2.50
6 BCi(s),JLe,SW,Killer Instinct, A:Misery,C:Ripclaw 2.50
7 BCi(s),JLe,SW, A:Cyberforce 2.25
8 BCi(s),JLe,SW, 2.25
9 BCi(s),JLe,SW, 2.25
Spec.#1 SrG(s),TC,SW,I:Destine, Pin-ups 3.50
TPB rep. #1-4,w/0 11.00

WILDC.A.T.S. TRILOGY
Image

1 BCi(s),JaL,V:Artemis 2.50
2 BCi(s),JaL,V:Artemis 2.25
3 BCi(s),JaL,V:Artemis 2.25

WILD FRONTIER
Charlton Comics
October, 1955

1 Davy Crockett 25.00
2 same 15.00
3 same 15.00
4 same 15.00
5 same 15.00
6 same 15.00
7 O:Cheyenne Kid 15.00

Becomes:

CHEYENNE KID

8 20.00
9 10.00
10 42.00
11 42.00
12 42.00
13 26.00
14 26.00
15 10.00
16 10.00
17 10.00
18 26.00
19 10.00
20 13.00
21 13.00
22 13.00
23 6.00
24 6.00
25 13.00
26 8.00
27 6.00
28 6.00
29 6.00
30 8.00
31 thru 59 @2.50
60 thru 98 @1.00
99 November, 1973 1.00

Wildstar #1 © Image Comics

WILDSTAR
Image

1 JOy,AG,I:Wildstar 2.25
1a Gold Ed. 75.00
2 JOy,AG 2.25
3 JOy,AG,V:Savage Dragon, D:Wildstar 2.25
4 JOy,AG,Last Issue,Pin-ups 2.25

WILD WEST C.O.W.-BOYS OF MOO MESA
Archie

1 Based on TV cartoon 1.25
2 Cody kidnapped 1.25
3 Law of the Year Parade, last issue 1.25

(Regular series)

1 Valley o/t Thunder Lizard 1.25
2 Plains, Trains & Dirty Deals 1.25

WILD WILD WEST
Millenium

1 2.95
2 thru 4 @2.95

WIN A PRIZE COMICS
Charlton Comics
February, 1955

1 S&K,Edgar Allen adapt. 200.00
2 S&K 150.00

Becomes:

TIMMY THE TIMID GHOST

3 30.00
4 20.00
5 20.00
6 10.00
7 10.00
8 10.00
9 10.00
10 10.00
11 20.00
12 20.00
13 thru 20 @5.00
21 thru 44 @4.00
45 1966 2.00

WINDRAGE

1 and 2 . . . . @1.25

WINTERWORLD
Eclipse

1 JZ,I:Scully, Wynn 1.75
2 JZ,V:Slave Farmers 1.75
3 JZ,V:Slave Farmers 1.75

WIREHEADS
Fleetway

1 . . . . 2.95

WITCHING HOUR
Millenium/Comico

1 Anne Rice adaptation 2.50
2 & 3 . . . . 2.50

Woody Woodpecker #1
© Harvey Publications

WOODY WOODPECKER
Harvey

1 thru 5 . . . . 1.25

WORLD OF WOOD
Eclipse

1 WW 1.75
2 WW,DSt(i) 1.75
3 WW 1.75
4 WW 1.75

WRATH
Malibu-Ultraverse

1 B:MiB(s),DvA,JmP,C:Mantra . . 2.25
2 DvA,JmP,V:Hellion 2.25
3 DvA,JmP,V:Radicals,
I:Slayer 2.25
4 DvA,JmP,V:Freex 2.25
5 DvA,JmP,V:Freex 1.95

WWF BATTLEMANIA
Valiant

1 WWF Action 2.50
2 . . . . 2.50
3 . . . . 2.50
4 . . . . 2.50
5 . . . . 2.50

WYATT EARP
Dell Publishing Co.
November, 1957

1 . . . . 30.00
2 . . . . 22.00
3 . . . . 20.00
4 . . . . 20.00
5 . . . . 20.00
6 . . . . 20.00
7 . . . . 20.00
8 . . . . 20.00
9 . . . . 20.00
10 . . . . 20.00
11 . . . . 15.00
12 . . . . 15.00
13 . . . . 15.00

X
Dark Horse

1 B:StG(s),DoM,JP,I:X-Killer 2.25
2 DoM,JP,V:X-Killer 2.25
3 DoM,JP,A:Pit Bulls 2.25
4 DoM,JP, ... 2.25
5 DoM,JP,V:Chaos Riders 2.00

XANADU
Eclipse

1 . . . . 2.00

XENO MAN

1 . . . . 1.75

XENOTECH
Mirage

1 I:Xenotech 2.75

XIMOS: VIOLENT PAST
Triumphant

1 JnR(s) 2.50
2 JnR(s) 2.50

XL

1 . . . . 1.25

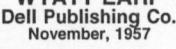

X-O Manowar #4
© Voyager Communications, Inc.

X-O MANOWAR
Valiant

0 JQ,O:Aric,1st Full
Chromium(c) 5.00
0a Gold Ed. 50.00
1 BL,BWS,I:Aric,Ken 35.00
2 BL(i),V:Lydia,Wolf-Class
Armor 25.00
3 I:X-Caliber,A:Solar 20.00
4 MM,A:Harbinger,C:Shadowman
(Jack Boniface) 23.00
5 BWS(c),V:AX 15.00
5a w/Pink logo 35.00
6 SD,V:Ax(X-O Armor) 10.00
7 FM(c),Unity#5,V:Pierce 5.00
8 WS(c),Unity#13,V:Pierce 5.00
9 Aric in Italy,408 A.D. 4.00
10 N:X-O Armor 4.00
11 V:Spider Aliens 3.50
12 A:Solar 3.50
13 V:Solar 3.50
14 BS,A:Turok,
I:Randy Cartier 4.00
15 BS,A:Turok 3.00
15a Red Ed. 28.00
16 V:The Mob 3.00
17 BL 3.00
18 JCf,V:CIA,A:Randy,I:Paul 2.75
19 JCf,V:US Government 2.75
20 A:Toyo Harada 2.50
21 V:Ax 2.50
22 Aria in S.America 2.50
23 Aria in S.America 2.50
24 Aria comes back 2.50
25 JCf,JGz,PaK,I:Armories,
BU:Armories#0 . . . . 4.00
26 JGz(s),RLv,F:Ken 2.50
27 JGz,RLe,A:Turok,Geomancer,
Stronghold,Livewire 2.50
28 JGz,RLe,D:X-O,V:Spider
Aliens,w/card 2.75
29 JGz,RLe,A:Turok,V:Spider
Aliens 2.50
30 JGz,RLe,A:Solar 2.50
31 JGz,RLe, ... 2.25
TPB rep.#1-4,w/X-O Manual . . . 11.00

YAKKY DOODLE & CHOPPER
Gold Key
December, 1962

1 . . . . 35.00

YIN FEI

5 . . . . 1.80
6 thru 11 . . . . @2.00

YOGI BEAR
Dell
Feb.-March, 1962

#1 thru #6, See Dell Four Color
7 thru 9 . . . . 30.00

Gold Key

10 . . . . 30.00
11 Jellystone Follies 30.00
12 . . . . 20.00
13 Surprise Party 30.00
14 thru 19 . . . . @20.00
20 thru 29 . . . . @14.00
30 thru 42 . . . . @10.00

YOGI BEAR
Charlton Comics
November, 1970

1 . . . . 25.00
2 thru 10 . . . . @15.00
11 thru 34 . . . . 10.00
35 January, 1976 . . . . 10.00

YOSEMITE SAM
Gold Key/Whitman
December, 1970

1 . . . . 15.00
2 thru 10 . . . . @6.00
11 thru 40 . . . . @3.00
41 thru 80 . . . . @2.00
81 February, 1984 . . . . 2.00

YOUNGBLOOD
Image

0 RLd.O:Youngblood,w/coupon

#7 . . . . 5.00
Oa without coupon 2.50
1 RLd,I:Youngblood(flipbook) . . 10.00
1a 2nd print.,gold border 3.00
2 RLd,I:Shadowhawk 8.00
3 RLd,I:Supreme 4.00

Young Indiana Jones #6
© Dark Horse Comics

YOUNG INDIANA JONES
Dark Horse

1 DBa,FS,TV Movie Adapt 3.25
2 DBa,TV Movie Adapt 2.75
3 DBa,GM 2.75
4 DBa,GM 2.75
5 DBa,GM 2.75
6 WW1,French Army 2.75
7 The Congo 2.75
8 Africa,A:A.Schweitzer 2.50
9 Vienna,Sophie-daughter of Arch-Duke Ferdinand 2.50
10 In Vienna continued 2.50
11 Far East 2.50
12 Fever Issue 2.50

YOUNGBLOOD
Image

0 RLd.O:Youngblood, w/coupon #7 . . . . 2.50
0a w/o coupon 2.50
0b Gold Coupon 75.00
1 RLd,I:Youngblood(flipbook) . . . 6.00
1a 2nd print.,gold border 3.00
2 RLd,I:Shadowhawk, Prophet 7.50
3 RLd,I:Supreme 3.00
4 RLd,DK,A:Prophet,BU:Pitt 3.00

YOUNGBLOOD BATTLEZONE
Image

1 BrM 2.25

YOUNGBLOOD STRIKEFILE
Image

1 JaL,RLd,I:Allies,A:Al Simmons (Spawn) 3.00
1a Gold Ed. 30.00
2 JaL,RLd,V:Super Patriot, Giger 2.75
2a Gold Ed. 30.00
3 RLd,JaL,DaM(i), A:Super Partiot 2.75
4 I:Overtkill 2.75

YOUNGBLOOD YEARBOOK
Image

1 CYp,I:Tyrax 2.75

Zen Intergalactic Ninja #3
© Archie Comics

ZEN INTERGALACTIC NINJA
Archie

1 Rumble in the Rain Forest prequel,inc.poster 1.25
2 Rumble in Rain Forest #1 . . . . 1.25
3 Rumble in Rain Forest #2 . . . . 1.25

Entity Comics

0 Chromium (c),JaL(c) 3.75
1 thru 2 . . . . 3.25

ZENITH PHASE II
Fleetway

1 thru 2 . . . . 1.95

ZERO PATROL
Continuity

1 EM,NA,O&I:Megalith 2.50
2 EM,NA 1.95
3 EM,NA,I:Shaman 1.95
4 EM,NA 1.95
5 EM 1.95
6 thru 8 EM . . . . @2.00

ZERO TOLERANCE
First

1 TV 3.50
2 TV 3.00
3 TV 2.25
4 TV 2.25

ZOONIVERSE
Eclipse

1 I:Kren Patrol 1.25
2 . . . . 1.25
3 . . . . 1.25
4 V:Wedge City 1.25
5 Spak vs. Agent Ty-rote 1.25
6 last issue 1.25

Zero Patrol #1 © Continuity Comics

ZORRO
Topps

0 BSf(c),DMG(s), ... 1.00
1 DMG(s) 2.75
2 DMG(s) 2.50
3 DMG(s) 2.50
4 MGr(c),DMG(s), ... 2.50

ZOT
Eclipse

1 . . . . 6.00
2 . . . . 3.00
3 . . . . 3.00
4 . . . . 3.00
5 . . . . 3.00
6 . . . . 2.00
7 . . . . 2.50
8 . . . . 2.00
9 . . . . 2.50
10 . . . . 2.00
10a B&W 6.00
10b 2nd printing 25
Original Zot! Book 1 . . . . 9.95
(Changed to B & W)

Hangin' on the Telephone with Jeff Smith

By 3BK

*Jeff Smith has taken the comic industry by storm. The easiest point of reference for non-*Bone *aficionados is the success of the* Teenage Mutant Ninja Turtles*-not since the appearance of the heroes on a half-shell hit the comics racks has a black-and-white independent comic caused such a stir. However, this reptilian reference may be damning the denizens of Boneville with faint praise. Smith brings us a rollicking adventure tale imbued with originality and fraught with overtones culled from such widely divergent sources as* The Lord of the Rings, Pogo, Popeye, *Carl Bark's classic Duck Adventures and* Moby Dick.

3BK: Why *Moby Dick*? [Editor's Note-When Fone Bone started his epic adventure, he packed a backpack containing Fone's favorite novel (*Moby Dick*), comics for Smiley Bone, and financial magazines for Phoney Bone. John.]

Jeff Smith: (Laughs) That joke is truth! I love *Moby Dick.* It really is my favorite book, and everytime I talk about it, people's eyes glaze over! Nobody wants to hear about *Moby Dick*!

3BK: It's funny because I have two favorite books, *Moby Dick* and *Huckleberry Finn*, and the guy who turned me on to *Bone* is always around when I start talking about *Moby Dick*, and he pipes in and says, "You're talking about that stupid book again!" So, it was just hilarious when that running joke was in *Bone*!

Jeff Smith: Nobody wants to hear about it! It's true!

3BK: It's great because when Fone starts telling Grandma about the wedding night chapter and she just falls asleep. I mean, I've had that conversation.

Jeff Smith: And they're asleep! I figure the time it takes people to fall asleep will get shorter and shorter, until pretty soon the Rat People will have Fone Bone cornered, and

Bone © Jeff Smith

he'll just turn and say, "Moby Dick" and they'll just fall over asleep.

3BK: That's beautiful! What were the comics he brought along for Smiley in the backpack?

Jeff Smith: I've had a lot of people ask me that. I was just making a comment about how the stupid one always has comics. It's kind of maddening how Zero in *Beetle Bailey* and Jughead in *Archie* read comics. Comics perpetuate their own myth that they're illiterate. But, they're not any specific comics.

3BK: When you and your wife first sat down and said, "Okay. We're going to do a monthly comic book, did you have x amount of dollars in the pot or a cut off point where if it hadn't worked you would go and try to work on the *Flintstones* or whatever?

Jeff Smith: Yeah, I owned my own animation studio and I sold that. My wife (Vijara) had a good-paying job, and we sat down together and I said, "I want to do six issues no matter what. Even if it's a bomb, I'm gonna promise myself to finish six issues and put them on the stands."

She backed me up, and we went for it, and *it was a bomb!* (Laughs)

The actual amount of money we had to put up wasn't that intense because you solicit in the catalogue, before you get orders. So you already know how many orders you have and the up-front money is fairly minimal because it's covered by the orders.

I actually went to a bank, showed them the nonreturnable orders, and said, "Give me a thirty-day loan!" But, basically, the profit was just enough to shovel back into the book to put out a new book. So, I definitely needed my wife's financial support (as well as emotional support)!

Last July, when things really started taking off, she finally quit her job and became my partner full-time. We figured that orders were going fast enough that if she came and helped me then, we'd make money, and if we waited the whole thing will go to hell.

BONE™
STILL NO SIGN OF THE TOWNSPEOPLE.
HEY! YA HEAR THAT, PHONEY? TH' COAST IS CLEAR!
LOOK AT HIM! WE GOT CHASED OUTTA BONEVILLE OVER TWO WEEKS AGO, AN' HE'S STILL MOPIN' AROUND!
...OH, WELL... I GUESS YOU CAN WHINE ALL YOU WANT, WHEN YER TH' RICHEST GUY IN TH' WHOLE TOWN.
AAAH!
OOPS! SILLY ME. EX-RICHEST!

3BK: Tell us a little bit about the beginnings of *Bone*. Where did he come from? When did you start drawing him?

Jeff Smith: When did I start drawing Fone Bone?

3BK: Yeah.

Jeff Smith: I first started drawing Fone Bone in kindergarten, or maybe even prekindergarten, I can't remember the year exactly. It was just a character. I used to draw lots of characters, in the same way that just about everybody in this business did when they were real little.

He (Fone Bone) was just one that stuck with me, and I kept drawing him. Shortly afterwards I came up with a supporting cast of characters, like Phoney Bone (who is sort of an anti-Fone Bone). Actually, Phoney Bone was started by a friend of mine who sort of drew an anti-Fone Bone character (hence "Phoney" Bone).

I drew him for a while, and then I kind of got over it by the time I got into sixth grade.

But I don't think that's anything different from most cartoonists; they're still reading comics, but they lose interest and get into "real" fields. Their teachers explain to them that "Cartooning is not real, and you have to get into math now."

I hung onto it, in the back of my mind, and got back into it again when I was in college.

3BK: When I first looked at *Bone*, I got the feeling that it might have been originally developed as a strip for a college paper. Was Bone ever used as a strip?

Jeff Smith: Yes.

3BK: Is there a collected set of those strips somewhere that might someday see publication or have they all been developed as a basis for the comic books?

Jeff Smith: Yes and no. I went to Ohio State University in 1982, and they had a daily newspaper called *The Lantern* with a circulation of like 50,000. I had previously been going to an art college where they didn't appreciate cartooning at all. So, I got the hell out of there.

They didn't appreciate cartooning at Ohio State either, but they did have a daily newspaper with this huge circulation. So, I went up to the editors and I said, "You know, I can't take any courses, I can't get a degree in cartooning, but you've got this newspaper where I could actually learn the tools of the trade I want to get into."

They looked over my submissions, which was basically *Bone* in a daily format.

3BK: Like four panels.

Jeff Smith: Yeah, your basic newspaper comic strip. They looked at the submissions, they liked it, and that was it; I did it every single day for four years.

I knew what I wanted to do-I wanted to do a daily comic strip. So I took this character I'd made up in kindergarten, and when I was developing the concept for the comic strip I took them out of a Boneville (or a Duckburg or Toontown kind of a world). So I transferred them to this valley with humans and dragons and monsters; that's when I got that all together, for the comic strip.

And then I did (I'm sorry, it took me a long time to get around to your question!) self-publish a paperback book, collecting the first year's strips together. That was my first experience with self-publishing.

3BK: That must have been excellent for discipline, sitting down and writing a strip every day. Or did you write like two weeks at a time?

Jeff Smith: It was pretty much every day. I worked my way through school, so I had to go to work, and then I had classes, then I did my schoolwork, and at about nine or ten at night I would start my strip for the next day. I had to submit it the next day, and it would run like two days later.

3BK: So, when you walked around the dorms, did you see it pinned up on refrigerators and stuff?

Jeff Smith: Yeah, I did. I don't really have a refrigerator-type of comic; it's not like *Family Circus* or anything. Despite the fact that it looks like a kiddie strip, it's not at all.

3BK: No; obviously not. Looking at your work, it's obvious that you've had some formal art training. What did you learn from your college art classes?

Jeff Smith: I did learn some stuff at college. But none of it really shows up in the comic; I didn't learn perspective or any of that kind of stuff. I learned a few color-theory things and I learned how to use certain tools. I learned that tools are very important. If I want to draw a comic, I don't just go to a store and buy a Repitograph so I won't have to learn how to use a dip pen or something.

I learned that if I'm going to do something, I'm going to have to go to the library, find books on cartooning, see what people talk about, and then go and get the right tools.

Pretty much all I got from college was...

3BK: Research skills?

Jeff Smith: Well, I learned how to take care of myself because I was completely rejected by everyone I met, every professor I ever had in college.

3BK: Did you ever try to sell *Bone* to Marvel or King Features Syndicate or any of the big guys?

Jeff Smith: I did try to sell to the newspaper syndicates.

3BK: Did they just dismiss you out of hand?

Jeff Smith: Most of them did; a couple of them didn't. King Features was really interested, Tribune Media Services was interested. I spent approximately two years working the strip over with them. They would say, "This isn't bad, but we don't really like the idea that it's an adventure strip. So, work up a whole new submission strip of gag-a-days." Which isn't really my forte!

I don't do comedy. If one of my characters says something funny, then he says something funny, and that's fine.

3BK: But only if it's in the context of the story?

Jeff Smith: I don't like to do three panels and *Buh dump bump*! But I tried it. I worked really hard trying to do what the syndicates wanted. I finally realized that I couldn't, and they realized that I couldn't! So we parted ways.

3BK: Who would you say was an influence on your art style or your storytelling style?

Jeff Smith: Some of the big influences on me really hit me when I was a lot younger. Reading the *Donald Duck* stories by Carl Barks (of course, we didn't know his name then).

3BK: He was the "Good Duck Artist."

Jeff Smith: Yeah, everybody called him that. I called him the "Long Story Artist" because his stories were always longer adventures. His storytelling in the exciting adventure mode really influenced me a lot. I was also influenced by the Bugs Bunny cartoons, especially by Friz Freleng and Chuck Jones. I've always loved Neal Adams and Joe Kubert.

3BK: Did you ever think about applying to the Kubert School when you were going to Ohio State?

Jeff Smith: I didn't know about it. Was it around it 1978?

3BK: I'm not really sure.

Jeff Smith: Well, if it was, I just didn't know about it. I didn't know there was a place you could go.

[Editor's Note: The Kubert School began in 1976 with twenty-one students. John]

3BK: I see a lot of Popeye in Grandma's face. Is that a conscious thing or are they just similar facial structures?

Jeff Smith: No, no, it is conscious. Grandma is Popeye, just like Fone Bone is Pogo.

3BK: Was there a Grandma in your life? Like a crazy aunt or grandmother?

Jeff Smith: There actually was a real Grandma Ben (her name wasn't Grandma Ben, I don't remember her real name). A girl I dated in high school, her grandmother raised steer, and she looked a lot like Grandma Ben, and she wore Adidas tennis shoes and she would just tear around that farm like nobody's business!

The cows would get across a creek (or somewhere they weren't supposed to be) and she would just say, "Damn! The cows are getting away!" She would just fling the gate open and this little old white-haired lady would go tearing flatout across the fields.

So, even though Grandma Ben is the most unbelievable character, she is the only one that is based on a real person.

3BK: Do you make an effort to keep *Bone* at a point where I'd feel comfortable giving this book to my nine-year-old nephew to read but that I can still read and enjoy as a thirty-two-year-old man?

Jeff Smith: I think that's just the way the characters work. I think, if anything, that I'm starting to get a little bit uncomfortable about how young the readers are. I decided early on, since I wanted to do comic strips and you can't really use swear words, I never got into that kind of a thing.

Right away I got into the challenge of trying to find a way to have the characters express, "Oh Shit!" without having them say "Oh Shit!" So it's clean, but only because I was originally shooting for a different medium that wouldn't let me be unclean. And I'm perfectly comfortable with that, I find *Krazy Kat* or *Pogo* to be completely adult entertainment and completely clean.

Sometimes it's actually a little more difficult, and I've had people argue and say it's easier to be clean.

3BK: That's ridiculous! Just in everyday life you have to exercise more vocabulary skills not to curse than you do to curse.

Jeff Smith: Right! It's one thing if you're talking pablum and not saying anything. But if you're going to write something engaging and still be clean, well, that's actually hard. I have a hard time doing that.

I think the reason the book is appealing to kids is because I made up the characters when I was young, and I have remained true to the comic book I wanted to have when I was young.

When I used to read comics, there was a certain comic book I wanted to read that wasn't there! I liked *Asterix the Gaul*, I liked *Uncle Scrooge* and *Pogo*, but they never really went on (and I don't really have a word for this) on a hard-core adventure.

3BK: A Quest?

Jeff Smith: Yeah, well, yeah! In a way, *The Lord of the Rings* is the about the closest thing to the concept. I read that in high school and I flipped out! There it was! That's the thing! Uncle Scrooge actually went on an adventure that had an ending and had consequences that changed him!

Carl Barks was doing an ongoing character, and he was doing it brilliantly. I wanted to do something that would have evolution, and an ending and consequences. And I've done that, and I guess that's why I'm seeing a lot of young readers. The reason I'm uncomfortable is that there is some responsibility in that.

3BK: Definitely!

Jeff Smith: That wasn't my intention; I'm just trying to tell a story. I'm going to stick to this, I'm going to tell a story and I don't care what kind of outside pressures I get. I've always said that from the beginning, even before it got popular, that whatever I do inside the pages of the comic book, that's the comic book I'm doing, come hell or high water.

I don't care if there's popular things putting pressure on it, like "Let's do toys and take some time off the book." Or "We're gonna do a Ted electric-toothbrush holder, and Ted hasn't been in the book for three issues so, by golly, you better put him in." I always said that I would never let the book be affected by pressures like that.

At the same time, I've got characters that do things, I've got characters that are greedy, I've got characters that smoke, and I'm not gonna let people come from the other end and

say, "Hey, you have a responsibility, you know. The dragon is smoking a cigarette there, and how dare you show a character smoking?"

What's inside the book is inside the book, and that's it. That's why I'm a little nervous about the younger readers because there's a responsibility there that I wasn't anticipating.

3BK: As a cartoonist without an editor, how do you keep continuity? Do you have *Bone* mapped out for the next two years? Do you have a giant "bible" you refer back to?

Jeff Smith: It's pretty much just in my head, but it is pretty well figured out. I worked out the whole story line once before when I was doing the college newspaper strip. I did that every day for four years, so that was quite a bit of material. I have the benefit of going back and saying, "Well, people laughed really hard at that joke, I'll use that one." Or "Nobody laughed at that, it was sophomoric, so I'll get rid of that."

I didn't finish the story in the college strip, so the first thing I did when I decided to do it as a comic book was I sat down and wrote the ending, I wrote the "big production" ending.

I mapped out, pretty tightly, the last three books of the series. So those are written in notebooks; nothing else is actually written down. I just have a very broad outline in my mind and I know it pretty much by heart.

I'm going into a story line now where Phoney Bone and Lucius (the big grumpy bar owner) do a little handshake bet, double or nothing on Phoney's debt to Lucius, sort of like the story about L. Ron Hubbard's bet.

The Hubbard story was that he and his science fiction writer buddies were in a bar and Hubbard bet that he could start up a cult.

3BK: Scientology?

Jeff Smith: Yeah. Dianetics. That was all started on a handshake in a bar! And he did it; he started up this cult. That's where I am taking off on this next story line: Phoney's going to bet that he can get people to give him money for nothing!

So, I know that I have this cult (or bet) story line coming up, but I don't have it mapped out that tightly because I want it to be spontaneous. I know what the bet is, I know what the climactic moment of the bet is, and I know what the resolution is. I can see that being two years worth of comic books. So, it's that loose.

3BK: You say you have a definite end in mind for *Bone*. Now be that five or ten or twenty years down the line, what would happen at that point?

Jeff Smith: Well, *Bone* the comic book would end. That would be it.

3BK: And then maybe Fone or Phoney Bone would do something else?

Jeff Smith: If I had another Bone story, I would do more Bone stuff. I have at least one other Bone project in my head that's fairly large scale. I figure the story I'm telling right now has something like eight more years to it.

3BK: Could Bone ever meet Cerebus or something like that?

OH, LISTEN! THE FIRST BIRDS OF SPRING! WE'LL HAVE YOU AND YOUR COUSINS BACK IN BONEVILLE BEFORE YOU KNOW IT!
....BONEVILLE....? ...WHAT'S BONEVILLE?

Bone © Jeff Smith

Jeff Smith: Yes, but not in the confines of the book. If Dave [Sims] wanted to have him in his book (I don't think he would), or if we did some separate thing. We've actually talked about doing stuff together.

3BK: Like a one-shot or a miniseries, maybe?

Jeff Smith: Inside the pages of *Bone*, I'm telling a story; and if Cerebus walked in it would really jolt the story.

3BK: You're right, it would be kind of ridiculous.

Jeff Smith: Well, the Bone Universe is complete. That's something that I work very hard at, that your disbelief is completely suspended and you believe completely in that world.

Dave and I are good friends, and we've talked about doing stuff together (nothing concrete), so we may do something and it would be a lot of fun. But it would have to be outside the confines of our books.

3BK: Do you think you could ever hand *Bone* over to somebody else for a couple of issues?

Bone © Jeff Smith

Jeff Smith: No. That's just a personal artistic choice of mine.

3BK: It seems to me that *Bone* would translate beautifully to animation. Are there any plans for that?

Jeff Smith: Not really. I've had some fairly serious conversations with quite a few animation studios. I'm not all that anxious to do limited television animation. Even though that's a hard thing to say when I'm talking to these studios that are putting a lot of work into these shows, most of them just look like shit!

I just don't want to do that; I'd rather just not have a TV show. Some of the people I'm talking to can do some really good stuff. I never say never.

I was in animation for about six years, so I believe it can be done. We'll see, but there is nothing in the works right now.

3BK: There has been some great animation done from comic books. I mean, *Akira* was phenomenal!

Jeff Smith: *Akira* was good, the *Batman* TV show is mind-numbingly well done. I mean, I wish it had more cels, more drawings per second but that's what I mean, there are ways to do good things without doing a feature movie. It is possible, but so much of it is done strictly for the movie with no care for the art at all.

3BK: Do you think we'll see a Bone action figure someday? Are you talking to somebody right now?

Jeff Smith: Someday. Well, yes and no. We (I say "we" because my wife Vijara is my business partner) get letters and proposals all the time! But we don't know that much about this stuff, so we're not calling anybody up and getting this stuff going. I mean companies are calling up from Germany and Finland, and what do we know about this stuff?

We're getting all these offers, but we're not really doing anything because we're trying to learn how it's done. We're not just going to jump in and sign a contract that's going to trap me. There's a lot of exciting things going on, but I'm just not in that much of a hurry to sell out. (Laughs)

3BK: In the last few months in *Comic Buyers Guide*, your name has come up in the letters page quite a bit when people were talking about distribution companies instituting fines for comic companies that didn't ship solicited products. The smaller comic book companies were saying that these fines could put them under, and if that happened, perhaps fans might miss out on the "next Jeff Smith." How do you feel about that?

Jeff Smith: To state this as briefly as possible, I don't feel there is any excuse for a late product, *none*. I support the thirty-day window that is now in place. This is a real business. I'm having a lot of fun drawing the comic (and that is the most important thing to me), but I have to stand up from my desk, shake myself, open my eyes, and say, "Okay, it's time to deal with business realities; there are commercial pressures at hand."

Be real about it. Go to the library and find out how businesses are run. It's just not an altruistic venture where "I'm going to do my stories and my art and the world will find them."

It's a real business. I worry that people think the world owes them a living and every artist who wants to have a crack at this can get a shot.

In fact, what is allowed now, for someone like me to just put an ad in a catalogue and if it works, it works-that's unbelievable. I can't really think of any other system (like records or movies) that's so simple. It's amazing!

My concern when they started to close things down was that I wanted to keep it open just a hair. I don't think we deserve extra breaks. My problem with some of the restrictions was that it was inequitable. It was claiming that there was a problem between publishers and retailers and that the distributors were going to take care of this problem with these penalties.

Those penalties didn't in any way address those problems they said they were addressing. Instead, it levied these huge fines on small publishers like Denis Kitchen and Gary Groth and even smaller single-title publishers. That was just inequitable!

And they did change that to something like three strikes and you're out, giving you three consecutive issues to get your shit back together.

3BK: It's interesting that you mention Denis Kitchen. Before when we were speaking about action figures, I was wondering why you didn't let a company like Kitchen Sink Press take care of all that marketing stuff.

Jeff Smith: I think that the whole point of self-publishing is to keep that control.

3BK: What do you think when you hear that a famous comic book artist like a Rob Liefeld or a Jim Lee is going to take a sabbatical from comics?

Jeff Smith: There's a lot of people who would give anything to do this job. But I have to say, I've been doing this for close to three years now, and it is exhausting! It is exhausting emotionally and physically. You have to go on the road. There's many things that I could never have imagined would take up so much of my time and my emotional energy.

I could see just wanting to stop. I don't want to sound ungrateful that the book is popular, but, every now and then, I'd like to stop for a minute. (Laughs) I can see taking a sabbatical, sure.

3BK: When you talk about emotional investment, is that the time you spend laboring over a book on the drawing board or is it a response to how the book is received? Or is once a book done it's done and you're on to the next one?

Jeff Smith: Oh, no. I secretly wait and see how it's received. The book goes out, and calls start filtering in from certain friends and people I trust, and I wait and hear what they have to say. It gets me excited if they're happy about the story.

3BK: So you must just be grinning ear to ear these days!

Jeff Smith: Certainly. I'm having a good time, no question.

Bone © Jeff Smith

A1 #2 © Atomeka Press

A1
Atomeka Press

1 BWs,A:Flaming Carrot,Mr.X. . . . 9.75
2 . . . . 9.75
3 . . . . 9.75
4 . . . . 5.95
5 . . . . 6.95
6a 4.95

ABC WARRIORS
Fleetway

1 thru 6 . . . . @1.95

ABUNDI SPECIAL

1 . . . . 2.50

AC ANNUAL
Aircel

1 . . . . 3.95
2 Based on 1940's heroes 5.00
3 F:GoldenAge Heroes 3.50
4 F:Sentinels of Justice 3.95

ACE COMICS PRESENTS

1 thru 7 . . . . @1.75

ACES
Eclipse

1 thru 5 . . . . @2.95

ACCIDENT MAN
Dark Horse

1 I:Accident Man 2.50

ACME

1 . . . . 1.95

ACTION FORCE

1 . . . . 1.75

ADAM AND EVE
Bam

1 . . . . 3.00
2 thru 10 . . . . @1.50

ADAM LOGAN

1 . . . . 1.50

ADOLESCENT RADIOACTIVE BLACK-BELT HAMSTERS
Eclipse

1 I:Bruce,Chuck,Jackie,Clint 2.50
1a 2nd printing 2.00
2 A parody of a parody 2.00
3 I:Bad Gerbil 2.00
4 A:Heap (3-D),Abusement Park . 1.50
5 Abusement Park #2 . . . . 1.50
6 SK,Abusement Park #3 . . . . . . 1.50
7 SK,V:Toe-Jam Monsters 1.50
8 SK 1.50
9 SK,All-Jam last issue 1.50

[2nd Series]
Parody Press

1 . . . . 2.50
2 Hamsters Go Hollywood 2.50

ADVENT

1 . . . . 1.75

ADVENTURES INTO THE UNKNOWN
A Plus Comics

1 AW 2.95
2 AW 2.95
3 AW 2.95
Halloween Spec. Reps. Charlton & American Comics GroupHorror 2.50

ADVENTURES OF B.O.C.

1 . . . . 1.50
2 . . . . 1.50
3 . . . . 1.50

ADVENTURERS
Aircel/Adventure Publ.

0 Origin Issue 2.50
1 with Skeleton 8.00
1a Revised cover 3.00
1b 2nd printing 2.00
2 Peter Hsu (c) 2.50
3 Peter Hsu (c) 2.50
4 Peter Hsu (c) 2.00
5 Peter Hsu (c) 2.00
6 Peter Hsu (c) 2.00
7 . . . . 2.00
8 . . . . 2.00
9 . . . . 2.00

ADVENTURERS BOOK II
Adventure Publ.

0 O:Man Gods 1.95
1 thru 9 . . . . @1.95

ADVENTURERS BOOK III

1A Lim.(c)Ian McCaig 2.25
1B Reg.(c)Mitch Foust 2.25
2 thru 6 . . . . @2.25

ADVENTURES IN MYSTWOOD

1 . . . . 3.00
2 . . . . 2.00
3 . . . . 2.00

ADVENTURES OF CHRISSY CLAWS
Heroic

1 thru 2 . . . . 3.25

ADVENTURES OF CHUK THE BARBARIC

1 . . . . 1.25

ADVENTURES OF LUTHER ARKWRIGHT
Valkyrie Press

1 . . . . 2.25
2 . . . . 2.25
3 . . . . 2.25
4 . . . . 2.25
5 . . . . 2.25
6 . . . . 2.25
7 . . . . 2.25
8 . . . . 2.25
9 . . . . 2.25

ADVENTURES OF MR. CREAMPUFF

1 . . . . 1.75

ADVENTURES OF MR. PYRIDINE

1 . . . . 2.25

ADVENTURES OF THEOWN

1 thru 3, Limited series . . . . . . @1.75

AESOP'S FABLES
Fantagraphics

1 Selection of Fables 2.25
2 Selection of Fables 2.25
3 inc. Boy who cried wolf 2.25

AFTERMATH

1 Type a, Partial map 4.50
1a Type b, Full map 2.00

AGENT ORANGE

1 . . . . 1.75
2 . . . . 1.75
3 . . . . 1.75

AGENT UNKNOWN
Renegade

1 . . . . 2.00

AGE OF HEROES

1 . . . . 1.25
2 . . . . 1.25
3 . . . . 1.25

AIRCEL

1 Graphic Novel year 1 . . . . 6.95

AIRFIGHTERS CLASSICS
Eclipse

1 O:Airboy,rep.Air Fighters#2 . . . . 3.00
2 rep.Old Airboy appearances . . . 3.00
3 thru 6 . . . . @3.95

AIRWAVES
Caliber

1 Radio Security 2.50
2 A:Paisley,Ganja 2.50
3 Formation of Rebel Alliance . . . 2.50
4 Big Annie,Pt. 1 . . . . 2.50
5 Big Annie, Pt 2 . . . . 2.50

A.K.A.: OUTCAST

1 . . . . 1.75

ALBEDO
Thoughts & Images

0 white cover, yellow drawing table Blade Runner 150.00
0a white(c) 85.00
0b blue(c),1st ptg 52.00
0c blue(c),2nd ptg 35.00
0d blue(c),3rd ptg 6.00
0e Photo(c),4th ptg.,inc. extra pages 4.00
1 SS,I:Nilson Groundthumper, dull red cover 44.00

Albedo #5 © Thoughts & Images

1a bright red cover 40.00
2 SS,I:Usagi Yojimbo 40.00
3 SS,Erma, Usagi 7.00
4 SS,Usagi 9.00
5 Nelson Groundthumper 8.00
6 Erma, High Orbit 7.00
7 . . . . 4.00
8 Erna Feldna 3.00
9 High Orbit,Harvest Venture 2.00
10 thru 14 . . . . @2.00

ALBEDO VOL II
Antartic Press
1 New Erma Story 2.50
2 E.D.F. HQ 2.50
3 Birth of Erma's Child 2.50
4 Non action issue 2.50
5 The Outworlds 2.50
6 War preparations 2.50
7 Ekosiak in Anarchy 2.50
8 EDF High Command 2.50

ALIEN DUCKLING
1 . . . . 2.00
2 thru 4 . . . . @1.75

ALIEN ENCOUNTERS
Fantagor
1 . . . . 1.25

ALIEN FIRE
Kitchen Sink Press
1 . . . . 3.50
2 . . . . 2.50
3 . . . . 2.00

ALIEN MUTANT WAR
1 . . . . 2.25

ALIEN NATION: A BREED APART
Adventure Comics
1 . . . . 3.00
2 . . . . 2.50
3 The 'Vampires' Busted 2.50
4 Final Issue 2.50

ALIEN NATION: THE FIRSTCOMERS
Adventure Comics
1 New Mini-series 2.50
2 Assassin 2.50
3 Search for Saucer 2.50
4 Final Issue 2.50

ALIEN NATION: PUBLIC ENEMY
Adventure Comics
1 'Before the Fall' 2.50
2 Earth & Wehlnistrata 2.50
3 Killer on the Loose 2.50

ALIEN NATION: THE SKIN TRADE
Adventure Comics
1 'Case of the Missing Milksop' . . 2.50
2 'To Live And Die in L.A' 2.50
3 A:Dr. Jekyll 2.50
4 D.Methoraphan Exposed 2.50

ALIEN NATION: THE SPARTANS
Adventure Comics
1 JT/DPo,Yellow wrap 4.00
1a JT/DPo,Green wrap 4.00
1b JT/DPo,Pink wrap 4.00
1c JT/DPo,blue wrap 4.00
1d LTD collectors edition 8.00
2 JT,A:Ruth Lawrence 2.50
3 JT/SM,Spartians 2.50
4 JT/SM,conclusion 2.50

Aliens #1 © Dark Horse Comics

ALIENS
Dark Horse
1 Movie Sequel,R:Hicks,Newt . . 35.00
1a 2nd printing 7.00
1b 3rd &4th printing 2.50
2 Hicks raids Mental Hospital . . . 24.00
2a 2nd printing 3.50
2a 3rd printing 2.50
3 Realize Queen is on Earth . . . 10.00
3a 2nd printing 2.50
4 Queen is freed, Newton on Aliens World 7.00
5 All out war on Aliens World 6.00
6 Hicks & Newt return to Earth . . 6.00
Aliens Book 1,rep.#1-#6 . . . . . . 24.95

ALIEN4 STRIKE FORCE
1 . . . . 1.95

ALIENS VS. PREDATOR
Dark Horse
0 PN,KS,Rep DHP#34-36 . . . . . 10.00

ALL-PRO SPORTS
All Pro Sports
1 Unauthorized Bio-Bo Jackson . . 2.50
2 Unauthorized Bio-Joe Montana . 2.50

ALPHA PREDATOR
1 . . . . 2.00

ALTERNATE HEROES
Prelude
1 and 2 . . . . @1.95

AMAZING COMICS
Premium
1 thru 9 . . . . @1.95

AMAZING CYNICALMAN
Eclipse
1 . . . . 1.50

AMAZING WAHZOO
1 RB 2.50
2 . . . . 1.75
3 . . . . 1.75

AMAZON WARRIORS
1 rep. 2.50

AMAZONS, THE
1 . . . . 2.95

AMERICAN, THE
Dark Horse
1 CW,'Chinese Boxes,'D:Gleason 8.00
2 CW,'Nightmares 4.50
3 CW,Secrets of the American . . . 4.00
4 CW,American vs.Kid America . . 4.00
5 A:Kiki the Gorilla 4.00
6 Rashomon-like plot 3.50
7 Pornography business issue . . . 3.50
8 Deals with violence issue 3.50
9 American Falls into a cult 3.50

AMERICAN PRIMITIVE
Spec. #1 . . . . 2.50

AMERICAN SPLENDOR
13 thru 15 . . . . @3.25
16 . . . . 3.95

AMUSING STORIES
Blackthorne
1 thru 3 . . . . @2.00

ANGEL OF DEATH
Innovation
1 thru 4 . . . . @2.25

ANGRY SHADOWS
1 . . . . 4.95

ANIMERICA
(Viz Comics)
1 F:Bubble Gum Crisis 2.95
2 F:Bubble Gum Crisis 2.95
3 F:Bubble Gum Crisis 2.95

ANIVERSE, THE
1 thru 3 . . . . @1.95

ANT BOY

1 . . . . 1.75
1a 2nd Printing 1.75
2 . . . . 1.75

ANTARES CIRCLE
Antarctic Press

1 . . . . 1.75
2 . . . . 1.75

A-OK
Antarctic Press

1 Ninja H.S. spin-off series 2.50
2 F:Paul,Moniko,James 2.50
3 Confrontation 2.50

APACHE DICK

1 thru 3 . . . . @2.25

APE CITY
Adventure Comics

1 Monkey Business 3.00
2 thru 4 . . . . @2.50

APEX PROJECT

1 . . . . 1.00

APPLESEED
Eclipse

1 MSh,rep. Japanese comic . . . 10.00
2 MSh,arrival in Olympus City . . . 5.00
3 MSh,Olympus City politics 3.00
4 MSh,V:Director 3.00
5 MSh,Deunan vs. Chiffon 3.00

Book Two

1 MSh,AAd(c),Olympus City 3.50
2 MSh,AAd(c),Hitomi vs.EswatUnit 3.00
3 MSh,AAd(c),Deunan vs.Gaia . . . 3.00
4 MSh,AAd(c),V:Robot Spiders . . 3.00
5 MSh,AAd(c),Hitome vs.Gaia . . . 3.00

Book Three

1 MSh,Brigreos vs.Biodroid 5.00
2 MSh,V:Cuban Navy 3.00
3 MSh,'Benandanti' 3.00
4 MSh,V:Renegade biodroid 3.00
5 . . . . 3.00

Book Four

1 MSh,V:Munma Terrorists 3.50
2 MSh,V:Drug-crazed Munma . . . 3.50
3 Msh,V:Munma Drug Addicts . . . 3.50
4 MSh,Deunan vs. Pani 3.50

APPLESEED DATABOOK
Dark-Horse

1 . . . . 3.50
2 . . . . 3.50

ARAMIS WEEKLY

1 mini-series 1.95
2 & 3 . . . . @1.95

AREA 88
Eclipse

1 I:Shin Kazama 3.00
1a 2nd printing 1.50
2 Dangerous Mission 2.00
2a 2nd printing 1.50
3 O:Shin,Paris '78 . . . . 2.00
4 thru 8 . . . . @2.00
9 thru 39 . . . . @1.50
40 and 41 . . . . @1.75
42 . . . . 2.00

ARGONAUTS
Eternity

1 thru 5 . . . . @1.95

ARGOSY
Caliber

1 'Walker' vs. Myth Beasts 2.50

ARIK KHAN
A Plus Comics

1 I:Arik Khan 2.50
2 . . . . 2.50

ARISTOCRATIC EXTRA-TERRESTRIAL TIME-TRAVELING THIEVES
Fictioneer Books

1 V:IRS 3.00
2 V:Realty 1.75
3 V:MDM 1.75
4 thru 12 . . . . @1.75

ARM
Adventure Comics

1 Death by Ecstasy Pt#1 . . . . 2.50
2 Death by Ecstasy Pt#2 . . . . 2.50
3 Death by Ecstasy Pt#3 . . . . 2.50

ARMADILLO ANTHOLOGY

1 & 2 . . . . @1.50

ARSENAL
SOL

1 . . . . 2.00

ART D'ECCO
FAN

1 . . . . 2.50

ARTHUR: KING OF BRITAIN
Tome Press

1 Saga of King Arthur Chronicled by Geoffrey of Monmouth 2.95

ASHES
Caliber

1 thru 5 . . . . @2.50

ASTONISH

1 thru 4 . . . . @1.25

ASTRON

1 . . . . 2.00

ASYLUM

1 . . . . 1.75
2 thru 4 . . . . @1.95

ATOMIC COMICS

1 . . . . 1.50

Becomes: MARK I

ATOMIC MAN

1 . . . . 3.00
2 . . . . 2.00
3 . . . . 1.75

ATOMIC MOUSE
A Plus Comics

1 A:Atomic Bunny 2.50

A TRAVELLER'S TALE
Antarctic Press

1 I:Goshin the Traveller 2.50
2 . . . . 2.50

ATTACK OF THE MUTANT MONSTERS
A Plus Comics

1 SD,rep.Gorgo(Kegor) 2.50

AV IN 3D
Aardvark Vanaheim

1 Color,A:FlamingCarot 6.00

AVENUE X
Innovation

1 Based on NY radio drama 2.50

AWESOME COMICS

1 thru 3 . . . . @2.00

B-MOVIE PRESENTS

1 thru 4 . . . . @1.70

BACK TO BACK HORROR SPECIAL

1 . . . . 1.50

BAD AXE

1 thru 3 . . . . @2.25

BADEBIKER

1 . . . . 2.50
2 . . . . 2.00
3 thru 5 . . . . @1.50

Badlands #1 © Dark Horse

BADLANDS
Dark Horse

1 I:Connie Bremen 3.50
2 Anne Peck, C.I.A. 3.00
3 Assassination Rumor 2.50
4 Connie heads South 2.50
5 November 22, 1963, Dallas . . . 2.25

BAD MOON

1 . . . . 3.00

BAD NEWS

3 . . . . 2.95

BAKER STREET
(Prev. color)
Caliber

3 . . . . 3.25
4 . . . . 1.95
5 Children of the Night Pt.1 . . . . . 1.95
6 Children of the Night Pt.2 . . . . . 1.95
7 Children of the Night Pt.3 . . . . . 2.50
8 Children of the Night Pt.4 . . . . . 2.50
9 Children of the Night Pt.5 . . . . . 2.50
10 Children of the Night Pt.6 . . . . 2.50

BAKER ST.: GRAPHITTI
Caliber

All comics prices listed are for *Near Mint* condition.

1 'Elemenary, My Dear' 2.50

BALANCE OF POWER
MU Press

1 thru 4 . . . . @2.50

BANETOWN

1 . . . . 1.50

BANYON OF THE HIGH FORTRESS

1 . . . . 1.95

BAOH
Viz

1 thru 8 . . . . @2.95

BARABBAS
Slave Labor

1 . . . . 4.50
2 thru 4 . . . . @1.50

BARBARIC FANTASY

1 . . . . 1.95
2 . . . . 1.95

BARBARIC TALES
Pyramid

1 . . . . 3.00
2 . . . . 1.70
3 . . . . 1.70

BARNEY THE INVISIBLE TURTLE

1 . . . . 1.95

BASEBALL SUPERSTARS
Revolutionary

1 Nolan Ryan 2.50

BASIL WOLVERTON'S FANTASIC FABLES
Dark Horse

1 thru 2 BW 2.50

BAT

1 . . . . 2.25

BATHING MACHINE

1 . . . . 2.50
2 . . . . 2.50
3 . . . . 2.50
4 . . . . 1.50

BATTLE ANGEL ALITA
Viz

1 I:Daisuka,Alita 2.75
2 Alita becomes warrior 2.75
3 A:Daiuke,V:Cyborg 2.75
4 Alita/Cyborg,A:Makaku 2.75
5 The Bounty Hunters Bar 2.75
6 Confrontation 2.75
7 Underground Sewers,A:Fang . . 2.75

BATTLE ANGEL ALITA II
Viz

1 V:Monsters 2.75
2 F:Alita 2.75

Book II

1 thru 2 . . . . 2.95

BATTLE ARMOR
Eternity

1 thru 4 . . . . @1.95

BATTLE AXE

1 . . . . 2.50
2 . . . . 2.95

BATTLE BEASTS
Blackthorne

1 thru 4 . . . . @1.50

BATTLE GROUP PEIPER
Caliber

1 Bio S.S.Lt.Col Peiper 2.95

BATTLETECH
(Prev. Color)

7 thru 12 . . . . @1.75
Ann.#1 . . . . 4.50

BATTLE TO DEATH

1 . . . . 1.80
2 . . . . 1.80
3 . . . . 1.80

BATTRON
NEC

1 WWII story 2.75
2 WWII contd. 2.75

BEAST WARRIOR OF SHAOLIN

1 thru 5 . . . . @1.95

THE BEATLES EXPERIENCE
Revolutionary

1 Beatles 1960's 3.00
2 Beatles 1964-1966 . . . . 2.50
3 . . . . 2.50
4 Abbey Road, Let it be 2.50
5 The Solo Years 2.50
6 Paul McCartney & Wings 2.50
7 The Murder of John Lennon . . . 2.50
8 To 1992, final issue 2.50

BECK AND CAUL
Gauntlet

1 I:Beck,Caul 2.95
2 thur 4 . . . . 2.95

BELLS OF KONGUR

1 . . . . 2.25

BESET BY DEMONS
Tundra

1 Short stories by M.McLester . . . 3.50

BEYOND MARS
Blackthorne

1 thru 5 . . . . @2.00

BIG BLACK KISS
Vortex

3 HC some color 3.75

BIG EDSEL BAND

1 FMc 1.75

BIG NUMBERS

1 BSz 6.00
2 BSz 5.50

BIG PRIZE
Eternity

1 . . . . 1.95

BILLI 99
Dark Horse

1 'Pray for us Sinners' 4.50
2 'Trespasses' 4.00
3 'Daily Bread' 4.00

BILLY NGUYEN PRIVATE EYE

1 . . . . 2.00
1a 2nd Printing 2.00
2 thru 6 . . . . @2.00

BIRTHRIGHT

1 thru 3 . . . . @2.00

BLACK BOW

1 . . . . 1.95

[Original] BLACK CAT

4 rep.. 2.00
5 A:Ted Parrish 2.00
6 50th Anniv. Issue 2.00
7 rep. 2.00

BLACK CROSS

Spec #1 . . . . 2.00
1a 2nd Print 1.75

BLACK KISS
Vortex

1 HC,Adult 7.00
1a 2nd printing 4.00
1b 3rd printing 1.25
2 HC 6.00
2a 2nd printing 3.00
3 HC 5.00
4 HC 4.00
5 HC 2.00
6 HC 2.00
7 thru 12 HC . . . . @1.50

BLACK MAGIC

1 . . . . 3.50
2 thru 4 . . . . @2.75

BLACKMASK

1 thru 6 . . . . @1.75

BLACK MOON

1 . . . . 2.50
2 thru 4 . . . . @1.50
5 . . . . 2.00

BLACK PHANTOM

1 . . . . 2.50

BLACK SCORPION
Special Studio

1 Knight of Justice 2.75
2 A Game for Old Men 2.75
3 Blackmailer's Auction 2.75

BLACK STAR

1 thru 4 . . . . @1.80

BLACKTHORNE 3 in 1

1 and 2 . . . . @2.00

BLACK ZEPPLIN
Renegade

1 . . . . 2.50
2 thru 6 . . . . @2.00

BLADE OF SHURIKEN
Eternity

1 thru 8 . . . . @1.95

BLADESMAN

1 . . . . 2.00

BLANDMAN
Eclipse

1 Sandman parody 2.50

BLAZING WESTERN
1 rep. 2.50

Blade of Shuriken #1 © Eternity

BLIND FEAR
Eternity
1 thru 4 . . . . @1.95

BLIP AND THE C CADS
1 . . . . 1.95

BLOOD AND GUTS
Aircel
1 . . . . 2.50
2 . . . . 2.50
3 . . . . 2.50

BLOODBROTHERS
Eternity
1 thru 4 . . . . @1.95

BLOOD IS THE HARVEST
Eclipse
1 I:Nikita,Milo 4.50
2 V:M'Raud D:Nikita? 2.50
3 Milo captured 2.50
4 F:Nikita/Milo 2.50

BLOOD JUNKIES
Eternity
1 Vampires on Capitol Hill 2.50
2 final issue 2.50

BLOOD OF DRACULA
1 thru 7 . . . . @1.75
8 thru 14 . . . . @1.95
15 +Record&Mask 3.50
16 . . . . 1.95
17 . . . . 2.25

BLOOD OF INNOCENT
Warp Graphics
1 thru 4 . . . . @2.50

BLOODWING
Eternity
1 thru 5 . . . . @1.95

BLOODY BOHES & BLACK-EYED PEAS
Galaxy
1 . . . . 2.00

BOB POWELL'S TIMELESS TALES
Eclipse
1 . . . . 2.00

BODY COUNT
1 . . . . 2.25
2 and 3 . . . . @1.95
4 . . . . 2.25

BOFFO LAFFS
1 1st hologram 4.00
2 thru 7 . . . . @2.00

BOGIE MAN: CHINATOON
Atomeka
1 I:Francis Claine 2.95
2 F:Bogie Man 2.95
3 thr 4 F:Bogie Man 2.95

BOGIE MAN: MANHATTEN PROJECT
Apocalypse
One Shot. D.Quale Assassination Plot 3.95

BOMARC: GUARDIANS OF THE I.F.S. ZONE
Spec. 1.95
Spec. 2 . . . . 1.95

BONE
Cartoon Books
1 I:Bone 150.00
1a 2nd printing 50.00
1b 3rd Printing 20.00
1c 4th printing 7.00
1d thru 1f 5th-7th printing . . . . @4.00
2 . . . . 85.00
2a 2nd printing 20.00
2b thru 2e 3rd-6th printing . . . . @3.00
3 . . . . 60.00
3a 2nd printing 10.00
3b thru 3d 3rd-5th printing . . . . @3.00
4 . . . . 38.00
4a thru 4c 2nd-4th printing . . . . @3.00
5 . . . . 30.00
5a thru 5c 2nd-4th printing . . . . @3.00
6 . . . . 25.00
6a thru 6c 2nd-4th printing . . . . @3.00
7 . . . . 20.00
7a,7b 2nd,3rd printing . . . . @3.00
8 . . . . 15.00
8a,8b 2nd,3rd printing . . . . @4.00
9 . . . . 12.00
9a 2nd printing 4.00
10 . . . . 8.00
11 . . . . 6.00
12 . . . . 4.00
13 . . . . 3.50
TPB rep.#1-4 . . . . 14.00

BONES
1 thru 4 . . . . @1.95

BOOGIE MAN
1 thru 4 . . . . @1.95

BOOK OF NIGHT
Dark Horse
1 CV 2.50
2 CV 2.00
TPB. Children of the Stars 12.95

BOOK OF THE TAROT
Caliber
1 History/Development o/t Tarot . . 3.95

BORDER GUARD
1 . . . . 2.00
2 . . . . 2.00

BORDER WORLDS
Kitchen Sink
1 adult 2.00
2 thru 7 . . . . @2.00

BORDER WORLDS: MAROONED
1 . . . . 2.00

BORIS' ADVENTURE MAGAZINE
1 and 2 . . . . @2.00

Boris the Bear #2 © Dark Horse

BORIS THE BEAR
Dark Horse
1 V:Funny Animals 3.00
1a 2nd printing 2.00
2 V:Robots 2.00
3 V:Super Heroes 2.00
4 Bear of Steel 2.00
5 Dump Thing 2.00
6 Bat Bear 2.00
7 Elves 2.00
8 LargeSize 2.50
9 Awol 2.00
10 . . . . 2.00
11 Comic Shop 2.00
12 thru 29 . . . . @2.00
30 thru 34 . . . . @2.50

BORN TO BE WILD
Eclipse
one shot. Benefit P.E.T.A. 10.95

BOSTON BOMBERS
Caliber
1 . . . . 1.95
2 . . . . 2.50

BOUNTY
1 'Bounty,''Navarro' Pt.1 . . . . 2.50
2 'Bounty,''Navarro' Pt.2 . . . . 2.50
3 'Bounty,''Navarro' Pt.3 . . . . 2.50

BOY AND HIS BOT
1 . . . . 2.00

 All comics prices listed are for *Near Mint* condition.

BRAT PACK
King Hell Publications
1 .... 7.00
1a 2nd printing 3.50
2 thru 4 .... @4.25
5 .... 4.00
Brat Pack Collection 13.00

BRICKMAN
1 .... 2.00

BRIKHAUSS
1 .... 1.75

BRINGERS
Blackthorne
1 .... 3.50

BROID
Eternity
1 thru 4 .... @2.25

BRONX
Aircel
1 A.Saichann Short Stories 2.50

BROTHER MAN
New City Comics
1 .... 5.00
1a 2.00
2 thru 7 .... @2.00

Bruce Jones: Outer Edge #1
© Innovation

BRUCE JONES: OUTER EDGE
Innovation
1 All reprints 2.50

BRUCE JONES: RAZORS EDGE
Innovation
1 All reprints 2.50

BRUTE
1 .... 2.00

BRYMWYCK THE IMP
Planet X Productions
1 .... 1.50

BUCE-N-GAR
RAK
1 .... 1.75
2 .... 1.75
3 .... 1.75

BUCK GODOT
Palliard Press
1 I:Buck Godot 2.95

BUCKWHEAT
1 .... 2.00
2 .... 2.00

BUFFALO WINGS
Antarctic Press
1 .... 2.50

BUG
Planet X Productions
1 .... 1.50
2 .... 1.50

BULLET CROW
Eclipse
1 .... 2.00
2 .... 2.00

BUMBERCOMIC
1 .... 1.00
2 .... 1.00

BURNING KISS
1 w/poster 4.95

BUSHIDO
Eternity
1 thru 6 .... @1.95

BUSHIDO BLADE OF ZATSICHI WALRUS
1 .... 3.00
2 .... 2.00

BY BIZARRE HANDS
Dark Horse
1 JLd(s), ... 2.50
2 JLd(s), ... 2.50
3 JLd(s), ... 2.50

CABLE TV
Parody Press
1 Cable Satire 2.50

CALIBER PRESENTS
(Prev. High Caliber)
1 TV,I:Crow 100.00
2 Deadworld 7.50
3 Realm 3.00
4 Baker Street 3.00
5 TV,Heart of Darkness, Fugitive 2.50
6 TV,Heart of Darkness, Fugitive 2.50
7 TV,Heart of Darkness, Dragonfeast 2.50
8 TV,Cuda,Fugitive 2.50
9 Baker Street,Sting Inc. 2.00
10 Fugitive, The Edge 2.50
11 Ashes,Random Thoughts 2.50
12 Fugitive,Random Thoughts 2.50
13 Random Thoughts, Synergist 2.50
14 Random Thoughts, Fugitive 2.50
15 Random Thoughts,Fringe 2.50
16 Fugitive, The Verdict 3.50
17 Deadworld, The Verdict 3.50
18 Orlak,The Verdict 3.50
19 Taken Under,Go-Man 3.50
20 The Verdict,Go-Man 3.50
21 The Verdict,Go-Man 3.50
22 The Verdict,Go-Man 3.50
23 Go-Man,Heat Seeker 3.50
24 Heat Seeker,MacktheKnife 3.50
Christmas Spec A:Crow,Deadworld Realm,Baker Street 50.00
Summer Spec. inc. the Silencers, Swords of Shar-Pei (preludes) 3.95

CALIBER PRESENTS
(One Shots)
Hybrid 2.50

CALIFORNIA GIRLS
Eclipse
1 thru 8 .... @2.00

CALIGARI 2050
1 Gothic Horror 2.25
2 Gothic Horror 2.25

CAMELOT ETERNAL
Caliber
1 .... 3.00
2 .... 2.50
3 .... 2.50
4 .... 2.50
5 Mordred Escapes 2.50
6 MorganLeFay returns from dead 2.50
7 Revenge of Morgan 2.50
8 Launcelot flees Camelot 2.50

CANADIAN NINJA
1 .... 1.50
2 .... 1.50

CAPT. CONFEDERACY
1 adult 8.00
2 .... 2.50
3 .... 2.00
4 .... 2.00
4a 1.50
5 thru 8 .... @2.00
9 thru 11 .... @1.75
12 .... 1.95

CAPT. CULT
1 .... 2.00

CAPT. ELECTRON
Brick Computers Inc.
1 .... 2.00
2 .... 2.25

CAPTAIN HARLOCK
Eternity
1 .... 3.00
1a 2nd printing 2.50
2 .... 2.50
3 .... 2.50
4 thru 13 .... @1.95
Christmas special 2.50

CAPTAIN HARLOCK DEATHSHADOW RISING
Eternity
1 .... 2.75
2 .... 2.50
3 .... 2.25
4 Harlock/Nevich Truce 2.25
5 Reunited with Arcadia Crew 2.25

CAPTAIN HARLOCK: THE MACHINE PEOPLE
Eternity
1 O:Captain Harlock 2.50

CAPTAIN JACK
Fantagraphics

1 . . . 4.00
2 . . . 2.50
3 . . . 2.50
4 thru 12 . . . @2.00

CAPT. OBLIVION

1 . . . 1.95

CAPTAIN PHIL
Steel Dragon

1 . . . 1.50

CAPTAIN SENTINEL

1 . . . 2.00

CAPTAIN THUNDER AND BLUE BOLT
Hero Graphics

1 New stories . . . 3.50
2 Hard Targets . . . 3.50

CARAVAN KIDD
Dark Horse

1 thru 10 . . . @2.50

[2nd Series]

1 thru 9 F:Miam . . . 2.50
10 . . . 2.50
Holiday Spec. . . . 2.50
Valentine's Day Spec. . . . 2.50

[3rd Series]

1 . . . 2.50

CARNIGE

1 . . . 1.95
2 . . . 1.95

CARTOON HISTORY OF THE UNIVERSE
Rip Off Press

1 Gonick art . . . 2.50
2 Sticks & Stones . . . 2.50
3 River Realms . . . 2.50
4 Old Testament . . . 2.50
5 Brains & Bronze . . . 2.50
6 These Athenians . . . 2.50
7 All about Athens . . . 2.50

CARTUNE LAND
Magic Carpet Comics

1 . . . 1.50

CASES OF SHERLOCK HOLMES
Renegade

1 thru 18 . . . @2.00
19 . . . 2.25

CASEY LACE

1 . . . 1.50

CAT & MOUSE
Aircel

1 . . . 4.00
2 . . . 3.00
3 thru 8 . . . @2.25
9 Cat Reveals Identity . . . 2.25
10 Tooth & Nail . . . 2.25
11 Tooth & Nail . . . 2.25
12 Tooth & Nail, Demon . . . 2.25
13 'Good Times, Bad Times' . . . 2.25
14 Mouse Alone . . . 2.25
15 Champion ID revealed . . . 2.25
16 Jerry Critically Ill . . . 2.25
17 Kunoichi vs. Tooth . . . 2.25
18 Search for Organ Donor . . . 2.25
Graphic Novel . . . 9.95

CAT CLAW
Eternity

1 O:Cat Claw . . . 2.75
1a 2nd printing . . . 2.50
2 thru 9 . . . @2.50

CAT-KIND

1 . . . 2.00

CELESTIAL MECHANICS
Innovation

1 thru 3 . . . @2.25

CEMENT SHOOZ

1 I:Cement Shooz . . . 2.50

CENTRIFUGAL BUMBLE-PUPPY

1 Adult . . . 2.25
2 thru 6 . . . @2.25
7 . . . 2.50

CEREBUS
Aardvark Vanaheim

0 . . . 3.00
0a Gold Ed. . . . 25.00
1 B:DS(s&a),I:Cerebus . . . 275.00
2 DS,V:Succubus . . . 150.00
3 DS,I:Red Sophia . . . 120.00
4 DS,I:Elrod . . . 90.00
5 DS,A:The Pigts . . . 78.00
6 DS,I:Jaka . . . 78.00
7 DS,R:Elrod . . . 78.00
8 DS,A:Conniptins . . . 40.00
9 DS,I&V:K'cor . . . 40.00
10 DS,R:Red Sophia . . . 40.00
11 DS,I:The Cockroach . . . 40.00
12 DS,R:Elrod . . . 40.00
13 DS,I:Necross . . . 33.00
14 DS,V:Shadow Crawler . . . 33.00
15 DS,V: Shadow Crawler . . . 33.00
16 DS, at the Masque . . . 27.00
17 DS,"Champion" . . . 27.00
18 DS,Fluroc . . . 27.00
19 DS,I:Perce & Greet-a . . . 27.00
20 DS,Mind Game . . . 27.00
21 DS,A:CaptCockroach,rare . . . 50.00
22 DS,D:Elrod . . . 27.00
23 DS,DuFort's school . . . 12.00
24 DS,IR:Prof.Clarmont . . . 12.00
25 DS,A:Woman-thing . . . 12.00
26 DS,High Society . . . 12.00
27 DS,Kidnapping of an Aardvark . . . 12.00
28 DS,Mind Game!! . . . 12.00
29 DS,Reprocussions . . . 10.00
30 DS,Debts . . . 10.00
31 DS,Chasing Cootie . . . 10.00
32 DS . . . 10.00
33 DS,DS,Friction . . . 6.00
34 DS,Three Days Before . . . 6.00
35 thru 50 DS . . . @6.00
51 DS,(scarce) . . . 16.00
52 DS . . . 6.00
53 DS,C:Wolveroach . . . 7.00
54 DS,I:Wolveroach . . . 9.00
55 DS,A:Wolveroach . . . 8.00
56 DS,A:Wolveroach . . . 8.00
57 DS . . . 5.00
58 DS . . . 5.00
59 DS,Memories Pt.V . . . 5.00
60 DS,more vignettes . . . 5.00
61 DS,A:Flaming Carrot . . . 6.00
62 DS,A:Flaming Carrot . . . 6.00
63 DS,Mind Game VI . . . 5.00
64 DS,Never Pray for Change . . . 5.00
65 DS,Papal Speech . . . 5.00
66 DS,Thrill of Agony . . . 5.00
67 thru 70 DS . . . @5.00
71 thru 74 DS . . . @4.00
75 DS,Terrible Analogies . . . 4.00
76 DS,D:Weisshaupt . . . 4.00
77 DS,Surreal daydream . . . 4.00
78 DS,Surreal daydream . . . 4.00
79 DS,Spinning Straw . . . 4.00
80 DS,V:Stone Tarim . . . 4.00
81 DS,A:Sacred Wars Roach . . . 4.00
82 DS,A:Tarim . . . 3.50
83 DS,A:Michele . . . 3.50
84 DS,Weisshaupt's Letter . . . 3.50
85 DS,A:Mick Jagger . . . 3.50
86 DS,A:Mick Jagger . . . 3.50
87 DS,Tower Climb . . . 3.50

Cerebus #80 © Aardvark Vanaheim

88 DS,D:Stone Tarim . . . 3.50
89 DS,A:Cute Elf . . . 3.50
90 DS,Anti-Apartheid(c) . . . 3.50
91 DS . . . 3.50
92 DS,A:Bill & Seth . . . 3.50
93 DS,Astoria in Prison . . . 3.50
94 DS,Rape of Astoria . . . 3.50
95 DS,Sophia-Astoria Dream . . . 3.50
96 DS,Astoria in Prison . . . 3.50
97 DS,Escape Planned . . . 3.50
98 DS,Astoria's Trial . . . 3.50
99 DS,Sorcery in Court . . . 3.50
100 DS,A:Cirin . . . 3.50
101 DS,The Gold Sphere . . . 3.00
102 DS,The Final Ascension . . . 3.00
103 DS,On the Tower . . . 3.00
104 DS,A:Flaming Carrot . . . 3.00
105 DS,V:Fred & Ethel . . . 3.00
106 DS,D:Fred & Ethel . . . 3.00
107 DS,Judge on the Moon . . . 3.00
108 DS,All History . . . 3.00
109 DS,O:Universe . . . 3.00
110 DS,More Universe . . . 3.00
111 DS,Cerebus' Fate . . . 3.00
112 DS,Memories . . . 3.00
113 DS,Memories . . . 3.00
114 DS,I:Rick nash . . . 3.00
115 DS,I:Pud Withers . . . 3.00
116 DS,Rick Meets Cerebus . . . 3.00
117 DS,Young Jaka Injured . . . 3.00
118 DS,Cerebus Apologizes . . . 3.00
119 DS,Jaka Opens Door . . . 3.00
120 DS,I:Oscar . . . 3.00
121 DS,Women Explained . . . 3.00
122 DS,lest History . . . 3.00
123 DS,Each One's Dream . . . 3.00
124 DS . . . 3.00
125 DS,C:Lord Julius . . . 3.00
126 DS,R:Old Vet'ran . . . 2.50
127 DS,Jaka Dances . . . 2.50
128 DS,L:Cerebus as Fred . . . 2.50
129 DS,Jaka's Story . . . 2.50

130 DS,D:Pud Withers 2.50
131 DS,Jaka Imprisoned 2.50
132 DS,A:Nurse 2.50
133 DS,I:Mrs. Thatcher 2.50
134 DS,Dancing Debate 2.50
135 DS,Jaka Signs 2.50
136 DS,L:Rick 2.50
137 DS,Like-a-Looks 2.50
138 DS,Maids'Gossip 2.50
139 A:Misogynist-roach 2.50
140 I:Old Oscar 2.50
141 A:Cerebus 2.50
142 C:Mick Jagger 2.50
143 DS,Oscars Forboding 2.50
144 DS,I:Doris 2.50
145 thru 150 DS . . . . @2.50
151 DS,B:Mothers & Daughters
Book 1 . . . . 6.00
152 DS,M & D cont. 4.50
153 DS,M & D cont. 4.00
154 DS,M & D cont. 4.00
155 DS,M & D cont. 4.00
156 DS,M & D cont. 3.00
157 DS,M & D cont 3.00
158 DS,M & D cont 3.00
159 DS,M & D cont. 3.00
160 DS,M & D cont. 3.00
161 DS,M & D cont 3.00
162 DS,E:M & D, Bk.1 . . . . 3.00
163 DS,B:Mothers & Daughters
Book 2 . . . . 2.75
164 DS,M & D Bk.2 contd,inc.
Tour Momentos 2.50
165 thru 168 DS,M & D
Bk.2 contd. . . . . @2.50
169 DS,M & D Bk.2 contd 2.50
170 DS,M & D Bk.2 contd 2.50
171 DS,M & D Bk.2 contd 2.50
172 DS,M & D Bk.2 contd 2.50
173 E:DS,M & D Bk.2 . . . . 2.50
174 B:M & D Bk.3 . . . . 2.50
175 M & D Bk.3 . . . . 2.50
176 M & D Bk.3 . . . . 2.50
177 M & D Bk.3 . . . . 2.50
178 thru 180 M & D Bk.3 . . . . . . 2.50
TPB Jaka's Story 25.00

CEREBUS CHURCH & STATE

1 DS rep #51 . . . . 2.25
2 thru 30 DS rep #52-#80 . . . . @2.00

CEREBUS COMPANION

1 . . . . 3.95

CEREBUS HIGH SOCIETY

1 thru 14 DS (biweekly) . . . . . @1.70
15 thru 24 DS rep. . . . . @2.00
25 DS rep. #50, final 2.00

CEREBUSJAM
Aardvark Vanaheim

1 MA,BHa,TA,WE,A:Spirit 15.00

CEREBUS REPRINTS

1A thru 28A DS rep . . . . @1.25
See also: Church & State
See also: Swords of Cerebus

CHAINGANG

1 . . . . 2.50
2 . . . . 3.50

CHAINSAW VIGILANTE
New England Press

1 Tick Spinoff 3.25

CHAMPION, THE

1 . . . . 2.50

CHAMPIONS

1 . . . . 2.25

CHARLIE CHAN
Eternity

1 thru 4 . . . . @1.95
5 and 6 . . . . @2.25

CHASER PLATOON
Aircel

1 Interstellar War 2.25
2 Ambush 2.25
3 New Weapon 2.25
4 Saringer Battle Robot 2.25
5 Behind Enemy Lines 2.25
6 . . . . 2.25

CHEERLEADERS FROM HELL

1 and 2 . . . . @2.50

CHEMICAL FACTOR

1 . . . . 1.75

CHEVAL NOIR
Dark Horse

1 DSt(c) 4.00
2 thru 6 . . . . @3.50
7 DSt(c) 3.50
8 . . . . 3.50
9 . . . . 3.50
10 80 page 4.50
11 80 page 4.50
12 MM(c) 3.95
13 thru 19 . . . . @3.95
20'Great Power o/t Chninkel' 4.50
21'Great Power o/t Chninkel' 3.95
22'Great Power o/t Chninkel'
concl. 4.50
23 inc."Rork','Forever War'
concl. 3.95
24 'In Dreams' Pt.1 . . . . 3.95
25 'In Dreams' Pt.2 . . . . 3.95
26 'In Dreams' Pt.3 . . . . 3.95
27 I:The Man From Ciguri
(Airtight Garage Sequel)
Dreams Pt.4 . . . . 2.95
28 thru 30 Ciguri,cont. . . . . @2.95
31 Angriest Dog in the World 2.95
32 thru 38 . . . . @2.95
39 In Search of Peter Pan 2.95
40 . . . . 2.95
41 F:Demon 2.95
42 thru 44 F:Demon . . . . @2.95
45 thru 47 . . . . 2.95
48 SwM(c), ... 2.95
49 thru 50 F:Rork 2.95

CHICAGO FOLLIES

1 . . . . 2.95

CHIPS & VANILLA

1 Spec. 1.75

CHIRON

1 and 2 . . . . @2.00

CHRONOS CARNIVAL
Fleetway

1 reps. 200 AD stories 7.95

CHUCK CHICKEN AND BRUIN BEAR
Jabberwocky

1 . . . . 3.00

CIRCUS WORLD

1 . . . . 2.50

CLIFFHANGER COMICS
AC Comics

1 rep. 2.50
2 rep. 2.50

CLINT

1 Trigon comics 3.00

CLINT THE HAMSTER
Eclipse

1 . . . . 2.50
2 . . . . 1.50

CLONEZONE
Dark Horse

Spec #1 . . . . 2.00

COBALT BLUE

1 Gustovitch Art 77 . . . . 10.00

COBRA
Viz

1 thru 6 . . . . @2.95
7 . . . . 3.25
8 V:SnowHawks 3.25
9 Zados 3.25
10 thru 12 . . . . @3.25

CODA

1 . . . . 3.00

CODENAME NINJA

1 and 2 . . . . @2.00

COLD BLOODED CHAMELEON COMMANDOS
Blackthorne

1 . . . . 2.00
2 . . . . 1.50
3 . . . . 1.50
4 . . . . 1.75
5 . . . . 1.75
6 . . . . 2.00
7 . . . . 2.00

COLE BLACK

1 Vol.I 15.00
2 Vol.I 10.00
3 Vol.I 10.00
4 Vol.I 10.00
5 Vol.I 12.00
1 Vol.II 3.50
2 Vol.II 2.00
3 Vol.II 1.50

COLONEL KILGORE
Special Studios

1 WWII stories 2.50
2 Command Performance 2.50

COLT
K-Z Comics

1 . . . . 5.00
2 pin-up by Laird 8.00
2 pin-up by Henbeck 2.00
3 . . . . 1.00
4 . . . . 1.00
5 . . . . 1.00

COMICS EXPRESS

1 thru 4 . . . . @2.95
5 thru 11 . . . . @3.95

COMING OF APHRODITE
Hero Graphics

1 Aphrodite/modern day 3.95

COMMAND REVIEW
Thoughts & Images

1 rep. Albedo #1-4 . . . . 6.00
2 rep. Albedo #5-8 . . . . 4.00
3 rep. Albedo #9-13 . . . . 4.00

COMPLETE FLUFFHEAD

1 . . . 2.00

Concrete #5 © Dark Horse

CONCRETE
Dark Horse

1 PC,R:Concrete . . . 12.50
1a 2nd printing . . . 3.00
2 PC,'Transatlantic Swim' . . . 6.00
3 PC . . . 4.00
4 PC . . . 3.50
5 PC,'ArmchairStuffed w/Dynamite' 3.50
6 PC,Concrete works on farm . . . 3.50
7 PC,Concrete grows horns . . . 3.50
8 PC,Climbs Mount Everest . . . 3.00
9 PC,Mount Everest Pt.2 . . . 3.00
10 PC,last Issue . . . 3.00

CONCRETE, A NEW LIFE
Dark Horse

1 . . . 3.50
Spec.Land & Sea,rep. . . . 3.25

CONCRETE: ECLECTICA
Dark Horse

1 PC,The Ugly Boy . . . 3.25
2 PC . . . 3.25

CONQUEROR
Harrier

1 . . . 3.50
2 thru 4 . . . @2.00
5 thru 9 . . . @1.75

CONQUEROR UNIVERSE
Harrier

1 . . . 2.75

CONSPIRACY COMICS
Revolutionary

1 Marilyn Monroe . . . 2.50
2 Who Killed JFK . . . 2.50
3 Who Killed RFK . . . 2.50

CONSTELLATION GRAPHICS
STG

1 thru 4 . . . @1.50

CONTINUM

1 . . . 1.50
2 . . . 1.75

CONTRACTORS
Eclipse

1 . . . 2.25

Corbo #1 ©

CORBO

1 . . . 1.75
2 . . . 1.75

CORMAC MAC ART

1 thru 4 . . . @1.95

COSMIC BOOK

1 . . . 1.95

COSMIC HEROES
Eternity

1 Buck Rogers rep. . . . 1.95
2 thru 6 . . . @1.95
7 . . . 2.25
8 . . . 2.25
9 . . . 2.95
10 . . . 3.50
11 . . . 3.95

COSMIC STELLAR REBELERS

1 thru 4 . . . @1.50

COSMOS

1 . . . 1.70
2 . . . 1.70

CRAZY MEN GO WILD

1 . . . 2.00

CREEPY
Dark Horse

1 KD,TS,GC,SL,Horror . . . 3.95
2 TS,CI,DC,Demonic Baby . . . 3.95
3 JM,TS,JG,V:Killer Clown . . . 3.95
4 TS,Final issue . . . 3.95

CRIME CLASSICS
Eternity

1 rep Shadow comicstrip . . . 1.95
2 thru 11 . . . @1.95
12 . . . 2.25

CRIME SMASHERS
Special Edition

1 . . . 1.80

CRIMSON DREAMS
Crimson

1 thru 11 . . . @2.00

CRITTER CORPS

1 . . . 1.50
2 . . . 1.50
3 . . . 1.50

CRITTERS
Fantagraphics Books

1 SS,Usagi Yojimbo,Cutey . . . 7.00
2 Captain Jack,Birthright . . . 4.50
3 SS,Usagi Yojimbo,Gnuff . . . 4.50
4 Gnuff,Birthright . . . 3.00
5 Birthright . . . 3.00
6 SS,Usagi Yojimbo,Birthright . . . 3.00
7 SS,Usagi Yojimbo,Jack Bunny . 3.00
8 SK,Animal Graffiti,Lizards . . . 2.50
9 Animal Graffiti . . . 2.50
10 SS,Usagi Yojimbo . . . 3.00
11 SS,Usagi Yojimbo, . . . 4.00
12 Birthright II . . . 2.00
13 Birthright II,Gnuff . . . 2.00
14 SS,Usagi Yojimbo,BirthrightII . 2.50
15 Birthright II,CareBears . . . 2.00
16 SS,Groundthumper,Gnuff . . . 2.00
17 Birthright II,Lionheart . . . 2.00
18 Dragon's . . . 2.00
19 Gnuff,Dragon's . . . 2.00
20 Gnuff . . . 2.00
21 Gnuff . . . 2.00
22 Watchdogs,Gnuff . . . 2.00
23 Flexi-Disc,X-Mas Issue . . . 4.00
24 Angst,Lizards,Gnuff . . . 2.00
25 Lionheart,SBi,Gnuff . . . 2.00
26 Angst,Gnuff . . . 2.00
27 SS,Ground Thumper . . . 2.00
28 Blue Beagle,Lionheart . . . 2.00
29 Lionheart,Gnuff . . . 2.00
30 Radical Dog,Gnuff . . . 2.00
31 SBi,Gnuffs,Lizards . . . 2.00
32 Lizards,Big Sneeze . . . 2.00
33 Gnuff,Angst,Big Sneeze . . . 2.00
34 Blue Beagle vs. Robohop . . . 2.00
35 Lionheart,Fission Chicken . . . 2.00
36 Blue Beagle,Fission Chicken . . 2.00
37 Fission Chicken . . . 2.00
38 SS,double size,Usagi Yojimbo . 2.75
39 Fission Chicken . . . 2.00
40 Gnuff . . . 2.00
41 Duck'Bill Platypus . . . 2.00
42 Glass Onion . . . 2.00
43 Lionheart . . . 2.00
44 Watchdogs . . . 2.00
45 Ambrose the Frog . . . 2.00
46 Lionheart . . . 2.00
47 Birthright . . . 2.00
48 Birthright . . . 2.00
49 Birthright . . . 2.00
50 SS,Neil the Horse,
UsagiYojimbo . . . 4.95
Spec.1 Albedo,rep+new 10pgStory 2.00

CROSSED SWORDS

1 95
2 95

CROSSFIRE
Eclipse

18 thru 26 DSp . . . @2.00

CROW, THE
Caliber

1 . . . 90.00
1a 2nd Printing . . . 25.00
1b 3rd Printing . . . 10.00
2 . . . 75.00

All comics prices listed are for *Near Mint* condition.

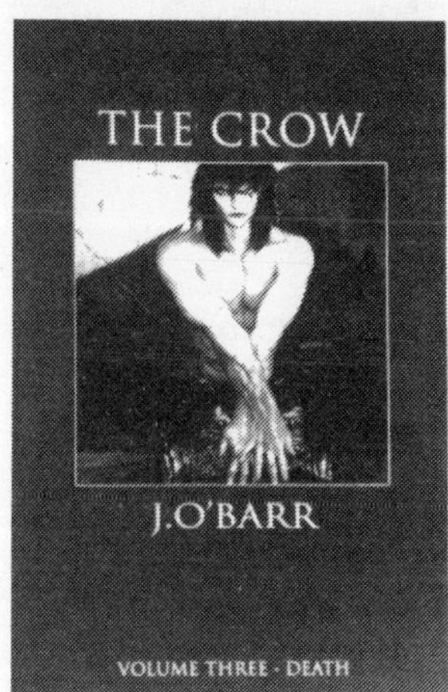

The Crow #3 © Caliber/J. O'Barr

2a 2nd Printing 20.00
2b 3rd Printing 7.50
3 .... 60.00
3a 2nd Printing 15.00
4 .... 50.00

Tundra

1 reps. Crow #1, #2 .... 20.00
2 and 3 .... @15.00
TPB 20.00

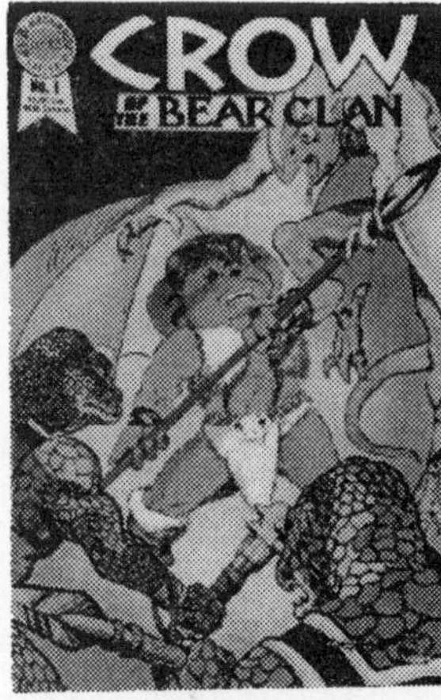

Crow of the Bear Clan #1 © Blackthorne

CROW OF THE BEAR CLAN
Blackthorne

1 .... 2.25
2 thru 6 .... @1.75

CRUSADERS
Guild

1 Southern Knights 10.00

CRUSADERS

1 .... 1.50
2 .... 1.50
3 .... 1.75
4 .... 1.75

CRY FOR DAWN

1 .... 50.00
1a 2nd Printing 6.00
1b 3rd Printing 2.25
2 .... 30.00
2a 2nd Printing 2.25
3 .... 20.00
4 thru 6 .... @5.00
7 Corporate Ladder, Rock A Bye Baby 3.00
8 Decay,This is the Enemy 3.00

CRY FOR DAWN: SUBTLE VIOLENTS

one shot F:Ryder 2.50

CRYING FREEMAN
Viz

1 .... 6.50
2 .... 5.50
3 thru 5 .... @5.00
6 thru 8 .... @4.50

CRYING FREEMAN II
Viz

1 .... 4.75
2 .... 4.00
3 .... 4.00
4 thru 6 .... @4.25
7 V:Bugnug 3.95
8 Emu & The Samurai Sword 3.95
9 Final Issue 3.95

CRY FREEMAN V
Viz

1 Return to Japan 2.75
2 A:Tateoka-assassin 2.75
3 .... 2.75
4 A:Bagwana 2.75
5 V:Tsunaike 2.75
6 V:Aido Family 2.75
7 V:Tsunaike 2.75
GN:Taste of Revenge 14.95

CRYPT

1 .... 1.95

CURSE OF THE ATOMIC WRESTLING WOMEN

1 .... 1.95

CURSE OF THE SHE-CAT

1 .... 2.50

CUTEY BUNNY

1 .... 8.00
2 thru 4 .... @4.00

Eclipse

5 .... 3.00

CYBER 7
Eclipse

1 .... 2.50
2 thru 5 .... @2.00

Book 2

1 thru 7 .... @2.00
8 thru 10 .... @2.50

CYBERHAWKS

1 .... 1.85
2 thru 4 .... @1.80

CYBORG GERBELS

1 English comic 4.00

CYCLOPS
Blackthorne

1 Mini-series 1.95
2 .... 1.95
3 .... 1.95

DAEMON MASK

1 .... 1.80

DAFFY QADDAFI
Comics Unlimited Ltd.

1 .... 2.00

DAIKAZU

1 .... 7.00
1a 2nd Printing 1.50
2 .... 3.00
2a 2nd Printing 1.50
3 .... 4.00
3a 2nd Printing 1.50
4 thru 7 .... @1.50
8 .... 1.75

DAMLOG

1 .... 1.80
1a 2nd printing 1.00
2 thru 5 .... @1.80

DANGEROUS TIMES

1 MK 2.50
2 MA(c) 2.00
2a 2nd printing 1.75
3 MR(c) 1.95
3a 2nd printing 1.95
4 GP(c) 1.95

DANGERWORLD

1 .... 1.00
2 .... 1.00
3 .... 1.00

DAN TURNER HOLLYWOOD DETECTIVE
Eternity

1 'Darkstar of Death' 2.50

DAN TURNER HOMICIDE HUNCH
Eternity

1 Dan Turner Framed 2.50

DAN TURNER THE STAR CHAMBER
Eternity

1 Death of Folly Hempstead 2.50

DARERAT

1 .... 1.95

DARK ADVENTURES

1 .... 1.25

DARK ANGEL SPECIAL

1 .... 1.75

DARK ASSASSIN

1 thru 3 .... @1.50

Vol. 2

1 thru 5 .... @2.00

DARK COMICS

1 .... 1.80
2 .... 1.80

DARK FORCE
Omega 7

1 A:Dark Force 2.00

DARK HORSE CLASSICS

1 Last of the Mohicans 3.95
2 20,000 Leagues under t/Sea . . . 3.95

DARK HORSE PRESENTS
Dark Horse

1 PC,I:Concrete 17.00
1a 2nd printing 3.00
2 PC,Concrete 11.00
3 Boris theBear,Concrete 10.00
4 PC,Concrete 9.00
5 PC,Concrete 8.00
6 PC,Concrete 7.00
7 I:MONQ 5.00

Dark Horse Presents #14
© Dark Horse

8 PC,Concrete 5.00
9 . . . . 5.00
10 PC,Concrete 5.00
11 . . . . 3.00
12 PC,Concrete 4.50
13 . . . . 3.00
14 PC,Concrete 4.00
15 . . . . 3.00
16 PC,Concrete 4.00
17 . . . . 3.00
18 PC,Concrete 4.00
19 . . . . 3.00
20 double,Flaming Carrot 5.50
21 . . . . 3.00
22 . . . . 3.00
23 . . . . 3.00
24 PCI:Aliens 30.00
25 thru 31 . . . . @3.00
32 . . . . 4.00
33 . . . . 3.00
34 Aliens 12.00
35 Predator 12.00
36 Aliens vs.Predator 15.00
36a painted cover 18.00
37 . . . . 2.50
38 . . . . 2.50
39 . . . . 2.50
40 . . . . 2.50
41 . . . . 2.50
42 Aliens 5.00
43 Aliens 4.00
44 . . . . 2.50
45 . . . . 2.50
46 Predator 4.00
47 . . . . 2.50

Dark Horse Presents #40
© Dark Horse

48 . . . . 2.50
49 . . . . 2.50
50 inc.'Heartbreakers' 2.50
51 FM(c),inc.'Sin City' 5.00
52 FM,inc. 'Sin City' 4.00
53 FM,inc. 'Sin City' 4.00
54 FM,Sin City;JBy Preview
of Next Men Pt.1 . . . . 10.00
55 FM,Sin City;JBy Preview
of Next Men (JBy) Pt.2 . . . . 8.00
56 FM,Sin City,JBy,Next MenPt.3
Aliens Genocide(prologue) . . . 6.00
57 FM,SinCity;JBy Next Men
Pt.4 . . . . 6.00
58 FM,Sin City,Alien Fire 3.00
59 FM,Sin City,Alien Fire 3.00
60 FM,Sin City 3.00
61 FM,Sin City 2.50
62 FM,E:Sin City 2.50
63 Moe,Marie Dakar 2.50
64 MWg,R:The Aerialist 2.50
65 B:Accidental Death 2.50
66 PC,inc.Dr.Giggles 2.50
67 B:Predator story(lead in to
"Race War"),double size 3.95
68 F:Predator,Swimming Lessons
(Nestrobber tie-in) 2.50
69 F:Predator 2.50
70 F:Alec 2.50
71 F:Madwoman 2.50
72 F:Eudaemon 2.50
73 F:Eudaemon 2.50
74 . . . . 2.50
75 F:Chairman 2.50
76 F:Hermes Vs. the Eye
Ball Kid 2.50
77 F:Hermes Vs. the Eye
Ball Kid 2.50
78 F:Hermes Vs. the Eye
Ball Kid 2.50
79 B:Shadow Empires Slaves . . . 2.50
80 AAd,I:Monkey Man & O'Brien . 6.00
81 B:Buoy 2.50
82 B:Just Folks 2.50
83 Last Impression 2.50
84 MBn,F:Nexus,E:Hermes Vs. the
Eye Ball Kid 2.50
85 Winner Circle 2.50
Fifth Anniv. Special DGi,PC,
SBi,CW,MW,FM,Sin City,
Aliens,Give Me Liberty 12.00
Milestone Ed.#1,rep.DHP#1 . . . . . 2.25
TPB rep.Sin City 15.00

DARK HORSE DOWN UNDER
Dark Horse

1 F:Australian Writers 2.50

DARK LORD
RAK

1 thru 3 . . . . @1.75

DARK REGIONS

1 . . . . 2.50
2 . . . . 2.50
3 Scarce 3.00
4 and 5 . . . . @1.50

DARK STAR

1 I:Ran 2.25
2 thru 3 . . . . @2.25

DARK VISIONS

1 I:Niort Stalker 1.70
2 thru 4 . . . . @1.70

DARK WOLF
Eternity

1 . . . . 1.95
2 . . . . 1.95
Volume 2
1 thru 14 . . . . @1.95
Annual #1 . . . . 2.25

DATA 6

1 . . . . 1.95
2 . . . . 1.95

DAZE & KNIGHT

1 . . . . 1.80

DAYS OF DARKNESS
Apple

1 From Pearl Harbor
to Midway 2.75
2 Pearl Harbor Attack,cont 2.75
3 Japanese Juggernaut 2.75
4 Bataan Peninsula 2.75

DEADFACE

1 . . . . 3.00
2 . . . . 2.50
3 . . . . 1.95

DEADFACE: DOING ISLANDS WITH BACCHUS
Dark Horse

1 rep. Bacchus apps. 2.95
2 rep. inc.'Book-Keeper of
Atlantis 2.95

DEADFACE: EARTH, WATER, AIR & FIRE
Dark Horse

1 Bacchus & Simpson in Sicily . . . 2.50
2 A:Don Skylla 2.50
3 Mafia/Kabeirol-War prep. 2.50
4 Last issue 2.50

DEADFISH BEDEVILED

1 . . . . 2.25

DEAD HEAT

1 . . . . 1.95

DEAD IN THE WEST
Dark Horse

1 TT,Based on Joe Landsdale

book 3.95

DEADLINE USA
Dark Horse
1 rep. Deadline UK,Inc. Tank Girl Johnny Nemo 9.95
2 inc. Tank Girl,Johnny Nemo 9.95

DEADKILLER
Caliber
1 Rep Deadworld 19 thru 21 2.95

DEADTALES
Caliber
1 'When a Body Meets a Body' 2.95

DEADTIME STORIES
1 AAd,WS 1.75

DEADWORLD
Arrow
1 Arrow Pyb 6.00
2 4.00
3 V:King Zombie 3.50
4 V:King Zombie 3.50
5 Team Rests 3.50
6 V:King Zombie 3.50
7 F:KZ & Deake, Graphic(c) 3.50
7a Tame cover 2.00
8 V:Living Corpse, Graphic(c) 2.50
8a Tame cover 2.00
9 V:Sadistic Punks, Graphic(c) 2.50
9a Tame cover 2.00
10 V:King Zombie, Graphic(c) 2.50
10a Tame cover 2.00
11 V:King Zombie, Graphic(c) 3.00
11a Tame cover 2.50
12 I:Percy, Graphic(c) 3.00
12a Tame cover 2.50
13 V:King Zombie, Graphic(c) 3.00
13a Tame cover 2.50
14 V:Voodoo Cult,Graphic(c) 3.00
14a Tame cover 2.50
15 Zombie stories,Graphic(c) 3.00
15a Tame cover 2.50
16 V:'Civilized' Community 2.50
17 V:King Zombie 2.50
18 V:King Zombie 2.50
19 V:Grakken 2.50
20 V:King Zombie 2.50
21 Dead Killer 2.50
22 L:Dan & Joey 2.50
23 V:King Zombie 2.50
24 2.50
25 (R:Vince Locke) 2.50
26 2.50
Caliber
1 thru 8 2.95

DEADWORD ARCHIVES
Caliber
1 Rep.Deadworld series 2.50

DEAD WORLD: BITS & PIECES
Caliber
1 Rep.1st Deadworld Story, Caliber presents #2 1.60

DEADWORLD: TO KILL A KING
Caliber
1 R:Deadkiller 2.95

DEATHBRINGER
1 thru 4 @1.60

DEATHDREAMS OF DRACULA
Apple
1 Selection of short stories 2.50
2 short stories 2.50
3 Inc. Rep. BWr,'Breathless' 2.50
4 short stories 2.50

DEATH HAWK
1 thru 6 @1.95

Death Hunt #1 © Eternity

DEATH HUNT
Eternity
1 1.95
2 1.95

DEATHQUEST
1 1.50

DEATH RATTLE
Kitchen Sink (Prev. Color)
6 2.00
7 EdGein 2.00
8 I:XenozoicTales 2.00
9 BW,rep. 2.00
10 AW,rep. 2.00
11 thru 15 @2.00
16 BW,Spacehawk 2.00
17 2.00
18 FMc 2.00

DEATH'S HEAD
Crystal
1 1.95
2 1.95
3 1.95

DEATH WATCH
1 1.75

DEATHWORLD
Adventure Comics
1 Harry Harrison Adapt. 2.50
2 thru 4 @2.50

DEATHWORLD II
Adventure Comics
1 Harry Harrison Adapt. 2.50
2 2.50
3 2.50
4 last issue 2.50

DEATHWORLD III
Adventure Comics
1 H.Harrison Adapt.,colonization 2.50
2 Attack on the Lowlands 2.50
3 Attack on the Lowlands contd. 2.50

DEFENSELESS DEAD
Adventure Comics
1 A:Gil 2.50
2 A:Organlegger 2.50
3 A:Organlegger 2.50

DELIRIUM
1 2.00
2 KG 2.00

DELTA SQUADRON
1 2.00
2 2.00

DELTA TENN
1 thru 11 @1.50

DEMON BLADE
1 1.75
2 1.95
3 1.95

DEMONHUNTER
Aircel
1 thru 4 @1.95

DEMON'S BLOOD
1 1.70
2 1.85

DEMON'S TAILS
Adventure
1 2.50
2 A:Champion 2.50
3 V:Champion 2.50
4 V:Champion 2.50

DEMON WARRIOR
1 thru 12 @1.50
13 1.75
14 1.75

DENIZENS OF DEEP CITY
Jabberwocky
1 thru 9 @2.00

DESERT PEACH
Thoughts & Images
1 thru 4 @2.00

DESTROY
Eclipse
1 Large Size 4.95
2 Small Size,3-D 4.95

DICK TRACY MAGAZINE
1 V:Little Face Finnyo 3.95

DICK TRACY MONTHLY
Blackthorne
1 thru 25 @2.00

DICK TRACY: THE EARLY YEARS
5 2.95
6 2.95
7 and 8 @3.50

DICK TRACY WEEKLY
26 thru 108 @2.00
Unprinted Stories #3 2.95

1 3-D Special 3.00
Spec. #1 . . . . 2.95
Spec. #2 . . . . 2.95
Spec. #3 . . . . 2.95

DIGGERS, THE
C&T

3 . . . . 1.75

DILLINGER
Rip Off Press

1 Outlaw Dillinger 2.50

DINOSAUR REX

1 . . . . 2.00
2 . . . . 2.00

DINOSAURS
Caliber

1 History of Dinosaurs 3.00

DINOSAURS FOR HIRE
Eternity

1 . . . . 3.00
1a Rep. 1.95
2 thru 9 . . . . @1.95
Fall Classic #1 . . . . 2.25

DIRECTORY TO A NON-EXISTENT UNIVERSE
Eclipse

1 . . . . 1.95

DIRTY-NAIL

1 . . . . 2.00

DIRTY PAIR

1 . . . . 5.00
2 . . . . 4.00
3 . . . . 3.00
4 end mini-series 2.50

Eclipse

reprint 1-3 . . . . 2.50
Vol 2 #1 . . . . 2.25
Vol 2 #2 . . . . 2.25
Vol 2 #3 . . . . 2.00
Vol 2 #4 . . . . 2.00
Vol 2 #5 . . . . 2.00

DIRTY PAIR: PLAGUE OF ANGELS
Eclipse

1 thru 5 . . . . @2.25

DIRTY PAIR: SIM EARTH
Eclipse

1 thru 4 . . . . 2.50

DISQUETTE

1 . . . . 2.50

A DISTANT SOIL
Warp Graphics

1 A:Panda Khan 5.00
2 . . . . 4.00
3 . . . . 3.00
4 . . . . 3.00
5 . . . . 3.00
6 thru 9 . . . . @2.00

Aria Press

1 thru 3 . . . . @2.00

DITKOS WORLD: STATIC
Renegade

1 SD 1.70
2 SD 1.70
3 SD 1.70

DR. GORPON
Eternity

1 I:Dr.Gorpon,V:Demon 2.25
2 A:Doofus,V:ChocolateBunny . . . 2.50
3 D:Dr.Gorpon 2.50

DR. RADIUM
Silverline

1 . . . . 3.00
2 . . . . 2.00
3 and 4 . . . . @1.50

DR. RADIUM: MAN OF SCIENCE
Slave Labor

1 And Baby makes 2,BU:Dr.Radiums' Grim Future 2.50

DOC WEIRD'S THRILL BOOK

1 AW 1.75
2 . . . . 1.75
3 . . . . 1.75

DOG

1 Military renegade 2.25

DOGAROO
Blackthorne

1 . . . . 2.00

DOMINION
Eclipse

1 . . . . 3.00
2 thru 6 . . . . @2.00

DOMINION
Dark Horse

TPB 1 . . . . 13.95

DOMINO CHANCE
Chance

1 1,000 printed 10.00
1a 2nd printing 3.50
2 . . . . 3.00
3 . . . . 3.00
4 . . . . 3.00
5 . . . . 3.00
6 . . . . 3.00
7 I:Gizmo 7.00
8 A:Gizmo 11.00
9 . . . . 2.50

[2nd Series]

1 . . . . 3.00
2 . . . . 1.95
3 . . . . 1.95

DONATELLO
Mirage

1 A: Turtles 12.00

DRACULA

1 . . . . 3.75
1a 2nd printing 2.50
2 . . . . 2.50
3 . . . . 2.50
4 . . . . 2.50

DRACULA IN HELL
Apple

1 O:Dracula 2.50
2 O:Dracula contd. 2.50

DRACULA: SUICIDE CLUB
Adventure

1 I:Suicide Club in UK 2.50
2 Dracula/Suicide Club cont. 2.50
3 Club raid,A:Insp.Harrison 2.50
4 Vision of Miss Fortune 2.50

DRACULA: THE LADY IN THE TOMB
Eternity

1 . . . . 2.50

DRAGONFORCE
Aircel
(Prev. Color)

8 thru 13 DK . . . . @2.50

DRAGONFORCE CHRONICLES
Aircel

Vol 1 rep. 2.95
Vol 2 rep. 2.95
Vol 3 rep. 2.95
Vol 4 rep. 2.95
Vol 5 rep 2.95

DRAGON OF THE VALKYR

1 . . . . 1.75
2 thru 4 . . . . @2.00

DRAGON QUEST

1 TV 15.00
2 TV 7.50
3 TV 6.50

Dragonring #1 © Aircel

DRAGONRING
[1st Series]

1 B.Blair,rare 110.00

Aircel

1 . . . . 3.50
2 . . . . 2.00
3 thru 6 . . . . @1.75

See Also Independent Color

DRAGON'S STAR

1 . . . . 1.75
2 . . . . 1.75
3 . . . . 2.00
4 . . . . 2.00

DRAGON WEEKLY

1 Southern Knights 1.75
2 . . . . 1.75
3 . . . . 1.75

DREAD OF NIGHT
Hamilton

1 Horror story collection 3.95
2 Json, inc.'Genocide' 3.95

DREAMERY
Eclipse

1 thru 13 . . . . @2.00

DRIFTERS AFAR

1 . . . . 1.70

DUCK & COVER

1 . . . . 2.00
2 . . . . 2.00

DUCKBOTS

1 . . . . 1.75
2 . . . . 1.75
3 . . . . 1.75

DUNGEONEERS

1 thru 8 . . . . @1.50

DURANGO KID

1 . . . . 2.50
2 . . . . 2.50

DUTCH DECKER

1 . . . . 1.95
2 . . . . 1.95
3 . . . . 1.95

DYNAMIC COMICS

1 . . . . 2.00
2 . . . . 2.00

EAGLE
Crystal

1 . . . . 5.00
1a signed & limited 7.00
2 thru 5 . . . . @2.75
6 thru 11 . . . . @2.25
12 . . . . 2.50
13 thru 17 . . . . @2.00

Apple

18 thru 26 . . . . @1.95

EAGLE: DARK MIRROR
Comic Zone

1 A:Eagle, inc reps 2.75
2 In Japan, V:Lord Kagami 2.75
3 . . . . 2.95
4 . . . . 2.95

EARTH LORE: LEGEND OF BEK LARSON
Eternity

1 . . . . 1.80

EARTH LORE: REIGN OF DRAGON LORD

1 . . . . 1.80
2 . . . . 1.75

EARTH: YEAR ZERO
Eclipse

1 thru 4 . . . . @2.00

EB'NN THE RAVEN
Now

1 . . . . 5.00
2 . . . . 3.00
3 . . . . 2.50
4 . . . . 2.00
5 thru 9 . . . . @1.50

EDDY CURRENT

1 thru 12 . . . . @2.00

EDGAR ALLAN POE

Tell Tale Heart 1.95
Pit & Pendulum 1.95
Masque of the Red Death 1.95
Murder in the Rue Morgue 1.95

EDGE

1 . . . . 3.00
Vol 2 #1 . . . . 3.00
Vol 2 #2 . . . . 3.00
Vol 2 #3 . . . . 3.00
Vol 2 #4 . . . . 2.00
Vol 2 #5 . . . . 2.00
Vol 2 #6 . . . . 2.00

Eightball #7 © Fantagraphics

EIGHTBALL
Fantagraphics

1 . . . . 12.00
2 . . . . 8.00
3 . . . . 7.00
4 . . . . 6.00
5 . . . . 5.00
6 . . . . 5.00
7 . . . . 5.00
8 . . . . 5.00
9 . . . . 4.00
10 . . . . 4.00
11 . . . . 3.50
12 F:Ghost World 3.25

ELECTRIC BALLET
Caliber

1 Revisionist History of Industrial Revolution 2.50

ELEGANT LADIES

1 . . . . 3.50

ELFLORD
[1st Series]

1 all rare 80.00
2 . . . . 65.00
3 . . . . 60.00
4 . . . . 50.00
5 . . . . 50.00
6 . . . . 80.00
7 . . . . 80.00
8 . . . . 80.00
9 thru 15 . . . . @50.00

ELFLORD
Aircel

1 I:Hawk 5.00
1a 2nd printing 3.50
2 . . . . 3.00
2a 2nd printing 2.00
3 V:Doran 3.00
4 V:Doran 3.00
5 V:Doran 2.00
6 V:Nendo 2.00
7 thru 13 . . . . @2.00
Compilation Book 4.95
(Vol 2, #1 to #24, see Color)
25 thru 31 . . . . @1.95
32 . . . . 2.50

ELFLORD CHRONICLES
Aircel

1 rep B.Blair 2.50
2 thru 8 rep . . . . @2.50

ELFQUEST
Warp Graphics

1 WP 42.00
1a WP,2nd printing 10.00
1b WP,3rd printing 6.00
1c WP,4th printing 4.00
2 WP 23.00
2a WP,2nd printing 5.00
2b WP,3rd printing 3.00
3 WP 23.00
3a WP,2nd printing 5.00
3b WP,3rd printing 3.00
4 WP 23.00
4a WP,2nd printing 5.00
4b WP,3rd printing 3.00
4c WP,4th printing 2.00
5 WP 23.00
5a WP,2nd printing 5.00
5b WP,3rd printing 3.00
6 WP 15.00
6a WP,2nd printing 4.00
6b WP,3rd printing 2.00
7 WP 12.00
7a WP,2nd printing 4.00
8 WP 12.00
8a WP,2nd printing 4.00
9 WP 12.00
9a WP,2nd printing 2.50
10 thru 15 WP . . . . @8.50
16 WP,I:DistantSoil 9.00
17 thru 21 WP . . . . @8.00

ELFQUEST: KINGS OF THE BROKEN WHEEL
Warp Graphics

1 WP 4.00
2 thru 9 WP . . . . @3.00

ELFQUEST: SEIGE AT BLUE MOUNTAIN
Warp Graphics/Apple Comics

1 WP,JSo 12.00
1a 2nd printing 3.00
2 WP 6.00
2a 2nd printing 3.00
3 WP 5.00
3a 2nd printing 2.00
4 thru 8 WP . . . . @4.00

ELFTHING
Eclipse

1 . . . . 3.00

ELFTREK
Dimension

1 . . . . 2.00
2 . . . . 1.75

ELF WARRIOR

1 . . . . 3.00

2 . . . . 2.50
3 thru 5 . . . . @1.95

ELIMINATOR
Eternity

1 'Drugs in the Future' 2.50

ELVIRA
Eclipse

1 Rosalind Wyck 2.50

ELVIS: UNDERCOVER

1 . . . . 2.00

EMERALDAS
Eternity

1 thru 4 . . . . @2.25

EMPIRE
Eternity

1 thru 4 . . . . @1.95

EMPIRE LANES
Comico

1 . . . . 2.95

EMPTY BALLOONS

1 . . . . 1.50
2 . . . . 1.50

Enchanted Valley #1 © Blackthorne

ENCHANTED VALLEY
Blackthorne

1 . . . . 1.75
2 . . . . 1.75

ENCHANTER
Eclipse

1 thru 3 . . . . @2.00

ENEMY LINES SPECIAL

1 . . . . 1.75

END, THE

1 . . . . 1.95

ENTROPY TALES

1 . . . . 2.00
2 Domino Chance 1.50
3 . . . . 1.50

EPSILON WAVE
Elite

1 . . . . 3.00
2 . . . . 2.00
3 thru 5 . . . . @1.60

EQUINE THE UNCIVILIZED
Graphspress

1 . . . . 4.00
2 . . . . 2.50
3 thru 6 . . . . @2.00

EQUINOX CHRONICLES
Innovation

1 I:Team Equinox, Black Avatar . . 2.25
2 Black Avatar Plans US conquest 2.25

ERADICATORS

1 RLm(1st Work) 5.00
1a 2nd printing 1.50
2 . . . . 2.50
3 Vigil 2.00
4 thru 8 . . . . @1.50

ERIN

1 . . . . 1.95

ESCAPE TO THE STARS
Visionary

1 thru 7 . . . . @1.25

[2nd Series]

1 . . . . 1.25
2 . . . . 1.25

ESCAPE VELOCITY

1 . . . . 1.50
2 . . . . 1.50

ESMERALDAS
Eternity

1 thru 4 . . . . 2.25

ETERNAL THIRST

1 . . . . 2.00
2 . . . . 2.00

ETERNITY TRIPLE ACTION
Malibu

1 F:Gazonga 1.95
2 F:Gigantor 2.50

EVIL ERNIE
Eternity

1 I&O:Evil Ernie (Horror) 5.00
1a Special Edition 2.95
2 Death & Revival of Ernie 4.00
3 Psycho Plague 3.00
4 . . . . 3.00
5 . . . . 2.50
TPB rep #1-5 . . . . 10.95

EX-MUTANTS
Amazing Comics

1 AC/RLm 5.00
1a 2nd printing 2.00

EC

2 . . . . 3.00
3 . . . . 2.00
4 . . . . 2.00
5 . . . . 2.00
6 PP 1.95
7 . . . . 1.95
8 . . . . 1.95
Annual#1 . . . . 1.95
Winter Special #1 . . . . 1.95

EX-MUTANTS: THE SHATTERED

EARTH CHRONICLES
Eternity

1 thru 3 . . . . @1.95
4 RLd(c) 2.75
5 RLd(c) 2.75
6 thru 14 . . . . @1.95

EXILE

1 . . . . 2.00
2 . . . . 2.00

EXTINCT
NEC

1 Rep Golden age stories 3.50

EXTREMELY SILLY

1 . . . . 4.00
1 Vol. II 1.25
2 Vol. II 1.25

EYEBALL KID
Dark Horse

1 I:Eyeball Kid 2.25
2 V:Stygian Leech 2.25
3 V:Telchines Brothers,last iss. . . 2.25

EYE OF MONGOMBO

1 . . . . 3.00
2 thru 5 . . . . @2.00

FAILED UNIVERSE

1 . . . . 1.75

FANBOYS

Spec #1 . . . . 2.00

FANTAESCAPE

1 . . . . 1.75
2 . . . . 1.75

FANTASCI
Warp Graphics-Apple

1 . . . . 2.50
2 . . . . 2.00
3 . . . . 2.00
4 . . . . 4.00
5 thru 8 . . . . @1.75
9 'Apple Turnover' 1.75

FANTASTIC ADVENTURES

1 thru 5 . . . . @1.75

FANTASTIC FABLES
Silver Wolf

1 . . . . 1.50
2 . . . . 1.50

FANTASY QUARTERLY

1 1978 1st Elfquest 65.00

FAT DOG MENDOZA
Dark Horse

1 I&O:Fat Dog Mendoza 2.50

FAT NINJA

1 . . . . 2.50
2 Vigil 2.50
3 thru 8 . . . . @1.50

FAUNA REBELLION

1 thru 3 . . . . @2.00

FAUST
North Star

1 Vigil 35.00
1a Vigil,2ndPrinting 5.00
1b Vigil,3rdPrinting 2.25
2 Vigil 23.00
2a Vigil,2ndPrinting 3.00

2b Vigil,3rdPrinting 2.25
3 Vigil 18.00
3a Vigil,2ndPrinting 2.25
4 Vigil 8.00
5 Vigil 6.00
6 Vigil 6.00
6a Faust Tour Book 40.00
7 Vigil 4.00
8 TV 3.50
9 TV,Love of the Damned 3.00
10 E:DQ(s),TV,Love o/t Damned . 3.00

FAUST VOL. II
REBEL

1 TV,Love of the Damned 2.50

FAUST PREMIERE
North Star

1 Vigil 45.00

FEM FANTASTIQUE
AC Comics

1 . . . . 1.95

Fem Force #46 © AC Comics

FEM FORCE
AC Comics
(See Color)

16 I:Thunder Fox 2.25
17 F:She-Cat,Ms.Victory, giant . . . 2.25
18 double size 2.25
19 . . . . 2.50
20 Giant,V:RipJaw,
Black Commando 2.50
21 V:Dr.Pretorius 2.50
22 V:Dr.Pretorius 2.50
23 V:Rad 2.50
24 A:Teen Femforce 2.50
25 V:Madame Boa 2.50
26 V:Black Shroud 2.50
27 V:Black Shroud 2.50
28 A:Arsenio Hall 2.50
29 V:Black Shroud 2.50
30 V:Garganta 2.50
31 I:Kronon Captain Paragon 2.75
32 V:Garganta 2.75
33 Personal Lives of team 2.75
34 V:Black Shroud 2.75
35 V:Black Shroud 2.75
36 giant,V:Dragonfly,Shade 2.75
37 A:Blue Bulleteer,She-Cat 2.75
38 V:Lady Luger 2.75
39 F:She-Cat 2.75
40 V:Sehkmet 2.75
41 V:Captain Paragon 2.75
42 V:Alizarin Crimson 2.75
43 V:Glamazons of Galaxy G . . . 2.75
44 V:Lady Luger 2.75
45 Nightveil Rescued 2.75
46 V:Lady Luger 2.75
47 V:Alizarin Crimson 2.75
48 . . . . 2.75
49 I:New Msw.Victory 2.75
50 Ms.Victory Vs.Rad,flexi-disc . . 2.95
51 . . . . 2.75
52 V:Claw & Clawites 2.75
53 I:Bulldog Deni,V:(Dick
Briefer's)Frightenstein 2.75
54 The Orb of Bliss 2.75
55 R:Nightveil 2.75
56 V:Alizarin Crimson 2.75

FEMFORCE: FRIGHTBOOK
AC Comics

1 Horror tales by Briefer,Ayers,
Powell 2.95

FEMME NOIRE

1 . . . . 2.00
2 . . . . 2.00

50'S TERROR
Eternity

1 thru 6 . . . . @1.95

FIGMENTS

1 . . . . 1.75
2 . . . . 1.75

FINAL CYCLE
Sirius

Graphic Novel 4.00
1 thru 4 . . . . @1.50

FINAL MAN

1 . . . . 1.50
2 . . . . 1.75
3 . . . . 1.75

FIRE TEAM
Aircel

1 . . . . 2.50
2 . . . . 2.50
3 . . . . 2.50
4 V:Vietnamese Gangs 2.50
5 Cam in Vietnam 2.50
6 . . . . 2.50

FISH POLICE
Fishwrap Productions
December 1985

1 1st printing 7.00
1a 2nd printing 3.00
2 . . . . 5.00
3 thru 5 . . . . @4.00

Comico Publ.

6 thru 12 . . . . @3.50
13 thru 17 **see Color issues**

Apple Publ.

18 thru 24 . . . . @2.50

FISH SHTICKS
Apple

1 . . . . 2.75
2 . . . . 2.75
3 . . . . 2.50
4 . . . . 2.50

FISSION CHICKEN

1 thru 5 . . . . @2.00

FIST OF GOD
Eternity

1 thru 4 . . . . @1.95

Fist of the North Star #1
© Viz Comics

FIST OF THE NORTH STAR
Viz Select

1 thru 3 . . . . @3.25
4 . . . . 1.95
5 . . . . 3.25
6 . . . . 2.95
7 . . . . 2.95

FITCH IN TIME
Renegade

1 . . . . 1.50

FLAME

1 Son of G.A.Flame 95

FLAMING CARROT
Aardvark Vanaheim

1 1981KillianBarracks 105.00
1a 1984 . . . . 56.00
2 . . . . 36.00
3 . . . . 25.00
4 thru 6 . . . . @18.00

Renegade

7 . . . . 13.00
8 . . . . 12.00
9 . . . . 12.00
10 . . . . 6.00
11 . . . . 5.00
12 . . . . 5.00
13 . . . . 4.00
14 . . . . 4.00
15 . . . . 4.00
15a 20.00
16 . . . . 4.00
17 . . . . 4.00

Dark Horse

18 . . . . 3.50
18a Ash-Can-Limited 12.00
19 thru 23 . . . . @2.00
24 . . . . 3.00
25 F:TMNT,Mysterymen 4.00
26 A:TMNT 2.00
27 TM(c),A:TMNT conclusion 2.25
28 . . . . 2.25
29 Man in the Moon,Iron City 2.50

Flaming Carrot #28 © Dark Horse

30 V:Man in the Moon 2.50

FLARE
Hero Graphics

1 thru 8 . . . . @3.95
9 F:Sparkplug 3.95
10 thru 12 . . . . 2.95

FLARE ADVENTURES
Hero Graphics

1 Rep 1st issue Flare 1.00
Becomes:

FLARE ADVENTURES/ CHAMPIONS CLASSICS

2 thru 15 . . . . @3.95

FLARE VS. TIGRESS
Hero Graphics

1 . . . . 3.50
2 . . . . 3.50

FLASH MARKS
Fantagraphics

1 . . . . 2.95

FLOATERS
Dark Horse

1 thru 5 From Spike Lee 2.75

FLOYD FARLAND
Eclipse

1 . . . . 2.95

FLYIN RALPH COMICS

1 75

FORBIDDEN KINGDOM

1 thru 11 . . . . @1.95

FORBIDDEN WORLDS

1 SD,JAp,rep. 2.50

FOREVER NOW

1 . . . . 1.50
2 . . . . 1.50

FOTON EFFECT

1 thru 5 . . . . @1.50

FOX COMICS

1 Spec. 2.95
25 . . . . 2.95
26 . . . . 3.50

FRAGMENTS

1 thru 3 . . . . @1.75

FRAN AN' MAABL

1 . . . . 2.50
2 . . . . 2.50

FRANKENSTEIN
Eternity

1 thru 3 . . . . @1.95

FRANKIES FRIGHTMARES

1 Celebrates Frank 60th ann 1.95

FRANK THE UNICORN
Fish Warp

1 thru 7 . . . . @2.00

FREAK-OUT ON INFANT EARTHS

1 Don Chin 1.75
2 Don Chin 1.75

FREAKS
Monster Comics

1 Movie adapt 2.50
2 Movie adapt.cont. 2.50
3 thru 4 Movie adapt. 2.50

FREE FIRE ZONE

1 thru 3 . . . . @1.75

FREE LAUGHS

1 . . . . 1.00

FRENCH ICE
Renegade Press

1 thru 15 . . . . @2.00

FRIENDS

1 thru 5 . . . . @2.00

FRIGHT
Eternity

1 thru 13 . . . . @1.95

FRINGE

1 thru 6 . . . . @2.50

FROM BEYOND
Studio Insidio

1 Short stories-horror 2.25
2 inc.Clara Mutilares 2.50
3 inc.The Experiment 2.50
4 inc.Positive Feedback 2.50

FROM HELL
Tundra

1 . . . . 4.95

Kitchen Sink
Volume Three

1 AMo(s) 3.95

FROM THE DARKNESS
Adventure Comics

1 thru 4 . . . . @2.50

FROM THE DARKNESS II BLOODVOWS
Cry For Dawn

1 R:Ray Thorn,Desnoires 2.50
2 V:Desnoires 2.50

FROM THE VOID

1 1st B.Blair,1982 . . . . 75.00

FROST

1 Heart of Darkness 1.95

FROST: THE DYING BREED
Caliber

1 Vietnam Flashbacks 2.95
2 Flashbacks contd. 2.95
3 Flashbacks contd. 2.95

FUGITOID
Mirage

1 TMNT Tie-in 12.00

FURRLOUGH
Antarctic Press

1 Funny Animal Military stories . . 2.95

FURY
Aircel

1 thru 3 . . . . @1.70

FUSION
Eclipse

1 . . . . 2.50
2 thru 17 . . . . @2.00

FUTURAMA
Slave Labor

1 thru 4 . . . . @1.75

FUTURE BEAT

1 . . . . 1.50
2 . . . . 1.50
3 . . . . 1.50

FUTURE COURSE

1 . . . . 1.75
2 . . . . 1.75
3 . . . . 1.75

FUTURE CRIME 98

1 . . . . 1.95

GAIJIN

1 thru 3 . . . . @1.95

GAJIT GANG

1 . . . . 1.95
2 . . . . 1.95

GAMBIT

1 . . . . 1.95
2 . . . . 1.95

GAMBIT & ASSOCIATES

1 thru 4 . . . . @1.75

GANTAR

1 thru 5 . . . . @1.75

GATEKEEPER

1 . . . . 2.50
2 and 3 . . . . @2.95

GATES OF THE NIGHT
Jademan

1 thru 4 . . . . @3.50

GATEWAY TO HORROR

1 BW 1.75

GENOCYBER
Viz

1 I:Genocyber . . . 2.75
2 . . . 2.75
3 thru 5 ToT . . . 2.75

GERIATRIC GANGRENE JUJITSU GERBILS
Planet X Productions

1 . . . 2.50
2 . . . 1.50

GERIATRIC MAN

1 . . . 1.75

GET LOST

1 . . . 1.95
1a signed (1200 copies) . . . 6.00
2 . . . 1.95
3 . . . 1.95

GHOSTS OF DRACULA
Eternity

1 A:Dracula & Houdini . . . 2.50
2 A:Sherlock Holmes . . . 2.50
3 A:Houdini . . . 2.50
4 Count Dracula's Castle . . . 2.50
5 Houdini, Van Helsing, Dracula team-up . . . 2.50

GHOULS

1 . . . 2.25

GIANT SIZE MINI COMICS
Eclipse

1 thru 4 . . . @1.50

G.I. CAT

1 . . . 1.50
2 . . . 1.50
3 . . . 1.50

G.I. MUTANTS

1 . . . 1.95
2 . . . 1.95

GIFT, THE
First

1 . . . 5.95

GIZMO
Chance

1 . . . 7.50

Mirage

1 . . . 5.50
2 . . . 2.50
3 . . . 2.00
4 thru 7 . . . @1.50

GIZMO & THE FUGITOID

1 . . . 1.75
2 . . . 1.75

GNATRAT
Prelude

1 . . . 5.00
2 Early Years . . . 2.00

GNATRAT: THE MOVIE

1 . . . 2.25

GNOSIS BRIDGE

1 . . . 1.50

GOBBLEDYGOOK
Mirage

1 1st series, Rare . . . 275.00
2 1st series, Rare . . . 275.00
1 TMNT series reprint . . . 12.00

Gobbledygook © Mirage Studios

GOD'S HAMMER

1 . . . 2.50
2 . . . 2.50
3 . . . 2.50

GODZILLA
Dark Horse

1 JapaneseManga . . . 3.50
2 thru 6 . . . @2.25
Spec #1 . . . 1.50

GOLDIGGER
Antarctic

1 Geena & Cheetah in Peru . . . 2.50
2 Adventures contd. . . . 2.50
3 Adventures contd . . . 2.50
4 Adventures contd . . . 2.50

GOLDEN FEATURES

1 thru 5 . . . @2.00

GOLDWYN 3-D
Blackthorne

1 . . . 2.00

GOLGO 13

1 thru 5 . . . @1.25

GO-MAN

1 thru 4 . . . @1.50
Graphic Novel 'N' . . . 9.95

GOOD GIRLS
Fantagraphics

1 adult . . . 2.00
2 thru 4 . . . @2.00

GOON PATROL

1 . . . 1.75

GORE SHRIEK
Fantagor

1 . . . 2.50
2 . . . 1.50
3 . . . 1.50
4 +Mars Attacks . . . 2.95
5 . . . 2.95
6 . . . 3.50
Vol 2 #1 . . . 2.50

GRAPHIC STORY MONTHLY

1 thru 5 . . . @2.95

GRAPHIQUE MUSIQUE

1 . . . 2.95
2 . . . 2.95
3 . . . 2.95

GRAVE TALES
Hamilton

1 JSon,GM, mag. size . . . 3.95
2 JSon,GM,short stories . . . 3.95
3 JSon,GM, inc.'Stake Out' . . . 3.95

GRENDEL
Comico

1 MW,Rare . . . 60.00
2 MW,Rare . . . 50.00
3 MW,Rare . . . 45.00

Grey #1 © Viz Select Comics

GREY
Viz Select

Book 1 . . . 5.00
Book 2 scarce . . . 5.50
Book 3 . . . 3.00
Book 4 . . . 3.00
Book 5 . . . 3.00
Book 6 . . . 2.50
Book 7 . . . 2.50
Book 8 . . . 2.50
Book 9 . . . 2.50

GRIFFIN, THE
Slave Labor

1 . . . 1.75
1a 2nd printing . . . 1.75
2 thru 4 . . . @1.75
5 . . . 1.95

GRINGO

1 . . . 1.95

GRIPS
Silver Wolf

1 Vigil . . . 20.00
2 Vigil . . . 16.00
3 Vigil . . . 11.00
4 Vigil . . . 9.00
Vol 1 #1 rep . . . 2.50
Volume 2

1 . . . . 2.50
2 . . . . 2.50
3 thru 6 . . . . @2.00
7 . . . . 2.25
8 . . . . 2.25
9 thru 12 . . . . @2.50

GRIPS ADVENTURE
1 double-size 2.50
2 thru 5 . . . . @2.00

GROOTLOTE
1 . . . . 2.00

GROUND POUND
1 JohnPoundArt 2.00

GROUND ZERO
Eternity
1 Science Fiction mini-series 2.50
2 Alien Invasion Aftermath 2.50

GRUN
1 . . . . 1.95
2 . . . . 1.95

GRUNTS
1 . . . . 1.50

GUERRILA GROUNDHOG
Eclipse
1 . . . . 1.50
2 . . . . 1.50

GUILLOTINE
Silver Wolf
1 and 2 . . . . @1.50

GUN FURY
Aircel
1 thru 10 . . . . @1.95

GUN FURY RETURNS
Aircel
1 . . . . 2.95
2 . . . . 2.95
3 V:The Yes Men 2.25

GUNS OF SHAR-PEI
Caliber
1 The Good,the Bad & the Deadly 2.95

HALLOWEEN TERROR
Eternity
1 . . . . 2.50

HALLOWIENERS
Mirage
1 . . . . 1.50
2 . . . . 1.50

HALO BROTHERS
Fantagraphics
Special #1 . . . . 2.25

HAMSTER VICE
Blackthorne
1 . . . . 3.50
2 . . . . 2.50
3 thru 11 . . . . @2.00

New Series
Eternity
1 and 2 . . . . @1.95

HAND SHADOWS
1 . . . . 2.00
2 . . . . 1.50

HARD-BOILED ANIMAL COMICS
1 . . . . 2.50

HARD LOOKS
Dark Horse
1 thru 10 AVs Adaptations . . . . @2.50
Book One 14.95

HARD ROCK COMICS
Revolutionary
1 Metallica-The Early Years 2.50

HAR HAR COMICS
1 . . . . 2.00

HARTE OF HARKNESS
Eternity
1 I:Dennis Harte,Vampire private-eye 2.50
2 V:Satan's Blitz St.Gang 2.50
3 Jack Grissom/Vampire 2.50
4 V:Jack Grissom, conc. 2.50

HARVEST
Spec. 3.00

HARVY FLIP BOOK
Blackthorne
1 . . . . 2.00
2 . . . . 2.00
3 . . . . 2.00

HATE
Fantagraphics
1 . . . . 25.00
2 . . . . 20.00
3 . . . . 15.00
4 . . . . 12.00
5 . . . . 10.00
6 . . . . 8.00
6a 2.25
7 thru 11 . . . . 6.00
12 . . . . 5.00
13 thru 15 . . . . 3.00

HEAD, THE
1 Old Airboy (1966) 2.00

HEADLESS HORSEMAN
1 . . . . 2.25
2 . . . . 2.25

HEARTBREAK COMICS
Eclipse
1 . . . . 1.50

HEAVY METAL MONSTERS
Revolutionary
1 'Up in Flames' 2.25

HELLBENDER
1 . . . . 2.25

HELL FOR LEATHER
1 and 2 . . . . @1.75

HELLHOUNDS
Dark Horse
1 I:Hellhounds 2.50
2 A:Hellhounds 2.50
3 A:Hellhounds 2.50
4 A:Hellhounds 2.50

HELLSTALKER
1 . . . . 2.25
2 . . . . 2.25

3 . . . . 2.25

HELLWARRIOR
1 . . . . 2.50
2 . . . . 2.50
3 . . . . 1.95
4 . . . . 1.95

HENRY V
Caliber
1 Play Adaption 2.95

HEPCATS
Double Diamond
1 . . . . 6.00
2 . . . . 5.00
3 . . . . 4.00
4 . . . . 3.50
5 . . . . 3.50
6 . . . . 3.50
7 thru 10 . . . . @3.00

HERALDS OF CANADA
1 . . . . 1.50
2 . . . . 1.50

HERCULES
A Plus Comics
1 Hercules Saga 2.50

HERCULES PROJECT
Monster Comics
1 Origin issue,V:Mutants 1.95

HEROES
Blackbird
1 . . . . 6.00
2 . . . . 3.00
3 . . . . 2.25
4 comic size 2.00
5 . . . . 2.00
6 . . . . 2.00
7 . . . . 2.00

HEROES' BLOOD
1 . . . . 1.95

HEROES FROM WORDSMITH
Special Studios
1 WWI,F:Hunter Hawke 2.50

HEROINES, INC.
1 thru 5 . . . . @1.75

HERO SANDWICH
Slave Labor
1 thru 4 . . . . @1.50
5 thru 8 . . . . @1.75
9 . . . . 1.95
Graphic Novel 7.95

HEY, BOSS
1 . . . . 1.50
2 . . . . 1.50

HIGH CALIBER
1 . . . . 4.00
2 . . . . 3.00
3 . . . . 2.50
4 . . . . 2.50
Becomes:Caliber Presents

HIGH SCHOOL AGENT
Sun Comics
1 I:Kohsuke Kanamori 2.50
2 Treasure Hunt at North Pole . . . 2.50
3 . . . . 2.50

HIGH SHINING BRASS
Apple

1 thru 4 .... @2.75

HIGH SOCIETY
Aardvark Vanaheim

1 DS,Cerebus 25.00

HITOMI
Antarctic Press

1 Shadowhunter,from Ninja HS .. 2.50
2 Synaptic Transducer 2.50
3 Shadowhunter in S.America 2.50
4 V:Mr.Akuma,last issue 2.50

HOLIDAY OUT

1 .... 2.00
2 .... 2.00
3 .... 2.00

HOMICIDE

1 .... 1.95

HONK
Fantagraphics

1 Don Martin 2.75
2 .... 2.75
3 .... 2.75

HONOR AMONG THIEVES

1 .... 1.50

HOODOO

Spec. 2.50

HOOHA COMICS

1 Mag. Size Animal
Anthology-500 print 15.00

HORDE

1 .... 2.00
2 .... 2.00

HORNET SPECIAL

1 .... 2.00

HOROBI
Viz

1 .... 4.00
2 thru 8 .... @3.75

Book 2

1 .... 3.50
2 D:Okado,Shoko Kidnapped 4.25
3 Madoka Attacks Zen 4.25
4 D:Abbess Mitsuko 4.25
5 Catharsis! 4.25
6 Shuichi Vs. Zen 4.25
7 Shuichi vs. Zen, conc. 4.25

HORROR

1 .... 2.95
2 .... 2.95

HORROR IN THE DARK
Fantagor

1 RCo,Inc.Blood Birth 2.00
2 RCo,Inc.Bath of Blood 2.00
3 RCo 2.00
4 RCo,Inc.Tales o/tBlackDiamond 2.00

HORROR SHOW
Caliber

1 GD,1977-80 reprint horror 3.50

HORSE

1 .... 2.95

HOT SHOTS

1 .... 1.95

2 .... 1.95

HOUSE OF HORROR
AC Comics

1 .... 2.50

HOWL
Eternity

1 .... 2.25
2 .... 2.25

HOW TO DRAW ROBOTECH BOOK

1 .... 2.00
2 .... 2.00

HOW TO DRAW TEENAGE MUTANT NINJA TURTLES
Solson

1 Lighter cover 15.00
1a Dark cover 5.00

HUGO
Fantagraphics

1 .... 4.00
2 .... 2.00
3 .... 2.00
4 .... 2.00

HUMAN GARGOYLES
Eternity

Book one 1.95
Book two 1.95
Book three 1.95
Book four 1.95

HUMAN HEAD
Caliber

1 Alice in Flames 2.50

HUMAN POWERHOUSE

1 .... 1.75
2 .... 1.75
3 .... 2.00

HUZZAH

1 I:Albedo'sErmaFelna 60.00

HYPE

1 .... 2.00
2 .... 2.00

I.F.S. ZONE

1 thru 6 .... @1.25

I AM LEGEND
Eclipse

1 Novel Adaption 5.95
2 Novel Adaption Cont'd 5.95
3 Novel Adaption Cont'd 5.95

IAN WARLOCKE

1 .... 1.50

ICARUS

1 thru 9 .... @1.70

ICON DEVIL

1 .... 2.00
2 .... 2.00

2nd Series

1 thru 5 .... @1.85

IDIOTLAND
Fantagraphic

1 .... 2.95

ILIAD II

1 .... 3.00
1a 2nd cover variation 3.00
2 .... 2.00
3 .... 2.00
4 .... 1.70

ILLUMINATUS

1 .... 2.00
2 .... 2.50
3 .... 2.50

IN-COUNTRY NAM

1 .... 1.75
2 .... 1.75
3 .... 1.75
4 .... 1.95
5 .... 1.95

INDEPENDENT COMIC BOOK SAMPLER

1 .... 1.50
2 .... 1.50

INK COMICS

1 thru 3 .... @2.50

INSANE

1 .... 1.75
2 .... 1.75

INVADERS FROM MARS
Eternity

1 .... 2.50
2 .... 2.50
3 .... 2.50

(Book II)

1 Sequel to '50's SF classic 2.50
2 Pact of Tsukus/Humans 2.50
3 Last issue 2.50

INVASION '55
Apple

1 .... 2.25
2 .... 2.25
3 .... 2.25

INVISIBLE PEOPLE
Kitchen Sink

1 WE,I:Peacus Pleatnik 2.95
2 WE,The Power 2.95
3 WE,Final issue 2.95

INVISION WORLD

1 .... 1.95

IRON HAND OF ALMURIC
Dark Horse

1 R.E.Howard adaption 2.00
2 A:Cairn,V:Yagas 2.25
3 V:Yasmeena,The Hive Queen .. 2.00
4 Conclusion 2.25

IRON SAGA'S ANTHOLOGY

1 thru 3 .... @1.75

ISMET

1 Cartoon Dog 12.00
2 .... 5.00
3 Rare 5.00
4 .... 5.00

IS YOUR BOOGEY-MAN LOOSE?

1 .... 2.95

ITCHY PLANET

3 .... 2.25

IT'S SCIENCE WITH DR. RADIUM
1 thru 7 .... @1.50
8 .... 1.75
9 .... 1.95
Spec #1 .... 2.95

Jackaroo #1 © Eternity

JACKAROO
Eternity
1 GCh 2.25
2 GCh 2.25
3 GCh 2.25

J.A.P.A.N.
1 .... 1.80

JACKFROST
1 .... 1.80
2 .... 1.95
3 .... 1.95

JACK HUNTER
Blackthorne
1 .... 3.50
2 .... 3.50
3 .... 3.50

JACK OF NINES
1 .... 1.25
2 thru 4 .... @1.50
5 .... 2.00

JACK THE RIPPER
1 thru 4 .... @2.25

JAKE TRASH
1 .... 3.95

JAM, THE
1 .... 2.00
2 .... 2.00
3 .... 2.25

JAM SPECIAL
1 .... 2.50

JANX
1 and 2 .... @1.00

JASON AND THE ARGONAUTS
Caliber
1 thru 5 .... @2.50

JAX AND THE HELL HOUND
1 thru 4 .... @1.75

JAZZ AGE CHRONICLES
1 thru 6 .... @1.50
7 .... 2.50

JCP FEATURES
1 1st MT;S&K,NA/DG rep.
A:T.H.U.N.D.E.R.Agents,TheFly,
Black Hood Mag.Size 4.50

JEREMIAH: BIRDS OF PREY
Adventure Comics
1 I: Jeremiah,A:Kurdy 2.50
2 conclusion 2.50

JEREMIAH: FIST FULL OF SAND
Adventure Comics
1 A:Captain Kenney 2.50
2 conclusion 2.50

JEREMIAH: THE HEIRS
Adventure Comics
1 Nathanial Bancroft estate 2.50
2 conclusion 2.50

JERRY IGERS FAMOUS FEATURES
Blackthorne
1 .... 3.00
2 thru 4 .... @2.00
Pacific
5 thru 8 .... @2.00

JIM
1 thru 3 .... @2.25
4 .... 2.50

JOE SINN
Caliber
1 I:Joe Sinn,Nikki 2.95
2 .... 2.95

JOHNNY ATOMIC
Eternity
1 I:Johnny A.Tomick 2.50
2 Project X-contingency plan 2.50

JOHNNY GAMBIT
4 .... 1.95

JONTAR
1 .... 1.75
2 .... 1.75
3 .... 1.75

JOURNEY
Aardvark Vanaheim
1 .... 13.00
2 .... 9.00
3 .... 8.00
4 .... 5.00
5 .... 3.00
6 .... 3.00
7 .... 3.00
8 thru 14 .... @2.50
Fantagraphics
15 .... 2.50
16 thru 28 .... @2.00

Journey #4 © Aardvark Vanaheim

JR. JACKALOPE
1 orange cover,1981 .... 8.00
1a Yellow cover,1981 .... 15.00
2 .... 8.00

JUDO JOE
1 and 2 .... @1.75

JUNGLE COMICS
Blackthorne
4 thru 6 .... @2.00

JUNGLE GIRLS
AC Comics
1 incGold.Age reps. 1.95
2 .... 1.95
3 Greed,A:Tara 2.75
4 CaveGirl 2.75
5 Camilla 2.75
6 TigerGirl 2.75
7 CaveGirl 2.75
8 Sheena Queen o/t Jungle 2.95
9 Wild Girl,Tiger Girl,Sheena 2.95
10 F:Tara,Cave Girl,Nyoka 2.95
11 F:Sheena,Tiger Girl,Nyoka ... 2.95
12 F:Sheena,Camilla,Tig.Girl 2.95
13 F:Tara, Tiger Girl 2.95

JUNIOR CARROT PATROL
Dark Horse
1 .... 2.00
2 .... 2.00

JUSTY
1 thru 9 .... @1.75

KAFKA
1 thru 5 .... @2.00
The Execution Spec. 2.25

KAMIKAZE CAT
1 .... 1.80
2 .... 1.95
3 .... 1.95

KAMUI
Eclipse
1 Sanpei Shirato Art 4.00
1a 2nd printing 2.50
2 Mystery of Hanbie 3.00
2a 2nd printing 1.50

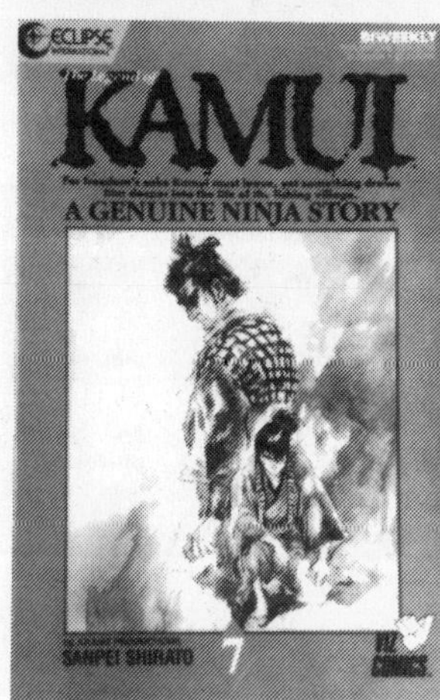

Kamui #7 © Eclipse

3 V:Ichijiro 2.00
3a 2nd printing 1.50
4 thru 15 . . . . @1.50
16 thru 19 . . . . @1.95
20 thru 37 . . . . @1.50

KAPTAIN KEEN

1 . . . . 1.75
2 . . . . 1.75
3 . . . . 1.75
4 . . . . 1.50
5 . . . . 1.50
6 . . . . 1.75
7 . . . . 1.75

KEIF LLAMA

1 thru 6 . . . . @2.00

KENDOR THE CREON WARRIOR

1 . . . . 1.50
2 . . . . 1.50

KID CANNIBAL
Eternity

1 I:Kid Cannibal 2.50
2 Hunt for Kid Cannibal 2.50
3 A:Janice 2.50
4 final issue 2.50

KID PHOENIX

1 . . . . 1.50

KIKU SAN
Aircel

1 thru 6 . . . . @1.95

KILGORE

1 thru 5 . . . . @2.00

KILLER OF CROWS

one shot, story of John Johnson . 2.50

KILLING STROKE
Eternity

1 British horror tales 2.50
2 inc.'Blood calls to Blood' 2.50

KIMBER
Antarctic Press

1 I:Kimber 2.50
2 V:Lord Tyrex 2.50

KINGS IN DISGUISE

1 thru 5 . . . . @2.00
6 end Mini-series 2.00

KIRBY KING OF THE SERIALS
Blackthorne

1 . . . . 2.00
2 . . . . 2.00
3 . . . . 2.00
4 . . . . 2.00

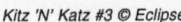

Kitz 'N' Katz #3 © Eclipse

KITZ 'N' KATZ

1 . . . . 3.50

Eclipse

2 . . . . 2.00
3 . . . . 1.50
4 and 5 . . . . @2.00

KIWANNI

1 . . . . 2.25
2 . . . . 1.75

KLOWN SHOCK
North Star

1 Horror Stories 2.75

KNIGHT MASTERS

1 thru 7 . . . . @1.50

KOMODO & THE DEFIANTS

1 thru 6 . . . . @1.50

KUNG FU WARRIORS
(Prev. ROBOWARRIORS)
CFW

12 . . . . 1.95
13 thru 19 . . . . @2.25

KURTZMAN KOMIX

1 . . . . 1.50

KWAR

1 . . . . 1.95

KYRA

1 . . . . 1.75
2 . . . . 1.75
3 . . . . 1.75
4 . . . . 2.00
5 . . . . 1.75

KZ COMICS

1 I:Colt 1985 . . . . 2.50

L.F.S. ZONE

1 . . . . 1.25

L.I.F.E. BRIGADE
Blue Comet

1 A:Dr. Death 1.50
1a 2nd printing 1.50
2 . . . . 1.50

LABOR FORCE
Blackthorne

1 thru 4 . . . . @1.50
5 thru 8 . . . . @1.75

LADY ARCANE
Heroic Publishing

1 thru 3 . . . . @3.50

LADY CRIME
AC Comics

1 Bob Powell reprints 2.75

LAFFIN GAS
Blackthorne

1 . . . . 2.50
2 thru 12 . . . . @2.00

LANCE STANTON WAYWARD WARRIOR

1 . . . . 1.50
2 . . . . 1.50

LANDRA
Polyventura Entertainment Group

1 . . . . 2.50

LAST DITCH
Edge Press

1 CCa(s),THa, ... 2.50

LAST GENERATION
Black Tie Studios

1 . . . . 6.00
2 . . . . 4.00
3 . . . . 2.25
4 . . . . 2.25
5 . . . . 2.25
Book One Rep. 6.95

LAST KISS, THE
Eclipse

Spec. 3.95

LATIGO KID WESTERN
AC Comics

1 . . . . 1.95

LAUGHING TARGET

1 . . . . 3.50
2 . . . . 3.50

LAUNCH

1 . . . . 1.75

LAUREL & HARDY

1 3-D 2.50

LAW

1 . . . . 1.75

LEAGUE OF CHAMPIONS
Hero Comics
(cont. from Innovation L.of C. #3)

1 GP,F:Sparkplug,Icestar 3.50
2 GP(i),F:Marksman,Flare,Icicle . . 3.50
3 . . . . 3.50
4 F:Sparkplug,League 3.50
5 Morrigan Wars Pt.#1 . . . . 3.50
6 Morrigan Wars Pt.#3 . . . . 3.50
7 Morrigan Wars Pt.#6 . . . . 3.50
8 Morrigan Wars Conclusion 3.50
9 A:Gargoyle 3.50
10 A:Rose 3.50
11 thru 12 . . . . 3.95
13 V:Malice 3.95
14 V:Olympians 3.95
15 V:Olympians 2.95

LEGEND LORE

1 and 2 . . . . @2.00
combined rep. 8.95

LEGION OF LUDICROUS HEROES

1 . . . . 2.00

LEGION X-I

1 McKinney 5.00
2 McKinney,rare 15.00
Volume 2
1 thru 4 . . . . @2.00

LEGION X-2

Vol 2 #1 . . . . 2.00
Vol 2 #2 . . . . 2.00
Vol 2 #3 . . . . 2.00
Vol 2 #4 . . . . 2.00

LENSMAN
Eternity

1 E.E.'Doc' Smith adapt. 2.25
2 . . . . 2.25
3 . . . . 2.25
4 . . . . 2.25
5 On Radelix 2.25
Spec #1 . . . . 3.95

LENSMAN: GALACTIC PATROL
Eternity

1 thru 7 . . . . @2.25

LEONARDO

1 TMNT 13.00

LIBBY ELLIS

1 . . . . 1.95
2 . . . . 1.95
Eternity
1 thru 4 . . . . @1.95

LIBERATOR
Eternity

1 thru 6 . . . . @1.95

LIBRA

1 . . . . 1.95

LITERACY VOLUNTEERS

1 Word Warriors 1.50
2 Quest for 1.50

LITTLEST NINJA

1 . . . . 1.80
2 . . . . 1.80

LIVINGSTONE MOUNTAIN
Adventure Comics

1 I:Scat,Dragon Rax 2.50
2 Scat & Rax Create Monsters . . 2.50
3 Rax rescue attempt 2.50
4 Final issue 2.50

LLOYD LLEWELLYN
Fantagraphics

1 Mag Size 4.00
2 Mag Size 2.25
3 Mag Size 2.25
4 Mag Size 2.25
5 Mag Size 2.25
6 Mag Size 2.25
7 Regular Size 2.25

LOCKE

1 . . . . 1.25
2 TD 1.25

LOCO VS. PULVERINE
Eclipse

1 Parody 2.50

LOGAN'S RUN
Adventure Comics

1 Novel Adapt 2.25
2 Novel Adapt 2.25
3 Novel Adapt 2.25
4 Novel Adapt 2.25
5 Novel Adapt 2.25
6 Novel Adapt 2.25

LOGAN'S WORLD
Adventure Comics

1 Seq. to Logan's Run 2.50
2 thru 5 . . . . @2.50

LOLLYMARS & LIGHT LANCERS

1 . . . . 1.75

LONER
Fleetway

1 Pt. 1 of 7 . . . . 1.95
2 Pt. 2 . . . . 1.95
3 Pt. 3 . . . . 1.95
4 Pt. 4 . . . . 1.95
5 Pt. 5 . . . . 1.95
6 Pt. 6 . . . . 1.95

LONE WOLF & CUB
First

1 FM(c) 9.00
1a 2nd printing 2.50
1b 3rd printing 1.50
2 . . . . 4.00
2a 2nd printing 2.00
3 . . . . 3.50
4 thru 10 . . . . @3.00
11 thru 17 . . . . @2.75
18 thru 25 . . . . @2.50
26 thru 36 . . . . @2.95
37 and 38 . . . . @3.25
39 120 Page 5.95
40 . . . . 3.25
41 MP(c), 60 page 3.95
42 MP(c) 3.25
43 MP(c) 3.25
44 MP(c) 3.25
45 MP(c) 3.25

LORD OF THE DEAD
Conquest

1 R.E.Howard adapt. 2.95

LOST ANGEL
Caliber

1 . . . . 3.50

Lone Wolf & Cub #8 © First Publ.

LOST CONTINENT
Eclipse

1 thru 5 . . . . @3.50

LOVE AND ROCKETS
Fantagraphics

1 HB,B&W cover, adult 85.00
1a HB,Color cover 45.00
1b 2nd printing 4.00
2 HB 18.00
3 HB 15.00
4 HB 15.00
5 HB 15.00
6 HB 7.50
7 HB 7.50
8 HB 7.50
9 HB 7.50
10 HB 9.00
11 HB 4.00
12 HB 4.00
13 HB 4.00
14 HB 4.00
15 HB 4.00
16 thru 21 HB . . . . @3.50
22 thru 39 HB . . . . @3.00
Bonanza rep. 2.95

LOVE FANTASY

1 . . . . 2.00

LUGH, LORD OF LIGHT

1 . . . . 2.50
2 . . . . 1.75

LUM*URUSEI YATSURA

1 Art by Rumiko Takahashi 2.95
2 . . . . 2.95
3 . . . . 2.95
4 . . . . 2.95
5 . . . . 3.25
6 thru 8 . . . . @2.95

M.C. GRIFFIN

1 . . . . 1.95

MACABRE

1 thru 2.00

MACH 1
Fleetway

1 I:John Probe-Secret Agent 1.95

MACK THE KNIFE
1 . . . . 2.50

MACKENZIE QUEEN
1 thru 5 . . . . @3.75

MACROSS II
Viz

1 Macross Saga sequel 2.75
2 A:Ishtar 2.75
3 F:Reporter Hibiki,Ishtar 2.75
4 V:Feff,The Marduk 2.75
5 . . . . 2.75
6 . . . . 2.75
7 Sylvie Confesses 2.75
8 F:Ishtar 2.75
9 V:Marduk Fleet 2.75

MAD DOG MAGAZINE
1 thru 3 . . . . @1.75

MAD DOGS
Eclipse

1 I:Mad Dogs(Cops) 2.50
2 V:Chinatown Hood 2.50
3 . . . . 2.50

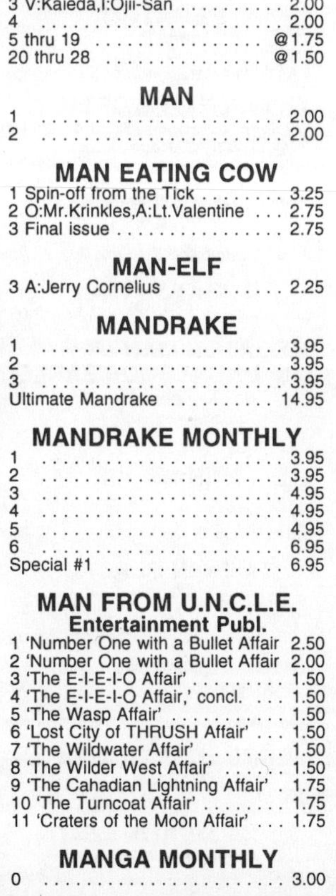

Maelstrom #1 © Aircel

MAELSTROM
Aircel

1 thru 5 . . . . @1.70
6 thru 13 . . . . @1.50

MAGGOTS
1 JSon, mag size 3.95
2 JSon, mag size 3.95
3 GM/JSon,inc.'Some Kinda Beautiful' 3.95

MAGNA-MAN: THE LAST SUPERHERO
1 . . . . 1.95
2 . . . . 1.95
3 . . . . 1.95

MAI, THE PSYCHIC GIRL
Eclipse

1 I:Mai,Alliance of 13 Sages 3.75
1a 2nd printing 2.00
2 V:Wisdom Alliance 2.00
2a 2nd printing 1.50

Mai, the Psychic Girl #7-#8 © Eclipse

3 V:Kaieda,I:Ojii-San 2.00
4 . . . . 2.00
5 thru 19 . . . . @1.75
20 thru 28 . . . . @1.50

MAN
1 . . . . 2.00
2 . . . . 2.00

MAN EATING COW
1 Spin-off from the Tick 3.25
2 O:Mr.Krinkles,A:Lt.Valentine . . . 2.75
3 Final issue 2.75

MAN-ELF
3 A:Jerry Cornelius 2.25

MANDRAKE
1 . . . . 3.95
2 . . . . 3.95
3 . . . . 3.95
Ultimate Mandrake 14.95

MANDRAKE MONTHLY
1 . . . . 3.95
2 . . . . 3.95
3 . . . . 4.95
4 . . . . 4.95
5 . . . . 4.95
6 . . . . 6.95
Special #1 . . . . 6.95

MAN FROM U.N.C.L.E.
Entertainment Publ.

1 'Number One with a Bullet Affair 2.50
2 'Number One with a Bullet Affair 2.00
3 'The E-I-E-I-O Affair' 1.50
4 'The E-I-E-I-O Affair,' concl. . . . 1.50
5 'The Wasp Affair' 1.50
6 'Lost City of THRUSH Affair' . . . 1.50
7 'The Wildwater Affair' 1.50
8 'The Wilder West Affair' 1.50
9 'The Cahadian Lightning Affair' . 1.75
10 'The Turncoat Affair' 1.75
11 'Craters of the Moon Affair' . . . 1.75

MANGA MONTHLY
0 . . . . 3.00

Mangazine #5 © Antartic Press

MANGAZINE
Antartic Press

1 newsprint cover 7.00
1a reprint 3.00
2 . . . . 5.00
3 . . . . 4.00
4 . . . . 2.00
5 . . . . 1.50

New Series

1 . . . . 3.00
2 . . . . 3.00
3 . . . . 1.75
4 . . . . 1.75
5 thru 7 . . . . @1.95
8 thru 13 . . . . @2.25
14 New Format 2.95
15 thru 17 . . . . 2.95

MANIMAL
1 EC,rep. 1.70

MAN IN BLACK CALLED FATE
1 . . . . 2.00

MAN OF RUST
Blackthorne

1 Cover A 1.50
2 Cover B 1.50

MANTUS FILES
Eternity

1 Sidney Williams novel adapt . . . 2.50
2 Vampiric Figures 2.50
3 Secarus' Mansion 2.50
4 A:Secarus 2.50

MARAUDERS OF THE BLACK SUN
1 . . . . 1.75
2 . . . . 1.75

MARCANE
Eclipse

1 Book 1,JMu 5.95

MARIONETTE
1 75

Man of Rust #1 © Blackthorne

MARK, THE
Dark Horse

1 . . . . 1.95
2 thru 7 . . . . @1.75

MARK I
(Prev.: Atomic Comics)

2 . . . . 1.50

MARTIANS

1 . . . . 2.00

MARTIAN SUMMERS

1 . . . . 1.75
2 . . . . 1.75

MASK
Dark Horse

0 'Who's Laughing Now' 5.50

MASKED MAN
Eclipse

12 . . . . 2.00

MASQUERADE
Eclipse

1 . . . . 1.50
2 . . . . 1.95
3 . . . . 1.95

MASTER

1 thru 4 . . . . @1.95

MATT CHAMPION

1 EC 2.00
2 EC 2.00

MAX OF REGULATORS

1 . . . . 5.00
2 . . . . 3.50
3 . . . . 3.50
4 . . . . 3.50

MAX THE MAGNIFICENT

1 . . . . 3.00
2 . . . . 2.00
3 . . . . 2.00

MAXWELL MOUSE FOLLIES

1 Large format (1981) 5.00
1a Comic Size(1986) 3.00
2 thru 6 . . . . @2.00

MAYHEM

1 thru 6 . . . . @2.50

MECHA
Dark Horse

1 thru 6 . . . . @1.75

MECHANOIDS
Caliber

1 . . . . 2.50
2 . . . . 3.50
3 . . . . 3.50

MECHOVERSE

1 . . . . 1.80
2 . . . . 1.50

MECHTHINGS

1 thru 5 . . . . @2.00

MEDUSA

1 . . . . 1.50

MEGATON
Megaton

1 JG(c),EL(1stProWork),GD,MG, A:Ultragirl,Vanguard 10.00
2 EL,JG(pin-up),A:Vanguard 8.00
3 MG,AMe,JG,EL,I:Savage Dragon 25.00
4 AMe,EL,2nd A:Savage Dragon (inc.EL profile) 20.00
5 AMe,RLd(inside front cover) . . . 5.00
6 AMe,JG(inside back cover), EL(Back cover) 5.00
7 AMe 4.00
8 RLd,I:Youngblood(Preview) . . . 25.00

MEGATON MAN

1 . . . . 2.00

MEGATON MAN MEETS THE UNCATEGORIZABLE X-THEMS
Jabberwocky

1 . . . . 2.00

MENAGERIE

1 . . . . 1.95
2 . . . . 1.95
3 . . . . 2.00

MEN IN BLACK
Aircel

1 . . . . 2.25
2 . . . . 2.25
3 . . . . 2.25

(Book II)

1 . . . . 2.50
2 . . . . 2.50
3 last issue 2.50

MERCHANTS OF DEATH
Eclipse

1 thru 5 . . . . @1.95

MERLIN
Adventure Comics

1 Merlin's Visions 2.50
2 V:Warlord Carados 2.50
3 . . . . 2.50
4 Ninevah 2.50
5 D:Hagus 2.50
6 Final Issue 2.50

[2nd Series]

1 Journey of Rhiannon & Tryon . . 2.50
2 Conclusion 2.50

MESSENGER 29

1 . . . . 1.50
2 . . . . 1.50

MESSIAH

1 . . . . 1.50

METACOPS
Midnight Comics

1 . . . . 1.95
2 . . . . 1.95

METAPHYSIQUE
Eclipse

1 NB,Short Stories 2.50
2 NB,Short Stories 2.50

METAL MEN OF MARS

1 . . . . 1.95

MIAMI MICE
Rip Off Press

1 1st printing 3.00
1a 2nd printing 2.00
3 . . . . 2.00
4 Record,A:TMNT 3.00

MICHELANGELO
Mirage

1 TMNT 17.00
1a 2nd Printing 4.50

MICRA
Fictioneer

1 . . . . 4.00
2 . . . . 3.00
3 . . . . 3.00
4 . . . . 2.00
5 . . . . 1.75
6 . . . . 1.75
7 . . . . 1.75
8 . . . . 2.25

MIDNIGHT
Blackthorne

1 thru 4 . . . . @1.75

MIDNITE SKULKER

1 thru 7 . . . . @1.75

MIGHTY GUY
C&T

1 thru 6 . . . . @1.50
Summer Fun Spec #1 . . . . 2.50

MIGHTY MITES
Continüm

1 I:X-Mites 1.95
2 . . . . 1.95

MIGHTY MOUSE ADVENTURE MAGAZINE

1 . . . . 2.00

MIGHTY THUN'DA KING OF THE CONGO

1 . . . . 2.50

MIGHTY TINY

1 thru 4 . . . . @1.75
5 . . . . 2.50
Mouse Marines Collection rep. . . . 7.50

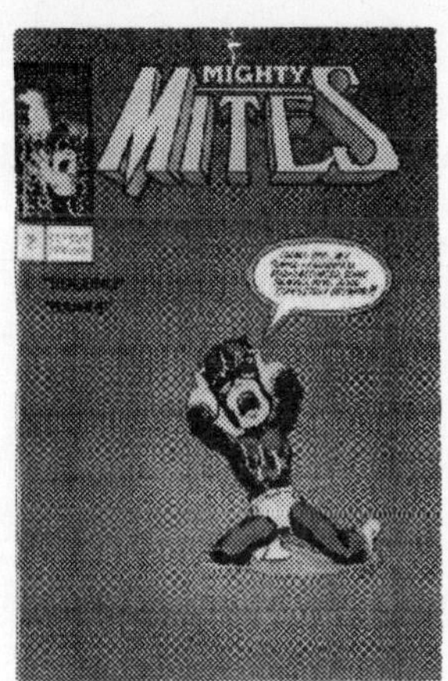

Mighty Mites #2 © Continüm

MIKE MIST MINUTE MYSTERIES
Eclipse

1 .... 3.00

MIRACLE SQUAD BLOOD & DUST
Apple

1 .... 1.95
2 .... 1.95
3 .... 1.95

MISSING BEINGS

1 Special 2.25

MISSING LINK

1 .... 1.70
2 .... 1.70

MISTER X
Vortex

Vol 2
1 thru 11 .... @2.00

MITES

1 .... 2.50
1a 1.90
2B 1.80
3 .... 1.80
4 .... 1.80

MODERN PULP
Special Studio

1 Rep.from January Midnight 2.75

MOGOBI DESERT RATS
Midnight Comics

1 I&O:Desert Rats 'Waste of the World' 2.25

MONSTER BOY
Monster Comics

1 A:Monster Boy 2.25

MONSTER FRAT HOUSE
Eternity

1 .... 2.25

MONSTER POSSE
Malibu

1 I:Monster Posse 2.50
2 I:P.O.N.E,Wack Mack Dwac's sister,D-Vicious 2.50

MONSTERS ATTACK

1 GM,JSe 2.00
2 GC 1.75
3 ATh,GC 1.49

MOONSTRUCK

1 .... 2.00

MOONTRAP

Special #1 .... 2.50

MORPHS

1 .... 2.00
2 .... 2.00
3 .... 2.00
4 .... 2.00

MORTAR MAN
Marshall Comics

1 I:Mortar Man 1.95
2 thru 3 .... 1.95

MORTY THE DOG

1 .... 2.00
1 digest size 3.95

MR. CREAM PUFF

1 .... 1.75

MR. DOOM

1 .... 1.95
2 .... 1.95

MR. FIXITT
Apple

1 .... 1.95
2 .... 1.95

MR. MONSTER
Dark Horse

1 .... 3.50
2 .... 2.50
3 Alan Moore story 2.50
4 .... 2.50
5 I:Monster Boy 2.00
6 .... 2.00
7 .... 2.00
8 V:Vampires (giant size) 4.95

MR. MYSTIC
Eclipse

1 Will Eisner 2.50

MS. TREE'S THRILLING DETECTIVE ADVENTURES
Eclipse

1 Miller pin up 4.00
2 .... 2.50
3 .... 2.00
Becomes:

MS. TREE

4 thru 6 .... @2.00
7 .... 2.50
8 .... 8.00
9 .... 2.00
Aardvark Vanaheim
10 thru 18 .... @2.00
Renegade
19 thru 49 .... @2.00
50 .... 4.50
1 3-D Classic 2.95

Ms. Tree #9 © Eclipse Comics

MUMMY, THE
Monster Comics

1 A:Dr.Clarke,Prof.Belmore 1.95
2 Mummy's Curse 1.95
3 A:Carloph 1.95
4 V:Carloph, conc. 1.95

MUMMY'S CURSE
Aircel

1 thru 4 .... @2.25

MURCIELAGA: SHE-BAT
Hero Graphics

1 Daerick Gross reps. 1.50
2 Reps. contd 2.95

MURDER
Renegade

1 SD 1.70
2 Cl(c) 1.70
3 SD 1.70

MURDER (2nd series)

1 .... 2.00

MUTANT FORCES

1 .... 1.50

MUTANT ZONE
Aircel

1 Future story 2.50
2 F.B.I. Drone Exterminators 2.50
3 conclusion 2.50

MYRON MOOSE FUNNIES

1 thru 3 .... @1.75

MYSTERY MAN
Slave Labor

1 thru 5 .... @1.75

MYSTICAL NINJA

1 .... 1.50

MYTH ADVENTURES
Warp Graphics

1 Mag size 1.50
2 thru 4 .... @1.50

5 Comic size ... 1.50
6 thru 11 ... @1.50
12 ... 1.75

MYTH CONCEPTIONS
Apple

1 ... 1.75
2 ... 1.75
3 thru 8 ... @1.95

MYTHROS

1 Mini series ... 1.50

NAIVE INTER-DIMENSIONAL COMMANDO KOALAS
Eclipse

1 ... 1.50

NATURE OF THE BEAST
Caliber

1 'The Beast' ... 2.95

Nausicaä of the Valley of Wind #6 © Viz Comics

NAUSICAÄ OF THE VALLEY OF WIND
Viz Select

Book One ... 4.50
Book Two ... 5.50
Book Three ... 4.00
Book Four ... 3.00
Book Five ... 2.50
Book Six ... 2.95
Book Seven ... 2.95
Part 2 #1 ... 2.95
Part 2 #2 ... 2.95
Part 2 #3 ... 2.95
Part 2 #4 ... 2.95

NAZ RAT
Eternity

1 ... 2.50
2 ... 2.00
3 ... 1.80
4 ... 1.80

NEAT STUFF

13 ... 2.50

Naz Rat #4 © Eternity

NEGATIVE BURN
Caliber

1 I:Matrix 7 ... 2.95
2 thru 3 ... 2.95

NEIL AND BUZZ

1 ... 2.00

NEIL THE HORSE
Aardvark Vanaheim

1 Art:Arn Sara ... 6.00
1a 2nd printing ... 2.00
2 ... 3.00
3 ... 4.00
4 ... 3.00
5 Video Warriors ... 2.00
6 Video Warriors ... 2.00
7 Video Warriors ... 2.00
8 Outer Space ... 2.00
9 Conan ... 2.00
10 ... 2.00

Renegade

11 Fred Astair ... 1.70
12 ... 1.70
13 ... 1.70
14 Special ... 3.00
15 ... 1.70

NEMESIS
Fleetway

1 thru 16 ... @1.95

NEO CANTON LEGACY

1 ... 2.00

NEOMAN

1 ... 1.75
2 ... 1.75
3 double-size ... 3.50

NEON CITY
Innovation

1 ... 2.25

NERVE

1 ... 2.50
2 ... 1.75
3 ... 1.50
4 ... 1.50
5 ... 1.50

NERVOUS REX

1 ... 3.00
1a 2nd printing ... 2.00
2 ... 3.00
3 ... 3.00
4 ... 2.50
5 thru 10 ... @2.00
GraphicNovel ... 3.50

NETHERWORLDS

1 ... 1.50
2 ... 1.50
3 ... 1.95
4 ... 1.95

NEW BEGINNINGS

1 ... 1.75
2 ... 1.75

NEW ENGLAND GOTHIC

3 ... 2.00

NEW ERADICATORS

Vol 2 #1 NewBeginnings ... 2.00
Vol 2 #2 NewBeginnings ... 2.00
Vol 2 #3 NewFriends ... 2.00

NEW FRONTIER
Dark Horse

1 From series in Heavy Metal ... 2.75
2 Who Killed Ruby Fields? ... 2.75
3 Conclusion ... 2.75

NEW FRONTIERS

1 CS(c) ... 3.00
1a 2nd Printing ... 1.75

NEW FRONTIERS
Evolution

1 A:Action Master, Green Ghost ... 1.95

NEW GOLDEN AGE

1 ... 1.50

NEW HERO COMICS
Pierce

1 ... 1.00
2 ... 1.00

NEW HUMANS
Eternity

1 ... 1.80
2 thru 15 ... @1.95
Annual #1 ... 2.95

NEW HUMANS

1 Shattered Earth Chron ... 1.95

NEW KIDS ON THE BLOCK
Harvey

1 ... 1.25

NEW L.I.F.E. BRIGADE

1 ... 1.80
2 ... 1.80
3 ... 1.80

NEW POWER STARS

1 ... 2.00

NEW REALITY

1 thru 6 ... @1.25

NEWSTRALIA
Innovation
(Prev. Color)

4 ... 2.25

5 . . . . 2.25

NEW TRIUMPH

1 . . . . 3.00
1a 2nd printing 1.75
2 thru 4 . . . . @1.50

NEW YORK CITY OUTLAWS

1 thru 5 . . . . @2.50

NEW YORK, YEAR ZERO
Eclipse

1 thru 4 . . . . @2.00

NEXUS
Capital

1 SR,I:Nexus,large size 35.00
2 SR,Mag size 15.00
3 SR,Mag size 7.00

NIGHT LIFE
Caliber

1 thru 7 . . . . @1.50

NIGHT MASTER

1 Vigil 5.50
2 Vigil 2.50
3 . . . . 1.50

NIGHT OF THE LIVING DEAD
Fantaco

0 prelude 1.75
1 based on cult classic movie . . . 4.95
2 Movie adapt,continued 4.95
3 Movie adapt,conclusion 4.95
5 . . . . 5.95

NIGHTSTAR

1 . . . . 2.50

NIGHT'S CHILDREN
Fantaco

1 . . . . 3.50
2 . . . . 3.50
3 . . . . 3.50

NIGHT STREETS
Arrow

1 . . . . 2.50
2 thru 4 . . . . @1.50

NIGHT VISITORS

1 . . . . 1.95

NIGHT WOLF

1 thru 4 . . . . @1.75

NIGHTVEIL'S CAULDRON OF HORROR

1 . . . . 2.50

NIGHTWIND

1 & 2 . . . . @1.95

NIGHT ZERO
Fleetway

1 thru 4 . . . . @1.95

NINGA-BOTS
Prelude

1 . . . . 2.00

NINJA
Eternity

1 . . . . 3.00

Ninja #5 © Eternity

2 thru 6 . . . . @1.80
7 thru 13 . . . . @1.95

NINJA ELITE

1 thru 5 . . . . @1.50
6 thru 8 . . . . @1.95

NINJA FUNNIES
Eternity

1 . . . . 1.80
2 . . . . 1.80
3 thru 5 . . . . @1.95

NINJA HIGH SCHOOL
Eternity

1 . . . . 1.75
2 thru 4 . . . . @1.50
5 thru 22 . . . . @1.95
23 Zardon Assassin 2.25
24 . . . . 2.25
25 Return of the Zetramen 2.25
26 Stanley the Demon 2.25
27 Return of the Zetramen 2.25
28 Threat of the super computer . 2.25
29 V:Super Computer 2.25
30 I:Akaru 2.25
31 Jeremy V:Akaru 2.25
32 V:Giant Monsters Pt.1 . . . . . . 2.50
33 V:Giant Monsters Pt.2 . . . . . . 2.50
34 V:Giant Monsters Pt.3 . . . . . . 2.50
35 thru 43 . . . . @2.50
Special #1 . . . . 2.95
Special #2 . . . . 2.95
Special #3 . . . . 2.95
Special #3 1/2 . . . . 2.25
Annual 1989 . . . . 2.95
Annual 3 . . . . 3.95

NINJA HIGH SCHOOL GIRLS
Antarctic Press

0 . . . . 2.75
1 rep. 2.75
2 rep. 2.75
3 thru 5 rep. 3.95

NINJA HIGH SCHOOL PERFECT MEMORY
Antarctic Press

1 thru 2 . . . . 4.95

NINJA HIGH SCHOOL SMALL BODIES
Antarctic Press

1 "Monopolize" 2.50

NO COMICS

1 . . . . 2.00
2 . . . . 2.00

NO GUTS, NO GLORY
Fantaco

1 One Shot, K.Eastman's 1st solo work since TMNT 2.95

NOMADS OF ANTIQUITY

1 thru 6 . . . . @1.50

NORMAL MAN
Aardvark Vanaheim

1 . . . . 4.00
2 thru 9 . . . . @2.50

Renegade

10 thru 19 . . . . @1.70

NORTHGUARD AND THE MANDES CONCLUSION

1 thru 3 . . . . @1.95

NOSFERATU
Dark Horse

1 The Last Vampire 3.95
2 . . . . 2.95

NULL PATROL

1 thru 2 . . . . @1.50

NYOKA THE JUNGLE GIRL
AC Comics

3 . . . . 2.25
4 . . . . 2.25
5 . . . . 2.50

OCTOBERFEST
Now & Then

1 (1976) Dave Sim 15.00

OFFERINGS
Cry For Dawn

1 Sword & Sorcery stories 2.75

OKTOBERFEST
Now & Then

1 (1976) Dave Sim 20.00

OFFICIAL BUZ SAWYER

1 . . . . 2.00
2 . . . . 2.00
3 . . . . 2.00
4 . . . . 1.50
5 . . . . 2.00
6 . . . . 2.00

OFFICIAL HOW TO DRAW G.I. JOE
Blackthorne

1 thru 5 . . . . @2.00

OFFICIAL HOW TO DRAW ROBOTECH
Blackthorne

12 . . . . 2.95
13 thru 16 . . . . @2.00

OFFICIAL HOW TO DRAW TRANSFORMERS

Blackthorne

1 thru 7 . . . . @2.00

OFFICIAL JOHNNY HAZARD

1 . . . . 2.00
2 . . . . 2.00
3 . . . . 2.00
4 . . . . 1.50
5 . . . . 2.00

OFFICIAL JUNGLE JIM

1 thru 5 AR,rep. . . . . @2.00
6 AR,rep. 1.50
7 thru 10 AR,rep. . . . . @2.00
11 thru 20 AR,rep. . . . . @2.50
Annual #1 . . . . 2.00
Giant Size 3.95

OFFICIAL MANDRAKE

1 thru 5 . . . . @2.00
6 . . . . 1.50
7 thru 10 . . . . @2.00
11 . . . . 2.50
12 . . . . 2.00
13 thru 17 . . . . @2.50
Annual #1 . . . . 3.95
King Size #1 . . . . 3.95
Giant Size #1 . . . . 3.95

OFFICIAL MODESTY BLAISE

1 thru 4 . . . . @2.00
5 . . . . 1.50
6 thru 14 . . . . @2.00
Annual #1 . . . . 3.95
King Size #1 . . . . 3.95

OFFICIAL PRINCE VALIANT

1 Hal Foster,rep. 2.00
2 Hal Foster,rep. 2.00
3 Hal Foster,rep. 2.00
4 Hal Foster,rep. 2.00
5 Hal Foster,rep. 2.00
6 Hal Foster,rep. 2.00
7 . . . . 1.50
8 thru 14 . . . . @2.00
15 thru 24 . . . . @2.50
Annual #1 . . . . 3.95
King Size#1 . . . . 3.95

OFFICIAL RIP KIRBY

1 AR 2.00
2 AR 2.00
3 AR 2.00
4 AR 1.50
5 AR 2.00
6 AR 2.00

OFFICIAL SECRET AGENT

1 thru 5 AW rep . . . . @2.00
6 AW 1.50
7 AW 2.00
8 AW 2.00
9 AW 2.00

OFFWORLDERS' QUARTERLY

1 . . . . 1.50

OF MYTHS AND MEN

1 . . . . 1.75
2 . . . . 1.75

OMEGA
North Star

1 1st pr by Rebel,rare 80.00
1a Vigil(Yellow Cov.) 27.00
2 . . . . 2.00

OMEN
North Star

1 . . . . 8.00
1a 2nd printing 2.00
2 thru 4 . . . . @3.50

OMICRON

1 . . . . 2.25
2 . . . . 2.25
3 . . . . 2.50

OMNIMAN

1 . . . . 2.00

OMNIMEN

1 . . . . 3.50

ONE SHOT WESTERN
Calibur

One Shot F:Savage Sisters, Tornpath Outlaw 2.50

ONLY A MATTER OF LIFE AND DEATH

1 . . . . 3.95

ON THE ROAD WITH GEORGE & BARBARA IN VACATIONLAND

1 . . . . 2.50

OPEN SEASON
Renegade

1 thru 7 . . . . @2.00

OPERATIVE SCORPIO
Blackthorne

1 . . . . 3.50

ORACLE PRESENTS

1 thru 4 . . . . @1.50

ORBIT
Eclipse

1 . . . . 3.95
2 . . . . 3.95
3 . . . . 4.95

ORIGINAL TOM CORBET
Eternity

1 Rep. Newspaper Strips 2.95
2 Rep. Newspaper Strips 2.95
3 Rep. Newspaper Strips 2.95

ORION
Dark Horse

1 SF manga-Masamune Shirow . . 2.50
2 F:Yamata Empire 2.95

ORLAK: FLESH & STEEL
Caliber

1 '1991 A.D.' 2.50

ORLAK REDUX
Caliber

1 . . . . 3.95

OTHERS, THE
Cormac Publishing

1 . . . . 1.50

OUT OF THIS WORLD

. . . . 3.50

OUTLANDER

1 . . . . 4.50
2 . . . . 3.00

The Others #1 © Cormac Publ.

3 . . . . 2.50
4 . . . . 2.50
5 . . . . 2.50
6 . . . . 1.95
7 . . . . 1.95
8 . . . . 2.25

OUTLANDERS
Dark Horse

1 . . . . 3.00
2 . . . . 2.50
3 thru 7 . . . . @2.00
8 thru 20 . . . . @2.25
21 Operation Phoenix 2.25
22 thru 30 . . . . @2.50
31 Tetsua dying 2.50
32 D:The Emperor 2.50
33 Story finale 2.50
#0 The Key of Graciale 2.75

OUTLANDERS: EPILOGUE
Dark Horse

1 . . . . 2.75

OVERLOAD
Eclipse

1 . . . . 1.50

OVERTURE

1 . . . . 2.25
2 . . . . 2.25

PAJAMA CHRONICLES

1 . . . . 1.50
2 . . . . 1.75
3 . . . . 1.75

PANDA KHAN

1 thru 4 . . . . @2.00

PAPER CUTS

1 E Starzer-1982 . . . . 17.50
2 . . . . 2.50
3 . . . . 2.50

PARTICLE DREAMS
Fantagraphics

1 . . . . 3.00
2 . . . . 2.25
3 . . . . 2.25
4 . . . . 2.25

5 . . . . 2.25
6 . . . . 2.25

PARTNERS IN PANDEMONIUM
Caliber

1 'Hell on Earth' 2.50
2 Sheldon&Murphy become mortal 2.50
3 A:Abra Cadaver 2.50

PARTS OF A HOLE
Caliber

1 Short Stories 2.50

PARTS UNKNOWN
Eclipse

1 I:Spurr,V:Aliens 2.50
2 Aliens on Earth cont. 2.50

PATRICK RABBIT

1 . . . . 2.00
2 . . . . 2.00
3 . . . . 2.00

PAUL THE SAMURAI
New England Comics

1 . . . . 2.75
2 . . . . 2.75
3 . . . . 2.75

PELLESTAR

1 . . . . 1.95
2 . . . . 1.95
3 . . . . 1.95

PENDULUM
Adventure

1 Big Hand,Little Hand 2.50
2 The Immortality Formula 2.50

PENGUIN AND PENCILGUIN

1 thru 6 . . . . @2.00

PENTACLE: SIGN OF 5
Eternity

1 . . . . 2.25
2 Det.Sandler,H.Smitts 2.25
3 Det.Sandler => New Warlock . . 2.25
4 5 warlocks Vs. Kaji 2.50

PETER RISK, MONSTER MASHER

1 thru 4 . . . . @2.00
5 . . . . 1.50

PHANTOM

1 . . . . 5.95
2 . . . . 5.95
3 . . . . 5.95
4 and 5 . . . . @6.95

PHANTOM OF THE OPERA
Eternity

1 . . . . 1.95

PHASE ONE
Victory

1 . . . . 3.00
2 . . . . 2.00
3 thru 5 . . . . @1.50

PHIGMENTS
Eternity

1 . . . . 5.00
2 . . . . 2.00
3 . . . . 1.95

PHONEY PAGES
Renegade

1 . . . . 1.70
2 . . . . 1.70

PIED PIPER OF HAMELIN
Tome

1 . . . . 2.95

PINEAPPLE ARMY

1 thru 10 . . . . @1.75

PINK FLOYD EXPERIENCE
Revolutionary

1 based on rock group 2.50
2 Dark Side of the Moon 2.50
3 Dark Side of the Moon, Wish you were here 2.50
4 The Wall 2.50
5 A Momentary lapse of reason . . 2.50

PIRATE CORPS!
Eternity

6 . . . . 1.95
7 . . . . 1.95
Spec. #1 . . . . 1.95

Piranha Is Loose! #1 © Special Studio

PIRANHA! IS LOOSE
Special Studio

1 Drug Runners,F:Piranha 2.95
2 Expedition into Terror 2.95

P.J. WARLOCK
Eclipse

1 . . . . 2.00
2 . . . . 2.00
3 . . . . 2.00

PLANET COMICS
Blackthorne (Prev. Color)

4 . . . . 2.00
5 . . . . 2.00

PLANET OF TERROR

1 BW 1.75

Planet of the Apes
© Adventure Comics

PLANET OF THE APES
Adventure Comics

1 WD,collect.ed. 7.00
1 2 covers 5.00
1a 2nd printing 2.50
2 . . . . 3.00
3 . . . . 2.75
4 . . . . 2.75
5 D:Alexander? 2.75
6 Welcome to Ape City 2.75
7 . . . . 2.75
8 Christmas Story 2.50
9 Swamp Ape Village 2.50
10 Swamp Apes in Forbidden City 2.50
11 Ape War continues 2.50
12 W.Alexander/Coure 2.50
13 Planet of Apes/Alien Nation/ Ape City x-over 2.50
14 Countdown to Zero Pt.1 . . . . . 2.50
15 Countdown to Zero Pt.2 . . . . . 2.50
16 Countdown to Zero Pt.3 . . . . . 2.50
17 Countdown to Zero Pt.4 . . . . . 2.50
18 Ape City (after Ape Nation mini-series 2.50
19 1991 'Conquest..' tie-in 2.50
20 Return of the Ape Riders 2.50
21 The Terror Beneath,Pt.1 . . . . . 2.50
22 The Terror Beneath,Pt.2 . . . . . 2.50
23 The Terror Beneath,Pt.3 . . . . . 2.50
Ann #1,'Day on Planet o/t Apes' . 3.50

PLANET OF THE APES BLOOD OF THE APES
Adventure Comics

1 A:Tonus the Butcher 3.00
2 Valia/Taylorite Connection 2.50
3 Ape Army in Phis 2.50

PLANET OF THE APES: FORBIDDEN ZONE
Adventure

1 Battle for the Planet o/t Apes & Planet o/t Apes tie-in 2.50
2 A:Juilus 2.50

PLANET OF THE APES: SINS OF THE FATHER
Adventure Comics

1 Conquest Tie in 2.50

PLANET OF THE APES URCHAKS' FOLLY
Adventure Comics

1 . . . . . 3.00
2 . . . . . 2.50
3 'The Taylorites' 2.50
4 Conclusion 2.50

PLANET 29
Caliber

1 A Future Snarl Tale 2.50
2 A:Biff,Squakman 2.50

PLANET X
Eternity

1 . . . . . 2.50

PLAN 9 FROM OUTER SPACE
Eternity

1 . . . . . 2.50
2 . . . . . 2.25
3 . . . . . 2.25

PLASMA BABY
Caliber

1 'Strange New World' 2.50

PLASTRON CAFE
Mirage

1 Eastman,Laird,RV,inc.North by Downeast 2.25

PLAYGROUND 1826
Caliber

1 . . . . . 2.50

POINT BLANK
Eclipse

1 thru 5 . . . . . @2.95

POLIS
Brave New World

1 I:Polis 2.50

PORK KNIGHT
Silver Snail

1 . . . . . 1.75

PORT
Silver Wolf

1 . . . . . 1.50
2 . . . . . 1.50

PORTABLE LOWLIFE

1 Real life Adventures 4.95

PORTIA PRINZ
Eclipse

1 thru 5 . . . . . @2.00

POSSIBLE MAN

1 . . . . . 1.75
2 . . . . . 1.75

POST BROTHERS
Rip Off Press

15 thru 18 . . . . . @2.00
19 . . . . . 2.50
20 . . . . . 2.50

POWER COMICS

1 Smart-Early Ardvaark 25.00
1a 2nd printing 8.00
2 I:Cobalt Blue 10.00
3 . . . . . 3.00
4 . . . . . 3.00
5 . . . . . 4.00

POWER COMICS
Eclipse

1 BB,DGb,Powerbolt 2.00
2 BB,DGb 2.00
3 BB,DGb 2.00

POWER CORPS

1 . . . . . 2.50
2 . . . . . 2.50

POWER PLAYS

1 . . . . . 1.75
2 . . . . . 1.75
3 . . . . . 1.75

POWER PRINCIPLE

1 thru 3 . . . . . @1.95

POWER STATION

1 . . . . . 1.75

POWER UNLIMITED

1 . . . . . 1.95

PRETEEN DIRTY GENE KUNG FU KANGAROOS
Blackthorne

1 . . . . . 1.50
2 . . . . . 1.50

PREY
Monster Comics

1 I:Prey,A:Andrina 2.25
2 V:Andrina 2.25
3 conclusion 2.25

PRICE, THE

1 Dreadstar mag. size 20.00

PRIME CUTS
Fantagraphics

1 adult 3.50
2 thru 6 . . . . . @3.50
7 thru 12 . . . . . @3.95

PRIMER
Comico

1 . . . . . 6.00
2 MW,I:Grendel 100.00
3 . . . . . 5.00
4 . . . . . 5.00
5 SK(1st work) 18.00
6 IN,Evangeline 18.00

PRIME SLIME TALES
Mirage

1 . . . . . 5.00
2 . . . . . 2.50
3 thru 6 . . . . . @1.50

PRINCE VALIANT

1 thru 4 . . . . . @4.95
Spec #1 . . . . . 6.95

PRINCE VALIANT MONTHLY

1 thru 6 . . . . . @3.95
6 . . . . . 4.95
7 . . . . . 4.95
8 . . . . . 4.95
9 . . . . . 6.95

PRIVATE EYES
Eternity

1 Saint rep. 1.95
2 . . . . . 1.95
3 . . . . . 1.95
4 . . . . . 1.95
5 . . . . . 1.95

PROBE

1 . . . . . 1.80
2 . . . . . 1.80

PROGENY

Spec 4.95

PROJECT: HERO

1 . . . . . 1.50
2 . . . . . 1.50
3 . . . . . 1.50

PROTOTYPE

1 . . . . . 1.75

PROWLER IN WHITE "WHITE ZOMBIE", THE

1 . . . . . 2.00

PRYDERI TERRA

1 . . . . . 1.75
2 . . . . . 1.75

PSI–JUDGE ANDERSON

1 thru 15 . . . . . @1.95

PSYCHOMAN
Revolutionary

1 I:Psychoman 2.50

Puma Blues #1 © Aardvark Vanaheim

PUMA BLUES
Aardvark Vanaheim

1 10,000 printed 4.50
1a 2nd printing 2.00
2 . . . . . 3.00
3 . . . . . 2.00
4 thru 19 . . . . . @1.70
20 Special 2.25

Mirage

21 thru 24 . . . . . @1.70
25 . . . . . 2.50
26 thru 28 . . . . . @1.75

PURGATORY USA

1 . . . . . 1.75
2 . . . . . 1.75
3 . . . . . 1.95

QUACK
Star Reach
1 . . . . . 2.00
2 . . . . . 2.00
3 . . . . . 2.00
4 Dave Sim 3.00
5 Dave Sim 3.00
6 . . . . . 2.00

QUADRO GANG
1 . . . . . 1.25

QUAZAR
1 . . . . . 2.00

QUEST PRESENTS
Quest
1 JD 1.75
2 JD 1.75
3 JD 1.75

RACE OF SCORPIONS
Dark Horse
1 A:Argos,Dito,Alma,Ka 2.25

RADIO BOY
Eclipse
1 . . . . . 2.00

RADREX
1 . . . . . 2.25
2 . . . . . 2.25
3 . . . . . 2.25

RAGNAROK
Sun Comics
1 I:Ragnarok Guy,Honey 2.50
2 The Melder Foundation 2.50
3 Guy/Honey mission contd. 2.50
4 I:Big Gossage 2.50

RAIKA
Sun Comics
1 thru 12 . . . . . @2.50

Ralph Snart Adventures #1
© Now Comics

RALPH SNART
Now
1 . . . . . 5.00
2 . . . . . 4.00
3 . . . . . 4.00
1 Vol. II 3.00
2 thru 10 . . . . . @1.50
Trade Paperback 2.95

RAMBO
Blackthorne
1 thru 5 . . . . . @2.00

RAMBO III
Blackthorne
1 . . . . . 2.00

RAMM
1 . . . . . 1.50

RAMPAGE ALLEY
1 . . . . . 1.75
2 . . . . . 1.75

RANMA 1/2
1 thru 2 . . . . . 2.75

RAPHAEL
1 TMNT 17.50
1a 2nd printing 7.50

RAT FINK
World of Fandom
1 color cover 2.50
2 color cover 2.50

RAW MEDIA MAGS.
Reb
1 TV,SK,short stories 5.00

REACTOMAN
1 thru 4 . . . . . @1.50
collection 4.95

REAGAN'S RAIDERS
1 thru 6 . . . . . @2.50

REAL LIFE
1 . . . . . 2.50

REALM
Arrow
1 Fantasy 7.50
2 . . . . . 4.00
3 . . . . . 3.00
4 TV,Deadworld 21.00
5 I:L.Kazan 2.00
6 thru 13 . . . . . @1.50
14 thru 18 . . . . . @1.95
19 . . . . . 2.50

REAL STUFF
Fantagraphic
1 thru 12 . . . . . 2.50

RED FOX
Harrier
1 scarce 6.00
1a 2nd printing 2.50
2 rare 5.00
3 . . . . . 3.00
4 I:White Fox 3.00
5 I:Red Snail 3.00
6 . . . . . 1.75
7 Wbolton 1.75
8 . . . . . 1.75
9 Demosblurth 1.75

RED & STUMPY
Parody Press
1 Ren & Stimpy parody 2.95

RED HEAT
Blackthorne
1 . . . . . 2.00

REDLAW
Caliber
1 Preview Killer of Crows 2.50

RED SHETLAND
Blackthorne
1 . . . . . 2.00

REID FLEMING
Blackbird-Eclipse
1 I:Reid Fleming 10.00
1a 2nd printing 5.50
1b 3rd printing 2.50
1b 4th printing 2.50
Volume 2
#1 Rogues to Riches Pt.1 . . . . . 6.00
#2 Rogues to Riches Pt.2 . . . . . 4.00
#3 Rogues to Riches Pt.3 . . . . . 3.00
#3a LaterPrinting 2.50
#4 Rogues to Riches Pt.4 . . . . . 3.00
#5 Rogues to Riches Pt.5 . . . . . 2.50

REIGN OF THE DARK LORD
1 . . . . . 1.80
2 . . . . . 1.80
3 . . . . . 1.80
4 . . . . . 1.95

RELENTLESS PURSUIT
1 . . . . . 2.00
2 . . . . . 1.75
3 . . . . . 1.95

RENEGADE
Rip Off Press
1 . . . . . 2.50

RENEGADE RABBIT
1 . . . . . 1.75
2 . . . . . 1.75

RENEGADE ROMANCE
1 . . . . . 2.00
2 . . . . . 3.50

RESISTANCE
1 . . . . . 1.95

RETALIATOR
Eclipse
1 I&O:Retaliator 2.50
2 O:Retaliator cont. 2.50

RETIEF
1 thru 6 . . . . . @2.00
[New Series]
1 thru 6 . . . . . @2.25

RETIEF OF THE CDT
1 . . . . . 2.00
2 . . . . . 2.00

RETIEF AND THE WARLORDS
Adventure Comics
1 Keith Laumer Novel Adapt. 2.50
2 Haterakans 2.50
3 Retief Arrested for Treason 2.50
4 Final Battle (last issue) 2.50

RETIEF: DIPLOMATIC IMMUNITY
Adventure Comics

1 Groaci Invasion. 2.50
2 Groaci story cont. 2.50

RETIEF: THE GIANT KILLER
Adventure Comics
1 V:Giant Dinasaur 2.50

RETIEF: GRIME & PUNISHMENT
Adventure Comics
1 Planet Slunch 2.50

RETROGRADE
Eternity
1 thru 4 . . . . @1.95

RETURN OF SKYMAN
1 SD 1.75

REVOLVER
Renegade
1 SD 1.70
2 thru 6 . . . . @1.70

Annual #1 . . . . 2.00

REVOLVING DOORS
Blackthorne
1 . . . . 1.75
2 . . . . 1.75
3 . . . . 1.75
Graphic Novel 3.95

RHAJ
1 . . . . 2.00
2 . . . . 2.00

RHUDIPRRT PRINCE OF FUR
1 . . . . 2.00

RICK GEARY'S WONDERS & ODDITIES
1 . . . . 2.00

RICK RAYGUN
1 . . . . 2.00
2 thru 8 . . . . @1.75

RING OF ROSES
Dark Horse
1 Alternate world,1991 . . . . 2.50
2 Plague in London 2.50
3 Plague cont.A:Secret Brotherhood of the Rosy Cross 2.50
4 Conclusion 2.50

RIO KID
Eternity
1 I:Rio Kid 2.50
2 V:Blow Torch Killer 2.50

RION 2990
Rion
1 . . . . 2.75
2 . . . . 1.50

RIP IN TIME
Fantagor
1 RCo,Limited series 3.00
2 RCo 2.00
3 RCo 2.00
4 RCo 2.00
5 RCo,Last 2.00

RIPPER
1 thru 5 . . . . @2.50

RISING STARS
1 . . . . 1.95

RIVIT: COLD-BLOODED COMMANDO FROG
1 . . . . 1.75

ROACHMILL
1 . . . . 5.50
2 . . . . 3.00
3 . . . . 3.00
4 . . . . 3.00
Dark Horse
1 thru 8 . . . . @3.50
9 and 10 . . . . @2.00

ROBIN HOOD
1 thru 3 . . . . @2.25

ROBIN RED
1 thru 3 . . . . @1.75

R.O.B.O.T. BATTALION 2050
Eclipse
1 . . . . 2.00

ROBOT COMICS
1 . . . . 1.50

ROBO WARRIORS
CFW
1 thru 11 . . . . @1.95
Becomes:

KUNG FU WARRIORS

ROBOTECH: INVID WAR
Eternity
1 No Man's Land 2.50
2 V:Defoliators 2.50
3 V:The Invid,Reflex Point 2.50
4 V:The Invid 2.50
5 Moonbase Aluce II 2.50
6 Moonbase-Zentraedi plot 2.50
7 Zentraedi plot contd. 2.50
8 A:Lancer 2.50
9 A:Johnathan Wolfe 2.50
10 . . . . 2.50
11 F:Rand 2.50
12 thru 13 . . . . 2.50

ROBOTECH: INVID WAR AFTERMATH
Eternity
1 thru 6 F:Rand 2.75

ROBOTECH II: THE MALCONTENT UPRISING
Eternity
1 thru 9 . . . . @1.95

ROBOTECH: RETURN TO MACROSS
Eternity
1 thru 5 . . . . 2.50

ROBOTECH II THE SENTINELS
Eternity
1 . . . . 3.50
1a 2nd printing 1.95
2 . . . . 3.00
2a 2nd printing 1.95
3 . . . . 2.00
3a 2nd printing 1.95
4 thru 16 . . . . @1.95
Book 2
1 thru 12 . . . . @2.25
13 thru 17 . . . . @2.25
Cyberpirates 1 . . . . 2.25
Cyberpirates 2 . . . . 2.25
Cyberpirates 3 . . . . 2.25
Cyberpirates 4 finale 2.25
Wedding Special #1 . . . . 1.95
Wedding Special #2 . . . . 1.95
Robotech II Handbook 2.50
Book Three
1 thru 8 V:Invid 2.50

ROBOTECH: UNTOLD STORIES
Eternity
1 . . . . 2.50

ROCITI'S REVENGE
1 . . . . 1.95

ROCK & ROLL COMICS
Revolutionary
1 Guns & Roses 7.50
1a 2nd printing 3.50
1b 3rd printing 2.00
1c 4th-7th printing 2.00
2 Metalica 5.00
2a 2nd printing 3.00
2b 3rd-5th printing 2.00
3 Bon Jovi 3.50
4 Motley Crue 4.00
5 Def Leppard 2.50
6 RollingStones 3.00
6a 2nd-4th printing 2.00
7 The Who 3.00
7a 2nd-3rd printing 2.00
9 Kiss 7.00
9a 2nd-3rd Printing 2.00
10 Warrant/Whitesnake 2.00
10a 2nd Printing 2.00
11 Aerosmith 2.00
12 New Kids on Block 7.00
12a 2nd Printing 2.00
13 LedZeppelin 2.00
14 Sex Pistols 2.00
See Independent Color

ROCKHEADS
1 . . . . 1.95

ROCKIN ROLLIN MINER ANTS
Fate Comics
1 As seen in TMNT #40 . . . . 2.25
1a Gold Variant copy 7.50
2 Elephant Hunting, A:Scorn,Blister 2.25
3 V:Scorn, Inc.,K.Eastman Ant pin-up 2.25
4 Animal Experiments,V:Loboto . . 2.25

ROCKOLA
1 . . . . 1.50

ROLLING STONES: THE SIXTIES
Personality
1 Regular Version 2.95
1a Deluxe Version,w/cards 6.95

ROSCOE THE DAWG
1 thru 4 . . . . @2.00

ROSE
Hero Graphics
1 From The Champions 3.50
2 A:Huntsman 3.50
3 thru 5 . . . . 2.95

ROTTWEILER
1 . . . . 1.50

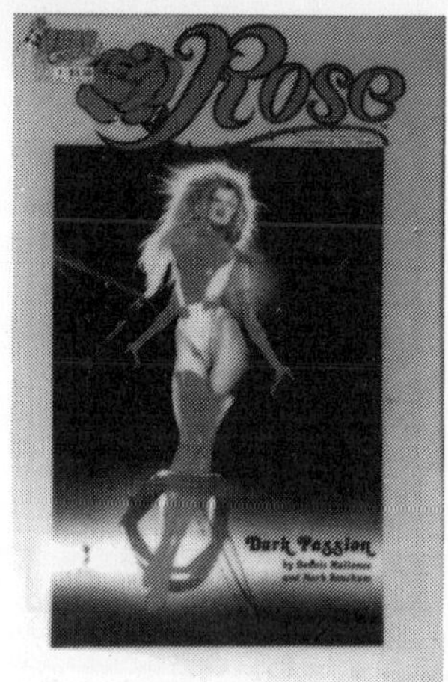

Rose #1 © Hero Graphics

2 . . . . 1.50

ROUGH RAIDERS
1 . . . . 1.80
2 . . . . 1.80
3 . . . . 2.00

ROULETTE
1 . . . . 2.50

ROVERS
Eternity
1 thru 7 . . . . @1.95

RUBES REVIVED
Fish Warp
1 . . . . 2.00
2 . . . . 2.00
3 . . . . 2.00

RUK BUD WEBSTER
Fish Warp
1 thru 3 . . . . @1.70

SAGA OF THE MAN-ELF
1 thru 5 . . . . @2.25

SAGA OF THE VON ERICH WARRIORS
1 . . . . 2.00

SALIMBA
Blackthorne
1 . . . . 3.50

SAMURAI (1st series)
1 . . . . 125.00
2 . . . . 60.00
3 . . . . 60.00
4 . . . . 60.00
5 . . . . 60.00

SAMURAI
Aircel
1 rare 9.00
1a 2nd printing 3.00
1b 3rd printing 2.00
2 . . . . 6.00
2a 2nd printing 2.50
3 . . . . 3.00
4 . . . . 3.00
5 thru 12 . . . . @2.00
13 DK (1st art) 5.00
14 thru 16 DK . . . . @4.00
17 thru 22 . . . . @2.00

[3rd series]
#1 . . . . 1.70
#2 . . . . 1.70
#3 . . . . 1.70
#4 . . . . 1.95
#5 . . . . 1.95
#6 . . . . 1.95
#7 . . . . 1.95
Compilation Book 4.95

SAMURAI FUNNIES
Solson
1 . . . . 2.00
2 . . . . 2.00
3 . . . . 2.00

SAMURAI PENGUIN
Solson
1 . . . . 3.00
2 I:Dr.Radium 2.00
3 . . . . 2.00
4 . . . . 1.50
5 FC 1.50
6 color 2.25
7 . . . . 2.25
8 . . . . 1.75
9 . . . . 1.75

SAMURAI 7
Gauntlet Comics
1 I: Samurai 7 . . . . 2.50

SAMURAI, SON OF DEATH
Eclipse
1 . . . . 3.95
1a 2nd printing 3.95

SANCTION 7
1 . . . . 1.95
2 . . . . 1.95

SANCTUARY
Viz
1 World of Yakuza 4.95
2 thru 4 . . . . @4.95
5 thru 9 . . . . @4.95

SANTA CLAWS
Eternity
1 'Deck the Mall with Blood and Corpses' 2.95

SAVAGE HENRY
Vortex
1 thru 13 . . . . @1.75

Rip Off Press
14 thru 15 . . . . @2.00
16 thru 24 . . . . @2.50

SAVIOR
1 thru 5 . . . . @1.95

SAX AND COMPANY
1 . . . . 1.50
2 . . . . 1.50

SCARAMOUCH
Innovation
1 . . . . 2.50

SCARLET IN GASLIGHT
1 A:SherlockHolmes 4.00
2 . . . . 3.00
3 . . . . 2.50
4 . . . . 2.50

SCARLET KISS: THE VAMPIRE
1 . . . . 2.95

SCIMIDAR
Eternity
1 . . . . 4.25
1a 2nd Printing 2.50
2 . . . . 3.00
3 . . . . 3.00
4 HotCover 3.50
4A MildCover 3.00

SCOUT HANDBOOK
Eclipse
1 . . . . 1.75

SCRATCH
Outside
1 . . . . 3.00
2 . . . . 2.00
3 . . . . 1.75
4 . . . . 1.75

SCREENPLAY
1 . . . . 1.75
2 and 3 . . . . @1.95

SCROG SPECIAL
1 . . . . 2.50

SECRET DOORS
1 . . . . 6.00
1a 2nd printing 2.00

SECRET OF THE SALAMANDER
Dark Horse
1 Jacquestardi, rep 2.95

SERPENT RISING
Gauntlet Comics
1 . . . . 2.95

SENTINEL
1 . . . . 1.95
2 . . . . 1.95
3 . . . . 1.95
4 . . . . 1.95

SERIUS BOUNTY HUNTER
1 thru 4 . . . . @1.75

SHADOWBLADE
1 . . . . 2.50
2 . . . . 2.50
3 . . . . 1.95
4 . . . . 1.95

SHADOWLAND
1 . . . . 2.25
2 . . . . 2.25

SHADOWALKER
Aircel
1 thru 4 . . . . @1.70

SHADOW LORD
1 . . . . 1.50

SHADOWMEN
1 . . . . 2.25

SHADOW OF THE GROUND
1 Groundhog 1.25

SHADOWS FROM THE GRAVE

1 . . . . . 2.00
2 . . . . . 2.00

Shanghaied #2 © Eternity

SHADOW SLAYER

0 . . . . . 1.95

SHADOW WARRIOR

1 . . . . . 1.60
2 . . . . . 1.60

SHALOMAN

1 thru 5 . . . . . @1.75

SHANGHAIED
Eternity

1 . . . . . 1.80
2 . . . . . 1.80
3 . . . . . 1.95
4 . . . . . 1.95

SHAOLIN: 2000

1 . . . . . 1.50

SHATTERED EARTH
Eternity

1 thru 9 . . . . . @1.95

SHATTERPOINT
Eternity

1 thru 4 Broid Mini Series . . . . @2.25

SHE-CAT
AC Comics

1 thru 4 . . . . . @2.50

SHERLOCK HOLMES
Eternity

1 thru 22 . . . . . @1.95

SHERLOCK HOLMES CASEBOOK
Eternity

1 . . . . . 2.25
2 . . . . . 2.25

SHERLOCK HOLMES: CHRONICLES OF CRIME AND MYSTERY
Northstar

1 'The Speckled Band' 2.25

SHERLOCK HOLMES OF THE '30's
Eternity

1 thru 7 . . . . . @2.95

SHERLOCK HOLMES: RETURN OF THE DEVIL
Adventure

1 V:Moriarty 2.50
2 V:Moriarty 2.50

SHERLOCK JUNIOR
Eternity

1 Rep.NewspaperStrips 1.95
2 Rep.NewspaperStrips 1.95

SHRED
CFW

1 thru 10 . . . . . @2.25

SHRIEK

1 . . . . . 4.95
2 . . . . . 4.95
3 . . . . . 7.95

SHRIKE

1 thru 6 . . . . . @1.50

SHURIKEN
Victory

1 Reggi Byers 6.00
1a 2nd printing 1.50
2 . . . . . 3.00
3 . . . . . 2.00
4 . . . . . 1.75
5 thru 13 . . . . . @1.50
Graphic Nov. Reggie Byers 8.00

SHURIKEN
Eternity

1 Shuriken vs. Slate 2.50
2 Neutralizer, Meguomo 2.50
3 R:Slate 2.50
4 Morgan's Bodyguard Serrate . . 2.50
5 Slate as Shuriken & Megumo . . 2.50
6 Hunt for Bionauts, final issue . . 2.50

SHURIKEN: COLD STEEL

1 . . . . . 1.95
2 . . . . . 1.95
3 thru 6 . . . . . @1.95

SHURIKEN TEAM-UP

1 thru 3 . . . . . @1.95

SIAMESE TWIN COMICS

1 . . . . . 2.50

SIDESHOW

7 . . . . . 3.50

SIEGEL & SHUSTER

2 . . . . . 1.70

SILENT INVASION
Renegade

1 . . . . . 4.00
2 thru 12, final issue . . . . . @2.00

SILVER FAWN

1 . . . . . 1.95

SILVER WING

1 . . . . . 1.00

SIMON/KIRBY READER

1 . . . . . 1.75

SINBAD

1 . . . . . 2.25
2 . . . . . 2.25
3 . . . . . 2.25
4 . . . . . 2.25

SINBAD: HOUSE OF GOD
Adventure Comics

1 Caliph's Wife Kidnapped 2.50
2 Magical Genie 2.50
3 Escape From Madhi 2.50
4 A:Genie 2.50

SIN CITY: A DAME TO KILL FOR
Dark Horse-Legend

1 FM(a&s),I:Dwight,Ava 4.00
2 FM(a&s),A:Ava 3.50
3 FM(a&s),D:Ava's Husband 3.50
4 FM(a&s), ... 3.50
5 FM(a&s), ... 3.50
6 FM(a&s),Final issue 3.25

SINNER

4 . . . . . 2.75
5 . . . . . 2.95
6 . . . . . 2.95

SKROG
Comico

1 . . . . . 3.00

SKULL

3 No price on cover 3.50

SLAUGHTERMAN

1 . . . . . 4.00
2 . . . . . 4.00

SLAVE GIRL

1 . . . . . 2.25

SNAKE
Special Studio

1 . . . . . 3.50

SNARF
Kitchen Sink

1 thru 10 . . . . . @2.00
10 (c)BE 2.00
11 thru 13 . . . . . @2.00

SNARL

1 . . . . . 2.50
2 . . . . . 2.50
3 . . . . . 2.50

SOCKETEER
Kardia

Rocketeer parody 2.25

SOLDIERS OF FORTUNE

1 . . . . . 1.95

SOLD OUT
Fantagor

1 . . . . . 1.75
2 . . . . . 1.75

SOLO EX-MUTANTS
Eternity

1 thru 6 . . . . . @1.95

SOLSON PREVIEW
Solson
1 .... 2.00

SOULFIRE
Aircel
1 mini-series 1.70
2 .... 1.70
3 .... 1.70

SOUL SEARCHER
1 thru 3 Peter David(s) 3.00

SOUTHERN KNIGHTS
1 See Crusaders
2 .... 8.00
3 .... 5.00
4 .... 5.00
5 thru 7 .... @4.00
Fictioneer
8 thru 11 .... @2.50
12 thru 33 .... @2.00
34 .... 2.25
35 The Morrigan Wars Pt.#2 .... 3.50
36 Morrigan Wars Pt.#5 .... 3.50
Annual #1 .... 2.50
DreadHalloweenSpec #1 .... 2.25
Primer #1 .... 2.25

SOUTHERN SQUADRON
Eternity
1 I:SQUAD 2.50
2 .... 2.25

SOUTHERN SQUADRON FREEDOM OF INFO. ACT.
Eternity
1 F.F.#1 Parody/Tribute cov. 2.50
2 A:Waitangi Rangers 2.50
3 .... 2.50

SPACE ARK
Apple
1 .... 2.75
2 .... 2.50
3 .... 1.75
4 .... 1.75
5 .... 1.75

SPACE BEAVER
Ten-Buck Comics
1 .... 2.50
2 .... 1.50
3 O&I:Stinger 1.50
4 A:Stinger 1.50
5 .... 1.50
6 O:Rodent 1.50
7 thru 12 .... @1.50

SPACED
1 I:Zip; 800 printed 40.00
2 .... 25.00
3 I:Dark Teddy 15.00
4 .... 15.00
5 and 6 .... @5.00
7 and 8 .... @2.00
Eclipse
9 .... 1.75
10 .... 1.75
11 .... 1.50
12 .... 1.50
13 .... 1.50

SPACE GUYS
1 .... 2.25

SPACEHAWK
Dark Horse
1 BW reps. 2.25
2 thru 4 BW .... @2.00

Space Beaver #3 © Ten-Buck Comics

5 BW 2.50

SPACE 34-24-34
1 .... 4.50

SPACE USAGI
Mirage Studios
1 Stan Sakai,Future Usagi 2.00
2 Stan Sakai,Future Usagi 2.00
3 Stan Sakai.Future Usagi 2.00

SPACEWOLF
Antarctic Press
1 From Albedo 2.50

SPARKPLUG
Hero Graphics
1 From League of Champions 2.95

SPATTER
1 .... 1.95
2 .... 1.95
3 .... 1.60
4 .... 2.00

SPEED RACER
1 .... 3.00
1a 2nd Printing 1.50

SPENCER SPOOK
A.C.E. Comics
1 .... 1.95
2 .... 1.95
3 thru 8 .... @1.75

SPICY TALES
1 thru 13 .... @1.95
14 thru 17 .... @2.25
Special #2 .... 2.25

SPIDER KISS
1 Harlan Ellison 3.95

SPINELESS MAN
Parody Press
1 Spider-Man 2099 spoof 2.50

SPIRAL CAGE
Renegade
Special 3.00

SPIRIT, THE
Kitchen Sink
1 WE,rep 5.25
2 WE,rep 4.25
3 WE,rep 4.00
4 WE,rep 4.00
5 WE,rep 3.00
6 WE,rep 3.00
7 WE,rep 3.00
8 WE,rep 3.00
9 WE,rep 3.00
10 WE,rep 3.00
11 WE,rep 3.00
12 thru 86 WE,rep .... @2.00

SPIRIT OF THE WIND
1 .... 2.00

THE SPIRIT: ORIGIN YEARS
Kitchen Sink
1 I:Denny Colt,Ebony White 2.95
2 I:Commissioner&Ellen Dolan 2.95
3 WE,Palyachi,The Killer Clown 2.95
4 WE,Orphans,Orang t/Ape Man 2.95
5 WE 2.95
6 WE,Kiss of Death 2.95
7 thru 8 WE 2.95

SPIRIT OF THE DRAGON
Double Edge
0 Dragon Scheme .... .75

SPITTING IMAGE
Eclipse
1 Marvel & Image parody 2.50

SPLAT
1 thru 4 .... @1.75

SPOTLIGHT
1 .... 1.50

STANLEY
1 .... 1.50

STARCHILD
Taliesin Press
0 .... 10.00
1 .... 15.00
2 .... 6.00
3 .... 4.50
4 .... 4.00
5 .... 3.00
6 .... 2.75
7 .... 2.50
8 .... 2.50

STARGATORS
1 .... 2.50
2 .... 2.50
3 .... 2.50

STAR JAM COMICS
Revolutionary
1 F:Hammer 2.50

STARJONGLEUR COLLECTION
1 .... 2.50
2 .... 2.50
3 .... 2.50

STAR BIKERS
1 .... 3.95
Special 2.00

STARK FUTURE
Aircel

1 .... 2.50
2 thru 7 .... @1.75
8 .... 2.00
9 thru 14 .... @1.70

STAR RANGERS

1 thru 3 .... @3.00
4 .... 1.95

BOOK II

1 .... 1.95
2 .... 1.95

STAR REACH

Star Reach

1 HC,I:CodyStarbuck 8.00
2 DG,JSn 2.00
3 FB 2.00
4 HC 2.00
5 JSon 3.00
6 GD,Elric 3.00
7 DS 5.00
8 CR,KSy 3.00
9 KSy 2.00
10 KSy 2.00
11 GD 2.00
12 MN,SL 2.00
13 SL,KSy 2.00
14 .... 2.00
15 .... 2.00
16 .... 2.00
17 .... 2.00
18 .... 2.00

STAR WOLF CONQUEROR

1 .... 2.00
2 .... 2.00

STARLIGHT

1 .... 1.95
2 .... 1.95

STARLIGHT AGENCY

Antartic Press

1 I:Starlight Agency 1.95
2 Anderson Kidnapped 1.95

STARLIGHT SQUADRON

Blackthorne

1 .... 2.00

STARSTRUCK

Dark Horse

1 Expanding Universe Pt1 .... 2.95
2 Expanding Universe Pt2 .... 2.95

STATIC

1 SD 1.50
2 SD 1.50
3 SD 1.50

STEALTH FORCE

1 thru 8 .... @.95

STECH

1 .... 1.50
2 .... 1.50

STEEL DRAGON STORIES

Steel Dragon

1 .... 1.50

STEPHEN DARKLORD

1 .... 1.75
2 .... 1.75
3 .... 1.75

STERN WHEELER

Spotlight

1 JA 1.75

STEVE CANYON

Kitchen Sink

1 thru 14 .... @5.00

STEVEN

1 .... 4.00
1a 2ndPrinting 2.95
2 .... 4.00
3 .... 2.95
4 and 5 .... @3.50

STICKBOY

Revolutionary

1 .... 2.00
2 thru 5 .... @2.50

STIG'S INFERNO

Vortex

1 .... 6.00
2 .... 3.50
3 .... 3.00
4 .... 3.00
5 .... 2.00

Eclipse

6 .... 1.75
7 .... 1.75

STING

Artline

1 .... 2.50

STINZ

Fantagraphics

1 .... 4.00
2 .... 4.00
3 .... 4.00
4 .... 4.00

[2nd series]
Brave New Words

1 thru 3 .... 2.50

STORMBRINGER

1 .... 2.00
2 .... 2.00
3 .... 2.00

STORMWATCHER

Eclipse

1 thru 4 .... @2.00

STRAND, THE

Trident

1 .... 2.50

STRANGE BEHAVIOR

Twilite Tone Press

1 LSn,MBr,Short Stories 2.95

STRANGE BREW

Aardvark Vanaheim

1 .... 5.00

STRANGE SPORTS STORIES

Adventure

1 thru 3 .... @2.50

STRANGE WORLDS

1 .... 3.95
2 .... 3.95
3 .... 3.95
4 .... 3.95

STRATA

Renegade

1 .... 3.00
2 .... 2.50
3 .... 1.70
4 .... 1.70
5 .... 1.70
6 .... 2.00

STRAW MEN

1 thru 5 .... @1.95
6 thru 8 .... @2.25

Street Fighter #1 © Ocean Comics

STREET FIGHTER

Ocean Comics

1 thru 4 limited series .... @1.75

STREET HEROES 2005

Eternity

1 thru 3 .... @1.95

STREET MUSIC

Fantagraphics

1 .... 2.75
2 .... 2.75
3 .... 2.95
4 .... 2.95
5 .... 2.50
6 .... 3.95

STREET POET RAY

1 .... 2.50
2 .... 2.00
3 .... 2.95
4 .... 2.95

STREET WOLF

1 limited series 2.00
2 .... 2.00
3 Last 2.00
Graphic Novel 6.95

STRIKER: THE ARMORED WARRIOR

Viz

1 Overture 2.75
2 V:Child Esper 2.75
3 Professor taken hostage 2.75

SUBURBAN HIGH LIFE

1 thru 5 .... @1.75

SUBURBAN NIGHTMARES

1 thru 4 .... @2.00

SUGAR RAY FINHEAD
Wolf Press
1 I&O Sugar Ray Finhead 2.50
2 I:Bessie & Big-Foot Benny the Pit Bull Man 2.95

SULTON
1 . . . . 1.50
2 . . . . 1.50
3 . . . . 1.50

SULTRY TEENAGE SUPERHEROES
1 thru 4 . . . . @2.00

SUNRISE
1 thru 4 . . . . @1.95

SUPERSWINE
Caliber
1 Parody, I:Superswine 2.50

SURVIVALIST CHRONICLES
Survival Art
1 . . . . 6.50
2 . . . . 6.50
3 . . . . 1.95

SWIFTSURE
Harrier Comics
1 . . . . 2.00
2 . . . . 2.00
3 thru 8 . . . . @1.75
9 . . . . 9.00
9a 2nd printing 1.75
10 . . . . 1.75
11 . . . . 1.95

SWORD OF VALOR
A Plus Comics
1 JAp,rep.Thane of Bagarth 2.50
2 JAp/MK rep 2.50

SWORDS AND SCIENCE
Pyramid
1 . . . . 1.70
2 . . . . 1.70
3 . . . . 1.70

SWORDS OF CEREBUS
Aardvark Vanaheim
1 rep. Cerebus 1-4 . . . . 18.00
1a reprint editions 10.00
2 rep. Cerebus 5-8 . . . . 12.00
2a reprint editions 8.00
3 rep. Cerebus 9-12 . . . . 12.00
3a reprint editions 8.00
4 rep. Cerebus 13-16 . . . . 12.00
4a reprint editions 8.00
5 rep. Cerebus 17-20 . . . . 12.00
5a reprint editions 8.00
6 rep. Cerebus 21-25 . . . . 12.00
6a reprint editions 8.00

SWORDS OF SHAR-PAI
Caliber
1 Mutant Ninja Dog 2.50
2 Shar-Pei 2.50
3 Final issue 2.50

SWORDS OF VALORS: ROBIN HOOD
A Plus Comics
1 rep. of Charlton comics 2.50

SYSTEM SEVEN
Arrow
1 thru 4 . . . . @1.50

T-BIRD CHRONICLES
1 . . . . 1.50
2 . . . . 1.50
3 . . . . 1.50

T-MINUS-ONE
1 . . . . 2.00
2 . . . . 2.00

TAKEN UNDER COMPENDIUM
Caliber
1 rep. Cal Presents #19-#22 . . . . 2.95

TALES FROM THE ANIVERSE
Arrow
1 7,400 printed 10.00
2 . . . . 4.00
3 10,000 printed 2.50
4 . . . . 2.50
5 . . . . 2.00
6 . . . . 1.50
7 Calamity 1.50

[2nd series]
Massive Comics Group
1 thru 3 . . . . 1.50

TALES FROM THE HEART
1 thru 5 . . . . @1.75
6 . . . . 1.95
7 . . . . 1.95

TALES OF BEANWORLD
Eclipse
1 . . . . 10.00
2 . . . . 4.00
3 . . . . 2.50
4 I:Beanish 1.50
5 . . . . 1.50
6 thru 20 . . . . @2.00

TALE OF MYA ROM
Aircel
1 . . . . 1.70

TALES OF ORDINARY MADNESS
Dark Horse
1 JBo(c),Paranoid 3.00
2 JBo(c),Mood 2.50
3 JBo(c),A Little Bit of Neurosis 2.50

TALES OF PIRACY SAVING GRACE
1 . . . . 1.95

TALES OF TEENAGE MUTANT NINJA TURTLES
1 . . . . 13.00
1B 2nd printing 3.00
2 . . . . 8.00
3 . . . . 5.00
4 . . . . 5.00
5 . . . . 5.00
6 thru 9 . . . . @4.00

TALES OF THE JACKALOPE
BF
1 . . . . 5.00
2 . . . . 3.00
3 and 4 . . . . @2.50
5 thru 9 . . . . @2.00

TALES OF THE NINJA WARRIORS
CFW
1 thru 14 . . . . @1.95
15 thru 19 . . . . @2.25

TALES OF THE PLAGUE
1 RCo 4.00

TALES THE STRIPED MAN KNEW
1 thru 4 . . . . @ 1.50

TALES TOO TERRIBLE TO TELL
1 thru 6 Pre-code horror stories @3.50

TALONZ
1 . . . . 1.75
2 . . . . 1.75

TAMMAS
1 . . . . 1.50

TANK GIRL
Dark Horse
1 Rep. from U.K.Deadline Mag. . . 4.00
2 V:Indiana Potato Jones 3.50
3 On the Run 3.00
4 . . . . 3.00

[2nd Series]
1 thru 2 . . . . 2.75
3 . . . . 2.75
4 Last issue 2.75

TANTALIZING STORIES
Tundra
1 F:Frank & Montgomery Wart . . . 2.25
2 Frank & Mont.stories cont. 2.25

TATTOOMAN SPECIAL
Fantagraphics
1 . . . . 2.75

TEAM NIPPON
Aircel
1 thru 7 . . . . @1.95

TEDDY & JOE
1 . . . . 1.50
2 . . . . 1.75

TEENAGE MUTANT NINJA TURTLES*
Mirage Studios
***Counterfeits Exist - Beware**
1 I:Turtles 250.00
1a 2nd printing 100.00
1b 3rd printing 35.00
1c 4th printing 20.00
1d 5th printing 4.00
2 . . . . 125.00
2a 2nd printing 18.00
2b 3rd printing 4.00
3 . . . . 50.00
3a 2nd printing 3.50
3b Special printing,rare 75.00
4 . . . . 30.00
4a 2nd printing 3.50
5 A:Fugitoid 18.00
5a 2nd printing 3.50
6 A:Fugitoid 16.00
6a 2nd printing 2.50
7 A:Fugitoid 15.00
7a 2nd printing 2.50
8 A:Cerebus 12.00
9 . . . . 10.00
10 V:Shredder 9.00
11 A:Casey Jones 8.00
12 thru 15 . . . . @7.00
16 thru 18 . . . . @6.00
19 Return to NY 6.00

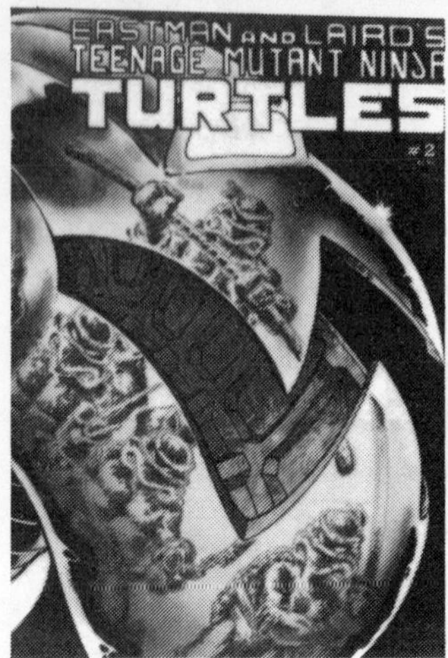

Teenage Mutant Ninja Turtles #2
© Mirage Studios

20 Return to NY 6.00
21 Return to NY,D:Shredder 6.00
22 thru 25 . . . . @4.00
26 . . . . 3.50
27 . . . . 3.50
28 thru 31 . . . . @3.00
32 . . . . 2.50
33 color, Corben 2.50
34 Toytle Anxiety 2.50
35 Souls Withering 2.50
36 Souls Wake 2.50
37 Twilight of the Rings 2.50
38 Spaced Out Pt.1, A:President Bush 2.50
39 Spaced Out Pt.2 . . . . 2.25
40 Spaced Out concl.,I:Rockin' Rollin' Miner Ants (B.U. story) 2.25
41 Turtle Dreams issue 2.25
42 Juliets Revenge 2.25
43 Halls of Lost Legends 2.25
44 V:Ninjas 2.25
45 A:Leatherhead 2.25
46 V:Samurai Dinosaur 2.25
47 Space Usagi 2.25
48 Shades of Grey Part 1 . . . . . . 2.25
49 Shades of Grey Part 2 . . . . . . 2.25
50 Eastman/Laird,new direction, inc.TM,EL,WS pin-ups 3.00
51 City at War #2 . . . . 2.25
52 City at War #3 . . . . 2.50
53 City at War #4 . . . . 2.50
54 City at War #5 . . . . 2.25
1990 Movie adaptation 6.50
Spec. The Haunted Pizza 2.25

TEENAGE MUTANT NINJA TURTLES TRAINING MANUAL

1 . . . . 5.00
2 thru 5 . . . . @3.00

TEKQ
Caliber

1 . . . . 2.95

TELL-TALE HEART & OTHER STORIES

1 . . . . 2.50

TERROR ON THE PLANET OF THE APES
Adventure Comics

1 MP,collectors edition 2.50
2 MP, the Forbidden Zone 2.50

TERROR TALES
Eternity

1 Short stories 2.50

Tex Benson #3 © Metro Comics

TEX BENSON
Metro Comics

1 thru 3 . . . . @2.00

TEYKWA

1 . . . . 1.75

THIEVES

1 thru 3 . . . . @1.50

39 SCREAMS

1 thru 6 . . . . @2.00

THIRTEEN O'CLOCK
Dark Horse

1 Mr.Murmer,from Deadline USA . 2.95

THIS MAGAZINE IS HAUNTED
A Plus Comics

1 . . . . 1.95

THORR SUERD OR SWORD OF THOR

1 . . . . 3.00
1a 2nd printing 2.00
2 . . . . 1.75
3 . . . . 1.50

THREAT

1 . . . . 5.00
2 . . . . 3.00
3 . . . . 2.00
4 . . . . 2.00
5 thru 10 . . . . @2.25

3 X 3 EYES
Innovation

1 Labyrinth o/t DemonsEyePt.1 . . 2.25
2 Labyrinth o/t DemonsEyePt.2 . . 2.25
3 Labyrinth o/t DemonsEyePt.3 . . 2.25
4 Labyrinth o/t DemonsEyePt.4 . . 2.25
5 Labyrinth o/t DemonsEye conc. . 2.25

THREE IN ONE

1 . . . . 1.75

THREE MUSKETEERS

1 . . . . 1.95
2 . . . . 1.95
3 . . . . 1.95

THREE ROCKETEERS
Eclipse

1 JK,AW,rep. 2.00
2 JK,AW,rep. 2.00

THRESHOLD OF REALTY

1 5,000 printed 2.50
2 thru 4 . . . . @2.00

THRILLKILL
Caliber

1 rep. Cal.Presents #1-#4 . . . . . . 2.50

THUNDER BUNNY

1 O:Thunder Bunny 2.50
2 VO:Dr.Fog 2.00
3 I:GoldenMan 1.75
4 V:Keeper 1.75
5 I:Moon Mess 1.75
6 V:Mr.Endall 1.75
7 VI:Dr.Fog 1.75
8 . . . . 1.75
9 VS:Gen. Agents 1.75
10 thru 12 . . . . @1.75

THUNDER MACE

1 Proto type-blue & red very rare:1,000 printed 15.00
1a four color cover 3.00
2 thru 5 . . . . @1.75
6 . . . . 2.00
7 . . . . 2.00
Graphic Novel, rep.1-4 . . . . 5.00

THUNDER SKULL

1 . . . . 1.95

TICK
New England Comics

1 BEd 45.00
1a 2nd printing 16.00
1b 3rd printing 6.00
1c 4th printing 2.50
2 BEd 25.00
2a 2nd printing 6.00
2b 3rd printing 4.00
2c 4th printing 2.50
3 BEd 11.00
3a 2nd printing 2.50
4 BEd 7.00
4a 2nd printing 2.50
5 BEd 6.00
6 BEd 3.50
7 BEd 3.50
8 BEd 3.50
8a Spec.No Logo edition 30.00
9 BEd,A:Chainsaw Vigilante, Red Eye 3.00
10 BEd 3.00
11 thru 12 BEd 2.75
Spec. Ed. #1, I:Tick 45.00
Spec. Ed. #2, 2nd App. Tick . . . 40.00

TICK:GIANT CIRCUS OF THE MIGHTY

1 A-O 2.75
2 P-Z 2.75
3 . . . . 2.75

TICK: KARMA TORNADO
1 . . . . . 3.25

TIGRESS
Hero Graphics
3 A:Lady Arcane 2.95
4 inc. B.U. Mudpie 2.95

TIGERS OF TERRA
1 6,000 printed 4.50
1a Signed & Num. 14.00
2 . . . . . 2.00
2a Signed & Num. 11.00
5 thru 7 . . . . . @3.50
8 thru 10 . . . . . @3.75

TIGER-X
Eternity
Special #1 . . . . . 2.25
1 thru 3 . . . . . @1.95

NEW SERIES
1 thru 4 . . . . . @1.95

TIME DRIFTERS
Innovation
1 thru 3 . . . . . @2.25

TIME GATES
Double Edge
1 SF series,The Egg #1 . . . . . 1.95
2 The Egg #2 . . . . . 1.95
3 Spirit of the Dragon #1 . . . . . 1.95
4 Spirit of the Dragon #2 . . . . . 1.95
4a Var.cover 1.95

TIME JUMP WAR
Apple
1 thru 3 . . . . . @1.95

TIME MACHINE
1 and 2 . . . . . @2.50

TIME OUT OF MIND
1 thru 4 . . . . . @1.85

TIME TRIPPER
1 . . . . . 2.00

TIME WARRIORS
Fantasy General
1 rep.Alpha Track #1 . . . . . 1.50
1a Bi-Weekly 75
2 75
3 75

TO BE ANNOUNCED
1 thru 6 . . . . . @1.50

TO DIE FOR
Blackthorne
1 . . . . . 2.00

TOM CORBETT SPACE CADET
Eternity
1 . . . . . 2.00
2 . . . . . 2.00
3 . . . . . 2.25
4 . . . . . 2.25

TOM CORBETT II
1 thru 4 . . . . . @2.25

TOM MIX HOLIDAY ALBUM
Amazing Comics
1 . . . . . 3.50

TOM MIX WESTERN
AC Comics
1 . . . . . 2.50
2 . . . . . 2.50

TOMMY & THE MONSTERS
1 thru 3 . . . . . @1.95

TOMMORROW MAN
1 R:Tommorrow Man 2.95

TONY BRAVADO
1 thru 3 . . . . . @2.00
4 . . . . . 2.50

TORG
Adventure
1 Based on Role Playing Game . . 2.50
2 thru 3 Based on Game . . . . . @2.50

TOR JOHNSON: HOLLYWOOD STAR
Monster Comics
1 Biographical story 2.50

TORRID AFFAIRS
1 . . . . . 2.25
2 . . . . . 2.95
3 . . . . . 2.95

TOTALLY ALIEN
1 . . . . . 17.00
2 . . . . . 12.00
3 . . . . . 8.00

TOUGH GUYS AND WILD WOMEN
Eternity
1 . . . . . 2.25
2 . . . . . 2.25

TRACKER
Blackthorne
1 . . . . . 2.00
2 . . . . . 1.75
3 . . . . . 2.00
4 . . . . . 2.00

TRANSIT
1 . . . . . 2.00
2 thru 6 . . . . . @1.75

TREKKER
Dark Horse
1 thru 4 . . . . . @1.50
5 and 6 . . . . . @1.75
7 . . . . . 1.50
8 O:Trekker 1.50
9 . . . . . 1.50

TRIAD
Blackthorne
1 . . . . . 1.75

TRIAL RUN
1 . . . . . 1.75

TRIARCH
Caliber
1 . . . . . 2.00

TRICKSTER KING MONKEY
1 thru 5 . . . . . @1.75

TRIDENT
1 thru 7 . . . . . @3.50
8 . . . . . 4.50

TRIO
1 . . . . . 1.50

TROLLORDS
1 1st printing 6.00
1a 2nd printing 2.00
2 . . . . . 3.00
3 . . . . . 2.00
4 thru 16 . . . . . @1.50
#1 special 1.75

TROLLORDS: DEATH & KISSES
1 . . . . . 1.95
2 thru 5 . . . . . @2.25

TROPO
1 and 2 . . . . . @2.00

Trouble with Girls #10 © Eternity

TROUBLE WITH GIRLS
Eternity
1 . . . . . 3.50
2 . . . . . 2.50
3 thru 14 . . . . . @1.95
15 thru 21 . . . . . @2.25
22 Lester's Origin 2.25
Annual #1 . . . . . 2.95
Graphic Novel 7.95
Graphic Novel #2 . . . . . 7.95
Xmas special 'World of Girls' 2.95

NEW SERIES
1 thru 4 see color
5 thru 11 . . . . . @1.95

TROUBLE WITH TIGERS
Antartic Press
1 NinjaHighSchool/Tigers x-over . 2.00
2 . . . . . 2.00

TRUE CRIME
Eclipse
1 thru 2 . . . . . 2.95

TRUFAN ADVENTURES THEATRE
1 . . . . . 8.00

2 3-D issue 5.00

TRYPTO THE ACID DOG
Renegade

1 . . . . 2.00

TUNESIA

1 . . . . 1.50

TURTLE SOUP

1 A:TMNT 6.00

TURTLES TEACH KARATE
Solson

1 . . . . 4.00
2 . . . . 3.50

TWILIGHT AVENGER
Eternity

1 thru 18 . . . . @1.95

TWIST
Kitchen Sink

1 . . . . 1.95
2 . . . . 2.00
3 . . . . 2.00

TWISTED TALES OF THE PURPLE SNIT
Blackthorne

1 . . . . 2.50
2 . . . . 2.00

2001 NIGHTS
Viz

1 . . . . 5.00
2 . . . . 4.00
3 thru 5 . . . . @3.75
6 thru 10 . . . . @4.25

TYLOR
Double Edge

0 The Egg 2.95

TYRANNY REX
Fleetway

GN reps. from 2000A.D. 7.95

ULTRA KLUTZ
Onward Comics

1 . . . . 2.50
2 thru 18 . . . . @1.50
19 thru 24 . . . . @1.75
25 thru 30 . . . . @2.00

UNCANNY MAN-FROG
Mad Dog

1 . . . . 1.75
2 . . . . 1.75

UNCENSORED MOUSE
Eternity

1 Mickey Mouse 10.00
2 Mickey Mouse 11.00

UNDERGROUND

1 . . . . 1.70

UNDERGROUND
Dark Horse

1 AVs(s) 4.25
2 AVs(s) 3.95
3 AVs(s) 3.95
4 AVs(s) 3.95

UNDIE DOG

1 . . . . 1.50

UNICORN ISLE
Genesis West

1 . . . . 2.50
2 . . . . 1.50
3 . . . . 1.50

Apple

4 thru 6 . . . . @1.75

UNICORN KINGS

1 . . . . 1.00
2 . . . . 1.00

UNION JACKS

1 thru 3 . . . . @2.00

UNSUPERVISED EXISTENCE

1 . . . . 2.00
2 . . . . 2.50
3 . . . . 2.50

UNTOLD ORIGIN OF MS. VICTORY

1 . . . . 2.50

UNTOUCHABLES

1 thru 20 . . . . @.75

USAGI YOJIMBO
Fantagraphics

1 SS 10.00
2 SS,Samurai 7.00
3 SS,Samurai,A:Croakers 5.50
4 SS 5.00
5 thru 7 SS . . . . @4.00
8 SS,A Mother's Love 4.00
9 SS 4.00
10 SS,A:Turtles 5.50
11 thru 18 SS . . . . @3.50
19 SS,Frost & Fire,A:Nelson Groundthumper 3.50
20 thru 21 SS . . . . @3.50
22 SS,A:Panda Khan 3.50
23 SS,V:Ninja Bats 3.50
24 SS 3.50
25 SS,A:Lionheart 2.50
26 SS,Gambling 2.50
27 SS 2.25
28 thru 31 SS,Circles Pt.1 . . . . @2.25
32 . . . . 2.25
33 SS,Ritual Murder 2.25
34 thru 37 . . . . @2.25
Spec#1 SS,SummerSpec, C:Groo 14.00

VAGABONDS

1 thru 3 . . . . @1.75

VALENTINO
Renegade

1 . . . . 1.70
2 . . . . 2.00
3 . . . . 2.00

VALOR THUNDERSTAR

1 and 2 . . . . @1.75

VAMPIRELLA
Dark Horse

1 'The Lion and the Lizard'Pt.1 . . 4.50
2 'The Lion and the Lizard'Pt.2 . . 3.95
3 'The Lion and the Lizard'Pt.3 . . 3.95
4 'The Lion and the Lizard'Pt.3 . . 3.95

VAMPIRELLA
Harris

1 DC,SL,Summer Nights,48page . 3.95

VAMPYRES
Eternity

1 thru 4 . . . . @2.25

VANGUARD: OUTPOST EARTH

1 and 2 . . . . @2.00

VARCEL'S VIXENS

1 thru 3 . . . . @2.50

VAULT OF DOOMNATION

1 . . . . 1.70

VENUS WARS
Dark Horse

1 Aphrodia V:Ishtar 3.00
2 I: Ken Seno 2.50
3 Aphrodia V:Ishtar 2.50
4 Seno Joins Hound Corps. 2.50
5 SenoV:Octopus Supertanks . . . 2.50
6 Chaos in Aphrodia 2.50
7 All Out Ground War 2.50
8 Ishtar V:Aphrodia contd. 2.50
9 Ishtar V:Aphrodia contd. 2.50
10 Supertanks of Ishtar Advance 2.50
11 Aphrodia Captured 2.50
12 A:Miranda,48pgs 2.75
13 Hound Brigade-Suicide Assault 2.25
14 V:Army 2.50
15 . . . . 2.50

Venus Wars II #11
© Dark Horse Comics, Inc.

VENUS WARS II

1 V:Security Police 2.75
2 Political Unrest 2.25
3 Conspiracy 2.25
4 A:Lupica 2.25
5 Love Hotel 2.25
6 Terran Consulate 2.25
7 Doublecross 2.25
8 D:Lupisa 2.95
9 A:Matthew 2.95
10 A:Mad Scientist 2.95
11 thru 15 V:Troopers . . . . @2.95

VERDICT
Eternity

1 thru 4 .... @1.95

VERSION
Dark Horse

1.1 thru 2.6 by H. Sakaguchi 2.75
2.7 by H. Sakaguchi 2.50

VIC & BLOOD
Renegade

1 RCo,Ellison 2.00
2 RCo,Ellison 2.00

VICKY VALENTINE
Renegade

1 thru 4 .... @1.70

VICTIMS
Silver Wolf

1 .... 1.50
2 .... 1.50

VICTIMS
Eternity

1 thru 5 .... @1.95

VIDEO CLASSICS

1 .... 3.50
2 .... 3.50

Vietnam Journal #2 © Apple Comics

VIETNAM JOURNAL
Apple Comics

1 .... 5.00
1a 2nd printing 3.00
2 .... 3.00
3 thru 5 .... @2.50
6 thru 13 .... @2.00
14 thru 16 .... @2.25

VIGIL: FALL FROM GRACE
Innovation

1 'State of Grace' 2.75
2 The Graceland Hunt 2.50

VIOLET STING ALTERNATE CONCEPTS

1 .... .95

VISION

1 I:Flaming Carrot 150.00
2 Flaming Carrot 50.00
3 Flaming Carrot 20.00
4 Flaming Carrot 15.00

VITAL-MAN

1 thru 3 .... @1.70

VITRUVIAM MAN

1 .... 2.50

VOX
Apple

1 thru 3 .... @1.95
4 .... 2.25
5 .... 2.25

WACKY SQUIRREL

1 thru 4 .... @1.75
Summer Fun Special #1 .... 2.00
Christmas Special #1 .... 1.75

WALKING DEAD
Aircel

1 thru 4 .... @2.25
Spec. 1 .... 2.25

WANDER

1 .... 1.75

WANDERING STAR

1 .... 2.00

WAR
A Plus Comics

1 .... 2.50

WARDRUMS

1 Adult 1.75
2 .... 1.75
3 .... 1.75

WARLOCK 5
Aircel

1 .... 6.00
2 .... 5.00
3 .... 6.00
4 .... 5.00
5 .... 5.00
6 thru 11 .... @4.00
12 .... 3.50
13 .... 3.50
14 thru 16 .... @2.00
17 .... 1.70
18 .... 1.75
19 thru 22 .... @1.95
Book 2 #1 thru #7 .... @2.00

WARLOCKS
Aircel

1 thru 3 .... @1.70
4 thru 12 .... @1.95
Spec #1 Rep. 2.25

WAR OF THE WORLDS
Eternity

1 TV tie-in 1.95
2 thru 6 .... @1.95

WARP WALKING
Caliber

1 'Quick and the Dead' 2.50

WARRIORS

1 .... 2.50
2 thru 7 .... @1.95

WARWORLD!
Dark Horse

1 .... 1.75

WAVE WARRIORS

1 .... 2.00

WAXWORK

1 .... 2.00

WAYWARD WARRIOR

1 .... 2.00

WEAPON FIVE

Spec. #1 .... 1.95

WEASEL PATROL
Eclipse

Spec. #1 .... 2.00

WEIRD MACABRE THRILLERS

1 .... 1.95

WEIRD ROMANCE
Eclipse

1 .... 2.00

WEREWOLF
Blackthorne

1 TV tie-in 2.00
2 thru 7 .... @2.00

WEREWOLF AT LARGE

1 thru 3 .... @2.25

WHAT IS THE FACE?
A.C.E. Comics

1 SD/FMc,I:New Face 1.95
2 SD/FMc 1.95
3 SD 1.75

WHISPERS & SHADOWS

1 8 1/2 x 11 .... 2.00
1a Regular size 1.50
2 8 1/2 x 11 .... 1.50
3 8 1/2 x 11 .... 1.50
4 thru 9 .... @1.50

WHITE LIKE SHE
Dark Horse

1 .... 2.95

WILD, THE

1 and 2 .... @1.50
3 thru 7 .... @1.75

WILD KNIGHTS
Eternity

1 thru 9 .... @1.95
Shattered Earth Chron. #1 ...... 1.95

WILDMAN

1 and 2 .... @1.50
3 thru 6 .... @1.85

WILD STARS

Vol 2 #1 .... 1.95

WILD THINGS

1 .... 2.00

WILD THINK

2 .... 2.00

WIMMINS' COMIX

13 and 14 .... @2.00

WIND BLADE
1 Elford 1st Blair 60.00

WINDRAVEN
Hero Graphics/Blue comet
1 The Healing,(see Rough Raiders) 2.95

WINDRAVEN
Heroic
1 . . . . 2.95

WITCH
Eternity
1 . . . . 1.95

WIZARD OF FOURTH STREET
Dark Horse
1 thru 4 . . . . @1.75

WIZARDS OF LAST RESORT
1 thru 3 . . . . @1.75
4 . . . . 2.00

WIZARD OF TIME
David House
1 . . . . 1.50
1a 2nd printing(blue) 1.50
2 and 3 . . . . @1.50

WOLF H
Blackthorne
1 and 2 . . . . @1.75

WORDSMITH
Renegade
1 . . . . 3.00
2 thru 6 . . . . @1.70
7 thru 12 . . . . @2.00

WORLD OF WOOD
Eclipse
5 Flying Saucers 2.00

WORLD OF X-RAY
1 . . . . 1.80
2 . . . . 1.80

WRAB
1 . . . . 2.95

WRAITH
Outlander
1 'Resurrected & the Damned' . . 1.75

WRONG COMIC
1 . . . . 1.70

WYOMING TERRITORY
1 . . . . 1.95

XANADU
Thoughts & Images
1 thru 5 . . . . @2.00

XENON
Eclipse
1 . . . . 3.00
2 thru 23 . . . . @1.50

XENOZOIC TALES
Kitchen Sink
1 . . . . 5.75
1aRep. 2.00
2 . . . . 3.50

Xenozoic Tales #1 © Kitchen Sink

2a Rep. 2.00
3 . . . . 3.00
4 . . . . 2.50
5 thru 7 . . . . @2.25
8 thru 12 . . . . @2.00

X-BABES VS. JUSTICE BABES
Personality
1 Spoof/parody 2.95

X-CONS
Parody Press
1 X-Men satire,flip cover 2.50

X-FARCE
Eclipse
One-Shot X-Force parody 3.00

X-MAS WITH SUPERSWINE
Spec 2.00

XMEN
1 Parody 1.50

X-THIEVES
1 . . . . 3.00
2 . . . . 1.75
3 . . . . 1.75

YAHOO
1 thru 3 . . . . @2.00

YAKUZA
Eternity
1 thru 5 . . . . @1.95

YARN MAN
1 . . . . 2.00

YAWN
Parody Press
1 Spawn parody 2.50

YIN-FEI
1 thru 4 . . . . @1.50

YOUNG HERO
1 . . . . 2.50
2 . . . . 2.50

YOUNG CYNICS CLUB
Dark Horse
1 . . . . 2.50

YOUNG MASTERS
1 thru 10 . . . . @1.75

ZELL THE SWORDDANCER
1 Steve Gallacci 5.50
2 . . . . 2.00
3 . . . . 2.00

ZEN, INTER-GALACTIC NINJA
1 thru 5 . . . . @1.75
6 thru 9 . . . . @2.00
X-mas Spec #1,V:Black Hole Bob 2.95

RA
[2nd Series]
1 'Down to Earth' 2.25
2 RA, A:Jeremy Baker 2.25

[3rd Series]
0 . . . . 2.95
1 thru 3 A:Niro . . . . @2.95
Sourcebook #1 . . . . 3.50

ZEN: MISTRESS OF CHAOS
1 . . . . 2.95

ZENITH: PHASE II
Fleetway
1 GMo(s),SY,Rep.2000 AD 1.95

ZERO & D.D.O.J.
1 . . . . 3.00

ZIG ZAG
1 . . . . 1.25
2 . . . . 1.25

ZOLASTRAYA AND THE BARD
1 thru 5 . . . . @1.70

ZOMBIE BOY
1 . . . . 1.50

ZOMBIE LOVE
1 . . . . 4.95

ZOMBIE WAR
1 thru 3 . . . . 3.95

ZONE
1 . . . . 1.95

ZONE CONTINUUM
Caliber
1 Master of the Waves 2.95
2 . . . . 2.95

ZORANN: STAR WARRIOR
1 . . . . 2.00

ZOT!
Eclipse
(#1-#10 See: Color)
11 New Series 2.50
12 thru 15 . . . . @2.50
16 A:De-Evolutionaries 2.50
17 thru 36 . . . . @2.00

ARE THERE ANY OTHERS FOOLISH ENOUGH TO TRY AND CHALLENGE THE LIVING TARIM?

MY POWER IS ABSOLUTE! NONE MAY STAND AGAINST ME!

CLASSICS ILLUSTRATED

GROWS UP

By Jeff Juliard

The comics industry is changing. What was once a newsstand phenomenon aimed at eight-to-ten-year-old's has become a twentysomething staple of America's entertainment industry.

Today there are stores that sell nothing but comics, and you can walk into any toy store and find entire aisles devoted to action figures of popular superheroes. Even America's holiest temples of consumerism, malls, have been invaded by new multistore comic shop chains. There is no doubt that the late twentieth century has seen this once tiny industry explode into a multi-million-dollar business.

One popular comic that has changed right along with the comic industry is *Classics Illustrated*. Once a small publisher of classic literature adapted to comics, Classics Illustrated is now the keystone of Classics International Entertainment, a publicly traded company with a chain of twenty-one retail comic book stores.

Mike Gold, Publisher and Editorial Director for Classics Illustrated, thinks part of *Classics Illustrated*'s staying power can be attributed to the role it has always played in exposing children to classic literature.

"They did a major piece on *Classics Illustrated* in *American Heritage Magazine* about a year ago," remembers Gold. "We were working on the company going public at the time, and it was really gratifying to see that type of coverage. We talked to the folks from the Smithsonian, got calls from educators, and really began to realize our role in history.

"*Classics Illustrated* really are a rite of passage, an awakening for younger readers into a whole area of literature that, certainly today, they are not predisposed to looking at. What I like about this whole *Classics Illustrated* thing is that not only are we taking comic book readers and exposing them to the world of fiction, but we're also taking students who aren't into fiction or into comic books and exposing them to both," Gold added.

Gold came to comics from journalism. A newspaper reporter, magazine writer, and editor, he began his comic career by consulting for comic book stores in Chicago. After helping found the Chicago ComiConn, he eventually worked for DC Comics as their first marketing person.

Between two stints at DC, he cofounded First Comics, which published popular titles such as *American Flagg*, *John Sable Freelance*, and *Grimjack*. First Comics picked up the logo, trademarks, and media rights to the original *Classics Illustrated* and began publishing them in 1991.

"The original First Comics suspended operations for a year or two while the company went through their metamorphosis into Classics International Entertainment," explains Gold. "I had left the company to go back over to DC and they brought me back as Publisher and Editorial Director for *Classics Illustrated*."

One of Gold's first moves was to bring back the original *Classics Illustrated* logo (the original First Comics Classics Illustrated books had replaced it with a newer one).

"I thought that was a marketing mistake," says Gold. "It was a beautiful logo, but everyone knew the original yellow-and-black logo. We moved away from the logo created in 1988 and restored the original logo. We also restored the issue numbers. I thought it was a very serious mistake on First's part to take those numbers off the cover. This is a medium that encourages collectibility. Now it will make it easier for people to go out there and collect *Classics Illustrated.*

"What's interesting is that we've done some test marketing on the newer versions of *Classics Illustrated* with the old logo and the issue numbers on them. They're selling about four times faster than the First Comics versions. We will be reprinting the stuff First had done but adding the logo and issue numbers. Then we'll move on from the issue #27 that they had done and do new stuff as well as sidebar series," Gold added.

The "sidebar series" he's talking about are projects for the educational market. Gold explains that by marketing *Classics Illustrated* to schools, he is once again following tradition.

"We're doing something that the original *Classics Illustrated* had done primarily back in the late '50s and '60s. They had another series of books under the *Classics Illustrated* imprint called *The World Around Us*. It highlighted real issues with fictional stories. We brought back *The World Around Us* series in conjunction with the Audubon Society. Our first story is called *Wolf Hunter* and it's about the decimation of the wolf in North America. It should be out the summer of 1994. Our educational marketing, television and print media marketing, and that stuff will probably begin to appear in late summer to early fall."

All of this represents a new and interesting challenge for Gold: to develop material for a unique segment of the comic-buying audience. "When I was at First Comics originally, in the early '80s, I really did not have the chance to go and develop books for the younger end of the market," says Gold. "First Comics was a direct-sale company, and we didn't do much newsstand distribution. At DC, the move was made towards focusing on that part of the industry as well. When I was there, DC's marketing department was disinterested in marketing comics geared to ten-to-fifteen year-olds. Here we have a company that's solely founded for the purpose of selling and marketing CI books for ten-to-fifteen year-olds. I'm having a lot of fun with it."

Still, getting a book like *Moby Dick* squeezed into forty four comic book pages is no small task! To do so, Gold assigns an editor to each book to figure out how to make it work. Although it is impossible to capture the entire book within the limited space, care is taken to provide a story with a beginning, middle, and end. This is done by focusing on certain elements of the story and highlighting them.

This type of story adaptation also fits the growing CD-ROM medium quite well. Gold and Classics International Entertainment are developing products for this market as well.

"It's not quite full animation like movie theaters and television, but it is an interactive form in which you can tell people stories visually (as well as with a narrative). It is similar to comics in that it's a synthesis of visuals and dialogue. A lot of people who don't know comics think of them as words and pictures, with the pictures illustrating the words. That's not true. I get kind of upset with artists who call themselves illustrators. They're not illustrating the story, they're telling the story. They're interpreting the story visually. There's a major difference. That's what makes comics unique. It's one of the few forms where you have that type of synthesis. We have that same communications form in CD-ROM. Clearly," says Gold, "it's like adapting a book for a movie."

So, why not go into television or movies? Apparently that idea had occurred to Gold as well. As of this writing, Classics International Entertainment has just finished a deal with Paramount to do a movie based on the First Comics character Badger. Gold speculates that television will be the medium for *Classics Illustrated*.

"The whole idea of coming up with *Classics Illustrated* programming is very comforting to a lot of television people," he says. "They're under a lot of fire for their children's programming and they're looking for something that will be high adventure, really entice the children, and yet have this educational ambience about it."

Aside from the television and movie deals and the CD-ROM development, Classics International Entertainment is still about publishing *Classics Illustrated;* but the new *Classics Illustrated* has also made efforts to appeal to a wider market. To that end, there have been spectacular works such as Bill Sienkiewicz's adaptation of Herman Melville's *Moby Dick* and Mike Ploog's telling of the Mark Twain classic *Tom Sawyer*. Gold is also considering offers to reprint collections of the older *Classics Illustrated* titles in hardcover form.

And, of course, there are the upcoming books. Although he was reluctant to reveal any specifics, the future of *Classics Illustrated* looks like it will include some interesting creative minds.

"What's going on right now is that I've approached quite a number of people with whom I've worked in the past," explains Gold. "I've gotten lists from each of them and everybody has three or four books that they want to do. Now the nightmare-and I've got a whole computer data base to deal with it-is to sort it out so that I can give each person one they want and not ace anybody out. It's almost a political issue as well as an editorial issue. I don't want to announce certain books and certain people because I haven't gotten around to finalizing that list."

But worrying over who gets what title is only half of the challenge. "Because they're doing a regular monthly book and they'll be doing CI on the side, it's going to take them a year to get one of those things done."

Whatever the arrangements, *Classics Illustrated* has a brisk pace planned for the future. Scheduling is going to be crucial! "We're producing two books every month because we have a book club," says Gold. "It's being advertised primarily on cable TV. You give us fifteen bucks or thirteen bucks, or something like that, and we send you five copies of the new *Classics Illustrated* and a poster, which Mike Grell drew for us. Then every month we ship you two more books. We shipped the first five in April 1994. So now we're shipping two books every month forever."

Add the book club to the television and movie projects, the CD-ROMs in development, and retail stores springing up all over the place, and you'll notice that Classics International Entertainment is poised to ride the comics boom into the next decade. Mike Gold has a pretty full agenda, but he says he enjoys it.

"It's great. Our stock has more than doubled, so our stockholders seem to be very happy, and that's wonderful because that gives us an enormous amount of freedom. I'm really enjoying it. After twenty years, it's like I've been able to have my cake and eat it, too."

Issued As Classic Comics
001-THE THREE MUSKETEERS
By Alexandre Dumas

10/41 **(---)** MKd,MKd(c), Original,10¢ (c) Price 3,500.00
05/43 **(10)** MKd,MKd(c), No(c)Price; rep 200.00
11/43 **(15)** MKd,MKd(c),Long Island Independent Ed; 150.00
6/44 **(18/20)** MKd,MKd(c), Sunrise Times Edition;rep ... 120.00
7/44 **(21)** MKd,MKd(c),Richmond Courrier Edition;rep 100.00
6/46 **(28)** MKd,MKd(c);rep 90.00
4/47 **(36)** MKd,MKd(c), New ClLogo;rep 40.00
6/49 **(60)** MKd,MKd(c),Cl Logo;rep 25.00
10/49 **(64)** MKd,MK(c),Cl Logo;rep 25.00
12/50 **(78)** MKd,MKd(c),15¢(c) Price; Cl Logo;rep 16.00
03/52 **(93)** MKd,MKd(c), Cl Logo;rep 15.00
11/53 **(114)** Cl Logo;rep 12.00
09/56 **(134)** MKd,MKd(c),New P(c),Cl Logo,64 pgs;rep 12.00
03/58 **(143)** MKd,MKd(c),P(c), Cl Logo,64 pgs;rep 11.00
05/59 **(150)** GE&RC New Art, P(c),ClLogo;rep 11.00
03/61 **(149)** GE&RC,P(c), Cl Logo;rep 7.00
62-63 **(167)** GE&RC,P(c), Cl Logo;rep 7.00
04/64 **(167)** GE&RC,P(c), Cl Logo;rep 7.00
01/65 **(167)** GE&RC,P(c), Cl Logo;rep 7.00
03/66 **(167)** GE&RC,P(c), Cl Logo;rep 7.00
11/67 **(166)** GE&RC,P(c), Cl Logo;rep 7.00
Sp/69 **(166)** GE&RC,P(c),25¢(c) Price,ClLogo, Rigid(c);rep 7.00
Sp/71 **(169)** GE&RC,P(c), Cl Logo,Rigid(c);rep 7.00

002-IVANHOE
By Sir Walter Scott

1941 **(---)** EA,MKd(c),Original . 1,300.00
05/43 **(1)** EA,MKd(c),word "Presents" Removed From(c);rep 175.00
11/43 **(15)** EA,MKd(c),Long Island Independent Edition;rep 130.00
06/44 **(18/20)** EA,MKd(c),Sunrise Times Edition;rep 100.00
07/44 **(21)** EA,MKd(c),Richmond Courrier Edition;rep 90.00
06/46 **(28)** EA,MKd(c),rep 80.00
07/47 **(36)** EA,MKd(c),New Cl Logo; rep 40.00
06/49 **(60)** EA,MKd(c),Cl Logo;r5p 21.00
10/49 **(64)** EA,MKd(c),Cl Logo;20p 18.00
12/50 **(78)** EA,MKd(c),15¢(c) Price; Cl Logo;rep 17.00
11/51 **(89)** EA,MKd(c),Cl Logo;rep 16.00
04/53 **(106)** EA,MKd(c),Cl Logo;rep 14.00
07/54 **(121)** EA,MKd(c),Cl Logo;rep 10.00
01/57 **(136)** NN New Art,New P(c),Cl Logo;rep 14.00
01/58 **(142)** NN,P(c),Cl Logo;rep . 6.00
11/59 **(153)** NN,P(c),Cl Logo;rep . 6.00
03/61 **(149)** NN,P(c),Cl Logo;rep . 6.00
62/63 **(167)** NN,P(c),Cl Logo;rep . 5.00
05/64 **(167)** NN,P(c),Cl Logo;rep . 6.00
01/65 **(167)** NN,P(c),Cl Logo;rep . 6.00
03/66 **(167)** NN,P(c),Cl Logo;rep . 6.00
09/67 **(166)** NN,P(c),Cl Logo;rep . 6.00
1968 **(166)** NN,P(c),Cl Logo;rep . . 6.00
Wr/69 **(169)** NN,P(c),Cl Logo Rigid(c);rep 6.00
Wr/71 **(169)** NN,P(c),Cl Logo,Rigid(c);rep 6.00

003-THE COUNT OF MONTE CRISTO
By Alexandre Dumas

03/42 **(---)** ASm,ASm(c),Original 900.00
05/43 **(10)** ASm,ASm(c);rep ... 175.00
11/43 **(15)** ASm,ASm(c),Long Island Independent Edition;rep 125.00
06/44 **(18/20)** ASm,ASm(c), Sunrise Times Edition;rep ... 110.00
06/44 **(20)** ASm,ASm(c),Sunrise Times Edition;rep 100.00
07/44 **(21)** ASm,ASm(c),Richmond Courrier Edition;rep 80.00
06/46 **(28)** ASm,ASm(c);rep 70.00
04/47 **(36)** ASm,ASm(c),New Cl Logo; rep 40.00
06/49 **(60)** ASm,ASm(c),Cl Logo;rep 25.00
08/49 **(62)** ASm,ASm(c),Cl Logo;rep 35.00
05/50 **(71)** ASm,ASm(c),Cl Logo;rep 16.00
09/51 **(87)** ASm,ASm(c),15¢(c) Price, Cl Logo;rep 14.00
11/53 **(113)** ASm,ASm(c), Cl Logo; rep 12.00
11/56 **(---)** LC New Art,New P(c), Cl Logo;rep 12.00
03/58 **(135)** LC,P(c),Cl Logo;rep . 6.00
11/59 **(153)** LC,P(c),Cl Logo;rep . 6.00
03/61 **(161)** LC,P(c),Cl Logo;rep . 6.00
62/63 **(167)** LC,P(c),Cl Logo;rep . 6.00
07/64 **(167)** LC,P(c),Cl Logo;rep . 6.00
07/65 **(167)** LC,P(c),Cl Logo;rep . 6.00
07/66 **(167)** LC,P(c),Cl Logo;rep . 6.00
1968 **(166)** LC,P(c),25¢(c) Price, Cl Logo;rep 6.00
Wn/69 **(169)** LC,P(c),Cl Logo, Rigid(c);rep 6.00

CI #4 *The Last of the Mohicans*
© Gilberton Publications

004-THE LAST OF THE MOHICANS
By James Fenimore Cooper

08/42 **(---)** RR,RR(c),Original .. 850.00
06/43 **(12)** RR,RR(c),Price Balloon Deleted;rep 175.00
11/43 **(15)** RR,RR(c),Long Island Independent Edition;rep 150.00
06/44 **(20)** RR,RR(c),Long Island Independent Edition;rep 125.00
07/44 **(21)** RR,RR(c),Queens Home News Edition;rep 100.00
06/46 **(28)** RR,RR(c);rep 90.00
04/47 **(36)** RR,RR(c),New Cl Logo; rep 40.00
06/49 **(60)** RR,RR(c),Cl Logo;re5 22.00
10/49 **(64)** RR,RR(c),Cl Logo;rep 20.00
12/50 **(78)** RR,RR(c),15¢(c) Price,Cl Logo rep 17.00
11/51 **(89)** RR,RR(c),Cl Logo;rep 16.00
03/54 **(117)** RR,RR(c),Cl Logo;rep 12.00
11/56 **(135)** RR,New P(c), Cl Logo; rep 12.00
11/57 **(141)** RR,P(c),Cl Logo;rep 13.00
05/59 **(150)** JSe&StA New Art, P(c), Cl Logo;rep 12.00
03/61 **(161)** JSe&StA,P(c),Cl Logo; rep 6.00
62/63 **(167)** JSe&StA,P(c),Cl Logo; rep 6.00
06/64 **(167)** JSe&StA,P(c),Cl Logo; rep 6.00
08/65 **(167)** JSe&StA,P(c),Cl Logo; rep 6.00
08/66 **(167)** JSe&StA,P(c),Cl Logo; rep 6.00
1967 **(166)** JSe&StA,P(c),25¢(c) Price, Cl Logo;rep 6.00
Sp/69 **(169)** JSe&StA,P(c),Cl Logo, Rigid(c);rep 6.00

005-MOBY DICK
By Herman Melville

09/42 **(---)** LZ,LZ(c),Original ... 950.00
05/43 **(10)** LZ,LZ(c),Conray Products Edition, No(c)Price;rep 175.00
11/43 **(15)** LZ,LZ(c),Long Island Independent Edition;rep 135.00
06/44 **(18/20)** LZ,LZ(c),Sunrise Times Edition;rep 125.00
07/44 **(20)** LZ,LZ(c),Sunrise Times Edition;rep 110.00
07/44 **(21)** LZ,LZ(c),Sunrise Times Edition;rep 100.00
06/46 **(28)** LZ,LZ(c);rep 80.00
04/47 **(36)** LZ,LZ(c),New Cl Logo;rep 40.00
06/49 **(60)** LZ,LZ(c),Cl Logo;re .. 25.00
08/49 **(62)** LZ,LZ(c),Cl Logo;rep . 30.00
05/50 **(71)** LZ,LZ(c),Cl Logo;rep . 20.00
09/51 **(87)** LZ,LZ(c),15¢(c) Price, Cl Logo;rep 16.00
04/54 **(118)** LZ,LZ(c),Cl Logo;rep 12.00
03/56 **(131)** NN New Art,New P(c), Cl Logo;rep 12.00
05/57 **(138)** NN,P(c),Cl Logo;rep . 6.00
01/59 **(148)** NN,P(c),Cl Logo;rep . 6.00
09/60 **(158)** NN,P(c),Cl Logo;rep . 6.00
62/63 **(167)** NN,P(c),Cl Logo;rep . 6.00
06/64 **(167)** NN,P(c),Cl Logo;rep . 6.00
07/65 **(167)** NN,P(c),Cl Logo;rep . 6.00
03/66 **(167)** NN,P(c),Cl Logo;rep . 6.00
09/67 **(166)** NN,P(c),Cl Logo;rep . 6.00
Wn/69 **(166)** NN,P(c),25¢(c) Price, Cl Logo, Rigid(c);rep 12.00
Wn/71 **(169)** NN,P(c),Cl Logo;rep 12.00

006-A TALE OF TWO CITIES
By Charles Dickens

11/42 **(---)** StM,StM(c),Original; 875.00
09/43 **(14)** StM,StM(c),No(c) Price; rep 175.00
03/44 **(18)** StM,StM(c),Long Island Independent Edition;rep 135.00
06/44 **(20)** StM,StM(c),Sunrise Times Edition;rep 125.00
06/46 **(28)** StM,StM(c);rep 75.00
09/48 **(51)** StM,StM(c),New Cl Logo; rep 40.00
10/49 **(64)** StM,StM(c),Cl Logo;rep 25.00
12/50 **(78)** StM,StM(c),15¢(c) Price, Cl Logo; rep 16.00
11/51 **(89)** StM,StM(c),Cl Logo;rep 14.00
03/54 **(117)** StM,StM(c),Cl Logo;rep 10.00

05/56 **(132)** JO New Art,New P(c), CI Logo;rep 14.00
09/57 **(140)** JO,P(c),CI Logo;rep . 6.00
11/57 **(147)** JO,P(c),CI Logo;rep . 6.00
09/59 **(152)** JO,P(c),CI Logo;rep 90.00
11/59 **(153)** JO,P(c),CI Logo;rep . 6.00
03/61 **(149)** JO,P(c),CI Logo;rep . 6.00
62/63 **(167)** JO,P(c),CI Logo;rep . 6.00
06/64 **(167)** JO,P(c),CI Logo;rep . 6.00
08/65 **(167)** JO,P(c),CI Logo;rep . 6.00
05/67 **(166)** JO,P(c),CI Logo;rep . 6.00
Fl/68 **(166)** JO,NN New P(c), 25¢(c)Price,CI Logo;rep 12.00
Sr/70 **(169)** JO,NN P(c),CI Logo, Rigid(c);rep 12.00

CI #7 Robin Hood
© Gilberton Publications

007-ROBIN HOOD
By Howard Pyle

12/42 **(---)** LZ,LZ(c),Original ... 650.00
06/43 **(12)** LZ,LZ(c),P.D.C. on(c) Deleted;rep 150.00
03/44 **(18)** LZ,LZ(c),Long Island Independent Edition;rep 125.00
06/44 **(20)** LZ,LZ(c),Nassau Bulletin Edition;rep 120.00
10/44 **(22)** LZ,LZ(c),Queens City Times Edition;rep 100.00
06/46 **(28)** LZ,LZ(c),rep 75.00
09/48 **(51)** LZ,LZ(c),New CI Logo;rep 35.00
06/49 **(60)** LZ,LZ(c),CI Logo;rep . 18.00
10/49 **(64)** LZ,LZ(c),CI Logo;rep . 16.00
12/50 **(78)** LZ,LZ(c),CI Logo;rep . 16.00
07/52 **(97)** LZ,LZ(c),CI Logo;rep . 14.00
03/53 **(106)** LZ,LZ(c),CI Logo;rep 13.00
07/54 **(121)** LZ,LZ(c),CI Logo;rep 12.00
11/55 **(129)** LZ,New P(c), CI Logo;rep 12.00
01/57 **(136)** JkS New Art,P(c);rep . 5.00
03/58 **(143)** JkS,P(c),CI Logo;rep . 6.00
11/59 **(153)** JkS,P(c),CI Logo;rep . 6.00
10/61 **(164)** JkS,P(c),CI Logo;rep . 6.00
62/63 **(167)** JkS,P(c),CI Logo;rep . 6.00
06/64 **(167)** JkS,P(c),CI Logo;rep . 7.00
05/65 **(167)** JkS,P(c),CI Logo;rep . 6.00
07/66 **(167)** JkS,P(c),CI Logo;rep . 6.00
12/67 **(166)** JkS,P(c),CI Logo;rep . 7.00
Sr/69 **(169)** JkS,P(c),CI Logo, Rigid(c);rep 6.00

008-ARABIAN KNIGHTS
By Antoine Galland

03/43 **(---)** LCh,LCh(c),Original 1,750.00
09/43 **(14)** LCh,LCh(c);rep 600.00
01/44 **(17)** LCh,LCh(c),Long Island Independent Edition;rep 500.00
06/44 **(20)** LCh,LCh(c),Nassau Bulletin Edition,64 pgs;rep .. 375.00
06/46 **(28)** LCh,LCh(c);rep 225.00
09/48 **(51)** LCh,LCh(c),New CI Logo; rep 225.00
10/49 **(64)** LCh,LCh(c),CI Logo;rep 200.00
12/50 **(78)** LCh,LCh(c),CI Logo;rep 160.00
10/61 **(164)** ChB New Art,P(c), CI Logo;rep 135.00

009-LES MISERABLES
By Victor Hugo

03/43 **(---)** RLv,RLv(c),Original . 550.00
09/43 **(14)** RLv,RLv(c);rep 175.00
03/44 **(18)** RLv,RLv(c),Nassau Bulletin Edition;rep 150.00
06/44 **(20)** RLv,RLv(c),Richmond Courier Edition;rep 125.00
06/46 **(28)** RLv,RLv(c);rep 95.00
09/48 **(51)** RLv,RLv(c),New CI Logo; rep 40.00
05/50 **(71)** RLv,RLv(c),CI Logo;rep 30.00
09/51 **(87)** RLv,RLv(c),CI Logo, 15¢(c)Price;rep 25.00
03/61 **(161)** NN New Art,GMc New P(c), CI Logo;rep 22.00
09/63 **(167)** NN,GMc P(c),CI Logo; rep 18.00
12/65 **(167)** NN,GMc P(c),CI Logo; rep 18.00
1968 **(166)** NN,GMc P(c),25¢(c) Price, CI Logo;rep 25.00

010-ROBINSON CRUSOE
By Daniel Defoe

04/43 **(---)** StM,StM(c),Original . 550.00
09/43 **(14)** StM,StM(c);rep 175.00
03/44 **(18)** StM,StM(c),Nassau Bulletin Ed.,'Bill of Rights'Pge.64;rep . 125.00
06/44 **(20)** StM,StM(c),Queens Home News Edition;rep 100.00
??/45 **(23)** StM,StM(c);rep 75.00
06/46 **(28)** StM,StM(c);rep 35.00
09/48 **(51)** StM,StM(c),New CI Logo; rep 25.00
10/49 **(64)** StM,StM(c),CI Logo;8ep 15.00
12/50 **(78)** StM,StM(c),15¢(c) Price, CI Logo;rep 13.00
07/52 **(97)** StM,StM(c),CI Logo;rep 12.00
12/53 **(114)** StM,StM(c),CI Logo;rep 12.00
01/56 **(130)** StM,New P(c),CI Logo; rep 12.00
09/57 **(140)** SmC New Art,P(c), CI Logo; rep 6.00
11/59 **(153)** SmC,P(c),CI Logo;rep 6.00
10/61 **(164)** SmC,P(c),CI Logo;rep 6.00
62/63 **(167)** SmC,P(c),CI Logo;rep 6.00
07/64 **(167)** SmC,P(c),CI Logo;rep 10.00
05/65 **(167)** SmC,P(c),CI Logo;rep 6.00
06/66 **(167)** SmC,P(c),CI Logo;rep 6.00
Fl/68 **(166)** SmC,P(c),CI Logo, 25¢(c)Price;rep 8.00
1968 **(166)** SmC,P(c),CI Logo,No Twin Circle Ad;rep 7.00
Sr/70 **(169)** SmC,P(c),CI Logo, Rigid(c);rep 7.00

011-DON QUIXOTE
By Miguel de Cervantes Saavedra

05/43 **(---)** LZ,LZ(c),Original ... 600.00
03/44 **(18)** LZ,LZ(c),Nassau Bulletin Edition;rep 175.00
07/44 **(21)** LZ,LZ(c),Queens Home News Edition;rep 125.00
06/46 **(28)** LZ,LZ(c);rep 75.00
08/53 **(110)** LZ,TO New P(c),New CI Logo;rep 22.00
05/60 **(156)** LZ,TO P(c),Pages Reduced to 48,CI Logo;rep ... 15.00
1962 **(165)** LZ,TO P(c),CI Logo;rep 8.00
01/64 **(167)** LZ,TO P(c),CI Logo;rep 8.00
11/65 **(167)** LZ,TO P(c),CI Logo;rep 8.00
1968 **(166)** LZ,TO P(c),CI Logo, 25¢(c)Price;rep 14.00

012-RIP VAN WINKLE & THE HEADLESS HORSEMAN
By Washington Irving

06/43 **(----)** RLv,RLv(c),Original 600.00
11/43 **(15)** RLv,RLv(c),Long Island Independent Edition;rep 175.00
06/44 **(20)** RLv,RLv(c),Long Island Independent Edition;rep 125.00
10/44 **(22)** RLv,RLv(c),Queens City Times Edition;rep 110.00
06/46 **(28)** RLv,RLv(c);rep 75.00
06/49 **(60)** RLv,RLv(c),New CI Logo;rep 25.00
08/49 **(62)** RLv,RLv(c),CI Logo;rep 23.00
05/50 **(71)** RLv,RLv(c),CI Logo;rep 20.00
11/51 **(89)** RLv,RLv(c),15¢(c) Price, CI Logo;rep 11.00
04/54 **(118)** RLv,RLv(c),CI Logo;rep 11.00
05/56 **(132)** RLv,New P(c), CI Logo; rep 12.00
05/59 **(150)** NN New Art;P(c), CI Logo; rep 12.00
09/60 **(158)** NN,P(c),CI Logo;rep . 6.00
62/63 **(167)** NN,P(c),CI Logo;rep . 6.00
12/63 **(167)** NN,P(c),CI Logo;rep . 6.00
04/65 **(167)** NN,P(c),CI Logo;rep . 7.00
04/66 **(167)** NN,P(c),CI Logo;rep . 6.00
1969 **(166)** NN,P(c),CI Logo, 25¢(c)Price,Rigid(c);rep 12.00
Sr/70 **(169)** NN,P(c),CI Logo, Rigid(c);rep 12.00

013-DR. JEKYLL AND MR.HYDE
By Robert Louis Stevenson

08/43 **(---)** AdH,AdH(c),Original 750.00
11/43 **(15)** AdH,AdH(c),Long Island Independent Edition;rep 200.00
06/44 **(20)** AdH,AdH(c),Long Island Independent Edition;rep 150.00
06/46 **(28)** AdH,AdH(c),No(c) Price; rep 110.00
06/49 **(60)** AdH,HcK New(c),New CI Logo,Pgs.reduced to 48;rep .. 40.00
08/49 **(62)** AdH,HcK(c),CI Logo;rep 35.00
05/50 **(71)** AdH,HcK(c),CI Logo;rep 20.00
09/51 **(87)** AdH,HcK(c),Erroneous Return of Original Date,CI Logo;rep .. 18.00
10/53 **(112)** LC New Art,New P(c), CI Logo;rep 18.00
11/59 **(153)** LC,P(c),CI Logo;rep . 7.00
03/61 **(161)** LC,P(c),CI Logo;rep . 7.00
62/63 **(167)** LC,P(c),CI Logo;rep . 7.00
08/64 **(167)** LC,P(c),CI Logo;rep . 7.00
11/65 **(167)** LC,P(c),CI Logo;rep . 7.00
1968 **(166)** LC,P(c),CI Logo, 25¢(c)Price;rep 8.00
Wr/69 **(169)** LC,P(c),CI Logo, Rigid(c);rep 7.00

014-WESTWARD HO!
By Charles Kingsley

09/43 **(---)** ASm,ASm(c),Original 1,350.00
11/43 **(15)** ASm,ASm(c),Long Island Independent Edition;rep 550.00
07/44 **(21)** ASm,ASm(c);rep ... 400.00
06/46 **(28)** ASm,ASm(c),No(c) Price; rep 350.00
11/48 **(53)** ASm,ASm(c),Pages reduced to 48, New CI Logo;rep 275.00

015-UNCLE TOM'S CABIN

By Harriet Beecher Stowe

11/43 **(---)** RLv,RLv(c),Original . 500.00
11/43 **(15)** RLv,RLv(c),Blank Price Circle, Long Island Independent Ed.;rep 200.00
07/44 **(21)** RLv,RLv(c),Nassau Bulliten Edition;rep 175.00
06/46 **(28)** RLv,RLv(c),No(c) Price; rep 90.00
11/48 **(53)** RLv,RLv(c),Pages Reduced to 48, New CI Logo;rep 40.00
05/50 **(71)** RLv,RLv(c),CI Logo;5ep22.00
11/51 **(89)** RLv,RLv(c),15¢(c) Price, CI Logo;rep 22.00
03/54 **(117)** RLv,New P(c),CI Logo, Lettering Changes;rep . . 12.00
09/55 **(128)** RLv,P(c),"Picture Progress"Promotion,CI Logo;rep 10.00
03/57 **(137)** RLv,P(c),CI Logo;rep . 6.00
09/58 **(146)** RLv,P(c),CI Logo;rep . 6.00
01/60 **(154)** RLv,P(c),CI Logo;rep . 6.00
03/61 **(161)** RLv,P(c),CI Logo;rep . 6.00
62/63 **(167)** RLv,P(c),CI Logo;rep . 6.00
06/64 **(167)** RLv,P(c),CI Logo;rep . 6.00
05/65 **(167)** RLv,P(c),CI Logo;rep . 6.00
05/67 **(166)** RLv,P(c),CI Logo;rep . 6.00
Wr/69 **(166)** RLv,P(c),CI Logo, Rigid(c);rep 12.00
Sr/70 **(169)** RLv,P(c),CI Logo, Rigid(c);rep 12.00

016-GULLIVER'S TRAVELS

By Johnathan Swift

12/43 **(----)** LCh,LCh(c),Original 450.00
06/44 **(18/20)** LCh,LCh(c),Queen's Home News Edition,No(c)Price;rep . 150.00
10/44 **(22)** LCh,LCh(c),Queen's Home News Editon;rep 125.00
06/46 **(28)** LCh,LCh(c);rep 75.00
06/49 **(60)** LCh,LCh(c),Pgs. Reduced To 48, New CI Logo;rep 30.00
08/49 **(62)** LCh,LCh(c),CI Logo;rep 19.00
10/49 **(64)** LCh,LCh(c),CI Logo;rep 14.00
12/50 **(78)** LCh,LCh(c),15¢(c) Price, CI Logo;rep 12.00
11/51 **(89)** LCh,LCh(c),CI Logo;rep 12.00
03/60 **(155)** LCh,New P(c),CI Logo; rep 6.00
1962 **(165)** LCh,P(c),CI Logo;rep . 6.00
05/64 **(167)** LCh,P(c),CI Logo;rep 6.00
11/65 **(167)** LCh,P(c),CI Logo;rep 6.00
1968 **(166)** LCh,P(c),CI Logo, 25¢(c)Price;rep 6.00
Wr/69 **(169)** LCh,P(c),CI Logo, Rigid(c);rep 6.00

017-THE DEERSLAYER

By James Fenimore Cooper

01/44 **(----)** LZ,LZ(c),Original . . 450.00
03/44 **(18)** LZ,LZ(c),No(c)Price;rep150.00
10/44 **(22)** LZ,LZ(c),Queen's City Times Edition;rep 110.00
06/46 **(28)** LZ,LZ(c);rep 75.00
06/49 **(60)** LZ,LZ(c),Pgs. Reduced to 48,New CI Logo;rep 30.00
10/49 **(64)** LZ,LZ(c),CI Logo;rep . 16.00
07/51 **(85)** LZ,LZ(c),15¢(c) Price, CI Logo;rep 14.00
04/54 **(118)** LZ,LZ(c),CI Logo;rep 12.00
05/56 **(132)** LZ,LZ(c),CI Logo;rep 11.00
11/66 **(167)** LZ,LZ(c),CI Logo;rep 11.00
1968 **(166)** LZ,StA New P(c),CI Logo, 25¢(c)Price;rep 14.00
Sg/71 **(169)** LZ,StA P(c),CI Logo, Rigid(c), Letters From Parents and Educators;rep 12.00

018-THE HUNCHBACK OF NOTRE DAME

By Victor Hugo

03/44 **(---)** ASm,ASm(c),Original Gilberton Edition 600.00
03/44 **(---)** ASm,ASm(c),Original Island Publications Edition . . 525.00
06/44 **(18/20)** ASm,ASm(c),Queens Home News Edition;rep 175.00
10/44 **(22)** ASm,ASm(c),Queens City Times Edition;rep 125.00
06/46 **(28)** ASm,ASm(c);rep . . . 100.00
06/49 **(60)** ASm,HcK New(c)8 Pgs. Deleted, New CI Logo;rep . . . 30.00
08/49 **(62)** ASm,HcK(c),CI Logo;rep 20.00
12/50 **(78)** ASm,HcK(c),15¢(c) Price; CI Logo;rep 16.00
11/51 **(89)** ASm,HcK(c),CI Logo;rep 12.00
04/54 **(118)** ASm,HcK(c),CI Logo;rep 21.00
09/57 **(140)** ASm,New P(c),CI Logo; rep 17.00
09/58 **(146)** ASm,P(c),CI Logo;rep 16.00
09/60 **(158)** GE&RC New Art,GMc New P(c),CI Logo;rep 7.00
1962 **(165)** GE&RC,GMc P(c),CI Logo; rep 7.00
09/63 **(167)** GE&RC,GMc P(c),CI Logo; rep 7.00
10/64 **(167)** GE&RC,GMc P(c),CI Logo; rep 6.00
04/66 **(167)** GE&RC,GMc P(c),CI Logo; rep 6.00
1968 **(166)** GE&RC,GMc P(c),CI Logo, 25¢(c)Price;rep 6.00
Sr/70 **(169)** GE&RC,GMc P(c),CI Logo, Rigid(c);rep 6.00

019-HUCKLEBERRY FINN

By Mark Twain

04/44 **(---)** LZ,LZ(c),Original Gilberton Edition 400.00
04/44 **(---)** LZ,LZ(c),Original Island Publications Company Edition 450.00
03/44 **(18)** LZ,LZ(c),Nassau Bulliten Editon;rep 175.00
10/44 **(22)** LZ,LZ(c),Queens City Times Edition;rep 125.00
06/46 **(28)** LZ,LZ(c);rep 85.00
06/49 **(60)** LZ,LZ(c),New CI Logo, Pgs.Reduced to 48;rep 30.00
08/49 **(62)** LZ,LZ(c),CI Logo;rep . 22.00
12/50 **(78)** LZ,LZ(c),CI Logo;rep . 15.00
11/51 **(89)** LZ,LZ(c),CI Logo;rep . 15.00
03/54 **(117)** LZ,LZ(c),CI Logo;rep 15.00
03/56 **(131)** FrG New Art,New P(c), CI Logo; rep6.00
09/57 **(140)** FrG,P(c),CI Logo;rep . 6.00
05/59 **(150)** FrG,P(c),CI Logo;rep . 6.00
09/60 **(158)** FrG,P(c),CI Logo;rep . 6.00
1962 **(165)** FrG,P(c),CI Logo;rep . 6.00
62/63 **(167)** FrG,P(c),CI Logo;rep . 6.00
06/64 **(167)** FrG,P(c),CI Logo;rep . 6.00
06/65 **(167)** FrG,P(c),CI Logo;rep . 6.00
10/65 **(167)** FrG,P(c),CI Logo;rep . 6.00
09/67 **(166)** FrG,P(c),CI Logo;rep . 6.00
Wr/69 **(166)** FrG,P(c),CI Logo, 25¢(c)Price, Rigid(c);rep 5.00
Sr/70 **(169)** FrG,P(c),CI Logo, Rigid(c);rep 5.00

020-THE CORSICAN BROTHERS

By Alexandre Dumas

06/44 **(---)** ASm,ASm(c),Original Gilberton Edition 450.00
06/44 **(---)** ASm,ASm(c),Original Courier Edition 400.00
06/44 **(---)** ASm,ASm(c),Original Long Island Independent Edition . . 400.00
10/44 **(22)** ASm,ASm(c),Queens City Times Edition;rep 165.00
06/46 **(28)** ASm,ASm(c);rep . . . 150.00
06/49 **(60)** ASm,ASm(c),No(c)Price, New CI Logo,Pgs. Reduced to 48;rep 125.00
08/49 **(62)** ASm,ASm(c),CI Logo;rep 115.00
12/50 **(78)** ASm,ASm(c),15¢(c) Price, CI Logo;rep 100.00
07/52 **(97)** ASm,ASm(c),CI Logo;rep 90.00

021-FAMOUS MYSTERIES

By Sir Arthur Conan Doyle
Guy de Maupassant
& Edgar Allan Poe

07/44 **(---)** ASm,AdH,LZ,ASm(c), Original Gilberton Edition . . . 650.00
07/44 **(---)** ASm,AdH,LZ,ASm(c), Original Island Publications Edition; No Date or Indicia . . 675.00
07/44 **(---)** ASm,AdH,LZ,ASm(c),Original Richmond Courier Edition . . . 600.00
10/44 **(22)** ASm,AdH,LZ,ASm(c), Nassau Bulliten Edition;rep . . 275.00
09/46 **(30)** ASm,AdH,LZ,ASm(c); rep 225.00
08/49 **(62)** ASm,AdH,LZ,ASm(c), New CI Logo;rep 150.00
04/50 **(70)** ASm,AdH,LZ,ASm(c), CI Logo;rep 135.00
07/51 **(85)** ASm,AdH,LZ,ASm(c), 15¢(c) Price,CI Logo;rep 100.00
12/53 **(114)** ASm,AdH,LZ,New P(c), CI Logo;rep 100.00

CI #22 The Pathfinder
© Gilberton Publications

022-THE PATHFINDER

By James Fenimore Cooper

10/44 **(---)** LZ,LZ(c),Original Gilberton Edition 350.00
10/44 **(---)** LZ,LZ(c),Original Island Publications Edition; . . 275.00
10/44 **(---)** LZ,LZ(c),Original Queens County Times Edition 275.00
09/46 **(30)** LZ,LZ(c),No(c) Price;rep 90.00
06/49 **(60)** LZ,LZ(c),New CI Logo, Pgs.Reduced To 48;rep 30.00
08/49 **(62)** LZ,LZ(c),CI Logo;re2 . 20.00
04/50 **(70)** LZ,LZ(c),CI Logo;rep . 16.00
07/51 **(85)** LZ,LZ(c),15¢(c) Price, CI Logo;rep 14.00
04/54 **(118)** LZ,LZ(c),CI Logo;rep 12.00
05/56 **(132)** LZ,LZ(c),CI Logo;rep 11.00
09/58 **(146)** LZ,LZ(c),CI Logo;rep 21.00
11/63 **(167)** LZ,NN New P(c),CI Logo; rep 17.00
12/65 **(167)** LZ,NN P(c),CI Logo;rep 17.00
08/67 **(166)** LZ,NN P(c),CI Logo;rep 17.00

023-OLIVER TWIST
By Charles Dickens
(First Classic produced by the Iger shop)

- 07/45 **(---)** AdH,AdH(c),Original 275.00
- 09/46 **(30)** AdH,AdH(c),Price Circle is Blank;rep ... 200.00
- 06/49 **(60)** AdH,AdH(c),Pgs. Reduced To 48, New CI Logo;rep ... 28.00
- 08/49 **(62)** AdH,AdH(c),CI Logo;rep ... 20.00
- 05/50 **(71)** AdH,AdH(c),CI Logo;rep ... 16.00
- 07/51 **(85)** AdH,AdH(c),15¢(c) Price CI Logo;rep ... 14.00
- 04/52 **(94)** AdH,AdH(c),CI Logo;rep ... 12.00
- 04/54 **(118)** AdH,AdH(c),CI Logo;rep ... 11.00
- 01/57 **(136)** AdH,New P(c),CI Logo; rep ... 12.00
- 05/59 **(150)** AdH,P(c),CI Logo;rep 9.00
- 1961 **(164)** AdH,P(c),CI Logo;rep . 9.00
- 10/61 **(164)** GE&RC New Art,P(c), CI Logo;rep ... 16.00
- 62/63 **(167)** GE&RC,P(c),CI Logo; rep ... 6.00
- 08/64 **(167)** GE&RC,P(c),CI Logo; rep ... 6.00
- 12/65 **(167)** GE&RC,P(c), CI Logo;rep ... 6.00
- 1968 **(166)** GE&RC,P(c),CI Logo, 25¢(c)Price;rep ... 6.00
- Wr/69 **(169)** GE&RC,P(c),CI Logo, Rigid(c);rep ... 6.00

024-A CONNECTICUT YANKEE IN KING ARTHUR'S COURT
By Mark Twain

- 09/45 **(---)** JH,JH(c),Original ... 300.00
- 09/46 **(30)** JH,JH(c),Price Circle Blank;rep ... 90.00
- 06/49 **(60)** JH,JH(c),8 Pages Deleted,New CI Logo;rep ... 25.00
- 08/49 **(62)** JH,JH(c),CI Logo;rep 20.00
- 05/50 **(71)** JH,JH(c),CI Logo;rep 14.00
- 09/51 **(87)** JH,JH(c),15¢(c) Price CI Logo;rep ... 12.00
- 07/54 **(121)** JH,JH(c),CI Logo;rep 11.00
- 09/57 **(140)** JkS New Art,New P(c),CI Logo; rep ... 11.00
- 11/59 **(153)** JkS,P(c),CI Logo;rep . 6.00
- 1961 **(164)** JkS,P(c),CI Logo;rep . 6.00
- 62/63 **(167)** JkS,P(c),CI Logo;rep . 6.00
- 07/64 **(167)** JkS,P(c),CI Logo;rep . 6.00
- 06/66 **(167)** JkS,P(c),CI Logo;rep . 6.00
- 1968 **(166)** JkS,P(c),CI logo, 25¢(c)Price;rep ... 6.00
- Sg/71 **(169)** JkS,P(c),CI Logo, Rigid(c);rep ... 64.00

025-TWO YEARS BEFORE THE MAST
By Richard Henry Dana, Jr.

- 10/45 **(---)** RWb,DvH,Original; . 300.00
- 09/46 **(30)** RWb,DvH,Price Circle Blank;rep ... 85.00
- 06/49 **(60)** RWb,DvH,8 Pages Deleted,New CI Logo;rep ... 30.00
- 08/49 **(62)** RWb,DvH,CI Logo;rep 20.00
- 05/50 **(71)** RWb,DvH,CI Logo;rep 15.00
- 07/51 **(85)** RWb,DvH,15¢(c) Price CI Logo;rep ... 12.00
- 12/53 **(114)** RWb,DvH,CI Logo;rep 11.00
- 05/60 **(156)** RWb,DvH,New P(c),CI Logo, 3 Pgs. Replaced By Fillers;rep 11.00
- 12/63 **(167)** RWb,DvH,P(c),CI Logo; rep ... 6.00
- 12/65 **(167)** RWb,DvH,P(c),CI Logo; rep ... 6.00
- 09/67 **(166)** RWb,DvH,P(c),CI Logo; rep ... 6.00
- Wr/69 **(169)** RWb,DvH,P(c),25¢(c) Price, CI Logo,Rigid(c);rep ... 6.00

CI #28 Michael Strogoff
© Gilberton Publications

026-FRANKENSTEIN
By Mary Wollstonecraft Shelley

- 12/45 **(---)** RWb&ABr,RWb & ABr(c),Original ... 650.00
- 09/46 **(30)** RWb&ABr,RWb &ABr(c), Price Circle Blank;rep ... 225.00
- 06/49 **(60)** RWb&ABr,RWb&ABr(c), New CI Logo;rep ... 65.00
- 08/49 **(62)** RWb&ABr,RWb & ABr(c), CI Logo;rep ... 75.00
- 05/50 **(71)** RWb&ABr,RWb & ABr(c), CI Logo;rep ... 40.00
- 04/51 **(82)** RWb&ABr,RWb &ABr(c), 15¢(c) Price,CI Logo;rep ... 25.00
- 03/54 **(117)** RWb&ABr,RWb & ABr(c),CI Logo;rep ... 14.00
- 09/58 **(146)** RWb&ABr,NS New P(c), CI Logo; rep ... 14.00
- 11/59 **(153)** RWb&ABr,NS P(c),CI Logo;rep ... 25.00
- 01/61 **(160)** RWb&ABr,NS P(c),CI Logo; rep ... 6.00
- 165 **(1962)** RWb&ABr,NS P(c), CI Logo; rep ... 6.00
- 62/63 **(167)** RWb&ABr,NS P(c), CI Logo; rep ... 6.00
- 06/64 **(167)** RWb&ABr,NS P(c), CI logo; rep ... 6.00
- 06/65 **(167)** RWb&ABr,NS P(c), CI Logo; rep ... 6.00
- 10/65 **(167)** RWb&ABr,NS P(c), CI Logo; rep ... 6.00
- 09/67 **(166)** RWb&ABr,NS P(c), CI Logo; rep ... 6.00
- Fl/69 **(169)** RWb&ABr,NS P(c),25¢(c) Price,CI Logo,Rigid(c);rep ... 6.00
- Sg/71 **(169)** RWb&ABr,NS P(c), CI Logo, Rigid(c);rep ... 6.00

027-THE ADVENTURES MARCO POLO
By Marco Polo & Donn Byrne

- 04/46 **(----)** HFl,HFl(c);Original . 300.00
- 09/46 **(30)** HFl,HFl(c);rep ... 85.00
- 04/50 **(70)** HFl,HFl(c),8 Pages Deleted, No(c) Price,New CI Logo;rep . 25.00
- 09/51 **(87)** HFl,HFl(c),15¢(c) Price,CI Logo;rep ... 15.00
- 03/54 **(117)** HFl,HFl(c),CILogo;rep 12.00
- 01/60 **(154)** HFl,New P(c),CI Logo;rep ... 11.00
- 1962 **(165)** HFl,P(c),CI Logo;rep . 6.00
- 04/64 **(167)** HFl,P(c),CI Logo;rep . 6.00
- 06/66 **(167)** HFl,P(c),CI Logo;rep . 6.00
- Sg/69 **(169)** HFl,P(c),CI Logo, 25¢(c)Price,Rigid(c);rep ... 6.00

028-MICHAEL STROGOFF
By Jules Verne

- 06/46 **(---)** AdH,AdH(c),Original 300.00
- 09/48 **(51)** AdH,AdH(c),8 Pages Deleted,New CI Logo;rep ... 90.00
- 01/54 **(115)** AdH,New P(c),CI Logo; rep ... 15.00
- 03/60 **(155)** AdH,P(c),CI Logo;rep 8.00
- 11/63 **(167)** AdH,P(c),CI Logo;rep 8.00
- 07/66 **(167)** AdH,P(c),CI Logo;rep 8.00
- Sr/69 **(169)**AdH,NN,NewP(c),25¢(c) Price, CI Logo,Rigid(c);rep ... 12.00

029-THE PRINCE AND THE PAUPER
By Mark Twain

- 07/46 **(---)** AdH,AdH(c),Original 500.00
- 06/49 **(60)** AdH,New HcK(c),New CI Logo,8 Pages Deleted;rep ... 30.00
- 08/49 **(62)** AdH,HcK(c),CILogo;rep 25.00
- 05/50 **(71)** AdH,HcK(c),CILogo;rep 15.00
- 03/52 **(93)** AdH,HcK(c),CILogo;rep 14.00
- 12/53 **(114)** AdH,HcK(c),CI Logo;rep ... 12.00
- 09/55 **(128)** AdH,New P(c),CI Logo; rep ... 12.00
- 05/57 **(138)** AdH,P(c),CI Logo;rep 6.00
- 05/59 **(150)** AdH,P(c),CI Logo;rep 6.00
- 1961 **(164)** AdH,P(c),CI Logo;rep . 6.00
- 62/63 **(167)** AdH,P(c),CI Logo;rep 6.00
- 07/64 **(167)** AdH,P(c),CI Logo;rep 6.00
- 11/65 **(167)** AdH,P(c),CI Logo;rep 6.00
- 1968 **(166)** AdH,P(c),CI Logo, 25¢(c)Price;rep ... 6.00
- Sr/70 **(169)** AdH,P(c),CI Logo, Rigid(c);rep ... 6.00

030-THE MOONSTONE
By William Wilkie Collins

- 09/46 **(---)** DRi,DRi(c),Original . 300.00
- 06/49 **(60)** DRi,DRi(c),8 Pages Deleted,New CI Logo;rep ... 40.00
- 04/50 **(70)** DRi,DRi(c),CI Logo;rep 20.00
- 03/60 **(155)** DRi,LbC New P(c), CI Logo;rep ... 45.00
- 1962 **(165)** DRi,LbC P(c),CI Logo; rep ... 16.00
- 01/64 **(167)** DRi,LbC P(c),CI Logo; rep ... 10.00
- 09/65 **(167)** DRi,LbC P(c),CI Logo; rep ... 7.00
- 1968 **(166)** DRi,LbC P(c),CI Logo, 25¢(c)Price;rep ... 6.00

031-THE BLACK ARROW
By Robert Louis Stevenson

- 10/46 **(---)** AdH,AdH(c),Original 275.00
- 09/48 **(51)** AdH,AdH(c),8 Pages Deleted,New CI Logo;rep ... 35.00
- 10/49 **(64)** AdH,AdH(c),CI Logo;rep ... 18.00
- 09/51 **(87)** AdH,AdH(c),15¢(c) Price;CI Logo;rep ... 15.00
- 06/53 **(108)** AdH,AdH(c),CI Logo;rep ... 14.00
- 03/55 **(125)** AdH,AdH(c),CI Logo;rep ... 12.00
- 03/56 **(131)** AdH,New P(c),CI Logo; rep ... 8.00
- 09/57 **(140)** AdH,P(c),CI Logo;rep 6.00
- 01/59 **(148)** AdH,P(c),CI Logo;rep 6.00
- 03/61 **(161)** AdH,P(c),CI Logo;rep 6.00
- 62/63 **(167)** AdH,P(c),CI Logo;rep 6.00
- 07/64 **(167)** AdH,P(c),CI logo;rep . 6.00
- 11/65 **(167)** AdH,P(c),CI Logo;rep 6.00
- 1968 **(166)** AdH,P(c),CI Logo, 25¢(c)Price;rep ... 6.00

032-LORNA DOONE
By Richard Doddridge Blackmore

12/46 **(---)** MB,MB(c),Original .. 300.00
10/49 **(53/64)** MB,MB(c),8 Pages Deleted,New CI Logo;rep 40.00
07/51 **(85)** MB,MB(c),15¢(c) Price, CI Logo;rep 26.00
04/54 **(118)** MB,MB(c),CI Logo;rep 16.00
05/57 **(138)** MB,New P(c); Old(c) Becomes New Splash Pge.,CI Logo;rep 12.00
05/59 **(150)** MB,P(c),CI Logo;rep . 6.00
1962 **(165)** MB,P(c),CI Logo;rep . 6.00
01/64 **(167)** MB,P(c),CI Logo;rep . 6.00
11/65 **(167)** MB,P(c),CI Logo;rep . 6.00
1968 **(166)** MB,New P(c),CI Logo; rep 14.00

033-THE ADVENTURES OF SHERLOCK HOLMES
By Sir Arthur Conan Doyle

01/47 **(---)** LZ,HcK(c),Original .. 825.00
11/48 **(53)** LZ,HcK(c),"A Study in Scarlet" Deleted,New CI Logo;rep ... 325.00
05/50 **(71)** LZ,HcK(c),CI Logo;rep 275.00
11/51 **(89)** LZ,HcK(c),15¢(c) Price,CI Logo;rep 225.00

034-MYSTERIOUS ISLAND
By Jules Verne
Last Classic Comic

02/47 **(---)** RWb&DvH,Original . 300.00
06/49 **(60)** RWb&DvH,8 Pages Deleted,New CI Logo;rep 30.00
08/49 **(62)** RWb&DvH,CI Logo;rep 20.00
05/50 **(71)** RWb&DvH,CI Logo;rep 32.00
12/50 **(78)** RWb&DvH,15¢(c) Price, CI Logo;rep 16.00
02/52 **(92)** RWb&DvH,CI Logo;rep 14.00
03/54 **(117)** RWb&DvH,CI Logo;rep12.00
09/57 **(140)** RWb&DvH,New P(c),CI Logo;rep 12.00
05/60 **(156)** RWb&DvH,P(c),CI Logo;rep 6.00
10/63 **(167)** RWb&DvH,P(c),CI Logo;rep 6.00
05/64 **(167)** RWb&DvH,P(c),CI Logo;rep 6.00
06/66 **(167)** RWb&DvH,P(c),CI logo;rep 6.00
1968 **(166)** RWb&DvH,P(c),CI Logo, 25¢(c)Price;rep 6.00

035-LAST DAYS OF POMPEII
By Lord Edward Bulwer Lytton
First Classics Illustrated

03/47 **(---)** HcK,HcK(c),Original 300.00
03/61 **(161)** JK,New P(c), 15¢(c)Price;rep 25.00
01/64 **(167)** JK,P(c);rep 9.00
07/66 **(167)** JK,P(c);rep 9.00
Sg/70 **(169)** JK,P(c),25¢(c) Price, Rigid(c);rep 10.00

036-TYPEE
By Herman Melville

04/47 **(---)** EzW,EzW(c),Original 135.00
10/49 **(64)** EzW,EzW(c),No(c)price, 8 pages deleted;rep 26.00
03/60 **(155)** EzW,GMc New P(c);rep 11.00
09/63 **(167)** EzW,GMc P(c);rep .. 8.00
07/65 **(167)** EzW,GMc P(c);rep .. 8.00
Sr/69 **(169)** EzW,GMc P(c),25¢(c) Price, Rigid(c);rep 7.00

037-THE PIONEERS
By James Fenimore Cooper

05/47 **(37)** RP,RP(c),Original .. 135.00
08/49 **(62)** RP,RP(c),8 Pages Deleted;rep 25.00
04/50 **(70)** RP,RP(c);rep 75.00
02/52 **(92)** RP,RP(c),15¢(c)Price; rep 15.00
04/54 **(118)** RP,RP(c);rep 12.00
03/56 **(131)** RP,RP(c);rep 12.00
05/56 **(132)** RP,RP(c);rep 12.00
11/59 **(153)** RP,RP(c);rep 8.00
05/64 **(167)** RP,RP(c);rep 8.00
06/66 **(167)** RP,RP(c);rep 8.00
1968 **(166)** RP,TO New P(c), 25¢(c)Price;rep 18.00

038-ADVENTURES OF CELLINI
By Benvenuto Cellini

06/47 **(---)** AgF,AgF(c),Original . 225.00

CI #38 Adventures of Cellini
© Gilberton Publications

1961 **(164)** NN New Art,New P(c); rep 15.00
12/63 **(167)** NN,P(c);rep 9.00
07/66 **(167)** NN,P(c);rep 9.00
Sg/70 **(169)** NN,P(c),25¢(c) Price, Rigid(c);rep 10.00

039-JANE EYRE
By Charlotte Bronte

07/47 **(---)** HyG,HyG(c),Original 200.00
06/49 **(60)** HyG,HyG(c),No(c)Price, 8 pages deleted;rep 30.00
08/49 **(62)** HyG,HyG(c);rep 25.00
05/50 **(71)** HyG,HyG(c);rep 22.00
02/52 **(92)** HyG,HyG(c),15¢(c) Price; rep 15.00
04/54 **(118)** HyG,HyG(c);rep ... 15.00
01/58 **(142)** HyG,New P(c);rep .. 16.00
01/60 **(154)** HyG,P(c);rep 14.00
1962 **(165)** HjK New Art,P(c);rep 16.00
12/63 **(167)** HjK,P(c);rep 16.00
04/65 **(167)** HjK,P(c);rep 14.00
08/66 **(167)** HjK,P(c);rep 14.00
1968 **(166)** HjK,NN New P(c);rep 32.00

040-MYSTERIES (The Pit & the Pendulum, The Adventures of Hans Pfall, Fall of the House of Usher)
By Edgar Allan Poe

08/47 **(---)** HcK,AgF,HyG,HcK(c), Original 500.00
08/49 **(62)** HcK,AgF,HyG,HcK(c), 8 Pages deleted;rep 225.00
09/50 **(75)** HcK,AgF,HyG, HcK(c);rep 185.00
02/52 **(92)** HcK,AgF,HyG,HcK(c) 15¢(c) Price;rep 135.00

041-TWENTY YEARS AFTER
By Alexandre Dumas

09/47 **(---)** RBu,RBu(c),Original 400.00
08/49 **(62)** RBu,HcK New(c),No(c) Price, 8 Pages Deleted;rep ... 30.00
12/50 **(78)** RBu,HcK(c),15¢(c) Price; rep 18.00
05/60 **(156)** RBu,DgR New P(c); rep 12.00
12/63 **(167)** RBu,DgR P(c);rep ... 6.00
11/66 **(167)** RBu,DgR P(c);rep ... 6.00
Sg/70 **(169)** RBu,DgR P(c),25¢(c) Price,Rigid(c);rep 6.00

042-SWISS FAMILY ROBINSON
By Johann Wyss

10/47 **(42)** HcK,HcK(c),Original 140.00
08/49 **(62)** HcK,HcK(c),No(c)price, 8 Pages Deleted,Not Every Issue Has 'Gift Box' Ad;rep 30.00
09/50 **(75)** HcK,HcK(c);rep 16.00
03/52 **(93)** HcK,HcK(c);rep 14.00
03/54 **(117)** HcK,HcK(c);rep 12.00
03/56 **(131)** HcK,New P(c);rep .. 12.00
03/57 **(137)** HcK,P(c);rep 11.00
11/57 **(141)** HcK,P(c);rep 11.00
09/59 **(152)** NN New art,P(c);rep 11.00
09/60 **(158)** NN,P(c);rep 6.00
12/63 **(165)** NN,P(c);rep 11.00
12/63 **(167)** NN,P(c);rep 7.00
04/65 **(167)** NN,P(c);rep 7.00
05/66 **(167)** NN,P(c);rep 7.00
11/67 **(166)** NN,P(c);rep 6.00
Sg/69 **(169)** NN,P(c);rep 6.00

043-GREAT EXPECTATIONS
By Charles Dickens

11/47 **(---)** HcK,HcK(c),Original 625.00
08/49 **(62)** HcK,HcK(c),No(c)price; 8 pages deleted;rep 315.00

044-MYSTERIES OF PARIS
By Eugene Sue

12/47 **(44)** HcK,HcK(c),Original 500.00
08/47 **(62)** HcK,HcK(c),No(c)Price, 8 Pages Deleted,Not Every Issue Has'Gift Box'Ad;rep 225.00
12/50 **(78)** HcK,HcK(c),15¢(c) Price; rep 200.00

045-TOM BROWN'S SCHOOL DAYS
By Thomas Hughes

01/48 **(44)** HFl,HFl(c),Original, 1st 48 Pge. Issue 110.00
10/49 **(64)** HFl,HFl(c),No(c) Price;rep 32.00
03/61 **(161)** JTg New Art,GMc New P(c);rep 12.00
02/64 **(167)** JTg,GMc P(c);rep ... 8.00
08/66 **(167)** JTg,GMc P(c);rep ... 8.00
1968 **(166)** JTg,GMc P(c), 25¢(c)Price;rep 8.00

046-KIDNAPPED
By Robert Louis Stevenson

04/48 **(47)** RWb,RWb(c),Original 90.00
08/49 **(62)** RWb,RWb(c),Red Circle Either Blank or With 10¢;rep .. 62.00
12/50 **(78)** RWb,RWb(c),15¢(c) Price; rep 16.00
09/51 **(87)** RWb,RWb(c);rep ... 14.00
04/54 **(118)** RWb,RWb(c);rep ... 12.00
03/56 **(131)** RWb,New P(c);rep . 11.00
09/57 **(140)** RWb,P(c);rep 6.00
05/59 **(150)** RWb,P(c);rep 6.00
05/60 **(156)** RWb,P(c);rep 6.00

1961 **(164)** RWb,P(c),Reduced Pge. Wdth;rep 6.00
62/63 **(167)** RWb,P(c);rep 6.00
03/64 **(167)** RWb,P(c);rep 6.00
06/65 **(167)** RWb,P(c);rep 6.00
12/65 **(167)** RWb,P(c);rep 6.00
09/67 **(167)** RWb,P(c);rep 6.00
Wr/69 **(166)** RWb,P(c),25¢(c) Price, Rigid(c);rep 6.00
Sr/70 **(169)** RWb,P(c),Rigid(c);rep 6.00

047-TWENTY THOUSAND LEAGUES UNDER THE SEA

By Jules Verne

05/58 **(47)** HcK,HcK(c),Original 110.00
10/49 **(64)** HcK,HcK(c),No(c) Price; rep 25.00
12/50 **(78)** HcK,HcK(c),15¢(c) Price; rep 20.00
04/52 **(94)** HcK,HcK(c);rep 18.00
04/54 **(118)** HcK,HcK(c);rep 15.00
09/55 **(128)** HcK,New P(c);rep . . 12.00
07/56 **(133)** HcK,P(c);rep 12.00
09/57 **(140)** HcK,P(c);rep 6.00
01/59 **(148)** HcK,P(c);rep 6.00
05/60 **(156)** HcK,P(c);rep 6.00
62/63 **(165)** HcK,P(c);rep 6.00
05/48 **(167)** HcK,P(c);rep 6.00
03/64 **(167)** HcK,P(c);rep 6.00
08/65 **(167)** HcK,P(c);rep 5.00
10/66 **(167)** HcK,P(c);rep 6.00
1968 **(166)** HcK,NN New P(c), 25¢(c)Price;rep 12.00
Sg/70 **(169)** HcK,NN P(c), Rigid(c);rep 12.00

048-DAVID COPPERFIELD

By Charles Dickens

06/48 **(47)** HcK,HcK(c),Original 110.00
10/49 **(64)** HcK,HcK(c),Price Circle Replaced By Image of Boy Reading;rep 25.00
09/51 **(87)** HcK,HcK(c),15¢(c) Price; rep 18.00
07/54 **(121)** HcK,New P(c);rep . . 12.00
10/56 **(130)** HcK,P(c);rep 7.00
09/57 **(140)** HcK,P(c);rep 7.00
01/59 **(148)** HcK,P(c);rep 7.00
05/60 **(156)** HcK,P(c);rep 7.00
62/63 **(167)** HcK,P(c);rep 6.00
04/64 **(167)** HcK,P(c);rep 6.00
06/65 **(167)** HcK,P(c);rep 6.00
05/67 **(166)** HcK,P(c);rep 6.00
R/67 **(166)** HcK,P(c);rep 11.00
Sg/69 **(166)** HcK,P(c),25¢(c) Price, Rigid(c);rep 6.00
Wr/69 **(169)** HcK,P(c),Rigid(c);rep 6.00

049-ALICE IN WONDERLAND

By Lewis Carroll

07/48 **(47)** AB,AB(c),Original . . 135.00
10/49 **(64)** AB,AB(c),No(c)Price;rep30.00
07/51 **(85)** AB,AB(c),15¢(c)Price;rep20.00
03/60 **(155)** AB,New P(c); rep 18.00
1962 **(165)** AB,P(c);rep 18.00
03/64 **(167)** AB,P(c);rep 15.00
06/66 **(167)** AB,P(c);rep 15.00
Fl/68 **(166)** AB,TO New P(c),25¢(c) Price, New Soft(c);rep 25.00
Fl/68 **(166)** AB,P(c),Both Soft & Rigid(c)s;rep 44.00

050-ADVENTURES OF TOM SAWYER

By Mark Twain

08/48 **(51)** ARu,ARu(c),Original 110.00
09/48 **(51)** ARu,ARu(c),Original 130.00
10/49 **(64)** ARu,ARu(c),No(c) Price; rep 25.00
12/50 **(78)** ARu,ARu(c),15¢(c) Price; rep 16.00
04/52 **(94)** ARu,ARu(c);rep 14.00
12/53 **(114)** ARu,ARu(c);rep . . . 12.00
03/54 **(117)** ARu,ARu(c);rep . . . 11.00
05/56 **(132)** ARu,ARu(c);rep . . . 11.00
09/57 **(140)** ARu,New P(c);rep . . . 9.00
05/59 **(150)** ARu,P(c);rep 11.00
10/61 **(164)** New Art,P(c);rep 6.00
62/63 **(167)** P(c);rep 6.00
01/65 **(167)** P(c);rep 6.00
05/66 **(167)** P(c);rep 6.00
12/67 **(166)** P(c);rep 6.00
Fl/69 **(169)** P(c),25¢(c) Price, Rigid(c);rep 6.00
Wr/71 **(169)** P(c);rep 6.00

CI #51 The Spy
© Gilberton Publications

051-THE SPY

By James Fenimore Cooper

09/48 **(51)** AdH,AdH(c),Original, Maroon(c) 100.00
09/48 **(51)** AdH,AdH(c),Original, Violet(c) 90.00
11/51 **(89)** AdH,AdH(c),15¢(c) Price; rep 20.00
07/54 **(121)** AdH,AdH(c);rep . . . 15.00
07/57 **(139)** AdH,New P(c);rep . . 11.00
05/60 **(156)** AdH,P(c);rep 6.00
11/63 **(167)** AdH,P(c);rep 6.00
07/66 **(167)** AdH,P(c);rep 6.00
Wr/69 **(166)** AdH,P(c),25¢(c)Price, Both Soft & Rigid(c)s;rep 14.00

052-THE HOUSE OF SEVEN GABLES

By Nathaniel Hawthorne

10/48 **(53)** HyG,HyG(c),Original 100.00
11/51 **(89)** HyG,HyG(c),15¢(c) Price; rep 20.00
07/54 **(121)** HyG,HyG(c);rep . . . 14.00
01/58 **(142)** GWb New Art,New P(c); rep 12.00
05/60 **(156)** GWb,P(c);rep 6.00
1962 **(165)** GWb,P(c);rep 6.00
05/64 **(167)** GWb,P(c);rep 6.00
03/66 **(167)** GWb,P(c);rep 6.00
1968 **(166)** GWb,P(c),25¢(c) Price; rep 6.00
Sg/70 **(169)** GWb,P(c),Rigid(c);rep 6.00

053-A CHRISTMAS CAROL

By Charles Dickens

11/48 **(53)** HcK,HcK(c),Original 125.00

054-MAN IN THE IRON MASK

By Alexandre Dumas

12/48 **(55)** AgF,HcK(c),Original 100.00
03/52 **(93)** AgF,HcK(c),15¢(c) Price; rep 20.00
09/53 **(111)** AgF,HcK(c);rep 30.00
01/58 **(142)** KBa New Art,New P(c); rep 12.00
01/60 **(154)** KBa,P(c);rep 6.00
1962 **(165)** KBa,P(c);rep 6.00
05/64 **(167)** KBa,P(c);rep 6.00
04/66 **(167)** KBa,P(c);rep 6.00
Wr/69 **(166)** KBa,P(c),25¢(c) Price, Rigid(c);rep 6.00

055-SILAS MARINER

By George Eliot

01/49 **(55)** AdH,HcK(c),Original 100.00
09/50 **(75)** AdH,HcK(c),Price Circle Blank,'Coming next'Ad(not usually in reps.);rep 25.00
07/52 **(97)** AdH,HcK(c);rep 15.00
07/54 **(121)** AdH,New P(c);rep . . 12.00
01/56 **(130)** AdH,P(c);rep 6.00
09/57 **(140)** AdH,P(c);rep 6.00
01/60 **(154)** AdH,P(c);rep 6.00
1962 **(165)** AdH,P(c);rep 6.00
05/64 **(167)** AdH,P(c);rep 6.00
06/65 **(167)** AdH,P(c);rep 6.00
05/67 **(166)** AdH,P(c);rep 6.00
Wr/69 **(166)** AdH,P(c),25¢(c) Price, Rigid(c);rep,Soft & Stiff 16.00

056-THE TOILERS OF THE SEA

By Victor Hugo

02/49 **(55)** AgF,AgF(c),Original 135.00
01/62 **(165)** AT New Art,New P(c); rep. 25.00
03/64 **(167)** AT,P(c);rep. 16.00
10/66 **(167)** AT,P(c);rep. 16.00

057-THE SONG OF HIAWATHA

By Henry Wadsworth Longfellow

03/49 **(55)** AB,AB(c),Original . . 100.00
09/50 **(75)** AB,AB(c),No(c)price,' Coming Next'Ad(not usually found in reps.);rep 25.00
04/52 **(94)** AB,AB(c),15¢(c) Price;rep 16.00
04/54 **(118)** AB,AB(c);rep 15.00
09/56 **(134)** AB,New P(c);rep . . 12.00
07/57 **(139)** AB,P(c);rep 6.00
01/60 **(154)** AB,P(c);rep 6.00
62/63 **(167)** AB,P(c),Erroneosly Has Original Date;rep 6.00
09/64 **(167)** AB,P(c);rep 6.00
10/65 **(167)** AB,P(c);rep 6.00
Fl/68 **(166)** AB,P(c),25¢(c) Price;rep 6.00

058-THE PRAIRIE

By James Fenimore Cooper

04/49 **(60)** RP,RP(c),Original . . 100.00
08/49 **(62)** RP,RP(c);rep 40.00
12/50 **(78)** RP,RP(c),15¢(c) Price In Double Circle;rep 20.00
12/53 **(114)** RP,RP(c);rep 14.00
03/56 **(131)** RP,RP(c);rep 12.00
05/56 **(132)** RP,RP(c);rep 12.00
09/58 **(146)** RP,New P(c);rep . . . 11.00
03/60 **(155)** RP,P(c);rep 6.00
05/64 **(167)** RP,P(c);rep 6.00
04/66 **(167)** RP,P(c);rep 6.00
Sr/69 **(169)** RP,P(c),25¢(c) Price; Rigid(c);rep 6.00

059-WUTHERING HEIGHTS

By Emily Bronte

05/49 **(60)** HcK,HcK(c),Original 105.00
07/51 **(85)** HcK,HcK(c),15¢(c)

Price; rep 26.00
05/60 **(156)** HcK,GB New P(c);rep 12.00
01/64 **(167)** HcK,GB P(c);rep 7.00
10/66 **(167)** HcK,GB P(c);rep 7.00
Sr/69 **(169)** HcK,GBP(c),25¢(c) Price, Rigid(c);rep 6.00

060-BLACK BEAUTY
By Anna Sewell

06/49 **(62)** AgF,AgF(c),Original 100.00
08/49 **(62)** AgF,AgF(c);rep 105.00
07/51 **(85)** AgF,AgF(c),15¢(c) Price; rep 22.00
09/60 **(158)** LbC&NN&StA New Art, LbC New P(c);rep 22.00
02/64 **(167)** LbC&NN&StA,LbC P(c); rep 15.00
03/66 **(167)** LbC&NN&StA,LbC P(c); rep 15.00
03/66 **(167)** LbC&NN&StA,LbC P(c), 'Open Book'Blank;rep . . . 42.00
1968 **(166)** LbC&NN&StA,AIM New P(c) 25¢(c) Price;rep 6.00

061-THE WOMAN IN WHITE
By William Wilke Collins

07/49 **(62)** AB,AB(c),Original, Maroon & Violet(c)s 100.00
05/60 **(156)** AB,DgR New P(c);rep 20.00
01/64 **(167)** AB,DgR P(c);rep . . . 15.00
1968 **(166)** AB,DgR P(c), 25¢(c)Price;rep 15.00

062-WESTERN STORIES (The Luck of Roaring Camp & The Outcasts of Poker Flat)
By Bret Harte

08/49 **(62)** HcK,HcK(c),Original 100.00
11/51 **(89)** HcK,HcK(c),15¢(c) Price; rep 22.00
07/54 **(121)** HcK,HcK(c);rep 15.00
03/57 **(137)** HcK,New P(c); rep 12.00
09/59 **(152)** HcK,P(c);rep 7.00
10/63 **(167)** HcK,P(c);rep 7.00
06/64 **(167)** HcK,P(c);rep 6.00
11/66 **(167)** HcK,P(c);rep 6.00
1968 **(166)** HcK,TO New P(c), 25¢ Price;rep 14.00

063-THE MAN WITHOUT A COUNTRY
By Edward Everett Hale

09/49 **(62)** HcK,HcK(c),Original 100.00
12/50 **(78)** HcK,HcK(c),15¢(c)Price In Double Circles;rep 25.00
05/60 **(156)** HcK,GMc New P(c); rep 22.00
01/62 **(165)** AT New Art,GMc P(c), Added Text Pages;rep 12.00
03/64 **(167)** AT,GMc P(c);rep 6.00
08/66 **(167)** AT,GMc P(c);rep 6.00
Sr/69 **(169)** AT,GMc P(c),25¢(c) Price, Rigid(c);rep 6.00

064-TREASURE ISLAND
By Robert Louis Stevenson

10/49 **(62)** AB,AB(c),Original . . 100.00
04/51 **(82)** AB,AB(c),15¢(c) Price;rep 22.00
03/54 **(117)** AB,AB(c);rep 17.00
03/56 **(131)** AB,New P(c);rep . . . 12.00
05/57 **(138)** AB,P(c);rep 6.00
09/58 **(146)** AB,P(c);rep 6.00
09/60 **(158)** AB,P(c);rep 6.00
1962 **(165)** AB,P(c);rep 6.00
62/63 **(167)** AB,P(c);rep 6.00
06/64 **(167)** AB,P(c);rep 6.00
12/65 **(167)** AB,P(c);rep 6.00
10/67 **(166)** AB,P(c);rep 11.00
10/67 **(166)** AB,P(c),GRIT Ad Stapled In Book;rep 64.00
Sg/69 **(169)** AB,P(c),25¢(c) Price, Rigid(c);rep 6.00

065-BENJAMIN FRANKLIN
By Benjamin Franklin

11/49 **(64)** AB,RtH,GS(Iger Shop), HcK(c),Original 100.00
03/56 **(131)** AB,RtH,GS(Iger Shop), New P(c) ;rep 15.00
01/60 **(154)** AB,RtH,GS(Iger Shop), P(c);rep 6.00
02/64 **(167)** AB,RtH,GS(Iger Shop), P(c);rep 6.00
04/66 **(167)** AB,RtH,GS(Iger Shop), P(c);rep 6.00
Fl/69 **(169)** AB,RtH,GS(Iger Shop), P(c), 25¢(c)Price,Rigid(c);rep . . 5.00

066-THE CLOISTER AND THE HEARTH
By Charles Reade

12/49 **(67)** HcK,HcK(c),Original 200.00

067-THE SCOTTISH CHIEFS
By Jane Porter

01/50 **(67)** AB,AB(c),Original . . . 90.00
07/51 **(85)** AB,AB(c),15¢(c) Price;rep 22.00
04/54 **(118)** AB,AB(c);rep 15.00
01/57 **(136)** AB,New P(c);rep . . . 12.00
01/60 **(154)** AB,P(c);rep 8.00
11/63 **(167)** AB,P(c);rep 8.00
08/65 **(167)** AB,P(c);rep 8.00

CI #68 Julius Caesar
© Gilberton Publications

068-JULIUS CAESAR
By William Shakespeare

02/50 **(70)** HcK,HcK(c),Original 100.00
07/51 **(85)** HcK,HcK(c),15¢(c) Price; rep 22.00
06/53 **(108)** HcK,HcK(c);rep 15.00
05/60 **(156)** HcK,LbC New P(c);rep20.00
1962 **(165)** GE&RC New Art, LbC P(c);rep 20.00
02/64 **(167)** GE&RC,LbC P(c);rep 6.00
10/65 **(167)** GE&RC,LbC P(c),Tarzan Books Inside(c);rep 6.00
1967 **(166)** GE&RC,LbC P(c);rep . 6.00
Wr/69 **(169)** GE&RC,LbC P(c), Rigid(c);rep 6.00

069-AROUND THE WORLD IN 80 DAYS
By Jules Verne

03/50 **(70)** HcK,HcK(c),Original 100.00
09/51 **(87)** HcK,HcK(c),15¢(c) Price; rep 22.00
03/55 **(125)** HcK,HcK(c);rep 15.00
01/57 **(136)** HcK,New P(c);rep . . 11.00
09/58 **(146)** HcK,P(c);rep 6.00
09/59 **(152)** HcK,P(c);rep 6.00
1961 **(164)** HcK,P(c);rep 6.00
62/63 **(167)** HcK,P(c);rep 6.00
07/64 **(167)** HcK,P(c);rep 6.00
11/65 **(167)** HcK,P(c);rep 6.00
07/67 **(166)** HcK,P(c);rep 6.00
Sg/69 **(169)** HcK,P(c),25¢(c) Price, Rigid(c);rep 6.00

070-THE PILOT
By James Fenimore Cooper

04/50 **(71)** AB,AB(c),Original . . . 90.00
10/50 **(75)** AB,AB(c),15¢(c) Price;rep 20.00
02/52 **(92)** AB,AB(c);rep 15.00
03/55 **(125)** AB,AB(c);rep 12.00
05/60 **(156)** AB,GMc New P(c);rep 8.00
02/64 **(167)** AB,GMc P(c);rep 8.00
05/66 **(167)** AB,GMc P(c);rep 8.00

071-THE MAN WHO LAUGHS
By Victor Hugo

05/50 **(71)** AB,AB(c),Original . . 125.00
01/62 **(165)** NN,NN New P(c);rep 65.00
04/64 **(167)** NN,NN P(c);rep . . . 60.00

072-THE OREGON TRAIL
By Francis Parkman

06/50 **(73)** HcK,HcK (c),Original . 70.00
11/51 **(89)** HcK,HcK (c),15¢(c) Price; rep 20.00
07/54 **(121)** HcK,HcK (c);rep . . . 15.00
03/56 **(131)** HcK,New P(c);rep . . 12.00
09/57 **(140)** HcK,P(c);rep 7.00
05/59 **(150)** HcK,P(c);rep 6.00
01/61 **(164)** HcK,P(c);rep 6.00
62/63 **(167)** HcK,P(c);rep 6.00
08/64 **(167)** HcK,P(c);rep 6.00
10/65 **(167)** HcK,P(c);rep 6.00
1968 **(166)** HcK,P(c),25¢(c)Price;rep6.00

073-THE BLACK TULIP
By Alexandre Dumas

07/50 **(75)** AB,AB(c),Original . . 225.00

074-MR. MIDSHIPMAN EASY
By Captain Frederick Marryat

08/50 **(75)** BbL,Original 225.00

075-THE LADY OF THE LAKE
By Sir Walter Scott

09/50 **(75)** HcK,HcK(c),Original . 70.00
07/51 **(85)** HcK,HcK(c),15¢(c) Price; rep 20.00
04/54 **(118)** HcK,HcK(c);rep 15.00
07/57 **(139)** HcK,New P(c);rep . . 12.00
01/60 **(154)** HcK,P(c);rep 6.00
1962 **(165)** HcK,P(c);rep 6.00
04/64 **(167)** HcK,P(c);rep 6.00
05/66 **(167)** HcK,P(c);rep 6.00
Sg/69 **(169)** HcK,P(c),25¢(c) Price, Rigid(c);rep 6.00

076-THE PRISONER OF ZENDA
By Anthony Hope Hawkins

10/50 **(75)** HcK,HcK(c),Original . 60.00
07/51 **(85)** HcK,HcK(c),15¢(c) Price; rep 20.00
09/53 **(111)** HcK,HcK(c),rep 15.00
09/55 **(128)** HcK,New P(c);rep . . 12.00
09/59 **(152)** HcK,P(c);rep 6.00

1962 **(165)** HcK,P(c);rep 6.00
04/64 **(167)** HcK,P(c);rep 6.00
09/66 **(167)** HcK,P(c);rep 6.00
Fl/69 **(169)** HcK,P(c),25¢(c) Price, Rigid(c);rep 6.00

077-THE ILLIAD
By Homer

11/50 **(78)** AB,AB(c),Original ... 60.00
09/51 **(87)** AB,AB(c),15¢(c) Price;rep 20.00
07/54 **(121)** AB,AB(c);rep 15.00
07/57 **(139)** AB,New P(c);rep ... 12.00
05/59 **(150)** AB,P(c);rep 6.00
1962 **(165)** AB,P(c);rep 6.00
10/63 **(167)** AB,P(c);rep 6.00
07/64 **(167)** AB,P(c);rep 6.00
05/66 **(167)** AB,P(c);rep 6.00
1968 **(166)** AB,P(c),25¢(c)Price;rep 6.00

078-JOAN OF ARC
By Frederick Shiller

12/50 **(78)** HcK,HcK(c),Original . 60.00
09/51 **(87)** HcK,HcK(c),15¢(c) Price; rep 20.00
11/53 **(113)** HcK,HcK(c);rep 15.00
09/55 **(128)** HcK,New P(c);rep .. 12.00
09/57 **(140)** HcK,P(c);rep 6.00
05/59 **(150)** HcK,P(c);rep 6.00
11/60 **(159)** HcK,P(c);rep 6.00
62/63 **(167)** HcK,P(c);rep 6.00
12/63 **(167)** HcK,P(c);rep 6.00
06/65 **(167)** HcK,P(c);rep 6.00
06/67 **(166)** HcK,P(c);rep 6.00
Wr/69 **(166)** HcK,TO New P(c), 25¢(c)Price, Rigid(c);rep 14.00

079-CYRANO DE BERGERAC
By Edmond Rostand

01/51 **(78)** AB,AB(c),Original,Movie Promo Inside Front(c) 60.00
07/51 **(85)** AB,AB(c),15¢(c) Price;rep 20.00
04/54 **(118)** AB,AB(c);rep 15.00
07/56 **(133)** AB,New P(c);rep ... 15.00
05/60 **(156)** AB,P(c);rep 12.00
08/64 **(167)** AB,P(c);rep 12.00

CI #80 White Fang
© Gilberton Publications

080-WHITE FANG
By Jack London
Last Line Drawn (c)

02/51 **(79)** AB,AB(c),Original ... 60.00
09/51 **(87)** AB,AB(c);rep 20.00
03/55 **(125)** AB,AB(c);rep 15.00
05/56 **(132)** AB,New P(c);rep ... 15.00
09/57 **(140)** AB,P(c);rep 6.00
11/59 **(153)** AB,P(c);rep 6.00
62/63 **(167)** AB,P(c);rep 6.00
09/64 **(167)** AB,P(c);rep 6.00
07/65 **(167)** AB,P(c);rep 6.00
06/67 **(166)** AB,P(c);rep 6.00
Fl/69 **(169)** AB,P(c),25¢(c) Price, Rigid(c);rep 6.00

081-THE ODYSSEY
By Homer
(P(c)s From Now On)

03/51 **(82)** HyG,AB P(c),Original 40.00
08/64 **(167)** HyG,AB P(c);rep ... 12.00
10/66 **(167)** HyG,AB P(c);rep ... 12.00
Sg/69 **(169)** HyG,TyT New P(c), Rigid(c);rep 12.00

082-THE MASTER OF BALLANTRAE
By Robert Louis Stevenson

04/51 **(82)** LDr,AB P(c),Original . 40.00
08/64 **(167)** LDr,AB P(c);rep ... 14.00
Fl/68 **(166)** LDr,Syk New P(c), Rigid(c);rep 14.00

083-THE JUNGLE BOOK
By Rudyard Kipling

05/51 **(85)** WmB&AB,AB P(c), Original 35.00
08/53 **(110)** WmB&AB,AB P(c);rep 7.00
03/55 **(125)** WmB&AB,AB P(c);rep 6.00
05/56 **(134)** WmB&AB,AB P(c);rep 6.00
01/58 **(142)** WmB&AB,AB P(c);rep 6.00
05/59 **(150)** WmB&AB,AB P(c);rep 6.00
11/60 **(159)** WmB&AB,AB P(c);rep 6.00
62/63 **(167)** WmB&AB,AB P(c);rep 6.00
03/65 **(167)** WmB&AB,AB P(c);rep 6.00
11/65 **(167)** WmB&AB,AB P(c);rep 6.00
05/66 **(167)** WmB&AB,AB P(c);rep 6.00
1968 **(166)** NN Art,NN New P(c), Rigid(c);rep 12.00

084-THE GOLD BUG & OTHER STORIES
(The Gold Bug-The Telltale HeartThe Cask of Amontillado)
By Edgar Allan Poe

06/51 **(85)** AB,RP,JLv,AB P(c), Original 100.00
07/64 **(167)** AB,RP,JLv,AB P(c);rep58.00

085-THE SEA WOLF
By Jack London

08/51 **(85)** AB,AB P(c),Original . 30.00
07/54 **(121)** AB,AB P(c);rep 5.00
05/56 **(132)** AB,AB P(c);rep 5.00
11/57 **(141)** AB,AB P(c);rep 5.00
03/61 **(161)** AB,AB P(c);rep 5.00
02/64 **(167)** AB,AB P(c);rep 5.00
11/65 **(167)** AB,AB P(c);rep 5.00
Fl/69 **(169)** AB,AB P(c),25¢(c) Price, Rigid(c);rep 5.00

086-UNDER TWO FLAGS
By Oiuda

08/51 **(87)** MDb,AB P(c),Original 30.00
03/54 **(117)** MDb,AB P(c);rep 6.00
07/57 **(139)** MDb,AB P(c);rep 6.00
09/60 **(158)** MDb,AB P(c);rep 6.00
02/64 **(167)** MDb,AB P(c);rep 6.00
08/66 **(167)** MDb,AB P(c);rep 6.00
Sr/69 **(169)** MDb,AB P(c),25¢(c) Price, Rigid(c);rep 6.00

087-A MIDSUMMER NIGHT'S DREAM
By William Shakespeare

09/51 **(87)** AB,AB P(c),Original . 30.00
03/61 **(161)** AB,AB P(c);rep 6.00
04/64 **(167)** AB,AB P(c);rep 5.00
05/66 **(167)** AB,AB P(c);rep 5.00
Sr/69 **(169)** AB,AB P(c),25¢(c) Price; rep 5.00

088-MEN OF IRON
By Howard Pyle

10/51 **(89)** HD,LDr,GS,Original .. 30.00
01/60 **(154)** HD,LDr,GS,P(c);rep . 6.00
01/64 **(167)** HD,LDr,GS,P(c);rep . 6.00
1968 **(166)** HD,LDr,GS,P(c), 25¢(c)Price;rep 6.00

089-CRIME AND PUNISHMENT
By Fyodor Dostoevsky

11/51 **(89)** RP,AB P(c),Original . 35.00
09/59 **(152)** RP,AB P(c);rep 6.00
04/64 **(167)** RP,AB P(c);rep 6.00
05/66 **(167)** RP,AB P(c);rep 6.00
Fl/69 **(169)** RP,AB P(c),25¢(c) Price, Rigid(c);rep 6.00

090-GREEN MANSIONS
By William Henry Hudson

12/51 **(89)** AB,AB P(c),Original . 35.00
01/59 **(148)** AB,New LbC P(c);rep 11.00
1962 **(165)** AB,LbC P(c);rep 5.00
04/64 **(167)** AB,LbC P(c);rep 5.00
09/66 **(167)** AB,LbC P(c);rep 5.00
Sr/69 **(169)** AB,LbC P(c),25¢(c) Price, Rigid(c);rep 5.00

091-THE CALL OF THE WILD
By Jack London

01/52 **(92)** MDb,P(c),Original ... 30.00
10/53 **(112)** MDb,P(c);rep 6.00
03/55**(125)**MDb,P(c),'PictureProgress' Onn. Back(c);rep 5.00
09/56 **(134)** MDb,P(c);rep 5.00
03/58 **(143)** MDb,P(c);rep 5.00
1962 **(165)** MDb,P(c);rep 5.00
1962 **(167)** MDb,P(c);rep 5.00
04/65 **(167)** MDb,P(c);rep 5.00
03/66 **(167)** MDb,P(c);rep 5.00
03/66 **(167)** MDb,P(c),Record Edition;rep 5.00
11/67 **(166)** MDb,P(c);rep 5.00
Sg/70 **(169)** MDb,P(c),25¢(c) Price, Rigid(c);rep 5.00

092-THE COURTSHIP OF MILES STANDISH
By Henry Wadsworth Longfellow

02/52 **(92)** AB,AB P(c),Original . 30.00
1962 **(165)** AB,AB P(c);rep 5.00
03/64 **(167)** AB,AB P(c);rep 5.00
05/67 **(166)** AB,AB P(c);rep 5.00
Wr/69 **(169)** AB,AB P(c),25¢(c) Price, Rigid(c);rep 5.00

093-PUDD'NHEAD WILSON
By Mark Twain

03/52 **(94)** HcK,HcK P(c),Original 32.00
1962 **(165)** HcK,GMc New P(c);rep 8.00
03/64 **(167)** HcK,GMc P(c);rep ... 6.00
1968 **(166)** HcK,GMc P(c),25¢(c) Price, Soft(c);rep 8.00

094-DAVID BALFOUR
By Robert Louis Stevenson

04/52 **(94)** RP,P(c),Original 32.00
05/64 **(167)** RP,P(c);rep 11.00
1968 **(166)** RP,P(c),25¢(c)Price;rep11.00

095-ALL QUIET ON THE WESTERN FRONT
By Erich Maria Remarque

05/52 **(96)** MDb,P(c),Original ... 75.00
05/52 **(99)** MDb,P(c),Original ... 60.00
10/64 **(167)** MDb,P(c);rep 16.00
11/66 **(167)** MDb,P(c);rep 16.00

096-DANIEL BOONE

By John Bakeless

06/52 **(97)** AB,P(c),Original 30.00
03/54 **(117)** AB,P(c);rep 5.00
09/55 **(128)** AB,P(c);rep 5.00
05/56 **(132)** AB,P(c);rep 5.00
----- **(134)** AB,P(c),'Story of Jesus'on Back(c);rep 5.00
09/60 **(158)** AB,P(c);rep 5.00
01/64 **(167)** AB,P(c);rep 5.00
05/65 **(167)** AB,P(c);rep 5.00
11/66 **(167)** AB,P(c);rep 5.00
Wr/69 **(166)** AB,P(c),25¢(c) Price, Rigid(c);rep 12.00

097-KING SOLOMON'S MINES

By H. Rider Haggard

07/52 **(96)** HcK,P(c),Original ... 30.00
04/54 **(118)** HcK,P(c);rep 8.00
03/56 **(131)** HcK,P(c);rep 5.00
09/51 **(141)** HcK,P(c);rep 5.00
09/60 **(158)** HcK,P(c);rep 5.00
02/64 **(167)** HcK,P(c);rep 5.00
09/65 **(167)** HcK,P(c);rep 5.00
Sr/69 **(169)** HcK,P(c),25¢(c) Price; Rigid(c);rep 6.00

098-THE RED BADGE OF COURAGE

By Stephen Crane

08/52 **(98)** MDb,GS,P(c),Original 30.00
04/54 **(118)** MDb,GS,P(c);rep ... 5.00
05/56 **(132)** MDb,GS,P(c);rep ... 5.00
01/58 **(142)** MDb,GS,P(c);rep ... 5.00
09/59 **(152)** MDb,GS,P(c);rep ... 5.00
03/61 **(161)** MDb,GS,P(c);rep ... 5.00
62/63 **(167)** MDb,GS,P(c),Erronously Has Original Date;rep 5.00
09/64 **(167)** MDb,GS,P(c);rep ... 5.00
10/65 **(167)** MDb,GS,P(c);rep ... 5.00
1968 **(166)** MDb,GS,P(c),25¢(c) Price, Rigid(c);rep 15.00

099-HAMLET

By William Shakespeare

09/52 **(98)** AB,P(c),Original 32.00
07/54 **(121)** AB,P(c);rep 5.00
11/57 **(141)** AB,P(c);rep 5.00
09/60 **(158)** AB,P(c);rep 5.00
62/63 **(167)** AB,P(c),Erroneusly Has Original Date;rep 5.00
07/65 **(167)** AB,P(c);rep 5.00
04/67 **(166)** AB,P(c);rep 5.00
Sg/69 **(169)** AB,EdM New P(c), 25¢(c)Price, Rigid(c);rep 12.00

100-MUTINY ON THE BOUNTY

By Charrles Nordhoff

10/52 **(100)** MsW,HcK P(c), Original 28.00
03/54 **(117)** MsW,HcK P(c);rep .. 5.00
05/56 **(132)** MsW,HcK P(c);rep .. 5.00
01/58 **(142)** MsW,HcK P(c);rep .. 5.00
03/60 **(155)** MsW,HcK P(c);rep .. 5.00
62/63 **(167)** MsW,HcK P(c),Erroneusly Has Original Date;rep 5.00
05/64 **(167)** MsW,HcK P(c);rep .. 5.00
03/66 **(167)** MsW,HcK P(c),N# or Price;rep 10.00
Sg/70 **(169)** MsW,HcK P(c), Rigid(c); rep 4.00

101-WILLIAM TELL

By Frederick Schiller

11/52 **(101)** MDb,HcK P(c),Original 28.00
04/54 **(118)** MDb,HcK P(c);rep ... 5.00
11/57 **(141)** MDb,HcK P(c);rep ... 5.00
09/60 **(158)** MDb,HcK P(c);rep ... 5.00
62/63 **(167)** MDb,HcK P(c),Erroneusly Has Original Date;rep 5.00
11/64 **(167)** MDb,HcK P(c);rep ... 5.00
04/67 **(166)** MDb,HcK P(c);rep ... 5.00
Wr/69 **(169)** MDb,HcK P(c)25¢(c) Price, Rigid(c);rep 5.00

102-THE WHITE COMPANY

By Sir Arthur Conan Doyle

12/52 **(101)** AB,P(c),Original ... 45.00
1962 **(165)** AB,P(c);rep 22.00
04/64 **(167)** AB,P(c);rep 22.00

103-MEN AGAINST THE SEA

By Charles Nordhoff

01/53 **(104)** RP,HcK P(c),Original 32.00
12/53 **(114)** RP,HcK P(c);rep ... 16.00
03/56 **(131)** RP,New P(c);rep ... 12.00
03/59 **(149)** RP,P(c);rep 12.00
09/60 **(158)** RP,P(c);rep 21.00
03/64 **(167)** RP,P(c);rep 9.00

104-BRING 'EM BACK ALIVE

By Frank Buck & Edward Anthony

02/53 **(105)** HcK,HcK P(c)Original 27.00
04/54 **(118)** HcK,HcK P(c);rep ... 5.00
07/56 **(133)** HcK,HcK P(c);rep ... 5.00
05/59 **(150)** HcK,HcK P(c);rep ... 5.00
09/60 **(158)** HcK,HcK P(c);rep ... 5.00
10/63 **(167)** HcK,HcK P(c);rep ... 5.00
09/65 **(167)** HcK,HcK P(c);rep ... 5.00
Wr/69 **(169)** HcK,HcK P(c),25¢(c) Price, Rigid(c);rep 5.00

CI #105 From the Earth to the Moon © Gilberton Publications

105-FROM THE EARTH TO THE MOON

By Jules Verne

03/53 **(106)** AB,P(c),Original ... 28.00
04/54 **(118)** AB,P(c);rep 5.00
03/56 **(132)** AB,P(c);rep 5.00
11/57 **(141)** AB,P(c);rep 5.00
09/58 **(146)** AB,P(c);rep 5.00
05/60 **(156)** AB,P(c);rep 5.00
62/63 **(167)** AB,P(c),Erroneusly Has Original Date;rep 5.00
05/64 **(167)** AB,P(c);rep 5.00
05/65 **(167)** AB,P(c);rep 5.00
10/67 **(166)** AB,P(c);rep 5.00
Sr/69 **(169)** AB,P(c),25¢(c) Price, Rigid(c);rep 5.00
Sg/71 **(169)** AB,P(c);rep 5.00

106-BUFFALO BILL

By William F. Cody

04/53 **(107)** MDb,P(c),Original .. 28.00
04/54 **(118)** MDb,P(c);rep 5.00
03/56 **(132)** MDb,P(c);rep 5.00
01/58 **(142)** MDb,P(c);rep 5.00
03/61 **(161)** MDb,P(c);rep 5.00
03/64 **(167)** MDb,P(c);rep 5.00
07/67 **(166)** MDb,P(c);rep 5.00
Fl/69 **(169)** MDb,P(c),Rigid(c);rep . 5.00

107-KING OF THE KHYBER RIFLES

By Talbot Mundy

05/53 **(108)** SMz,P(c),Original .. 30.00
04/54 **(118)** SMz,P(c);rep 5.00
09/58 **(146)** SMz,P(c);rep 5.00
09/60 **(158)** SMz,P(c);rep 5.00
62/63 **(167)** SMz,P(c),Erroneusly Has Original Date;rep 5.00
62/63 **(167)** SMz,P(c);rep 5.00
10/66 **(167)** SMz,P(c);rep 5.00

108-KNIGHTS OF THE ROUND TABLE

By Howard Pyle

06/53 **(108)** AB,P(c),Original ... 30.00
06/53 **(109)** AB,P(c),Original ... 36.00
03/54 **(117)** AB,P(c);rep 5.00
11/59 **(153)** AB,P(c);rep 5.00
1962 **(165)** AB,P(c);rep 5.00
04/64 **(167)** AB,P(c);rep 5.00
04/67 **(166)** AB,P(c);rep 5.00

109-PITCAIRN'S ISLAND

By Charles Nordhoff

07/53 **(110)** RP,P(c),Original ... 32.00
1962 **(165)** RP,P(c);rep 9.00
03/64 **(167)** RP,P(c);rep 9.00
06/67 **(166)** RP,P(c);rep 9.00

110-A STUDY IN SCARLET

By Sir Arthur Conan Doyle

08/53 **(111)** SMz,P(c),Original . 100.00
1962 **(165)** SMz,P(c);rep 46.00

111-THE TALISMAN

By Sir Walter Scott

09/53 **(112)** HcK,HcK P(c),Original 45.00
1962 **(165)** HcK,HcK P(c);rep ... 6.00
05/64 **(167)** HcK,HcK P(c);rep ... 6.00
Fl/68 **(166)** HcK,HcK P(c), 25¢(c)Price;rep 6.00

112-ADVENTURES OF KIT CARSON

By John S. C. Abbott

10/53 **(113)** RP,P(c),Original ... 50.00
11/55 **(129)** RP,P(c);rep 6.00
11/57 **(141)** RP,P(c);rep 6.00
09/59 **(152)** RP,P(c);rep 6.00
03/61 **(161)** RP,P(c);rep 6.00
62/63 **(167)** RP,P(c);rep 6.00
02/65 **(167)** RP,P(c);rep 6.00
05/66 **(167)** RP,P(c);rep 6.00
Wr/69 **(166)** RP,EdM New P(c), 25¢(c)Price, Rigid(c);rep 12.00

113-THE FORTY-FIVE GUARDSMEN

By Alexandre Dumas

11/53 **(114)** MDb,P(c),Original .. 65.00
07/67 **(166)** MDb,P(c);rep 25.00

114-THE RED ROVER

By James Fenimore Cooper

12/53 **(115)** PrC,JP P(c),Original 65.00
07/67 **(166)** PrC,JP P(c);rep . . . 25.00

115-HOW I FOUND LIVINGSTONE
By Sir Henry Stanley

01/54 **(116)** SF&ST,P(c),Original 65.00
01/67 **(167)** SF&ST,P(c);rep . . . 30.00

116-THE BOTTLE IMP
By Robert Louis Stevenson

02/54 **(117)** LC,P(c),Original . . . 70.00
01/67 **(167)** LC,P(c);rep 25.00

117-CAPTAINS COURAGEOUS
By Rudyard Kipling

03/54 **(118)** PrC,P(c),Original . . . 50.00
02/67 **(167)** PrC,P(c);rep 15.00
Fl/69 **(169)** PrC,P(c),25¢(c) Price, Rigid(c);rep 12.00

118-ROB ROY
By Sir Walter Scott

04/54 **(119)** RP,WIP,P(c),Original 65.00
02/67 **(167)** RP,WIP,P(c);rep . . . 25.00

119-SOLDERS OF FORTUNE
By Richard Harding Davis

05/54 **(120)** KS,P(c),Original . . . 65.00
03/67 **(166)** KS,P(c);rep 15.00
Sg/70 **(169)** KS,P(c),25¢(c) Price, Rigid(c);rep 12.00

120-THE HURRICANE
By Charles Nordhoff

1954 **(121)** LC,LC P(c),Original . 60.00
03/67 **(166)** LC,LC P(c);rep 30.00

121-WILD BILL HICKOCK
AUTHOR UNKNOWN

07/54 **(122)** MI,ST,P(c),Original . 25.00
05/56 **(132)** MI,ST,P(c);rep 6.00
11/57 **(141)** MI,ST,P(c);rep 6.00
01/60 **(154)** MI,ST,P(c);rep 6.00
62/63 **(167)** MI,ST,P(c);rep 6.00
08/64 **(167)** MI,ST,P(c);rep 6.00
04/67 **(166)** MI,ST,P(c);rep 6.00
Wr/69 **(169)** MI,ST,P(c),Rigid(c);rep 6.00

122-THE MUTINEERS
By Charles Boardman Hawes

09/54 **(123)** PrC,P(c),Original . . . 25.00
01/57 **(136)** PrC,P(c);rep 6.00
09/58 **(146)** PrC,P(c);rep 6.00
09/60 **(158)** PrC,P(c);rep 6.00
11/63 **(167)** PrC,P(c);rep 6.00
03/65 **(167)** PrC,P(c);rep 6.00
08/67 **(166)** PrC,P(c);rep 6.00

123-FANG AND CLAW
By Frank Buck

11/54 **(124)** LnS,P(c),Original . . . 25.00
07/56 **(133)** LnS,P(c);rep 6.00
03/58 **(143)** LnS,P(c);rep 6.00
01/60 **(154)** LnS,P(c);rep 6.00
62/63 **(167)** LnS,P(c),Erroneusly Has Original Date;rep 6.00
09/65 **(167)** LnS,P(c);rep 6.00

124-THE WAR OF THE WORLDS
By Herbert George Wells

01/55 **(125)** LC,LC P(c),Original . 45.00
03/56 **(131)** LC,LC P(c);rep 6.00
11/57 **(141)** LC,LC P(c);rep 6.00
01/59 **(148)** LC,LC P(c);rep 6.00
05/60 **(156)** LC,LC P(c);rep 6.00
1962 **(165)** LC,LC P(c);rep 6.00
62/63 **(167)** LC,LC P(c);rep 6.00
11/64 **(167)** LC,LC P(c);rep 6.00
11/65 **(167)** LC,LC P(c);rep 6.00
1968 **(166)** LC,LC P(c),25¢(c) Price; rep 6.00
Sr/70 **(169)** LC,LC P(c),Rigid(c);rep 6.00

125-THE OX BOW INCIDENT
By Walter Van Tilberg Clark

03/55 **(---)** NN,P(c),Original 30.00
03/58 **(143)** NN,P(c);rep 6.00
09/59 **(152)** NN,P(c);rep 6.00
03/61 **(149)** NN,P(c);rep 6.00
62/63 **(167)** NN,P(c);rep 6.00
11/64 **(167)** NN,P(c);rep 6.00
04/67 **(166)** NN,P(c);rep 6.00
Wr/69 **(169)** NN,P(c),25¢(c) Price, Rigid(c);rep 6.00

126-THE DOWNFALL
By Emile Zola

05/55 **(---)** LC,LC P(c),Original,'Picture Progress'Replaces Reorder List 25.00
08/64 **(167)** LC,LC P(c);rep 5.00
1968 **(166)** LC,LC P(c),25¢(c) Price;rep 9.00

127-THE KING OF THE MOUNTAINS
By Edmond About

07/55 **(128)** NN,P(c),Original . . . 25.00
06/64 **(167)** NN,P(c);rep 9.00
Fl/68 **(166)** NN,P(c),25¢(c)Price;rep 9.00

128-MACBETH
By William Shakespeare

09/55 **(128)** AB,P(c),Original . . . 32.00
03/58 **(143)** AB,P(c);rep 6.00
09/60 **(158)** AB,P(c);rep 6.00
62/63 **(167)** AB,P(c);rep 6.00
06/64 **(167)** AB,P(c);rep 6.00
04/67 **(166)** AB,P(c);rep 6.00
1968 **(166)** AB,P(c),25¢(c)Price;rep 6.00
Sg/70 **(169)** AB,P(c),Rigid(c);rep . 6.00

129-DAVY CROCKETT
AUTHOR UNKNOWN

11/55 **(129)** LC,P(c),Original . . . 70.00
09/66 **(167)** LC,P(c);rep 40.00

130-CAESAR'S CONQUESTS
By Julius Caesar

01/56 **(130)** JO,P(c),Original . . . 25.00
01/58 **(142)** JO,P(c);rep 6.00
09/59 **(152)** JO,P(c);rep 6.00
03/61 **(149)** JO,P(c);rep 6.00
62/63 **(167)** JO,P(c);rep 6.00
10/64 **(167)** JO,P(c);rep 6.00
04/66 **(167)** JO,P(c);rep 6.00

131-THE COVERED WAGON
By Emerson Hough

03/56 **(131)** NN,P(c),Original . . . 25.00
03/58 **(143)** NN,P(c);rep 6.00
09/59 **(152)** NN,P(c);rep 6.00
09/60 **(158)** NN,P(c);rep 6.00
62/63 **(167)** NN,P(c);rep 6.00
11/64 **(167)** NN,P(c);rep 6.00
04/66 **(167)** NN,P(c);rep 6.00
Wr/69 **(169)** NN,P(c),25¢(c) Price, Rigid(c);rep 6.00

132-THE DARK FRIGATE
By Charles Boardman Hawes

05/56 **(132)** EW&RWb,P(c), Original 25.00
05/59 **(150)** EW&RWb,P(c);rep . . 9.00
01/64 **(167)** EW&RWb,P(c);rep . . 9.00
05/67 **(166)** EW&RWb,P(c);rep . . 9.00

133-THE TIME MACHINE
By Herbert George Wells

07/56 **(132)** LC,P(c),Original . . . 45.00
01/58 **(142)** LC,P(c);rep 8.00
09/59 **(152)** LC,P(c);rep 8.00
09/60 **(158)** LC,P(c);rep 8.00
62/63 **(167)** LC,P(c);rep 8.00
06/64 **(167)** LC,P(c);rep 8.00
03/66 **(167)** LC,P(c);rep 8.00
03/66 **(167)** LC,P(c),N# Or Price;rep 8.00

CI #133 The Time Machine © Gilberton Publications

12/67 **(166)** LC,P(c);rep 8.00
Wr/71 **(169)** LC,P(c),25¢(c) Price, Rigid(c);rep 10.00

134-ROMEO AND JULIET
By William Shakespeare

09/56 **(134)** GE,P(c),Original . . . 25.00
03/61 **(161)** GE,P(c);rep 6.00
09/63 **(167)** GE,P(c);rep 6.00
05/65 **(167)** GE,P(c);rep 6.00
06/67 **(166)** GE,P(c);rep 6.00
Wr/69 **(166)** GE,EdM New P(c), 25¢(c)Price, Rigid(c);rep 21.00

135-WATERLOO
By Emile Erckmann & Alexandre Chatrian

11/56 **(135)** GrI,AB P(c),Original 25.00
11/59 **(153)** GrI,AB P(c);rep 5.00
62/63 **(167)** GrI,AB P(c);rep 5.00
09/64 **(167)** GrI,AB P(c);rep 5.00
1968 **(166)** GrI,AB P(c),25¢(c) Price; rep 5.00

136-LORD JIM
By Joseph Conrad

01/57 **(136)** GE,P(c),Original . . . 25.00
62/63 **(165)** GE,P(c);rep 5.00
03/64 **(167)** GE,P(c);rep 5.00
09/66 **(167)** GE,P(c);rep 5.00
Sr/69 **(169)** GE,P(c),25¢(c) Price, Rigid(c);rep 5.00

137-THE LITTLE SAVAGE
By Captain Frederick Marryat

03/57 **(136)** GE,P(c),Original . . . 25.00
01/59 **(148)** GE,P(c);rep 5.00
05/60 **(156)** GE,P(c);rep 5.00
62/63 **(167)** GE,P(c);rep 5.00
10/64 **(167)** GE,P(c);rep 5.00
08/67 **(166)** GE,P(c);rep 5.00
Sg/70 **(169)** GE,P(c),25¢(c)

Price, Rigid(c);rep 5.00

138-A JOURNEY TO THE CENTER OF THE EARTH

By Jules Verne

05/57 **(136)** NN,P(c),Original ... 35.00
09/58 **(146)** NN,P(c);rep 5.00
05/60 **(156)** NN,P(c);rep 5.00
09/60 **(158)** NN,P(c);rep 5.00
62/63 **(167)** NN,P(c);rep 5.00
06/64 **(167)** NN,P(c);rep 5.00
04/66 **(167)** NN,P(c);rep 5.00
1968 **(166)** NN,P(c),25¢(c)Price;rep 5.00

139-IN THE REIGN OF TERROR

By George Alfred Henty

07/57 **(139)** GE,P(c),Original ... 28.00
01/60 **(154)** GE,P(c);rep 5.00
62/63 **(167)** GE,P(c),Erroneusly Has Original Date;rep 5.00
07/64 **(167)** GE,P(c);rep 5.00
1968 **(166)** GE,P(c),25¢(c)Price;rep 5.00

140-ON JUNGLE TRAILS

By Frank Buck

09/57 **(140)** NN,P(c),Original ... 25.00
05/59 **(150)** NN,P(c);rep 5.00
01/61 **(160)** NN,P(c);rep 5.00
09/63 **(167)** NN,P(c);rep 5.00
09/65 **(167)** NN,P(c);rep 5.00

141-CASTLE DANGEROUS

By Sir Walter Scott

11/57 **(141)** StC,P(c),Original ... 25.00
09/59 **(152)** STC,P(c);rep 5.00
62/63 **(167)** StC,P(c);rep 5.00
07/67 **(166)** StC,P(c);rep 5.00

142-ABRAHAM LINCOLN

By Benjamin Thomas

01/58 **(142)** NN,P(c),Original 25.00
01/60 **(154)** NN,P(c);rep 5.00
09/60 **(158)** NN,P(c);rep 5.00
10/63 **(167)** NN,P(c);rep 5.00
07/65 **(167)** NN,P(c);rep 5.00
11/67 **(166)** NN,P(c);rep 5.00
Fl/69 **(169)** NN,P(c),25¢(c) Price, Rigid(c);rep 5.00

143-KIM

By Rudyard Kipling

03/58 **(143)** JO,P(c)Original 25.00
62/63 **(165)** JO,P(c);rep 6.00
11/63 **(167)** JO,P(c);rep 6.00
08/65 **(167)** JO,P(c);rep 6.00
Wr/69 **(169)** JO,P(c),25¢(c) Price, Rigid(c);rep 6.00

144-THE FIRST MEN IN THE MOON

By Herbert George Wells

05/58 **(143)** GWb,AW,AT,RKr,GMC P(c), Original 32.00
11/59 **(153)** GWb,AW,AT,RKr,GMC P(c); rep 6.00
03/61 **(161)** GWb,AW,AT,RKr,GMC P(c); rep 6.00
62/63 **(167)** GWb,AW,AT,RKr,GMC P(c); rep 6.00
12/65 **(167)** GWb,AW,AT,RKr,GMC P(c); rep 6.00
Fl/68 **(166)** GWb,AW,AT,RKr,GMC P(c), 25¢(c) Price,Rigid(c);rep 6.00
Wr/69 **(169)** GWb,AW,AT,RKr,GMC P(c), Rigid(c);rep 6.00

145-THE CRISIS

By Winston Churchill

07/58 **(143)** GE,P(c),Original ... 26.00
05/60 **(156)** GE,P(c);rep 6.00
10/63 **(167)** GE,P(c);rep 6.00
03/65 **(167)** GE,P(c);rep 6.00
1968 **(166)** GE,P(c),25¢(c)Price;rep 6.00

146-WITH FIRE AND SWORD

By Henryk Sienkiewicz

09/58 **(143)** GWb,P(c),Original .. 26.00
05/60 **(156)** GWb,P(c);rep 9.00
11/63 **(167)** GWb,P(c);rep 9.00
03/65 **(167)** GWb,P(c);rep 9.00

147-BEN-HUR

By Lew Wallace

11/58 **(147)** JO,P(c),Original ... 26.00
11/59 **(153)** JO,P(c);rep 30.00
09/60 **(158)** JO,P(c);rep 6.00
62/63 **(167)** JO,P(c),Has the Original Date;rep 6.00
----- **(167)** JO,P(c);rep 6.00
02/65 **(167)** JO,P(c);rep 6.00
09/66 **(167)** JO,P(c);rep 6.00
Fl/68 **(166)** JO,P(c),25¢(c)Price, BothRigid & Soft (c)s;rep 15.00

148-THE BUCKANEER

By Lyle Saxon

01/59 **(148)** GE&RJ,NS P(c), Original 25.00
----- **(568)** GE&RJ,NS P(c),Juniors List Only;rep 9.00
62/63 **(167)** GE&RJ,NS P(c);rep . 6.00
09/65 **(167)** GE&RJ,NS P(c);rep . 6.00
Sr/69 **(169)** GE&RJ,NS P(c),25¢(c) Price, Rigid(c);rep 6.00

149-OFF ON A COMET

By Jules Verne

03/59 **(149)** GMc,P(c),Original .. 25.00
03/60 **(155)** GMc,P(c);rep 6.00
03/61 **(149)** GMc,P(c);rep 6.00
12/63 **(167)** GMc,P(c);rep 6.00
02/65 **(167)** GMc,P(c);rep 6.00
10/66 **(167)** GMc,P(c);rep 6.00
Fl/68 **(166)** GMc,EdM New P(c), 25¢(c)Price;rep 15.00

150-THE VIRGINIAN

By Owen Winster

05/59 **(150)** NN,DrG P(c),Original 40.00
1961 **(164)** NN,DrG P(c);rep ... 12.00
62/63 **(167)** NN,DrG P(c);rep ... 11.00
12/65 **(167)** NN,DrG P(c);rep ... 11.00

151-WON BY THE SWORD

By George Alfred Henty

07/59 **(150)** JTg,P(c),Original ... 40.00
1961 **(164)** JTg,P(c);rep 11.00
10/63 **(167)** JTg,P(c);rep 11.00
1963 **(167)** JTg,P(c);rep 11.00
07/67 **(166)** JTg,P(c);rep 11.00

152-WILD ANIMALS I HAVE KNOWN

By Ernest Thompson Seton

09/59 **(152)** LbC,LbC P(c),Original 40.00
03/61 **(149)** LbC,LbC P(c),P(c);rep 6.00
09/63 **(167)** LbC,LbC P(c);rep ... 5.00
08/65 **(167)** LbC,LbC P(c);rep ... 5.00
fl/69 **(169)** LbC,LbC P(c),25¢(c) Price,Rigid(c);rep 5.00

153-THE INVISIBLE MAN

By Herbert George Wells

11/59 **(153)** NN,GB P(c),Original 45.00
03/61 **(149)** NN,GB P(c);rep 7.00
62/63 **(167)** NN,GB P(c);rep 6.00
02/65 **(167)** NN,GB P(c);rep 6.00
09/66 **(167)** NN,GB P(c);rep 6.00
Wr/69 **(166)** NN,GB P(c),25¢(c) Price,Rigid(c);rep 6.00
Sg/71 **(169)** NN,GB P(c),Rigid(c), Words Spelling'Invisible Man' Are' Solid'Not'Invisible';rep 6.00

154-THE CONSPIRACY OF PONTIAC

By Francis Parkman

01/60 **(154)** GMc,GMc P(c),Original40.00
11/63 **(167)** GMc,GMc P(c);rep . 15.00
07/64 **(167)** GMc,GMc P(c);rep . 15.00
12/67 **(166)** GMc,GMc P(c);rep . 15.00

155-THE LION OF THE NORTH

By George Alfred Henty

03/60 **(154)** NN,GMc P(c),Original 42.00
01/64 **(167)** NN,GMc P(c);rep .. 11.00
1967 **(166)** NN,GMc P(c),25¢(c) Price; rep 11.00

CI #160 The Food of the Gods
© Gilberton Publications

156-THE CONQUEST OF MEXICO

By Bernal Diaz Del Castillo

05/60 **(156)** BPr,BPr P(c),Original 32.00
01/64 **(167)** BPr,BPr P(c);rep 7.00
08/67 **(166)** BPr,BPr P(c);rep 7.00
Sg/70 **(169)** BPr,BPr P(c),25¢(c) Price; Rigid(c);rep 6.00

157-LIVES OF THE HUNTED

By Ernest Thompson Seton

07/60 **(156)** NN,LbC P(c),Original 35.00
02/64 **(167)** NN,LbC P(c);rep ... 14.00
10/67 **(166)** NN,LbC P(c);rep ... 14.00

158-THE CONSPIRATORS

By Alexandre Dumas

09/60 **(156)** GMc,GMc P(c), Original 35.00
07/64 **(167)** GMc,GMc P(c);rep . 14.00
10/67 **(166)** GMc,GMc P(c);rep . 14.00

159-THE OCTOPUS

By Frank Norris

11/60 **(159)** GM&GE,LbC P(c), Original 32.00
02/64 **(167)** GM&GE,LbC P(c);rep 12.00
166 **(1967)** GM&GE,LbC P(c),25¢(c) Price;rep 12.00

160-THE FOOD OF THE GODS
By Herbert George Wells
01/61 **(159)** TyT,GMc P(c),Original 30.00
01/61 **(160)** TyT,GMc P(c),Original; Same Except For the HRN# . . 25.00
01/64 **(167)** TyT,GMc P(c);rep . . 12.00
06/67 **(166)** TyT,GMc P(c);rep . . 12.00

161-CLEOPATRA
By H. Rider Haggard
03/61 **(161)** NN,Pch P(c),Original 45.00
01/64 **(167)** NN,Pch P(c);rep . . . 16.00
08/67 **(166)** NN,Pch P(c);rep . . . 16.00

162-ROBUR THE CONQUEROR
By Jules Verne
05/61 **(162)** GM&DPn,CJ P(c), Original 32.00
07/64 **(167)** GM&DPn,CJ P(c);rep 12.00
08/67 **(166)** GM&DPn,CJ P(c);rep 12.00

163-MASTER OF THE WORLD
By Jules Verne
07/61 **(163)** GM,P(c),Original . . . 32.00
01/65 **(167)** GM,P(c);rep 12.00
1968 **(166)** GM,P(c),25¢(c) Price;rep 12.00

164-THE COSSACK CHIEF
By Nicolai Gogol
1961 **(164)** SyM,P(c),Original . . . 35.00
04/65 **(167)** SyM,P(c);rep 12.00
Fl/68 **(166)** SyM,P(c),25¢(c) Price;rep 12.00

165-THE QUEEN'S NECKLACE
By Alexandre Dumas
01/62 **(164)** GM,P(c),Original . . . 35.00
04/65 **(167)** GM,P(c);rep 12.00
Fl/68 **(166)** GM,P(c),25¢(c) Price;rep 12.00

166-TIGERS AND TRAITORS
By Jules Verne
05/62 **(165)** NN,P(c),Original . . . 60.00
02/64 **(167)** NN,P(c);rep 16.00
11/66 **(167)** NN,P(c);rep 16.00

167-FAUST
By Johann Wolfgang von Goethe
08/62 **(165)** NN,NN P(c),Original 90.00
02/64 **(167)** NN,NN P(c);rep . . . 50.00
06/67 **(166)** NN,NN P(c);rep . . . 50.00

168-IN FREEDOM'S CAUSE
By George Alfred Henty
Wr/69 **(169)** GE&RC,P(c), Original, Rigid (c) 80.00

169-NEGRO AMERICANS THE EARLY YEARS
AUTHOR UNKNOWN
Sg/69 **(166)** NN,NN P(c), Original,Rigid(c) 80.00
Sg/69 **(169)** NN,NN P(c), Rigid;rep 60.00

See Also:
Independent Color Listings

CLASSICS

ILLUSTRATED GIANTS
An Illustrated Library of Great Adventure Stories -(reps. of Issues 6,7,8,10) . . . 800.00
An Illustrated Library of Exciting Mystery Stories -(reps. of Issues 30,21,40,13) 850.00
An Illustrated Library of Great Indian Stories -(reps. of Issues 4,17,22,37) . 725.00

CLASSICS ILLUSTRATED JUNIOR
501-Snow White and the Seven Dwarves 70.00
502-The Ugly Duckling 40.00
503-Cinderella 24.00
504-The Pied Piper 16.00
505-The Sleeping Beauty 16.00
506-The Three Little Pigs 16.00
507-Jack and the Beanstalk 16.00

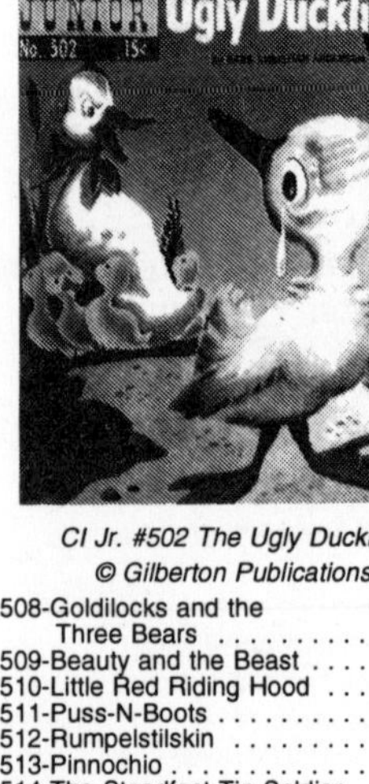

CI Jr. #502 The Ugly Duckling
© Gilberton Publications

508-Goldilocks and the Three Bears 16.00
509-Beauty and the Beast 16.00
510-Little Red Riding Hood 16.00
511-Puss-N-Boots 16.00
512-Rumpelstilskin 16.00
513-Pinnochio 24.00
514-The Steadfast Tin Soldier . . 32.00
515-Johnny Appleseed 16.00
516-Alladin and His Lamp 24.00
517-The Emperor's New Clothes 16.00
518-The Golden Goose 16.00
519-Paul Bunyan 16.00
520-Thumbelina 24.00
521-King of the golden River . . . 16.00
522-The Nightingale 11.00
523-The Gallant Tailor 11.00
524-The Wild Swans 11.00
525-The Little Mermaid 11.00
526-The Frog Prince 11.00
527-The Golden-Haired Giant . . 11.00
528-The Penny Prince 11.00
529-The Magic Servants 11.00
530-The Golden Bird 11.00
531-Rapunzel 16.00
532-The Dancing Princesses . . . 11.00
533-The Magic Fountain 11.00
534-The Golden Touch 11.00
535-The Wizard of Oz 32.00
536-The Chimney Sweep 11.00
537-The Three Faires 11.00
538-Silly Hans 11.00
539-The Enchanted Fish 24.00
540-The Tinder-Box 24.00
541-Snow White and Rose Red . 16.00
542-The Donkey's Tail 16.00
543-The House in the Woods . . 11.00
544-The Golden Fleece 32.00
545-The Glass Mountain 16.00
546-The Elves and the Shoemaker 11.00
547-The Wishing Table 11.00
548-The Magic Pitcher 11.00
549-Simple Kate 11.00
550-The Singing Donkey 11.00
551-The Queen Bee 11.00
552-The Three Little Dwarves . . 16.00
553-King Thrushbeard 11.00
554-The Enchanted Deer 11.00
555-The Three Golden Apples . . 11.00
556-The Elf Mound 11.00
557-Silly Willy 28.00
558-The Magic Dish 28.00
559-The Japanese Lantern 28.00
560-The Doll Princess 28.00
561-Hans Humdrum 11.00
562-The Enchanted Pony 24.00
563-The Wishing Well 11.00
564-The Salt Mountain 11.00
565-The Silly Princess 11.00
566-Clumsy Hans 11.00
567-The Bearskin Soldier 11.00
568-The Happy Hedgehog 11.00
569-The Three Giants 11.00
570-The Pearl Princess 7.00
571-How Fire Came to the Indians 9.00
572-The Drummer Boy 14.00
573-The Crystal Ball 14.00
574-Brightboots 14.00
575-The Fearless Prince 16.00
576-The Princess Who Saw Everything 24.00
577-The Runaway Dumpling . . . 32.00

CLASSICS ILLLUSTRATED SPECIAL ISSUE
N# United Nations 225.00
129-The Story of Jesus 40.00
132A-The Story of America 35.00
135A-The Ten Commandments . 40.00
138A-Adventures in Science . . . 32.00
141A-The Rough Rider 32.00
144A-Blazing the Trails 32.00
147A-Crossing the Rockies 40.00
150A-Royal Canadian Police . . . 35.00
153A-Men, Guns, and Cattle . . . 35.00
156A-The Atomic Age 30.00
159A-Rockets, Jets and Missles 30.00
162A-War Between the States . . 70.00
165A-To the Stars 40.00
166A-World War II 45.00
167A-Prehistoric World 45.00

AMAZING DOPE TALES
Greg Shaw

1 Untrimmed black and white pages, out of order;artist unknown . 110.00
2 Trimmed and proper pages . . . 95.00

AMERICAN SPLENDOR
Harvey Pekar
May, 1976

1 B:Harvey Pekar Stories, HP,RCr,GDu,GBu 12.00
2 HP,RCr,GDu,GBu 6.50
3 HP,RCr,GDu,GBu 6.00
4 HP,RCr,GDu,GBu 5.50
5 HP,RCr,GDu,GBu 5.00
6 HP,RCr,GDu,GBu,GSh 4.50
7 HP,GSh,GDu,GBu 2.50
8 HP,GSh,GDu,GBu 2.00
9 HP,GSh,GDu,GBu 2.75
10 HP,GSh,GDu,GBu 2.75
11 . . . . 3.00
12 . . . . 4.50
13 . . . . 3.25
14-19 . . . . 3.50
20 E:Harvey Pekar Stories 4.00

ANTHOLOGY OF SLOW DEATH
Wingnut Press/Last Gasp

1 140 pgs, RCr,RCo, GiS, DSh,Harlan Ellison VB,RTu 37.00

APEX TREASURY OF UNDERGROUND COMICS, THE
Links Books Inc.
October, 1974

1 . . . . 35.00

APEX TREASURY OF UNDERGROUND COMICS –BEST OF BIJOU FUNNIES
Quick Fox
1981

1 Paperback,comix,various artists 21.00

ARCADE THE COMICS REVUE
Print Mint Inc.
Spring, 1975

1 ASp,BG,RCr,SRo,SCW 16.50
2 ASp,BG,RCr,SRo 12.00
3 ASp,BG,RCr,RW,SCW 8.50
4 ASp,BG,RCr,WBu,RW,SCW . . 8.50
5 ASp,BG,SRo,RW,SCW 7.50
6 ASp,BG,SRo,RCr,SCW 7.50
7 ASp,BG,SRo,RCr,SCW 7.50

BABYFAT
Comix World/Clay Geerdes
1978

1 B:8pg news parodies, one page comix by various artists 4.50
2 same 3.00
3 same 3.00
4 same 3.00
5-9 same 3.00
10 thru 26 same . . . . @2.00

BATTLE OF THE TITANS
University of Illinois SF Society
1972

1 Sci-Fi;VB,JGa 42.50

BEST BUY COMICS
Last Gasp Eco-Funnies

1 Rep Whole Earth Review;RCr . . 3.50

BEST OF BIJOU FUNNIES, THE
Links Books Inc.
1975

1 164 pgs,paperback 235.00

BEST OF RIP-OFF PRESS
Rip Off Press Inc.
1973

1 132 pgs paperback,SCW, RCr,SRo,RW 24.00
2 100 pgs,GS,FT 27.50
3 100 pgs,FS 10.75
4 132 pgs,GiS,DSh 13.00

BIG ASS
Rip Off Press
1969-1971

1 28 pgs,RCr 75.00
2 RCr 42.00

Bijou Funnies #1
© Bijou Publ. Empire

BIJOU FUNNIES
Bijou Publishing Empire
1968

1 B:JLy,editor;RCr,GS SW 285.00
2 RCr,GS,SW 85.50
3 RCr,SWi,JsG 52.00
4 SWi,JsG 30.00
5 SWi,JsG 33.50
6 E:JLy,editor,SWi,RCr,JsG . . . 27.00
7-8 . . . . 26.00

BINKY BROWN MEETS THE HOLY VIRGIN MARY
March, 1972
Last Gasp Eco-Funnies

N# Autobiography about Growing up w/a Catholic Neurosis,JsG . 22.50
2nd Printing:only text in bottom left panel 12.00

BIZARRE SEX
Kitchen Sink Komix
May, 1972

1 B:DKi,editor,various artists 27.00
2 . . . . 22.00
3 . . . . 16.00
4-6 . . . . @11.00
7 . . . . 4.00
8 . . . . 3.50
9 Omaha the Cat Dancer,RW . 16.50

BLACK LAUGHTER
Black Laughter Publishing Co
Nov 1972

1 James Dixon art 64.00

BLOOD FROM A STONE (GUIDE TO TAX REFORM)
New York Public Interest Research Group Inc.
1977

1 Tax reform proposals 8.50

BOBBY LONDON RETROSPECTIVE AND ART PORTFOLIO
Cartoonist Representatives

1 . . . . 19.50

BOBMAN AND TEDDY
Parralax Comic Books Inc
1966

1 RFK & Ted Kennedy's struggle to control Democratic party 35.50

BODE'S CARTOON CONCERT
Dell
Sept, 1973

1 132 pgs; VB 27.50

BOGEYMAN COMICS
San Fransisco Comic Book Co., 1969

1 Horror,RHa 55.00
2 Horror,RHa 42.00

The Company & Sons

3 . . . . 31.00

BUFFALO RAG/THE DEAD CONCERT COMIX
Kenny Laramey
Dec 1973

1 Alice in Wonderland parody . 55.00

CAPTAIN GUTS
The Print Mint
1969

1 Super patriotV:Counter culture 26.50
2 V:Black Panthers 19.00
3 V:Dope Smugglers 19.00

CAPTAIN STICKY
Captain Sticky
1974-75

1 Super lawyer V:Social Injustice 17.50

CARTOON HISTORY OF THE UNIVERSE
Rip Off Press
September, 1978

1 Evolution of Everything; B:Larry Gonick 6.50
2 Sticks and Stones 6.50
3 River Realms-Sumer & Egypt . 6.50
4 Part of the Old Testament . . . 4.50
5 Brains and Bronze 4.50
6 Who are these Athenians 3.75

CASCADE COMIX MONTHLY
Everyman Studios
March, 1978

1 Interviews,articles about comix & comix artists 6.50
2 same 6.50
3 same 6.50
4 thru 11 . . . . @3.00
12 thru 23 . . . . @2.25

CHECKERED DEMON
Last Gasp
July, 1977

1 SCW 13.00
2 SCW 8.50
3 SCW 6.50

CHEECH WIZARD
Office of Student Publications, Syracuse U
1967

n/n VB 120.00

CHICAGO MIRROR
Jay Lynch/Mirror Publishing Empire
Autumn, 1967

1 B:Bijou Funnies 45.00
2 same 35.00
3 same 115.00

COLLECTED CHEECH WIZARD, THE
Company & Sons
1972

n/n VB 55.00

COLLECTED TRASHMAN #1, THE
Fat City & The Red Mountain Tribe Productions

n/n SRo 32.50

COMICS & COMIX
October, 1975

1 . . . . 12.00

COMIX BOOK
Magazine Management Co.,Inc.
October, 1974

1 Compilation for newsstand distribution 14.50
2 . . . . 9.00
3 . . . . 9.00

Kitchen Sink Enterprises

4 . . . . 14.50
5 . . . . 8.50

COMIX COLLECTOR, THE
Archival Press Inc.
December, 1979

1 Fanzine 5.00
2-3 Fanzine 4.00

COMMIES FROM MARS
Kitchen Sink Enterprises
March, 1973

1 TB 32.50

Last Gasp

2 thru 5 TB . . . . @9.50

COMPLETE FRITZ THE CAT
Belier Press
1978

n/n RCr,SRo,DSh 49.50

CONSPIRACY CAPERS
The Conspiracy
1969

1 Benefit Legal Defense of the Chicago-8 . . . . 79.00

DAN O'NEIL'S COMICS & STORIES
VOL.1 1-3
Company & Sons

1 B:Dan O'Neill 45.00
2-3 . . . . 30.00

1971

VOL.2 1-3

1 . . . . 6.50
2 . . . . 4.50
3 E:Dan O'Neill 4.50

DAS KAMPF
Vaughn Bode
May, 1963

N# 100 Loose pgs. 750.00
2nd Printing 52pgs.-produced by Walter Bachner&Bagginer,1977 9.50

Freak Brothers #1, © Gilbert Shelton

DEADBONE EROTICA
Bantam Books Inc.
April, 1971

n/n 132 pgs VB 42.50

DEADCENTER CLEAVAGE
April, 1971

1 14 pgs 38.00

DEATH RATTLE
Kitchen Sink Enterprises
June, 1972

1 RCo,TB 25.00
2 TB 19.00
3 TB 16.00

DESPAIR
The Print Mint
1969

1 RCr 33.00

DIRTY DUCK BOOK, THE
Company & Sons
March, 1972

1 Bobby London 25.00

DISNEY RAPES THE 1st AMENDMENT
Dan O'Neil
1974

1 Benefit Air Pirates V:Disney Law suit; Dan O'Neill 8.50

DOPE COMIX
Kitchen Sink Enterprises
February, 1978

1 Drugs comix;various artists 7.50
2 same 5.75
3-4 LSD issue 4.00

DOPIN DAN

Last Gasp Eco-Funnies
April, 1972

1 TR 12.00
2 TR 8.50
3 TR 8.50
4 Todays Army,TR 7.50

DR. ATOMIC
Last Gasp Eco-Funnies
September, 1972

1 B:Larry S. Todd 12.00
2 and 3 . . . . @10.00
4 . . . . 7.50
5 E:Larry S. Todd 4.75

DR. ATOMIC'S MARIJUANA MULTIPLIER
Kistone Press
1974

1 How to grow great pot 7.50

DRAWINGS BY S.CLAY WILSON
San Francisco Graphics

1 28 pgs 185.00

DYING DOLPHIN
The Print Mint
1970

n/n 14.50

EBON
San Francisco Comic Book Company

1 Comix version; RCr 20.00
1 Tabloid version 18.00

EL PERFECTO COMICS
The Print Mint
1973

N# Benefit Timothy Leary 27.00
2nd Printing-1975 . . . . 4.00

ETERNAL TRUTH
Sunday Funnies Comic Corp

1 Christian Comix 19.50

EVERMUCH WAVE
Atlantis Distributors

1 Nunzio the Narc; Adventures of God 60.00

FABULOUS FURRY FREAK BROTHERS, THE
COLLECTED ADVENTURES OF
Rip Off Press #1
February, 1971

1 GiS 70.00

FURTHER ADVENTURES OF
Rip Off Press #2

1 GiS,DSh 47.50

A YEAR PASSES LIKE NOTHING WITH
Rip Off Press #3

1 GiS 17.00

BROTHER CAN YOU SPARE $.75 FOR
Rip Off Press #4

1 GiS,DSh 12.00

FABULOUS FURRY FREAK BROTHERS, THE
Rip Off Press #5

1 GiS,DSh 9.50

SIX SNAPPY SOCKERS FROM THE ARCHIVES OF
Rip Off Press #6

1 GiS 5.25

FANTAGOR
1970

1 (Corben), fanzine 90.00
1a (Last Gasp) 22.00
2-3 . . . . 20.00
4 . . . . 30.00

THE ADVENTURES OF FAT FREDDY'S CAT,
Rip Off Press
February, 1977

1 . . . . 14.00
2 . . . . 4.50
3 . . . . 6.00
4 . . . . 5.00
5 . . . . 2.50

FEDS 'N' HEADS COMICS
Gilbert Shelton/Print Mint
1968

N# I:Fabulous Furry Freak Bros.; Has no 'Print Mint' Address 24 pgs. 350.00
2nd printing,28 pgs. 55.00
3rd printing,May, 1969 . . . . 45.00
4th printing,Says 'Forth Printing' 17.50
5th-12th printings . . . . @8.00
13th printing 6.50
14th printing 4.75

FELCH
Keith Green

1 RW,SCW,RCr 40.00

FEVER PITCH
Kitchen Sink Enterprises
July, 1976

1 RCo 20.00

Jabberwocky Graphix

2 250 signed & numbered 14.50
3 400 signed & numbered 13.50
4 . . . . 8.50

50'S FUNNIES
Kitchen Sink Enterprises
1980

1 Larry Shell, editor,various artists 5.00

FLAMING CARROT COMICS
Kilian Barracks Free Press
Summer/Autumn, 1981

1 Bob Budden,various artists . . . 8.50

FLASH THEATRE
Oogle Productions
1970

1 44 pgs 37.50

FLESHAPOIDS FROM EARTH
Popular Culture Exploitation Press
December, 1974

1 36 pgs 33.00

THE COMPLETE FOO!
Bijou Publishing
September, 1980

1 RCr, Charles Crumb, r:Crumb brothers fanzines 30.00

FRITZ BUGS OUT
Ballentine Books
1972

n/n RCr 50.50

Fantagor #4, © Fantagor

FRITZ THE CAT
Ballentine Books
1969

n/n RCr 100.00

FRITZ THE NO-GOOD
Ballentine Books
1972

n/n RCr 45.00

FRITZ: SECRET AGENT FOR THE CIA
Ballentine Books
1972

n/n RCr 39.00

FUNNY AMINALS
Apex Novelties/Don Donahue
1972

1 RCr 50.00

GAY COMIX
Kitchen Sink Enterprises
September, 1981

1 36 pgs 7.50
2 36 pgs 5.00

GEN OF HIROSHIMA
Educomics/Leonard Rifas
January, 1980

1 Antiwar comix by Hiroshima survivor Keiji Nakawaza 9.50
2 same 6.50

GHOST MOTHER COMICS
John "Mad" Peck
1969

1 SCw,JsG 47.50

GIMMEABREAK COMIX
Rhuta Press
February, 1971

2 48 pgs, #0 & #1 were advertised,but may not have been printed . . 95.00

GIRLS & BOYS
Lynda J. Barry
1980

1 B:12 pgs with evdanyk,atile Bparyeart 800
2 thru 10 same . . . . @6.50
11 thru 20 same . . . . @4.50
20 thru 25 same . . . . @3.50

GOD NOSE
Jack Jackson/
Rip Off Press
1964

N# 42 pgs. 995.00
2nd printing,Pinkish(c);44p 60.00
3rd printing,Blue Border(c) 30.00
4th printing,Red Border(c) 15.00

GOTHIC BLIMP WORKS LTD.
East Village Other/
Peter Leggieri
1969

1 VB,Editor,various artists . . . 185.00
2 same 145.00
3 KDe,editor 135.00
4 KDe,editor 130.00
5-7 KDe,editor . . . . @125.00
8 various artists 185.00

GREASER COMICS
Half-Ass Press
September 1971

1 28 pgs, George DiCaprio 17.50

Rip Off Press
July 1972

2 George DiCaprio 10.00

GRIM WIT
Last Gasp
1972

1 RCo 35.00
2 RCo 25.00

HAROLD HEAD, THE COLLECTED ADVENTURES OF
Georgia Straight
1972

1 . . . . 45.00
2 . . . . 10.00

HARRY CHESS THAT MAN FROM A.U.N.T.I.E.
The Uncensored Adventures
Trojan Book Service
1966

N# 1st Comix By & For Gay Community 100.00

HEAR THE SOUND OF MY FEET WALKING....
Glide Urban Center
1969

1 Dan O'Neill, 128 pgs 65.00

HISTORY OF UNDERGROUND COMIX
Straight Arrow Books
1974

1 Book by Mark James Estren about Underground Comix 30.00

HOMEGROWN FUNNIES
Kitchen Sink
1971

1 RCr 39.00

HONKYTONK SUE, THE QUEEN OF COUNTRY SWING
Bob Boze Bell
February, 1979

1 BBB 7.00
2-3 BBB 5.00

IKE LIVES
Warm Neck Funnies
1973
1 20 pgs,Mark Fisher 10.00

INSECT FEAR
Last Gasp
1970
1 SRo,GiS,RHa,JsG 75.00
Print Mint
1970-1972
2 . . . . 30.00
3 . . . . 20.00

IT AIN'T ME BABE
Last Gasp Eco-Funnies
July. 1970
n/n First all women comix
Womens Liberation theme . . 32.50

JAPANESE MONSTER
Carol Lay
July, 1979
1 8pgs, Carol Lay 5.00

JESUS LOVES YOU
Zondervan Books/Craig Yoe
1972
1 Christian, RCr 29.50

THE NEW ADVENTURES OF JESUS
Rip Off Press
November 1971
1 44 pgs, FSt 50.00

JIZ
Apex Novelty
1969
1 36 pgs; RCr, SRo, VMo, SCW; hand trimmed and unevenly stapled . . 45.00

JUNKWAFFEL
The Print Mint
1971
1 VB 30.00
2 VB 25.00
3 VB 22.00
4 VB,JJ 18.00

KANNED KORN KOMIX
Canned Heat Fan Club
1969
1 20pgs 8.00

KAPTAIN AMERIKA KOMIX
Brief Candle Comix
March 1970
1 anti U.S. involvement in Laos . 27.50

KING BEE
Apex/Don Donahue & Kerry Clark
1969
1 RCr,SCW 100.00

KURTZMAN COMIX
Kitchen Sink Enterprises
September, 1976
1 HK,RCr,GiS,DKi,WE 12.50

LAUGH IN THE DARK
Last Gasp
n/n KDe,RHa,SRo,SCW 14.00

LENNY OF LAVEDO
Sunbury Productions/Print Mint
1965
N# Green(c);1st Joel Beck-a . . 545.00
2nd printing, Orange(c) 390.00
3rd printing, White(c) 195.00

THE MACHINES
Office of Student Publications
Syracuse University
1967
1 VB 125.00

THE MAN
Office of Student Publications
Syracuse University
1966
1 VB 155.00

MAGGOTZINE
Charles Schneider
May, 1981
1 Various Artists,conceptual
maggot stuff 3.50

MANTICORE
Joe Kubert School of Cartooning & Graphic Arts Inc.
Autumn, 1976
1 Fanzine,various artists 7.50

MEAN BITCH THRILLS
The Print Mint
1971
1 SRO 7.00

MICKEY RAT
Los Angeles Comic Book Co.
May, 1972
1 Robert Armstrong 32.50
2 same 29.00
3 same 9.50

MOM'S HOMEMADE COMICS
Kitchen Sink Enterprises
June 1969
1 DKi, RCr 125.00
The Print Mint
2 DKi 35.00
Kitchen Sink Enterprises
3 DKi,RCr 17.00

MONDAY FUNNIES, THE
Monday Funnies
1977
1 8pgs,various artists 6.50
2 16pgs,various artists 9.00
3 16pgs,various artists 6.50
4 16pgs,various artists 5.50

MONDAY FUNNIES, THE
Passtime Publications
July-August, 1980
1 thru 8 Marc L.Reed . . . . @4.00

MOUSE LIBERATION FRONT
COMMUNIQUE #2
August, 1979
1 SRo, SCW, VMo,DKi; Disney's suit against Dan O'Neil's Air Pirates . . 9.50

MOONCHILD COMICS
Nicola Cuti
1968
0 Nicola Cuti 27.00
2 Nicola Cuti 27.00
3 Nicola Cuti 75.00

MOONDOG
The Print Mint
March, 1970
1 All George Metzer 11.00
2 same 6.50
3 and 4 . . . . @3.75

MORE ADVENTURES OF FAT FREDDY'S CAT
Rip Off Press
January, 1981
1 GiS 14.00

MOTOR CITY COMICS
Rip Off Press
April, 1969
1 RCr 155.00
2 RCr 110.00

MR. NATURAL
San Fransisco Comic Book Co.
August, 1970
1 RCr 85.00
2 RCr 40.00

NARD N' PAT, JAYZEY LYNCH'S
Cartoonists Cooperative Press
March, 1974
1 Jay Lynch 7.00
2 Jay Lynch 4.50
Kitchen Sink Press
1972
3 . . . . 10.00

NEVERWHERE
Ariel Inc.
February 1978
1 RCo 17.50

NICKEL LIBRARY SERIES
Gary Arlington
1 1 pg heavy stock colored paper, Reed Crandall 5.00
2 Kim Deitch 1.50
3 Harrison Cady 1.50
4 Frank Frazetta 3.00
5 Will Eisner 3.00
6 Justin Green 1.50
7 C.C. Beck 3.00
8 Wally Wood 3.00
9 Winsor McCay 1.50
10 Jim Osborne 1.50
11 Don Towlley 1.50
12 Frank Frazetta 3.00
13 Will Eisner 3.00
14 Bill Griffith 1.50
15 George Herriman 1.50
16 Cliff Sterrett 1.50
17 George Herriman 1.50
18 Rory Hayes & Simon Deitch . . 1.50
19 Disney Studios 1.50
20 Alex Toth 1.50
21 Will Eisner 1.50
22 Jack Davis 1.00
23 Alex Toth 1.50
24 Michele Brand 1.50
25 Roger Brand 1.50
26 Arnold Roth 1.50
27 Murphy Anderson 2.00
28 Wally Wood 3.00
29 Jack Kirby 4.00
30 Harvey Kurtzman 3.00
31 Jay Kinney 1.50
32 Bill Plimpton 1.50
33 . . . . 1.50
34 Charles Dallas 1.50
35-39 . . . . 1.50
40 Bill Edwards 1.50
41 Larry S. Todd 1.50
42 Charles Dallas 1.50
43 Jim Osborne 1.50
43 1/2 Larry S. Todd 1.50
44 Jack Jackson 1.50
45 Rick Griffin 1.50
46 Justin Green 1.50
47 Larry S. Todd 1.50
48 Larry S. Todd 1.50

49 Charles Dallas 1.50
50 Robert Crumb 3.00
51 Wally Wood 3.00
52 Charles Dallas 3.00
53 Larry S. Todd 1.50
54 Larry S. Todd 1.50
55 Charles Dallas 1.50
56 Jim Chase 1.50
57 Charles Dallas 1.50
58 Larry S. Todd 1.50
59 Dave Geiser 1.50
60 Charles Dallas 1.50

ODD WORLD OF RICHARD CORBEN–
Warren Publishing
1977

1 84pgs paperback 20.00

O.K. COMICS
Kitchen Sink Enterprises
June, 1972

1 Bruce Walthers 7.00
2 Bruce Walthers 7.00

O.K. Comics #12, © O.K. Comics

O.K. COMICS
O.K. Comic Company
1972

1 Tabloid with articles,reviews,nudie cuties photos 27.50
2 thru 18 . . . . @18.75

ORACLE COMIX
Thru Black Holes
Comix Productions
October, 1980

1 Michael Roden 2.50
2 Michael Roden 2.50

PENGUINS IN BONDAGE
Sorcerer Studio/
Wayne Gibson
July, 1981

1 8pgs,Wayne Gibson 2.75

PHANTOM LADY
Randy Crawford
June, 1978

1 Sex funnies 4.50

PHUCKED UP FUNNIES
Suny Binghamton
1969

1 ASp; bound insert in yearbook 400.00

PINK FLOYD, THE
October, 1974

1 sold at concerts 27.50

PLASTIC MAN
Randy Crawford
May, 1977

1 Sex funnies,RandyCrawford . . 4.00

PORK
Co-op Press
May, 1974

1 SCW 11.00

PORTFOLIO OF UNDERGROUND ART
Schanes & Schanes
1980

1 SRo,SCW,VMo,RW and many others 13 loose sheets in folder, 32pg book, 1200 signed and numbered 75.00

POWERMAN AND POWER MOWER SAFETY
Frank Burgmeir, Co.
Outdoor Power Equipment

1 VB; educational comic about power mower safety 185.00

PROMETHIAN ENTERPRISES
Promethian Enterprises
Memorial Day, 1969

1 B:Jim Vadeboncuor editor . . 72.00
2 same 60.00
3 -5 . . . . @25.00

PURE ART QUARTERLY
John A. Adams
July, 1976

1 16pgs,All John A.Adams 8.50
2-5 same . . . . @8.50
6 thru 10 same . . . . @5.00
11 thru 14 same . . . . @3.50

QUAGMIRE COMICS
Kitchen Sink Enterprises
Summer, 1970

1 DKi,Peter Poplaski 11.00

RAW
Raw Books
1980

1 36pgs,10pgs insert 310.00
2 36pgs,20pgs insert 185.00
3 52pgs,16pgs insert 155.00
4 44pgs,32pgs insert,Flexi disk record 125.00

R. CRUMB'S COMICS AND STORIES
Rip Off Press
1969

1 RCr 75.00

RAWARARAWAR
Rip Off Press
1969

1 GSh 55.00

RED SONJA & CONAN "HOT AND DRY"
Randy Crawford
May, 1977

1 Sex funnies,Randy Crawford . 3.50

REID FLEMING WORLD'S TOUGHEST MILKMAN
David E. Boswell
December, 1980

1 . . . . 6.00

RIP OFF COMIX
Rip Off Press
April, 1977

1 GiS,FSt,JsG,DSh 17.50
2-5 GiS,FSt . . . . @6.00
6 thru 10 . . . . @4.25

ROWLF
Rip Off Press
July, 1971

1 RCo 55.00

RUBBER DUCK TALES
The Print Mint
March, 1971

1 Michael J Becker 12.00
2 Michael J Becker 11.00

S. CLAY WILSON TWENTY DRAWINGS
Abington Book Shop Inc.
1967

N# (a),Cowboy(c) 460.00
(b),Pirate(c) 460.00
(c),Motorcyclist(c) 460.00
(d),Demon(c) 460.00
(e),Deluxe with all 4 variations on same(c) with Gold Embossed Lettering 675.00

SAN FRANSISCO COMIC BOOK
San Fransisco Comic Book Co.
January-February, 1970

1 . . . . 120.00
2 . . . . 20.00
3 . . . . 17.50
4-6 . . . . 12.00

SAVAGE HUMOR
The Print Mint
1973

1 . . . . 4.00

SAY WHAT?
Loring Park Shelter
Community Cartooning Workshop
April, 1979

1 B:Charles T. Smith,editor, various artists 7.00
2-6 same 6.50

SCHIZOPHRENIA, CHEECH WIZARD
Last Gasp Eco-Funnies
January, 1974

1 VB 30.00

SEX AND AFFECTION
C.P. Family Publishers
1974

1 Sex Education for Children . . . 5.50

SHORT ORDER COMIX
Head Press/Family Fun
1973

1 50 cents,36pgs. 8.50
2 75 cents,44pgs 2.25

SKULL COMICS
Last Gasp
March, 1970

1 Horror,RHa 47.00
2 GiS,DSh,RCo 25.50
3 SRo,DSh,RCo 14.00
4 DSh,Lovecraft issue 14.00
5 SRo,RCo,Lovecraft issue . . . 14.00
6 RCo,Herman Hesse 14.00

SLOW DEATH FUNNIES
Last Gasp
April 1970

1 Ecological Awarness & Red Border on (c) 47.00
2nd-4th Printings White Border(c) 10.00
2 Silver(c);1st edition' pgs 34 . . . . 85.00
2b Non Silver(c);Says 1st Edition pgs 34 . . . . 20.00
2nd Amorphia Ad on pg 34 . . . . 6.75
3rd Yellow Skull on (c) 5.00
4th 'Mind Candy For the Masses' Ad on pg. 34 . . . . 5.00
5th $1.00(c) price 3.50
3 thru 5 . . . . @12.00
6 thru 10 . . . . @4.50

SMILE
Kitchen Sink Enterprises
Summer, 1970

1 Jim Mitchell 13.50
2 Jim Mitchell 12.00
3 Jim Mitchell 11.00

SNARF
Kitchen Sink Enterprises
February, 1972

1 DKi,editor,various artists 24.50
2-5 same . . . . @15.00
6 thru 9 same . . . . @6.50

SNATCH COMICS
Apex Novelties
1968

1 RCr,SCW 295.00
2 RCr,SCW 145.00
3 RCr,SCW,RW 65.00

SNATCH SAMPLER
Keith Green
1979

n/n RCr,SCw,RW,RHa 32.00

SPACE INVADERS COMICS, DON CHIN'S
Comix World/Clay Geerdes
April, 1972

1 8pgs 4.00

SPASM!
Last Gasp Eco-Funnies
April, 1973

1 JJ 15.00

STONED PICTURE PARADE
San Francisco Comic Book Co. 1975

1 RCr,SRo,SCW,WE 20.00

SUBVERT COMICS
Rip Off Press
November, 1970

1 SRo 25.00
2 SRo 20.00
3 SRo 12.00

TALES OF SEX & DEATH
Print Mint
1971

1 JsG,KDe.RHa,SRo 32.50
2 JsG,KDe.RHa,SRo 19.50

THRILLING MURDER COMICS
San Francisco Comic Book Co.1971

1 SCW,KDe,RCr,SRo,Jim Arlington,editor 24.50

2 (TWO)
Keith Green
February, 1975

1 SCW 7.00

VAMPIRELLA
Randy Crawford
June, 1978

1 Sex Funnies 3.50

VAUGHN BODE THE PORTFOLIO
Northern Comfort Communications
1976

1 VB,16pgs 125.00

VAUGHN BODE PRODUCTIONS PORTFOLIO #1
Vaughn Bode Productions
1978

1 VB,10 pgs 35.00

VAUGHN BODE'S CHEECH WIZARD THE COLLECTED ADVENTURES OF THE CARTOON MESSIAH
Northern Comfort Communications
1976

1 VB,88pgs 55.00

VAUGHN BODE'S DEADBONE THE FIRST TESTAMENT OF CHEECH WIZARD,
Northern Comfort Communications
1975

1 VB 65.00

VIETNAM

N# 20pgs. Role of Blacks in the War,TG Lewis 125.00

WEIRDO
Last Gasp Eco-Funnies
March, 1981

1 RCr 10.00
2 RCr 10.00
3 RCr 10.00

WEIRDO, THE
Rodney Schroeter
October, 1977

1 B:Rodney Schroezer,1pg 4.50
2 88pgs 4.50
3 44pgs 4.50

WIMMEN'S COMIX
Last Gasp Eco-Funnies
November, 1972

1 All women artists&comix 10.75
2 same 10.75
3 same 10.00
4-7 same . . . . @6.75

WONDER WART-HOG AND THE NURDS OF NOVEMBER
Rip Off Press
September, 1980

1 GiS 15.00

WONDER WART-HOG, CAPTAIN CRUD & OTHER SUPER STUFF
Fawcett Publications
1967

1 GiS,VB 22.00

YELLOW DOG
The Print Mint
May, 1968

1 4pgs,RCr 30.00
2 8pgs,RCr 25.00
3 8pgs,RCr 25.00
4 8pgs,RCr,SCW 25.00
5 8pgs,RCr,SCW,KDe 25.00
6 thru 12 . . . . @25.00
13/14 52pgs RCr,Jay Lynch . . . 12.00
15 Don Scheneker,editor 59.00
16 . . . . 55.00
17 thru 24 . . . . @15.00

YOUNG AND LUSTLESS
San Fransisco Comic Book Co.
1972

1 BG 15.50

YOUNG LUST
Company & Sons
October, 1970

1 BG,ASp 27.00
2 BG 15.00
3 BG,JsG,RCr,ASp 12.00
4 KDe,BG,SRo 10.50
5 BG,SRo 7.50
6 SRo,KDe 5.50

Yow #2, © Last Gasp

YOW
Last Gasp
April, 1978

1 BG 5.75
2 BG 4.75

becomes:

ZIPPY

3 BG 6.50

ZAP COMIX
Apex Novelties
October, 1967

0 RCr 325.00
1 RCr 325.00
2 RCr,SCW 90.00
3 RCr,SCW,VMo,SRo 55.00
4 VMo,RW,RCr,SCW.SRo,GiS 55.00
5 RW,GiS,RCr,SCW,SRo 50.00
6 RW,GiS,RCr,SCW,SRo 25.00
7 RW,GiS,RCr,SCW,SRo 18.50
8 RW,GiS,RCr,SCW,SRo 10.00
9 RW,GiS,RCr,SCW,SRo 12.00

Bibliography

Daniels, Les. *Comix: A History of Comic Books in America*. New York, NY: Bonanza Books, 1971.

Gerber, Ernst. *The Photo Journal Guide to Comic Books*. Minden, NV: Gerber Publishing, 1989. Vols. 1 & 2.

Gerber, Ernst. *The Photo Journal Guide to Marvel Comics*. Minden, NV: Gerber Publishing, 1991. Vols. 3 & 4.

Goulart, Ron. *The Adventurous Decade*. New Rochelle, NY: Arlington House, 1975.

Goulart, Ron. *The Encyclopedia of American Comics*. New York, NY: Facts on File Publications, 1990.

Goulart, Ron. *Over 50 Years of American Comic Books*. Lincolnwood, IL: Mallard Press, 1991.

Hegenburger, John. *Collectors Guide to Comic Books*. Radnor, PA: Wallace-Homestead Book Company, 1990.

Kennedy, Jay. *The Official Underground and Newave Price Guide*. Cambridge, MA: Boatner Norton Press, 1982.

Malan, Dan. *The Complete Guide to Classics Collectibles*. St. Louis, MO: Malan Classical Enterprises, 1991.

O'Neil, Dennis. *Secret Origins of DC Super Heroes*. New York, NY: Warner Books, 1976.

Overstreet, Robert. *The Official Overstreet Comic Book Price Guide*. New York, NY: The House of Collectibles, 1991. 22nd Edition.

Rovin, Jeff. *The Encyclopedia of Super Heroes*. New York, NY: Facts on File Publications, 1985.

Rovin, Jeff. *The Encyclopedia of Super Villians*. New York, NY: Facts on File Publications, 1987.

Thompson, Don & Maggie. *The Golden Age of Comics, Summer 1982*. Tampa, FL: New Media Publishing, 1982.